The Oxford Companion to

American
Food and Drink

Editorial Board

The Oxford Companion to

American Food and Drink

Edited by Andrew F. Smith

OXFORD
UNIVERSITY PRESS

OXFORD
UNIVERSITY PRESS

Oxford   New York

Auckland Bangkok Buenos Aires Cape Town Chennai
Dar es Salaam Delhi Hong Kong Istanbul Karachi Kolkata
Kuala Lumpur Madrid Melbourne Mexico City Mumbai Nairobi
São Paulo Shanghai Taipei Tokyo Toronto

Copyright © 2007 by Oxford University Press, Inc.

Published by Oxford University Press, Inc.
198 Madison Avenue, New York, New York, 10016
http://www.oup.com/us

Oxford is a registered trademark of Oxford University Press

Library of Congress Cataloging-in-Publication Data

The Oxford companion to American food and drink / Andrew F. Smith, editor.
   p.   cm.
Includes bibliographical references and index.
ISBN-13: 978-0-19-530796-2 (hardcover : alk. paper)
1. Food–Encyclopedias.   2. Cookery, American–Encyclopedias.
3. Food habits–United States–Encyclopedias.   I. Smith, Andrew F., 1946–

TX349.O94 2007
394.1′20973—dc22

                                                    2006032303

9 8 7 6 5 4 3 2 1

Printed in the United States of America
on acid-free paper

Contents

EDITOR'S PREFACE   vii

COMMON ABBREVIATIONS   x

ACKNOWLEDGMENTS   xi

CONTRIBUTORS   xiii

ENTRY TITLES BY SUBJECT   xix

THE OXFORD COMPANION TO
AMERICAN FOOD AND DRINK   1

FOOD BIBLIOGRAPHY   643

DRINK BIBLIOGRAPHY   645

FOOD FESTIVALS   646

FOOD-RELATED MUSEUMS   650

FOOD PERIODICALS   651

FOOD-RELATED ORGANIZATIONS   652

FOOD WEBSITES   654

INDEX   655

PICTURE CREDITS   693

Editor's Preface

What is American food? Is it traditional foodstuffs, such as maize, beans, squash, domesticated in the Americas? Is it warmed-over British fare, such as meat, potatoes, puddings, and sandwiches? Or perhaps is it special holiday treats—turkey, cranberries, corn on the cob, candied sweet potatoes, or Christmas cookies? Is it ethnic foods brought by continuous waves of immigrants—tacos, pizza, spaghetti, and fortune cookies—and bastardized in America? Is it fast food—hamburgers, french fries, pizza, or hot dogs? Or commercial products—Lay's potato chips, Hershey bars, Campbell's soups, Good Humor ice creams, Betty Crocker cake mixes, Minute Maid frozen orange juice, Swanson TV dinners, or Coca-Cola? Or is it the haute cuisine of America's best restaurants like Delmonico's and Per Se in Manhattan? Perhaps the new, emerging "California cuisine" à la Wolfgang Puck, Alice Waters, Thomas Keller, and Jeremiah Towers is the essence of edible in America? What about those foods discussed in *Gourmet, Bon Appetite,* or *Saveur*? Or the cooking programs on PBS or the Food Network? Maybe the foods cited in the more than twenty thousand cookbooks and other food books published annually in the United States are the real thing?

The Oxford Companion to American Food and Drink broadly and eclectically defines American food and drink as the foods and beverages consumed in the United States. It is a smorgasbord foodscape filled with creative entrepreneurs, overworked consumers, well-intentioned reformers, and competing culinary elites. It is composed of numerous ingredients, diverse flavors, unique dishes, ever-changing modes of preparation, expanding methods of distribution, and the usual and unusual ways Americans eat. In addition, this *Companion* examines the underlying processes and broad trends, such as urbanization, industrialization, suburbanization, and globalization, that have determined what Americans eat today.

Food has profoundly affected the American continent, beginning in prehistoric times, when Old World hunters came to the New World seeking big game, to modern times, in which American agriculture helps feed the world. Food has profoundly shaped our society: It has influenced population growth and migrations, dictated economic and political changes, expanded commerce, inspired poems and literature, and precipitated the evolution and invention of certain lifestyles. The desire for food served at particular times and in specific ways has caused the creation of new technologies, from the earliest canning efforts to microwave ovens. Food was at the core of American medicine in the nineteenth century, and dietary concerns remain an important component of medical practice today. Food has also been an important weapon in war.

Well-fed armies usually defeat hungry ones, as illustrated by the Civil War; conversely, wars have altered our eating habits by introducing new foods and processes and by creating new uses for old foods. After the Civil War, for instance, peanuts went from a slave food to one of America's first national snack foods, and canned food went from an expensive luxury to a low-cost everyday product. Chocolate bars became popular due to military procurement policies during World War I. And Coca-Cola marched along with the American military to the farthest reaches of the globe during World War II.

Beyond nutritional value, food has psychological and emotional value. Consuming foods and beverages gratifies pleasure and relieves stress. Depending on the circumstance, with whom one eats and under what conditions could be a family get-together, a romantic encounter, a business matter, a status enhancer, or a religious experience. Finally, food is security and power: Those who have it survive and thrive; those who don't languish and die.

Food is America's most important business and its largest export. Never before in the history of the world has one group of people had so much influence over the culinary lives of others. American food surpluses have saved millions of lives in other nations, and American farm subsidies and tariffs have caused economic havoc and political upheaval in Africa and Southeast Asia. Other countries are rapidly expanding their exports to the United States, and American food corporations are rapidly expanding abroad. American fast food companies are increasing their operations in other countries while they are contracting their operations in the United States. Some of these corporations are at the forefront of genetic engineering research and applications. As a consequence of this technology, the world may either be on the verge of a great culinary revolution or perhaps a genetic catastrophe.

The idea of an "American cuisine" is not a new phenomenon. Although the dominant culinary style in the original thirteen colonies was English, Americans adapted to new environmental conditions by creating a cuisine entirely their own. In the four centuries since the English colonies were established in North America, American cookery has been greatly modified by climatic and environmental conditions in the New World, the availability of new ingredients, and numerous adoptions and adaptations from the cookery of immigrants from a multitude of nations, cultures, and religions. American food has never stopped changing, and this constant innovation is perhaps its hallmark. The pace of culinary change in America and the world is accelerating, and it will likely continue to do so in the future.

Until recently, America's food history has been largely told by newspaper reporters, magazine writers, and television producers. Some writers have taken the easy way out and presented nice stories—repeating culinary fakelore—rather than spend the time and energy to discern significant underlying patterns. Since the 1980s, however, magazines, popular journals, and television programs have increasingly paid serious attention to American food and drink. This attention reflects growing interest in this field. Many Americans want to know more about food: they examine commercial food labels, worry about nutrition, seek quality foods and beverages. Amateur and professional cooking schools and programs have rapidly proliferated. Restaurateurs and chefs visit farmers' markets, buy fresh produce from local growers, and take pride in the quality foods served in their establishments. Some Americans have joined food-related organizations, buy from artisanal bakers, and even engage in culinary tourism. More and more Americans want healthy food as well as food that tastes good.

Simultaneously, academics have begun to see the culinary experience as worthy of professional exploration. Numerous articles have appeared in academic and popular journals; graduate students have completed theses and dissertations on food-related topics; courses and culinary programs have emerged at many universities; and serious books on culinary topics are released regularly.

What has emerged is the broad-based, eclectic, and electric field of culinary studies. The field involves academicians from diverse disciplines, but it is also peopled with museum curators, professional chefs, independent scholars, cookbook authors, food writers, librarians, advocates, and a growing number of foodies. When their diverse body of work is sifted and amalgamated, a fascinating tale of American food and drink unfolds. It is action-packed, buzzing with home cooks and fancy restaurateurs, family farmers and corporate giants, captains of industry and street vendors, mom-and-pop grocers and massive food conglomerates, burger barons and vegetarians, the hungry and the affluent, hard-hitting advertisers and health food advocates, those who make medical claims and home economists, slow food promoters and fast food consumers, along with ethnic and religious groups of every flavor.

A Note to the Reader

The intent behind the *Oxford Companion to American Food and Drink* is to make this body of knowledge available to the public. The *Companion* has been designed in such a way as to combine historical, descriptive, and analytical articles with synthetic and interpretive essays. Although the book is organized alphabetically, there are several types of entries within:

- Chronological surveys that look at American history during different time periods from the pre-Columbian era to the early twenty-first century.
- Product entries that focus on a specific food or drink, such as tomatoes, Manhattans, club sandwiches, Moxie, Twinkies, breakfast cereal, and anadama bread.
- Contributions of ethnic, religious, cultural, and racial groups to American culinary life, such as those by African Americans, German Americans, Mexican Americans, Chinese Americans, Seventh-Day Adventists, Muslims, Catholics, and Jews.
- Biographies of important contributors to American food and drink, including chefs, corporate leaders, critics, food writers, cookbook authors, cookery bibliographers, and others whom the editors considered influential on American culinary life.
- Corporate histories and commercial products, including junk foods and fast foods, that have dramatically reshaped American culinary life for the last century and will likely continue to do so for the foreseeable future.
- Political and social movements, such as temperance, Prohibition, vegetarianism, the drive for pure food, and the organic food movement.

The entries in the *Companion* are arranged alphabetically. More than two hundred contributors have sought to write in clear language with a minimum of technical vocabulary. The articles give important terms and titles in their original languages, with English translations when needed. To guide readers from one article to related discussions elsewhere in the *Companion*, cross-references appear after many articles. There are also cross-references within the body of a few articles, while blind entries direct the user from an alternate form of an entry term to the entry itself. For example, the blind entry for "Train Food" tells the reader to look under "Dining Car." This *Companion* is not intended to be comprehensive and it does not include every possible topic. It covers a wide range of topics, but it only scratches the surface of most. It is not intended as the final word on American food and drink. Because the study of American food and drink is rapidly expanding, it is anticipated that this work will be revised regularly to include new works and perspectives.

ANDREW F. SMITH, JANUARY 2007

Common Abbreviations Used in This Work

AI, adequate intake

AID, Agency for International Development

AVA, American Viticultural Area

BATF, Bureau of Alcohol, Tobacco, and Firearms

B.C.E, before the Common Era (= B.C.)

BLT, bacon, lettuce, and tomato sandwich

CARE, Cooperative for American Relief Everywhere

C.E., Common Era (= A.D.)

DRI, dietary reference intake

EAR, estimated average requirement

FDA, Food and Drug Administration

NAFTA, North American Free Trade Agreement

PL, Public Law

RDA, recommended daily allowance

UNICEF, United Nations International Children's Emergency Fund

USFA, United States Food Administration

USDA, United States Department of Agriculture

WHO, World Health Organization

Acknowledgments

M any individuals could be singled out for their assistance in producing this *Companion*. I would like especially to thank Barry Popik, whose online research that appears in the archives of the American Dialect Society was used by many writers. He was always willing to answer questions and respond to inquiries.

Many thanks to those who contributed to the illustration program. Meryle Evans, Kit Barry, Cathy Kaufman and the Institute of Culinary Education, and Barbara Kuck provided invaluable assistance in locating and gaining permission to use many illustrations. Kit Barry, Rynn Berry, Steve Heller, Barbara Kuck, Georgia Maas, John C. Campbell, Howard Paige, Bonnie Slotnick, and Mark H. Zanger, among others, allowed us to use images from their own collections. Joe Zarba took several photographs in the New York area.

On a personal note, I'd like to thank Bonnie Slotnick, who commented on all my entries and pointed out foolish mistakes of grammar as well as of content. I also thank the writers who contributed entries and the associate editors for the time they spent designing and selecting entries, identifying and guiding authors, and reviewing and editing entries. It was a personal joy and professional pleasure to work with them all.

Finally, I thank the staff at Oxford University Press, especially Ben Keene, Katie Henderson, Christina Carroll, Dena Ratner, Martin Coleman, and Karen Horton. Without their effort, enthusiasm, and encouragement, this *Companion* would never have been completed.

Contributors

PAULINE ADEMA
Food Writer, Dallas, Texas
Foodways

GARY ALLEN
Food Writer, Kingston, New York
Armour, Philip Danforth; Chile; Crab Boils; Cream Cheese; Food Websites; Ginger Family; Mint Family; Mustard Family; Onion Family; Parsley Family; Prepared Herb and Spice Mixtures; Saint Patrick's Day; Sarsaparilla and Wintergreen; Sinclair, Upton; Sweet Spices

JEAN ANDERSON
Cookbook Author and Journalist, Chapel Hill, North Carolina
Food Processors

HEA-RAN L. ASHRAF
Department of Food and Nutrition, Southern Illinois University
Diets, Fad

JOSEPHINE BACON
Writer, Editor, and Translator, London
Chickpeas; Jennie June; Olives; Partridge; Passover; Pastrami; Salsify; Squash

VIRGINIA K. BARTLETT
Independent Scholar, Hingham, Massachusetts
Cooking Manuscripts; Food Periodicals; Leslie, Eliza; Periodicals; Radio/TV Food Shows

LINDA BASSETT
Department of Culinary Arts, North Shore Community College, Massachusetts
Howard Johnson; Johnson, Howard

AMY BENTLEY
Department of Nutrition and Food Studies, New York University
Historical Overview: World War II; Stewart, Martha

JENNIFER SCHIFF BERG
Department of Nutrition and Food Studies, New York University
Egg Cream

RYNN BERRY
Author of *Food for the Gods: Vegetarianism and the World's Religions*
Animal Rights; Fletcherism; North American Vegetarian Society; Rawfoodism; Veganism; Vegetarianism

LINDA MURRAY BERZOK
Independent Scholar, Tucson, Arizona, and Stephentown, New York
Dairy; Fusion Food; Jell-O Molds; Obesity; Southeast Asian Food

MARIAN BETANCOURT
Food Writer, Brooklyn, New York
Cheese, Moldy; Cuba Libre; Hearts of Palm; Moxie; Scandinavian and Finnish American Food, sidebar on *Finnish Pulla; Snapple*

CHARLOTTE BILTEKOFF
Ph.D. Candidate, American Civilization, Brown University
Quaker Oats Man

DANIEL BLOCK
Department of Geography, Sociology, Economics, and Anthropology, Chicago State University
Butter; Buttermilk; Dairy Industry; Milk

HENRY BONNER
Food Writer, St. Mary's City, Maryland
Crab Cakes

ANNE L. BOWER
Department of English, Ohio State University
Community Cookbooks

BARRETT P. BRENTON
Department of Sociology and Anthropology, St. John's University, Jamaica, New York
Food Stamps; Health Food; Hunger Programs; International Aid; Organic Food

ROBERT W. BROWER
Chef and Attorney, El Sobrante, California
Adulteration; Food and Drug Administration; Good Housekeeping Institute; Kellogg Company; Law; Molasses; North American Free Trade Agreement; Pasties; Pizza; Pizzerias; Saltwater Taffy; Valentine's Day

THOMAS BURFORD
Orchard and Nursery Consultant, Monroe, Virginia
Apples; Cider; Johnny Appleseed; Myths and Folklore

JOSEPH M. CARLIN
Founder and Owner, Food Heritage Press, Ipswich, Massachusetts
Aseptic Packaging; Automats; Bars; Beatrice; Birdseye, Clarence; Birdseye Corporation; Borden;

Clams; ConAgra; Concentrated Orange Juice; Culinary Historians of Boston; Food-Related Organizations; General Foods; General Mills; Historiography, sidebars on *Food History Organizations and Culinary History Groups; Kraft Foods; Krispy Kreme; Meals on Wheels; Milk Packaging; Nestlé; Puddings; Punch; Saloons; Taverns; Waxed Paper; Wiley, Harvey*

JOHN F. CASSENS
President, Cassens Consulting Company, Fort Lee, New Jersey
Flavorings

HUDSON CATTELL
Editor, *Wine East,* Lancaster, Pennsylvania
Wine: Eastern U.S. Wines

ANN CHANDONNET
Independent Scholar, Juneau, Alaska
Alaska; Honey

SHIRLEY E. CHERKASKY
Founder, Culinary Historians of Washington, D.C.
Food-Related Museums

ANDREW COE
Food Writer, Brooklyn, New York
Lamb and Mutton; Phosphates; Seltzer; Soda Drinks

ALFREDO MANUEL DE JESUS OLIVEIRA COELHO
Agro-Montpellier, University of Montpellier, France
Water, Bottled; Water, Imported

STEVEN M. CRAIG
New York Epicurean
Gallo, Ernest and Julio; Mondavi, Robert; Robert Mondavi Co.; Wine: Later Developments; Wine Barrels; Wine Bottles; Wine Casks; Wine Cellars; Wine Glasses; Wine-Tasting Rooms

JAMES CRAWFORD
Curator, Canajoharie Library and Art Gallery, Canajoharie, New York
Beech-Nut

FRED CZARRA
Food Writer, St. Mary's City, Maryland
Fried Oysters, Pepper, Black; Stuffed Ham

TOM DALZELL
Independent Scholar, Berkeley, California
Slang, Food

CHARLES DANIEL
Department of Biology, University of
California, Santa Cruz
Chicken

MITCHELL DAVIS
James Beard Foundation, New York City
*Restaurant Awards and Guides; Restaurant Critics
and Food Columnists; Restaurants*

SALLY S. DEFAUW
Independent Scholar, De Kalb, Illinois
Corn Syrup

DALE DEGROFF
Master Mixologist, Institute for Culinary
Education, New York
*Cocktails; Collins; Mai Tai; Sazerac; Screwdriver;
Singapore Sling; Whiskey Sour; Zombie*

LISA DELANGE
Researcher and Writer, New York City
Sherry; Vermouth

JONATHAN DEUTSCH
Department of Tourism and Hospitality,
Kingsborough Community College, City
University of New York
Chuck Wagons; Firehouse Cooking

PAUL DICKSON
Writer, Garrett Park, Maryland
Combat Food; Space Food; Toasts; Toothpicks

SUSAN FEAKES DORSCHUTZ
Technical Editor and Writer, Rodale Institute,
Kutztown, Pennsylvania
Organic Gardening

ELIZABETH McCANTS DRINNON
Writer, Macon, Georgia
Stuckey's

CAROLYN EASTWOOD
Author of *Near West Side Stories: Struggles
for Community in Chicago's Maxwell Street
Neighborhood*
Street Vendors

REBECCA L. EPSTEIN
Department of Film, Television, and Digital
Media, UCLA
Film, Food in

ASTRID FERSZT
Writer, London and Albuquerque, New Mexico
Biotechnology; Drying; Fermentation

RIEN T. FERTEL
Food Writer, New York, New York
Jambalaya

HOPE-MARIE FLAMM
Writer, New York City
Mimosa

CHERYL FOOTE
Author of *Women of the New Mexico Frontier,
1846–1912*
Pinole; Southwestern Regional Cookery

CHERYL FORBERG
Author of *Stop the Clock! Cooking: Defy Aging
with Natural Healing Comfort Foods*
Sorghum Flour; Sorghum Syrup

LINDA CAMPBELL FRANKLIN
Artist, Writer, and Collector, Baltimore
*Apple-Preparation Tools; Biscuit Cutters; Bread-
Making Tools; Butter-Making Tools and Churns;
Cabbage Cutters and Planes; Can Openers; Cheese-
Making Tools; Cherry Pitters or Stoners; Chopping
Knives and Food Choppers; Coffee Makers, Roasters,
and Mills; Containers; Cookie Cutters; Cornbread
Baking Pans; Corn-Preparation Tools; Cupboards
and Food Safes; Dishwashing and Cleaning Up;
Doughnut-Making Tools; Egg-Preparation Tools;
Flytraps and Fly Screens; Frying Baskets; Graters;
Juicers; Kettles; Lunch Boxes, Dinner Pails, and
Picnic Kits; Mortar and Pestle; Nutcrackers and
Grinders; Nutmeg Graters; Peach Parers and
Stoners; Pot Holders; Potato-Cooking Tools; Pressure
Cookers; Sieves, Sifters, and Colanders; Timers,
Hourglasses, Egg Timers; Toasters; Turnspit Dogs;
Waffle, Wafer, and Pizelle Irons*

REBECCA FREEDMAN
Writer, White Plains, New York
Freeze-Drying

ELLEN J. FRIED
Research Associate, Rudd Center for Food
Policy and Obesity, Yale University
Hemp

ELYSE FRIEDMAN
Author of *Dial-Out, Dine-In: Chicago Restaurants
That Deliver*
Cooperatives; Kitchen Gardening

RACHELLE E. FRIEDMAN
Independent Scholar, New York City
*Historical Overview: Revolutionary War to the
Civil War*

JIM FUTRELL
Author of *Amusement Parks of New Jersey*
Amusement Parks

FRAN GAGE
Food Writer and Cookbook Author, San
Francisco
Eggs

RANDY GARBIN
Roadside Magazine, Jenkintown, Pennsylvania
Diners; Roadside Food

JUDITH H. GERJUOY
Independent Scholar, Helsinki, Finland
Apple Pie

CAROLYN M. GOLDSTEIN
Industrial Historian, Somerville, Massachusetts
Home Economics

DARRA GOLDSTEIN
Department of Russian, Williams College
Periodicals, sidebar on *Gastronomica; Russian
American Food*

ALEXANDRA GREELEY
Author of *Asian Soups, Stews, and Curries*
Bread Machines; Coconuts

CAROL A. GREENBERG
Proprietor of Cornucopia, Brattleboro,
Vermont
Etiquette Books

FRED GRIFFITH
Coauthor of *Nuts! Recipes from around the
World That Feature Nature's Perfect Ingredient*
Chestnuts; Garlic; Onions

LINDA GRIFFITH
Coauthor of *Nuts! Recipes from around the
World That Feature Nature's Perfect Ingredient*
Chestnuts; Garlic; Onions

MADGE GRISWOLD
Editor, *The Peripatetic Epicure*, Tucson, Arizona
Library Collections

MARK C. GRUBER
Wine and Spirits Instructor, Northwestern
University
Whiskey

BARBARA HABER
Food Historian, Winchester, Massachusetts
*Child, Lydia Maria; Culinary History vs. Food
History*

CAROL MIGHTON HADDIX
Food Editor, *Chicago Tribune*
Cookbooks and Manuscripts: 1970s to the Present

ANNIE S. HAUCK-LAWSON
Department of Health and Nutrition
Services, Brooklyn College
Polish American Food

CORINNA HAWKES
Consultant, International Food Policy
Research Institute
*Farm Subsidies, Duties, Quotas, and Tariffs;
Sanders, Colonel; Transportation of Food*

JOANNE LAMB HAYES
Food Writer and Historian, New York City
Lincoln, Mrs.; Richards, Ellen Swallow; Vitamins

KAREN HESS
Independent Scholar, New York City
*French Fries: Historical Overview; Jefferson,
Thomas; Lowenstein, Eleanor; Randolph, Mary;
Simmons, Amelia; Wilson, Mary Tolford*

LYNN HOFFMAN
Independent Scholar, Philadelphia
Brewing

DAVID GERARD HOGAN
Department of History, Heidelberg College
*Alcoholism; Budweiser; Fast Food; Hamburger;
Kentucky Fried Chicken; Pizza Hut; Prohibition;
Take-Out Foods; Temperance; Wendy's; White
Castle; World's Fairs*

PEGGY L. HOLMES
Writer and Farmer, Chillicothe, Illinois
Soybeans

TONYA HOPKINS
Food Writer and Wine Consultant, Brooklyn,
New York
*Fruit Wines; Kwanzaa; Rum; Wine, Hot Spiced;
Wine Coolers; Wineries*

ROGER HOROWITZ
Center for the History of Business,
Technology, and Society, Hagley Museum
and Library, Wilmington, Delaware
Meat

LYNN MARIE HOUSTON
Independent Scholar, Covington, Louisiana
Airplane Food; Kitchens: 1800 to the Present

SHARON HUDGINS
Author of *The Other Side of Russia: A Slice of Life in Siberia and the Russian Far East*
Chili; Salsa

PHYLLIS ISAACSON
James Beard Foundation, New York
Beard, James

JANET JARVITS
Independent Scholar, Pasadena, California
Brown, Helen Evans

VIRGINIA SCOTT JENKINS
Author of *Bananas: An American History*
Bananas; Chesapeake Region, Food and Drink of the; Eggnog; Halloween; Ice; Sally Lunn; Syllabub

RICHARD J. JENSEN
Senior Adviser to the President, University of Nevada, Las Vegas
Farm Labor and Unions

LIZA JERNOW
Cookbook Author and Food Stylist, New York City
Birthdays; Gibbons, Euell; Heirloom Vegetables; Highball

EVE JOCHNOWITZ
Ph.D. Candidate, Department of Performance Studies, New York University
Borden, sidebar on Elsie the Cow; Community-Supported Agriculture; Jewish Dietary Laws; Matzo

SHARON KAPNICK
Food Writer and Sommelier, New York City
Jolly Green Giant; Pillsbury Doughboy; Tschirky, Oscar

DAVID KARP
Food Writer, Venice, California
Cactus; Citrus; Dates; Fruit; Kiwis; Persimmons; Plums; Pomegranates

KAREN KARP
Director, Karp Resources, New York City
Settlement Houses; Soup Kitchens

ROBERT KAUFELT
Proprietor of Murray's Cheese, New York City
Cheese: Recent Developments

CATHY K. KAUFMAN
Institute of Culinary Education, New York City
Appetizers; Bakeries; Carrots; Ceramics Definitions; Chicken Cookery; Christmas; Cooking Schools: Twentieth Century; Cooking Techniques; Cordials, Historical; Creams, Dessert; Cucumbers; Custards; Dining Rooms and Meal Service; Easter; Flowers, Edible; Glassware; Historical Dining Reenactment; Hotel Dining Rooms; Lady Baltimore Cake; Lady Fingers; Leeks; Lenox Company, The; Mushrooms; New Year's Celebrations; Nouvelle Cuisine; Pastries; Plates; Restaurant Labor Unions; Restaurants, sidebar on The Rise of Restaurants; Sauces and Gravies; Sprouts; Sugar Beets; Sunflowers; Trencher; White House

PATRICIA M. KELLY
Editor, Culinary Historians of Boston newsletter, Dorchester, Massachusetts
Milkshakes, Malts, and Floats; Soda Fountains

C. T. KENNEDY
Fruit Grower and Attorney, San Francisco
Blackberries; Figs; Grapes; Mulberries; Pears; Quince

PAMELA GOYAN KITTLER
Food, Culture, and Nutrition Consultant, Sunnyvale, California
Broccoli; Insects; Kvass; Weddings

STEVEN KOLPAN
Wine Studies and Gastronomy, Culinary Institute of America
Champagne

KEVIN R. KOSAR
Editor, AlcoholReviews.com
Cider, Hard; Vodka

BETH KRACKLAUER
Food Writer, Brooklyn, New York
Taffy

BRUCE KRAIG
Roosevelt University, Chicago (Emeritus), and President, Culinary Historians of Chicago
Archer Daniels Midland; Brady, Diamond Jim; Hearn, Lafcadio; Hines, Duncan; Hot Dogs; Ice Creams and Ices, sidebar on Ice Cream Cone and the St. Louis World's Fair; Luncheonettes; Pigs; Sara Lee Corporation; Swift, Gustavus Franklin; Turnips; Vienna Sausage

MICHAEL KRONDL
Independent Scholar, New York City
Advertising; Crisco; Fats and Oils; Lard and Shortening; Margarine; Post Foods; Vegetable Oils

PETER LaFRANCE
Publisher, BeerBasics.com, Brooklyn, New York
Amber Lager; Amber Red Ale; Barley Wine Ale; Beer; Beer Cans; Brown Ale; Coors Brewing Company; Light Lager; Low-Carbohydrate Light Lager; Märzen/Oktoberfest; Microbreweries; Miller Brewing Company; Pale Ale; Pilsener; Premium Lager; Stout; Strong Pale Ale

DESMOND R. LAYNE
Department of Horticulture, Clemson University
Pawpaw

HYON JUNG LEE
M.A. Candidate, Gallatin Program, New York University
Korean American Food; Salt and Salting

JAMES C. LEE
Independent Scholar, Lookout Mountain, Georgia
Poke Salad

DAVID LEITE
Food Writer and Editor, New York City
Burger King; Chorizo; Kale; Swanson

WALTER LEVY
Independent Scholar, Accord, New York
Picnics

WILLIAM G. LOCKWOOD
Department of Anthropology, Michigan State University
Midwestern Regional Cookery

YVONNE R. LOCKWOOD
Michigan State University Museum
Midwestern Regional Cookery

LUCY M. LONG
Department of Popular Culture, Bowling Green State University
Myths and Folklore

JANICE BLUESTEIN LONGONE
Curator of American Culinary History, Clements Library, University of Michigan
Cookbooks and Manuscripts: To 1860 and Cookbooks and Manuscripts: From the Civil War to World War I

SYLVIA LOVEGREN
Independent Scholar, Midland Park, New Jersey
Barbecue; Breakfast Foods; Bridge Luncheon Food; Bubble Tea; Bully Beef; Chafing Dish; Chipped Beef; Cream Soda; Department of Agriculture, United States; Fondue Pot; Historical Overview: To the Early 1960s and Historical Overview: 1960s to the Present; Irish Coffee; Muslim Dietary Laws; Passenger Pigeon; Pure Food and Drug Act; Refrigerators; Root Beer; Slow Cookers; Tea, sidebar on Boston Tea Party

CATHY LUCHETTI
Independent Scholar, Oakland, California
Frontier Cooking of the Far West

ROBYNNE L. MAII
Food Writer and Chef, New York City
Hawaiian Food

MAURICE MANRING
Independent Scholar, Columbia, Missouri
Aunt Jemima

ANDREW MARIANI
Independent Scholar, Morgan Hill, California
Apricots; Cherries; Peaches and Nectarines

LISA B. MARKOWITZ
Department of Anthropology, University of Louisville
Farmers' Markets

MIMI MARTIN
Department of Nutrition, Food Studies, and Public Health, New York University
Prison Food

RENEE MARTON
Chef Instructor and Food Writer, New York, New York
Fannie May; Licorice; LifeSavers; M&M Milk Chocolate Candies; Oh Henry!; Schraft's; Sees Candies

MARTY MARTINDALE
Host of FoodSiteoftheDay.com, Largo, Florida
Barley; Bread, Sliced; Sassafrasses

KEVIN T. McINTYRE
Department of Southeast Asian Studies,
University of California, Berkeley
*Food Stamps; Health Food; Hunger Programs;
International Aid; Organic Food*

MATT McMILLEN
Writer, Washington, D.C.
Frozen Food; TV Dinners

ANNE MENDELSON
Author of *Stand Facing the Stove: The Story of the
Women Who Gave America the Joy of Cooking
Cookbooks and Manuscripts: From World War I to
World War II; Historical Overview: From World War
I to World War II; New York Food; Rombauer, Irma*

BECKY MERCURI
Food Writer, Rushford, New York
*Club Sandwich; Cookbooks and Manuscripts: From
World War II to the 1960s; Cookies; Cooking Contests;
Culinary Institute of America; Dagwood Sandwich;
Denver Sandwich; Dr Pepper; Food Festivals; French
Dip; Gyro; Hoagie; Hot Brown Sandwich; Italian
Sausage Sandwich with Peppers and Onions; Monte
Cristo Sandwich; Muffaletta Sandwich; Oyster Loaf
Sandwich; Panini; Philadelphia Cheesesteak
Sandwich; Pimiento Cheese Sandwich; Po'Boy
Sandwich; Reuben Sandwich; 7 Up; Sloppy Joe;
Wraps*

VIRGINIA MESCHER
Independent Scholar, Burke, Virginia
Switchel

ELLEN MESSER
Departments of Anthropology and
International Studies, The George
Washington University, and School of
Nutrition Science and Policy, Tufts University
Potatoes

JACKIE MILLS
Independent Scholar, Jackson Heights, New
York
Southern Regional Cookery, sidebar on *Moon Pie*

JENNIFER MINNICK
Independent Scholar, New York City
Batidos; Beer Mugs; New Orleans Syrup

MARY MOONEY-GETOFF
Independent Scholar, Northampton,
Massachusetts
Boston Cooking School; Fireless Cookers; Parloa, Maria

ROBIN M. MOWER
Independent Scholar, New York City
*Cherry Bounce; Coffee Substitutes; Johnson and
Wales; Lemonade; Maple Syrup; Orange Flower
Water; Ratafia; Rose Water; Spinach*

MARYANNE NASIATKA
Researcher and Writer, Plymouth, Michigan
Uncle Ben

JOAN NATHAN
Author of *Jewish Cooking in America*
Bagels; Jewish American Food

MARION NESTLE
Department of Nutrition, Food Studies, and
Public Health, New York University
Politics of Food

JACQUELINE M. NEWMAN
Queens College (Emerita), and Editor, *Flavor
and Fortune*
*Chinese American Food; Chinese New Year;
Chinese Regional Foods; Fortune Cookies*

KARA NEWMAN
Independent Scholar, New York City
Historical Overview: World War I; Twinkies

LUCY NORRIS
Cookbook Author and Independent Scholar,
Portland, Oregon
Pickles; Pickling

MAURA CARLIN OFFICER
Independent Scholar, Gloucester,
Massachusetts
Eggplants

BEATRICE OJAKANGAS
Independent Scholar, Duluth, Minnesota
Scandinavian and Finnish American Food

SANDRA L. OLIVER
Food Historian and Founding Editor of *Food
History News*
*Abalone; Anchovies; Bass; Blackfish; Carp; Catfish;
Chemical Leavening; Cisco; Crab; Crappie;
Crayfish; Eel; Fish, Freshwater; Fish, Saltwater;
Flat; Flounder and Sole; Food History News;
Freshwater Aquaculture; Great Lakes Commercial
Fishery, The; Grunion; Haddock; Halibut; Herring
and Sardines; Lobster; Mackerel; Monkfish; Mullet;
Mussels; New England; Perch; Pickerel; Pike;
Pollock; Red Snapper; Salmon; Sauger; Scallops;
Sea Mammals; Sea Turtle; Sea Urchins; Seaweed;
Shad; Shellfish; Ship Food; Shrimp and Prawns;
Smelt; Squid; Sturgeon; Sunfish; Swordfish;
Terrapin; Tilapia; Trout; Walleye; Whale Meat and
Whale Oil; Whitefish*

LYNNE M. OLVER
Editor, The Food Timeline, Morris County
Library, Whippany, New Jersey
Mock Foods

JANE C. OTTO
Food Consultant, Culinary Adviser, and
Pastry Chef, Encino, California
Liquor Cabinets; Tailgate Picnics

HOWARD PAIGE
Author of *Aspects of African American Foodways*
African American Food: To the Civil War

RUSS PARSONS
Food Columnist, *Los Angeles Times*
Ranhofer, Charles

BOB PASTORIO
Independent Scholar and Food Writer,
Swoope, Virginia
*Bistros; Chemical Additives; Distillation; Fourth of
July; Humor, Food; Poetry, Food; Songs, Food; Stills*

MARK PENDERGRAST
Independent Scholar, Essex Junction,
Vermont
*Coca-Cola; Coffee; Coffee, Decaffeinated; Coffee,
Instant; Coffeehouses; Cola Wars; Folgers; Maxwell
House; Nestlé,* sidebar on *Nestlé Coffee Products;
Starbucks*

CHARLES PERRY
Staff Writer, Food Section, *Los Angeles Times*
Middle Eastern Influences on American Food

MARGE PERRY
Food Writer and Journalist, Tenafly, New Jersey
Irradiation; Packaging

MATTHEW PETERSEN
Food Writer, Chicago, Illinois
Little Caesars

ROSS PETRAS
Independent Scholar, Midland Park, New
Jersey
Department of Agriculture, United States

KIM PIERCE
Food Writer, Dallas, Texas
*Blue Bell; Bundt Cake; Chicken Fried Steak;
Center for Science in the Public Interest; Enchilada,
Fried Chicken; Hoppin' John; Slow Food U.S.A.*

JEFFREY M. PILCHER
Department of History, University of
Minnesota, Minneapolis
Mexican American Food

THOMAS PINNEY
Author of *A History of Wine in America from the
Beginnings to Prohibition*
Wine: Historical Survey; Wine Books

SUSAN McLELLAN PLAISTED
Proprietor, Heart to Hearth Cookery, and
Director of Foodways, Pennsbury Manor,
Morrisville, Pennsylvania
*Corn; Middle Atlantic States; Tastykake; Whoopie
Pie*

KIRK W. POMPER
Principal Investigator of Horticulture,
Kentucky State University
Pawpaw

COLLEEN JOYCE PONTES
Writer, Bronx, New York
Gas Grill; Sandwich Trucks

BARRY POPIK
Independent Scholar, Austin, Texas
Chicken Cookery, sidebar on *Chicken à la King*

LESLEY PORCELLI
Food Writer; Brooklyn, New York
Devil's Food

JAMES D. PORTERFIELD
Independent Scholar, State College,
Pennsylvania
Dining Car; Harvey, Fred; Pullman, George

MARICEL PRESILLA
President, Gran Cacao Company; Chef-owner
of Zafra, Hoboken, New Jersey
*Chocolate: Recent Developments; Cuban
American Food*

GAVRIEL PRICE
Food Writer, New York, New York
Orthodox Union and Food

KATHLEEN PURVIS
Food Editor, *Charlotte Observer*
Funeral Food

Mustard; Nathan's Famous; New England Confectionary Company (NECCO); Nuts; Oats; Okra; Onion Rings; Orange Juice; Oreos; Oscar Mayer; Pancakes; Peach Melba; Peanut Butter; Peanuts; Pepperidge Farm; Peter Paul Candy Company; Pineapple; Pine Nuts; Pistachios; Popcorn; Popeyes; Popsicle; Poultry and Fowl; Pumpkins; Redenbacher, Orville; Reese's Peanut Butter Cups; Rice; Ronald McDonald; Root Beer, sidebar on Hires Root Beer; Roy Rogers; Royal Crown Soda; Salads and Salad Dressings; Sandwiches; Sangria; Sbarro; Shakey's; Smorgasbord; Snacks, Salty; Snickers; Sonic; Soups and Stews; Soy Sauce; Stoves and Ovens: Gas and Electric; Submarine Sandwiches; Subway; Sweet Potatoes; Taco Bell; Tacos; Tamales; Tastee-Freez; Thanksgiving; Thomas, Dave; Tomatoes; Tombstone Pizza; Tootsie Roll; Tuna; Turkey; Vanilla; Venison; Watermelon; Waters, Alice; Wheat; Wienerschnitzel; Yum! Brands, Inc.

JEFFERY SOBAL
Division of Nutritional Sciences, Cornell University
Food and Nutrition Systems

MARK F. SOHN
Culinary Analyst, Pikeville, Kentucky
Appalachian Food

GERD STERN
Cheese Importer and Consultant and Media Producer
Cheese: Historical Overview

BOB STODDARD
Independent Scholar, Claremont, California
Pepsi-Cola

DAN STREHL
Author of *Encarnación's Kitchen: Mexican Recipes from Nineteenth-Century California*
Pinedo, Encarnación

HELEN H. STUDLEY
Cookbook Author and Food and Travel Writer, New York City
Buffalo; Claiborne, Craig

CHARLES L. SULLIVAN
Author of *A Companion to California Wine: An Encyclopedia of Wine and Winemaking from the Mission Period to the Present*
Wine: California Wines

JEAN TANG
Independent Scholar, New York City
Tang

JOHN MARTIN TAYLOR
Cookbook Author and Owner of HoppinJohns.com, Charleston, South Carolina
Southern Regional Cookery

GERRY THOMAS
Writer, deceased
TV Dinners, sidebar on *TV Dinners: A Firsthand Account*

RUTH TOBIAS
Food Writer, Boston
Beans; Brandy; Cafeterias; Corned Beef; Crullers; Dressings and Stuffings; Eating Disorders; Ginger Ale; Hot Toddies; Old-Fashioned; Pickles, Sweet; Roadhouses; Sarsaparilla; Toast

ELISABETH TOWNSEND
Freelance Writer and Photographer, Concord, Massachusetts
Breakfast Drinks; Juice Bars; Low-Calorie Syrup

ALISON TOZZI
Independent Scholar, Brooklyn, New York
Historical Overview: Victorian America to World War I

ALEXA VAN DE WALLE
Marketing Consultant and Writer, New York City
Clarifying

BRIAN WANSINK
Director, Cornell University Food and Brand Lab, Ithaca, New York
Food Marketing

SCOTT WARNER
Food Writer, Chicago
Bayless, Rick; Pépin, Jacques; Puck, Wolfgang; Szathmary, Louis; Trotter, Charlie; Willan, Anne

NAHUM J. WAXMAN
Proprietor, Kitchen Arts & Letters, New York City
Recipes

LYNN WEINER
College of Arts and Sciences, Roosevelt University, Chicago
Baby Food

JAY WEINSTEIN
Author of *The Everything Vegetarian Cookbook*
Bottling; Jelly Rolls; Karo Syrup; Plastic Bags; Rice Cookers; Water

LAURA B. WEISS
Food Writer, New York, New York
Mozzarella; Pumpkin Pie

JAN WHITAKER
Independent Scholar, Northampton, Massachusetts
Tea

MERRY WHITE
Department of Anthropology, Boston University
Japanese American Food

PAT WILLARD
Writer, Brooklyn, New York
Communal Gatherings and Integration; Homemade Remedies; Pies and Tarts

JACQUELINE BLOCK WILLIAMS
Author of *The Way We Ate: Pacific Northwest Cooking 1843–1900*
Arbuckle's; Camas Root; Mint Julep; Pacific Northwest; Pennell, Elizabeth

MICHAEL KARL WITZEL
Author of *The American Drive-In*
Drive-Ins

IZABELA WOJCIK
James Beard Foundation, New York City
Bialy

WENDY A. WOLOSON
Program in Early American Economy and Society, The Library Company of Philadelphia
Candy and Candy Bars; Hershey Foods Corporation; Sugar; Weddings, sidebar on Wedding Cakes

CAROLYN WYMAN
Independent Scholar, Philadelphia
Jell-O; Spam

SANDRA YIN
Associate Editor, American Demographics
Combat Food, sidebar on Military Slang; Dr. Brown's; Nabisco; Plastic Covering

CAROLIN C. YOUNG
Author of *Apples of Gold in Settings of Silver: Stories of Dinner as a Work of Art*
Anadama Bread; Silverware; Tupperware

RUSSELL ZANCA
Department of Anthropology, Northeastern Illinois University
Central Asian Food

MARK H. ZANGER
Independent Scholar, Boston
African American Food: Since Emancipation; Alcohol and Teetotalism; American Chop Suey; Baked Alaska; Bierocks; Booyah; Brownies; Brunswick Stew; Buffalo Chicken Wings; Calas; Campbell, Tunis G.; Caribbean Influences on American Food; Cassava; Chiterlings; Clams Casino; Coush-Coush; Cowpeas; Datil Chile; Ethnic Foods; Fudge; Funnel Cakes; German American Food; Hermit Cookies; Hot Tamales; Hominy Grits; Hush Puppies; Iberian and South American Food; Indian Pudding; Italian American Food; Johnnycakes and Hoecakes; Knish; Liberty Cabbage; Macaroni and Cheese; Natchitoches Meat Pies; Pennsylvania Dutch Food; Pretzel; Shoo-Fly Pie; Succotash; Scrapple; Tamale Pie; Vichyssoise; Yummaretti

Entry Titles by Subject

This topical outline offers an overview of the Encyclopedia, with entries listed in the following subject categories. Some entries appear in more than one category.

The History of American Food
The Geography of American Food
Ethnic and Cultural Cuisines
Types of Food Staples
Cooked and Processed Foods
Drinks and Beverages
Preparing, Serving, and Distributing Food
Meals and Eating
Food and Culture
Holidays
Education, Organizations, and Food Writing
Cookbooks and Manuscripts
Food and Society
Food and Drink Corporations
Politics, Policy, and Issues
Science, Health, and Fads
Biographies

THE HISTORY OF AMERICAN FOOD

Culinary History vs. Food History
Historical Overview
  The Colonial Period
  The Revolutionary War
  From the Revolutionary War to the
    Civil War
  The Civil War and Reconstruction
  From Victorian America to World War I
  World War I
  From World War I to World War II
  World War II
  From World War II to the Early 1960s
  From the 1960s to the Present
Historic Dining Reenactment
Historiography
  FOOD-HISTORY ORGANIZATIONS
    (sidebar)
Myths and Folklore
  JOHNNY APPLESEED (sidebar)
  ROBERT GIBBON JOHNSON AND THE
    TOMATO (sidebar)
  THE ICE CREAM CONE AND THE SAINT
    LOUIS WORLD'S FAIR (sidebar)

Periodicals
  GASTRONOMICA (sidebar)
  FOOD HISTORY NEWS (sidebar)
Pioneers and Survival Food
Prohibition
Tea
  BOSTON TEA PARTY (sidebar)
Temperance

THE GEOGRAPHY OF AMERICAN FOOD

Alaska
Appalachian Food
California
Chesapeake Region, Food and Drink
  of the
Frontier Cooking of the Far West
Hawaiian Food
Middle Atlantic States
Midwestern Regional Cookery
New England
New York Food
Pacific Northwest
Puerto Rican Food

Southern Regional Cookery
Southwestern Regional Cookery

ETHNIC AND CULTURAL CUISINES

Ethnic Foods
African American Food
  To the Civil War
  Since Emancipation
    THE HERITAGE OF SOUL FOOD (sidebar)
Cajun and Creole Food
Caribbean Influences on American Food
Central Asian Food
Chinese American Food
Cuban American Food
Dutch Influences on American Food
French Influences on American Food
Fusion Food
German American Food
Iberian and South American Food
Indian American Food
Italian American Food
Japanese American Food
  CALIFORNIA ROLLS (sidebar)

Jewish American Food
Knish
Matzo
Korean American Food
Mexican American Food
Enchilada
Hot Tamales
Tacos
Tamales
Middle Eastern Influences on American
    Food
Native American Foods
    Before and After Contact
    Spiritual and Social Connections
    Technology and Sources
Nuevo Latino Cuisine
Pennsylvania Dutch Food
Shoo-Fly Pie
Yummasetti
Polish American Food
Russian American Food
Scandinavian and Finnish American Food
    FINNISH PULLA (sidebar)
Smorgasbord
Southeast Asian American Food

TYPES OF FOOD STAPLES
Fruits and Vegetables

Apples
Apricots
Artichokes
Asparagus
Avocados
Bananas
Beans
Blackberries
Blueberries
Broccoli
Cabbage
Cactus
Camas Root
Carrots
Cassava
Cauliflower
Celery
Cherries
Chickpeas
Chile
Citrus
Cowpeas
Cranberries
    CRANBERRIES IN HISTORY (sidebar)
Cucumbers
Currants
Dates
Datil Chile
Eggplants
Endive
Figs
Flowers, Edible
Fruit

Garlic
Grapes
Hearts of Palm
Hemp
Kale
Kiwis
Leeks
Lettuce
Melons
Mulberries
Mushrooms
Okra
Olives
Onions
Pacific Northwest
    WAPATO (sidebar)
Parsnips
Pawpaw
Peaches and Nectarines
Pears
Peas
Persimmons
Pickles
Pickles, Sweet
Pineapple
Plums
Poke Salad
Pomegranates
Potatoes
Pumpkins
Quince
Radishes
Ramps
Raspberries
Rhubarb
Salsify
Soybeans
Spinach
Sprouts
Squash
Strawberries
Sugar Beets
Sunflowers
Sweet Potatoes
Tomatoes
Turnips
Vegetables
Watermelon

Grains

Barley
Corn
Oats
Rice
Sorghum Flour
Supawn
Wheat

Nuts and Peanuts

Almonds
Brazil Nuts

Cashews
Chestnuts
Filberts
Macadamia Nuts
Nuts
Peanuts
Pecans
Pine Nuts
Pistachios
Walnuts

Dairy

Buttermilk
Cheese
    Historical Overview
    Later Developments
Cheese, Moldy
Dairy
Milk
Milk, Powdered
Velveeta

Fats and Oils

Butter
Crisco
Fats and Oils
Lard and Shortening
Margarine
Vegetable Oils

Fish and Seafood

Abalone
Aquaculture
Bass
Blackfish
Carp
Catfish
Clams
Crab
Crab Cakes
Crappie
Crayfish
Eel
Fish
    Freshwater Fish
    Saltwater Fish
    Saltwater Shellfish
Fish and Chips
Flounder and Sole
Freshwater Aquaculture
Grunion
Halibut
Herring and Sardines
Lobster
Lobster Rolls
Mackerel
Monkfish
Oysters
Perch
Pickerel

Pike
Pollock
Red Snapper
Sauger
Scallops
Seafood
Sea Mammals
Sea Turtle
Sea Urchins
Shad
Shrimp and Prawns
Smelt
Squid
Sturgeon
Sunfish
Swordfish
Tilapia
Trout
Tuna
Whale Meat and Whale Oil
Whitefish

Meat and Poultry

Buffalo
Butchering
Chicken
Chicken Cookery
Chili
Duck
Eggs
Game
Goose
Insects
Lamb and Mutton
Meat
Partridge
Passenger Pigeon
Pig
Poultry and Fowl
Turkey
Venison

COOKED AND PROCESSED FOODS

Breads

Anadama Bread
Bagels
Bialy
Bran Muffins
Bread
    TOAST (sidebar)
Bread, Sliced
Chemical Leavening
Hardtack
Scandinavian and Finnish American Food
    FINNISH PULLA (sidebar)

Processed Meats

American Chop Suey
Buffalo Chicken Wings
Bully Beef
Chicken McNuggets
Chicken Fried Steak
Chipped Beef
Chitterlings
Chorizo
Cincinnati Chili
Corned Beef
Fried Chicken
Hot Dogs
Pastrami
Pepperoni
Salami
Sausage
Scrapple
Spam
Stuffed Ham
Vienna Sausage

Prepared and Cooked Dishes

Bierocks
Booyah
Brunswick Stew
Burrito
Canapé
Casseroles
Chicken Cookery
    CHICKEN À LA KING (sidebar)
Clams Casino
Coush-Coush
Crab Cakes
Dressings and Stuffings
Dumplings
Enchilada
Fermentation
    FERMENTED FOOD (sidebar)
French Fries
   Historical Overview
   The Twentieth Century
Fondue
Frogs' Legs
Frozen Foods
    TV DINNERS (sidebar)
    TV DINNERS: A FIRSTHAND ACCOUNT
    (sidebar)
Hot Tamales
Hush Puppies
Indian Pudding
Jonnycakes and Hoecakes
Knish
Liberty Cabbage
Lobster Roll
Macaroni and Cheese
Melba Toast
Mock Foods
Mulligan Stew
Natchitoches Meat Pies
Pancakes
Pizza
Poke Salad
Sauces and Gravies

CHARLES RANHOFER'S BREAD SAUCE
    (sidebar)
Soups and Stews
Succotash
Tacos
Tamales
Tamale Pie
Vichyssoise
Yummasetti

Salads and Salad Dressings

Jell-O
Salads and Salad Dressings

Sandwiches and Wraps

Club Sandwich
Dagwood Sandwich
Denver Sandwich
French Dip
Gyro
Hamburger
Hoagie
Hot Brown Sandwich
Italian Sausage Sandwich with Peppers
   and Onions
Monte Cristo Sandwich
Muffaletta Sandwich
Navajo Tacos
Oyster Loaf Sandwich
Panini
Philadelphia Cheesesteak Sandwich
Pimiento Cheese Sandwich
Po'Boy Sandwich
Reuben Sandwich
Sandwiches
Submarine Sandwiches
Sloppy Joe
Wraps

Spices and Flavorings

Flavorings
Ginger Family
Mint Family
Mustard Family
Onion Family
Parsley Family
Pepper, Black
Prepared Herb and Spice Mixtures
Salt and Salting
Sarsaparilla
Sarsaparilla and Wintergreen
Sweet Spices
Vanilla

Sweeteners

Corn Syrup
Honey
Karo Syrup

Low-Calorie Syrup
Maple Syrup
Molasses
New Orleans Syrup
Sorghum Syrup
Sugar
Sweeteners

Condiments

Condiments
Ketchup
Mayonnaise
Mustard
Peanut Butter
Salsa
Soy Sauce

Breakfast Foods

Breakfast Foods
    AVENA (sidebar)
Calas
Cereal, Cold
Goetta
Hominy Grits

Dessert Foods

Entry Titles
by Subject
_____

xxii

Apple Pie
Baked Alaska
Brownies
Bundt Cake
Cakes
Cheesecake
Cream
Creams, Dessert
Crullers
Custards
Election Cake
Frito-Lay
    FRITO PIE (sidebar)
Fudge
German American Food
Grasshopper Pie
Jelly Rolls
Lady Baltimore Cake
Ladyfingers
    SHOOFLY PIE (sidebar)
New England Regional Cookery
    COFFEE GELATIN (sidebar)
Pies and Tarts
    CHESS PIE (sidebar)
Puddings
    HASTY PUDDING (sidebar)
Peach Melba
Pumpkin Pie
Southern Regional Cookery
    MOON PIE (sidebar)
Twinkies
    DEEP-FRIED TWINKIES (sidebar)
Weddings
    WEDDING CAKES (sidebar)

Sweets

Baby Ruth
Butterfinger
Cakes
Candy and Candy Bars
    PENNY CANDY (sidebar)
    JELLY BEANS (sidebar)
Chocolate
  Historical Overview
  Later Developments
Cookies
Cracker Jack
Devil's Food
Doughnuts
Fortune Cookies
Funnel Cakes
Girl Scout Cookies
Good & Plenty
Gum
Gummy Candy
Hermit Cookies
Ice Cream and Ices
Jelly Bean
Jelly Rolls
Juice Bars
Just Born
Klondike Bar
Krispy Kreme
Ladyfingers
LifeSavers
Liquorice
M & M Milk Chocolate Candies
Marshmallow Fluff
Milky Way
Moon Pie
Oh Henry!
Oreos
Pastries
Popsicle
Reese's Peanut Butter Cups
    REESE'S PIECES (sidebar)
Sally Lunn
Saltwater Taffy
See's Candies
Shoo-Fly Pie
Snickers
Taffy
Tootsie Roll
Twinkies
Whoopie Pie

Salty Snacks

Crackers
Dips
French Fries
  Historical Overview
  The Twentieth Century
Onion Rings
Pasties
Peanuts
Popcorn
Pretzel
Snack Food

DRINKS AND BEVERAGES
Non-Alcoholic Beverages

Birch Beer
Breakfast Drinks
Bubble Tea
Buttermilk
Chocolate Drinks
Cider
Coffee
Coffee, Decaffeinated
Coffee, Instant
Coffee Substitutes
Cream Soda
Dr. Brown's
Dr. Pepper
Egg Cream
Frappes
Fruit Juices
Ginger Ale
Hot Toddies
Ice
Ice Cream Sodas
Kool-Aid
Lemonade
Milk
Milk, Powdered
Milkshakes, Malts, and Floats
Moxie
Nestlé
    NESTLÉ COFFEE PRODUCTS (sidebar)
Orange Flower Water
Orange Juice
    CONCENTRATED ORANGE JUICE
    (sidebar)
Orange Julius
Phosphates
Root Beer
    HIRES ROOT BEER (sidebar)
Rose Water
Sarsaparilla
Sassafrasses
Seltzer
7-UP
Snapple
Soda Drinks
Switchel
Tang
Tea
Water
Water, Bottled
Water, Imported

Wine

Champagne
Fruit Wines
Sangria
Wine

Historical Survey
Later Developments
Eastern U.S. Wines
California Wines
Wine, Hot Spiced
Wine Coolers

Alcohol and Alcoholic Beverages

Alcohol and Teetotalism
Amber Lager
Amber Red Ale
Applejack
Barley Wine Ale
Beer
Beer, Corn and Maple
Brown Ale
Bourbon
Brandy
Cider, Hard
Cordials
Cordials, Historical
Gin
Grog
Light Lager
Low-Carbohydrate Light Lager
Moonshine
Pale Ale
Pilsener
Premium Lager
Prohibition
Ratafia
Rum
Sherry
Spruce
Stout
Strong Pale Ale
Tequila
    MESCAL (sidebar)
Vermouth
Vodka
Whiskey

Cocktails and Mixed Drinks

Bloody Mary and Virgin Mary
Boilermaker
Brandy Alexander
Cherry Bounce
Cocktails
Collins
Cuba Libre
Eggnog
Grasshopper
Highball
Irish Coffee
Lime Rickey
Mai Tai
Manhattan
Margarita
Martini
Mimosa

Mint Julep
Old Fashioned
Punch
Sazerac
Screwdriver
Singapore Sling
Syllabub
Tequila Sunrise
Whiskey Sour
Zombie

Ethnic Drinks

Batidos
Coconuts
Kvass
Pinole
Sorrel

Drink Processes

Brewing
Clarifying
Distillation
Fermentation
Stills

PREPARING, SERVING, AND DISTRIBUTING FOOD
Food Preparation

Adulterations
Bakeries
Cooking Techniques
Fermentation
Frozen Food
Kitchens
    Early Kitchens
    1800 to the Present
Microbreweries
Packaging
Wineries
Yeast

Food Preparation and Serving Equipment

Ale Slipper
Apple-Preparation Tools
Beer Barrels
Beer Cans
Beer Mugs
Biscuit Cutters
Blenders
Bread Machines
Bread-Making Tools
Butter-Making Tools and Churns
Cabbage Cutters and Planes
Can Openers
Chafing Dish
Cheese-Making Tools
Cherry Pitters or Stoners

Chopping Knives and Food Choppers
Coffee Makers, Roasters, and Mills
Containers
Cookie Cutters
Cooking Containers
Cooking Equipment: Social Aspects
Corks
Cornbread Baking Pans
Corn-Preparation Tools
Cupboards and Food Safes
Dishwashing and Cleaning Up
Doughnut-Making Tools
Dutch Ovens
Egg-Preparation Tools
Fireless Cookers
Flytraps and Fly Screens
Fondue Pot
Food Processors
Freezers and Freezing
Frying Baskets
Frying Pans, Skillets, and Spiders
Gas Grill
Glassware
Graters
Grinders
Hearth Cookery
Iceboxes
Ice Cream Makers
Ice Cream Molds
Jell-O Molds
Juicers
Kettles
Kitchens
    Early Kitchens
    1800 to the Present
Liquor Cabinets
Lunch Boxes, Dinner Pails, and Picnic Kits
Mason Jars
Microwave Ovens
Milk Packaging
Mortar and Pestle
Nutcrackers and Grinders
Nutmeg Graters
Pancake Pans
Peach Parers and Stoners
Pie-Making Tools
Plates
    THE LENOX COMPANY (sidebar)
    CERAMICS DEFINITIONS (sidebar)
    THE TRENCHER (sidebar)
Potato-Cooking Tools
Pot Holders
Pots and Pans
Pressure Cookers
Refrigerators
Rice Cookers
Sieves, Sifters, and Colanders
Silverware
Slow Cookers
Stoves and Ovens
    Wood and Coal
    Gas and Electric

Timers, Hourglasses, and Egg Timers
Toasters
Turnspit Dogs
Waffle, Wafer, and Pizelle Irons
Wine Barrels
Wine Bottles
Wine Casks
Wine Cellars
Wine Glasses

Food Processing and Preserving

Bottling
Canning and Bottling
Drying
Freeze-Drying
Packaging
Pickling
Plastic Bags
Plastic Covering
Preserves
Salt and Salting
Smoking
Tupperware
Waxed Paper

Food Distribution

Automats
Chuck Wagons
Convenience Stores
Cooperatives
Delicatessens
Farmers' Markets
Grocery Stores
Sandwich Trucks
Street Vendors
Take-Out Foods
Transportation of Food
Vending Machines

MEALS AND EATING

Appetizers
Barbecue
Birthdays
Breakfast Foods
Bridge Luncheon Food
Clambake
Crab Boils
Funeral Food
Meal Patterns
Picnics
Tailgate Picnics
Weddings

Restaurants and Eating Places

Automats
Bars
Beer Gardens
Beer Halls

Bistros
Boardinghouses
Cafeterias
Coffeehouses
Diners
Dining Rooms, Table Settings, and Table
    Manners
Drive-Ins
Fast Food
Hotel Dining Rooms
Juice Bars
Luncheonettes
Midwestern Regional Cookery
        THE BEST SINGLE RESTAURANT IN THE
            WORLD? (sidebar)
Oyster Bars
Pizzerias
Restaurants
        THE RISE OF RESTAURANTS (sidebar)
Roadhouses
Roadside Food
Saloons
Settlement Houses
Soda Fountains
Soup Kitchens
Taverns
Wine-Tasting Rooms

Festivals, Events, and Special Venues

Amusement Parks
Communal Gatherings
Cooking Contests
Food Festivals
Fund-Raisers
Märzen/Oktoberfest
Pillsbury Bake-Off
White House
        MARTIN VAN BUREN AND THE "GOLD
            SPOON" SPEECH (1840) (sidebar)
        DINNER AT THE WHITE HOUSE, 5 P.M.,
            DECEMBER 19, 1845 (sidebar)
        BUY AMERICAN, OR AT LEAST DECORATE
            AMERICAN (sidebar)
World's Fairs

Institutional Food

Airplane Food
Combat Food
Dining Car
Firehouse Cooking
Prison Food
School Food
Ship Food
Space Food

FOOD AND CULTURE

Drinking Songs
Film, Food in
Humor, Food

Literature and Food
Poetry, Food
Slang, Food
Songs, Food

HOLIDAYS

Christmas
Easter
Fourth of July
Halloween
Kwanzaa
New Year's Celebrations
Passover
Saint Patrick's Day
Thanksgiving
        PRESIDENT'S THANKSGIVING PROCLAM-
            ATION, 2003 (sidebar)
Valentine's Day
Washington's Birthday

EDUCATION, ORGANIZATIONS, AND FOOD WRITING

Boston Cooking School
Celebrity Chefs
Cooking Schools
    Nineteenth Century
    Twentieth Century
Culinary Historians of Boston
Culinary Institute of America
Food History News
Good Housekeeping Institute
Historiography
        FOOD-HISTORY ORGANIZATIONS
        (sidebar)
Home Economics
International Association of Culinary
    Professionals
Johnson and Wales
Library Collections
North American Vegetarian Society
Orthodox Union
Periodicals
        GASTRONOMICA (sidebar)
Radio and Television
Restaurant Awards and Guides
Restaurant Critics and Food Columnists
Wine Books

COOKBOOKS AND MANUSCRIPTS

Advertising Cookbooklets
    and Recipes
Cookbooks and Manuscripts
    From the Beginnings to 1860
    From the Civil War to World War I
    From World War I to World War II
    From World War II to the 1960s
    From the 1970s to the Present
    Community Cookbooks

Children's Cookbooks
Cooking Manuscripts
Recipes

FOOD AND SOCIETY

Advertising
Canning and Bottling
    HOME CANNING (sidebar)
Cooking Equipment: Social Aspects
Counterculture, Food
Gender Roles
Dining Rooms, Table Settings, and Table
    Manners
Etiquette Books
Foodways
Frozen Foods
    TV DINNERS
    TV DINNERS: A FIRSTHAND ACCOUNT
        (sidebar)
Health Food
Jewish Dietary Laws
Kitchen Gardening
Measurement
Muslim Dietary Laws
Nouvelle Cuisine
Organic Gardening
Radio and Television
Rawfoodism
Slang, Food
    MILITARY SLANG (sidebar)
    SODA FOUNTAIN AND DINER SLANG
        (sidebar)
Slow Food Movement
Toasts
Toothpicks
Veganism
Vegetarianism

FOOD AND DRINK CORPORATIONS

A&W Root Beer Stands
Arbuckles'
Arby's
Archer Daniels Midland
Baskin-Robbins
Beatrice
Beech-Nut
Ben and Jerry's
Big Boy
Birdseye Corporation
Blimpie International, Inc.
Blue Bell
Borden
    ELSIE THE COW (sidebar)
Boston Market
Breyers
Budweiser
Burger King
Cadbury Schweppes
California Pizza Kitchen
Campbell Soup Company
Carl's Jr.
Carvel Corporation
Chuck E. Cheese Pizza
Church's Chicken
Coca-Cola
Cola Wars
ConAgra
Coors Brewing Company
Dairy Queen
Dairy Industry
Delmonico's
Del Monte
Domino's
Dunkin' Donuts
Famous Amos
Folgers
Franchising
Frito-Lay
Gallo, Ernest and Julio
General Foods
General Mills
Good Humor
Häagen-Dazs
Hardee's
Heinz Foods
Hershey Foods Corporation
Hostess
Howard Johnson
Hunt's
In-N-Out Burger
Jack in the Box
Just Born
Keebler
Kellogg Company
Kentucky Fried Chicken
Kraft Foods
Little Ceasars
Lüchow's
Mars
Maxwell House
McDonald's
Miller Brewing Company
Mondavi Wineries
Mrs. Fields' Cookies
Nabisco
Nathan's Famous
Nestlé
    NESTLÉ COFFEE PRODUCTS (sidebar)
New England Confectionary Company
    (NECCO)
Oscar Mayer
Pepperidge Farm
Pepsi-Cola
Peter Paul Candy Company
Piggly Wiggly
Pillsbury
Pizza Hut
Popeyes
Post Foods
Roy Rogers
Royal Crown Cola
Sara Lee Corporation
Sbarro
Shakey's
Sonic
Starbucks
Stuckey's
Subway
Swanson
Taco Bell
Tastee-Freez
Tastykake
Tombstone Pizza
Wendy's
Wienerschnitzel
White Castle
Yum! Brands, Inc.

Advertising Icons and Fictitious Characters

Aunt Jemima
Betty Crocker
Campbell Soup Kids
Jolly Green Giant
Mr. Peanut
Pillsbury Doughboy
Popeyes
Quaker Oats Man
Rastus
Ronald McDonald
Uncle Ben

POLITICS, POLICY, AND ISSUES

Advertising
Department of Agriculture,
    United States
Farm Labor and Unions
Farm Subsidies, Duties, Quotas,
    and Tariffs
Food and Drug Administration
Food Marketing
Food Stamps
Hunger Programs
International Aid
Law
Meals on Wheels
McDonaldization
North American Free Trade
    Agreement
Politics of Food
Pure Food and Drug Act
Radio and Television
School Food
Settlement Houses
Soup Kitchens

SCIENCE, HEALTH, AND FADS

Alcoholism

Aquaculture
Aseptic Packaging
Baby Food
Biotechnology
Center for Science in the Public
    Interest
Chemical Additives
Community-Supported Agriculture
Diets, Fad
Eating Disorders
Fletcherism
Food and Nutrition Systems
Freshwater Aquaculture
Heirloom Vegetables
Homemade Remedies
Irradiation
Nutrition
Obesity
Organic Food
Politics of Food
Veganism
Vegetarianism
Vitamins

BIOGRAPHIES

Armour, Philip Danforth
Bayless, Rick

Beard, James
Beecher, Catharine
Birdseye, Clarence
Bitting, Katherine
Brady, Diamond Jim
Brown, Helen Evans
Campbell, Tunis G.
Carver, George Washington
Child, Julia
Child, Lydia Maria
Claiborne, Craig
Farmer, Fannie
Fisher, M. F. K.
Gibbons, Euell
Graham, Sylvester
Harvey, Fred
Hearn, Lafcadio
Hines, Duncan
Jefferson, Thomas
Jennie June
Johnson, Howard
Karcher, Karl N.
Kellogg, John Harvey
Lagasse, Emeril
Leslie, Eliza
Lincoln, Mrs.
Lowenstein, Eleanor
Mondavi, Robert

Oscar Mayer
Parloa, Maria
Pennell, Elizabeth
Pépin, Jacques
Pinedo, Encarnación
Prudhomme, Paul
Puck, Wolfgang
Pullman, George
Randolph, Mary
Ranhofer, Charles
Redenbacher, Orville
Richards, Ellen Swallow
Rombauer, Irma
Rorer, Sarah Tyson
Sanders, Colonel
Simmons, Amelia
Sinclair, Upton
Stewart, Martha
Swift, Gustavus Franklin
Szathmary, Louis
Thomas, Dave
Trotter, Charlie
Tschirky, Oscar
Waters, Alice
Wiley, Harvey
Willan, Anne
Wilson, Mary Tolford
Yan, Martin

A&W Root Beer Stands

On June 20, 1919, Roy Allen opened a root beer stand in Lodi, California, brewing the beverage from a recipe he had bought from an Arizona pharmacist. Allen's gimmick was to freeze the glass mugs so that the root beer would stay icy cold to the last drop. He offered these frosty mugs of his home-brewed special root beer for a nickel. Things went well, and Allen soon opened more stands in Stockton and Sacramento; one of these outlets was a drive-in—a novel concept in those early years of the automobile age. "Tray-boys" and "tray-girls" (later called carhops) took orders and served customers, who never had to step out of their cars. In 1920 Allen took Frank Wright, an employee at the Stockton stand, as his partner; combining their initials, they called the company A&W Root Beer. After opening A&W stands in California, Utah, and Texas, Allen eventually bought out Wright, trademarked the A&W Root Beer logo (an arrow and target), and began to franchise his operation.

Unlike many franchises, A&W thrived during the Depression: By 1933 A&W had 170 outlets, and by 1941 there were 260 A&W Root Beer stands nationwide. World War II, with its labor shortages and sugar rationing, took its toll, but once the war ended, A&W began to grow anew. In the 1950s, Roy Allen sold the business to the Nebraskan Gene Hurtz, who formed the A&W Root Beer Company. Within ten years, the number of A&W outlets had increased to more than two thousand. The first A&W Root Beer outlet opened in Canada in 1956, followed by the first stands in Guam and the Philippines in the early 1960s.

At about this time, A&W was sold to the J. Hungerford Smith Company, which had manufactured the concentrate for the beverage almost from the first. Three years later, United Fruit Company (later renamed United Brands Company) acquired the firm. Within this structure, the company name was changed to A&W International and, in 1971, to A&W Beverages, Inc. At that time, the beverage was test-marketed in bottles and cans in California and Arizona, and subsequently distributed nationally, along with sugar-free, low-sodium, and caffeine-free versions. In 1974 the company introduced its mascot, "The Great Root Bear."

In 1975 the National Advisory Council of the National A&W Franchisees Association (NAWFA) formed an elected board—the first time in industry history that franchisees had a voice in the formation of their contract. A standardized restaurant menu was created in 1978. The new A&W Great Food Restaurants included salad bars and ice cream bars along with hot dogs, hamburgers, and other family fare. At the same time, A&W Restaurants, Inc., a wholly owned restaurant franchise subsidiary, was formed.

The shopping-mall and real-estate tycoon A. Alfred Taubman purchased A&W Restaurants, Inc., in 1982, and opened new franchises in malls and shopping centers. Smaller "A&W Hot Dogs and More" restaurants were added to franchisees' options. By the mid-1980s, the company had expanded its operations into several Southeast Asian countries, with an office in Malaysia serving as the center for A&W's international operations. In October 1993, A&W Beverages, Inc., became part of Cadbury Beverages, Inc. In the early twenty-first century A&W Beverages continued under the ownership of Plano, Texas–based Dr Pepper/Seven Up, Inc., the largest non-cola soft drink enterprise in North America and the largest subsidiary of London-based Cadbury Schweppes.

BIBLIOGRAPHY

Funderburg, Anne Cooper. *Sundae Best: A History of Soda Fountains.* Bowling Green, OH: Bowling Green State University Popular Press, 2002.

Jakle, John A., and Keith A. Sculle. *Fast Food: Roadside Restaurants in the Automobile Age.* Baltimore: Johns Hopkins University Press, 1999.

Langdon, Philip. *Orange Roofs, Golden Arches: The Architecture of American Chain Restaurants.* New York: Knopf, 1986.

ANDREW F. SMITH

Abalone

Now considered a luxury shellfish, abalone is found on the Pacific Rim and along the coast of California. The commercial abalone fishery was closed in 1997, although some abalone is taken in a sport fishery north of San Francisco, and it is being farm raised. In earlier times, abalone was taken by Native Americans. In the mid-nineteenth century the Chinese in California fished for abalone, drying and salting the meat for export to China and selling the shells, which were the chief object of the few Anglo-Americans involved in the fishery. The shells were polished and used for inlay, jewelry, mantle ornaments, and soap dishes. When the shallow-water abalone fishery was closed in approximately 1900, Japanese American divers fished for abalone in the subtidal zone.

The Latin species name for abalone, *haliotis*, means "sea ear" and refers to the shape of the creature. The name "abalone" comes from the Spanish word *aulon* or *aulone*. There are nine species of abalone, but the primary food species are the red and pink, or pinto, abalone, the red being harvested commercially in California, and the pinto being harvested in British Columbia, Canada, and Alaska. Red, pink, and green abalone are farm raised. Most abalone are considered suitable for harvest when the shells are approximately four inches long. The shellfish must be cooked very quickly, usually panfried, or else it toughens.

SANDRA L. OLIVER

Additives, *see Chemical Additives*

Adulteration

Adulteration is the practice of adding unsafe amounts of chemical preservatives to foods and drinks, or adding color to conceal inferior or deteriorated food and drink products, or mixing inexpensive foods and drinks with expensive ones so as to reduce costs, or substituting inexpensive foods and drinks for expensive ones. Adulteration has played a large role in the history of American food and drink; the public's demand for federal protection from unscrupulous and dishonest producers and manufacturers at the beginning of the twentieth century led to the breakthrough passage in 1906 of both the Pure Food Act and the Meat Inspection Act.

Industrialization and Fraud

Although adulteration of American food and drink existed during the eighteenth century, it was not prevalent until the end of the nineteenth century, after dramatic changes had taken place in the nation's food industry. Before the end of the Civil War in 1865, most food was obtained locally. Americans knew where their food was made and who made it. The distance between producer and consumer was usually the length of a handshake—a distance that ensured the quality of most food products by means of the producer's personal guarantee.

After the Civil War, as industry moved people from rural to urban areas, cities grew and Americans became distant from the producers and manufacturers of their food. By 1875 a national railroad system transported food from farms and ranches to centrally located urban processing locations; in turn, the railroads carried jarred, tinned, and paper-packaged food to distant consumers. America had developed a national commerce in food. Few consumers knew how their food was produced, manufactured, or handled.

Taking advantage of this situation, many food companies developed inexpensive goods as fraudulent substitutes for more costly ones, thereby decreasing costs and increasing profits. In addition, the distance food traveled and the time that elapsed between production and sale created significant problems with respect to preservation. Food producers addressed these problems by using various chemical additives to prevent decomposition, hide decay, restore natural color, and modify flavor.

By the end of the nineteenth century, most American food and drink was adulterated. Against this wave of corporate irresponsibility there arose in the United States a movement supporting a return to pure food. The leader of this effort was Dr. Harvey W.

Wiley, the chief of the Department of Agriculture's Bureau of Chemistry. He and his staff chemists proved that most of America's food was adulterated for producers' economic benefit. These chemists and their supporters concluded that America needed a federal law prohibiting adulteration.

For approximately twenty-five years, between 1879 and 1905, the pure food movement was unsuccessful in its attempts to get a national pure food law passed by Congress. During that period more than one hundred bills were introduced in Congress; all of them failed under lobbying pressure from food and liquor manufacturers.

Forces of Change

In 1906 two significant events drove Congress to pass a federal pure food law. First, Dr. Wiley finished a controlled study of the effects of chemical preservatives on healthy people. Twelve young men volunteered to eat their meals at the Bureau of Chemistry in Washington, DC. They agreed to eat pure food only; however, the volunteers also took capsules that contained increasing doses of chemical preservatives. For this reason, the press gave the volunteers the melodramatic title "the Poison Squad."

When Dr. Wiley testified before the House of Representatives in February 1906, he reported that the volunteers suffered various degrees of illness, including stomach pain, dizziness, nausea, and significant weight loss. Nine of the twelve had to drop out of the experiment because of illness. The "Poison Squad" experiments proved to many Americans that chemical preservatives were harmful to their health. Second, in the same month, Upton Sinclair's novel *The Jungle* was published. In *The Jungle*, Sinclair exposed the evils of immigrant victimization in Packingtown—the stockyards and slaughterhouses of Chicago. Although Sinclair's novel was not about pure food, American readers focused their attention on the dozen or so pages of the book that described the unsanitary conditions in the slaughterhouses, the limited scope of federal meat inspections, and the ineffectualness of inspectors.

President Theodore Roosevelt read *The Jungle* in March 1906. Concerned about the adverse economic impact of Sinclair's novel on American meat exports, Roosevelt decided that a law was needed authorizing complete control over the meatpacking process by federal inspectors. This law, called the Meat Inspection Act, was passed by the Congress.

Meanwhile, the Senate had passed a pure food bill, but the leadership of the House decided that the bill was too controversial and slated it to die quietly in committee without reaching the House floor for a vote. President Roosevelt obtained the release of the pure food bill from committee. Pushed along by Roosevelt, the impetus of the meatpacking reform legislation, and the pure food reformers, it finally passed Congress.

President Roosevelt signed both bills into law on June 30, 1906.

The Pure Food Act of 1906

The Pure Food Act prohibited the introduction into interstate commerce of any food that was adulterated or misbranded. The statutory definition of adulteration was broad. It included the addition of any substance that diminished the food's quality or reduced its strength; the use of a fraudulent substitute; the removal of any valuable part of the food; the concealment of any damage or inferiority by coloring, coating, or staining; the addition of any poisonous or deleterious ingredient; and the incorporation of any filthy, decomposed, or putrid animal or vegetable substance into the food.

Enforcement of the Pure Food Act of 1906 and its successor, the Federal Food, Drug, and Cosmetic Act of 1938, greatly decreased the adulteration of food during the twentieth century. Adulteration has not been eliminated, however. In addition, uninspected imported food containing unregulated, excessive amounts of chemical preservatives presents a significant risk of illness. In the early twenty-first century, it remained to be seen whether the federal government would muster sufficient resources to defeat the continuing problem of adulteration.

[See also Food and Drug Administration; Law; Pure Food and Drug Act; Sinclair, Upton; Wiley, Harvey.]

BIBLIOGRAPHY

Sinclair, Upton. *The Jungle*. Introduction and notes by James R. Barrett. Urbana: University of Illinois Press, 1988.

Wiley, Harvey W. "The Pure Food Battle; Looking Backward and Forward." In *1001 Tests of Foods, Beverages, and Toilet Accessories, Good and Otherwise*. Revised ed. New York: Hearst's International Library Co., 1916.

ROBERT W. BROWER

Advertising

American food culture has been influenced by advertising like no other in history. The process began with the Industrial Revolution, but by the 1920s most of the marketing and advertising techniques we would recognize today were already in place. There were billboards and newspaper ads; promotional gimmicks, premium giveaways and direct mail; attractive store displays and enticing packaging promising new and improved health, wealth, and motherhood. Experts, celebrities, cartoon characters, and even plain-Jane regular folk pitched everything from canned soup to fake lard. And by the end of the 1920s, even the brand new mass medium of radio had been enlisted to sell the reinvented American diet.

The earliest form of advertising, placards identifying a particular business, had appeared in America by the mid-seventeenth century. The most prominent of these signboards promoted inns, taverns, and coffeehouses, often with an iconic picture rather than text. This idea lives on in McDonald's golden arches.

By the early eighteenth century, print advertising was beginning to make inroads, first in the form of broadsides and leaflets that might be posted on trees, posts, and buildings and, somewhat later, as actual advertisements in newspapers. Those began to show up around 1704, when the *Boston Newsletter* began publication. For many years, advertising consisted of little more than lists of merchandise.

But the era between the Civil War and World War I changed everything, as the country was completely transformed in ways that made advertising as we now know it possible. The railroads united America into one national market, while national magazines now reached into every home. A skyrocketing urban population meant that many could no longer cultivate their own supper, and as a result a cash market for not only food but also consumer goods exploded.

For some the Industrial Revolution meant science and progress, but many found the changes unsettling. The farm folk who crowded into the cities—whether from Massachusetts or Calabria—could no longer count on their traditional culture to tell them what to eat. In the countryside farmwomen had been just as productive as men, but in the capitalist economy the husband was required to be the sole breadwinner while the wife was expected to do the shopping. Women had to be taught their new role as consumers. No wonder the advertisers had such a receptive audience.

As late as the 1880s, most advertisements still performed the traditional function of informing consumers about the availability, costs, and characteristics of goods. Patent medicine sellers and soap manufacturers however, pioneered a fresh approach that was more purely based on hype. The soap ads made luxury, glamour, and wholesomeness as much a selling point as cleanliness, while the patent medicine notices promised bogus cures for everything from neuralgia to baldness. Coca-Cola was first sold as a patent medicine, promoted as "The Ideal Brain Tonic," in an 1892 ad headline.

The cereal industry subsequently copied the nostrum sellers' lead, placing notices full of testimonials in national magazines, advertising cures for vague maladies, even putting on circuslike public displays. Kellogg's Corn Flakes, Post Grape Nuts, and Quaker Oats were all originally promoted as health foods. Grape Nuts was even advertised as an alternative to surgery for an inflamed appendix and recommended for consumption, malaria, and loose teeth. Even foods like chocolate and beer were hyped for their healthfulness. Later, in the 1920s, vitamins were all the rage, even if their function was barely understood. Accordingly, Sunkist oranges were promoted for their "Vitamines [sic] and rare salts and acids."

FOOD PRODUCTS

FRAY=BENTOS

In the little South American Republic of Uruguay is the birth place of Liebig Company's Extract. The factory which in 1865 consisted of one small workshop, now occupies a whole town in the vicinity of the rich cattle fields, where freshness of raw material, cleanliness and economy of working, and scientific experience, unite to produce the extract which the world's doctors, nurses, housekeepers and cooks, stamp by their universal approval as being unapproached in concentration, flavor and efficacy.

LIEBIG COMPANY'S EXTRACT
OF BEEF

WHITE LABEL SOUPS

20 Varieties ready for use.

Concentrated White Label Soups

7 Varieties, ready for dilution and use. 10¢ can makes 6 plates.

An exquisite blending of flavors with strength. Our booklet explains, free. Note Helmet trade-mark and Kansas City on package.

ARMOUR PACKING CO.
DEPARTMENT R
KANSAS CITY, U.S.A.

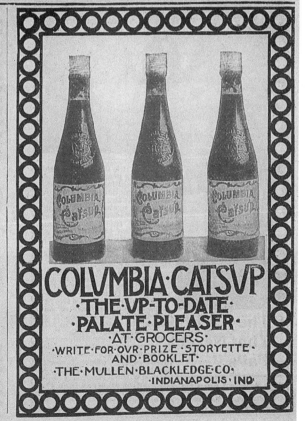

COLVMBIA·CATSVP
·THE·VP-TO-DATE·
·PALATE·PLEASER·
AT·GROCERS·
·WRITE·FOR·OVR·PRIZE·STORYETTE·
·AND·BOOKLET·
·THE·MULLEN·BLACKLEDGE·CO·
·INDIANAPOLIS·IND·

Advertisements from the November 1899 issue of The American Monthly Illustrated Review of Reviews.

MAGIC YEAST RAISES

MAGIC YEAST

OUR DAILY BREAD

"A SQUARE MEAL"

A Magic Yeast advertisement.

from barns to railroad cars to the white cliffs of Dover. Sample boxes and premium give-aways drove the point home.

Companies like Royal Baking Powder came to dominate their respective markets by massive promotional expenditures, spending $500,000 for advertising in 1893 alone.

Initially, there had been a great deal of customer resistance to the packaged foods the wary shoppers could not examine, smell, and taste. The large national manufacturers explicitly took advantage of these fears by promoting the purity, safety, and healthfulness of their brand in both their packaging and print material. Royal Baking Powder always came with the tagline "Absolutely Pure." Jell-O was "Approved by the Pure Food Commissioners."

In the post–Civil War era, entirely new foods like Jell-O, breakfast cereal, and even eating chocolate had to be introduced to an ignorant public. In the case of Post, Quaker, and Kellogg's advertising often cost more than what was in the box. Will Kellogg once spent one third of his funds on a *single page* in the widely circulated *Ladies' Home Journal* to promote his Corn Flakes. The demand for chocolate exploded only when companies led by Hershey started to sell and market their inexpensive candy bars.

It was not only new foods that had be explained. Over the years, consumers also had to be taught that they needed appliances like toasters, blenders, microwave ovens, and food processors.

When it came to educating the public about new food products, premium cookbooks were popular with manufacturers and consumers alike. These promotional guides, cooked up in the test kitchens of companies who manufactured products like Tabasco hot sauce, Carnation condensed milk, Nestlé's chocolate and, of course, Campbell's soup, influenced the cooking of several generations. Often, the recipes developed for the cookbooks migrated to the package itself. Nestlé first printed the Toll House Cookie recipe on the back of its chocolate bars.

Company recipes also appeared in publications such as *Ladies' Home Journal, Women's Home Companion,* and *Good Housekeeping,* side by side with the articles. Often, the recipes in the ads outnumbered the recipes in the editorial. Not that it made so much difference; many of the dishes developed at the magazines were barely distinguishable from those in the advertisements.

From the beginning, it was recognized that women were the target of all this advertising since they were the ones buying food and kitchen products. Accordingly, the pitches were presented with delicate drawings, pastel colors, and serif typefaces. In an attempt to appeal to consumers' presumed maternal feelings, young children have often appeared in ads of every kind from the Morton's salt girl to the Campbell's kids. Sex has also been long used to sell products from Cool Whip to wine

By the 1970s foods were hyped as lowering cholesterol and decreasing the incidence of various cancers, and promoted as salt-reduced, low-fat, and sugar-free. The trend got a further boost during the deregulatory climate of the 1980s and 1990s, when the government allowed advertisers much broader leeway in making health claims. In this new environment, Kellogg's All-Bran as well as Lipton Tea could be pitched as cancer fighters, and packaged butter promoted as containing "zero carbs."

Proprietary packaging came in the late nineteenth century. Up until then, most goods had been sold in bulk, but the new food manufacturers like Heinz and Nabisco realized that they could maximize their profits by selling under their own brand in attractive packages emblazoned with their name.

One of the earliest basic commodities to have a national brand identity was Quaker Oats, mainly due to an ad campaign that placed the company's logo on everything coolers. As early as 1912, an ad for Nabisco Sugar Wafers featured an illustration of a shirtless Hiawatha, a demure Indian maiden sheltered behind his buff torso.

Advertisers not only explained how to seduce and keep a husband but also how to raise and feed the resulting baby. Commercially prepared baby food first came on the market in the 1870s and the campaign to convince mothers of its superiority knew no bounds. Manufacturers of processed baby food also produced child-care guides with recipes. Since these guides were often written by physicians, women came to trust the brand-name foods for which the pamphlets were produced.

As appealing as advice from "experts" might be, food manufacturers have often sought to imbue their brand-name product with personality by using, or inventing, an icon or spokesperson to hawk their wares. A very early example of this was Baker's Chocolate's "La Belle Chocolatiere"—introduced in 1825. One of the best-known icons was the African American character on Aunt Jemima pancakes, based on a real person hired to flip flapjacks at the 1893 Chicago World's Columbian Exhibition. Over the years, children and celebrities have been popular, but even animals—like Tony the Tiger on Kellogg's Frosted Flakes—were roped in as spokesbeasts.

Needless to say, everything advertisers have claimed has not always been strictly true. The federal government recognized this when they passed the first Pure Food and Drug Act into law in 1906. Subsequent legislation strengthened the regulations through the 1970s but in the 1980s and 1990s the rules were once again relaxed. The 1994 Dietary Supplement Health and Education Act explicitly *restrained* the government from regulating many health claims.

The government itself has occasionally paid for advertising to get its view across. At the time of the world wars, Washington promoted the use of alternatives to foods needed by the boys at the front. Nutrition has also been a focus. In 1917 the U.S. Department of Agriculture published *How to Select Foods*, the first of many pamphlets intended to educate the public. By the 1990s, the government efforts mostly focused on promoting a lower fat, higher carbohydrate diet that was illustrated as a food "pyramid." Yet not surprisingly, the results were lackluster given that the annual educational budget of the USDA was not even half of what McDonald's spent on print and broadcast ads at the time.

Broadcasting arrived in the 1930s with radio, but it was television that would deliver a truly mass audience for the advertisers. In the early days of radio, ad agencies not only created advertising messages but—before the establishment of networks—even produced the actual programs. At first, the main form of advertising took the form of sponsorship, but soon spot ads became ubiquitous. Print ads drove home the connection between a particular program and its sponsor.

The postwar era not only tore up the landscape to make room for suburban subdivisions but also concomitantly transformed shopping patterns, ways of eating, and even socializing rituals. The new jumbo-sized supermarkets required bigger, bolder packaging and eye-catching displays. The car culture created a demand for fast food. The new houses springing up everywhere needed plenty of kitchen appliances. Of course the most popular appliance was a television; by 1960, 90 percent of American households had one.

Television advertising reflected the times. In the 1950s, the Cold War could be enlisted to sell Ovaltine with spots featuring "Captain Midnight" in his high-tech bunker. The youthful aspirations of the Vietnam generation were probably best expressed in a 1971 Coca-Cola commercial where a huge chorus sang "I'd like to teach the world to sing / In perfect harmony / I'd like to buy the world a Coke / And keep it company / That's the real thing." Since the sexual revolution of the 1970s, sex has been used much more blatantly to attract viewers' attention with commercials verging on soft porn.

The arrival of TV now meant that even preliterate children were targeted for ads. Commercials aimed at children were carefully constructed to catch their attention, thus they often feature other kids, fuzzy animals, and especially cartoon characters. As a result kids wield increasing influence on what the family eats. In the 1990s a survey of kids aged six to fourteen reported that about two-thirds exerted "some" to "a lot" of influence on the family's choice of restaurant. No wonder that fast food restaurants have gone out of their way to make themselves attractive with playgrounds and toy giveaways that are in turn cross-marketed with television or movie characters. Then, once the kids are old enough to go to school, logo-emblazoned soft-drink dispensers are ubiquitous.

Since the 1970s, advertising has begun to appear on just about any medium that would accommodate it, from t-shirts and baseball caps to parking meters and public restrooms. Corporate sponsorship took over the once countercultural rock concerts with brands like Coke, Pepsi, and Bacardi Rum subsidizing tours. Movie producers began to charge for product placement in films. Perhaps the most successful was the use of Reese's Pieces candy in the movie E.T. (1982), which resulted in a sales increase of 85 percent.

It has been estimated that in the early 1970s the daily number of ads targeted at the average American was 560; by 1999 this number had jumped to 3,000.

Television too has changed. What used to be an undifferentiated mass medium controlled by only three networks began to transform, in the 1970s, into a smorgasbord of hundreds of channels. These channels were designed around delivering a particular demographic to advertisers, whether children, teenagers, women, African Americans, Hispanics, or any other niche market. In reaching out to these new audiences, the commercials actually depicted people of color for the first time without the early stereotypes. Some, like the home shopping channels, even dispensed with the programs to dedicate themselves to commercials 24/7. For those particularly interested in cooking and eating, the Food Channel delivered food manufacturers a particularly engaged viewership. With the Internet, advertisers saw the chance to customize their message to individual households.

The contemporary American diet is largely a result of the advertising and marketing that has nurtured it over the last 120 years. Our gulp-and-go lifestyle may have originated long before the advent of corn flakes and Gatorade, but it cannot be denied that the hundreds of billions spent each year on advertising have influenced our eating habits. The world is following suit.

BIBLIOGRAPHY

Carson, Gerald. *Cornflake Crusade*. New York: Rinehart, 1957.

Guber, Selina S., and Jon Berry. *Marketing to and through Kids*. New York: McGraw-Hill, 1993.

Hill, Daniel Delis. *Advertising to the American Woman, 1900–1999*. Columbus: Ohio State University Press, 2002.

Krondl, Michael. *Around the American Table: Treasured Recipes and Food Traditions from the American Cookery Collections of the New York Public Library*. Holbrook, MA: Adams, 1995.

Nestle, Marion. *Food Politics: How the Food Industry Influences Nutrition and Health*. Berkeley: University of California Press, 2002.

Norris, James D. *Advertising and the Transformation of American Society, 1865–1920*. New York: Greenwood Press, 1990.

Strasser, Susan, *Satisfaction Guaranteed: The Making of the American Mass Market*. New York: Pantheon, 1989.

MICHAEL KRONDL

Advertising Cookbooklets and Recipes

Since the mid-nineteenth century, recipes have been used to sell products. At first, recipes were incidental to the products advertised. Publishers hoped that readers interested in the recipes would see and buy the advertised products. As the century progressed, advertisers became much more sophisticated, and recipes often called for the use of the products that were being advertised.

In many ways, advertising cookbooklets reflect the broader advertising industry that developed in the nineteenth century. During the 1850s advertising companies promoted products such as soap. As food processors became important toward the end of the century, the advertising profession turned its attention to selling brand-name foods and drinks, such as Quaker Oats and Coca-Cola. By the beginning of the twentieth century, advertising accounted for 25 percent of the total budget of many food processors.

FOOD SURPRISES

Food Surprises from the Mirro Test Kitchen (c. 1920).

Patent Medicine Cookbooklets
The first such recipes appeared in patent medicine cookbooklets and almanacs. The intent of these small pamphlets was to promote manufacturers' medical products to housewives. The booklets usually included descriptions of products or services and testimonials from satisfied customers. The recipes usually had little to do with the medical products being sold. Good examples include *Mrs. Winslow's Domestic Receipt Book*, published annually from 1861 to 1879, which promoted the medicines of Jeremiah Curtis and John I. Brown of Boston. An even longer series was the *Ransom's Family Receipt Book*, published annually from 1868 to 1925, which promoted the medicines of David Ransom and Company of Buffalo, New York. Both annuals were thirty-six-page pamphlets that were about half recipes and half advertising and testimonials. Druggists distributed them free to customers, who saved them for future reference. Another famous patent medicine maker who also produced cookbooklets was Lydia Pinkham. Her Vegetable Compound for "female complaints" was widely advertised, and tens of thousands of

copies of dozens of different cookbooklets were distributed by the company that bore her name. This genre declined after the Pure Food and Drug Act of 1906 knocked many patent medicines off the market.

Product Cookbooklets
After the Civil War another category of product-sponsored publications appeared. These publications promoted specific foods or culinary equipment. When the U.S. Patent Office began registering trademarks and slogans, the use of brand names and attractive labels grew. Around the same time, a drop in the price of paper and the invention of the rotary press made possible high-speed, low-cost printing. With major advances in color lithography and photography in the late 1800s, brand-name food manufacturers began advertising nationally by buying ad space in magazines and by publishing pamphlets. These pamphlets encouraged customers to request particular brand-name products at local grocery stores rather than to accept unbranded bulk goods. Local stores, in turn, were encouraged to purchase products

directly from manufacturers. This system eliminated the need for middlemen or brokers and reduced prices for retailers and for customers. The recipes in these booklets usually featured the company's products, and these recipes were often reprinted in newspapers, magazines, and cookbooks.

Among the early producers of advertising cookbooklets were manufacturers of cookery equipment. In the 1870s Granite Iron Ware distributed cookery booklets that encouraged the use of the company's pots and pans. Granite Iron Ware was followed by Agate Iron Ware, whose cookbooklets were particularly attractive. Other manufacturers followed, including makers of meat grinders, stoves, and electrical appliances, such as refrigerators, freezers, bread machines, and microwave ovens.

Ingredient-Based Cookbooklets
In many cases, the advertised food products were simply the old generic commodities with new brand names. Because brand-name products required advertising and expensive packaging, they cost more than generic products. Manufacturers had to offer reasons why housewives should purchase their products rather than generic products. Hence, the "new and improved" shibboleth became commonly associated with food advertising campaigns. In addition, many products claimed health benefits.

Many food products, however, were new creations or inventions and had no generic equivalent. In these cases manufacturers had to create a demand for their products. Also, housewives had to be shown how to use these products. As these were showcase recipes, they were often developed by professionals. Two successful early examples include the Shredded Wheat Company and the Genesee Pure Food Company. The Shredded Wheat Company produced a series of advertising cookbooklets provocatively titled *The Vital Question* (1899), featuring dozens of creative uses of shredded wheat; the Genesee Pure Food Company published cookbooklets that included a wide variety of recipes incorporating Jell-O.

Early producers of advertising cookbooklets turned to well-known cookery experts. For instance, Fannie Farmer, the principal of the Boston Cooking School, first published *The Horsford Cook Book* (1895), an advertising booklet promoting the baking powder made by Rumford Chemical Works in Rhode Island. All recipes in the booklet were subsequently incorporated into the popular first edition of her *Boston Cooking-School Cook Book* (1896). Sarah Tyson Rorer wrote advertising cookbooklets for the Marvelli Company (1900), the Liebig Company (1905), the Fairbanks Company (1910), and the Perfection Stove Company (1926). Janet MacKenzie Hill, the editor of the *Boston Cooking-School Magazine*, published dozens of advertising cookbooklets, such as *The Story of Crisco with Two Hundred Recipes* (1914) produced by Procter and Gamble.

A promotional book of recipes distributed by Campfire Marshmallows.

Many early promotions claimed that their products saved consumers time and energy. Then the focus shifted to economy and nutrition. In 1931 *Favorite Recipes of the Movie Stars* suggested a new direction for advertising cookbooklets—using movie stars to push products. In 1933 General Mills published the cookbooklet *Betty Crocker's 101 Delicious Bisquick Creations as Made and Served by Well-Known Gracious Hostesses, Famous Chefs, Distinguished Epicures, and Smart Luminaries of Movieland,* which included many recipes signed by Hollywood movie stars. Two years later, General Mills offered *Let the Stars Show You How to Take a Trick a Day with Bisquick as Told to Betty Crocker.* Of course, the "as told to Betty Crocker" tag is disingenuous, as she was a fictional character invented by General Mills in 1922. Betty Crocker was not the first fictional character intended to sell food products. Probably the first was trademarked in 1877, and the image of a Quaker originally graced the label of a whiskey bottle. This image was more successfully used to sell Quaker Oats, one of the first cardboard-packaged foods in America. Other successful fictional characters, such as Aunt Jemima and Uncle Ben, were also created about the same time.

Children's fantasy characters emerged to promote the sale of particular products. America's sweetener during the nineteenth century was molasses. As the price of sugar decreased, sugar sales boomed, and molasses sales declined. By the 1920s molasses manufacturers had to advertise to attract customers. Brer Rabbit was borrowed from children's literature to sell molasses. The strategy did not work, and molasses has since been relegated to the

position of a minor sweetener. Promotional cookbooklets targeted at children were common, such as *The Little Gingerbread Man* (1923), published by the Royal Baking Powder Company.

In addition to those booklets published by individual manufacturers to sell specific products, advertising cookbooklets were also produced by agricultural and business associations interested in promoting generic products. Calavo, an association of California avocado growers, published recipes encouraging consumers to incorporate avocados in many different dishes. Power companies published cookbooklets encouraging customers to use electrical kitchen appliances.

The single descriptive characteristic of advertising cookbooklets is their diversity. Some were no more than small, one-page, folded brochures while others were actually full-fledged books with hard bindings. As all were intended to sell products, many were written by professionals. As the companies that manufactured the products needed to guarantee that the recipes worked, the recipes were excellent examples of how their products could be used. Hence the recipes in advertising cookbooklets were occasionally much better than those that appeared in regular cookbooks, as were the recipes that manufacturers placed on their labels or inserted into advertisements in newspapers and magazines.

Distribution

Companies circulated cookbooklets in a variety of ways. Some gave them away with their products by inserting them into boxes. Cookbooklets connected with cooking equip-

ment, such as stoves, refrigerators, or choppers, took the form of instruction booklets, providing as a bonus recipes for foods that could be prepared or served using the equipment. Other companies distributed the booklets free through retail outlets. One of the most common ways of distributing booklets was to mention them in a magazine advertisement or on the product package. A cookbooklet would be sent to customers free or for the price of postage. This method gave manufacturers the customer's address, and that customer could then be targeted for future unsolicited product advertising.

In general, advertising cookbooklets were often enticing and usually included illustrations of products, of the foods produced by the recipes, of prizes the company had won at fairs and expositions, or occasionally of company headquarters or the factory, demonstrating its modernity and cleanliness. Early booklets were relatively simple, black-and-white affairs with few illustrations. As time progressed, these booklets became more colorful, elaborate, and attractive. Most were filled with lively anecdotes, engaging advice of the era, and amusing quotes praising the products. The booklets introduced new color processing techniques in drawings and photographs. Color was used as an eye-catcher to promote products and whet the appetite for the depicted meal or recipe. For instance, the Jell-O cookbooklets published by the Genesee Pure Food Company offer some of the best illustrations, including some by Norman Rockwell, who was more famous for his *Saturday Evening Post* covers.

Some cookbooklets were die cuts, shaped like the product or another image related to the company. The Campbell Soup Company, for instance, issued *Campbell's Condensed Tomato Soup* (1914) shaped partly like a tomato soup can. Penick and Ford published a cookbooklet promoting its molasses partly in the shape of Brer Rabbit.

Tens of thousands of advertising cookbooklets were published, and many have survived. Unfortunately, no comprehensive bibliography of advertising cookbooklets has been published. There are an estimated 100,000 cookery pamphlets and leaflets in known collections, and this estimate is probably low. While the success of advertising cookbooklets to sell products is difficult to determine, manufacturers obviously believe they are important. Many companies, including General Foods, General Mills, the Campbell Soup Company, and H. J. Heinz, continue to publish booklets, and it is likely that advertising cookbooklets will continue to be part of food manufacturers' advertising repertoire.

[See also ADVERTISING; COOKBOOKS AND MANUSCRIPTS.]

BIBLIOGRAPHY

Cagle, William R., and Lisa Killion Stafford. *American Books on Food and Drink*. New Castle, DE: Oak Knoll Press, 1998.

Norman, Sandra J., and Karrie K. Andres. *Vintage Cookbooks and Advertising Leaflets*. Atglen, PA: Schiffer, 1998.

Smith, Andrew F. "Advertising and Promotional Cookbooks." *The Cookbook Collectors' Exchange* (September–October 1999): 5–9.

ANDREW F. SMITH

African American Food: To the Civil War

The study of African American food can be broken into two areas: The first deals with its origin in the homelands in Africa during the seventeenth to the nineteenth centuries, and the other deals with its development in America.

Most African Americans trace their descent to the west coast of Africa or inlands drained by large rivers to that coast, a vast expanse of land where diverse Africans grew their staple crops: yams were the staple of the Ashanti, the Yoruba, and the Ibo; plantain (and later cassava) was favored by the tribes of the Congo and Angola; rice, millet, and eventually maize pleased the tribes of present-day Senegambia, Sierra Leone, Ivory Coast, and Liberia.

Some other foods and spices in the region during this period included sorghum, black-eyed peas, sesame seeds, Bambara groundnuts, eggplant, okra, spinach, cabbage, kidney beans, mushrooms, onions, maize, tomatoes, mustard greens, collard greens, lima beans, cucumbers, sugar cane, sweet potatoes, bananas, lemons, mangoes, limes, peaches, coconuts, watermelons, wild game, wild ducks, goats, pigs, chicken, guinea hens, cattle, shrimp, cod, flounder, catfish, crab, salt, Melegueta pepper, coriander, ginger, saffron, thyme, sage, sweet basil, mint, parsley, curry, hazelnuts, and kola nuts.

The cooking utensils included iron pots and pans, leaves of the banana and papaya plants, clay bowls, and gourds. The pots were used to make soups and stews; the leaves were used to wrap meats, puddings, and bread, which were then steamed or cooked buried in hot cinders.

Grating stones along with mortar-and-pestle were used to grind rice, corn, yams, beans, millet, cassava, seeds, or nuts. The African cook used these ground ingredients as a paste to thicken soups and sauces, or as a flour to make breads, bean fritters, and bean cakes. For frying purposes, she used the extracted oil from shea nuts, coconuts, peanuts, and palm nuts.

She grilled meats by impaling them with sharp, thin strips of wood or iron rods, then sauced them over an open pit with lime, or lemon juice, and peppers. Gourds were used as mixing bowls, jugs, drinking cups, measuring cups, storage containers, and spoons. She served her meals in wooden saucers or banana leaves.

HOTEL KEEPERS,

HEAD WAITERS,

AND

HOUSEKEEPERS' GUIDE.

BY TUNIS G. CAMPBELL.

BOSTON:
PRINTED BY COOLIDGE AND WILEY,
12 WATER STREET.
1848.

A portrait and the title page from Tunis G. Campbell's Hotel Keepers, Head Waiters, and Housekeepers' Guide *(Boston, 1848).*

Not all of these foods were available to any one tribe, although they all were in the region during the period.

Once the African cook was transplanted into America, her culinary efforts were directed toward pleasing the palate of those who owned her service. This was, indeed, a challenge to the African cook, but not an impossible task, as the foods and cooking techniques of West Africa were similar to those in the colonies. Although African American cooks distinguished themselves in the kitchens of farm homes in the New England colonies and the Middle Atlantic and, as caterers, sold their pleasing preparations to the public, owned oyster houses, restaurants, and taverns during the period of slavery, it was the Big House cook and the field hand cooks who were among the most numerous cooking practitioners of the times, interpreting, defining, and contributing to America's nascent but ever-evolving cuisine.

On Colonel Lloyd's plantation in Maryland where Frederick Douglass was born in February 1817, sumptuous dishes were prepared by the Big House cook for Colonel Lloyd's table. These included dishes of ducks, guinea fowls, turkey, beef, veal, mutton, perch, drums, trout, oysters, and crabs, which were garnished with asparagus, celery, cauliflower, eggplants, beets, lettuce, parsnips, peas, radishes, cantaloupes, and melons—all prepared for the most demanding palates of not only the Lloyd family, but also of their many friends and guests.

Foods common to the field hand's table contained those that were rationed to the slave, that which he grew on his own plots, or game caught or trapped in the surrounding woods, and fish netted or hooked in the nearby lakes and streams. Some of these foods were johnnycake, greens, cornmeal dumplings, hoecakes, cornbread, sweet potatoes, fried fowl, rice, fish, cakes, pies, tarts, cookies, turnip greens, cabbage, nuts, molasses, peach cobblers, apple dumplings, whole hogs, sheep, beef, cheese, candy, coffee, custards, and so forth. They cooked to please themselves and their families.

The knowledge of African Americans about different manners of food service in the period was not passed down through the century simply by word of mouth. Three authors recorded their knowledge on cookery matters in early books: Robert Roberts's *House Servant's Directory*, published in 1827; Tunis G. Campbell's *Hotel Keepers, Head Waiters, and Housekeepers Guide*, published in 1848; and Mrs. Abby Fisher's *What Mrs. Fisher Knows about Old Southern Cooking*, published in 1881.

Roberts's book provided advice in the management of prominent homes, which included how servants are to perform their assignments; the art of waiting on tables; instructions for cleaning plate, brass, steel, glass, lamps, and so forth; some friendly advice to cooks; and some useful recipes for salad sauce, mustard sauce, currant jam, ginger beer, and

The Heritage of Soul Food

The expression "soul food" is a term grafted from the expression "soul music," which in the 1960s referenced black artists noted for their soulful blues and rhythmic music. The term "soul" was applied also to artists noted for their culinary skills, particularly to field-hand cooks in antebellum America, who performed culinary miracles with foods then thought to be too common for the master's table. These included the South's cheapest staples, such as black-eyed peas, yams or sweet potatoes, collard greens, dandelion greens, turnip greens, chitterlings (the small intestines of hogs), hog maws (the stomach of the hog), ham hocks, trotters (the feet of the hog), hog jowl (the cheek of the hog), cornbread, and so on.

The numerous African American authors who wrote soul food cookbooks in the 1960s (and even in the twenty-first century) invariably listed a wide range of foods, many of which were made from corn, such as cornbread, spoon breads, corn muffins, hot corn cakes, crackling bread, hush puppies, griddlecakes, batter cakes, corn dodgers, corn on the cob, grits, hominy, corn pudding, fried corn, or stuffing for poultry. Other dishes included beaten biscuits, buttermilk biscuits, salmon croquettes, fried oysters, frogs' legs, fried shrimp, fried or stewed catfish, codfish balls, crab cakes, conch salad, country-fried chicken, smothered chicken, chicken and dumplings, chicken salad, and chicken feet soup. Preparations were made from practically all parts of the hog except the squeal— thus fried tripe, barbecued pig feet, fried ham with cream gravy, salt pork and cream gravy, hog's-head cheese, fried or smothered pork chops, neck bones and rice, salt pork and black-eyed peas, fried spareribs, spareribs and lima beans, ham hocks and beans, ham hocks and turnip greens, pig snouts, and pig tails. And the list goes on with peanut cookies, tea cakes, fried or smothered steak, hamburger meat pie with red bean sauce, beef and rutabaga, beef gumbo, pot roast of beef, short ribs of beef, candied yams, fried sweet potato cakes, apple fritters, rice custards, sweet potato pie, lemon meringue pies, chess pie, pecan pie, egg custard pies, molasses pies, fried fruit pies, old-fashioned pound cakes, bourbon pecan cakes, coconut cakes, marble cakes, hash brown potatoes, fried green tomatoes, baked corn and tomatoes, baked eggplant, butter beans, succotash, fried grits, jambalaya, hoppin' John, smothered cabbage, okra gumbo, brussels sprouts, okra and tomato soup, and oxtail soup.

Because African Americans played such a prominent role as the cook-practitioners of the South, interpreting and imposing their preferences in the kitchen on their own and other people's foodways, it is reasonable to view the boundaries between soul food and so-called southern food as extremely blurred; and one is most cautious in saying, if one must, that " 'soul food' is more a determinant based on who cooked it than what was cooked."

HOWARD PAIGE

Hoe cakes and hush puppies.

lemonade. Roberts's prominent position in the culinary trades brought with it community leadership. He sponsored and addressed national abolitionist meetings.

Campbell's book was similar to Roberts's book in that it also contained the best advice to domestics in carrying out their various chores in prominent homes and hotels. He made his purpose abundantly clear on the very first page of his book: "As, truly, order is Heaven's first law, it becomes our duty to aim at, if we cannot attain it, in all things." Campbell offered a wide range of recipes in his book—a total of ninety-eight—covering

hotel dinner dishes, sauces, desserts, cornbread, buckwheat cakes, dumplings, and more. Campbell did not accept a subservient position for himself in America, nor did he advocate such for his compatriots. In 1848 he was already an active abolitionist, and during and after the Civil War, he went south to organize freed slaves during Reconstruction.

Fisher's book contained a total of 152 recipes that she most likely learned in a plantation kitchen in South Carolina. In 1880, at the San Francisco Mechanics' Fair, she was awarded two medals, one for her pickles and sauces and another for her jellies and

Sylvia's, a restaurant that has been serving its famous soul food in Harlem, New York City, since 1962.

[See also African American Food: Since Emancipation; Campbell, Tunis G.; Kwanzaa; Leslie, Eliza; Mortar and Pestle; Southern Regional Cookery.]

preserves. Some of her other recipes included croquettes, sponge cakes, lamb or mutton chops, blackberry rolls, crab salads, and clam chowder soup.

Bibliography

Franklin, John Hope. *From Slavery to Freedom: A History of Negro Americans.* New York, 1967.

Hall, Robert L. "Savoring Africa in the New World." In *Seeds of Change,* edited by Herman J. Viola and Carolyn Margolis. Washington, DC: Smithsonian Institution Press, 1991.

Harris, Jessica. *African American Heritage Cooking.* New York: Simon and Schuster, 1995.

Hess, Karen L. *The Carolina Rice Kitchen: The African Connection.* Columbia: University of South Carolina Press, 1992.

Meltzer, Milton. *The History of the American Negro, In Their Own Words.* New York: Crowell, 1964.

Paige, Howard. *Aspects of Afro-American Cookery.* Southfield, MI: Aspects, 1987.

Howard Paige

African American Food:
Since Emancipation

Although slavery had ended in most northern states by 1830, rising tides of prejudice and the arrival of new groups of European immigrants pushed free people of color out of many trades. One sector that remained open to African Americans was food service: in private homes, as independent caterers, as street merchants, and as cooks and waiters in commercial hotels and restaurants.

The caterers in particular were social leaders and noted abolitionists. W. E. B. Du Bois described the situation in 1840s Philadelphia, but there were similar developments in New York and Boston: "the whole catering business…transformed the Negro cook and waiter into the public caterer and restaurateur, and raised a crowd of underpaid menials

to become a set of self-reliant, original business men, who amassed fortunes for themselves and won general respect for their people."

Philadelphia caterers developed reputations for particular dishes, such as terrapin stew and chicken croquettes, which were both seen as African American specialties, and which were also prestigious foods on the tables of socially prominent white families. By the 1850s, the Philadelphia cookbook author Eliza Leslie was acknowledging that she had gathered recipes from southern cooks, including many "dictated by colored cooks of high reputation in the art." White writers have praised African American cooks and food ever since, but their abilities have also been described as mysterious, innate, nonintellectual, untrained, and secretive. In deliberate contrast, African American food writers have both described their multisensory approach to cooking and seasoning and presented careful measurements, from the first recipes published by Robert Roberts in 1827 to the present day.

African Americans continued to dominate the catering business in northeastern cities into the 1890s and competed notably in Chicago; Washington, DC; and even as far west as San Francisco after the Civil War. African American caterers also held positions of respect in southern cities throughout the era of segregation.

The Civil War did not end all the perils of the black community, north or south, but it did spread the reputation of African American culinary art. Northern soldiers were sometimes welcomed into the homes of free people of color. White southerners were deprived of imported foods by the naval blockade, but pleasantly surprised by what their remaining slave cooks could do with locally grown produce such as sweet potatoes, black-eyed peas, rice, collard greens, and corn-meal. The stereotypes of slave cooks as mistresses of the Big House kitchen have

been backdated from the late nineteenth century, but their basis in fact really arose only during the Civil War period and in the economic depression of the South after the war. Prior to that time, the role of slave cook was more often to cook imported delicacies by recipes dictated by the mistress of the house. After that time, African American cooks fused the two traditions of southern food into regional delicacies.

Since emancipation, economic opportunities for African Americans have varied, but food service has almost always been a possibility, and sometimes the only possibility. For African American males, the railroads provided service employment, including positions as high as head chef, and several railroad chefs went on to write cookbooks, from Rufus Estes at the turn of the twentieth century to Leonard E. Roberts in the 1960s. African Americans were also chefs in restaurants, even and perhaps especially, segregated restaurants. African American men were regarded as the masters of all schools of slow-cooked barbecue and were sought-after cooks at wealthy estates and hunting camps.

Free African Americans continued their prewar efforts as street vendors despite increasing immigrant competition. They were identified with Creole breakfast fritters called "callas" in New Orleans, with Nagadoches meat pies in northern Louisiana, with pepper pot soup and peanut brittle in Philadelphia, and with "hot tamales" (fresh and warm, not spicy) all over the southern states. They sold peanuts, pralines, produce, seafood, and groceries door-to-door.

Within the African American community, tastes persisted for African foods like yam, black-eyed peas, okra, and guinea hen; as well as for the foods of slavery times made from pork and cornmeal; as well for as the fancier southern foods for special occasions like peach pie or tea cakes; as well as for the small game of the South like raccoons and opossums and snapping turtles; but special efforts were made for Sunday dinners and church suppers, with competing pies, potato salads, fried chicken, and barbecue. This layering of hungers reflects the zigzag social progress of African Americans. The African American community was always multicultural, with clear differences between the Gullah-Geechee rice table of the Carolina lowlands and sea islands, and the Creole dishes of Louisiana.

But the community became even more multicultural with the addition of Afro-Caribbean immigrants in the 1920s. With the civil rights movement of the 1950s and 1960s, "soul food" became an interest for white liberal cooks, although segregationists in the South had enjoyed a modified version for more than a century. (The term "soul" for essential "blackness" seems to date from the 1930s and printed references to "soul food" from 1964.)

Within the African American community, the ethnic revival of the 1980s, set off in part by the television miniseries *Roots,* inspired many African American families to investigate African recipes. By the 1990s, Pan-Africanism and a more sophisticated feeling for the African Diaspora developed, and many families found jerk chicken, or Dominican fried chicken, or Trinidadian roti in restaurants catering to Afro-Caribbean immigrants. Recent immigrant communities from Nigeria, Ethiopia, Eritrea, Egypt, Haiti, the Dominican Republic, Cuba, Honduras, and Guyana have also enriched the common pot, the church buffet, school pot-luck, and the restaurant table. Urban markets now sell goat meat and Caribbean seafoods as well as tropical roots, plantains, African cowpeas, and prepared Jamaican meat pies. The Pan-Africanist holiday of Kwanzaa has become widely popular, with its New Year's Eve feast incorporating African and Diaspora dishes.

Another phenomenon within the African American community in the last thirty years has been an interest in dietary reform. This might be traced to the unusual food rules of the Nation of Islam (which add to the restrictions of orthodox Islam strictures against fried foods, hot breads, most cornbread, and pie crust), or to the fasting and vegetarian reducing diets promoted by the political activist Dick Gregory. A much wider circle more casually rejects pork, and urban barbecue establishments in African American neighborhoods now generally offer beef ribs as an alternative to pork ribs. Wide publicity of diet-related health problems has led to a general effort from chefs to homemakers in substituting smoked turkey for bacon as a flavoring in many dishes, and in reducing sugar and salt in traditional "soul food."

[See also AFRICAN AMERICAN FOOD: TO THE CIVIL WAR; APPALACHIAN FOOD; AUNT JEMIMA; BARBECUE; CARIBBEAN INFLUENCES ON AMERICAN FOOD; CARVER, GEORGE WASHINGTON; CHESAPEAKE REGION, FOOD AND DRINK OF THE; DINING CAR; KWANZAA; MUSLIM DIETARY LAWS; RASTUS; SOUTHERN REGIONAL COOKERY; STREET VENDORS; UNCLE BEN.]

BIBLIOGRAPHY

Du Bois, W. E. B. *The Philadelphia Negro: A Social Study*. New York: Lippincott, 1899. http://www2.pfeiffer.edu/~lridener/DSS/DuBois/pnchiv.html.

Roberts, Robert. *The House Servant's Directory*. Boston: Munroe and Francis, 1827. Facsimile, Waltham, MA: Gore Place Society, 1977.

MARK H. ZANGER

Airplane Food

United Airlines, a pioneer in the industry, was the only airline to serve meals on trays from the beginning of commercial aviation. While other airlines had copilots passing out sandwiches to passengers, United employed uniformed stewardesses to serve cold chicken. Many airplane travelers in the early days of the aviation industry's food service complained of how often chicken was served; American Airlines was even nicknamed "the fried chicken airline." Passengers derided chicken as a cheap food option; industry professionals found that chicken's versatility responded well to the demands of in-flight food service.

By 1936 American Airlines stewardesses were filling service trays with food from very large thermoses containing hot food prepared in advance—usually by the airport café—and offering real dishware and flatware to boot. Food would stay hot in the containers for about one to two hours, with no need for reheating. The thermos approach was succeeded by a system of using large casseroles, which provided the advantage of loading meals already plated and hot. Food often stayed heated for many hours with this system, however, and food quality suffered, along with menu choices. Then, around 1945, Pan American worked together with Clarence Birdseye and the Maxson Company to create the convection oven, which would allow frozen foods to be heated on board the aircraft. Maxson called the first convection oven it designed the Whirlwind Oven: it had a heating element in front of a fan and held six meals. Soon afterward, the microwave oven was developed; it has since become the industry standard in aircraft food service preparation.

The first meal trays were served on pillows on passengers' laps, until trays had been developed with lids that would serve to elevate the food in front of the passengers. Finally, fold-out service trays were installed in the seat backs. The three-course meal that has become the standard for airplane food trays grew out of the creation by United Airlines in 1937 of the first functional airplane kitchen, conceived in an effort to improve the quality of food offered during flight. United brought in managers and chefs from hotels to redesign their food service. Don Magarrell, one such hotel manager hired by United, began to supervise the preparation of gourmet meals in the airline's kitchen facilities on the ground and is responsible for the design of the standard three-course airline meal, a design devised to comport with the dimensions of the meal trays:

> In the center of [Magarrell's] twenty-four-by-thirty-inch mock-up was a twelve-inch depression—that was for the main dish. Laid on at the right were coffee, cream, and sugar. Salad in a paper cup took the upper center, dessert the upper left corner, and appetizer the upper right, and there were little holes for salt and pepper shakers. What then emerged from the atelier of Industrial Designers, Incorporated, was a flat, rigid artifact of pressed pulp, light and disposable, but strong enough to hold things in place in choppy air. A cunningly shaped cover, in matching white with blue and buff stripes, fitted over it. (Solberg, *Conquest of the Skies*, p. 220)

The first successful frozen three-course meal fitting the tray's specifications—consisting of meat, potatoes, and vegetables—was marketed by the Maxson Company; the meals were sold to Pan American Airways in 1946.

As the twentieth century progressed, two elements affected the continuing development of airplane food: America became more tolerant of a diversity of eating habits, and a greater diversity of people began using airplanes as a means of travel. To respond to these trends, airlines began offering a greater variety of types of meals that responded to religious, ethnic, or health requirements with respect to food. As of 1995 a trade journal reported that American Airlines offered all of these food options for their in-flight service:

> children's meal...bland/soft (suitable for those with ulcers); diabetic; gluten-free (no wheat, rye, barley, oats, which people with celiac disease cannot digest); low calorie; lactose-free (no milk products); low carbohydrate; low fat and low cholesterol; low sodium; Moslem; Hindu; Kosher; vegetarian; and strict vegetarian (excludes milk products and eggs). (cited in Gottdeiner, *Life in the Air*, p. 103)

During the late 1990s and early 2000s airlines began doing away with meal service on their flights so as to reduce the price of their tickets; some offered cold meals in packs that passengers picked out of coolers as they boarded the aircraft. Passengers grumbled at the bag of peanuts or pretzels served as a snack in place of a real meal, but the market for cheaper tickets remained strong. Many passengers began bringing food on board, most often from the fast food restaurants in airports. Now a few discount airlines sell meals to passengers on board their flights. The sale of airplane meals for profit is perhaps one of the most significant changes in the history of airplane food.

[See also BIRDSEYE, CLARENCE.]

BIBLIOGRAPHY

Gottdiener, Mark. *Life in the Air: Surviving the New Culture of Air Travel*. Lanham, MD: Rowman and Littlefield, 2001.

Haynes, Karla, ed. *Sky Chefs: From the Beginning*. Arlington, TX: Sky Chefs, 1992.

McCool, Audrey C. *Inflight Catering Management*. New York: Wiley, 1995.

Parrott, Philip J. *The History of Inflight Food Service*. Miami Springs, FL: International Publishing Company, 1986.

Solberg, Carl. *Conquest of the Skies: A History of Commercial Aviation in America*. Boston: Little, Brown, 1979.

LYNN HOUSTON

Alaska

A line of salmon tails sticking out of the dirt is an appetizing sight to an Alaskan, especially if the tails come off easily in his hand. This means the fish have ripened into an enigmatic dish known as "stink fish," eaten raw. The line of tails is the fast food version of the dish. The more time-consuming version, meant to be harvested months later, is a cache pit, lined with wild celery leaves and then filled with salmon or salmon heads. Beauty is in the tastebuds of the eater, or, as Cervantes put it in *Don Quixote*, "Hunger is the best sauce." A whale grounded on the beach meant good eating to early Alaskans.

Finding food is crucial to survival. Thus, in prehistoric Alaska, villages or seasonal camping spots were often named after resources. For example, the Taku River derives its name from the Tlingit word meaning "where geese gather." The Athabascan village of Telida gets its name from the fall run of whitefish or *telia*; Telia-da means "place of whitefish."

Fifteen to forty thousand years ago, Asian people walked across a land bridge to the place later called "Alaska." Their long migration was a natural extension of their following herds of grazing mammals, which they ate. Those who made Alaska their permanent home gradually evolved into separate cultures. They became the four major anthropological groups of the state: Eskimos, Aleuts, Athabascans, and Northwest Coast Indians (Tlingit, Haida, and Tsimshian, fishermen of the coast and hunters of the rain forest).

Until Russian and European explorers made contact in the 1700s, Alaska natives ate what was at hand. Eskimos chowed down on bowhead whale, walrus, and seal, along with seabird eggs. Aleuts searched tide pools for shellfish, octopus, and seaweed; they speared seals from kayaks and downed birds with arrows. Athabascans dined on moose, caribou, bear, beaver, muskrat, geese, ducks, and fish. Tlingit, Haida, and Tsimshian consumed steelhead, salmon, herring, halibut, and venison. Menus were seasonal, depending on the migration of caribou, the nesting of birds, and the spawning of fish.

Greens and edible roots supplemented meals. Depending on the habitat, natives enjoyed greens like rosewort, beach asparagus, goosetongue (*Plantago maritima*), pink plume (*Polygonum bistorta*), and king's crown (*Sedum rosea*). They brewed hot drinks from evergreen shrubs, such as Labrador tea (*Ledum* species). Food was eaten raw, frozen, fermented, smoked, dried, or boiled. Hundreds of variations are possible by combining methods. Half-dried salmon, for example, is an Aluutiq dish; salmon is simmered with wild onions before it is ready to store.

Clay cooking pots were known to only a few Eskimo groups; most Alaskans roasted their food on spits or boiled it in baskets. Cooking baskets were woven of split spruce roots; those roots swell when wet, making the baskets watertight. Rocks heated in the fire were added and the contents stirred until the food was done. Tongs removed cooled rocks and added new, hot ones. Preservation of food for the lean months of winter was paramount. Food was dried or smoked; if that was impossible, blubber or whale roasts were frozen in "ice cellars," holes dug in the permafrost. Tlingit packed berries into wooden forms to make "bricks" and strung dried clams on willow withes. Tsimshian preserved wild crab apples in the rendered fat of eulachon or candlefish. Sealskins were hollowed out like gourds to form "pokes," skin bottles in which willow leaves or small birds were stored with oil, which tenderized them. At Barrow during winter months, one can still see haunches of caribou perched frozen on the roof, safe from dogs, and mallards hanging by their necks from front-porch railings.

Celebrations meant Eskimo ice cream or *aguduk*. The Eskimo cook whips seal oil until it is creamy and then folds in freshly fallen snow and tundra roots. The Athabascan version is whipped caribou-leg marrow, cooked meat flakes, and berries. *Aguduk* was served on festive occasions, such as a young man's first successful polar bear hunt or a wedding. Oil from hooligan, seal, or whale was a diet staple, used to soften dried foods and add vitamins, along with a taste something like that of anchovy dip.

Russian fur hunters and settlers introduced new foods—barley, rice, buckwheat, Chinese tea, and flour—as well as a new kitchen tool, the oven. The Aleuts quickly mastered piecrust and began baking pirog, a "fish pie" of salmon, hard-boiled eggs, rice, and onion, enclosed in pastry. The Russians also introduced rudimentary agriculture, with crops like cabbage, radishes, turnips, and potatoes. Walrus stew slowly changed from a simple pot of meat and broth to something complicated, with potatoes and macaroni.

After the United States purchased Alaska in 1867, paddle wheelers began regular journeys up great inland rivers with supplies like dried beans, sugar, oranges, apples, and canned milk. Gold rush prospectors survived mostly on beans and biscuits, often cooked by novices. The author Rex Beach, on a trip to Candle near Nome, where gold was discovered in 1901, wrote in his autobiography *Personal Exposures* (1940), "If the weather wasn't bad it promised to become so and we talked abut little else except that, and indigestion."

To avoid the curse of underdone beans along the gold rush trail, portable soup became the savior of the hour. Beans and bear grease were stewed to tenderness on the stove; then the kettle was allowed to freeze. Next, the soup was dumped from the pot in a lump and stored in a burlap sack. When dinner was needed an ax was applied to the lump, and a few chunks were thawed and heated.

Holidays were celebrated with feasts of roast ptarmigan, sourdough bread, canned pineapple, plum duff, and spaghetti concocted of moose rump roast, goose grease, and dried soup vegetables. Prospectors who lingered to become settlers learned to adapt local ingredients to recipes of the lower forty-eight states. They made ketchup with currants or cranberries, piecrust with black-bear lard, butter with caribou marrow, and mincemeat with moose. Alaskan cuisine continues to evolve, but it is easy to glimpse its roots when a friend brews rose hips with whole cloves for tea, or when mason jars of hooligan oil sit side by side with beadwork on bazaar tables.

[See also RUSSIAN AMERICAN FOOD.]

BIBLIOGRAPHY

Chandonnet, Ann. *The Alaska Heritage Seafood Cookbook*. Anchorage, AK: Alaska Northwest Books, 1995.

Kari, Priscilla Russell. *Tanaina Plantlore. Dena'ina K'et'una: An Ethnobotany of the Dena'ina Indians of Southcentral Alaska*. Fairbanks, AK: Alaska Native Language Center, 1987.

Qawalangin Tribe of Unalaska. *Unalaaskam Qaqagan Qasudaa, "Good Unalaska Food" Cookbook*. Unalaska, AK, 1998.

Paul, Frances Lackey. *Kahtahah*. Rev. ed. Anchorage, AK: Alaska Northwest Books, 1996.

ANN CHANDONNET

Alcohol and Teetotalism

At the time of European exploration and settlement of the United States, Native Americans frequently drank fresh water. This surprised the Europeans, who at home and on ship drank ale, wine, spirits, or (regionally) cider with every meal—men, women, children, and babies. In Europe most urban water sources were dangerously polluted.

Alcoholism is hard to describe in a society in which everyone drinks at every meal. But the colonies had laws against public drunkenness and attempted to pass laws about trading liquor to the Indians—both only sporadically enforced. Apple trees were more reliable croppers than barley, so cider replaced beer for many American families. Drinks were also brewed from molasses, maple syrup, and corn.

Problems with alcohol increased in the eighteenth century, as inexpensive spirits became more common in commerce. Rum was produced for trade in Boston and Philadelphia. Pennsylvania Dutch and Scotch-Irish immigrants put their brewing and distilling know-how to American corn and rye, creating the first American whiskeys.

The first American temperance movements appeared toward the end of the century. In some cases these were branches of temperate British denominations, such as the Methodists, but a nondenominational temperance movement began around the time of the American Revolution, with a 1788 convention that suggested using only beer and cider, under the slogan "Despise Spiritous Liquors as Anti-Federal."

In the Early American period temperance became associated with a series of reform issues that also included abolition of slavery, women's suffrage, public education, and health food. One might specifically give up rum, because sugar was harvested by slaves. Or one might, like Sylvester Graham and the Alcott family, give up leavened bread, because yeast produces alcohol in the action of "putrefaction."

By the 1840s Catharine Esther Beecher, whose minister father founded a temperance movement, thought "it proper to use wine and brandy in cooking, and occasionally for medicinal purposes." In her 1840s cookbook she produced the first nonalcoholic, noncaffeinated recipes for children. Almost all of the new religious denominations that began in America took up aspects of temperance: Seventh-Day Adventism and the Mormon Church, both founded in Early American times, avoid alcoholic beverages and caffeinated drinks. Christian Science, drawing on Adventist ideas of health food, discourages alcohol.

Although prohibition was enacted in a few states for short periods of time before the Civil War, early temperance was a matter of individual conscience. Given that early American cookbooks use wine and spirits in almost every recipe, including cakes and cookies, it is possible to follow the idea of temperance when sweet cider or vinegar is included as a substitution in recipes for mincemeat, syllabub, cakes, plum pudding, or summer drinks. Sweet cider is given as an alternative in minced pie in *American Cookery* by Amelia Simmons (1795).

Baking powder was promoted by some temperance enthusiasts as a replacement for demon yeast in breads and cakes. Temperate travelers or students could stay at Grahamite boardinghouses and hotels, which were both vegetarian and yeast-free.

Historical statistics suggest a spike in alcohol consumption around 1860, with levels of consumption not reached again until the period from 1906 to 1915. After the Civil War the reform coalitions began to diverge, but temperance and women's rights were still strongly connected. A wave of direct attacks on saloons in the early 1870s launched prohibition as a militant movement. The Women's Christian Temperance Union, founded in 1874, pressed not only for suffrage and temperance but also for prohibition, reaching out to rural and religious women.

Prohibition was a women's issue that made men nervous in the 1870s, as shown by the widespread public mockery of Mrs. Rutherford B. Hayes as "Lemonade Lucy" after she banned liquor from White House receptions. By 1890 the temperance position was respectable enough for a temperance punch to be included in *Statesmen's Dishes and How to Cook Them*, a recipe book edited by Mrs. Benjamin Harrison. The movement focused ever more on beverage alcohol, with published recipes for temperance punch and canned unfermented grape juice—the communion wine of dry denominations, promoted by Thomas Welch of Vineland, New Jersey. It is also in the last quarter of the nineteenth century that the British term "teetotaler" (coined in the 1830s for total abstainers) entered American discourse.

The emphasis on individual and family temperance became political with the collection of circulating pledge cards on which young people signed an oath never to drink. The large numbers of these pledge cards were communicated to politicians, and candidates found themselves polarized between "wets" and "dries." Among the wets were working-class immigrants for whom the saloon was a community institution.

National prohibition did not take effect until 1919 and was repealed in 1932. "Near beer" with 3.2 percent alcohol was permitted, as was home brewing and limited commercial wine making for religious use. Prohibition also marked the introduction of oversalted cooking wine. Illegal imported liquor turned American tastes to blended Scotch and Canadian whiskeys. Cocktails, blending often-crude spirits with wines, juices, and flavorings, proliferated and remained part of American taste through the 1960s. Cookbooks of the 1920s have alcohol-free recipes for drinks, often with a winking reference to how much liquor had been used in former times. Many local breweries never reopened after Prohibition, and numerous American vineyards were replanted with fruit trees. American wines did not again become nationally popular until the 1970s. This was followed by a revival of craft brewing in the mid-1980s and a revival of retro-cocktail drinking in the 1990s.

Some localities retained prohibition after 1932. But most antialcohol activism since has used the individual-recovery model of Alcoholics Anonymous (founded 1935). The failure of Prohibition and the hardships of the Depression and World War II produced a tacit pro-alcohol culture in the 1950s and 1960s, with cookbooks published on how to use wine and spirits in every course and manuals entirely on how to mix drinks. Suburban homes included a bar in the basement, so one could have a kind of saloon in one's own home. Government statistics suggest a spike in alcohol consumption in 1946, with a general rise through the 1950s and 1960s to unprecedented levels in the 1970s and 1980s.

Political opposition to alcohol revived in the 1990s with movements for more severe punishments for drunk driving. There has been some overall decline in alcohol consumption by Americans age fourteen and over since 1992. Some surveys indicate that about one-fourth of all American adults are lifelong abstainers, 60 percent drink at times, and between 5 and 20 percent are binge drinkers or alcoholics.

[See also ALCOHOLISM; BEECHER, CATHARINE; GRAHAM, SYLVESTER; PROHIBITION; TEMPERANCE.]

BIBLIOGRAPHY

Oliver, Sandra L. *Saltwater Foodways.* Mystic, CT: Mystic Seaport Museum, 1995.

Zanger, Mark H. *The American History Cookbook.* Bridgeport, CT: Greenwood, 2003. This book was originally commissioned for school libraries.

MARK H. ZANGER

Alcoholism

Alcoholism, also known as Alcohol Dependence Syndrome, is a general term describing many types of alcohol abuse and alcohol dependence. The National Council on Alcohol and Drug Dependence defines alcoholism as a "chronic disease...characterized by a continuous or periodic impaired control over drinking, preoccupation with the drug alcohol, use of alcohol despite adverse consequences, and distortions in thinking, most notably denial." Other authorities contend that alcoholism is not actually a disease, but rather a symptom of other physical and psychological disorders. Despite moral, medical, or philosophical disagreements about the problem, alcoholism is understood to be an individual's compulsive craving for and overconsumption of alcohol.

Both the recognition and condemnation of alcoholism date back through thousands of years of recorded history. Though most cultures around the world used alcohol for recreation, religious ceremony, and medicine, virtually all created taboos against its overuse and dependency. Ancient Greek, Hebrew, and early Christian writings celebrated the role of wine in sacred worship, while consistently warning against the evils of the overindulgence in alcohol. In his Analects, Confucius even spoke about "trouble with alcohol." Throughout world history, each culture defined its own acceptable parameters for alcohol consumption and devised sanctions against chronic or excessive drunkenness. Nevertheless, some individuals in almost every society continued to habitually abuse alcohol, despite ridicule, punishment, and deteriorating health. The excessive drinking of gin became so rampant in England that Parliament in 1751 imposed exorbitant taxes on all hard liquor to stem consumption.

In early America, Protestant religious groups often stressed sobriety, usually allowing moderate alcohol use, but meting out harsh punishments for those who remained persistently drunk. Puritan New Englanders condemned chronic alcohol abuse both as a moral evil itself and even more practically as an economic burden on the resources of their community. Puritans prized productivity and personal virtue and often severely punished chronic drunkards who could not work to provide for themselves or their families. Over the years, controversy over appropriate alcohol use continued in American society, frequently pitting newly arrived Catholic immigrants against native-born Protestant groups, who differed in their definitions of what constituted alcohol abuse. In essence, alcoholism was often culturally defined, with one group's idea of chronic drunkenness simply being another's idea of recreation. Social and political movements continued to attack excessive drinking throughout the late eighteenth and early nineteenth centuries, eventually culminating in an unsuccessful national prohibition of alcohol from 1920 to 1933.

Despite varying cultural perspectives, the concept of alcoholism—that some members of every society just could not control their drinking—was clearly understood for thousands of years. Alcoholism became only formally identified as a serious health problem in the late nineteenth century, as physicians scientifically defined categories of diseases and dysfunction. In an 1879 study, H. Maudley first described "alcoholic insanity," "chronic alcoholism," and "dipsomania," which he defined as "well-marked mental degradation, if not actual mental derangement which shows itself in a fierce morbid craving for alcoholic stimulants and is greatly aggravated by indulgence." Debates raged throughout the twentieth century about the possible physiological or psychological roots of alcoholism; whether alcoholism was a single problem or, rather, numerous disassociated problems. All of these same controversies still exist in the early 2000s, but a notable consensus quickly formed around E. M. Jellinek's 1960 study, *The Disease Concept of Alcoholism*. In this study, Jellinek identifies five categories of alcoholics, each with their own unique physiological origins, patterns of drinking, and adverse health effects. Most important, Jellinek's work reinforced both the medical diagnosis and the popular understanding that alcoholism was a real physical and psychological problem, or disease, instead of an avoidable moral failing. Other medical and psychological research continues, however, which advances still more differing theories about the nature and manifestations of alcoholism, with many studies focusing on the role of genetic predisposition.

Treatment for alcoholism is as varied as the theories explaining it. Severely addicted alcoholics experience intense and often dangerous withdrawal symptoms when detoxified. Treatment often includes a month-long hospital stay. Physicians prescribe drugs to alcoholics that either deter the craving for alcohol or cause unpleasant physical effects, such as nausea, when alcohol is consumed. In the late twentieth century, physicians began to use a variety of new antidepressant medications to treat underlying chemical imbalances in the brain that may cause the alcoholic to drink. The clinical assumption behind this course of treatment adheres to the argument that alcoholism is more symptomatic of other ills than a disease in itself.

By far the most popular treatment program for alcoholism is Alcoholics Anonymous. Self-described as a worldwide fellowship of men and women who help each other to stay sober, it is a mutual help program for recovering alcoholics. Alcoholics Anonymous was founded in 1935 by the stockbroker and alcoholic Bill Wilson. Wilson envisioned a network of small support groups to aid other alcoholics. Today, over 100,000 of these groups meet worldwide. Laying out a twelve-step recovery program, Alcoholics Anonymous stresses the importance of taking responsibility for past behavior, staying anchored in the reality of the present moment, and relying both on other alcoholics and a spiritual "higher power" to achieve continued sobriety. While among the first to acknowledge the disease nature of alcoholism, Alcoholics Anonymous places its emphasis on member spirituality and self-determination rather than on medical solutions.

Alcoholism remains a pervasive and expensive problem in the United States. The National Institute on Alcohol Abuse and Alcoholism says that alcohol abuse costs about $166.5 billion each year. Research continues in an effort to discover the sources of alcoholism and to find ways to minimize problem drinking. Despite now being securely defined medically as a disease, alcoholism still carries with it a stigma of immorality, deviance, or character flaw.

[**See also** ALCOHOL AND TEETOTALISM; PROHIBITION; TEMPERANCE.]

BIBLIOGRAPHY
Dodes, Lance M. *The Heart of Addiction: A New Approach to Understanding and Managing Alcoholism and Other Addictive Behaviors*. New York: HarperCollins, 2002.
Edwards, Griffith. *Alcohol: The World's Favorite Drug*. New York: St. Martin's, 2002.
Hartigan, Frances. *Bill W: A Biography of Alcoholics Anonymous Cofounder Bill Wilson*. New York: Thomas Dunne/St. Martin's, 2000.
Lender, Mark Edward, and James Kirby Martin. *Drinking in America: A History*. Rev. ed. New York: Free Press, 1987.
Olson, Nancy. *With a Lot of Help from Our Friends: The Politics of Alcoholism*. Lincoln, NE: Writers Club Press, 2003.

DAVID HOGAN

Ale Slipper

The ale slipper, also known as an ale boot, or less commonly an ale shoe, is a boot-shaped vessel with a pouring spout, a handle, and sometimes a hinged cover that is used to heat beverages in hot coals. Ale slippers are made of tin-lined copper, tin, or cast iron and were in use in the British Isles by the sixteenth century. They came to the New World with early colonists and were used to heat mulled wine, ale, and cider, as well as caudles, possets, and gruels. Ingredients were combined in the ale slipper and then the toe was pushed into glowing embers. The heated drink was poured into a mug or cup before being consumed.

Ale slippers were common equipment in taverns and possibly in homes. Nineteenth-century American cookbooks indicate that the same hot ale preparations were being prepared at home, but in "pots," suggesting that the ale slipper had become obsolete as the fireplace gave way to the cookstove.

[**See also** CIDER; HEARTH COOKERY; POTS AND PANS.]

BIBLIOGRAPHY
Franklin, Linda Campbell. *From Hearth to Cookstove*. 5th ed. Iola, WI: K. P. Krause, 2003.
Seymour, John. *Forgotten Household Crafts: A Portrait of the Way We Once Lived*. New York: Knopf, 1987.

BOB SIMMONS

Almonds

The almond (*Prunus amygdalus*) is botanically related to the cherry, peach, plum, and apricot. It probably originated in Asia Minor and has been consumed since prehistoric times.

Almonds were particularly important during the Middle Ages; at that time, marzipan, a sweet almond-paste confection, was introduced by Arabs into western Europe. Recipes using almonds appear in medieval English cookery manuscripts. Almonds were first planted in coastal California by Franciscan missionaries in the eighteenth century, but the growing conditions were not suitable. In the 1850s, almond trees were successfully cultivated in California's Central Valley.

Almonds are the most important and the most versatile of all tree nuts and have the largest share of the world's tree nut trade. In addition to being a popular and nutritious snack, almonds are used for making flavorings, macaroons, marzipan, salads, baked goods, and confections, such as coconut-almond and chocolate-almond candy bars. All commercial American almonds are grown in California, which also supplies more than 70 percent of all the almonds consumed in the world.

[**See also** CALIFORNIA; CANDY AND CANDY BARS; NUTS.]

ANDREW F. SMITH

Amber Lager

This style of beer evolved from emulating the Märzen, also known as Oktoberfest, style beer, developed in Vienna, Austria. In 1841 the Viennese brewer Anton Dreher introduced a new beer with a reddish, coppery color and a full malt character. The popular acceptance of this new beer made a great impression on brewmaster Gabriel Sedlmayr at the Spaten brewery in Munich. He was soon brewing his version of that beer and calling it Märzen ("March beer"). Today, Anton Dreher's style of beer is no longer brewed in Vienna, while Sedlmayr's beer continues being brewed as "Oktoberfest" beer.

American brewers, both large and small, brew variations of the "Vienna" style, with enough of a unique character to claim a distinctive style of their own. What makes the American version unique is lighter body and less hop flavor. The color of the beers comes from the use of darker Crystal malts, Vienna malts, Munich malts, and occasionally darker malts such as British Amber, Chocolate, and Black malt.

The Coors Brewing Company markets George Killian's Irish Red, which is neither Irish nor red. Many smaller breweries produce amber lagers still loosely based on the Vienna style but have largely reduced the style to a copper-colored lager, more caramel flavored than paler beer with a pronounced citrus American hop character. The Association of Brewers' 2004 Beer Style Guidelines state that, "This is a broad category in which the hop bitterness, flavor, and aroma may be accentuated or may only be present at relatively low levels, yet noticeable." Typical alcohol content is 4.8–5.4 percent by volume.

[**See also** BEER.]

PETER LaFRANCE

Amber Red Ale

American Amber Ale, also known as American Red Ale, is the top-fermenting version of the American Style Amber Lager. It is particularly popular because of the fruity-ester aroma, bright copper color, and slightly sweet flavor. This style is more aromatic and has more of an aggressive flavor profile than that associated with the American Style Amber Lager. The aroma of apple, pear, and cherry comes from the top-fermenting ale yeast used to ferment these beers. American brewers use particular American grown and developed hops (usually Cascade) to impart a citric, almost grapefruit impression to both the aroma and the flavor. This flavor profile is unique to this style.

Garrett Oliver, in his book *The Brewmasters Table*, writes that

> Darker versions of American pale ale are sometimes referred to as amber beers, or, even more vaguely, just "amber." To some extent, amber ale is a catch-all term and therefore difficult to pin down. You can expect these beers to be copper colored and show more caramel malt flavor than paler beers. They are sometimes fuller bodied and can be fairly fruity. Almost all will show some citrus American hop character.

The Association of Brewers' 2004 Beer Style Guidelines state that this style of beer is "characterized by American-variety hops used to produce high hop bitterness, flavor, and medium to high aroma. Amber ales have medium-high to high maltiness with medium to low caramel character. They should have medium to medium-high body." Most of these beers have alcohol content between 4.5 and 6 percent by volume.

[**See also** BEER.]

PETER LaFRANCE

American Chop Suey

American food culture was formed in an environment that was resource-rich and labor-poor. There has always been a premium on one-pot sautés or quick stews, and these have sometimes acquired fanciful names like slumgullion (perhaps from Salmagundi), or mulligan stew (perhaps from slumgullion), or Finnish American *mojaka* (perhaps from mulligan stew). In old New England, a random collection of smothered meat and potatoes was known as potato bargain or necessity mess. A quasi-Italian casserole from Columbus, Ohio, spread across the country as Johnny Mazzetti with numerous variations. During the Great Depression, the names of foreign mixed dishes, such as goulash, hodgepodge (perhaps from *hachepôt*), or chop suey, were applied to quick assortments of meat, vegetables, and potatoes, and sometimes even to desserts with mixed ingredients.

American chop suey, however, eventually became somewhat standardized, especially in institutional catering, as a stew or casserole of beef, celery, and macaroni—none of which

seems especially Chinese. Chinese restaurant chop suey was itself a poorly defined American invention and basically another mixed stew. A likely origin for American chop suey is the recipe for Chop Suey Stew in the 1916 *Manual for Army Cooks*, an urtext for many institutional foods of the twentieth century. The army recipe could be made with either beef round or pork shoulder, beef stock, barbecue sauce, and salt. By 1932 the Navy's cookbook had added cabbage and green peppers. *Practical Home Economics* (1919) has a recipe entitled "Chop Suey" that adds tomatoes and parsley and omits the onions and cabbage.

All these early recipes leave out soy sauce but suggest serving the stew over rice. More recent recipes simplify the service by dropping the rice and mixing in cooked macaroni, but they tend to restore some amount of soy sauce unless using Italian tomato sauce. As distinct from Chinese restaurant chop suey, American chop suey in the early twenty-first century is usually made with beef instead of pork; the vegetables are usually restricted to celery and onions; and macaroni often replaces rice.

[**See also** CHINESE AMERICAN FOOD.]

MARK H. ZANGER

Spaghetti Chop Suey

1 Package Mueller's Spaghetti	3 Cups tomatoes
2 Tablespoons butter	1 Teaspoon salt
1 Green pepper, chopped	1 Teaspoon sugar
2 Onions, chopped	¼ Teaspoon pepper
1½ Cups chopped celery	½ Pound round steak, ground

Boil the spaghetti for 9 minutes in 4 quarts rapidly boiling water to which 1 tablespoon salt has been added. Drain. Melt the butter in a frying pan, add the green pepper, onions and celery, and cook slowly for 15 minutes, stirring constantly. Add the tomatoes, salt, sugar and pepper and continue cooking until the mixture thickens. Then add the well-drained spaghetti and cook slowly for 20 minutes. Fry the round steak in small cakes. Just before serving, crumble over the top of the mixture. Serve piping hot. Mushrooms may be substituted for the steak. Macaroni may be used instead of the spaghetti if desired.

One of a line of "happy heat-and-eat choices for buon appetito" from Prince Treasury of Italian Recipes, *1960s.*

Amusement Parks

The roots of today's amusement parks date back to the 1500s, when so-called pleasure gardens began opening on the outskirts of major European cities. In addition to primitive rides, these gardens featured shows, fireworks, and numerous concession stands selling food and novelties. While there is little written about the food that the pleasure gardens served, most likely it was simple to store and to prepare and easy for customers to consume while walking around enjoying the other attractions. These traits continue to guide amusement park food choices to this day.

As America became increasingly urbanized in the mid-1800s, people began clamoring for ways to escape the crowded, dirty conditions that characterized cities of the time. Entrepreneurs responded by opening American versions of the European pleasure gardens. These amusement parks tended to develop in two major forms: seaside resorts and picnic parks. Seaside resorts were best embodied by Coney Island in Brooklyn, New York, which was the heart and soul of the amusement park industry during the late 1800s and early 1900s and featured three major amusement parks and dozens of smaller attractions.

According to legend, Charles Feltman invented the hot dog, a staple of amusement park food, at Coney Island in 1867. Feltman went on to open a large, elaborate restaurant at the resort, ceding the hot dog business to other concessionaires—including Nathan Handwerker, who opened Nathan's at Coney Island in 1916. It quickly became the most popular stand at Coney Island by selling hot dogs for a nickel, half the price of its competitors. Nathan's remains a popular Coney Island institution.

Picnic parks were popularized by trolley companies, which sought a way to generate ridership on evenings and weekends. Although most customers brought a picnic lunch to enjoy in the park's groves, concession stands were plentiful as well. The most popular items included hot dogs and hamburgers; popcorn, peanuts, and Cracker Jack; lemonade; and ice cream. Most of these stands were operated by independent concessionaires who leased space from the park owners.

Another popular item throughout the industry, particularly in areas with a large German population, was beer, which was served in elaborate beer gardens. In fact, many early amusement parks were developed by brewers like Schlitz and Pabst.

After peaking at fifteen hundred in 1919, the number of amusement parks in the United States entered a period of decline in the 1930s and the 1940s and was reduced to fewer than four hundred. But the complexion of the industry was forever changed in 1955 when Disneyland opened in Anaheim, California, kicking off the theme-park era. With Disneyland's tightly controlled themed environments and high levels of maintenance, the nature of food service changed. To maintain standards, control shifted from concessionaires to the park operators themselves. While a few once-popular items like roasted peanuts fell by the wayside, as the mess they created did not meet standards of cleanliness, customers continued to seek out food that could be quickly served and easily consumed, and many of the traditional favorites remained.

Theme parks being an all-day destination, however, most include some sort of cafeteria or restaurant offering full meal service, although alcohol was typically forbidden. The popularity of such dining facilities is generally limited—with a few exceptions, such as Epcot Center at Walt Disney World, Florida, where fine dining is a key part of the experience.

As of the early twenty-first century, there are approximately six hundred parks attracting over 300 million visitors, who spend approximately $11 billion annually. Food accounts for approximately one-fourth of park revenues, and approximately 80 percent of a park's food revenue typically comes from 20 percent of the products. On average, parks tend to have between fifteen and twenty food outlets.

Amusement parks have continued to add new items to reflect changing customer habits. Ethnic items such as nachos, pizza, and egg rolls can be found in many amusement parks along with more healthful alternatives, such as salads and frozen yogurt, although traditional fare such as hot dogs, hamburgers, ice cream, funnel cakes, and cotton candy still dominate.

Parks have also become much more focused on offering greater value to customers. Some, such as Cedar Point in Sandusky, Ohio, feature all-you-can-eat buffets, and many places have combo meals, much like fast food restaurants. In 2000 Holiday World in Santa Claus, Indiana, set a new industry standard when it offered free soft drinks to their patrons.

Another dominant trend in amusement park food service has been the addition of branded foods. Parks not only promote particular food brands such as Coke and Pepsi; increasingly, they incorporate entire fast food franchises. While some parks—like Paramount's Kings Island in Kings Island, Ohio, near Cincinnati—emphasize local chains, others, such as Dorney Park in Allentown, Pennsylvania, feature national franchises.

[See also BEER; BEER GARDENS; Cracker Jack; FAST FOOD; HOT DOGS; LEMONADE; PEANUTS; POPCORN.]

BIBLIOGRAPHY

Adams, Judith A. *The American Amusement Park Industry: A History of Technology and Thrills*. Boston: Twayne, 1991.

Samuelson, Dale. *The American Amusement Park*. St. Paul, MN: MBI, 2001.

JIM FUTRELL

Anadama Bread

This yeast bread made with cornmeal and molasses originated on the North Shore of Boston. The Cape Ann towns of Rockport and Gloucester are among those that claim to have invented it. According to competing popular legends, a farmer—or a local fisherman—grew tired of eating the cornmeal-and-molasses porridge that his wife incessantly prepared for him. He dumped flour and yeast into the bowl and threw it in the oven, grumbling, "Anna, damn her!" Others say it was Anna who got so fed up with her husband that she left him; returning home, her distraught husband threw random ingredients into her unfinished cornbread, muttering, "Anna, damn her!" More appreciative versions claim that Anna's spouse pronounced his defining epithet with pride as he munched thick slices of her tasty bread, or that Anna's tombstone fondly read, "Anna was a lovely bride, but Anna, damn 'er, up and died." The bread is also known as amadama bread, allegedly derived from the irate husband who cried, "Where am 'er, damn 'er?" when his wife was away.

These stories, traceable in written form only to the nineteenth century, are repeated by local restaurants and bakeries that serve anadama bread. The bread's varying legends reveal a simple, home-cooked regional food. Whether created by a colonial settler, who added flavorful indigenous ingredients to an English yeast bread, or by a post-Revolutionary housewife, in a community whose cuisine harked back to seventeenth-century English cooking, anadama bread embodies the fierce local pride and deep English roots of the North Shore of Boston. The Arnold Bread Company produced a commercial variety until the late twentieth century; Klink's Baking Company in South Hamilton, Massachusetts, still distributes it to local grocery stores.

[See also BREAD.]

BIBLIOGRAPHY

Bowles, Ella Shannon, and Dorothy S. Towle. *Secrets of New England Cooking*. New York: Barrows, 1947.

CAROLIN C. YOUNG

Anchovies

Anchovies (*Engraulis encrasicolus*, *E. ringens*, and *Anchoa hepsetus*) are small but important food fish that are found in the Atlantic Ocean, the Pacific Ocean, the Mediterranean Sea, and the English Channel. The primary anchovy for cookery is the Mediterranean variety. These anchovies are almost always preserved and used as a flavoring agent in cookery, with even very early cookbooks calling for them. Filleted, salted, and packed in cans with oil, they are also made into a paste sold in tubes. Modern recipes call for anchovies on pizza, in Caesar salad, in salad dressings, and in a variety of sauces often used on blander fish.

SANDRA L. OLIVER

Animal Rights

A significant force for dietary change in North America has been the animal rights movement. It does not take much imagination to realize that if animals had rights they would invoke those rights in a court of law to prevent humans from turning them into pâté de foie gras, veal, steak, bacon, crabcakes, buffalo wings, lamb chops, filets of sole, and so on. The corollary of the animal rights movement is the spread of ethical vegetarianism, which among younger generations of Americans is proceeding apace.

From the inception, some of the most potent animal activists in America have also been dietary reformers like the Quaker abolitionist and ethical vegetarian Benjamin Lay, author of *All Slave Keepers That Keep the Innocents in Bondage Apostates* (1737); the abolitionist and animal advocate Bronson Alcott, who founded America's first vegan commune, Fruitlands (1843); Curtis Freshel, inventor of an early bacon substitute called Bacon-Yeast; and his wife, Emarel Freshel, founder of the Millennium Guild and author of an early animal-rights vegetarian cookbook, *The Golden Rule Cookbook* (1906). However, it really was not until the 1974 publication of Peter Singer's *Animal Liberation*—which contained a selection of vegetarian recipes—that the animal rights movement—and the ethical vegetarianism that it spawned—began to stir from centuries of lethargy and inertia. As Singer observed, in the first 1,970 years of the Christian era only 240 works on the moral status of animals had been published, but since 1970 the number of works published on this subject has risen into the tens of thousands and is growing exponentially. In 1976 a breakthrough in animal rights history was achieved by Henry Spira, whose protests against the American Museum of Natural History's cat experiments succeeded in stopping a funded research project. Spira followed this with a campaign to pressure major cosmetic manufacturers to stop animal-testing their products. In 1998, shortly before his untimely death, Spira, a one-man animal rights crusade, and a supreme pragmatist, was negotiating with the fast food industry to institute humane conditions for the rearing and slaughtering of animals for food. In 1977 Paul Watson founded the Sea Shepherd Conservation Society, which takes direct action to foil illegal fishing and whaling practices on the high seas. Animal rights did not start to crystallize as a social movement until the 1980s.

A watershed year in its history in the United States was 1981. It marked the founding of People for the Ethical Treatment of Animals (PETA). That same year saw the founding of the Farm Animal Reform Movement. FARM started an annual spring event, the Great American Meatout, that is modeled after the Great American Smokeout (an attempt to rid Americans of their smoking habit). Farm Sanctuary, a refuge for abused farm animals, started in 1986. Nearly all these animal rights organizations have published ethical vegetarian cookbooks to entice people to eat fruits and vegetables instead of animals. In 1993 PETA published the best-selling vegan (no flesh, eggs, dairy, or honey) cookbook, *The Compassionate Cook: Please Don't Eat the Animals*. In 2005 Friends of Animals (founded in 1957) published *Dining with Friends: The Art of North American Vegan Cuisine*. In the late 1980s, as a portent of their impact on the meat-eating habits of North Americans, animal rights groups began to denounce the wearing of fur, and as a result fur wearing has gone permanently out of vogue. The number of hunters has declined from a peak of 21 million in 1981 and is now estimated to number 13 million. The number of trappers has declined from 800,000 in 1981 to 100,000 today. In 1990 Karen Davis started United Poultry Concerns, the first sanctuary for poultry, an animal whose cause had been overlooked—unjustly so, in view of the fact that chickens make up 95 percent of the 10 billion animals slaughtered for food in the United States each year. Davis is the author of a vegan cookbook entitled *Instead of Chicken, Instead of Meat* (1999), which offers vegan alternatives to traditional poultry and egg recipes.

Such books as *The Case for Animal Rights* (1983); *Slaughterhouse* (1997); *Ethics into Action* (Peter Singer's biography of Henry Spira) (1998); *Rattling the Cages: Toward Legal Rights for Animals* (2000); and *Dominion* (2002) have

given an enormous impetus to the spread of ethical vegetarianism in the U.S.

BIBLIOGRAPHY
Sculley, Matthew. *Dominion: The Power of Man, the Suffering of Animals, and the Call to Mercy.* New York: St. Martins, 2002.

RYNN BERRY

Appalachian Food

Traditional Appalachian foods include the many-layered dried-apple stack cake; soup beans or pinto beans boiled with pork; chicken and slick dumplings served with gruel; white half-runner green beans boiled for long periods with salt pork or pork side meat; and feather-light biscuits covered with white sausage gravy. Appalachians take pride in preparing apple butter, deviled eggs, pork barbecue, and fried apple pies, and they speak reverently about their eggs scrambled with poke, their fried morel mushrooms or dryland fish, and their white lightning or moonshine, a high-alcohol-content drink poured from quart-sized canning jars. The corn that yields moonshine is also the source of cornbread, roasted ear corn, fried corn, hominy, and grits. This list of diverse Appalachian foods could go on for hundreds of items, eventually comprising the wild, garlic-like green ramps dug from the ground in March and the highly perfumed tropical pawpaw

A cookbooklet of Appalachian recipes issued by Christian Relief Services in Vernon, Virginia, in 1992.

fruits that fall from small trees in September. It would also have to include wild meats such as bear, venison, squirrel, and turtle, but it might not include foods associated with the South such as rice and crabmeat.

This discussion of Appalachian food is limited to the Central and Southern Highlands of the Appalachian region, a mountainous area that stretches from the Maryland panhandle through southwestern Ohio, West Virginia, eastern Kentucky and Tennessee, western Virginia and North Carolina, and northeastern portions of Georgia. One other defining comment: Traditional Appalachian food did not develop in commercial test kitchens, cookbook writers' homes, or cooking schools. It is food from the soil, hearth, and home, and its roots predate the arrival of Christopher Columbus.

Pre-Columbian Period

A nomadic people, likely arriving from Asia, settled the Appalachian region some twelve thousand or more years ago, and they developed food traditions that continued until the industrial revolution. They ate mastodon and giant tortoise. They hunted, fished, and gathered. Then the earth warmed, the mastodon and tortoise died off, and their diet changed. About ten thousand years ago, native Appalachians ate white-tailed deer, turkeys, squirrels, and raccoons. They also enjoyed hickory nuts, black walnuts, acorns, grapes, berries, and persimmons.

The most prominent Native American foods of this region are corn, beans, pumpkins, and squash, but these became important much later, because rather than being gathered in the wild, they were grown.

Once Europeans settled the region, native food habits began to change. In the 1950s the Museum of the Cherokee Indian in Cherokee, North Carolina, sponsored Indian feasts that illustrated the mixture of native and European foods that had become characteristic of the region. For example, dinners featured boiled corn mush, baked cornbread loaves or pones, fresh young-ear gritted cornbread, thick and salty cornmeal gravy, rolled flat-flour dumplings boiled with dry beans or chicken, succotash of lima beans and corn, butter beans boiled with onions, flavorful dried leather breeches (green beans) boiled with side meat, fried crease greens, watercress, and squirrel gravy served over biscuits. Also included were dishes with wild blackberries, huckleberries, raspberries, elderberries, plums, cherries, ground cherries, persimmons, fox grapes, muscadine grapes, and gooseberries. The mix of foods served at these dinners illustrates that although Europeans influenced Appalachian food, native Appalachians had an even greater impact on European habits.

Frontier Period

From the beginning of the nineteenth century and until the coming of railroads and industry about eighty years later, European settlers were often isolated and independent. To survive in the Appalachian frontier, they cleared fields, built cabins, and cooked with cast-iron cookware. In early mountain cabins the fireplace and open hearth provided heat for both the house and the cooking.

A grand dinner during this period might include elk backstrap steaks, venison stew, greens fried in bear grease, and ashcakes. Ashcakes are a cornbread rolled in ashes and baked, not in a pan but near the coals on the hearth. Corn on the cob and Irish and sweet potatoes were cooked in the same fashion. After a dessert of fruit pie or sweet cake, a bottle was passed and a shot of whiskey taken. Appalachian settlers prided themselves on quality foods, and occasionally the table was set in high fashion and the meal served with hot biscuits, fresh butter, honey, strawberry preserves, mixed pickles, rich milk, cream, tea, and coffee.

From this period, dried apples, peach leather (a sheet of dried fruit puree), and shuck beans have remained popular. Native Appalachians taught settlers to use wild greens—and some of these, including creases, dandelions, dock, fiddleheads, lambs-quarters, poke, purslane, ramps, shepherd's purse, spring beauty, and watercress—are well known today. But during this period wild meat and animal fats were more important than greens. Settlers ate buffalo, bear, elk, deer, razorback hogs, turkey, fox, raccoon, and the meat of many more wild animals. Pork and beef were raised to supplement wild game.

Industrial Period

The impact of industrialization on Appalachia was uneven, with some communities modernizing quickly and others maintaining traditional ways long into the twentieth century. In some areas one- and two-room schools were the norm until the late 1950s, and a rural lifestyle was dominant. Those living in the country often worked in mines and factories but continued to raise livestock, with chickens and new vegetable varieties such as sweet corn becoming new frontier traditions. They canned meats, fruits, and vegetables.

Families were large, and so were the dinners. Such dinners, while family oriented, are diverse, reflecting the varied nationalities of immigrants to Appalachia—whose population comprises people from Germany, Greece, Hungary, India, Ireland, Italy, Mexico, Poland, Russia, Scotland, and the Ukraine. Appalachia during the late frontier and industrial periods did not have a homogeneous style of eating or cooking, and this fact is illustrated again and again in community-based cookbooks. Poles, for example, prepared pierogi, crullers, and pickled herring. Russians brought sweet nut and poppy seed breakfast rolls. Italians cooked gnocchi and stromboli. Germans brought to the region orange cookies and sauerkraut salad. Many of these recipes, while associated with particular ethnic groups, are now widely known throughout Appalachia.

An example is the stack cake, also called the dried-apple stack cake. It stores well, slices thin, and looks classy, comprising six to twelve ginger-flavored layers covered with a spicy apple sauce. The sauce soaks into the cake, softening it and allowing the flavors to mingle.

[See also CANNING AND BOTTLING; COMMUNITY COOKBOOKS; DUMPLINGS; GAME; HARDTACK; MOONSHINE; NATIVE AMERICAN FOODS: BEFORE AND AFTER CONTACT; PAWPAW; PICKLING; RAMPS; SALT AND SALTING; SOUTHERN REGIONAL COOKING.]

BIBLIOGRAPHY

Dabney, Joseph E. *Mountain Spirits: A Chronicle of Corn Whiskey from King James' Ulster Plantation to America's Appalachians and the Moonshine Life.* New York: Scribners, 1974.

Dabney, Joseph E. *Smokehouse Ham, Spoon Bread, and Scuppernong Wine: The Folklore and Art of Southern Appalachian Cooking.* Nashville, TN: Cumberland House, 1998.

Page, Linda Garland, and Eliot Wigginton. *The Foxfire Book of Appalachian Cookery: Regional Memorabilia and Recipes.* New York: Dutton, 1984.

Sohn, Mark F. *Mountain Country Cooking: A Gathering of the Best Recipes from the Smokies to the Blue Ridge.* New York: St. Martin's, 1996.

Steelesburg Homemakers Club. *Appalachian Heritage Cookbook.* Radford, VA: Commonwealth, 1984.

MARK F. SOHN

Appetizers

Appetizers and hors d'oeuvres—the latter literally meaning "outside of the work"—assume a wide variety of forms in American dining. Late-twentieth-century dictionaries treat appetizers and hors d'oeuvres—popularly understood to be bite-sized finger foods offered at cocktail parties and receptions—as synonyms. Americans also use "appetizer" to indicate the first course eaten when seated at table in a three-course (appetizer, main course, dessert) meal.

Hors d'Oeuvres in History

Virtually all cultures have indulged in preprandial morsels designed to whet the appetite for more substantial fare, and there is remarkable consistency across cultures in offering salty foods as stimulants. The ancient Greeks and Romans sampled bits of fish, seasoned vegetables, cheeses, and olives, while the Renaissance Italian writer Platina recommended thin rolls of grilled veal to stimulate the appetite for food and drink. Wealthy Frenchmen picked at *hors d'oeuvre* throughout fancy meals from the late seventeenth through the mid-nineteenth centuries, when little plates and their suggested contents—ranging from oysters, stuffed eggs, and pâtés to slices of beef tongue or braised quails—were shown on table layouts illustrating dinners served *à la française*. Those Americans who emulated that French model made a variety of hors d'oeuvres (the plural is used only in English) part of the American table and offered them throughout the meal as a palate refresher, until the desserts were served.

Styles of service changed radically in the nineteenth century, evolving to the successive, multicourse structure of formal contemporary meals. The role of hors d'oeuvres in

A recipe booklet issued by Canape Parade, Scarborough, New York, 1932.

the structure of a meal changed as well. Although simple hors d'oeuvres, such as olives, radishes, celery, and nuts, remained on the table throughout the meal, by the late nineteenth century, more complicated hors d'oeuvres, sometimes called "dainty dishes"—such as small pastry cases filled with bits of meat in creamy sauce—had become a separate course after the soup was served. The term "appetizer" seems to have appeared nearly simultaneously in England and America in the 1860s simply to provide an Anglophone equivalent for the French *hors d'oeuvre*.

By the 1890s both appetizers and hors d'oeuvres could appear within the same elegant menu. Abby Buchanan Longstreet's *Good Form Dinners, Ceremonious and Unceremonious, and the Modern Methods of Serving Them* (1896) describes appetizers as an optional first course, preceding soup, that is set on the table prior to a party's entering the dining room. These appetizers were most often raw oysters or clams, but they might be small canapés, such as caviar on toast. Mrs. Longstreet assumed that celery, salted nuts, and the like would fill the table throughout the meal, and she directed the host to place these "various *hors-d'oeuvres* within reach of each guest, these appetizers serving to fill in the time between courses."

The Americanization of Hors d'Oeuvres: The Cocktail Hour and Streamlined Menus

The introduction of the predinner cocktail hour in the early twentieth century changed Americans' view of hors d'oeuvres. Before World War I, guests at a dinner party were presumed to arrive punctually and to proceed almost immediately into the dining room. If cocktails were served, they opened the dinner, accompanying a plated appetizer, once everyone was seated at the table. This custom had changed by the 1920s, when racy hostesses served hors d'oeuvres as "accompaniments for the liquid refreshment that dodges prohibition conscientiously and yet is flavorsome enough to make the quarter hour before dinner less solemn and uninteresting than it sometimes proves" (Eaton, p. 124). After the repeal of Prohibition, the modern cocktail party burst on the scene, with a slew of recipes for hors d'oeuvres to help absorb the liquor.

Until about 1940, "fine dining" restaurant menus tended to use French terminology in organizing the successive courses—at least for those courses that did not have a handy English translation, such as hors d'oeuvre, entrée, and entremets. But a simpler model for a "proper" meal was emerging from the 1920s on, consisting of only three courses. A term being needed to pigeonhole the many types of dishes being offered, the generic category "appetizers" began to appear, denoting the first of three courses. Appetizers broadly included soups, salads, and savory pastries, all of which had appeared as separate courses—although in smaller portions—in nineteenth- and early-twentieth-century meals. Middle-class cookbooks, such as Alice Bradley's *Menu-Cook-Book* (1936), also began to suggest "a first course or appetizer for every dinner, as it seems to add much pleasure to the meal.... This course may be omitted if it seems to be the extra item that means too much work."

Influences beyond the French

Americans who have not assimilated the Anglo-French style of dining have different appetizer traditions. Perhaps most familiar is the Italian antipasto, meaning "before the meal." The dishes serving as the antipasto vary with the cook's budget and regional heritage; they may be modest grilled vegetables or rich cured meats. The eastern Mediterranean and Middle Eastern *mezze* (derived from the Persian for taste or relish), found wherever Greek and Arab populations settled, typically present baba ghanoush, *tzanziki*, hummus, and *taramasalata*, all scooped with bits of flat breads. The Scandinavian-inspired smorgasbord ("table of buttered bread") groans under small, open-faced sandwiches covered with herring, salmon, and other fishes and may serve as a meal in itself. Authentic Russian *zakuska* can be found in Brighton Beach, Brooklyn, where plates brimming with smoked and cured fishes, pickled and stuffed vegetables, meat-filled pastries, and the omnipresent caviar vie for table space among frosty bottles of vodka. The tapas bar is at home in cities with a Spanish population, allowing patrons to snack on small plates of marinated vegetables and seafood and the signature chorizo and *jamón*, while imbibing sherry, sangria, or cocktails. Chinatowns bustle with dim sum ("so close to my heart") trolleys delivering little baskets of dumplings, spareribs, and the like, which can be eaten for breakfast or lunch, but never dinner.

The universal appeal of a variety of little "tastes" coupled with a relaxing drink has encouraged "grazing" as a restaurant trend, beginning in the late twentieth century: diners compose a meal from dishes offered in appetizer-sized portions. Appealing primarily to a youthful, urban clientele, these grazing bars often fuse diverse cultural influences in their menus and offer more "tastes" than a traditional three-course meal.

[**See also** DINING ROOMS AND MEAL SERVICE; FRENCH INFLUENCES ON AMERICAN FOOD.]

BIBLIOGRAPHY

Beard, James. *Hors D'Oeuvre and Canapés, with a Key to the Cocktail Party.* New York: Barrows, 1940. A good general collection of recipes, this book is divided into chapters for different categories (hot, cold, sandwiches, canapés, first courses), each of which is introduced by a brief essay on the different functions served by hors d'oeuvres.

Eaton, Florence Taft. "Varied Hors d'Oeuvres." *Delineator* 109, no. 31 (November 1926): 31, 124. A very interesting article addressed to the middle class, which includes recipes and techniques and explains the multiple functions of hors d'oeuvres.

CATHY K. KAUFMAN

Applejack

Applejack, an American type of apple brandy, was widely produced during the colonial period of American history. In New England applejack was the most commonly consumed brandy. It was made by placing hard cider in wooden barrels and exposing them to freezing temperatures during winter. The water in the hard cider froze on the top of the barrel and was removed, leaving a stronger fermented concentrate in the barrel, along with other residues. In the middle colonies and the upper southern colonies, where temperatures were not cold enough to use the freezing method, applejack was made by distilling hard cider. It competed with peach and other brandies.

Applejack had a reputation for its strong kick, which was illustrated by its many colloquial names, such as "cider oil," "essence of lockjaw," and, because New Jersey produced large quantities of it, "Jersey Lightening." George Washington enjoyed apple brandy, and Abraham Lincoln served it in his tavern in Springfield, Illinois. The consumption of applejack declined during the nineteenth century and almost disappeared during the twentieth century. The major reason for the decline was that the freezing method retained unpleasant apple residue and oils.

The alcoholic content of applejack has varied greatly through the years, depending on the method used to make it. By the early twenty-first century all commercial applejack was made through distillation, which produces a product that is about 70 proof. It is usually aged for two years before consumption; other apple brandies are aged for a much longer period. For instance, French calvados is frequently aged about twenty years. The major commercial producer of applejack, Laird and Company of Scobeyville, New Jersey, which began making the brandy in 1780, uses the distillation method. The company has published a cookbook, *AppleJack: The Spirit of Americana*, filled with recipes using applejack in food and drinks. [**See also** BRANDY; CIDER, HARD.]

BIBLIOGRAPHY

Laird and Company. *AppleJack: The Spirit of Americana*. Brick, NJ: Strand Printery, 1992.

Watson, Ben. *Cider Hard and Sweet: History, Traditions, and Making Your Own*. Woodstock, VT: Countryman Press, 1999.

Weiss, Harry B. *The History of Applejack or Apple Brandy in New Jersey from Colonial Times to the Present*. Trenton: New Jersey Agricultural Society, 1954.

ANDREW F. SMITH

Apple Pie

The typical American pie made from uncooked apples, fat, sugar, and sweet spices mixed together and baked inside a closed pie shell descends from fifteenth-century English apple pies, which, while not quite the same, are similar enough that the relationship is unmistakable. By the end of the sixteenth century in England, apple pies were being made that are virtually identical to those made in America in the early twenty-first century.

Apple pies came to America quite early. There are recipes for apple pie in both manuscript recipes and eighteenth-century English cookery books imported into the colonies. Amelia Simmons's *American Cookery* (1796) contains two different recipes for apple pie, one flavored with rose water or wine. The anonymous *New American Cookery*, published in 1805, contains a recipe for dried-apple pie.

Apple pies can vary in many ways: the type of sweetener used, if any; the type of fat; the type of crust, whether solid or made of crumbs; the use of such extra ingredients as raisins, lemon juice, or almonds; and the choice of spices. While the most common apple pie in America is the two-crust pie, there are other versions as well, including one-crust pies and pies with bottom crusts and crumb toppings. One-crust pies have been found in the United States since at least 1820. Mary Randolph's *The Virginia House-Wife* (1824) contains a recipe for Baked Apple Pudding, which is an apple pie variant that has already-baked apples, butter, sugar, eggs, and lemon rind baked further in a one-crust pie shell.

Apple pies rapidly became an iconic part of the American culture, witnessed by the cliché "as American as apple pie." In Louisa May Alcott's *Little Men* (1886), one of the first things Jo teaches her niece Daisy to cook is an apple pie. Even imitation ones were devised. In the 1930s a mock apple pie recipe, which used Ritz crackers instead of apples, was printed on Ritz cracker boxes. In 1968 McDonald's added an apple pie dessert to its menu.

Apple pies have been eaten not only as a dessert. In the nineteenth century, apple pie was also a common breakfast food among Yankees and people in rural communities, prompting Ralph Waldo Emerson's alleged comment, "Well, what is pie for?" The use of pie as a breakfast food had declined by the end of the nineteenth century.

Although homemade apple pies were most common through the early twentieth century, bakeries and grocery stores in urban settings started offering apple pies for sale in the nineteenth century. In the early twentieth century, a woman by the name of Mrs. Smith, who baked pies that her son then marketed, turned her pie company, Mrs. Smith's pies, into a mass-market industry. It still exists today. Others did the same, and by the mid-twentieth century frozen apple pies became available.

Apple pies are often served with a topping. The two most common are vanilla ice cream, first served with the title "à la mode" in the 1890s, and cheese. The poet Eugene Field in the late nineteenth century praised the latter combination in a poem asking, "the Lord to bless me with apple pie and cheese."

[**See also** APPLE-PREPARATION TOOLS; APPLES; DESSERTS; RANDOLPH, MARY; SIMMONS, AMELIA.]

BIBLIOGRAPHY

Hechtlinger, Adelaide. *The Seasonal Hearth*. Woodstock, NY: Overlook Press, 1977.

Simmons, Amelia. *American Cookery*. Hartford, CT: Hudson and Goodwin, 1796.

JUDITH H. GERJUOY

Apple-Preparation Tools

As eighteenth-century American apple orchards expanded throughout the colonies, demand increased for mechanical aid in preparing the seasonal harvest for cider, preserves, and drying. By the 1780s or 1790s, belt-driven, bench-mounted, wooden devices made paring quicker. Seated astride the bench, with one hand the operator cranked a shaft with an apple on its pronged tip while pressing a sharp-bladed shaver against the fruit. The first parer patent, in 1803, was for a simple wood and iron device clamped to a tabletop. Homemade adaptations during the next forty years led to mass-produced cast-iron peelers with replaceable, bolted-together parts, gears that increased the apple's turning speed, and blades held firmly against the fruit with a spring. A simple lathe-type apple parer, "The White Mountain," first patented in 1880, was still made in the early 2000s.

Improvements to several geared parers added the ability to core, segment or slice, and ultimately eject an apple in less than three seconds. Large and small versions satisfied both commercial and home canners.

Before the mid-nineteenth century, corers were made of carved bone or wrought iron. Tin corers took their place, some with wooden knobs that protected the user's palm. Tin coring and segmenting (usually quartering) tools with sharp edges were used by pushing against an apple on a cutting board.

[**See also** APPLEJACK; APPLE PIE; APPLES.]

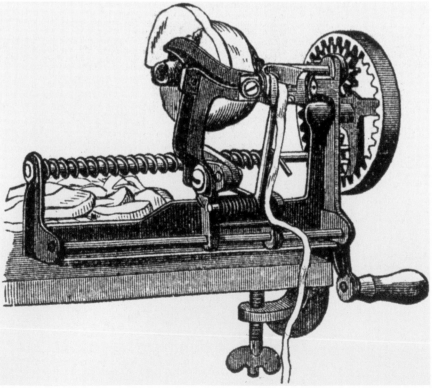

An illustration of an apple parer from Housewife's Library *(Philadelphia, 1883), p. 290.*

BIBLIOGRAPHY

Franklin, Linda Campbell. *300 Years of Kitchen Collectibles*. Iola, WI: Krause Publications, 2003.

Thornton, Don. *Apple Parers*. Moss Beach, CA: Thornton House, 1997.

LINDA CAMPBELL FRANKLIN

Apples

Apples are in the family Rosaceae and constitute the genus *Malus*. It is speculated that the cradle of the apple is in Asia Minor and that the fruit resulted from a millennia-old evolutionary cross of an Asiatic crab apple and a European crab apple. The science and study of the apple is pomology, a word that also applies to the study of fruit in general.

Malus pumila, the domestic apple we know from supermarket shelves, is not a native fruit of America. A few native crab apples, notably *M. augustifolia* and *M. coronaria*, were found by the colonists. Seeds, buds, and small plants of the apples of the British Isles and Europe trickled into the temperate zones of the New World to establish the apple as a food commodity. By the middle of the seventeenth century there were apple orchards with thousands of trees, planted not for eating but for cider production.

Every seed in every apple is a new variety; thus, the planting of the seeds out of a named variety from abroad in the rich soil of the colonies would produce many different varieties. Trueness to name was unimportant, because the purpose of the apple in new America was exclusively to produce juice for cider. Production was so successful that by 1820 cider not only was the national beverage but also became a currency, a major commodity for barter.

From the great cider orchards of America, where tens of thousands of trees were planted from the random seeds collected from the cider presses, a tree occasionally would produce a fruit with desirable eating qualities. Cider seedling orchards were the natural breeding laboratories for the selection of more pleasing apple varieties for eating for culinary purposes. Buds from the acclimated varieties were grafted to unknown-variety seedlings; when they had been established for a few years in the first American fruit tree nurseries, orchards with named apple selections were planted for the first time in America.

By 1850 thousands of named apple varieties for fresh eating, cooking, drying, pickling, and making cider, apple butter, applesauce, vinegar, wine, and even livestock food were listed in nursery catalogs. There was considerable diversity of varieties in New England, the Middle Atlantic, the upper Midwest, and the Northwest, and there were even a few adapted to the warmer regions of the Deep South. In 1905 W. H. Ragan's *Nomenclature of the Apple: Catalog of Known Varieties Referred to in American Publications from 1804–1904* listed seventeen thousand apple varieties grown in America.

In the first half of the twentieth century, because of developments in transportation and fruit-storage facilities as well as the disappearance of the diversity once found on family farms and orchards, thousands of varieties were abandoned. In the 1920s and 1930s alcohol prohibition, the proliferation of pests and diseases, and the emergence of the soft-drink industry furthered the decline of the golden age of the apple in America.

The agricultural skill of fruit propagation by grafting disappeared with the orchards, as marketing and sales came under the control of larger and larger nurseries focused on fewer and fewer varieties. The dozen or so commercial varieties marketed in the second half of the twentieth century were chosen by producers for high volume and trouble-free bearing, low mechanical damage, long shelf life, and, above all, cosmetic impact. The approaching monoculture solidified with the appearance of the Red Delicious and its three hundred look-alike strains. The stereotypical apple had emerged, and it would dominate the apple industry until the 1960s, when other commercial varieties from abroad began to be introduced.

Apples: The Immigrant Fruit

History repeated itself in the "re-appleing" of America. New varieties from Japan, New Zealand, and Australia, notably Gala, Braeburn, Pink Lady, and Fuji, trickled in to

An illustration of families picking and barreling apples.

begin the fragmentation of the Delicious monoculture. The consumer demanded apples with better flavor. In the development of new varieties, research stations began to consider taste as a major characteristic. Apple varieties of the past, like the Newtown Pippin, Roxbury Russet, Grimes Golden, Northern Spy, and Arkansas Black, returned to commerce, at least on a small scale.

Thirty-five states grow apples commercially, with the largest production in Washington, New York, Michigan, California, Pennsylvania, and Virginia. In 2002 the total bearing acreage in the United States was 404,950 acres. The sale value exceeded $1.3 billion. The number-one apple variety harvested is still the Red Delicious, though its market share is shrinking steadily. The Golden Delicious remains in second place. Some other prominent commercial varieties are Braeburn, Cortland, Empire, Fuji, Gala, Ginger Gold, Goldrush, Granny Smith, Honeycrisp, Jonagold, Jonathan, McIntosh, Mutsu, Pink Lady, Rome, Suncrisp, Winesap, and York. One hundred or more other varieties have lesser commercial value; many are popular regionally, among them the Baldwin, Grimes Golden, Macoun, Newtown Pippin, Stayman, Gravenstein, and Wealthy.

Physical characteristics of apples vary considerably, with skin colors that range from all hues of whites to reds, greens, browns, and yellows. Striping, mottling, and speckling can cover all or just a small area of the skin surface. The shapes are enormously diverse, and sizes may range from that of a small pea to that of a large grapefruit. Inside, the flesh can be very dense or open grained. Seeds may be white, green, yellow, brown, tan, or red. The stems vary from chunky to threadlike, and they can be just long enough to hold the fruit to the stem or two inches in length. When the apples are mature, the flavors may range from extremely bitter to saccharine sweet and contain varying amounts, singly or in combination, of acid, tannin, and sugar as well as trace elements. A medium-sized dessert apple has about eighty calories.

The apple is a portable fruit that can be conveniently stored from a few days to many months under a controlled environment. Some varieties exude a natural coating, often described as greasy or waxy, that protects the fruit from desiccation. The wood of the apple is used for heating, flavoring meats by its smoke, and furniture making. The versatile fruit continues to be consumed in a variety of forms. [**See also** APPLEJACK; CIDER.]

BIBLIOGRAPHY

Beach, S. A. *The Apples of New York*. Albany: New York Agricultural Experiment Station, 1905.

Manhart, Warren. *Apples for the 21st Century*. Portland, OR: North American Tree Company, 1995.

Morgan, Joan, and Allison Richards. *The New Book of Apples: The Definitive Guide to Apples, Including over 2,000 Varieties*. 2nd ed. London: Ebury Press, 2002.

THOMAS BURFORD

Apricots

The apricot, *Prunus armeniaca*, once thought to be native to Armenia, is actually indigenous to China, where it has been cultivated for at least four thousand years. Its culture spread through Asia by ancient travelers along the Silk Road and reached the Mediterranean during Roman times. In America, Thomas Jefferson set out apricot trees in his orchard at Monticello as early as 1778, and the British explorer George Vancouver found apricot trees growing at the Spanish mission of Santa Clara, California, in 1792. The apricot, with its early-blooming habit, flourishes in the soil and climate of California. There, after the gold rush, the world's largest apricot industry developed in areas relatively free of spring frosts, which is the limiting factor for commercial production east of the Rockies.

In the early years most of California's production was dried or preserved by canning. Major varieties included Royal Blenheim and Moorpark. These traditional varieties were considered the most delectable of fruits, with soft, juicy, aromatic flesh; rich flavor; and a delicate balance of sweetness and acidity. In the 1970s and 1980s growers shifted to apricots with firmer flesh, both for the fresh market and processing; thus, the Castlebrite and Patterson varieties, which have larger, firmer fruit but more acidic flavor, began replacing the older varieties. Urbanization of older growing districts, reliance on varieties of lesser quality, and foreign competition led to a steady decline in California's apricot industry, as Turkey overtook California in dried apricot production and Spain and Greece took the lead in canned apricots. Since the late 1990s, newer varieties like Tomcot, Goldensweet, and Robada, which combine rich flavor with good shipping qualities, are increasingly being planted in California and the Northwest.

The apricot is truly a versatile fruit. It is consumed fresh, canned, conserved, and dried. It is very high in vitamins C and A, containing as much as one hundred times more vitamin A than is found, on average, in most other fruits. The rich sweet-tart flavor of apricots makes them a favorite filling for old-fashioned fried pies, a comfort food and dessert staple in the southern United States for generations. [**See also** CALIFORNIA; FRUIT.]

BIBLIOGRAPHY

Wickson, E. J. *The California Fruits and How to Grow Them*. 6th ed. San Francisco: Pacific Rural Press, 1926.

ANDREW MARIANI

Aquaculture

Aquaculture is the cultivation of fish, shellfish, and plants under controlled conditions in oceans, lakes, ponds and rivers. It was first practiced in China thousands of years ago, and that country still has the most extensive aquaculture in the world, producing an estimated 70 percent of all farmed seafood. Aquaculture rapidly expanded throughout the world during the late twentieth century:

In 2004, aquaculture accounted for more than 25 percent of all aquatic foods consumed in the world. Aquaculture is one of the fastest-growing segments of the U.S. and global agricultural economies.

In the United States, fish were farmed during the nineteenth century, but aquaculture did not become an important commercial activity until the 1960s and 1970s. The initial interest was in producing commercial items, such as salmon and shrimp. As more efficient and cost-effective techniques were developed, the number of species under cultivation expanded. Now salmon, trout, catfish, sea bass, oysters, and mussels are farmed in U.S. waters. As of 2004, the value of aquaculture production in the United States exceeded $1.13 billion per year.

By 2004, almost 40 percent of all shrimp production in the world came from aquaculture, mainly in developing countries. Other species, such as striped bass, haddock, hake, halibut, cod, arctic char, clams, and scallops, are increasingly being farmed. There has been a real boom in aquaculture since the 1970s—a shift that has been tagged the "blue revolution." Proponents believe the growth of aquaculture will be as successful as the "green revolution" has been for farmers in the developing world.

The explosive growth of the aquaculture industry has generated mounting criticism over its social, economic, and environmental consequences. Critics have many concerns. One is about escapees from fish farms. For instance, Atlantic salmon farmed in British Columbia have been inadvertently released into the Pacific and some environmentalists believe that the Atlantic salmon will cause problems for Pacific salmon. There are also many environmental concerns, such as habitat interactions and water quality. Critics say that fish farms generate high levels of disease and parasites that infect wild fish stocks living in waters near the fish farms. And it has been observed that farm-raised seafood lacks the flavor and texture of seafood harvested from the wild. Aquaculture opponents also cite health concerns such as the use, in developing countries, of fungicides and parasiticides that are banned in the United States. These can persist in the flesh of the fish and cause harm when eaten.

Proponents point to the dwindling stocks of many wild fish and shellfish species. Aquaculture, they say, reduces fishing pressure on wild stocks and allows ecosystems to replenish them over time. Proponents also point out that fish require much less feed than do cattle, swine, or poultry, and therefore help preserve other food supplies.

BIBLIOGRAPHY

Kelly, Anita M., and Jeffrey Silverstein, eds. *Aquaculture in the 21st Century*. Bethesda, MD: American Fisheries Society, 2005.

Stickney, Robert R. *Aquaculture: An Introductory Text*. Cambridge, MA: CABI, 2005.

ANDREW F. SMITH

Arab American Food, *see Middle Eastern Influences on American Food*

Arbuckles'

Creating a business requires courage, determination, and imagination. John Arbuckle, a Pittsburgh grocer, had them all. In 1860 Arbuckle entered the wholesale grocery business McDonald and Arbuckle, begun by his brother Charles, his uncle Duncan McDonald, and his friend William Roseburg. The uncle and friend left the business, and John and Charles assumed charge. By 1868 John Arbuckle's formula for a tasty roasted coffee and his keen business expertise had revolutionized the coffee industry. William Ukers, writing in *All about Coffee*, calls Arbuckle "the original national-package-coffee man" (p. 447).

Until the mid-nineteenth century people purchased green coffee beans, which had to be roasted and ground before the drink could be brewed. Although a few firms advertised that they sold ground coffee "guaranteed to retain its strength and flavor for years" (as advertised in the *St. Louis Missouri Republican*, March 30, 1850), the product did not live up to the promise. Unscrupulous manufacturers often mixed chicory, sawdust, or bran with the coffee. Moreover, successful roasting was difficult, because freshly roasted beans quickly lost the volatile oils that give coffee flavor and aroma. A good cup of coffee meant daily roasting until 1868, when Arbuckle perfected a glutinous mixture made of Irish moss, gelatin, isinglass, white sugar, and eggs for preserving the freshness of roast coffee. Subsequent formulas contained only sugar and eggs. Arbuckle packaged the beans in one-pound "little paper bags like peanuts" (Fugate, p. 30). In 1873 Arbuckle combined hearty Rios and Santos beans to produce a blend called Ariosa. It was the first successful national brand of packaged coffee in the United States. The trademark, a drawing of an angel floating in the air, became famous.

To persuade consumers to purchase his brand, Arbuckle hired an army of agents to write orders. The coffee was publicized with colored folksy handbills, trading cards, and coupons redeemed for premiums. The coupons printed on the package had a cash value of one cent. As consumers began sending in coupons and collecting premiums, such as silverware, china, towels, and curtains, houses, especially in the West, took on an "Arbuckles" decor. The catalog describing the gifts was a "wish book" for many. Ahead of his time, Arbuckle had the catalog printed in Spanish so Spanish-speaking aficionados could order their gifts.

Westerners, mainly cowboys and Indians, had a particular fondness for Ariosa coffee. They liked the convenience that eliminated roasting, the light weight of the packages compared with large bags of beans, and the guarantee of a consistently good cup of coffee.

Arbuckles' was so successful that in the 1880s the company established branches in New York, Kansas City, and Chicago as well as ports in Brazil and Mexico. The company ac-quired its own fleet of seagoing vessels to transport coffee beans from field to factory and entered the sugar-refining business. Thirty-five years after developing a successful roasting process, John Arbuckle improved his own method by patenting a coffee roaster that used hot gases to suspend coffee beans in superheated air.

In 1937 the General Foods Corporation acquired a number of Arbuckle Brothers brand names, including Yuban, which had been served only to dinner guests by John Arbuckle. Having disappeared from the market by 1944, the Ariosa brand, the "Coffee That Won the West"—packaged with a stick of peppermint, a favorite premium—was resurrected in 1993.
[See also COFFEE.]

BIBLIOGRAPHY

Fugate, Francis L. *Arbuckles: The Coffee That Won the West*. El Paso: Texas Western Press, 1994. A history of how one man and one company set about solving the task of making a consistently good cup of coffee. Includes extensive photographs and illustrations.

Ukers, William H. *All about Coffee*. New York: Tea and Coffee Trade Journal Company, 1935. A comprehensive history of the coffee industry. Includes a coffee chronology, coffee dictionary, and a bibliography of more than two thousand authors and titles.

JACQUELINE BLOCK WILLIAMS

Arby's

In 1949 Forrest Raffel and his younger brother Leroy bought their uncle's Youngstown, Ohio, restaurant equipment business and formed Raffel Brothers, Inc. Observing the restaurant trade, the Raffels saw a place in the market for an upscale fast food outlet serving something other than hamburgers. One rainy night, as they queued up at a popular sandwich shop for 79-cent roast beef sandwiches, it occurred to the brothers that they could create a fast food chain around that menu item. They chose the name "Big Tex," but it was already in use, so instead they spelled out the initials of Raffel Brothers (RB) to produce "Arby's."

The first Arby's opened in Boardman, Ohio, in 1964. The brothers franchised their first operation within a year of opening the Boardman restaurant. The chuck-wagon-style building and the natural wood and stone decor evoked the Old West. The neon sign at the roadside was in the shape of a giant ten-gallon hat. The original menu offered 69-cent roast beef sandwiches, potato chips, and iced tea. At the time, fast food hamburgers were priced at around 19 cents, but the Raffels were hoping for a more upscale clientele. They added items such as Reuben Turkey Sandwiches, Fresh Wraps, Chicken Sandwiches, and Curley Fries to the menu.

In 1976 Royal Crown Cola Company of Atlanta, Georgia, purchased Arby's. The first overseas Arby's opened in Tokyo in 1981, and by 1988 there were more than two thousand Arby's restaurants worldwide. In 1991, responding to consumer concerns, the chain introduced a light menu that offered seven meals each under 300 calories. In 1996, the company bought T. J. Cinnamons Classic Bakery, a chain specializing in breakfast foods, snacks, and desserts. The first dual-branded Arby's/T. J. Cinnamons restaurant opened in 1997. Today, there are more than 3,400 Arby's restaurants worldwide.

BIBLIOGRAPHY

Jakle, John A., and Keith A. Sculle. *Fast Food: Roadside Restaurants in the Automobile Age*. Baltimore: Johns Hopkins University Press, 1999.

Langdon, Philip. *Orange Roofs, Golden Arches: The Architecture of American Chain Restaurants*. New York: Knopf, 1986.

ANDREW F. SMITH

Archer Daniels Midland

With 275 processing plants worldwide, 22,000 employees, and official sales of more than $20 billion at the end of the millennium, the Archer Daniels Midland Company is one of the world's leading agribusinesses. Headquartered in Decatur, Illinois, the self-styled "Supermarket to the World" processes soybeans, wheat, corn, peanuts, rice, barley, and various oil seeds and converts cocoa into "value-added products" for human and animal consumption. The company is also a world leader in nutraceuticals (vitamins E and C, choline, soy isoflavones, and others) and bioproducts, especially ethanol fuels. It is a thoroughly modern company that grew because of innovation, business prowess, and the close links it forged with government policymakers at home and abroad.

The union of two flaxseed-crushing companies founded in the nineteenth century, Archer Daniels joined with Midland Linseed in 1923 to become America's largest producer of linseed oil. It was a conservative company located in Minneapolis, Minnesota, but broke from usual milling company practices when it established a research laboratory in the 1930s. From it came the first edible soy protein and soy lecithin, the main emulsifier in many food products. After World War II, ADM grew to be the number-one soybean producer, selling some seven hundred items to industries ranging from food to printing, gasoline, pharmaceuticals, and even a cake mix called Airy Fairy.

Archer Daniels Midland took on its modern form beginning in 1966, when Dwayne and Lowell Andreas, and eventually other members of their family, were invited to take control of the company. Raised on a farm in Iowa, the Andreas brothers were already highly successful in the growing agribusiness industry. Dwayne Andreas came to head the company, moved it to Decatur, and led it to its preeminent position as the leader in soybean oil; high fructose corn syrup, a critical ingredient of many processed foods, especially soft drinks; and textured soy protein. A percipient businessman, Andreas saw market demands and was able to adjust the company's products to meet them. These products range from chicken and cattle feeds to pasta, hydroponic vegetables, meat substitutes (the Boca Burgers line), soy milk, pet foods, and low-calorie sweeteners.

With its mission "to unlock the potential of nature to improve the quality of life" (admworld.com), ADM has been a leader in cogenerated, environmentally friendly, power plant–based products that fight diseases and has dealt with problems of world hunger. The image of good corporate citizen was tarnished in the 1990s by scandals that were all too common in American business at the time. Seeming to reflect the company's culture, a former president is reported to have said, "Our competitors are our friends. Our customers are the enemy" (Lieber, 2000).

In the late 1990s ADM was fined a record $100 million for price-fixing. Several company officials were found guilty of other acts of price-fixing in federal court and sentenced to heavy fines and jail sentences. The company has also been accused of lavishing gifts and campaign funds on politicians—presidents, senators, and members of Congress—who, in turn, have protected ADM's interests. Sugar subsidies and ethanol production are two policy areas most often mentioned. ADM remains a corporate powerhouse with strong political connections. Like other agribusiness entities, it will doubtless grow ever larger in the twenty-first century.

BIBLIOGRAPHY

Archer Daniels Midland. www.admworld.com. Corporate website.

Kahn, E. J., Jr. *Supermarketer to the World: The Story of Dwayne Andreas, CEO of Archer Daniels Midland.* New York: Warner Books, 1991.

Lieber, James B. *Rats in the Grain: The Dirty Tricks and Trials of Archer Daniels Midland.* New York: Four Walls Eight Windows, 2000.

BRUCE KRAIG

Armour, Philip Danforth

Born in 1832 on a farm in Stockbridge (now Oneida), New York—close to the Erie Canal—Philip Danforth Armour was uniquely prepared to recognize and capitalize on the integration of agriculture, technology, and transportation systems. His foresight and entrepreneurial zeal made him a prototype for modern agribusiness and, along the way, changed the way Americans eat.

As a young man, Armour went to California in search of gold. He used the capital he acquired to open his first meatpacking plant, in Milwaukee in 1859. Business acumen was an essential part of Armour's success. He sold barrels of salt pork to the Union armies during the Civil War—until he saw that the war was coming to an end. At that point Armour sold all his inventory at forty dollars a barrel, watched the market collapse, and then bought it back for five dollars a barrel. In 1879 Armour purchased 150,000 barrels of pork intended for foreign markets at eight dollars a barrel and then resold it in the United States for fourteen dollars a barrel. Armour learned early on to control the flow of key materials, and he

became a major speculator in grain futures. Recognizing that the Union Stockyards and the Chicago rail hub (which had opened in 1865 and 1870, respectively) made Chicago's location pivotal in the transfer of goods from the Great Plains to the markets of the east, Armour relocated his operations there in 1875.

Armour's use of emerging technologies, in both processing and transportation, was among his most important contributions. Armour was one of the first to develop a processing line (a precursor of Ford's assembly line—or, in Armour's case, a disassembly line) to prepare the carcasses of hogs. Armour was an early proponent of canning and sold huge quantities of canned meats. In 1886 his company was the first in the

packing industry to hire a full-time chemist—Dr. Herman B. Schmidt—for the purpose of finding profitable uses for all the waste products of the plant. Soap, glue, upholstery, stuffing, and fertilizer were produced and marketed. It was said at the time that Armour had a use for "everything but the squeal" (Geib).

Armour's early plants made use of natural ice, but by the 1880s artificial ice (already in use in Milwaukee's breweries) was the standard. A decade later all Armour plants were refrigerated. Armour was mistaken in his belief that his brother Joseph was the first to develop refrigerated railroad cars (Gustavus Swift did so, in 1879), but he made good use of them.

An image from an 1893 stereograph, "Cutting up the hogs, Armour's great packing house, Chicago, U.S.A."

Armour, the consummate meat monopolist, was pitted against the railroad monopolists. The railroad companies preferred to ship live cattle, because profits were dependent on the volume, not the market value, shipped. The railroads also were reluctant to accept the added complications of keeping refrigerated cars iced. In 1889 Armour was successful in persuading the railroads to ship dressed beef. By the end of his life, in 1901, more than six thousand refrigerated cars carried the Armour logo.

[**See also** CANNING AND BOTTLING; PIGS; SWIFT, GUSTAVUS FRANKLIN; TRANSPORTATION OF FOOD.]

BIBLIOGRAPHY

Geib, Paul. E. "Everything But the Squeal: The Milwaukee Stockyards and Meat-packing Industry." *Wisconsin Magazine of History* 78 (1994): 2–23.

Leech, Harper, and John Charles Carroll. *Armour and His Times.* New York and London: Appleton-Century, 1938.

Sinclair, Upton. *The Jungle.* New York: Heritage Press, 1965.

GARY ALLEN

Artichokes

The globe artichoke (*Cynara scolymus*), which originated in the Mediterranean basin, is a member of the thistle family. Artichokes were eaten by the ancient Greeks and Romans, who served them in a sauce of honey and vinegar. North African Arabs improved the artichoke during Europe's Dark Ages and introduced the new version into Muslim-controlled parts of southern Italy. During the Renaissance the improved artichoke became highly prized first in Italian and later in French cookery. Artichokes were also introduced into England at this time, and recipes for them appear in British cookbooks. Martha Washington's *Booke of Cookery*, a manuscript once owned by George Washington's wife, contains a seventeenth-century recipe titled "To Make Hartichoak Pie."

Globe artichokes, also called French artichokes or green artichokes, were grown in Virginia as early as the 1720s and in New England around the time of the Revolutionary War, when they may have been introduced by allied French soldiers. Instructions for growing artichokes regularly appeared in gardening books beginning in 1806. Early American cookbooks occasionally published recipes with artichokes as ingredients. N. K. M. Lee's *The Cook's Own Book* (1832), for example, featured five recipes, including two for boiling and dipping the leaves in butter and two for preserving artichoke hearts.

Before the Civil War, artichokes often appeared on the tables of wealthy Virginia planters. After the war, artichoke recipes frequently appeared in American cookbooks. In 1868 *quartiers d'artichauts lyonnaise* were featured on the menu of a Delmonico's banquet honoring Charles Dickens.

Artichokes were grown in California and Louisiana in the eighteenth century but were not a successful commercial crop. In the 1890s Italian farmers in northern California's

Half Moon Bay planted the crop, and beginning in 1904 boxcar loads of artichokes were sent east from California to supply the needs of artichoke lovers on the East Coast—at that point, mainly Italian immigrants. The first American pamphlet published about artichoke canning was prepared by A. W. Bitting in the 1920s.

The first American artichoke cookbook was R. E. Scammell's *Thistle Eaters Guide* (1969), and it has been succeeded by several others, including Patricia Rain's *The Artichoke Cookbook* (1985) and A. C. Castelli's *The Sensuous Artichoke* (1998). Fresh artichokes are usually boiled or steamed and served with a butter-based sauce for dipping. Artichoke hearts—fresh, canned, or frozen—are served on their own and used in salads, casseroles, and pizzas.

In 1922 Italian farmers began cultivating artichokes in the Salinas Valley of California. Castroville, home to artichoke growers, packers, and processors, calls itself "the Artichoke Capital of the World" and celebrates this claim with an annual artichoke festival. Today all artichokes produced commercially in the United States are grown in California.

[**See also** CANNING AND BOTTLING; ITALIAN AMERICAN FOOD.]

BIBLIOGRAPHY

Bitting, A. W. *The Artichoke.* Baltimore: Canning Trade, n.d.

Castelli, A. C. *The Sensuous Artichoke: Magic of the Artichoke.* Riverdale, NY: Castelli Associates, 1998.

Rain, Patricia. *The Artichoke Cookbook.* Berkeley, CA: Celestial Arts, 1985.

Scammell, R. E. *Thistle Eaters Guide.* 6th ed. Lafayette, CA: Floreat Press, 1970.

ANDREW F. SMITH

Aseptic Packaging

The first invention was likely a device for carrying food. Hunters and gatherers needed to lighten the burden of bringing food back to a central camp. These early camps were undoubtedly located near water, because the means of transporting liquids was still a long way off. As populations grew and were forced to move farther away from a secure source of water, the need to carry liquids became urgent. Skins and shells, followed by pottery and ceramics and then glass, metals, and plastics, became the materials needed for storing, preserving, and transporting liquids. In 1989 the Institute of Food Technologists, an organization of food scientists devoted to improving the production and distribution of food, selected aseptic packaging as "the most significant food science innovation of the past fifty years" (Mermelstein, 2000). Most consumers do not recognize the term "aseptic packaging," but they instantly recognize this packaging concept as the familiar "juice box." This revolutionary packaging system first appeared in U.S. supermarkets in the 1970s. Aseptic packaging is defined as "the filling of

a commercially sterile product into sterile containers under aseptic conditions and sealing of the containers so that reinfection is prevented" (Robertson, p. 51). Aseptic packaging is more than just a container; it is a system that allows food manufactures to fill a sanitized package with a sterile food product in a hygienic environment. The word "aseptic" means that unwanted organisms have been eliminated from the packaging system.

Ruben Rausing in Sweden reportedly conceived the concept for holding milk in a container made from a paperboard composite. The original package had a tetrahedral shape and was called a Tetra Pak. This new technology was married to aseptic technology, and a new industry was born. The box-shaped package that is so widely available is a laminate of six layers of three materials: paperboard, 70 percent; polyethylene, 24 percent; and aluminum, 6 percent. Each layer of material serves a specific purpose. The single layer of paperboard provides mechanical rigidity. The aluminum foil layer acts as a gas and light barrier. The outer polyethylene layer protects the ink layer and enables the package flaps to be sealed. Two inner layers of polyethylene provide a liquid barrier, and another layer binds the aluminum to the paperboard. When it is sealed, the container can preserve milk, soy beverages, juice, soup, sauce, wine, tea, and many other products for months without refrigeration or artificial preservatives.

Aseptic processing is not limited to retail food items. Aseptic bulk storage and transportation systems that can hold up to 1 million gallons of products such as orange juice have been designed. These large commercial systems allow food manufactures to harvest fruit and vegetables at optimum growing periods, partially process the food, and store it for final processing at a later time. Innovations in plastic technology and plasma-discharge silica-coating technology offer the promise that more foods will be packaged in efficient aseptic packages during the twenty-first century.

[**See also** CONTAINERS; COOKING CONTAINERS; PACKAGING.]

BIBLIOGRAPHY

Brody, Aaron L. "Thinking outside the Box: Tetra Pak's Past and Future." *Food Technology* 56, no. 11 (November 2002): 66–68.

Mermelstein, Neil H. "Aseptic Bulk Storage and Transportation." *Food Technology* 54, no. 4 (April 2000): 107–109.

Robertson, Gordon L. "The Paper Beverage Carton: Past and Future." *Food Technology* 56, no. 7 (July 2002): 46–52.

JOSEPH M. CARLIN

Asparagus

This perennial garden vegetable (*Asparagus officinalis*) is a member of the Lily family. Native to the East Mediterranean area, the name is derived from the Persian word *asparag*, meaning sprout. Originally, asparagus was quite tall and spindly, resembling contemporary wild asparagus, but by the eighteenth century fatter-stemmed varieties had evolved. The cultivated form of this plant has been developed through selective breeding to produce a number of varieties that shade from white to purple.

For centuries, the British have known the vegetable as sparrow grass, a term that English and Dutch colonists to New England brought in their cookbooks in the 1700s along with their asparagus seeds. Amelia Simmons in her *American Cookery* (1796) considers the asparagus an "excellent vegetable" and recommends the largest available. Her cooking instructions include the lovely refinement to "tie them up in small even bundles…and boil them up quick; but by overboiling they will lose their heads." Miss Eliza Leslie's *Directions for Cookery* (1828) advised cooks that ham should always be accompanied by a green vegetable, such as asparagus. Virtually all nineteenth-century cookbooks recommend serving asparagus on toast, accompanied by melted butter and usually lemon or orange slices. More contemporary recipes for asparagus feature it either as a hot side dish (minus the toast) or as a cold salad, although asparagus has found its way into soups, sauces, pickles, and such nouvelle cuisine conceits as asparagus ice cream.

Asparagus has been a kitchen garden crop since colonial times but has also been readily naturalized in sandy soils along riverbanks, lakeshores, and seacoasts. Commercial cultivation took off only in the nineteenth century, with improved plants and means of transporting the perishable vegetable to urban markets. Among the most popular variety was Conover's Colossal Asparagus, a fat-stemmed asparagus developed in New York that is recommended to home gardeners as an "heirloom" variety in the twenty-first century.

California has grown asparagus since the 1850s; the white asparagus first used for canning came entirely from that state. In the early 2000s California led the nation in asparagus production with a harvest of over 50,000 metric tons annually, or 70 percent to 80 percent of the annual total. Most of

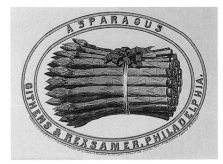

An asparagus advertisement from Githens & Rexsamer.

---

this is marketed as fresh asparagus. The remainder of the major U.S. commercial asparagus crop is raised in Washington and Michigan, where the crop is often frozen or canned.

[**See also** HEIRLOOM VEGETABLES; LESLIE, ELIZA; SIMMONS, AMELIA; VEGETABLES.]

BIBLIOGRAPHY

Cornell University. *Department of Horticulture at Cornell University*. http://www.hort.cornell.edu. The vegetable research and extension program provides agricultural producers and the general public with current science-based information and production practices.

Michigan Asparagus Advisory Board. *Welcome to Asparagus Online*. http://www.asparagus.org. This site has the answer to almost any asparagus-related question, including details on the National Asparagus Festival.

SARA RATH

Aunt Jemima

Aunt Jemima pancake flour, the first nationally distributed ready-mix food and one of the earliest products to be marketed through personal appearances and advertisements featuring its namesake, was created by combining advances in manufacturing and distribution with popular nostalgia for the antebellum South.

The self-rising pancake flour was created by a pair of speculators, Chris Rutt and Charles Underwood, in St. Joseph, Missouri, in 1889. The duo had purchased a bankrupt mill and planned to make it successful by developing a new product that would spur demand for their flour. Despite their lack of culinary expertise, or perhaps because of it, the two settled on developing a foolproof and less labor-intensive pancake batter that would require only the addition of water. They experimented with a variety of recipes in the summer of 1889 before settling on a mixture of wheat flour, corn flour, lime phosphate, and salt.

The product was originally named "Self-Rising Pancake Flour" and sold in bags. In the fall of 1889 Rutt was inspired to rename the mix after attending a minstrel show, during which a popular song titled "Old Aunt Jemima" was performed by men in blackface, one of whom was depicting a slave mammy of the plantation South. The song, which was written by the African American singer, dancer, and acrobat Billy Kersands in 1875, was a staple of the minstrel circuit and was based on a song sung by field slaves.

Rutt and Underwood sold their milling company to a larger corporation owned by R. G. Davis of Chicago. He transformed the local product into a national one by distributing it through a network of suppliers and by creating a persona for Aunt Jemima. Davis hired Nancy Green, a former Kentucky slave and cook in a Chicago kitchen, to portray Aunt Jemima in that city's 1893 World's Columbian Exposition. She served pancakes from a booth designed to look like a huge flour barrel and told stories of life as a cook on an Old South plantation. Her highly publicized appearance spurred thousands of orders for the product from distributors. Davis also commissioned a pamphlet detailing the "life" of Aunt Jemima. She was depicted as the actual house slave of one Colonel Higbee of Louisiana, whose plantation was known across the South for its fine dining—especially its pancake breakfasts.

The recipe for the pancakes was a secret known only to the slave woman. Sometime after the war, the pamphlet said, Aunt Jemima was remembered by a Confederate general who had once found himself stranded at her cabin. The general recalled her pancakes and put Aunt Jemima in contact with a "large northern milling company," which paid her (in gold) to come north and supervise the construction of a factory to mass-produce her mix. This surprisingly durable fable formed the background for decades of future Aunt Jemima advertising.

The Advertising Campaign

The basic story was fleshed out and brilliantly illustrated through an advertising campaign in North American women's magazines during the 1920s and 1930s. The ads were the work of James Webb Young, a legendary account executive at the J. Walter Thompson advertising agency in Chicago, and N. C. Wyeth, the well-known painter and illustrator of such books as *Treasure Island* and *The Last of the Mohicans*. The full-page color advertisements ran regularly in *The Ladies' Home Journal*, *Good Housekeeping*, and the *Saturday Evening Post* and told tales of the leisure and splendor of the plantation South, complete with grand balls, huge dinners, and visitors

"I'se in town, Honey!"
Reg. U. S. pat. off.

America's most famous recipe

New ways in which millions of women are using it to make delicious pancakes, waffles and muffins

A recipe pamphlet depicting Aunt Jemima issued by the Quaker Oats Company, mid-twentieth century.

dropping in from across the region. Not too subtly, Aunt Jemima Pancake Mix, a labor-saving product, was marketed with comparisons to a time and place when some American white women had access to the ultimate labor-saving device: a slave. A line from a 1927 product display read, "Make them with Aunt Jemima Pancake Flour, and your family will ask where you got your wonderful southern cook."

After Aunt Jemima's debut in 1893, her character was played by dozens of women in radio and, eventually, television commercials and in appearances at schools and county fairs. After Nancy Green, the original actress, died in 1923, she was replaced as Aunt Jemima by Anna Robinson, a darker-complected and heavier (at 350 pounds) woman. The image on the box and in ads was adjusted to resemble her more closely. Later, the actresses Aylene Lewis and Edith Wilson portrayed the mammy in some advertisements. Lewis also played the role at Aunt Jemima's Pancake House in Disneyland, which opened in 1957.

However, the advertising icon, always a source of criticism in African American newspapers, came under increasing scrutiny in the 1950s and 1960s as first the civil rights movement and then the black power movement reached their respective crests. Local chapters of the National Association for the Advancement of Colored People began pressuring schools and fair organizers not to invite Aunt Jemima to appear. In 1967 Edith Wilson became the last woman to play Aunt Jemima in advertisements when the Quaker Oats company, which had owned the product since 1925, fired her and canceled its television campaign. Quaker Oats also took Aunt Jemima's name off the Disneyland restaurant in 1970; Aylene Lewis was the last woman to portray Aunt Jemima on the company's behalf.

Revising the Image

Throughout the 1960s Quaker Oats lightened Aunt Jemima's skin and made her look thinner in print images. In 1968 the company replaced her bandanna with a headband, slimmed her down further, and created a somewhat younger-looking image. She still appeared in print advertisements but without the heavy reliance on the southern plantation settings and largely without a speaking role. In 1989 Quaker Oats made the most dramatic alteration yet to Aunt Jemima's appearance, removing her headband to reveal a head full of graying curls and adding earrings and a pearl necklace. The company said it was repositioning the brand icon as a "black working grandmother."

In 1993 Quaker Oats debuted a series of television ads for the pancake mix featuring the singer Gladys Knight as a spokeswoman and using Aunt Jemima's face only sparingly. The ads had a very short run, and Aunt Jemima continues to hold a low profile in the advertising world, even though she consistently ranks as one of the most recognizable trade names in North America. Aunt Jemima pancake mix and syrup remain market leaders in the United States, and in the 1990s Quaker Oats even licensed the use of her name and image for a line of frozen breakfast products manufactured by another firm. Despite the controversy surrounding her image in the late twentieth century, Aunt Jemima remains one of the most successful advertising icons of our time.

[**See also** ADVERTISING.]

BIBLIOGRAPHY

Kern-Foxworth, Marilyn. *Aunt Jemima, Uncle Ben, and Rastus: Blacks in Advertising, Yesterday, Today, and Tomorrow.* Westport, CT: Greenwood, 1994.

Manring, M. M. *Slave in a Box: The Strange Career of Aunt Jemima.* Charlottesville: University Press of Virginia, 1998.

MAURICE MANRING

Automats

Before McDonald's, there was the Horn and Hardart Automat. On December 22, 1888, Joe Horn and Frank Hardart opened their first lunchroom at 39 South Thirteenth Street in Philadelphia, opposite Wanamaker's Department Store. Customers flocked to their lunchroom to sip their "gilt-edge" coffee, prepared in the French-drip method made popular in New Orleans, Louisiana.

At the turn of the twentieth century the company learned about a new Swiss invention called the "waiterless restaurant" or the "automatic." The first machine they purchased was manufactured in Germany and installed at 818 Chestnut Street in Philadelphia on June 9, 1902. In 1912 John Fritsche, the chief engineer for Horn and Hardart, designed a more efficient machine with rectangular glass doors that could be opened by a knob. The customer would walk down a wall of these windows, select a hot or cold item, insert a nickel, and turn the knob; the door would then spring open to reveal the food. Behind the bank of glass doors an efficient team of women kept the slots filled with food.

The company opened its first Automat in New York City in 1912. Horn and Hardart commissioned the glass sculptor Nicola D'Ascenzo, who had designed the windows for the Cathedral Church of St. John the Divine in New York City, to create a stained-glass window two stories high. The ceiling contained elaborate carvings, and the customers sat at tables topped with Carrara glass. At the time there was probably no other place in the United States where a person could have a nickel cup of coffee and a nourishing meal in that much splendor. Forty-two Automats were operating in New York City by 1932, and another forty-six had opened in Philadelphia.

All food was prepared in a central commissary and delivered to the Automats daily. To meet the demands of their customers, retail stores were opened in 1922 so that people could have their favorite Horn and Hardart prepared food at home.

The Oxford Dictionary of Word Histories defines fast food as "food served in catering outlets where it is kept hot or semi-prepared ready to serve quickly." Based on this definition alone, Horn and Hardart can be credited with starting the fast food revolution in America.

To promote the Automat in the late 1930s the company started *The Horn and Hardart Children's Hour* on WCAU radio in Philadelphia, with the slogan "less work for mother." It became one of the longest-running shows on radio and television. Bernadette Peters, Frankie Avalon, Eddie Fisher, and Bobby Rydell got their starts on this program.

Joe Horn and Frank Hardart understood the need of customers for a familiar and clean environment and a quick meal at low cost, with no tipping. What they did not expect was that the Automat would be a rendezvous for celebrities and a cultural icon immortalized in both song and movies. The image of two children inserting nickels into the slots under cakes and pies, as their chauffeur held their coats, graced the February 26, 1938, cover of the *New Yorker*. Doris Day is pictured standing next to a bank of Automat glass doors in the movie *That Touch of Mink* (1962). Other scenes filmed in Automats are in *Affair with a Stranger* (1953), with Victor Mature and Jean Simmons, and *Just This Once* (1952), with Peter Lawford and Janet Leigh.

In the 1980s most Horn and Hardart Automats were converted to Burger Kings. The last Automat closed in Philadelphia on May 12, 1990, and nearly a year later the last Automat in New York City closed on April 8, 1991.

Before the Automat disappeared entirely, a thirty-five-foot section of an ornate Automat with mirrors, marble, and marquetry was installed in the Smithsonian's National Museum of American History.

[**See also** LUNCHEONETTES.]

BIBLIOGRAPHY

Diehl, Lorraine B., and Marianne Hardart. *The Automat: The History, Recipes, and Allure of Horn and Hardart's Masterpiece.* New York: Potter, 2002.

JOSEPH M. CARLIN

Avena

"Avena" means "oats" in both Latin and Spanish. It is also the name of a gruel consumed as a breakfast drink in Latin America and by Latinos in the United States. Rolled oats or oat flour is steeped or boiled in milk, fruit juice, or water and often sweetened with sugar or honey. Crushed fruit and spices, especially cinnamon, may be added. The drink is served either hot or cold in the

same manner as corn-based *atole* and pinole, which have been staples in the Central American diet since before the introduction of oats from Europe.

BOB SIMMONS

Avocados

The avocado (*Persea americana*) originated in the broad geographical area stretching from the eastern Mexican highlands to the Pacific Coast of Central America. In pre-Columbian times avocados were disseminated to other places in Central America and Peru. Its seeds have been found in archaeological sites in Mexico dating to 6000 B.C.E. The Aztecs consumed avocados in a variety of ways, one of which was to make a sauce base called *ahuaca-mulli* or guacamole, which consisted of mashed avocados with chopped tomatoes and New World onions.

Three distinct avocado subspecies have emerged: Mexican, Guatemalan, and Antillean (or lowland). Lowland avocados were disseminated to the Caribbean region soon after the Spanish conquest of Central America and were subsequently introduced into Southeast Asia. The avocado was introduced into the region that became the United States from three directions: from Hawaii early in the nineteenth century (the fruit was common on Oahu by 1855); from Florida before 1850, probably from Cuba; and from California before 1856, perhaps by a gold rush participant who traveled through Central America. By the end of the nineteenth century avocados had become popular, and an extensive avocado trade had bloomed between the Caribbean region and East Coast cities.

To compete with companies importing avocados, Floridians in the early twentieth century planted the first American commercial avocado orchards. But it was in California that the avocado industry flourished. Eleven years after avocados were first grown commercially in Altadena, California, by Carl Schmidt in 1911, growers formed a cooperative association called Calavo, which eventually dominated the industry. California produces 95 percent of the avocados grown in the United States.

Soon after its formation, Calavo published an advertising booklet that contained recipes and encouraged readers to consume avocados in diverse ways. Calavo subsequently published numerous such works. Many of the recipes were later published in noncommercial sources, including magazines, newspapers, and cookbooks. Avocados were used mainly in salads, sandwiches, and cold soups, because avocado pulp becomes bitter when heated.

Avocado cuisine flowered beginning in the 1920s. The 1933 *Sunset All-Western Cook Book* featured twenty-eight avocado recipes. From that date on, avocado recipes were published in almost all mainstream American cookbooks. The first noncommer-

HALF SHELL...with your favorite dressing

SALADS • COCKTAILS • ENTREES • SPREADS • DESSERTS

The Calavo Book of Popular Avocado Recipes, *published by Calavo Growers of California (Los Angeles, 1949).*

cial cookbook to focus entirely on avocado cookery was Judy Hicks and Mims Thompson's *The Alluring Avocado: Recipes Hot and Cold* (1966). A great diversity of avocado recipes were published, including unusual ones for guacamole, avocado candy, avocado ice cream, and even cooked avocados.

The Fuerte avocado, which matures in winter, is the green-skinned variety that built the industry, but the summer-ripening Hass dominates production, because it holds up better in shipping, is high in oil, and turns black when ripe. By 2002 an estimated 43 percent of all U.S. households were purchasing avocados annually. Consumption increased in part because of the growing popularity of guacamole, a dish featured in Mexican American cookery. The United States produced 225,000 tons of avocados in 2002 and was the second-largest avocado producer in the world after Mexico. Despite record production, importation of avocados from Caribbean countries and South America is common in the United States in the early twenty-first century.

[**See also** ADVERTISING COOKBOOKLETS AND RECIPES; DIPS; MEXICAN AMERICAN FOOD.]

BIBLIOGRAPHY

Whiley, A. W., B. Schaffer, and B. N. Wolstenholme, eds. *The Avocado: Botany, Production, and Uses.* New York: CABI International, 2002.

ANDREW F. SMITH

Avocados

B

Baby Food

Historically, babies were fed with breast milk provided by their own mothers or wet nurses. Solid foods were usually not introduced until the fourth month or later. However, the decades from the mid-nineteenth to mid-twentieth centuries saw a shift in infant feeding practices, as bottled formula and manufactured baby foods were widely adopted. The rise of industrialism and consumerism transformed infant feeding, accompanied by lively public discourse over the meaning of motherhood, child rearing, and nutrition.

New practices of infant feeding were brought about in part by industrialization, which led to a rise in the numbers of working mothers, and innovations in the mass production and distribution of canned goods. By the late nineteenth century, the growth in advertising enabled the rapid introduction of new food products to American consumers.

These changes were accompanied by shifting ideologies of motherhood. Before the early twentieth century, many believed that "natural motherhood" and proper child development favored breast milk as the best food for babies. Child-rearing texts advocated that supplemental foods should be plain and natural because they affected infant development; feeding infants with "stimulating" salty or spicy foods, for example, could lead to nervous adults.

At the same time, nineteenth-century physicians and reformers believed that some babies were malnourished because of nutritional deficiencies in their mother's milk, and that cow's milk was a poor substitute because of the transmission of disease. In 1867 the Swiss merchant Henri Nestlé invented the first artificial infant food, and within twenty years several brands of infant foods, mostly grain mixtures to be mixed with milk or water, followed. Perhaps the most widely used of these was Mellin's Food, developed by the English chemist Gustav Mellin in the late 1860s. There was also Borden's condensed milk, invented by Gail Borden as a remedy for poor infant health. In 1924, Moores and Ross Milk Company created a milk-based infant formula, known as Franklin Infant Food, which was renamed Similac in 1927.

The adoption of these formulas was reinforced by the growing belief in so-called "scientific motherhood," which emphasized the importance of medical expertise. "Maternal instinct" was considered old-fashioned and unsound; doctors were to "prescribe" breast-feeding or bottle-feeding to mothers.

Advice manuals, such as Benjamin Spock's *The Pocket-Book of Baby and Child Care*, first published in 1946, encouraged mothers to feed babies on precise schedules, weigh them before and after feeding, and follow complicated procedures for sterilizing bottles and preparing formula. If breast-feeding their babies, mothers were to wean them to formula by three to seven months of age. Many of the companies producing baby food and formula, including Gerber, Mellin's, and Bordens, circulated free booklets on child care emphasizing scientific approaches to infant feeding.

The notion that infant formula was equal to if not superior to mother's milk took hold in America. Where 80 percent of American infants had been breast-fed before 1920, by 1948 only 38 percent of babies were breast-fed at one week of age, declining to 18 percent by 1956. At the same time, the age at which solid foods were introduced dropped from about seven months in 1920, to four to six weeks by the 1950s. As a result, the market for both infant formula and baby food expanded rapidly.

The adoption of manufactured formula and baby foods was not universal. Some women urged a return to more natural forms of infant feeding, including the La Leche League, a voluntary association founded in 1956 to promote "good mothering through breast-feeding." Yet while the La Leche League advocated that babies be breast-fed on demand as long as possible—at least a year, and preferably longer—most American women who breast-fed did so for far shorter periods.

By the late 1920s, commercially canned baby food was introduced and quickly adopted by American consumers. Conditions were favorable: advertising had become widespread, the cost of canned foods had fallen, and experts recommended the addition of fruits and vegetables to the infant diet. The Gerber Company initiated this revolution by expanding the scope of the canned foods industry. According to Gerber company history, Dorothy Gerber laboriously hand-strained vegetables for her seven-month-old daughter, Sally, and urged her husband Daniel to consider manufacturing strained baby food. In 1928 the company introduced strained peas, prunes, carrots, and spinach to the market, and launched an advertising campaign featuring a sketch of an infant known as the Gerber Baby. Beech-Nut, a company that had been formed to market ham and bacon, introduced thirteen varieties of strained baby foods sold in glass jars in 1931. That same year, Heinz, a company begun in 1869 to manufacture horseradish, added baby food to its product line.

Public concerns with food additives developed by midcentury. The American Medical Association disapproved the addition of vitamins and minerals to canned baby food during World War II. Debates over additives during the 1960s focused on corporate practices that included sweetening baby food to please the palates of mothers. Another tension developed in 1977 when a consumer boycott against the Nestlé Corporation was launched to protest Nestlé's promotion of infant formula in developing countries that lacked the technology to use formula effectively.

By the beginning of the twenty-first century, commercial baby food and formula defined infant feeding in the United States. Only 33 percent of American babies were breastfed at six months. The most widely used infant formula was Enfamil, manufactured by Mead Johnson. Fifteen percent of American families prepared baby food at home, with the majority purchasing baby food—a $1.25 billion a year industry. Multinational corporations purchased the three largest baby food brands. Squibb acquired Beech-Nut in 1968, and was in turn bought by Nestlé of Switzerland. In 1994 the Swiss drugmaker Sandoz purchased Gerber and then merged with Ciba-Geigy to form Novartis. Heinz sold its U.S. baby food businesses to Del Monte Foods. By 2002 the Gerber brand held a 77 percent market share among mass retailers of baby food, with rivals Beech-Nut and Heinz following far behind at 11 percent of market share apiece.

BIBLIOGRAPHY

Apple, Rima. *Mothers & Medicine: A Social History of Infant Feeding, 1890–1950.* Madison: University of Wisconsin Press, 1987.

Bentley, Amy. "Inventing Baby Food: Gerber and the Discourse of Infancy in the United States." In *Food Nations: Selling Taste in Consumer Societies*, edited by Warren Belasco and Philip Scranton, 92–112. New York: Routledge, 2002.

Van Esterik, Penny. *Beyond the Breast-Bottle Controversy.* New Brunswick, NJ: Rutgers University Press, 1989.

LYNN WEINER

Baby Ruth

In 1916 Otto Y. Schnering of Chicago founded a bakery, food, and wholesale candy business in Chicago. The candy products soon outstripped the bakery items in popularity, and Schnering changed the company's name to reflect this, calling it the Curtiss Candy Company (Curtiss was his mother's maiden name). One of his products was the Kandy Kate bar—a pastry center topped with nuts and coated with chocolate. In 1920, Schnering changed the formula, devising a filling of peanuts covered with nougat, and he changed the name to "Baby Ruth." Within two years of its creation, the "Baby Ruth" bar was sold nationwide.

The candy bar's popularity convinced Babe Ruth, the baseball star, to form his own company, called the George H. Ruth Candy Co.; his plan was to market the "Babe Ruth Home Run Bar." Curtiss sued for breach of copyright infringement. Babe Ruth claimed that Curtiss was using his name without permission. Curtiss maintained that their candy bar was named after President Grover Cleveland's daughter, Ruth, and had nothing to do with the Babe. But Ruth Cleveland was born in 1891 and died of diphtheria in 1914. Cleveland himself died in 1908. Putting aside the questionable taste of naming a candy bar after a president's child who had died in childhood, few young candy buyers would have recognized Ruth's name, but everybody knew Babe Ruth, the nation's most popular baseball player. Still, the Curtiss Candy Company won their suit. When Babe Ruth was informed, he reportedly retorted, "Well, I ain't eatin' your damned candy bar anymore!"

The Baby Ruth bar was a huge success, thanks mostly to Schnering's promotional ability. He chartered an airplane and "airlifted" the bars by parachute over the city of Pittsburgh. He later expanded his drops to cities in more than forty states. At the same time, the company began advertising in national magazines. These proclaimed that Baby Ruth was the "Sweetest Story Ever Told," and that it was "the world's most popular candy." Later, the doctor caring for the Dionne Quintuplets (born in 1934 in Canada) endorsed Baby Ruth as the only candy given to the little girls.

Schnering had to build another factory, then another, to keep up with demand for Baby Ruths. These plants consumed five or six train carloads of peanuts every day. By 1927, the Curtiss facilities were the largest of their kind in the world, operating twenty-four hours a day. Baby Ruth had become the largest selling five-cent confection in America (during the Depression, Schnering also marketed a smaller penny bar). This position was solidified in 1929, when Curtiss began sponsoring the CBS radio program "The Baby Ruth Hour." The Curtiss Candy Company was sold to Standard Brands in 1930.

BIBLIOGRAPHY

Broekel, Ray. *The Chocolate Chronicles*. Lombard, Illinois: Wallace-Homestead Book Company, 1985.

Richardson, Tim. *Sweets: A History of Candy*. New York: Bloomsbury, 2002.

Smith, Andrew F. *Peanuts: The Illustrious History of the Goober Pea*. Urbana: University of Illinois Press, 2002.

ANDREW F. SMITH

Bagels

A bagel is a round yeast roll with a hole in the middle. A true bagel is completely plain and made with white wheat high-gluten flour, and then boiled in water and baked. Boiling the dough reduces the starch content and gives the bagel its outer sheen and hard crust. The

An assortment of the unmistakable rolls at La Bagel Delight, Brooklyn, New York.

word "bagel" possibly derives from *beigen*, German for "to bend," or the Middle High German *bougel* or *buegel*, meaning a twisted or curved ring or bracelet.

In ancient Egypt there was a hard cracker with a hole in the middle called *ka'ak* that can be seen as an ancestor of the bagel. From Egypt, ancestry can be traced to classical Rome and to what is now Italy and then to France, where there is a boiled and baked anise-flavored bread, similar to a bagel. Eventually, precursors of the bagel made their way to Russia and Poland. The first Jewish community in Poland, established by invitation and charter in the thirteenth century, probably brought *biscochos*, a ring-shaped cookie or cracker, with them dating from the Roman period.

It is in Poland where some say the present-day bagel was born. Mentioned as early as 1610 in the community regulations of Kraków, Poland, bagels, symbolic of the endless circle of life, were given as a gift to women in childbirth. There is another theory tracing them to 1683 Vienna, where bakers created stirrup-shaped buns in honor of their deliverance from the Turks by the Polish King John Sobieski; *buegel* is the Austrian word for stirrup. Yet another theory is that bagels were invented as an economical food for poor people because the hole saved on ingredients.

The Beigel family of Kraków, Poland, bread bakers for centuries, tells a story that may explain why the bagel is boiled. Eastern European Jews were particularly careful about their meats, fish, and breads, allowing only Jewish bakers to bake for them. Most Jews earned their living as peddlers and when traveling the countryside could not eat bread, the most holy of foods, because it had not been blessed. Jewish dietary laws dictated that bread could not be eaten until after hands were washed and a blessing said. But because clean water was rarely available when they were traveling, the men had to go hungry. By having their dough boiled first, rather than baked, bagels fell outside the category of traditional bread. Consequently, the ritual hand-washing and blessing was not required before eating for a time.

Many bagel bakers came to the United States with the mass of eastern European Jewish immigrants at the turn of the twentieth century. The hole in the center of the bagel enabled bakers to sell their wares on the streets of the Lower East Side of New York by threading dozens of bagels on long sticks that they could carry to customers. By 1907 the International Beigel Bakers' Union was created, joining together three hundred bagel bakers. Only sons of union members could be apprenticed to learn the secrets of bagel baking in order to safeguard the culinary act. Until the late 1950s, bagels were handcrafted in small two- or three-person cellar bakeries on New York's Lower East Side. The oven was built so low that a pit two or three feet deep had to be dug in front of it for the person working the oven. To remove the bagels, they used a twelve-foot *shalivka*, which was a board with a knifelike edge that slid under the bagel and helped toss it into a chute.

By the mid-1920s the number of bagel bakeries had begun to decline as Jews turned away from their old folk customs. Then in 1951 a Broadway comedy, *Bagels and Yox*, put the word "bagel" into mainstream magazines, such as *Time*. That same year *Family Circle* included a recipe for bagels. This was also the time when bagels were paired with toppings like cream cheese, sweet butter, and smoked salmon. Although bagels had always been a food reserved for Sunday mornings and were thought of as a Jewish dish, this new recognition in major magazines began popularizing them throughout America.

When Murray Lender joined his father's bagel business in 1955, he began expanding the business and making bagels a mainstream food item by packaging bagels to sell in supermarkets. He also began to experiment with bagels flavored with onions, egg, and pumpernickel flour. In 1962 Lender's bought and made operational the first bagel-making machine and began freezing bagels, which they marketed nationally under the Lender's brand.

In the twenty-first century, bagels have been completely assimilated into American food culture and can be found everywhere in supermarkets and national bakery chains, such as Dunkin' Donuts, Einstein's Bagels, and Bruegger's Bagel shops. Bagels are mostly steamed and offered in every conceivable flavor, from the more traditional pumpernickel or onion, to the sweetened blueberry or chocolate chip versions, as well as many other flavors in between. Of all Jewish foods, the bagel has become the most mainstream, enjoyed by people not only in the United States but also worldwide.

[**See also** BIALY; JEWISH AMERICAN FOOD; JEWISH DIETARY LAWS.]

BIBLIOGRAPHY

Kirshenblatt-Gimblett, Barbara. *Getting Comfortable in New York: The American Jewish Home, 1880–1950*. New York: Jewish Museum, 1990.

Nathan, Joan. *Jewish Cooking in America*. Updated ed. New York: Random House, 2001.

Nathan, Joan. *Jewish Holiday Baker*. New York: Schocken Books, 1997.

Nathan, Joan. *Jewish Holiday Kitchen*. New York: Schocken Books, 1985.

JOAN NATHAN

Baked Alaska

Baked Alaska is a dessert of ice cream surrounded by insulating cake and/or meringue, which can then be heated or even flambéed and brought to the table as a hot dessert that is cold inside. The general idea seems to have been developed by chefs in the eighteenth century, and linked to two Americans at the turn of the nineteenth century. Thomas Jefferson is supposed to have served an ice cream dessert encased in hot pastry in 1802; while Count Rumford, an American Tory who had moved to Europe, supposedly developed an "omelette surprise" using meringue in Monaco in 1804.

The name may date from as early as the 1850s, but the clear chain begins with the U.S. Alaska purchase of 1867. Delmonico's Restaurant in New York was serving a dish called "Alaska Florida"—banana and vanilla ice cream on a base of Savoy biscuit encased in meringue and browned for two minutes in a hot oven—as early as 1876, and the recipe was published by the chef Charles Ranhofer in his 1894 cookbook, *The Epicurean*. A visiting British journalist, George Augustus Sala, ordered one in 1879, and found the contrast unpleasant: "you go on discussing the warm cream soufflé till you come, with somewhat painful suddenness, on the row of ice."

Mrs. Rorer called a simplified version "Alaska Bake" in her 1886 *Philadelphia Cook Book*. Barry Popik has found New York menu references to "Baked Alaska" from 1888, and that name appears on a printed recipe by Fannie Farmer in 1896. The concept survives in "fried ice cream" or "tempura ice cream" served as a dessert in Chinese, Mexican, or Japanese restaurants in the United States today.

BIBLIOGRAPHY

Sala, George Augustus. *America Revisited: From The Bay Of New York to The Gulf of Mexico.* London: Vizetelly, 1883. Reprint. New York: Arno, 1974.

MARK H. ZANGER

Bakeries

Bread bakeries heralded the dawn of civilization. Often government-run or regulated because of the importance of a reliable supply of this staple food, bakeries flourished in Egypt, Mesopotamia, and the Greco-Roman world as well as throughout medieval and early modern Europe. Indeed, wherever villages grew to a critical mass, bakers made and sold fresh, perishable bread. Within a generation of the establishment of successful colonies in America, commercial bakeries had opened in Plymouth, Massachusetts (no later than 1640), New Amsterdam (by 1645), and New Haven, Connecticut (by 1650). However, most baking in America was done at home until the mid-twentieth century, when the balance shifted to favor store-bought products.

Typically the village baker ran a one-man operation reminiscent of his European forefathers. His living quarters adjoined his oven and workspace, with only a small retail area, because colonial bakeries tended to produce to order. From the mid-seventeenth through the mid-nineteenth centuries, many local authorities regulated bakers through assizes of bread that established quality and price controls.

The baking industry grew slowly through the mid-nineteenth century: in 1700 Philadelphia boasted seven bakers serving a population of 4,500, probably the densest concentration of bakers then in America, and 150 years later, the *Census of Manufacturers of 1850* reported a paltry 2,027 bakeries in the entire United States, employing fewer than seven thousand workers to produce the country's commercial supply of breads, sweet and savory pastries, and crackers. Most bakeries remained small, constrained by limited urban markets, the practical difficulties of distributing a perishable product, and arduous preindustrial production techniques that had changed little since the Roman Empire and kept the price of bakery goods relatively high. The convenience of store-bought breads and pastries was a luxury unavailable to the estimated 85 percent of the population living rurally in 1850. Moreover, even when the commercial product was available, Americans generally preferred home-baked goods, especially the South's oven-warm breads and biscuits.

Notable exceptions to the one- or two-person bakeshops were the ship bread (or hardtack) bakers, who produced dry, unleavened, nearly imperishable breads that fed the colonial merchant fleets, the overland western expansion, and the armies (especially during the Civil War). These crackerlike commodities had no tradition of home production, did not stale, and were easier to produce and distribute than leavened breads, sparking the first larger-scale American baking operations virtually from their inception as adjuncts to flour milling. The ship bread was purchased in large volumes by wholesalers, who resold the product to ships' operators, pioneering expeditions, and grocers; ship bread manufacture, combined with flour milling, was second in economic importance only to tobacco in the middle and southern colonies. These bakers evolved into the behemoth modern cookie and cracker industry.

Changes in ovens and the introduction of mechanical mixers and dough shapers brought an industrial efficiency and uniformity to the bakers of perishable goods starting in the late nineteenth century and continuing through the twentieth. Furthermore, by 1900 approximately 40 percent of the population lived in cities, easing distribution issues. Servantless housewives had less time to devote to the perceived drudgery of baking, especially breads. The 1890s hygienic innovation of wrapping loaves individually in waxed paper for transporting from factory to store also led to greater acceptance of commercial loaves. As incomes rose in the early twentieth century, so did the consumption of purchased bakery goods: by 1930 as much as 60 percent of all bread was purchased, although many housewives still preferred to bake their cakes and

The interior of a bakery at Homestead, Iowa, 1920s.

pastries. The Great Depression temporarily interrupted the growth in the baking industry, which revived during and after World War II, when most bread and, increasingly, pastries were purchased either directly from small-scale bakeries or from grocery stores retailing products from wholesale operations.

Bakeries have played a role in perpetuating ethnic foodways, creating new ones (for example, blueberry bagels), and defining class norms. Wherever significant immigrant populations congregated, mom-and-pop bakeries produced distinctive old-country breads and pastries to satisfy the physical and emotional needs of recent arrivals and to maintain ethnic identities in subsequent generations. At the opposite end of the spectrum are the French bakeries that appeared in the early Federal period, especially in Washington, DC, serving the transient diplomatic trade. These bakeries and their counterparts in other cities allowed an aspiring or upper-class clientele in the nineteenth century to demonstrate what was viewed as urbane taste. In the last quarter of the twentieth century, the revival of interest in artisanally produced foods encouraged many small-scale bakers to penetrate urban and affluent areas. Exquisitely handcrafted loaves and specialty pastries of astounding variety come at a price: by the early twenty-first century, in major metropolitan markets well-heeled clients were paying pay five dollars or more for their daily bread.

[**See also** BREAD; CAKES; CRACKERS; HARDTACK; PASTRIES.]

BIBLIOGRAPHY

Leslie, Eliza. *Seventy-five Receipts for Pastry, Cakes, and Sweetmeats.* Boston: Munroe and Francis, 1828.

Glezer, Maggie. *Artisan Baking across America.* New York: Artisan, 2000.

Panschar, William G. *Baking in America: Economic Development.* Evanston, IL: Northwestern University Press, 1956.

CATHY K. KAUFMAN

Baking Powder, *see Chemical Leavening*

Bananas

Bananas are tropical or subtropical plants of the genus *Musa* that bear clusters of long yellow or reddish fruit. There are sixty-seven species and more than two hundred varieties

Chiquita Banana was a trademark of the United Fruit Company. Recipe book, 1950.

item until the introduction of steamships, the extension of the railroad throughout the United States, and the availability of refrigeration. These innovations made it possible to cut the time in transit and to keep the fruit at a constant temperature to slow the ripening process. By the mid-1880s consumers could find red and yellow bananas in the markets of New York, Philadelphia, and Boston. At the end of the nineteenth century bananas were available in many parts of the United States, although they were expensive and considered a luxury outside the port cities of the East Coast. Fruit importing companies knew that they had a profitable item if they could only find a consistent supply of the fruit abroad and expand their markets at home.

American fruit companies taught Americans to eat bananas and encouraged the people of the Caribbean basin to grow bananas on a commercial basis. Local banana growers in Jamaica, Cuba, and elsewhere expanded cultivation of bananas in response to the increasing North American demand for the fruit. The United Fruit Company was the first to achieve a constant, year-round flow of bananas to North American cities. By 1920 United Fruit had become one of the largest enterprises in the United States. The company had a vertically integrated network of plantations, refrigerated steamships, and railroad cars to produce, transport, distribute, and market bananas.

The large banana companies set up marketing divisions and education programs to persuade Americans that bananas were an essential item to be eaten every day. Bananas lost their status as a luxury food and were transformed through low price, year-round availability, and abundance into comfort food for children and the elderly and health food for athletes and dieters. The fruit that had been introduced to the Americas as a food for slaves and became an exotic luxury for wealthy and well-traveled North Americans in the nineteenth century entered the twentieth century as an inexpensive food for the poor as well as a food of the health-conscious middle and upper classes.

Bananas became widely available in the United States at roughly the same time that discoveries were being made concerning calories, germs, and vitamins. Changing notions about sanitation, diet, and disease led to incorporation of the newly available fruit into American medicine. Bananas were advertised successfully as the fruit in the germproof wrapper, as full of essential vitamins, and as a diet food. In the 1930s bananas were promoted for use in the treatment of diarrhea, ulcers, colitis, tuberculosis, diabetes, obesity, malnutrition, fertility problems, celiac disease, scurvy, and gout. The American Medical Association approved bananas for general promulgation to the public in 1931.

In the nineteenth century bananas were served raw with dessert, but by 1900 American cooks were experimenting with bananas to produce a variety of dishes, including

of bananas. Cultivated as early as 1000 B.C.E. in the rain forests of Southeast Asia, bananas were taken to the Near East and Africa by Arab traders in the seventh century. In 1516 the Catholic missionary Friar Tomas de Berlanga landed on the island of Hispaniola (Haiti and the Dominican Republic) and planted bananas as the least expensive and most satisfactory food for the growing African slave population. When he became bishop of Panama, Friar Tomas took banana plants with him to the mainland. Bananas spread rapidly through Central America, Mexico, and southern Florida, so rapidly that later observers believed the banana to be native to the New World.

The first English colonists of Roanoke Island, off the coast of what became North Carolina, brought banana stocks with them from the Caribbean islands, but the bananas did not thrive in the nontropical climate. Bananas were growing on the Hawaiian Islands when the islands were visited by Captain James Cook in 1799, and the fruit became an export crop in the nineteenth century. Despite several attempts in Florida and California, commercial banana plantations on the mainland United States have not been successful.

Before the 1880s most residents of the United States had never seen or eaten a banana. Although they found a ready market in schooner days, bananas remained a luxury deep-fried banana fritters, baked bananas served with meat, and banana ice cream. In 1910 an advertisement showed a bowl of sliced bananas with a small amount of cereal being spooned over it. Soon it became more common to add sliced bananas to a bowlful of breakfast cereal. On cereal is perhaps the most common way in which Americans at the beginning of the twenty-first century consume bananas, despite decades of effort by fruit companies to include the fruit in all meals and between-meal snacks.

Latrobe, Pennsylvania, is credited with being the home of the banana split, which was first served in 1904. Banana splits became widely popular soda fountain treats in the 1920s and remain popular. Banana bread is said to have been invented by a Depression-era housewife in search of a way to make extra money at home. Banana pudding with vanilla cookies embedded in it has also become an American staple and is often found at diners, supermarket salad bars, and restaurants featuring "home cooking."

Banana puree was first produced commercially in 1966 and is used to flavor sherbet, ice cream, eggnog, yogurt, and cottage cheese. It is also used in banana bread, cake, tarts, muffins, doughnuts, icing, and cream pie and is found in a variety of baby food products. Banana powder is used in dry mixes and crunch toppings, and banana extract is used to flavor beverages, dairy products, and bakery products. Bananas are included in commercial products such as barbecue and other sauces, glazes, gravy, soups, and salad dressings as a flavor builder and thickening agent.

Imported bananas have been the one of the least expensive fruits in the grocery store for more than a century. Bananas also are the most widely consumed fruit in the United States. Per capita consumption of bananas increased from twenty-one pounds in 1979 to 28.4 pounds in 2000, representing a triumph of distribution, advertising, and marketing.

[See also BABY FOOD; BREAKFAST FOODS; CARIBBEAN INFLUENCES ON AMERICAN FOOD; CEREAL, COLD; DESSERTS; FRUIT; HAWAIIAN FOODS; HEALTH FOOD; HOMEMADE REMEDIES; PUDDINGS; TRANSPORTATION OF FOOD; TWINKIES.]

BIBLIOGRAPHY

Abella, Alex. *The Total Banana: The Illustrated Banana—Anecdotes, History, Recipes, and More!* New York: Harcourt, Brace, Jovanovich, 1979.

Gowen, S. R., ed. *Bananas and Plantains*. London: Chapman and Hall, 1995. The most comprehensive reference.

Jenkins, Virginia Scott. *Bananas: An American History*. Washington, DC: Smithsonian Institution Press, 2000.

Langley, Lester D., and Thomas Schoonover. *The Banana Men: American Mercenaries and Entrepreneurs in Central America, 1880–1930*. Lexington: University Press of Kentucky, 1995.

Robinson, J. C. *Bananas and Plantains*. Wallingford, U.K.: CAB International, 1996.

VIRGINIA SCOTT JENKINS

Barbecue

Barbecue is a method of slow-cooking meat over coals. Most authorities agree that both the word "barbecue" and the cooking technique derive from the Taino and Carib peoples of the Caribbean and South America. The Spanish conquistadores reported natives of Hispaniola roasting, drying, and smoking meats on a wooden framework over a bed of coals, called a *barbricot*, which the Spaniards pronounced *barbacoa*. It was the low heat of the coals and the consequent slowness of the process that set the New World method apart from previous cooking methods.

Styles of Barbecue

The oldest form of American open pit barbecue is practiced all along the flat coastal plain of the southeastern United States where the English colonists originally settled. What is called the "pit" is constructed either by digging a hole in the ground or by making a wide, shallow container, and placing a rack on top. A whole dressed hog is split and placed on the rack. Hardwood logs are burned down to coals in a separate fireplace and then these hot coals are continuously shoveled under the meat, which cooks anywhere from eight to fourteen hours, depending on the fire and the pitmaster. It is an extremely laborious process. No sauce is used on the meat nor is the meat basted while it cooks, although some pitmasters will allow a dry-seasoning rub before the meat goes on the rack to cook. When the meat is so tender that it is ready to fall off the bone, the pig is taken off the rack, the meat is "pulled" into shreds or chopped fine, then splashed with a thin, sharp sauce of vinegar and red pepper. This barbecue will sometimes be served as is, but it is most often topped with some coleslaw and additional sauce and sandwiched into a soft, white bun. Sweetened iced tea is the preferred beverage, and hush puppies are a typical side dish.

Whole-hog barbecues with a simple vinegar sauce can still be found in the rural areas of Georgia and South Carolina, but in the urban areas shoulder and rib barbecues are more common. South Carolina is famous for its unusual yellow mustard–based barbecue sauce, but Georgia's sauce, while tomato-based, also has a distinct mustard component. South Carolina is also known for serving Brunswick stew with its barbecue, along with sweetened iced tea.

Mississippi, Tennessee, and Alabama also have the occasional whole-hog barbecue, but again shoulder and ribs are more common. It is in Kentucky that the first real break from the pork barbecue tradition takes place, for Kentucky is the home of barbecued mutton. There are a number of theories as to why mutton is so popular there. One theory suggests that because of the Wool Tariff of 1816, raising sheep became profitable in Kentucky

at about the same time the sheep-loving Welsh were migrating into the area.

In Oklahoma, Missouri, Kansas, and Texas, beef became the meat of choice for barbecue, and the style of cooking changed as well. Blacks, both free and slave, moved into the area from the Southeast in the 1800s and brought old-style pit barbecue with them. (Interestingly, most pork barbecue restaurants in Texas are still run by African Americans.) Another influence was that of the Mexican *barbacoa*, a pre-Columbian technique of slow-cooking pieces of meat wrapped in leaves in earth-covered pits. Added to this, nineteenth-century cowboy cooks found that long cooking over coals turned tough beef from range cattle into edible meat. Lastly, the German and eastern European immigrants who came to Texas in the 1800s brought with them a liking for certain cuts of meat and sausage, and these cuts were quickly incorporated into western-style barbecue.

All of these differing influences met in Texas and the West and combined to create a new style of barbecue using beef, as well as such other available meats as goat. Western-style barbecue tends to be "closed pit," in which the cooking container is covered, using indirect heat rather than live coals under the meat, and features a great deal more smoke than the older southeastern style. It is in closed pit barbecue that the telltale smoke ring appears. This is a pinkish ring just inside the meat that forms as part of a chemical reaction between the smoke and the moisture in the meat. This is considered a good thing in the West but a sign of over-smoking on the Eastern seaboard.

In parts of Texas, the very smoky beef is cooked and served without any sauce at all. Side dishes are different, as well: crackers, Texas toast (Texas-size garlic bread), and beans are common accompaniments. In Kansas and Missouri, where beef brisket "burnt ends" are a favorite, a very spicy tomato-based barbecue sauce is common. Side dishes are likely to include spicy barbecued beans. Western barbecue is served with either iced tea or beer, depending on the locale and the attendees.

Chicago is one of the few areas outside the South that has developed its own unique barbecue culture, featuring heavily smoked pork ribs, shoulders, and other cuts, served with a spicy tomato-based sauce. In other urban centers, such as New York, Los Angeles, and Seattle, fairly authentic African American-owned barbecue "joints" may be found, but these areas have not yet developed their own styles of barbecue.

The Future of Barbecue

At the beginning of the twenty-first century, interest in old-fashioned barbecue was at an all-time high. Barbecue contests became wildly popular. Two of the largest contests were the American Royal Barbecue Contest in Kansas City and the Memphis in May Contest, which started in the 1980s as relatively small, local barbecue cook-offs: each of these contests now draws crowds of over 100,000. The rising popularity of the study of American culinary history has sparked an interest in indigenous and historical cooking methods, such as barbecue. As a result, the number of books published about barbecue had grown from virtually none prior to 1990 to well over thirty by the early 2000s.

[See also Cooking Techniques; Fund-Raisers; Hearth Cookery; Meat; Southern Regional Cookery; Southwestern Regional Cookery.]

BIBLIOGRAPHY

Browne, Rick, and Jack Bettridge. *Barbecue America: A Pilgrimage in Search of America's Best Barbecue.* Alexandria, VA: Time-Life, 1999.

Elie, Lolis Eric. *Smokestack Lightning: Adventures in the Heart of Barbecue Country.* New York: Farrar, Straus and Giroux, 1996.

SYLVIA LOVEGREN

Barley

A grass in the genus *Hordeum*, barley is cultivated mostly for animal feed and as a key ingredient in beer. Barley is also used in private kitchens in the making of soup, cereal, and gluten-free bread. Archeologists studying Sumeria in southern Mesopotamia discovered remnants of wild barley, *Hordeum spontaneum*, dating to approximately 8000 B.C.E. Resembling oatmeal, barley grains were used as a basic unit in the Sumerian measuring system. Cultivated barley was important to the Egyptians dating to 5000 B.C.E. Barley bread and beer made from fermented barley were everyday nourishment for Egyptian slaves who built the pyramids. Much later, the medieval English used barley bread as a trencher, which served as a platter, bowl, plate, and serving dish.

Ancient Hebrews revered barley as one of seven special species along with wheat, grapes, figs, pomegranates, olives, and date honey. In 2800 B.C.E. the Chinese held barley to be one of five sacred plants along with rice, wheat, millet, and soybeans. At the beginning of the Common Era, wheat became the favorite grain of the rich. Wheat was popular because it contained more gluten than other grains, affording lighter and moister bread. The poor continued to eat barley bread. By 1602 barley was being planted in North America. Pennsylvania settlers added limestone water to barley; once fermented, the concoction was distilled and made into whiskey.

In the making of beer, whole, unrefined barley is soaked until it sprouts. During soaking, proteins within the bran convert to enzymes that change starches to sugars. Next the barley is dried to prevent further sprouting and is lightly cooked. The resulting malt is crushed and combined with warm water, and the conversion of starch to sugar begins. Addition of yeast to malt leads to fermentation, which results in alcohol. In beer production, hops are added to the barley malt.

In the twenty-first century dominant producers of barley are Australia, Russia, and Canada. The United States ranks fourth and is followed by France. Barley grows in three varieties: two-rowed and six-rowed and an irregular type found in Ethiopia. Because it is drought resistant, barley can be sown in spring and fall. In countries with severe climates, such as Tibet, only one crop a year is possible.

Rich in carbohydrates and containing protein, barley is low in fat and contains no cholesterol. Barley also supplies potassium, calcium, iron, B vitamins, and fiber. Hull-less barley contains the most protein, is chewier and has a richer flavor than other forms. Pearled barley has had the husk, bran, and germ removed and is used widely as flour, grits, powder, groats, and flakes. Patent barley, which is ground from pearl barley, is used commercially to make thickener and baby cereal.

Barley is a central part of the diet of many cultures. In Britain, aleberry or barley berry is a favorite dessert. Stale barley bread is boiled in mild ale until quite thick, sweetened with honey, and served with cream. In the mountains of France, *boulon* is served as a hard bread with a soupy casserole for dunking. Tibetan monks prepare *tsampa*, a porridge of toasted barley ground into flour and blended with yak butter and boiling tea.

[See also Beer; Bread; Distillation; Whiskey.]

BIBLIOGRAPHY

Bumgarner, Marlene Anne. *The New Book of Whole Grains: More than 200 Recipes Featuring Whole Grains, Including Amaranth, Quinoa, Wheat, Spelt, Oats, Rye, Barley, and Millet.* New York: St. Martin's Griffin, 1997.

Wood, Rebecca. *The Splendid Grain: Robust, Inspired Recipes for Grains with Vegetables, Fish, Poultry, Meat, and Fruit.* New York: Morrow, 1997.

MARTY MARTINDALE

Barley Wine Ale

Originally called "Strong Ale" in England, American specialty or "craft" brewers, interested in developing high alcohol content brews, have created a unique American style of barley wine. American Style Barley Wine Ale is not only a very strong, top fermented ale, with an alcohol content that can range from about 8.5 percent up to 14 percent by volume, but is also more aggressively flavored than the original English version.

English-Style Barley Wine Ale is traditionally high in alcohol content, ruddy copper to dark brown in color, and full bodied with deep residual malty sweetness. The essence of this brew is a complexity of sensations that involved warm alcohol and fruity-ester characters, balanced by the perception of low to medium bitterness, with a caramel and sherry-like aroma and flavor.

Brewmaster Garrett Oliver, in his book *The Brewmasters Table*, notes that "The American version is a peacock display of malty power and bright hop flavor. Subtlety and balance, the hallmarks of British brewing, are often tossed out the window when American brewers brew barley wine."

The Association of Brewers' 2004 Beer Style Guidelines determine the major differences between the English and American styles of barley wine to be the "assertive bitterness and extraordinary alcohol content. Hop aroma and flavor are at medium to very high levels." The alcohol content of this style is usually between 8.4 and 12 percent by volume.

[See also Beer.]

PETER LaFRANCE

Bars

Bars, taverns, saloons, pubs, taprooms, clubs, cafés, and cocktail lounges all fall within the larger context of what can be called "commercial leisure spaces." The definition for each of these different drinking places is not precise, and the elements that distinguish them blur at the boundaries.

One element found in all of these places is the bar. The bar is generally viewed as a wooden counter, longer than it is wide, over which alcoholic beverages or other refreshments are served. The person who pours the drinks or pulls the tap is the bartender; the woman who carries drinks to the table is the barmaid or cocktail waitress. Almost anything that comes in contact with the wooden counter picks up the prefix of "bar." The bowls of peanuts and pretzels on the bar are called bar mixes or bar snacks. Patrons sit on bar stools and if they spill their drink, the towel used to wipe it up is called a bar mop.

Another universal element is that bars are nocturnal establishments, places where people go to drink and eat, generally after work. Drinking during daylight hours carries a negative image in the minds of many Americans. The idea of a three-martini lunch signifies excess and waste.

Nightclubs (1940s and 1950s), go-go clubs (1960s), and discos (1970s) were also nocturnal drinking establishments. When they flourished, they were viewed as places to visit after dinner or the theater, even after bar hopping, to continue drinking and dancing. Bars that operated illegally during Prohibition (1920 to 1933) were called speakeasies. They were everything your neighborhood pub or bar was not.

Colonial taverns dispensed expensive distilled liquors, imported wines, and bowls of punch from a small room called a bar or cage bar. This bar was generally constructed in one corner of the main room. It was open on two sides except for wooden bars that ran from the top of the counter to the ceiling. A small

A bartender prepares for customers at the Park Slope Ale House in Brooklyn, New York.

section of the obstructing grate could be lifted or lowered from within the cage. The tavern keeper entered the enclosed space from a back door. In this small space he mixed the punches, decanted wine, and measured out spirits into tankards and mugs while at the same time protecting his investment from breakage or theft. Patrons did not drink at this bar but carried their drinks to a table.

The modern bar and saloon, along with the concept of the hotel and restaurant, slowly evolved out of the inns and taverns that served the needs of the colonies for food, drink, and lodging during the seventeenth and eighteenth centuries. These public arenas were copied from British inns and taverns that had been part of the social structure since medieval times. Taverns were places where people came to socialize and interact. Just as they were necessary then to provide shelter, food, and entertainment for the traveler, they exist in the twenty-first century for the same reasons.

With the explosion in the number of Americans traveling abroad in the second half of the nineteenth century, bars modeled after English and Irish pubs become popular in American cities. "Pub," short for "public house," was the British designation for a casual neighborhood bar. The signboard hanging outside to identify it as a drinking place might be the only outward indication that it was not a private house.

In some cities, particularly Philadelphia, neighborhood bars were called taprooms and catered mostly to blue-collar workers. Many of these neighborhood institutions started off as private homes. When retrofitted for serving food and drink, the first floor was divided into taproom, public parlor, bar, and kitchen. Private living quarters were located on the second and third floors.

Male patrons entered the bar directly from the main street but women entered the public parlor from a side door. Above this door might be a sign that read Ladies Entrance or Ladies Invited.

Bar proprietors competed with each other by putting out elaborate repasts to attract so-called barflies and beer hounds. During the early part of the twentieth century and the second half of the nineteenth century the free lunch was not limited exclusively to bars and saloons. The Waldorf, Knickerbocker, Biltmore, and Plaza hotels in New York also provided a free lunch, but the ten-cent mugs of beer in these establishments were out of reach of the working class. At these upscale hotels the lunch counter might offer chicken salad, lobster Newburg, melted cheese on toast, cold corned beef, or sliced Virginia ham.

At bars that catered to the working class with five-cent beers, patrons could choose from tomatoes, scallions, beans, radishes, or sausages. Some offered a complete New England boiled dinner and two beers, all for the price of a dime. Barkeepers kept a close eye on what customers were eating. It was an unwritten law that patrons invest at least fifteen cents in beers if they were going to partake of the free lunch. Bouncers kept a close eye on hungry drinkers.

Before Prohibition took effect in the 1920s it seemed to some that there was a bar on every corner. After Prohibition, bars did not return in the same numbers because soda fountains, drugstores, and even cigar stores gobbled up the spots vacated by the barrooms. The stores that replaced the bar were more profitable because drugstore customers, except when they stopped for a malted milk at the soda fountain, did not linger. In contrast, saloons made money only when their customers stayed to drink.

The triangular martini glass with an olive in it is internationally recognized as the symbol for "bar."

[**See also** ALCOHOL AND TEETOTALISM; ALCOHOLISM; BEER HALLS; MICROBREWERIES; PROHIBITION; ROADHOUSES; SALOONS; TAVERNS; TEMPERANCE; WINE-TASTING ROOMS.]

BIBLIOGRAPHY
Rector, George. *The Girl from Rector's*. Garden City, NY: Doubleday, Page, 1927.
Ryder, Bethan. *Bar and Club Design*. New York: Abbeville, 2002.

JOSEPH M. CARLIN

Baskin-Robbins

Californian Irvine Robbins and his brother-in-law, Burt Baskin, formed a partnership in 1946 to sell premium ice cream. Robbins had run the Snowbird Ice Cream Store in Glendale, serving twenty-one flavors of ice cream. Baskin had also owned an ice cream parlor, called Burton's, in the Los Angeles area. Within a year, Baskin and Robbins began to franchise their operation, and within three years the chain had grown to eight stores.

In 1953 the company advertised "31 flavors" of ice cream, thereby trumping the twenty-eight flavors served at Howard Johnson's. At Baskin-Robbins, customers so disposed could try a different flavor every day of the month. The company also created topical treats to celebrate holidays or current events, such as the "Lunar Cheesecake" offered at the time of the 1969 moon landing. Flavors were rotated throughout the year, with certain selections going "on vacation" to make room for new flavors.

Baskin and Robbins intentionally designed their outlets so that customers would not stay on the premises long. Most customers ate their ice cream outside; for those who wanted to eat inside, the stores had a few uncomfortable chairs to further discourage lingering.

Baskin-Robbins's first franchise outside of California opened in Phoenix in 1959. Burt Baskin died in 1967, and the company was sold to United Fruit, who continued running it until 1973, when it was sold to the London-based J. Lyons & Co., Ltd. As of 2005, there are about 2,500 Baskin-Robbins stores in the United States and a similar number in fifty other countries.

[**See also** ICE CREAMS AND ICES.]

BIBLIOGRAPHY
Funderburg, Anne Cooper. *Chocolate, Strawberry, and Vanilla: A History of American Ice Cream*. Bowling Green, Ohio: Bowling Green State University Popular Press, 1995.

ANDREW F. SMITH

Bass

The designation "bass" is applied to a great many fish, true bass being saltwater fish such as grouper and striped bass. The freshwater food fish most often called bass include

A store sign in Bayside, New York—one of over 12,000 Dunkin' Brands Inc. restaurants around the world.

[**See also** BLENDERS; CARIBBEAN INFLUENCES ON AMERICAN FOOD; FRUIT; MILKSHAKES, MALTS, AND FLOATS.]

BIBLIOGRAPHY

Farrell-Kingsley, Kathy. "Florida Fusion." *Vegetarian Times* 228 (August 2001): 42–46.

Raichlen, Steven. *Miami Spice: The New Florida Cuisine.* New York: Workman, 1993.

JENNIFER MINNICK

Bayless, Rick

Rick Bayless refers to himself as a gringo from Oklahoma, yet he has become one of America's leading emissaries of Mexican cuisine thanks to his odyssey as an award-winning chef, restaurateur, author, TV personality, salsa manufacturer, and teacher. Bayless was born in Oklahoma City in 1953 into the fourth generation of a family of restaurateurs and food people. His great-grandparents were the first grocers in the state of Oklahoma, and his parents ran the family barbecue restaurant. Bayless demonstrated his own culinary bent when, on his tenth birthday, he asked his parents to buy him Julia Child's *Mastering the Art of French Cooking*.

Although without Mexican roots, Bayless has said he had felt a spiritual connection to Mexico from childhood. He began studying Spanish when he was twelve and organized a family vacation to Mexico when he was fourteen. On arrival there, he said he felt like he had come home. He pursued an undergraduate degree in Spanish language and literature and Latin American culture at the University of Oklahoma and a master's degree in linguistics at the University of Michigan. He had nearly completed his Ph.D. in anthropological linguistics at Michigan when he decided to leave academia and devote himself full time to teaching cooking classes, running a catering business, and hosting *Cooking Mexican*, his first PBS show in 1979.

In the early 1980s, Bayless began a five-year, 35,000-mile grassroots exploration of Mexico's diverse regional cuisine. He visited local markets, home kitchens, and street vendors, taking notes with a scholar's zeal. In 1987, with his treasure chest of recipes, Bayless published with his wife, Deann, *Authentic Mexican: Regional Cooking from the Heart of Mexico*. Considered a classic, the book is still in print in the early 2000s. Immediately following the book's publication, Bayless opened Frontera Grill, a casual seventy-seat restaurant near downtown Chicago that he decorated with festive, contemporary Mexican art.

Bayless chose Chicago because of its large Mexican population and excellent Mexican markets. Working closely with local farmers and purveyors, Bayless showcased the bold, vibrant flavors of authentic Mexican cuisine, such as complexly spiced moles, light citrus marinades, grilled quail, smoky chilies, and cilantro-enhanced dishes, not the soft, heavy food, covered with melted cheese, which he said the majority of Americans mistakenly

largemouth or bigmouth, smallmouth, and spotted bass, and sunfish. One traveler to America in 1800, John Maude, observed "Bass...is a favorite word with the Americans; they not only call trees by this name, but five or six distinct kinds of fish."

Bass are typically medium-to-large, white-fleshed, and mild-flavored. Some are commercially fished, and others make good sport fish. Like many favored fish, bass has been introduced beyond its usual range and is farm raised for stocking ponds and lakes. The largemouth bass (*Micropterus salmoides*) is a major warm-water sport fish but is found in cooler northern waters as well. Largemouth bass, so called because the jaw line extends well past the eyes, averages approximately one to one and a half pounds in the north but is larger in southern waters, growing as large as five pounds. The Florida largemouth bass (*M. salmoides floridanus)* is the largest largemouth. The smallmouth bass (*Micropterus dolomieui)* is somewhat smaller than the largemouth bass.

Bass is considered an excellent game fish and is fished in tournaments. Trophy bass weighing ten pounds are rare, although they were less unusual in the past, and are likely to be mounted rather than eaten. Largemouth bass may pick up flavor from their habitat, as do other wild fish. Some largemouth bass has what is described as a weedy or grassy flavor, which can be countered by skinning, seasoning, and deep-frying it. Bass from clean, clear water with woody cover usually has a milder flavor, and smallmouth bass is less likely to acquire off flavors.

In early cookery books, recipes for bass often do not specify which of many possible basslike fish might have been available in different regions of the country. For example, New Englanders liked striped bass, which in the South is called rockfish. Some fish in the family *Serranidae* that are usually called groupers also end up with "bass" in the common name. Stripers were introduced to the West Coast in the 1800s, and a hybrid of wild striped bass and white bass is farm raised.

Bass meat is white, lean, and flaky and can be prepared many different ways, as most white-fleshed fish are. Bass is usually filleted and baked, stuffed, broiled, fried, or grilled. Bass generally was prepared in the same manner as cod, pollock, and haddock. It can be baked or stewed; it is also used in chowders and as fillets for all sorts of fish dishes. Smaller bass and groupers can be cooked whole.

SANDRA L. OLIVER

Batidos

Batidos are tropical fruit shakes consisting of crushed ice, fruit, a sweetener, and milk or water. The ingredients can be blended with ice or served over crushed ice. Typical fruits include banana, guava, mamey, pineapple, sweetsop, papaya, mango, passion fruit, and tamarind. Derived from the Spanish word meaning "to beat," these light, frothy drinks originated as thirst quenchers in tropical climates. In the early twenty-first century batidos are becoming popular in the United States wherever there are large Latin American and Caribbean immigrant communities.

Two modern devices have aided the popularity of batidos: the blender and the refrigerator. Before blenders, all ingredients except ice were beaten by hand, and the resulting mixture was poured over crushed ice. Freezers make ice storage possible and allow milk, a primary ingredient, to stay fresh in warm climates. Before the widespread availability of refrigerators, sweetened, condensed milk—a dairy product needing no refrigeration—was often used in batidos.

believed was true Mexican. Frontera Grill was an immediate success. In 1989 Bayless opened Topolobampo, a seventy-five-seat fine-dining restaurant, adjacent to Frontera.

As he came to prominence, Bayless began winning numerous awards, including the 1995 James Beard Award as Outstanding Chef in the United States. He appeared as a guest on Julia Child's *Cooking with Master Chefs*. He was a founder, and later chairman, of the Chef's Collaborative, a nationwide group that promotes sustainable agriculture. He started his own company, Frontera Foods, which produces sauces and salsas from regional recipes. In the early 2000s, he launched his second PBS series, *Mexico—One Plate at a Time*, and authored his fourth cookbook. He was also training professional chefs throughout the world. Bayless says he intends to continue his crusade to make authentic Mexican cuisine accessible to the home cook and to help Americans appreciate Mexican food for the world-class cuisine it is.

[See also CHILD, JULIA; MEXICAN AMERICAN FOOD.]

BIBLIOGRAPHY
Davis, Dawn. *If You Can Stand the Heat: Tales from Chefs and Restaurateurs*. New York: Penguin, 1999.
Dornenburg, Andrew, and Karen Page. *Dining Out: Secrets from America's Leading Critics, Chefs, and Restaurateurs*. New York: Wiley, 1998.
Shore, Debbie, Catherine Townsend, and Laurie Roberge. *Home Food: 44 Great American Chefs Cook 160 Recipes on Their Night Off*. New York: Potter, 1995.

SCOTT WARNER

Beans

Beans and bean products are diet staples worldwide. The history of beans in the Americas in general and the United States in particular is highly colorful—literally, involving brown pintos, black beans, red beans, black-eyed peas, navy beans, and more (with a great deal of crossover). Most varieties of beans are grown in the United States, whether or not they are indigenous.

Taxonomy

Beans are of the order Fabales and the family Leguminosae, or Fabaceae, commonly known as legumes or pulses—terms applicable both to the plants as a whole and to their edible pods and seeds. Beans inhabit several genera, but the most important for culinary study are *Phaseolus*, *Vigna*, *Vicia*, and *Glycine*. In these genera are almost all the most familiar species. For example, among beans familiar yet not native to the Americas are *Glycine maximus*, the soybean so crucial to the Asian diet; *Vigna unguiculata*, the African cowpea or black-eyed pea; and *Vicia faba*, the European broad-bean or fava bean, which arrived in America with the colonists. American species generally belong to the genus *Phaseolus*, such as *Phaseolus coccineus*, the runner or scarlet bean; *Phaseolus lunatus* (also called *Phaseolus limensis*), the lima or butter bean; and *Phaseolus vulgaris*,

whose many varieties fall under the umbrella term "haricot bean." (The French appellation's resemblance to the Aztec word, *ayacotl* or *ayecotl*, is coincidental.) *Phaseolus vulgaris* includes black (turtle) beans, white (cannellini) beans, green (snap, French, or string) beans, navy (pea) beans, kidney beans, pinto beans, flageolets, and more (these terms sometimes overlap). Beans may also be classified by their growth patterns: Pole or garden beans are borne on vines; bush or field beans come from low-growing plants.

History

Archaeological evidence shows that beans were among the world's first domesticated plants. It is estimated that Amerindian tribes began cultivating bean crops anywhere from 7000 to 3000 B.C.E. Throughout the precolonial Americas, beans were among a handful of foods that constituted daily fare—the others being corn, which forms a complete protein in combination with beans; squash; and, from Mexico southward, tomatoes and chilies. As Sophie D. Coe notes in *America's First Cuisines*, the Aztecs and Maya developed customs and created dishes involving beans that are recognizable as part of U.S. culinary heritage. (The Incas, whose repertoire was limited to the lima bean for which Peru's capital is named, had lesser influence.) For instance, the Mesoamerican Maya were partial to the black bean or *buul*, which they boiled with chilies and, typically, paired with corn, using the cooked beans to fill stone-ground, stone-griddled tortillas or in cornmeal-thickened stews. The Aztecs used myriad *P. vulgarius* specimens, adding them to *atolli*—corn pulp boiled with lime—or mashing them as modern-day Mexicans do *frijoles refritos*.

Like those of what we now call Latin America, the indigenous peoples of so-called Anglo America also contributed to the evolution of bean cookery. Tribes that practiced husbandry, such as the Hopi and Papagos in the southwest and the Iroquois in the northeast, grew several varieties of beans—and even worshipped them in ceremonial bean dances or festivals. Typically, the harvested beans were dried, then simmered, stewed, or baked. Two dishes in particular found lasting popularity not only with natives across tribal lines but also with colonists: succotash and baked beans. Just as its English name is a simplification of similar-sounding Indian names, succotash, still common in the South, is often boiled down (literally) to two ingredients—lima beans and corn—from its original hodgepodge. Baked beans, as the natives prepared them, were combined with maple sugar and bear fat in a pit filled with hot stones or ashes. Settlers replaced the pit with a pot, the maple sweetener with molasses, and the bear fat with hog fat—and finally ignored altogether the dish's origins, instead crediting Bostonians with its invention, who did in fact adopt and adapt it so wholeheartedly that their city earned the moniker "Bean-

A drawing of Low's New Champion bush bean, from Aaron Low's Illustrated Retail Seed Catalogue and Garden Manual, *1887.*

town." By the end of the nineteenth century, baked beans—which then contained tomato sauce as well—had become a popular canned item.

Usage

Late-twentieth-century patterns of U.S. immigration, in conjunction with increased awareness of the virtues of plant-based diets, have encouraged the introduction of a variety of bean products. Most notably, Americans' exposure to Asian foods has broadened considerably. Hence soybean goods that once seemed alien are now widely available. Just as tofu, or bean curd, has proven an efficient meat substitute, soy "milk," "cheese," and "ice cream" are becoming familiar dairy alternatives.

The most representative bean dishes in the United States, meanwhile, tend to involve multicultural fusion rather than wholesale importation. Tex-Mex cookery is, as the expression goes, full of beans—indispensable for burritos, enchiladas, and tacos, be they boiled or refried with lard. The same is true of New Mexican cuisine, which merges the foodways of the Pueblo Indians with those of the local Hispanic population. In Louisiana, the traditions of French-Canadian settlers, African slaves, and Native Americans have resulted in a wealth of Cajun and Creole bean dishes—from limpin' Susan, also known as red beans and rice, to hoppin' John, a combination of black-eyed peas and rice flavored with pork, customarily served on New Year's Day.

[See also AFRICAN AMERICAN FOOD: SINCE EMANCIPATION; CAJUN AND CREOLE FOOD; CARIBBEAN INFLUENCES ON AMERICAN FOOD; CHINESE AMERICAN FOOD; JAPANESE AMERICAN FOOD; MEXICAN AMERICAN FOOD; NATIVE AMERICAN FOODS; SOYBEANS.]

BIBLIOGRAPHY
Coe, Sophie D. *America's First Cuisines*. Austin: University of Texas Press, 1994.

RUTH TOBIAS

Beard, James

Often referred to as the father of American gastronomy, James Beard (1903–1985) crusaded for appreciation of American cuisine, no matter how humble. Through cookbooks, a cooking school, personal appearances, and groundbreaking television programs, Beard popularized the art of home cooking in general and American cooking in particular.

Born on May 5, 1903, in Portland, Oregon, to Elizabeth and John Beard, James Beard learned about Oregon's natural bounty during summers at the beach and by haunting local food markets. In 1923 Beard was expelled from Reed College, in Portland, and he began to pursue his first love, the theater. He lived abroad for several years, studying voice and acting. Beard returned to the United States in 1927, intent on a theatrical career. To supplement his earnings, he began a catering business and with friends in 1937 opened a small shop called Hors d'Oeuvre Inc.

Writing was Beard's strength. Throughout his career, he contributed articles and columns to *Woman's Day*, *Gourmet*, and *House and Garden*, among others, encouraging readers to appreciate their American roots. Beard wrote twenty-seven cookbooks, many of which were best sellers. *Hors d'Oeuvre and Canapés* (1940) was followed by *Cook It Outdoors* (1941). Reflecting Americans' migration to the suburbs, the latter offered plans for a build-it-yourself barbecue pit. After World War II, Beard wrote *Fowl and Game Cookery* (1944), *The Fireside Cookbook* (1949), *Paris Cuisine* (1952), *James Beard's Fish Cookery* (first edition published in 1954 under the title *Fish Cookery*), *How to Eat Better for Less Money* (1954; with Sam Aaron, of the Sherry-Lehmann wine store), *The Complete Book of Outdoor Cookery* (1955; with Helen Evans Brown), and *The Casserole Cookbook* (1968).

Beard made television history in 1946 when he hosted television's first cooking show, NBC's *Elsie Presents James Beard in "I Love to Eat,"* Elsie being the Borden cow. Beard's national exposure led to commercial endorsements for Birds Eye, Green Giant, and Planters. Beard advised the food service giant Restaurant Associates for many years beginning in 1954, when it opened innovative themed restaurants such as the Latin American La Fonda del Sol (1960) and the Forum of the Twelve Caesars (1957), an opulent recreation of ancient Rome. Both demonstrated Beard's "food as theater" philosophy.

In New York in 1955 the James Beard Cooking School opened in Beard's home in Greenwich Village. Beard taught cooking for the rest of his life there as well as at a branch of his home school, in Seaside, Oregon; at women's clubs; at other cooking schools; and at civic clubs around the United States. To a country just becoming aware of its culinary heritage Beard advocated good food passionately prepared with fresh, wholesome ingredients. *The James Beard Cookbook* (1959), a paperback originally priced at seventy-five cents and positioned at cash registers, introduced millions to classic American and international dishes. *James Beard's American Cookery* (1972) reflected Beard's encyclopedic knowledge of American cuisine. Beard's joyous approach to food and cooking is epitomized in *James Beard's Theory and Practice of Good Cooking* (1977), in which he writes, "Cooking is primarily fun and…the more [people] know about what they are doing, the more fun it is" (p. vii). When he died at age eighty-two on January 21, 1985, James Beard left a legacy of American culinary authenticity to home cooks and professional chefs.

[**See also** CELEBRITY CHEFS; COOKBOOKS AND MANUSCRIPTS: FROM WORLD WAR II TO THE 1960S; COOKING SCHOOLS; RADIO/TV FOOD SHOWS.]

BIBLIOGRAPHY

Beard, James. *Delights and Prejudices*. New York: Atheneum, 1964.

Beard, James, in collaboration with José Wilson. *James Beard's Theory and Practice of Good Cooking*. New York: Knopf, 1977.

Clark, Robert. *The Solace of Food: A Life of James Beard*. Hanover, NH: Steerforth, 1996.

Jones, Evan. *Epicurean Delight: The Life and Times of James Beard*. New York: Simon and Schuster, 1990.

PHYLLIS ISAACSON

The cover of the first edition of James Beard's American Cookery, *published in 1972.*

Beatrice

George Haskell, a bookkeeper with the Fremont Butter and Egg Company, purchased the company's Nebraska plant when the company folded in 1891. He renamed it the Beatrice Creamery Company. In 1901 the company adopted the trademark Meadow Gold for its butter.

From an early date, Beatrice was a leader and innovator in the dairy business. It is reported to have been the first company to package butter in sealed cartons. The company pioneered the use of aluminum foil milk caps and was an early innovator in the marketing of homogenized milk. In 1931 Beatrice was the first company to advertise its ice cream products nationally.

In an attempt to expand its product line, the company purchased La Choy, a producer of Asian foods, in 1943. La Choy was founded in 1922 by Wally Smith and Ilhan New, who met while attending the University of Michigan. New, a Korean by birth, and Smith, a grocery store owner in Detroit, set out to sell bean sprouts packaged in glass jars. In a new round of acquisitions Beatrice purchased the Krispy Kreme doughnut chain in 1975 and added sandwiches, a retail mix that failed. A group of investors, led by one of the chain's most successful franchisees, purchased the company in the 1980s.

In 1984 Beatrice Food purchased Hunt-Wesson Inc., a large food products company in California. By 1985 Beatrice in turn was purchased in what was then the largest leveraged buyout in history. Beatrice, along with Hunt-Wesson and La Choy, was sold to ConAgra Inc. Besides being a case study in acquisition and diversification within the food industry, Beatrice has become a slimmer and more focused company.

[**See also** CONAGRA; DAIRY; DAIRY INDUSTRY; MILK PACKAGING.]

BIBLIOGRAPHY
International Directory of Company Histories. 55 vols. Chicago: St. James Press, 2003.

JOSEPH M. CARLIN

Beecher, Catharine

Catharine E. Beecher (1800–1878) was a social innovator who helped to reshape women's roles in the mid-nineteenth century and whose writings continued to guide an idealized image of middle-class urban women for decades to come. Beecher's authority derived from her membership in a famous family of activists and reformers and from her own extensive pioneering of education for single professional women and married women at home. Beecher wrote and lectured widely on women's issues, intermingling what was sometimes extreme conservatism with farseeing change.

In *Treatise on Domestic Economy* (1841), Beecher expanded on the inherited Calvinist belief that women's true destiny was marriage and home. She encouraged women to develop their presumed gender-specific talents for religiosity, morality, aesthetics, and nurturing, areas in which women were considered superior to men. Beecher saw in the female "profession" of homemaking a role parallel and balancing to that of urban men in factories, shops, and offices. Women were thus

charged with creating a beautiful, serene, and smoothly run home, a haven for husbands distressed by the anxiety-filled business world. Expected to display her husband's success at moneymaking, a woman was to create a stylishly decorated home, to dress modishly, and to set a fashionable table. This "glorification" of women separated them from the public sphere and consequently was a rejection of women's suffrage.

Although its framework was conventional, the *Treatise* included a number of food-related innovations. With an eye to efficiency, Beecher discussed health, kitchen fires, and care of the kitchen, cellar, and storeroom. Cookery was a major arena. Beecher's cookbook (*Domestic Receipt Book*, 1846) emphasized basic traditional cooking, baking, and preserving but tempered them with modernizing innovations, such as the new cookstove, cream of tartar, and the home ice cream maker. Beecher included many more regional recipes than was usual at the time, perhaps because of her wide-flung lecture circuit. On one page alone she lists Pennsylvania flannel cakes, Kentucky corn dodgers, and Ohio corn cakes. Beecher's recipe for birthday pudding (a layered bread pudding with apples) encouraged the new rituals and elaboration of birthday celebrations, and her temperance drinks represented an early voice in what would become a major movement. Much ahead of her time, Beecher detailed efficient work routines for the kitchen, furnishing plans, and recommendations for cooking utensils. Beecher included lengthy chapters on dining etiquette, such as table setting, food presentation, servant training, and service (the *service à la Française* buffet style).

In 1869 Catharine collaborated with her sister Harriet Beecher Stowe in writing an update of the *Treatise*, titled *The American Woman's Home*. Among other topics, *Home* offered expanded plans for kitchen efficiency and recommended new factory-made furnishings and utensils.

Despite her strong voice for married women's place in the home, Catharine Beecher never married. Her own life's example of the independent single woman working professionally to improve the lot of others (in part through food, in part through education) may seem to be a contradiction but nevertheless figured in the creation of the new range of choices opened to twentieth-century women.

[**See also** HOME ECONOMICS.]

BIBLIOGRAPHY
Beecher, Catharine. *Domestic Receipt-Book: Designed as a Supplement to Her Treatise on Domestic Economy.* New York: Harper, 1846.
Rugoff, Milton. *The Beechers: An American Family in the Nineteenth Century.* New York: Harper and Row, 1981.
Sklar, Kathryn Kish. *Catharine Beecher: A Study in American Domesticity.* New York: Norton, 1976.

ALICE ROSS

Beech-Nut

Between 1891 and 1946 the Beech-Nut Packing Company grew from a regional business to a nationally significant corporation because of its diverse product line and innovative marketing techniques. It tried to portray itself as a small company appealing to women, children, and families, and it frequently succeeded in doing so.

The Beech-Nut Packing Company was founded in 1891 as a meatpacking plant in Canajoharie, New York. Most of the initial investment came from two local families, the Lipes and the Arkells. When the board of directors chose the officers for the new company, then known as the Imperial Packing Company, Bartlett Arkell was designated president and Walter Lipe chosen to be vice president. The company was named after the hotel in New York where Arkell lived at that time. From the start, Imperial Packing produced bacon, sliced ham, and beef under two brand names, Erie and Beech-Nut. In 1898 Imperial Packing reincorporated as Beech-Nut Packing Company. Informal corporate histories suggest that the change occurred after the executives held a contest at the plant to select a less formal, more national name for the company.

At the time the company was founded, New York State had the strictest laws in the country for regulating the food-processing industry. The company emphasized food purity and lack of adulteration in its products, in both advertising campaigns and packaging. The public was allowed and encouraged to visit the plant, and most of the early products were packed in glass jars so that customers could see the products they were buying.

The plant expanded at a single location in Canajoharie for the first ten years of its existence, until a fire in 1903 destroyed the smokehouse. The rebuilding of the company in 1903–1905 also saw the expansion of the product line to include chewing gum, hard candy, jams and jellies, coffee, peanut butter, ketchup, and mustard, all made before World War I. (See the accompanying table for specific dates of product manufacture.)

Growth of the Company between the Wars

By 1900 Beech-Nut not only was vacuum packing most of its food products in glass jars but also was including, as a seal, a rubber gasket it had patented that year. This ensured a very long shelf life for the company's products.

A Beech-Nut advertisement, 1905.

Although there have been improvements in the manufacturing methods and materials used to seal glass jars since that time, the basic canning process remains similar.

By 1910 a single building was too small for the company's manufacturing needs, and a second plant was built in Canajoharie. By 1920 Beech-Nut was also making gum and coffee at the Bush Terminal Building in Brooklyn, New York, and had acquired a plant in San Jose, California, to make jams and jellies. In 1924 the company added a plant in Rochester, New York, for coffee and tomato juice.

In 1919 a fire at the Equitable Life Building at 120 Broadway in New York City all but destroyed the Beech-Nut offices and corporate records. Most of the company executives moved to Canajoharie, although Bartlett Arkell maintained a New York City office on Broadway at Fortieth Street for the rest of his life. In the 1920s and 1930s the company was at its most adventurous in terms of advertising. The use of commercial artists such as Norman Rockwell and Cushman Parker established the company's association with women and families. Celebrities such as Chef Oscar of the Waldorf-Astoria, the aviator Amelia Earhart, and the boxer Jack Dempsey also were involved in advertising promotions for the company. Radio spots were used on the program *Chandu the Magician.* Lifestyle spots advertised that Beech-Nut offered "everything for breakfast but the eggs."

At about this time Beech-Nut sued the Lolliard Tobacco Company, a Virginia firm, for copyright and trademark infringement. Lolliard used a very similar logo and the name "Beechnut" for one of its brands of chewing tobacco. The case, which reached the U.S. Supreme Court in 1924, determined that two companies could use almost identical trademarks as long as the products were different. The finding, which is a major, and still valid, legal precedent with respect to trademarks, was a setback for Beech-Nut.

In 1932, after two years of test marketing, Beech-Nut introduced a line of strained baby food for younger children and a line of junior foods for older ones. Company brochures from the 1930s suggest that the products were marketed for convenience and to replace home-strained food at about the time that mothers had traditionally introduced foods other than milk to their infants' diets. Packing this type of food in glass jars eased consumer worries about the purity of the product. Along with candy, baby food is Beech-Nut's best-known product line and the only one still manufactured in Canajoharie.

Between the world wars, Beech-Nut salesmen generally tried to sell as many different products as they could to small, family-owned groceries, offering free window displays, better discounts, and racks to store owners who took the entire company line. Federal Trade Com-

mission efforts to fine and discontinue this practice failed in court. Although Beech-Nut had to close its San Jose plant and discontinue some product lines, the company remained stable during the Depression, surviving mostly on gum and candy sales. Not every product the company introduced at this time was successful. It made soda for just three years and oyster sauce for only two.

World War II and Later Years

The Beech-Nut company had to alter some of its lines to fulfill government contracts during World War II. Most of the extra wartime production involved the making of K Ration—a packaged line of emergency foods developed for the armed services. All but the chewing gum was produced elsewhere and shipped to Canajoharie, where the various parts were assembled into a finished meal. Beech-Nut Gum was added to each meal prior to shipping. A small machine shop and freeze-drying plant were added to Beech-Nut's regular manufacturing facilities as well.

In 1946 Bartlett Arkell passed away, and within ten years the company was sold to LifeSavers. Its focus became more specialized, and it made fewer and fewer products. By 1960 baby food and candy were the two main products; coffee was a distant third. A baby-food plant, which opened in San Jose in 1947, was the only new plant built after the war, before the LifeSaver merger.

The 1956 acquisition of Beech-Nut by LifeSavers brought about a short-lived boom for the company. It expanded aggressively in the 1960s, buying several additional businesses and building a large plant in Michigan. By 1967 the company was in serious financial trouble, and that year it sold its holdings to Squibb. Since that time, Squibb has divested all of the various divisions, which are each owned by several other national and international companies.

[See also BABY FOOD; PURE FOOD AND DRUG ACT.]

BIBLIOGRAPHY

"Beech-Nut Packing." *Fortune,* November 1936, 85–93.

Hughes, Lawerence. "Beech-Nut Keeps the Kettle Boiling." *Sales Management,* August 1950.

JAMES CRAWFORD

Beer

The traditional brew house consists of a gristmill, (which grinds grain into small pieces called grist), a mash tun (a large vessel where the grist and hot water are combined to make a porridge, or mash), a copper (a large boiler, traditionally made of copper because of its ability to conduct heat, in which the liquid, or wort, from the mash tun is flavored with hops), a fermenter (a large vessel in which the first fermentation takes place), conditioning tanks (vessels that contain the fermented and carbonated brew) and a kegging or bottling line—unless, as in a brewpub, the beer is

drawn to the tap directly from the conditioning tanks.

The History of Beer

There is some debate as to whether grain was first cultivated specifically for use in brewing beer or baking bread. However, there is no doubt that the earliest days of the brewing of fermented grain beverage took place around in 8000 B.C.E., in the Middle East, between the Euphrates and Tigris rivers.

The Sumerian version of beer parlors received special mention in the Code of Hammurabi in the eighteenth century B.C.E. Stiff penalties (death by drowning) were dealt out to owners who overcharged customers or who failed to notify authorities of criminals in their establishments.

When this grain beverage found its way to Egypt, it was considered a drink for only the royal. This beer was made of grain, ginger, and honey, sweetened with date sugar.

The Greeks called the Egyptian beer a barley wine and introduced it to the Romans, who passed it to other civilizations as they traveled through Europe. In northern Europe, where grain grew in abundance, the preference for beer was a result of agricultural whim. Where grapes grew in abundance, wine was the beverage of choice.

Evidence of the early history of brewing in Europe is meager but reveals that brewing was done by women as part of maintaining a proper household. The entire family drank fermented beverages made from grain. They were nutritious and not nearly as dangerous as drinking the contaminated waters found near most towns and villages.

After the Roman Empire, the monasteries of Europe were the sole providers of healers, teachers, preachers—and beer.

The first recorded mention of hops in relation to brewing is in the twelfth-century writing of Hildegard, the Benedictine nun who was abbess of Rupertsberg, near Mainz, Germany. She specifically suggested that hops retarded spoilage of beer. With the growth of cities and the greater use of roads, sea-lanes, and caravan routes, the market for beer became intercontinental.

Early American Brewing

The arrival of the *Mayflower* at Plymouth Rock in 1620 was not intended. The ship's original destination was what was then called Hudson's River, but because of less-than-perfect navigation and other problems while crossing the Atlantic Ocean, the vessel arrived off the coast of Cape Cod. The captain and crew insisted that the passengers disembark there, because if more time were spent looking for another site there would not be enough beer to supply the crew for the trip back to England.

In 1630 Captain Robert Sedgwick opened the first of the New England breweries in Charlestown, now part of greater Boston. In nearby Cambridge, home of Harvard

A crowded New York City bar in 1919.

University, Nathaniel Eaton was dismissed as president in 1639 when he failed to maintain the students' beer supply.

In 1632 the West India Company opened a brewery on Brouwers (Brewers) Straet in lower Manhattan. By 1657 the number of breweries on Brouwers Straet discharging their effluent into the street made it necessary to pave it with cobblestones and change its name to Stone Street.

The commercial breweries of colonial North America were primarily urban and supplied nearby taverns and the inhabitants of the town with potable beverages that ranged from small beer, a barely alcoholic brew, to full-strength brews of between 6 and 7 percent alcohol by volume. In rural areas home brewing and cider making provided the family with potable beverages.

Clipper ships offered an opportunity to bring "lager" yeast to the United States. Lager (anaerobic) yeast could not survive the long sea voyage from Europe to North America. Ale (aerobic) yeast, a far hardier organism, was, and is, less fragile. When lager beer reached the market in the United States in the nineteenth century, it was regarded for some time as little more than a novelty. With the development of industrial refrigeration that could produce it, and with the immigration of central Europeans, Germans, and Czechs, who had a thirst for it, lager beer soon eclipsed traditional ale.

Wars, the Great Depression, and Prohibition

From 1861 through 1865, the demand for machinery and raw materials during the Civil War sapped resources. But the rebound of industry can be seen when, in 1867, there

were 3,700 breweries in operation in the United States producing 6 million barrels of beer. Two years later, with the completion of a transcontinental railroad, the market for goods and the ability to provide mass-produced packaged goods would propel the industry forward until, in 1873, breweries in the United States numbered 4,131 and were turning out 9 million barrels of beer annually. One year later the Woman's Christian Temperance Union was founded.

In 1900 the Woman's Christian Temperance Union member Carrie Nation challenged the public imagination when she allegedly took a hatchet and proceeded to chop at the bar of the Carey Hotel in Wichita, Kansas. Four years later a resolution to prohibit liquor through a constitutional amendment lost narrowly in the House of Representatives.

By 1916 twenty-three states had gone dry. In 1917 the United States entered World War I, and the District of Columbia passed its own prohibition legislation. With the onset of war all distilleries were closed by the Food Control Law and the brewing industry was also restricted. On the eleventh hour of the eleventh day of the eleventh month of 1918, World War I ended. Just over two months later, on January 16, 1919, the Eighteenth Amendment to the United States Constitution was ratified. Prohibition began one year later.

Repeal of Prohibition

Prohibition began to recede into history in March 1933, in the depths of the Great Depression, when the Cullen Bill was passed, allowing states that did not have state prohibition laws to sell 3.2 percent beer and placing a five-dollar per barrel tax on that

beer. Then, on April 17, 1933, the legalization of beer took effect with the passage of the Twenty-first Amendment.

On December 3, 1933, U.S. citizens took their first legal drinks in fourteen years. Of the 1,568 breweries in operation in 1910 (brewing over 63 million barrels a year), only 750 reopened when Prohibition was ended in 1933. Production in that year was just over 2 million barrels. By the end of June, 31 breweries were back in full operation. One year later, 756 breweries were meeting the demands of a thirsty nation. The brewing industry recovered gradually, reaching production of just over 55 million barrels when World War II broke out.

After World War II—The Rise of the Brewing Giants

The postwar years were a time of prosperity for most North Americans. There was an optimistic belief that there was no limit to the expansion of science, technology, democracy, or economy. The economy of size was undeniable. Larger size meant lower overhead cost per item and ease of production. Gradually the small, local breweries that survived Prohibition had to close because they could not compete with the cans of beer distributed across the country by national brewers and sold for half the price of locally bottled beer. Then regional brewers folded under the onslaught of nationwide advertising on radio and television, designed to create a demand for national products. It came down to fewer than one hundred breweries in the United States—and Anheuser-Busch, Miller, Schlitz, and Pabst owned three-quarters of them. By 1969 canned beer outsold bottled beer.

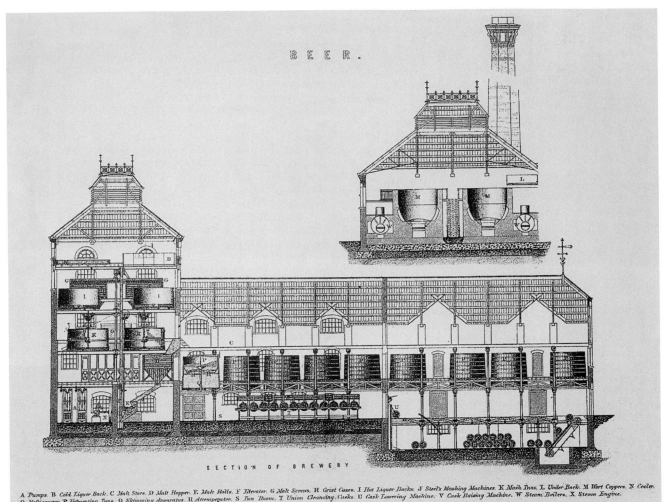

BEER.

SECTION OF BREWERY

A *Pumps*. B *Cold Liquor Back*. C *Malt Store*. W *Malt Hopper*. F *Malt Rolls*. F *Elevator*. G *Malt Screws*. H *Grist Cases*. I *Hot Liquor Backs*. J *Steel's Mashing Machines*. K *Mash Tuns*. L *Under Back*. M *Wort Coppers*. N *Cooler*.
O *Refrigerator*. P *Fermenting Tuns*. Q *Skimming Apparatus*. R *Attemperator*. S *Tun Room*. T *Union Cleansing Casks*. U *Cask Lowering Machine*. V *Cask Raising Machine*. W *Steam Boilers*. X *Steam Engine*.

A cross-section of a brewery from the nineteenth century illustrates the stages involved in creating beer.

The Microbreweries

The year 1969 was also a turning point for the small, local brewery that had a reputation, a good product, but no more money. That year, Fritz Maytag, of the family better known for home appliance manufacturing, took ownership of the Anchor Brewing Company in San Francisco. It was not obvious at the time, but a brewing revolution had begun.

Americans were beginning to demand quality in their beverage alcohol. In 1973 a brewer named Jack McAuliffe sold his first pint of New Albion ale, brewed at the New Albion Brewery in Sonoma, California, the first "microbrewed" beer since Prohibition.

The New Albion Brewery would only last five years, from 1977 to 1982. But it would take less than twenty years for the microbrew industry to grow to more than 2,500 breweries and brewpubs offering more than 10,000 different beers.

[See also ALCOHOL AND TEETOTALISM; ALCOHOLISM; ALE SLIPPER; BARS; BEER; BEER, CORN AND MAPLE; BEER BARRELS; BEER CANS; BEER GARDENS; BEER HALLS; BEER MUGS; BIRCH BEER; BOILERMAKER; BOTTLING; BUDWEISER; CANNING AND BOTTLING; COORS BREWING COMPANY; FERMENTATION; MICROBREWERIES; MILLER BREWING COMPANY; PROHIBITION; ROOT BEER; STOUT; TAVERNS; TEMPERANCE; YEAST.]

BIBLIOGRAPHY

Baron, Stanley Wade. *Brewed in America: A History of Beer and Ale in the United States*. Boston: Little, Brown, 1962.

Baum, Dan. *Citizen Coors: An American Dynasty*. New York: Morrow, 2000.

Jackson, Michael. *Michael Jackson's Beer Companion: The World's Greatest Beer Styles, Gastronomy, and Traditions*. Philadelphia: Running Press, 1993.

LaFrance, Peter. *Beer Basics: A Quick and Easy Guide*. New York: Wiley, 1995.

Lathrop, Elise. *Early American Inns and Taverns*. New York: Arno Press, 1977.

Lender, Mary Edwards, and James Kirby Martin. *Drinking in America: A History*. New York: Free Press, 1982.

Plavchan, Ronald Jan. *A History of Anheuser-Busch 1852–1933*. New York: Arno Press, 1969.

Rice, Kym S. *Early American Taverns: For the Entertainment of Friends and Strangers*. Chicago: Regnery Gateway, 1983.

Smith, Gregg. *Beer in America: The Early Years, 1587–1840: Beer's Role in the Settling of America and the Birth of a Nation*. Boulder, CO: Siris Books, 1998.

Vaizey, John. *The Brewing Industry, 1886–1951: An Economic Study*, for the Economic Research Council. London: Pitman, 1960.

PETER LAFRANCE

Beer, Corn, and Maple

Pre-Classic Maya farmers were probably the first people to brew beer from maize, doing so around 2600 B.C.E. The Maya used fermentation as one method of releasing vital amino acids stored in the grain. Other indigenous North American peoples fermented maize to make it more nutritious but used it as leavening and flavoring for maize breads, gruels, "soft" drinks, and broths. In 1587 English colonists at Roanoke made beer from maize, most likely the first brewed in what is now the United States. Beer was the beverage of choice in seventeenth-century America, a habit and technology inherited from a mother country whose drinking water supply was chronically contaminated. By 1620 Virginia boasted European brewhouses, which produced maize beer for local consumption.

Imports of beer and barley crops for beer freed "corn mash" for distillation into bourbon whiskey, but corn beer continued to be used during shortages and emergencies. In the Civil War, Union soldiers brewed corn beer in Confederate prison camps to augment rations and prevent scurvy. Corn was widely used as an additive in the commercial beers that came to dominate the North American brewing industry in the late nineteenth century. Corn helps to produce the distinct flavor of mass-marketed American beers.

Southeastern Native Americans used the sap of the sugar maple tree to flavor "sagamite," or wood ash hominy, and to increase yeast production in fermented maize dishes. Europeans were quick to appreciate maple as a sweetener and as a fermenting agent. Alone or combined with maize, maple made a beer of variable potency, and fermented with native persimmons it made a sweet fruit wine. Maple beer is brewed as a regional New England specialty. Like maize, maple is used as a flavoring and fermenting agent in the microbrewery renaissance.
[See also Beer; Corn; Distillation; Maple Syrup.]

BIBLIOGRAPHY

Fussel, Betty. *The Story of Corn: The Myths and History, the Culture and Agriculture, the Art and Science of America's Quintessential Crop.* New York: North Point Press, 1992. A social and scientific history of corn combined with a family history and memoir. The author describes a worldwide pursuit of "corn culture." The use of corn in the American South is mentioned briefly.

ESTHER DELLA REESE

Beer Barrels

It is likely that the barrel of ironbound wooden staves used to hold beer during its secondary fermentation originated with the "beer pails" of the Vikings. A barrel is a thirty-six-gallon cask made from metal by machines or out of white oak by a "tight cooper," a craftsman who specializes in making casks that will hold liquid. Stainless steel and aluminum barrels first came into use in the United States in the 1930s, almost completely replacing oak casks by the 1970s.

Although lighter and more efficient in production of a uniform brew suitable for the mass market, metal barrels do not impart the flavor that cask conditioning does. To compensate, commercial brewers use additives to imitate the natural carbonation and unique body imparted by oak. The success of "traditional method" microbreweries has encouraged a return to oak-cask fermentation both commercially and by home brewers. Cask-conditioned beers are called "real ales."
[See also Brewing.]

BIBLIOGRAPHY

Smith, Larry D. *The Cooper.* 2001. http://www.motherbedford. com/Cooper.htm. A visually informative website about the craft of coopering in early America.

ESTHER DELLA REESE

Beer Cans

Attempts to can beer before 1930 were unsuccessful. What made canning beer difficult was that the beer can had to be able to withstand pressures over 80 pounds per square inch (psi). Food products require between 25 and 30 psi. A greater challenge was finding a can lining to protect the beer from what brewers called "metal turbidity," a chemical reaction that ruined the beer. The American Can Company developed a breakthrough in 1934 when it produced the flat, or punch-top, can with a lining made from "Vinylite," a Union Carbide product. The package was trademarked as "Keglined" on September 25, 1934.

On January 24, 1935, in Richmond, Virginia, the first twelve-ounce cans of Krueger Special Beer went on the market. The Gottfried Krueger Brewing Company of Newark, New Jersey, supplied the beer, and the American Can Company provided the technology. That first year of beer in cans ended with over 200 million cans having been sold. By then twenty-three brewers had begun using cans. The competition soon included the Continental Can Company, which introduced the "cone-top" can in an effort to fill the need of brewers who wanted to use can technology on their bottling lines. The cone-top beer can all but disappeared during the 1950s.

In July 1935 it was announced that Pabst Export Beer would be canned. One month later G. Heilemann Brewing Company of La Crosse, Wisconsin; Berghoff Brewing Company of Fort Wayne, Indiana; and Bridgport Brewing Company of Albany, New York, were also canning their beer. During World War II rationed metal was directed toward the war effort, forcing brewers to package their beer almost entirely in bottles. The exception was beer packaged especially for the overseas troops. Many of the cans exported overseas for the war effort were painted in the army's traditional olive drab color. Even the can tops and bottoms were painted this color, to avoid reflecting light at night and possibly giving an easy target to the enemy.

From the beginning, the beverage can was made from three pieces of metal: a sleeve with separate top and bottom. It was not until 1959 that Coors introduced the first all-aluminum beverage can and launched a recycling program, offering a penny for every returned can. The Schlitz Brewing Company offered the next significant development when it introduced the pull-tab can to the market in March 1963. This inventive package was later made safer for the beer drinker and more ecologically friendly by the development of the stay-tab, introduced in the mid-1970s.
[See also Beer, Coors Brewing Company.]

BIBLIOGRAPHY

Baron, Stanley. *Brewed in America.* Boston: Little, Brown, 1962.

Ronnenberg, Herman. *Beer and Brewing in the Inland Northwest, 1850–1959.* Moscow: University of Idaho Press, 1993.

Skilnik, Bob. *The History of Beer and Brewing in Chicago, 1833–1978.* St. Paul, MN: Pogo Press, 1999.

PETER LaFRANCE

Beer Gardens

Beer gardens were introduced to the United States by German immigrants, who also brought with them lager beer, the familiar light-colored, effervescent beverage. In the days before refrigeration, brewers planted trees to cool the ground above the cellars where aging lager was kept cold. In good weather, beer was sold to the public in the "garden." The Germans believed that beer was best enjoyed in social settings, preferably with food, fresh air, and music. They gathered in outdoor venues planted with groves of trees and filled with rows of tables. Beer gardens were places where people from all social classes could mix on an equal basis. Everyone was welcome, including women, children, and non-Germans. Prices were kept low to allow even those of modest means to visit often.

America's first beer gardens were opened in the middle of the nineteenth century by breweries seeking to attract more customers. Over the years, beer gardens grew increasingly elaborate. The largest offered entertainment such as Wild West shows, dance halls, menageries, and lavish nighttime light displays. Beer gardens such as the Schlitz Palm Gardens and Pabst Park, both in Milwaukee, Wisconsin, are considered the forerunners of theme parks. In some cities with large German populations, especially New York, huge, parklike indoor establishments were built that offered lager beer and live entertainment year round. As a result, the term "beer garden" came to be interchangeable with "beer hall." Outdoor beer gardens offering traditional food and entertainment are found in a number of communities with German American populations. Blob's Park in Jessup, Maryland, claims to have introduced Oktoberfest to America, staging the nation's first such celebration in 1947.
[See also Amusement Parks; Beer Halls; German American Food.]

BIBLIOGRAPHY

Gabaccia, Donna R. *We Are What We Eat: Ethnic Food and the Making of Americans.* Cambridge, MA: Harvard University Press, 1998.

Oldenberg, Ray. *The Great Good Place: Cafes, Coffee Shops, Bookstores, Bars, Hair Salons, and Other Hangouts at the Heart of a Community.* 3rd ed. New York: Marlowe, 1999.

PAUL RUSCHMANN

Beer Halls

Throughout history, people have gathered in public places to drink beer and converse. But in post–Revolutionary War America, the beer hall, both the term and the institution, fell into disfavor. It became unfashionable for large numbers of people to drink beer socially, and beer was associated with idleness. That all changed in the middle of the nineteenth century, when waves of German immigrants arrived. Beer and a place to drink it were essential to their community life. The towns in which Germans settled soon had breweries and, later, beer halls similar to those in which they had drunk back home. The Germans were uncomfortable in "American" taverns, by which they usually meant Irish bars: dark establishments patronized exclusively by men. Germans viewed drinking places as extensions of the home. Their beer halls were well lit and filled with large tables where groups, often working-class families, drank together and ate traditional food, such as sausages, sauerkraut, Bismarck herring, rollmops, and sauerbraten.

The beer Germans brought with them was different from the dark, rich, English-style ales Americans had consumed since colonial times. German beer was a light colored—and less potent—beverage called lager, so named because it required long fermentation in a cool place (the word is derived from *lagern*, meaning "to store"). Americans, especially the young, quickly took a liking to lager. Beer hall proprietors, many of whom were German, catered to the newfound taste for lager. In some cities they built establishments with high ceilings and filled them with trees and plants in an effort to capture the atmosphere of an outdoor park—even in winter. Although they were roofed and enclosed, these establishments were commonly referred to as "beer gardens." After the Civil War there were an estimated three to four thousand beer halls in New York City alone. The largest, such as the Atlantic Beer Garden, entertained customers with shooting galleries, billiard rooms, and bowling alleys in addition to music and dancing.

Americans considered beer halls more wholesome than taverns because the halls had gemütlichkeit, an atmosphere of intimacy and comfort. Men brought their wives and children; patrons drank slowly; the practice of buying rounds was unheard of; beer only was served; and, most important, violence was not tolerated. Some observers promoted beer as a beverage of moderation and held up the Germans as examples of temperance. Nevertheless, the presence of children in beer halls and the practice of drinking on Sundays offended many Americans. Prohibition, wartime hostility toward Germans and their culture, and assimilation of German Americans into mainstream culture led to the near extinction of beer halls.

Even though it adopted German beer, over time the United States dropped the amenities associated with German beer halls. After the repeal of Prohibition, most drinking establishments were modeled after the Irish bar. The concept of the beer hall survived, however, especially in the Midwest. Beer halls of the early twenty-first century include the Brauhaus, in Chicago; the Dakota Inn Rathskeller, in Detroit, Michigan; and the Essen Haus, in Madison, Wisconsin. A number of small breweries, such as the Pennsylvania Brewing Company, in Pittsburgh, and the Weeping Radish, in Maneto, North Carolina, offer modern versions of the German beer hall. The world's most famous beer hall, the Hofbraühaus, of Munich, has a location in the Cincinnati, Ohio, area, and the Kaltenberg Castle Brewery, of Bavaria, has a beer hall in Vail, Colorado.

[See also BEER GARDENS; GERMAN AMERICAN FOOD.]

BIBLIOGRAPHY

Gabaccia, Donna R. *We Are What We Eat: Ethnic Food and the Making of Americans.* Cambridge, MA: Harvard University Press, 1998.

Oldenberg, Ray. *The Great Good Place: Cafes, Coffee Shops, Bookstores, Bars, Hair Salons, and Other Hangouts at the Heart of a Community.* 3rd ed. New York: Marlowe, 1999.

PAUL RUSCHMANN

Beer Mugs

Beer mugs are lidless, handled drinking containers made of materials that include glass, earthenware, pewter, and stoneware. Before the development of sturdy glass and stoneware, wooden and earthenware mugs were used. In the late seventeenth century in England, strong, leaded glass was developed, but throughout Europe, pewter and German stoneware remained the materials of choice. In England in the mid-nineteenth century, pressed glass technology and lifting of the glass excise tax led to the creation and acceptance of the modern glass beer mug.

Colonial Americans imported mugs from Germany and England and produced them at local pottery and pewter factories. As were all drinking vessels of the time, these mugs were marked according to official capacity standards to ensure that the drinker received the measure of drink paid for. Around the time of the Revolutionary War, with the breakdown of communication between America and England, pewter fell out of use because tin could no longer be imported. In the early twenty-first century mugs are made predominately of stoneware and glass but are also made with other materials, such as plastic. Both the temperature and the material of a mug can affect the flavor of the beer. Some beer drinkers enjoy drinking beer from room-temperature stoneware mugs, whereas others prefer icy-cold plastic mugs.

[See also BEER; BEER BARRELS; BEER CANS; BEER GARDENS; BEER HALLS.]

BIBLIOGRAPHY

Kirsner, Gary. *The Beer Stein Book: A 400 Year History.* Coral Springs, FL: Glentiques, 2000.

Noël Hume, Ivor. *Here Lies Virginia: An Archaeologist's View of Colonial Life and History.* Charlottesville: University Press of Virginia, 1994.

Stratton, Deborah. *Mugs and Tankards.* London: Souvenir, 1975.

JENNIFER MINNICK

Ben & Jerry's

Ben Cohen and Jerry Greenfield, two elementary school friends who dreamed of owning an ice cream company, took a correspondence course in ice cream making from Penn State University and then invested $12,000 to turn a former gas station in Burlington, Vermont, into a manufacturing plant. Ben & Jerry's Homemade Ice Cream and Crêpes opened in Burlington in 1978. Ben & Jerry's flavors capitalized on the newly popular concept of

Heath Bar Crunch as it first appeared to consumers in the 1980s.

"mix-ins," folding chunks of chocolate, nuts and the like into various basic flavors. Ben & Jerry's became a local favorite, and the company began marketing the brand to supermarkets. After receiving an out-of-court settlement from food industry giant Pillsbury (which had, in an attempt to freeze out the newcomer, tried to restrict retailers to one choice in the premium ice cream category, hoping their Häagen-Dazs brand would prevail), Ben & Jerry's ice cream rose to national popularity with innovative blends with memorable names like Chubby Hubby, Chocolate Chip Cookie Dough Ice Cream, and Cherry Garcia (named after the rock star Jerry Garcia). Promoting their use of all-natural ingredients and the company's eco-friendliness helped cement the product's relationship with its baby-boomer fans. The farmers who supplied dairy products to the company pledged not to use bovine growth hormone (BGH). The ice cream cartons were made from recycled paper. The company donated a percentage of profits to charity.

Cohen and Greenfield decided to take the company public to raise additional capital for growth. Unfortunately, this allowed investors to take control. Cohen and Greenfield attempted to regain control of the company but failed. In August 2000, Ben & Jerry's was bought by the Unilever conglomerate, which also owns the Dove and Breyer's ice cream brands. In 2002 the Center for Science in the Public Interest accused Ben & Jerry's of using artificial flavors, hydrogenated oils, and other "unnatural" ingredients, and the "All Natural" tagline was removed from packages and advertising. Today, with flavors with unusual names, such as Phish Phood and Chunky Monkey, the brand continues to be extremely popular, especially in urban markets.

[See also ICE CREAMS AND ICES.]

BIBLIOGRAPHY

Funderburg, Anne Cooper. *Chocolate, Strawberry, and Vanilla: A History of American Ice Cream.* Bowling Green, Ohio: Bowling Green State University Popular Press, 1995.

Lager, Fred. *Ben & Jerry's, the Inside Scoop: How Two Real Guys Built a Business with Social Conscience and a Sense of Humor.* New York: Crown Publishers, 1994.

ANDREW F. SMITH

Benne, *see Fats and Oils*

Berries, *see Blackberries; Blueberries; Fruit; Raspberries; Strawberries*

Betty Crocker

One of the most famous Americans who never lived, Betty Crocker was "born" in 1921, a child of necessity. The Washburn-Crosby Company, makers of Gold Medal flour, had run a promotional contest, and along with thousands of entries came hundreds of baking questions. Previously, a small staff had answered consumer correspondence over their own signatures, but the onslaught of queries called for the creation of a fictional spokeswoman to sign the letters. Company directors chose the names Betty ("one of the most familiar and most companionable of all family nicknames"), and Crocker (surname of recently retired director William G. Crocker). Betty's "signature" was developed from samples submitted by female employees.

In 1924 Washburn-Crosby began broadcasting the *Betty Crocker Cooking School of the Air* on its Minneapolis radio station, WCCO. Later aired nationally, the program was written (and originally hosted) by Marjorie Husted. In 1951 Adelaide Hawley, an actress, was the first to portray Betty Crocker on television. A number of actresses took the role when the *Betty Crocker Magazine of the Air* was broadcast nationally in the 1950s.

The first product to bear the Betty Crocker name was a soup mix, in 1941. The first Betty Crocker cake mix was introduced in 1947. The *Betty Crocker Cook Book of All-Purpose Baking*, a soft-cover promotional item, was published in 1942. The comprehensive *Betty Crocker's Picture Cook Book*, one of the most successful and beloved American cookbooks, was published in 1950, and more than 1 million copies were in print by 1951. So began a dynasty of Betty Crocker books, booklets, and other publications. Keeping up with the times, the Betty Crocker website, launched in 1997 and retooled in 2001, offers recipes, advice, product information, cookbooks, kitchen equipment, tableware, and gifts.

Beginning in the 1920s Betty Crocker had been depicted in print ads by various artists. In 1936 Neysa McMein, a prominent painter, was commissioned to create an official portrait. According to General Mills, the image was not a portrait of an individual but was an

A holiday advertisement for Betty Crocker cake mixes in 1952 attributes "that special homemade goodness" to the addition of eggs by the cook.

artful composite of the staff of the home service department. The Betty Crocker making her debut on the Softasilk cake flour box in 1937 was a severe young matron with a distant gaze, slightly pursed lips, and crisp white ruching at the neckline of her red dress. The portrait has been updated seven times since 1955. In 1957 a touch of gray appeared at Betty's temples, rendering her sweetly motherly. The 1965 incarnation was distinctly younger, reminiscent of Jacqueline Kennedy. The 1996 seventy-fifth-anniversary Betty Crocker, painted by John Stuart Ingle, is an olive-skinned career woman who might be part Asian, Latin, or African American. The watercolor, based on the digital "morphing" of photographs of seventy-five American women chosen by General Mills as embodying the characteristics of Betty Crocker, was engineered for broad demographic appeal.

The Betty Crocker red spoon, a symbol first used on packages in 1954, has all but supplanted the Betty Crocker image on products and in advertising.

In 1945 Betty Crocker was identified by *Fortune* as the second most popular woman in America (after Eleanor Roosevelt). She was named one of the top ten advertising icons of the twentieth century by *Advertising Age*. Betty Crocker products, adapted for the tastes of local markets, are sold in Canada, the United Kingdom, Europe, Australia, the Middle East, and Asia.

[**See also** GENERAL MILLS.]

BIBLIOGRAPHY

Betty Crocker. http://www.bettycrocker.com. Information about Betty Crocker food products, books and other publications, and catalogs of home products.

Inness, Sherrie A., ed. *Kitchen Culture in America*. Philadelphia: University of Pennsylvania Press, 2001.

BONNIE J. SLOTNICK

Bialy

The bialy is a type of bread roll, consumed as an alternative to the bagel. Typically three to four inches in diameter, it has a depressed center and a doughy, chewy circular rim flecked with chopped onions. The dough is made with high-gluten flour, fresh baker's yeast, salt, and water. Both bialys and bagels are associated with Jewish American culinary traditions. However, the awareness and popularity of bagels have reached a national level, while bialys remain virtually unknown.

Bialys differ from bagels in four significant ways: ingredient content, manufacturing process, general appearance, and flavor. Unlike bagel dough, bialy dough does not have added sugar or sweeteners. Bialys are baked, whereas bagels are kettle-boiled and then baked. Bialys have a signature depression, but never a hole. And bialys are always doughy and have the taste of onion, while bagels are available in a variety of flavors.

The bialy originated in the city of Bialystok, in what is now northeastern Poland, although no one can definitively claim its creation or give the date when it was first made. Before World War II, Bialystok was a thriving city with a majority Jewish population, one of the largest in Poland. The word "bialy" is derived from the Yiddish *bialystoker kuchen*, *kuchen* referring to a baked good such as a cake. Jews from the Bialystok area were nicknamed *bialystoker kuchen fressers*, or prodigious *kuchen* eaters. Bialys were baked primarily by Jewish bakers and were a staple of the Jewish diet. They were commonly spread with butter or soft farmer cheese, either on top or on the bottom. They were never cut. Children often ate them with halvah, a sweet sesame paste. The original bialys were large—roughly six to nine inches in diameter—with a wider and crisper indent and a generous topping of chopped fresh onions and poppy seeds. Bakers used special rolling pins to create the depressed center.

Pogroms and the Holocaust dispersed the remaining European Jews throughout the world. Many immigrated to New York City's Lower East Side. From the 1920s on, *bialystoker* bakers set up numerous bialy productions in that area; only one, Kossar's, survived into the twenty-first century. Bialys are no longer made or known in Poland. To *bialystokers* around the world, the bialy is more than just a lost bread; it has come to represent a lost culture.

[**See also** BAGELS; JEWISH AMERICAN FOOD; POLISH AMERICAN FOOD.]

BIBLIOGRAPHY

Sheraton, Mimi. *The Bialy Eaters: The Story of a Bread and a Lost World*. New York: Broadway Books, 2000.

Wisniewski, Thomas, et al. *Jewish Bialystock and Surroundings in Eastern Poland*. Massachusetts: Ipswich, 1998.

IZABELA WOJCIK

Bierocks

Bierocks—also known as bierrocks, bierochen, cabbage busters, runzas, German rocks, kraut Bierocks or kraut Runzas—are stuffed breads filled with a hash of beef, cabbage, and onions. There are also versions with sauerkraut or other vegetarian fillings. Under whichever name, they are the canonical dish of Germans from Russia and Ukraine who settled the prairie states in the late nineteenth century. Their descendents may be the largest ethnic group in North Dakota. The name "Bierocks" is a Germanized pronunciation of the Russian "pirog" (pie), or the Turkish "beorek"—the apparent origins of these savory treats. "Runza" means "a bun" in Low German. The bun shape is the most traditional, but pasties and turnovers are also common, and there are squares, triangles, and recently a "runza casserole," analogous to a tamale pie.

Like Cornish pasties, bierocks have survived in America because they were packable lunches for workers employed far from home. Also like Cornish pasties, bierocks lent themselves to commercial production and crossed over to regional popularity—in this case as runzas in Nebraska and surrounding states. In Nebraska they are popular snacks at college football games, and there is even a chain of Runza fast food restaurants, founded in 1949. In the restaurants the flavors have somewhat diversified to offer Swiss cheese and mushroom as well as the condiments associated elsewhere with hamburgers. They are popular dishes at church suppers and fundraisers wherever Germans from Russia have settled, and by the late twentieth century were often made at home with frozen bread dough.

MARK H. ZANGER

Biotechnology

Biotechnology uses living organisms or biological processes to generate products. Yogurt and beer are unrelated, but both are formed using microorganisms (bacteria in yogurt, yeast in beer). Antibiotics (produced by molds) also are products of biotechnology.

One aspect of biotechnology has generated more public attention: recombinant DNA (rDNA) technology, known as genetic engineering. Before the 1999 World Trade Organization meeting in Seattle, Washington, many Americans had not heard the words "frankenfoods," "biopiracy," and "genetically modified organism," or "GMO." Few knew they were eating genetically engineered foods.

Biotechnology in food production is controversial. American farmers who plant GM crops cannot always export those crops. Many American food manufacturers use GM ingredients; others have banned them. Consumers are starting to take more notice of biotechnology and how it affects their food.

Genetic Engineering

Early agriculturalists learned that their crops and animals made copies of themselves. Oddities occurred such as Jacob's spotted sheep (Gen. 30:32–43). Plants or animals were chosen for desired characteristics and bred. Offspring with those characteristics were bred again until the trait "bred true."

How this worked was unknown until the mid-nineteenth century. In 1856 Gregor Mendel, a Moravian monk, examined the pea plants growing in the garden of his monastery. Mendel was able to establish that heredity followed patterns and that certain outcomes could be predicted. The offspring, as a group, would exhibit a particular trait in definite ratios. Mendel couldn't identify that unit of heredity.

That unit became known as a "gene." Each gene is a set of instructions for producing a molecule. These instructions are strung along structures known as "chromosomes." Genes and chromosomes are made of DNA (deoxyribonucleic acid). Cells use DNA and its relative, RNA (ribonucleic acid), to store information needed to run the cell and reproduce.

DNA has only four components, assembled in linear arrangements (sequences) to make genes. Modern technology allows genetic engineers to isolate or synthesize genes and "cut and paste" them into the DNA of another organism. One needs the desired gene and a host organism (soybeans, for example) that will take up the DNA. If properly done, the new piece of DNA works in its new location. The organism uses the inserted DNA to make the protein specified by the foreign gene.

Taking up DNA is one step. The new DNA must slip correctly into the host DNA. Cells that have taken up and incorporated the new DNA must be identified. Selection is usually done by "markers" attached to the inserted DNA. Common markers are antibiotic-resistance genes, although these are being phased out. Pesticide resistance can be identified by growing the cells in the presence of the pesticide. Cells that survive probably have the required gene.

The final stage is to produce a complete organism. Under the right conditions, plants regenerate from single parental cells. Generating whole animals from engineered cells is more complicated, but can be done. Organisms so altered are called "transgenic." Another popular name is "genetically modified organism." Plants or animals bred by conventional methods are genetically modified relative to their wild ancestors, but are not considered transgenic. They would not normally carry genes from an unrelated species.

Purpose of Genetic Engineering

With careful choice of breeding stock, desirable traits can be improved in successive generations. The process is slow. Breeders can take years to establish a new line. The cost of the process could make overall profits small. Genetic engineering can cut the time required.

Another attraction of gene transfer is the ability to add new traits. Bt (*Bacillus thuringiensis*), a bacterial insecticide long used by organic gardeners, has been engineered into some commercial crops. Human insulin is produced by engineered bacteria. Allergens or toxins may be removed. Novel foods or new flavors can be generated by rDNA technology. Any combination is possible, but not all combinations are useful. The final product must be profitable to producers, acceptable to consumers, and must present no harm.

One goal of plant genetic engineering is nitrogen fixation. Certain bacteria can use atmospheric nitrogen directly for nutrition. The most familiar examples are the bacteria that live in the roots of legumes, such as beans, peas, and clover. Engineering this trait into other plants could save farmers huge quantities of nitrogen fertilizer. However, nitrogen fixation is a multigene trait, and not all of the genes have been identified.

Regulation of Biotechnology

Three government agencies regulate transgenic organisms in the United States: the Department of Agriculture (USDA), the Environmental Protection Agency (EPA), and the Food and Drug Administration (FDA). A product may be regulated by more than one agency. The agencies generally base decisions on information supplied by producers.

Foods that are the result of biotechnology need not be labeled as such, provided there are no hidden hazards. Use of the term "genetically modified" or "GM" on labels is not allowed. The FDA considers that all foods are genetically modified from their wild-type ancestors and that to label foods as such is "misleading" ("Guidance for Industry," http://www.cfsan.fda.gov/~dms/biolabgu.html). Research with FDA focus groups indicates that consumers want such information. Almost all participants felt bioengineered foods should be labeled as such, as is done in the European Union.

Obtaining approval for a transgenic foodstuff can be a lengthy and expensive process. Only the largest companies can complete the process and remain profitable. In addition, approval in the United States does not ensure approval overseas. American companies must obtain similar approvals from any importing country.

Biotechnology on the Farm

The first genetically engineered vegetable grown and released for sale in the United States was the Flavr Savr tomato. The tomato was approved by the USDA in 1992, commercialized in 1994, and withdrawn from the market in 1996. Yields had been low with little consumer interest.

The Roundup Ready soybean (Monsanto) was the first commercially successful GM crop in the U.S. Approval was granted in 1994, and the first commercial fields were planted in 1996. The beans are engineered to resist a widely used herbicide, glyphosate. The resistance also was engineered into corn, cotton, sugar beets, rapeseed (canola), and wheat. Farmers can spray the herbicide on fields with little or no damage to crops. Approximately 70 percent of the soybeans grown in the United States in 2002 were engineered to be herbicide resistant.

Another strategy is to engineer plants to produce their own pesticide, such as Bt. The molecules are toxic to many insects. Bt has been engineered into corn, cotton, soybeans, potatoes, tomatoes, and other crops. Not all have been approved for commercial production. Most engineered corn, soybeans, and cottonseed oil are used in animal feed and processed foods.

Another aspect of farm biotechnology is production of transgenic plants and animals for substances used in medicine, known colloquially as "pharming." Although yeast and bacteria are used in this way, these organisms cannot form many human or animal proteins properly. Inserting genes for the production of biochemicals into plants and animals can result in abundant "manufacture" of those molecules. Milk can be drunk as is, or a fruit can be consumed as usual. An example is the GM banana system being designed to deliver vaccines. The bananas can be eaten raw, and vaccines produced in them may not be as perishable as conventional vaccines.

Development of pharming has been slow. Pharmed products must meet the standards for any drug marketed. There are concerns about mixing of pharmed products with conventional products. Milk or crops of a given type look much the same. Should pharming become commercially viable, pharmaceuticals must not end up on consumers' plates without their consent.

Biotechnology at the Supermarket

American supermarkets contain foods with GM ingredients. Consumers may be unaware of this, because such labeling is restricted. The first product of genetic engineering in the U.S. food supply was Chy-Max chymosin, (Pfizer) approved by the FDA in 1990. It is a version of vegetarian rennet, used to make certain cheeses. Approximately 60 percent of all U.S. cheeses are produced with GM chymosins; some may be labeled "vegetarian."

Processed foods, such as bakery products, heat-and-serve meals, and breakfast cereals all contain a variety of GM corn- and soybean-derived ingredients. The FDA considers these ingredients to be "substantially equivalent" to their non-GM counterparts.

Vegetable oils are being engineered to be more heart friendly and to have better properties. The nutritional characteristics will be changed. The GM oils (such as cottonseed) must be labeled as being altered in composition.

Genetically engineered fruits and vegetables are extremely rare on market shelves; few have been approved for commercialization in America. As of 2002 cantaloupes, potatoes, radicchio, squash, papaya, sugar beets, corn, soybeans, and tomatoes were the only fruits and vegetables given FDA approval. Corn products sold directly to consumers are unlikely to be biotechnology versions. Only a small percentage of U.S. engineered corn is sweet corn, and no popcorn varieties have been approved. Americans rarely use fresh soybeans, other than as the snack edamame, popular since the late 1990s.

Future Foods or Food Fights?

Most American farms are small and family owned, but don't always provide a living for their owners. In 1997 approximately 70 percent of farms brought in less than fifty thousand dollars; the average cost of production was about seventy thousand dollars. Between 1992 and 1997 total cropland and the number of farms decreased approximately 1.5 percent nationwide. More food must be grown in less space by fewer growers.

Genetically engineered crops can be a tool for increasing production on less farmland. Crops can be developed for conditions previously considered unsuitable for agriculture. Yields can be increased by manipulation of the relevant genes. Biotechnology can be considered a route to "cleaner," less-polluting agriculture.

The "agrobiotechnology" companies were confident that their products would revolutionize farming and the food industry. These companies learned that although everyone needs to eat, not everyone wants to eat engineered food. Abundant food production is good, but "dumping" surpluses can disrupt farming in poor countries. The chemical companies turned "life-science" companies were caught off guard by consumer attitudes.

Companies tended to present their patented, licensed, genetically engineered crops as the only solution to world hunger. Factors such as politics, poverty, and trade regulations have been ignored.

To protect intellectual property rights, GM seeds are not sold outright to farmers. Seed may not be saved or exchanged with another grower. Growers must sign documents and pay a licensing fee. Initial licenses from Monsanto prohibited the use of any brand of glyphosate beside Roundup. That restriction was overturned in the courts.

Agrobiotech companies inspect farms looking for license violations. That does not sit well with farmers. Poor farmers worldwide may find it difficult to deal with complicated licenses and will find themselves bound to third parties who will. GM crops have not always performed well in less-than-ideal conditions, and farmers have sued for compensation.

Importers have begun paying premiums to American growers for non-GM crops. Consumers in many countries expect GM foods to be labeled as such, while American producers (not consumers) object. This discrepancy can lead to trade disputes.

The organic food industry has benefited obliquely from biotechnology. The National Organic Program does not allow GM foods to be certified as organic. Consumers who do not want to eat GM foods can choose organic. This has increased the production of organically raised foods in America.

Biotechnology has a role to play in food production, if managed sensibly and responsive to consumer demand.

[**See also** DEPARTMENT OF AGRICULTURE, UNITED STATES; FOOD AND DRUG ADMINISTRATION.]

BIBLIOGRAPHY

Ag BioTech InfoNet. http://www.biotech-info.net.

Animal and Plant Health Inspection Service. http://www.aphis.usda.gov.

Charles, Daniel. *Lords of the Harvest: Biotech, Big Money, and the Future of Food.* Cambridge, MA: Perseus, 2001.

Cooper, Ann, with Lisa M. Holmes. *Bitter Harvest: A Chef's Perspective on the Hidden Dangers in the Foods We Eat and What You Can Do about It.* New York: Routledge, 2000.

Cornell University Public Issues Education Project. http://www.geo-pie.cornell.edu.

Council for Biotechnology Information: http://www.whybiotech.com.

Cummins, Ronnie, and Ben Lilliston. *Genetically Engineered Food: A Self-Defense Guide for Consumers.* New York: Marlowe, 2000.

Durant, John, Martin W. Bauer, and George Gaskell. *Biotechnology in the Public Sphere.* London: Science Museum, 1998.

Gaskell, George, and Martin W. Bauer, eds. *Biotechnology 1996–2000: The Years of Controversy.* London: Science Museum, 2001.

Lambrecht, Bill. *Dinner at the New Gene Café: How Genetic Engineering Is Changing What We Eat, How We Live, and the Global Politics of Food.* New York: St. Martin's, 2001.

Lurquin, Paul F. *High Tech Harvest: Understanding Genetically Modified Food Plants.* Boulder, CO: Westview, 2002.

Martineau, Belinda. *First Fruit: The Creation of the Flavr Savr Tomato and the Birth of Biotech Foods.* New York: McGraw-Hill, 2001.

McHughen, Alan. *Pandora's Picnic Basket: The Potential and Hazards of Genetically Modified Foods.* Oxford and New York: Oxford University Press, 2000.

Organic Trade Association. http://www.ota.com.

Pence, Gregory E. *Designer Food.* Lanham, MA: Rowman and Littlefield, 2002.

U.S. Department of Agriculture Statistics. http://www.nass.usda.gov/census.

U.S. Environmental Protection Agency. http://www.epa.gov.

U.S. Food and Drug Administration. http://vm.cfsan.fda.gov.

U.S. Food and Drug Administration. "Guidance for Industry: Voluntary Labeling Indicating Whether Foods Have or Have Not Been Developed Using Bioengineering." http://www.cfsan.fda.gov/~dms/biolabgu.html.

Wilmut, Ian, Keith Campbell, and Colin Tudge. *The Second Creation: Dolly and the Age of Biological Control.* New York: Farrar, Straus and Giroux, 2000.

ASTRID FERSZT

Big Boy

In 1936 Robert Wian opened a ten-stool diner called "Bob's Pantry" in Glendale, California. After a promising start, Wian expanded the place into a combination coffee shop and drive-in. Observing that the hamburgers at the nearby White Castle hamburger stand seemed skimpy, Wian bid for attention by making a double-decker burger: He split a sesame-seed bun in three and tucked two burgers in between. This more substantial sandwich was originally called the "Fat Boy," but Wian soon changed the name to "Big Boy." In 1937 he renamed the restaurant itself "Bob's Big Boy." Its icon was a plump, saucer-eyed boy in red and white checked overalls with the words "Big Boy" emblazoned across his chest, holding aloft a double-decker hamburger. A 12-foot statue of the Big Boy was placed in front of each restaurant in the chain.

As Wian expanded his operation, new units generally included indoor seating as well as drive-in service. He also franchised the restaurant, giving franchisees the freedom to substitute their own name for "Bob's." The Frisch Company opened Frisch's Big Boys throughout the Midwest, and "Azar's Big Boy" could be found in Colorado. It was not an integrated operation, but a contractual relationship that funneled Wian royalties (2 percent on gross sales) in exchange for the use of the "Big Boy" logo and the double-decker sandwich. The company also prepared and distributed to franchisees comic books, coloring books, and games to entertain children at its restaurants.

The flagship meal at Bob's was the "Combo," with a Big Boy hamburger, fries, and a small salad. Still, by the 1960s Big Boy found it hard to compete with the large, lower-priced fast food operations, such as McDonald's, Burger King, and Wendy's. In 1984 the company attempted to revitalize its image by doing away with the Big Boy statues and logo. Customers complained, and the company held a public poll on whether to retain the Big Boy: the overwhelming vote was in favor of keeping the familiar icon.

Today, the chain is owned by Robert Liggett, who renamed it "Big Boy Restaurants International." Liggett moved the headquarters to Warren, Michigan. Today, the company has about five hundred Big Boy Restaurants in the United States and Japan.

BIBLIOGRAPHY

Langdon, Philip. *Orange Roofs, Golden Arches: The Architecture of American Chain Restaurants.* New York: Knopf, 1986.

ANDREW F. SMITH

Birch Beer

Birch beer, a beverage made with the sap of birch trees, first became popular in America in the 1880s and 1890s, during the temperance movement. Many soft drinks, including ginger ale, sarsaparilla, spruce beer, root beer, cherry smash, and Coca-Cola, were developed and mass-marketed during this time. Because they contained no alcohol, these beverages were billed as family drinks. That some of these sodas were said to have healing properties helped spur sales. For example, ginger ale was supposed to cure nausea and help digestion; sarsaparilla was said to be a blood purifier; and early versions of Coca-Cola were billed as hangover and headache cures. By the late 1800s, many sodas were being bottled for mass distribution. The crimped metal cap was patented in 1892, enabling more than one hundred bottles per minute to be easily sealed.

The first birch beers were homemade, brewed without a standard recipe. All contained at least some portion of sap from birch trees, also called birch water. The trees, usually sweet birch or black birch, were tapped in the early spring, around the end of February or beginning of March, similar to the way maples are tapped to make maple syrup. A hole was drilled in the tree, and a spile (tube) was inserted to let the sap run into a bucket. Although it did not contain much flavor, the raw sap was used to replace plain water in drink recipes.

Early versions of birch beer contained yeast and were left to ferment, making them alcoholic. Birch wine was made with birch sap that was boiled down, fermented, and stored in casks stopped with bungs. Other ingredients in birch beer varied but could include sassafras, honey, juniper, and vanilla. Birch bark or small birch twigs sometimes were added to give the brew a stronger birch flavor.

Birch beer is similar to root beer but typically is less sweet and less carbonated. The natural flavor of birch sap and twigs is similar to wintergreen. Modern formulas for birch beer usually include flavor extracts as well as benzoate of soda as a preservative. Because sassafras root was a suspected carcinogen, the U.S. government banned use of the root in the 1960s. Sassafras extract is permitted as a flavoring. Food coloring is sometimes added to birch beer to make it red. White birch beer is a clear, colorless variation.

Birch beer never gained the cult following of other temperance drinks, such as Moxie and Dr Pepper. Birch beer is a regional specialty, sold mostly in the mid-Atlantic states and New England. It is especially popular in the Pennsylvania Dutch country. Companies that have been making birch beer since the late nineteenth century include the Kutztown Soda Co. in Pennsylvania, and Boylan's in New Jersey. Birch beer is experiencing a comeback because several beverage companies are reviving old-fashioned American sodas.

[**See also** BOTTLING; ROOT BEER; SARSAPARILLA; SODA DRINKS.]

BIBLIOGRAPHY

Brown, John Hull. *Early American Beverages.* Rutland, VT: Tuttle, 1966.

Cresswell, Stephen. *Homemade Root Beer, Soda, and Pop.* Pownal, VT: Storey, 1998.

Devito, Carlo. *The Everything Beer Book*. Holbrook, MA: Adams, 1998.

CLARA SILVERSTEIN

Birdseye, Clarence

Clarence Birdseye, the inventor and pioneer in frozen foods, was born in Brooklyn, New York, on December 9, 1886. Until he died on October 8, 1956, Birdseye never came in from the cold. According to family legend, an ancestor saved the life of an English queen by shooting an attacking hawk through the eye, thereby earning the name "Birds Eye." Clarence Birdseye attended Amherst College but was forced to leave school for lack of money. As a struggling student, Birdseye recounted the day he passed a spring hole and saw thousands of small frogs. He wondered what the frogs were good for, so he sold them to the Bronx Zoo for $115. This ability to look at the familiar and see opportunity was a creative trait Birdseye never lost.

Birdseye went to Labrador, Canada, to work as a fur trapper and to conduct a fish and wildlife survey as a field naturalist for the U.S. government. On August 21, 1915, on a visit to Washington, DC, Birdseye married Eleanor Garrett, whose father was a founder of the National Geographic Society. The Birdseyes and their newly born son, Kellogg, returned to Labrador to live in a remote shack. While Clarence traveled by dogsled to acquire furs, Eleanor tended the winter traps.

In Labrador, Birdseye discovered that foods frozen quickly in the frigid Artic air kept their flavor. He experimented by putting cabbages in his baby's bath pan, adding salt water, and exposing the pan to the frigid winds. As a result, the family had green food all winter.

Upon returning to the United States, Birdseye took a job as assistant to the president of the U.S. Fisheries Association. It disturbed him to see fish in melted ice water, a medium that promoted bacterial growth. In September 1922 Birdseye began development of a commercial method for quickly freezing food. His tools were primitive—an electric fan, buckets of brine, and ice. Birdseye moved to Gloucester, Massachuetts, in 1925 to be near a supply of fresh fish and founded the General Seafoods Corporation to produce "frosted foods." His method of quick freezing produced small ice crystals that did not damage the structure of food. When thawed, the food retained its original flavor, texture, color, and taste. After Birdseye sold the company it was renamed General Foods Corporation. Birdseye stayed with General Foods to supervise its frozen foods laboratory. Over his career Birdseye was granted almost three hundred patents.

Birdseye was very modest about his accomplishments. "I did not discover quick-freezing. The Eskimos had used it for centuries, and scientists in Europe had made experiments along the same lines I had. What I accomplished . . . was merely to make packaged quick-frozen food available to the public" (Nickerson). Birdseye was also an early pioneer in the area of food dehydration. He called his new food processing method "anhydration" and the product "waterless foods."

An inventor in the mold of Benjamin Franklin and Thomas Edison, Birdseye was an adventurer, explorer, scientist, promoter, and naturalist. His contributions revolutionized the way food was marketed, not only in the United States but also throughout the world. Without Birdseye's creative thinking, there would have been no TV dinners in the 1950s. [See also BIRDSEYE CORPORATION; FROZEN FOOD; TV DINNERS.]

BIBLIOGRAPHY

Nickerson, Jane. "News of Food: New and Better Way to Process Food by Anhydration Announced by Birdseye." *New York Times*, November 14, 1945.

JOSEPH M. CARLIN

Birdseye Corporation

Freezing food for later consumption was not a new idea in twentieth-century America. The English philosopher-statesman Francis Bacon had long ago experimented with stuffing chickens with snow. Clarence Birdseye, while working in Labrador, Canada, observed that foods frozen quickly at low temperatures had superior quality. Upon returning to the states he perfected a method for rapid freezing that did not destroy the cellular structure of foods.

Birdseye founded the Birdseye Seafood Company in 1919 in New York City, where he began processing fish fillets at a facility near the Fulton Fish Market. In 1925 Birdseye founded the General Seafoods Corporation in Gloucester, Massachusetts, to be closer to a steady supply of fresh fish. His successful technique was to pack fresh fish in five-inch by three-inch by two-inch retail cartons and to place the cartons between two metal plates in contact with calcium chloride brine flowing at a very low temperature. The frozen cartons were packaged in cellophane. Birdseye was one of the first people to use cellophane as a moisture-vapor seal to prevent dehydration of frozen food. By 1928 he was able to apply this technique to meat, poultry, and shellfish in commercial quantities. Birdseye's success coincided with the development of home refrigeration and freezing units.

A major influence on Clarence Birdseye and the future of frozen food was Marjorie Merriweather Post, daughter of the founder of the Postum Company. Post is reported to have enjoyed eating frozen goose on board her yacht when it tied up in Gloucester for provisioning. Her chef told her that the goose had been frozen for several months. Post urged her second husband, Edward F. Hutton, to talk to the inventor of this frozen goose. Impressed, Post persuaded the board of directors of the Postum Company to purchase Birdseye's company. The deal was made in 1929, when Postum together with the Goldman-Sacks Trading Corporation bought Birdseye's patents and trademarks for $22 million. The new company was called the General Foods Corporation. The Birdseye name was kept as a corporate trademark but split into two words: "Birds Eye."

The first sale of frozen foods—Birdseye preferred to call his invention "quick-frozen foods"—to the public took place on March 6, 1930, in Springfield, Massachusetts, at Davidson's Market and Bakery. This step was bold because at the time consumers thought frozen foods were low-grade. Another problem faced by retailers was the high cost of freezer cabinets and the electric current needed to run them. By 1933 there were only 516 retail outlets for frozen foods in America.

In the early twenty-first century Birds Eye Foods is owned by Agrilink Foods, a $1 billion national food-processing company that markets a variety of product lines of branded, private-label frozen food products. Birds Eye is the flagship brand for the company. [See also BIRDSEYE, CLARENCE; GENERAL FOODS; POST FOODS.]

BIBLIOGRAPHY

Guinane, Joseph E. "I Remember 'Bob' Birdseye." *Quick Frozen Foods* (March 1960): 317–320.

JOSEPH M. CARLIN

Birthdays

Birthdays are milestones in the evolution of an individual or a group. In ancient times they occasioned feasting and entertainment but solely among the upper echelons of societies. Birthday cakes were not then part of the celebrations, although special sweets abounded. Centuries would pass before celebrations of birthdays and saint's days would find a place in popular culture, a result of the medieval church's new practice of recording births. Subsequently local European birthday rituals developed according to national cultural differences and were brought by various ethnic groups to colonial America, where they eventually merged into a new form.

The dominant English culture in America shaped birthday patterns for some time. Colonial birthdays were enjoyed by privileged adults, who feasted well, or, at the very least, shared a glass of wine and a small slice of fruitcake with friends. Children's parties echoed the adult formats. After the War of Independence, patriots honored the Founding Fathers on their birthdays. George Washington's birthday, for example, was celebrated locally in many communities, and the special foods served were either those known as his favorite dishes or others named for him. This kind of birthday-holiday survives in the commemorations of Abraham Lincoln and Martin Luther King Jr.

In the new age of democracy, birthdays did not remain class-limited. As the nineteenth century progressed, a number of factors reshaped the events. The growth of

A card depicting a birthday cake, published by L. Prang in 1886.

themes. Beautifully hand-colored, molded ice creams could be ordered to suit the guest list, such as military and patriotic themes for boys and dolls and flowers for girls.

The Candles

Small, colored candles became an integral part of the American birthday cake. An American style guide of 1889 directed, "At birthday parties, the birthday cake, with as many tiny colored candles set about its edge as the child is years old, is, of course, of special importance." The modern use of candles on a special cake may be connected to the German tradition of *Kinderfest*, dating from the fifteenth century, a time when people believed that on birthdays children were particularly susceptible to evil spirits. Friends and family gathered around protectively, keeping the cake's candles lit all day until after the evening meal, when the cake was served. The candles were thought to carry one's wishes up to God. This German observance was brought to colonial Pennsylvania and was later reinforced by the influence of British-German fashions from Queen Victoria's court.

The British contribution to American birthdays was the model of dramatic Christmas pudding presentations. Almost identical to the Cratchit family's ritual in Dickens's *A Christmas Carol*, the iconic American cake is aflame with candles instead of brandy and makes the same entrance into a darkened dining room, promising to fulfill anticipations of sugared delight. Ultimately candles would be made in novel shapes, sizes, and colors, and add to the cake's decor.

The Cake

Although fruitcakes and rich, yeasted cakes were the traditional English festive cakes, the modern form of the birthday cake originated in American kitchens in the mid-nineteenth century. In contrast to their European counterparts, American women were active home bakers, largely because of the abundance of oven fuel in the New World and the sparsity of professional bakers. By the later 1800s, home bakers were spurred further by several innovations. The cast-iron kitchen stove, complete with its own quickly heated oven, became standard equipment in urban middle-class homes. Women in towns had more discretionary time compared to farm women, and they had an expanding social life that required formal and informal hospitality. Sugar, butter, spice, and flour costs were dropping. Improved chemical leavening agents, baking powder among them, enabled simpler and faster baking and produced a cake of entirely different flavor and texture. A cake constructed in layers, filled and frosted, became the image of the standard birthday cake. One observer of the early 1900s compared bubbly soap lather to "the fluffiness of a birthday cake" and snowy, frost-covered hills to iced birthday cakes.

industry, elevated urban material standards, and emerging middle-class culture made more elaborate birthday celebrations increasingly attractive. Changing notions of the nature of childhood stimulated a new style of young people's parties. Enterprising manufacturers saw great financial possibilities in the accoutrements of birthdays, such as special room and table decorations, foods, entertainments, party favors, and hats. Typical was the early twentieth-century party game of Pin the Tail on the Donkey, requiring the purchase of colorful paper accessories. This game was almost as necessary as blowing out candles and making secret wishes, cutting the formulaic cake and serving it with ice cream, and receiving gifts.

Ice cream and cake became defining elements, whether after a meal or as the centerpiece of a party. By the late 1800s ice cream had become available to those of almost all income levels and was featured at any festivity. Fancy ice cream shops delivered their frozen wares to birthday parties, while some people cranked ice cream churns at home to make their own. After the turn of the twentieth century, a number of confectioneries stocked small pewter ice cream molds of varied patterns and

Cutting the birthday cake after the candles have been blown out.

Ornamentation

Writing on birthday cakes began with professional bakers and caterers, who were proliferating in growing cities. The cakes of the late 1800s were decorated with inscriptions like "Many Happy Returns of the Day" and the celebrant's name, a tradition that continues into the twenty-first century. Sometimes the cake was home baked but then decorated by a specialist. A typical inscription might read, "Mabel Smither July 8th 1885 from Dick and Lizzie." The phrase "Happy Birthday" did not appear on birthday cake messages until the popularization of the now-ubiquitous song "Happy Birthday to You" (1910). Cookbook authors began to recommend decorating with birth dates and names and offered instruction on how to make colored frostings with such ingredients as parsley and beets. Some taught home bakers to make their own pastry bags, which were used to dispense the decorative frostings. By 1958 A. H. Vogel had begun to manufacture preformed cake decorations. Inexpensive letters, numbers, and pictorial images, such as flowers or bows, with matching candleholders were standard supermarket offerings.

The Twentieth-Century Birthday Industry

In the course of the twentieth century, the homemade birthday cake depended increasingly on purchased cake mixes. The use of mixes was reinforced by such guides as *The Cake Mix Doctor*. Available in white, spiced, and devil's food flavors, these mixes made suitable birthday cakes. In the twenty-first century many adults thought of cake mixes when they remembered the so-called homemade birthday cakes of their childhoods.

Commercial novelty cakes found a new direction. In the late 1930s Carvel, combining traditional party ice cream with cake, developed ice cream cakes often made in cartoon character shapes. Cakes of unusual size were newsworthy, for example the 128,238-pound cake honoring the one-hundredth birthday of Fort Payne, Alabama. In the early 2000s, the American emphasis on individualism found expression in vegetarian or vegan cake recipes, special interests, favorite flavors of cakes, or even life-size portraits in cake, increasing the province of professional party designers. Cakes are often made in a format or with designs expressing the celebrant's interests,

such as golf, football, or gardening. Despite the attractions of the new professionalism in the birthday industry, numbers of how-to publications such as *The Birthday Cake Book* and *Colette's Birthday Cakes* seemed to indicate that baking from scratch and homemade birthday parties were still alive in American culture.

[**See also** Bakeries; Cakes; Crisco; Ice Creams and Ices; Washington's Birthday.]

BIBLIOGRAPHY

Byrn, Anne. *The Cake Mix Doctor*. New York: Workman, 1999.

Lewis, Percy, and A. G. Bromley. *The Victorian Book of Cakes*. New York: 1903. Reprint, New York: Random House, 1991.

Rorer, Sarah Tyson. *Mrs. Rorer's Cakes, Icings, and Fillings*. Philadelphia: Arnold and Company, 1905.

LIZA JERNOW

Biscuit Cutters

Biscuits that were no longer hard, like sea biscuits or beaten biscuits, appeared with the early-nineteenth-century use of homemade potash, pearl ashes, and subsequent commercial baking sodas and powders. It was customary from the 1840s or so to the mid-twentieth century for farm housewives and family cooks to make fresh biscuits for at least one meal a day. An inverted tumbler twisted against the dough can cut a biscuit, but it pinches the edge and keeps the biscuit from rising fully. A sharp-edged cutter did not have to be twisted. Until the 1870s, biscuit cutters were either pieced tin or carved wood circles, with or without a handle, similar to cookie cutters.

The ideal of quickly cutting as many biscuits as possible out of each rolled-out sheet of dough spurred inventors. By the late nineteenth century, two types of multiple cutters were in use. Rolling types of tin or aluminum (looking somewhat like toy lawnmowers), which would cut at least two biscuits with each revolution of the wheel, to which the cutting edges were attached, were made from the 1880s to the 1930s. A tin and wood rocker type that cut four biscuits with one rocking movement across the dough was manufactured in the late 1880s and 1890s by the inventor and manufacturer Henry Sidway, who also made rolling types.

BIBLIOGRAPHY

Franklin, Linda Campbell. *300 Years of Kitchen Collectibles*. 5th ed. Iola, WI: Krause Publications, 2003.

LINDA CAMPBELL FRANKLIN

Bison, *see Buffalo*

Bistros

The original French incarnation of bistros featured *cuisine de grand-mère*, or grandmother's cooking. Bistro foods and wines are robust, rustic, and plentiful. Bistros serve simple dishes, presented simply and priced inexpensively, as would be expected in neigh-

borhood restaurants that cater to nearby residents. Bistros in France still preserve their social-center feeling.

No one is certain where the name "bistro" came from. There are several apocryphal tales to explain it, but none is convincing. One theory says that Russians living in Paris in 1815 shouted "bistrot," meaning faster, while they waited for food, and the French adopted the term. The only problem with that idea is that "bistro" did not enter written French until the 1880s, and the variant "bistrot" did not enter the language until the 1890s.

Others suggest that the name comes from *bistrouille*, which refers to eau-de-vie, or perhaps from the verb *bistrouiller*, which means to make a sort of cobbled-together "wine" from alcohol, water, and other ingredients. Most lexicographers do not accept any of these explanations.

Ignoring the source of the name, another idea is that bistros were originally *café-charbons*, or shops that sold coal and firewood. They were places where locals could meet for a glass of wine or a cup of coffee. After a time, owners began to serve family-style dishes to their guests, according to the legend.

Irrespective of the origins of the name, early in the twentieth century the concept of neighborhood restaurants serving plain but good foods and wines was well established in France. The spirit of French bistro life is generosity, simplicity, and earthy lustiness. Portions are liberal and are often served in large bowls or on platters family-style for all at the table to help themselves. Menus change infrequently in French bistros, and the plat du jour is often the same thing on corresponding days each week.

In the United States there was not that same sort of cultural push to create the bistro in the French style. The diversity that immigrants brought pushed casual dining in a completely different direction. The American parallels to the idea of the French bistro have two major incarnations of the style in the United States—one rather sophisticated and one much more homey.

The urban bistro is less a social center than a casual restaurant emphasizing sophisticated food and drink. Urban bistros often feature fancier service ware and presentations than their French namesakes, and they have a more variable menu. Menus in the upscale bistros generally change to suit the seasons, and specials are usually changed more frequently. Offerings reflect adventuresome preparations using a wide variety of raw materials and techniques.

The other variation is home-style restaurants that would never be called bistros. Their hallmark is that they offer inexpensive food in casual settings. They include a wide range of restaurant concepts, from country operations in rural areas with a homey feel to places featuring foreign cuisines. Typically, service is very informal, portions are large, and prices are low.

Like "trattoria" and "pub," "bistro" has become as much a marketing term as a designation of a type of restaurant. It became fashionable in the 1980s to so name restaurants for the social cachet to be gained.

[**See also** RESTAURANTS; TAVERNS.]

BIBLIOGRAPHY

Mariani, John. *America Eats Out: An Illustrated History of Restaurants, Taverns, Coffee Shops, Speakeasies, and Other Establishments That Have Fed Us for 350 Years.* New York: Morrow, 1991.

Wells, Patricia. *Bistro Cooking.* New York: Workman, 1989. Well-researched and comprehensive source of anecdotal information and recipes.

ROBERT PASTORIO

Bitting, Katherine

Katherine Golden (1869–1937) was born in Canada, but her family later immigrated to the United States. She received her BS from the State Normal School in Salem, Massachusetts; studied bacteriology at the Massachusetts Institute of Technology in Cambridge; and received an MS from Purdue University in Lafayette, Indiana. While completing her master's thesis, she worked at the Purdue Agricultural Extension Station, and in 1893 she became an assistant professor, teaching biology, structural botany, and bacteriology. At Purdue, she met and married Arvil Bitting, who had previously served as veterinarian to the Agricultural Experiment Station in Florida for three years. He received a doctorate in veterinary medicine from Iowa State College in 1895. After graduation he began teaching veterinary medicine at Purdue University while studying medicine at the Indiana Medical College. He received his MD in 1900 but never practiced medicine.

The marriage between Arvil Bitting and Katherine Golden launched a successful personal and professional partnership that lasted four decades. In 1906 Arvil Bitting became a special agent for the U.S. Department of Agriculture, stationed at Lafayette. The following year he became an inspector for the Bureau of Chemistry. In September 1907 Katherine Bitting was appointed to the position of microbotanist in the bureau and was assigned to work with her husband. Their first joint project was to determine how to make ketchup without the use of added preservatives.

The Bittings established a laboratory and a model ketchup factory in their home in Lafayette. In all, they analyzed more than sixteen hundred bottles of ketchup. In addition, they visited dozens of factories that made tomato pulp and twenty ketchup factories. As homemade ketchup stayed fresh for a much longer period after opening than did their experimental ketchup, the Bittings began collecting ketchup recipes from magazines, journals, cookbooks, and other sources and testing them in their laboratory. In 1907,

after numerous experiments, the Bittings devised a method for producing preservative-free ketchup that would keep almost indefinitely under normal household conditions; their system became the standard for making ketchup. The method increased the amount of sugar and vinegar in the ketchup, thus creating a thick and sweet product. In January 1909 Arvil Bitting published their initial findings, *Experiments on the Spoilage of Tomato Ketchup.* Six years later the Bittings published two additional monographs bound together: Arvil Bitting's *Ketchup: Methods of Manufacturer* and Katherine Bitting's *Microscopic Examination.*

In the 1920s the Bittings left the Bureau of Chemistry to work for the National Canners Association, Arvil as a food technologist and Katherine as a microanalyst. She later worked as a biologist with the Glass Container Association. Based on their knowledge of the canning process, Arvil published his major work, *Appertizing; or, The Art of Canning,* in 1937.

From their early years the Bittings collected food-related books. Their collection grew over the years to include the French edition of Nicolas Appert's *L'art de conserver les substances animales et végétales (1810),* which Katherine Bitting translated into English as *The Book for All Households; or, The Art of Preserving Animal and Vegetable Substances for Many Years* and published in 1920. During the 1930s she began assembling a bibliography of their collection. She died before it saw print, but her husband published her *Gastronomic Bibliography* posthumously in 1939. It has endured as a major American culinary resource. Even more significant, the Bittings donated their extensive cookbook collection to the Library of Congress, and it is a significant legacy accessible to researchers.

[**See also** CANNING AND BOTTLING; KETCHUP.]

BIBLIOGRAPHY

Bitting, A. W. *Appertizing; or, The Art of Canning: Its History and Development.* San Francisco: Trade Pressroom, 1937.

Bitting, A. W., and K. G. Bitting. *Ketchup: Methods of Manufacture* and *Microscopic Examination.* Lafayette, IN: Murphey-Bivins Company Press, 1915.

Bitting, Katherine. *Gastronomic Bibliography.* San Francisco: Halle-Cordis Composing Room and Trade Freeroom, 1939.

ANDREW F. SMITH

Blackberries

The blackberry of common speech is not one, but some two dozen species of plants in the genus *Rubus*, native to America, Europe, and Asia. All have in common a fruit composed of drupelets (small, round, juicy parts) arranged on a pithy central core. It is this core, which detaches intact from the fruit stem, that distinguishes blackberries from the other group of bramble species, the raspberries; in blackberries, the adherence of drupelets to the core gives the fruit a solidity lacking in raspberries. Since blackberries do not decompose when heated, they are suitable for cooking.

In horticultural terms, blackberries are divided between upright and running types. Upright-growing blackberries are found east of the Rocky Mountains; attain a height of seven feet; and, in the wild, form dense, impenetrably thorny clumps. Modern breeders have produced thornless forms, which have made blackberry culture more popular in the eastern states. Formerly, blackberry fanciers and the markets relied on wild-collected berries. By the early twenty-first century, certain states—Arkansas, in particular—had a considerable cultivated blackberry industry. Blackberries, no longer limited to

A label for preserved blackberries.

rural availability at farm stands, have become an article of long-distance commerce. Modern varieties are large and durable, with a long shelf life; however, they often lack the characteristic "wild" flavor sought by many.

Running blackberries, known as dewberries in the lower South, are a group of species, chiefly of Pacific Coast origin, that trail along the ground. Olallieberry and Himalayan (synonym "Theodor Reimers"), which runs wild in the West, are typical, but there exist many other forms, often hybridized with the raspberry, such as boysenberry, youngberry, marionberry, loganberry, and Lucretia. The parent species are all susceptible to winter cold and most are intolerant of great heat, so commercial culture is limited to the West and lower South. These species, with their rich, acid flavor, provide the frozen blackberries of commerce. Preserved berry juices as a beverage, formerly an article of commerce, are now uncommon. Blackberries, often strained of their large seeds, are used in conserves and in cooked desserts, such as pies.

[See also FRUIT; PACIFIC NORTHWEST.]

BIBLIOGRAPHY

Daubeny, Hugh A. "Brambles." In *Fruit Breeding*. Volume 2: *Vine and Small Fruits*, edited by Jules Janick and James N. Moore, 109–190. New York: Wiley, 1996.

Galetta, Gene J., and David G. Himelrick. *Small Fruit Crop Management*. Englewood Cliffs, NJ: Prentice Hall, 1990.

C. T. KENNEDY

Blackfish

The blackfish (*Tautoga onitis*), which feeds on shellfish and crabs, is known by the names black trout, black ruff, tautog, black porgy, oysterfish, and chowderfish. It is most plentiful between the Chesapeake Bay north to Cape Cod, but it has a range from Nova Scotia to South Carolina. Native Americans used the fish, and it was the object of inshore fisheries in earlier times. Amelia Simmons mentions blackfish in the first American cookbook, *American Cookery* (1796), though she does not comment on an ideal way of preparing the fish. The name chowderfish, however, is consistent with the tautog's reputation for firm flesh, though the fish can also be grilled and baked.

SANDRA L. OLIVER

Blenders

The modern blender, a familiar electric appliance that blends, chops, grates, purees, and liquefies foods, was invented by Stephen Poplawski in 1922 to make soda fountain drinks. In 1935 the popular bandleader Fred Waring teamed up with inventor Frederick Osius to improve the appliance, marketing the Waring Blender (originally Blendor) as a revolutionary bartending tool. By the 1950s blender manufacturers' cookbooks contained recipes for everything from soups and canapés to cakes and ice creams and, in a

sign of the times, more than a few recipes for gelatin desserts and molded salads. *The Blender Cookbook* of 1961 promised to revolutionize Americans' cooking habits with "exciting new ideas, short cuts, and magic recipes that will take the drudgery out of cooking and make it a pleasure."

That same year, in *Mastering the Art of French Cooking*, Julia Child, Louisette Bertholle, and Simone Beck taught millions of Americans how to make emulsions like mayonnaise and hollandaise with the electric blender, though of the latter they warned that "the blender variety lacks something in quality... perhaps because of complete homogenization." But, they continued, "as the technique is well within the capabilities of an 8-year-old child, it has much to recommend it."

The emergence of the food processor later threatened the supremacy of the blender, but cooks soon realized the blender's superiority for certain tasks, such as liquefying solids, pureeing solids with liquids, and preparing smoothies and frozen drinks. The standard blender consists of a covered jar (usually glass or, for bar use, metal) fitting securely on top of a motorized base, with four sharp blades that make thousands of rotations per minute. While modern blenders often come with electronic touch-pad controls, sleek new jar designs, and a multitude of speeds, one test by *Cook's Illustrated* found that basic, old-fashioned models outperformed newer designs. Newer hand-held immersion blenders, some of which even crush ice, are also growing in popularity.

[See also FOOD PROCESSORS.]

BIBLIOGRAPHY

Child, Julia, Louisette Bertholle, and Simone Beck. *Mastering the Art of French Cooking*. New York: Knopf, 1961.

Schur, Sylvia, ed. *New Ways to Gracious Living: Waring Blendor Cook Book*. Winsted, CT: Waring Products, 1957.

Seranne, Ann, and Eileen Gaden. *The Blender Cookbook*. Garden City, NY: Doubleday, 1961.

MERYL S. ROSOFSKY

Blimpie International Inc.

In 1964 three friends in Hoboken, New Jersey—Tony Conza, Peter DeCarlo, and Angelo Baldassare—opened the first Blimpie sandwich shop. The name "blimpie" was derived from "blimp"—the inflatable airships, based at the Lakehurst Naval Air Station, that were a common sight in the skies over New Jersey at the time. Even more than a submarine, a blimp has a plump ovoid shape, making the name appropriate for a well-stuffed sandwich. Blimpie shops offered sandwiches akin to the familiar "hero," filled with meats, cheeses, and salad. Sandwich prices ranged from 35 to 95 cents, considerably more than fast food hamburgers at the time, but the market accepted the product and the prices, and Blimpie's became a national and then an international brand.

As of 2004, there were almost sixteen hundred Blimpie locations across the United States and in more than ten other countries.

BIBLIOGRAPHY

Conza, Tony. *Success: It's a Beautiful Thing; Lessons on Life and Business from the Founder of Blimpie International*. New York: Wiley, 2000.

ANDREW F. SMITH

Bloody Mary and Virgin Mary

The Bloody Mary is a cocktail made with vodka, tomato juice, lemon juice, Worcestershire sauce, cayenne pepper, and salt. Folklore attributes the origin of the Bloody Mary to Ferdinand "Pete" Petiot, a bartender at Harry's Bar in Paris. Petiot purportedly first mixed vodka with tomato juice in 1921. After Prohibition ended in 1933, Petiot moved to the United States and became a bartender at the King Cole Bar at New York's St. Regis Hotel, where he added Worcestershire sauce and pepper to the recipe. Petiot named the drink either after a girlfriend called Mary or after Mary Tudor, the mid-sixteenth-century Catholic queen of England, who killed many Protestants during her reign. In any case, the Bloody Mary was born—or so the story goes.

While the story is plausible, it is unlikely. An essential Bloody Mary ingredient is tomato juice, which was not available commercially until 1929. Decades earlier, chefs had experimented unsuccessfully with juicing tomatoes. When juiced, tomato solids quickly separate and settle at the bottom of a can or glass. This problem was not solved until John Kemp and his son Ralph, of Frankfort, Indiana, began experimenting with breaking tomato pulp into minute particles that floated in the juice. They did this with a viscolizer, a machine used in making ice cream. After four years of work, the Kemps finally succeeded in 1928, and the following year they began manufacturing the first commercial tomato juice. Tomato juice was an instant hit with the American public. The H. J. Heinz Company and the Campbell Soup Company moved into high gear to produce and promote their own brands of tomato juice, and by 1935 more than eight million cases of tomato juice were sold in America.

It may never be known who first paired tomato juice with vodka, but two other claims have some plausibility. The first is that it was invented in the 1930s at New York's 21 Club by a bartender named Henry Zbikiewicz, who was charged with mixing Bloody Marys. A second claim attributes its invention to the comedian George Jessel, who frequently visited the 21 Club. The first known recipe for the Bloody Mary was published in Lucius Beebe's *Stork Club Bar Book* (1944). Beebe, a columnist for the *New York Herald Tribune*, mentioned the Bloody Mary in December 3, 1939: "George Jessel's newest pick-me-up which is receiving attention from the town's paragraphers is called a Bloody Mary: half tomato juice, half vodka."

Six months later Beebe again associated the Bloody Mary with Jessel. Jessel knew John G. Martin, a member of the Heublein family, which owned G. F. Heublein and Company. The company acquired Smirnoff Vodka after Vladimir Smirnoff's death in 1939. The Bloody Mary made its national debut in a magazine advertisement that appeared in late 1955 featuring George Jessel, who declared that he had invented the cocktail. Whether or not Jessel invented the Bloody Mary, his advertisement popularized the Bloody Mary nationwide, and the cocktail was on the road to stardom. To exploit the interest, Bloody Mary bars have been launched by restaurants, permitting customers to construct their own cocktail with various garnishes. It is one of the few cocktails drunk at breakfast or brunch.

By the beginning of the twenty-first century, the Bloody Mary was America's most popular cocktail, which has contributed to an increase in the sale of vodka. By the 1970s vodka was outselling bourbon in most states. For those unable or unwilling to make their own Bloody Marys, commercial mixes have been manufactured, such as McIlhenny's Tabasco Bloody Mary Mix, which claims to use the original 1934 recipe. For those who prefer their Bloody Marys without the vodka, the Virgin Mary has been served since the 1970s. [**See also** VODKA.]

BIBLIOGRAPHY

O'Hara, Christopher B. *The Bloody Mary: A Connoisseur's Guide to the World's Most Complex Cocktail.* New York: Lyons, 1999.

Smith, Andrew F. *Souper Tomatoes: The Story of America's Favorite Food.* New Brunswick, NJ: Rutgers University Press, 2000.

ANDREW F. SMITH

Blue Bell

Founded in 1907, the Brenham Creamery Company was a dairy farmers' cooperative that took over an abandoned cotton gin in rural Brenham, Texas, and started making butter from surplus cream. In 1911, it added ice cream, making just two gallons a day. This was packed in ice and salt in a large wooden tub for delivery by horse-and-buggy. But the cooperative was on the verge of failure in 1919 when E. F. Kruse, a respected local teacher, was asked to take over as general manager. His leadership reversed the company's fortunes.

In 1930 he changed the name to Blue Bell Creameries in honor of his favorite wildflower. Unlike other businesses, the company did well during the Depression, when a double-dip nickel cone became the one treat many people could still afford. The advent of refrigerated delivery trucks in 1936 gave the company another boost, facilitating wider distribution to retail outlets. By 1958 the product was so successful that Blue Bell ceased butter production to concentrate on ice cream. The company's carefully nurtured homespun image began taking shape in 1960, when it entered Houston, its first big-city market. Blue Bell capitalized on a positive impression of the "little creamery from Brenham," and in ensuing years found a receptive audience for its wholesome, sometimes quirky image. The tagline, "the best ice cream in the country," also resonated with devotees, who developed cultlike loyalty.

Blue Bell introduced its best-selling flavor, Homemade Vanilla, in 1969 after a salesman suggested it needed something that would taste like old-fashioned, hand-cranked ice cream. Its popular Cookies 'n Cream was introduced in 1978. Still, the company expanded slowly, nurturing its premium ice cream as carefully as its image: To ensure quality, it created its own cold storage centers and distribution network. In 1986 Blue Bell became the first major ice cream manufacturer to make a "lite" frozen dessert with NutraSweet. When the company began moving into neighboring states Oklahoma and Louisiana in 1989, it quickly gained dominance. In 2005, with distribution still limited to seventeen states, Blue Bell ranked third in sales behind Breyer's and Dreyer's. Today, Blue Bell makes more than three hundred flavors and products, including ice cream novelties, frozen yogurt, and low-fat and diet ice cream. The original plant was listed in the National Register of Historic Places in 1990, and Kruse's descendants still run the company. Blue Bell was a fixture in both Bush White Houses.

BIBLIOGRAPHY

Boisseau, Charles. "Blue Bell Creameries, Brenham's Homespun Hero, Gets a Ringing Endorsement from Its Fans as It Licks the Competition with Just a Tiny Taste of the National Ice Cream Market." *Houston Chronicle*, Sept. 1, 1996.

Handbook of Texas Online. "Blue Bell Creameries." http://www.tsha.utexas.edu/handbook/online/articles/BB/dibgi.html

KIM PIERCE

Blueberries

The blueberry is a fruit native to America, whose popularity has soared since its domestication began in the early twentieth century. At that time, a scientist for the U.S. Department of Agriculture, Frederick Coville, working in conjunction with a grower, Elizabeth White of Whitesbog, New Jersey, began studying the conditions required by the plant and selecting and breeding varieties. Despite its small size, the blueberry is not a berry but a pome, as are apples and pears.

Three types are grown commercially. Lowbush blueberries, *Vaccinium angustifolium*, are native to the northeastern United States. The plants spread by underground stems and grow only about a foot high; they are small, sweet, and often powdery blue. The bulk of the commercial crop is destined for canning and pie fillings. These blueberries are harvested mostly from tamed wild stands. Highbush blueberries, *V. corymbosum*, which are native to the East Coast, grow as six- to ten-foot-high bushes. So-called southern highbush blueberries are adapted to areas with mild winters and provide the earliest harvests. The latest-ripening blueberries, rabbiteyes (*V. asheii*), are native to the Southeast and are borne on fifteen-foot-tall bushes.

Blueberry plants' unusual soil requirements have limited their commercial cultivation to where they are native or where soil is otherwise naturally suited. Blueberries require soils that are very acidic, very high in humus, and consistently moist and well aerated. Important production areas include New Jersey, North Carolina, Michigan, Maine, and the Canadian Maritime Provinces. Production also has spread to California, where early-season harvests are possible in soils amended to suit the plants. [See also FRUIT.]

BIBLIOGRAPHY

Eck, Paul, and Norman F. Childers, eds. *Blueberry Culture.* Piscataway, NJ: Rutgers University Press, 1966.

McClure, S., and L. Reich. *Rodale's Successful Organic Gardening: Fruits and Berries.* Emmaus, PA: Rodale Press, 1996.

Reich, Lee. *Uncommon Fruits for Every Garden.* Portland, OR: Timber Press, 2004.

LEE REICH

Boardinghouses

Throughout history people have needed to live apart from their families for a variety of reasons. Colonial travelers traditionally resorted to taverns, inns, and, since the nineteenth century, to hotels. However, during the nineteenth and twentieth centuries industrialization and the growth of American cities stimulated a considerable movement of people, rich and poor. Many were relocating from farms to industrial centers; others were immigrants from abroad in search of work. The sudden demand for inexpensive housing was unprecedented and contributed to the development of the boardinghouse. Usually the province of women, keeping a boardinghouse was one of the first cash-economy jobs recommended as suitable for women.

The boardinghouse institution began as a middle ground between the financial need of a married, middle-class woman and the prevalent "doctrine of separate spheres" that forbade her to work in the public marketplace. Sometimes the extra income enabled a young family to meet mortgage payments on a house; at other times it meant survival for a widow with no business training or the skills for succeeding in the male business world. Taking in lodgers allowed women to support themselves with the only capital they had—a house with empty bedrooms and their own domestic skills. Ideally, women provided boarders with a bed (sometimes shared), ample meals, laundry, and a degree of personal assistance, although standards varied widely.

Types of Boardinghouses

One of the earliest forms of boardinghouses in nineteenth-century America evolved in frontier towns that were developing rapidly into small cities. Lodgers coming from farms for jobs in town were often absorbed into the keeper's family routines and treated like distant relatives. They attended church with their host families and socialized together, partaking in meals that were very like the farm cuisine of their own families.

In contrast, company boardinghouses were organized by large mills, as exemplified by the textile mills of Lowell, Massachusetts, begun in the 1820s. Their experimental arrangements were far more ambitious and impersonal than the small family operations. Built as part of the mill complex, they accommodated between twenty and forty lodgers each, often six in a room. Although at this time women did not usually leave home for careers, mill owners sought to attract young farm girls of good families by instituting a series of rules and curfews; the presumably safe and moral environment was presided over by salaried boardinghouse keepers. Keepers were allotted limited budgets for expenses, based on the numbers of lodgers they had, and they competed for boarders on the reputation of their tables, a situation that sometimes resulted in financial distress. For example, Lucy Larcom, the daughter of a Lowell boardinghouse keeper, described in her memoirs her mother's inability to compromise her fine culinary taste with the company's allocations and her constant difficulties in supporting her children.

Keepers bought their provisions from local shops and vendors, many of whom maintained delivery routes. Boardinghouse cuisine was typical of New England and of necessity leaned heavily on inexpensive staples, such as potatoes and beans, and on seasonal products merchandized by nearby farmers and fishermen. Local salmon was cheap and readily available and was overused to the point that keepers were forced to promise their boarders not to serve it more than once a week. Many staples, including flour, sugar, salt cod, and fresh and preserved meats, were shipped from Boston to meet the large demand.

Meal schedules accommodated the Lowell Mill bell system. Work began seasonally with sunrise, and a half hour was allotted to breakfast. The noon bell announced the dinner break, during which time the girls literally ran across the street to their boardinghouses (intentionally placed nearby to save time), where a hot family-style meal awaited. Girls ate as fast as they could before the work bell rang again only forty-five minutes later. A simple evening supper, the most relaxed meal of the day, provided the only time to linger over desserts and tea.

Other kinds of small, job-related boardinghouses were established for the convenience of employers and their tenants, sometimes because of the lack of appropriate nearby accommodations. Under the master-journeyman-apprentice system, the master's wife boarded her husband's young trainees. Apprentices did not pay directly for such services, but boarding was considered part of their reimbursement for labor. In addition, a master boatbuilder might take in one of his unmarried craftsmen, or a milliner might offer room and board to a female assistant for whom there were few housing alternatives. Keeping hired hands on ranches and farms and boarding itinerant "mechanics" (artisans) of the countryside fell into this arrangement. Cuisine in such cases was entirely regional and often abundant, standard fare.

Throughout the nation ethnic boardinghouses developed to accommodate the succeeding waves of immigration and factored in the survival of cultures. Immigrant families living in the tenements of large coastal cities rented some of their meager space to "greenhorns" from home. The lodgers were sometimes family members or friends from home who boarded temporarily until they could learn the language and find their feet in the job market. A boarder might have slept in a temporary bed in the corner of an already crowded kitchen and shared the family's familiar ethnic cooking, thereby maintaining cultural prescriptions and taboos. The landlady bought her ingredients at food shops, open markets, or pushcarts run by immigrants. Thus, a kosher Jew could purchase food in compliance with the dietary laws of *kashruth* (keeping kosher) and also maintain such traditional foods as salt herring and potatoes, Italians could find the fixings for *pasta e fagiole* (pasta and beans), Asians could buy special kinds of rice, blacks in the north could cook the okra or black-eyed peas they had been used to eating in the South, and western Basques could make and eat their own sourdough breads and lamb shanks.

Another kind of urban boardinghouse of the mid-nineteenth century was dedicated to groups with special orientations or professions. One could find accommodations specifically for actors, sailors, artists, spiritualists, medical students, and others, and sometimes the menu was essential. For example, Graham boardinghouses were tailored to the needs of the often famous advocates of Sylvester Graham's dietary theories, serving the requisite vegetarian diet and avoiding stimulants of all kinds (red meat, spices, sugar, spirits, and caffeine).

With an entirely different focus, expensive and luxurious urban boardinghouses sheltered the wealthier people of all ages. Young married couples of means sometimes preferred the carefree life of this kind of lodging, as it offered freedom from domesticity, a pleasant interlude before "taking up housekeeping." The keepers of these establishments, who were also from privileged backgrounds and aware of fashion, set a stylish tone with their furnishings, table appointments, and menus. The food was often extravagant and may have boasted a French influence. The new "service à la Russe," which required ostentatious place settings and servants, was de rigueur. Such boardinghouses were later replaced by residential hotels.

Before the end of the nineteenth century, summer boardinghouses in the countryside or at the waterfront hosted people escaping the heat and discomfort of the cities. Visitors may have been working people with one week a year for vacation or an entire family of more means enjoying a three-month stay. Their meals were based on the wholesome and fresh yield of the keeper's barnyard, orchard, and garden, and they were entertained by such bucolic entertainments as fishing, berry picking, and ice cream making. A seasonal vacation boardinghouse demanded intensive work from the keeper's entire family, but many earned enough to carry them through the winter and secure their children's futures.

By the turn of the twentieth century, certain boardinghouse keepers with a high priority on cuisine had developed their own natural aptitudes or had hired a talented cook. Their fine meals were in high demand, and dinners were offered on a subscription basis to others in the community. They were among the first kinds of restaurants for middle-class and rural diners, who were otherwise limited to meals at home. Their influence sometimes spread far beyond their locales. For example, Craig Claiborne, the cookbook author and first and longtime food editor of the *New York Times*, absorbed the high standards of his mother's southern boardinghouse kitchen, and James Beard, the influential cooking educator and author from the West Coast, similarly learned and disseminated the elements of fine cooking and new Asian influences prevalent where he lived.

The American boardinghouse has largely disappeared, a victim of affluence, more varied job choices for women, increasing mobility, the rise of motels, the wide availability of fast food, and the growth of good middle- and working-class restaurants. Only a few echoes of its once common culture remain in folklore—as, for example, in the phrase "boardinghouse reach" to describe unmannerly conduct at the dining table, the repeated lampooning of squalid or pretentious boardinghouses in such 1930s comics as "Our Boarding House," and this song of the Great Depression:

In the boarding-house where I live, everything is
* green with mold.*
Grandma's hair is in the butter, silver threads
* among the gold.*
When the dog died, we had hot dogs, when the cat
* died, catnip tea,*
But when the landlord kicked the bucket, oh, that
* was too much for me.*
(I don't like hash).

[**See also** GRAHAM, SYLVESTER.]

BIBLIOGRAPHY

Dublin, Thomas. *Women at Work: The Transformation of Work and Community in Lowell, Massachusetts, 1826–1860.* New York: Columbia University Press, 1979.

Echeverria, Jeronima. *Home Away from Home: A History of Basque Boarding Houses.* Reno: University of Nevada, 1999.

Gunn, Thomas Butler. *The Physiology of New York Boarding Houses.* New York: Mason Brothers, 1857.

ALICE ROSS

Boilermaker

A boilermaker is a shot of whiskey with a beer chaser, although it may also be a glass of beer with a shot of whiskey in it—sometimes dropped in, shot glass and all. (The latter version is also known as a Depth Charge.) Some aficionados say that the drink is meant to be imbibed all in one slug, but this practice is unusual. The particulars vary by region, bar, and bartender.

The Boilermaker originated in the 1890s in the mining camps of Butte, Montana, as the "Sean O'Farrell." The powerful, ten-cent Sean O' was served only as miners came off their shifts. Bartenders all over the United States imitated the drink, dubbing it the Boilermaker for reasons that remain unknown. The name may have come from the "head of steam" feeling that the drink generates, or perhaps it was a favorite drink of men who worked as boilermakers. The U.S. heavyweight boxing champion from 1899 to 1905, James Jackson Jeffries, was nicknamed "the Boilermaker," and perhaps the drink name stems from a similar tough, manly sense of the word. (Purdue University's football team has had the name "Boilermakers" since 1891.)

The main purpose of this workingman's drink is to take a great deal of alcohol into one's system as quickly as possible. It is not a drink only for men, though—Myrna Loy's character in the movie *Airport 1975* drinks a few to take her mind off a hair-raising flight. Recipes for boilermaker barbecue sauce, baked beans, jambalaya, and the like incorporate whiskey and beer with the more usual ingredients.

[See also BEER; WHISKEY.]

BIBLIOGRAPHY

Reynolds, Edward B., and Michael Kennedy. *Whistleberries, Stirabout, Depression Cake: Food Customs and Concoctions of the Frontier West.* Helena, MO: Three Forks, 2000.

JESSY RANDALL

Booyah

Booyah is a thick mixed stew that demonstrates how American ethnic food can include dishes that would be completely alien in recipe or usage to past generations. Groups of Belgian American Walloons settled around Door County (Green Bay), Wisconsin, in the 1850s, bringing with them a dish of clear bouillon served with rice. The hen that had been boiled to obtain the bouillon made an-

other meal the next day. Sometime in the 1930s, men took over the dish and turned it into a thick soup full of boned chicken meat and vegetables (and often served with saltines) at the annual Belgian American kermis harvest festival. The pots became larger, the men used a canoe paddle to stir the soup, and "booyah" became the name of the event as well as the central dish.

By the 1980s, booyah was served at church fund-raisers, at a midsummer ethnic festival for visitors, and on Green Bay Packer football weekends. Secret recipes and "booyah kings" have been added to make booyah a male-bonding ritual like those surrounding barbecue, chili con carne, burgoo, and Brunswick stew—the latter two soup-stews being highly similar to booyah.

It is possible that booyah has features of other Belgian soups, such as *hochepot*. It often happens that American ethnic dishes begin to accumulate features of several old-country dishes. It also may be that booyah is not descended from Belgian bouillon at all. Around Saint Cloud, Minnesota, Polish Americans believe that "bouja" is an old Polish soup, and men make it much as Belgian Americans do in Door County, Wisconsin, but flavored with pickling spices. An early published recipe (1940) describes "boolyaw" as a French Canadian dish from the hunting camps of Michigan. A more recent Wisconsin cookbook called it an old German recipe. The dish has gone from a thin soup made by women at home to a thick stew made by men for communal events. An Italian American might mistake booyah for minestrone, yet Belgian Americans in Wisconsin believe it is named for Godfrey of Bouillon, a leader of the First Crusade. The fruit tarts served for dessert at booyah feasts are made by women much as they were in Eastern Belgium in the early nineteenth century.

MARK H. ZANGER

Borden

At one time the Borden company was America's largest dairy business. Gail Borden Jr., the founder of the Borden Condensed Milk Company, was born in Norwich, New York, in 1801. He died in 1874, leaving behind a thriving business, two sons, and a host of inventions and patents.

Borden worked as a surveyor during the 1820s and moved to Texas in 1829. For a time he edited the *Telegraph and Texas Register,* a newspaper founded by his brother and another partner to serve as the voice of the government of Texas when it was still a republic. Some claim that Borden wrote the famous headline "Remember the Alamo." He turned his creative mind to inventing and soon came up with ideas for the lazy Susan and the prairie schooner, a sail-powered wagon. But the invention for which he is best known is a process using a vacuum evaporator to kill bacteria in fresh milk. He is reported to have committed

A Borden advertising piece in the shape of a milk-delivery van circa 1890.

himself to finding a safe milk product after witnessing several children die on board ship after drinking contaminated milk. He borrowed the idea for using a vacuum evaporator from the Shakers, who used this technology to preserve fruit. Charles Page and Henri Nestlé also used vacuum evaporators to start their companies. In time, both of these companies would combine to form the Nestlé Company. Borden called his unique product "condensed milk."

In 1857 Borden established a small company to produce his new product. Borden received financing from Jeremiah Milbank, and in 1858 they formed a partnership called the New York Condensed Milk Company. The product came on the market at the same time national magazines were condemning "swill milk" produced under unsanitary conditions in city dairies.

Borden's first major orders came from the U.S. government, which ordered condensed milk to feed the troops during the Civil War. In a patriotic spirit Borden adopted the American bald eagle as his trademark. In 1930 Borden introduced Elsie the Cow as the company's mascot and brand identity. Elsie went on to become one of the best-loved trademarks in the country.

In 1919 the company changed its name to the Borden Company and throughout the twentieth century purchased a number of smaller companies to capture supermarket shelf space. Many of the companies acquired have remained regional brands, but others have catapulted into national brands, including Snow's seafood chowders, Wyler's bouillon, RealLemon lemon juice, Cracker Jack candied popcorn, Pennsylvania Dutch egg noodles, Drake Bakeries, and Campfire marshmallows.

In 1929 the company acquired a small company that made glue from casein, a by-product of skim milk. From this initial beginning in the adhesives business the company's specialty chemicals businesses grew. In 2001 Borden sold its domestic and overseas food businesses to become Borden Chemical Inc.

[See also CRACKER JACK; DAIRY; DAIRY INDUSTRY; MILK PACKAGING; NESTLÉ.]

BIBLIOGRAPHY

International Directory of Company Histories. 55 vols. Chicago: St. James, 2003.

JOSEPH M. CARLIN

Elsie the Cow

Elsie, the world-famous "spokesbovine" of the Borden Milk Company, first began appearing in newspaper and radio advertisements in the 1930s. In these early appearances Elsie is clearly a cow. She stands on all fours; she does not wear clothes, except for a garland of daisies around her neck; and her face is squarish and cowlike, with a broad mouth and big eyes.

At the New York World's Fair of 1939–1940 Borden's enormous and enormously successful exhibit featured the Rotolactor, a turntable device on which cows rode while attached to milking machines. Many fairgoers asked the guides which cow was Elsie. It was in response to these inquiries that the Borden Company decided to choose the handsomest Jersey cow at the fair and introduce her as Elsie. The company put Elsie herself on display, and in the second year of the fair an exhibit entitled Elsie in Her Boudoir became part of the Borden exhibit.

Over the years Elsie became less of a cow and more of a girl. Her udder was last seen in 1940. Her face became narrower and more human and her eyes more heavily lashed. In 1941 Elsie stood up on her hind legs and began wearing dresses or aprons with a cinched waist that gave her an enviable hourglass figure (for a cow). Andy Warhol chose Elsie, along with Marilyn Monroe, as the subject for one of his paintings of American icons.

Special thanks to Christine Iadorosa.

BIBLIOGRAPHY

Miller, I. C. "What Makes a World's Fair Exhibit Click?" *Food Industries* (January 1940): 44–48; (February 1940): 55–59.

EVE JOCHNOWITZ

Boston Cooking School

The Boston Cooking School began as a charitable endeavor by the Women's Educational Association to teach cooking to poor women. Begun with seven students, it widened its scope to include homemakers, and by 1882 there were nearly four hundred students.

Volunteer women ran the school, but the beginning teaching staff consisted of experienced teachers. Joanna Sweeney, who had given cooking classes in Boston, and Maria Parloa, a noted cooking authority and author, were the first two teachers. They trained Mary Lincoln, who then became another teacher. She became well known for her *Mrs. Lincoln's Boston Cook Book*, written as a text book for her classes. Fannie Farmer, who became principal in 1894, was first a pupil and then an assistant principal.

The school offered a First Course (Plain Cooking), a Second Course (Richer Cooking), and a Third Course (Fancy Cooking), as well as twelve lessons for nurses. The school also became well known for its sickroom cookery classes and taught Harvard Medical School students for many years.

The school had considerable influence on cooking through these classes; it also trained teachers of cooking. Parloa taught the first normal course for prospective teachers. The school received many invitations for graduates of its training course to open cooking schools in other cities.

The Boston Cooking School Magazine spread ideas about cooking to the general public. Fannie Farmer's *The Boston Cooking-School Cook Book* became very popular, going through several revisions and reprintings.

Despite its many successful ventures, the Boston Cooking School taught its last course in 1903. Farmer had opened her own school in 1902, and the older school was unable to compete. However, though in existence for only some twenty years, the Boston Cooking School had a wide influence on American cooking.

[**See also** FARMER, FANNIE; LINCOLN, MRS.; PARLOA, MARIA.]

BIBLIOGRAPHY

Lincoln, Mary J. *Mrs. Lincoln's Boston Cook Book*. Boston: Roberts Brothers, 1893. Contains a listing of the foods taught in the twelve lessons of each of the courses of instruction at the Boston Cooking School.

Shapiro, Laura. *Perfection Salad: Women and Cooking at the Turn of the Century*. New York: Farrar, Straus and Giroux, 1986.

MARY MOONEY-GETOFF

Boston Market

Arthur Cores and Steven Kolow opened the first Boston Chicken restaurant in 1985 in Newton, Massachusetts, specializing in rotisserie chicken and a selection of side dishes in a cafeteria setting. The company was sold to George Nadaff in 1989, and during the next

An advertisement for a cooking school in American Cookery, June–July 1917.

four years he opened thirty-five new locations in the Northeast. In 1995 Boston Chicken's menu was expanded to include turkey, ham, and meatloaf, and the name was changed to Boston Market. The chain grew rapidly during the mid-1990s, with an advertising campaign that promoted their take-home meals as a way of bringing back family dinner in a busy household. In 1999 H. J. Heinz began producing "Boston Market Home Style Meals," which were glorified TV dinners. In 2001 McDonald's Corporation purchased the chain, which consisted of 751 restaurants. Outlets were upgraded and a new format, the Rotisserie Grill restaurant, was launched in 2003. Boston Market is part of McDonald's subsidiary, "Golden Restaurant Operations," which also includes Donato's Pizza and Chipotle Mexican Grill.

BIBLIOGRAPHY

Striffler, Steve. *Chicken: The Dangerous Transformation of America's Favorite Food.* New Haven : Yale University Press, 2005.

ANDREW F. SMITH

Bottling

Historic finds indicate that the art of making glass bottles was well known throughout the ancient world when the Egyptians were producing them in 1400 B.C.E. Their glass was made in much the same ways as it is in the twenty-first century, by heating a mixture of sand, lime, and other minerals to a temperature of 2500°F. Naturally occurring glass, such as obsidian and rock crystal, had been used for art in the Stone Age. By 300 B.C.E., the Syrians had perfected the blowpipe, and blown-glass bottles were common. Rapid progress in bottling followed the early Renaissance introduction of standard-size corks to fit glass bottles. In the mid-sixteenth century, bottles fitted with wax seals were status symbols for the nobility of Europe, with every family marking their private bottles with its own seal. The first American glass house began producing blown-glass bottles in Jamestown, Virginia, in 1608. By 1650, adaptations introduced from England, including flanged bottlenecks and screw-on metal caps sealed with resin or pitch, improved the seal, enabling bottlers to maintain carbonation in beer.

Demand for bottled products by the late 1700s led to glass shortages, and customers were asked to bring glass of any kind back to glass production houses. While customers were still often expected to bring bottles back to the bottler for refilling, large-scale glass recycling had begun. The debut of the modern champagne bottle in 1757, with a flared cork affixed in a flanged bottle top with wire webbing, made possible the bottling of much higher-pressure contents than ever before. This opened the door to commercial packaging of sparkling mineral waters and beers, although results were inconsistent and leakage was a problem.

The introduction of the porter bottle, commonly known as a beer bottle, in 1820 standardized packaging shape. Bottles had to be stored on their sides to keep their corks from drying out and leaking. Around the same time, carbonated water sold as a health tonic and sometimes flavored with fruit juice was introduced by Townsend Speakman under the name Dr. Physick's Soda Water. Popularity of flavored soda water grew over the next forty years, spreading across America until nearly every city could claim its own soda fountain. Root beer, a descendant of colonial birch beer, made its appearance in the 1840s and achieved national renown when Charles E. Hires introduced bottled Hires Root Beer in 1870. Numerous capping methods were in use in the late 1800s, including marbles tied into the necks of bottles and the Hutchinson closure, an internal stopper held in place by the pressure of a carbonated beverage, which was opened by pushing the stopper inward.

The invention of the crown cork cap by William Painter in 1892 revolutionized the bottling industry. His single-use, cork-lined metallic cap eliminated problems that had plagued the bottling industry for centuries, including leakage and contamination. He patented his process, which is widely used one hundred years later, and formed the Crown Cork and Seal Company. His 1898 invention the Crown Soda Machine, which mixes sodas, fills bottles, and caps them in one integrated process, is the standard equipment used by modern bottlers.

Cans had been used for food products since the mid-1800s but were not sturdy enough to package liquids under pressure.

Prior to Prohibition, breweries like Anheuser-Busch and Pabst had experimented with canning. But contact with metal spoiled the beer, a condition known as metal turbidity. The idea was shelved until better can liners were brought to the market by the American Can Company in 1934 in the form of a Union Carbide product called Vinylite, a plastic. The can had obvious advantages over glass bottles in terms of surface area available for advertising. Punch-top, cans, requiring a special opener, were eclipsed for a time by cap-sealed, or cone-top, cans, which could be used with existing bottling infrastructure. Crown Cork and Seal, after purchasing the Acme Can Company of Philadelphia in 1936, introduced the most advanced cone-top model, known as the Crowntainer, which consisted of a well-sealed two-piece structure, capped with the same crown cap as the company used on its glass bottles. Opinions flared into battles between adherents of glass or metal packaging, with can fans pointing out the deleterious effects of light on beer and bottle believers arguing that metal made beverages taste skunky. The shipping and storage advantages of flattop cans spelled the end of the cone-top era by the early 1950s. The cans have become highly prized collectibles.

The advent of the zip-tab can in 1962 rejuvenated can sales by eliminating the need for a special can opener. Environmental concerns about litter and the danger of the sharp tabs to children led to the development of push-top cans in the late 1970s, in which the tab remains attached to the container after opening. While glass bottles remain popular among beer drinkers, the introduction of cheaper disposable plastic bottles in the late 1970s eclipsed glass in the packaging of soft drinks.

[**See also** ASEPTIC PACKAGING; CAN OPENERS; CANNING AND BOTTLING; CORKS; MASON JARS; MILK PACKAGING; SELTZER; WATER, BOTTLED; WINE BOTTLES.]

BIBLIOGRAPHY

American Society of Mechanical Engineers. "The Crown Cork Cap and Crown Soda Machine 1892 and 1898." May 25, 1994.

Bates, Paul W. "History of the Beverage Can." Millersville, TN: Museum of Beverage Containers and Advertising, 1996.

JAY WEINSTEIN

Bourbon

Bourbon, a style of whiskey that can legally be made only in the United States, must be distilled from a mash containing a minimum of 51 percent corn and aged in new, charred, oak barrels for a minimum of two years. It gained its name from Bourbon County, Kentucky, where, in the late 1700s, flatboats were loaded with barrels of local whiskey that were then transported to cities in the South. There it became known as whiskey from Bourbon and, eventually, bourbon whiskey.

Although the Whiskey Rebellion against taxes introduced on spirits in 1791 took place in Pennsylvania, it is pertinent, since it drove

Bottling

60

some distillers into Kentucky, where bourbon was born. In 1794, after numerous riots resulting in tax collectors' being tarred and feathered and their houses burned, President George Washington, for the first time in the history of the United States, mustered troops to fight their own countrymen and quell the uprising. The rebellious distillers lost the battle without a great deal of violence; those who agreed to pay taxes were pardoned, and others were imprisoned until they settled their debts.

One drink that is usually associated with bourbon is the mint julep (although the original base spirit of this classic was, in all probability, peach brandy), a drink described in 1803 as "a dram of spirituous liquor that has mint in it, taken by Virginians of a morning." Another famous bourbon-based cocktail is the old-fashioned, a drink said to have been created at the Pendennis Club in Louisville, Kentucky, and introduced to New York at the old Waldorf-Astoria by Colonel James E. Pepper, a Kentucky whiskey distiller, in the late 1800s.

Ulysses S. Grant was known to have been enamored of bourbon, and during the Civil War, when it was brought to President Abraham Lincoln's attention that Grant might be drinking too much, Lincoln reportedly asked what brand of whiskey Grant drank, so that he could send some to his other generals. After becoming president, though, Grant was once again connected to bourbon when Benjamin Helm Bristow, secretary of the treasury, initiated an investigation into what became known as the Whiskey Ring, a group of people, including Grant's secretary, General Orville E. Babcock, who were accused of keeping for themselves a percentage of the taxes paid by bourbon distillers.

Grant himself testified at Babcock's trial, and Babcock was acquitted, but General John McDonald, a regional supervisor of the Internal Revenue Service, was found guilty of the crime and sentenced to three years in prison and a fine of five thousand dollars. Upon his release, McDonald accused Grant, in a book, *Secrets of the Great Whiskey Ring*, of being directly involved with the Whiskey Ring, and the scandal was said to have been largely responsible for Grant's loss of the next election.

Various other scandals have plagued the bourbon industry, and legal pressure in the late 1800s brought down what was known as the Whiskey Trust, a conglomerate of sorts that sought to control the whole industry. Also, because unscrupulous profiteers offered adulterated whiskey bearing "bourbon" labels, Colonel Edmund Haynes Taylor Jr., a reputable distiller, teamed up with John G. Carlisle, then secretary of the treasury, to lobby for the Bottled-in-Bond Act, which was passed in 1897. The act stipulated that bonded whiskey must be aged for at least four years in government-supervised warehouses and bottled at 50 percent alcohol by volume, thus giving legitimate bourbon

An advertisement for Hunter's Own Bourbon.

producers a way to differentiate their whiskey from those not made to high standards. Further standards of identity that clarified the definition of true bourbon were enacted in acts of Congress in 1907 and 1909.

Although some bourbon distilleries remained in business during the years of Prohibition (1920–1933) by keeping pharmacists supplied with what was known as medicinal whiskey, available by prescription only, the majority of American whiskey producers went out of business. During this time a great quantity of blended whisky from Canada was smuggled into America, and when Prohibition was repealed, the American public had grown used to these lighter products.

Although it was once again legal to distill bourbon, this change in taste, coupled with the fact that the newly distilled whiskey had to be aged before it could be sold, gave the public even more time to grow used to lighter whiskeys. Also, many people switched to rum and gin—both spirits that had increased in popularity during Prohibition. Hence, bourbon sales declined and remained low, to a large extent, right up until the 1980s.

During the last two decades of the twentieth century, relatively high priced single-malt scotches became popular, partly because the American public had reduced its intake of distilled spirits. Instead, many Americans spent their money on small quantities of high-quality, expensive products. In the late 1980s, the

bourbon industry took note of this phenomenon and began to introduce more premium whiskeys of its own; in this way, bourbon once again became popular with the American public. The market in the early twenty-first century boasted more bottlings than at any time since the onset of Prohibition.

Along with the influx of these new, bolder bourbons came descriptive phrases used to market them. "Single-barrel" bourbon, meaning whiskey that is from a single barrel (most bourbons are the product of mingling together whiskeys from many barrels) had been around prior to Prohibition, but the term was not used after repeal until 1984, when Blanton's Bourbon was introduced. Other companies followed the trend, and more single-barrel bourbons appeared in a relatively short time.

The first "small-batch" bourbon, Booker's, was released in 1988, and this was a term that would cause some controversy. The Jim Beam Brands company, which issued Booker's bourbon, defined the term as "rare and exceptional bourbons married from a cross-section of barrels in the rack house" and went on to explain that the whiskey was picked from certain spots in their aging warehouses where bourbon seemed to mature better than in other places. Master distillers from other companies agreed that this phenomenon existed, but not all companies that started to use the phrase "small-batch" stuck to Beam's definition. Maker's Mark, for example, claimed that, since it distilled in smaller quantities than any other distillery at the time, its bourbon was a true small-batch whiskey, and other companies followed suit, creating their own definitions of the term. Most bourbon aficionados agree that whiskeys bearing the "small-batch" designation on their label are high-quality products but that an age statement, showing how long the bourbon had spent in the barrel, is far more important as a guide to high quality.

In 2002 America's bourbon distilleries numbered ten: Barton, Jim Beam, A. Smith Bowman, Buffalo Trace, Early Times, Four Roses, Heaven Hill, Labrot and Graham, Maker's Mark, and Wild Turkey. The A. Smith Bowman plant is in Virginia, and all the rest are based in Kentucky. Jack Daniel's and George Dickel whiskeys, though commonly mistaken for bourbons, are Tennessee whiskeys, both produced in Tennessee. These whiskeys are differentiated from bourbons by a filtration through sugar-maple charcoal before aging, which adds a distinctive "sooty sweetness" to the final products.

[**See also** DISTILLATION; PROHIBITION; WHISKEY.]

BIBLIOGRAPHY

Barr, Andrew. *DRINK: A Social History of America.* New York: Carroll and Graf, 1999.

Harwell, Richard Barksdale. *The Mint Julep.* Charlottesville: University Press of Virginia, 1985.

Murray, Jim. *Classic Bourbon, Tennessee, and Rye Whiskey.* London: Prion, 1998.

GARY AND MARDEE HAIDIN REGAN

Brady, Diamond Jim

The phrase "Gilded Age" appears in histories of the later nineteenth century and is often accompanied by pictures of obese, bearded men, their bulging stomachs covered in white and black evening clothes stuck through with diamond pins and draped with gold chains. Captains of industry and finance, they are often seated at saturnalian tables, symbols of an age of coarse materialism, massive corruption, and unbridled greed. Of them all, none was more emblematic than the grand gourmand of his, and perhaps any, age, Diamond Jim Brady.

James Buchanan Brady, the son of an immigrant Irish saloon keeper, was born on the Lower East Side of Manhattan in 1856. Raised in the slums of New York City and without much formal education, the plump lad left home at age eleven for a bellhop job at the St. James Hotel. Always jovial, smart, and hungry, he learned how to ingratiate himself with wealthy patrons and how to behave among them. Hired by the New York Central Railroad at age fifteen, Brady rose to become a salesman for a railroad equipment company, thus beginning his career as America's first "supersalesman." Through sharp dealing, a keen business sense, and financial tips from his many well-placed friends, Brady

made (and spent) millions and entered the ranks of America's newly rich.

Diamond Jim's feeding bouts are the stuff of legend, especially when he dined with his great (platonic) friend, the incomparable American beauty Lillian Russell. Breakfasts consisted of several dozen oysters, chops, steaks, eggs, and pancakes, all washed down with quarts of milk and orange juice. Twelve-course dinners always consisted of balanced food groups—fish and fowl; oysters and clams; canapés; turtle soup; several lobsters; roasted meats; refreshing sherbet; and a course of canvasback duck, terrapin, and fresh asparagus followed by mousses, cakes, pies, and fruit topped off with two to five pounds of his favorite chocolates. Russell could and sometimes did match him dish for dish, after shedding her corset.

Like the aristocracy of medieval and early-modern Europe, Brady's eating was a spectator sport. He held court at Rector's and the other great New York restaurants, sharing gargantuan meals and demanding every new dish that he had heard about. At Chicago's Columbian Exposition in 1893, watching Brady and Russell eat mountains of fresh corn at Rector's Marine Café was as popular an event as any on the celebrated midway, according to the press.

Conspicuous consumption was the mark of the man; diamonds, he reckoned, were a salesman's best friend. To sell high-priced goods, one had to look the part, both in bearing and attire. Of his twenty thousand diamonds and six thousand other precious stones, he said, "Them as has 'em, wears 'em." The same explanation held for his three hundred plus pounds. Still, he was the soul of generosity, constantly giving lavish gifts. He founded the nation's first urological institute (where he had had surgery for kidney stones) and, on his death in 1917, left almost all his wealth to charities. While the Vanderbilts and Rockefellers built dynasties, Diamond Jim became the model and caricature of a society built on eternal salesmanship and never-ending consumption.

BIBLIOGRAPHY

Burke, John. *Duet in Diamonds: The Flamboyant Saga of Lillian Russell and Diamond Jim Brady in America's Gilded Age.* New York: Putnam, 1972.

Jeffers, H. Paul. *Diamond Jim Brady: Prince of the Gilded Age.* New York: Wiley, 2001.

BRUCE KRAIG

Brandy

From bucks to fixes, flips to fizzes, smashes to sours and slings, Americans have taken the venerable Old World spirit known as brandy and turned it into something all their own—a cocktail-hour favorite. The word "brandy" derives from the Dutch *brandewijn,* or "burnt wine," a reference to the heat-based distillation process that yields spirit from a fermented mash of fruit—primarily grapes, though apples, berries, and

some stone fruits yield notable variations. The reasonable consensus among historians is that brandy originated with the Dutch, who were trading in it by the sixteenth century, although the French managed within decades to take the concept and run with it, all the way to Cognac. Today, French brandies set the standard, while several other European countries, Spain foremost, dabble in its manufacture as well—not only as an end product but as an additive, whereby it fortifies wines like port, sherry, and Madeira; the long-standing practice both preserves and boosts the alcohol content of such wines, which were thus highly popular in the era of maritime trade.

Although there are now several domestic brands, even imported brandy could always be counted on to help put the "spirit" in "American spirit." For instance, one much disputed, but no less beloved bit of folklore finds Manhattan being baptized in brandy, as the beverage with which the English explorer Henry Hudson plied the Delaware Indians he met there in 1609; in honor of the hilarity that ensued, Hudson's new associates named the spot Manahachtanienk, which translates roughly as "the place where we got drunk." Thus did the Big Apple spring from grapes. True or not, brandy was undeniably a factor in the shaping of convivial customs that were a literal and symbolic departure from those overseas. For Europeans, brandy is inherently postprandial, best served neat in snifters as a digestif; in the United States, however, it functions as often as not as an ingredient in mixed drinks—which themselves form the nucleus around which our drinking culture revolves. In the colonial and Revolutionary War eras, taverns served brandy-based toddies and sweetened punches such as shrub to warm tummies and kindle republican ardor.

In modern times, from the cocktail lounge to the cocktail party, Americans have mixed company in conjunction with drinks, whose supposedly salubrious effects become irrelevant compared with their socially lubricating effects. (In fact, it may even be possible to draw a link between the appearance of the cocktail and the disappearance of alcohol, brandy included, from the American doctor's kit bag—the frivolity of the one being incommensurate with the sobriety, so to speak, of the other as a restorative.)

At any rate, among brandy's more illustrious cocktail credits are the orange-tinged sidecar (said, oddly enough, to be an invention of Harry's New York Bar—in Paris); the crème de menthe–spiked stinger; the sweetly spiced brandied coffee known in New Orleans as *café brûlot;* the brandy Alexander, which incorporates heavy cream and crème de cacao in an appeal to dainty tastes; and even the original mint julep (in which, however, it was ultimately replaced by bourbon).

The label from a bottle of Jarvis Medicinal Blackberry Brandy.

The United States—as represented by California, where the stateside industry resides almost exclusively—also differs from Europe (as represented by France) with respect to modes of production. While under penalty of law the French must use only white grapes (and the Cognacais only certain types thereof), Californians have access to any state-grown grape, although Thompson Seedless and Flame Tokay predominate. And whereas the most celebrated French brandies must undergo a laborious double-distillation process in copper pot stills or alembics, California makers have contented themselves, by and large, with the continuous or patent still, the results being both more expedient and more consistent—hence, one might say, more in keeping with American values. (There are exceptions among top-tier producers, such as Germain-Robin and Jepson.) Relatively painless government regulations include minimums on the duration of oak aging (two years) and the percentage of alcohol (30 percent, or 60 proof), which most respected producers not only meet but, in fact, exceed.

The U.S. brandy industry has not always, however, enjoyed such freedom from federal interference. Its birth and early growth in the 1850s and 1860s—with which the French émigré Jean-Louis Vignes, the German immigrants Charles Kohler and John Frohling, and the Hungarian-born Colonel Agoston Haraszthy are all associated, although Spanish missions had long been doubling as private distilleries—was hobbled by prohibitive taxation and exacting fines, the latter often leveled against those who engaged in fraudulent labeling practices precisely in order to evade the former. Such shenanigans on both sides dogged the industry for decades. Eventual tax repeals, however, and the Pure Food and Drug Act of 1906 undid some of the early damage. By the early years of the twenty-first century, with the insult and injury of Prohibition all but forgotten, California brandies were slowly earning a vastly improved reputation.

[**See also** BRANDY ALEXANDER; COCKTAILS; SHERRY.]

BIBLIOGRAPHY

Carosso, Vincent P. *The California Wine Industry: A Study of the Formative Years.* Berkeley and Los Angeles: University of California Press, 1976.

Grossman, Harold J. *Grossman's Guide to Wines, Beers, & Spirits* 7th rev. ed. New York: Wiley, 1983.

Pinney, Thomas. *A History of Wine in America: From the Beginnings to Prohibition.* Berkeley and Los Angeles: University of California Press, 1989.

RUTH TOBIAS

Brandy Alexander

The brandy Alexander, which rose to popularity as a Prohibition-era after-dinner drink, consists of brandy, crème de cacao, and cream, shaken with ice and sometimes garnished with nutmeg. It was originally known as the Alexander cocktail, made with gin in place of brandy. Perhaps the most notorious "girl drink," the brandy Alexander is cloyingly sweet, like a chocolate milkshake. (The nonalcoholic, "mocktail" version of the brandy Alexander is a blend of milk, chocolate syrup, and soda water—in other words, a chocolate egg cream.)

A 1934 issue of *Esquire* included the Alexander on its list of the ten worst cocktails of the preceding decade, with other "pansies" like the Pink Lady and the Clover Club. The drink has survived, however, into the twenty-first century: the international chain restaurant T.G.I. Friday's serves it in hot, cold, and "frozen" versions, the last with ice cream, whipped cream, and chocolate shavings. The flavor has also endured in the form of brandy Alexander pie, invented in 1933, when Prohibition was repealed and people could go back to using liqueurs in foods. The pie is a blend of crème de cacao, brandy, whipped cream, and chocolate in a graham-cracker or cookie-crumb crust.

[**See also** BRANDY; COCKTAILS.]

BIBLIOGRAPHY

Lanza, Joseph. *The Cocktail: The Influence of Spirits on the American Psyche.* New York: St. Martin's, 1995.

JESSY RANDALL

Bran Muffins

Bran muffins would seem like a natural American health food, since American food faddists had been concerned about overrefined flour since Sylvester Graham in the 1820s. However, health food writers were satisfied with wholewheat "Graham gems" (smaller muffins) for the rest of the nineteenth century, during which wheat bran by itself was mostly fed to animals. (Muffins until the very end of that century were thick pancakes like English muffins.) The first printed recipe for a bran muffin may well be that in Fannie Farmer's *Food and Cookery for the Sick and Convalescent*, published in 1904. Miss Farmer liked the recipe well enough to include it in her final work, the 1912 *A New Book of Cookery*, but it went into general use mainly through high school home economics texts written in the teens of the twentieth century.

ANDREW F. SMITH

Brazil Nuts

Brazil nuts (*Bertholletia excelsa*) originated in the tropical forests of Brazil, Bolivia, Peru, Colombia, and Venezuela. The Brazil nut tree has hardly been domesticated, and hence nearly all nuts are harvested by hand from wild trees. Indigenous peoples in South America ate Brazil nuts from their forests. Europeans first encountered them in the sixteenth century. The earliest known shipment of Brazil nuts to the United States occurred in 1810, when a small quantity was exported to New York. Larger quantities were imported after the Civil War. By 1873, 3 million pounds of Brazil nuts were imported into the United States. Large, meaty Brazil nuts, which are very high in fat, are eaten raw, roasted, and salted and are an important component in mixed nuts. They are used in bakery and confectionery.

[**See also** CANDY AND CANDY BARS; NUTS.]

ANDREW F. SMITH

Bread

The history of bread in America is complex, encompassing the traditions of Native Americans and of myriad immigrant groups, each of whom brought to the American table their own breads. Many of these traditional breads have been modified, and new types or unique variations of bread have emerged in the United States. Finally, American entrepreneurs have commercialized many types of bread and have changed the breads in the process.

The main grain cultivated by Native Americans in pre-Columbian times was corn. They removed the tough outer covering from the kernels by soaking them in lye ash and water, and then ground the kernels in mortars and pestles. From this ground hominy, Native Americans made bread by patting the dough into flat disks and cooking them on heated rocks; or they wrapped the dough in leaves and buried it in hot ashes.

An ancient source of nutrition and nourishment, bread in the United States is made from a variety of grains including corn, wheat, rye, or, pictured here, oats and barley.

Early English colonists brought Old World grains, including barley, oats, rye, and wheat, but, as many colonists were ill equipped for and unskilled in farming, their first crops were initially unsuccessful. The Native Americans taught the colonists to grow corn and prepare it for the table resulting in corn pone, johnnycake, and cornbread. Rye thrived in New England, and it was mixed with cornmeal to produce a dark, dense bread called "Injun 'n' Rye"; this local staple later evolved into Boston brown bread.

While these breads were heavy and sustaining, they did not satisfy the bread hunger of British and European immigrants who wanted wheat bread. Wheat is rich in gluten, which gives dough a plastic quality that allows it to entrap the air bubbles created by yeast or other leavening. When the dough is baked, the walls of these tiny air pockets become rigid, so the bread retains its inflated form after the trapped air has cooled again. Varieties of wheat were naturalized into America, and by the mid-seventeenth century, it was readily available throughout the colonies.

Professional Bakers
Colonial bakers were similar to their European counterparts. Many had immigrated to America from Europe and taught the baking trade to apprentices in their new home. Bakeries were usually one-man operations. Bread was sold unwrapped over the counter and later in paper bags.

By most accounts, baker's bread was considered inferior to homemade bread until the twentieth century. Home bakers made bread in relatively small batches with the best ingredients they could afford. But commercial bakeries were subject to market forces: local laws controlled the price and characteristics of baker's bread. To make a profit, bakers cut costs by altering ingredients and methods and occasionally through using adulterations, such as powdered chalk or plaster to make the bread whiter and heavier.

Demographics, however, were on the side of commercial bakers. As urbanization and real income increased, home baking decreased. Urban life required a different allocation of women's time. Well-to-do women spent more time at churches, schools, and social organizations. They could easily afford to purchase their bread rather than spend tedious hours baking at home. Less affluent women, who worked in sweatshops and at other grueling jobs, had less time for baking bread, and they did not teach their daughters how to bake.

Urbanization also created the concentration of potential customers that made the mass distribution of bread financially viable. Bakers could sell their goods retail, or they could distribute their bread to grocery stores. City dwellers were able to pay for the ease and convenience of buying baker's bread; and women's tasks shifted from making things to buying things.

Not everyone was happy with these changes. One person who was particularly upset was Sylvester Graham, who advocated the use of coarse, unbolted flour for bread. He was so popular that bread made in this way was called "Graham bread." Graham collected his thoughts about bread and published them in his *Treatise on Bread and Bread-Making* (1837), which was the first book published in America solely focused on the subject. He criticized the way wheat was grown, objecting to the use of fertilizers, believed that bolting largely eliminated the healthful bran from the flour. He believed that only the housewife should bake bread, as he was concerned with the quality and wholesomeness of baker's bread.

Leavenings
Until the mid-nineteenth century, both commercial and home bakers used wild yeast, which grows naturally when moistened flour is left exposed to the air. Although bakers and brewers knew the effects of yeast, it was not until 1855, when Louis Pasteur (and others working independently) proved that yeast caused fermentation. From these discoveries, others learned how to isolate single yeast cells and select pure cultures with particular characteristics.

Yeast was not the only leavening agent used in bread; various forms of what we now call baking powder evolved over the course of the nineteenth century, including saleratus (bicarbonate of potash); tartaric acid, a byproduct of wine making, which when refined into a powder is called cream of tartar; and bicarbonate of soda. As no fermentation was necessary, the dough was ready for the oven in minutes rather than hours.

Loss of Taste
Traditional flour milling released the oils from the wheat germ, which quickly turned rancid, a process that was exacerbated by the heat generated by high-speed roller mills used during the 1880s. So millers installed blowers and other devices to rid the flour of bran and germ. This created bright white flour that had a long shelf life. In the process, the flour was robbed of much of its nutrition and flavor. To compensate for the loss of flavor, bakers began to increase the amount of sugar used in the dough. and use milk and shortening. A dense, chewy crust was one of the casualties of these changes, and commercial bread became softer, sweeter, moister, and whiter.

Home Bread Making
Breads made from corn, rye, rice, and oats regularly appeared in American cookbooks, as did recipes for wheat breads containing other ingredients, such as potatoes, squash, beans, and pumpkin. About the same time, recipes using buttermilk and sour milk as well as soda and other leavenings were also published. As the flour produced by roller mills began to dominate the marketplace, cookbook authors revised their recipes, calling for more sugar to be added in bread making. The addition of sugar vitiates fermented bread, encouraging puffiness, a flaccid crumb, and a soft crust, and gives the bread a sweet taste.

Toasters

Since colonial times, Americans have used toasters that held slices of bread upright near an open fire, at first on open hearths and later in wood and coal stoves. At the beginning of the twentieth century, electric toasters began to be sold, and their popularity led to the development of the bread slicer. The problem with slicing bread mechanically was not how to cut the bread, but how to hold the slices together until the bread was wrapped. Many devices were tried, including rubber bands, string, and wire pins. These were abandoned in favor of a device developed in 1928 by Gustav Papendick, a St. Louis baker, which provided for a collapsible cardboard tray. With Papendick's device, the loaf was fitted into the tray and held firmly while being sliced, and then the entire unit, slices and tray, were wrapped together.

Johnnycake

Johnnycake has its origin in an oaten bread called jannock (later bannock) in parts of England. These names evolved into "johnnycake" and later to "journey cake" in England. In America, johnnycakes were made from whatever grain, such as corn, rice, wheat or oats, was available. Since they could be made on any hot surface and did not require an oven, johnnycakes became a common food among the poor.

Sourdough Bread

Sourdough breads have been consumed since antiquity. The word "sourdough" goes back to Middle English, and recipes for such breads appear in English cookbooks beginning in the seventeenth century. Sourdough bread is made with wild yeast and bacteria that give a slight sour taste to the bread. As yeasts and bacteria vary with location, sourdough breads differ as well. San Francisco has become famous for its sourdough bread.

Hot Dog and Hamburger Buns

The production of commercial hot dog buns, long, soft rolls tailored to the size of the popular sausage, began during the early 1870s. The hot dog bun is frequently credited erroneously to Charles Feltman, a baker who opened a restaurant at Coney Island about 1874. Billy Ingram, who started the White Castle hamburger chain in 1921, is usually identified as the inventor of the commercial hamburger bun. He maintained standardization among the different chains by centralizing bun-baking operations.

Pumpernickel

Pumpernickel is a dense, slightly sour traditional dark rye bread brought to the United States by German immigrants. Commercial pumpernickel is usually made from refined rye flour and wheat flour, colored with caramel or other additives.

Soda Bread

Soda bread is a light loaf leavened with bicarbonate of soda. Soda bread was made in America during the 1830s. It had become known as Irish soda bread by the latter part of the nineteenth century.

Parker House Rolls

Parker House rolls originated during the 1870s at Boston's Parker House Hotel, which opened in 1856. They are made by folding a butter-brushed round of dough in half; when baked, the roll has a pleasing abundance of crusty surfaces. Recipes for Parker House rolls first appeared in cookbooks during the 1880s.

Croissants

The croissant is a crescent-shaped breakfast roll made from a very buttery dough resembling puff pastry. It is said to have been created by Viennese bakers or by Budapest bakers to celebrate the late-seventeenth-century defeat of the Turks, whose symbol was the crescent. No primary evidence has surfaced to support these contentions. It became part of French culinary traditions in the mid nineteenth century. The first known introduction of croissants into the United States was not until after World War I; croissants became increasingly popular beginning in the 1960s, and in the early 2000s stuffed croissants were served as breakfast sandwiches by fast food outlets.

Wonder Bread

The bread symbolic of this period is Wonder Bread. This originally unsliced bread was first baked by the Taggart Baking Company of Indianapolis about 1920. Taggart was acquired by Continental Baking Company in 1925. Wonder Bread was first sold sliced in 1930, and during the decade extensive promotion was carried out on its behalf. Wonder Bread was produced at a full-scale bakery at the New York World's Fair in 1939 and was the sponsor of popular radio programs. In 1941 Wonder Bread was advertised as "enriched" with vitamins and minerals and was advertised on children's radio and television programs. During the 1950s, the tag line "Wonder Bread Builds Strong Bodies 8 Ways," came into use. In the 1960s, when a backlash arose against overly refined food products, Wonder Bread became a prime target for criticism.

ANDREW F. SMITH

A selection of some of the many varieties of bread available at Zabar's, a deli and specialty food shop that serves roughly 40,000 customers daily on New York's Upper West Side.

Other types of bread were developed in the United States based on culinary traditions from other countries, such as the bagel and bialy, which were based on eastern European traditions. Challah is the bread eastern European Jews traditionally eat on the Sabbath and on holidays. Portuguese sweet bread (*pao doce*), which is similar to Hawaiian sweet bread, became popular during the mid-twentieth century. Tortillas from Mexico and pita from the Mediterranean became part of American culinary traditions during the twentieth century, although they did not become mainstream until after World War II. By the end of the war, most Americans were buying their bread rather than baking it at home.

Recent Developments

Wheat milling removed the bran, germ, and oil from the flour, and then the flour was bleached. This created a bright white flour that appealed to consumers and extended the flour's shelf life, which pleased grocers. That this white flour and the bread made from it lacked important nutritional components was a concern by the end of the nineteenth century. Nutrition experts began to object to removing the germ and bran and commercial bakeries began to enrich white bread with B vitamins, such as thiamine (vitamin B_1), riboflavin (B_2), and niacin (B_3), as well as iron, folate, and calcium.

Large commercial bakers produced the greatest proportion of the bread eaten in America. It was not until the 1970s that a backlash developed against the bland, standardized flavor and texture and limited nutritional value of commercial bread. Home bread baking enjoyed a renaissance, and since the 1970s many communities have enjoyed the products of small artisanal bakeries. One group supporting this trend has been

the Bread Bakers Guild of America, which has also attempted to raise the standards of artisanal bread baking.

[**See also** ANADAMA BREAD; BAGELS; BAKERIES; BIALY; BREAD, SLICED; BREAD MACHINES; BREAD-MAKING TOOLS; CORNBREAD BAKING PANS; DUTCH OVENS; FARMER, FANNIE; FERMENTATION; GRAHAM, SYLVESTER; LINCOLN, MRS.; MATZO; PILLSBURY; RANDOLPH, MARY; RORER, SARAH TYSON; SALLY LUNN; SANDWICHES; SIMMONS, AMELIA; STOVES AND OVENS: GAS AND ELECTRIC; STOVES AND OVENS: WOOD AND COAL; TOAST; TOASTERS; WAXED PAPER; YEAST.]

BIBLIOGRAPHY

Dupaigne, Bernard. *The History of Bread*. New York: Abrams, 1999.

Jacob, H. E. *Six Thousand Years of Bread: Its Holy and Unholy History*. Garden City, NY: Doubleday, Doran, 1944.

Panschar, William G. *Baking in America*. Evanston, IL: Northwestern University Press, 1956.

Storck, John, and Walter Dorwin Teague. *A History of Milling Flour for Man's Bread*. Minneapolis: University of Minnesota Press, 1952.

ANDREW F. SMITH

Bread, Sliced

The earliest barley bread appeared in about 10,000 B.C.E. It was a flatbread less than one inch thick and required no slicing. Later, wheat, rye, and leavening agents were introduced, making much larger loaves that needed to be torn by hand or sliced with a knife. At the beginning of the twentieth century, an Iowa-born inventor, Otto Frederick Rohwedder, recognized that the slicing of entire loaves would be helpful. He struggled for twenty-six years before his machine went on the market in Battle Creek, Michigan, in 1928, earning him the title "Father of Sliced Bread." During the process, Rohwedder knew that slicing the bread was not his only goal.

He needed to devise a way to hold the slices next to one another for portability and longer-lasting freshness. First, he tried hat pins, which joined several slices to each other. He soon discovered that this method was not practical. His final solution was to create a slicing machine that also wrapped all the slices together.

Wonder Bread placed the first commercially sliced bread on the market in 1930. Within five years North Americans were consuming more sliced than unsliced bread. This popularity helped increase the demand for Charles Strite's spring-loaded, pop-up toaster, invented in 1926, which went along with the popularity of the lunch counter, with its grilled cheese sandwiches, BLTs, and club sandwiches. Later, a St. Louis baker, Gustav Papendick, improved on Rohwedder's design by devising a cardboard tray, which he placed between the bread and the wrapper to stabilize the loaves. Presliced bread was still considered a dispensable luxury in 1943, when the U.S. secretary of agriculture banned the manufacture of metal bread-slicing machines to release materials for use in World War II.

[**See also** BREAD; TOAST; TOASTERS.]

BIBLIOGRAPHY

Jacob, H. E. *Six Thousand Years of Bread: Its Holy and Unholy History*. Translated by Richard and Clara Winston. 1944. Reprint, New York: Lyons and Burford, 1997.

MARTY MARTINDALE

Bread Machines

Long considered a twentieth-century marvel, the automatic bread-making machine debuted at the end of the nineteenth century. Created by a Massachusetts inventor named Joseph Lee, the prototype of the modern bread maker mixed and kneaded ingredients with commendable speed. But in the late twentieth century the Japanese—not traditionally bread-eating or bread-making people—further developed the concept: Zojirushi Corporation marketed the Home Baker in 1988, an all-in-one bread-making appliance that proofs, mixes, kneads, rises, shapes, and bakes the bread dough within hours. This appliance enables amateur cooks to create their own gourmet loaves without the manual labor and guesswork characteristic of making bread.

Several manufacturers have competed with Zojirushi to capture the home bread-baking market. Despite slight variations, machines operate similarly and generally include a nonstick loaf pan—sizes and shapes may vary from manufacturer to manufacturer—a kneading paddle, heating coil, and timer. The cook has only to select the appropriate bread recipe, measure and add the ingredients to the loaf pan, set the timer, and push a switch. After several hours, the bread has baked and is ready for cooling, slicing, and eating. Success depends used hearth griddles over coals and wrought-iron turners. More complex European yeasted breads depended on large brick ovens, covered bake kettles, or Dutch ovens heated with flames or glowing embers. Their overnight risings required large, wooden, lidded dough troughs and bowls or earthenware containers with cloth coverings. Heavy tin (actually tinned sheet-iron) bowls made with close-fitting but ventilated lids became available before the Civil War.

Although loaves were traditionally "cast" directly on the oven floor, cast-iron bread pans saw occasional use during the eighteenth century. Nineteenth-century cookstoves required bread pans, first manufactured in earthenware and tin. By the 1880s enameled tin (agate ware, for example) had eliminated problems of breakage, rust, and cleaning (though not chipping); this was followed by twentieth-century improvements in aluminum and, later, Pyrex.

The real change came when inventors in the third quarter of the nineteenth century patented tin and cast-iron dough "machines" that used hand-turned, geared cranks to move paddles through the dough as it was manipulated in a semblance of hand-mixing and kneading. When thoroughly combined, the paddles were withdrawn and the container (which came in a range of sizes to make one loaf or several) was covered and set in a warm place for rising. These machines were called dough mixers, dough brakes, bread mixers, and bread machines. By the 1930s large electric countertop or stand mixers were available to housewives, with attachments for mixing and kneading bread dough. Since the 1990s electric bread makers have accomplished the mixing, rising, and baking of bread, while their automatic timers can start and finish the process at any time of day or night.

Commercial neighborhood bread bakeries thrived in colonial cities almost from their start. After the American Civil War they proliferated with evolving assembly-line and moving-belt production, ovens, and improved bread slicers, providing the forerunners of the familiar packaged, sliced, and airy loaves sold in modern times.

[**See also** BREAD MACHINES; MIXERS.]

BIBLIOGRAPHY
Franklin, Linda Campbell. *300 Years of Kitchen Collectibles.* 5th ed. Iola, WI: Krause, 2003.

LINDA CAMPBELL FRANKLIN

Breakfast, *see Meal Patterns*

Breakfast Drinks

At the beginning of the twentieth century a growing number of patent-medicine peddlers exploited customers who wanted to lose weight regardless of their health. They began selling the forerunners to liquid diets and instant breakfast drinks. These patent medicines ranged from the harmless Jean Down's Get Slim mixture of pink lemonade

The Wonder Book of Good Meals, *distributed by the Continental Baking Company at the Century of Progress Exposition, Chicago, 1933–1934.*

on following the manufacturer's detailed instructions carefully and on other factors outside the machine's control, such as the quality of ingredients, humidity, and air temperature.

With practice, cooks may confidently develop their own recipes, but several bread-making cookbooks offer recipes suitable for all brands of bread machines. While most machines generally work equally well with quick breads and yeast breads, some of the more expensive and sophisticated models include instructions on making jams, cakes, and pizzas.

BIBLIOGRAPHY
Hensperger, Beth. *The Bread Lover's Bread Machine Cookbook.* Boston: Harvard Common Press, 2000.
Vance, Glenna, and Tom Lacalamita. *Bread Machines for Dummies.* New York: Hungry Minds, 2001.

ALEXANDRA GREELEY

Bread-Making Tools

From earliest civilizations, the technology of bread baking has been relatively simple. European colonists brought a tradition of unleavened flatbreads, adapted to New World ingredients, and baked in the fire's embers as ash cake. Alternatively, cornmeal johnnycakes to less benign remedies, such as the 1930s Helen's Liquid Reducer Compound, which encouraged dieters to gargle away their fat with a mixture of peppermint, bleach, and hydrogen peroxide. Dr. Stoll's Diet Aid was the first of these new diet drinks that got their start in the 1930s and have been reincarnated in each subsequent decade.

Liquid diets replaced patent medicines when science became more sophisticated and the Food and Drug Administration (FDA) became more powerful, clamping down on hucksters and their useless remedies. Breakfast drinks marketed as liquid diets at the turn of the twenty-first century included Carnation Instant Breakfast, Ensure, Herbalife, Naturslim, Metrecal, Sustacal, Resource, Boost, Nutrament, Sweet Success, Nutrilite, Nutrasoy, Go Lean, and Slim-Fast. Resembling milkshakes, the liquid diets are powders or canned drinks that include protein, vitamins, minerals, and other dietary supplements. Powders are combined with water, juice, milk, or other liquids; canned drinks require no preparation.

These beverages were first developed as a way for sick and weak patients to get some nutritional sustenance, and they were recommended by doctors and dietitians. Metrecal was one of the early beverages created for people trying to gain weight and was introduced to the public in 1959 as one of the first high-energy, high-protein drinks. It became popular as a meal replacement for dieters, known as the "Metrecal for Lunch Bunch." Trying to rekindle interest in similar products in the late 1960s, Mead Johnson Nutritionals also created Nutrament, promoted as a recovery drink for athletes, and Boost, a meal replacement or snack for healthy adults and for weight gain in cases of illness or surgery.

Introduced about twenty-five years ago, Slim-Fast now promotes their product with a plan that promises weight loss. According to researchers, Slim-Fast is effective in "long-term weight loss and weight maintenance" (Chernitsky, 1999). But staying on the Slim-Fast plan or other liquid diets longer than a couple of weeks may deprive the body of necessary nutrients found only in food. Many of these vitamins, minerals, fibers, phytonutrients, fats, and carbohydrates are contained only in whole foods.

Two-income households, longer workweeks, and a faster pace of life have become the American norm, leaving less time and requiring more energy for meal preparation. The drink manufacturers take advantage of baby boomers' worry about age-related slowing down, by equating healthful eating with their products and touting their nutritional benefits. Convenience is another selling point—portable cans or cartons are easily tucked into a briefcase, purse, or athletic bag. The old adage "breakfast is the most important meal of the day" partly explains why American adults continue to turn to simple solutions such as breakfast drinks. Whatever the concern—diet, health, or convenience—the market for breakfast drinks remains strong. [See also BREAKFAST FOOD; DIETS, FAD.]

BIBLIOGRAPHY

Chernitsky, Laura. "Slim-Fast® and Weight Loss." 1999. http://www.vanderbilt.edu/AnS/psychology/health_psychology/healthpsych.HTM.

Pilcher, Jeffrey M. "Food Fads." In *The Cambridge World History of Food*, edited by Kenneth F. Kiple and Kriemhild Coneè Ornelas, vol. 2:1492–1493. New York: Cambridge University Press, 2000.

Schwartz, Hillel. *Never Satisfied: A Cultural History of Diets, Fantasies, and Fat.* New York: Free Press, 1986.

ELISABETH TOWNSEND

Breakfast Foods

In the early years of the European settlements, the Native Americans showed the colonists how to grow Indian corn, or maize, and how to turn it into cakes and pones, or stew it into porridge or "mush," as the natives called it. When fat was available, slices of cold mush could be fried to a nutritious crispness. As soon as the colonists had sweeteners, such as molasses, maple syrup, or honey, they used them to add interest and calories to their corn-based preparations.

The breakfast drink of choice for most in the colonies was either hard cider or low-alcohol small beer. At that time it made a great deal of sense: water was often polluted; milk was considered a drink only for babies; fruit juices were unavailable. With prosperity, Americans would add coffee, tea, and chocolate to their breakfasts.

Regional Breakfasts

In New England, breads, meats (especially salt pork), and fruit pies became part of the breakfast menu, as did the cornmeal-based porridge, hasty pudding. The breads were often cornmeal mixed with other grains, such as rye 'n' injun (corn-and-rye bread) or brown bread (steamed bread made with rye, corn, and wheat).

An advertising flier issued by the Shredded Wheat Co. of Niagara Falls, New York, in 1916.

In the Mid-Atlantic colonies the early Dutch settlers brought waffles to the breakfast table, which were served with maple syrup or the molasses that was appearing as a result of the slave trade in the West Indies. Dutch *oliebollen* (oil balls)—doughnuts without the hole—were also common. Yeast-raised buckwheat pancakes became popular in New England and the Mid-Atlantic and their popularity spread west as the country grew.

In the southern colonies, plantation owners and the well-to-do enjoyed luxurious breakfasts. With servants or slaves to help with the cooking, the southern kitchen became famous for its breakfasts: beaten biscuits (so called because the dough was literally beaten for thirty minutes or more), grits with butter, fried ham, redeye gravy, spoon bread or hominy soufflé, eggs and toast, grilled chicken or game, fried shrimps or oysters, and many types of sweetbreads. With the advent of chemical leavens, biscuits, corn breads, and cakes all became popular breakfast fare. When Louisiana became part of the growing country in 1803, rich contributions were made to the breakfast table, including French doughnuts, or beignets; *calas* (deep-fried rice cakes dusted with powdered sugar); and *pain perdu* (French toast), all served up with Louisiana-style café au lait enriched with bitter chicory. The Louisiana breakfast also likely featured pork sausage, grits and grillades (braised beef or veal with gravy), biscuits, and eggs.

In the West, cornmeal mush or cornmeal and pork scrapple were typical breakfast fare, often served with whatever sweetener could be obtained. Fresh fruit was hard to find, but dried apples became the basis for many a pie in the 1800s. Pork was ubiquitous in the farming areas, and river-caught fish were common on the breakfast table. In the Southwest, chicken-fried steak, which turned leathery range-raised beef into tender fried morsels, was a favorite served with cream gravy, biscuits or potatoes, and boiled coffee.

Land of Plenty
As the country grew richer, breakfasts grew more luxurious, including treats such as cinnamon rolls, sticky buns, and Sally Lunn—a cake-like yeast bread. Toast was served with butter and preserves but also as milk toast or as "buttered toast"—toasted bread dipped in a sort of butter gravy. Bread could also be made into French toast or deep fried for Mennonite toast. Also popular were biscuits made with sour milk and soda or with sweet milk and baking powder. Biscuits were as likely to be split and covered with creamed chipped beef, a northern specialty, or fried chicken with gravy in the South. Pancakes were frequently made with rice and cornmeal as well as wheat or buckwheat. Some cooks served sweet fritters dusted with powdered sugar, while others passed syrup or molasses and butter.

Bacon, salt pork, sausages, and ham were the most widely eaten breakfast meats, but there were others, depending on the region of the country. In New England corned beef hash or codfish balls, in the Mid-Atlantic region creamed chipped beef or a porterhouse steak, in the South fried chicken or chicken hash, and in the Midwest and West pan-fried fish, broiled oysters, liver and bacon, or lamb chops might grace the breakfast table. Eggs—sunny-side up, over easy, scrambled, or soft- or hard-boiled—potatoes in many different guises, fruit in compotes or in sparkling jellies or preserves, and even a vegetable or two, along with pies or doughnuts and cookies, would make a hearty meal.

Manufactured Foods
To counter this landslide of rich food, health sanitariums in the late 1800s came up with whole-grain breakfast cereals, such as John Harvey Kellogg's Granula—twice-baked graham cracker nuggets. Kellogg and his brother then worked on a process for pressing cooked grain between rollers, resulting in the world's first flake cereal. The Kellogg Company of Battle Creek, Michigan, marketed Granose Flakes in 1895, the foundation for what would become the largest manufacturer of ready-to-eat cereals in the world.

One of Kellogg's patients was Charles William Post, who started a company in Battle Creek as well, selling ersatz coffee based on toasted wheat and molasses, which he called Postum. Post's "Grape Nuts" was a huge hit as a breakfast cereal.

Many other breakfast foods were marketed during this time. In 1889 Aunt Jemima pancake mix went on the market. The Quaker Oats Company started selling their breakfast oats in 1891, followed by Cream of Wheat. Malt-O-Meal hot cereal was marketed in 1919 and the first packaged, sliced bacon in 1924. Wheaties, the "Breakfast of Champions," also was introduced in 1924, followed in 1928 by Rice Krispies and, in 1930, by two biscuit mixes, Jiffy and Bisquick.

Bananas had been the rage in the 1890s, but canned fruits became popular at the end of the century as well, with canned pineapple becoming particularly fashionable in the 1920s. With the discovery of vitamins, canned fruit juice became a common addition to the breakfast table. The crowning achievement, of course, in fruit juice history and perhaps a defining moment in the American breakfast came with the development of frozen orange juice after World War II.

Immigrants—from Breakfast Doughnut to Breakfast Bagel
At the beginning of the twentieth century, immigrants introduced many new breakfast foods: bagels were contributed by eastern European Jews, as were the lox atop them. Frozen bagels made by agribusinesses eventually became available across the country. Blintzes—thin pancakes wrapped around a cheese filling and usually garnished with fruit compote—became a regular breakfast

Workers label and inspect cereal at the Quaker Oats Factory in Cedar Rapids, Iowa; mid-twentieth century.

item at such chains as International House of Pancakes and Denny's.

Throughout the Southwest *huevos rancheros* became a standard breakfast dish, usually served with refried beans and tortillas. The Mexican influence was also felt with the introduction of the breakfast burrito—a tortilla wrapped around eggs, salsa, sausages, and chiles. The Denver omelet—an omelet folded over a mix of ham and peppers—became a breakfast staple as well.

Modern Breakfast Tables
In 1964 Kellogg introduced Pop-Tarts, the first successful toaster pastry. Carnation's Instant Breakfast was introduced in 1965, the same year Tang took the kid's breakfast market by storm. In the mid-twentieth century, diners and truck stops served breakfast to the thousands of Americans on the move, as did the increasingly popular International House of Pancakes and Waffle House, both of which got their start in the 1950s. McDonald's restaurants, purveyors at the time of lunch and dinner menus, decided to offer three meals a day with the introduction of the Egg McMuffin in 1972.

Another modern breakfast trend was that for supersweet cereals. During the 1940s cereal companies introduced a few mildly sweetened cereals aimed squarely at the children's market, but that push accelerated greatly in the 1950s. Kellogg introduced Frosted Flakes in 1952 and Fruit Loops in 1963, General Mills gave us chocolate-flavored Cocoa Puffs in 1958, and Post brought Fruity Pebbles and Cocoa Pebbles to the market in 1971. Many cereals hardly seemed to be food any longer, but were simple sugary snacks.

Whole-grain granolas became popular in the early 1970s and a number of natural bakeries started producing alternative cereals and baked goods. One of the health food movement's biggest sellers was the granola bar. Kellogg and General Mills picked up on that trend very quickly and were soon selling their own brands of cereal bars. Technology also gave us microwavable instant hot cereal, some already in its own plastic breakfast cup.

In contrast to the luxurious breakfasts of old—bacon, creamed chicken, buckwheat pancakes, biscuits and homemade jellies—many Americans fuel up on instant convenience foods before rushing out the door. Others break their fast on cereal, coffee, and, if they are health conscious, some fruit. Still others, sadly, eat no breakfast at all.

[See also Aunt Jemima; Bagels; Breakfast Drinks; Cereal, Cold; Doughnuts; Dutch Influences on American Food; Fruit Juices; Hasty Pudding; Kellogg Company; Maple Syrup; Post Foods; Sally Lunn; Scrapple; Waffle, Wafer, and Pizelle Irons.]

BIBLIOGRAPHY

Graber, Kay, ed. *Nebraska Pioneer Cookbook*. Lincoln: University of Nebraska Press, 1974. A compilation of nineteenth-century sources.

Weaver, William Woys. *Sauerkraut Yankees: Pennsylvania Dutch Foods and Foodways*. Mechanicsburg, PA: Stackpole Books, 2002. A look at the foodways of early Pennsylvania Dutch Germans.

SYLVIA LOVEGREN

Brewing

Fermentation happens when yeast attacks a solution of sugar dissolved in water. Yeast eats sugar, gives off alcohol and carbon dioxide, and creates chemicals called esters, which are volatile flavor compounds. Being volatile means that esters evaporate easily and, in doing so, make themselves available to the sense of smell. Esters derive from the combination of organic acids and the alcohols formed during fermentation. Most of the fruity aromas of beer (and, indeed, many of the fruity aromas of fruit) come from esters. In bread making, the alcohol evaporates during baking; in wine making, the carbon dioxide is released into the air; and in beer making, both products are preserved.

Barley is starchy, and before it can be fermented, the starch has to be converted to sugar. The conversion involves a bit of deception. First, the grain is warmed and dampened. In an environment that mimics spring, the barley sprouts. This sprouting, or "malting," as it is known in the trade, converts the barley's hard starch into a soft, soluble one. It also develops useful enzymes. These sprouts are then baked, and the heat of baking kills the sprout. A short, cool kilning makes pale, light-flavored malt; longer, hotter roasting adds a toasty flavor and darker color to the grain.

To convert the soft starch to fermentable sugar, the grain is crushed and soaked in water, and the water is heated to about 150°F in a process called "mashing," which occurs in huge copper kettles called "mash tuns." The heating activates enzymes that make vitamins for the yeast and contribute to the beer's head. It also kick-starts the enzymes that will convert the soft starch into fermentable sugar. The fermentable sugar dissolves into the hot water.

This sugary water, called "wort," is moved to a new kettle and boiled with hop flowers. The hop plant grows all over the beer-making world in dozens of different varieties. Hops may be added at any time after the boil is complete, in a process called dry-hopping.

The hops in the boiling beer contribute bitterness through the extraction of alpha acids and also act as a preservative. The cooler temperatures preserve the aroma of the hops without extracting any more alpha acids. Each variety of hops has a distinctive aroma and capacity to impart bitterness, and a beer may contain more than one kind of hops. The wort is then cooled, inoculated with yeast, and fermented.

All these various choices in the brewing create different recipes for beer. If a wine's flavor is the product of the soil and climate where the grape is grown, a beer's flavor is the product of its recipe. Some of these recipes are very similar to one another, and among the cognoscenti these families of recipes and their beers are each called a beer style. Beer styles commonly produced in the United States include lagers, pilsners, pale ales, and stouts.

[See also Barley; Beer; Beer, Corn and Maple; Yeast.]

LYNN HOFFMAN

Breyers

William A. Breyer began selling ice cream in Philadelphia in 1866 and opened a retail ice cream store in 1882. After his death, his wife and sons incorporated and expanded the business, opening a manufacturing plant in 1896. The company's logo is a sweetbrier leaf. Breyer's Ice Cream Company became a division of the National Dairy Products Corporation in 1926. The company was acquired by Kraft, and then in 1996, Unilever, which combined it with the Gold Bond–Good Humor Ice Cream Company. In 1993 the company was renamed Good Humor–Breyer's Ice Cream Company. Breyer's brand is one of America's most consumed ice creams.

BIBLIOGRAPHY

Funderburg, Anne Cooper. *Chocolate, Strawberry, and Vanilla: A History of American Ice Cream*. Bowling Green, Ohio: Bowling Green State University Popular Press, 1995.

ANDREW F. SMITH

Bridge Luncheon Food

Although the roots of the card game of bridge go back at least to the early sixteenth century, the game itself, a variant of whist, did not come into being until the end of the nineteenth century. When and by whom the first bridge luncheon was given is not known, but it is probable that bridge's rapid rise in popularity at the turn of the twentieth century in combination with the emerging club movement made it a natural way for a middle-class woman to entertain her female friends.

One of the earliest mentions of a luncheon featuring bridge occurred in Mary E. Wilkins Freeman's *The Winning Lady*, published in 1909. By 1922 Emily Post's *Etiquette* included advice on how long a guest was expected to stay at a bridge luncheon. Since bridge luncheons were almost always strictly feminine affairs, the food and drink tended to be light and dainty. A typical menu from a 1933 cookbook was cream of mushroom soup, frozen cheese salad with fruit mayonnaise, pocket rolls or ginger muffins, coconut cake or cherry angel food, coffee, and chocolate peppermints. The book noted "a smart bridge luncheon may be served easily" on the card tables (*All about Home Baking*, 1933). Some hostesses served small sandwiches, biscuits, or cookies cut out in club, heart, diamond, or spade shapes, while others had special sets of table linens decorated in card-suit themes or even similarly decorated bridge luncheon plate-and-cup sets designed to fit comfortably around the small tables. Manufacturers also obliged the hostess with bridge mix, candy and nut assortments, in this period.

By the end of the 1990s bridge luncheons were perhaps not as ubiquitous as they had been from the 1920s to the 1960s, owing to the card game's declining popularity and the rise in the numbers of women working outside the home, yet they could still be a popular way to entertain. A 2002 symphony orchestra bridge luncheon fund-raiser featured an updated menu of wild mushroom tartlets, roasted red pepper soup, lobster salad with minicroissants, pear tart, and champagne cocktails.

BIBLIOGRAPHY

Adams, Joan. *Foodarama Party Book*. New York: Kelvinator Institute, 1959. Distributed by E. P. Dutton.

Editors, General Foods Corporation. *All about Home Baking*. New York: General Foods Corporation, 1933.

MacDougall, Alice Foote. *Coffee and Waffles*. Garden City, NY: Doubleday, Page, 1926.

SYLVIA LOVEGREN

Broccoli

Broccoli is paradoxical. It is identified in American consumer surveys as the vegetable most often eaten to promote good health, yet it is these same protective factors (particularly glucosinolates) that make broccoli bitter tasting and widely disliked. Unopened flower heads on thick stalks form broccoli (*Brassica oleracea*), which is botanically undifferentiated from cauliflower and is similar to cabbage sprouts. It is also related to brussels sprouts, turnips, and other cool-weather vegetables, all members of the Cruciferae family. Although its origins are lost to history, broccoli has long been associated with Italy. It was prized by the Romans, and the term "broccoli" is derived from the Italian word *brocco*, meaning "little branches." The sprouting type, often called Italian broccoli, is most common, though a strain with a cauliflower-like head is available.

Colonists introduced broccoli to the United States in the early eighteenth century. It was mentioned in *A Treatise on Gardening by a Citizen of Virginia*, written by a Williamsburg resident, John Randolph, around 1765. Broccoli was also planted in Thomas Jefferson's garden at Monticello. Recipes for broccoli appear in a number of cookbooks found in America in the eighteenth and nineteenth centuries, such as Hannah Glasse's *The Art* of *Cookery Made Plain and Easy* (both in the original 1747 English edition and the 1805 American edition). Lettice Bryan's *Kentucky Housewife* (1839) contains recipes for both sprouting and head broccoli. Broccoli did not gain widespread availability, however, until the 1920s, when the first commercial crops were grown by Italian immigrants in California.

The popularity of broccoli increased in the late 1970s, when the health benefits of cruciferous vegetables were reported. An excellent source of vitamin C, beta-carotene, folate, potassium, calcium, and dietary fiber, broccoli also contains numerous phytochemicals, such as sulforaphane, which are considered potent cancer-fighting compounds. American broccoli consumption rose by more than 900 percent in the last quarter of the twentieth century, nearing eight pounds per person annually.

[**See also** VEGETABLES.]

BIBLIOGRAPHY

Drewnowski, Adam, and Carmen Gomez-Carneros. "Bitter Taste, Phytonutrients, and the Consumer: A Review." *American Journal of Clinical Nutrition* 72 (2000): 1424–1435.

Lucer, Gary. "Broccoli: Super Food for All Seasons." *Economic Research Service USDA Agricultural Outlook* (April 1999): 8–12.

PAMELA GOYAN KITTLER

Brown, Helen Evans

Helen Evans Brown (1904–1964) was an internationally known food expert and a prolific author not only of magazine articles, some as contributing editor to *Sunset Magazine*, but also of cookbooks. Helen Brown's most stunning literary achievement was the classic *West Coast Cook Book* (1952). The book documented and collected the best recipes of the Pacific states and employed tools not widely used in food writing at that time: historical detail, bibliographic reference, and social commentary. The book awakened Americans to the rich bounty of the Pacific coast and bridged the gap between the earlier chatty, nonscholarly voice in such American cookery books as *Joy of Cooking* (1931) and the later, more authoritative voice heard in books like James Beard's *American Cookery* (1972).

Helen Brown's reputation as a cooking and food expert dated from the middle 1930s. The excellent food and hospitality of her Pasadena home attracted publishers, authors, and food experts from all over the world. Brown's husband, Philip, a rare-book dealer, acted as her typist, taster, and editor. He was also the librarian who built her extensive and eventually famous culinary library.

At the height of her career, Brown was known to New York foodies as "the West Coast food establishment." She was a well-connected member of the food community. Her professional associations included Julia Child, Albert Stockli, Craig Claiborne, and Helen McCully, but Brown's most famous associate was James Beard. Beard and Brown formed a friendship when he wrote her a fan letter after reading *West Coast Cook Book*. The two had a lifelong association. They wrote each other twice weekly about matters culinary and otherwise, took trips together to enjoy food, and spent evenings at the Brown house socializing over food and cookbooks. Brown's name appears in the dedication to Beard's treatise *American Cookery* and they cowrote a book on outdoor cookery. Brown was an assertive, intelligent woman who shared Beard's enthusiasm for American cuisine. Beard was deeply attached to her. She functioned somewhat as an older sister. She was unerringly supportive in his professional endeavors and was concerned especially about his health and professional reputation. Hers was the voice of reason he would listen to. The two of them championed the burgeoning reputation of American regional cuisine until Brown died suddenly in 1964, her life cut short by cancer.

[**See also** BEARD, JAMES; CALIFORNIA; PACIFIC NORTHWEST.]

BIBLIOGRAPHY

Beard, James. *Love and Kisses and a Halo of Truffles: Letters to Helen Evans Brown*. Edited by John Ferrone. New York: Arcade, 1994.

JANET JARVITS

Brown Ale

Brown Ale is the quintessential British ale style. It evolved from the original crude brews concocted for home consumption. There is some anecdotal evidence that this lighter than normal brew was developed prior to 1300 in Britain. What made this brew unique was the color, not the specific grains used to brew it. The earliest, most primitive version of this brew ranged in color from amber to rich brown with an alcohol content between 2.6 percent and 3.3 percent by volume.

Eventually two types of British Brown Ale developed. The "London style" developed into a full-colored brew, related to Dark Mild, Porter, and Stout. A slightly different Brown Ale, very dark in color, almost opaque, sweet and low in alcohol content, developed a far greater following and became popular with brewers and imbibers all over England.

American Brown Ale, sometimes called California Brown, or Texas Brown, is markedly hoppier than the English variety.

The Association of Brewers 2004 Beer Style Guidelines state that "American brown ales range from deep copper to brown in color. Roasted malt caramel-like and chocolate-like characters should be of medium intensity in both flavor and aroma. American brown ales have an evident hop aroma, medium to high hop bitterness, and a medium body." The average alcohol content ranges from 4 to 6.5 percent by volume.

[**See also** BEER.]

PETER LAFRANCE

Brownies

Brownies are bar cookies, usually chocolate, baked in square or rectangular cake pans. Although in the early 2000s some brownies seemed as rich and dense as fallen chocolate cakes, the original brownie recipes by Fannie Farmer were based on her cookie recipes, and she initially baked them in fluted marguerite molds or "small, shallow, fancy cake tins" as individual cakes. The original brownies had no leavening, except for an egg or two, and little flour, but were so rich with butter and melted chocolate that they baked up softer than other cookies, a distinction that is sometimes lost among the many soft or underbaked cookies of the twenty-first century. Fannie Farmer's first brownie recipe published in 1896 produced a confection that was colored and flavored with molasses. Each brownie had a nut placed at its center. All early brownies contained chopped nuts as well.

Brownies took their name from the mobs of nocturnal "little people," or Brownies, who were the subjects of Palmer Cox's cartoons and poems, which began appearing in the early 1880s. Cox's Brownies also inspired elf-shaped chocolate candies sold in the 1897 Sears catalog, an 1898 marble cake fiddled with straws (the cook used hay straws to pull the darker batter into lines) to make the image of an elf in every slice, and eventually Eastman Kodak's comparatively elfin portable cameras, as well as the younger level of the Girl Scouts called Brownie Scouts (1916).

The first chocolate brownie recipe was also published by Fannie Farmer in her 1905 revision of the *Boston Cooking-School Cook Book*. The proportions are similar to her 1896 chocolate cookie recipe, except that she radically reduced the amount of flour. In the chocolate recipe she specified a "7-inch square pan." As her assistant Janet M. Hill had remarked earlier of the molasses brownies, "The mixture is rather stiff, but spreads in baking." In fact, if you follow the 1907 directions of Maria Willett Howard [Hilliard] to "spread on buttered sheets and bake ten to fifteen minutes," the batter is apt to drip over the edge of the sheets.

Howard, who had been trained by Fannie Farmer, was then employed by the Walter Lowney chocolate company. She enriched Farmer's chocolate brownie recipe with an extra egg, creating Lowney's Brownies. She then varied the recipe by adding an extra square of chocolate and named them Bangor Brownies. This last recipe apparently started the idea that brownies had been invented by housewives in Bangor, Maine. The leading advocate of the Bangor theory of brownie origin was Mildred Brown Schrumpf, aptly nicknamed "Brownie," born in Bangor in 1903. Unfortunately, Mrs. Schrumpf's best piece of evidence that brownies began in Bangor was a *Girl's Welfare Cook Book* published there in 1912. This is not only seven years post-Farmer, but the recipe contributed by Marion Oliver for "Brownies, Chocolate" to that cookbook is almost exactly the same as the two-egg recipe for Lowney's Brownies, not Bangor Brownies. Oliver also contributed a recipe for "Brownies, Molasses" evidently taken from the Farmer cookbook. *The You-and-I Cook Book*, published in Bangor in 1905, has no brownies in it at all, although "A.M.T." provided a version of Fannie Farmer's chocolate cookies.

Maria Howard may have considered the Bangor Brownies, which were to be baked in a cake pan (unlike her Lowney's Brownies), to be descended from a recipe for Bangor Cake in Maria Parloa's *Appledore Cook Book* (1872), which was a white sheet cake. Another explanation for the myth that brownies began in Maine may be that "Bangor Brownies" was a mistake for "Brockton Brownies." The September 1906 Brockton [Mass.] *Hospital Cook Book* anticipates one of Howard's recipes. But the Brockton women's recipe used a second egg, as did Lowney's Brownies, whereas the Bangor Brownies used one egg, and three ounces of chocolate. And Brockton, then the shoe capital of New England, failed to produce a Brownie Schrumpf.

In fact, the two-egg Lowney's Brownies was the recipe most often reprinted in New England community cookbooks before 1912. It was renamed Brownies II in Cora Perkins's 1915 revision of the Fannie Farmer cookbook. In 1908 Maria Parloa, one of Farmer's teachers, developed a three-egg version with a little baking powder, called Fudge Squares, for Walter Baker and Company, a Boston chocolate manufacturer in competition with Lowney's. Ruth Wakefield slightly reduced the flour in her *Toll House Tried and True Recipes* (1936).

Molasses brownies persisted in commerce at least as late as the third edition in 1926 of *Baker's Weekly Recipes*, but chocolate and nuts endure as the basic brownie. Spices, raisins, and molasses were combined in an early Philadelphia hybrid recipe, but only tentatively were the nuts replaced by chocolate chips (first marketed in 1939), candies, or raisins. By the 1950s, butterscotch or vanilla brownies were described as "blonde brownies," underscoring the primacy of chocolate. Recipes were categorized as "fudgey" or "chewy," a difference produced mainly by fiddling with baking times and temperatures. "Cakey" brownies require more flour and leavening, such as the reaction of buttermilk and baking soda, or are made from commercial cake mixes with added butter and eggs.

Contemporary brownies vary considerably. One Internet site listed 569 different recipes in late 2003. Flavor variations include chocolate mint, white chocolate, mocha or coffee, peanut butter, raspberry truffle, and even ginger-chocolate. Mix-ins, beyond or replacing the original walnuts, include almonds, apricots, cherries, chocolate chips (or butterscotch or vanilla chips), coconut, currants, dates, hazelnuts, macadamia nuts, orange peel, peanuts, raisins, and candies, such as brickle bits, chocolate-covered espresso beans, Heath bars, miniature marshmallows, M&Ms, or whole Snickers bars.

Attempts to make brownies more healthful include substituting carob for cocoa; using applesauce, prune butter, bananas, pumpkin, or zucchini to replace butterfat; and mixing in fiber in the forms of bran, cornmeal, oatmeal, or raisins. Some recipes substitute honey or caramel candies for the sugar or brown sugar; James Beard tried maple syrup.

Modern nonchocolate variations include Amish apple brownies, "beige" or praline brownies (made with brown sugar), cinnamon (also added to chocolate), and carrot-bran. Common color contrasts are marble brownies (usually with vanilla cheesecake) or "black and white" brownies (often layered with coconut).

By analogy, any bar cookie with a chocolate layer can be described as a brownie, such as frosted brownies (sometimes vanilla frosting on chocolate or vice versa), and banana, orange, or vanilla cream brownies. Brownie recipes clearly not for children include Black Russian brownies made with vodka and coffee liqueur.

Perhaps the most extreme commercial variation is a brownie pizza promoted in the 1990s by Kraft foods. This is a round, thin brownie shell covered with sliced fruit like a fruit tart. The official illustration shows kiwi and strawberry slices—a long reach from Fannie Farmer's elfin cakes, each with its walnut half placed delicately at the center.

[**See also** BOSTON COOKING SCHOOL; CHOCOLATE; COOKIES; FARMER, FANNIE.]

BIBLIOGRAPHY

Dennett, Mabel Freese, ed. *Girl's Welfare Cook Book: Containing Practical Recipes and Favorite Dishes*. Bangor, ME: Press of the Furbish Printing Company, 1912. First documented Bangor, Maine, brownies.

Farmer, Fannie Merritt. *The Boston Cooking-School Cook Book*. Boston: Little, Brown, 1896. First recipe for brownies.

Farmer, Fannie Merritt. *The Boston Cooking-School Cook Book*. Boston: Little, Brown, 1905. Addition of chocolate brownies.

Walter Baker and Company Limited. "Choice Recipes." Dorchester, MA, 1908.

MARK H. ZANGER

Brunch, *see Meal Patterns*

Brunswick Stew

Like Kentucky burgoo and booyah, Brunswick stew is a thick, catch-all, soup-stew made by men stirring very large kettles with canoe paddles. Like its cousins, it has an early association with hunting camps, a historic involvement with political rallies, and a contemporary association with large gatherings and barbecue. Although there are competing stories about its origins and divergent recipes, all trails lead back to Native American stews of corn, beans, and game like the original succotash, and generally via African American slave cooks.

The likeliest origin is Brunswick County, Virginia, and there is little reason to doubt the attribution to "Uncle" Jimmy Matthews, slave and hunting-camp cook of Dr. Creed Haskins, later a member of the Virginia state legislature. Native American cooking techniques and recipes such as hoecakes often persisted among African American slaves, many of whom had Native slave ancestors. The "official" Virginia story is that in 1828, while Haskins and his friends hunted larger game, Matthews made up a pot of squirrel stew thickened with onions and stale bread. Matthews later was engaged to make a vast pot of stew for a political rally, perhaps for President Andrew Jackson.

In favor of this story is the repetition of squirrel as the canonical ingredient in Brunswick stew, and chicken as a common substitute. Against the story is that Matthews's original dish lacked corn and beans, which are present in almost all later versions, and would have been characteristic of the standing Native American stew. Supporting this story is that a very early printed recipe was titled "Virginia Stew" as published in the *Southern Recorder* of Milledgeville, Georgia, in 1862.

Brunswick, Georgia's claim is that the first kettle of Brunswick stew was produced there in 1898. The Georgia version of Brunswick stew is usually based on a combination of beef and pork (apparently a hog's head was an early favorite), and it is spicier than Virginia recipes. It often accompanies barbecue. In favor of Georgia is an extensive and continual use of the name in association with political rallies and church suppers. Another plus for Georgia is the witty recipe attributed to the Georgia humorist Roy Blount Jr.: "Brunswick stew is what happens when small mammals carrying ears of corn fall into barbeque pits." The alpha-male stewmakers of Georgia are known as "stew dogs."

The third claimant is Brunswick, North Carolina. North Carolina recipes tend to share the strong tomato influence of Georgia Brunswick Stew, and its frequent use as a side dish at barbecue restaurants. But the meats run toward the Virginia recipe of chicken, and the thought that it really ought to be squirrel. An unusual thickening adjunct in North Carolina is rice.

Besides the meats (and sometimes bacon or salt pork) and the corn and beans (often lima beans), modern recipes may include red and green peppers, a great many onions, potatoes, summer squash, okra, or even fruit. The universal ideal is that the stew ends up thick enough to hold up a spoon.

[**See also** SOUPS AND STEWS]

MARK H. ZANGER

Bubble Tea

Invented by street vendors in Taiwan in the early 1980s, bubble tea was originally a mix of tea, milk, and ice shaken to produce frothy bubbles. It became popular with children, and fruit flavors and purees were added to the mix. Finally, vendors included marble-sized dark tapioca pearls, which are now considered characteristic of true bubble tea. Bubble tea, also called *boba* drink, is usually served in a clear cup, showing off the dark tapioca bubbles, with a fat straw wide enough to suck up the chewy tapioca. Flavors range from the original tea with milk to mango, coconut, peach, peppermint, red bean, papaya, watermelon, and every common or exotic flavor sellers can devise. Bubble tea has spawned variants such as Thai bubble tea, made with sweetened condensed milk, and bubble coffee. Bubble tea first appeared in the United States in California in the mid-1980s, but by the year 2000 the fad was spreading across the country.

BIBLIOGRAPHY
Bubble Tea Supply. http://www.bubbleteasupply.com.

SYLVIA LOVEGREN

Budweiser

The most popular beer in the world, Budweiser is the flagship brand for the Anheuser-Busch Companies Inc. A lager beer of very mild flavor, Budweiser helped set industry standards for American brewing, became one of the most identifiable brands among all consumer products, and dominated beer marketing for over a century.

Budweiser is part of a long brewing tradition. In 1860 the German immigrant Eberhard Anheuser bought a struggling St. Louis brewery and, with his son-in-law Adolphus Busch, made it a thriving company. Under primarily Busch's leadership, the Bavarian brewery strove to serve a national market, an unusual idea in an era of local and even neighborhood breweries. In 1863, for example, there were 2,004 breweries operating in the United States, collectively making 2 million barrels of beer. To facilitate creating such a national brand and shipping it great distances, Busch devised a network of roadside icehouses to cool railcars filled with his beer. Years later he would pasteurize his product and invest in a fleet of refrigerated freight cars.

Upon creating this system to cool barrels of beer while in transit, Busch and his friend Carl Conrad developed a new brand of beer in 1876 to be shipped nationally. Naming it Budweiser, Busch made his new beer a rather light amber lager, a bottom-fermenting brew, using the yeast strain *Saccharomyces uvarum*. Brewed cooler and fermented longer than either ales or stouts, his Budweiser and other lagers were clearer and lighter, appealing more to the American palate.

Busch's Budweiser was an immediate success, soon selling well in cities throughout the Midwest. As Busch changed his company's name to the Anheuser-Busch Brewery in 1879, his Budweiser was already competing with the other burgeoning national brands, especially rival Pabst Brewing Company's Blue Ribbon Beer. For the remainder of the nineteenth century Anheuser-Busch and Pabst competed to be the dominant "ship-

per," the slang term of the era for nationally shipping brewers. National expositions and fairs featured elaborate pavilions funded by both companies, and taste-judging contests often dissolved into bitter disputes. In 1896 Busch introduced another national brand, Michelob, which he described as a "draught beer for connoisseurs," and by 1901 was brewing a combined total of 1 million barrels of beer each year (Smith).

Despite Adolphus Busch's death in 1913, his company's growth continued unabated until 1920, when the temperance movement's political efforts culminated in a national prohibition of alcoholic beverages. His son, August A. Busch Sr., assumed the helm, pivoting production over to a line of nonalcoholic items, including carbonated soft drinks, corn syrup, ice cream, and baker's yeast—a product that became an enormously profitable industry leader and continued in the Anheuser-Busch line until 1988. These diverse consumer products sustained profitability until Prohibition ended in 1933, when the company immediately resumed beer production. To celebrate the return to brewing, Busch included a team of matching Clydesdale workhorses as part of Budweiser's marketing campaign. These huge horses would come to symbolize the Budweiser brand, and Anheuser-Busch constantly maintained a herd of over two hundred for public display and enjoyment in parades and fairs.

Budweiser remained a national leader throughout the century, earning the status in 1957 of being the world's best-selling beer. The advent of television closely tied the brand name Budweiser with American sports, largely because of Anheuser-Busch's sponsoring of thousands of televised events and games. This strategic use of television advertising confirmed the popular perception of Budweiser as America's "national beer." Its continued success spawned Bud Light in 1982, a lower-calorie version brewed with a different ratio of malt and hops, targeted at health- and weight-conscious consumers.

Bud Light's subsequent success as the second-best-selling beer in the United States, trailing only its parent, led to the introduction of additional Budweiser spin-offs twelve years later, Bud Ice and Bud Ice Light. This expanded Budweiser family extended the beer market even further; by 2002 the company was producing more than 100 million barrels per year and collectively accounting for over 20 percent of all beer sold in the United States. The brand continues to become more and more ingrained in American culture, its Clydesdales a traditional feature of many community events and its Super Bowl advertising an annual event in itself.

[See also ADVERTISING; BEER.]

BIBLIOGRAPHY
Hernon, Peter, and Terry Ganey. *Under the Influence: The Unauthorized Story of the Anheuser-Busch Dynasty.* New York: Simon and Schuster, 1991.
Plavchan, Ronald. *A History of Anheuser-Busch, 1852–1933.* New York: Arno, 1975.
Price, Steven D. *All the King's Horses: The Story of the Budweiser Clydesdales.* New York: Viking, 1983.
Smith, Gregg. *Beer: A History of Suds and Civilization, Mesopotamia to Micro-Breweries.* New York: Avon, 1995.

DAVID GERARD HOGAN

Buffalo

The scientific name of buffalo is *Bos bison*, commonly known as bison, which in turn is used interchangeably with American buffalo, or buffalo for short. The largest terrestrial mammals on the North American continent, buffalo were the center of life for the Plains Indians. These majestic animals provided them with food, clothes, and shelter, and they served as a basis for the Indians' spiritual life.

When the Europeans arrived, they found buffalo on the plains in awesome numbers, their estimated total varying from 30 to 70 million. Pushing west to find a way to the Pacific coast, members of the Lewis and Clark expedition reported that upon reaching the heart of buffalo country, they encountered buffalo in such numbers that the animals were beyond counting. Other reports record that during the "running season," buffalo herds congregated into such masses as literally to blacken the prairies for miles.

However, by 1800 the herds east of the Mississippi River were nearly gone, most likely having been killed to protect the newly developed homesteads in that region. With westward expansion of the American frontier, systematic reduction of the plains herds began around 1830, when unregulated buffalo hunting became the chief industry of American migrants to the plains. Organized groups of hunters killed buffalo for hides, meat, or trophy. By 1900 fewer than one thousand buffalo remained.

Thanks to the efforts of a handful of dedicated conservationists, the federal government finally stepped in to help save the noble beast from extinction. Budding ranchers discovered that the genetically strong buffalo are able to thrive year-round anywhere there is adequate forage, water, and space. Efficient grazers, buffalo eat only top grass and do not damage the ecosystem the way cattle do, making buffalo the ideal environmentally correct animal for the twenty-first century. Buffalo herds are being farm-raised in nearly every state of the union. In addition, about fifty-one Native American tribes are actively engaged in restoring the American bison to its rightful range.

Bulls weigh up to 2,200 pounds, and cows weigh up to 1,000 pounds. Despite their size, buffalo have amazing mobility and are able to sprint at great speed. Male and female are characterized by an overdeveloped front portion and tapered hindquarters. Their huge head and hump, covered with dark brown, woolly hair, contrasts sharply with their small hips. Buffalo cows travel in herds of related animals while the mature males either roam alone or in small groups. The cows are very protective of their young and will become aggressive if they are threatened. Newborn calves are tawny to buff colored and darken over time.

Roaming free, raised without growth hormones or antibiotics, buffalo is a splendid source of red meat. High in protein and low in fat, tasty buffalo is the meat of choice of a large number of consumers and is featured in many fine American restaurants. Frozen buffalo meat is available in many supermarkets or may be ordered from one of the specialty mail order houses, many of which are owned by dedicated ranchers who are bent on restoring the balance of nature.

[See also FRONTIER COOKING OF THE FAR WEST; MIDWEST; NATIVE AMERICAN FOODS: BEFORE AND AFTER CONTACT.]

BIBLIOGRAPHY

Intertribal Bison Cooperative. http://www.intertribalbison.com.

National Bison Association. http://www.bisoncentral.com.

HELEN H. STUDLEY

Buffalo Chicken Wings

Buffalo chicken wings are divided into two pieces (the wingtips discarded), then fried and coated with a mild, oil-based hot sauce; and served with a blue cheese dressing and celery sticks. They were invented by Teressa Bellissimo October 30, 1964, at the Anchor Bar, in Buffalo, New York, and became famous though a 1980 *New Yorker* magazine story by Calvin Trillin. Trillin joked that no one even in Buffalo knew what to do with the celery sticks and blue cheese dressing. The only variation in the recipe or presentation since 1964 is that Bellissimo broiled the wings for some period before switching to a simple deep-fry. Trillin's article also mentions the influence on Buffalo wing cuisine of African American cook John Young, who was well-known in Buffalo in the 1960s for breaded whole wings fried and served with a spicy "mambo sauce."

No food origin story is ever simple, and even this recent and well-recorded event has three versions: 1. The wings were a spontaneous snack for Bellissimo's son Frank and friends; 2. The wings were a Friday-midnight inspiration for Catholic customers who had not had meat all-day; 3. The wings had been delivered in error instead of necks and backs for spaghetti sauce or stock, and were salvaged as appetizers.

Buffalo retirees in South Florida opened a second region to the wings in the 1980s, and they were taken national by the Florida-based Hooter's chain in 1983, followed by Domino's Pizza and Pizza Hut in the 1990s. National television advertising by these chains that feature quick-delivery pizza thus turned a bar snack into a national favorite associated with televised sports. However, the original Anchor Bar and its rival, Duff's, continue to sell vast quantities of the wings to locals and culinary pilgrims in Buffalo.

BIBLIOGRAPHY

Trillin, Calvin. *Third Helpings*. Boston: Ticknor and Fields, 1983.

MARK H. ZANGER

Bully Beef

"Bully beef" is the name used primarily by British and British colonial soldiers for canned corned beef. Most sources indicate that the name came into use during World War I when troops noticed the words *bouilli boeuf* (French for "boiled beef") on the cans. However, an Australian source says the term derived from the canned salt beef supplied from Booyoolee Station to men working in the outback in the 1870s. The workers called this ration "Booyoolee beef," which was shortened to bully beef.

Although references to bully beef turn up chiefly in British, South African, Australian, Jamaican, New Zealand, and Canadian sources, American soldiers also used the term. In 1932 a group of World War I veterans formed the Last Buddies' Bully Beef Club, whose symbol was a bottle of cognac and a can of bully beef. During World War II one Michigan soldier wrote that the only rations that survived a supply-plane drop were the cans of bully beef.

[See also COMBAT FOOD; CORNED BEEF; SLANG.]

BIBLIOGRAPHY

American Heritage Dictionary of the English Language. 4th ed. New York: Houghton Mifflin, 2000.

"Bully Beef on Thanksgiving." *Holland Sentinel*, November 27, 1997.

SYLVIA LOVEGREN

Bundt Cake

Originally, Bundt was a trademark for a fluted-and-scalloped tube pan. Today it is a generic term for any cake made with bundt-style bakeware. The bundt pan was created by H. David Dalquist in Minneapolis in 1950, according to Nordic Ware, a division of Northland Aluminum Products, which Dalquist founded. A group of Jewish women from the local Hadassah asked if he could make a more practical "bund pan" for their *bundkuchen* than the fragile ceramic or heavy, cast-iron versions from Europe. The chemical engineer, whose fledgling company made Scandinavian cookware and pastry molds, agreed to try. He developed a light, sturdy cast-aluminum model of the pan that improved on its centuries-old design. Dalquist added a "t" to the word "bund," German for "gathering," and trademarked it in 1951. The bundt pan skyrocketed to fame in 1966 after the Texan Ella Helfrich used it to create her Tunnel of Fudge cake, which won second prize in that year's Pillsbury Bake-Off. Sales of the pan soared. In 1985 federal courts declared the term generic. By the time of Dalquist's death in 2005, Nordic Ware had sold nearly 50 million bundt pans in addition to 10 million of variations on the original.

BIBLIOGRAPHY

Hahn, Trudi. "Bundt Pan Inventor H. David Dalquist Dies." *Star Tribune*, January. 6, 2005.

Herbst, Sharon Tyler. *The New Food Lover's Companion*. New York: Barron's Educational Series, 1995.

Hotta, Syugo. "A Linguistic Exploration of Foreign Terms in Trademarks." Master of Laws thesis.

Gendreau, Y. ed. *Intellectual Property: Building Aesthetics and Economics/Propriété intellectuelle: Entre l'art et l'argent*. Montreal: Themis, 2006.

KIM PIERCE

Burger King

In 1954 James W. McLamore and David Edgerton founded Burger King of Miami Inc. in Miami, Florida. The company, which had 11,450 restaurants in fifty-eight countries by the early twenty-first century, played an important role in shaping the fast food industry, standardizing its practices, and developing task-specific machinery, such as the "Miracle Insta Machine," which broiled hamburgers and toasted buns.

Burger King's first restaurant, which was located in Miami, sold eighteen-cent hamburgers and eighteen-cent milkshakes, along with twelve-ounce and sixteen-ounce sodas. Three years later the best-selling Whopper sandwich was introduced for thirty-seven cents. In 1958 the company turned to advertising, and the campaign featuring the memorable tagline "Home of the Whopper" was launched. Seen as an alternative to McDonald's hamburgers, which were fried, the Whopper was touted as superior because it was "flame-broiled."

From the recognition gained from the ad campaign, McLamore and Edgerton secured national and international franchising rights. The first stores to open outside the continental United States were in Puerto Rico in 1963. The company's growth caught the attention of Pillsbury Company, which in 1967 acquired Burger King as a subsidiary for $18 million. In 1988 Grand Metropolitan PLC acquired Pillsbury and its subsidiaries, including Burger King, for $5.79 billion. The following year Grand Metropolitan acquired Wimpy restaurants, two hundred of which were converted to Burger King franchises by mid-1990. In 1997 Grand Metropolitan merged with Guinness to create a new company called Diageo PLC. In December 2002 Diageo sold its Burger King holdings for $1.5 billion to the buying consortium of Texas Pacific Group, Bain Capital, and Goldman Sachs Capital Partners.

For almost thirty years Burger King's menu remained unchanged until, in an attempt to keep pace with competitors and food trends, the company began offering new food items, such as the Bacon Double Cheeseburger (1982); salad bars (1983); breakfast featuring the Croissan'wich (1985), French Toast Sticks (1986), and Cini-minis

Buffalo Chicken Wings

74

(1998); Chicken Tenders (1986); Bagel Sandwiches (1987); Chicken International sandwiches (1988); the BK Broiler (1990), a flame-broiled chicken sandwich; spicier, crisper french fries (1997); the Chicken Club sandwich (1999); and the first Whopper line extension, the Chicken Whopper (2002).

Since the 1990s criticism has been leveled at Burger King by nutrition experts, citing the company's encouragement of poor eating habits in adults and especially children. The critics considered Burger King's food too high in saturated fat. The company responded by switching to 100 percent vegetable oil for frying french fries, 1 percent low-fat milk, and reduced-fat mayonnaise in its ingredients list. The launch of the 2002 BK Veggie, a nonmeat alternative that boasts Burger King's signature flame-broiled flavor, was another attempt to cater to modern tastes.

One criticism that Burger King and other fast food companies have not been able to counter is that the inexpensiveness of its products, the ubiquitousness of its stores, and the ease of purchase, made especially convenient by drive-through windows, have contributed to altering—and, some have said, eroding—the tradition of the American family dinner.
[**See also** FAST FOOD.]

BIBLIOGRAPHY
Burger King. http://www.burgerking.com.
Schlosser, Eric. *Fast Food Nation: The Dark Side of the All-American Meal*. New York: HarperCollins, 2002.

DAVID LEITE

Burrito

The burrito, which means "little donkey" (burro), is a large flour tortilla rolled around a filling such as beans, meat, or cheese, along with vegetables and salsa. David Thomsen and Derek Wilson, authors of *¡Burritos!* (1998) believe that the modern burrito originated "in the dusty borderlands between Tucson and Los Angeles." The first located mention of burritos in America, however, appeared in Erna Fergusson's *Mexican Cookbook*, published in 1934 (Fergusson's recipes were from New Mexico). Wherever they may have been invented, burritos were a specialty of Los Angeles's famed El Cholo Spanish Café in the 1930s, and they became a mainstay elsewhere in the Southwest by the 1950s. In the 1960s burritos were popular nationwide, and in the 1970s fast food chains such as Taco Bell, El Pollo Loco, and Chipotle featured them. Ready-made burritos, to be reheated in the store's microwave, were sold in 7-Eleven convenience stores. The McDonald's Breakfast Burrito—sausage and eggs wrapped up in a tortilla—transformed the burrito into a breakfast food. Several fast food chains, such as Burritoville and the Green Burrito, have named themselves after their flagship product.

BIBLIOGRAPHY
Smith, Andrew F. "Tacos, Enchiladas, and Refried Beans: The Invention of Mexican-American Cookery." In *Cultural and Historical Aspects of Foods*, edited by Mary Wallace Kelsey and ZoeAnn Holmes, 183–203. Corvallis: Oregon State University, 1999.
Thomsen, David, and Derek Wilson. *¡Burritos!* Salt Lake City, Utah: Gibbs-Smith, 1998.

ANDREW F. SMITH

Butchering

The word "butcher," from the French *boucher*, dating back to the thirteenth century, is synonymous with slaughtering and meatpacking. Butchering entails dismembering animals and fowl and salvaging their parts for sale or consumption.

As evidenced by 300,000-year-old artifacts in Tornalba, Spain, Cro-Magnons pioneered butchering tools. The first butchering tools discovered in America belonged to the Clovis culture of ancient New Mexico (11,000 B.C.E.). Early natives butchered primarily bison and turkey as diet staples until cattle were introduced in the 1500s by the Spanish and then by the British.

Different animals were butchered according to the seasons, such as spring lamb or autumn pigs. In rural communities, much of the operation was concentrated in the late fall and early winter, as farmers slaughtered animals that would strain limited winter pasturage and feed stores and whose flesh could be preserved through such techniques as salting and smoking. Butchery was a year-round activity in urban markets where, through the nineteenth century, quadrupeds were either "walked" or shipped by rail and slaughtered on premises. Skilled artisan butchers slaughtered and dressed fresh meats for consumers; some accounts estimate eleven minutes to slaughter and dress an entire ox.

Large-scale commercial butchering started in the Chicago stockyards in the 1800s, setting standards on quality and innovation for the rest of the world. Kansas City, Kansas, served by major cattle trails, became the next major player. In the 1850s the meat mogul Philip Armour organized slaughterhouses in both cities and introduced high-speed, mass butchering technologies to serve dinner tables and pioneered the use of by-products for glue, fertilizer, lard, gelatin, and margarine production.

Butchering practices profited tremendously when technology and standardization of processes improved efficiency and reduced reliance on expensive skilled workers. In the late 1800s ice-cooling and refrigerated railroad cars facilitated yearlong butchering activities, shipping products instead of live animals to distant markets. Overhead rails, power lifts, and assembly-line production compartmentalized the work of slaughtering thousands of animals daily and enabled the Armour, Cudahy, Merrell, and Swift companies profitably to introduce canned meats for consumer meal preparations. World War I and World War II introduced American standards and enhanced global butchering practices.

Meat inspection, essential to butchering, was first documented in the Hebrew Bible as part of Mosaic law. Federal enforcement was enacted in 1891. Owners applied questionable and often dangerous techniques for profits and circumvented meat inspection laws. To instigate more effective regulations, Upton Sinclair published *The Jungle* in 1906, exposing the appalling conditions of meat production and slaughterhouse workers. The Meat Inspection Act (1906) and the Pure Food and Drug Act (1906) were passed to protect consumers, but butchering practices improved only when President Lyndon B. Johnson signed the Wholesome Meat Act (1967) and the Wholesome Poultry Act (1968), which mandated federal standards for butchering practices.

A nineteenth-century print showing the steps involved in butchering turkeys.

Before 1938, slaughterhouse owners adopted tactics that isolated butchers, minimized communication for any coordinated reaction, and shielded from the public the appalling conditions of meagerly paid workers. Subsequently, the United Packinghouse Workers Union emerged to defend workers. The titans retaliated by distancing themselves from unions into rural environs, where cattle were fed and housed. Kansas, with access to feedlots, railroad tracks, and rivers, emerged as the butchering industry leader.

At the beginning of the twenty-first century, the butchering industry was composed of low-paid immigrants operating high-tech plants in rural areas for such conglomerates as Iowa Beef Processing (IBP), Smithfield, Armour-Swift, ConAgra, and Tyson. In addition to immigrant workers, skilled butchers were operating service counters in independent stores and meat departments of large chain grocers in urban and suburban areas. Relatively few independent butcher shops still exist where the customer can request a special cut or watch steaks being trimmed from a primal quarter, and these shops tend to be found in affluent communities and ethnic neighborhoods.

[See also Armour, Philip Danforth; ConAgra; Meat; Pig; Sinclair, Upton; Swift, Gustavus Franklin.]

BIBLIOGRAPHY

"How New York Is Fed." *Scribner's Monthly*, October 1877. Reprint, *Journal of Gastronomy* 4 (spring 1988): 62–80.

Rixson, Derrick. *The History of Meat Trading*. Nottingham, UK: Nottingham University Press, 2000.

Toussaint-Samat, Maguelonne. *A History of Food*. Translated by Anthea Bell. Cambridge, MA: Blackwell Reference, 1993.

U.S. Department of Agriculture. *Official United States Standards for Grades of Slaughter Cattle*. Washington, DC: Agricultural Marketing Service, 1989.

KANTHA SHELKE

Butter

Americans are not known for eating prodigious amounts of butter. In 2001 they consumed an average of 4.9 pounds of butter per person, almost five four-stick packs. While this is much more than is eaten by residents of Latin American and Asian countries, it is far less than the quantity eaten by most western Europeans. German consumption that year averaged almost three times that of Americans, and French consumption, the highest in the world, was almost four times as high.

Moderate and declining butter consumption has been a long-standing trend. In 1937, when margarine consumption was quite low and butter was still produced on many farms, the average American ate 16.7 pounds of butter a year. This total is much higher than the 2001 figure, but rates in other English-speaking countries, such as New Zealand, Canada, and the United Kingdom, were even higher.

Americans may not eat as much butter as most Europeans, but the United States has a large butter industry that produced over 1 billion pounds a year by 2000. Almost all of this production takes place off-farm, in large factories. For much of the history of the nation, however, butter making was a farm activity. Butter was generally made from leftover cream during the summer months, when milk production was high. While some of this butter was marketed, much of it was used on the farm. The first creameries (butter factories) appeared in Upstate New York in the late 1850s and early 1860s. These were small plants that generally contained a springhouse, filled with pans for separating cream from skim milk, and a churning area.

Industrial Butter Production

The industrialization of butter production truly took off in the last decade of the nineteenth century, promoted by the invention of the mechanical cream separator. Earlier, the size of creameries had been constrained by the time needed to wait for the cream to rise to the top of the separating vats. The mechanical cream separator allowed cream to be separated out from whole milk in a matter of minutes rather than days, and creameries could start butter production with cream rather than whole milk.

Factory production of butter rose from 29 million pounds in 1879 to 627 million in 1909 to over 1 billion in 1921. With this rise, dominant brands appeared. In the nineteenth century butter was marketed mainly in tubs and portioned out by the grocer to individual buyers. In 1898 the first packaged butter was marketed by Beatrice Creamery Company, the predecessor of Beatrice Foods. Aside from Beatrice, many of the early leaders in packaged butter were meatpacking companies, such as Swift and Armour, who entered the business through their production of margarine. There were few differences in the packaging of butter and margarine, so these companies attempted to control sales of both products.

The hold of these companies over the market was lessened in the 1920s with the passage of the Capper-Volstead Act, which awarded farm cooperatives antitrust protection. Dairy cooperatives, in particular, Minnesota-based Land O'Lakes, began to market their products aggressively, directly to consumers. Their butter was produced from "sweet cream" rather than sour. Using soured cream was thought to be essential in creating flavorful butter, but it also increased perishability. Making butter from sweet cream quickened production and extended the distance from the manufacturing plant that butter could be sold, but it also may explain the charges of tastelessness that are often levied against American butter. Most butter by this time was made from pasteurized milk and also iced in transit. These and other innovations in hygiene allowed less preservative salt to be added.

The butter that Land O'Lakes sold in the 1920s, lightly salted in one-pound containers with four prepackaged bars, differed little from its product sold by the end of the twentieth century. Land O'Lakes also asked the federal government to send an inspector directly to its plants to certify that its butter met the highest standards. Previously, butter had been scored at the mercantile exchanges. The company included in its packages a certificate of inspection from the U.S. butter inspector. A race to promote quality followed, and soon premium butter of 93 score or higher, from pasteurized milk with few defects in taste, became the standard for retail marketing.

Butter and Margarine

Since that time, consumption and production of butter in the United States have fallen, primarily owing to rising consumption of margarine. Margarine was developed in the nineteenth century, but consumption paled compared with that of butter, partly as the result of home butter production by farmers but also because of taxes and regulations on margarine. Margarine consumption rose quickly during World War II, because of quotas on butter, and truly took off following the war. Margarine production surpassed that of butter in 1958 and nearly doubled butter production in 1969. Total butter production peaked in 1940 at over 2.2 billion pounds a year but dropped to less than half this amount by 1975.

Margarine outsold butter because it was cheaper, usually costing about one-quarter to one-half the price of butter. During the 1980s margarine was also promoted as healthier than butter. Questioning of this theory by researchers in the late 1990s may help account for a consequent modest rise in butter consumption. Nevertheless, Americans consume about one-third as much butter per capita as they did in 1940. Several innovations have been introduced. Margarine-butter "blends" have appeared. Premium quality butters, including American artisan and imported European products, are sold at specialty stores. In general, however, the appearance and packaging of American butter have been amazingly stable since the period of innovation that ended in the 1920s. Perhaps as a result, consumers often tie butter to a less industrialized age of food production.

[See also Dairy; Fats and Oils; Margarine.]

BIBLIOGRAPHY

Hunziker, Otto Frederick. *The Butter Industry*. 3rd ed. LaGrange, IL: Otto Frederick Hunziker, 1940.

Riepma, S. F. *The Story of Margarine*. Washington, DC: Public Affairs Press, 1970.

Selitzer, Ralph. *The Dairy Industry in America*. New York: Magazines for Industry, 1976.

DANIEL BLOCK

Butterfinger

In 1926 Otto Schnering, owner of the Curtiss Candy Company of Chicago, invented the Butterfinger candy bar, a honeycomb-textured, peanut-butter-flavored bar covered with chocolate. The name for the candy bar was reputedly selected in a public contest: "Butterfingers" is a term used by sports fans to describe an athlete who muffs an easy catch. Schnering got his new product off to a flying start by including Butterfingers in some of his famous airplane "candy drops," an idea he originally conceived to publicize the Baby Ruth candy bar. The Curtiss Candy Company was sold and ended up as an RJR Nabisco brand. In 1989 Nestlé bought Butterfinger brand. Nestlé's has co-branded with others, and Butterfinger candy bits, for instance, are included in Duncan Hines Candy Shop Brownies.

BIBLIOGRAPHY

Brenner, Joël Glenn. *The Emperors of Chocolate: Inside the Secret World of Hershey and Mars*. New York: Broadway Books, 2000.

Broekel, Ray. *The Chocolate Chronicles*. Lombard, IL: Wallace-Homestead Book Company, 1985.

ANDREW F. SMITH

Butter-Making Tools and Churns

Butter is made by agitating cream until it emulsifies. The high fat content of cream makes butter possible. This agitation is best accomplished with a churn, which until the mid-nineteenth century was typically a vessel of wood or glazed ceramic. Later in the century churns were sometimes metal. Churns could hold as little as three pints of cream or as much as sixty gallons. Churns also had different designs. Some worked by moving a perforated dasher up and down through the cream for hours until it emulsified. Others had a turbinelike dasher that was cranked. Sometimes the whole churn rocked or revolved rather like a washing machine. After 1900, small, glass, tabletop churns with hand-cranked gears were introduced. These prepared butter for at most a few days' use. Dairies, on the other hand, used huge churns that required external power sources, such as windmills or treadmills using animals, to move the dasher.

After the butter had formed in the churn, it needed to be removed and "worked" to remove the last traces of buttermilk and to mix in salt if desired. A wooden butter fork or spade transferred the butter from the churn to either a wooden bowl where it was worked with a butter ladle, or to a butter worker, which was a traylike device with a corrugated or flat wooden arm that was moved back and forth over the butter.

When the butter was ready for serving, a pair of corrugated wooden paddles could be used to form fancy butter balls. The butter might also be pressed into carved molds that produced a design, which could even include advertising, on the top. Plain molds existed that made a simple rectangular log of butter. Levered iron and wire butter slicers were patented after 1900 to slice pats from stick butter.

[**See also** BUTTER; BUTTERMILK; DAIRY; DAIRY INDUSTRY; MILK.]

BIBLIOGRAPHY

Franklin, Linda Campbell. *Three Hundred Years of Kitchen Collectibles*. 5th ed. Iola, WI: Krause, 2003.

Kindig, Paul E. *Butter Prints and Molds*. West Chester, PA: Schiffer, 1986.

Van Vuren, Robert E., and Barbara S. Van Vuren. *Molds and Stamps: A Guide to American Manufacturers with Photo Identifier*. Napa, CA: Butter Press, 2000.

LINDA CAMPBELL FRANKLIN

Two wooden butter molds.

Buttermilk

Despite its name, buttermilk lacks butter. Traditionally, buttermilk was the liquid left over after fat had been separated out of cream for making butter. It has a distinct, lightly sour flavor. Buttermilk has been drunk and used in American cooking since colonial times. Dutch settlers in New York had it with their breakfasts. In the early 1800s, New York City peddlers sold buttermilk at three cents a quart. It was sometimes resold as pot cheese, a combination of buttermilk, butter, salt, and sometimes sage.

Buttermilk was important to early farmers because it was an economically valuable by-product of the cheese- and butter-making process. In the early twentieth century another by-product use was created when a process was developed to make cultured buttermilk by adding lactic acid bacteria to skim milk. At the time, skim milk was relegated primarily to feeding farm hogs.

Today, buttermilk is used in the United States mainly as an ingredient in cooking. Buttermilk pancakes and biscuits connote wholesomeness and old-time cooking. Buttermilk consumption figures show that this old-fashioned label is not incorrect. In 1909, the average American consumed over seven gallons of buttermilk a year. In the early 2000s, Americans consumed less than one gallon annually. This trend is ongoing. Buttermilk sales halved between 1975 and 2002. Buttermilk's downfall may be its name. Although it is usually fat-free, declines in consumption have paralleled those for whole milk, as consumers increasingly avoid fatty foods. In addition, buttermilk consumption may be falling as Americans find less time for cooking homemade biscuits and pancakes.

[**See also** BUTTER; DAIRY; DAIRY INDUSTRY; MILK.]

BIBLIOGRAPHY

Selitzer, Ralph. *The Dairy Industry in America*. New York: Books for Industry, 1976.

DANIEL BLOCK

C

Cabbage

Native to Europe, wild cabbage is a parent plant of many cultivated vegetables, including broccoli, brussels sprouts, cabbage, cauliflower, collards, kale, and kohlrabi. The domesticated cabbage (*Brassica oleracea capitata*) consists of large leaves that form a compact globular head. There are three major types of cabbage. The most popular in the United States are the smooth-leaved green (sometimes so pale that is almost white) and red (magenta to purple) cabbages. The third type, Savoy, which has finely crimped leaves that form a looser head, is less common.

The earliest European settlers on North America's eastern shores brought cabbage seeds with them, and cabbage was a general favorite throughout the colonies. The Dutch who founded New Netherland (New York State), for instance, grew cabbage extensively along the Hudson River. They served it in their old-country ways, often as *koolsla* (shredded cabbage salad). This dish became popular throughout the colonies and survives as coleslaw. In New Jersey and Pennsylvania, German immigrants grew cabbage to make their traditional sauerkraut.

By the 1880s cabbage and its cousins had fallen from favor with the upper crust because of the strong sulfurous odors these vegetables give off when cooking. Marion Harland, hoping to change public opinion, offered a dish she called "Ladies' Cabbage"—finely chopped boiled cabbage baked in a rich, creamy sauce. American fiction writers often described lower-class homes as smelling objectionably of cabbage. But this sturdy and versatile vegetable never disappeared from middle-class kitchens.

Later immigrants to American shores brought different cabbage varieties and diverse recipes with them. For instance, stuffed cabbage, sweet-and-sour red cabbage, and cabbage soups came from central and eastern Europe. Wisconsin produces more cabbage than any other state; the crop is used mainly in the production of sauerkraut. Florida is the leading state for winter and spring production of fresh market cabbage.

BIBLIOGRAPHY

Dalton, Dennis E. *Sauerkraut Cook Book: One Nation under Sauerkraut*. St. Petersburg, FL: privately printed, 1980.

Weaver, William Woys. *Sauerkraut Yankees: Pennsylvania German Foods and Foodways*. Philadelphia: University of Pennsylvania Press, 1983.

ANDREW F. SMITH

Fottler's Improved Early Brunswick Cabbage.

Premium Flat Dutch Cabbage.

Improved Savoy.

Henderson's Early Summer.

Wakefield Cabbage.

Stone-Mason.

MR. LOW:—Those seed I got of you last season done splendid, we have the largest cabbage in the country I believe. Everything done well. LONG FALLS CREEK, KY., MARCH 20th. W. I. CARRAWAY.

Cabbages offered for sale in a seed catalog.

Cabbage Cutters and Planes

A wooden plank with a hole cut into it for an adjustable steel blade is called a cabbage plane or cabbage cutter. In America, it dates back at least to the eighteenth century. Sometimes the planks were carved with a date, a fancy cutout hanging hole, initials, or even a heart at one end. Such a tool is much safer to use than a chopping knife when slicing and shredding a large, unwieldy, and heavy head of cabbage. In fact, many were made with a box enclosure for the cabbage, to use in passing it back and forth over the very sharp blade.

Shredded cabbage was used for making Dutch slaw, German sauerkraut, or Irish "bubble and squeak," a sort of casserole of boiled, then fried, beef, potatoes, and cabbage. When making sauerkraut, the cabbage plane could be set up directly over the storage keg or small barrel, ready for adding salt for the fermenting. Small planes with an adjustable blade have long been used for slicing cucumbers, squash, and root vegetables. [See also CABBAGE.]

BIBLIOGRAPHY

Franklin, Linda Campbell. *300 Years of Kitchen Collectibles*. 5th ed. Iola, WI: Krause, 2003.

LINDA CAMPBELL FRANKLIN

Cactus

Most botanists think that the family of plants called Cactaceae is native to the New World. Those cactus species indigenous to the southwestern United States were used for food by the original inhabitants, but only one, *Opuntia ficus-indica*, plays a significant role in American commerce. The fruits, once known as tunas or prickly pears, are mostly marketed to North Americans as cactus pears; they come in many colors, but the leading commercial variety, grown near Salinas, California, and harvested in fall and winter, has a greenish-red peel and red pulp. The spines are rubbed off before sale. The flesh, which contains numerous seeds, is juicy, with a mild flavor reminiscent of watermelon. The fruits are generally eaten fresh; traditionally, they were also juiced and made into a sweetened paste, called *queso de tuna* in Spanish. In addition, the thick, fleshy cactus pads, called *nopalitos*, are stripped of their spines and used as a vegetable in salads, egg and meat dishes, soup, and pickles. Since about the year 2000 several California growers have established plantings of another species, *Hylocereus undatus*, known as *pitahaya*, *pitaya*, and dragon fruit, which has large, spineless, flaming pink fruit with white flesh and small seeds.

BIBLIOGRAPHY

Nobel, Park S., ed. *Cacti: Biology and Uses*. Berkeley: University of California Press, 2002.

DAVID KARP

Cadbury Schweppes

Cadbury Schweppes is a leading global confectionery company and the world's third largest soft drink manufacturer. The firm's roots go back to 1783, when Jean Jacob Schweppes improved a process for manufacturing carbonated water and formed the Schweppes Company in Geneva, Switzerland. Shortly thereafter, he set up a factory in England for the production of soda water and seltzers. Schweppes moved the company to England in 1792, and the company manufactured soda water, mainly for medicinal purposes. In 1870 Schweppes began bottling Tonic Water and Ginger Ale. The company opened its first factory in America in 1884. The company continued to expand its global operations, particularly after World War II.

In 1824 John Cadbury opened a store in Birmingham, England, which sold coffee, tea, and chocolate. Cadbury, a Quaker and a strong supporter of temperance, believed that these products were good alternatives to alcoholic beverages. In 1831 Cadbury began manufacturing cocoa and drinking chocolate, and by 1866 the company produced eating chocolate. In 1879 Cadbury opened a new community called Bournville, where modest houses were provided for workers in the chocolate factory. Bournville pioneered several novel labor practices, such as paid holidays and vacations, insurance programs, and night-school classes for employees. The Bournville factory produced handmade bonbons, chocolate-covered nougat and other chocolate candies. Cadbury began producing milk chocolate in 1897. In 1919 Cadbury merged with J. S. Fry and Son, another major British chocolate maker. After the merger, the new company continued to grow globally throughout the twentieth century.

In 1969 Cadbury and Schweppes merged to form Cadbury Schweppes. Its subsidiary, Cadbury Schweppes Americas Beverages (CSAB) is headquartered in Plano, Texas. It includes the following brands: Canada Dry, Hires Root Beer, 7-Up, Dr Pepper, RC Cola, A&W Root Beer, Diet Rite, Snapple, Mott's Apple Juice, Sunkist Soda, Hawaiian Punch, and Slush Puppie frozen drinks. The acquisition of Adams Confectionery, makers of Halls cough drops and Trident, Dentyne, and Bubbas chewing gum, made Cadbury Schweppes the world's second largest manufacturer of gum.

BIBLIOGRAPHY

Williams, Iolo Aneurin. *The Firm of Cadbury, 1831–1931*. London: Constable, 1931.

ANDREW F. SMITH

Cafeterias

In its heyday the American cafeteria was a sociological as well as a culinary phenomenon. Although it was christened with the Spanish word for "coffee shop," it is rather a buffet—a self-service operation on a relatively large scale. Efficient and economical, it provided a solution to various logistical problems arising in the transition between a primarily agrarian and an essentially urban-industrial society: as fewer and fewer people worked on either their own land or their own time, and scheduled lunch breaks made midday commutes home impractical, the need for eateries that were conveniently located within commercial districts and streamlined for speed—as well as thrift—increased. This need was first met in the 1880s with the opening of the Exchange Buffet in New York City (met, that is, for men, to whom the place catered exclusively). It gained credence across the country in the next decade, boosted by an exhibition at the 1893 Chicago World's Fair—where the term "conscience joint" was

coined in a nod to the honor system by which patrons settled the check—and by the efforts of such entrepreneurs as the brothers Samuel and William Childs, who are credited with introducing the system of lines and trays that defines the modern cafeteria.

Where expedience in a restaurant is a virtue, food preparation and selection are sure to be mere formalities—or informalities, for that matter. Cafeteria fare generally resembles that of any other casual American-style eatery, from coffee shop to truck stop. Cheap, hearty (but seldom heart-healthy) quick fixes abound, from snack items like burgers, fries, and malts to entrées like fried chicken or spaghetti and meatballs. These meals come complete with starchy sides, the occasional boiled vegetable, and a bowl of Jell-O or a slice of pie for dessert. As for beverages, soda, juice, coffee, and the like are typical; alcohol is less so.

Like the bland food, the cafeteria setting is instantly recognizable in its very anonymity. Granted, this was not always the case; in the first half of the twentieth century, cafeterias were distinguished (from other genres, if not from one another) by their swanky, or at least imitation swanky, interiors. As the ethic and aesthetic of the fast food franchise began to affect the restaurant industry as a whole, however, the look changed. By the end of the twentieth century vast dining rooms, identically decorated and awash in oranges, beiges, and browns, were filled with vinyl booths and booster chairs negotiated by busboys and waitstaff with more or less limited duties, such as seating, filling drink orders, or transacting payment. Diners line up at long counters or steam tables fitted with sneeze guards and slide rails, lading their trays as they go; the level of counter service varies, but the standard practice is to station employees at the hot buffet while keeping cold items, such as salads and desserts, within customers' own reach.

Still, if sameness in the sense of homogeneity has always been the name of the cafeteria game, sameness in the sense of stagnation has not. Spin-offs have periodically thrived, from the vending-service "automats" of the early twentieth century to the smorgasbords of the 1960s to the salad bars of the 1970s and 1980s; cafeteria chains have also flourished, beginning with the Childs brothers' New York–based operations at the turn of the century and eventually migrating south and west. In fact, while the original urban model has all but disappeared in the shuffle of fast food establishments, its roadside offspring have fared comparatively well in those areas of the country where automobility is a necessity, offering as they do a somewhat more formal, yet still affordable, alternative to the burger chains (hence their folkloric popularity with churchgoing crowds on Sunday). Indeed, according to Ruth Kedzie Wood (Jakle and Sculle, p. 33), California was known for a time as the "Cafeteria Belt," while the Deep South to this day fairly teems with Morrison's, Furr's, Piccadillys, and Luby's. Although these places command only a small share even of these regional markets, they continue to attract certain segments of the population steadily, namely, retirees and middle- to lower-middle-class families.

Noncommercial Venues

Of course, the rise of the automobile spurred a steady exodus of individuals and the industries that service them from city centers to rapidly forming bedroom communities; but the commercial cafeteria's shift from urban, worker-oriented environs to suburban, family-oriented ones may be linked even more specifically to its development and image in noncommercial sectors. Initially, the impersonal, assembly-line nature of the cafeteria was deemed disruptive to the family unit, breaching the sanctity of the sit-down dinner hour, at the same time that it was conducive to productivity in its emphasis on rapid lunch-hour turnover. Granted, from a managerial standpoint, the root of the problem—the midday scattering of employees from the workplace itself, regardless of the length of the lunch break—had yet to be addressed. But since the advantages of the cafeteria system—relatively low costs and, hence, a potentially superb cost-benefit ratio—were not in question, the solution, it seemed, was simply to install it onsite. Thus did the company lunchroom evolve, becoming commonplace by the 1920s. Of course, its commercial counterpart in the vicinity waned accordingly, and the owners of such establishments were forced to rethink the nature of their enterprise.

Meanwhile, cafeterias were proving effectual in another unexpected context—schools. Concerns about child malnutrition around the turn of the twentieth century had prompted various philanthropic organizations to set up shop within schools to furnish students with balanced lunches; eventually, the schools themselves became legally responsible for such provisions and the cafeteria-style facilities proper to them. Their success in this venture is highly debatable; time-honored children's jokes about mystery meat and fish sticks have given way to much more serious misgivings regarding corporate takeovers of school lunchrooms, whereby students have on-campus access to the same junk food they have long gravitated toward off campus.

Still, for much of the twentieth century, cafeterias were equated vis-à-vis school-lunch programs with wholesomeness. For that matter, they are probably the type of eatery most closely connected with social services in general and with the moral commitment presumably required to coordinate them, from hospitals to armed service camps to soup kitchens. The patina of charity and even patriotism thus covering cafeterias further explains the steadfastness of their reputation among many Americans in those areas of the country where a belief in hospitality and a bent for conservatism coexist.
[See also ROADSIDE FOOD; SCHOOL FOOD.]

BIBLIOGRAPHY
Bryan, Mary de Garmo. *The School Cafeteria*. New York: Crofts, 1936.
Jakle, John A., and Keith A. Sculle. *Fast Food: Roadside Restaurants in the Automobile Age*. Baltimore: Johns Hopkins University Press, 1999.
Mariani, John. *America Eats Out: An Illustrated History of Restaurants, Taverns, Coffee Shops, Speakeasies, and Other Establishments That Have Fed Us for 350 Years*. New York: Morrow, 1991.
Pillsbury, Richard. *From Boarding House to Bistro: The American Restaurant Then and Now*. Boston: Unwin Hyman, 1990.

RUTH TOBIAS

Cajun and Creole Food

The vast area spanning the Gulf of Mexico and eventually known as the Louisiana Territories was settled in 1699, when French colonists first touched its shores. Since then, peoples from Europe, Africa, Asia, and Latin America have left their mark on the region and inspired two original culinary traditions: the Creole cuisine of New Orleans and the Cajun food of the surrounding bayous and prairies.

From Criollo to Creole

The word "Creole" is derived from the Spanish word *criollo*, which means "native to the place," and was probably first used in the sixteenth century to describe Spanish children born in Spain's South American and West Indian colonies. In its broadest meaning, "Creole" designates anyone from New Orleans. The term also refers to the original cuisine of New Orleans.

When the first settlers arrived in Louisiana, they surely relied on traditional French cooking techniques and any foodstuffs that had survived the voyage. Soon, though, the challenges of colonial life forced adaptation and a reliance on the hunting, fishing, and farming techniques learned from Indian nations, such as the Choctaws and Chitimachas. Among the Choctaw's lasting contributions to Creole cuisine was the introduction of filé (dried and powdered sassafras leaves) as a flavoring and thickening agent in soups and stews. It is almost certain that African slaves and Europeans other than the French were already influencing the flavors of the pot as well.

Gumbo, Quintessential Creole Classic

The word "gumbo" derives from the Angolan term *kingombo*, which means okra. The term also refers to a French patois spoken in the West Indies and a separate French dialect used in Louisiana, but gumbo has come to signify for Americans the rich soup for which Louisiana is famous.

Some aficionados consider gumbo a simple adaptation of the French recipe for bouillabaisse. Others suggest different influences. The Choctaws, for example, may have shared a recipe for boiled seafood that influenced gumbo's development. Gumbo may bear its strongest resemblance to African and West Indian okra soup recipes. In time, though, gumbo soup took on a more generic meaning and could refer to various soups made with or without the actual vegetable.

Spain Acquires a Neglected Colony

In 1762 France secretly granted New Orleans and nearby lands to Spain. Although the colony was in trouble, the Spanish transformed New Orleans into a commercial hub. Spain retained control over Louisiana until 1800.

The recipe for jambalaya, a highly seasoned rice casserole, has long been considered a Spanish contribution to Creole menus. Numerous sources trace the recipe's inspiration to paella, a signature rice dish of Valencia. Later scholarship asserts that jambalaya is closer to the rice dishes of Provence, France, called pilau.

Moros y Cristianos, a Spanish dish of highly seasoned black beans and plain white rice, is often cited as the inspiration for the classic New Orleans dish of red beans and rice. As with jambalaya, though, there is debate on this point, as some scholars look more to the African roots of the women who prepared the dish for clues to its origins.

Despite decades of Spanish influence, New Orleans retained a distinctively French personality. This is true in large part because the Castilians opened Louisiana's gates wide to new settlers, including members of the French nobility who escaped the revolution of 1789 and French refugees who fled the crown's colony at Saint Domingue (Haiti) in the 1790s during a slave uprising.

Antoine Amedee Peychaud, an apothecary in New Orleans and himself a French refugee from Saint Domingue, is credited with the invention of the cocktail. In 1793, as the legend goes, at his French Quarter shop, Peychaud introduced a tonic of cognac and bitters that he served in a French egg cup, or *coquetier*. Peychaud's creation is said to have inspired a bit of slurring in the words of those who imbibed, thereby securing the cocktail's place in the English lexicon. Peychaud's potion inspired the creation of other famous Crescent City drinks such as the Sazerac cocktail and the Ramos gin fizz.

Cajuns

In 1755 the French Acadians fell victim to the colonial struggle for control of North America and were ordered by the British to leave Canada. Thousands returned to France; others did not. The first Acadians arrived in Louisiana around 1765. Although some put down roots in New Orleans, the majority settled on nearby lands. The term "Cajun," a corruption of "Acadian," did not come into use until the nineteenth century.

A Creole cookbook entitled Mme Begué and Her Recipes: Old Creole Cookery.

American Influence

The incorporation of Louisiana into the United States in 1803 precipitated a flood of American influence. The resulting boom in trade, especially along the Mississippi River, ushered in a golden era of commerce and migration that forever changed the region. The increased trade also spiked the demand for slaves, whose talent for mixing diverse cultures and tastes on a single plate was considered unsurpassed.

During this period, black women called *pralinieres* could be found on the streets of New Orleans selling confections like the Creole praline. The French praline, a sugared almond, bears the name of César duc de Choiseul, comte Du Plessis-Praslin, the French marshal and diplomat who took credit for creating the tiny sweet. The Creole version, a candy patty made with pecans and cane sugar, actually bears little resemblance to the French praline and may compare more closely to creamy confections made in various Latin American countries.

Although a process of Americanization continued until the early twentieth century, the Gulf Coast region of Louisiana never lost its distinctively Gallic flair. In Cajun country, where the use of the French language was once suppressed in schools, a council was established in 1968 to promote its use. Likewise, the efforts of chefs like Paul Prudhomme ignited a craze for Cajun in the 1980s and cast an international spotlight on the region's French-inspired food and culture.

Menu cards at the famous French Quarter restaurant called Arnaud's (established in 1918) still carry the founder's festive missive: "At least once a day...one should throw all care to the wind, relax completely and dine leisurely and well." Conveying more than a philosophy on dining, Arnaud Cazenave's words express a timeless outlook on life in New Orleans. The Cajuns also have preserved their traditions of living and eating simply but well. Together, Cajun and Creole food represent a blurring of cultural lines and a marriage of flavors that is uniquely and unmistakably American.

[See also AFRICAN AMERICAN FOOD; CASSEROLES; COCKTAILS; FRENCH INFLUENCES ON AMERICAN FOOD; NATIVE AMERICAN FOODS; PRUDHOMME, PAUL.]

BIBLIOGRAPHY

Gutierrez, C. Paige. *Cajun Foodways.* Jackson: University Press of Mississippi, 1992.

Hall, Gwendolyn Midlo. *Africans in Colonial Louisiana: The Development of Afro-Creole Culture in the Eighteenth Century.* Baton Rouge: Louisiana University Press, 1992.

The Original Picayune Creole Cook Book. New Orleans: Times-Picayune Publishing, 1966. First published in 1901.

Prudhomme, Paul. *Chef Paul Prudhomme's Louisiana Kitchen.* New York: Morrow, 1984.

AMANDA WATSON SCHNETZER

Like the first French settlers, the Acadians relied on native Indians for information about indigenous foods. Over time, they also interacted with the Spanish, the French Creoles, and an array of other immigrants. They also intermingled with Africans, both slave and free.

The humble crawfish (known more widely as crayfish) owes its rise to stardom to the Cajuns and is perhaps most notably identified with étouffée. Literally meaning "smothered," étouffée in Cajun parlance is a one-pot stew that spotlights a single main ingredient, such as crawfish or shrimp. An étouffée may or may not begin with a roux, but it will always start off with green peppers, onions, and celery sautéed in the pan. Peeled crawfish tails and either water or stock are added to the mix, which is covered with a lid and cooked down until the main ingredient becomes tender.

Cakes

From the beginning of the nineteenth century through the middle of the twentieth, cake was the reigning passion of American women, and the cakes that American women devised, in all their glorious tastes and textures, stunning colors, and imposing forms, constituted a world-class repertory.

The Early English Roots of American Cake

Cake came to America with the first English settlers primarily as great cake, a lightly spiced, lightly sweetened, fruited bread something like today's raisin bread baked in the large, or great, size of approximately fifty pounds. In colonial America, great cake was particularly associated with harvest festivals, thanksgiving feasts, university commencement days, and, above all, with election day, the day on which local representatives to the colonial courts were chosen. Smaller versions of this cake, meant to be served at election day teas, remained part of American cookbook literature until the early twentieth century.

Around the turn of the eighteenth century, the plum cake (later called fruitcake) came to America from England. This cake, raised by beating air into butter and eggs, was much richer and sweeter than the old yeast-raised celebration cakes. It was baked in large sizes for weddings, smaller sizes for parties celebrating Christmas and Twelfth Night. Also newly arrived from England in the eighteenth century were the pound cake, which was basically a small plum cake without fruit, and the Savoy Cake, a type of sponge cake.

The American Fine Cakes of the Early Nineteenth Century

At the fancy evening parties of the early nineteenth century, cake was a principal attraction. The long party table covered with a white cloth typically bore a row of different "fine cakes" down the center. Initially these cakes were plum cake, pound cake, and sponge cake. But, by the 1830s, supper tables also included uniquely American cakes spun out of pound cake and sponge cake. The two new pound cake offshoots were to be particularly important to American cake baking. They were the stunningly white lady cake, made with egg whites rather than whole eggs and flavored with bitter almonds, and the deep yellow golden cake, made with egg yolks and flavored with orange or lemon. The fashion was to bake both cakes for supper tables to highlight the contrast in color.

Cake was also the main offering at the informal company teas that women staged, particularly around the New Year. In most households, women opted for less expensive, quicker, easier cakes to serve at such teas. American women devised two new cake families for tea. Both were off-shoots of pound cake, and both depended on a secret ingredient pioneered by American housewives: pearl ash, an alkaline leavening similar to today's baking soda. Pearl ash allowed women to make cake with less butter and fewer eggs than pound cake required—and pearl ash also made strenuous beating of the batter unnecessary. One of the new cake families comprised various cakes flavored with spice, raisins, and currants. These were often named for American patriots (Washington, Madison, Harrison, Jefferson) or American cities (Boston, Rutland,

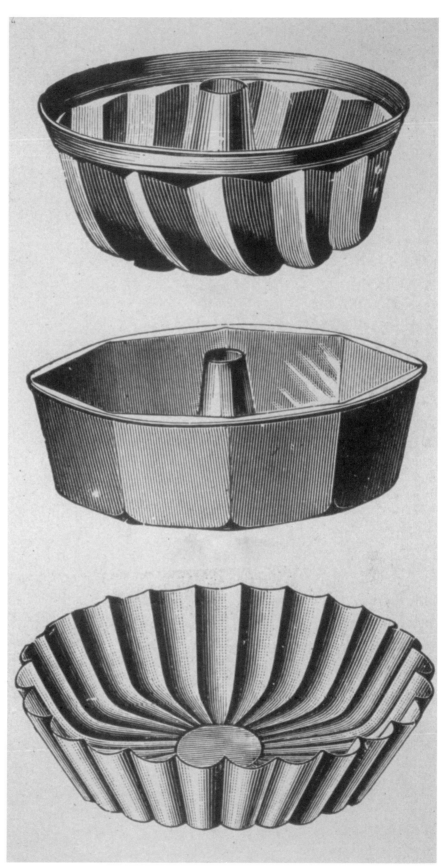

From top to bottom: Turks' head cake mold, octagon cake mold, and scalloped cake pan.

20 Wonderful Cakes
made by the new
KRAFT OIL METHOD

A cookbooklet of cake recipes issued by Kraft.

Dover). The other new cake was "cup cake," which proved to be one of the most important cakes in American cake-baking history. The cake was so named because its ingredients were measured by the cup (which was more convenient than weighing) and because, at least initially, it was baked in small cups, which facilitated the rising of inexpensive, quickly made batters. Soon enough, cup cake came to be baked in large sizes as well.

The New Cakes of the Stove Era
By 1850 most American households had forsaken the ancestral kitchen hearth in favor of the enclosed iron stove. Because the stove oven was much easier to manage than the fireplace oven and Dutch oven, cake baking became more accessible to ordinary middle-class women. Middle-class women, however, found the hearth-era recipes for pound cake, lady cake, and golden cake too expensive, time-consuming, and labor-intensive for

their means. Cookbook authors responded to their plight. By the 1850s, cookbook authors outlined many thriftier, simplified recipes for fine cakes. These cakes were basically pound cakes, lady cakes, and golden cakes reconfigured along the lines of cup cake—that is, the ingredients measured rather than weighed, butter and eggs reduced to modest quantities, the beating process shortened and streamlined, and, crucially, the batter raised with chemical leavening.

By the end of the Civil War a new American cake age had dawned. There were now essentially three American cake families: the traditional rich cakes such as fruitcake and pound cake; the new chemically leavened butter cakes; and the sponge cakes. The butter cakes were of three principal types: whole egg cakes (such as 1-2-3-4 cake), egg white cakes, and egg yolk cakes. There was also a new white sponge cake on the scene, commonly called "angel cake."

The New Cake Forms of the Stove Era
By the 1870s America had entered its legendary Gilded Age, when grandiloquent Frenchified styles of cooking, dining, and entertaining were in vogue among the wealthy, styles that were imitated, albeit on a humbler scale, by middle-class women. Much grander party cakes were required for this new age, and they promptly materialized: the marble cake, which had dark swirls; the jelly cake (or roll), which was a conflation of the jelly cake with the fashionable French roll cakes of the day; and the layer cake. The earliest layer cake recipes were outlined in southern cookbooks published immediately after the Civil War. Most often called "white mountain cake," the cakes typically consisted of four to six layers of yellow or white butter cake filled and frosted with meringue icing.

By the 1880s the vogue for layer cakes had spread across the United States, and new layer cakes developed. Almost as popular as white mountain cake were layer cakes filled with "caramel," a glossy, sticky-chewy cooked syrup made with brown sugar, milk, butter, and, in some recipes, chocolate. Caramel fillings were succeeded in the 1890s by fudge fillings and frostings, which were similar to caramel except that the syrup was beaten after cooking and so became soft and creamy. The long time American fascination with spiced, fruited, dark-colored cake also found expression in new layer cakes. A favorite conceit entailed sandwiching a dark cake layer between two yellow or, better, white layers. Such was the plan behind ribbon cake, metropolitan cake, Neapolitan cake, Prince of Wales cake, Dolly Varden cake, Jenny Lind cake, and others.

The Cakes of the Twentieth Century
By the 1930s marketing forces increasingly ruled American kitchens and steered the course of American cake. American homemakers were using cake recipes found in newspaper and magazine advertisements, on box tops and product inserts, and in booklets published by companies that produced flour, sugar, vegetable shortening, baking powder, chocolate, nut meats, flavoring extracts, dried fruits, and other products. The preparation of all dishes, including cakes, became less expensive, quicker, easier, and more approachable.

When the occasion was fancy, American women gravitated toward either roll cakes or angel cake, which some particularly ambitious bakers hollowed out and filled with gelatinized mousse and frosted with whipped cream. Angel cake was difficult to prepare, and American bakers were grateful when Betty Crocker unrolled, with great fanfare, a brand-new cake that was every bit as moist and tender and every bit as tall as angel cake but was much easier to make. It was the chiffon cake, invented in the 1920s by Harry Baker, a Los Angeles insurance salesman turned Hollywood caterer. Baker sold the formula to General Mills in the 1940s. The secret of Baker's formula was cooking oil, a then unheard-of ingredient in cake.

While Baker was perfecting chiffon cake, the large food companies were simplifying the mixing of butter cakes. The standard procedure was to "cream" (that is, soften and aerate) the butter and sugar, to beat in the eggs one at a time, and then to add the dry ingredients (flour, leavening, and salt) in increments alternating with the milk. A General Foods baking booklet of the 1930s described a quicker, easier way, often called the "muffin method," in its recipe for busy day cake, a yellow butter cake. By the 1940s the major flour mills were publishing many recipes for cakes mixed this way. But American women did not embrace the muffin method, likely because, working with a spoon or rotary egg beater, as most women then still did, they were unable to beat the batter sufficiently to achieve good results. The muffin method, now called the two-stage method (dry, then wet), is better known today due in large measure to Rose Levy Beranbaum's *The Cake Bible* (1988), a highly popular cookbook in which it was featured. Using electric mixers, Beranbaum's readers can be assured of success.

Faux butter cakes made with cooking oil and mixed muffin style appeared sporadically in cookbooks in the 1950s. Such recipes were not widely used, however, until the introduction of carrot cake in the 1960s. Carrot cake was an oil cake that blended the old American predilection for spiced, raisin-studded cake with the health consciousness of the late twentieth century. It was a tremendous hit. By the 1980s there were uncountable recipes for oil cakes in cookbooks. Many of these cakes were made with fruits or vegetables, such as applesauce, bananas, pumpkin, and chopped pineapple, but some were simply yellow cakes or chocolate cakes. These so-called dump-and-mix cakes not only were extremely quick and easy to make, but, just as important, they also were moist, at least if sufficient oil was used. Truly dry cake has never been liked. "Dump-and-mix" has not entirely conquered American cake baking. Rich pound cakes and Bundt cakes, which often are soaked in syrup to give them the sought-after moistness, are much in vogue today.

Cake is not really all that difficult, but decades of reliance on store-bought cakes and cake mixes have rendered American home bakers, particularly younger ones, helpless before even the simplest recipes.
[**See also** ADVERTISING COOKBOOKLETS AND RECIPES; BETTY CROCKER; CHILD, LYDIA MARIE; DESSERTS; FARMER, FANNIE; JELLY ROLLS; LADY FINGERS; LESLIE, ELIZA; SIMMONS, AMELIA.]

STEPHEN SCHMIDT

Calas

Calas are fried rice cakes, sugared for use as breakfast bread in New Orleans. They were made by African American women, who sold them from wooden bowls carried on top of their heads, mostly in the second half of the nineteenth century. Recipes and references at the end of that period by *The Picayune's Creole Cook Book* (1901) and *La Cuisine Creole* (1903) by Celestine Eustis are nostalgic in tone,

recording the street cry, "Bel calas tout chauds." The first printed recipe is for "callers" in the 1885 *Creole Cookery*, by the Christian Women's Exchange of New Orleans. That is, unless one counts two similar recipes for "rice puffs" in the 1847 *The Carolina Housewife*. Carolina-style rice cookery was taken up wholesale in Louisiana when rice began to be grown there in the 1880s.

The name, however, is almost certainly African, deriving from a series of cowpea-based fritters generally called "akara" or "akra" (sometimes "akla") in West Africa, and "acras" in much of the Afro-Caribbean diasporas, but "callas" in Curaçao. The beans are painstakingly soaked and the skins are rubbed off to give the fritters a pure white color. In Trinidad and Haiti, salt-cod fritters—also snow white—also are called acras. The lengthy description in the *Picayune's Creole Cook Book* noted that in former (perhaps slavery) times, the calas women pounded the rice in mortars, an African technique.

BIBLIOGRAPHY

Hess, Karen. *The Carolina Rice Kitchen: The African Connection*. Columbia: University of South Carolina Press, 1992.

MARK H. ZANGER

California

Nomadic groups of peoples originating in Asia first visited what is today California beginning about 12,000 B.C.E. These groups were followed by successive waves of peoples, some of whom settled permanently. Their diets reflected the local climate and ecology. In the northwestern California rain forest, salmon and trout were the major protein source, while groups living along the coast hunted sea mammals and gathered shellfish. For those living east of the Sierras, the staple food was the pine nut, especially the nut of the piñon pine. In the southern deserts, mesquite beans and the leaves of the century plant provided food. California Indians living along the lower Colorado River in southeastern California practiced agriculture, and raised corn, beans, and squashes.

Beginning in 1769, Spain supported the establishment of missions, military strongholds, and small civilian colonies from San Diego to north of San Francisco. These colonists brought with them many plants and domesticated animals from Mexico, including almonds, apples, apricots, beans, chilies, dates, figs, grapes, lentils, maize, olives, tomatoes, walnuts, and wheat, as well as chickens, cows, goats, sheep, and domesticated turkeys. Spanish settlements in California were isolated and remained small by the time Mexico gained its independence in 1821. The main foods consumed during California's Mexican period were beef, frijoles (beans), and tortillas.

Americanization

When war erupted between Mexico and the United States in 1846, American soldiers supported by local Mexicans quickly seized California. When gold was discovered in

A Sun-Maid raisin recipe booklet issued by the California Associated Raisin Co., Fresno, 1921.

1848, thousands of prospectors headed for California's gold mining regions. These groups overwhelmed the small population of California and they brought their own culinary ideas with them. As the gold rush brought new wealth to the region, San Francisco restaurants became increasingly elaborate. Meals were hearty, such as a breakfast composed of beefsteak, flapjacks, bacon, stewed apples, rolls, butter, and coffee. During the late nineteenth and early twentieth centuries, northern California's restaurants continued to improve. A restaurant guide published in 1914 lists French, Spanish, German, Italian, Mexican, Chinese, and Japanese establishments, as well as fish restaurants and hotel restaurants.

Lacking a similar infusion of wealth to spur rapid growth, southern California grew more slowly and its early culinary achievements were limited. With its population growing after the completion of railroads and the advent of Hollywood, Los Angeles also began to develop good restaurants, such as the Brown Derby, which opened in 1926, that catered to movie stars.

Agriculture and Canning

While gold was the reason immigrants poured into California in the late 1840s and 1850s, agriculture was the reason many remained. California's climate and soil were ideal for a variety of crops, particularly fruits,

A premium card distributed with Arbuckles' Ariosa Coffee in the late 1880s.

vegetables, and nuts, and for raising cattle, poultry, and sheep. With the completion of the transcontinental railroad in 1869, California became a net exporter of canned goods. With the invention of the refrigerated railroad car in the 1880s, fresh produce could be shipped east. Some of America's largest food companies, such as Hunt's, Del Monte, and Sunsweet, were launched in California. Sales increased threefold by World War II.

Salad plants grew easily in California. It is no surprise that California has been considered the "land of salads" since the late nineteenth century. With the development of early varieties of sturdy head lettuce in the 1890s, it became possible to ship California-grown lettuce across the nation. In the early 2000s, California and Arizona raise about 80 percent of America's lettuce. Olives became an important commercial crop by the end of the nineteenth century. At that time, Californians cured green olives in brine, creating a unique flavor. California has become the center for many other fruits and vegetables, such as artichokes, garlic, raisins, avocados, dates, almonds, walnuts, and pistachios. In the early 2000s, virtually the entire commercial crops of these plants came from California.

California Wine

Despite the rapid development of the wine industry in the state, there was little demand even in California, and the wine industry almost disappeared during Prohibition. This changed beginning in the 1930s, when winemakers began to call the wines by the varietal names of the grapes, such as Zinfandel and Cabernet Sauvignon. Some vintners earned excellent reputations, and by the 1980s California wines were competing successfully with the best French wines.

California Cookery

California's cuisine was influenced by foods, recipes, and traditions brought by Americans from the eastern United States. California's first cookbooks were written mainly by Americans from the eastern states. At the turn of the twentieth century, California restaurant chefs began writing cookbooks. Substantial tomes demonstrated a wide range of dishes from classical French to typical American food. California home cooking was also developing in the first half of the twentieth century, and dishes reveal a distinctive California cuisine in formation, as well as creations with Chinese, Japanese, and Mexican influences.

Of all the foreign influences on California's foodways, the Mexican contribution is the most important. Taco recipes appeared in California cookbooks beginning in 1914. During the twentieth century, a distinctive so-called Cal-Mex cookery evolved, which included guacamole and the burrito. During the twentieth century, ethnic food from around the world became common California fare as immigrant groups moved into the state, including Italians, Basques, Japanese, Chinese, Koreans, and more recently Southeast Asians.

Fast Food

By the mid-twentieth century, California food was ready to explode onto the national scene. One of the ways it did so was through fast food. Bob's Big Boy opened in Glendale during the 1930s. As Bob's Big Boy franchised its operation, it expanded throughout California and then across the United States. In 1951 a businessman named Robert O. Peterson opened the first Jack in the Box restaurant in San Diego. In the 1950s Glen Bell decided to experiment with the fast-food preparation of tacos. After several attempts, in 1962 he launched Taco Bell in Downey, California. The most important fast-food operation, however, was launched by Richard and Maurice McDonald, who opened a hamburger drive-in in San Bernardino, California, that applied assembly-line efficiency to the restaurant business. McDonald's has become a worldwide enterprise.

In 1971 Alice Waters launched her restaurant Chez Panisse in Berkeley. Waters served simple French food with a particular emphasis on the traditions of Provence. As time went on, she began experimenting with local ingredients. She changed her menu daily, focusing on the freshest and best seasonal ingredients. James Beard and many other food writers wrote about Alice Waters, raising Chez Panisse to national prominence. Chez Panisse served a number of dishes that came to be identified with California cuisine. Waters was one of the first American restaurateurs to partner with local farmers, ensuring them a market for the finest produce they could grow, and as the twenty-first century opened she had become an outspoken advocate of sustainable agriculture, a key factor in the continued success of California cuisine. Chefs from Chez Panisse went out on their own and made many additional contributions to American culinary life. Jeremiah Tower launched Stars in San Francisco. The former Chez Panisse chef Mark Miller launched the Coyote Café in Santa Fe, New Mexico.

Other innovators contributed to the California culinary revolution. Wolfgang Puck, Austrian-born, became famous as the chef at Ma Maison in Los Angeles in 1981. He subsequently opened Spago in Hollywood and had restaurants in many cities in the early 2000s. Puck became known for his California-style brick-oven pizza. During the 1990s Puck marketed frozen versions of his California-style pizzas as well as other gourmet specialties.

At the beginning of the twenty-first century, the California culinary style continued to embrace inventive cooking methods that showcased the highest quality fresh, seasonal, and native ingredients.

[See also ARTICHOKES; AVOCADOS; BROWN, HELEN EVANS; CELEBRITY CHEFS; CITRUS; DEL MONTE; DRIVE-INS; FAST FOOD; GRAPES; HUNT'S; LETTUCE; MCDONALD'S; MEXICAN AMERICAN FOOD; OLIVES; PINOLE; PUCK, WOLFGANG; TACO BELL; TOMATOES; WATERS, ALICE; WINE: CALIFORNIA WINES; WINERIES.]

BIBLIOGRAPHY

Balls, Edward K. *Early Uses of California Plants*. Berkeley and Los Angeles: University of California Press, 1962.

Kuh, Patric. *The Last Days of Haute Cuisine: America's Culinary Revolution*. New York: Viking, 2001.

Linsenmeyer, Helen Walker. *From Fingers to Finger Bowls: A Sprightly History of California Cooking*. San Diego: Union-Tribune Publishing, 1972.

Pinedo, Encarnación. *The Spanish Cook: Selected Recipes from El Cocinero Español*. Edited and translated by Dan Strehl. Pasadena, CA: Weather Bird, 1992.

Smith, Andrew F. "Tacos, Enchiladas and Refried Beans: The Invention of Mexican-American Cookery." In *Cultural and Historical Aspects of Foods*, edited by Mary Wallace Kelsey and ZoeAnn Holmes, 183–203. Corvallis: Oregon State University, 1999.

Strehl, Dan, ed. *One Hundred Books on California Food and Wine*. Los Angeles: Book Collectors, 1990.

ANDREW F. SMITH

California Pizza Kitchen

In 1985, Rick Rosenfield and Larry Flax opened the first California Pizza Kitchen (CPK) in Beverly Hills, California. Rosenfield and Flax created unusual pizzas with toppings such as BBQ Chicken, which differed greatly from traditional Italian American pizza. Its "lite" toppings were attractive to health-conscious consumers. The CPK also serves pasta, salads, sandwiches, soups, and desserts. As of 2004, there were 156 CPK full-service restaurants. In addition, the company created smaller "ASAP" outlets, which offer a pared-down menu in a fast-food setting. CPK pizzas are also available frozen in many supermarkets. CPK does not franchise in the United States, but it does internationally. The CPK has released two cookbooks; the profits generated are given to charities.

BIBLIOGRAPHY

Flax, Larry, and Rick Rosenfield, *The California Pizza Kitchen Cookbook*. New York: Macmillan 1996.

Jakle, John A., and Keith A. Sculle. *Fast Food: Roadside Restaurants in the Automobile Age*. Baltimore: Johns Hopkins University Press, 1999.

ANDREW F. SMITH

Camas Root

Two species of camas, the common *Camassia quamash* and the less common *C. leichtlinii*, grew profusely in the grassy meadows of the Pacific Northwest. Explorers such as Meriwether Lewis noted that the bulb resembled an onion and had a sweet taste. A member of the lily family, the edible camas is an herbaceous perennial with large, glutinous bulbs covered with a membranous brown skin. It was a staple food of the Indians, who considered camas plots valuable personal property.

To distinguish the blue-flowering edible camas from the white-flowering death camas, which grows in the same areas, Indian women harvested the bulbs during or soon after flowering. A three- or four-foot-long hardwood stick, sharpened at one end and fitted with an antler horn handle, was their digging tool. After gathering a large quantity, the women layered a rock-lined steaming pit with branches of such plants as salal, moss, camas, and dirt. Water poured into a hole furnished the steam. When cooked, the camas was soft, blackish, and sweet. It could then be molded into cakes and baked in the sun or on heated stones to preserve it for later use. This prolonged cooking process, one to three days depending on the quantity, breaks down the long-chain sugar inulin and makes the bulbs more digestible. A communal feast celebrated the camas harvest.

[See also NATIVE AMERICAN FOODS; PACIFIC NORTHWEST.]

BIBLIOGRAPHY

Pojar, Jim, and Andy MacKinnon. *Plants of the Pacific Northwest Coast: Washington, Oregon, British Columbia, and Alaska*. Edmonton, Canada: Lone Pine, 1994.

Thwaites, Reuben Gold, ed. *Original Journals of the Lewis and Clark Expedition 1804–1806*. Reprint, New York: Antiquarian, 1959.

JACQUELINE BLOCK WILLIAMS

Campbell, Tunis G.

In *The Philadelphia Negro*, W. E. B. Du Bois praised the African American caterers of the 1840s, who "aided the Abolition cause to no little degree." Although the caterers assumed a subservient manner, they were independent businesspeople of means who led their community toward liberation. No individual more successfully embodied this duality than Tunis Campbell (1805-1891). Born in New Jersey, and educated in a Long Island Episcopal school where he was the only black student, Campbell became an African Methodist Episcopal Church elder, headwaiter, temperance preacher, baker, abolitionist, and author of the second cookbook published by an African American; he was elected leader of three predominantly African American Georgia counties for eleven years. In the 1840s he had preached equality and self-help on lonely New York street corners, and he went on to organize among newly freed slaves on the Carolina Sea Islands in the 1860s and in Georgia into the late 1870s.

Campbell's *Hotel Keepers, Head Waiters, and Housekeepers' Guide* was published in Boston in 1848, with supporting letters from the owners of Howard's Hotel in New York and the Adams House Hotel in Boston. In it, he honored the tradition—begun by Robert Roberts—of teaching African American servants how to succeed through polite service. At the same time, he outlined a style of dining room organization on military models, to make "an entire change in hotel-keeping and waiting." In light of Campbell's career, it is impossible to overlook such comments as, "Men should be instructed to hold themselves erect, and upon a squad drill they should be taught a regular step, the same as a military company."

Recipes fill more than half the book to enable waiters to increase their versatility and employability. Most of the recipes are for the kinds of game dishes and sauces served in early American hotels; however, a dish of stewed gizzards and the opening recipe for cornbread—with carefully detailed proportions that refute the stereotype of African American cooks never measuring—may be the first instances of published recipes for African American food, to be used by African Americans.

During the Civil War, Campbell was an active partner in Davies and Company, Unfermented Bread Manufacturers in what is now Manhattan's East Village. At that time temperance activists were concerned about the yeast and alcohol in conventional bread. Temperance was part of a group of reform issues that included the abolition of slavery and advocacy for women's suffrage. Unable to enlist in the army, Campbell eventually secured a commission to organize freed slaves to farm, attend school, and serve in militia companies in the Carolina Sea Islands.

Campbell's work continued under military auspices after the Civil War. He eventually had to relocate hundreds of people to the Georgia mainland, where he was able to register them to vote, secure land titles, and rebuild schools and churches. He was elected to the Georgia constitutional convention, state senate, state legislature, and more enduringly as justice of the peace in three counties. He lobbied in Washington for congressional reconstruction, the Fifteenth Amendment, and the Ku Klux Klan Act.

In 1876 white authorities imprisoned him over malpractice in two county legal cases in which he had sentenced white offenders, and he served a year in prison on a chain gang. He was made to eat hard corn cakes and undercooked bacon but later was able to obtain better meals from an Atlanta Hotel and cakes from his wife. He left Georgia, but he returned briefly to aid the losing Republican cause in the 1882 election. He died in Boston in 1891.

[See also COOKBOOKS AND MANUSCRIPTS: To 1860; DINING ROOMS AND MEAL SERVICE; HOTEL DINING ROOMS; TEMPERANCE.]

BIBLIOGRAPHY

Campbell, Tunis Gulic. *Freedom's Shore: Tunis Campbell and the Georgia Freedmen*. Athens: University of Georgia Press, 1986.

Campbell, Tunis Gulic. *Hotel Keepers, Head Waiters, and Housekeepers' Guide*. Boston: Coolidge and Wiley, 1848.

Campbell, Tunis Gulic. *Sufferings of the Rev. T. G. Campbell and Family in Georgia*. Washington, DC: Enterprise, 1877. Excerpted in *First Person Past: American Autobiographies*, edited by Marian J. Morton and Russell Duncan, vol. 2. St. James, NY: Brandywine, 1994.

MARK H. ZANGER

Campbell Soup Company

Joseph Campbell, born in Bridgeton, New Jersey, joined Abraham Anderson as a partner in a tomato canning and preserving firm established in Camden in 1869. Beginning with canned peas and asparagus, the two men added many other kinds of canned and preserved foods. One of their more important products was the beefsteak tomato, which they aggressively advertised using the trademarked image of a gigantic tomato carried on the shoulders of two men. In 1876 Anderson and Campbell received a medal for their preserving at the Philadelphia Centennial Exposition. When difficulties arose between the partners, Campbell bought Anderson out and acquired new partners. One was Arthur Dorrance from Bristol, Pennsylvania. In 1891 Dorrance and Campbell incorporated in

New Jersey as the Joseph Campbell Preserve Company, which canned and bottled preserves, jellies, meats, fruits, sauces, vegetables, and other goods.

The company grew and flourished, even in the five depression years from 1892 to 1897. It advertised its canned goods as the "best in the world." If a local grocer did not stock Campbell's products, the company supplied samples directly to the consumers in the area, putting pressure on local retailers. By the 1890s the company produced more than two hundred products, one of which was canned ready-to-serve soup. Arthur Dorrance's son, John T. Dorrance, a chemist trained in Germany, was hired at Campbell's Camden laboratory in 1896 to improve the quality of soup. He concentrated on producing condensed soups. Within a few months of his arrival, he had come up with five condensed soups: tomato, chicken, oxtail, vegetable, and consommé, which were released in 1897.

The following year the company adopted the famous red-and-white labels. The uncluttered design prominently displayed the name of each Campbell's condensed soup. The condensed soups were successful, and Dorrance expanded his work, conducting experiments to determine how best to maintain uniformity of flavor and how to reduce waste caused by can spoilage. In the year that John Dorrance arrived at Campbell, the company had lost sixty thousand dollars. One year after the introduction of condensed soups, the firm became profitable. The soup division expanded, while the other sectors declined in importance. Most of Campbell's other products were phased out, and the major effort focused on condensed soup. In recognition of its importance, the company changed its name in 1921 to the Campbell Soup Company.

Initially, Campbell soup retailed for ten cents a can. It was sold to retailers at the same price, leveling the playing field for smaller operations that did not warrant volume discounts. The profit generated for the Campbell Soup Company was less than a quarter-cent per can. For larger stores, it meant that Campbell soup was a loss leader; that is, stores sold it at a loss to bring in customers who bought other items at a profit for the store. Campbell raised the price of a can to twelve cents in 1925—a price that remained constant for decades.

Advertising

There were many reasons for Campbell's rapid and consistent growth, but, most important, the company knew how to advertise and market its products. Newspaper and streetcar advertising were initially used, followed by magazine advertising, which gave Campbell's much broader exposure. Its major advertising image was the Campbell Kids, created by Grace Drayton in 1904. The company advertised extensively in newspapers and magazines and on radio and television when the Depression hit in the 1930s, and the company's advertising budget shot up to $3.5 million. During the 1930s the Campbell Soup Company introduced the jingle "M'm! M'm! Good!"

Another very effective way of advertising was through regular offerings of cookery pamphlets and cookbooks emphasizing how soups could be enhanced or used as ingredients to make other dishes. Campbell's published its first advertising cookbooklet in 1910 and has subsequently put out dozens of such items. The recipes that appear in these booklets frequently were reprinted in newspapers, magazines, and cookbooks. In 1994 the Campbell Soup Company was inducted into the Marketing Hall of Fame. It is one of the leading advertisers in the United States.

Globalization and Diversification

The Depression had profound effects on Campbell. While the company had exported its soup abroad for decades, many countries put up protectionist barriers to help local manufacturers during the Depression. For instance, Canada protected its manufacturers from American competition by increasing the import rate for duties on canned goods in 1930. Campbell responded by organizing a subsidiary in Canada, the Campbell Soup Company Ltd. For similar reasons, Campbell's Soups Limited was organized in the United Kingdom in 1933 and quickly became one of the United Kingdom's greatest suppliers of tomato and other soups. These first subsidiaries in other countries were followed after World War II by many more. In addition, the Campbell Soup Company has acquired companies in other countries, such as Liebig in France and Erasco in Germany.

The Campbell Soup Company's first major diversification was into tomato juice, which reversed the sole focus on soup making. Shortly after World War II ended, the company made another logical addition when it purchased V8 juice from Standard Brand. Campbell has been diversifying ever since. Its other American food brands are Swanson, V8 and V8 Splash juices, Pace Mexican sauces, Prego pasta sauces, Godiva chocolates, and Pepperidge Farm, which makes Gold Fish crackers and Chocolate Chunk and Milano cookies. Although the company is still headquartered in Camden, it closed its manufacturing operation at that site in 1900. Its main tomato-processing operations are located in California. Soup remains Campbell's flagship product, and the company is still the largest soup manufacturer in the world.

[See also ADVERTISING; CAMPBELL SOUP KIDS.]

BIBLIOGRAPHY

Collins, Douglas. *America's Favorite Food: The Story of Campbell Soup Company.* New York: Abrams, 1994.

Packaged Facts. *The International Soup Market.* New York: Packaged Facts, 1996.

Smith, Andrew F. *Souper Tomatoes: The Story of America's Favorite Food.* New Brunswick, NJ: Rutgers University Press, 2000.

ANDREW F. SMITH

Campbell Soup Kids

During the early twentieth century the Joseph Campbell Company, forerunner to the Campbell Soup Company, began to advertise its products nationally. They were advised to market their products to women through "child appeal." Theodore Wiederseim, an employee of Ketterlineus Lithographic Manufacturing Company in Philadelphia, was asked for suggestions. He recommended the services of his wife, Grace Drayton, a staff artist for the *Philadelphia Press and Evening Journal* and a freelance illustrator of children's books. She had been sketching little round-faced, rosy-cheeked children for years, and she adapted them for the company's purposes, creating what would become known as the Campbell Kids.

The Campbell Kids first appeared on streetcar advertisements in early 1905. Along with the illustrations appeared light and sometimes humorous advertising verses. The Kids were so successful that the company used them in black-and-white magazine advertisements in the September 1905 issue of *Ladies' Home Journal* and later in the *Saturday Evening Post.* The company added a touch of red to their artwork in 1906 and commenced full-color advertising in the 1920s.

The Campbell Kids were first sold as dolls in 1910, under license to the E. I. Horseman Company. They were subsequently marketed by other companies, including Montgomery Ward and Sears. Dolls were one of the first of numerous products to bear the Campbell Kids' likeness: the Kids appeared on balloons, bells, bridge tallies, calendars, canisters, cards, clips, clocks, cookbooklets, cookie jars, cutting boards, dolls, games, can covers, decals, die-cuts, dishes, figurines, hats, jewelry, lamps, lapel buttons, lunch boxes, markers, mugs, music boxes, napkins, ornaments, pails, playing cards, pins, planes, plaques, plates, posters, puzzles, salt and pepper shakers, silverware, T-shirts, thermometers, thermoses, timers, toys, waste cans, watches, and water bottles, to name a few.

Until 1921 the Kids appeared in almost every Campbell advertisement. Thereafter, they were downplayed in Campbell's advertising. They appeared in fewer than 10 percent of the company's ads by the early 1950s. In 1954 this trend was reversed as Campbell's commemorated the Kids' fiftieth birthday. Campbell's licensed thirty-four companies to manufacture Kids products, which included beach balls, doll carriages, rubber stamps, paper napkins, toy vacuum cleaners, wallpaper, and yo-yo's. This campaign commenced with a seven-page advertisement in a November 1954 issue of *Life* magazine and climaxed with the release of over half a million Campbell Kids dolls. Simultaneously, the Campbell Kids were featured on television promotions.

Over the years, the Campbell Kids were updated and modernized. Their clothes kept pace with changing fashion. The thousands of products featuring the Campbell Kids are eagerly sought by collectors, and some are quite valuable. By any standard, the Campbell Kids are one of the most successful American advertising icons.

[**See also** ADVERTISING; CAMPBELL SOUP COMPANY.]

BIBLIOGRAPHY

Collins, Douglas. *America's Favorite Food: The Story of Campbell Soup Company.* New York: Abrams, 1994.

Smith, Andrew F. *Souper Tomatoes: The Story of America's Favorite Food.* New Brunswick, NJ: Rutgers University Press, 2000.

ANDREW F. SMITH

Canapé

Canapés are bite-size items served as an appetizer or hors d'oeuvre. They usually consist of a small piece of bread (plain or toasted), a cracker, or a diminutive pastry shape topped with something savory, such as caviar, cheese, meat, poultry, or seafood, often in the form of a creamy spread. Canapés originated in France (the word, meaning a sofa or couch, suggests the way the topping rests on the base), and they commonly appear in nineteenth-century French cookbooks. British cookbooks published recipes for them by the end of that century, and American cookbooks included them by the early twentieth century.

Canapés are typically passed on a tray before a meal or at cocktail parties, and they can be easily eaten in one or two bites by guests who are standing and holding drinks. In the United States, canapés (along with cocktail parties) became popular during the 1920s and 1930s, when dozens of books were published with recipes for them. The first cookbook that focused solely on canapés was Rachel Bell Maiden's *The Canapé Book* (1934). One of the best-known cookbooks featuring canapé recipes is James Beard's first book, *Hors d'Oeuvre and Canapés, with a Key to the Cocktail Party* (1940).

BIBLIOGRAPHY

Beard, James. *Hors d'Oeuvre and Canapés, with a Key to the Cocktail Party.* New York: Barrows, 1940.

Maiden, Rachel Bell. *The Canapé Book.* New York: Appleton-Century, 1934.

ANDREW F. SMITH

Candy and Candy Bars

Sweetmeats—comfits, candied nuts, preserved fruits—came to America in the eighteenth century, imported from Britain and France. "Sugar-candy" was first advertised in the 1730s by refiners who also sold other grades of sugar. A rarity in the eighteenth century, sugar was considered a luxury until the 1830s, when it became cheaper to produce and distribute.

A promotional booklet issued by the Franklin Sugar Refining Company shows several boxes of their product in an illustration of a taffy pull.

Druggists used hard sugar to coat medicines; confectioners copied their formula, selling the hard candy lozenges without the medicine. In 1847, the English firm Joseph Fry & Son developed the first true edible solid chocolate. In 1879, Henri Nestlé produced the first milk chocolate bar and Rudolphe Lindt vastly improved the texture of solid chocolate. Before the end of the nineteenth century, solid chocolates were produced mostly by skilled French immigrants for a luxury market; most chocolate was available only as a pulverized powder, incorporated in baked goods or reconstituted with sugar and warm milk to make a beverage.

Nineteenth-century reformers responded negatively to candy's increasing popularity. They claimed that candies were adulterated and would lead children to more harmful vices such as drinking as smoking. They blamed mothers, too, for both indulging in too many sweets themselves and also for weakening their children by appeasing them with sweets.

By the end of the nineteenth century sweets had become ubiquitous in the American diet. The Stephen F. Whitman Company, founded in 1842, was the first to manufacture solid chocolates on a large scale. Other similar brands included Brach's (specializing in caramels and founded in 1904) and Fannie May Candies (established in 1920). In 1896 Austrian immigrant Leo Hirshfield first made Tootsie Rolls (named after his daughter's nickname). David L. Clark developed his Clark Bar as a confection for soldiers during World War I. With partners, Peter Paul Halajian founded Peter Paul candies in 1919, producing the Mounds Bar beginning in 1922 and the Almond Joy in 1948. Trade organizations such as the National Confectioners Association, Chocolate Manufacturers Association, and Retail Confectioners International were also founded to promote the production and distribution of confectionery.

Milton Hershey (1857–1945) was the most successful candy maker in the country. In 1893, Hershey installed state-of-the-art chocolate-making equipment in his Lancaster, Pennsylvania, factory and began manufacturing affordable chocolates, the first person to do so. Hershey's success was his production of milk chocolates, whose mild flavor was more palatable to the American public, especially children. The Hershey's Chocolate Bar became the most popular candy in America. Although its size fluctuated over time, it cost five cents until 1970.

Hershey's chief competitor in the twentieth century was the Mars Company (founded by Frank Mars). Among other products, Mars manufactured the Milky Way Bar (introduced to the market in 1924), Snickers (1930), 3 Musketeers (1932), and the Mars Bar (1936). Frank Mars's son Forrest E. Mars Sr. founded M&M Ltd. in 1940, and manufactured M&M's—candy-coated chocolate bits (1941), and Peanut M&M's (1954). Dominating the American chocolate industry, Mars and Hershey's together controlled 75 percent of the retail candy market by the late twentieth century. The Swiss company Nestlé Inc. introduced its Milk Chocolate Bar and one with almonds in 1919, the Crunch bar in 1938, and its $100,000 Bar in 1966.

Other sweet treats also gained popularity at the end of the nineteenth century. Chewing gum was first popularized by William Wrigley Jr., who introduced Juicy Fruit gum and Wrigley's Spearmint gum in 1893. Cracker Jack, a mixture of caramel-coated popcorn and peanuts, also first appeared in 1893, marketed by F. W. Rueckheim; toy prizes were included in the boxes from 1912 on. Two other popular coated candies were Goobers, chocolate-coated peanuts (1925), and Raisinets, chocolate-covered raisins (1927). The first Life-Savers appeared in 1912 and starting in 1924 were offered in fruit flavors. Red Hots,

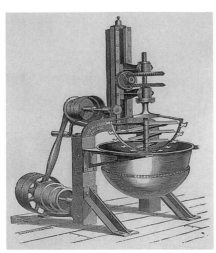

An illustration of a candy mixer from the Thomas Mills and Bro. catalog, 1930.

the candy industry to generate revenue. Candy Day, renamed Sweetest Day, was invented by the National Confectioners' Association around 1916; it continues to be celebrated, mostly in the Midwest.

By the twentieth century candy was so essential to the American life and diet that chocolate bars comprised part of soldiers' rations during the two World Wars. It also became an integral part of American leisure pursuits. Cotton candy was consumed at baseball games and local fairs. Confections such as Jujubes, Junior Mints, and M&M's were eaten during movies at the cinema. Candy also became an important part of merchandising. Children's products such as baseball cards came packaged with sticks of bubble gum. Saccharine products such as cereal were often packaged with small premiums meant for children.

Because they rely so heavily on novelty, confections express contemporary fads and interests. Candy containers are often shaped as popular consumer commodities. In addition, candies count as important product tie-ins for television and movies. Candy cigars and cigarettes, once wildly popular among children, were censored in the late twentieth century due to antitobacco campaigns, and were only available from companies producing "nostalgia" candies. The diet fads of the late twentieth century inspired more "healthy" sweet alternatives, such as the Granola Bar, introduced in 1975 by General Mills, and "power bars," supposedly high-energy fitness bars popular since the 1990s. Boutique confections—fancy hand-made chocolates and hard candies—also became popular and were marketed in upscale urban areas, while traditionally expensive chocolates such

introduced in 1932, were flavored with cinnamon and spicy hot. Also popular were the sweet-and-sour Smarties (1949) and SweeTarts (1963). And Pez, short for pfefferminz (peppermint), with its novel plastic dispenser, was invented in 1927 by the Austrian Eduard Haas.

Popular gelatin-based sugar candies included jelly beans, which had become an Easter staple by the 1930s. Henry Heide Inc. first marketed Jujubes and Jujyfruits in 1920; Just Born Inc. introduced Mike and Ike, fruit-flavored jellied capsules, in 1940, and Hot Tamales in 1950. Jelly Belly Jelly Beans, considered "gourmet" candies and first introduced in 1976 by the Herman Goelitz Candy Company, came in many flavors from the sweet to the savory, and could be combined to make more complex flavors. Gummy bears and gummy worms, popular beginning in the 1980s, were also manufactured by the Goelitz Company.

Holidays generate the most candy sales, and Halloween is the largest candy holiday. The National Confectioners Association estimated 2003 sales from trick-or-treat candy to be about $6.9 billion, even though parental anxieties about food tampering remain. Easter is the second largest candy holiday. Just Born Inc. founded in 1923, began making sugar-coated, chick-shaped marshmallow "Peeps" in 1953. The quintessential winter holiday treat, candy canes, are thought to have first decorated American Christmas trees in the late 1840s; they became striped with red and white in the 1920s. Edible solid chocolates in fancy boxes became the staple Valentine's Day gift beginning in the last quarter of the nineteenth century. One Valentine's candy, "conversation hearts," produced by the New England Confectionery Company (NECCO) beginning in 1866, bore printed expressions such as "Be true," "Be kind," and "Be mine." The National Confectioners Association estimated that 36 million heart-shaped boxes of chocolates would be sold for Valentine's Day in 2003. Other holidays were wholly devised by

Penny Candy

Penny candies, the first goods children spent their own money on, were also the first confections to reach a mass audience in America. By the late 1830s sugar's increasing availability and decreasing price enabled confectioners to profitably produce sugary drops without the medicine typically found in druggists' stocks. Unlike exclusive confections marketed to elite adults, these "penny candies," often sold ten to a dozen for a penny, were aimed at the palates of working-class children, for whom a penny was in reach. By the early 1850s individual candy men could readily obtain the machinery and raw materials necessary to profit from making batches of candy in greater quantities. Revolving steam pans enabled boiling sugar and water to reach the correct molten consistency without burning, and candy "presses" shaped and separated the saccharine masses into a marketable product. Because they did not need to be as skilled as fine confectioners, candy men could therefore run successful, if modest, neighborhood businesses.

Penny candies introduced nineteenth-century children to the world of consumption by teaching them how to be good future consumers; they were the bane of the period's reformers, who feared that a taste for candy inculcated in the young would lead to intemperate behavior as adults. Brightly colored and often displayed in shop windows in glass jars, penny candies (also called "toys") often came in the shape of familiar consumer products, such as shoes, boats, hats, and purses; confectioners also offered candies shaped as cigars, cigarettes, and even gin bottles.

From the beginning, candy store operators, who depended on narrow profit margins and a capricious audience, relied on novelty to entice their customers, presaging later marketing techniques aimed at children. "Prize packages," popular after the Civil War, sensationally promised an often chintzy item in every box of candy, a technique used in the twentieth century to sell Cracker Jack and sugar-laden cereals. Cardboard and glass candy containers—themselves shaped like popular material objects—also enticed children but were often too costly for the poor.

By the early 1870s penny candies were ubiquitous, appearing not only in candy shops but in tobacco stores and five-and-dimes, and at newsstands and movie theaters. By the mid-twentieth century the penny candy as such no longer existed except as more expensive nostalgic root beer barrels, cinnamon-hot fireballs, and flavored candy sticks. But later candy manufacturers continued to use marketing techniques established in the nineteenth century. Sweets aimed at young people continued to stress novelty; some candies featured tie-ins to the mass media, referencing popular cartoon characters or action heroes.

Like their nineteenth-century counterparts, candies of the late twentieth century also tapped into children's desire to be more adult and often came in forms imitating desirable adult goods. Bright candy lipstick and jewelry, for example, allowed little girls to imitate their mothers. And cigarettes made of chocolate and bubble gum were popular throughout the twentieth century until concern about tobacco effectively removed them from store shelves.

BIBLIOGRAPHY

Woloson, Wendy. *Refined Tastes: Sugar, Consumers, and Confectionery in Nineteenth-Century America.* Baltimore: Johns Hopkins University Press, 2002.

WENDY A. WOLOSON

as Godiva began being mass distributed to department stores and local shops. The subject of popular songs, books, and even films, candy has become a cultural icon.

By the end of the twentieth century, most smaller candy companies had been bought by larger ones. Hershey Foods Corp. purchased Peter Paul in 1988 and Leaf North America in 1996, gaining ownership of Good & Plenty, Jolly Rancher, Whoppers, Milk Duds, Heath, and PayDay. In the late 1990s it bought out the longtime family-owned Henry Heide Inc., taking over Jujyfruits and Wunderbeans in the process. Hershey and other confectionery companies also established subsidiaries selling dog food, pasta, and rice, among other products. And according to the U.S. Department of Commerce, Americans consumed $17.8 billion worth of confections (some 6.2 billion pounds) in 2004.

BIBLIOGRAPHY

Brenner, Joël Glenn. *The Emperors of Chocolate: Inside the Secret World of Hershey and Mars.* New York: Random House, 1999.

Broekel, Ray. *The Great American Candy Bar Book.* Boston: Houghton Mifflin, 1982.

Coe, Sophie D., and Michael D. Coe. *The True History of Chocolate.* London: Thames and Hudson, 1996.

Lopez, Ruth. *Chocolate: The Nature of Indulgence.* New York: Abrams, 2002.

National Confectioners Association. www.candy-usa.org.

Schmidt, Leigh Eric. *Consumer Rites: The Buying and Selling of American Holidays.* Princeton: Princeton University Press, 1995.

Woloson, Wendy. *Refined Tastes: Sugar, Consumers, and Confectionery in Nineteenth-Century America.* Baltimore: Johns Hopkins University Press, 2002.

WENDY WOLOSON

Canning and Bottling

The marvels of modern canning and bottling operations are the result of millennia of humankind's efforts. From prehistoric times, humans have tackled the problem of how to preserve surplus foods for use in times of want. Numerous ways were developed, from drying food in the sun to salting food in containers. Other early preserving techniques included smoking, sugaring, and freezing food in ice or snow. These techniques were employed for hundreds of years with little alteration.

Home-canned fruits and vegetables, Box Elder County, Utah, 1940.

Home Canning

Food preservation was not new when Mason invented his "fruit jar" (1858), but it had never achieved the relatively safe and durable vacuum seals of home canning. Incidentally timed to coincide with the new availability of inexpensive sugar, it offered average homemakers their first opportunity (economically) to put up a year's supply of summer products for winter use. In addition, the process was simplified by the use of the popular cookstove and such adjunct implements as canning kettles, racks, wide-mouth funnels, and lifters.

Home canning surpassed the earlier preservation methods of salting or drying. Out-of-season fruits and vegetables, far less expensive than comparable commercially canned foods, could be eaten with much greater frequency and brought great improvement in nutritional health.

Home-canned foods were the closest thing to fresh fruits and vegetables, which were not yet distributed nationally out of season. Year-round meals were more likely to include additional vegetable courses, sweet desserts of fruits in their syrups, cakes and pies with berry fillings, and flavored beverages, homemade beers, and soda pop. In addition, seasonally butchered or hunted meats and fish were sometimes put up in large canning jars, albeit most frequently on farms.

"Putting up" became a major concern of women, whether on farms or in towns or cities. Preserved foods were judged at local fairs for color, texture, (sometimes flavor), and pleasing arrangements within the jar, and good results earned high status for a woman. Cookbooks began to include entire chapters on home canning, and eventually the process became the sole focus of such works as Mrs. Rorer's *Canning and Preserving* (1887).

The large job of home canning required expanded spaces in which to do the work. Summer kitchens were now built to accommodate the heavy summer and fall undertakings, while at the same time distancing the increased and excessive heat from the house. Some were added to the house itself as a second kitchen, but sometimes they were little more than free-standing lean-tos in the yard. They were fueled by means of cast-iron cookstoves, which were simply moved from the winter kitchen, and sometimes by oil stoves, small kerosene burners that were intended to handle canning demands.

ALICE ROSS

This state of affairs changed in the early nineteenth century. In 1795 the French government offered a prize for an improved method of conserving food. Nicolas Appert began experiments on different methods of preserving food. The best technique, he concluded, was boiling and sealing food in a container without air. Appert packed fruits, vegetables, meats, and other foods into wide-mouthed glass bottles and then heated them for various lengths of time in a bath of boiling water. The openings were sealed with a stopper made of cork tightly wired to the bottle. He wrote up his conclusions, which were published in France in 1810 and two years later in England and the United States as *The Art of Preserving.* The British built on Appert's methods, choosing tin for containers rather than glass.

American Bottles and Cans

In the United States commercial bottling operations did not commence until the arrival of experienced English canners. The first was William Underwood, an English pickler, who landed in New Orleans in 1817 and decided to trek across the country on foot. Two years later he arrived in Boston, where he launched the firm later known as the William Underwood Company. Underwood canned luxury goods and ships' provisions, including oysters, lobsters, fish, meats, soups, fruits, and a few vegetables. By 1821 he was shipping plums, quinces, currants, barberries, cranberries, pickles, ketchup, sauces, jellies, and jams packed in glass to South America. During the next thirty years many small bottling factories were launched from Maryland to Maine, but the three major canning areas were Baltimore, New York, and Portland, Maine.

Another early packing firm was operated by Ezra Daggett and his son-in-law, Thomas Kensett, who packed salmon, lobsters, and oysters in New York City starting in about 1819. In 1825 they applied for a tin canning patent, the first in the United States. Canning with tin was difficult and expensive. These operations were labor intensive, for everything was made entirely by hand. The food was placed in the can, and the lid was soldered in place. The can was then placed in a water bath for five hours, a hole in the lid providing a means for the steam to escape. When the bath was finished, the hole was soldered, and the can was sealed airtight. These techniques were not well understood, and problems emerged, including bursting cans and contamination, which often resulted in illness or death to those consuming the contents. The American public was leery both of the high price of canned goods and their high spoilage rates and health threats. As canning in tin and bottling in glass were two very different processes, requiring different machinery and raw materials, specialization developed by the mid-nineteenth century.

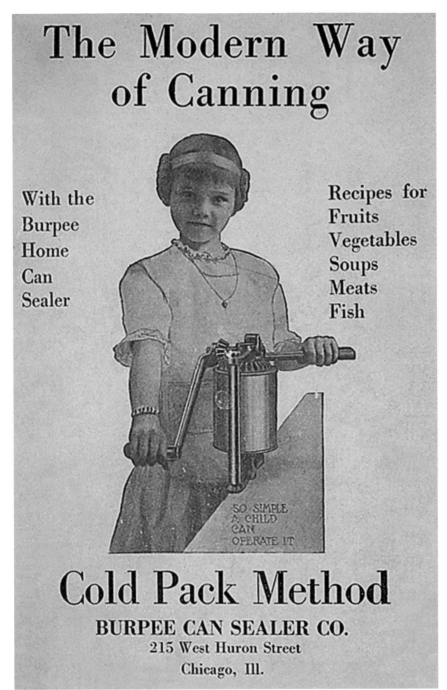

The Modern Way
of Canning

With the
Burpee
Home
Can
Sealer

Recipes for
Fruits
Vegetables
Soups
Meats
Fish

SO SIMPLE
A CHILD
CAN
OPERATE IT

Cold Pack Method

BURPEE CAN SEALER CO.
215 West Huron Street
Chicago, Ill.

Canning instructions and recipes issued by the Burpee Can Sealer Company.

Civil War

By 1860 canned goods were an expensive specialty item consumed by few Americans. In the following year American canners greatly sped up the processing of food by heating cans in a solution of calcium chloride and reducing the time the cans remained in a water bath. This and other innovations caused the canning industry to leap ahead during the Civil War. The federal government began purchasing small amounts of canned goods in 1863; this action primed the pump, and canneries sprang up across northern states. The quality of these operations improved, as did their efficiency, which lowered costs. The result was that millions of Americans were exposed to canned goods, including Confederate soldiers, who often raided Union supply trains. The demand for canned goods grew after the war, and the upward spiral continued. Where 5 million cans were put up annually in 1860, the figure was six times greater a decade later. By the 1880s canned foods were commonly available in most grocery stores throughout the nation.

Home Canning

At the end of the summer many farmers and gardeners found themselves with a glut of fruit and vegetables. Canning with tin was difficult for individuals, and bottling was complicated and often unsuccessful. The need for easier means of preserving food in the home led to new techniques and devices for home canning. One important innovation was devised by New Jersey–born John L. Mason, who had set up a metalworking shop in New York. On November 30, 1858, Mason patented the glass jar and zinc lid. The screw-on lid pressed down on a rubber gasket sealed out air. It greatly simplified home bottling and made it possible to reuse glass jars, thus revolutionizing fruit and vegetable preservation in the home. As the jars were relatively inexpensive, their popularity soared, and by 1860 mason jars were shipped throughout the United States. Home canning was important through the mid-twentieth century. Because of the low cost of canned and bottled commercial foods and a busy urban way of life, most Americans have forgotten the art of home canning.

Canning and Bottling Revolutions

Canning technology took a major leap forward with the invention of the "sanitary can" in the early twentieth century. It built on previous inventions, such as the double-seamed cans first manufactured in 1859, and was used in Europe for canning food shortly thereafter. A thick rubber gasket similar to those used on mason jars was placed between the end and body, and the end was crimped to the body by rollers. This method was demonstrated at the Columbian Exposition in 1893 in Chicago. But the rubber ring was cumbersome and costly. Charles M. Ams lined the edge of the can end with rubber cement, greatly reducing the amount of rubber used and simplifying the sealing process. It was dubbed the "sanitary can." Ams continued to improve the process and by 1903 had developed a line of commercial machines that revolutionized the canning industry.

In the late nineteenth century bottling manufacturers faced serious problems related to glass and capping technology: heating filled bottles to temperatures above 200°F resulted in enormous breakage, but if the contents were not heated above this temperature, they were not sterilized. The contents had to be heated first and then poured into the bottles and corked. As the contents cooled, the corks were unable to maintain the vacuum. Air was sucked through and around the cork, and spoilage commenced. In the early part of the twentieth century researchers developed improved glass bottles that were shatterproof at higher temperatures. Researchers also concluded that vacuum-sealed bottles were absolutely essential. Hence, corks were covered with a metal cap that effectively sealed the bottle from contact with outside air. This type of bottle was especially important in the soda industry. Another major advance was the development of the screw cap, which enabled consumers to open bottles and reseal them for subsequent use.

Challenges and Opportunities

Despite the spectacular success and rapid expansion of the bottling and canning industry, all was not well in the food-packaging world. Since the industry's inception, contamination and adulteration had been alarming problems. These afflictions became more menacing and more visible as the industry expanded. Fly-by-night manufacturers filled cans and bottles with low-quality products or toxic ingredients, and illness and death resulted. These abuses spurred on the movement to enact pure food laws in states and attempt to pass legislation in Congress beginning in 1876. Federal efforts were not successful until June 1906, when Congress passed the Pure Food and Drug Act. While passage of the act did not immediately end all abuses, serious problems sharply declined subsequently.

By 1900 most middle-sized communities in America were home to one or more canners. The Pure Food and Drug Act required food processors engaged in interstate trade to adhere strictly to proper health and safety procedures. This made it more difficult for small and medium-sized canners to survive, and many closed or were bought out. Slowly the canning and bottling industry has been consolidating into large conglomerates, such as the H. J. Heinz Company, Campbell Soup, Del Monte, Kraft Foods, PepsiCo, and Coca-Cola. Smaller canners and bottlers have survived, and many thrive in niche or regional markets.

Larger canning operations have advantages of scale. They can invest in state-of-the-art equipment, ensuring maximum efficiency at the lowest possible price. Some large plants are able to manufacture millions of cans or bottles daily. Large canners can also invest in national distribution networks and extensive advertising campaigns, which have greatly increased sales of canned and bottled goods. Finally, large conglomerates have the ability to expand to markets in other countries.

[**See also** MASON JAR; PRESERVES; PURE FOOD AND DRUG ACT.]

BIBLIOGRAPHY

Bitting, A. W. *Appertizing; or, The Art of Canning: Its History and Development.* San Francisco: California Trade Pressroom, 1937.

Collins, James H. *The Story of Canned Foods.* New York: Dutton, 1924.

May, Earl Chapin. *The Canning Clan: A Pageant of Pioneering Americans.* New York: Macmillan, 1937.

Smith, Andrew F. *Souper Tomatoes: The Story of America's Favorite Food.* New Brunswick, NJ: Rutgers University Press, 2000.

ANDREW F. SMITH

Canola, *see Fats and Oils*

Can Openers

The earliest can openers were not like those with the revolving cutting blades we know. Early cans, from the 1830s to the 1870s, had filling holes over which caps were soldered or cemented tight after boiling. Until the 1850s, cans were opened by chiseling a new hole in their tops.

The first patented opener in the United States dates from 1858. It has a piercing bar that is hammered into the tin to make a starter hole into which a rocking cutter blade is inserted. The simplest can openers work the same way in the twenty-first century. Because cans came in so many sizes and shapes, it was useful to be able to adjust the distance between piercing bar and cutting blade; many patents were designed this way. A rocking-blade "sardine opener" was made to open boxy sardine cans and had a relatively small blade, which allowed it to go around the corners. Powerful metal-cutting shears called sardine shears, with small, sharp blades, could be used for sardine cans, corned beef cans, or even stovepipes. In the 1880s and 1890s, openers with round frames and rotating blades were made for the increasingly more standardized, cylindrical, commercial cans. The major collector of can openers in the United States has over five thousand different designs. Obviously, consumers have never thought their can openers worked perfectly.

[See also CANNING AND BOTTLING.]

BIBLIOGRAPHY

Franklin, Linda Campbell. *Three Hundred Years of Kitchen Collectibles.* 5th ed. Iola, WI: Krause, 2003.

LINDA CAMPBELL FRANKLIN

Caribbean Influences on American Food

The Caribbean influence on North American food has been continual for millennia, as Native Americans and their foods migrated up the Gulf Coast or possibly came island hopping to Florida. The clear chain of influence began in 1492, as the varieties of maize, beans, chilies, squash, peanuts, and cassava collected by the Spanish expeditions to the Caribbean would return to North America with every European visitor and with African slaves as early as the abortive Spanish settlement of South Carolina in the 1520s. By 1565 the Spanish had sent large expeditions through the American southeast, and set up forts from St. Augustine, Florida, to as far north as Cape Fear, North Carolina—largely to forestall French, British, and Dutch rivals. In the process, the Spanish introduced European, Caribbean, and African foods, including pigs, chickens, watermelons, peaches, oranges, coconut palms, and sweet potatoes, all of which remained with Native Americans, African Americans, and other European settlers of the Southeast and Gulf coasts.

As the English, French, and Dutch established or conquered their own Caribbean colonies in the early 1600s, trade between the Caribbean and North American colonies increased. By the late 1600s, New England's economy had become organized around supplying food and forest products to the sugar plantations in the Caribbean, engendering the development of New England cod fisheries and salt works, plantation maize production by slaves in Rhode Island, rum and sugar refineries in Massachusetts, the triangular slave trade, and the periodic appearance of chocolate (from British Jamaica), coconuts, oranges, and pineapples on the tables of wealthy Anglo-American merchants.

One of the lasting legacies of the sugar trade with the Caribbean was the American sweet tooth—cheap sugar was as much an emblem of American freedom and prosperity as cheap meat. The by-product of the refineries—molasses—flavored Boston baked beans, Indian pudding, and hermit cookies. Caribbean coffee, cocoa, and spices have influenced the palates and tables of all Americans.

The Brawta Café in Brooklyn, New York, specializes in Jamaican food.

Certain Caribbean islands were used in the slave trade as centers for sorting, training, and trading. Thus many slaves arrived in the North American colonies and the early United States after some period in the Caribbean, and with some experience of Caribbean foods and cooking. One culinary example is southern coush-coush, made from cornmeal, but likely derived from African couscous via Barbadian coo-coo. Another example is hoppin' John, a bean pilaf served throughout the southern states on New Year's Day for good luck. It is also called by that name in the Bahamas, and the same dish brings the same New Year's good luck as *arroz con gandules* in Puerto Rico.

Even as the other European colonists gave way to the British and then to the new United States, Caribbean foodstuffs persisted, such as the datil chili, a variety of habanero localized in St. Augustine; or the mirliton, a tree fruit similar to summer squash and still popular in Louisiana.

West Indian immigrants such as Alexander Hamilton were prominent in the American Revolution, but some were also cooks, such as the mixed-race New York innkeeper Samuel Fraunces, who eventually served George Washington as presidential chef. Someone like Fraunces probably developed the Philadelphia version of Jamaica pepper pot stew at about the same time. From the 1840s another African Caribbean immigrant, Peter Augustin (or Augustine), was a leading caterer in Philadelphia, famous for chicken croquettes that may have been based on African Caribbean–style bean or codfish fritters. The Haitian Revolution had sent French colonists, free "Creoles of color," and their slaves primarily to Francophone New Orleans but also as far north as Philadelphia, where the Haitian Creoles are thought to have introduced peanut brittle.

Some of the earliest modern Caribbean migrations to the United States were of Cuban cigar factories and their workers, established in Tampa and Key West, Florida, and East Harlem by the 1890s. Puerto Ricans went to Hawaii as contract sugar workers in the 1890s; some remain, contributing *pasteles* (plantain tamales wrapped in banana leaves), fried plantains, and fried pork rinds to Hawaiian "local food."

American trade and political involvement in the Caribbean increased migration of Caribbean peoples to the United States, especially of African Caribbeans to the eastern states. At the same time, Florida and the Caribbean islands became accessible to North American tourists. Miami vacationers and retirees encountered tropical foods, and by the 1970s could wander into Cuban American restaurants. Those who sailed or flew to Cuba or Puerto Rico brought back tourist-trade cocktails, such as the daiquiri and rum punch, and later the Cuba libre and piña colada (invented in 1948 at the San Juan Hilton). While a Cuban-style black bean

soup or a Puerto Rican–derived *arroz con pollo* were still exotic dishes at 1950s North American dinner parties, they had arrived and were somewhat popular among military families.

World War II opened Gulf Coast port jobs to Caribbean people, who replaced Americans (and Puerto Ricans) who had gone to war. In the concentrated migration of Puerto Ricans to the United States in the 1950s, many immigrants came to New York City and the northeastern states. Although some Puerto Rican rice and bean dishes became known outside the community, there was more mainstream culinary interest in the 1960s wave of Cuban refugees, who established more restaurants serving black bean soup, roast fresh ham, fried plantains, and pressed sandwiches made with three kinds of pork.

With the opening of immigration laws in the late 1960s, substantial immigrant communities of Jamaicans, Dominicans, Trinidadians, Guyanese, Honduran and Belizan Garifuna, and others joined the Cubans and Puerto Ricans in American port cities from Houston, Texas, to Boston. Along with the worldwide popularity of reggae music, there was a confluence of interest in Jamaican meat pies and jerk barbecue, Trinidad-style roti, fried plantains, and every national variety of rice and beans. By the 1990s Caribbean dishes could be found in relatively authentic versions in immigrant neighborhoods, in upscale or "nuevo Latino" versions served by enterprising (and often Anglo) chefs, and in more casual form in African American neighborhood cafes or at the Kwanzaa Karamu feast. The hot sauce vogue of the 1990s renewed interest in the Caribbean habanero pepper, one of the hottest of all chilies. Jamaican hot sauces, Cuban sandwiches, and Dominican fried chicken have since reached the North American mainstream, at least in eastern coastal cities.

These immigrant foods so far from home close a circle, for when Columbus first made contact with Caribbean Taino Indians on Hispaniola (the present Dominican Republic), he was given cassava bread and chilies, which the Spanish heard described as "axi." In any Dominican bodega in New York City, the same foods can still be discovered, labeled "pan de casabe" and "achies."

BIBLIOGRAPHY

Cook, Evelyn, comp. *West Kauai's Plantation Heritage: Recipes and Stories for Life from the Legacy of Hawaii's Sugar Plantation Community.* Edited by Elizabeth Hahn. Waimea, HI: West Kauai Community Development Corporation, 2002.

Steele, Ian K. *Warpaths: Invasions of North America.* New York: Oxford University Press, 1994.

MARK H. ZANGER

Carl's Jr.

Carl's Jr. was launched in 1956 by fast food pioneer Karl Karcher of Anaheim, California. After a visit to the McDonald's operation in San Bernardino, California, Karcher decided

to develop a fast food chain of his own. Initially, two outlets were opened in Anaheim and nearby La Brea. Because they were "mini" versions of Carl's, a restaurant Karcher already owned, he called them Carl's Jr. Within ten years, the company had twenty-four outlets in southern California. To supply its franchisees, Carl's Jr. began purchasing ingredients, processing them and delivering them to outlets.

The company incorporated as Carl Karcher Enterprises Inc. (CKE) in 1966. Two years later, the company began an expansion plan that created a new enlarged version of the Carl's Jr. restaurants, complete with attractive architecture, larger dining rooms, and piped-in music. The main menu items were hamburgers, hot dogs, fries, and malts. By 1975, the company had about one hundred outlets in California. The first out-of-state restaurant was opened in 1979. In 1981 the company went public. CKE sold Carl's Jr. franchises nationwide. The company began to diversify its menu to include a Western Bacon Cheeseburger, breakfast items, and a chicken sandwich. During the 1990s, Carl's Jr. joined with the Green Burrito chain, which CKE eventually acquired. It also acquired Hardees, La Salsa Fresh Mexican Grill, and Taco Bueno. The corporation has also co-branded with Texaco gas stations, and many Carl's Jr. outlets were placed inside Texaco gas stations. In 2004, CKE restaurants had more than 3,400 outlets.

BIBLIOGRAPHY

Karcher, Carl, and B. Carolyn Knight. *Never Stop Dreaming: The Story of Carl Karcher Enterprises.* San Marcos, California: Erdmann, 1991.

Schlosser, Eric. *Fast Food Nation: The Dark Side of the All-American Meal.* New York: Houghton Mifflin, 2001.

ANDREW F. SMITH

Carp

Carp (*Cyprinius carpio*) was introduced to North America as a food fish in the late 1870s, although sources do not agree on whether the fish is native to Asia or to Europe. Because it is tolerant of relatively warm water, carp has been ideal for pond raising and can live as long as twenty years, quickly growing to a length as great as two feet in seven years. In North America, the largest reported carp caught was sixty pounds, although the common size is between one and two feet with a weight of eight to ten pounds.

Carp was once part of the commercial fishery of the Mississippi River basin. In other places where the fish are numerous, carp is an important food fish. Carp has become widely distributed in freshwater from Canada to the New Mexico border and from coast to coast. The English and Europeans find carp a fine sport fish because it is a strong fighter. In 1653 in *The Compleat Angler*, Izaak Walton described carp as "the Queen of Rivers: a stately, a good and a very subtle fish." But Americans have tended to disregard carp for sport or eating. Carp flesh is lean and white, somewhat coarse, and like catfish, it can assume the flavor of muddy water if raised in it. Carp is the fish most often used in making gefilte fish, the mixture of fish, matzo meal, and sometimes onion that is formed into balls and poached. Carp also can be baked, steamed, or battered and fried.

SANDRA L. OLIVER

Carrots

The carrot (*Daucus carota*) most likely originated in Afghanistan as a yellow or purple root. Its earliest dispersal, possibly via the Greeks, is uncertain, but there is some evidence that colorful central Asian varieties were cultivated in the Hellenistic Mediterranean, becoming extinct after Rome's fall. The vegetable spread (or was reintroduced) to the Middle East, Europe, India, and China by the Arabs, starting in the eleventh century. The Dutch crossed the old Afghani varieties in the late seventeenth century creating the brilliant orange root that is associated with most modern carrots, botanically subgrouped as *D. carota sativus*.

Adding to the confusion of early carrot history is the wild white carrot (also classed *D. carota*) that is native to Europe and was subsequently naturalized in America. Now popularly known as Queen Anne's lace, and most famous for its ornamental flower, the woody root has been used interchangeably with its visually similar cousin, the parsnip (both are members of the Apiaceae family). The late-fourth-century Roman cookery book of Apicius lists recipes suitable for either carrots (presumably wild and cultivated) or parsnips, advice repeated nearly fifteen hundred years later in Lettice Bryan's *The Kentucky Housewife* (1839) that "carrots may be cooked in every respect like parsnips."

English carrots were the first to be introduced into the colonies, accompanying colonists to Jamestown in 1609 and early Pilgrims to Massachusetts no later than 1629, where they grew "bigger and sweeter" than anything found in England. Dutch Mennonites brought orange and scarlet carrots with them into Pennsylvania, from whence they slowly spread through the rest of the colonies. Amelia Simmons's *American Cookery* (1796) describes yellow, red, and orange carrots, preferring the yellow of "middling siz'd, that is, a foot long and two inches at the top end." Carrots were easily transported, and they became popular vegetables with truck farmers, who brought them into urban markets from outlying areas by the end of the colonial period.

All parts of the carrot have culinary uses. The roots are most commonly eaten raw or pickled in salads and as hors d'oeuvres; boiled, roasted, fried, or mashed as vegetable side dishes; pureed or chopped for soups and stews; extracted into juices; or baked into sweet cakes and puddings. Considered an aromatic (along with onions and celery), carrots

add subtle sweetness to stocks and sauces. The lacy green leaves can be used in salads and as an herb, while the aromatic seeds function as a spice. Carrots traditionally were ascribed tonic properties, thought to be good for the stomach. Teas made from wild carrots have been used for bladder and kidney ailments. During World War II carrots were dehydrated, treated with carbon dioxide or nitrogen, and shipped to troops overseas to supply dietary carotene. Pennsylvania folk medicine prescribed the wild seeds as a postcoital contraceptive.

Most of the carrots in contemporary markets are orange descendants of the two varieties introduced by the Mennonites. Specialized carrots, including the gourmet baby sizes, have been developed through selective breeding. Shapes range from small spheres through stumpy cylinders to long tapers and colors shade from pale whites to deep violet; some are variegated. Although fresh carrots form the largest segment of the American market, with California and Colorado the leading producers, carrots also withstand canning and freezing reasonably well.

[See also HOMEMADE REMEDIES; KITCHEN GARDENING; SIMMONS, AMELIA; VEGETABLES.]

BIBLIOGRAPHY

Facciola, Stephen. *Cornucopia II: A Source Book of Edible Plants.* Vista, CA: Kampong, 1998.

Hedrick, U. P., ed. *Sturtevant's Edible Plants of the World.* New York: Dover, 1972. Reprint of *Sturtevant's Notes on Edible Plants.* Albany, NY: Lyon, 1919.

Weaver, William Woys. *Heirloom Vegetable Gardening.* New York: Holt, 1997.

CATHY K. KAUFMAN

Carvel Corporation

In 1934 Thomas Carvel, a salesman who sold ice cream at fairs and beach resorts, opened a retail ice cream shop in Hartsdale, New York. The following year, he perfected the product that would make his fortune: soft-serve ice cream, dispensed from a freezer of his own invention. Carvel was operating three stores when World War II started. After the war, he formed two companies: the Carvel Corporation and the Carvel Dari-Freeze Stores, which he immediately began to franchise. Within five years, he had generated 125 franchise stores from Maine to Florida. As part of the franchise package, he included plans for a drive-up Carvel stand with a forward-tilting facade under a roof that pitched upward toward the street. It was a singularly visible and welcoming design. To help franchisees, he established the "Carvel College of Ice Cream Knowledge," which was referred to as "Sundae School."

Location is the key to the success of a roadside franchise. Carvel believed that the best place for a Carvel stand was on a secondary highway where traffic moved along fairly slowly, in an area with a large enough population that the store could generate repeat customers. To help identify profitable spots,

"location engineers" were called in. They used counters to determine the number of motorists and pedestrians who passed a given location each day.

Over the years, the Carvel product line expanded to include hundreds of products, from 10-cent ice cream cones to elaborate custom-decorated ice cream cakes such as "Fudgy the Whale" and "Cookie Puss." Carvel introduced an ice cream sandwich that replaced the usual wafers with two chocolate chip cookies.

In 1992 Carvel began distributing its ice cream to supermarkets. In 2001 the company was sold to Roark Capital Group, a private equity firm, and three years later, it was acquired by FOCUS Brands, along with Cinnabun.

BIBLIOGRAPHY

Funderburg, Anne Cooper. *Chocolate, Strawberry, and Vanilla: A History of American Ice Cream.* Bowling Green, Ohio: Bowling Green State University Popular Press, 1995.

Jakle, John A., and Keith A. Sculle. *Fast Food: Roadside Restaurants in the Automobile Age.* Baltimore: Johns Hopkins University Press, 1999.

ANDREW F. SMITH

Carver, George Washington

George Washington Carver's early life is shrouded in myth and legend. He was probably born in the spring of 1865 in a one-room cabin on a farm in Newton County, Missouri. His mother had been a slave; his father was unknown to him. The owners of the farm were Moses and Susan Carver, German immigrants. Along with his mother, George was abducted as an infant by night riders who carried him off to Arkansas. Moses Carver found George and traded a horse valued at three hundred dollars for him—or so legend relates.

Carver never saw his mother again, and the childless Carvers became his foster parents. George was sickly as a child, so he was assigned household chores and learned to read. The Carvers encouraged him to get an education. He worked his way through high school and then enrolled in Simpson College in Indianola, Iowa. In 1891 he transferred to Iowa State College of Agriculture and Mechanical Arts at Ames. Working his way through college, Carver received a bachelor's degree in 1894, after which he was given faculty status while pursuing graduate work. He received a master of agriculture degree in 1896. Carver was particularly interested in botany and mycology, but he also painted.

In 1896, Booker T. Washington offered Carver a position at the Tuskegee Institute in Alabama. Washington wanted Carver to head the new agriculture department. Carver accepted the position and spent the remainder of his forty-six years at the institute. During the first twenty years he focused his research on a variety of food plants, including tomatoes, sweet potatoes, and cowpeas. Carver's work earned him election to membership in Great Britain's Royal Society of Arts in 1915.

Smith, Andrew F. *Peanuts: The Illustrious History of the Goober Pea*. Urbana: University of Illinois Press, 2002.

ANDREW F. SMITH

Cashews

Cashews (*Anacardium occidentale*) are native to tropical South America. The Portuguese introduced cashews to East Africa, Indonesia, and India, where they quickly spread to the Malabar coast and southwestern India. The Spanish introduced cashews to their colonies in the Caribbean, Central America, and the Philippines. Cashews were first imported into the United States shortly after the Civil War. Although their origins are in the New World, cashews are not a major crop in any country of the Americas. In the early twenty-first century, India led the world in production. Raw or roasted, salted or not, cashews are favorites for snacking, and they are the most important dessert nut after almonds. Cashews are lower in fat than other commonly consumed nuts.

[**See also** ALMONDS; BRAZIL NUTS; NUTS.]

ANDREW F. SMITH

Cassava

Most North Americans know cassava only in the form of tapioca pudding, but it is an American domesticate that is a staple for an estimated 500 million people in ninety-two countries, mostly in tropical Africa and Asia as well as South America. Cassava (also known as manioc or yucca) is the tuber of a large shrub, *Manihot esculenta*. The word "cassava" comes from the Taino Indian word for cassava bread, a stiff flatbread offered to Columbus by the Taino Indians on Hispanola. Cassava bread is still produced in the Dominican Republic and is widely available in urban bodegas in New York and other East Coast American cities. The original domestication was probably in Brazil, where cassava meal, *farinha*, is still part of every meal. Cassava was a staple of the Mayan empire and had reached Peru and Argentina before the arrival of Columbus. The Taino preferred it to maize, and their other name, "Arawaks," means "eaters of meal."

Cassava is an unusual domesticate, in that the raw roots of most varieties contain fatal amounts of prussic acid. Thus the Indians had to devise methods of grating, soaking, pressing, boiling, drying, and roasting to produce edible starches and syrups. (Some inferior varieties can be peeled and boiled like potatoes.) Cassava became a slave staple in Brazil and was disseminated by the Portuguese to central Africa, by the Dutch to Indonesia, and by the Spanish to the Philippines. Cassava was probably grown in parts of Florida, the Carolinas, and Virginia to feed slaves, but the written record is unclear. The earliest reference in English is Thomas Harriot's account of 1585–1586; he described the food of the Indians of the outer banks of the Carolinas: "*Coscúshaw*, some of our company tooke to bee that kinde of roote which

While at Tuskegee, George Washington Carver published a bulletin that included 105 ways of preparing peanuts "with the hope that the city folk will find the diet not only wholesome, satisfying, healthful and appetizing, but very economical."

Carver paid little attention to peanuts during his early years at Tuskegee. The minor exception was a small experiment he conducted in 1903, using peanuts as swine feed. However, in late 1915 Carver decided to publish a bulletin on peanuts. The boll weevil had destroyed Alabama's cotton crop, and many farmers had begun to convert to peanuts. Peanuts had several distinct advantages over other potential cash crops, especially for sharecroppers. If the peanuts could not be sold, sharecroppers would at least have something nutritious to eat during the winter. Shortly after the publication of the bulletin, Carver began conducting experiments and developing products from peanuts.

When Congress held hearings on a peanut tariff, Carver was asked to testify. He performed well, and his national popularity soared. He continued to develop peanut products, reportedly more than three hundred items, including chili sauce, candy, salad oils, oleomargarine, cheese, instant coffee, beverages, paint, cattle feed, and milk substitute. Carver was criticized at the time for his failure to commercialize his peanut discoveries, and few were ever converted to practical uses.

Carver died on January 3, 1943. Although America was again embroiled in a world war, newspapers, magazines, and Americans of all races paused to show their respect for him. He has been portrayed as an African American role model ever since in school textbooks and in children's books, many of which have stressed Carver's connection with the peanut.

[**See also** PEANUTS.]

BIBLIOGRAPHY

Holt, Rachham. *George Washington Carver: An American Biography*. Garden City, NY: Doubleday, Doran, 1944.

McMurry, Linda O. *George Washington Carver: Scientist and Symbol*. New York: Oxford University Press, 1982.

the Spaniards in the West Indies call *Cassauy*, whereupon also many called it by that name." If this was true cassava, it might have been brought there by far-ranging Tainos or, more likely, by the Spanish Carolina colonists of 1526, whose one hundred African slaves rebelled and joined the Indians near the Pee Dee river.

Thomas Jefferson's 1787 *Notes on the State of Virginia* lists cassava as a domestic plant but gives the Latin name of an entirely different species. The last and northernmost reference is Mary Randolph's 1824 description in *The Virginia House-Wife* of a rice johnnycake "nearly as good as cassada [sic] bread." It is thus possible that Virginia plantations had been quietly growing and processing cassava for more than two hundred years, but, more likely, Randolph's cassava bread was imported from the West Indies. The durable flatbreads had become a ship's supply and conquistador marching ration as early as the 1500s.

Manioc starch (Brazilian arrowroot) was used as a pudding thickener in colonial and early America, and pearl tapioca, primarily from Indonesian plantations, became a popular thickener for puddings and pies in the United States in the mid-nineteenth century. Since the 1950s cassava has reentered the United States as a boiled or fried root (yucca) with migrant populations from Puerto Rico, refugees from Cuba, and immigrants from Brazil (*mandioca*) and the Dominican Republic. Honduran and Belizan Garifuna (descendants of Africans and indigenous peoples of the West Indies) in Los Angeles, New Orleans, and Brooklyn, New York, use cassava to thicken stews and for toast breads. Cassava syrup, *cassareep*, is the crucial ingredient in Jamaican pepper pot, and Brazilian *farinha* is sold to Nigerian Americans as well as Brazilian immigrants.

[See also CARIBBEAN INFLUENCES ON AMERICAN FOOD; NATIVE AMERICAN FOODS.]

BIBLIOGRAPHY

Randolph, Mary. *The Virginia House-Wife*. With historical notes and commentary by Karen Hess. Columbia: University of South Carolina Press, 1984.

MARK H. ZANGER

Casseroles

The name for the food comes from the container in which it is cooked. A casserole (from a Greek word meaning "cup," a Latin word meaning "ladle" and "pan," and an Old French word *casse*, which eventually evolved into *cassole*) is a cooking vessel made of ovenproof material. Ceramic or metal, the casserole usually has a lid and is suitable for long, slow cooking in an oven where it holds at least two ingredients that are subjected to a constant temperature and continuous basting. The typical casserole container is round, may vary in depth, and if decorative may be placed on the buffet or dining table when the meal is served. It is also a favorite at American potluck

suppers, summer picnics, and anywhere a "hot dish to pass" is requested of guests.

Casserole cookery has been around since prehistoric times, when it was discovered that cooking food slowly in a tightly covered clay vessel softened fibrous meats and blended succulent juices. It is an unsophisticated method and can withstand a bit of neglect. If the casserole is not removed from the oven immediately it will not be ruined. With the addition or subtraction of leftovers or inexpensive cuts of meat, the casserole is flexible and economical in terms of both ingredients and effort. The classic casserole, a French dish, was originally made with a mound of cooked rice. Fannie Merritt Farmer's *Boston Cooking-School Cook Book* (1896) had one casserole recipe, for Casserole of Rice and Meat, to be steamed for forty-five minutes and served with tomato sauce. In the twentieth century, casseroles took on a distinctive American identity. During the depression of the 1890s, the economic casserole provided a welcome way to stretch meat, fish, and poultry. Certain items were also scarce during World War I and leftovers were turned into casserole meals. The same was true during the Great Depression of the 1930s, when busy housewives and small kitchens eventually made the casserole convenient fare. For many the cherished comfort foods of childhood include the ubiquitous tuna-potato chip casserole bound together with Campbell's Cream of Mushroom Soup (an absolute boon for housewives when it was introduced in 1934), a Tater Tot Casserole (cook's choice of creamed soup, plus hamburger and Tater Tots) or the good old green bean casserole (green beans, cream of mushroom soup, and french fried onion rings), a Thanksgiving dinner requirement almost as necessary as pumpkin pie.

To prepare food *en casserole* initially denoted culinary sophistication to American cooks, but immigrants brought their own casserole recipes to the New World in the nineteenth century, and favorite ethnic and regional classics evolved. The New England cookstove often held a simmering casserole of baked beans and molasses. In the southern United States jambalaya was popular. Ethnic influences and regional tastes adapted the Greek or Turkish moussaka with acceptable modifications. In South Carolina and Georgia, rice plantations and an abundance of shrimp brought about a casserole that combined both. Yankee Oyster Pie, a casserole native to the northeastern coast of the United States, layers oysters and oyster crackers with plenty of cream, butter, and Worcestershire sauce. Hungarian goulash is enjoyed everywhere. A truly original concoction, the King Ranch Casserole, with chicken, cheese, tortilla chips, and cream of mushroom and cream of chicken soup is, according to the magazine *Texas Monthly*, "the clubwoman's contribution to Texas cuisine."

[See also ADVERTISING COOKBOOKLETS AND RECIPES; CAMPBELL SOUP COMPANY; COOKING TECHNIQUES; POTS AND PANS.]

BIBLIOGRAPHY

Kaufman, William I. *The Art of Casserole Cookery*. New York: Doubleday, 1967.
Vilas, James. *Crazy for Casseroles*. Boston: Harvard Common Press, 2003.

SARA RATH

Catfish

A member of the family Ictaluridae, catfish is a warm water fish that has long been well regarded for food and sport. Catfish also is farm raised. Channel catfish (*Ictalurus punctatus*) is the most widely farm-raised fish in the United States. All wild catfish are descendants of catfish that originated east of the Continental Divide. The native western catfish is apparent only in the geologic record. Catfish has an odd appearance. Its barbels, which resemble whiskers, and sharp, spiny fins are venomous and capable of causing injury.

There once was a commercial trawl fishery for catfish on the Great Lakes, but sportfishing on the Great Lakes and in the Mississippi basin accounts for most of the wild catfish caught for food. Channel catfish is raised in ponds, mostly in the Mississippi delta. The catfish business sputtered in the delta in the 1960s but had a resurgence in the 1980s and 1990s. At that time an industry-wide effort was made to develop a freezing and transportation infrastructure for the product together with marketing efforts to promote farm-raised catfish. Fast food franchises using large quantities of catfish helped support the industry.

Wild catfish can have a muddy flavor, but farm-raised catfish flesh can be flavorless, an attribute sought by catfish growers, who maintain laboratories for testing the flavor of sample fish from a pond full of the fish. When the right flavor is reached the pond is harvested. These fish are suitable for preparation as fish fillets, often breaded for deep-fat frying. Catfish fries and shrimp and crayfish boils are fish-based social events in the South, matching whitefish boils on the Great Lakes.

SANDRA L. OLIVER

Cauliflower

Cauliflower (*Brassica oleracea botrytis*) is one of the cultivated varieties of the cabbage plant. The vegetable is picked in the bud stage, before it blossoms, and only the florets are consumed—these are the small, tightly packed buds that make up the head. Cauliflower is a close relative of broccoli, but unlike the leaves of broccoli, cauliflower's leaves cover the flower head as it grows, keeping the florets from producing chlorophyll and turning green.

Cauliflower may have originated in the Middle East, and it has been grown in Italy since the fifteenth century. It was subsequently distributed to other parts of Europe and was cultivated in North America by the

A cauliflower seed advertisement.

late 1600s. By the late eighteenth century, recipes were published in American cookbooks for boiling, frying, or stewing cauliflower; early recipes were also offered for pickling, and pickled cauliflower was served when fresh vegetables were unavailable and as a condiment. In the nineteenth century, cauliflower cookery expanded. Sometimes boiled in milk to gentle its flavor, cauliflower was sauced, usually with a butter or white sauce, and served as a side dish with meats; it was also sieved to make creamy soups.

Cauliflower was baked and browned in a cheese sauce, folded into omelets, and served (cooked, chilled, and dressed with mayonnaise or vinaigrette) as a salad. Raw cauliflower, fairly tough on the digestive system, became a component of crudités platters served with dips during the late twentieth century. The first cauliflower cookbooklet was published by Arthur A. Crozier in 1891, and cauliflower has been featured in later cookbooks, such as Charlotte Snyder Turgeon's *Of Cabbages and Kings Cookbook* (1977).

White cauliflower is more abundant in the United States, but orange and purple cauliflowers are sold. Some markets stock broccoflower, which is light green in color and milder and sweeter in flavor than either broccoli or cauliflower.

ANDREW F. SMITH

Celebrity Chefs

Celebrity chef is the title given to people who are famous for cooking in public. Although the term did not gain widespread use until the 1990s, it is generally applied to all well-known cooks and chefs of the past and present. It is a role characterized by status, rather than a particular function, in a culture in which food has become a form of popular entertainment. There are many types of celebrity chefs—from restaurateur-activists to cooking-show host-authors—and, collectively, they appeal to a broad spectrum of American society. Popularized through the mass multimedia, including twenty-four-hour television programming, cookbooks, consumer magazines, and the Internet, they have become prominent public figures in our culture.

Postwar to 1970s

Chefs, Hollywood celebrities, and radio personalities were in the public eye before the mid-twentieth century, their images publicized through cookbooks, advertising pamphlets, and other food-product endorsements. But the phenomenon of the celebrity chef stems from two cultural forces of the post–World War II era: the emergent food consciousness in America and the development of the mass media. The watershed event in the rise of the celebrity chef was the debut of Julia Child as *The French Chef* in 1962. From its first local broadcast, the show rapidly became a national sensation, and she became universally recognized by her given name, Julia, and her sign-off, "Bon appétit." When her image appeared on the cover of *Time* magazine (November 25, 1966), the accompanying article read, "Julia Child's TV cooking shows have made her a cult from coast to coast and put her on a first-name basis with her fans."

Julia Child's broad fan base was made up of a generation of new consumers of a gourmet culture that developed from the economic boom and increased social and physical mobility after World War II. Affluence, automobiles, and new restaurants across the country gave the middle class newfound access to eating out as a leisure activity, while increased air travel put international dining within reach of more Americans. Popular cookbooks, general interest and food magazines, and radio and television programs also widely promoted the idea of food as a source of pleasure for the average American. Julia Child captivated the nation's attention because she reconceived haute cuisine as an affordable luxury for the general public. French cuisine, the order of the day in the finest restaurants, was what socially mobile people aspired to eat in and outside of the country. The allure of French food was further heightened by the glamour surrounding the Francophile First Lady Jacqueline Kennedy, whose hiring of the French chef René Verdon in 1961 made front-page news.

Julia Child was not the first television cooking teacher. For example, James Beard, a successful cookbook author, instructor, *Gourmet* magazine contributor, and product spokesperson, had starred in the spot *Elsie Presents James Beard in "I Love to Eat"* from 1946 to 1947 on the NBC network. His and other early programs introduced cooking shows to the television audience. By the 1960s, with televisions in many more American homes, *The French Chef* revolutionized the cooking program as a form of entertainment.

Although Julia Child was an unlikely television star, she quickly rivaled the popularity of the best-known food personality in America of the period, the fictional character Betty Crocker. Child's onscreen persona tempered her patrician background with a disarming lack of pretense. She reassured her audience while demonstrating the pleasures of cooking and eating well. Her wit and unedited goof-ups on the program made *The French Chef* not only educational but also engaging and funny. The mass media played a pivotal role in turning the television cook Julia Child into a national superstar. Her successful cookbook, *Mastering the Art of French Cooking*, which had been published in 1961, further bolstered her public image. In turn, sales of the book surged. Publicity only increased with the publication of a second volume in 1970, which coincided with a new *French Chef* series. From *TV Guide* to *House and Garden* to the *New Yorker*, it was the rare magazine that did not feature her. Likewise, newspapers across the country ran articles about her, especially when she was in the area for book tours, cooking demonstrations, honorary dinners, and charity events.

The media attention showered on Julia Child, which expanded her influence and status, is one of the hallmarks of the celebrity chef. For her part, Child wrote companion cookbooks to *The French Chef* series, granted countless interviews in her homes in Cambridge, Massachusetts, and Provence, France, and contributed to national publications. It is also significant that although Child never endorsed specific products, her publicity inspired waves of purchasing, cooking, and eating behaviors, which accelerated the gourmet food trend throughout the country.

1970 to the Twenty-first Century

With the success of *The French Chef*, public television expanded its offerings of cooking programs. Some of them included other ethnic cuisines popular in the 1970s, notably Chinese and Italian. Joyce Chen, a Chinese immigrant restaurant owner, and Margaret and Franco Romagnoli, Italian cookbook authors and restaurateurs, hosted their own programs. They were exceptional because they were chefs in the classical sense, that is, they were the heads of kitchens, as well as public figures. But audiences have never recognized a distinction between chefs and nonchefs. Television cooking stars, such as Graham Kerr of *The Galloping Gourmet*, and cookbook authors, such as the *New York Times*'s Craig Claiborne, are all considered celebrity chefs.

Social changes through the late 1970s and into 1980s further entrenched the status of food in American culture. More full-time

How to Cook Better
with Planters French-Process Peanut Oil
by JAMES BEARD

America's foremost food authority, Beard is a consultant to famed restaurants, TV star, author of "The Fireside Cookbook", "How to Eat Well on Less Money", "The James Beard Cookbook", "Outdoor Cooking".

James Beard, shown here in 1961 on the cover of a recipe booklet issued by Planters Peanuts, was one of the first celebrity chefs.

working women put a premium on cooking at home, while more cookbooks were published each year. Dining out continued to connote status, and new magazines, such as *Food and Wine*, spurred the public passion for the next dining trend. Health concerns spawned vegetarian cookbooks, including *The Moosewood Cookbook*, and diet-conscious magazines, such as *Cooking Light*. The paradox of the predominant interest in food in general society is that while it steadily increased, the number of home-cooked meals decreased—a trend that has continued.

The 1980s is the period often noted as the food revolution in the United States. It is also significant for the widespread name recognition accorded to American chefs for the first time. Two California chefs, in particular, Alice Waters and Wolfgang Puck, received major media coverage when the West Coast became the focus of national culinary interest. As attention turned to the country's other regional cuisines, working chefs, including Paul Prudhomme, Larry Forgione, and Mark Miller, gained prominence. *Cooking with the New American Chefs*, published in 1985, profiled these three chefs, along with twenty others. Although they were not yet called "celebrity chefs," the enhanced status of the American-made chef contributed significantly to the celebrity chef phenomenon. Organizations within the culinary profession, several of which were founded during the 1980s, also spotlighted chefs by publicly honoring them. The annual James Beard Foundation awards, for example, are called "the Oscars of the food world."

The creation of the Food Network in 1993 was the final breakthrough in the era of the celebrity chef. It not only capitalized on the entertainment value of cooking on television but also firmly established food as pop culture. Cooking, which once had been a common, private activity, became public performance. And those who cooked had become a new brand of cultural hero to a wide range of classes, age groups, and tastes in America.

Emeril Lagasse, one of the first stars created by the Food Network, is a model of the celebrity chef. Like Julia Child, Lagasse is widely recognized by first name only, as is his catchphrase, "Bam!" In addition to his many television series, he manages a conglomeration of commercial and media enterprises that includes restaurants and cookbooks, cookware lines, a website, prime-time television programs, documentaries, guest appearances, and charity events. He is one of many cult figures in the large and growing pantheon of celebrity chefs.

[See also BEARD, JAMES; CHILD, JULIA; CLAIBORNE, CRAIG; LAGASSE, EMERIL; PRUDHOMME, PAUL; PUCK, WOLFGANG; RADIO/TV FOOD SHOWS; WATERS, ALICE.]

BIBLIOGRAPHY
Brenner, Leslie. *American Appetite: The Coming of Age of a National Cuisine.* New York: HarperCollins, 1999.
Fitch, Noël Riley. *Appetite for Life: The Biography of Julia Child.* New York: Doubleday, 1997.
Kuh, Patric. *The Last Days of Haute Cuisine.* New York: Viking Penguin, 2001.

LYNNE SAMPSON

Celery

The crisp, mild-flavored celery eaten in the early twenty-first century is a descendant of a bitter wild celery (*Apium graveolens*), called smallage, that is indigenous to Europe, the Middle East, and South Asia. In the ancient Mediterranean, the seeds and roots of this plant were used by the Greeks and Romans, mainly as spices and flavorings. In the seventeenth century, the bitterness was bred out, and the stalks and leaves began to be served in salads and as cooked vegetables in Europe. This improved variety was grown in England by 1644 but was not introduced into America until the following century.

Celery became an important food in America by the early nineteenth century. Four varieties were noted in Bernard M'Mahon's *The American Gardener's Calendar* (1806). Celery stalks were used for a variety of culinary purposes: fried or stewed and sauced and served as a vegetable, added to soups and sauces (the latter used especially for turkey and other fowl), and immersed in seasoned vinegar for pickles. Celery glasses, serving pieces that held celery stalks, became important during the first two decades of the nineteenth century. These pieces were made from glass or silver and initially took a variety of urn shapes. Around the 1890s the flatter plate or dish became popular, supplanting glasses, stands, and vases for celery.

By the late nineteenth century, raw celery stalks were served as appetizers and as an ingredient in salads, such as Waldorf salad. Celery seeds and leaves were used as a flavoring. Celery salt, consisting of dried, pulverized celery stalks mixed with salt, was added to America's spice shelf by the 1870s. In the twentieth century, celery became still more popular. By midcentury, a succession of diet fads made the crisp stalks a favorite food for weight watchers, and a false rumor circulated that celery had "negative calories" (that chewing it burned more calories than the celery supplied to the body). Lengths of celery stalks filled with cream cheese became a popular appetizer during the 1950s. Filled with peanut butter and topped with a row of raisins, celery stalks became "ants on a log," a children's favorite. In the 1960s, a celery stalk became a requisite garnish for a Bloody Mary cocktail. Celery sticks are also a standard accompaniment to Buffalo wings.

The main variety of celery consumed in the United States is Pascal, which was first cultivated in 1874 in Michigan. California is the largest celery producer, followed by Florida. Celery seed for seasoning is generally imported from Asia.

[See also BLOODY MARY AND VIRGIN MARY; CALIFORNIA; HEALTH FOOD; PEANUT BUTTER; PICKLES; PICKLING; POULTRY AND FOWL; SALADS AND SALAD DRESSINGS; TSCHIRKY, OSCAR; TURKEY.]

ANDREW F. SMITH

Center for Science in the Public Interest

The Center for Science in the Public Interest is a nonprofit consumer advocacy organization that has been instrumental in changing policy and passing laws concerned with food safety, nutrition, and alcohol in the United States. Some of its more sensational public campaigns have included calling fettuccine Alfredo a "heart attack on a plate" and revealing that Chinese kung pao chicken is as bad nutritionally as a McDonald's Quarter Pounder. CSPI's lobbying was a key factor in passing the Nutrition Labeling and Education Act of 1990, which requires the Nutrition Facts panel on virtually all food and beverages. More recently, CSPI succeeded in getting trans fats added to the Nutrition Facts panel, an issue it raised in 1994 that became law in 2006. Earlier, CSPI acted to get warning labels for pregnant women on alcoholic beverages and to enact a ban on deceptive food advertising.

The Center for Science in the Public Interest was founded in 1971 by current executive director Michael Jacobson and two other scientists, Albert Fritsch and Jim Sullivan, who met while working with the consumer advocate Ralph Nader. Jacobson has a doctorate in microbiology. CSPI's original goal was to encourage scientists to become more active in the social issues of the day. When the two cofounders left in 1977, CSPI's focus was tightened to its present priorities. The organization has targeted both policymakers and the public with its research and information.

Its aggressive approach and especially its more publicity-oriented research have produced a backlash from culinary and nutrition experts as well as the food and restaurant industry, beginning in the early 1990s. But its impact, for better or worse, on nutrition awareness and the way foods are made, marketed, and sold in America, is undisputed. Its nutrition newsletter, which goes out ten times a year to 900,000 subscribers (as of 2005), accounts for most of its financial support.

BIBLIOGRAPHY
Center for Science in the Public Interest. www.cspi-net.org.
Food Safety and Inspection Service, U.S. Department of Agriculture. www.fsis.usda.gov/OPPDE/Comments/05-019N/05-019N-1.pdf

KIM PIERCE

Central Asian Food

Central Asian culinary influences in the American diet are historically minor but are starting to grow as Americans travel to Central Asia and as more and more Central Asians settle in the United States. Central Asian or Turkestani (mainly from former Soviet Central Asia and China's Xinjiang/Sinkiang province) immigrant communities have existed in the United States, mainly in Brooklyn and New Jersey, since the Russian Revolution in 1917. Many of these early Central Asian immigrants fled the Russian empire, first spending time in Afghanistan, Iran, China, and Turkey before immigrating to the United States. Since the 1930s steadily growing numbers of Turks, Persians, and Afghans have come to the United States following patterns such as the flight of Soviet Jewry (mid-1970s), the Iranian Revolution (1979), and the Soviet invasion of Afghanistan (1980). Substantial Turkish immigration to the United States followed World War II. It can be further divided into eras and classes: the first wave, mainly through the mid-1970s, comprises typical immigrants seeking a better life and less repressive states. Since the 1970s Turks coming to America typically have been young and accomplished professionals, people demanding higher-quality and more authentic restaurant culture.

The heart of former Soviet Central Asian culinary culture lies in New York—mainly the boroughs of Brooklyn and Queens. Most but not all of the clientele remain first-generation

Central Asians, predominantly Bukharan Jews, Tajiks, and Uzbeks. Los Angeles and Seattle also boast a number of Central Asian eateries with a wider multiethnic appeal. Southern California is home to greater numbers of Iranians and Afghans than Central Asians, but similarities in culinary lifeways mutually reinforce one another. Since the 1970s Seattle has had a sister-city relationship with Tashkent, the capital of Uzbekistan, and the University of Washington has had a very active Central Asian studies program, which has brought many Central Asians to Seattle.

Probably the most widely accepted and enjoyed Central Asian food in America is yogurt (a Turkish word; in Turkish the "g" is not pronounced). Of course, the consumption of yogurt is so widely spread throughout Europe that it is easy to forget its origins as a product of the Eurasian steppe. One yogurt drink is slowly catching on in large cities, such as Chicago and Los Angeles, and in large university towns that support Near Eastern or Central Asian communities. The drink is *airan* (Turkish) or *doh* (Persian), and it is a watered-down yogurt drink, sometimes served with salt, ice, and herb flavorings, such as basil or cilantro. It is available not only in restaurants but also as a packaged good in specialty ethnic groceries. On hot days in Iran, Turkey, or Uzbekistan, *doh* or *airan* stands are ubiquitous.

Pilafs, generally available since the end of World War II in American supermarkets in the form of packaged dry mixes, are widely obtainable throughout the Near East and Central Asia, where they are known as *palov* or *osh*. These hearty rice stews—which typically include copious amounts of carrots, mutton and mutton fat or beef and vegetable oil, cumin, and garlic—are served in Central Asian eateries on the coasts and in Chicago.

Increasingly, the Uzbek and Tajik variety of bread, known as *obi* or *patir non* (or naan), is gaining a wider audience, owing to its wonderful textures, aroma, and flavor. It resembles some of the best types of naan found in Indian or Pakistani restaurants but tends to have an even crisper and firmer crust. Bread lovers in coastal cities such as New York and Los Angeles are becoming familiar with this world-class bread.

Curiously, some of the best foodstuffs in Central Asia, including soups, noodle dishes, and large dumplings, seem to have their origins in western China—Xinjiang to be exact. Whereas in Central Asia the status of Uyghur cooks is legendary, Americans are just barely learning of the various ethnic cum national distinctions extant in Central Asia. It will probably be some time before localized Central Asian culinary traditions become better known in North America.

Afghan dishes, themselves an interesting fusion of northern Indian and Iranian ingredients with many local variants, have been attracting Americans to dining establishments since the 1970s. Renewed interest in Afghan cuisine accompanies the "War on Terror." Breads, kabobs, yogurt sauces, and vegetarian dishes, including those made with eggplant, okra, and squashes, tend to be among the favorites.

Most Central Asians are Muslims, so pork does not appear on their tables. Lamb and mutton are often the basis for cherished dishes. Americans on the whole do not consume large quantities of lamb, much less mature mutton, and certainly not the famous fat-tailed sheep beloved of the Central Asian homeland. For that reason, among others, authentic Central Asian cuisine has been and will remain a niche cuisine. No doubt, clever restaurateurs will modify their menus for American tastes and, like their Greek counterparts, emphasize beef and poultry dishes.

Overall, the influence of Central Asian culinary types in American gastronomy mainly operates through restaurants and cookbooks. Since journalism seems to be the primary vehicle by which discussion of relatively unknown cuisines is spread in America, people who try such foods often do so after reading restaurant reviews. Others who are getting out the word and slowly helping influence mainstream eating patterns are the increasingly popular chowhound-type organizations, which make use of the Internet to spread the news.
[**See also** Lamb and Mutton.]

BIBLIOGRAPHY
Algar, Ayla E. *Classical Turkish Cooking: Traditional Turkish Food for the American Kitchen.* New York: HarperCollins, 1991.
Shaida, Margaret. *The Legendary Cuisine of Persia.* London: Grub Street, 2000.
Visson, Lynn. *The Art of Uzbek Cooking.* Hippocrene Books, 1999.

RUSSELL ZANCA

Ceramics Definitions

Ceramics is the umbrella term for items fashioned from clay and hardened by heat. *Earthenware* is created from clays containing various impurities that limit the firing temperature to between 800°C and 1100°C and often richly color the ware. Earthenware is less sturdy than items fired at higher temperatures, and the vessel that results remains porous unless a glaze is applied. The relatively low temperature allows for a wide range of minerals (including lead) and colors in the glazes, which do not fuse to the body. Earthenware is susceptible to chipping.

Maiolica and *delft* are tin-glazed earthenwares, both of which were imported to America before 1650; very generally speaking, the former originates in Spain or Italy, the latter in Holland or England. *Faïence* is the French equivalent.

Creamware and *pearlware*, created by Englishman Josiah Wedgwood in the 1760s and 1770s, were highly popular cream-colored and white earthenware, widely imported in elegant dinner sets.

Majolica is nineteenth-century whimsical lead-glazed earthenware, frequently molded in floral, vegetal, or animal motifs and glazed to mimic nature's colorings.

Stoneware is fashioned from clay with fewer impurities, permitting a higher firing temperature (1200°C–1300°C), which encourages vitrification. The pieces are nonporous and stronger than earthenware, but not so sturdy as porcelain. Rhenish stoneware was used in the colonies by 1650 (distinct from the salt-glazed stoneware manufactured in England); Huguenot immigrants started domestic production no later than the 1720s. Fine English stoneware was especially popular in colonial America between 1720 and 1770.

Porcelain, originating in China in the fifth century, is a specialized mixture of clays permitting the highest firing temperatures, over 1300°C. True (hard-paste) porcelain contains the china clays kaolin and petuntse. Coveted for its beauty, porcelain was technically challenging to make, and the first efforts in Europe in the early eighteenth century resulted in soft-paste porcelain, which contains little or no kaolin, is fired at a slightly lower temperature, and lacks the translucence of most true porcelain. The demand for Chinese porcelain was so great that Chinese potters made export porcelain specifically for Western consumers. The decoration on export porcelain steadily declined in the eighteenth and early nineteenth centuries, as growing demand tolerated mediocre craftsmanship. American efforts to make true porcelain started around 1738, although none were commercially successful until the late nineteenth century.

CATHY K. KAUFMAN

Cereal, Cold

Ready-to-eat (or cold) cereal is an American invention that grew out of the health reform movement of the late 1800s. Sanatoriums built during this period served grain-based cereals as part of food regimens intended to offer relief for sufferers of dyspepsia, a chronic digestion problem caused by the high-protein diets of the time. During the late 1880s and early 1890s several independent, ready-to-eat cereal companies were developed from the products created by these institutions. Cold cereals were one of the first modern convenience foods, and the companies they formed became the foundations of several of today's largest American food conglomerates.

At his sanatorium in Battle Creek, Michigan, Dr. John Harvey Kellogg (1852–1943) created a cereal named Granola, made of wheat flour, cornmeal, and oatmeal. It was so successful that by 1889 he was selling approximately two tons of it per week. Experimenting with other grains, Dr. Kellogg and his brother, W. K. (Will) Kellogg (1860–1951), then developed a process to form crisped, wheat flakes, creating the first flaked breakfast food, Granose Flakes, in 1895. At the same time, in the early 1890s, Henry Perky (1843–1906) created a

THE CHOICEST FOODS IN THE WORLD
AMERICAN BREAKFAST CEREALS.

A.B.C. WHITE OATS. A.B.C. WHITE WHEAT.
A.B.C. BARLEY FOOD. A.B.C. MAIZE.

An advertisement for American Breakfast Cereals.

machine that extruded strands of boiled wheat that could then be formed and baked into Shredded Wheat biscuits. He sold the cereal door to door in Colorado, then expanded east in 1895, finally moving to a huge factory in Niagara Falls in 1902.

Although Kellogg had passed up an offer to buy Perky's company in 1894, a decision he later regretted, the Kellogg brothers continued to devise new products including a flake made from corn, in 1898, called Sanitas Toasted Corn Flakes. Will Kellogg then added sugarcane, over his brother's objections, and sales of the newly named Kellogg's Toasted Corn Flakes soared. After working for his brother for twenty-two years, Will separated the cereal company from the sanatorium in 1906, forming the Battle Creek Toasted Corn Flake Company, which became the Kellogg Company in 1925.

Charles (C. W.) Post (1854–1914) also opened a Battle Creek sanatorium, in 1897, where he had created Grape-Nuts cereal, a granulated, twice-baked nugget, for his Post-um Cereal Company (renamed General Foods in 1929). Post, an innovative advertiser, was one of the first to used national ad campaigns, coupons, premiums, and samples to make Grape-Nuts a success. His next product was a flaked corn cereal originally called Elijah's Manna, although he was forced to change its name to Post Toasties in 1908 by outraged clergymen.

During this period Battle Creek was a magnet for cereal makers, attracting more than forty breakfast food companies in the early 1900s. By 1911 that city alone produced 107 brands of corn flakes as brands proliferated. Dr. Alexander P. Anderson (1862–1943) spent years perfecting a technique to puff rice, which he solved in 1902 by shooting kernels of rice from a cannon. He then sold his process to Quaker Oats, which introduced Puffed Rice cereal in 1905. Kellogg introduced All-Bran, labeled "a natural laxative cereal," in 1916 and Rice Krispies in 1928, and the Washburn Crosby Company (later General Mills) perfected bran flakes, creating Wheaties in 1921.

Although the number of cereal companies declined in the following decades, the number of brands continued to grow. General Mills unveiled Kix, a puffed cereal coated with vitamins, Cheerios (originally called Cheerioats) debuted in 1941, shortening its name in 1946, and Post's Raisin Bran appeared in 1942. The first presweetened cereal, Ranger Joe Popped Wheat Honnies, arrived in 1939, and versions from the big cereal companies followed—Post's Sugar Crisp, in 1949; Kellogg's Sugar Corn Pops in 1950, which was a newly sweetened version of the 1930s Corn Pop; and Frosted Flakes in 1952. General Mills joined the sugar bandwagon in 1954 with Trix, which at that time contained more than 46 percent sugar.

But what really sold the often similar-tasting cereals were advertisements and promotions. The first singing radio commercial, touting Wheaties, aired on Christmas Eve in 1926, and by 1929 a national radio campaign, directed toward children, was launched. Television opened up a new medium to reach the public, and by the early 1950s Kellogg was sponsoring television shows for both children and adults, and the other manufacturers soon followed. Children, however, were the desired audience, and animated characters that had been created for cereal boxes began to star in their own cartoon series, until 1969, when the Federal Communications Commission ruled that characters associated with a product, (either real or animated), could not appear on children's shows. Even so, the cereal advertisers were not deterred, and by 1976, 43 percent of all the Saturday morning commercials were promoting high-sugar breakfast cereals.

By the 1970s and 1980s, adults were again experiencing a renewed interest in the benefits of high-fiber diets, and new brands entered the marketplace. Cereals previously only available in health food stores began to enter the mainstream. Not only were smaller brands making inroads into the sales of the large manufacturers, but by 1996 consumers began to purchase store-brand cereals, motivated by price, not by taste, causing the major cereal companies, led by Post, to slash prices by as much as 28 percent.

As consumers' interest continued shifting toward whole grains and natural foods, General Mills introduced Sunrise in 1999, the first mainstream organic cereal, and smaller companies, like Arrowhead Mills and Cascadian Farms (owned by General Mills), also began infiltrating the supermarket shelves with natural products. Multi-ingredient fortified cereals, such as Kellogg's Smart Start, appeared in 1998, and cereals targeted expressly toward women, such as General Mills's Harmony, containing calcium, soy, antioxidants, and folic acid, followed in 2000.

Although ready-to-eat cereal accounted for approximately 35 percent of all American breakfasts in 2001, sales of the $8.5-billion cereal industry had begun a slight decline. Hoping to maintain their dominance, all the major manufacturers introduced breakfast bar versions of their cereals, containers for eating cereals on the go, and cereals fortified with vitamins. By 2005 the large manufacturers converted many familiar brands to whole grains, whose consumption was encouraged by the USDA guidelines for healthier eating, hoping to revive flat sales. The cereal industry continues to evolve, continually changing with the times, altering its products to reflect Americans' changing tastes and eating habits. [See also Breakfast Foods; General Mills; Graham, Sylvester; Kellogg, John Harvey; Kellogg Company; Post Foods.]

BIBLIOGRAPHY

Bruce, Scott, and Bill Crawford. *Cerealizing America: The Unsweetened Story of American Breakfast Cereal.* Boston: Faber and Faber, 1995.

Carson, Gerald. *Cornflake Crusade.* New York: Rinehart, 1957.

JOY SANTLOFER

Chafing Dish

"Chafing dish" derives from the French *chauffer*, meaning "to heat." The chafing dish's history goes back at least as far as classical times, when Cicero described a "kind of saucepan of Corinthian brass.... This simple and ingenious vessel possesses a double bottom, the uppermost one holds the light delicacies ... and the fire is underneath" (Lovegren). It was used in medieval times as well, for delicately warming foods and medicines.

In 1720 a wealthy American ordered six small brass chafing dishes to be sent from England for his daughter's wedding gift, but it is likely that the implement, common in

Three-pint nickel-plated chafing dish.

Europe, had been brought to American shores long before that date. By the early 1800s the chafing dish had taken its modern form of an elegant silver-plated dish set over a spirit lamp. It went through a period of great popularity during the 1890s, when the renowned Waldorf-Astoria hotel served after-theater chafing-dish suppers to such celebrities as J. P. Morgan and Lillian Russell. The Gay Nineties chafing-dish fad was so strong that special sets of tablecloths and matching napkins became popular, and a great number of American cookbooks were written on the subject.

After losing steam during the 1920s and 1930s, the chafing dish again became chic after World World II, owing to the rise of informal entertaining, the lack of servants, and the desire to add a touch of glamour to everyday life. Popular dishes included beef Stroganoff, Swedish meatballs, crêpes suzette, cherries jubilee, cheese fondue, and sukiyaki.

BIBLIOGRAPHY

Hess, Karen, ed. *Martha Washington's Booke of Cookery.* New York: Columbia University Press, 1981.

Kinsley, H. M. *One Hundred Recipes for the Chafing Dish.* New York: Creative Cookbooks, 2001. Reprint of the 1894 edition.

Lovegren, Sylvia. *Fashionable Food: Seven Decades of Food Fads.* New York: Macmillan, 1995.

SYLVIA LOVEGREN

Champagne

Champagne is a wine produced only within the eponymous region of France, as specified and delimited by the Appellation d'Origine Contrôlée (AOC) laws. It is a sparkling wine, the overwhelming majority of which is white, made exclusively from three legal grapes: Pinot Noir, Pinot Meunier, and Chardonnay. Champagne has had a long presence in America; it was shipped through English wine merchants and brokers into the colonies starting in about 1735, coinciding with the very beginning of the international Champagne trade. By the 1850s, vintners in Ohio were making the first American sparklers.

Champagne must be made by the *méthode champenoise,* meaning that the second fermentation, which produces the bubbles, must occur in the same bottle that is sold to the consumer. Producers of Champagne have gone to great lengths to protect the name "Champagne" from imitators making sparkling wines outside the official AOC zone, and many countries both within and outside of Europe have signed international trade agreements not to use the term "Champagne" (or for that matter, *méthode champenoise*) on their labels or in their advertising.

The United States and Champagne

The United States is not a signatory to these agreements. Although not alone in its refusal to recognize the patrimony of Champagne as geographically and historically French, membership in that group is shrinking. The United States is by far the most powerful wine-producing nation that does not acknowledge that true Champagne is unique. Indeed, in the United States "Champagne" is a generic but legal label term for any wine with bubbles. This state of affairs has led to great confusion in the American wine market, which appears to be exactly what the Champagne imitators had in mind when they adopted the name of a famous wine-producing region to describe a style of wine.

The use of "Champagne" as a generic label is no different from calling any white swill-in-a-box "Chablis" or any red wine from a jug "Burgundy." Since the end of Prohibition in

1933 and until 1997 (when for the first time, varietal label wines accounted for a greater proportion of sales than generics), the American wine industry was built on popular, mostly drinkable, inexpensive wines with generic labels. True Chablis, the glorious unoaked Chardonnay made from grapes grown on chalk soils in the coolest climate in Burgundy, is still a tough sell in the American wine market because of the image of Chablis as a cheap jug wine. The image problem for Champagne is even worse.

Undrinkable wines made from excess Thompson Seedless grapes, and nearly undrinkable wines made from excess Chenin Blanc, are subjected to the Charmat bulk process, first employed around 1913 in Ohio, California, and New York. Although interrupted by Prohibition, Charmat bulk processing resumed in the 1930s, with various technical improvements. In the processing of the early 2000s, the wine is sealed in an anaerobic tank and pumped up with carbon dioxide, forming bubbles as large as those in ginger ale. A flavoring dosage is added and the wine is bottled under continuous pressure. This finished product, often featuring a plastic stopper, will sell extremely cheaply. The label will of course include the name of the producer (often a wholly fictitious French winegrower, whose name may be Jean or André), and the product name "Champagne." Most domestically produced sparklers are this Charmat plonk.

Many Americans will complain that Champagne gives them a headache or stomach trouble. When asked if they have ever tried true Champagne their interrogator can expect a blank look in answer to the question, because quite a few neophyte wine drinkers have limited their consumption of sparkling wines to cheap imitations of Champagne. Often these wines are consumed at catered events, where they are drunk out of modified sherbet glasses, or coupes, that are also used to create the popular "Champagne Fountain."

Champagne versus Sparklers
The informed American consumer can at least choose from wines made from a better selection of grapes, and a wine that is hopefully made by the transfer method, not Charmat bulk processing. In the transfer method, the second fermentation does indeed happen in a bottle, but then thousands of bottles of this bubbly wine are poured into a tank, a dosage is added, and the wine is poured back into bottles. Wines labeled as "fermented in the bottle" are made by this process, which was developed in Germany for its *Sekt* sparklers. The American versions of these wines are drinkable, even enjoyable, but despite their label, they are not, and will never be, true Champagne.

It is important to note that some good, inexpensive Champagne alternatives without misleading labels have flooded the American market, led by Cava from northeastern Spain,

which is made by the actual *méthode champenoise*, most often in a true brut style, from white Macabeo, Xarello, and Parellada grapes. Cavas outsell Champagne in the American market and are the single largest sparkling import. Fruity and refreshing Prosecco from Veneto, Italy, is a pleasing Charmat-produced alternative. The French have joined the American domestic production, making sparklers in California's North Coast American Viticultural Area (AVA). Domaine Chandon is owned by Moët, Domaine Carneros by Taittinger, Mumm Cuvée Napa by Mumm, Pacific Echo by Veuve Clicquot, and Roederer Estate (the finest of the five) by Louis Roederer.

Méthode Champenoise Wines
Excellent vintage-dated, estate-bottled *méthode champenoise* wines are made, in the early 2000s, by American-owned Iron Horse in the Green Valley of Sonoma County. The artisan Milla Handley in the Anderson Valley of Mendocino also makes fine sparklers. Schramsberg of Napa Valley labels at least some of their fine wines as "Napa Valley Champagne." The late Jack Davies, who with his wife, Jamie, founded Schramsberg in 1965 as the first sparkling-wine producer in the Napa Valley, originally created the label to needle the neighboring French interlopers, and that label stands in the early twenty-first century.

Argyle sparklers (although owned by Petaluma of Australia) come from Oregon's Willamette Valley. Washington State's Domaine Ste. Michelle produces thousands of cases of fine *méthode champenoise* wines. In New Mexico, Gruet produces quality sparklers and North Carolina's Biltmore Estate Brut is justifiably famous. In New York State's Finger Lakes, Glenora makes extraordinary sparkling wines by the classic method (so does Konstantin Frank Vinifera Winery, but it is labeled "Champagne"). Americans generally do not successfully export their sparklers, and market share for American *méthode champenoise* wines is less than 10 percent of the domestic market for sparklers.

Perhaps the last word on this touchy subject should be left to someone who was born in the United States, but loved true Champagne so much that Pol Roger named its *cuvée de prestige* in his honor. In 1918, as World War I was coming to a close, Sir Winston Churchill proclaimed, "Remember, gentlemen, it's not just France we are fighting for, it's Champagne!"

[See also WINE; WINERIES.]

BIBLIOGRAPHY
Brennan, Thomas. *Burgundy to Champagne: The Wine Trade in Early Modern France*. Baltimore: Johns Hopkins University Press, 1997.
Faith, Nicholas. *The Story of Champagne*. New York: Facts on File, 1989.
Simon, André. *The History of Champagne*. New York: Octopus Books, 1971.
Sutcliffe, Serena. *Champagne: The History and Character of the World's Most Celebrated Wine*. New York: Simon and Schuster, 1989.

STEVEN KOLPAN

Cheese:
Historical Overview
There is no evidence that any of the Native American tribes milked animals. In 1611 "sixe good shippes, men, provisions and cattle" arrived to replenish the Jamestown, Virginia, colony, which had been chartered in 1606. Farther north the Massachusetts colonists were joined in 1623 by the ship *Anne*, which contained both goats and cattle. It is unlikely that any of the "Holland Cheeses" listed as provisions on the *Mayflower* remained when the ship reached shore, but it is purported that fresh goat and cow cheeses were made early in Plymouth Plantation.

In the history of early immigrations to the Americas, agricultural skills that included cheese making were among the assets brought by settlers from their native countries to the New World. Whether they were Spanish missionaries moving north from Mexico into California, Netherlanders settling "Nieuw Amsterdam," or part of the subsequent flows of Italians, French, Russians, and other nationals, each group craved the foods, including cheeses, that were specific to its traditional ethnicity.

In the colonial period cows gave low yields of milk, and most cheese production was a family affair. Cheddar was the style of choice for both New Englanders and New Yorkers. Taking its name from England's Cheddar Gorge, "cheddaring" was a method of milling or cutting curd, enhancing the drying process as well as acidification. Cheddar cheeses are made worldwide and represent a large percentage of U.S. cheese production.

Cheese production expanded in the mid-nineteenth century. Credit is given the Williams family of Rome, Oneida County, New York, for the organization of a farmers' milk cooperative. The cooperative's cheddar plant began production in 1851. In the late nineteenth century a factory in Verona, New York, started shipping cheeses to England. The Crowley cheese plant of Vermont claims to have the longest operating history in the United States.

Although Wisconsin is known as America's Dairyland, it was not until 1841 that Anne Pickett opened the first cheese factory in that state. By 1864 Chester Hazen of Ladoga, Wisconsin, was using the milk of three hundred cows for cheese making, and in 1886 the University of Wisconsin offered short courses for dairy farmers and cheese makers. Both the American Dairy Association and the Wisconsin Dairymen's Association were formed in the late nineteenth century.

In 1921 Wisconsin was the first state to adopt an official cheese-grading program. Approximately fifteen hundred Wisconsin cheese plants produced more than 500 million pounds of cheese annually in the mid-twentieth century. In the early twenty-first century milk from approximately seventeen thousand Wisconsin dairy farms, 90 percent of which is used to make approximately 2 billion pounds of cheese annually, represents almost one-fourth of annual U.S. cheese production. Wisconsin traditionally had small dairy farms that milked twenty to one hundred cows each. A national pattern starting in the late twentieth century, however, is toward the large-scale economy of highly automated milking herds, numbering as many as one thousand or more high-yield cows. By 2003 California dairy farms had surpassed Wisconsin farms in annual milk production.

Only a few cheeses originated in America. Among those varieties are Wisconsin brick and colby. Wisconsin is the only state with a master cheese maker certification program. One of those masters is Joe Widmer, the third-generation proprietor and maker of Widmer's brick cheese in the small town of Theresa. The name "brick" is not a description of the cheese's shape; it refers to the building bricks used as weights to press the liquid whey from the cheese curds. Widmer continues to use the bricks used by his grandfather and father. The Widmer family also has maintained the "washed rind" bacterial culture used to produce the characteristic pungent and aromatic flavors that develop as brick cheese is aged.

Colby is the name of a Wisconsin city and the name of a cheese type made since 1885. In that year a cheddar maker named Joseph Steinwand varied his normal procedure by washing the curds with cold water. The result was a more open textured, granular, moister cheese, which Steinwand named after the nearby city. Colby quickly gained popularity as a milder, economically produced variety of cheddar. Both colby and brick cheeses are mass marketed under these generic labels.

In the twentieth century advances in the technology of cheese production made possible the construction and operation of ever larger and more automated plants. James Kraft, like many cheese sellers, was troubled by the perishability of his product. Kraft experimented, grinding up cheddar, adding emulsifying salts, heating the mixture, and then pouring the results into forms. In 1917 Kraft sold the first canned processed cheese to the U.S. Army. From then on the Kraft Cheese Company developed a full line of processed cheese products, Velveeta (1928) and Cheez Whiz (1952) among them, that culminated in the individually wrapped slice.

In the early twenty-first century processed cheese competes with mozzarella for the largest annual sales numbers. Distinct from the classic cooked and stretched *pasta filata* Italian mozzarella, the cheese produced in the United States is mostly a brined product used to make ever-increasing quantities of

Admirers of President Andrew Jackson presented him with a 1,400-pound wheel of cheese shortly before he left the White House in 1837. When Jackson invited members of the public to eat the cheese it was finished within two hours.

fresh and frozen pizza. A cheese anomaly is the term "American cheese." This term refers to a type of cheese akin to cheddar and includes American processed varieties, the irony being that much of this processed food is made from imported products.

An increase in the growth of small specialty cheese making began in the late twentieth century in the United States. The American Cheese Society counts approximately two hundred farms and plants engaged in so-called artisanal activity. Many of these cheese makers buy milk from farmers or cooperatives, but quite a few make "farmstead cheese," a term used somewhat loosely to mean cheese made of cow, goat, or sheep milk from the farm where the cheese is made. Beginning with the early settlements, most cheese in America carried the names of European varieties, but Cypress Grove Humboldt Fog, Cowgirl Creamery Mount Tam, and Capriole Wabash Cannonball demonstrate a trend of naming new American cheeses for American regions. Oregon Tillamook, dating to the first years of the twentieth century, is an early example.

In the 1970s annual per person cheese consumption reached eighteen pounds. Early in the twenty-first century Americans consume more than thirty pounds of cheese per person per year. Travel abroad, attention from the news media, the interest of hotel and restaurant chefs, and the spread of specialty food outlets have contributed to this increase, but the most important factor has been the interest of consumers in the quality and variety of a national product.

[See also CHEESE: RECENT DEVELOPMENT; CHEESE-MAKING TOOLS; DAIRY; DAIRY INDUSTRY; KRAFT FOODS; MILK; PIZZA.]

BIBLIOGRAPHY

Cheese Importers Association of America. *Cheese Importers Association of America Yearbook, 2003–2004.* New York: CIAA, 2004.

Eekhof-Stork, Nancy. *The World Atlas of Cheese.* Edited by Adrian Bailey. London and New York: Paddington, 1976.

Selitzer, Ralph. *The Dairy Industry in America.* New York: Magazines for Industry, 1976.

GERD STERN

Cheese:
Recent Developments

The new American renaissance in artisan cheese making began around 1980 but has really taken off since the mid-1990s.

There are a number of factors that have led to this, though two in particular stand out. The first is the disillusionment with the industrially produced foods that had become ubiquitous all over America, which were beginning to be known for their low grade, unhealthy, tasteless ingredients. Second, the upsurge in foreign travel gave many more people the opportunity to try unfamiliar cheeses made in the European artisanal tradition.

Americans began to go to Europe, and there they discovered, largely unaltered, the artisan cheese making industry: small producers and dairies producing unpasteurized cow, goat, and sheep's cheeses all over the continent. The cheesemaker's craft had not died out or lost its place in society or the cuisine of the region, and was not seen as an unhealthy way to eat as it was in America, where numerous diets and advice on cholesterol had made cheese the enemy.

Recently, there has been a movement in America to return to our traditional cheese making traditions and methods, and there

A selection of cheeses at a gourmet retailer in Brooklyn, New York.

are now hundreds of small, artisan producers the length and breadth of the country. They are particularly concentrated in Vermont, Wisconsin, and northern California, where they have had support from the state, university, or trade groups. These are young, keen cheese enthusiasts who have not necessarily had any connection with the farming industry before.

In the last ten years the number of entries in the annual judging of the American Cheese Society has gone from under a hundred to almost one thousand, so it is not inaccurate to describe the phenomenal growth in the cheese market as a renaissance. All those who invest their time and talent in the industry are determined that this should continue and that artisanal cheese making should become a safe tradition rather than a fad or a trend.

Since 2000, another interesting development has been the appearance of the restaurant cheese board, where many of the serious restaurateurs have begun offering a cheese course and become more knowledgeable about the cheeses they serve and their provenance.

In numerous recent studies, a low-fat diet has been shown to have little impact on health, and people are beginning to understand the positive health benefits from eating good cheese regularly, particularly the artisan-made unpasteurized cheeses which also have the best flavor.

As the variety of artisanal cheeses has increased, so have the outlets from where they are sold. Wholefoods markets, specialist cheese counters, and farmers markets have been at the forefront of the trend, and have offered their customers a more sophisticated knowledge of the product. This is unquestionably related to the upsurge of the organic movement, and the desire to eat things that not only are better for you, but taste better too.

There has definitely been a downturn in popularity in French cheeses, matched by the upturn in popularity of artisan-made American cheeses as they continue to improve and as raw milk French and European cheeses get more difficult to obtain. There is a sixty-day rule in America, whereby raw milk cheeses have to be at least that old to qualify for importation, and recently this rule has become far more rigidly enforced than it was in the past. (The cheese mongers believe that the only effective control of American ship-

ping ports has been the virtual elimination of raw milk cheese!)

Spain and Portugal continue to grow slowly in terms of specialty cheese sales, whereas cheeses from England, Ireland, and Wales have flattened out.

If present trends continue, Italy will surpass France. In most specialty cheese shops the top sellers continue to be Parmigiano Reggiano and fresh mozzarella. Sales of cheddar and brie continue to keep their place at the top of the list.

Some of the artisan producers are beginning to gain some local, and in rare cases, national, renown, and have begun to brand products that they do not produce themselves. As long as their premier concern is the quality of the product, this can only enhance their profitability and help make the artisan cheese maker successful and viable rather than marginal in business terms.

There is pressure from the large dairy industry to make all cheese pasteurized regardless of its age as this makes controls from the various food boards and authorities easier and does not inhibit export sales. Australia, for example, bans all unpasteurized cheese. This would be unthinkable in France where every village, however small, has one if not more small dairies making unpasteurized cheese. There would probably be a second French Revolution if anyone tried to ban raw-milk cheese, but the countries who do not have such an unbroken tradition of good food and cheese making, such as England and Ireland, are finding it increasingly difficult to satisfy the stringent new health and safety laws that are neither desirable, necessary, nor financially viable for them to carry out.

It remains to be seen whether the small artisanal farms can survive and remain economically viable. Most small farms sell their milk to gigantic co-ops, who in turn control the market. There is very little institutional support for conversion to artisan cheese production, and many dairy farmers lack the sophisticated knowledge of what the market wants and what it is looking for. It is also difficult to learn the art of cheese making if you live outside the main cheese producing areas in the United States. Teaching cheese making is concentrated in Wisconsin, Vermont, and northern California. In New York State however, which has an enormous dairy industry and good dairy universities, artisan cheese making is virtually moribund, and six thousand dairy farms are slated to go out of business by 2015.

American food distribution has involved successfully solving problems of infrastructure historically; i.e. transporting and shipping perishable products at a reasonable price. Yet while industrial distribution is extremely sophisticated, artisan cheeses are still shipped in the old-fashioned, most expensive method, being case by case using Fed Ex or similar services. Since the cost of these cheeses is already more expensive than their

European counterparts, which are still, despite recent regulations, often heavily subsidized, retail prices of American farm cheeses makes them inaccessible to a large section of their potential market.

This is one of the problems that the new generation of artisan cheese makers will surely be determined to solve, so that their skills and talents and our cheese making heritage will not be in danger of being lost to the nation yet again now that it has been recovered and transformed so successfully.

[**See also** CHEESE: HISTORICAL OVERVIEW; CHEESE-MAKING TOOLS; CHEESE, MOLDY; DAIRY; DAIRY INDUSTRY; FRENCH INFLUENCES ON AMERICAN FOOD; VELVEETA.]

BIBLIOGRAPHY

Baboin-Jaubert, Alix. *Handbook of Cheese*. London: Hachette Illustrated, 2003.

Graham, Peter. *Classic Cheese Cookery*. London: Grub Street, 2003.

Jenkins, Steven. *Cheese Primer*. New York: Workman, 1996.

Michelson, Patricia. *The Cheese Room*. London: Penguin, 2001.

Slow Food Editore. *Italian Cheese*. Bra: Slow Food Arcigola Editore, 1999–2000.

ROBERT KAUFELT

Cheese, Moldy

Like wine and truffles, moldy cheeses are products of the damp, dark underworld. Legend has it that the first moldy cheese was discovered thousands of years ago when an absent-minded shepherd left his curds and bread in a cave while he was off chasing sheep. The shepherd returned to find a moldy sandwich but was so hungry he ate it anyway. Since then, moldy cheeses such as Roquefort, Gorgonzola, English Stilton, and Danish blue have been developed by Europeans into gourmet fare. Government licenses assure a cheese is the genuine article. Aficionados of moldy cheese have included Pliny the Elder, Charlemagne, and Casanova, who considered the cheeses an aphrodisiac.

People who love the earthy zest of moldy cheeses—primarily called blue cheeses—crumble the cheese over salad, stir it into scrambled eggs, melt it on hamburgers, use it in pasta and on pizza, and eat it as is with a stack of water crackers. Few cheeses offer as many menu possibilities, from a sliced apple and Stilton appetizer to an elegant, not too sweet dessert mousse. Not all blue cheeses are smelly, crumbly lumps; some are mild, creamy, and even sweet.

The aroma and taste of moldy cheeses depend on the intensity of the cure and the type of mold. The shape, size, and surface of the cheese, and the microclimate of the curing cellar also affect the outcome. The type of milk used to make the cheese is an important factor. For example, sheep provide the milk for Roquefort, and a red sheep is imprinted on the wrapper. Milk from Holstein cows is used for most moldy cheese made in the United States.

The earliest makers of blue cheese used bread to begin production of the distinctive mold and then waited patiently for the veins of mold to grow and spread naturally between the curds. In later times mold growth is often induced with penicillium spores (related to the mold that produces the antibiotic penicillin but not known to cause the allergic reaction penicillin can). White-hatted "cheese ripeners" still use bread to inoculate wheels of Roquefort with mold spores. After repeated salting by hand during the first three to five days of preparation (to make the cheese firm on the outside), the cheese is pricked so that oxygen essential to mold growth can penetrate the wheel. Veins of mold range in color from pale blue to deep green. Roquefort is aged for three months in neat rows on oak benches in limestone caves in Combalou, in southwestern France. The caves have a constant temperature, high humidity, and optimal air circulation.

Maytag blue is the most famous of the American-born moldy cheeses. It was developed at Iowa State University in 1941 from the Holstein cows on the family farm of Fritz Maytag, an early-twentieth-century settler who became known as an appliance king. An Iowa State professor who helped develop the cheese had worked in the dairy industry in Denmark, where Saga blue cheese was developed. Maytag blue is a dense, crumbly cheese with a spicy and creamy flavor. It is hand made in small batches in Newton, Iowa, and aged for six months in caves on the side of a hill where the natural molds and yeast live. Some of the Holsteins that produce the milk for Maytag blue cheese are direct descendants of the original 1919 prizewinning herd.

Another cave-produced cheese was developed in the early 1940s in an old railroad tunnel that cut through Stumphouse Mountain in South Carolina. The abandoned tunnel caught the attention of a professor in the dairy department of Clemson Agricultural College of South Carolina (later Clemson University), who began experimenting with a Roquefort-style cheese made with milk from the Clemson herd of 680 Holsteins. World War II and scarce milk supplies interrupted production, but Operation Blue Cheese resumed in 1953. The cheese was manufactured on campus and cured in the tunnel, which was thirty miles away. Production was directed by a graduate of Iowa State University.

Clemson blue cheese is an artisan cheese, made the old-fashioned way. Each 288-gallon vat holds a batch of approximately 240 pounds, which is salted, waxed, and aged for six months. When the cheese is ready, each hoop is scraped and packaged by hand. Eventually the college duplicated the conditions of the cave on campus, so the need to transport cheese to the tunnel and back ended, and the tunnel became a tourist site. Other small artisan moldy cheeses are made where the breeds of cows needed are available, such as the Colorado foothills and Minnesota.

Although they vary in color from white to creamy yellow, moldy cheeses should never be brown. The veining ranges from the palest blue to dark hues of green. If the veining looks gray or dusty, the cheese is past its prime. Whether a creamy or a dry variety, the cheese should be firm. Cheese that looks cracked, mushy, or weepy should not be purchased.

Consumers need to ask for a taste before buying moldy cheese. A good blue always is flavorful but never is sour or harsh. The older the cheese, the more pungent the flavor and the more dense the veining. Roquefort, for example, sometimes overly salted for the export market, so consumers sensitive to sodium need a taste. The riper the cheese, the more difficult it is to slice. Cheese is easier to cut when cool. A knife used to serve cheese should be dipped in hot water to melt the cheese fat. A cheese wire is the better tool. Roquefort-style cheeses simply crumble. Pressing the cheese through a strainer and combining it with cream, lemon juice, and oil produces the famous Roquefort salad dressing.

Like an aromatic, full-bodied red wine—its most worthwhile accompaniment—moldy cheese needs to breathe, because the mold is a living thing, and the cheese continues to ripen. If the cheese is wrapped in plastic, the wrapping must be changed often. Moldy cheeses can be refrigerated for several weeks, but they taste better when allowed to warm to room temperature.
[See also CHEESE; CHEESE-MAKING TOOLS; DAIRY; MILK.]

BIBLIOGRAPHY
Betancourt, Marian. "Singing the Blues." In *Phila-delphia* magazine, August 1991.
Department of Food Science and Human Nutrition, Clemson University. www.clemson.edu.

MARIAN BETANCOURT

Cheesecake

Tarts, pies, and pastries filled with various types of cheese have been common throughout Europe and the Middle East since ancient times. The English and other European colonists introduced their versions of cheesecake into North America, and cheesecake recipes were included in colonial cookery manuscripts, such as those used by the William Penn family in Pennsylvania, dated about 1694, and that of Harriot Pinckney Horry in South Carolina, dated 1770. The family recipe book used by Martha Washington beginning in 1794 contained three cheesecake recipes, two of which call for making fresh curds using new milk and rennet. The third thickens cream with eggs and butter.

Immigrants from southern and eastern Europe introduced their cheesecake traditions into the United States in the late nineteenth and early twentieth centuries. Italian cheesecake, for instance, is made with ricotta

cheese. Russian *pashka* is a molded dessert—a pyramid of sweetened creamy cheese—served at Easter. Eastern European cheesecakes are made with cottage cheese or farmer cheese, and some are baked in yeast-dough crusts.

America's favorite, New York–style or "Jewish-style" cheesecake, relies for its dense richness on cream cheese, which became available toward the end of the nineteenth century. The New York City restaurants Lindy's and Junior's became famous for their cheesecakes, and restaurants nationwide followed suit with similar cakes. The classic is made of cream cheese sweetened with sugar, enriched with eggs and cream, flavored with vanilla, and baked in a crumb, cookie dough, or sponge-cake crust. It is sometimes dressed up with fruit toppings—cherry, blueberry, strawberry, pineapple—and new variations are constantly appearing: chocolate swirl, mocha, pumpkin. An unbaked "icebox" cheesecake with a gelatin-thickened filling is a convenient shortcut; and there are yogurt cheesecakes for the fat-conscious and tofu cheesecakes for the vegan.
[See also CAKES; NEW YORK FOOD.]

BIBLIOGRAPHY
Bovbjerg, Dana, and Jeremy Iggers. *The Joy of Cheese-cake.* Woodbury, NY: Barron's, 1980.
Zisman, Larry, and Honey Zisman. *The 50 Best Cheesecakes in the World: The Recipes That Won the Nationwide "Love That Cheesecake" Contest.* New York: St. Martin's, 1993.

ANDREW F. SMITH

Cheese-Making Tools

Soft and hard cheeses are made after curd, which is solid, is separated from whey, which is liquid. Cheese baskets or cradles have been used for centuries to drip off whey. These devices were woven of natural materials, usually strips of oak splint. Cheese drainers were colander-like vessels of ceramic and later of punctured sheet metal. Some cheese drainers had a weighted lid that rested on top of the curds. A large cheese press was needed to apply great pressure to make a large, hard cheese. The cheese press resembled a sawhorse to which was attached a round wooden container that had holes in the bottom and a long wooden lever that pushed a presser against the curds in the container. The first U.S. patent for a cheese press was granted in 1812, and many patented and homemade presses followed. Fancy tin egg cheese and cottage cheese strainer molds in heart and other shapes were made in the 1850s to 1870s in Pennsylvania. Long, thin, flexible steel cheese knives and whips have been used since the middle of the nineteenth century to break curds into large or small pieces for soft cheeses. The knives are used in the making of hard cheeses to mix in thickening and curdling agents, such as rennet, as well as salt and coloring and to break up the curds to make the cheese smooth.
[See also CHEESE.]

BIBLIOGRAPHY

Franklin, Linda Campbell. *300 Years of Kitchen Collectibles.* 5th ed. Iola, WI: Krause, 2003.

LINDA CAMPBELL FRANKLIN

Chefs and Cookbooks, *see Celebrity Chefs; Radio/TV Food Shows*

Chemical Additives

Extra ingredients have been added to foods for millennia to make preparation easier, to preserve, to enhance appearance and scents, to thicken, to improve nutritive value, to create intoxicants, and to add apparent social value (as gold leaf on foods). Some additives have been toxic, like mercuric compounds painted on foods to make them white and pretty, and bits of brass added to the cooking water of vegetables to brighten the color. Others have been added inadvertently and have resulted in illness or death.

According to the American governmental agency responsible for additives, the Food and Drug Administration (FDA) in the Department of Health and Human Services, a food additive is "any substance the intended use of which results or may reasonably be expected to result—directly or indirectly—in its becoming a component or otherwise affecting the characteristics of any food." This definition includes any substance used in the production, processing, treatment, packaging, transportation, or storage of food.

Few chemical additives were in wide use until relatively recent times. Today, the FDA lists more than six thousand additives that can be deliberately or coincidentally added in production, handling, and packaging.

Chemical Food Additives in American History

Since the 1800s crusaders have tried to persuade the government to create and administer regulations about food sanitation, purity, and adulteration. Little was done until muckraking articles and novels, such as *The Jungle* by Upton Sinclair portraying the horrors of the meatpacking industry, inflamed public indignation and helped set the stage for congressional action. Common use of toxic preservatives and dyes in foods as well as quack claims for worthless and dangerous patent medicines were the triggering issues. In 1906 the Food and Drug

An advertisement for Aurora brand macaroni notes its superior quality and artificial coloring.

Act was passed. The Meat Inspection Act was enacted on the same day. The next year, certified color regulations were promulgated to standardize colors and make sure the ones used were safe.

Through the next three decades, small steps were taken to deal with the issues of food safety. In 1930 the Bureau of Chemistry became the Food and Drug Administration and was given broader authority. In 1949 the FDA published guidance for the industry for the first time. Titled *Procedures for the Appraisal of the Toxicity of Chemicals in Food* (and informally called Guidance to Industry), it came to be known as the "black book" in the food production industry. In 1958 the Food Additives Amendment was enacted, and the list of "Generally Recognized as Safe" food additives was published. In the late 1960s the agency was given additional responsibility for sanitation standards for handling milk, shellfish, food service, and interstate travel facilities, and for preventing poisoning and accidents.

The "Everything Added to Food in the United States" (EAFUS) database, administered by the FDA, contains administrative, chemical, and toxicological information on more than two thousand substances directly added to food in the following categories: direct, secondary direct, color additives, generally recognized as safe (GRAS), and prior-sanctioned substances.

The Federal Food, Drug and Cosmetic Act (FFDCA) of 1938 defines a food contact substance as "any substance intended for use as a component of materials used in manufacturing, packing, packaging, transporting, or holding food if such use is not intended to have any technical effect in such food." This includes adhesives and components of coatings, paper and paperboard components, polymers, and adjuvants and production aids. In general, these are substances that may come into contact with food as part of packaging, handling, or processing equipment but are not intended to be added directly to food.

Common Uses of Additives

Different types of food products call for different types of additives. Many foods include more than one additive to address the multiple considerations that consumers expect, and many additives perform more than one function. Often two or more additives serve the same general purpose but have slightly different characteristics that, when combined, create a synergistic effect, modifying or amplifying each other's effects. Looking at the four applications of food additives in some detail gives a sense of the process whereby foods are designed or adapted to modern industrial opportunities.

1. To impart or maintain desired consistency in the finished product. Both manufacturers and consumers have preferences and expectations about food. Consumers say that baked goods and mixes should be able to reach the table with a sense of freshness and moisture. Salad dressings, ice cream, and processed cheeses are expected to be smooth and emulsified (nonseparating). Consumers expect coconut to stay moist on the shelf. Foods are expected to have a good "mouthfeel." Table salt has to pour freely to be used easily.

Food gums, like alginates, carrageenan, pectin, guar gum, and xanthan gum, can thicken and gel foods, adding viscosity to beverages and helping to solidify puddings and other spoonable desserts. Ingredients like maltodextrin can also help provide thickness and body in liquids and help retain moisture in baked goods. Such emulsifiers as lecithin, monoglycerides, and diglycerides help hold oil and water combinations together, as in salad dressings and cheeses, but they can also help foods retain moisture and are antifoaming agents.

Sweetened, flaked coconut has a combination of additives to keep it tasting and feeling fresh, including sugar, water, propylene glycol (to preserve freshness and give a moist mouthfeel), salt, and sodium metabisulphite (a preservative to maintain whiteness). Sodium aluminosilicate is added to salt to keep it free pouring, but it is also used with whole, broken, or flaked grain, including rice, other sugars and syrups (such as brown sugar or maple syrup), herbs, spices, seasonings (including salt substitutes), and condiments (such as seasoning for instant noodles).

2. To improve or maintain the nutritive value of the food. Many foods are enriched by the addition of minerals and natural and synthetic vitamins. Sometimes foods are enriched to replace nutrients lost in processing; at other times additives are included to improve the nutrient profile, as, for example, when vitamins A and D are added to milk. Products containing added nutrients must be so labeled. Additives can be found in wheat products, including flour, bread, biscuits, breakfast cereals, and pasta. These additives include niacin, reduced iron, thiamine mononitrate, riboflavin, and folic acid, all essential nutrients. Cornmeal products are often enriched with the same additives that are found in flour.

Margarine is a complex formulation made up in great measure of additives. The following are ingredients in a typical margarine product: partially hydrogenated soybean oil (to make the product solid), liquid soybean oil (to keep it spreadable), water (to approximate butter), salt (for flavor and a slight degree of preservation), whey (from milk, for flavor), soy lecithin (to emulsify the oil and water), vegetable monoglycerides and diglycerides (to help emulsify), sodium benzoate (as a preservative), citric acid (as a preservative and a flavoring agent), artificial flavor, vitamin A (palmitate), and beta-carotene (for color). Iodized salt is enriched with iodine to prevent goiter in the general population. The condition has virtually disappeared since the introduction of the product.

3. To maintain palatability and wholesomeness of packaged foods. Several families of chemical additives help retain freshness and retard spoilage in processed foods (caused by mold, air, bacteria, fungi, or yeast), and they are not interchangeable, even when chemically similar. Propionic acid and its salts are a good example: Although both calcium propionate and sodium propionate are equally effective antimicrobial agents, calcium propionate is used throughout the world as a preservative in bread production. It can act as a calcium enricher, contributing to total calcium in the diet, and its use in preference to sodium propionate will result in slightly lower sodium levels in the bread. By contrast, sodium propionate is favored over calcium propionate in cake production because added calcium can interfere with the leavening, or rising action, of the cake.

4. To enhance flavor or impart a desired color. The first group of flavor additives to consider is the oldest—herbs and spices, such as cloves, ginger, cinnamon, and nutmeg as well as fruit flavors derived from the flesh or peels (for example, limonene, an oil from the skins of citrus fruit). Some herbs and spices provide both flavor and color (to varying degrees), such as turmeric, saffron, and annatto seeds.

It is difficult to find a processed food that has not had some enhancement of flavors and color. Foods ranging as far and wide as spice cake and gingerbread, soft drinks, yogurt, soup, candies, baked goods, cheeses, jams, and chewing gum all contain flavor enhancers, and most will also have some color added.

[**See also** Chemical Leavening; Honey; Preserves; Salt and Salting; Sugar; Sweeteners; Vitamins.]

BIBLIOGRAPHY

Food and Drug Administration. http://www.fda.gov/.

McGee, Harold. *On Food and Cooking: The Science and Lore of the Kitchen.* 2nd ed. New York: Scribners, 2004.

Robert Pastorio

Chemical Leavening

The North American predilection for speed and innovation spurred the nineteenth-century adoption of chemical leavenings in common baking and so laid the groundwork for prepackaged mixes. A flurry of experimentation through the 1800s with combinations of chemicals known to work as leavening agents resulted in the most common and popular modern types. Along the way, there was much controversy and confusion about the dangers of using the agents and charges and countercharges of ingredient adulteration.

An advertisement for Hecker's Perfect Baking Powder, 1890s.

Chemical leavenings replaced yeast and beaten egg whites. A blending of acid and alkali creates the gas required to raise batter or dough, usually accomplished by introducing an alkali to acid ingredients in the batter or by adding both an acid and an alkali to the ingredients. Since basic principles of chemistry were understood by the late eighteenth century, conscious product development led to the use of these products.

Earliest Use

The use of pearl ash was in all likelihood one of the professional secrets of European bakers. Peter Rose, historian of colonial Dutch American culinary practices, theorizes that in mid-eighteenth-century Albany, New York, the practice leaked out from bakers to home cooks. The first recorded mention of pearl ash use in America was in Amelia Simmons's *American Cookery*, published in 1796, though the practice was surely established by that time.

Pearl ash is potassium carbonate, refined from potash, which was derived from plant material ashes—in England from pea and bean stalks and in America usually from wood. Potash, widely used in wool manufacturing, was made by boiling lye leached from ashes. Subjected to intense heat in an oven or reverberatory furnace, carbon was burned away from potash, leaving the lighter-colored alkaline pearl ash. For pearl ash to work in baking, it had to be combined with an acid ingredient, usually molasses or milk (sometimes sour milk), wine, or lemon, and required thorough mixing.

Saleratus (from *sal*, meaning salts, and *aeratus*, meaning aerating) was a term in use from the 1830s through the early twentieth century to describe a variety of products, including potassium bicarbonate and sodium bicarbonate, used as rising agents. There were plant and, increasingly, mineral sources for

saleratus, particularly as methods were developed for using sea salt as a source.

The term "baking soda" occurs in cookery books in the 1850s, referring to sodium bicarbonate, which formerly had been called saleratus and was a by-product of salt or, in some cases, was refined from naturally occurring alkalis. It, too, had to be used with sour milk, buttermilk, or molasses. Some of the earliest products easily clumped in dampness, so they had to be stored dry and carefully powdered before use.

Cream of tartar is bitartrate of potassium, an acid product used in combination with the alkalis to aerate batters. Originally derived from the lees of wine, it was expensive until nonorganic sources were developed. Its costliness accounted for much adulteration of the product in the later nineteenth century.

Baking powder was developed as a self-contained, premixed acid-and-alkali combination product. For the last half of the nineteenth century, cookbooks called for both baking soda and cream of tartar in baking and by the 1850s occasionally referred to "yeast powders" (baking soda and cream of tartar wrapped separately but sold together), an early form of baking powder. Recipes continued to call for baking soda and cream of tartar even into the 1900s, but increasingly baking powder is specifically mentioned.

To make baking powder, the acid and alkali ingredients were typically mixed in proper proportion with a starch filler to prevent lumping. The nature of the acid determined the type of baking powder. Phosphate powders were made with calcium phosphate, tartrate powders with cream of tartar, and alum powders from a calcined double phosphate of aluminum.

There were many confusing, sometimes alarmist, claims made by competing baking powder companies, which proliferated in the last two decades of the nineteenth century and the first decade of the twentieth century. Unscrupulous manufacturers fluffed out baking powders with inert or poor-quality ingredients. Various claims were made about healthfulness, purity, reliability, and digestibility. Most modern baking powders have their origins in the last half to last quarter of the 1800s, including Rumford, Davis, and Clabber Girl.

Besides these basic rising agents, there were other types in use during the 1800s. Most, but not all, of them have largely fallen out of use, including baking ammonia, Rochelle salts, powdered alum (used with baking soda), and hartshorn. With the favored acids and alkalis all coming from various sources, and used in various combinations with each other and other ingredients, the chemical leavening picture between 1850 and 1880 still can be very confusing, as it must have been to the cooks of the era as well. Nevertheless, they were widely adopted as a cheap and easy alternative to eggs or yeast, and the harm to flavor seems not to have been much regretted.

[See also CAKES.]

BIBLIOGRAPHY
The best historical information about baking powders comes from grocer's manuals and descriptions of manufacturing processes.

De Voe, Thomas F. *The Market Assistant, Containing a Brief Description of Every Article of Human Food Sold in the Public Markets of the Cities of New York, Boston, Philadelphia, and Brooklyn; Including the Various Domestic and Wild Animals, Poultry, Game, Fish, Vegetables, Fruits &c., &c., with Many Curious Incidents and Anecdotes.* Detroit: Gale Research, 1975. Reprint of the 1867 first edition.

Felker, Peter H. *The Grocer's Manual, Containing the Natural History and Process of Manufacture of All Grocer's Goods.* Claremont, NH: Claremont Manufacturing, 1878.

SANDRA L. OLIVER

Cherries

Wild forms of both the sweet cherry (*Prunus avium*) and the sour cherry (*P. cerasus*) grow along the eastern Mediterranean, especially in southeastern Europe and Asia Minor, the regions of origin for both species. The species name for sweet cherry, *avium*, refers to birds, the agents largely responsible for the distribution of the seed and therefore the spread of both species. Hybrids of the two species, commonly called Duke cherries, are also cultivated to a limited extent but are not significant commercially in the United States.

The sweet cherry apparently was first domesticated in ancient Greece. Although it has been cultivated for more than two thousand years, it remained for much of that time a plant for the home garden, not one cultivated for the market. Both sweet and sour cherries were introduced to America by early settlers in the Northeast and later were distributed into states such as Virginia and Carolina and then expanded into the Midwest and, finally, to the Pacific Coast. There, in Oregon, the Lewelling family introduced the Bing cherry. This popular, firm-fleshed variety, together with improvements in transportation and the advent of refrigeration, helped establish the modern sweet cherry industry by making it possible to ship fresh cherries to distant markets.

Sweet cherries are classified into two general groups. One type, a class of soft, juicy cherries, is called a heart or a gean, and the other is called a *bigarreau*, a French term that initially referred to the variegated color of the fruit but now applies to any sweet cherry with firm flesh, regardless of color. A typical heart is Black Tartarian, a soft, richly flavored cherry, very delicate when ripe and suitable only for nearby markets. The *bigarreau* type includes the crisp-textured Bing and Rainier cherries, which account for most of the nation's sweet cherry production, concentrated in the Northwest and California. Sweet cherries are also grown in New York and Pennsylvania.

The bane of sweet cherry growers even in the more arid parts of the West is rainfall at harvest, which can be devastating some years, inducing fruit of susceptible varieties like Bing to crack. Sweet cherries also are traditionally harvested with their stems, and this is accomplished only by costly hand labor, thus making sweet cherries one of the most expensive fresh fruits on the market. While the Bing is the mainstay of the industry, there are new varieties maturing earlier and later than Bing, thus extending the marketing season; there are also new self-fertile types and others with some resistance to rain cracking. The Rainier is a light-fleshed but highly blushed sweet cherry growing in popularity as a high-quality dessert fruit.

Sweet cherries are primarily sold for fresh consumption, but they are also used in cherries jubilee, a classic dessert made of a saucy cherry flambé poured over ice cream. Maraschino cherries, used in fruit cocktail, drinks, and fruit cakes, are made of sweet cherries that are artificially flavored and colored, mostly of the Royal Ann variety.

The tart, or sour, cherry industry began in the mid-nineteenth century and is centered in Michigan. The Montmorency is the primary variety and can be harvested mechanically. Used mostly for culinary purposes, tart cherries are excellent for cherry pies and preserves; however, a new, sweeter variety from Hungary, the Balaton cherry, shows great potential for fresh market and juice. Both species of commercial cherries are relatively high in vitamin C and antioxidants and appear to provide both antigout and anti-inflammatory benefits.

[See also PACIFIC NORTHWEST.]

BIBLIOGRAPHY
Webster, A. D., and N. E. Looney, eds. *Cherries: Crop Physiology, Production, and Uses.* Wallingford, U.K.: CAB International, 1996.

Hedrick, U. P. *The Cherries of New York.* Albany, NY: Lyon, 1915.

ANDREW MARIANI

Cherry Bounce

Cherry bounce is best known as an American cordial that is homemade at all socioeconomic levels by crushing wild black cherries or cultivated sour cherries together with their pits, sugar, and the alcohol of choice and then letting the mixture mature. The well-to-do colonial New Englander or Virginian opted for rum or brandy; other southerners preferred whiskey. Modern-day Louisiana Cajuns accept only bourbon, while cherry-rich Wisconsin claims vodka as the spirit of choice.

In late seventeenth-century England, "cherry-bouncer" might refer to any "mingled" drink or punch. By the mid-1700s cherry bounce was often indistinguishable from cherry brandy (although it was sometimes spiced with cinnamon or nutmeg). Indeed, it is probable that the name "bounce" was intended to foil tax collectors: in the eighteenth and nineteenth centuries (and in early twentieth-century rural Maryland) one meaning of "bounce" was to lie or swindle. Before its near-synonymous association with cherries, "bounce" sometimes also referred to other fruit-flavored cordials (e.g., blackberry brandy) and to an eighteenth-century combination of spruce beer and wine drunk by some New Hampshire fishermen.

[See also CORDIALS; CORDIALS, HISTORICAL; RATAFIA.]

ROBIN M. MOWER

Cherry Pitters or Stoners

Cherry pies can be enjoyed fully only when the eater is confident that there are no pits to break the teeth. Homemade pronged sticks were used to push a pit through a cherry. In 1863 a cherry pitter was patented in the United States. The device was a cast iron, horseshoe-shaped frame with three legs, a hopper, and a crank. Cherries were poured slowly into the hopper while the user turned a crank to move a ribbed wheel that rubbed the stones out and away while the mangled fruit was channeled into a bowl. A cherry pitter patented in 1870 was a box and frame that held twenty cherries. The device was fitted with a hinged presser and twenty wooden dowels that pushed out the twenty stones at the same time. Later patents generally followed the 1863 concept. By 1890 handheld stoners with a spring-action prong were being used to push stones from one cherry at a time. This type continues to be manufactured.

[See also CHERRIES.]

BIBLIOGRAPHY
Franklin, Linda Campbell. *300 Years of Kitchen Collectibles.* 5th ed. Iola, WI: Krause, 2003.

LINDA CAMPBELL FRANKLIN

Chesapeake Region, Food and Drink of the

The Chesapeake Bay is bordered by Maryland and Virginia. It is rich in seafood, and salt marshes provide food and winter quarters for migrating birds and waterfowl. The region's temperate climate favors vegetable and fruit growing. Native Americans grew corn, sweet potatoes, melons, and a variety of squash and beans. They harvested strawberries, blackberries, persimmons, acorns, hickory nuts, and black walnuts, and hunted deer, turkeys, and small game. They also ate oysters, crabs, and fish. In 1607, the first permanent English colony was established at Jamestown, Virginia. St. Mary's City, first capital of the Maryland colony, was founded in 1634. European settlers brought with them cattle, sheep, pigs, and chickens, and European grains, fruits, and vegetables. Peanuts, black-eyed peas, okra, and watermelon were introduced from Africa.

The colonial-era tobacco plantation society was noted for its tradition of lavish hospitality. Enslaved African cooks combined the foods of America, Europe, and Africa to create a regional cuisine. Fried chicken may have had its origins in Africa. Sweet potato biscuits and corn breads come from the Indian tradition. Corn pudding, spoon bread or batter bread, hominy, grits, and sweet potato and pumpkin pies, were all adaptations using local ingredients. Brunswick stew (made with squirrel, onions, chicken, lima beans, corn, okra, and tomatoes) might have originated in Brunswick County, Virginia.

Pork is a common ingredient in Chesapeake region cooking. As early as 1639, dry-cured Virginia hams had a distinctive flavor that rivaled Europe's best. Today, vegetables and game are cooked with salt pork. Pie crusts and biscuits often are made with lard as shortening. Stuffed fresh ham is a traditional Easter dish, cooked with spring greens packed into slits cut in the meat. Maryland beaten biscuits are traditionally served with a thin slice of dry-cured Smithfield or Virginia ham.

In the eighteenth century, a few wealthy landowners owned fishing nets to catch herring in the rivers. The fish were preserved by salting as food for slaves and the poor. Not until the mid-nineteenth century were fish caught in quantity for growing urban markets. Today, planked shad is popular at annual shad festivals. Shad roe is a delicacy. Rockfish, known elsewhere as striped bass, is eaten stuffed and baked. Eels, the second largest commercial fin fish catch in Maryland, are not consumed locally; most of the catch is exported to Europe and Asia.

European colonists made apple and peach cider, peach brandies, and fruit cordials. Rye whiskey production centered in Maryland and Pennsylvania, where Scotch-Irish immigrants settled. Rye whiskey, for many years America's most popular spirit, remained the dominant whiskey type in Maryland and southern Pennsylvania well into the twentieth century.

The nation's first railroad was built from Baltimore and connected with the Ohio River by 1853, providing new markets for the products of the Chesapeake region. Market hunting sent wild geese, and other waterfowl, to the markets of large cities.

Fishermen rake for oysters in the Chesapeake Bay despite stormy conditions.

Canvasback ducks, fed on wild celery in Chesapeake marshes, were internationally acclaimed as one of America's great wild foods. Trappers caught muskrat for their fur, but local residents esteemed the flesh as well. Diamondback Terrapin, a member of the turtle family, were once so plentiful that they were common food for slaves. By the late 1800s, terrapin had become scarce, and terrapin soup and stew, flavored and served with Madeira or sherry wine, was fashionable.

An oyster packinghouse established in Baltimore in 1834 was the first to use hermetically sealed tin canisters (or "cans") for shucked oysters, fruits, and vegetables. In 1860, Baltimore fed the nation with seafood and locally grown fruits and vegetables, especially oysters, peaches, tomatoes, and corn. Thirty-four Baltimore companies provided canned goods for the Union army. By 1868, there were eighty oyster packinghouses in Baltimore. Raw oysters, oyster stew, scalloped oysters, fried oysters, oyster fritters, and ham and oyster pie remain popular in the region.

Eastern Shore farmers grew peaches, melons, tomatoes, and all sorts of vegetables for the canneries. Maryland was the leading tomato canning state in the nation until the 1940s, when Eastern Shore farmers shifted their efforts to raising poultry and to growing corn and soybeans for poultry feed. By the late twentieth century, the Delmarva Peninsula was one of the most highly concentrated poultry-raising areas in the world.

On the fishing boats of the bay, all-male crews developed a tradition of good eating with inexpensive ingredients, often prepared by black men. The custom of melting sharp cheese in hot coffee both lightened the coffee when there was no fresh milk, and provided melted cheese for hard biscuits. Watermen relished salt fish for breakfast, cooked with potatoes, onions, and salt pork. Bean soup with hot biscuits or fry bread and molasses was a staple midday meal. Stewed chicken or dried lima bean soup with slick dumplings, or cornmeal dumplings known as dodgers, remain popular.

German immigrants brought with them a taste for sauerkraut. In Baltimore, sauerkraut is a necessary compliment to Thanksgiving turkey (with oyster stuffing), and sauerkraut salad is a popular dish. Sauerbraten, or sour beef, is another regional favorite. There were more than two dozen breweries in Baltimore alone in the 1890s. German breweries also operated in Washington, DC, and Norfolk, Virginia, until Prohibition in 1920 closed most of them. Beer is served with steamed crabs, crab cakes, soft-shell crabs, oysters, fried fish, and barbecued foods, and is used for steaming shellfish and fish, and as a braising agent for meats, cabbage, sausages, and sauerkraut.

In the twentieth century, blue crabs took the place of oysters in the economy and cuisine of the Chesapeake region. With declining oyster harvests, and scares over polluted shellfish in the 1920s, many watermen and packinghouse owners shifted their focus to the harvesting and marketing of blue crabs. A good cook knows at least twenty ways to prepare crabs, including crab cakes, crab soups, deviled crabs, Crab Imperial, and Crab Norfolk. Soft-shell crabs are served whole in sandwiches. Maryland and Virginia companies now import crabs and crab meat from Asia and Mexico, as well as Texas, Louisiana, and the Carolinas to keep pace with consumer demand.

In the 1950s, commercially harvested soft-shell clams, both fresh and frozen, were sent to New England markets. Maryland state agencies promoted local consumption of soft-shell clams, (known as maninose or manos) with a festival in 1971, but overharvesting defeated their efforts. Hard-shell clams from southern Virginia waters are found in chowders and stews.

Desserts have changed very little since the eighteenth century. Puddings made from rice, bread, and crackers are still favorites, as are custard pies (baked pudding in a pie shell). Elegant dessert jellies of the eighteenth and nineteenth centuries have been replaced by Jell-O. Chess pies (originally containing cheese) are a Virginia specialty, filled with a mixture of butter, sugar, raisins, eggs, and black walnuts or hickory nuts. Ginger cookies and gingerbread date back to colonial days. Peach cobbler and strawberry-rhubarb pie are favorites on Maryland tables. Regional cakes include Kossuth Cake, created to honor the 1851 visit of Hungarian patriot General Lajos Kossuth, Lady Baltimore cake (also claimed by Savannah, South Carolina), Lord Baltimore cake, and Smith Island seven-layer chocolate-frosted cakes.

[**See also** BREWING; CANNING AND BOTTLING; CLAMS; CRAB BOILS; CRAB CAKES; GAME; OYSTERS; PIES AND TARTS; SCRAPPLE; SEAFOOD.]

BIBLIOGRAPHY

Dutton, Joan Parry, commentator. *The Williamsburg Cookbook.* Williamsburg, VA, 1975.

From a Lighthouse Window: Recipes and Recollections from the Chesapeake Bay Maritime Museum. St. Michaels, MD: Chesapeake Bay Maritime Museum, 1989.

Stieff, Frederick Philip. *Eat, Drink, & Be Merry In Maryland: An Anthology from a Great Tradition.* New York: Putnam, 1932.

Warner, William W. *Beautiful Swimmers: Watermen, Crabs, and the Chesapeake Bay.* New York: Little, Brown, 1976.

VIRGINIA SCOTT JENKINS

Chestnuts

In the nineteenth century in the eastern part of the United States the chestnut was everyone's free food. Chestnuts fell in profusion from the branches of 4 billion trees and were there on the forest floor for the taking. Farmers allowed their pigs to roam free to fatten on the mast of the forest, the edible nuts and fruits that fall from the trees and bushes. The American chestnut was also an important source of quality lumber for construction and furniture making. In Europe and Asia cousins of the American chestnut played a similar role in the lives of the people.

In the first half of the twentieth century a blight that came to America with imported Asian trees virtually destroyed the American chestnut. In Europe there was a similar blight, although it was not nearly as savage. The Asian varieties were much more resistant and escaped major damage. The typical chestnuts roasted on an open fire are probably from Asian chestnut trees—either trees from Asia or Asian trees planted in America. The Asian trees do well in orchards but because they are short and bushy they do not do well in forests of tall straight trees. The American Chestnut Foundation has been having some success in breeding the blight resistance of the Asian tree into the surviving American chestnut trees.

The chestnut is not an ordinary fat-laden tree nut. It has much less oil than pecans, walnuts, and almonds and much more carbohydrate. Sometimes called "the bread of the mountain," the chestnut was often ground into flour for cooking. And in northern Italy, before explorers brought corn from the New World, ground chestnuts were the key to the early polenta. The chestnut, once free for the taking, is today a luxurious treat. The sweet-soaked marrons of France and Italy are a sought-after treasure at holiday time. The wonderfully fragrant roasting chestnuts that are sold on the streets of Milan or Lyon or New York City are coveted by buyers willing to pay whatever it takes to get a bagful.

[**See also** NUTS.]

BIBLIOGRAPHY

Bhagwandin, Annie. *The Chestnut Cook Book: Recipes, Folklore, and Practical Information regarding the Most Diverse of Culinary Nuts.* Onlaska, WA: Shady Grove Publications, 1996.

Griffith, Linda, and Fred Griffith. *Nuts: Recipes from around the World That Feature Nature's Perfect Ingredient.* New York: St. Martin's Press, 2003.

LINDA GRIFFITH AND FRED GRIFFITH

Chicken

Charles Darwin identified the wild jungle fowl of Southeast Asia, *Gallus gallus*, as the biological forerunner of the domestic chicken, *Gallus domesticus*. These ancestral birds still exist both in their native areas and as escapees from domesticated and cockfighting flocks. As discomforting as cockfighting may seem to most Americans in the twenty-first century, it remains widespread among many cultures, having been called the most popular sport ever known to man (and it is almost exclusively a masculine pastime). One school of thought suggests that domesticating birds for cockfighting predated the development of the chicken and the egg as food and facilitated the birds' original adoption as a staple of the table.

The time of the chicken's domestication is lost in prehistory, but no doubt it was relatively early in the history of agriculture. Chickens apparently spread from Southeast Asia through cultural diffusion and as a trade item. Whether moved as cargo on beasts of burden, or carried below decks as part of the virtual barnyard on merchant and naval ships to provide meat and eggs for the captain's table, chickens spread to Egypt and ports throughout the world, including Europe, England, and eventually the Americas.

In Egypt references to chickens are attributed to the Second Dynasty. In the early fourteenth century B.C.E. Egypt was a technologically advanced and highly inventive society, adapted to the mass production and distribution of food. The Egyptians built incubators of clay brick, in which the attendants kept the incubation temperature correct with constantly burning fires, using their own skin to judge the warmth, about 105 degrees Fahrenheit. These incubators, one of the most remarkable inventions of the time, could hatch ten or fifteen thousand chicks at once. It is only in recent years that production of this magnitude was approached in the West.

The Chicken Reaches America

The worldwide migration of the chicken was hugely successful. The birds' compact size and obvious utility on and off ships made them ideal immigration partners with the earliest Spanish and English colonists in the sixteenth and seventeenth centuries, although some contend that chickens reached the New World, specifically South America, through earlier contacts. By virtue of their adaptability to a variety of environments, chickens are now found throughout America, from the blustery shores of Maine to the warmth of Baja California. They also thrive on the islands of Hawaii. It is amazing to observe them scratch at the poorest soil, somehow finding enough sustenance not only to stay alive but also to raise their chicks and to help provide for the family table. Although chickens are not generally found on the boulevards of cities or the manicured streets of suburbia, it is not uncommon to find them kept as pets in city apartments.

In the eighteenth and early nineteenth centuries the general public began to take an interest in science, becoming a part of the so-called scientific revolution. From the mid-nineteenth through the early twentieth centuries, American amateur agriculturalists developed different breeds by selecting the birds that showed desirable characteristics and, through brother-sister mating, establishing a line that eventually bred true. Setting aside the difficult techniques of genetic engineering, this is very much the same method in use in the early 2000s. The popularity of selective breeding, coupled with the exchange of particular chickens between individual breeders, produced some truly beautiful and quite astonishing birds. This fad, dubbed "Hen Fever" by one of its proponents, led to shows where the public could inspect these unusual birds—one 1849 exhibition brought together 1,023 breeds and attracted thousands of enthusiastic viewers. The newspapers contained accounts of "rare and curious and inexpressibly beautiful examples of poultry." Others of these special breeds were selected for their fighting abilities, as cockfighting continued to be a popular sport, particularly in the American South.

The Industrial Chicken

The urbanization of the population in America in the late nineteenth century led to "improvements" in the production of birds for meat and eggs. With every American consuming an average of eighty pounds of chicken per year, with an estimated total value of $40 billion, the chicken industry became more centralized and vastly more efficient. Hens, in the twenty-first century, can be housed in buildings containing 250,000 birds. In many cases the buildings have no windows, so the birds are denied the pleasure of even a bit of sunlight. Each hen shares a cage with six or seven others. The cages themselves are stacked six to seven on top of each other, and each is so scandalously small that a hen cannot do that most natural act in the class Aves—spread her wings, flutter them a bit, and relax contentedly.

In most cases when eggs are selected for hatching they are placed on a mechanical contrivance that rotates them regularly while maintaining the optimum temperature for hatching. Nature, of course, does it quite differently. Biologists now understand that "broodiness," nesting on eggs until they hatch in favor of laying new ones, is the result of an increased production of the pituitary hormone prolactin.

Nutritional Value

Nutritionally the chicken and egg are almost certainly the most readily and universally available source of food in both industrialized and emerging areas. The flesh of the chicken has no known special nutritional qualities that distinguish it from other sources of meat. The most striking feature of the chicken is its white breast meat, characterized by the absence of the oxygen-binding protein, myoglobin. The myoglobin gives the flight muscles the ability to scavenge oxygen from the blood with greater efficiency. Chickens do not migrate and are not well adapted for long flights, their activities being mainly terrestrial during the day. By contrast, in birds that migrate long distances and for which endurance is an essential survival characteristic, such as ducks and geese, the breast is dark because of its high content of myoglobin. The chicken's white breast has the sprinter's advantage, however, being characterized by very powerful "fast twitch fibers" that are capable of launching even a heavy-bodied bird into a tree or onto a roost for the night. There is no significant nutritional difference between the two types of flesh, beyond the larger amount of iron present in the myoglobin-rich dark meat.

The egg is virtually a complete food, used as the main source of materials and energy during the chick's embryonic development. Compared to most other eggs, particularly those of mammals, it is huge. The ova needed to produce several thousand elephants would fit comfortably within even a small hen's egg. This size is another reason the chicken's egg is such a good source of nutrition.

There are interesting cultural differences with respect to what a proper egg should look like when cracked open. The yolk from a local U.S. franchise-type restaurant has a pale yellow color. Overseas, yolks with much deeper coloring are found, deriving from the yellow pigment carotene. The carotene can come from marigolds, which are often one of the components of chicken feeds, or from green plants, such as grasses, which account for the beautiful color of eggs from free-range chickens. Similar feed manipulations are used to vary the skin tones of industrially produced chickens, from creamy white to more golden hues.

[**See also** CHICKEN COOKERY; EGGS; KENTUCKY FRIED CHICKEN; POULTRY AND FOWL; SANDERS, COLONEL.]

BIBLIOGRAPHY

Burnham, George. *The History of the Hen Fever*. Boston: James French, 1885.

Jull, M. A. "The Races of Domestic Fowl." *National Geographic* (April 1927): 379–452.

Smith, Page, and C. W. Daniel. *The Chicken Book*. Boston: Little Brown, 1975.

CHARLES DANIEL

Chicken Cookery

Seventeenth- and eighteenth-century descriptions of colonial foodways ignored the chicken for the most part. In the earliest manuscripts to enter America there are, of course, chicken recipes for roasts, stews, and pies, and none other than Governor William Byrd II was dining on the iconic southern dish of fried chicken at his Virginia plantation by 1709. But most culinary descriptions praise the abundant wild game that so caught visitors' eyes and make scant mention of the barnyard fowl. Nor do platters of chicken occupy prestigious spots on the meticulously diagrammed table layouts; these, too, were reserved for wild birds and game. This is not to suggest that chickens were not widely eaten; virtually every colonial American archaeological site shows evidence of chicken consumption. Chicken merely suffered an image problem, possibly attributable to its husbandry.

Unlike the manly and aristocratic hunting of game, tending, slaughtering, and cleaning barnyard chickens was work for women and children. A few imported English books offered advice on raising chickens, but little appeared domestically until C. N. Bement's *American Poulterer's Companion* (1843). The common chicken was known by the unappetizing moniker "Dung-hill" fowl. Amelia Simmons, in *American Cookery* (1796), judges the ubiquitous dunghill only "tolerable," and she then cryptically notes that "*chickens*, of either [unspecified] kind are good, and the yellow leg'd the best, and their taste the sweetest." N. M. K. Lee, in *Cook's Own Book* (1832), disagrees, preferring the black-legged fowls for roasting.

By the nineteenth century, cookbook authors assumed that many of their readers would purchase poultry rather than raise their own. Shoppers were advised to differentiate between young and old chickens by the softness of the breastbone, the stiffness of the feet, and the color and smoothness of the legs and comb, all relevant indicia at a time when selections could be poked and heads and feet still came attached. Even with a market chicken, the cook faced the tedious task of cleaning it by picking out the pinfeathers and singeing the flesh to remove the last delicate down.

For those raising and slaughtering their own fowl, Sarah Josepha Hale, in *The Good Housekeeper* (1841), recommends hanging the poultry to tenderize it before cooking: one night in summer, while "in cold weather it may be kept a much longer time to advantage." Preservation was only a modest issue in the days before ice boxes. Unlike larger animals, chickens could be consumed without waste promptly after slaughter. If a chicken starts to "become musty before you want to cook it," Mrs. Hale recommends placing a skinned onion or a bit of charcoal in the cavity.

Recipes recommended different sizes and ages of chickens for particular preparations. Capons, or castrated young roosters, were particularly prized for their generous size

Chicken à la King

There's nothing royal about Chicken à la King, which is an entrée of cubed cooked chicken breast in a cream sauce that is dotted with pimento and mushrooms and often flavored with Madeira or a similar wine. An early claim for its invention appeared in 1915 in the obituary of William King, who had worked as a cook at Philadelphia's fashionable Bellevue Hotel around 1895. King included truffles and red and green peppers in his recipe.

Under the more pedestrian name "creamed chicken," similar recipes appeared in cookbooks beginning in the late nineteenth century. Peas are often added to the sauce in these recipes, and the sauced chicken is served over hot toast, biscuits, or waffles. The first located recipe titled "Chicken à la King" appeared in Paul Richard's *The Lunch Room* (1911). The name quickly became popular, and the dish became a standard menu item in all kinds of restaurants, upscale and down, especially tearooms that catered to women, since this dish could be eaten in a most ladylike way without picking up a knife.

BIBLIOGRAPHY

New York Tribune, March 5, 1915, p. 9.

BARRY POPIK AND ANDREW F. SMITH

and fatty flesh. Roasting times seem short by contemporary standards and may be attributable to the intense heat of hearth cookery and the scrawnier eighteenth- and nineteenth-century free-range birds, compared with the industrially produced broiler chickens available in the twenty-first century. The stewing recipes resemble current practices.

One of the most common recipes for chicken from the eighteenth through the mid-twentieth centuries was the fricassee, a white or brown stew of small chickens lightly bound with egg yolks, and, by the nineteenth century, often enriched with milk or cream. In a nod to increasing delicacy (an elegant term for Victorian squeamishness) at table, later nineteenth-century hostesses would remove the head and, less frequently, the feet before serving roasted birds; in the earlier nineteenth century, cooks were instructed that the head of roasted fowls "should be turned under the wing, like a turkey." Southern tables were noted for pilaf, chicken cooked with rice; the dish spread throughout the country in the nineteenth century and remains popular. Among the most diverse and interesting chicken recipes through the first half of the nineteenth century are those found in Lettice Bryan's *The Kentucky Housewife* (1839).

In the later nineteenth century, the emerging railroad networks eased the transportation of chickens to hatcheries and markets, helping launch an incipient poultry industry. The number of chickens in America more than doubled in the decade between 1880 and 1890, from 102 million birds to over 250 million, although much of the industry focused on egg-layers rather than table birds. "How-to" poultry manuals proliferated and cookbooks offered proportionately more chicken recipes, as the availability of game birds declined in the late nineteenth and early twentieth centuries. The United States Department of Agriculture (USDA) encouraged home rearing of chickens during both World Wars, viewing a small flock of ten hens as an efficient recycler of table scraps, producer of many dozen eggs per year, and supplier of meat to a country severely strained by wartime shortages.

But market chickens remained dear, generally costing more than beef through World War II, because chicken flocks could be devastated by disease and parasites. One mark of the chicken's enhanced status and relative expense was Herbert Hoover's 1928 campaign promise of prosperity that would be measured by "a chicken in every pot." Working with the USDA in breeding experiments, poultry farmers in the 1930s began raising broiler chickens (ranging up to five pounds) for the commercial market, culminating in the "Chicken of Tomorrow" contest in 1948, designed to engineer a meatier, faster-growing bird. The experiments were successful, but the size of commercial chicken farms would be limited until growers could control

diseases and parasites with the introduction of the first effective drugs in the 1950s.

Drugs, coupled with higher-protein and vitamin-enriched feeds, inaugurated large-scale chicken production, most famously by Tyson Foods and Perdue Farms. Chicken became an inexpensive, year-round staple. The smaller nuclear family of the mid-twentieth century made the chicken an ideally sized roast. Butchered chickens, sold prepackaged as breasts, wings, legs, or thighs, further eased the housewives' burden. Pierre Franey's "60 Minute Gourmet," a nationally syndicated column from the 1970s and 1980s, depended heavily on the widely available, quick-cooking breast to put tasty dishes on the table in what was then considered record time.

Chicken maintains a prominent place in American cookery, shown by the huge number of chicken recipes found in cookbooks, including a number of "365" books that offer a different chicken preparation for each day of the year. Consumers concerned with food safety, especially the *salmonella* bacteria associated with chickens and eggs, and gourmands looking for perceived deeper flavor, have encouraged smaller, free-range production of chickens, harking back to the preindustrial production of the nineteenth century. Like the nineteenth-century market, these chickens are significantly more expensive than their industrial counterparts. [**See also** CHICKEN; KENTUCKY FRIED CHICKEN; POULTRY AND FOWL; SANDERS, COLONEL.]

BIBLIOGRAPHY

Percy, Pam. *The Complete Chicken: An Entertaining History of Chickens.* Stillwater, MN: Voyageur, 2002.

CATHY K. KAUFMAN

Chicken Fried Steak

Chicken fried steak most likely developed as a way to make a tough cut of beef more palatable: The first step in preparation is pounding a cutlet to tenderize it. Then, mimicking the technique for Southern fried chicken, it is either dredged in flour or dipped in batter before being fried in hot oil in a cast-iron skillet. A cream, or milk, gravy made from the drippings is spooned on top.

There are several theories about chicken fried steak's origins. One holds that it developed in cattle country—Texas and the Midwest—before beef was as tender as it is today. Another holds that it descended from *Wienerschnitzel*, courtesy of the Germans who settled in Central Texas starting in the 1830s. Recipes resembling chicken fried steak are not uncommon in historical cookbooks. In *The Kentucky Housewife* (1839), a recipe for frying beef steaks starts with cutlets from the tough chuck and rump. It instructs the cook to "beat them tender, but do not break them or beat them into rags." The cutlets are then dredged in flour and fried in "boiling lard." Instructions for making a cream gravy follow.

Whatever its origins, chicken fried steak was well established in home kitchens by 1932, when a reader submitted a menu featuring "Chicken Fried Steak With Cream Gravy" to *The Dallas Morning News*. In 1936, the year of the Texas centennial, the same newspaper reported that the president of the Dallas Restaurant Men's Association had received cards and letters from out-of-towners praising his and other restaurants: "To them a chicken-fried steak, smothered in brown, creamy gravy is the tops in foods." The first known recipe that refers to Chicken Fried Steak by name appears in the *Household Searchlight Recipe Book* (1949), published in Topeka, Kansas. "Country fried steak" and "chicken fried steak" are sometimes used interchangeably.

BIBLIOGRAPHY

Bryan, Mrs. Lettice. *The Kentucky Housewife.* Cincinnati: Shepard and Stearns, 1839.

Gee, Denise. "Dueling Steaks." In *Cornbread Nation 1: The Best of Southern Food Writing*, ed. John Egerton for the Southern Foodways Alliance. Chapel Hill: University of North Carolina Press, 2002.

KIM PIERCE

Chicken McNuggets

During the 1970s, chicken consumption greatly increased in the United States, largely because of fast food chains such as Kentucky Fried Chicken, Chicken Delight, and Church's Chicken. At the same time, the medical profession praised the health advantages of chicken over hamburgers. This caused a stir in the fast food industry, and in 1979 Fred Turner, McDonald's chairman, set out to devise a chicken product that could easily be eaten while driving, as many people ate their fast-food burgers. It took six months to produce McNuggets, small pieces of reconstituted chicken held together by stabilizers, breaded, fried, frozen, and shipped to the outlet, where they were reheated. The original McNugget formula contained ground skin in addition to chicken meat, and the McNuggets were fried in oil. When tested by McDonald's technicians, a serving of six McNuggets had twice as much as fat as a Big Mac. When McNuggets were made with skinless chicken instead, they weighed in at 16.3 grams fat compared to 32.4 grams for the Big Mac. McDonald's contracted with Tyson Foods to supply them with the chicken for the new product, and when Chicken McNuggets debuted in 1983, their success was such that McDonald's became the second-largest purchaser of chicken in the United States. Other fast food chains came up with their own "clones" of the McNugget, such as Chicken Tenders.

Although McNuggets were tasty, easy to eat on the run, and especially appealing to children, they were not the healthy alternative to hamburgers that they might have been. Cooked in oil, their saturated fat content rivaled that of a hamburger. When this information became public, the chain switched to vegetable oil in response to consumer pressure, but added beef extract to the McNuggets during manufacturing to retain their familiar taste.

The continued popularity of McNuggets has changed the way poultry is raised and processed in the U.S. In 1980, most chickens were sold whole; today a large percentage are processed into cutlets or nuggets. In 1992, for the first time, American consumption of chicken surpassed that of beef.

BIBLIOGRAPHY

Schlosser, Eric. *Fast Food Nation: The Dark Side of the All-American Meal.* New York: Houghton Mifflin, 2001.

ANDREW F. SMITH

Chickpeas

The chickpea (*Cicer arietinum*) is a legume or pulse. It is one of the oldest foods known to humankind, having been among the first crops cultivated—along with wheat and barley—in the Fertile Crescent (modern Iraq) around 4000 B.C.E. The chickpea is a large, round seed, slightly pointed at one end, and grooved down the center. It is a larger relative of the garden pea, but there is only one to a pod. Because of its taproot system, the chickpea can withstand drought conditions by extracting water from deep in the soil. This allows it to thrive in dry climates. Although the color varies widely when grown in the Mediterranean, in the United States, it is almost always light brown when ripe.

The chickpea was first brought to the New World by the Spanish and Portuguese conquerors and has become one of the basic ingredients of Mexican cooking. It is known in the southwestern states as the garbanzo bean from the Spanish for "chickpea," *garbanzo*. However, the chickpea also reached the United States with later immigrants, chiefly from Italy (where chickpeas are known as *ceci*), the Middle East, and the Indian subcontinent (where two varieties are grown: *besan* and the smaller variety, *channa*).

The chickpea prefers a relatively cool, dry climate so it is a useful winter crop to alternate with cereals. Half of the chickpeas eaten in the United States are grown in California. The rest come from eastern Washington State, Idaho, and Montana.

The chickpea is extremely versatile, hence its popularity. When ground into flour and mixed with olive oil and tahini, it is known as hummus, a Middle Eastern dish that has become a universally popular appetizer. In Mexican cooking, chickpeas are added to stews, such as *ropas viejas* and *cocido*, and they are used similarly in Spain, India, and France. Common uses in the United States are in soups, vegetable combinations, or as a component of salads.

The chickpea is highly nutritious—containing about 20 percent protein, 5 percent fat, and 55 percent carbohydrate, as well as malic and oxalic acid—and it has become a favorite among health-conscious Americans.

[**See also** BEANS; PEAS.]

BIBLIOGRAPHY

"Grain Legumes as Alternative Crops." Proceedings of a symposium sponsored by the Center for Alternative Crops and Products. University of Minnesota, July 23–24, 1987.

McNair, James. *James McNair's Beans and Grains.* San Francisco: Chronicle Books, 1997.

South Dakota State University. *Chickpeas: A Potential Crop for the Midwest.* Bulletin 698. Brookings, SD: Agriculture Experiment Station, 1986.

JOSEPHINE BACON

Child, Julia

Julia Child (1912–2004) became the most celebrated American cook and an important cultural figure in a public career spanning more than forty years. Her appealing blend of education and entertainment in the groundbreaking television series *The French Chef* introduced classical cooking techniques, exotic ingredients, and specialty equipment to mainstream America in the 1960s and 1970s. As a popular television personality, cookbook author, and mentor, Child elevated the status of cooking, shaped modern notions of food, and contributed to the development of the culinary profession throughout the second half of the twentieth century.

Child's success as a media star was often attributed to her charming wit and uninhibited nature. The oldest daughter of a well-to-do family, Julia McWilliams was born in Pasadena, California, and graduated from Smith College in Northampton, Massachusetts, in 1934. A position with the Office of Strategic Services during World War II took her to posts in Asia,

A portrait of Julia Child, a popularizer of French cooking techniques.

where she met her husband, Paul Child, who later became her collaborator. Her culinary career began at the age of thirty-seven, when the Childs moved to Paris and she enrolled in the Cordon Bleu cooking school.

Child's first cookbook, *Mastering the Art of French Cooking*, was the product of her collaboration with two Frenchwomen, Simone Beck and Louisette Bertholle. The three were partners in a Paris cooking school called L'Ecole des Trois Gourmandes, and its insignia decorated the blouse Child later wore on *The French Chef*. The book's long route to publication is part of publishing lore. Ten years in the making and rejected by Houghton Mifflin, its contracted publisher, *Mastering the Art of French Cooking* was ultimately published by Knopf in 1961 to great acclaim. The best-selling cookbook was the first to popularize the principles of French cooking to a broad-based American audience. Thorough instructions and consideration of available ingredients set a new standard in cookbook writing, a model for the many cookbooks on ethnic cuisines that followed in the 1970s.

Child achieved her greatest influence through television. Although it was initially broadcast on a Boston public television station, *The French Chef* quickly became a national sensation, watched by men and women, noncooks and cooks, and won the first of its five Emmy Awards in 1965, a landmark event for educational television. Its popularity was due in part to Child's sense of humor and the mistakes she handled with aplomb. Statuesque, with an unmistakable warbling voice, her manner and gaffes were frequently exaggerated and widely parodied. *The French Chef*, which aired from 1963 to 1973, created the celebrity called "Julia" and institutionalized the televised cooking show.

Her role as an educator was paramount to the show's success and popularity. She approached haute cuisine with a sense of fun and fearlessness and emphasized simplicity over snobbery. Although she strayed from French cooking in successive series, she remained devoted to teaching home cooks the pleasures of preparing a meal—and to public television. She was also instrumental in the development of the American Institute of Wine and Food and the International Association of Culinary Professionals. She became a mentor to many chefs and was a role model for women in the field.

Soon after receiving the French Legion of Honor and just before her ninetieth birthday, Child left her home in Cambridge, Massachusetts, and the famous kitchen that was the set for her last three cooking shows to return to southern California. In recognition of her role in American social history, the Smithsonian Institution acquired her original kitchen with nearly all of its contents, including the pegboard wall of pans and the Garland stove, and reinstalled it in the National Museum of American History in 2002.

[See also CELEBRITY CHEFS; COOKBOOKS AND MANUSCRIPTS: FROM WORLD WAR II TO THE 1960S; COOKBOOKS AND MANUSCRIPTS: 1970S TO THE PRESENT; RADIO/TV FOOD SHOWS.]

BIBLIOGRAPHY

Beck, Simone, Louisette Bertholle, and Julia Child. *Mastering the Art of French Cooking*. New York: Knopf, 1961.

Fitch, Noël Riley. *Appetite for Life: The Biography of Julia Child*. New York: Doubleday, 1997.

Greenspan, Dorie. *Baking with Julia*. New York: Morrow, 1996.

LYNNE SAMPSON

Child, Lydia Maria

The daughter of a baker known for his Medford Crackers, Lydia Maria Francis was born near Boston in 1802 and grew up to become part of that city's intellectual scene. She eventually married David Child, a dedicated reformer. Mrs. Child also became an ardent reformer and was known especially for writing the antislavery book *An Appeal in Favor of That Class of Americans Called Africans* (1833). To support herself and her impractical husband, Child lived by her pen, and in 1829 she published one of the most popular and successful domestic books of the nineteenth century, *The Frugal Housewife*. Retitled *The American Frugal Housewife* when it was sold in England and Germany, the book does not give an accurate image of its author, who projected herself as a middle-aged housewife with a brood of children. In fact, Child was only twenty-six when the book was published, remained childless throughout her marriage, and lived a public life at a time when women were expected to confine themselves to domestic pursuits.

Child's theme of frugality clearly appealed to her reading public; by 1832 *The Frugal Housewife* had gone into seven editions. The book has a sober, cheeseparing tone, with recommendations to feed the family with scraps that otherwise would have been directed to the garbage pail and careful instructions for cooking the cheapest cuts of meat. "Calf's head should be cleansed with very great care," Child explains. "It is better to leave the wind-pipe on, for if it hangs out of the pot while the head is cooking, all the froth will escape through it." Her memorable aphorisms include admonishments such as, "Look to the grease pot, and see that nothing is there which might have served to nourish your own family or a poorer one." The book is an extended lecture on the morality of parsimony.

The money she earned from writing popular books was used to fund projects that the Childs hoped would correct social injustices. To this end, David Child, who knew nothing about farming, set off to Northampton, Massachusetts, to start a sugar beet farm. Like other antislavery reformers of their day, the Childs believed that if sugar beets could be grown throughout the United States, then

the Caribbean sugarcane plantations—major incentives for perpetuating slavery—could be made obsolete. Unfortunately, David Child's attempt at farming only put him further into debt, causing his wife to work even harder by writing novels, children's books, magazine articles, and poems in addition to political treatises.

At the time of Child's death in 1880, the poet John Greenleaf Whittier wrote, "Wherever there was a brave word to be spoken, her voice was heard, and never without effect." While her zealous opposition to slavery should define her legacy, she is most remembered for a line from her poem "A Boy's Thanksgiving Day," published in *Flowers for Children*, volume 2 (1844): "Over the river, and through the wood, to Grandfather's house we go," which is sung by schoolchildren all over America each November.

[See also COOKBOOKS AND MANUSCRIPTS: TO 1860; SUGAR BEETS.]

BIBLIOGRAPHY

Clifford, Deborah Pickman. *Crusader for Freedom: A Life of Lydia Maria Child*. Boston: Beacon Press, 1992.

Karcher, Carolyn L. *The First Woman in the Republic: A Cultural Biography of Lydia Maria Child*. Durham, NC: Duke University Press, 1994.

BARBARA HABER

Children's Cookbooks

The European cookbook tradition brought by settlers to the first American colonies did not include children's cookbooks. This literary genre is a relatively recent phenomenon that originated in the late nineteenth century, a time when domestic training for girls was reinforced by social ideals, increased leisure time and affluence among the middle class, and the new home economics movement. The first juvenile cookbooks were written in entertaining and sometimes fanciful styles to secure children's interest, teach cookery, and sugarcoat a substantial measure of morality, manners, obedience, religion, and social responsibility. As in the late 1800s, children's cookbooks continue to reflect contemporary social issues and child-rearing philosophies.

Using the ploy of fictionalized stories for girls, the first cooking instructions for children were set into the plot as the action dictated. Recipes appeared as conversations between young friends or mothers and daughters. As exemplified by Ella Farman Pratt's volume *The Cooking Club of Tu-Whit Hollow* (1885), standard recipes such as those for soft cake or fruitcake were presented following the traditional anecdotal style everyone used to teach cooking skills to the next generation.

The use of fictional settings in children's cookbooks continued for some decades, although the balance between story content and recipes shifted. Jane Eayre Fryer's *Easy Steps in Cooking; or, the Mary Frances*

Cookbook; or, Adventures among the Kitchen People (1912) keeps a story line but stresses cookery. Anthropomorphized kitchen utensils in cartoonlike drawings verbalize the cooking hints.

By the 1920s, home economics had found a place in public school curricula. Clara Ingram Judson wrote a series of children's cookbook texts, among them, *Cooking without Mother's Help* (1920). Judson's *When Mother Lets Us Cook* (1919) was a straightforward collection of recipes with only the occasional diversion of presenting basic rules in poetry form. As her series of texts progressed, the illustrations became more educational, and Judson adapted the new emphasis on science by presenting recipes in modern form (utensils, ingredients, and processes listed separately).

By the 1930s simple cookbooks had become more accessible both financially and instructionally. Louise Price Bell's paperback *Kitchen Fun: Teaches Children to Cook Successfully* (1932) used large-format pages, print, and measurements; she diagrammed measuring cups and spoons for ease in fractional amounts and produced a book of simple recipes that a young reader could handle alone or in school. Under the combined influence of ongoing immigration and new melting pot theories, Gertrude I. Thomas's *Foods of Our Forefathers in the Middle Colonies, 1614–1776* (1941) offered a text on American cultural history through recipes.

Increasing commercialism prompted the publication of free or giveaway promotional cookbook pamphlets. In 1905 Pillsbury issued *A Little Book for a Little Cook* by L. P. Hubbard. After World War II, Westinghouse offered schools its text *Sugar an' Spice and All Things Nice* (1951) by Julia Kiene. In 1957 the classic *Cook Book for Boys and Girls* by Betty Crocker began its long series of reprints and revisions, all sprinkled with advertisements.

In the 1970s a new emphasis on creativity brought books like the award-winning Tomie de Paola's *Pancakes for Breakfast* (1978), extended the readership of children's cookbooks to preschoolers, and raised the publication of cookbooks to an art form. Newer cookbooks ask children to see food in larger contexts: survival basics, science in the kitchen, ethnicity, holidays, health, vegetarianism, and just plain fun.

[See also COOKBOOKS AND MANUSCRIPTS: FROM THE CIVIL WAR TO WORLD WAR I; HOME ECONOMICS.]

ALICE ROSS

Chile

Chile, comprising various *Capsicum* species, is also known as chili, chilli, chilly, pepper, green pepper, pod pepper, red pepper, and countless regional and varietal names. "Chile" is the only accepted spelling in New Mexico, where they take their chiles very seriously (and which distinguishes it from "chili," which usually refers to uniquely American dishes made with chiles, such as chili con carne).

Capsicum is part of the Solanaceae, a New World family of plants that includes potatoes, tomatoes, eggplants, tobacco, and a number of poisonous plants (such as the nightshades). Genetic evidence points to a beginning near Bolivia for the *Capsicum* genus, but the plants have been introduced to every arable part of the globe. In frost-free Tropical America it is a perennial—but it is grown as an annual in most of the United States.

Columbus, the first European to experience this New World phenomenon, wrote in his journal on 15 January 1493, "there is much *Axí*—their pepper, much stronger than [our] pepper, and everyone refuses to eat without it, for they find it very healthful; in Hispaniola, it's possible to fill fifty caravels each year with it." Columbus had sailed west specifically to find a shortcut to the source of spices—such as pepper—so, when he encountered this new hot spice, he naturally thought of it as pepper. Hence, the confusion over names that persists between these unrelated species.

In the United States, most of the chiles consumed are cultivars of the *Capsicum annuum* species, including all the sweet peppers (bell peppers, cubanelles, Italian frying peppers, and pimentos) as well as a wide range of hot peppers, such as anaheims, cherry peppers, jalapeños, cayennes, and serranos. These varieties are usually seen fresh or pickled.

Some chiles are also dried. Deep green poblanos, when dried, become anchos. Anchos, along with mulattos (an almost black variety of ancho) and pasillas (literally, "little raisins," slender, aromatically fruity, dark chiles) are used in combination to make chili con carne and the popular Mexican import Mole Poblano.

Commercial "chile powder" is usually a mixture of chile (primarily the relatively mild ancho, which is dried poblano), and other spices—along with some silicon dioxide (fine sand) to prevent caking.

Thick-fleshed jalapeños don't dry well, so they are smoked to produce chipotles—sold whole, ground or canned ("en adobo," a thick pungent sauce of tomatoes, garlic, onions and oil), as well as in countless salsas, sauces, and other condiments. Chipotles, with their slowly emerging heat and rich smoky flavor, have become American favorites. In fact, the name recognition of these dried chiles has helped a national fast-food chain (Chipotle Mexican Grill, owned by McDonald's since 1998) emerge as a serious competitor to Pepsico's Taco Bell.

Capsicum annuum is the primary species used in the United States, but it is certainly not the only one. *C. chinense* varieties include habaneros (which, despite the name, are not from Havana, but from Mexico), the closely related Scotch bonnets of the Caribbean, and the regional datil peppers that grew wild in the region around St. Augustine, Florida.

These are among the hottest peppers in the world, with the Red Savina cultivar achieving Scoville ratings (a standardized rating system for chiles' hotness) of 577,000—by comparison, typical jalapeños are rated at about 4,000, or 10,000 for the more concentrated chipotles.

C. frutescens is represented by the Tabasco pepper. Originally from Mexico, the peppers were grown in New Iberia, Louisiana, by the Avery family for the production of the famous hot sauce named for the peppers. Today, much of the crop comes from Honduras, but the sauce is still made the same way—by fermentation with vinegar, under a thick layer of Avery Island salt—by the original family-owned business.

C. pubuscens (rocoto) is less well-known to American chile-fanciers, but should be immediately recognizable by its dark seeds and violet-colored flowers—all other species have white flowers and pale seeds. The last species of the genus, *C. baccatum*, is the familiar golden yellow Aji of Peru. It is virtually unknown in the United States, except by the hot pepper fanatics who call themselves "chileheads."

American public interest in hot sauces has led to the creation of literally thousands of brands. Some, like Louisiana, Frank's, and Crystal, are imitations of the original red Tabasco. Others, however, making use of the Caribbean Scotch bonnet, tend to be thickened with a mixture of prepared mustard and pureed carrots. These are heavy, bright yellow condiments, extremely hot but with a fruity perfume that is characteristic of all the habaneros. Chipotles, of course, are everywhere—even Tabasco has a chipotle-based sauce. Some companies, in pursuit of even more heat, have added pure capsaicin oleoresin—the refined essence of the chiles' fire—to make truly incendiary concoctions, such as Dave's Insanity and Endorphin Rush (the latter's name refers to the euphoria caused by the body's release of natural opiate-like compounds in response to perceived pain caused by capsaicin).

The chiles for Spanish and Hungarian paprikas arrived in their respective countries, well before 1600, by very different routes. Spain's were brought, by Columbus and later navigators, from the Caribbean, Mexico, and Peru. Hungary's arrived overland via Ottoman Turks, who got them from Arab and Indian traders, who got them from Portuguese navigators, who in turn got them from what is now Bahia, Brazil. Consequently, the flavors of the paprikas from the two major producing countries are very different. American paprika is used primarily as a reddish garnish (because, unlike Spanish and Hungarian paprikas, it has little flavor).

The "heat" of chiles is mainly due to the alkaloid capsaicin—but also to a number of minor capaicinoids that create differences in the location, duration, and kind of burning sensations. Perhaps because of chiles' reputation as hot, hence wild and uncontrollable—traits that some mild-manned people believe they would like to emulate—marketers have tried to capitalize on chiles' "bad boy" image. However, advertising "hotness" and convincing people to willingly experience the extreme burn of some chiles are very different matters. Consequently, the agricultural scientists at Texas A & M developed a variety of jalapeño with no heat at all—allowing the timid to affect unmerited levels of machismo.

[**See also** PREPARED HERBS AND SPICE MIXTURES.]

BIBLIOGRAPHY

Andrews, Jean. *Peppers: The Domesicated Capsicums.* Austin, TX: University of Texas Press, 1984.

Facciola, Stephen. *Cornucopia II, A Sourcebook of Edible Plants* (second edition). Vista, CA: Kampong Publications, 1999.

GARY ALLEN

Chili

Chili is a dish consisting of meat (usually beef, coarsely ground or finely cubed) cooked in fat and then slowly simmered with red chilies (hot-spicy *Capsicum* peppers, fresh or dried, or both), a liquid such as water or meat stock, and seasonings such as cumin, garlic, oregano, and salt. Its consistency is halfway between a thick soup and a stew. Although other ingredients such as onions and tomatoes are often added, chili's primary constituent is meat.

Chili as we know it originated in the American Southwest, most likely in the region that became the state of Texas. Culinary historians think that chili began as a peasant dish prepared by poor people using cheap, inferior cuts of meat cooked together with other inexpensive, readily available ingredients, primarily peppers and onions. They also agree that chili is an American, not Mexican, dish—although

Chile peppers drying in front of an adobe house in Isleta, New Mexico.

chili is associated closely with the Mexican population in Texas, and dishes similar to chili can be found in Mexico, particularly in the north. In 1997, in recognition of chili's long-standing and deep-rooted connection with Texas, the state's legislature declared chili to be the "Official Texas State Dish."

Texas chili—affectionately known as "a bowl of red"—is a one-dish meal traditionally served in a plain, heavy bowl and eaten with a spoon. Beef is the preferred meat, although game (especially venison) is also sometimes used. Purists insist that Texas chili should never contain beans, but many Texans like their chili with beans (usually pinto beans), either added to the chili itself or served in a separate small bowl on the side. Chili garnishes can include crumbled soda crackers, chopped raw onions, fresh or pickled jalapeño peppers, or a combination of these.

Beyond the Lone Star State

In the late 1800s chili's popularity began spreading to other parts of the United States. By the 1920s "chili parlors" or "chili joints"—small, inexpensive, hole-in-the-wall diners—were opening across America. Although the number of chili parlors declined during World War II, more chili parlors began to open again in the 1950s, only to be eventually replaced by the inexpensive hamburger chains that were also being built around the country.

As the popularity of chili spread throughout America, recipes for this dish evolved to reflect the ingredients and taste preferences of local cooks in different parts of the country. From a simple Texas stew of meat and hot peppers, served in a bowl, chili also developed into a topping for several other foods: rice, spaghetti, macaroni, corn chips, hamburgers, and hot dogs. The list of possible ingredients expanded too, so that you can find dishes called "chili" that are made with pork, bacon, sausage, lamb, mutton, or poultry; a

variety of vegetables and beans; tomato juice, coffee, beer, whiskey, or tequila; thickeners such as flour, *masa harina*, or cracker meal; sugar, nuts, or unsweetened cocoa or chocolate (for adding depth to the flavor); and such garnishes as sour cream, diced avocados, shredded cheese, and snipped chives. There are even vegetarian versions of chili, usually made with several kinds of beans to provide the protein.

Outside Texas some regional versions of chili have attained recognition in their own right. Cincinnati's famous "five-way chili" is composed of a layer of spaghetti on a shallow oval plate, topped with a layer of chili sauce made with ground beef seasoned with cinnamon, cardamom, allspice, and cloves. This is covered with a layer of kidney beans, followed by a layer of chopped raw onions and one of shredded cheddar cheese. "Two-way," "three-way," and "four-way" versions are eaten as well, which are merely the same dish with fewer layers of ingredients, always starting with a base of spaghetti and a topping of chili sauce. Oyster crackers are the traditional garnish.

In some parts of the Midwest any chili served with pasta is called a "chili mac." The chili can be a topping for cooked pasta (usually macaroni) or mixed with the pasta before serving. And chili even turns up as a filling for Cornish miner chili pasties in Michigan's Upper Peninsula.

The state of New Mexico lays claim to its own dish, called *chile*, which is made primarily of red or green peppers stewed with onions, garlic, other herbs and spices, and water or meat stock. The consistency of a thick sauce, New Mexico *chile* can be eaten on its own, used as a sauce to garnish other dishes, or included as an ingredient in other recipes. New Mexico's *chile verde* (green *chile*) is made with any of several varieties of fresh New Mexican green peppers, which are first roasted and peeled. *Chile colorado* (red *chile*) is

Jalapeño peppers are frequently used as a spicy garnish in chili.

made with dried, ripe New Mexican red peppers—whole, crushed into flakes, or ground into powder. These types of processed green and red New Mexican peppers are also major ingredients in *chile* stews containing meats such as pork, beef, lamb, mutton, or poultry, and starches such as garbanzo beans, corn, or *posole* (hominy).

Chili Products

Chili powders—commercial or homemade—are a pungent blend of spices, including powdered dried red peppers (mild, medium, or hot, or any combination of these) mixed with ground cumin, dried Mexican oregano, garlic powder, salt, and sometimes other spices. Powdered *ancho* peppers are usually the primary ingredient, and cumin gives all chili powder mixtures their characteristic taste. The first commercial chili powders were manufactured and marketed in Texas in the early 1890s. These spice mixtures made chili easier to prepare and ultimately helped spread the popularity of this dish to other parts of America where dried red peppers were not as commonly available as in the Southwest.

By the early 1900s commercially canned chili was being produced in several parts of the United States. This new convenience food in a can also helped spread the popularity of chili around the country, although many cooks still consider canned chili to be greatly inferior to homemade. By 1980 chili was one of the best-selling canned foods in America; in the early twenty-first century most of the chili eaten in the United States comes out of a can. Commercial frozen chili is also available. [**See also** CINCINNATI CHILI; SOUTHWESTERN REGIONAL COOKERY.]

BIBLIOGRAPHY

Bridges, Bill. *The Great Chili Book*. New York: Lyons and Burford, 1994.

DeWitt, Dave, Mary Jane Wilan, and Melissa T. Stock. *Hot and Spicy Chili*. Rocklin, CA: Prima, 1994.

Hudgins, Sharon. "Red Dust: Powdered Chiles and Chili Powder." In *Spicing Up the Palate: Studies of Flavourings—Ancient and Modern*. Proceedings of the Oxford Symposium on Food and Cookery 1992. Edited by Harlan Walker. Totnes, U.K.: Prospect Books, 1993.

Jameson, W. C. *The Ultimate Chili Cookbook: The History, Geography, Fact, and Folklore of Chili*. Plano, TX: Republic of Texas Press, 1999.

O'Hara, Christopher B. *The Ultimate Chili Book.* Guilford, CT: Lyons, 2001.

Stern, Jane, and Michael Stern. *Chili Nation: The Ultimate Chili Cookbook with Recipes from Every State in the Nation*. New York: Broadway Books, 1998.

Tolbert, Frank X. *A Bowl of Red*. Garden City, NY: Doubleday, 1966.

SHARON HUDGINS

Chinese American Food

Food and eating, intellectual and sensual, are important parts of Chinese life, maintained over millennia. The Chinese retain past experiences and incorporate some foreign customs and commodities. Among them is an early belief that those who eat raw or uncooked food and do not consume large amounts of grain are not Chinese. Another is that meals must have more *fan* (rice and other grains) and lesser amounts of *cai* (*tsai*) or vegetables, meats, and other foods. Yet another, that meals incorporate the five basic Chinese flavors: acid, salt, sweet, bitter, and pungent.

The Chinese believe food is more than just nourishment. It helps prevent and treat disease. Chinese food, preparation, and dishes maintain bodily harmony using a duality of forces called *yin* and *yang*. In addition, food is consumed and transformed into life's energy or *Qi*.

Chinese Immigration

The name "China" translates to Middle Kingdom, a vast land of 3.7 million square miles. In the twenty-first century with 1.2 billion people, it is the world's most populous nation; 57 million more live outside the country. According to the 2000 United States census, the Chinese are the largest Asian immigrant group. In 1830, the first American census to count Asian populations, there were but three Chinese.

Changing Chinese Immigrant Food Habits

After several generations, the Chinese in the United States eat differently than they did in their homeland. Some immigrants seek the American dream and eat many Western foods. A few years later, they typically revert to serving traditional Chinese meals at dinnertime, festivals, and life-cycle events such as birthdays, weddings, and funerals. When these immigrants go back to eating more Chinese food, they prepare dishes from the Chinese regions they came from.

First-generation American-born Chinese eat more Western foods at weekday breakfasts and lunches and many more Chinese-tasting dinner foods. Subsequent generations, particularly those living away from Chinatown areas, eat more Western-style foods at all meals. They maintain some Chinese eating habits and prepare foods with Chinese tastes, particularly at festivals and meals celebrating life-cycle events. The more Chinese the immigrants speak, the greater their Chinese food influences.

Early and Later Chinese Immigrants

The Chinese were the first Asian group to come to the United States in significant numbers. Most came from south China in and around Canton (Guangzhou). By the end of 1852, about twenty thousand males came to their *gum san*, or "Golden Mountain." They gave America this name because they planned to pan for gold and return home rich. In 1865, the Central Pacific Railway Company brought thousands to help build the transcontinental railroad. Prior to these immigrations, perhaps only one hundred or so Chinese lived in the United States.

Mr. Wonton in Brooklyn, New York, one of nearly 40,000 Chinese restaurants across the United States.

Over the next two dozen years, up to 250,000 more Chinese men arrived. Then in 1882, the Chinese Exclusion Act made it illegal for more Chinese laborers to enter the United States. It also prohibited naturalization of earlier arrivals. After 1882, additional laws restricted immigration. Then, in 1943 these acts were repealed.

Early Chinese Food in the United States

With mining and railroad work no longer available, and discrimination against Chinese at its peak, many Chinese found work as cooks. They later opened restaurants serving foods of their native land to other Chinese and those willing to try Chinese food. In the 1860s and 1870s, Chinese immigrants became involved in fishing and farming, producing foods for Asian restaurants and markets.

Among those who opened Chinese eateries, rare was a trained cook, more rare someone who knew fine Chinese food. The immigrants were poor working-class men serving foods remembered from southern China. They knew eating rice and noodles best, and being hungry. To them, meat meant pork; chicken was a luxury, beef rarely encountered, and lamb virtually unknown. In the United States, they found their American customers liking beef, chicken, and other meats, so they prepared and served southern Chinese dishes with lots of animal protein. Chinese restaurants still emphasize more meat and serve fewer vegetables than is common in China.

Changing Chinese Food Availability

Immigrants from elsewhere in China did not arrive in large numbers until after Congress rescinded the Chinese Exclusion Acts. Before the 1940s, most Chinese food was Cantonese-style, cooked by southern immigrants from Guangzhou. After 1965, immigration restrictions eased and newer immigrants came from all over China. In 1981 when they eased even more, immigrants came from all over China, Taiwan, and Hong Kong, and from Southeast Asia and Latin America. By the beginning of the twenty-first century there were about 3.5 million legal Chinese immigrants in the United States, plus many undocumented residents.

Since these changes in immigration law, those from many other regions introduced foods of China's more than twenty provinces

A nineteenth-century print of a busy Chinese kitchen.

and three major urban jurisdictions (Beijing, Guangzhou, and Shanghai). The foods of China's ethnic minority populations, such as Muslims, Mongols, and Hakka, also came to Chinese restaurants and Chinese homes.

Chinese Food in Homes

With more women among the immigrants, emphasis on Chinese family life increased. The immigrants, particularly those with more disposable income, maintained more traditional eating habits. Seeing family and friends meant more rituals revolving around food. For example, once a week many Chinese families ate in a Chinese restaurant after buying their weekly Chinese groceries in a Chinatown. Often they ate small southern Chinese dishes called *dim sum* (which means "dot the heart").

Now, Chinese food is widely available. Many Chinese foods are produced in the U.S., many more imported. Examples of both include Chinese sausages, cuttlefish, dried bean curd, dried oysters, bamboo shoots, ginger, black mushrooms, preserved duck eggs, many different soy and bean sauces, birds' nests, water chestnut flour, fish fins (including those of shark), lily buds, and a plethora of different Chinese greens.

Chinese Foods and Food Behaviors

The importance of food to Chinese Americans, as with the Chinese population, cannot be overemphasized. They believe nothing is more important than eating. What they prepare and consume depends on availability, geography, and family economics. But no matter the food, the dietary staple remains grain, primarily rice or wheat. Pork, the most commonly consumed meat, is eaten in small amounts. Vegetables are consumed in large quantities, and dairy products are rarely part of the diet.

Most Chinese Americans attempt to make everything taste Chinese, even if the ingredients are not. Outside the home, Chinese food is the second most popular ethnic cuisine (after Italian), and one-third of all U.S. ethnic restaurants are Chinese. As the Chinese population grows, so do the number and size of their restaurants. Merchants are importing more Chinese foodstuffs for them and for Asian and American supermarkets.

Chinese American Food in the Future

Chinese families maintain the central role of food in their lives. In the United States more than in China, they eat out more often in Chinese and other restaurants and celebrate family and banquet meals in them. Chinese New Year gatherings are the major attachment to their Chinese roots, and fewer Chinese maintain other traditional practices. The first American-born generation is changing considerably, as are younger generations of Chinese in China and in other countries. All are consuming more fast food and lots of carbonated soda, and bringing Western foods into their homes.

Families of professionals acculturate faster than the less affluent; but rich or poor, in China and elsewhere, Chinese are purchasing more frozen and take-out foods and doing less cooking. Chinese Americans eat more red meat and larger amounts of all meats, drink more coffee and less tea, and consume more sugar and fat than their ancestors did. They exhibit other Western ways at home including not cutting foods into small pieces before cooking. When eating out, they order fewer duck and chicken feet, offal, and "thousand-year eggs" (actually processed for about one hundred days).

Main Meals

Especially at dinners, Chinese Americans still eat lots of rice or noodles and have smaller *cai*, or meat and vegetable dishes, to accompany them. At celebration or banquet meals the reverse is true, and only one main dish is eaten at a time. During ordinary meals all dishes are eaten together.

Most Chinese still eat three meals daily and combine little meat with one or more vegetables when making a *cai* dish. Many snack two or three times each day, a practice rarely done in China. They still consider meals eaten with family ordinary and meals eaten away from home as special. Younger Chinese Americans neither make time nor know how to prepare special foods. They eat less meat than typical Americans and eat lots of ice cream, pizza, and pastries, items never part of traditional Chinese diets.

Chinese who adopt more American foods and Western behaviors are sometimes called "bananas," meaning they are yellow on the outside, white within. Others call them "bamboo sticks," indicating lack of roots in either culture. Recently, second- and later-generation Chinese who do not speak, read, or write Chinese keep fewer Chinese customs but are beginning to transmit some cultural heritage to children and grandchildren. They buy them Chinese cookbooks and subscribe to Chinese food magazines such as *Flavor and Fortune*.

Extensive interest in food and food behaviors are characteristic of the Chinese. They spend a larger proportion of their income on food than do other Americans. They maintain respect for the elderly and continue to offer elders the best foods at special meals. When greeting another person, they still ask *mi fan* (have you eaten) and continue to observe some mother-country and regional diet and health practices.

For all Chinese, no matter where they came from, main meals revolve around a staple carbohydrate that accounts for 60 to 80 percent of calories. This staple is rice or rice noodles in Guangzhou (Canton) and all areas except the north, where wheat and other grains are consumed more. There are other regional differences, mostly differentiated by compass points, or discussed by province, region, or ethnic minority population.

Chinese Food and Health

Chinese philosophically balance their meals for optimum health. At every meal they have lots of grain or *yin*, considered cold, mild, and bland with lesser amounts of *cai* (*tsai*) which is *yang* or hot, rich, strong, and spicy. They call foods and illnesses "conditions" and classify them by this duality. With a *yin* condition, Chinese recommend eating a *yang* food, and vice versa. While they cannot always verbalize which disease or food is *yin* or *yang*, practice has taught traditional combinations, and when ill they consume the correct pairing.

Besides adherence to this duality, there are cultural traditions in the Chinese humoral theory of food. For example, Chinese do not serve elders cold foods such as bean sprouts and white turnips. They know older people have weak blood. As the wrong foods can weaken it further, they give them hot foods such as ginger to strengthen the heart, a *yang* organ. They give new mothers hot foods for thirty days postpartum, including eggs, chicken soup, liver, and gingerroot, and encourage them to avoid most fruits and vegetables because they are cold or *yin*.

Chinese Assimilation

Chinese assimilate less rapidly than most other ethnic groups. Those who live in or near a Chinatown maintain more traditional health practices. They also have lower incidences of alcohol abuse than do second- and third-generation Chinese Americans.

Many cookbooks have been published about Chinese food, fewer books or articles about Chinese food behavior. Publications confirm soup still the beverage of choice, special foods being purchased for the elderly, and special foods served at life-cycle events and banquets.

Chinese Americans in the United States

California and New York have the largest Chinese populations and the largest number of Chinese eateries and markets for Chinese food. In 2001, California had about a million and a half Chinese residents; New York about half that number. The next most populous states, in decreasing order, are Hawaii, Texas, New Jersey, Massachusetts, Illinois, and Washington.

Chinese food is changing in China, the United States, and everywhere. Newer U.S. immigrants maintain more traditions and have greater availability of Chinese foods than before. Everywhere, Chinese are changing what they think is "Chinese food" and what Chinese food they eat. The Chinese American population is projected to triple by 2020. The characteristics that will define Chinese food at that time are unknown because different cultural values impact Chinese people and their food. In the past, the Chinese have traditionally exhibited resistance to food habit assimilation. No one knows if they will continue to do so.

[**See also** CHINESE NEW YEAR; CHINESE REGIONAL FOODS; DUCK; DUMPLINGS; FORTUNE COOKIES; RICE; SOYBEANS; SOY SAUCE.]

BIBLIOGRAPHY

Anderson, E. N. *The Food of China*. New Haven, CT: Yale University Press, 1988.

Newman, Jacqueline M. *Chinese-American Foods, Customs, and Culture*. Beijing, China: Chinese Dietetic Culture Society, 1998.

Newman, Jacqueline M. *Chinese Cookbooks: An Annotated English-Language Compendium/Bibliography*. New York: Garland, 1987.

Newman, Jacqueline M. *Food Culture in China*. Westport, CT: Greenwood, 2004.

Pan, Lynn, ed. *The Encyclopedia of the Chinese Overseas*. Cambridge, MA: Harvard University Press, 1999.

Simoons, Frederick J. *Food in China: A Cultural and Historical Inquiry*. Boca Raton, FL: CRC Press, 1991.

Wu, David Y. H., and Sidney C. H. Cheung. *The Globalization of Chinese Food*. Honolulu: University of Hawaii Press, 2002.

JACQUELINE M. NEWMAN

Chinese New Year

Chinese New Year *(Xinnian) is* a lunar festival falling between January's end and early February. This most important Chinese holiday used to continue for fifteen days until Lantern Festival. It begins with a feast on New Year's Eve; children and elders gather to see the old year out and eat Buddha's Delight, a dish of eight vegetables, wishing for a lucky year. They also enjoy *baozi*, dumplings made by the hundreds before New Year's Day. Some only eat vegetable foods this night, their dumplings filled with mushrooms, bamboo shoots, and cellophane noodles; others have shrimp, pork, and vegetables in their dough wrappers. Various fillings in glutinous rice balls are served in soup. New Year Cakes made with sweet rice are eaten then and all the holiday. A whole fish may be served, symbolizing prosperity; meat dishes rarely are.

Dressing in new clothes and visiting relatives and friends during the first days of the New Year is commonplace, as is bringing cakes, tangerines, and other sweets to symbolically say: May your family be prosperous and successful and have a sweet year. At home and when visiting, children kowtow to their elders and receive red envelopes with money inside. In some parts of China people enjoy different foods; their tables and visits can overflow with other symbolic foods such as pomegranates, their seeds a wish for many children; lotus root, wishing long life; oranges, tangerines, and kumquats, symbolizing wealth, good fortune, and happiness; and bamboo, offering longevity and strength.

The day before the New Year, old pictures of door gods are removed, and new ones replace them. Couplets written near or below them welcome the New Year and wish for good fortune. On New Year's first days, dragon dances are commonplace accompanied by gongs, loud drums, and exploding firecrackers. These are to chase away evil spirits. A newer notion is to gather monies from merchants to help less fortunate folk.

Traditional New Year festivities ended on Lantern Festival, a day when children and adults made lanterns, paraded with them, and put them outside their homes. There were riddles and couplet contests, floats made, and competitions for all of them. This culminating New Year holiday is of lesser importance in and outside China; Chinese New Year is not.

JACQUELINE M. NEWMAN

Chinese Regional Foods

China, a large country, has many different climates and foods in its different regions. These make for regional differences there and among immigrants living in the United States. Those studying them say they play a minor role; bigger divisions are by the compass points of south, east, west, and north.

Cantonese and Southern Chinese Foods

People from Canton (now called Guangzhou) and nearby Toisan were the first Chinese to immigrate to the United States. They defined America's understandings about Chinese food. At home and away, they like roasted meats, a minimum of sauces, and very fresh foods. Their primary cooking technique is stir-frying; but they also steam, steep, boil, roast, cook in soy sauce, clear-simmer, stew, deep-fry, blanch and/or cold-mix, salt, smoke, and pickle foods. Their main starch is rice and rice flour noodles. In China, these make up seventy percent of their calories; in the United States about fifty percent. At banquets or special meals, southerners love dishes such as birds' nests, sharks' fins, and others with expensive ingredients. Ordinary meals can include fried rice and egg rolls; and dim sum (little dishes that "dot the heart") at breakfast and lunch.

Shanghai and Eastern Chinese Food

Foods of this region are growing in popularity in the United States. They have rich flavor and some delicacy, many red-cooked with different soy sauces, black vinegars, and sugars. They also come from the provinces of Gansu, Zhejiang, and Fujian; the latter are America's newest immigrants. Meals from Fujian include two or more soups and/or stewed and red dishes; their color comes from red lees left after making red rice–based wines. Eastern dishes can include sweet and sour fish fillets, lion's head, eel in brown sauce; and crossing bridge noodles.

Sichuan and Western Chinese Food

Foods from this region are spicy, pungent, and flavorful, most from the Sichuan and Hunan provinces and surrounding areas. Many use lots of black and Sichuan pepper (also known as fagara of the genus *Xanthoxylum*), chilies, and piquant bean sauces. Dishes from this region can be oily; double cooked, with smoky tea flavors; and incorporate nuts, cloud ear mushrooms, and chicken fat. Western Chinese foods include dishes such as hot and sour soup, twice-cooked pork, orange beef, and cold sesame noodles.

Beijing and Northern Chinese Food

Cooking in this region is the most varied in China and among Chinese American immigrants. It is associated with the capital and lands north of the Chang River (Yangtze). Wheat and other grains are used more than rice. Most dishes incorporate onions, garlic, and scallions, though Buddhist monks avoid them, believing they increase sexual energy. A popular banquet dish, Peking duck, is roasted and served with buns or pancakes filled with crisp duck skin, *hoisin* sauce, and shredded scallions or cucumbers. The meat and bones are made into other dishes served later at the same meal. Northern dishes use lots of wine, have strong flavors, can be smoked or salty, or can include considerable ground white pepper. Lamb, rarely eaten in the rest of China, is grilled or stir-fried to the delight of Muslim, Mongol, and other non-Han populations. Popular dishes can be noodles, sweet and sour fish, steamed buns, chicken velvet, and dumplings.

[See also CHINESE AMERICAN FOOD.]

JACQUELINE M. NEWMAN

Chipped Beef

Chipped beef, or dried beef, is made from the lean cuts of top round, bottom round, or sirloin tip or knuckle. The beef is brined, then dried and sometimes smoked to preserve the meat, before being shaved—or chipped—into thin pieces. The end product's light weight and resistance to decay have made it the ideal food for wayfarers for centuries, as well as the perfect ration for soldiers and sailors. Creamed chipped beef on toast was served so often in U.S. military mess halls during World War II that it came to be known by the earthy name "shit on a shingle."

[See also COMBAT FOOD; MEAT; SHIP FOOD.]

BIBLIOGRAPHY
Lovegren, Sylvia. *Fashionable Food: Seven Decades of Food Fads*. New York: Macmillan, 1995.

SYLVIA LOVEGREN

Chitterlings

Chitterlings or chitlins, are an old European name for the intestines of hogs (or a sausage made from them). All pork butchering, generally a winter activity, provides plenty of chitterlings and a stomach (hog maw or ponce) which require lots of cleaning and then can be made into sausages or stews. All peasant cultures have dishes of both types, just as Native Americans had recipes for the innards of buffalo. Uniquely in the United States, the slave system directed all choice cuts and smoked hams to a small privileged class of owners and overseers, while assigning all the chitterlings, hog maws, and lesser parts to African American slaves.

Thus chitterlings, usually cleaned and stewed with vinegar and hot pepper, became a boundary dish in plantation areas of the southern states. Even after the Civil War, when white southerners took up many items of African-influenced food and evolved the myth of the kitchen-tyrant black cook, chitterlings—because of the cooking smells and gutter associations—remained outside the canon of "southern food." (In poorer areas of the white south, chitterlings had their ordinary place among other kinds of pork offal.)

So chitterlings became an iconic item of soul food, a boundary dish, which African Americans came to relish, but which remained a symbol of both identity and oppression. Until the late 1970s, pledges to white fraternities at UNC were taken to a soul food restaurant and forced to eat chitlins. For those who relish them, the art of cooking chitlins is to clean them carefully but not too carefully, to remove some fat, but not all the fat, as some slight redolence of decay is essential to the relish of otherwise rather tasteless tripe.

The dualistic situation of chitterlings led to pride in Depression-era black church fundraisers called "chitlin struts," to identification with the "chitlin circuit" of segregated black theaters and musical venues, and to euphemisms like "wrinkled steak" and "Kentucky oysters." A twentieth-century dish is deep-fried chitlins, a dish not so different in intent from the old Yankee dish of broiled tripe in mustard sauce.

BIBLIOGRAPHY
Council, Mildred. *Mama Dip's Kitchen*. Chapel Hill: University of North Carolina Press, 1999.

MARK H. ZANGER

Chocolate:

Historical Overview

Chocolate, a product derived from the fruit of the cacao tree (*Theobroma cacao*), originated in the New World. In pre-Columbian times, the Olmec and Maya peoples of Central America figured out how to bring out the rich flavor of cacao beans through a complicated process that involved fermenting and roasting. Christopher Columbus encountered the cacao bean—which he mistook for a type of almond, noting that it was highly prized by the natives—on his fourth voyage in 1502, on the island of Guanaja, off Honduras. Hernán Cortés, during his invasion of Mexico in 1519, found the Aztec emperor and nobles consuming vast quantities of cacao in the form of a dense, frothy beverage thickened with cornmeal and flavored with chilies, vanilla, spices, and other additions. Cacao beans were introduced before 1585 into Spain. A beverage made from ground beans combined with sugar, vanilla, and water became a favorite drink of kings and nobles. This beverage was disseminated from Spain throughout Europe, reaching England by 1657.

Colonial Americans acquired large quantities of cacao beans from the West Indies, and drinking chocolate was served as a hot beverage by the late seventeenth century. Since it was also a popular drink in Mexico, cacao beans were imported into the Spanish possessions in California, Florida, Louisiana, and the Southwest prior to these lands being acquired by the United States. As in Mexico and Europe, chocolate was consumed mainly in beverage form, although consumption never reached the levels later attained by tea or coffee in America.

The processing of cacao beans in America did not begin until the mid-eighteenth century. One early chocolate manufacture was James Baker, who in 1765 had financed John Hannon's chocolate business. In 1780 Baker began producing "Baker's" chocolate in Dorchester, Massachusetts. His son, Walter Baker, continued to expand the business, which eventually became Walter Baker and Company. It was sold to General Foods in 1927; a number of products, notably solid baking chocolate, are still sold under the Baker name in the early 2000s.

Attempts were first made to convert cacao into a solid in the late eighteenth century, but the result was a dry, brittle bar. In 1815, the Dutch chemist Coenraad Van Houten developed a process to make chocolate easier to mix with water in order to make a beverage. He pressed out most of the fat and then put the resulting dry cocoa through an alkalizing process. His cocoa powder, patented in 1828, became known as Dutch chocolate; it was darker in color and milder in flavor. Dutch cocoa powder changed the way hot chocolate was prepared and also simplified the manufacture of chocolate in solid form.

American cookbooks throughout the nineteenth century included an expanding array of recipes made with chocolate. Although early chocolate cakes were made to serve with drinking chocolate, rather than containing the ingredient themselves, chocolate was the dominant flavor in blancmanges, creams, cream pies, custards, éclairs, jellies, jumbles, macaroons, puddings, soufflés, syrups, and tarts. In addition to its use in hot beverages, it was also used to make frappes, chocolate ice water, and even wine with a chocolate flavor. Chocolate ice cream became popular, as did chocolate syrups for soda-fountain creations. Chocolate-iced yellow or white cakes were among the first uses of chocolate in cake baking, but subsequently cocoa or solid chocolate became an important ingredient in cakes and cookies themselves. Chocolate was used extensively in home candy making; fudge, chocolate drops, dipped bonbons, and chocolate-coated nuts were popular. Although the price of chocolate declined throughout the nineteenth century, chocolate was frequently adulterated and extended with peanuts, oats, or powdered rice, or colored with annatto.

Chocolate candies and the techniques that made them were imported from Europe, particularly from England, France, Switzerland, and Austria during the late nineteenth century. As European chocolate-making discoveries filtered into the United States during the nineteenth century, chocolate manufacturing rapidly expanded. Confectioners began coating candy with chocolate. By the 1870s, chocolate-covered candy and chocolate caramels were important American businesses.

Walter M. Lowney, a candy maker from Boston specializing in handmade chocolates, exhibited his wares at Chicago's Columbian Exposition in 1893. Milton S. Hershey, a caramel maker from Lancaster, Pennsylvania, visited Lowney's exhibit, and at the exposition Hershey also viewed the chocolate-making machinery manufactured by Lehmann and Company of Dresden, Germany. He ordered the machinery and, early in 1894, created the Hershey Chocolate Company as a subsidiary of his caramel business. In addition to chocolate coatings, the company produced breakfast cocoa, sweet chocolate, and baking chocolate. In 1900, Hershey sold the Lancaster Caramel Company, but retained the chocolate-manufacturing equipment and the rights to manufacture chocolate. In 1903, he moved to the heart of Pennsylvania's dairy country and began to build the world's largest chocolate-manufacturing plant, which opened two years later. Hershey's success pointed the way for other manufacturers, and many followed during the early twentieth century. Over the past one hundred years, more than forty thousand different candy bars have been manufactured in the United States. The most successful have contained chocolate.

Most Americans identify chocolate as their favorite flavor, and cookbooks featuring chocolate recipes are perennial best sellers. High on America's homemade chocolate hit parade are devil's food cake, fudge cake, German chocolate cake, brownies, and Toll House cookies. [**See also** BROWNIES; CANDY AND CANDY BARS; CHOCOLATE: RECENT DEVELOPMENTS; CHOCOLATE DRINKS; COMBAT FOOD; COOKIES; DESSERTS; FRAPPES; FUDGE; HALLOWEEN; HERSHEY FOODS CORPORATION; ICE CREAMS AND ICES; ICE CREAM SODAS; MARS; MILKSHAKES, MALTS, AND FLOATS; VALENTINE'S DAY.]

BIBLIOGRAPHY

Brenner, Joël Glenn. *The Emperors of Chocolate: Inside the Secret World of Hershey and Mars.* New York: Broadway Books, 2000.

Broekel, Ray. *The Chocolate Chronicles.* Lombard, IL: Wallace-Homestead, 1985.

Coe, Sophie D., and Michael D. Coe. *The True History of Chocolate.* New York: Thames and Hudson, 1996.

ANDREW F. SMITH

Chocolate:
Recent Developments

Throughout the twentieth century, chocolate was mostly eaten in America in the form of highly sweetened, mass-produced candy, often bought in individually wrapped bars from vending machines or corner stores, and later, supermarkets. Among the most important manufacturers were Hershey's and Mars. Chocolate in several forms (bitter, bittersweet, or sweet, in tablets or chips) was also manufactured on a large scale for cooking purposes, the most popular producer being the old New England firm of Walter Baker. Drinking chocolate was generally made with cocoa powder, the solid component of cacao from which the fat has been extracted.

The taste preferences that American chocolate was meant to meet were simple and unadventurous. The cacao beans themselves (predominantly of the hardy *forastero* type, from plantations in West Africa or Brazil) were chosen, roasted, and processed for consistent, mild, sweet candies. When Americans wanted elegant, high-end eating chocolate, they generally thought of imported Swiss brands, such as Lindt.

The situation began to change in the 1970s and 1980s, when American consumers showed interest in darker chocolate (often Belgian or French) as both cooking ingredient and candy. But it was not until the 1990s that Americans started to explore European *couvertures*—

Early-twentieth-century advertisement for Hershey's bitter chocolate.

high-quality chocolates made with greater percentages of cacao and less sugar—and become fascinated with chocolate's new-world roots and the baroque flavor combinations linked to its pre-Columbian past.

Trends and Innovations in Chocolate Making

There are several issues with which American consumers became concerned with respect to chocolate quality:

- The quality and origin of the cacao itself, with a rediscovery of so-called flavor beans belonging to the superior *criollo* and *trinitario* strains or certain unusual *forasteros*
- The fermentation and roasting processes, which develop deep and refined chocolate flavors while modulating the bitterness and astringency of raw cacao
- The highest possible proportion of cacao to other ingredients, especially sugar. In the new paradigm, the aim was to preserve as much pure, natural cacao flavor as possible, unmasked by oversweetening, overroasting, or the common alkalization process that manufacturers used to suppress unwanted bitterness, astringency, and acidity in bulk beans

Possibly spurred by the examples of the influential French manufacturer Valrhona and the Venezuelan Chocolates El Rey (the latter having been introduced in the United States in 1995), artisanal American chocolatiers began producing chocolate with such selling points as beans of carefully selected origin, sometimes single-variety or single-estate from Venezuela (South America's premier producer of quality beans); high cacao content; and a lack of the alkalis or added "fillers" and artificial flavors common in mass-produced commercial chocolate. Beginning in the late 1990s firms such as the tiny San Francisco–based Scharffen Berger and Guittard Chocolates, an established San Francisco firm founded in the late nineteenth century, began manufacturing boutique lines of chocolate products made from custom blends of flavor beans and high cacao content. The success of these efforts and the continuing influence of innovative European manufacturers have inspired at least half a dozen other small producers to experiment with high-cacao artisanal chocolates from select beans. Some have gone even further, reaching back into chocolate's pre-Columbian and European past to devise such products as complexly spiced drinking chocolates inspired by Aztec or colonial Spanish recipes, chili-laced balls of ground cacao like those used for grating in parts of Latin America, or unusual perfumed combinations.

There are only two important modern innovations in chocolate technology—a trend toward crushing the cacao beans into coarse fragments, or "nibs," before, rather than after, roasting them and a switch to faster, more powerful conching machines to agitate the semiliquid ground chocolate to improve the final flavor and texture. There are more changes in store. The American chocolate industry is absorbing the impact of a new breed of premium chocolates along with other culinary and social developments. Although the industry as a whole began moving toward greater consolidation in the early years of the twenty-first century, with major processing operations (for example, nib roasting and grinding) in the hands of only nine American companies, a few of the major manufacturers are either considering or taking steps toward launching boutique-style high-cacao-content chocolates with select beans or chocolates with higher cacao content. Other issues that transcend technology are certain to affect American chocolate.

Other Concerns

Organic farming and sustainable agriculture have become a focus of interest. Certified organic cacao is being raised by growers in several Latin American and African countries, in response to demand from concerned consumers. The integrated use of renewable resources in tropical forest habitats is an allied issue that U.S. companies such as Mars and cacao organizations such as the World Cacao Foundation have sought to address through experimental projects in several producing countries.

There is also the question of human rights abuses. In response to exposés of harsh labor conditions (among them, forced exposure to toxic pesticides) and the coercive use of child labor in Ivory Coast and other cacao-growing West African nations, the major American

chocolate companies have begun monitoring conditions on plantations that supply them. The international lobbying group the Fair Trade Federation began pressuring manufacturers to buy cacao only from sources that guarantee plantation workers safe working conditions and a minimum wage that is not dependent on speculator-driven market price fluctuations. Artisanal manufacturers and organic chocolate companies are leading the campaign to certify cacao produced under fair and humane conditions.

Chocolate's effects on health are the subject of much study. Reacting to people's interest in comparatively high-fat, low-carbohydrate weight-maintenance diets and the related issues of epidemic obesity and diabetes, the major American manufacturers have worked to develop products made with reduced sugar content (a trend that was anticipated by the makers of high-end boutique chocolates) or with other noncaloric sweeteners tested for flavor, safety, and suitability for use in cooking.

At the same time, an increasingly sophisticated medical understanding of the origins of cardiovascular disease is yielding surprising insights into the therapeutic properties of chocolate. With support from Mars, chocolate came under intense study as a strikingly rich source of compounds known as "flavonoids." Two subclasses of these compounds, "flavanols" and "procyanidins" (present in large amounts in some dark chocolates and cocoa powder made with beans that have not been overly fermented, alkalized, or roasted at high temperatures), demonstrate antioxidant and anticlotting activity, along with an ability to improve arterial blood flow. At least one major company (Mars) is switching to cacao beans processed with a proprietary method that retains high concentrations of these beneficial substances; products made with these beans bear the trademark "Cocoapro" (from cacao and procyanidins). The ongoing research on chocolate's health benefits is bound to change the way chocolate is manufactured, marketed, and consumed for years to come.

[**See also** Candy and Candy Bars; Chocolate; Hershey Foods Corporation.]

BIBLIOGRAPHY

Brenner, Joel. *The Emperors of Chocolate: Inside the Secret World of Hershey and Mars.* New York: Broadway Books, 2000.

Coe, Sophie D., and Michael D. Coe. *The True History of Chocolate.* New York: Thames and Hudson, 1996.

Presilla, Maricel. *The New Taste of Chocolate: A Natural and Cultural History of Cacao with Recipes.* Berkeley, CA: Ten Speed Press, 2001.

MARICEL PRESILLA

Chocolate Drinks

The Olmec civilization made a beverage from the roasted and ground seeds of *Theobroma cacao* (cocoa tree) as early as 1600 B.C.E. The Maya and Aztec continued the practice, instructing Spanish conquistadores on how

An early twentieth century advertisement for Bournville Cocoa.

to process the raw cacao beans. In 1528 Hernán Cortés brought cacao to the Spanish court, where the Mesoamerican delicacy quickly was adopted. The royal physicians praised it as a food and medicine, and King Philip successfully kept cacao away from the rest of Europe until 1655, when Great Britain took control of his cacao plantations in Jamaica. By 1657 the first of many chocolate houses had opened its doors in London.

American colonists took quickly to the fashionable chocolatl. Beans imported from the West Indies were roasted and ground into a liquid paste. Spices like vanilla and nutmeg and aromatics like ambergris were added to the cocoa as it was ground. The resulting liquor was mixed with water, spirits, or milk, and sweetened with sugar. After heating, the drink was skimmed to remove cacao butter and then beaten to a froth to lighten the remaining fat and mitigate any bitterness from faulty fermentation.

Hand grinding often resulted in chocolate-lover's elbow, a complaint that may have brought the money-making potential of cacao to the attention of Dr. James Baker of Dorchester, Massachusetts. In 1764 Baker opened the first successful American chocolate business in partnership with the Irish immigrant chocolate maker John Hannon. Baker's hot chocolate sustained pioneers on the Oregon Trail and bolstered the morale of Union troops in the Civil War, becoming so ubiquitous that its name is still confused with a type of chocolate rather than a brand.

Domenico Ghirardelli arrived in San Francisco for the gold rush in 1849, but instead struck a chocolate bonanza. In 1865 Ghirardelli's factory discovered cacao butter would separate from the roasted beans if they were left hanging in a bag in a warm room. This broma processing remains in common use. At the end of the Civil War, Americans were drinking cocoa, made from Dutched cacao and sold in cakes or powdered; hot chocolate, made from Baker's chocolate bars; and Broma.

America's relationship with chocolate was changed forever when, in 1893, the successful caramel manufacturer Milton Hershey saw a demonstration of the new Swiss conche machine and other European innovations at the World's Columbian Exposition in Chicago. By 1900 Hershey's milk chocolate candy bar had begun the industry that would make Americans think of chocolate as something to eat—preferably while drinking a chocolate soda.

In 1832 pharmacies began selling carbonated artificial mineral water as a therapeutic drink. Pharmacists soon added herb and fruit syrups to increase its healthfulness and marketability. The first use of chocolate syrup with soda water is unknown, but the earliest nationally recognized chocolate soda was the turn-of-the-century New York egg cream, made with Fox's U-Bet chocolate syrup, milk, and seltzer.

Consumers wanted soda water available in their own kitchens, and entrepreneurs raced to be the first to accommodate them. By the early 1920s the bottling industry had advanced sufficiently that manufacturers and retailers could offer homepaks, the forerunner of the six-pack. Many of the bottles were filled with noncarbonated Yoo-hoo chocolate drink. Popular through the early 1970s, Yoo-hoo and other nostalgia sodas are enjoying a new popularity.

In 1926 Hershey capitalized on the soda fountain and ice cream parlor boom by marketing cocoa syrup, renamed chocolate syrup in time to compete with Bosco Chocolate Syrup for the hearts and wallets of the baby boomers of the post–World War II generation. By 1956 Hershey was helping tuck children in at night with instant hot cocoa, a happy amalgamation of cocoa powder, milk powder, and sugar.

International producers began influencing the American market in 1930, when the Swiss-owned Ovaltine began sponsoring the popular radio adventure *Little Orphan Annie*. The Nestlé company followed in 1948 with the introduction of Nestlé Quik.

In the 1970s individual servings of chocolate-flavored soy milk began to appear in the American market, providing an alternative for the health conscious and lactose intolerant. Convenience drove the market in the 1980s, and beverage manufacturers obliged with off-the-shelf chocolate milk and powdered breakfast drinks for those on the go. In the 1990s chocolate diet drinks appeared along with energy-boosting drinks, which took a leaf from the pharmaceutical marketing slogans of the 1890s.

Current trends resemble the customized mixtures of cacao beans of the eighteenth and early nineteenth centuries. Inspired by the success of boutique coffees, restaurants and chocolate makers are producing gourmet chocolate for a new generation's drinking pleasure.

[**See also** CHOCOLATE; HERSHEY FOODS CORPORATION; SODA DRINKS.]

BIBLIOGRAPHY

Coe, Sophie D., and Michael D. Coe. *The True History of Chocolate*. New York: Thames and Hudson, 1996.

ESTHER DELLA REESE

Chopping Knives and Food Choppers

Chopping knives have been used to cut everything from raw vegetables to chunks of meat. There are a few types, but all have relatively wide or deep blades, unlike a paring knife, for example. A few look like cleavers, with the blade and handle on the same horizontal plane, but most have handles on top, to utilize vertical force. Handles are either T-shaped with one tang or have a grip with two tangs—one at each end of the blade, for more control. Some chopping knives have two or even three blades, often curved along the bottom, giving them the nineteenth-century moniker "rug cutters," a nickname shared by rocking chairs. In the 1920s one was made with a spring-action T-handle, adding force. Chopping knives were used with cutting boards or wooden cutting bowls. Early nineteenth-century ones may be fancy and made with figural cutouts in the deep blade.

Mechanical food choppers date from the 1860s on. Forerunners of food processors, they often had a set of blades for different purposes. Basically, there is a cast-iron frame with cranked gears that move the chopping blades up and down while the geared container (with wooden bottom) revolves. Used for vegetables and meat, they were often called "hashers."

[**See also** FOOD PROCESSORS.]

BIBLIOGRAPHY

Franklin, Linda Campbell. *300 Years of Kitchen Collectibles*. 5th ed. Iola, WI: Krause, 2003.

A chopping knife with its characteristic wide blade.

Lasansky, Jeannette. *To Draw, Upset, and Weld: Work of the Pennsylvania Rural Blacksmith, 1742–1935*. Lewisburg, PA: Oral Traditions, 1980.

LINDA CAMPBELL FRANKLIN

Chorizo

Chorizo, Spain's ubiquitous sausage, is usually made of chopped pork, sweet or hot paprika, crushed red peppers, and garlic. It is available in two forms: a soft variety for cooking and a cured, hard variety that is sliced and served as a tapa. Spanish chorizo differs significantly from the plumper, juicier Mexican chorizo, which is made of freshly ground pork and a chili-spice blend, and from Portuguese *chouriço*, which contains less paprika and more garlic and includes wine. In America, Spanish chorizo is popular in areas with large Hispanic populations. It has caught the attention of top chefs and often is used as a bold flavor counterpoint, especially in fusion cuisine.

[**See also** SAUSAGE; SOUTHWESTERN REGIONAL COOKERY.]

BIBLIOGRAPHY

Davidson, Alan. *The Oxford Companion to Food*. Oxford: Oxford University Press, 1999.

DAVID LEITE

Christmas

For most Americans Christmas rivals Thanksgiving for indulgence. Unlike Thanksgiving, however, Christmas is more than a single meal. Specialty Christmas foods permeate the month-long holiday season. Titles such as *Old-Fashioned Christmas Cookbook* and *Twelve Days of Christmas Cookbook* recall Christmases past, and gingerbread men, plum puddings, and cookies are part of culinary tradition. Homemakers have covered Christmas tables in red and green since the late nineteenth century, and holiday dishes bearing the image of Santa Claus or evergreens have been marketed since the 1930s.

All this would stun a time traveler from the early nineteenth century. When Philadelphia's *Democratic Press* asked in 1810, "Shall we have Christmas," the question was not merely rhetorical. The answer depended on one's religion and ethnicity and ranged from a resounding "No!" through modest acknowledgement of the day to a patchwork of holidays. Starting with the feasts of Saint Lucy and Saint Nicholas in early December and continuing through Twelfth Night on January 6, many disparate threads have now been woven into a season-long American Christmas mantle. Yet it was only in the mid-nineteenth century that December 25 became a widespread, governmentally sanctioned holiday. At that same time, a formulaic Christmas dinner swept the nation that would last through the end of the nineteenth century, only to fade in the twentieth. Unlike the iconic Thanksgiving comestibles, which anchor that singularly American holiday regardless of one's ethnicity, there is nothing

The William G. Bell Company, manufacturers of canned spiced seasoning, issued advertising cards such as this one showing a Christmas delivery in the late nineteenth century.

A collection of readers' favorite recipes from Woman's Day *magazine, "Holiday Cakes and Cookies."*

originally American about Christmas except Santa Claus and candy canes. Christmas's multicultural roots have meant that Americans of different regions, classes, and ethnic groups celebrate with different foodstuffs.

Christmas before the 1840s

English, Dutch, and German colonists approached the December holidays differently. Even among the English expatriates, attitudes toward Christmas varied according to religious sect. William Bradford, the Puritan governor of Plymouth Colony, in 1621 chastised non-Puritans for their revelries on "the day they call Christmasday." Because nothing in the Bible identified December 25 as Christ's birthday, Puritans viewed that date as simply another workday. There were no special foods, church services, or commemorations, an attitude shared by many Protestant denominations well into the nineteenth century. Puritans railed against mincemeat pie as "idolatrie in a crust." The spices in the pie were believed to signify the luxuriously exotic gifts of the magi and to evoke popery. From 1659 to 1681 it was illegal to celebrate Christmas in Massachusetts, there being a five-shilling penalty for doing so. Analogous penalties were threatened against Dutch colonists who celebrated Saint Nicholas Day on December 6. In the seventeenth century the Reformation government in Amsterdam tried to squelch the perceived disorder that arose from people congregating in public with "any kind of candy, eatables or other merchandise." Most of the early Dutch settlers in America celebrated nonreligious New Year's Day with open houses, but there were only pockets of private Saint Nicholas observances.

Some early colonists in America did welcome Christmas. In the eighteenth century, German colonists in Pennsylvania brought branches, precursors of the evergreen Christmas tree, into the house and then decorated them with wafers, honey cakes, gingerbreads, cookies, apples, and marzipan. Descriptions (including criticism from Quakers, who shared the Puritans' attitude) abound of Philadelphians' extravagant early-nineteenth-century Christmas balls. Elegant collations fortified weary dancers with cold meats, terrapin, oysters, and pyramids of sweetmeats and creams. The celebrations were lavish, but the foods served were not distinctively associated with Christmas.

Southern colonists were largely Anglican with a few French Huguenots. Their Christmas festivities focused more on revelry than on food, Christmas hunts and games being the main entertainment. Outdoor parties adjourned to plantation homes for copious dinners, but these were "no otherwise than common," given the luxurious standards of the households. In 1709 the guests of the Virginia governor William Byrd II sat down to a typical southern spread of "turkey and chine, roast apples and wine, tongue and udder" as well as many other meats and sea-

food. Holiday observances might extend through Epiphany with "great pyes" and Twelfth Night cakes but little else to distinguish the tables.

Heavy drinking and gifts of liquor marked colonial and frontier celebrations. At wealthy plantations eggnog often was drunk in bed on Christmas morning. Christmas in the South coincided with completion of the harvest. With the exception of the cooks and a few essential house workers, many (but by no means all) slaves were relieved of their labors and given a Saturnalian break for feasting, drinking, and revelry. This celebration followed the custom of the English country gentry who were the forebears of Anglican southerners. In England the local squire hosted a Christmas feast for the extended community that contributed, directly or indirectly, to the running of the household. Through the Civil War, the plantation owner often prepared his personal concoction for eggnog in a large punch bowl and then distributed a cup to each guest and plantation dependent in much the same spirit as the wassail bowl had been passed in England.

Christmas Dinner in the Mid-Nineteenth Century

In the mid-nineteenth century, cultural changes in America led to a fundamental shift in the nature of Christmas observances from bawdy and rowdy public frolics to sentimental Victorian domesticity. Popular literature such as *The Sketch-Book of Geoffrey Crayon, Gent.* (1819) by Washington Irving and the 1823 poem "A Visit from Saint Nicholas" piqued an antiquarian interest in Christmas. Christmas demanded a dinner with family that was special but within the economic reach of most Americans. Because no single cultural Christmas tradition monopolized American foodways, the unifying model for the American Christmas dinner of the middle to late nineteenth century was supplied by Charles Dickens in *A Christmas Carol* (1843).

Although Dickens did not invent the idea of serving turkey at Christmas (it had always been one of many foods on festive American tables), his extraordinarily popular novella was a remarkable case of life imitating art. Most American food writers in the late nineteenth and early twentieth centuries prescribed a Christmas dinner of roast turkey with gravy, mashed potatoes, sage and onion stuffing, and plum pudding. Unlike the controversial mincemeats, the plain menu described by Dickens largely lacked religious connotations and thus assuaged sectarian differences. Civil War diaries brimmed with descriptions of efforts to procure the "Christmas turkey." These accounts were matched by mid-nineteenth-century Minnesotans' careful recording of the prices of Christmas turkeys imported by sleigh from Iowa and Illinois. Those who could not afford turkey (a relatively expensive bird in the late nineteenth century) could follow the advice to the frugal offered by Marion Harland (the pseudonym of Mary Virginia Hawes Terhune) in *Breakfast, Dinner and Supper* (1897) that they enjoy the less expensive boiled goose. The charitable gesture whereby the character Ebenezer Scrooge sends the largest turkey in the poulterer's window to replace a scrawny goose was allegedly emulated by a Vermont factory owner on hearing Dickens read *A Christmas Carol* in Boston in 1867. This man reportedly was so moved that he broke with his Puritan tradition of opening his factory on Christmas Day. The following year, the factory owner instituted the tradition of giving a holiday turkey to each employee. By the 1880s the concept of a proper Christmas dinner for all led charities to host Christmas dinners for the urban poor, especially orphans, and for immigrants cloistered on Ellis Island. All served turkey as the main, "Americanizing" course, a tradition that continues in holiday soup kitchens.

Christmas Dinner in the Twentieth Century

By the late nineteenth century, some cookery writers tentatively suggested alternatives for those who wanted something out of the ordinary. Although roast turkey remained a popular centerpiece, turkey farmers such as Horace Vose found that the Christmas market demanded much smaller birds than the Thanksgiving market. Food writers suggested that other meats might supplement or even supplant the American bird. Terhune, writing for a more affluent readership in *House and Home* (1889), recommended a "noble" saddle of venison in lieu of the "provincial" turkey that must appear on Thanksgiving. She wrote that Christmas turkey was required only if "your culinary conscience or the family appetite demand the sacrifice of the Bird of Plenty." Other writers suggested steak, meatloaf, and veal curry. Even the somewhat conservative Good Housekeeping Institute by the late 1920s suggested crown roast of pork as an alternative to turkey.

As the importance, although not necessarily the form, of Christmas dinner was being established, newly invented dishes emulated the secular symbols of the holiday. Alice Bradley, the principal of Fannie Farmer's cooking school, in 1936 described Christmas pear salad. The recipe called for cutting a pear into the shape of a Christmas tree, dressing it with green mayonnaise, decorating it with slivered almond "candles," and then garnishing the result with cubes of cream cheese "presents" and with "ribbons" painted with food coloring. Others cooks used grapefruit salad to mimic wreaths by coating the edges of grapefruit shells with tinted green sugar and garnishing the fruit cup with maraschino cherry "poinsettias." Later cookbooks often incorporate red and green foods into Christmas menus.

Regional and ethnic influences tailor Christmas foods to local preferences, so it is impossible to identify a universal American Christmas. In the South barbecue and chili are added to the Christmas table, and in the Southwest tamales are served. Italian Americans may eat a seven-course fish dinner on Christmas Eve. French Americans have imported the "thirteen desserts," said to represent each participant in the Last Supper. New Orleans continues to specialize in yeasted Twelfth Night cake, and many Japanese Americans serve white rice with turkey. Cookie exchanges, parties for the purpose of swapping homemade cookies, are becoming a tradition. Once-common foods such as mincemeat are now specifically associated with the holiday.

Although the modern Christmas menu is mutable, there lingers an undercurrent of nostalgia for the ancient feast described by Irving in the chapter in *The Sketch-Book* titled "The Christmas Dinner." The feast at Bracebridge Hall, complete with boar's head and wassail bowl, was knowingly anachronistic when Irving wrote and was too opulent to be mimicked on most American tables. Yet affluent Americans have patterned entertainments after this "medieval" feast since the mid-nineteenth century, children's dress-up pageants paying homage to the traditional foods. Adults also have indulged in the fantasy: Since 1927 the Ahwahnee Hotel in Yosemite National Park, in California, has held Bracebridge dinners at Christmas. Tickets are assigned by lottery, averaging fifteen thousand entries for three hundred spots. The photographer Ansel Adams was the original pagentmeister for the costumed fete that loosely adapts Irving's dinner to contemporary tastes: tenderloin of pork and filet mignon stand for the aristocratic boar's head and baron of beef.

[**See also** Eggnog; New Year's Celebrations; Thanksgiving; Turkey.]

BIBLIOGRAPHY

Bauer, John E. *Christmas on the American Frontier, 1800–1900.* Caldwell, OH: Caxton, 1961.

Kaufman, Cathy. *Nurturing a Holiday: Christmas Foods in Eighteenth and Nineteenth Century America.* In *The Proceedings of the Oxford Symposium on Food and Cookery 2003*, edited by Richard Hosking.

Marling, Karal Ann. *Merry Christmas! Celebrating America's Greatest Holiday.* Cambridge, MA: Harvard University Press, 2000.

Nissenbaum, Stephen. *The Battle for Christmas.* New York: Random House, 1996.

Restad, Penne *Christmas in America.* New York: Oxford University Press, 1995.

Weaver, William Woys. *The Christmas Cook: Three Centuries of American Yuletide Sweets.* New York: HarperCollins, 1990.

CATHY K. KAUFMAN

Chuck E. Cheese Pizza

Nolan Bushnell, who had worked as games division manager of an amusement park, developed one of the first hugely successful video games, "Pong." In 1972 Bushnell and Ted Dabney founded Atari, which was sold to Warner Communications in 1976. While working for Warner Communications, Bushnell created Chuck E. Cheese's Pizza Time Theatre; the first such outlet opened in 1977 in San Jose, California. It featured pizza, one hundred video games, and animated entertainment with life-size robots, including Chuck E. Cheese, a giant mouse with his trademark cigar.

Bushnell left Atari but bought Pizza Time Theatre from Warner Communications. He marketed Pizza Time Theatre, and by 1983 there were more than two hundred nationwide outlets. Robert L. Brock, president of Topeka Inn Management, signed a co-development agreement with Bushnell, which gave Brock exclusive franchising rights for Pizza Time Theatres in several states. Topeka Inn Management created a subsidiary called Pizza ShowBiz to help launch the new franchises.

Brock declared the co-development agreement void and in 1980 opened the ShowBiz Pizza Place in Kansas City, Missouri. It was similar to Pizza Time Theatre. Bushnell sued Brock for breach of contract, and the lawsuit was settled out of court with ShowBiz paying Pizza Time Theatre a portion of its profits for fourteen years.

During the late 1970s, both Pizza Time and ShowBiz enjoyed success and both restaurants rapidly expanded their operations. In the 1980s Pizza Time's profits plunged and in 1984, it filed for bankruptcy. ShowBiz Pizza Place bought it out. During 1986 profits begin to increase, and the company changed its name to CEC Entertainment Inc., headquartered in Irving, Texas. As of 2005, there were 498 Chuck E. Cheese outlets, which operate in forty eight states and four countries.

[**See also** Pizza; Pizzerias.]

BIBLIOGRAPHY

Langdon, Philip. *Orange Roofs, Golden Arches: The Architecture of American Chain Restaurants.* New York: Knopf, 1986.

ANDREW F. SMITH

Chuck Wagons

The invention of the chuck wagon is attributed to the legendary rancher Charles "Chuck" Goodnight. In 1866, he designed a four-wheeled wagon of wide gauge for transporting supplies and preparing food. The notable feature of the chuck wagon is a cabinet or "chuck box" in the rear, filled with small supplies and bearing a fold-down table for food preparation. The chuck wagon was a significant development not only in forming and institutionalizing the "cowboy cuisine" of fact and lore but also in enabling, in part, the grand cattle drives of the cowboy heyday in the American West.

Ranching and Driving in Context

The short but colorful heyday of the American cowboy began after the Civil War and ended gradually with the privatization and fencing in of the West from the 1880s until the early twentieth century. It is estimated

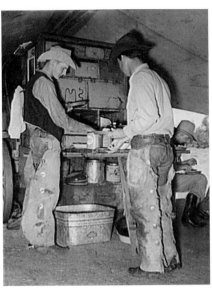

Cowboys near Spur, Texas, serve themselves at the chuck wagon in May 1939.

that in Texas alone in 1860 there were some 3.5 million wild cattle grazing the unfenced land, the descendants of a few ancestors brought to the Americas by conquistadors and settlers. After the Civil War ended, freed slaves, former soldiers already hundreds of miles from home, other men with marital, legal, or financial problems, and young boys looked to the American West for their fortunes or at least for a good steak dinner cut from one of the millions of wild cattle.

The fortune, if there was to be one, was found in rounding up these wild cattle, claiming them, and leading them to a major city, where they could be sold and consumed or shipped by rail to another population center. These early cowboys, working alone or in small groups, typically cooked for themselves a meal of beef, coffee, and perhaps some pinto beans ("frijoles"); if they were wealthy enough, they might have a Mexican or black hired hand to handle the cooking and other chores.

As was true throughout American agricultural history, the independent cowboy with a small herd of cattle could not be financially successful compared with the owners of what is considered the "ideal herd size" by economies of scale. The larger outfits were orchestrated by entrepreneurial ranchers like Goodnight, who had the capital and political clout to buy off or kill potential enemies on the trail. Furthermore, they could guarantee wages despite the volatility of beef prices, which could change dramatically over the months-long cattle drive. All of these early ranching outfits had the need for a mobile commissary to feed their staffs during the long cattle drives. While the idea of having a victual wagon with a designated cook traveling along the trail was a natural development, it was Goodnight's modifications to a traditional wagon that institutionalized the chuck wagon.

Coosie and the Chuck

Goodnight's wagon soon became the standard across the West, and a cook could move from one outfit to another without noticing significant changes in the commissary or the food system. In the wagon, often under a canvas roof, were stored the nonperishable foods and the men's bedrolls. The typical larder included frijoles, coffee beans (usually Arbuckles' brand, which came with a peppermint candy awarded to the man who volunteered to grind), molasses, flour, dried fruit, and canned tomatoes. Under the wagon in a hide attached to the bottom, called a "coonie" (from the Spanish *cuña*, or "cradle"), were stored firewood, pots, Dutch ovens, and aging beef wrapped in canvas. In the chuck box one could find small items like spices, flatware (called "eating irons"), a bottle of whiskey for medicinal use, medicines, matches, and other incidentals.

With this wagon developed the cuisine of the cowboy, which revolved around the "three B's"—beef, beans, and bread. The beef, cowboys agreed, should preferably be steaks from the hindquarter of a heifer, fried in tallow until well done; the beans, pintos or navy; the bread, sourdough biscuits (the starter well coddled by the cook and also accredited to Goodnight, who is said to have picked up the knack from his mother). With this meal the men drank strong, boiled black coffee. If the cook was in a pleasant mood and feeling ambitious, there may have been a dessert, such as a cobbler or stewed dried fruit. "Chuck" was used to indicate any sort of meal, and colorful nicknames were ascribed to nearly every ingredient and preparation: sinker (biscuit), lick (molasses), mop (gravy), calf slobber (icing), alkali water (coffee), moonshine (rice), skunk eggs (onions), and music roots (sweet potatoes, said to cause flatulence).

The most famous distinctly cowboy food was "son of a bitch stew," almost ceremoniously prepared whenever a calf was slaughtered. While the muscle meat was best aged for a few days in the coonie, the organs—namely, brain, sweetbreads, liver, heart, tripe, and the key ingredient, marrow gut (or margut, a four-foot tube that connects the cow's stomachs and contains a milky fluid of partially digested grass)—would spoil immediately and so were cooked into stew with tomato, onion, and chilies.

Linked inextricably with the story of the chuck wagon is the tale of the stereotypical camp cook, often dubbed "coosie," from the Spanish *cocinero*. Coosie was notoriously temperamental, often in trouble with the law, and of dubious culinary skill. A good cook was a treasure on the trail and a major perquisite. The men would go out of their way to keep a good cook happy by cleaning his dishes, gathering firewood, and, most important, respecting the cook's domain, the chuck wagon. A good cook could lure cowboys to work for the tastier outfits. Even

a bad cook, though, was respected on the trail, as a cowboy complaining about the food or inciting the cook to quit would be promptly rewarded with his apron and "gouch hook" (pothook) and asked to demonstrate how things should be done. Both derisively and lovingly called "old woman" or "old lady" (Adams, p. 54), the cook "was doctor, dentist, and older brother, and it was he who dosed the cowboys when they were ill, heard them when they were depressed, or amused them when they were bored" (Durham and Jones, *The Negro Cowboys*, p. 50).

Although a diet based on the "three B's" may seem monotonous to our modern culinary sensibilities, cowboy cuisine as a whole became distinct and unified and reduced from its nuances in history and lore. Like Coosie and the foods themselves, the chuck wagon has become institutionalized as an icon of the American West.

[**See also** ARBUCKLES'; BEANS; CHILI; SLANG, FOOD.]

BIBLIOGRAPHY

Adams, Ramon F. *Come an' Get It: The Story of the Old Cowboy Cook*. Norman: University of Oklahoma Press, 1952.

Cano, Tony, and Ann Sochat. *Chuck Wagon Heyday: The History and Color of the Chuck Wagon at Work*. Canutillo, TX: Reata, 1997.

Durham, Philip, and Everett L. Jones. *The Negro Cowboys*. Lincoln: University of Nebraska Press, 1983.

Hughes, Stella. *Chuck Wagon Cookin'*. Tucson: University of Arizona Press, 1974.

JONATHAN DEUTSCH

Church's Chicken

In 1952, George W. Church Sr., a retired incubator salesman, created the first "Church's Fried Chicken to Go" in downtown San Antonio, Texas. It was a low-overhead operation that offered only take-out service, but Church's was distinguished by its extra-large chickens.

At first, Church only sold fried chicken; french fries and jalapeños were added in 1955. It later added fried okra, coleslaw, mashed potatoes, corn on the cob, and honey butter biscuits. When George Church died in 1956, four outlets were open. Family members took over the operation, and by 1962 the chain had grown to eight locations in San Antonio. The company began to expand beyond San Antonio. The Church family sold the company in 1968, and the following year, Church's Fried Chicken Inc. became a publicly held company. At the end of 1969, over one hundred Church's restaurants were in operation in seven states. Between 1969 and 1974, Church's grew by an additional 387 restaurants. International expansion began in 1979, with the announcement of the first Church's in Japan, and the company subsequently established locations in countries under the brand name Texas Chicken.

In 1981, Church's merged with Popeyes. In 1992, America's Favorite Chicken Company, since renamed AFC Enterprises Inc. became the parent company to Church's Chicken. In 2004, the Atlanta-based Arcapita Inc. bought Church's Chicken from AFC Enterprises Inc. As of 2005, Church's was the third-largest chicken franchise company in the United States.

[See also CHICKEN.]

BIBLIOGRAPHY

Jakle, John A., and Keith A. Sculle, *Fast Food: Roadside Restaurants in the Automobile Age*. Baltimore: Johns Hopkins University Press, 1999.

ANDREW F. SMITH

Cider

In America the word "cider" most often means juice right out of the apple, sweet juice. With the growing interest in fermenting sweet juice to develop an alcoholic drink, the products are being redefined. Buyers are often confused, because in the American marketplace cider has for many years meant a sweet, unfermented juice.

Besides fermented apple juice, there are several drinks with an apple base that have quenched the thirst of Americans for centuries. Low-quality sweet cider paved the way for the emergence of the soft drink industry. Before regulation, this roadside jugged juice often was not only watered down but also made from apples that had fallen from the tree, poorly washed or not washed at all, and pressed from a single variety that does not make a tasty cider, especially the Red Delicious. Many small orchardists take great pride in blending apples with the elements of acid, tannin, and sugar for a quality sweet cider.

Ciderkin is made by overnight soaking of the pomace, the residue left after most of the juice is removed from the apple, and then repressing it and fermenting this "wash" in the traditional way. It is very delicate, with a light apple taste, and is sometimes called cider wash or cider water. It was often served to children and, frequently, spices were added to elevate the flavor.

Scrumpy was made occasionally by colonists who came to America from England. It is a rough, strong, dry cider, ready for consumption after a few months of fermentation. There are recipes that add raisins and raw meat to the juice.

[See also APPLEJACK; APPLES; CIDER.]

BIBLIOGRAPHY

Orton, Vrest. *The American Cider Book: The Story of America's Natural Beverage*. New York: Farrar, Straus and Giroux, 1973.

Watson, Ben. *Cider Hard and Sweet: History, Traditions, and Making Your Own*. Woodstock, VT: Countryman Press, 1999.

THOMAS BURFORD

Cider, Hard

The word "cider" has its roots in ancient Hebrew. *Sheker*, which means strong drink, was translated into the Greek *sikera*, the Latin *sicera*, and then the French *cidre*. The English called it *cyder* or cider.

Hard cider has been produced since at least 1200 C.E., owing, in part, to the ease with which it can be made. Because of the natural yeasts that exist on apples, apple juice, if left at room temperature, will ferment. This is one reason why grocery stores keep fresh apple juice chilled—to prevent it from turning into hard cider. Cider probably began as a farmer's drink. Apples were knocked from trees or, in the case of *scrumpy* (*scrump* originally meant "shriveled"), old, overripe apples were gathered off the ground. Traditionally, the apples are milled into a pulp (or *pomace*) from which the juice is pressed.

The Normans brought cider to England. By the seventeenth century it was so beloved that the English wrote poems and songs about cider. On Old Twelfth Night (January 17) field laborers would quaff cider and dance around the best apple trees, exhorting them to grow good apples. The English carried hard cider to America. It became very popular in the northeastern colonies, where apple trees were plentiful. Americans considered cider a health booster and a safer beverage than available water, so they consumed it throughout the day. From field laborers to American presidents, nearly everyone drank cider.

In the mid-nineteenth century, beer and then spirits and wine gained popularity, and cider consumption declined. Hard cider saw a resurgence in the 1980s, making way for dozens of new brands. They are more refined and variegated, and some have added flavors like cranberry. Cider also can be found on tap in many bars and in bottles at numerous retailers.

[See also APPLEJACK; APPLES; CIDER.]

BIBLIOGRAPHY

Watson, Ben. *Cider, Hard and Sweet: History, Traditions, and Making Your Own*. Woodstock, VT: Countryman Press, 2000.

KEVIN R. KOSAR

Cincinnati Chili

A popular fast food found principally in the region around Cincinnati, Ohio, Cincinnati chili is made of ground beef cooked in a tangy, tomato-based sauce. It is served over spaghetti and dressed with beans, onions, and cheese. Cincinnati chili was developed in the early 1920s by a Macedonian immigrant, Athanas "Tom" Kiradjieff, and his brother, John, and served at their small Cincinnati restaurant, which became known as Empress Chili owing to its location next door to the Empress burlesque house.

The Kiradjieff brothers originally served their uniquely spiced sauce over steamed frankfurters on buns, in imitation of the style popularized at New York's Coney Island

```
•••••••••••••••••••••
SKYLINE CHILI
Carry Out Menu

                                    1/2 PINT  PINT
Chili Plain ..........................  1.30   2.25
Chili Spaghetti .....................  1.15   1.95
Chili Beans .........................  1.15   1.95
3-Way-Chili - Spaghetti, Cheese ....  1.55   2.35
4-Way-Chili - Spaghetti, Onions,
                            Cheese ..  1.70   2.50
5-Way-Chili - Spaghetti, Onions,
                    Beans, Cheese ...  1.75   2.55
Extra Chili .........................   .15    .30
Extra Crackers ......................          .10

            •••••

Coney Islands .......................          .65
Coney Islands with Cheese ...........          .75
Order of Cheese .....................          .40
Order of Onions .....................          .15

            •••••

Ice Tea .......................  .35 & .45 & .50
Soft Drinks ...................  .35 & .45 & .50
Coffee & Hot Tea ...................  .35 & .40
Sanka ..............................        .35
Hot Chocolate ......................  .35 & .45
Milk ..........................  .45 & .70 & .90

• BY PHONING YOUR ORDER THERE'S NO WAITING •
    U.S. GOVT. INSPECTED MEATS, EST. 1691
```

A 1980s take-out menu from Cincinnati's famous Skyline Chili, a restaurant opened by Nicholas Lambrinides, a Greek immigrant to the United States.

amusement park in the early part of the twentieth century. Their frankfurters were known as coneys and, sometimes, chili dogs. When grated cheddar cheese is added to the sandwich, it becomes a cheese coney. Raw chopped onions are another garnish, and hot sauce is often applied at the table.

The Kiradjieffs' sauce became popular and was soon served by itself in a bowl rather than as a topping for frankfurters. Embellished by combinations of condiments, Cincinnati chili spawned a unique chili jargon. A one-way is plain chili with oyster crackers on the side. Chili served over a plate of spaghetti becomes a two-way. Add grated cheddar cheese to the spaghetti and sauce to create a three-way. Raw chopped onions or kidney beans make a four-way chili. Spaghetti, cheese, onions, and kidney beans add up to a five-way. Experienced diners order by nickname.

A distinguishing characteristic of Cincinnati chili is that the beef is simmered directly with the other ingredients rather than undergoing a preliminary browning, although recipes vary. Unlike western and Texas-style chili, Cincinnati chili does not rely on whole chilies for heat, finding its warmth from cayenne, commercial chili powder, or cumin instead. It has a sweeter, more subdued flavor that is spicy but not hot. The Kiradjieff brothers drew from the familiar seasonings of their native Macedonia when they created Cincinnati chili. In addition to oregano and bay leaf, the sauce hints of allspice and cinnamon, seasonings frequently used in Balkan and other eastern Mediterranean cuisines. There is also an exotic whiff of chocolate.

Cincinnati Chili

129

Others adopted the idea of the original Empress Chili line, notably the Greek immigrant Nicholas Lambrinides, who began Skyline Chili in the late 1940s. While there remains a brisk rivalry among chili brands, Skyline has become the dominant name in chili throughout the region. Recipes for each clan's spice blends are closely guarded secrets passed down to family members, and chili devotees are fiercely loyal to their favorite brand.

Cincinnati chili traditionally is served in chili parlors, small, utilitarian restaurants devoted almost exclusively to selling chili. Most Cincinnati chili parlors are owned by leading chains such as Empress or Skyline, although there are several independent restaurants. Frozen or canned chili produced by the major brands is available in supermarkets, and dried seasoning packets of the secret spice blends are also sold in area stores. [**See also** CHILI; COOKING CONTESTS.]

BIBLIOGRAPHY

Bridges, Bill. *The Great American Chili Book.* New York: Rawson, Wade, 1981.

DuSablon, Mary Anna. *Cincinnati Recipe Treasury: The Queen City's Culinary Heritage.* Athens: Ohio University Press, 1989.

MARY SANKER

Cisco

Cisco (*Coregonus artedi*), like whitefish, with which it is sometimes confused, is found in northern waters, south to Ohio and Illinois. In the salmon family, cisco also is found in the Minnesota River because of introduction there, although it is not native to that river. Cisco is smaller than whitefish, a record catch in Minnesota being a four-pounder from Big Sandy Lake. Cisco is fished both for sport and commercially. There were at one time in the Great Lakes seven species of cisco, six of which disappeared when alewives invaded the lakes. Because the alewife population has declined in the Great Lakes, the one surviving species of cisco has recovered well enough to be fished commercially. Cisco is also called tullibee (a name given it by the fur traders), chub, and lake or freshwater herring. Cisco appears in markets in the round and smoked. It is suitable for steaming, frying, and broiling.

SANDRA L. OLIVER

Citrus

The many forms of commercial citrus all descend primarily from three original species native to Asia: citron (*Citrus medica*), an ancestor of the lemon; pummelo (*C. grandis*), a giant parent of the grapefruit; and mandarin (*C. reticulata*), which includes tangerines and similar fruits. Citrus cultivation in the area that would become the United States dates from the Spanish exploration and settlement of Florida in the sixteenth century; it reached Louisiana around 1700 and California with the arrival of Franciscan friars in 1769.

With the advent of steam transportation in the mid-nineteenth century, citrus was imported from Mexico, the West Indies, and Italy. Large-scale commercial cultivation began in Florida and California in the 1870s and 1880s, when the extension of railroads allowed fresh fruit to be shipped to major eastern and midwestern markets.

At first, growers planted many seedling trees, which are easy to propagate but take up to a decade to come into bearing and are not always true to the type of the parent. In the second half of the nineteenth century nurserymen and growers imported scores of varieties, which they grafted onto rootstock, making possible the marketing of true citrus varieties.

In 2002 the United States ranked second to Brazil among citrus-producing nations, with 1.05 million bearing acres, of which Florida had 727,600; California, 268,000; Texas, 29,100; and Arizona, 28,600.

The sweet orange (*C. sinensis*), believed by scientists to be a natural hybrid of pummelo and mandarin, is the leading citrus fruit in the United States, which produces three classes of oranges in commercial quantities: common oranges, a large and diverse group that includes Valencia and juice oranges; navel oranges, which have small, rudimentary secondary fruits embedded in the blossom (bottom) end and are usually seedless; and blood oranges, pigmented with anthocyanins, which impart a distinctive red coloration and berry flavor to the flesh.

The Valencia, the most widely grown orange variety in the United States and the world, was sent from England to California in 1876 and to Florida the next year. It is well colored and flavored and very late in season, maturing in late spring through autumn of the year after it flowers. By 2002 Florida grew 82 percent of the nation's Valencia crop on 300,500 bearing acres, but 97 percent of its harvest went to processing; California grew most of the rest, but in the same year 82 percent of its harvest went to the fresh market.

Juice oranges, such as Hamlin and Pineapple, are early and midseason varieties, maturing from late September into February. Florida grows most of the nation's crop on an estimated 267,235 acres (as of 2002); the vast majority goes to processing.

The navel orange, imported from Brazil to Washington, D.C., in 1870 and sent to Riverside, California, several years later, is the nation's leading fresh citrus variety. Large, seedless, and easy to peel, the navel at its best has a smooth, deep-orange rind, and intense, sweet-tart flavor, unsurpassed among oranges. In 2002 California had 127,500 bearing acres, mostly in the San Joaquin Valley, and accounted for 86 percent of the nation's crop. California-grown navels, at peak from January to March, offer high levels of sugar and acidity, a proper balance between the two, and rich aromatics. In addition to being consumed fresh and as juice, oranges are used in salads, savory dishes, and desserts such as cakes and ices.

Grapefruit (*C. paradisi*) arose in the seventeenth century in the West Indies, as a hybrid of sweet orange and pummelo. All modern grapefruit derive from seeds or plants brought to Florida in 1809. Early varieties, notably Duncan, had whitish flesh and rich flavor, but many seeds; Marsh, a nearly seedless mutation discovered in about 1860, long dominated Florida's commercial shipments, which began in the 1880s. In the early twentieth century, growers in Florida and Texas discovered pink-fleshed, seedless mutations such as Ruby, which, along with later red-fleshed varieties, such as Rio Red and Star Ruby, dominate production. Most of the remaining white grapefruit goes for processing.

America, which had 138,300 bearing acres of grapefruit in 2002, is by far the world's largest producer of the fruit. The best growing areas, Florida and the lower Rio Grande valley of Texas, have humid conditions and high total heat units during the growing season. Grapefruit is primarily consumed as a fresh fruit, in juice, and in fruit salad.

America is the world's second-largest producer of lemons, after Argentina, with 64,300 bearing acres in 2002, mostly in California and Arizona. The two main varieties, Eureka and Lisbon, both came to prominence in the 1870s; they are similar and are marketed interchangeably.

In coastal California lemon trees flower and fruit year-round, but overall lemon production peaks in winter, as for most citrus. Since demand increases in summer—for lemonade and for wedges to squeeze in alcoholic beverages—packinghouses have mastered the science of storing lemons, which are picked green and held for months in climate-controlled rooms.

Mandarins, popularly often called tangerines, have thin skin and delicate pulp. They were introduced in the 1840s to Louisiana, but they have always been a secondary crop in America. There were 38,600 bearing acres in 2002, of which Florida had the majority and California and Arizona the rest. The classic Florida "Christmas tangerine," Dancy, has superb aroma and flavor and an edible rind, but it was replaced toward the end of the twentieth century by Fallglo and Sunburst, which are brightly colored but of mediocre eating quality. Satsumas, early-season, seedless varieties, are grown in California and along the Gulf Coast. Most mandarins are eaten fresh.

The two chief varieties of lime (*C. aurantifolia*) both have greenish, acid pulp and are usually sold with green rinds, although they turn yellow when fully ripe. The Mexican, or Key, lime, is small, round, and seedy; the Persian, or Bearss, lime is larger and seedless. Limes are used to flavor sweet items such as sorbet; to "cook" fish with its acid in seviche dishes; to add zest to soft and alcoholic drinks; and in a dessert classic, Key lime pie. [**See also** FRUIT; FRUIT JUICES.]

BIBLIOGRAPHY

Jackson, Larry K., and Frederick S. Davies. *Citrus Growing in Florida*. 4th ed. Gainesville: University Press of Florida, 1999.

McPhee, John. *Oranges*. New York: Farrar, Straus and Giroux, 1967.

Walheim, Lance. *Citrus: Complete Guide to Selecting and Growing More Than 100 Varieties*. Tucson, AZ: Ironwood Press, 1996.

DAVID KARP

Claiborne, Craig

Food editor, restaurant critic, cookbook author, and gracious host, Craig Claiborne (1920–2000) was instrumental in leading millions of meat-and-potato Americans to the table of fine cuisine. As food editor of the *New York Times* and the country's foremost restaurant critic, he introduced gastronomically sheltered Americans to the greatest chefs of France, Italy, and Asia and, through his recipes and more than twenty books, encouraged home cooks to broaden their culinary horizons.

Born in Mississippi, Claiborne graduated in 1942 from the University of Missouri, where he studied journalism. Aided by the GI Bill after discharge from the navy, he fulfilled his lifelong dream and entered the prestigious École Hôtelière near Lausanne, Switzerland, to study classic French cooking.

He started his culinary journey as a receptionist at *Gourmet* magazine and eventually moved up to become one of its editors. In 1957 he broke journalistic ground by landing the position of food editor at the *New York Times*, a post traditionally held by women. He was the first restaurant critic with a solid background in food preparation, rating a restaurant rigorously on its food. Known for his gentlemanly authoritarian manner, he showed a hitherto unfamiliar respect for chefs and restaurateurs. He hated pretension and sloppy or overbearing service, and his eye for detail could make even tough restaurateurs wince. In 1972 he gave up restaurant criticism for the *Times* to start a short-lived newsletter with his colleague Pierre Franey, whom he had known since 1959, when Franey was a chef at Henri Soulé's celebrated Le Pavillon. When Franey left Le Pavillon, he began accompanying Claiborne on his restaurant rounds and developed recipes for Claiborne's food columns.

Claiborne's most notorious caper was an American Express–sponsored unlimited-expense dinner for two. Reporting on the thirty-one-course, four-thousand-dollar dinner that he and Franey consumed at Paris's *Chez Denis* restaurant made headline news and brought thousands of letters of protest. Claiborne returned to the *Times* in 1974 to concentrate on writing about food and chefs. The cooking took place in the enormous kitchen of his East Hampton home, with Franey developing recipes for the *New York Times Magazine* and later for the Living Section.

A portrait of food critic and author Craig Claiborne.

Their collaboration led to seven books for the *Times*, among them *Classic French Cooking*, *Veal Cookery*, *Craig Claiborne's "The New York Times" Cookbook*, and *Craig Claiborne's Gourmet Diet*, written after his doctor advised him to limit his salt and fat intake.

An avid traveler, Claiborne had a knack for identifying fresh talent and frequently bolstered a young chef's career by giving him or her exposure in the *Times*. Among those who benefited from his foresight were French chefs like Paul Bocuse, Roger Vergé, Alain Ducasse, Jean Troisgros, and Gaston Lenotre, as well as the Italian cookbook writer Marcella Hazan and the Cajun chef Paul Prudhomme.

A Feast Made for Laughter chronicles the dining and cooking adventures encountered along the way. At heart a Francophile, he was open to other cuisines, including those of Brazil, Mexico, and China. He had a talent for demystifying the formality of cooking and made it accessible to all, as in *The Chinese Cookbook*, written with Virginia Lee. *Memorable Meals* is his collection of meals shared with his wide range of friends, including his nearly legendary New Year's Eve dinners. Among other books are *Craig Claiborne's Kitchen Primer*, *Elements of Etiquette*, and *Craig Claiborne's Southern Cooking*, in which he pays homage to his southern roots.

[**See also** CELEBRITY CHEFS; COOKBOOKS AND MANUSCRIPTS: 1970S TO THE PRESENT; PRUD-HOMME, PAUL.]

BIBLIOGRAPHY

Claiborne, Craig. *A Feast Made for Laughter*. New York: Holt, 1983.

HELEN H. STUDLEY

Clambake

Generations of historians incorrectly record that the New England clambake is the survival of a native custom learned by the first English colonists. Archaeological and historical evidence supports clam eating by Native Americans, but not by the newcomers, who identified them with "savagery." Clams were a starvation ration to the Europeans, who used the abundant shellfish to feed pigs.

The clambake myth arose from the social and political changes brought about by American independence. The new nation needed an icon of its unique cultural identity, and an "ancient ritual" featuring indigenous food provided it. It is no accident that the popularity of the clambake exploded after the Civil War, when a new national myth was again created. Plymouth replaced Jamestown as the cradle of America, and the "New England" clambake became an American institution.

The advent of mass transportation in the late nineteenth century gave businessmen the opportunity to turn the clambake into a tourist industry. Rhode Island entrepreneurs were so successful that the first printed recipe for a "clambake" gives that state credit for the custom. Clambake "pavilions" quickly spread across New England. Often combined with equally popular picnics, clambakes worked especially well as fund-raisers and political rallies, a role they continue to fill.

No longer exclusive to New England, clambakes seem to require only that the clams be cooked by steam. A "traditional" clambake occurs in a pit dug in the sand of the beach where the clams are gathered. The pit is lined with rocks, and a fire is built over them. When the rocks are white hot, they are covered with layers of seaweed, clams, and other foods. A wet tarp is laid over all until the food is cooked. Items typically included on the menu are lobster, corn, white potatoes, clam chowder, and cold beer.

[See also CLAMS; NEW ENGLAND; PICNICS.]

BIBLIOGRAPHY

Neustadt, Kathy. *Clambake: A History and Celebration of an American Tradition*. Amherst: University of Massachusetts Press, 1992.

ESTHER DELLA REESE

Clams

The poor clam has taken a back seat to the regal oyster. While oysters starred as Oysters Rockefeller at city restaurants, clams either were used as bait or served fried at roadside clam shacks. While clams lack the regal image of the oyster, they still represent a valuable fishery product. Five species of clams make

An illustration of a chowder party on Fire Island, New York, by John Worth, published in Harper's Weekly in 1873.

up the bulk of the U.S. commercial harvest: surf clam (*Spisula solidissima*), ocean quahog (*Arctica islandica*), hard-shell clam (*Mercenaria mercenaria*), soft-shell clam (*Mya arenaria*), and Manila clam (*Tapes philippinarum*).

Before Europeans arrived in America, Native Americans harvested clams. Huge piles of clamshells or kitchen middens identify old Indian campsites. Native Americans used the hard-shell clam, also known as a quahog, as a source of food and medium of exchange and for sealing friendships. The purple part of the shell, along with the white part of periwinkle shells, were fashioned into beads, strung on sinew, and made into belts called wampum. For a time during the colonial period, individual beads and ornamental wampum belts were used as money.

Surf clams and ocean quahogs are dredged from the ocean depths and represent by far the largest harvest. The hard-shell clams—also called littleneck, cherrystone, or chowder depending on the size—are consumed raw or minced for use in chowders. Hard-shell clams are harvested by hand with tongs or by dredging. Soft-shell clams are gathered at low tide by spading with a fork. It is a slow and laborious process, but clamming provides an important source of income for some New England coastal residents.

Understanding the names under which clams are sold is like untangling a fishnet. *M. arenaria*, the eastern soft-shell clam, is served as fried clams at roadside clam shacks throughout New England. Some cookbooks refer to them as the common clam, longneck, long clam, sand gaper, old maid, maninose (nannynose), belly clam, or squirt clam. Since the nineteenth century it has been listed on restaurant menus as the Ipswich clam after Ipswich Bay, with its highly productive clamming flats. Ipswich, Massachusetts, is a commercial center for clam processing and wholesale distribution. Since 1935 tourists have made the pilgrimage to Ipswich to eat fried clam bellies at the Clam Box.

When East Coast production falls behind demand, clams are shipped from Washington State, where small amounts of soft-shell clams are harvested. It is estimated that most soft-shell clams are consumed "within five miles of the coast from Boston to Bar Harbor, Maine." The first canneries in the United States were established along the coast, and marine products made up a substantial part of what was canned. Burnham and Morrill opened the first clam cannery about 1870 at Pine Point, Maine.

On the West Coast, early pioneers found a host of new clam species to duplicate the chowders, bisques, clam pies, and fritters they remembered from New England. They had a group of small clams called the butter (*Saxidomus giganteus*), Pismo (*Tivela stultorum*), the western jackknife clam (*Tagelus californianus*), and the horse clam (*Tresus nuttallii*). They also had the giant geoduck (*Panopea abrupta*), pronounced "gooey-duck," a Nisqually Indian phrase meaning "to dig deep." Genevieve A. Callahan's *Sunset All-Western Cook Book: How to Select, Prepare, Cook, and Serve All Typically Western Food Products* (1933) describes this clam as a "legless, headless duck, the shells forming the wings and the wrinkled, mottled skin representing the down on the neck and breast." With this abundance of Pacific Coast clams, traditional New England recipes take on new names such as Pacific Coast Clam Chowder and Oregon Clam Bisque.

[See also CLAMBAKE; NEW ENGLAND; SEAFOOD; SHELLFISH.]

BIBLIOGRAPHY

Peterson, James. *Fish and Shellfish*. New York: Morrow, 1996.

Davidson, Alan. *North Atlantic Seafood*. New York: Viking, 1979.

Dore, Ian. *Shellfish: A Guide to Oysters, Mussels, Scallops, Clams, and Similar Products for the Commercial User*. New York: Van Nostrand Reinhold, 1991.

JOSEPH M. CARLIN

Clams Casino

Clams casino is an appetizer of clams baked in the shell with bacon and green pepper. In southern New England today, it usually is also stuffed with breadcrumbs, possibly an influence of Italian stuffed mussels. The classic presentation of two soft shell clam bellies has also been widely replaced by a single littleneck or cherrystone on the half-shell. A widely reprinted error in a food encyclopedia had it invented in New York City in 1917. The town of Narragansett, Rhode Island, however, has reclaimed the dish. *Providence Journal* reporter Arline A. Fleming sent food historians back to the sources for an August 2005 article that establishes that the original dish was invented in 1894 by Julius Keller at Louis Sherry's Narragansett Casino for socialite Mrs. Paran Stevens. Research by Barry Popik had found the recipe in a professional dictionary of about 1908 and on a 1916 restaurant menu in Washington, DC.

MARK H. ZANGER

Clarifying

To "clarify" means to clear a liquid of solid particles. The purpose of clarifying is to make a liquid clear, preserve food, or remove a taste. Early recipes for clarifying sugar, butter, molasses, stocks, jellies, beer, and wine demonstrate various techniques. Typically, recipes involve introducing some sort of clarifying agent, frequently egg whites, and careful straining to filter impurities. While modern production techniques and changing tastes have eliminated the need to clarify most foods, a few, such as butter and stock, are still clarified for particular culinary applications.

Martha Washington's *Booke of Cookery and Booke of Sweetmeats*, written in the days before white sugar was common (probably between 1550 and 1625; the text is based on an old manuscript passed down to Washington), opens with a recipe for clarified sugar. "Take a pinte of faire water & beat ye white of an egg…put a pound of sugar in to it & let it boyle…. There will rise a black scum…take it off until it is very clear, & then streyne it through A Jelly Bag or wet cloth" (p. 225). Similar recipes appeared throughout the mid-nineteenth century in works such as Catharine Beecher's *Domestic Receipt-Book* (1846).

Recipes for "calf's-feet jelly" require egg whites to clarify the stock. Typical is Eliza Leslie's recipe in *Seventy-five Receipts for Pastry, Cakes, and Sweetmeats* (1832), in which the whites and small bits of eggshell are mixed with stock. Leslie instructs the reader to "boil it hard for five minutes,…pour it hot into the bag (made of white flannel) and let it drip through into the dish" (p. 539). Broths for aspic and consommé are still clarified by a similar process.

Selected Receipts of a Van Rensselaer Family, 1785–1835 offers several clarifying techniques, including using milk to clear spiced wine, adding a piece of burned chalk to keep a barrel of beer "brisk and clear" (p. 42), and preserving butter (for up to a year) by melting it with an onion and letting the particles settle to the bottom. Modern cooks still clarify butter to extend its shelf life and increase its smoke point by melting it to remove the fragile milk solids.

BIBLIOGRAPHY

Kellar, Jane Carpenter, Ellen Miller, and Paul Stambach. *Selected Receipts of a Van Rensselaer Family, 1785–1835*. Albany, NY: Historic Cherry Hill, 1976.

Leslie, Eliza. *Seventy-five Receipts for Pastry, Cakes, and Sweetmeats*. Bedford, MA: Applewood Books, 1989. Reprint of the original 1832 edition.

Washington, Martha. *Martha Washington's Booke of Cookery and Booke of Sweetmeats*. Transcribed and edited by Karen Hess. New York: Columbia University Press, 1995.

ALEXA VAN DE WALLE

Club Sandwich

The club sandwich typically is composed of three slices of toast, spread with mayonnaise, that separate a filling of sliced turkey, ham, or chicken along with sliced tomato, strips of crispy fried bacon, and lettuce. The origin of the sandwich is unknown. The first recipe appears as Club-House Sandwiches in Sarah Tyson Rorer's *Sandwiches* (1894). In the late 1890s it was a popular item at the casino owned by Richard Canfield, "America's Greatest Gambler," in Saratoga Springs, New York. The casino's dining room was known for its fine cuisine and for its gambler's buffet, which provided delicious food for those who wanted minimum interruption of their gaming pursuits. By 1896 the club sandwich appeared on the menus of such New York City establishments as the Waldorf-Astoria Hotel and the Windsor Hotel. The club sandwich remains a ubiquitous item on restaurant luncheon menus.

[See also SANDWICHES.]

BIBLIOGRAPHY

Mercuri, Becky. *Sandwiches That You Will Like*. Pittsburgh, PA: WQED Multimedia, 2002.

Rorer, Sarah Tyson. *Sandwiches*. Philadelphia, PA: Arnold and Company, 1894.

BECKY MERCURI

Cobbler, *see Pies and Tarts*

Coca-Cola

Invented in 1886 by an Atlanta pharmacist, John S. Pemberton, Coca-Cola is the second-best-known term on earth (after "OK") and is the most widely distributed single product in the world. As a symbol of the American consumer lifestyle, the drink has significance and power far beyond its fizzy sugar-water contents.

Coca-Cola evolved from Pemberton's French Wine of Coca, a cocaine-laced wine beverage sold in imitation of the extremely popular Vin Mariani. When Atlanta voted in November 1885 to go "dry" the following year, Pemberton revised his formula, removing the wine and adding an assortment of essential flavoring oils, caramel for color, and a large amount of sugar. Along with coca leaf and kola nut extract—the respective sources of cocaine and caffeine and the origin of the drink's name—these ingredients made up Coca-Cola syrup, which was then mixed with carbonated water to make a popular drink in an era of resplendent soda fountains offering a wide variety of flavors.

But Coca-Cola was also a patent medicine, a popular "nerve tonic" to cure neurasthenia, a mythical disease supposed to afflict high-strung housewives and businessmen. The beverage was also touted as a headache and hangover cure. When Pemberton died in 1888, a fellow Atlanta pharmacist, Asa Candler, who believed that Coca-Cola helped his migraines, secured the rights to the formula in a convoluted, somewhat shady series of transactions. Frank Robinson, who had worked for Pemberton, named the drink, wrote the flowing script for the logo, marketed the drink for Candler, and wrote most of the advertising. By 1899 it was a national soda fountain drink, with branches and syrup factories in Dallas, Chicago, Los Angeles, Philadelphia, and New York.

Up to that time Coca-Cola was only a soda fountain drink. Fearful of spoilage and spillage, Candler saw no future in bottles, so in 1899 he gave away the bottling rights to Benjamin Thomas and Joseph Whitehead, two lawyers from Chattanooga, Tennessee, with the stipulation that they buy syrup only from the Coca-Cola Company. These "parent bottlers" established a successful network of Coca-Cola bottlers, and the drink became available everywhere to everyone, including African Americans, who in those days were excluded from soda fountains.

By the turn of the century Coca-Cola's cocaine content, though very small, was causing problems, because the supposed wonder drug of 1886 was then seen as an addictive scourge. Owing to racism, it was also blamed for unrest among southern blacks. Bowing to social pressure, Candler took the cocaine out of Coca-Cola in 1903, though coca leaf extract with its cocaine content removed remains in the formula.

With missionary zeal, Coca-Cola salesmen and bottlers pushed the beverage as a magical elixir. With equal fervor, food faddists and temperance women fought against Coca-Cola, claiming that its caffeine was bad for children and adults. Candler survived a 1911 government lawsuit prompted by Dr. Harvey Wiley, head of the U.S. Food and Drug Administration, but the company stopped using children under the age of twelve in its advertising and cut the caffeine content in half.

As Candler grew older, he gave most of the company stock to his children, who sold the company in 1919 for $25 million to a consortium of bankers headed by the Atlanta wheeler-dealer Ernest Woodruff. In the

A Coca-Cola advertising card circa 1905.

inflationary post–World War I period, the price of sugar soared, throwing the company into crisis and conflict with its independent bottlers, whose contract called for a fixed syrup price. When Woodruff attempted to abrogate the contract, a protracted lawsuit ensued. It was finally settled with a sliding price for the sugar content.

The Woodruff Era

Robert Woodruff, Ernest's charismatic thirty-three-year-old son, took over as president in 1923. Known as "the Boss," he ruled the company, passing on every major decision until his death at the age of ninety-five in 1985. Woodruff forbade negative, defensive advertising and, with the help of Archie Lee's "Pause That Refreshes" slogan and Haddon Sundblom's Coca-Cola Santa Claus paintings, he made Coca-Cola an all-American drink. By the time of World War II, it had become a

symbol of the American way of life. During the war Coca-Cola for the military was exempted from sugar rationing, and Coke employees were given pseudo-military status in order to bottle the drink behind the lines. This gave Coca-Cola an invaluable foothold for international expansion following the war.

Meanwhile, Pepsi-Cola emerged as a major contender. It had thrived during the Depression as a cheap alternative to Coke, but that had given it a lower-class stigma. In the 1950s and 1960s Pepsi sought a more vital, upscale image, focusing on the baby boom generation. The conservative Woodruff refused to respond for a long time, but in 1955 he permitted the introduction of King Size Coke to match Pepsi ounce for ounce, and in the 1960s the company sold alternate drinks, such as Sprite, Tab, and Fanta.

Because of its symbolic weight and ubiquity, Coca-Cola was particularly subject

to political forces. In the postwar world, Communists spread rumors that the drink caused health problems and that a German Coca-Cola plant was a secret atom bomb factory. When the company rejected an Israeli franchise in 1966, American Jews protested. After the company rushed to correct the problem, the Arabs boycotted Coke products. The company was politically well connected in the United States, however. Woodruff had helped elect President Dwight Eisenhower, who shared ownership in Latin American bottling plants, and a later president, Jimmy Carter, relied heavily on the Coca-Cola Company's expertise for inside information in foreign countries.

Goizueta's Changes

By the time the Cuban expatriate Roberto Goizueta took over as chief executive officer in 1981, Coca-Cola was widely perceived as a sleeping giant, a conservative company living largely on its past accomplishments. Pepsi was making inroads. Goizueta announced that there would be no sacred cows, no sacred formulas. For the first time, the company took on debt. Goizueta violated tradition by having the company assume equity positions in bottlers around the world, approving the introduction of Diet Coke, with its previously forbidden use of the main drink's name, and, finally, in 1985, daring to change the formula of Coca-Cola itself. New Coke turned out to be a disaster, but even that blunder worked out well in the end, when the market share of the reintroduced Coca-Cola Classic increased.

By the time Goizueta died of cancer in 1997, the revitalized company's market share had exploded from $4.3 billion when he took over to $145 billion, and Coke products accounted for half of the world's soft drink sales. Since then, the company has had problems, largely owing to a troubled world economy. During his brief, stormy tenure as CEO, Doug Ivester mishandled a health scare in which the company had to withdraw its supposedly contaminated drinks in Belgium and other European countries, although independent scientists concluded that the panic, nausea, and dizziness—classic symptoms of psychosomatic illness—were probably caused by mass hysteria. Ivester resigned in 1999 and was replaced by an Australian, Douglas Daft. In the twenty-first century, the drink Coca-Cola remains extremely important, but the company is shifting with the times to offer a wider variety of noncarbonated beverages, such as Fruitopia and its bottled water, Dasani.

[**See also** ADVERTISING; COLA WARS; SODA DRINKS.]

BIBLIOGRAPHY

Allen, Frederick. *Secret Formula: How Brilliant Marketing and Relentless Salesmanship Made Coca-Cola the Best-Known Product in the World.* New York: HarperBusiness, 1994.

Greising, David. *I'd Like the World to Buy a Coke: The Life and Leadership of Roberto Goizueta.* New York: Wiley, 1998.

Pendergrast, Mark. *For God, Country, and Coca-Cola: The Definitive History of the Great American Soft Drink and the Company That Makes It.* 2nd ed. New York: Basic Books, 2000.

MARK PENDERGRAST

Cocktails

The first recorded definition of the cocktail appeared on May 13, 1806, in *The Balance and Columbian Repository,* published in New York City. In a comical letter written to the editor, a reader inquired about what the cocktail consisted of and whether the name was "expressive of the effect which the drink has on a particular part of the body." The editor replied:

> Cocktail is a stimulating liquor composed of spirits of any kind, sugar, water, and bitters—that is vulgarly called bittered sling and is supposed to be an excellent electioneering potion, inasmuch as it renders the heart stout and bold at the same time that it fuddles the head. It is said also to be of great use to a Democratic candidate; because, a person having swallowed a glass of it is ready to swallow anything else.

The one ingredient that differentiated the cocktail from other mixed alcoholic drinks that preceded it was the emergence of a new product called bitters. Made from distilled spirits infused with spice, fruit, and botanical ingredients, bitters are highly concentrated flavor additives. Although bitters contain as much as 40 percent alcohol, they are designated as a food additive and in the nineteenth century were sold as medicinal tonic, a designation that allowed the purveyors to avoid the high tax on spirits. The three most widely used bitters are Angostura, Peychaud's, and the bitters line from Fee Brothers in Rochester, New York.

Technology

The soul of the American cocktail is ice. Ice was a luxury enjoyed only by the wealthy early in the nineteenth century, so the artificial ice machines were especially important to cocktail development. By the 1880s artificial ice was affordable at even modest drinking establishments.

In the 1830s another development that dramatically changed the distilling industry was the invention of the Coffey, or column, still in Ireland. This permitted distillers to produce spirits faster and more cheaply than ever before. This new technology precipitated the emergence of the large commercial distiller.

Recipe

In 1862, in the middle of this growth, a colorful figure named Jerry Thomas entered the scene with a book and a mission. The book was *How to Mix Drinks; or, The Bon Vivant's Companion.* It was a compilation of recipes from around the country and Europe, using spirits and wines in many categories of mixed drinks. The mission was to popularize the sprit-based mixed drinks Thomas had dedicated his life to compiling. Buried in the pages of this groundbreaking book with the flips and sangarees was a small category called "Cocktails and Crustas." The cocktail was a strong spirit, a sweet ingredient, and bitters. Only thirteen cocktails and crustas were listed in the book along with 223 other concoctions, so it was a relatively small category. By the end of the nineteenth century, however, the word "cocktail" had become the generic word for all mixed spirit drinks.

A similar phenomenon occurred with the word "martini." The martini cocktail, narrowly defined, is a combination of gin, vermouth, and an olive or a twist of lemon. Actually the martini cocktail has gone through substantial evolution as well, from a much sweeter version in the nineteenth century, with additional ingredients like bitters, to the vodka martini of the late twentieth century. Among a younger group of drinkers, "martini" describes any drink served with alcohol in the classic V-shaped martini glass.

Products from Europe figured prominently in early cocktail recipes, and some actually defined the classic cocktails that still reign as the superstars of the category. The two most widely known and classic of the cocktails from the nineteenth century are the martini and the Manhattan; both use vermouth, which was originally formulated in the late eighteenth century in Turin, Italy. Curaçao, from the Bols distillery, was an important sweet ingredient in the earliest cocktails even before vermouth was available in America, and some of the raw materials for both curaçao and vermouth were from the New World. The bitter oranges of Curaçao and the spices from South America and the Caribbean are ingredients that made the round trip and became the cornerstones of the cocktail culture.

Cocktails are shaken or stirred, rolled or muddled; they are dry or sweet, creamy or frozen. They are perfect or dirty; they are up or over. But one thing they are not is weak. There is an hour reverentially dedicated to them. Parties are named after them. Thousands of designers have created vessels exclusively to showcase them or shake them. They are truly American, a gift to the beverage culture of the world.

[**See also** BOURBON; BRANDY; MANHATTAN; MARTINI; RUM; STILLS; TAVERNS; VERMOUTH; WHISKEY.]

BIBLIOGRAPHY

Barr, Andrew. *Drink: A Social History of America.* New York: Carroll and Graf, 1999.

Brown, John Hull. *Early American Beverages.* Rutland, VT: Tuttle, 1966.

Farmer, J. S., and W. E. Henley. *Slang and Its Analogues.* New York: Arno Press, 1970.

DALE DEGROFF

Coconuts

Probably natives of tropical Asia or Melanesia, coconut palms (*Cocos nucifera*) flourish in tropical areas where their stately trunks (sometimes averaging one hundred feet in height) and their swaying, rustling leaves have become synonymous with beach holidays. The palm's hard, brown nut reportedly earned its name when Spanish and Portuguese explorers likened the three eyes of the coconut shell to the face of a smiling goblin, or "coco." Cited in Samuel Johnson's 1775 *Dictionary of the English Language*, the word was once spelled "cocoanut," but over time the "a" was dropped, possibly to avoid confusion with the word "cocoa."

Credit for the coconut palm's global dispersal belongs to ancient traders, explorers such as Marco Polo, and seafarers who carried along the coconut as a source of both food and beverage. But the coconuts themselves may have played a role in their migration. The durable nut readily floats and can easily travel along ocean currents to land on tropical beaches miles away from its point of origin.

Just when the coconut palm appeared on American shores is open to debate, but some accounts tell that on southern plantations coconut meat was used for making the

A cookbooklet issued by the Franklin Baker Company, 1923.

holiday dessert ambrosia. In the late 1860s, a Pennsylvania farmer traveling along the Florida coast spotted three coconut palms growing wild on the shores of what is now Miami beach and decided to relocate there to try growing and harvesting coconuts. A decade later, accounts state, Florida's Palm Beach received its name when the vessel *Providencia*, bound from Havana to Europe, washed ashore with its load of coconuts in 1878.

Although all coconut palms look generally alike, numerous cultivars do exist and are distinguished by differences in size, color, meat and liquid content, and shape of the nut. The nut is probably the most valuable aspect of the coconut palm and has multiple uses. It can provide a cooling, clear liquid to quench thirst (including the alcoholic drink toddy, derived from the sap); a firm, white flesh to enhance savory or sweet dishes; an oil for frying and conversion into such industrial products as soaps and fuel; a coarse husk for cooking fuel; and a hard outer shell for household items like kitchen utensils and hair ornaments. No wonder John F. Kennedy felt gratitude for the hard-shelled nut. Stranded in the Pacific during World War II, Kennedy scratched a plea for rescue on a coconut shell, which natives found and took to the Americans. That coconut later became part of Kennedy's White House collection.

Coconut milk, extracted from the nut's mature meat, plays a significant role in the cuisines of several countries, including India, Southeast Asia, the Caribbean, and coastal Africa. For all its seeming blandness, versatile coconut milk offers its own culinary alchemy. It smoothes out flavors in fiery dishes, adds a subtle sweetness, and can double as cream, milk, or thickener. Because of its high fat content, thick coconut cream, which is the liquid produced from the first pressing of coconut meat, can also be used as an oil for frying.

Coconut milk should not be mistaken for the slightly opaque liquid that sloshes around in a young or immature coconut's cavity. This watery fluid can be extracted by cracking open the coconut's top and then sipping the coconut water with a straw or pouring it into glasses. Coconut water quenches thirsts in hot climates, and according to at least one old wives' tale, drinking it may help prevent skin from aging.

Although rarely an ingredient in North Asian or other northern kitchens, coconut milk is a staple in most tropical countries where natives understand its properties and worth. Southeast Asian and southern Indian cooks find coconut milk almost indispensable, using it in every course from soups and curries to salads, beverages, and desserts. Its widespread use in the American kitchen may be traced to the foresight of the Philadelphian Franklin Baker, who in the late 1890s processed the meat from a bulk shipment of coconuts, giving both home and professional cooks access to dried, shredded coconut for use in confections and other dishes.

Beyond the nut itself, the entire tree yields useful resources. Its roots and fibers provide herbal remedies; its trunk furnishes timber for building; and its dried fronds, or leaves, form thatching for buildings. No wonder Sanskrit writings describe the coconut palm as *kalpa vriksha*, or the tree which gives all that is necessary for living.

[**See also** Candy and Candy Bars; Caribbean Influences on American Food; Fats and Oils; Indian American Food; Southeast Asian Food.]

BIBLIOGRAPHY

Davidson, Alan. *The Penguin Companion to Food*. New York: Oxford University Press, 2002.

Passmore, Jacki. *The Encyclopedia of Asian Food and Cooking*. New York: Hearst, 1991.

Stobart, Tom. *The Cook's Encyclopedia: Ingredients and Processes*. Edited by Millie Owen. New York: Harper and Row, 1981.

ALEXANDRA GREELEY

Coffee

Coffee is the second most valuable legally traded commodity on earth, after oil, and it has long been the beverage of choice to jumpstart Americans on the go.

On the mountainsides of Ethiopia, the native understory coffee tree grows under the rain-forest canopy. There are many species of coffee plant, but only two have proved to be commercially viable. *Coffea arabica*, the original Ethiopian species, considered superior in taste, accounts for 75 percent of world consumption. It grows best on mountainsides in mild tropical climates. *Coffea canephora*, also known as robusta, has twice the caffeine, is more disease resistant, endures hotter temperatures, and has a more bitter taste.

No one is sure when humans first used the coffee tree, which produces the alkaloid caffeine as a natural pesticide. The drug laces coffee leaves and cherries. Probably in the fifteenth century, someone roasted, ground, and steeped the pits in hot water to produce the drink we know as coffee.

By the sixteenth century, Arab coffeehouses were popular meeting places featuring gaming, erotic rendezvous, and seditious poetry. For many years, the Arabs held a monopoly on coffee. As coffee achieved popularity in Europe in the seventeenth century, however, the Dutch broke the monopoly, growing coffee in Java and Ceylon (Sri Lanka). The French, too, began to grow coffee in the Caribbean, the Spanish in Central America and Colombia, and the Portuguese in Brazil. Today coffee grows in a girdle around the earth between the Tropics of Cancer and Capricorn.

Coffee in America

American colonists preferred tea until the Boston Tea Party of 1773, after which it became a patriotic duty to switch to coffee. American coffee consumption grew in the first half of the 1800s. The Civil War increased the American desire for coffee on both sides of

Coffeepots from top: tin tea pot, tin coffee boiler, tin mess can.

the conflict—Union soldiers lived on it, while Confederates yearned for the real thing instead of roasted dandelion roots.

In 1864 Jabez Burns invented the self-emptying roaster. The brothers John and Charles Arbuckle, Pittsburgh wholesale grocers, bought a Burns machine and began to sell preroasted coffee in one-pound paper bags. Arbuckle Brothers' main coffee brand, Ariosa, was wildly successful, particularly with cowboys in the American West.

Early Coffee Brands

In the late nineteenth century, coffee became an international commodity, and speculation in coffee beans made and lost fortunes. A boom-bust cycle commenced, plaguing the coffee industry ever since. When prices are high, farmers plant more trees, which take four years to produce a good crop. Then there is too much coffee, and the price plummets. Farmers cannot just rip up coffee trees and plant corn, so they continue to harvest, but they neglect fertilizing and pruning. Over time the glut subsides, the price goes up, and the cycle starts again.

Other coffee firms arose. James Folger, who arrived in San Francisco in 1850 at the age of fourteen, roasted coffee for gold prospectors. San Francisco also provided a home for two other major roasters, Hills Brothers and MJB Coffee. In Boston, Caleb Chase and

Coffee pots from top: tin French coffee filter biggins, and heavy tin coffee biggins, with faucet.

James Sanborn founded Chase and Sanborn in 1878. Joel Cheek, a Kentucky traveling salesman who moved to Nashville, Tennessee, created a blend he called Maxwell House Coffee, named after a prestigious Nashville hotel, in 1892. All of these new coffee brands used increasingly sophisticated advertising to sell their products.

Coffee is a notoriously fragile product. Once roasted, it stales quickly if exposed to oxygen. With the mass production and retailing of preroasted, preground coffee, something was both gained and lost. The product was uniform, likely to contain real coffee, and easy to use. But it was also stale, unlike home-roasted beans.

Twentieth-Century Developments

As coffee consumption swelled around the turn of the twentieth century, health faddists such as John Harvey Kellogg and C. W. Post preached that caffeine was harmful. In response, coffee firms offered defensive ads that frequently made matters worse.

The coffee firms also had to contend with two new competitors: price-cutting chain stores such as the A&P, and door-to-door peddlers. World War I boosted American coffee consumption, as soldiers in the trenches valued the caffeine hit, even if it came via newly invented instant coffee. In the Roaring Twenties, Prohibition advanced coffee as a nonalcoholic alternative, and coffeehouses proliferated in American cities. Those brands that advertised widely did well, but Arbuckle Brothers refused to mount a national campaign and went into decline. Many family businesses gave way to corporations. Chase & Sanborn became a part of Standard Brands, while General Foods snapped up Maxwell House Coffee.

During the Depression, the automat, with its robotic fresh-brewed nickel cup, appealed to frugal consumers, and coffee, an affordable luxury, continued to sell, as radio gave coffee advertising a vital new medium, with *The Maxwell House Show Boat* and *Major Bowes Amateur Hour*, sponsored by Chase & Sanborn.

Cheapened Blends and the Rise of Specialty Coffee

World War II increased the use of instant coffee, this time with improved Nescafé from Swiss-based Nestlé, followed by American brands. After the war, instant coffee sales took off, even with poor taste from reconstituted inferior robusta beans. As coffee roasters engaged in price-cutting wars, they also cheapened their regular blends. Coffee lost the baby boomers to Coke and Pepsi.

In the 1960s, a new generation of small, grassroots batch roasters (as opposed to mass continuous roasting) started the modern "specialty coffee" movement, exemplified by Starbucks Coffee, founded in 1971 in Seattle.

Today many consumers buy high-quality arabica beans, grinding them at home for a superior cup. Others go to Starbucks or the many other specialty coffeehouses. But the majority of coffee is still sold in cans by the four largest coffee companies—Philip Morris (Maxwell House), Procter & Gamble (Folgers), Nestlé (Taster's Choice and others) and Sara Lee.

Despite increased awareness of social issues involved with coffee and much publicity for fair trade beans, which guarantee a decent price to certified coffee cooperatives, coffee continues to suffer from a boom-bust cycle in which poor coffee farmers suffer.

[**See also** ARBUCKLES'; COFFEE, DECAFFEINATED; COFFEE, INSTANT; COFFEEHOUSES; COFFEE MAKERS, ROASTERS, AND MILLS; COFFEE SUBSTITUTES; COMBAT FOOD; FOLGERS; IRISH COFFEE; MAXWELL HOUSE; MIDDLE EASTERN INFLUENCES ON AMERICAN FOOD; NESTLÉ.]

BIBLIOGRAPHY

Pendergrast, Mark. *Uncommon Grounds: The History of Coffee and How It Transformed Our World.* New York: Basic Books, 1999.

MARK PENDERGRAST

Coffee, Decaffeinated

From its earliest history, there were health concerns regarding coffee and its effects. In 1511 the Arab governor of Mecca closed the coffeehouses, partly on medical advice that, like wine, coffee contained a harmful drug. In 1679 a French doctor asserted in a pamphlet that coffee produced "general exhaustion, paralysis, and impotence" (Pendergrast, p. 9).

Caffeine was first isolated from green coffee beans in 1820 and proved to consist of three methyl groups around a xanthine molecule; among other things, it mimics the neurotransmitter adenosine, which aids sleep. When a caffeine molecule gets to a receptor first, it prevents adenosine from doing its job, thus keeping people awake longer. Caffeine affects some people more than others, and excessive coffee consumption can lead to lack of sleep and irritability, which explains the appeal of decaffeinated coffee.

Ludwig Roselius was convinced that his father, a professional coffee taster in Bremen, Germany, had died prematurely because of his excessive caffeine intake. Roselius steamed green coffee beans and then flooded them with benzol; he patented this decaffeination process in 1906, selling Kaffee Hag in Germany, Sanka ("sans caffeine") in France, and Dekafa in the United States.

In the early 1980s coffee was implicated as a possible cause of birth defects, benign breast lumps, pancreatic cancer, and heart disease.

Coffee Gelatin

Coffee gelatin is one of the original recipes at Durgin-Park, a Boston restaurant that dates back to 1827—"Established before you were born," as the slogan goes. The restaurant used to serve straightforward Yankee fare to workers at Boston's Faneuil Hall, and still serves classics like prime rib, Yankee pot roast, baked beans, and Indian pudding. Originally, coffee gelatin was considered a poor person's dessert, because it used leftover coffee. The recipe is nothing more than reheated coffee, sugar, and unflavored gelatin stirred together and refrigerated until firm. It is served in bowls with homemade whipped cream on the side. Customers, especially old-timers, also like to pour cream on top and gently stir for a café au lait effect. Eaten plain, the coffee gelatin is much less sweet than any fruit-flavored gelatin from a packaged mix, a humble ending to a traditional New England meal.

BIBLIOGRAPHY

Stern, Jane, and Michael Stern. *The Durgin-Park Cookbook: Classic Yankee Cooking in the Shadow of Faneuil Hall.* Nashville, TN: Rutledge Hill Press, 2002.

CLARA SILVERSTEIN

Sales of decaffeinated coffee rose dramatically. The standard method of decaffeination used methylene chloride, which left virtually no chemical on the roasted bean, but a new "Swiss water process" appealed to the health conscious, as did treatment with carbon dioxide. While the taste was not equal to that of regular coffee, it had improved substantially.

Health fears about caffeine gradually subsided as the early epidemiological studies failed to be replicated. Most doctors give the nod to moderate consumption of regular coffee, but for those people who react badly to caffeine or who do not wish to become addicted and suffer withdrawal headaches or who want to drink coffee just before bedtime, decaffeinated coffee provides an alternative.

[See also Coffee; Coffee, Instant; Coffee Substitutes; Middle Eastern Influences on American Food.]

BIBLIOGRAPHY

James, Jack E. *Understanding Caffeine: A Biobehavioral Analysis.* Thousand Oaks, CA: Sage Publications, 1997.

Pendergrast, Mark. *Uncommon Grounds: The History of Coffee and How It Transformed Our World.* New York: Basic Books, 1999.

Weinberg, Bennett Alan, and Bonnie K. Bealer. *The World of Caffeine: The Science and Culture of the World's Most Popular Drug.* New York: Routledge, 2001.

MARK PENDERGRAST

Coffee, Instant

There are many possible claimants for maker of the first soluble coffee. In 1771 the British granted a patent for a "coffee compound," and in the late nineteenth century a Glasgow firm invented Camp Coffee, a liquid "essence." In 1900 the Tokyo chemist Sartori Kato made a version of instant coffee, as did the St. Louis roaster Cyrus Blanke with his Faust Instant Coffee in 1906 and, independently and simultaneously, the German-Guatemalan Federico Lehnhoff Wyld. In 1910 a Belgian named George Washington refined coffee crystals from brewed coffee, calling it G. Washington's Refined Coffee, which was very popular with soldiers during World War I.

All of these early instants used the "drum method," in which brewed coffee was boiled down to crystals. In 1938 Nestlé launched Nescafé, made by spraying coffee liquid into heated towers, and this produced a better cup. Although still lacking the body, aroma, and flavor of real coffee, it helped a new generation of soldiers survive World War II. After the war, instant coffee became popular in America, prompting an increase in the growth of inferior robusta beans used for the cheap blends used for soluble coffee. Aggressive advertising—millions of tiny "flavor buds" supposedly released with Maxwell House Instant Coffee—pushed sales.

In 1964 freeze-dried coffee provided a superior instant coffee, and in subsequent years more arabica beans have been used for instant coffees of higher quality. In the early 1990s a highly successful Taster's Choice (made by Nestlé) television ad campaign featured a serial soap opera approach in which Tony wooed Sharon with the right freeze-dried brand. Nonetheless, no instant coffee can compare to a fresh-brewed cup.

[See also Coffee; Combat Food; Maxwell House.]

MARK PENDERGRAST

Coffeehouses

Beginning with the *kaveh kanes*, as fifteenth- and sixteenth-century Arab establishments were known, coffeehouses have provided a place for people to socialize over a cup of coffee and a bite to eat. The coffeehouse combined with café has a longer European pedigree, but the American Revolution was planned in Boston's Green Tavern, a coffeehouse that also served ale. In the 1950s smoky, atmospheric coffeehouses in cities such as San Francisco and New York fueled hipsters and beatniks. In the Vietnam War era, GI coffeehouses outside army bases promoted antiwar sentiments. By the end of the twentieth century the coffeehouse boom based on espresso-milk drinks had given Americans an appreciation for safe places to meet or sip nonalcoholic beverages in contemplative solitude.

[See also Coffee; Middle Eastern Influences on American Food.]

BIBLIOGRAPHY

Pendergrast, Mark. *Uncommon Grounds: The History of Coffee and How It Transformed Our World.* New York: Basic Books, 1999.

MARK PENDERGRAST

Coffee Makers, Roasters, and Mills

Harvested coffee beans are roasted to bring out the flavor. The first U.S. coffee roaster patent was granted in 1833 and the next in 1840, followed by about seventy-five more during the next thirty years, all of sheet metal or cast iron. Roasters were of two basic types: revolving drums with a side crank or stirring pans with a lid crank. All had stirring wings or fingers to agitate the berries constantly. Most roasters were used atop ranges, but one from 1866 was a cast-iron, round-bottom "kettle" with three peg legs and a crank in the lid, set over coals or hearth embers. A few were portable and came mounted on their own little stoves.

After roasting, coffee beans are ground—to a consistency from coarse to fine—to make coffee in a coffee boiler, percolator, or biggin (drip style). Early mills may have been cylindrical brass mills, like spice mills, originating in the Middle East. The first U.S. coffee mill patent was granted in 1798, eight years after the patent office's establishment—it was the twenty-sixth patent granted. It was not until 1832 that another mill was patented, and that by a company—Parker Brothers—that made coffee mills until 1932. Mills proliferated as inventors tried to make one that would not grind the beans twice.

Box or lap mills were smallish boxes, with hoppers and cranks on top. Grounds fell into a drawer below. A side mill was rather like half a hopper mounted to a board or cupboard so as always to be ready to use. Canister-top mills held beans in a closed container and were usually wall mounted. Countertop mills had heavy cast-iron frames, one or two side wheels turned by a crank, and large closed hoppers on top. The largest were for stores. All coffee mills had screw adjustments to set fineness of grounds. Electric mills appeared in the 1930s as attachments to stand mixers. Also in the 1930s grocery stores had electric mills with adjustable settings for customers to grind bags of selected roast coffee beans. Small electric mills are still the most popular, but old-style box mills are sold to customers who shun electricity.

The method of coffee making is considered as important as grinding and is as hotly contested as it was during the nineteenth and twentieth centuries. Biggins—the original drip maker that was invented about 1800 in Paris by Mr. Biggin—were made in the United States for seventy to eighty years; some were arranged to drip hot water slowly through a fine strainer holding fine grounds and, later, a cloth and then a paper filter. Percolators were common by about 1910; in these coffee makers boiling water roiled up a tube and drained down through coarse grounds. The flavor was stronger, because the coffee kept boiling. In coffee boilers—large, lighthouse-shaped kettles in which coarse grounds were boiled directly in water—the coffee was "cleared" with eggshells to take away the muddiness and poured off after settling. This type is seen around the campfire in old Western movies. Many so-called coffeepots are actually serving pieces and may be fancy tin, enameled iron, silver plate, or china.

[See also Coffee; Middle Eastern Influences on American Food.]

BIBLIOGRAPHY

Franklin, Linda Campbell. *300 Years of Kitchen Collectibles.* 5th ed. Iola, WI: Krause Publications, 2003.

Fumagalli, Ambrogio. *Coffeemakers: Macchine da Caffè, 1800–1950, American and European.* San Francisco: Chronicle Books, 1995.

Kvetko, Edward, and Douglas Congdon-Martin. *Coffee Antiques.* Atglen, PA: Schiffer, 2000.

White, Michael L., and Judith A. Sivonda. *Antique Coffee Grinders: American, English, and European.* Atglen, PA: Schiffer, 2001.

White, Michael L., and Derek S. White. *Early American Coffee Mills: Patent History and Guide for Collectors.* Yardley, PA: WhiteSpace, 1994.

LINDA CAMPBELL FRANKLIN

Coffee Substitutes

Wartime blockades, taxes, temperance movements, religions, health-food adventists, and the very great expanse and rough terrain of the country itself (leading to high

A Universal Coffee Percolator that appeared in a catalog in 1915.

barley, cornmeal, millet, and grain sorghum), figs, seeds (the Kentucky coffee tree, grape, locust, persimmon, okra, and cotton), parsnips, field peas, walnuts, crushed walnut shells, pumpkin shells, corn, corn cobs, and soybeans.

Advertisers began to brand coffee in the late 1860s, but by the end of the nineteenth century, coffee's commoditization had left it open to unscrupulous adulteration. Prodded by popular concern about just what it was that they were drinking, as well as by critical attitudes (many saw coffee as an "evil drug"), some people believed that the time was ripe for introducing a "pure food" commercial substitute. But these businessmen advertised against the odds: memories of "war coffee" remained strong.

One successful businessman, Charles William (C. W.) Post, prevailed. During a brief stay at Dr. John Harvey Kellogg's sanitarium in Battle Creek, Michigan, in 1891, Post was served Caramel Cereal Coffee (which the doctor himself described as "a very poor substitute for a very poor thing," made from bran, molasses, and burned bread crusts). In 1895 C. W. introduced his own coffee substitute, Postum Cereal Food Coffee ("Postum"). By 1900 a half-dozen rival "healthy" coffee substitutes included Grain-o and Graino, but C. W. Post out-advertised them all, to build Postum into an enduring brand.

[**See also** COFFEE; COFFEE, DECAFFEINATED; POST FOODS.]

ROBIN M. MOWER

Colanders, *see Sieves, Sifters, and Colanders*

Colas, *see Soda Drinks*

Cola Wars

The so-called cola wars began shortly after Coca-Cola was invented in 1886 by Dr. John S. Pemberton, an Atlanta pharmacist, although two popular regional drinks—Moxie in Massachusetts and Dr Pepper in Texas—actually preceded Coke by a year. In the 1894 corporate report for the Coca-Cola Company, Asa Candler, who made a success of the beverage after Pemberton died, complained of various "bogus substitutes" (Pendergrast, p. 62). The imitators were led by J. C. Mayfield, a former Pemberton partner, who sold Yum Yum and Koke, and his former wife, Diva Brown, who sold My-Coca. Each claimed to have the original Coca-Cola formula.

By the turn of the century eighty cola drinks were trying to ride on Coca-Cola's successful coattails, including Afri-Kola, Chero-Cola, Dope (a nickname for Coca-Cola, because of its former cocaine content), Kaw-Kola ("Has the Kick"), Pepsi-Cola, Vani-Kola, and Wise-Ola. Encouraged by the passage of the Trademark Law of 1905, Coca-Cola's lawyer Harold Hirsch began to sue imitators, in the process practically creating modern American trademark law while filing an average of one case per week. He won most of his cases, based on a competitor's similar label, script, or name. To help differentiate the Coca-Cola

transportation costs) have all challenged Americans' taste for coffee. Chicory ("coffee-weed") roots, roasted and ground, had long been used to extend or adulterate coffee in Europe as well as in America. But ingenuity stepped up to adversity. Americans found substitutes—some better than others—in barley, sweet potatoes, acorns, beets, grains (rye, bottle from all others, in 1916 the company adopted a trademark "hobble skirt" bottle, with a slim waste and bulging top and bottom.

Of all the imitators, the most tenacious was Pepsi-Cola, invented in 1894 in New Bern, North Carolina, by the pharmacist Caleb Bradham. By World War I the drink had achieved modest success, with franchised bottlers in half the states. Caught in the wildly swinging sugar market of 1920, however, Bradham went bankrupt. The firm was purchased by a Wall Street speculator named Roy Megargel, who failed to make it thrive. Twice Coke refused to purchase the troubled Pepsi remains. In 1931 Charles Guth, who owned a chain of candy stores with soda fountains, became infuriated that Coca-Cola would not sell him its syrup at discount. He bought most of the ownership of Pepsi and began selling it in his stores. In 1934 he began to sell Pepsi in recycled twelve-ounce beer bottles for a nickel, the same price Coke charged for a 6.5-ounce drink. Sales boomed, particularly among poor people.

Guth lost the company over a lawsuit, and the canny businessman Walter Mack took over in 1939. Mack approved a lilting bit of doggerel that became the first smash-hit radio jingle. "Pepsi-Cola hits the spot / Twelve full ounces, that's a lot / Twice as much for a nickel, too / Pepsi-Cola is the drink for you."

John Sibley, the frustrated Coca-Cola lawyer who took over from Hirsch, sued in the United States and elsewhere. Pepsi countersued. Finally, in 1941 Coca-Cola's president, Robert Woodruff, cut a deal with Walter Mack, recognizing Pepsi's trademark in the United States. Sibley felt betrayed and quit as Coca-Cola counsel soon afterward.

During World War II, Coca-Cola aced Pepsi by securing an exemption from sugar rationing for all Coke served to the military. Coca-Cola men were designated "technical observers," whose work behind the lines setting up bottling plants was deemed vital to the war effort. Although Walter Mack complained bitterly, Pepsi did not receive the same treatment. In response, Mack set up three huge Pepsi-Cola Servicemen's Centers in Washington, San Francisco, and New York, where soldiers could find a free Pepsi and other services.

In 1949 the former Coca-Cola executive Al Steele joined Pepsi and, under his leadership in the 1950s, Pepsi began to shed its lower-class image, with perky Polly Bergen singing "Pepsi-Cola's up to date" on television spots. Steele also reformulated the oversweetened drink to make it taste more like Coke. As Pepsi gained ground, Coca-Cola's boss Robert Woodruff refused to match Pepsi ounce for ounce at the same price, and no one inside Coke headquarters in Atlanta ever spoke the "P" word, referring to Pepsi only as the "Imitator" or the "Competition." Finally, in 1955, Woodruff allowed King Size Coke to match Pepsi.

The wars between Coca-Cola and Pepsi produced some of the most entertaining television advertisements of the modern era.

Pepsi came up with "Come Alive, You're in the Pepsi Generation," attempting to claim the baby boomers. Coke responded with "Things Go Better with Coca-Cola" and then, in a simultaneous appeal to tradition and hippies, "It's the Real Thing." In 1971 Coca-Cola's Hilltop commercial, filmed on an Italian hill, featured young people from around the world singing about buying the world a Coke and living in perfect harmony.

In 1975 in Dallas, Pepsi held a miserable 4 percent of the soft-drink market, behind native Dr Pepper and Coke. In desperation, Pepsi launched "the Pepsi Challenge," showing candid shots of die-hard Coke consumers astonished to discover that they preferred Pepsi in blind taste tests. The ads outraged Coca-Cola and, when secret blind taste tests inside company headquarters revealed that a slim majority *did* prefer Pepsi, Coke chemists began to work on a revised formula.

Meanwhile, the pattern for Coca-Cola and Pepsi ads was set. "Coke Is It," which made its debut in 1981, featured Coca-Cola itself as the star of the ads, fueling all-American good times at pep rallies and other wholesome events. Pepsi relied more on celebrity endorsements, lifestyle ads, and edgy humor, hiring the pop singers Michael Jackson and Madonna to push the drink.

No matter what ads Coke ran, the market share of Coca-Cola continued a slow decline. In 1985 Coke's chief executive officer, Roberto Goizueta, approved a new formula that beat Pepsi in taste tests. Pepsi's president, Roger Enrico, declared victory, saying, "The other guy just blinked," and proclaiming a companywide holiday (Pendergrast, p. 351). New Coke was a media and business disaster, as many consumers refused even to taste it, horrified that the symbol of America was being changed. When Coke brought back Coca-Cola Classic three months later, however, it *gained* market share on Pepsi.

Since the New Coke debacle, Coca-Cola has struggled to come up with an effective advertising campaign, while Pepsi continues to hammer at youthful, hip-hop, in-your-face themes. Nonetheless, Coca-Cola is still number one, and Pepsi is the perennial we-try-harder number two, particularly in the international market. Other drinks, such as Royal Crown Cola, may beat both of them in taste tests, and nouveau Virgin Cola may try to grab market share, but Coke and Pepsi remain the two top of-mind drinks in the cola wars.

[**See also** ADVERTISING; COCA-COLA; DR PEPPER; PEPSI-COLA.]

BIBLIOGRAPHY

Allen, Frederick. *Secret Formula: How Brilliant Marketing and Relentless Salesmanship Made Coca-Cola the Best-Known Product in the World.* New York: HarperBusiness, 1994.

Enrico, Roger, with Jesse Kornbluth. *The Other Guy Blinked: How Pepsi Won the Cola Wars.* New York: Bantam, 1986.

Pendergrast, Mark. *For God, Country and Coca-Cola: The Definitive History of the Great American Soft Drink and the Company That Makes It.* 2nd ed. New York: Basic Books, 2000.

MARK PENDERGRAST

Collins

A Collins is a drink made with strong spirits, carbonated water, sugar, lemon juice, and ice. There are two different Collins drinks that appear in the classic recipe books: the Tom Collins and the John Collins. The John Collins was traditionally made with Holland gin, and the Tom Collins was made with Old Tom sweetened gin.

John Collins was a headwaiter at Limmer's Hotel and Coffee House on Conduit Street in London and is credited with the invention of the Collins. Limmer's Hotel is mentioned in *Reminiscences of Captain Gronow . . . Being Anecdotes of the Camp, the Court, and the Clubs, at the Close of the Last War with France,* written in 1814, and was clearly open for most of the nineteenth century, but it is unclear when John Collins worked at Limmer's. An early mention of the drink in print, possibly the first, was in the *Australasian Newspaper* from Victoria, Australia, on February 24, 1865. This was in reference to "that most angelic of drinks for a hot climate—a John Collins (a mixture of soda water, gin, sugar, lemon, and ice)."

The John Collins is commonly prepared with American whiskey. Since Old Tom gin has not been produced since the 1960s, the Tom Collins is now made with London dry gin. The category of Collins drinks has grown to include the Michael Collins with Irish whiskey, the Pedro Collins with rum, and the Pierre Collins with cognac or brandy. One guess is that the Collins, which requires carbonated water, would have gained popularity around the mid-nineteenth century, when machinery for producing carbonated water dispensed from a soda fountain became affordable to the average merchant.

In *Modern American Drinks,* George J. Kappeler has an unusual take on the preparation of a Collins. He muddles the lemon wedges and sugar together. Generally, the preparation of a Collins is fairly simple: sugar and lemon juices are dissolved together, and a shot of gin is added. The drink is served over ice in a tall chimney or Collins glass and topped with soda water. The Collins differs from a gin fizz in that it calls for a fruit garnish and is served in a taller chimney glass.
[**See also** COCKTAILS; GIN.]

BIBLIOGRAPHY

Farmer, J. S., and W. E. Henley. *Slang and Its Analogues.* New York: Arno Press, 1970.

Kappeler, George. *Modern American Drinks: How to Mix and Serve All Kinds of Cups and Drinks.* Akron, OH: Saalfield, 1895.

Mew, James, and John Ashton. *Drinks of the World.* New York: Scribner and Welford, 1892.

SaskyCom. http://www.sasky.com.

DALE DEGROFF

Combat Food

At the beginning of the Revolutionary War, individual colonies fed their own militias, but as the army increased in size, it soon became apparent that it would have to develop a better system to feed itself. The first legislation fixing components of the military ration was a resolution, passed by the Continental Congress on November 4, 1775, calling for one pound of beef, three quarters of a pound of pork, or one pound of salt fish per day, along with three pints of peas or beans per week or the equivalent portion of vegetables. The ration also called for milk, rice, or Indian meal, and either spruce beer, cider, or molasses plus soap and candles. Though not bad on paper, in reality the ration commonly fell far short of what it was supposed to be. Items like vegetables and milk disappeared often. Moreover, the food came uncooked so the soldiers had to prepare it themselves. The many stories of deprivation, starvation, and remarkable determination were a major legacy of the Revolutionary War. Congress revised the ration in 1790 by taking out vegetables and other perishables and replacing them with two ounces (raised to four ounces in 1798) of rum, brandy, or whiskey. One critic wrote, "fatal experience has taught…that a greater proportion of men have perished with sickness in our armies that have fallen by the sword." Yet this kind of thinking set the tone for the next hundred years.

Civil War and Spanish-American War

During the Civil War, the Union Army ration was still basically a meat-and-bread diet. Hardtack, a baked mixture of flour and water, was often soaked in cold water overnight then fried in grease for breakfast. Beans or rice were the primary vegetable component. In addition to coffee (or tea) and sugar, the ration included salt and vinegar. Troops also occasionally received condensed milk, reaping the benefit of Gail Borden's condensing process. Confederate troops suffered from a constant and critical lack of provisions, a situation caused primarily by a sparse, one-crop economy and a federal blockade, and which many believe contributed to their defeat. In 1898, when the Spanish-American War began, the situation quickly turned nightmarish. Many men became ill from eating bad beef. Vegetables,

The dinner (lunch) unit included biscuits, a cheese product, a confection, lemon juice powder, sugar, chewing gum, and cigarettes. Soldiers were also served a breakfast unit and a supper unit.

Military Slang

army strawberries—prunes
battery acid—coffee
bokoo soused—very drunk
bug juice—Kool-Aid and other powder-based fruit drinks
bullets—beans
buzzard—chicken or turkey
cackleberry—egg
canned cow—canned condensed milk
canteen—a liquor store on a military base
chow—food, a meal
chow down—to eat
chowhound—first in line at the mess
"come and get it"—the time-honored call of the mess sergeant
desecrated vegetables—dried or dessicated vegetables
fly light—to miss a meal
gut-packings—food, rations
hardtack—a baked mix of flour and water, soaked in cold water overnight and fried in grease for breakfast
hooch—hard liquor. According to the early-twentieth-century author and critic H. L. Mencken, it comes from an Eskimo home-brew called hoochino.
java—coffee
joe—coffee
kitchen police, K.P.—those assigned to menial clean-up duties
lurp—Long Range Patrol Ration, consisted of precooked freeze dried entrees, could be cold, dry, or warm
meal refusing to exit, meal rejected by Ethiopia—meal ready to eat (M.R.E.)
moo juice—milk
mud—coffee
mystery meat—meat that lacks clear identity
rabbit food—greens, especially lettuce
repeaters—beans, sausages, refers to the gas they produce
shrapnel—Grape Nuts
tube steak—hot dog

BIBLIOGRAPHY

Dickson, Paul. *Chow: A Cook's Tour of Military Food.* New York: New American Library, 1978.

Dickson, Paul. *War Slang: American Fighting Words and Phrases from the Civil War to the Gulf War.* New York: Pocket Books, 1994.

SANDRA YIN

whether fresh or canned, spoiled before making it to the troops, and many units were forced to live on a diet of coffee, hardtack, and fatty bacon for weeks at a time. In the period after the war, the federal government saw the need for vast improvement. In 1905, the first school for cooking and baking was established at Fort Riley, Kansas, acknowledging the need for a professional approach to food preparation.

World War I and World War II

By World War I, there was a noticeable improvement in the quality and variety of the ration. Doughboys received standard ration items like beef and beans, but also a wide assortment of canned goods, among them soups, condensed milk, butter, cheese, sweet potatoes, spices, candy, and cigarettes. By the end of the war, the American army was being called the best fed on earth. Some of the reasons for this improvement were the ability to better handle and process perishable food in the field, successful and widespread use of dehydrated vegetables, and the creation in France of an official garden service to supply the men with fresh provisions. While there was nothing lavish about the food, it was as if the nation was finally willing to allow its army to eat fairly well and fight on a full stomach. World War II marked major departures in the feeding of troops. In addition to an even wider variety and higher quality in general, special food packs became available for specific situations. The C ration, with a caloric value of 3,700, was intended for operational needs of three to twenty-one days under combat conditions. Billed as the "balanced meal in a can," Cs were bulky and came in packs of six twelve-ounce cans; three were meat concoctions and three contained bread. Sugar, instant coffee, and candy were also included. The D ration was intended exclusively for survival. A "quick energy" emergency pack to be used for very short periods of time, when nothing else was available, it consisted of three four-ounce, nearly unpalatable chocolate candy bars artificially flavored and fortified with sucrose, skim milk, cacao fat, and raw oatmeal flour. The K ration, beyond doubt the most famous and well remembered of the World War II emergency rations, was developed under the leadership of Dr. Ancel Keys (hence the "K") of the University of Minnesota. It was initially designed as a lightweight, nutritional blitz ration for paratroopers, tank soldiers, and others who needed something more substantial than a D or less bulky than a C ration.

The Korean War

By 1950 continued advances meant that forward combat troops usually got two hot meals a day. Rolls and pastries were baked close to the front, and dehydrated mashed potatoes were so well prepared the troops actually preferred them to fresh.

Fresh Food and Lightweight Rations

During the initial period of American involvement in the Vietnam War, the provisioning of American troops was on a par with that of the Korean War, but as the war intensified and U.S. buildup continued, the ability to feed the men became so sophisticated that it almost seemed incongruous for wartime conditions. Soldiers at fire-support bases could begin their day with fresh cooked eggs to order and end it with a double-dip ice cream cone. If, however, weather, hostile action, or terrain made it impossible to get hot, freshly prepared meals to units in the field, there were still combat rations. Most important were the MCI (for Meal, Combat, Individual), which was a more nutritionally balanced descendant of the C ration, and the new Long Range Patrol ration (dubbed "Lurp"), a remarkably lightweight, compact ration that could be flexibly packaged because it had no cans. The key components were eight precooked, freeze-dried entrees (such as chicken stew or beef hash) that could be turned into hot meals with the addition of hot water. The Lurp also came with a sweet, cereal, coffee, cream, sugar, toilet paper, matches, and a plastic spoon. The staple ration of the Gulf War was the Meal, Ready-to-Eat (MRE), which in the early 1980s replaced the MCI and the Lurp as the standard individual military operational ration. The book-sized MRE is a lightweight, self-contained, flexibly packaged meal for U.S. soldiers and marines in the field. It is used by the services to sustain individuals during operations that preclude organized food-service facilities.

[**See also** CANDY AND CANDY BARS; COFFEE, INSTANT; HARDTACK.]

BIBLIOGRAPHY
Dickson, Paul. *Chow: A Cook's Tour of Military Food.* New York: New American Library, 1978.

PAUL DICKSON

Communal Gatherings and Integration

America has always been a country of banquets. From the Pilgrims' 1621 feast with the Native Americans to latter-day spaghetti nights at local fire stations, social gatherings centered around a meal have been and remain an essential component of American life.

The earliest communal gatherings grew from the country's settlement period when, in exchange for much-needed help in building homes and completing farm tasks, even the poorest households were expected to offer a well-dressed table. These practical gatherings fostered an important sense of community among groups of settlers, encouraged integration, and, later in U.S. history, promoted a spirit of national unity. Outsiders were incorporated into the fold, news was shared, problems were solved, and laws and communal standards were formed and devised.

All kinds of events provided an excuse to meet around the table: market and court days were high points of early town life, for both news gathering and socializing, and often incorporated bake sales and cakewalks to benefit some local need; the long trip back home after the end of church services made hearty breakfasts nearly essential. Colonial diaries are filled with reports of arduous work being rewarded with such high-flinging socials as barn raising, corn husking, apple drying, and apple butter parties. Southern traditions such as cemetery and church cleanings always brought people out for a noon meal. Quilting bees were held indoors and mainly among women. Hog killing was a particularly inclusive affair: men did the butchering; women cleaned the entrails and rendered lard; children helped scrape the hair off the hides and prepare the feet and ears. Afterward, everyone sat down to a feast.

Communal dinners also hold a long-honored and important civic role. From the first democratic election, American politicians understood their best chance to capture an audience was to give them a meal. Perhaps the most famous of these political feasts was the barbecue thrown by the newly elected governor of Oklahoma, Jack Callaway Walton, on January 8, 1923. Proclaimed as the largest barbecue of its day, Walton's party lasted three days and the more than 250,000 guests consumed a railcar-full each of Alaskan reindeer, cattle, chickens, rabbits, and buffalo.

Many American gatherings developed a regional flavor. Indeed, individual traditional gatherings, even within a state, may vary widely in character, with almost ironclad rules that have been passed down and govern everything from the food preparation to presentation. Two of the most common examples of these variations may be seen in the recipes for clam chowder and Brunswick stew. For traditional chowder, cooks along the northern Atlantic coast add cream to the broth, in the mid-Atlantic stir in tomatoes, and below the Mason-Dixon Line scorn both. In Georgia, Brunswick stew includes pork or beef as the base, while in Virginia squirrel, rabbit, or chicken are the only proper meats at any self-respecting Brunswick party.

PAT WILLARD

Community Cookbooks

Community cookbooks (CCBs)—also known as charity, regional, and fund-raising cookbooks—evolved during the American Civil War, in conjunction with fund-raising "Sanitary Fairs." Cookbooks to benefit northern and southern veterans, widows, and orphans of war followed, and the form was adopted by religious and philanthropic groups. Most nineteenth-century CCBs were created and printed locally, although women's groups adapted each others' designs. Commercial companies that assisted women in compiling,

Enjoying barbecued elk at a community picnic by the lake, 1915.

publishing, distributing, and often, sadly, standardizing their cookbooks came on the scene in the 1930s.

CCBs have always been valued for revealing what people "really eat"; as keepsakes linking individuals to their ancestors, institutions, and communities; and as souvenirs of visits to particular regions. The Tabasco Company (Avery Island, Louisiana) celebrates CCBs via its annual Community Cookbook Awards and Walter S. McIlhenny Hall of Fame Awards for CCBs selling over 100,000 copies.

Margaret Cook authored the first bibliography of CCBs and delved into their origin (1971). Subsequently, culinary historians and academics have focused on more than the recipes in these cookbooks: women's values that prompted involvement in charitable/reformist causes; desires to assimilate into or differentiate themselves from mainstream society; class affiliations and aspirations; interests in maintaining community; and abilities to use this genre to tell history, demonstrate creativity, and promote female agency (see Bower, Kirschenblatt-Gimblett, and Theophano).

Older CCBs usually contain prefatory matter attesting to the "tried and true" nature of dishes included, along with caveats concerning a book's modest goals or its authors' lack of professional culinary training. Yet women compilers frequently assert the importance of their homemaker role. The 1876 *Centennial Buckeye Cook Book* (First Congregational Church, Marysville, Ohio) is dedicated to "the plucky housewives of 1876, who master their work instead of allowing it to master them." Here we see the adoption of the domestic science movement and the notion that home management is just as important as the public work of men.

Some early CCBs—such as *The Ladies' Handbook* (Old South Church, Windsor, Vermont, 1880s), which contains rules for "Religious and Table Etiquette" and medicinal, household cleaning, and other guides as well as food recipes were organized loosely, without any real table of contents. Others were more organized, like the *Buckeye Cook Book*, with a full table of contents in its first edition and, in later editions, a detailed index. Special sections for menus and for "foreign foods" were also components of some books.

Advertisements included in most early CCBs establish that women had a central economic role as consumers. Soliciting such ads, moving cookbooks through publication, and marketing them provided an introduction to the life of business and publicity. Some bolder women used CCBs to trumpet their rights and values. For example, *The Woman Suffrage Cook Book* (Boston, 1886) includes recipes by Lucy Stone and other leading suffragists, words of advice from Julia Ward Howe, and a section on "Eminent Opinions on Woman Suffrage," containing quotations from Plato, Louisa M. Alcott, Emerson, and others.

As more women entered public life, CCBs changed, revealing negotiations with conflicting roles and new technologies. A book like *Who Says We Can't Cook!*, from the National Women's Press Club (1955), stresses the women's professional roles as journalists, but assures readers that the women are excellent hostesses. A number of recipes use canned foods or such items as "1 roll prepared snappy cheese" (p. 38), and titles of recipes often indicate speed or efficiency, as with "Angel in a Hurry" and "Favorite Quick and Easies."

Other CCBs put more stress on traditional values, even as they incorporated canned soup and Jell-O into some recipes. *Virginia Cookery— Past and Present* (Women's Auxiliary, Olivet Episcopal Church, 1957), emphasizes continuity with past traditions through its emphasis on historical characters and events, inclusion of a manuscript cookbook from the Lee and Washington families, and excerpts from "Old Virginia" cookbooks. Elaborate Junior League cookbooks like *Stop and Smell the Rosemary* (1996) combine sophisticated format and photographs, cosmopolitan and traditional recipes, and introductory material highlighting the role of gracious entertaining.

Fund-raising cookbooks also demonstrate their authors' attitudes toward assimilation into mainstream society or their need to sustain a particular heritage. Jewish CCBs began in the nineteenth century, but one of the most famous, *The Way to a ... Man's Heart* (1903), later published as *The Settlement Cook Book*, has had enduring popularity. The book contains much typical German-Jewish fare but includes recipes using shrimp, bacon, and other items Orthodox Jews would not eat; it is assimilationist in tone. In contrast, the 1937 *At Home on the Range* (Westchester Ladies' Auxiliary in support of the United Home for Aged Hebrews, New Rochelle, N.Y.)—like many later Jewish cookbooks—contains a more Orthodox selection of foods and a section on foods and rituals for religious holidays like Rosh Hashanah and Succoth. This book is less assimilationist, working overtly to maintain Jewish identity.

After World War II, more CCBs concentrated on ethnic pride and food specialities. The 1953 *Woman's Glory: The Kitchen* (Slovenian Women's Union of America, Chicago) aimed to "serve as an instructor to the Slovenian women of today who wish to include in their homemaking dishes for which their mothers have always been famous" (preface). Cookbooks like *Espanola Valley Cookbook: Recipes from Three Cultures, Spanish, Anglo, Indian* (women of the Espanola Hospital Auxiliary, 1974), have become common. In such CCBs women authors become cultural historians; a book's foreword and chapter introductions educate readers about a group's cultural traditions. African American women, similarly, have created CCBs that feature aspects of their historical background; an early example is the 1958 National Council of Negro Women's *Historical Cookbook of the American Negro* (followed in the 1990s by four more recipe collections based on African American and African traditions).

More recently, children have created CCBs as have some men's groups. The 1987 *Out of Our Kitchen Closets: San Francisco Gay Jewish Cooking* demonstrates the adaptability of the CCB form for community building and outreach. While CCBs are still reliable as fundraisers and repositories of beloved dishes, they have also become valued as part of our material culture, telling us much about the people who put them together.

BIBLIOGRAPHY

Bower, Anne L. "Bound Together: Recipes, Lives, Stories, and Reading," and "Cooking Up Stories: Narrative Elements in Community Cookbooks." In *Recipes for Reading: Community Cookbooks, Stories, Histories*, edited by Anne L. Bower, pp. 1–14; 29–50. Amherst, MA, 1997.

Cook, Margaret. *America's Charitable Cooks: A Bibliography of Fund-Raising Cook Books Published in the United States (1861–1915)*. Kent, OH, 1971.

Kirshenblatt-Gimblett, Barbara. "Recipes for Creating Community: The Jewish Charity Cookbook in America." *Jewish Folklore and Ethnology* 9 (1987): 8–20.

Theophano, Janet. *Eat My Words: Reading Women's Lives through the Cookbooks They Wrote*. New York: Palgrave, 2002.

ANNE L. BOWER

Community-Supported Agriculture

Community-supported agriculture (CSA) connects farmers with local consumers in a mutually beneficial agreement that creates a sense of community. To start a CSA collective, a group of buyers in an urban setting forms an association with a local farm, usually organic, and agrees to buy shares of the farm's crop for the growing season. The buyers pay in advance for their shares (or futures) to cover the farmer's costs; then during the harvest season the farmer delivers whatever was cut that week to a designated pickup point in the city.

The benefits of CSA for the farmer are that the buyers pay in advance and agree to accept a portion of the risks and benefits of the growing season. For example, if there is a failure in the pumpkin crop, the buyers get fewer (or no) pumpkins. If there is a bumper crop of tomatoes, they get extra tomatoes. Having sold the entire crop before the farming season, the farmer is free to concentrate on the work of farming and land stewardship. The benefits of CSA for the buyers are that each week through the summer and fall they receive a selection of the freshest and ripest produce at costs significantly below the market price. They also get the benefit of connecting directly with the land on which their food is grown. Many CSA farmers include a letter with the week's supply of vegetables explaining the harvest and how the weather has affected the crop. Some organize outings on which sharers visit the farm or volunteer a day's work harvesting.

Teikei (partnership) ventures originated in 1965 in the Kanagawa prefecture in Japan, when a group of two hundred homemakers organized to ask a local family farm about providing milk at reduced prices if they pledged to pay in advance. This cooperative grew into the Seikatsu Club, which by the late twentieth century connected more than 20 million Japanese consumers with local producers. In 1985 Robyn Van En, the owner of the Indian Line Farm in western Massachusetts, organized the first such collective in the United States and named the venture "community-supported agriculture." As of 2002 more than one thousand independent organic farms in the United States were supported by CSA collectives. Organizations such as Just Food in New York City and the Hartford Food Collective in Connecticut connected farms with buyers, as well as arranging for sliding-scale systems of payment, food stamps, and the distribution of uncollected produce to local food banks.

[**See also** COOPERATIVES.]

BIBLIOGRAPHY

Nabhan, Gary Paul. *Coming Home to Eat: The Pleasures and Politics of Local Foods.* New York and London: Norton, 2001.

Van En, Robyn. "Eating for Your Community." In *In Context: A Quarterly of Humane and Sustainable Culture* 42 (Fall 1995): 29–32.

EVE JOCHNOWITZ

ConAgra

144

ConAgra

Healthy Choice, Banquet, Armour, Blue Bonnet, Parkay, La Choy, Butterball, Slim Jim, Chef Boyardee, and Orville Redenbacher are brand names for some of America's most recognized food products. But few Americans outside the food industry know that they are all produced by ConAgra Foods, the second-largest food processing company in terms of retail sales.

This food-processing giant started out in 1919, when Alva Kinney bought four grain milling companies in central Nebraska. He operated them successfully as Nebraska Consolidated Mills (NCM) until he retired in 1936. His successor, R. S. Dickinson, followed the example of other midwestern millers, such as General Mills and Pillsbury, and expanded into prepared foods, made profitable by the postwar boom. Company research led to the successful development of a cake mix. In 1953 NCM entered into an agreement with Hines-Park Foods to market the cake mix under the Duncan Hines label.

In 1971 the company changed its name to ConAgra, meaning in partnership with the land, to better reflect the new direction of the company. In 1980 ConAgra acquired Banquet Foods Company to expand the market for chicken produced in its Georgia-based Dalton Poultry Company, which ConAgra had purchased in 1963.

During the 1980s the company aggressively moved into the frozen seafood and red meat markets by acquiring the Taste O' Sea brand and by purchasing the Armour Food Company. ConAgra expanded under the leadership of its next president, Michael Harper, but the job took its toll on him. Harper suffered a heart attack in 1985. During his recovery his wife prepared him a bowl of low-fat but spicy chili made from turkey. It came to him in a flash that healthy food can also taste good. After four years of development, the line of Healthy Choice products was announced—one of the most successful food brands introduced by an American food company since the 1960s.

During the 1990s ConAgra bought a slew of companies, including Beatrice in 1990 as well as the Slim Jim brand of meat snacks, Fleischmann's margarine, and Egg Beaters egg substitute, all in 1998. In 2000 ConAgra added Chef Boyardee pasta products, PAM cooking spray, Gulden's mustard, Bumble Bee seafood, and Jiffy Pop popcorn to its long list of brand name products.

Average American consumers may not recognize the name ConAgra, but they have one or more of the company's products in their kitchen.

[**See also** BEATRICE.]

BIBLIOGRAPHY

International Directory of Company Histories. 55 vols. Detroit: St. James, 2003.

Encyclopedia of Consumer Brands. 3 vols. Edited by Janice Jorgensen. Detroit: St. James, 1994.

JOSEPH M. CARLIN

Concentrated Orange Juice

Oranges must ripen on the tree, between December and June, before they can be picked. In Florida, 98 percent of all oranges are harvested by hand after testing determines that the ratio of Brix (soluble sugar content) to acidity is just right. The ripe oranges are transported to a processing plant, washed, and graded, and the juice is extracted. Next the peel, pulp, and seeds are removed. The juice can be pasteurized for "not from concentrate" products or it can go into vacuum evaporators, where most of the water is removed. The concentrated orange juice is then chilled and frozen. It is packaged into cans for sale in supermarkets or shipped by tanker truck to dairies, to be reconstituted with fresh water and packaged into cardboard cartons, glass bottles, or plastic jugs.

John M. Fox, the founder and president of the Minute Maid Company, is credited with developing frozen orange juice concentrate in the 1940s. He used a technique he had seen demonstrated during World War II to dehydrate penicillin and blood plasma. Fox intended to make a soluble orange juice powder but it had a bad taste. However, by adding water to the reduced concentrate, the juice had a fresh-squeezed taste. An advertising agency in Boston, the city famous for its minutemen, created the name "Minute Maid," to emphasize the product's convenience and ease of preparation. The company was sold to Coca-Cola in 1960.

BIBLIOGRAPHY

Encyclopedia of Consumer Brands. Edited by Jonice Jorgenson. Vol. 1: *Consumable Products.* Detroit: St. James, 1994.

JOSEPH M. CARLIN

Condiments

The term "condiment" originally meant pickled or preserved foods. By the beginning of the twenty-first century it was broadly applied to a variety of substances that enhance, intensify, or alter the flavor of other foods. Condiments can enhance delectable foods and make bland or unsatisfying foods palatable. Condiments have been used by Americans since colonial times, but they have changed over the centuries. The earliest condiments were salt, pepper, seeds, and herbs. In colonial times only the middle and upper classes could afford many condiments, and the ones that were used were simple: salt, pepper, butter, jams, jellies, mustard, sugar, and molasses.

During the nineteenth century the use of table condiments such as ketchup and mayonnaise became common, as did opposition to the use of condiments. The food reformer Sylvester Graham in his *Lectures on the Science of Human Life* (1839) banned condiments, including mustard, ketchup, pepper, cinnamon, and salt, because they were "all highly exciting and exhausting." In 1835 William Alcott launched a campaign against condiments, which he defined as substances used "to season or give relish to dishes which would be otherwise less agreeable to the taste." In addition to banning the condiments cited by Graham, Alcott also opposed spices (ginger, fennel, cardamom, mace, nutmeg, and coriander) and flavorings (molasses, garlic, cucumbers, pickles, gravies, sauces, lettuce, and horseradish). Alcott considered them to be disgusting and indecent "powdered drugs." Dio Lewis, a Harvard-trained physician, campaigned around the country against the use of condiments. In his *Chastity; or, Our Secret Sins* (1874), he proclaimed, "Everything which inflames one appetite is likely to arouse the other also. Pepper, mustard, ketchup and Worchestishire [sic] sauce—shun them all. And even salt, in any but the smallest quantity, is objectionable; it is such a goad toward carnalism."

Graham, Alcott, and Lewis lost their campaign, and the use of condiments grew dramatically in the twentieth century as their cost to consumers decreased. Condiments became classified in several nonexclusive categories: salt and spices, such as pepper and cinnamon; bread spreads, such as butter, jellies, jams, and honey; table sauces, such as ketchup, mayonnaise, and mustard; vegetables, such as pickles, onions, and horseradish; beverage sweeteners and flavorings, such as sugar and cream; salad dressings, such as vinegar and oil; dips, such as french onion dip; and ethnic condiments, such as soy sauce, Japanese horseradish or wasabi (*Eutrema wasabi*), and chutney.

Salt and Spices

Historically, the two most common condiments in America have been salt and pepper. Salt was the early colonists' most important condiment, and was used as a preservative and a seasoning on a wide range of foods. In early colonial times domestic production did not meet demand, and salt was imported from England, France, Spain, and the West Indies. In the early eighteenth century, salt deposits were located in the British North American colonies. During the American Civil War, northern armies controlled the major salt deposits and the South was cut off from them, causing severe problems in the preservation of food and the making of gunpowder.

Black pepper (*Piper nigrum*), a product of Asia, was expensive in colonial America. It was imported as early as 1629 and was commonly used by the middle and upper classes. Pepper was not available to the masses until improved production techniques and less expensive transportation made it an affordable condiment in the late nineteenth century.

Red pepper (*Capsicum*), a product of the Americas, was commonly employed in dried form in making ketchup, sauces, and pickles beginning in the nineteenth century. It was less expensive than black pepper until the twentieth century and it was more pungent. Condiments made from chilies, such as Tabasco sauce and crushed red pepper flakes, had become popular table condiments by the beginning of the twenty-first century.

Other spices, such as nutmeg, mace, cloves, ginger, and cinnamon, were imported into America and integrated into American cookery. Curry powder, a diverse combination of spices, also was used in American recipes by the nineteenth century. These spices mainly were used in cooking and not as table condiments; the exceptions were cinnamon, which was shaken on toast, and nutmeg, which was sprinkled on eggnog and other beverages.

Bread Spreads

Butter, jellies, jams, preserves, conserves, fruit butters, and honey were used by Europeans on their bread, toast, and pastries well before they migrated to the Americas; these condiments were used regularly in America from colonial times. In North America, the Europeans found a new sweetener—maple sap—which was converted into syrup by boiling. By 1664 maple syrup was being used on flapjacks, pancakes, waffles, and other foods.

Table Sauces

By the early 2000s the major table condiments were ketchup, mustard, hot sauce, and mayonnaise. Mustard seeds arrived with European colonists and were converted into powdered form and sold in stores by the eighteenth century. Ketchup became an important condiment in America during the late eighteenth and early nineteenth century, but mayonnaise did not emerge until the last decade of the nineteenth century. The use of all three condiments increased as they became interconnected with the rise of fast foods, particularly hot dogs, hamburgers, and french fries.

Other table condiments entered America during the nineteenth century, including A1 Steak Sauce, Harvey's Sauce, The Gentleman's Relish, and Worcestershire sauce, all of which were British imports, and Tabasco sauce, which was produced after the Civil War by the McIlhenny family on Avery Island, Louisiana. In the twentieth century, commercial barbecue sauce became a table condiment in many restaurants.

Horseradish (*Armoracia rusticana*) was integrated into English cookery before the arrival of English colonists in America, and was used regularly as a seasoning and condiment in colonial times. Horseradish was commercialized and made into a table condiment in the nineteenth century. The most prominent manufacturer of horseradish was the H. J. Heinz Company.

Vegetables

Vegetables historically have been converted into condiments, including pickled cucumbers, onions, ginger, horseradish, sauerkraut, piccalilli, and a variety of relishes. In addition, fresh vegetables came to be served as condiments, including sliced tomatoes and sliced or diced onions, which frequently were employed on sandwiches.

Beverage Sweeteners and Flavorings

After salt and pepper, the most popular condiment at the end of the twentieth century was sugar. However, sugar was expensive in colonial America, and honey and molasses were used more commonly. As sugar prices declined during the nineteenth century, it was used in greater quantity in a greater diversity of cookery, such as baking. As a condiment, sugar was particularly important added to bitter beverages, such as tea, coffee, and chocolate. Sugar and honey also were employed in making other condiments such as jams, jellies, preserves, and marmalades. Likewise, milk, cream, and lemon were used to flavor beverages.

Salad Dressings

In colonial times, vinegar and oil was the most prevalent salad dressing. As salads became more important as the nineteenth century ended, salad dressings increased in diversity. By 1900 dozens of different dressings were employed on various salads. Beginning in the late nineteenth century, salad dressings were commercialized, and seven major salad dressings emerged: russian, italian, blue cheese, thousand island, french, caesar, and ranch.

Simply stated— you get more flavor, more eating and drinking pleasure, from products that bear the TABASCO® trademark.

An advertisement for Tabasco products.

Dips

Humans have been dipping food into sauces for millennia, but the commercial category of dips can be traced to the 1950s, when Lipton began a promotional campaign to combine their french onion soup mix with sour cream or cream cheese as dips for potato and corn chips. Since then, hundreds of commercial dips have been manufactured; by far, salsa has been the most important. While it had been made in America since the early nineteenth century, its use exploded during the 1980s and continued to increase during the following decade. By the mid-1990s salsa outsold ketchup. Although it slipped subsequently in its ratings, in the early 2000s salsa remained as one of America's most important condiments.

Ethnic Condiments

During the second half of the twentieth century, ethnic sauces greatly changed the world of American condiments. These sauces were purveyed by restaurants and cookbooks, and promoted by their American manufacturers. A short list of common ethnic condiments includes: soy sauce, duck sauce, pickled ginger, oyster sauce, wasabi paste, guacamole, chutney, curry, and fish sauce. Dozens of other ethnic condiments are commonly available throughout America.

Continued Use of Condiments

In the twentieth century, the use of condiments in America expanded mainly because of their decrease in cost. The downside of the widespread dissemination of certain condiments was standardization. This loss of diversity was offset by the infusion of new condiments generally introduced by immigrants. Gradually, ethnic condiments became part of the culinary mainstream. American condiments have greatly influenced the world as many have been transported into other cuisines through American fast food establishments.

[**See also** BUTTER; DIPS; HONEY; KETCHUP; MAPLE SYRUP; MAYONNAISE; MOLASSES; MUSTARD; PEPPER, BLACK; PICKLES; SALADS AND SALAD DRESSINGS; SALSA; SALT AND SALTING; SUGAR.]

BIBLIOGRAPHY

Costenbader, Carol W. *Mustards, Ketchups, and Vinegars: Making the Most of Seasonal Abundance.* Pownal, VT: Storey Communications, 1996.

Smith, Andrew F. *Pure Ketchup: A History of America's National Condiment, with Recipes.* Washington, D.C.: Smithsonian Institution, 2001.

Solomon, Jay. *Condiments!: Chutneys, Relishes, and Table Sauces.* Freedom, CA: Crossing, 1990.

ANDREW F. SMITH

Coney Island, see Amusement Parks

Containers

Most food before and after preparation has to be kept in a container to protect it from insects, rodents, or just the moisture in the air. In particular, staples—flour, sugar, salt, ground meal, spices, coffee, and tea—historically were stored in bulk in close-fitted containers. Tea and some spices were so expensive in the eighteenth and early nineteenth centuries that the small containers in which they were stored were kept locked. The earliest American food containers were barrels, baskets, boxes, canisters, and ceramic crocks or jugs. The first American patent for any kind of container was issued in 1811, for barrel staves and lids.

Barrels and kegs were made by coopers out of wooden staves, usually oak or cedar, which were bound by bentwood straps and later metal hoops. They were airtight enough to store dry foods such as flour or fresh foods such as apples packed in straw. The wood swelled when wet, so coopered wares were also watertight and leakproof for foods such as sauerkraut or cider. Various coopered wood containers, from buckets and firkins to barrels and hogsheads, also were used as dry or liquid measures; the more or less standard capacities differed based on the contents. A hogshead, for example, held 63 liquid gallons or 7.2 firkins.

Baskets were made of wood splints, especially oak or hickory, or of reeds, rushes, willow, or other plant materials that could be bent and woven. Sizes ranged from a half-pint, a quart, and a peck (8 quarts) to a bushel (32 quarts).

Boxes first were made of wood in the United States. Some had joined corners like case-furniture drawers and some were bentwood—nailed or pegged to wood bases and lids, and oval or round. Shakers made the most notable bentwood boxes, in sizes from tiny for dried herbs or pastilles to quite large for cheeses. Often these boxes were painted.

By about 1810 tin boxes, which had been imported from Wales, began to be made on a large scale in the United States. They were varnished or japanned with special coatings to keep them from rusting. Thirty years later square and round tins with lids were used to sell food, especially staples. By the 1880s decorated tin canisters were sold in sets. At the turn of the century, glass and ceramic canisters were made in sets for spices, sugar, salt, flour, meal, and soda. Matching sets of canisters, decorated and with the stenciled name of the food contents, became popular in the

1920s when the idea of a decorated kitchen, instead of just a functional kitchen, was touted in women's magazines. Color schemes such as red and yellow or green and cream could be echoed by colorful canisters. In the twentieth century, figural cookie jars made in the shape of animals, people, or houses became popular.

Crocks of stoneware (heavy ceramic with a salt glaze, created by throwing salt into the kiln during firing) were used for storing butter and soft cheese in the springhouse or cellar. Draped with a wet cloth, which cooled as the water evaporated, such crocks effectively stored foods at low temperatures before the advent of iceboxes and refrigerators. Salt glaze is impervious to acids, so such crocks were used widely for pickled foods. Jars, jugs, and bottles of glass and various ceramics (stoneware, earthenware, redware) were used by the eighteenth century for storing liquids and also dry staples. Corks, carved wooden plugs, and even corncobs were used to stopper jars and jugs throughout the nineteenth century.

Spice cabinets made like fine furniture, with many drawers and locked doors, were used in the eighteenth and early nineteenth centuries. These cabinets evolved by the 1880s into wooden wall-mounted little chests of drawers with a drawer for each spice. They were mostly made of oak, and reproductions imported from Germany were made at least until the 1950s. Similar tin spice chests also were used. Compartmentalized tin containers called spice boxes were popular in the 1800s. Round or rectangular, they were japanned inside and out and had hinged lids with a hasp for a lock and a carrying handle. Inside there were either sectional divisions or small lidded cans for at least four, and usually six to eight, necessary spices: allspice, cloves, nutmeg, ginger, cinnamon, mustard seeds, peppercorns, and mace. Usually there was a small nutmeg grater built in or detachable from the lid. By 1880 tin boxes sometimes included room for bottled extracts. Also by then commercially prepared and ready-to-use spices and flavorings were sold in small tins (later in cardboard and tin boxes, to store on shelves or wall-hung racks). These were chromolithographed with decorative images so that housewives would keep the container in use and be reminded of the brand.

[See also MASON JARS.]

BIBLIOGRAPHY

Franklin, Linda Campbell. *300 Years of Kitchen Collectibles.* 5th ed. Iola, WI: Krause, 2003.

Hine, Thomas. *The Total Package: The Evolution and Secret Meanings of Boxes, Bottles, Cans, and Tubes.* Boston: Little, Brown, 1995.

Leybourne, Douglas M., Jr. *The Collector's Guide to Old Fruit Jars.* North Muskegon, MI: Altarfire, 2000.

Roerig, Fred, and Joyce Herndon Roerig. *The Collector's Encyclopedia of Cookie Jars.* 3 vols. Paducah, KY: Collector Books, 1991–1998.

LINDA CAMPBELL FRANKLIN

Convenience Stores

Beginning in the 1920s, self-service supermarkets began to displace small neighborhood grocery stores in the United States, and during the next twenty years, tens of thousands of small stores went out of business. For major grocery shopping, supermarkets offered lower prices and a greater variety of products. Still, a shopper needing just a few common items, such as bread and milk, might not want to travel to the supermarket (which might be miles away) or deal with long lines at the checkout stands. Ironically, this created a niche for small, local markets offering the most frequently purchased groceries. These grew modestly until World War II and rapidly expanded after the war. Their main reason for success was their fast service—the customer was in and out of the store in minutes, having picked up a missing ingredient for that evening's meal or the makings of the next morning's breakfast.

In 1927 the Southland Ice Company of Dallas began selling milk, eggs, and bread, and then slowly expanded its line of packaged and canned items. The store began to expand to other locations and it began to franchise its operation. The company also began to increase its geographic reach—first in Texas, then around the country, and finally throughout the world. Southland Ice called these "Tote'm stores," since customers "toted" away their purchases. In 1946, the company renamed the stores "7-Eleven," reflecting their hours of operation, 7 A.M. to 11 P.M. The outlets were usually located on the edge of town, surrounded by a small parking lot.

Beginning in 1964, 7-Eleven began selling coffee to go; it later added the syrup-and-ice drinks called Slurpees (1966); oversized soft drinks—the 32-ounce Big Gulp (1980), and 64-ounce Double Gulp—and hot dogs (1988). Today the chain sells 100 million hot dogs every year. In 1991, 7-Eleven introduced its World Ovens pastries. Today, the stores sell about 60 million freshly baked doughnuts and pastries annually; the blueberry muffin is the perennial best seller. The nearly 2 million consumers who visit a 7-Eleven store each day to buy last-minute groceries, on-the-go meals, snacks, and drinks make 7-Eleven one of the world's largest food purveyors.

Dozens of smaller convenience stores operate around the United States. Many chains started as businesses in other fields, often as dairy farms, such as the Isaly family, who owned the Mansfield Pure Milk Company in Mansfield, Ohio, where they invented the Klondike ice cream bar. The Isly dairy store began selling the Klondike bars and began to expand the the goods that they sold, such that they became a convenience store chain operating in Ohio, western Pennsylvania, and West Virginia. By the 1940s, the Isaly family had seven dairy plants that supplied more than three hundred Isaly dairy stores.

In 1972, the company was sold to a group of investors, who believed that the Klondike bar was more profitable than its labor-intensive stores. A few stores remain, but the bar has been produced by the conglomerate Unilever since 1993.

Another convenience store chain was Cumberland Farms, which began in Cumberland, Rhode Island, in 1939. It expanded into gas stations after World War II and then began selling a limited line of dairy products and groceries in the stations. As of 2005, it was the largest convenience store chain in the Northeast with more than 1,100 outlets, and it still produces its own line of dairy products. The Millville Manufacturing Company, a New Jersey–based textile company with mills in several states, opened a convenience store in 1964 called Wawa in Folsum, Pennsylvania. As of 2005, the chain operated five hundred stores in Virginia, Pennsylvania, New Jersey, Delaware, and Maryland.

Royal Farms Convenience Stores, launched in 1959, operates in Maryland, Virginia, and Delaware. Skinny's, founded in 1974 in Abilene, Texas, operates in twenty-eight north Texas cities. The Town & Country Food Stores chain, established in Austin, Texas, in 1958, operates in east Texas and New Mexico. The Rhodes Companies launched its first convenience store location in Cape Girardeau, Missouri, in 1979, and its Rhodes 101 Stops, complete with drive-up windows, operate throughout Missouri. Likewise, many gas stations first offered Coca-Cola and other beverages for sale in vending machines, and later have opened convenience stores for motorists. As of 2005, there were an estimated 125,000 convenience stores in the United States.

BIBLIOGRAPHY

Bainbridge, Robert E. *Convenience Stores and Retail Fuel Properties: Essential Appraisal Issues*. Chicago: Appraisal Institute, 2003.

Butko, Brian. *Klondikes, Chipped Ham, and Skyscraper Cones: The Story of Isaly's*. Mechanicsburg, PA: Stackpole Books, 2001.

Thompson, Maria M., and Donald H. Price. *Wawa*. Charleston, SC: Arcadia, 2004.

ANDREW F. SMITH

Cookbooks and Manuscripts:
To 1860

Early settlers carried manuscript and printed cookbooks with them to the New World. Once they arrived, they continued to acquire European cookbooks, by purchase here or abroad, and wrote their own cookery manuscripts. It appears that America came late to cookbook publishing. Native Americans had been cooking on the continent for millennia and Europeans and Africans had been preparing meals in America for more than one hundred years before the first cookbook was printed in the English colonies. The first formal cookbook of American imprint was Eliza Smith's *The Compleat Housewife* (1742) published by William Parks of Williamsburg, Virginia. It was reprinted from an earlier English cookbook, but Parks made some attempt to fashion it to American tastes and circumstances by deleting certain recipes, "the ingredients or materials for which are not to be had in this country." Other English cookbooks were published in America, but none seriously attempted to reach an American audience for another fifty years.

Twenty years after the American Revolution, Amelia Simmons published her *American Cookery* (1796), generally acknowledged as the first cookbook written by an American. Although many of the recipes in *American Cookery* are outright borrowings from British cookery books of the period, especially Susannah Carter's work, it also contains new and distinctly American recipes. Its originality lies in its recognition and use of truly American produce. There are five recipes using cornmeal: three for Indian pudding, one for johnnycake or hoecake, and one for Indian slapjacks. Other American innovations were the use of corncobs for smoking bacon and the suggestion of cranberry sauce as an accompaniment to roast turkey. Perhaps the most far-reaching innovation was the introduction of pearl ash (similar to potash), a well-known staple in the colonial American household, as a chemical leavening in dough. This practice eventually resulted in the compounding of modern baking powders.

Development of American Classics

Two conflicting trends became evident during the sixty years following the publication of *American Cookery*. English and other European works continued to be reprinted regularly in the United States, often with special sections or adaptations for the American audience. But increasingly, cookbooks written by Americans for Americans were capturing the market.

The next major U.S. cookbook after *American Cookery* was Mary Randolph's *Virginia House-Wife* (1824). This first regional American cookbook was extremely popular, with at least nineteen printings prior to the Civil War, and is still in print. It includes recipes for truly regional items including ones for ochra soup, catfish, barbecue, and gumbo, among many others.

In the 1820s and 1830s, the cookery works of Eliza Leslie and Lydia Maria Child dominated the cookbook scene. They exemplified a major trend in nineteenth-century American cookbook publishing: the domination of the field by an influential and remarkable group of women who were not only recognized culinary authorities but also were active in all the major cultural and societal concerns of their day.

In the 1840s and 1850s, new culinary authorities, almost all American women, emerged: Sarah Josepha Hale, Mary Hooker Cornelius, Mrs. T. J. Crowen, Mrs. A. L. Webster, Esther Allen Howland, and Catharine Beecher. Their works were often printed in many editions and were of great import in influencing the development of scientific kitchen planning, which blossomed after the Civil War.

Trends in Topics and Authors

Certain trends and themes appear in the published cookbooks of the first half of the nineteenth century. Among these are a preoccupation with sweets and desserts, economy and frugality, management and organization, diet and health, vegetarianism, and regional American cooking. These trends are evident in such influential works as Leslie's *Seventy-five Receipts for Pastry, Cakes, and Sweetmeats* (1828), Child's *The Frugal Housewife* (1829), H. L. Barnum's *Family Receipts* (1831), Sylvester Graham's *Treatise on Bread, and Bread-Making* (1837), and William Alcott's *Vegetable Diet* (1849).

Following Randolph's 1824 work on Virginia cooking, many other regional American cookbooks appeared: Lettice Bryan's *The Kentucky Housewife* (1839), Phineas Thornton's *The Southern Gardener and Receipt Book* (1840), Philomelia Hardin's *Every Bodys Cook and Receipt Book: But More Particularly Designed for Buckeyes, Hoosiers, Wolverines, Corncrackers, Suckers . . .* (1842), Howland's *New England Economical Housekeeper* (1844), and Sarah Rutledge's *The Carolina Housewife* (1847). Regional recipes abound in these works. For example, Hardin's book, published in Cleveland, Ohio, contains many locale-specific recipes: Buckeye Dumplings (Ohio), Wolverine Junket (Michigan), Hoosier Pickles (Indiana), and Corncrackers' Pudding (Kentucky). Rutledge's book, published in Charleston, South Carolina, has about two dozen recipes for rice-based breakfast breads and cakes, plus recipes for a rice soup, several pilafs, and many rice desserts, and includes detailed instructions for preparing and boiling rice.

Two works by African American authors also were published prior to the Civil War: Robert Roberts's *The House Servant's Directory* (1827) and Tunis Campbell's *Hotel Keepers, Head Waiters, and Housekeepers' Guide* (1848). Although each has recipes, these are not mainly cookbooks, but rather manuals written by professional men to teach others how to manage large private households or hotel and restaurant dining rooms.

Popular Publishing Forms

Large compendiums, usually in encyclopedia form, were very popular in this early period of American culinary imprints. They present a wide variety of information, including recipes as well as advice on household management, medical cures, food preservation, beverage and dairy production, farming and laundry chores, etiquette, home furnishings, and child care. The earliest of these culinary encyclopedias, which were compiled from British, Continental, and American sources and often reprinted, include Mrs. N. K. M. Lee's *The Cook's Own Book* (1832), Thomas

AMERICAN COOKERY,

OR THE ART OF DRESSING

VIANDS, FISH, POULTRY and VEGETABLES,

AND THE BEST MODES OF MAKING

PASTES, PUFFS, PIES, TARTS, PUDDINGS,
CUSTARDS AND PRESERVES,

AND ALL KINDS OF

CAKES,

FROM THE IMPERIAL PLUMB TO PLAIN CAKE.

ADAPTED TO THIS COUNTRY,

AND ALL GRADES OF LIFE.

By Amelia Simmons,

AN AMERICAN ORPHAN.

PUBLISHED ACCORDING TO ACT OF CONGRESS.

HARTFORD:

PRINTED BY HUDSON & GOODWIN.

FOR THE AUTHOR.

1796.

The title page of the 1796 edition of Simmons's book—the first representative collection of English-American cuisine—was in common usage until the early nineteenth century.

Webster's *An Encyclopædia of Domestic Economy* (1845), and Elizabeth Ellet's *The Practical Housekeeper* (1857). Ellet's book covers the house and its furniture, duties of the mistress and the servant, the storeroom and marketing, "domestic manipulation," bills of fare, perfumery and toilet, infusions and cosmetics, pomades, vinegars, and soaps, and provides a family medical guide as well as "five thousand practical receipts and maxims"; it is illustrated with five hundred wood engravings.

Beginning in 1828, translations from the French and reprints of noted English works on French cookery also were printed with some regularity. In 1846 three major French cookbooks were published: Madame Utrecht-Friedel's *The French Cook,* Charles Francatelli's *French Cookery: The Modern Cook,* and Louis-Eustache Audot's *French Domestic Cookery.* Likewise, German cookbooks, both in English and in translation, continued to be published especially in the Pennsylvania Dutch community.

Recipes for the housewife also were available in sources other than printed cookbooks, especially in the new women's magazines such as *Godey's Lady's Book* (founded in 1830) and in the ubiquitous and popular almanacs. *Godey's* influential editor, Sarah Josepha Hale, wrote many cookbooks and campaigned to establish Thanksgiving as a national holiday. Almanacs also included recipes and were of a multitude of kinds; some were agricultural; some were in support of causes, especially of temperance; and some were simply gift books. Examples are Turner's *The House-Keeper's Almanac* (1842), *The Lady's Annual* (1842), and *Fisher's Temperance House-Keeper's Almanac* (1843).

Additional Sources

Another group of books of importance in early America concern milk, cheese, and dairying. Although most dairying and milk processing chores were the housewife's responsibility, all of these books and pamphlets were written by American or British male authorities. The books are practical how-to guides on home dairy management, stressing the importance of cleanliness and consistency of technique for the production of increased and better quality product. An excellent example is Joshua Johnson's twelve-page pamphlet called *The Art of Cheese-Making* (1801). There are about a dozen similar early works on dairying recognized in the relevant bibliographies.

Most of the early trends in American cookbook publishing continued after 1860, although whole new genres of cookbooks increasingly became available.

[**See also** BEECHER, CATHARINE; CAMPBELL, TUNIS G.; COOKBOOKS AND MANUSCRIPTS: FROM THE CIVIL WAR TO WORLD WAR I; COOKING MANUSCRIPTS; GRAHAM, SYLVESTER; LESLIE, ELIZA; RANDOLPH, MARY; SIMMONS, AMELIA.]

JANICE BLUESTEIN LONGONE

Cookbooks and Manuscripts: From the Civil War to World War I

Many societal changes influenced the history of American cookbooks after 1860: the Civil War, the Industrial Revolution, the change from a rural to an urban society, large waves of immigration, the westward expansion, the changing role of women, and the increasing knowledge of and interest in scientific diet and nutrition.

New Postwar Publishing Forms

The first change was a legacy of the Civil War, when women's charitable organizations compiled and sold cookbooks to raise funds to aid war victims. The first known charity cookbook, *A Poetical Cook-Book* (1864), was published to benefit a sanitary fair in Philadelphia. When the war ended, these organizations turned their charitable attentions to other causes. From 1864 to the beginning of World War I more than five thousand such books were published. They preserved regional recipes and traditions and their proceeds benefited diverse causes including those of both local interest (churches, libraries, orphanages) and those with a national and political agenda (suffrage, temperance, the formation of women's organizations.) They reveal the increasing diversity of women's activities outside the home as well as the growth of advertising as a way of reaching the consumer. Working on these cookbooks taught women organizational skills and was one way for them to participate in the great public life of the nation.

Another major explosion in post–Civil War cookbooks was the growth of promotional and advertising literature. The new national food and equipment companies began publishing millions of copies of pamphlets (culinary ephemera) and hardcover books that provided instructions, hints, recipes, illustrations, and general diet and nutrition advice to convince readers to buy packaged, brand-name products. The success of this technique was phenomenal.

Other major developments were the growth of the domestic economy, home economics, scientific cookery, and cooking-school movements as well as the fight for pure food and drug laws. Juliet Corson, Sarah Tyson Rorer, Mary Lincoln, Fannie Farmer, Maria Parloa, Marion Harland, and Janet McKenzie Hill continued in the footsteps of the great culinary authorities of the pre–Civil War era. Corson, the founder of the New York Cooking School, was particularly interested in feeding the poor and authored a number of influential pamphlets such as *Fifteen Cent Dinners for Workingmen's Families* (1878) which she distributed free of charge to those in need. Rorer, the founder of the Philadelphia Cooking School, published more than one hundred books and pamphlets; was part owner of *Table Talk,* a gastronomic monthly; and was the domestic editor of the *Ladies' Home Journal* for four-

teen years. Lincoln, in addition to her work at the Boston Cooking School and on many books, was the culinary editor of the *American Kitchen Magazine* and active in educational clubs and women's organizations. Farmer, of the Boston Cooking School and Miss Farmer's School of Cookery, taught and lectured throughout the United States and became the best known of the nineteenth-century cooks. Her *Boston Cooking-School Cook Book* (1896) is one of the all-time best sellers in the field. Janet McKenzie Hill, a graduate of the Boston Cooking School, founded the *Boston Cooking School Magazine* in 1896 and was its editor until shortly before her death in 1933. Along with Parloa and Harland, these women became role models for generations of women who became professionals making a living in the culinary arts.

During this era, consumer issues, adulteration, and agitation for pure food and drug laws as well as an increased interest in vegetarianism, diet, and nutrition, all produced a voluminous body of literature.

Immigration and Ethnic Recipes

Prior to 1920, the American housewife could purchase books on the cuisine of dozens of other cultures, sometimes in English, sometimes in the original language, and sometimes with bilingual text. These works include the first Jewish cookbook published in America, Esther Levy's *Jewish Cookery Book* (1871); the charity cookbook *St. Paul's Bazaar-Kochbuch und Geschaeftsfuehrer* (1892); the bilingual *Svensk-Amerikansk Kokbok* (1895); May E. Southworth's *One Hundred and One Mexican Dishes* (1906); Sara Bosse and Onoto Watanna's *Chinese-Japanese Cook Book* (1910); and K. D. Shastri's *Hindu Dietetics* (1917). In addition, foreign and ethnic foods, foodways, and recipes were introduced to American housewives by countless articles in women's magazines; virtually every culture and country was represented.

Professional Publications

The Hotel Monthly Press of Chicago produced an enormous variety of practical professional guides in many editions following the turn of the century. In addition, it published several classics written by the most renowned chefs of the era including, from Delmonico's restaurant in New York City, Charles Ranhofer's *The Epicurean* (1894), which offers the best picture of fine restaurant dining in Victorian America.

Fairs and Expositions

Among the most popular destinations of this era when Americans were beginning to travel by train or car (and the source of a fine body of regional cookbooks) were the many fairs and expositions held throughout the country. A remarkable cookbook came out of the fair held in Philadelphia to

THE
HOUSE SERVANT'S DIRECTORY,
OR
A MONITOR FOR PRIVATE FAMILIES :
COMPRISING
HINTS ON THE ARRANGEMENT AND PERFORMANCE OF
SERVANTS' WORK,
WITH GENERAL RULES FOR
SETTING OUT TABLES AND SIDEBOARDS
IN FIRST ORDER ;
THE ART OF WAITING
IN ALL ITS BRANCHES ; AND LIKEWISE HOW TO CONDUCT
LARGE AND SMALL PARTIES
WITH ORDER ;
WITH GENERAL DIRECTIONS FOR PLACING ON TABLE
ALL KINDS OF JOINTS, FISH, FOWL, &c.
WITH
FULL INSTRUCTIONS FOR CLEANING
PLATE, BRASS, STEEL, GLASS, MAHOGANY ;
AND LIKEWISE
ALL KINDS OF PATENT AND COMMON LAMPS :
OBSERVATIONS
ON SERVANTS' BEHAVIOUR TO THEIR EMPLOYERS ;
AND UPWARDS OF
100 VARIOUS AND USEFUL RECEIPTS,
CHIEFLY COMPILED
FOR THE USE OF HOUSE SERVANTS ;
AND IDENTICALLY MADE
TO SUIT THE MANNERS AND CUSTOMS OF FAMILIES
IN THE UNITED STATES.

By ROBERT ROBERTS.

WITH
FRIENDLY ADVICE TO COOKS
AND HEADS OF FAMILIES,
AND COMPLETE DIRECTIONS HOW TO BURN
LEHIGH COAL.

BOSTON,
MUNROE AND FRANCIS, 128 WASHINGTON-STREET.
NEW YORK,
CHARLES S. FRANCIS, 189 BROADWAY.
1827.

The title page of the 1827 edition of the House Servant's Directory.

celebrate America's Centennial in 1876: *The National Cookery Book* issued by the Women's Centennial Committee. It offers a splendid picture of contemporary regional American cookery. *Favorite Recipes: A Columbian Autograph Souvenir* (1893) was issued at the World's Columbian Exposition held in Chicago in 1893. From the Cotton States and International Exposition held in Atlanta in 1895 came the *Tested Recipe Cook Book*, which attempted to preserve old southern traditions. For the Louisiana Purchase Exposition held in St. Louis in 1904, Sarah Tyson Rorer published the *World's Fair Souvenir Cook Book*. From the Panama-Pacific International Exposition held in San Francisco in 1915 emerged the *Pan-Pacific Cook Book,* which captured the international character of that city with recipes from sixty countries from Algeria to Venezuela.

Pre–Civil War Trends Continued

A prominent example of the continuing interest in sweets and desserts is the comprehensive *The Art of Confectionery* (1866). Its 44 chapters in 346 pages cover, in exquisite detail, every aspect of the subject. Baking, candy, and confectionery works, for and by both the professional and the amateur, continued to appear in great numbers.

Cookbooks by doctors continued to be popular. For example, the many editions of works by the medical doctor Alvin Wood Chase of Ann Arbor, Michigan, sold more than 4 million copies. Pamphlets touting a wide variety of patent medicines also increased astronomically. These concoctions, often worthless nostrums, were peddled at fairs and door-to-door by salesmen and quacks. Some American carbonated beverages got their start as patent medicines. Many other types of almanacs were published in all parts of the country.

Culinary encyclopedias also continued to be issued in great numbers. Representative are Mrs. E. F. Haskell's *The Housekeeper's Encyclopedia...in All Branches of Cookery and Domestic Economy* (1861), Henry Hartshorne's *The Household Cyclopedia of General Information Containing over Ten Thousand Receipts* (1871), and Artemas Ward's compilation of *The Grocer's Encyclopedia* (1911), an exhaustive and "informative compendium of useful information concerning foods of all kinds."

Regional and Sectarian Cookbooks

The burst of regional American and sectarian cookbooks continued unabated. The South, which has, perhaps, America's most enduring cookery heritage, added glorious cookbooks to those available before the Civil War. Some of the books can be classified as Reconstruction literature and were written to teach southern homemakers how to keep their traditions alive in the "altered" postwar circumstances of loss of slaves and

servants in the home. More importantly, these works reflected southern pride in the regional culinary history; other books were written simply to preserve the old recipes and traditions. This splendid body of literature includes from the South: Annabella P. Hill's *Mrs. Hill's Southern Practical Cookery* (1867); M. L. Tyson's *The Queen of the Kitchen, Old Maryland Receipts* (1874); Marion Cabell Tyree's *Housekeeping in Old Virginia* (1879); and Lafcadio Hearn's *La Cuisine Creole* (1885); and from the rest of the country: Lucia Gray Swett's *New England Breakfast Breads* (1891); *Buckeye Cook Book* (1876); *The Kansas Home Cook-Book* (1874); *The Trans-Mississippi Home Maker* (1898); *Good Housekeeping in High Altitudes* (1888); and *California Recipe Book* (1872).

African American authors were represented in greater numbers after the Civil War. These publications include, among others, two scarce items authored by African American women. The earliest, Malinda Russell's *A Domestic Cook Book* (1866), was written by a free woman of color; Abby Fisher, author of *What Mrs. Fisher Knows about Old Southern Cooking* (1881), was by an emancipated slave who left the South after the Civil War to make a new life in California.

Additional Culinary Literature

New genres of culinary books and magazines began to be published in increasing numbers during this period. Books on markets, for example Thomas DeVoe's *The Market Book* (1862) and *The Market Assistant* (1867); gastronomic literature, for example George H. Ellwanger's *The Pleasures of the Table* (1902); and children's cookbooks, for example Jane Fryer's *The Mary Frances Cook Book* (1912) all became a regular part of the culinary publishing industry. Newly formed general women's magazines, such as *The Woman's Home Companion* (founded 1873), *Ladies' Home Journal* (1883), and *Good Housekeeping* (1885), all carried articles on cooking and entertaining. These were joined by many others specifically culinary in nature, some for the professional and others for the homemaker. All broadened America's culinary horizons and choices.

In the years between 1860 and World War I, the ferment of culinary publishing mirrored the dramatic changes and innovations characterizing all areas of American life, both in breadth and intensity. The eddies and currents of the diverse cultural, societal, and scientific movements made this one of the most exciting and seminal periods in American cookbook history. Cookbook publishing in the twenty-first century is beholden to this formative era.

[**See also** ADVERTISING COOKBOOKLETS AND RECIPES; COMMUNITY COOKBOOKS; COOKBOOKS AND MANUSCRIPTS: TO 1860; COOKING MANUSCRIPTS; COOKING SCHOOLS; WORLD'S FAIRS.]

JANICE BLUESTEIN LONGONE

Cookbooks and Manuscripts:
From World War I to World War II

At the start of World War I, few American households owned more than one or two cookbooks and these were not central to most kitchen activity. The Boston area still retained an importance in instructional food writing inherited from the early days of the New England Kitchen and the Boston Cooking School. The best-known American cookbook was *The Boston Cooking-School Cook Book* (1896) by Fannie Farmer, who had died in 1915. Its very fine predecessor and rival, *Mrs. Lincoln's Boston Cook Book* (1884) by Mary J. Lincoln, went out of print after 1919. Revisions of the Farmer book were overseen until 1930 by her sister, Cora Perkins, and thereafter by Perkins's daughter-in-law, Wilma Lord Perkins. A few other veterans of the nineteenth-century New England scientific cookery movement—notably Janet McKenzie Hill, the longtime editor of *The Boston Cooking School Magazine*, and Alice Bradley, Farmer's successor as the principal of Miss Farmer's Cooking School—continued to publish widely for several decades, but their books seldom aimed for universal manual status or stressed claims of scientific method. Despite the huge prestige of dietetics at this time, too much emphasis on the subject was coming to mark a cookbook as stuffy and dated. By the early 1940s even Wilma Lord Perkins was trying to make *The Boston Cooking-School Cook Book* match current preferences with dashes of added warmth, personality, and attention to new products or fashions.

New Classics and Niches

By the 1920s, New York City was the main hub of food-writing activity. Enterprising service or shelter magazine publishers and home economics institutes, both there and elsewhere, set about creating encyclopedic, up-to-date, all-purpose manuals to challenge *Boston* as the nation's preeminent kitchen bible. Efforts of this kind include Ida C. Bailey Allen's *Mrs. Allen's Cook Book* (1917) and *Mrs. Allen on Cooking, Menus, Service* (1924), which was reissued in 1932 as *Ida Bailey Allen's Modern Cook Book*; Isabel Ely Lord's *Everybody's Cook Book* (1924), a work developed at the Pratt Institute in Brooklyn; *America's Cook Book* (1937), compiled by the Home Institute of the *New York Herald Tribune*; *The American Woman's Cook Book* (1938), edited by Ruth Berolzheimer and produced at the Culinary Arts Institute in Chicago; *The New American Cook Book* (1941), edited by Lily Haxworth Wallace; an enormous revision of *The Good Housekeeping Cook Book* (1942); and the *Woman's Home Companion Cook Book* (1942). The most serious competitors to Fannie Farmer, however, were productions by midwestern amateurs. From 1936 through the late 1990s, Irma Rombauer's *The Joy of Cooking* was issued by one of the few remaining midwestern publishers, Bobbs-Merrill. The many reissues of *The Settlement Cook Book* (1901), compiled by Mrs. Simon Kander, remained based in Milwaukee, Wisconsin, until 1954. With its strong German Jewish emphasis, *Settlement* was probably the most important cookbook for many American Jews during this period.

While the big kitchen manuals duked it out, cookbook publishers began exploiting specialized marketing niches. Works devoted to particular corners of a subject now seen as vast and complex multiplied. An audience developed for food-related books meant as bedtime reading or gift ideas rather than answers to concrete domestic needs. Some authors applied themselves to one specialty subject after another; among the best known were the tireless Ida Bailey Allen and the mother, daughter-in-law, and son team of Cora, Rose, and Bob Brown.

The following list is by no means a complete roster of the numerous subcategories that developed:

- Books directed to special needs or circumstances like wartime food rationing, financial straits, dietary limits, two-person households, cramped kitchenettes, or working-women's schedules. Some of the best known are *Cooking for Two* by Janet McKenzie Hill (1909; frequently reissued until 1968), *Macy's Cook Book for the Busy Woman* (1932) by Mabel Claire (published under different titles for distribution through several department stores and newspapers), and *How to Cook a Wolf* (1942) by M. F. K. Fisher (inspired by World War II shortages).
- Books for cooks/readers and nostalgia buffs, with or without recipes. These sprang from an increasing sense of food as something to be not just cooked and eaten but recalled, contemplated, discussed, and dreamed of. The strong breaks with an earlier America represented by World War I and Prohibition helped create an audience for evocations of the past including *The Girl from Rector's* (1927) and *The Rector Cook Book* (1928) by George Rector, *Peacock Alley* (1931) by James R. McCarthy, and *The Old-Time Saloon* (1931) by George Ade. A taste developed for other forms of vicarious culinary experience: food mavens' anthologies like *The Bed-Book of Eating and Drinking* (1943) by Richardson L. Wright, culinary reminiscences like the charming *The Country Kitchen* (1936) by Della T. Lutes, and protean food-for-thought musings like M. F. K. Fisher's *Serve It Forth* (1937), *Consider the Oyster* (1941), and *The Gastronomical Me* (1943).
- Media tie-ins and celebrity cookbooks. *Feeding the Lions: An Algonquin Cookbook* (1942) by Frank Case of New York City's Algonquin Hotel was an agreeable instance of the latter. Several of the former were sparked by radio shows, including *One Hundred Four Prize Radio Recipes* (1924) by Ida Bailey Allen, *Aunt Sammy's Radio Recipes* (1926; several reissues) by the USDA. Bureau of Home Economics, and *The Mystery Chef's Own Cook Book* (1934) by John MacPherson, an industrial engineer

who moonlighted as radio's "Mystery Chef."

- Books on parties and entertaining. The best of this genre was the sophisticated *June Platt's Party Cookbook* (1936) by the popular *House Beautiful* columnist.
- Works devoted to a single ingredient or class of ingredients, cooking appliance, menu category, theme, or gimmick. Notable single-subject books included *Ida Bailey Allen's Wine and Spirits Cook Book* (1934), *Herbs for the Kitchen* (1939) by Irma Goodrich Mazza, *Hors d'Oeuvre and Canapés* (1940) by James Beard, and *Casserole Cookery* (1941) by Marian and Nino Tracy.
- Works on foreign cuisines and haute cuisine. A sprinkling of these appeared in the 1920s; interest gathered in the next decade, perhaps reflecting a Depression-fed yearning for luxury and cosmopolitan adventure. Books on particular cuisines or geographical areas include *Good Food from Sweden* (1939) by Inga Norberg, the still-insightful *South American Cook Book* (1939) by the Browns, *Cook at Home in Chinese* (1938) by Henry Low, and the extraordinarily illuminating *How to Cook and Eat in Chinese* (1945) by Buwei Yang Chao. Among the globe-trotting anthologies published between the wars, *The Questing Cook* (1927) by Ruth A. Jeremiah Gottfried was the most perceptive and the *World Wide Cook Book* (1939) by Pearl V. Metzelthin the most ambitious. Works evincing a growing American taste for epicurean flourishes and fanfare include the Nero Wolfe mysteries of Rex Stout (beginning in 1934 with *Fer-de-Lance*), *The Art of Good Living* by André Simon (first American edition 1930), *Cooking à la Ritz* (1941) by Louis Diat, *Gourmet Dinners* (1941) by G. Selmer Fougner (the *New York Sun's* wine columnist), and an English translation of Escoffier's *Guide Culinaire* (1941).
- Explorations of America's culinary heritage. The post–World War I vogue for both automobile and armchair tourism, aided by surges of popular interest in colonial and pioneer history as well as American folk culture, found expression in many cookbooks. Because cookbooks were largely irrelevant to the cooking of African Americans, recent immigrants, rural women, many of the elderly, and poor people in general, this flowering generally sheds little light on their experience. There are, however, some valuable documents of regional cooking including *Southern Cooking* (1928; first trade edition 1941) by Henrietta Dull, *The Savannah Cook Book* (1933) by Harriet Ross Colquitt, *Good Maine Food* (1939) by Marjorie Mosser, *Hawaiian and Pacific Foods* (1940) by Katherine Bazore, *Mrs. Appleyard's Kitchen* (1942) by Louis Andrews Kent, *Cross Creek Cookery* (1942) by Marjorie Kinnan Rawlings, and several *Sunset* magazine recipe collections by Genevieve A. Callahan culminating in *The California Cook Book for Indoor and Outdoor Eating* (1946). The most illuminating coast-to-coast surveys of the time are *The National Cook Book* (1932) by Sheila Hibben, which appeared in a revised version in 1946 as *American Regional Cookery*; *Through the Kitchen Door* (1938) by Grace and Beverly Smith and Charles Morrow Wilson;

and *New York World's Fair Cook Book: The American Kitchen* (1939) by Crosby Gaige (a remarkable state-by-state compilation of recipes collected by each state's home economists).

[See also BOSTON COOKING SCHOOL; BEARD, JAMES; FARMER, FANNIE; FISHER, M. F. K.; PROHIBITION; ROMBAUER, IRMA.]

BIBLIOGRAPHY

Clark, Robert. *The Solace of Food: A Life of James Beard*. South Royalton, VT: Steerforth, 1996.

Mendelson, Anne. *Stand Facing the Stove: The Story of the Women Who Gave America the Joy of Cooking*. New York: Scribners, 2003.

ANNE MENDELSON

Cookbooks and Manuscripts:
From World War II to the 1960s

Between 1945 and 1969, writers of culinary literature found an enthusiastic audience, and publishers issued a steady stream of cookbooks that responded to Americans' growing interest in food and cooking. Some publications served as guides to basic cooking, while others launched the cook on an exciting adventure to foreign lands and flavors. Among the thousands of cookbooks that rolled off the presses over the twenty-five-year period following World War II, several stand out. The result is a representative body of classical culinary literature that exemplifies the diversity of the period.

1945 to 1949: A Culinary Awakening

Among a host of general cookery manuals used throughout the period from 1945 to 1970, Irma Rombauer's *The Joy of Cooking*, first published in 1931, was one of the most popular. Rombauer delivered her eminently practical recipes in a personable, chatty style that resulted in a classic manual destined to sell more than 15 million copies.

America's fascination with California, home to a burgeoning population made up, in large part, of former servicemen and their families, was rewarded with Genevieve Callahan's *The California Cook Book* (1946). Americans were reminded of the tantalizing dishes that could be prepared on outdoor grills, a concept that had been touted by James Beard in *Cook It Outdoors* (1941) on the eve of America's entry into World War II.

African Americans had long influenced the cookery of America. However, little credit was given to the African American influence on American cookery until the publication of Freda De Knight's classic *A Date with a Dish: A Cook Book of American Negro Recipes* (1948). De Knight dispensed with the stereotypical mammy in the southern kitchen and clearly illustrated the culinary diversity and accomplishments of African American cooks.

After World War II Americans became extremely interested in international and ethnic cuisine. Dione Lucas, the founder of Le Cordon Bleu cooking school in New York, was teaching Americans to cook classic French recipes; in 1947 her compilation *The*

Cordon Bleu Cook Book was published. Those looking for guidance in Chinese cooking turned to Buwei Yang Chao's *How to Cook and Eat in Chinese* (1945). It was recognized for its clarity and authenticity, and Americans learned the technique of stir-frying.

The brightest flower in America's postwar culinary bouquet was M. F. K. Fisher, whose passion, wit, and sensuality toward food made her the nation's first lady of food writing. It was through her work that Americans began to appreciate food as more than simple sustenance. *Here Let Us Feast: A Book of Banquets* (1946) presents a deliciously whimsical argument for celebrating life's great moments with fine food and drink.

Dichotomy of the 1950s

The 1950s also saw the publication of important new cookbooks dedicated to the exploration of regional American cooking. *The Southern Cook Book* (1951) was the result of Marion Brown's efforts to compile a representative selection of southern recipes culled from charitable cookbooks and professional cooks.

Gourmet Era of the 1960s

During the 1960s, two-income households necessarily limited time spent by parents in the kitchen. Women who found themselves trapped in an endless whirlwind of domestic chaos thus greeted the publication of Peg Bracken's *The I Hate to Cook Book* (1960) with relief.

At the other end were cookbooks published during the 1960s that represented the gourmet era. *Mastering the Art of French Cooking* (1961) by Simone Beck, Louisette Bertholle, and Julia Child turned out to be a culinary landmark. The American-born Child single-handedly revolutionized American home cooking with her precise instructions that taught Americans how to prepare French cuisine. Child's television debut in 1963 clearly reinforced the fact that cooking could be fun. By the time *The French Chef Cookbook* was released in 1968, Americans had been converted to the delights of French cooking.

In 1968 Time-Life Books launched its seminal twenty-seven-volume *Foods of the World* series. Authored by the top food writers of the time, each volume is an in-depth, well-researched exploration of the culture and history of a particular cuisine accompanied by authentic recipes. Notable volumes published in 1968 include *American Cooking* by Dale Brown, *The Cooking of Provincial France* by M. F. K. Fisher, *The Cooking of Italy* by Waverley Root, and *The Cooking of Vienna's Empire* by Joseph Wechsberg.

Amid the racial strife of the 1960s African Americans demonstrated renewed pride and interest in the documentation of their recipes and foodways. During the late 1960s the term "soul food" appeared to describe traditional African American food. Amid a flurry of new African American cookbooks, the first commercial use of "soul food" in a title appeared in *Soul Food Cookery* (1968) by Inez Yeargan Kaiser.

The health food movement advocated back-to-nature living and cooking. The first food-related book in this vein was Euell Gibbons's *Stalking the Wild Asparagus* (1962). The idea of foraging for food caught on, and it was incorporated into the natural food and vegetarian movements. By 1969 they had their first cookbook. *The Alice's Restaurant Cookbook*, written by Alice May Brock, advocates improvisation and creativity by cooking with fresh, natural foods on a daily basis.

By 1969 Americans had traveled through a decade that began with the romance and glamour of Julia Child and French cooking and ended with the comparative austerity of the natural food movement. Even a quick glance back to 1945 provides ample proof that an enormous array of new foods and cooking techniques, as well as a new culinary sophistication, had been embraced by the end of the 1960s. America's endless curiosity, a rapacious appetite, and the arrival of new immigrant groups from Asia promised that even more diversity and change would come in the following decades.

[**See also** AFRICAN AMERICAN FOOD; BEARD, JAMES; CHILD, JULIA; FISHER, M. F. K.; FRENCH INFLUENCES ON AMERICAN FOOD; GIBBONS, EUELL; HEALTH FOOD; ROMBAUER, IRMA.]

BECKY MERCURI

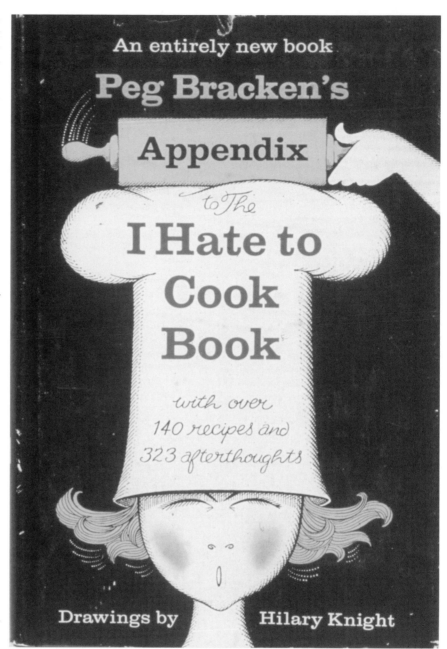

The appendix to the I Hate to Cook Book *(New York, 1966).*

Cookbooks and Manuscripts:
1970s to the Present

America is fascinated with food. And cookbooks feed the fascination. The last thirty years of the twentieth century, for example, brought a proliferation of cookbooks so dramatic that few could keep count. The momentum grew from the early 1970s to the year 2000, when about one thousand cookbooks were published.

As the 1970s began and Americans were shrugging off the swinging sixties, Julia Child continued her mission via television to bring French cooking to those Americans ready to graduate from frozen foods and macaroni and cheese from a box. Child's *Mastering the Art of French Cooking* (1961), written with Simone Beck and Louisette Bertholle, was still selling well. She continued her popular cooking shows and later went on to write *The Way to Cook* (1989) and *Cooking with Master Chefs* (1993).

With Julia at their side, Americans embraced all things French throughout the 1970s. Craig Claiborne also helped spread the Gallic gospel through his work as food editor and critic for the *New York Times*. He wrote *Classic French Cooking* (1970) with chef Pierre Franey, simplifying French cuisine for readers. Claiborne and Franey would continue writing and influencing American cooks for the next three decades.

While learning what went into those French cooking pots, Americans also discovered the best ways to chop, julienne, and whip those ingredients into shape, thanks to Jacques Pépin, a transplanted French chef and teacher. His book *La Technique: The Fundamental Techniques of Cooking; An Illustrated Guide* (1976) focused on step-by-step photographs and directions.

Meanwhile, a group of young French chefs had been experimenting with what they called nouvelle cuisine, a way of cooking that spurned the heavy-handed sauces and techniques of classical French cuisine à la Auguste Escoffier. *Michel Guérard's Cuisine*

Cover of Mollie Katzen's Moosewood Cookbook *(1977).*

Minceur (1976) was one influential cookbook from the movement. Soon American cooks were mimicking the style, and nouvelle cuisine went on to influence cooking in America for decades.

But fancy French food was not the only pursuit in the 1970s. As the economy worsened, cooks began looking more closely at food costs. Books on supermarket shopping, bargain foods, and the virtues of hamburger (365 ways!) filled bookstore shelves. Perla Meyers wrote *The Seasonal Kitchen: A Return to Fresh Foods* (1973), a book preaching the economies inherent in cooking with foods during their peak season. It became a forerunner of later works emphasizing farmers' markets, sustainable farming, and natural foods.

And as nutritional research made advances, an onslaught of books on diet regimens, food additives, and healthful eating began in the 1970s and continues today. Vegetarian cookbooks touted brown rice, tofu, and sprouts. *Diet for a Small Planet* (1971) examined the American system of food production and found it lacking. The author, Frances Moore Lappé, warned against America's wasteful process of raising meat for food while many in the rest of the world starved. Americans jumped onto this health bandwagon, beginning the long-running dichotomy of enjoying the newfound pleasures of the table—à la Child—while worrying about the correctness of what they were eating.

Meanwhile, America's own food heritage gained appeal with writers. Foremost among them was James Beard, the author and cooking teacher often called the father of American cooking. *James Beard's American Cookery* (1972), was part history lesson, part cookbook, and brought a down-to-earth approach to regional and national foods such as potpies, cheeseburgers, and potatoes O'Brien.

Also in the early 1970s, a series from Time-Life Books wove together the culture and cuisine of America's regions. Later, Evan Jones tackled a more historical account of American cooking in his landmark *American Food: The Gastronomic Story* (1975). With help from his wife, Judith, an editor at Knopf Publishing, Jones captured the transformation of American regional cookery to a more national uniformity.

One region, the South, had a propensity for fine cooking that created a batch of worthy cookbooks, especially in the 1980s—among them, John Egerton's *Southern Food: At Home, on the Road, in History* (1987), Bill Neal's *Southern Cooking* (1985), and *Nathalie Dupree's Southern Memories: Recipes and Reminiscences* (1993). America's love affair with Cajun and Creole cooking began with the publication of *Chef Paul Prudhomme's Louisiana Kitchen* (1984). Prudhomme did more for spreading the Cajun gospel (remember blackened redfish?) than any other culinary preacher before or since.

Another preacher, of the African American influence on southern cooking, was Edna Lewis. She wrote *The Taste of Country Cooking* (1976), a mouthwatering book that sets forth

the traditions of raising and cooking food on her family's farm in Freetown, Virginia, a town founded by former slaves. Other African American collections followed, including Norma Jean and Carole Darden's *Spoonbread and Strawberry Wine: Recipes and Reminiscences of a Family* (1978), and Jessica Harris's *The Welcome Table: African-American Heritage Cooking* (1995).

General cookbooks also continued selling well through the decades. In the 1970s and 1980s new editions appeared of *The Better Homes and Garden Cookbook*, *The Joy of Cooking*, *The Fannie Farmer Cookbook*, and *The Pillsbury Cookbook*. The comprehensive *Doubleday Cookbook: Complete Contemporary Cooking* by Jean Anderson and Elaine Hanna began its bid for classic status in 1975.

Although French cuisine remained a popular topic for books, Americans' tastes were expanding with every visit overseas or every meal at burgeoning ethnic restaurants. They turned to cookbooks to duplicate those exciting flavors from overseas. The enticing series *Foods of the World* from Time-Life Books in the late 1960s and early 1970s quickly became collectibles.

Diana Kennedy shared her extensive knowledge of Mexican food in *The Cuisines of Mexico* (1972). It was considered to be the ultimate reference to the country's ingredients and classic dishes. Later, the Chicago chef Rick Bayless and his wife, Deann Groen Bayless, continued the mission with *Authentic Mexican: Regional Cooking from the Heart of Mexico* (1987).

Couscous and Other Good Food from Morocco (1973) was Paula Wolfert's first book, and it opened America's eyes to the exotic dips, stews, and desserts of that North African country. Wolfert continued her explorations of Mediterranean cooking into the 1990s with books about southwestern France and the eastern Mediterranean.

In the same fashion, the cooking teachers Marcella Hazan and Giuliano Bugialli introduced Americans to the joys of Italian food. Hazan wrote *The Classic Italian Cook Book: The Art of Italian Cooking and the Italian Art of Eating* (1973), followed by *More Classic Italian Cooking* (1978). Bugialli wrote a series of excellent, historically authentic cookbooks: *Giuliano Bugialli's Classic Techniques of Italian Cooking* (1982) and *Giuliano Bugialli's Foods of Italy* (1984). Carol Field and Lynne Rossetto Kasper followed in Hazan's and Bugialli's paths, writing excellent books in the 1980s and 1990s that captured the Italian style.

More Americans began traveling to Asia in the 1980s and 1990s, bringing back a taste for Pacific Rim foods. Notable books helped fuel their interest, including Elizabeth Andoh's *An Ocean of Flavor: The Japanese Way with Fish and Seafood* (1988) and Nicole Routhier's *The Foods of Vietnam* (1989). The impressive *Hot, Sour, Salty, Sweet: A Culinary Journey through Southeast Asia* (2000) had a winning formula of travel, research, and photography from authors Jeffrey Alford and Naomi Duguid.

The boom times of the last quarter of the twentieth century also allowed consumers to leave their kitchens. Moving from one glitzy restaurant to the next, the so-called foodies created a new celebrity: the chef. Restaurateurs and chefs marketed themselves as never before—with cookbooks and television shows. One of the first impressive efforts was *Jean-Louis, Cooking with the Seasons* (1989) by Fred J. Maroon with recipes by Jean-Louis Palladin. Many others have followed, and the trend continues.

While a fascination with cooking and chefs continued, a new generation of noncooks came of age in the 1980s. Food professionals began writing books to help the new generation get a grip on entertaining and basic cooking. One of the most popular books of the 1980s was *The Silver Palate Cookbook* (1982), written by Julee Rosso and Sheila Lukins with Michael McLaughlin. More than 2.5 million copies of their first book are in print.

The mid-1990s also saw a number of retro-revival cookbooks, as publishers updated some of their old titles to appeal to younger cooks. *The Boston Cooking-School Cook Book*, first written in 1896 by Fannie Farmer, was revised almost one hundred years later by Marion Cunningham as *The Fannie Farmer Cookbook* (1990). The still popular *Joy of Cooking* went through a massive update, in which the original work by Irma Rombauer and Marion Rombauer Becker was rewritten by food professionals around the country.

In the late 1990s and early 2000s, hundreds of books touted quick cooking as an answer to the increasing time demands of families. At the same time, Americans yearned for comfort dishes of the past. Books like *Recipes from Home* (2001) by David Page and Barbara Shinn and *Back to the Table: The Reunion of Food and Family* (2001) by Art Smith helped satisfy our nostalgia.

Nothing, though, is more comforting than baked goods. Books on chocolate, cakes, pies, and artisan breads arrived—all answered the growing obsession for home-baked goods. *In the Sweet Kitchen: The Definitive Baker's Companion* (2001) by Regan Daley was one award-winning book that took bakers by the hand with its extensive directions.

From sweet to savory, cookbooks continue to reflect the changing American culture. And despite the growth of recipes online in the 2000s, cookbooks remain popular. For cooking enthusiasts, it seems, following a printout can not compare to that battered, but coveted, cookbook ready to hand down to the next generation.

[**See also** BARBECUE; BAYLESS, RICK; BEARD, JAMES; CAJUN AND CREOLE FOOD; CELEBRITY CHEFS; CHILD, JULIA; CLAIBORNE, CRAIG; COOKBOOKS AND MANUSCRIPTS: FROM WORLD WAR II TO THE 1960S; FARMERS' MARKETS; FRENCH INFLUENCES ON AMERICAN FOOD; FUSION FOOD; HEALTH FOOD; NOUVELLE CUISINE; SLOW FOOD U.S.A.;

Frontispiece to the Mary Frances Cook Book by Jane Allen Boyer (Philadelphia, 1912), a publication meant for children.

SOUTHERN REGIONAL COOKERY; STEWART, MARTHA; TROTTER, CHARLIE.]

BIBLIOGRAPHY

Barile, Mary. *Cookbooks Worth Collecting*. Radnor, PA: Wallace-Homestead, 1994.

Haber, Barbara. *From Hardtack to Home Fries: An Uncommon History of American Cooks and Meals*. New York: Free Press, 2002.

Lovegren, Sylvia. *Fashionable Food: Seven Decades of Food Fads*. New York: Macmillan, 1995.

Theophano, Janet. *Eat My Words: Reading Women's Lives through the Cookbooks They Wrote*. New York: Palgrave, 2002.

CAROL MIGHTON HADDIX

Cookie Cutters

After cookie dough is rolled out, cookie cutters sometimes are used to shape the dough before baking. At their simplest, cookies cutters are round and indistinguishable from biscuit cutters. At their fanciest, they cut an outline and impress a design on the top, for example, leaf-shaped cutters with veins. Pieced tin cutters, which, according to folklore were fashioned from scraps by traveling tinkers, have been made since the 1840s; they may have been made earlier in Pennsylvania by European immigrants with a cookie-shaping heritage. The first U.S. patent for a cake cutter (cookies were called "cakes" in the 1800s) was issued in 1857. Early cookie cutters usually were made of tin, or occasionally of wrought iron or copper. They were one-of-a-kind creations until about 1870, when mass-produced sets were made in the United States or imported, particularly from Germany. Housewives often kept a dozen or more strung on a cord, ready for use.

Tin cutters may have flat backs to strengthen the thin bent outline, with airholes to easily release the dough. Simple outlines may be braced only with strips of tin. Backed or backless cutters may have strap handles. By the 1880s rolling cutters, which cut several designs with one turn, were made. Stamped aluminum cutters came next. The first plastic cookie cutters were made in the 1940s and had the same features as tin ones: a strap handle, bracing, airholes, and even the interior shallow impression lines.

The shapes of cookie cutters have long reflected changing popular culture—people, flowers, everyday objects, animals, holiday characters such as Belsnickel (an early German version of Santa Claus), geometrics, playing card suits, and patriotic symbols. In the twentieth century, a multitude of commercial figures based on cartoons came out. The huge variety of available cookie cutters has encouraged housewives to buy new sets and singles. [**See also** BISCUIT CUTTERS; COOKIES.]

BIBLIOGRAPHY

Franklin, Linda Campbell. *300 Years of Kitchen Collectibles*. 5th ed. Iola, WI: Krause Publications, 2003.

Lasansky, Jeannette. *To Cut, Piece, and Solder: The Work of the Rural Pennsylvania Tinsmith, 1778–1908*. Lewisburg, PA: Union County Oral Traditions Project, 1982.

Wetherill, Phyllis Steiss. *Cookie Cutters and Cookie Molds: Art in the Kitchen*. Exton, PA: Schiffer, 1985.

LINDA CAMPBELL FRANKLIN

Cookies

Cookies are a favorite American sweet, made from a dough of flour and sugar that contains a relatively high ratio of fat, such as butter, vegetable shortening, or margarine. The dough typically is flavored with various combinations of spices, extracts, chocolate, fruits, and nuts and is baked in the form of small, thin cakes.

Origin and Evolution of American Cookies

The macaroon is one of the earliest of cookies still known in modern times. It probably originated in Italy. From there the macaroon spread to France and Holland and crossed the channel to England. Early English and Dutch immigrants first introduced the cookie to America in the 1600s. While the English primarily referred to cookies as small cakes, sweet biscuits, or tea cakes, or by specific names, the Dutch called them *koekjes*, a diminutive of *koek* (cake). Etymologists note that by the early 1700s, "koekje" had been Anglicized into "cookie" or "cookey," and the word clearly had become part of the American vernacular. Amelia Simmons's *American Cookery* (1796), the first American cookbook, gave two recipes for "Cookies."

America's First Homemade Cookies

In early America, cookies were made in home kitchens and were considered special treats because of the high cost of sweeteners. The most popular of these early cookies were jumbles, a spiced butter cookie, and macaroons, based on beaten egg whites and almonds. *Apeas*, a rolled cutout cookie made with caraway seeds, sometimes called "seed cakes," were also popular.

Because gingerbread was relatively inexpensive and easy to make, it was one of the most popular early cookies and remained so in subsequent centuries. In cookie form it is often called "hard" gingerbread to distinguish it from the softer cake version. Gingersnaps are a variation of molasses-flavored gingerbread, and they likely got their name because of their crispy texture and tops that crinkle when baked. The Quaker Oats Company is credited with popularizing the oatmeal cookie by including various recipes on oatmeal packages over the years. Later additions to the basic recipe include raisins, nuts, and chocolate chips.

America's repertoire of cookie recipes grew, and one new cookie included peanut butter. Ruth Wakefield's *Toll House Tried and True Recipes* (1937) calls for rolling peanut butter–flavored dough into nut-sized balls and pressing them with a fork in crisscross fashion. Baking chocolate was melted before its incorporation into cookie dough until the 1930s, when Wakefield, the owner of the Toll House Inn in Whitman, Massachusetts, created the "Toll House Chocolate Crunch Cookie," which later became known as the chocolate chip cookie. When sales of semisweet chocolate soared in New England, Nestlé investigated, and in 1939 the company introduced semisweet chocolate morsels and signed a contract with Wakefield allowing the company to print her recipe on every package. The chocolate chip continues its reign as America's favorite homemade cookie.

Commercialization of the Cookie

Sugar prices steadily declined during the nineteenth century, and by the 1880s, sugar was an affordable commodity. By the turn of the century sugar was a dominant ingredient in American cooking, most notably in sweets such as cookies. The increasing popularity of cookies, accompanied by affordable sugar and new technologies, caught the attention of manufacturers, who began mass production of many of America's most popular cookies around the turn of the twentieth century. The Fig Newton, a soft cookie filled with fig jam, was one of the first commercially baked products in America. The Kennedy Biscuit Company of Massachusetts began manufacturing Fig Newtons in 1891. The company commonly named its products after towns in the Boston area, and the new fig cookie was named for the community of Newton.

During the late 1800s cookies shaped like animals were imported from England, and it was not long before small American bakeries began to imitate the product, which they called "circus crackers" or "animals." In 1898 several of those regional bakeries merged to form the National Biscuit Company (later Nabisco). In 1902 the company renamed the cookies "Barnum's Animals," and because packaging was key to successful national marketing, the product was released for the Christmas holidays in a box designed as a circus wagon complete with a string for hanging on the tree. Animal Crackers, as they later became known, still are sold in the famous box.

In 1912 the National Biscuit Company introduced two other cookies: the Lorna Doone, which was probably named after the Scottish heroine of the 1869 novel of the same name, and the "Oreo Biscuit," consisting of two rounds of chocolate sandwiched together with a rich cream filling. Oreos were created in response to the Hydrox cookie, which was launched in 1910 by Sunshine Biscuits. Backed by superior marketing and distribution, and a name that was more felicitous, Nabisco's Oreos became the leader of the chocolate sandwich cookie category and the largest-selling cookie in the world. According to Nabisco, more than 450 billion have been produced for worldwide consumption since the cookie's introduction in 1912.

Commercial Cookie Production Diversifies

Manufacturers eventually added cookie mixes to their product lines. After World War II General Mills introduced its "GingerCake and Cooky Mix." In 1953 Pillsbury introduced its "Chocolate Chip Cookie Mix." In 1957 Pillsbury introduced its refrigerated cookie dough, called "Ice Box Cookies," in three flavors: butterscotch nut, crunchy peanut, and coconut. Chocolate chip and sugar cookies soon followed, and Americans eventually could choose from a broad range of both refrigerated and frozen cookie dough.

Chocolate chip cookies reigned as the most popular cookie in America, and enterprising cookie bakers moved in to capitalize on it, each claiming to have the ultimate chocolate chip cookie. Wally Amos introduced his Famous Amos version in 1975, followed by Debbi Fields's launch of her first Mrs. Fields Chocolate Chippery cookie boutique in Palo Alto, California, in 1977, a move that led to a nationwide chain of cookie stores.

Thousands of recipes, hundreds of cookie cookbooks, and dozens of commercially baked cookies attest to the continued popularity of this sweet, all-American snack. Billions of cookies, both home- and commercially made, are consumed annually by more than 95 percent of American households. The cookie is honored every October, which is designated as National Cookie Month. [**See also** CHOCOLATE; DESSERTS; DUTCH INFLUENCES ON AMERICAN FOOD; NABISCO; SUGAR.]

BIBLIOGRAPHY

Brenner, Leslie. *American Appetite: The Coming of Age of a Cuisine*. New York: Bard, 1999.

Weaver, William Woys. *The Christmas Cook: Three Centuries of American Yuletide Sweets*. New York: HarperPerennial, 1990.

BECKY MERCURI

Cooking Containers

The technology of working basic materials changed little during the eighteenth and early nineteenth centuries, despite strong stylistic changes. Objects were made by individual craftsmen with the same kinds of hand tools their great-great-grandfathers had used. Production revolved around hand methods and hand power. Although local craftsmen often made pieces to order for local customers, larger workshops employed many highly skilled workmen capable of tremendous speed and precision developed through constant repetition.

Equipment for the hearth is made out of various materials, which are chosen for a variety of characteristics; among these might be cost, availability, performance, desirability, and fashion. Raw materials may be divided into three categories: metals, clays, and organics (animal components and wood).

Metal Containers

The most common metal used in cooking was wrought iron. Its advantages are high strength, low cost, toughness, and abundance. It also has the highest melting point of the common metals. Unfortunately, it is only a moderate heat conductor, will not heat evenly enough for dry cooking or sauces, and runs the risk of scorching. Thin pans can heat very quickly and are good for frying or warming liquids. Iron is excellent for andirons, fire tongs, trivets, grills, forks, and spoons. It has no dangerous effect on food, although leaving an iron spoon in acidic foods for extended time can alter flavor. Iron will readily oxidize (rust) if left in wet conditions.

Cast iron, or pig iron, is composed of iron with 2 percent to 4 percent carbon added. This was the cheapest metal available in the eighteenth century; its greatest drawback was its extreme brittleness. Cast iron is the slowest heat conductor of all the common metals. The pieces commonly made from cast iron are pots, griddles, firebacks, stoveplates, Dutch ovens, teapots, and occasionally andirons. Because cast iron is somewhat porous, it will gradually absorb oil and grease until eventually it develops a smooth, nonstick, durable surface.

Steel is composed of iron and less than 1 percent carbon. It can be hardened dramatically and this gives it excellent edge-holding ability and stiffness. The main drawback of steel was its high cost, so the amount used was limited in each piece. Usually a small amount of steel was welded to the end of an iron tool, giving the advantages of both the economy of iron and the hardness of steel. Cleavers are a good example, as most of the tool could be iron as long as the edge was steel. It was also used in common table cutlery.

Tin is lightweight and easy to work with. As tin melts at approximately 450°F, tinware is actually composed of wrought iron sheets with a thin coating of tin on the surface. Tin was well suited to vessels and containers, such as washpans, storage canisters, teapots, inexpensive saucepans, drinking cups, funnels, and molds. It was also used for reflector ovens, though some care was needed to avoid melting the solder. In addition, tin was often chosen for field use, both military and civilian.

Pewter is a relatively soft metal, composed mostly of tin. Pewter was a popular choice for plates, tankards, teapots, spoons, and other common eating utensils. Its low melting point and softness make it unfit for cooking utensils. Copper is strong and easy to forge. It is one of the fastest heat conductors, making it ideal for saucepans, water boilers, and teapots. However, its relatively high cost limited extensive use to more prosperous kitchens. One serious drawback to using copper is the toxic nature of copper oxide. To avoid health risk, vessels are usually coated inside with tin.

"Brass" was the name given to a range of copper-based metal alloys. These alloys are good heat conductors and are well suited for use in saucepans, skillets, and posnets. Forged brass sheeting is used for lighter vessels, such as teapots, kettles, and small utensils like ladles, graters, and tinderboxes.

Cookware. Redware, so called because of the natural red-brown color of the clay it was made from, was the lowest-fired pottery and the most porous. It was sealed with glazes that required lead, a health hazard. It had the distinct advantage of easy cleaning, and its even heat transmission reduced thermal-shock breakage caused by uneven expansion. Once heated through, it sustained fairly high cooking heats. It performed well in stew pots, small three-legged frying pans, posnets and pipkins (small saucepans), cups and dishware, storage containers, bowls, churns, pie plates, pitchers, and decorative molds. In the early 1800s, lead-glazed, molded yellowware began to replace redware.

Stoneware, made of an expensive high-fired clay, was dense, durable, and lead-free, but it was a poor conductor of heat. More likely to crack when heated, it was suitable for storage jugs and drinking steins. Although its American manufacture dated from the 1630s, its great popularity began in the mid-nineteenth century.

In the twenty-first century, ceramic cookware is increasingly available as commercial and hand-crafted casseroles, stove-top teapots, and small skillets, strengthened against thermal shock by the addition of perlite (grit) or lithium.

Dinnerware. The wealthiest households of the eighteenth century sought more colorful, decorative, and delicate styling. European, and then American, potteries produced low-fired majolica, faience, and creamware. Among the favorites were Chinese porcelains and Dutch Delft. English Wedgwood and Staffordshire were available in different qualities at different prices. Nineteenth-century industrialization introduced mechanized

Advertisement for Lalance and Grosjean Agate Nickel-Steel Ware, circa 1903.

methods which increased the production of high-fired porcelain and whiter dinnerware. In the early 1900s, reoccurring movements that attempted alternately to embrace technological innovation or to celebrate nostalgia, or even to synthesize both, brought a new kind of ceramics to the dining table. Influenced by the early Bauhaus movement and its explorations of modernistic shape and glaze, ceramics appeared as hand-constructed bowls and platters. Succeeding styles evolved into art nouveau, art deco, and, after World War II, a domestic artist-craftsperson movement. Since the 1960s, there has been a focus on natural materials and ethnic handcrafts, produced as casseroles, serving bowls, platters, mugs, pitchers, and tea sets.

Wood

Early kitchens were furnished with a wide range of hand-fashioned wooden utensils. The most common included implements, bowls, containers, tools, baskets, tubs, cabinetry (food safes, dressers), or common tableware. Cutting boards and wooden spoons continue to be produced; however, in the late twentieth century such synthetic materials as plastics became common. Most exotic woods were being reserved for serving platters and bowls.

Glass

Glass-blowing developed commercially in eighteenth-century New Jersey, where good-quality silica sand abounded. Limited by fragility and little heat tolerance, glass was used for wine and spirits bottles, carafes, pitchers, drinking tumblers, stemware, punch bowls and cups, decorative serving pieces, and jelly glasses. Home canning jars (the first were produced by Mason in 1858) and inexpensive glassware were introduced by the 1860s.

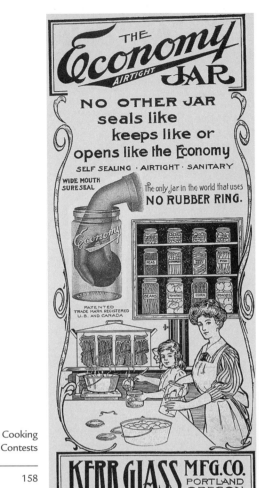

Kerr Glass Manufacturing Company advertisement, 1910.

Heat-tolerant Pyrex (1915) was used for bakeware and mixing bowls, followed mid-century by Anchor Hocking and Fire King ovenware. [**See also** APPLE-PREPARATION TOOLS; BEER BARRELS; BISCUIT-MAKING TOOLS; BREAD-MAKING TOOLS; BUTTER-MAKING TOOLS AND CHURNS; CABBAGE CUTTERS AND PLANERS; CHEESE-MAKING TOOLS; CHERRY PITTERS OR STONERS; CHOPPING KNIVES AND FOOD CHOPPERS; CONTAINERS; CORN-PREPARATION TOOLS; DOUGHNUT-MAKING TOOLS; DUTCH OVENS; EGG-PREPARATION TOOLS; FRYING PANS, SKILLETS, AND SPIDERS; KETTLES; MASON JARS; PANCAKE PANS; PIE-MAKING TOOLS; POTATO-COOKING TOOLS; POTS AND PANS; SIEVES, SIFTERS, AND CULANDERS; SILVERWARE; WAFFLE, WAFER, AND PIZELLE IRONS; WINE BARRELS.]

BIBLIOGRAPHY

Barons, Richard, and Devere Card. *The American Hearth*. Binghamton, NY: Broome County Historical Society, 1976.

Cullity, Brian. *Slipped and Glazed: Regional American Redware*. Sandwich, MA: Heritage Plantation of Sandwich Museum, 1991.

DeVoe, Shirley Spaulding. *The Art of the Tinsmith*. Exton, PA: Schiffer, 1981.

Fennimore, Donald L. *Metalwork in Early America*. Wilmington, DE: Henry Francis DuPont Winterthur Museum, 1996.

Ketchum, William C., Jr. *American Stoneware*. New York: Holt, 1991.

Neumann, George. *Early American Antique Country Furnishings*. New York: McGraw Hill, 1984.

PETER ROSS

Cooking Contests

Cooking contests are an American pastime, annually attracting thousands of participants. The culinary equivalent of sporting events, they fall into three categories: those held as part of fairs and festivals; those sponsored by food manufacturers as promotional events, such as the Pillsbury Bake-off Contest; and those that celebrate distinctive, all-American foods. Many cooking contests feature monetary prizes, while others benefit charity. The most famous American cook-offs include several state fair and food festival cooking competitions and major-league events like the Pillsbury Bake-off Contest and barbecue and chili competitions.

Cooking Competitions at State Fairs and Food Festivals

America's agricultural fairs, established in the early 1800s, sponsored America's oldest cookery competitions, based on home canning and preserving, showcasing vital skills for housewives of the time. Baking contests, featuring breads and pies, were added, and the winners received ribbons in recognition of their prowess in the kitchen. As fairs spread throughout the country on both a county- and statewide basis, cooking exhibits and contests also proliferated.

Nearly two centuries after the establishment of agricultural fairs, Americans still compete in fair cooking contests. From the New York State Fair's pie competition to the pickling and preserves contest at the California State Fair, the domestic arts are celebrated. Various new categories, such as Tex-Mex and heart-healthy cooking, have been added along with divisions for various age groups. Major food manufacturers sponsor many of the contests, and cash prizes often are awarded in addition to ribbons. Many of the fair organizations periodically publish cookbooks featuring winning recipes.

Food festivals, held in ever-increasing numbers throughout the United States, typically pay tribute to a regional crop, a food product, or even a special ethnic dish. Many of America's food festivals originated around the turn of the twentieth century, with hundreds having been added over the years. They often feature cooking contests that showcase special foods or ingredients.

At the Wild Blueberry Festival in Machias, Maine, the state's Wild Blueberry Commission sponsors a cooking contest for the best overall entry in a wide variety of categories featuring Maine's favorite berry. Oysters take center stage at the National Oyster Cook-off, held as part of the St. Mary's County Oyster Festival in Leonardtown, Maryland. The innovative use of cornmeal, a southern staple, is rewarded with handsome cash prizes at the National Cornbread Festival and World Championship Cornbread Cook-off in South Pittsburg, Tennessee. America's heartland features the country's favorite dessert at Pie Day in Braham, Minnesota, where flaky-crusted pies are entered in a contest designed to ensure that pie making does not become a lost art. In Gilroy, California, the annual Garlic Festival includes the Great Garlic Cook-off, one of America's most famous festival cooking contests.

Pillsbury Bake-off Contest

The Pillsbury Bake-off Contest, the premier manufacturer-sponsored cooking contest in America, was first held in 1949. Known initially as the Grand National Recipe and Baking Contest, it was held annually (except for 1965) until 1976 and then subsequently every two years. Selected recipes are tested, and one hundred finalists are chosen to prepare their recipes for judging by a panel of food experts. The grand prizewinner receives $1 million.

In 1999 Pillsbury created the Bake-off Hall of Fame, a collection of the most popular winning recipes, such as "Dilly Casserole Bread," "French Silk Chocolate Pie," "Peanut Blossom Cookies," and "Tunnel of Fudge Cake." Pillsbury donated the collection, which includes contest materials and memorabilia, to the Smithsonian Institution's National Museum of American History.

Competition Barbecue

Barbecue aficionados engage in formal barbecue cook-offs, which have grown from a few dozen in the mid-1980s to more than five hundred annual events attended by some five million people. The pinnacle of serious all-American barbecue is represented by three major competitive events known as MiM, the Royal, and the Jack.

The World Championship Barbecue Cooking Contest, held in Memphis, Tennessee, as part of a month-long celebration known as Memphis in May (MiM) is the largest annual pork barbecue competition in the world, with more than thirty-nine tons of pork served each year.

Since 1980 the American Royal Barbecue has been held as part of the annual American Royal Livestock, Horse Show, and Rodeo in Kansas City, Missouri. The Royal is officially sanctioned by the Kansas City Barbecue Society (KCBS), which established the de facto standard judging rules for barbecue cook-offs. Barbecue categories include brisket, pork ribs, chicken, and pork shoulder or Boston butt.

The tiny town of Lynchburg, Tennessee, is home to the Jack Daniel Distillery and the Jack Daniel's World Championship Invitational Barbecue. A comparative cook-off newcomer, the Jack began in 1988, but it quickly established itself as a serious barbecue event. To win the Jack's championship title, teams are required to demonstrate expertise in four of the following categories: whole hog, pork ribs, pork shoulder, chicken, and beef brisket.

Chili Wars

American chili cooking competition is as heated and volatile as the debate surrounding the origin of chili and what constitutes a proper "bowl of red." Such debates sparked the first chili cook-off, which was held in 1967 in the abandoned mining town of Terlingua, Texas. Over the years, the original organization that sponsored Terlingua split into three separate camps, resulting in the three major chili championships.

The Terlingua International Chili Championship is staged annually during the first weekend in November at Rancho CASI de los Chisos. It is sponsored by the Chili Appreciation Society International (CASI), an organization formed after the first Terlingua cook-off in 1967. Terlingua hosts a second cook-off that also is held the first weekend of November: the Original Terlingua International Frank X. Tolbert–Wick Fowler Memorial Championship Chili Cookoff, which takes place four miles away from CASI's cook-off. The event is named for two of CASI's original founders, who split off to form their own organization in 1983. "The Cookoff," as it is commonly known, celebrates authentic Texas chili. The International Chili Society (ICS) cook-off is held annually during the first weekend of October, and entrants compete in divisions for traditional red chili and *chile verde*.

America's interest in cook-offs continues to grow. Whatever the reason, the cook-off is a uniquely American institution that has become deeply ingrained in our social culture and foodways.

[**See also** BARBECUE; CHILI; FOOD FESTIVALS; PILLSBURY BAKE-OFF.]

BIBLIOGRAPHY
Mercuri, Becky. *Food Festival, U.S.A.: Red, White, and Blue Ribbon Recipes from All 50 States*. San Diego, CA: Laurel Glen, 2002.
Pillsbury Bake-off. http://www.bakeoff.com.

BECKY MERCURI

Cooking Equipment, Social Aspects of

It is impossible to separate the materials of cookery and dining from the cultures that produced them. The constructs of regional and cultural world views, value systems, environmental, social, cultural, and physical aspects of the things with which we surround ourselves are clues, but they must be seen as a whole. For the sake of this discussion, they will be examined one by one.

Worldview

The prevailing philosophies of a society determine the significance of its material objects. Among many American colonists, materialism was a high priority, and ownership of more objects of good quality was an important goal. Unfettered desire for wealth existed early among southern English planters growing tobacco, corn, and rice, the Spanish of the Southwest growing Mexico-derived corn, beans, and tomatoes, the Dutch in the Northeast with their homeland cuisine, and the French throughout the Mississippi River Valley with their love of cream and wine, to name a few.

Culture dictated choice of objects. For example, English American colonists traditionally rejected the "excessive" richness and the sensuality of French foods and their *accoutrements*, while Thomas Jefferson, influenced by his experience in France, trained his chef in French cookery.

Religion was a factor. The eighteenth-century Amish ate simply, believing that life should be conducted in surroundings that permitted full attention to their relationship to God. Other groups who emigrated for religious regions came with different beliefs about eating: they included English Puritans and Quakers (and later Shakers), German and French Huguenots (who ate well), and French Jesuits (who followed the Catholic fast-feast day calendar).

Nationality counted, too. The faith of Dutch Calvinists supported frugal daily meals, but their feasts revolved around excessive dining. Although they took pride in displays of gleaming copper and brass (and porcelains in later periods), their kitchens were often modest and their cooking artless. Shakers were unencumbered by such dualities. They were eminently practical, and limited themselves to few possessions.

However, their communal kitchens were well stocked with modern (for the time) technologies, often of their own invention. Concerned with communalism and efficiency, their equipment accomplished quantity cookery without unnecessary work, in such pieces as "arch kettles" (built-in stew pots of different sizes) or "griddle stoves" (griddles installed permanently over their own enclosed fireboxes). They were famous for their design and craftsmanship in cheese and spice boxes.

Economics

A family's economic place within a community may be analyzed by its possessions and judged by its estate inventories, a mandatory listing of possessions after the death of the head of the family. These suggest that a hearth qualified as a kitchen cooking fireplace when it contained a cast-iron cauldron (a three legged bulbous pot with a swinging bail handle), a fry pan, and a cast-iron water kettle (mistakenly called a tea-kettle). The more average families might then have a

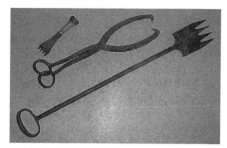

Ice tongs and two chippers: nineteenth-century tools used for handling ice at home.

tin reflecting oven and a Dutch oven or two, a grid-iron (grill), an iron griddle, and lots of tin and ceramic cookware and dishware. The upper class added to these a salamander (a footed, thick plate of iron at the end of long handle, heated glowing red and passed over the food to toast or broil it), and a clock jack (a large wind-up tool that turned the meat on a spit, placed before the fire and over a dripping pan). Its dinnerware was more likely pewter, mixed with colorful import China basins, platters, and tea sets, Stratfordshire pasteware, and Delftware.

Geography, Ethnicity, and Folk Art

Rural and urban wealth took different forms. Farming required that one's wealth was tied up in land, buildings, equipment, stock, and so on, limiting cash flow, and was not always available for kitchen improvements. City dwellers generally worked for cash, and budgeted expenditures accordingly with an eye to fashion and efficiency.

Geographically, natural assets (such as rivers) provided transportation for objects to be bought and sold, and river-bottom land, being more fertile, produced more lucratively. On the ever-changing frontier, a few manufactured goods were supplemented by large numbers of handmade kitchen and farming tools. With nineteenth-century industrialization and rapid growth, city dwellers were earlier to acquire new technological advances, among them the cookstove, refrigerators, canning supplies, and gadgetry, and were more sensitive to changing kitchen and dining room styles.

Geographical location was often associated with ethnic settlements in which food-related objects were shaped or decorated distinctively. For example, Pennsylvania Dutch redware was often decorated with hearts, birds, and flowers, whereas the English of New York, New Jersey, and Connecticut preferred waved line patterns; Carolinian African Americans used disk-shaped, flat rice fanners, different from New England winnowers with handles and uneven rims. These distinctions began to blur by the 1750s, when English imports of the products of its Industrial Revolution began to replace local forms.

Comparison of Estate Inventories

LOWER AND UPPER CLASS KITCHEN AND DINING ROOM OBJECTS

Gavin Pludge, Hempstead, NY, 1735

	Pounds	Shillings
to pewter brass tin earthen and knifes & forks	08	03
To 5 Iron Pt & kettle two trammils & other Iron things	02	18
1 case of bottles and other glass things	01	10

Mordacay Gomez, New York City, 1750

		ounces
1 Large Silver Tankard		44 ½
1 Ditto		30 ½
1 Ditto		242 ⅛
1 Large silver Cup & Cover		358 ⅞
1 Large Coffe Pott & handle		25
1 Silver Tea Pott & handle		11 ½
1 Silver Mugg		9
1 Silver ?		49 ¾
1 Large Silver Salver		29
2 Salters		
1 Porringer		
1 Spice Box		
1 Milk Pott		
1 Sugar		
1 Small Tea & . . .		
2 Tea spoons & Shovel	[the group]	32 oz ¼
11 Large Spoon		
3 Tea Spoons		
1 Salt Shovel	[the group]	22 oz ½
1 Table Silver spoon		
1 Punch strainer		
1 Punch ladle & wood handle		
1 Supe spoon large		
1 Silver chafingdish & handle	[the group]	41 oz ⅜

1 paire bellows
1 Doz Pewter Plates
1 Brass Toggin Iron
12 New Knives
12 New forks
2 Iron Pott hooks
3 Tea Kittles

2 fry pans
2 Grid Iron
2 frying pans
1 Brass Morter & Pestle
1 Wooden ditto
1 Little brass sauce pan
1 Old brass Skiullet
1 Chaffin Dish
1 Copper . . . pot
1 ? chocolate ditto
1 Old Tin Coffee pott
6 Pewter Dishes old, large & small
24 Plates
4 Iron Potts
1 Brass Ladle
Two Brass ? of the Potts
4 Brass Kittles large & small
1 Iron Chopping knife
2 tinned pooding pans
3 Old Iron potts
3 Pewter porringers
2 Funnels
1 Small brass pepper boc
35 knives
25 forks
1 Pewter bason
1 Large China Pott. broaken
21 China plates, broken & whole
16 Chocolate Cups, ditto
25 Tea Cupps
27 Sawcers
1 China sugar box
1 Tea Pott broek d

Courtesy of the Gomez Mill House Museum, Newburgh, New York

History and Fashion

Fashion and its timing are closely tied to economics. Usually, fashion was made by the upper classes and worked its way down, and only occasionally moved the other way.

Timing was often of the essence. For example, the replacement of the urban hearth with a cookstove in the 1830s suggested a family on the cutting edge, whereas the same replacement some forty years later had entirely different connotations. Nineteenth-century gentry, desiring to differentiate itself from lower levels of society, adopted *service á la Russe*. Replacing the earlier glorified seated buffet, it embraced the series of courses that required endless chinaware, goblets, silver-ware, and specialized serving pieces. With the advent of national catalog shopping such as Sears, Roebuck (turn of the twentieth century), matched sets became available to the middle class, along with simple gas and electric appliances, chafing dishes (1920–1950), fondue pots (1960s and 1970s), and powerful mixers (1980s). Dishwashers and microwave ovens have been elevated to necessity status. As the twenty-first century opened, kitchens furnished with the state-of-the-art appliances and cabinetry had become the ideal.

[**See also** CHAFING DISH; FONDUE POT; FOOD PROCESSORS; GLASSWARE; ICEBOXES; MICROWAVE OVENS; PLATES; REFRIGERATORS; SILVERWARE; STOVES AND OVENS.]

BIBLIOGRAPHY

Belden, Louise Conway. *The Festive Tradition: Table Decoration and Desserts in America 1650–1900.* New York: Norton, 1983.

Franklin, Linda Campbell. *Three Hundred Years of Kitchen Collectibles,* 5th ed. Iola, WI: Krause, 2003.

Schlereth, Thomas J. *Material Culture Studies in America.* Nashville, TN: American Association for State and Local History, 1982.

ALICE ROSS

Cooking Manuscripts

Every person who cooks has a manuscript cookbook. It may not be a tidy copybook written in a fine Spenserian hand, as so many early American manuscripts were. Scribbles and indecipherable notes may decorate the pages. It could be a file folder stuffed full of clippings and handwritten recipes from friends. Or, in the early 2000s, the computer may be the family cookbook. Whatever the system, a cookbook is highly personal, revealing much of the cook's taste, family preferences, and skills, and it frequently opens a window on the life of the author.

In early America, female literacy was not a priority, so few written records by women are extant. But those books that survive, each one unique, say a great deal about the life of American women from the seventeenth century through the twenty-first.

Handwritten Cookbooks

Many British women emigrating to the New World brought along perhaps their most precious possession, a personal cookbook, often a wedding gift, almost certainly passed down through the family, with recipes frequently written in more than one hand. Some surviving manuscripts contain an interesting combination of English and American recipes that often require detective work in order to discover the provenance. Some eighteenth-century manuscripts at first glance appear to be English, but recipes for American ingredients, such as Indian meal and cranberries, give away their true origins.

Frequently the recipes share space with other enterprises, such as an account book of either household expenditures or a family business. Polly Lathrop, who lived in Saybrook and Norwich, Connecticut, from 1779 until 1817, kept meticulous accounts of her boardinghouse roomers ("Mr. Ezra L. Hommedieu came to bord [sic] October 10, 1804), as well as her income as a seamstress

("Maid [sic] a gingham frock for Mary 47 cents"). Hattie A. Sachs, the recording secretary of the National American Woman Suffrage Association, kept detailed minutes of the proceedings at the group's annual convention in Akron, Ohio, but only half of her notebook contains association business. On the back of almost every page are menus for elaborate dinners and more modest luncheons, along with many recipes, including sweet-and-sour fish, horseradish sauce, and maple parfaits.

Common Characteristics

Although each cookbook is an individual record of some aspects of a woman's life, many have characteristics in common. The manuscript is often anonymous: no date, no name, no town, simply a collection of kitchen wisdom compiled by a woman whose major priority was taking care of her family. These books have been well used, pages stained, brown with age and spilled food, some frayed at the edges. In the center of a worn copybook a child has scribbled a mysterious drawing. A neatly bound nineteenth-century volume includes a calendar from a farmer's almanac pasted inside the front cover. Handwritten comments are attached to some recipes: "Very nice," "Tried and didn't like it," "Add more milk."

These books reveal what was important to the housewife and her family. The vast majority of manuscripts, at least until the early 1900s, include medical information. Women, especially on the frontier, were often without benefit of what medical help existed at the time. It is no wonder that they collected numerous and often bizarre prescriptions for ailments ranging from mad dog bites to cures for cancer; new treatments for cholera and scarlet fever clipped from newspapers; and handwritten notations on cures for whooping cough, rattlesnake bites, indigestion, consumption, nausea, and a host of other ailments. Appended to some is the brave declaration, "Never fails." Likewise, household hints abound: how to clean kid gloves, mend a black satin dress, make a yellow dye, de-flea a pig, remove wine stains from a carpet, make liquid shoe blacking, mend broken china, bleach bed linens, banish bedbugs.

Because many women in the early days of the Republic were educated poorly, if at all, words were often spelled phonetically. Thus it is not uncommon to find "plumb pudding," "warfels," "cramburys," "linnen," "blomong (blanc mange)" and "flat-jacks."

Until the mid-twentieth century, directions are skimpy, if given at all, and measurements are far from accurate, usually requiring a teacup of this or a handful of that. A list of ingredients for a cake or cookies may omit flour entirely, since the experienced housewife supposedly knew that she must add a sufficient amount of

flour to make a proper batter. Cooking times are rare, and the overwhelming number of recipes in early manuscripts are for sweets—candy, pie and cake, pudding and jelly—with far fewer directions for everyday meat and vegetables.

Tucked between the Pages

Manuscript cookbooks are full of surprises. Many display newspaper clippings pasted in, but not always of recipes. Poems, prayers, household hints, almanacs, and farm information abound, as well as scribbled recipes on torn sheets of note paper tucked into the pages, waiting to be properly entered at another time. Pressed flowers drop out; checks, knitting directions, letters, menus, grocery lists—the accumulation of a housewife's hours. A newspaper clipping of a poem, "To My Brother," tucked into the 1833 Pittsburgh copybook of Mrs. Boggs asks him to think of her in times of trouble, and is pasted beside a newspaper story about the battleship *Sumpter.* A poem, "On the Loss of a Child in Infancy," begins, "Our beauteous child we laid among the silence of the dead."

Sources

Fortunately, culinary historians, such as Karen Hess and Janet Theophano, have recognized the importance of these manuscripts and rescued many from oblivion, editing and publishing them to present a picture of the person and her time. In her edition of *Martha Washington's Booke of Cookery,* Hess not only provides recipes but also digs deeply into genealogical mysteries, giving us a rich picture of the Washington household. Many important manuscripts are available to scholars, housed in special collections in universities and historical societies. Those interested in family cookbooks should search the attic or garage for these tattered journals that were once considered of no value. Now they deserve a second look, as an irretrievable part of America's history.

[**See also** ADVERTISING COOKBOOKLETS AND RECIPES; HOMEMADE REMEDIES; LIBRARY COLLECTIONS.]

BIBLIOGRAPHY

Hess, Karen. *Martha Washington's Booke of Cookery.* New York: Columbia University Press, 1981.

Theophano, Janet. *Eat My Words: Reading Women's Lives through the Cookbooks They Wrote.* New York: Palgrave, 2002.

VIRGINIA K. BARTLETT

Cooking Schools:
Nineteenth Century

Four different types of cooking schools emerged in America during the nineteenth century. The first was an expansion of the pastry lessons offered by experts during the eighteenth century. The shift between private

The British traveler George Augustus Sala commented in the 1880s on the "schools of cookery for young ladies" that were springing up in American cities.

lessons and public courses was made by Elizabeth Goodfellow, who opened a pastry shop in Philadelphia in 1808. She subsequently offered lessons, which turned into formal classes offered to the public, and thus established America's first cooking school. Goodfellow never published a cookbook, but her course of study is known through her students. One of her pupils, Eliza Leslie, collected Goodfellow's recipes and published them as *Seventy-Five Receipts for Pastry, Cakes, and Sweetmeats* (1828). After Goodfellow's death in 1851, the cookbook *Cookery as It Should Be* (1853) was compiled by an unidentified "pupil of Mrs. Goodfellow." Despite Leslie's complaints that many of the book's recipes had not come from Goodfellow, the cookbook went through at least four editions.

Celebrity Chef Cooking Schools

The second type of cooking school was a European import. Its proponent was Pierre Blot, a Frenchman who immigrated to the United States about 1855. Claiming to have been the editor of *Almanac Gastronomique* in

Paris, he lectured on the culinary arts. In 1863 he published his first book, *What to Eat, and How to Cook It; Containing over One Thousand Receipts*. Two years later, he launched a cooking school called the Culinary School of Design and called himself the professor of gastronomy. Blot's second book, *Hand-Book of Practical Cookery*, first was published in 1867, and he followed it up with a series of articles on culinary topics in *Galaxy* magazine, which gave him great visibility. With the financial assistance of Commodore Vanderbilt's daughter, Blot opened the New York Cooking School, which was America's first French cooking school. It mainly catered to the wealthy and lasted only a few years, but the celebrity chef cooking school reemerged during the twentieth century.

Cooking Schools for Working-Class Women

In addition to offering classes for middle-class women who wanted to learn the latest cooking techniques, Juliet Corson also targeted unemployed working-class women,

with the hope that after taking cookery courses they might find employment as domestics. Beginning in 1872, she began lecturing on cooking at charitable institutions in New York City. In November 1876 she launched the city's second New York Cooking School, which offered a series of twelve lessons. Based on her lectures, Corson wrote *The Cooking Manual of Practical Directions for Economical Every-Day Cookery* (1877) and *Cooking School Text Book and Housekeepers' Guide to Cookery and Kitchen Management: An Explanation of the Principles of Domestic Economy Taught in the New York Cooking School* (1879), which became the textbook for subsequent cooking schools. Her establishment was so successful that she received inquiries from many cities around the nation, including Philadelphia and Boston, on how to start and manage cooking schools.

In Philadelphia, the New Century Club invited Matilda Lees Dods, a graduate of the South Kensington Cooking School in London who had taught at the Culinary College in Edinburgh, to lecture on cooking. Her lectures were so successful that the New Century Club decided to open a cooking school. Elizabeth Devereaux agreed to teach courses, and one of her star pupils was Sarah Tyson Rorer. When Devereaux left in 1880 over a contract dispute, Rorer, who was a cousin of the school's founders, replaced her. The course of study consisted of twenty-four demonstration lectures. After three years of running the New Century Cooking School, Rorer left to establish the Philadelphia Cooking School, which flourished from 1882 until 1903. *Mrs. Rorer's Philadelphia Cook Book: A Manual of Home Economics* (1886) largely was based on her courses offered at the school.

Similar events to those in Philadelphia were underway in Boston. In 1878 the Boston Cooking School was launched under the auspices of the Women's Education Association. Maria Parloa was the first teacher. The program consisted of three private lessons and three group lessons each week. Twenty-four lessons constituted a course. One of Parloa's pupils was Mary J. Lincoln. When Parloa resigned from the school to write a book, Lincoln became the principal, a position she retained until 1885. Lincoln's books, the *Boston Cooking-School Cook Book* (1884) and *Boston School Kitchen Text-Book, Lessons in Cooking for the Use of Classes in Public and Industrial Schools* (1887), were used by other cooking schools and were cited extensively by leaders of the home economics movement.

One of Lincoln's students was Fannie Merritt Farmer, who became the assistant principal and later the principal when Lincoln left. Farmer's *Boston Cooking-School Cook Book* (1896), a revision of Lincoln's book, became one of the most popular cookbooks ever published in the United States. Graduates of the Boston Cooking School included

Lucy Allen, Alice Bradley, and Janet McKenzie Hill, who also went on to become successful authors. Many graduates also contributed editorial columns to the *Boston Cooking School Magazine*. Farmer left the school and in 1902 opened Miss Farmer's School of Cookery, which survived her death in 1915 and continued until 1944.

Collegiate Programs and Schools

The final type of cooking school to emerge during the nineteenth century was based at colleges and universities. The interest in cooking schools also influenced college programs. These originally were intended to prepare women for life as homemakers and later were vocationally directed. The first known cookery program at a college was at Iowa Agricultural School at Ames (later Iowa State University); in 1876 the school offered a course in domestic economy, which included cooking. The teacher was Mary B. Welch, who convinced the college administration that the school should offer cookery courses. A kitchen was constructed, and in 1878 Welch began teaching the course using Corson's cookbook as a text. About this time, many other collegiate cooking programs were begun, including ones at Kansas State Agricultural College at Manhattan (later Kansas State University) and the Illinois Industrial University, which started a School of Domestic Science in 1878. Its course of study included dietetics, household science, chemical structure of bread making, and many other topics. Many graduates of these college programs taught in public schools, and many became leaders of the home economics movement in America.

[**See also** BOSTON COOKING SCHOOL; COOKING SCHOOLS: TWENTIETH CENTURY; FARMER, FANNIE; HOME ECONOMICS; LESLIE, ELIZA; LINCOLN, MRS.; PARLOA, MARIA; RORER, SARAH TYSON.]

BIBLIOGRAPHY

Longone, Jan. "Professor Blot and the First French Cooking School in New York." *Gastronomica* (Spring 2001): 65–70 and (Summer 2001): 53–59.

Shapiro, Laura. *Perfection Salad: Women and Cooking at the Turn of the Century*. New York: Holt, 1987.

Weigley, Emma Seifrit. *Sarah Tyson Rorer: The Nation's Instructress in Dietetics and Cookery*. Philadelphia: American Philosophical Society, 1977.

ANDREW F. SMITH

Cooking Schools:
Twentieth Century

In the first half of the twentieth century, cooking schools for housewives and their domestics were little changed from their nineteenth-century predecessors. But at mid-century, cooking schools changed fundamentally, as the market for cookery instruction expanded into three new territories. First was the truly revolutionary emergence of vocational schools for training professional cooks. Second, hobbyist-cooks began exploring an astonishing diversity of culinary instruction that exceeded the scope of late-nineteenth-century cooking schools. Third, celebrity chef demonstrations and "cooking school vacations" became a new form of entertainment for affluent cooks.

Vocational Instruction

Before 1946, no one in America went to school to learn to be a restaurant chef. Americans saw most paid cooking as a low-status vocation to be picked up on the job, and what little culinary training existed was either haphazard or given in a rarified, academic context. Representative was Cornell University's Department (now School) of Hotel Administration, designed to give budding hospitality executives a passing familiarity with cookery that would enable them to supervise, rather than actually toil in, professional kitchens. The actual running of America's fine dining establishments was generally left to French and German immigrant chefs who had trained through arduous European apprenticeships. They peopled their kitchens with other immigrants or untrained Americans with few employment opportunities.

The founding of the International Hotel Workers Union in 1911 planted the first seeds of formal culinary education on American soil. Touting cooking as a "profession," rather than mere "slavish drudgery," culinary activists such as Joseph Dommers Vehling (himself a German immigrant and product of several European apprenticeships) stressed the need to educate cooks formally. Unions offered enrichment classes to their members (many of whom continued to be immigrant workers), and union newspapers published testimonials from cooks about the classes' value. The classes were sporadic, without overarching curricula, and one needed to be a working cook and union member already to take advantage of these opportunities.

During Prohibition the economics of running restaurant kitchens without the lubricant of alcoholic beverage profits brought increasing attention to a chef's managerial talents. The American Culinary Federation, founded in 1929 to advance the culinary profession, urged the adoption of an apprenticeship system, ideally one that would "sandwich" hands-on experience with theoretical classroom instruction. World War II temporarily quashed the ACF's efforts, but the war ultimately encouraged professional cooking schools through the G.I. Bill's promise of education for returning veterans. The New Haven [Connecticut] Restaurant Institute opened in 1946, premised on the assumptions that cooking could be a respectable, middle-class occupation for veterans and that professional cooks needed theory and management training in addition to practical skills. Now known as the Culinary Institute of America, or the "other" CIA, the school

An instructor offers advice to students at the Institute of Culinary Education, New York.

relocated to an impressive campus in Hyde Park, New York, in 1970. It became the first degree-granting culinary institution, awarding two-year associate degrees in occupational studies or applied science, and, since 1993, has awarded four-year baccalaureates in professional studies, with students majoring in either culinary or pastry arts management. Generally considered the preeminent, and certainly the pioneer, professional cooking school in America, by 2003 there was plenty of competition, with nearly five hundred American programs in different aspects of the hospitality industry.

The training of cooks for professional kitchens is constantly evolving and reflects changing attitudes. Some culinary associations support structured apprenticeships in lieu of, or in addition to, classroom study. Schools offer separate programs for cookery, pastry and baking, and business-oriented management skills. The label chosen to describe the training programs varies, from "vocational" to "professional" or "career," the latter reassuring to those paying $25,000 or more for tuition. This nomenclature chasm illustrates the centuries-old debate about the precise status of cookery—art, science, craft, or labor.

Cookery has entered academia through Boston University's graduate-level Master's of Liberal Arts in Gastronomy and New York University's Department of Nutrition, Food Studies, and Public Health. Although neither program is designed to train professional chefs, both take an interdisciplinary approach to the study of food in society that includes fine cookery and related topics.

Recreational Cooking Classes

Whether as adult education adjuncts to secondary schools and colleges, private schools set up to teach cooking exclusively, or add-ons to restaurant and hotel kitchens, cooking classes reached unprecedented cadres of eager students in the second half of the twentieth century. The catalyst was television, with luminaries such as James Beard and Julia Child, who popularized "cooking as fun" to the increasingly affluent, post–World War II generation. A lucky few attended Beard's own cooking school, operated out of his townhouse in New York's Greenwich Village from 1955 through the mid-1980s; for others, an exploding number of worldwide venues for cookery instruction has been catalogued in Shaw Associates' *The Guide to Cooking Schools*, published annually since 1988, which covers both professional and hobbyist programs. Recreational schools report that, at least in urban, affluent areas, hobbyist classes have seemed immune to economic fluctuations, as food-obsessed amateurs of the past twenty years try to develop skills to emulate celebrity chefs.

Cooking-as-entertainment has led to a resurgence of the celebrity chef instruction pioneered by Pierre Blot. Some of the country's most prestigious chefs travel widely to lecture and demonstrate their signature dishes to packed audiences. A typical example is the teaching kitchen De Gustibus, located in Manhattan's Macy's Department Store, which has hosted many of the prominent names in the food world, both American and foreign, since its founding in 1983.

Another take on celebrity chef instruction is quite exclusive: the opportunity for amateurs to apprentice in preeminent restaurant kitchens, working at simpler stations and absorbing first hand the balletic operations of professional kitchens. Among the restaurants that have opened their doors (the students pay richly, albeit sometimes to charities, for the privilege) are Charlie Trotter's in Chicago and Le Bernardin in New York City.

Finally, culinary instruction can be the centerpiece of a vacation. Depending on one's palate, Americans flock to the Napa Valley, quaint villages in Tuscany or the South of France, exotic Bangkok, or other pleasing destinations to absorb cookery and local culinary culture. Even Walt Disney teaches the Mickey Mouse set with fruit kabobs assembled by four-year-old Escoffiers.

BIBLIOGRAPHY

Focus on Culinary Education. The National Culinary Review, June 1998, pp. 21–28.

The Guide to Cooking Schools. Coral Gables, FL: Shaw Associates, c. 1988–.

Klein, Camille. *The Professional Cook: His Training, Duties, and Rewards*. New York: Helios Books, 1965.

Scotto, Charles. *What to Do about Apprentices for Our American Kitchens? Reviewing the Various Methods Followed to Assure Trained and Efficient Future Workers*. Hotel Bulletin and Nation's Chefs, 46, (June 1931): 543–544.

CATHY K. KAUFMAN

Cooking Techniques

Cookery transforms raw ingredients into finished dishes by altering the temperature and the moisture content of foods. Most cookery chooses between wet or dry heat, applied directly (by submersion in a liquid or by contact with a heat-conducting metal) or indirectly (by contact with heated air).

The basic wet heat cooking methods are boiling (with its variations, stewing and poaching) and steaming. The basic dry techniques are roasting, baking, grilling (and its cousin, broiling), and pan-frying or sautéing. Deep-frying, in which food is submerged in fat, is a dry technique; wet techniques require a water-based liquid. Many dishes combine two or more techniques sequentially, such as sautéing meat before stewing it. Occasionally techniques merge, such as cooking custard in a water bath, which is a baking-poaching hybrid.

For centuries cooks used equipment that had changed little since the introduction of chimneys in medieval Europe. During the nineteenth and early twentieth centuries, dramatic changes in kitchen equipment eased much of the arduous physical labor required by hearth cookery. The underlying cooking techniques changed little; what did change, however, was the language used to describe the various techniques.

The Wet Heat Techniques

From the seventeenth through much of the nineteenth century, "boiling" most frequently labeled any wet heat cookery. But "boil" did not always have the contemporary cook's understanding of water volcanically erupting at 212°F. Cookbooks distinguished among fast and slow boils, or what contemporary cooks would call poaching, simmering, braising, or boiling, depending on the amount of heat. Myriad other details within the recipes, such as placing sealed vessels in the hearth's embers, adjusting the position of the vessel from the fire, varying the amount of liquid to be used, and even the instruction to cook *slowly*, indicate boiling was the imprecise name for all wet heat cookery. Historic names for boiled dishes include ragoos, fricassees, or the ubiquitous "à la mode."

Wood- or coal-fired stoves required significant effort to stoke fires and to manipulate dampers to attain gentle heat for stewing. With the introduction of thermostatically controlled electric and gas stoves in the early twentieth century, housewives could braise simply by flicking a switch, making braising a labor-saving technique, particularly if the stew is assembled in an attractive casserole dish that doubles as a serving piece, saving washing an extra pan.

Steaming, cooking in trapped vapors, was an identified technique no later than the 1850s, when potato steamers that fit on the stovetop were listed as an essential part of the *batterie de cuisine*. Poaching completely submerges food in relatively cool (about 140–170°F) liquids to gently cook items. The technique was especially popular in the nineteenth through early twentieth centuries, when every well-equipped kitchen had a special "fish kettle," an oblong pan with a removable, perforated insert that cradled large cuts, such as a side of salmon or beef filet, that were then presented whole at table. With changing service styles, such presentations are generally relegated to catered buffets.

The Dry Heat Techniques

Before the twentieth century, cooks unambiguously distinguished among roasting, baking, and broiling. The language was precise because each technique required specific equipment, and none was interchangeable. As kitchen technology changed, rather than abandon the vocabulary, Americans changed their definitions of these terms.

Most striking is roasting. Any critter roasted in 1650 was mounted on a turning spit in front of a hearth, aided by a reflector oven to reflect heat back onto the food. Moisture freely evaporated, resulting in crisp

Grilling meat at the Institute of Culinary Education, New York.

crusts on the meat. The modern "roast" is cooked inside a tightly closed chamber, bathed in steam. The differences are obvious: *The Virginia Housewife* (1824) states that, "No meat can be well roasted, except on a spit turned by a jack, and before a steady, clear fire—other methods are no better than baking." While hearth roasting was a living memory, nineteenth-century writers condemned oven roasting as inferior, but by the turn of the twentieth century, "oven roasting" was the norm. Contemporary idiom dictates that one "roasts" a chicken but "bakes" a cake, even though both dishes may be placed in the identical oven, set at the identical temperature, for an identical time. Convection ovens, introduced to residential kitchens in the late 1980s, contain a fan to circulate air, mimicking some of the air currents of hearth roasting.

Hearth broiling was accomplished by rubbing gridirons with a bit of fat and heating them before the open fire. Thin cuts of meat were placed on the hot metal for a quick "broil." Modern grill pans on a stovetop accomplish much the same result, although modern cooks call it "grilling." Modern ovens often contain "broilers," that is, open gas flames, exposed electrical elements, or infra-red heating units that use indirect, but intense, heat to cook food placed immediately below, a technique unavailable to pre-twentieth-century cooks.

The biggest change in frying and sautéing since the colonial kitchen has been the substitution of compact saucepans set on stovetops for the long-handled pans set on trivets or made with stubby legs that were heated by the hearth's glowing coals.

Lost Cookery Techniques

Modern refrigeration has eliminated the need for much home salting, corning (brining), smoking, canning, preserving, potting, and pickling; cooks now purchase these items rather than prepare them at home and the techniques have fallen into desuetude.

Changes in raw ingredients and dietary theories account for the loss of other techniques. Larding, in which meat is pierced with strips of fat before roasting or braising was relatively common through the early twentieth century for lean meats, particularly beef and tough game birds. Barding wraps lean mean with thin leaves of fat or bacon to add flavor and richness. Both are rare in our fat-phobic times.

Indigenous Techniques

The term "barbecue" appears in American sources by the mid-seventeenth century and derives from *barbacoa*, the word used by the Taino of Haiti to describe an apparatus of sticks straddling a pit fire that roasted, grilled, and smoked foods. It soon referred to outdoor social gatherings as well as to the cooking technique. *The Kentucky Housewife* (1839) has an early barbecue recipe involving

a preparatory salt-and-molasses rub that could be at home in contemporary recipes. Barbecuing is America's cult culinary pastime; aided by kettle smokers and outdoor gas grills, barbecuing has become a catchall term for outdoor cookery.

Plank cookery affixes fish, frequently shad or salmon, shellfish, or fowl to a hardwood board that traditionally was held before an open fire, although nowadays the plank might be placed in an oven for cooking. The foods absorb a bit of the woody flavor.

Cooking without Heat

Some cookery requires no heat at all, such as whipping cream or emulsifying eggs, oil, and vinegar into mayonnaise. Health food gurus have periodically recommended a diet of raw or "living" foods, that is, foods never subjected to heat in excess of 118°F, the point at which certain enzymes are believed to be compromised. Breads and cakes are made from an amalgam of dried fruits, ground nuts, and cereals, held together by oil or honey and allowed to dry in the sun or dehydrate in a carefully moderated oven. Juicing, blending, marinating, and sprouting round out raw cookery.

BIBLIOGRAPHY

Beard, James. *James Beard's Theory and Practice of Good Cooking*. New York: Knopf, 1977. Reprint, Weathervane Books, 1990.

Colicchio, Tom. *Think Like a Chef*. New York: Clarkson Potter, 2000.

Culinary Institute of America. *The Professional Chef*. 7th ed. New York: Wiley and Sons, 2002.

Kamman, Madeleine. *The New Making of a Cook: The Art, Techniques, and Science of Good Cooking*. New York: Morrow, 1997.

McGee, Harold. *On Food and Cooking*. New York: Collier, Macmillan, 1984.

Plante, Ellen M. *The American Kitchen 1700 to the Present: From Hearth to Highrise*. New York: Facts On File, 1995.

Trotter, Charlie, and Roxanne Klein. *Raw*. Berkeley: Ten Speed, 2003.

CATHY K. KAUFMAN

Cookout, see *Historical Overview: World War II to the Early 1960s*

Cooperatives

Food cooperatives, or co-ops, have a long history of helping American consumers to improve the quality of their lives. They are nontraditionally structured businesses that are owned, democratically controlled, and operated to serve the needs of the consumers who use them. Members invest limited capital in order to start or join the co-op. As members they share in the benefits or profits generated by the business. Co-ops differ from traditional corporations in that each shareholder has only one vote regardless of the number of shares owned. Although food co-ops in the United States differ widely in the philosophy, size, and services offered, they are generally socially and environmentally conscious organizations.

A notice board at Park Slope Food Co-op, a cooperative that was established in Brooklyn, New York, in 1973.

More than 750 million people participate in cooperatives worldwide.

Cooperative buying groups or clubs, also known as preorder co-ops, are usually informal nonprofit organizations made up of individuals and families who have come together to save money on groceries and gain greater control over the choice and quality of food available to them. Goods ranging from organic and natural foods to standard grocery items are purchased in bulk from wholesale suppliers or farmers and then are divided among co-op members. Members manage the ordering, buying, and distribution of goods. The number of buying clubs in the United States is large, far exceeding that of retail co-ops.

Retail consumer food cooperatives range from storefront natural food stores to multi-outlet supermarkets. Many storefront food co-ops began as buying clubs, which then expanded in response to membership growth and increased sales volumes.

Cooperative food warehouses or wholesales serve as the distribution component of the co-op system, supplying retail co-ops and buying clubs with goods and services, thus enabling them to combine their collective buying power. The warehouses generally offer a wide variety of natural and organic foods as well as other groceries.

Origins of the Cooperative Movement

The modern consumer cooperative originated in nineteenth-century Great Britain. It was a response to the depressed economic conditions brought about by the Industrial Revolution, which effectively did away with the prevailing rural agrarian way of life in England. The depression of the 1840s also caused widespread unemployment and crushing poverty, especially in many newly industrialized urban areas. Corrupt company stores controlled most of the food supply, selling contaminated food at inflated prices.

Cooperative businesses were seen as a solution to the desperate conditions of the time, and many ventures were attempted. None, however, experienced any lasting success. In 1844 a group of twenty-eight unemployed craftspeople called the Rochdale Pioneers Equitable Society established a cooperative grocery store on Toad Lane in Rochdale, England. Influenced by the ideas of socioeconomic theorists such as Robert Owen and Dr. William King, the Pioneers codified a set of basic organizational principles for operating a cooperative business. Despite enormous odds, their enterprise proved extremely successful: by the 1860s more than four hundred Rochdale-inspired cooperatives were operating across England. The Rochdale principles of cooperation spread rapidly to other industrial nations with similar success.

Food Cooperatives in the United States

Cooperative activity in America dates back to the days of the early colonists. In 1752 Benjamin Franklin organized the first successful cooperative in the United States, the Philadelphia Contributorship for the Insurance of Houses from Loss by Fire. During the nineteenth century, cooperative experiments such as the Grange were widespread, with the majority resulting in failure. Immigrants from Finland and Bohemia who were familiar with the Rochdale cooperative principles established the first successful American food cooperatives in the early twentieth century.

The economic hardships and food shortages of the Great Depression of the 1930s spurred a wave of food co-op organizing. Buying clubs provided a way for consumers to reduce high grocery costs by combining their money and buying food in bulk. The Federal Emergency Relief Administration also promoted buying clubs as a method of self-help. Consequently, food co-ops from this period are referred to as New Deal or old-wave co-ops. For the most part the co-ops faded away as economic conditions improved. A small number of the Depression-era buying clubs, however, expanded into large supermarkets, which were still operating successfully after more than fifty years.

The tumultuous political, social, and cultural forces of the late 1960s and 1970s brought renewed interest in food co-op experimentation. New-wave food co-ops assumed many forms, from buying clubs (also called food conspiracies) and storefronts to worker collectives and communes. Radically different in style and substance from its New Deal predecessor, the new-wave co-op provided an innovative forum for addressing many diverse countercultural issues such as alternative health and nutrition and political activism. Great value was placed on natural, organic, and unprocessed foods, many of which were sold in bulk—an unheard-of practice at the time. The co-ops also provided a vehicle to connect countercultural consumers with the producers of the locally or regionally produced foods they required. The ecology movement of the early 1970s further increased the market for the co-ops, as did the high food prices caused by inflation. Food co-ops also were established by government agencies such as Volunteers in Service to America to assist the urban poor. It is estimated that 5,000 to 10,000 food co-ops were established in the United States between 1969 and 1979. Poor business management caused the majority to fail eventually; however, approximately three hundred of the new-wave co-ops still live on with varying degrees of success.

Influence of the American Food Co-op Movement

The widespread practice of community support for sources of sustainably grown food and family farms and farmers' markets is firmly rooted in the co-op movement. As such, the co-ops made a fundamental contribution to changing the American food system.

Further, by expanding Americans' awareness of the importance of unprocessed, whole, and organic food, the co-ops introduced a viable alternative to the products and experience of mainstream shopping. Food retailing also was changed as a result of the introduction of bulk foods made available for individual consumption. In addition, the food co-ops were pioneers in the areas of food labeling, consumer education, and environmentalism.

[See also COMMUNITY-SUPPORTED AGRICULTURE; COUNTERCULTURE, FOOD; FARMERS' MARKETS.]

BIBLIOGRAPHY

Belasco, Warren J. *Appetite for Change: How the Counterculture Took on the Food Industry.* Ithaca, NY: Cornell University Press, 1993.

The Co-op Handbook Collective. *The Food Co-op Handbook: How to Bypass Supermarkets to Control the Quality and Price of Your Food.* Boston: Houghton Mifflin, 1975.

Cox, Craig. *Storefront Revolution: Food Co-ops and the Counterculture.* New Brunswick, NJ: Rutgers University Press, 1994.

ELYSE FRIEDMAN

Coors Brewing Company

The Coors brewery was founded in 1873, just west of Denver, Colorado, by the twenty-six-year-old German immigrant Adolph Coors and his partner, Jacob Schueler. Coors invested $2,000 in the venture, and Schueler added the remaining $18,000 needed to purchase the eleven acres where the brewery first was built. In 1880 Coors, the proud father of his first child, a daughter, bought out Schueler; brewing production had doubled by 1887, when Coors's children numbered six, and the brewery was rolling out seven thousand barrels of beer a year.

When Coors had to borrow money in the late 1890s to cover debts and expenses, he vowed that once his debts were paid off he would never borrow money again. This sense of self-reliance continued to permeate the organization long after his death. In the early 1900s Coors purchased a porcelain business, which kept the company afloat during Prohibition, when the brewery produced malted milk and near beer. While the company was still a regional brewery, in 1959 Coors introduced the first all-aluminum two-piece beverage can. Reflecting the spirit

Adolph Coors Co. engaged in talks to merge with the Canadian brewing company Molson Inc.

of its founder, Coors launched a recycling program, offering a penny for every returned can.

Until the 1970s, Coors existed with just one product sold in eleven western states, but the company entered the twentieth-century marketing wars when it introduced Coors Light, "The Silver Bullet," in 1978. Three years later, in an attempt to take market share from the imported beer market segment, Coors introduced George Killian's line of products, which included Irish Red Lager, Irish Brown Ale, and Wilde' Honey Ale. This initiative was followed by the introduction of Coors Extra Gold (1985), Coors Arctic Ice, Coors Arctic Ice Light, and Coors Cutter (1991).

The growth of small breweries in the United States inspired Coors to introduce Winterfest, a specialty lager brewed in limited quantities for distribution during the holiday season. It became available nationally in 1987, after first being introduced in Colorado in 1986. In the mid-1990s Coors used its Sand Lot Brewery at Coors Field to produce the Blue Moon line to win over beer drinkers who had created a growing market for craft beers or microbrews. The Blue Moon products included Belgian White Ale, Honey Blonde Ale, Nut Brown Ale, Raspberry Cream Ale, and Harvest Pumpkin Ale. Coors's nationwide introduction in 1994 of Zima, a clear, carbonated alcoholic malt beverage, made news in the advertising industry, as it was one of the first of the nonbeer sparkling malt beverages to hit the U.S. market.

In 1990 Coors purchased its first brewery outside of Colorado, a Stroh Brewery Company plant in Memphis, Tennessee. In addition to its Denver headquarters and the Memphis brewery, Coors also has a brewery in Zaragoza, Spain, a packaging facility near Elkton, Virginia, and a Korean joint venture. It has about sixty-two hundred employees worldwide. The Coors family retains 100 percent of the company's voting stock, while 50 percent of the nonvoting stock is publicly traded.

[See also BEER; BREWING; MICROBREWERIES.]

BIBLIOGRAPHY

Baum, Dan. *Citizen Coors: An American Dynasty.* New York: Morrow, 2000.

LaFrance, Peter. *Beer Basics: A Quick and Easy Guide.* New York: Wiley, 1995.

Van Wieren, Dale P. *American Breweries II.* West Point, PA: Eastern Coast Breweriana Association, 1995.

PETER LAFRANCE

Cordials

Cordials, sometimes referred to as liqueurs or schnapps, are made from distilled spirits flavored with fruits, herbs, spices, or other botanicals; sweetened with sugar, honey, or other agents; and diluted with wine, water, or other liquids bearing less alcohol than spirits. Cordials are one of the earliest forms of distilled beverages and frequently were used as medicines, since it was believed that the curative properties of certain herbs could be preserved in spirits. Benedictine, for example, is an herbal cordial that was developed in 1510 by the Benedictine monk Dom Bernardo Vincelli. Chartreuse, another herbal liqueur, first was made in 1737 by Carthusian monks, who still make this cordial. Early cordials were used both as potable medicines and as liquid ointments for bathing wounds.

Cordials can be made in many different ways. Sometimes the botanicals or flavoring agents are distilled into the spirit, sometimes they are added to the spirit and left to infuse, and sometimes less expensive bottlings are made merely by adding flavorings, such as citrus oil, to the base product. By law, effective in 1936, U.S. commercial cordials must contain a minimum of 2.5 percent sugar.

The use of cordials has changed drastically over the years. Although they have been used as an ingredient in mixed drinks since at least the mid-1700s, more often they were served neat as after-dinner drinks until the latter half of the twentieth century. Cream liqueurs, such as Baileys Irish Cream, were not created until the early 1970s when a way to stabilize cream in distilled products was discovered, and they contributed greatly to the world of mixed drinks as ingredients in cocktails such as the B52. Before this time, however, liqueurs were used to make brandy Alexanders, pink squirrels, sidecars, and golden dreams, and curaçao, an orange-flavored cordial, was an ingredient in some of the first Manhattan recipes published in the late 1800s.

Triple sec, another orange-flavored cordial, is perhaps the most important liqueur in the world of American mixology, since it is used in many popular drinks such as the margarita, sidecar, kamikaze, cosmopolitan, and metropolitan. Other cordials such as Amaretto, an almond-flavored liqueur; Chambord, flavored with black raspberries; crème de menthe; crème de cacao; Drambuie; Grand Marnier; and Kahlúa are also integral to the bartender's craft.

Jägermeister, an herbal cordial from Germany, became very popular in the 1990s when it was served ice-cold as a shooter, and many other cordials also became fashionable at that time and were consumed in a similar fashion. Produced in many different flavors such as root beer, butterscotch, ginger, and even bubble gum, these were favored by younger drinkers at bars and parties across the nation.

Although some cordials are made in the United States, they are mainly generic items such as triple sec, curaçao, crème de menthe, and crème de cacao. The more easily recognizable brand names such as Drambuie, Kahlúa, Disaronno, and Galliano are all imported.

More recently new cordials such as green apple schnapps have been used by bartenders to create runaway hit cocktails such as the green apple martini—perhaps the most popular new drink of 2001. The craze for cocktails that started in the 1990s has done much to increase the popularity of cordials, and new flavors are being introduced on a regular basis.

[See also COCKTAILS; CORDIALS, HISTORICAL.]

GARY AND MARDEE HAIDIN REGAN

Cordials, Historical

Rummage through an American's liquor cabinet from the seventeenth through the nineteenth centuries and you likely would find an assortment of homemade cordials. Made from a mixture of distilled liquor, usually brandy but occasionally whiskey or rum, heavily sweetened, and distinctly flavored fruit juices or aromatics, the cordial was left to infuse, often for weeks or months, before being filtered for the most elegant translucence. The alcohol kick varied. Lettice Bryan's recipes in *The Kentucky Housewife* (1839) dilute the brandy with two or three parts fruit juice or herbal syrup, depending on the flavor. Mary Randolph's recipes in *The Virginia House-Wife* (1824) recommend diluting the brandy "to the strength of wine" or, in the case of her stronger lemon cordial, diluting the brandy by half. Most robust is Mrs. Harriott Pinckney Horry's 1770 recipe for Golden Cordial, which infuses lemon rind and flavorings into undiluted brandy.

Cordials historically played a dual role, as part of the medical arsenal and as a pleasant sociable nip. Recipes for physicians' "cordiall waters" and "cordiall powders," found in collections such as Martha Washington's *Booke of Cookery and Booke of Sweetmeats* (which dates to the mid-seventeenth century), were some of the few arrows in the housewife's quiver for treating diseases, especially those of the heart. Robert Roberts's *The House Servant's Directory; or, A Monitor for Private Families* (1827) offers a "strong anise-seed water" that is "a fine stomachic." Even those inclined to temperance, such as Sarah Josepha Hale in *The Good Housekeeper; or, The Way to Live Well, and to Be Well While We Live* (6th ed., 1841), reluctantly conceded that liquors might be "necessary, sometimes, as a medicine, but never, never consider them a necessary item in housekeeping."

Yet Americans in the eighteenth and nineteenth centuries did consider cordials necessary, drinking them neat with or following dessert. Sipped from small cordial cups and saucers or delicately proportioned stemmed glasses, each with a capacity of 1.5 ounces or less, cordials were savored digestives.

Americans began to consume cordials differently during the nineteenth century. With the development of cocktails, cordials became ingredients in more complicated drinks. Bartenders' guides inventoried the array of cordials needed for a full-service bar. Works such as Christian Schultz's *Manual for the Manufacture of Cordials, Liquors, Fancy Syrups, &c., &c.* (1862), appended to Jerry Thomas's *The Bon Vivant's Companion; or, How to Mix Drinks* (1862), gave professional formulas for manufacturing cordials. European imports such as kirsch, curaçao, and Chartreuse, many of which are still popular, flooded the American market. These standardized products could yield consistently flavored mixed drinks. Although still served after dinner, cordials increasingly were shaken into predinner libations.

Commercially manufactured cordials dominated the twentieth-century liquor cabinet. Recipes for homemade cordials, however, still could be found in books such as Magnus Bredenbek's *What Shall We Drink? Popular Drinks, Recipes, and Toasts* (1934), which evokes the old-fashioned tradition that "cordials really take the place of sweets and should be sipped with exquisite relish, hardly more than moistening the lips at each raising of the glass."

[See also COCKTAILS; CORDIALS.]

BIBLIOGRAPHY

Bredenbek, Magnus. *What Shall We Drink? Popular Drinks, Recipes, and Toasts.* New York: Carlyle House, 1934.

Johnson, Sharon Peregrine, and Byron A. Johnson. *The Authentic Guide to Drinks of the Civil War Era, 1853–1873.* Gettysburg, PA: Thomas, 1992.

CATHY K. KAUFMAN

Corers, *see Apple-Preparation Tools*

Corks

Cork was probably first used as a wine stopper by the ancient Romans, who, despite their discovery, more commonly closed their amphorae with clay or wood sealed with gypsum. The modern cork tradition reportedly dates to the seventeenth century, when Dom Perignon plugged one of his bottles of bubbly with a piece of bark. By the eighteenth century, corks had become the stopper of choice.

Corks are made from the bark of the cork oak tree (*Quercus suber*), which is harvested by hand every nine or ten years and is a renewable resource. These natural corks are well suited to their primary purpose of keeping wine in and air out, and traditionalists love the ritual and romance associated with them. But that tradition is threatened, as a number of prominent wineries turn to synthetic corks, which do not crumble, dry out, or run the risk of cork taint. This unwanted "corkiness," caused by the moldy-smelling compound 2,4,6-trichloro anisole (TCA), affects one in twelve bottles of wine and costs wine producers as much as $10 billion every year.

In some places, corks are being supplanted by the formerly déclassé screw cap. In the United States, consumer resistance is preventing broader adoption of corkless bottles, though environmentalists fear that it is only a matter of time before the centuries-old cork forests of such Mediterranean countries as Portugal (the origin of 85 percent of wine corks) succumb to lack of demand.

BIBLIOGRAPHY

Prial, Frank J. "Wine Talk: A Secret about Corks Is Out of the Bottle." *New York Times*, February 3, 1999.

Prial, Frank J. "Wine Talk: Now in the Best Bottles—Plastic." *New York Times*, August 8, 2001.

MERYL S. ROSOFSKY

Corn

Corn is both one of the most familiar and one of the least understood of America's common plants. Most Americans can identify corn yet consume corn unknowingly in hundreds of foods. It is one of the most easily identifiable grain plants to the eye, but its story is complex and full of mystery and much debate.

The use of the word "corn" is peculiar to the United States. "Maize" is used in most other countries. Europeans who were accustomed to the names wheat corn, barley corn, and rye corn for other small-seeded cereal grains referred to the unique American grain maize as Indian corn. The term was shortened to "corn," which has become the American word for the plant.

Basically, maize is an annual grass of the Maydeae family consisting of two genuses: *Tripsicum* and *Zea*. *Zea* has two major species: *Zea mays*, American corn, and *Zea diploperennis*, perennial *teosinte*. *Zea mays mexicana*, the annual variety of *teosinte*, is the closest botanical relative to maize and still grows as a wild annual in Central America. That maize is a New World plant from the Central American area is almost universally accepted. But the actual plant origin remains a mystery. There are three recognized theories about the origins of maize: the ancestor of maize is annual *teosinte*; maize evolved from a wild extinct

A nineteenth-century advertising card showing corn people.

maize; and maize derived from the hybridization of both *teosinte* and *tripsicum*.

Another mystery still shrouding the wild ancestry of corn is its inability to disperse seeds and hence its dependence on the intervention of man. Maize plants bear large seed heads (ears). The whole ear is covered by husks, which created an interdependence of corn and man present long before European contact. All other grasses, wild or cultivated, can reseed themselves naturally. Corn's seed-bearing ear is unique in the plant kingdom, preventing seed-dispersal by wind, birds, or other means. For the perpetuation of corn the seeds must have the spaced planting that only man can provide.

Types of Corn

Mature corn seeds (kernels) consist of three main parts: the germ, the endosperm, and an outer hull (pericarp). The many varieties of corn can be classified into six major types: dent, flint, flour, sweet, pod, and popcorn. Dent corn gets its name from the dent (depression) on the dried, mature kernel as a result of the shrinking of the soft, floury starch between the hard starch in the endosperm of the kernel. Dent is the corn fed to livestock. Flint corn has a smooth kernel and either a complete absence of soft starch or a limited amount fully surrounded by hard endosperm. The flour corn kernel resembles the kernel of the flint in size and shape but soft starch predominates so the kernel can be easily crushed into flour. Sweet corn has kernels that are easily recognized by their wrinkled exterior. Their sweetness is the result of a genetic defect in metabolism

preventing the sugars from being completely transformed into starch. Pod corn is the most primitive and together with popcorn possibly one of the oldest types of maize. Each kernel of pod corn is enclosed in a glume or husk. Pod corn is not of any commercial importance. Popcorn has small, hard kernels with a high proportion of hard starch. The major characteristic trait of popcorn is its ability to explode and produce a white flake when the raw kernels are exposed to heat.

The Dissemination of Corn

Most scientists believe that the earliest maize domesticated was of the pod-pop variety in the area of Central America about eight thousand years ago. But by the time of sixteenth-century European exploration, the Native Americans had developed the other four categories of maize: flint, dent, sweet, and flour. The dissemination of corn into what is geographically now the United States was slow. Flint corn spread from western Mexico into the southwestern United States and then proceeded northward and eastward. Dent corn was the predominant corn disseminated from the American southwest to the southern states. Probably the only two races of maize that populated the eastern seaboard prior to European contact were the eight-rowed flint corn of the north and the dent corn of the south.

A second major movement of corn began in the late 1700s, as settlers migrated to the Ohio Valley and to the mid-continent prairie, which became the corn belt of today. As the settlers migrated with their corn seed, the Southern Dent and the Northern Flint were brought into close proximity to naturally hybridize to form a new dent variety that has become the world's most important crop.

Corn has now become a basic food plant of modern American civilization. Corn feeds the nation—or more precisely the nation's animals that are the basis of the American diet. As the population increased in this country, the need to increase the production of corn became mandatory and was met with corn's ability to hybridize. Controlled hybridization for increase yields, earlier maturity, and resistance to disease and drought began to be developed and utilized in the beginning of the twentieth century.

Corn as Food

Throughout American history there has been a great diversity in the preparation and use of corn as food. Native Americans parched corn by roasting it in ashes or processed the kernels with lye water prepared from ashes or lime to remove the hulls for whole hominy that is easier to grind. In the Southwest, the most common process was to boil the corn in lime solution prior to grinding the grain into a fine masa. The process of nixtamalization (alkaline processing of kernels) loosens the

Corn

168

Two diners eat corn on the cob.

hulls, increases the nutritional content of the grain by improving the amino acid balance and making the niacin content more available, and ensures that a flexible, flat tortilla can be made.

Whole hominy (great hominy) is the result of the alkaline (lye) process of removing the hulls. But the word "hominy" refers to dried and hulled maize kernels, coarsely ground and prepared for use. The term "grits" or hominy grits, usually of white corn, refers to fine-ground hominy used to prepare "the potatoes of the South."

Cornbread was the initial staff of life in America. Early American cornbreads included corn pone, hoecakes, johnnycakes, ash cakes, bannocks, and dodgers. A simple cornbread was made of cornmeal, water or milk, and perhaps salt, sugar, and fat. Later recipes for cornbread are more elaborate, mixing cornmeal with wheat flour and sometimes raising agents. Spoon breads were soft, rich corn breads made with milk, butter, and egg and best eaten with a spoon.

During the nineteenth century, food industries began the production of corn syrup, corn oil, and cornstarch from corn, and corn became less identifiable in the diet. Americans can avoid all visible corn products, fresh corn, canned or frozen corn, corn flours and cornstarch and still be eating invisible corn products at almost every meal. Indeed a supermarket without corn would be little more than just fresh fruits and vegetables with a fish counter.

[See also BEER, CORN AND MAPLE; CORN-PREPARATION TOOLS; CORN SYRUP; MEXICAN AMERICAN FOOD; NATIVE AMERICAN FOODS; POPCORN; SOUTHERN REGIONAL COOKERY; SOUTHWESTERN REGIONAL COOKERY.]

BIBLIOGRAPHY
Fussell, Betty. *The Story of Corn.* New York: Knopf, 1992.
Parker, A. C. *Iroquois Uses of Maize and Other Food Plants.* Ontario, Canada: Iroqrafts, 1994.

Smith, Andrew F. *Popped Culture: A Social History of Popcorn in America.* Columbia: University of South Carolina Press, 1999.

SUSAN MCLELLAN PLAISTED

Cornbread Baking Pans

Cornmeal recipes abounded in the nineteenth century: cornbread was very popular all over the country. It was baked in cast-iron skillets, some of which had divisions or partitions that formed wedge-shaped sections of cornbread. By about 1900 cast-iron stick pans that made long, thin sticks of cornbread were in use. By the 1920s several foundries were making mold pans with more or less realistic corncob cups. Some of these pans were called "corn-" or "wheat-stick" pans. The most interesting pans look as if the casting molds to make them were created with actual corncobs, each kernel is so individualistic.

[See also CORN.]

BIBLIOGRAPHY
Franklin, Linda Campbell. *300 Years of Kitchen Collectibles.* 5th ed. Iola, WI: Krause, 2003.

LINDA CAMPBELL FRANKLIN

Corned Beef

All-American as beef in most forms may be, corned beef has never quite managed to shed its Old World image. Even the name sounds quaint—"corn" being a bygone English synonym for "granule," a reference to salt as the product's active ingredient. To complicate matters, the English themselves prefer the term "salt beef" (or "pickled beef") to distinguish the cured brisket (or other comparable cut) found in delicatessens from the canned loaf found on supermarket shelves; in the United States, however, "corned beef" applies to both items.

The history of corned beef is likewise confusing. Salting as a mode of food preservation is as ancient and widespread as civilization itself, such that the genesis of any one product is hard to pinpoint. For instance, the consensus is that salt meat was well and widely known in Europe by the Middle Ages, but opinions continue to differ as to whether the origins of corned beef per se lie in the British Isles and, more specifically Ireland, or in central and eastern Europe and, in particular, among the Ashkenazi Jews. It is clear, however, that Ireland created and led the market in exportation of corned beef until the nineteenth century, when the canning industry emerged in England and opened doors for the cattlemen of South America, who came to dominate production of canned corned beef—although its heyday passed with World War II, at least among civilians. (Consumption is still notable among British and U.S. armed forces.)

Techniques for salting meat vary, from dry salting, a method based on topical application and absorption, to wet salting, whereby the meat is immersed in brine. These procedures, which can take days to complete, are also known as curing and pickling, respectively. For corned beef the latter process is key, although it is often preceded by the former; brines may contain sugar, saltpeter, and spices in varying amounts.

What does not vary much is the way in which corned beef brisket is traditionally prepared: it is simmered with a blend of seasonings that may include garlic, peppercorns, bay leaf, tarragon, mustard, parsley, thyme, marjoram, cloves, nutmeg, or allspice. It can then be served hot, accompanied by onions, potatoes, and the like, or cold, with copious condiments from horseradish to sweet relish. Corned beef and cabbage is the most famous version—one with Irish roots but American blossoms—eaten especially on Saint Patrick's Day, when it forms the centerpiece for the proverbial New England boiled dinner.

Strangely, this peasant dish appeared regularly on the elaborate menus of America's grand hotels in the nineteenth century. Its even more humble relatives have taken different routes: from the hash houses of the period to modern-day greasy spoons, corned beef hash, frequently paired with eggs, remains a staple, while the Reuben, a classic deli sandwich of sliced corned beef piled high on rye with Swiss cheese, sauerkraut, and thousand island dressing, continues to inspire heated debate between Nebraskans and New Yorkers as to its birthplace.

[See also SAINT PATRICK'S DAY.]

BIBLIOGRAPHY
Shephard, Sue. *Pickled, Potted, and Canned: How the Art and Science of Food Preserving Changed the World.* New York: Simon and Schuster, 2000.

RUTH TOBIAS

Corn Oil, *see Fats and Oils*

Corn-Preparation Tools

From the early days of the United States, corn was grown for livestock feed and human consumption. For livestock, husked ears of corn were usually dried and stored in corn cribs—ventilated structures that were open invitations to rats. Husking pegs or corn huskers were short metal or wooden rods, pointed on the end and often fitted to a leather strap that was worn around the hand so that the peg and sometimes a hook for pulling off the husks were in the palm of the hand. The first of dozens of U.S. corn hullers (huskers) was patented in 1836; previously they were homemade.

The first U.S. corn sheller, patented in 1815, was followed by many more from the 1830s to the 1920s. When dried ears were fed into the hopper, it knocked off the hard kernels—for seed or for grinding into meal. In the 1840s so-called unrefined folks ate corn on the cob with butter and salt. Others believed the kernels must be slit open, releasing the milky juices and making the corn digestible. Corn graters (colloquially called "gritters") "creamed" the corn by slitting the kernels and expressing the contents; these tools were made as early as the 1840s to 1850s. Some were small, flat tables with grating blades, something like cabbage cutters. Corn cutters dating from the 1870s were cylindrical metal devices with rows of sharp teeth, pulled over fresh ears of corn.

[See also CORN; CORNBREAD BAKING PANS.]

BIBLIOGRAPHY

Franklin, Linda Campbell. *300 Years of Kitchen Collectibles*. 5th ed. Iola, WI: Krause, 2003.
Moffet, Jim. *American Corn Huskers: A Patent History*. Sunnyvale, CA: Off Beat Books, 1996.

LINDA CAMPBELL FRANKLIN

Corn Syrup

Corn syrup is a clear, colorless sweetener made from cornstarch. In the refining of cornstarch, a chemical breakdown by heat, acid, enzymes, or any combination of the three results in dextrose or starch sugar. More complete conversion of the starch yields a sweeter syrup.

In the food industry the beneficial properties of corn syrup are myriad. In ice cream, corn syrup improves body and texture and prevents ice crystal formation. With baked goods, it regulates the rate of fermentability in yeast doughs. Corn syrup lends a chewy texture to many candies and chewing gum. Its browning characteristics promote crust color in baked products. When used with other sugars, corn syrup controls crystallization. Naturally hygroscopic, it readily absorbs moisture and adds pliability to many foods. Above all, it has replaced cane sugar as a food sweetener.

The first attempts at converting corn into a sweetener resulted from the Molasses Act of 1733. Molasses was taxed heavily and the colonists sought a cheap substitute. War between France and Great Britain in 1806 led to the British blockade of France's West Indies cane producers. Napoléon I offered a monetary reward for a natural sugar replacement and the Russian chemist K. S. Kirchhof

produced a sweet syrup from potato starch by adding sulfuric acid. Kirchhof's technique of acid hydrolysis of starch was applied to corn in the mid-1860s. At the same time, commercial production of corn syrup began in the United States with the Union Sugar Company in New York City and a decade later with the American Glucose Company of Buffalo, New York.

In the 1870s economic conditions made the production of dextrose from corn profitable, and new markets for corn syrup opened up in the baking, candy, and brewing industries. During World War I, sugar shortages led to an increased dependence on corn syrup, as confectioners, bakers, and jam and jelly producers replaced cane or beet sugar in their formulas. The development of a process for the purification and crystallization of dextrose in 1921 allowed corn sweeteners to compete more fully with sugar.

Using enzymes to hydrolyze cornstarch, the major corn refiner A. E. Staley Manufacturing Company marketed a product called Sweetose in 1938 that was 60 percent as sweet as sugar. Twice as sweet as regular corn syrup and three times more fluid, it was used in candies and fruit packing, then later in jams, jellies, preserves, and ketchup.

In 1967 new Japanese enzyme technology brought about a revolution in corn syrup development. High fructose corn syrup was made by a more complete hydrolysis of glucose to fructose. IsoSweet, a high fructose corn syrup developed by Staley, was approximately 92 percent as sweet as sugar.

In the early 1970s imported sugar made up almost 60 percent of U.S. sugar demand. Prices quadrupled and food processors increased their use of IsoSweet. In 1974 Coca-Cola used IsoSweet to replace 25 percent of the sugar in its minor flavors. Corn syrups in food processing took off after 1978, when Staley developed a 55 percent fructose syrup, which was essentially as sweet as sugar. By the mid-1980s corn syrups had replaced sugar as the sweetener of choice for the soft-drink industry. As of 2002 corn syrup sweeteners comprised more than 55 percent of the U.S. nutritive sweetener market.

By the early 2000s corn sweeteners were under attack by critics who claimed that the rise in American obesity was partly the result of an overuse of cheap sweeteners in fast foods. Soft-drink servings, for example, rose from a standard eight ounces to twenty ounces, and many other foods experienced the same kinds of expansion.

[See also SODA DRINKS; SWEETENERS.]

BIBLIOGRAPHY

Forrestal, Dan J. *The Kernel and the Bean: The 75-Year Story of the Staley Company*. New York: Simon and Schuster, 1982.
Fussell, Betty. *The Story of Corn*. New York: Knopf, 2004.

SALLY S. DEFAUW

Counterculture, Food

Great strides were made in American agriculture during the twentieth century. Farmers were able to increase production with newly available pesticides, herbicides, petrochemical fertilizers, and hormones that were developed to prevent disease and maximize yield of both plants and animals. Farmers also increased mechanization and irrigation, and more of them specialized in growing a single crop or raising only one type of animal, abandoning the diversity characteristic of American family farms. Each of these changes required major financial investments, and once the improvements were made, the cost of food production declined. Many small farmers could not compete, were unable to make a living, and sold out to large corporate operations. Similarly, food companies began consolidation during this period, and the result was the emergence of a few corporate food giants.

Concerns

Despite increases in production and decreases in prices, concerns about corporate agriculture and food processing had been expressed since the 1930s. Jerome I. Rodale, for instance, launched the magazine *Organic Gardening and Farming*, which emphasized composting, soil building, and biological control of pests. Organic farming was best practiced on a small scale: farmers and customers would deal directly with each other in farmers' markets, and the middle level, including shippers, wholesalers, and supermarket owners, would be eliminated. Rodale was also concerned with nutrition, and he

Ballantine/Cookbook 24711/$1.95

THE MILLION COPY
BEST SELLER
*NOW
COMPLETELY
REVISED
AND UPDATED*

HIGH PROTEIN
MEATLESS COOKING
Diet
for a
Small
Planet

Frances Moore Lappé

Illustrations by Kathleen Zimmerman & Ralph Iwamoto

The cover of Frances Moore Lappé's landmark 1971 publication.

launched *Prevention* magazine in 1950 to offer advice on healthy eating. This concern was shared by others, such as Adele Davis, who emphasized the role of diet in a healthy life, recommended specific food regimens for various ailments, and advised avoidance of most processed foods, artificial additives, and chemical fertilizers.

Counterculture Food Movement

The food counterculture, best described by Warren Belasco in his book *Appetite for Change: How the Counterculture Took on the Food Industry, 1966–1988*, included a broad cross section of individuals and groups opposed to corporate agriculture and corporate manufacturing of food. Many participants in the counterculture eschewed foods grown with chemicals or processed with additives.

One solution was food co-ops, which were self-run by members who each contributed a certain amount of time to the project. Natural foods were touted as healthier and tastier than processed foods. Co-ops were initially no-frills sources for staples such as brown rice, whole-grain bread, herbal tea, nuts, seeds, beans, dried fruit, honey, and soy products, and later added natural cheeses, yogurt, organically grown fruits and vegetables, pure juices, granolas, oils, and vitamin and mineral supplements. There were an estimated five to ten thousand food co-ops in America by the 1970s.

The counterculture discouraged the consumption of meat for a number of reasons. Some vegetarians based their diets on the teachings of Buddhism and Hinduism. Others pursued macrobiotics, a rigorous system of purification of the diet based on Taoist thought. Some members of the counterculture saw a vegetarian diet as a way to improve one's health and help fight hunger in America and around the world. The popularity of this view can be attributed in part to Frances Moore Lappé, who was concerned about the vast amount of acreage devoted to growing feed grain for livestock and popularized the theory of protein complementarity. According to this theory, one could creatively combine beans, seeds, grains, and dairy products to meet daily protein needs without resorting to ecologically wasteful meat. Lappé's book, *Diet for a Small Planet* (1971), explained that by feeding vegetable protein to animals rather than directly to humans, Americans were wasting scarce protein resources at a time when much of the world was going hungry or suffering from serious nutritional deficiencies.

Countercultural Legacies

The counterculture spurred interest in food and nutrition. Because many participants distrusted the establishment, which included food companies and the FDA, there was a clear need for improved research, and groups, such as the Center for Science in the Public Interest, emerged to research and publish

eye-opening nutritional analyses and critiques of fast food and convenience foods.

Some enterprises launched by those in the counterculture food movement have survived and thrived. Erewhon, for instance, was founded as a cooperative in 1966 to supply Boston-area followers of the macrobiotics gurus Michio and Aveline Kushi. Erewhon became one of the largest retailers, manufacturers, and distributors of natural foods in the United States. Celestial Seasonings, started in 1969 in Boulder, Colorado, offered herbal teas that were additive free and organically grown or gathered in the wild. Celestial Seasonings is the largest purveyor of herbal teas in the United States.

The counterculture food movement greatly increased interest in vegetarianism. The North American Vegetarian Society was founded in 1974, and several vegetarian magazines, such as *Vegetarian Times*, have large numbers of subscribers.

Counterculture food concerns increased interest in organic gardening, which has blossomed since the 1970s. Associated with organic gardening has been a movement to preserve family farms by connecting people in cities with small farmers in surrounding areas. One such effort was the growth of greenmarkets in cities. In these urban markets, local farmers sell their produce directly to customers.

Another effort to connect farmers to consumers is community-supported agriculture, which appeared in the United States in the mid-1980s. Community-supported agriculture was championed as a way for farmers and community members to work together to create a local food system whereby the farmers produce vegetables, fruits, meats, and related products and sell them directly to community members.

Issues raised by the counterculture food movement persist in concerns about the globalization of food and the resistance to genetically modified foods. The slow food movement, which embodies many of the original concerns, was launched in 1986 by Carlo Petrini as a response to the opening of a McDonald's restaurant in Rome. Slow Food U.S.A., which was launched in 1999, has ten thousand members. It is dedicated to saving America's food heritage and to supporting and celebrating the food traditions of North America.

[**See also** BIOTECHNOLOGY; CHEMICAL ADDITIVES; COMMUNITY-SUPPORTED AGRICULTURE; COOPERATIVES; FARMERS' MARKETS; FAST FOOD; FOOD AND DRUG ADMINISTRATION; FOOD AND NUTRITION SYSTEMS; HEALTH FOOD; ORGANIC FOOD; ORGANIC GARDENING; SLOW FOOD U.S.A.; TRANSPORTATION OF FOOD; VEGETARIANISM.]

BIBLIOGRAPHY

Belasco, Warren J. *Appetite for Change: How the Counterculture Took on the Food Industry, 1966–1988*. New York: Pantheon, 1989.

Davis, Adele. *Let's Eat Right to Keep Fit*. New York: Harcourt, 1954.

Dragonwagon, Crescent. *The Commune Cookbook*. New York: Simon and Schuster, 1972.

Lappé, Frances Moore. *Diet for a Small Planet*. New York: Ballantine, 1971.

Nestle, Marion. *Food Politics: How the Food Industry Influences Nutrition and Health*. Berkeley: University of California Press, 2002.

ANDREW F. SMITH

Coush-Coush

Coush-coush is a Louisiana breakfast dish, a corn mush made like hasty pudding from fresh cornmeal or leftover cornbread. Although it is now most associated with Cajun country cooking, it was once the universal camp meal of the Confederate Army (called simply "coush"). It could be made in a skillet from a ration of cornmeal or from stale cornbread. And yet, the origins of coush-coush point to three continents of the African diaspora.

The name almost certainly comes from African couscous, usually today a wheat-based steamed pasta, but also a name for millet, the small grain the pasta resembles. When American maize was introduced to Africa by the Portuguese, it often took the place of millet or sorghum in mushes or polentas. The most closely related dish to Louisiana coush-coush is cou-cou or "turn corn" from Barbados, a cornmeal mush that also contains okra, another marker for African origins. Barbados was the central depot of the British slave trade, and it is easy to see how cou-cou could have been named after a similar African mush, and the name taken by slaves to Louisiana.

Brazilian and Cape Verdean *cuscux* are also corn puddings, usually turned out into molds or balls like cou-cou. Since the earliest slave trade was Portuguese, it is likely that these dishes are older branches of the family tree of coush-coush. Since coush-coush is a mush or pudding, and couscous is now a steamed pasta, it may be that the Brazilian dish is the original, and that Native Brazilian slaves traded to the Caribbean or even to Louisiana carried the recipe under a similar Native name or adopted the African name known to their African slave spouses. American foods and recipes, especially from Brazil, were often taken back to Cape Verde, which had been settled as a station for the Portuguese slave trade.

MARK H. ZANGER

Cowpeas

Cowpeas—also known in the United States as bird peas, black-eyed peas, cornfield peas, conch peas, Congo peas, crowder peas, pigeon peas, red peas, southern peas, whip-poor-will peas, zipper peas, *gandules* (Puerto Rico), and simply "peas"—are various warm-weather beans, descended from the wild African cowpeas *Vigna unguiculata*. Cultivated varieties were developed as early as 3000 B.C.E. in Africa and came to the Americas with the slave trade. They remained a popular slave food, as reported in a southern journal in

1850: "There is no vegetable of which negroes are more fond than of the common field pea" (quoted in Breedon, p. 98).

The best-known dish of cowpeas is South Carolina's hoppin' John, a pilaf of rice and beans and usually pork or bacon, probably of African or Afro-Caribbean origin. The dish is thought to bring good luck when eaten at New Year's. In West Africa cowpeas are soaked to remove the skins and ground to make creamy-white fried or steamed cakes. There is some evidence of African-style cowpea preparations retained in Georgia through the nineteenth century. Neo-African cowpea cakes have entered the United States via Key West, Florida (where they have been known by an anglicized Cuban name, *bolos*, since at least 1948), and are found among the recent immigrant communities of Afro-Cubans, Haitians, Brazilians, and Nigerians.

[See also PEAS.]

BIBLIOGRAPHY

Hess, Karen. *The Carolina Rice Kitchen: The African Connection.* Columbia: University of South Carolina Press, 1992.

MARK H. ZANGER

Crab

Valuable fisheries have formed around several species of American crab. The early history of crab consumption reflects highly regional tastes, although in more recent times many crabs are caught, packed, and shipped to all parts of the United States. Because of the labor-intensive effort of harvesting crabs, in colonial times the meat was used in small amounts (as was most shellfish) in soups, stews, sauces, and, like other flaked fish, in small fried cakes. Some recipes suggested that other shellfish could be substituted for crab.

Blue crab ranges from Delaware to Florida, but that from Chesapeake Bay is most famous. The most popular way to prepare blue crabs is to boil them in seasoned water. Eating blue crab in the rough is a favorite recreational pastime. Soft-shell crabs are those that have shed their shells. They are cooked to be eaten whole, often in a sandwich. Blue crabs have long been a commercial fishery. The meat, and the famous she-crab soup of the Chesapeake region, is canned and distributed across the United States. The principal blue crab fisheries are in Maryland and Louisiana.

Snow crab, sometimes called queen crab (as opposed to king crab), from the colder waters of the North Atlantic and North Pacific oceans, appeared on the market in the 1960s. Snow crabs are caught in pots and with tangle nets, which are set by multiple-boat operations that obstruct the crabs' migration across the seabed. Snow crabs vary in size from one and one-half to five pounds and sometimes measure two feet from pincer tip to pincer tip. The crabs have worthwhile body meat, although the main object is the leg meat. The fishery is managed with quotas

for the annual catch. Atlantic Canada is the center of the fishery, but a large fishery exists in Alaska, the crabs being sold cooked and frozen across the United States.

Alaska king crab is highly prized for its large meaty claws and legs, which can have a span of up to ten feet. In this fishery, which poses dangers to fishermen, six- to seven-hundred-pound pots set with herring bait are attached to long buoy lines. The pots are hauled in sometimes heavy seas in late fall and early winter around the Aleutian Islands and in the Bering Sea. The crabs, usually only male red, blue, or golden king crabs, are usually taken ashore alive but are processed soon after, the legs, called "sections," being cooked and frozen. These large crabs are highly desirable because of the ratio of meat to time spent picking it and because the large, well-flavored chunks of meat are good in salads, sandwiches, pasta, and Asian dishes. A great deal of king crab is sold to Japan. Although the fishery is managed, king crabs are nearly overfished, and seafood conservationists caution against overconsumption.

Dungeness crab is found on the Pacific coast from Mexico to Alaska in a fishery that usually opens in December, putting the fishers at risk of bad weather to get the earliest crab to market. The fishery, which is well managed, extends roughly from the central California coast to the Gulf of Alaska, centered between northern Washington State and northern Oregon. Only male Dungeness crabs may be legally caught, and the species is considered abundant. This crab averages approximately two pounds at commercial size and yields one-fourth of its weight in meat, approximately twice the yield of a blue crab.

Rock crab ranges from Labrador, Canada, to Florida. Although the crabs have good-tasting meat, extremely hard shells make rock crab an unattractive fishery. The crabs sometimes are a by-catch of lobstering along the New England coast. The meat is picked out of legs and claws for sale in traditional crab dishes such as salads, crab rolls, and crab cakes.

SANDRA L. OLIVER

Crab Boils

Blue crabs, *Callinectes sapidus*, are native to the western Atlantic, from New England to the Gulf coast of Florida—but nowhere are they more abundant or more abundantly enjoyed than in the vicinity of Chesapeake Bay. Half of all the blue crabs caught in the United States are captured by Chesapeake watermen along its four thousand miles of shoreline. Since the 1850s watermen have harvested oysters in the winter months. The oyster catch is declining, but each year up to 100 million pounds of crabs are caught between April and fall.

During crab season, crab houses flourish around the bay. At the beginning of the twenty-first century at least seventy-five crab houses surrounded the bay and the Potomac estuary, serving all sorts of crab dishes—but

A typical serving of Maryland boiled crabs.

none more popular than the traditional Maryland crab boil.

"Crab boil" is something of a misnomer because the crabs are not boiled but steamed over water, beer, vinegar, or some combination thereof. Crab boils' distinguishing features are their informality—cooked crabs are usually served without plates on paper-covered tables with no utensils other than small wooden mallets for cracking the shells—and their salty-spicy crust, which clings to diners' fingers and calls for lots of cold beer.

The spice blend is sprinkled on the crabs as they are placed in the steamer, and the lid is quickly replaced so that the crabs do not escape. Many places use their own spice blends, but Old Bay Seasoning is most often the choice. The seasoning was invented in Baltimore in 1939 by the German immigrant Gustav Brunn; its primary ingredient is celery salt, but the peppery mixture includes many other spices. Old Bay was sold to McCormick and Company in 1990.

[See also SEAFOOD.]

BIBLIOGRAPHY

Blue Crab Archives. http://www.blue-crab.org.

Warner, William W. *Beautiful Swimmers.* Boston: Little, Brown, 1976.

GARY ALLEN

Crab Cakes

The crab cake is an important Chesapeake Bay regional dish, using the meat from the ubiquitous blue crab. The dish's origin has been attributed to Boston, Massachusetts; New York City; Wilmington, Delaware; and Baltimore, Maryland. All are possible. Starting in 1820 the harvesting of the tidal waters of the eastern seaboard, particularly oysters, became the engine of the area's prosperity, which, despite the Civil War, lasted up to the beginning of the twentieth century. The crab cake has evolved along with America's eating habits over the last two hundred years to become a multifaceted dish demonstrating the influence of Afro-American and French cooking. It is possible that the first crab cake was cooked in emulation of the New England codfish cake, substituting crabmeat for salt cod; or by a black slave cook on a Maryland tidewater plantation; or by a European trained chef at some hotel or club in Baltimore. Within reason it was probably a combination of all three, and may well have occurred in Baltimore.

By 1850 Baltimore had become the center of the seafood canning industry, particularly oysters and crabmeat. The crab cake has as many individual interpreters as there are cooks. But there are five common denominators: one, a pound of picked-over crabmeat; two, a binder, such as eggs or mayonnaise; three, seasonings, such as parsley, onion, green pepper, salt and pepper, mustard, Worcestershire sauce, Old Bay Seasoning, and so on; four, fillers (not obligatory), such as bread crumbs, crushed crackers, or mashed potato; and five, cooking, such as deep fat frying, pan frying, or sautéing. The crab cake's main ingredient was the uncooked crabmeat, which required cheap but fairly skilled labor to extract the fresh, as opposed to cooked, meat from the crab. It was an extreme smelly and soggy job, but by the 1870s a place like Baltimore had many indigent blacks and immigrant Irish and Italians to work for the canners. Also, because of the money to be made, local entrepreneurs set up canning operations by the late nineteenth century in Maryland towns around the Chesapeake Bay such as Cambridge, Tighman Island, Oxford, Crisfield, Solomons, and Shady Side. By 1930 most of them were gone as a result of the Depression and changing eating and food buying habits. The Maryland crab cake can now be bought frozen.

[**See also** CHESAPEAKE REGION, FOOD AND DRINK OF THE; CRAB.]

BIBLIOGRAPHY

Frederick Philip Stieff. *Eat, Drink, and Be Merry in Maryland*. Baltimore: Johns Hopkins University Press, 1932.

From a Lighthouse Window. St. Michaels, MD: The Chesapeake Bay Maritime Museum, 1989.

300 Years of Black Cooking in St. Mary's County. Leonardtown, MD: Bicentennial Edition, 1976.

HENRY BONNER

Cracker Jack

During the 1870s the German immigrants Frederick and Louis Rueckheim sold popcorn on the streets of Chicago. They began to experiment with combining popcorn with several other products. When the Columbian Exposition opened in Chicago in 1893, they sold a confection composed of popcorn, molasses, and peanuts, which they prepared in a small factory. After the exposition, orders for the confection rose. The Rueckheims increased production, repackaged the product so that it would stay fresh, named it Cracker Jack, and promoted it nationwide. Conflicting stories as to how "Cracker Jack" acquired its name have surfaced. The most commonly told story goes as follows. While sampling and tasting the new confection, John Berg, a company salesman, purportedly exclaimed: "That's a crackerjack." Frederick Rueckheim looked at him and said, "Why not call it by that name?" Berg responded, "I see no objection." Rueckheim's decisive reply was "That settles it then." The story is probably apocryphal as,

at that time, the term "crackerjack" was a commonly used slang that meant first-rate or excellent.

Cracker Jack was soon sold in snack bars at circuses, fairs, and sporting events. In 1908 the lyricist Jack Norworth and the composer Albert von Tilzer immortalized Cracker Jack in their song, "Take Me Out to the Ball Game" with the lyrics: "Buy me some peanuts and cracker-jack / I don't care if I never get back." Unlike other fad foods, Cracker Jack survived. Throughout the early twentieth century the company expanded, opening operations in Canada and the United Kingdom. By 1913 Cracker Jack was the world's largest-selling commercial confection. A major reason for its longevity was extensive national advertising, specifically focused at children. In 1912 a small toy was included in every package. The little sailor boy and his dog were first used in advertisements in 1916, and three years later they appeared on the Cracker Jack box. They were based on a picture of Frederick Rueckheim's grandson with his dog, named Bingo. His grandson, Robert, died of pneumonia shortly after the package was introduced.

In 1970 Cracker Jack was enjoyed in 24,689,000 homes, or 41 percent of all American households. Then other companies began manufacturing Cracker Jack–like snacks, and Cracker Jack sales declined. By the 1990s Cracker Jack ranked behind its competitors in sales.

[**See also** ADVERTISING; POPCORN.]

BIBLIOGRAPHY

Piña, Ravi. *Cracker Jack Collectibles with Price Guide*. Atglen, PA: Schiffer, 1995.

Smith, Andrew F. *Popped Culture: A Social History of Popcorn in America*. Columbia: University of South Carolina Press, 1999.

ANDREW F. SMITH

Crackers

Crackers started out as thin, crisp, nonsweet, bite-sized flat breads. The making of crackers was among the first food industries in America. During the eighteenth century, cheap, hard crackers called "ship's bread," "ship's biscuits," and later, "hardtack" were widely manufactured for use on ships and for those migrating westward. These large, sturdy crackers, made only of flour and water—no shortening—kept for a very long time. One of the earliest brand-name foods was Bent's water crackers, which were initially manufactured in 1801 by Josiah Bent, a ship's bread baker in Milton, Massachusetts. The Bent Company continues to manufacture these crackers.

Crackers were packed in barrels and sold to grocery stores and restaurants. Recipes for simple crackers appeared in early American cookbooks. These crackers were little more than baked flour and water and were not made with fermented dough. By the 1840s three major cracker varieties made with short-

ening had been introduced: the soda cracker, the butter cracker, and the round sugar biscuit. During the 1850s a new product, the graham cracker, was likely first manufactured by Russell Thacher Trall, a follower of Sylvester Graham and the author of *The New Hydropathic Cook-book* (1854). Graham crackers were made with graham flour—coarsely milled, unbolted whole wheat flour—and were intended for use by those following the dietary regimen advocated by Sylvester Graham. Graham crackers made commercially contain sugar and other ingredients Sylvester Graham likely would not condone.

During the Civil War, the northern armies and navy were supplied with hardtack. To meet the greatly increased demand, cracker bakers constructed continuously fired, revolving-reel ovens, which greatly increased output. They also installed mixing machines, dough brakes, rolling machines, automatic dough cutters, and stamps for cutting the dough into various shapes. After the Civil War, sales of hardtack declined, but crackers made with sugar became popular. Commercial production of crackers increased when compressed yeast became available in America in the late 1860s. In the nineteenth century crackers were generic products, sold from open barrels, so the crackers were exposed to air, dust, moisture, odors, and the depredations of flies and mice. In the South the term "cracker" was used as a pejorative term for poor whites, particularly in Georgia.

The era of the generic crackers ended in 1898 with the formation of the National Biscuit Company, the forerunner of Nabisco. The company had been formed by a merger of several companies and at the time controlled approximately 70 percent of the American cracker industry. The new company introduced wrapping and packaging machines for their new brand-name product, Uneeda biscuits. To promote these crackers, National Biscuit launched the first major national advertising campaign for a food product, emphasizing a particular advantage: The crackers were sealed in a moisture-proof package that kept them dry, crisp, and unspoiled. In the first full year of the campaign National Biscuit sold 120 million packages of Uneeda biscuits. Another cracker in the National Biscuit product line almost from the company's beginning was the Premium saltine, a square soda cracker. Salt-topped Ritz crackers, made with considerably more shortening than other crackers, were first manufactured in 1935.

After World War II the cracker industry expanded along with the rest of the snack food field. As Americans broadened their tastes, new technology made possible a greater variety of flavors and shapes. Crackers are flavored with onion, herbs, and spices and topped with sesame or poppy seeds. No longer only rectangular or round, crackers may be triangular, oval, scalloped, and fish shaped. In response to market demand, some crackers, including saltines, are made in low-sodium versions, and a few manufacturers have reduced the amount of hydrogenated fat in their products. Crackers are eaten with soups and chowders, softened in milk, and served as a snack food and for dipping. [See also GRAHAM, SYLVESTER; HARDTACK; NABISCO; SNACKS, SALTY.]

BIBLIOGRAPHY

Cahn, William. *Out of the Cracker Barrel*. New York: Simon and Schuster, 1969.

Crackers. New York: Mintel, 2003.

Manley, Duncan J. R. *Technology of Biscuits, Crackers, and Cookies*. 3rd ed. Boca Raton, FL: CRC, 2000.

Panschar, William G. *Baking in America*. Evanston, IL: Northwestern University Press, 1956.

ANDREW F. SMITH

Cranberries

Cranberries (*Vaccinium macrocarpon*), native to bogs and swamps of the northeastern United States and adjacent parts of Canada, were cultivated by Native Americans long before white settlers arrived. Commercial farming, by management of native stands, began early in the nineteenth century on Cape Cod, Massachusetts. The plant enjoys cool summers and requires soils that are very acidic, sandy, moist, and rich in humus. Suitable sites, which have also been developed in Wisconsin and the Pacific Northwest, are furnished with dikes and drainage ditches for water management, important for periodically flooding fields for winter cold protection, harvest, and irrigation.

Although more than 150 cultivars exist, the market is dominated by four—Early Black, Howes, Searles, and McFarlin—which were all selected from the wild in the nineteenth century. The cultivars differ mostly in such characteristics as harvest date and yield. Flavor differences are insignificant, especially for a fruit that is consumed only after processing, so varieties are not marketed by name.

Cranberry plants are woody evergreens whose low stature, thin stems, half-inch leaves, and small blossoms give the plant a delicate appearance. So-called runner stems creep along the ground, forming roots wherever they contact moist soil. In lieu of pruning, cranberry bogs are covered every few years with a two-inch depth of sand, which rejuvenates plants by stimulating formation of new roots on covered portions of stems. The flowers, poised like white cranes on the stalks (the inspiration for the name "crane berry," which became "cranberry") are self-fruitful. Fruits ripen from 60 to 120 days after flowering, depending on the cultivar.

Cranberries are harvested either dry or wet. All the vines are trained in the same direction for dry harvest, and the berries are popped off the vines as they are combed with a rake. Fields are flooded for wet harvest, and special machinery is used to beat the berries from the vine. The dislodged berries float and can then be gathered together for harvest. The bulk of the cranberry crop is sold processed. Fresh fruits keep well and will ripen and redden to some degree even off the vine. The fruit, which is high in vitamin C, is processed into sauces, juices, relishes, and, of course, jelly, the traditional accompaniment to the Thanksgiving turkey.

BIBLIOGRAPHY

Da, M. "Cranberry Management." In *Small Fruit Crop Management*, edited by Gene J. Galletta and David G. Himelrick, 334–362. Englewood Cliffs, NJ: Prentice Hall, 1990.

LEE REICH

Crappie

Crappie is a small fish in the family Centrarchidae, which also includes bass and sunfish, and is a popular sport and food fish. Among sport fishers who call themselves "panfish anglers," black crappie (*Pomoxis nigromaculatus*) and white crappie (*Pomoxis annularis*) are favorites.

Crappie is found all over the United States, but black crappie originated in eastern America. It has been introduced to the western states, as has white crappie, which used to inhabit a range from New York to the Dakotas and south toward Texas. Black crappie prefers cold water but tolerates warmer, more saline water. Although it is found along the Gulf of Mexico and some East Coast areas, black crappie is more populous in northern lakes. White crappie is found more commonly in the South in freshwater rivers, lakes, and bayous.

Crappie eat other small fish, freshwater shellfish, and plankton. The fish seldom grow larger than half a pound to one pound. Record sizes for crappie are four or five pounds. The small size makes crappie ideal for panfrying, although the fish usually is dressed to remove tail, head, and fins before cooking.

SANDRA L. OLIVER

Crayfish

Crayfish also are known as "crawfish," "crawdads," "mudbugs," and, in France, *écrevisses*. In 1887, George Brown Goode wrote about this freshwater crustacean as follows: "Although fresh water crayfish are very abundant in any portions of the United States, they are seldom used as food, and, in fact, there appear to be only two regular markets for their sale, New York and New Orleans. One of the principal uses to which they are put is for garnishing fish dishes in hotels and restaurants." Goode reported that crayfish was such an inconsequential fishery that one could not collect statistics on it. It was known, however, that the crayfish appearing in New York came from Washington, DC, and the Potomac River as soon as the ice was out and from Milwaukee, Wisconsin. Crayfish, a close relative of the lobster, were similarly shipped and sold live. "Crayfish are probably more commonly eaten in New Orleans than in any other American city," Goode observed, "and yet they are seldom seen in the markets there in large quantities."

Crayfish grow to be as long as six inches. There are many species, not any one of which in the United States can support a commercial fishery except along the Atchafalaya River in Louisiana, where red swamp and white river crayfish are harvested. Crayfish farming is gradually providing more and more product, and the United States and China are the major producers. Red swamp crayfish (*Procambarus clarkii*) is the major farmed species, and Louisiana and Minnesota are centers for producing it, often in rotation with rice.

For the Cajuns of Louisiana, crayfish are a prime identity marker. Crayfish cookery was well developed in France, where the European crayfish is raised and harvested. In the Mississippi basin, crayfish are indispensable for use in gumbo, étouffée, and crayfish bisque. Boiled in seasoned water, crayfish are eaten straight from the shell, sometimes during social events called crayfish boils.

SANDRA L. OLIVER

Cream

Cream is a dairy product, rich in fat and skimmed from milk, usually cow's milk. Cream contains all the main constituents of milk but in different proportions, especially butterfat. The fat globules in cream are lighter than the rest of the milk so they naturally cluster and float, rising to the surface when whole milk is left to stand. Once skimmed by hand, commercial cream now is separated by centrifugal force in a mechanical separator that rotates at 5,400 revolutions per minute. Jersey cows yield more cream per

---

Cranberries in History

Native Americans introduced cranberries to New England colonists, who quickly adopted them into their cookery. John Josselyn reported in *New England Rarities Discovered* (1672) that "The *Indians* and *English* use them much, boyling them with Sugar for Sauce to eat with their Meat; and it is a delicate Sauce especially for roasted Mutton; Some make Tarts with them as with Goose Berries." In 1728 cranberries were identified as a food that children could eat between meals. America's first cookbook author, Amelia Simmons, recommended in *American Cookery* (1796) that turkey be served with cranberries, a connection likely made since early colonial times. During the nineteenth century, cranberries were used extensively in pies, sauces, jellies, jams, preserves, puddings, dumplings, marmalades, and ketchup. Cranberries were also mashed and made into a beverage called "cranberryade."

ANDREW F. SMITH

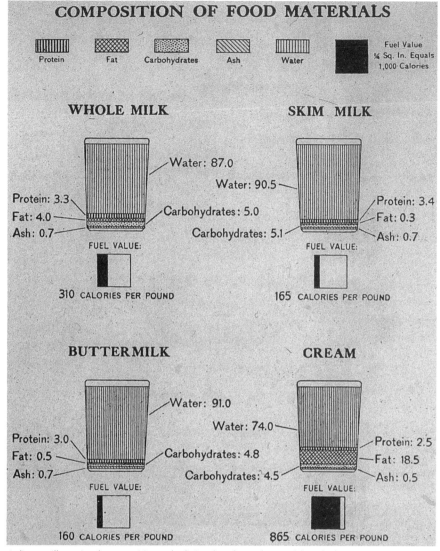

COMPOSITION OF FOOD MATERIALS

Protein | Fat | Carbohydrates | Ash | Water | Fuel Value ¼ Sq. In. Equals 1,000 Calories

WHOLE MILK

Water: 87.0
Protein: 3.3
Fat: 4.0
Ash: 0.7
Carbohydrates: 5.0

FUEL VALUE:

310 CALORIES PER POUND

SKIM MILK

Water: 90.5
Protein: 3.4
Fat: 0.3
Ash: 0.7
Carbohydrates: 5.1

FUEL VALUE:

165 CALORIES PER POUND

BUTTERMILK

Water: 91.0
Protein: 3.0
Fat: 0.5
Ash: 0.7
Carbohydrates: 4.8

FUEL VALUE:

160 CALORIES PER POUND

CREAM

Water: 74.0
Protein: 2.5
Fat: 18.5
Ash: 0.5
Carbohydrates: 4.5

FUEL VALUE:

865 CALORIES PER POUND

A diagram illustrating the composition and caloric value of several types of dairy food.

gallon of milk than a Holstein and were popular in the nineteenth century. But the demand for milk eventually caused yield to be more important than butterfat, and thus the prevalence of the black-and-white-spotted Holstein, America's most popular and productive dairy cow.

The natural thickness of cream depends on the fat content. Single cream has a minimum butterfat content of 18 percent, but its thickness also can be manipulated by manufacturing processes to produce whipping cream (35 percent butterfat), clotted cream (55 percent butterfat), and half-and-half (10 percent butterfat). Sour cream, found in the grocery store's dairy case, is made from pasteurized, homogenized single cream, has a butterfat content of 18 percent, and is soured by the addition of a starter—a bacterial culture that grows in the cream and converts lactose, the natural milk sugar, into lactic acid. Cream also can be found bottled, canned, and preserved by ultra-high temperature (UHT) processing, but may have a slightly cooked flavor.

The preservation and availability of cream was a dilemma for early American housewives. The richness of the milk varied with the weather and cream would spoil unless measures were taken to keep it fresh. The traditional English technique for preserving cream (pour milk into shallow pans until the cream has risen, then heat it to 82°F for half an hour and allow to cool overnight) was adopted in America with few modifications. Lettice Bryan's *The Kentucky Housewife* (1839) includes a technique for boiling sugar-sweetened cream, bottling it with corks dipped in melted rosin, and storing it in a cool place such as a root cellar. Pioneer women sometimes invoked myth and superstition to blame the cream for going sour (thunder and lightning) or butter for being slow to form (pixies in the churn). In North Carolina they called for someone with an ugly face to peer into a cream jar and clot the cream.

Cream is widely used in baking and confectionary, soups and sauces, and desserts, where it is an essential ingredient whether frothily whipped or frozen into ice cream. It

is the basic component of butter and is important in cream cheese and acidulated creams, such as mascarpone and crème fraîche, which originated in Europe but later were manufactured in America as well.

Cream is integral to many beverages, from the Elizabethan syllabub, brought to America and popular through the nineteenth century, to cocktails such as the grasshopper. It is the epitome of coffee additives, memorialized by the singer Ruth Etting in the 1929 recording of the love song "You're the Cream in my Coffee." The famous egg cream soda fountain confection first produced in New York City contains neither eggs nor cream.

[See also BUTTER; CREAMS, DESSERT; DAIRY; MILK; SYLLABUB.]

BIBLIOGRAPHY
Rath, Sara. *About Cows.* Minocqua, WI: NorthWord, 1987.

SARA RATH

Cream Cheese

The term "cream cheese" generally refers to spreadable, cow's-milk cheeses, originally with a high butterfat content (though many versions now substitute various gums and gelling agents to produce a low-fat, yet spreadable, cream cheese). An early version of cream cheese was, strictly speaking, not even cheese (as it was not made from curds)—it was nothing more than cream hung to dry in cheesecloth until thickened. Some precursors of cream cheese were true cheeses, however. Some European cheeses—such as Neufchatel and Marscarpone—had similar properties: like our cream cheese, they were served young—with their lactic tanginess unmellowed by aging, but they were not the same as American cream cheese.

Like many other products of American industry and imagination, cream cheese was invented, or discovered, due to a fortuitous combination of accident, luck, the current technological environment, and the entrepreneurial urge to increase profits by imitating the success of others.

In the post Civil War period, New York State's Catskill Mountains were in need of a new industry. Dairy farming was one of the few forms of agriculture that was feasible in the bare rocky soil that was left after its forests were cut down to provide hemlock bark for the tanneries that supplied the Union Army with leather. However, the area's dairy farmers could not sell all their fresh milk in nearby New York City's vast market because there was not yet adequate refrigeration available. Therefore, one of the oldest forms of preservation of dairy products, cheese making, soon became an important part of the region's economy.

A domestic version of Neufchâtel had already been produced, in New Jersey, in 1870, but Charles Green (an Orange County cheesemaker) thought he could produce a better one, at a lower cost. In 1872, he brought a European cheese maker to the village of Chester as a consultant on the production of the soft French cheese.

However, William A. Lawrence overheard Green's lesson (local legend says he was lurking under an open window). Lawrence tested the recipe—using twice the required amount of cream. He began producing his creation, which was sent to Philadelphia, where it was packaged as "Star Brand Cream Cheese."

At the end of the nineteenth century, the most fashionable marketing name in the United States was "Philadelphia," so the cheese was not named after its birthplace in the rural Catskills. The Empire Cheese Factory, in South Edmeston, New York, registered the brand name "Philadephia Cream Cheese" in 1885. The company name was changed to "The Phenix Cheese Corporation" in 1924 (the modernized name referred to the original factory that had burned, and been rebuilt, in 1900). Kraft purchased the company, as well as its successful brand name, "Philadelphia," in 1928. Its familiar foil-wrapped bricks, bearing the name of a city that had little to do with its provenance, have become the standard for American creamcheese.

The proximity of Jewish immigrants on New York City's Lower East Side and the Catskills' dairy farmers led to the creation of two very American takes on Old World foods: New York-style cheesecake and bagels "with a schmeer" (a thick slathering of cream cheese).

BIBLIOGRAPHY
Stamm, Eunice R. *The History of Cheesemaking in New York State: The History of Cheesemaking in the Empire State from the Early Dutch Settlers to Modern Times.* Endicott, NY: Lewis Group, 1991.

GARY ALLEN

Creams, Dessert

Dessert creams are sweet dishes incorporating cream or egg whites, usually whipped, into a flavorful base. Highly popular in America in the eighteenth and nineteenth centuries, creams were a ubiquitous treat on English and French tables no later than the seventeenth century and were transported to American shores as domestic dairying grew.

Creams were made easily at home, requiring only a pan set over a heat source, a fork or whip to create the volume, and a way of cooling the mix. Creams were originally and most typically flavored with fruits, nuts, coffee, or tea, although chocolate and vanilla debuted in the nineteenth century. Recipes fell into two basic categories, and the texture ranged from a spoonable, thick sauce to a billowy cloud.

The simplest recipes are essentially enriched medieval nut milks: cream was boiled with ground nuts until thickened and then strained into glasses for chilling. Much more common were cream recipes based either on whipped eggs, particularly whites, or whipped

cream. Some recipes used both. These creams, decoratively tinted in pastels, could be spooned into glasses or elaborate jelly dishes and chilled, or frozen into ice cream. Highly perishable, creams were elite and effete, referred to as "the little end of nothing whittled down."

By the early twentieth century, readily available commercial gelatin added to the base created Bavarian creams, which are sturdy enough to unmold and slice. Even with the gelatin, however, creams, unless frozen, were never good candidates for commercial production and transportation. Requiring fresh whipped eggs or cream, they remained a homemade dessert, although the shrinking number of recipes in twentieth-century cookbooks attests to their declining popularity.
[**See also** CREAM; DESSERTS; EGGS.]

BIBLIOGRAPHY
Belden, Louise Conway. *The Festive Tradition: Table Decoration and Desserts in America, 1650–1900.* New York: W. W. Norton, 1983.

CATHY K. KAUFMAN

Cream Soda

Cream soda is a carbonated soft drink whose main ingredients are water, sweetener, and vanilla. Although some bottlers use cane sugar for the creamiest texture, most varieties are made with high fructose corn syrup. Cream soda is naturally clear, but most are colored with caramelized sugar, which also adds a slight flavor. Red cream soda has been popular occasionally, and there has even been a vogue for blue cream soda.

There are a number of explanations for the name "cream soda." The most obvious is the soda's creamy feel in the mouth. Another possibility is that some recipes call for cream of tartar, which adds to the creaminess of the drink. And, last, some people believe that it was originally called "ice cream soda," because it tastes as though it were made from vanilla ice cream.

Carbonated vanilla drinks were known in the United States as cream soda by 1854. Gray's Brewing of Wisconsin has been selling its cream soda since 1856. Although cream soda has captured only a small piece of the soft-drink market and has sometimes been considered an older person's drink, bottlers have been going after a younger market with hand-crafted cream sodas using more expensive ingredients, such as Tahitian vanilla and exotic honeys.
[**See also** SODA DRINKS.]

SYLVIA LOVEGREN

Creole Food, *see Cajun and Creole Food*

Crisco

In 1911 the Procter & Gamble Company of Cincinnati, Ohio—until then best known for Ivory soap—introduced "An Absolutely New Product. A Scientific Discovery Which

A Crisco advertisement.

[would] Affect Every Kitchen in America. Something that the American housewife had always wanted" (Krondl, p. 266). It was Crisco. P&G was well placed to manufacture hydrogenated vegetable shortening, because the technology to make soap is substantially the same. Moreover, the company had been in the shortening business since at least 1870, when lard was part of its line.

Crisco was launched with one of the most comprehensive and successful advertising campaigns of all time. The shortening was hailed as modern and pure, playing on the public's fears concerning the unhygienic practices found in the meatpacking plants where commercial lard was processed. Advertisements extolled the immaculate factory housed "in a specially designed building lined with tile and flooded with sunshine" (Krondl, p. 272). The fat was individually packaged to safeguard it from contamination. In addition, numerous premium recipe collections were produced, including a kosher cookbook in 1933. P&G's literature quoted Rabbi Margolies of New York stating that "that the Hebrew Race has been waiting 4,000 years for Crisco" (Krondl, p. 267). However, the most important selling point to Jew and Gentile alike was that Crisco was considerably cheaper than butter or even lard.

Over the years the brand name has been used for vegetable oil (from 1960) as well as vegetable sprays (from 1995). Since 1991 Crisco has been sold in butter-sized sticks beside the original tubs. Perhaps more remarkable, though, was the introduction of butter-flavored shortening in 1981—this from a company that had once claimed that "upon thousands of pages, the words 'lard' and 'butter' [had] been crossed out and the word 'Crisco' written in their place" (Krondl, p. 267).

BIBLIOGRAPHY
Krondl, Michael. *Around the American Table: Treasured Recipes and Food Traditions from the American Cookery Collections of The New York Public Library.* Holbrook, MA: Adams, 1995.

MICHAEL KRONDL

Croly, Jane Cunningham, *see Jenny June*

Crullers

In essence, a cruller is a twisted piece of deep-fried sweet dough. It originated with the Dutch, who named it for its distinctive shape (the verb *krullen* means "to curl"). In practice, especially U.S. practice, exceptions and variations abound—not only among the Dutch Americans whose forebears are credited with introducing the cruller to New York, but also among bakers of Scandinavian, Austrian, and Polish descent, each with their own twist (if you will) on the recipe. No ingredient save flour is completely indispensable, not even butter, sugar, milk, or eggs. Flavorings run the gamut from cinnamon, nutmeg, cardamom, lemon, and vanilla to wine, whiskey, rum, and even rose water (a suggestion from the seminal nineteenth-century cookbook author Eliza Leslie). The namesake shape is only one of many crullers may take. Various recipes specify diamonds, braids, corkscrews, cigars, rectangles, and even rings (whereupon they are dead ringers for doughnuts). Some are plain, others are glazed, dusted with sugar, or topped with syrup or jam. Finally, crullers are known by a slew of alternative names, including twist cakes, love knots, matrimony knots, angel wings, and Henriettes. Leslie knew them additionally as wonders, and Louisiana Cajuns proffer *croquignoles*.

[**See also** DOUGHNUTS; DUTCH INFLUENCES ON AMERICAN FOOD; PASTRIES.]

BIBLIOGRAPHY

Rose, Peter G., trans. and ed. *The Sensible Cook: Dutch Foodways in the Old and the New World*. Syracuse, NY: Syracuse University Press, 1989.

RUTH TOBIAS

Cuba Libre

"Cuba Libre" was shouted over raised glasses in bars in the United States and Cuba during and after the Spanish-American War. The combination of Cuban rum with the newly invented American Coca-Cola seemed natural for a drink. The Cuba Libre became Cuba's national cocktail and is widely consumed in South Florida. It is made with rum, Coca-Cola, and a dash of Key lime juice; it is served over ice in a chilled highball glass with a lime wedge. Many bartenders naturally put a lime wedge in a rum and Coke even when the drink is not ordered by its original name.

[**See also** COCA-COLA; COCKTAILS; RUM.]

MARIAN BETANCOURT

Cuban American Food

Located barely ninety miles from Key West, Florida, Cuba is the largest island nation in the Caribbean. It is a slender, crocodile-shaped land with fertile soil and a moderate tropical climate. The cuisine of the island was created by the native Taino (Arawak) Indians and transplanted peoples from four continents: Caribbean Indians and some from Florida brought to work in the mines, Spanish colonists, African slaves, Chinese contract workers, French refugees from Haiti, and peasants from Jamaica and Haiti.

Two events have marked the history of Cuba and defined its cuisine: the Spanish conquest and settlement, which lasted more than four hundred years, and the socialist

A sign in the window of Las Americas Restaurant in Hoboken, New Jersey, advertises fritas Cubanas.

revolution that began in 1959. Cuban cuisine formed almost biologically through the cross-fertilization of successive waves of peoples and cultures under Spanish colonial rule. The cuisine has preserved more of a Mediterranean character than many other Latin American cuisines. There is little use of the hot peppers or cilantro as in Mexican and some Andean cooking and relatively little use of corn. The corn that is used is prepared simply: fresh in tamales and both fresh and dried in sweet and savory porridges (*harina de maiz* and *tamal en cazuela*). The basis of most Cuban dishes is a classic Spanish *sofrito* (sauce base) made of sautéed garlic, onion, and green pepper and often enriched with bacon or Spanish sausage (chorizo) and a touch of beer or wine. Cubans seldom cook meat, fish, or game before seasoning it with adobo, a paste made with a mixture of an acid medium, such as lime, sour orange, or vinegar, and crushed garlic, pepper, salt, cumin, and oregano. Permanent food shortages and the concurrent erosion of traditional foodways have been part of the fallout of the revolution and accompanying international tensions.

Cuba's proximity to the United States and the cultural and political ties that have joined the two countries since the Spanish-American War in the 1890s turned the United States into the natural destination for Cubans seeking political asylum. José Martí and hundreds of Cuban exiles had relocated to Key West and Tampa, Florida, and New York City before the war. Cubans first came to the United States in large numbers after the 1959 revolution, arriving on chartered planes sponsored by the U.S. government. When the Cuban government stopped the legal exodus, immigrants swam across Guantánamo Bay to find refuge at the American naval base ("Gitmo") or risked their lives crossing the

Straits of Florida by boat or on flimsy rafts. The first wave of post-1959 immigration was composed of affluent Cubans, mostly from Havana and the western provinces of the island. Exiles from all regions of the country and representing all social groups and occupations gradually began arriving in large numbers. The 2002 U.S. Census estimated that 1,241,685 Cubans, including exiles born in Cuba and their U.S.-born descendants, live in United States. Although Cubans live all over the United States, most have settled in Dade County, Florida, particularly in Miami, and in Hudson County, New Jersey. The trend is for retired Cubans living in the Northeast to move to Florida. Immigration of Cubans in the early 1960s transformed Miami, which was once little more than a tropical vacation enclave, into a durable and cosmopolitan city. Most Cubans had left behind family, friends, and material possessions but clung strongly to their cultural identity. Unable to return to Cuba legally for more than a decade, Cubans were unique among Hispanics living in the United States for their speedy assimilation into mainstream society coupled with a strong attachment to Cuba, its music, and its cuisine.

The Cuban exodus to Florida had a historic precedent. During the war of independence at the turn of the nineteenth century, Cuban political dissidents, mostly cigar makers, sought refuge in Key West. This tiny island at the tip of Florida became a lively Cuban enclave with cultural centers and restaurants, cigar factories where novels were read to workers as was traditionally done in Cuba, and a distinct Cuban cuisine. After Cuba gained its independence from Spain, Key West became the gateway for citrus fruits and avocados ferried from Cuba. These foods were transported north by train by Martin Brooks, the founder of Brooks Tropicals, a prominent grower and distributor of tropical fruits and vegetables in the Redlands of Homestead, Florida. After 1935 Brooks began to grow avocados and tropical fruits from Cuban seed in the fertile fields of Homestead, just south of Miami. In the 1960s newly arrived Cuban farmers, mostly from Las Villas, planted tropical tubers and fruits, such as yucca (cassava), sweet potato, malanga coco, and mamey, near those same fields, changing the landscape and providing the raw materials for a transplanted Cuban cuisine.

Cuban restaurants sprang up all over Miami and wherever Cubans settled. Small restaurants and cafeterias keep the home fires burning by serving traditional foods: black beans, roast pork seasoned with adobo marinade, tender yucca doused in the garlicky table sauce called *mojo*, twice-fried green plantain (*tostones*); tropical juices and milkshakes; pressed Cuban sandwiches with layers of ham, pork, swiss cheese, and a pickle; and creamy flan sweetened with condensed milk. There also are numerous bakeries where people gathered for their daily *cafecito cubano* (inky espresso served in tiny cups) and sweet guava pastries. In the bakeries, Cubans also buy their traditional flaky bread for sandwiches and order elaborate, towering cakes for a girl's *fiesta de quince* or "sweet fifteen" party. From Boston to Hialeah, from New Jersey to Las Vegas, Cuban restaurants and cafeterias have a sameness that Cubans find comforting. Two dishes from other Latin American nations have become firmly established on the menus of Cuban restaurants. Argentinean-style skirt steak, which is generically listed as *churrasco* is served with *chimichurri*, a mildly spicy Argentinean table sauce. *Tres leches*, a trifle cake made popular by Nicaraguans in Miami, consists of a simple sponge cake soaked in three milks: condensed, evaporated, and heavy cream.

The usual restaurant menus do not represent the original range of Cuban regional dishes. At home, Cubans continue to cook traditional foods, but like other immigrant groups, they have also embraced American convenience foods and fast food, diversifying their diets with other ethnic cuisines, particularly Chinese and Italian. Although Cubans constitute only 3.7 percent of the total Hispanic population in the United States, Cuban food is the second most influential Latin cuisine in this country after Mexican cooking. Cuban food and drinks, particularly the *mojito*, a lemony rum cocktail perfumed with crushed mint leaves, have begun to stir the imagination of Latino and American chefs. Cuban food has been represented in the United States for a very long time with no major consequences and little crossover, except for black bean soup, Cuban sandwiches, and some rum cocktails, such as the daiquiri. Havana's fabled reputation as the playground of the rich and the watering hole of

the Americas has contributed to a revival of the Cuban cocktail tradition. One result of interest in Cuban culture is the emergence of restaurants that play on the mythology of Cuba's elusive and fun-filled past. Old cigar labels, Cuban paraphernalia, and decor reminiscent of sultry street corners in Havana become props for Cuban cuisine of the imagination—at best, American fusion with a thin tropical veneer. A more genuine revival must await freer communication between chefs in the United States and the Cuban culinary tradition back on the island.

[See also CARIBBEAN INFLUENCES ON AMERICAN FOOD.]

BIBLIOGRAPHY

Presilla, Maricel. "The Making of the Cuban Culinary Tradition." *Journal of Gastronomy* 3 (Winter 1987/1988): 44–53.

Presilla, Maricel. "Miami Cubans." In *The Food of Miami: Authentic Recipes from South Florida and the Keys*, edited by Caroline Stuart, 16–18. Boston: Periplus, 1999.

Presilla, Maricel. "My Eternal Cuba." *Saveur*, December 1999.

Rodriguez, Douglas. *Nuevo Latino*. Berkeley, CA: Ten Speed, 1995.

MARICEL PRESILLA

Cucumbers

The cucumber, *Cucumis sativus*, is a subtropical annual originating in India. Domesticated by the seventh century B.C.E., the cucumber soon spread to China and the ancient Mediterranean world. Galen ascribed diuretic properties to cucumbers but cautioned that overindulgence produced a "wretched juice that is the cause of malignant fevers."

The Romans spread the cucumber through the empire; the plant thrived in Mediterranean areas. Seeds have been found at Roman sites in Britain, although archaeologists debate whether cucumbers were a luxury import or were grown at villas of the rich during classical times, as they would have required fancy cold frames or other agricultural techniques to flourish in the chilly British climate. By the sixteenth century, cucumbers were a fad foodstuff in England: aristocrats built cold frames and hothouses, developing what would become heirloom varieties from experiments in forcing stock.

Cucumbers first arrived in the New World with the Spanish, landing in Haiti in 1494. They spread quickly to Florida and then through Native American populations ranging as far west as the Great Plains. Cucumbers were introduced separately in the north. Sometimes called "cowcumber" in British and early American sources, allegedly because the cucumber's perceived indigestibility made it fit only for cows, both British and Dutch colonists boasted of the cucumber's success in sultry colonial summers. Related to but distinct from cucumbers are gherkins, *C. anguria*, which were introduced into America only in 1793 but which spread quickly as a

reliable crop free from the insects that plagued *C. sativus*.

Cucumbers are most frequently pickled or used raw in salads with vinaigrettes or "high" seasonings. In the nineteenth century cucumbers were often stewed and flavored with gravy, fried, stuffed, or even added to cold soups as part of a Spanish gazpacho. Cucumbers are also sautéed, creamed, or served with rich butter sauces, and they are used decoratively in thin slices to simulate fish scales on large sides of cold, poached salmon.

Cucumbers have maintained a reputation for indigestibility, with different preparation tricks suggested to reduce the danger. In *The American Frugal Housewife* (1829), Lydia Maria Child recommends slicing cucumbers thinly and soaking them in cold water to take out "the slimy matter, so injurious to health." Thomas J. Murrey gives precisely the opposite advice in *Salads and Sauces* (1884), in which he blames digestive difficulties on removing the natural juices; he urges peeling the skins and dousing the juicy remains copiously with oil.

Early Americans appreciated the different varieties of cucumbers. In *American Cookery* (1796), Amelia Simmons identifies preferred uses for the "many kinds": prickly (she is likely referring to the gherkin, *C. anguria*); tender whites; and smooth, bright green ones. In 1806 Bernard M'Mahon identified eight varieties in his authoritative *The American Gardener's Calendar*. Modern American growers generally classify cucumbers by their culinary purposes: either pickling or slicing, with greenhouse (also known as European), Middle Eastern, and Oriental groupings further dividing the slicing category. Those subgroups include many cultivars that have been bred for different qualities: seedlessness and digestibility, flavor and smooth skin, and crispness. The Southeast, along with California, leads in growing slicing cucumbers, while Michigan and North Carolina lead in growing pickling cucumbers.

[See also PICKLES; VEGETABLES.]

BIBLIOGRAPHY

Phipps, Frances. *Colonial Kitchens, Their Furnishings, and Their Gardens*. New York: Hawthorn Books, 1972.

Weaver, William Woys. *Heirloom Vegetable Gardening*. New York: Holt, 1997.

CATHY K. KAUFMAN

Culinary Historians of Boston

The Culinary Historians of Boston, founded by Barbara Ketchum Wheaton and Joyce Toomre, was the first group of its kind and has been meeting every month of the academic year since 1980. The first meeting took place on May 29 with a brown-bag lunch under a maple tree in Radcliffe Yard. Most of those who came to that first meeting did not know one another but had heard about the founding meeting by word of mouth. Wheaton recalls that it was a very informal but enthusiastic get-together.

Those first members came from a variety of academic and work backgrounds, a pattern that has continued.

One common theme shared by the members of the group was the desire to expose the misinformation that had been published about food and to set a standard for excellence for doing food and culinary research.

Some of those early members included Barbara Haber, a bibliographer of women's history and a curator of printed books at the Schlessinger Library; Ann Robert, a French restaurateur; Joyce Toomre, a college professor and a specialist in Russian cookery; Ruth Palombo, a dietitian at Massachusetts General Hospital; David Miller, an expert on the history and manufacture of metalwork, especially molds; Tom Lam, a graduate student studying the life and work of Ellen Swallow Richards; and Nina Simonds, an expert on Chinese cookery.

Since the beginning, the final event for the year has been a period banquet. At the first banquet members prepared recipes from *Savoring the Past: The French Kitchen and Table from 1300 to 1789* by Barbara Wheaton. Other dinners have included a Roman banquet, an 1830s American picnic, a Civil War banquet, a Russian banquet, and an Indonesian feast.

After a quarter of a century some of the original members were still attending the monthly meetings. At the beginning of the twenty-first century the Culinary Historians of Boston was continuing as a nonprofit organization dedicated to the study of foodways. Members around the country receive a newsletter with announcements of meetings, accounts of previous meetings, notices of new books, and information on exhibits and food-related conferences.

[**See also** CULINARY HISTORY VS. FOOD HISTORY.]

JOSEPH M. CARLIN

Culinary History vs. Food History

Until relatively recently, the study of food was pursued almost exclusively in America by independent scholars who call themselves "culinary historians" and commonly share a deep interest in ingredients, recipes, and cooking techniques. A growing number of academic scholars now see themselves as "food historians" who may ignore cooking as such but study food to illuminate such broad areas as immigration history, the history of science and technology, and contemporary culture and society.

In *Sweetness and Power* (1985), the anthropologist Sidney Mintz created an influential interdisciplinary model for food historians by combining field work with Caribbean sugarcane workers and a study of the social, economic, and political history of sugar as a major agricultural product. The historian Harvey Levenstein soon followed with *Revolution at the Table* (1988), relating changing eating habits in the United States between 1880 and 1930 to immigration, urbanization,

developing technologies, and the growth of the corporate food industry. In *Paradox of Plenty* (1993), Levenstein showed how the American diet was shaped by cultural, political, and economic forces since the 1930s. The American Studies professor Warren Belasco in *Appetite for Change* (1989) analyzed how corporate America profitably co-opted such counterculture foods as brown rice and whole wheat bread that had symbolized radical opposition to capitalism in the 1960s.

The impact of immigration on American food is the focus of geography professor Richard Pillsbury's *No Foreign Food* (1998), which explores dietary changes from colonial times to the present. In the same year, Donna Gabaccia, a specialist in immigration and women's history, published *We Are What We Eat*, which also looks at the impact of ethnicity on American eating habits. The historian Hasia Diner in *Hungering for America* (2001) contrasts the food experiences of the Irish, Italians, and Jews in the Old World and America, and explores how preserving ancestral foodways forged ethnic community and identity in the United States.

By the late 1990s academic food studies focusing on women's history proliferated. Amy Bentley's *Eating for Victory* (1998) examines American women's important roles relative to food in supporting the nation during World War II and its aftermath. In addition to three essay collections, Sherrie Inness offered her own study, *Dinner Roles* (2001), on the deep connections between American women and food throughout the twentieth century. The literary scholar Doris Witt connects African American studies, cultural studies, and food history in *Black Hunger* (1999), exploring the relationship between African American women and food in literature, art, and advertising. In *Eat My Words* (2002), the folklorist Janet Theophano dignifies cookbooks as a literary genre, showing the importance of food not only to women's history but also to human history.

Culinary historians have commonly been curious about the origins of different dishes and gone on to investigate such related subjects as the specific foods people raise and how foods move from one culture to another. The methodology of these largely independent scholars is well illustrated in the work of Karen Hess, renowned for her facsimile editions of *Martha Washington's Booke of Cookery* (1981), *The Virginia House-wife* (1984), *What Mrs. Fisher Knows about Old Southern Cooking* (1995), and the *Carolina Rice Cook Book*, compiled by Mrs. Samuel G. Stoney, included in *The Carolina Rice Kitchen* (1992). In all of these works, Hess provides historical contexts for the recipes and important conclusions about the cookbook writers. In *The Carolina Rice Kitchen*, for instance, she establishes the connections between the South Carolina rice culture and the early African American cooks who introduced such dishes as rice and bean pilafs.

Like Hess, William Woys Weaver sees cookbooks as cultural artifacts, as demonstrated in his facsimile edition of *A Quaker Woman's Cookbook* (1982). Originally published in 1845, the book served as a handbook for inexperienced young wives who knew little about cookery. To Weaver, it is a rich source of information about the role of Quaker women in the Middle Atlantic region of nineteenth-century America. Weaver has also written on Pennsylvania Dutch cooking and Pennsylvania German foods in *Sauerkraut Yankees* (1983) and *Pennsylvania Dutch Cooking* (1993). In *America's First Cuisines* (1994), another independent scholar, Sophie Coe, used her anthropological training to contribute to our understanding of pre-Columbian civilizations—Aztec, Maya, and Inca—after examining the writings of early Spanish settlers and remnants of their cooking vessels.

Culinary historians learn of one another's work through their publications and by attending the growing number of meetings and conferences that have been held since the early 1980s. The first such gathering, the Oxford Symposium on Food and Cookery, organized by the British food historian Alan Davidson, brought together an international group that continues to meet in Oxford, England. Since then, culinary history groups have sprung up across the United States, typically inviting outside speakers who are recognized authorities on food topics and often staging period meals to illustrate how food was grown, cooked, and served in the past. Amateur researchers also enjoy comparable cooking demonstrations held at living-history museums throughout the country.

Professional scholars attend their own conferences such as the annual joint meeting of the Association for the Study of Food and Society and the Agriculture, Food and Human Values Society. Moreover, academic historians are sometimes dismissive of culinary historians and their "womanish" concern with recipes and hands-on cooking. Yet without an understanding of what is involved in food preparation—the labor, equipment and ingredients—academics risk serious errors of fact and interpretation. Standard ingredients familiar to cooks, such as nasturtiums in salads or candied violets in cake decorating, may strike academic scholars as unusual and exotic. Or they may not appreciate why ordinary families employed servants in nineteenth-century America without knowing how demanding cooking was in kitchens of that era. In time it may be universally recognized that knowledge of how dishes are prepared, served, and eaten is indispensable to the proper study of food. When that happens, the terms "food historian" and "culinary historian" will become a distinction without a difference, and research on food by academic and independent scholars will become richer and deeper as well as more accurate.

[**See also** CULINARY HISTORIANS OF BOSTON; HISTORICAL DINING REENACTMENT; HISTORIOGRAPHY.]

BIBLIOGRAPHY

Flandrin, Jean-Louis, and Massimo Montanari. *Food: A Culinary History from Antiquity to the Present.* English edition by Albert Sonnenfeld. New York: Columbia University Press, 1999.

Neuhaus, Jessamyn. *Manly Meals and Mom's Home Cooking: Cookbooks and Gender in Modern America.* Baltimore: Johns Hopkins University Press, 2003.

Zanger, Mark H. *The American History Cookbook.* Westport, Greenwood, 2003.

BARBARA HABER

Culinary Institute of America

The Culinary Institute of America (CIA) is the only residential college in the world with a curriculum devoted entirely to the culinary profession. First known as the New Haven Restaurant Institute, it was founded in 1946 in New Haven, Connecticut, as a vocational training school for World War II veterans. Demand for food-service professionals in a burgeoning industry sparked rapid expansion, and in 1947 the cooking school moved to larger quarters and was renamed the Restaurant Institute of Connecticut. In 1951 the school became known as the Culinary Institute of America.

Continued growth in the food industry placed increased demand on facilities, and in 1970 the CIA moved to Hyde Park, New York. St. Andrew-on-Hudson, a former Jesuit seminary, was purchased, and it served as the nucleus around which the campus was built. In 1995 the CIA expanded to the West Coast, purchasing the former Christian Brothers Winery-Greystone Cellars in the Napa Valley of California.

The CIA offers bachelor's and associate's degree programs in culinary arts and baking and pastry arts as well as continuing education for wine and food professionals. Research and study of nutritional cooking are centered at the CIA's General Foods Nutrition Center, and the culinary collection at the Conrad N. Hilton Library serves both students and food scholars. The CIA is the only school authorized to administer the American Culinary Federation's master chef certification program. The Learning Resources Center produces and maintains instructional videotapes for the culinary profession.

Students staff the CIA's five Hyde Park restaurants, gaining hands-on experience in all venues of food preparation and service. The restaurants, which are open to the public, have garnered several industry awards for outstanding cuisine. The Escoffier Restaurant, specializing in modern interpretations of classic French cuisine, was the recipient of *Restaurants and Institutions* magazine's coveted Ivy Award.

[See also COOKING SCHOOLS.]

BECKY MERCURI

Cupboards and Food Safes

Convenience for cooks and protection from pests are the driving forces in storing food. From the beginning of American kitchens, containers, bowls, and tools have been stored on shelves or in built-in or freestanding cupboards with shelves and drawers. Before refrigeration various foods were kept in food "safes."

Cupboards fixed to kitchen walls were often fitted with sliding shelf-boxes for storing such items as cleaning supplies and closed bins of meal and flour. Freestanding cupboards held preparation tools as well as tableware and serving pieces. Sometimes such cupboards were called "dressers." In 1869 Catharine Beecher and her sister, Harriet Beecher Stowe (author of the antislavery novel *Uncle Tom's Cabin*, 1852), published *The American Woman's Home.* It depicts a practical kitchen layout with fixed shelves, some below the work surfaces, laden with boxes and tins.

Meat and other food safes are wooden, furniture-like cases with one or more shelves, with or without legs, and with punctured tin or wood panels or screening for air circulation and insect protection. They could be fixed to joists or set where convenient in kitchen or pantry. An amusing household hint was to put each leg of a food safe in a container of water to deter ants. The most notable U.S. food safes are pie safes, sometimes decoratively painted and with ornamental patterns in the punctured tins.

From the late 1800s to the 1930s freestanding cabinets (generally known as "Hoosier" cabinets because so many brands came from Indiana) with shelves, storage bins, and enameled work surfaces were popular. Some had pullout dough boards, and even coffee grinders and flour sifters were built into them.

[See also KITCHENS.]

BIBLIOGRAPHY

Franklin, Linda Campbell. *300 Years of Kitchen Collectibles.* 5th ed. Iola, WI: Krause, 2003.

Kennedy, Phillip D. *Hoosier Cabinets.* Indianapolis, IN: privately published, 1989.

LINDA CAMPBELL FRANKLIN

Currants

Currants are making a comeback in America, after once having gone out of favor for being implicated as alternate hosts for a white pine disease. They are plants of northern regions, thriving where summers are cool.

Red and white currants are different-colored forms of hybrids of *Ribes rubrum, R. sativum,* and *R. petraeum.* They became popular in northern Europe in about the fifteenth century and were one of the first plants brought over by early colonists to America. Into the early part of the twentieth century, red currants were a significant crop and were grown, for example, between apple trees in New York's Hudson Valley for sale locally and for shipment to New York City.

Red and white currants are generally concocted into a beautiful, translucent jelly, although some varieties are tasty when eaten fresh.

Black currants, mostly of the *Ribes nigrum* species, are susceptible to the pine disease, although resistant varieties have been bred. Black currants first came into favor in Europe in the sixteenth century, as a medicinal plant whose fruits are recognized as a potent source of vitamin C. The robust raw flavor does not appeal to everyone, but it makes a delectable jam and juice and is the fruit flavoring for cassis. The clove currant, *R. odoratum,* is a native American black currant that was once valued for the spicy fragrance of its yellow, trumpet-shaped blossoms; its aromatic, sweet-tart fruit is larger than that of the European black currant. "Dried currants" are not made from currants but from grapes.

BIBLIOGRAPHY

Reich, Lee. *Uncommon Fruits for Every Garden.* Portland, OR: Timber, 2004.

LEE REICH

Custards

Custards are a combination of eggs and milk or cream, with additional flavorings added, either sweet or savory, and gently cooked until thickened. Cooking techniques vary. Stirred custards, misleadingly called "boiled" (as boiling curdles the texture and is usually considered a fault), are made in a pan over a heat source and result in a rich but pourable sauce. Baked custards are gently cooked in an oven until they become a solid gel. Virtually all European cuisines have had some form of custard since the late medieval period; most—such as boiled pudding sauces (often called "crème anglaise") from England and flan from Spain—have found their way into American kitchens with successive waves of immigrants.

Historically custards were frequently baked in a crust, forming an important component of medieval meat pies. Recipes for such dishes came to America in colonial manuscripts and continue to appear under the name of "quiche." Quiche enjoyed a brief renaissance in the 1970s, one that was squelched by the assertion that "real men don't eat quiche."

Perhaps custard's most popular form is crème brûlée, which rocketed to cultlike status in restaurants in the 1980s and 1990s. Home cooks emulated, purchasing tiny torches for caramelizing the custard's crackling sugar lid. Had they read the "receipt" for burnt custard in *The Kentucky Housewife* (1839) by Lettice Bryan, they would have used a red-hot shovel or a salamander to singe the sugar.

[See also CREAM; EGGS.]

CATHY K. KAUFMAN

D

Dagwood Sandwich

The Dagwood sandwich was the creation of the *Blondie* cartoonist Murat "Chic" Young. In the late 1930s fans first witnessed its construction when Blondie's husband, Dagwood Bumstead, clad in his famous polka-dot pajamas, threw open the refrigerator and built a sandwich based on any and all ingredients that came to hand. In 1947 the recipe appeared in Young's *Blondie's Soups, Salads, Sandwiches Cook Book* as the "Skyscraper Special," and it included sardines and baked beans, along with suggestions for other somewhat incompatible foods. The term "Dagwood" is used for any large, multilayered sandwiches, like hoagies or submarines, consisting of various cold cuts, fillings, and condiments.
[**See also** HOAGIE; SANDWICHES.]

BIBLIOGRAPHY

Mercuri, Becky. *Sandwiches That You Will Like.* Pittsburgh, PA: WQED Pittsburgh, 2002.

BECKY MERCURI

An advertisement for St. Charles Evaporated Cream, late nineteenth century.

Dairy

Each American consumes five hundred pounds of dairy products a year, including milk, butter, buttermilk, cream, sour cream, cheese, ice cream, milk sherbet, and yogurt, making dairy the largest food group by weight in the nation's diet. These foods provide 75 percent of the calcium in the diet, especially important for pregnant, nursing, and menopausal women. On the other hand, the high fat content of dairy foods elevates levels of LDL cholesterol, which contribute to heart disease. About 50 million Americans, most notably African and Asian Americans and American Indians, are lactose intolerant and cannot drink milk without adverse reactions.

Milk: America's "Perfect" Food

Milk is a symbol of American national identity and, with its whiteness and presumed perfection, a reminder of mother's milk. The United States produces 38 billion gallons a year, the raw material for almost all dairy foods, making the country the greatest milk-producing country in the world. California, Wisconsin, New York, Pennsylvania, and Minnesota are the leading states.

Cheese

The United States is the world's largest cheese producer, manufacturing 8.5 billion pounds in 2001. The top five cheese-making states are Wisconsin, Minnesota, California, Idaho, and New York. The most consumed American original cheese is Cheddar. Other well-known ones include Colby, Monterey Jack, Swiss, Brick, Liederkranz, Limburger, and Tillamook.

Goat's milk cheese has a tangy flavor derived from a higher percentage of medium- and small-chain fatty acids than are found in cow's milk. It has better digestibility and more calories, calcium, and vitamin A. Cottage cheese, known in the early nineteenth century as "pot cheese," is made from whole, part-skimmed, or skimmed milk.

History

Dairying was introduced to the New World in 1611 by settlers of Jamestown, Virginia, who brought the first cows from England. The English, Dutch, and Germans who settled the Northeast brought traditions of dairy farming and butter- and cheese-making.

Milk was not consumed as a beverage but used in cooking. Milk drinking emerged as a food habit only in the mid-nineteenth century in urban areas, when it began to be substituted for breast milk. Lack of pasteurization, however, resulted in a high infant mortality rate.

Pasteurization was introduced in 1895 but not mandated until 1912 by New York State and adopted elsewhere slowly. It so altered the taste of milk that many consumers refused to drink it. The dairy industry set about convincing the urban public that milk was clean and tasty by opening dairy lunch restaurants, where a few quick dishes, like milk toast, and rice and milk, were served along with steaks and chops. By the 1940s, the average American drank over a pint of milk a day, double the amount of the 1880s, and milk had become a staple of the nation's diet.

Regional and Ethnic Influences on Dairy

Not surprisingly, the development of dairy cuisine emerged where the industry was pioneered. New York State was the leading dairy state in 1839, producing almost one-third of all products for the country. Dairy dishes in the nineteenth century in the Northeast included clam chowder, bread puddings, ice cream, chipped beef with milk gravy on toast, and scalloped dishes.

The industry moved quickly to the Midwest, with Iowa surpassing New York in 1890 in production and Wisconsin soon taking the lead. In the heartland, dairy cookery called "white cuisine" was developed by German and Swiss German immigrants. Dishes included cheese, milk, butter, white sauces, white meat (milk-fed veal), white beer (*weisse bier*, made with sour milk), and homemade cottage cheese.

During the immigration of the early Industrial Revolution (1785–1830), western and northern Europeans, especially Swedes, Norwegians, and Finns, settled in the Midwest. Scandinavians introduced complicated butter-rich baking to make light and fragile cakes and cookies.

During the late Industrial Revolution (1875–1905), eastern and southern Europeans—Russians and Jews—migrated into industrial centers. Jewish immigrants who settled the Lower East Side of New York introduced Kosher dairy restaurants to conform to religious dietary laws, which stipulate separation of meat and dairy. Dishes included New York cheesecake, with a cream cheese filling and graham cracker crust; kugel (noodle pudding), with sour cream or cottage cheese; and egg cream, a milk, seltzer, and chocolate syrup drink. Although cream cheese was invented in France in 1872, the marketing opportunity as a complement to New York bagels was quickly exploited. Italians, who settled mostly in New York and Philadelphia, introduced numerous cheeses, including Parmesan, Asiago, Romano, provolone, ricotta, and mozzarella, as well as Italian cheesecake made with ricotta and pizza with mozzarella.

Changes in Dairy Consumption

In 1983, whole-milk consumption fell from its 1950 peak of forty gallons per person to nineteen, more than a 50 percent decline. Consumers were concerned that saturated fat in dairy products raises LDL ("bad" cholesterol), increasing risk of coronary artery disease. In the early 1960s, Americans began replacing whole-milk products with low-fat versions containing between 0.5 and 2 percent milk fat and eating less butter.

Move toward Organic Milk

In 1993 the Food and Drug Administration approved the first agricultural biotechnology product, recombinant bovine growth hormone (rBGH). When injected into cows, it increases milk yield by 50 percent. In 2001 less than one-third of all dairy farmers were using the substance, primarily because of strong consumer concern about possible adverse effects although there is no scientific evidence.

As a result of the introduction of rBGH and treatment of sick cows with antibiotics, the organic milk industry has grown 50 to 80 percent annually since the early 1990s.

Politics of Dairy

In an effort to reverse the thirty-year decline in milk consumption, the $75 billion dairy industry has consistently pushed for higher government recommended daily intake. The fifth edition of the USDA *Dietary Guidelines for Americans*, released in 2000, suggests that the two to three daily servings be fat-free or low-fat.

As a result of these efforts, milk consumption has increased to twenty-eight gallons annually among children, the highest level in ten years; among teens, a rise of 3 percent was the first in this age group in five years. Dairy remains an important category in the American diet.

[See also BUTTER; BUTTERMILK; CHEESE; DAIRY INDUSTRY; DEPARTMENT OF AGRICULTURE, UNITED STATES; FOOD AND DRUG ADMINISTRATION; ICE CREAMS AND ICES; JEWISH DIETARY LAWS; MILK; MILK PACKAGING.]

BIBLIOGRAPHY

DuPuis, E. Melanie. *Nature's Perfect Food: How Milk Became America's Drink.* New York: New York University Press, 2002.

Nestle, Marion. *Food Politics: How the Food Industry Influences Nutrition and Health.* Berkeley: University of California Press, 2002.

Visser, Margaret. "Butter—and Something 'Just as Good' " and "Ice Cream: Cold Comfort." In her *Much Depends on Dinner: The Extraordinary History and Mythology, Allure and Obsessions, Perils and Taboos, of an Ordinary Meal*, 83–114 and 285–322. Toronto, Canada: McClelland and Stewart, 1986.

Whitaker, Jan. "Dairy Lunches." *Newsletter of the Culinary Historians of Boston* 12, no. 1 (1991): 5–8.

LINDA MURRAY BERZOK

Dairy Industry

The dairy industry is one of the highest-value agricultural sectors in the United States. Its story is highlighted by *increasing* production and industrialization and *decreasing* numbers of both dairy farms and cows. The beginning of American industrial dairying came in 1851, when a cheese maker in upstate New York contracted for his neighbors' milk in order to create a larger and more efficient cheese plant. By the 1860s the practice swept through New York, was adopted by the butter industry, and began to penetrate other areas of the country. Industrialization was slowed somewhat until a hand separator was intro-

duced in 1885 that allowed for faster separation of cream from milk. Another important innovation was the Babcock test, developed in 1890, which allowed farmers and factory-owners to quickly test for fat content. Since farmers were paid according to the volume of fat in their milk, they were now surer of their payments.

At the same, the dairy industry was transformed through the development of laws and processes that protected milk from contamination. Fresh milk was a great vector for epidemics. To stop the contamination, two methods were put into place: pasteurization, which heated milk to destroy germs, and certification, which carefully inspected leading dairy farms to "certify" their ability to produce milk for the city. Pasteurization was much cheaper and won out, but certification also affected the industry, as cities adopted long lists of regulations to which farmers had to adhere to gain a license to send fluid milk to the city. By 1917 many cities required both pasteurization and inspection.

During and after World War I, high prices led many dairy farmers, particularly in fluid-milk-production regions, to invest in improved technology, including milking machines, trucks, and tractors. Production began to rise, but farmers also became more indebted. A fall in prices in 1921 led to the beginning of the agricultural depression. This state of affairs was combated somewhat in 1922 by the passage of the Capper-Volstead Act, which gave agricultural cooperatives antitrust protection. Farmers, who previously had been price takers, were able to negotiate with dealers for higher prices. Larger cooperatives soon began manufacturing and marketing their own products. At the same time, modernization continued to take place among processors, with milk plants growing larger and larger, truck pickup of milk replacing rail in all but the largest cities, and pasteurization and sanitary rules, such as testing for tuberculosis, becoming standard. This situation came to a sudden halt when the economic downturn expanded from agriculture to the rest of the American economy in late 1929. Consumers refused to pay high prices for milk and began to go to alternative sources, in particular "cash and carry stores" that often worked outside the cooperatives. Dealers had to cut prices, but they were locked into contracts with cooperatives, which were loath to lower prices for their members. Often cooperatives struck, withholding their milk from the city. In many cases the National Guard was called out to protect milk entering the city. The response of the federal government to this crisis was the milk marketing order system, which sets minimum prices to producers in fluid markets that ask to be regulated. The government also began buying stocks of cheese, butter, and dried milk when the overall milk price fell too low.

Following World War II, the modernization of the American dairy industry truly took off. The milk-marketing program and government dairy purchases stabilized dairy prices. Strikes became almost nonexistent. Farmers and dealers were more able to invest in new equipment and grow. Between 1945 and 1978 the number of commercial dairy farms dropped from 602,000 to 168,000. At the same time, total production per cow more than doubled. Great changes also took place off the farm. Pasteurization and bottling became almost entirely automated. The number of plants declined from more than eight thousand in 1945 to just over one thousand in 1981. In the same space of time, the amount of product per plant had increased more than twelve times. While national dairy firms had existed in earlier times, between 1957 and 1980 the number of local firms declined sharply, from almost five thousand to less than one thousand. Cooperatives merged. In 1957 there were 455 cooperatives, but in 1980 there were only 45.

At the end of the twentieth century, the dairy industry was both larger and smaller than ever before. The value of products shipped annually by the fluid-milk industry alone (including fluid milk, yogurt, cream, and cottage cheese) was over 23 billion dollars. While the numbers of dairy employees, plants, farms, and cows all declined rapidly, total milk production in 2000 was twenty billion pounds higher than 1990. In general, the number of dairy farms fell precipitously but the remaining farms became larger and more industrial at an amazingly fast pace. In 1998 there were more than forty thousand fewer dairy farms than in 1993, but the total number of dairy farms with more than two hundred cows rose by 590. Concentration also occurred among dairy-processing companies. In 1997 there were 405 fluid-milk-industry companies in the United States, 120 fewer than just five years earlier.

While production increased, per-capita sales of most dairy products declined. Exceptions to this were yogurt and cheese. Consumption of mozzarella, in particular, almost tripled between 1980 and 2000, as Americans ate more pizza. The places of production shifted west. Wisconsin and New York remained centers of dairy farming, but in 1993, California overtook Wisconsin as the nation's leading dairy state. In 1997 average herd size in California was 530 compared with just 59 in Wisconsin.

Despite these trends, all small dairy farms have not disappeared. There remain some niches, including organic and directly marketed products, in which "craft" methods are profitable. Particularly in New England and New York, states and communities have attempted to protect their small-dairy-farm tradition. While concentration and industrialization will continue, the future of the dairy industry may also include growth of alternative producers.

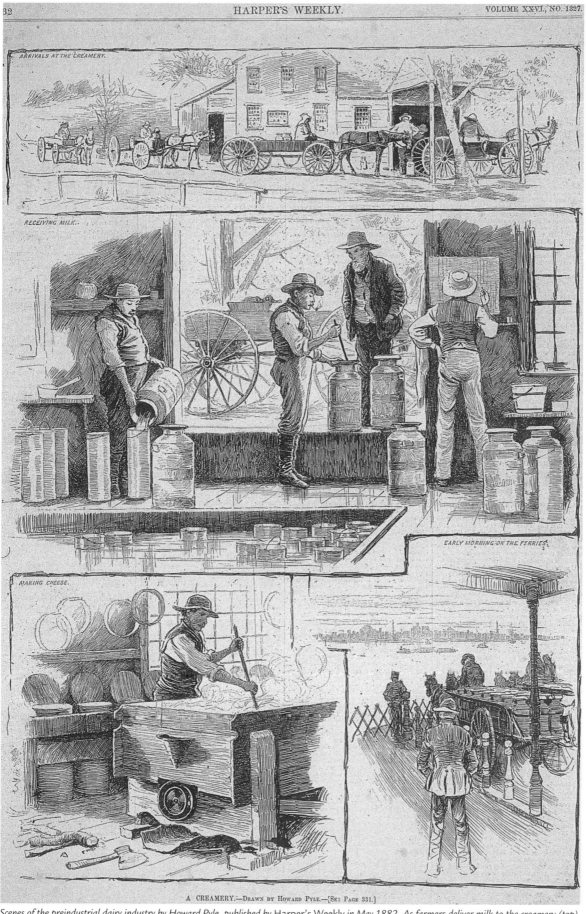

A CREAMERY.—Drawn by Howard Pyle.—[See Page 331.]

Scenes of the preindustrial dairy industry by Howard Pyle, published by Harper's Weekly *in May 1882. As farmers deliver milk to the creamery (top), the milk is poured into the creamery's containers (middle). A worker makes cheese (bottom left). Milk cans are brought to the city by ferry (bottom right).*

[See also BUTTER; BUTTERMILK; DAIRY FOODS; ICE CREAMS AND ICES; MILK; MILK PACKAGING.]

DANILE R. BLOCK

Dairy Queen

John F. McCullough began selling ice cream in 1927. A few years later, he and his son, H. A. "Alex" McCullough, founded the Homemade Ice Cream Company in Green River, Illinois. After some experimentation, John McCullough concluded that ice cream would be more flavorful if served at a temperature higher than the normal 5°F, as cold temperatures numb the taste buds. The McCulloughs began experimenting with what would later be called soft-serve ice cream. They found that when it contained about 6 percent butterfat and was served at 18°F., the ice cream still held its shape. In 1938, feeling that they had found a winning flavor blend, they asked a friend who owned a ice cream store to test market their soft-serve product with his customers. It was a hit. Before the McCulloughs could commercialize it, though, they needed a machine to make large quantities of the soft-serve ice cream. They approached manufacturers, but none were interested in designing and manufacturing such a machine.

The McCulloughs then heard about Harry M. Oltz, a hamburger stand proprietor in Hammond, Indiana, who claimed to have invented a continuous freezer that made it possible to serve ice cream at 20 degrees. The McCulloughs met with Oltz and gained manufacturing rights to his machine, which Alex McCullough perfected. F. J. McCullough fine-tuned the ice cream mix and found a manufacturer for it. They named their new product "Dairy Queen," as they believed that it would be the crowning jewel of the dairy industry. In June 1940, Sherb Noble, an ice cream store owner in Kankakee, Illinois, acquired a franchise and opened his first Dairy Queen stand in nearby Joliet. Noble opened additional outlets, but by the time World War II broke out, there were still only ten Dairy Queens.

The McCulloughs informally licensed operators to control territories for cash, and did not include royalties as part of the arrangement. Operators purchased the continuous freezers and the mix from the company and displayed the Dairy Queen logo, and that was about it. The parent company did not set operating standards and did not offer business support to franchisees, which meant that there was considerable variation among outlets.

The war halted expansion as materials for making the continuous freezer were needed for the war effort. But after the war, the McCulloughs sold 50 percent of Dairy Queen to Harry Axene, who aggressively pushed the franchising aspect of the operation. Axene charged franchisees a small up-front fee along with royalties on all Dairy Queen ice cream that was sold. Dairy Queen grew quickly, from 17 outlets in 1946 to 2,600 in 1955, most of which were seasonal operations, closed during the winter months. Each franchise was indepen-

dently owned, which led to a new company motto: "Nationally Known, Locally Owned." The company also began expanding abroad, opening its first franchise outside the United States in Saskatchewan, Canada, in 1953. The changes instituted by Axene did not solve Dairy Queen's corporate problems. To counter the lack of corporate structure, franchisees formed the Dairy Queen National Trade Association (later renamed International Dairy Queen) in 1948. It purchased back many territories from franchisees and launched a national training school for operators. One attendee at the association's first meeting was Ray Kroc, who sold Multimixers, which made multiple milkshakes simultaneously, to Dairy Queen operators. Kroc later launched the national franchise operation for McDonald's.

The Dairy Queen National Trade Association expanded the menu to include malts and milkshakes, banana splits and other items. Many Dairy Queen stands also served more substantial food, so in 1958 the "Brazier" food line, consisting of broiled hamburgers and hot dogs, was launched. The 1960s saw the introduction of a new Dairy Queen building prototype, called the "Country Fresh" design, which was a walk-in store with a red, gabled "barn" roof.

Dairy Queen's most successful product was the Blizzard—soft-serve ice cream, crushed cookies (such as Oreos), and candy (such as M&Ms) blended together. It was test marketed in 1984 and was officially introduced in 1985.

Unlike most other fast food chains, Dairy Queen targeted America's small towns. As the company has continued to expand and diversify—purchasing Karmelkorn Shoppes Inc. and Orange Julius of America—it has established more outlets in urban areas. In January 1998, International Dairy Queen Inc. and its subsidiary companies were purchased by Warren Buffett's investment group, Berkshire Hathaway Inc. As of 2005, Dairy Queen had more than 5,900 restaurants in the United States and twenty other countries.

[See also ICE CREAMS AND ICES.]

BIBLIOGRAPHY

Funderburg, Anne Cooper. *Chocolate, Strawberry, and Vanilla: A History of American Ice Cream.* Bowling Green, Ohio: Bowling Green State University Popular Press, 1995.

Otis, Caroline Hall. *The Cone with the Curl on Top: Celebrating Fifty Years, 1940–1990.* Minneapolis, Minn.: International Dairy Queen, 1990.

ANDREW F. SMITH

Dates

The date is the fruit of a palm tree, *Phoenix dactylifera*, native to the deserts of North Africa and the Middle East. In the late nineteenth century settlers in the American Southwest noted that parts of the area enjoyed similar conditions, suitable for growing dates—fierce heat, access to water, and dry weather during harvest in late summer and autumn. They planted seeds from imported dates, but these seedling trees mostly bore inferior fruits; only after plant explorers from the U.S. Department of Agriculture and private nurseries brought back offshoots of superior varieties from the Middle East in 1900 and over the next two decades did commercial cultivation begin.

Most American date production comes from two California districts, the Coachella Valley, southeast of Palm Springs, and the Bard Valley, near Yuma, which together had 4,300 bearing acres as of 2002; there are also several hundred producing acres in southwestern Arizona. The harvest takes place from August to December. The major varieties are Deglet Noor, typically picked fully dried and later rehydrated; Medjool, a large, luscious fruit that is increasing in popularity; and Barhi, sometimes marketed in the *khalal* stage, when it is yellow, crunchy, mildly astringent, and the fruit is at maximum size. Virtually all dates are sold in the dried *tamar* stage, in which the fruit has dried to a fairly firm consistency, but connoisseurs prefer fruits in the softer *rutab* stage (soft, moist, and delicious), available at local markets in California and by mail order. Very high in sugar content, dates have been consumed since the nineteenth century as dessert fruits and in cakes, cookies, and puddings.

[See also FRUIT; MIDDLE EASTERN INFLUENCES ON AMERICAN FOOD.]

BIBLIOGRAPHY

Heetland, Rick I. *Date Recipes.* Phoenix, AZ: Golden West, 1993.

Popenoe, Paul B. *The Date Palm.* Coconut Grove, FL: Field Research Projects, 1973.

DAVID KARP

Datil Chile

The datil chile, grown in and around St. Augustine Florida, is the oldest and perhaps the only variety of habanero (*Capsicum chinense*) naturalized in what is now the United States. Its fiery flavor is associated with the Minorcan ethnic group that was first settled in British Florida in 1768, and the name means "date"—the shape of all chinensis chilies—in Catalan. It was long thought that the Minorcans had brought the pepper from the Mediterranean, but there were no habanero types cultivated in Europe at the time. They may have acquired it in their initial coastal settlement at New Smyrna, Florida, or through later Caribbean trade. Minorcan descendants in and around St. Augustine use the chopped pepper directly or via a spicy vinegar in pilaus and seafood stews, and there are several local commercial brands of datil-based hot sauce.

MARK H. ZANGER

Delicatessens

"Delicatessen" is a German word meaning to eat delicacies; in Germany it referred to a retail store selling specialty food items. Nineteenth-century German delicatessens sold raw, pickled, roasted, spiced, and smoked hams, sausages, fowl, fish, and venison, as well as the heads and feet of calves, sheep, and swine. They also offered prepared salads made from chicken, herring, or potatoes, as well as raw and cooked sauerkraut and pickles of all descriptions. Frequently, a wild boar's head, the quintessential symbol of the feast, was placed in the window of the shop to symbolize the abundance within.

German immigrants introduced the delicatessen to the United States. According to Artemas Ward, a chronicler of the nineteenth-century grocery trade, the first delicatessen in America opened on Grand Street in New York City around 1868. At that time Manhattan's Lower East Side had a substantial German immigrant population. Delicatessens attracted not only German Americans but also a wide variety of others who were enticed by foreign and gourmet-type foods. During the late nineteenth century, delicatessens filled the gap between butcher shops, which mainly sold uncooked meats, and general grocery stores, which mainly sold generic and packaged goods. Delicatessens quickly spread to other cities. By 1910 they were common throughout urban America and ubiquitous in New York City. Delicatessens have traditionally been family owned. They tended to be smaller and to sell fewer items than grocery stores.

The first American delicatessens sold cooked, ready-to-eat meats, poultry, and fish, as well as specialty products, such as cheeses, teas, mushrooms, caviar, olive oil, pickled foods, and imported canned goods. Later, delicatessens sold tuna and chicken salad sandwiches and salads, such as coleslaw and potato salad. Originally, the prepared foods were taken out and consumed elsewhere, but as delicatessens thrived and expanded, some made a place for customers to sit down and eat in the store, particularly at lunch. The German deli had largely disappeared by World War I.

During the 1880s larger numbers of Jewish immigrants began moving into New York and other eastern cities. Some Jews opened delicatessens that paralleled German delicatessens. If the delicatessen was kosher, only meat and pareve (neutral) foods were served. These offerings eventually included chicken soup, corned beef, gefilte fish, lox, knishes, pastrami, chopped liver, tongue, and garlic pickles. If kosher laws were not followed, the menu expanded in the 1920s to include bagels, bialys, cream cheese, and Jewish-style cheesecake. Delis also popularized Jewish-style breads, notably rye and pumpernickel. Famous kosher or Jewish-style delicatessens include Katz's, the Carnegie Deli, and the Second Avenue Deli in New York City; Shapiro's Deli in Indianapolis, Indiana; Eli's Stage Deli in Chicago; and Langer's and Canter's in Los Angeles. During the mid-twentieth century some delicatessens became full-fledged restaurants and remained delica-

Abe Lebewohl's 2nd Ave. Deli, located on Second Avenue at Tenth Street in Manhattan, had been serving kosher delicacies since 1954 before it closed in early 2006.

tessens in name only. Although Jewish delicatessens still survive and thrive in major cities, their heyday has passed.

Delicatessens were the birthplace of some prepared foods that reached national markets. Around the turn of the twentieth century, a delicatessen owner in Philadelphia produced large batches of mayonnaise in the back of his store. Sold under the name Mrs. Schlorer's, it was the first commercial mayonnaise brand. It was so successful that the owner began producing other products and created the Schlorer Delicatessen Company to market and distribute them. Richard Hellmann, a German immigrant, opened a delicatessen in New York City in 1905. He began selling commercial mayonnaise in 1912 under his own name and later expanded his product line.

Still others created businesses that catered to delicatessens. Frank Brunckhorst, for instance, began supplying other New York delicatessens in 1905. At the time, competition was heavy. Brunckhorst opened a manufacturing plant in Brooklyn in 1933 and sold his products under the brand name Boar's Head. Boar's Head Provision Company has become one of the largest suppliers of prepared meats to delicatessens and supermarket deli counters.

During the mid-twentieth century, mainstream America adopted many traditional "deli" specialties. Supermarkets incorporated delis into their operations, and many foods sold in delicatessens—such as pastrami, corned beef, and lox—have become popular American foods. For those who want old-fashioned deli flavors and aromas in their homes, several cookbooks have preserved the recipes, such as *Deli: 101 New York–Style Deli Dishes, from Chopped Liver to Cheesecake* (1985) by Sue Kreitzman and *Second Ave Deli Cookbook: Recipes and Memories from Abe Lebewohl's Legendary New*

York Kitchen (1999) by Sharon Lebewohl and Rena Bulkin.

The name "delicatessen" remains an important component of American cities, but the term is used loosely today. As new immigrants—Italians, Greeks, Puerto Ricans, West Indians, Asians, Russians, and Mexicans—moved into American cities, many found that deli proprietorship was one way to enter American economic life. Some delis serve foods similar to those of the past, and most have incorporated culinary treats from their different homelands. For instance, some Korean Americans frequently sell kimchi and other Asian delicacies. Other "delis" are small grocery stores that may or may not sell prepared food. There are more delicatessens than ever, and several chains franchise "New York" delis throughout America, although many are related to traditional delicatessens in name only.

[**See also** CORNED BEEF; GERMAN AMERICAN FOOD; JEWISH AMERICAN FOOD; MAYONNAISE, PASTRAMI; RESTAURANTS.]

BIBLIOGRAPHY

Lebewohl, Sharon, and Rena Bulkin. *The 2nd Ave Deli Cookbook: Recipes and Memories from Abe Lebewohl's Legendary New York Kitchen*. New York: Villard, 1999.

ANDREW F. SMITH

Delmonico's

For nearly a century, from the early 1830s until the 1920s, Delmonico's was the place for New York City's rich and famous to eat and be seen. Often credited with the introduction of French haute cuisine to Americans, it was founded by John Delmonico, a sea captain from Ticino in the Italian-speaking part of Switzerland who settled in New

York in 1825 and opened a wine shop near the Battery. In 1828 he opened a café, Delmonico & Brother (John's brother Peter, a pastry cook, had emigrated to work with him) at 23 William Street; the menu offered pastries, confections, tea, coffee, chocolate, and liqueurs. In 1831 the Delmonicos hired a French chef, who prepared potages, ragoûts, and other hot dishes; thus, Delmonico's became one of the city's first "restaurants" in the true sense of the word—an eating house where one went to be "restored" with rich broth and other sustaining fare. A year later the Delmonicos' nephew Lorenzo (destined to lead the family business into its golden age) joined them, followed by three more nephews brought over from Switzerland.

That first restaurant burned in the great fire of 1835, but the new Delmonico's, opened in 1837 at Beaver and South William Streets, became a true palace of haute cuisine, right down to the marble pillars that flanked its entrance. By 1838 a seven-page Carte du Restaurant Français offered a staggering selection of soups, hors d'oeuvres, salads, omelets, meats, seafood, and game; a choice of eighteen vegetables (including uncommon ones, such as eggplant and artichokes); the exotic Macaroni à l'Italienne (translated on the English side of the menu as "Macaroni with gravy"); a rich array of pastries, soufflés, cheese, and fruits; and no fewer than fifty-seven wines and two dozen liqueurs.

Moving uptown as the city grew northward, Delmonico's was variously located on Broad Street (hard by the stock exchange); Broadway at Chambers Street; Broadway and Pine Street; Fifth Avenue and Fourteenth Street; Fifth Avenue and Twenty-sixth Street; and, finally, at Fifth Avenue and Forty-fourth Street, where it opened in 1897 and closed for good in 1923.

From the time Lorenzo Delmonico assumed the helm in 1845, Delmonico's waxed ever more luxurious and exclusive. Food quality was paramount: Lorenzo's early-morning market purchases were complemented by fine fruits and vegetables grown on the family's 220-acre Brooklyn farm, established to supply the restaurant's needs. Charles Dickens was feted at Delmonico's in 1868; the first debutante to meet society in a public place (not a private home) made her debut there in 1870. During the 1880s and 1890s the Four Hundred—the cream of New York society—dined at Delmonico's on oysters by the dozen, terrapin soup, roast canvasback duck, and endless rivers of Champagne. The restaurant served parties of Vanderbilts, Astors, and Belmonts and frequently hosted the music-hall star Lillian Russell and her constant companion, "Diamond Jim" Brady, renowned for his insatiable appetite.

Delmonico's produced some memorable culinary celebrities and creations. The Swiss émigré Alessandro Filippini, having worked his way up through Delmonico's kitchens, published several cookbooks, including The Table (1889), a comprehensive manual of high-class home cooking. In 1894, Charles Ranhofer, another Delmonico's chef, published The Epicurean, a massive manual of restaurant cooking that enshrines the taste of those times. Some dishes associated with the restaurant are lobster Newberg, Delmonico steak, Delmonico potatoes, chicken à la King, and baked Alaska.

[See also BRADY, DIAMOND JIM; RANHOFER, CHARLES; RESTAURANTS.]

BIBLIOGRAPHY

Filippini, Alessandro. The Table: How to Buy Food, How to Cook It, and How to Serve It. New York: Webster, 1889.

Ranhofer, Charles. The Epicurean. 1893. Reprint, New York: Dover, 1971.

Thomas, Lately. Delmonico's: A Century of Splendor. Boston: Houghton Mifflin, 1967.

BONNIE J. SLOTNICK

Del Monte

Eighteen California packers, representing about half of the fruit canners in California, formed the California Fruit Canners Association in 1899. Seventeen years later the association incorporated under the name California Packers Association (Calpak); its premier brand was Del Monte. It was not until 1967 that the Calpak name was phased out and the company used only "Del Monte."

From the beginning, the company expanded its operations and packed a vast array of products, including peaches, baked beans, olives, berries, squash, sweet potatoes, peppers, and cranberries, as well as dried fruit, jams, and jellies. It also aggressively marketed its products. In 1914 the company produced a silent film, The Winning of a Peach, which may have been the first industrial promotion film produced in the United States. In 1917 Calpak enlisted the culinary expert Marion Harris Neil to write an advertising cookbooklet, Good Things to Eat, featuring Del Monte products. The company has regularly published cookbooklets ever since. Early print advertisements announced that Del Monte was "not a label, but a guarantee." During the 1920s the company expanded its operations into an array of other canning businesses, including tuna and coffee.

Del Monte survived the Depression by belt-tightening and increased advertising. When the United States entered Word War II, Calpak sent 50 percent of its canned fruits and vegetables to the military. Because of the wartime shortage of metals for cans, some domestic products were sold in glass containers.

After the war Calpak launched a $50-million expansion program and initiated a national advertising campaign. One beneficiary of this campaign was Del Monte Catsup. Calpak had bottled ketchup since 1916, but it was not a particularly important product. After Del Monte acquired the Edgar H. Hurff Company of Swedesboro, New Jersey, its national ketchup production took off. In 1948 Del Monte first advertised its ketchup nationwide. An advertisement in Collier's asked,

An advertisement for Del Monte canned fruits and vegetables from the back cover of The Del Monte Fruit Book (1929).

"Catsup? Now Try It Del Monte Style!" Later, Del Monte ketchup highlighted that it used pineapple vinegar, which gave its ketchup a special zesty flavor.

Del Monte established operations in Hawaii shortly after its founding. During the 1930s it created the Philippines Packing Corporation. After World War II, Calpak increased its sales to foreign countries, and by 1965 exports topped $96 million. Del Monte has continued to expand its operations and exports abroad.

In 1979 Del Monte merged with RJ Reynolds Industries. During the following two decades there were several ownership changes. In 1999 Del Monte Foods became a publicly traded company. The company added new products and acquired companies with other product lines. In 1998 Del Monte acquired Contadina, which sold foods of Italian heritage. It also began to manufacture Orchard Select and Sunfresh citrus and tropical fruit. In March 2001 it acquired the S&W brand of beans, condiments, fruits, and vegetables. At the beginning of the twenty-first century, Del Monte was one of the largest producers and distributors of processed fruit and vegetable products in the United States.

[See also CANNING AND BOTTLING; KETCHUP.]

BIBLIOGRAPHY

Braznell, William. California's Finest: The History of the Del Monte Corporation and the Del Monte Brand. San Francisco: Del Monte Corporation, 1982.

Smith, Andrew F. Pure Ketchup: The History of America's National Condiment. Columbia: University of South Carolina Press, 1996.

ANDREW F. SMITH

Denver Sandwich

The Denver sandwich, also known as the Western sandwich, is composed of toasted white bread encasing an omelet filled with diced ham, onion, and green pepper. Several tales have been written as to the origin of the Denver sandwich, but as yet none has been confirmed. Some say that it was developed to disguise the tainted taste of no-longer-fresh eggs carried by pioneers or of eggs that were later hauled into settlements in the West. A second theory states that the sandwich was developed by chuck-wagon cooks as a snack to be carried in the saddlebags of cowboys. Finally, James Beard noted in *James Beard's American Cookery* (1972) that Chinese cooks working in logging camps and railroad gangs concocted it as an Americanized version of egg foo yong. The first identified print reference to date is from a 1918 restaurant industry publication. The Denver, known as a "cowboy" in diner lingo, is common on American menus throughout the country, and it may actually be America's oldest breakfast sandwich.

[See also BEARD, JAMES; BREAKFAST FOODS.]

BIBLIOGRAPHY
Mercuri, Becky. *Sandwiches That You Will Like*. Pittsburgh, PA: WQED Pittsburgh, 2002.

BECKY MERCURI

Department of Agriculture, United States

The United States Department of Agriculture (USDA) has grown over the past 150 years from a small government office to a cabinet-level bureaucracy with over 100,000 employees. In addition to agriculture, the USDA has had an enormous impact on American cooking and nutrition, helping transform the American diet. The USDA is divided into seven large agencies: Farm and Foreign Agricultural Services; Food, Nutrition, and Consumer Services; Food Safety; Marketing and Regulatory Programs; Natural Resources and Environment; Research, Education, and Economics; and Rural Development. Under each large agency are many smaller services; together, these groups constitute the largest single agricultural organization in the world, devoted to agricultural research and aid and the dissemination of agricultural information. The USDA's specific functions are enormously broad, ranging from lending programs for farming cooperatives to forestry to home economics and human nutrition. The focus here is on those areas with a direct influence on the American diet.

Early Years
On May 15, 1862, Abraham Lincoln signed a bill creating the Department of Agriculture. In 1889 the Department of Agriculture was made an executive agency whose chief, the secretary of agriculture, was given cabinet status. In the same year, the Land Grant Education Act was passed, offering public lands to each state for the establishment of colleges of agriculture. As the land grant colleges became established, they began relying on USDA publications for their scientific instruction. A special Bureau of Home Economics Office

was created under it to disseminate scientific research. Since 1916, the department has issued nutritional guidelines in the form of the *Food Guide Pyramid* pamphlet. The department also made its food recommendations directly known to the public. For example, the USDA radio service broadcast a talk show in the 1920s. *Aunt Sammy's Daily House-keeper's Chat* was popular, and the associated cookbook became a byword in rural areas. In 1926–1927 alone more than forty thousand "Aunt Sammy's" cookbooks were distributed, further advancing the cause of scientific nutrition.

Food Safety
In 1883, Harvey Wiley, a chemist from Purdue University, was hired to head the Bureau of Chemistry at the USDA, and he began a long campaign for general U.S. food-safety standards. After a series of food-poisoning scandals and the publication of Upton Sinclair's exposé of the meatpacking industry, *The Jungle*, the Pure Food and Drug Act of 1906 and the accompanying Meat Inspection Act were passed. Inspection and regulation fell to the Bureau of Chemistry, renamed in 1930 the Food and Drug Administration; in 1940 the FDA passed out from the USDA, eventually becoming a part of the Department of Health and Human Services.

Agricultural Diversity
The USDA aid to farmers comes in many forms. It has worked to enhance agricultural yields and to decrease costs. This has led, however, to charges that the USDA has discouraged crop diversity by focusing the bulk of farm research on a limited number of traditional crops. USDA farm aid for specific agricultural crops comes in many forms. Government price supports guarantee certain prices for specified agricultural commodities through regulated purchases by the USDA Commodity Credit Corporation. Price supports prevent the laws of supply and demand from working normally; they artificially keep certain crops at high levels of production and certain types of farmers in business. All of this USDA aid has been extremely successful—especially for a few important commercial crops.

In the early 2000s this situation began to change. Biodiversity and food diversity are becoming big business, and in this area, too, the USDA has had a role. Its agricultural research programs have developed new seeds and produced new foods throughout its history. For example, over 70 percent of all citrus fruits grown in the United States are varieties developed by the USDA Agricultural Research Service. The USDA also has had a role in introducing new crops to formerly unpromising regions. Early in this century, in one instance, USDA scientists produced an alfalfa variety that could survive harsh midwestern winters and so helped produce the green mainstay of a huge new dairy industry in this region.

Social Programs
The USDA also has a direct role in feeding many millions of Americans, particularly through the Food and Nutrition Service (FNS). One of six Americans in the early 2000s received some sort of food assistance from the FNS. Two forms of assistance are noteworthy: the Food Stamp program and the School Lunch program. The School Lunch program was created in 1946 to provide nutritionally balanced and low-cost meals to children from low-income families in schools across the United States; the food is provided by the USDA from agricultural surpluses or via donation or through cash subsidies. Meals must meet federal nutritional guidelines, although one study by the USDA has found that many schools violate that standard and offer meals that contain more fats and fewer nutritious items than is required.

The Food Stamp program is another cornerstone of the USDA. Eligible recipients are provided with coupons or Electronic Benefit Transfer (EBT) cards that can be used in lieu of cash for buying food. As may be expected, providing Food Stamps increases not only recipients' overall food consumption but also their consumption of certain foods, especially meat, milk, and chicken.

Organic Foods
The USDA also has had an impact on the American diet in the "natural versus artificial" foods debate: on the one hand approving the irradiation of foods to enhance preservation, and on the other implementing standards for organic agricultural food products and monitoring agricultural chemicals in the groundwater. Interestingly, a USDA scientist, C. V. Riley, was one of the pioneers in the 1880s of biological pest controls now favored by organic farmers. This role in organic farming is not really surprising, given the USDA's size, breadth, and energy: it is a huge bureaucracy with a wide-ranging mandate, and it has had an enormous impact, for better and sometimes for worse, in all areas of American agriculture and food.

[See also FARM SUBSIDIES, DUTIES, QUOTAS, AND TARIFFS; FOOD AND DRUG ADMINISTRATION; FOOD AND NUTRITION SYSTEMS; FOOD STAMPS; LAW; NUTRITION; PURE FOOD AND DRUG ACT; SCHOOL FOOD.]

BIBLIOGRAPHY
Levenstein, Harvey. *Revolution at the Table*. New York: Oxford University Press, 1988.
United States Department of Agriculture. http://usda.gov.

SYLVIA LOVEGREN AND ROSS PETRAS

Desserts
The final course served at meals, dessert is most often a prepared sweet, such as pudding, pie, or cake, although fresh fruit, nuts, or cheeses may be served. The word "dessert" derives from the French *desservir*, to remove what has been served or clear the table, and was popularized

How to Make *Delicious* RENNET-CUSTARDS *and smooth* ICE CREAM

Recipes using Junket Rennet Dessert Powder and Tablets issued by Chr. Hansen's Laboratory, 1936.

in England after the restoration of Charles II in 1660. The English also adopted fashionable French desserts and incorporated them with the traditional sweets that, by Tudor and Stuart times, were served in England as a final course at formal meals. Both traditions were transported to North America, where colonists, using native fruits and other ingredients as well as imported foods, replicated many of the familiar desserts of home.

Rich planters and merchants entertained lavishly during the colonial era, and dessert assumed great importance as the conclusion of an impressive meal or a late evening party. The easy availability of sugar, spices, exotic fruits, nuts, and wines from the extensive Atlantic shipping trade allowed for a wide range of desserts.

Sweetmeats of preserved fruit as well as cake and creams were very popular. Throughout the colonial era and the early years of the republic, icehouses provided year-round ice and cold storage, and creams of all sorts remained in fashion through the early twentieth century. Only ice cream, however, continued to be served regularly through the remainder of the century. Fresh fruit, when available, was presented at the dessert table through the early twentieth century. Almonds, walnuts, and other nuts were served as well.

While usually not served at parties in wealthier households, pie was regularly eaten as a family dessert, and making "paste" was an important part of the housewife's activities.

By the end of the nineteenth century, pie was consumed in many households on a daily basis and continued to be a popular dessert throughout the twentieth century.

Pudding moved from the forefront of the meal to the last course, as grain and vegetable puddings gave way to sweeter dishes, such as Indian pudding, a variation on traditional English grain puddings made from ground corn and molasses. By the end of the nineteenth century, puddings were made with vanilla and chocolate as these flavorings became popular. Thrifty bread and rice puddings continued to be popular through the twentieth century.

Gingerbread was an old favorite commonly eaten in America through the nineteenth century, either as a cake in the American style or rolled flat and baked hard in the older English tradition. Other cakes were popular and most often were baked in deep bowls. Layered cakes did not appear until the nineteenth century.

Little sugar cakes and seedcakes came to be known as "cookies," a word derived from Dutch settlers in New York who had brought their fondness for *koekjes* from the Lowlands. Jumbles were twisted ropes of dough, either baked like cookies or deep-fried. As doughnuts, they now are more often eaten as breakfast food.

While the early desserts derived from the English colonists, many desserts came from the large German population, particularly in Pennsylvania. The Pennsylvania Dutch continue to be known for shoofly pie, special Christmas cookies, and pastries.

The English, French, German, and Dutch were significant in forming American dessert traditions, but other cultures also contributed to the richness of the American dessert table. Native Americans mixed ground corn with crushed strawberries to create a crude strawberry shortcake and also traditionally introduced early settlers to maple syrup as well as pumpkin. In the South, African slave cooks baked benne wafers made with sesame seeds brought from Africa. Sweet potato and bean pies substituted for the rich man's pecan pie, and southern cooks mixed fresh coconut and oranges to create ambrosia, a popular holiday dessert. Puffy, deep-fried sopaipillas have been eaten in the Southwest for over two hundred years. Cardamom and ginger of Southeast Asia are used in contemporary American desserts as well as in traditional favorites. Italian cannoli and Greek baklava are widely available, and Jewish rugalach is a bakery staple throughout urban America.

Until the beginning of the twentieth century, dessert-making was tedious work. Boiling calves feet for gelatin, purifying sugar, making butter, beating batters, and steaming puddings all required extensive time. Open hearths, primitive stoves, and the dangers of cooking fires made preparation of all meals, not just dessert, extremely hard work. Many desserts could not be stored for any length of time, thereby requiring daily preparation.

By the late nineteenth century, innovations in stoves and ovens led to widespread baking of cakes and cookies. The easy availability of commercial sugar, leavening agents, gelatin, and uniformly milled flour allowed housewives to create desserts in a few hours, a boon to servantless households. Affordable and available refrigeration allowed gelatins, puddings, and creams to be made ahead and stored at home.

The Great Depression of the 1930s and the shortages imposed by rationing during World War II made desserts luxuries for many, while others used ingenuity to create simple, inexpensive sweets for their families. By the 1950s cake mixes, instant puddings, and flavored gelatin powders had transformed the American dessert table. Ice cream was more popular than ever because of the prevalence of freezers in every home. Packaged cookies, given shelf life with preservatives, became readily available, as did commercially packaged cupcakes and doughnuts. Frozen pies and piecrusts meant that pie baking was a lost art, and fewer people made desserts from scratch.

The diet and health concerns of the late twentieth century led to the decline of desserts served at home, except for celebrations and special occasions. Recreational "gourmet" cooking inspired by Julia Child and other celebrity cooks called for elegant conclusions to dinner parties. Restaurant desserts came to be extravagant demonstrations of the pastry chef's art, dramatically presented on individual plates rather than served from traditional dessert carts or sliced from one cake or pie. At the same time, low-fat and low-calorie desserts dominated the freezer sections of supermarkets and recipe columns of popular magazines at the end of the twentieth century.

Intermarriage of ethnic and religious groups, mass marketing, and the fluid mobility of American society have produced increasing uniformity in American desserts, yet regional favorites are found still throughout the country. Cooks and pastry chefs continue to refine traditional desserts to suit contemporary tastes, while increasing globalization and changing immigration patterns are introducing new flavors and traditions to the American dessert table.

[**See also** CAKES; COOKIES; DUTCH INFLUENCES ON AMERICAN FOOD; FRENCH INFLUENCES ON AMERICAN FOOD; GERMAN AMERICAN FOOD; ICE CREAMS AND ICES; NUTS; PIES AND TARTS; PUDDINGS; SUGAR.]

BIBLIOGRAPHY

Belden, Louise Conway. *The Festive Tradition: Table Decoration and Desserts in America, 1650–1900.* New York: Norton, 1983.

Weaver, William Woys. *The Christmas Cook: Three Centuries of American Yuletide Sweets.* New York: HarperPerennial, 1990.

MARY SANKER

Devil's Food

It started out as a cake, and is still most commonly known as a cake, but "Devil's Food" has also become a flavor name that can be used to describe any moist, chocolaty baked good. Where did this curious name come from?

In 1902 appeared the first published recipes for Devil's Food cake, one in *Mrs. Rorer's New Cook Book*, and the other in *The New Dixie Receipt Book* (the latter was subtitled, "Fit for Angels"). Prior to the 1880s, chocolate was not a common ingredient in cake baking in the United States. In fact, chocolate was thought of as little more than the key ingredient to the warm beverage—that is, hot chocolate—until the late 1870s, when improvements in processing cocoa resulted in a much smoother and more delicious chocolate, suitable to be eaten on its own. Subsequently, a nationwide taste for eating chocolate took off, and chocolate eased its way into the baker's pantry, first as a flavoring for frosting: In the 1880s and early 1990s, "chocolate cake" for the most part implied a yellow cake with chocolate frosting. As recipes for cakes with chocolate in the actual batter began to appear, we can presume that a new name was warranted, in order to differentiate from the less chocolaty chocolate cakes of the past. Indeed, chocolate-battered cake recipes published prior to 1902 often had modifiers in their titles, such as Miriam Cooper's "black chocolate cake" published in *The Home Queen Cookbook* in 1898. As for the term "Devil's Food," one has to note that Angel Food cake, a snowy-white, light sponge cake with little or no cooking fat, had already been popular for several decades. Considering the degree to which the new rich, dark chocolate cake was a polar opposite of Angel Food cake; and given the use of the culinary term "devilled" to refer to a dark or richly spiced dish; and finally, given the general whimsy with which cakes born of the nineteenth century were named, the evolution of Devil's Food was all but inevitable.

So what makes a chocolate cake a Devil's Food cake? Some consider the two synonymous, but those who do differentiate usually include more chocolate or cocoa in their Devil's Food recipes: In a 1914 manual for commercial bakers, a chocolate cake includes 3 ounces of cocoa, while a Devil's Food cake of similar proportions uses 10 ounces. And there is always a cooking fat present, whether butter, lard, oil, or shortening. As is a degree of humor: As one old Baker's Chocolate manual suggests, concluding its Devil's Food recipe, "Spread with Divinity Frosting."

BIBLIOGRAPHY

Coe, Sophie D., and Michael D. *The True History of Chocolate*. London: Thames and Hudson, 1996.

Morton, Marcia, and Frederic Morton. *Chocolate: An Illustrated History*. New York: Crown, 1986.

LESLEY PORCELLI

Diets, Fad

A "fad diet" is a scheme of eating that enjoys temporary and sometimes enthusiastic popularity. Usually created by one person or the product of a religious movement, these diets are meant to improve the practitioners' health, vitality, and appearance. Such diets often either limit or emphasize one particular

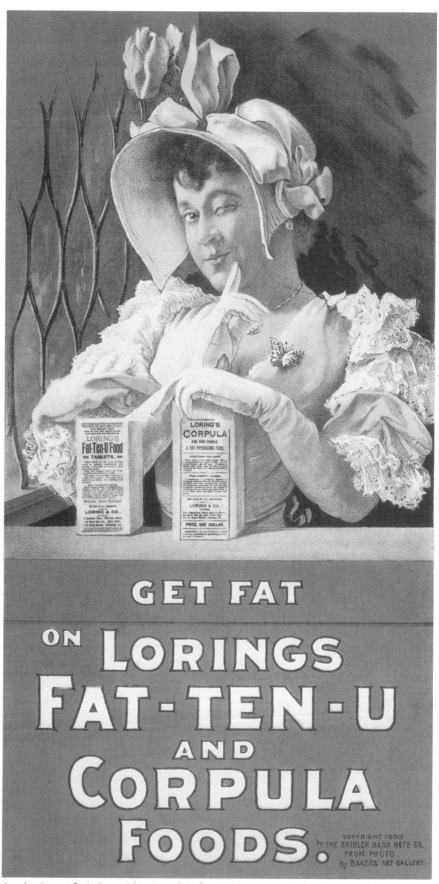

An advertisement for Lorings weight-gain products from 1895 contrasts with the advice commonly sold today.

food or type of food. The origin of American food faddism is commonly attributed to the health movement of the 1830s. William Sylvester Graham, who championed the use of graham (whole wheat) flour, was a leading figure in the movement. Posed against professional medicine, the movement sought a more natural, less complicated lifestyle based on several key elements: a simple, vegetarian diet using whole grains and daily exercise to promote physiological and spiritual reform. Highly seasoned food, rich dishes, and meat were considered stimulating, sinful food. James C. Jackson, one of Graham's disciples, advocated hydropathy, also known as water-cure, as an addition to Graham's health reform. Jackson's invention of Granula, made of graham flour and water, was said to be the first cold breakfast cereal.

Like patent medicines, fad diet plans abounded in the nineteenth century, and some led to major food companies. John Harvey Kellogg was formally trained in medicine, performed surgical procedures, and wrote tracts about his health-reform ideas. Kellogg was a Seventh-Day Adventist and a vegetarian, and like his coreligionists, he believed that the body is a temple of the Holy Spirit. Adventists founded a religious colony and sanitarium at Battle Creek, Michigan, often called "the San," where Kellogg's wealthy clients "detoxified" with enemas and high-fiber diets, including corn flakes and granola, a baked and ground mixture of oatmeal and cornmeal. By 1899 the Kellogg Company's cornflakes had become a multimillion-dollar business. Their chief competitor, among many, was Charles W. Post, a former Kellogg patient. Post's wheat and barley Grape Nuts, a supposed cure for appendicitis, malaria, consumption, and loose teeth, also became a nationally sold product. Both Kellogg and Post came to dominate the breakfast food industry throughout the twentieth century.

Bernarr Macfadden took a slightly different road to wellness. Known as the "Father of Physical Culture," he was a lifelong advocate of physical fitness through natural food, outdoor exercise, and the natural treatment of disease. The core of his philosophy held that impurities in the blood from poor diet and lack of proper exercise were the real causes of ailments. Fruits, vegetables, and whole grains were the keys to good health, but white bread was one of the worst things a person could eat. Believing that almost all diseases could be cured by correct fasting, Macfadden advocated fasting both on a regular basis and during illness. Macfadden was a genius at self-promotion, and his influence is still present in the health food industry, literature, and clinical practice.

In the 1930s George Ohsawa, a Japanese philosopher, developed Zen macrobiotics. It is a belief based on the laws of yin and yang described in the ancient Buddhist philosophy. An extremely restrictive diet regimen, this diet consists of whole cereal grains;

locally and organically grown vegetables; small amounts of soups; beans; sea vegetables; and meat, fish, and fruit in limited amounts. Popular from the 1960s into the 1980s, this dietary concept has been criticized as having been developed without the benefit of scientific evidence, but its principles have made their way into mainstream healthy-diet literature and practice.

Fruitarianism is a subcategory of the holistic health doctrine of Natural Hygiene and is related to an ascetic form of vegetarianism called "vegan." Fruitarians believe that eating only fruit is the highest moral concept of nutrition because less destruction of life is required to obtain fruits than other types of foods. Choice of foods for fruitarians is limited only to raw fruits. However, nuts, some fermented cereals, olive oil, and honey are allowed in less restricted regimens.

Weight-Loss Industry and Fad Diets
The numbers of overweight adults and obesity in the United States increased from 45 to 55 percent from 1960 to 1994, when the figure reached more than 97 million. From 1991 to 1998 obesity increased in every state, regardless of gender, race, age, or educational level. Total costs (medical costs and lost productivity) attributable to obesity amounted to an estimated $99 billion in 1995. By 2000 the national obesity rate was pegged at 28 percent. Serious health risks, such as cardiovascular disease and diabetes, together with social stigma, drove many Americans to seek fast-working weight-loss programs. As a result a wide variety of fat reducing diets appeared on the market. By the turn of the millennium, Americans were spending more than $30 billion on diet products and diet plans each year. Weight-loss fad diets may work for a short period at first due to extremely low caloric intake, but their effectiveness may be difficult to maintain in the long run.

Fad diets can be categorized into five groups: food-specific diets; high-protein, low-carbohydrate diets; high-fiber, low-calorie diets; liquid diets; and fasting. An example of a food-specific diet is the popular cabbage soup diet. These diet plans rely heavily on a specific food or food group and thereby do not provide healthy eating habits and are not nutritionally balanced. High-protein, low-carbohydrate diets such as the Dr. Atkins' New Diet Revolution, the Zone Diet, the Scarsdale Medical Diet, and the Protein Power Diet, were on the market from the early 1970s and remained popular. These diets are based on the principle that eating excessive carbohydrates causes production of excessive amounts of insulin, leading to obesity and other health risks. Critics claim that high-protein foods are often high in saturated fat and cholesterol and thereby may increase risks of coronary heart disease and kidney problems. High-fiber, low-calorie diets promote eating vegetables for their low caloric content and the feeling of satisfaction.

However, eating more than fifty to sixty grams a day can cause cramping, bloating, and diarrhea. Liquid diet products, such as Slim Fast and Sweet Success, were on the market as early as 1930s. Although convenient, replacing regular meals with these products does not advocate healthy eating and requires medical supervision. Fasting has been practiced historically by various religions as an accompaniment to religious reflection and meditation. However, fasting deprives the body of nutrients; weakness, lightheadedness, and medical problems may result.

Religion, health, fashion, and social and individual psychologies have all been important factors in the appearance of fad diets. Each diet scheme has its own internal logic that is related to external "facts," be they religious belief or scientific evidence, and therefore can appeal to general consumers. For all of these reasons, fad diets will likely continue to appeal to a wide body of Americans.

[See also CEREAL, COLD; HEALTH FOOD; KELLOGG COMPANY; KELLOGG, JOHN HARVEY; NUTRITION; POST FOODS; VEGETARIANISM.]

BIBLIOGRAPHY

Herbert, Victor, and Stephen Barrett. *Vitamins and "Health" Foods: The Great American Hustle.* Philadelphia: Stickley, 1981.

Schwartz, Hillel. *Never Satisfied: A Cultural History of Diets, Fantasies, and Fat.* New York: Free Press, 1986.

Whorton, James C. *Crusaders for Fitness: The History of American Health Reformers.* Princeton, NJ: Princeton University Press, 1982.

HEA-RAN L. ASHRAF

Diners

In 1872, a street vendor from Providence, Rhode Island, named Walter Scott converted a horse-drawn freight wagon into a self-contained food-service facility. Noting that most restaurants closed in the early evening, Scott parked his wagon outside the offices of the *Providence Journal*, dispensing simple hot meals, sandwiches, pie, and hot coffee. The immediate success sparked a growing number of competitors and an industry of constructing such wagons for operation by others.

Observing Scott's operation on a rainy evening in 1880 inspired Samuel Messer Jones of Worcester, Massachusetts, to start his own business building larger wagons that provided indoor seating, thus also establishing that city as the birthplace of the diner-building industry. His new business constructed and operated a small fleet of wagons serving late-night shift workers, agricultural fairs, and other public events. Subsequent Worcester entrepreneurs, Charles H. Palmer and T. H. Buckley, Charlie Gemme, and others, constructed larger and increasingly ornate wagons for sale to others to operate.

With more cities banning mobile lunch wagons, citing concerns related to public safety, Patrick Tierney in New Rochelle, New York, established his own company in 1905 to build stationary lunch wagons for permanent locations. Jerry O'Mahony in Bayonne, New Jersey, followed suit in 1917, soon claiming the construction of a "diner a day." From the 1920s until World War II the industry grew, adding to its roster dozens of new companies—most in New Jersey—to serve a growing fast food trade. During this time, construction quality hit its stride, incorporating all relevant technological and construction advances in a continual effort to trump the competition. For the enterprising operator willing to work very hard for long hours, the diner industry offered a turnkey restaurant operation on credit for a 10 percent down payment. If business outgrew the existing diner, operators could trade in old structures for newer, larger, and more capable units.

The iconic stainless-steel diner first hit the roadsides in the early 1940s, as builders used the material to advance both design and function of their product. Always stressing the cleanliness and efficiency of diners, builders used durable, smooth-surfaced materials, such as porcelain enamel, polished laminates, and ceramic tile, during a period regarded as the diner's golden age.

Designed to serve full meals in a short time, the diner's profitability demanded high turnover. Menus then consisted mainly of meat-and-potatoes fare, with roasts, soups, stews, and other meat dishes among the best sellers. Larger operations also featured fresh-baked desserts. Diners located in ethnic neighborhoods offered specialties that reflected the local market.

Until World War II the diner remained primarily a male preserve, since men dominated the industrial workforce. Although dining out remained a relative rarity by modern-day standards, savvier operators attracted women customers seeking a break from cooking for their families, stressing their diner's cleanliness, comfort, and affordability. During World War II many women entering the workforce landed behind the counters of the neighborhood diner for the first time. Unlike their counterparts in the factories, however, the waitress became a permanent practitioner in the trade.

As diners left the cities and mill towns for more suburban locations after the war, the demand to make them ever larger led to the development of the first multisectioned, prefabricated restaurants. The industry could build and ship units that accommodated one hundred customers or more, in buildings transported by road or occasionally by rail, theoretically to any location in the country.

By the 1950s diners still had their counters, but they shed other Victorian vestiges, such as wood and tile, for a completely modernized appearance using stainless steel, Formica, and terrazzo. Menus in larger diners usually incorporated full breakfasts, lunches, and dinners. At the busier locations, these diners rarely closed. Customer demographics often incorporated all walks of American society, with the industry systematically

The Cheyenne Diner at Thirty-third Street and Ninth Avenue offers comfort food in the heart of New York City.

building the first restaurant type that catered to whole families based on modular, prefabricated construction. In this way, diners helped establish the American habit of dining out.

Diner owners traditionally consisted of families or individuals seeking relatively easy entry into the restaurant trade. A wave of Greek immigration in the 1950s established the dominance of their ethnicity in the industry. Although some units shipped to other parts of the country, the industry's northeastern locus meant that relatively few diners landed west of Cleveland, Ohio, or south of Baltimore, Maryland. By the late 1950s the introduction of national chains such as Howard Johnson's, franchising, and fast-food burger stands loomed as the industry's biggest threat, eventually displacing the diner from its role as family restaurant. As the industry squeezed profits through efficiency and scale, the family-run, full-service diner faced marginalization, thriving only in local niches and markets.

By 1964 diner design shed the transportation metaphor, by adopting first early-American themes and then Mediterranean, colonial, rococo, or "modern" styling. Menus expanded with seating capacity to provide several aspects of American cuisine, including but not limited to Greek, Italian, eastern European, southern, and other specialties. The larger operations strove to serve almost anything at anytime, while smaller, older diners in the struggling mill towns and on bypassed highways contracted into breakfast and lunch operations, owing to the decreased need for prep work and lack of demand.

The diner's revival began in the mid-1970s, with the almost simultaneous establishment of upscale diners, the publication of diner-related book titles, and the growing

ubiquity of diner iconography in the mass media. This higher profile attracted people who were increasingly bored with homogeneous fast food meals and nostalgic for basic meals in locally owned establishments. As people rejected the haute cuisine of the 1980s during the recession of the early 1990s, the American diner serving "comfort food" started a trend in the industry.

By the late 1990s larger restaurant chains made their own forays into the field. Denny's led the way with their brand-new, factory-built structures introduced in 1997, followed by a new McDonald's Diner in Kokomo, Indiana, which opened in 2001. Still, as it has for more than a century, the classic local diner continues to provide inexpensive home-cooked meals to the hungry patron.

[See also FAST FOOD; LUNCHEONETTES; RESTAURANTS; ROADSIDE FOOD; SODA FOUNTAINS.]

BIBLIOGRAPHY

Baeder, John. *Diners*. New York: Abrams, 1995.

Butko, Brian, and Kevin Patrick. *Diners of Pennsylvania*. Mechanicsburg, PA: Stackpole Books, 1999.

Gutman, Richard J. S. *American Diner Then and Now*. 2nd ed. Baltimore: Johns Hopkins University Press, 2000.

Witzel, Michael Karl. *The American Diner*. Osceola, WI: MBI, 1999.

RANDY GARBIN

Dining Car

From their inception in 1831, American railroads wrestled with techniques for feeding passengers. Early passengers, plagued by long delays caused by derailments, faulty equipment, and the lack of signaling devices to control train movements, resorted to foraging for food, packing meals of varying quality and scent, or buying food of questionable quality from vendors at stations.

Engraving of a dining car from the nineteenth century.

Eventually passengers could purchase food from an onboard "news butcher" who passed through the train selling all manner of sundries, or at scheduled stops at stations outfitted with eating houses established for the purpose. However, as the industry continued to consolidate, regional trunk lines formed between 1865 and 1900 to connect major cities, and competition among them for passengers and shippers intensified. With train speeds exceeding a mile a minute, it became inconvenient to stop a train every several hours so that passengers could eat.

In July 1866 the industrialist and inventor George M. Pullman introduced the first railroad car designed for preparing and serving food to passengers in transit. Named the President, the car was built in the Aurora, Illinois, shops of the Chicago, Burlington and Quincy Railroad. The "hotel car" consisted of the patented Pullman face-to-face sleeping-car seating and had mountings for a table that could be inserted between the seats at mealtimes. The car had a small (three feet by six feet) kitchen at one end. Two years later Pullman introduced the dining car Delmonico, which was outfitted with a fully equipped eight-foot by eight-foot kitchen. Meals were served as in a restaurant, usually with a waiter for each "section" consisting of two tables that seated either four and two or four and four passengers. A steward supervised.

Dining car kitchens evolved to measure approximately eight feet by fifteen feet, typically containing a range and a broiler with fire boxes beneath and warming shelves above. Other equipment included a coffeemaker with cup warmer, steam table, carving board, refrigerator, two sinks, and a pastry table. The kitchen had storage space for ingredients, pots and pans, cooking utensils, dishes, and ice, coal, and charcoal. In this space three cooks and a chef prepared all portions for as many as two hundred people

per meal for each of three meals a day. An adjoining pantry measuring approximately eight feet by twelve feet held the items needed for making salads, serving bread, and preparing drinks, as well as the dishes and tableware needed for completing setup and service. Compact and efficient, dining car kitchens inspired the architects and designers who first constructed apartment buildings.

Seen as a promotional necessity by the railroads, the dining car showcased a railroad's approach to service and offered some of the best cuisine available in America. Railroads attracted top chefs to create menu items, instruct in their preparation, and supervise their success. American tastes expanded because passengers from all walks of life and from throughout the land could experience culinary achievements only found otherwise in expensive restaurants and hotels in the big cities. Dining cars introduced regional ingredients to a national audience, from the Idaho potato (Union Pacific) to the Great Big Baked Apple (Great Northern). Railroads test kitchens found many uses for items transported by the respective company's freight department, such as cantaloupe pie (Texas and Pacific) and curried rice (Southern Pacific). Railroads pioneered the food service manual, standardization of preparation and portions, and the use of quality ingredients and fewer preparation steps to ensure quality and prompt service, all hallmarks of restaurant chains in the twenty-first century. Common food products such as Bisquick baking mix (Southern Pacific) and square sandwich bread (Pullman) and preparation aids such as pressed sawdust logs (Union Pacific) originated in dining cars.

Amtrak, the National Railroad Passenger Corporation, operated all intercity passenger trains in the early 2000s. Amtrak's food service cars fall into three categories. Café or lounge cars, found in all trains, offer snack

items, beverages, and packaged salads, sandwiches, and entrées, some warmed in microwave ovens. Full dining cars come in two configurations. Heritage and Viewliner cars, which are one level high, enable operation through tunnels in and out of New York and Washington, DC, and resemble the floor plans of the earliest dining cars. Superliner, or bilevel, cars for western trains consist of a ten-foot by forty-foot kitchen on the lower level and a seventy-two-seat dining room on the upper level, which is serviced by dumbwaiters.

[See also BREAD, SLICED; HARVEY, FRED; PULLMAN, GEORGE.]

BIBLIOGRAPHY

Menchen, August. *The Railroad Passenger Car: An Illustrated History of the First Hundred Years with Accounts by Contemporary Passengers.* Baltimore: Johns Hopkins University Press, 2000.

Porterfield, James D. *Dining by Rail: The History and the Recipes of the Golden Age of American Railroad Cuisine.* New York: St. Martin's Griffin, 1998.

JAMES D. PORTERFIELD

Dining Rooms and Meal Service

Formal dining rooms were the province of the elite in colonial and new nation America. Only the wealthy possessed spacious houses, extensive tablewares, and the knowledge of how to use them. But material and cultural changes had started in the eighteenth century that, by the 1870s, would make the dining room the epitome of middle-class prosperity and exemplar of the democratically optimistic belief that learned etiquette could be a social equalizer.

Ironically, no room did more to point out class distinctions within America. Moreover, no sooner had the dining room come to symbolize idealized domesticity than its pull as the family's magnet started to weaken. During its first year of publication in 1885, *Good Housekeeping* magazine tackled the challenge of luring the family to shared meals in the cloistered dining room when the tantalizing world beyond beckoned. By the 1920s, anthropologists rued frenzied modern life and the decline of the at-home family dinner even in small-town America, a lament that continues in the contemporary press.

Spaces for Eating

To dedicate a room exclusively to eating is a luxurious allocation of space. Most seventeenth-century homes were one or two rooms, wherein all cooking, eating, sleeping, and working took place. At mealtimes a trestle table was assembled in the main room and then broken down to make room for other activities. By the early eighteenth century, influenced by European models, house plans for moderately prosperous town houses might identify a "dining room" or "dining parlor," but those rooms were used for other functions as well: Hepplewhite's *The*

Cabinet-Maker's and Upholsterer's Guide (1794) recommended furnishing a dining parlor with a sofa and pier tables, substituting a dining table only if the room was to be used "exclusively" for dining.

By the mid-nineteenth century, rising standards of living coupled with etiquette books and household manuals fueled the vogue for dining rooms among the middle class. With up to 8 percent of the labor force working as domestics, there were plenty of hands to polish silver and glassware and wait table. Even Manhattan's new-fangled, space-saving apartments, built in the 1870s as the next step up from tenement life, dedicated a room to formal dining. But with early-twentieth-century industrialization, domestic service plummeted. The servant shortage made it necessary to rethink the physical structure of middle-class homes to function in the emerging servantless society.

Early-twentieth-century designers and architects responded with laborsaving designs and open floor plans that eased the flow from kitchen to dining area. Going even further, industrial designers Mary and Russel Wright's 1950 *Guide to Easier Living* proposed to revamp suburban living and entertaining. With chapters entitled "The Vanishing Dining Room," and "The New Hospitality," the Wrights eliminated tablecloths, place mats, and cloth napkins, limited utensils to a maximum of one knife, fork, and spoon per diner, and suggested that guests pitch in and wash the dishes afterward, aided by plastic aprons for men and women.

Nowadays, as more people require home offices, dedicating floor space to an old-fashioned dining room fits fewer American lifestyles, and the formal room is once again becoming an emblem of the wealthy. For middle-class America, flexible "great room" plans combine kitchen, living, and dining spaces into a communal area reminiscent of the colonial American home, albeit on a more spacious scale.

Serving the Elite Meal

Table settings and meal service styles have changed radically from the seventeenth century, when colonists might eat a one-course dinner of steaming pottage from a communal dish by scooping bites with a spoon, a bit of bread, or one's fingers. Conspicuously absent was a dining fork, and often individual plates and cups for the poorer and middling classes. One's eating utensil (spoon or fingers) returned unwashed to the common trough, although unwritten etiquette sanctioned precisely how each diner divided the dish. Those who had individual plates and drinking vessels were considered refined.

By the mid-eighteenth century, a consumer revolution was bringing more and better quality plates, glasses, and utensils to American tables. Wealthy diners aspired to eat in the "French" style, in which a dinner was divided into two main courses plus a

The industrialist and horse fancier C. K. G. Billings hosted a dinner in the ballroom of Sherry's restaurant in New York on March 28, 1903. Guests ate off dining trays attached to the saddles. At the end of the dinner, the horses were served oats.

separate dessert course. Much like contemporary Thanksgiving boards, each course consisted of many dishes placed on the table simultaneously.

French service was a feast for the eye and was highly interactive, as guests served themselves and others from the dishes nearest them. The host and hostess asked each guest what he would prefer and prepared or directed that a plate be filled with the guest's choices, which usually was delivered by servants. One started eating immediately upon being served, without waiting for others. Attentive hosts noticed when a guest had finished what was on his plate and inquired to what the guest would be helped, never uttering the words "next" or "more" or "another": noticing how much a person ate was vulgar. In most instances, the guest passed the plate for refills, but one unresolved etiquette question was whether the fork and knife journeyed with the plate as it was passed, or remained at one's place. Holding utensils when one was not actively eating was poor form, but it was also rude to soil the cloth with them. Some suggested leaning the utensils on bread, but the most common solution was to slide one's knife and fork onto the plate at right angles, the set traveling as a precarious trio. Eighteenth century plates were a bit deeper than modern ones, helping to stabilize the utensils.

In the 1830s, French service began to give way to dining *à la russe*, which had become the elites' preferred dining style by the 1880s. A meal served *à la russe* did not place platters on the table but instead presented individual courses, often fifteen to twenty in succession, to each diner, which the diner could accept or

decline. Many Americans, accustomed to the heavily laden tables of French service, objected, typified by former New York City Mayor Philip Hone's reaction to his first meal *à la russe* in January 1838:

> The table, covered with confectionery and gew-gaws, looked like one of the shops down Broadway in the Christmas holidays, but not an eatable thing. The dishes were all handed round; in my opinion a most unsatisfactory mode of proceeding in relation to this important part of the business of a man's life. One does not know how to choose, because you are ignorant of what is coming next, or whether anything more is coming. Your conversation is interrupted every minute by greasy dishes thrust between your head and that of your neighbor, and it is more expensive than the old mode of shewing a handsome dinner to your guests and leaving them free to choose.

Others thought Russian service delightful for relieving "host and guest...of every kind of responsibility. Dish after dish comes round, as if by magic; and nothing remains but to eat and be happy."

Russian service was a red-letter day for conspicuous consumption, as the number of objects thought necessary to serve the meal exploded. Fresh dishware met each course, and the most extravagant tables varied the china to surprise the diner with novel objects, such as majolica oyster plates, footed bouillon cups, and crescent-shaped salad plates to cradle plates holding game. Each course demanded flatware ergonomically engineered to be the most subtly efficient way of consuming a particular food. Different wines were served every few courses, and glasses of

Napkins

Napkins have been used since at least the classical Roman world, when guests brought cloths to dinner to wrap up leftovers—the original doggy bag. Seventeenth century European elites were dazzled at table by damask napkins intricately folded into flora or fauna. Contemporaneous Plymouth colonists, who ate without dining forks, wiped their soiled fingers on more plebeian linen. Napkins were one of the first "luxuries" listed in the simplest colonial decedent's estate. Yet Americans by no means universally used napkins, and it was not simply a question of cost. With the spread of the dining fork, some assumed that the napkin was superfluous.

Mid-nineteenth-century etiquette books explained what to do if no napkin was provided: as finger licking was never acceptable, the gentleman unfortunately had to choose between smearing the tablecloth and gallantly whipping out his handkerchief. The disagreeable consequence of the latter action, of course, was that the gentleman then had to stuff the besmirched fabric back in his pocket. Many exasperated writers queried why the napkin had not been universally adopted, and a few tried to shame the recalcitrant by labeling them indispensable. The Napkin Question was sufficiently open in the 1850s that Mrs. Ellet's *The Practical Housekeeper* (1857) gives detailed, illustrated instructions for seven decorative folds, telling the housekeeper to place the bread under the convoluted napkin on the dinner plate. She then blithely states that if dinner napkins are not used, the proper place for the bread is to the left of the plate.

Although napkins became ubiquitous after the Civil War, essayists could rely on them for a knowing laugh. An 1879 article in *The Nation* delighted in fathers who liked to mortify "their aspiring daughters by remarks in peculiarly aggravating circumstances about the frivolousness of napkins." Issues still arose about their proper size and color. White or ivory, denoting purity and cleanliness, were the only acceptable hues for a dinner napkin through the nineteenth century, although colored napkins enlivened the fruit course, when the juicy fruits might leave indelible stains. Colored (read potentially soiled) napkins otherwise were never permitted. This strict rule was relaxed first for ladies' "color" luncheons at the turn of the twentieth century, when pastel linens matching the meal's theme color were encouraged. Colors, especially tied to holidays, eventually filtered to dinner. Finally, in a complete inversion of tradition, the painfully chic have applauded the introduction of black napkins that leave no uncool lint on the laps of black-clad hipsters.

In addition to playing chameleon, napkins have shrunk. Thirty-inch squares (suitable for decorative folding) have given way to the now-standard twenty to twenty-two inch dinner square, impossibly small to contort into elaborate shapes. Luncheon napkins are even smaller, at about fourteen inches square, with cocktail napkins, developed to meet the needs of twentieth-century cocktail parties, the tiniest of all, at about eight inches square.

Paper napkins appeared no later than 1915, when they were critiqued in Lucy Allen's *Table Service*. Tolerated for family meals by the 1930s, fastidious hostesses still considered them insulting to guests, as they bespoke a lack of effort. Nonetheless, good quality paper napkins, particularly with the host's monogram, gained acceptance at that time for informal entertaining. Paper is still shunned for formal meals.

CATHY K. KAUFMAN

varying shapes, colors, and sizes showcased the selections.

Dining for the Aspiring

Middle-class Americans wanted to emulate the wealthy, but the lacked the wealthy's phalanx of European-trained servants. Catharine Beecher's *Domestic Receipt Book* (1858) addressed to

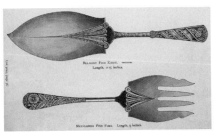

Belmont fish knife and Mayflower fish fork: two examples of specialized silverware.

"young and inexperienced housekeepers" hosting a "plain, substantial" but emphatically *not stylish* dinner, offered a pragmatic model suitable to a bourgeois household with two cooks and one experienced waiter. The meal visually resembled simplified French service: host and hostess portioned at the table, and the waiter delivered filled plates. However, each important food was served on a fresh plate. For a dinner for twelve, Miss Beecher recommends a minimum of three dozen dinner plates, "to allow one plate for fish, and two for two changes of meat for each guest. Some would provide more." Three dozen dessert plates, one dozen saucers, two dozen dessert forks and knives, and one dozen dessert spoons were needed to sample the multiple desserts. These quantities would have been astounding to all but the wealthiest fifty years earlier; here, they are considered minimums for a merely respectable dinner.

By the last quarter of the nineteenth century, aspiring households attempted "course dinners" adapted mainly from the Russian model. Mary F. Henderson's *Practical Cooking and Dinner Giving* (1877) proposed a "stylish" dinner for those of moderate means consisting of soup, fish, roast, possibly followed by game, then salad (simple greens, vegetables, or even a lobster mayonnaise), cheese, and dessert. Mrs. Henderson reassures the budget conscious that, with a little practice, one cook can easily prepare this dinner, with desserts purchased from the confectioner's shop. For Mrs. Henderson, course service was essential even for the quotidian family repast: "If one has nothing for dinner but soup, hash, and lettuce, put them on the table in style: serve them in three courses, and one will imagine it a much better dinner than if carelessly served."

The middle classes soon discarded these pretensions. The twentieth-century doyenne of formal etiquette, Emily Post, sympathized with "Mrs. Three-in-One," the aspiring homemaker trying to perform as cook, maid, and hostess. In *The Blue Book of Social Usages* (1st ed., 1922), she proposed chafing-dish dinners supplemented by preset cold salads and desserts, eliminating the need to fetch while entertaining. And if a dining area and even a dining table are lacking in a tiny apartment, Sharon Dlugosch's 1990 *Table Setting Guide* recommends filling the plates in the kitchen and inviting guests to pick one up and convene around the coffee table or desk.

BIBLIOGRAPHY

Ames, Kenneth L. *Death in the Dining Room and Other Tales of Victorian Culture.* Philadelphia: Temple University, 1992.

Becker, Hazel T. "Four Dining-room-less Houses." *Better Homes and Gardens,* June 1926.

Gillies, Mary Davis. "*What Women Want in Their Dining Rooms of Tomorrow: A Report of the Dining Room of Tomorrow Contest.*" New York: McCall's Corp., 1945.

Grover, Kathryn, ed. *Dining in America: 1850–1900.* Rochester, NY: University of Massachusetts/Margaret Woodbury Strong Museum, 1987.

Mayhew, Edgar de N., and Minor Myers, Jr. *A Documentary History of American Interiors from the Colonial Era to 1915.* New York: Scribners, 1980.

Sprackling, Helen. *Customs on the Table Top.* Sturbridge, MA: Old Sturbridge Village, 1958.

CATHY K. KAUFMAN

Dinner, *see Meal Patterns*

Dinner Pails, *see Lunch Boxes, Dinner Pails, and Picnic Kits*

Dips

Humankind has been dipping solid food into semiliquid complements for thousands of years, but it was not until the second half of the twentieth century that commercial dips emerged as an important category of food. Credit for this shift goes to the Thomas J. Lipton Company, which mounted a massive promotional campaign in the 1950s featuring dips made from its dried onion soup mix combined with sour cream or cream cheese. At that time Lipton sponsored Arthur Godfrey's popular *Talent Scouts* radio and television program, and these dips were advertised extensively on the weekly show. Lipton also distributed tens of thousands of hanging cards to retailers, promoting these dips, and provided dip recipes on millions of their packages.

While the Lipton dips could be served with many foods, such as carrots and celery, the major host foods were salty potato and corn chips, which were also extensively marketed during the 1950s. Within six months of its release in 1952, sales of Lipton soup mix skyrocketed. Lipton's success encouraged other manufacturers to enter the commercial dip world, and new product lines emerged. One was the fondue, which had originated in Switzerland as an egg-and-cheese casserole into which bread was often dipped. During the 1950s fondue morphed into a way of making dips, and fondue pots became a major selling item in America. In 1952 some fondue recipes replaced the cheese with oil, and chunks of skewered meats were cooked and dipped into sauces. By 1964 fruit was being dipped into heated chocolate. Fondue became the culinary hit for parties during the 1960s and 1970s.

Many successful commercial dips have been based on strong flavors. By far the most successful dips, for instance, were drawn from the Mexican culinary heritage, such as chili, guacamole, and salsa. Guacamole, a combination of mashed avocados, chili, garlic, and other ingredients, became popular in America during the late nineteenth century, consumed as a salad. During the 1930s Calavo, the California association of avocado growers, began publishing pamphlets that included directions for making guacamole. Subsequent recipes encouraged the use of pieces of tortilla to scoop up the dip. After World War II potato chips were recommended as guacamole dippers. Guacamole did not become a prominent dip until the commercial production of larger and thicker corn chips in the 1960s and the adoption of this combination in Mexican-style restaurants in the United States. In the 1960s Calavo produced the first commercial guacamole, which was subsequently sold to restaurants and grocery stores.

Another dip originating in Mexican culinary traditions is salsa, generally composed of chili peppers, tomatoes, vinegar, and flavorings. Salsas are diverse and traditionally were intended as condiments for other foods, such as tacos and enchiladas. Their use as a dip was championed by Mexican restaurants in the United States, which served salsa with tortilla chips. Soon the combination became an American staple. The first known manufacturer of salsa was Pace Foods of San Antonio. Its owner, Dave Pace, experimented with bottling salsa in 1947 and finally succeeded in perfecting the formula the following year. His success encouraged other manufacturers to produce salsa, including Old El Paso and Ortega. The salsa market exploded during the 1980s and continued to grow in the following decade. During the 1990s salsa briefly outsold ketchup, which shook up the condiment world.

By the end of the twentieth century, hundreds of commercial dips were sold, and by 2002 this category of foods had sales of $1.5 billion per year. In addition, thousands of dip recipes appear in cookbooks for fish, poultry, dairy, meat, fruits, and vegetables. Among the most famous dips are ones made from beans, clams, crabs, and cheese. Americans have also adopted and adapted dips from other cuisines, such as soy sauce from Japan and China, *quesa* from Mexico, *satay* sauce from Thailand, curry-based dips from India and Indonesia, seasoned olive oil from Italy and Spain, and fish sauces from Southeast Asia. The major host foods for dips remain chips, bread sticks, and vegetables such as celery and carrots.

[See also CONDIMENTS; FONDUE POT; SALSA; SNACKS, SALTY.]

BIBLIOGRAPHY

France, Christine. *The Complete Book of Sauces, Salsas, Dips, Relishes, Marinades, and Dressings.* New York: Lorenz Books, 2001.

Stock, Dawn. *The Encyclopedia of Homemade Dips.* Philadelphia: Courage Books, 1996.

ANDREW F. SMITH

Dishes, *see Plates*

Dishwashing and Cleaning Up

In cleaning up after cooking, sanitation is the major concern, but food that is stuck on pans also interferes with cooking. Useful patinas on cast-iron wares, deliberately and slowly built up from grease and carbonized food, act like a Teflon coating. For centuries, until the 1850s or so, most cooking fat and grease was saved to make soap. Farm wives scraped plates into slop jars to feed their pigs well into the twentieth century.

Along with dishpans, dish mops, and drainers, tools included scouring sands, brushes, scrapers, and chain cloth pot cleaners. In the eighteenth and nineteenth centuries, knives were placed on long scouring boards so that fine polishing grit could be rubbed on the blades. Cranked knife cleaners came in the 1860s. Clamshells were used as early pot scrapers; by the 1880s scrapers were made of metal in odd shapes so that corners fit the contours of different pans.

In the twenty-first century, just as scouring pads and powdered cleansers have early precedents, so do electric dishwashers: an early mechanical (though not electric) dishwasher was patented in 1891 by a Mrs. Stevens shortly followed by a see-through glass dishwasher invented by Josephine Cochrane.

[See also KITCHENS.]

Rising Sun and Sun Paste stove polish advertisement from 1898.

BIBLIOGRAPHY

Franklin, Linda Campbell. *300 Years of Kitchen Collectibles.* 5th ed. Iola, WI: Krause, 2003.

LINDA CAMPBELL FRANKLIN

Distillation

Distillation is the process of controlled heating of a mixture to separate the more volatile from the less volatile parts, then cooling and condensing the vapor to make a purer substance. The word "distill" comes from the Latin *destillare*, meaning to drip.

There are hints about oils and "essences" in books of the Ayurvedas from India c. 3000 B.C.E., and distilled rice or barley liquor was consumed there as early as 800 B.C.E. Egyptians distilled oils for perfumes and medicines as early as 2500 B.C.E. Chinese alchemists used distillation in approximately the sixth century B.C.E. These peoples used distillation primarily for alchemy and transmutation of various substances. Arabs developed the technology that shaped European distillation until the Middle Ages. The basic piece of equipment for distillation was the alembic.

Until the Middle Ages, distillation was used for alchemical and medical purposes. Europeans began to distill alcohol in larger quantities for its health-giving properties. The name "water of life" appears in almost all European languages; related terms include aqua vitae, aquavit, eau-de-vie, and *uisquebeatha* or *uisce beatha*, the parent of the word "whiskey."

As a medicine, alcohol was amended with roots, berries, leaves, stems, and even animal components. The fifteenth century saw the change of distilled alcohol from a pharmaceutical product to a beverage. Wine was distilled to concentrate the alcohol and was called *brannten Wein*, or burned wine, in German. The Dutch variant of that name, *brandewijn*, provides us with the word "brandy." Grain beers were distilled in Celtic lands between 1100 and 1300 to create whiskey, or "whisky," depending on where it is from. Scotland alone spells the product without the "e."

American settlers made familiar beers and wines as well as some new ones based on new raw materials. Sugarcane was readily available to make rum. Barley and rye were used for whiskey in the North. Corn was common throughout the South and gave rise to the unique American whiskey called bourbon, either with a "sweet mash" of all-fresh ingredients or a "sour mash" in which some of a prior batch was added for a fuller flavor.

Whereas until the nineteenth century distillation of beers and wines (called the "wash") was accomplished in pot stills that required shutting down, emptying, and cleaning after each batch, modern distilling is most often accomplished in column stills that deliver a continuous stream of distillate from a continuous input of wash. The advantages of the column still are the quantity of distillate produced and the ease of operation. A disadvantage is that the distillate contains less of the flavor elements and so produces a relatively mild tasting product. These grain neutral spirits are used to make other infused or flavored liquors and blended whiskeys.

Americans consumed beer, wine, and distilled alcohol in the 1970s in the approximate volume ratios of 100 units of beer to 10 units of distilled spirits to about 7 units of wine. In the 1980s wine sales pushed ahead of distilled spirits. Approximate ratios in the late twentieth century were beer, 100 units; wine, 8.5 units; distilled spirits, 5.6 units. The decline is both in percentage consumed and in actual volume.

[See also BEER; BOURBON; BRANDY; WHISKEY.]

BIBLIOGRAPHY

McGee, Harold. *On Food and Cooking: The Science and Lore of the Kitchen.* 2nd edition. New York: Scribners, 2004. The most authoritative book on the science and history of culinaria.

ROBERT PASTORIO

Domino's Pizza

In 1961, brothers Thomas S. and James Monaghan purchased Dominick's, a pizzeria in Ypsilanti, Michigan. Eight months later, James traded his share to his brother for a used car. The first franchise was sold within a few years. In 1965 Tom Monaghan renamed the business Domino's Pizza. The company expanded and it opened its two hundredth franchise in 1978. Monaghan located many outlets in towns with a military installation or college.

One reason for their success was home delivery, which had not been possible with other fast foods, such as hamburgers, which quickly lose their appeal as they cool. Pizza, however, can be kept hot (Domino's used the "Heat Wave," a special bag, to accomplish this) long enough to be delivered. When Domino's main competitor, Pizza Hut, began offering home delivery, Domino's promised customers that if their pizza was not delivered in less than thirty minutes, there would be no charge for the order.

In the 1980s, the first Domino's outside the United States opened in Winnipeg, Canada. In 2005 Domino's had more than seven thousand stores in sixty-one countries. The company has localized many of its products. In Japan, for instance, the company's best seller is a pizza with mayonnaise, potatoes, and ham or bacon. In Hong Kong, it's a pizza with Cajun spices

with small marinated cooked cubes of meat. Domino's is the country's second largest pizza chain after Pizza Hut.

[See also PIZZA; PIZZERIAS.]

BIBLIOGRAPHY

Monaghan, Tom, with Robert Anderson. *Pizza Tiger.* New York: Random House, 1986.

ANDREW F. SMITH

Doughnut-Making Tools

The center holes in the deep-fried cakes known as doughnuts (also called *oliekoecken,* fried dough, or dough nuts in the 1800s) have been accomplished with gadgets since at least the 1850s. The first cake cutter patent, in 1857, shows a strap-handled, round cutter for cookies plus an insert piece to be snapped on to cut center holes. In 1867 a patent was issued for a rolling "confectionery" cutter that had rolling-pin-like handles and cut two with every revolution. An 1876 spring-activated cutter was placed on dough, the center knob was depressed to cut a hole quickly, and the cutter sprang back. In 1954 an almost identical ejection cutter was patented. Also in the 1870s cookie dough presses, consisting of a tube and a plunger, were widely used for making jumbles. Similar tools continued to be made through the 1930s but were finally called "doughnut presses." Such presses were filled with dough, and the doughnuts were expressed directly into the boiling fat.

[See also COOKIE CUTTERS; DOUGHNUTS.]

BIBLIOGRAPHY

Franklin, Linda Campbell. *300 Years of Kitchen Collectibles.* 5th ed. Iola, WI: Krause, 2003.

LINDA CAMPBELL FRANKLIN

Doughnuts

Doughnuts are deep-fried cakes with a long European history and roots in still earlier Middle Eastern cuisine. They were introduced to America by the Dutch in New Netherlands as *oliekoecken* (oil cakes or fried cakes). Made of yeast dough rich in eggs and butter, spices, and dried fruits, their sweetness came from the fruit and the final dusting of sugar. The dough was often somewhat sticky (additional flour toughened and masked the spicy and buttery flavors) and was dropped as blobs off the end of a spoon into hot rapeseed oil (canola). The resulting doughnuts took the form of irregular balls, at some point called *oliebollen,* or oil (fried) balls. They were eaten during the Dutch Christmas season, which extended through New Year's to Twelfth Night (January 6), and for special occasions throughout the year. Once in the New World, the Dutch replaced their frying oil with the preferred lard (far more available here), as it produced a tender and greaseless crust.

Other ethnic groups brought their own doughnut variations. Moravians of Pennsylvania and South Carolina made *fastnachts,* generally associated with Shrove Tuesday

observances, and the French established beignets in New Orleans. Ultimately, the English American cooks adopted them as well. By 1845 doughnuts appeared in American cookbooks as staples, and the weekly Saturday baking (breads, cakes, and pies) included doughnut frying.

In this same antebellum period, two changes in technology contributed to a basic alteration in the doughnut. Chemical leavening (notably baking powder) was substituted for the yeast, producing a more cakelike and less breadlike product. In the same era inexpensive tin doughnut cutters with holes were manufactured commercially and sold widely. Before the end of the century they were distributed as commercial giveaways, a testament to continuing interest in doughnut making. Home cooks had adopted the form and textures dictated by the technology, but continued to fry both kinds.

Throughout the twentieth century doughnuts remained popular at home and in coffee shops. During World War II they were associated with mass-produced canteen snacks and USO hospitality for GIs. The familiar twentieth-century jelly doughnut, now the Israeli Hanukkah icon *sufganyot,* has made its way into Jewish American homes. Sustained doughnut popularity is reflected in such successful chains as Dunkin' Donuts and Krispy Kreme, although doughnuts are prepared only rarely in home kitchens.

[See also BREAKFAST FOODS; DOUGHNUT-MAKING TOOLS; DUTCH INFLUENCES ON AMERICAN FOOD.]

ALICE ROSS

Dr. Brown's

Dr. Brown's is a line of sodas best known for Cel-Ray, a celery soda. A brand with distinct regional appeal, it can be found in New York City and major soft-drink markets where New Yorkers have relocated. The cans claim that Dr. Brown's has been sold since 1869. Whether there really was a Dr. Brown who founded the brand is obscured by time. The sodas were produced by Schoneberger & Noble, a New York–based drink company, which originated the brand.

By 1910 its labels advertised "Dr. Browns [sic] Celery Tonic," made with crushed celery seeds, as a "pure beverage for the nerves" that "strengthens the appetite and aids digestion." By 1928 the American Beverage Corporation had produced and bottled the brand. In the 1930s it was advertised in local Jewish newspapers and on the radio. In the 1950s Food and Drug Administration objections to the use of the word "tonic" led the company to change the name to Cel-Ray. Dr. Brown's is also known for its black cherry soda and vanilla-flavored cream soda.

The sodas enjoyed a wide Jewish following in New York delis in the early twentieth century. But in the early 1980s, as Jewish delis in New York vanished, the company expanded distribution to include delis, gourmet shops, and restaurants in major markets around the country, bringing a formerly "ethnic" drink into the mainstream. Canada Dry Bottling Company of New York acquired Dr. Brown's in 1982.

[**See also** CREAM SODA; FOOD AND DRUG ADMINISTRATION; SODA DRINKS.]

BIBLIOGRAPHY
Hillinger, Charles. "Drink of the Deli People: Dr. Brown's Cream Soda Making Its Mark Outside of New York." *Los Angeles Times*, July 4, 1986.
Turan, Kenneth. "Cel-Ray Is on the Way: Ethnic Tonic, or a Way of Life?" *Washington Post*, December 28, 1977.

SANDRA YIN

Dr Pepper

Dr Pepper is a soft drink created in 1885 by a pharmacist from Waco, Texas, named Charles Alderton. The American soft-drink industry, which began in the 1830s, had developed steadily as the result of antiliquor pressure from the temperance movement. Local pharmacies had become popular gathering spots for refreshments, and pharmacists naturally developed innumerable new soft-drink flavors. Alderton supplemented his pharmaceutical duties at Morrison's Old Corner Drug Store by serving its soda-fountain customers. Fascinated by the various carbonated beverages, he developed a successful new combination of flavors that patrons called "a Waco," in reference to its local affiliation. Wade B. Morrison, owner of the drugstore, reportedly named it Dr Pepper after a former employer named Dr. Charles T. Pepper in Rural Retreat, Virginia.

By 1891, demand outstripped the amount of Dr Pepper that Morrison's drugstore could supply, and Morrison formed a partnership with Robert S. Lazenby, a Waco beverage chemist. They formed the Artesian Manufacturing and Bottling Company, and they also struck a deal with Sam Houston Prim, owner of a bottling plant in Dublin, Texas. Dr Pepper was introduced at the 1904 World's Fair Exposition in St. Louis, but despite national exposure, the company remained a regional operation, selling primarily to the southern and southwestern markets. Not until 1963, when a United States District Court ruled that Dr Pepper was not a cola, was the firm able to circumvent franchise contract conflicts with Pepsi-Cola and Coca Cola and sell Dr Pepper to independent bottlers nationwide.

In 1986 Dr Pepper merged with the Seven-Up Company. In 1995 Cadbury Schweppes of London, England, purchased the company. By the end of the twentieth century Dr Pepper / Seven-Up was the largest North American purveyor of non-cola soft drinks, with about 16 percent market share. Dr Pepper's advertising slogans have ranged from "King of Beverages" (1910–1914) to "Old Doc" (1920s–1930s) and then to "the friendly Pepper-Upper" (1950s). In response to changing times, the 1970s marked the slogan "the most original soft drink ever in

the whole wide world," followed by the famous 1977 campaign "Be a Pepper." In 2002, the company launched its promotional "Be You" campaign.

Two museums celebrate Dr Pepper. The Dr Pepper Museum and Free Enterprise Institute is located in the 1906 Artesian Manufacturing and Bottling Company building in downtown Waco. Donated by the Dr Pepper Company in 1988, it is listed in the National Register of Historic Places as the "Home of Dr Pepper." Exhibits teach the history of soft drinks and the free-enterprise economic system. Old Doc's Soda Shop, located in Sam Houston Prim's original Dr Pepper bottling plant in Dublin, Texas, also serves as a shrine to the product. This is the only facility licensed to manufacture Dr Pepper with the original formula calling for cane sugar, rather than the high fructose corn syrup adopted by the soft-drink industry in the 1970s. In the United States, Dr Pepper serves as a cocktail mixer as well as an ingredient in numerous home-cooked dishes, such as cakes, candies, jellies, desserts, molded salads, breads, and marinades.

[**See also** ADVERTISING; COLA WARS; SODA DRINKS.]

BIBLIOGRAPHY
Rodengen, Jeffrey L. *The Legend of Dr Pepper/Seven-Up.* Fort Lauderdale, FL: Write Stuff Syndicate, 1995.

BECKY MERCURI

Dressings and Stuffings

Important as it is to America's festive culinary traditions, "dressing" is a term that wants some pinning down. Above all, whether it is interchangeable with "stuffing" is a matter of continual debate. On the one hand, insofar as "dressing" came into use in the nineteenth century as a prim euphemism for the latter term, we can assume it is equivalent. On the other hand, the verbs "to dress" and "to stuff" have historically connoted distinct culinary procedures—the one having to do with the cleaning and preparing of the carcasses of fish or fowl and the other with the making of fillings of all sorts. In this light, dressing might be viewed as a subtype in the more general category of stuffing, namely, one related directly to meat cookery—whereby filling the animal cavity with various ingredients would simply constitute a later step in the dressing process. This verb-based distinction accords to some extent with the popular notion that, technically, stuffing is the mixture actually inserted into the animal to be consumed, while dressing is the same mixture cooked separately, "on the outside." At any rate, "stuffing" is the dominant term, while "dressing" inheres in regional vocabularies, particularly in the South and Southeast.

When it comes to recipes, however, dressing is all over the map. A central component of the Thanksgiving repast (among others), it ultimately reflects all manner of culinary

considerations, from basic technique to ethnic background to regional and national custom. For instance, to the extent that there is such a thing as a classic American recipe for dressing, it is the one that draws on our Anglo heritage to include white bread, sage, and sausage—a bland combination that nonetheless happens to pair especially well with turkey, the standard centerpiece of our holiday meal. That said, one of the very distinctions between British and U.S. culture that, for better or worse, Americans have chosen to emphasize is an "anything goes" attitude—such that we might as soon deem "classics" those recipes that must once have seemed boldly experimental: oyster dressing from the Gulf Coast of Louisiana, say, or Minnesotan wild rice stuffing. By the same token, we are quick to appropriate as "new" ideas that, to the immigrants who introduce them, are anything but novel; we may give our dressing an Italian makeover with ingredients like truffles, chestnuts, and pancetta or add dried fruits for Germanic flair. Thus, future classics may exist even among today's quirkiest-seeming dressings, from southwestern versions using blue cornbread, green chilies, and pine nuts to Caribbean-style mixtures of curried chickpeas and rice.

Of course, questions of taste aside, it is not exactly the case that anything goes in the preparation of dressing. After all, dressing serves a specific culinary function—it helps maintain, or even enhances, the moisture content of the meat containing it; its ingredients, then, must strike a balance between absorbent starch and absorbefacient fat. What is more, because it makes contact with potentially contaminating raw meat juices, care must be taken to ensure that the dressing is fully cooked before it is served. The unfortunate upshot is that fears of food-borne illness—instilled in part by an anxious United States Department of Agriculture via a media that loves a good scare—have led many to abandon the practice of stuffing meats altogether.

[**See also** THANKSGIVING; TURKEY.]

BIBLIOGRAPHY
Baker, James W., and Elizabeth Brabb. *Thanksgiving Cookery.* New York: Brick Tower, 1994
Rodgers, Rick. *50 Best Stuffings and Dressings.* New York: Broadway Books, 1997.

RUTH TOBIAS

Drinking Songs

American drinking songs fall into two main categories, with much overlap: songs about drinking (with lines like "It's beer, beer, beer that makes me wanna cheer") and songs generally sung when one is drinking or drunk. They are almost always loud, boisterous, and long. ("Ninety-Nine Bottles of Beer on the Wall" is seldom sung from start to finish—an earlier version had only forty-nine bottles.) Often, they are sentimental or profane. These songs are usually sung slightly out of tune in large groups, with the understanding that sober people are too repressed to sing them, but, fortified with alcohol, singers can drape arms around one another's shoulders and let loose.

The earliest American drinking songs were mostly imported from Great Britain. Robert Burns's "Auld Lang Syne," based on a seventeenth-century Scottish folk song, was still sung in 2002 by American New Year's revelers. Others were quintessential American folk songs, such as "Clementine" and "I've Been Working on the Railroad." Two drinking songs that appear regularly in published collections are "Little Brown Jug" ("My wife and I live all alone / In a little brown hut we call our own, / She loves gin and I love rum, / Tell you what, don't we have fun?") and "Frankie and Johnnie" ("He was her man, but he done her wrong"). Dean Henry Aldrich's seventeenth-century verse on drink is also a classic:

> If on my theme I rightly think,
> There are five reasons why I drink,—
> Good wine, a friend, because I'm dry,
> Or lest I should be by and by,
> Or any other reason why.

Drinking songs usually exist in several versions, each more ribald than the last. Published drinking songs tend to be toned down, with "dirty" words removed. Some songs even make a joke out of this, like "The Crayfish in the Chamber-Pot," which begins with obscene rhymes and then backs off ("Children, children, hear your mother grunt, / The crayfish in the chamber pot has got your mother's…nose").

Drinking songs are often familiar tunes with new lyrics, like "I want a beer just like the beer that pickled dear old dad" (sung to the tune of "I Want a Girl"). Some have become so well known that children sing them on the playground or at summer camp: "Be Kind to Your Web-Footed Friends" (to the tune of John Philip Sousa's "The Stars and Stripes Forever") or "Great Green Gobs of Greasy Grimy Gopher Guts" (to the tune of "The Old Gray Mare"). The most famous example, of course, is Francis Scott Key's "The Star-Spangled Banner," the national anthem of the United States, which is based on "To Anacreon in Heaven," an eighteenth-century drinking song from a London social club.

In the late nineteenth century the American temperance movement countered with songs of its own, like "Father, Come Home," from the temperance play *Ten Nights in a Bar-Room*, and "Touch Not the Cup" (to the tune of "Long, Long Ago"). Lord Charles Neaves responded, in turn, with "I'm Very Fond of Water: A New Temperance Song":

> I'm very fond of water,
> I drink it noon and night
> … But I forgot to mention—
> 'Tis best to be sincere—
> I use an old invention
> That makes it into Beer.

Many twentieth-century drinking songs are college- or club-specific, like "The Engineers' Drinking Song" from MIT ("We are, we are, we are, we are, we are the Engineers / We can, we can, we can, we can demolish forty beers") or "What Do We Do with a Drunken Alien" (to the tune of "What Shall We Do with a Drunken Sailor"), sung around the campfire at pagan festivals or at science fiction convention parties.

The twentieth century has yielded a few drinking songs with known composers and one official set of lyrics, like "Madeira, M'Dear" by Michael Flanders and Donald Swan, "An Irish Ballad" by Tom Lehrer, "Margaritaville" by Jimmy Buffett, and "Escape (The Pina Colada Song)" by Rupert Holmes. In the late twentieth century, American bars began purchasing Japanese karaoke machines, which allowed patrons to sing along to recorded music. Performing popular songs solo, and watching your friends do the same, became one more form of musical entertainment to accompany drinking.

[**See also** BEER; TEMPERANCE.]

JESSY RANDALL

Drive-Ins

"People in their cars are so lazy that they don't want to get out of them to eat!" The proclamation still rang as true at the end of the twentieth century as it did when the candy and tobacco magnate Jessie G. Kirby first uttered the words in 1921. At the time, he was trying to interest Reuben W. Jackson, a physician from Dallas, Texas, in investing in a new idea for a roadside restaurant—a sort of fast-food stand, although he did not call it that.

Introducing America's New Motor Lunch

Kirby's idea was simple: Patrons were to drive up in their automobiles and make their food requests from behind the wheel. At the curbside a young lad would take the orders directly through the window of the car and then deliver the food and beverages the very same way. It was a novel way to dine. Customers could remain in their cars and consume their meals while still sitting in the front seat.

Of course, the Roaring Twenties was an era ripe for such a brazen idea. Adventurous folk perched atop flagpoles, danced the Charleston at around-the-clock marathons, and consumed illegal bathtub gin at speakeasies. During Prohibition, freedom of travel emerged as the new thrill, fueled by automobile ownership that soared from 6 million to 27 million motorcars by the decade's end.

The automobile was America's newest fad, and people hit the highways for many reasons, including recreation, romance, adventure…and to get a bite to eat. When Kirby and Jackson's Texas "Pig Stand" beckoned cars to pull off the busy Dallas–Fort Worth Highway in the fall of 1921, hordes of Texas motorists tipped their ten-gallon hats to what the highway billboards called

"America's New Motor Lunch." Here was the ultimate dining-in-your-car experience, positioned strategically between the cities of Dallas and Fort Worth, Texas.

Good Food and Innovative Service

The star of the show was the "Pig Sandwich," Kirby and Jackson's contribution to the emerging culinary category known as "fast food." Prepared with tender slices of roast pork loin, pickle relish, and barbecue sauce layered inside a bun, the entrée quickly gained a loyal following and became the soon-to-be chain's signature (and later trademarked) sandwich. A frosty bottle of Coca-Cola or Dr Pepper, another Texas original, washed down the savory motoring meal.

At the Pig Stand the dining arrangements followed the menu's simplicity. Unlike conventional sit-down restaurants of the era, the Pig Stand offered an atmosphere where patrons did not have to contend with stuffy waiters and formal table etiquette and the exorbitant prices that accompanied them. A simple board-and-batten shack housed a small galley for food preparations, and a detached barbecue pit was used to prepare the pork. With no need to dress for dinner, service workers, such as delivery men, taxi drivers, and tradesmen, could grab a meal on the go, without being concerned about appearances. Whether a person arrived in a Model T Ford or a Duesenberg did not matter. Both the patron and the car were king.

But the casual atmosphere was not the only attraction. From the beginning, the fleet-footed lads who took the orders and delivered food became the focus of the drive-in's appeal. Donning white shirts, white hats, and black bow ties, the eager carboys were a sight to see, routinely jumping into action before arriving vehicles rolled to a complete stop. "As soon as they saw a Model T start to slow down and tires turn towards the curb, they'd race out to see who could jump up on the running board while the car was still moving," recalled Richard Hailey, successor to the pork sandwich dynasty and president of Pig Stands Inc. with headquarters in San Antonio, Texas. Vying for tips, the nation's first automotive food servers became a phenomenon, and the term "carhop" was coined to describe the flashy combination of waiter, busboy, cashier, and daredevil.

America Embraces the Drive-In

As the carhop replaced the soda jerk as the new hero of recreational dining, the reputation of the Pig Stands spread. As the stands were propelled beyond the borders of Texas by one of the first franchise arrangements in the industry, the number of locations quickly multiplied. Between 1921 and 1934 more than one hundred Pig Stand drive-in restaurants were constructed in Alabama, Arkansas, California, Florida, Louisiana, Mississippi, New York, Oklahoma, and Texas.

Innovation followed growth. In 1931 California Pig Stand Number 21 achieved a milestone when it pioneered the concept of "drive-through" car service with the first drive-up window. The customers eased their cars up to the window, issued their food orders, grabbed their lunches from the cook, and returned to the roadway. With its year-round sunny climate and car-filled boulevards, California proved to be particularly well suited for dining with one's motor running. During the 1930s surface streets like Sepulveda Boulevard, Cahuenga, and the Sunset Strip emerged as a haven for restaurants that catered to the car crowd. By the time Pig Stand Number 27 opened in Los Angeles, savvy restaurateurs saw the opportunity to make big money with a proven format. Featuring multilayer ziggurats, rooftop pylons, and miles of neon, new drive-ins like Bob's Big Boy, Carpenter's, Dolores, Herbert's, Simon's, Stan's, McDonnell's, Mel's, Roberts Brothers, and Van de Kamp's trumped the Pig Stands with the architectural styling of art deco and streamline modern.

In the decades to come, Pig Stands and their raft of imitators continued to fine-tune the basic format of drive-in service. When automobiles became more streamlined and lost their running boards, carhops strapped on roller skates in an effort to speed up service. Electronic intercom systems came into vogue during the 1960s and replaced the human element with vacuum tubes and wiring. Gradually, as automobiles became faster and highways wider, the novelty of carhop service wore off.

The motoring public grew increasingly impatient with carhop service, despite the best efforts by drive-in operators to enhance the customer experience. Even with a speaker box that was conveniently mounted to take one's order, customers still had to wait for someone to walk out and bring them their food, collect their money, and bring back the change (eyed by carhops as a potential tip).

By the 1970s it was clear that the drive-through window was superior in terms of its speed, simplicity, and practicality. Not surprisingly, many of the emerging burger chains embraced it as the best way to serve customers in their cars. While the number of drive-in restaurants that used carhop service dwindled, the clever service innovation originated by the Texas Pig Stands became integral to the new wave of American fast food eateries. Although the format had evolved since those early days of the drive-in, Kirby's prophetic words stood the test of time. By the early years of the twenty-first century, the public's desire to order, pick up, and eat an affordable meal—while still seated in their automobile—was as strong as ever.

[**See also** Fast Food; Roadside Food.]

BIBLIOGRAPHY

Langdon, Philip. *Orange Roofs, Golden Arches: The Architecture of American Chain Restaurants.* New York: Knopf, 1986.

Witzel, Michael K. *The American Drive-in: History and Folklore of the Drive-in Restaurant in American Car Culture.* Osceola, WI: Motorbooks International, 1994.

Witzel, Michael K. *Drive-in Deluxe.* Osceola, WI: Motorbooks International, 1997.

MICHAEL KARL WITZEL

Drying

The microorganisms that normally inhabit fresh foods require water in order to multiply. Removing that moisture prevents spoilage and prolongs the storage life of foodstuffs; dried foods also weigh less and occupy a smaller volume. An ancient technique, drying is very easy and cheap. Before canning and refrigeration, it was an important method of food preservation. Drying can be accomplished with direct sunlight or dry air. The chile *ristras* of the Southwest are an example of simple drying; whole chiles are strung into garlands and hung outdoors to dry.

Applying heat is an easier way to dry foods where sunlight or dry air is not plentiful. Foods can be dried at home in ovens, special dehydrators (bought or built at home), or even in the microwave. Commercial drying methods include freeze-drying (where water is removed from frozen foods under vacuum) and spray-drying (by spraying liquids into columns of hot air). Herbs and instant coffee and tea are often freeze-dried, and powdered milk is typically spray-dried.

Dried foods retain much of their nutritional value, although some vitamins are lost with heat or air exposure. Properly dried foods can be stored without refrigeration, provided that moisture and insects are kept out. Even with the availability of canning, refrigeration, and freezing, home production of dried foods is still common. The use of dried foods in traditional regional recipes, such as the Pennsylvania Dutch dish *schnitz und knepp* ("slices and buttons," made with dried apples, ham, and dumplings), can be done by choice rather than necessity.

[**See also** Coffee, Instant; Freeze-Drying; Milk, Powdered.]

BIBLIOGRAPHY

Hobson, Phyllis. *Making and Using Dried Foods.* Pownal, VT: Storey Communications, 1994.

McClure, Susan, ed. *Preserving Summer's Bounty.* Emmaus, PA: Rodale, 1998.

ASTRID FERSZT

Duck

The word "duck" is a generic term for small, web-footed birds of the Anatidae family, especially the genera *Anas, Aythya,* and *Cairina.* Ducks are generally smaller than other members of this order, which includes geese and swans. Ducks are found throughout the world. They are good swimmers and flyers but are awkward on land. Ducks in the Old World and the New World have been captured and used for food since prehistoric times.

Pair of Rouen ducks.

The mallard (*Anas boschas*) was probably domesticated in China in approximately 1000 B.C.E. and spread throughout the Old World in ancient times. Ducks became an important food, served particularly on the tables of the wealthy and on special occasions by other classes. Europeans introduced domesticated ducks into the New World, where they have thrived since colonial times.

The New World also had many species of wild ducks, but only the Muscovy (*Cairina moschata*) was domesticated. By the time Europeans arrived, the Muscovy duck was widely distributed throughout the tropical regions of Central and South America. The Spanish probably introduced it into the Caribbean, and the Portuguese introduced it into West Africa, where it thrived. The slave trade introduced the Muscovy duck into British North America. Archaeological evidence has surfaced demonstrating that slaves raised and consumed these fowl and later introduced them to the rest of America. By the 1840s the Muscovy duck was widely distributed throughout America. It survived as a commercial poultry item in the United States until the late nineteenth century but then largely disappeared as chicken and turkey began to dominate the poultry market.

Domesticated ducks were raised on a small scale on farms and were herded to market, usually with the help of specially trained dogs. An advantage of raising ducks was that these birds foraged and consumed food not eaten by other poultry. In addition, duck feathers were used for clothing and bedding. Canvasback ducks were raised on the Potomac and Susquehanna rivers in the early nineteenth century and later were shipped to all major East Coast cities and to Europe. Likewise, the Cayuga duck was bred in central New York and after the completion of the Erie Canal became available in East Coast cities. It was sandy and pond-filled Long Island, however, that became the center of early American duck raising. Long Island farms had easy access to the market in New York City, and Long Island green duckling became an important food in America.

In the mid-nineteenth century, duck breeding became an important business, and American efforts to improve the quality of ducks were greatly enhanced by the introduction of the Pekin duck (*Anas domesticus*) from China in 1873. Almost all commercial production uses strains of this variety. The American duck industry is concentrated in the Midwest—Wisconsin, Indiana, and Illinois. The duck industry is small compared with the chicken and turkey industries. Commercial ducks are generally sold frozen. There is also a niche market for duck eggs.

Ducks were served for special occasions, such as Thanksgiving and Christmas. Most nineteenth-century American cookbooks contain recipes for preparing ducks for the table. N. K. M. Lee's *Cook's Own Book* (1832) lists twelve recipes, including instructions for roasting, stewing, hashing, and boiling ducks. Several recipes contain directions for duck stuffing, which is similar to that for other fowl. Duck cookery was especially important among French American chefs, and numerous duck recipes appeared in their cookbooks. For example, Felix Déliée's *Franco-American Cookery Book* (1884) included forty-four duck recipes, including dishes with peas, onions, turnips, jellies, cranberries, anchovies, and assorted sauces and stuffings. Likewise, *The Picayune Creole Cook Book* (1901) featured many duck recipes. These included recipes for specific types of ducks, such as the canvasback (*Aythya valsineria*), which acquired its name for the coloring on its back, teal (*Anas crecca*), and widgeon (*Anas americana*). Ducks were served with a variety of other foods, including peas, oranges, and carrots. Despite the diversity of recipes and the quality of preparation, duck never achieved the popularity in America that it had in Europe. Duck recipes largely disappeared from American cookbooks in the early twentieth century, and ducks are mainly sold in specialty shops and French restaurants.

With the introduction of *magret* (boneless breast of the Moulard duck) in the 1980s through small East Coast breeders, duck has made a comeback. This resurgence coincides with a culinary shift toward the use of rare duck meat by upscale restaurants and ambitious home cooks.

[See also CHICKEN; CHRISTMAS; DRESSINGS AND STUFFINGS; FOWL; FRENCH INFLUENCES ON AMERICAN FOOD; GAME; GOOSE; THANKSGIVING; TURKEY.]

BIBLIOGRAPHY

Batty, Joseph. *Domesticated Ducks and Geese.* Mildhurst, UK: Beech, 1996.

Dohner, Janet Vorwald. *The Encyclopedia of Historic and Endangered Livestock and Poultry Breeds.* New Haven, CT, and London: Yale University Press, 2001.

ANDREW F. SMITH

Dumplings

Dumplings are plump, delicious, and unpretentious foods that defy precise definition. Even Maria Polushkin, in her *Dumpling Cookbook*, despairs that "no one seems to be very sure just what is and what is not a dumpling."

What is certain is that dumplings originated in Asia, and four regions of the world have contributed American adaptations: England invented the Norfolk dumpling, the archetypal and most authentic dumpling, according to the British; Central Europe contributed flavored and filled dumplings; and Italy was the home of ravioli and gnocchi. The American-Asian dumpling connection includes the multiplicity of dim sum, a Cantonese snack named for a phrase that means to touch the heart.

Adding to the dumpling distress, no one seems to know the actual derivation of the word. Dictionaries offer the dismal "origin obscure." Early American usage included "dumperling," as in "a mess er turnip-greens an' dumperlin's" (1877). The actual word "dumpling" appeared in print in America for the first time at the beginning of the seventeenth century to denote a small ball of boiled or steamed dough. That kind of dumpling probably evolved when a bread-making farm wife dropped a walnut-sized piece of dough into a simmering liquid, where it fell to the bottom of the pot like a lump of lead, then rose, puffed and beautiful, light and savory, to the top. Polushkin divides dumplings into "dropped dumpling" and "filled dumpling," with the seventeenth-century version unquestionably falling into the "dropped" category.

The dropped dumpling—usually a mixture of flour, eggs, and butter with herbs, spices, and other ingredients sometimes added to the basic dough—is simmered or boiled in liquid. Parsley dumplings (all-purpose, all-American, according to Polushkin) are prepared with stew, soup, chowder, fricassee, or ragout. Matzo balls (*knaydelach* is Yiddish for dumplings) are simmered in chicken broth or chicken stew and are traditionally served at the Passover Seder; they are also eaten year-round. Leftovers are incorporated in bread dumplings and mashed potato dumplings. Spaetzle—tiny, buttery German dumplings ("spaetzle" means little sparrows)—are made with a spaetzle mill and can be eaten as a meal by themselves. Liver dumplings (*leberkloesse*), dumplings made with finely-chopped liver, are popular in the South, where they are served Austrian style in a light broth or with sautéed onions. *Kluski*, Polish dumplings, are served with pot roast or stewed chicken. Elegant French quenelles are dropped dumplings. So are gnocchi, straddling the fine line that divides pasta from dumplings.

The filled dumpling basically consists of flour and water, sometimes with egg and a little shortening, rolled out and cut into circles or squares. A small amount of the filling goes in the center, and the edges are tightly sealed before the dumpling is boiled, fried, or steamed. Kreplach—Jewish dumplings stuffed with meat, cheese, or kasha (buckwheat groats)—are in the filled dumpling category. So is the knish, a kind of potato and flour dumpling stuffed with mashed potato and onion, chopped liver, or cheese; "knish" comes from the Polish word for dumpling. Empanadas from Argentina, ravioli and tortellini from Italy, and even wonton and egg rolls from China are popular dumplings in this category.

Early Moravian records indicate that pork and dumplings was a common dish eaten at the main meal of the day in the Carolinas during the eighteenth century. Polish pierogi—filled dumplings containing cheese, butter, potato, spinach, or onion—were brought to central Canada by Ukranian immigrants in the late 1800s. Joe Booker stew, made of lean beef, vegetables, and parsley dumplings, was a favorite dish during Maine winters when men came in from cutting ice or chopping down trees—but just as with the dumpling, no one seems to know who Joe Booker was.

For dessert, sweet-pastry dumplings might consist of an apple, cored and baked inside a snug pocket of dough. A special favorite of early Carolina settlers, the apple dumpling was made from cored apples filled with cinnamon and sugar, then snuggled in a jacket of puff pastry and boiled. Each apple dumpling was served with melted butter and sprinkled with sugar.

On Chinese New Year it is traditional to eat dumpling soup on the first day of the five-day celebration. Whoever bites into the dumpling with the surprise inside is sure to have good luck throughout the coming year.

A peculiar claim to dumpling diversity may be discovered in the frozen food section of American grocery stores; the pizza dumpling, a dumpling filled with Italian pizza ingredients, is manufactured by a Korean firm.

Closely related to dumplings are fritters, deep-fried batter that may include additional ingredients like vegetables, mushrooms, cheese, oysters, or shrimp. Calas, the traditional deep-fried yeasted fritters from New Orleans, Louisiana, are made with rice, eggs, vanilla, and nutmeg, and are served hot with thick coffee.

Doughboys (the nickname given to American soldiers in World War I) may or may not be related to a kind of flour-based dumpling that developed into the doughnut and was in use by the late eighteenth century.

[See also CHINESE AMERICAN FOOD; DOUGHNUTS; GERMAN AMERICAN FOOD; ITALIAN AMERICAN FOOD; JEWISH AMERICAN FOOD; SOUPS AND STEWS.]

BIBLIOGRAPHY

Polushkin, Maria. *The Dumpling Cookbook.* New York: Workman, 1977.

SARA RATH

Dunkin' Donuts

William Rosenberg dropped out of school at fourteen. Among other odd jobs he held around his native Boston, he delivered telegrams for Western Union and was employed as a door-to-door salesman. During World War II work was plentiful, and he saved $1,500 in war bonds. Aftre the war, he cashed in the bonds and borrowed an additional $1,000 to start a business that sold coffee, sandwiches, and baked goods from converted telephone trucks at worksites in suburban

In 1950 Bill Rosenberg opened the first Dunkin' Donuts shop in Quincy, Massachusetts.

Boston. Within three years, his company, called Industrial Luncheon Services, was operating 140 trucks. Observing that doughnuts were always in high demand, in 1948 he opened a small doughnut shop called the Open Kettle in Quincy, Massachusetts. Two years later, he renamed his shop Dunkin' Donuts. In 1955, he sold his first franchise; by 1966 there were enough shops around the country that Rosenberg set up "Dunkin' Donuts University" to help franchisers run their businesses. By 1968 there were 334 outlets; by 1986, there were 6,900. In 1970, the company opened its first outlet abroad, in Japan. Dunkin' Donuts began to advertise on television in 1978. In 1983 they had an incredible success with a commercial showing "Fred the baker" (played by Michael Vale) arising before dawn and mumbling, "Time to make the doughnuts" as he made his way to his Dunkin' Donuts shop. This was honored by the Television Bureau of Advertising as one of the five best commercials of the 1980s.

In addition to a choice of dozens of different kinds of doughnuts and crullers, Dunkin' Donuts sells "Munchkins," bite size spheres supposedly made from the dough punched from the centers of the doughnuts (they are not, really). In 1996 the company began selling freshly baked bagels and breakfast sandwiches made from them. In 2002 it introduced espressos, lattes, and cappuccinos and began stressing the quality of its coffee in television commercials.

Dunkin' Donuts bought the Mister Donut chain, the nation's second largest, in 1990. The French-based multinational Allied Lyons bought Dunkin' Donuts and in 1994 joined Pedro Domecq to create Allied Domecq, owners of Baskin-Robbins (as well as Mumm's and Perrier-Jouet Champagne). As of 2005, there were more than 5,500 Dunkin' Donuts outlets in thirty nations. The

company sells an estimated 6.4 million doughnuts per day totaling 2.3 billion per year.
[See also DOUGHNUTS.]

BIBLIOGRAPHY

Jakle, John A., and Keith A. Sculle. *Fast Food: Roadside Restaurants in the Automobile Age.* Baltimore: Johns Hopkins University Press, 1999.

ANDREW F. SMITH

Dutch Influences on American Food

The history of the Dutch colony New Netherland begins in 1609. In that year Henry Hudson explored the Hudson River, as it was later named, on behalf of the Dutch East India Company. His aim was to find a northern passage to Asia. Through his explorations the Dutch claim to a vast area between New England and Virginia was established. This claim reached from the Connecticut River to the Delaware Bay. In 1621 a charter with exclusive trading rights in the Western Hemisphere was given to the Dutch West India Company. In 1626 the island of Manhattan was purchased; in 1664 the English took over New Netherland, and, with the exception of a brief interlude in 1673-1674, the area remained in British hands until the American Revolution. In only seven brief decades, those persistent settlers managed to entrench themselves in their new homeland.

The Dutch colonists brought with them seeds and tree stock as well as horses, cows, pigs, and other domesticated animals. The settlers contributed the foodstuffs we so readily associate with the Hudson River Valley: vegetables such as cabbage, carrots, peas, onions, parsnips, and turnips; herbs such as parsley, rosemary, and chives; and fruits such as apples, pears, and peaches. In his 1665 book *A Description of the New Netherlands*, Adriaen van der Donck reports that they all "thrive well." By

1679 a traveler notes that he has never seen finer apples. He particularly enjoyed the Newtown Pippin, the Esopus (in the area of Kingston, New York), the Spitzenburgh, and the Poughkeepsie Swaar apples. Some of these old varieties are still grown in the orchards of the Hudson Valley. A century later the Swedish botanist Peter Kalm marveled in his diary at peach trees bearing such abundant fruit that roaming pigs gorged themselves.

Diaries and inventories show that the Dutch also brought with them the implements used for cooking those familiar foods cultivated in the New World. For example, Margareta van Slichtenhorst Schuyler (1630-1711) owned a brass "poffer" (silver-dollar pancake) pan as well as a waffle iron, according to the inventory of her estate. The twelve thousand assorted documents that remain from the Dutch period, partly translated by the New Netherland Project in Albany, make it clear that the settlers wanted to re-create their life in the Netherlands in New Netherland.

Dutch Contributions

Doughnuts, pretzels, coleslaw, pancakes, waffles, wafers, and, above all, cookies are all part of America's culinary heritage brought to New Netherland by the Dutch in the seventeenth century. The Dutch words *koolsla* and *koekje* were even adopted into American English with only slight transformations. *Kool* (pronounced like "cole") means cabbage, and *sla* means salad; together they became our American "coleslaw." The Dutch *koekje* (the "oe" is pronounced like "oo"), which is the diminutive of *koek*, a flat, not highly risen baked good, forms the root of the American word "cookie." The British call cookies "little cakes," or "biscuits." The first American cookbook, Amelia Simmons's *American Cookery*, published in 1796, features several cookie recipes, and Americans have loved cookies ever since.

Bread was the mainstay of the Dutch diet. It was consumed with butter or cheese for breakfast, paired with meat or a stew for the midday main meal, and served with the evening's dish of porridge. At holiday time, festive breads such as the *duivekater*, made with white flour and sugar, were given to the poor, as the deacon's accounts of the Reformed Church in Brooklyn show. Bread was even used in trade with Native Americans. Court records contain an account of a case in which a Beverwijck (Albany) baker was charged with selling a sugar bun to a Mohawk Indian in a period when, owing to grain scarcity, such sales were forbidden. To protect the population, government ordinances in the colony (or, as the Dutch called it, "the province"), as well as in the homeland, closely regulated the price, sale, and quality of bread. The same can be said of beer, the common drink before tea and coffee became fashionable at the end of the seventeenth century.

The typical meal pattern consisted of breakfast, along with midday, afternoon, and evening meals. Breakfast was mainly bread and butter or cheese. Beer was the usual drink for all meals. On the farms, buttermilk was drunk as well. The midday meal was the main meal of the day, made up of no more than two or three dishes. The first was often a *hutspot* (or hotchpotch), a one-pot dish of meat and vegetables; the second dish might be some sort of fish or a meat stewed with prunes and currants; and the third might be fruit, as well as cooked vegetables and cakes or savory pies. On the farm this midday meal was often simply a porridge, bread, and meat. A few hours after the midday meal, between two and three o'clock, some bread with butter or cheese was eaten. The last meal of the day, usually a porridge or leftovers of the noon meal and bread, was served just before bedtime.

For people used to eating porridge, it was easy to get used to the Native American cornmeal mush called *sapaen*, made from ground corn and water. The Dutch added milk to it, and it became an integral part of the Dutch-American diet. *Oliekoecken*, deep-fried dough balls filled with apples and raisins, were the edible symbols of the Dutch in America and the forerunners of the doughnut. They were always served at gatherings, church socials, or festive occasions. Descendants of the settlers continued the foodways of their ancestors. They might have forgotten the native tongue, but they did not forget the taste of the foods of their forebears and continued to enjoy the pastries and other items connected with feasts and holidays well into the nineteenth century and even up to the present day. Recipes for those familiar Dutch foods can be found in the hand-written manuscript cookbooks, spanning more than three centuries, that belonged to the descendants of families such as the Van Rensselaers of Albany, the Van Cortlandts of Croton-on-Hudson, or the Lefferts of Brooklyn. The Dutch touch left a lasting mark on the American kitchen.

[**See also** BEER; BREAD; BREAKFAST FOODS; COOKBOOKS AND MANUSCRIPTS: TO 1860; DOUGHNUTS; HISTORICAL OVERVIEW: COLONIAL PERIOD TO THE REVOLUTIONARY WAR; NATIVE AMERICAN FOODS.]

BIBLIOGRAPHY

Rose, Peter G., trans. and ed. *The Sensible Cook: Dutch Foodways in the Old and the New World.* 2nd ed. Syracuse, NY: Syracuse University Press, 1998. Includes a translation of a seventeenth-century Dutch cookbook.

Van der Donck, Adriaen. *A Description of the New Netherlands*, edited by Thomas F. O'Donnell. Syracuse, NY: Syracuse University Press, 1968. Reprint of the first English translation, published in 1841.

PETER G. ROSE

Dutch Ovens

The term "Dutch oven," as used here, refers to an American pot of European ancestry, a small, portable, cast-iron oven that has evolved to accommodate changing fuel sources since the eighteenth century. This is to distinguish it from the English use of the same term, which refers to what Americans call tin-reflecting ovens or side-wall fireplace brick ovens. The derivation of the term is similarly unclear, perhaps referring to legendary Dutch frugality (far less fuel required) or perhaps early Dutch expertise in casting iron, but it is probably an American designation. In any case, the American Dutch oven has been valued for its combination of steaming and baking, stewing, and braising.

Eighteenth-century American Dutch ovens were designed for the hearth, where they were heated with glowing embers. The high rims of their heavy lids held the glowing fuel on the top. Additional heat was provided by piles of coals underneath, and the oven's three legs held it at a good height above the heat source. Dutch ovens hung over the heat from swinging bail handles or were maneuvered by C-shaped handles on their sides. They were made in different sizes—the smallest was simultaneously pot and oven, while the larger ones could also contain pans of food.

American Dutch ovens can be traced to seventeenth-century Europe in such still-life paintings as Harmen Van Steenwyrk's *Skillet and Game* (1646). These examples were somewhat shallow and graceful and were often used as tart pans. Others, probably limited to wealthier families, were made of bronze or copper, exemplified by French *daubieres* (stew pans). An English version called the "bake kettle" varied, in that it was sometimes a round-bottomed, straight-sided kettle that hung covered over the heat and at other times was a flat-bottomed hanging kettle called a "yetling" in the West Country of England and a "bastable" in Ireland. These kettles were

A simple illustration of a Dutch oven.

often found in remote European rural areas with little access to commercial bakeries or enough wood to fuel home brick ovens. Bats of smoldering peat or other fuel substitutes were placed above and below. Peat produced lower temperatures than wood; its use resulted in heavy and moist breads that required additional drying.

American Dutch ovens were manufactured in the colonies in the eighteenth century—the Pine Grove Furnace (Pennsylvania) produced three sizes. No longer limited to affluent kitchens, they were inevitably made of cast iron and figured in such dishes as overnight beans, stewed or potted meats, tea cakes, cornbreads, pies, and puddings.

By the mid- to late nineteenth century, early American manufacturers of cast-iron implements were producing variations of hearth Dutch ovens called "spiders" (frying pans) and ovens that retained their legs and high-rimmed heavy lids. At the same time, in response to the proliferation of the woodstove, new dome-lidded, flat-bottomed forms, sometimes porcelain lined, were offered by such noted manufacturers as Griswald (Pennsylvania), who added such innovations as self-basting lids. Legs and high-rimmed lids had become obsolete with the passing of the kitchen hearth, but twentieth-century ovens, also called casseroles, continued to be popular kitchen equipment and are still essential adjuncts to the pot roasts and stews we honor as slow food.

[**See also** CASSEROLES; FRYING PANS, SKILLETS, AND SPIDERS; HEARTH COOKERY; SLOW COOKERS; SOUPS AND STEWS.]

BIBLIOGRAPHY

Ragsdale, John G. *Dutch Ovens Chronicled: Their Use in the United States.* Fayetteville: University of Arkansas Press, 1991.

ALICE ROSS

E

Easter

Easter celebrates spring and the resurrection of Christ. For observant Catholics, it also ends Lent, the forty-day penitential period beginning on Ash Wednesday that, until the mid-twentieth century, greatly influenced the diet of Catholics worldwide. Beginning in the seventh century, Catholics were expected to abstain from eating all animals and animal products during Lent, except on Sundays. Over time, the Roman Catholic Church relaxed these strictures to permit eating fish (ninth century) and dairy products (fifteenth century), although meat and poultry remained forbidden. In 1966 all fasting obligations were removed except for those related to Ash Wednesday and Good Friday. The Eastern Orthodox Church continues Lenten fasts. Protestants traditionally do not fast, but there is a growing movement among some American Protestants, as well as Catholics, to relinquish a favored treat, frequently chocolate, caffeine, or pastry.

The history of Easter celebrations in America parallels the controversies surrounding Christmas. Puritan sects viewed Easter dimly, as a holiday that smacked of popery. Until the mid-nineteenth century, only certain Protestants and the relatively small handful of Catholics in America venerated Easter as a religious feast. American folk observations of Easter (the name derives from an Anglo-Saxon goddess of fertility or spring, Eostre, whose sign was the rabbit), however, date back to the eighteenth century and greatly influence contemporary celebrations. The Pennsylvania Dutch imported the *Oschter Haws*, or Easter Hare, who delivered colored eggs to good children (or rabbit pellets to the naughty) who put out their hats for a "nest." By the early nineteenth century, entire Pennsylvania Dutch villages would turn out with gaily decorated Easter eggs to play games, including egg eating contests and "picking" eggs, in which young gladiators would butt eggs until one competitor's egg broke. For good health, the Pennsylvania Dutch ate wild greens, especially dandelion, on Maundy Thursday. They gathered eggs laid on Good Friday for consumption on Easter, for use in folk medicine, or as talismans against evil spirits. A favorite Pennsylvania Dutch Easter bread depicts a rabbit in the preposterous posture of laying an egg.

By the later nineteenth century, most Protestant groups had eased their opposition to Easter, and Sunday-dress Easter parades became a national pastime. The renamed Easter Bunny visited children, and confectioners began producing special sweets for the holiday, especially candy eggs to replace the dyed hens' eggs. Seasonal treats included marzipan, chocolate eggs, garishly colored jelly beans, and, more recently, "Peeps" (tinted marshmallow chicks and bunnies), all stuffed into the Easter baskets that replaced the hare's nest.

In the late nineteenth and early twentieth centuries, Catholic immigrants maintained Easter culinary rituals with overtly religious symbolism. Slovenian and Polish immigrants brought baskets of food to churches for blessings on Holy Saturday. The baskets contained hams and sausages (representing Christ incarnate), eggy breads (a Eucharistic allusion), vinegar (recalling the sponge soaked with the cheap sour wine, or posca, that was offered to Christ on the cross), a sugar or butter lamb (evoking Christ as the Lamb of God), and horseradish (denoting Christ's bitter sorrows).

Significantly, horseradish also plays an important role in the Jewish Passover feast, reinforcing the connection between Passover and Holy Week—considered by some the "Christian Passover." Another link is the Paschal Lamb, believed to have been eaten at the Last Supper, widely thought to have been a seder. Not only did the lamb become a Christian symbol, but also the Hebrew "Pesach" provides the common etymology for both Easter and Passover in many languages.

Special Easter breakfasts, popular from the early twentieth century, prominently feature egg dishes or foods shaped as eggs, such as delicately tinted blancmange puddings molded in blown-out eggshells. Unlike the formulaic dinners touted as "traditional" for Thanksgiving and, to a lesser extent, Christmas, there is no archetypical American Easter dinner. Moreover, according to one 1959 survey, only 75 percent of respondents judged a family Easter dinner very or somewhat important, compared to 94 percent for Christmas and 97 percent for Thanksgiving. Relatively few cookbooks or magazines published before the mid-twentieth century suggest Easter menus; those that do favor ham, with lamb running a close second. Other meats and even salmon had muscled their way onto Easter menus by the late twentieth century. Eggs may appear as starters for Easter dinner, in rich hollandaise sauce enrobing asparagus, as hard-cooked eggs garnished with caviar, or even as *oeufs en gelée.*

With Americans' increasing interest in ethnic cuisines, mainstream magazines offer recipes for "traditional" Easter meals from such Roman Catholic and Eastern Orthodox strongholds as Italy, Poland, Ukraine, and

Children dismantling a giant chocolate Easter egg, nineteenth-century print.

Greece. Common to all of these menus are massive, yeasted enriched cakes and breads. Hot cross buns—currant-studded, sweetened rolls decorated with royal icing crosses—are a more diminutive Holy Week treat.

[**See also** CANDY AND CANDY BARS; CHRISTMAS; EGGS; PASSOVER.]

BIBLIOGRAPHY

Cohen, Hennig, and Tristram Potter Coffin, eds. *The Folklore of American Holidays: A Compilation of More Than 600 Beliefs, Legends, Superstitions, Proverbs, Riddles, Poems, Songs, Dances, Games, Plays, Pageants, Fairs, Foods, and Processions Associated with over 140 American Calendar Customs and Festivals.* 3rd ed. Detroit: Gale, 1999.

Shoemaker, Alfred L. *Eastertide in Pennsylvania: A Folk Cultural Study.* Kutztown, PA: Pennsylvania Folklife Society, 1960.

CATHY K. KAUFMAN

Eating Disorders

Currently, somewhere between 5 million and 10 million Americans suffer from eating disorders. Typically, they are young women, although numbers are rising among females of all ages, including children, as well as among men. Broadly speaking, what is at stake in an eating disorder is a sense of control, both of oneself and of one's surroundings—a vexed issue for females in a patriarchal capitalist setting (even, if not especially, in a postfeminist era). The notion of self-possession, of a full-fledged identity, becomes bound up with the image of a fully grown body and its needs; when psychological disposition and family dynamics render these bindings particularly uncomfortable, an eating disorder may develop. Most common are anorexia, bulimia, and binge-eating disorder.

Anorexia

Extreme restriction of food intake, drastic weight loss, and a pattern of obsessive-compulsive behaviors involving diet, elimination, and exercise—to the exclusion of many other activities—are the hallmarks of anorexia nervosa. Aside from emaciation itself, the systemic complications it presents may include amenorrhea, anemia, early-onset osteoporosis, and/or hypotension leading, ultimately, to heart arrhythmia and heart failure.

The psychological profile of a typical sufferer of anorexia might read as follows: She is a female (as are nine of every ten) in her teens or early twenties, with a middle- or upper-middle-class background. The proverbial good girl, she demonstrates the perfectionism and painful modesty—especially regarding sexuality (namely, her own)—indicative of self-esteem issues. Theories as to why these issues should translate into preoccupations with thinness vary, but many of them consider the extent to which size, power, and sexuality have been conceptually linked throughout history.

While exaggeratedly full-figured fertility totems (such as the Venus of Willendorf) abound among prehistoric peoples, the heroines of the patriarchal civilization that is the Judeo-Christian West are markedly asexual, from the Virgin Mary to the medieval-era martyrs who exhibited "anorexia mirabilis," as it was known early on (that is, miraculous lack of appetite). On the one hand, the latter's ritual fasts bespoke purification, renunciation of the multivalent appetite that rendered Eve, and by extension womankind, the original sinner. On the other, as Caroline Walker Bynum notes, these sainted women, like modern-day anorexia sufferers, often came from relatively wealthy households, where their rigidly prescribed roles as nurturers revolved around food; by avoiding it—except, perhaps, when donating their families' own store to the poor—they could appear pious while covertly protesting the materialism and attendant sexism of the status quo. Apparently suspecting as much, the church ultimately discouraged women's fasting practices. With the Enlightment came added skepticism about these so-called "fasting girls," this time scientific in nature. By the late nineteenth century, physicians (and, eventually, psychologists) were treating self-starvation as a pathology rather than a supernatural phenomenon.

In today's secular world, preservation of the patriarchal status quo still obtains. That the mid-to-late-century rise of the feminist movement and the entry of women into the workplace concurred with a shift in the female beauty ideal—from the voluptuousness of sex symbols like Marilyn Monroe to the slim, prepubescent profiles of sixties fashion icons like Twiggy—strikes few as coincidental, though interpretations vary. Does the current ideal emulate boyishness in an attempt to embody, literally, the workforce? Or does it cling to girlishness as a conciliatory gesture, in order to lessen any perceived threat to male privilege and power that might provoke a backlash? Either way, it implies that woman's place remains in the home—at least insofar as her characteristic curves cannot enter the historically male public sphere with her.

Obviously, social factors are not in themselves sufficient to explain anorexia; if they were, every woman in industrialized society—and no man, for that matter—would be affected, rather than an estimated 1 percent. Treatment generally focuses on the psychological factors, taking a multipronged approach that may include individual or group psychotherapy, behavioral therapy, nutrition counseling, and medication.

Bulimia

Episodes of seemingly uncontrollable eating, or binges, distinguish bulimia nervosa from anorexia. By the standard definition, a binge entails the consumption of food far beyond the body's caloric requirements in a disproportionately brief time period, two hours being the duration usually named.

The person with bulimia—also most likely a young female—generally experiences crippling feelings of guilt and shame following a binge. To compensate, she will restrict her intake all the more; exercise compulsively, sometimes for hours per session; or purge—induced vomiting and laxative abuse being especially common methods. Over time, the binge-purge cycle can wreak havoc on the digestive system, leading to kidney, liver, and esophagus damage, as well as electrolyte imbalances that potentially cause heart failure.

As with anorexia, most explanations for bulimia run along a psychoanalytic-biochemical axis. It is currently believed that certain neurochemicals and hormones do effect a linkage between mood and appetite; serotonin, for instance, appears to regulate feelings of well-being, including satiety. Hence that class of antidepressants known as "selective serotonin reuptake inhibitors," or SSRIs, is frequently prescribed to patients with eating disorders, who may underproduce the chemical.

Binge-Eating Disorder

The third major type of eating disorder is binge-eating disorder, otherwise known as compulsive overeating. Like bulimia, it involves episodes of abnormal food intake that stem from and sustain low self-esteem; unlike bulimia, it does not involve purgation. Sufferers from this disorder—of whom there are believed to be millions—are thus likely to be overweight.

Of course, excess weight is itself a U.S. epidemic; studies released in the early twenty-first century indicated that as many as two in three Americans were overweight, one in three being clinically obese. Yet overeating, in and of itself, is not symptomatic of mental illness; it is only when the practice exacts a heavy emotional as well as physical toll on the practitioner, who despises her behavior but feels compelled to repeat it, that consultation with a therapist first and foremost, and not simply a dietitian, is likely in order.

[**See also** Obesity.]

BIBLIOGRAPHY

Abraham, Suzanne, and Derek Llewellyn-Jones. *Eating Disorders: The Facts.* 5th ed. New York: Oxford University Press, 2001.

Brumberg, Joan Jacobs. *Fasting Girls: The Emergence of Anorexia Nervosa as a Modern Disease.* Cambridge, MA: Harvard University Press, 1988.

Chernin, Kim. *The Hungry Self: Women, Eating, and Identity.* New York: Times Books, 1985.

RUTH TOBIAS

Eel

Eels (*Anguilla rostrata*) have an amazing life cycle, called catadromous, which begins with birth in the Sargasso Sea in the Atlantic Ocean. They drift on the Gulf Stream as transparent or "glass" eels to freshwater rivers and lakes, where they grow to be elvers and adults. Adult eels migrate back to the Sargasso Sea to spawn and die.

As food, eel is not much appreciated in America, although historically it was speared and trapped by Native Americans and English colonists. The Indian nation name "Algonquin" means "at the place of spearing fishes and eels." In the nineteenth century eel was caught to add variety to the diet and was most esteemed by European immigrants, particularly those from Germany, France, Italy, and the Netherlands. Asians value eel very highly. Since the 1970s, a market for elvers in Japan, China, Taiwan, and Korea has supplied eel for pond raising to adult size. The demand collapsed in the 1980s but returned in the 1990s, making elvers one of the most valuable per pound catches. In some parts of the United States, there is a concern that the elver harvest is too great and that not enough eels find their way to the streams and lakes. The season for elvers usually is limited to three months in the spring, and hand dip nets, or fykes, must be used.

Most modern fishers regard eels as a nuisance, although there is a small sport fishery for these fish. Eel flesh is oily, like that of mackerel, and it is good smoked, fried, and prepared in spicy stews. Earlier in American history, eel was roasted on spits, made into pies, and pickled.

SANDRA L. OLIVER

Egg Cream

The egg cream, a seemingly simple beverage, is produced from only three ingredients—milk, seltzer, and chocolate syrup—and contains neither eggs nor cream. While folklore, more so than fact, defines the egg cream's history, the origin and popularity of the drink indisputably belong to New York City.

The egg cream, originally a drink associated with eastern European Jewish immigrants, quickly became a beverage so linked to New York that it serves as one of the city's most recognizable icons. Almost exclusive to soda fountains and ice cream parlors, this New York specialty has been around since the 1920s, with popularity surging from the 1930s to the 1950s and then waning during the 1960s and 1970s, as soda fountains and ice cream parlors disappeared.

Because the drink contains neither eggs nor cream, the manner in which it got its name interests us. Perhaps the most widely accepted story is that Louis Auster, a Lower East Side candy shop owner, invented it during the 1890s and named it after the white foam layer on top, which moderately resembles beaten egg whites. The drink soon caught on, and its popularity swelled. Stanley Auster, the last known Auster family member, maintained that egg creams never contained either eggs or cream.

According to another piece of folklore, "soda jerks" (those who work in soda fountains) first created the egg cream, using syrup made from eggs and adding cream to give the drink a richer taste. Legend has it that sometime later, milk and sugar-based syrup replaced these ingredients, but the name remained. In a 1906 version of the historical text *The Standard Manual of Soda and Other Beverages*, an egg cream recipe includes a preparation with egg yolks, cream, syrup, seltzer, and vanilla, but few egg cream enthusiasts give much credence to this recipe.

A third legend is that the name "egg cream" was merely a marketing gimmick. Producers could now replace costly ice cream sodas and malteds, favored during the 1930s, with inexpensive egg creams. One final legend speculates that "egg cream" resulted from a poorly pronounced English translation of the French *chocolat et crème* by the Yiddish actor Boris Thomashevsky; because the correct pronunciation of "*et crème*" is "ay krem," the drink slowly evolved into "egg cream."

Disregarding the egg and cream controversy, most New Yorkers agree that customary egg creams call for a mixture of chocolate or vanilla syrup, chilled milk, and seltzer. There is much debate, however, over who originated—and therefore who owns—the egg cream. Legend states that Brooklyn soda jerks begin with syrup, follow with milk, and end with seltzer, ensuring a "milky white" foam. Their Bronx counterparts begin with syrup thoroughly mixed with seltzer and completed with milk, generating a brownish head.

Like many nostalgia foods, egg creams began enjoying a newfound surge in popularity and consumption in the 1990s that continues today. A proliferation of egg creams has appeared on restaurant and diner menus. No longer quintessentially Jewish, egg creams are consumed throughout the United States.

[See also CHOCOLATE DRINKS; DAIRY; ICE CREAM SODAS; JEWISH AMERICAN FOOD; NEW YORK FOOD; SELTZER; SODA DRINKS; SODA FOUNTAINS.]

JENNIFER SCHIFF BERG

Eggnog

Rich and creamy dessert drinks, such as eggnog and syllabub, reflect the English heritage in America, especially in the South. In England posset was a hot drink in which the white and yolk of eggs were whipped with ale, cider, or wine. Americans adapted English recipes to produce a variety of milk-based drinks that combined rum, brandy, or whiskey with cream. The first written reference to eggnog was an account of a February 1796 breakfast at the City Tavern in Philadelphia. Beginning in 1839 American cookbooks included recipes for cold eggnogs of cream, sugar, and eggs combined with brandy, rum, bourbon or sherry, sprinkled with nutmeg. Southerners enjoyed a mix of peach brandy, rum, and whiskey.

Eggnog has been served at holiday parties since the nineteenth century and is a tradition of Christmas and New Year's celebrations throughout the United States. In the nineteenth century eggnog was also a nourishing drink prepared for invalids, especially fever patients. A commercial nonalcoholic version is available in the dairy cases of grocery stores beginning in mid-October. Canned eggnog can be purchased year-round. During the winter holidays, eggnog is used to flavor ice cream, pancakes, french toast, cheesecake, breads, and cookies.

[See also CHRISTMAS; HOT TODDIES; NEW YEAR'S CELEBRATIONS; SYLLABUB.]

VIRGINIA SCOTT JENKINS

Eggplants

Few foods can lay claim to causing insanity, acting as an aphrodisiac, and serving as a dental cosmetic. Eggplant, *Solanum melongena*, lays claim to all of the above and much more. Although most often considered a vegetable, eggplant is actually a fruit. Technically it is a berry and a member of the nightshade family. It is possibly this botanical relationship to belladonna, the deadly nightshade, that prompted early Europeans to dub eggplant the "mad apple" on the premise that it could cause insanity. Quite a contrary view emerged, however, as the "apple of love" was sought after as an aphrodisiac in sixteenth-century Spain. Eggplant was also used as a cosmetic in the fifth century A.D. in China, where women used eggplant skins to make a black dye. As was the fashion of the day, women then used the dye to stain and polish their teeth until they took on a metallic sheen.

Eggplant, as it is known in America and was once known in Britain, is so named because the earliest variety to arrive in England in the sixteenth century was small and white, similar to a hen's egg. Eggplant is also widely known by its French name, aubergine.

Today eggplant is available in countless shapes and colors. The migration of eggplant can be roughly traced through the name "aubergine," which derives from the Catalan *alberginera*, the Arabic *al-b jinj n*, and the Persian *badin-gan*; the Arabic and Persian terms derive from the Sanskrit *vatin-ganah*. *Vatin-ganah* translates to "wind-go." Food historians have debated whether the word means that it does or does not cause flatulence. The Italian name, *petonciano*, may shed some light on this debate as *petonciano* translates to "fart."

It is virtually universally accepted that the eggplant was first cultivated in India some four thousand to five thousand years ago and was likely cultivated for ornamental purposes because of its attractive leaves and flowers. It is also probable that eggplant was first consumed as food in India. From India, eggplant was most likely introduced to China and then to the Middle East by Arab traders in the seventh century A.D., and possibly as early as the fourth century A.D. The Moors then introduced eggplant to Spain in the early eighth century A.D. By the thirteenth century, eggplant had made its way to Italy and then to the rest of Europe, brought on trade ships carrying spices and other goods from the East.

How and when eggplant first arrived in America is a subject of dispute. Early Spanish conquerors of Mexico and the Caribbean may have been the first to introduce eggplant to the Americas in the sixteenth century. Eggplant may also have been introduced to America by African slaves. According to one story, the eggplant was introduced to America by Thomas Jefferson. With its striking violet flowers and gray leaves, eggplant was grown for its ornamental as well as food value.

Despite having arrived in the Americas with or soon after the first European settlers, eggplant is often considered an ethnic food. In *Heirloom Vegetable Gardening* (1997), William Woys Weaver notes that Americans have been slow to expand their taste for eggplant. Weaver speculates that this lack of popularity may be due to the eggplant's horticultural weaknesses, including a rather finicky need for hot summer nights in order to fruit, as well as its susceptibility to the flea beetle and such fungi as fusarium and verticillium wilt.

The eggplant is most commonly associated with foods of the Far East, the Middle East, and the Mediterranean, although many of these foods have become commonplace in America. Eggplant parmesan is an Italian favorite in America. Moussaka is an import from Greece, and baba ghanoush is from the Middle East. Eggplant is also a key ingredient in the French classic ratatouille.

There are few preparations of eggplant considered distinctly American. One such preparation is fried eggplant, a southern specialty that appears in *The Virginia House-wife* (1824), in which Mary Randolph likens fried eggplant to soft-shell crabs. Rather than salting eggplant to extract the allegedly bitter juices, as is the standard contemporary practice, nineteenth-century American cookbooks recommend parboiling eggplant before the final cooking process. Another common American preparation is baked eggplant mashed with butter and topped with bread crumbs, served both at breakfast and at dinner.

[See also CHINESE AMERICAN FOOD; HEIRLOOM VEGETABLES; INDIAN AMERICAN FOOD; MIDDLE EASTERN INFLUENCES ON AMERICAN FOOD.]

BIBLIOGRAPHY

Weaver, William Woys. *Heirloom Vegetable Gardening: A Master Gardener's Guide to Planting, Growing, Seed Saving, and Cultural History.* New York: Holt, 1997.

MAURA CARLIN OFFICER

Egg-Preparation Tools

Eggs are used so many ways in cooking that all sorts of specialized utensils and gadgets have been developed to prepare them. In the earliest American colonies the equipment was simple. For boiling, a pan with room for water to cover the egg was enough. For frying, a three-legged skillet or even a griddle was used, along with a wide, flat-bladed turner, which was also used for flatbreads and pancakes. For beating eggs, peeled twigs, forks, or even spread fingers were used.

In the 1870s, perhaps earlier, wire racks for more than one egg were manufactured and widely used. A center vertical handle meant that the rack, with six, eight, or even more eggs held in wire cups, could be lowered into boiling water and then safely extracted after boiling and used to serve eggs at the breakfast table.

Egg openers are scissor-action devices to cut the shell at the smaller end, so that a soft- or hard-boiled egg can be eaten directly out of the shell. Egg slicers and wedgers have been made since the 1870s. These items have a slotted space for a peeled hard-boiled egg and a hinged or sprung frame tightly strung with fine wires that is passed through the egg to slice it as desired. For poaching, low pans were made in the late 1800s; each had a rack pierced with holes to hold the raw eggs in boiling water. Lift-out, tab-handled inserts made it easy to slip the eggs onto a plate. Other free-standing egg-poaching cups could be used with any pan.

Wire whisks became available in the nineteenth century for every kind of culinary need, from candy making to cream whipping to beating eggs. They are essentially a bundle of looped wires secured to a handle. They may be flat, somewhat like a flat spoon with the bowl made of wire, or they may have wires held together to form a rounded or egg-shaped ball. When beating eggs for meringues, chefs prefer deep, round-bottomed bowls and whisks.

The most inventiveness is displayed in the mechanical eggbeater. The first ones were patented in the 1860s; these operate by rotary action, like many other devices that use a cranked gear to spin the useful end many times per revolution of the crank. Based on the way a whisk, with many wires, works by cutting through the egg, four to eight thin blades or "wings" were spun through the egg. Variations have included rotary turbine beaters that were designed scientifically, with small bent blades at the bottom that would constantly move the beaten egg up the sides of the container to go through the blades again and again. Many rotary eggbeaters came with their own bowls. There were also one-handed eggbeaters worked by a squeeze-action handle, and simple cheap beaters with a knob that was quickly slid up and down a twisted central rod, causing the rod and attached beater blades to revolve one way, then the other. Most of these drill-action devices date from the 1880s through the 1920s.

The cranked-gear, rotary type of eggbeater with whisklike blades has mostly won out, and is still made. Electric beaters came into use in the 1930s; they had heavy motors and were set into their own fitted bowls, like small mixers. Later electric beaters were lightweight and portable, useful in any container or bowl.

[See also EGGS; FRYING PANS, SKILLETS, AND SPIDERS.]

BIBLIOGRAPHY

Franklin, Linda Campbell. *300 Years of Kitchen Collectibles.* 5th ed. Iola, WI: Krause, 2003.

Thornton, Don. *The Eggbeater Chronicles: The Stirring Story of America's Greatest Invention.* 2nd, enlarged ed. Moss Beach, CA: Thornton House, 1999.

LINDA CAMPBELL FRANKLIN

Eggs

Although the eggs of quail, duck, and other birds are prized, by far the majority of eggs consumed in America are chicken eggs. Early European colonists brought egg layers with them, but they were not particularly productive. In the middle 1800s interest in poultry breeding paved the way for the development of chicken breeds suited to specific tasks, such as producing eggs. The raising of chickens became so popular during the latter half of the nineteenth century that virtually every American farm had flocks of chickens.

Industrialization of the Egg

Although commercial hatcheries have been in operation since 1873, it was Petaluma, California, that mastered the industrial production of chickens and eggs. In 1879 Lyman Byce and Isaac Dias of Petaluma invented an incubator that took over the hens' hatching chore. Soon other enterprising locals began making commercial incubators. Petaluma ascended to world-class status as the home of the largest egg ranch, Corliss, in 1918 and the largest hatchery, Must Hatch, in 1929.

Other discoveries contributed to the commercialization of egg production. The single-comb white leghorn, for instance, was found to be the best egg layer. The invention of the trap nest, a device that held a hen in a compartment until her egg could be identified as belonging to her, further refined egg production: prolific egg layers were chosen as breeders. The introduction of artificial lighting in chicken coops also increased egg production by simulating long hours of daylight, when hens lay the most eggs. Farmers added conveyor belts to dispense feed and collect the eggs.

These changes meant that the chickens were confined to coops. As a result, chickens became more susceptible to disease because of the crowded conditions, leading to the development of vaccines and antibiotics. The large number of eggs also meant that machines replaced hands to wash, grade, and pack them. Electronic eyes replaced human eyes, and artificial sources of light replaced candles. Gradually, larger operations began supplying most of the country's eggs; the small farmer could not compete.

Present-day farmers raise hens with good laying records; their eggs are shipped to hatcheries, where they are pampered at precise temperature and humidity levels in artificial incubators. Once hatched, the chicks are shipped to farms, where they reach egg-laying age. Then they are moved again to the modern-day version of a hen house, where more than a million hens may live out their days.

Eggs are graded by diminishing quality as AA, A, or B, although only grades AA and A are sold in retail stores. (Grade B eggs go to large food service operations or to egg-breaking facilities for use in egg products.) The difference depends on the proportion and thickness of the white and the strength of the yolk membrane. Eggs are also sized by the weight of a dozen in the shell, and these sizes range from jumbo to peewee, with jumbo and extra large being the most popular.

In addition to being sold in the shell, eggs are pasteurized, either whole or separated, and sold for industrial use to ice cream manufacturers and large-scale bakeries. The customers can specify further treatment—added salt or sugar or whipping aides to help the whites froth. Eggs can also be frozen or dried and powdered. The call for dried eggs to feed the troops during both world wars of the twentieth century provided a major source of income for the egg industry.

Smaller farms still exist, where chickens have room to move, and some eat only organic feed, qualifying their eggs as organic. Some eggs have brown shells; the color is determined by the breed of chicken and has nothing to do with the taste—Rhode Island Reds lay brown eggs. Taking the organic feed one step further, various farmers give their chickens docosahexaenoic acid, an omega-3 fatty acid, which is intended to boost the nutritional content of the eggs.

Once thought of as an almost perfect source of food, eggs suffered a blow in the 1980s when the amount of cholesterol in eggs was implicated in the development of heart disease. In later years the disease-producing bacterium *Salmonella enteritidis*, found inside some eggs, prompted more caution. The egg industry stepped up controls to ensure good sanitation in all aspects of production. They also embarked on an education program that emphasizes refrigeration, cleanliness during preparation, and adequate cooking. Very few cases of salmonella infection are caused by eggs.

Eggs as Myths and Symbols

In addition to their use for food food, eggs symbolize life and rebirth in Easter and Passover celebrations. Historically, eggs were forbidden during Lent, so people saved them to eat on Easter Sunday, sometimes incorporating them into rich breads. Often, these breads had hard-cooked eggs, which were sometimes dyed, nestled in the dough. These traditions are kept alive in America and are exemplified by various Easter sweet breads, like Greek *lambrópsomo*, Russian *kulich* and *choerek*, French *echauds aux œufs de Pâques*, and Italian *colomba* (also *colomba de Pasqua*), an Easter bread baked in the shape of a dove. In addition to eggs and butter, most of these special breads also contain fruits, nuts, and spices. A roasted egg is part of the Passover seder, celebrating rebirth and regrowth.

Quintessential American Egg

Historically, a particularly important use of eggs was in baking; bake sales were (and still are) common fund-raisers for church and school groups. The advent of agricultural fairs let women compete and win ribbons for the best cake, just as their husbands collected honors for livestock.

Today eggs remain important in America. As a breakfast food, eggs are often simply poached, fried, or scrambled, but for fancier presentations, they are whipped into omelets or topped with hollandaise sauce.

[See also COMBAT FOOD; DEPARTMENT OF AGRICULTURE, UNITED STATES; EASTER; EGG-PREPARATION TOOLS; FOOD SAFETY; PASSOVER.]

BIBLIOGRAPHY
Lowry, Thea S. *Empty Shells: The Story of Petaluma, America's Chicken City.* Novato, CA: Manifold, 2000.
Newall, Venetia. *An Egg at Easter.* London: Routledge and Kegan Paul, 1971.
Smith, Page, and Charles Daniel. *The Chicken Book.* Athens: University of Georgia Press, 2000.

FRAN GAGE

Election Cake

One of the best excuses for a large party in colonial times involved elections: all of the colonies enjoyed some degree of elected representation, whether for legislators or even governors. Traveling to polling places over seventeenth- and eighteenth-century roads could be arduous, however, and men tended to stay in the polling towns for several days to await the result and to socialize with distant neighbors. Among the foods served at these mass gatherings were grandly proportioned, yeasted "Great Cakes" similar to ones that the colonists' English forbearers had baked for religious and folk festivals. Particularly in the Puritan and Congregationalist North, secular holidays like Election Day substituted for religious holidays like Epiphany or Christmas. The cakes associated with these Catholic and Anglican rites in the Old World were applied to secular gatherings in America.

The first published recipe for Election Cake is in Amelia Simmons's *American Cookery* (2nd ed., 1796). With "Thirty quarts flour, 10 pound butter, 14 pound sugar," and dried fruits, spices and yeast in comparable measure, the cakes were baked in large brick ovens supported by great hoops. By the end of the nineteenth century, elections had become routine, polling places more frequent, and transportation easier. Mass public celebrations linked to the vote declined, and large Election Cakes disappeared. Small versions occasionally are baked as nostalgic curiosities.

BIBLIOGRAPHY
Ross, Alice. "Election Cake." *Journal of Antiques and Collectibles*, Oct. 2003. Also at http://www.journalofantiques.com/Oct03/hearthoct03.htm.
Schmidt, Stephen. "Why Cake? Why Hartford?" *Yankee* 65 (May 2001): 22–26.

CATHY K. KAUFMAN

Enchilada

An enchilada consists of a corn tortilla dipped in a chile sauce to soften it, then rolled around a filling such as cheese, chicken or meat. Tortillas and chiles were staples of Mexico's indigenous peoples, dating to pre-Columbian times, and the Mayan dish *papadzules* ("food of the nobles") could be considered a proto-enchilada. Tortillas were spread with two sauces: one made from squash seeds and pungent *epazote* tea, and the other made with whole habaneros simmered in tomato puree. Lacking cheese, cooks filled them with hard-boiled bird eggs. Centuries later, Mexicans brought their foodways north as they settled what would become the southwestern United States. But the first known Mexican-American enchilada recipe was published not in the Southwest. It was discovered in the *Centennial Buckeye Cook Book* assembled by the women of the First Congregational Church in Marysville, Ohio (1876). The recipe was contributed by Anson Safford, the territorial governor of Arizona, who wrote, "Any one who has ever been in a Spanish speaking country will recognize this as one of the national dishes, much as the pumpkin pie is a New England specialty."

By the 1880s, Mexican dishes and references to enchiladas were making their way into regional books across the American Southwest. In *The Alamo City Guide* (1882), Stephen Gould described enchiladas among the dishes that Mexicans served in San Antonio's busy plaza. *Santa Barbara Recipes*, published by the Ladies of the First Congregational Church (1888), included a four-page "Spanish Recipes" section, in which a recipe for enchiladas appears. References to enchiladas increase dramatically after this time.

Today enchiladas are ubiquitous throughout the Southwest. In California, enchiladas may be served with a tomato-based, red-chile sauce. In Texas, they're commonly filled with cheese and onions, and smothered in chile-cumin gravy. In New Mexico, enchiladas are often stacked, Sonoran-style, with a *chile verde* (green chile) sauce. Cheese and beef fillings are relatively modern, as cattle arrived in the Americas with the Spanish, who conquered Mexico in 1521.

[See also MEXICAN AMERICAN FOOD.]

BIBLIOGRAPHY
Pilcher, Jeffrey M. *¡Que vivan los tamales! Food and the Making of Mexican Identity.* Albuquerque: University of New Mexico Press, 1998.
Smith, Andrew F. "Tacos, Enchiladas, and Refried Beans: The Invention of Mexican-American Cookery." Food Resource Symposium: Cultural Aspects of Food. Oregon State University, 1999. Presentation.

KIM PIERCE

Endive

Endives (*Cichorium endivia*) are foliage greens native to the Mediterranean (where they once grew wild). Cultivated first by the Egyptians, endives were later introduced to the United States from Europe, possibly by German or Dutch immigrants. There are two basic endive types. Curly leaf cultivars grow low to the ground and feature pretty, ruffled, prostrate leaves around a creamy yellow heart. Broadleaf cultivars grow larger and taller and have coarse, crumpled leaves with speared tips. Escarole is an example of a broadleaf endive. Among the few winter greens, endives are often used raw in salads, and many varieties may be cooked as side dishes. The coarse outer leaves of the broadleaf endives are generally used in soups or stews.

Endives are closely related to chicories (*C. intybus*)—a relationship made confusing by the fact that the English call the curly leaf endive "chicory" (the French call it *chicorée frisée*), while what is known as "Belgian endive" is actually a variety of chicory. Both endives and chicories have a strong, slightly bitter taste. To prevent them from bolting or becoming excessively bitter, the plants are blanched before harvest by covering their centers or by tying their leaves together to keep out the light.

Among the principal chicory types are heading, loose leaf, forced, and root. Some varieties of chicory—favored particularly in Italy—are grown for their roots, which are boiled and sliced. The coffee substitute known as chicory is made from dried, ground Magdeburg root chicory.

Through the late eighteenth century, endives tended to appear more often as a hobby of gentlemen farmers than as part of kitchen gardens or market crops. By the mid-nineteenth century, endives were commercially cultivated around urban areas for luxurious French restaurants and caterers. By the 1870s and 1880s recipes for endive salads begin to appear in American cookbooks. These vegetables still retain a slightly exotic mystique and, depending on the variety, may be associated with Belgian, French, and especially Italian cuisines. [See also SALADS AND SALAD DRESSINGS; VEGETABLES.]

BIBLIOGRAPHY

Bittman, Sam. *The Salad Lover's Garden*. New York: Doubleday, 1992.

Rubatzky, Vincent E., and Mas Yamaguchi. *World Vegetables: Principles, Production, and Nutritive Values*. 2nd ed. New York: Chapman and Hall, 1997.

KAY RENTSCHLER

Ethnic Foods

Americans today can claim identification with hundreds of ethnic groups and Native American nations, and can buy a multitude of ethnic foods in supermarkets and restaurants. There are two distinct meanings to the phrase "ethnic food" in the United States today: food that is cooked and served to express membership in one's own ethnic group, and food that is identified with an ethnic group different from one's own. Eating off the first menu feeds a hunger for belonging, in particular the need to persist in some minority identity while joining in the wider American culture. The story of American ethnic food eaten among fellow group members—or served proudly to outsiders at a church supper or folk fair—is about the survival of group feelings. The second menu feeds a hunger to know "the other," and reflects the pendulum swings of mainstream American culture and changing attitudes toward eating outside the home and toward foods and people that are "different." The rise of mass media and frequent American migrations have accelerated the processes by which ethnic foods change in America, how some become mainstream foods without losing their ethnic identity, and how in-group foods continue to be transformed.

Both kinds of ethnic food can be described in degrees of authenticity, but it may be more useful to see them on a spectrum of cultural tradition and innovation. Some of the most modernized or "Americanized" foods may convey the strongest feelings of belonging for in-group members, while restaurant-goers may choose what is most foreign to them as the most authentic ethnic food, regardless of whether this food is still widely used by ethnic group members. Ethnic restaurant food is not exactly like ethnic home cooking, but it can be as conservative as old-country dishes. Among third-generation

EATING AS A FINE ART.
(*From the "New York Daily Graphic."*)

An illustration—steeped in nineteenth century stereotypes—of ethnic eating habits.

Americans and later immigrant groups, ethnic restaurants are often a reserve of ethnic dishes that are no longer made at home, perhaps because they require too much labor. Ethnic restaurants provide more established immigrant groups a place in which to celebrate life-cycle events with ethnic feasts.

This collision of authenticities is perhaps most easily examined in regard to Native American foods. Many outsiders believe that the most authentic Indian foods are tribe-specific dishes that date from before contact with Europeans. Contemporary Indians, who often live and work outside Indian reservations, may well treasure opportunities to hunt and gather and cook wild foods in the way of their ancestors, but they may have stronger feelings about more recent family recipes with more Pan-Indian origins, such as fry bread, which usually contains no ingredient native to the hemisphere.

Ethnicity and ethnic food in America predate Columbus but became more prominent as diverse European powers colonized what became the United States, often drawing on minorities and subject peoples to fill a need for labor. Roger Williams wrote in 1644 about the ethnic differences in a dish of corn meal mush later familiar to colonists as "hasty pudding" and known to local Indians as *nasaump*: "From this the English call their samp...and eaten hot or cold with milk or butter, which are mercies beyond the natives' plain water." After the American Revolution, the United States increasingly became a nation of immigrants. The prevailing view has gone back and forth many times between accepting diversity in people and foods, or requiring that ethnic groups conform to a simplified national identity and a bland, non-diversified diet.

It is important to note that not all ethnic groups are immigrant groups. Some are aboriginal or multiracial groups; some formed in North America from immigrant groups; some arrived in North America as slaves; and some ethno-religious groups were founded in the United States or substantially changed here. New ethno-religious groups such as the Mormons and the Black Muslims were founded with dietary regulations that led to distinctive dishes (honey-wheat bread and bean pie, respectively) in only a few generations.

Immigrants to the United States have almost always had to adjust to a new life in which foodstuffs are less expensive and kitchen time is shorter than what they knew elsewhere. Most groups have therefore selected dishes that are easily assembled and quickly cooked, especially one-pot casseroles and sandwiches. Almost every group has increased its use of meat and intake of calories. And each group has also limited complex traditional cooking and baking, perhaps to only Sunday or a few annual holidays. Ethnic foods are Americanized over time with increasing amounts of beef (replacing other meats), sugar, baking powder, and potatoes.

An early-twentieth-century photograph of an Italian American immigrant market.

Dishes must be easy to eat and tend to become softer and whiter to conform to Anglo-American ideals. Ethnic flavors are combined and dishes seem to accumulate flavors from several recipes as if to get the entire ethnic table and all four seasons onto one plate. Corn, chilies, beans, and squash are added or substituted. Tomatoes (and canned tomatoes) are increased in amount or substituted for other acidic ingredients, such as vinegar, lemons, and yogurt.

Such "modernization" of ethnic dishes is a global phenomenon, but has occurred especially rapidly in the United States. Most immigrant groups tend to follow a three-generational pattern of initial acceptance of "American food" followed by reversion to foreign food as imported ingredients become available; a second-generation that is bilingual and eats ethnic food only on visits to parents; and a third generation that loses the language but revives the cuisine. Most exceptions to this pattern have been formed by the historic waves of discrimination and progress for ethnic groups of color and Native Americans, which make for more complex and layered foodways.

Ethnic food served to mainstream American clients in restaurants has generally been pressed into Anglo-American meal patterns, quicker, easier to eat, and with a main course of discrete meat, vegetables, and starch on the same plate. Ethnic dishes which pass into mainstream use are subject to a process described by William and Yvonne Lockwood (describing the Cornish pasty of Upper Michigan) as "diversification to standardization and, finally, to rediversification." The rediversification may be a combination of flavors from related ethnic dishes, such as the "everything bagel," or a postethnic transformation, such as the blueberry or jalapeño bagel. Ethnic foods have progressed variously into the mainstream through factory and school lunch exchanges, church bazaars, and small restaurants, eventually becoming regional foods—such as pierogi in western Pennsylvania, pasties in Upper Michigan, Polish-style fish in Chicago, and pastrami in New York—and even becoming nationally loved American foods. Among the latter are pizza, bagels, spaghetti with tomato sauce, taco chips, salsa, hummus, pita, and yogurt, all of which were available only in urban ethnic markets or restaurants or private homes in 1960.

Ethnic foods also can move from group to group. The winter succotash eaten in Plymouth well into the nineteenth century was barely modified from Native stews made from lye hominy and shell beans, usually with preserved meat. It was listed on the menu of the 1769 Forefathers Day dinner of the Old Colony Club in Plymouth, Massachusetts. At that dinner, Anglo-American men went to a local inn and dined on a number of Native American dishes that were, for them, symbols of their English forefathers and what the settlers had eaten in the early years of the Plymouth colony. On the symbolic level, the diners were expressing Anglo-American ethnicity by eating non-British foods, perhaps even symbolically consuming the Indians' food as they had taken over their village and corn fields.

At the extreme of both assimilation and nonassimilation, Chinese American restaurants invented entire menus of heavily Americanized food by the 1890s while offering a more authentic menu written in Chinese characters, sometimes posted on the wall as an apparent decoration, a practice that continues in urban Chinatowns today.

Restaurant ethnic food also undergoes changes. Nachos were invented for a party of Anglo-American visitors by Ignacio "Nacho" Anaya in a Mexican border town in the 1940s.

This dish consisted of neat canapés of tortilla chips, cheese, and jalapeño peppers. Nachos made their way onto every "authentic" Mexican restaurant menu in America by the 1960s, but by 1990, the original form of the appetizer had become unrecognizable, with added ingredients such as refried beans, sour cream, onions, salsa, black beans, and kernels of corn piled on the chips in a messy heap. By 2000 "nacho" had become an adjective for the flavor of Mexican spices, as in "nacho cheese" and "nacho popcorn." Because they were never Mexican American home food, nachos are unlikely to be revived in their original or "authentic" form, but they may take on new flavors and a new ethnic life in the future.

There have been periods of increased respect for diversity, including culinary diversity, as early as the American Revolution, when the Scotch-Irish and Pennsylvania Dutch minorities were communities relatively undivided by residual loyalties to Great Britain. The United States' centennial in 1876 and bicentennial in 1976 were both followed by national debates in which some Americanizers wanted to reform ethnic diets, whereas others were newly stimulated by the diversity in the kitchen and were curious to add regional and ethnic dishes to mainstream cookbooks. The success of the civil rights movement, the loosening of immigration restrictions, and the many cultural changes of the 1960s and 1970s set off an ethnic revival that peaked in the 1980s, probably around the time of the 1983 television presentation of Alex Haley's *Roots*. For many third-generation white ethnics, the 1980s also saw a revived interest in genealogy, European tourism, and old-country recipes.

Ethnic recipes can be identified in the earliest American cookbooks. Cookbooks by and for ethnic minorities first appeared in the mid-nineteenth century. Multiethnic cookbooks for outsiders began to appear around the turn of the twentieth century. Although there is surprisingly little true fusion food, many American families today have a multiethnic recipe list derived from multiple heritages, exchanges with neighbors, and selections from ethnic dishes encountered in restaurants.

BIBLIOGRAPHY

Zanger, Mark H. *The American Ethnic Cookbook for Students*. Phoenix, AZ: Oryx, 2001.

Zanger, Mark H. *The American History Cookbook*. Westport, CT: Greenwood, 2003.

MARK H. ZANGER

Etiquette Books

The dining room has been the primary testing and proving ground of etiquette in America. Changing table etiquette—the proper use of furniture and tableware, appropriate menus and recipes, and the specifics of table service and deportment—has been a guide to social and cultural values and the various strata of the population. In colonial America wealthier classes set styles and fashions; later the newly emerging middle classes, striving to become accepted into society, followed their lead.

Regardless of period, codified etiquette was partly a statement of gentility and status and partly a way to avoid social confusion. Table manners were essentially conventions devised to make people comfortable, often in an upwardly mobile environment. Every aspect of dining had a carefully prescribed ritual. With more complex table settings, and several sets of flatware, guests who knew that the table was set according to menu began with the flatware placed on the outside and worked inward. With these conventions, diners could focus on conversation and fine food—essentially the purpose of the meal.

Table manners emerged as the final test of refinement, character, and good breeding, and correct behavior at the table became essential for entry into proper society. During the nineteenth century social gaps narrowed, and the social elite protected their place by devising more complex rules, maintaining class distinctions by keeping manners mysterious to the lower classes. Many parents observed the rituals of the table daily, and it was vital to their children's education. They consulted the burgeoning number of etiquette books describing deportment and behavior at the table.

These books existed in Europe before the settling of America and were brought to the colonies by wealthy settlers. A scion of an upper-class Virginia family transcribed a French book of conduct when a schoolboy. George Washington's *Rules of Civility & Decent Behaviour in Company and Conversation* (1774) was a list of 110 rules—seventeen dealing with table manners.

Newcomers in small towns, cities, or farms on the shifting frontiers lived differently. They rarely had individual plates, cups, or spoons, carried their own knives to the table and often used communal flatware or their fingers. Cleanliness was a luxury, with little need for the manners and formality of the elite. This table behavior was observed by the English traveler Frances Trollope in *Domestic Manners of the Americans* (1832). She bemoaned the crude and loathsome manners of American visitors.

The growth of cities, the new cash economy, and the emerging middle class ushered in an entirely different mentality. The ideology "The Doctrine of Separate Spheres" directed that the mission of men was monetary success and that of their wives was to display their wealth. Etiquette books found a new and growing market.

Eliza Leslie, in *The House Book* (1840), described how to set the table and how to wait on it, and how to prepare for a dinner party from a domestic housekeeper's point of view. The American character of table etiquette did not truly begin to evolve until the American Industrial Revolution (c. 1850). By the late nineteenth century, stylish manners were indispensable.

E. G. Storke's *The Family and Householder's Guide* (1859) was for the everyday housewife. Storke presented suggestions for a family keeping few, or even no domestics, complete with diagrams for setting the table properly. Other authors of the time were Eliza Farrar, Catherine Sedgwick, Lydia Maria Child, and Sarah Josepha Hale. Their books covered every aspect of the behavior of dining—predinner etiquette, correct ways to enter the dining room, proper seating arrangements, handling of food and wine, use of utensils, suitable dinner conversation, and the appropriate duties and behavior of servants.

At the end of the century it was important to maintain the complex ceremonies of dining and deportment, to own the right accoutrements, and use them correctly.

America became the land of the hostess. Mrs. Mary Elizabeth Wilson Sherwood's *Manners and Social Usages* (1884) addressed the new audience of social achievers. She identified those who had recently made fortunes, exemplified them to excess, and described those who saw themselves as having native refinement and taste as the rightful arbiters of manners.

Formal and elegant dinners as models lasted into the early twentieth century. After World War I and the upheaval of the country's social structure, etiquette manuals became more informal and simpler. Emily Post's *Etiquette in Society, in Business, in Politics, and at Home* (1922) was readable, and assumed all people would want to know how to behave correctly. Her unique writing style provided guidance to the socially uncertain. She recognized that there were many whose commercial success required the ability to deal with social situations for which they were not prepared. Her book was famous, went through twelve editions, sold 12 million copies, and was used as a textbook. Her trademarked name remains an authoritative voice for twentieth-century taste and manners.

After World War II, American women became house proud, and new appliances freed up their time for entertaining. Table items appeared on shop lists known as brides registries that were maintained in shops for couples about to marry and set up house. *The Joy of Cooking* (1953 edition), by Irma S. Rombauer and Marion Rombauer Becker, devoted a chapter to entertaining and table service for the "untried hostess" that included suggestions for setting and serving every type of meal. The latter part of the century into the twenty-first century was represented by the syndicated columnist "Miss Manners" (Judith Martin), expressing manners for a society that had lost its civility. Her system of manners was demanding, unbending, and precise, and her writings enthusiastically read and followed.

Entertaining continued to become more informal, but the kitchen and dining room with state-of-the-art equipment still conferred high status, as did gourmet skills. The newly prosperous needed ways to display it, and outfitting a proper table with the right expensive china, crystal, flatware, and linens, became almost mandatory.

Most American families, limited by complicated schedules and time constraints, rarely assembled around the dinner table, hardly enough to impart rituals to youngsters. Dining etiquette became pointless in the pervasive fast food culture, although it was still recommended as a way of projecting success and savoir faire. Microwaved meals, take-out food, and eating on the run made the dining ritual so casual that it required little in the way of table manners. Guides to socializing became obsolete for those who ate alone.

At the beginning of the twenty-first century there are still those who choose etiquette as a means to acquire and reflect standing and privilege.

[**See also** CHILD, LYDIA MARIA.]

BIBLIOGRAPHY

Aresty, Esther B. *The Best Behavior: The Course of Good Manners—from Antiquity to the Present—as Seen through Courtesy and Etiquette Books.* New York: Simon and Schuster, 1970.

Visser, Margaret. *The Rituals of Dinner: The Origins, Evolution, Eccentricities, and Meaning of Table Manners.* New York: Grove Weidenfeld, 1991.

CAROL A. GREENBERG

Etiquette
Books

211

Famous Amos

In 1975, Wally Amos, a talent agent with the William Morris Agency, opened the Amos Chocolate Cookie Company on Hollywood's Sunset Boulevard in Los Angeles. He called his brand "Famous Amos," and his was the nation's first gourmet chocolate chip cookie store. His cookie was simply a variation of the classic Nestle's Toll House Cookie, but Amos was a good promoter with plenty of big-name contacts who helped him promote his store and his products. In the 1970s, Bloomingdale's began selling his cookies and the *New York Times* published an article about them.

The company was successful enough that in 1983 Wally Amos published a memoir, *The Famous Amos Story: The Face that Launched a Thousand Chips.* But despite his fame, the company was floundering. In 1984, a controlling interest was acquired by investors. Wally Amos gave up the right to use his name commercially and became an employee of the company. The company was sold twice more by 1988. Wally Amos left the company and in 1992 started selling baked goods, such as muffins, under the brand "Uncle Noname." In 1994, Wally Amos told his distressing story in another book, *The Man with No Name,* and he has continued to publish additional inspirational books since then. In 1999 he changed the name of his new company to Uncle Wally's, Inc.

President Baking Company acquired Famous Amos in 1992 and in 1998 it was acquired by the Keebler Company, which in turn was acquired by Kellogg's in 2001. Despite the corporate changes, Famous Amos cookies are still selling well, reported at about $100 million per year in 2004.

BIBLIOGRAPHY

Amos, Wally, with Leroy Robinson. *The Famous Amos Story: The Face that Launched a Thousand Chips.* Garden City, NY: Doubleday, 1983.

ANDREW F. SMITH

Fannie May

A classic tale of success, downfall and renewal, Fannie May candies started life with H. Teller Archibald, who opened the first store in Chicago, Illinois, in 1920. Archibald Candy Corp. established itself in Chicago as a leading manufacturer and retailer of chocolates and confections. For the next decade and a half, new shops opened regularly and by 1935, four dozen shops in Illinois and neighboring states had opened. As ingredients became scarce during World War II, handcrafted boxed chocolates were difficult to produce in quantity. Maintaining quality was difficult, and continuing use of original recipes resulted in reduced product quantity and store closings. Debt increased, and business faltered. The Thorne family ran the company during the 1970s and 1980s (in 1980, after Denton Thorne died, his wife Jean Thorne and financial officer John Hughes took over the company). Ownership changed again in 1992, when the Jordan Company took over the Fannie May Candy Shops. In 2002, the company filed for Chapter 11, seeking bankruptcy protection following a string of acquisitions that led to an unsustainable debt load. In 2004 Alpine Confections, Inc., bought Fannie May and Fanny Farmer brands. Both companies are wholly owned subsidiaries of Alpine Confections Inc. Plans include the reopening of all 228 Fannie May stores in Chicago. Pixies, introduced in 1946 and made of caramel and nuts with a chocolate coating, are once again available to throngs of fans. Other well-known Fannie May favorites include Trinidads (crunchy, coconut-covered chocolates, introduced in 1970), Nut Fudge, and Mint Meltaways, as well as vanilla buttercreams and chocolate truffles.

[**See also** CANDY AND CANDY BARS.]

RENEE MARTON

Farm Labor and Unions

Throughout American history there has been a constant effort made to increase the amount and improve the quality of farm products. To achieve these goals, farmers needed a predictable supply of workers, but the needs of growers and those of workers often conflicted. Agricultural workers have consistently faced similar problems in all sections of the country: low wages, unpredictable employment and a transient lifestyle, poor housing and medical care, exposure to chemicals and pesticides, onerous demands of employers, and the potential loss of jobs because of mechanization.

In their search for laborers, growers have imported workers and then isolated them, keeping them separate from society at large and the members of other ethnic groups so that they could not unite and organize. Farmers have also taken advantage of federal programs that allowed them to import temporary workers from poor areas like Mexico, Jamaica, and Puerto Rico.

The search for workers has forced growers to recruit people of many different ethnic groups, including Africans in the eighteenth century. After the Civil War, Chinese laborers in California were the first large group of farm workers, but in 1882 a law prohibited the importation of more Chinese labor. Japanese workers were next, but they were not easily subjugated, and many became independent farmers. Growers then turned to East Indians, Koreans, Middle Easterners, Filipinos, and Mexicans.

Unionization in agriculture resulted from the consolidation of smaller agriculture holdings into large farms. The owners and their supporters crushed early organizing efforts. Workers received little support from the American Federation of Labor (AFL) because they were unskilled laborers. The AFL was composed of skilled workers who were organized into unions based on their craft (such as carpentry, cigarmaking, plumbing). Because unskilled workers performed a variety of tasks, they could not be organized by individual craft, so the AFL was not interested in working with them. The unskilled workers often turned to more radical unions, like the Industrial Workers of the World (IWW), an affiliation that frequently led to violence. In 1913, for example, a violent dispute occurred near Wheatland, California. Owners of a ranch recruited more workers than they needed and forced them to live in squalid conditions, which prompted IWW leaders to organize. Police tried to break up a rally, leading to a riot that killed four people. IWW leaders were jailed, and the strike was broken. In the 1930s, the Cannery and Agricultural Workers Industrial Union, an outgrowth of the Communist Party's Agricultural Workers Industrial League, led a series of strikes, but again there was violence. In 1933, a posse composed of police and growers fired on a crowd of workers in Pixley, California, killing two. There were other unsuccessful organizing efforts during the 1930s, such as those of the Southern Tenants Farmers' Union among workers in the southern cotton fields.

In 1935, the National Labor Relations Act guaranteed the right of employees to join unions, free from reprisals by employers. Farmworkers were excluded from the act, however. In many areas, farm workers were also exempt from state regulations. During the 1930s, a massive wave of poor whites migrated to California because the dust bowl conditions in the Midwest made it impossible for them to make a living on farms in that region. These workers vied for the same jobs as other farmworkers, creating a glut of available labor and making it possible for employers to pay lower wages. Many of these individuals from the Midwest entered the military or took industrial jobs during World War II, so the growers again turned to Mexico. In 1942, the United States and Mexico created the bracero program, which allowed American growers to recruit large numbers of temporary Mexican workers.

One union achieved its goals during the 1930s. In 1937 the Congress of Industrial Organizations (CIO) chartered the International Longshoremen's and Warehousemen's Union (ILWU) in Hawaii. The ILWU led a successful dock strike and then turned to organizing agricultural workers. The union improved working conditions by forcing growers to mechanize their farms and created a powerful political alliance with the Democratic Party. Although many growers have moved their operations to the Philippines, Taiwan, South Korea, Thailand, Malaysia, and other countries where wages are lower, the union remains active in Hawaii, even though its membership has declined. In 1963 Cesar Chavez formed the United Farm Workers (UFW) during an era of economic expansion that was more conducive to unionizing than the 1930s had been. The bracero program was ending, and Chavez received support from religious leaders, students, organized labor, and liberal activists. Chavez's tactics included a national boycott of California grapes and lettuce so effective that it persuaded growers finally to sign union contracts. Chavez worked to limit the use of pesticides on crops and negotiated agreements on the introduction of machinery in agriculture. The UFW also organized in Arizona, Texas, and Florida.

The Farm Labor Organizing Committee (FLOC) was created in 1979 to represent workers in the Midwest. The union adopted many UFW tactics and faced similar issues, such as mechanization, controlling pesticide use, and the elimination of child labor. In 1994 FLOC affiliated itself with the AFL-CIO. Unions continue to adapt to new developments in agriculture, such as genetically engineered crops, and, at the same time, work toward their traditional goals. Because they represent the labor force still needed to produce the nation's food, unions will continue to play a vital role in American life. [See also FARM SUBSIDIES, DUTIES, QUOTAS, AND TARIFFS.]

BIBLIOGRAPHY

Barger, W. K., and Ernesto M. Reza. *The Farm Labor Movement in the Midwest: Social Change and Adaptation among Migrant Farm Workers.* Austin: University of Texas Press, 1994.

Edid, Maralyn. *Farm Labor Organizing: Trends and Prospects.* Ithaca, NY: ILR, 1994.

Hall, Greg. *Harvest Wobblies: The Industrial Workers of the World and Agricultural Laborers in the American West, 1905–1930.* Corvallis: Oregon State University Press, 2001.

Mooney, Patrick H., and Theo J. Majka. *Farmers' and Farm Workers' Movements: Social Protest in American Agriculture.* New York: Twayne, 1995.

RICHARD J. JENSEN

Farm Subsidies, Duties, Quotas, and Tariffs

Farm subsidies, tariffs, and quotas are policy instruments used by the United States to support agricultural prices and to protect agriculture from foreign competition. Subsidies are payments made to farmers to support crop prices. Tariffs—or customs duties—are taxes levied on goods when they pass across national boundaries, usually made on imported goods and collected by the government of the importing country. Quotas are a government-imposed limit on the amount of a product that can be grown for the domestic market (production quotas) or, in international trade, on how much of a specific product can be imported or exported (quantitative restrictions).

Brief History

Subsidies became the cornerstone of American agricultural policy in the 1930s. Net farm incomes had fallen drastically in the Great Depression, and the solution, according to President Franklin D. Roosevelt, was to limit production as a way to boost prices. In 1933 he signed the Agricultural Adjustment Act, setting production quotas and authorizing subsidies for farmers in return for reducing crop acreage. Although they were originally intended as a crisis measure, subsidies became locked into American agricultural policy in the following decades and remain so today. Under commodity programs, farmers receive direct cash payments to make up the difference between the market price and a guaranteed price per bushel of commodity. Indirect subsidies also are provided, to limit production. While the Federal Agriculture Improvement and Reform Act of 1996 (the "farm bill") intended to change the direction of agricultural policy by reducing subsidies, direct payments increased once more in the 2002 Farm Bill.

Agricultural tariffs have an older history. The first tariff act was signed in 1789, with the purpose of raising revenues. Tariffs on imported agricultural goods were imposed in the 1920s and, to further protect domestic agriculture, raised to prohibitively high levels under the 1930 Smoot-Hawley Tariff Act. After a fierce trade war, the Reciprocal Trade Agreements Act of 1934 reversed the high-tariff policy. By the early years of the twenty-first century, the United States had relatively low tariffs on imported agricultural products—an average of 12 percent, compared with a global level of 62 percent. Along with subsidies, the United States tends to favor quotas as a means of protecting domestic agriculture, measures that are more restrictive than tariffs.

Farm subsidies, quotas, and tariffs are considered the enemy of free trade. For international institutions such as the World Trade Organization, they are anathema to the globalization of the world economy. In 1994 the General Agreement on Tariffs and Trade, originally signed in 1947, was renegotiated to include agricultural products for the first time. The resultant Agreement on Agriculture required the conversion of quotas to tariffs and the reduction of tariffs and defined the type and level of spending permitted on domestic subsidy programs. The United States also signed the North American Free Trade Agreement (NAFTA) with Canada and Mexico in 1994. Under NAFTA all non-tariff barriers to agricultural trade between the United States and Mexico were eliminated, and many other tariffs were eliminated or phased out more gradually.

Effect on American Food

Farm subsidies, quotas, and tariffs have had profound impacts on agricultural production and trade in the United States. In turn, they also have influenced the American diet. Corn is one example. Federal subsidies of corn are among the highest of any commodity, amounting to $30 billion between 1996 and 2001. By the beginning of the twenty-first century, 80 million acres of land were being used for growing corn, 14 million more than in 1970. As a result, corn became cheap and plentiful. Corn is used to feed animals bred for meat. It is converted into high-fructose corn syrup and used as a substitute for sugar. It also is processed into starch, flour, and corn oil for use in prepared foods. The "cornification" of the American diet is palpable. The low cost of corn cheapened the meat supply and drove a threefold increase in the consumption of corn products between 1970 and the turn of the century. Corn is used in everything from cookies to soda.

Consider, in this respect, the Coca-Cola Company. As a cost-saving measure, the company switched to 100 percent corn sweeteners in the 1980s and so was able to sell larger bottles at no extra cost. For Coke, the problem with sugar was that it cost more than corn, a result, in part, of another measure intended to protect American farmers: quotas. Under the federal sugar program, only a certain quota of sugar can be imported. Above this quota, all sugar imports are subject to a prohibitively high tariff. The lack of real competition with other sugar producers boosts the price paid to producers—but costs domestic sweetener users $1.9 billion a year.

Tariffs have also affected the American food supply. After the implementation of NAFTA, Americans began to eat more imported food, especially fruits and vegetables. With lower tariffs affording a competitive advantage, Mexico became the largest supplier of fresh and frozen fruit in the United States, providing a steady supply of limes, melons, grapes, strawberries, mangos, and papayas year-round. Tariffs are also used as a weapon in "food wars." In 1996, for example, Florida tomato growers demanded that tariffs be placed on tomato and bell pepper imports from Mexico, claiming that they were losing $1 billion a year. In 1999 the United States retaliated against a European Union ban on hormone-treated U.S. beef, imposing $116.8 million worth of 100 percent tariffs on such gourmet foods as Roquefort cheese, Dijon mustard, and fresh truffles. [See also COCA-COLA; CORN; NORTH AMERICAN FREE TRADE AGREEMENT.]

BIBLIOGRAPHY

Watkins, Kevin, and Penny Fowler. *Rigged Rules and Double Standards: Trade, Globalization, and the Fights against Poverty.* Oxford: Oxfam, 2002.

CORINNA HAWKES

Farm Stands, *see Farmers' Markets*

Farm
Subsidies,
Duties,
Quotas, and
Tariffs

214

Farmer, Fannie

Fannie Merritt Farmer emerged from the domestic science movement to become the most famous cooking expert of her time, in part by harnessing the brisk, businesslike methods of "scientific cookery" to a cuisine of sweetness and affluence. She was born in Boston on March 23, 1857, to the bookish family of a struggling printer. A bout of childhood polio cut short her education and left her with a limp, making her an unlikely candidate for either marriage or a career. At age thirty-one she decided to attend the Boston Cooking School, whose graduates were busy across the country teaching in public schools, settlement houses, and other institutions dedicated to raising society's morals by improving women's domestic skills. She did so well that she became principal of the school in 1894.

A gifted and ambitious teacher, she brought the school to its height of success, especially after the publication of her landmark work, *The Boston Cooking-School Cook Book* (1896). Farmer borrowed liberally from an earlier text produced by the school's first principal, Mary Lincoln, in 1884, but the new book had an entirely different personality. It remained a comprehensive, science-based teaching manual, but unlike many of her colleagues, Farmer was interested chiefly in helping women serve appealing meals, not in turning the home kitchen into a chemistry lab. So she shortened the scientific explanations and added a decorative overlay to Lincoln's plainspoken recipes. Fashionable dishes inspired by New York restaurants were introduced, salads proliferated and became more fanciful, and a new section devoted to chafing-dish recipes appeared. Yet a pedagogical spirit reigned, notably on the subject of measuring. The school had introduced standardized measuring cups and spoons in the mid-1880s, but Lincoln's book still referred to "rounded" or "heaping" spoonfuls and cupfuls. Farmer wanted to make sure that even beginners could measure accurately. "A cupful is measured level," she instructed. "A tablespoonful is measured level. A teaspoonful is measured level." The regular deployment of a knife to level the surface of a cup or spoon was one of Farmer's lasting contributions to the American kitchen.

In 1902 Farmer left the Boston Cooking School and opened Miss Farmer's School of Cookery. Her lively, practical lessons in all aspects of home cooking drew so many students that the school soon had four kitchens and ten teachers. Classes in sickroom cookery were a specialty, as they had been at the Boston Cooking School. Farmer knew from experience the importance of feeding invalids properly and for years taught the subject herself at Harvard Medical School.

Farmer traveled and lectured widely and contributed a monthly column to the *Woman's Home Companion*. She also wrote five more books: *Chafing Dish Possibilities* (1898), *Food and Cookery for the Sick and Convalescent* (1904), *What to Have for Dinner* (1905), *Catering for Special Occasions, with Menus and Recipes* (1911), and *A New Book of Cookery* (1912). On January 15, 1915, she died in Boston of arteriosclerosis. Over the next six decades *The Boston Cooking-School Cook Book* went through eleven editions and sold nearly 4 million copies.

[**See also** Boston Cooking School; Cookbooks and Manuscripts: From the Civil War to World War I; Measurement.]

A portrait of Fannie Farmer, the "Mother of Level Measurements."

BIBLIOGRAPHY

Shapiro, Laura. *Perfection Salad: Women and Cooking at the Turn of the Century*. New York: Farrar, Straus and Giroux, 1986.

Laura Shapiro

Farmers' Markets

Since the 1970s, farmers' markets have blossomed across the United States. According to the U.S. Department of Agriculture, in the 1960s there were only about one hundred markets, while by 2002 more than 3,100 were in operation. These markets vary greatly in size and scope. Some, like the Dane County Market in Madison, Wisconsin, are beloved local institutions drawing thousands of shoppers each Saturday to browse among hundreds of stalls stocked with Asian greens, heirloom apples, and homemade pasta. Others consist of a handful of producers selling tomatoes, peppers, and sweet corn in church parking lots. Both kinds of markets offer to consumers a selection of fresh, local produce, typically far surpassing what can be found in supermarkets, in a cheery, social setting. For small farmers, this kind of direct marketing offers both an alternative to dealing with large-scale commodity markets and the possibility of receiving much higher returns on their products.

Although contemporary markets are a novelty for most Americans, they hark back to the colonial era, when farmers hauled their produce and meat into nearby urban centers to sell to city residents. As Lisa Hamilton (2002) recounts, the historic demise of direct marketing follows the development of the modern industrial food system. With the expansion of cities and transportation systems in the nineteenth century, growers were pushed farther away from their urban customers. These longer distances, and the ascendance of intermediary food handlers, increased the likelihood of spoilage. More and more, markets were viewed as unhygienic and old-fashioned, in contrast to the modernity associated with new processing technologies like canning and new forms of distribution such as grocery stores. While markets continued to play a role in urban commerce through the late nineteenth and early twentieth centuries, particularly in the West and in smaller towns, the dramatic rise of mass retailing, followed by the economic hardships of the Great Depression and the food shortages of World War II, contributed to their disappearance from the national landscape.

The resurgence of farmers' markets is linked to disenchantment with, and a search for alternatives to, the agro-industrial system that originally precipitated their decline. In the mid-1970s concerns about the environmental consequences of conventional agriculture, the quality and safety of food, and the future of family farmers spurred the markets' reappearance. Currently, markets not only have proliferated but are increasingly regarded as a means of "relocalization" of food production and distribution. Although the 67,000 producers who sell at markets represent only a sliver of the country's 2 million farmers, these markets, ideally, counter the dominance of agribusiness by promoting a series of linked environmental, economic, and social benefits. By supporting small farmers, including many organic growers, the markets encourage sustainable agricultural practices and permit a larger proportion of each food dollar to remain within the local area. In many instances, the higher returns of successful retailing enable family farmers to stay in operation, which contributes to the overall prosperity of rural and peri-urban communities. For city dwellers, purchasing fresh-picked produce directly from a favorite farmer not only presages culinary pleasures but also creates a new sense of personal connection with agriculture and the environment, especially when repeated weekly. The prospect of finding a variety of fresh, local food draws people to markets. Farmers work hard to meet consumer expectations through close attention to customer preferences and innovation in their own production and marketing strategies. For example, with smaller, more frequent plantings farmers can bring popular fruits and vegetables to market at their prime. Diversification is important as well, both in offering varieties of the same item and in introducing new ones. Farmers, on the lookout for the next

hot product, have played a key role in acquainting consumers with "new" foods such as buffalo meat or hitherto unknown or forgotten varieties of hot peppers, radishes, tomatoes, and pears. Generous samples and preparation suggestions serve to educate shoppers and generate demand. Diversification extends to the elaboration of foods and nonfood crops, in ways that add value to products and entice customers. Many vendors set out ready-to-eat foods—salsa, persimmon pudding, focaccia, and corn chowder—alongside their produce displays. Herb growers lengthen their selling season by packaging infusions and potpourris and preparing flavored vinegars. Others specialize in jams, fruit butters, honey, and baked goods (including vegetarian dog biscuits). The cumulative visual and olfactory panoply, often enhanced by the presence of flower producers selling bouquets and hanging plants, creates a festive atmosphere that, in itself, becomes one more reason for shoppers to abandon their local supermarket.

[See also Food Marketing; Organic Food.]

BIBLIOGRAPHY

Corum, Vance, Marcie Rosenzweig, and Eric Gibson. *The New Farmers' Market: Farm-Fresh Ideas for Producers, Managers, and Communities*. Auburn, CA: New World, 2001.

Hamilton, Lisa M. "The American Farmers Market." *Gastronomica* 2, no. 3 (2002): 73–77.

LISA B. MARKOWITZ

Fast Food

Fast food commonly consists of freshly prepared and wrapped food items sold across counters or through automobile drive-up windows. Often referred to as "quick-service food" in the restaurant industry, fast food usually is served in a short amount of time, ranging from seconds to several minutes. Although many fast food restaurants offer customer seating, table service is rare. Varying widely in food type, fast food encompasses most meats, ethnic cooking styles, and cooking methods. Hamburgers dominate the industry, but other types of fast food include hot dogs, pizza, roast beef, pasta, chicken, and fish, in addition to a wide variety of ethnic specialties. Although the meal offerings and types of service vary, fast food commonly is inexpensive fare packaged for carry out and delivered quickly.

Vendors have sold foods to passersby on the roadside and city streets all around the world for thousands of years. Usually fast, inexpensive, and handheld, such foods were long popular for their convenience and cost. Fast food during the nineteenth century in the United States varied by region, ranging from fatty German sausage dominating northern cities to filled tortillas in the Southwest. By the early 1900s pushcart vendors sold sausages, stews, and meatballs to industrial workers outside factory gates. Although popular among urban workers, foods sold by these vendors never became mainstream fare.

Urban dining became a transitional phase between patronizing pushcart vendors and eating at fast food restaurants. Often constructed from old streetcars, diners served working-class customers inexpensive short-order meals usually cooked to order. The menu selection at diners varied, but fried foods predominated, and speed and quantity often were emphasized over taste.

The precise origin of modern fast food is in dispute, and competing theories are based on regional boosterism. Stories, usually lacking credible evidence, credit numerous individuals as the "inventors" of both the hot dog and the hamburger. Most verifiable is Walter Anderson's founding of a hamburger stand on a busy street in Wichita, Kansas. Five years later Anderson had a partner, Billy Ingram, an insurance broker, and the stand had grown into the White Castle System of Eating Houses. Quickly saturating the Wichita market, White Castle spread across the Midwest and ultimately defined itself as a "national institution" by the late 1920s. Setting a standard for fast food, Anderson and Ingram offered a streamlined menu of hamburgers, Coca-Cola, and coffee, emphasizing take-out, larger-quantity purchases "by the sack." White Castle succeeded by offering uniformly high quality food, obsessive cleanliness, and courteous customer service in all stores.

The 1920s, an era of increasing prosperity and burgeoning technology, witnessed the rise of many large national companies, including grocery stores, processed food makers, and soft-drink bottlers. At first cautious, consumers soon accepted these larger companies, eventually prizing "name brands" over locally produced items. White Castle succeeded in becoming both the leading nationally known chain and for a while even a synonym for fast food hamburgers. The success of White Castle spawned countless imitators, who closely copied White Castle's architecture, hamburgers, company name, and even its advertising slogan. For the next two decades, fast food hamburger outlets in the United States were largely in urban neighborhoods and usually resembled Anderson and Ingram's White Castle model. Formal recognition of the place of the fast food hamburger in society came in 1929, when the president of the American Restaurant Association proclaimed the hamburger and apple pie "America's foods."

Widespread poverty during the Depression caused stagnation in the growth of the fast food industry. Few new restaurants opened, and a shrinking customer base forced fast food chains to contract or close. Notable exceptions were the openings in 1936 of the California-based Big Boy chain, which offered a popular double-decked, two-patty hamburger, and in 1939 of the original McDonald's restaurant. Even the growth of these chains was slow, first confronted by Depression-era hardships and then in the early 1940s by wartime food shortages and rationing of commodities. World War II further decimated the fast food industry by diverting the labor force to the military and to more lucrative jobs in the defense industry. Existing chains shrank to a fraction of their prewar size, many closing altogether. Prosperity after the war did not immediately revitalize fast food. Many chains were in shambles, and fears of food rationing continued. Rebuilding was a slow process. Regional chains of small, eat-in restaurants filled the void, especially in small towns and rural areas. Some urban fast food hamburger outlets survived, but postwar inflation dictated higher prices and decreased business.

The fast food industry rebounded in the 1950s with the development of modern suburbia. As veterans and their growing families fled traditional city neighborhoods, new fast food hamburger chains quickly followed. By the end of the decade, McDonald's and Burger King restaurants became fixtures at suburban crossroads, selling burgers, french-fried potatoes, and milkshakes to hungry customers. Both Ray Kroc, of McDonald's, and Jim McLamore, of Burger King, sought to build one of their franchised restaurants in every American town and actively worked toward that goal. They largely succeeded, opening hundreds of new outlets each year throughout the 1950s and 1960s. Consumers flocked to these restaurants, possibly viewing them as part of their modern, faster-paced lifestyle. While Burger King battled McDonald's for market share, Burger Chef restaurants joined the frantic competition, and Arby's, Kentucky Fried Chicken, and Taco Bell were not far behind. Introducing items such as roast beef, chicken, and tacos, these newest restaurants thrived, opening the door for countless other specialties. The term "fast food" was no longer synonymous with the hamburger alone. It became a generic term for describing many foods sold in a take-out style.

The fast food industry experienced turmoil in the late 1960s and early 1970s that caused even large chains to merge or fold, often edged out by the two industry leaders. As the field narrowed, McDonald's and Burger King gained even greater dominance, making it extremely difficult for new chains to compete. Some new companies, however, did successfully enter the market. Opening his Wendy's chain in defiance of the odds in 1969, Dave Thomas, a former KFC executive, offered consumers a bigger, more expensive burger, the popularity of which quickly earned Wendy's third place in the industry. Thomas's unexpected success and the continued prosperity of McDonald's and Burger King faced fresh challenges in the latter half of the 1970s. Environmentalists, health advocates, and unions attacked fast food companies about their products, trash, and labor practices. Some critics condemned the fried burgers, potatoes, fish, and chicken

An illustration of the perils of fast food from Life magazine, 1907.

as health hazards, claiming these foods responsible for both obesity and poor nutrition. Others focused on how the fast food industry's packaging materials, such as plastic foam containers and aluminum or plastic wrap, were not biodegradable in garbage landfills. Labor activists criticized how the major chains maximized their profits by hiring teenage employees at very low wages. Despite these attacks, Americans continued to flock to fast food outlets in ever-increasing numbers.

Although conscious of health risks, by 2002 the average American consumer ate some type of fast food 16.4 times each month. Fast food remains popular because it tastes good and is inexpensive, predictable, and convenient. Americans may also eat fast food because it is a cultural norm, the American ethnic food. Fast food, especially the hamburger, is the most consumed type of food in the United States and is closely identified around the world as the centerpiece of distinctly American cuisine. In a nation com-

posed of diverse ethnic backgrounds, the hamburger has emerged as the culinary common ground of a newly synthesized American ethnicity.

"Fast food" transcends the area of food, having become a broadly applied term describing other types of products and services. Meanings range from simple descriptions of speed and convenience of service to derogatory references of superficiality or low quality. Social critics often use "fast food" as a metaphor for deriding the homogeneity and commercialism of modern society. If the critics are correct, the usage signifies that good or bad, fast food is an important central factor in American culture.

[See also BURGER KING; DINERS; KENTUCKY FRIED CHICKEN; MCDONALD'S; STREET VENDORS; TACO BELL; TAKE-OUT FOODS; WENDY'S; WHITE CASTLE.]

BIBLIOGRAPHY
Langdon, Philip. Orange Roofs, Golden Arches: The Architecture of American Chain Restaurants. New York: Knopf, 1986.

Mariani, John. *America Eats Out*. New York: Morrow, 1991.

Tennyson, Jeffrey. *Hamburger Heaven: The Illustrated History of the Hamburger*. New York: Hyperion, 1993.

DAVID GERARD HOGAN

Fats and Oils

There used to be a time when fat was good and the advertisers of Crisco could tout their product because it would induce little girls to eat *more* fat. Needless to say the consensus has changed. In the postwar era, opinion began to look more critically at dietary fat in general and the composition of certain cooking fats in particular. In the 1950s and 1960s, cholesterol was implicated as a risk factor for heart disease leading many health professionals to advise against eating the highly saturated animal fats and tropical oils that appeared to boost blood cholesterol. This, of course was a bonanza for margarine manufacturers who up until this point had only price to recommend their product over butter. Now margarine was the healthy alternative. But not for long.

As science further refined its opinions about the composition of fats, oils high in monounsaturated and polyunsaturated fat became the new darlings of the mainstream press and marketers alike. New strains of rapeseed, a relative of mustard, which had been pressed for industrial oil for hundreds years in Europe was now lauded for its extremely low saturated fat content. It was not, however, until 1988 when the FDA allowed the product to shed its unsavory name in favor of "canola" that its sales hit the big time.

Olive oil was similarly promoted for its healthful qualities. Yet while Americans used increasing quantities of olive oil in their cooking, many found they did not actually like the taste. Seeing a marketing opportunity, manufacturers concocted a "light" olive oil that had much of the flavor refined out of it.

While rising health concerns led companies to reformulate their cooking oils and spreads (McDonald's stopped using beef fat in its fryers, Proctor & Gamble converted its Puritan-brand oil from a soybean blend to all canola oil), the holy grail of the American food industry was to create a fat that had all of its flavor and texture attributes but without the calories. To this end, in 1991, A. E. Staley Manufacturing introduced Stellar, a corn-based product meant to replace oil in margarine, baked goods, and so forth. The faux fat joined Nutrasweet's dairy-derived Simplesse, which had been developed to simulate high-fat flavor in the company's line of frozen desserts.

The most notorious of these fat substitutes, Olestra, was introduced in 1996 by Procter & Gamble under the brand name Olean. This pseudofood is, chemically speaking, an actual fat but it is formulated in such a way that it is indigestible and thus passes right through the body without entering the blood stream. In spite of the mostly negative publicity the product received on its denouement, it soon made its quiet way into potato and corn chips.

Even while some companies were trying to create fake fats, food scientists discovered a new villain. The trans fatty acids created in hydrogenating vegetable oil to make most margarines and shortening were found to be just as bad as saturated fat. Margarine producers scrambled to reformulate their fats, in some cases adding ingredients that were supposed to decrease blood cholesterol. In 2004 even the makers of Crisco introduced a line without any trans fats.

Designs by C. E. Emerson Jr. for two advertising pieces for Heinz products, 1918.

[**See also** AFRICAN AMERICAN FOOD; BUTTER; BUTTER-MAKING TOOLS AND CHURNS; CORN; DAIRY INDUSTRY; OBESITY; PEANUTS; PIGS; SOYBEANS; SUNFLOWERS.]

MICHAEL KRONDL

Fermentation

Fermentation is an ancient technique of food transformation and preservation. It is a natural part of metabolism and one way for microorganisms to derive energy from certain nutrients. Uncontrolled fermentation can render foods unpalatable or inedible. Encouraging the growth of benign bacteria and fungi inhibits spoilage—or disease-causing microorganisms, which must compete for nutrients. Fermentation generates various molecules, including alcohols and acids. These give fermented foods their complex flavors and odors. Altering conditions, such as salt or sugar content, temperature, humidity, or oxygen level, can alter those flavors. Most "natural" fermentations stop when the original food source has run out (the sugars in grape must, for example) or when conditions inhibit the fermenting organism (as acids accumulate in yogurt). Adding more nutrients or removing waste products can keep the process going if needed.

Some fermentations rely on a single microorganism: the carefully selected cultivated yeasts used in commercial production of alcohols. Others rely on a mixture: the wild yeasts and bacteria used to produce various sourdough breads. Sourdoughs (or sauerkrauts, cheeses, salamis, or pickles) made in different locations will have slightly different microorganisms, even though similar starting ingredients have been used. This contributes to the individuality of these products. Commercial producers control their domesticated organisms to avoid such variations.

Fermented foods contain many of the proteins and minerals, and some of the vitamins, of their starting materials. Some foods are felt to be more digestible after fermentation, as the offending polysaccharides have been processed. Fermented foods are not entirely immune to spoilage, although such contamination is often obvious prior to consumption.

[**See also** BEER; CHEESE; WINERIES; YEAST.]

BIBLIOGRAPHY

Campbell-Platt, G. *Fermented Foods of the World*. London and Boston: Butterworths, 1987.

Wood, Brian J. B., ed. *Microbiology of Fermented Foods*. 2nd ed. 2 vols. Dordrecht: Kluwer, 1997.

ASTRID FERSZT

Festivals and Fairs, *see Food Festivals*

Figs

Essentially Mediterranean fruits, figs (*Ficus carica*) prosper only in warm, dry climates. In the southeastern United States, fig plantings suffer from excessive humidity, exposure to rain, and occasional freezing injury. In the United States, figs are grown commercially in large plantings only in California. The fig tree is the northernmost representative of the tropical banyans. The fruit develops inside-out: The stem forms the skin and encloses the sweet, edible pulp and seeds.

Fresh figs rarely appear in supermarkets. They are found more often in specialty fruit shops and also directly from the grower in areas of local production, including on the Delmarva Peninsula and southern seaboard (near Chesapeake Bay) and in Florida. The fruits are palatable only when fully ripe, when the interior pulp has softened to a jelly-like condition. Full ripeness is indicated by soft skin and limp stems. In such a state, the fruit is exceptionally perishable, and refrigeration is an absolute necessity. In poor seasons with little heat, even fully ripe fruit can be insipid.

The most widely grown cultivars in the United States are Brown Turkey and Bruns-wick (synonym in Texas, Magnolia), but the finest (Excel, White Adriatic, and Bourjassotte Noire) are found only in California. Dried figs, partially rehydrated in loose-filled plastic pouches, are produced in the Merced-Fresno district of that state in the Black Mission (dark-skinned) and Calimyrna (light-skinned) varieties. The former is common as a fresh fruit in California, although not of the highest quality; the latter is the Sari Lop of the Izmir district of Turkey and an outstanding, but rare, item as a fresh fruit. Tinned and, more often, bottled figs are a specialized commodity also in California and are made exclusively of the Italian Dottato variety (locally named Kadota).

[See also CALIFORNIA; FRUIT.]

BIBLIOGRAPHY
Ferguson, Louise, Themis Michailides, and Harry H. Shorey, "The California Fig Industry." Horticultural Reviews 12 (1990): 409–490.

TODD KENNEDY

Filberts

Filberts (or hazelnuts) are native to both the New World and the Old World. The two species of hazel trees indigenous to United States are *Corylus americana*, which grows primarily in the East, and *C. cornuta*, which ranges from the Atlantic to the Pacific. The nuts of both were consumed by Native Americans and early European colonists. However, filberts from the New World are small, with thick shells, and inferior in quality; the nuts have little commercial value. The European hazel (*C. avellana*) is the source of most commercial nuts. Hazelnuts have been an important human food since prehistoric times. The ancient Romans praised them, and hazelnuts were grown in Britain in Roman times. The seeds were sent to Massachusetts in 1629, and filberts were being sold in New York City by 1771. Oregon leads the nation in hazelnut production. Filberts are enjoyed as snacks,

and their sweetness is used to advantage in baked goods and other desserts, often in combination with chocolate.

[See also NUTS.]

BIBLIOGRAPHY
Gerspacher, Lucy. *Hazelnuts and More*. Portland, OR: Graphic Arts Center, 1995.
Oregon Filbert Commission. *A Treasury of Prize Winning Filbert Recipes*. 3rd ed. Tigard, OR: Oregon Filbert Commission, 1973.

ANDREW F. SMITH

Film, Food in

Food has been appearing in film since the medium took shape. From turn of the nineteenth century, a silent short film by the Lumière Brothers shows a baby eating cereal and then, to her distress, making a huge mess. In another, a thick wave of men exit and reenter a factory as they break and return from lunch—an image that defined the new industrial era. These everyday-life moments involving food have never faded from film; if we are to relate to film characters, they must at least eat and drink like the rest of us.

But film in the United States has done more than present typical eating habits; over the history of cinema, food in American film has encompassed a wide range of meanings, including sex, gender, ethnicity, and social class.

To date, the largest body of written work on the subject centers on non-American films. *Le Grande Bouffe* (1972), *Tampopo* (1986), *Babette's Feast* (1987), and *Like Water for Chocolate* (1992) are among the movies regularly invoked. However, American-made "food films" have started to catch on in re-

cent years, *Big Night* (1997) and *Soul Food* (1997) among them.

Aesthetics, of course, are essential. Improvements in cinematography over the past thirty years have enhanced the technical art of food styling so that food on film looks good enough to eat. With its lavish displays of Sicilian delicacies, *The Godfather* (1972) was a pioneer in this area, a consequence of an Italian American director (Francis Ford Coppola) and writer (Mario Puzo) seeking not only visual splendor but also culinary authenticity.

Regarding content, genre films are indeed food-dependent. Westerns rely on saloons for brawls, and comedies such as *Who Is Killing the Great Chefs of Europe?* (1978) and Italian Mafia film spoofs (the ridiculous *Godson* [1998], the sublime *Freshman* [1990]) deliver food as a recipe for laughs, especially when edibles are thrown, regurgitated, or ignited. The same is true of teen sex comedies, such as *American Pie* (1999), in which food is a recipe for sexual exploration and humiliation. Food as a comedic prop for social commentary can be traced back to Charlie Chaplin's *Modern Times* (1936), in which an "eating machine" serves as a metaphor for the sterile perils of the Machine Age, and in the silent Keystone Kops films in which social oppression gets a literal pie in the face. Meanwhile, horror and thriller films often depict food taboos: *The Silence of the Lambs* (1991) and *Alive* (1993) exploit cannibalism, whereas science fiction films, from *Soylent Green* (1973) to *The Matrix* (1999), compel us to probe deeper and to ask, What do we mean by "food," anyway? How do we define eating behaviors as savage or civilized?

James Cagney roughly offers Mae Clarke a grapefruit kiss in The Public Enemy, *1931.*

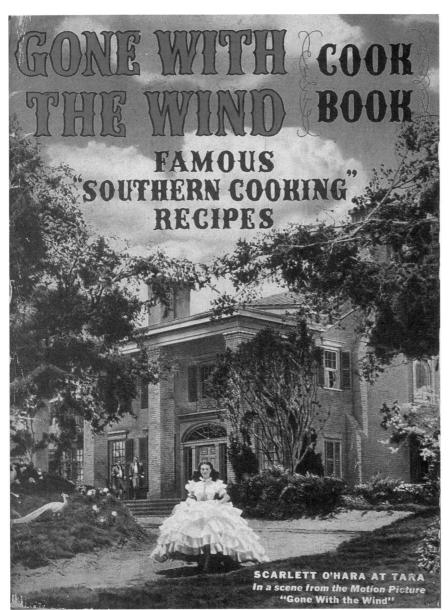

Famous "Southern Cooking" Recipes

SCARLETT O'HARA AT TARA
In a scene from the Motion Picture
"Gone With the Wind"

The Pebeco Toothpaste Company issued this cookbooklet tie-in with Gone with the Wind, *an MGM movie directed by Victor Fleming.*

Food is often noteworthy even in films where it is relegated to the background. Jack Nicholson's famous request in *Five Easy Pieces* (1970) left us forever eager to challenge the phrase "no menu substitutions," and Sally's fake orgasm at a deli in *When Harry Met Sally* (1989) made us all want "what she's having."

In some cases, a film's food scenes serve as a key to structure: Coppola's *Godfather* trilogy consistently alternates between lavish ceremonies involving food and equally visceral killings, and in junk-food-laden, neo-noir *Pulp Fiction* (1993), each meal forecasts a violent plot turn.

Food and Filmmakers

Narrative mechanics and symbolism aside, food and eating scenes can also be tempting, as a practical matter, for filmmakers. Dialogue scenes are easy to shoot at a table, and dining scenes typically bring out subtleties of place and persons.

As in narrative cinema, food in documentaries humanizes characters and provides detail. Documentarians, however, do not determine the comestibles; rather, food and eating is organic to the events being filmed. *Chulas Fronteras* (1976) and *Garlic Is as Good as 10 Mothers* (1980) are among Les Blank's celluloid celebrations of diverse food types and rituals.

Film, Food, and the Culture

At the end of the twentieth century, a mounting interest in food history and culture led to merchandise inspired by food in film. Although celebrity-penned cookbooks have always been popular, the director Martin Scorsese, whose cinematic portraits of Italian Americans have included many a plate of pasta, helped his mother, Catherine, produce *Italianamerican: The Scorsese Family Cookbook*, including film stills and stories from the sets where Catherine would regularly feed the cast and crew. In a wackier tribute, *The Star Wars Cookbook* (1998), released in tandem with *Star Wars, Episode 1: The Phantom Menace* (1999), offers concoctions not in the film but inspired by its story. (Skywalker Smoothie, anyone?)

Of course, Hollywood film and food are natural companions. The documentary *Off the Menu: The Last Days of Chasen's* (1998) shows how from the industry's beginnings, gossip and allure grew from establishments where stars ate, drank, and greeted their fans. Hollywood restaurants also became places for making "deals over meals." From Elizabeth Taylor's legendary demands for Chasen's chili on the set of *Cleopatra*, to the caricature wall at the Brown Derby, to the celebrity-owned Planet Hollywood and post-Oscar parties at famed eateries Morton's and Spago, the interconnectedness of Hollywood film and food has routinely fed the masses.
[**See also:** Radio/TV Food Shows.]

BIBLIOGRAPHY

Barr, Terry. "Eating Kosher, Staying Closer: Families and Meals in Contemporary Jewish American

Not until the 1980s did food begin to take center stage as plot and motive in American films. Two main types developed: the ethnic-based food film and the weight-preoccupied one. Terry Barr has designated a "Jewish cinema"—including *Avalon* (1987) and *Crimes and Misdemeanors* (1989)—that recapitulates stereotypes about Jewish eating traditions and yet reveals how food aided assimilation into Anglo-Saxon Protestant culture. But a common pitfall of such works is that food becomes another way to reduce ethnic (or nonwhite) culture and differences to a matter of "taste."

Other films show the trials and traumas of obesity, such as *Heavy* (1995) and *What's Eating Gilbert Grape?* (1993). *Eating* (1990) deliberates on women's physical insecurities and food obsessions. Perhaps it is no coincidence that as diet and exercise fads appeared faster and more furiously, there was a significant increase in films that catered to the gastronomically tortured. No doubt *Chocolat* (2000) and its cinematic cousins tapped into audiences' deep emotional and physical hunger through a zero-calorie viewing experience.

Aside from pornography, in which the use of food in sexual acts is far from unusual, filmmakers often use food for sexual innuendo. Highly explicit was Adrian Lyne's *9-1/2 Weeks* (1986), with its kinky, food-based sex play that upped the ante set twenty years earlier in the British release *Tom Jones* (1963). Of course, more tamely, food preparation and service often reveals gender roles. *Chocolat* (2000), for example, reasserts the idea that a woman's power depends on her talents in the kitchen.

Cinema." *Journal of Popular Film and Television* 24, no. 3 (Fall 1996): 134–144.

Goodwin, Betty. *Chasen's, Where Hollywood Dined: Recipes and Memories*. Santa Monica, CA: Angel City Press, 1996.

Loukides, Paul, and Linda K. Fuller, eds. *Beyond the Stars III: The Material World in American Popular Film*. Bowling Green, OH: Bowling Green University Popular Press, 1993.

Westfahl, Gary, George Slusser, and Eric S. Rabkin, eds. *Foods of the Gods: Eating and the Eaten in Fantasy and Science Fiction*. Athens: University of Georgia Press, 1996.

REBECCA L. EPSTEIN

Firehouse Cooking

Firehouse cooking has become entrenched in American popular culture. Firefighters conspicuously shop en masse, write cookbooks, and demonstrate their recipes on television. Excluding food-service professionals, perhaps no other occupation is so deeply and publicly involved in shopping, cooking, and eating as part of their work lives. Although each city has a slightly different story, New York City typifies and has influenced the evolution of firehouse cooking as a significant social fixture.

Historical Framework: New York as a Model

The Fire Department of New York was established in 1865 when funds were first allotted for standardizing the numerous community-supported volunteer companies in the New York area. Early professional firefighters worked and lived together in the firehouse, originally working nine twenty-four-hour days followed by a tenth day off. The firefighters were allotted three hours of breaks per day, which could be divided among one, two, or three meals, depending largely on the distance between the firehouse and the firefighter's home. These breaks would be suspended in the event of a major fire. Early professional firefighters walked or bicycled home or to local diners for meals and cooked in the firehouse only for festive occasions. The most common of these occasions was the Saturday night chowder, for which pots, utensils, and items of decor were collected from firefighters' homes, and the men chipped in for the food to have a firehouse-cooked meal open to family and friends.

Despite the existence of festive firehouse cooking in the nineteenth century, however, cooking did not begin to become a part of everyday firehouse life until the 1920s, a period of major change for the fire department. Many developments during this period dramatically changed the nature of firefighting and firehouse life. Perhaps most significant was the decision to change from a one-platoon system to a two-platoon system, whereby firefighters would work alternating twelve-hour shifts. This change eliminated meal breaks, prompting the firefighters to bring food from home or have it delivered by family, friends, or neighborhood children.

Along with these dramatic shifts came changes borne of practical considerations. A newly horseless engine house gave firefighters more space and a cleaner environment—they had been congregating and sleeping in a loft above the stable in most firehouses. In some houses, firefighters installed rudimentary kitchens in the room where the stable had been, using equipment and utensils brought from home or purchased with pooled funds. The firefighters began pooling food as well and later appointed one man as cook on alternating days when things were calm.

Both the union and the city were impressed by firefighters' initiative in the kitchen. The union saw cooking as a way to regain the fraternal sentiment lost in the change from voluntarism to a tightly regulated paramilitary structure and to improve the quality of the working day. The department administrators saw the cooking as a way to keep the men together and away from alcohol, women, and other distractions of meal breaks. With such rare and powerful support of both the union and the department, firehouse cooking was becoming an institution in the United States.

Obstacles and Functions

Firehouse cooking has endured despite the presence of many obstacles. Most fire departments have never financially supported firehouse cooking. Firefighters negotiate the menu among themselves, ride the fire truck to shop together for food so that if they receive a call they are ready to abandon their carts at the market and respond to the emergency, and divide the cost of each meal among those present. Moreover, firefighters contribute to a commissary fund to provide staple ingredients and to fund necessary maintenance of the kitchen equipment.

Another obstacle to firehouse cooking is the unpredictable nature of firehouse life. Dennis Smith, a New York City firefighter, wrote, "I once kept a running account of how many meals I could eat in the firehouse without interruption. It went for three and a half months, and in that time I never ate one uninterrupted meal" (*Report from Engine Co. 82*). Furthermore, firefighters receive no training with regard to food and cooking, other than its nutritional aspects, which can produce some unsavory results among the new recruits.

Although the obstacles to firehouse cooking may be significant from a material standpoint, firehouse meals have important social functions that in a corporate environment might be called "acculturation," "diversity training," and "feedback sessions." One study of a firefighter training class and the students' placement in the field showed that housekeeping chores, especially cooking, served as "proving grounds" for new recruits (Chetkovich, *Real Heat*). In the urban fire department it is not sufficient to perform well at the fire ground or to master the book knowledge. One has to prove oneself competent and active in firehouse culture. This may include learning one another's cultural tastes and experiences, adapting to the meal system at each firehouse, and recovering from the day, most typically in the kitchen and at the table. Working together smoothly in the relaxed atmosphere of the firehouse kitchen is seen as insurance that the group will be able to work well in the stressful emergency environment.

Although it may endure as an icon of popular culture, firehouse cooking has value behind the closed doors of the firehouse. Firefighters never know which meal will be their last and may feel this more saliently than most people do. Firefighters tend to celebrate the everyday, and negotiating the intricacies of the meal, cooking elaborate meals together, and eating in a raucous and convivial atmosphere are important to this outlook.

[**See also** COOKING EQUIPMENT, SOCIAL ASPECTS OF; KITCHENS.]

BIBLIOGRAPHY

Chetkovich, Carol. *Real Heat: Gender and Race in the Urban Fire Service*. New Brunswick, NJ: Rutgers University Press, 1997.

Zurrier, Rebecca. *The American Firehouse: An Architectural and Social History*. New York: Abbeville, 1982.

JONATHAN DEUTSCH

Fireless Cookers

The principle of cooking with retained heat has been known for its usefulness in many times and many cultures. Peasants wrapped pots of partially cooked food in heavy feather beds. Well insulated, the food would continue to cook until the family returned from the fields to a hot meal. Native Americans used heated stones for clam bakes. Logging camps baked beans over hot stones in pits. Farmers carried fireless cookers into the fields

Delicious Fireless Cooked Dishes, *issued by the Toledo Cooker Company in 1919.*

so they could enjoy a hot meal at noon. Immigrants to America used their iceboxes as fireless cookers during the winter. Campers have used their sleeping bags to cook with retained heat.

Commercial fireless cookers were made with one to three wells in a tightly insulated covered box. A thick disk of preheated soapstone was placed under the pot in the cooker. Commercially made cookers were used at home, in institutions, and in the armed forces. Several cookers that crossed the plains in covered wagons can be seen in western museums. The advantage for westering cooks was that the food and pot could be made very hot over the fire after the breakfast foods had been removed. A fire did not have to be built to provide the family with a hot meal when they stopped at noon.

Fireless cookers were so popular in the early years of the twentieth century that a U.S. Department of Agriculture farmers' bulletin published in 1916 contained much information about fireless cookers. It presented directions for making a cooker at home as well as illustrations and recipes with suggestions on how to use the cooker. In that era, there were numerous publications on fireless cookers. The U.S. Experiment Station Office in 1914 produced the *Illustrated Lecture on the Homemade Fireless Cooker*, which was accompanied by thirty-six lantern slides. State experiment stations also published booklets on this method of cooking.

A simple type of fireless cooker called the "hay box" was easily made at home. This device was used in England and the United States. A sturdy wooden box with a hinged top was lined with several inches of hay on the sides and bottom, allowing room for a pot and several inches on the top for a pillow or hay enclosed in a casing to completely cover the top of the box. Hot food was placed in a pot with a minimum of airspace and set in the box. When the lid was closed the hay box could be put aside to cook for hours. Pots with no handles or flip-down handles and tight fitting lids with recessed knobs were well suited for this type of cooker. Other insulating materials, such as newspaper or cork, also could be used. In later years plastic foam and packing "peanuts" could be adapted for use as insulating materials.

Many campers use hay boxes, which are particularly suited for cooking rice and other grains and cereals, stews, soups, and other foods cooked in liquid that adapt well to slow cooking. The cooker is made with a heavy cardboard box. The bottom and sides are lined with thick aluminum foil, and the box is filled with hay, into which a pot containing hot food is nestled. A pillow fits completely over the pot and hay, and when the lid is closed, cooking proceeds without further attention.

There are many advantages to fireless cookers. They conserve fuel, because after the initial period of heating the pot and the food, no additional source of fuel is needed. Food can be safely left to cook while the family is away. Foods do not burn or "cook down" because there is no loss of moisture. Slow cooking is economical because less tender cuts of meat can be used.

As modern stoves and electrical cooking appliances came into use fewer and fewer cooks continued to use fireless cookers. Advertisements for commercial cookers disappeared from newspapers, and directions for using them disappeared from recipe books. Yet the idea was not entirely lost. In the late 1940s, interest was revived by the publication of *Fireless Cooking: A Traditional Energy-Efficient Method of Slow Cooking*. In a humorous article in *Ms* magazine in 1982, titled "The Strangest Dinner Party I Ever Went To," Alice Walker related arriving for dinner but finding no odors of cooking food emanating from the kitchen. She was puzzled until the hostess uncovered the pot from the fireless cooker and served a delicious meal. Similar in many ways to the modern slow cooker and its many advantages for working people, the fireless cooker can still function in modern kitchens as a low-energy time saver.
[**See also** PIONEERS AND SURVIVAL FOOD; SLOW COOKERS.]

BIBLIOGRAPHY

Kirschner, Heidi. *Fireless Cookery: A Traditional Energy-Efficient Method of Slow Cooking*. Seattle, WA: Madrona, 1981.

MARY MOONEY-GETOFF

Fish:
Freshwater Fish

Freshwater food-fish are the object of both fish farming and recreational fishing. Commercial freshwater fisheries and sportfishing often overlap, and both must deal with the effects of overfishing, pollution, and loss of spawning habitat to shoreline development. Freshwater fisheries occupy lakes, streams, and rivers above the fall line, where tidewater cannot go.

In North America, commercial fishing of any consequence for wild stocks of fish occurs mostly on the Great Lakes and in large rivers. The commercial advantage, which is considerable in some places, to fishing on smaller streams and lakes is derived from interest in sportfishing. Many states and small localities support the sport fishery through stocking as well as wildlife and environmental protections. Freshwater sportfishing enthusiasts have created a market for species-specific magazines, websites, and businesses that sell lures and other equipment and bait. Lodges and camps, boat rentals, and guides further serve freshwater-fishing enthusiasts.

The common names of freshwater fish, like those of saltwater fish, are highly regional and obscure a world of biological difference. Confusingly, the same name is applied to various fish and is sometimes applied to similar saltwater fish. For example, bass and perch both have saltwater counterparts.

On the job at New York's Fulton Fish Market during the spring of 1943.

Freshwater fish have appeared in cookbooks since the early days of America, but the recipes do not convey the natural variety and frequency of the fish. A small number of fish are named in the books; otherwise, the general label "fish" is used. The size of the fish and nature of the bones and flesh determine its suitability for various culinary procedures. White flesh and bland-flavored fish are favored. Small fish are usually consumed as panfish, that is, fried or broiled, and larger fish are filleted. The catch of some freshwater fish prompts outdoor festivities such as crayfish boils, fish fries, and fish boils.
[**See also** BASS; CARP; CATFISH; CISCO; CRAPPIE; CRAYFISH; EEL; FISH: SALTWATER FLAT FISH; PERCH; PICKEREL; PIKE; SALMON; SAUGER; SHELLFISH; SMELT; STURGEON; SUNFISH; TERRAPIN; TILAPIA; TROUT; WALLEYE; WHITEFISH]

BIBLIOGRAPHY

Active Angler. http://www.activeangler.com.
Behnke, Robert J. *Trout and Salmon of North America*. New York: Free Press, 2002.
Froese, R., and D. Pauly, eds. *FishBase*. http://www.fishbase.org/search.cfm.
Sorenson, Eric. *The Angler's Guide to Freshwater Fish of North America*. Stillwater, MN: Voyageur, 2000.
Waszczuk, Henry. *The Complete Guide to North American Freshwater Game Fishing*. Toronto: Fenn, 1992.

SANDRA L. OLIVER

Fish:
Saltwater Flat Fish

Until the mid-twentieth century, the size, texture, bone structure, and oiliness of a fish determined its use in the American kitchen. Wherever settlers landed, they viewed any unfamiliar fish and shellfish with an eye toward what familiar seafood it resembled. They then would cook it in a comparable manner, merely adopting the new fish and adapting its preparation to what they already knew. The view of fish and shellfish from the kitchen broke into several categories of use that did not change much from the earliest settlement through the middle of the twentieth century.

Most fish were poached, fried, or baked. (Early cookbooks that recommend "boiling" fish usually caution the cook not to let the fish boil hard; because the fish were simmered more than boiled, most modern cooks would call the process poaching.) In the hearth cooking era, large fish were sometimes tied to a board and roasted before the fire in a process sometimes called planking, but when stove cookery superseded open fires, most cookbooks acknowledged that baking tended to dry out fish, and cooks who chose to bake were obliged to baste, serve with a sauce, or otherwise ensure moisture. Leftover fish was flaked up, the bones were carefully removed, and the meat was rewarmed in a sauce or made into fish cakes.

Small fish were usually fried, broiled, or grilled. Chowders called most often for white, firm-fleshed fish, and soups often used shellfish. During the mid- and later nineteenth century, certain fish and shellfish were favored for salads, and some shellfish were cooked and stuffed back into shells for presentation.

The average size of saltwater fish caught has changed over time. As a species is heavily fished, the older, larger fish are thinned out and the younger, smaller fish are left and may never achieve the size of the earlier catch. Because so many culinary decisions are based on fish size, the way some fish were prepared in earlier times is different from the present methods for some species.

Large, Solid Fish with Few Bones
Americans who liked a centerpiece entrée used meaty, large fish with bones that were easy to find and remove. Salmon, sturgeon, halibut, and, later, swordfish and tuna were poached or roasted, either whole or in large steak or roastlike pieces weighing several pounds. Codfish heads and shoulders, in the days when the cod was landed weighing upwards of thirty pounds, were also cooked and presented whole. These fish were usually served with a sauce, often containing anchovies or shellfish, such as lobster, oyster, crab, or shrimp.

Medium-to-Large White, Firm-Fleshed Fish
Some fish that once fit this category no longer do because overfishing has left mostly smaller fish of the species. Cod, both salt and fresh; cusk; striped bass, known as rockfish in the South; haddock; pollock; tautog, or blackfish; mullet; drum; sheepshead; bream; red snapper; and recently, John Dory; Pacific cod; orange roughy; and Chilean sea bass have all shared this category. They have been baked, boiled, and stewed whole as well as put into chowders, and their fillets have been baked and broiled. Leftovers have been warmed up in cream sauces, scalloped, or mixed with potatoes and made into fish cakes or croquettes.

Many early cookbooks advise cooks to use fish without specifying which type, which shows this category to possess fairly elastic culinary interpretations. Fish migrate, so most fish would have appeared in market or at the end of a fishing pole only seasonally. A cook had to be flexible.

Medium-to-Large Oily-Fleshed Fish
Many of the fish in this category—shad, mackerel, bluefish, salmon trout, small salmon, eels, and others—were less popular table fish. Most Americans, historically and to the present, prefer bland, white-fleshed fish to the oilier, dark-fleshed fish. This group, however, contained sport fish and the famous anadromous fishes that Americans fished for family as well as commercial use.

Anadromous fish include alewives, salmon, and shad, which spawn in freshwater but live their adult lives in the sea. They appeared in springtime in great abundance in the seventeenth and eighteenth centuries as well as in the nineteenth century until many large rivers and streams were dammed for power. They were relatively easy to harvest as they surged upstream. Whether early New Englanders netting alewives, Philadelphians scooping up shad, or Native Americans in the Northwest harvesting salmon, the annual appearance of the fish caused tremendous excitement as fishermen took advantage of the opportunity. In the case of shad, the roe was often as much the object of the fishery as the flesh, which was famous for its boniness.

Many fish in this category were salted; some were subsequently smoked. The oily flesh took up salt well, and when the fish were smoked, they did not dry out unpleasantly. For the same reason, these fish were good for baking, roasting, or planking; they were also suitable for broiling. Eels could even be spitted to cook before a hearth fire.

Small White- or Oily-Fleshed Fish
This category included many fish, all of which could have been described as "panfish" because their small size allowed them conveniently to fit into a frying pan. Small and tinker (juvenile) mackerel, perch, herring, flounder, alewife, sole, smelt, and several freshwater fish fit this category of quickly cooked fish, though some were also filleted and are suitable for baking. Usually these fish were too thin or bony for convenient use in soups and stews. Some could be grilled. Some, such as alewives, herring, and mackerel, were caught commercially and salted or smoked, which accounts for their appearance inland in cookbooks published in places far from the sea.

[See also ALASKA; ANCHOVIES; BASS; BLACKFISH; FISH: FRESHWATER FISH; FLOUNDER AND SOLE; GRUNION; HADDOCK; HALIBUT; HERRING AND SARDINES; MACKEREL; MONKFISH; MULLET; PACIFIC NORTHWEST; PERCH; POLLOCK; RED SNAPPER; SALMON; SEA MAMMALS; SEA TURTLE; SEAWEED; SHAD; SHELLFISH; SOUPS AND STEWS; SQUID; STURGEON; SWORDFISH; WHALE MEAT AND WHALE OIL]

Pamphlet issued by the Madam Brand Crab Company.

BIBLIOGRAPHY
Davidson, Alan. *North Atlantic Seafood: A Comprehensive Guide with Recipes.* 3rd ed. Berkeley, CA: Ten Speed Press, 2003.
Davidson, Alan, ed. *The Oxford Companion to Food.* 2nd ed. Oxford: Oxford University Press, 2006.
Oliver, Sandra L. *Saltwater Foodways: New Englanders and Their Food at Sea and Ashore, in the Nineteenth Century.* Mystic, CT: Mystic Seaport Museum, 1995.

SANDRA L. OLIVER

Fish and Chips
The combination of battered and fried fish (frequently cod or other white fish) with chips (known in the United States as french fries) originated in the United Kingdom in the mid-nineteenth century. Joseph Malin is credited with opening the first combined fish and chip shop in London in the 1860s. Fish and chips are commonly served with malt vinegar. In the United Kingdom, fish and chips are served in an estimated eight thousand fish and chip shops and the combination is considered the UK's national dish. It is popular in Australia, Canada, Ireland, New Zealand, and South Africa.

Despite the importance of fish and chips elsewhere, it did not become an important food combination in the United States until after World War II, when many restaurants that specialized in fish began serving them. Legal Seafoods, one of the more prominent chains, served them beginning in 1950, when it opened its first restaurant in Cambridge, Massachusetts.

Two fast food chains that served fish and chips in America were launched in 1969. One was Arthur Treacher's Fish & Chips, which opened its first restaurant in Columbus, Ohio. The chain was named after the British actor who came to the United States in 1928 and appeared frequently on Merv Griffin's television show during the 1960s. Arthur Treacher served as a spokesperson for the company in its early years. Arthur Treacher's chain claimed to have purchased the recipe for its fish and chips from Malin's, the chip shop in London. It used Atlantic cod as a base for its fish and chips. In the 1980s, the price of Atlantic cod skyrocketed and the company suffered; as a result, the troubled company changed hands repeatedly. In 1998 a partnership was formed with Pudgie's Famous Chicken, Miami Subs, and Nathan's Famous. In selected locations, the Arthur Treacher's menu is served at these franchises.

The second fish and chips fast food chain was Long John Silver's, which was launched in 1969 by Jerrico Inc. of Lexington, Kentucky. The name of the chain was derived from a character in Robert Louis Stevenson's *Treasure Island*. The first outlet proved successful and franchising began the following year. The architecture for the chain was intended to resemble a building from an early American fishing village. Initially, Long John Silver's featured fried battered fish and grilled fish along with fries and coleslaw. Its menu evolved to include seafood, chicken, sandwiches, salads, and desserts.

In 1989 senior management and a New York investment firm acquired Jerrico and its subsidiaries in a leveraged buyout. Long John Silver's had difficult times and it went bankrupt in 1998. The following year it was merged with A&W Root Beer to form Yorkshire Global Restaurants, based in Lexington, Kentucky. Yorkshire Global Restaurants, in turn, was purchased by Tricon Global Restaurants (now Yum! Brands) in 2002. As of 2005, there were twelve hundred Long John Silver's restaurants in the United States, two hundred in multibranded restaurants, and thirty-three in other countries. It is the largest fast food fish chain in America.

Other American fast food chains that sell fish and chips include Cedric's Fish and Chips, H. Salt Fish and Chips, and Ivar's in the Pacific Northwest. In addition, independent fish and chips shops have opened up in the United States, such as the Chip Shop in Brooklyn, which invented deep-fried Twinkies.

BIBLIOGRAPHY

Jakle, John A., and Keith A. Sculle, *Fast Food: Roadside Restaurants in the Automobile Age*. Baltimore: Johns Hopkins University Press, 1999.

Walton, John K. *Fish & Chips and the British Working Class 1870–1940*. London and New York: Leicester University Press, 1992.

ANDREW F. SMITH

Fisher, M. F. K.

For more than fifty-five years, Mary Frances Kennedy Fisher, a self-styled third-generation journalist and widely acclaimed "poet of the appetites," crafted essays, stories, and articles that changed the character of culinary writing across America. Born on July 3, 1908, in Albion, Michigan, Fisher was the daughter of Rex Brenton Kennedy and Edith Oliver Holbrook, who in 1912 settled in Whittier, California, when Rex Kennedy became part owner and editor of the *Whittier News*.

Fisher attended private boarding schools, Illinois College, Whittier College, and Occidental College before continuing her education in 1929 at the University of Dijon, France, as the newly married Mrs. Alfred Fisher. The Fishers returned to California in 1932 and lived in Laguna Beach, doing odd jobs and writing. M. F. K. Fisher's first published article, "Pacific Village," appeared in *Westways* in 1934.

The pleasures of the table as well as the legends and lore of culinary history in cookbooks as old as *Apicius de re Coquinaria* and as influential as *Mrs. Beeton's Book of Household Management* were the subjects of Fisher's first book, *Serve It Forth* (1937). In *Consider the Oyster* (1941), Fisher distracted her second husband, Dillwyn Parrish, from the pain of Buerger's disease by writing about the legendary bivalve. Survival and dining well in wartime were Fisher's preoccupation in *How to Cook a Wolf* (1942). A year later in *The Gastronomical Me* she took the measure of her powers when she re-created her gastronomically satisfying moments at home and abroad and used food as a surrogate for easing basic human longings. A series of articles for *Gourmet* magazine about Fisher's experiences living in Hollywood and her third marriage, to Donald Friede, became *The Alphabet for Gourmets* (1948).

By the time these quintessential Fisher books were collected in *The Art of Eating* in 1954, M. F. K. Fisher had distinguished herself as a solo voice in gastronomical writing, distancing herself from the early-twentieth-century American gastronomers—Joseph Wechsberg, Alexis Lichine, Lucius Beebe, and A. J. Liebling—and from the pattern of food writing that concentrated on nutritional information, balanced meals, and entertaining tips. Innovative, autobiographical, and nostalgic, Fisher defined gastronomy as the art of eating and drinking with intelligence and grace, and she wrote about it in her own inimitable style. Extensively published in *House Beautiful* and *Gourmet* in the 1940s and in *The New Yorker* in the 1960s and 1970s, Fisher also contributed to *Vogue*, *Westways*, *Ladies Home Journal*, the *Atlantic Monthly*, *Esquire*, *Coronet*, and *Holiday*.

In the late 1940s, Fisher's literary reputation grew with an anthology of culinary selections from great literature, called *Here Let Us Feast: A Book of Banquets* (1946), the novel *Not Now But Now* (1947), and a translation of Brillat-Savarin's *Physiology of Taste* (1949). After periods of residency in France, Fisher added other places to her repertoire and published books on Aix-en-Provence, Marseilles, and Dijon. By the late 1960s, she revisited the foods of her growing-up years as well as the accumulated recipes that had served her well and published the cookbook *With Bold Knife and Fork* (1969) and a memoir of her childhood, *Among Friends* (1970). It was with the publication of Time-Life's *The Cooking of Provincial France* (1968), however, that Fisher became more actively associated with the rising stars of America's culinary community—James Beard, Julia Child, and Craig Claiborne.

When North Point Press reissued many of Fisher's books in the 1980s, recognition and honors, including election to the American Academy of Arts and Letters in 1991, came her way, and Last House, Fisher's unique home in the Sonoma Valley, attracted both established and aspiring members of the culinary establishment. After a ten-year struggle with Parkinson's disease, M. F. K. Fisher died on June 22, 1992, her literary reputation secured and her contribution to the art of eating recognized.

[**See also** CALIFORNIA; COOKBOOKS: FROM WORLD WAR II TO THE 1960S; MYTHS AND FOLKLORE; PERIODICALS; RESTAURANT CRITICS AND FOOD COLUMNISTS.]

BIBLIOGRAPHY

Ferrary, Jeannette. *Between Friends: M. F. K. Fisher and Me*. New York: Atlantic Monthly Press, 1991.

Reardon, Joan. *M. F. K. Fisher, Julia Child, and Alice Waters: Celebrating the Pleasures of the Table*. New York: Harmony, 1994.

JOAN REARDON

Flavorings

The term "flavoring" encompasses a range of definitions. General dictionaries define "flavoring" as "a particular sensation as perceived after placing a substance in the oral cavity," whereas the U.S. Food and Drug Administration provides the detailed explanation, "Flavoring means any substance, the function of which is to impart flavor, which is derived from spice, fruit or fruit juice, vegetable or vegetable juice, edible yeast, herb, bark, bud, root, leaf or similar plant material, meat, fish, poultry, eggs, dairy products, or fermentation products thereof." Flavor has olfactory (smell) and gustatory (taste) components. The Monell Chemical Senses Center indicates, "It has long been established that our sense of taste detects four basic sensations—sweet, salty, sour and bitter. More recently, increasing consensus has developed for the addition of a fifth class of taste sensation: umami, sometimes described as brothy."

The term "flavor" is used ambiguously by consumers. For example, a stew may be perceived as having a good flavor because it contains spice, whereas strawberry Jell-O may be thought to have a good flavor even though it does not contain any spice. Flavors occur in foods in several different ways: they may be present already in a food, such as the banana flavor of a banana; the cook may add ingredients to flavor a food, such as using Bing cherries with duck or white wine with fish; a cook may use a commercial, store-bought flavoring extract to flavor a food, such as adding vanilla extract to whipped cream; a food already may contain a flavor that has been added by a food manufacturer. Food manufacturers use commercial flavors purchased from flavor manufacturers, such as International Flavors and Fragrances, Givaudan, and Firmenich.

Flavors can be categorized as natural, artificial, natural and artificial, and natural with other natural flavors (WONF). Flavor chemists usually attempt to re-create flavors of foods found in nature. Natural flavors only can contain flavoring components derived from the named flavor. For example, natural lemon flavor contains components from lemons such as lemon juice and lemon oil. Artificial flavors usually contain a chemical that is the main characteristic flavor of the natural materials. Vanillin, characteristic of the flavor of vanilla, and benzaldehyde, characteristic of the flavor of cherries, both can be produced chemically. Using these flavor chemicals causes a flavor to be labeled artificial.

The U.S. Food and Drug Administration has the ultimate responsibility for the safety of foods and flavors. The 1958 Food Additive Amendment to the Pure Food Act established a law requiring that all ingredients added to food must be safe. An independent expert panel reviews the safety of flavor ingredients and establishes the ingredients' status as generally recognized as safe (GRAS). Flavors are used at very low levels in foods, usually at one to ten parts per million.

Use of Flavorings in the Home

Before 1850 Americans flavored their own foods and beverages using local and foreign sources of flavorings such as rum, fruit juice, and spices. By the mid-nineteenth century, food and beverage products containing commercial flavors started to appear in the United States. The addition of flavorings to whiskey, to simulate aging, was one of the first uses of a flavored product. Flavored ice cream was first produced commercially in 1841 in Baltimore. Coca-Cola was first sold in 1886. McCormick started selling flavor extracts directly to the consumer in 1900, and Jell-O became available in 1901.

The American consumer experienced a proliferation of flavored products throughout the twentieth century; in 2004 the U.S. flavor industry sold more than $2 billion of flavors. Coca-Cola and Pepsi added new flavors to their traditional cola line. Formerly exotic flavors such as mango, kiwi, and Irish coffee became commonplace. Flavor companies continued to attempt to duplicate the flavor and aroma of fresh-brewed coffee for instant coffee, improve the fresh-squeezed

flavor of orange juice, and capture the flavor of fruit on the vine.

History of the U.S. Flavor Industry

The U.S. flavor industry has its roots in the United Kingdom and Europe. Beginning in the early 1700s, natural plant and fruit extracts, essential oils, and distillates were prepared and sold. U.S. companies started using and manufacturing commercial flavors around 1850. Early flavors contained components derived from natural materials such as fruits and spices. One of the first synthetic aroma chemicals to be used in flavorings was citral, a chemical found in lemon that is characteristic of lemon flavor. The isolation, synthesis, and production of citral in the United States first occurred around 1900. Vanillin (vanilla) and cinnamic aldehyde (cinnamon) also became commercially available in the United States in the early 1900s.

It was common to ship European flavors to New York City as early as 1797. Most U.S. flavor companies started in a four-square-block area near the South Seaport (East River) in lower Manhattan. There were seventy-two flavor and essential flavor oil companies in New York City in 1927; only eighteen of these companies were in existence under same name in 1977. Four companies from that 1927 list (Givaudan, A. M. Todd, Ungerer and Company, and Manheimer) were in existence at the beginning of the twenty-first century.

There are now more than two hundred U.S. flavor suppliers. Most flavor companies moved from New York City to New Jersey by 1950. Givaudan purchased a number of companies through the years and ranks as the number-one U.S. flavor company. International Flavors and Fragrances is second. New Jersey is the leading state for flavor sales. Cincinnati, Ohio, the site of Givaudan's headquarters, is the leading city.

Development of New Commercial Flavors

The advent of the use of gas liquid chromatography (GLC) in 1960 to 1970 greatly expanded the flavor chemist's ability to identify new volatile chemicals in food. This led to a significant increase in the number of new flavors created by flavor companies. Research into flavor chemistry earned Nobel Prizes in 1910, 1939, and 2001.

Food and beverage companies develop new products to meet a real or perceived consumer need or want and drive the flavor companies to develop flavors for new products and to improve the flavors of existing products. Flavor salespeople identify flavor needs for food and beverage companies. Flavor application chemists determine which existing flavors meet the needs of the food or beverage manufacturer. If necessary, flavor chemists create a new flavor. The food or beverage company requests flavor samples from two or more flavor suppliers, and then

it conducts consumer tests to determine the acceptability of the product or flavor. Once the product is marketed, the process of improving the flavor or reducing its cost begins.

More than six thousand new food and beverage products were introduced in 2003, and many of those products contained flavors. The trend is for the consumer to purchase more and more different types of flavored products, which bodes well for the creative and highly competitive U.S. flavor industry.

[**See also** CHEMICAL ADDITIVES.]

BIBLIOGRAPHY
Carlin, J. M. "Eating and Drinking in the Early Republic." *Nutrition Today* 33, no. 2 (March/April 1968): 71–76.
Dorland, Wayne E., and James A. Rogers, Jr. *The Fragrance and Flavor Industry*. Mendham, NJ: W. E. Dorland Company, 1977.

JOHN F. CASSENS

Fletcherism

One of America's earliest weight-reduction experts and food reformers was a rotund "Mr. Five-by-Five" named Horace Fletcher (1849–1919). An immensely successful businessman, Fletcher had amassed an outsize fortune by the age of forty, but his health had not similarly prospered. At forty, all his hair had turned white, and he was calamitously fat. On his five-foot-five frame, he carried 205 pounds. Worst of all, no longer could Fletcher, who had been noted for his prodigious strength and athleticism as a young Dartmouth College undergraduate, even take a short walk or climb a flight of stairs without puffing and straining. He felt, he said, "like a thing fit but to be thrown on the scrap-heap." So in his late forties—because medical nostrums had been unavailing—he decided to try to cure his health problems on his own. He recounts his triumphal progress in two books, *The ABZ of Our Own Nutrition* and *How I Became Young at 60*.

In 1898, while ruminating on an article on human dentition that had been written by the British statesman Sir William Gladstone, Fletcher had a eureka experience. Gladstone opined that as Nature had equipped humans with thirty-two teeth, Nature must have intended that each bite of food should be chewed thirty-two times—one chew for each tooth. Although Gladstone's dubious inference seems a bit of a non sequitur, Fletcher fearlessly elaborated it into a whole system of eating. Its cardinal precepts include: eat only when you are hungry; eat only those foods that your appetite craves; stop eating when your hunger abates; chew each morsel of food until it loses its flavor; and liquids should be chewed before each swallow.

Using himself as a test subject, Fletcher began to chew each morsel of food thirty-two times. At the end of the experiment, Fletcher found that the food seemed to vaporize on the tongue. What's more, he found that his appetite for food diminished the more he chewed. Within a few months, not only had he shed his considerable avoirdupois, tipping the scales now at 160 pounds (a weight that he maintained for the rest of his life), but he also had recovered his youthful energy and strength. His strength now rivaled that of Yale and West Point oarsmen, against whom the middle-aged Fletcher competed in exhibition strength contests.

When Americans learned that they could lose weight simply by masticating vigorously, Fletcherism swept the country. A number of fin-de-siècle American luminaries such as novelist Henry James and his brother, the philosopher William James; Yale professors Russell Chittenden and Irving Fisher; author Elbert Hubbard; publisher Bernarr Macfadden; author Upton Sinclair; and Dr. John "Cornflakes" Kellogg became ardent Fletcherites. Dr. Kellogg even posted a big sign in the dining room of his vegetarian sanitarium that urged his patients to F-L-E-T-C-H-E-R-I-Z-E, a verb that, along with the noun "fletcherite," Dr. Kellogg himself had coined. Although not their author, the Great Masticator was proud to discover that in 1910 his two eponyms had been included as entries in *Webster's International Dictionary*.

When Fletcher found that meat offered the greatest resistance to being liquefied through chewing, he stopped eating meat, and recommended that earnest followers of his regimen do likewise. Because Fletcherism promoted a vegetarian diet, Fletcher—along with Kellogg, Sinclair, and Macfadden—is credited with turning Americans in the direction of fleshless eating in the early decades of the twentieth century. Fletcherism also contributed to the growth of the nascent American raw foods movement, as Fletcher deplored the eating of "savr'y stews" and other overcooked dishes; rather, he held that food should either be unfired or lightly cooked in order to give the teeth and jaw muscles an adequate workout.

Although Fletcherism was a food fad that eventually ran its course, Americans continued to masticate their food well into the 1940s. However, Fletcher's insight that slowing down the process of eating promotes increased weight loss, enhanced enjoyment of food, and improved digestion forms the basis of most modern weight-loss programs.

BIBLIOGRAPHY

Green, Harvey. *Fit for America: Health, Fitness, Sport, and American Society.* New York: Pantheon, 1986.

RYNN BERRY

Floats, *see Milkshakes*

Flounder and Sole

Flounder and sole are part of a large category of flatfish, to which even halibut belong, that have been caught commercially in American inshore fisheries probably since the eighteenth century and sold in urban markets. These fish did not reach large-scale commercial importance until the later nineteenth century. Many of these fish, especially the summer flounder, are becoming scarce, and conservationists seek to protect them.

There are many common names for this group of fish, *Pleuronectiformes*, which around the world includes over five hundred species caught in every ocean. Called flounder, sole, turbot, sand dab, fluke, and plaice, many of these fish move into estuaries in summer and are caught recreationally by hook and line. Among the most desirable as food fish are winter, summer, and yellowtail flounder.

Most of these are filleted and are good for baking or broiling; they are also used as panfish or are stuffed and rolled. In nineteenth-century cookbooks, the words "sole" and "turbot" often seem to describe a method of preparing a white-fleshed fillet rather than to specify preparation of a particular species. For example, there is no true American sole in the family *Soleidae*, but the word "sole" is used to describe a way of preparing flounder.

SANDRA L. OLIVER

Flowers, Edible

Edible flowers, the most popular being nasturtiums, pansies, marigolds, violets, and roses, have enjoyed a renaissance that began in the 1980s. Far from being only an ornamental conceit of nouvelle cuisine, edible flowers were being used in American kitchens by the mid-seventeenth century for both culinary and medicinal purposes. English colonists were primarily responsible for introducing flowers into American cooking; cookery manuscripts and colonial-era cookbooks contain a wide range of recipes. Traditionally, flowers have been pickled or used fresh, like herbs, to add color, texture, and very subtle flavor to salads; infused into wines, cordials, syrups, and teas; made into conserves and jellies; or candied and added to desserts and confections. More recently, Italian Americans have popularized zucchini blossoms stuffed with anchovy and mozzarella and deep-fried in a light batter.

Flowers are especially difficult to transport in peak condition, and with the decline in kitchen gardens as a ready supplier of produce, flower cookery also declined in the twentieth century, if not earlier in urban areas. The resurgence of urban farmers' markets and the increasing popularity of gourmet stores in the last quarter of the twentieth century reintroduced edible flowers as an ingredient.

Not all flowers are edible, most notably the beautiful but poisonous lily of the valley. Because of the fragility, potential danger, and sheer inconvenience of using fresh or candied flowers to decorate ceremonial cakes, an entire confectionery subspecialty has spawned legions of skilled artisans who fashion realistic-looking flowers from sugar-based pastes such as *pastillage*, fondant, or marzipan, delicately tinted to mimic or even better Mother Nature.

[See also ORANGE FLOWER WATER; ROSE WATER.]

CATHY K. KAUFMAN

An illustration of nasturtiums from the Burpee Seed catalog, 1914.

Flytraps and Fly Screens

Woven wire screening was manufactured as early as the 1830s in the United States, in Connecticut, and was used to screen the sides and doors of food safes and to make sieves. Cheesecloth was used to cover serving dishes on the table until woven wire dish covers—round and oval domes of screening with metal rims, in many sizes—became available in the 1850s. In the early twenty-first century, similar covers of flexible cloth are marketed for outdoor dining. After the 1890s, window screens became fairly common, but most houses were not screened until the late 1920s. Window screens reduced the need to protect containers and dishes from flies. Other nineteenth-century tools in the battle against fly-borne diseases were flyswatters; wind-up fly fans with long-reaching gauzy wings, which were set on dining or worktables; baited flytraps of glass or wire mesh with funneled openings from which flies could not escape; and sticky coils of paper.

[See also INSECTS.]

BIBLIOGRAPHY

Franklin, Linda Campbell. *300 Years of Housekeeping Collectibles.* 5th ed. Iola, WI: Krause Publications, 2003.

LINDA CAMPBELL FRANKLIN

Folgers

Folgers, one of the two dominant mass-market American coffees, originated in San Francisco in 1850, when fourteen-year-old James Folger arrived with his two older brothers. The Folger boys, from a long line of Nantucket whalers, sought their fortune in the California gold rush, but James, the youngest, went to work for Pioneer Steam Coffee and Spice Mills. By the age of twenty-four, Folger was a full partner. He survived bankruptcy in 1865, paid off all his debts, and thrived with J. A. Folger and Company. After

Folger died in 1889, his son carried on. The salesman Frank Atha opened a Folger's outlet in Texas, while the main plant supplied the West. In 1906 Folger's was the only coffee roaster to remain standing through the San Francisco earthquake. During the Depression, Folger's sponsored *Judy and Jane*, a daytime radio soap opera, and in World War II, James Folger III was appointed to the War Production Board. The war swelled California's coffee-drinking population, because many who had migrated to work in the war plants stayed, as did disembarking veterans.

Looking for a brand to compete with Maxwell House, Procter & Gamble purchased Folger's in 1964, taking over one of the last family-owned coffee companies and dropping the possessive apostrophe. The relaxed, personal style of the firm gave way to marketers with fat briefcases. With a major cash infusion, Folgers television advertisements, featuring Mrs. Olson, an omniscient Swedish busybody, saved marriages by showing up with a can of Folgers coffee. In a later campaign, Procter & Gamble produced effective commercials with the tag line "The best part of waking up is Folgers in your cup," but the coffee in the can left a great deal to be desired, containing an unspecified amount of cheap robusta beans.

A boycott mounted against Folgers in 1990 because of its purchase of El Salvadoran beans during a time of death squad activity helped lead to a peaceful settlement of that country's civil war. In 1995 Procter & Gamble purchased the specialty roaster Millstone, which sells all-arabica whole beans.

[**See also** ADVERTISING; COFFEE; POLITICS OF FOOD.]

BIBLIOGRAPHY

Pendergrast, Mark. *Uncommon Grounds: The History of Coffee and How It Transformed Our World*. New York: Basic, 1999. Comprehensive business and social history.

Swasy, Alecia. *Soap Opera: The Inside Story of Procter & Gamble*. New York: Times, 1993.

MARK PENDERGRAST

Fondue

The term "fondue" comes from the French word for "melted," and the word is applied to a number of dishes that feature melted cheese. Fondue recipes were published in the United Kingdom by 1828 and in the United States beginning in 1832, but early "fondue" recipes are often for cheese soufflés. The French chef Pierre Blot, who opened America's first French cooking school in the 1860s, writes in his *Hand-Book of Practical Cookery* (1863) that fondue is the "favorite dish in Italy and in Switzerland where it originated."

Recipes for fondue soufflés, sometimes with chicken and beef added, continued to be published in the United States throughout the nineteenth and early twentieth centuries. The chafing dish became popular in the late nineteenth century, and at least some recipes for fondue gave instructions for the familiar Swiss-style dish: melting cheese and then dipping bread into it. Historically, melted Gruyere or Emmenthaler—also known as Swiss cheese—was combined with a white wine to make the classic Swiss fondue *neuchâteloise*. Emmenthaler cheese was imported into the United States during the early twentieth century, but it was not until the 1950s that cheese fondue was popularized by chef Konrad Egli of the Chalet Swiss Restaurant in New York. His diverse approach, which included heating cubes of meat in oil and later fruit in hot chocolate, stretched the notion of fondue but contributed to the fondue party rage in America beginning in the late 1960s.

During the late 1960s, there was a rage for fondue parties, and no self-respecting hostess lacked a fondue pot with its attendant "canned heat" over which the pot was kept warm, and a set of color-coded fondue forks (so that American standards of culinary hygiene could be upheld). The alternative to cheese fondue was called fondue bourguignonne—oil was heated in the pot and small cubes of meat cooked in it. The favored dessert for such a meal (or any company meal) was chocolate fondue—melted chocolate into which cubes of pound cake or strawberries and chunks of other fruits were dipped. Beginning at that time, dozens of books were published on fondue cooking, such as Ed Callahan's *The Fondue Cookbook* (1968). Books include recipes as well as safety tips and proper etiquette at fondue parties.

[**See also** FONDUE POT.]

ANDREW F. SMITH

Fondue Pot

A fondue pot is a pot that goes over a small portable heating element, such as an alcohol burner or candle. Fondue pots may come with accessories such as a stand for the pot, a diffuser for the heating element, a tray, and fondue forks for dipping. The pots also may be electrified. The oldest and most traditional fondue pot is the *caquelon*, which is made of earthenware. The *caquelon* is heavy and has a wide bottom (as with most glazed ceramic and enameled iron pots), which ensures the steady, even heat ideal for temperamental cheese fondues and chocolate fondues. Heavy stainless steel or enameled iron pots are used for hot oil and broth fondues.

During the 1950s and 1960s, when fondue first became widely popular in the United States, stainless pots in Scandinavian modern designs were fashionable. These gave way to enameled pots in decorator colors such as harvest gold and avocado green and finally to wildly patterned pots by artists such as Peter Max. In the 1970s, fondue pots were a popular wedding gift. Out of fashion for twenty years, fondue and its pots made a comeback in the late 1990s. Sales of Le Creuset brand cast-iron pots surged 20 percent, Williams-Sonoma reintroduced fondue pots in its holiday cata-

The cover of a fondue cookbooklet.

log, and West Bend added an extra large Entertainer pot to its line.

[**See also** CHEESE; CHOCOLATE; FONDUE; POTS AND PANS; WEDDINGS.]

BIBLIOGRAPHY

Lovegren, Sylvia. *Fashionable Food*. New York: Macmillan, 1995.

SYLVIA LOVEGREN

Food and Drug Administration

The Food and Drug Administration (FDA) is an agency of the Department of Health and Human Services of the executive branch of the U.S. government. The FDA is authorized to enforce federal laws and make regulations pertaining to food production and food safety. With the exception of meat, poultry, and some egg products, which are under the jurisdiction of the U.S. Department of Agriculture (USDA), the FDA regulates the production, manufacture, processing, packaging, labeling, and distribution of all U.S. food shipped in interstate commerce and all food imported to or exported from the United States.

Although the FDA has been an agency within Health and Human Services since 1979, the beginnings of the FDA can be traced to 1862, when Congress passed a law establishing the Department of Agriculture and an 1863 appropriation authorizing funds "for the purpose of establishing a laboratory, with the necessary apparatus for practical and scientific experiments in agricultural chemistry." First called the Division of Chemistry and in 1901 renamed the Bureau of Chemistry, the laboratory focused its work on the identification of food products that were adulterated or were fraudulent substitutes. For example, in 1879 the bureau reported the fraudulent substitution and sale of yellow-dyed oleomargarine for true butter.

In 1883 Dr. Harvey Washington Wiley (1844–1930) became the sixth chief chemist of the Bureau of Chemistry. For more than twenty years, Wiley fought for congressional passage of a federal pure food law. When the Pure Food Act was finally passed by Congress and signed into law in 1906, Wiley's Bureau of Chemistry was chosen as the federal agency to examine all foods to determine whether they were adulterated or contaminated or were misbranded fraudulent substitutes. To accomplish this assignment, the first federal food and drug inspectors were selected and appointed in 1907. Thus the Bureau of Chemistry added a law enforcement function to its role as a scientific and research institution.

Although the 1906 law had criminal penalties, the primary enforcement mechanism was confiscation. Adulterated, contaminated, and substitute foods were seized by the inspectors and removed from the marketplace. Initial enforcement of the law by the Bureau of Chemistry led to successful prosecutions involving many adulterated or substitute foods: watered milk, short-weight cheese, cheese labeled "full cream" made from skim milk, decomposed and putrid eggs, artificially colored and chemically preserved jams and jellies, "pure" olive oil mixed with cottonseed oil, artificially colored imitation vinegars labeled "pure," contaminated ketchup, artificially colored and flavored "pure" lemon and vanilla extracts, and ground pepper made solely from other ingredients. However, the failure of Congress to authorize the USDA to adopt standards of identity or standards of purity for many foods seriously weakened the law. Without a standard of identity or purity, it was difficult to prove in court that a food was adulterated or a substitute.

Internal agency disputes about the legality of certain chemical preservatives led to Wiley's resignation from the Bureau of Chemistry in March 1912. He joined the Good Housekeeping Institute as director of its Bureau of Food, Sanitation and Health. At the Good Housekeeping Institute, Wiley continued his crusade for pure food, periodically reporting in *Good Housekeeping* magazine on the status of the government's efforts to regulate the food supply.

The Bureau of Chemistry was reorganized in 1927 to separate its scientific agricultural research function from food law enforcement. As part of the reorganization, the Food, Drug, and Insecticide Administration was established as the law enforcement agency within the USDA. Renamed the Food and Drug Administration in 1930, the agency continued to enforce the Pure Food Act of 1906. The passage of the Federal Food, Drug, and Cosmetic Act of 1938 significantly expanded the enforcement powers of the FDA. Under the 1938 law, the FDA was authorized to go to court to obtain injunctions to prevent illegal foods from reaching the marketplace. In addition, the 1938 law gave the FDA the authority to promulgate food standards. By 1960 FDA food standards were applied to half the food sold in the United States. In 1940, to promote consumer confidence, the FDA was transferred from the Department of Agriculture to the Federal Security Agency. In 1953 the FDA became part of the Department of Health, Education, and Welfare, which in 1979 was renamed the Department of Health and Human Services.

The FDA makes its own regulations for the efficient enforcement of federal food laws. In addition to regulations, the FDA may also make general statements of policy, guidelines, advisory opinions, and recommendations. As a result of this comprehensive regulatory power, the FDA has a wide-ranging influence on American food. The FDA has the power and responsibility to ensure that all imported food (except meat and poultry, which are regulated by the USDA) meets federal standards. After receiving notice of the arrival of an imported food from the U.S. Customs Service, the FDA inspects and obtains samples of the product for laboratory evaluation. The food product is detained at the border pending the FDA's determination of compliance. If it does not comply with all federal laws and regulations, the product must be removed or destroyed.

The FDA has found that pure food is not necessarily safe food. In 2001 the Centers for Disease Control and Prevention reported that each year 76 million Americans become ill from eating unsafe food. Of those, 325,000 are hospitalized and 5,000 die. To address the problem of food-borne illness in the United States, the FDA has instituted a number of programs designed to ensure the safety of the entire food production chain, often called "farm to table." Prevention-oriented programs such as the Hazard Analysis and Critical Control Point (HACCP) system have been established for seafood, fresh fruits and vegetables, sprouts, unprocessed juice, and eggs. Surveillance and outbreak response programs include mandatory recalls of contaminated food products to prevent further exposure and scientific investigations to identify causation so that the problem does not reoccur. The FDA in collaboration with other governmental entities, industry representatives, and consumer advocates conducts educational programs to inform consumers about the importance of proper sanitation, cooking, and storage to decrease the number of deaths and cases of illness caused by food-borne pathogens.

[See also ADULTERATION; DEPARTMENT OF AGRICULTURE, UNITED STATES; FOOD AND NUTRITION SYSTEMS; FOOD SAFETY; GOOD HOUSEKEEPING INSTITUTE; LAW; NUTRITION; ORGANIC FOOD; PURE FOOD AND DRUG ACT; TRANSPORTATION OF FOOD; WILEY, HARVEY.]

BIBLIOGRAPHY

Hilts, Peter J. *Protecting America's Health: The FDA, Business, and One Hundred Years of Regulation*. New York: Knopf, 2003.

ROBERT W. BROWER

Food and Nutrition Systems

The American food and nutrition system is a set of processes transforming raw materials into foods that are consumed to provide nutrients for health. Considering the whole system provides a broad perspective, viewing food chains and food webs within food contexts.

Food Chain

A food and nutrition chain is a sequence of stages flowing into each other. Food chains examine the full life cycle of foods, with upstream and downstream pathways.

Resource Inputs. Many resources are needed to produce foods. Biophysical inputs include seeds, animals, water, soil, energy, feed, fertilizer, and so on. Socioeconomic inputs include knowledge, money, effort, skills, and so on. Drought, erosion, economic depression, and disease epidemics may deprive food systems of essential resources.

Food Production. Production propagates plants and animals. Hunting and gathering has been largely supplanted by agriculture. Industrialization has led to the production of staple foods by large corporations, although small family farms continue to produce many foods.

Food Processing. Processing transforms crops and animals into foodstuffs and foods. Crude processing includes cleaning, sorting, and other simple modifications. Most foods are further processed by food manufacturing that mills, combines, heats, cools, preserves, and packages foods.

Food Distribution. Food distribution makes foodstuffs and foods available for consumer purchase. Most U.S. food is distributed through supermarkets and other types of markets or is sold by the food-service industry in restaurants and other outlets. Some people gather and exchange their own foods, or use emergency food distribution sources such as food pantries and soup kitchens.

Food Acquisition. Acquisition occurs as consumers procure foods at distribution outlets that transfer foods between the food industry and consumers. Acquisition may involve shopping for groceries, selecting a restaurant, or being given foods by family or friends.

Food Preparation. Preparation involves diverse cooking activities that include cleaning foodstuffs, combining ingredients, heating/cooling, and serving. Preparation follows formula of cuisines by combining ingredients, flavorings, cooking, and eating behavior appropriate for a particular food culture.

Food Consumption. Consumption occurs as individuals and families select and eat meals and snacks. Conventional meal patterns are changing as people skip meals, combine meals, or graze on snacks. Food ingestion begins the incorporation and use of nutrients in the body.

Digestion. Digestion begins with chewing to break up food and mix it with saliva. Swallowing moves food to the stomach, where digestive fluids chemically break down the food. Absorption selectively diffuses nutrients through the walls of the small intestine into the body. Excretion of feces and urine completes passage of food through the body.

Transport. Nutrient transport moves macronutrients (proteins, carbohydrates, fats, and alcohol) and micronutrients (vitamins and minerals) throughout the body by the circulatory system to sites where nutrients will be used or stored.

Metabolism. Metabolism occurs as each nutrient is used in physiological processes in the body. Nutrients produce energy, contribute to growth and repair, and prevent nutrition-related diseases. Both deficiencies and excesses of nutrient supplies and stores disrupt body functioning and can lead to disease.

Health Outputs. Health is an output of the food and nutrition system. Major causes of death in the United States are based partly on intake of foods containing adequate but not excessive levels of nutrients, including heart disease, stroke, diabetes, cancer, and liver disease. Population health is influenced by the way in which foods are produced, processed, distributed, acquired, prepared, and consumed.

Food Web

Food webs are interrelationships between individuals and groups involved with food and nutrition. Roles in food webs including farmers, grocers, cooks, food servers, dietitians, and many others.

The food web consolidates agriculture, food processing, food retailing, and food service. Small farms are being replaced by large agricultural corporations. Local food processors are integrating into global food corporations. Community food distributors are declining as national chains develop networks of supermarkets and hypermarkets. Independent restaurants are being replaced by restaurant chains and fast food franchises.

Workers in the U.S. food and nutrition system are increasingly specialized and isolated from each other. Distancing between food workers and consumers is also occurring. Food terms reflect differing interests across the food web: farmers produce crops, processors purchase commodities and manufacture products, grocers buy and sell merchandise, shoppers purchase foodstuffs, cooks gather ingredients and prepare dishes, consumers eat foods in meals, dietitians examine nutrient levels, and physicians treat diseases.

Food Contexts

Food contexts are environments within which the food and nutrition system operates. Contexts influence inputs into the system and receive outputs from the system. The

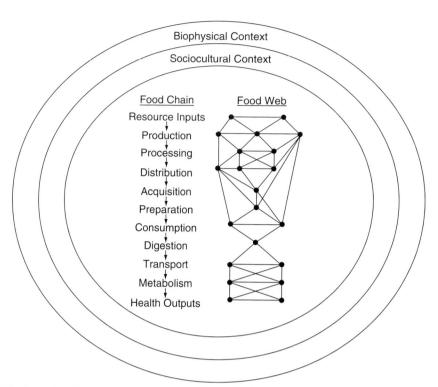

The food and nutrition system: food chains, food webs, and food contexts.

U.S. food and nutrition system has evolved from local "foodsheds" to a global system.

Sociocultural contexts include cultural, economic, political, and other social components of society that interact with the food and nutrition system. For example, economic systems offer markets for food products, establish prices for energy and other commodities used by the system, and establish interest rates for financing activities in the system. Similarly, laws and regulations influence how foods are grown, handled, served, and eaten.

Biophysical contexts include physical, biological, geological, and other material components of the world. Concerns exist about the ecological sustainability of the current energy-intensive U.S. food and nutrition system that relies on nonrenewable resources. Waste and by-product outputs occur at every stage of the system and must be disposed of, recycled, or reused as agricultural refuse, food processing by-products, food products that cannot be distributed, kitchen scraps, and human waste.

Conclusion

The food and nutrition system includes a wide scope of interrelated processes that link stages in the food chain from agriculture to health, integrate components of the food web across many food sectors, and embed the system in contexts such as the economy and the environment. The U.S. food and nutrition system is characterized by industrialized agricultural production linked with extensive food processing and widespread distribution to consumers who often do not cook for themselves and frequently eat away from home. This leads to high-fat and low-fiber

intake, which promote chronic diseases. Holistic thinking about the American food and nutrition system offers a broad perspective, identifies specific pathways, and reveals links between diverse aspects of agriculture, food, eating, nutrition, and medicine.

[**See also** COMMUNITY-SUPPORTED AGRICULTURE; CONAGRA; COOKING CONTAINERS; COOPERATIVES; DEPARTMENT OF AGRICULTURE, UNITED STATES; FOOD AND DRUG ADMINISTRATION; GROCERY STORES; HUNGER PROGRAMS; NORTH AMERICAN FREE TRADE AGREEMENT; ORGANIC FOOD; POLITICS OF FOOD; PURE FOOD AND DRUG ACT; RESTAURANTS; TRANSPORTATION OF FOOD.]

BIBLIOGRAPHY

Sobal, Jeffery. "Food System Globalization, Eating Transformations, and Nutrition Transitions." In *Food in Global History*, ed. R. Grew, 171–193. Boulder, CO: Westview, 1999.

Sobal, Jeffery, Laura K. Khan, and Carole Bisogni. "A Conceptual Model of the Food and Nutrition System." *Social Science and Medicine* 47 (1998): 853–863.

JEFFERY SOBAL

Food Festivals

Around the turn of the twentieth century, many of America's early harvest festivals were transformed into food festivals that celebrated pride in regional commercial crop production. Combined with an increase in commercial preservation and packaging and the growth of competitive marketing strategies, festivals celebrating local foods, grown or manufactured, evolved into promotional venues. Many such festivals are formally sponsored by trade organizations or manufacturers and thus serve as powerful advertising and marketing tools in an increasingly competitive global economy. Some food festivals serve to celebrate holidays or culinary traditions of the past, paying tribute to ethnic cultures and special dishes or to foodways, such as the collection of maple syrup in the spring or the making of apple butter in the fall, that are rapidly vanishing from modern America. Despite the commercial aspect of food festivals, a single strong link to the past is prevalent.

Every state in America hosts food festivals. The greatest number of such events is staged in California, followed by Texas and the Midwestern states, a pattern that mirrors demographics related to food production and harvesting. Local community groups, clubs, and religious organizations often oversee these events, and usually volunteers staff them. Other food-related festivals are held through the efforts of museums and historical societies. As they have grown and increased in popularity, food festivals are increasingly managed by professionals in concert with corporate sponsorship.

Festivals commonly feature food in several ways. Displays provide both education and promotional opportunities. Cooking competitions and demonstrations illustrate the diverse uses of various foods and ingredients. Tastings, formal meals, and snack vendors provide the opportunity for festival visitors to become familiar with new foods and dishes. Attendees can purchase food items from associated farmers' markets, auctions, and vendors. The eating contests that are often part of the festivities provide amusement.

Harvest and Promotional Festivals
A large percentage of American food festivals celebrate local crops or industries, and they serve as promotional opportunities with attendant economic benefits. Nearly every fruit and vegetable produced in the United States is showcased in at least one festival. Castroville, California, hosts an annual Artichoke Festival. The National Apple Harvest Festival in Arendtsville, Pennsylvania, promotes apples with heritage demonstrations of cider pressing and apple butter cooking. Cherry production in Traverse City, Michigan, is so important to the local economy that it is celebrated in an eight-day extravaganza called the National Cherry Festival. Rockland hosts the Maine Lobster Festival, where visitors feast on lobster steamed in the world's largest lobster cooker. The oyster is honored at St. Mary's County Oyster Festival in Leonardtown, Maryland. Among numerous maple syrup events is the Parke County Maple Syrup Festival in Rockville, Indiana. Visitors partake of sausage and pancakes drenched in maple syrup, and they can purchase syrup and other maple products. In West Virginia, the wild ramp, a form of leek, is a harbinger of spring.

Commercially manufactured foods are often celebrated at food festivals. Wisconsin is known for cheese and for bratwurst, a spicy pork sausage of German origin. In Little Chute, the Great Wisconsin Cheese Festival showcases the huge variety of quality cheeses produced in the state, and dedicated fans of cheesecake enjoy winning delicacies entered in the homemade cheesecake contest.

Heritage and Regional Celebrations
America's regional food specialties are showcased at food festivals throughout the country. The South, for example, is noted for corn production, which goes hand in hand with hog raising. The National Cornbread Festival in South Pittsburg, Tennessee, pays homage to "the bread of the South." Cornbread is popular not only because it is a local product but also because it can be baked quickly during the heat of summer. Turnip greens and barbecue, other southern favorites, are served as typical accompaniments to the corn bread. Grits, another corn product favored in the South, are celebrated at the World Grits Festival in St. George, South Carolina. Both commercially ground and stone-ground grits are served as side dishes with regional breakfast and lunch specialties. Hispanic heritage and cultural pride are the focus of events surrounding the International Tamale Festival in Indio, California. Nearly a half million tamales, a beloved part of Hispanic Christmas celebrations, are consumed by visitors. Vendors offer creations ranging from traditional tamales based on meat and savory blends of chilies to vegetarian and sweet dessert tamales. Perhaps the most famous dish of southern Louisiana is gumbo, created by Creole and Cajun cooks. At the annual Bridge City Gumbo Festival, both devotees and initiates enjoy more than two thousand gallons of the stewlike dish. Gumbo, based on a fat and flour mixture called a roux, contains celery, green pepper, onions, and various spices. It is enhanced with shellfish, sausage, fish, game, or poultry and thickened with okra or filé powder.

Fund-Raising, Communal Identity, and Holiday Festivals
Food festivals are often held for fund-raising designed to benefit various charitable organizations. Rhode Island's May Breakfasts provide an interesting example of this type of festival. The May Breakfast dates to 1867, when the Oak Lawn Baptist Church in Cranston initiated it. Held throughout the state during May, which is heritage month, the breakfasts are sponsored by religious and community groups, who serve traditional repasts that include Rhode Island's traditional johnnycake (always spelled "jonnycake" in South County), made from a variety of hard corn grown only in the region.

America's food festivals continue to grow in popularity. Like the National Buffalo Wing Festival in New York State, which commemorates the chicken wings that originated at the city's Anchor Bar, there is always something new to celebrate when it comes to food and fun. Each festival provides a sense of heritage and community in an increasingly fractured world.
[See also Ethnic Foods; Food Marketing; Fund-Raisers.]

BECKY MERCURI

Food History News

Food History News (*FHN*), first published in June 1989, is one of the longest-standing publications dealing with the subject of food history. With a small circulation, it has an influence far beyond its size, enjoying an eclectic readership consisting of food writers, historic cooks, military reenactors, chefs, academics, and food professionals of all sorts, as well as a substantial general readership.

The publication explores topics dealing with North American food history since the early seventeenth century. Topics have ranged from fairly esoteric discussions—for example, traditional uses of mutton or wild fowl—to those with a wider interest, such as food and health, gentility and refinement, and popular foods such as apples and doughnuts. *FHN* typically includes a section devoted to food in military history, another for announcements and reader queries, and an ongoing column dedicated to the history of a particular dish or ingredient, ranging from bran muffins to salt-rising bread, from chemical leavenings to sugar.

With the growing use of the Internet, *FHN* established a website, www.foodhistorynews.com, with a calendar of events, food history resources, a guide to products and services for food historians, and a searchable directory of international food and beverage museums. The weekly updated "Editor's Notebook" offers news about people and events, book reviews, and links to sites related to food history. *Food History News* is published four times a year.

SANDRA L. OLIVER

Food Marketing

Food marketing brings together the producer and the consumer. It is the chain of activities that brings food from "farm gate to plate." The marketing of even a single food product can be a complicated process involving many producers and companies. For example, fifty-six companies are involved in making one can of chicken noodle soup. These businesses include not only chicken and vegetable processors but also the companies that transport the ingredients and those who print labels and manufacture cans. The food marketing system is the largest direct and indirect nongovernment employer in the United States.

The Three Historical Phases of Food Marketing
There are three historical phases of food marketing: the fragmentation phase (before 1870–1880), the unification phase (1880–1950), and the segmentation phase (1950 and later). In the fragmentation phase, the United States was divided into numerous geographic fragments because transporting

Pumpkins. *These squashes' thick skins mean they can be stored over the winter, making them a favorite staple of the American pioneers. Pumpkin pie, a uniquely American dish, originates from those first early winters. Over 50 million pumpkin pies are baked in the U.S. each year, mostly during Thanksgiving.*

Clockwise from top: An American Diner. *Since its inception in 1872, the diner has evolved from a horse-drawn cart into a national institution.*

Nathan's Famous Inc. *Known for its raucous promotions for close to a century, Nathan's hot dog eating contests still take place every Fourth of July on Coney Island.*

Ice cream sign. *Originally reserved for the rich, democracy and the advent of the domestic freezer changed ice cream into a treat that anyone could lick for a nickel.*

Milkshake. *In the 1950s the soda fountain call for a milkshake was "shake one," modified by the flavor at the end. A strawberry milkshake was ordered by shouting "shake one in the hay."*

Popcorn. *The American Indians who domesticated maize were the first people to make popcorn, long before Columbus reached America. The invention of the steam powered popcorn wagon in 1885 transformed it into one of the United States' most beloved fair foods.*

MAMMOTH CAVE SPRINGS PURE COPPER WHISKEY.

CHASE & SANBORNS "SEAL BRAND" COFFEE. SERVED EXCLUSIVELY AT THE WORLD'S FAIR. FOR SALE BY OLIVER MOORE.

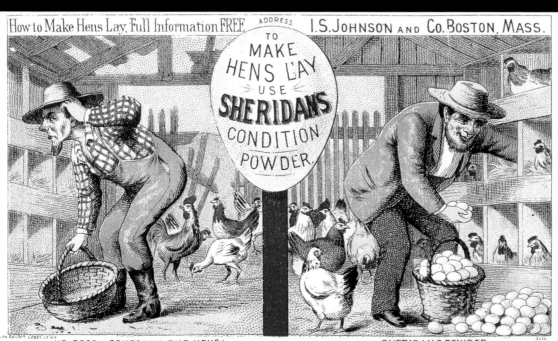

How to Make Hens Lay, Full Information FREE. ADDRESS I.S. JOHNSON AND Co. BOSTON, MASS.

TO MAKE HENS LAY USE SHERIDANS CONDITION POWDER.

NO EGGS? CONFOUND THE HENS!

AH? THE SHERIDANS POWDER DID IT!

Clockwise from top left:
Advertisement for Mammoth Cave Springs Whiskey. *Whiskeys specific to the U.S. include wheat and American blended whiskey.*

Honey Advertisement. *Even the earliest advertisements for sweets, such as this ad for honey, were directed at children.*

Sheridan's Powder Advertisement. *A popular powder that promised to encourage stubborn hens to lay, from the early 1900s.*

Coffee Advertisement. *Many companies successfully took advantage of the hype surrounding the 1939 World's Fair.*

Facing Page: Watermelon Advertisement. *As featured on the back cover of D.M. Ferry and Co.'s Seed Annual catalog, 1883.*

Lobster. Considered the specialty in many New England restaurants, lobster was once so plentiful that the refuse from lobster canneries along the Atlantic Coast was given to farmers as cheap fertilizer. Lobster has since been added to the list of species of seafood that need protection.

Clockwise from top: Preparing Dessert in the White House. *From Taft's banquets to Eisenhower's TV dinners, First Menus reflect changing tastes nationwide.*

Wedding Cake. *A highly decorated white cake became the norm for most American weddings by the early twentieth century.*

Turkey. *A vital protein source for American Indians and colonists alike, turkey remains a centerpiece on contemporary tables.*

Farmers' Markets. *The number of farmers' markets in the U.S. expanded from fewer than 100 in the 1960s to over 3,000 in 2002.*

food was expensive, leaving most production, distribution, and selling locally based. In the unification phase, distribution was made possible by railroads, coordination of sales forces was made possible by the telegraph and telephone, and product consistency was made possible by advances in manufacturing. This new distribution system was led by meat processors such as Armour and Swift in Midwestern cities and by companies such as Heinz, Quaker Oats, Campbell Soup, and Coca-Cola, which sold their brands nationally. Advertising in print media and direct marketing through demonstrations at stores and public venues were among the prime marketing tools. The initial Crisco campaign, in 1911, was an example. In the segmentation phase (1950 and later), radio and television advertising made it possible for a wider range of competing products to focus on different benefits and images and thus appeal to different demographic and psychographic markets. Distribution via the new national road system strengthened national brands.

Two Views of Food Marketing: The Production Focus and the Consumer Focus

There are two basic views of food marketing: production focus and consumer focus. The production-focused view is an institutional one that is primarily concerned with producing a food as efficiently as possible and transporting it so it can eventually be sold. In this perspective, "marketing" is basically a distribution activity.

In contrast to this production perspective, the consumer-focused view involves understanding what exactly consumers want and providing it to them in a form, in a message, and at a profitable price. Whereas a production focus is typically not flexible enough to anticipate consumer demands and interests, a consumer focus necessitates this skill.

The Food Marketing Mix and the Four Ps of Marketing

The four components of food marketing are often called the "four Ps" of the marketing mix because they relate to product, price, promotion, and place. One reason that food manufacturers receive the largest percentage of the retail food dollar is that they provide the most differentiating, value-added service. The money that manufacturers invest in developing, pricing, promotion, and placing their products helps differentiate a food product on the basis of both quality and brand-name recognition.

Product. In deciding what type of new food products a consumer would most prefer, a manufacturer can either try to develop a new food product or try to modify or extend an existing food. For example, a sweet, flavored yogurt drink would be a new product, but milk in a new flavor (such as chocolate strawberry) would be an extension of an existing product. There are three steps to both developing and extending: generate ideas, screen ideas

for feasibility, and test ideas for appeal. Only after these steps will a food product make it to national market. Of one hundred new food product ideas that are considered, only six make it to a supermarket shelf.

Price. In profitably pricing the food, the manufacturer must keep in mind that the retailer takes approximately 50 percent of the price of a product. A frozen food sold in a retail store for $4.50 generates an income of $2.25 for the manufacturer. This money has to pay for the cost of producing, packaging, shipping, storing, and selling the product.

Promotion. Promoting a food to consumers is done out of store, in store, and on package. Advertisements on television and in magazines are attempts to persuade consumers to think favorably about a product, so that they go to the store to purchase the product. In addition to advertising, promotions can also include Sunday newspaper ads that offer coupons such as cents-off and buy-one-get-one-free offers.

Place. Place refers to the distribution and warehousing efforts necessary to move a food from the manufacturer to a location where a consumer can buy it. It can also relate to the place within a store that it is located.

Segmenting Consumers on the Basis of Taste and Preference

The third historical phase of food marketing was built on the notion of market segmentation. This means that consumers have different tastes and different preferences. Many groups of people have different views and different preferences for any given food—lamb, for example. The vegetarian segment does not eat lamb, nor does the segment of meat eaters who do not like the odor of lamb. Certain ethnic segments eat lamb only in stews and in combination with other foods; other segments eat it only on special holidays. Another segment is those who enjoy fine dining and eat only young lamb that is tender and served in restaurants.

To believe that all lamb is the same and should be marketed in a generic or one-size-fits-all manner would miss many of the marketing opportunities within these segments. Different marketing efforts should be targeted at different segments. The ethnic segment could be targeted through butcher shop promotions. Those preparing holiday dinners could be reminded of lamb through in-store ads, and those who do not eat lamb might be reintroduced to it with a new version that has been produced in a manner that reduces the characteristic smell. Aficionados of fine dining would be targeted by efforts in the distribution chain to promote lamb to finer restaurants.

The food marketing system in the United States is an amazingly flexible one. Consumer focus helps marketers anticipate the demands of consumers, and production focus helps them respond to changes in the market. The result is a system that meets the ever-changing demands of consumers.

Atkins low-carbohydrate breakfast and granola bars at a grocery store in Burbank, California.

[See also ADVERTISING; ADVERTISING COOKBOOKLETS AND RECIPES; COOKING CONTAINERS; COMMUNITY-SUPPORTED AGRICULTURE; DAIRY INDUSTRY; FARMERS' MARKETS; GROCERY STORES; MILK PACKAGING; PACKAGING; TRANSPORTATION OF FOOD.]

BIBLIOGRAPHY

Belonax, Joseph J. *Food Marketing.* Boston: Pearson Custom, 1999.

Tedlow, Richard S. *New and Improved: The Story of Mass Marketing in America.* New York: Basic Books, 1990.

Wansink, Brian. *Marketing Nutrition: Soy Functional Foods, Biotechnology, and Obesity.* Champaign: University of Illinois Press, 2005.

Wansink, Brian. *Mindless Eating.* New York: Bantam Dell, 2006.

BRIAN WANSINK

Food Processors

When America's first food processor was unveiled at the national housewares exposition in Chicago in January 1973, it barely caused a ripple. With a blocky base about half the size of a shoe box, a broad clear plastic work bowl, and a fierce S-shaped blade some six inches across, the appliance was dismissed as an oversized, overpriced electric blender, even though it came with slicing and shredding disks. But Carl G. Sontheimer, the man behind the machine, was undaunted. A retired electronics engineer from Greenwich, Connecticut, and an accomplished hobby cook, Sontheimer knew that his food processor could revolutionize the way America cooked.

In 1971, Sontheimer and his wife, Shirley, had seen a small, powerful multipurpose machine put through its paces at a housewares show in Paris. Called Le Magimix, this was a home version of Le Robot-Coupe, the heavy-duty food processor that French chefs found indispensable for chopping, slicing, shredding, and puréeing—for making everything from flaky puff pastry to feathery fish dumplings. The Sontheimers were so impressed with Le Magimix that Carl tracked down its inventor, Pierre Verdun, who had also created Le Rebot-Coupe. Obtaining distribution rights for Le Magimix, Sontheimer bought a dozen of the machines and shipped them home. In his garage workshop, Sontheimer took the machines apart, analyzed them, and put them back together. Then he and his wife kitchen-tested them. Sontheimer reconfigured the slicing and shredding disks, improved the torque, added safety features, streamlined the overall design, and gave it a new name: Cuisinart.

After the disappointing Chicago debut of the Cuisinart, Sontheimer contacted American's principal food writers and cookbook authors, gave each of them a personal demonstration, and quickly proved his point: The food processor was a supremely versatile machine that could spare the home cook endless tedium. It could shortcut the preparation of complicated classics and even speed the making of coleslaw and hash browns.

Soon the Cuisinart was being praised on television and in print. It was the miracle worker every cook had to have. In no time, nearly every appliance manufacturer introduced its own food processor. The exception was KitchenAid, whose standing electric mixers had long been the standard by which all others were judged. The company's attitude was wait and see. And what it saw was that few of the processors rushed to market could match the Cuisinart for stamina, dependability, and versatility. Within a few years, most of them had disappeared.

Sontheimer continued to improve the Cuisinart throughout the 1970s and 1980s. Pulse buttons were added, and work bowls grew larger as did their feed tubes, making it possible to slice entire oranges and tomatoes. Accessories proliferated, including thick and thin slicing disks, coarse and fine shredding disks, french fry cutters, citrus reamers, egg whips, and pasta makers.

In 1988, Sontheimer sold Cuisinart to a group of investors who the next year sold it to the Conair Corporation, of Stamford, Connecticut, a major manufacturer of household appliances. In 1994, KitchenAid at long last launched its own line of food processors—sleek machines in a range of sizes that had touch-pad controls and plenty of prowess; some models had miniature bowl and blade inserts, most in designer colors. In response to the competition from KitchenAid, Cuisinart introduced a new generation of food processors—streamlined machines with quick-to-clean keypad switches and gentle dough modes for kneading yeast breads. Carl Sontheimer did not live to see the new Cuisinarts. He died in 1998 at the age of eighty-three, but by then the "white elephant" he had introduced at the Chicago housewares show in 1973 had revolutionized the way America cooked.

[See also BLENDERS; CHOPPING KNIVES AND FOOD CHOPPERS; GRATERS; KITCHENS.]

BIBLIOGRAPHY

Anderson, Jean. *Process This! New Recipes for the New Generation of Food Processors Plus Dozens of Time-Saving Tips.* New York: William Morrow, 2002.

JEAN ANDERSON

Food Safes, *see Cupboards and Food Safes*

Food Safety, *see Chemical Additives; Department of Agriculture, United States*

Food Stamps

The food stamp program is a federal initiative aimed at alleviating hunger and food insecurity in the United States. A version of the program first operated between 1939 and 1943, when the U.S. Secretary of Agriculture was authorized to promote domestic consumption of foods as a way to reduce surplus agricultural commodities. The current program was authorized in 1959 and began as a pilot project in 1961 under the administration of President John F. Kennedy. At the urging of President Lyndon Johnson, Congress made food stamps a permanent federal program in 1964, though states and counties were permitted to decide how they would participate. By the early 1970s Congress established uniform eligibility requirements, and by 1975 all states and counties took part in the program.

Food stamps provide direct support to low-income people for the purchase of foods in a low-cost diet developed by the U.S. Department of Agriculture (USDA). Recipients may purchase breads, cereals, dairy products, meat, fish, poultry, fruits, and vegetables, among other foods, but are prohibited from using the stamps to purchase such items as alcohol, tobacco products, other nonfood goods, and ready-to-eat foods intended to be consumed in a store. Food stamps traditionally were issued as denominated paper coupons; the program has added electronic benefit transfers, which move funds from the recipient's federal account to that of the retailer. At present, 85 percent of food stamp benefits are issued by this means.

Participation in the food stamp program peaked in March 1994 at nearly 28 million people, approximately 10 percent of the U.S. population. Since then, it has declined significantly, owing to welfare reform efforts of 1996, which limited the number of eligible people; placed time limits on benefits for unemployed, able-bodied, childless adults; and required all healthy, fit adults to meet certain work requirements. Eligibility for most legal immigrants also was eliminated, but then the Farm Bill of 2002 restored many of those benefits.

An enduring criticism of the program is that many eligible low income people do not participate for a variety of reasons, such as stigma and shame associated with participation, lack of knowledge about eligibility, and difficulty in meeting state administrative requirements for signing up for the program. Research suggests that although the food stamp program has not eliminated hunger in America, it has, on the whole, benefited low-income households by increasing the availability of nutritional foods and raising the level of intake of certain nutrients within household diets. Critics of this research, however, have pointed out that distribution patterns among households and differential food-purchasing power based on geography contribute to varied results. Other critics have asserted that food stamps are to blame, in part, for the growing obesity epidemic among the poor, because individual food purchases are not regulated by nutritional content.

The program has been the subject of long-standing complaints about fraud and abuse. The Government Accounting Office, for example, determined that recipient fraud between 1988 and 1993 totaled nearly $2 billion. Such fraud has undercut public support for the food stamp program and left it politically vulnerable to numerous efforts throughout its history to tighten eligibility, cut back the number of participants, and decrease the size of the program's budget. [See also DEPARTMENT OF AGRICULTURE, UNITED STATES; HUNGER PROGRAMS.]

BIBLIOGRAPHY

Berry, Jeffrey M. *Feeding Hungry People: Rulemaking in the Food Stamp Program.* New Brunswick, NJ: Rutgers University Press, 1984.

Eisinger, Peter K. *Toward an End to Hunger in America.* Washington, DC: Brookings Institution Press, 1998.

Ohls, James C., and Harold Beebout. *The Food Stamp Program: Design Tradeoffs, Policy, and Impacts.* Washington, DC: Urban Institute Press, 1993.

BARRETT P. BRENTON AND
KEVIN T. MCINTYRE

Foodways

Foodways is a noun that is used to denote general food habits of a familial, regional, cultural, or ethnic group. Foodways refers to overall patterns of food use, including methods of procurement, preparation, presentation, and consumption. More specifically, the term refers to tangible and intangible—and often taken-for-granted—forces that shape how people prepare and serve food, including especially attitudes, customs, traditions, and ritualistic protocol. Foodways connotes actual foodstuffs as well as, perhaps more important, the various historic, symbolic, political, social, religious, economic, and cultural factors that influence food choice and use.

The term is widely used by social scientists and nutritionists. Historically, nutritionists and dietitians tended to focus on foodways as a group's dietetic system, with less regard for sociocultural forces that influence patterns of consumption. Until recently, it was primarily anthropologists and folklorists who studied foodways as part of the larger system of culture. With the emergence of the interdisciplinary fields of food studies and food history, foodways increasingly are recognized as worthy of focused study in and of themselves as a fundamental component of the cultural systems within which they are practiced, and as markers of identity.

The term's origins are unclear. Some scholars erroneously attribute "foodways" to the American folklorist Don Yoder, who embraced the term in the 1970s to replace the term "folk cookery." Use of "foodways," however, predates the 1970s, and Yoder recognized that; he cited a 1961 publication by John Honigman that considered the foodways of a native Canadian population. Honigman's work, which first appeared in 1948, likely drew on the 1941 work of another anthropologist, John William Bennett, whose treatise concerned subsistence economy and foodways, or general food habits of a population.

In the 1940s, the term "foodways" appeared in government documents and was used by government officials under the auspices of the National Nutritional Conference for Defense (1941), which was concerned with modifying American patterns of food consumption. As a factor in national defense, the term was used synonymously with "food habits."

Slightly modified, the word takes on biological significance. Foodway can refer to the physical location in the back of the mouth where food goes as it is swallowed. Within the medical and biological sciences, "foodway" has, since at least 1904 when the term appeared in an American medical journal, referred to part of the alimentary canal.

Especially when used by historians and social scientists, the term most often is used with a modifier—for example, American foodways, regional foodways, or southern foodways—thus lending a bit more specificity to a very broad and important concept. The term's breadth and ambiguity enhance its appeal among those interested in talking about, studying, documenting, and possibly modifying socioculturally informed patterns of food use.

PAULINE ADEMA

Forks, see Silverware

Fortune Cookies

Fortune cookies, thought to be Chinese, actually were born in America. Their soft circles of baked dough are folded in half over a paper message, usually a fortune. American as apple pie, they were popularized in Chinese restaurants after World War II, and have made their way around the world.

Chinese often associate a special food with a particular holiday or event. There was a food used for carrying messages during the fourteenth-century Moon Festival. Its mes-

sage, inserted in Moon Cakes, had the intent of overthrowing Mongol invaders. Time and place for a proposed uprising was in many cakes distributed by a Taoist priest and others. However, the fortune cookie is in no way related to this famous uprising nor to any moon cake.

The origin of the fortune cookie is elusive, perhaps shared, born in California, and related to Asian immigrants. A Japanese landscape architect, Sumiharu Hagiwara-Nagata, is said to have introduced them in 1914 at a garden he designed in San Francisco to accompany tea. That garden is now the Golden Gate Park Japanese Tea Garden. Although Sumiharu believed that he was the first to make them, he did give credit to the Chinese for successful marketing.

The baker David Jung is said to have invented fortune cookies in Los Angeles some time around 1918. Also a preacher, he handed them out to the poor and homeless containing not fortunes but biblical messages of hope and encouragement. Later, Jung started the Hong Kong Noodle Company and continued to produce them. In the early 1930s, the first to make them on the East Coast was William T. Leong and his Key Fortune Cookie Company.

Each of these manufacturers hand-folded their fortune cookies, often with the help of chopsticks. In the late 1960s, San Franciscan Edward Louie, owner of the Lotus Fortune Cookie Company, invented a machine to fold them.

In the late 1970s, someone decided that the fortune cookie needed its own day. Like many things about the fortune cookie, year, month, and day are shrouded in mystery. Many say the date was September 13, others place the date some time between April and September. There was a mock court case to determine the California city of origin; San Francisco won. No one contested or confirmed the date for fortune cookie celebrations.

Companies on both coasts and in between and some in other countries now make these treats of flour, sugar, and flavoring. Wonton Food Inc., using the trade name Golden Bowl, is the world's largest manufacturer, making more than 4 million a day. With one exception, all of their manufacturing lines are automated. The automated line makes fortune cookies with special messages for occasions such as weddings and birthdays. Billy Wilder's 1966 movie *The Fortune Cookie* distributed fifteen thousand with the message, "There's a marvelous picture in your future."

The fortune in each cookie can be English or bilingual, depending on the country of sale. Many have smiley faces, jokes, advice, lottery numbers, and fortunes on their paper strips. According to the Powerball Lottery Commission, in 2005 more than a hundred winners in several states used numbers from those printed on Golden Bowl fortune cookies.

Wonton Food Inc. which began as the Wonton Noodle Company, changed its name in the 1980s. In 1993 they began producing fortune cookies in a country that never knew them, China. They learned that these cookies are not as popular in China as in the United States.

[**See also** CHINESE AMERICAN FOOD.]

JACQUELINE M. NEWMAN

Fourth of July

The Continental Congress of the United States declared independence from England in its convention in Philadelphia on July 4, 1776. At first, celebrations were scattered and sporadic but, as years passed, the tradition of parades, picnics, and pyrotechnics was born and thrived.

There are no official national holidays in the United States. Holidays are left to the states and municipalities to decree and observe. There is, therefore, no federally designated or mandated Fourth of July holiday for all Americans but only many, many local events. In 1870 Congress, which can only decree the days that its offices close, established the Fourth of July as a holiday, but without pay, for federal employees and the District of Columbia. In 1938 Congress amended it to be a holiday with pay. Congress has since modified the law further in consideration of changing times.

The First Fourths

Picnics or, at least, outdoor activities were natural events, given the midsummer weather, although the grand public displays with lengthy parades and large celebrations had to wait for the war with the British to be over and the country to grow. Some of the first organized celebrations occurred at the public readings of the Declaration of Independence. The earliest of these were held in Philadelphia, followed shortly by Williamsburg, Virginia; Trenton, New Jersey; and New York, where a statue of King George III of England (1738-1820) was torn down to be recast into bullets. In places across the nation where the Declaration was publicly read, people shouted their huzzas, fired their muskets, and pulled down British flags and other emblems.

As early as 1777, celebrations were occasionally raucous events. It became customary within a few years to fire thirteen cannonades to commemorate the number of colonies and drink thirteen toasts. In Philadelphia, leaders put together an extravagant event for Congress and guests to mark the first year. A newspaper reported that in attendance were "President and Supreme Executive Council, and Speaker of the Assembly of this State, the General Officers and Colonels of the army, and strangers of eminence, and the members of the several Continental Boards in town." The day included the ringing of bells, crowds that cheered the parades, music and fireworks, and a dinner accompanied by

A rug from Shelburne, Vermont, commemorates Independence Day.

more music and the drinking of many toasts, all while the new nation's colors dressed up armed ships and galleys in the harbor.

Food was always an integral part of the celebration. Early dinners were held in taverns, coffeehouses, public buildings, schools, and homes, and the meals provided opportunities for socializing and neighborliness in the largely rural nation. These festivities became rather large-scale events in just a few years, and many were held outdoors in parks and other areas where there were trees for shelter and springs for water. They often drew hundreds of people and became increasingly more sumptuous as the eighteenth century ended and the nineteenth began. Menus might include several meats (usually beef, pork, mutton, and game), poultry (including chickens, turkeys, pheasant, and other birds), vegetables and fruit in season, with a wide selection of desserts including cakes, pies, cobblers, and other baked goods. The events grew so large that tickets were frequently necessary so that the providers would know how much food to prepare and so that the size of the venue could be established and controlled.

As urban environments grew and became more settled, parks were created and were often the places where the people could assemble for the day's observances. Vendors set up booths and sitting areas in which they sold food and drink. According to newspaper accounts, in 1824, in what would later become New York's Central Park, some of the booths sold "baked beans, roast pig and punch, custards and clam soup" (*New York Daily Advertiser*, July 5, 1824, p. 2).

In Smithfield, Virginia, in 1855, the *Daily Southern Argus* reported the city's efforts, beginning the day before, to prepare all that was necessary for a large celebratory feast.

> Tuesday was a great "preparation day" in Smithfield, for the Democratic jubilee and banner presentation was to take place on Wednesday. Chickens and ducks were decapitated by the hundred; fat pigs, lambs and calves, were slaughtered by the dozen, [sic] and a number of busy cooks were engaged in preparing immense bacon hams, and large joints and sides of fresh meat, as well

as untold quantities of pies, puddings and cakes for the long tables that were spread for the numerous guests expected from Norfolk, Portsmouth, and elsewhere on the glorious Fourth.

As the nation expanded and moved westward, the celebrations continued with local, seasonal foods and celebrations suited to the setting. In Sacramento, California, the first Fourth of July celebration was held in 1849. During the Civil War and its aftermath celebrations were more subdued, generally, but that changed with the centennial in 1876 when there were many very large events with strong political elements. For the bicentennial, in 1976, the celebration featured the usual sorts of public events with an added layer of spectacular extras like a sixty-nine-thousand-pound birthday cake in Baltimore, while in Florida, 7,241 people became naturalized American citizens simultaneously, the largest single group in American history to that date to do so.

The celebrations have remained the midsummer holiday for all Americans, with picnics, barbecues, and fireworks as the essential ingredients. Gatherings in parks with parades, entertainment, fairground amusements, and kiddie rides, which are matched with a large selection of foods to choose from, remain part of the culture of most small towns across the United States.

Because of the shift toward urban and suburban growth, family and neighborhood gatherings are more frequent than in the past. People live in denser settlements than when the United States was a farming nation, and it has become easier to socialize with neighbors. The greater ethnic diversity of the American public ensures that new foods continue to arrive on the holiday table. Colonial Americans were largely limited to fresh, seasonal foods, but food choices have evolved with technology, and options have increased greatly. Well over two centuries have passed since the first Fourth of July, and although some of the ingredients have changed, the tradition of celebrating remains.

[**See also** BARBECUE; ICE CREAMS AND ICES; PICNICS; WATERMELON.]

BIBLIOGRAPHY

Heintze, James R., ed. and comp. *Fourth of July Celebrations Database*. http://gurukul.american.edu/heintze/fourth.htm. American University. Washington, DC.

Travers, Len. *Celebrating the Fourth: Independence Day and the Rites of Nationalism in the Early Republic*. Amherst: University of Massachusetts Press, 1997.

BOB PASTORIO

Fowl, *see Poultry and Foul*

Franchising

The system of franchising began in the United States during the mid-nineteenth century, when get-rich quick schemes abounded. The concept started with manufacturers who wanted to expand retail operations without spending their own capital, and franchisees who want to start their own business without risking everything on a new idea.

The American beverage industry began to franchise during the early twentieth century. The Coca-Cola Company began franchising bottlers in 1899. By 1921, there were more than two thousand bottlers throughout the nation. A&W Root Beer franchised its first outlet in 1924. It sold territorial franchises, in which franchisees were given a vast territory, such as a major city, a state, or a group of states. They then could sell franchises to others in a pyramid scheme. While A&W root beer quickly achieved national prominence, the system of territorial franchises had serious problems other than the image problem described above. One A&W franchisee was J. Willard Marriott, who bought the franchise for Washington, DC., in 1927. He went on to create one of America's largest hotel chains, Marriott Corporation, which later created the franchise fast food chain Roy Rogers.

In 1925, Howard Johnson bought a drugstore with a soda fountain. He invented a range of twenty-eight ice cream flavors and began selling them at roadside stands, which proved very popular during the summer. In 1935, he opened his first roadside coffee shop; within six years, there were 150 franchises. Howard Johnson's coffee shops had similar architecture and an immediately identifiable orange roof. The company retained 50 percent control of each new franchise, and Johnson required franchisees to buy exclusively from him. This maintained the quality of the food, which was crucial for the success of the chain. During the 1950s, the company expanded to include motels.

Following World War II, franchising took off, fueled in part by former soldiers returning from the war who were looking for investment opportunities. The fast food establishments that emerged during the 1950s were largely dependent on franchising. Franchises catered to the rapidly growing suburbs, and they spread to every small town in America and subsequently to almost every country in the world. Dairy Queen was one of the earliest success stories: Harry Axene had begun franchising soft-serve ice cream parlors after World War II; by the time he left the company in 1948, there were twenty-five hundred outlets. Dunkin' Donuts, Baskin-Robbins, Chicken Delight, Burger King, Jack in the Box, and Kentucky Fried Chicken all began franchising in the early 1950s.

Richard and Maurice McDonald began franchising McDonald's in 1952. They advertised in national restaurant trade magazines and quickly acquired twenty-one franchisees, mainly in Southern California. Ray Kroc saw the advertisements, visited the McDonald brothers, and was impressed with what he saw. In 1954, he signed an agreement to franchise the operation nationally. In 1955, Kroc sold his first franchise to himself, and opened an outlet in Des Plaines, Illinois. Kroc also sold some franchises to members of his country club, but he quickly concluded that he needed a different type of franchisee—not investors, but people who wanted to operate their own restaurants. McDonald's general avoidance of territorial franchises—arrangements that relinquished control over large geographic areas—was a reason for its early success.

At the time, other chains demanded large franchise fees and sold off rights to entire territories. They made money by selling supplies directly to their franchisees. Kroc kept the initial franchise fee at a very low $950. Kroc's business partner, Harry J. Sonneborn, who had developed his franchising expertise as a Tastee-Freez executive, created the mechanism for financial control of franchisees. McDonald's purchased or leased the property for most of its American franchisees. The property was then leased to franchisees at a hefty profit. If franchisees refused to obey the franchise contract, McDonald's could evict them. By 1969, a McDonald's franchise cost $53,000. Other fast food restaurants followed a similar path: Burger King and Hardee's grew quickly in their early years as a result of franchising.

Franchising got a big boost when federal loans became available from the Small Business Administration. This made it possible for potential franchisees to launch their business with federal funds. Between 1967 and 1979, the Small Business Administration guaranteed eighteen thousand franchise loans, 10 percent of which ended in default.

Today, fast food is considered a mature business in the United States: the American market is pretty well saturated. Franchisers have placed new franchises closer to existing ones, which franchisees call encroachment. Their sales and profits decline when new franchises are opened nearby. Another problem relates to product sourcing, whereby franchisees are required to purchase products only from the franchiser or designated suppliers, often at inflated prices.

The legal basis for franchising has emerged over the past century and it remains subject to judicial reinterpretation. Many unscrupulous promoters were attracted to restaurant franchising; numerous franchise schemes were attempted, and many verged on fraud. One serious abuse was pyramiding of territorial licenses, in which a licensee holding franchise for a broad geographical area sublicensed rights to others, who in turn sold them to others. All along, the licensors had no real intention of operationally supporting franchisees; they just wanted the initial fees. Congress stepped in during the 1960s and began passing legislation to regulate franchising. The Federal Trade Commission requires that franchisers provide lengthy disclosure statements for franchisees. Contracts often require franchisees to waive legal rights to file complaints. Once the contract is signed, franchisees are on their own. Franchisees must obey corporate directives, whether or not they were spelled out in the contract.

[See also Fast Food.]

BIBLIOGRAPHY

Birkeland, Peter M. *Franchising Dreams: The Lure of Entrepreneurship in America*. Chicago: University of Chicago Press, 2002.

Dicke, Thomas S. *Franchising in America: The Development of a Business Method, 1840–1980*. Chapel Hill: University of North Carolina Press, 1992.

Luxenberg, Stan. *Roadside Empires: How the Chains Franchised America*. New York: Viking, 1985.

ANDREW F. SMITH

Frappes

A frappe is what Bostonians call a thick blend of ice cream, milk, and flavorings—known more commonly as a milkshake. The word comes from the French verb *frapper*, which means to shake. A frosted is another name for a milkshake, as is a velvet. Around the turn of the twentieth century, when ice was a new commodity, a frosted was soda with ice in it, according to Ed Marks of Lititz, Pennsylvania, founder of the Ice Screamers, a national group devoted to ice cream memorabilia. Rhode Islanders call their version of the milkshake a cabinet. Some other New Englanders use "frappe," but the word seems to be primarily a Boston locution. In Boston, "milkshake" means a glass of milk with flavorings, shaken until frothy and containing no ice cream. This was the original definition of a milkshake. In the 1880s and 1890s, ice cream was added only occasionally. Milkshakes containing ice cream became more common around 1915.

To make things extra confusing, the term "frappé," with the accent mark, refers to a frozen slush made without dairy products. Fannie Farmer's 1896 *Boston Cooking-School Cookbook* defined a frappé as "water ice frozen to a consistency of mush." A recipe for clam frappé called for twenty clams to be steamed open, then the pot liquor cooled and frozen to a mush. Farmer's recipe for café frappé called for a beaten egg white, coffee, water, and sugar. It was frozen and served with whipped cream in special frappé glasses. Even though Farmer was based in Boston, the glossary of frozen desserts in her cookbook did not define the frappe as a milkshake. Soda fountain guides from the 1910s described frappes as half-frozen sherbets or well-shaken ice cream sodas. Some frappes from this era had nicknames, including ping-pong, buffalo, flinch, and delmonico. It is unclear when the concept of a frappe as a milkshake came into popular use, but this information suggests it was after 1920.

In the Boston area in the early twenty-first century, ice cream parlor frappes usually contain at least equal proportions of milk and ice cream, plus flavorings such as chocolate or coffee syrup. They can sometimes be ordered extra thick. When ice cream parlors were most popular, frappes were prepared in stainless steel containers in commercial mixers. Anything that could not fit into one tall glass was poured into a second glass or left on the side for the customer to use for a refill. In the early twenty-first century, a frappe is often served in a paper cup with a straw, although the thick consistency sometimes makes a spoon more suitable.

Milkshakes originated nationally in the soda fountains of the 1880s and 1890s. One early recipe called for sweetened and flavored milk, carbonated water, and a raw egg, shaken by a special machine. In the early twentieth century, milkshakes became standard soda fountain fare, along with sundaes and ice cream sodas.

[See also Egg Cream; Ice Cream Sodas; Ice Creams and Ices; Milkshakes, Malts, and Floats; Soda Fountains.]

BIBLIOGRAPHY

California Culinary Academy. *Ice Cream and Frozen Desserts*, p. 36. San Ramon, CA: Ortho, 1988.

Damerow, Gail. *Ice Cream! The Whole Scoop*. Lakewood, CO: Glenbridge, 1996.

Funderburg, Anne Cooper. *Chocolate, Strawberry, and Vanilla*. Bowling Green, OH: Bowling Green State University Popular Press, 1995.

Marks, Ed. "Don't Shake the Cabinet or You'll Spill the Frappe." *The Scoop*, Winter 1998.

CLARA SILVERSTEIN

Freeze-Drying

Freeze-drying, also known as lyophilization, is a method of food preservation by which frozen items are dehydrated in a vacuum. During this process, foods are placed in a pressure chamber and undergo sublimation, whereby ice converts directly from a solid to a gaseous state. Moisture quickly escapes as vapor, and the dried items are left with a porous texture. Unlike many other drying approaches, freeze-drying allows the final product to largely retain its shape, size, flavor, and nutritional makeup.

The principles behind freeze-drying have been applied for centuries. The ancient Incas used a form of this preservation technique by storing their food in the heights of the Andes mountains. There the temperature, low pressure, and high altitude effectively freeze-dried the food supplies. It was not until World War II that the process became industrialized, when it was developed to preserve blood plasma for the war effort. In the 1950s through 1970s, the Army Natick Labs, in Natick, Massachusetts (now called the U.S. Army Natick Soldier Center), was instrumental in developing and refining the process of freeze-drying food products.

Because they rehydrate easily and have an extended shelf life, freeze-dried products are well suited for packaged goods, from liquids such as coffee and juices to dried fruit in cereals and components of soup mixes. The National Aeronautics and Space Administration has used freeze-drying in the development of foods for the U.S. space program.

[See also Cooking Containers; Space Food.]

BIBLIOGRAPHY

Francis, F. J. *Encyclopedia of Food Science and Technology*. New York: Wiley, 2000.

Potter, Norman N. *Food Science*. Westport, CT: AVI, 1986.

REBECCA FREEDMAN

Freezers and Freezing

Freezing slows bacterial growth and reduces spoilage. Humankind has understood for millennia that freezing preserves food, but only in the past few centuries has this process come under human control. In colonial times, ice was used to cool cellars, but ice cooling had many limitations. Ice was bulky and required expensive transportation, large insulated storage facilities, and a massive distribution system. When the ice melted, the moisture frequently promoted the growth of mold and bacteria. Equally important was that ice was effective only when it was in direct contact with food.

By the 1880s, cooling systems based on absorption and condensation revolutionized the industry. It encouraged the vast expansion of trade in frozen food, for it allowed slaughtering and butchering of livestock close to where it was raised. The frozen meat then was shipped to cities hundreds of miles away. Because this system required large amounts of capital, the livestock industry became centralized, and major meatpackers, such as Swift and Armour, emerged during this period.

Advantages and Disadvantages

The development of frozen foods offered a variety of advantages. It encouraged regional specialization. Fruits and vegetables could be grown in the best climate and soil and then frozen and shipped great distances. Because frozen foods were stored, farmers and distributors could sell their products when they could obtain the highest prices. For consumers, freezing expanded year-round food choices because the availability of produce was no longer limited to its growing season. Freezing of food tended to stabilize prices. Because waste at the point of origin was eliminated, use of frozen food saved on transportation and storage. Frozen foods were particularly useful for restaurants. A small kitchen could supply a diverse demand, and restaurant chains could centralize their cooking, thereby lowering costs.

The limitations of frozen foods were that they required expensive freezing plants, special packaging, transportation, warehouses, and retail stores. Frozen food companies also had to educate the public about their products, because there was extensive opposition to frozen food. Many people did not like the taste or smell of thawed food; and still others complained about the expense. There was some justification for these complaints during the years when the process of freezing was in its infancy. Some companies froze inferior-quality food because it was impossible for consumers to tell the difference between good and bad food at the point of sale. Some retailers thawed or refroze foods before sale, thus speeding deterioration. Experimentation on frozen food and made recommendations on matters such as the rapidity with which foods needed to be frozen, methods of freezing, storage temperature, dehydration, and the length of time that frozen foods could be held without spoilage.

Package design was also important both to prevent dehydration during storage and to attract consumers. Clarence Birdseye—perhaps the best-known name in the industry—began quick-freezing food in 1923. His major contribution was not the process of freezing but the invention of moisture-proof packaging, which allowed foods to be frozen faster and kept them from disintegrating when thawed. Birdseye sold his company to General Foods. Under the brand name Birds Eye, General Foods invested the capital necessary to promote and market frozen food. Other companies began to compete, but sales were insignificant until the late 1930s, largely because of the Depression and the unwillingness of grocery stores to invest one thousand dollars for a freezer that held relatively little product.

Electric Refrigerators and Freezers

Electric refrigerators had been marketed since the 1890s, but none was successful until the Guardian Frigerator Company manufactured the Frigidaire in 1916. The company was purchased by General Motors Corporation, which began to mass-produce refrigerators. The small freezer section of the Frigidaire held ice trays and had room for little else. The size of the freezer section of refrigerators steadily increased as commercial frozen foods became common.

Stand-alone freezers were marketed during the 1920s, but they were beyond the reach of most Americans. After World War II, home freezers became more common as the price declined and the number of frozen foods available in grocery stores grew. During the 1950s, freezers became common in American homes. At the same time, most grocery stores had large self-service freezers, which offered consumers convenient access to everything from frozen peas to ice cream.

Frozen Food

Before World War II the main frozen foods were peas, beans, corn, spinach, berries, cherries, apples, and peaches. After the war an avalanche of new frozen foods hit the market, including Sara Lee cakes, Quaker Oats waffles, Swanson chicken potpies, and Birds Eye fish sticks. The most successful of all postwar frozen foods was orange juice, which had first been marketed unsuccessfully during the 1930s. By the early 1950s, orange juice accounted for 20 percent of the frozen food market. As the volume of sales of frozen foods increased, the price declined. A landmark in frozen food history was the TV dinner, first produced by Swanson in 1953.

Microwaves and Frozen Food

The wedding of microwaves and frozen food was the next major leap forward. The microwave oven made it possible for frozen foods to be cooked in minutes, a particularly useful feature in restaurants. At first the market was not big enough to encourage food processors to cater to the needs of microwave oven users. This situation had changed by the 1970s, when more than 10 percent of all American homes had microwave ovens.

The frozen food industry has continued to grow. As of 2001, 26.6 billion dollars worth of frozen food products were sold to consumers, and an additional $40 billion were sold to restaurants, cafeterias, hospitals, schools, and other outlets.

[See also ADVERTISING COOKBOOKLETS AND RECIPES; AIRPLANE FOOD; BIRDSEYE CORPORATION; BIRDSEYE, CLARENCE; CAMPBELL SOUP COMPANY; COCA-COLA; FISH: SALTWATER FLAT FISH; FOWL; FROZEN FOOD; FRUIT; GROCERY STORES; H. J. HEINZ COMPANY; ICE; ICEBOXES; ICE CREAMS AND ICES; MEAT; MICROWAVE OVENS; REFRIGERATORS; RESTAURANTS; SWANSON; TRANSPORTATION OF FOOD.]

BIBLIOGRAPHY

American Frozen Food Institute. http://www.food-infonet.com/outside.asp?path=http://affi.com /factsat_aglance.asp.

Williams, E. W. *Frozen Food: Biography of an Industry*. Boston: Cahners, 1963.

ANDREW F. SMITH

French Dip

The french dip sandwich is composed of a french roll dipped in meat juices and filled with slices of roast beef, pork, ham, turkey, or lamb. Philippe Mathieu, a French immigrant, created the "french dipped sandwich" in 1918. The proprietor of a Los Angeles sandwich shop, Philippe the Original, Mathieu accidentally dropped a roll into the roast drippings as he prepared a beef sandwich for a hungry policeman. The policeman later returned with several friends, all requesting "dipped" sandwiches. It is not known whether the sandwich was named for the french roll on which it was made, for the Frenchman who created it, or for the police officer, whose last name was "French," but its popularity quickly spread. The french dip sandwich continues to be served at Philippe the Original and at restaurants nationwide.

[See also SANDWICHES.]

BIBLIOGRAPHY

Mercuri, Becky. *Sandwiches That You Will Like*. Pittsburgh, PA: WQED, 2002.

BECKY MERCURI

French Fries:

Historical Overview

Whether crispy strips or crackling, paper-thin chips, french fries came to the United States from France. American legend suggests that they were "invented" in Saratoga Springs, New York, in the early 1850s, but recipes for

Freezers and Freezing

236

deep-frying exceedingly thin slices of raw potato had long been appearing in published French works, at least as early as 1795–1796 with the anonymous, revolutionary *La Cuisinière Républicaine*. In 1824 Mary Randolph gave a recipe "To Fry Sliced Potatoes," in which she directs that raw potatoes should be "cut in shavings" before frying them in lard "over a quick fire…till they are crisp," so it would seem that even in the United States, paper-thin, deep-fried potatoes were known decades before they were introduced as "Saratoga chips." Indeed, directions for deep-frying sliced raw potatoes appear in a document in Thomas Jefferson's hand that clearly dates from the years 1801–1809, his years in the President's House when he had a French chef and *maître d'hôtel* in attendance; there can be little question that Randolph got her recipe from the Jefferson family, one that was plagiarized throughout the century. In both France and America, early published recipes call for very thin slices of raw potato to be deep-fried until crackling crisp, but some authorities believe that deep-fried strips of potatoes had been sold by vendors on the bridges of *vieux Paris* well before the appearance of the recipe of 1795–1796, citing *pommes de terre Pont-Neuf*, the crispy, thin strips found in any Paris bistro today; apparently they were regarded as plebeian, as indeed they still are.

[**See also** FRENCH INFLUENCES ON AMERICAN FOOD; FRENCH FRIES, TWENTIETH CENTURY; POTATOES.]

KAREN HESS

French Fries:
Twentieth Century

Throughout the nineteenth century, potatoes were fried in a variety of shapes and sizes. During the 1870s, some types of fried potatoes were standardized into particular shapes and sizes. Those that were round and extremely thin became potato chips. Those that were long, rectangular, and approximately one-fourth of an inch thick became "french fried potatoes," a name that had been shortened to "french fries" by 1918.

By the early twentieth century, french fries were served in cafés, diners, and roadside eateries. Although franchised fast food establishments had been around since the 1920s, french fries did not become an important part of their menu until World War II, when rationed meat became scarce and fast food hamburger stands sought alternatives. When the war ended, french fries were well established on the fast food menu, along with hot dogs, hamburgers, and sodas.

When it began to grow in the 1960s, the McDonald's restaurant chain needed a way to distribute its already famous french fries. Working with the Simplot potato company in Idaho, McDonald's devised new methods of freezing raw potatoes while keeping their flavor and texture. Other chains emulated this method, and french fries became the single most popular fast food in America. Similar methods were used for the home market; annual sales had grown to more than 1 billion dollars by 2000.

[**See also** FAST FOOD; FREEZERS AND FREEZING; FRENCH FRIES: HISTORICAL OVERVIEW; FROZEN FOOD; MCDONALD'S; POTATOES; RESTAURANTS.]

ANDREW F. SMITH

French Influences on American Food

By the time America was settled in the seventeenth century, the French dominated professional cookery in western Europe. They created cooking implements, defined food terms, and systematically ordered cooking processes. To foster their culinary empire, they established an apprentice system intended to prepare young men to become chefs. The English aristocracy hired French chefs, or English chefs trained in France, such as Robert May, author of *The Accomplished Cook* (1685). However, most of the English were suspicious of French cookery. Specifically, French food was "dishonest," the British believed, as its sauces, gravies, and other "made dishes" were designed to disguise the poor quality of French meat, poultry, and fish. Also, the French ate unusual and even repugnant foods, such as snails and frogs legs, which horrified English sensibilities.

Authors of many eighteenth-century British cookbooks expressed strong anti-French views. E. Smith's *The Compleat Housewife* (1728), for instance, reproached the reader with, "To our disgrace, we have admired the French tongue and French messes." Copies of *The Compleat Housewife* were regularly imported into the colonies, and in 1742 it became the first cookbook published in America. The English author Hannah Glasse also railed against French cooks in *The Art of Cookery Made Plain and Easy* (1747): "the blind folly of this age, that would rather be imposed on by a French booby, than give encouragement to a good English cook!" Glasse does include some French recipes in her work. On one she comments: "This dish I do not recommend; for I think it an odd jumble of trash." Copies of Glasse's *Art of Cookery* were commonly imported into America, and it was one of most popular cookbooks during the colonial period.

The English were by far the largest group to settle the American colonies, and their cooking traditions and culinary prejudices dominated early America. Initially, many Americans held the same anti-French view as did the English, even though a large number of French immigrants, such as the Huguenots in South Carolina and French Canadians in New England, settled in America. The French controlled Canada and claimed the entire Old Northwest and the Mississippi Valley. Protestant American colonists had fought French Catholics in several wars, of which the French and Indian War (1754–1764) was the most

The cover of Francois Tanty's La Cuisine Francaise: French Cooking for Every Home, Adapted to American Requirements *(Chicago, 1893).*

important. Thanks to this war, the English gained control of all French territories east of the Mississippi River and all of Canada. A number of French Canadians, called Acadians or Cajuns, chose to migrate to Louisiana; others were deported by the British.

When Glasse's *Art of Cookery* (1805) was finally published in the United States, the negative comments regarding French cookery were omitted. American views toward the French and their food had changed dramatically during the previous two decades. During the Revolutionary War, the French had become allies of the American colonies. French troops introduced some Americans to French cookery. American exposure to French cookery expanded further after the French Revolution of 1789, when many nobles and their chefs fled France. Some moved to England; others came to the United States. One of these was the epicure and author Jean-Anthelme Brillat-Savarin. While in America, he visited Jean Baptiste Gilbert Payplat dis Julien, another French refugee, who had opened a public eating house in Boston in 1794. Other French restaurants opened in New York, Philadelphia, Baltimore, and Charleston.

Almost simultaneous with the French Revolution was the slave uprising in Haiti. Many French and Creoles, along with their slaves and servants, immigrated to New York, Boston, Charleston, Philadelphia, and New Orleans. They brought their culinary traditions with them, and some opened restaurants. The result of the French and Creole immigration to America was that some French culinary traditions were adopted by many upper-class Americans, and French food was often served at fashionable dinner parties.

Franco-American soup cookbooklet from the early twentieth century.

The French Influence from Louisiana

Thomas Jefferson, who had served as American ambassador to France (1785–1789) before becoming president (1801–1809), had a great interest in French cooking. When he lived in France, he took advantage of this opportunity to explore French cookery. When he moved into the White House, he brought along a French chef. Jefferson's acquisition of Louisiana in 1803 gave further impetus to the increasing popularity of French food. Louisiana was home to French and Haitian immigrants, Creoles, Cajuns, African Americans, and Native Americans; they combined to create a culinary cauldron that influenced early American cookery and has continued to do so ever since. Creole cuisine shows the French influence in its use of roux, stocks, and adaptations of classic sauces; traditional French seafood soups evolved into gumbo, made with local shrimp, crawfish, and oysters.

French Cookbooks in America

The French influence also filtered into America through cookbooks. Louis Eustache Ude, the cook of Louis XVI, who had fled to England during the French Revolution, published *The French Cook* (London, 1813); this book demonstrated the elegant cooking that was the mark of a fashionable household. It was published in Philadelphia fifteen years later, the first of many French cookbooks in America. Other nineteenth-century books of French cookery published in the United States include Eliza Leslie's translation of *Domestic French Cookery* (1832), Mme. Utrecht-Friedel's *La petite cuisinière habile* (1840), the first French language cookbook published in America, and Louis Eustache Audot's *La cuisinière de la campagne et de la ville*, which was translated into English and published in America as *French Domestic Cookery* (1846). Charles Elmé Francatelli, Queen Victoria's maître d'hôtel, was born in London of Italian heritage, but he studied under the legendary French chef Marie-Antoine Carême. Francatelli's *French Cookery* was first published in the United States in 1846.

French Restaurants

By the early nineteenth century, the French influence was clearly visible on the menus of America's restaurants. Most Americans ate at home during the late eighteenth and early nineteenth centuries. Taverns, saloons, public houses, and inns served mainly travelers. Restaurants were opened toward the end of the eighteenth century, mostly by French refugees. Their clientele consisted of businessmen and an increasingly affluent upper class. In 1827 Joseph Collet opened a French restaurant on the lower floor of his Commercial Hotel on Broad Street in New York. Eight years later, Collet sold his hotel and restaurant to the Swiss émigrés John, Peter, and Lorenzo Delmonico. The Delmonico brothers had established a café and pastry shop in New York in 1827, and ten years later they opened what became known as Delmonico's Restaurant. From its inception it offered a variety of French dishes. Delmonico's was only one among many of the restaurants in American cities that served French food during the nineteenth century.

So prestigious was French cooking in nineteenth-century America that many American chefs claimed to have been born in France, although most were not even trained in French cookery. For the same reason, French culinary terms such as "café," "filet," "fricassee," "meringue," and "entrée" commonly appeared on restaurant menus. Some words changed in meaning when used in America—the word "entrée," for instance, came to mean a main course, whereas in France it means a small dish served between main courses. French food words were further popularized in the United States during the 1850s, when some wealthy American families employed French chefs.

After the Civil War, the chefs in America's most prestigious restaurants were French or French-trained. Several of them published cookbooks during the late nineteenth century. Felix Déliée, who cooked at the New York Club and the Union and Manhattan Clubs, published *The Franco-American Cookery Book* in 1884. Charles Ranhofer, chef at Delmonico's, wrote *The Epicurean* (1896); Oscar Tschirky, maître d'hôtel at the Waldorf, wrote *The Cook Book of Oscar of the Waldorf* (1896). Another influential Frenchman was Auguste Escoffier (1846–1935), who connected with César Ritz to create Ritz hotels beginning in 1890. Escoffier's *Guide culinaire*, translated as *A Guide to Modern Cookery* (1907), was regularly published in the United States.

The French influence in American cooking schools and professional culinary organizations is also apparent. Elizabeth Goodfellow opened a cooking school in Philadelphia during the early nineteenth century and included French cookery in the course of studies. One of her star pupils, Eliza Leslie, translated and published *Domestic French Cookery*, which was based on a French cookbook published in Belgium by Sulpice Barué. Pierre Blot (1818–1874) immigrated to the United States about 1855, where he wrote articles and two cookbooks, *What to Eat, and How to Cook It* (1863), and *Hand-Book of Practical Cookery* (1867), which went through several editions. He also founded the New York Cooking Academy, which was America's first French cooking school. French cookery in some form has been a part of the course of studies of most American cooking schools.

French Influences in the Twentieth Century

During the twentieth century, French cuisine continued to influence American cookery. Elizabeth Pennell, M. F. K. Fisher, and Julia Child spent time in France and brought their discoveries back to the United States. Julia Child, along with Simone Beck and Louisette Bertholle, published *Mastering the Art of French Cooking* (1961), and two years later Child began her stint on the WGBH television program *The French Chef*, which ran on Public Television for two hundred episodes with reruns that were being broadcast in the early 2000s. This program introduced her version of French cooking into American homes and clearly sparked an interest in French cooking in America. Her sign-off, "bon appétit" has become a part of America's vocabulary. Simultaneously, French chefs and French-trained chefs, such as Jacques Pepin and Emeril Lagasse, have flooded into the United States to dazzle Americans with French cooking on other television series. Other Americans used their experience in France to criticize American cooking rather than convince Americans that they should learn how to cook a bastardized form of French cookery.

As the twenty-first century began, most American cooking schools used classic French cookery as the basis for their training. In addition, Americans continued to go to France to study the culinary arts. An association, Les dames d'Escoffier International, was launched in 1978 to honor women who have achieved excellence in the food, beverage, and hospitality professions. In 1984 the French Culinary Institute was founded in New York with the expressed purpose of combining classic French techniques with American inventiveness.

Nouvelle cuisine, a term coined in 1973 by the French restaurant critics Christian Millau and Henri Gault, stressed use of the best local ingredients rather than elaborate preparations. It rejected unnecessarily complicated and pretentious dishes and encouraged seasonal and available ingredients. It encouraged creativity and experimentation. Nouvelle cuisine was introduced into the United States by a number of chefs and restaurateurs. One was Alice

Waters, who in 1971 opened Chez Panisse in Berkeley, California. At first, Waters served simple French food with a particular emphasis on the traditions of Provence. As time went on, she began experimenting with local ingredients. While a chef at Chez Panisse, Jeremiah Tower began adopting the principles of nouvelle cuisine into his cookery. Another apostle of nouvelle cuisine was Wolfgang Puck, the Austrian-born chef at Ma Maison in Los Angeles. His *Modern French Cooking for the American Kitchen* (1981) was among America's best-selling "French" cookbooks. The efforts of Waters, Tower, Puck, and many other chefs have helped create a culinary renaissance in America.

[**See also** Cajun and Creole Food; Celebrity Chefs; Child, Julia; Child, Lydia Maria; Delmonico's; Fisher, M. F. K.; Jefferson, Thomas; Lagasse, Emeril; Leslie, Eliza; Nouvelle Cuisine; Prudhomme, Paul; Puck, Wolfgang; Ranhofer, Charles; Simmons, Amelia; Tschirky, Oscar; Waters, Alice.]

BIBLIOGRAPHY

Gabaccia, Donna R. *We Are What We Eat: Ethnic Food and the Making of Americans*. Cambridge, MA: Harvard University Press, 1998.

Hess, John, and Karen Hess. *The Taste of America*. Urbana: University of Illinois, 2000.

Trubek, Amy B. *Haute Cuisine: How the French Invented the Culinary Profession*. Philadelphia: University of Pennsylvania Press, 2000.

Zanger, Mark H. *The American Ethnic Cookbook for Students*. Phoenix, AZ: Oryx Press, 2001.

ANDREW F. SMITH

Freshwater Aquaculture

In America, farm raising of food fish is geared toward five basic species, three of which are freshwater: catfish, trout, and tilapia. Salmon and shrimp, the other two main food fishes, are largely saltwater raised, although there are freshwater salmon. Beyond fish for food, there is considerable farm raising of sport fish species, including trout, largemouth bass, catfish, red ear and bluegill sunfish, and striped bass. Crayfish, which is valued as food, and other small fish, such as minnows, are farm raised but are used more to supply the bait market than as food. The potential for raising some of the sport fish for food may increase as farm-raising technology improves.

SANDRA L. OLIVER

Fried Chicken

Fried chicken is an American specialty based on Medieval and Renaissance fricassee recipes, as reinforced, refined, and improved by African American cooks. It has had many meanings over the course of American history, from an aristocratic banquet dish in colonial Virginia, to a Sunday dinner after church for ordinary Americans, to fast food and even a snack food. Recent immigrants have added new forms and flavors, and perhaps restored some of the oldest forms of fried chicken cookery from Southeast Asia, where the chicken was originally domesticated.

The apparent origins of American fried chicken all return to the Mediterranean basin, early endowed with the three basics: iron pots, large quantities of animal and/or vegetable fat, and chickens. By the late medieval period, the technique of cutting up chickens and frying them before braising in a sauce had appeared in French culinary manuscripts, and in 1490 took the term "friquasée" from a combination of the words to "fry" and "break." Long before this, iron pots, vegetable oils, and chickens were in similar use in sub-Saharan Africa, reinforced by a trans-Saharan caravan trade with the Mediterranean basin.

Some but not all fricassee recipes in British and Scottish renaissance manuscripts begin with frying pieces of chicken in oil. The seventeenth-century cooking manuscript that was passed down to Martha Washington has two such fricassee recipes, the first of which pan fries two cut-up chickens in a half-pound of butter before adding some water to stew and finishing into an egg-yolk bound sauce.

The cookbook Martha Washington actually used, *The Art of Cookery* by Hannah Glasse, starts a "Brown Fricasey" with a breaded fried chicken we would recognize more clearly: "You must take your Rabbits or Chickens and skin them, then cut into small Pieces, and rub them over with Yolks of Eggs: Have ready some grated Bread... [mixed with spices]... and then roll them in it." These breaded pieces of chicken are then fried "of a fine brown" in butter, before stewing the pieces in a gravy with mushrooms and pickles. Glasse's was the most popular British cookbook in colonial Virginia, and was reprinted twice in early America.

Glasse's recipe almost certainly influenced the first printed American recipe for "Fried Chickens," in the 1824 *The Virginia House-Wife*, by Mary Randolph: "Cut them up as for the fricassee, dredge them well with flour, sprinkle them with salt, put them into a good quantity of boiling lard, and fry them a light brown, fry small pieces of mush and a quantity of parsley nicely picked to be served in the dish with the chickens, take half a pint of rich milk, add to it a small bit of butter with pepper, salt, and chopped parsley, stew it a little, and pour it over the chickens, and then garnish with the fried parsley."

One can see that the fried chicken step of the fricassee recipe was becoming more important, whereas the ensuing braise was becoming a matter of making a simple gravy. (Note also the first recipe for "hush puppies" as a side dish.) The gravy persisted in printed recipes for fried chicken into the early twentieth century, eventually becoming fixed as "fried chicken Maryland."

Something else was also happening, both in the big house kitchen at Mt. Vernon and at the professional kitchen of Mrs. Randolph's boardinghouse. The actual cooks were African American slaves with some of their own ideas about chickens and how to cook them.

The first to dictate her own recipe was Mrs. Abby Fisher, who learned to cook during the 1860s in South Carolina and Alabama, and whose recipe, published in 1881, uses a simple dip of flour, implies rather more frying fat, and finishes with a simplified gravy that is as thin as soup.

African slaves had come to the Americas with a culture that considered poultry a prestigious food. (Live chickens are still handed to honored guests in some African villages.) As slaves, they were sometimes able to raise and cook or sell poultry, especially in the Chesapeake area, where they dominated the market. For most of the nineteenth century, in most markets chicken was more expensive, and thus more prestigious, than pork. Big house cooks might cook fricassees with the mistress reading from a printed cookbook, or might be trusted to fry chicken by their own favorite means. Deep-fat frying then, as now, was dangerous and hot work, and the mistress would not undertake it herself. But on larger plantations where slaves were more carefully managed, chicken dishes were only available to most slaves as special treats around Christmastime, or when the chickens were stolen and cooked surreptitiously. Almost everyone had access to iron pots and plenty of lard, however.

When master went hunting or later became a soldier in the Civil War, fried chicken was considered a durable food that could be sent to men several days away. The process of frying sterilized and sealed the pieces of chicken. After the war, the high and low dishes of southern food were increasingly combined into a regional food broadly accepted by both white and black southerners. For free African Americans, however, fried chicken (still usually with gravy) became a symbol of gentility like tea cakes and was often reserved for Sunday dinner. This eventually became a stereotype, and in the 1970s and 1980s some African Americans would not eat fried chicken in mixed groups as a protest.

Increasing mobility kept up the need for travel foods, and traveler's restaurants near railroad depots or highways served fried chicken. Railroad dining cars (with black cooks under white supervision, but increasingly with black chefs) served fried chicken, too. More detailed recipes gradually dropped the gravy or made it separately but Africanisms could be observed: washing the chicken pieces in lemon juice, brining them in saltwater (a North Carolina regional variation), soaking them in water or buttermilk, and increasing the seasoning of the breading or the gravy.

By the 1940s, Harland Sanders, a white Kentucky café owner, had developed a mixture of flour with eleven herbs and spices and was experimenting with pressure cookers to decrease the frying time. In 1952, at the age of sixty-five, he went on the road selling franchises of his cooking method, and founded a global empire, known as Kentucky Fried Chicken.

Although home pressure cookers were revived in the 1970s and again in the 1990s, inconvenience and health concerns have turned most American home cooks to "oven fried" chicken, or to catering with fast food fried or rotisserie chickens. Buffalo Chicken wings have become a national fad with their own chain restaurants, and recent immigrants from East Asia and the Caribbean have brought fried chicken traditions of their own to restaurants where outsiders find immediate comfort in what they think of as a classically American dish.

BIBLIOGRAPHY

Edge, John T. *Fried Chicken: An American Journey.* New York: G.P. Putnam's Sons, 2004.

Hess, Karen. *Martha Washington's Book of Cookery.* New York: Colombia University Press, 1981.

Randolph, Mary. *The Virginia House-Wife; a facsimile of the first edition, 1824, along with additional material from the editions of 1825 and 1828, thus presenting a complete text.* Historical notes and commentaries by Karen Hess. Colombia: University of South Carolina Press, 1984.

KIM PIERCE

Fried Oysters

The tidewater Chesapeake oyster is known to be smaller and more tasty than its northern and western neighbors. In this Mid-Atlantic region, oysters were historically offered with a question: "fried, stewed, or nude?" Fried oysters are more common in this region than the other two offerings.

The basic twentieth-century recipe for fried oysters is a quart of oysters, three eggs, one-quarter cup of milk (or water), cracker meal or bread crumbs, and salt and pepper. Drain the oysters, beat the eggs and add salt, pepper, and milk, dip in egg mixture, then fry in one inch of fat, shortening, or cooking oil in a frying pan or deep fryer until brown. Buttermilk can be added to make the batter a little sour, which enhances the flavor of the oyster. Pancake mix or cornmeal may be used as well as flavorings such as Old Bay Seasoning, garlic powder, and Cajun seasonings. An oyster fritter can be made by substituting flour and baking powder for cracker meal or bread crumbs and using milk and melted butter as well as the egg, salt, and pepper.

Varieties of fried oyster can be seen in Asia and Latin America, and include tempura batters, sesame seed, and ginger sauces, as well as West Indian Hot Pepper Sauce on beer battered oysters.

[See also OYSTER BARS; OYSTERS.]

BIBLIOGRAPHY

Chestory: The Center for the Chesapeake Story. www.chestory.org.

FRED CZARRA

Frito-Lay

Herman W. Lay was a salesman for Sunshine Biscuit Company, but during the Depression he lost his job. In 1932, Lay was hired by Barrett Foods, a snack food firm in Atlanta, Georgia, and began selling peanut butter sandwiches in southern Kentucky and Tennessee. Lay was an aggressive businessman and began acquiring distributorships. When Barrett's founder died in 1937, Lay bought the company, which included plants in Atlanta and Memphis, Tennessee. Popcorn, manufactured in Nashville, Tennessee, was the first product to have the "Lay's" brand name. Lay also manufactured potato chips.

Lay's potato chip sales increased during World War II mainly because snack foods that contained sugar and chocolate were unavailable because of rationing. After the war, Lay fully automated his potato chip manufacturing business and diversified its products. The firm had become a major regional snack food company by the end of World War II. In 1945, Lay met Elmer Doolin, who manufactured Fritos corn chips in San Antonio, Texas. Doolin granted Herman Lay a license to distribute Fritos. The two companies also cooperated on other products. For example, Cheetos cheese-flavored snacks were invented by the Frito company and were marketed by Lay in 1948.

When Doolin died in 1959, his Frito company merged with Lay's company, creating Frito-Lay Inc., headquartered in Dallas, Texas. The merged company continued to grow. By the end of the 1960s, Frito-Lay was the dominant company in the snack world. In 1965, Frito-Lay merged with Pepsi-Cola Company, creating PepsiCo. The newly merged company launched many products. In 1966, Frito-Lay introduced Doritos corn chips, which the company claimed tasted like authentic tostadas. Doritos became popular nationwide as the era of the Anglo corn chip dawned. By the early twenty-first century, Doritos had become the largest-selling snack food in the world.

The main target of Fritos advertising was children. A cartoon character, the Frito Kid, was launched in 1953. In 1958, the company launched a campaign featuring "Munch a bunch of Fritos corn chips." In 1963, with growing awareness of niche markets, Frito-Lay introduced the Frito Bandito, a move that appalled the Mexican American community. The Frito Bandito soon disappeared.

Frito-Lay continued to innovate and develop new products. For example, in 1958 the company produced Ruffles potato chips, a thick chip with ridges made especially for dipping. In 1988, Frito-Lay introduced Chee-tos cheddar cheese flavored popcorn and launched a major promotion campaign starring Chester Cheetah, a cartoon character aimed at children and young adults. Rold Gold brand pretzels were introduced in 1989 and were subsequently promoted by "Pretzel Boy," portrayed by the actor Jason Alexander of the *Seinfeld* television series. In 1993, Doritos Thins brand tortilla chips were introduced nationally with Chevy Chase as the celebrity spokesman.

Frito-Lay has acquired other food companies, such as Cracker-Jack in 1997. By 2000, Frito-Lay had become the largest snack food conglomerate in the world.

[See also FRITO PIE; MEXICAN AMERICAN FOOD; POPCORN; POTATOES; SNACKS, SALTY.]

BIBLIOGRAPHY

Guenther, Keith J. "The Development of the Mexican-American Cuisine." In *Oxford Symposium 1981: National and Regional Styles of Cookery; Proceedings,* edited by Alan Davidson. London: Prospect, 1981.

Smith, Andrew F. "Tacos, Enchiladas and Refried Beans: The Invention of Mexican-American Cookery." In *Cultural and Historical Aspects of Foods,* edited by Mary Wallace Kelsey and ZoeAnn Holmes, 183–203. Corvallis: Oregon State University, 1999.

ANDREW F. SMITH

Frito Pie

Frito pie consists of beef or bean chili, cheese, onions, and jalapeños layered over Frito corn chips. The dish traditionally was served directly inside the corn chip bag, but because the bag has become thinner, the dish is usually served on a plate. Although, or perhaps because, Frito pie is a quintessential road food from the southwestern United States, its origins are undetermined. Both Texas and New Mexico claim to have created Frito pie. The dish gained renown at the Woolworth lunch counter in Santa Fe, New Mexico. According to the Dallas-based Frito-Lay company, the mother of Elmer Doolin, the founder of Frito-Lay, invented the dish in 1932. The latter is the most likely answer, because snack food companies have a history of creating recipes with their products to increase sales. Frito pie is essentially an Americanized version of the Mexican tostada—corn tortillas topped with ingredients similar to those used in Frito pie.

[See also FRITO-LAY; MEXICAN AMERICAN FOOD; ROADSIDE FOOD; SNACKS, SALTY; SOUTHWEST.]

JEAN RAILLA

Frogs' Legs

Frogs' legs, considered a delicacy by the French in the seventeenth century, were introduced into England by French chefs (and by English chefs trained in France). A recipe for frogs' legs with saffron was published in the English edition of *The French Cook* by Francis Peter LaVarenne (1653), and subsequent English cookbooks included similar recipes.

The Dutch also ate frogs' legs, and it is likely that Dutch settlers ate them in New Netherland (later New York), but no evidence has surfaced indicating that English colonists dined on frog. When the War for American Independence broke out, American colonists came into contact with the French military, which became an ally. According to an eighteenth-century observer of American life, Americans believed that the French virtually lived on frogs. Bostonians served frogs to French naval officers, who broke into laughter when they found a whole frog in their soup.

By the mid-nineteenth century, frogs' legs were sold in markets in many American cities. In 1863, Pierre Blot, author of the *Hand-Book of Practical Cookery,* wrote that frogs' legs were formerly "eaten by the French only, but now, frog-eating has become general, and the Americans are not behind any others in relishing that kind of food." Despite such enthusiastic pronouncements, frogs' legs were mainly served in upper-class, French-dominated restaurants from Cajun and Creole restaurants in New Orleans to the Poule d'Or in San Francisco to Delmonico's in New York. Recipes for frogs' legs—fried, stewed, creamed, fricasseed, and broiled, in white sauce, gumbo, soup, and salad—appeared in American cookbooks beginning in the latter half of the nineteenth century. By the 1930s, dozens of farms, particularly in Florida, raised frogs to supply the American market. Today, frogs' legs remain a specialty item, offered mainly in French restaurants and rarely to be found in retail markets.

ANDREW F. SMITH

Frontier Cooking of the Far West

The earliest Americans to explore the Rocky Mountains were the trappers, traders, and mountain men, whose presence began as early as 1803, and who were well established west of the Rockies by 1820. Mountain men spent their summers drying elk meat, basting venison in its own fat, or trading with the Blackfeet or Sioux for dried salmon. For sweetening, they plucked succulent berries from vast quantities of cherries, plums, and berries growing wild in the mountains. Bears supplied meat to last an entire year when jerked or turned into pemmican—a compressed "packet" of meat flakes and berries, dried over a slow fire, pounded to powder and smothered in a thick coat of melted bear grease. Jerked meat was sun dried on strings, then packed away in saddlebags, where it would stay unspoiled for months on a long journey.

Winter's heavy snows often forced the mountain men to find leaner fare, often raccoon, pine bark boiled as tea, or dried juniper berries still on the bush. In the Pacific Northwest, they dug camas root and pounded it into a flat mound of dough. If dried, it turned into a thin, slightly sweet cookie.

The military was at the forefront of a crucial influx into western territories. Soldiers were sustained at mealtime by paltry portions of coffee, hardtack, raw salt pork, and the interminable soaked beans. Military provisions were bland and monotonous; meats arrived in camp worm-ridden, beans and potatoes were tainted with mold, and the hardtack had been nibbled by mice. By the 1870s, the army's organized supply network prompted a quicker distribution of canned goods and out-of-area specialties. This increased use of canned goods offered a more varied selection, including the ubiquitous tinned oysters—one of the most popular "delicacies" in the West. Overland emigrants traveled west in the greatest numbers from 1840 to 1860, usually headed for California. Food prepared and eaten around an open

fire was extraordinarily different from the familiar foods of home. Women gathered wild grapes and berries in abundance, including delicious strawberries; seedy, pink gooseberries tasting of grapes; cranberries; sarvis berries, and the amber yellow salal berries or salmonberries, too tart to eat without cooking, and related to the raspberry. Thick clusters of mesquite beans from the thorny, lime-green bush were ground into flour and eaten as "bread fruit."

White beans were an overland traveler's mainstay, simmered through the night or buried in a "bean pit" to cook in a tightly covered kettle, perhaps a Dutch oven. Laced with bones, vegetables, and savory meat scraps, such as salt pork, the beans were ready for breakfast or dinner the following day. Pocket soup was made of bones or meat—usually veal, beef, or pig's trotters—cooked into a broth and strained, with the remaining broth cooked again to the consistency of a thick, often bland, glue. Emigrants knew that a pound of bacon went as far as three pounds of beefsteak and that pork was popular because it kept well as smoked ham or bacon or salt pork. The summer season offered wild berries, whereas winter offered greater ease in hunting and preserving game. Small game abounded year-round—woodchucks, prairie chickens, myriad birds, rabbits, squirrels, raccoons, and opossums.

In the Great Plains, canned goods such as peaches or tomatoes could be purchased at trading posts, bringing the impact of technology to bear in the most remote reaches of the country. Bread was baked in a Dutch oven. Bread starters, or a "sponge" of sourdough, salt, and yeast, were a treasured brew of secret ingredients, nurtured and tended like a child. Yeast often fermented and turned sour in the heat.

During the Gold Rush, 1849–1860, a major segment of the overland emigration headed toward the gold and silver regions of California and Nevada. Mining camps served monotonous fare, usually hardtack biscuits washed down with coffee. In the early camps, scurvy was rampant and could be countered only by the antiscorbutic effects of lime juice, wild lettuce, potatoes with vinegar, or even, in desperation for what little citrus might be found, orange marmalade. As the mines prospered, the number of western hotels grew—many serving luxurious helpings of elk steak, codfish balls, roast grizzly, and fish chowder stewed in claret. California forty-niners often feasted on salmon, easily caught in the Sacramento River. Coffees, chocolates, and cakes were common, whereas cash-poor miners dined on Chinese chop suey. Rambunctious California miners invented the Hangtown fry, an egg and oyster dish, as well as the oyster cocktail.

The most colorful arrival on the far frontier was the cowboy, whose heyday lasted from the end of the Civil War until the mid-1880s. Cowboy fare varied according to the

Cowboys eat near a chuck wagon in Arizona, 1907.

whims of the cook, who dished up chuck for hard-worked men. Any cook unable to whip up the trailside favorites—hot breads; mallet-softened meat dredged in flour, called chicken-fried steak; beans; and peaches from the can—did not last long. A well-funded outfit enjoyed luxury items, such as pickles and spices, whereas an imaginative chef might add green purslane, a succulent green potherb, or cactus buds, fried up like green beans and used to deter scurvy. A savory buffalo hump stew would be laced with onions or "cracklin'" cornbread with pork skin flavoring.

On farms, ranches, and homesteads, there was an abundance of game to augment the usual mealtime portions. As rural communities stabilized, so did the food supplies, including cattle and poultry. Many farms kept cattle, adding milk, curds, and cheese to the daily menu, while truck gardens, established usually after the farm had been settled for several years, offered a seasonal bounty—tomatoes, snap beans, melons, and squash. Wheat flour might be milled locally or trundled by horse from the nearest general store.

Many adapted to the new foods of the new terrain, and regional preferences held sway. Southwestern settlers used the ubiquitous jalapeño to spice barbecued meat, red beans, and agarita jam, pressed from the pungent berry of the sharp-tipped agarita bush. They embraced the Spanish legacy of savory *carne seca*, spicy jerked beef, that was quickly adopted by the new Anglo-Californians. Barbecued meat, spit-roasted over an open fire, was popular, as was *colache*, or vegetable succotash, spiced with garlic, olive oil, and green chilies. Favorite of all were tortillas, tamales, and *chile con carne*.

Urbanites found that life in the western towns and cities eventually offered as varied a diet as that of the East. They could pick and choose from a wealth of supplies, from fresh green peas to imported pâté, supplied by a growing railway network that linked small, localized markets to city shoppers. Fashionable magazines instructed women in the newest dessert developments, such as bananas cut lengthwise and heaped with whipped cream or lavish main course dishes, such as saddle of mutton covered in an "iced" topping of cooled meat drippings with the white top fat skimmed off, remelted, and spread over the meat in a smooth, white coat. For urbanites, Continental dining arrived with delicious little side offerings of French foods—hors d'oeuvres, sauced vegetables, dense meat stocks, scalded calves feet for jelly, and desserts such as constructed gilt cakes, bonbons, and fondue, often savored at popular outdoor cafés.

Many Asians flooded into the West after the gold boom, bringing with them foods and cooking styles based on their culinary roots. Using inexpensive vegetables, Asian immigrants added a savory cooking style that was healthy and cheap. Chop suey houses served rice and hot, brewed tea, as well as stir-frying and steaming. Boiled tea protected the Chinese from waterborne diseases, and many Chinese also brewed up local roots and barks for medicine, flavorings, and spices.

Other immigrants to America brought their favorite foods: Italians settled in northern California and Nevada, introducing pasta and meat dishes and enjoying lentils. Texas Germans made wurst from fatty venison or pork mixed with coarse salt, pepper, and saltpeter. Jewish immigrants, some salesmen, some farmers, brought garlic-flavored pickles and gunnysacks filled with kasha, in case they ran out. African Americans migrated into Iowa after emancipation, and later came to California, bringing traditional southern cooking practices, such as rice and black-eyed pea concoctions. Black sharecroppers wrapped meat in cabbage leaves and baked it in the ashes, or smoked meat over apple wood or sassafras. Black cooking introduced peanuts, molasses, and sesame seeds as well as salads made of wild greens. Women ground corn husks into meal to make bread—anything to keep from starving.

Good food was both cause and means of celebration, and the lexicon of "plain cookin'" on the frontier encompassed savory or plain, salted or sweet. The pioneering process turned cooking, American-style, into a savory blend of spices, herbs, flavors, and techniques that combined the Old World and the New World. Foods mirrored not only the land and the region but also the outlook, status, and tastes of frontier cooks.

[See also BARBECUE; BUFFALO; BUTTERMILK; CALIFORNIA; CHINESE AMERICAN FOOD; COFFEE; PACIFIC NORTHWEST; RESTAURANTS.]

BIBLIOGRAPHY

Conlin, Joseph R. *Bacon, Beans, and Galatines: Food and Foodways of the Western Mining Frontier.* Reno: University of Nevada Press, 1986.

Lucetti, Cathy Lee. *Home on the Range: A Culinary History of the American West.* New York: Villard, 1993.

Ross, Nancy Wilson. *Westward the Women.* New York: Knopf, 1944.

Stratton, Joanna L. *Pioneer Women: Voices from the Kansas Frontier.* New York: Simon and Schuster, 1981.

CATHY LUCHETTI

Frosting, *see Cakes*

Frozen Food

After more than thirty years as publisher of the trade journal *Quick Frozen Foods*, E. W. Williams described an American utopia of frozen dinners: "Where can a consumer buy its equivalent in a restaurant? It is economical, saves dishes and cooking. It is the perfect answer to modern living." These comments appeared in 1970 in Williams's book *Frozen Foods.* By that time, frozen foods had become a staple in the American diet. Sales had climbed from 150 million dollars in 1940 to 7 billion dollars three decades later. Retailers numbered in the hundreds in the mid-1930s. Fifteen years later, there were two hundred thousand. In 1928, during the industry's infancy, 1 million pounds of fruits and vegetables were frozen; in 1946, 860 million pounds. For all this, one man is primarily responsible: Clarence Birdseye.

Birdseye was born in Brooklyn, New York, in 1886. As a young man, he lived in Labrador, in northeastern Canada. There, in the region's subzero temperatures, he stored meat and fish outside, where it promptly froze. When thawed, Birdseye noticed, it tasted freshly caught. Predicting a great market for quickly frozen foods, he founded General Seafoods in 1924 on a shoestring budget. On the eve of the Great Depression, the Postum Company and the Goldman Sachs Trading Company together acquired General Seafoods and Birdseye's patents for $22 million. They called the new company General Foods.

Growth of an Industry

An early obstacle to sales was the American public's association of frozen foods with poor quality and spoilage. Marketers were tasked with creating new perceptions, and the first step was dissociation. General Foods dubbed the new products "frosted" foods and sold them under the brand name Birds Eye, claiming only the freshest of foods were frozen, equal in flavor to and superior in convenience to fresh foods.

Quick freezing was more than a gimmick. Before Birdseye, freezing methods were too slow to prevent the loss of nutritious proteins, vitamins, and salts. Ice crystals that formed during slow freezing caused a chemical reaction that resulted in drier, tougher meat. Slow freezing also led to oxidation of fats, which turns meat rancid. The quicker the freezing, then, the less damage done. Birdseye's revolutionary method extended the shelf life of many foods.

On March 6, 1930, at a Springfield, Massachusetts, market, the first Birds Eye frosted foods went on sale: peas and spinach, raspberries, loganberries, and Oregon Bing cher-

A woman restocks a dispenser claiming to sell "garden fresh" frozen foods.

ries. Seasonal foods such as strawberries now could be purchased anywhere and at any time during the year. In the coming years, American food and eating habits were transformed.

The nascent frozen foods industry faced an obstacle that was exacerbated by the sour economic climate of the 1930s: how to convince retailers that frozen foods were not simply a fad and that buying expensive freezer cabinets was a wise investment. Still, by 1940, one year after the first precooked frozen meals appeared on the market, the number of retail stores equipped to sell frozen foods had increased to fifteen thousand, a thirty-fold increase over seven years. Despite the increase, retail sales of frozen foods accounted for only approximately 10 percent of the total amount of frozen food sales. Sales were limited to urban centers, primarily on the East Coast. Why? Placed in ice cream cabinets, the new products were hardly given the visibility they needed to become a familiar part of the grocery landscape.

Frozen Food Comes Home

Throughout World War II, frozen foods made advances on the home front. According to Williams, "Tin went to war; frozen foods stayed at home" (*Frozen Foods*). Tin was needed for the war effort. Frozen foods, however, were packaged in nonessential materials, including parchment, cellophane, paper bags, cardboard, and waxed paper bags. Frozen foods were taken off the rationing list a year and a half before canned goods. Prepared frozen foods were not rationed at all.

In September 1945, the first television program featuring frozen foods was produced. Representatives of Marshall Field's, the Chicago department store and program sponsor, demonstrated how to prepare frozen foods. American housewives, the target audience, were told that frozen foods offered more time away from the stove. Over the next decade, items such as french fries, fish sticks, waffles, and baked goods appeared. By the mid-1950s, a quarter million retail stores were selling one thousand frozen food products. Ten years later, that number had grown to nearly twenty-five hundred. The selection was not restricted to meat and potatoes. Hot tamales, chili con carne, and enchiladas were frozen, as were blintzes and potato pancakes, chow mein and chop suey.

Here to Stay

Frozen food became a market mainstay. The industry experimented with package sizes and design, Eskimos and huskies giving way to pictures of the vegetables themselves. Pour-and-store bags were introduced in 1959, allowing consumers to cook only the amount they wanted. One packaging innovation and catchy design caught the market in 1954: the Swanson TV dinner. The all-American dinner—in a three-section aluminum tray containing turkey with gravy and dressing, peas, and sweet potatoes—radically changed the way Americans eat. By 1960 annual sales of frozen dinners, TV and otherwise, surpassed $200 million.

The next several decades saw many emerging trends. Frozen ethnic cuisines became big business as companies such as Deep Foods in New Jersey began to offer the growing immigrant community a taste of home. Meals for weight-conscious consumers, such as Weight Watchers, Lean Cuisine, and Healthy Choice, entered the market. Frozen pizza became a constant, as did rising annual sales figures. After surpassing $5 billion in 1965, sales increased tenfold over the next three decades.

In 1967 the introduction of the compact home microwave oven confirmed the future of frozen foods. Frozen foods, which had always been marketed as convenience foods, were finally matched with a technology that made that claim indisputable. And on March 6, 1984, the fifty-fourth anniversary of the first retail sales of frozen foods, President Ronald Reagan declared National Frozen Food Day, "in recognition of the significant contribution which the frozen food industry has made to the nutritional well-being of the American people."

[See also BIRDSEYE CORPORATION; BIRDSEYE, CLARENCE; FREEZERS AND FREEZING; GENERAL FOODS; GROCERY STORES; HISTORICAL OVERVIEW: WORLD WAR II; ICEBOXES; MEAT; MICROWAVE OVENS; PACKAGING; REFRIGERATORS; SWANSON.]

BIBLIOGRAPHY

Gabaccia, Donna R. *We Are What We Eat: Ethnic Food and the Making of Americans*. Cambridge, MA: Harvard University Press, 1998.

Hess, John L., and Karen Hess. *The Taste of America*. Urbana, IL, and Chicago: University of Illinois Press, 2000.

Inness, Sherrie A. *Kitchen Culture in America: Popular Representations of Food, Gender, and Race*. Philadelphia: University of Pennsylvania Press, 2001.

Shephard, Sue. *Pickled, Potted, and Canned: How the Art and Science of Food Preserving Changed the World*. New York: Simon and Schuster, 2000.

Williams, E. W. *Frozen Foods: Biography of an Industry*. Boston: Cahners, 1970.

MATT McMILLEN

Fruit

Only a few fruits now of commercial importance, including blueberries, cranberries, strawberries, and cactus pears, are indigenous to the United States. Before the arrival of European settlers, Native Americans commonly gathered raspberries, blackberries, and strawberries that grew wild in openings in the forest. They also ate many species of wild grapes, blueberries, cranberries, native persimmons, and mulberries. Native species of plums, typically smaller and more astringent than cultivated imported species, as well as crab apples and chokecherries, grew from coast to coast.

Fruits in Colonial America

European settlers brought with them the fruits familiar in their homelands, including apples, pears, quinces, peaches, nectarines, apricots, cherries, and plums. There were some grafted trees in seventeenth-century American plantings, but for the most part the numerous small orchards planted in the colonies consisted of seedlings. By the early eighteenth century, grafting and budding were practiced. In the beginning, most of the named varieties that were grown were imported from Europe, but over time more and more varieties of native origin, such as Roxbury Russet, Rhode Island Greening, and Newtown Pippin apples, were propagated from the few superior seedlings.

Apples and peaches were the fruits most commonly grown in the colonies. Apples were grown chiefly for cider, which was a common drink of rich and poor, used for farmers' own consumption and for sale, trade, and export. Both apples and peaches were commonly used for distilling brandy and as fodder for livestock. Some farmers used ovens to dry tree fruits and berries, which stored and shipped well.

Expansion of Fruit Culture in the Nineteenth and Twentieth Centuries

Over the course of the nineteenth century, fruit cultivation spread westward, and the number and extent of orchards and nurseries increased dramatically. By the middle of the century, commercial fruit culture had become well established as cities grew and transportation facilities improved. Fresh fruit became more readily available in urban areas. Many people had previously believed that the consumption of fresh fruits led to disease, but in the nineteenth century, diet reformers preached the virtues of simple, natural, plain foods. Men of wealth and culture took a great interest in growing and appreciating fruit.

Apples and peaches continued to be the leading fruits and came to be grown more commonly as grafted varieties. Commercial cultivation of native grape varieties, centered in western New York State and nearby areas, surged after the introduction of the Concord variety in the 1850s. At this time, too, cultivation of strawberry and bush fruits became more popular.

Starting in the mid-nineteenth century, the expansion of railways and the development of the compound steamship engine made bulk cargo economical. Orange cultivation in Florida and California expanded

Picking blueberries in Lehigh County, Pennsylvania, in the 1920s.

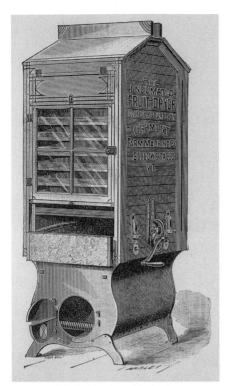

A pneumatic fruit drier pictured in the Vermont Farm Machine Catalog, *1900.*

rapidly in the decades after 1870. Lemon and grapefruit plantings followed after 1880. In the last decades of the nineteenth century, stone fruit production surged in California.

In the late nineteenth and early twentieth centuries, the deliberate, systematic breeding of new fruit varieties became more common. The most celebrated inventor, Luther Burbank of Santa Rosa, California, developed the modern market plum. Plant explorers such as David Fairchild, Walter Swingle, and Frank Meyer combed the world and brought back plants and seeds of new fruits and varieties. In the early twentieth century, cultivation of subtropical fruits such as avocados, dates, figs, persimmons, and pomegranates boomed in California.

The organizational, economic, and scientific bases of fruit growing evolved as it became big business. Instead of diversified plantings, farmers more often cultivated large blocks of single fruit crops. Traditional districts surrounding metropolitan markets yielded to distant growing areas with lower costs of production. Growers organized marketing cooperatives to secure better prices for their crops and negotiate railroad rates. To ship fruit long distances, large growers and cooperatives established special fruit packing houses.

Over the course of the nineteenth century, as the cost of containers dropped, fruit canning became common in American homes. Consumption of dried fruits such as prunes, peaches, and apricots increased dramatically, because it could be easily shipped and marketed year-round. Frozen fruit, including frozen juice concentrate, however, became popular only in the mid-twentieth century, as processing techniques advanced and consumers bought freezers. Fruit shifted from being a relative rarity and luxury in the mid-nineteenth century to being a staple of the American diet in the mid-twentieth century.

Trends in Modern Fruit Production and Marketing

In the twentieth century, several factors combined to greatly extend the season of fresh fruits, so that many came to be available year-round. For example, fresh peaches once were sold in the Northeast from late July to October, but the harvest from California and the Southeast arrives starting in April or early May, whereas imports from the southern hemisphere fill the market from November to April. Fruit breeders have devised early- and late-maturing varieties. In addition, handlers have perfected techniques of storing fruit under modified atmospheric conditions (low oxygen and high carbon dioxide), which slows respiratory metabolism, allowing some fruits, such as apples, to be held for a year or more.

Since the mid-1970s, although overall per capita consumption of fruit held steady, fresh fruit consumption increased 23 percent, from 102 pounds annually in 1976 to 125.7 pounds in 2001. During the same period, consumption of both canned and dried fruits declined 23 percent. Educated and affluent consumers especially became more interested in a healthful, varied diet, and producers responded by supplying larger quantities and a greater diversity of fresh fruits.

In the 1980s and 1990s, technology played an increasing role in fruit distribution and marketing. Stickers, affixed at the packing house to many fruits, enabled checkout clerks to speedily and accurately identify fruits and varieties. Produce marketers responded to consumers' demand for convenience by offering "ready-to-eat" fresh-cut fruits, such as sliced melon and pineapple.

Some farmers and consumers have responded to the industrialization of fruit production by circumventing conventional commercial pathways. Small growers have sought to market their fruit directly to consumers through farm stands and farmers' markets, which have multiplied in recent decades. Production of organically grown fruit, driven by consumer concern about pesticide use and the sustainability of agricultural practices, has surged to the point that many commercial produce companies have established large organic plantings. For the most part, however, the compromises of commerce that make fruit readily available often degrade its quality.

[**See also** APPLES; APRICOTS; AVOCADOS; BANANAS; BATIDOS; BIOTECHNOLOGY; BLACKBERRIES; BLUEBERRIES; CACTUS; CALIFORNIA; CANNING AND BOTTLING; CHERRIES; CIDER; CITRUS; COCONUTS; COOPERATIVES; CRANBERRIES; CURRANTS; DATES; FARMERS' MARKETS; FIGS; FOOD SAFETY; FRUIT JUICES; FRUIT WINES; GRAPES; IRRADIATION; KIWIS; MELONS; MULBERRIES; NUTS; OLIVES; ORGANIC FOOD; ORGANIC GARDENING; PEACHES AND NECTARINES; PEARS; PERSIMMONS; PINEAPPLES; PLUMS; POMEGRANATES; PUMMELO; QUINCE; RASPBERRIES; RHUBARB; STRAWBERRIES; TOMATOES; TRANSPORTATION OF FOOD; VEGETABLES; WATERMELONS.]

BIBLIOGRAPHY

Hatch, Peter J. *The Fruits and Fruit Trees of Monticello.* Charlottesville: University Press of Virginia, 1998.

Hedrick, Ulysses Prentiss. *A History of Horticulture in America to 1860, with an Addendum of Books Published from 1861–1920.* Portland, OR: Timber, 1988.

Knee, Michael, ed. *Fruit Quality and Its Biological Basis.* Boca Raton, FL: CRC, 2002.

Stoll, Steven. *The Fruits of Natural Advantage.* Berkeley: University of California Press, 1998.

Upshall, W. H., ed. *History of Fruit Growing and Handling in United States of America and Canada 1860–1972.* University Park, PA: American Pomological Society, 1976.

DAVID KARP

Fruit Juices

Old World fruits were introduced in America by European settlers in the sixteenth and seventeenth centuries. The Spanish introduced citrus trees, such as lemons, limes, and oranges, into Florida and the Caribbean, and the fruits were regularly exported to British North America. The English, French, and German colonists introduced other fruits, including apples, cherries, plums, and pears. Native fruits, such as elderberries, cranberries, and huckleberries, rounded out the early American fruit basket. In addition to being eaten fresh, these fruits were pressed or squeezed into juice. Apples, lemons, and oranges were the main juice fruits, but currants, grapes, peaches, pineapples, plums, raspberries, and strawberries also were used for juice. Beginning in the nineteenth century, the most common way of serving fruit juice was with added sugar and water in the form of "ades," such as appleade, lemonade, orangeade, and strawberryade. These juices were sometimes served ice-cold and called "sherbet." For a lighter drink, a few spoonfuls of these sweetened juices were stirred into cold water. By the nineteenth century, a wide range of fruit juices was used to flavor ice cream and soda fountain drinks.

Fruit juices also were cooked with a large quantity of sugar and preserved for future use, mainly for use in cooking and baking. In addition, juices were fermented into flavorful vinegars, and they were used in alcoholic and temperance beverages, including shrubs, which were composed of fruit juice plus spirits or vinegar. Most fruit juices were fermented to produce alcoholic beverages such as hard cider, perry (made from pears), wine, brandy, including applejack, and cordials.

In the home, fruit was juiced by hand until 1930, when the first commercial juicing machine was marketed by Norman Walker, who encouraged a diet of raw food and juices.

An advertisement for grape juice offers dry and sweet varieties of "nature's tonic."

Juicing became popular in America during the 1970s. Smoothies, thick drinks consisting of fresh fruit blended with milk, yogurt, or ice cream, became popular in the 1980s. Juice bars, which frequently serve smoothies, were launched in the early 1990s in health food stores and quickly evolved into major independent businesses.

The first nonalcoholic fruit juice sold commercially was made from grapes. In 1869 Thomas Bramwell Welch of Vineland, New Jersey, a Methodist minister who strongly favored temperance, manufactured what he called "unfermented wine" intended for sacramental use. Welch was unsuccessful in his attempt to replace wine in church services, and he stopped making the juice in 1873. His son Charles Welch revived the idea two years later, marketing Welch's Grape Juice as a temperance beverage with the slogan "The lips that touch Welch's are all that touch mine." It was the beginning of the pasteurized fruit juice industry in America. Welch Foods has been bottling, canning, and freezing juice and selling jelly and other related products ever since.

When the citrus industry was launched in Florida and California in the 1880s, growers canned and bottled fruit juice in addition to selling the fresh fruit, but sales of juice were limited. In 1907 California citrus growers banded together in a cooperative called the California Fruit Growers Exchange, which later sold its products under the brand name Sunkist. In 1920 the cooperative began to advertise that its products contained vitamins (first identified in the previous decade), particularly emphasizing vitamin C. Three years later, the co-op distributed 100 million promotional brochures. Florida growers followed Sunkist's lead, emphasizing the therapeutic qualities of lemons and oranges. The sales of fruit juice increased threefold within two decades, and fruit juice became a breakfast mainstay. In addition, fruit juices, especially apple juice, became an important component of babies' diets and children's lunches.

A new addition to the fruit juice market was frozen juices, which were first marketed during the 1930s. During World War II scientists developed a process for making powdered orange juice. After the war, the powdered juice concentrate was marketed by Florida Foods Corporation. It was not greatly successful, but then the company launched a new line of frozen juice under the brand name Minute Maid, and sales skyrocketed. The company changed its name to the Minute Maid Company. Minute Maid was acquired by the Coca-Cola Company in 1960. Canned fruit juices are sold in vending machines and stores along with soda pop.

[**See also** Applejack; Brandy; Cider; Citrus; Fruit; Fruit Wines; Juice Bars; Juicers.]

BIBLIOGRAPHY
Chazanof, William. *Welch's Grape Juice: From Corporation to Co-Operative.* Syracuse, NY: Syracuse University Press, 1977.

Merlo, Catherine. *Heritage of Gold: The First 100 Years of the Sunkist Growers, Inc., 1893–1993.* Los Angeles: Sunkist Growers, n.d.

Andrew F. Smith

Fruit Wines

Wines made from the fermented juice of any fruit except grapes are known as fruit wines. Berry, citrus, melon, tree fruits (apple, cherry, peach, pear, and plum), and dried fruit such as raisins are used in home recipes and at commercial wineries throughout America to make wine. Most fruit requires the addition of sugar, water, acid, and yeast nutrients to trigger the fermentation process and achieve the alcohol level of wine, between 7 percent and 15 percent by volume. Yeast converts sugar to alcohol, and more sugar may be added for sweetness.

Grapes do not generally require these additions as they are naturally high in sugar, water, bacteria-resistant tartaric acids and yeast. Some producers of grape wine add sweeteners, fruit flavoring, and sometimes carbonation to make what are commonly called pop wines. Such products designed to appeal to young, casual wine drinkers or those seeking sweeter tastes are not true fruit wines in the strictest sense.

Because most edible fruits have the potential to ferment without human intervention, winelike fruit beverages have a global history dating back to humanity's earliest origins. Peoples throughout Africa, Asia, Europe, the Americas and the world's archipelagoes are all known to have made wines from indigenous fruits historically, and many still do so. Ancient Egyptian pomegranate wines and Mesopotamian date wines are among the earliest documented examples. Many European colonists and pioneers who settled what is today the United States had come from northern regions where grapes were not primary crops, so they were accustomed to making fermented concoctions from apples, wild berries, and grains.

Before mass production of American consumer goods, homemade fruit wine was an integral part of American cookery, like canning and preserving foodstuffs to last beyond a harvest. As in cooking, recipes and techniques varied greatly, but there were key requirements: crushed fruit, sugar, gallons of water (usually boiled), active yeast components, clean utensils to avoid contamination, good ventilation, large, airtight storage vessels, and space to store them at appropriate temperatures. In addition, time and diligence were needed to carry out the multistep wine-making process: several days for flavor extraction, fermentation and storage transfer; siphoning, over the course of a few weeks; and weeks or months after bottling and corking for the wine to develop.

Before Prohibition and after its repeal, fruit wines were sold at general stores in small towns throughout America, notably in rural areas and in the South. During Prohibition, much fruit wine was made in American homes, due in large part to clauses in federal law that allowed families to make up to two hundred gallons per year of fruit "juice" (that sometimes fermented) for personal use. As efficient wine-making equipment was often unavailable or expensive, this practice continued on many American farms and fruit orchids, further underlining the strong association of fruit wines with country living.

By the end of the twentieth century, the making of fruit wines had become an American hobby supported by numerous societies and websites linking enthusiasts to information and technological advances that foster quality wine making. Nevertheless, most fruit wine in the United States is produced and sold at wineries, generally using locally grown fruit. Many wineries cooperate with local tourist enterprises to promote seasonal fruit wines at county harvest festivals. Outside of this context, one of the most popular fruit wines consumed in the United States is plum wine, available at many Japanese restaurants and some retail liquor stores.

[**See also** Fermentation; Fruit; Fruit Juices; Wine: Historical Survey; Wineries; Yeast.]

BIBLIOGRAPHY
Darden, Norma Jean, and Carole Darden. *Spoonbread and Strawberry Wine: Recipes and Reminiscences of a Family.* New York: Doubleday, 1994.

Vargas, Patty, and Rich Gulling. *Country Wines: Making and Using Wines from Herbs, Fruits, Flowers and More.* Pownal, VT: Storey Communications, 1992.

Tonya Hopkins

Frying Baskets

When deep-frying foods, cooks need a safe way to remove cooked food from dangerously hot fat. With a frying basket, a cook lowers cut-up food into the fat all at once

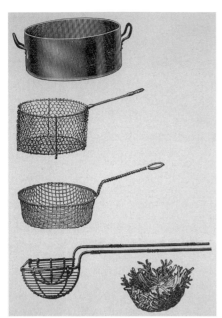

Imported (second from top), domestically produced (middle), and bird's nest frying baskets.

and then removes it as soon as cooking is complete. In the late 1800s, paired, close-fitting baskets—called bird's-nest baskets—were used for frying various sizes of "nests" of cooked noodles or rice that were filled with other foods before being served. Large deep-fryer sets comprised a stamped-iron kettle and a high, fixed hoop from which was hung a removable wire or perforated basket. These devices were commonly used for frying large batches of foods such as crullers, doughnuts, and potatoes.

[**See also** CRULLERS; DOUGHNUT-MAKING TOOLS; DOUGHNUTS; FRYING PANS, SKILLETS, AND SPIDERS; POTATO-COOKING TOOLS.]

BIBLIOGRAPHY
Franklin, Linda Campbell. *300 Years of Kitchen Collectibles*. 5th. ed. Iola, WI: Krause Publications, 2003.

LINDA CAMPBELL FRANKLIN

Frying Pans, Skillets, and Spiders

The first colonists in America brought with them and used frying pans and skillets developed over centuries of forging and casting in Europe. Early American foundries, beginning in 1646 with the Saugus Mill in Massachusetts, produced similar designs—a shallow pan with a long handle and three legs, designed for perching above fireplace embers. Some, lacking legs, worked on high cooking trivets. The variant term "spider," whimsically derived from the pan's long handle, body, and legs, originated in early New England and spread regionally after 1800. The related term "skillet" seems to have been less precise—sometimes referring to a deeper, three-legged, long-handled saucepan called, at the time, a "posnet," and sometimes to the frying pan.

By the middle of the nineteenth century, industry had adapted to the stovetop, manufacturing legless frying pans with shorter handles of wood or metal. By the late 1800s, sheet-iron and cast-iron pans, called "skillets," "fry pans," "frying pans," "spiders," and "deep fryers," were being made with new finishes; some pans were manufactured of cast aluminum to reduce weight. Many incorporated pouring lips and secondary tab handles, heat rings, grease moats, and self-basting domed lids, often available in diameters from 4.5 inches to more than 16 inches. Cheaply made thin skillets, in use by the 1900s, were popular, despite poor quality. Twentieth-century advances included electric frying pans in the 1950s and coatings of Teflon, to prevent food from sticking to the pan, in the 1960s.
[**See also** COOKING TECHNIQUES; KETTLES; POTS AND PANS.]

BIBLIOGRAPHY
Franklin, Linda Campbell. *Three Hundred Years of Kitchen Collectibles*. 5th ed. Iola, WI: Krause, 2003.
Smith, David G., and Chuck Wafford. *The Book of Griswold and Wagner*. 2nd ed. Atglen, PA: Schiffer, 2000.

ALICE ROSS AND
LINDA CAMPBELL FRANKLIN

Fudge

Fudge, typically chocolate but commonly marketed in dozens of flavors, is a candy made by boiling a sugar mixture until it makes a soft ball when dropped into ice water, or reaches 234°F to 238°F at sea level, and then stirring to make a soft candy. Soft candy was known as fondant in classical French confectionery, but fondant is mostly used as a soft center for candies dipped in chocolate or a harder candy mixture. In America, early fudge was strongly associated with the "seven sisters" women's colleges of the 1890s. Students at the colleges spread the popularity of fudge by bringing it to their homes. The name probably developed in 1888 at Vassar College, in Poughkeepsie, New York, and refers to an expression young women might have used instead of swearing. Fudge was something that homesick girls at school could make in their dormitories late at night using a spirit lamp borrowed from the chemistry laboratory, a gaslight, or a chafing dish—a popular gadget at the time. When Fannie Farmer recorded a fudge recipe in 1906, it was not in her practical *Boston Cooking-School Cook Book* but in her more casual book, *Chafing Dish Dainties*.

The first published recipe for "fudges" (for approximately ten years, one square was "a fudge" and a plateful were "fudges") may have been that in the 1893 cookbook produced by the women's building at the Columbian Exposition in Chicago. A 1908 pamphlet published by Walter Baker Company, the chocolate maker, contained recipes for eight kinds of fudge, including Vassar fudge, Smith College fudge, and Wellesley marshmallow fudge, contributed by Janet McKenzie Hill.

Soft candies in general have a documented existence well before 1888, and brown-sugar fudge in particular has a clear line of descent from Mexican sweets perhaps a century older or more. By the 1890s, brown-sugar fudge was known to American college women as penuchi, penuche, ponouche, penucio, and panocha. The term "panocha" was used as early as 1870 in a federal report describing a sweet distributed on Indian reservations to the detriment of the health of the Indians. *Panocha* (or *panucho*) was Mexican-border Spanish for a round corn pancake or johnnycake, and by analogy the name was applied to a round cake of soft sugar candy with nuts. Such candy is still made in Mexico and is known as *cajeta* (because it is packed in small boxes) or *palenqueta* (because it naturally spreads out like a plaque). The same candy is called a praline in New Orleans, which was under Spanish rule for most of the late eighteenth century. (The original French pralines are nuts with a sugar coating.) Any recipe for New Orleans pralines can be used to make fudge, and vice versa. The main difference is that brown-sugar fudge is poured into pans and cut into squares, whereas New Orleans pralines are poured onto marble slabs and are more or less round.

Many nineteenth-century recipes for caramels can be used to make fudge, because instructions are unclear about how long to boil the candy. By the 1870s, there were American recipes for "soft candy" that specified cooking to the soft-ball stage, stirring the candy as it cooled to make it smoother, or using a combination of the two techniques. A recipe for "soft candy" that can be made by children appeared in the 1878 cookbook *Six Little Cooks*.

Early fudge was thought to be an easy candy to make, because it required relatively less boiling than hard candies and toffee. Softer than caramels, fudge was easier to eat. But preparation of fudge can be tricky, especially without an accurate thermometer. Results are affected by both weather and altitude. (Boiling temperature also varies by altitude.) Sometimes fudge does not stiffen, and sometimes it is granular.

By the 1900s, fudge was a staple in candy stores across America, especially at summer resorts in New England and on Mackinac Island, Michigan, where it became a celebrated local specialty. Divinity, which is made by a technique that combines those for nougat, fudge, and Italian meringue (marshmallows), became popular around the same time. There was a recipe for divinity in the *New York Times* by 1907, and this confection became more popular in the southern states. A number of nontraditional soft candies not based on boiling sugar are sometimes called fudge. Among them are the quick or no-cook fudges that were developed in the 1950s (including the recipe widely attributed to Mamie Eisenhower), mashed-potato candy, peanut butter candy, and freezer frosting fudge. Early flavors other than chocolate and brown sugar were maple sugar, vanilla, butterscotch, candied fruit, coconut, and fudge layered in two flavors and colors. More recent additions are coffee, peanuts, various fruits such as strawberries, and liquor flavorings.

[See also CANDY AND CANDY BARS; CHAFING DISH; CHOCOLATE; FARMER, FANNIE; MEXICAN AMERICAN FOOD; SUGAR.]

BIBLIOGRAPHY

Bening, Lee Edwards. *Oh, Fudge: A Celebration of America's Favorite Candy.* New York: Henry Holt, 1990.

MARK H. ZANGER

Fund-Raisers

At the time of European settlement in the New World, the male-driven church and state together managed the governmental, economic, and social aspects of life. Church funds were gathered by a system of levies and donations. People in need, lacking other resources, became the responsibility of the community. The nineteenth century generally disrupted this tradition. As part of the shift to a more secular, mercantile, and urban culture in the North, male involvement was replaced by the fund-raising of urban, middle-class, home-centered women. With discretionary time available for local church, charitable, and reform work, women used traditional cookery skills to raise funds for the church—missionary support and building maintenance—and for addressing such community concerns as education, clean water, prison, housing reform, and the needs of the poor. Although the century idealized and emphasized women's private role, the public, philanthropic contributions of women were usually applauded as well. Many women's projects eventually evolved into national charities such as the Red Cross.

A community would sometimes raise a minister's salary by means of the quarterly donation party. The entire congregation gathered in the large home of one of its wealthier members to enjoy an evening of conviviality. Women prepared and donated their best dishes, counting on the resulting good spirits to loosen purse strings and produce a significant sum. During the Civil War, various social gatherings, among them "oyster suppers," raised large sums for soldiers and hospitals. Such efforts inspired the United States Sanitary Commission, which started in New York in 1861. This large organization with its many branches ran hospitals and soup kitchens with funds raised at ambitious fairs where the donated items on sale included food.

The late nineteenth century was a time of ice cream socials, festivals, fairs, and complex church suppers. At first, donated foods were brought from home, but, as churches built their own kitchens, menus expanded. Some churchwomen raised funds by preparing conference banquets. As these events became increasingly successful financially and socially, they were undertaken by secular groups such as the Grange, an organization of farm families. These food-based fund-raisers are still important social events in local communities nationwide, offering fine traditional ethnic and regional cuisines.

Charity cookbooks served a similar function. Instituted at Sanitary Fairs to raise funds for the victims of the Civil War, they became one of the more common philanthropic strategies across the country. Although most of them were compiled by church groups, they were published also for secular charitable causes such as the temperance movement, suffrage, hospitals, and schools. They are still going strong.

The Woman's Exchange movement provided another way of using food to raise money, this one through a self-help system for middle-class women in need of support. Begun in 1832, the exchanges sold their handmade products anonymously (protecting their donors from embarrassment), keeping only a small percentage to cover their overhead. Some exchanges developed restaurants and raised funds with fashionable and popular meals; others distributed catalogs of nonperishable foods nationwide, and they, too, compiled cookbooks. They remained viable well into the twentieth century.

At the turn of the twenty-first century, the gender lines had blurred and the practice of fund-raising with food had become a useful tool universally. Community fund-raisers, cookbooks and even some exchanges survived. The most common examples of the practice were Girl Scout Cookies, pancake breakfasts, clambakes, bake sales, raffled cooking lessons and dinners, restaurant donations, and political banquets.

[See also COMMUNITY COOKBOOKS; GENDER ROLES; SETTLEMENT HOUSES.]

BIBLIOGRAPHY

Burdett-Coutts, Baroness Angela Georgina, ed. *Woman's Mission: A Series of Congress Papers on the Philanthropic Work of Women, by Eminent Writers.* Chicago International Exhibition of Women's Work. London: Low Marston, 1893. Facsimile edition, Cheshire, UK: Portrayer, 2002.

Ross, Alice. "Ella Smith's Unfinished Community Cookbook: A Social History of Women and Work in Smithtown, New York 1884-1922." In *Recipes for Reading: Community Cookbooks, Stories, Histories,* ed. A. L. Bower. Amherst: University of Massachusetts Press, 1997.

ALICE ROSS

Funeral Food

In the American South, people used to say that a man's standing in the community could be judged by the number of plates his widow had to return after his funeral. The bounty of foods spread out for mourners in the South is legendary, fondly chronicled in novels and short stories. As the folk artist Kate Campbell sang in "Funeral Food," in 1998, "We sure eat good when someone dies." Fried chicken, baked ham, potato salad, deviled eggs, rolls, pound cake, and endless pies filled the home, brought by friends, family, and neighbors.

Funeral food is more than a southern ritual. All over America, funeral food is both comforting and practical, giving mourners something to do, surrounding the bereaved with proof that life goes on, and relieving the family of the burden of feeding guests. In many regions, the best-known funeral foods are casseroles—familiar, practical, and transportable. Utah is known for "funeral potatoes," a mixture of hash browns, sour cream, and cream soup that is topped with a cornflake crust. The dish is so common that it was one of the images used on pins for the 2002 Winter Olympics in Salt Lake City.

In the early twenty-first century, the fried chicken may be takeout and the ham is spiral cut, but the impulse to accompany mourning with food is the same as it always has been. That funeral food is less likely to come from busy neighbors and more often from restaurants and caterers is, in a sense, a return to old ways. Providing food and edible mementos at funerals has always been a business. In the eighteenth and nineteenth centuries, funeral tokens, particularly funeral biscuits, were used in many communities. Like the cake slices given to departing wedding guests, funeral biscuits stamped with symbolic images were given as tokens or were served after the funeral, often with wine. William Woys Weaver, in his book *America Eats: Edible Forms of Folk Arts* (1989), records many designs, including hearts, cherubs, and hourglasses. Providing food for mourners who traveled long distances was such a burden that it was sometimes accounted for in eighteenth- and nineteenth-century estate inventories. In the North Carolina Archives in Raleigh, the historian James Jordan III found the following in the 1779 inventory of the estate of Timothy Clear, a New Bern merchant: "(In the trunks) No. 3 a case with 10 bottles three of them full of wine—expended at his funeral...No. 6 one iron-bound case, key found, contains 11 bottles, 6 full wine...used at his funeral...one half of one keg used...ditto."

Not all funeral foods have disappeared. Funeral pie is still found in Amish and Pennsylvania Dutch communities. According to some sources, the simple filling of raisins and sugar is made from inexpensive staples a homemaker would have had available at any time of the year. However, some historians note that before the twentieth century, raisins had to be seeded. Going to the trouble to make a raisin-baked pie showed how much the cook valued the deceased. The following are examples of rituals that continue in some form among ethnic groups in the United States.

Jewish

Se'udat havra'ah (various spellings), the Jewish meal of condolence, is loving and practical. The first meal served to the bereaved after the burial, *se'udat havra'ah*, is prepared by friends or relatives from their own food. This practice can be seen as life giving: Because the foods are prepared by others, mourners are obligated to eat. Many of the foods served are symbolic. Round foods are often used, to signify the continuance of life. Commonly used foods are round breads, such as challah, and lentils, used both for their round shape and because of a tradition that lentils were prepared by Isaac after he heard of the death of his father, Abraham. Hard-boiled eggs are served without salt. The eggs symbolize the cycle of life, and the lack of salt may symbolize the end of tears. Salt on the Passover seder table represents the tears of Hebrew slaves.

Mexican

Mexican funerals may include treasured foods, such as mole and tamales, but it is the annual commemoration of those who have died that is best known. In Mexico *Dias de las Muertos* (Days of the Dead) is a weeklong community event leading up to All Souls Day, November 2. Because the dead are often returned to Mexico for burial, it is a much smaller observance in the United States. In communities with small or developing Mexican communities, Day of the Dead may be noted only as a folk festival. The traditional bread, *pan de muertos*, can be found in cities with large enough Mexican populations to support traditional bakeries. Lightly sweet and covered with sugar, the bread is made in various shapes, including bodies decorated with lumps of dough that represent the skeleton and round shapes that represent the soul.

Italian

Italians mark All Souls Day with special cookies. Called *fave dei morti* (beans of the dead) and *osso dei morti* (bones of the dead), these are very hard, dry cookies, often containing chunks of almonds and shaped to resemble beans or bones. The beans have various meanings. Some stories connect them to immortality and the underworld. In other explanations, fava beans were used to weight the eyes of the dead. *Osso dei morti*, with a dry texture resembling chunks of bone, are more common in Italian-American bakeries and are sold all year despite their macabre name.

Chinese

In Chinese communities, ancestors are honored participants in the lives of the living. At funerals symbolic foods are taken to the grave as a last offering—piles of oranges to symbolize good luck and roasted chickens or ducks to represent a whole life. After being offered to the deceased, these dishes or duplicates may be served to mourners as a way of sharing a last meal with the loved one. On the first anniversary of the death, on the person's birthday, or during the spring festival of Ching Ming, the food offerings may be repeated.

Greek

Rather than food brought by others, a unique food served at Greek funerals is made by the family of the deceased and given to mourners. *Koliva* (or *kolyva*) is a sprouted wheat salad, taken from Jesus's words in John 12:24: "Unless a wheat grain falls in the earth and dies, it remains alone; but if it dies, it bears much fruit." Preparation of *koliva* is a two-day process that ideally involves the family. Wheat is soaked overnight and then boiled and mixed with toasted sesame seeds, raisins, nuts, parsley, and sometimes pomegranate seeds. Sometimes sweetened, the mixture is dried, shaped in a mound, covered with bread crumbs, and topped with confectioners' sugar. The top is decorated with icing or Jordan almonds in the sign of the cross and the deceased's initials. The *koliva* is taken to the church and distributed after the funeral as a symbol of immortality and resurrection.

[**See also** CAKES; CASSEROLES; CHINESE AMERICAN FOOD; ETHNIC FOOD; ITALIAN AMERICAN FOOD; JEWISH AMERICAN FOOD; MEXICAN AMERICAN FOOD.]

BIBLIOGRAPHY

Kolatch, Alfred. *The Jewish Mourner's Book of Why.* Middle Village, NY: David, 1993.

Levine, Rabbi Aaron. *To Comfort the Bereaved.* Northvale, NJ: Aronson, 1996.

KATHLEEN PURVIS

Funnel Cakes

Funnel cakes are circles of fried dough made lacy and very crisp by pouring a light batter into hot oil with a funnel, stopping the hole with a finger between pastries. In the United States, they are associated with Pennsylvania Dutch celebrations and street fairs, and are sold at sporting events. The idea has probably been invented several times, as it appears in medieval Anglo-Norman and Old English cooking manuscripts as "mincebek," "blaunche escrepes," or "cryspes"—all deep-fried fritters created by making a hole in a bowl.

Although Anglo-American cookbooks preserve many recipes for fritters, the particular trick of swirling in the batter through a funnel or bowl-with-hole seems to have been abandoned, and did not reappear until a Pennsylvania Dutch cookbook of the 1930s gave a recipe for "funnel cakes." A likely source that does use the technique is the recipe for Schneebälle (Snowballs) in the German-language cookbook of Henrietta Davidis, first published in 1844, widely reprinted in the United States (in German) from 1879, and partially translated into English (but without the expressed fried pastry recipe) in 1896.

BIBLIOGRAPHY

Frederick, J. George. *The Pennsylvania Dutch and Their Cookery.* New York: Business Bourse, 1935. Reprint, *Pennsylvania Dutch Cook Book,* New York: Dover 1971.

MARK H. ZANGER

Fusion Food

The term "fusion cuisine," the major American culinary trend of the twentieth century, was coined in the 1970s to describe the combining of ingredients, flavors, and culinary techniques from two or more cultures to create new dishes. The Florida chef Norman Van Aken takes credit for inventing the phrase, borrowed from jazz vernacular, in which fusion means a blending of jazz with other musical elements, such as rock. Continuing this musical analogy, the *New York Times* food critic William Grimes described fusion at its best as "the culinary version of counterpoint, in which precisely defined flavors talk back and forth to each other rather than blending into a single smooth harmonic effect; it keeps 'your palate on edge.'"

Fusion has progressed from confusing and even offensive to acceptance and mainstream, especially in metropolitan areas and among people under thirty. Menu descriptions of fusion dishes can sound jarring: rare duck breast with hot and sweet pineapple fried rice and white pepper ice cream (Jean-Georges Vongerichten, Vong, New York City); seared Maine scallops nestled in a shell served with potato cabbage puree and red wine black bean sauce (Wolfgang Puck, Chinois on Main, Santa Monica, California); *mofongo*-stuffed roasted breast of chicken with very black beans and homestead mango chutney (Norman Van Aken, Norman's, Coral Gables, Florida); lobster roll wrapped in slivers of pear with a drizzling of sevruga caviar, potato foam, and a shot glass of ginger ale granité (Marcus Samuelsson, Aquavit, New York City and Minneapolis, Minnesota).

Television cooking shows, particularly *East Meets West with Ming Tsai* with Chinese-American chef Ming Tsai, have introduced home chefs to the concept. Tsai combines traditional Chinese flavors and techniques with contemporary American foods. For Thanksgiving 2002, for example, he devised a recipe for brining cut-up turkey, deep frying it in a wok, and serving the dish with a cranberry dipping sauce containing rice wine vinegar and ginger.

Origins

Although "fusion" is an American term, the trend has antecedents in French nouvelle cuisine of the 1970s, in which Gallic chefs rejected traditional rich sauces in favor of lighter dishes and fresh ingredients. Undercooked, crisp vegetables were served with fruit-based as well as wine-reduction sauces. French master chefs such as Paul Bocuse visited the Orient for inspiration. The French were already versed in the East-West concept because of colonization of Indochina (Vietnam, Cambodia, and Laos). The blending of compatible ingredients and techniques formerly isolated in Asian or European kitchens paved the way for experimentation.

The challenge was taken up in California in the 1970s and 1980s, when chef Alice Waters of Chez Panisse restaurant began fashioning her groundbreaking combinations of elements. Among her signature dishes are duck confit pizza with sun-dried tomatoes and calzone stuffed with goat cheese, fresh herbs, and prosciutto.

For the French chef Jean-Georges Vongerichten, famous for his signature "Thailoise" Franco-Asian cuisine served at his Vong restaurant in New York, the turning point came when he opened a French restaurant in Bangkok, Thailand. There, he became fascinated with local flavors such as lemongrass, fish sauce, ginger, curry pastes, and coconut milk. This experience changed his food forever.

Fusion owes much to broader cultural changes that chefs reflected in their cooking. In the late 1960s in America, people began eating less fat in response to health warnings. Global economy and increased tourism in the 1960s and 1970s exposed Americans to new culinary cultures in other parts of the world. This phenomenon helped foster an intense interest in ethnic food in the 1980s. Changed immigration patterns brought an influx of people, particularly from parts of Asia, to the United States. They brought along their culinary customs and habits, opened restaurants, and began to sell the exotic ingredients of their native cuisines. Culinary globalization produced an international melting pot in which various culinary cultures blended, not neatly bounded but bleeding into each other. High-end chefs and restaurant owners discovered that cultural diversity sells, allowing diners to participate in culinary tourism without leaving home. Fusion has moved beyond East-West cuisine to include Central and South American, Moroccan, and other national culinary identities.

The Japanese American poet David Mura points out that multiculturalism is a fact in the modern world in the arts as well as becoming the departure point for cutting-edge cuisine.

Fusion versus Confusion

The products of fusion cuisine are not always harmonious on the palate or universally appreciated. Many detractors discredit this style of cooking for having more to do with sensation and novelty than integrity. These purists argue that individual ethnic flavors become diluted and that fusion undermines generations of culinary traditions that have culminated in the signature flavors, spices, and herbs that make each cuisine distinctive. Some critics feel fusion is often carelessly practiced by chefs who combine too many elements and have only superficial knowledge of the individual cuisines involved.

Albert Sonnenfeld, English-language editor of *Food: A Culinary History* (1999), is not opposed to fusion per se, simply the way it is practiced in America, where, he believes, the use of too many ingredients and confusion of ingredients with flavor leads to "clashing flavors." In Europe, by contrast, Sonnenfeld has found that chefs understand that less is more.

In his book *Near A Thousand Tables: A History of Food* (2002), Felipe Fernandez-Armesto, historian and professor at Oxford University, England, has called fusion cuisine "Lego cookery," made possible only by the availability of worldwide produce and resources, mix-and-match elements that arrive in kitchens in processed form. Far from inventive, he claims that fusion operations are nothing more than factories.

Most fusion chefs agree that it is essential to have a deep understanding of the individual culinary traditions before fusing. Many culinary educators maintain that it is only after a solid grounding in French techniques at the undergraduate level that a chef is ready to take on the study of the cooking methods of Asia or Mexico, for example. Finally, good fusion cuisine must "work" on the palate with flavors, textures, and techniques that complement each other.

[See also CALIFORNIA; CELEBRITY CHEFS; CHINESE AMERICAN FOOD; ETHNIC FOODS; FRENCH INFLUENCES ON AMERICAN FOOD; NOUVELLE CUISINE; RESTAURANTS; SCANDINAVIAN AND FINNISH AMERICAN FOOD; SOUTHEAST ASIAN FOOD; SOUTHWEST REGIONAL COOKERY.]

BIBLIOGRAPHY

Carpenter, Hugh, and Teri Sandison. *Fusion Food Cookbook*. New York: Artisan, 1994.
Grimes, William. "A Fearless Chef with an Artistic Streak." *New York Times*, May 23, 2001.
Tsai, Ming, and Arthur Boehm. *Blue Ginger: East Meets West Cooking with Ming Tsai*. New York: Clarkson Potter, 1999.

LINDA MURRAY BERZOK

G

Gallo, Ernest and Julio

Ernest (1909-) and Julio Gallo (1910-1993), although brought up in a grape-growing and wine-making family, did not start what is America's largest wine empire until after the mysterious deaths of their parents in 1933. The Gallo family had continued to grow grapes throughout Prohibition for "home wine making," and the murder-suicide—the official verdict of the deaths on June 21, 1933—has been shrouded with questions. The Prohibition era was a time of widespread lawlessness, and it would have been very difficult for a significant grape grower to have avoided contact with unsavory elements. This was especially true in California, where organized crime from the East Coast and Midwest was establishing itself in everything from film unions to clandestine alcohol production. The "accidental death" of the film star Thelma Todd in 1935 led to a great deal of unwanted publicity on this issue and the corruption of many California institutions and industries.

Soon after their parents' deaths, the Gallo brothers obtained a permit to produce fifty thousand gallons of wine. When Prohibition ended several months later, the brothers, unlike most of their neighbors, had a large inventory to sell legally. In 1935 production was 350,000 gallons, and by 1936 the Gallos had built a storage facility with a capacity of 1.5 million gallons. This huge growth was the result of strong management. Ernest did the front-office work of marketing and planning, and Julio was in charge of wine crafting and land management. Their philosophy was to establish control over as many aspects of production as possible, so the Gallos began acquisition of transportation, bottling, printing, and marketing companies. The business plan was so successful that by 1950 the Gallos had one of the largest wine production capacities in the United States. Production increased to the extent that in 1992 storage capacity in the four primary Gallo facilities was estimated to be 330 million gallons, or 660 times the capacity in 1933. Gallo has remained a private family business. One out of every four bottles of wine purchased in the U.S. market is a Gallo brand.

Despite its success, the Gallo family was not immune to tragedy and family acrimony. One of Julio's sons committed suicide. Ernest and Julio were estranged from their younger brother, Joseph Jr. In addition, they sued Joseph Jr. and won, in a trademark infringement case over Joseph's use of the Gallo name for his cheese business. Julio Gallo was killed in a jeep accident in 1993 at the age of eighty-three. To give the family's point of view of these events, the Gallo family released *Ernest and Julio: Our Story* (1994) in response to an expose, *Blood and Wine: The Unauthorized Story of the Gallo Wine Empire* (1993), by Ellen Hawkes.

Until 1974 core wine production at Gallo was either generic, mass-produced wines or sweet, fortified wines, such as the lemon-flavored white port marketed as Thunderbird. These sweet wines sold in pint bottles were controversial because many of those who bought them did so to become quickly and inexpensively intoxicated. In the early days Gallo marketers had secured the most favorable shelf space in the urban package stores that catered to this market, and Gallo came to dominate the market. The change in direction to premium varietal wines was an important change in marketing strategy.

As a result of Gallo's change in focus to varietal wines, thousands of acres were turned to production of premium grapes and development of brands such as Dry Creek, Anapuma, Zabaco, Indigo Hills, Marcelina, and Frei Brothers, new brands seemingly being added monthly. A large portion of the shelf space of local wine stores is devoted to Gallo, albeit under many brand names. The economy of scale allows Gallo to buy high-quality products, pay good wages, and not use grapes it believes are inferior to its standard. The prevalence of Gallo products, however, makes it difficult for other companies to compete for shelf space and can lead to creation of many labels without meaningful difference in the product inside the bottles—much as generic products established the family fortune. The wines have met with critical acclaim and in terms of price to quality ratio are among the best values on the market. In 1993 Ernest Gallo told the *Wine Spectator* that his firm's historic entry into the premium wine market was an attempt to make the best possible wine in America and that the venture was driven by "largely a matter of personal satisfaction" and "certainly it's not for the profit."

Because the United States is a market in which 11 percent of wine buyers buy most of the wine and because of competition from producers in countries where land and production costs are considerably less expensive than in the United States, Gallo is seeking to boost its sales abroad. Because U.S. wine exports account for less than 4 percent of production, the venture represents a vast new market for the dominant American wine maker. The success of two of Julio's grandchildren, Gina and Matt Gallo, at the Dry Creek and Marcelina vineyards seems to indicate that the company will remain "in the family."

[See also WINE: HISTORICAL SURVEY; WINE: RECENT DEVELOPMENTS; WINERIES; WINE: CALIFORNIA WINES.]

BIBLIOGRAPHY

Gallo, Ernest and Julio, with Bruce B. Henderson. *Ernest and Julio: Our Story.* New York: Times Books, Random House, 1994.

Hawkes, Ellen. *Blood and Wine: The Unauthorized Story of the Gallo Wine Empire.* New York: Simon & Schuster, 1993.

STEVEN M. CRAIG

Game

Virtually all American Indians hunted game, including beaver, birds, buffalo, deer, elk, mountain sheep, prairie dogs, rabbits, raccoons, reindeer, and seals. In addition to meat, animals provided fur and skin for clothing, shelter, bedding, shoes, and storage containers, and animal parts were used for ceremonial and religious purposes.

The New World was particularly well endowed with edible fowl. Native Americans prized ducks, geese, partridges, pheasants, pigeons, and seabirds. Nonmigrating land birds, such as ruffed grouse and wild turkey, were plentiful and these birds were particularly important during the winter, when other food sources were scarce. Native Americans captured wildfowl with nets and snares and occasionally shot them with arrows. The hunting lifestyle was modified with the introduction of agriculture, which was adopted by some Native Americans, but even those engaged in farming continued to hunt game where possible.

The introduction of the horse by the Spanish in the sixteenth century greatly improved the American Indians' ability to hunt game. The Plains Indians became highly proficient at tracking and hunting buffalo on horseback. Likewise, the introduction of firearms greatly improved Native Americans' ability to acquire game.

European Colonists

At the beginning of the colonial era, North America teemed with game and wildfowl. After the first few years, colonists became proficient at trapping and hunting, and game became an extremely important food source for early Americans. The main advantage of wild game and fowl was that, unlike domesticated animals, they cost nothing to maintain. In addition, many birds and wild animals were crop pests, and killing them increased farm yields.

The four most important game animals were in colonial and early America were the deer, bear, buffalo, and wild turkey. Deer was by far the most important. It was plentiful throughout the colonies and was relatively easy to hunt. Venison was on the menu in almost all European settlements in eastern America. The common deer had become scarce in populated areas even before the American Revolution. By the end of the nineteenth century, deer had largely

Shoppers select game in a scene depicting Washington Market, New York City.

disappeared from New England. Deer remained an important food source in rural areas and in the South and West. Western hunters brought deer to market in eastern cities. By 1900 deer had become rare even in many western states, and state game laws had largely forbidden deer hunting. The result was the virtual elimination of venison from the American diet.

In early colonial America, brown and black bears were numerous, and their meat was an important food source in the eastern colonies. Rendered bear fat was used for shortening, and most frontier homes contained a deerskin bag of bear oil. Black bear meat was occasionally sold in eastern markets during the early nineteenth century but largely disappeared by the middle of the century.

In the early colonial era, buffalo roamed throughout much of eastern North America. The buffalo was an extremely important food source simply because of its large size. Colonists prepared buffalo in the same manner as did Native Americans: broiled on wood cinders or buffalo chips with wood ash rather than salt used as a flavoring. Buffalo were hunted with such skill that by 1770 they had disappeared from America east of the Mississippi River, but they remained an important food source on the Great Plains. During the late 1860s, William F. Cody was hired to supply buffalo meat to work crews constructing the eastern part of the transcontinental railroad, which was completed in 1869. Cody was so successful at hunting buffalo that he acquired the moniker "Buffalo Bill." The arrival of the railroads and increased European settlement on the Great Plains diminished the buffalo population as many of the animals were killed for sport. During the nineteenth century, hunters and sportsmen slaughtered them in huge numbers. By 1891 only 540 buffalo were known to have survived.

Small Game and Wildfowl

Over the centuries, Americans have eaten an astonishing array of game animals and birds. Large birds, such as cranes and swans, were so prized that they had largely disappeared from the East Coast by 1750. Wild turkeys were initially an important food source for early European colonists. At the beginning of European settlement, an estimated 10 million wild turkeys roamed eastern America. Wild turkeys were sought after throughout the nineteenth century. As wild turkeys became rarer during the nineteenth century, they also became more highly valued. By 1900, wild turkeys had vanished completely from twelve states and were fast disappearing elsewhere. By the Great Depression, there were only approximately thirty thousand wild turkeys in America.

Wild ducks were plentiful, and early colonists ate them often. Canvasback ducks, for example, wintered along the shores of Chesapeake Bay, where the wild celery they fed on flavored their flesh. Canvasbacks commanded high prices. Smaller birds caught or shot for food included blackbirds, blue jays, crows, herons, larks, orioles, plovers, quail, reedbirds, robins, sandpipers, snipes, turtledoves, and woodcocks. An excellent source of dietary protein, wild birds were sometimes kept in cages to be fattened for later slaughter. Other wildfowl also disappeared from America. The brant, which was still seen in the 1870s along the East Coast, had almost disappeared by the 1880s. The canvasback duck became nearly extinct.

One of the most important small birds on nineteenth-century tables was the pigeon. Most cookbooks contained directions for trussing and cooking these birds. Pigeon was eaten in every conceivable way—roasted, boiled, braised, broiled, stewed, and fricasseed. During some times of the year, pigeon was the most common food in many midwestern and southeastern areas of America. The most colorful and common of these birds was the passenger pigeon, which numbered an estimated 5 billion before European colonization. Passenger pigeons wintered along the southern coasts, where they were easily caught. Throughout the nineteenth century, these birds were caught by the millions. Because the supply was abundant, passenger pigeons made inexpensive food for the poor; leftovers were given to hogs. Passenger pigeons had been killed in such profusion that by the 1870s public anger led individual states to ban their slaughter. These laws were not effective, and by 1909 only two passenger pigeons remained alive. By 1914, the species was extinct.

Frontiersmen and trappers killed and ate a wide variety of animals, some of which became important culinary items. Beaver, for example, was trapped mainly for its fur, but frontiersmen also considered it tasty. A particular delicacy was beaver tail, which was frequently dried and shipped to market along with the pelt. Small game was particularly important for slaves and the rural poor.

Slaves, poor whites, and frontiersmen commonly ate opossum, raccoon, porcupine, rattlesnake, squirrel, and occasionally skunk. Even smaller animals found their way onto America's tables. On the frontier, frogs' legs were eaten when nothing else was available, but beginning in the mid-nineteenth century, frogs' legs were fashionable. Likewise, snails were enjoyed by those familiar with French cookery. Grasshoppers were occasionally consumed in the West, but only when there was nothing else to eat.

Return of Game

In parts of Appalachia and the rural South, venison, bear, wild turkey, and squirrel remained staple foods for decades, but generally game faded from the American culinary scene in the early twentieth century, although game occasionally appeared on the menu at swank restaurants.

The 1937 passage of the Federal Aid in Wildlife Restoration Act placed an excise tax on hunting equipment. The proceeds were designated for the management and restoration of wildlife and their habitats. The program has been largely responsible for the recovery of deer, elk, antelope, beaver, black bear, duck, giant Canada goose, elk, bighorn sheep, and other species. Three exemplary success stories are those of the wild turkey, white-tailed deer, and buffalo. The first efforts to reintroduce wild turkeys took place in the late 1930s. By the 1950s, the wild turkey population in New England had begun to increase. There are an estimated 5.6 million wild turkeys in America. Likewise, the white-tailed deer population is estimated at approximately 18 million. In the early twentieth century, conservationists and ranchers began taking steps to save the buffalo. Buffalo is no longer an endangered species and has become a sought-after food because it is leaner than beef. A number of ranchers raise buffalo for meat, and the numbers in public and private herds combined are more than 350,000 head.

The change in circumstances for some wild animals increased culinary interest in game. Although game generally disappeared from mainstream cookbooks in the latter part of the twentieth century, specialty game cookbooks have become a major genre since the 1930s. Game has returned to the table. Wild turkey, venison, and farm-raised buffalo are sold in specialty stores throughout the United States.

[See also BUFFALO; NATIVE AMERICAN FOODS: BEFORE AND AFTER CONTACT; NATIVE AMERICAN FOODS: TECHNOLOGY AND FOOD SOURCES; POULTRY AND FOWL; TURKEY.]

BIBLIOGRAPHY

Arnold, Samuel P. *The Fort Cookbook: New Foods of the Old West from the Famous Denver Restaurant; 190 Recipes for Game, Buffalo, Elk, and Much Standard Fare.* New York: HarperCollins, 1997.

Haines, Francis. *The Buffalo: The Story of American Bison and their Hunters from Prehistoric Times to the Present*. Norman and London: University of Oklahoma Press, 1995.

Webster, Harold. *The Complete Venison Cookbook*. Brandon, MS: Quail Ridge, 1996.

ANDREW F. SMITH

Garlic

For centuries, people have attributed medicinal qualities to garlic. More recently, scientists have studied garlic's potential for healing. No one can say with certainty that the risk of heart disease or cancer is reduced by eating garlic, but it is certain that garlic improves the flavor of food.

Garlic has long had a bad image. Garlic, like all alliums, contains sulfurous compounds that can burn the mouth and eyes and leave a powerful smell on the breath. (Many believed that garlic was strong enough to repel a vampire.) The English writer John Ruskin called garlic a "strong class barrier," good for laborers, perhaps, but nothing that would be brought into a decent kitchen. Amelia Simmons, in the first America cookbook, wrote, "Garlicks, tho' used by the French, are better adapted to the uses of medicine than cookery." In 1896 Oscar Tschirky, better known as Oscar of the Waldorf, put 3,455 recipes in his famous cookbook, but only one featured garlic. Sixty-five years later, when Craig Claiborne's *New York Times Cookbook* appeared, things were starting to change. Although only two of the fifteen hundred recipes in the book contained the word "garlic" in the title, there were dozens of others in which a clove or two had made its way onto the page (sometimes qualified as optional).

The food writer James Beard made a made major contribution to getting garlic on the map. In 1954 Beard wrote about an old Provençal recipe that called for cooking a chicken with forty cloves of garlic. Thousands of his readers tried it and liked it. At about the same time, the social critic Russell Lynes, in his famous discourse on highbrow and lowbrow phenomena, wrote about how the upscale cook might rub a wooden salad bowl with a clove of garlic to make the lettuce taste better. Whether for health or culinary reasons, the use of garlic in the United States has quadrupled since the early 1970s.

Most of America's garlic is grown in the Central Valley of California. More than 90 percent of the garlic used in the United States is the California Early or the California Late variety. These are solid, long-lasting softneck varieties that lend themselves to braiding. Most California garlic is processed in Gilroy in a huge plant, packaged as dried garlic powder or flakes, and shipped in long cartons to major food processors. In most other places, hardneck varieties of garlic rule. They grow a tough stem that comes up from the middle of the head. As the plant matures, the stem circles around and forms a small bulb called a "scape." The scape is removed so that it will not use resources that should go to the bulb. Often the tender scapes are marketed to Asian restaurants and cooked as a delicacy. Sometimes hardneck garlic is harvested early, before the cloves form in the heads, and it is coveted as green garlic.

Although they have developed thousands of onion cultivars, plant breeders have not been able to do the same with garlic, which does not produce seed. Garlic growers must put aside at least 10 percent of their crop to be broken into cloves for October planting. Strains of garlic that grow in one place for a long time develop particular characteristics. The garlic may be red or purple or blue. There may be a lot of cloves or just a few. The heads may be big or small. Some are hotter than others. But there is consistency in the strain. If that same garlic were grown in a new place, a new set of characteristics might evolve. The garlic responds to different soil conditions, different day lengths, different climates, and different altitudes. Although hundreds of garlic varieties are grown around the world, local growing conditions make each variety unique. Scientists are conducting research on shaping the garlic of the future and on getting garlic to produce true seed.

Like many of the alliums, garlic originally grew in south central Asia in what some call the "garlic crescent." The original genetic material has disappeared. Garlic was carried by migrating populations all around the Mediterranean. Early Egyptians, Greeks, and Romans used garlic as both medicine and food. Not a truly nutritious food, garlic is approximately 60 percent moisture, 30 percent carbohydrate, a small amount of protein, and traces of vitamins and minerals. Whether garlic is food or medicine continues to be debated.

[**See also** CALIFORNIA; HOMEMADE REMEDIES; SIMMONS, AMELIA; TSCHIRKY, OSCAR.]

BIBLIOGRAPHY

Aaron, Chester. *Garlic Is Life*. Berkeley, CA: Ten Speed, 1996.

Bergner, Paul. *The Healing Power of Garlic*. Rocklin, CA: Prima, 1996.

Crawford, Stanley. *A Garlic Testament*. Albuquerque: University of New Mexico Press, 1998.

Engeland, Ron L. *Growing Great Garlic*. Okanogan, WA: Filaree, 1991.

Griffith, Linda and Fred. *Garlic Garlic Garlic*. Boston: Houghton Mifflin, 1998.

Harris, Lloyd J. *The Book of Garlic*. Reading, MA: Addison-Wesley, 1988.

LINDA AND FRED GRIFFITH

Gas Grill

Modern Home Products (MHP), founded by Walter Koziol in the 1950s, invented the first outdoor gas grill and brought it to market in 1960. MHP was the first company to offer affordable residential outdoor gas lighting to the homeowner. This business grew and inspired Koziol to explore other ways to use gas outdoors. MHP produced the first outdoor gas barbecue grill, called Perfect Host, a 22.5-inch round steel grill on a portable cart supplied with either natural or liquid propane gas. By 1964 the first rectangular grills with rust-free solid aluminum construction were produced, and this design continues to be the industry's most popular.

By 1989 sales of gas grills had more than doubled, surpassing sales of charcoal grills almost two to one, according to the Barbecue Industry Association. Unlike briquette-fired grills, gas grills emulate indoor cooking ranges with more precise control of cooking conditions, which makes them very popular. According to the Hearth, Patio and Barbecue Association, because of the great taste of food cooked outdoors, easy cleanup, and informal mode of entertainment, 69 percent of gas grill owners cook out year-round. Although hamburgers, steak, hot dogs, and chicken breasts remain popular nationally, outdoor cooking styles vary regionally—from pork in the Carolinas to Cajun spices in the Deep South to lighter fare such as vegetables and fish on the West Coast.

[**See also** STOVES AND OVENS.]

COLLEEN JOYCE PONTES

Gender Roles

From the earliest records, prehistoric gender divisions in food work were divided according to those who were to be fed. Women (gatherers, later agriculturists), tied to their homes by young children, cooked for the family by serving up wet meals of stews and soups. The men (hunters), cooking on special occasions for men in the community, dry roasted meats out of doors. Each used their own equipment. Feasts and festivals combined the efforts of both. The same kind of gender divisions continued through the early European civilizations, and then through the Dark Ages, the Middle Ages, and the Renaissance, and were carried across the Atlantic Ocean to the American colonies. The English gender system prevailed in colonial American cooking, as in everything else.

American Colonial Cookery

The English common law system, transplanted to the American colonies, limited the role of married, white Anglo-Saxon, middle-class women to that of the household. Their private position as family cooks was secondary to that of their husbands, who represented their family unit in political and social matters. They were not allowed to own outright the equipment they needed to provide food, and only maintained the use of pots and pans, to be restored to the oldest son after their death. They were also denied the opportunity to run a public business on their own—running a tavern, a food shop, and catering, for example.

The men were required to grow the large crops and hunt, and to participate in outdoor political affairs. Men also took on the public ownership of taverns and performed as chefs

On the left side of this lithograph from the 1890s, the wife cooks while the husband reads a newspaper.

for the higher echelons of society. They ran specialized food shops, among them bakeries and butcher shops. Single women were allowed to run a business but only as a secondary choice to marriage.

Lower-class and upper-class women did not follow these rules: the lower because they had to work to survive, and the upper because they did not participate in household work.

Nineteenth-Century Cookery

With the growth of cities and the Industrial Revolution, men and women began leaving the farm and participating in the new urban cash economy. A new social division took over—the men aspired to a new goal, the self-made man, and his wife took on the duties of "homemaker." The cash he earned provided her with the tender for buying necessities, and she became a shopper. No longer burdened by the need to produce foods, she broadened her range of menus and recipes, following a quickly instituted fashion, that, in many cases, of simplified French cookery. Middle-class women began to write cookbooks, the first being Amelia Simmons's *American Cookery* (1796). Her landmark work was followed by increasing numbers of other such works, all by women in need of sustenance. They also conducted cooking schools, perhaps the first being that of Mrs. Goodfellow, of Philadelphia. With the expanding cities, restaurants became more popular, taking over the services of eighteenth-century tavern kitchens. The chefs were male, as before; their underlings were men or women. However, there were the beginnings of a few small restaurants and cafés owned by women, some of them married.

The new home economics movement had begun before the Civil War, and some women were teaching cookery in the spreading private colleges and the new land-grant schools. Some of their students became home economics teachers in grade schools, where they taught boys and girls daily from grade one. Others,

following the lead of Catharine Beecher, promoted and taught in the new women's colleges; Beecher put forth a new design of kitchens, wrote a cookbook, and generally promoted domestic roles. By the end of the nineteenth century, the Boston Cooking school was training nutritionists and educators. On a more modest level, women ran boardinghouses, often dependent on the quality of the table for reputation and fees. Some housed such fine kitchens as to serve patrons who did not live in, and were among the best small-town restaurants. A few women also invented or improved on cooking equipment. For example, Nancy M. Johnson patented the ice cream machine in 1843. Waves of immigration provided a labor force of married women with their own domestic experience, and many hired out as cooks to middle-class households or worked in canning factories.

Philanthropy was another role gender-assigned to women. Raising money by cooking and baking for festivals and suppers benefited political and social organizations such as churches, the Grange, the Red Cross, libraries, the Women's Christian Temperance Union, suffragists, and Women's Exchanges. During the Civil War, the Sanitary Commissions expanded these. Women's endeavors straddled the gap between men's and women's work, opening way for women in the public field.

Men's work expanded as well. The large-scale, geographic production of foods (as, for example, the grain fields of the Northwest, and the raising and slaughtering of pigs in the Midwest) were amazingly prolific. Men also ran small food shops, which became more and more specialized. By the end of the nineteenth century, urban areas contained bakeries and butcher shops. In smaller communities, general stores contained departments dedicated to food—prepackaged breads, tin cans, packed crackers, and so on, as well as products bartered from local farms. Pierre Blot, a cooking teacher and author from France, wrote a work on simplified French

cookery for Americans; Sylvester Graham, inspired by German research in nutrition, put forth his own theories on the subject: an antistress vegetarian diet that eschewed caffeine, sugar, spices, and meats, which combated the anxiety and stresses of city life. And the growing universities developed nutrition departments.

At the same time, the relocating male French chefs, displaced from France at the end of the turn of the nineteenth century, flocked to New York and became the basis of the new restaurant scene.

The Twentieth Century

The beginnings of the new century saw gender roles associated with food continuing in the directions already established. Men persevered in corporate undertakings and ran the chain stores. A&P expanded during the twentieth century, competing with Grand Union, Piggly Wiggly, and Krogers. Large food corporations merged and remerged, forming international networks of male production and trade. Men also maintained strong gender lines, participating at home by gardening, and earning their living as greengrocers, importers, and retailers of essential ethnic specialties for their communities.

When it was financially possible, women stayed home and cooked, transmitting both culture and nutrition to their families. Italian women, for example, were especially dedicated to home cooking, as family was the center of their culture, and food was the glue that held it together.

World War I brought the victory garden and government booklets on how to cook without the wheat, sugar, and butter which were being sent to the men fighting abroad. After the war, the success of the automobile and improved roads set the paths for tearooms and roadside cafes, perhaps modifications of the boardinghouse. Women ran these street-side institutions at which "dainty" menus were the rule (they specialized in fashionable salads and layer cakes), and that led to urban women's restaurants such as Schraffts. The Great Depression followed, and once more women's skills were more marketable, including their work as domestic cooks.

Conditions during World War II were similar to those of the first war, but in this case women worked to replace men and staff the war industry, and managed to cook with ration coupons for staples. After the war, Americans returned to "normalcy": women gave the jobs back to men and returned home to have families.

By the 1960s, Julia Child and her two French associates had published their mammoth two-volume work, *Mastering the Art of French Cooking*, and Julia Child's television series had begun. Child created a bridge between men's professional food and female home cooking. California-based Alice Waters (who gardened, wrote, and cooked for her restaurant Chez Panisse, featuring freshly picked, natural foods), Mollie Katzen, of Ithaca, New York (author, owner, and cook for the cooperative vegetarian restaurant Moosewood), and Lidia Bastianovich of New York City (author, owner, and cook for the Italian restaurant "Felidia") all followed Child's example.

By 2000, the field became more level, and gender less of an issue. Professional cooking schools accept equal numbers of men and women. Recent laws require home economics classes for both girls and boys. Men still dominate the corporations, and women the kitchen, but to a lesser degree. Fast foods, convenience foods, and takeout foods have softened the home gender division. Men are more likely to do hobby cooking on weekends, for entertainment's sake. In short, what began as a strict dichotomy has blurred and is moving closer to a situation without male and female limitations.

[See also BEECHER, CATHARINE; BOARDING-HOUSES; BOSTON COOKING SCHOOL; CHILD, JULIA; CHILD, LYDIA MARIA; COOKING SCHOOLS; DELMONICO'S; FUND-RAISERS; HOME ECONOMICS; LESLIE, ELIZA; LINCOLN, MRS.; PARLOA, MARIA; RANDOLPH, MARY; RESTAURANTS; ROADHOUSES; RORER, SARAH TYSON; SETTLEMENT HOUSES; SIMMONS, AMELIA; STREET VENDORS; TAVERNS; TEMPERANCE.]

BIBLIOGRAPHY

Counihan, Carole M. and Steven Kaplan. *Food and Gender: Identity and Power*. New York: Routledge, 1889.

Inness, Sherrie A., ed. *Cooking Lessons: The Politics of Gender and Food*. Lanham, MD: Rowman and Littlefield, 2001.

Matthews, Glenna. *"Just a Housewife:" The Rise and Fall of Domesticity in America*. New York: Oxford University Press, 1987.

ALICE ROSS

General Foods

The General Foods Company can date its beginning to 1895 when C. W. Post created the Postum Cereal Company to market Postum, a coffee substitute made out of wheat bran and molasses. He got the idea for the substitute while a patient at the Battle Creek Sanatorium operated by the Kellogg brothers.

In 1897, Post introduced a cereal that he called Grape-Nuts. This was followed in 1904 by Elijah's Manna, a cornflake cereal that would not be a hit with consumers until it was renamed Post Toasties. On Post's death in 1914, Marjorie Merriwether Post, his daughter, took over the company and began to create what would be General Foods. Ms. Post married Edward F. Hutton, an investment broker, in 1920. By 1923, he was chairman of the Postum Cereal Company.

In 1925, the company acquired the Jell-O Company and in quick order added Swans Down cake flour, Minute tapioca, Baker's coconut, Baker's chocolate, and Log Cabin syrup to an expanding list of consumer products. Maxwell House coffee was added in 1928, and the following year Postum purchased the General Foods Company from Clarence Birdseye, the man who had perfected a successful method for quick freezing food. To reflect the diverse product mix under the control of the company the name was changed to the General Foods Company. Over the next thirty years, more brand names were added, including Gaines Dog Food and Yuban coffee. Shortly after World War II ended, Maxwell House instant coffee was introduced. Other successful products included Kool-Aid, Tang, Crystal Light, 4 Seasons salad dressing, Oscar Mayer meat products, and Open Pit barbecue sauce.

General Foods is a case study in how large companies acquire and assimilate smaller food companies. General Foods has been called the "prototypical American food processor." It was acquired and assimilated itself in 1985 when the tobacco giant Philip Morris bought General Foods. In 1989, General Foods and Kraft, which Philip Morris had bought the year before, were combined to form a food products division called Kraft General Foods. In 1995, the name was shortened to Kraft Foods Inc.

[See also BIRDSEYE CORPORATION; CEREAL, COLD; COFFEE; COFFEE SUBSTITUTES; COFFEE, INSTANT; JELL-O; KELLOGG COMPANY; KRAFT FOODS; MAXWELL HOUSE; POST FOODS.]

BIBLIOGRAPHY

Paulakepos, Paula, ed. *International Directory of Company Histories*. Vol. 7. Detroit: St. James Press, 1993, p. 272.

JOSEPH M. CARLIN

General Mills

In 1866, Cadwallader Washburn opened a flour mill in Minneapolis, Minnesota, calling it the Minneapolis Milling Company. In 1869, Charles A. Pillsbury, another Minneapolis miller, established his flour mill across the Mississippi River from Washburn's. A century and a half later, these two competing firms would become one company. When John Crosby joined Washburn's business in 1877 the company changed its name to the Washburn Crosby Company. In 1880, after winning the gold, silver, and bronze medals at the first International Miller's Exhibition, the Washburn Crosby Company changed the brand name of its best flour to Gold Medal. After acquiring twenty-seven other milling operations, the company incorporated as General Mills in 1928. At the time, it was the largest flour-milling company in the world.

In 1921, General Mills introduced Betty Crocker to the world, a fictional spokeswoman, originally created as a persona and a pen name to answer consumer letters. Betty Crocker was to become one of the most successful brand names ever introduced by an American food company. It was more than a name; it was a face, a signature, and a radio voice. For many people Betty Crocker really existed.

In 1933, the company scored another advertising success with the slogan "Wheaties—The Breakfast of Champions." However, the company's flagship cereal has always been Cheerios, first created in 1941 as "Cheerioats" but renamed several years later. In 1995, the successful formula was supplemented with sugar-frosted Cheerios. Pursuing strength in the breakfast-food market General Mills purchased the Chex and Cookie Crisp cereal brands, along with Chex Mix snacks, making it the second-largest ready-to-eat cereal company in America, just behind Kellogg.

After World War II, consumers demanded products that required less time to prepare. In response, General Mills introduced Betty Crocker cake mixes in 1947 and presweetened cereals in 1954. Building on its strong base of brand name cereals and convenience foods, such as Cheerios, Chex, Cocoa Puffs, Kix, Total, Trix, Yoplait yogurt, and Hamburger Helper, the company expanded by acquiring Lloyd's Barbeque Company, a maker of refrigerated, microwave-ready entrées.

The company acquired the Red Lobster seafood chain in 1970 and in 1983 created the Olive Garden Italian restaurant chain, but in 1995 it sold the restaurant division to its shareholders to create Darden Restaurants Inc. In 2001 General Mills acquired Pillsbury, which had begun as the mill across the river more than one hundred years earlier, to create one of the world's largest food companies.

[See also BETTY CROCKER; CAKES; CEREAL, COLD; PILLSBURY; WHEAT.]

BIBLIOGRAPHY

"General Mills." In *International Directory of Company Histories*, edited by Jay P. Pederson. Vol. 36. Chicago: St. James Press, 2001.

JOSEPH M. CARLIN

Genetically Modified Food, see Biotechnology

German American Food

According to U.S. census data, German Americans are the largest American ethnic group. Because Germany was not a united country until the 1870s, German American identity was defined by language rather than by national origin. German speakers from many different countries have been counted as German Americans. Between 1790 and 1910, more than 10 percent of all Americans spoke German. But because Germany was an enemy country in both world wars, German American identity has been muted, and descendents of German-speaking immigrants often identify with national origins outside Germany or with ethnoreligious groups.

Because the German presence has been so large and continuous, German Americans do not always receive credit for all-American foods such as casseroles, cheesecake, cream

2 Years.   HANS SCHLOPPENBERG.

A nineteenth-century cartoon shows a German immigrant, Hans Schloppenberg, who has found work as a waiter in a tavern.

cheese, cream soups, hot dogs, jelly dough-nuts, meatballs, meat loaf, milk gravy, potato salad, pretzels, sauerkraut, sticky buns, whoopie pies, and numerous types of pickles, cakes, and cookies. American beer is lager—like German beer and unlike British ale. The German American ethnic group is so large that it has become involved in almost every other kind of American food, from the Moravian cookies of North Carolina to the many uses of Spam on Hawaiian tables. Especially among the immigrants of the 1840s and 1850s, German Americans included many professional bakers, brewers, butchers, chefs, grocers, restaurateurs, and wine merchants who dispersed to farm and frontier as well as major cities. German Americans started wineries in New York and Missouri as well as the well-known Midwestern breweries.

The major founding stock German American population was the Pennsylvania Dutch, who were distinguished from later immigrants by a uniquely American dialect of Low German and by their prominent Protestant sects. Another distinctive subgroup is Germans from Russia, who in the 1870s began homesteading the prairie states. The major story of German American food and drink has been how so much of it has become assimilated as characteristically American mainstream, whereas many dishes have remained recognizably German American.

German-owned restaurants outside Pennsylvania arose first to feed the immigrants of the 1840s and 1850s and were regarded as cheap, unreliable, and somewhat exotic. After the Civil War, more elaborate saloons, beer halls, Weinstuben, and function rooms appeared, which appealed to the general American public. These establishments popularized not only Rhine wines and lager beer but also a variety of sausages, breads, and cakes. German American saloons offered an extensive free lunch, with emphasis on salty hams and pickles, which were thought to increase beer sales. Some of these places survived Prohibition by becoming sit-down restaurants and serving near-beer. German restaurants were popular in most American cities, even those without large German American communities.

German American identity has been greatly muted since World War I, when more than twenty states passed laws against using the German language in public meetings or schools. Prohibition meant the end of many more German American saloons and restaurants.

Although many German American foods have been assimilated into the American mainstream, many distinctively German American dishes have persisted. In some cases, such as the Salzburger raisin bread of Savannah, Georgia, the ethnic identity of a dish has outlived the group that produced it, in this case, an eighteenth-century Austrian settlement. Many Pennsylvania Dutch dishes developed in the United States, such as shoofly pie, continue to be recognized as ethnic rather than general American food. Sauerbraten and rouladen, among the most common German American dishes in contributed cookbooks, have been popular on German American tables since the 1840s yet continue to be viewed as German American food.

Pennsylvania Dutch Food, The Forty-Eighters, and Other Early Immigrants

The Pennsylvania Dutch came from many parts of the German-speaking world and belonged to many Protestant sects as well as mainstream Lutheran and Reformed churches. They moved into inland valley farms up and down the Appalachians and across the mountains to Ohio and Indiana. They were joined by Moravians settling around Winston-Salem, North Carolina, and by ten thousand Hessian deserters during the American Revolution. Pennsylvania German food was noted for the quality of the farm produce, dairy products, and baked goods before the American Revolution and continues to be so noted in the early twenty-first century.

Great numbers of German Americans arrived in the United States during the 1840s and 1850s, with a peak in 1854. Those fleeing the failure of the 1848 uprisings were known as "forty-eighters." This group, consisting mostly of speakers of High German, did not connect with the Pennsylvania Dutch farmers and more often settled in eastern and Midwestern cities. A contingent of German Jews was included in this group, and they were joined by continuing waves of immigrants. Another peak occurred in the 1870s, motivated by Bismarck's laws against socialists and Catholics. These "new immigrant" German Americans settled heavily in Mid-Atlantic and Midwestern cities, including Baltimore, Philadelphia, Cincinnati, Pittsburgh, St. Louis, and, above all, Chicago and Milwaukee. In these cities, German-speaking communities were so large that they retained a sense of regional foods from Bavaria, Prussia, or Bohemia.

The forty-eighters reinforced large breakfasts, lentil soup, liver dumplings, Wiener schnitzel, steak tartare, sauerbraten with potato pancakes and red cabbage, rouladen, knockwurst, bratwurst, liverwurst, hasenpfeffer, Black Forest cake, *Lebkuchen*, *Schnecken*, strudel, and many cookies. Baked goods especially have been welcomed into the American mainstream, sometimes with translated names such as "cinnamon stars," "sand tarts," "cinnamon buns," "sticky buns," and "pepper nuts." Despite their culinary contributions, German Americans in the Midwest were subject to some of the most extreme wartime rhetoric and were stigmatized into the 1960s for eating brains and blood sausage.

Although German-language cookbooks were written and published in the United States as early as the 1840s, Milwaukee editions of German cookbooks, such as that of Henriette Davidis, were popular in German American homes of the late nineteenth century. Many German Americans were eager to embrace American foods, so later and posthumous editions of Davidis have translated recipe titles. A number of nineteenth-century American cookbooks were translated into German. Many cookbooks by German Americans appeared in the twentieth century. Titles ranged from the barely adapted German recipes of the frequently reprinted *The Art of German Cooking and Baking* (1909) by Lina Meier to the deliberate Americanization of the first *The Way to a Man's Heart* (1901), later known as *The Settlement Cookbook*. A number of German American recipes were included in *The Joy of Cooking* by Irma Rombauer.

Although German immigration has been continuous, a third distinctive group began coming to the United States in the 1870s. These immigrants were Germans who had been invited to relocate in Russia, Ukraine or eastern Europe in the seventeenth and eighteenth centuries. In the United States, Germans from Russia initially did not connect closely with either of the previous German American populations but set up their own settlements in the prairie states, becoming the largest ethnic minority in North Dakota. The most typical dish of Germans from Russia has been stuffed breads, known as *bierocks*, or *kraut runza*.

German American Foods in the Mainstream

Many of the mainstream American foods influenced by German Americans date to colonial and early American times. These dishes are poorly documented because the influence began at the fringes of Pennsylvania Dutch farm country and worked toward cities. Prominence in dairy farming suggests German American influence on the American love of cream soup and the preference for milk gravy in the farm country of Pennsylvania, Indiana, and upstate New York. Although there are medieval references in England to cream cheese, the modern American form was developed by German Americans in Philadelphia. Much the same can be said about modern American cheesecake, developed by German Jews in New York City.

The case of sauerkraut is much clearer because fermented cabbage was not a part of British or French foodways. Three-bean salad, popular since the 1950s, is a direct transcription of German *Bohnensalat*. Casseroles were not unknown in British and French cooking and may have been described in ancient Rome, but the American love of casseroles and "hot dishes" seems to emanate from Pennsylvania Dutch ovens and is strongest in the heavily German American Midwest.

Like casseroles, cookies and doughnuts are an area of overlap between German and Scandinavian cuisines. Therefore it is difficult to trace whose spice cookie or jelly doughnut (*Berliner kransen* in Swedish) is the original. Philadelphia scrapple is generally thought to have been developed by German American butchers. German American butchers also get the credit for marketing goetta (pork-oatmeal loaf) and "city chicken" (a ground pork roast) in Cincinnati. These butchers likely played an important role in the switch from veal loaf to American, beef-based meat loaf in the 1880s. German-style chopped raw steak was the first popular form of steak tartare in the United States, and a German-language cookbook from Milwaukee contained a recipe for a steak tartare sandwich, although the popular American name "cannibal sandwiches" did not appear until later. To complete the ground meat dishes, there are widely remembered Swedish, Danish, and Norwegian meatballs, but *Königsberger Klopse* appeared first and in greater numbers than the other forms. Probably the only kind of chopped meat dish German Americans did not help originate is hamburger, which first came to America in a British cookbook as "Hamburgh Sausage" and then appeared on a Delmonico's menu. In calling the dish "Hamburgh Sausage" the London publisher of Hannah Glasse's cookbook apparently considered chopped beef a German food. The hot dog is evidently a German-style cooked wurst, although not authentically a frankfurter (from Frankfort) or a wiener (from Vienna). The bun, added for American convenience but not unprecedented in Germany, makes the sandwich an American hot dog.

Sticky buns, associated with Philadelphia, are fluffy versions of *Schnecken*. The significant and early German settlement in southern Texas suggests a strong association between Wiener schnitzel and chicken-fried steak, as well as a possible influence of goulash soup on the addition of cumin to San Antonio chili.

The ancestry survey of the 1990 U.S. census showed a dramatic increase in the number of citizens claiming German ancestry and corresponding decreases in the projections for other German-speaking immigrant groups. The ancestry survey of the 2000 U.S. census suggested a decrease in the number of respondents claiming German descent, as it did in a number of white immigrant groups. However one reads this data, German food is overdue for a revival on American home and restaurant tables.

[**See also** BEER; BEER HALLS; BIEROCKS; ETHNIC FOOD; GOETTA; MIDDLE ATLANTIC STATES; SALOONS; SCRAPPLE.]

BIBLIOGRAPHY
Frederick, J. George. *The Pennsylvania Dutch and Their Cookery*. New York: Business Bourse, 1935. Reprint, *Pennsylvania Dutch Cook Book*, New York: Dover, 1971.

Weaver, Nevilee Maass. *Rezepte: German-Texan Culinary Art*. Austin, TX: Eakin, 1999.

Weaver, William Woys. *Pennsylvania Dutch Country Cooking*. New York: Abbeville, 1993.

Weaver, William Woys. *Sauerkraut Yankees: Pennsylvania German Foods and Foodways*. Philadelphia: University of Pennsylvania Press, 1983. A translation of the 1851 Pennsylvania Dutch cookbook, *Die Geschickte Hausfrau*.

MARK H. ZANGER

Gibbons, Euell

Euell Gibbons held a number of arbitrary occupations in the course of his life. He was at different times a hobo, a cowboy, a beachcomber, a surveyor, a boat builder, a newspaperman, a schoolteacher, a farmer, an educator, an author, and a spokesperson for Grape-Nuts cereal. But he is best known for being the man who taught America to forage for food in the wild.

Many European cuisines still rely heavily on foraging. For example, the French and Italians are infatuated with mushroom hunting, but modern Americans have not had a deep interest in gathering wild foods. Following Gibbons, great American chefs such as Alice Waters and organizations such as the Slow Food Movement revived the concepts of respect for and exchange with nature and the environment. Early American Indians relied wholly on foraging and hunting for their sustenance. They believed in life lived in harmony with nature. Gibbons imparted this credo to the American public and was awarded an honorary degree by Susquehanna University in 1972.

Gibbons was born in 1911 and raised in Clarksville, Texas, until the family moved to New Mexico when he was eleven. Legend tells us that by the time he was a teenager he supplemented the family's food supply by hunting, trapping, and foraging, which he had learned to do from his mother. He would leave for the forest with a knapsack in the morning and return in the evening to feed his family from a bag full of wild, edible items.

He left home at the age of fifteen for the Northwest. Once there, Gibbons wandered, supporting himself by working at odd jobs and foraging. He served in the army for two years, from 1934 to 1936. While he was in the army, he married his first wife, Anna Swanson; they had two boys and had divorced by 1945. Although he had joined the Communist Party in the 1930s, he later renounced his Red membership. Gibbons moved to Hawaii after his stint in the army, where he worked in a shipyard. After the war he became a beachcomber, finishing his high school degree, attending the University of Hawaii, and marrying his second wife, Freda Fryer. The couple taught on Maui until 1953 when they joined the Religious Society of Friends (Quakers) and moved back to the East Coast to teach in Quaker schools. It was there that Gibbons began to write what he thought was going to be a novel. However, when he handed in his manuscript, his publisher told him: "Take the novel out. Leave the wild food in." The result was *Stalking the Wild Asparagus*, published in 1962. It was immensely popular, taken up by those drawn to the back-to-nature movement, and it established Euell Gibbons as the authority in the area of wild food.

In 1963, the Gibbons family moved to a farm in Troxelville, Pennsylvania, where Gibbons wrote six other books: *Stalking the Healthful Herbs*, *Stalking the Blue-Eyed Scallop*, *Beachcombers Handbook*, *Stalking the Good Life*, *Stalking the Far Away Places*, and *Euell Gibbons' Handbook of Edible Wild Plants*. Gibbons wrote articles for magazines including *National Geographic* and *Organic Gardening and Farming*. He made television appearances in Grape Nuts cereal commercials, on *The Tonight Show Starring Johnny Carson*, and *The Sonny and Cher Show*. Gibbons died in 1975 of a heart attack at the age of sixty-four.

[**See also** COOKBOOKS: FROM WORLD WAR II TO THE 1960s; SLOW FOOD MOVEMENT; WATERS, ALICE.]

LIZA JERNOW

Gin

Gin, a juniper-flavored distilled spirit (although many other botanical ingredients are now used in its production), takes its name from *genièvre*, the French word for "juniper." It is often said that gin was first created in the mid-seventeenth century by Franz Deleboe (1614–1672), also known as Dr. Sylvius, a professor at the University of Leiden; however, some sources claim that similar juniper-based spirits were first made by Italian monks and used in attempts to combat the bubonic plague (1347–1350), as juniper was known to be a diuretic and one of the symptoms of the plague was enlarged glands in the groin. It is clear that the spirit was being made before Deleboe is said to have created it, because English mercenaries helping the Dutch in their war with Spain introduced gin to England in the late 1500s. It is possible that Deleboe's recipe was the first to use grain rather than fruit as a base. Grain is the base of all gins made in the twenty-first century.

Two styles of gin—Old Tom, a sweetened spirit, and dry gin—were both popular as cocktail ingredients in the United States by 1862, when Jerry Thomas, a celebrated bartender of the time, published the world's first cocktail recipe book, *How to Mix Drinks; or, The Bon-Vivant's Companion*. Whiskey, however, was the spirit of choice among Americans until Prohibition was enacted in January 1920. Using industrial alcohol and oil of juniper, bootleggers during Prohibition found it relatively simple to make a crude form of gin. Whiskey was much more difficult to replicate. So scofflaws during the so-called Noble Experiment, including many women who had been banned from most bars before Prohibition, preferred to drink gin when they visited speakeasies or threw cocktail parties at home. Even after Prohibition was repealed in December 1933, gin retained its popularity, especially as the main ingredient in the dry martini cocktail.

In the 1940s, when vodka was first widely marketed in the United States, gin began a very slow decline in popularity. Advertisers told Americans that vodka would leave them "breathless," whereas gin was fairly easy to detect on the breath. Some martini drinkers began switching to the less-aromatic spirit, especially when it was still acceptable to partake of three-martini lunches and return to work in the afternoon. Not until the 1980s, after Absolut vodka introduced a very seductive advertising campaign, did gin really fall from favor in this country. Meanwhile, Bombay, a gin introduced to America in the 1950s, was lurking in the background.

Most gins have a highly perfumed taste with juniper flavors predominating, but Bombay is far subtler, and this style of gin started to gain in popularity in the mid- to late 1990s. Gin producers targeted vodka drinkers by wooing them with a softer style of gin that was easier to acquire a taste for than the bolder bottlings on the market, and this tactic appeared to have been relatively successful by the early 2000s. Many more gins have been introduced—some touting ingredients never before known as gin flavorings, such as cucumbers—to attract people who were not enamored of the bolder styles of regular gin. Many gins are available in the United States; the most popular brands at the beginning of the twenty-first century included Beefeater, Bombay, Bombay Sapphire, Boodles, Gordon's, Hendrick's, Plymouth, Tanqueray, and Tanqueray No. 10.
[See also COCKTAILS; MARTINI.]

BIBLIOGRAPHY
Brown, Gordon. *Classic Spirits of the World.* New York: Abbeville Press, 1996.
Kinross, Lord. *The Kindred Spirit: A History of Gin and the House of Booth.* London: Newman Neame, 1959.
Lord, Tony. *The World Guide to Spirits, Aperitifs and Cocktails.* New York: Sovereign Books, 1979.

GARY AND MARDEE HAIDIN REGAN

Ginger Ale

Ginger ale—a carbonated beverage sweetened and flavored with extract of ginger root (or imitations thereof)—serves as the transitional link between the home-brewed alcoholic small beers and small ales of old and modern-day mass-produced soft drinks. Small beers had been prevalent for centuries as affordable, if far less potent, alternatives to commercial alcoholic brews. Derived from almost any part of almost any plant available in England and colonial America, small beers and ales were generally presumed to be tonic in contrast to civic water supplies, which were believed to be potentially toxic. Ginger beer, which peaked in popularity in the early nineteenth century, was certainly considered to be healthy: Ginger's reputation as a counterirritant and digestive aid, among other things, was firmly entrenched in folk medicine.

At the same time, the rage for natural mineral springwater fueled the development of artificially carbonated water or soda water. The first name in soda water manufacture was Jacob Schweppe, who set up shop in Geneva and London in the late eighteenth century. His ingenuity inspired chemists for decades to come, who added to his achievement by adding flavor, including, by the mid-nineteenth century, ginger. The company Schweppe founded—a multinational corporation in the twenty-first century—went on to become the foremost producer of ginger ale.

Although the precise circumstances of its invention remain unknown, ginger ale, also called ginger champagne or gingerade, achieved immediate fame throughout the British Isles and overseas as a product of Belfast. There may have been a few American antecedents. Kenneth F. Kiple and Kriemhild Coneè-Ornelas cite a sixteenth-century source that refers to a Native American concoction containing ginger boiled with cinnamon; however, the early date is suspect, as ginger is not indigenous to the New World. The same authors and others also allude to switchell, a curious-sounding colonial American beverage made by combining ginger with molasses and vinegar.

The role Americans played in the soda revolution is better known. Stateside pharmacists invented the soda fountain itself, the popularity of which surged throughout the nineteenth century. Over the course of the century, the health benefits of soda water were eclipsed by its refreshing qualities, just as had happened in the case of small beer. As the soda fountain became a form of entertainment, a destination in itself, the beverages it dispensed were increasingly drunk for pleasure rather than health.

And so it was with ginger ale, which occupied the top of the flavor-popularity charts from the moment of its introduction until the 1940s, with home consumption increasing as the bottling and, eventually, canning industries grew. Vernor's was the first American manufacturer of note. Ginger ale was also employed as a mixer in such classic cocktails as the buck and the highball, Prohibition notwithstanding, as well as the Shirley Temple, a nonalcoholic favorite of children. (The rum-based dark and stormy, meanwhile, traditionally is made with alcoholic ginger beer.)

Around the mid-twentieth century, however, colas began to dominate the market through the promotion of a youthful, all-American image. Ginger ale, by contrast, came to be associated with an old-school if not Old-World quaintness, and at the beginning of the twenty-first century its share of soft-drink sales was all but negligible, despite modestly successful attempts to innovate with new flavors, such as raspberry and grape.
[See also BEER; COCKTAILS; SODA DRINKS; SODA FOUNTAINS; WATER, BOTTLED.]

BIBLIOGRAPHY
Funderburg, Anne Cooper. *Sundae Best: A History of Soda Fountains.* Bowling Green, Oh: Bowling Green State University Popular Press, 2002.

RUTH TOBIAS

Ginger Family

Ginger and Turmeric are rhizomes, and cardamom seeds, of tropical Southeast Asian perennials of the family Zingiberaceae.

Cardamom (*Elettaria cardamomum*) seeds are used with meats, poultry, sausages, pickles, soups, stews—curries, or Arabic dishes—and Scandinavian and Dutch baked goods.

Ginger (*Zingiber officinale*), ground, is used in baking, candies, and condiments. It provides warmth to ginger ale and root beer. Fresh green ginger is essential in most tropical cuisines. Thai, Caribbean, Chinese, Indian, and Indonesian food would be unthinkable without it.

Turmeric (*Curcuma domestica*) is usually seen as a powder in the United States. Because of its intense yellow color, turmeric is sometimes used as a substitute for saffron.
[See also PREPARED HERB AND SPICE MIXTURES.]

BIBLIOGRAPHY
Allen, Gary. *The Herbalist in the Kitchen.* Champain: University of Illinois Press (forthcoming).
Bailey, L. H. *Hortus Third: A Concise Dictionary of Plants Cultivated in the United States and Canada.* New York: Macmillan, 1976.

GARY ALLEN

Girl Scout Cookies

The Girl Scouts were founded in 1912, and within five years, cookie sales were part of the program. The cookies were homemade initially, and the project taught the girls about baking and business while it generated funds for their scouting activities. In 1922, Florence E. Neil, a local troop director in Chicago, published the first "official" cookie recipe in the *American Girl*, the Scouts' own magazine. At first, the homemade cookies were packed in waxed paper bags and sold door to door by the girls. In the 1930s, Girl Scout councils began selling commercially baked cookies, and in 1936 the national Girl Scout organization began licensing commercial bakers to produce cookies. The following year, many Girl Scout councils sponsored cookie sales.

During World War II, when flour, chocolate, sugar, and butter were rationed, the Girl Scouts suspended cookie sales, but after the war, they resumed selling. In the 1950s, three varieties of Girl Scout cookies were sold: sandwich cookies (vanilla- or chocolate-filled), shortbread (baked in the shape of the Girl Scout symbol, they were also called Trefoils), and chocolate mint cookies (Thin Mints). In the 1960s, sales of Girl Scout cookies went way up, and additional varieties became available, including peanut butter cookies (also called Do-si-dos or Savannahs) and Samoas (also called Caramel deLites). The perennial favorite is Thin Mints.

The First Lady, Grace Coolidge, smiles as she eats cookies presented by a New York Girl Scout troop.

Concerns for the nutritional content of Girl Scout cookies became an issue during the 1990s, and new low-fat and sugar-free cookies were added to the line. In the twenty-first century trans fats were the new dietary concern, and the Girl Scouts have strongly encouraged their bakers to produce cookies free of trans fats. As of 2005, annual sales of Girl Scout cookies are estimated to be $400 million, which makes them one of the most successful fund-raising devices in history. It is estimated that this income covers one half of the annual expenses of most local councils.

BIBLIOGRAPHY

Degenhardt, Mary, and Judith Kirsch. *Girl Scout Collectors' Guide: A History of Uniforms, Insignia, Publications, and Memorabilia.* 2nd ed. Lubbock: Texas Tech University Press, 2005.

ANDREW F. SMITH

Glassware

Glass-making is an ancient process of melting silica, usually from sand, with an alkali to form a malleable compound that hardens on cooling. Whether discovered in one location or several, by the fifteenth century B.C.E. glass was known in Egypt and Mesopotamia and thereafter spread to the Mediterranean region and China. Various metals were often added to mimic precious stones because it was technologically impossible to make colorless glass. Drinking glasses were a luxury, made by the arduous process of dipping a core mold into molten glass. With the invention of glassblowing in Rome in the first century B.C.E., glass vessels became more affordable and common. European glassblowing declined with the fall of Rome but was revived, most impressively, in medieval Venice.

By the seventeenth century, glass-making was an active, competitive industry with many centers. Even the American colonies, which were rich in the raw materials needed to make glass, briefly engaged in the manufacture of glass. The purpose of the colonial glass factories, which were funded by entities such as the English Board of Trade, was to manufacture glass for the European market. Jamestown (1608 and 1621), Salem, Massachusetts (c. 1639–1643), New Amsterdam (c. 1650–1674), and Philadelphia (c. 1683) had small glassworks. All failed, largely because of undercapitalization and the perils of transatlantic shipping.

Most early colonists drank their beverages from sturdy woodenware or pewter, but wealthy colonists imported luxury glassware for wine and spirits. Glass purchases tended to follow colonial trade patterns. English colonists bought British glass, and those in New Amsterdam bought Holland glass. An occasional bit of Venetian glass appeared in the richest homes. Glass sales were tied to liquor consumption: one Albany merchant bemoaned poor glass sales in 1657, blaming the slow market on that year's shortage of wine.

In 1739, Caspar Wistar rekindled the American glass industry with a glasshouse in Salem County, New Jersey, that was devoted to utilitarian windows, colored bottles, and a few items of tableware. Other early glassworks, founded by Henry William "Baron" Stiegel (active in Pennsylvania, 1763–1774) and John Frederick Amelung (active in Maryland, 1784–1794), produced blown and molded drinking vessels (mugs, goblets, tumblers, flips, and wine glasses), cruets, decanters, and other table glass. These manufacturers relied on highly skilled British and European glassworkers, who made items in different styles to satisfy the different tastes of Dutch, German, and English colonists. Although these businesses all succumbed to better-priced British competition, the economics changed after the War of 1812. Manufactories followed settlers west, supplying local markets with basic glass needs. Manufacturers near eastern cities produced luxurious tableware.

Most early wine glasses were quite small by later standards owing to the way wine was served at elegant dinners. Before the 1830s, wine glasses and water glasses were typically kept on a sideboard and delivered by a servant to each diner upon request. The diner would drain the glass and return it to the servant, who would wash the glass and await the next beverage request. With changing service styles, diners started to leave their glasses on the table. By 1840, etiquette books were suggesting several glasses for each diner, including individual water tumblers, one or more wine glasses of different shapes for different wines, and small water bottles at each place so that diners could independently replenish their water glasses. Decanters, cruets, and casters continued to be placed on the table for communal use.

The forests of glasses on dining tables were made possible, in part, by one of America's most important contributions to glass technology: the perfection of machine-pressed glass. In the late 1820s and early 1830s, various American factories improved the existing mechanical processes so that good-quality glass could be produced with comparatively little skill. Semiskilled American workers supplanted trained European craftsmen in manufacturing all but luxury glass. Output tripled and costs fell, quickly making pressed glass an affordable refinement. The pressing technology opened a new design vocabulary that included intricate, lacy patterns, bull's-eye borders, and figurative motifs. Pressed glass was quickly adapted for propaganda: Presidential candidates distributed appropriately embossed plates, flasks, and other items as campaign mementoes, and Manifest Destiny found expression in the popular "Westward Ho" pattern, which incorporated stylized animals and images of Native Americans.

Modestly priced pressed glass thoroughly penetrated the middle classes by the 1850s and the working classes by the 1880s, so that the affluent needed a distinguishing product. It came in the 1880s in the form of brilliant cut glass. Combining high-silica sand, which had been discovered in western Massachusetts, with lead oxide produced glass of extraordinary brilliance that could imitate the finest eighteenth-century English leaded glass. Although it was wildly popular in upper-middle-class markets, particularly among men, brilliant cut glass lost its cachet after World War I.

With the successful complete automation of pressed-glass factories in the 1920s, attractive table glass became affordable for all. Glassmakers needed to invent new glass products to capture the public's purse. Adapting technology used in railroad signal lights, the Corning Glass Works pioneered thermal shock-resistant glass that could go from refrigerator to oven to table. First offered in 1915 through its Pyrex ovenware line, this multifunctional glassware capitalized on the efficiency espoused by the home economics movement. Pyrex was expensive and marketed to well-heeled women who were up-to-date in domestic science. Changes in the design, manufacture, and marketing of Pyrex brought it to the masses by the late 1930s, and it remains a staple item.

After World War II, competition from modernized European and Asian factories forced many of the remaining American luxury glass manufacturers out of business. With the trend to increasingly casual entertaining, postwar consumers purchased a large numbers of glasses, but they were often inexpensive novelty items or were made of plastic and paper. "Good crystal" decreased in importance as a status symbol. The final twentieth-century development was an extraordinary increase in the size and capacity of glasses, especially for wine. Modern oenophiles can opt for gargantuan twenty-eight-ounce bowls that permit lusty swirling of Bacchus's gift.

Although most American glass follows long-established forms, there were a few distinctly American innovations. One was the glass cup plate, which was designed to protect the table from trickles of tea when the hot drink was poured from a handleless cup into a deep saucer for cooling. Tea drinkers needed a place to rest their cups as they sipped delicately from their saucers. Other American creations are specially shaped glasses for martinis and for ice cream sundaes and sodas.

[**See also** Dining Rooms, Table Settings, and Table Manners; Wine Glasses.]

BIBLIOGRAPHY

Blaszczyk, Regina Lee. *Imagining Consumers: Design and Innovation from Wedgwood to Corning.* Baltimore and London: Johns Hopkins University Press, 2000.

Gardner, Paul Vickers. *Glass.* Washington, DC: Cooper-Hewitt/Smithsonian Institution, 1979.

McKearin, George S., and Helen McKearin. *American Glass.* New York: Bonanza, 1989.

Palmer, Arlene. *Glass in Early America.* Winterthur, DE: Winterthur Museum, 1993.

Spillman, Jane Shadel. *Glassmaking: America's First Industry.* Corning, NY: Corning Museum, 1976.

CATHY K. KAUFMAN

Goetta

A seasoned mixture of oatmeal and meat, usually pork, goetta (rhymes with "meta") is traditional breakfast fare of southwestern Ohio and northern Kentucky. The origin of the word "goetta" is unknown. It was used at the end of the nineteenth century in Cincinnati, Ohio, and nearby Covington, Kentucky, where goetta was popularized by German immigrants, although the local Irish population supposedly also ate it. Goetta probably began as a way to extend pork scraps by frugal German workers in Cincinnati's extensive pork-packing industry. Goetta is very similar to the Pennsylvania Dutch dish scrapple, which uses cornmeal rather than oatmeal, and is derived from the German tradition of meat puddings prepared at butchering time from meat remnants bound together with grains.

Goetta is prepared by first slowly cooking it in a pot to a thick, gluey consistency, then pouring it into a pan and chilling it. When served, goetta is unmolded from the pan, sliced, and fried. As breakfast food, it replaces bacon or sausage and often appears with eggs. It is sometimes used as a stuffing and modern cooks seek new applications, such as pizza toppings.

Area butchers began producing goetta and selling it as a winter specialty. A few commercial firms currently provide most of the goetta in the Cincinnati region, which is available fresh and frozen at local supermarkets. Renewed interest in regional foods has sparked an appreciation of this humble food, and an annual goetta festival in Covington, Kentucky, celebrates the enduring popularity of goetta.

[**See also** Breakfast Foods; Dressings and Stuffings; Food Festivals; Scrapple.]

BIBLIOGRAPHY

DuSablon, Mary Anna. *Cincinnati Recipe Treasury: The Queen City's Culinary Heritage.* Athens: Ohio University Press, 1989.

MARY SANKER

Good & Plenty

First produced by the Quaker City Confectionery Company in Philadelphia in 1893, Good & Plenty, ovoid licorice pieces coated in a pink or white candy shell, is believed to be the oldest brand-named candy in the United States, although the name was not trademarked until 1928. Good & Plenty became part of American culture when it was advertised nationally beginning in 1950. Television jingles such as "Choo-Choo Charlie" became favorites with children. The Good & Plenty brand now belongs to the Hershey Company.

BIBLIOGRAPHY

Richardson, Tim. *Sweets: A History of Candy.* New York: Bloomsbury, 2002.

ANDREW F. SMITH

Good Housekeeping Institute

Founded in 1900 in Springfield, Massachusetts, as the Good Housekeeping Institute Experiment Station, for the evaluation of food products and, a few years later, of household appliances, the Good Housekeeping Institute is one of America's premier consumer-protection and quality-assurance facilities. Products that do not satisfy the requirements of the institute's product testing and approval programs are not allowed to advertise in *Good Housekeeping* magazine.

The institute's work supplies the essential foundation for the Good Housekeeping Consumers' Refund Replacement Policy, which in every issue of the magazine warrants that "if any product that bears our Seal or is advertised in this issue [of our magazine]...proves to be defective within two years from the date it was first sold to a consumer, we, Good Housekeeping, will replace the product or refund the purchase price." After *Good Housekeeping* magazine was purchased by William Randolph Hearst in 1912, the institute moved to New York City, where it was still located at the beginning of the twenty-first century.

The Good Housekeeping Institute played a significant role in twentieth-century American food history. Before the passage of the Pure Food and Drug Act in June 1906, the institute tested food products to determine their purity. Every month, *Good Housekeeping* printed a "Roll of Honor for Pure Food Products," listing foods that were unadulterated. In 1910, in response to the spread of electricity, the electrification of the American home, and the development of electric appliances, the institute established test kitchens to determine which electric appliances were safe and effective. The names of reliable products were published in the magazine along with a seal that stated, in part, "Tested and Approved by the Good Housekeeping Institute."

After Dr. Harvey W. Wiley was hired as head of the institute's Bureau of Food, Sanitation, and Health in 1912, the institute broadened its scope to study all aspects of food and health; the results of these studies were also published in the magazine. Between 1912 and his death in 1930 Dr. Wiley authored or coauthored more than 175 articles on pure food and health that were published in *Good Housekeeping.* Many of these articles discussed proper nutrition with a special focus on babies and children. American women trusted Dr. Wiley, and this trust, in part, accounted for the popularity and success of the institute and the magazine. During the Great Depression, the institute developed recipes and menus designed to maximize the nutritional value of meals while keeping the cost of food low, and in World War II the institute helped Americans by providing strategies to deal with food shortages. Finally, with the advent of the Internet, the institute placed its Buyer's Guide on the Web at http://www.goodhousekeeping.com, allowing free access to anyone interested in consumer information about general cookware, flatware and tools, and kitchen appliances, among other things.

In the early 2000s, the Good Housekeeping Institute had separate departments for food, nutrition, home care, chemistry, consumer and reader services, engineering, food appliances, and textiles. The institute continued to evaluate a wide variety of food and household products, publishing the results of those evaluations in the magazine as "Taste Tests" and "Institute Reports."

[See also FOOD AND DRUG ADMINISTRATION; PURE FOOD AND DRUG ACT; WILEY, HARVEY.]

ROBERT W. BROWER

Good Humor

In 1910, the candymaker Harry Burt of Youngstown, Ohio, introduced the Good Humor Sucker, an ice cream on a stick. His reason for selecting the name was that he believed that humors determined one's disposition. Burt made the ice cream at home and then began delivering it to stores in his automobile.

When the Eskimo Pie became a national sensation in 1921, Burt began experimenting with chocolate-dipped ice cream. He put a chocolate-coated rectangle of ice cream on a wooden stick to make it less messy to eat, and called it the Good Humor Ice Cream Sucker. Burt applied for two patents, but he didn't wait until the application was approved. He immediately began selling his ice cream bars, packed in ice, from trucks that drove around Youngstown with bells clanging to announce their presence. After Harry Burt died, the company was bought by a group of Cleveland businessmen in 1926. They created the Good Humor Corporation of America and began franchising the operation. They needed funds to expand, and approached the New York financier Michael J. Meehan, who gained control of the company.

The company's trademark was the Good Humor man, a friendly ice cream vendor dressed in a clean white uniform with a white hat who drove through America's neighborhoods with bells a-jingle, attracting a stream of children as he went. Good Humor men worked on commission and did especially well during the summer. They became such an important component of American culture that they appeared in magazines, comics, and radio programs. The movie *The Good Humor Man* (1950), starring Jack Carson, popularized the company and the Good Humor bar. The company stopped selling its ice cream from trucks in 1976, although some private contractors continued driving Good Humor trucks after this date. The products are now sold in stores.

The Meehan family sold the company to Thomas J. Lipton Inc. in 1961. Today, the brand is part of Unilever, an Anglo-Dutch company.

[See also ICE CREAMS AND ICES.]

BIBLIOGRAPHY

Funderburg, Anne Cooper. *Chocolate, Strawberry, and Vanilla: A History of American Ice Cream.* Bowling Green, Ohio: Bowling Green State University Popular Press, 1995.

ANDREW F. SMITH

Goose

Geese are large, web-footed birds of the family Anatidae, including the genera *Anser* and *Branta*. Geese have heavier bodies and longer necks than ducks but are smaller than swans. There are two dozen species worldwide, but the domesticated gray goose (*Anser domesticus*) derives from only two species, the wild gray goose and the greylag goose (*Anser ferus* and *Anser anser*). By 3000 B.C.E., geese were common in China and the Middle East. They were raised in ancient Egypt and have been part of everyday life in western Europe since prehistoric times. Geese are easily raised, and they consume foods, including many weeds, not eaten by other animals. In Europe, geese were highly valued for their eggs, meat, grease, and feathers. In England, geese were usually eaten on special occasions, such as Michaelmas and Christmas.

European settlers brought domesticated geese (*Anser domesticus*) to the New World. The Pilgrim goose was brought from England by early colonists. Embden geese were imported in 1821, followed shortly thereafter by Bremen geese. Chinese geese were imported by the 1840s, as was the African or Guinea goose, which was the largest breed in mid-nineteenth-century America. These imported birds contributed to extensive breeding efforts to produce larger and meatier geese.

Geese were generally prepared for the table in the same manner that turkeys and ducks were. They were roasted, boiled, or used as ingredients in savory pies. Like other poultry, geese were stuffed with almost every conceivable concoction, from traditional chestnut fillings to those composed of onions, potatoes, and sauerkraut. Geese were usually served on special occasions, such as Thanksgiving and Christmas. Recipes for preparing geese were published in American cookbooks, ranging from Amelia Simmon's recipe in her *American Cookery* (1796) entitled "To boil a Turkey, Fowl or Goose" to Felix Déliée's eight complex recipes in his *Franco-American Cookery Book* (1884).

Domesticated geese never achieved the culinary popularity in America that they did in Europe, however, perhaps because of the plentiful supply of wildfowl in America and the availability of low-cost and less greasy turkey. Since 1890 the consumption of geese in America has steadily declined, and recipes for preparing geese have generally disappeared from American cookbooks. Wild geese do remain a highly favored menu item among hunters, and recipes for their preparation appear in specialty cookbooks.

Geese were generally raised in small flocks on farms, but some commercial raising of geese did go on in Rhode Island in colonial times. These birds were usually driven to markets in towns during the fall. In the nineteenth century, geese were raised in the South and the Midwest mainly for their feathers, which were used for down comforters and featherbeds. Wing feathers were used for quill pens. Live geese were plucked several times during the summer. This practice, considered cruel and inhumane, did not stop until the early twentieth century, when demand for the feathers declined.

[See also CHRISTMAS; DRESSINGS AND STUFFINGS; DUCK; POULTRY AND FOWL; THANKSGIVING; TURKEY.]

Bremen or Emden geese.

BIBLIOGRAPHY

Batty, Joseph. *Domesticated Ducks and Geese.* Mildhurst, UK: Beech Publishing House, 1996.

Dohner, Janet Vorwald. *The Encyclopedia of Endangered Livestock and Poultry Breeds.* New Haven, CT, and London: Yale University Press, 2001.

ANDREW F. SMITH

Graham, Sylvester

His name lives on in a nursery cookie, but Sylvester Graham (1794–1851), one of America's earliest and most vocal advocates of dietary reform, left a far larger legacy: the concept that a vegetarian diet of natural and largely raw foods—whole grains, vegetables, fruits, and nuts—can restore and maintain health. Graham campaigned for pure, unadulterated food at a time when baker's bread might contain copper sulfate, plaster, or alum. And in an era predating scientific knowledge of carbohydrates, protein, fat, and fiber, he insisted that processing, milling, sifting, and overcooking stripped food of its most important components. Although mocked in his day, Graham's theories foreshadowed much modern nutritional knowledge.

The Connecticut-born Graham was ordained a Presbyterian minister in New Jersey; his first congregation was in Philadelphia, where he mingled with and learned from Quakers, temperance advocates, and vegetarians—notably, members of the Bible Christian Church, an English sect that had established a church in Philadelphia. As a traveling temperance lecturer, Graham studied the physiological effects of alcohol.

Sylvester Graham advocated a diet based on fruits, vegetables and foods made, like his crackers, from coarsely ground grain.

He also researched the effects of foods on the human body, leading to his espousal of a vegetarian diet with particular emphasis on firm, crusty bread—home-baked from coarsely ground, unbolted (not sifted) whole-wheat flour—and raw fruits and vegetables. Unadulterated, unprocessed, uncooked foods were preferable: "The simpler, plainer and more natural the food…the more healthy, vigorous and long lived will be the body," Graham wrote.

Increasing urbanization in early-nineteenth-century America promoted emotional and mental stress among city-dwellers, who suffered a virtual epidemic of dyspepsia, or indigestion, as they bolted down the era's fast food (meat and potatoes doused with greasy gravy and spicy condiments and washed down with whiskey or beer) in ever more bustling surroundings. Graham believed that such a diet was overstimulating, irritating to the digestive organs, and responsible for kindling unhealthy passions and desires. He developed an Edenic diet: what Adam and Eve ate was good enough for modern man. Foods forbidden as highly stimulating included meat (especially pork), shellfish, fatty sauces, salt, spices, sugar, coffee, tea, highly flavored condiments, and alcohol. Advocating a regimen of fresh air, exercise, and personal cleanliness and inveighing against corsets and featherbeds, Graham pronounced that proper food calmed the senses while providing the jaws, teeth, and digestive organs with healthy exercise.

As a wave of cholera swept American cities in the early 1830s, Graham lectured to audiences desperate to learn how diet could help prevent disease. The mid-1830s saw the founding of Graham societies (promoting his brand of dietary reform) and Graham hotels (serving his recommended fare),

which flourished in American cities. Graham flour, bread, and crackers—some of the first health foods—hit the market. Newspapers and magazines, including the *Graham Journal of Health and Longevity*, popularized Graham's theories. The Shakers adopted Graham's diet for a time, hoping that it would help their members adhere to their vows of celibacy. Other Graham followers were Bronson Alcott, cofounder of the utopian (and vegan) Fruitlands community in Massachusetts; Horace Greeley; and John Harvey Kellogg and Will K. Kellogg of Battle Creek sanatorium fame. Although Graham's unrelenting dogmatism and his sometimes excessive zeal on the lecture platform made him subject to scorn and ridicule by some members of the press and the public, from a modern perspective it is obvious that he was many, many decades ahead of his time.

[See also HEALTH FOOD; KELLOGG, JOHN HARVEY; VEGETARIANISM.]

BIBLIOGRAPHY

Giedion, Siegfried. *Mechanization Takes Command.* New York: Norton, 1969.

Nissenbaum, Stephen. *Sex, Diet, and Debility in Jacksonian America: Sylvester Graham and Health Reform.* Westport, CT: Greenwood, 1980.

BONNIE J. SLOTNICK

Grapes

Although the Old World was first to exploit it, the grape vine is a particularly American plant. Only one species of grape is to be found wild in Europe, while there are few places in temperate North America, from Canada to Mexico, without a native grape species. North America is the center of diversity for the grape. Twenty grape species are found there, and nowhere else.

American grapes found their first culinary use in the Native Americans' pemmican, a confection of animal fats, fruits, and shredded meats. No doubt grapes were also consumed fresh, although very few vines produced tasty fruits. Viking explorers named their Newfoundland landfall Vinland, for the vines there; early colonists from England remarked on the bounty of grapes in their new home—and also their acrid flavor. These grapes, called *labrusca*, as a class, have two outstanding characteristics: a thick skin that separates readily from the berry and a highly pungent aroma, described as foxy.

Introducing the wine grape of Europe (*Vitis vinifera*) to America was a matter of policy in the colonies, along with other commodities for export, such as rice, sugar, and olives. That attempts at introduction were not successful is evidenced by Thomas Jefferson's correspondence with Europe, seeking more robust as well as finer varieties of grape. Lack of success is explained not only by the occasionally harsh winters of the Atlantic seaboard but also by the numerous pathogens specific to the vine, such as the phylloxera root aphid, mildew, black rot,

and, above all, Pierce's disease, a lethal bacterial, to all of which most native American species had developed resistance or immunity, but to which the European grape had none at all.

American Hybrids

Until the 1850s, grapes of dessert quality remained a luxury for those few who maintained a greenhouse to grow varieties of European origin. At about that time, certain experimenters started to hybridize the few European grapes then known with wildlings selected from the American forests. These hybrids, although still far from perfect in hardiness and productivity, were a revelation that the future of American grape culture lay in seedlings of European and American species combined by hybridization. The first generations of American hybrid grapes were the basis of a wine industry founded on the Ohio River near Cincinnati, and later on Lake Erie and in upstate New York, which survived until National Prohibition.

Concord is considered the type for all *labrusca* grapes. It is dark-skinned, adaptable to most of the East and Midwest, and still accounts for nearly half the eastern grape production, notwithstanding its very modest eating quality. Niagara is a yellow-skinned counterpart, of higher value for dessert. Catawba is the most-grown red-skinned type, although it ripens very late in the season, too late for most of America. All three are used in the making of bottled juice, and the tonnage of Concord devoted to manufacture of jellies is formidable indeed. Hybrid varieties are preferred for dessert use by knowledgeable grape fanciers. Delaware grapes are first among these, forming small clusters of small berries. Jefferson and Iona grapes are also fine red grapes. Brilliant and Steuben are fine varieties of black and Seneca of white.

During the late nineteenth and early twentieth centuries, French nurserymen believed hybrids between American species and local grapes would prove the salvation of French vineyards from phylloxera. During these years, very many such hybrids were created and proved competent producers of fair wines, but not wines of the accustomed standard. These hybrids were later introduced to New York, Virginia, and elsewhere. In those areas, dessert grapes of these French hybrids, although small, are sometimes available for fresh market and are highly prized over American hybrid grapes, whose slipping skins and foxiness they lack.

The market prevalence of California table grapes that lack seeds has led some state experiment stations, notably in Arkansas and New York, to begin breeding programs featuring crosses between American hybrids and the seedless grapes of California. The resulting progeny—Interlaken, Himrod, Remailly, Reliance, Venus—derive either from the sultana type and share their very neutral flavor or from Black Monukka and are likewise imperfectly seedless. They are

From left to right: Brighton, Moore's Diamond, and Eaton grapes.

rapidly driving older seeded varieties of greater character from the marketplace.

California Grapes

The *V. vinifera* of Europe was introduced to California in the late eighteenth century to produce altar wines for the missions. The easy growth of this species under California conditions impressed later immigrants from the eastern states and a wine industry soon developed. The market was limited for dessert fruit until the advent of the refrigerated railway car in the 1880s. At that point, grape plantings in the Modesto and Fresno districts expanded, chiefly in varieties of character and flavor: White Malaga, Ahmeur bou Ahmeur (as Flame Tokay), Alphonse Lavallee (as Ribier), Olivette Blanche, and Muscat of Alexandria.

At the same time, the sultana type of *V. vinifera*, which has no seeds, was planted for sun-drying, especially in the southern San Joaquin valley. There the grape experiences extremely low humidity and no rains before October. It was discovered by the 1930s that the popular Sultanina Bianca (grown as Thompson Seedless) was a versatile fruit. If picked immature, before turning fully yellow in color, it has sufficient acid to make a pleasant dessert fruit, and one without seeds. When fully ripe, it is of high sugar content and useful for making the cheapest of wines, as well as for drying. By the 1980s, it and the many progeny of the sultana type, such as Perlette, Flame Seedless, Fantasy Seedless, Ruby Seedless, and certain varieties proprietary to large industrial growers, had displaced nearly all the seeded true table grapes in American commerce.

For drying purposes, the Black Corinth type of *V. vinifera*, a quite distinct small seedless grape, is grown for production of the so-called currants of commerce. At the turn of the twenty-first century, fresh fruit of this variety was sold as a novelty under the false name, champagne grape. The traditional dried Muscat of Alexandria had vanished from nearly all American supermarkets. Typically, these were processed to remove the seeds, and the result-

ing product was lubricated with grapeseed oil to prevent consolidation in the package. Black Monukka produces a tough raisin of high acidity and character, with occasional seeds. An innovation has been the breeding of sultanas named DOV (dried on vine) that can dry while attached to the severed vine and then be mechanically gathered. A very small secondary industry evolved in the Fresno area for production of grape derivatives, such as verjus and grape syrup, or so-called molasses. These products rarely leave California.

The Muscadine

In the southern states, where the conventional American hybrid and European grapes cannot be grown, the Muscadine grape (*V. rotundifolia*) is at least as important in the market and in local culture. Muscadines have a tan, green, or purple-black slipping skin that is tough and papery and never eaten; the berry is pulpy and cohesive and must be chewed. The aroma is higher than in the American hybrid grapes. Scuppernong is the best-known variety and indeed is the oldest American grape variety on record, dating from the early eighteenth century. Other varieties have had far shorter lives, as private individuals are still engaged in breeding superior fruit and wine varieties of Muscadines.

[*See also* CALIFORNIA; CHAMPAGNE; CURRANTS; FRUIT; FRUIT WINES; INSECTS; WINE: CALIFORNIA WINES; WINE: EASTERN U.S. WINES]

BIBLIOGRAPHY

Hedrick, U. P. *The Grapes of New York*. Albany: New York Agricultural Experiment Station, 1908.

Winkler, A. J., James A. Cook, W. M. Kliewer, and Lloyd A. Lider. *General Viticulture*. Berkeley: University of California Press, 1962.

C. T. KENNEDY

Grasshopper

In the 1930s, the grasshopper, supposedly named for the jumpy effect it produced, was a temperance drink made of lemon juice, orange juice, a raw egg, sugar, and ice.

The alcoholic version, probably invented in the 1960s, was an after-dinner drink of crème de menthe, crème de cacao, and heavy cream, shaken with ice and strained into a cocktail glass. It became a sweet and minty "girl drink," named for its color. The grasshopper had fallen out of favor by the early twenty-first century but was still available in a frozen, ice cream version, the "Flying Grasshopper," at the international T. G. I. Friday's chain.

"Grasshopper" has since become a descriptor for mint-flavored or green-colored desserts, such as grasshopper pie, which appeared soon after the drink. It is a frothy, mint-green dessert of crème de menthe, crème de cacao, whipped cream, and beaten egg whites in a graham-cracker or cookie-crumb crust, served chilled. Variations on grasshopper pie include versions made with lime gelatin, pistachio pudding, Oreo cookies, cream cheese, or marshmallows. One can also find recipes for grasshopper brownies, grasshopper bars, grasshopper milkshakes, and the like, usually incorporating crème de menthe. In 2002 the menu of the chain restaurant Denny's listed a "Grasshopper Sundae" and a "Grasshopper Blender Blaster," both nonalcoholic mint desserts.

[*See also* COCKTAILS; DESSERTS.]

JESSY RANDALL

Graters

Foods such as raw root vegetables, hard cheese, and baking chocolate can be reduced to shreds by hand with a grater. Grating reduces food to a more easily chewed, cooked, or melted state and produces flavorful tidbits to mix thoroughly through a dish. Small bits of food are removed with each rubbing across a surface made rough with punctures—holes with sharp, raised edges.

Graters have existed for centuries. Most are metal (wrought iron, sheet iron, tin, sometimes brass). Some have a flat or curved surface fixed to a wire frame that forms a grip or a prop to position it over a mixing bowl or other receptacle. Others are half-rounds fixed to a small board. Box graters are built into the top of a wooden box so that the gratings fall within. Some graters are freestanding cylinders or open-ended boxes, with various size grating holes on different sides. Graters with tiny burrs are called zesters and are used for grating the rind, or zest, of citrus fruits. Mechanical graters with cranks and revolving grating drums were patented in the 1850s for corn, vegetables, and nutmeg.

[*See also* CORN-PREPARATION TOOLS; NUTMEG GRATERS.]

BIBLIOGRAPHY

Franklin, Linda Campbell. *300 Years of Kitchen Collectibles*. 5th ed. Iola, WI: Krause, 2003.

LINDA CAMPBELL FRANKLIN

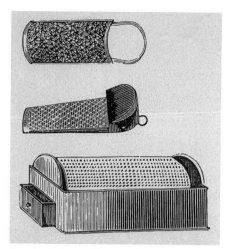

From top to bottom: tin grater, heavy nutmeg grater, and box grater.

Great Lakes Commercial Fishery, The

At one time, the Great Lakes were an isolated environment. Because of the extraordinary fall line of the Niagara River, no species of fish that had not been in the Great Lakes at the retreat of the glaciers could enter the lakes from an ocean or river. The fish population included lake trout, whitefish, lake herring, seven species of lake chub, yellow perch, sturgeon, shiner, sucker, burbot, round whitefish, and sculpin. The French explorer Antoine Laumet de La Mothe, sieur de Cadillac, observed Native Americans fishing for whitefish. The Native Americans used nets, weirs to trap migratory fish, and, particularly on rapids or falls entering the lakes, dip nets. They favored large trout, walleye (yellow pike), and sturgeon.

In the nineteenth century, cisco, also known as lake herring and chub; lake trout; whitefish; yellow perch; and sturgeon constituted the major commercial fisheries on the Great Lakes. George Brown Goode wrote in the 1880s that the pound net fishery was most important on Lake Superior and Lake Michigan and at the western end of Lake Erie, delivering to market the most valuable fresh fish. The gill net fishery was next most important but required the strongest fishery and navigational skills on the lakes and was even conducted through ice in winter. In the upper lakes, the most important gill net catches were trout and whitefish. Elsewhere, lake herring, pike bass, sturgeon, trout, and whitefish were most important. Seine fishing was conducted in the summer for sturgeon, bass, herring, sucker, mullet, and whitefish. Not all fish were used as food; alewives, for example, were used for meal and oil. Ice fishing on Saginaw Bay in the later 1800s tended more to sport, utilizing hook and line or a spear. A small city of icehouses sprung up on the frozen lake, and in one instance, even a billiard table was hauled out. In summer there was much hand-line sportfishing on the lakes.

Great Lakes commercial fisheries peaked in 1899. Commercial fisheries inevitably were overfished despite artificial propagation of whitefish by the U.S. Fisheries Commission. But the main difficulty on the lakes was the introduction of exotic species, against which the native species had no protection from predation or competition for habitat. Invasions began as early as 1829 with the completion of the Welland Canal, which connected Lake Erie to Lake Ontario and the Saint Lawrence River. Sea lamprey, alewife, and white perch entered the lakes via canals. Other species, such as zebra mussels, came later in ballast water in vessels. Still others such as rainbow and brown trout, chinook and coho salmon, and carp were deliberately introduced.

The lamprey invasion proved to be disastrous to lake trout, destroying most of them by the 1950s and injuring many other fish populations. The alewives that entered the Great Lakes were food for trout. When the trout population collapsed, an alewife fishery developed but caused the elimination of six of seven chub species. Herring, yellow perch, and emerald shiner almost disappeared. Without a predator, the alewives overpopulated and the shores of the lakes were littered with dead fish. An alewife fishery supplying fish meal and oil has brought the population under control.

SANDRA L. OLIVER

Grinders

Mechanical grinders saved time and required relatively little physical strength and thus were a vast improvement over women's age-old chore of pounding and chopping foodstuffs by hand. Among the first grinders to be developed to deal with new food imports into Europe were those for spice and coffee. By the late seventeenth century, small, geared, forged-iron grinders were designed with an upper holding hopper, hand-cranked grinding surfaces, and a lower collecting chamber. This basic design continued to be used during the next centuries. As costs of spice and coffee dropped, inexpensive casings of wood or tin replaced the iron grinders. Electric versions appeared in the last decades of the twentieth century in response to gourmet interest in the freshest flavors.

By the early 1800s, a second form of grinder was developed for making sausages. Strong wooden cases fitted with screwlike bores coarsely chopped the meats. Still cranked by hand, the core's rows of iron pegs pushed the meat against arrays of small sharp knives embedded in the box walls. By the mid-1800s, the design was re-created in cast iron as small tabletop grinders. The late 1800s saw the household cast-iron meat grinder, fitted with a choice of nozzle plates for different grades of coarseness, clamped to the kitchen table. Made by many different companies, the Enterprise models were probably the most famous and survived well into the twentieth century.

[**See also** NUTCRACKERS AND GRINDERS.]

ALICE ROSS

Grits, *see Corn*

Grocery Stores

For almost three hundred years, public markets were the primary retail and wholesale food source for urban Americans. In rural areas, even self-sufficient farmers needed to buy some food products, such as salt and sugar. All-purpose country stores sold necessities and, occasionally, luxury items.

As American towns grew into cities, small grocery stores emerged to accommodate residents who lived too far from the city center to shop conveniently at the public markets. These were small, family-owned stores that stocked mainly staple foods, such as flour, grains, and sugar, which were sold from barrels or sacks. Customers requested what they wanted, and the clerks then retrieved the items. The rapid growth of cities accelerated the trend away from the crowded public markets to grocery stores, and by the early twentieth century, public markets had been almost entirely replaced by grocery stores.

Grocery Chain Stores

In 1859 George F. Gilman, a prosperous New York businessman, and George H. Hartford started selling tea in New York City. They decided to buy tea in bulk directly from the source in China and sell directly to the customer, thereby eliminating the middleman, dramatically lowering the retail price. Their system was so successful that by 1865 Hartford and Gilman had five small stores in New York City, thus creating what would become America's first grocery chain. When the transcontinental railroad was completed in 1869, Gilman and Hartford named their company the Great Atlantic and Pacific Tea Company, subsequently shortened to A&P.

A&P expanded and by 1925 it owned 14,034 stores. Other entrepreneurs saw the success of A&P and emulated its operation. In 1872, the Grand Union Company was founded in New York. Bernard H. Kroger began a Cincinnati-based chain store operation in 1883. In 1916 in Memphis, Tennessee, Clarence Saunders

A meat counter in Greendale, Wisconsin, 1939.

launched the Piggly Wiggly grocery store and with it the revolutionary concept of self-service. Customers collected their own groceries, placed them in small hand baskets, and took them to a cashier. Self-service reduced labor costs, as fewer clerks were needed to serve customers.

Chain stores had many advantages over the independents. The chains usually had better insurance, so when struck by a fire or other catastrophe they could still reap profits from their other stores while reconstruction was in progress. Chain stores also were able to survive economic hard times by closing financially troubled stores while keeping the more successful locations open. Furthermore, they had the wherewithal to analyze and select the best sites for stores and to establish new outlets when the opportunity arose. Chain stores could hire buyers who specialized in certain product lines; their job was to maximize volume purchases and thereby reduce unit costs. To capture control of wholesale prices, some grocery chains launched their own store brands, which eliminated the middleman and further reduced overhead costs. The chains could afford advertising, and when radio became available they were able to advertise regionally and then nationally. The independent grocer hardly stood a chance against the chain stores.

Supermarkets

The chain-store system and the self-service concept shaped the supermarket. The term "super market" originated in southern California during the 1920s. Two chains—Ralph's Grocery Company and Alpha Beta Food Markets—constructed stores that covered five thousand square feet—ten times the size of traditional grocery stores.

The California model spread throughout the nation. In 1930 Michael Cullen launched King Kullen, in Jamaica, New York. Cullen profited by reducing prices and increasing

The entrance to a supermarket in Corpus Christi, Texas, December 1940.

volume. By the mid-1930s supermarkets were overtaking both chains and independent grocers. The A&P and other chains responded by closing their smaller stores and opening supermarkets. Independent grocers were unable to make the switch, and tens of thousands went out of business during the late 1930s and early 1940s.

The conversion from small stores to large supermarkets was hastened by the Depression. Customers saw supermarkets as a practical means of saving money. They were willing to forego the pleasant atmosphere of the neighborhood grocery for the lower prices they found in supermarkets. World War II slowed the growth of supermarkets, but the postwar growth of supermarkets was tremendous. The variety of inventory grew with the number of stores: In the 1940s, an average supermarket carried three thousand different items; by the late 1950s this had increased to fifty-eight hundred. By the 1970s, supermarkets stocked more than ten thousand items.

Technological Advances

Several advances in technology greatly enhanced supermarket shopping. The grocery shopping cart was invented by Sylvan Goldman in 1937 for his Standard Food Stores in Oklahoma City. The cart made it easy for customers to move their purchases from the cash register to their automobiles in the store's parking lot. A larger cart was an enticement to buy more. In 1947 "telescoping" shopping carts, which could be fitted into other empty carts, thus creating a more compact way of storing them, were first used. By 1956, 80 percent of all new supermarkets had piped-in music and air-conditioning, and many supermarkets provided special areas and rides for small children. Prices were stamped on items to reduce the time clerks spent writing down prices on each item, and price tags were installed on shelves so that consumers could easily see the cost of each product. Cash registers were redesigned to itemize purchases on the customer's receipt. To increase checkout speed, cashiers were trained to keep their eyes on the product price stamps, not the cash register keyboard. In 1967 the first bar code scanner was installed in a Kroger's supermarket in Cincinnati. Although not commonly used until the 1980s, bar codes combined with computer analysis revolutionized supermarket inventories and increased the ability to track and analyze customers' purchases.

During the first few years of the twenty-first century, supermarkets diversified their product lines as organic, vegetarian, and ethnic foods became popular. As food became a global business, with foods shipped from thousands of miles from producer to consumer, United States supermarkets set the world standards.

[See also DELICATESSENS; FARMERS' MARKETS; FOOD MARKETING; PIGGLY WIGGLY; TEA; TRANSPORTATION OF FOOD.]

BIBLIOGRAPHY

Kahn, Barbara E., and Leigh McAlister. *Grocery Revolution: The New Focus on the Consumer.* Reading, MA: Addison Wesley Longman, 1997.

Marnell, William H. *Once Upon a Store: A Biography of the World's First Supermarket.* New York: Herder, 1971.

Seth, Andrew, and Geoffrey Randall. *The Grocers: The Rise and Rise of the Supermarket Chains.* 2nd ed. Dover, NH: Kogan Page, 2001.

Walsh, William I. *The Rise and Decline of the Great Atlantic and Pacific Tea Company.* Secaucus, NJ: Lyle Stuart, 1986.

Zimmerman, M. M. *The Super Market: A Revolution in Distribution.* New York: McGraw-Hill, 1955.

ANDREW F. SMITH

Grog

Rum had become a staple ration in the British navy by the late seventeenth century. On August 21, 1740, the British vice admiral Edward Vernon ordered that the rum ration be mixed with water to reduce drunkenness. English sailors named this mixture "grog" in honor of Vernon, who was called "Old Grog" because of the cloak he wore, which was made of grogram, a thick blend of silk, wool, and mohair. In 1756 the dilution of rum with water was institutionalized in British naval regulations. George Washington's home, Mt. Vernon in Virginia, was named by Washington's elder half-brother, Lawrence, who had served under Admiral Vernon in 1740.

The American navy adopted grog, which was a part of a seaman's ration until it was discontinued in 1862. Over the years, the quantity of rum and water varied, producing "two-water grog" or "three-water grog," depending on the dilution. Other alcoholic beverages, such as arrack, were frequently substituted for the rum in grog, and sometimes other ingredients, such as sugar and lime, were added.

Grogshops had sprung up in American ports before the Revolutionary War. They were frequented by sailors and were considered among the most unsavory establishments in American cities. As the price of whiskey declined during the nineteenth century, it was often substituted for rum. Grogshop owners sometimes adulterated the whiskey in the grog with logwood (a dye), berries, tobacco, and strychnine. Raw eggs were also occasionally added to grog, and this may have been the origin of the American drink, egg 'n' grog or eggnog, which emerged in the United States during the nineteenth century and remains a favorite at Christmastime and on New Year's Day.
[See also RUM.]

BIBLIOGRAPHY

Brown, John Hull. *Early American Beverages.* Rutland, VT: Charles E. Tuttle, 1966.

Pack, James. *Nelson's Blood: The Story of Naval Rum.* 3rd ed. Annapolis, MD: Naval Institute Press, 1995.

ANDREW F. SMITH

Grunion

The grunion is a small fish that is found on the California coast between around Morro Bay to part way down the Baja peninsula. Its spawning habits, like those of anadromous fishes, have made it prey to humans. The grunion comes ashore at high tide, in Southern California always at night, in schools of males and females during the full and new moons. The females open a place in soft, watery sand and lay eggs. The males, finding a female doing so, wind themselves around the female and supply milt to fertilize the eggs. When they are done, the fish flop themselves back into the water, leaving the eggs to hatch and wash out to sea in a high tide about ten days later.

The grunion may be caught only by hand. Rolled in cornmeal and fried, it is considered a panfish. The grunion is protected, and conservation steps taken include a "no-take" season from March to May as well as efforts to discourage beach grooming with rakes, which disturbs the grunion eggs.

SANDRA L. OLIVER

Guacamole, *see Dips and Spreads*

Gum

People have been chewing gumlike wax, resin, and latex for thousands of years. American Indians introduced American colonists to the pleasures of chewing the fragrant resin from spruce trees. By the mid-nineteenth century, sweetened paraffin was commonly chewed. Modern commercial chewing gum got its start when the Mexican general Antonio de Santa Ana (who as president of Mexico had tried to put down the revolt in Texas), was exiled in the 1860s. When he came to the United States, he brought chicle—a latex from the sapodilla tree that Mexicans liked to chew. Santa Ana approached a man named Thomas Adams with the chicle in hopes that there might be some commercial use for it. Adams tried to make toys and other products from the substance, but nothing worked. Finally, in 1869 he realized that it had an elasticity and resilience that made it satisfying to chew. At the time Americans chewed flavored paraffin-based gum, called White Mountain. Adams's first gum, which had no added flavoring but was sweetened, was mass-produced beginning in 1871. It was wrapped in tissue and sold for a penny a stick. Adams introduced flavored gums beginning in 1884 and gumballs the following year; by 1888, they were sold in vending machines.

Other manufacturers began producing gum. John Colgan began manufacturing Taffy Tolu Chewing Gum in 1879. Dr. Edward Beeman marketed pepsin gum, said to improve digestion, in 1891. Thomas Wrigley Jr. put Wrigley's Spearmint and Juicy Fruit gums on the market in 1893. In 1899, a dentist named Franklin V. Canning introduced Dentyne Gum and Chiclets.

Bubble gum was invented in 1928 by Walter E. Diemer, an accountant for the Fleer Chewing Gum Company in Philadelphia. He experimented with formulas for chewing gum and found one that stretched more easily and was less sticky than most. It was marketed by Fleer as Double Bubble gum. The rights to this gum were bought by Marvel Entertainment Group, who packaged it with trading cards (most famously, baseball cards) until the late 1980s. In 1988, the rights for Double Bubble gum were sold to Concord Confections, which manufactured bubble-gum gumballs.

The Topps Gum company, which started in Brooklyn in 1939, began marketing Bazooka Bubble Gum after World War II. In 1953, the company began placing baseball cards in each package. Bazooka Bubble Gum quickly became the largest selling gum. Sugarless gum was produced in the 1950s, but these were usually sweetened with cyclamates, which was banned by the Food and Drug Administration (FDA) in 1972. Aspartame became the main sweetener for sugar-free gums. Wrigley was the first American gum manufacturer to begin selling its products abroad. As of 2004 gum made up about 25 percent of the total candy sales in the United States.

BIBLIOGRAPHY
Redclift, Michael R. *Chewing Gum: The Fortunes of Taste.* New York: Routledge, 2004.
Richardson, Tim. *Sweets: A History of Candy.* New York: Bloomsbury, 2002.

ANDREW F. SMITH

Gummy Candy

Colorful, chewy, sweet, gelatin-based gummy candies were invented by Hans Riegel during the early 1920s in Germany. It is the gelatin that gives gummies their elasticity. Riegel, the owner of the German candy company Haribo, produced gummy bears, which were widely sold in Germany before World War II. Gummy candies were imported into the United States during the 1960s. The Brock Candy Company and the Goelitz Candy Company both claim to have been the first American companies to produce gummy candy about 1980. In 1982, Haribo began marketed gummy bears in the United States. Their fanciful shapes appealed to adults as well as children. Gummy bears became an instant classic in the United States in the 1980s. Trolli, another German candy manufacturer, introduced gummy worms in lurid colors in 1990s, and they were also a big hit.

Gummy candy comes in a variety of flavors, including strawberry, lemon, pineapple and orange. Sour flavors are particular popular. New varieties of gummy candies are now on the market, including chocolate-covered gummy candy from Sweden and vitamin enriched gummies. In 2002, the convenience store 7-Eleven teamed up with Dayhoff to produce the "Candy Gulp" cups, which were filled with Juicee Gummee gummi bears. The reclosable cups fit nicely into cup holders in cars and they promptly became the chain's largest candy seller.

Young children have particularly enjoyed gummy candy and a number of publishers, including Walt Disney Productions, have used characterizations of gummy bears in children's books and an animated series.

BIBLIOGRAPHY
Traxler, Hans. *The Life and Times of Gummy Bears.* New York: HarperPerennial, 1993.

ANDREW F. SMITH

Gyro

The gyro sandwich is most likely the invention of Greek immigrants who, sometime around the 1970s, adapted the cooking of their homeland as a way to earn a living by providing ground meat in a new manner, one that would tempt the sandwich-loving American public. Ground lamb or beef, or a mixture of both, is seasoned with herbs and spices and molded around a vertical spit that rotates before a flame. The word "gyro" means ring or circle, and the sandwich was thus named for the spinning spit on which it is prepared. As the meat cooks and forms a crust on the outside, it is shaved off, placed in pita bread, and served with lettuce, onion, tomato, and *tzatziki*, a yogurt sauce flavored with garlic and cucumber. Gyros have become so popular since their introduction that they can be found in major cities throughout most of the United States.

[**See also** SANDWICHES; STREET VENDORS.]

BIBLIOGRAPHY
Mercuri, Becky. *Sandwiches That You Will Like.* Pittsburgh, PA: WQED, 2002.

BECKY MERCURI

H

Häagen-Dazs

Reuben Mattus, a high-school dropout, emigrated from Poland to New York City and worked with his mother, who sold fruit ices and ice cream pops from a horse-drawn cart in the Bronx before World War II. The family business began manufacturing ice cream and distributing it to grocery stores. It prospered through the Depression and World War II. By the 1950s, large ice cream makers, such as Breyers and Bordens, undersold small local producers so severely that supermarkets switched to the national brands. Mattus felt that large manufacturers were compromising their products' quality to reduce the price; he saw a niche for ultra-rich, top-quality ice cream and hoped that there would be customers willing to pay more for it.

In 1960 Mattus formed a company of his own. His wife came up with the name Häagen-Dazs, which conveyed an image of Denmark (although the words are not Danish—they are not any language at all), which he believed had a positive image in the United States. He started with three basic flavors—vanilla, chocolate, and coffee—and sold pint cartons to small shops in Manhattan. Mattus mixed very little air into his ice cream and to give it a rich taste it was made with a high butterfat content. It was also made from all-natural ingredients without preservatives or additives.

Eventually he began distributing throughout the East Coast, and finally, nationwide. He experimented with new flavors, and decided to open up Häagen-Dazs retail outlets in 1976.

The Häagen-Dazs brand was a success, and others imitated Mattus and began manufacturing premium ice cream with foreign sounding names. One such clone was Frusen Gladje, which had originated with Richie Smith, an ice cream manufacturer who also distributed Dolly Madison ice cream. Häagen-Dazs has outlasted Frusen Gladje and other copycat products. Reuben Mattus sold Häagen-Dazs to the Pillsbury Company in 1983, and since then, the brand's product lines have expanded to include ice cream bars, frozen yogurt, and sorbet. As of 2005, Häagen-Dazs ice cream was sold in fifty-four countries.

[See also ICE CREAMS AND ICES.]

BIBLIOGRAPHY

Funderburg, Anne Cooper. *Chocolate, Strawberry, and Vanilla: A History of American Ice Cream*. Bowling Green, OH: Bowling Green State University Popular Press, 1995.

ANDREW F. SMITH

Haddock

A handsome ground fish in the family Gadidae with cod and pollock, haddock (*Melanogrammus aeglefinus*) was valued for its firm, white flesh with its capacity for being salted and smoked to make finnan haddie. Old-time New England fishermen used to recall a day before haddock was appreciated, but it was fished in the late eighteenth century and more widely caught in the nineteenth and twentieth centuries. In *History and Methods of the Fisheries* (1887), George Brown Goode reports that in the mid-1800s salted and dried haddock was nicknamed "skulljoe" on Cape Cod. Finnan haddie was named for the town of Findon, Scotland, where haddock was salted and smoked commercially, although the process caught on in New England and was widely spread in Portland, Maine.

By the end of the nineteenth century, haddock was regarded as the ideal chowder fish, but it was useful for all purposes. In the twentieth century haddock was caught for fillets, as was cod, and in the 1920s haddock actually exceeded cod in tons caught. It is as stressed a fishery as cod, flounders, and other white-fleshed fish.

SANDRA L. OLIVER

Halibut

The halibut (*Hippoglossus hippoglossus* and *H. stenolepis*), in the same Pleuronectidae family as other flatfish such as flounder, reached popularity in the nineteenth century, when the size of the individuals sometimes reached heroic proportions of six hundred pounds. Caught in northern Atlantic waters, inshore for many years but eventually on the Georges Bank as a commercial fishery in the mid-1800s, halibut was iced and shipped coastwise to the South and even inland by rail, which helps to account for cookbook writers across the country including halibut cooking directions. On the West Coast, the Pacific halibut is today an important fishery both commercially and recreationally, whereas the East Coast halibut fishery is mostly depleted.

Halibut has a firm, sometimes dark flesh; large, easy-to-find bones; and a meaty texture when cooked. Because the individual fish were so large, halibut was almost always sold as steaks, which can be fried or baked. Some halibut was salted and smoked, and when halibut became hard to find, salted and smoked sturgeon was substituted for it.

Like many fish, the halibut caught are smaller than they were at one time. For example, the average Pacific halibut weighs between thirty and forty pounds, whereas three hundred pounds was once a common size.

SANDRA L. OLIVER

Halloween

Halloween may be the only American holiday that is not associated with a particular feast or recipe. Nineteenth-century Irish immigrants brought the October 31 celebration to the United States. On that night, it was traditional to give soul cakes to visitors to their households in return for promises to say prayers on behalf of dead relatives. They also put lanterns made from vegetables in the windows to welcome ghosts and wandering souls. In Ireland and Scotland, these candlelit lanterns were carved from large turnips or potatoes, and in England from beets, but in the United States immigrants used the larger native pumpkins.

Carved pumpkin jack-o'-lanterns are an integral part of Halloween festivities, but they are seldom eaten. The specially bred pumpkins, which can range in size from one to over one thousand pounds, are hollowed out and carved with holes to represent eyes, nose, and mouth. When a lighted candle or flashlight is placed inside, the pumpkin's face glows in the dark. Smaller species of cheese pumpkin, pie pumpkin or sweet pumpkin, which have sweeter, less watery flesh, are used for making pies, soups, and breads. Some people save the seeds to dry, roast, and salt as a snack. Roasted, salted pumpkin seeds can be purchased commercially as well.

American harvest festivals called play parties were a precursor to the modern Halloween. In the mid-nineteenth century, Snap Apple Nights or Nut Crack Night parties were celebrated in some regions of the United States with games, such as dunking for apples or fortune-telling with nuts, that symbolized the end of the harvest season.

Ducking for Apples

Children duck, or bob, for apples on this early-twentieth-century embossed postcard.

A Halloween postcard, circa 1909.

Bobbing for apples was a British folk tradition in which young, unmarried people tried to bite an apple that was floating in water or hanging from a string without using their hands. The first person to bite into one would be the next to marry. For a Nut Crack Night party, pairs of walnuts were set on the hearth near the fire by courting couples. If the heated nuts bounced around and cracked open, they foretold a troubled relationship, but if the nuts roasted quietly, the relationship would be smooth.

In the late nineteenth century, middle-class Americans looking toward their Celtic heritage rediscovered (and reinvented) Halloween customs and made them respectable. Beginning in the 1870s, articles on Halloween appeared in periodicals that encouraged a new, more uniformly celebrated Victorian fete. By the twentieth century, Halloween parties for both children and adults had become a common way to mark the day, with games like bobbing for apples, festive costumes, and refreshments that included cider, doughnuts, candy corn, popcorn balls, and apples.

Candies made in the shape of corn kernels and pumpkins commemorated the harvest season. The Wunderle Candy Company of Philadelphia was the first to commercially produce candy corn in the 1880s. The sons of German immigrant Gustav Goelitz, founder of Goelitz Confectionery Co., began commercial production in 1898 in Cincinnati, Ohio. The company he founded claims to be the oldest manufacturer of the holiday icon. Brach's in Chicago began manufacturing the small, soft, triangular and tricolor (orange, yellow, and white) candies in the late 1920s. By the 1990s, the company was turning out 30 million kernels a day. In 2001, candy corn manufacturers sold more than 20 million pounds, or approximately 8.3 billion kernels.

Before World War II, Halloween pranks were the norm, while families hosted small parties at home for young children. During the war years, little candy was available because of sugar rationing. In the 1950s, Halloween evolved into a family- and neighborhood-centered holiday directed mainly at the young, in an attempt to discourage teenage pranksters. Home bakers produced pumpkin or witch cookies, shaped with newly available cookie cutters, and devil's food cupcakes frosted with orange and black icing.

The ancient Halloween ritual of trick or treat was revived as a relatively inexpensive way for the new postwar suburban communities to share the Halloween celebration. It became a child's right and privilege to go from house to house filling a pillowcase with apples, popcorn balls, and candy. The tradition of Trick-or-Treat for UNICEF began in 1950 when Philadelphia schoolchildren collected money in decorated milk cartons to help the world's children through the United Nations Children's Fund. Trick-or-Treat for UNICEF spread across the country, and as the twenty-first century opened millions of children participated each year in Halloween-related fund-raising campaigns in the United States, Canada, Ireland, Mexico, and Hong Kong.

Door-to-door trick-or-treating became less popular at the end of the twentieth century when fabricated urban legends grew up about poisoned candy and neighbors who gave children apples containing razor blades or needles. Many communities and churches tried to redirect the holiday to well-chaperoned indoor parties and some children were not allowed to eat noncommercial, unpackaged treats.

In addition to holiday candy and games, Americans play with their food at Halloween by creating party foods in the shape of pumpkins, black cats, ghosts, and witches. Jack-o'-lantern cheese balls are consumed, along with quantities of candy. Many enjoy foods that are frightening or disgusting, such as candy worms in chocolate pudding dusted on top with crushed chocolate-cookie crumbs to look like dirt, licorice spiders, pretzel witch fingers with almond fingernails, or ice cubes containing stuffed olives that simulate eyes. Food is used as a substitute for human body parts in haunted houses, a popular party game or community fund-raiser. Visitors to the haunted house are blindfolded and told to put their hands in bowls of cooked pasta representing intestines, dried apricots representing ears, or peeled grapes representing eyeballs. Gourmets experiment with pumpkin soups, seasonal vegetables, and unusual sauces.

In the 1990s, Americans spent an estimated $6.9 billion annually on Halloween, making it the country's second-largest commercial holiday next to Christmas. By the late twentieth century, the holiday had changed again from a children's festival to an all-ages extravaganza. By the early 2000s, Halloween had become a bigger holiday for candy consumption than Valentine's Day, Christmas, or Easter. Miniature candy bars, produced especially for Halloween, were popular with trick-or-treaters, and candy corn continued to outsell all other nonchocolate Halloween candy.

[**See also** Candy and Candy Bars.]

BIBLIOGRAPHY

Bannatyne, Lesley Pratt. *Halloween: An American Holiday, An American History.* New York: Facts on File, 1990.

Halloween: Bewitching Treats, Eats, Costumes and Decorations. New York: Lorenz Books, Anness Publishing, 1999.

Virginia Scott Jenkins

Ham, *see Pigs*

Hamburger

The hamburger is the single most popular food item consumed in the United States, with Americans eating billions of them each year. Originally known as the hamburger sandwich, hamburgers commonly consist of a flattened patty of ground beef placed between two halves of a white flour bun. To enhance the flavor, hamburger eaters routinely adorn their grilled or fried ground beef patties with a variety of possible cheeses, vegetables, and sauces, creating a seemingly endless combination of tastes. French-fried potatoes and carbonated soft drinks traditionally accompany the burgers, creating America's favorite fast-food meal. In fact, this burger-and-fries feast is viewed worldwide as American food.

The hamburger's exact origins are vague. Explanations of its roots are based more on myth than on verifiable fact. Chopping or grinding up meat before eating it is possibly as old as our species, dating far back into prehistory. Food historians offer numerous, often contradictory, accounts of where the hamburger originated, but most trace it to northern Germany, which had a similar beef sausage. The hamburger, in turn, accompanied the massive wave of German immigrants coming to America during the early to mid-nineteenth century. Their ethnic dish of seasoned ground beef appeared on the menu of New York City's elite Delmonico's restaurant in 1834, featured as the Hamburg Steak. By the latter half of the century, American cookbooks included recipes for Beefsteak à la Hamburg and for the identical, yet Americanized, Salisbury steak.

How the hamburger became a popular part of the mainstream American diet is also in question, as competing tales credit its introduction to several different entrepreneurs. Residents of New Haven, Connecticut, insist that the immigrant Louis Lassen began selling hamburgers from his lunch wagon by

1900. Another hamburger legend has Charlie Nagreen serving the first true hamburger at a fair in Seymour, Wisconsin, in 1885. The Akron, Ohio, native Frank Menches is locally acclaimed for serving the world's first hamburger at his local Summit County Fair. Menches, however, also claims credit for inventing the ice cream cone. Seemingly more verifiable was the work of the Texan Fletcher Davis, who probably sold what he termed hamburgers to fairgoers at St. Louis's 1904 Louisiana Purchase Exposition. Regardless of who was first, the early hamburger did not immediately gain a popular following, remaining either somewhat of a "fair food," or an inexpensive snack sold to workers from food carts at factory gates.

One factor that may have hindered the hamburger's popularity was the common distrust of the meat industry in the early twentieth century, prompted by the 1906 publication of Upton Sinclair's *The Jungle*. Sinclair's book exposed the unsanitary and dangerous conditions in meat-processing plants, discouraging meat consumption. Ground meat was even more suspect, since at that time most meat was only ground up after it had begun to spoil. Butchers regularly ground their unsold meat, keeping it salable longer by adding chemical preservatives to the mix. The ground meat also commonly included a high percentage of animal fat and undesirable organ tissue. With such a dismal reputation, only the most impoverished consumers resorted to purchasing and consuming ground meat. Although inexpensive, ground beef patties long remained on the margin of the American diet.

The hamburger finally became popular in the 1920s because of the intensive marketing campaign by an upstart restaurant chain in Wichita, Kansas. In 1921, Billy Ingram and Walter Anderson opened the White Castle System of Eating Houses, featuring a five-cent hamburger as their primary offering. (In fact, another Midwestern legend credits the White Castle cofounder and fry cook Walter Anderson with actually creating the first flattened hamburger patty on a bun.) Ingram realized the great profit potential from selling hamburger sandwiches. To persuade customers that the hamburger was safe to eat, Ingram aggressively marketed the concepts of cleanliness and purity by whitewashing his buildings' exteriors, using only gleaming stainless steel counters and fixtures, and constantly grinding good, fresh cuts of beef within customers' sight. Ingram later even commissioned a medical school study that indicated that hamburgers were a highly nutritious food. He succeeded in popularizing his hamburgers, both by stressing their purity and nutritional value and by offering them at an inexpensive price. Ingram also encouraged customers to purchase numerous burgers at one time, and to take them home "by the sack." This take-out format became the norm for most of their transactions and

The Union Stockyards gate in Chicago, the last stop for cattle entering Armour's packing plants. The stockyards are now long gone, and the gate is all that remains.

the precedent for modern fast food. White Castle quickly spread eastward across the Midwest in the early 1920s and was already firmly established in New York City by 1929.

Countless imitators of White Castle's buildings, products, name, and even slogan soon sprang up throughout the United States, extending the sudden popularity of the hamburger sandwich from coast to coast. White Tower overlapped White Castle's territory in the Midwest and East, and Crystal's and Little Tavern became the dominant hamburger chains in the South. By the end of the 1920s, the hamburger craze had completely saturated the restaurant market, so much so that the president of the American Restaurant Association announced in 1929 that the hamburger and apple pie had become America's favorite foods. The rate of hamburger consumption continued to grow, even during the Depression-era economic hardships of the 1930s. In fact, innovators even expanded beyond the White Castle–style burger, offering customers new and different variations. Most significant was the introduction in California of Bob Wian's Big Boy, a double-stacked, two-patty burger sandwich, including cheese, an extra layer of bread, lettuce, mayonnaise, and relish. The hamburger boom continued up until the beginning of World War II, when the restaurant industry was suddenly crippled by labor and food shortages. Workers either joined the military or took higher-paying war production jobs, leaving hamburger restaurants without employees. Compounding this labor void was a program of national food rationing that severely limited the availability of meat, coffee, and sugar. The hamburger industry began to rebound after the war ended, making a slow recovery in the late 1940s.

In the 1950s, the hamburger gained a new following, becoming the most popular food of burgeoning suburbia. Shedding their ethnic identities along with their urban neighborhoods, new suburbanites stressing conformity embraced the hamburger as their common food. Hamburger stands appeared soon after suburban housing tracts, making their products readily available to the young families of the Baby Boom. Nationally franchised chains, such as McDonald's and (Insta-) Burger King, began to edge out local and regional chains by the late 1950s, becoming the dominant force in suburban hamburger sales. By the mid-1960s, McDonald's emerged as the industry leader, dominating most market areas and introducing most of the industry's product innovations. Serving many millions of its inexpensive round, one-ounce burgers, with the already popular combination of ketchup, mustard, onion, and pickle condiments, McDonald's set the standard for what consumers expected from a hamburger. Its only variation on the hamburger was the cheeseburger, created by adding a slice of American cheese to the top during cooking.

By the 1970s, however, both McDonald's and the other leading chains offered a wide variety of oversized burgers. Most popular among this new generation of hamburgers was McDonald's two-tiered Big Mac—essentially a modified Big Boy burger—and Burger King's Whopper, featuring a larger beef patty topped by a gooey salad mix of lettuce, onion, pickles, mayonnaise-based sauce, and tomato slice. Dave Thomas's Wendy's chain first appeared in 1969, selling only bigger hamburgers, all made-to-order for each customer from a long list of possible condiments. Eventually, other companies sold burgers topped with everything from chili to bacon to bean sprouts, customizing their sandwiches to suit regional, ethnic, and trendy preferences.

The hamburger went from the margin of society to the mainstream during the twentieth century, becoming America's undisputed culinary favorite. More than simply a popular food, the hamburger emerged as a symbol of American culture, and even as a key aspect of American ethnicity. Hailed as "the" American food, ever-expanding multinational restaurant chains efficiently market the hamburger all around the globe.

BIBLIOGRAPHY

Hogan, David Gerard. *Selling 'Em by the Sack: White Castle and the Creation of American Food.* New York: New York University Press, 1997.

Jakle, John A., and Keith A. Sculle. *Fast Food: Roadside Restaurants in the Automobile Age.* Baltimore: Johns Hopkins University Press, 1999.

Kroc, Ray, with Robert Anderson. *Grinding It Out: The Making of McDonald's.* Chicago: Contemporary Books, 1977.

DAVID GERARD HOGAN

Hardee's

In 1960, Wilbur Hardee in Greenville, North Carolina opened the first Hardee's restaurant. It featured fifteen-cent charco-broiled hamburgers, soft drinks, french fries, and milkshakes. Later, biscuits were added to the menu. In 1961 J. Leonard Rawls and James Carson Gardner bought out Wilbur Hardee. They took out advertisements and quickly expanded their operations, particularly in small towns in the South. Fourteen years later, Hardee's had more than nine hundred outlets, housed in modular buildings that reportedly took just six hours to erect. At first, these buildings had red and white stripes, like McDonald's, but then the company shifted to a brown-and-orange color scheme like Burger King's. The company also purchased a bakery and suppliers of seafood and frozen hamburger patties. Hardee's was one of the first fast food chains to sell stock on the open market. In 1977, Imasco, the Canadian tobacco, food, and retail conglomerate, began buying Hardee's stock, and in 1980 it took over Hardee's, which by then had 2,141 outlets. The chain expanded to Central America and the Middle East and absorbed many Burger Chef restaurants when that chain folded. In 1990, Hardee's acquired the Roy Rogers chain, and Hardee's was, in turn, acquired by Carl's Jr. in 1997. Hardee's outlets feature Carl Jr.'s symbol—a five-pointed yellow star with the happy face. As of 2005, there were 3,200 Hardee's outlets. [**See also** FAST FOOD.]

BIBLIOGRAPHY

Jakle, John A., and Keith A. Sculle, *Fast Food: Roadside Restaurants in the Automobile Age.* Baltimore: Johns Hopkins University Press, 1999.

ANDREW F. SMITH

Hardtack

For centuries, hard breads made of flour and water and baked into round, oval, or square shapes have accompanied travelers on long treks, soldiers in military campaigns, and sailors at sea. Hardtack's first important North American role was in sustaining crews and passengers of European vessels en route to the New World and as a ration in the ensuing seaborne trade. Ship's bread continued to feed seamen well into the twentieth century. Hardtack also was known as biscuit, crackers, ship's bread or biscuit, hard bread or biscuit or crackers; soft tack was fresh bread.

Military biscuit predated the independent United States, serving armies in both Europe and North America and was an important ration for the Continental Army in the

This piece of hardtack from the Spanish-American War was autographed by enlisted men from Pennsylvania and mailed home to Pine Grove by George Heiser, one of the soldiers.

Revolutionary War (1775–1783). General George Washington constantly asked the baking superintendent Christopher Ludwick for large quantities to feed his campaigning soldiers, and the Revolutionary private Joseph Martin was served biscuit "hard enough to break the teeth of a rat."

This durable foodstuff achieved iconic status during the American Civil War (1861–1865). The three-inch-square hardtack symbolized the hardship and singularity of a soldier's life, providing a tangible wartime and postwar link among veterans. Nicknames abounded: angle cake, cast-iron biscuits, teeth dullers, McClellan pies, Lincoln pies. Soldiers' correspondence, diaries, and postwar literature, evincing both fondness and antipathy, show that hardtack held a special place in the soldiers' collective consciousness. Capt. Francis Donaldson, of the 118th Pennsylvania, expressed this mixed attitude, writing in April 1862 of "the despised sheet iron cracker." Only six months later Donaldson noted, "I can make as enjoyable a meal on [hard] crackers as others can on roast chicken and trimmings." Hardtack appeared in verse, too. "Short allowance prevailed throughout the brigade. The men changed the words of a song which goes 'Hard times! Come again no more,' [Stephen Foster, 1854] into the following, and sang it with much vigor and vim:

> 'Tis the voice of the hungry,
> Hardtack, hardtack,
> Come again once more!
> Many days I've wandered,
> from my little tent door
> Crying hardtack, hardtack
> Come again once more!"

Hardtack's special connotation both preceded and postdated the American Civil War. Soldiers sent or took samples home, and many are now in museum collections across the country. Other souvenir examples exist, such as an inscribed 1784 British ship's biscuit in the National Maritime Museum collections, Greenwich, England, and a Spanish-American War hardtack sent to Pine Grove, Pennsylvania, bearing the date "May 7 1898" along with the names of the correspondent and his four messmates. Hardtack remained an important part of World War I army campaign rations (1917–1918) and continued to feed American soldiers on field maneuvers into the 1930s.

[See also COMBAT FOOD; SHIP FOOD.]

BIBLIOGRAPHY

Billings, John D. *Hardtack and Coffee.* New York: Time-Life Books, 1982, originally published 1887, 112–120.

Oliver, Sandra L. *Saltwater Foodways: New Englanders and Their Food, at Sea and Ashore, in the Nineteenth Century.* Mystic, CT: Mystic Seaport Museum, Inc., 1995.

Rees, John U. "Cooking with Biscuit and Hard Tack in Camp." *Food History News* 8, no. 4 (spring 1997): 4–5.

Rees, John U. " 'Hard Enough to Break the Teeth of a Rat': Biscuit and Hard Bread in the Armies of the Revolution." *Food History News* 8, no. 4 (spring 1997): 2–6.

JOHN U. REES

Harvey, Fred

Frederick Henry Harvey (1835–1901), a restaurant entrepreneur, immigrated to New York City from England at age fifteen in 1850. He found work in restaurants there and in New Orleans, before moving to St. Louis, where he and a partner opened a restaurant in 1857. The outbreak of the Civil War in 1861, combined with the dishonest behavior of Harvey's partner, left his business in ruins and him unemployed. He eventually found work as a railway mail clerk on the Hannibal & St. Joseph Railroad (1862), which later became part of the Chicago, Burlington, & Quincy Railroad (CB&Q). There he experienced firsthand the often squalid conditions and chicanery that greeted passengers on trains scheduled to stop "twenty minutes for refreshments" at designated stations, which was at that time the primary means of feeding people traveling long distances by rail.

His sensibilities as a gourmand were outraged at what he saw and what he had to consume, so Harvey drew on his experience as a restaurateur to come up with a better idea. He proposed building eating houses at intervals that would allow trains to stop at times appropriate for dining. At each stop, passengers would be offered a clean and handsomely furnished dining room, with Irish linen and English silver at table, ample portions of well-prepared food, and efficient and courteous service. His plan to carry this out included preferred shipping arrangements for foodstuffs over the host railroad, offering attractive salaries to noted chefs of the day who joined his firm, and, eventually, hiring young women to serve as waitresses.

Harvey's employer, the CB&Q, turned this proposal down. Harvey next approached the Atchison, Topeka, & Santa Fe Railway (AT&SF), then building a line between Kansas and southern California. Through negotiations with that railroad and its existing food vendor, Harvey acquired the food concession at the depot in Topeka, Kansas, in 1876. From there, he and his heirs and successors went on to establish fifty-two lunch and dining rooms, the Harvey Houses, twenty-three hotels, and thirty newsstands, a majority of them in association with the AT&SF. Meanwhile, when the AT&SF began running dining cars on their long distance trains in 1888, Harvey negotiated to staff and provision those eating establishments as well. When the AT&SF acquired rail access to the rim of the Grand Canyon, Harvey created, in 1903, the recreational and boarding accommodations there. His firm eventually also established corporate and public eating establishments that stretched from Cleveland, Ohio, to Los Angeles, California.

Harvey's contributions to American culinary history are of a pioneering nature. His establishments and his reputation for quality played a critical role in attracting riders to the Santa Fe system. He created centralized menu planning, which assured that passengers on the AT&SF would never encounter identical selections when traveling. He established standards for excellence in food and service that applied to an extensive chain of restaurants, with the result that patrons could be assured of a certain high-quality meal experience wherever they encountered a Harvey operation. Perhaps his most unique contribution is an outgrowth of his desire to offer exceptional service. He is credited with populating the American Southwest with thousands of educated, adventuresome, attractive, and single young women—the Harvey Girls waitresses—early in the region's settlement history, earning him the title "civilizer of the West."

[See also DINING CAR; JOHNSON, HOWARD; PULLMAN, GEORGE.]

BIBLIOGRAPHY

Haber, Barbara. "The Harvey Girls: Good Women and Good Food." In *From Hardtack to Home Fries: An Uncommon History of American Cooks and Meals,* 87–106. New York: Free Press, 2002.

Henderson, James David. *Meals by Fred Harvey.* Fort Worth: Texas Christian University Press, 1969.

Poling-Kempes, Lesley. *The Harvey Girls: Women Who Opened the West.* New York: Paragon House, 1989.

JAMES D. PORTERFIELD

Hasty Pudding

Hasty pudding was basically a stirred cornmeal porridge that became a symbol of classlessness and independence in eighteenth-century America. It was known at every hearth of the time, regardless of class or ethnic origin. Its reference in "Yankee Doodle," a song of the Revolutionary War period—"And there we saw the men and boys/as thick as hasty pudding"—testifies that it was so widely known that it could be used as a simile.

Likewise, the Connecticut poet Joel Barlow, contributing to the American literary genre born after the Revolutionary War, wrote a long, mock-epic poem, "The Hasty Pudding," extolling the dish. Somewhat tongue in cheek, he not only gave detailed cooking instructions but also sentimentalized the dish's virtues as a wholesome food of the new democracy and the "common man."

The porridge that the American colonists called hasty pudding combined European and Native American traditions. European settlers had been accustomed to making their porridges from the European grains—wheat, oats, rye, and barley—whereas Native Americans used indigenous New World corn (maize) for their sagamite. As corn was easier to grow and more bountiful than the Old World grains, settlers made expedient substitutions and adapted their own cuisines to corn. Everyone, it seems, made cornmeal porridges—the New York and New Jersey Dutch, the Delaware Swedes, the Pennsylvania Germans, and the New England and Virginia English. It was served with milk and molasses for breakfast or supper, according to the tastes of each ethnicity; for example, the Dutch, who loved sour flavors, drowned their "sappaen" in buttermilk.

The English version, also called mush, took the name hasty pudding because of its ancient pudding origins. In a technique conceived in the middle ages, a rather complex mixture of assorted meats, grains, fruits, and spices was tied in a cloth or "pudding bag" and boiled in a large pot for as long as twelve or fourteen hours to cook through. With time, the nature of puddings diversified and simplified; one offshoot led to American hasty pudding.

Such transitional puddings as An Excellent Pudding, described in *The Closet of Sir Kenelme Digbie Opened* (London, 1669), required only a manageable hour in a bake oven, a significant change in technology. The pudding bag had been dispensed with, and the dish's character was more like bread pudding. In the next century, Hannah Glasse's Flour Hasty-Pudding (1747) was stirred on the hearth in a process akin to that for making porridge, but it was still called pudding and it cooked faster than the traditional plum puddings which were still boiled in a pudding bag.

The nineteenth century brought American Eliza Leslie's *Directions for Cooking* (1837) and its then-old recipe for Indian Mush, a porridge in fact and name ("Indian" meant cornmeal). She stressed the importance of constant stirring with a "pudding stick," a long, slim, wooden paddle, and up to two hours of cooking. A symbol of patriotic pride at the time of the centennial celebrations, hasty pudding continued as a breakfast staple throughout the nation until the development of still-faster twentieth-century cereals.

[**See also** Cookbooks and Manuscripts: To 1860; Corn; Ethnic Food; Historical Overview; Leslie, Eliza; New England; Puddings.]

BIBLIOGRAPHY

Barlow, Joel. "The Hasty Pudding." In *The Works of Joel Barlow, In Two Volumes, Volume II: Poetry.* Edited by William K. Bottorff and Arthur L. Ford. Gainesville, FL: Scholar's Facsimiles and Reprints, 1970.

ALICE ROSS

Hawaiian Food

Food of Hawaii can be separated into two categories: Hawaiian food, the food of the native islanders, and local food, the eclectic blend of the cuisines of later settlers. Before explorers, missionaries, and immigrants arrived, Hawaiian food consisted of fresh ingredients that were prepared raw or cooked simply, using broiling, boiling, and roasting techniques. Protein sources included poultry, pig, and dog. Fish and other seafood, such as turtles, sea urchins, limpets, and shellfish, were also consumed but in modest quantities.

Bananas, coconuts, breadfruits, and mountain apples are native to the islands and were a big part of the Hawaiians' diet. Other tropical fruits, such as pineapples, mangoes, gooseberries, passion fruits, guavas, and avocados, were introduced to the islands in the 1800s. Although there were few vegetables available, most of the daily calories came from the starchy tuber *kalo* or taro, which was usually boiled and then pounded into a paste called *poi.* Sweet potatoes might also be pounded but were more often roasted like yams.

Poi is something of miracle food because of its long shelf life and nutritional content. When freshly pounded, poi is at its sweetest. If a more sour poi is desired, it needs to ferment a few days. *Kalo*'s heart-shaped pliable leaves, *lu'au*, are also edible. The *lu'au* can be wrapped around morsels of meat then roasted, or they can be boiled plain as a spinach-like side dish. (The word *lu'au* became the name of the great feast because of the Hawaiians' favorite stewlike dish consisting of tender *lu'au* leaves and coconut milk baked with chicken or squid.) Because sweet potato greens were the only other green vegetable available, a large variety of seaweeds supplied essential vitamins and minerals to the Hawaiians' diet.

Local food was a product of the cultural melting pot in Hawaii. In the early 1800s, missionaries from New England were the first large group of immigrants to settle in the islands. They brought salted meat and salted salmon. When the pineapple and sugar industries exploded, more human labor was needed. Because the Hawaiian population had declined so rapidly because of diseases contracted from the missionaries, immi-

The American Can Company issued this cookbooklet by Isabel N. Young in 1935.

grants from Japan, China, Korea, Okinawa, the Philippines, Puerto Rico, and a large number of Portuguese from the Atlantic islands flocked to Hawaii seeking to fill the jobs. Smaller groups of immigrants from Samoa, Tonga, Vietnam, and Thailand soon followed.

As each ethnicity adapted their cuisine to the readily available ingredients and as dishes were borrowed and exchanged between groups, local food was born. The Chinese brought their leafy vegetables, rice, ginger, and chopsticks. The Japanese introduced charcoal grilling or hibachi, as well as stewed meat and fish dishes, tofu, and the ubiquitous teriyaki sauce. Yeast cakes and breads like *pao doce* (sweet bread) and *malasadas* (doughnuts) from the Portuguese became favorite island treats. The Portuguese also shared their love for rich bean soups and spicy *linguica*, or sausage. With the Koreans came pungent ingredients like garlic, onions, and red pepper. And the Filipinos shared dishes that were braised in vinegar, like pork adobo.

As these cultures worked side by side, a cuisine and a language were born: local food and pidgin. Through the decades, certain dishes from each ethnicity became staples and are prepared and loved in most homes in the twenty-first century. Cooking techniques and ingredients were exchanged and adapted to reflect the melding of so many ethnicities. A typical island gathering might include a hodgepodge of dishes: *sh yu* chicken (a Chinese-style braised dish named for its essential ingredient—Japanese soy sauce), Korean-style barbecued meat, Spam *musubi* (slices of fried Spam sandwiched between layers of short-grained rice and wrapped with nori or dried laver sheets), chicken chow mein, *manapua,* or *char siu bao* to the Chinese (sweet buns stuffed with minced roast pork),

kalua pig (Hawaiian smoked roast pork), *lomi lomi* salmon (salted salmon with diced onions and tomatoes), and potato and macaroni salad dressed with a liberal amount of mayonnaise.

Desserts and sweets are equally diverse. The island favorites include a Hawaiian coconut pudding called *haupia*, which is present at every *lu'au*, and shaved ice with syrup, which is generally consumed after a long day at the beach. There are about fifty different flavored syrups to choose from. Locals also like to eat shaved ice stuffed with vanilla ice cream and adzuki beans (sweet red beans usually stuffed in Japanese sweet rice cakes called *mochi*).

[**See also** Chinese American Food; Japanese American Food; Korean American Food; Pineapple; Soy Sauce; Sweet Potatoes.]

BIBLIOGRAPHY

Corum, Ann Kondo. *Ethnic Foods of Hawaii.* Honolulu: Bess Press, 2000.

Laudan, Rachel. *The Food of Paradise: Exploring Hawaii's Culinary Heritage.* Honolulu: University of Hawaii Press, 1996.

ROBYNNE L. MAII

Hazelnuts, *see Filberts*

Health Food

Historically, health food claims have originated from divine inspiration, promoting public health, and capitalist profit. Today, it is difficult for most consumers to separate food faddism from the constantly changing and often contradictory nutritional and health information coming from the scientific community.

Perhaps the individual most noted for ushering in a modern age of healthy-eating food reform and vegetarianism in America was Sylvester Graham (1794–1851). Graham, a Presbyterian minister, became a crusader for proper eating and temperance believing that a vegetarian diet was the one that God had intended. His name is perhaps best associated with developing a high bran flour subsequently baked into a thin flat bread, the graham cracker.

By the mid-nineteenth century, the influence of Graham and other reformers led to the establishment of the American Vegetarian Society. The agenda of these health reformers was the promotion of a vegetable diet and to campaign against the newly emerging industrialized food processing industry. This industry has been a focal point of criticism by health food proponents ever since.

Following Graham, a series of utopian communities and health reformers continued a tradition of Christian vegetarianism and temperance. Most notable was Ellen G. White (1827–1915), who helped establish the Seventh-day Adventist Church and the promotion of spiritual vegetarianism. Under her tutelage, church member Dr. John Harvey Kellogg (1852–1943) developed in Michigan the expansive Battle Creek Sanitarium and its vegetarian regimen.

Cornflake Crusaders

In time, Kellogg created a health food marketing empire based on "biological living," a theory that extolled the virtues of his inventions, cornflakes and granola. Eventually his business ideals led to severed relations with the church. In 1906, the Battle Creek Toasted Corn Flake Company was incorporated under the management of his younger brother, William Keith Kellogg (1860–1951), who developed the cornflake that became a breakfast staple. The era of the cornflake crusaders also witnessed the start of companies founded by Charles William Post (1854–1914), known for developing Postum, Post Toasties, and Grape-Nuts (essentially graham flour bread broken into bits). More than forty other cereal companies were also in operation in Battle Creek during that time.

By the early twentieth century, the influence of health reformers was challenged by the development of nutritional science and the discovery of vitamins and other essential nutrients. The passage of the 1906 Pure Food and Drug Act also supposedly protected consumers from fraudulent health claims. Lobbying efforts for the act were clearly influenced by the 1906 publication of *The Jungle* by Upton Sinclair, a book that depicted the horrific conditions of America's meatpacking industry. The 1906 Act also led to the creation of the Food and Drug Administration (FDA) which oversees the U.S. food and drug industry. Over the years, additional legislation provided more protective clauses. In the 1990s, however, the loosening of FDA labeling regulations regarding nutritional supplements and health claims has supported a growing billion-dollar industry in the United States.

Vitamin Pushers

In the mid-twentieth century, Adelle Davis (1904–1974) emerged as one of the first mass media spokespersons for "popular nutrition." In books such as *Let's Eat Right to Keep Fit* (1954), she extolled the virtues of natural foods and dietary supplements, especially vitamins. Criticized for lacking scientific proof, Davis nevertheless sold over 10 million copies of her various books and still has her supporters today. The so-called vitamin pushers continue to promote high doses of various vitamins to restore and maintain health. One of the best-known advocates for vitamins was the Nobel laureate Linus Pauling (1901–1994), who believed that megadoses of vitamin C could even cure the common cold.

As other social movements captured America in the 1960s and 1970s so did a litany of ideas on alternative eating with a concomitant growth of vegetarianism and organic foods. Jerome Rodale (1898–1971), a pioneer of the organic food movement beginning in the 1940s and founder of *Prevention* magazine, promoted the growing of fruits and vegetables without the use of pesticides and artificial fertilizers and the virtues of health foods in America.

The late twentieth century saw the reemergence of the physician as spokesperson for novelty diets and health-food cures. Perhaps the best known is Dr. Robert C. Atkins (1930–2003), whose 1972 book *Dr. Atkins' Diet Revolution* was a million-copy best seller. His original high protein/low carbohydrate approach to weight loss and healthy living waned by the 1980s as the evils of saturated fat and cholesterol became known. But cycles come and go, and as the public's fear of cholesterol subsided in the 1990s, *Dr. Atkins' New Diet Revolution* (1992) also became a bestselling book, only to slowly subside again after his death in 2003, replaced by a host of other low-calorie, low-carbohydrate, and food-combining dietary plans (e.g., *The Scarsdale Diet* (Tarnower), *The Zone* (Sears), *Protein Power* (Eades and Eades), *The South Beach Diet* (Agatston), and a nod to our "caveman" ancestors with *The Origin Diet* (Somers) and *The Paleolithic Prescription* (Eaton, Shostak, and Konner). The frequent appearance of new weight-loss diets is a testament to their repeated failure. Their mere novelty may explain why dieters tend to ignore the mundane message promoted by most health professionals who simply advise people to eat smaller portions of a well-balanced diet.

Specific labeling of foods such as medicine has come full circle in the form of nutraceuticals and functional foods that target specific ailments, often with claims that they are working with an individual's own genetic makeup. Health foods are a growing multibillion-dollar industry in the United States but still cater in most part to those who can afford their premium cost. Although the mainstream food-processing industry keeps reducing the prices of "supersized" food products with empty calories, the cost of healthy eating rises. At any nutritional supplement store or full-service organic food and health store, products that represent the entire history of both health foods and fads are on sale: tablets, powders, and extracts of royal jelly; bee pollen; spirulina; kelp; garlic; ginseng; unprocessed, unbleached, organically grown granola; and a host of other products that can be cooked from scratch or popped in the microwave.

[See also Food and Drug Administration; Graham, Sylvester; Kellogg Company; Kellogg, John Harvey; Nutrition; Organic Food; Post Foods; Pure Food and Drug Act; Sinclair, Upton; Vegetarianism.]

BIBLIOGRAPHY

Barrett, Stephen, and Victor Herbert. *The Vitamin Pushers: How the "Health Food" Industry Is Selling America a Bill of Goods.* Amherst, NY: Prometheus Books, 1994.

FDA Consumer Magazine. http://fda.org.gov/fdac.

Whelan, Elizabeth M., and Frederick J. Stare. *Panic in the Pantry: Facts and Fallacies about the Food You Buy.* Amherst, NY: Prometheus Books, 1992.

Barrett P. Brenton and Kevin T. McIntyre

Hearn, Lafcadio

In writing *La cuisine créole* (Creole cookery), Patricio Lafcadio Tessima Carlos Hearn—journalist, sometime novelist, and unsuccessful restaurateur—tapped into and celebrated New Orleans's heterogeneous culture. The landmark 1885 cookery book was the first to describe the cosmopolitan Creole cuisine, which blends the characteristics of the American, French, Spanish, Italian, West Indian, and Mexican traditions.

At first glance, Lafcadio Hearn seemed an unlikely cookbook author. Born on a Greek island in 1850, the son of a minor British bureaucrat, he was reared by a rigidly religious aunt in Dublin, Ireland. Small in stature (five feet three), extremely nearsighted, one eye virtually blind and the other bulged to double normal size, he was frail, often ill, and almost constantly in pain. His extreme shyness and often irritable personality are thought to have influenced his morbid, gothic interests and writings. But Hearn's timidity also made him a keen and unobtrusive observer.

Coming to America, Hearn took a job as a reporter for the *Cincinnati Enquirer* in 1871. He wrote what have been described as "weird romantic stories" and eventually became a star crime reporter after writing about a murder case in "horripilating" detail. In 1876 he was sent to New Orleans to report on the disputed presidential election results in Louisiana. Immediately taken with the exotic city he described it as "fading, moldering, crumbling…a dead bride crowned with orange flowers." He would remain there for a decade working for low wages as a newspaperman and becoming a seminal figure in establishing New Orleans as a unique cultural center.

Hearn found the French market, with its colorful denizens, market cries, and foods, exactly to his liking. He came to know the people of the city, from intellectuals to the common folk, and wrote about them voluminously, including a large number of sayings in the Creole dialect, which he called gumbo French. Hearn got a friendly publisher to print them for the Cotton States Exposition of 1884 (in a volume he named after *gumbo z'herbes*, the traditional New Orleans dish), along with a historical guide and a cookbook. The books were not printed in time for the exposition, and they failed, save for one: *La cuisine créole*.

The recipes in the book came from the wives of two friends and were perhaps influenced by the cuisine of the African Creoles who fascinated him. Most of the recipes are American—pies and pastries for example—and made plain for use in ordinary households. However, the collection includes key ingredients and dishes that distinguish this sophisticated cookery: jambalaya, crayfish, court bouillon (a fish dish in a rich, roux-based sauce), and gumbos, many with okra. In *La cuisine créole*, Hearn located food at the core of a people's culture. Its publication marked the beginning of a wave of nineteenth-century cookery books that preserved and popularized singular cuisines in their historical place.

Two years after publishing *La cuisine créole* and its sister volumes, Hearn left New Orleans forever. By 1890, he had found his way to Japan where he became world famous for his writings about that country, especially collections of ghost tales and folklore. He died there in 1905.

[**See also** AFRICAN AMERICAN FOOD: SINCE EMANCIPATION; CAJUN AND CREOLE FOOD; COOKBOOKS AND MANUSCRIPTS; FRENCH INFLUENCES ON AMERICAN FOOD; SOUTHERN REGIONAL COOKERY.]

BIBLIOGRAPHY

Hearn, Lafcadio. *La cuisine créole.* New York: W. H. Coleman, 1885. Reprinted, with a foreword by Hodding Carter, as *Lafcadio Hearn's Creole Cook Book. With the Addition of Drawings and Writings by Lafcadio Hearn during his Sojourn in New Orleans from 1877 to 1887: A Literary and Culinary Adventure.* Gretna, LA: Pelican, 1990.

Starr, S. Frederick, ed. *Inventing New Orleans: Writings of Lafcadio Hearn.* Jackson: University Press of Mississippi, 2001.

BRUCE KRAIG

Hearth Cookery

Hearth cookery refers to the cooking and baking done directly over or in front of a kitchen fire. It has played a major role in human existence for millennia. The earliest skills for managing the heat of fire, embers, and ash enlarged the scope of edible foods. The long span of years ahead brought mastery of the use of clay, bone, wood, stone, and leather. Copper, bronze, and iron were added. During this time, the range of cooked items

Firebacks, heavy plates of cast iron propped against the brick, reflect heat efficiently and protect the hearth from heat damage.

(boiling, frying, grilling, roasting, toasting, and baking) changed relatively little, although complexity of sauces grew among the wealthy.

The first immigrants to the New World came with knowledge of fireplaces and hearths, as well as the equipment used in them. Despite varying ethnic preferences in the design of the hearth (for example, the Germans used raised hearths and the English used flat hearths), the techniques of cookery remained the same for roughly 250 years. Almost every kitchen had a stone, brick, hardened mud, or clay fireplace with a paved floor and an apron jutting out into the room (the hearth). Brick ovens had their doors in the back wall of the fireplace, sharing access to the chimney with the hearth. Everyone cooked or baked under conditions that the modern eye would find primitive, and everyone was comfortable with them. Although there was a fair amount of drudgery—lifting heavy pots, and so on—and the additional effort of making and maintaining the fire, the results were often fine and to some minds better than those obtained in the twenty first century.

Most basic was the wood. Gathered in the wintertime when snow made pulling the sledges easier, it was split and aged for a year to make it fit for cooking. People knew the burning properties of different woods, for example, that Osage orange burned at a very high temperature, oak and hard fruit and nut woods were fine, and that pine deposited pitch in the chimneys and caused dangerous fires. Hearth fires were started quickly by hitting a steel striker against a sharp piece of flint stone, creating sparks. These were caught in some fine tinder—often tow left

from carding flax—and used to ignite gradually larger pieces. It was so simple and fast that there was no need to carry coals from a neighbor's home.

Controlling the heat was the next challenge. Fires continually changed, burning down or up, and the cook needed to maintain even temperatures. This was achieved by moving the pots in and out or up and down (when swung from a trammel or a swinging crane), or by moving the fire to place it appropriately. The temperature of the pot was judged by the feel of the heat on one's hand and sensory memory.

Cooking Styles and Implements

Ash cooking was the simplest form of hearth cookery. It required placing the food either on or in the embers, sometimes tempered with ash. The ash, accumulated over time, provided a thick bed in which to cook. The food was sometimes wrapped in green leaves, such as cabbage or corn, which offered steam and a suggestion of flavor. Once finished, the food was dusted off or washed, if necessary.

Pots were often mounted on three legs, useful for straddling the coals. They also had swinging bail handles attached on the upper sides, used for hanging them over the fire from suspended hooks. Those without legs and handles were perched on cooking trivets of various sizes and shapes and that worked like three-legged pots. Many had lids to keep flying ash out. The most efficient of all was the cast-iron Dutch oven, which had legs and often a swinging bail handle, and a high-rimmed lid edge. This ingenious portable oven straddled embers (coals) on the hearth and held another scoop or two of embers on the top. Skillets on high legs

Dutch ovens were common in American kitchens and had myriad uses. The heavy rimmed lid held coals above, while the legs suspended the oven above piles of coals.

fried well, and gridirons and griddles placed over coals did a good job of pan-baking and grilling. There were copper jelly pans and bronze preserving pans, tin and ceramic posnets (saucepans).

Roasting gear ranged from a string to a wall-mounted mechanical clock jack. These offered ways to keep the meats turning in front of the fire, over a dripping pan. Midway was the tin reflecting oven, which required that the spitted, skewered, and trussed meat be turned by hand so that it would remain in a stationary position until it was time to secure it in another position. Standing spits held small birds and roasts at an adjustable height.

Women's work was safe enough to prevent their burning up in flames. The fibers used then were wool and linen, and neither flamed. Instead, they smoldered, leaving a small hole near the hem. The more critical injuries came from tipped kettles and infected burns.

Cuisine

Despite its so-called primitive qualities, the hearth actually turned out diverse and delicious foods, depending on the skill of the cook and her access to ingredients. Cookbooks of the time described a wide array of traditional dishes ranging from simple to complex. The foods ranged from ash cake or corn breads to elaborately sauced "made dishes" and included everything from soup to nuts. George Washington's professional chef, Philadelphian Samuel Fraunces, served banquets and feasts of period haute cuisine, unconstrained by the hearth. Family meals generally depended on their ethnic background—Dutch, German, Native American, and largely English, brought from the old country in handwritten manuscript collections or printed cookbooks, or written in the United States.

The ingredients were, for the most part, those grown on home farms, with a few luxurious cheeses, spices, sugars, and preserves ordered by those of means from European sources. And Native American foods—corn, beans, and squash or pumpkins—found their way into the menus.

The End of Hearth Cooking

The nineteenth-century cookstove signaled the gradual demise of the American cooking hearth. By 1850, most urban middle-class families had made the change. However, some folk continued to make do with the hearth, particularly in such remote areas as Appalachia.

In the last few decades, hearth cookery has undergone a renaissance of sorts and has become interesting to reenactors, living history museums, academicians, chefs, and hobbyists.

BIBLIOGRAPHY

Franklin, Linda Campbell. *Three Hundred Years of Kitchen Collectibles*. 5th ed. Iola, WI: Kraus Publications, 2003.

Phipps, Frances. *Colonial Kitchens, Their Furnishings and Their Gardens*. New York: Hawthorn Books, 1972.

Plante, Ellen M. *The American Kitchen: 1700 to the Present*. New York: Facts on File, 1996.

Rubel, William. *The Magic of Fire*. Berkeley, CA: Ten Speed Press, 2002.

ALICE ROSS

Hearts of Palm

Hearts of palm, an expensive delicacy, were served at fancy hotel restaurants early in the 1900s. But in Florida, where this luxury item was known as swamp cabbage, hearts of palm were so widely consumed during the Great Depression that the state of Florida had to enact laws to protect the palmetto tree, the source of these tender hearts. The Pulitzer Prize–winning author and Florida resident Marjorie Kinnan Rawlings loved this indigenous plant but seldom served it because she loved the environment more. "You cannot have your palm and eat it, too," she said. According to Rawlings, only an expert knew how to cut down the cabbage palm and strip the bark to get to the crisp, white, tender core. The Florida bear, she claimed, was one of those experts, because she had found palms slashed by sharp claws "and the hearts torn out as though by giant forks." Rawlings, who named cooking as her only vanity, wrote about swamp cabbage in her memoir and her cookbook, *Cross Creek Cookery*, which was still in print in the early 2000s.

The palmetto, or cabbage palm (*Sabal palmetto*), is tall, tough-barked, and graceful. It flourished for thousands of years throughout Central and South America. Columbus discovered the Carib Indians using the bark and leaves for houses. They ate the core of the young plants and the nuts of the mature tree. Today this tree is grown as a cash crop harvested after one year, when it reaches a height of five feet.

Hearts of palm are slender, ivory colored, and delicately flavored and resemble white asparagus without tips. Their texture is firm and smooth, and they taste a bit like artichoke. Each stalk is about four inches long and can range in diameter from pencil-thin to one to one and a half inches. In the United States, they are available fresh only in Florida. Canned hearts of palm are packed in water and are sold in gourmet markets and many large supermarkets. They can be refrigerated in their own liquid for up to a week in a nonmetallic container.

Hearts of palm can be deep-fried or used in salads and in main dishes. Rawlings also loved them sliced thinly and soaked for an hour in ice water, then drained and served with french dressing or tart mayonnaise. "The flavor is much like chestnuts," she said. In *Cross Creek Cookery*, Rawlings based her recipes on fresh hearts of palm. She made swamp cabbage camp-style by simply boiling the palm hearts slowly in as little water as possible, with several slices of white bacon. She also simmered them tightly covered, for forty-five minutes or "until meltingly tender, and until most of the moisture has been absorbed." She liked to heat them to simmering in the cream from her cow, Dora. "Prepared this way, heart of palm is fit for a king," she said.

[See also GIBBONS, EUELL; SALADS AND SALAD DRESSINGS.]

MARIAN BETANCOURT

Heirloom Vegetables

Heirloom vegetables are the produce of plants grown from original seeds. In the last decades of the twentieth century and into the next millennium, old and often forgotten varieties of food plants garnered renewed interest among gardeners and the grocery-shopping public. Although they are called heirlooms, no regulated nationwide standard has ever existed for them, though most experts agree on a general definition: The plant variety must have been introduced before 1951, which was when plant breeders began to hybridize inbred plant lines, and it must have been grown from a variety at least one hundred years old. The plant also must have been open-pollinated by natural means, such as wind, dew, insects, or birds.

Before seeds were bought from catalogs or from seed merchants, they were saved from one crop in order to plant the next and shared with neighbors and family. Before European colonization, North America had few varieties of indigenous domesticated food plants but had a fair amount of wild or semidomesticated species. People emigrating from the Old World, including Africa, as far back as the sixteenth century, brought seeds with them to America. When the seeds were planted, many of them were able to adapt to the new weather and soil conditions. These hardy species brought considerable genetic diversity to the New World. As a result of centuries of natural adaptation, many heirlooms are resistant to different forms of blight and can survive bad soil and climate extremes.

Americans' interest in cultivating, developing, and preserving numerous varieties of native and newly acclaimed imported food and ornamental plants goes back to the seventeenth and eighteenth centuries. Scientists, such as John Bartram of Philadelphia and Thomas Jefferson, experimented with new varieties, while farmers, such as the Pennsylvania Dutch, were more practically minded and focused on their kitchen gardens. The post–Civil War period saw the rise of commercial seed growing. Most heirloom vegetables and their quirky names, as announced in colorful catalogs, for example, Esopus Spitzenburg apples, Kentucky Wonderbowl beans, and Boothby's Blonde cucumbers, date from the years after 1865 when American industrialization and urbanization were on the rise.

Truck farms, supplied by seed companies, proliferated and remained a major source of food for urban populations until after World War II. Some heirloom vegetables remained on these farms, but streamlined production methods led to modern single-variety and genetically manipulated vegetables and fruits. Fully industrialized farms that raised single crops, which were shipped hundreds or thousands of miles across the country, took over the market. Efforts at genetic modification concentrated on adapting plants for shipping and on streamlining production values, not on developing flavor, therefore modern industrialized farm products cannot match the flavors of heirlooms. In addition, commercial farms strive for uniformity in their plants. For example, all the tomatoes on a factory farm must be picked at the same time, because it limits production overhead, so ideally they should all ripen at the same time. Genetic engineers have induced this process. Genetic engineers have also produced modified plant varieties (genetically modified organisms, or GMOs) to ship well, maintain certain uniform appearances, and have longer shelf lives. Modifying vegetables to yield a higher profit margin produces vegetables that may look bright and ripe on store shelves but which lack flavor. Winter-grown tomatoes shipped to northern cities provide a classic and reviled example. The flavor of summer once found in perfectly ripened August fruits has been lost.

American heirloom enthusiasts' concern with GMOs goes beyond a lack of flavor, however. Environmental awareness and activism has led to interest in heirloom produce. Concerns about the planet's biological sustainability and possible dangers inherent in gene modification technology became widespread, especially among younger Americans, in the early twenty-first century. Activists were concerned with biodiversity and with perpetuating the small farms and gardens that they favored. They noted that most commercial farms that supplied the nation's food practiced monoculture, that is, they planted only one or two species that had been genetically modified at a time. Based on such historical precedents as the Irish potato famine of the 1840s, when Irish potatoes, of Peruvian origin, were not resistant to a blight unintentionally brought from Mexico, activists argued that some common GMOs were resistant to only one form of blight rather than many different kinds.

Furthermore, critics claimed, agribusinesses created so-called terminator seeds that produce plants that do not produce their own seeds. This not only limits biodiversity but also controls or halts natural food crop reproduction. Activists are concerned that farmers may become completely reliant on seed companies for crop reproduction. In reply, corporations, such as Monsanto, argued that all food plants throughout history have been genetically manipulated, that their genetically modified seeds had been extensively tested, were safe, and were the only means by which burgeoning world populations could be fed. If plant species had been lost, it was because of human population rise, not because of the planting of manipulated crops. The vigorous debate was going on worldwide without resolution at the beginning of the twenty-first century.

The reduction of the genetic-plant repository inspired the formation of historical farms and open-air museums to maintain heirloom varieties. For instance, a historical farm or an open-air museum might grow a kitchen garden of the same heirloom plants (from heirloom seeds) that had been planted in that same spot in colonial times. Seed-saving organizations, the earliest founded in 1895 in Russia, preserved diverse genetic-heritage seeds, focusing on heirloom plant varieties headed for extinction. The Seed Savers Exchange and Seeds of Change were among the best-known genetic repositories in the early 2000s. Seeds were either kept in suspended animation or planted to perpetuate the genetic stock. Whereas seed savers worked with government agencies, open-air museums, and living history farms, their main focus was to maintain an ongoing genetic repository. Heirloom enthusiasts tended to support smaller farmers as well.

People who love heirloom vegetables do so for many reasons, including taste, curiosity, and environmental consciousness. Beginning in the late 1970s, Americans renewed their romance with gourmet food and cooking; chefs and epicureans were constantly seeking out unusual ingredients and flavors, and heirlooms suited these new cooks' fancies. Alice Waters's restaurant Chez Panisse in Berkeley, California, and her cookbooks became a touchstone for the culinary aspects of a new heirloom movement.

For the weekend gardener, there are many seed companies that boast "antique" or "heirloom" on the labels of their products. True heirloom seeds are also always labeled "open pollinated." These seeds produce plants from an older seed stock with an unaltered, high-quality gene line that will grow the flavorful tomato, squash, or corn of yore. Unlike their commercial counterparts, heirloom vegetables are variegated to be patchy in color and to differ in taste. Some are oddly shaped and sized. Heirloom fans choose some squash for their sweet flesh, beans for their decorative flowers, or beets for their stripes. The rich, sweet flavor of a Brandywine tomato or the peppery crunch of a rocket leaf or a Persia Broadleaf Cress is unrivaled.

[See also BIOTECHNOLOGY; WATERS, ALICE.]

BIBLIOGRAPHY

Seed Savers Exchange. http://www.seedsavers.org/.

Weaver, William Woys. *Heirloom Vegetable Gardening.* New York: Henry Holt, 1997.

LIZA JERNOW

Hemp

Hemp is a member of cannabis family. One of the first cultivated plants, consumption by ancient Chinese, Egyptians, and Romans ranged from peasants' hemp porridge to fried sweet desserts. The female cannabis flower, which contains the psychotropic substance tetrahydrocannabinol (TCH) is not used in producing food. The seed, or nut, is the source of hemp oils and flour.

The 1954 Alice B. Toklas cookbook recipe for "Haschich Fudge" promised "euphoria and brilliant storms of laughter" and cemented the marriage of hemp and marijuana in the American psyche. The trend toward whole grain consumption that began in the 1960s continued in the 1970s and 1980s, as did the quest for healthier diets. Early 1990s advocates promoted hemp as ecologically sustainable and a nutritional powerhouse based on its profile of omega-6 and omega-3 essential fatty acids that rivaled flaxseed and tasted far better than fish oils.

Renewed worldwide interest has rejuvenated hemp cultivation in thirty-three countries and spurred development of THC-free grocery-basket items including hemp-based waffles, salad dressing, snack bars, corn chips and veggie burgers. Hemp foods, even when legal, have the unusual appeal of being both healthy and illicit, a reputation other foods can't match. Growing hemp, however, remains illegal in the United States.

BIBLIOGRAPHY

Conrad, Chris. *Hemp: Lifeline to the Future: The Unexpected Answer for Our Environmental and Economic Recovery.* Los Angeles: Creative Xpressions Publications. 1993.

Toklas, Alice B. *The Alice B. Toklas Cookbook.* New York: Harper & Row, 1954. Foreword by M. F. K. Fisher, Harper & Row, 1984.

ELLEN J. FRIED

Hermit Cookies

Hermit cookies today are soft, square molasses cookies with raisins, especially popular in New England. Perhaps they resemble the brown robes of a hermit. But the earliest printed recipes, in the late 1870s, are for round, white, spiced teacakes with chopped raisins. Perhaps hermits were kept in a cookie jar to hand out to mendicants? Perhaps they were identified with Moravian spice cookies (*Hernhutter* in German)? The white sugar form persisted in recipes through the 1920s. Thrifty home cooks must have substituted brown sugar from the start, and many American foods have tended to become softer and easier to eat. The molasses recipe appears around 1900, but the first standard New England cookbooks to use molasses were in the late 1920s. The flavor and texture hearken back to colonial English teacakes and American soft gingerbread, as well as nineteenth-century molasses cookies. The origin of the name remains a mystery.

MARK H. ZANGER

Hero, *see Hoagie; Sandwiches*

Herring and Sardines

Herring (*Culpea harengus*) belong to the same family of fish that includes shad, alewives, and sardines, although they do not spawn in freshwater. They school in huge numbers and were fished for commercially in Europe and off the New England and Middle Atlantic coasts. Their oily flesh made them ideal for salting and smoking, which meant that they were shipped inland for sale.

Some plantation owners arranged for catches of herring, which were salted to be food for slaves, but herring consumption was relatively low in America until more immigrants arrived, especially from the British Isles, Germany, and Scandinavia. Several products made from herring included hard or red herring, bloaters, kippers, and bucklings. Immature herring were canned in the same manner as true sardines (*Sardinia pilchardus*), when imported sardines from France became fashionable in the later 1800s. Although sardines were a favorite in saloons and bars in the twentieth century, sardine consumption took a nosedive during Prohibition. Sardine packing hung on through the end of the twentieth century in Maine, but most sardines eaten in America come from herring canned in Canada and Scandinavia.

SANDRA L. OLIVER

Hershey Foods Corporation

Hershey's, the brand named after the company's founder and longtime leader, Milton Snavely Hershey (1857–1945), is synonymous with American chocolate. Known as the "Henry Ford of chocolate makers," Milton Hershey introduced mass-manufacturing to solid chocolate, bringing to the general public a once-luxurious product.

After an initial foray into candy manufacturing, Hershey was inspired by state-of-the-art chocolate-making machinery he saw at the 1893 World's Columbian Exposition. He purchased the machinery after the exposition's close. A year later, the Hershey Chocolate Company was born, operating alongside his Lancaster Caramel Company (founded in 1887). Hershey sold his caramel company in 1900 for $1 million but kept the chocolate manufactory, making it the center of a new business, which produced solid chocolates, breakfast cocoa, and baking chocolate. In 1902, Hershey purchased land in rural Derry Township, Pennsylvania, and began erecting a utopian community. By 1904, the chocolate business was in full production, aided by ready supplies of fresh milk, local limestone for building, and a reliable labor force in the hardworking Pennsylvania Dutch.

Until Hershey offered an affordable product, edible chocolate was only available to the very wealthy who frequented elite confectioners. Streamlined production technologies decreased the price of chocolates and increased their availability. Hershey's signature nickel bar, while ever changing in size, remained the same price from its introduction in the mid-1890s to 1969. The incorporation of milk transformed chocolate's bittersweet taste and dark complexion, creating a sweeter, mellower product that was more suited to the American palate. Hershey's earliest product lines included chocolate novelties, such as cigars and cigarettes, and milk chocolate bars, plain and with almonds. Introduced in 1907, Hershey's famous chocolate kisses, bite-sized pieces wrapped in foil, gained their so-called identification plumes (slips of tissue paper emblazoned with the company name) in 1921. The company expanded its own lines and acquired other confectionery companies, eventually producing Reese's Peanut Butter Cups, Twizzlers, Jujubes, Good & Plenty, and Milk Duds, among other candies.

Milton Hershey's philanthropy motivated the development of his chocolate empire. His unified company town and community, a utopian vision, was completed in 1904, effectively insulated from urban ills such as poverty and crime. In addition to the factory, Hershey built modern workers' housing, an amusement park, community center, golf course, department store, bank, public garden, and entertainment center. When Milton's wife, Kitty, died in 1918, Hershey donated the entire estate, including all the company stock, to the Hershey Trust in order to maintain the Hershey Industrial School, a school for orphan boys founded by the couple in 1909. During World War I, Hershey set up a nearly identical factory town in Cuba that produced sugar in response to American supply shortages. During the Depression, he instituted private public-works initiatives within Hershey, Pennsylvania, resulting in the building of, among other things, a stadium and community center.

Until the end of the twentieth century, when it was overtaken by Mars, Hershey's remained the most successful American chocolate company, and the town's other attractions, like Hershey Park and Chocolate World, helped sustain its earnings. In the late 1990s, the Hershey Trust was worth more than $5 billion. Prospects of selling the trust in the early twenty-first century stirred national controversy, indicating the degree to which people well beyond the region cared about the Hershey legacy.

[See also AMUSEMENT PARKS; CANDY BARS AND CANDY; CHOCOLATE; CHOCOLATE; RECENT DEVELOPMENTS; MARS.]

BIBLIOGRAPHY

Brenner, Joel Glenn. *The Emperors of Chocolate: Inside the Secret World of Hershey and Mars.* New York: Random House, 1999.

Snavely, Joseph R. *Milton S. Hershey, Builder.* Hershey, PA: J. R. Snavely, 1934.

Winpenny, Thomas R. "Milton S. Hershey Ventures into Cuban Sugar." *Pennsylvania History* 62, no. 4 (1995): 491–502.

WENDY WOLOSON

Highball

This classic American drink is half whiskey, half carbonated water. There are two stories about how it got its name, both related to the metal ball that railroad stationmasters would hang high on a pole in the station to signal "full speed ahead" to locomotive engineers. Patrick Gavin Duffy, the barman at the Ashland House in 1890 and the author of *The Official Mixer's Manual* (1934), claimed that he named his highball after the speed with which it could be assembled. Another story from around the 1890s says the highball was created by John Slaughtery, a barman at a Saint Louis railway saloon, whose railroad employee customers had only a short break, during which they wanted a drink they could consume quickly.

At the time of its invention, the highball was a remarkable novelty. People had not mixed cocktails, probably because no one wanted to dilute good liquor when plenty of bad liquor already came that way. Although the classic drink itself is no longer very popular, the glass named after it, the tall, narrow-mouthed highball glass, which holds eight to twelve ounces of liquid, remains the most common shape in American barware.

[See also BARS; COCKTAILS; WHISKEY.]

LIZA JERNOW

Hines, Duncan

Now best known as a cake-mix brand name, Duncan Hines was once the most widely recognized name in American food. Hines's importance for the latter half of the twentieth and early twenty-first centuries is twofold: as the author of immensely popular guides to American restaurants, which were the forerunner of all the dining guides that would appear in succeeding decades, and, more significantly, as the name on cake mixes and related products. Hines was a prototype for one of the most effective and widely used marketing ploys in the period—branded food celebrity.

Born in 1880 in Bowling Green, Kentucky, Hines began his paid professional life as a traveling salesman for a printing firm in 1905. His avocation was the kind of home-style cooking he recalled from his boyhood on his grandparents' farm, while his passion was cleanliness. Over the next thirty years, Hines and his wife, Florence, collected notes detailing the best of the restaurants they encountered on the road. Word of mouth gave him a reputation as an expert on good eating with exacting standards. His often-quoted remark was to the point: "The library paste served as gravy in some short-order places was a personal insult." And if a restaurant was not scrupulously clean, he would not even enter it. Besieged by callers after a newspaper article on his efforts appeared in the Chicago press, he created cards listing his 167 favorite restaurants across thirty states for the 1935 Christmas season. That led to even more requests, which he answered by publishing the first edition of his guide, *Adventures in Good Eating*, in 1936, which sold for one dollar. Sales from this, together with *Lodging for a Night*, and two cookery books, were such—one half million copies a year—that Hines retired from his traveling salesman's route to take up full-time restaurant reviewing and writing.

Hines's reviews were about places on America's roads. These were mostly small-town eating establishments—tearooms in the South, diners, and, later, a restaurant chain he lauded constantly as a model of cleanliness and good food, Howard Johnson's. Hines promoted well-cooked, down-home American regional food. The "Recommended by Duncan Hines" sign became a valuable marketing tool for lodgings and restaurants and at the same time forwarded Hines's agenda of promoting well-made American dishes and sanitary restaurants. Although to later commentators Hines's tastes might appear to have been provincial, his ideas of regional cookery have come full circle among American chefs in the early 2000s.

In 1949, Roy Park, a friend and public relations director for a farmers' cooperative that would become Agway, persuaded Hines, then sixty-nine years old, to allow the company to use his name as a brand. Within a short time, Hines-Park foods had licensed two hundred products to some ninety manufacturers. Soon Duncan Hines's name and face on packaged foods were ubiquitous on America's food-store shelves, in advertising, and on television. From fancy preserves to cookware and appliances, Hines was the arbiter of good cooking because of his "discriminating" taste. The cake mix is a prime example of his marketing power. Unlike other mixes, it did not contain dehydrated eggs. Eggs had to be added because, as Hines said, "strictly fresh eggs make a bigger, better cake." All the major cake-mix makers followed suit. Hines died in 1959, a famous man, now largely unremembered save for a logo bearing his name, but he was the immediate progenitor of all the Martha Stewarts, Emeril Lagasses, and Wolfgang Pucks who have followed.

[**See also** CAKES; HOWARD JOHNSON.]

BIBLIOGRAPHY

Hatchett, Louis. *Duncan Hines: The Man behind the Cake Mix*. Mercer, GA: Mercer University Press, 2001.

Hines, Duncan. *Duncan Hines' Food Odyssey*. New York: Crowell, 1955.

Schwartz, David M. "Duncan Hines: He Made Gastronomes out of Motorists." *Smithsonian* 15 (November 1984).

BRUCE KRAIG

Historical Dining Reenactment

Making history come alive is the goal of the living history museums and historical reenactment groups. Before social history gained academic respect in the 1960s, traditional scholars accused living history museums of entertaining the public with sentimental myths about bygone days. This charge is still levied today but with less justification at the preeminent sites, as historians, archaeologists, anthropologists, and other specialists have made living history museums laboratories for testing theories about quotidian past life.

Most living history museums belong to ALHFAM, the Association for Living History, Farm and Agricultural Museums. ALHFAM members use preindustrial horticultural techniques, raise heritage breeds (defined as fewer than one thousand animals annually registered in North America and that usually were found in America before the twentieth century), and cook and brew in period kitchens according to period recipes.

Colonial Williamsburg is America's best-known living history museum, founded in the late 1920s when John D. Rockefeller Jr. underwrote the restoration of the Virginia capital's historic buildings to their late-seventeenth- and eighteenth-century glories. Soon thereafter, the town was populated with costumed "interpreters" who demonstrated or discussed Williamsburg's eighteenth century culture with visitors. In 1983 Williamsburg created a Department of Historic Foodways, running demonstration kitchens and offering specialized programs in butchery and curing, brewing, hearth cookery, and chocolate. Archaeological digs in the Chesapeake area have investigated both slave and white colonial foodways; these are conducted behind the scenes, with the results of interest to specialized scholars. Williamsburg's "historic" taverns are geared to tourist refreshment. The menus are heavily adapted to suit modern equipment, service constraints, health codes, and contemporary palates.

Plimoth Plantation in Massachusetts has rebuilt the village as it is believed to have existed in 1627, largely through the efforts of the archaeologist James Deetz and the vernacular architectural specialist Henry Glassie, who pioneered using seventeenth-century techniques and tools to reconstruct the settlement. Plimoth opened its stockades in 1972 to Jay Anderson, an expert in Stuart yeoman foodways, who spent several weeks brewing "Shakespeare's" beer according to seventeenth-century East Anglian receipts and living within the confines of the stark plantation. Anderson acknowledged that the "unremitting hard physical work punctuated by meals of boiled salt fish and sour porridge," wore him "down in body and mind." Visitors to Plimoth fare better in the plantation's public eateries. Especially noteworthy are the Thanksgiving dinners that include adaptations of seventeenth-century foods (forks discouraged) as well as Victorian menus (forks encouraged).

Plimoth launched an ambitious and controversial Native American program in the early 1970s, growing flint corn following slash-and-burn land clearing and cooking road kill by indigenous techniques. Although interrupted during the 1980s, the program as currently configured represents Wampanoag life and agriculture. It is staffed and directed by Native Americans, although the site does

A historic dining reenactment in Lafayette, Indiana.

not use the costumed role-playing found in the 1627 village.

Other institutions focusing on Native American foodways include Arizona's Coronado National Memorial, where school groups experiment with Zuni foodways, grinding corn with a mano and metate and tasting other indigenous foods. Other sites, however, are more concerned with entertainment than education and have not incorporated rigorous scholarship, offering recipes for fried "Indian Tacos" made from sugar, milk, self-rising wheat flour and canned corn.

The Hancock Shaker Village, located in Pittsfield, Massachusetts, and affiliated with the New England Heritage Breeds Conservancy, and Old Sturbridge Village in Sturbridge, Massachusetts, both offer dining experiences in period settings. Old Sturbridge offers lessons in 1830s etiquette, such as using the flat blade of the knife to convey food to one's mouth, rather than the awkward two-tined forks then popular in New England. The Conner Prairie Settlement in Noblesville, Indiana, re-creates a frontier village circa 1836 with an ethnically mixed population resettled from New England, the Hudson River Valley, and Kentucky. Conner Prairie visitors can assist interpreters in preparing a hearth-cooked dinner using recipes from works such as *The Kentucky Housewife* (1839).

Amateur Reenactment

Historical reenactment groups unite amateurs with a keen interest in a particular historical era to reenact life "as it might have been." They don period-style dress and use period technologies to prepare meals that are often supported by considerable research.

The Society for Creative Anachronism is an international organization with over twenty-eight thousand members, founded in Berkeley, California, in 1966. The group is organized along a feudal structure with seventeen different kingdoms, each ruling more localized baronies, cantons, and shires. They gather to "*selectively* recreate medieval culture, choosing elements of the culture that interest and attract us," and admit that the feasts are usually unabashedly skewed interpretations of pre-1600 dining, as few people choose to impersonate starvers, who eat only porridge and wild greens. Feasts are run by a selected "feastocrat," who has demonstrated historical cooking experience within the organization. SCA members have produced meaningful research on pre-1600 foodways by translating medieval and Renaissance cookery texts, publishing pamphlets on herbs, brewing, and cookery under the rubric of "The Compleat Anachronist," sourcing out hard-to-find ingredients, sharing copies of rare cookery texts that would largely be unavailable, and experimenting with ancient technologies by reenacting feasts in the open field.

Most other reenactment groups in America generally focus on one of two main themes: the Revolutionary War or the Civil War. These groups reenact battles and can be quite accurate in their efforts to simulate soldiers' foodways during various campaigns. Civil War groups use records of the actual rations prescribed for soldiers, with mess officers requisitioning foodstuffs from a commissary and setting up field kitchens comparable to those that would have been found under battle conditions. The reenactments distinguish between officers' and enlisted men's foodways: officers had to pay for their food and their reenacted meals focus on more elegant comestibles, again using period recipes.

The Past Masters in Early American Domestic Arts interpret domestic skills and processes in the English colonies circa 1681–1783, with a special emphasis on the American Revolutionary period. The *Past Masters News*, a quarterly publication, contains many food-related articles, and several of the members regularly speak at ALHFAM events and have published well-researched books and articles on colonial gardening and household receipts.

BIBLIOGRAPHY

Anderson, Jay. *Time Machines: The World of Living History.* Nashville, TN: The American Association for State and Local History, 1984.

Association for Living Historical Farms and Agricultural Museums. http://www.alhfam.org.

Kruger, John D. *Behind the Public Presentations: Research and Scholarship at Living History Museums of Early America. William and Mary Quarterly,* 3rd ser. (1991) 48: 347–385.

Leon, Warren, and Margaret Piatt. *Living-History Museums.* In *History Museums in the United States,* ed. W. L. and R. Rosenzweig. Urbana and Chicago: University of Illinois Press, 1989.

Living History News: A Common Passion Connecting Reenactors and Living Historians of All Time Periods. http://www.heritagebooks.com/.

The Civil War Reenactors. http://www.cwreenactors.com.

The Revolutionary War Reenactors. http://www.revwar.com/reenact/.

The Society for Creative Anachronism Inc. http://sca.org/welcome.html.

CATHY K. KAUFMAN

Historical Overview:
Colonial Period to the Revolutionary War

From the beginning of European colonization, the population of eastern North America was culturally, linguistically, religiously, and racially diverse. There were hundreds of Native American groups as well as British, Dutch, Swedish, German, and French immigrants; and slaves were brought from Africa. Although each of these groups contributed to colonial life, English culture put down the deepest roots in America. English settlers not only were the most numerous but also maintained connections with England.

Throughout the colonial period, most Americans lived on farms, which were generally self-sufficient. Those who lived in small towns acquired their food in public markets and occasionally maintained their own gardens. The few colonists who lived in cities such as Philadelphia, Boston, and New York had fairly sophisticated foods available, both from the hinterlands and from abroad.

In addition to rural and city differences, diverse climatic and soil conditions created different culinary regions, which roughly divided the colonies into New England (New Hampshire, Massachusetts, Rhode Island, and Connecticut), the middle colonies (New York, New Jersey, and Pennsylvania), and the southern colonies (Delaware, Maryland, Virginia, North and South Carolina, and Georgia). A fourth culinary region was the frontier, which during colonial times began approximately one hundred miles inland from the Atlantic Ocean. Those living on the frontier were largely dependent on hunting, fishing, and trapping.

Colonial America began with the founding of the first permanent English colony in North America at Jamestown, Virginia, in 1607. They barely survived because of poor provisioning, the failure of European plants to grow in the New World, and the lack of skills. Other European settlers, such as the Dutch in New Amsterdam, were better provisioned, skilled, and equipped, but even they initially depended largely on the cultivation of American plants, fishing, and hunting for their survival. Within a decade of the beginning European settlements, however, food was plentiful.

American Vegetables

By far the most important plant food in pre-Columbian America was maize. Native Americans taught English colonists how to grow, harvest, dry, store, and prepare corn, and it quickly became a staple food of the colonial diet. The second most important New World vegetable was domesticated beans, which were widely distributed throughout the Americas before the arrival of Europeans. Squash, including pumpkins, were the third important group of vegetables.

Native Americans introduced colonists to a variety of other New World plants. Cranberries, groundnuts, Jerusalem artichokes, and sunflower seeds were all consumed. Nuts, such as American chestnuts, filberts, hickory nuts, and black walnuts, were gathered and served after meals. Colonists, particularly in frontier areas, also gathered wild foods, such as acorns, elderberries, grapes, leeks, onions, plums, pokeweed, and strawberries. Blackberries, blueberries, and huckleberries were sun-dried Indian style and substituted for currants and raisins.

Many vegetables from Africa and South America were brought to colonial tables by slaves. In the southern colonies, many slaves were permitted to have their own gardens, which supplemented their basic food rations, so vegetables, such as okra, cassava, sweet potatoes, yams, peanuts, melons, and sesame seeds, had been little used in England became popular in the American South in the eighteenth century.

Game, Fowl, Seafood, and Domesticated Animals

Before sufficient stocks of domestic cattle and poultry had been raised, the colonists harvested the abundant game, fowl, fish, and seafood they found in their new land. European settlers quickly became proficient at trapping, hunting, and fishing. Game—deer, bear, buffalo, and wild birds—were extremely important food sources throughout the colonial period. Likewise, colonists feasted on fish and seafood taken from rivers and coastal waters. The favorite fish included catfish, salmon, shad, sturgeon, and trout. Also plentiful was shellfish, such as oysters, crabs, clams, lobsters, turtles, and shrimp.

The most important meat animal in colonial America was the pig. Pigs and hogs thrived throughout the English colonies, but particularly in the South. Pigs were generally turned loose in the woods, where they fed on mast and other food sources and rapidly multiplied. Pork was relatively easy to preserve by salting, pickling, and smoking. In addition, pigs provided lard, which was used for frying and baking.

The colonists imported cows, which supplied milk, butter, cheese, and, occasionally, meat and hides. Dairy farming was so successful that New England exported butter and cheese. Colonists drank tea with milk, and consumed quantities of butter, milk, buttermilk, and cheese. When cattle herds became large enough, fresh meat had to be sold within a few hours of slaughter. In the countryside, where most people lived, beef cattle were butchered in early winter. Domesticated poultry, particularly chickens, ducks, geese, and turkeys, were also important food sources during the colonial period. In addition to meat, hens provided eggs, and feathers for bedding.

Grains, Fruit, and Vegetables

The colonists were fortunate in that Europe and New England and the middle colonies had similar climates, making possible the transfer of many Old World plants to America. Rye and oats were successfully grown and quickly became important grains in New England. Wheat flourished in the middle colonies from New York to Virginia, and by the mid-seventeenth century, these colonies became known as the "bread colonies." Slaves from West Africa who were familiar with rice cultivated it in low-country South Carolina and Georgia and helped to incorporate that grain into American colonial cuisine.

Colonists successfully transplanted many common European vegetables, such as beets, cabbage, carrots, onions, peas, and turnips. Colonists also planted asparagus, chives, cabbage, cauliflower, cucumbers, endive, garlic, leeks, lettuce, shallots, and spinach in kitchen gardens. Vegetables not consumed

A nineteenth-century print entitled The Pilgrims' Dinner Interrupted.

fresh were preserved for future use by drying, canning, pickling, and cellaring. In colonial times, sweet potatoes were cultivated in the South. White potatoes were introduced during the late seventeenth century but did not become an important food until the following century.

Early colonists established orchards at an early date, and within twenty years of initial settlements, orchards were in full production in all colonies. Depending on climatic conditions and the region, colonists grew apples, cherries, currants, peaches, pears, plums, pomegranates, and quinces. Fruit was eaten fresh, made into tarts and pies, fermented and distilled into alcoholic beverages, and dried.

Colonists planted melons soon after colonization, and these fruits proliferated throughout America. Figs, nectarines, oranges, and pomegranates grew on the coastal plain from South Carolina to Florida. Citrus and pineapples were imported from the Caribbean, but they were expensive.

Salt and Sweeteners

The most important preservative in the colonies was salt, which was needed to preserve meat and fish. The English colonies never produced enough salt from seawater, inland salt springs, salt licks, and mining of small deposits of salt, so much salt had to be imported. Native Americans sold or traded salt to colonists.

There were few natural sweeteners in North America. Maple sap and later maple syrup were used in limited quantities as sweeteners in the northern and middle colonies. Wild honey was collected. Colonists imported refined cane sugar from Europe and later the Caribbean. It remained expensive throughout the colonial period. A less expensive alternative sweetener was molasses, an end product of sugar refining.

Meal Patterns

English colonists usually ate three meals a day. These meals varied by region and season and by the religion and social station of the diners. Breakfasts frequently consisted of leftovers, bread and butter, or porridge; occasionally eggs, beef, pork, fish, or cheese; and fruit. The English drank tea, the Germans coffee; beer and cider were common. Chocolate was occasionally drunk. Dinner was served at midday and included a buffet-like series of meats, fish, side dishes, bread, butter and jam. The meal was concluded with fruit and nuts or cheese. Sweet dishes were offered at afternoon tea or on special festive evening occasions. Served with the meal were several alcoholic beverages, such as beer, cider, and wine. Supper, a light meal served in the early evening, consisted of porridge or soup and a dessert, usually cheese, fruit, nuts, or pastries. The well-to-do had complicated menus, whereas the poor ate whatever was inexpensive and at hand.

Alcoholic Beverages

Rum was introduced into North America from the West Indies around 1651. When importation of inexpensive molasses began, New Englanders began to distill their own rum. Because rum was inexpensive, its use quickly spread among all classes. Whiskey was commonly made from corn and other available grains. Many colonists favored mixed drinks, of which there were many types, such as flips—sweetened beer strengthened with rum; posset, made from spiced hot milk and ale or beer evolved into eggnog; shrubs, composed of citrus juice and various spirits; hot toddies, made of liquor, water, sugar, and spices; cherry bounce, made from cherry juice and rum; punch, composed of rum, citrus juice, sugar, water, and spices; and sangaree, made of wine, water, sugar, and spices.

Copper pots were used in the eighteenth century for making fruit preserves.

[See also BEANS; BEER; CIDER; CORN; DAIRY; FISH: FRESHWATER FISH; FISH: SALTWATER FLAT FISH; POULTRY AND FOWL; FRUIT; KITCHENS: EARLY KITCHENS; MILK; NATIVE AMERICAN FOODS: BEFORE AND AFTER CONTACT; NATIVE AMERICAN FOODS: TECHNOLOGY AND SOURCES; POTATOES; RICE; RUM; SALT AND SALTING; SHELLFISH; SQUASH; SUGAR; SWEET POTATOES; VEGETABLES; WHEAT; WHISKEY.]

BIBLIOGRAPHY

Carlo, Joyce W. *Trammels, Trenchers, Tartlets: A Definitive Tour of the Colonial Kitchen.* Old Saybrook, CT: Peregrine, 1982.

Conroy, David. *In Public Houses: Drink and the Revolution of Authority in Colonial Massachusetts.* Chapel Hill: University of North Carolina Press, 1995. Published for the Institute of Early American History and Culture, Williamsburg, VA.

Hess, Karen, ed. *Martha Washington's Booke of Cookery.* New York: Columbia University Press, 1981.

Hooker, Richard J., ed. *A Colonial Plantation Cookbook: The Receipt Book of Harriott Pinckney Horry, 1770.* Columbia: University of South Carolina Press, 1984.

Salinger, Sharon V. *Taverns and Drinking in Early America.* Baltimore: Johns Hopkins University Press, 2002.

ANDREW F. SMITH

Historical Overview:
Revolutionary War Food

Food commodities played their part in the political upheaval that characterized British North America in the 1760s, 1770s, and 1780s. Taxes and tariffs on these commodities went to replenish British government coffers. The most notorious duty, the 1773–1774 Tea Act, was levied to prop up the East India Company and became a crucial catalyst for rebellion when it inspired the Boston Tea Party. Less militant citizens engaged in political action by refusing to drink tea. Some friends of the American cause, however, could not give up the "pernicious weed" and purchased it under the table rather than using ersatz tea or other substitutes. Wartime mobs seized tea or threatened merchants who charged exorbitant prices for it, but tea, along with coffee and chocolate, remained popular with Americans during the War for Independence (1775–1783).

Wartime Shortages and Soldiers' Rations

Occasional wartime shortages caused difficulties, and food riots, long a fact of life in England and France, occurred more than thirty times in America. Causes ranged from local hoarding to inflated prices. Molly Gutridge of Marblehead, Massachusetts, circulated a broadside poem (c. 1779) that mentioned many foods connected to rioting, as well as trouble with dietary staples. One verse states, "It's hard and cruel times to live" and goes on to lament,

> For salt is all the Farmer's cry,
> If we've no salt we sure must die.
> We can't get fire nor yet food,
> Takes 20 weight of sugar for two foot of wood,
> We cannot get bread nor yet meat,
> We see the world is nought but cheat...
> All we can get it is but rice
> And that is of a wretched price...
>
> We now do eat what we despis'd...
> We must go up and down the Bay.
> To get a fish a-days to fry.
> We can't get fat were we to die.
> Were we to try all thro' the town,
> The world is now turn'd up-side down.

Soldiers, too, had to eat, and cultural considerations, actual or ideal, affected the components and quantities of Continental Army rations. In February 1778, Timothy Pickering noted that less meat would be necessary if troops ate more soups, but, he reflected, "No people on earth eat such quantities of flesh as the English," and "nothing but the example of the [American] officers would possibly avail to effect this matter, and perhaps the attempt [to reduce the meat ration] could not be made without the danger of mutiny." The original ration, which was based on that of the British, illustrates what foods were considered necessary to sustain American soldiers and provides insight into society's staples. The hoped-for per diem allotment included one pound of beef or fish or three-quarter's of a pound of pork, one pound of bread or flour, one pint of milk per day, one quart of spruce beer or cider. Each man per week was entitled to three pints of peas, beans, or other vegetables, one-half pint of rice or one pint of Indian meal, and nine gallons of molasses for one hundred men. Meat and flour, with occasional vegetables, became army staples, while supply difficulties caused milk, beer, cider, and molasses to be dropped.

Other foods, more often seen in civilian life, were sometimes issued. For seven months in 1780, New Jersey soldiers stationed in their home state received extraordinary state stores consisting of rum, sugar, and coffee in substantial quantities, and small amounts of chocolate, tea, pepper, and vinegar. After a winter of reduced rations at Valley Forge, in April 1778 fish, bacon, and peas or beans were added to the daily allotment. Four months later, soft and hard breads, as well as butter, were being issued. When flour rations were reduced in November 1779, additional portions of meat, beans, potatoes, and turnips were issued.

Foraging and Feasting

Although scarcity was hardly an everyday occurrence Revolutionary soldiers' suffering is popularly synonymous with food dearth. Colonel Josiah Harmar wrote about shortages on August 22, 1780, "Provisions extreme scarce; only half a Lb. Meat in three days." Three days later he wrote, "This movement of our... [troops] is occasioned through dire necessity, the Army being on the point of starving." In hard times soldiers often subsisted on fire cake, the "sodden cakes" described by one man as "Flower... Wet with Water & Roll[ed]... in dirt & Ashes to bake... in a Horrible Manner." As hardtack later became a symbol connected to Civil War service (1861–1865), so fire cake was for the Continental soldier.

Soldiers' narratives also provide insights into civilian foodways. Near Woodbridge, New Jersey, Colonel Israel Shreve wrote, "I Rode All over this Village through the Gardens in search of Asparigas [but] found none, All the Beds being Cut that Day by the soldiers." General George Washington authorized foraging for wild "vegetables" at Middlebrook, New Jersey. His list included common and french sorrels, lamb's-quarters (or goosefoot), and watercresses. He went on to recommend to the soldiers the constant use of greens, "as they make an agreeable sallad, and have the most salutary effect." During 1776 at Fort Ticonderoga, New York, a soldier wrote of having chocolate, "Milk Porrage," and supawn (boiled corn meal and water) on different days. Joseph Joslin served as a wagon driver for the Continental army in Connecticut. His diary lists foods eaten at local taverns and private homes in and around Danbury in 1777 and 1778, including Indian pudding, milk porridge, johnnycake, potatoes, fried pumpkin, codfish, scallops, and "a good Supper Pork beef turnips tators Bread Sider Butter Cheese Puden appelpy nuts & milk." General George Washington's rather elegant meals at West Point in August 1779,

> had a Ham (sometimes a shoulder) of Bacon, to grace the head of the table; a piece of roast Beef adorns the foot; and a small dish of Greens or Beans... decorates the center. When the Cook has a mind to cut a figure... we have two Beef-stake-Pyes, or dishes of Crabs in addition.... Of late, he has had the surprizing luck to discover, that apples will make pyes.

Regional foods could pose problems for outsiders. Colonel Henry Lee remembered that in South Carolina, "Rice furnished our substitute for bread, which... was very disagreeable to the Marylanders and Virginians, who had grown up in the use of corn or wheat bread." Luigi Castiglioni, traveling through the United States from 1785 to 1787, wrote,

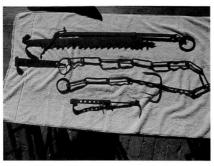

Adjustable forged iron trammels were hung in the fireplace; the terminal hook that held the cooking pot could be raised or lowered to regulate the heat.

Ordinarily, edible rice is given no other preparation except to boil it in water and take it this way to the table, where it is mixed with fresh butter. In the country it is used boiled in this manner at lunch and dinner. However, certain thin cakes are also made of it, which are served in the morning with tea or coffee, and it is also prepared in many other ways. The cracked rice serves as food for the negroes.

Food-related taxes had instigated the eight-year struggle for independence, and it was another food trade issue, American access to the Newfoundland Banks fisheries and the right to dry the catch onshore, that held up the peace negotiations in 1782 and 1783. Hostilities ceased when those rights, and other concessions, were won.

[**See also** Cookbooks and Manuscripts: To 1860; Hardtack; Supawn; Tea.]

BIBLIOGRAPHY

Cometti, Elizabeth. "Women in the American Revolution." *New England Quarterly* 20, no. 3 (September 1947): 335–337.

Morgan, Kenneth. "The Organization of the Colonial American Rice Trade." *William and Mary Quarterly*, 3rd ser., 52, no. 3 (July 1995): 432–452.

Rees, John U. " 'The Foundation of an Army Is the Belly.' North American Soldiers' Food, 1756–1945." In *ALHFAM: Proceedings of the 1998 Conference and Annual Meeting.* Vol. 21. Bloomfield, OH, Association for Living History, Farm and Agricultural Museums, 1999. http://revwar75.com/library/rees/index.htm.

Smith, Barbara Clark. "Food Rioters and the American Revolution." *William and Mary Quarterly*, 3rd ser., 51, no. 1 (January 1994): 3–38.

JOHN U. REES

Historical Overview:
Revolutionary War to the Civil War

After the American Revolution, Americans had many styles of eating. For many average farm families, pork and grain along with dried beans composed most of the diet for much of the year. However, wealthy slave owners were able to sustain a luxurious, British style of dining little changed from colonial times. Urban workers had access to a variety of foods, although they might not have been able to afford them every day. Merchant families in port cities were able to participate in a global food economy that brought them occasional access to tropical fruits, European wines, curries from India, and varieties of coffee and tea.

The notion that early Americans ate unseasoned food and avoided milk, fruits, and vegetables is actually a late Victorian one that got wrongly attached to early Americans after the nation's centennial in 1876. The detailed cookbook recipes are lavish with nutmeg, mace, cinnamon, pepper, and lemon juice where contemporaries wrote "spice to taste." Tomatoes, broccoli, and new varieties of vegetables and fruits enjoyed popularity in a vogue for experimental farming in the 1830s. But poor Americans took advantage of the foods local to their areas, and some rural families were still living on very few seasonal foods, eating the same thing until it ran out, during the late winter-to-spring lean period. Regional variations persisted; in New England, for instance, wheat was difficult and expensive to grow and thus barley, rye, oats, and corn were substituted, even after the opening of the Erie Canal brought western wheat to market in the 1820s. In coastal regions, Americans ate oysters and lobsters as well as other fish. Although lobsters were not yet regarded as a luxury, an oyster frenzy hit the nation in the mid-nineteenth century when those living inland clamored for them. The delicacy was shipped by rail to the heartland to be served in oyster houses and sold by street peddlers. All over the country, shellfish was served raw, baked, fricasseed, in soups, and in pies. The railroads also lengthened the seasons for urban cooks and made for more reliable supplies of strawberries and other delicacies.

Class also dictated diet. Wealthier Americans of course ate better and more varied diets than members of the working classes. Many tried to emulate European tastes, eating a wider range of foods, which required more complicated preparations. The presence of servants to cook for wealthier families made cooking and eating more pleasurable. Working-class Americans favored cheap and easily prepared foods. A popular dish among laborers was blood pudding, a mixture of pork or beef blood mixed with chopped pork stuffed into casing. Pigs were especially cheap and easy to raise; they did not require feeding or other care. When New York City banned pigs from roaming the streets, housewives protested the ban by fighting back with their brooms.

Americans of every stripe enjoyed a great variety of sweets and beverages. Access to sugar for American refineries had been an issue in the Revolution, and cheap rum, sugar, and molasses were among its victories. Pork and beef were often cured with molasses. Americans developed a sweet tooth. A wide variety of desserts were popular in America. Gelatin—or gelatine, as it was spelled in the nineteenth century (prepared with calf's foot-jelly, isinglass from sturgeon, and increasingly faked with arrowroot or cornstarch)—was a popular pudding. Yeasted cakes and pound cakes began to yield to the taller, layered cakes as baking powders became more widely marketed, sometimes with a temperance endorsement. Pies were still popular for their durability and ease of baking, but the most popular and exciting dessert was ice cream. This delicacy offered an opportunity to display one's access to the improved ice cutting and distribution developed in this period in New England, especially on the Fourth of July holiday. During and after the War of 1812, when the price of British-monopoly tea rose and coffee from Brazil and the Caribbean became more affordable, the traditionally British drink fell out of favor. Nineteenth-century housewives produced a large variety of drinks at home: beers from barley, ginger, spruce, sassafras, maple syrup, and molasses; and wines from local and imported grapes and berries, as well as cordials and punches. Drink was as much a part of American life as food was, and in the late eighteenth and early nineteenth centuries, alcoholism was regarded as a great problem in America. Liquor, most often whiskey and cider, was a regular part of everyday meals and social gatherings.

Food and the Industrial and Transportation Revolutions

Changes in technology and transportation changed American foodways. Refrigeration, in particular improvements in icehouses, allowed meat, poultry, and fruit to be kept longer. Machinery that cut ice more easily, better insulation techniques (such as packing ice in sawdust), as well as falling ice prices made keeping food cold a more viable option. By the mid-nineteenth century, icehouses were common on farms. The ice chest was patented in 1803, and cold storage warehouses appeared in 1858. Americans began to consume different foods as a result of refrigeration; perhaps the best example is fresh milk, which had become a health hazard because it spoiled so quickly.

It also became possible to transport foods greater and greater distances. The appearance of steamboats beginning in 1807 meant that foodstuffs could be transported long distances; by 1830 they were widely in use. Roads and canals also facilitated the exportation of food. Prices dropped as a result of new transportation methods. Flour, which had been scarce along the eastern seaboard, became cheaper and more readily obtainable. Railroads had an even greater impact. The rails brought a wider variety and better quality of foods to Americans. Once-exotic or limited-season fruits and vegetables (especially peaches) were more commonplace in the middle of the country. The appearance of clipper ships at mid-century meant that pineapples,

A handmade sausage grinder typifies the pre-industrial implements that would be superseded by cast-iron equipment made industrially after the Civil War. The wooden core set with iron "pushing nails" seen here guided the meat into small knives embedded in the frame, eventually pushing the completed sausage out below.

bananas, and coconuts, if not eaten every day, were available to middle-class consumers along the eastern seaboard.

Feeding the Slaves

The amount and types of food that masters allotted to slaves differed from that which slaves prepared and ate. Their owners were concerned with providing only enough nourishment to enable slaves to work as much as possible. The mainstays of the slave diet were pork and corn, both of which were plentiful in the South. The typical ration, set in the eighteenth century, was a peck of corn per slave per week. This was varied locally with broken rice, sweet potatoes in season, and other starches. The diet of pork and corn allowed the adult slave to consume approximately forty-five hundred calories per day. Although this amount seems excessive in a modern diet, surviving photographs of African Americans, who were, with little exception, slim, suggest that this intake was necessary to sustain them as they worked "from sun-up to sun-down." The typical diet was both monotonous and not especially healthful, because pork and corn, while providing protein and carbohydrates, lack many vitamins. To vary their food choices (and to a lesser extent to provide more nutrition), slaves hunted, fished, trapped, stole, and grew their own foods whenever possible. Other masters, especially as plantations evolved and became larger, thought that it was inefficient to have slaves working to feed themselves and so provided a better ration, or delegated certain slaves to cook in the fields or in communal kitchens for the children. When and where they could, slaves added okra, cabbage, squash, peas, and rice, as well as grouse, squirrels, raccoons, possums, fish, alligators, turtles, and groundhogs.

Some female slave cooks, and a handful of males, reigned supreme among the house servants and were able to assert some authority. Some slave cooks had other slaves to assist them in the kitchen, as meals were often elaborate productions. The cook alone had access to exotic and expensive supplies, and she alone helped the plantation mistress entertain in grand southern style, thereby solidifying the reputation of both. Masters and their families liked French and English food and were forced to embrace local dishes only with the naval blockade of the Civil War. The stereotype of the skilled slave cook also seems to have developed mostly after the Civil War, when African Americans could compete for paid positions in the fewer wealthy southern families, and when more white southerners had developed a taste for African-derived dishes and seasonings.

[See also African American Food: To the Civil War; Alcohol and Teetotalism; Beecher, Catharine; Child, Lydia Maria; Cookbooks and Manuscripts: To 1860; Cooking Manuscripts; Fourth of July; Graham, Sylvester; Ice; Jewish Dietary Laws; Kitchens; Leslie, Eliza; New Year's Celebrations; Randolph, Mary; Simmons, Amelia; Temperance; Thanksgiving; Transportation of Food.]

BIBLIOGRAPHY

Fox-Genovese, Elizabeth. *Within the Plantation Household: Black and White Women of the Old South.* Chapel Hill: University of North Carolina Press, 1988.

Nissenbaum, Stephen. *The Battle for Christmas: A Cultural History of America's Most Cherished Holiday.* New York: Knopf, 1996.

Rorabaugh, W. J. *The Alcoholic Republic: An American Tradition.* New York: Oxford University Press, 1979.

Theophano, Janet. *Eat My Words: Reading Women's Lives through the Cookbooks They Wrote.* New York: Palgrave, 2002.

Travers, Len. *Celebrating the Fourth: Independence Day and the Rites of Nationalism in the Early Republic.* Amherst: University of Massachusetts Press, 1997.

RACHELLE E. FRIEDMAN

Historical Overview: Civil War and Reconstruction

The Civil War (1861–1865) and Reconstruction (1863–1877) eras bridged old and new pathways. Western expansion, industrial innovation, and foreign immigration all had their effects. Large-scale immigration into the West began in the 1840s, exposing Native Americans to Anglo foods, and vice versa. Native cultures suffered and European foodways gradually prevailed. The Lakota Sioux medicine man Sitting Bull referred to this when advising against assimilation in 1867: "The whites may get me at last . . . but I will have good times till then. You are fools to make yourselves slaves to a piece of fat bacon, some hard-tack, and a little sugar and coffee."

Soldiers' Food

Society's idea of the daily food needed for basic sustenance was reflected in the U.S. Army Civil War ration (1861–1864):

twelve ounces of pork or bacon, or, one pound and four ounces of salt or fresh beef; one pound and six ounces of soft bread or flour, or, one pound of hard bread, or, one pound and four ounces of corn meal; and to every one hundred rations, fifteen pounds of beans or peas, *and* ten pounds of rice or hominy; ten pounds of green coffee, or, eight pounds of roasted (or roasted and ground) coffee, or, one pound and eight ounces of tea; fifteen pounds of sugar; four quarts of vinegar; . . . three pounds and twelve ounces of salt; four ounces of pepper; thirty pounds of potatoes, when practicable, and one quart of molasses.

Whenever possible, troops supplemented government rations with found or purchased foods, such as ripe or unripe fruits and vegetables, or pies, cakes, and canned goods bought from sutlers (mobile storekeepers). Civil War soldier-cooks tried to imitate homemade fare, making soup, stew, hash, pudding, flapjacks, fried cakes, corndodgers, boiled or roasted corn, succotash, baked beans, lobscouse, and applesauce. How close these dishes came to the home-cooked original is open to question. In 1862 Private Wilbur Fisk from Vermont voiced a theme common to soldiers' cooking: "These . . . boys . . . out-Graham Sylvester Graham himself, in his most radical ideas of simplicity in diet. . . . Coarse meal, cold water and salt have been the ingredients composing many a meal for us, which a thanksgiving supper, in other circumstances, will scarcely rival."

Soldiers' humorous epithets signaled the importance of food: "dough bellies" (infantrymen), "chicken thieves" (cavalrymen), "Soft Breads" (Army of the Potomac soldiers), "pound-cake brethren" (easy-living soldiers), "coffee coolers" (stragglers), "Virginia rabbits" (pigs), "desecrated" (dessicated) vegetables, and a "square meal" (hardtack). Hardtack came to symbolize the soldier's life. Some men thought it inedible at first, but most came to agree with Lieutenant Fred Chapman, Twenty-ninth United States Colored Troops: "two pieces of hard-tack with a slice of raw, fat salt pork between—not a dainty meal, but solid provender to fight on." Major Frederick Hitchcock of Pennsylvania described a popular hardtack preparation. "'Lobskous' . . . consisted of hardtack broken up and thoroughly soaked in water, then fried in pork fat."

Preserving increased in the nineteenth century as glass fruit jars began to replace earlier preserving methods such as cast iron pots.

A sutler's bombproof "Fruit and Oyster House" on the front line in Petersburg, Virginia, 1864–1865.

Cornmeal was a southern staple, and "cush" was a dish associated with Confederate troops. Sergeant William W. Heartsill from Texas described it in October 1863: "Well dinner is ready…prepared in this manner, chop up a small quantity of fat bacon into a frying pan, get the grease all out of it, put in a quart of water, when it boils crumble in cold corn bread and stir until dry, and you are ready for a dinner of 'CUSH.'" Another Texan, Second Lieutenant Robert M. Collins, added that "'cush'… with some of the corn-bread burned to a black crisp, out of which we make coffee, was fine living." Real coffee, a prerequisite of Federal fare, having replaced the alcohol ration in October 1832, was often traded to southern soldiers for tobacco.

Alcohol was occasionally issued, and both officers and men continually sought other sources. Cornelia Hancock, a Quaker nurse from New Jersey, alluded to its widespread use in July 1864: "I introduced [brother William] to all my friends. They, of course, invited him to drink some whiskey which he refused to do…a very rare thing in the army." Sergeant Cyrus Boyd, Fifteenth Iowa Volunteers, told of soldiers' behavior in Tennessee in January 1863: "I took a ramble thro' Memphis.…Whiskey O Whiskey! Drunk men staggered on all the streets.…The streets were full of *drunk* men. The men who had fought their way from [Fort] Donelson to Corinth and who had met no enemy able to whip them now surrendered to Genl *Intoxication*." Widespread alcohol consumption fueled the temperance movement. The Prohibition Party was founded in 1869, and the 1873–1874 Woman's Crusade resulted from years of female activism against alcohol consumption and traffic.

Civilians' Food

For wartime southerners, deprivation and make-do were the order of the day. Game animals, fish, and eggs replaced beef and pork, one wag remarking that a "hundred ways of cooking an egg became well-known in the Confederacy." Preserves made with sor-

ghum, instead of sugar, "had a twang." Rice bread was called secession bread. And rye and other coffee substitutes were used. Occasionally meals were reminiscent of prewar plenty. Mary Chestnut of Charleston wrote in April 1861, "The supper was a consolation—*pâté de foie gras* salad, *biscuit glacé* and *champagne frappé*." She wrote from Richmond, "*Christmas Day, 1863*…We had for dinner oyster soup, besides roast mutton, ham, boned turkey, wild duck, partridge, plum pudding, sauterne, burgundy, sherry, and Madeira. There is life in the old land yet!"; and on "*February 1st*.[1864]—Mrs. Davis gave her 'Luncheon to Ladies Only'…Gumbo, ducks and olives, chickens in jelly, oysters, lettuce salad, chocolate cream, jelly cake, claret, champagne, etc."

The nurse Cornelia Hancock's letters home to New Jersey show the variety of dishes possible in an 1864 Virginia army hospital. From Brandy Station, dated February 11, "Today the men had for their breakfast oysters, meat and breads. For dinner, soup, Turkey broth, corn and lima beans. For supper oysters, farina, bread, and butter. So you see, although out of the world we are of the world." She continues on March 2, "We had what is called here a splendid dinner— Ham, Eggs, Oyster pie, Roast Beef and Potatoes, peach tarts and cup custards." From City Point on July 4, "a real Fourth dinner, potatoes, beef, onions, canned peach pie, and corn starch pudding." And on July 18, "Twice have I given ice cream to my patients."

Canned Goods and Meatpacking

Large city-centered populations needed quantities of long-lasting, easily stored foodstuff. Armies on the march had the added requirement of portable, compact comestibles. Although not an army-issue item, canned foods began to fill those needs. In 1870, Captain T. J. Wilson, tasked by the army to study the quality of American canned goods, wrote:

> Ten years ago Baltimore…cou'd boast no more than half a dozen packing establishments (there are now, December, 1867, at that place, from twenty-five to thirty).…Hermetically sealed goods at that day sold for fabulous prices, and were consumed by a few only. The outbreak of the Rebellion, in 1861, brought about a sudden and remarkable change. Manufactories sprung up everywhere, and the demand for the supply for the army, through sutlers, became enormous.

A 1924 study noted that at the war's onset in 1861: "Probably five million cans of everything [was annually produced].… In 1870…the output reached thirty million cans.…Factories could not be built fast enough to supply customers.…Canneries were started inland for the first time, at Cincinnati, Indianapolis, and other places."

Wartime demand for meat fueled the growth of the western beef business. As a major rail hub, and because of the Mississippi River blockade, Chicago benefited. By 1865, the new 320-acre Chicago Union Stock Yards were operating, attracting to the city the large meatpacking firms of Armour, Swift, Morris, and Hammond. According to the Chicago Historical Society, by 1900 Chicago's meatpacking industry employed more than 25,000 people and produced 82 percent of the meat consumed in the United States. The 1872 institution of meat coolers allowed year-round meatpacking, and the adoption of refrigerated rail cars in 1882 meant that processed meats could be transported over long distances.

Canned goods and refrigerated beef had become commonplace items at the supper table by the century's end. The U.S. Army subsisted on both in Cuba, Puerto Rico, and the Philippines in 1898.

[**See also** ARMOUR, PHILIP DANFORTH; CANNING AND BOTTLING; COFFEE SUBSTITUTES; COMBAT FOOD; COOKBOOKS AND MANUSCRIPTS: FROM THE CIVIL WAR TO WORLD WAR I; GRAHAM, SYLVESTER; HARDTACK; SOUTHERN REGIONAL COOKERY; SWIFT, GUSTAVUS FRANKLIN; TEMPERANCE; TRANSPORTATION OF FOOD.]

BIBLIOGRAPHY

Collins, James H. *The Story of Canned Foods*. New York: Dutton, 1924.

Massey, Mary Elizabeth. *Ersatz in the Confederacy: Shortages and Substitutes on the Southern Homefront*. Columbia: University of South Carolina Press, 1993.

Rees, John U. " 'The Foundation of an Army Is the Belly.' North American Soldiers' Food, 1756–1945." In *ALHFAM: Proceedings of the 1998 Conference and Annual Meeting*, vol. 21. Bloomfield, OH: Association for Living History, Farm, and Agricultural Museums, 1999.

JOHN U. REES

Historical Overview:
Victorian America to World War I

As the Industrial Revolution brought America into the machine age, its impact on agriculture transformed the way food was produced, purchased, and consumed. In the years from 1880 to the beginning of World War I, the American public began to change from a nation of producers to a nation of consumers. Everything from the way that food was grown, processed, and packaged to the manner in which it was distributed, purchased, and consumed was affected, as the marriage of science and agriculture created a more efficient, mechanized, and industrialized food system.

In the beginning of this period, the main processed foods available to consumers were items such as crackers, white flour, and refined sugar, produced locally and sold in bulk at the general store. For the most part, food processing was done in the home, with canned and preserved foods. It was during this era, however, that many of the commercially processed foods that have become mainstays of the American diet were developed by large food corporations.

The transition from the local and regional foodways of Victorian America to the national and international markets of the modern food system was made possible by advances in agriculture, transportation, and food processing, as well as the marketing and advertising revolutions of the era. By the time World War I began, nationally branded, mass-produced products that were individually wrapped, packaged, and canned were being purchased on a cash-and-carry basis from markets stocked with a wide array of processed goods—a far cry from the way that Americans were buying food just a few decades earlier.

Advances in Agriculture

The union of science and agriculture is one of the defining characteristics of this period. An era of research and testing in the agricultural sphere dramatically increased production on American farms, increased the nation's food supply, and hastened the movement from the local food system to the industrial model. The starting point of this development was the federal Hatch Act of 1887, which established agricultural experiment stations and funded the agricultural research that led to widespread efficiency in farming methods and hardier strains of hybrid seeds for wheat, corn, soybeans, and other crops.

Between 1875 and 1915, the U.S. production of most staple crops doubled, and wheat production tripled. Dairy farming also increased, as ranchers developed ways to produce stronger animals, and the corn and hog belts expanded as larger tracts of farmland were purchased farther and farther west. This led to lower prices on agricultural products, making more items affordable to all Americans. Farmers needed to produce more to make the same profits. The movement toward larger acreages, mechanization, and crop specialization was underway.

Transportation and Distribution

With the completion of the first transcontinental railroad in 1869 and the increased use of the refrigerated railroad car, railroads became a key factor in the industrialization of food. They enabled food to be shipped across the country and lessened the importance of local and regional markets. The improved transportation system increased the availability and affordability of meat products, allowed fruits and vegetables from warm climates to be marketed far from the farms, and made it possible for dairy products to be carried to market without spoilage. As a national market for food became a reality, new types of crops were designed to withstand the journey to market.

Food Processing

New technologies were created to capitalize on agricultural advances, and by the end of this period, food processing would account for 20 percent of the nation's manufacturing,

Advertisement for the New Empire stove, c. 1875.

mostly dominated by several large companies. As food companies sought to create demand for their products they realized that one way to do this was by replacing items traditionally produced in the home with those mass-produced in factories.

Packaging, Branding, and Advertising

The shipment of food outside of local areas required some kind of package in which the product could be protected from damage. By 1879 machines were producing flat, foldable cardboard boxes that were branded and labeled to differentiate one company's product from the next.

To take full advantage of the economies of scale of mass production, more goods than consumers actually needed or demanded were being produced; corporations increasingly relied on advertising to create that demand. It was during this period that Americans saw the rise of national brands and big corporations with enormous advertising budgets. These changes dramatically affected the way that food was sold and purchased once it got to market. The independent general store of the Victorian era gave way first to the grocery chain stores, where individually packaged goods with fixed prices replaced the need for clerks to dole out bulk items and determine their price.

Purchasers for chain groceries such as the A&P usually acquired goods for several stores at a time; therefore, they sought out larger producers, further encouraging large-scale mass production. Small farmers who could not compete were forced to take factory jobs in urban areas, thus becoming part of the industrial economy. Every facet of the industrial food system thrived as more people moved off the farm and depended on industry for what they ate.

Food Purity

The processing of food far from the source of its production raised concerns about food safety. In the early 1900s, the United States government recognized the need to regulate the food industry. The Pure Food and Drug Act of 1906 called for the labeling of ingredients in packaged food and prohibited the sale of mislabeled or adulterated products.

As the nation's food supply became more industrialized, there was a growing disconnection between Americans and the food they consumed. In these decades, many Americans went from producing their own food, or at the very least consuming food produced locally, to purchasing food from places they had never even visited. Grocery stores from the East Coast to the West began selling identical products, and the food industry became increasingly consolidated. The remarkable changes in the food production and distribution system permanently affected the nation's eating habits and eventually wreaked havoc on the environment.

[**See also** ADVERTISING; ARMOUR, PHILIP DANFORTH; CAMPBELL SOUP COMPANY; CANNING AND BOTTLING; COOKBOOKS AND MANUSCRIPTS: FROM THE CIVIL WAR TO WORLD WAR I; FOOD MARKETING; GROCERY STORES; H. J. HEINZ COMPANY; KELLOGG COMPANY; PILLSBURY; POST FOODS; TRANSPORTATION OF FOOD.]

BIBLIOGRAPHY

Coppin, Clayton A. and Jack High. *The Politics of Purity: Harvey Washington Wiley and the Origins of Federal Food Policy.* Ann Arbor: University of Michigan Press, 1999.

A Warming Cup

of hot bouillon, so refreshing after exercise, is quickly and easily made from

Van Camp's

CONCENTRATED SOUPS

Tomato, Chicken, Bouillon, Vegetable, Mock Turtle, Ox Tail, Beef, Consomme, Mullaga-tawny, Cream of Celery, Chicken Gumbo and Tomato Okra,

all piquantly spiced and seasoned, cooked, ready to heat. No water in the can. Dilute when you heat it. Sold by grocers at ten cents a can, making a quart of soup. Sample can of either kind, with recipe book, for six cents in stamps.

**VAN CAMP PACKING CO.,
356 Kentucky Ave., Indianapolis, Ind.**

"Old woman, old woman, whither so high?"
"To answer this telegram sent from the sky;
The mandate of Jove, whom none may defy,
Directs me this sample instanter to bring,
For proven on earth a most excellent thing,
It must suit the taste of the Olympian King."

Send for FREE booklet on "Salads: How to Make and Dress Them," giving many valuable and novel recipes for Salads, Sand-wiches, Sauces, Luncheon Dishes, etc. Sample, 10 cents.   **E. R. DURKEE & CO., 121 Charlton Street, New York.**

For mutual advantage when you write to an advertiser please mention this magazine.

Advertisements for Van Camp's soups and Durkee salad dressing that appeared in the American Monthly Illustrated Review of Reviews *in November 1899.*

Magdoff, Fred, John Bellamy Foster, and Frederick H. Buttel, eds. *Hungry for Profit: The Agribusiness Threat to Farmers, Food, and the Environment.* New York: Monthly Review Press, 2000.

Shapiro, Laura. *Perfection Salad: Women and Cooking at the Turn of the Century.* New York: Farrar, Straus & Giroux, 1986.

Strasser, Susan. *Satisfaction Guaranteed: The Making of the American Mass Market.* Washington, DC: Smithsonian Press, 1995.

Williams, Susan. *Savory Suppers and Fashionable Feasts: Dining in Victorian America.* Knoxville: University of Tennessee Press, 1996.

ALISON TOZZI

Cover of a packet of recipe cards with picnic foods suitable for transportation by automobile, 1920s.

Historical Overview:
World War I

By the time the United States entered World War I in April 1917, the war had been raging for three years and food was desperately needed to supply America's European allies. American civilians were urged to conserve food by increasing production, cutting waste, and substituting plentiful for scarce foods in their diet. President Woodrow Wilson placed exports of foodstuffs, fuel, iron, and steel under government control as war matériel. Congress passed the Food and Fuel Control Act (Lever Act), and the future U.S. president Herbert C. Hoover, who had served as chairman of the Commission for Relief in Belgium, was appointed to head the U.S. Food Administration in 1917. Hoover exhorted U.S. farmers with the slogan, "Food can win the war."

The government instituted limited control over the production and distribution of food during the war but did not ration food for civilians at first. For example, the government limited sugar purchases by industrial manufacturers, wholesale producers, and retailers, while encouraging domestic consumers to use sugar in home canning to preserve as much food as possible. Consumers were entitled to purchase sugar in twenty-five-pound quantities for that purpose, and to minimize waste. Rather than rationing, Hoover's early mandate was to persuade Americans to cut back voluntarily on consumption of beef, wheat, and other foodstuffs that were needed by U.S. and Allied troops in Europe.

U.S. wheat prices rose precipitously in the spring of 1917 as Allied governments, American millers, and speculators bid up prices on the Chicago Board of Trade. The Grain Corporation, part of Hoover's U.S. Food Administration, bought, stored, transported, and sold wheat and fixed its price at $2.20 per bushel under the terms of the Lever Act.

Although certain areas of Europe, most notably Belgium, suffered from food shortages throughout "The Great War," the United Kingdom was hit harder by labor shortage than by food shortage in the early years. Although luxury goods such as alcoholic beverages, sugar, cheese, and butter were scarce and expensive, staples such as bread, milk, and beef were still relatively available thanks to generous subsidies. It was not until late 1917 and early 1918—in retrospect, the period deemed to be the height of distress for Europe—that rationing was instituted. Before 1918 British civilians were encouraged to conserve foodstuffs, but institutionalized rationing began in January 1918, beginning with sugar and continuing with meat and butter.

The United States only began its conservation measures after the country entered World War I. During wartime, a greater effort became necessary in order to feed U.S. citizens, send provisions to soldiers in Europe, and supply much of the food of U.S. Allies, both civilian and military. U.S. sugar rationing began in mid-1918, with each citizen allowed eight ounces per week. Sugar prices soared, and the black market for consumer goods proliferated. Hoover established special conservation days, urging Americans to eat no wheat on Mondays and Wednesdays, no meat on Tuesdays, and no pork on Thursdays and Saturdays. He also asked citizens to eat whole wheat "victory bread" in place of white bread. To replace the factory-canned vegetables that were sent overseas to feed soldiers and the Allies, people were urged to raise vegetables in vacant lots or yards, called "liberty gardens," in order to bring fresh, home-canned, and dried produce to the table. For many Americans, the wartime restrictions resulted in a more nutritious diet of whole wheat bread, less sugar, and more fresh vegetables than usual.

World War I helped move the baking of bread from the home to commercial bakeries as more women took work outside the home, leaving less time for baking. Besides, the government asked both bakers and the public to bake with flours that combined several grains, mixtures that were difficult for householders to obtain. Home cooks developed new and imaginative ways of using low-grade war flour and wheat substitutes in their recipes. They used syrup and molasses instead of sugar and found substitutes for lard, butter, and meat to feed their families; the relatively new vegetable shortening, Crisco, became a substitute for butter or lard, and peanut butter emerged as a protein substitute for meat.

Hoover's Food Administration sponsored a major education campaign to familiarize people with calories, vitamins, proteins, carbohydrates, the values of fruits and vegetables, and the best means of canning, preserving, and drying foods. A multitude of pamphlets, posters, advertisements, and other documents were produced to help teach the rules of substitution and persuade Americans that eating less would not harm their health and might even improve it. Even the press, schools, and clergy pitched in to preach what became known as "the doctrine of the clean plate."

World War I gave many Americans their first taste of vegetarian meals as home cooks introduced dishes like bean loaf to the dinner menu to replace meat loaf. Soybeans, later a staple of vegetarian diets, also gained space in Americans' awareness, if not yet on most dinner tables. For example, in 1918 U.S. Secretary of Agriculture David F. Houston issued a circular entitled, "Use Soy-Bean Flour to Save Wheat, Meat, and Fat." It included recipes for "victory bread," soybean "meat loaf," and soybean "mush croquettes." However, few U.S. farmers produced soybeans, few facilities existed to process the beans, and few stores carried soybean products. Soybeans were produced more widely starting in 1920.

Although U.S. consumers observed voluntary rationing, or "conservation," during the war, consumers in some western European countries were subject to compulsory rationing. Some scholars, such as Amy Bentley, in her book *Eating for Victory*, suggest that voluntary rationing during World War I did not work for everyone. Better-educated and more affluent Americans observed no-wheat and meatless days, but immigrants and those in the working classes were less likely to do so and in many cases ate more meat as their incomes rose. These inconsistent conservation habits also contributed to rampant price inflation, panic about food supplies, hoarding of food, and black-market sales of scarce food items.

On November 11, 1918, World War I ended in an armistice. "Hunger does not breed reform; it breeds madness," said President Wilson in his Armistice Day address to Congress. All food regulations were suspended in the United States by December 1918 but remained in effect in Britain and Europe for several months thereafter.

[**See also** INTERNATIONAL AID; NUTRITION; PEANUTS; SOYBEANS.]

BIBLIOGRAPHY

Bentley, Amy. *Eating for Victory: Food Rationing and the Politics of Domesticity.* Urbana and Chicago: University of Illinois Press, 1998.

KARA NEWMAN

Historical Overview:
Word War I to World War II

The 1920s and 1930s saw an expanding parade of food-related fashions, reflecting an explosive growth of discretionary spending choices in the first age of "consumerism," or the view that public purchasing/using-up/repurchasing habits were the lifeblood of national productivity. A multiplicity of inexpensive food products appeared, including catchily named cold breakfast cereals, nickel candy bars, frozen snacks, bottled sauces, prepackaged bread, processed cheese, instant mixes for puddings and baked goods, canned or bottled fruit juices, and many new canned foods from soups to sauces. Modern mass communications helped keep people poised to buy: national radio networks and news wire services, syndicated newspaper features, movies, expanded journalistic "lifestyle" coverage, and aggressive national advertising campaigns—often presented in several media at once—contributed to a larger consumer awareness of brand names. Food journalists,

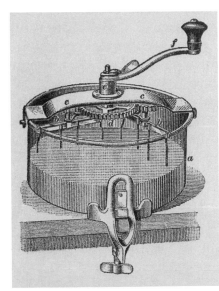

Diagram of a cake mixer.

notably Clementine Paddleford in the *New York Herald-Tribune*, eagerly filled the role of trend-spotters and (often) commercial cheerleaders.

At the same time, two fundamental changes took place in American food-shopping habits. One was triggered by a decrease in the number of foods being commonly sold loose or in bulk, in comparison to those in labeled packages (including cans). This went hand in hand with the advent of self-service stores, beginning in 1916 with the nation's first Piggly Wiggly in Memphis. The first supermarkets appeared in the 1930s. Self-service shopping helped cement the importance of brand-name canned and packaged foods, which in turn blurred consumers' appreciation of local or seasonal variability as a factor in food choices. Partly through the medium of commercial canning, this period also brought a number of ethnic dishes into mainstream kitchens in somewhat Americanized versions: among others, ravioli, enchiladas, chili con carne, goulash, and chop suey.

The multiplication of food choices extended to eating out, which had now become a recreational activity open to all classes in different forms. Automobiles aided in this expansion, fostering the appearance of local eateries in even small or mid-sized towns. By 1930, most middle-class and working-class people had a range of inexpensive restaurant options including coffee shops, drugstore or five-and-dime lunch counters, cafeterias, diners, Chinese or Italian eateries, "tea shoppes," hamburger joints, soda fountains, and places devoted to local specialties like "shore dinners." People with cars could choose from drive-ins, roadhouses, ice cream stands, chili shacks, and visual-gimmick establishments like restaurants in the shape of giant hot dogs.

Household-engineering experts meanwhile were leading a shift toward small, compact kitchens—often geared to little more than can-opener cookery—with modern gas or electric stoves, well-insulated iceboxes or mechanical refrigerators, and labor-saving small appliances such as electric toasters and mixers. Another cadre of experts sought to read lessons in dietetics to the nation. Striving to capitalize on a wave of breakthroughs in nutritional understanding that had begun at about 1912 with early vitamin research, they assumed an unprecedented degree of visibility as spokespersons for public health policy. Orthodox nutritional advice, however, played out against successive waves of weight-loss fads largely triggered by an obsession with fashionable slenderness that started around 1910 and has not ceased since.

The troubled course of American agriculture was interwoven with these shifts in food habits and dietary emphases. Large government-spurred increases in crop production during World War I rapidly turned into chronic and financially ruinous postwar *over-*production. This perennial crisis coincided

with a severe rural depopulation trend (urban residents outnumbered rural for the first time in the 1920 national census) and a shrinking farm labor pool. Although grain farmers confronted a series of price collapses, others found opportunity in horticultural crops that were receiving a good nutritional press (e.g., citrus fruits and green vegetables) or that promised to transcend specialty-market appeal and reach a larger public (broccoli, zucchini, avocados, and artichokes, among others). The genetic diversity of most food plants shrank between the wars, a consequence of increasingly mechanized industrial-scale farming with a view to factors like high yield, transportability, and predictably uniform quality.

In the years spanning the two world wars, the federal government's influence on farming and food grew rapidly, along with government-sponsored gains in the public role of nutrition experts. During the war effort of 1917–1918, the Food Administration under Herbert Hoover launched a strategic food-management campaign that included voluntary rationing of meat, refined wheat flour, and sugar as well as increases in crop production. Almost as soon as the war was over, a far more drastic intervention into private consumption habits began through the Volstead Act of 1919, which put most distillers and some luxury restaurants out of business while aiding the rise of eating places not dependent on liquor or wine sales and encouraging the growth of the soft-drink industry. The repeal of Prohibition in 1933 heralded a growth in pricy gastronomic fashion, bon vivant journalism (culminating in the launch of *Gourmet* magazine in 1941), and chic wining-and-dining spots.

Despite the long postwar crisis in farm prices, the federal government did not intervene until 1933, when still worse price collapses coincided with the Dust Bowl soil-erosion catastrophe. The Roosevelt administration at last responded with measures including farm price supports, acreage-reduction and soil-conservation initiatives, and the Rural Electrification Act of 1936. World War II brought new rationing measures (this time compulsory); a restriction on metal sales that left commercial canners unable to obtain metal and spurred the "victory garden" drive; some price controls; and nutritional-education efforts that sought to give people the most nutrients for the buck and steer them to alternative sources of protein.

The immediate aftermath of the war roused widespread dissatisfaction among consumers, as massive foreign food-relief programs coincided with a bitterly resented inflation of domestic food prices after the end of price controls. As the nation recovered from several decades' worth of crises including the two wars, Prohibition, and the Depression, the American table was poised to become a battleground of nutritional, economic, cultural, and moral interests, as well as a potential counter in international politics.

[See also ALCOHOL AND TEETOTALISM; CALIFORNIA; DELMONICO'S; DEPARTMENT OF AGRICULTURE, UNITED STATES; DIETS, FAD; FARM SUBSIDIES, DUTIES, QUOTAS, AND TARIFFS; GROCERY STORES; PIGGLY WIGGLY.]

BIBLIOGRAPHY

Bentley, Amy. *Eating for Victory: Food Rationing and the Politics of Domesticity.* Urbana: University of Illinois Press, 1998.

Poppendieck, Janet. *Breadlines Knee-Deep in Wheat: Food Assistance in the Great Depression.* New Brunswick, NJ: Rutgers University Press, 1986.

Schwartz, Hillel. *Never Satisfied: A Cultural History of Diets, Fantasies, and Fat.* New York: Free Press, 1986.

Strasser, Susan. *Satisfaction Guaranteed: The Making of the American Mass Market.* New York: Pantheon, 1989.

Strasser, Susan. *Waste and Want: A Social History of Trash.* New York: Metropolitan, 1999.

ANNE MENDELSON

Historical Overview:
World War II

During World War II (1941–1945), the mandatory rationing of food in the United States was a vital part of the war effort. Whereas rationing ensured a sufficient, if unexciting, diet for Americans, it also helped instill for many a sense of public commitment to the war. By complying with rationing and even producing and preserving their own food, Americans increased their initial commitment, making it easier for them to support an extended and devastating world war. Although Americans managed to modify their food consumption to the strictures of wartime rationing, such changes were short-lived. After the war's end, a booming postwar economy helped to hasten the return to familiar eating patterns, and Americans increased their consumption of such high-status foods as expensive cuts of red meat even beyond prewar levels.

As the United States thrust itself full force into World War II, government officials immediately recognized the need for rationing programs and price controls, especially for food, to offset the possibility of spiraling inflation, ferocious black markets, and inequitable distribution of goods. Price controls and rationing would keep prices down, allowing all, not just the wealthy, to afford food that otherwise would demand exorbitant prices. Distributing food equitably was important politically. During the war, U.S. farmers produced 50 percent more food annually than they had during World War I. Yet much of this prodigious output was earmarked for wartime distribution: to the U.S. military, to Allied countries, and to formerly Axis-occupied territories.

Rationing Implemented

In May 1942, sugar was rationed, with meat and other foods soon to follow. The Office of Price Administration (OPA), as the overseer of rationing, sought a system that would curb

Harold B. Rowe, director of the Office of Price Administration's Food Rationing Division, indicates the point values of various processed foods, February 1943.

Americans' consumption but would still allow people choice and control over their food. Although sugar and coffee were rationed according to the stamp method, under which consumers would relinquish a stamp to purchase an allotted amount every few weeks, the government introduced a more complicated point system for rationing meat, fats, and processed foods, which allowed the consumer a reasonable amount of control over the family's diet.

The War on the Kitchen Front

Government propaganda and commercial advertising declared the homemaker's kitchen a war zone, turning it into a public arena. Cooking and shopping for food became, according to the media, political and patriotic acts. Because women were the traditional family food procurers, part of their patriotic duty was to avoid hoarding food or buying on the black market. Yet women felt a heightened concern for the well-being of their immediate families as well. Home and kitchen thus served not only as a public battlefront but also as a refuge from battle.

Home Front Food Production: Victory Gardening and Canning

The government encouraged Americans to grow and eat their own fruits and vegetables, in large part to allow most commercially grown and canned produce for the armed forces, the Allies, and newly liberated countries. By 1943, 20 million households produced more than 40 percent of vegetables Americans consumed, and 4.1 billion jars of food were preserved at home and community canning centers. Americans embraced victory

gardening and canning as quintessential symbols of home front sacrifice and patriotism, allowing citizens to feel they were making a real contribution to the war effort. Furthermore, victory gardening and canning were touted as a way to renew or strengthen community ties during this global crisis.

Setting Official Standards for Healthy Eating: The Basic Seven

To promote knowledge of healthy eating, the government established an educational campaign called the Basic Seven. The Basic Seven outlined the different categories of foods Americans should eat daily for optimum health. Government officials regarded the Basic Seven as a way in which housewives could learn about proper nutrition without having to know much about specific nutrients. Basic Seven accurately assessed the need for different vitamins but gave no clues about the amounts of fat, for instance, that one should consume daily. That butter had a category of its own is telling.

Effects of Food Rationing

Although during the war Americans cut down on their consumption of sugar, coffee, butter, and choice cuts of red meat, wartime food rationing did not significantly alter Americans' long-term eating habits or the structure of their meals. What changed was Americans' perception about food and its abundance during wartime. Americans worried that food rationing, combined with tight domestic supplies, could lead to severe food shortages and hence inadequate nutrition. Despite periodic hoarding of coffee, sugar, and red meat, food rationing seemed to work: food was distributed relatively equitably, and Americans had surprisingly full larders. In a public opinion poll taken in May 1943, almost two-thirds said their meals had been no different since extensive rationing had gone into effect; three-fourths indicated that the size of their meals had remained the same. This is not to suggest that World War II rationing was not needed. With up to 50 percent of some foodstuffs being sent overseas, mandatory food rationing assured Americans that they would get their fair share of the nation's food supply.

Food and Beverage Products Prominent in World War II

In addition to vitamin-enriched flour and bread products, recipes for sugarless desserts, and the tepid promotion of soy products and "variety meats" as substitutes for the more familiar steaks and chops, World War II also spurred the consumption of such manufactured products as Spam, margarine, and Coca-Cola. Although developed in the 1930s, Spam was catapulted into the American and international spotlight during World War II. An unrationed, easily transportable meat product high in fat and salt that had an indefinite shelf life, Spam was popular both at home and abroad. Americans stocked their cupboards with Spam, and the government shipped it by the ton to its allies. As a result, Spam became a common and desirable ingredient in Hawaii. Margarine, until the war heavily restricted by the dairy states, rose to prominence as a result of wartime rationing of butter. Coca-Cola similarly acquired national and international fame as a result of World War II. Strategic product development and acclaimed advertising campaigns that cleverly cultivated the relationship between Coca-Cola, Americanism, and patriotism, cemented its popularity both at home and abroad. By the end of the war, Coke had become an international symbol of the United States.

[See also Advertising; Coca-Cola; Cookbooks and Manuscripts: From World War I to World War II; Food and Nutrition Systems; Kitchen Gardening; Spam.]

BIBLIOGRAPHY

Anderson, Karen. *Wartime Women: Sex Roles, Family Relations, and the Status of Women during World War II*. Westport, CT: Greenwood, 1981.

Bentley, Amy. *Eating for Victory: Food Rationing and the Politics of Domesticity*. Urbana: University of Illinois Press, 1998.

Hayes, Joanne Lamb. *Grandma's Wartime Kitchen: World War II and the Way We Cooked*. New York: St. Martin's Press, 2000.

Ward, Barbara McLean, ed. *Produce and Conserve, Share and Play Square: The Grocer and the Consumer on the Home-Front Battlefield during World War II*. Portsmouth, NH: Strawberry Banke Museum, 1994.

Weiner, Mark. "Democracy, Consumer Culture, and Political Community: The Story of Coca-Cola during World War II." *Food and Foodways* 6, no. 2 (1996): 109–129.

AMY BENTLEY

Historical Overview:
World War II to the Early 1960s

During the lean years before and during World War II, Americans had to be careful about what they ate. After the war, Americans seemed to indulge in everything they had been missing for so long, particularly meat. Demand for meat was so high that farmers depleted their grain stocks to fatten their animals, whereas some even went so far as to butcher their breeding stock. In 1947, Americans set a forty-year record for meat consumption.

Although pork was always popular, the preferred meat by far was beef. Roasts, of course, were considered to be luxurious fare, perfect for special occasions or Sunday dinner, yet still prized for their leftover possibilities. But by far the most prestigious meat was steak, thick T-bones and porterhouse for no-nonsense good eating, and tender filet mignons for gourmet dining.

Less expensive was ground beef, which had become a popular, stretchable, and low-ration-point protein source during the war. A favorite way of serving ground beef was as meat loaf. One of the most common ways to serve ground beef was as hamburgers and the popular place to eat them was at drive-ins. Americans flocked to drive-ins in record numbers, gobbling up burgers, fries, shakes, and floats while watching the carhops run, or sometimes skate, from car to car.

In 1948, two drive-in owners, Richard and Maurice McDonald of San Bernardino, California, got rid of their carhops, cut their menu drastically, and opened service windows where customers had to walk up to order. They also cut the price of their hamburgers. By 1952, they were selling over 1 million hamburgers a year. In 1955, they began franchising nationally with Ray Kroc, who bought the brothers out in 1961. Many other self-service fast food restaurant chains got their start in the 1950s. Church's Chicken and Kentucky Fried Chicken both opened in 1952; Jack in the Box and Burger King opened in 1951 and 1953 respectively; Shakey's Pizza opened in 1954; Gino's opened in 1957, and Pizza Hut in 1958; and the first Dunkin' Donuts opened in 1950.

Backyard Barbecue

In 1951, the Kingsford Chemical Company took over the production of Ford charcoal briquettes, the same year that George Stephen made his first kettle-shaped covered grill, which would become the number-one grill in the country under the name Weber Kettle. In 1953, Sears, Roebuck started selling the Big Boy grill for the then fairly princely price of seventy-nine dollars. Hot dogs also saw a tremendous rise, from 750 million pounds per year in 1950 to over 1 billion pounds per year in 1960. Much of the increase was due to the popularity of the backyard barbecue. Kebabs, or skewer cookery, on the barbecue also was a passion.

A Jell-O box from the 1950s.

Side dishes of choice included garlic bread, especially easy now that aluminum foil was available; three-bean salad made with canned beans; baked beans, also mostly made with canned beans that were doctored with ketchup, mustard, and molasses; corn on the cob; and potato salad. Another popular item was the baked potato—often wrapped in foil and cooked on the side of the grill—topped off in the new California style with sour cream and chives.

America Goes International

During the 1950s, many Americans visited Europe and fell in love with French cuisine. Writers such as James Beard, Dione Lucas, and M. F. K. Fisher wrote about the food of France, as did the highbrow *Gourmet* magazine, which had gotten its start in 1941 and seemed to focus almost entirely on international cuisine. French onion soup became a popular restaurant dish, usually garnished with a raft of toasted french bread sporting a load of melted Gruyère-type cheese. Duckling à l'orange, coq au vin, and boeuf bourguignon were three popular dishes, frequently made at home by ambitious cooks. Other cooks, a little less sure of themselves, might nevertheless perk up a familiar American beef stew with a slightly daring flick of garlic or an even more daring splash of wine. The most adventurous eaters might try frogs' legs or escargots on a trip to a French restaurant.

Some of the most popular "gourmet" dishes of the period were not necessarily French, but they sounded sophisticated. Beef stroganoff first became chic in the 1940s, and by the 1950s it was considered an essential party dish, helped along by the fact that it could be made in the fashionable chafing dish. Chicken divan—made with chicken, broccoli, béchamel sauce, and hollandaise sauce—also was a favorite party dish. Tomato aspic, although not at all French, continued its vogue as a necessary adjunct to many a fancy meal.

In addition to French and quasi-French cookery, Italian cooking—meaning mostly spaghetti and meatballs and fettuccine Alfredo—was considered quite gourmet. Chinese and Japanese dishes owed a great deal to the fascination with Hawaii. Teriyaki and sukiyaki were big fads in the 1950s, the sukiyaki often being

A Campbell advertising piece distributed in Canada, 1950s.

cooked table side in the new electric skillets. Cantonese Chinese food enjoyed a huge boom: Egg foo yong, barbecued pork (*cha sui*), Chinese spareribs, almond chicken, sweet and sour pork, and Chinese-style duck were all fashionable and ubiquitous dishes.

Cocktail Parties

Whereas many Americans were serving milk with dinner and punches made from ginger ale and lime sherbet for adult parties during the 1950s, a large group was going all out for home cocktail parties. So popular were cocktail parties that a whole industry grew up around gag gifts related to drinking. Cocktails included the standard Manhattans, whiskey sours, rickeys, fizzes, Collinses, and old-fashions, but particularly popular was the martini.

Food at a cocktail party was primarily of the "nibble" variety. Popular items were Swedish meatballs, sweet and sour meatballs, Vienna sausages, *rumaki*, crackers with fancy cheeses, celery stuffed with cream cheese, salted nuts, cheese straws, and cocktail canapés. Potato chips and dips were extremely popular, especially clam dip. Also wildly popular was California dip, which apparently got its start in 1954, when an unnamed California cook took Lipton's dried onion soup mix and mixed it with sour cream. Another ubiquitous feature at cocktail parties was the cheese ball.

Changing American Home

As American families gathered nightly around the television, the need for dining areas that were adjacent to the set became apparent. Food that was easily eaten while watching television also became important. Swanson introduced its frozen TV dinners in 1953, with a box that was designed to look a television. The TV tray, a folding tray table, followed swiftly so that the family without a dining area near the television would not have to miss a single episode of their favorite show during mealtime.

As the Eisenhower postwar era ended, a new era was getting under way with the young President Kennedy and his chic wife. The Kennedys' "Camelot" presidency was widely credited with bringing a new sophistication, particularly French sophistication, to the American culinary landscape. With all their international traveling and gourmet clubs in the 1950s, Americans were ready to embrace this new lifestyle. Other forces besides the Kennedys and their French chef in the White House kitchen contributed as well.

In 1957 Craig Claiborne joined the *New York Times* as a restaurant reviewer, startling his readers with his detailed and frank reviews. In 1961 Claiborne produced *The New York Times Cook Book*, a massive, authoritative, and hugely popular compendium of mostly sophisticated recipes. That same year the first *Mastering the Art of French Cooking*, written by Julia Child with Simone Beck and Louisette Bertholle, debuted. In the following year Child's cooking show, *The French Chef*, premiered and would nearly single-handedly revolutionize American home cooking.

As the 1950s ended and the 1960s began, the split between those who were willing to cook complicated dishes from scratch and those who preferred to whip up family meals from processed ingredients was widening. In 1950, only 23 percent of married women worked outside the home. By 1960, that number had risen to nearly 32 percent. The feminist movement was also gaining momentum. In 1963, the housewife and mother of three Betty Friedan published *The Feminine Mystique*, which examines what was missing from women's, especially suburban women's, lives. Lack of time for working women was an important factor in the ready acceptance of convenience foods, but there was also a mid-century fascination with the very idea of modernity.

[See also BARBECUE; BEARD, JAMES; CHILD, JULIA; CHINESE AMERICAN FOOD; COCKTAILS; COOKBOOKS AND MANUSCRIPTS: FROM WORLD WAR II TO THE 1960S; DIPS; FRENCH INFLUENCES ON AMERICAN FOOD; HAWAIIAN FOOD; JAPANESE AMERICAN FOOD.]

BIBLIOGRAPHY

Lovegren, Sylvia. *Fashionable Food: Seven Decades of Food Fads.* New York: Macmillan, 1995.

Mariani, John. *America Eats Out: An Illustrated History of Restaurants, Taverns, Coffee Shops, Speakeasies, and Other Establishments That Have Fed Us for 350 Years.* New York: Morrow, 1991.

Schremp, Gerry. *Kitchen Culture: Fifty Years of Food Fads.* New York: Pharos Books, 1991.

SYLVIA LOVEGREN

Historical Overview:
1960s to the Present

From 1960 to 2000, the American food scene changed radically. It went from primarily home-based food preparation to the widespread custom of buying premade food for home consumption. Simultaneously, as people were less and less likely to cook at home on a regular basis, the complexity of the recipes that they did cook went up, and the appliances in the underused home kitchen began to resemble those in a restaurant. The types of foods available changed dramatically as well.

1960s and 1970s

Although homemakers had been using canned and frozen convenience foods for years by the 1960s, a new idea began to creep in during that decade: canned or frozen food was better than homemade food. It was faster, more modern, and more space age. The idea that gourmet meals could be whipped up on a moment's notice with canned or frozen ingredients took off like wildfire.

Cooking as a glamorous leisure time hobby also was a 1960s idea. One favorite of cooking hobbyists was flaming food, such as crêpes Suzette, café brûlot, and cherries jubilee. Gourmet food hobbyists did not eat only flambéed food, of course. Some of the other favorite elegant dishes of the time were green beans amandine—often canned or frozen green beans topped with almonds browned in margarine—crepes, and beef Wellington. Also in the 1960s came fondue. First there was cheese fondue. Then came beef fondue and, finally, Conrad Egli's creation, chocolate fondue. *Look* magazine called it the "new hip dip."

The interest in gourmet cooking coincided with the rise of Julia Child. Although her first cookbook came out in 1961, it was not until Child's television show aired in 1963 that her fame really took off. If Child used a new utensil or new ingredient on her show, that new item would be sold out at stores around the country the following week.

At the end of the 1960s, the health food movement, supported by baby boomer hippies, got underway, as well. Organic, locally grown foods, whole or unprocessed foods, and the exploration of vegetarian cuisines started their rise in popularity during this period.

Gourmet cooking, whether from scratch, from cans, or organic, remained fashionable in the 1970s. Quiche was hugely popular, both at brunch and as an easy, easy-to-serve, gourmet item for buffets. Italian food had long been considered quite chic and just a tad daring in the United States, but by the 1970s tomato-based sauces and traditional dishes such as spaghetti and meatballs were considered a little old-fashioned. But pasta dishes with rich and creamy white sauces became all the rage. Spaghetti carbonara with a sauce of butter, cheese, cream, and bacon was one rich dish that was very popular, as was fettuccine Alfredo, made with butter, cheese, and sometimes cream. One of the most fashionable dishes was pasta primavera.

Although Chinese food had been available and popular at restaurants in most towns across the United States for years, it became very fashionable for Westerners to cook

THE
VEG-ALL
I'M
TOO TIRED
TO COOK
BOOK

Busy consumers too tired to cook were encouraged to use Veg-All canned vegetables in this cookbooklet issued by the Larsen Company in the 1980s or 1990s.

Chinese at home during the 1970s. Tofu was just becoming widely available, and frozen pea pods were in all the supermarkets. At the same time, the wok came out of import stores and started appearing in mainstream kitchen shops.

Japanese cooking also rose in popularity during the 1970s. The first Benihana of Tokyo opened in New York City in 1964, and by the middle of the next decade Japanese steak houses had appeared across the country. With their comfort level with Japanese food rising, young Americans started venturing into sushi bars.

One of the most important developments in the 1970s was the American counterpart to the French nouvelle cuisine revolution. American nouvelle owed some of its existence to French reforms, but it was as much a product—or by-product—of the health food movement of the 1960s as well. Alice Waters opened Chez Panisse in Berkeley, California, in 1971, with the revolutionary idea of showcasing fresh, seasonal, and local ingredients.

The 1980s–1990s

By the 1980s, "California cuisine," as exemplified by Alice Waters and Jeremiah Tower in northern California and Michael McCarty and Wolfgang Puck in Los Angeles, was all the rage. This style was characterized by fresh ingredients, often with a Mediterranean or Mexican slant, light sauces, grilling (often over mesquite), beautiful yet informal presentation, and usually high prices as well. Some of the items that were characteristic of California cuisine were warm goat cheese salad, cream of corn soup, roasted whole heads of garlic served on toasts, and designer pizzas.

Culinary Associations

Before 1975, roughly, there were few organizations, associations, or venues where professional chefs and others interested in the serious study of food could meet and discuss ideas. This changed in large part because of the explosion in the number of people needed to manage an expanding food-service industry, which in turn led to the growth of a national network of professional cooking schools to meet the demands of that industry. As a result, professionals found a need to form a variety of associations with a variety of purposes. Some of them are listed here.

American Culinary Federation
10 San Bartola Drive
St. Augustine, FL 32086
904-824-4468
800-624-9458
Fax: 904-824-4758
www.acfchefs.net
Culinarians dedicated to promoting their profession through education, apprenticeship, and certification. Local chapters throughout the country.

The American Institute of Wine and Food (AIWF)
304 West Liberty Street, Suite 201
Louisville, KY 40202
502-992-1022
Fax: 502-589-3602
www.aiwf.com
Educational organization devoted to improving the appreciation and understanding of food and drink.

American Personal Chef Association
4572 Delaware Street
San Diego, CA 92116
800-644-8389
Fax: 619-294-2436
www.personalchef.com

Association for Living History, Farm, and Agricultural Museums (ALHFAM)
8774 Route 45 NW
North Bloomfield, OH 44450
http://www.alhfam.org
ALHFAM is the museum organization for those involved in living historical farms, agricultural museums, outdoor museums of history and folklife, and those museums—large and small—that use living history programming.

The Association for the Study of Food and Society (ASFS)
ASFS is a multidisciplinary international organization dedicated to exploring the complex relationships between food, culture, and society. Its members, who approach the study of food from numerous disciplines in the humanities, social sciences, and sciences as well as in the world of food beyond the academy, draw on a wide range of theoretical and practical approaches and seek to promote discussions about food that transgress traditional boundaries. Search the Internet for current address and membership information.

Food and Culinary Professionals
P. O. Box 46998
Seattle, WA 98146
http://www.foodculinaryprofs.org/index.htm
FCP is a Dietetic Practice Group of the American Dietetic Association whose members are committed to developing food expertise throughout the profession of dietetics. *Tastings*, a newsletter, is published quarterly.

Foodways Section of the American Folklore Society
American Folklore Society
4350 North Fairfax Drive, Suite 640
Arlington, VA 22203
703-528-1902
http://www.afsnet.org
Publishes *Digest: An Interdisciplinary Study of Food and Foodways*

International Association of Culinary Professionals (IACP)
304 West Liberty Street, Suite 201
Louisville, KY 40202-3011

502-581-9786
Fax: 502-589-3602
http://www.iacp.com
Association provides continuing education and development for its members who are engaged in the areas of culinary education, communication, or in the preparation of food and drink. This organization has a food history section.

The James Beard Foundation
The Beard House
167 West Twelfth Street
New York, NY 10011
212-627-2308
http://www.jamesbeard.org
James Beard is recognized by many as the father of American gastronomy. The foundation celebrates the country's culinary artists, provides scholarships and educational opportunities, serves as a resource for the industry, and offers members the opportunity to enjoy the delights of fine dining.

Radcliffe Culinary Friends.
Schlessinger Library
10 Garden Street
Cambridge, MA 02138.
Publishes *Radcliffe Culinary Times*, which often has articles by and appealing to food historians.

Research Chefs Association
5775 Peachtree-Dunwoody Road
Building G, Suite 500
Atlanta, GA 30342
404-252-3663
Fax: 404-252-0774
http://www.culinology.com
This is the leading professional community for food research and development. Its members are the pioneers of the discipline of culinology, the blending of culinary arts and the science of food.

San Francisco Professional Food Society (SFPFS)
268 Bush Street, Number 2715
San Francisco, CA 94104
415-442-1999
Fax: 415-358-5960
http://www.sfpfs.com

A forum for food and beverage professionals to come together to exchange information and promote social interaction.

Slow Food U.S.A.
434 Broadway, Sixth Floor
New York, NY 10013
212-965-5640
Fax: 212-226-0672
http://www.slowfoodusa.org
Slow Food U.S.A. is an educational organization dedicated to stewardship of the land and ecologically sound food production; to the revival of the kitchen and the table as centers of pleasure, culture, and community; to the invigoration and proliferation of regional, seasonal culinary traditions; and to living a slower and more harmonious rhythm of life. The Italian association was founded in 1986 and the international movement was founded in Paris in 1989.

Southern Foodways Alliance
Center for the Study of Southern Culture
Barnard Observatory
University of Mississippi
Oxford, MS 38677
662-915-5993
http://www.southern foodways.com/index.shtml
Established in 1977 at the University of Mississippi, the center has become a focal point for innovative education and research by promoting scholarship on every aspect of Southern culture.

The kiwi became a star attraction in new American cooking, and consumption of the fruit increased sevenfold from 1980 to 1985. Other exotics that became popular during that period, many of them introduced by Fried's Produce in California, were the passion fruit, mango, star fruit, radicchio, blood oranges, enokidake mushrooms, blue potatoes, mesclun, arugula, Tahitian vanilla, lemongrass, and green peppercorns.

The next trend to hit was southwestern cooking. This style included Cal-Mex, Tex-Mex, and Santa Fe styles. Beans, corn (especially blue corn), chilies, cilantro, jicama, limes, and squash blossoms all become fashionable ingredients, and everyone seemed to have a special recipe for fresh salsa. In addition to the California and southwestern food crazes, foodies went wild for Cajun cuisine in the 1980s. One of the reasons was the Louisiana chef Paul Prudhomme, who in March 1980 created his signature dish, blackened redfish, which actually led to the fish being placed on the endangered species list. Cajun-style restaurants opened across the country, offering such dishes as duck gumbo or spot prawn jambalaya.

Italian food became even more popular than it had been in the 1970s. Particularly chic were colored pastas—tinted with tomato or spinach, or even such as exotics as beets, saffron, herbs, or squid ink. Pasta salads, which seem to be more an American than an Italian invention, also became a huge fad. Polenta cast off its humble beginnings as food for poor people and was served at nearly every trendy restaurant in the 1980s. The simple foods of Tuscany were very fashionable, and recipes for Tuscan beans seemed to be on every magazine cover.

On the dessert cart, anything made with chocolate could be found. Chocolate decadence cake was extremely fashionable, as were chocolate truffles, fruits dipped in chocolate, and tortes and cakes covered in chocolate ganache. Double-chocolate brownies were a common treat, even at expensive restaurants. White chocolate also became a common ingredient in trendy desserts.

At the end of the 1980s, with the sharp drop in the stock market, American "comfort food" or "retro food" was In: fried chicken, mashed potatoes and gravy, meat loaf, Jell-O salads, grilled cheese sandwiches, lemon meringue pie, and chocolate cake. Yet fewer and fewer Americans were eating food cooked at home from scratch. The microwave oven was finally becoming a real presence in the American kitchen, and over 760 microwavable food products were introduced in 1987 alone. By 1989, over 40 percent of American families reported bringing home a complete meal twice a month or more.

Hot chilies became very popular in the early 1990s and "mouth surfing," as eating the hottest chilies was known, became something of a sport. The incendiary habañero chili, over one

Culinary History Groups

Until the Culinary Historians of Boston was founded in the early 1980s, there were few opportunities for those interested in the history of food or the culinary arts to meet. Some of these early food historians were chefs, such as Louis Szathmary, who operated the Bakery Restaurant in Chicago, and Barbara Ketchum Wheaton, the author of *Savoring the Past*, who worked outside the food field but had an abiding interest in all things culinary.

During the early 1980s, word spread about this new Boston group, which held their monthly meetings in one of the residence halls at Harvard University in Cambridge. Other groups soon sprang up around the country and outside the United States. In 2004, the Culinary Historians of Tasmania announced their formation.

The following is a list of known organizations in the United States. The Internet is the best place to start a search for a current contact person, or one can go to http://www.foodhistorynews.com for an up-to-date list of culinary history groups.

Culinary Historians of Ann Arbor
Ann Arbor, Michigan
Founded in 1983 by Jan Longone, a well-known food historian and dealer in antiquarian culinary publications. The group also publishes a quarterly newsletter.

Culinary Historians of Boston
Cambridge, Massachusetts
http://www.culinary.org/chb/index.htm
A bimonthly newsletter is published; meetings are monthly.

Culinary Historians of Chicago
Chicago, Illinois
http://www.culinaryhistorians.org
Founded in 1993 as a nonprofit educational organization committed to the study of the history of food and drink in human cultures. The members are from a wide range of competencies: from everyday cooks or amateur historians to those in academia.

Foodways Group of Austin
Austin, Texas
Founded by the food writer Alice Arndt, cofounder of the Houston Culinary Historians, and Glenn Mack of the Culinary Academy of Austin. The purpose of this group is for local food lovers to explore food and foodways of the past and present, in Texas and around the world.

New Orleans Culinary History Group
New Orleans, Louisiana
http://www.tulane.edu/~wclib/culinary.html

Culinary Historians of Hawaii
Honolulu, Hawaii

Historic Foodways Society of the Delaware Valley
The society began in October 1994 with a gathering of more than thirty people interested in preserving the rich foodways culture of the communities along the Delaware River. The organization is devoted to exploring the rich, diverse culinary heritage of the region including southeastern New York, Pennsylvania, New Jersey, Delaware, and Maryland's Eastern Shore.

Culinary Historians of New York
New York, New York
www.culinaryhistoriansny.org

Culinary Historians of Southern California (CHSC)
Los Angeles, California
http://www.lapl.org/central/science.html#Culinary
CHSC was founded in 1995 for scholars, cooks, food writers, nutritionists, collectors, students, and others interested in the study of culinary history and gastronomy.

Culinary Historians of Washington, DC
Washington, District of Columbia
http://www.chowdc.org/index.html
Their newsletter, *ChoWLine*, is published nine times each year. It contains monthly reports on the organization's meetings and provides information on upcoming meetings, food-related events, publications, and films.

Mediterranean Culinary Historians of Houston (MCHH)
Houston, Texas
MCHH was founded to merge the growing academic field of culinary history with popular interest in Mediterranean cuisine and diet.

JOSEPH M. CARLIN

hundred times hotter on the Scoville index than the jalapeño, became extremely fashionable, but not everyone was able to eat it. Hot chilies appeared in salsas, curries, chutneys, and sambals, all of which became ubiquitous relishes. Caribbean cooking also became popular, particularly Jamaican foods, such as the very hot and spicy "jerk" " chicken.

One of the most controversial fads of the 1990s was so-called fusion cuisine. Americans had always been fusion cooks, melding the techniques and recipes they brought from the old country with the ingredients they found in the New World. But in the 1980s, adventurous chefs started blending French and Japanese ingredients and techniques to produce intentionally shocking tastes. By the 1990s, the idea of deliberately mixing cuisines was common even in chain restaurants, resulting in such odd sounding dishes as Szechuan chicken alfredo.

Expensive professional grade stoves and refrigerators became very popular in the 1990s. Yet it was not unusual for these appliances to be used only for special occasions. As willing as they were to try new and unusual foods, many American families were not cooking those foods themselves. By the end of the 1990s, nearly 70 percent of women were working outside the home. The number of households using microwave ovens grew from 8 percent to over 80 percent. Many supermarkets cut back on the actual "groceries" they stocked and expanded their lines of ready-to-eat foods. And although 74 percent of grocery shoppers in 2001 indicated that they had a home-cooked meal at least three times a week, a rising proportion of "home-cooked" food was really "home-heated" convenience food. It seems likely that the number of from-scratch, homemade meals will only decline as Americans move through the twenty-first century.

[See also CAJUN AND CREOLE FOOD; CARIBBEAN INFLUENCES ON AMERICAN FOOD; CHILD, JULIA; CHINESE AMERICAN FOOD; COCKTAILS; DIETS, FAD; FAST FOOD; FATS AND OILS; FRENCH INFLUENCES ON AMERICAN FOOD; ITALIAN AMERICAN FOOD; JAPANESE AMERICAN FOOD; JELL-O; KITCHEN GARDENING; KIWIS; MEXICAN AMERICAN FOOD; MICROWAVE OVENS; ORGANIC FOOD; ORGANIC GARDENING.]

BIBLIOGRAPHY
Lovegren, Sylvia. *Fashionable Food: Seven Decades of Food Fads.* New York: Macmillan, 1995.
Mariani, John. *The Dictionary of American Food and Drink.* New York: Hearst Books, 1994.
Schremp, Gerry. *Kitchen Culture: Fifty Years of Food Fads.* New York: Pharos Books, 1991.
SYLVIA LOVEGREN

Historiography

For the past fifty years, American Foodways have been examined by historians in works such as Richard Osborn Cummings's *The American and His Food: A History of Food*

Habits in the United States (1946) and Richard J. Hooker's *Food and Drink in America: A History* (1981), both of which remain excellent general resources for American culinary history.

Since the 1950s, a major change has emerged in the approach to food history. In France, the *Annales* school (named after the journal *Annales: économies, sociétés, civilisations*) criticized traditional historians who focused only on high politics and events at the expense of long-term historical structures and dynamics. The *Annales* school also believed that historians should supplement traditional historical methods with those from the social sciences. Their emphasis on material culture meant that food was an appropriate and significant topic for historical investigation. The *Annales* school influenced American historians and several American historians have focused specifically on food.

This approach to food history has expanded rapidly since the mid-1990s. Individual professors have incorporated culinary topics into traditional courses and scholars have formed groups, such as the Association for the Study of Food and Society, to examine particular aspects of food. The result of this activity has been the rapid expansion of culinary history as an academic topic. This growth is reflected in the increasing number of culinary courses and interdisciplinary programs, such as those offered by the Department of Nutrition and Food Studies at New York University and Boston University's Master of Liberal Arts in Gastronomy. Centers, organizations, programs, and conferences have encouraged academic research into food and drink, and numerous articles have appeared in academic journals. Likewise, the number of food-related theses and dissertations has increased and the number of books published on related topics has mushroomed. Several university presses, such as those at Oxford, Columbia, Cambridge, University of Illinois, and University of California, have developed extensive lists of scholarly works on food.

Content and Methods

Culinary historians, like other scholars exploring the broader field of food studies, have focused on different contents, explored different culinary processes, and employed different methods. Some historians have focused on culinary ingredients or products, for example, Virginia Scott Jenkins's research into the history of bananas. Others, such as Ken Albala in *Eating Right in the Renaissance* (2002), have examined particular historical periods, while others have focused on histories of national cuisines, such as Richard Osborn Cummings's *The American and His Food: A History of Food Habits in the United States* (1946) and Richard J. Hooker's *Food and Drink in America: A History* (1981). Still others have focused on specific topics, such as Alison J. Clarke's *Tupperware: The Promise of Plastic in 1950s America* (1999).

The methods used in culinary history include the traditional academic ones of observation, text analysis, linguistics, botany, zoology, and DNA studies, travelers' putative eyewitness reports, self-reports of individuals from within a culture, historical records, and archaeological evidence among others. But there are also methods unique to culinary history, such as actually preparing the recipe, whether written, orally communicated, or inferred from archaeological, literary, and other primary sources. The cookbook, a collection of written recipes, is an important manifestation of culinary history, but until recently it was rarely mentioned in traditional academic discourse. In many ways, the recipe itself is a means by which to explore the past. Much is to be learned from the past by trying to re-create it.

American Journals, Newsletters, and Reenactors

Several American culinary history newsletters and journals have been inaugurated since 1984. As the twenty-first century opened, journals with culinary history content were emerging, the most important of which were *Gastronomica: The Journal of Food and Culture* published by the University of California Press; *Food History News* published by Sandra Oliver in Isleboro, Maine; and *Flavor and Fortune*, a quarterly publication of the Institute of the Science and Art of Chinese Cuisine. Likewise, culinary history organizations had begun to thrive in many American communities, such as Ann Arbor, Austin, Boston, Chicago, Houston, Los Angeles, New York, Philadelphia, San Francisco, and Washington, DC.

Yet another segment of the culinary history field are the "practitioners" and "reenactors" who participate in culinary history programs, such as those sponsored by members of the Association for Living History, Farm and Agricultural Museums (ALHFAM). They engage in preserving the culinary heritage of the past by attempting to duplicate recipes or food practices of different historical periods.

Food museums have opened throughout the world, such as the Wyandot Popcorn Museum in Marion, Ohio. Some museums have taken to the Internet and have become virtual museums, such as the New York Food Museum. Food has also become an important topic for many traditional museums. Several major television series focusing on the history of food and drink have been aired, generating wide popular interest.

What has emerged is a broad-based, interdisciplinary, diverse field of culinary history that counts scholars from a variety of disciplines, such as sociology, anthropology, women's studies, religion, political science, geography, environmental studies, culinary arts, psychology, ethnobotany, literary criticism, food technologists, and those sciences related to health and nutrition. In addition to academics, the field embraces professional chefs, food writers, librarians, independent scholars, historical reenactors, cookbook authors, and just plain old foodies.

[*See also* HISTORICAL DINING REENACTMENT; HISTORICAL OVERVIEW.]

BIBLIOGRAPHY

Bitting, Katherine. *Gastronomic Bibliography*. San Francisco: Halle Cordis Composing Room and Trade Freeroom, 1939.

Brown, Eleanor, and Bob Brown. *Culinary America: Cookbooks Published in the Cities and Towns of the United States of America during the Years from 1860 through 1960*. New York: Roving Eye Press, 1961.

Cagle, William R., and Lisa Killion Stafford, *American Books on Food and Drink*. New Castle, DE: Oak Knoll Press, 1998.

Cook, Margaret. *America's Charitable Cooks: A Bibliography of Fund-Raising Cook Books Published in the United States (1861–1915)*. Kent, OH: np, 1971.

Lincoln, Waldo. *American Cookery Books 1742–1860*. Worcester, MA: The Society, 1929.

Lowenstein, Eleanor. *Bibliography of American Cookery Books, 1742–1860*. Worcester, MA: American Antiquarian Society, 1972.

Smith, Andrew F. "False Memories: The Invention of Culinary Fakelore and Food Fallacies." In *Proceedings of the Oxford Symposium on Food and Cookery 2000*, edited by Harlan Walker. Devon, UK: Prospect Books, 2001.

ANDREW F. SMITH

H. J. Heinz Company

In 1869 at the age of twenty-five, Henry J. Heinz helped launch a pickle and horseradish preserving company in Sharpsburg, Pennsylvania. The business expanded quickly, but when the depression hit in 1875, the company went into bankruptcy. Two months later, the company emerged from the ashes under the nominal control of Henry's brother and cousin. Under Henry's direction, the business thrived. By 1888, Heinz had paid off the debts incurred during the bankruptcy, bought out his brother and cousin, and named the firm H. J. Heinz Company. The company rapidly expanded operations and distribution facilities throughout the United States.

Heinz expanded its product line to include sauerkraut, vinegar, pepper sauce, chili sauce, apple butter, baked beans, tomato soup, sweet pickles, pickled onions, and pickled cauliflower. Around the turn of the twentieth century, H. J. Heinz selected the slogan "57 Varieties" because he liked the number fifty-seven. The slogan was similar to those selected by other companies at the time, although it did not reflect the firm's product line—Heinz produced more than fifty-seven products.

Although Heinz had made the condiment since 1873, ketchup was initially not among the company's more important product lines. This status changed during the 1880s. Heinz began patenting ketchup

A commemorative booklet issued by the H. J. Heinz Company in 1926.

newspapers during the early twentieth century and later advertised on radio. Advertisements and cookery pamphlets contained recipes for the use of Heinz ketchup that were supplied by the Heinz home economics department.

With the launch of aggressive advertising campaigns by Hunt's and Del Monte after World War II, Heinz's market share for ketchup began to fade, and Heinz's U.S. profits fell to an all-time low, leading Heinz executives to greatly increase their advertising budget. Billboards, prevalent during the preceding decades, were abandoned. Half-minute color television commercials became the company's primary advertising vehicle. One of the most innovative commercials featured a ketchup-pouring race, which highlighted the phrase "thick and rich," the narrator commenting, "Heinz loses, Heinz always loses." The second commercial was "the plate test" in which no fluid ran out of the bottle because Heinz ketchup was thicker and richer than the other brand. These commercials were successful. By 1971, the Heinz market share had rebounded to 34 percent. It continued to increase, and in the first few years of the twenty-first century, the Heinz market share exceeded 50 percent.

Globalization and Diversification

Almost from its inception, Heinz was extremely interested in making sales outside the United States. Heinz regularly displayed its products at international food exhibitions. Before the end of the nineteenth century, Heinz sold ketchup extensively in Canada and the United Kingdom and had established agencies in Antwerp, Belgium, Sydney, Australia, and Bermuda. By 1899, new agencies had been established in Mexico City, Mexico, Liverpool, England, and the Canadian cities of Toronto and Montreal. By 1907, Heinz was shipping products in five-gallon cans and forty-six-gallon wooden casks to England, Australia, New Zealand, South Africa, South America, Europe, Japan, and China. In 1910, Heinz built its first factory outside the United States in Leamington, Ontario, Canada. Heinz has continued to expand abroad. Headquartered in Pittsburgh, Pennsylvania, in 2004 Heinz had two hundred major operations worldwide.

Like other food companies, Heinz has diversified. It is one of the world's leading marketers of branded foods. In addition to the Heinz brand, the company operates twenty other brand names. In 1963 Heinz acquired StarKist, which controls 50 percent of the tuna market. Ore-Ida was acquired in 1965 and commands 45 percent of the packaged potato market. Other major Heinz brands include Weight Watchers Foods and Boston Market. The 9 Lives and Kibbles 'n Bits operations make Heinz one of the largest pet food manufacturers. Heinz is also a major

manufacturer of baby food. In 2002 Heinz spun off StarKist, 9 Lives, and other subsidiaries to Del Monte Foods Company. Heinz produces more than five thousand different products annually. Its 2001 revenue was $9.43 billion, making Heinz one of the world's largest food companies.

Heinz's flagship product continues to be ketchup. Heinz is the largest ketchup manufacturer, producing more than 1 billion ounces per year. Heinz has continued innovations of its ketchup, including the development of a plastic squeeze bottle for home use and a single-serve container for commercial use. During the late 1990s, Heinz introduced alternative-color varieties of its popular condiment, bringing out EZ Squirt green ketchup, which was followed by purple ketchup. These products made headlines around the world, and they captured the imagination of children, who are the main users of ketchup.

[**See also** ADVERTISING; ADVERTISING COOKBOOKLETS AND RECIPES; CANNING AND BOTTLING; CONDIMENTS; DEL MONTE; FOOD MARKETING; KETCHUP; PICKLES; PICKLING; PURE FOOD AND DRUG ACT; TUNA.]

BIBLIOGRAPHY

Alberts, Robert C. *The Good Provider: H. J. Heinz and His 57 Varieties.* Boston: Houghton Mifflin, 1973.

Dienstag, Eleanor Foa. *In Good Company: 125 Years at the Heinz Table (1869–1994).* New York: Warner, 1994.

Smith, Andrew F. *Pure Ketchup: The History of America's National Condiment.* Columbia: University of South Carolina Press, 1996.

ANDREW F. SMITH

Hoagie

Sandwiches based on Italian rolls or French bread and filled with multiple layers of ingredients are known by various names throughout the United States, including hoagie, hero, submarine, Italian sandwich, grinder, bomber, torpedo, rocket, spuckie, wedge, and zeppelin. These made-to-order sandwiches originally consisted of cold cuts, cheese, and lettuce garnished with a choice of tomatoes, onion, pickles, or peppers and dressed with mayonnaise, oil, or mustard. Fillings were later expanded to include other choices, such as tuna, meatballs, sandwich steaks, and various vegetarian options.

The hoagie is the earliest sandwich of this type. Legend credits its creation to the Philadelphia sandwich shop proprietor Al De Palma, who introduced the sandwich as the "hoggie" in 1936. De Palma reportedly chose the name after witnessing a friend devour a large sandwich and thinking that he was a hog to eat it all once. As competitors in the Philadelphia area copied his sandwich and sold it under various names, including hoagie, hogie, and horgy, De Palma responded by proclaiming himself "The Original Hoggie

---

COLUMN 1 (continued from earlier):

bottles in 1882. By 1890, Heinz had hit on what became the world-famous combination of keystone label, neckband, screw cap, and octagonal bottle, although he continued to explore other shapes and labels. Soon after the turn of the twentieth century, Heinz had become the largest tomato ketchup producer in America, by 1905 producing more than 5 million bottles of ketchup. By 1908, Heinz ketchup sales had reached $2.5 million, a phenomenal amount by the standards of the day.

Before 1903, Heinz ketchup was medium-bodied with average acidity. Like most other manufacturers, Heinz added coal-tar coloring as well as benzoic and salicylic acids to ketchup. Also like most of its competitors, Heinz used nontomato ingredients in ketchup. To meet new state pure-food laws, Heinz began experimenting with canning techniques that did not include preservatives. When the Pure Food and Drug Act passed in June 1906, Heinz decided to produce all its foods without preservatives.

Advertising

A major reason for Heinz's success was advertising. As early as 1888 the company was printing small cards promoting its products. Heinz also displayed products at fairs all over the United States, setting up large booths. In 1899 in Atlantic City, New Jersey, Heinz built an ocean pier that featured cooking demonstrations, free samples, and lectures. Heinz placed advertisements on streetcars and billboards and soon became one of the largest outdoor advertisers in the United States. Heinz began advertising in magazines and

Man." By 1950, the various spellings started to disappear, and the sandwich became commonly known as the hoagie. It was declared the "Official Sandwich of Philadelphia" in 1992.

Meanwhile, word of the hoagie spread, and by 1939 New York had its own version of the sandwich. Known as the hero, it was popular among visitors to Coney Island. Around 1940, the submarine became the local rendition of the hoagie in restaurants along the mid-Atlantic coast.

As the popularity of these large, multilayered sandwiches increased throughout the United States during the 1950s and 1960s, they became known by different names on a regional basis. Hoagie is used in Pennsylvania and New Jersey, whereas in New York City they are referred to as heroes. In Maine, they are known as Italian sandwiches, and in Massachusetts, Rhode Island, Connecticut, and Vermont they are usually called grinders. Spuckie is a term for the sandwich unique to the Boston area. Submarine is commonly used throughout the United States, whereas other names, including bomber, rocket, wedge, zeppelin, and torpedo, can be found in various areas throughout the country.

[**See also** ITALIAN AMERICAN FOOD; SANDWICHES.]

BIBLIOGRAPHY

Mercuri, Becky. *Sandwiches That You Will Like*. Pittsburgh, PA: WQED, 2002.

BECKY MERCURI

Home Economics

In the late nineteenth century, industrialization and urbanization placed the American home in a state of flux. To guide homemakers through this transition, a group of mainly middle-class women launched an educational reform movement. In 1899, they organized a meeting in Lake Placid, New York, to propose the term "home economics" for a new field of study that would enable homemakers to perform domestic work more efficiently and manage household budgets more economically. In 1909, this group established the American Home Economics Association (AHEA) to promote a vision of private family life that was predicated on a public role for this new group of women professionals.

Food was a central, but not exclusive, concern for home economists. All household activities—including cleaning, managing the family budget, and even child rearing—represented opportunities for these women to model the home on the new industrial order and infuse it with moral ideals. Still, the selection, purchase, and storage of foodstuffs, and the preparation and serving of meals, received special emphasis in home economists' quest for "right living" based on rationality. In part because food occupied the single largest expense in all but the most

generous family budgets, the movement's founder, Ellen Swallow Richards, and her colleagues understood the American diet as a focal point for reforming American domestic life.

New findings in chemistry, physiology, and bacteriology provided not only reassuring answers but also opportunities for many of these women to pursue scientific careers. Although the specific instruction varied according to the individual teacher and her audience, most home economists emphasized the quantifiable aspects of foods and their constituent parts rather than taste and pleasure. Efficiency in fueling the human body, economy in purchasing ingredients, and sanitation in preservation were the main goals of the home economists' lessons about food. By incorporating these values into a new understanding of a homemaker's responsibility for her family's food consumption, home economists helped ordinary women navigate the expanding body of scientific and technological information about food in the twentieth century.

Scientific Cookery and Social Reform

The movement got its start after the Civil War, when reformers fastened on the diet as the means of combating the social problems of the day: poverty, crime, intemperance, and labor unrest. Domestic scientists established urban cooking schools in many northeastern cities to promote economical and healthful ways of preparing food among immigrant women. At the New England Kitchen in Boston and at the Women's Laboratory at the Massachusetts Institute of Technology, Richards taught women to consider food in scientific terms. She devoted much of her career to studying the chemical processes involved in cooking and digesting food, and trained a cohort of younger women who went on to become administrators and professors of home economics departments at the new state land-grant colleges. In these programs, home economists served as important interpreters of nutritional science to an expanding body of female students. In addition, Richards's chemical analyses of food adulteration and water contamination drove many early home economists to campaign for government regulation of food safety and to lobby for the passage of the Pure Food and Drug Act of 1906.

World War I was a watershed for home economists and their authority as experts on nutrition and food. The U.S. Food Administration, established to send food to the American military and the Allied civilian population in Europe, enlisted home economists to promote food conservation and popularize new ideas about nutrition. Home economics professors, teachers, and students developed recipes that gave precise definitions of meatless meats, sugarless sweets, and bread without wheat. They

A Home Economics class at the Horace Mann Institute, Tulsa, Oklahoma, 1917.

also introduced the concept of food value and the principle of substituting one food for another. By emphasizing each food's contribution to an individual's diet, these recipes showed homemakers that substitutes were not only possible but also healthy. Through hundreds of cookbooks, pamphlets, newspaper and magazine articles, and lesson plans—as well as live cooking and canning demonstrations—home economists brought scientific cookery into the cultural mainstream.

Status and Expertise

Home economists' enhanced wartime reputation as food experts enabled them to secure postwar places in higher education and in the agricultural research establishment. The growth of home economics departments in state land-grant colleges and a few private universities and the creation of an Office of Home Economics in 1915 and, by 1923, a Bureau of Home Economics, inside the U.S. Department of Agriculture further supplied home economists with institutional contexts for building a research program around consumption, with a considerable emphasis on food.

From within these institutions, home economists converted the subjects of food and nutrition into an academic study. As a group, home economists concentrated their efforts on defining an *applied* science of nutrition that they could call their own. This broad field injected an element of empirical study and science into just about every aspect of food and its use in the home. Nutritional food values, food preservation and storage, dietary planning and budgeting, and recipe development—investigated according to the principles of chemistry, bacteriology, and physics—all had a place in home economists' nutritional research agenda.

Nutrition Education as Social Service

By 1940, home economics had acquired a distinctive place in the curriculum at four-year and junior colleges, high schools, and elementary schools. Mature homemakers in rural areas received informal instruction from home demonstration agents through

A poster produced by the Illinois WPA Art Project publicizes evening classes in Winnetka, Illinois, 1941.

served on these committees, where they played a key role in developing the first official recommended daily allowances (RDAs) of vitamins, carbohydrates, and calories, and translated these dietary guidelines into terms that homemakers could understand and use.

Product Development and Promotion
An elite group of home economists found jobs in the expanding consumer product industries of the 1920s and 1930s. As early as the 1880s, domestic scientists had provided consulting services for a number of companies, but many food processors stepped up the practice during World War I and relied on home economists to ally their brand-name products to the patriotic cause of food conservation. After the war, corporate managers created a more permanent place for home economists because they saw them as a means of getting closer to female consumers. Home economists' dual identity—as women and as scientists—perfectly suited the needs of these managers. By 1940, the AHEA's business section included more than six hundred members working as permanent employees in more than four hundred private enterprises, including utility companies, women's magazines, restaurants, manufacturers of household equipment, and retail firms. These women helped to correlate supply and demand for many elements of the modern kitchen.

Home economists also helped corporate managers to understand consumers' views of their products. Before marketing and market research emerged as distinct functions of business management after World War II, home economists gathered information about consumer preferences and shared them with corporate managers. By testing products from the user's perspective, home economists also contributed regularly to the development of manufactured food products as well as kitchen appliances and other cooking utensils.

Expertise under Fire
Beginning in the 1960s, home economists came under fire from a wide range of social critics. Feminists accused the movement of chaining women to the domestic sphere; consumer advocates accused its members of selling out to corporate powers. Food writers criticized home economists for overemphasizing nutrition and neglecting the taste of food and blamed them for the poor state of the American diet. Although subsequent generations of home economists eventually joined the newer trends and altered collective priorities, the failure of the profession to keep up with changing values in the 1960s and 1970s left an indelible mark.

Throughout the twentieth century, home economists used their authority as food experts to exert a powerful influence over what families ate. Through education,

the agricultural extension service. In addition, the Bureau of Home Economics disseminated many of the results of its studies directly to women through government bulletins, written correspondence, and *Aunt Sammy's Radio Program*.

National emergencies gave home economists the opportunity to provide important social service in times of need. During the Great Depression and World War II, food was a public issue. Economic hardship and national preparedness triggered renewed interest in healthy eating and food

conservation on the part of government leaders as well as many homemakers—particularly middle-class women who had the time and money to do the planning and work required.

When the military draft during World War II revealed that many potential soldiers were unfit for service because of malnutrition, the National Research Council established committees to determine dietary needs and to explore ways of adjusting food habits to meet those needs. Leading home economists and nutrition experts research, and the development and promotion of manufactured food products and appliances, home economists played a key role in defining the modern kitchen. By framing food in terms of health, economy, efficiency, and cleanliness and by teaching women how to achieve these goals, they made nutritious eating—along with packaged food products, gas and electric cooking, mechanical refrigeration, and cooking by the book—a hallmark of middle-class identity.

[See also Betty Crocker; Cookbooks and Manuscripts: From World War I to World War II; Department of Agriculture, United States; Ethnic Food; Food and Nutrition Systems; Health Food; Historical Overview: Victorian America to World War I; Lincoln, Mrs.; New England; Richards, Ellen; Vitamins.]

Carolyn M. Goldstein

Homemade Remedies

Until concrete scientific advances began to occur in the late nineteenth century, professional medical treatment in America was frequently unavailable and when available was ineffectual and occasionally brutal and dangerous. By necessity and choice, many Americans preferred to treat illnesses and injuries at home. Many home medical practitioners were women who concocted remedies and potions with herbs from their gardens. Knowledge of such preparations and their proper administration were considered an essential part of a girl's overall education. The first settlers from England and the Continent were well versed in herbal remedies, with recipes handed down from mother to daughter, or found in popular household books, such as Culpepper's *Complete Herbal and English Physician* (1652). Healing herbal plants were cultivated alongside vegetables in kitchen gardens and considered just as important to a family's survival, harvested to be brewed into teas and soups; mixed in with oats for fortifying gruels; and steeped for use as medicinal soaks and first-aid ointments.

Invalid Cooking

The reality of American life, whether in the fast-growing cities, or out across the vast plains, was that, for rich and poor alike, disease was rampant. In addition to remedies found in published books, family household accounts and individual diaries often listed them. A fine example of these personal records are those left behind by the wealthy New York Van Rensselaer family women, who wrote out cures for everything from sore throats (rue steeped in rum) and earaches (a roasted onion pressed, still warm, to the afflicted ear), to frozen limbs (rub with warm goose grease). Other common household remedies included black cherry bark, blackberries, allspice, and rhubarb to alleviate diarrhea and dysentery; turpentine, camphor, laudanum, and peppermint to battle cholera.

Separate from these cures, however, was a repertoire of recipes, often known as "invalid cooking," that were expressly used to feed and restore the sick and convalescent and were listed in almost every cookbook printed throughout the nineteenth and early twentieth centuries. Examples of these recipes include wine whey (white wine mixed with boiling water to form curds); lightly spiced oatmeal gruels, saps (milk toast), and beef teas (essentially the bloody drippings of a flank steak); Irish moss puddings, wine-infused jellies, and flavorful broths. Directions for making and serving these dishes were precise. To lessen any chance of contamination, these dishes were made in small batches from the freshest ingredients available. Patients were served small amounts at regular intervals, and the tray on which the dishes were brought to the sickroom were to be arranged, as one author noted, as "a dainty Dresden watercolor of delicate hues and harmonious tints."

The Invasion of Quackery

Although invalid cooking, in itself, may have been beneficial to patients, most homemade remedies were not. This, however, did not stop the creation (and incredible prosperity) of an industry whose purpose was to promote dubious—and often dangerous—patented medicines to the gullible public. What was particularly American about this development was its convergence of commercialism, democratic individualism, entertainment, and even religious fervor.

Medicine and tent shows crisscrossed the country, providing the populace with lively entertainment in the form of instant cures for everything from baldness and lameness to cancer—all by drinking a potion or submitting to electric shocks. Drug preparations could be bought at general stores or from mail-order catalogs. Some were even prescribed and dispensed by doctors who found them convenient and certainly no less damaging than common medical procedures. Many of these preparations were a corruption of old recipes—mixtures of herbs and roots—fortified with hefty measures of alcohol or narcotics (and sometimes both). Although users certainly felt better for a time, these elixirs produced their own ills—poisoning, addiction, and even death. And yet patented medicines proliferated, encouraged by outlandish advertising campaigns, and by the fact that they were often cheaper and less invasive than a doctor's visit. With no laws to hinder them, medicine companies made vast fortunes promoting such brands as Lydia Pinkham (for female complaints); Parker's Tonic (which claimed to cure consumption and asthma as it rejuvenated blood); and Belle tablets (for dyspepsia).

Pure Food and Drug Act of 1906

The regulation of patented medicine came about through the efforts of muckraking journalists who called attention to the dangers of these potions, which resulted in public pressure on Congress. In 1906, a reluctant Congress passed the landmark Pure Food and Drug Act, giving birth to the Food and Drug Administration (FDA) and to laws requiring the strict governance of the food and drug industries. The act also forbade anyone from obtaining prescriptions except from a licensed doctor and required warning labels on all habit-forming medicines. In addition, all medicines had to be certified by the FDA, a certification that most patented medicines failed, and consequently most were banned from the market.

Homemade remedies, and even some patented medicines, survive in the twenty-first century, protected by cultural and ethnic preferences. Since 1960, there has been renewed interest in natural and Native American medicines, and various ethnic groups, especially those from the Caribbean, China, and Asia, have brought to America their ancient reliance on medicinal herbs. Many of these are gaining increasing respect and acceptance from the established medical communities.

[See also Food and Drug Administration; Health Food; Pure Food and Drug Act.]

BIBLIOGRAPHY

Anderson, Ann. *Snake Oil, Hustlers and Hambones: The American Medicine Show.* Jefferson, NC: McFarland, 2000.

Willard, Pat. *A Soothing Broth.* New York: Broadway Books, 1998.

Pat Willard

Hominy Grits

Hominy grits today are the favorite starch of much of the American South, eaten with butter for breakfast and as a side dish for lunch and dinner. Certain combinations, such as shrimp and grits in the Carolinas (the states of highest consumption) or grits and grillades (braised beef steak) in Louisiana, are classics. Baked cheese grits (sometimes with added sausage) is on every list of essential Soul Food. Hominy (from Virginia Algonkian 'rockahominy' meaning "boiled corn") grits (from Old English *greot*, "crush") is now a mush made with fine-ground corn meal—usually white, that has been treated with alkali to remove the skins and improve the vitamin content. The term "nixtamalization" for this technology was coined from the Aztec by food historian Sophie Coe. However, at various times and places hominy has meant cracked or ground corn without nixtamalization.

Historically, lye hominy was part of the oral "cookbook" of every Native American tribe that grew corn. It must have been among the first foods offered to European explorers, but the explorers were male fortune-seekers who did not pay a lot of attention to native culinary technology. Thus, some of the first maize used to replace sorghum in polentas in Europe and Africa was not nixtamalized and caused the niacin-deficiency disease pellagra. Pellagra was identified among poor farmers in the American South in 1902 and persists in some parts of India.

Nevertheless, there is a fairly clear line from Native American sofkey (a hot drink of southern tribes now often made with "instant grits") and Cherokee/Appalachian whole-grain hominy (pozole in Mexico and the southwestern states) through African American "hog and hominy" dishes, to today's grits. A northern dish of whole-grain lye hominy and beans persisted regionally as Plymouth succotash.

Corn hulls also could be removed by pounding dried corn without nixtamalization, and either kind of dried corn could be reduced to grits with a sapling-sprung mortar pounding a tree-stump pestle—the whole rig was called a "hominy block" or "samp mill," equipment taken directly from Native American and African originals.

[**See also** Corn.]

BIBLIOGRAPHY

Zanger, Mark H. *The American History Cookbook.* Westport, CT: Greenwood Press, 2003.

MARK H. ZANGER

Honey

Honey is the fragrant, thick, syrupy creation of honeybees (*Apis mellifera*) that can be flavored by the type of bloom growing most profusely where the bees gather their nectar. Consumers can find honeys flavored with the blossoms of wildflowers, sage, thyme, rosemary, lavender, heather, apple, orange, clover, grapefruit, tupelo, buckwheat, and alfalfa. Buckwheat honey is one of the darkest, in both color and flavor; grapefruit is one of the lightest. Artisanal honeys are available in limited quantities. Blueberry and cranberry are popular in the Northeast. Sage and mesquite rule in the West, whereas eucalyptus and manzanita are prized in California.

Orchardists who keep domesticated bees to fertilize fruit blossoms net a second crop, honey, from the hives set out among the fruit trees. Over the course of a worker bee's lifetime, the bee makes less than one-twelfth of a teaspoon of honey. Bees store honey in combs, collections of six-sided wax cells. Honey can be purchased in combs but is much more expensive than bottled honey, which has been separated from the wax by heat and centrifuge. The wax is recycled in candles, cosmetics, furniture polish, and in sewing applications.

Honey is mentioned as an ingredient in the earliest Roman cookbooks. From ancient times until the eighteenth century, honey was the main form of sweetener in Europe and the American colonies. (Molasses, maple sugar, and maple syrup also were used in America.) Clarified sugar from sugarcane was so expensive that it was sold by the ounce, by apothecaries. A German chemist discovered beet sugar in 1747. Barley sugar was common into the 1940s but is seldom manufactured in the early twenty-first century.

Honey's virtues are many. It has greater sweetening power than sugar. It combines levulose and dextrose, both quickly absorbed by the bloodstream and thus is a source of quick but lasting energy. Unlike white sugar, honey contains vitamins and minerals. Its antimold enzyme is useful in canning and preserving, and it can also be used as an antiseptic on minor cuts. Finally, it helps to keep yeast breads and pastries moist longer than those baked with other sweeteners.

In medieval times, honey was fermented with water to make a drink called mead. In colonial America and through the nineteenth century, honey was commonly used in switchel, a haymaker's drink, and as a base for homemade vinegar. Honey is pleasant added to a cup of hot tea, smeared on toast, scones, or biscuits, or drizzled over morning oatmeal. Salad dressings and vinaigrettes are the better for it.

Honey can be substituted for white sugar in any recipe by using about half the quantity. However, honey in a recipe can cause the cookies, cakes, or breads to brown more quickly than if beet or cane sugars were incorporated, and bakers must be vigilant so that sweets do not burn. Should honey crystallize, it can be reliquefied by setting the honey jar in a pan of warm water, or briefly heating the jar in a microwave.

Children under a year of age should not be fed honey or soothed with nipples dipped in honey, because it may contain bacterial spores that could cause infant botulism—a rare but serious disease. Adults and children over one year of age are routinely exposed to, but not normally affected by, botulism spores. Honey is slightly laxative, and some people find it indigestible. For most people, however, it is an aromatic addition to the daily diet.

[**See also** Sugar; Sugar Beets; Sweeteners; Switchel.]

BIBLIOGRAPHY

Rosenbaum, Stephanie. *Honey: From Flower to Table.* New York: Chronicle, 2002.

ANN CHANDONNET

Hoppin' John

Hoppin' John is South Carolina's signature dish. Made with rice and peas, it is eaten throughout the South for good luck on New Year's Day, typically accompanied by greens and cornbread. The dish has its roots in South Carolina's low country rice culture, which flourished under the experienced hands of rice-growing slaves from West Africa, who had prepared similar concoctions in their homeland. Most often, the legumes were cowpeas, or black-eyed peas (*Vigna unguiculata*), a common field crop in the South that was used both as food and animal feed. Congo peas, or pigeon peas (*Cajanus cajan*), also found their way into the dish, but never green or yellow field peas (*Pisum sativum*).

A recipe for hoppin' John appears in *The Carolina Housewife* (1847) by Sarah Rutledge, calling for "one pint of cow (or red) peas, 1 pint of rice, 1 pound of bacon." Although first a slave dish, its inclusion in a book written for southern ladies signals its acceptance in upper-class kitchens. Most subsequent recipes vary little from the original: Some call for salt and pepper, some for onion, and some for red pepper (cayenne), which was cheaper than expensive, imported black pepper. Historians have suggested that the name is a corruption of the French *pois de pigeon*. But in her master work, *The Carolina Rice Kitchen* (1992), the culinary historian Karen Hess proposes a different etymology whereby *bahatta kachang*, Hindi- and Malagasy-rooted words, respectively, meaning cooked rice and legumes, eventually became hoppin' John when people substituted similar sounds for words they could neither pronounce nor understand.

BIBLIOGRAPHY

Hess, Karen. *The Carolina Rice Kitchen: The African Connection.* Columbia: University of South Carolina Press, 1992.

Taylor, John Martin. *Hoppin' John's Lowcountry Cooking: Recipes and Ruminations from Charleston and the Carolina Coastal Plain.* New York: Houghton Mifflin, 1992.

Thorne, John. Personal communication, 2005.

KIM PIERCE

Hostess

The Taggart Baking Company of Indianapolis, maker of Wonder Bread, began making chocolate cupcakes in 1919. These cakes did not contain the white filling until after World War II. Taggart Baking Company was acquired by Continental Baking Company in 1925. Continental wanted additional products to sell to grocers, and in 1927 they hit on sponge cakes used for making strawberry shortcake. Continental gave the brand name of "Hostess" to its new line of individual-sized cake products.

Although shortcakes sold well during strawberry season, Continental sought year-round sellers. One of their creations, which debuted in 1930, was Twinkies—cream-filled sponge cakes that are still the most popular Hostess product. Other individually packaged Hostess items are chocolate cupcakes, Ding-Dongs, Ho Hos, Suzy Qs, Sno Balls, and individual fruit pies. Continental advertised these products extensively and in the 1970s created cartoon characters to represent them—Twinkie the Kid, Happy Ho Ho, King Ding Dong, Captain Cupcake, and Fruit Pie the Magician. The company began an unusual promotional campaign in 1991, when it produced "Hostess Turtles Pies" before the release of the movie *Teenage Mutant Ninja Turtles II*. These pies were advertised as "Fresh from the sewers to you!"

In 1995, Interstate Bakeries Corporation, headquartered in Kansas City, Missouri, acquired Continental Baking Company. This made Interstate the largest wholesale maker of cake in the United States. Interstate faltered during the first few years of the twenty-first century, when the Atkins and other low-carb diets became popular. In 2004, Interstate Bakeries filed for bankruptcy protection under Chapter 11. The company continues to operate under the protection of the court.

BIBLIOGRAPHY
Bundy, Beverly. *Century in Food: America's Fads and Favorites.* Portland, OR: Collectors Press, 2002.

ANDREW F. SMITH

Hot Brown Sandwich

The Hot Brown is an open-faced sandwich based on toasted white bread on which thin slices of turkey or chicken, ham, crisp bacon, and sliced tomato are layered. A rich cheese sauce, usually made from cheddar, is spooned over the top. Sprinkled with grated parmesan cheese, the sandwich is quickly broiled until bubbling hot. Fred K. Schmidt, chef at the Brown Hotel in Louisville, Kentucky, created the Hot Brown to serve famished guests following the nightly dinner dances featured at the hotel after it opened in 1923. The sandwich was so popular that it was added to the hotel's luncheon menu along with a cold version, composed of rye bread, chicken or turkey, lettuce, sliced tomato, and hard-boiled egg and served with thousand island dressing. Long revered as a favorite sandwich of the upper South, the Hot Brown, or a variation of the original, is found on menus throughout the United States.

BIBLIOGRAPHY
Mercuri, Becky. *Sandwiches That You Will Like.* Pittsburgh, PA: WQED Multimedia, 2002.

BECKY MERCURI

Hot Dogs

Hot dogs are smoked, cooked sausages composed of pork, beef, chicken, or turkey, singly or in combination. Most hot dogs are made from emulsified or finely chopped skeletal meats, but some contain organs and other "variety" meats. Water, fat (roughly 30 percent), and seasonings, such as salt (about 1–1.5 percent), garlic, sugar, ground mustard, nutmeg, coriander, and white pepper, are other ingredients. Hot dogs can be made in natural gut casings, but most are skinless, stuffed in a cellulose wrapper that is stripped off after cooking. But the hot dog is more than just a sausage.

From the end of the nineteenth century and well into the second half of the next, the hot dog was America's chief iconic food item. Originally an ethnic food, it may have been America's first industrially produced, portion-controlled, and mass-marketed meat product. Widely sold in public venues such as ballparks, boardwalks, and fairs to consumers from every social and economic strata, its mythic attributes might best be summed up in the phrase, "America's great democratic food."

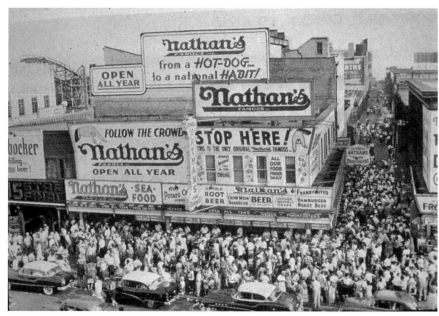

Nathan's on Coney Island has been selling its famous hot dogs since 1916.

The real and legendary histories of the hot dog are tied to the history of modern America. Wieners and frankfurters, as their interchangeable names reveal, are descended from European sausages: Viennese (Wiener) sausages are slim, white, finely ground, or emulsion-made sausages, usually containing at least 30 percent veal. Frankfurters contain some beef, are spicier, heavier, and more coarsely ground than wieners. Both were brought to America in the nineteenth century, by mainly German-speaking Central European immigrants. German beer gardens became common in American cities by the 1860s as did their staple foods: sausages, bread, and potatoes. Sausages served with bread took to the streets with pushcarts in that decade and soon became Americanized as sandwiches. Charles Feltman's sausages, sold with rolls and sauerkraut at his famous Coney Island stand in 1871, were an early example. Nathan's, serving hot dogs in buns with french fries, founded in 1916, is the most famous of all stands.

What went into the casings had always been a subject of wry speculation. Ditties such as, "Oh Hagenbeck [the name changes according to the singer], oh Hagenbeck, how could you be so mean to grind up all those doggies in your hot dog machine?" The earliest known joke of this type dates to 1860. That German butchers kept sausage-shaped dogs—dachshunds, recognized by the American Kennel Club in 1885—might have added to the legend. From these associations, German-style sausages came to be called hot dogs. In the mid-1890s, students at Yale and Princeton were using the term. Apparently applied first to young dandies, or perhaps good athletes, at Yale, it migrated to sausages by 1894 or 1895. One sausage wagon was even called "The Kennel Club." The term

"hot dog" was certainly popularized by such originators of slang phrases as the sports cartoonist T. A. Dorgan (TAD) early in the twentieth century.

Chopped or encased ground pork products (for example, hot links) were already staples of the American table, but the rising popularity of German-style sausages attracted major meat packers, such as Swift, Armour, Wilson, and Cudahy. Before the Pure Food and Drug Act of 1906 and later labeling laws, sausages had often been convenient ways to use scraps and offal. Rising technology permitted mass-processing: power meat choppers appeared in the 1860s (1868, the first steam-powered one); mixers, improved choppers, powered sausage stuffers, and linkers in the 1890s; and in the early twentieth century more potent grinders and mixers that could handle large amounts of meat. Mechanically operated smokers simplified and increased production. So popular had sausages become that, in the late 1880s, companies such as John Morrell in Cincinnati sent hog casing to Chicago to be processed and then returned for stuffing. Chicago and New York sausage companies began importing large amounts of sheep casings in the 1890s, mainly from Australia. Today, natural-cased sausages account for only 5 percent of the market.

Small-scale butchers—such as Oscar Mayer, founded in 1883 in Chicago and later headquartered in Madison, Wisconsin—grew into large local and regional producers. A niche-market producer before World War II, Oscar Mayer emphasized purity and quality. Its products were made exclusively from skeletal meats. Other local producers, such as the Jewish packers of New York and Chicago, emphasized meaty all-beef products with an aura of purity from their kosher associations. The latter makers, like many bratwurst producers in the upper Midwest, geared their production to the food-service industry. Sabrett in New York and Vienna Beef in Chicago were the main suppliers of urban hot dog carts and stands in the early 2000s, whereas large-scale companies, Bryan in the South, Oscar Mayer, Hygrade (Ballpark), Armour, Swift, and others, had considerable presence in supermarkets. These hot dogs differ greatly from the older varieties in formulas and usage.

The hot dog was marketed largely as a fun food, playing its role in cookouts, amusement parks, and ballgames. Marketing campaigns carried out by large centralized food producers before World War I made the hot dog the great American fast food. By the 1920s, the phrase "weenie roast" had passed into common usage. Oscar Mayer in the 1930s exemplified such marketing. The company hired a small person to bring Little Oscar, a cartoon character created for print advertising, to life. Little Oscar drove "the famous wienermobile," a car designed to look like a wiener as a way of publicizing hot dogs. Little Oscar, intended to appeal to families, was a newly minted myth devised to sell a food product. After World War II campaigns pitching hot dogs as a convenience food were directed toward the home market, especially children. Jingles, such as "I wish I were an Oscar Mayer wiener" and "Armour hot dogs, the dogs kids love to bite," became imbedded in American popular culture.

The rise of national hamburger chains, and, to some extent, pizza and taco purveyors after World War II eclipsed hot dogs as Americans' fast foods of choice. Hot dog stands remained local, mainly in urban areas such as Mobile and Birmingham, Alabama, Chicago, New York, and Los Angeles. Nevertheless, by the turn of the twenty-first century, hot dog sales were strong with more than 1.25 billion pounds of all types sold in retail stores alone. The hot dog remained an icon of American life as commemorated in the advertising slogan: "Baseball, hot dogs, apple pie and Chevrolet."

[See also AMUSEMENT PARKS; ARMOUR, PHILIP DANFORTH; GERMAN AMERICAN FOOD; STREET VENDORS; SWIFT, GUSTAVUS FRANKLIN.]

BIBLIOGRAPHY

Cohen, Gerald, ed. "Compiling Material for a Book on Hot Dog—Part I: Bibliography." Comments on Etymology 33, no. 3 (December 2003).

Graulich, David. The Hot Dog Companion: A Connoisseur's Guide to the Foods We Love. New York: Lebhar-Friedman Books, 1999.

BRUCE KRAIG

Hotel Dining Rooms

Hôtel means "town mansion" in French. When Americans began building grand public accommodations in the nineteenth century, these hotels were called "palaces of the people." More than feeding guests, the hotel dining room showcased upwardly mobile, status-conscious, public leisure in a uniquely egalitarian, American context. As the editors of the Weekly Mirror observed about the Hotel Astor, "The distinguished, the fashionable, the dressy and handsome may all dine without peril of style in the public table. But,—since so may the opposites of all these, and anybody else who is tolerably dressed and well behaved,—the public table is the tangible republic."

Taverns, inns, and "ordinaries" had fed and sheltered travelers along colonial thoroughfares, but these spots catered primarily to the community and often accommodated transients indifferently. These establishments would lay copious dishes of the house's choosing on communal tables at fixed hours. The cost of these meals was included in the room charge—what came to be known as the "American plan." To the extent that one toured for pleasure or required extended lodging, one might sojourn at a boarding house, taking meals in comparatively modest surroundings with limited public access.

Hotels were different. The largest hotels sported imposing architecture, billiards rooms, theaters, shops, and capacious dining rooms that seated hundreds at a time. Although many early hotel dining rooms copied the tavern model, the most elegant hotels, including the Tremont House, which opened in Boston in 1829, offered guests the choices of when and what to eat. The Tremont grouped guests into small parties of six or eight, delicately serving individual dishes from a sideboard. Similarly, the Astor House in New York boasted that although its dining room kept regular meal hours in the traditional style, it also would serve "Dinners for one or more at any hour. In short, we take pleasure in providing for the wants of our patrons, regardless of the hour." The Astor even had its own press for printing menus, novelties in themselves but necessary for this individual service. The European plan, whereby room and food charges were separate, had evolved by the middle of the 1840s. Use of the European plan slowly spread through the nineteenth century, but the American plan remained common.

Nineteenth-century hotel dining rooms filled four distinct niches. First, hotels such as the block-long City Hotel, which opened in New York in 1794, sprouted in the commercial districts of larger cities and served emerging business communities. Well-heeled businessmen who could not travel home for the midday meal dined on the hotels' original "businessman's lunch."

Second, the grandest hotels were entertainments in themselves and had a near-monopoly as sites for banquets and elegant dining. Often staffed by European chefs and waiters, the hotels broadcast sophistication. Dinners were choreographed with military precision. A gong summoned guests for dinners at which waiters in unison removed silver domes covering the various dishes,

A hotel dining scene from the nineteenth century.

creating a public spectacle akin to the most opulent dinners in private homes. The great expense of the food generally was compensated by liquor sales. Prohibition effectively killed the hotel dining rooms, and in the changed economy of the 1930s, restaurants, rather than hotels, became the sites of culinary excellence.

Third, hotels great and small were long-term residences. Before America's first apartments were built in the 1870s in New York, the cost of elegant urban homes and housekeeping increased dramatically. Well-to-do, permanent boarders, single persons and families alike, accounted for one-half of the hotel occupancy in the mid-nineteenth century and often took meals in the public dining rooms.

Fourth, hotel dining rooms were a progressive public venue for ladies, who generally were not welcome in restaurants, particularly unescorted, until the late nineteenth century. Hotel etiquette and service differed from that in private homes, as detailed by authors such as Eliza Leslie and Tunis G. Campbell. Both of these authors emphasized the egalitarian nature of the hotel tables. Leslie observed that, "Nobody 'sits below the salt'. And every one has an equal chance of obtaining a share of the nicest articles on the table."

On the other side of the social coin, hotels were a battleground for fledgling labor unions in the early twentieth century. Carefully timed walkouts by waiters at the most elegant establishments left bewildered patrons in dinner jackets to serve themselves. When cooks joined the fray, shutting down the immense kitchens, management was forced to negotiate. Labor unions continue to organize vast hotel staffs. Hotel dining rooms no longer command their extraordinary place in the pantheon of American eateries. For the cost of a nineteenth-century dinner, they allowed old and new money, women, and the socially aspiring to "rub elbows and pick their teeth at a public table."

[See also BOARDINGHOUSES; RESTAURANTS; TAVERNS; TSCHIRKY, OSCAR.]

BIBLIOGRAPHY

Hamilton, Thomas. Men and Manners in America. New York: Kelly, 1968. Reprint of the 1833 edition with additions from the edition of 1843.

Josephson, Matthew. Union House, Union Bar: The History of the Hotel and Restaurant Employees and Bartenders International Union AFL-CIO. New York: Random House, 1956.

Williamson, Jefferson. *The American Hotel.* New York: Arno, 1975. The original edition was published in 1930.

Cathy K. Kaufman

Hot Tamales

By the time of European settlement, almost all Native American farmers had corn, beans, and squash, and an oral "cookbook" of at least one hundred corn recipes. Maize-based mushes and hearth breads were taken on by the settlers as soon as the shipborne foods ran out, but boiled leaf breads, although universally reported among Native Americans, were not adapted, probably because they were not in use even by rural or backward communities in Europe. Thus, the Virginia colonists noticed that "they lap yt [fresh corn off the cob] in rowlls within the leaves of the corne, and so boyle yt for a deyntie," but they did not take the time to do likewise. Cherokee "broadswords" and "dog-heads," or Iroquois wedding breads (paired like dumbbells) might be eaten and described by visitors, but apparently were not adapted by colonial farmers other than a few intermarried pioneers. Tamale-like leaf breads were steamed and roasted in contemporary Africa, and some native leaf breads may have persisted in the slave quarters for a time but are not recorded.

Only in what are now the southwestern states were local leaf breads incorporated into the colonial diet, and the early Spanish and Mexican colonists did so under the Aztec name, tamales.

"Hot tamales" was the street vendor's cry when tamales swept back east across the southern United States as a street snack in the late nineteenth and early twentieth centuries. These tamales were "hot" because the larded cornmeal from which they were made held the heat of steaming; they were not necessarily spicy. The few printed recipes in American cookbooks show either moderate Mexican-style spicing, as in a California contributed recipe of 1887, or almost none—one "Spanish pepper" to four cups of cornmeal and a chicken—as in *Mrs. Gillette's Cook Book* of 1899.

Tamales were sold by African American youths, and the recipes may have varied according to where they sold them. Later, American tamales did become spicier, as seen in the restaurant tamales of the twenty-first century that survive in some southern localities, as well as in canned tamales once sold by Texas chili canners but now produced only by Hormel. In contrast to most Mexican tamales, Americanized tamales were often served with a spicier sauce or chili gravy. Recent immigrants have brought blander Central American and Caribbean tamales into storefront restaurants but do not sell them in the street, where Columbian-style *arepas* are now the only native American stuffed cornbreads on sale in a few coastal cities.

Mark H. Zanger

Hot Toddies

To many Americans, who know the toddy only as a steaming après-ski pick-me-up, the term "hot toddy" may seem redundant. Yet it makes a legitimate distinction, for the cool toddy does exist. Both of these drinks reflect the climate of their birthplace; indeed, toddies may even be defined by their usefulness in countering the effects of extreme temperature.

The cool version has its origins in the tapped and fermented sap of certain tropical palms, for which British colonialists in India developed a taste and a name, toddy, derived from the Hindi word *tārī*. The word traveled from the outposts of the British Empire to sultry plantation-era America, where Dixie gentlemen adopted it for their own combination of rum, sugar or molasses, and nutmeg, which was mixed with hot water and then cooled. It was also known as bombo, or, on occasion, bimbo.

The hot toddy hails from eighteenth-century Scotland, where a similar mixture of spirits (namely malt whiskey), hot water, sugar or honey, and lemon, plus spices, such as nutmeg, cinnamon, cloves, or mace, was touted as a cure for colds—although its application was, not surprisingly, far more general. The name, in this case, is said to refer to Tod's Well in Edinburgh from whence the water came. Scottish affection for the drink is particularly evident in the gadgetry contrived specially for its preparation, including kettles, ladles, and lifters. (The lifter, which was usually made of glass, resembled a decanter but functioned like a ladle, transferring the beverage in question from punch bowl to drinking vessel.)

The hot toddy's popularity must have spread fast, if the lore that would-be American revolutionaries took courage from rounds of toddies (which were often heated by pokers straight from the tavern hearth) holds any truth. Certainly, Americans adopted the drink wholeheartedly, down to the toddy-stick (an implement akin to a muddler, flat at one end and knobbed at the other) with which it was stirred. In colonial New England, however, rum or brandy often replaced the whiskey—and the punch bowl itself often precluded glassware, as drinking from a common vessel was considered properly sociable among tavern patrons. Although for all the democracy of the gesture, it should be noted that toddy contained two ingredients—citrus and sugar—that commanded high prices at the time. It was therefore not quite the drink of the people. New Orleanians, for their part, boast of their favorite French-born son Antoine Peychaud's experiments with bitters-laced toddies as leading to the invention of the cocktail around the turn of the nineteenth century.

Meanwhile, a few variations on the theme help stretch the definition of a hot toddy, from the blazer—a toddy that is not merely heated but actually ignited—to hot buttered rum, which floats a pat of butter on its surface. Such drinks are typically served in a short-stemmed glass with a handle that is itself known as a toddy.

[**See also** Homemade Remedies; Cocktails and Taverns.]

BIBLIOGRAPHY

O'Hara, Christopher B. *Hot Toddies.* New York: Clarkson Potter, 2002.

Rice, Kym S. *The Early American Tavern: For the Entertainment of Friends and Strangers.* New York: Fraunces Tavern Museum in conjunction with Chicago: Regnery Gateway, 1983.

Ruth Tobias

Howard Johnson

Howard Johnson was a mid-twentieth-century phenomenon, an American company that pioneered concepts of food service and hospitality still in use in the twenty-first century. Superpremium ice cream, restaurant franchises, turnpike service stops, commissary-based restaurant production, quality control, and customer service were formulated by the founder, Howard Deering Johnson, beginning with one corner drugstore in the oceanside Wollaston section of Quincy, Massachusetts, south of Boston. In 1925, the twenty-seven-year-old businessman turned his newsstand into a thriving delivery service, then set his sights on improving the soda fountain. He developed the first superpremium commercial ice cream using natural flavoring and cream with twice the butterfat content. Depending on the source, the story goes that Johnson either improved on his mother's recipe or purchased the formula from a pushcart operator. In any event, his new, larger portions were distinctively sculpted with a specially designed ice cream scoop.

Johnson sold his ice cream cones for a nickel from a growing series of wooden stands situated directly on the beach. By 1928, sales grossed $240,000 and the original flavors, vanilla, chocolate, and strawberry, gradually increased to twenty-eight. A high-quality hot dog was added to the beachfront menu. Clipped at either end, notched down the center, and cooked in butter, it was presented in a buttered, toasted roll, cradled in a cardboard holder with scalloped edges, and renamed a "frankfort."

In early 1929, Johnson opened a full-service restaurant in a new ten-story building in downtown Quincy. The menu included typical New England fare, such as fried clams, chicken potpies, and baked beans, in addition to the popular frankforts and ice cream and huge sodas that were topped with an oval cookie embossed with the company logo.

The Franchise

Just as the fledgling company was poised for expansion, the stock market crashed. Banks were not lending, but Johnson conceived of the idea of a franchise. In return for an initial investment, Johnson would provide the design,

A Howard Johnson restaurant.

menu, standards, and food products, while the investor/franchisee/property owner reaped most of the profits. The first franchise opened in Orleans, Massachusetts, on Cape Cod in the depths of the Great Depression. A simple white clapboard colonial house, trimmed in turquoise, it featured three dormers, multipaned windows, a cupola with a clock and weathervane in the shape of Simple Simon and the Pieman, the company logo. A bright orange roof ensured maximum visibility.

Johnson outlined hitherto unknown standards of cleanliness and service that ranged from procedures for scrubbing to staff comportment in the "Howard Johnson Bible." He enforced them strictly during personally conducted surprise inspections. In an era when roadside-dining facilities consisted of diners, teahouses, and small eateries of questionable quality, Johnson stressed dependability.

By 1940 the established company, with two hundred roadside eateries in the eastern United States, bid on and won, in rapid succession, exclusive rights to build restaurants on the Pennsylvania, Ohio, and New Jersey turnpikes. When World War II brought a halt to leisure motor travel, most of the outlets closed. The company kept solvent by providing meals for war workers and educational institutions.

At the war's end, America was poised for travel: gas rationing ended, cars rolled off assembly lines, and a baby boom filled new housing tracts and suburbs outside city limits. A system of interstate highways was under construction, and although the highways were business-free, Howard Johnson built restaurants at the exits. The company claimed the road, adopting the slogan "Landmark for Hungry Americans" and the family-friendly nickname "HoJo's."

With a shortage of trained chefs, the company established the large central commissary to produce and portion food, thus ensuring standardization throughout the franchises. As the U.S. economy and family travel flourished, the turnpike restaurants reaped great profits. The company added motor lodge franchises with a restaurant on each property.

The Next Generation

In 1959, Johnson turned operations over to his son, Howard Brennon Johnson, remaining as chairman and treasurer, and in 1961 the company was publicly traded on the New York Stock Exchange. Jacques Pepin, formerly personal chef to the French president Charles DeGaulle, oversaw the central commissary from the 1960s to 1970. Applying his French training, he learned the work of every station, beginning by flipping burgers in the largest restaurant in the chain on Queens Boulevard, New York City. Pepin recalled that era as "my American apprenticeship, learning about mass production and marketing." Pepin, along with his fellow French chef Pierre Franey, worked on product development. Under their leadership simple macaroni and cheese bubbled in preportioned oval casseroles; vats of creamy clam chowder were tasted and tested; and mass-produced fried clam strips, without the highly perishable bellies, were developed to maintain fresh Cape Cod seafood flavor. Home convenience products were developed for sale in supermarket freezers.

The company opened Red Coach Grills for the business traveler and the casual Ground Round. But after Howard Deering Johnson died in 1972, the company began to fail. In the late 1970s, an energy crisis, oil embargo, and inflated fuel prices brought the automobile travel that made up 85 percent of the company's business to a standstill. New competing food outlets, such as McDonald's, Burger King, and Kentucky Fried Chicken, streamlined Howard Johnson's concepts and were able to feed the population faster and cheaper. Holiday Inn, Ramada Inn, and Marriott built newer, more comfortable hotels. Inside the company, unsupervised, unscrupulous franchisees cut corners. According to Pepin, "after Johnson's death in 1972, the company lost its raison d'etre. The restaurants became obsolete; the food quality deteriorated."

In 1979, Imperial Group of Great Britain acquired both the company-owned and independent operations, a total of 1,040 restaurants and 520 motor lodges, for $630 million, then sold them, except for Ground Round, to Marriott, which in turn sold off the company-owned franchises to Prime Motor Inns. The independent franchise owners incorporated and hired the former U.S. Attorney General Griffin Bell to negotiate with Marriott and Prime Motor Inns.

In the early 2000s, Franchise Associates Inc. retained ownership of the original recipes. The company produced Howard Johnson's signature products for retail sale, such as Macaroni and Cheese, TenderSweet Fried Clams, Chicken Croquettes, and Toastees at Fairfield Farm Kitchens in Brockton, Massachusetts, and bulk ice cream at The Ice Cream Club in Boynton Beach, Florida. Cendant Corporation operated the midprice hotel chain under the name Howard Johnson (without the " 's").

The last original Howard Johnson's Restaurant in Massachusetts closed in March 2002. Fewer than a dozen restaurants remained in the twenty-first century, one in New York City's Times Square. A number of websites are devoted to Howard Johnson's lore and memorabilia.

[*See also* Burger King; Clams; Ice Cream and Ices; Johnson, Howard; McDonald's; Roadside Food; White Castle.]

Linda Bassett

Humor, Food

"Waiter, waiter! Bring me a crocodile sandwich, and make it snappy!"

Food humor probably has as long a history as food. What passes for humor, however, has changed over the years. A kind of humor modern Americans would find strange or even unnerving marked the banquets of the Romans and continued through the Middle Ages. From ancient Rome came "flying pies" immortalized in the nursery rhyme about "four and twenty blackbirds baked in a pie." These pies consisted of empty shells with lids baked separately that, after baking and cooling, had birds put inside them to be released in the banquet hall for the amusement and entertainment of the guests.

In Renaissance Italy, Ascanio Sforza invited his fellow cardinals to a banquet where there were bones sculpted from sugar and the drinking cups were shaped like skulls. Another frequent joke was to have a sculpture at a wedding feast of the bride in childbirth. Perhaps mercifully, no pictures survive of such sculptures, although frequent references to them exist in old writings.

In colonial America, there was "grinning for cheese," a popular contest at fairs and markets in which, in what would seem a cruel joke, people would grin widely. The contestant with the fewest teeth would be the winner and given cheese as a prize—perhaps the source of "say cheese" for photographs.

Food humor has often taken the form of jokes, songs, and skits. Consider the song "Yankee Doodle" with its humorous reference to a dandy with a feather in his hat as a "macaroni." Many songs mention items of food and drink, like "mountain dew" with its moonshine reference or "red beans and rice" with its New Orleans flavor.

In contemporary America, food humor falls into several loosely defined and often overlapping categories: the two-story story, the tall story, wordplay including the pun, and the essay. "There are two laws in the universe: The law of gravity, and everyone likes Italian food," said Neil Simon. This is a two-story story. The setup implies a certain kind of conclusion, an expansion on the beginning, but the punch line delivers a different and contrasting one. Most of the "waiter, waitress" jokes fall into this category. "Waiter, waiter, what's this fly doing in my soup?" "The backstroke, I believe, sir." There are countless variations on that theme: "Waiter, there's a dead fly in my soup." "What do you expect for a dollar, a live one?" A variation: "Waitress, there's a fly in my soup!" "Well, keep quiet about it or everyone will want one." And yet another variation on the concept: "Waitress, I'll have my bill now." "How did you find your steak, sir?" "Oh, I just moved the potato and there it was."

A tall tale is a story that has a larger-than-life situation and exaggerated details that describe things as greater than they really are. The classic tall stories are exemplified by tales about Paul Bunyan and his blue ox, Babe, Johnny Appleseed, or Pecos Bill. One such tells about watermelons growing so fast that they were "drug round the garden and had their skins wore off" by the friction "so when the vine decided to rest, they done sat there all red and ready to eat."

Wordplay is pivotal in many types of humor. For example: "The new chef from India was fired a week after starting the job. He kept favoring curry." Or: "A Zen Buddhist walks into a pizza parlor and says, 'Make me one with everything.'" Puns are a form of wordplay. A famous one transforms the observation "The pun is the lowest form of wit" into "The bun is the lowest form of wheat." There are riddles that use plays on words: What was green and a great trick shooter? Annie Okra. And there are true puns: "Waiter, there's a hair in my honey." "It must have dropped off the comb, sir!"

Longer food-related stories featuring puns and wordplay have been making the rounds on the Internet. An excerpt from one of the more popular ones is:

Pillsbury Dough Boy Dead at 71
Veteran Pillsbury spokesman Pop N Fresh died yesterday of a severe yeast infection....The graveside was piled with flours as longtime friend Aunt Jemima delivered the eulogy, describing Fresh as a man who "never knew how much he was kneaded."...Fresh is survived by his second wife; they have two children and one in the oven. The funeral was held at 2:25 for 20 minutes.

The following essay usually appears as an article for a newspaper or magazine and runs to several hundred words. An edited excerpt from one example (which appeared in the *Waynesboro News-Virginian*):

Spoilage Simplified
Many people ask me how to know how long to keep food in the refrigerator. A good question. Something we should all know for maximum safety and to prevent the need to use power tools to clean the veggie crisper.

Let's list a variety of things to consider in the specific cases of the most common foods we all have. There are some commonsense things you already know. Even the most hardened kitchen-avoider will know much of this stuff. But it's good to have reminders, don't you think?

FOOD SPOILAGE INDICATORS
THE GAG PROTOCOL—Anything that makes you gag may safely be considered spoiled. Except for leftovers from what you cooked for yourself within the past 48 hours. Or if it contains okra. Or if you're watching an old Jerry Lewis movie.

DAIRY PRODUCTS—Milk is spoiled when it looks like yogurt. Yogurt is spoiled when it looks like cottage cheese. Cottage cheese is spoiled when it starts to look like beige spackle. All cheese is just spoiled milk anyway, so don't get too strange about that whole idea. It can, however, grow pretty green fur. Once I saw pink fur. I controlled my desire for cheese that day.

EGGS—When something, anything, is pecking its way out of the shell, the egg is probably past its consumption ideal. You'd better hope it's a chicken working so hard if it came from your fridge and came with 11 kindred ovals.

[See also LITERATURE, FOOD AND; MYTHS AND FOLKLORE.]

BIBLIOGRAPHY

Jillette, Penn, and Teller. *How to Play with Your Food*. New York: Random House, 1992.

Lileks, James. *The Gallery of Regrettable Food*. New York: Crown, 2001.

Steingarten, Jeffrey. *The Man Who Ate Everything*. New York: Vintage, 1997.

ROBERT PASTORIO

Hunger Programs

Historically, efforts to alleviate hunger in the United States have been initiated and supported by both private and public sectors of society. Nearly every faith-based organization in America provides funds or direct services for feeding the hungry. The Salvation Army, for example, began providing food aid with its first mission to the United States in 1880. Other major, nonprofit charitable groups include Meals on Wheels, begun in 1954 to provide food to the country's homebound residents, and Second Harvest, the nation's largest domestic hunger-relief organization, which operates as a network of over two hundred food banks and food-rescue programs.

Before the 1930s, most food aid came from community-based charitable groups and local government support. Unable to meet the enormous demand imposed by the Great Depression, when breadlines and soup kitchens for the destitute and unemployed witnessed unprecedented need, such aid was supplemented through several New Deal programs providing temporary relief. The largest of these was the National Social Security Act of 1935, which, in addition to providing a supplementary pension to retirees, included a provision for Aid to Dependent Children (ADC), later Aid to Families with Dependent Children (AFDC), a major program in what became known as welfare. Various food-distribution programs were also put into place. Although many federal programs had their roots in the Depression years and shortly thereafter, most of those specific to food aid did not gain much momentum until the War on Poverty began during President Lyndon Johnson's administration in the 1960s.

Federal programs include those that came into being with the Food Stamps Act (1964), the most extensive hunger-prevention initiative. The National School Lunch Act (1946), later expanded to the Summer Food Service Program (1968), and the School Breakfast program (1975) were meant to provide nutritional security for America's youth. The Supplemental Food Program for Women, Infants, and Children (WIC) (1974), a voucher program, provided health benefits and nutritional education to low-income mothers and children up to age five. The Child and Adult Care Food Program (CACFP) provided nutritious meals and snacks to those in need. The Emergency Food Assistance Program (TEFAP) (1990) was another form of aid, this coming through distribution of surplus commodities to individuals and community agencies. In the early 2000s, an additional federal hunger program was administered by the U.S. Department of Health and Human Services' (USDHHS) Office of Community Services (OCS). The Community Food and Nutrition Program (CFNP) provided funding to a number of antihunger organizations for food distribution and nutrition education.

The U.S. government's responsibility for monitoring hunger in America was redefined in 1999 with the implementation of the USDA's standardized measures of food security and hunger in conjunction with the U.S. Census Bureau. A report titled "Household Food Security in the United States, 2001" by the USDA Economic Research Service found that almost 11 percent of American households were food-insecure at some time during the year and that in 3.5 million households, at least one member went hungry because there was not enough food to go around.

The key issue permeating the history of hunger programs in the United States relates to whether these programs should function as emergency food relief or as entitlements. This has set up a debate, much like that concerning welfare generally. One side sees food assistance as a form of charity that should be provided on a temporary basis and then only to the neediest. Any kind of entitlement, or anything beyond emergency assistance, under this argument, is ripe for fraud and abuse and provides no incentive for leaving the program. Therefore, nonprofit charitable organizations and local governments, not the federal government, should provide all additional needed support. Because of such reasoning, the governmental programs that have traditionally gained strongest bipartisan support are those targeting children and the elderly.

The other side of the debate believes that structural inequalities continue to contribute both to poverty and hunger in America. Unless these underlying concerns are addressed, hunger and poverty will never decrease. In this argument, public assistance is not a matter of charity but a matter of social justice: individuals have a right, or entitlement,

A farmer gathers provisions from the Surplus Commodities Committee, St. Johns, Arizona, 1940.

to a minimum standard of living, including food assistance, in a civilized society.

The nongovernmental voluntary programs that continue a tradition of soup kitchens, food pantries, and food banks are under constant pressure to bridge the gap left by government programs. This is especially true for feeding the homeless, who, without a permanent address or phone number, often find it difficult to secure federal food aid. The ultimate contradiction for hunger programs in the United States is that as nongovernmental programs increase in size and number with the growing demand for hunger relief, many lawmakers feel justified in making cuts in federally funded initiatives. Although large numbers of the U.S. population are not starving, millions do go hungry. Given the affluence of American society, that this should be the case, especially for children, raises basic issues of human rights.

[**See also** DEPARTMENT OF AGRICULTURE, UNITED STATES; FOOD STAMPS; MEALS ON WHEELS; SOUP KITCHENS.]

BIBLIOGRAPHY

Eisinger, Peter K. *Toward an End to Hunger in America.* Washington, DC: Brookings Institution Press, 1998.

Poppendieck, Janet. *Sweet Charity? Emergency Food and the End of Entitlement.* New York: Viking, 1998.

BARRETT P. BRENTON AND
KEVIN T. MCINTYRE

Hunt's

In 1888, Joseph and William Hunt launched a small preserving business in Santa Rosa, California. Two years later, it was incorporated as the Hunt Brothers Fruit Packing Company. During their first year, they canned thirty thousand cases. They expanded in the following years and outgrew their canning facility. In 1896, the brothers moved their operation to Hayward, California. At the turn of the century, they produced an extensive line of fruit and vegetable products. However, they did make one major mistake: shortly after Hawaii was acquired by the United States, Hunt Brothers was offered exclusive importing rights for Hawaiian pineapple but passed up the opportunity, because they did not think that pineapples would be popular with the American public.

The Hunt Brothers chose not to join the California Fruit Canners Association, a cooperative that later marketed Del Monte brand foods. They did, however, join the Pure Food Manufacturers Association, along with the Beech-Nut Packing Company, H. J. Heinz, and Charles Gulden, in an attempt to raise the standards of the canning industry.

By the early 1940s, Hunt Brothers was a regional canner known mainly in the West. The Hunt Brothers sold their operation to Norton Simon in 1943. Simon had previously acquired Val Vita Food Products, a small orange juice–canning factory in Fullerton, California. Through advertising, he had increased Val Vita's sales dramatically within a few years and he hoped to do the same with Hunt Brothers. In 1945, Simon merged Hunt Brothers with Val Vita to form Hunt Foods.

To promote his new company, Simon targeted tomato sauce for major promotion. The slogan, "Hunt—for the best," appeared along with color illustrations of Hunt's Tomato Sauce in major women's magazines in 1946. These advertisements also featured recipes for dishes with tomato sauce as the key ingredient. Simon also printed tomato sauce recipes inside millions of matchbook covers. This campaign propelled Hunt Foods from a regional business into a national brand. Coupled with the company's campaign featuring tomato sauce, Simon also began promoting Hunt's Tomato Catchup, later changed to "Ketchup." Precisely when Hunt's began producing ketchup is unknown, but it took off after Hunt Foods acquired the E. Prichard Company in Bridgeton, New Jersey, in 1948, which had manufactured Pride of the Farm ketchup. Hunt Foods was extremely aggressive in their ketchup marketing during the 1950s. In addition, Simon introduced new lines of convenience foods, including Manwich, Skillet dinners, and snack packs.

By the 1950s, the company claimed to be the largest processor of tomato-based products in the world. It increased its tomato products to include spaghetti sauce and barbecue sauce. To promote its tomato products, Hunt Food published advertising cookbooklets, such as *Hunt's Complete Tomato Sauce Cookbook* (1976).

Simon merged Hunt Foods with the Wesson Oil and Snowdrift Company to create Hunt-Wesson Foods in 1960. Eight years later, Hunt-Wesson Foods became a major group of Norton Simon Inc. which in turn was acquired by ConAgra, based in St. Louis. By the late twentieth century, Hunt Foods manufactured only tomato products, such as barbecue sauce, ketchup, sauce, paste, and puree, as well as diced, stewed, and crushed tomatoes. By the twenty-first century, ConAgra was the second-largest U.S. food conglomerate behind Kraft Foods.

[**See also** CANNING AND BOTTLING; CONAGRA; KETCHUP; TOMATOES.]

BIBLIOGRAPHY

Hunt's. http://www.hunts.com/A01AboutHunts.jsp? mnav=about.

Mahoney, David J. *Growth and Social Responsibility: The Story of Norton Simon Inc.* New York: Newcomen Society in North America, 1973.

ANDREW F. SMITH

Hush Puppies

Hush Puppies are fried cornmeal dumplings or croquettes, usually made and served along with fried chicken or fried fish. Because deep fat frying is strongly associated with African American cooking, hush puppies probably began as soul food, perhaps as a lagniappe to use up the extra dredging meal for kitchen slaves. The term has not been found in print before the 1910s, which also argues for a soul food origin. There is a persistent folk etymology that the dumplings were thrown to quiet barking dogs.

But a very early printed recipe, in Mary Randolph's 1824 *The Virginia House-Wife,* for "fried chicken" specifies that one should also fry small pieces of mush with parsley, and gives a brief recipe for making cornmeal mush. So perhaps these irresistible fried snacks were once named "mush puppies." Yet another story is that salamanders were known as "mud puppies" in the southern states, and eaten fried as a poverty food. Because hush puppies were often fried with catfish, perhaps the corn "dogs" were simply a complement to the filleted "cats." Here's a new one: "Hush" is an old Scottish term for Atlantic lumpfish, which might have been applied somewhere in the South to freshwater catfish, and then the leftover batter from a catfish fry could produce "hush puppies."

The shape varies from round to roughly conical, or the football shape of corn dodgers, but perhaps finger-shaped (like shorter hot dogs) is the most common. Most recent recipes don't use mush, but a simple cornmeal batter, spiced with salt and pepper, and possibly chopped onion or green onion.

MARK H. ZANGER

Hush
Puppies

309

Iberian and South American Food

The influence of Iberian and South American foodways on North American food have been continual. The Caribbean islands had been populated from the South American mainland, and thus the maize, chilies, squashes, sweet potatoes, cassava, peanuts, and pineapples first presented to Spanish explorers were South American varieties. Mexican foodstuffs—some also originally domesticated or improved in South America—such as maize, tomatoes, haricot beans, turkeys, and localized varieties of peppers, cacao, and peanuts quickly followed. The new foods were altered across the Mediterranean, selected for more northern climates, and returned to North America with colonists from Spain, France, Holland, England, and even Sweden. With the Spanish conquests in South America came white potatoes, lima beans, and other strains of maize and haricot beans. Because they were grown at high altitude in the Andes, these crops were more suited to northern Europe and the northern colonies in America. The white potato may have been first brought to Florida or Virginia in the sixteenth or seventeenth century, but it appeared in most American colonies with the eighteenth-century influx of the Protestant Irish ethnic group now known as the Scotch-Irish, who were growing "Irish potatoes" in their settlement of Londonderry, New Hampshire, by the 1720s.

Portuguese explorers and colonists introduced maize, cassava, sweet potatoes, and peanuts to Africa, and thus many African slaves arrived in North America with a taste for and knowledge of these originally Native American foods. The early Iberian contact with Africa and primary involvement in setting up the transatlantic slave trade left enduring influences via African American food. Iberians probably reinforced African techniques such as deep fat frying, marinating foods in vinegar, and making rice into pilafs. The Iberian slave trade also introduced African or Africanized plants, such as coconut palm, cowpeas, rice, and watermelon; and animals, such as guinea hens, to Florida and the Caribbean. From there, these foods diffused to the British American colonies.

The North American colonies were not self-contained units but part of global trading networks that brought many Iberian foods to them—peacefully during periods when England, France, or the Netherlands traded with Spain or Portugal; through privateering in times of war; and often by illicit trade or smuggling.

Basques may have been fishing and whaling in Newfoundland before the time of Columbus and were well established there by the early sixteenth century, when the fishery was dominated by Iberians. Spanish and French Basques were so prominent in Newfoundland cod fishing that Mi'kmaq and other Algonquian Indian languages absorbed Basque vocabulary. The interchange influenced Native cooking by providing metal pots and hatchets and thus may have affected the mainstream development of chowders and maple syrup. Basque names are prominent in all Spanish colonization in the Americas, but Basque-speaking shepherds began coming to the Americas as contractors in the mid-nineteenth century. In the twentieth century, some of their boardinghouses became public restaurants, providing ethnic flavor to the Rocky Mountain states. The French Basque omelet called *pipérade* may have been an influence on the "western" omelet and the Denver sandwich made from it.

The best-known Spanish colonies in what became the United States are Saint Augustine, Florida (founded 1565) and Santa Fe, New Mexico (founded 1608). Most of the California missions date from the mid- to late eighteenth century. Saint Augustine was turned over to the British in 1765, but the population of Catalan-speaking Minorcans recruited by the British (who had taken over their Mediterranean island homeland at the same time) remained, and still retain recipes for Easter cheese cakes, chowders of local shellfish, and dishes that use *datil* chilies.

The Spanish colonies in New Mexico had to be abandoned for almost twenty years after the Pueblo Revolt of 1680 but then developed a considerable Iberian identity that has persisted for more than three hundred years. New Mexico Hispanics enjoy "Mexican food" but preserve many old Iberian foodways, such as noodle soups and wheat breads baked in beehive ovens.

The Spanish dominion over Louisiana (1765–1803) likely introduced pralines (from similar Mexican sweets), possibly jambalaya, and probably the empanada-shaped turnovers that survive as "Natchitoches meat pies." The Spaniards encouraged colonization by Canary Islanders in Texas who may have introduced the characteristic cumin to Texas chili. Iberian influence in early California was reinforced by gold seekers and ranchers from South America, some only a generation or two out of Spain. Both Argentine dishes and some old Iberian noodles (*fideos*), meatballs (*albondigas*), and fish dishes persisted in the mix of Californian cuisine.

In the mid-nineteenth century, communication between the two coasts of North America was primarily by ship around South America. There was exchange of people and foods at every port of call around South America. Gentleman farmers and progressive seed merchants from the United States visited South America in search of seeds. The first real popcorn in the United States probably came from Chilean seed, and most of the beans now grown in the United States have primarily South American DNA. Before and after the Spanish-American War, the United States acquired a number of immigrants from Cuba, Puerto Rico, and the Philippines, some of whom were Iberian-born and all of whom brought Spanish food, such as rice dishes and egg-rich sweets, along with the Creole foods of their native regions.

Although Portugal did not successfully colonize North America, there was a notable minority of Portuguese, mostly Jewish, in the New Netherlands colony. A later and even larger colony of Iberian Jews settled in Charleston, South Carolina. Both of these colonies, along with Iberian Jews in London, helped to introduce deep-fried fish and what came to be called "french toast" to the Anglo-American table.

A community of Portuguese and Cape Verdean immigrants developed in the whaling ports of Massachusetts in the 1780s. This community was reinforced by continual immigration.

The recipe for a Cape Verdean bean pilaf called *jagacida* or "jag" was published as a regional Massachusetts dish in English as early as 1939. The dish is still regional specialty, along with kale soup, linguica and chorizo sausages, and eggy sweet bread. The sausages and sweet bread have become regional dishes in Hawaii, where Portuguese were among the earliest contract workers on the sugar plantations.

Since the loosening of immigration restrictions in the late 1960s, South American immigrants have come to the United States to escape civil strife or to work, often in restaurants. Brazilians have started restaurants of mainstream appeal based on the *parilladas* of Rio de Janeiro, where assorted grilled meats are carried on swords and carved at tableside. Argentine steakhouses have opened periodically in New York and Los Angeles. In "Neuvo Latino" fusion food, enterprising chefs have made elaborate dishes out of Peruvian ceviches and stews, the Ecuadorian potato stew *locro,* Venezuelan Christmas bread, and newly available ingredients such as passion fruit, cherimoya, plantain, and yucca.

[See also AFRICAN AMERICAN FOOD UP TO THE CIVIL WAR; APPALACHIAN FOOD; CAJUN AND CREOLE FOOD; CARIBBEAN INFLUENCES ON AMERICAN FOOD; CHOCOLATE; PINEDO, ENCARNACIÓN.]

BIBLIOGRAPHY

Coe, Sophie D., and Michael D. Coe. *The True History of Chocolate.* New York: Thames and Hudson, 1996.

Steele, Ian K. *Warpaths: Invasions of North America.*
New York: Oxford University Press, 1994.

MARK H. ZANGER

Ice

Ice has been used to preserve food and cool beverages for thousands of years. Wealthy Europeans brought their appreciation of icy desserts and iced drinks with them to the New World. Archaeologists at Jamestown, Virginia, found ice pits dating from as early as the seventeenth century. The colonists cut ice from ponds, lakes, and rivers during the winter and stored it in caves and underground cellars to last through the hot summer months. In the eighteenth century, icehouses, which were more efficient than cellars, provided cold storage, as well as preserving ice for chilling food and drink and making ice cream. Ice was advertised for sale in Philadelphia newspapers as early as 1784, and Europeans visiting Philadelphia and Baltimore in the 1790s reported that Americans drank water with ice and that containers of ice were used to cool hotel rooms.

The first recorded cargo of ice was shipped from New York to Charleston, South Carolina, in 1799, and between 1805 and 1860 Frederick Tudor, a Boston merchant, grew rich shipping harvested ice from Massachusetts ponds overseas. Tudor, known as the Ice King, promoted the construction and use of ice chests, sent agents to help establish businesses selling ice cream, extolled the virtues of ice for preserving food, and promoted the sale of carbonated water, which he thought tasted better cold. He even offered bar owners free ice for a year if they agreed to sell iced drinks at the same price as warm ones. In spite of Tudor's enthusiasm for cold drinks, some customers resisted because they believed that ice disguised bad liquor or diluted the effects of alcohol.

By the 1850s, ice was available in most urban places that were near rivers or served by railroads, and the widespread availability of ice at a reasonable price allowed the middle classes to use large quantities. By the 1880s, every well-equipped kitchen contained a patented icebox or ice chest, which was supplied almost daily by local refrigeration plants. In 1895, more than fifteen hundred ice wagons served customers in Brooklyn and New York City.

Seafood and dairy products packed with ice were transported in refrigerated railroad cars from the 1840s to the 1860s. The refrigerated transport of meat came later. Until the late 1860s, local butchers had slaughtered their own animals and chilled the meat in walk-in cold-storage boxes supplied with lake or river ice. Frozen meat was common in colder climates, where farmers and ranchers butchered their cattle and sheep in early winter, then packed the meat in outside cold boxes filled with ice and snow. The first shipload of commercially frozen beef was transported in 1869 from Indianola, Texas, to New Orleans, Louisiana, where it was served in hospitals, hotels, and restaurants. However, not everyone was in favor of frozen meat. Many considered it unsanitary, dangerous, or even poisonous, and some states attempted to put the new cold-storage warehouses out of business.

In 1867, J. B. Sutherland, of Detroit, Michigan, patented an insulated railroad car with bunkers for ice at each end, with the result that food was no longer packed in ice. This development made it possible to regulate the temperature by adding ice or by putting heaters in the bunkers in the winter. Gustavus F. Swift, who had founded a meatpacking business in Chicago in 1875, is generally credited with having commercialized the system of shipping fresh meat in refrigerated railroad cars. By 1892, over 100,000 refrigerated railroad cars transported dairy products, fruit, vegetables, meat, and fish.

The natural ice harvest peaked in 1886 at 25 million tons, and then began to decline as mechanical refrigeration took the place of natural ice. In 1911 the United States boasted nearly two thousand artificial ice plants serving the general public, in addition to the dedicated plants supplying meat packers, breweries, ice cream manufacturers, and other businesses requiring large quantities of ice. Despite advances in mechanical ice making and refrigeration, the natural ice trade between Maine and southern ports lasted well into the twentieth century.

The invention of small electric refrigerators was fatal to many large, established ice companies. In 1914, Fred W. Wolf Jr. invented a refrigerating machine, the Domestic Electric Refrigerator (DOMELRE) with an ice cube tray, and in 1918 Frigidaire became the first affordable, mass-produced electric household refrigerator. The first flexible metal ice cube tray, which fit the small freezer compartments of the new electric and gas-powered refrigerators, was invented by Guy L. Tinkham in 1933. The rural electrification movement that began in the 1930s brought electricity to

Cutting ice in Lehigh County, Pennsylvania, in the 1920s.

Examples of ice shavers from the 1922 catalog of the Crandall Pettee Company, New York.

rural as well as urban dwellers and made it possible for small businesses to make their own ice and to run their own freezers. The mass production of modern refrigerators with large freezers began after World War II, and automatic ice makers appeared in the 1960s. Nevertheless, commercial ice companies continue to provide ice for the fishing industry, as well as ice cubes for parties and the coolers of campers, sailors, and picnickers.

[See also ICEBOXES; REFRIGERATORS; SWIFT, GUSTAVUS FRANKLIN.]

BIBLIOGRAPHY

Anderson Jr., Oscar Edward. *Refrigeration in America: A History of a New Technology and Its Impact.* 1953. Reprint, Port Washington, NY: Kennikat Press, 1972.

Woolrich, W. R. *The Men Who Created Cold: A History of Refrigeration.* New York: Exposition Press, 1967.

VIRGINIA SCOTT JENKINS

Iceboxes

Ice was the original refrigerant and at one time was big business. During the nineteenth century, thousands of Americans made their living in the ice industry. Some cut ice from ponds and lakes to sell. Others manufactured equipment for the industry. Some shipped ice all over the world, and others delivered it from door to door. Still, ice had its drawbacks. It was often scarce or expensive, and, worst of all, it melted. To slow the melting, people mixed it with salt, layered it with straw, covered it with sawdust, or wrapped it in old blankets or carpets. They built ice pits and icehouses in which to store it, and they bought iceboxes, which also were called "refrigerators."

Many iceboxes were handsome paneled, hardwood cabinets fitted with brass hinges and locks. Others were of a plainer design. The interiors were lined with zinc, galvanized metal, or porcelain and were insulated with charcoal, cork, or fiber. One compartment held large blocks of ice; the others were for food. The ice could last for a day or more if the door to the ice compartment was not opened too often. Iceboxes for home use were made in a variety of sizes, from three to five feet high and from two to three feet wide or even larger. Horizontal ice chests were from two to three feet high and from two to three and one-half feet wide. Larger iceboxes were made for grocers and restaurateurs.

Iceboxes kept foods cold but not frozen, so chefs, confectioners, and cooks for the elite had a special, smaller icebox for ice cream and other frozen treats. The French term for this smaller icebox was *cave*; it also was known as an ice safe, freezer box, freezing box, or (confusingly) an icebox. The *cave* was a simple oblong box made of metal and lined with sheet iron or zinc. The space between the box and the lining was filled with charcoal, sawdust, or fibers for insulation. The *cave* had movable tin shelves to allow for the storage of several small ice cream molds or a few tall ones. It also had holes near the bottom to

allow the melted ice to drain out. *Caves* were available in a variety of sizes and held from one to several quarts of ice cream.

Caves were intended to keep items frozen for a few hours or even overnight, provided they were not opened frequently during that time. They allowed cooks and confectioners to make and even decorate fancy molded ice creams ahead of time without having them melt before being served or sold. After filling the molds with ice cream, cooks placed them in the *cave*, heaped salted ice over and around them, and left them until it was time to unmold and serve the ice cream. Some small *caves* had handles and could be used to transport ice cream to picnics and garden parties.

Electric refrigerators were introduced in the early part of the twentieth century. By the end of World War II, *caves* and iceboxes had become obsolete, and the demand for ice was melting away. By the end of the century, the industry still supplied ice to supermarkets and convenience stores, and consumers occasionally bought bags of ice for a party, but ice was no longer a big business.

[See also FREEZERS AND FREEZING; ICE; ICE CREAMS AND ICES; REFRIGERATORS.]

BIBLIOGRAPHY

Jones, Joseph C., Jr. *America's Icemen: An Illustrative History of the United States Natural Ice Industry, 1665–1925.* Humble, TX: Jobeco Books, 1984.

Israel, Fred L., ed. *1897 Sears Roebuck Catalogue.* New York: Chelsea House Publishers, 1968.

Selitzer, Ralph. *The Dairy Industry in America.* New York: Dairy and Ice Cream Field and Books for Industry, 1976.

Wheaton, Barbara Ketcham. *Victorian Ices & Ice Cream.* New York: Metropolitan Museum of Art, 1976. A reprint of the 1885 edition of *The Book of Ices* by Agnes B. Marshall, with an introduction and annotations by B. K. Wheaton.

JERI QUINZIO

Ice Cream Makers

In the eighteenth century, ice cream was a rare and expensive treat in the United States, enjoyed only at the most genteel gatherings. However, there was nothing elegant about the process by which it was made. Home cooks and professional confectioners alike faced the same difficulties. First, they had to obtain ice, chip it into manageable pieces, and mix it with salt. They put the ice-and-salt mixture into a large wooden tub or bucket. Then they mixed the ingredients for their ice cream; poured the mixture into a metal freezing pot with a cover, called a *sorbetière*; secured the cover; and set the pot in the tub. *Sorbetières* made of pewter or even silver could be purchased, but some cooks simply used any pot with a cover.

To make creamy—rather than icy—ice cream, the pot had to be shaken and turned continuously by hand. In addition, every now and then the person making the ice cream had to stop, open the pot, scrape the frozen ice cream off the sides, blend it into the

An advertisement for the White Mountain freezer, circa 1885.

mixture, close the pot, and begin turning it again. This process was repeated until the ice cream was ready. It was cold, difficult work—the task of slaves, servants, or lowly confectioners' helpers.

In 1843, an American, Nancy M. Johnson, revolutionized ice cream making. She invented (and patented as U.S. patent 3254) an ice cream freezer with a crank outside the tub that was attached to a dasher, or paddle, inside the freezing pot. The person making the ice cream turned the crank, and the dasher churned the ice cream mixture, automatically scraping the sides of the pot. Johnson's invention involved less work and made better ice cream. Best of all, it democratized ice cream, since it allowed even those who lacked servants and helpers to make it.

Johnson's invention led to others, and both home and commercial ice cream making expanded rapidly. Commercial ice cream makers used horse-powered treadmills, steam engines, and finally electric motors to churn ever-larger quantities of ice cream. Eventually, home cooks switched to electric ice cream makers, although hand-cranked models remain the stuff of nostalgic memories. Thanks to the ice cream maker, by the twentieth century, ice cream was an everyday treat, enjoyed by all.

[See also ICE; ICE CREAMS AND ICES.]

BIBLIOGRAPHY

David, Elizabeth. *Harvest of the Cold Months: The Social History of Ice and Ices.* Edited by Jill Norman. New York: Viking, 1995.

Lincoln, Mrs. D. A. *Frozen Dainties.* Bedford, MA: Applewood Books, 2001. A facsimile of the 1889 booklet published by the White Mountain Freezer Company.

JERI QUINZIO

Ice Cream Molds

A bowl heaped with ice cream was enough to dazzle dinner guests in early-eighteenth-century America. But once the novelty of having ice cream wore off, American cooks began to emulate Europeans by sending ice cream to the table in disguise. In the nineteenth century, they molded and decorated ice creams to resemble anything from a wedge of cheese to a melon with a slice cut out to contrast its green exterior with its pink center, and from a bouquet of flowers to a stalk of asparagus.

The ice cream molds themselves were crafted from pewter, copper, or tin and shaped to resemble fruits, vegetables, animals, and flowers. They were made in single-serving, quart, and banquet sizes. Home cooks could buy simple molds at the general store or from catalogs. Confectioners and caterers used elaborate, often multipart, molds.

To mold the ice cream, cooks chilled the molds, packed them full of ice cream, and put them in a small icebox, called a *cave* from the French (as in *cave à glace*), on a bed of salted ice. Then they heaped up more ice around the molds inside the *cave* and left the molds to firm up. After removing the molds from the *cave*, wiping off the ice mixture, and dunking the molds in warm water, they turned out the ice cream. It could be served immediately, put back in the *cave* to be served later, or decorated.

Although home cooks molding ice cream for a special occasion might line a fluted mold with vanilla ice cream and fill the center with strawberry, professionals went to far greater lengths. After they unmolded the ice cream, they embellished it. They tinted ice cream "lemons" with yellow coloring made with saffron and painted ice cream "cucumbers" with green coloring made from spinach. They tucked real leaves and stems into the tops of ice cream "fruits" and served them in baskets sculpted from sparkling ice. They wrapped ice cream "asparagus" in ribbons and brushed colored sugar over ice cream "peaches" to give them a delicate fuzz. The practice of molding ice creams, if not the attention to fine detail, continued throughout the twentieth century, as large-scale manufacturers offered both ready-made and custom ice creams molded into a variety of shapes for holidays, birthdays, and banquets.

[**See also** Desserts; Ice; Ice Creams and Ices.]

BIBLIOGRAPHY

Funderburg, Anne Cooper. *Chocolate, Strawberry, and Vanilla: A History of American Ice Cream.* Bowling Green, OH: Bowling Green State University Popular Press, 1995.

JERI QUINZIO

Ice Creams and Ices

Ice cream did not originate in America. But America can take credit for transforming it from a royal treat to a democratic dessert.

Ice cream's origins go back to the sixteenth century, when Italian scientists discovered they could intensify the natural coldness of ice by mixing it with salt. Soon, European confectioners began experimenting with freezing, and created the first ices and ice creams. To make them, they mixed ice or snow with salt in a large pail, then poured the ice cream mixture into a covered pot called a *sorbetière*, and placed it in the pail. In order to make smooth ice cream, they had to take the *sorbetière* out of the pail occasionally, open it, stir the mixture, recover the container, and put it back in the pail. It was cold, hard, time-consuming work. Nevertheless, by the eighteenth century, confectioners were making ices and ice creams in flavors that included orange blossom, jasmine, and rose, then molding them into the shape of fruits and flowers. They were royal desserts, made for royalty.

America's first families also were ice cream fans. George Washington owned "a Cream Machine for Making Ice," and Thomas Jefferson's papers include his handwritten recipe for vanilla ice cream. A few confectioners sold ice cream in America, most offering one or two flavors and making others to order. But until the mid-nineteenth century, the average person could not afford ice cream. Ice was not always affordable or available, nor was cream. Sugar was costly. Most important, making ice cream was too laborious for households without servants or slaves.

Ice Cream for All

Ice cream became more democratic after 1846 when Nancy Johnson, an American, invented an ice cream freezer suitable for home use. Johnson's freezer featured a crank and a dasher, or churn, inside the freezing pot, so the ice cream mixture could be stirred without opening the pot. The freezer made ice cream making easier. At the same time, it was more affordable because the price of sugar had dropped, and ice was more widely available.

The cost of buying ice cream went down when wholesalers went into the business. Jacob Fussell, a Baltimore dairyman, led the way. Others followed, and after the Civil War ended, the business expanded rapidly. In 1859, national production was estimated at four thousand gallons. Ten years later, it was 24,000 gallons. By the turn of the century, Americans were gobbling up five million gallons a year.

Ice cream was served at home and in restaurants. It teamed up with cake at birthday parties. Specialized ice cream utensils became fashionable, as did serving ices as palate cleansers between dinner courses. Vendors on city streets screamed "ice cream," and kids came running, pennies clutched in their hands. The ice cream soda became so popular a magazine called it "our national beverage." Ice cream sundaes, sandwiches, Popsicles, and other innovations followed. In 1920, Harry Burt of Ohio invented the "Good Humor Ice Cream Sucker," a chocolate-covered ice cream on a stick. He also was the first to sell ice cream from trucks, decked out with jingling bells.

Perhaps the most popular innovation was the ice cream cone, supposedly invented at the 1904 World's Fair in St. Louis. The legend is that a vendor selling ice cream in small glass dishes

Three types of ice cream mold.

Ice cream trucks typically sell manufactured bars, sandwiches, and popsicles.

could not wash them fast enough to keep up with demand. So Ernest Hamwi, a wafer-maker, rolled his wafers into cones and filled them with ice cream. However, Italo Marchiony, who sold lemon ices from a pushcart in New York, had previously applied for a patent on an ice cream cone mold. And, for years, European confectioners had filled wafer cones with whipped creams and later ice creams. But those were ice cream cones on a silver platter. America popularized the ice cream cone one licks outdoors on a summer day.

A New Era for Ice Cream

In 1920, America prohibited alcohol and started an ice cream boom. Consumption went up by more than 100 million gallons when the country went dry. Ice cream parlors replaced corner saloons. Breweries stopped producing beer and started making ice cream.

The repeal of Prohibition and the Great Depression of the 1930s sent sales plummeting, but by the end of the decade ice cream was back and selling better than ever. New manufacturing and refrigeration methods made it possible to make ice cream faster and to store it longer. During World War II, the government deemed it a necessity for America's fighting forces, and the U.S. military became the world's largest ice cream manufacturer.

When the war and gas rationing ended, Americans took to the road. They drove to Dairy Queen, Carvel, and Tastee Freeze for new soft-serve ice creams, and they stopped at Howard Johnson's for ice cream cones. Howard Johnson had opened his first ice cream stand in 1925 with three flavors of hand-cranked ice cream—vanilla, chocolate, and strawberry. By the 1950s, he had four hundred restaurants and twenty-eight flavors. Neighborhood ice cream parlors and drugstore soda fountains couldn't compete.

In the 1950s, Americans began shopping at supermarkets, buying packaged ice cream, and storing it in their new home freezers. Supermarket ice cream was cheap and readily available, but often it was not very good. Manufacturers made ice cream with artificial colors and imitation flavors, and they whipped a lot of air into it. In 1960, the American ice cream maker Reuben Mattus created a high-fat ice cream he named Häagen-Dazs for its European sound and gourmet appeal. Mattus discovered that consumers would pay more for high-quality ice cream, and ushered in the premium ice cream market.

At the turn of the twenty-first century, Americans consumed twenty-three quarts of ice cream per person, per year, more than people in any other country. They could choose from light, reduced-fat, low-fat, nonfat, regular, premium, and superpremium ice creams, as well as sherbets, sorbets, gelati, frozen yogurts, and innumerable novelty frozen desserts. They could even buy orange blossom, jasmine, and rose ice creams. The same flavors eighteenth-century confectioners made for royalty are blossoming again for everyone, thanks to the democratization of ice cream.

[See also Birthdays; Dairy Industry; Desserts; Flowers, Edible; Freezers and Freezing; Howard Johnson; Ice; Ice Cream Makers; Ice Cream Molds; Ice Cream Sodas; Iceboxes; Jefferson, Thomas; Johnson, Howard; Milk; Milkshakes, Malts, and Floats; Refrigerators; Soda Fountains.]

BIBLIOGRAPHY
Funderburg, Anne Cooper. *Chocolate, Strawberry, and Vanilla: A History of American Ice Cream.* Bowling Green, OH: Bowling Green State University Popular Press, 1995.
Kelly, Patricia M., ed. *Luncheonette: Ice Cream, Beverage, and Sandwich Recipes from the Golden Age of the Soda Fountain.* New York: Crown, 1989.
Wheaton, Barbara Ketcham. *Victorian Ices and Ice Cream.* New York: Metropolitan Museum of Art, 1976. A reprint of the 1885 edition of *The Book of Ices* by Agnes B. Marshall, with an introduction and annotations by B. K. Wheaton.

JERI QUINZIO

Ice Cream Sodas

By the early nineteenth century, cold carbonated waters that imitated waters from famous spas were sold in the United States on street corners in major cities and towns, in drug store soda fountains, and in lush surroundings such as those of the Tontine Coffee House in New York City. While they were initially drunk as curative beverages, ice cream sodas rapidly came to be viewed as refreshing treats.

Flavored syrups were added to carbonated waters beginning in the early 1800s. These flavored beverages caught on quickly, and the number of flavorings grew from a handful

---

Ice Cream Cone and the St. Louis World's Fair

The sweet equivalent of the sandwich, the ice cream cone belongs to one of America's favorite food categories, the handheld wrapped dish in which filler and wrapping are eaten together. Like many other iconic American dishes, ice cream cones were made for public eating and became popular in venues such as seaside resorts, fairs, and carnivals at the turn of the nineteenth century.

The classic cone is a wheat-based wafer baked in an iron mold and then rolled into a cone shape with a pointed bottom. The wafer is a venerable dish, dating to the European Middle Ages. Its more immediate antecedent in the United States is the waffle, which was brought to North America by Dutch immigrants in the seventeenth century. As in Europe, ice cream, which had become popular throughout colonial America, was often eaten with sweet wafers. The earliest written recipe yet discovered for a "cornet with cream" comes from England and appears in *Mrs. A. B. Marshall's Cookery Book* (1888), written by a then guru of French cookery. Marshall's recipe calls for flour, eggs, ground almonds, and orange water, and suggests that the ice cream should be eaten from the cone with a utensil.

The other style of ice cream cone, a plain wafer baked with a flat bottom, was introduced to the general public in 1904 at the St. Louis World's Fair, which celebrated the centennial of the Louisiana Purchase, although it may not have been invented there. The most common tale about the origin of the ice cream cone says that a Syrian immigrant named Ernest A. Hamwi had a concession at the fair for *zalabia*, a waffle of Persian origin. His stand was set up next to an ice cream stand, and Hamwi (or a Lebanese acquaintance named Abe Doumar) suggested rolling the waffles and filling them with ice cream. Thus was the "cornucopia" born. Hamwi soon thereafter worked with a Cornucopia Waffle Company and set up several other companies in later years.

The first cone-making mold to be patented was invented in New York City in 1903, the year before the St. Louis World's Fair. Italo Marchiony, an Italian ices maker and pushcart vendor, wanted a replacement for the glass cups in which he sold his ices in the area around Wall Street. His device made flat pastries that were rolled on the spot by pushcart vendors. Marchiony later claimed that he had come up with the idea in 1896, and this is generally conceded to be the date of the origin of the cone.

Nevertheless, the St. Louis fair made the ice cream cone popular, and, despite Hamwi's invented history, it appears that there were so many waffle vendors and ice cream makers cheek by jowl at the event that the idea of the cornucopia, which already existed in New York, probably occurred to many vendors, perhaps Hamwi among them. Paper cones for ice cream had appeared by at least the 1850s.

Within a few years, ice cream cone making had become industrialized. Frederick Bruckman patented a machine to make rolled cones in 1912, and in the 1920s molded cones with flat bottoms, modeled on Marchiony's design, were perfected by the Maryland Baking Company in Baltimore. By the late 1920s, at least one-third of all ice creams sold in the United States were in industrially made cones.

BIBLIOGRAPHY
Dickson, Paul. *The Great American Ice Cream Book.* New York: Atheneum, 1972.
Liddel, Caroline, and Robin Weir. *Ices: The Definitive Guide.* London: Hodder & Stoughton, 1994.

BRUCE KRAIG

Ice cream paraphernalia.

early in the century to hundreds by the end. Sweet cream or sweet cream syrup could also be added, creating what were called "ice cream sodas" or "iced cream sodas," although they did not actually contain ice cream. That these beverages were considered healthy is indicated by Gustavus Dows's 1861 advertisement promoting his soda fountains: "to preserve your health during the warm season, drink from two to five glasses of Dow's Ice Cream Soda Water Daily!"

The man most often associated with the creation of the ice cream soda as it is known today is Robert Green, who operated a small soda fountain at the semicentennial celebration of the Franklin Institute in Philadelphia in 1874, selling soda water flavored with various syrups and sweet cream. When Green ran out of cream, he purchased some vanilla ice cream from a nearby confectioner to use instead. Returning to his stand, Green found customers waiting and, instead of melting the ice cream, he scooped it into the beverages.

In Green's own account of the origin of the soda, which he provided years later, he recalls that when he realized that his small fountain could not compete with a more elaborate one, he decided that he had to come up with something new, a soda with ice cream. He offered young people free sodas to try his creation. They did, loved it, and spread the word. A number of other people laid claim to the creation of the soda, but it was Green who popularized it. He even directed that "originator of the ice cream soda" be engraved on his tomb.

Sipping ice cream sodas had become a national pastime by the 1890s, although not without initial opposition. Soda fountain proprietors worried that the ice cream soda

took too long to assemble and too long to consume. However, sodas became so popular that the soda fountain industry soon promoted them vigorously, providing formulas and diagrams of new creations. A few religious leaders initially viewed sipping sodas on Sunday as sinful, but temperance advocates saw the soda as a good alternative to alcoholic beverages, and church opposition faded.

Ice cream sodas in endless variety were soon sold in every soda fountain in the country. They ranged from simple chocolate and strawberry sodas to the black cow, made from root beer syrup, vanilla ice cream, soda water, and whipped cream, to the fancifully named Minnehaha and Floradora Brandy sodas. Ice cream sodas represent a simpler time in America's history, when families, dating couples, and neighbors gathered at the local soda fountain to sip and socialize.

[*See also* CHOCOLATE DRINKS; SODA DRINKS; SODA FOUNTAINS.]

BIBLIOGRAPHY

Funderburg, Anne Cooper. *Sundae Best: A History of Soda Fountains.* Bowling Green, OH: Bowling Green State University Popular Press, 2002.

Kelly, Patricia M., ed. *Luncheonette: Ice-Cream, Beverage, and Sandwich Recipes from the Golden Age of the Soda Fountain.* New York: Crown, 1988.

Wheaton, Barbara Ketcham. *Victorian Ices & Ice Cream.* New York: Metropolitan Museum of Art, 1976. A reprint of the 1885 edition of *The Book of Ices* by Agnes B. Marshall, with an introduction and annotations by B. K. Wheaton.

JERI QUINZIO

Iced Tea, *see Tea*

Indian American Food

There is a common saying in northern India, "*Kosa kosa pai pani badale chara kosa pai bani,*" meaning "Every two miles the water doth change and every four the dialect." This Hindustani proverb hints at a popular geography of taste where *pani*, water, is a metonym for taste. Food in India is essentially regional, as is the case with every major country, especially one as large, geographically fragmented and culturally diverse as India. India has twenty-five (mostly) linguistically differentiated states. Language is a good indicator of culinary difference.

In most societies, there are numerous sites where cooking develops. Some of the important locations of culinary creativity in India have been imperial courts, temples, commercial eating establishments, and domestic households. Each of these institutions puts food to a different use. For instance, the essential point of court cuisine is to display power through the consumption of elaborately prepared foods using expensive ingredients, such as sugar, ice, spices, and meats. This is the realm of rich curries using ghee, cardamom, clove, and saffron, typically the cuisine of Delhi in northern India, called Mughlai food. The Mughals have had such a

disproportionate impact on imaginings of commercial Indian haute cuisine because they dominated the subcontinent just before the arrival of the British, and Indian food is a product of Indian nationalism.

If courtly cuisine is dominated by Delhi-centered regimes, then street foods are marked by numerous regional variations: savory samosas in the north; sweet and salty fried legumes in western India; sour and savory crêpes (*dosa*) in south India; and desserts made from farmer's cheese in the east. These foods often serve as metonyms for cultural regions. Each of the subregions, such as Punjab and Uttar Pradesh in the north, has its own cuisine with its distinctive spice mix, fat base, cooking methods, utensils, cutting and grinding implements, complex carbohydrate core, protein fringe, and legume.

Beyond the court and the marketplace, another site of culinary creativity is the domestic hearth. This is where spices, salt, and sugar are used much more sparingly, partly as a result of poverty, and partly because there is no need either to impress vassals and patrons or to extend shelf life. Eastern India, which has neither been the center of Indian politics nor as highly urbanized as the western region around Surat and Mumbai (Bombay), is almost exclusively the realm of domestic cooking. It is quite difficult, for instance, to buy Bengali food in the preeminent Bengali city of Kolkata (Calcutta).

The regional and social variety of Indian cuisines is not reflected in the cooking of Indian American restaurants. Most serve a version of northern Indian Mughlai cuisine. Southern Indian restaurants and menu items such as *dosas* and *idlis* have become visible in the United States since the late 1990s. Typically, the main courses are Mughlai, whereas some of the appetizers are from western India, such as *bhel puri*. Indian restaurants appear to confine themselves to one or two kinds of food, much as Italian American restaurants did until the last decade of the twentieth century.

Most Indian restaurants in the United States are entrepreneurial ventures of Punjabis and Gujaratis. This is because they migrate with fewer professional credentials but better familial networks than other South Asians, such as Bengalis from West Bengal. Hence, Punjabis and Gujaratis are more likely to use small ethnic businesses as routes of upward mobility. Therefore, it is the northern (Punjabi) and western (Gujarati) aesthetic that dominates American Indian restaurant cuisine. In an interesting complication, many Bengalis from Bangladesh (not from the Indian state of West Bengal) also work in these restaurants, because they have even fewer professional credentials. Thus, in the same way as the Chinese have come to dominate sushi restaurants, Bangladeshi sojourners cater Mughlai food, in Punjabi restaurants, to

Americans seeking Indian food—partly because of the shape of the labor market and partly because they believe that Americans will not know the difference.

Domestic Cooking

To say something about Indian American domestic cooking, it is necessary to abandon the category "Indian" and look more closely at the linguistic subset such as Bengali Americans.

For a typical Bengali American, breakfast is either milk and cereal or toast. Bengalis prefer tea over coffee, which is predictable for people coming from a state including a region called Darjeeling. Lunch, consumed at or near the workplace, is a salad or a slice of pizza, sometimes a sandwich. It is dinner that remains in the realm of "tradition." Rice, *dal*, and fish cooked in a sauce with *panch phoron* (a Bengali five-spice mix of fenugreek, onion seed, fennel, cumin, and mustard seed) are often eaten for dinner. Contrary to stereotype, most Bengalis, like most Indians, are *not* vegetarians.

It is, of course, an exaggeration to say that dinner remains wholly "traditional." Take, for instance, the appetizer for a typical Sunday dinner: ground turkey croquettes cooked with chopped garlic, ginger, onion, and fresh cilantro. Turkey is hardly a traditional Bengali ingredient. Yet it is cooked in a typically Bengali form, with ground turkey replacing ground goat meat. Any meat in Bengali cuisine is usually cooked with the trinity of wet spices: onion, ginger, and garlic.

Then there is the more explicit intermingling of American and Bengali cuisines, for example, when the menu includes roast chicken, steamed rice, and apple juice. There is a pervasive "Bengaliness" in all this mixing up. Rice continues to be the core of the evening meal. The animal protein is important but remains a fringe item in terms of calories. The carbohydrate core and the animal-protein fringe are paired with the third defining element, *dal*, or legume soup, which is sparsely spiced. The animal-protein fringe, in contrast, is highly spiced as is typical in Bengali cuisine. The spices and herbs are drawn mostly from within the Bengali repertoire and the cooking processes are typically limited to sautéing, stewing, and braising, which are basic Bengali notions of "cooking."

Furthermore, the greatest change can be seen in the elements that are peripheral to the Bengali conception of the "meal," that is, turkey replacing goat meat in the appetizer, juices and soda replacing water, and strawberry shortcake simulating a Bengali dessert. This perhaps is because the most radical changes are confined to the accompaniments that the "meal" can still be defined as Bengali.

Thus, dinner has changed in two directions: new ingredients, such as turkey, are absorbed into old culinary paradigms; and the use of old constituents, such as rice and

fish, are insisted upon. One absorbs change and the other accentuates tradition in a new context. With breakfast and dinner, it is as if Bengalis have divided up the day into what they characterize as moments of "modernity" and moments of "tradition," both perceived as good and necessary in their separate places. This complementary duality toward the "modern" and the "traditional" is central to the identity of the Bengali middle class. The Indian migrant has long been threatened and seduced by the promise of modernization, and he has acted on those concerns in organizing his food practices in the United States.

[See also Ethnic Foods; Herbs and Spices; Muslim Dietary Laws; Rice; Vegetarianism.]

BIBLIOGRAPHY

Achaya, K. T. *Indian Food: A Historical Companion.* Delhi: Oxford University Press, 1994.

Khare, R. S. *Culture and Reality: Essays on the Hindu System of Managing Foods.* Simla: Indian Institute of Advanced Studies, 1976.

Ray, Krishnendu. *The Migrant's Table. Meals and Memories among Bengali American Households.* Philadelphia: Temple University Press, 2004.

Krishnendu Ray

Indian Pudding

Indian pudding is one of the oldest celebratory foods of North America. At present, it is generally regarded as an old New England dish and consists of yellow cornmeal baked with milk and molasses, often eggs, sometimes spiced with ginger, and often served with ice cream. As such, it represents the American evolution of a typical British pudding, with native maize meal substituted for other grains, and cheap molasses commemorating colonial and early American tastes in a way that was reinforced in a revival of regional foods in the late nineteenth century. However, the dish also is included in at least fifteen Native American cookbooks published in the twentieth century. How Indian pudding evolved is a question that divides food historians and can perhaps best be understood with a model of Native-colonial collaboration.

Many popular books project Indian pudding as a dish Indians made in earth ovens with maple syrup that was simply taken over by New England settlers. There is no support for this in either the archaeological record nor the writings of explorers or colonists, nor in Native oral histories. Beginning with Karen Hess in the 1977 *The Taste of America*, food historians corrected this view, pointing out: "Now, anyone who had read English cookbooks of the seventeenth century would recognize that these [three recipes for Indian Pudding in the first American-authored cookbook] are not Indian puddings but English boiled and baked puddings using Indian—i.e. corn—meal." Cornmeal was known as Indian meal in early America where speakers of British English still used the word "corn" for any grain. And in fact, some nineteenth-

century American recipes are for "Indian Meal Pudding."

Certainly, the technique of the first published recipes supports the picture of English and Scottish housewives substituting corn meal for European grains in typical European bagged-and-boiled or oven-baked puddings. Before European contact, New England Indians used neither technique and had no access to milk or molasses.

However, they did make and sometimes even bake cornmeal mushes that could be either sweetened or fortified with fat. So, from a Native point of view, Indian pudding was simply a case of adapting newly available milk and molasses, and eventually oven baking, to typical Native sweetened and/or fortified mushes.

None of the Native names of these mushes passed over to Indian pudding, but the names did pass over for unsweetened mushes: samp in New England, suppawn in New Netherlands, hominy and sofkey in the southern coastal colonies, and sagamite in the French colonies. Descriptions by explorers and settlers confirm that these Native cornmeal mushes were often fortified or sweetened, and colonial diaries indicate that the typical table service of plain cornmeal mush or "hasty pudding" was often accompanied with butter or molasses or both.

The Spanish explorers of the southwestern states encountered a liquid mush or thick drink of hominy grits they knew from Mexico as atole but that the Native Americans in what became the United States knew as "sofkey." In Mexico, it was sweetened with honey, maguey syrup, parched cornmeal, and even cacao. (In the present southwestern states, it survives under the Aztecan names of atole, pinole, and champurado.) When the English explorer Captain Arthur Barlow tasted some on Roanoke Island in 1584, he described it as "some wheat like furmentie." Because Barlow compared this Indian wheat to English frumenty (and not to porridge or pottage), we can guess that it was fortified with something sweet and/or fatty, since frumenty might have used milk, almond milk, egg yolks, or ale. Barlow mentions grapes and melons at the same feast, and some other possible Native additions besides honey are hickory or pecan milk, boiled maple or grape sap, duck or turtle eggs, animal fats, or even crudely fermented corn or grape liquids.

A closer observer, Roger Williams, in his 1643 *Key to Language of America*, notes: "atti-taash—*Hurtle-berries*, Of which there are divers sorts sweete like Currants. ... Sautaash are these Currants dried by the *Natives*, and so preserved all the yeare, which they beat to powder, and mingle it with their parcht meale, and make a delicate dish which they cal *Sautáuthig*; which is as sweet to them as plum or spice cake to the *English*." Therefore, this was an instant mush mix of parched corn (itself somewhat sweet) and powdered, dried blueberries.

By 1672, John Josselyn, just returned from Maine, records that "The *Indians* dry them in the Sun, and sell them to the *English* by the bushell, who make use of them instead of Currence, putting of them into Puddens, both boyled and baked, and into Water Gruel." So in Maine, at least, Native Americans were now part of the colonial food supply system, and settlers were using the blueberry-mush recipe in pudding bags and molds. In a later book, Josselyn mentions an Indian in the dairy business as well, that settlers had learned from Indians to make a sweet drink from cornstalks, and the Indian use of dried eggs to thicken broth.

Meanwhile, in 1673, Father Marquette enjoyed a fortified pudding-like mush in the Midwest: "The first course was a great wooden platter full of sagamité,–that is to say, meal of Indian corn boiled in water, and seasoned with fat." Colonial Americans of all backgrounds also tended to serve the Indian pudding first, to fill up before the meat came out. Poor families might do this at all three meals.

These early accounts show that Native Americans made pudding-like dishes of corn meal mush and available sweeteners and oils. Later, anthropologists collected many recipes for sweetened corn mushes, often used as ceremonial treats for weddings or secret society rituals, using sprouted grain, honey, or local sweeteners. But, increasingly, Native Americans were trading with settlers and acquiring milk and molasses. Natives were indentured or enslaved, and learned to make European puddings as kitchen servants well into the eighteenth century. Natives also entered European society and acquired wide tastes in later colonial times as sailors, seasonal farm laborers, mercenary soldiers, and caterers. For example, the January 5, 1719, *Boston News Letter* advertised for sale an Indian woman who "can sew, wash, brew, bake, spin, and milk cows."

By 1749, Pehr Kalm, a Swedish botanist visiting Canada, found acculturated Huron with all the tools for making "Indian Pudding" living in Quebec: "These Indians have the French their patterns in several things, besides the houses. They all plant maise; and some have small fields of wheat and rye. Many of them keep cows. They plant our common sun-flower in their maize fields, and mix the seeds of it into the sagamite, or maise-soup."

Although molasses is universal to New England Indian pudding, milk is not. One of the earliest written recipes, by the New England–born Tory Count Rumford, is for a bagged pudding without milk. Southern cookbooks from the early nineteenth century generally do not include milk. And Elizabeth Lea's Maryland cookbook uses almost no sweetener–a little sugar and dried peaches–and adds molasses only as a sauce. Two antebellum southern cookbooks have recipes for sweetened and enriched version of sofkee. North and south, many poor farmers (and likely most farming native Americans) sweet-

ened their mush pudding with local sweeteners—maple syrup and sugar, sorghum molasses, boiled cider—into the twentieth century, and these alternatives did not reach printed cookbooks.

Ice cream became an important celebratory dish in the early nineteenth century as ice became available in the summer. It was added to Indian pudding to strike a patriotic note for the Fourth of July. Throughout the nineteenth century, the puddings became sweeter, with a more pronounced flavor of molasses. Food historians Keith Stavely and Kathleen Fitzgerald, in *America's Founding Food*, trace this to a colonial revival after the nation's centennial celebrations in 1876, in which the flavor of molasses—once stigmatized as cheap sweetener for the poor—became a patriotic symbol for New Englanders. Other patriotic symbols, including much of the Thanksgiving dinner, also have Native associations, and so the idea of Indian pudding as a dish taken directly from the Indians would have fit right in with serving it as a symbol of Anglo-American identity.

The dish also evolved in printed cookbooks. One could add the milk late to a baked pudding to make a custardlike top. Eggs and spices are mentioned, a long list of berries, and a dried-apple version. In the twentieth century, rustic New Englanders developed a "mock Indian pudding"–wheat toast or bread pudding flavored with molasses and custard.

MARK H. ZANGER

In-N-Out Burger

A striking exception in the pantheon of American fast food chains, In-N-Out Burger, founded in 1948 in Baldwin Park, California, has never been sold or franchised. When Harry and Esther Snyder opened their first hamburger stand, it was a family-owned enterprise—and, with 150 outlets as of 2005, it remained so. The Snyders didn't open a second stand until 1951, and at the time of Harry Snyder's death, in 1976, there were still only eighteen In-N-Out Burger outlets. (The original stand, now closed, may become the In-N-Out Museum.)

There was nothing revolutionary about In-N-Out's menu in 1948–it was the usual selection of burgers, fries, soda, and shakes—but the Snyders were among the first to offer drive-through service, using a version of the two-way speaker system found at most chains today. The same familiar foods are still available at In-N-Out, with the intriguing addition of a "Secret menu" that can be viewed on the company's website. Some of the options found there are the "3×3"–a cheeseburger with three patties and three slices of cheese—and the "Animal Style" burger, made with a beef patty cooked in mustard.

In-N-Out operates its own meat-packing facility and delivers the ground beef to its outlets in refrigerated trucks; there are no microwaves, freezers, or heat lamps in the

restaurants. The burgers are all beef, the fries made with potatoes cut in the store, and the shakes are made from real ice cream. To help maintain its high standards, the company trains managers at the In-N-Out "University." The pay scale is significantly above minimum wage, and workers are offered a comprehensive benefits package.

[**See also** FAST FOOD.]

BIBLIOGRAPHY

Schlosser, Eric. *Fast Food Nation; the Dark Side of the All-American Meal.* Boston & New York: Houghton Mifflin Company, 2001.

ANDREW F. SMITH

Insects

Lobsters, crabs, and shrimp are esteemed foods in the United States, but grasshoppers, termites, and caterpillars are not. All are arthropods with tough, segmented exoskeletons and high-protein muscle tissue. Yet many Americans define ocean-living shellfish as edible and land-dwelling insects as inedible. Just the mention of eating "bugs" can prompt the gag reflex.

This aversion to insects as food is not shared globally. Entomophagy, meaning "insect eating," is widespread, providing approximately 10 percent of protein consumed worldwide. Baby bee appetizers in Japan, mopane worm casserole in South Africa, scorpion soup in China, and grasshopper tacos in Mexico are examples of entomophagy. The American attitude toward entomophagy has its roots in Europe, when, during the Middle Ages (1000 to 1400 B.C.E.), meat, especially beef and pork, became so abundant that even the poor had plenty of protein without foraging for insects. It is theorized that only regions of the world with scarce or difficult-to-hunt protein sources and a geography unsuited to raising domesticated animals developed extensive entomophagy. In Europe and the United States, where protein is ample, insects are usually associated with dirt, disease, crop destruction, decomposition, biting or stinging, teeming, and other attributes that bring forth loathing and disgust.

A young boy inspects an hors d'oeuvre prepared with an insect before eating it at New York's Museum of Natural History.

In the United States, nineteenth-century ethnographic data demonstrate that entomophagy was important in certain Native Americans groups, especially those living in the Great Basin and southwestern desert areas. Locusts and grasshoppers were particularly popular. The Shoshone formed a large circle called a surround and beat the ground with sticks, herding the grasshoppers into a large pit. The Ute used a similar technique, driving them toward hot coals. The Washo would set the prairie grasses aflame to collect locusts. Both insects were enjoyed roasted with salt (likened to shrimp) and pulverized to make a flour used in porridge or bread. Pandora moth caterpillars were commonly smoked out of trees and roasted for immediate consumption, or air-dried for future use. Shore fly larva collected from alkaline lakes, crickets beaten out of bushes, and larva scooped from anthills were other insect favorites.

In this same period, some Plains settlers consumed grasshoppers following destruction of crops by swarms of the insect, but others starved because of entomophagy prejudice. A few U.S. authors began to question the rationality of ignoring insect protein sources, especially during food shortages. In 1885, a small book titled *Why Not Eat Insects?* by Vincent Holt suggested that the addition of insect dishes to the diet was a matter of common sense and of reason conquering fashion. Anticipating deprivation during World War I, some scientists recommended that research on insect palatability be undertaken by college departments of home economics and by the U.S. Department of Agriculture. Concern that the world's food supply was running out popularized Ronald Taylor's book on entomophagy *Butterflies in My Stomach* (1975) and his booklet *Entertaining with Insects; or, The Original Guide to Insect Cookery* written in 1976 with Barbara Carter. Increasing interest in a unique dining experience resulted in a number of late-twentieth-century publications, including the *Eat-a-Bug Cookbook* by David George Gordon (1998) and *Man Eating Bugs: The Art and Science of Eating Insects* by Peter Menzel and Faith D'Aluisio (1998).

Canned insects are sometimes available in ethnic markets. However, American entomophagy in the twenty-first century is primarily limited to tequila-flavored lollipops with mealworms, chocolate-covered ants, other candied insect novelties, and the occasional instructional menu created by entomologists for their students. Unintentional insect eating is more common. The Food and Drug Administration regulates the amount of whole insects, fragments, and larva or eggs allowed in food, such as ten aphids in five hundred grams (about one pound) of raspberries that are frozen or canned, three hundred fragments in that same amount of chocolate, and five fly maggots in that amount of tomatoes used for tomato paste, pizza sauce, or juice. In most cases, the insects

are processed and become an undetectable addition to the product.

Pound for pound, edible portions of insects provide high-quality protein that is typically lower in fat and higher in other nutrients, such as calcium and iron, than protein from meat, poultry, or fish. Entomologists note that some insects convert their feed to body tissue more efficiently than vertebrates, at rates nearly double those of chicken and five hundred times higher than cattle. It has been suggested that mass production of insects could ease world hunger. Entomophagy should be limited to commercial insects because of the potential for contamination by pesticides and toxins; people sensitive to shellfish also may be allergic to insects.

[**See also** ADULTERATIONS; ASEPTIC PACKAGING; GIBBONS, EUELL; NATIVE AMERICAN FOOD: TECHNOLOGY AND SOURCES; PIONEERS AND SURVIVAL FOOD; PURE FOOD AND DRUG ACT.]

BIBLIOGRAPHY

Bodenheimer, Friedrich S. *Insects as Human Food: A Chapter in the Ecology of Man.* The Hague: W. Junk, 1951.

De Foliart, Gene R. *The Human Use of Insects as Food: A Bibliographic Account in Progress.* http://www.food-insects.com. 2002.

Harris, Marvin. *Good to Eat: Riddles of Food and Culture.* New York: Simon & Schuster, 1985.

Sutton, Mark Q. *Insects as Food: Aboriginal Entomophagy in the Great Basin.* Menlo Park, CA: Ballena Press, 1988.

PAMELA GOYAN KITTLER

International Aid

Signed into law in 1954, Public Law (PL) 480 has served as the most significant instrument of food aid in U.S. foreign policy. The program has three parts. Title I, overseen by the U.S. Department of Agriculture, makes government-to-government sales of agricultural commodities (such as wheat, rice, corn, and soybeans) on long-term credit to developing countries. Title II, administered by the Agency for International Development (AID), makes donations by the U.S. government of agricultural commodities for international humanitarian food needs to other governments, intergovernmental agencies, and public and private nongovernmental organizations. Title III, also administered by AID, supports economic development by donating agricultural commodities, which recipient countries then sell on the domestic market, using the proceeds for development programs.

Public Law 480 arose from the poor economic conditions in Europe following World War II. American agriculture had produced large surpluses sufficient to supply U.S. domestic needs and those of European countries. As European agriculture recovered in the early 1950s, overproduction in the United States created economic uncertainty and the consequent need to expand markets in lieu of curtailing U.S. agricultural production. The Agricultural Trade Development and Assistance Act of 1954, which authorized

Poster created by the National Association of Ice Industries for the United States Food Administration during World War I.

PL 480, was designed to dispose of federal surplus agricultural commodities, expand international trade, and create new foreign markets via economic development in developing nations. The act also furthered the U.S. geopolitical interests of the Cold War. Congressional desire to use "food as a weapon" of foreign policy to stop the global spread of communism was explicitly reflected in debate on S. 2475, which became PL 480.

An overt emphasis on humanitarian food aid did not emerge until 1958 when Senator Hubert Humphrey (D-MN) sought revisions to the law in a report entitled "Food and Fiber as a Force for Freedom." Humphrey sought to rename the law the Food for Peace Act, a name that remains current in the early 2000s, and to redirect the focus from economic support of the agricultural sector in the United States, toward the promotion of international welfare, peace, and freedom. With Cold War objectives still in place, PL 480 played an unambiguous role in helping those countries considered politically friendly to the foreign policy interests of the United States. For these reasons, critics refer to PL 480 as the "Food as a Weapon" program. Congress later redefined the program's goals, directly linking food aid to countries demonstrably affected by food shortages. Public Law 480 continued, as the twenty-first century opened, to be defined in part by commitments to development and expansion of export markets for U.S. agricultural commodities, as well as by promoting political goals.

In its initial years, the Food for Peace program accounted for one-quarter to one-third of all U.S. agricultural exports. Largely through PL 480, the U.S. by the early 1960s had come to supply over 95 percent of all international food aid, a figure that declined by nearly half in the following decade. PL 480 continues to serve as a major source of humanitarian food assistance. In fiscal year 2002, the program provided 2.7 million metric tons of food totaling nearly $595 million, making the United States the single largest government contributor of international food aid.

Critics of PL 480 have pointed to several, sometimes contradictory, concerns with the program. Some stress the tendency of PL 480 to flood the markets of less-developed countries with large surpluses of U.S. agricultural commodities, thereby threatening the indigenous agricultural base and economy. Others argue that certain recipient governments have relied heavily on PL 480 contributions to insulate and support local agricultural sectors that in some cases actually could benefit from greater modernization. Still others note that PL 480 has served as a major governmental subsidy for U.S. agricultural interests. Concerns over genetically modified U.S. food aid have also been raised in some recipient countries.

Supporters of the program, including the World Food Program, CARE, and the Coalition for Food Aid, view PL 480 as vital in the continuing effort to feed populations facing serious threats to food security. For them, compassion fatigue and declining American support in the 1990s for foreign food aid signal troubles for ongoing humanitarian efforts.

[**See also** Department of Agriculture, United States; Hunger Programs; Nutrition.]

BIBLIOGRAPHY
Cathie, John. *The Political Economy of Food Aid*. New York: Palgrave Macmillan, 1982.
FASonline. http://www.fas.usda.gov/food-aid.html. Describes food aid programs under PL 480 and other initiatives of the U.S. government.

Kevin T. McIntyre and
Barrett P. Brenton

International Association of Culinary Professionals

In 1978, culinary educators launched the Association of Cooking Schools. In 1990, the name was changed to the International Association of Culinary Professionals (IACP). It is a professional society of individuals employed in the culinary industry. Since 1986, IACP has given awards to authors of outstanding cookbooks and beverage publications, and awards for excellence in food journalism.

IACP is one of the largest associations of culinary professionals in the United States. As of 2005, the association has more than four thousand members in thirty-five countries. The IACP holds an annual national conference and distributes publications, such as the quarterly publication *Food Forum* and special publications, such as Delores Custer's *The Art of Food Photography: A Retrospective from the 1950s through the 1990s* (1990s), Madge T. Griswold's *A Selective Guide to Culinary Library Collections in the United States* (2001), and Griswold's *For the Love of Food: Recipes and Stories from the Chefs of the IACP* (2005). IACP's philanthropic partner is The Culinary Trust, which gives grants to food writers, administers scholarships for students studying at culinary schools, and preserves culinary heritage. IACP and the Trust are headquartered in Louisville, Kentucky.

Andrew F. Smith

Irish Coffee

Although people have been lacing coffee with alcohol for years, Irish coffee, a drink of slightly sweetened hot coffee that is fortified with Irish whiskey and served with a blanket of whipped cream floating on top, was supposedly invented in the winter of 1943 by Joe Sheridan, chef at Foynes Airport in Limerick, Ireland. The story goes that Sheridan, after hearing that a flight bound for New York had turned back as a result of bad weather, mixed up a special drink to warm the exhausted passengers. Among the travelers was the writer Stanton Delaplane, who liked the concoction so much that he brought the recipe back to Jack Koeppler, bartender at the Buena Vista Hotel in San Francisco. Koeppler and Delaplane tried to re-create the drink, but the whipped cream kept sinking to the bottom. Koeppler eventually visited Sheridan in Ireland and learned the threefold secret of floating the cream—the coffee must be lightly sweetened, the cream must be both fresh and softly whipped, and the cream must be poured into the hot coffee over the back of a spoon.

Irish coffee became a staple after-dinner drink in the United States in the 1950s. Its popularity peaked in the 1970s, when seemingly endless variations using sweeter liqueurs came into vogue. Although it is no longer a huge fad, Irish coffee remains a classic cold-weather drink.

[**See also** Coffee.]

BIBLIOGRAPHY
Lovegren, Sylvia. *Fashionable Food: Seven Decades of Food Fads*. New York: Macmillan, 1995.
Mariani, John F. *The Dictionary of American Food and Drink*. New Haven: Ticknor and Fields, 1983.

Sylvia Lovegren

Irradiation

Irradiation is a process in which food is exposed briefly to a radiant energy source in an effort to kill harmful bacteria, eliminate insect pests, inhibit further maturation of fresh foods, extend shelf life, and sterilize packaging materials. Similar to sending luggage through an airport scanner, the food is passed in containers quickly through a radiation field. Commercial irradiation equipment uses gamma rays, electron beams, or X-rays. Federal rules require irradiated foods to be labeled as such. Irradiating food does not eliminate all risk of food-borne illness, and proper handling is still required.

Scientists first studied radiation in the 1930s, but shortly after World War II research efforts increased as the U.S. Army sought a means of reducing field troops' dependence on refrigeration. By the 1950s, research took a new turn when the Eisenhower administration's Atoms for Peace program explored irradiation as a way of killing insects on fruits and vegetables.

Combined with simultaneous studies in other countries, the research found the most important benefit of irradiation to be the control of harmful food pathogens. It was not until 1963 that the FDA approved the first commercial use of irradiation for wheat and wheat flour. As is still true in the early 2000s, the approval came with strict guidelines for the maximum amount, or dose, of radiation allowed, as measured in kiloGrays, or kGy.

It took another twenty years for the FDA to approve additional commercial uses of the process. In 1983, irradiating spices and dry vegetable seasonings became permissible for the purpose of decontaminating and controlling insects and microorganisms. Two years later, dry and dehydrated enzyme preparations were added to the list of products approved for irradiation, and, in 1986, the FDA approved pork for irradiation in an effort to control *Trichinella spiralis* parasites. It took six more years for approval to be granted for use on poultry, and it was not until 2000 that the federal government added raw meat and meat products to the list of foods that could be irradiated to control pathogen microorganisms.

Consumer understanding and acceptance of irradiation has by no means kept up with the government's approval of the process, although consumer acceptance has increased. In 1993 a national Gallup poll found that over 60 percent of consumers were extremely

The radura symbol on a package means the food has been subjected to irradiation.

concerned that irradiated food might cause cancer or other illness. By 1998–1999, a survey of adult consumers by the Foodborne Diseases Active Surveillance Network (Food-Net) showed 50 percent of their participants were willing to buy irradiated foods. But the study further showed that the percentage decreased greatly when the cost of irradiated food was higher than that of nonirradiated food.

The amount of food irradiated in the United States will be limited, according to the U.S. Department of Agriculture's *Food Safety Economics,* by manufacturers' perception of public attitude toward irradiation. As the twenty-first century began, irradiation equipment was very costly, and food manufacturers were unlikely to make the investment as long as they perceived consumers were unwilling to buy irradiated products.

[**See also** ASEPTIC PACKAGING; FOOD SAFETY; MICROWAVE OVENS.]

BIBLIOGRAPHY

Frenzen Paul D., Alex Majchowicz, Jean C. Buzby, and Beth Imhoff. "Consumer Acceptance of Irradiated Meat and Poultry Products." *Issues in Food Safety Economics*. USDA/ERS.

MARGE PERRY

Italian American Food

Among the six largest ethnic groups in modern America, Italian Americans were the last to arrive in substantial numbers, faced a great deal of discrimination as immigrants, and have the most popular ethnic cuisine by every measure: restaurant meals, supermarket sales, published cookbooks, and recipes in contributed cookbooks. Contemporary American youth of all backgrounds love pasta and pizza; the most refined gourmets seek out exotic Italian regional specialties like *ventresca tuna, farro,* and fennel pollen.

All of this would surprise the typical Italian immigrant family of one hundred years ago, who might well know none of the foods mentioned above, nor even think of themselves as Italian. Southern Italy and Sicily, the origin of most Italian Americans, did not join the Kingdom of Italy until 1861. Italian immigrants seemed to come directly from rural villages to American port cities, mostly between the years 1900 to 1924—when most of the farmland in the United States had been taken. Thus people of peasant background were crowded into "Little Italy" urban neighborhoods and may have learned that they were "Italian" instead of Sicilian or Abruzzese from immigration officials or social workers.

Italians in service of Spain, Portugal, and England were the among the first to lead expeditions to the Americas, and these expeditions were also partially financed by Italian capital. Reports on the new continents—including significant botanical information and samples—went directly to Venice, Florence, and Genoa. Later, there were scattered Italian artisans in the British colonies, including Philip Mazzei, who came to Virginia in 1773 and became a close associate of Thomas Jefferson. Although Mazzei's attempts to grow wine grapes in Virginia failed, he became a Revolutionary diplomat in Italy and sent Jefferson seeds and plants. Jefferson himself traveled in northern Italy in 1787 and sent his associate William Short to Naples a year later to collect a pasta mold and to study cheese making and possibly ice creams. Some of this activity may have resulted in the recipes "To Make Polenta" and "To Make Vermicelli" in *The Virginia Housewife* (1824).

Of the American foodstuffs sent to Europe, tomatoes, bell peppers, and summer squash were significantly improved in Italian gardens before returning to North America with colonists. Other Italian vegetables, such as heading broccoli, were not widely eaten in the United States until marketed in the 1930s by Italian American growers, and arugula—a weed in Italy—only became part of the American gourmet vocabulary in the 1990s.

The first lasting Italian American communities were founded by north Italians in the nineteenth century. The largest was in northern California, where they were involved in the early Napa Valley wineries, the San Francisco fishing fleet, and the developing agriculture of a Mediterranean climate region in which they could grow artichokes, cardoons, olive trees, and familiar herbs. Northern Italians were early restaurateurs on the East Coast, especially in New York City, but the restaurants, such as the famous Delmonico's, served predominantly French food for most of the nineteenth century.

One of the most remarkable things about Italian American food becoming the favorite ethnic delight of the United States is how seldom Italian immigrants had eaten most of those dishes in their homeland. Many immigrants recalled eating meat only three times a year: at Christmas, at Easter, and at the *festa* of the local saint. These celebrations, with food preparations beginning well ahead of time and food shared among all members of society, were so significant that Italian American immigrants were able to restore an entire cuisine from those memories.

The *festas* for local saints, with a brass band and parade, remained a rallying point for regional identity in American immigrant neighborhoods. At the same time, the *festas* have increasingly become street parties that serve as meeting points for people from different parts of the old country.

As late arrivals, Italian Americans appeared more alien to mainstream Americans than other immigrants, and were stigmatized for their accents, their appearance,

A cookbook with recipes attributed to the opera singer Luisa Tetrazzini (1871–1940), distributed by the Sunday American.

and even for their use of herbs and garlic in cooking. Unsupervised Italians were known to gather apparently inferior foods, such as mussels and dandelions, from the urban wild. Unwittingly abetted by urbanization, Italian families resisted Americanization with imported foodstuffs, rooftop gardens, and multigenerational Sunday dinners.

Most immigrant groups quickly adopted American foods for the workplace lunches and weeknight suppers. Italian Americans were able to produce and commercialize American sandwiches with Italian flavors and to retain Italian foods for weeknight meals. Men and women working outside the home at first carried what they could approximate of the Italian fieldworker's ration of chunks of hard bread, sausage, and cheese. Inevitably bakeries and groceries made these ingredients up into sandwiches known by a variety of regional names: "submarine sandwiches," "subs," "spuckies," "Dagwoods," "grinders," "heroes," "hoagies," "muffalettas," "Garibaldi sandwiches," and sometimes "rockets," "torpedoes," "bombers," and (formerly) "zeppelins." Not all of these sandwiches have Italian names, but most are understood as Italian American food, even when purveyed by Greek Americans, or when made of tuna salad.

Italian American sandwiches crossed over quickly to mainstream use not only because they fit American rapid lunches but also because there were numerous Italian street vendors and restaurateurs to sell them. Immigrant youth were pressed into service as peanut vendors, so much so that Italian

An advertisement for La Cosechera Italian Macaroni Company.

Italian
Sausage
Sandwich
with Peppers
and Onions

322

Americans founded the Planter's Peanut Company to supply them. Italians sold Italian sausages, American hot dogs, Italian ices, American ice cream bars, Italian sandwiches, American sandwiches, espresso, cappuccino, and American coffee from pushcarts, market stalls, luncheonettes, candy stores, coffee shops, bakeries, groceries, and eventually restaurants, supermarkets, and shopping malls (arguably invented by the DeBartolo brothers).

To cross over, Italian home cooking had to be transformed, but even in its most Americanized version it has always been recognizably Italian. If the multicourse pattern of Italian meals did not fit into the rapid pace of American dining, Italian American restaurants put the meat course into or next to the pasta course, with a salad on the side. Thus was born spaghetti and meatballs, but also seafood *fra diavolo* and the unfortunate, limp side-dish pasta with a meat entrée. To get more meat on the table, a Lenten dish such as eggplant parmigiana was redone with what was then the cheapest meat in the market to become veal parmigiana.

Northern Italian restaurateurs had already set useful precedents, introducing pasta and the Bolognese form of tomato sauce with meat. The northerners had also introduced minestrone, a catchall soup from Genoa, cioppino in California, and an identification of Italian food with cheap red wine that survived even Prohibition.

Southern Italian immigrants were employed as waiters and cooks at northern Italian establishments and soon branched out on their own. By the 1930s, there were an estimated ten thousand Italian restaurants in New York City, perhaps one-third of all restaurants there. Pizza bakeries, which had appeared to sell this Neapolitan flatbread at the turn of nineteenth century, were still exotic even to most Italian Americans and did not spread into the American mainstream until after World War II, when the long campaign for Italy had familiarized many servicemen with the food of Naples, the main liberty port.

Espresso bars, daily meeting places for Italian American men, had few non-Italian customers until they became gathering places for beatniks in San Francisco's North Beach in the 1950s. However, by the early 2000s, American teenagers of all backgrounds knew the difference between cappuccino and caffe latte.

From the 1900s until well into the 1980s, the stereotypical Italian restaurant had red-and-white checkered tablecloths and candles stuck into straw-covered empty Chianti *fiaschi*; they served cheap red wine and pasta with red sauce. The crossover decade for Italian food in America was the 1980s, when a previous consensus about elaborate French-style food that had held for almost two hundred years collapsed. The baby boomer generation of Americans, reared on pizza and taken out to suburban spaghetti houses, cooked pasta and sauce in their first apartments, preferred the price/value ratio of Italian restaurants when dining out, and used upscaled Italian food as the new standard for special occasion dining. The immediate attraction of Italian food for the postwar generation was the unmistakable burst of flavor, whether it was the raw garlic and hit of fresh basil in blender pesto, the nutty cheese flavors of imported parmesan or gorgonzola in a slow-cooked risotto, or the citric accents of fennel seed and lemon peel in a Sicilian tomato sauce. As the yuppies invested in better clothing, the red sauce dishes were superseded by a restaurant category openly described as "white-sauce Italian" or "northern Italian." However, each successive recession brings a revival of "red-sauce Italian" restaurants, serving America's favorite ethnic food.

[See also CALIFORNIA; DAGWOOD SANDWICH; GALLO, ERNEST AND JULIO; ETHNIC FOODS; GARLIC; HOAGIE; ITALIAN SAUSAGE SANDWICH WITH PEPPERS AND ONIONS; MONDAVI, ROBERT; ROBERT MONDAVI CO.; MUFFALETTA SANDWICH; PANINI; PEANUTS; PEPPERONI; PIZZA; PIZZERIAS; SALAMI; SETTLEMENT HOUSES; TOMATOES; WAFFLE, WAFER, AND PIZELLE IRONS; WINERIES.]

BIBLIOGRAPHY

Barr, Nancy Verde. *We Called It Macaroni: An American Heritage of Southern Italian Cooking*. New York: Knopf, 1990.

Diner, Hasia. *Hungering for America: Italian, Irish, and Jewish Foodways in the Age of Migration*. Cambridge, MA: Harvard University Press, 2001.

Goode, Judith, Janet Theophano, and Karen Curtis. "A Framework for the Analysis of Continuity and Change in Shared Sociocultural Roles for Food Use: The Italian-American Pattern." In *Ethnic and Regional Foodways in the United States: The Performance of Group Identity*, ed. Linda Keller Brown and Kay Mussell. Knoxville: University of Tennessee Press, 1984.

MARK H. ZANGER

Italian Sausage Sandwich with Peppers and Onions

Grilled Italian sausage, served in an Italian roll and topped with fried peppers and onions, is found throughout most of the United States, but it is especially popular in the Northeast and Chicago areas where Italian immigrants originally settled. Preserved meats in the form of sausages have a long history in Italy, so the Italians naturally brought their sausage-making skills to America. Initially, Italian sausage, composed of pork flavored with garlic and anise or fennel seed, was made for home consumption or for sale within Italian communities. American troops returning home from World War II brought with them a taste for many foreign foods, including Italian, and in the 1950s and 1960s the taste for both mild and hot sausages spread to a wider public. Soon, Italian sausage sandwiches, topped with peppers and onions, were being sold at many church and public events and at amusement parks. That tradition continues, and the sandwich is a featured food at festivals, fairs, and ballparks.

[**See also** AMUSEMENT PARKS; ETHNIC FOOD; FOOD FESTIVALS; ITALIAN AMERICAN FOOD; SAUSAGE.]

BIBLIOGRAPHY

Mercuri, Becky. *Sandwiches That You Will Like*. Pittsburgh, PA: WQED Multimedia, 2002.

BECKY MERCURI

Bread peddlers on Mulberry Street in New York City, circa 1900.

Italian
Sausage
Sandwich
with Peppers
and Onions

Jack Daniels, *see Bourbon*

Jack in the Box

Jack in the Box was founded in San Diego, California, by Robert O. Peterson in 1950. Initially, Jack in the Box served only hamburgers, french fries, and milkshakes. Although the company experimented with other products, such as tacos and sandwiches, the hamburger remained the number-one menu choice. In 1951, Jack in the Box was sold to the San Diego Commissary Co., which later changed its name to Foodmaker, Inc. Franchises were sold mainly in southern California. Jack in the Box was one of the first fast food chains to systematically incorporate drive-through windows equipped with two way intercoms for ordering. By the late 1960s, the chain maintained 870 outlets.

In the 1970s, Jack in the Box began to pattern itself after McDonald's. Its advertisements in 1975, amid the so-called burger war, ended with "Watch out, McDonald's!" By 1979, the company had expanded to 1,100 units. It reorganized in 1979 by dropping some outlets and diversifying the menu. In the early 1970s, Jack in the Box began serving breakfasts, and it was the first fast food chain to add salads to its menu.

Jack in the Box has continued to grow, even after an event that might have ruined the company: In 1993, four customers died and more than one thousand people became sick from undercooked hamburgers contaminated with lethal bacteria.

In 1968, Foodmaker, Inc., became a wholly owned subsidiary of Ralston Purina. In 1985, Ralston Purina sold the company to a group of investors, including managers of Foodmaker, Inc. The company changed its name to Jack in the Box, Inc., in 1999. In 2002, it cobranded with a convenience store called Quick Stuff. The following year, Jack in the Box acquired Qdoba Restaurant Corporation, which operates the Qdoba Mexican Grill chain. As of 2005, Jack in the Box was the fifth largest hamburger chain in America, with 1,670 outlets nationwide.

[**See also** Fast Food.]

BIBLIOGRAPHY

Jakle, John A., and Keith A. Sculle. *Fast Food: Roadside Restaurants in the Automobile Age.* Baltimore: Johns Hopkins University Press, 1999.

Langdon, Philip. *Orange Roofs, Golden Arches: The Architecture of American Chain Restaurants.* New York: Knopf, 1986.

ANDREW F. SMITH

Jambalaya

A rice-based mélange of meats, seafood, vegetables, herbs, and spices, jambalaya is a representative fare of southern Louisiana cooking. Jambalaya, like its ancestral dish the Spanish paella, is versatile in preparation and composition. Commonly used as a leftover dish, jambalaya embodies all of the common Cajun and Creole flavors and ingredients.

Jambalaya predates the arrival of both the Cajun and Creole cultures. Spanish settlers who arrived in the early eighteenth century most likely introduced rice-centric dishes, such as paella, to Louisiana. Rice, the central component of paella, imported from the West Indies by the French since 1718, grew in abundance along the Mississippi River. However, the other traditional ingredients of paella were not found in Louisiana. Creoles replaced paella's clams, mussels, and squid with the indigenous oysters, shrimp, and, less frequently, crawfish. The Cajuns added andouille, a spicy smoked sausage, and fresh ham as substitute for the Spanish cured variety. The name jambalaya, like its flavors, combines words from several languages; *jambon* translates in French to ham, and *yaya* is a West African word for rice.

Traditional jambalaya begins with the browning of meat in oil or fat. Common to most all Cajun and Creole dishes, the Holy Trinity of onion, celery, and bell pepper together with garlic is added to the meat. Stock, brought to a boil then allowed to simmer, furnishes the base. Other vegetables such as mushrooms and green onions and liberal amounts of spices (bay leaf, salt, pepper, Tabasco) are added before any seafood. Rice added last, either raw or cooked, forges a substantially hearty dish. New Orleans–style Creole jambalayas, referred to as "red," incorporate tomatoes, usually canned sauce or diced. Cajun cooks renounce the use of tomatoes in jambalaya, thus classified as "brown."

Jambalaya might be most well known from its popularization in Hank Williams's country song about Cajun life, "Jambalaya (On the Bayou)". The residents of Gonzales, Louisiana, celebrate the annual Jambalaya Festival each May.

[**See also** CAJUN AND CREOLE FOOD.]

BIBLIOGRAPHY

Folse, John D. *The Encyclopedia of Cajun & Creole Cuisine.* Gonzales, LA: Chef John Folse and Company, 2004.

Gutierrez, C. Paige. *Cajun Foodways.* Jackson: University Press of Mississippi, 2004.

RIEN T. FERTEL

Japanese American Food

In the history of Japanese immigration and Japanese American experiences, foodways have illustrated both continuity and change. Foods represent family rather than national identity, and increasingly refer to generations of life in America rather than to roots in Japan. Japanese communities in Hawaii since the 1880s, on the west coast of the mainland, in the internment camps during World War II, and in postwar dispersals across mainland America demonstrate the maintenance, adaptation, and innovation of diet in these groups.

Chief among the factors of identity in Japanese American populations is generation. The issei, or first-generation Japanese Americans, were born in Japan and emigrated to America in the late nineteenth century. The first to come were *dekasegi*, temporary migrant workers whose goal was to return to their families in Japan. Most migrants were of peasant origin. Their numbers increased after 1882, when Japanese immigrants began to replace Chinese laborers, then barred by the Exclusion Act of 1882. In Hawaii, Japanese worked under contract on plantations; on the mainland, they first worked on the railways and in mines. These workers did not see the overseas sojourn as a new beginning for themselves but as support for those left behind.

A national heritage was rarely invoked, as even within Japan, local, regional ways of doing things were more meaningful than being Japanese. Over time in America, one's identity became tied to family in America, not family in Japan, and its foodways included idiosyncratic, atraditional adaptations, such as one grandmother's habit of using shreds of fresh ginger in a baked lasagna.

Family foods, such as shoyu (soy sauce) hot dogs and Spam musubi (a block of sushi rice topped with a slice of Spam and encircled with a strip of nori) became objects later of nostalgia among second- and third-generation Japanese Americans. Shoyu hot dogs—hot dogs seasoned with brown sugar and shoyu and sautéed with onions and bell peppers—were created out of necessity by families with scant resources. Immigrant families traveling from difficult lives in Japan to difficult ones in America would scarcely in any case have such iconic foods as sushi or elaborate kaiseki (tea ceremony meals), diverse and expensive. Identity foods for such people are foods of deprivation and shared hardship. Ideas of "authentic" had to wait until relative affluence gave a family the means to aspire to such food, but, by that time, family foods had adapted to local foodways and ingredients.

Adaptation seemed to some nisei (second generation) necessary, especially to those living far from concentrated populations of Japanese Americans. Assimilation was difficult, however much a family might espouse American foodways to show their acceptability (white bread, large amounts of meat, long-cooked vegetables, for example) because of racism and "cultural stereotyping."

School had a strong influence on the second generation. For the sake of children who wanted to fit in at school, lunchboxes would often contain a mix of foods. Wanting

California Roll

California rolls, consisting of avocado, imitation crabmeat, and mayonnaise encased in rice with sesame seeds on the outside, are an excellent example of Japanese American food. The rolls were invented by Japanese chefs in Los Angeles during the 1970s for Americans who were squeamish about eating raw fish. California rolls became a popular addition to Japanese restaurant menus in the United States during the 1980s, and they were eventually exported back to Japan, although many sushi purists eschew them, as they are not a traditional Japanese food.

ANDREW F. SMITH

to be approved, children might ask for an "American" sandwich lunch from home that did not contain "smelly pickles" and that they might be able to trade at lunchtime. Some children, by contrast, found Japanese foods highly tradeable.

For most older Japanese Americans, a meal is not a meal without rice. Intermarriage and geographic assimilation in the third and fourth generations may have changed tastes, but an electric rice cooker is an essential appliance in most Japanese American homes, where there also would be a bottle of soy sauce on the table at any meal.

Between 1885 and 1895, more than thirty thousand Japanese came to work in Hawaii. The first were menial casual workers, who came empty-handed with a dream of striking it rich or at least working hard to send money home to indigent families in Japan. By the early 1890s, most were contract workers, coming from Kumamoto, Hiroshima, and Yamaguchi. Regional identity was strong and sometimes divisive. One woman reared in Hawaii recalled her mother saying "You had better learn to cook as we do—not like those people down the road from Kumamoto: they mix their foods all up, it's messy!" By 1893, 70 percent of the 32,000 plantation workers (mostly in sugar cane) were Japanese. By 1900, the plantation populations included Portuguese (often foremen), Chinese, Filipinos, Koreans, Okinawans, and Puerto Ricans. By 1924, when the Oriental Exclusion Act was passed, the total number of Japanese migrants was 220,000. Only in 1952 were Japanese residents allowed American citizenship; many by then were second- or third-generation residents.

The early immigrants were men, but after 1900 "picture brides" (women introduced through go-betweens in Japan and known to the men only through letters and photographs) began to arrive to marry workers. Families began to settle in Hawaii and to remain there after workers completed their labor contracts.

Plantations and other communities in Hawaii were mixing bowls of races and cultures in which people shared their foods. The mixture of traditions found its way to the lunch wagons, food stalls, and *okazuya*, the Japanese Hawaiian delicatessens selling a variety of prepared foods. What came to be known as the "plate lunch" or "mixed plate" included foods of all the populations of Hawaii: scoops of rice, potato salad, and macaroni salad, surmounted by Portuguese beef stew, chicken teriyaki, hamburgers, Filipino egg rolls (lumpia), Chinese noodles, Korean and Japanese pickles, chorizo sausages, and endless other possibilities.

For the large numbers of workers coming from Hawaii to the west coast, Chinese workers acted as mentors and, as in Hawaii, taught the Japanese men working by their side how to cook. The association between Chinese and Japanese workers produced "Japanese chop suey" and "Japanese chow mein," which became emblems of acculturation. The word "chow" came to mean food, in everyone's vocabulary. The food of the years of hard labor in mines, railroads, and farming was the quintessential thin dumpling soup, *dango jiru*. After families were established, the elder males would make this soup to teach children of the character-building "bad old days." The dumplings of flour floating on greasy thin soup (greasy when a bit of bacon was available) was a reminder of heritage in America, not Japan.

In urban communities of Japanese, such as those in Los Angeles, San Francisco, and Seattle, whatever common issei culture there was soon was challenged by children and grandchildren. Foods reflected the generational divide: one meal did not suit the tastes of both, and so mealtime began to symbolize acculturative tendencies as sandwiches, pasta, and hamburgers were added to the basic miso soup and rice. Parents tried to maintain a family-first standard for high quality in such emblematic foods as shoyu. One Los Angeles resident noted "We used Chinese shoyu for our restaurant but saved the Japanese for the family."

The Fourth of July picnic became a big event for Japanese American families—not as an indicator of patriotism but as an occasion when everyone was free to be together. The most important holiday meal among Japanese American families, however, was on New Year's Day, and most Japanese American families tried to create something "really Japanese" for this event.

New Year's meals demanded hospitality and visiting. The women cooked for days beforehand and greeted visitors at home while men did most of the required visiting. A typical spread would include baked fish, chicken curry, rice, onishime, (a kind of stew), and, of course, sake. Communities would sometimes pool their resources in a potluck event in community halls, including hibachis for grilling steaks and other nontraditional foods. This kind of celebration released the women for card games, which themselves became a New Year's tradition. One observer noted that anything happening on New Year's Day in America became a New Year's instant tradition.

On February 19, 1942, Franklin Delano Roosevelt issued Executive Order 9066, placing Japanese Americans under a double exile. Eventually, over 120,000 Japanese (64 percent of whom were American citizens) were housed in internment camps in the western interior. Taken from their homes, these people had to make a home life in very difficult conditions, and food became all the more emblematic of home—and deprivation.

Accounts by interned people referred to the loss of the sense of family in the communal mess halls. Randomly housed together, people of different social classes, generations, backgrounds, and occupations, tried to preserve family integrity. Parents would tell children to stay close to them in mess hall lines and at the long trestle tables, attempting to mark a spot for "home" at the table, keeping children from "unsuitable" others. But, soon, especially adolescent children would band together and leave the parents' "home space." One woman reported that it was wonderful to be bold enough to say to her mother "You didn't make this food; I don't have to sit with you!" and go off to eat with her peers. Older people complained that "nothing was like family anymore" as the young enjoyed friendships and romances independently, paradoxically finding freedom in camp life.

There were stories of filial respect and solidarity in the camps as well. One told of a woman who sank into a depression in the camp, caused by her inability to be a good food provider for her family. What she missed most was *unagi* (eel). Her son headed out to the barren desert near the barbed-wire perimeter and killed a rattlesnake, which skinned and grilled with shoyu, was a rough approximation of an eel—and cheered the mother greatly.

Although school occupied the young in camps, other family members worked on the farms that interned people created in the very poor soil of the camps, growing onions, radishes, beans, potatoes and, later, more "Japanese" foodstuffs such as gobo (burdock) and daikon (giant white radish). The food in the camps was barely palatable. Shoyu was the only condiment available. A typical evening meal consisted of a boiled potato, a canned Vienna sausage, and bread and margarine.

Camps traded food, once they had begun gardens and organized food manufacturing. This shared labor allowed for more diverse menus. This self-reliance was encouraged by superintendents of camps, especially because many foods were strictly rationed during the war. Menus from Tule and Gila River camps give evidence that food was an object of contention and shortages of rice in particular a cause for alarm. To avoid unrest and the food riots and resistances that occurred in several camps, superintendents asked cooks to "serve rice to older people, bread to the younger" and noted that, for example, "After October 15, the rice harvest will be in, be sure to tell people that there WILL be rice!"

Attempts to create a Japanese New Year's meal in camp varied. In 1943, camp menus revealed that mulligan stew was the centerpiece, but by 1944, a more elaborate menu was prepared and in 1945, several days of New Year's meals were included. January 4, 1945, was the fourth day in a row that year that the midday meal was almost completely Japanese, a fish and vegetable tempura meal with nori, rice, pickles, and boiled daikon with dried shrimp. After the war, these communities chafed under discriminatory language and fought for reparations for the internment experience and the loss of property. For many, eating Japanese American foods became a political statement. A preference for Japanese foods over Japanese American foods among fourth and later generations (many of whom do not speak Japanese) may perplex their older relatives for whom the foods evolved in America have become "family" and "identity" foods. The popularization of "Japanese food" across America has led to what has been called the "sushi-ization" of America, a general understanding of Japanese foods such as sushi that has little to do with Japanese American communities and their foodways.

[See also HAWAIIAN FOOD; NEW YEAR'S CELEBRATIONS; RICE; SOY SAUCE; SPAM.]

BIBLIOGRAPHY

Fugita, Stephen. *Japanese American Ethnicity: The Persistence of Community.* Seattle: University of Washington Press, 1997.

Japanese American National Museum. *From Bento to Mixed Plate: Americans of Japanese Descent in Multicultural Hawai'i.* Los Angeles: Japanese American National Museum, 1997.

Kendis, Kaoru Oguri. *A Matter of Comfort: Ethnic Maintenance and Ethnic Style among Third Generation Japanese Americans.* New York: AMS, 1989.

Laudan, Rachel. *The Food of Paradise: Exploring Hawai'i's Culinary Heritage.* Honolulu: University of Hawai'i Press, 1996.

Masumoto, David Mas. *Harvest Son: Planting Roots in American Soil.* New York: Norton, 1998.

MERRY WHITE

Jefferson, Thomas

Thomas Jefferson was born on April 13, 1743, at Shadwell, Albemarle County, Virginia, and died on the Fourth of July 1826 at Monticello. He penned the Declaration of Independence, championed the cause of separation of church and state, served as ambassador to France from the United States (1785–1789), and became the third president of the United States, serving two terms (1801–1809). He was also a most illustrious epicure and may be said to have introduced elements of eighteenth-century royalist cuisine to America, this by two paths: During his years in Paris (1784–1789), he had the enslaved James Hemings trained as a chef, who in turn trained his brother Peter. Further, during his terms of presidency, Étienne LeMaire and Honoré Julien served Jefferson in their respective capacities as maître d'hôtel and chef de cuisine; Edy, described as Mr. Jefferson's "favorite cook," learned her craft in the kitchen of the President's House. Recipes attributed to LeMaire and Julien turn up in the culinary manuscripts kept in later years by Jefferson's granddaughters and great-granddaughter. Those attributed to LeMaire, in particular, confirm Jefferson's detailed descriptions of many dishes, these in his own hand. What is remarkable is the fact that these recipes came into the hands of Mrs. Mary Randolph, a cousin of Jefferson and a sister of Thomas Mann Randolph, the husband of Jefferson's daughter Martha Jefferson Randolph. They show up in her work *The Virginia House-wife* (1824), those attributed to LeMaire in particular—some with long, identical tell-tale phrases. Thus, Mrs. Randolph may fairly be described as the amanuensis of the French cuisine at the President's House during Jefferson's terms of office. The imprint of royalist French cuisine is especially strong in Virginia because of the vast and continuing influence of *The Virginia House-wife*.

Jefferson's passion for French cuisine was such that Patrick Henry accused him of forsaking his "native vittles," but in a note to his daughter Martha Jefferson Randolph he wrote: "Pray enable yourself to direct us here how to make muffins in Peter's method. My cook here cannot succeed at all in them, and they are a great luxury to me." This was in 1802, when he was ensconced at the President's House with a French chef in the kitchen.

But Jefferson's real passion was gardening. His copious and meticulously kept notes in his *Garden Book* and *Farm Book* serve as the bible of all those who would know about gardening and food in eighteenth and early nineteenth-century Virginia. He cadged seeds and cuttings from acquaintances far and wide, including France, Italy, and England, cultivating rare varieties like radicchio di Pistoia, recently reintroduced to the United States. He devoted a great deal of effort to acclimating the olive and benne (*Sesamum orientale*) to Virginia, but was unsuccessful. All this was in addition to his passion for wines. Furthermore, LeMaire's records, kept in his capacity as maître d'hôtel during Jefferson's terms at the President's House in Washington, take careful note of all purchases at the public market in Georgetown, day after day, purchase by purchase, complete with prices. These records are invaluable in showing the extraordinary breadth of choice of vegetables and other foodstuffs that were available at a public market in the first decade of the nineteenth century.

[See also FRENCH INFLUENCES ON AMERICAN FOOD; HEIRLOOM VEGETABLES; RANDOLPH, MARY; SOUTHERN REGIONAL COOKERY; WINES, EASTERN U.S.]

BIBLIOGRAPHY

Betts, Edwin Morris, ed. *Thomas Jefferson's Farm Book.* Charlottesville: University of Virginia Press, 1987.

Betts, Edwin Morris, ed. *Thomas Jefferson's Garden Book 1766–1824: With Relevant Extracts from His Other Writings.* Philadelphia: American Philosophical Society, 1944.

Betts, Edwin Morris, and James Bear Jr., eds. *The Family Letters of Thomas Jefferson.* Columbia: University of Missouri Press, 1966.

KAREN HESS

Jell-O

Jell-O is the brand name of a dessert mix of colored and flavored sugar and crystallized gelatin, made by Kraft Foods, Inc. When mixed with water and chilled, it becomes a food that wobbles like rubber, looks like translucent plastic, and tastes like fruit. Although Jell-O sales peaked in the 1960s and some gourmets consider it déclassé, most hospitals, diners, school cafeterias, church potlucks, and holiday tables in America offer Jell-O, either alone or in one of thousands of recipe variations featuring fruit, nuts, miniature marshmallows, and any number of real and imitation dairy products.

Jell-O was invented in 1897 in LeRoy, New York, by a carpenter named Pearle Wait. Wait also made and sold patent medicines, so he knew how to add colorings and flavorings to prettify products of unsavory origins—such as the boiled calves feet used to make gelatin. He also was undoubtedly familiar with the powdered, unflavored gelatin products that had entered the market in the mid-1800s as recipe ingredients. Wait was the first to add color and flavor to the crystallized gelatin to create a stand-alone dessert mix.

Wait's wife, May, named the product Jell-O by attaching to the word "jell" the "O," a popular ending for product names at the time. In fact, another patent medicine maker in LeRoy, Orator Woodward, had become wealthy selling a cereal-based coffee substitute called Grain-O.

Wait peddled raspberry-, lemon-, orange-, and strawberry-flavored Jell-O door to door not very successfully for less than two years and then sold the business to Woodward, his patent medicine competitor, for $450. At first, Woodward had little more success than Wait. Woodward was so discouraged that one day in 1900 he offered to sell the whole Jell-O business to his plant superintendent for $35. The employee refused, and that turned out be a lucky break for Woodward, because he soon identified and solved the problem that was hindering sales.

Recipe for Success

At the time, virtually all dishes were prepared from basic ingredients; homemakers did not know what to do with a food that was almost ready to serve and needed no recipes. So Woodward gave them recipes. In 1902, Woodward's Genesee Pure Food Company produced the first of a subsequent flood of Jell-O recipe booklets. Woodward's nattily dressed salesmen, driving spanking new rigs drawn by dappled gray horses, delivered the new recipe booklets to every house in a town. Then, and only then, would the salesmen approach the local grocer to tell him about a new dessert mix that would soon be in great demand.

These direct sales were then supplemented by print ads featuring a little girl, whose image conveyed how much kids loved Jell-O and how easy it was to make. The Jell-O Girl appeared in ads and recipe books for almost twenty-eight years—at first in photographs and later, after the model grew up, in illustrations by Rose O'Neill, the artist who designed the Kewpie doll. Norman Rockwell and Maxfield Parrish also created Jell-O ads at the height of their artistic careers. Magazine illustrators of that era were well-paid celebrities who moved freely between commercial and noncommercial work. The Jell-O domestic scenes and still lifes they painted in the 1920s rival fine art in beauty and technique and were often displayed in magazines as museum oil paintings with the word Jell-O appearing discreetly in the plaque on the frame.

By 1923, Jell-O sales so dominated the Genesee Pure Food Company that the firm's name was changed to the Jell-O Company. In 1925, the company was sold to a former rival in the coffee substitute business, Postum, for an exchange of stock valued at $84 million. Postum reduced Jell-O's price and scored record sales but not record profits. Jell-O was then in direct competition with cheaper brands, including Royal, which by 1934 was sponsoring a popular radio show featuring Fanny Brice, the singer. Jell-O fought back with Jack Benny, whose Sunday night radio comedy show became an immediate hit. Within a few months, Jell-O sales soared to the highest level since the company, which by then was marketing more than 150 different products under the name General Foods, bought the business.

Jell-O Jingles and Jokes

For the next eight years, as many as 40 million Americans tuned in to hear Benny's "Jell-O again" greeting, the five-note ascending "J-E-L-L (pause) O" jingle, and jokes about announcer Don Wilson's "wiggly waist" and "six-delicious-flavors sway." Show skits also frequently mentioned Jell-O. Benny's January 1935 spoof of the French classic *The Count of Monte Cristo* was called *The Count of Monte Jell-O*, for instance. General Foods took Benny off the Jell-O campaign in 1942 because wartime sugar shortages restricted Jell-O production. Nevertheless, Jack Benny and Jell-O were inextricably linked to each other in the minds of many Americans for decades.

Jell-O sales at the time also benefited from the newly popular electric refrigerators with their more consistent cooling abilities, and from Jell-O's growing popularity as a salad ingredient. During the Depression, a Jell-O salad was considered an elegant and inexpensive way to stretch leftover foods.

When World War II and its sugar shortages ended, American housewives resumed their Jell-O cooking with renewed enthusiasm and unprecedented creativity. In fact, there was hardly anything a 1950s hostess could do that would impress her guests more than to serve a beautiful molded Jell-O dish. Popular molds included Under-the-Sea Salad (layers of lime Jell-O, pears, and cream cheese), Sunshine Salad (lemon Jell-O, crushed pineapple, and shredded carrots), Cranberry Waldorf Salad (cherry Jell-O, jellied cranberry sauce, apples, celery, and nuts) and Crown Jewel Dessert (colored cubes of Jell-O set against a backdrop of real or artificial whipped cream to resemble stained glass).

In 1963, the best of the 1950s Jell-O recipes were collected in *The Joys of Jell-O*, a 250-recipe cookbook that came out again and again, in eleven editions. The 1960s also produced the famous slogan "There's always room for Jell-O." It was featured in a series of ads that showed families eating dinner, and it positioned Jell-O as the perfect light ending to the huge meals common in those prosperous times.

Those ads helped propel Jell-O to its late 1960s sales peak of four boxes per person per year. Jell-O sales declined after that, mainly as a result of competition from more convenient snack cakes and frozen desserts and because of the huge increase in the number of women working outside the home who had less time to make elaborate molded gelatin desserts. The gourmet and natural-foods movements also made mainstream America wary of processed convenience foods like Jell-O. In addition, Jell-O's image suffered from twin bar fads of the 1980s: alcohol-spiked portions of Jell-O; and Jell-O wrestling, scantily clad women tussling on a Jell-O "mat."

Bouncing Back as a Snack

In 1990, Jell-O did come up with a big sales success, a recipe for a gummy, candylike snack called Jigglers. The recipe requires four times the usual amount of Jell-O, and the result can be cut into shapes like cookies, thus making it a perfect means of cultivating young Jell-O fans. Jell-O sales increased by 7 percent the first year of the Jigglers promotion; that banner year also saw the first Jell-O gelatin ads by Bill Cosby, the comedian and longtime Jell-O Pudding spokesman. Even more important at a time when dessert eating was in decline and on-the-go snacking was on the rise, Jigglers could be eaten by hand.

The Smithsonian Institution honored Jell-O with a daylong mock academic conference held on April Fool's Day 1991. In 1997, the historical society in Jell-O's birthplace of LeRoy, New York, opened the world's only museum dedicated to Jell-O facts and artifacts. As the twenty-first century began, Jell-O sales were highest in the Midwest and Utah. Food experts attribute Jell-O's popularity in Utah to the state's extensive Mormon population with large families, low alcohol consumption, and compensating high sugar intake. Whatever the reason, a pin depicting a bowl of lime gelatin proved to be one of the most popular souvenirs of the 2002 Salt Lake City Winter Olympics.

New flavors and mold giveaways remained at the core of official company promotional efforts. In 2002, Jell-O expanded its line of already-made Jell-O gelatin snacks in supermarket refrigerator cases to include tubes of gelatin that can be eaten without a spoon. In fact, Jell-O marketing efforts are clearly aimed at the many Americans who have more room for Jell-O in their hearts and stomachs than time in their schedules to make it.

[See also ADVERTISING COOKBOOKS AND RECIPES; COFFEE SUBSTITUTES; DESSERTS; GENERAL FOODS; JELL-O MOLDS; KRAFT FOODS; RADIO/TV FOOD SHOWS.]

BIBLIOGRAPHY

Shapiro, Laura. *Perfection Salad: Women and Cooking at the Turn of the Century*. New York: Holt, 2001.

Wyman, Carolyn. *Jell-O: A Biography: The History and Mystery of America's Most Famous Dessert*. San Diego: Harcourt, 2001.

CAROLYN WYMAN

Jell-O Molds

Aluminum molds produced and stamped by the Jell-O Company have become kitchen collectibles, more often hung on walls than used for the salads they were designed to shape. The prototype dates back to fourteenth-century England, where noble households fashioned flavored "jellies" in copper molds. In early America, copper molds lined with tin to prevent food poisoning were commissioned from the local tinsmith. In 1902, the Jell-O Company distributed instructions for having "your tinner" fashion a "mould."

At about that time, however, the need for mass production of Jell-O molds became apparent. The domestic science cooking movement decreed that salads—so naturally unruly—should become neat and contained, and the best way to accomplish that was to encase the salad in gelatin and the gelatin in a mold. Although it is not known when or where the first Jell-O mold of stamped aluminum was made, the Jell-O Company began offering free molds to consumers around

1908. Aluminum had the advantage over copper because it was lighter, cheaper, and did not require periodic retinning. Between 1925 and 1930, as the molds gained in popularity, Jell-O sold about a million at a nominal price.

The next big boost came in the 1930s, when gelled or "congealed" salads—savory and sweet—achieved staple status. About one-third of all cookbook recipes of the time were gelatin based. Studded with bits of vegetables, canned fruit, marshmallows, nuts, cottage or cream cheese, and other foods, the molded concoctions were promoted during the Great Depression as an elegant way to package leftovers. This trend continued into the 1940s, and the *Joy of Cooking*, published in 1946, contained sixty-nine recipes requiring molds.

During the 1950s, the most impressive food a hostess could serve was a towering, molded Jell-O salad, but by the 1960s culinary fashions had changed. Women hung up their molds, perhaps because the pouring of colored layers of Jell-O and the placing of bits of food in a preordained design were tedious chores, and the unmolding precarious and challenging. Sales of Jell-O fell off during the 1970s and 1980s. In 1995, however, the company introduced a successful new mold, the plastic Jiggler Egg form, to make snacks for children. Collectors covet classic molds such as Jell-O's Bridge Set, but most of the company's aluminum forms are worth not much more than five dollars.

[**See also** DESSERTS; JELL-O; SALADS AND SALAD DRESSINGS.]

BIBLIOGRAPHY

Better Homes and Gardens. *The Joy of Jell-O Molds: 50 Festive Recipes from the Classic to the Contemporary.* Des Moines, IA: Meredith, 1998.
Franklin, Linda Campbell. *300 Years of Kitchen Collectibles.* Florence, AL: Books Americana, 1997.
Wyman, Carolyn. *JELL-O: A Biography, The History and Mystery of America's Most Famous Dessert.* San Diego, New York, London: Harcourt, 2001.

LINDA MURRAY BERZOK

Jelly Bean

Jelly beans are small fruit-flavored candies. Made from sugar, coloring and flavoring, and gelatin, the egg-shaped candies are chewy on the inside, with a firm outer shell.

The earliest print reference to jelly beans is dated 1886; it was promoted as a Christmas treat. In those days, jelly beans were commonly sold in bulk from glass jars, or from vending machines that dispensed a handful for a penny. It wasn't until the 1930s that jelly beans were sold as Easter candy—someone had noted their obvious resemblance to eggs. Today, they're sometimes identified as "jelly bird eggs" at Eastertime.

Jelly beans have long been made by major candy companies such as Brach's and Just Born, but the candy was transformed in the 1970s by the Herman Goelitz Candy Company, founded by Gustav Goelitz in Belleville, Illinois, in 1869 as an ice cream and candy store. Goelitz purportedly invented candy corn around 1900, and in 1976 his successors began turning out gourmet "Jelly Belly" beans, made with natural flavors. The mini beans come in about fifty flavors, including pear, chocolate pudding, watermelon, root beer, and buttered popcorn, which is reportedly the most popular flavor. Although priced considerably higher than traditional jelly beans, Jelly Bellies were a huge success, and the firm was renamed the Jelly Belly Candy Company. Now located in Fairfield, California, the company also makes "Bertie Bott's Every Flavour Beans" named after a product mentioned in the Harry Potter series of books by J. K. Rowling. The company also makes "sports beans," which are intended to be eaten during exercise.

Jelly beans went into politics when Ronald Reagan became governor of California in 1966. He liked jelly beans and always had a large glass jar of them on his desk in Sacramento. When he became president, he carried on the tradition in the White House.

[**See also** CANDY.]

BIBLIOGRAPHY

Richardson, Tim. *Sweets: A History of Candy.* New York: Bloomsbury, 2002.

ANDREW F. SMITH

Jelly Rolls

Jelly rolls, also known as Swiss rolls or jelly cakes, consist of a sponge cake coiled around a jelly filling. They are usually sliced crosswise to reveal an attractive spiral pattern and are occasionally used as the decorative exterior for a charlotte (a molded cake filled with custard or fruit or Bavarian cream.). The spiral cross-sections of jelly roll line a handsome exterior for this gelatin-set mousse. The earliest reference to them has been found in several cookbooks published immediately after the American Civil War, but they are thought to have arisen at the same time the genoise sponge cake appeared in mid nineteenth century France. Common fillings include currant jelly, pastry cream, apricot preserve, and raspberry jam. Baking pans designed for cooking the thin sheets of batter used for jelly rolls have flat bottoms and one-inch-high straight sides. Called "jelly-roll pans" by consumers, they have become standard baking equipment in commercial kitchens, where they are referred to simply as "sheet pans." "Jelly roll" and "honey pot" were popular slang euphemisms for female genitalia at the turn of the twentieth century, and it is likely that the famous jazz pianist Jelly Roll Morton acquired his nickname from playing in bordellos.

[**See also** CAKES; CREAMS, DESSERT; DESSERTS; PRESERVES.]

JAY WEINSTEIN

Jennie June

Jane Cunningham Croly (1829–1901), the journalist and cookbook author known as "Jennie June," was born in Market Harborough, Leicestershire, England. Her family emigrated to the United States in 1841, settling first in Poughkeepsie and afterward in or near Wappingers Falls, New York. She married David G. Croly, a reporter for the *New York Herald*, in 1856.

Under her nom de plume of Jennie, Mrs. Croly was a pioneer woman in the workplace. She was a prolific writer, the first woman journalist to have her articles syndicated, and also invented the syndication of readers' responses. Despite having to run a lavish household and bring up five children, her output was enormous, and she contributed to almost every important publication of the time. She edited *Demorest's* magazine for twenty-seven years and was both editor and owner of *Godey's Magazine* and *The Home-Maker. The Cycle* was her own creation and property. Many of her writings were collected into book form.

Jennie June wrote almost exclusively on homemaking subjects, which found a large audience among the women of the emerging American middle class of the post–Civil War era. Her manual of needlework and stitchery was published in 1885. As a founding member of Sorosis, one of the first organizations in the American Women's Club, Jennie June wrote a history of the movement in 1898.

Jennie June's main contribution to American cooking was the publication in 1866 of *Jennie June's American Cookery Book*, described on the title page as "containing upwards of twelve hundred choice and carefully tested receipts; embracing all the popular dishes, and the best results of modern science, reduced to a simple and practical form."

The book is modeled on contemporary British cookbooks (though it is fairly short by their standards, consisting of only 399 pages), including hints on general household management, with separate chapters "for invalids, for infants [and] one on Jewish cookery." There are also separate chapters of contributions from Sorosis and from the Oneida Community, a religious community in Oneida, New York, that practiced a form of free love. Another section of the book is entitled "Favorite Dishes of Distinguished Persons," from which we learn that "President Grant is very fond of scrambled eggs and fried ham" and that Queen Victoria (referred to simply as "Victoria") "loves boiled mutton and caper sauce and is also very partial to a cup of tea." In the preface to a new edition in 1878, Jennie June wrote: "All that I have to beg of young housekeepers is that they will try [the recipes] with their own hands, and not turn them over to the tender mercies of Bridget. It is not the personal extravagance of American women that is sapping the foundation of American homes. It is the disintegrating quality of our domestic service."

[See also COMMUNITY COOKBOOKS; COOKBOOKS AND MANUSCRIPTS: AMERICAN COOKBOOKS FROM THE CIVIL WAR TO WORLD WAR I; PERIODICALS.]

BIBLIOGRAPHY

Woman's Press Club of New York City. *Memories of Jane Cunningham Croly, "Jennie June."* New York: G. P. Putnam's Sons, 1904.

JOSEPHINE BACON

Jewish American Food

The story of Jewish food in America begins in 1654, when twenty-three Sephardic Jews arrived in New Amsterdam. Their basic recipes of stew and fish fried in olive oil, beef and bean stews, almond puddings, and egg custards came directly from the Iberian Peninsula. Once in America, most Jewish colonists observed the laws of kashruth in their homes. Some of their dishes, such as cod or haddock fried "Jewish style" (that is, in olive oil, not lard), soon became popular among non-Jews.

German Jewish Immigrants and Their Foods

Of the 10 million immigrants to this country between the years 1830 and 1880, 3 million were Germans and 200,000 were Jews from German-speaking lands. The most important German Jewish center of commerce, culture, and cuisine was Cincinnati, Ohio. By the end of the nineteenth century, these Jews had become American-German-Jewish, and this triethnicity played itself out in both culture and cuisine. In Jewish homes, foods such as chicken noodle or vegetable soup, roast chicken, and goose graced tables for Friday night dinner or Sunday lunch when the entire family gathered together.

These immigrants brought with them marvelous kuchen, breads, and tortes. Jewish communities from Bavaria carried their own German regional recipes such as *Lebkuchen* or *Dampfnudeln*, a wonderful brioche-like cake soaked in caramel and served with a vanilla sauce. Surely it was no coincidence that Cincinnati became the home of Fleischmann's yeast and Crisco, a vegetable-based shortening.

Changes in American Jewry and Its Cuisine

In nineteenth-century America, traditional Jews were having a hard time. Because laws prohibited shops from being open on Sunday, Jews usually had to keep their shops open on Saturday (the Jewish Sabbath) and often postponed their Sabbath meals to Sunday dinner.

Isaac Mayer Wise, the leader of the Reform movement in Judaism, called for the dietary laws to be recognized as an archaic relic of the past. Wise's ambivalence toward the laws of kashruth, and the growing gap within the Jewish community with regard to the dietary laws, contributed to the final schism between traditional and Reform American Jews. On July 12, 1883, the graduation of the first class of American rabbis was celebrated with an eight-course dinner for two hundred people at the Highland House in Cincinnati.

While Reform Jews were tasting American produce, their family recipes were becoming regionalized. In Mississippi and Alabama, pecans replaced almonds in tortes and cookies; in Ohio, molasses or brown sugar replaced honey in *schnecken*; in Washington State, salmon appeared instead of carp in gefilte fish on Sabbath tables; and in Louisiana, hot pepper and scallions were used instead of mild ginger in matzo balls. Crossover foods were already beginning to affect the non-Jewish public as well, appearing with greater frequency in mainstream American nineteenth-century cookbooks.

Eastern European Jewish American Cuisine

Between 1881 and 1921, approximately 2.5 million Jewish immigrants from Eastern Europe entered the United States. They crowded into New York's Lower East Side, Chicago's West Side, Boston's North End, and South Philadelphia. As the immigrants adjusted to new food habits, they quickly forgot some of the foods of their poverty, like *krupnick*, a cereal soup made from oatmeal, sometimes barley, potatoes, and fat. If a family could afford it, milk would be added to the *krupnick*; if not, it was called "*soupr mit nisht,*" or supper with nothing. Bagels, knishes, or herring wrapped in newspaper were taken to the sweatshop.

Orthodox Jews clung to their old traditions, including kashruth. The butchers, bakers, and pushcart peddlers of herring and pickles soon became small-scale independent grocers, wine merchants, and wholesale meat, produce, and fruit providers.

Innovations in Jewish American Food Inspired by the Second Wave of Immigrants

The first national Jewish women's organization, the National Council of Jewish Women, was founded in the fall of 1893. By 1900, its 7,080 members in fifty-five cities helped support mission and industrial schools for poor Jewish children along with cooking classes in the settlement houses. Council cookbooks, such as *The Settlement Cook Book*, were put out nationwide, with proceeds helping to support their projects. Other organizations followed suit.

While the women's organizations were working to help the less fortunate, another revolution was taking place—that of food technology and scientific discovery. Slowly the kitchen was transformed. Not only was Heinz producing its bottled ketchups and fledgling companies making kosher canned foods, but companies were manufacturing a white vegetable substance resembling lard— the shortening that would change forever the way Jewish people cooked. The inventions of cream cheese, rennet, junket, Jell-O, Coca-Cola, nondairy creamer, pasteurized milk, phyllo dough, and frozen foods would all affect the way Jews cooked in America.

With the growth of food companies, delicatessens, school-lunch programs, and restaurants, both American food and American Jewish food became more processed and more innovative.

Kashruth and American Jews. As the latest wave of Eastern European Jews became more Americanized, they began trying new dishes, like macaroni and cheese and canned tunafish casseroles. Jewish cookbooks included recipes for Creole dishes, for chicken fricassee using canned tomatoes, and for shortcut kuchen using baking powder. At the turn of the twentieth century, the Union of

East Side Glatt Kosher Butcher on Grand Street in New York City.

Orthodox Jewish Congregations, the umbrella organization for Orthodox Jews, was established. In 1923, it created its women's branch and the Union's official kashruth supervision and certification program was introduced.

Jewish Food from World War II Onward
Political and economic upheavals in the decades after World War II brought to the United States more Jews who had been persecuted in other countries by regimes unfriendly to them. These Mediterranean Jews have enriched the tapestry of Jewish cuisine, contributing new "Jewish" dishes such as Syrian tamarind-flavored meat pies, fresh cumin-accented carrot salads from Morocco, and Israeli falafel. Americans are attracted to their cuisines because of the many vegetable-based dishes—the kind of cooking that is in keeping with American's new dietary trends.

The end of the twentieth century saw a small transformation in Jewish food. Since the 1980s, kosher food has enjoyed an astonishing revival from coast to coast. To many Americans, the word "kosher" is synonymous with better and safer. But most Americans do not even know—nor do they care—that they are "buying kosher" when they pick up a box of Pepperidge Farm cookies or a bottle of Heinz ketchup, only two of the thousands of kosher products that are on the market today.

With nearly six million Jews, the United States is the major cultural center of the Jewish world outside of Israel. Immigrants to America adapted most of their foods to the culture of their new home. In doing so, they enriched their adopted homeland. Sweet challah bread, overstuffed deli sandwiches of pastrami and corned beef, large bagels filled with cream cheese and lox, New York cheesecakes, and even bagel sushi—rice wrapping wasabi, lox, and cream cheese—are today as American as apple pie.

American Jewish Foods—Or What Passes for Them
Babka. Babka is an eastern European-style cake made from an egg-and-butter yeast-based dough, often filled with raisins, chocolate, or cinnamon sugar and nuts. It is sold in most bakeries today, and is served as a dessert and as a coffee cake at brunches.

Bialys. Bialys, similar to bagels but without holes, are made with only water, yeast, salt, and flour—the same ingredients as New York bagels but in different proportions. The soft bialy dough is formed into small rounds, which are patted down. Bialys need a long, slow rising period. Later, a thumb indents the center and fills it with diced onions and sometimes poppy seeds before it is baked in a very hot oven.

The bialy's origin is not clear, but bialys are suspected to be from the Middle East. In Poland and Russia, Jews ate a Bialystoker *tsibele pletzel*, a flat onion bread originally from the city of Bialystok, Poland. It came in two sizes: a larger version, called an "onion board" in English, and a smaller version called simply a *pletzel.* One hypothesis as to how bialys got their name is that Jewish bakers in the United States made *pletzel*, and their bosses, perhaps thinking that "*pletzel*" sounded too much like "pretzel," decided to name the American "*pletzel*," after its place of origin. Bialys, unlike most bagels today, are still made by hand, although a roll maker, invented in the 1930s, has increased production tremendously.

Blintzes. Thin pancakes filled with cheese and traditionally eaten at the springtime holiday of Shavuoth, blintzes are of Russian-Polish origin. Suspiciously like French crêpes or Chinese egg-roll wrappers, blintzes, or *blinchiki*, were often filled with shredded leftover brisket to make a complete meal or to serve as an accompaniment to chicken soup. They also were filled with farmer's or pot cheese for a dairy meal. In this country, many people add richer cream cheese.

Brisket. Brisket is a cut of beef from the breast muscles and other boneless tissues from the forequarter. It is often braised in liquid and covered, or it can be cured in salt water and spices and served as corned beef. Almost every country has its own variation of brisket.

Burek. Burek or *burekas* are turnovers of Turkish origin, often filled with cheeses or other savory mixtures.

Challah. Challah, originally thought of as the portion of bread thrown in the oven as an offering in the Temple of Jerusalem, is now known as the special bread reserved by Jews for the Sabbath. In biblical times, however, the Sabbath bread was probably more like our present-day pita. Through the ages and as Jews moved to different lands, the loaves used for the Sabbath varied geographically. Eastern European immigrants put challah on the gastronomical map in the United States.

Sugar was added to challah in the late nineteenth and early twentieth century, when all breads were sweetened in the United States; sugar was a sign of affluence. Some restaurants in the United States today, Jewish and non-Jewish, serve challah french toast as a breakfast or brunch dish.

Cholent. Call it cholent, *chamin, sk'eena,* or *adafina,* this Jewish Sabbath luncheon stew made from beans, meat, and onions is a dish that has distinguished Jewish cooking since the fourth century. Every wave of Jewish immigration to the Americas has its own form of this Sabbath dish, adding rice, barley, potatoes, and the like.

Ethrog. An *ethrog* is the fruit of a citron, a citrus fruit similar in appearance to a lemon but less round and more oval-shaped. It is used with the *lulav,* a traditional festive palm branch, in celebrating Sukkoth, the autumn harvest festival.

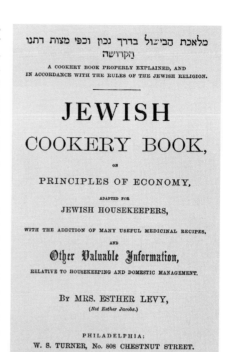

The title page of Esther Levy's Jewish Cookery Book, *1871.*

Gefilte Fish. Gefilte fish, basically a poached fish ball with filler (composed of bread crumbs or matzo meal), was served on the Sabbath and holidays by eastern European Jews; it is traditionally made from whitefish, pike, and carp. Gefilte fish can also describe a stewed or baked whole fish stuffed with a mixture of the fish flesh, bread or matzo crumbs, eggs, and seasonings. Today, gefilte fish mixings are often sold frozen. Gefilte fish is commonly eaten by American Jews today on the Jewish New Year and Passover and still, often, on the Sabbath.

Griebenes. Cracklings from goose fat and goose skin, usually salted.

Hamantaschen. Hamantaschen are filled triangular-shaped cookies eaten at Purim, a holiday that usually falls toward the end of the winter and that celebrates the Jews' salvation from the clutches of an evil Persian minister. The cookies, made with either yeast-based or butter-based dough, are often filled with sweet fruits, poppy seeds, or nuts.

Haroseth. Haroseth is a pastelike mixture of fruit, nuts, cinnamon, and wine eaten during the Passover Seder; it is often spread over matzo. Traditionally, this mixture represents the mortar that the Israelites used in building during their slavery in Egypt. In the United States, it is usually made with walnuts or pecans, apples, sweet wine, sugar, and occasionally cinnamon.

Kasha Varnishkes. Kasha varnishkes was a dish prepared for special occasions by Russian Jews. Made from sautéed onions, buckwheat groats (kasha), and square, shell, or

A butcher at work in East Side Glatt Kosher Butcher in New York City.

they became visible Jewish food. Today's knishes have gone mainstream, come in a variety of flavors, and are even available at "kosher-style" delis in shopping-mall food courts.

Kreplach. Kreplach, similar to Chinese wontons or Italian tortellini, are triangular pockets of noodle dough filled with chopped meat or cheese. They are boiled and eaten with chicken soup, or fried and eaten as a side dish. Kreplach arrived in Europe either when the khazars brought it to Polish lands or Jews brought it from trading expeditions in China.

Kugel. Kugel, meaning pudding, is the Sabbath "extra" food that goes along with stew or cholent. Kugels are made from bread crumbs and flour, potatoes, vegetables, noodles, and other ingredients and can be sweet or savory.

Latke. Latke means "pancake" in Yiddish, but most commonly it refers to a potato pancake eaten during the wintertime holiday of Hanukkah, when fried foods are served to commemorate the miracle of the holiday. Potatoes, inexpensive and easy to grow, were and are a common food in Eastern Europe, where Jews celebrated by eating latkes made from grated potatoes. Although some people take shortcuts, buying dehydrated or frozen grated potatoes or even frozen latkes, designer, freshly made potato pancakes have become popular in chic restaurants as well as in kosher and "kosher-style" delis.

Lekakh. Lekakh is the Yiddish word for honey cake, traditionally served on Rosh Hashanah (the Jewish New Year), and during the fall holiday season and eaten throughout the year as well. *Lekakh* often appears as a sweet treat on happy occasions, such as a birth or a wedding.

Lokshen. Lokshen is Yiddish for egg noodle, often eaten with stews or in kugels.

Lox. Lox, meaning "salmon," comes from the German word *Lachs*. In the late nineteenth century in the United States, "lox" referred to salt-cured salmon from the Pacific Ocean. In this period, before refrigeration, lox was not smoked but cured—in a heavy salt brine as a preservative—and then placed in large wooden casks. A large portion of this lox was shipped to Europe; some remained in New York, where it was soaked in water before eating. It was enjoyed largely by the Jewish community of the Lower East Side. With the advent of refrigeration and freezing, salmon came both frozen and in a mild salt cure before being smoked.

Smoked or cured salmon is not of Jewish origin but has come to be thought of as such because so many Jewish immigrants ate it, especially with cream cheese and bagels. Nova (*Nova Scotia*) salmon, cured in a wet brine of sugar and salt before being smoked, is available throughout the United States.

bow tie–shaped noodles (*varnishkes*), it is often eaten on Purim. Kasha is usually made from coarse cracked buckwheat but can also be made from barley, millet, oats, or wheat or from a mush made from one or more of those grains. Kasha was the common staple food for poor Jews in Romania; buckwheat is the grain most indigenous to Russia. Whole buckwheat groats, when they are cooked with water, milk, or broth, make a hearty, nourishing porridge.

Kishke. Kishke, literally a stomach casing from beef or fowl, is a delicacy when filled with a savory stuffing, usually composed of matzo meal or flour, chicken fat, and onion. The stuffed casing is then roasted. Nowadays, the casing is made from plastic.

Knaidlach. Knaidlach, or matzo ball dumplings, are composed of matzo meal, eggs, chicken fat, and sometimes ground almonds. They are served in soups.

Knishes. Knishes are round or square pieces of leavened dough that are folded over a savory meat, cheese, or potato filling. They can be baked or fried. Potato, kasha, liver, or cheese knishes may once have been a celebratory food in the Ukraine, where the potatoes were encrusted in a flaky pastry. But on New York's Lower East Side—specifically on lower Second Avenue, nicknamed "Knish Alley"—the knish became a convenient hot finger food that sweatshop workers could buy and take to work for a filling snack or lunch. Knishes were often sold outside, so

Smoked salmon from other parts of the world, such as Ireland, Scotland, and Denmark, is frequently dry-cured with rubbed salt before it is smoked.

Mamaliga. *Mamaliga* is a Romanian version of polenta, a very thick cornmeal mush. Corn was brought back to the Old World by explorers after they discovered America. Apparently, only Italy and Romania showed any interest in this versatile food; they turned it into polenta and *mamaliga*, respectively. *Mamaliga* is often served with various kinds of cheese on top. Because of the Jewish prohibition against mixing milk products with meat, *mamaliga* could not be served at a restaurant that served meat. Without cheese, it can be served, dipped in gravy, with pot roast as a side dish.

Matzo. Matzo is an unleavened, cracker-like bread that symbolizes both oppression and freedom. It is eaten by Jews at Passover, the springtime festival of freedom celebrating the Exodus from Egypt. Matzo is made without yeast and is quickly baked, so as to recall that the Jews fleeing from Egypt had no time to let their bread rise or to bake it properly. Originally, matzo was round and a lot thicker than the crispy, machine-made matzo sold in stores today.

There are special rules involved in making matzo. No yeast can be used, and the unbleached flour is carefully monitored for impurities, from the time the wheat is reaped (for handmade, so-called *shemurah*—or specially guarded—matzo) or from the time it is brought to the mill (for regular, machine-made matzo) until a finished product is produced. The water used for baking matzo must sit for twenty-four hours, with no foreign elements allowed to contaminate it.

Certain mills are designated and carefully cleaned so as to be suitable for grinding Passover flour, and special blessings are recited by the workers as the flour is ground. According to Jewish law, the mixing of the flour and water, the kneading on one side so no rising occurs, the piercing of holes, and the baking must take no more than eighteen minutes to the emergence of the finished product from the oven. If any more time is taken to make the matzo, the bread will rise, rendering it unsuitable for Passover.

Matzo is eaten at the seder, the ceremonial dinner eaten on the first night of Passover (on the first two nights, among traditional Jews in the Diaspora). On the seder table, three pieces of matzo are placed one above the other—to symbolize, according to one interpretation, the division of the Jewish people into *kohanim* (priests), *levi'im* (Levites), and Israelites (everyone else). At the beginning of the seder, the middle matzo is divided; the larger part, or *afikomen* (meaning "dessert" in Greek), is put aside and hidden. The *afikomen* should be the last food eaten at the meal. Matzo is also one of the first foods eaten at the seder, and a matzo sandwich is eaten shortly thereafter.

Petcha. *Petcha*, calf's-foot jelly, is a Sabbath afternoon dish. The custom of eating jelly reflects the idea that in the time of redemption even the feet will be elevated; the Sabbath is said to give the faithful a taste of the world to come, so "food made of feet" was eaten in anticipation. Practically, the calf's foot, like the African American delicacy made from hog heads and feet called "head cheese" or souse, is an inexpensive cut of meat, and for poor Eastern European Jews, like their poor African American counterparts, this jelly was another way to stretch what meat was available.

Pierogi. Pierogi are small pastries stuffed with savory fillings, frequently potatoes. Most countries have a version of these, variously called empanadas, *burekas*, pasties, or turnovers.

Rugelach. Rugelach is a horn-shaped rolled cookie that has been eaten for at least the last century. It is made in both a pareve (nonmeat, nondairy) and a buttery fashion. Rugelach usually consists of a dough with a cream-cheese-and-flour base, rolled with a sweet fruit, cinnamon, or chocolate filling. Cream cheese was an American addition to the rugelach dough, as are many of the innovative fillings used today. The cream cheese dough may have been developed by the Philadelphia Cream Cheese Company because the dough is often called "Philadelphia cream cheese dough." Cookbook writer Maida Heatter put rugelach on the culinary map with her grandmother's recipe; Heatter's is the rugelach most often found in upscale bakeries nationwide. Rugelach is often served at Hanukkah, as it is traditional then to eat sweets with cheese or sour cream. These cheese sweets represent the cakes that Judith allegedly fed the evil general Holofernes before she killed him.

Sambusak. *Sambusak* are crescent-shaped pastries of Middle Eastern origin, filled with savories. Sambusak, along with *burekas*, are among the many finger foods that Middle Eastern Jews brought with them to the United States. These pastries, originally filled with Syrian goat cheese, can also be made with muenster cheese, Balkan kashkeval cheese, or any other type of hard cheese that can be grated. Indian, Iraqi, and Persian Jews also eat *sambusak*, filling them most often with potatoes or chicken.

Schmaltz. Schmaltz is rendered poultry fat, obtained from the bird by frying the solidified fat until it is liquefied. Traditionally used for frying, schmaltz has been replaced, in large part, by modern conveniences like Crisco and other vegetable-based shortenings.

Schnecken. Schnecken are cakelike sweets served as desserts or at brunches. They are composed of a buttery yeast or cream-cheese dough rolled with nuts, sugar, cinnamon, and sometimes raisins. The dough is sliced and then baked, usually in a honey or brown-sugar-and-butter syrup. *Schnecken*, when made with yeast, have become the American pecan roll, caramel cinnamon roll, or sticky bun. Pecans and brown sugar have replaced almonds, walnuts, and honey.

Sufganiyot. *Sufganiyot* are doughnuts, often filled with jelly, which are an Israeli Hanukkah tradition. *Sufganiya*, a modern Hebrew word, comes from the Greek *sufgan*, meaning "puffed and fried."

Taiglach or Teyglakh. *Taiglach* are pieces of fried dough coated in honey, traditionally served at festive holidays and events such as Rosh Hashanah (the Jewish New Year), Sukkoth, Simchas Torah, Hanukkah, Purim, weddings, and births.

Tsimmes. *Tsimmes* is a sweetened, baked combination of vegetables or meat and vegetables, often made with dried fruits. It is stew-like and often eaten on the Sabbath and Sukkoth, the fall harvest holiday. In Yiddish, *tsimmes* means a big fuss made over someone. [See also BAGELS; BIALY; CHEESECAKE; DELICATESSENS; EGG CREAM; ETHNIC FOOD; JEWISH DIETARY LAWS; MATZO; NEW YORK FOOD; PASSOVER; SARA LEE CORPORATION.]

BIBLIOGRAPHY

Kafner, Stefan. *A Summer World: The Attempt to Build a Jewish Eden in the Catskills, from the Days of the Ghetto to the Rise and Decline of the Borscht Belt.* New York: Farrar, Straus & Giroux, 1989.

Nathan, Joan. *Jewish Cooking in America.* New York: Knopf, 1994.

Nathan, Joan. *The Jewish Holiday Baker.* New York: Shocken, 1997.

Schoener, Allon. *The American Jewish Album, 1654 to the Present.* New York: Rizzoli, 1983.

JOAN NATHAN

Jewish Dietary Laws

Kashruth, the Jewish dietary laws, shapes the everyday life of those who observe it. Observance of the dietary laws separates Jews from non-Jews and is intended to imbue the most mundane activities with holiness and significance. (The English word "kosher" reflects the Western, Yiddish pronunciation of the Hebrew word *kasher*, meaning fit or suitable.)

The cryptic and complicated prohibitions of Leviticus regarding animal food have been expanded by centuries of rabbinic commentary to apply to almost any food one might encounter. Any food that has been handled, processed, or packaged must be subject to strict rabbinic supervision; even some raw vegetables must be meticulously examined for bugs and dirt.

The laws of kashruth as outlined in the Hebrew Bible fall into three basic categories: prohibition of the consumption of blood, prohibition of the consumption of certain categories of animals, and the prohibition(s) regarding combinations of milk and meat products.

Blood. Consumption of blood is prohibited in Leviticus 17:14 on the grounds that an animal's blood is its life. In practice, this requires that meat must be thoroughly soaked and salted to remove any blood before it can be cooked, and eggs must be examined for blood spots before they may be added to a recipe.

Forbidden animals. Certain categories of animals are forbidden in the Hebrew Bible. Among sea creatures, only fish with fins and scales are suitable for consumption (Leviticus 11:9–12 and Deuteronomy 14:9–10). The Hebrew Bible provides a list of prohibited birds in Leviticus 11:13–19 and Deuteronomy 14:11–18; because the forbidden birds are scavengers and birds of prey, all such birds came to be regarded as unclean, and prohibited. Among land creatures, only ruminants, animals with split hooves that chew the cud, are suitable (Leviticus 11:3–8 and 20–27 and Deuteronomy 14:4–8 and 19–20).

The combination of milk and meat. A most important facet of the observance of kashruth, and the one that most distinguishes a kosher kitchen, is the separation of milk and meat products. This practice is traced to the three instances in the Pentateuch (Exodus 23:19, Exodus 34:26, and Deuteronomy 14:21) in which the children of Israel are forbidden to cook a goat in the milk of its mother. Whether these verses are the source of the prohibition remains a matter of dispute. In practice, meat and milk products are never cooked or prepared together and never served at the same meal. Kosher kitchens have completely separate sets of cookware, dishware, and cutlery for handling meat and milk products.

The details of the observance of the dietary laws cannot all be inferred from the Hebrew Bible itself nor from the Talmud, a multivolume elaboration on the commandments of the Torah or Pentateuch completed in the sixth century. The immediate source upon which *poskim,* rabbis who decide questions of Jewish law, base Jewish practice is the *Shulkhan Arukh* (or "Set Table"), compiled in the middle of the sixteenth century by Rabbi Joseph Caro (published 1565), and expanded with the commentaries of Rabbi Moses Isserles.

The Jewish Dietary Laws in America

Jewish immigrants to the United States in the seventeenth, eighteenth, and nineteenth centuries attempted with varying degrees of success to re-create the infrastructure that had enabled supervision of kosher food in Europe. By the late nineteenth century, many American Jews had shrugged off the strictures of kashruth entirely. In 1887, Rabbi Moses Weinberger wrote that *shokhtim* (ritual slaughterers) in America were entirely unsupervised, and although there were some *shokhtim* who were honest in their work, in general the kashruth of meat in America was not to be trusted.

In 1888, in an attempt to allay the anarchic situation present in the kosher meat business, Rabbi Jacob Joseph, the first and only Orthodox chief rabbi of New York City, instituted a stamp system under which all poultry that had been subject to proper rabbinic supervision would be certified kosher and stamped with a lead tag, or *plumba.* The intention was to assure Jewish consumers that they could trust their butchers, but the cost of the tags—one cent apiece—caused outrage. The Yiddish press compared the stamps to the *karobka,* punitive taxes levied on kosher meat in czarist Russia.

In 1902, in response to a 50 percent increase in the wholesale price of kosher beef (raising the retail price from twelve cents to eighteen cents per pound), Fanny Levy and Sarah Edelson, Jewish homemakers perhaps inspired by the resistance of Jewish women in the labor movement, went from door to door to persuade their neighbors not to buy kosher meat. On May 15 of that year, thousands of Jewish women broke into kosher butcher stores on the Lower East Side and threw meat onto the sidewalks, doused it with gasoline, or otherwise made it inedible. Two weeks later religious authorities formally endorsed the boycott—which finally ended in mid-June, when the retail price of kosher beef fell to fourteen cents a pound.

Coca-Cola received kashruth certification from an Atlanta rabbi in 1915 after the Coca-Cola company agreed to remove tallow-derived glycerin from its formula. (In order to be made privy to the list of ingredients in the Coca-Cola secret formula so that he could certify Coca-Cola as kosher, the rabbi had to swear that he would never reveal them.)

In the United States, the Union of Orthodox Jewish Congregations, commonly called the "OU" and represented by a letter U inside a letter O, is the most well known certifier of kosher foods. The Orthodox Union created the "OU" symbol in 1923; this trademarked symbol unobtrusively marks prepared and packaged foods that have been certified as kosher by the Union. (The first product to be graced with the symbol was Heinz vegetarian baked beans.) It was to be many years, however, before the "OU" symbol caught on.

In 1933, the Orthodox Union instituted a newsletter with a "kashruth column" to respond to the queries of Jewish homemakers trying to make sense of the staggering abundance of foods to be found in America. Today, the Orthodox Union certifies as kosher a quarter of a million products manufactured in sixty-eight countries. About 20 percent of kosher foods are certified by smaller organizations or local rabbinical associations.

[**See also** JEWISH AMERICAN FOOD; PASSOVER.]

BIBLIOGRAPHY

Cohn, Jacob. *The Royal Table: An Outline of the Dietary Laws of Israel.* New York: Bloch Publishing Co., 1936.

EVE JOCHNOWITZ

Johnny Appleseed

Johnny Appleseed is the name legend ascribes to John Chapman, an apple-tree nurseryman and frontiersman who was born in Leominster, Massachusetts, on September 26, 1774, and died near Fort Wayne, Indiana, on March 18, 1845. His father, Nathaniel, was a carpenter and farmer who served in the Continental army during the Revolutionary War; his mother, Elizabeth Symonds, died when John was two years old, and he was raised by relatives.

During the 1790s, Chapman and his half-brother, Nathaniel, traveled westward into Pennsylvania a number of times, planting small nurseries of apple trees from seeds collected at commercial cider presses in Pennsylvania. In the first decade of the nineteenth century, John Chapman, then in his middle twenties, traveled alone into Ohio to plant nurseries ahead of settlers encouraged to develop the West by federal homesteading policy.

In 1798, Congress had granted public land ranging from 160 to 2,240 acres to settlers who indicated they would permanently occupy it. One sign of such intention was the planting of an orchard. Chapman, as a land developer, selected dozens of suitable nursery sites, fenced them in, sowed the apple seeds, and returned periodically to maintain the nursery and to sell or give trees to the homesteaders. These seedlings enabled the development of profitable orchards in the Ohio Valley.

Chapman did not develop particular varieties of apples by grafting but used a method of seeding orchards based on the Van Mons theory, which claimed to improve the apple quality. The theory named for Jean Baptiste Van Mons (1765–1842) was based on seed selection and successive planting generation after generation to regenerate a rapid, uninterrupted, direct line of descent. He also may have rejected grafting on the religious principle that grafting or budding interfered with the work of God.

As every seed in every apple represents a potential new variety, Chapman's selection of seeds from successful strains produced hundreds of new varieties, including Black Annette, Franklin, Ohio Nonpareil, Western Beauty, and Ingram. Orchardists and newcomers in developing towns along the Ohio and Mississippi rivers bought and established orchards of these new acclimated varieties.

Early in the 1800s, Chapman became a self-ordained missionary of the Church of the New Jerusalem, a Christian church based on the biblical writing of Emanuel Swedenborg, the Swedish philosopher and theologian. The dress, demeanor, and behavior that generated many myths about Chapman probably resulted from this spiritual expression.

Chapman was a highly organized businessman who would, at the same time, bury money for future use, barter for clothes that did not fit him, give trees to those who could not pay, and converse with Native Americans in their languages. Many of the legends about him come from an article, "Johnny Appleseed, a Pioneer Hero," by W. D. Haley, in an 1871 issue of *Harper's New Monthly Magazine*. Along with many nonlegendary nurserymen in the same business, Johnny Appleseed took the seeds from the apple presses of the East and established the foundation of the orchards of the West.

[**See also** APPLES; FRUIT; MIDWEST; MYTHS AND FOLKLORE.]

BIBLIOGRAPHY

Price, Robert. *Johnny Appleseed: Man and Myth*. Bloomington: Indiana University Press, 1954.

THOMAS BURFORD

Johnson, Howard

Howard Deering Johnson (1897–1972), the only son of a Boston tobacconist, was born in Quincy, Massachusetts, a small industrial city bordering Boston on the south. The family lived in the middle-class, seaside Wollaston neighborhood. After serving in France during World War I, Johnson returned to take over his deceased father's failing shop. Three years later, in 1922, Johnson liquidated its assets, assumed the debt, and purchased a small corner drugstore that sold patent medicine, newspapers, tobacco, and candy. To make the business viable, he expanded the newspaper section to include a delivery service employing seventy-five boys. Then the self-professed ice cream aficionado, who consumed a cone every day of his life, turned his attention to the marble-topped soda fountain. He improved on the commercial ice creams of the day by manufacturing a product with twice the butterfat content. Different sources state that the formula was based on his mother's recipe or one that Johnson purchased from an elderly street vendor.

The ice cream became the cornerstone of the business, and he gradually expanded from the standard chocolate, vanilla, and strawberry to twenty-eight flavors. To make purchase convenient for sunbathers, he built small wooden stands along the beachfront where he sold ice cream cones for a nickel. By 1928, the Johnson's ice cream business alone was grossing $240,000 in sales. With the profits, he opened a restaurant featuring New England family-style specialties, such as clam chowder and chicken potpie, in a new ten-story granite building that still stood in downtown Quincy in the early 2000s.

During the Great Depression when banks were reluctant to give loans, Howard Johnson continued to expand his company by creating the concept of the restaurant franchise. For a small investment, he supplied every aspect of the business from facility design to food products, including the use of his name on the logo. The first was in Orleans, Massachusetts, on Cape Cod. Operating investors reaped

large profits and the enterprise grew rapidly, numbering two hundred restaurants by 1940.

All but twelve of the restaurants closed with the advent of World War II, but Johnson kept the company alive by providing meals for the military and educational institutions. After the war, Howard Johnson continued to apply the central commissary concept to the restaurant business ensuring quality and uniformity. Many products, including Tendersweet Clam Strips and HoJo Cola, were trademarked.

Anticipating highway expansion, he bid on and won exclusive rights to build the restaurants on the Pennsylvania, Ohio, and New Jersey turnpikes. He recorded a code of quality and cleanliness in the "Howard Johnson Bible" and upheld it through surprise inspections. He continued expansion by building motor lodges beside his restaurants located nearby new interstate highway exit ramps, bringing travelers the same standards in lodging that they had come to expect in the restaurants.

Johnson and his wife, Marjorie Smith, had two children, Dorothy Johnson Weeks and Howard Brennon Johnson. His son succeeded him in 1959 and took the company public in 1961. Although Johnson Sr. remained as chairman and treasurer, he devoted increasing time to acquiring art and sailing aboard his sixty-foot yacht. At his death in 1972, he maintained residences in Boston, Miami Beach, and Manhattan.

[**See also** BURGER KING; CLAMS; ICES AND ICE CREAM; HOWARD JOHNSON; MCDONALD'S; ROADSIDE FOOD; SANDERS, COLONEL; SODA FOUNTAINS; WHITE CASTLE.]

LINDA BASSETT

Johnson, Robert Gibbon, and the Tomato

On Sunday, January 30, 1949, the CBS radio network broadcast a "reenactment" of Robert Gibbon Johnson eating the first tomato in the United States, an event that supposedly took place in Salem, New Jersey, in September 1820. According to the broadcast, which was on the CBS *You Are There* series, until Johnson's moment in 1820 Americans considered the tomato poisonous. Johnson, one of Salem's most prominent citizens, had imported tomato seeds from South America and planted them in his garden. When the plants produced fruit, Johnson announced that he intended to eat a tomato on the courthouse steps. On the appointed day, as the CBS version told it, hundreds of onlookers gathered to watch Johnson eat a tomato—and die a painful death. Johnson sank his teeth into the tomato but did not die. His brave act shocked the crowd and changed the course of American culinary history. Thanks to Johnson's courage, Americans started eating tomatoes—or so the story went.

The CBS broadcast was not the first telling of this tale. The earliest known version of it appeared in the *Salem County Handbook* (1908), when William Chew, who was to become

publisher of the *Salem Standard and Jerseyman*, asserted that Johnson brought tomatoes to Salem in 1820. That unremarkable fact might have remained a simple, obscure nugget of Salem lore had not Joseph S. Sickler, an amateur local historian, added something to it and recounted the story to Harry Emerson Wildes, who included it in his nationally acclaimed book *The Delaware* (1940). Using Sickler's account, Wildes wrote that Johnson had dared to eat a prize tomato publicly on the courthouse steps. Stewart Holbrook, in his *Lost Men of American History* (1946), dramatized Wildes's version by creating imaginary dialogue for the event. Then Sickler, as historical consultant to CBS for the broadcast, embellished the story further.

Versions of the legend have appeared in professional and scholarly journals; in several publications of historical societies; in *Scientific American*, *Horticulture*, the *New Yorker*, and similar magazines; and in prestigious newspapers, including the *New York Times*. Dozens of cookbooks and food books have retold it. Yet no primary evidence has surfaced indicating that this story has any basis in fact.

The myth of Johnson and the tomato became enshrined as legend for several reasons. First, it rings true and is difficult or impossible to disprove. Second, the story seems to explain why Americans, who formerly thought that the tomato was poisonous, began eating it. Third, some residents of Salem believed the story would make their community famous, and they therefore kept telling the tale to reporters and authors. Finally, the writers found the story attractive: as there were no primary sources for it, writers could—and did—embellish the narrative to give punch to their writing. The story of Johnson eating the first tomato in America made good reading—and bad history.

[**See also** MYTHS AND FOLKLORE; TOMATOES.]

BIBLIOGRAPHY

Smith, Andrew F. "The Making of the Legend of Robert Gibbon Johnson and the Tomato." *New Jersey History* 108 (Fall/Winter 1990). 59–74.

Smith, Andrew F. *The Tomato in America: Early History, Culture and Cookery*. Columbia: University of South Carolina Press, 1994.

ANDREW F. SMITH

Johnson and Wales

Johnson and Wales University was founded as a business school in 1914 in Providence, Rhode Island, by Gertrude I. Johnson and Mary T. Wales, but it soon attained full-fledged associate degree–awarding status. In 1973, the university opened the College of Culinary Arts. Four campuses—in Norfolk, Virginia; North Miami, Florida; Denver, Colorado; and Charlotte, North Carolina—were added over the next thirty years. Associated sites include Vail, Colorado, and Göteborg,

offers undergraduate degrees in culinary
nutrition, food marketing, food-service entrepreneurship, and food-service management.
Master's degrees are also offered in accounting,
financial services management, hospitality administration, international trade, marketing,
organizational leadership, and teaching.

The private, nonprofit, accredited coedu-
cational institution trains restaurant chefs
and professionals in all areas of the food-
service industry. Students learn industrial,
contractual, and resort food-service operations through a combination of general academic, professional skill, and career-focused
courses. The practical curriculum of laboratory classes and academic studies is augmented by the Distinguished Visiting Chef
Program, designed to expose students to the
techniques and philosophies of internationally recognized chefs who visit the university
to lecture and demonstrate.

In 1989, one of the visiting chefs, the late
Louis Szathmary of Chicago, donated to the
university his entire collection of priceless culinary memorabilia. The collection is housed
in the Johnson and Wales University Culinary
Archives and Museum at the Providence
campus.

[See also CELEBRITY CHEFS; COOKING SCHOOLS;
CULINARY INSTITUTE OF AMERICA; RISE OF RESTAUR-
ANTS, THE; SZATHMARY, LOUIS.]

ROBIN M. MOWER

Jolly Green Giant

The Jolly Green Giant towers over most other
advertising icons. The original giant dates to
1925, when the Minnesota Valley Canning
Company wanted to sell a new kind of pea
that was tender, sweet, and tasty. But it was
also wrinkled, oblong, and huge, and
small June peas were popular at the time.
To overcome market resistance, Minnesota
Valley cleverly capitalized on the size of the
peas by calling them Green Giant and putting
a symbolic giant on the label.

The first giant looked quite different from
the one that the world now knows. Based on a
character in a Grimm fairy tale, the original
figure sported a bearskin and a scowl. He was
white and hunched over, and seemed more like
a dwarf than a giant. In 1935, Leo Burnett's
Chicago advertising agency provided a much-
needed makeover and created a giant with better posture, green skin, a leafy outfit, and a big
smile. Accompanying the smile was the addition of "Jolly" to the Green Giant's name.

Burnett also invented a valley for the giant
to preside over and gave him a responsibility
to rule it well. Part of his job there is quality
control, to ensure that only top-notch vegetables are grown and marketed under his
watch. Although all he ever says is "Ho, ho,
ho," he is positioned as the authority figure,
as befits someone of his stature. The supporting characters, or Valley Helpers, quote him
in commercials and convey his knowledge and
concerns to consumers. He has explained, for
example, that peas must be picked at the

*Historical re-enactors in historically inaccurate costumes outside the house of Colonel Robert Gibbon Johnson
in Salem, New Jersey, commemorate a nonevent. According to legend, Johnson proved that tomatoes are not
poisonous by eating a basket of them on the steps of the Salem County courthouse in 1820. He didn't.*

Sweden, the latter for programs in business
and hospitality.

With more than five thousand students enrolled at its various campuses, the College of
Culinary Arts is the largest food-service educa-

tor. In 1993, Johnson and Wales became the first
school in America to offer a bachelor of science
in the culinary arts. In addition to the associate
degree and the bachelor of science in culinary
arts and in baking and pastry arts, the university

fleeting moment of perfect flavor, that beans should be cut on a slant, and that niblet corn needs to be vacuum-packed.

The Jolly Green Giant's role has changed over the years. After his makeover, he appeared more often in print ads. He came to symbolize not only the pea but the company as well, and in 1950 Minnesota Valley Canning Company changed its name to Green Giant Company. In 1959, the giant made his TV advertising debut, and, soon after, spoke his first "Ho, ho, ho." In 1972, he was blessed with an enthusiastic and outgoing apprentice, Sprout, a giant in training. The Jolly Green Giant has instructed Sprout in the ways of vegetables and the ways of the valley, nurturing the little fellow just as he nurtures the vegetables in his care. In 1993, the giant tried semiretirement, quitting all ads and appearing only on labels. But on his seventy-fifth birthday, in 2000, the advertisers brought him back to work in print ads with slogans like "Give peas a chance" and "I stand for goodness (In fact I haven't sat down since 1925)."

The Jolly Green Giant represents a successful and enduring advertising campaign. *Advertising Age* considers the giant to be the third most recognized ad icon of the twentieth century, after the Marlboro Man and Ronald McDonald. Green Giant has become the largest vegetable brand in the world. Its vegetables are marketed in twenty-six countries, and the giant appears in such far-flung places as Greece, China, Japan, Israel, and Saudi Arabia.

[See also ADVERTISING; CANNING AND BOTTLING; CORN; PEAS; VEGETABLES.]

BIBLIOGRAPHY

McGrath, Molly Wade. *Top Sellers, U.S.A: Success Stories behind America's Best-Selling Products from Alka Seltzer to Zippo.* New York: Morrow, 1983.

SHARON KAPNICK

Johnnycakes and Hoecakes

Corn-based hearth breads were, along with cornmeal mush, the two Native foods most important to European colonists and early American farmers, and hoecakes became the staple food of African slaves and many poor farmers through the nineteenth century. Rhode Island johnnycakes are still regionally popular. When they are cooked as simple unleavened pancakes from ground Narragansett white cap corn, water, and salt, they are almost exactly the way they were eaten by Native Americans for millennia. George Washington's favorite breakfast at Mount Vernon was described as three simple mush cakes but "swimming in butter and honey."

One part of the Native American recipe that has persisted is that the cornmeal is usually scalded with boiling water into a mush or batter before cooking. This technique was noted by seventeenth-century English colonists in Virginia and Connecticut, and is also mentioned in almost all of the nineteenth-century recipes ascribed to slave or ex-slave cooks, who were considered masters of the dish. It seems likely that the technique was transmitted directly from early Native American slaves (mostly female, whereas the first African slaves were mostly male) to their African American descendents. The Native breads were cooked on flat stones like grills over the fire (as some Native American breads in Arizona are still baked) or by radiant heat on split wood planks propped up near an open fire. Some also were wrapped in leaves and buried in ashes or cooked in ashes which were then brushed off. All of these techniques were previously known to European settlers, as methods used for unleavened hearth breads by very poor rural people in Europe, who might, however, replace the cooking stones with iron pots or griddles. The radiant-heat, planked-flatbread method persisted with the two most popular forms, johnnycakes and hoecakes, until stoves replaced most open fireplaces in the second half of the nineteenth century.

The most important change to the Native recipe was the addition of eggs, salt, sugar, cream, lard, ham fat, milk, or leavening to make lighter and richer pancakes and cornbreads. But the plain ash cakes, fire cakes, hoecakes, johnnycakes, corn dodgers, corn pones, mush cakes, spider breads (a spider was a fireplace frying pan with legs), bannocks, Indian (meal) flapjacks, or Indian water cakes in native style persisted in many localities well into the twentieth century. By the time of printed cookbooks in the nineteenth century, the names were almost interchangeable, and interchangeably applied to crude or improved hearth cakes, pancakes, and leavened cornbreads alike. Today, johnnycake is a Rhode Island specialty, corn pones are mostly southern, and bannocks are generally Native American flatbreads, especially across Canada.

Unlike the cornmeal mushes, most of the hearth breads did not keep their Indian names. Corn pone, from the Virginia Algonkian "apan" ("baked") is the exception. Other names came from similar European flat breads: bannock from a Scottish barley cake; johnnycake probably from a Lancashire oatcake called a jannock. Both British names may derive from the Latin "panicium" ("of bread") or "panicum" ("millet"). The folk etymology "journey cake" is too commonly cited to be entirely discarded, although it has been frequently recorded that corn breads taste much better hot than cold, and thus are rather poor travel rations. However, johnny cake (the usual spelling outside Rhode Island) has the widest geographic spread, as there were southern johnnycakes made from rice or hominy corn, and an Australian form as well.

The most common and uniquely American name is "hoe cake," traced at least back to a 1750s Pennsylvania diary. Putting an agricultural tool over the fire to make lunch would weaken the temper of the tool, so if hoecakes were baked on actual hoes, they were probably propped up like the wooden johnnycake boards. Printed recipes almost always describe the dish as cooked on hoes *in former times,* which leads to a suspicion that the term may really go back to the Old English word "hoe" or "hough" for a hillock or hill-shaped piece of land, and described the shape of the crude loaf rather than the cooking implement. Against this, food historian Sandra Oliver has located a Williamsburg, Virginia, newspaper ad for "bake hoes," which implies there may have been specific hoecake baking tools apart from weeding hoes. Certainly some eighteenth- and nineteenth-century hoes had large enough blades to bake on, or against.

MARK H. ZANGER

Juice Bars

Juice bars, a billion-dollar business, began modestly in 1926 in Los Angeles when Julius Freed opened a shop selling fresh orange juice. His real estate agent, Bill Hamlin, a former chemist, suggested an all-natural mixture that gave the orange juice a creamy, foamy consistency. It contained orange juice, water, egg whites, vanilla extract, sugar, and ice. When Freed and Hamlin started selling the new beverage, sales soared from twenty dollars to one hundred dollars a day, and a name for the product arose from the way customers asked for the drink: "Give me an orange, Julius." By 1929, Orange Julius had grown into a chain with one hundred stores in the United States.

The macrobiotic vegetarianism fad in the mid-1960s stirred up the juice-bar business with the creation of smoothies, originally a mixture of fruit, fruit juice, and ice sold in the back of health-food restaurants and stores. Steve Kuhnau started a health-food store in 1973, offering nutritious, energy-packed smoothies as an alternative to the ubiquitous high-fat food of New Orleans and to help resolve his own health problems. In 1987, Kuhnau and his wife, Cindy, cofounded one of the major smoothie companies, Smoothie King Franchises Inc. A competitor, Jamba Juice Company, began in 1990 in California as a store that offered fresh-fruit smoothies, fresh squeezed juices, bread, and pretzels.

By the end of the twentieth century, regional and independent juice bars had sprouted up across the country, often selling coffee, tea, sandwiches, bagels, soups, and salads, as well as juice. Juice bars became prominent at the front of many health-food restaurants and stores, health clubs, and chains such as Wild Oats Markets Inc. and Whole Foods Markets Inc. Mobile smoothie stations in carts and kiosks make the drinks even more available and less expensive to purvey.

Changes in American culture increased the growth of juice bars. With a faster pace of life consumers look for nutritious, convenient, portable snacks or meal replacements, and the aging population searches for an energy elixir as zealously as athletes seek fast replenishment after exercise.

Beverages sold in juice bars are a good source of both dairy products and the recommended five-a-day servings of fruit and vegetables. They are often high in calories, ranging from 250 to over 500, many of which are from sugars. They also have a different nutrient combination than a complete meal does.

Juice bars try to make their drinks appealing with names such as Kiwi Berry Burner, Jamba Powerboost, and Bounce Back Blast. Juice bars serve beverages that may contain exotic fruit juices, organic juices, unusual Russian winter wheatgrass, seaweed, or vegetables. Many dessert-style smoothies contain milk; ice cream or ice milk; yogurt or frozen yogurt; sorbet; or soy, rice, or nut milk. Nutritional supplements may be added. Even tea and coffee are sometimes mixed with juice, fruit, and supplements.

In 2002, as the juice and smoothie business surpassed $1 billion in sales for the first time, there were about 3,500 juice bars in the United States. Smoothie King and Jamba Juice dominate the industry, but Orange Julius, owned by International Dairy Queen Inc., survives, with more than 370 franchises nationwide and internationally.

[See also COUNTERCULTURE, FOOD; DESSERTS; DIETS, FAD; FRUIT JUICES; HEALTH FOOD; VEGETARIANISM.]

BIBLIOGRAPHY

Wilbur, Todd. *Top Secret Recipes: Creating Kitchen Clones of America's Favorite Brand-Name Foods.* New York: A Plume Book, 1993.

Titus, Dan. *Smoothies! The Original Smoothie Book: Recipes from the Pro's.* Chino Hills, CA: Juice Gallery Multimedia, 2000.

ELISABETH TOWNSEND

Juicers

In order to remove as much juice as possible from citrus fruit, a ribbed or ridged rounded cone that fits inside the halved fruit can be used. From the outside of the fruit, pressure alone, or pressure and rotation combined, squeeze out the juice, seeds, and some of the pulp. Such a ridged cone is called a *reamer*; it is usually fitted with a raised slotted rim to separate seeds from juice and is either positioned over a receptacle or is designed as an all-in-one saucer with handle and pouring lip. Most are molded glass or plastic; the first patented one dates to 1889.

Old juicers are usually levered or cranked. Simple levered types have two hinged handles and date to about 1870. On one side is a convex dome; opposing it is a cavity with drip holes. As the handles are closed, the fruit is squeezed and juiced. In more complex levered juicers, half a citrus fruit on a convex reamer is squeezed with a levered concave presser. In others, a quarter of citrus fruit is put into a hopper and a levered presser folds and crushes it—much as it would be in your hand. Some cranked juicers move the reamer around the inside of the fruit while it is tightly held by a levered presser. Electric juicers have been used since the 1930s. There are small wedge squeezers for lemon used at the table or bar. Dating to the 1930s or so, they are still made.

Nineteenth-century juice presses for berries or raw meat were essentially metal boxes with holes in the bottom and a heavy screw-levered pressing plate. Meat juice—that is, blood—was used for invalid food until the early twentieth century.

BIBLIOGRAPHY

Franklin, Linda Campbell. *300 Years of Kitchen Collectibles.* 5th ed. Iola, WI: Krause, 2003.

LINDA CAMPBELL FRANKLIN

Juices, *see Fruit Juices*

Just Born

Samuel Born, a Russian immigrant, arrived in New York in 1910. He invented a machine that automatically inserted sticks into lollipops, thereby revolutionizing the lollipop industry. In 1917, he opened a retail candy store in Brooklyn. In 1923, Born started his own manufacturing company, along with his brothers-in-law, Irv and Jack Shaffer. They named their company Just Born. In 1932, the company relocated to Bethlehem, Pennsylvania, and three years later it acquired the Maillard Corporation, which made hand-decorated chocolates, crystallized fruits, Venetian mints, jellies, and "the best bridge mix in the country."

Just Born sold popular candies such as Mike and Ike (first manufactured in 1940) and Hot Tamales (introduced in 1950). In 1953, the company bought the Rodda Candy Company of Lancaster, Pennsylvania, which specialized in marshmallows and jelly beans. With Rodda's equipment, Just Born was able to create Marshmallow Peeps—brightly colored marshmallow chicks that have become an Easter tradition. Sam Born's son joined the company in 1946, and he helped to mechanize the marshmallow forming process. In 1977, the company expanded its jelly bean line to include Teenee Beanee Jelly Beans. In the mid-2000s, Just Born produced more than 4.2 million Peeps each day and remained a family-owned company.

[See also CANDY.]

BIBLIOGRAPHY

Richardson, Tim. *Sweets: A History of Candy.* New York: Bloomsbury, 2002.

ANDREW F. SMITH

Kale

Kale is a member of the *Brassica oleracea* species, *acephala* group, also known as Old World cabbages. This headless vegetable originated in the Mediterranean countries and was the main greenstuff of the poor in Europe until the Middle Ages, when headed cabbages were cultivated. The name is derived from the Scottish term for the plant, which is *kail*. In the United States, collard greens, a form of kale, is a staple in southern cooking, but otherwise kale is underused by most American cooks. It is eaten primarily by Americans from northern Europe and Iberia, where kale is most often encountered.

[**See also** CABBAGE; SOUTHERN REGIONAL COOKERY.]

BIBLIOGRAPHY

Schneider, Elizabeth. *Vegetables from Amaranth to Zucchini: The Essential Reference.* New York: William Morrow, 2002.

DAVID LEITE

Karcher, Carl

Carl N. Karcher (1917–) was born near Upper Sandusky, Ohio. His father was sharecropper and the family moved frequently. Carl dropped out of school and worked long hours in the fields. When an uncle in Anaheim, California, offered him a job in 1936, he accepted. Arriving in southern California, Karcher was amazed at the number of hot dog stands on the street corners, and he thought he might do well running a stand himself. He borrowed $311 and bought a hot dog cart, which was so successful that he bought a second stand. By the end of World War II, he owned four stands. In January 1945, Karcher opened a restaurant called Carl's Drive-In Barbecue. His business soared after the war.

During the 1950s, Karcher visited the McDonald's brothers restaurant in San Bernardino. His visit convinced him to open his own fast food restaurant, and the first Carl's, Jr. opened in 1956. Karcher quickly opened many more outlets in California, and ten years later the company incorporated as Carl Karcher Enterprises, Inc. (CKE). In the 1980s, it went public and began selling franchises nationwide. The 1990s were difficult for CKE, and the company ended up in debt. At this time, Karcher proposed making a deal with Green Burrito, a Mexican restaurant chain in California. The CKE Board opposed the deal and ousted Karcher in 1993. Nine months later, he engineered a takeover and had the Green Burrito plan adopted. The corporation turned around in 1997, and CKE purchased Hardee's, thus becoming the fourth largest hamburger chain in the world.

[**See also** CARL'S, JR.; FAST FOOD.]

BIBLIOGRAPHY

Karcher, Carl, and B. Carolyn Knight. *Never Stop Dreaming: The Story of Carl Karcher Enterprises.* San Marcos, CA: Robert Erdmann Publishing, 1991.

Schlosser, Eric. *Fast Food Nation; the Dark Side of the All-American Meal.* New York: Houghton Mifflin Company, 2001.

ANDREW F. SMITH

Karo Syrup

Southern cuisine owes much to the Corn Products Refining Company of New York and Chicago, inventor of Karo Corn Syrup, a liquid sugar produced from cornstarch. The bottled flavoring, not as sweet as cane sugar, with the consistency of honey, is essential to numerous down-home recipes. Pecan pie cannot be made without it. Before its introduction in 1902, housewives carried jugs to the grocery store for refilling from barrels. These barrels contained various regional brands of corn syrup, but not the crystal-clear Karo we know today. The origins of the name are shrouded in mystery. Some company historians believe the chemist who invented it named it after his wife, Caroline. Others trace the name back to an earlier brand name, Kairomel.

Karo is a prime example of successful advertising. Within a year of its first appearance, the company was running full-page ads in *Ladies' Home Journal* touting the purported wholesomeness of the syrup, though its value as a source of nutrition differs little from cane sugar. A massive quarter-million-dollar publicity blitz in 1910 (unprecedented in scale at the time), including distribution of a free cookbook of Karo recipes, made Karo a household word even before many people had tried it. In the early 1930s, the wife of a corporate sales executive devised a recipe of corn syrup, sugar, eggs, vanilla, and pecans baked in a pie shell, which became the now-famous pecan pie. A variant of that recipe, without pecans, became another southern favorite known as chess pie. In 1934, in still another marketing coup, the company enlisted the Dionne quintuplets, born in Callander, Ontario, for what became a decade-long endorsement by the internationally famous girls.

Capitalizing on the popularity of syrups as toppings for breakfast foods, the company launched "waffle syrup" to compete with much more expensive genuine maple syrup. The company's original light and dark corn syrups continued to gather a following for their usefulness in the manufacture of homemade hard candies, baked goods, and desserts. The light syrup is clarified and decolorized and contains vanilla for flavor. The dark syrup has the flavor and color of caramel and a stronger taste.

In the latter part of the twentieth century, corn and corn products began to replace other staple foodstuffs in the United States, especially in increasingly popular processed foods. Starches, meal, and alcohol derived from corn were substituted for more expensive products as modern farming technology made corn production more efficient. In 2001, a trade dispute erupted between the United States and Mexico over Mexico's assertion that American manufacturers were illegally dumping corn syrups onto the Mexican market, depressing that country's cane sugar industry. It was an early test of the terms of the North American Free Trade Agreement (NAFTA) and was settled by a World Trade Organization (WTO) panel decision in favor of the United States. Eventually, corn syrup eclipsed cane sugar as the prevalent sweetening agent in soft drinks and processed foods (replacing cane sugar in Coca-Cola in 1985, for example).

Although the commercial use of corn syrup has increased dramatically, fewer people than ever are manufacturing candies in the home. Karo is widely distributed for commercial use and, although regional brands exist, it remains the only brand available in grocery stores nationwide.

[**See also** ADVERTISING; ADVERTISING COOKBOOKS AND RECIPES; BREAKFAST FOODS; CLARIFYING; COCA-COLA; CORN SYRUP; PIES AND TARTS; SOUTHERN REGIONAL COOKERY; SUGAR.]

JAY WEINSTEIN

Kashruth, *see Jewish Dietary Laws*

Keebler

Godfrey Keebler opened a neighborhood bakery in Philadelphia in 1853. By the beginning of the twentieth century, Keebler products were distributed regionally, and operations were gradually expanded into other states. In 1924, Keebler joined with other bakeries to form the United Biscuit Company of America in order to compete more effectively with the nation's largest cookie and biscuit manufacture, the National Biscuit Company (Nabisco). By 1944, United Biscuit consisted of sixteen bakeries located from Philadelphia to Salt Lake City. In 1966, Keebler Company became the official corporate name and the brand name for all products.

Keebler advertising and packaging featured the characters "Ernie Keebler" and the "Keebler Elves," who explained in television commercials that the cookies were baked in the Hollow Tree in Sylvan Glen. The Elves, known for making "Uncommonly Good" products in a "magic oven," are among the best-recognized advertising characters in America.

In 1996, Keebler acquired the Sunshine brand, makers of Hydrox chocolate sandwich cookies. To compete more effectively with Oreo cookies manufactured by Nabisco, Keebler decided to change Hydrox's flavor and renamed the cookie "Droxies." Through its Little Brownie Bakers subsidiary, Keebler is also a leading licensed supplier of Girl Scout Cookies. Keebler's brands include Cheez-Its, Chips Deluxe, Famous Amos, Fudge Shoppe, Keebler, Plantation, Sunshine, and Town House. Keebler was acquired by the Kellogg Company in 2001. Keebler is the second-largest cookie and cracker brand in the country.

BIBLIOGRAPHY

Cahn, William. *Out of the Cracker Barrel; From Animal Crackers to Zu Zu's.* New York: Simon and Schuster, 1969.

ANDREW F. SMITH

Kellogg, John Harvey

No single individual influenced American eating habits during the early twentieth century more than Dr. John Harvey Kellogg (1852–1943). Born in Tyrone, Michigan, one of sixteen children, Kellogg studied medicine at Bellevue Hospital College in New York and in 1876 was asked to manage the Western Reform Institute in Battle Creek, Michigan. The Institute was a small health clinic specializing in hydrotherapy; it was sponsored by the Seventh-Day Adventists, who encouraged a vegetarian diet.

Kellogg changed the Institute's name to the Sanitarium (although it was occasionally referred to as the Sanatorium), and under his guidance it thrived. America's rich and famous flocked to the Sanitarium. Over the years, its patients included Henry Ford, J. C. Penney, Thomas Edison, and President William Howard Taft.

At the Sanitarium, Kellogg enforced a vegetarian regimen and sought to develop new vegetarian products. He was also a strong

An illustration of Kellogg by Glory Brightfield published in Rynn Berry's Famous Vegetarians and Their Favorite Recipes.

believer in the importance of thorough mastication of food. Patients with sore teeth, missing teeth, or no teeth had difficulty chewing hard substances, such as zwieback, then a common food in hospitals. To make such substances easier to chew, Kellogg ground them up into small pieces or granules.

Subsequent experiments with pressing grains and nuts between rollers led to successes with flattened kernels of wheat and maize that were baked in the oven and emerged as flakes. Kellogg also developed substitutes for meat and dairy products. In an attempt to find an alternative to dairy butter, he invented nut butters which were quickly adopted by vegetarians and then became known to the broader public. Peanuts were inexpensive, so peanut butter soon became an American fad food.

To promote and advance his medical theories, John Harvey Kellogg wrote more than fifty books and thousands of articles and lectured to hundreds of thousands of Americans throughout the nation in over five thousand public presentations. He was not averse to making money on his discoveries and he created a number of businesses to sell his products, but he had little personal interest in running the companies. He selected his younger brother, Will K. Kellogg, to manage several of them, including the Toasted Corn Flake Company. John Harvey Kellogg was unwilling to conduct the marketing necessary to compete with the imitators that had sprung up, so a split developed between the brothers.

John Harvey Kellogg was originally the majority stockholder, but he had distributed stock to the Sanitarium physicians. Will Kellogg bought up the stock, took control of the company, and renamed it the Kellogg Company. Will then put his signature on the product boxes and later, to enhance sales, added sugar and other nutrients to the cereal. The estranged brothers did not speak to each other for years, and battled in court, but in the end Will won.

The Sanitarium began to lose money in the Depression, and it closed in 1942. John Harvey Kellogg died the following year, aged ninety-one. His influence on America's breakfast table endures.

[See also BREAKFAST FOODS; FOOD AND NUTRITION SYSTEMS; HEALTH FOOD; KELLOGG COMPANY; NUTRITION; PEANUT BUTTER; VEGETARIANISM.]

BIBLIOGRAPHY

Carson, Gerald. *Cornflake Crusade.* New York: Rinehart, 1957.

Powell, Horace B. *The Original Has This Signature—W. K. Kellogg.* Englewood Cliffs, NJ: Prentice Hall, 1956.

ANDREW F. SMITH

Kellogg Company

Founded in 1906 by Will Keith Kellogg (1860–1951) as the Battle Creek Toasted Corn Flake Company, the Kellogg Company develops, manufactures, and promotes high-fiber, low-fat, ready-to-eat breakfast cereals such as Kellogg's Corn Flakes, All-Bran, and Rice Krispies. These cereals are primarily whole grains that have been cooked, flaked, and then toasted. They reflect a long-standing corporate tenet that convenient, low-cost, nutritious breakfast cereals can improve health.

Although the Kellogg corporate doctrine has a scientific basis, the company has historical roots in the religious principles of the Seventh-Day Adventist Church, which established the Western Health Reform Institute at Battle Creek, Michigan, in 1866. Later renamed the Battle Creek Sanitarium, this facility functioned as a retreat, hospital, and spa, focusing on a vegetarian menu and dietary counseling. The vegetarian diet represented a form of abstinence, a religious response to the high-fat, low-fiber American diet prevalent in the late nineteenth century.

Dr. John Harvey Kellogg (1852–1943), a prominent Seventh-Day Adventist, was chief physician at the Battle Creek Sanitarium; his brother Will was business manager. One goal of the Kellogg brothers was to develop a ready-to-eat breakfast cereal for their patients. In 1894, after experimenting unsuccessfully for several years, the brothers accidentally discovered a way to make a ready-to-eat whole-grain cereal. Wheat grains were first boiled, then soaked in water for several days to hydrate. Prolonged soaking allowed the moisture within each kernel of wheat to equalize. When the cooked, soaked grains were passed through rollers, they formed large thin flakes, which the brothers named "Granose" partly because the rollers were the same ones they used to make their "Granola." Granose was not only very popular at the Battle Creek Sanitarium but also sold by mail order.

In 1902, the brothers created a ready-to-eat, malt-flavored cornflake. Called Toasted Corn Flakes, this cereal was crisper and tastier than the wheat flakes. In 1906, after breaking with his brother and the sanitarium, Will Kellogg founded his own company to manufacture and promote Toasted Corn Flakes. The product was a huge financial success but Will Kellogg was less concerned with money than with providing Americans with healthful breakfast food. Recognizing the importance of fiber to a good diet, Will Kellogg in 1916 introduced All-Bran, the gold standard of high-fiber cereals. Other Kellogg bran cereals followed: Bran-Flakes (1923), Raisin Bran (1942), Bran Buds (1961), and Cracklin' Bran (1976).

In 1941, the Kellogg Company started adding extra nutrients to its breakfast cereals. Special K, a fat-free flaked-rice cereal introduced in 1955, was "fortified" with seven vitamins and minerals. Launched in 1966, Product 19, so-named because it was the nineteenth Kellogg cereal product, is enhanced with thirteen added vitamins and minerals. In 1998 the company went even further with Smart Start: of the fourteen

An All-Bran ad from the back cover of The Housewife's Almanac: A Book for Homemakers (1938), published by Kellogg.

vitamins and minerals added to it, ten supply 100 percent of the recommended daily requirement. The company introduced Smart Start Soy Protein in 2004. The addition of cinnamon-flavored soy granola clusters to Smart Start makes the cereal heart-healthy because soy protein is known to lower blood cholesterol.

In 1923, Will Kellogg created a Home Economics Services Department within the company. This department developed free educational materials so that home economics teachers could provide school children with information about the benefits of low-fat, high-fiber breakfast cereals. To interest children in its cereals, the Kellogg Company created cartoon characters as advertising symbols for some of its products: Tony the Tiger for Frosted Flakes; Snap! Crackle! Pop! for Rice Krispies; and Toucan Sam for Fruit Loops. Somewhat controversially, the company adds artificial sweeteners to some of its products. However, in 2004, in response to consumer demand, Kellogg introduced reduced-sugar versions of two of its popular children's cereals: One-Third Less Sugar Frosted Flakes and One-Third Less Sugar Fruit Loops.

As a result of diversification in the 1990s and with the acquisition of Keebler Foods in 2001, the company's products include a wide variety of snack and convenience foods. The complete product line generated sales of nearly $9 billion in 2003, with sales in more than 180 countries. Kellogg employs 25,000 people, with manufacturing facilities in seventeen countries. Kellogg's net income for 2003 was $787 million.

To promote "the health, happiness and well-being of children," Will Kellogg established the W. K. Kellogg Child Welfare Foundation in 1930. Later renamed the

W. K. Kellogg Foundation, it is primarily funded by a trust that holds Kellogg Company shares of stock donated by Will Kellogg in 1934. The foundation holds about 30 percent of the company stock; as a result, every purchase of a Kellogg product generates money for the foundation, making it one of the world's largest private philanthropic foundations.

[See also Advertising; Advertising Cookbooklets and Recipes; Breakfast Foods; Food and Nutrition Systems; Health Food; Home Economics; Kellogg, John Harvey; Nutrition; Vegetarianism.]

BIBLIOGRAPHY

Kellogg Company. *A Citizen's Petition: The Relationship between Diet and Health.* Battle Creek, MI: Kellogg Company, 1985.

Kellogg Company. *http://www.kelloggs.com.*

ROBERT W. BROWN

Kentucky Fried Chicken

Kentucky Fried Chicken, a franchised restaurant chain founded by Colonel Harland Sanders, introduced chicken to the fast food marketplace, thereby starting a diversification of fast food content and challenging the singular dominance of the hamburger. The success of Sanders's brand also increased the overall popularity of chicken as a mainstream American food, causing a surge in domestic chicken production and consumption. Not to be overshadowed by his company's achievements, Harland Sanders himself became a legendary figure in American advertising and, in a broader sense, in American cultural history.

Born in Indiana in 1890, Harland Sanders worked at several jobs growing up, including as a streetcar conductor, as a soldier in Cuba, as a railroad fireman, and on a farm. As a

young man he studied law, sold insurance, worked on a steamboat, and held court as a justice of the peace in Little Rock, Arkansas. Finally Sanders settled on selling tires and operating an automobile service station on the busy U.S. Route 25 in Corbin, Kentucky.

In 1930, Sanders began serving meals to hungry travelers stopping at his station, and he quickly discovered that his food—especially his seasoned fried chicken, which he made in a pressure cooker—was more popular and profitable than gasoline or tires. He expanded the business to a restaurant and motel across the street from his service station, and the growing fame of his chicken eventually attracted the acclaim of the celebrity food critic Duncan Hines. As a result of this national exposure, Kentucky governor Ruby Laffoon bestowed on Sanders the title of Kentucky Colonel.

Sanders's initial success proved short-lived, however. In 1955, Interstate 75 opened up three miles to the west of Corbin and diverted the heavy traffic from his restaurant. Forced to auction off his property, and reduced to living on a Social Security retirement check of $105 each month, Sanders set out to franchise his popular chicken recipe and cooking technique. In black formal attire and sporting a gold-tipped cane, Sanders drove a white Cadillac from state to state, pitching his franchise offer to restaurant owners and other potential investors. His secret recipe, he claimed, was "a blend of eleven herbs and spices." He cooked his fried chicken for investors, and, thanks to his smooth salesmanship, usually left with a handshake agreement for a new franchise. Under his standard franchising arrangement, restaurateurs agreed to pay him five cents for each Kentucky Fried chicken sold.

His nickels soon began to add up; he had more than six hundred franchisees under contract by 1963. The following year, already seventy-four years old, Sanders sold his company for $2 million to investors led by John Y. Brown and Jack Massey. Colonel Sanders remained as the company's "good will advisor," and, changing to a white suit, became a popular, familiar figure in print and television advertisements. The company boomed under Massey and Brown's direction, selling shares publicly on the New York Stock Exchange in 1966, and growing in size to 3,500 company-owned or franchised outlets by 1970.

In 1971 Brown sold out to Heublein Inc. for $285 million. A distiller and food manufacturer, Heublein proved ill-prepared to operate fast-food restaurants. Profits fell and fewer new franchisees signed up. Fortunes rebounded, however, when R. J. Reynolds acquired Heublein in 1982. Four years later, in 1986, RJR Nabisco sold KFC to PepsiCo Inc. for $840 million. In addition to its beverage business, PepsiCo understood the fast food industry, having owned the Taco Bell and Pizza Hut chains since the 1970s. Eventually, PepsiCo combined those two chains, KFC, A&W

All-American Restaurants, and Long John Silver's into an independent subsidiary called Tricon Global Restaurants Inc. In 2002, PepsiCo changed the name Tricon Global to Yum! Brands Inc. At that point, it was the world's largest restaurant company, with a combined total of 32,500 units worldwide.

Despite this succession of corporate owners, KFC maintained its identity and Harland Sanders continued as spokesman, still traveling a quarter million miles each year to promote the company, until his death in 1980. At the beginning of the twenty-first century, KFC had more than ten thousand outlets and was growing most rapidly outside the United States. In 2002, the company opened its seven hundredth restaurant in China, only fifteen years after starting business there. The "Colonel's Chicken" is standard fare around the globe, but his recipe's "eleven herbs and spices" remain a closely guarded secret.

[See also Advertising; Chicken; Fast Food; Hamburger; Hines, Duncan; Roadhouses; Sanders, Col.]

BIBLIOGRAPHY

Jakle, John A. *Fast Food: Roadside Restaurants in the Automobile Age*. Baltimore: John Hopkins University Press, 1999.

Thomas, R. David. *Dave's Way: A New Approach to Old Fashioned Success*. New York: Berkley Publishing Group, 1992.

DAVID GERARD HOGAN

Ketchup

The word "ketchup" conjures up an image of the thick, sweet, tomato-based condiment that American teenagers deploy indiscriminately on most of their foods. Although almost every restaurant and café in the United States provides easily accessible bottles of tomato ketchup—often standing on each table next to the salt and pepper shakers—Americans did not invent ketchup, which was originally not thick, or sweet, or made from tomatoes.

The concoction takes its name from the Mandarin word *k-tsiap*, which refers to a fermented sauce made from soybeans. British explorers, colonists, and traders came into contact with the sauce in Southeast Asia, and upon their return to Europe they attempted to duplicate it. As soybeans were not grown in Europe, British cooks used such substitutes as anchovies, mushrooms, walnuts, and oysters. British colonists brought ketchup to North America, and Americans continued experimenting, using a variety of additional ingredients, including beans and apples.

Tomato ketchup may have originated in America. It was widely used throughout the United States in the early nineteenth century and small quantities of it were first bottled in the 1850s. After the Civil War, commercial production of ketchup rapidly increased and, although other ketchups were manufactured, tomato ketchup became the most important version. In 1891, a writer in the *Merchant's Review* declared it to be the "sauce of sauces." In 1896, the *New York Tribune* reported that tomato ketchup was America's national condiment, available "on every table in the land." A 1901 study found ninety-four different brands of tomato ketchup being sold in Connecticut alone. The authors reported that ketchup was the "most popular bottled table sauce" in America, that it was "found on the tables of nearly every hotel and restaurant," and was "consumed in large quantities in families." More than eight hundred different ketchups have been identified as manufactured before 1915, and this is probably only a fraction of the total number actually bottled in America.

Up until about 1900, ketchup was mainly used as an ingredient for savory pies and sauces, and to enhance the flavor of meat, poultry, and fish. It then became famous as a condiment following the appearance of three major host foods: hamburgers, hot dogs, and french fries. A leading commercial producer at the time was the H. J. Heinz Company, which first sold tomato ketchup in 1873. By 1890, Heinz had hit on the famous brand-image combination of keystone label, neckband, screw cap, and octagonal bottle. The ketchup bottle itself has become a culinary icon throughout the world. In the early years of the twentieth century, the H. J. Heinz Company was the largest tomato ketchup producer, and when the century ended it was still in that position.

Another ketchup manufacturer, the Del Monte Corporation of San Francisco, had begun bottling ketchup by 1915 and rapidly expanded production during the 1940s. Yet another producer was the Hunt Brothers Packing Company, which began making ketchup during the 1930s. Heinz, Del Monte, and Hunt are the three largest ketchup producers in the world.

Virtually all ketchup was originally packed into glass bottles, except for commercial ketchup, which was sold in large cans. This changed in the 1970s when the H. J. Heinz Company introduced the Vol-Pak, a plastic bag filled aseptically with ketchup. Designed for food-service operations and restaurants, the bag was kept on a rack to refill plastic bottles conveniently. The Vol-Pak soon replaced cans. During the 1980s, two additional packaging innovations appeared: the single-serving ketchup pouch, which increased in sales from half a million cases to 5 million cases in just ten years; and the squeezable plastic ketchup bottle, which was easier to use than a glass bottle and almost unbreakable. By 2000, 60 percent of all ketchup in the United States was sold in plastic containers.

The consumption of ketchup has expanded along with the proliferation of fast food restaurants, where it is dispensed in single-serving pouches or in large plastic reservoirs with push pumps. Americans alone purchase 10 billion ounces of ketchup per year, averaging out to

An advertisement for Blue Label ketchup, early twentieth century.

about three bottles per person. Worldwide, more than 840 million fourteen-ounce bottles alone are sold annually.

By the end of the twentieth century, ketchup was ubiquitous. Its usage had expanded rapidly throughout Latin America, Europe, Australia, and East and Southeast Asia. Few other sauces or condiments have transcended local and national culinary traditions as thoroughly as tomato ketchup. With the global growth of fast-food chains, the consumption of ketchup is likely to escalate. Some denounce it as an American culinary atrocity and others condemn it as a promoter of global homogenization. Still others view it as the Esperanto of cuisine.

[See also Aseptic Packaging; Bottling; Condiments; Fast Food; H. J. Heinz Company; Packaging; Soybeans; Tomatoes.]

BIBLIOGRAPHY

Smith, Andrew F. *Pure Ketchup: A History of America's National Condiment*. Columbia: University of South Carolina Press, 1996.

ANDREW F. SMITH

Kettles

The term *kettle* appears most often in early cooking manuscripts referring to pots used for preserving and candying that were generally made of earthenware, bronze, or copper, materials that did not darken acidic food. They were open pots with straight or slanted sides and swinging or "falling" bail handles for suspension over coals or flames, and they were well suited for efficient evaporation. Other kettles made of cast iron worked better for long, slow, moist cookery of stews, soups, and porridges. By the late seventeenth century the term was sometimes used synonymously with *pot*, and thus either word might have referred to the same utensil. For the most part, kettles had flat bottoms. Kettles sometimes were made with a pouring lip on one edge and a tipping handle partway down the opposite side.

In the 1830s, a manufactory of brass kettles—Israel Coe and Company—thrived in America's brass-producing state, Connecticut. In 1851, H. W. Hayden, of Waterbury, Connecticut, patented a new method of manufacturing brass preserve kettles. His process for spinning brass on a wooden form mostly put an end to the pieced-brass kettles with dovetailed joins. The Hayden spun-brass kettles were made in sizes from two to fourteen gallons and they retained the old-fashioned wrought-iron bail handle. By the 1890s, many kettles were made in enameled sheet iron that had been stamped into shape before enameling; others were produced in cast iron with enameled interiors, which made them almost impervious to acidic foods. From about 1900 on, spun- and cast-aluminum kettles were made, but these are only satisfactory when heavy enough to accommodate the long, slow cooking for which kettles are still needed.

[**See also** POTS AND PANS; PRESERVES.]

BIBLIOGRAPHY

Franklin, Linda Campbell. *300 Years of Kitchen Collectibles*. 5th ed. Iola, WI: Krause Publications, 2003.

Greguire, Helen. *The Collector's Encyclopedia of Graniteware Colors, Shapes, and Values*, Book 2. Paducah, KY: Collector Books, 1993.

LINDA CAMPBELL FRANKLIN AND
ALICE ROSS

KFC, *see Kentucky Fried Chicken*

Kitchen Gardening

A steadfast symbol of sustenance, well-being, and American self-sufficiency, kitchen gardening has played a vital role in the evolution of America's cultural and culinary heritage for nearly four hundred years. As the American diet has evolved over time to accommodate ever-shifting priorities and the introduction of a variety of new foods, so has the kitchen garden followed suit.

Early American Kitchen Gardens

The kitchen garden was a mainstay of early American life and was mandated by law as early as 1624. A necessity for enduring the many hardships common to life in the New World, the kitchen garden, along with the hearth, served as the hub of the early American colonial home. A no-nonsense food production area designed for function rather than aesthetics or pleasure, the kitchen garden produced plants used for food and flavorings, in herbal medicines, for dyes, for air freshening, and for insect repellent. The division of labor mandated that women of the time feed and attend to their families' medical needs while the majority of men practiced large-scale crop farming.

The early American culinary garden was typically divided into four (or more) symmetrical square or rectangular raised beds divided by two narrow intersecting paths in the tradition of the English cottage garden, known as the four-square design. The raised beds helped warm the soil for early planting and encouraged drainage. Traditionally, the food garden was planted within close proximity to the home and to a water source, and the garden was surrounded by a protective enclosure, such as a fence, in order to keep animals out. Kitchen gardens varied in size from one-fourth of an acre in the North to six or more acres in the South. Planting and harvesting were done according to the phases of the moon and the astrological calendar.

Many of the seeds and plants used in early American kitchen gardens were brought from the Old World in an effort to duplicate the gardens left behind. Culinary gardens of the time often contained lettuce, beets, peas, asparagus, celery, cucumbers, radishes, sorrel, kidney beans, broccoli, and cauliflower. Culinary herbs included chives, leeks, mint, fennel, marjoram, tarragon, savory, parsley, borage, and thyme. Such pharmaceutical herbs as chamomile, hyssop, angelica, betony, clary sage, feverfew, licorice, rue, and valerian were grown. Kitchen gardens of the northern colonies relied heavily on root vegetables, such as turnips, parsnips, onions, carrots, and (eventually) potatoes, as they could be preserved through the cold winters in the mandatory root cellar. Cabbage was among the most highly prized plants for its hardiness and keeping qualities. The more temperate climate of the South allowed for greater flexibility in plant selection, which included such greens as spinach and collards. The indigenous populations had also introduced the settlers to such important native foods as corn, runner beans, pumpkins, squash, and Jerusalem artichokes, which were gradually integrated into their diet.

Thomas Jefferson's kitchen garden at Monticello in Charlottesville, Virginia, and that of George Washington at Mount Vernon, Virginia, are two examples of formal, early American kitchen gardens that have remained under cultivation.

African Slaves and the Kitchen Garden

Enslaved Africans were frequently allocated personal garden plots, enabling them to supplement their food rations while growing the foods they preferred. African cooks also were responsible for food preparation in the large

Order envelope of Aaron Low, Seed Grower, Essex, Massachusetts, 1880s. Low's catalogs included illustrations of vegetables, an order form, and advertisements from agricultural implement sellers.

southern plantation houses, allowing them to introduce a variety of new foods to the American table. These included peanuts, black-eyed peas, sesame (also known as benne), okra, sweet potatoes, yams, watermelon, rice, sorghum, eggplant, and tomatoes. Over time, these foods became integral parts of the American diet while contributing to the development of a distinct cuisine.

The Good Life

The importance of kitchen gardening declined in the later nineteenth century as the dominant agrarian way of life gave way to rapid urbanization. Consequently, for the first time in U.S. history, the population began buying produce from retail grocers rather than cultivating it themselves. Many people left the cities for the newly created post–Civil War suburbs, seeking relief from such urban problems as crime and epidemics. Gardening was promoted as a therapeutic activity while vegetables were recognized for the contribution they made to good health. Thus, the opportunity to cultivate a kitchen garden was an acknowledged factor in the appeal of the suburban "good life." However, hybrid seeds sold by new commercial seed catalogs and chemical fertilizers now

War Gardens Victorious

Every War Garden a Peace Plant—
NATIONAL WAR GARDEN COMMISSION
— Charles Lathrop Pack, President.   WASHINGTON, D.C.

A poster distributed by the National War Garden Commission around 1919.

replaced the time-honored practice of seed saving and using composted manure.

"Planting for Freedom"

Escalating prices, food shortages, and economic hardships of World War I triggered a major wave of kitchen gardening across the United States. The National War Commission, created in 1917, encouraged citizens of all economic classes to contribute to the domestic war effort by growing liberty gardens (later known as victory gardens). Liberty gardens (1917–1920) frequently took the form of community gardens, also known as allotment gardens, cultivated on large, open spaces, such as vacant city lots or railroad yards. Despite its enormous success, the end of the war prompted the demise of the liberty garden program.

The Great Depression of the 1930s also inspired a revival of culinary gardening as rampant unemployment and widespread poverty among the middle classes spurred the development of government-sponsored community "relief" gardens (1930–1939).

During World War II, kitchen garden cultivation was regarded as a patriotic duty. Providing a way for the population to feel involved in the war effort, the victory gardens also served as a self-help solution to deal with food shortages and rationing. Americans were urged to grow and preserve as much of their own food as possible in order to make commercially grown produce available to the troops overseas. It is estimated that nearly 20 million victory gardens were planted during World War II. In 1944 alone, more than one-third of the country's vegetables were grown in victory gardens. The end of the war, coupled with the return of national prosperity, signaled an end to the kitchen gardening movement.

Back to Nature

In the early 1960s, growing concern over the environmental impact of chemical fertilizers and pesticides gave birth to the organic gardening movement. The energy crisis, high food prices brought about by inflation, and widespread disenchantment with mass-produced foods all contributed to a renaissance in both culinary and community gardening in the early 1970s.

Modern Kitchen Gardening

A 1998 Harris Poll ranked gardening as America's most popular leisure activity. With over 31 million Americans taking part and thousands of books, articles, and television programs devoted to the subject, kitchen gardening has become a significant influence on modern American popular culture. In addition, a worldwide movement seeks to preserve genetic diversity by restoring to their former prominence heirloom seeds thought to have been lost through hybridization. Cooking creatively with vegetables and herbs from the kitchen gar-

den remains an important culinary trend among restaurant chefs and home gardeners alike.

[**See also** HEIRLOOM VEGETABLES; ORGANIC GARDENING.]

BIBLIOGRAPHY

Tucker, David. *Kitchen Gardening in America: A History.* Ames: Iowa State University Press, 1993.
Weaver, William Woys. *Heirloom Vegetable Gardening: A Master Gardener's Guide to Planting, Seed Saving, and Cultural History.* New York: Holt, 1997.

ELYSE FRIEDMAN

Kitchens:
Early Kitchens

In the earliest English American settlements, relatively small "kitchens" were truly the heart of the house. Life was conducted around the fire; everyone knew how to make a fire with a steel striker, a sharp-edged flint stone, and enough tinder. Originating from the packed dirt floor, central fireplace, and thatched roof that allowed the smoke to exit, developed the brick, stone, or wattle and daub (mud and branches) chimney, hearth, and bake oven. This was how things remained for some 250 to 300 years.

The architecture of the kitchen depended on a number of factors. Apart from basic shelter and climate conditions, it reflected social views, economic status, and familiar European styles. For example, English Americans located their fireplaces and chimneys on interior walls for back-to-back hearths and more efficient heating. The Dutch hearth was built against a stone exterior wall, without jambs (fireplace side walls), and a "fender" (a canopy leading to the chimney) high on the wall to catch the smoke. Most used floor-level hearths, although the Germans in Pennsylvania had raised hearths, and the clay and tile of the Spanish directed building styles in the American southwest.

Regional and Social Variations

Conditions in the colonies also determined the kitchen's architectural form. Pioneering cabins—one-roomed log cabins—were often the first to be built in any region, and may have had sod roofs and a fireplace. At the other extreme, southern plantations developed a unique response to heat and danger of the kitchen fire and the sensory evidence of cookery, moving the work out of the house into a series of sheds or small buildings. For those who could not manage this luxury, one-room huts resembling the early colonial style sufficed for slaves; the middle-class farmer made do with something in the middle. In Louisiana and Carolina dogtrot cabins, the kitchen was separated from the second room by a wide breezeway, all under a common roof.

In northeastern cities, where plot size was limited, kitchens were frequently removed to a cellar area, moving the smells, sights and sounds down rather than out. This arrange-

An illustration of the kitchen at the Governor's Palace in Williamsburg, Virginia.

ment had certain benefits for the cook: the temperature was cooler in summertime and the stored foods and chores were closer to hand. These included butchering and meat processing, storage of root vegetables and fruit, butter and cheeses, wine, beer, and cider.

Large bulkhead doors were necessary to allow the entry and removal of large items. Bake ovens were important kitchen features. Although they were sometimes built freestanding, out of doors, they were more likely to be found just behind the fireplace, with a door opening between them at the front face of the chimney. By the eighteenth century, the oven door had moved to the side jamb, and, by the early nineteenth, to the front wall of the jamb. This later fireplace had the advantages of ash pits and interior flues with sliding doors to carry away the waste. The oven was heated by lighting a good fire inside it (the smoke came out into the fireplace and then up the chimney), and when it was deemed hot enough, the remaining ash, ember, and unburned wood was raked out onto the fireplace floor, the food inserted with a long-handled peel, and the door closed.

Implements and Furnishings

The basic cooking implements of the early kitchens was simple. People made as many as they could at home, using wood, bone, or leather. Iron was expensive in the seventeenth and early eighteenth centuries, so it was owned in limited quantities, according to means. Far

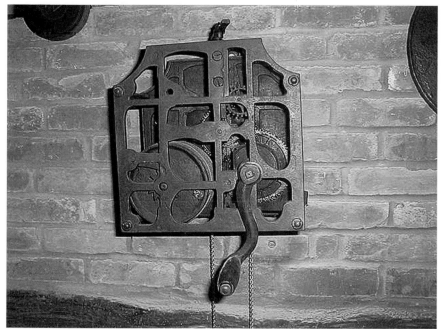

The clock jack was the epitome of cooking equipment of the eighteenth century. Its pulley served as an early rotisserie, driving the spitted meats on the hearth. Handmade by a skilled blacksmith, it commanded high prices and was only available to wealthier or commercial kitchens of the time.

more common was earthenware, inexpensive and made locally, and well suited to simple frying and stewing. The early 1700s brought the tin industry, and tin artifacts became common. The swinging crane, the large arm from which to hang pots, offered an improvement over the earlier trammels that hung from lug poles high in the chimney.

A minimal kitchen also needed an all-purpose, cast-iron, cauldron-shaped pot; it was made in varying sizes, sat on three legs or hung from a swinging bail handle. Griddles and three-legged frying pans were also found everywhere, as were broiling gridirons (sometimes forged in a standing position), water kettles, and posnets (saucepans). Toasters were important to the English, as were salamanders (broilers), thick plates of iron, preheated and passed over the food. As the eighteenth century progressed, modestly priced tin reflecting ovens achieved simpler and faster roasting. And everyone cooked with long-handled meat forks, ladles, skimmers, turners, and spoons.

Kitchen furnishings expanded as the cookware did. Pioneering families had few tables; children ate sitting on the floor. The table was a multitasking item, accommodating cooking, dining, and other work. With time came longer tables and chairs for all, simple open shelving for utensils, and ultimately dressers for storing dishware and lockable "pie safes" for important meats or cheeses. Closets were rare. Farm kitchens were extended with "dirty kitchens," lean-to enclosures behind the fireplace that held the oven, in which were stored work tools, bulky cooking equipment, and occasionally food.

By the early 1800s American cities were on the rise, beginning a transition to the new urban culture that would replace rural ways. Urban homemakers were no longer deeply involved in producing and preserving foods, as their husbands provided cash and those items were purchased. Their kitchens changed in character, and there was a long period of overlap as the fireplace and cookstove were in use. The range of equipment, storage, and furnishings began to reflect industrial changes, and the first waves of mass migration, beginning with the Irish, became a source of hired help.

During these centuries, the social nature of the kitchen changed from the one all-purpose work, eating, socializing, and sleeping room to the single-purpose cooking and eating room. The movement of men's work to the city and of children to compulsory education left the kitchen to the women. Still a social gathering place, it was no longer a family workspace.

[**See also** CUPBOARDS AND FOOD SAFES; DUTCH INFLUENCES ON AMERICAN FOOD; FRYING PANS, SKILLETS, AND SPIDERS; HEARTH COOKERY; STOVES AND OVENS; TURNSPIT DOGS.]

BIBLIOGRAPHY

Harrison, Molly. *The Kitchen in History*. New York: Scribner's, 1972.

Phipps, Frances. *Colonial Kitchens, Their Furnishings, and Their Gardens*. New York: Hawthorn, 1972.

Plante, Ellen M. *The American Kitchen, 1700 to the Present: From Hearth to Highrise*. New York: Facts on File, 1995.

Smallzreid, Kathleen Ann. *The Everlasting Pleasure: Influences on American Kitchens, Cooks, and Cooking from 1565 to 2000*. New York: Appleton Century Crofts, 1956.

ALICE ROSS

Kitchens:
1800 to the Present

Early industrial growth and technologies escalated during the antebellum period, crowding kitchens with equipment, storage, and furnishings. There was a long period of overlap during which both fireplaces and cookstoves were used, sometimes in the same room. By the 1840s and 1850s, cookstoves had been enlarged and perfected and were commonly accepted in urban middle-class households. Rural kitchens were not modernized at this time.

1850–1900

With the onset of the American Industrial Revolution (ca. 1850), the numbers of manufactured kitchen goods continued to rise. Gadgetry became extremely desirable, and many inexpensive tools, from apple peelers to canning equipment and egg beaters to shaped baking pans competed with reasonably priced tableware for storage space. The storage problem urgently required solutions in the face of more complex and stylish cooking, baking, and newly instituted home canning.

One of the earliest figures to shape women's new roles and responsibilities was Catharine Beecher. Beecher's seminal works (*Treatise on Domestic Economy*, 1841, and *The American Woman's Home*, 1869) promoted innovative theories on kitchen management, design, and efficiency. Beecher suggested rearranged workspaces, new furnishings, and simplified traffic patterns. In a similar work, *The Philosophy of Housekeeping*, published in 1869, Joseph B. and Laura E. Lyman contributed the notion of the L-shaped kitchen plan, charting an imaginary "triangle" between major workspaces.

In addition to the central, all-purpose worktable, kitchens were furnished with free-standing jam cupboards and food safes like the Hoosier cabinet. This freestanding cabinet had special shelves, drawers, and compartments for cutlery and linens; dispensing bins; and a pullout work shelf. Cast-iron hand pumps, which sometimes were installed indoors, eliminated the heavy work of hauling well water. In addition, the refrigerator, invented in the 1830s, was improved and marketed widely in association with the new ice industry. However, few of these innovations were incorporated into the kitchens of poor neighborhoods and remote rural areas.

1900–1945

In the early twentieth century, wood- and coal-burning cookstoves were replaced with gas and electric ranges that became available in 1910 but were not easy or practical to use until 1913, when the automatic oven temperature regulator was invented. Electric ranges were not in general use for another two decades.

Electricity was added to kitchens slowly but steadily. A good deal of work—beating and mixing, for example—was still done manually. In the 1920s and 1930s, sinks, refrigerators, and ranges were freestanding, but most urban kitchens had electricity, and electric stoves gained favor. The first automatic dishwashers, although not common in average homes, were built in next to the sinks of the well-to-do.

From the 1920s on, kitchen design began reflecting the concern for sanitation promoted by home economists. Walls were made of easily cleaned materials: improved paints made them easier to maintain, and the wooden wainscoting popular in the 1880s and 1890s was done away with. Instead of oilcloth, sheets of decorative linoleum were used throughout the kitchen like throw rugs to cover less sanitary brick and wood flooring. Those who could afford it applied shining tile to their kitchen floors and walls. Before furnishings became secondary to built-ins, most kitchens with adequate space had a second worktable in the middle of the room. The top surface was made of an easy-to-clean material, such as zinc, enamel, or porcelain.

A new concept in the previously utilitarian workspace suggested that a degree of socializing might be conducted in the kitchen. Designers and manufacturers recommended the use of color in the kitchen to add warmth and a note of personal style, and sponging, a decorative painting technique, was used on kitchen floors. In 1927 Westinghouse offered a selection of new porcelain-enamel ranges that had no legs and came in a variety of colors. Art nouveau curves of the early twentieth century were replaced in the 1930s and 1940s with the classic straight lines of art deco. By 1930 the eastern cities had been introduced to sinks built in to countertops. The lazy Susan, a rotating round shelf, was invented in 1933. These kitchen fashions spread slowly, reaching middle-class homes of the Midwest after World War II.

Advertisement for Frigidaire refrigerators that appeared in Good Housekeeping, *1929.*

1945–2000

After World War II, every kitchen needed increased electrical service to meet the demands of new appliances and electrical equipment. Even newly built kitchens were, before long, in need of more outlets.

The postwar kitchen renewed its social function. After the war, women left their wartime jobs to raise families and reverted to their earlier kitchen orientation. In the new American suburbia, housewives welcomed an open floor plan that allowed them to supervise children. In their new automobile-centered communities homeowners wanted their kitchens to be near the driveway for unloading groceries and informal neighborhood visiting.

Informal kitchen islands surrounded by stools became an alternative to breakfast nooks. "Warm" wood replaced "cold" metal. The 1970s brought built-in ovens, countertop ranges, and countertop microwave ovens.

A long period of economic affluence permitted faster-paced fashions. The bicentennial of 1976 inspired the country look—idealized and romanticized images of colonial life. The 1980s revived the Victorian look. Soon thereafter came high tech, a spin-off of the industrial images of commercial kitchens, and a modernist style known as "city slick," which featured the most advanced kitchen technology. In the late twentieth and early twenty-first centuries, marble countertops, restaurant stoves with powerful exhaust fans, convection ovens, garbage disposals, and dishwashers, previously limited to the privileged, have become commonplace and are marketed as having quiet operation and ecological advantages. Despite the preoccupation with kitchen design, a large part of the population uses their kitchens less. Many families no longer eat meals together and rarely use their kitchens as social family centers.

[See also BEECHER, CATHARINE; CUPBOARDS AND FOOD SAFES; DISHWASHING AND CLEANING UP; GENDER ROLES; HOME ECONOMICS; ICEBOXES; KITCHENS: EARLY KITCHENS; MICROWAVE OVENS; REFRIGERATORS; STOVES AND OVENS: GAS AND ELECTRIC; STOVES: WOOD AND COAL.]

BIBLIOGRAPHY

Campbell Franklin, Linda. *Three Hundred Years of Kitchen Collectibles.* 5th ed. Iola, WI: Krause, 2003.

Celehar, Jane H. *Kitchens and Gadgets 1920–1950.* Radnor, PA: Wallace-Homestead, 1982.

Celehar Jane H. *Kitchens and Kitchenware.* Radnor, PA: Wallace-Homestead, 1985.

Harrison, Molly. *The Kitchen in History.* New York: Scribners, 1972.

Plante, Ellen M. *The American Kitchen: 1700 to the Present—From Hearth to Highrise.* New York: Facts on File, 1995.

Smallzried, Kathleen Ann. *The Everlasting Pleasure, Influences on American Kitchens, Cooks, and Cooking from 1565 to 2000.* New York: Appleton-Century-Crofts, 1956.

LYNN MARIE HOUSTON

A drawing of an early ice-cooled refrigerator.

Kitchenware, see *Frying Pans, Skillets, and Spiders; Pots and Pans; Sieves, Sifters, and Colanders*

Kiwis

Native to East Asia, the kiwifruit (*Actinidia deliciosa*), or Chinese gooseberry, was first commercially cultivated in the early twentieth century in New Zealand and has been exported to the United States since the 1960s. Domestic plantings of kiwi vines began in the late 1960s, chiefly in California, where there were 4,500 bearing acres in 2002. The leading variety, Hayward, is a bit larger than an egg, with tan, fuzzy skin, and green, tart-sweet flesh. The harvest is in late autumn, but the fruits store well and are available throughout the year. They are eaten fresh, in fruit salads, and in desserts such as tarts and cakes.

A closely related species, *A. chinensis*, has yellow flesh. Sweeter and more complex than the Hayward, with hints of mango, melon, and citrus flavor, it was first exported from New Zealand in 2000 and was soon being planted by California farmers. There are also several species of hardy kiwis with grape-size fruits that are grown on a small scale from Oregon to Pennsylvania.

BIBLIOGRAPHY

Hasey, Janine K., and R. Scott Johnson, eds. *Kiwifruit Growing and Handling.* Oakland: University of California Press, 1994.

Warrington, I. J., and G. C. Weston, eds. *Kiwifruit Science and Management.* Wellington, New Zealand: Ray Richards, 1990.

DAVID KARP

Klondike Bar

The Klondike Bar, a square block of vanilla ice cream encased in a chocolate coating, was created around 1922 by the Isaly family, who owned the Mansfield Pure Milk Company in Mansfield, Ohio. The product was probably named after the Klondike River in the Yukon, made famous by a gold rush in the 1890s. The bars were made by hand at the family's store outside Youngstown, Ohio; at first they were made on a stick, and were offered in several different flavors. Klondike Bars were later produced by the Isaly Dairy Company of Pittsburgh, founded in 1931.

Until the 1970s, Klondike Bars were sold only in Ohio, western Pennsylvania, and West Virginia. In 1972, the company was sold to a group of investors. The Clabir Corporation purchased the company in 1977 and expanded distribution to Philadelphia, Florida, New York, and New England. In 1982, the company began a national advertising campaign featuring the jingle, "What would you do for a Klondike Bar?" It quickly became America's largest selling novelty ice cream bar, surpassing competitors such as Eskimo Pie. In 1993, the Isaly Klondike Company was acquired by Unilever and folded into a subsidiary that also sold Good Humor bars and Breyers ice cream.

BIBLIOGRAPHY

Butko, Brian. *Klondikes, Chipped Ham & Skyscraper Cones: The Story of Isaly's.* Mechanicsburg, PA: Stackpole Books, 2001.

ANDREW F. SMITH

Knish

The knish is a canonical item of Jewish American food, which has had three transformations over the twentieth century. The name comes from Ukrainian Yiddish (the verb 'to crease'), and seems to have reached the United States only with the large numbers of Russian, Ukrainian, and Belarusian Jewish immigrants to New York City around 1900. It is a form of piroshky: baked pastry originally folded over (creased) mashed potatoes, buckwheat, sauerkraut, mushrooms, or meat mixtures. In New York, however, the knish became a pan-Jewish food and the shape was restricted to that of a round bun, with the usual fillings reduced to mashed potatoes or buckwheat, as the function shifted to a hot snack sold on the streets of the garment district for a worker's hot lunch. An early entrepreneur was Yonah Schimmel, a Romanian Rabbi who sold potato knishes dressed with mustard from a pushcart on the Lower East Side and Sundays at Coney Island but established his own bakery in 1910 next to a Yiddish theater.

The round, potato-stuffed knish became an American Yiddish metaphor for stupidity ("the brains of a knish"), unexpected good fortune ("to be hit with a knish"), and sexual favors ("looking for some knish.") As Jewish Americans progressed into the middle class, knishes became an ethnic signifier at catered life-cycle celebrations, and diversified in shape to include square and rectangular and in size to include tiny hors d'oeuvres. Meat and liver fillings returned to reflect increased affluence.

Since the 1990s, commercial knishes have rediversified with flavors such as sauerkraut, onion, cabbage, and cheese that have been reinforced by recent immigrants from Eastern Europe; and also with postethnic flavors such as broccoli, spinach, vegetarian chili, toasted onion, roasted garlic and "southwestern rice & bean."

MARK H. ZANGER

Knives, *see Silverware*

Kool-Aid

Kool-Aid concentrated soft-drink mix was created by Edwin Perkins, head of the Perkins Products Company of Hastings, Nebraska. The firm manufactured a wide array of products and sold them through mail order. In 1920, Perkins marketed his first soft-drink concentrate, Fruit Smack, a syrup that consumers mixed with water and sugar to produce a sweet beverage. It proved successful, but the four-ounce glass bottles were heavy and often broke in the mail. Inspired by the tremendous success of Jell-O dessert powder, Perkins decided to sell a powdered beverage concentrate in paper packets. All the customer had to do was mix the powder with water and sugar.

In 1927, the first Kool-Aid packets sold through the mail for ten cents apiece. The original six flavors were cherry, grape, lemon-lime, orange, raspberry, and strawberry. As the sales of Kool-Aid increased, Perkins phased out his other products and concentrated on marketing Kool-Aid. By 1929, it was sold in stores throughout the United States. During the Depression, Perkins lowered the price of Kool-Aid to five cents a packet and launched a major national advertising campaign aimed at children. Perkins subsequently developed additional Kool-Aid products, including pie fillings and ice cream mixes, but they were not successful. During World War II, sugar rationing restricted the consumption of Kool-Aid, but, after the war, sales of Kool-Aid took off again, and the product enjoyed its heyday in the 1950s.

In 1953, Perkins sold his company to General Foods Corporation, which added root beer and lemon flavors in 1955 and sweetened Kool-Aid in 1964. In 1988, General Foods merged with Kraft Inc., and the merged company launched new product lines, such as Kool-Aid Slushies and ready-to-drink Kool-Aid Splash. When Kool-Aid celebrated its seventy-fifth anniversary in 2002, a permanent exhibition of product memorabilia and history was inaugurated at Hastings Museum of Natural and Cultural History, in Hastings, Nebraska.

For many Americans, Kool-Aid evokes images of childhood, refreshment, and innocent summer fun. Its longtime advertising image, a smiling face drawn in the condensation on an icy pitcher of Kool-Aid, has become a national icon.

[See also FLAVORINGS; GENERAL FOODS; JELL-O; KRAFT FOODS.]

BIBLIOGRAPHY

Hastings Museum of Natural and Cultural History, Hastings, NE. http://www.hastingsmuseum.org/koolaid/history.htm.

ANDREW F. SMITH

Korean American Food

Korean cuisine is richly endowed with fermented foods, hundreds of vegetable and wild green dishes, grains, soups, teas, liquors, confections, and soft drinks. Traditional *hanjongshik* literally means "full course Korean meal." It is invariably accompanied by a huge, steaming bowl of soup or stew and features grilled fish or meat and many vibrant side dishes. Korean food is seldom deep-fried like Chinese food; it is usually boiled or blanched, broiled, stir-fried, steamed, or pan-fried with vegetable oil. Vegetables are parboiled and seasoned with spices that specifically complement the main dish. It is said that the vegetables ought to be mixed, seasoned, and soaked by hand to improve the taste. Unlike Western cuisines, where courses are served one after the other, Korean dishes are served all at once—some at room temperature, others piping hot, and many, in fact,

Knishes and other ethnic fast food on Coney Island Avenue in Brooklyn, New York.

while still cooking, as anyone who has seen the giant clam in a spicy Korean stew (*chigae*) can attest.

Types of Korean Food

Boiled rice, often mixed with barley, corn, or other grains, is a staple of the Korean diet. Rice and grains can be together into gruel, then served as a choice delicacy. Along with ginseng, porridge has served as a medicinal dish for the ailing for thousands of years.

Soups, known as *guk* or *tang*, are usually composed of meat, vegetables, fish, seaweed, clams, and beef bones, tripe, and other internal organs. Stews and casseroles contain less water and feature more ingredients than soups.

Gui and *jeon* are dishes prepared by either broiling on a spit or directly on a grill. The notorious *bulgogi*, which literally means "fire beef," is thinly sliced and marinated beef and ribs. *Jeon* is a popular pan-fried dish. Chopped meats, fish, or vegetables are covered with flour, dipped in beaten egg, then pan-fried. Koreans are fond of raw meat and fish on special occasions. Raw and parboiled dishes are said to complement sturdy Korean libations, especially *soju*, or potato vodka, and beer.

Tteok is steamed rice flour in the form of a cake. These traditional cakes are used in ceremonial rites honoring ancestors during holidays and festivities. *Hangwa* are light and crispy traditional sweets made of rice flour and mixed with honey. *Hwachae*, served as refreshments with dessert, are traditional Korean fruit-based drinks. A sweet rice drink or a cinnamon fruit punch are common palate refreshers after a spicy Korean meal.

Kimchi

A Korean meal without kimchi is unthinkable. Today, there are more than 160 kimchi variations, differentiated by regional specialties and by season. Fresh and lively flavors are preferred for a light summer kimchi, while more intense, often garlicky or briny flavors, are suitable for winter kimchi. One question, however, persists: is the kimchi in the United States comparable to the authentic version found in the homeland?

One native Korean recently traveling in Texas observed: "The kimchi I am having at the hotel has less pickled shrimp and clams in it, so it tastes very plain, which means ... terrible. A good kimchi should have that strong smelly socks stink. And kimchi is not a hot food. It may look hot. Some Mexican food here is hotter."

And that is just one kimchi style. Not surprisingly, kimchi styles vary greatly across the United States. Korean Americans have brought different kimchi recipes from their native Korean regions and then have adapted them with available regional ingredients.

In early Korea, kimchi was simply a mass of pickled vegetables. Salt-preserved vegetables are assumed to have very long history according to Korean literature, which suggests that Koreans had pickled vegetables as early as the seventh century. Later, around the twelfth century, various additives began to flavor kimchi. Then, in 1592, red peppers were introduced to kimchi during Hideyoshi's invasion of Korea. It is assumed that red pepper was used in an effort to conserve valuable salt. Hot red pepper contains capsaicin, which accelerates the process of fermentation and implants a particular taste and texture. Around the nineteenth century, cultivation of cabbage for winter kimchi became systematized. The tradition continues in the twenty-first century, as Korean cooks still prepare winter kimchi from late November through early December during a nationwide annual event called *kimjang*.

Fermentation has long played a role in the preservation of nutrients in vegetables and fish in Korea. The Korean peninsula is largely mountainous, home to hundreds of wild vegetables. The Korean climate ranges from the dry and frigid winters of the north to the nearly tropical conditions in parts of the south. Accordingly, early Koreans developed methods of preserving food with salt. One process, known as *yumjang*, had been developed to keep vegetables during cold winters when fresh vegetables were scarce. In the cold northern regions, kimchi was traditionally prepared with powdered red pepper and strong salted fish. In the warmer southern areas, kimchi was typically prepared with simple powdered red pepper and salt. The purity and quantity of salt, the salinity of the brine, the duration of the salting process, and the temperature of the pickled mass all influence the taste of kimchi.

Tropical conditions of the south also perfected a brining technique. Koreans still preserve fish, their internal organs and eggs, and clams with salt until they become fermented. *Jjim* is prepared by putting ingredients and seasonings into an earthenware pot and steaming at low heat. Glazing in soy sauce, or in *gochuchang*, a red pepper paste, is a time-honored technique that preserves food for weeks. These intensely salty but tasty side dishes are also unique base flavorings for kimchi and other dishes.

Korean Americans

Aside from having introduced so-called Korean barbecue and kimchi to Americans, Korean immigrants have contributed *doenjang*, a paste made of soybeans, and *gochujang* to Asian markets in the States. These fermented staples, along with soy sauce, are indispensable to Korean cookery. Immigrants often chuckle as they recount stories of stowing jars of *doenjang* and *gochujang* in their luggage during their migration overseas. By 1888, a small number of Korean students, political exiles, ginseng merchants, and migration laborers began to arrive on American shores. The first major wave of immigrants reached Hawaii from 1903 to 1905, when a total of 7,226 Koreans arrived in as contract laborers for sugar plantations. The second wave of Koreans arrived between the Korean War of 1950–1953 and 1965, as war orphans or wives and relatives of American servicemen who had been stationed in Korea. Koreans began to immigrate to the United States in larger numbers after the Immigration Act of 1965 removed quotas based on national origin. From 1976 to 1990, an annual average of 30,000 to 35,000 Koreans immigrated to the United States.

Korean Americans have found employment as greengrocers in the United States and also operate a fair number of liquor stores, fish markets, and restaurants. Koreans happened to enter the fish market business as an extension of their greengroceries. In New York City during the 1980s, ownership of fish markets began to change hands, along with the selection of fresh fish. As a result, fried shrimp, clams, fish and chips, and even sushi and sashimi became widely available at Korean fish markets. Typically, the owner serves as the cashier, while two or more workers clean and slice the fish. The experience has been the training ground for many who go on to become sushi chefs in Japanese and Korean restaurants.

Even with thirty or so Korean cookbooks published in the United States, Korean cookery has yet to truly influence American cuisine. Korean restaurants are generally clustered in Korean neighborhoods around the country, satisfying Koreans who crave comfort foods. In the last several years, Pan-Asian and Asian fusion restaurants have started to casually represent such Korean staples as kimchi and *bulgogi*. These restaurants, found in hip metropolitan enclaves, cater to a smattering of adventurous eaters. In Manhattan, the area around Thirty-Second Street between Broadway and Fifth Avenue, known as K-town, boasts a wide array of restaurants, markets, and coffeehouses, featuring talents of Korean chefs from every region. Han Ah Reum Asian Market in Manhattan is a leading Korean American food retailer, with fifteen outposts in New York, New Jersey, Pennsylvania, Maryland, and Virginia, which has served the Korean American community since 1982. At Korean greengrocers in New York City, kimchi is often found as an international delegate at the salad bar, next to, say, German potato salad or Italian lasagna. Go to any Korean American household for Thanksgiving dinner, and, inevitably, kimchi stands as a proud side dish, as important to the family as the turkey itself.

[**See also** FERMENTATION; FUSION FOOD; PICKLING; SALT AND SALTING; SOY SAUCE.]

BIBLIOGRAPHY

Hepinstall, Hi Shooshin. *Growing Up in a Korean Kitchen: A Cookbook*. Berkeley, CA: Ten Speed Press, 2001.

The Wonderful World of Korean Food. Seoul: Korean National Tourism Organization. 2001.

HYON JUNG LEE

Kosher, *see Jewish Dietary Laws*

Kraft Foods

In 1903, James L. Kraft noticed that grocers traveled daily to the cheese market to buy cheese for their stores. Recognizing an opportunity, he started a wholesale cheese distribution business in Chicago that brought the cheese to the grocers. His four brothers joined him in 1909 and they incorporated the fledgling business as J. L. Kraft and Brothers Company.

Kraft used innovative and aggressive advertising to promote its line of thirty-one varieties of cheese. Kraft was one of the first food companies to use color advertisements in national magazines. In 1914, the company opened its first cheese factory. At the beginning of the twenty-first century, Kraft Foods had evolved into the largest food company in the United States.

When James Kraft started his business, cheese was produced in large wheels. When cut, cheese has a tendency to spoil quickly at room temperature, which was a problem at a time when most grocers and consumers had little access to refrigeration. Kraft came up with the idea in 1915 of a cheese that did not spoil as quickly. He created a blended, pasteurized cheese, which he called "process cheese," and packaged it in small tins. The sale of 6 million pounds of cheese to the U.S. Army during World War I ensured the fortunes of the company.

The company changed its name to Kraft Cheese Company in 1924 and soon after merged with the Phenix Cheese Corporation, the maker of Philadelphia Brand cream cheese (introduced in the United States in 1880). In 1928, the company introduced Velveeta pasteurized process cheese spread and Miracle Whip salad dressing, adding Kraft caramels in 1933. In 1937, Kraft's famous macaroni and cheese dinner was launched, followed by Parkay margarine in 1940. Kraft again became a major food supplier to the armed forces during World War II. To market their growing list of products, the company sponsored the *Kraft Musical Review* on radio in 1933, which evolved into the *Kraft Music Hall* hosted by Bing Crosby. In 1947, the company created the *Kraft Television Theatre*, the first network program on television.

New products continued to appear in the postwar era. In 1952, Kraft introduced Cheez Whiz, which for some replaced the provolone cheese that was a traditional topping for a Philadelphia cheesesteak. In 1965, Kraft introduced individually wrapped cheese slices. Light n' Lively yogurt came on the market in 1969.

In 1988, the Philip Morris Company, because of a shrinking tobacco market, purchased Kraft, just as they had purchased the General Foods Corporation in 1985. In 2000, Philip Morris acquired the Nabisco Company. In the early 2000s, there is probably not a refrigerator or cupboard in America that does not have one or more brand name products distributed by Kraft Foods. Some of these brands include Post cereals, Oscar Mayer meat products, Maxwell House coffee, Life Savers, Kool-Aid, Jell-O, Planters Nuts, Ritz crackers, and Snackwells low-fat cookies and crackers.

[See also CEREALS, COLD; CHEESE: LATER DEVELOPMENTS; CRACKERS; GENERAL FOODS; JELL-O; KOOL-AID; MAXWELL HOUSE; NABISCO; PHILADELPHIA CHEESESTEAK SANDWICH; POST FOODS; VELVEETA.]

BIBLIOGRAPHY

"Kraft Foods Inc." In *International Directory of Company Histories*, ed. Jay P. Pederson. Vol. 45. Chicago: St. James Press, 2002.

"Kraft General Foods Inc." In *International Directory of Company Histories*, ed. Lisa Mirabile. Vol. 2. Chicago: St. James Press, 1990.

JOSEPH M. CARLIN

Krispy Kreme

"When Krispy Kremes are hot, they are to other doughnuts what angels are to people," quipped the southern humorist Roy Blount Jr. in the *New York Times Magazine*. Krispy Kreme doughnuts are marketed at retail shops with the familiar green roof and red-glazed brick exterior and the distinctive sign Hot Doughnuts Now. When the sign is lit, freshly made doughnuts can be seen moving along an overhead conveyor belt.

Joe LeBeau, a French chef in New Orleans, is credited with developing this yeast-raised doughnut sometime before the Great Depression. He sold the business in 1935 to Vernon Rudolph who took the business to Winston-Salem, North Carolina. For a short time in the 1970s, the Beatrice Foods Company operated Krispy Kreme without success. Krispy Kreme was purchased from Beatrice in the 1980s by one of Krispy Kreme's largest franchisees. In 2003, the company had 310 stores in 41 states, Canada, and Australia. Their doughnuts were never hotter!

BIBLIOGRAPHY

Blount, Roy, Jr. "Southern Comfort." *New York Times Magazine*. September 8, 1996.

"Krispy Kreme Doughnut Corporation." In *International Directory of Company Histories*, ed. Tina Grant and Jay P. Pederson. Vol. 21. Detroit: St. James Press, 1998.

JOSEPH M. CARLIN

Kroc, Ray, *see McDonald's*

Kvass

Kvass, from the Russian word for "leavened," is the quintessential Russian beverage. It is brewed from traditional fundamentals of the diet, either black rye bread or beets, providing a significant secondary source of nutritionally rich foods in a drinkable form. Similar to beer, kvass is thinner and only slightly fizzy, with a flavor that is both sweeter and tangier. Black-currant leaves, caraway, mint, and fruit such as lemons and raisins are sometimes added. The technique for brewing kvass dates back to ancient Mesopotamia, when ale was prepared from baked grain loaves. Because of the short fermentation period, two to three days, the alcoholic content of kvass is low, typically 0.7 to 2.2 percent.

Kvass has been made in Russia and surrounding eastern European nations for centuries. It was originally a home-brewed beverage associated with the poor, consumed with meals, and added to some dishes, such as soups. Its popularity increased during the early 1900s as small-scale commercial production began. It became widely available from small, truck-mounted kegs on urban corners, especially in summer. Some Russians consider kvass good for digestion and a cure for hangovers. In the United States, kvass concentrate is available for home use; kvass is also sometimes found in the refrigerator section of Russian delicatessens, sold in used two-liter soda bottles.

[See also BREWING; ETHNIC FOODS; FERMENTATION; RUSSIAN AMERICAN FOOD.]

BIBLIOGRAPHY

Volokh, Anne. *The Art of Russian Cuisine.* New York: Collier Books, 1983.

PAMELA GOYAN KITTLER

Kwanzaa

Kwanzaa is a nonreligious, African American cultural holiday celebrated annually from December 26 through January 1. The word "Kwanzaa" is derived from the Swahili phrase *"matunda ya kwanza"* (first fruits of the harvest), and the nomenclature for the holiday comes from this East African language as well. The holiday was created in 1966 in Southern California by Dr. Malauna Karenga, an African American scholar who later became a professor of African Studies at California State University, Long Beach. Karenga's inspiration for Kwanzaa drew from the time before Africans were enslaved on American soil and reclaims and affirms lost cultural traditions, imagery, history, symbolism, philosophy, values, and spirituality. The unifying week of commemoration Karenga created serves to instill seven core African-inspired values. These seven principles are known as the *Nguzo Saba* and uphold the holiday's main purpose, which is to strengthen familial and communal bonds. The *kinara* (candleholder) is a main icon in which a different colored candle (three red, three green, and one black in the middle) is lit daily to illuminate each principle: *Umoja* (Unity), *Kujichagulia* (Self-Determination), *Ujima* (Collective Work and Responsibility), *Ujamaa* (Cooperative Economics), *Nia* (Purpose), *Kuumba* (Creativity), and *Imani* (Faith). On each of Kwanzaa's seven days, the corresponding principle is the central theme for daytime and evening activities, including crafting and giving gifts (*zawadi*) or making and sharing memorable meals (*karamu*). In the early twenty-first century, Kwanzaa was embraced by an estimated

28 million people of African descent around the globe honoring a common heritage, and its popularity continues to grow.

Kwanzaa and Harvest

The concept of Kwanzaa is linked to sustenance and agrarian rites, as it is a creative synthesis of the many African harvest rituals practiced across the continent during ancient and modern times. At these "first fruits celebrations," people come together to harvest crops (*mazao*) of fruits, vegetables, and produce and to give thanks for the bounty of their efforts. Like Kwanzaa, these African festivals typically last seven to nine days, occurring at the end of one year and the beginning of a new.

Food imagery is woven throughout the fabric of the holiday and shows up prominently on the Kwanzaa table. An African basket or wooden bowl of fruits and vegetables represents the crops and serves as the centerpiece. Another symbol, *muhundi* (corn) has special relevance in many African societies as a fundamental food staple that also represents the human life cycle. During Kwanzaa, ears of corn represent the children of a household, extended family, or community. The unity cup (*Kikombe cha umoja*) is used for the ancient African practice of pouring libations for the ancestors using water, juice, or wine.

The Kwanzaa Feast

People celebrate Kwanzaa in unique and creative ways using food to cultivate and share old and new traditions. Some try a different cuisine each day, highlighting regional fare from the African diaspora: the African continent, the Caribbean Islands, Central and South America, and the American South. Families or groups of friends might take turns hosting an afternoon brunch or a dinner each night of the week. Community organizations host banquets in major cities throughout the nation, notably the annual Kwanzaa *Karamu* in Los Angeles, traditionally hosted and attended by Dr. Karenga himself, along with representatives from his organization, Us.

The holiday culminates in a glorious *Karamu* feast that takes place on December 31, the evening of the sixth day (*Kuumba/Creativity*). This is when extended family, friends, and neighbors come together for a ceremonial, communal meal. Most *Karamu* festivities begin or end with the candle-lighting ceremony amid an African motif with a red, black, and green color scheme. The decor usually features tables covered with African fabrics, woven table and floor mats, the *mazao* centerpiece, and African masks and art on the walls. Guests often dress in African attire representing many nationalities. More elaborate events might incorporate African drumming, music, dancers, storytelling, and history lessons. Participants might also forgo Western dining protocol, opting for floor seating and a traditional African etiquette of eating with one's hands or using flatbreads and other food items for gathering up bite-size portions.

The Kwanzaa Menu

Although there is no set menu, it is customary to serve African and African-influenced foods for any Kwanzaa meal. Indigenous African foodstuffs and those introduced to the Americas from Africa are common: black-eyed and pigeon peas, cassava, yams or yuccas, chilies and peppers, coconuts, dates, eggplants, figs, leafy greens, okra, peanuts or groundnuts, rice, sesame seeds, sweet potatoes, tomatoes, watermelons. A full-course meal could highlight one national cuisine, a broader or regional theme (soul food, Caribbean cuisine, West African dishes), or a multinational selection of African-influenced dishes from different continents.

Hearty stews, one-pot dishes, and rice pilaus resonate throughout the African diaspora and as main courses for Kwanzaa. Ghanaian groundnut stew, West Indian or South African curry dishes, Philadelphia pepper pot soup, Louisiana jambalaya, Nigerian *jollof* rice, and Senegalese *thiebou dienne* (national fish and rice dish) are among the many examples. Fish and shellfish (indicative of coastal origins) are popular, as is chicken served in a variety of international ways, such as Jamaican jerk, Senegalese *yassa*, or southern fried. Starch or vegetable side dishes might consist of cabbage, couscous, or candied yams, baked or fried plantains, and fritters made from flour mixed with minced fish, meats, or pureed beans. A wide variety of breads can accompany the Kwanzaa meal from buttermilk biscuits to Ethiopian *injera*, Native American fry bread, and numerous breads made from cornmeal (spoon bread, hush puppies, corn pone, cornbread, hoe cakes, cracklin' bread, johnnycakes, ash cake, batter bread). Popular beverages include (mostly tropical) fruit juices and drinks, Jamaican ginger beer, and rum punch for adults. Fruit-based desserts are quite common, ranging from simple pieces of fruit to ambrosia or fruit salad and apple, berry, or peach cobblers. Sweet potato and bean pies, bread puddings, and *benne* (sesame seed) or coconut cakes are also popular, as are assorted Kwanzaa cookies.

Labor-intensive dishes reserved for special occasions naturally find their way onto the Kwanzaa menu, such as New Orleans seafood gumbo at Christmas, Puerto Rican *pasteles* for the holiday season, or Cuban tamales for New Year's Day. Dishes with folkloric significance are eaten, for example, the Gullah and southern black food traditions of eating collard greens with black-eyed peas or hoppin' John (black-eyed peas with rice) on New Year's Day for good luck and prosperity throughout the new year. Pork dishes are sometimes not appropriate for Kwanzaa meals because of the strong influence of black American Muslim dietary laws that render pork taboo. However, religious diversity does not interfere with the Kwanzaa ideal of promoting Unity (*Umoja*) and Collective Work and Responsibility (*Ujima*) by having dishes prepared by many different cooks or organizing the meal as a potluck that enriches an already festive holiday season.

[**See also** AFRICAN AMERICAN FOOD; CAJUN AND CREOLE FOOD; CARIBBEAN INFLUENCES ON AMERICAN FOOD.]

BIBLIOGRAPHY

Copage, Eric V. *Kwanzaa: An African-American Celebration of Culture and Cooking*. New York: Morrow, 1991.

Harris, Jessica B. *A Kwanzaa Keepsake*. New York: Simon and Schuster, 1995.

Karenga, Maulana. *The African American Holiday of Kwanzaa: A Celebration of Family, Community, and Culture*. Los Angeles, CA: University of Sankore Press, 1988.

Karenga, Maulana. *Kwanzaa: A Celebration of Community and Culture: Commemorative Edition*. Los Angeles, CA: University of Sankore Press, 2002.

TONYA HOPKINS

L

Ladles, see Silverware

Lady Baltimore Cake

Lady Baltimore Cake is an achingly sweet white layer cake held together with a sugary boiled and beaten filling spiked with nuts and dried or candied fruits. It is frosted with boiled meringue flavored with almond and vanilla extracts and lemon. Although some have suggested that the cake can be traced back to Dolley Madison, the towering, layered sponge cake suggests late-nineteenth-century origins. Legend places it as a specialty of a Charleston, South Carolina, restaurant later renamed "The Lady Baltimore Tea Room" in honor the cake.

Lady Baltimore Cake was catapulted to fame in Owen Wister's 1906 novel *Lady Baltimore*, in which the cake figured as a tearoom offering and as a wedding cake. The Charleston dame Alicia Rhett Mayberry is credited with baking the cake for Wister, but no published recipes seem to predate the novel. Recipes appeared in print soon thereafter, such as in Rufus Estes's *Good Things to Eat* (1911). Traditionally made with three layers, the April 1928 issue of *Pictorial Review* assured hostesses that a sufficient dessert course could be a single, dramatic Lady Baltimore Cake, rather than multiple offerings fashionable through the 1920s. Closely related is the Lord Baltimore Cake, a yellow cake that has macaroons added to the Lady Baltimore filling.

[**See also** CAKES.]

BIBLIOGRAPHY

Fertig, Judith M., *All American Desserts*. Boston, MA: Harvard Common Press, 2003.

Lovegren, Sylvia, *Fashionable Food: Seven Decades of Food Fads*. New York: Macmillan, 1995.

CATHY K. KAUFMAN

Lady Fingers

Lady fingers are dry, airy cakes, often with a sugary crust, which are made by piping a stiffly whipped egg-and-flour batter into diminutive oblongs. The sponge batter used for lady fingers was developed in Europe by the seventeenth century to produce Naples or Savoy biscuits. Introduced to colonial America under those names, the cakes often were baked in specially designed tins or paper cases of varying sizes and shapes. The term "ladies' fingers" was used in America no later than the 1820s, although recipes continue for Savoy biscuits, in which one puts the batter "into the biscuit funnel, and lay it out about the length and size of your finger."

Lady fingers have no strong ethnic identity and can be used in most recipes requiring sponge cake, from trifle to charlotte to tiramisu. They substitute for chemically leavened biscuits in fruit shortcakes, garnish ice cream, and grace trays of petits fours.

[**See also** CAKES; DESSERTS.]

BIBLIOGRAPHY

Carson, Jane. *Colonial Virginia Cookery: Procedures, Equipment, and Ingredients in Colonial Cooking*. Williamsburg, VA: Colonial Williamsburg Foundation, 1985. Distributed by the University Press of Virginia, Charlottesville.

Weaver, William Woys. *The Christmas Cook: Three Centuries of American Yuletide Sweets*. New York: HarperPerennial, 1990.

CATHY K. KAUFMAN

Lagasse, Emeril

Emeril Lagasse (1959–) is a popular television chef and a star of the Food Network since 1993. Noted for his theatrical cooking style and audience rapport, he has hosted several cooking series and made regular appearances on network television. *Emeril Live!*, with its live audience and studio band, has the elements of a late-night entertainment program. In many ways Lagasse is the embodiment of the age in which chefs have become as famous as rock stars. His catchphrases—"Bam!" and "Kick it up a notch"—are as familiar to Americans as Julia Child's "Bon appétit" was to television viewers in the 1960s and 1970s.

Of Portuguese and French Canadian descent, Lagasse was born in Fall River, Massachusetts. He began his culinary arts education at a vocational high school and completed it at Johnson and Wales University in Providence, Rhode Island, in 1978. After training in restaurants in France and the northeast United States, Lagasse settled in New Orleans and became the executive chef of Commander's Palace. There he adopted Creole cooking, which became the basis for the menu at his own successful restaurant, Emeril's, opened in 1990. His infusion of Portuguese and Vietnamese influences into Creole and Cajun cooking was a style he defined in his first cookbook as *Emeril's New New Orleans Cooking* (1993). He has established restaurants in New Orleans, Las Vegas, Orlando, and Atlanta and published numerous cookbooks.

Lagasse was the first professional chef to star in a television sitcom. His overwhelming popularity has resulted in a stream of enterprises and commercial partnerships, including signature lines of cookware and knives, sauces, salad dressings, and wines.

[**See also** CELEBRITY CHEFS.]

LYNNE SAMPSON

Lamb and Mutton

Lamb and mutton are the meats of the domesticated sheep (*Ovis aries*). The meat is termed "lamb" from birth until about eighteen months, when the characteristics of the flesh, bones, and joints begin to change. By about two years, the meat becomes mutton, with a higher percentage of fat and a richer flavor. Like all red meats, lamb and mutton are high in proteins, amino acids, B vitamins, niacin, zinc, and iron. Despite their many positive culinary and nutritional

Chef Emeril Lagasse holds a plate of food in the kitchen of his restaurant in New Orleans, Louisiana.

characteristics, the meats have never found much favor with American palates.

Domestic sheep were first brought to the New World by the Spanish conquerors of Florida and New Mexico. Settlers also carried them to the English and Dutch colonies in Virginia, Massachusetts, and New York. Although the first sheep were dual-use breeds producing both meat and wool, for the next three centuries American sheep would be bred primarily for their wool. The early colonists were poor shepherds, and their sheep ran wild, allowing many to be taken by Indians or eaten by wolves and other predators. Sheep that survived were harvested mainly for their wool. Their meat was poor and never became as popular as it remained back in Europe. When it was cooked, mutton (it was not economical to slaughter lambs) was usually prepared in the English style, in chops, roasted or boiled, often covered with a sour sauce. Martha Washington's *A Booke of Cookery* includes a roast or boiled leg of mutton served with a sauce made from currants, barberries, herbs, verjuice (the sour juice of grapes, crab apples, or other unripe fruit), and sugar.

In 1801, a handful of merino sheep, a breed known for its fine wool, were smuggled out of Spain and taken to the United States. Within decades, the majority of American ewes had merino blood in them, the wool industry boomed, and sheep covered states such as Massachusetts, Vermont, and Pennsylvania. Unfortunately, merinos were inferior mutton sheep and did not improve the quality of the meat on American tables. Travelers from England, where mutton was a staple, often complained of the poor quality of what mutton they could find. Mrs. Harriet Martineau said of her fare in Tennessee, "The dish from which I ate was, according to some, mutton; to others, pork. My own idea is that it was dog."

Nevertheless, as wool production rose, there were more sheep to harvest for meat. Sheep farmers even had large enough flocks to cull some of the young ones, and for the first time numbers of "spring lambs" (probably from six months to a year old) began to appear in the market. The meat cost about 50 percent more than mutton and at first was mainly a seasonal specialty sold in expensive restaurants. In elite New York City restaurants such as Delmonico's, the roast saddle of mutton was joined by spring lamb with mint sauce and *cotelettes d'agneau à la jardinière*.

By 1900, the United States was home to a record 61 million head of sheep, the vast majority used solely for wool production. The center of sheep production moved westward, first to Illinois and Iowa and eventually to Texas, California, Wyoming, and other western states. The merino breed, which was notoriously delicate, had been strengthened by the introduction of Rambouillets, larger and hardier French merinos. (By the early 2000s, nearly all American sheep contained at least 50 percent Rambouillet blood.) The Rambouillets also produced better meat, which was advantageous because the wool market tended to go through cycles of boom and bust. In wartime, soldiers needed wool for their uniforms, and business skyrocketed. During peacetime, however, foreign wool became more competitive, so sheep producers were glad to have meat as a secondary product.

After World War I, Americans developed a taste for lamb, whereas mutton was considered coarse, stringy, and "woolly." More delicate than mutton, lamb needed gentler cooking methods, such as those that produced roasted leg of lamb, broiled lamb chops, or Irish stew. At the table, the roast or broiled meat was usually served with mint sauce or jelly, which American palates seemed to like because it masked the distinctive flavor of the meat. During the 1930s, lamb and mutton rose to over 6 percent of American red meat consumption, a record but still far behind pork and beef. Most of this was in the urban Northeast, where Americans of Jewish or Mediterranean ancestry kept up Old World culinary and religious traditions that included lamb. Greek Americans served baby or suckling lamb six to ten weeks old at their Orthodox Easter celebrations, whereas lamb dishes were the main course at Jewish Passover feasts.

Lamb and mutton consumption rose even further during World War II, although not always willingly. Sheep production had skyrocketed owing to wool demand, whereas tons of pork and beef were being sent to soldiers and allied nations. Because of rationing on the home front, often the only meat sold by butchers was low-grade lamb and mutton. By the end of the war, many consumers had vowed to swear off both of them. During the postwar economic boom, consumption of sheep products plummeted. Prosperity meant people could afford beef, and so steak and hamburgers appeared on every American table. Meanwhile, the American wool market crashed in the face of cheap imports, and the number of sheep fell from 57 million in 1945 to less than 5 million by the beginning of the twenty-first century. Sheep producers adapted their flocks to this new reality by cross-breeding them with mutton breeds, so that they would be primarily mutton sheep with wool as the secondary product. (There is also a small but growing dairy sheep industry producing mainly artisanal cheeses.)

But paralleling the decline in the wool market, by the early 2000s Americans were consuming less than a pound of lamb a year per capita. That decline was tied to the decline of consumption of all red meats, as a result of their perceived health risks. What lamb and mutton does get to American tables comes increasingly from Australia and New Zealand, the world's largest lamb producers. Most of the meat is served as chops or roasts in individual homes, but lamb has also found a niche as a luxury item in the nation's "white tablecloth" restaurants. Chefs offer it as chops or rack of lamb or in nouvelle cuisine preparations that emphasize the delicateness of the meat. Unfortunately for aficionados of its rich flavor, mutton has almost vanished. It retains a tiny foothold in a few old-style steakhouses where it usually appears as mutton chops. It is the preferred barbecue meat of Owensboro, Kentucky. And it survives in the culinary traditions imported by recent immigrants from the Middle East and South Asia.

[See also MEAT.]

BIBLIOGRAPHY

Olney, Richard, ed. *Lamb: The Good Cook*. New York: Time-Life, 1981.

Wentworth, Edward Norris. *America's Sheep Trails*. Ames: Iowa State College Press, 1948.

Wing, Joseph E. *Sheep Farming in America*. Chicago: The Breeder's Gazette, 1912.

ANDREW COE

Lard and Shortening

Lard came to America with the first colonists. When the first Europeans set up their stockades in North America they filled them with pigs and cows, the four-legged factories that would produce virtually all the cooking fat used in this country up until the industrial revolution.

Pork fat was by far the most common shortening throughout the colonial era and well into the antebellum period of the young republic. It was used for frying, for breads, biscuits, and cakes, and even as a dressing for vegetables. Before the advent of refrigeration, most of the nation's pork was salted and the fattier parts were used for flavoring stuffings as well as stews. Bacon, and the drippings that it would yield, were a prized ingredient. In this agrarian society, lard was rendered at home and kept in the cool confines of the aptly named larder successfully for many months. The crisp crust that lard produces in frying was particularly appreciated in the South where, it has been suggested, black cooks adapted West African frying techniques to create regional specialties such as fried chicken and hush puppies. Certainly lard was much more available below the Mason-Dixon Line than in New England, where dairy and beef cattle were the more common form of livestock.

Cows not only provided butter but were also a source for suet, deemed an essential ingredient in the many steamed, boiled, and baked puddings beloved by colonists from the British Isles. Nonetheless, in spite of the occasional recipe that begins "fry out suet" as a way of obtaining a shortening for sautéing, cow fat never enjoyed the popularity of lard.

Price and religion also made it difficult for everyone to savor a lard-rich pie crust. As increasing numbers of Americans moved from a self-sufficient rural setting to newly industrialized cities of the late nineteenth century, they had to pay cash for the cooking fats that, on the farm, had been a substantially free by-product of livestock husbandry. Then, as large numbers of Eastern European Jews passed through Ellis Island, a new market was crying out for a kosher substitute for pig fat. As a result, an array of more economical ersatz butters, commercially processed lard, and newly perfected vegetable oils were developed and marketed. Giant food processors such as Armour used the by-products of their meatpacking business to sell industrially rendered lard for cooking and soap making. By the turn of the twentieth century, food scientists had learned not only to add extra hydrogen atoms to make liquid oil solid at room temperature (thus the term "hydrogenated"). This is what the soap-making company Proctor & Gamble did when they cooked up Crisco and introduced it in 1911. Finally, here was a vegetable oil–based lard that was sufficiently cheaper than the real thing.

Yet today, for many recipes, lard continues to retain favor in parts of the old confederacy. And, in recent years, Latino cooks have imported their penchant for the lard that is used in their native cuisines. Mexican American cooks, for example, seek out pork fat for the texture and flavor it imparts to everything from tamales and flour tortillas to refried beans and moles. It seems that lard is here to stay.
[**See also** FATS AND OILS.]

MICHAEL KRONDL

Latin American Food, see *Cuban American Food; Iberian and South American Food; Mexican American Food; Puerto Rican Food; Southwestern Regional Cookery*

Law

The production, distribution, and sale of food in the United States is controlled by a complex structure of interrelated federal, state, and local laws and regulations. These laws and regulations are designed to ensure that the American food supply is safe and that consumers are not defrauded. With the exception of home consumption of homegrown food, all food in the United States is subject to some type of law or regulation.

Scope of Federal Legislation
The federal government's power to regulate food comes from the U.S. Constitution. When the Constitution was written in 1787, the founders wanted the federal government to promote and encourage commerce among the states. To prevent individual states from setting up unreasonable barriers to commerce, the commerce clause of the Constitution gave the federal government the right to control interstate commerce. By statute, interstate commerce is defined as commerce between any state or territory and any place

outside the state or territory. Federal control starts when food enters into interstate commerce and ends when food is delivered to the ultimate consumer. Because the courts interpret interstate commerce broadly, the power of the federal government over food is virtually complete.

The federal government also has the right to control all foreign food imports, all American food exports, and food commerce within the District of Columbia.

Development of Federal Food Laws
Because the United States did not have a significant interstate commerce in food until after the Civil War, the first federal food laws concerned the export and import of food products. The first food law specifically regulating interstate commerce, however, was the Meat Inspection Act of 1891. This law authorized federal inspection of all cattle, sheep, and hogs in interstate commerce "prior to their slaughter" and, thereafter, the marking or stamping of those meat products from animals "found to be free of disease, and wholesome, sound, and fit for human food."

The scope of the 1891 law was narrow. It did not give federal inspectors the power to address the generally unsanitary conditions in the meat processing and meatpacking industry. The description of these conditions in Upton Sinclair's novel *The Jungle* led to passage of the Meat Inspection Act of 1906.

Although Congress was aware of the movement of adulterated food in interstate commerce, the first comprehensive Pure Food Act was not passed until 1906. Passage of such a law by Congress did not go unchallenged. Many people thought that the federal government did not have the authority under the commerce clause of the Constitution to regulate adulterated food. They argued that only states had the right to set standards and regulate the quality of food. That dispute was resolved in a series of cases decided by the U.S. Supreme Court between 1911 and 1918. The Supreme Court confirmed that Congress had the power to regulate interstate commerce in food and seize adulterated products that were "outlaws of commerce." Although there were some problems with enforcement and interpretation of the Pure Food Act of 1906, the power of the federal government to prohibit the introduction, movement, and delivery of adulterated and misbranded food in interstate commerce was never again seriously questioned.

The full extent of the federal government's power over interstate commerce in food found expression in the Federal Food, Drug, and Cosmetic Act of 1938. For most foods in interstate commerce, this comprehensive law explicitly authorized the establishment of federal definitions and standards of identity, federal standards of quality, and federal container standards for

the amount of fill. Adulterated foods were broadly defined to prohibit any food that was "injurious to health" from entering into interstate commerce. In addition, fraudulent substitutes and all other forms of economic adulteration were prohibited. The act mandated that certain minimum information be printed on a label, and it prohibited false or misleading labeling and the use of names of foods not represented in a product unless labeled "imitation." Although there have been some substantive amendments since its passage, including the Miller Pesticide Amendment of 1954, the Food Additives Amendment of 1958, and the Color Additive Amendment of 1960, the 1938 act remains the backbone of federal regulation of U.S. food.

State and Local Regulation
Although the federal government regulates imported food and all food moved in interstate commerce, states still retain the right to pass laws governing foods that are placed into interstate commerce. Any state rule or regulation that does not conflict with federal law is allowed to stand.

Many states have laws and regulations designed to protect economically important local food products. California, for example, has specific laws and regulations that protect its avocado, navel orange, and Valencia orange industries. California also has specific regulations for bottled water, butter, eggs, honey, ice, olive oil, organic foods, tomatoes, and wine grapes.

Local government regulation of food focuses primarily on food safety at local retail food facilities and establishments. Food facilities may include vending machines, produce stands and farmers' markets, ice cream and taco trucks, and any other stationary or mobile food-preparation unit. Food facility permits are required, and the permit application, issuance, and inspection process is designed to ensure that a local retail food establishment conforms to all local and state food safety laws. A facility that violates the laws may be cited and risk having its permit to operate revoked.

State and local retail food safety laws direct that food be pure and free from contamination, adulteration, and spoilage. Regulations therefore establish standards for food storage, food handling, sanitation, and hygiene. For example, most state and local regulations require that potentially hazardous foods, like meat, seafood, and eggs, be held at or below 41°F or at or above 140°F (to prevent the growth of bacteria), that certain foods be cooked to minimum temperatures (for example, ground beef to 157°F), that utensils and cutting boards be cleaned and sanitized when switching between foods to prevent cross-contamination, and that food handlers wash their hands with hot water and soap for at least twenty seconds at specified times.

[See also ADULTERATIONS; PURE FOOD AND DRUG ACT.]

BIBLIOGRAPHY

Levenson, Barry M. *Habeas Codfish: Reflections on Food and the Law*. Madison: University of Wisconsin Press, 2001.

ROBERT W. BROWER

Leeks

Leeks (*Allium ampeloprasum porrum*) are cylindrical onions with a white base that bleeds into green leaves. They can be fried as a vegetable, braised or boiled as a vegetable or salad, and used to flavor soups, stews, and stocks.

Colonial Americans seem to have made little use of cultivated European leeks. John Josselyn's *New England's Rarities Discovered* (1672) praised indigenous "wild Leekes," probably *Allium canadense*, "which the Indians use much to eat with their fish," and other early sources talk about gathering the wild plant. Some early American cookbooks may have envisioned leeks, wild or cultivated, in braised onion recipes, as they specify "the white kind" or suggest cooking the onion with some of the tender green attached. Mrs. N. K. M. Lee's *Cook's Own Book* (1832) uses them for seasoning but asserts, "they are very rarely brought to table." Only two varieties of leeks appear in Bernard M'Mahon's 1815 seed catalog.

Leeks grew modestly in popularity in the later nineteenth century, when numerous French cultivars were introduced and more recipes appeared in French-influenced cookbooks. Although easily found at supermarkets, leeks remain bit players in American cookery.

[See also HEIRLOOM VEGETABLES; ONIONS.]

BIBLIOGRAPHY

Weaver, William Woys. *Heirloom Vegetable Gardening*. New York: Holt, 1997.

Phipps, Frances. *Colonial Kitchens, Their Furnishings, and Their Gardens*. New York: Hawthorne, 1972.

CATHY K. KAUFMAN

Legal Issues, *see Law*

Lemonade

Lemonade, which in its simplest form is a drink made from lemon juice, sugar, and water, has a history dating back to at least the thirteenth century, when Arab cookery books offered recipes for drinks made from lemon syrup. The Mongols enjoyed a sweetened lemon drink preserved with alcohol, and the Persians enjoyed *sharbia*, from which the English "sherbet" derives. By the mid-seventeenth century, the drink was popular in Europe when *limonadiers*, street vendors in France, sold lemonade at modest prices. A lemonade recipe appears in the 1653 English translation of LaVarenne's *The French Cook*.

Lemonade arrived in America no later than the eighteenth century, imported from the various European cultures of immigrants. Recipes varied widely. One might begin by bruising sugar and lemon rind together; another added a single sliced lemon directly into water; yet another required a large quantity of juice. Many started off with lemon and sugar syrup, which could be bottled and stored for later use. Some added milk, and others clarified cloudy lemon juice by adding an egg and then straining the liquid. Mary Randolph's *The Virginia Housewife* (1824) included an iced lemonade recipe that is actually a sherbet. The popularity of homemade aerated, or effervescing, lemonade paralleled the rise of commercially available lemon-flavored soda water. By the 1860s, several bartender's guides contained "lemonade" recipes that packed a wallop from the various wines and spirits added to the sweetened lemon juice.

But lemonade's image underwent a transformation engendered by the temperance movement, which turned lemonade into a genteel Victorian drink. The First Lady Lucy Webb Hayes, a teetotaler, forbade virtually all alcohol in the White House of the 1870s, thus garnering the moniker "Lemonade Lucy." Modern technology also helped the juice flow: household juice extractors, a vast improvement over the gadgets of the past, appeared in the second half of the nineteenth century. Hostesses conspicuously served front-porch visitors from pitchers specifically designed for the beverage. They also brought the beverage along on picnics. Lemonade's popularity rose unabated, prompting the 1901 New Orleans *Times-Picayune's Creole*

American Flag leeks from the 1894 catalog of Peter Henderson & Company, New York.

Cook Book to proclaim, "Lemonade is among the most delightful and most commonly used of all Fruit Waters."

Lemonade also was considered a tonic, served to those suffering from colds (hot "flax-seed lemonade") or to invalids. The Shakers, an American religious sect, read in the April 1881 issue of their *Manifesto*, that "lemonade is one of the healthiest and most refreshing drinks of all drinks; suitable for almost all stomach and bowel disorders and excellent in most sicknesses." Lemonade also proved useful in the westward expansion, particularly in the forms of dried "portable lemonade" and "lemon sugar," for which recipes appeared in many cookbooks. A photographer along the Union Pacific noted in his 1869 diary that he "used a good deal of 'portable lemonade'" to counter the brackish taste of the local river water.

As the twenty-first century opened, lemonade flourished at all points along a commercial and culinary spectrum: from instant powder and imitation lemonades that historically relied for tartness on essence of lemon, lemon oil, and tartaric or citric acid, to the frozen concentrate introduced in 1950s, to ready-to-drink supermarket varieties, to homemade "front-porch lemonade," to flavor variations such as ginger, blackberry, or pineapple.

[See also FRUIT JUICES; INVALID COOKERY; TEMPERANCE.]

ROBIN M. MOWER

Lentils, *see Beans*

Leslie, Eliza

Although Eliza Leslie's cookbooks were reprinted dozens of times, Leslie maintained that her first love was fiction, finding herself drawn to it even as a child. Born the eldest of five children in Philadelphia in 1787, she was educated primarily at home by her father, a self-taught watchmaker and mathematician, who counted Thomas Jefferson and Benjamin Franklin among his friends and fellow members of the American Philosophical Society. When he died in 1803, he left the family virtually penniless, and Eliza, at the age of sixteen, and her mother were forced to open a boardinghouse in order to support the family.

Leslie's first commercial success resulted from attending the Philadelphia cooking school of Mrs. William Goodfellow, where she took copious notes. At her brother's behest, she collected them in *Seventy-five Receipts for Pastry, Cakes and Sweetmeats* by "A Lady from Philadelphia." Published in 1827, this became one of America's earliest and most popular cookbooks.

Leslie took great pleasure in writing fiction, particularly juvenile stories about American children. Her stories for adults, which often punctured America's social pretensions and pointed out the defects of American manners, appeared in most of the day's leading magazines. Despite her prefer-

ence for fiction, she admitted that most of her income came from the many editions of her books on domestic economy. After the success of *Seventy-Five Receipts*, she published *Domestic French Cookery* (a translation, 1832), the *Domestic Cookery Book* (1837), *Directions for Cookery in Its Various Branches* (1837), *The House Book* (1840), *The Ladies' Receipt Book* (1846), *Miss Leslie's New Cookery Book* (1857), and several volumes on etiquette. Although Leslie never acknowledged her cooking teacher in her books, the publication of *Mrs. Goodfellow's Cookery as It Should Be* in 1865 is widely believed to be the work of Eliza Leslie.

Leslie's success depended in large measure on her concern for American housewives. She declared that all the ingredients and utensils necessary for her recipes were available in the United States. She drew heavily on such easily obtained foods as pumpkin, cranberries, clams, wild grapes, green corn, and Indian meal, with recipes for baked Indian pudding, flannel cakes, johnnycakes, and Indian bread. She professed to believe in accurate measurements and provided tables of equivalencies, recommending an accurate scale and a set of tin cups in graduated sizes. Leslie sometimes violated her own precepts, however, calling for "a teacup of sugar" or "a small wineglass of brandy." Lists of ingredients preceded each recipe in her early books, but she later strayed from this model and reverted to the more conventional style of combining ingredients and directions into one or two paragraphs. Some of her recipes were clearly British and French in origin, but each book remains firmly American in style, with recipes for Federal cake, Connecticut cake, election cake, catfish, Yankee tea cakes, and okra.

Leslie never married, supporting herself by her writing. She lived the last few years of her life at the U.S. Hotel in Philadelphia, holding court for a wide variety of celebrities, friends, and relatives. Leslie had a reputation as a somewhat difficult curmudgeon, as she was often abrupt and critical, yet she devoted much of her time to charity and those close to her described her as warm and loving.

[See also COOKBOOKS AND MANUSCRIPTS: AMERICAN COOKBOOKS TO 1860.]

BIBLIOGRAPHY
Haven, Alice B. "Personal Reminiscences of Miss Eliza Leslie." *Godey's Lady's Book* (April 1858): 344–350.

VIRGINIA K. BARTLETT

Lettuce

Lettuce is any plant of the genus *Lactuca*. Its wild ancestors were commonly distributed in Europe and Asia in prehistoric times. A semi-wild type called spindly lettuce grows in the Mediterranean, which suggests that lettuce cultivation probably began there. Ancient Egyptians, Greeks, and Romans cooked lettuce and also served it raw. Cultivated lettuce (*Lactuca sativa*) was grown throughout Europe during the Middle Ages and the Renaissance,

and it was among the first old-world plants introduced into the New World.

Both leaf and head type lettuces were commonly grown in colonial and early American times. Lettuce was highly perishable and was available only locally in season. However, lettuce became more readily available in the twentieth century with the development of crisphead lettuce (iceberg is the most familiar). With sturdy leaves forming a compact, round head, these lettuces can be transported over long distances without damage. Distributed by railroad from California and Arizona, lettuce became an important year-round food in America. During the 1920s and 1930s its production tripled.

Lettuce was the main ingredient in salads, from the ubiquitous lettuce and tomato salad to the Caesar salad, and in sandwiches, from the BLT to the hamburger sandwich.

The most commonly consumed varieties are iceberg and the long-leaved romaine (also called cos). With salads becoming more prominent in the American diet, butterhead lettuces, such as Bibb and Boston, and loose-leaf lettuces, such as red leaf, are gaining a wider audience. Most recently, the gourmet "mesclun" mixes of baby lettuces have become common in restaurants and even supermarkets, where industrially produced, prewashed bags of mesclun and other lettuces offer consumers unprecedented ease in preparing salads at home.

[See also SALADS AND SALAD DRESSINGS.]

BIBLIOGRAPHY
Book of Lettuce and Greens. rev. ed. Burlington, VT: National Gardening Association, 1985.
Ryder, Edward J. *Lettuce, Endive, and Chicory*. New York: CABI Publishing, 1999.

ANDREW F. SMITH

Liberty Cabbage

Supposedly Americans renamed sauerkraut as "liberty cabbage" during World War I. But it may never have happened. The only known contemporary source, a November 30, 1918, *New York Times* article quoted by Paul Dickson in *War Slang*, actually refers to a postwar distribution of abandoned "liberty cabbage" in U.S. Army messes in Europe.

An early and reliable retrospective source, the 1919 *The American Language* by H. L. Mencken, says that the renaming was a short-lived local experiment.

MARK H. ZANGER

Library Collections

Libraries in the United States that contain major culinary collections vary greatly in their holdings. Some concentrate on contemporary material, while others have very old material or collections focused on specific areas. Large culinary collections suitable for serious research most often reside at major universities or independent research libraries, though a few exceptions are found in public libraries and professional culinary schools.

Collections in Universities and Public Institutions

The Arthur and Elizabeth Schlesinger Library on the History of Women in America at the Radcliffe Institute for Advanced Studies at Harvard University, Cambridge, Massachusetts, maintains a collection of more than sixteen thousand cookery books. This is an excellent culinary research resource, especially when supplemented by the holdings of the Widener Library in early and rare culinary material in the collection of the Houghton Library, both at Harvard. The University of Iowa holds a portion of the great library of the late chef Louis Szathmary of Chicago, which includes many rare and unusual works.

Hale Library, on the campus of Kansas State University in Manhattan, Kansas, is rich in early materials, which are housed in its Special Collections Department. The collection contains early English works. The general collection of the library is also strong in cookery books and related material that make possible studies in the social history of food.

There are culinary collections at two universities in Bloomington, Indiana. The Lilly Library at the University of Indiana at Bloomington has both depth over several hundred years and breadth in areas of concentration. It is especially strong in American, English, French, German, and Italian material from early times to the present. The Main Library at Indiana University at Bloomington has significant holdings in Chinese, Japanese, and Korean cuisines.

The Library of Congress, in Washington, DC, serves the same function for the United States that the British Library does for the United Kingdom and the Bibliothèque Nationale for France. Like these two, the Library of Congress is considered the library of last resort for researchers who are expected to try all other resources first. The Library of Congress holds an extraordinary collection of community cookbooks and also much locally specialized material.

The culinary collection of Michigan State University holds many of these. The collection also has an unusual profile, holding some early English and French works in the original and is also strong in the cooking of Africa and in Jewish cookery.

The Los Angeles Public Library, the library for the City of Los Angeles, California, Science and Patents Division, has substantial holdings in Pacific Rim cookery, as well as many books on Mexican and African cookery and a wide representation of books on barbecuing that cover aspects from slow-cooked pit barbecue to grilling and smoke cooking. America's California-style cookery is also a strong feature of the collection, as are the foods of the American South and Southwest and the Caribbean.

The collection of the New York Academy of Medicine in New York City contains material on the history of cookery, gastronomy, nutrition, and dietetics. The collection contains some very old and rare materials, including a ninth-century manuscript written by Apicius, *De re culinaria. Libri I–IX,* on vellum.

The New York Public Library, the library of the city of New York, has extensive culinary holdings in its Research Division. The collection is especially strong in American cookery and in early and contemporary African, English, French, and Italian cuisines.

The Blagg-Huey Library on the campus of Texas Women's University at Denton, Texas, is strong in general cookery of the late twentieth and early twenty-first centuries, including American, English, French, and Mexican works. The collection focuses on cooking in the home and contains broad representations of community and organization cookbooks, recipes accompanying equipment and products, and the publications of county extension services. The library includes a large representation from the American Southeast, Louisiana, and Texas.

The Penrose Library of the University of Denver in Denver, Colorado, holds over eight thousand volumes of culinary material, divided between the main stacks and the Special Collections Department. The Special Collections holdings are strong in nineteenth- and twentieth-century American materials and the collection has some very early European works in excellent condition.

A large number of works related to food and cooking are dispersed throughout the collections of the University of Michigan. The collections are especially strong in American foodways and American culinary literature. It also has online access to all of the culinary material in the Early English Books Online collection. But what are most remarkable are the large holdings in original languages pertaining to Japanese, Chinese, and other East Asian cuisines.

The University of Pennsylvania libraries, home for the culinary collection of the late Esther Aresty, hold many pre-1800 American works, including some very early volumes and manuscripts. There are also early works on English cooking. Other cuisines especially well represented are Mexican, Brazilian, and Indic.

Library Collections at Culinary Schools

The Conrad Hilton Library at the Culinary Institute of America in Hyde Park, New York, displays exceptional breadth in modern-day cuisine and books on ethnic and regional cookery. Much of this information is available in translation for the student who does not read languages other than English, although some books are in other languages. The library provides an excellent base for a comparative study of cuisines of the early 2000s. Modern editions of some early texts are also available.

The Culinary Archives and Museum of Johnson and Wales University in Providence, Rhode Island, holds a vast number of books, periodicals, and ephemera valuable to a culinary researcher. Among these are the collection of rare books donated by Paul Fritsche and many books and ephemera from the collection of the late chef Louis Szathmary and other prominent persons in the culinary field.

Many other libraries in the United States have fine culinary collections. An examination of their online catalogs is the place to begin for readers interested in working in one of these libraries. Many require special permission for visitors to use them. It is also necessary to determine the location of a book and verify how long it may take to retrieve it from off-site storage before setting out to use the library.

[**See also** COOKBOOKS; MANUSCRIPTS.]

BIBLIOGRAPHY

Bitting, Katherine Golden. *Gastronomic Bibliography.* San Francisco: Halle-Cordis Composing Room and Trade Freeroom, 1939.

Cagle, William R. *A Matter of Taste: A Bibliographical Catalog of International Books on Food and Drink.* 2nd ed. New Castle, DE: Oak Knoll Press, 1999.

Cagle, William R., and Lisa Killion Stafford. *American Books on Food and Drink.* New Castle, DE: Oak Knoll Press, 1998.

Feret, Barbara L. *Gastronomical and Culinary Literature.* Metuchen, NJ, and London: Scarecrow Press, 1979.

International Association of Culinary Professionals Foundation. http://www.iacpfoundation.com.

MADGE GRISWOLD

Licorice (Liquorice)

Licorice is the name for the roots and rhizomes of a small leguminous shrub (*Glycyrrhiza glabra*), native to Europe, Asia, and the Americas. Europeans colonists brought licorice to America; they used it for medicinal purposes. Licorice was and still is used for coloring and flavoring in beer, gingerbread, liquor, and tobacco. M and F Worldwide is the world's largest producer of licorice products. Although 70 percent of licorice sales are used to flavor and color tobacco products, licorice products are sold worldwide to confectioners, food processors, cosmetic companies, and pharmaceutical manufacturers. Although the extract is extremely sweet, it contains bitter flavor compounds that are tempered by the addition of more sweeteners. Licorice penny candy was available in grocery stores. Licorice paste (extract, sugar, thickeners, and colorings) is the base for Good & Plenty, first marketed in 1893 by Quaker City Confectionary Company, later acquired by Hershey Foods in 1996. Twizzlers were first made in 1929 by Y and S Candies, which became the National Licorice Company, and also merged with Hershey Foods Company in 1977. Twizzlers are still thought of as a licorice candy; however, there is no licorice in them other than in the black version.

Advertisement for Heide's candies from 1901.

LifeSavers

Clarence Crane, a chocolatier from Cleveland, Ohio, had a problem. his chocolates melted when the temperature rose, so he decided to make a hard candy that wouldn't melt during the summer. In 1912, after noticing a hand-operated pill-making machine in use at a pharmacy, he used a similar machine to make LifeSavers, which resembled their nautical namesake: a small, hard, round candy with a hole in the middle. The original flavor was mint. Crane packaged LifeSavers in cardboard boxes; however, the glue seeped onto the candy, and grocers refused to stock it. One year later, Crane sold the rights to Life-Savers to a purportedly unsuspecting Edward Noble, owner of Mint Products Company of New York, for $2,900. Noble repackaged the mints in tin foil wrappers and sold them for a nickel. Grocers still refused to stock Life-Savers, so Noble sold them to bars, where the displays were placed next to the cash register. The mint candies were a real lifesaver to those who wanted to disguise the alcohol on their breath. In 1915, United Cigar Store placed Lifesaver displays in their stores, and success was assured. Lifesavers are thought to be the first impulse-buy food item.

LifeSavers were made manually until 1919, when mass production machinery was acquired. Noble marketed LifeSavers to drug and grocery stores, encouraging placement of candy displays next to the cash register. For ten years, there was one flavor: Pep-O-Mint LifeSavers. Five flavor LifeSavers (orange, lemon, cherry, pineapple, lime) started holeless; by 1929, holes were added. Ten years later, all five flavors were combined in one package: the Five Flavor LifeSavers Roll. By 1969, the plant in Hamilton, Ontario, produced twenty flavors. In 1956, LifeSavers acquired Beech-Nut Company, and was itself acquired by Nabisco, later by Kraft Foods, and finally in 2005 by the Wrigley Company, which has recently changed the Five Flavor LifeSavers Roll flavor line-up to reflect current tastes: watermelon, cherry, pineapple, raspberry, and orange. As of the early 2000s, 550 million rolls are produced annually.

RENEE MARTON

Light Lager

This style of beer was developed to meet consumer demand for a beer that was low in both calories and carbohydrates. That market segment, the largest segment of the beer market in the United States, is less than demanding when it comes to balance of flavors, taste, or aroma profiles. They want basic, mildly alcoholic, low calorie beverages.

The style has been described as; "a watery interpretation of the Pilsener style …," "An American term, indicating watery Pilsener-style beer …," and "Thin stuff, the equivalent of traditional English small beer …"

A "regular beer" has about 138 calories per twelve-ounce bottle. Light beers have between 95 and 102 calories in a

Strawberry and other fruit flavors, despite being called licorice candy, have no licorice in them. The American Licorice Company, founded by Martin Kretchmer in Chicago in 1914 and still run by family members, makes Red Vines, Super Ropes, and other chewy textured candies, which can be extruded. Snaps and Twists are still made the slow old-fashioned way: batch process, with a higher concentration of licorice extract than that used in the continuous process method, used for newer flavors, such as Sour Punch and Blue Raspberry. Children in particular like the fruit flavored sticks, twists, and strips. Sugar, and, more recently, artificial sweeteners, are used to make many products that may contain licorice extract, whether original or synthetic. Most licorice candy manufactured today is synthetically flavored. Licorice flavored candies—whether real or by association—are gaining in popularity at present because there is usually no fat used in the manufacturing process.

RENEE MARTON

A lithograph recommends lager beer as a national drink, a healthy drink, a family drink, and a friendly drink.

twelve-ounce bottle. Essential to "light" beer is the fact that alcohol contributes 7.1 calories per gram, and can be made in only two ways: with special enzymes to convert unfermentable dextrin (at 4.1 calories per gram) to fermentable sugars, which will convert to alcohol, or just by adding water.

The U.S. government has yet to step in and legislate what brewers might call light beer. Canadian regulations specify that light beer, ale, stout, porter, and malt liquor must have 3.2 to 4 percent alcohol by volume content.

The Association of Brewers' 2004 Beer Style Guidelines states, "These beers are extremely light straw colored, light in body, and high in carbonation. Flavor is very light/mild and very dry. Hop flavor, aroma and bitterness is negligible to very low. Alcohol by volume is between 3.5–4.4 percent."

PETER LaFRANCE

Lime Rickey

The lime rickey is a nonalcoholic, sweet, refreshing lime soda, sometimes made with actual lime pulp, and sometimes augmented with cherry or raspberry. The term can also refer to a drink of rum, coconut syrup, cream, and lime juice shaken with ice and served in a half coconut, but this recipe is less common. The nonalcoholic lime rickey was sold at soda fountains and ice cream shops possibly as early as the 1920s. (Other lime drinks, such as lime cola and green river, were particularly popular around 1918.) In the 1940s, Seaman's Beverages began selling a mass-market, bright-green bottled version of the lime rickey that was still available in Canada in 2002. In the United States by that time, lime, raspberry-lime, and cherry-lime rickeys were generally available only in Boston and New England ice cream shops and diners. For a time, the lime rickey was served at the American chain restaurant Friendly's.

Originally, a rickey was any iced alcoholic drink mixed with lime and carbonated water, the most popular being the gin rickey. That drink owes its name to Colonel Rickey, an 1890s lobbyist in Washington, DC, who frequented a tavern called Shoemaker's and liked lime juice with his liquor. By 1906, bartenders were serving gin, brandy, whiskey, and vermouth rickeys.

[**See also** COCKTAILS; SODA DRINKS.]

JESSY RANDALL

Lincoln, Mrs.

Mary Johnson Bailey Lincoln (Mrs. David. A. Lincoln), cooking teacher, cookbook author, and first principal of the Boston Cooking School, was born July 8, 1844, in South Attleboro, Massachusetts. Hired in 1879 by the Cooking School Committee of the Women's Education Association to teach at the Boston Cooking School, Mary J. Lincoln had no professional training as a cook or a teacher. She had been a Boston homemaker until she was suddenly forced to earn a living to alleviate financial difficulties caused by her husband's ill health. Mrs. Lincoln rose to the occasion by translating her experience in running a kitchen in her own home into a career as one of the most famous late-nineteenth- and early-twentieth-century American cooking teachers.

When the committee hired her, they stipulated that she take two weeks of classes at the school before starting her job. Lincoln did take several classes in "fancy dishes" from Joanna Sweeney and attended a single demonstration by Maria Parloa, the previous term's teachers, before assuming the positions of both principal and teacher at a salary of seventy-five dollars a month. She remained at the school until 1885, when she resigned to devote all of her time to writing, editing, and lecturing.

The Boston Cooking School never attracted home cooks from immigrant neighborhoods, as had been its intended purpose, but during Mrs. Lincoln's tenure it became a Boston institution training a small number of household cooks and a greater number of their bosses in "plain cooking," "richer cooking," and "fancy cooking." In addition, the "normal" course (referring to normal schools) produced many cooking teachers, supervisors of school and hospital kitchens, tearoom operators, private caterers, and nutrition lecturers. A pioneer of household economics, Mrs. Lincoln offered her students orderly, clearly written, detailed, and extremely thorough information on nutrition, table service, teaching, and "rational cooking." She promoted the movement toward scientific measurement during her tenure at the school. Indeed, her first cookbook, which became the school's primary text, contained detailed directions for using the measuring equipment available at the time. Fannie Farmer, who graduated from the Boston Cooking School and later became its most famous principal, had studied from that text and built on Mrs. Lincoln's foundation when she perfected and popularized the system of level measurements with standard cups and spoons that is still used in America today.

After leaving the Boston Cooking School, Mary J. Lincoln wrote for *American Kitchen Magazine*, was coeditor of *New England Kitchen Magazine* with Anna Barrows, and promoted products that she felt were "pure foods." Her books include *Mrs. Lincoln's Boston Cook Book* (1884), *Mrs. D. A. Lincoln's Boston School Kitchen Text-Book; Lessons in Cooking for the Use of Classes in Public and Industrial Schools* (1884), *Mrs. Lincoln's Cook Book: What to Do and What Not to Do in Cooking* (1896), *The Home Science Cookbook* (1902), *What to Have for Luncheon* (1904), and *Home Helps: A Pure Food Cook Book* (1911). Most were reissued many times, and the textbook Mrs. Lincoln wrote for the Boston public school system's cookery classes set the model for domestic science programs in schools all across the country.

[**See also** BOSTON COOKING SCHOOL; FARMER, FANNIE; MEASUREMENT; PARLOA, MARIA.]

BIBLIOGRAPHY

Krondl, Michael. *Around the American Table: Treasured Recipes and Food Traditions from the American Cookery Collections of the New York Public Library.* Holbrook, MA: Adams, 1995.

Shapiro, Laura. *Perfection Salad: Women and Cooking at the Turn of the Century.* New York: Farrar, Straus and Giroux, 1986.

JOANNE LAMB HAYES

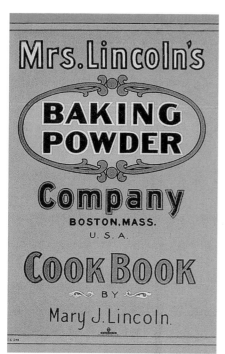

Cover of Mary J. Lincoln's baking powder cookbook.

Liquor Cabinets

Liquor cabinets were introduced in Europe during the fifteenth century as a means of keeping alcohol under lock and key in public houses or as a way to transport small quantities of alcohol. In colonial America, cellarettes—freestanding cabinets or chests—crafted from wood and fitted for bottles were among the more common objects for storing wine, Scotch, whiskey, and rye. During the Revolutionary War, officers' cellarettes were outfitted with more elaborate accessories, such as hand-blown crystal decanters, pitchers, glass funnels, shot glasses, and drinking goblets. Cellarettes remained in use through the Civil War and well into the twentieth century in public houses and private homes.

During the federal period (1788–1825), liquor cabinets began to give way to more conventional storage facilities that would become a standard for design: upright cupboards, sideboards, and breakfronts. These were crafted from mahogany and sometimes included marble tops. "Pedestal-end" sideboards incorporated a separate, freestanding cellarette.

Prohibition (1920–1933) generated an active underground movement of illegal alcohol consumption, as well as new methods for keeping illegal alcohol safe. Storage facilities ranged from subterranean storerooms to revolving faux walls ("libraries") in drinking establishments and private homes. Cellarettes enjoyed a renaissance, in the form of new variations that included trompe l'œil cabinetry designed to transform ordinary household furnishings—drop-leaf tables, bookshelves, and end tables—into objects that could conceal contraband substances.

The beverage cart was invented in the 1930s as a means of serving alcohol to passengers traveling by rail, cruise ship, and air or to guests enjoying hospitality in private homes. Upright cupboards, sideboards, and breakfronts were transformed into lavish lacquered wooden (burled walnut or bird's-eye maple, for example) objects with mirrors, etched glass, and halogen lights. Cabinet doors folded out into drop-down shelves; ample space was provided for the storage of alcohol and bar accessories, chrome or silver juicers, and Bakelite "martini-picks."
[See also COCKTAILS.]

BIBLIOGRAPHY

A Dram of History presented by Dr. David "The Scotch Doc" McCoy. http://www.scotchdoc.com/tsd/seminars/dramhist.html.

Montgomery, Charles F. American Furniture: The Federal Period (1788–1825), in the Henry Francis du Pont Winterthur Museum. New York: Viking Press, 1966.

JANE C. OTTO

Literature and Food

Americans consume stories the way they consume food, voraciously, and American fiction reflects this gastronomic and literary passion with its artistic, symbolic representations of food production and consumption, of food rituals and feasts. The Canadian novelist Margaret Atwood explains in The CanLit Foodbook that "eating is our earliest metaphor, preceding our consciousness of gender difference, race, nationality and language. We eat before we talk" (p. 2). Food becomes the social basis of most human interchanges, experiences, and communication, and, as symbol, encodes multiple languages of signification that examine power, gender, value, and creativity in literature.

In both real life and literature, food is oftentimes more than nourishment; Joyce Carol Oates notes in (Woman) Writer that "food…is a kind of poetry….it seems scarcely to exist in itself but rather as an expression of metaphor" (p. 310), functioning as a symbol of success or failure, of wealth or poverty, of civilization or savagery; sometimes it displays a taste of the sacred in the profane and is frequently a text of self-discovery. The language of food-as-symbol in literature allows the reader to get at the uncertainties and unknowns of life by examining food tropes about power, self, and cultural expressions. As Kim Chernin observes in The Hungry Self, "an obsession with food is always, at heart, an expression of some attempt to bring about either profound personal transformation or entry into collective life and its spiritual meanings" (p. 168).

Immigrants: Anzia Yezierska

America and American literature began as a melting pot of other nationalities and narratives. The best example of food-as-metaphor is found in the New World fictions of Anzia Yezierska, an eastern European Jewish immigrant. Writing in a tenement on the Lower East Side of New York during the early decades of the twentieth century, Yezierska announces her predilection for food in such titles as Hungry Hearts (1920) and Bread-Givers (1925). For her, cultural assimilation is mirrored in the adoption of American food and foodways; mealtimes and table manners symbolically measure one's integration into the New World. For Yezierska's heroines, to be American is to abandon Old World energetic cooking and relishing of food and to conform, instead, to a stereotype of simpering ineffectuality and fasting; ironically, to become an American is to be hungry in the new land of plenty for her characters.

The Northeast: Edith Wharton and Gloria Naylor

In a reverse immigration movement, the American novelist Edith Wharton transplants Americans from the New World to the Old; in The House of Mirth (1905) her Americans remain Americans no matter what the geography. In the heart of the gastronomically rich European scene, they search for un-foreign food, which underscores their Yankee snobbery. Descended from Old World Puritan stock, Wharton's Yankees devour whatever is not new as they eat well-cooked, Old World style peas and terrapin. They remain powerful in their isolationism. Yezierska's characters forget their birth nationalities to become Americans; Wharton's always remember they are Americans no matter where they are geographically.

Gloria Naylor, a black writer from New York, urges her protagonists to define themselves racially by the foods they do not eat. In her 1985 novel, Linden Hills, her characters remove themselves from their African American heritage by binging and purging or starving themselves to death. In order to assimilate into the white world, they must erase their blackness and their appetites for black food; instead of greasy pork ribs, collard greens, deep-fried catfish, and the like, her characters nibble lettuce and cucumbers, dabs of fish, and cottage cheese. Maxwell Smyth in Linden Hills so controls his food that he lives his life in the bathroom, a prisoner to his elimination of clear, white foods in his attempt to negate his natural blackness. Bulimia and anorexia define Naylor's African American characters.

Southern Women Writers

African American foods and identity also filter into southern literature. Perhaps more than in any of the other regional literatures, the southern narrative is a story of growing up, and it is defined by its symbolic food matrix of southern plenty and well-being; the self-discovery narratives and the tables of these rites of passage stories groan with the antebellum comfort foods of fried chicken, ham, greens, gravy, and gumbo. It is southern women writers especially who put their signature on this regional literature. For Eudora Welty, Flannery O'Connor, Fannie Flagg, and Anne Tyler, to name a few of the most prominent, the kitchen becomes the heart and soul of the southern narrative and the female narrator its fertile nurturer.

The Midwest: Willa Cather and Ernest Hemingway

Plains narratives also reinscribe the feminine. The archetypal author here is Willa Cather, who examines the relationship between immigrants, the land, and the self in her many novels. Her descriptions of food are as detailed as any aesthetic description of a work of art, and her theme is always food as a gesture of love. *My Ántonia* (1918), for example, opens and closes in a kitchen; three of its five sections are organized around food production: growing crops in a wild land; establishing a community that will provide these crops to the world; and creating a secure home in this new country. Like Yezierska, Wharton, and others, Cather defines the narrating self in terms of the region and its food.

The most American of accents, the most American of foods, and perhaps the most American of narratives come from the heartland of America: the Midwest. The quintessential figure here is Ernest Hemingway, who was born in Illinois. He incorporates all regions and all accents in his fictions and uses food as a code to heighten or intensify a moment of adventure in his fiction. From celebratory food in *The Sun Also Rises* (1926) to last suppers in *A Farewell to Arms* (1929) from the meals in *A Moveable Feast* (1964) to the nonexistence of meals in *To Have and Have Not* (1937), the shared communion of food or lack thereof symbolizes the relationship between the characters and the world. Hemingway's archetypal protagonist, Nick Adams, celebrates his union with himself and nature with a meal by the Big Two-Hearted River, thus providing one of the quintessential food-as-self metaphors in American literature.

To examine food as metaphor in American literature concisely is to look to the geography of the United States. Like William Butler Yeats's observation that one cannot tell the dancer from the dance, so one cannot separate American literature from its regional food roots; foodways and literary byways become one. [**See also** MIDWEST; SETTLEMENT HOUSES; SOUTHERN REGIONAL COOKERY.]

BIBLIOGRAPHY

Atwood, Margaret, comp. *The CanLit Foodbook: From Pen to Palate, a Collection of Tasty Fare.* Toronto: Totem, 1987.

Chernin, Kim. *The Hungry Self: Women, Eating and Identity.* New York: Harper, 1985.

Oates, Joyce Carol. "Food as Poetry." In *(Woman) Writer*, pp. 310–315. New York: Dutton, 1988.

MARY ANNE SCHOFIELD

Little Caesars

Founded in 1959 by former minor league shortstop Mike Ilitch and his wife, Marian, Little Caesars is a carryout pizza chain with franchises throughout the United States and Canada. Before opening the first Little Caesars, Ilitch prepared pizzas at a Detroit nightclub and did informal research at local pizza restaurants when on the road with the Tigers' farm team. After receiving a career-ending injury, Ilitch worked to build $10,000 in capital and borrowed $15,000 to fulfill his dream of opening a pizza shop. The first restaurant was originally called Little Caesars Pizza Treat and was located in a strip mall in the Detroit suburb of Garden City. "Little Caesar" was Marian's pet name for Mike.

The marketing ploy of selling two pizzas for the price of one is eponymous of the company's U.S. trademarked slogan, "Pizza! Pizza!" Although Ilitch Holdings, which also owns various development, entertainment, and sports enterprises (including the Detroit Tigers), made over $1 billion in 2004, Little Caesars has lost its spot as the third-ranking franchised pizza business to Papa John's and its snack bar contract with Kmart. In the first quarter of 2005, customer satisfaction in the chain dropped 1.3 percent.

In recent years, the company has also had legal difficulties with franchise owners over the procurement of supplies from the corporate owned Blue Line distribution and has a had both a positive and a negative reaction to its "Hot and Ready" $5 premade pizza promotion. Still family owned, Mike Illich handed over the Little Caesar mantle to his son, Christopher, in 2004, after an internal power struggle between the younger Illich and his sister Denise. [**See also** PIZZA, PIZZERIAS.]

BIBLIOGRAPHY

Garber, Amy. "Little Caesars Nails Pre-made Pies." *Nation's Restaurant News*, September 29, 2003.

MATTHEW PETERSEN

Lobster

Considered a luxury item in most seafood restaurants, cold-water lobster trapped in Maine and Canadian waters is shipped around the United States for consumption. There have been attempts to farm-raise lobsters in Hawaii and elsewhere. Some lobster trappers claim that even wild lobsters are accidentally farmed because they feed on bait from the bags placed in traps. Gradually rotting bait floats out into the surrounding waters, where the lobsters eat it. The lobsters creep into and out of the traps to feed there as well. Eventually the lobsters grow so large they cannot leave the traps, which have net openings as a conservation feature. Even so, American lobster trappers are required to measure the lobsters and throw back both undersize and oversize ones.

For more than one hundred years, New England lobster trappers have managed to follow various practices that have conserved lobster populations. Yet from the settlement of America to the present, average lobster size

has declined. Lobsters had commercial value early. They were trapped and brought ashore in New England cities, where they were often cooked immediately to prevent spoilage and sold door to door. As early as the mid-eighteenth century, as reported by the Swedish naturalist Peter Kalm in 1749, lobsters were transported alive to Boston and New York in well vessels—boats with seawater flowing through portions of the hull, which contained the shellfish. That practice continued into the nineteenth century.

The establishment of lobster canneries along the New England coast in the mid-nineteenth century made the product available inland for salads, sauces, and bisques. Cannery refuse, sold to farmers as compost, may account for the oft-repeated claim that lobsters were so plentiful they were plowed into fields. The fishery was active along the New England coast for two hundred years but declined in the twentieth century along the southern New England coast. In the early twenty-first century, Penobscot Bay, on the coast of Maine, and adjacent areas report the greatest catches. Canadian and Maine trappers vie over the lobster populations in the eastern Gulf of Maine and argue about the appropriate and sustainable harvest size. Some seafood conservation groups have put American lobster on the list of species that need protection.

SANDRA L. OLIVER

Lobster Roll

A lobster roll is a sandwich that is found in two distinct versions. The first and more popular of the two contains a cold lobster salad made of diced, steamed lobster meat, celery, onion, mayonnaise, and chives. The second interpretation of the sandwich is composed of warm chunks of steamed lobster meat, including tail, claw, and knuckle meat that are simply drenched in butter. Both are served on split-top hot dog buns. The buns are often toasted in both renditions of this dish. They are most commonly served with pickles and chips or shoestring fries. The lobster roll, whether made with butter or mayonnaise, can be found in restaurants and seafood shacks up and down the North Atlantic coast. There is no geographical boundary that divides these two types of sandwiches. Legal Seafood, a popular chain restaurant in the Northeast, serves both versions.

Although residents of Maine claim to have invented the butter version of the lobster roll, the Lobster Roll Restaurant on Long Island, New York, claims to have invented the mayonnaise version in the 1960s. No matter who the inventor, this seafood sandwich is definitely a twentieth-century creation, as the hot dog bun, the yeast top-split bun, did not appear in production in American culinary history until 1912.

BIBLIOGRAPHY

Charles, Rebecca *Lobster Rolls and Blueberry Pies.* New York: Regan Books, 2003.

TRICIA L. WILLIAMS

Low-Calorie Syrup

For centuries, people mixed sugar with water or fruit juice to create syrups used as sweeteners or flavorings or to deliver medications. Artificial sweeteners opened the door for the low-calorie and sugar-free market, starting with saccharin, discovered in 1879. Its use became widespread when sugar was rationed during World War I and World War II.

Before the 1960s, dietetic products were sold to people on medically restricted diets, such as diabetics. But, during the 1960s, when people became more health conscious, and during the 1970s fitness boom, so-called light products, meaning low calorie or low fat, became more popular. By 2003, with over 65 percent of Americans, more than 135 million people, overweight, both dieters and low-calorie converts had incorporated light products into their lives.

Low-calorie breakfast syrups often use artificial maple flavoring. Other low-calorie syrups for desserts and beverages, for instance, include flavors ranging from chocolate and vanilla to fruit to liquors, nuts, and spices. Food and beverage manufacturers have many newer artificial sweeteners with a wide range of sweetness, supplying few or no calories, to choose from. They may combine them or use them singly. Syrups made from these artificial sweeteners satisfy a strong demand for safe, low-calorie, tasty foods and beverages, because Americans still want to eat their favorite foods but without the calories.

ELISABETH TOWNSEND

Low-Carbohydrate Light Lager

The development of American low-carbohydrate light lager is credited to Dr. Joseph L. Owades. In 1960, he was hired by Rheingold Breweries in Brooklyn. In 1967, he developed a beer called Gablinger's Diet Beer, using a process that removed the starch from beer, making it lower in carbohydrates and calories. His process and recipe were later sold to Meister Brau.

In 1972, Miller bought rights to the Meister Brau line of products, including "lite beer." Although lite beer cost less to produce than regular beers, the Miller Brewing Company positioned it as a premium beer. Miller's goal was to convince the public that the low-calorie beer was as suited for men as it was for women. Not only did Miller achieve this goal, it broke ground in the brewing industry by developing the lo-calorie/low-carbohydrate beer and made it a national best seller.

This style of beer is one of the most popular beers sold in the United States. The total U.S. beer market in 2004 was 209.9 million barrels of beer, according to the Beer Institute. Four of the top five market share beers were "light" beers. According to the Beverage Marketing Corporation, in 2004, "The 10 biggest domestic brands accounted for 68.0% of total U.S. beer volume. The leading lights accounted for 45.1% of that volume, leaving about 22.9% for the leading regular beers."

According to the Association of Brewers' 2004 Beer Style Guidelines, "These beers are extremely light straw colored, light in body, and high in carbonation. They should have a maximum carbohydrate level of 3.0 gm per 12 oz. (356 ml). Flavor is very light/mild and very dry. Hop flavor, aroma and bitterness is negligible to very low." Alcohol content by volume is between 3.5 and 4.4 percent.

PETER LAFRANCE

Lowenstein, Eleanor

Eleanor Lowenstein (1909–1980) was a definitive bibliographer of culinary Americana and seller of rare cookery books. A native of New York City, she held forth many years in the Corner Book Shop on lower Fourth Avenue, a mecca for cooks and food historians. A chosen few were occasionally invited to browse in her fabled private holdings.

[See also COOKBOOKS AND MANUSCRIPTS: AMERICAN COOKBOOKS TO 1860.]

BIBLIOGRAPHY

Lowenstein, Eleanor. *Bibliography of American Cookery Books, 1742–1860.* 3rd ed. Worcester, MA: American Antiquarian Society, 1972. Based on *American Cookery Books, 1742–1860* by Waldo Lincoln.

KAREN HESS

Lüchow's

In the 1880s, when New York City's Union Square was a cultural crossroads—home to the Academy of Music, Steinway Hall, and Tony Pastor's Music Hall—Lüchow's German restaurant was the haunt of musicians, actors, and writers who came for the pigs knuckles, sauerbraten, bratwurst, roast goose, schnitzel, and Würzburger beer and stayed for the gemütlichkeit. Notables who were seen at Lüchow's included O. Henry, H. L. Mencken, Theodore Dreiser, Lillian Russell, John Barrymore, Enrico Caruso, Richard Strauss, and Victor Herbert, who for four years led the resident string ensemble in Viennese favorites. Even when the beer stopped flowing—Prohibition spelled the end for many establishments—Lüchow's hung on. The day Prohibition was repealed, one thousand guests came to quaff seidels of Würzburger.

Lüchow's was founded by August Guido Lüchow, who came to New York from Hanover, Germany, in 1879. Within a few years he had bought the beer hall at 110 East Fourteenth Street where he had worked as a waiter. Part of Lüchow's charm was its decor. The oak-paneled walls were covered with European paintings, photographs of celebrated customers, and elaborate mirrors. The Hunt Room had twenty-one mounted deer heads, and in the Nibelungen Room there were murals representing scenes from Wagnerian opera. Hundreds of beer steins lined the walls. At holiday time, the restaurant hosted the city's tallest indoor Christmas tree.

In the 1950s, a number of old-fashioned dishes that had not been served since the 1920s were reinstated by the new owner Leonard Jan Mitchell, who also revived the old festivals—Bock Beer, May Wine, Venison, and Goose—with special menus and music. Mitchell also compiled *Lüchow's German Cookbook,* published in 1952. Like many old-fashioned German restaurants across America, the restaurant closed its East Fourteenth Street doors in 1982. Following a brief revival in a midtown location, Lüchow's closed for good.

[See also GERMAN AMERICAN FOOD.]

BIBLIOGRAPHY

Mitchell, Leonard Jan. *Lüchow's German Cookbook.* Garden City, NY: Doubleday, 1952.

BONNIE J. SLOTNICK

Lunch, *see Meal Patterns*

Lunch Boxes, Dinner Pails, and Picnic Kits

In the eighteenth and early nineteenth centuries, farmers, miners, laborers, schoolchildren, and city workers carried meals (especially the midday dinner now called lunch) in wooden boxes or wrapped in oiled paper or cloth. Tinplate boxes made by tinkers were used in the early 1800s, as were reused tin biscuit boxes.

In the 1850s, meals began to be carried in fitted metal pails and boxes. Most of these containers were made of sheet metal, tinplated to be sanitary and resist rust, and formed into stacked compartments or pails within pails. They had metal handles and bands or leather straps. Most contained a drinking cup. Workers carrying their tinboxed meals were referred to in a trade newspaper (*The Metal Worker,* 1882) as the "tin pail brigade." Miners sometimes used large fitted tin trunks, which held meals for a whole crew. Some city workers of the 1880s and 1890s carried small stamped and decorated lunch or sandwich carriers, which were disguised to look like books or little satchels. In the 1880s and later biscuits and tobacco sometimes were sold in colorful lithographed tin boxes, which could be used for lunch boxes after their original contents were gone. Invented in 1892, glass-lined vacuum bottles or thermoses kept liquids hot or cold. Children's lunch kits with thermoses and the familiar workers' lunch kits shaped like little barns with a pullout drawer for the thermos and cup were in wide use by the 1920s.

Picnic kits—usually baskets fitted with tin plates, cups, flatware, and thermoses—became common by about 1910, as automobiles gave people an easy way to travel into the countryside for recreation. Children's lunch boxes were decorated amusingly with appealing characters as early as 1902, but most were made after 1930. The first children's lunch box with a cartoon character on it appeared in 1935 and depicted Mickey Mouse, but it was not until 1950, with decals of television's Hopalong Cassidy, that decorated children's lunch boxes became hugely popular. Decades later many lunch kits were made either of plastic or insulated fabric. Take-out fast food largely made lunch boxes for workers obsolete.

[**See also** Containers; Picnics; Tailgate Picnics.]

BIBLIOGRAPHY

Aikins, Larry. *Pictorial Price Guide to Metal Lunch Boxes and Thermoses.* Gas City, IN: L-W Book Sales, 1994.

Franklin, Linda Campbell. *300 Years of Kitchen Collectibles: A Price Guide for Collectors, with 60 Color Pictures and 400 Black and White Illustrations.* 5th ed. Iola, WI: Krause, 2003.

Woodall, Allen, and Sean Brickell. *The Illustrated Encyclopedia of Metal Lunch Boxes.* West Chester, PA: Schiffer, 1992.

LINDA CAMPBELL FRANKLIN

Luncheonettes

Strictly speaking, luncheonettes are small restaurants, the suffix implying size, where light meals are served at lunchtime. The term does not always refer to freestanding dining spots but could mean food-service counters within other establishments, such as Woolworth's five-and-ten stores.

Restaurants specializing in midday meals appeared in America with industrialization and the intensification of office work in cities and towns. In the early to mid-nineteenth century, the concept of lunch, dining away from home during the workday, became regulated by the clock as was work itself. Eating fast had long been an American characteristic, but quick service was now required when lunch breaks might last only thirty minutes.

Lunch service for people engaged in business dates to the mid-eighteenth century, when a New York City tavern offered it, only to be accused of destroying home life. The real progenitors of the fixed-location lunch places were street vendors who served urban populaces, as they still do, notably in New York City. They served varieties of raw and cooked foods, from oysters to sausages. Quick service counters may have emerged

A crowded lunch counter in nineteenth-century New York.

with railroads in the 1850s; food counters were introduced in Chicago in 1852 or 1854 with the new connections to its western hinterlands. The food counters were typically horseshoe shaped, later with high stools, to minimize the number of servers needed.

The idea spread to cities, especially catering to middle class people and to the growing numbers of women who were entering the workforce as clerical staff. H. M. Kohlsaat opened a "dairy lunch room" in the Loop in Chicago specifically as a safe place for young women to dine quickly and cheaply. His restaurant featured swivel stools, the later standard for the industry. By the early twentieth century, entrepreneurs, such as John Raklios, had set up chains of "luncheonettes" in Chicago and across urban America. The name, coming from "luncheon," suggested a better grade of dining than the blunter "lunch" or "lunch counter."

The food served in early luncheonettes was hot, mostly meats (chicken à la king and chipped beef on toast after World War I), but with cheese and egg dishes along with coffee and teas. By the 1920s, menus had begun to offer lighter fare. A 1934 pulp

novel describes one such as place "a roadside sandwich joint, like a million others." Ham, grilled cheese, BLT, egg salad, tuna salad, perhaps grilled hamburgers (with or without cheese), tuna melts, and others were sandwich staples. Many were served on toast, not available until commercial toasters came into use in the 1920s. Soups, from chicken noodle to tomato, reheated from food service cans, were also featured. For healthier fare, salads—such as ham, chicken, macaroni, and tuna—were served with iceberg lettuce and unripe tomatoes. However, some dishes were regional; grits were almost always on southern luncheonette menus. Some lunch places, drugstore lunch counters especially, became soda fountains serving national or regional soft drinks and ice cream creations.

With the advance of national fast food chains, beginning in the later 1950s, classic luncheonettes have mostly disappeared from the American dining scene. Some remain as nostalgic reminders of a past life but usually with modernized menus.

[**See also** Restaurants; Sandwiches; Soda Fountains.]

BRUCE KRAIG

Macadamia Nuts

The macadamia nut tree (*Macadamia integrifolia*) originated in the rain forests of Queensland, Australia, and was first domesticated in 1858. In 1882, William Purvis brought the first macadamia nut trees to Hawaii, and they were widely planted in the islands. The horticulturist Walter Storey introduced macadamia trees to California, and other states have attempted to grow them. However, most of the world's commercial macadamias are still grown in Hawaii. Creamy-fleshed macadamias are the highest in fat and calories of all tree nuts; they are usually enjoyed on their own but are also incorporated into candies, cookies, and luxurious desserts.

[**See also** HAWAIIAN FOODS; NUTS.]

BIBLIOGRAPHY

Shigeura, Gordon T., and Hiroshi Ooka. *Macadamia Nuts in Hawaii, History and Production*. Honolulu: Hawaii Institute of Tropical Agriculture and Human Resources, College of Tropical Agriculture and Human Resources, University of Hawaii at Manoa, 1984.

ANDREW F. SMITH

Macaroni and Cheese

Macaroni and cheese is one of the most popular meals among all Americans, from toddlers to senior citizens reaching back for "comfort food." What differentiates it from most Italian pasta dishes is that the macaroni—most typically tubular "elbows"—is first boiled quite soft, then baked with cheese sauce to almost a smooth paste of simple starch and melted cheese, perhaps with a contrasting crust of browned crumbs.

The early history of pasta is still controversial, although it is agreed that it was widespread in medieval Italy well before Marco Polo. A 1986 survey by Corby Kummer suggested the earliest pasta was in ancient China, and that it was known in the Middle East early in the Common Era. Clifford A. Wright, focusing on the diffusion of durum wheat, puts the origin in the Arab world. Certainly pasta dressed with cheese is described in most surviving medieval cooking manuscripts, including the British *Forme of Cury*, which gives a recipe for "macrows." There are two versions of baked vermicelli puddings (but neither with cheese) in Hannah Glasse's mid-eighteenth-century cookbook, the most popular British cookbook in colonial Virginia. Anglo-American macaroni of the colonial period was imported from Italy, and most probably overboiled and overbaked, as the practice is denounced in Kitchiner's *The Cook's Oracle* in the late 1820s.

Not long after the American Revolution, Thomas Jefferson imported pasta-making equipment from Italy, and the first American pasta factories were established by French chefs fleeing the French revolution. One of these, Louis Fresnaye of Philadelphia, was handing out a printed recipe for "vermicelli baked like pudding" with cheese as early as 1802. But the center for early American macaroni and cheese was Virginia, and Mary Randolph's 1824 recipe, possibly influenced by her connections with Jefferson, is the clear ancestor of what became a Southern regional dish, an African American specialty, a railroad dining-car classic, and a national favorite—always as a vegetable or side dish. By 1906, a high-society recipe from Philadelphia began, "Boil the macaroni one hour and quarter in salt and water, until the macaroni falls apart when lifted of pierced by the fork." Later, it notes, "The secret of success lies in the boiling, and if it is not very tender, it should boil another 15 minutes. This will be a revelation to lovers of good macaroni."

As Italian immigrants began to advance the use of pasta to a main dish with meat and tomato sauce, macaroni and cheese (or in England "Macaroni Cheese") became a shelf-stable convenience food with Kraft's 1937 introduction of "Kraft Dinner"—"A meal for four in nine minutes for an everyday price of 19 cents." Although the recipe on the box suggested baking for 15 minutes with a topping of breadcrumbs, the crust and the baking step were increasingly sacrificed for speed. Sales jumped during World War II when it was both a convenience food and a meat-meal substitute for only one ration point.

In the early twenty-first century, macaroni and cheese is still the category leader, and Kraft is still the market leader, claiming sales of seven million boxes per week. Organic and discounted competition have encouraged Kraft to market new shapes based on cartoon characters and a more healthful formulation without trans fats and with added vitamins, calcium, and some whole grain—both aimed at children and teenagers, who have always loved the bland richness of macaroni and cheese.

MARK H. ZANGER

Mackerel

Because they are an oily fleshed fished, mackerel (*Scomber scombrus* and *S. japonicus*) do not meet with as much favor as other fish, and seafood sections of large supermarkets do not often display fresh mackerel. In the nineteenth and twentieth centuries, mackerel were served, as were herring, as a "relish" at breakfast, supper, or tea, and they are often smoked and used as hors d'ouvres. Mackerel flesh is tender, blue-gray, and rich in omega-3 fatty acids. These fish are very good grilled or fried as panfish.

Mackerel was an important East Coast fishery in the eighteenth and nineteenth centuries but declined considerably in the twentieth century. Beginning as a hook-and-line fishery, it progressed to jigging, and by the mid-1800s, mackerel were purse seined, which dramatically increased the catch. Dressed aboard the fishing vessel, mackerel were split, salted, and sold even inland in the United States. Among saltwater fish, mackerel appears nearly as frequently in early cookbooks as salt codfish.

Along the East and West coasts, where mackerel school in summer, they are popular among recreational fishermen and are relatively easy to catch because they will bite at almost anything, even bare hooks. They have great ranges, from the Mediterranean to the North Sea, all along the Atlantic, and from Mexico to Alaska. On the Pacific Coast they are called chub mackerel.

Jack mackerel, *Trachurus symmetricus*, are important commercial fish, often canned and distributed widely as inexpensive protein. In the early twentieth century, commercial fishermen made relatively little distinction between chub and jack mackerel.

SANDRA L. OLIVER

Mai Tai

Victor Bergeron, also known as Trader Vic, tells the following story about the mai tai in his book *Trader Vic's Bartender's Guide*. He was experimenting at the bar of his original *Trader Vic's* location in Emeryville, California, with a fine sixteen-year-old Jamaican rum he had purchased. When he finished he served the drink to his friends from Tahiti, Ham and Carrie Guild. After tasting the drink, Carrie raised her glass and said, "*mai tai roa ae*," which means out of this world, the best in Tahitian. "That's the name of the drink," replied Bergeron. He often said it was "One of the finest drinks I ever concocted."

Many years later, in 1970 over drinks with Jim Bishop, a syndicated newspaper columnist and Donn Beach, his biggest competitor and the pioneer of the tiki drinks craze, Bergeron admitted that Donn had come up with the original mai tai. In actuality, the two recipes are completely different.

Bergeron's mai tai is a sweet and sour rum drink; the sweet ingredients are orange curacao and orgeat syrup, a milky almond flavored syrup used extensively in Italian baking. The sour ingredient is fresh lime juice. Don the Beachcombers' recipe calls for a Jamaican and a Cuban rum mixed with grapefruit, lime, Cointreau, and falernum along with a dash of bitters and a dash of Pernod. To make a mai tai, combine 2 ounces of aged rum, $\frac{3}{4}$ ounce of orange curaçao, ¾ ounce of lime juice, and ¼ ounce of orgeat syrup. Shake well with ice and strain into an old-fashioned glass filled with ice. Garnish with mint sprigs and a piece of lime. [See also COCKTAILS; RUM.]

BIBLIOGRAPHY
Bergeron, Victor J. *Trader Vic's Rum Cookery and Drinkery*. New York: Doubleday, 1974.
Bergeron, Victor J. *Trader Vic's Bartender's Guide*. New York: Doubleday, 1972.

DALE DEGROFF

M&M Milk Chocolate Candies

Forrest Mars noticed, while in Spain during the Spanish civil war (1936–1937), that soldiers ate pieces of chocolate covered with a crisp sugar coating—the chocolate pieces did not melt. He (son of founder of the Mars candy company) and partner Bruce Murrie (son of the president of Hershey chocolate company) opened a factory in England to produce chocolate candies coated with a hard sugar shell. Another purported influence on the development of M&M's is Smarties—an English sugar-coated chocolate confection launched in 1937 by the Rowntree company. Forrest Mars and R. William Murrie combined their last names to create M&M candies. Their company eventually merged with Mars, Inc. M&M chocolate candies started production in 1940. The original colors were red, yellow, green, orange, brown, and violet. The candies were sold in a brown plastic bag; peanut M&M's were launched in 1954, in a bright yellow bag.

Relations between the two partners became strained; Mars bought out Murrie for $1 million in 1949. By the early 1950s, annual sales of M&M's topped $3 million. Product placement on the new television shows *Howdy Dowdy* and the *Mickey Mouse Club* helped to increase sales dramatically. By 1956, sales topped 40 million. Mr. Plain and Mr. Peanut cartoon characters were part of the advertising campaign, and M&M's became the most popular candy in America.

While M&M's were available nationally after 1941, they were popularized after World War II because they were part of soldiers' rations, thereby creating a huge customer base. They were easy to eat, and didn't melt. This led to one of the most famous advertising slogans: "The Milk Chocolate Melts in Your Mouth—Not in Your Hand." M&M's are still part of the MREs (meals-ready-to-eat) that form part of a soldier's daily food kit.

In 1960, red, yellow, and green colors were added to the mix. Orange arrived in 1976. From the mid-1970s to the mid-1980s, Mars removed red M&M's from the mix, as a result of an FDA recall of red food dye coloring. Later, the FDA reversed its decision, and the color was reinstated. To keep pace with competitors, other products have been introduced over the years: peanut butter M&Ms', almond chocolates candies, and MINIS Mega Tubes. M&M Peanuts are the most popular candy today. Global sales of all M&M products generate annual revenue of more than $2 billion. In 1995, the introduction of blue M&M's resulted from a mass marketing campaign involving 10 million votes for this color. Removing colors temporarily, and having M&M's available in black and white, are short-term sales tactics that have been used. Interactive relationships with consumers are used today via M&M stores and websites—the individualizing of consumer taste.

In 1982, M&M's were launched into space on the space shuttle. They could also have been used to introduce a space alien to the human world: ET, the extraterrestrial. However, believing that this film idea was not likely to be successful, they turned down the opportunity to use M&M's to create a trail for the alien to follow. In 1984 and 1992, M&M's were the official snack of the Olympic Games. Today, M&M chocolate candies are part of Masterfoods, Inc.—a division of Mars, Inc. [See also CHOCOLATE.]

RENEE MARTON

Manhattan

One of the most important drinks in the world of the cocktail-mixing bartender, the Manhattan, created by an unknown mixologist, probably in the 1870s, was one of the first cocktails to utilize vermouth as a balancing agent. Originally made with straight rye whiskey, sweet vermouth, bitters, and a dash of curaçao or maraschino liqueur, the recipe has changed, though not substantially, over the past century or more.

The first cocktail book to be printed, *How to Mix Drinks; or, The Bon-Vivant's Companion* (1862) by Jerry Thomas, contained no mention of the Manhattan, but his next book, *The Bar-Tender's Guide; or, How to Mix all Kinds of Plain and Fancy Drinks* (1887), contained a recipe for the drink, and this time span coincides with the growth of sales of vermouth in the United States. Sweet vermouth became popular before dry vermouth, to the point where many recipe books before 1900 called for "vermouth" without differentiating between the two types. After that time, cocktail books started to call for either vermouth or dry vermouth, thus indicating that the sweet variety was more commonly known.

Thomas's recipe calls for twice as much vermouth as whiskey, but in 1906 a book by Louis Muckensturm, *Louis' Mixed Drinks with Hints for the Care and Service of Wines*, reversed the ratios, and the whiskey became the base of the drink. Since then, apart from myriad variations on the theme, the Manhattan has not changed a great deal.

After the repeal of Prohibition in 1933, Americans started to refer to blended Canadian whiskey as rye, since the Canadians used much rye in their formula at that time, and it was far easier to find than straight American rye. Blended Canadian whiskey became the base of the drink, but the formula stayed pretty much the same. During the 1980s and 1990s, when bourbon was enjoying a resurgence in popularity, many people started to order bourbon Manhattans and shied away from the Canadian version. This was also the period when bitters began to be omitted from the formula, but for no apparent reason other than perhaps a little laziness on the part of American bartenders.

The Manhattan is one of the most difficult drinks to make correctly, mostly because, in order to achieve proper balance in the cocktail, the mixologist must take into consideration the style of whiskey being used and also the brand of vermouth. Whiskeys and vermouths vary fairly drastically from one bottling to the next, so a keen knowledge of ingredients is required in order to make a good Manhattan cocktail. [See also COCKTAILS; VERMOUTH.]

BIBLIOGRAPHY
Behr, Edward. *Prohibition: Thirteen Years That Changed America*. New York: Arcade Publishing, 1996.
Grimes, William. *Straight Up or On the Rocks: The Story of the American Cocktail*. New York: North Point Press, 2001.
Johnson, Harry. *New and Improved Illustrated Bartender's Manual*. New York: Harry Johnson, 1900.

GARY AND MARDEE HAIDIN REGAN

Maple Syrup

During the six-week "maple moon" of consistently warm, sunny days and cold nights in late winter, sap flows through sugar maples (*Acer saccharum*) and black maples (*Acer nigrum*) from eastern Canada to Minnesota and as far south as Kentucky. Since at least the mid-1500s, North American Indians and early European forest travelers drank the clear, barely sweet liquid, which was at times their only source of nourishment.

Anthropologists and historians debate the point, but it is probable that the Indians were the first both to tap maple trees and to distill their sap into syrup. Sap was collected through carved wooden spigots ("spiles") inserted into ax cuts in the tree. The colonists learned both the method of making syrup and an appreciation for the sweetener from the Indians.

Maple sugar takes a lot of work to produce. Sap is less than 3 percent sugar; thirty-two to forty gallons of sap boil down to just one gallon of syrup, and eight gallons of syrup boil down further to make one pound of maple sugar. But, historically, maple sugar may have been more useful than maple syrup.

Early colonists liked their desserts sweet, but they also liberally doused savory dishes with sweeteners. However, even muscovada, the coarsest brown cane sugar, was costly. Pragmatic Americans used the cheapest source available, maple sugar or syrup from nearby woods, to appease a sweet tooth.

Nineteenth-century print of couples collecting and tasting maple syrup.

To many seeking a more neutral alternative, this "Indian melasses," also known as "Indian sugar," was avoided because of its relatively strong taste. To other mid-eighteenth- and nineteenth-century settlers, such as the Quakers, maple sugar was a morally acceptable alternative to cane sugar, which they boycotted. They abhorred the New England–African–Caribbean triangle trade of sugar and molasses, rum, and slaves on which they believed many East Coast fortunes were based.

It was not until the eighteenth century, however, that maple syrup and sugar gained widespread use. These remained popular until the end of the nineteenth century. Several factors then conspired to restrict the use of these sweeteners. Among them were a decline in the price of other competing sugars, increased labor costs, a preference for commodity foods, and the introduction of cheaper imitation syrups.

This quintessential North American sweetener (Canada is by far the largest producer) has captured the imagination of pancake eaters but not their taste buds or their wallets: an estimated 90 to 95 percent of Americans have never tasted the real thing. Today's pancake syrups are far removed from maple sap. By law, only syrups containing at least 2 percent of maple syrup may use the words "maple syrup." Some so-called maple syrups contain only artificial flavorings. Pure maple syrup is graded according to color (and, at least in Vermont, by depth of flavor). Grades are variously named, from light and delicate (Fancy Grade A Light Amber, for example) through a more robust midrange (Grade A Medium Amber, Grade A Dark Amber, and Grade B) to a commercial grade.

Recipes featuring maple syrup include the favorite of New England schoolchildren: hot maple syrup poured over clean snow to congeal into "sugar on snow," "wax sugar," or "gum sugar." Maple syrup sweetened New Englanders' baked beans, was drizzled over 1880s flannel cakes, and flavored a 1913 Texas ice cream recipe. Maple walnut pie rivals the South's popular cane- or corn-syrup-sweetened pecan pie.

Maple syrup has a unique—and delicious—character. As early tasters noted, it cannot be used as a generic sweetener. It can be tricky to cook with; some cooks suggest treating it as a flavoring rather than a sweetener. But it remains prized. As the Vermont senator George Aiken is said to have observed, "You can bribe anyone in Washington with a quart of maple syrup."

[See also NATIVE AMERICAN FOOD; NEW ENGLAND; SWEETENERS.]

BIBLIOGRAPHY

Lawrence, James M., and Rux Martin. *Sweet Maple: Life, Lore, and Recipes from the Sugarbush.* Shelburne, VT: Chapters, 1993.

Nearing, Helen, and Scott. *The Maple Sugar Book.* New York: John Day, 1950.

ROBIN M. MOWER

Margarine

Since its inception, margarine has had to define itself in opposition to butter, at first as a cheaper and then as a healthier alternative. Hippolyte Mège Mouriès, a French chemist, concocted the first margarine out of beef suet and milk in 1869. Two years later, he sold his process to Jurgens (later merged with Unilever), a Dutch dairy company that found a ready market for its synthetic butter in industrial Europe's working class. These early margarines were made mostly of imported American animal fats, a cheap by-product of the booming midwestern meatpacking industry. In 1873, an American patent was granted to Mège Mouriès, who intended to expand production to the United States. There was, however, already competition in New York, where the U.S. Dairy Company had begun production of "artificial butter" by that same year.

The butter substitute was so successful that state laws were passed as early as 1877 to protect state dairy interests. Within ten years, even Congress got into the act, passing a bill taxing and regulating the margarine industry. By this point, more than thirty factories were churning out margarine. It was particularly the yellow dye added to the many ersatz butters that drew the lawmakers' ire. As a consequence, by 1902 thirty-two states had banned yellow margarine. And once again Washington followed suit, this time by increasing the tax on tinted margarine fivefold. In order to bypass government regulation, purveyors began to provide little capsules of food coloring to knead into the fat. By the 1930s, even the armed forces and other federal agencies were barred from using margarine for anything but cooking purposes. Although the campaign against margarine began to let up during the food shortages and rationing of World War II, it was not until 1967 that Wisconsin became the last state to repeal restrictions on margarine.

The composition of margarine has changed with technology. Early margarine got its butterlike texture from naturally occurring, highly hydrogenated animal fats and tropical oils, which remain firm at room temperature. By 1910, the chemistry of hydrogenating vegetable oils had been perfected, and soon it was possible to produce margarine from virtually any oil. In the United States, peanut and cottonseed oil led the way, but tropical oils, milk, and even a little real butter might be added to the mix. Not surprisingly, some of the earliest producers were companies that had a firm grasp of the chemistry of fat from their experience manufacturing soap, for example, Lever Brothers of New York.

Margarine consumption received a tremendous boost in the late 1960s, when butter and other fats high in cholesterol were deemed practically homicidal and the public was enjoined to turn to margarine as a healthier alternative. As a result, millions of people made the switch. In 1930, per capita consumption of margarine was only 2.6 pounds while butter was 17.6 pounds. On the cusp of the twenty-first century, the average American ate 8.3 pounds of margarine and only 4.2 pounds of butter.

At the moment that margarine's ascendancy over butter seemed unassailable, new research in the 1990s once again muddied scientific opinion. It appeared that the trans-fatty acids, which result when oils are hydrogenated to form solid stick margarine, might pose even greater health hazards than the naturally occurring, saturated fat in butter. What little agreement existed steered the health-conscious consumer toward margarines that are the softest in consistency because they are the least likely to raise the

Jelke Good Luck Margarine recipe booklet, 1927.

levels of cholesterol associated with heart disease.

As the twenty-first century opened, margarine continued to see gains as producers tinkered with their formulas. The grocery dairy cases were full of butter substitutes: some that actually included butter or other dairy products, most made from some half dozen edible oils, while others even contained pharmaceuticals that promised to lower cholesterol. Chemistry clearly held sway over the fat of the land.

BIBLIOGRAPHY

International Margarine Association of the Countries of Europe. http://www.imace.org/margarine/history. htm.

National Association of Margarine Manufacturers. http://www.margarine.org.

Tanner, John. "Unilever's History." *New Internationalist,* June 1987.

MICHAEL KRONDL

Margarita

The margarita, a cocktail made of tequila, triple sec or Cointreau, and lime juice served in a salt-rimmed glass, was popularized by Victor J. Bergeron in his chain of Señor Pico restaurants in California during the 1960s. Bergeron went to Mexico to find a recipe but concluded that Mexicans drank tequila straight and did not like tequila cocktails. So Bergeron adapted recipes borrowed from other American restaurateurs. By 1973, his Señor Pico restaurants sold more tequila than did any other restaurant in the world.

Although Bergeron popularized the margarita, he did not invent it. Several different origin stories for margaritas have circulated. According to Marion Gorman and Felipe de Alba's *The Tequila Book,* one story traces the margarita to the bar at the Caliente Race Track in Tijuana, Mexico, about 1930. Another

credits Doña Bertha, owner of Bertha's Bar in Taxco, Mexico, with the invention of a drink that later evolved into the margarita. The former Los Angeles bartender Daniel Negrete claims to have originated the cocktail in 1936 at the Garcí Crespo Hotel in Puebla, Mexico, naming it after a girlfriend called Margarita. Although the margarita may have started out in bars, it quickly spread to Mexican restaurants. Los Angeles's El Cholo café served margaritas a few years after opening in 1927. Another contender for the title of originator was Margarita Sames, who made the drink for houseguests in 1948 while living in Acapulco, Mexico. Yet another story credited Pancho Morales, a bartender in Tommy's Place in Juárez, with the invention of the drink in 1942.

Whatever its origins, the margarita cocktail quickly spread throughout America during the 1960s. It became a staple in Mexican restaurants in the United States. In Mexico, restaurants that attracted the American tourist trade adopted margaritas. From the original margarita, Anglo tastes encouraged adaptations. Mariano Martinez Jr. purportedly assembled the first frozen margarita with crushed ice in 1971 at Dallas's El Charro Bar. In an attempt to hide tequila's taste, since not everyone liked it, the strawberry margarita and other flavor sensations appeared in bars and restaurants. As the twenty-first century opened, the margarita was one of America's most popular cocktails.

BIBLIOGRAPHY

Bergeron, Victor J. *Trader Vic's Pacific Island Cookbook with Side Trips to Hong Kong, Southeast Asia, Mexico, and Texas.* Garden City, NY: Doubleday, 1968.

Smith, Andrew F. "Tacos, Enchiladas and Refried Beans: The Invention of Mexican-American Cookery." In *Cultural and Historical Aspects of Foods,* ed. Mary Wallace Kelsey and ZoeAnn Holmes. Corvallis: Oregon State University, 1999.

ANDREW F. SMITH

Markets, *see Farmers' Markets; Grocery Stores*

Mars

Mars, Inc., one of the largest family-owned businesses in the United States and a global confectionery giant, began when Frank C. Mars (1883–1934) launched the Mar-O-Bar Company in 1911, making buttercream candies in his home in Tacoma, Washington. In 1920 Mars moved his company to larger quarters in Minneapolis, introducing Snickers (minus the chocolate coating) and Milky Way (1922) candy bars. Relocating again outside Chicago and renamed Mars Candies in 1926, the company prospered even during the Depression, when it successfully introduced Mars Almond Bar, chocolate-covered Snickers, and 3 Musketeers.

Forrest Mars (1904–1999) worked with his father at Mars Candies, but they had a tumultuous relationship. The younger Mars was sent to England in the early 1930s to start

his own company, aided by a sum of cash and the world rights for Milky Way candy bars from his father. Forrest, a driven perfectionist, first worked incognito in Swiss chocolate factories to learn more about candy making. In England, he produced a sweeter Milky Way, called a Mars Bar, building a successful candy company in addition to a canned pet food company, Pedigree.

Forrest returned to the United States in 1940, founding M and M Limited in Newark, New Jersey, with Bruce Murrie, the son of a Hershey executive. Borrowing the idea of a hard sugar shell from the British candy, Smarties, they created a chocolate candy—M&M's—that could be sold during the warm summer months when melting was a problem. M&M's became so popular that they were included in soldiers' rations during World War II. The company began using the ad slogan "Melts in your mouth, not in your hand" in 1954, the same year they introduced M&M Peanuts.

The 1960s was a decade of expansion. New plants were built in New Jersey and in Europe. Frank Mars's original company, Mars Candies, was merged with his son's in 1964. The consolidated company was named Mars, Inc. Although it was already the largest dog-food packer in the world, in 1968 Mars acquired another dog food company, Kal-Kan Foods Inc.

During the 1970s and 1980s Mars fought Hershey Foods for the leadership of the candy industry, a fight ultimately won by Hershey's in the United States. The era also saw the introduction of many new products: Bounty Bars, Combos, Starburst, Skittles, and Twix Cookie Bar. Mars also acquired the Dove Bar in 1985 (a hand-dipped ice cream bar with a thick chocolate coating developed by Leo Staphanos in Chicago in 1956) and created ice-cream versions of 3 Musketeers, Milky Way, and Snickers. The company, which also owned Uncle Ben's Rice, successfully introduced Uncle Ben's Rice Bowls, frozen, microwave dinners, in the late 1990s.

At the start of the twenty-first century, remaining family owned and notoriously secretive, the company, based in McLean, Virginia, was jointly run by Forrest Mars Sr.'s children, John and Jacqueline Badger Mars. (Another son, Forrest Jr., retired in 2000.) The Mars family had become one of the richest families in the United States.

[See also CANDY BARS AND CANDY; CHOCOLATE.]

BIBLIOGRAPHY

Brenner, Joel Glenn. *The Emperors of Chocolate.* New York: Random House, 1999.

Grant, Tina, ed. *International Directory of Company Histories.* Vol. 40. Farmington Hills, MI: Gale, 2001.

JOY SANTLOFER

Marshmallow Fluff

Marshmallow Fluff is a spreadable marshmallow cream developed in the Boston area around 1915 and produced since the 1920s at Durkee-Mower Incorporated in Lynn,

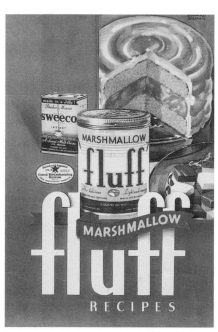

Recipe booklet for Marshmallow Fluff tested and approved by the Good Housekeeping Bureau.

Massachusetts. Marshmallow confections were first made by the French, who in the nineteenth century added whipped egg whites and sugar to the sticky sap from roots of the marshmallow plant (*Althaea officinalis*). The gooey result was called "*paté de guimauve.*" Before that, the sap, harvested from the roots of the plant, was used in northern Europe as a type of gum. During the eleventh century and through the Middle Ages, the mallow sap was also dispensed as a cure for colds.

The original Fluff recipe came from Archibald Query, a Boston-area man who made batches of it in his kitchen. He sold it door to door until the ingredients became too scarce during World War I. After the war, veterans H. Allen Durkee and Fred L. Mower pooled their savings and bought the recipe from Query for five hundred dollars. Durkee and Mower called their early product "Toot Sweet Marshmallow Fluff," a pun on the French expression *tout de suite*, which translates as "right away," and sold it door to door. The "Toot Sweet" was dropped, but the "Fluff" caught on with customers. In the late 1920s, Durkee and Mower began selling their product at retail stores and advertising in Boston newspapers. The first factory opened in 1929. From 1930 through the late 1940s, the company's *Flufferettes* show on the Yankee radio network attracted listeners from around New England.

Although Durkee-Mower also made Sweeco hot chocolate mix (originally Rich's Instant Sweet Milk Cocoa) for nearly thirty years, Fluff has remained its primary product. Recipes that use Fluff have become American classics. Never Fail Fudge, developed with Nestlé in 1956 from First Lady Mamie Eisenhower's recipe, is still reprinted on

Fluff labels. The peanut butter–Fluff combination, officially named the "Fluffernutter" in the 1960s, is still a lunchbox favorite in the early twenty-first century. Fluff is also made in raspberry and strawberry flavors, sold around the United States and internationally. [See also FUDGE; PEANUT BUTTER.]

BIBLIOGRAPHY

McLaughlin, Michael. *The Back of the Box Gourmet.* New York: Simon and Schuster, 1990.

Marshmallow Fluff. http://www.marshmallowfluff.com.

CLARA SILVERSTEIN

Martini

During the 1990s, the word "martini" became synonymous with the word "cocktail" and, in the early 2000s, was used to describe almost any drink served in a V-shaped cocktail glass, also known as a martini glass. The original martini appeared in cocktail recipe books during the 1880s and was made with Old Tom gin (a sweetened spirit), sweet vermouth, bitters (often orange-flavored bitters), and sometimes a little maraschino liqueur. A drink calling for identical ingredients, known as the Martinez, also appeared in cocktail books of that same era.

Some recipes for the Martinez instructed only that one should make it "like a Manhattan substituting Old Tom for the whiskey," indicating that the drink was merely a variation on the Manhattan. Dry martinis, made with dry gin, dry vermouth—usually in equal proportions—and orange bitters, did not appear in cocktail books until the years surrounding the turn of the twentieth century. There are many theories about why the name "Martinez" was changed to "martini," but the most likely answer is that the company marketing Martini and Rossi vermouth changed the name by advertising the drink in American newspapers. Sales of that brand of vermouth were massive compared with sales of other brands at the time, and the company has in its archives a 1906 newspaper advertisement that substantiates this claim.

Orange bitters remained an ingredient in the dry martini right up to, and even after, the years of Prohibition (1920–1933). Even during the so-called Great Drought, at least one book, printed in 1926 and "issued for the St. Botolph Society," detailed a martini that called for two parts gin to one part vermouth. This ratio was adhered to in many cocktail books published shortly after Prohibition was repealed. The bitters did not disappear from the drink in most books until the 1950s. This was also the time when gin became by far the main ingredient of the martini—sometimes comprising as much as seven-eighths of the drink. In 1958, *The Fine Art of Mixing Drinks*, by David Embury, mentioned that some bartenders were merely coating the interior of the cocktail glass with vermouth, shaking the vermouth out so that hardly any remained, and then adding

cold gin; still others were employing atomizers to add minuscule amounts of vermouth to the dry martini.

The same book by Embury also states that the vodka martini had reared its head by this time and comments: "It is hard to conceive of any worse cocktail monstrosity than the Vodka Martini." According to Barnaby Conrad III, author of 1995's *The Martini*, the earliest written mention of the vodka martini occurred in Ted Saucier's cocktail book *Bottoms Up* in 1951. Conrad wrote, "The recipe for a 'Vodkatini' was contributed by Jerome Zerbe, photographer and then society editor of *Town and Country.* Zerbe called for ⅘ jigger of Smirnoff vodka and ⅕ jigger of dry vermouth to be stirred with ice; the garnish was a twist of lemon peel." Substituting another liquor for the gin in a martini was also detailed by Embury, who allowed that martinis could be made with spirits such as rum and even tequila, and he included recipes for variations on the drink that called for other ingredients, such as sherry, curaçao, and crème de cassis.

The martini has often been used in literature and film to bring a sense of sophistication to a character. Lowell Edmunds's book *Martini, Straight Up*, published in 1998, explores this use in depth. Some famous people have used the drink to express how "American" something is. For example, President Gerald Ford said in a 1978 speech to the National Restaurant Association, "The Three Martini lunch is the epitome of American efficiency. Where else can you get an earful, a bellyful, and a snootful at the same time?"

Writers have also been known to wax lyrical on the subject of martinis. Bernard DeVoto claimed in his 1948 book *The Hour* that "you can no more keep a Martini in the refrigerator than you can keep a kiss there. The proper union of gin and vermouth is a great and sudden glory; it is one of the happiest marriages on earth and one of the shortest-lived." And the poet Ogden Nash gave us his take on the drink in his famed verse, "A Drink with Something in It":

> There is something about a Martini,
> A tingle remarkably pleasant;
> A yellow, a mellow Martini;
> I wish that I had one at present
>
> There is something about a Martini,
> Ere the dining and dancing begin,
> And to tell you the truth,
> It is not the vermouth—
> I think that perhaps it's the gin.

The 1971 edition of *Playboy's Host and Bar Book*, written by Thomas Mario, included recipes for martini variations that called for strawberry liqueur, sambuca, pineapple juice, lime juice, and even cream, so it is hardly surprising that by 2000 the word "martini" had become an acceptable substitute for the word "cocktail." But the debate on the question whether "martini" was a logical synonym for "cocktail" raged in the barrooms of America. At the turn of the twenty-first century, it was not uncommon to be offered a menu full of all manner of cocktails when ordering a martini at a bar, and the so-called purist who desired a mixture of gin and dry vermouth had to specify a dry gin martini. The vodka martini, meanwhile, grew in popularity until by the 1990s many bartenders claimed that the vodka version outsold the gin-based variety by at least ten to one.

Garnishes for the martini have varied over the years, but the 1906 book *Louis' Mixed Drinks with Hints for the Care and Service of Wines*, by Louis Muckensturm, suggests a twist of lemon peel, and the 1912 book *Hoffman House Bartender's Guide: How to Open a Saloon and Make It Pay* calls for a cherry or an olive as well as a lemon twist, although the recipe in that book is for a martini made with Old Tom and sweet vermouth. The Gibson, a dry gin martini garnished with cocktail onions, was reportedly created at New York's Players Club in the 1930s, but recipes for the drink without the onion garnish appeared in Jacques Straub's *Drinks*, published in 1914, as well as Tom Bullock's 1917 book *The Ideal Bartender*. In the twenty-first century, all manner of garnishes made their way into martinis, and it was possible at some bars to order the drink served with caper berries, cornichons, or even pickled quail eggs.

[See also COCKTAILS; GIN; VERMOUTH.]

BIBLIOGRAPHY

Connrad, Barnaby, III. *The Martini: An Illustrated History of an American Classic.* San Francisco: Chronicle Books, 1995.

GARY AND MARDEE HAIDIN REGAN

Märzen/Oktoberfest

In 1810, the first Oktoberfest was held in Munich's "village green" to celebrate the wedding of Prince Luitpold of Bavaria and his bride the Bavarian Queen Theresia. It was such a fun wedding that the citizens of Munich have celebrated it every year since (with only two or three years when political and military events overshadowed the celebration).

Oktoberfest, the beer, was introduced in 1872 when the Spaten brewery began offering what they called Ur-Märzen the "original" Märzen. The beer grew out of collaboration between Spaten's Gabriel Sedlmayr and Anton Dreher of Vienna, hence the term Vienna beer.

The story begins in 1841, when Viennese brewer Anton Dreher began brewing a new beer. It had a reddish, copper color and a sweet malt character. It was an immediate success. Dreyer's Vienna beer did not go unnoticed by Gabriel Sedlmayr at the Spaten brewery in Munich. He was soon introduced his own version, a beer called Märzen ("March beer"). It was an amber-red, malty, medium alcohol content, crystal clear, and bottom fermented with lager yeast. The result

of this fermentation is a style of beer with a richer malt aroma than flavor, and slightly more hop flavor than aroma.

Traditionally, it is brewed in March and stored in a cold environment (lagered) until late September when Oktoberfest actually begins.

According to the *Association of Brewers' 2004 Beer Style Guidelines*, "The American style of this classic German beer is distinguished by a comparatively greater degree of hop character. Oktoberfests can range from golden to reddish brown. Malt character should be light-toasted rather than strongly caramel (though a low level of light caramel character is acceptable). Bread or biscuit-like malt character is acceptable in aroma and flavor. Sweet maltiness should dominate over a clean, hop bitterness. The bitterness should not be aggressive or harsh. Hop aroma and flavor should be notable but at low to medium levels." Alcohol content should range between 5.3 and 5.9 percent by volume.

PETER LAFRANCE

Mason Jars

The mason jar—a glass canning jar with a sealable metal lid—revolutionized fruit and vegetable preservation in the home, freeing Americans from earlier, more complicated and less reliable processes of preserving fruits and vegetables. It was the invention of John L. Mason of New Jersey, who had a metalworking shop on Canal Street in New York City. On November 30, 1858, when he was twenty-six years old, Mason patented a self-sealing zinc lid to fit preserving jars. A rubber gasket between the glass lip and zinc lid completed the seal. The inexpensive screw-on lid greatly simplified the canning process and made jars genuinely reusable. As the jars had wide mouths, they were easy to fill. Although his name remained on the jar, Mason's control of his invention was short lived. In 1859, he sold his patent to Lewis R. Boyd, who owned the Sheet Metal Screw Company of New York. Boyd made additional improvements, one of which separated the zinc lid from the contents of the jar. As the jars were easy to use and comparatively inexpensive to produce, their popularity soared, and mason jars were shipped throughout the United States during the 1860s.

In 1871, Boyd's company was merged with others to form the Consolidated Fruit Jar Company. Since then, numerous companies have manufactured mason jars, and containers very similar to Mason's original are still in use. Several improvements to Mason's design have been developed over the years. The most important is credited to Alexander H. Kerr, who founded the Hermetic Fruit Jar Company in 1903. Kerr invented a two-piece lid composed of a flat metal disk with a rubber gasket attached to its underside; a threaded metal band, which overlapped the disk, screwed onto the jar and held the lid in place. Once the jar was filled, sterilized, and cooled, the

Advertisement for Payne's fruit preserves, which used mason jars. Reprinted in Mason Jar Centennial, 1858–1958.

disk was sealed to the jar, and the threaded band could be removed and used for canning another batch. This innovation was employed in the "economy" jar, which has been manufactured ever since.

In addition to improving home canning, the mason jar also provided the inspiration for major advances in commercial canning. Commercial food processors confronted problems similar to those of home canners. In the late nineteenth century, commercial canners, who packed food into metal cans, began using thick rubber gaskets similar to those used in mason jars. The rubber rings, however, were cumbersome and costly. Charles M. Ams came up with the idea of lining the rim of the tin can with a rubber cement. This innovation greatly reduced the amount of rubber required and sped up the canning process. The result contributed to the creation of the "sanitary can," which simplified and sped up the sealing process, revolutionizing can manufacture and use.

[See also CANNING AND BOTTLING; PACKAGING.]

BIBLIOGRAPHY

Creswick, Alice. *The Fruit Jar Works.* 2 vols. N. Muskegon, MI: Leybourne, 1995.

Toulouse, Julian H. *Fruit Jars.* Camden, NJ: Nelson, 1969.

ANDREW F. SMITH

Matzo

Matzo is the unleavened bread baked in great haste by the children of Israel on the eve of their flight from Egypt (Exodus 12:8). Every year at Passover, or the Feast of Unleavened

Bread, the eating of matzo and the purging of all leavened products from the home commemorate this flight (Exodus 12: 15–39, 13: 6–7, and 23:15). Unleavened bread is the only food the children of Israel are actually commanded to eat in the Hebrew Bible. In this sense, matzo is the most Jewish food there is. The foods that are called Jewish foods are almost always the regional foods from areas where Jews have settled in large numbers. These Jewish foods may be different from the local non-Jewish food, but they bear more resemblance to non-Jewish food of their own region than to Jewish food from far away. The exception is matzo. Every Jewish community has some variation of matzo. The variations in shape and thickness, however, are minor, since the laws of matzo manufacture are so very specific. All matzo must be prepared in less than eighteen minutes from the moment water comes into contact with flour to the moment the fully baked matzo emerges from the oven.

For most of its three-thousand-year history, matzo was made only by hand in an exhausting and very expensive process. Because matzo was so expensive, it was generally eaten only on Passover and only by Jews. In the middle of the nineteenth century, with the invention of machinery for matzo manufacture, matzo producers promoted their product as suitable for the whole year.

The first major American matzo concern was started in 1883, when Regina Horowitz Margareten and her husband, Ignatz Margareten, immigrated to Manhattan from Hungary. Their families opened a grocery store on Willett Street on the Lower East Side of New York City. They baked their own matzo for themselves their first year, and the next year they produced extra matzo for sale in their store. A few years later, they abandoned the grocery store to devote themselves to the baking of matzo.

In 1888, Rabbi Dov Ber Manischewitz opened the B. Manischewitz company in Cincinnati, Ohio, to provide reliably kosher matzo in the West. A few years later, he opened a second factory in New Jersey and made Manischewitz a national brand. Manischewitz matzo became the best-known and best-selling American matzo, thanks to the company's aggressive campaign to market matzo as a year-round food. The hallmark of this campaign was the commercials on Yiddish-language radio written and recorded by the great Yiddish lexicographer, playwright, and performer Nahum Stutchkoff. In these brilliant spots for Manischewitz American Matzos, Stutchkoff always emphasized the combination of Jewish and American virtues that made Manischewitz matzo unique. In one memorable ad for Tam Tam crackers, Stutchkoff noted that the crackers had two great virtues: a Jewish heritage and an American upbringing. He could have been speaking about his listeners' own children.

By the end of the twentieth century, the Streit's company, founded in 1925, was the only major American matzo company still located in Manhattan.

Most of the matzo consumed in the Americas and worldwide is machine-made. There are, however, still matzo bakeries in New York, Montreal, and Israel that make hand matzo. This matzo is called *shmura matzo*, or guarded matzo, to reflect the fact that it is under rabbinic supervision at every point in the process from the harvesting and milling of the wheat to the baking of the matzo.

[See also JEWISH AMERICAN FOOD; JEWISH DIETARY LAWS; PASSOVER.]

EVE JOCHNOWITZ

Maxwell House

Maxwell House Coffee, one of the two dominant mass-market American coffees, was the creation of Joel Owsley Cheek, a rural Kentucky native who served as a drummer, or traveling salesman, for a wholesale grocery firm. In 1884, he moved to Nashville, Tennessee, and in 1892 approached the Maxwell House, a prestigious Nashville hotel, with his special blend of coffee. Impressed with consumer reaction, the hotel manager allowed Cheek to name his blend after the establishment.

Cheek quit his job in 1893 and formed a partnership with John Neal. The Cheek-Neal Coffee Company established a successful business in the Nashville area, opening additional roasting facilities in Houston, Texas; Jacksonville, Florida; and Richmond, Virginia, by 1916. Six of Cheek's eight sons joined the firm. Cheek was a gracious boss who truly cared for his employees and believed that coffee was a boon to humankind. He was also a master marketer. He adopted the slogan "Good to the Last Drop" in 1920, claiming that Teddy Roosevelt had used the phrase in reference to Maxwell House Coffee. General Foods purchased Maxwell House in 1928, taking the brand national with ads featuring southern hospitality. During much of the Depression the *Maxwell House Show Boat* was the top rated radio show, with favorite characters slurping the coffee audibly throughout the program.

During World War II, Maxwell House produced patriotic print ads extolling the lift the troops got from instant and regular coffee. In the postwar era, Instant Maxwell House ads claimed that its crystals "burst instantly into that famous good-to-the-last-drop flavor," although it tasted only remotely like regular coffee. General Foods also began to put cheaper robusta beans into the regular Maxwell House blend.

In 1960, television viewers saw the now-classic Maxwell House percolator ad, with its perky theme music. The company introduced Maxim, the first freeze-dried instant coffee, in 1964. The following year saw the introduction of the sexist "Be a Maxwell Housewife"

commercials, in which a patronizing husband taught his wife to make coffee. Later, the down-home Aunt Cora character touted Maxwell House to counter Folgers's Mrs. Olson.

Despite some heartwarming commercials over the years, General Foods failed to understand or to take advantage of the specialty coffee movement. It pulled innovative 1983 spots featuring the comedian Jerry Seinfeld, and it mishandled the 1985 introduction of whole beans in supermarkets, in part because it distributed to warehouses rather than following the lead of small specialty roasters, who sent out individual supervisors to put freshly roasted beans directly on shelves. Late in 1985, the tobacco giant Philip Morris, looking to diversify in the face of hostility to cancer-causing cigarettes, bought General Foods. Philip Morris also owned Gevalia, a high-quality Swedish coffee roaster, and Jacobs Kaffee, the major German brand, among others.

[See also COFFEE; COFFEE, INSTANT.]

BIBLIOGRAPHY

Pendergrast, Mark. *Uncommon Grounds: The History of Coffee and How It Transformed Our World.* New York: Basic Books, 1999.

MARK PENDERGRAST

Mayonnaise

Mayonnaise is a thick sauce traditionally composed of egg yolk beaten up with oil, vinegar, and seasonings. How mayonnaise acquired its name has been debated for years, and the only general agreement is that the word "mayonnaise" was popularized by the French. Historically, mayonnaise was based on aioli—a Catalan and Provençal sauce that combined olive oil, eggs, and garlic. In the late eighteenth century, the French whipped the egg and slowly added oil. The lecithin in the egg yolks acted as an emulsifier and broke the oil into droplets. Mayonnaise became one the five foundation sauces of classical French cookery. It is an adaptable ingredient, used in many dishes and other sauces.

Mayonnaise was mentioned in cookbooks published in the United States by 1829, but it did not become an important condiment until the end of the nineteenth century. The major reason for this delay was the high cost of imported olive oil. Several factors contributed to the increase in the popularity of mayonnaise in America during the last few decades of the nineteenth century. One was the use of mayonnaise in upscale American restaurants, such as Delmonico's in New York, by French chefs during the latter part of the nineteenth century. Another factor was a decrease in olive oil's price, owing to production of domestic olive oil in Florida and California. Yet another reason was that mayonnaise was used to make salad dressings and other condiments, such as tartar sauce. Indeed, the main use of mayonnaise during the late nineteenth century was on salads and as an accompaniment to cold fish and meats. There had been a vast increase in American interest in fresh green salads, caused in part by a transportation revolution that made it possible to grow salad vegetables in California and Florida and transport them long distances year-round. During the twentieth century, mayonnaise replaced butter as a sandwich spread. Along with the hamburger, American mayonnaise rose to global prominence.

Recipes for making mayonnaise and for using it as an ingredient in other dishes began to appear regularly in American cookbooks by 1880 and in cookery magazines shortly thereafter. Depending on the ingredients, the results of these recipes differed in color (white, yellow, green, or red), taste (garlic, horseradish, or red pepper), and content (salmon, lobster, or chicken). Mayonnaise recipes were targeted for specific use on salads, poultry, fish, shellfish, and meats.

Commercial Mayonnaise Production

Mayonnaise separates and easily spoils and does not survive the bottling process. Commercial mayonnaise therefore differs greatly from that which is made fresh. The first known attempt to make a commercial mayonnaise occurred in 1907, when a delicatessen owner in Philadelphia named Schlorer mixed up a batch of his wife's mayonnaise in the back of his store and added preservatives. He marketed it as "Mrs. Schlorer's Mayonnaise," and it led to the creation of the Schlorer Delicatessen Company, which produced commercial salad dressings, including mayonnaise. In 1911, Schlorer trademarked his mayonnaise. The company began producing advertising cookbooklets featuring mayonnaise during the 1920s.

Schlorer's competition came from four major firms: Hellmann's, Best Foods, Kraft, and Blue Plate. The German immigrant Richard Hellmann opened a delicatessen in New York City in 1905, and his wife's recipe for mayonnaise was featured in salads sold in the store. In 1912 Hellmann began to sell mayonnaise in wooden containers. Later, he marketed two versions of mayonnaise in glass jars, around one of which he put a blue ribbon. There was such a great demand that Hellmann designed a Blue Ribbon label, which was trademarked in 1926. In the same year Hellmann produced his first advertising cookbooklet, which encouraged customers to incorporate his mayonnaise into various dishes. In 1932, Richard Hellmann Inc. was acquired by Best Foods Inc.

In about 1912, Gold Medal Mayonnaise Company began producing mayonnaise in California. In 1923, it merged with Nucoa to form Best Foods. Best Foods began publishing advertising cookbooklets featuring its mayonnaise by 1927. When Richard Hellmann's firm was acquired by Best Foods in 1932, Hellmann's mayonnaise was sold east of the Rockies and Best Foods mayonnaise

in the west. Both Best Foods and Hellmann's are now part of Unilever. In New Orleans the Southern Cotton Oil Company, a subsidiary of Wesson-Snowdrift, produced mayonnaise in 1929 under the name Blue Plate Food. Through several mergers, Blue Plate Mayonnaise remains a regional product marketed in the South.

Kraft introduced Miracle Whip at the 1933 Century of Progress World's Fair in Chicago. The company was founded in 1903 by James L. Kraft, who sold cheese in Chicago, Illinois. By 1914, the company had begun manufacturing its own cheese. When Miracle Whip was introduced, Kraft launched a major food advertising campaign, including a weekly two-hour radio show. At the end of this introductory period, Miracle Whip outsold all brands of mayonnaise. In the late 1980s, Kraft introduced Miracle Whip Light and Miracle Whip Cholesterol Free. In 1991, Miracle Whip Free, with no fat at all, was launched. Mayonnaise is a major American condiment: in 2000, Americans purchased more than 745 million bottles of mayonnaise. American mayonnaise is increasingly sold in other countries, which can be attributed, in part, to the global spread of American fast food.

[See also Advertising Cookbooklets and Recipes; Condiments; Salads and Salad Dressings.]

BIBLIOGRAPHY

Association for Dressings and Sauces. http://www.dressings-sauces.org/index.html.

SBI Market Profile: Salad Dressings and Mayonnaise. New York: Specialists in Business Information, 1996.

ANDREW F. SMITH

McDonald's

When Ray Kroc, a salesman, met two drive-in restaurant operators, Richard and Maurice McDonald, in 1954, America's foodscape changed forever. Richard and Maurice

McDonald, born in New Hampshire, moved to southern California to make their fortune in 1930. After several jobs, they opened a hot dog stand and later graduated to a barbecue drive-in.

Origins

In 1948, the brothers opened a hamburger drive-in in San Bernardino, California, which applied assembly-line efficiency to the restaurant business. They eliminated carhops and waitresses and did not have indoor tables. Customers ordered their food at an outdoor window and ate it in their cars. The menu was limited to a few items: fifteen-cent hamburgers, nineteen-cent cheeseburgers, french fries, milkshakes, and sodas. Their hamburgers came with ketchup, mustard, chopped onions, and two pickles. All food was served in disposable paper wrappers and paper cups. The brothers sped up the process of making hamburgers through a series of innovations; for example, they assigned some workers to make and wrap the food while others took orders, prepared the drinks, and packed the food into paper bags. They purchased Multimixers, which made five milkshakes simultaneously, to speed up the preparation of drink orders.

The McDonald brothers called this the Speedee Service System. It reduced expenses, permitting the McDonald brothers to sell hamburgers at a lower price. The brothers believed that the increased volume of customers would lead to greater profits. Their efforts to streamline their system and mass-produce hamburgers paid off. In 1951, they grossed $275,000.

As efficient as their internal operation was, the McDonald brothers concluded that they could do even better with a new floor plan. They also wanted a more distinctive exterior architectural design to distinguish their drive-in from the hundreds of other

A McDonald's drive-in, sometime after 1958, when 100 million burgers had already been sold.

fast-food establishments in southern California. Their new plan called for a forward-sloping front and walls painted in red and white stripes. Richard McDonald came up with the idea of constructing yellow or "golden" arches right through the building's roof.

Even before their new design was constructed, the McDonald brothers franchised their operation. This permitted others to build McDonald's drive-ins based on the model developed in San Bernardino. Those receiving franchises paid the McDonald brothers an up-front fee and a percentage of their sales. In 1953 newly designed franchises opened in Phoenix, Arizona, and Downey, California.

All the early McDonald's drive-ins attracted crowds. One visitor to the San Bernardino operation was Ray Kroc, born in 1902 in Oak Park, Illinois. After a variety of odd jobs, he had settled on selling Lily paper cups. After seventeen years of selling cups successfully, he launched the Prince Castle Sales Corporation. Its main product was the Multimixer for soda fountains and restaurants. He also sold Multimixers to many fast food franchisees, including Dairy Queen and Tastee Freez. These customers had given Kroc a deeper understanding of the fast food business and some knowledge of the problems related to franchising. In the early 1950s, increased competition had reduced the sales of Multimixers and Kroc needed new outlets. He was surprised to learn that a small San Bernardino drive-in had bought eight Multimixers. His curiosity aroused, Kroc visited the McDonald brothers in 1954.

Kroc saw the potential of the McDonald's operation immediately. Ever the optimist, Kroc met with the brothers and signed an agreement allowing him to sell McDonald's franchises nationwide. In the mid-1950s, franchising consisted mainly of assigning territories to franchisees for huge up-front fees. Kroc had a better idea. He avoided territorial franchises by selling one store franchise at a time, thereby controlling the number of stores a licensee could operate. He also required strict conformity to operating standards, menus, recipes, prices, trademarks, and architectural designs.

On April 15, 1955, Kroc opened his first McDonald's in Des Plaines, Illinois. It was intended as a model operation to attract franchisees. It worked. By the end of 1957, there were thirty-seven McDonald's. Two years later, the total had reached over one hundred. In 1961, Kroc bought out the McDonald brothers for $2.7 million.

The early success of McDonald's rested in part on the managers selected to oversee operations. Kroc's mantra was "Quality, Service, Cleanliness, and Value," which he tried to instill in every franchisee. Kroc was also so committed to training managers that he established Hamburger University, which offered a degree in "Hamburgerology." The first class of fifteen graduated in February 1961. By the early 2000s, sixty-five thousand managers had graduated.

Kroc expanded his operation throughout America. Within a decade of his first encounter with the McDonald brothers, Ray Kroc had revolutionized fast food service through further automation, improved franchising, and national advertising, which began in 1966. The company's promotional campaigns have targeted youth primarily. Ronald McDonald, a created clown character, was invented to be the national spokesperson in 1966, and McDonald's began opening children's Playlands shortly thereafter. It has tied in much of its marketing with major children's motion pictures. McDonald's Happy Meal, inaugurated in 1979, packages its food with toys. At the beginning of the twenty-first century, 96 percent of American children recognize Ronald McDonald, and McDonald's is the world's largest toy distributor.

Innovation and Globalization
Kroc's success encouraged the growth of other fast food chains, which readily adopted McDonald's methods. To keep ahead of the competition, McDonald's has developed new products regularly, such as the Big Mac with its two patties, introduced in 1968. Other innovations include the Quarter Pounder, the McDLT, and the McLean Deluxe, a 90 percent fat-free hamburger. In 1983, McDonald's introduced Chicken McNuggets, consisting of reconstituted chicken delivered to franchises frozen and then reheated before serving.

McDonald's opened its first Canadian drive-in in 1967. Its success convinced Kroc that McDonald's should expand aggressively to other countries. It has continued to expand abroad ever since. Kroc had originally envisioned one thousand McDonald's operations in the United States. When he died in 1984 at the age of eighty-one, there were 7,500 McDonald's outlets worldwide.

By 1994 McDonald's counted more than 4,500 restaurants in seventy-three foreign countries. At the opening of the twenty-first century, there were more than thirty thousand restaurants in about 121 countries. McDonald's operated over one thousand restaurants in Japan alone. The most popular restaurant in Japan, measured by volume of customers, was McDonald's. In the early 2000s, the world's largest McDonald's was in business near Red Square in Moscow, where a Big Mac lunch cost the equivalent of a week's paycheck. McDonald's boasted 127 restaurants in China—one of which overlooked Tiananmen Square in Beijing. McDonald's international sales were $15 billion out of a total of almost $32 billion.

In part because of McDonald's success, the company has been criticized on a variety of issues. When it was charged with promoting junk food, the company began selling salads, reduced the fat content of its hamburgers, and changed the way it made its french fries. When charged with causing harm to the environment, McDonald's encouraged recycling, purchased more than

$4 billion of recycled materials for its own operations, replaced its Styrofoam containers with more biodegradable material, and refused to buy beef from Brazil, thus helping to protect the rain forests.

McDonald's also has been charged with having adverse effects on local cultures and businesses around the world. McDonald's success abroad has caused deep resentment in others who see the company as a symbol for the United States and who believe that the expansion of McDonald's threatens local culinary traditions. In France, the sheep farmer Jose Bove demolished a McDonald's restaurant that was nearing completion. Similar actions have occurred in other European countries. McDonald's has pointed out that its foreign operations are locally owned and most ingredients used in McDonald's restaurants are produced in the country where the franchise resides.

The study of McDonald's has become a hot academic topic. Many popular works have tried to dissect the company's success and examine its influence. Among the more famous studies are George Ritzer's *The McDonaldization of Society* (1993), which examines the social effects of McDonald's in the United States; Benjamin Barber's *Jihad vs. McWorld* (1995), which uses McDonald's as a global symbol for modernization; and Eric Schlosser's *Fast Food Nation: The Dark Side of the All-American Meal* (2001), which looks at the seamier side of fast food. Dozens of other works have examined McDonald's worldwide impact.

By the end of the twentieth century, one of every eight American workers had, at some point, been employed by McDonald's. Globally McDonald's served an estimated 20 million customers every day. It was the world's largest purchaser of beef, and its french fries required 7.5 percent of America's entire potato crop. McDonald's was one of the world's most famous brand names.

[**See also** Drive-Ins; Fast Food; French Fries: Twentieth Century; Hamburger; Ronald McDonald.]

BIBLIOGRAPHY

Gould, William. *Business Portraits: McDonald's*. Lincolnwood, IL: VGM Career Horizons, 1996.

Kroc, Ray, with Robert Anderson. *Grinding It Out: The Making of McDonald's*. Chicago: St. Martin's, 1987.

Love, John F. *McDonald's: Behind the Arches*. Rev. ed. New York: Bantam, 1995.

Ritzer, George. *The McDonaldization of Society*. Newbury Park, CA: Pine Forge Press, 1993.

Schlosser, Eric. *Fast Food Nation: The Dark Side of the All-American Meal*. Boston and New York: Houghton Mifflin, 2001.

ANDREW F. SMITH

McDonaldization

The term *McDonaldization* was coined by Jim Hightower in his book *Eat Your Heart Out* (1975). Hightower was a farm activist who warned that fast food threatened independent businesses and family-owned farms. He believed that the practices of international fast food chains, such as McDonald's, were creating a food economy dominated by giant corporations. According to Hightower, "Not only are hams becoming uniformly bland, but so is American taste. Not only are local beers disappearing, but so is local identity."

The term was picked up and popularized in academic circles by the sociologist George Ritzer, whose book *The McDonaldization of Society* (1993), examined the social effects of McDonald's in the United States. McDonald's rigorously controlled the appearance of each of its outlets, as well as their menus, equipment, procedures, advertising, suppliers, and polices. McDonald's success had given rise to many imitators, not only in fast food industry, but throughout America's retail economy. Ritzer defined McDonaldization as "the principles by which the fast-food restaurant are coming to dominate more and more sectors of American society and of the world." The principles included efficiency, predictability, and control. According to Ritzer, McDonald's exhibits "the irrationality of rationality." Ritzer attacked the fast food industry for its homogenizing influence on American eating habits. He reports that customers and employees are "socialized into, and have internalized, the norms and values of working and living in a McDonaldized society."

McDonald's and other fast food chains have set up shop in the rest of the world, and the phenomenon has been studied by a number of scholars, including James L. Watson, whose *Golden Arches East: McDonald's in East Asia* (1997) examined the effects of McDonald's in Japan, Korea, China, and Southeast Asia. Many other academic articles and books have been written on McDonaldization, notably *McDonaldization Revisited: Critical Essays on Consumer Culture* (1998), edited by Mark Alfino, John S. Caputo, and Robin Wynyard. Globally, the term McDonaldization is broadly used to mean the acceptance of Western eating (and other) habits in other countries.

BIBLIOGRAPHY

Alfino, Mark, John S. Caputo, and Robin Wynyard, eds. *McDonaldization Revisited: Critical Essays on Consumer Culture.* Westport, CT: Greenwood Publishing Group, 1998.

Hightower, Jim. *Eat Your Heart Out: Food Profiteering in America.* New York: Crown Publishers, [1975].

Ritzer, George. *The McDonaldization of Society.* Rev. ed. Thousand Oaks, CA: Pine Forge Press, 1996.

Ritzer, George. *The McDonaldization Thesis: Explorations and Extensions.* London; Thousand Oaks, CA; and New Delhi: Sage Publications, 1998.

Smart, Barry, ed. *Resisting McDonaldization.* London; Thousand Oaks, CA: Sage, 1999.

ANDREW F. SMITH

Meal Patterns

American meal patterns over the past four centuries have varied across different regions of the country and have been determined by an individual's occupation, social class, gender, ethnicity, and personal preferences. Seasons, holidays, and the weekly round of activities also played a part in determining what is eaten when.

All meals, whether served at home or in a restaurant, are structured events. Seating arrangements often reflect status. Rituals, including prayers and other formal components of meals, are often observed. Etiquette rules for eating became commonly accepted, and divergence from these rules reflects badly on the rule breaker. Most dinners follow a typical pattern from savory to sweet. Meals also move from simple salads to more complex foods, the desserts often being the most difficult dish to prepare. Dinners served on special occasions, such as birthdays, weddings, and holidays, often connect the individuals to the wider social fabric.

Colonial Times
In colonial times, American meal patterns followed European practices, in which the extended family participated in meals, which occurred three times a day: the standard meals were breakfast, dinner, and supper. As the first meal of the day, breakfast literally broke the fast. It was eaten immediately on rising or a few hours later, after the earliest chores had been completed. A summer breakfast might consist of dishes like bread, rice, milk-pudding, cheese, cold meat, smoked fish, fowl, and fresh berries; milk, cider, coffee, tea, or chocolate were common breakfast beverages. Cold weather called for a heartier meal that might include toast soaked in milk, warm muffins, barley cakes, buckwheat cakes, waffles, mush, hominy, or baked pumpkin.

Working men and schoolchildren returned home for dinner, the main meal of the day, which was traditionally served in the early or late afternoon. For the upper classes, this could be a formal and lengthy meal replete with multiple courses of meats, poultry, seafood, vegetables, followed by lavish sweets such as flummeries, trifles, or whipped syllabub. Middle-class dinners would be somewhat pared-down versions of the upper-class meal. The lower classes, poor farmers, indentured servants, and slaves ate what they could produce on their own or afford to buy, usually simple fare such as a pudding or mush, game, stews, soups, and home-grown vegetables.

Supper, the last meal of the day, was light and, sometimes, optional. It was eaten in the early evening. In some regions and at certain times of year, supper was similar to breakfast; in New England, for example, pie was eaten at both meals. In other settings, supper was composed of dinner leftovers, or a simple soup, plus dessert.

For women who kept house, and for the servants and slaves of those who did not, this traditional meal pattern required hours of hard work. They had to rise early (4 A.M. was not unusual) to prepare the hearth or stove fire, cook and serve breakfast, and clean up afterward; preparation for the next meal began almost immediately. To keep food on the table there was also marketing, gardening, baking, and preserving to be done—in addition to other rigorous household chores such as keeping the stove clean and doing the laundry.

The Nineteenth Century
The traditional meal pattern began to change during the mid-nineteenth century, in part as a result of the growth of cities and the shifting occupations of American men. The first meal to change was dinner. As towns and cities grew, it became more difficult for workers to return home for dinner at midday as the distance between the home and the place of work increased. Workers earning an hourly wage did not have paid lunch breaks, so they tended to eat as quickly as possible. And if a husband and wife both worked, a relaxed noontime meal at home with the family was out of the question.

Dinner, the most important meal of the day, moved to the evening, when the family could dine together at a more leisurely pace. The midday repast came to be called lunch (shortened from "luncheon") and evolved into a small, light, and frequently rushed meal—often something brought from home in a tin pail or a brown bag, or a quick bite in a workplace cafeteria. Sandwiches, soups, and salads became common luncheon foods.

Although somewhat more the masters of their own schedules, professionals, such as doctors, lawyers, and businessmen, rarely had time to home for a long afternoon meal. So they ate large, hearty breakfasts and big dinners, and skipped lunch or ate something light at work. By contrast, sometimes business was conducted over an extended lunch similar to the dinners of earlier years, but these meals were eaten in restaurants, not at home. Middle- and upper-class women, once they no longer had to spend the morning preparing the family dinner, were now free to seek out their own social activities, such as women's clubs, which frequently met at a member's home for lunch. These ladies' lunches—usually dainty fare because there were no men present—became a field for social competition as each hostess attempted to outdo the last with clever table decorations, color-coordinated foods, and favors.

To fill the void between lunch, usually consumed at noon, and dinner, usually eaten at 8 P.M. in upper-class homes, afternoon tea was served at 4 or 5 P.M. Having the main meal of the day served late in the evening necessitated a shift in breakfast, as many people who eat a late and heavy dinner were not hungry for a big breakfast. Lighter breakfasts, consisting of fruit, bread, coffee, or tea, became common at the end of the nineteenth century. For those of the leisure class who were inclined to sleep late, a hybrid meal called "brunch" became popular. Eaten in late morning or early afternoon,

Late nineteenth-century lithograph of a family meal.

brunch could consist of breakfast foods such as eggs and waffles, or could be made up of heartier foods such as would normally be served at lunch. Alcoholic beverages made with breakfast juices (mimosas, Bloody Marys, and screwdrivers) became a standard accompaniment. Brunch became a meal for relaxing on weekends, whether eaten in a restaurant or enjoyed with guests at home.

By the late nineteenth century, the evening meal became the major meal of the day; it evolved into an occasion for entertaining. Among the affluent, dinner was served later and the offerings were much more sumptuous than they had been. Most meals contained meat, particularly beef, which became abundant as cattlemen in the western states and territories began raising and transporting cattle to markets thousands of miles away.

The Twentieth Century

Yet another major shift in American meal patterns was caused by the rise of commercial food processors. The breakfast food industry challenged the traditional morning menu with quick-cooking and ready-to-eat cereals such as granola, rolled oats, grape nuts, and cornflakes. These new products, promoted as healthful, began to replace the traditional, heavier breakfast foods. During the 1920s, the orange juice industry used the same technique of stressing the healthful qualities of orange juice as a breakfast drink and within a decade, fruit juice became a major breakfast food fad throughout America.

The rise of the snack food industry around the turn of the twentieth century wrought a major change in American eating habits. Eating between meals was a new option. Confections, candy, and roasted nuts, which had previously been available only at fairs, circuses, and other special events, were now widely available for on-the-spot consumption and to keep on hand at home. As the twentieth century progressed, breakfast

often became a quick downing of a commercial drink something like a milk shake or the consumption of a breakfast bar while running out the door.

After World War II, the American meal pattern changed yet again. With men away at war and women taking their places in the work force, getting a family meal on the table was a challenge. Prepared, processed, canned, frozen, or dehydrated foods requiring little kitchen time were a boon to the working mother. Toward the end of the twentieth century, the microwave oven took center stage as the source of hot meals at home and in the workplace. At the same time, Americans were increasingly eating their meals away from home, and cafeterias, lunch counters, cafes, restaurants, and fast food outlets flourished.

Snacking became increasingly common as the century progressed, and the "three squares" diminished in importance. Eating a series of small meals and snacks throughout the day—"grazing" or "noshing"—became popular in some circles in the 1980s; it was thought to be more healthful than sitting down to three heavy meals a day.

BIBLIOGRAPHY

Barbara Haber. *From Hardtack to Home Fries: An Uncommon History of American Cooks and Meals.* New York: Free Press, 2002.

Levenstein, Harvey A. *Revolution at the Table: The Transformation of the American Diet.* New York and Oxford: Oxford University Press, 1988.

ANDREW F. SMITH

Meals on Wheels

There is an old folk saying that goes, "Old John would half-starve were there no woman to prepare his meals; old Nellie would starve if she had no one to share her cooking." Until the middle of the twentieth century many elderly people, living alone and isolated from families and friends, died prematurely from hunger and malnutrition. The situation changed for the better for some elderly people

in January 1954, when a group of volunteers at the Lighthouse, a settlement house in the Kensington area of Philadelphia, started to deliver noontime meals, five days a week, to elderly, isolated shut-ins. They modeled their program after a civil-defense program started by the Women's Voluntary Services in Great Britain to feed the aged during the blitz. As word about Philadelphia's so-called meals-on-wheels spread, communities across the country began their own volunteer programs. More than three hundred of them started over the next twenty years.

The idea for using federal dollars to expand this service took root at the 1961 White House Conference on Aging. The deciding event that finally prompted action was the publication in 1965 of the shocking findings from a national food-consumption survey conducted by the U.S. Department of Agriculture. This study found that as many as 6 million to 8 million older persons might have deficient diets. A task force on nutrition was created to develop both administrative and legislative recommendations for correcting the problem. In 1968, Congress appropriated $2 million to fund a national demonstration to determine whether a nationwide model for feeding older people was feasible. Twenty-three demonstration programs tested two potential models for providing meals to older people: meals taken to the home, called home-delivered meals, and meals served in group settings, called congregate meals. The home-delivered–meals model was clearly derived from existing meals-on-wheels programs. The congregate program took as its model the meals programs operated in the Jewish settlement houses located on the Lower East Side of Manhattan.

On March 22, 1972, a law was passed creating the Elderly Nutrition Program to be administered nationwide by the Administration on Aging, then part of the U.S. Department of Health, Education, and Welfare, now the Department of Health and Human Services. The purpose of the program was to provide lifesaving meals to elderly people at nutritional risk. Meals were to be both served in a congregate setting and delivered to the home. This new program grew out of the social activism that paralleled America's soul-searching in the 1960s during America's involvement in the Vietnam War and the struggles of the civil rights movement. Providing nutritious meals to America's elderly was viewed as just one of the many actions society needed to take to provide a safety net for America's most vulnerable.

In 2003, more than 300 million meals were delivered to the elderly under this program. About half of these meals were delivered to people at home. Since the creation of Meals on Wheels as a federal program in 1972, it has continued to grow, as an army of volunteers carries out the work of Little Red Riding Hood, delivering meals to America's elderly.

[See also EATING DISORDERS; HUNGER PROGRAMS; INVALID COOKERY.]

BIBLIOGRAPHY

"Meals on Wheels: A New and Progressive Step in the Care of the Aged." *What's New*, no. 203 (1957). Special Christmas Issue published by Abbott Laboratories, North Chicago, IL.

Bechill, William D., and Irene Wolgamot. *Nutrition for the Elderly: The Program Highlights of Research and Development Nutrition Projects Funded under Title IV of the Older Americans Act of 1965.* Washington, DC: U.S. Department of Health, Education, and Welfare, Administration on Aging, 1973.

JOSEPH M. CARLIN

Measurement

Throughout history, food measurements have had more to do with experience and judgment than objective amounts. However, when needed in the English American colonies, they followed a loose and variable adaptation of the English imperial system. Originally based largely on weight, they gave way to volume measurements by the late nineteenth century, at about the same time a single American standard was adopted.

Weight and Volume

Colonial food measurements in the commercial and household arenas were developed to meet different needs. Commercial transactions were regulated by law to ensure honest dealings and depended on carefully calibrated equipment. Eighteenth-century tavern owners, for example, were legally obliged to buy and use sets of official measures for dispensing cider, wine, beer, ale, and spirits in familiar volume units—gallons, half gallons, quarts, pints, cups, and gills.

Likewise, seventeenth- and eighteenth-century barrels were required to meet regional standards of size and were labeled appropriately. In New York City, pipes contained at least 120 gallons of wine, hogsheads 60 gallons, and quarter casks 30 gallons. Molasses hogsheads held 63 gallons and the casks for dried salt fish held 31½ gallons. Others, equally specific, held meat, cider, beer, salt, rum, bread, ship's biscuit, and flour.

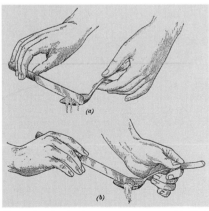

Illustration showing how to use a spoon and knife to measure ingredients.

Home cooking was more concerned with ensuring desired amounts and achievable quality. Colonial American cooks measured with a kinesthetic system that suggested amounts and depended on the cook to adjust them according to experience, the knowledge of flavor principles, and the properties of food. As both measuring equipment and ingredients were inconsistent, cooks learned to determine the correct amounts pragmatically, according to the look, feel, smell, taste, and even sound at various steps of the recipe. The food itself indicated when quantities, handling, or timing were sufficient; a competent cook achieved consistently good results. Cooks' training, whether involving a professional master and apprentice or home-based mother and daughter, relied on close supervision, oral instruction, demonstration, and hands-on practice. The written recipes of period cookbooks, invoking the same methods, were used chiefly by the affluent and literate.

Another factor in the success of the measurement system lay in the fact that local foodways were dominated by a single ethnic tradition and their cooking repertoires were familiar, limited, and fairly standard. English or Dutch cookbooks were used by those already versed in basic preparations. For example, the common instruction, "Put in flour until it is enough," although inadequate for modern cooks, made sense to someone of the right cultural grounding.

This system of sensory measurement was entirely appropriate to home-based cultures with limited technology, familiarity with foodstuffs, enough time for daily cooking, and a high regard for meals. The favored measurement technique for solids was by weight, as balances and steelyards (arm and fulcrum) required minimal technology and had calibrated weights. Liquids were estimated by volume, using drinking cups and eating spoons of inconsistent sizes, and small amounts were gauged by tasting.

Nineteenth-century cookbook authors faced the challenge of transmitting an oral tradition in written form. Unable to instruct by demonstration, they refined their measurement systems. For example, a recipe for bread in Mary Randolph's *The Virginia House-Wife* (1824) requires one quart of flour and then, as an afterthought, explains that a quart of flour weighs 1¼ pounds.

An exponential rise in the number of printed recipes followed. Cookbooks, women's magazines, newspaper columns, and advertising handouts disseminated large numbers of unfamiliar recipes and an expanding, evolving cuisine, reinforcing the need for dependable, clear instructions. At the same time, more women, unschooled in cookery at home, were involved in education and jobs. New authors, increasingly writing for inexperienced brides, recognized the importance of complete and accurate measurements and measured by volume, finding it easier to use.

It was not until the mid- to late nineteenth century that standardized equipment for volume measuring was mass-produced and distributed. Influenced by the new field of science and early nutrition research, cooking schools rewrote traditional American recipes in more precise volume units. Mary J. Lincoln's *Boston School Kitchen Text-Book* (1887), one of the most important pioneering efforts, defines a standardized cup as "just half a pint (beer measure)," a clear adaptation of legal volume, and instructs, "A cupful is all the cup will hold without running over, —full to the brim." Her "scant cupful is within a quarter of an inch of the top," and various spoon measurements are defined as rounded or level. Fannie Merritt Farmer's 1896 revision further recommends the use of inexpensive (and then widely available) graduated tin or agate measuring cups and spoons.

In the early twentieth century, newly required public-school classes in home economics taught scientific measurement methods to generations of boys and girls. Lincoln and other early proponents of standardization knew the value of cooking by experience and believed the consistent use of measurements was a stepping-stone toward that experience, but later practitioners focused with such zeal on the new scheme that it became the only correct way. Although it overshadowed a tried-and-true system for achieving good results, it nevertheless served home cooks exploring new cuisines, ethnic and international cookery, and the sophisticated creations of gifted chefs.

At the end of the twentieth century, the "outdated" measuring systems began to be reinstated. Involvement with international cooking brought weight measurement and kitchen scales to American homes, particularly as many cooks believed them to be more accurate. American descendants of immigrants, eager to recreate the ancestral foods of their childhoods, learned the sensory techniques of their aging relatives. It seems that Americans are using the best of all systems.

Heat and Time

Heat measurement is another aspect of cookery. For millennia, cooks have judged the heat of the hearth by its feel on the skin, the look of embers and flames, the bubbling sounds of frying, the telltale indication of white brick-oven walls after the soot burns off, and how long it takes to brown a cube of bread. Thermometers and then thermostats were largely twentieth-century advances and permitted the cook almost to ignore stove or oven progress.

Time measurements have long depended on experience and estimations, the desired result, an inner time sense, clocks and watches, perhaps even the position of the sun. Modern timers have freed the busy cook from close watching. Timing has taken on new meanings: menu construction often is based on the time available in a busy day; the twenty-minute meal has restructured family dinners.

Eighteenth-Century Measurement by Weight

French Biskits: "Having a Pair of clean Scales ready, in one Scale, put three new-laid Eggs, in the other Scale put as much dried flour, an equal Weight with the Eggs, take out the Flour, and as much fine Powder-sugar. ..."

Glasse, Hannah. The Art of Cookery, Made Plain and Easy. London: 1747.

Historical American Measuring

4 even saltspoons = 1 teaspoon
4 teaspoonfuls = 1 tablespoon
4 teaspoonfuls = 1 wineglass, or 1/4 cup
8 tablespoons = ½ cup, or ½ gill
2 gills or 1 cup = ½ pint
4 gills or 2 cups = 1 pint
2 pints = 1 quart
4 quarts = 1 gallon
1 even tablespoon of butter or lard = 1 ounce
1 heaping tablespoon of butter or lard = 2 ounces
butter the size of a walnut = 1 ounce
butter the size of an egg = 2 ounces
1 even cupful of butter = ½ pound
1 pint of liquid = 1 pound
1 pint finely chopped meat = 1 pound
1 cupful raisins (stemmed) = 6 ounces
5 nutmegs = 1 ounce
1 teaspoon (heaping) ground spice = ¼ ounce
2 teaspoons (rounded) mustard = ¼ ounce
The standard cup in all cooking recipes is the ordinary kitchen cup, which is larger than a teacup, but not so large as a breakfast cup. It holds exactly half a pint.

Taken from Served in Sayville *(1909), published by the Sayville Congregational Church in Long Island, New York.*

Modern American Measures

Dry Measures by Volume
3 teaspoons = 1 tablespoon
2 tablespoons = 1 ounce
8 ounces (or 16 tablespoons) = 1 cup
2 cups = 1 pint
2 pints = 4 cups = 1 quart
4 cups = 1 quart
4 quarts = 1 gallon

Liquid Measures
1 gallon = 4 liquid quarts
1 liquid quart = 2 liquid pints
1 liquid pint = 4 liquid gills

Avoirdupois Weight
16 ounces = 1 pound

ALICE ROSS

[See also COOKBOOKS AND MANUSCRIPTS: AMERICAN COOKBOOKS FROM THE CIVIL WAR TO WORLD WAR I; COOKBOOKS AND MANUSCRIPTS: AMERICAN COOKBOOKS TO 1860; HOME ECONOMICS; RECIPES; TIMERS, HOURGLASSES, AND EGG TIMERS.]

BIBLIOGRAPHY

Carlin, Joseph M. "Weights and Measures in Nineteenth-Century America," *The Journal of Gastronomy* 3, no. 3 (Autumn 1987).

ALICE ROSS

Meat

America has been a meat-eating nation from the days of the Native American hunter-gatherer societies. Annual per capita meat consumption reached approximately 150 pounds in the early 1700s and remained at the level, give or take 20 percent, until the 1950s.

Pork was America's favorite and most widely consumed meat until the twentieth century. The flesh could be preserved through materials easy to obtain and use—salt, sugar, and smoke—and thus stored for later consumption in an era without home refrigeration. The principal cured pork product before 1900, barrel pork, consisted of the pig's trunk (less its limbs) cut into pieces small enough to place in a barrel filled with a brine solution usually composed of salt, saltpeter, and sugar or molasses. Hams (rear legs) and front shoulders often were dry cured, sprinkled with salt, saltpeter and sugar rather than immersed in a liquid solution, then smoked to complete the curing process. Sometimes, farmers separated the ribs from the pig's belly and cured the latter as bacon. Fresh pork remained a highly seasonal dish, a fall or winter treat accompanied by curing the rest of the animal for later use.

For fresh meat, eighteenth- and nineteenth-century Americans vastly preferred beef. As in Europe, however, fresh meat consumption was predominantly was an urban phenomenon until the twentieth century. Rural Americans had only occasional access to fresh beef. In an era before refrigeration, fresh meat could be regularly found only in towns large enough to develop stable livestock markets and a slaughterhouse business. The varieties of beef sold in urban settings meant most nineteenth-century city dwellers could obtain this meat in some form. Elites might favor rib roasts and loin steaks, but poorer folks still could obtain tougher beef for soups and stews. Cured beef was an undesirable form of meat at the bottom of American's meat hierarchy.

Beginning in the 1820s, entrepreneurs discovered that, whenever possible, it was cheaper to move the slaughterhouses and meat processing facilities to the animal than to ship livestock to major population centers. So long as the meat could be kept from spoiling and transported economically, large-scale production facilities near livestock sources permitted economies of scale in meat production. Until well after the Civil War, these processes were limited to cured pork. Advantageously situated river cities such as Cincinnati became the nation's leading pork packing centers in the 1830s, 1840s, and 1850s. The expansion of the railroad network allowed Chicago to become the "hog butcher to the world" following the American Civil War.

The application of refrigeration to production and distribution altered the stature of beef in American foodways after 1900. The development of the ice-cooled railroad car in the 1880s permitted radical separation of slaughter from consumption, allowing slaughterhouses to be located considerable distances from those who ate their products. By World War I, the distribution networks of the five dominant Chicago-based meatpacking firms touched 25,000 American communities. Nationalizing beef production made fresh beef more widely available for Americans as consumers no longer had to rely on local livestock sources to obtain it. Traditional cuts and consumer preferences

Nineteenth-century print of shoppers in a meat market.

persisted as beef consumption spread. Steaks and roasts remained intractably perched on the top of the status hierarchy despite persistent efforts from meat producing firms, retailers, and home economists to stimulate more diverse use of cuts.

Although modern beef remained essentially unchanged, twentieth-century pork was radically different than nineteenth-century varieties. The focal points for innovation, bacon and ham, occupied different places in the pork hierarchy. Hams were the elite pork products while bacon was a common meat. Firms tried to reduce ham production costs and expand the demand for bacon.

Through production innovations meatpacking companies fundamentally changed American ham. Once slowly cured for months, after 1920 firms introduced "artery" pumping to inject water-based brine solutions into hams, plugging nozzles into the joint's circulatory system to speed delivery of the curing agent. Soon hams that once took three months to cure were ready for sale within five days. As meat flavor was large part a result of slow ripening under conditions that inhibited uncontrolled bacterial growth, the fast cure did not give sufficient time for the meat to age and develop a traditional taste. The hams of the 1960s might not have seemed like hams to eighteenth-century consumers. Wet cured and less inoculated with salt than their predecessors, hams became softer and sweeter—or blander, depending on taste preferences. But if their character changed, their elite place in the pork hierarchy did not.

Bacon changed fundamentally as well. Traditional dry cure techniques for bacon—slowly drying and smoking the bellies—were too slow for modern production demands. Thousands of pounds could be cured more efficiently in watery brine solutions instead. By the early twentieth century, only "fancy" bacon was made through traditional dry cure methods. Bacon then experienced a second transformation that expanded its appeal across socio-economic lines. Until the 1910s, bacon left the packinghouse as cured slabs of four to ten pounds. Beginning in 1915, packing firms began to incorporate slicing machines into bacon operations. In the 1950s, needle cure injection methods similar to artery pumping of hams reduced the still considerable bacon curing times to a few days, whereas clear packaging protected the meat from the deteriorating effects of air and light. By the mid-1960s, sliced bacon was a true national meat whose appeal crossed income levels. It was no longer a lower-class meat; slightly over 60 percent of all families purchased bacon, with higher income groups slightly more likely to do so than lower.

Barrel pork, once America's preeminent meat, simply disappeared as a consumption option shortly after World War II. Fresh pork rose from the ashes of barrel pork's demise. Cuts that had previously been cured, or available fresh only at certain times of the year, were widely obtainable by the 1960s. By the twenty-first century, Americans ate more fresh than cured pork, a dramatic reversal of our nation's historic preference for pork in cured forms.

In 2000, Americans ate more meat than at any point in America history by consuming 195 pounds per person. However, the composition of their preferred meats was quite different from that of the eighteenth century. On an annual per capita basis, beef led at 64.5 pounds per person. Pork, once America's leading meat, trailed behind at 47.7 pounds. Chicken consumption reached 53 pounds, far higher in the early twentieth century. Fish accounted for 15 pounds, turkey another 13.5 pounds, and lamb barely 1 pound. Americans still like their meat—and evidence indicates we will remain a meat eating nation for the foreseeable future.

[See also ADULTERATIONS; ARMOUR, PHILIP DANFORTH; ASEPTIC PACKAGING; BURGER KING; BUTCHERING; CHICKEN; CHIPPED BEEF; CORNED BEEF; DRYING; FOWL; FREEZERS AND FREEZING; GAME; GOETTA; HAMBURGER; LAMB AND MUTTON; MCDONALD'S; PICKLING; PIG; POPEYES CHICKEN AND BISCUITS; REFRIGERATORS; SALT AND SALTING; SANDERS, COLONEL; SAUSAGE; SCRAPPLE; SINCLAIR, UPTON; SMOKING; SOUPS AND STEWS; SPAM; STUFFED HAM; SWIFT, GUSTAVUS FRANKLIN; TRANSPORTATION OF FOOD; VIENNA SAUSAGE; WHITE CASTLE.]

BIBLIOGRAPHY

Broadway, Michael, and Donald Stull. *Slaughterhouse Blues: The Meat and Poultry Industry in North America.* New York: Wadsworth, 2003.

A cooking class prepares meat at the Institute of Culinary Education, New York.

Hilliad, Sam Bowers. *Hog Meat and Hoecake: Food Supply in the Old South, 1840–1860.* Carbondale: Southern Illinois University Press, 1972.

Horowitz, Roger. *Meat in America: Taste, Technology, Transformation.* Baltimore: Johns Hopkins University Press, 2005.

Horwitz, Richard P. *Hog Ties: Pigs, Manure, and Mortality in American Culture.* New York: St. Martin's Press, 1998.

Walsh, Margaret. *The Rise of the Midwestern Meat Packing Industry.* Lexington: University Press of Kentucky, 1982.

Williams, William H. *Delmarva's Chicken Industry.* Georgetown, DE: Delmarva Poultry Industry, 1998.

ROGER HOROWITZ

Melons

Melons originated in Africa and have been cultivated in the Middle East and Europe since prebiblical times. They were introduced to the New World by Christopher Columbus in 1494. The term "melon" refers to members of the species *Cucumis melo*, which sometimes are referred to as muskmelons, cantaloupes, or winter melons. The term does not include other species such as watermelon (*Citrullus lanatus*) or jelly melon (*Cucumis metuliferus*).

Charles Naudin, a French botanist, determined in the mid-nineteenth century that various melons previously considered to be different species easily can be crossed and therefore all belong to the same species. He classified them into different groups, including the group commonly called cantaloupe in the United States and the group *inodorus*. Cantaloupes have a netted rind and a separation layer on the stem that causes an abscission or the natural separation of the fruit from the vine when it is mature. Melons of the *inodorus* group have a smooth rind and lack a separation layer for abscission.

Cantaloupe varieties are about twice as popular with growers and consumers as those of the *inodorus* group. The disease-resistant cantaloupe variety PMR 45 was popular throughout the second half of the twentieth century, but has been superseded by Top Mark and other F1 hybrid varieties that also have heavy fruit netting, which enables them to be shipped across the country. Varieties that have large fruit with sparse netting, such as Iroquois, do not ship as well but often are grown in eastern states and marketed locally.

Varieties of the *inodorus* group include honeydew, casaba, and canary. Most have green or white flesh. They are called winter melons because they have a long storage life, enabling them to be shipped from growers in western states to markets thousands of miles away. The honeydew variety was introduced from France a century ago and has been an important commodity in America ever since then. Honeydew fruit have a smooth, cream-colored rind and green flesh with a high sugar content and delectable flavor. Honeydew melons can be stored for two weeks or more at 45°F and 85 to 90 percent relative humidity.

Orange-fleshed cantaloupe varieties predominate, but in the early 1900s melons of this group with green flesh were more popular. The orange color is caused by the presence of beta-carotene, a precursor to vitamin A that is an antioxidant and has nutritional and health benefits. Orange-fleshed melon varieties provide much more vitamin A than melons with green flesh. Melons are mostly water (more than 90 percent), but have significant amounts of niacin and vitamins A and C.

Melons most often are served fresh as a dessert, sometimes à la mode, and are a colorful addition to salads. They occasionally are processed by being frozen in syrup and are even used in soups, salsa, ice cream, and alcoholic drinks.

All melons are of inferior quality if they are harvested before full maturation. Looking at the separation layer of cantaloupes in the market can provide an indication if they were harvested too soon. When melons are fully mature, they have a smooth, round area where the fruit formerly was attached to the plant. Melons harvested before the half-slip stage, when more than half of the stem attachment area is jagged, seldom are of desirable flavor. The appearance of the stem attachment area for melons that abscise is one indication of maturity. Others include aroma, softness, and the color of the fruit.

An important quality attribute is sugar content. The total soluble solids measurement, mostly sugars, needs to be above 11 percent to meet U.S. Fancy and 9 percent for U.S. No. 1 grades. Honeydew melons generally have more sugar than cantaloupes and California requires by law that they have at least 10 percent soluble solids. Melons are grown in every American state, but the leading states for commercial production are California, Arizona, Texas, and Georgia. Most melons are produced in the spring and summer months. Prices received by growers are significantly lower in the summer. The consumption of melons in the United States is increasing.

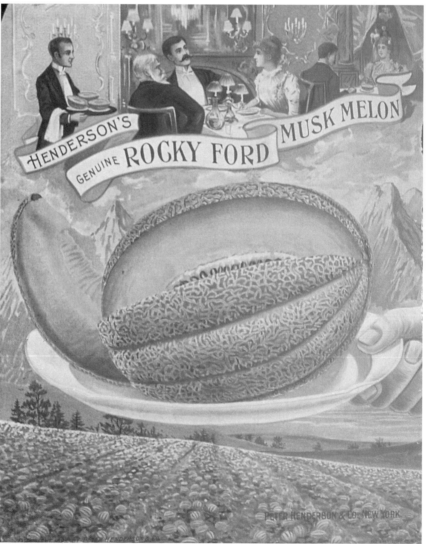

An elegant label that appeared on Rocky Ford musk melons.

[See also FRUIT; WATERMELON.]

BIBLIOGRAPHY

Goldman, Amy. *Melons: For the Passionate Grower.* New York: Artisan, 2002.

Robinson, R. W., and D. S. Decker-Walters. *Cucurbits.* New York: CAB International, 1997.

RICHARD ROBINSON

Mexican American Food

The foods of Mexican Americans are simultaneously one of the oldest regional cuisines in the United States and one of the newest immigrant contributions to this multicultural nation. Although Native American and Hispanic influences survive in the Southwest, new immigrant communities have taken root as far away as Atlanta and New York City. Most people in the United States encounter Mexican food neither in isolated towns nor in urban immigrant enclaves but, rather, in sub-

urban restaurants and fast food outlets where the cooking bears little resemblance to dishes served south of the border. Between settled tradition and immigrant adaptation, appropriation and McDonaldization, the experience of Mexican Americans encompasses the entire history of food in the United States.

For Mexican Americans, fusion cuisine is not a trendy new discovery but a historical process reaching back for centuries. Following the conquest of Mexico, Native American and Spanish cooking traditions blended to form a "mestizo" cuisine, which varied widely between regions. The foods of the Southwest were part of a predominantly Hispanic *norteño* tradition, with wheat tortillas rather than indigenous corn, fewer vegetables and more European meats, particularly beef, and relatively uncomplicated chile pepper sauces compared with the intense *moles* prepared farther south.

Mexican Cookery for American Homes was published by the Gebhardt Chili Powder Company of San Antonio, Texas, in 1943.

Although foods cross easily over the U.S.-Mexican border, considerable variety exists from one state to the next. Tex-Mex cooking, found in northeastern Mexico as well as Texas, is noted for the predominance of beef and tiny, lethal *chiltepín* peppers. Notwithstanding the stereotype of fajitas, the true heart of the cuisine is the chili gravy, not a beef stew but rather a pan gravy made with small amounts of ground beef and served over enchiladas and tamales. The foods of the Sonoran desert, including the Mexican state of the same name and southern Arizona, likewise emphasize beef, often dried as *carne seca*. Burritos, another Sonoran tradition, are wrapped in giant flour tortillas and mildly spiced with Anaheim pepper sauces. The much hotter New Mexico chile pepper, also grown in Chihuahua, southern Colorado, and northern Arizona, forms the basis for another regional variant. Used either fresh and green (*chile verde*) or dried and red (*chile colorado*), the peppers are served thick as an enchilada sauce or with broth, pork, and vegetables as a stew. Finally, Cal-Mex cooking is a relatively modern creation, in contrast to the deep roots of other southwestern styles, created by new immigrants and flavored by memories of the Californio ranching society that existed before 1848. The fish taco, for example, was discovered by surfers such as Ralph Rubio while vacationing in Baja California.

Following the U.S. invasion of 1846–1848, Mexican American foods were appropriated by Anglo corporations and consumers. This process can be seen through the history of San Antonio chili, which was originally a simple *mole* spiced with red chiles, cumin, and oregano—ingredients available to Mexican settlers on the northern frontier. In the 1880s, Hispanic vendors, known as "Chili Queens," began setting up tables in San Antonio plazas to sell their spicy stews to Anglo tourists arriving by train. The dish gained national attention at the 1893 World's Columbian Exposition in Chicago and was industrialized by nonethnic businessmen such as the German immigrant William Gebhardt. Already tamed-down for Anglo palates, chili underwent further alterations, with the side order of beans dumped into the mixture, and spread on hot dogs. Meanwhile, back in San Antonio, after a long struggle with city inspectors, the original chili stands closed down as a supposed health hazard in the late 1930s.

Despite these indignities, Mexican Americans insisted on the value of their food, and used the home economics movement as a way of claiming cultural citizenship. Beginning in the 1930s in New Mexico, the descendants of colonial settlers such as Cleofas M. Jaramillo and Fabiola Cabeza de Vaca Gilbert published cookbooks in order to counter inaccurate descriptions of local foods. A courageous blind Mexican immigrant to San Francisco, Elena Zelayeta, likewise published cookbooks and taught classes to support her family. These works sought to counter stereotypes of Mexican food as unhealthy and unsanitary, and to gain acceptance within the broader society.

Mexican American cooks nevertheless had to adapt their foods to appeal to Anglo customers. The combination plate, rarely seen in Mexico but one of the mainstays of Mexican American restaurants, fulfilled Anglo expectations by combining snack foods such as tacos, enchiladas, and tostadas into a formal meal. Anglo demands for a full plate of food, as opposed to the Mexican preference for separate, smaller courses, encouraged cooks to combine the main dish with rice (usually eaten before the main course) and beans (after). Numbering the combination plates relieved non-Spanish speakers of the need to pronounce what they were eating, a strategy also taken by Chinese cooks seeking a crossover clientele.

Despite the best efforts of ethnic cooks, Mexican American food did not achieve a national presence until taken over by corporations such as Taco Bell. The breakthrough in Mexican fast food came by prefrying corn tortillas in order to speed up production, thus creating the prototype for the hard taco shell. Mexican-style food was thereby released from the need for fresh tortillas, which tied it to the ethnic community, and spread throughout the country and around the world. Supermarket sales of tortillas, chips, salsas, and other Mexican American foods have also been dominated by Anglos since Elmer Doolin purchased the formula for Fritos corn chips from a nameless Mexican American in 1932 and Dave Pace began bottling salsa in 1948.

In contemporary America, Spanish has become the lingua franca of the restaurant world, as migrants provide essential labor in French, Chinese, and American as well as Mexican restaurants. The harsh conditions of undocumented kitchen workers in upscale restaurants are matched by the self-exploitation of families struggling to maintain taquerías in ethnic barrios and of commissary vans drivers who deliver Mexican food to factories across the country. These workers will never appear on the Food Channel, but they nevertheless represent the future, not just of Mexican American but of all American cuisine.

BIBLIOGRAPHY

Pilcher, Jeffrey M. ¡Que vivan los tamales! Food and the Making of Mexican Identity. Albuquerque, N.M., 1998.

JEFFREY M. PILCHER

Microbreweries

The microbrewery industry, as we know it in this country, began in July 1965, when Fritz Maytag purchased an interest in the Anchor Steam Brewery (est. 1896) of San Francisco, California. Maytag's rescue of the company and its turnaround into a thriving firm were to prove an inspiration to an entire generation of followers. In January 1983, the United States could boast of just fifty-one companies operating only eighty breweries that provided fewer than twenty-five nation-

The Park Slope Ale House in Brooklyn, New York, specializes in microbrews.

ally distributed brands. Not before or since has the United States had fewer commercial breweries in operation. Just thirty years later, there were more than twelve hundred breweries, producing some five thousand different beers. There are more different styles of beer made in the United States than in any other country in the world, and it all happened over a remarkably short period of time.

As Maytag said, "We are all friends in fermentation," and so it was in California in the mid-1960s. People with money and an appreciation of fine wine began investing in California real estate, developing vineyards. They invested, they planted, and they waited for California to become another Bordeaux. The vines grew and produced fine grapes, the weather was predictable, and then the Internal Revenue Service revised the "Limited Partnership" provisions that made investing in ventures like cattle futures and boutique wineries very profitable. Even with the shakeout of financially distressed wineries at the end of the twentieth century, there was a good amount of world-class wine flowing from the Napa, Sonoma, and Mendocino valleys of California. The success of the wineries caught the attention of others. These were people who knew what well-made, fresh beer tasted like. It was a demand waiting to be satisfied.

Jack McAuliffe was stationed at a military base in Scotland while on active duty with the U.S. Navy in the mid-1970s. His appreciation of the local ales was restrained by the size of his paycheck. To compensate, he took up the local custom of home brewing. When he returned to the United States, he continued home brewing. He got so good at it that in 1977, just one year before federal legislation was passed legalizing home brewing, he was toasting his partners Suzy Stern and Jane Zimmerman, of the New Albion Brewing Company in Sonoma, with the first pints of ale that marked the rebirth of the small-brewing

industry in the United States, lost because of Prohibition. That year the first U.S. microbrewery," with an annual production of two hundred barrels, began producing British-style ale and a stout. Their market was limited, but their reputation flourished in the friendly climate of the California wine country.

The Microbrew Boom

In fact, import beers were beginning to find increasing favor with consumers who were returning from their travels overseas and demanding the same full-flavored beers they had enjoyed in Europe. These consumers demanded foods and beverages of quality, and they knew quality. They defined "quality" by a product's ingredients, not by the brand name. This search for quality continues unabated.

If Jack McAuliffe was the father of the U.S. microbrewing industry, then Bert Grant gets the credit for making the brewpub, a brewery with a restaurant or a restaurant with a brewery, part of the North American food service business. It was in 1982 when, for the first time since Prohibition, Bert Grant's Yakima Brewing and Malting Company was permitted not only to sell beer at the brewery but also to serve food. The brewpub was born. Two years later, in 1984, the small breweries (breweries that produce fewer than fifteen thousand barrels of beer annually) began to spread, including Riley-Lyon in Arkansas, Boulder in Colorado, Snake River in Idaho, Millstream in Iowa, Columbia River in Oregon, Kessler in Montana, and Chesapeake Bay in Virginia. That same year, on the East Coast, New York City could boast of a microbrewery when Manhattan Brewing Company opened its doors in the SoHo neighborhood and Jim Koch established the Boston Beer Company in Boston.

The growth of the microbrew industry in 1990 included the opening of the Dock Street Brewing Company in Philadelphia, Pennsylvania. That year the Sierra Nevada Brewery, in

Chico, California, became the first micro-brewery to break into the regional ranks when its production reached 31,000 barrels of beer. The Association of Brewers, a trade association of brewers, reckons that the term "microbrewery" is applied to breweries producing less than 15,001 barrels of beer annually. The "regional" breweries produce between 15,001 and two million barrels of beer annually. In 1990, Wendy Pound and Barbara Groom opened the Lost Coast Brewery & Café. Just four years later, in 1994, California could boast of eighty-four microbreweries or brewpubs, more breweries than were in operation in the entire United States in 1984. By 1995 approximately five hundred breweries were in operation in the United States, and the numbers continued to grow at a pace of three or four per week. The next year there were more than one thousand microbreweries and brewpubs rolling out over 5 million barrels annually. That was also the year that a record 333 new brewpubs and microbreweries opened for business.

According to statistics provided by the Association of Brewers, by 1977, the opening of 218 new microbreweries pushed the total number of microbreweries to 1,320, and total production to 5,573,427 barrels of beer. However, one year later, 77 new breweries were only able to increase total production by 1,844 barrels, as larger microbreweries closed at the same time smaller "pub-breweries" opened their doors. The growth of pub-breweries (restaurants with on-premise breweries producing beer for on-premise consumption) would soon outpace the traditional microbreweries that brewed, bottled, and kegged beer for consumption in restaurants, taverns, and the home. The result was an interesting situation of more breweries opening while the total number of barrels of beer produced would remain stable. The result of the shake-out was a slowing down in the growth of the number of breweries and brewpubs. By 1999 there were 1,147 microbreweries producing 5.8 million barrels of more than five thousand brands of beer. One year later the number of breweries remained stable, but the amount of beer they were brewing had grown by 300,000 barrels. From those first pints of ale served by Jack McAuliffe in 1977, the microbrewing segment of the U.S. brewing industry grew over twenty-five years to include more than fourteen hundred breweries and brewpubs producing more than 6 million barrels of beer and maintaining a $3 billion share of the $51 billion annual U.S. production.

[See also Beer; Beer Barrels.]

BIBLIOGRAPHY
Baron, Stanley. *Brewed in America*. Boston: Little, Brown & Company, 1962.
Ronnenberg, Herman. *Beer and Brewing in the Inland Northwest, 1850–1959*. Moscow: University of Idaho Press, 1993.
Skilnik, Bob. *The History of Beer and Brewing in Chicago (1833–1978)*. St. Paul, MN: Pogo Press, 1999.

PETER LAFRANCE

Microwave Ovens

The microwave oven emerged from radar experimentation during World War II. Percy Spencer, an employee of the Raytheon Corporation of Waltham, Massachusetts, walked in front of a magnetron that was emitting microwaves and discovered that microwaves had heating properties. After the war Spencer patented the process of heating food by conveying it under two parallel magnetrons. Two years later, William M. Hall and Fritz A. Gross, who were coworkers of Spencer's, patented a microwave heating device enclosed in an oven. The prototype microwave oven constructed by Spencer in 1946 cost approximately $100,000. In 1947, Raytheon began constructing commercial ovens, calling them Radaranges. The main use of these ovens was heating cold sandwiches and other foods. Because these early microwave ovens cost in excess of three thousand dollars, sales were mainly limited to restaurants, railroads, cruise ships, and vending-machine companies.

Home Use

In the 1950s, Raytheon dominated the microwave oven field. It was the principal manufacturer of magnetrons, but it licensed other companies, such as Hotpoint, Westinghouse, Kelvinator, Whirlpool, and Tappan, to manufacture ovens. In 1952, Tappan Company engineers who were experts in cooking developed an experimental commercial microwave oven intended for home use, but it proved impractical. Tappan continued to experiment and in October 1955 introduced the first domestic microwave oven. Designed to fit on top of a conventional oven, the microwave oven retailed for $1,295. It was marketed as an "electric range" with a cool oven that had the unique ability to reheat food. The Hotpoint division of General Electric unveiled its electronic oven in 1956. Both the Tappan and the Hotpoint ovens generated enthusiasm, but sales were dismal mainly because of the high price. In addition, specially packaged microwavable foods did not yet exist.

What turned the microwave oven into a common kitchen appliance was the invention in 1965 of a compact, low-cost magnetron by Keishi Ogura of the New Japan Radio Company. Raytheon acquired Amana Refrigeration, which developed the first affordable household Radarange, in 1967. The $495 unit was well received, and it launched a microwave oven revolution in American kitchens. In 1965, Litton caused a similar revolution with its Model 500, which was used on TWA airplanes. By 1970, Litton dominated the sale of microwave ovens to restaurants.

Obstacles to Adoption

Despite the early successes, the microwave oven industry faced serious challenges. The first involved persuading the American public that microwave ovens were safe. Safety concerns were raised after a federal government report issued in 1970 stated that microwave ovens leaked microwaves. New standards were developed, and microwave oven manufacturers developed safer ovens, but consumers remained concerned about potential risks. However, by 1975, microwave ovens were outselling gas ranges.

The second challenge had to do with food packaging. Microwave oven manufacturers had to persuade food processors both to take advantage of microwave technology in their product development and to repackage products for microwave use. Foil wrappers, for example, blocked microwaves and damaged ovens. When Americans began to purchase microwave ovens in the 1970s, food processors began producing microwave-safe cookware and microwavable food products. By the early twenty-first century, most American kitchens had microwave ovens, and thousands of microwavable products were being sold in the United States. The two major uses of microwave ovens are to reheat food and to pop popcorn. Several culinary experts have encouraged broader use of microwave ovens because of findings that vegetables retain more nutrients cooked in a microwave oven than when cooked in conventional ovens.

[See also AIRPLANE FOOD; POPCORN; SHIP FOOD; STOVES AND OVENS: GAS AND ELECTRIC; TRAIN FOOD; VEGETABLES; VENDING MACHINES.]

BIBLIOGRAPHY
Behrens, Charles W. "The Development of the Microwave Oven." *Appliance Manufacturer* 24 (1976): 70–72.
Buderi, Robert. *The Invention That Changed the World: How a Small Group of Radar Pioneers Won the Second World War and Launched a Technological Revolution*. New York: Simon and Schuster, 1997.

ANDREW F. SMITH

Middle Atlantic States

The Middle Atlantic States includes the states of Pennsylvania, New Jersey, New York, and Delaware. These states share a history of Native American tribes that were replaced by European settlements, colonization, and immigration. The unique Mid-Atlantic cuisine is Native American fare combined with the adaptations and preferences of these many European immigrants.

The Mid-Atlantic cuisine is as varied as the European settlers of the region were diverse in nationality and food customs. The earliest settlers in the Hudson and Delaware river valleys were Dutch and Swedish in the seventeenth century. The English gained political control but did not dislodge the earlier Dutch settlements that continued their customs and traditional foodways. When William Penn, an English Quaker, was granted a charter for

Pennsylvania in 1681, his thoughts on religious freedom attracted immigrants from central Europe, the Germans (Pennsylvania Dutch), and Scotch-Irish (Protestant Irish) with their distinctive eating styles. This was in contrast to the Quakers of the West Jersey colony (southern New Jersey) who were directly from England and desired to replicate their traditional diet in a new land.

As Europeans arrived in the Mid-Atlantic region, they found the Native Americans thriving on the bounties of the indigenous foods of the region—wild turkey, deer, clams, oysters, mussels, scallops, crabs ducks, geese, turtles, catfish, eels, salmon, shad, trout, and sturgeon. Wild fruit included blueberries, cranberries, grapes, and beach plums. And, in the villages, gardens planted with corn, beans, and squash. Food was bountiful with more meat and protein foods than the average European colonist was accustomed to. But to many of these new settlers, much of this food was strange. In the short term, many of the Europeans adapted to the Native American foods but the long-term goal was to bring their farm crops to this land.

One of the first European introductions to the Mid-Atlantic region was wheat. In 1626, the Dutch planted wheat in New Netherlands (New York). Wheat was the chief agricultural product in New York State from the first Dutch settlements until the building of the Erie Canal in 1821, and considered New Jersey's staple crop in the eighteenth century. During the first half of the nineteenth century, New York and Pennsylvania were the two leading states in wheat production, but after the introduction and expansion of the railroad by the 1860s, a cheaper, better wheat was then available from the western states and dominated the market.

Apples were also introduced to the Mid-Atlantic region in the seventeenth century. Apple seeds imported from England were planted in New Jersey as early as 1632. Other fruit trees were introduced but apple trees were by far the most economically significant. New Jersey's reputation for cider making was unique among the Mid-Atlantic colonies. And not only cider was being made but an immigrant from Scotland, William Laird, in 1698, began to distill cider into apple brandy (applejack).

Europeans also wanted their beef and dairy cattle that were familiar. The raising of beef cattle began in New York with the Dutch in New Netherland, who brought their black and white cattle in the seventeenth century. The cuisine brought to the Mid-Atlantic region by the English and Welsh was based on dairy. The most important sauce was the white sauce that incorporated butter or milk thickened with flour. But it was not until the nineteenth century when dairying became an industry. All the Mid-Atlantic states are currently leading producers of milk in this country. With dairying came cheese making, and New York now leads all other states in the production of cheese.

An Amish couple cuts up beef for canning, near Honey Brook, Pennsylvania, March 1942.

Swedish settlers along the lower Delaware never numbered more than a few hundred and had little impact on Mid-Atlantic foodways. The early Dutch settlements were larger and had more influence on the cuisine of the region. The Germans or Pennsylvania Dutch (a corruption of the German word Deutsch for German) have left an enduring and distinctive imprint on Mid-Atlantic foodways.

Philadelphia

Philadelphia's culinary tradition is based on the foodways of the English Quakers with later influences of the foods of the French, the Pennsylvania Dutch, and Italian Americans.

The early Quakers who founded Philadelphia were not drab in either appearance or foods. Their dishes reflected Britain's colonial days with the use of ingredients imported from Europe and the West and East Indies such as spices, sugar, rose and orange flower water, almonds, and currants.

Along with the affinity for spices went a sweet tooth. Philadelphians loved desserts and ice cream. Philadelphia became noted for its excellent ice creams that were influenced by French ice cream but different without an egg base.

Other Philadelphia specialties continue to survive. The Pennsylvania Dutch scrapple is so associated with Philadelphia that, in spite of its rural origins, it is referred to as Philadelphia scrapple and frequently served for breakfast. The Philadelphia pepper pot, which was hawked in the city's streets in milk cans in the nineteenth century and consisted of tripe, veal knuckle, vegetables, herbs, and spices, is still a desired Pennsylvania Dutch–influenced dish. Another Philadelphia specialty of French influence, which has not

fared well with the passing of time, is snapper soup with tender morsels of snapping turtle meat in a thick liquid flavored with Sherry or Madeira. But common on the Philadelphian scene are two food traditions: the Philadelphia soft pretzel and the Philadelphia cheese steak. The origins of the Philadelphia soft pretzel are attributed to the Pennsylvania German pretzel-making tradition. The essential and irreplaceable ingredient of a Philadelphia cheese steak is the Italian roll. The Italian Americans settled in South Philadelphia in the late nineteenth century and one of their culinary gifts to the city was the crusty, yeasty Italian roll. A true Philly cheese steak outside of Philadelphia is virtually impossible without a South Philadelphian Italian roll.

New Jersey: The Garden State

New Jersey was a garden state, as its nickname implies, from the time of first settlement until the present. The seeds and plants that were early European agricultural experiments thrived in the temperate climate and fertile farmlands. There is no part of the state that is more than 125 miles from New York City and Philadelphia. Thus, historically, most of the garden produce has been grown for these two excellent markets. Over 150 crops are grown commercially in New Jersey with tomatoes as the state's leading crop. Peaches are the most valuable fruit crop in the state with major peach orchards in the southern part of the state. New Jersey also ranks among the leading states in the production of blueberries and cranberries.

But in the middle of this agricultural and industrial state is a region known as the New Jersey Pine Barrens that covers about one-third of the state. This region is unsuitable for conventional agriculture or development.

Scenes of garden farming in New Jersey by Paul Frenzeny, Harper's Weekly, August 25, 1883: conveying goods to market (top left), berry vendors waiting for a train at Carlstadt (top right), gathering watercress (middle left), gathering mushrooms above ground (middle center), and below ground (bottom left), hotbeds and greenhouse (bottom center), and preparing celery for market (bottom right).

The self-sufficient inhabitants of this area are called Pineys. The foodways of the Pinelands is much like the rural cookery in other parts of the United States but it is unique to New Jersey. The customs of traditional hunting and gathering are valued and the family garden plot is the next best source of food. The key virtues of the Pineys are attachment to the land and self-sufficiency.

In striking contrast to the New Jersey Pineys are the New Jersey–born scientists that have made the state famous for discoveries in agricultural research. The scientific work on hybridization has resulted in new, improved varieties of peaches, tomatoes, and sweet potatoes. These improved varieties have increased yield but fewer of New Jersey's vegetables go to nearby city markets and more go to canning and frozen food processing plants. New Jersey is one of the leading states in the canning of vegetables. Canned tomatoes in their many forms are the largest single food canned. The Campbell Soup Company, noted for its advertisement that housewives could not keep house without Campbell's Tomato Soup, was born in Camden, New Jersey.

New York
The European settlers and immigrants to New York State found fertile fields and a climate conducive to many crops. Apples and grapes are the two leading fruit crops. The grapes support a flourishing wine industry. New York State is second only to California in the production of wine. New York is also a leading producer of maple syrup ranking just behind Vermont and Maine.

The cooking of New York has been influenced by immigrant fare with the Dutch, English, and Germans settling in the region with foodways similar to that of Pennsylvania. Another English influence was brought to New York when Mother Ann, founder of the Shakers, came to Watervliet in 1774. Plain, wholesome food eaten in moderation was considered a preventative against indigestion and was central to the Shaker faith. The Shakers were among the first to advocate for the greater inclusion of fruits and vegetables and whole grains in the diet. Shakers extended the growing season by a unique rotation of crops to have fresh vegetables available for more months in the year. Shakers used herbs profusely and advertised herbs to world's people (non-Shakers) to improve the flavor of food, to stimulate the appetite and to add charm and variety to ordinary dishes. Shakers were also among the first to insist on the inclusion of the whole-wheat kernel ground for flour for its health promoting qualities.

Many central Europeans arrived in New York during the late 1800s including the Poles who settled in the Buffalo area. Bagels, introduced by the Poles, were paired with an 1872 New York invention, cream cheese, and

popularized throughout the nation in the 1990s. The Buffalo area is also attributed with the evolution of the Buffalo wings, chicken wings that are deep-fried, highly spiced, and traditionally served with celery and blue cheese dressing. These wings were popular in Buffalo-area bars in the 1960s.

Delaware
In the eighteenth century, agriculture was the dominant activity of Delawareans and grain was the main agricultural product. Corn and wheat were the primary crops then, but, as the population grew and new agricultural lands were open in the west, grain farming declined. Some new crops were introduced but, unlike the other Mid-Atlantic states, most attempts at diversification of agriculture were unsuccessful until the nineteenth century when peaches became the money crop for the state. At that time, Delaware became known as the Peach State. The peach-growing boom peaked about 1870 and declined steadily after 1900. In the twentieth century, the broiler chicken industry replaced the peach as the dominant agricultural industry.

The Middle Atlantic States—Pennsylvania, New Jersey, New York, and Delaware—are populated by immigrants or descendants of immigrants. This culinary melting pot has absorbed all the flavors of the millions of immigrants of hundreds of ethnic backgrounds over three centuries and blended them into the rich diverse cuisine of the Middle Atlantic States.

[See also APPLEJACK; APPLES; BAGELS; BEER; BORDEN; CAMPBELL SOUP COMPANY; CAMPBELL SOUP KIDS; CANDY BARS AND CANDY; CANNING AND BOTTLING; CHEESE; CHESAPEAKE BAY; CHICKEN COOKERY; CHOCOLATE; CIDER; DAIRY; DAIRY INDUSTRY; DUTCH INFLUENCES ON AMERICAN FOOD; FISH: FRESHWATER FISH; FISH: SALTWATER FLAT FISH; GERMAN AMERICAN FOOD; HERBS AND SPICES; ICES AND ICE CREAMS; MOLASSES; NATIVE AMERICAN FOOD; PHILADELPHIA CHEESE STEAK SANDWICH; PICKLES; PICKLES, SWEET; PICKLING; PIES AND TARTS; PIG; SCRAPPLE; SHELLFISH; SUPAWN; TOMATOES; WINES, EASTERN U.S.]

BIBLIOGRAPHY
Gerstell, Richard. *American Shad in the Susquehanna River Basin: A Three-Hundred-Year History.* University Park: Pennsylvania State University Press, 1998.
Gillespie, Angus K. "A Wilderness in the Megalopolis: Foodways in the Pine Barrens of New Jersey." In *Ethnic and Regional Foodways in the United States: The Performance of Group Identity*, ed. Linda Keller Brown and Kay Mussell, 145–168. Knoxville: University of Tennessee Press, 1984.
The Sensible Cook: Dutch Foodways in the Old and the New World. Translated and edited by Peter G. Rose. Syracuse, NY: Syracuse University Press, 1989.
Weaver, William Woys. *Sauerkraut Yankees: Pennsylvania Dutch Foods and Foodways.* 2nd ed. Mechanicsburg, PA: Stackpole Books, 2002.

SUSAN MCLELLAN PLAISTED

Middle Eastern Influences on American Food
The Middle East is where so many crops, such as wheat, barley, onions, peas, and lentils, were domesticated in ancient times, as well as animals, including sheep and probably cattle, that its influence on America's European heritage was immense, if hard to trace. It is generally agreed that Egypt gave the world leavened bread, and beer was the everyday beverage of both Egypt and Mesopotamia. In the Middle Ages, the Arabs carried sugar, the techniques for the making of candy and syrups, and probably also the idea of rice pudding from India. They passed on the eggplant from India, too, adding their own technique of salting it before frying (a dish they called *badhinjan buran*).

The Persians invented the favorite medieval Arab sweet *lauzinaj*, which we know as marzipan, and the Moors experimented with various ways of making puff pastry, some with Arab names and some with Spanish, reflecting the lively cultural interaction of Moorish Spain. In Anna Martellotti's study of *Il Liber de ferculis di Giambonino da Cremona*, an Arab recipe collection that a Spanish cleric translated into Latin in the thirteenth century, Martellotti argues that the word "aspic" comes from the Arabic "as-sikbaj" through Latin forms, such as "assicpicium." *Sikbaj* was a dish of meat stewed with vinegar, and its broth certainly does become a jelly when it cools. The Arabic source of the *Liber de ferculis* even defined jelly (*hulam*) as the broth of *sikbaj*.

Coming to America
Some Middle Eastern dishes—pilaf, for instance—came to America by way of other countries and cuisines. The English had developed a taste for this Persian dish (spelling it "pillaw") in India, where they learned to wash the rice scrupulously to remove surface starch, boil it until nearly done, and then steam it for up to half an hour so that all the grains fluffed and separated. They brought it to South Carolina when they started rice plantations there. (They also brought a sweet drink called julep, from the Persian Arabic "jullab.") Pilaf is the origin of the Carolina dish perloo, and what southern cooks call dry rice is also pilaf.

Stuffed cabbage came from central Europe, which very likely got it from the Turks. The Swedes even borrowed their word for it, "dalma," from the Turkish "dolma." Strudel seems clearly descended from Turkish filo pastries, such as baklava. The most widely traveled dish was the Moorish *samak munashsha*, fish dipped in batter before frying. In the seventeenth century, Sephardic Jews brought the recipe to England, where it became known as Jewish fish (Thomas Jefferson admired the recipe), and eventually it became one-half of the favorite English fast food, fish and chips. Meanwhile, Portuguese missionaries had taken batter-fried fish to Japan, where it metamorphosed into a variety of seafood and vegetable tempuras.

Immigrants started coming to the United States from the Ottoman Empire in the 1870s; the vast majority at that time were either Armenians or Arab Christians from Syria and Lebanon. On the whole, their foods remained confined to their own communities, though some influenced their neighbors' cooking without Americans' realizing that these were Middle Eastern foods.

The 1960s

Conscious borrowings from the Middle East began around 1960, when Greece became a fashionable tourist destination (and setting for movies). This was the era of shish kebab marinated in red wine (Americans usually made it with beef, rather than lamb, but always included onions, peppers, and tomatoes on the skewer in the Greek manner), stuffed grape leaves and a particular recipe for moussaka, which covered the meat and eggplant stew with a thick, custardy béchamel sauce. This was when avant-garde American cooks discovered filo pastry and made not only baklava but also a host of novel hors d'oeuvres and finger foods with it.

Later in the 1960s, tourists visiting Israel encountered a number of Middle Eastern dishes that had been brought there by Jewish refugees. Among them were sandwiches wrapped in pocket bread (always known in America by its Hebrew name, "pita"); the sesame-flavored chickpea paste, hummus; the parsley and bulgur salad, tabbouleh; and the fried bean paste balls called falafel. Over the years, they have become standard cafeteria and fast food dishes, and in the late 1990s there was a craze for wrap sandwiches that were as often made with pita as with tortillas.

Vegetarians and health-foodies seized on these Israeli dishes passionately, helping to popularize them. The health-conscious were also enthusiastic about bulgur wheat, often under the misapprehension that it was a form of whole wheat when, actually, the bran and germ have been removed. But bulgur is certainly a convenient food. Having been cooked and dried before being cracked, its starch has already converted into a digestible form so that it does not even have to be cooked again (it is used raw in tabbouleh). In the 1990s, Americans discovered couscous, a grain that is also quickly cooked; however, in this incarnation it was typically cooked by boiling, rather than steaming it in the North African way.

Anonymous Borrowings

There had already been Middle Eastern borrowings on an unconscious, folk level. Rice-A-Roni is a dish of rice mixed with toasted pasta that has been popular since the Middle Ages under such names as *rizz bi-sha'riyya* and *sehriyeli pilav*. The founder of the Rice-A-Roni company had learned to make the dish in childhood from his Armenian neighbors. In the Midwest, there is a positive cult for a dish variously called taverns, maid-rights, or loosemeats. It is ground beef fried loose, not in a patty but in such a way that all the tiny bits of meat are separate. This is an ancient dish that every Turkish-speaking nation from the Mediterranean to western China cooks; the Turkish word for it, "*kiyma*," shows up in the names of various dishes on Greek and Indian menus. It was introduced to the Midwest by an Arab restaurateur.

According to a well-known story, the ice cream cone was invented at the 1904 Columbian Exposition (popularly known as the St. Louis World's Fair) by a Syrian immigrant named Ernest Hamwy who ran a booth selling a pastry called *zalabiya*. Unlike the coiled fritter of this name, which in most Middle Eastern countries is made by pouring a thin stream of batter into boiling oil, Hamwy's Syrian version was a flat wafer with a grid-patterned surface that was cooked between hot irons. The story continues that a neighboring ice cream vendor on the midway ran out of serving cups and Hamwy obliged by rolling up *zalabiyas* into cones. The ice cream cone is claimed by many fathers, however. Other Syrian or Turkish immigrants (little distinction was made at the time) named Abe Doumar, Nick Kabbaz, and David Avayu also said they invented the ice cream cone. They were not the first to serve ice cream in a cone—the prominent English ice cream maker Agnes Marshall had been using ice cream cones made from rolled-up wafers since the 1880s—but the ice cream cone craze that swept the country began at the World's Fair, and all those claiming to have invented the cone were Middle Easterners.

There may be even more unrecognized Middle Eastern influences, because immigrants from the Middle East have generally preferred not to stress their ethnic identity. The father of the dancer Robert Joffrey was a refugee from Afghanistan who ran a chili parlor in Seattle during the early twentieth century using a recipe that had touches of Middle Eastern spicing. Joffrey's father sold his popular recipe to one of the major canning companies (the family no longer remembers which one), so countless people have had, in effect, Afghan chili without ever knowing it.

[**See also** ALMONDS; APRICOTS; CHICKPEAS; COFFEE; ETHNIC FOODS; HEALTH FOOD; JEWISH AMERICAN FOOD; MUSLIM DIETARY LAWS; PISTACHIOS; RICE; SUGAR; VEGETARIANISM; WORLD'S FAIRS.]

BIBLIOGRAPHY

Anawalt, Sasha. *The Joffrey Ballet: Robert Joffrey and the Making of an American Dance Company*. New York: Scribners, 1999.

Marlowe, Jack. "Zalabia and the First Ice Cream Cone." *Aramco World Magazine*, July/August 2003.

CHARLES PERRY

Midwestern Regional Cookery

Geographically, the Midwest is that area between the Ohio River and the Great Plains. Some would include the Great Plains states. A great many of the people who originally settled this area came from New York, New Jersey, and Pennsylvania. Immigrants coming directly from Europe soon followed. Many features that define Midwest traditional foodways today are due to these immigrants.

Vegetables and Fruit

Native American inhabitants first cultivated corn, and corn farming extends through most of the region today. A nice ear of boiled or roasted corn, slathered with butter, minutes away from the field where it grew, is one of the great Midwestern culinary treats and is paid proper respect in regional culture. It is no coincidence that the corn dog and cornflakes both originated in the Midwest.

Another example of Native American influence on Midwestern foodways is wild rice. It grows in northern lakes in Minnesota and Wisconsin (as well as Ontario) and hand-harvested, is regarded a gourmet food, especially outside the region, but it is also used in everyday soups, salads, and casseroles.

Certain fruits have become specifically identified with the Midwest. With the felling of forests in the 1800s, farmers planted fruit trees, especially apple trees. The Midwest is

---

The Best Single Restaurant in the World?

African American Henry Perry opened Kansas City's first barbecue establishment about 1908. Working out of an old trolley car, he practiced the art of making slow-smoked ribs. Texas-born Charlie Bryant and his son Arthur learned these techniques from Perry and opened their barbecue establishment, named Charlie Bryant's, in 1927. Charlie died in 1952, and the restaurant was continued by Arthur, who became known as the "Barbecue King" in Kansas City. The restaurant was located near Kansas City's Municipal stadium—later the home of the Kansas City Chiefs—and became a popular eating establishment. It received national recognition in 1974 when Kansas City native Calvin Trillin declared in a tongue-in-cheek *New Yorker Magazine* article that Arthur Bryant's barbecue was the single best restaurant in the world. Arthur Bryant died in 1982, and his restaurant was eventually sold to a management group, which has subsequently opened a second establishment at the Ameristar Casino.

ANDREW F. SMITH

where the legend of Johnny Appleseed (a.k.a. John Chapman) is rooted and best remembered. Apple cider is an all-time favorite, and making apple butter is an old tradition. Cider mills and pick-your-own orchards are scattered through the area and provide popular excursion sites, especially in the fall. Sour cherry orchards, established by early homesteaders in northwest Michigan, spawned a range of traditions and foods (preserves, dried cherries, juice, pies, soups) maintained and prized throughout the region. Since 1988, cherries have even been utilized as an extender in ground meat to improve its nutritional value. The climate tempered by Lake Michigan makes Michigan the leading producer of tart cherries.

Pie is one of the dishes most frequently associated with the Midwest. Local and regional specialties include sour cream raisin, buttermilk, vinegar, and fruit, especially apple, cherry, blueberry, and rhubarb. The fried pies of southern cuisine are also traditional in areas of the Midwest adjacent to the South. Pie is eaten not only for dessert and snacks but is also regarded by many as excellent breakfast food.

Pork

Pork is frequently the meat of choice, and receives much attention in the culinary culture. Pigs are slaughtered in winter, and headcheese, country ham, bacon, and many kinds of sausage are prepared in kitchens, sheds, and butcher shops across the region. *Goetta*, a specialty of the greater Cincinnati region, is a mixture of ground pork (and sometimes beef) scraps, steel-cut oats, and seasonings that is cooked, molded, cooled, and then sliced and fried.

Barbecue is plentiful in homes and restaurants and at community festivals and cook-offs. Across the northern portion of the Midwest, barbecue means ribs with a sweet, mildly spiced, ketchup-based sauce, a style particularly associated with Chicago, but the city most renowned for barbecueis Kansas City, Missouri.

The pork chop—grilled, fried, baked, smoked, or stuffed—also constitutes a popular home and restaurant meal. Some restaurants feature one-pound pork chops. A favorite lunch across Iowa, and extending into the neighboring states of Nebraska, Illinois, Indiana, is the tenderloin sandwich: a slice of tenderloin (conscientious cooks slice their own) pounded very thin (the thinner the better) and dipped in flour (some add a bit of cornmeal for crunch) before frying. It is most often eaten on a hamburger bun with the usual sandwich condiments, but the same tenderloin is offered as a main course with mashed potatoes.

Fish

All along the Mississippi River, fried catfish is an especially popular dish. In the northern half of the Midwest, the site not only of the five Great Lakes but also countless smaller

Photograph of the Chicago Stockyards taken in the late nineteenth century.

lakes, rivers, and streams, fish takes center stage. Fish was a crucial resource for both the original Native population and the settlers who intruded on them. Commercial fishing is important in the region's economy. Midwesterners use a wide variety of fish, including whitefish (the principal commercial fish); lake, brook, and rainbow trout; perch pike; pickerel; burbot; mullet; catfish; muskellunge; sturgeon; chub; suckers; bass; bluegill; and smelt and salmon (both introduced from saltwater), prepared in an even wider variety of ways: fried, baked, grilled, planked, smoked, pickled, boiled, and steamed, using innumerable specific recipes, but more often with no recipe at all. Planked whitefish, for example, is a traditional manner of preparation still offered in some upscale restaurants in the Great Lakes area. Smoked fish is one of the traditional delicacies of the region, appreciated by tourists,

visiting sports enthusiasts, and local inhabitants. Smoked lake trout, chub, and whitefish are the most popular, but even suckers, little used otherwise, are good smoked. Fish smoking is both a commercial and a private enterprise. The liver and roe of whitefish are special delicacies. Few whitefish livers make it to market, however, because commercial fishermen tend to keep them for themselves. They dredge them in flour and sautee them in butter, perhaps with onions or mushrooms.

Fish boils are important group activities around the Great Lakes, much like pig roasts in the southern part of the Midwest. Fish boils are the most institutionalized in Door County, a peninsula in northeastern Wisconsin. Fishermen host smaller events, often cooking the results of that day's catch in camp. The Friday fish fry is an important institution throughout much of the area.

Built as a tribute to the agriculture of South Dakota, the original Corn Palace in Mitchell was established in 1892.

Bratwurst

Bratwurst is found throughout much of the Midwest, but it is especially associated with Sheboygan, Wisconsin, where it is the focus of much local pride and cultural elaboration. The Sheboygan brat is a charcoal-grilled, coarsely ground pork sausage, customarily served on a hard roll with butter and fried onions. It is often ordered as a pair, two brats on a single roll. There are numerous variants: some parboil in beer before grilling, some even make it into a patty, sans casing. It is a popular bar food and a common picnic food, and it is offered by numerous streetside carts, stands, and restaurants. Fairs and carnivals of the region always include at least one bratwurst stand.

Cudighi is a specialty of the Negaunee-Ishpeming area of northern Michigan. In 1936 an Italian immigrant opened a sausage stand between the family barbershop and the bar from which came many of his customers. He served homemade Italian sausage with a secret spicing in a sandwich with an American-style sandwich dressing of mustard, ketchup, and chopped onions. He called it gudighi. His son opened a bar in the post–World War II period, when pizza was first becoming universalized, and he distinguished his sandwich from his father by forming the meat into a patty and dressing it with pizza sauce and mozzarella cheese. In this form it became ubiquitous, being offered in nearly every restaurant in the area except franchises. Butcher shops and grocers offer a variety of *cudighi*-related products: *cudighi* meat either in bulk or already formed into patties, in three degrees of spiciness; turkey *cudighi*; cold and hot *cudighi* sandwiches; packages of *cudighi* buns; store-made sauces to dress *cudighi* sandwiches; and packages of mixed spices to combine with meat for *cudighi*.

The pasty was originally brought to the region by tin miners who came from Cornwall in the mid-nineteenth century. In this region it became standardized: chopped or ground beef, or beef and pork, potatoes, onions, and rutabaga or carrots baked in a pie-crust turnover. New variants, including chicken and vegetarian, have become common. The pasty is ubiquitous throughout the region and has taken on great symbolic significance as a marker of regional pride.

The *paczki* is the Polish version of the jelly doughnut, which are eaten at Carnival before Lent. *Paczki* are made of a yeast dough rich with eggs and butter and best fried in lard (though vegetable oil is usually used). Traditionally, they were made to use up all the lard and eggs in the home before Lenten fasting. They are still made for the pre-Lenten season, but eating them no longer has anything to do with being either Polish or Catholic. Available until the 1980s only at Polish bakeries and church and community celebrations, *paczki* can be found at non-Polish bakeries and even at most chain supermarkets in the area. Traditionally prepared without filling or filled with prune butter, *paczki* are also made in the Midwest with a half-dozen different fruit jam fillings and custard. Recently, *paczki* are becoming the focus of local annual festivals and parades on Shrove Tuesday, or Paczki Day.

Toasted ravioli, a specialty of St. Louis, Missouri, are beef ravioli that have been deep fried. They have no precedent in Italy but are the creation of an Italian American restaurateur and have spread throughout the community. Similarly, deep-fried sauerkraut balls are a specialty of northern Ohio and apparently were developed by members of the large German American population there, although nothing like them exists in Germany. Likewise, Italian beef sandwiches are a local specialty of Chicago, though there is little about them that is Italian other than the ethnicity of those who owned the earliest sandwich shops. They consist of thinly sliced beef *au jus* on a crusty roll, usually dressed with spicy *giardiniera* or roasted peppers.

Macedonian immigrants in the industrial cities of the northern Midwest began to season American chili with the sweet spices of the eastern Mediterranean and to serve it as a sauce, along with chopped onions and mustard, on a hot dog sandwich. They called this a coney, after Coney Island, although hot dogs are served there in quite a different style. The coney has become the dominant hot dog style throughout the northern Midwest, except in Chicago, which has its own distinctive hot dog (an all-beef wiener on a poppy seed bun, dressed with mustard, onions, bright green piccalilli relish, tomato and lettuce, celery salt, and a couple of port peppers). Coney stands are abundant across the area.

[**See also** BARBECUE; BEANS; CHEESE; CINCINNATI CHILI; CORN; CRANBERRIES; DAIRY INDUSTRY; FISH, FRESHWATER; FUND-RAISERS; GERMAN AMERICAN FOOD; GOETTA; GRAPES; MAPLE SYRUP; MIDDLE EASTERN INFLUENCES ON AMERICAN FOOD; MILK; MUSHROOMS; MYTHS AND FOLKORE, *sidebar on* JOHNNY APPLESEED; PASTIES; PERSIMMONS; PIG; POLISH AMERICAN FOOD; RUSSIAN AMERICAN FOOD; SCANDINAVIAN AND FINNISH FOOD; SOYBEANS.]

YVONNE R. LOCKWOOD AND WILLIAM G. LOCKWOOD

Stability and Change in Midwestern Foodways

Culture is always changing, always evolving; so, too, are food and foodways. Although many food traditions of the early inhabitants of the Midwest are still intact, the region continues to attract new settlers who bring with them new resources, ingredients, and cuisines. Sometimes a process of culinary adoption, adaptation, and amalgamation occurs, and, finally, regional foodways develop. By contrast, although food traditions can be quick to adapt and change in new contexts, they also are resistant to change and held onto tightly. Thus, newer food traditions coexist with foods and food habits dating from an earlier time. However Midwestern food is described, the picture will look somewhat different in the future.

[**See also** BARBECUE; BEANS; CHEESE; CINCINNATI CHILI; CORN; CRANBERRIES; DAIRY INDUSTRY; FISH: FRESHWATER FISH; FUND-RAISERS; GERMAN AMERICAN FOOD; GOETTA; GRAPES; MAPLE SYRUP; MIDDLE EASTERN INFLUENCES ON AMERICAN FOOD; MILK; MUSHROOMS; MYTHS AND FOLKORE, *sidebar on* JOHNNY APPLESEED; PASTIES; PERSIMMONS; PIG; POLISH AMERICAN FOOD; RUSSIAN AMERICAN FOOD; SCANDINAVIAN AND FINNISH FOOD; SOYBEANS.]

BIBLIOGRAPHY

Hachten, Harva. *The Flavor of Wisconsin*. Madison: State Historical Society of Wisconsin, 1981.

Isern, Thomas D. "Bierocks." In *The Taste of American Place*, ed. Barbara G. Shortridge and James R. Shortridge, 135–137. Lawrence: University of Kansas Press, 1998.

Kaplan, Anne R., Marjorie A. Hoover, and Willard B. Moore. *The Minnesota Ethnic Food Book*. St. Paul: Minnesota Historical Society Press, 1986.

Lockwood, Yvonne R., and Anne R. Kaplan. "Upper Great Lakes Foodways." In *Smithsonian Folklife Cookbook*, ed. Katherine Kirlin and Thomas Kirlin, 172–211. Washington, DC: Smithsonian, 1991.

Lockwood, Yvonne R., and William G. Lockwood. "Pasties in Michigan: Foodways, Interethnic Relations, and Cultural Dynamics." In *Creative Ethnicity*, ed. Stephen Stern and John Allan Cicala, 3–20. Logan: Utah State University Press, 1991.

YVONNE R. LOCKWOOD AND WILLIAM G. LOCKWOOD

Military Food, *see Combat Food*

Milk

Milk was not always the American staple that it became in the twentieth century. Although cows were present in Jamestown by 1611, milking in early America was a seasonal event, occurring almost entirely in spring and summer, when vegetation was abundant. The milk itself was mainly turned into longer-lasting products, such as cheese and butter. For the next two centuries, fresh milk was somewhat of a seasonal luxury, particularly in the warm South.

Until the nineteenth century, most of the cows providing cities with milk were primarily pastured behind urban homes, in neighborhood pastures such as Boston Common, or on nearby farms. As cities grew and became more densely settled, lack of room and sanitation problems led to a decline in pasture space. The major issue of the time involved in-city "swill dairies," attached to breweries and distilleries. The cows were fed the grain mash that was left over after distilling and fermentation. Although this practice was an effective way for brewers and distillers to recycle waste, city-dwellers objected to both the dreadful conditions in which the cows were kept and the idea that their children were drinking milk produced by "drunk" cows. By 1862, it was outlawed in New York State. Many other states and cities followed suit.

By the end of the nineteenth century, almost all the milk drunk in the largest U.S. cities arrived from surrounding areas by rail. The increased distance from which this milk was sourced and increased awareness about both the nutritional benefits of milk and its ability to act as a vector for disease made milk a focus of Progressive-era urban reformers. Milk was chosen as "the perfect food" because of a combination of its ability to provide numerous nutritional benefits at a relatively low price to growing urban populations. In addition, ties between milk and western European culture and the connection between milk and motherhood and purity helped it to become a part of standard Americanization techniques.

Moving farms outside the city made farmers more anonymous to urban consumers and more difficult to control by urban authorities. Adulteration issues appeared, such as milk skimmed and then whitened with chalk. Even worse cases involved tainting milk with formaldehyde so it would not sour. Outlawing adulteration was the focus of most early milk laws. At the same time, milk delivery services became widespread and dominated milk distribution during the first three decades of the twentieth century. These services were increasingly controlled by large milk dealers.

During the first three decades of the twentieth century, the amount of milk drunk by the average American increased markedly. In New York City, for example, between 1890 and 1930 sales of milk and cream rose at approximately double the rate of population growth. Such growth would not have been possible if public health officers and the dairy industry had not dealt with the fact that milk was a vector of disease. Two remedies appeared to solve the problem. Certification involved the creation of a long list of strict requirements for farmers providing milk to a city. A commission, usually composed of physicians, certified farms as pure producers. Pasteurization involves the heating of milk to kill pathogenic bacteria. Although both movements influenced regulation, pasteurization was ultimately more popular, because it was less expensive and did not impose heavy restrictions on farmers.

Until the 1930s, milk markets were locally regulated. Farmers providing milk to cities often were upset by the perceived strictness of city and state health regulations and by the terms of milk contracts. The need for farmers to have daily buyers for their milk forced them into annual contracts, often at unfavorable terms. The Capper-Volstead Act of 1922 gave farmer cooperatives antitrust protection, which allowed them to demand higher prices for milk. These better terms became more difficult to receive during the Great

Paul Frenzeny's illustrations of dairying activities appeared in Harper's Weekly *on September 2, 1882.*

Depression as prices and demand fell. Dealers were under pressure from upstarts who sold to stores and did not have to pay for home delivery. This situation led to "milk strikes" during the 1930s, whereby farmers withheld their milk from cities.

The federal solution to the problem of milk pricing was the milk marketing order program, authorized by Congress in 1937. This program allows dairy farmers serving particular cities to agree to be federally regulated. The federal government then sets a floor on

the price received by farmers for fluid milk within that "milkshed" (the area that provides a city with milk). This program, greatly revised, continues to guide the milk market in most of the United States.

By 1940, milk faded from the headlines and became a trusted staple of the American diet. Dairy products and milk in particular became and remained a cornerstone of federal nutrition advice. Despite this, per-capita consumption of milk has declined since World War II. Estimated consumption of

A poster promoting milk produced by the Federal Art Project for Cleveland Division of Health in 1940.

milk in 1946 was 267 pounds a year per person, increasing from 151 pounds in 1926. Consumption was steady throughout the 1950s and 1960s but then declined to 233 pounds in 1981 and 190 pounds in 2001. The type of milk sold also has changed. Whereas in 1946 most milk sold was whole, in 2001 more reduced and lowfat milk was sold than whole.

The decline in milk consumption per capita is due at least in part to increased immigration from Latin America and Asia, both of which are low-milk-drinking areas. However, such a large decline likely has additional sources, including a declining focus on milk drinking as an "Americanization" tool and increased consumption of soda. In response to this trend, the dairy industry has developed new flavored and sugared milks in easy to "chug" containers and developed new marketing techniques directed at younger consumers. Finally, current industrial dairying methods have inspired outcry among consumers that parallel the "dirtying of a pure product" discussions of the late nineteenth century. As a result, new, usually more expensive milk products, such as organic milk and premium delivery services, have become increasingly popular.

[**See also** ADULTERATIONS; BORDEN; DAIRY; DAIRY INDUSTRY; MILK PACKAGING; MILK, POWDERED; PURE FOOD AND DRUG ACT; TRANSPORTATION OF FOOD.]

BIBLIOGRAPHY

Cohen, Robert. *Milk: The Deadly Poison.* Englewood Cliffs, NJ: Argus, 1997.

DuPuis, E. Melanie. *Nature's Perfect Food: How Milk Became America's Drink.* New York: New York University Press, 2002.

Manchester, Alden C. *The Public Role in the Dairy Economy: Why and How Governments Intervene in the Milk Business.* Boulder, CO: Westview, 1983.

Selitzer, Ralph. *The Dairy Industry in America.* New York: Dairy and Ice Cream Field and Books for Industry, 1976.

DANIEL BLOCK

Milk, Powdered

Marco Polo gets the credit for introducing powdered milk to Europe. His journals contain a lively account of thirteenth-century Mongols dehydrating skimmed mare's milk in the sun, creating a transportable, durable food. Modern technology has mechanized production, but the process of reducing milk to a powder has not changed. Defatted milk has its water content removed through evaporation, leaving a residue containing the proteins, vitamins, and minerals present in whole milk. Properly stored, powdered milk will keep its maximum nutritional value for up to four years. Because of its long shelf life, its portability, and the ease of reconstitution, it is a favored ration for hunters, hikers, survivalists, relief agencies, and the military.

Britain issued a patent for manufacturing dried milk in 1855. In 1869, Henri Nestlé perfected the process in Switzerland, and the United States issued a patent for producing it in 1872. The product was initially unpopular because of the food adulteration scandals that rocked the last part of the nineteenth century. Consumers were leery of how easily the powder could be cut or replaced entirely by other substances, like plaster of Paris. However, necessity brought it into wide use during World War II both on the battlefield and on the home front. Powdered milk became a staple of relief agencies operating in the postwar world.

Powdered milk found its niche in America in partnership with other ingredients to make foods like bread, instant cereal, and a variety of other convenience and ready-made foods. It achieved what is arguably its starring role in Pennsylvania in 1895, when the entrepreneur and candymaker Milton Hershey applied Henry Ford's assembly line to the formula for milk chocolate he had created based on the Swiss method of combining conched chocolate with powdered milk. The result was a smooth, consistent flavor of chocolate that is still a mass-market best seller.

Powdered milk is a mainstay of chocolate milk mixes, instant breakfast drinks, and numerous "instant" puddings, dips, and dressings, as well as a major supplement to livestock feed.

[**See also** BREAKFAST DRINKS; DIPS; HERSHEY'S; MILK; NESTLÉ; PUDDINGS.]

BIBLIOGRAPHY

Tannahill, Reay. *Food in History.* rev. ed. New York: Crown Publishers, 1989.

ESTHER DELLA REESE

Milk Packaging

For most of human history, milk was kept in its original package, the cow's udder, until it was needed. On the farm this meant that the cow was milked daily. In the city, cows were walked to the customer's door and milked on the spot. Some cows were milked at a central location in the city, and the milk was quickly delivered in metal pails. Customers came out with pitchers and bowls to receive the milk. During hot weather some of this milk spoiled, became contaminated, and in some places was a major source of milk-borne diseases, such as tuberculosis, diphtheria, and dysentery.

As populations grew, particularly in the cities, the pressure to find more efficient methods of packaging and distributing milk became a priority. The New York Dairy Company is thought to have been the first dairy to use a factory-made milk bottle around 1875. In 1878, the Lester Milk Jar received a patent as a milk container. In 1880, a glass milk bottle with a glass lid held in place with tin clips was patented. But the bottle that was to be the standard for most of the twentieth century was a milk bottle with a cap seal, which permitted the user to reseal the bottle with a paper disk. Milk bottles were embossed with the name of the dairy in order to ensure that they found their way back to be reused. Until the 1960s, the cream in the milk floated to the top of the bottle and was used in coffee or reserved for making whipped cream. Homogenization (breaking up the butterfat into particles that stay in suspension) became standard at this time, and the layer of cream at the top disappeared.

Through the 1950s, it was the milkman who delivered milk in heavy glass bottles. With a car, the modern housewife could purchase milk in paper cartons at convenient supermarkets. These containers were at first covered with wax to make the carton waterproof. These paper-based milk containers first appeared in California around 1906, but it was not until 1915 that John Van Wormer, a toy factory owner, received a patent for his paper milk carton. It took him ten years to develop a machine that could fold, glue, fill, and seal the cartons at the dairy. He called his paper milk container Pure-Pak, "pure" because it could be discarded after one use. By 1934, the Ex-Cell-O Corporation owned the rights to the Pure-Pak system. They introduced the tab on the side of the gable so it could be lifted for pouring. Before this innovation, consumers had to use a knife to open the top of the container. By the 1970s, the one-gallon plastic jug had become the standard milk container. The paper carton, its waxing replaced by a polyethylene laminate, is still widely used for half-pint servings, mostly in schools and vending machines.

[**See also** ASEPTIC PACKAGING; MILK.]

BIBLIOGRAPHY

Moyer, Judith. "From Dairy to Doorstep." *Historic New England*, Fall 2001.

JOSEPH M. CARLIN

Advertisement for Grandmother's A&P Condensed Milk.

Milkshakes, Malts, and Floats

In the late nineteenth century soda fountains all over the United States offered a variety of sweet concoctions. Among the most popular from the late nineteenth century on were malteds, milkshakes, and ice cream floats.

Malted milk powder was introduced in 1887 by William Horlick of Racine, Wisconsin, who marketed the powder in association with his brother James, an English apothecary. Malted milk, consisting of whole dried milk, malted barley, and wheat flour was intended to be dissolved in hot water and was used as a dietary supplement for infants. It also was considered useful for treating intestinal problems.

Soda fountain operators began adding malted milk powder to their flavored beverages, selling cold malted milk shakes in the summer and hot in the winter. Malted milk beverages were viewed as healthy, complete meal drinks that had particular appeal for men who preferred hearty, rich beverages to dainty ones. The temperance movement helped promote malteds as a good alternative to alcoholic beverages and thus as a draw for male customers at soda fountains.

Another invention that promoted the popularity of malteds was the development of various types of blenders in the late nineteenth and early twentieth centuries. The blender allowed soda jerks to create smoother, richer drinks than they could by hand and added to the showmanship that was integral to the soda fountain experience. In the 1920s, one malted milk powder manufacturer offered a free blender to any soda fountain that ordered a substantial amount of its malted milk powder.

Malteds were so popular that some soda fountains were called malt shops. Soda jerks used a special lingo when malts were ordered. "Twist it, choke it, and make it cackle" was an order for a malted with an egg or malted nog. Among the most popular malteds and their code calls were "black and white," a chocolate malted with vanilla ice cream; "burn one," a chocolate malted milk; and "burn one all the way," a chocolate malted with chocolate ice cream. As with other soda fountain beverages, the varieties were limitless.

Like malteds, milkshakes became popular in the late 1800s. They also were viewed as health drinks because they contained syrup along with the milk or the milk and ice cream. In different parts of the country milkshakes were called by different names. For example, a shake in most of New England was called a "frappe," but in Rhode Island it was a "cabinet." The variety of shakes was endless, chocolate and strawberry being the most popular. A more complex shake was the brown cow, which included chocolate syrup, milk, and root beer, and an unusual one was the prune juice shake. The basic soda fountain call for a milkshake was "shake one," modified by the flavor, such as "shake one in the hay"—a strawberry milkshake. Milkshakes could be shaken by hand, but as with malteds, the blender provided a thicker, smoother shake—and a show.

Ice cream floats are a form of ice cream soda. The differences lies in when the ice cream is added to the beverage. In a float the syrup is put into the glass, milk, if being used, is added, and then soda water is drawn into the glass so that a small amount of space is left at the top for the floating of ice cream and a bit more syrup. In making an ice cream soda, the ice cream is added when the glass is half to three-quarters full, and topped off with carbonated water. The most familiar popular floats were made with root beer or Coca-Cola. A black or brown cow was a root beer float.

[See also BATIDOS; BLENDERS; EGG CREAM; FRAPPES; ICE CREAM SODAS; ICES AND ICE CREAMS; MILK; PHOSPHATES; ROOT BEER; SELTZER; SODA DRINKS; SODA FOUNTAINS.]

BIBLIOGRAPHY

Funderburg, Anne Cooper. *Sundae Best: A History of Soda Fountains.* Bowling Green, OH: Bowling Green State University Popular Press, 2002.

Kelly, Patricia M., ed. *Luncheonette: Ice-Cream, Beverage, and Sandwich Recipes from the Golden Age of the Soda Fountain.* New York: Crown, 1988.

PATRICIA M. KELLY

Milky Way

In 1923, Frank Mars, a candymaker in Minneapolis, introduced the Milky Way bar, and distributed it locally. The Milky Way bar consisted of a center of malt-flavored nougat and caramel with a chocolate-coating that kept the candy bar fresh. It was bigger than other candy bars, such as the Hershey's Chocolate Bar, then on the market, but cheaper to make because it had only half as much chocolate. In 1924, Milky Way was marketed nationally and its sales topped $800,000 in the first year. In 1935, Milky Way was advertised as "the sweet you can eat between meals." Milky Way remains one of America's largest selling candy bars. Until the 1960s, all the chocolate in the Milky Way bar was supplied by its major competitor Hershey.

Forest Mars, Frank Mars's son, claimed that he gave his father the idea for the candy bar. Frank Mars booted Forest Mars out of Mars Inc. in 1932. Forrest was given $50,000 and the foreign rights to the Milky Way bar. He moved to England, where he launched Mars, Ltd. One of his first products was the Mars Bar—a slightly sweeter version of the American Milky Way bar. It was the first successful combination bar sold in the United Kingdom. During the 1960s, Forest Mars gained control of Mars Inc., and combined the operations of his companies.

BIBLIOGRAPHY

Brenner, Joël Glenn. *The Emperors of Chocolate: Inside the Secret World of Hershey and Mars.* New York: Broadway Books, 2000.

ANDREW F. SMITH

Miller Brewing Company

In 1855, Frederick Miller, an immigrant from Germany, bought the Menomonee Valley Brewery, a Milwaukee brewery also known as the Plank Road Brewery, which had been founded seven years earlier by Frederick Charles Best. The company remained in the hands of the Miller family until the late 1960s, when the head of the family was killed in an airplane crash. Philip Morris and Company purchased Miller in 1970. In 1972, Miller bought rights to the Meister Brau line of products, including one called Meister Brau Lite beer. Although Lite Beer cost less to produce than conventional beer, Miller positioned the product as a premium beer. The formula for Lite Beer from Miller continued to prove a winner, especially because of widespread, aggressive marketing. Miller's goal was to persuade the public that the low-calorie beer was as suited for men as it was for women. Miller not only achieve this goal but also broke ground in the brewing industry by developing low-calorie and low-carbohydrate beer and making it a national best seller.

In 1973, Miller's advertising agency, McCann-Erickson, was given the Lite Beer from Miller account. The usual brand research found that the beer drinkers of Anderson, Indiana, where the product was test marketed, gave Lite Beer an extremely high approval rating. The decision was made conduct a nationwide campaign with a television advertisement that is considered a classic. The commercial featured lovable Matt Snell, a well-known former football player, and the slogan "New Lite Beer from Miller is all you ever wanted in a beer…and less." That was the start of an advertising campaign that turned Miller Lite into a national institution and started the revolution in "light beer"—beer low in calories and carbohydrates.

By 1978, Miller passed Schlitz and Pabst to take second place to Anheuser-Busch, which had become the first brewer to sell 40 million barrels of beer a year. Soon the two top brewers were producing more than 50 percent of the beer sold in America, largely at the expense of smaller, independent breweries. In 1993, Miller test-marketed a clear beer, which failed in every way. In an attempt to expand the market and distribution of imported products with established reputations, Miller in 1995 acquired a stake in Canada's Molson and Mexico's FEMSA breweries. In May 2002, South African Breweries bought Miller Brewing Company from Philip Morris for $3.6 billion in stock, renaming the company SABMiller. This transaction allowed SABMiller to begin importing South African Breweries Pilsner Urquell beer to the United States and SABMiller to promote Miller products internationally.

[See also ADVERTISING; BEER; BREWING; BUDWEISER; COORS BREWING COMPANY.]

BIBLIOGRAPHY

Baron, Stanley. *Brewed in America*. Boston: Little Brown, 1962.

LaFrance, Peter. *Beer Basics*. New York: Wiley, 1995.

Rhodes, Christine P., ed. *The Encyclopedia of Beer*. New York: Henry Holt, 1995.

PETER LAFRANCE

Mimosa

The mimosa is one of America's first designer cocktails. It is the American version of a Buck's fizz. Invented in Britain in the 1920s, the Buck's fizz is made up of equal parts orange juice and champagne plus another, disputed ingredient, such as gin, brandy, or Cointreau. Sometime in the 1940s or 1950s, the drink appeared in the United States without the disputed extra ingredients and was called the "mimosa." One Hollywood legend has it that the mimosa was introduced to the United States by the British film director Alfred Hitchcock (Miller et al., *Champagne Cocktails*). As the story goes, Hitchcock added champagne to orange juice at a luncheon and presented it to fellow guests as a hangover cure. Perhaps this is why the mimosa is the drink of choice for brunch. The sweet and effervescent

cocktail has proved the perfect accompaniment to everything from croissants and muffins to eggs and smoked salmon. In an interesting twist, as the designer cocktail reemerged on the scene in the late twentieth century, bartenders across the United States once again began to put their signatures on the mimosa by adding an additional ingredient such as tangerine juice or Cointreau.

[See also CHAMPAGNE; COCKTAILS.]

BIBLIOGRAPHY

Brown, Jared, Don Gatterdam, and Anistatia Miller. *Champagne Cocktails*. New York: Harper Collins, 1999.

HOPE-MARIE FLAMM

Mint Family

The Mint (*Lamiaceae*) family provides many of the culinary herbs—over forty species. They are perennials (except as noted). Among the mint family members most used in the United States are:

Basil (*Ocimum basilicum*) is a familiar annual in America. Popular cultivars include anise, black opal, citriodorum, lettuce leaf, licorice, and purple ruffles.

Mint (*Mentha* species), also known as peppermint and spearmint. The many species and varietals are native to the Old World, but found almost everywhere. Its cool scent and hot taste are unmistakable.

Oregano (*Origanum vulgare*), occasionally found fresh in the supermarkets but is most commonly seen dried. Often, the "oregano" sold in the grocery store is actually a form of marjoram (*O. majoran*).

Rosemary (*Rosmarinus officinalis*), an evergreen woody herb, with an aromatic resinlike scent. Native around the Mediterranean, it grows in frost-free herb gardens everywhere.

Sage (*Salvia officinalis*). There are dozens of cultivars and other species of *Salvia*—not all of which have culinary value.

Summer Savory (*Satureja hortensis*) and Winter Savory (*Satureja montana*). Summer Savory is an annual, and is the species usually found on supermarket spice shelves. Both are used with dried beans.

Thyme (*Thymus vulgaris* and *Thymus serpyllum*), two of many species that are closely related, botanically and in culinary use.

[See also PREPARED HERB AND SPICE MIXTURES.]

BIBLIOGRAPHY

Allen, Gary. *The Herbalist in the Kitchen*. Champain: University of Illinois Press, (forthcoming).

Bailey, L. H. *Hortus Third: A Concise Dictionary of Plants Cultivated in the United States and Canada*. New York: Macmillan, 1976.

GARY ALLEN

Mint Julep

Far from their Kentucky home, two men traveling to the California gold mines in the early 1850s gathered snow left over from the past winter and prepared "mint juleps in abundance" (Morgan, 1959). They were, like so

many others in Kentucky, Virginia, Georgia, and elsewhere planning on carrying on the tradition of banishing the cares of the day with a frosty drink made with mint, ice, sugar, and whiskey. In the antebellum South, a mint julep was compared with sipping the nectar of the gods. Although the recipe sounds simple, preparing it requires a carefully observed ritual.

"Julep," according to the *Oxford English Dictionary*, comes from the Arabic *julab* or Persian *gul-ab* (rose water). The French adapted the word to *julep*. A citation in the *OED* from as early as 1400 describes a julep as a medicinal "syrup made only of water and sugar." Americans in Virginia, according to Richard Barksdale Harwell, the author of *The Mint Julep*, added spirits in 1787 and mint in 1803 and originated the mint julep. Deciding that the English might like this new version, Captain Frederick Marryat, who had been traveling in America, reintroduced the mint julep to the English in 1837. Marryat noted that the mint julep is "one of the most delightful and insinuating potations that ever was invented" (Harwell, *The Mint Julep*).

The first mint julep recipes called for brandy or rum, but local whiskey, frequently home-distilled rye and bourbon soon became the spirits of choice. Charles Joseph Latrobe, who described the mint julep in 1833 at a meeting of the Anti-Temperance Society in Saratoga, Florida, declared the mint must be unbruised. Jerry Thomas, in *How to Mix Drinks*, which was published in 1862, called for bruising the mint. The issue is still being debated. Both Latrobe and Thomas called for filling a tumbler or glass with shaved ice. Preparation of mint julep is seeped in ceremony and is a symbol of southern hospitality. Harwell quotes Judge Soule Smith, a Lexington, Kentucky, attorney in the late nineteenth century, praising the drink as "the very dream of drinks, the vision of sweet quaffings. The bourbon and the mint are lovers" (Harwell, p. 34).

Although the mint julep is appreciated throughout the South, Kentucky, proud of its bourbon, popularized the drink in the twentieth century. The year and date are unknown, but a letter written by Judge Soule Smith in the late nineteenth century makes clear that Kentucky bourbon should be the whiskey of choice for a mint julep. The tradition is upheld each year at the Kentucky Derby. Mint julep in a glass marked "Kentucky Derby" was first served in the dining room at Churchill Downs, home of the derby, in 1938. The vessel was an ordinary water glass, but patrons kept it as a souvenir and established a tradition. The next year proper julep glasses were used. Official Kentucky Derby glasses are collectors' items. Kentucky distilleries vie for the distinction of having their bourbon poured into the mint juleps served on derby day.

[See also BOURBON; COCKTAILS.]

BIBLIOGRAPHY

Harwell, Richard Barksdale. *The Mint Julep*. Charlottesville: University of Virginia Press, 1975.

Morgan, Dale L., ed. *The Overland Diary of James A. Patterson*. Denver: Old West Publishing, 1959.

JACQUELINE BLOCK WILLIAMS

Mock Foods

Mock foods are an insight into America's national heritage. This culinary genre was introduced to colonial America by European cooks versed in the ancient arts of presentation and food substitution. American mock foods were created when colonial cooks plied these skills to reconcile Old World recipes with New World ingredients. Recipes evolved according to immediate need, technological advancement, cultural advancement, economic necessity, and health concerns. In the eighteenth and nineteenth centuries, American mock foods centered on practical substitutions. In the late nineteenth century, creations featured more complicated, showy foods. In the twentieth century, mock foods often showcased manufactured products promoted by food companies. What makes a food "mock" is not a simple question to answer.

Mock can denote substitution of a primary ingredient. Perhaps the most famous mock food is mock turtle soup, immortalized by Lewis Carroll in *Alice's Adventures in Wonderland*. Mock goose (leg of pork), mock duck (leg of lamb), and "mock oysters" (corn fritters) were known to Americans in the nineteenth century. In the twentieth century, recipes for mock chicken were variously composed of pork, peanuts, tuna, or veal.

Mock can mean that a food tastes like another. The mock apple pie known to most Americans was introduced in the 1930s by the National Biscuit Company (Nabisco) as a promotion for Ritz crackers. This recipe evolved from mid-nineteenth-century imitation apple pies and mock mince pies, which were made with soda crackers, sugar, and spices. Crackers have a history of approximating apple pie in both texture and taste.

Mock foods may look like other foods. Upscale caterers throughout time have used food to create complicated, edible works of art. American culinary artists have been known to disguise entire hams as Easter eggs, create fantastic beasts from bread, and sculpt national icons from pâté. In the twentieth century, American homemakers decorated holiday tables with pineapple peacocks and cheese ducks.

Mock foods can be economical approximations of more expensive foods. Depression-era and wartime cooks relied on mock foods to stretch budgets. American cookbooks printed in these lean years were filled with less-expensive alternatives to traditional favorites. In some cookbooks, the word "mock" was featured in the index, facilitating recipe identification. Fannie Farmer's 1939 *Boston Cooking-School Cook Book* listed nineteen recipes under this heading.

Mock Foods List

Soups
Mock bouillon—canned tomatoes, diced vegetables, and spices, 1923
Mock fish chowder—fish chowder without the fish, 1918
Mock St. Germain soup—diced salt pork, canned condensed pea soup, and two cups of bouillon, 1942
Mock turtle soup—calf's head, 1824

Sauces and Dressings
Mock hollandaise—hot cream cheese, egg yolks, lemon juice, and mayonnaise, 1958
Mock maple syrup—brown sugar, water, salt, and vanilla, 1939

Meats and Eggs
Mock chicken—breaded & fried peanuts and sweet potatoes, 1925
Mock chicken drumsticks or "city chicken"—veal and pork on skewers, 1946
Mock chicken salad—cubed pork, 1923
Mock chicken salad—cubed veal, 1956
Mock chicken sandwiches—tuna, 1931
Mock duck—shoulder of lamb, the shank shaped to look like a duck's bill, 1884
Mock duck—stuffed tenderloin or flank steak, 1958
Mock goose—leg of pork, 1877
Mock sausages—pureed lima beans, cracker crumbs, heavy cream, and spices fried in oil, 1923
Mock veal cutlets—baked lentils, peanuts, graham cracker crumbs, tomatoes, and spices, 1925
Mock venison—mutton served with gravy and currant jelly, 1844

Seafood
Mock crab sandwich—grated cheese, creamed butter, mustard, and anchovy paste served hot, 1929
Mock crabs—canned corn, cracker crumbs, milk, and spices baked in butter, 1923
Mock oysters—corn fritters shaped like oysters, 1844
Mock oysters—mushrooms dipped in egg and bread crumbs and then fried, 1902
Mock scallops—halibut cut in the shape of scallops, breaded and deep fried, 1939
Mock terrapin—chicken, white sauce, eggs, sherry, and spices, 1939

Vegetables and Starches
Mock artichokes—white turnips, 1902
Mock macaroni—crackers soaked in milk and used for casseroles, 1828
Mock olives—unripe plums preserved in brine, 1918

Desserts
Mock angel cake—two egg whites instead of the usual eight to ten, 1923
Mock charlotte—cornstarch, sugar, eggs and water served with custard sauce, 1902
Mock cheese blintzes—cottage cheese, Uneeda biscuits, eggs, milk, and butter, 1958
Mock cherry pie—cranberries and raisins, 1923
Mock cream—milk, cornstarch, eggs, and butter, 1910
Mock cream pie—eggs, flour, and milk poured over puff paste and cooked in the oven, 1847
Mock Devonshire cream—cream cheese, cream, and sugar, 1956
Mock Indian pudding—whole wheat bread, milk, molasses, and butter, 1923
Mock mince pie—crackers rolled fine, water, vinegar, molasses, sugar, currants, and spices, 1877
Mock pistachio ice cream—vanilla with almond extract and green food coloring, 1931
Mock toasted marshmallows—gelatin, water, sugar, egg whites, vanilla, and stale macaroons, 1939

Candy
Mock almonds—stale bread cut in almond shapes, brushed with butter, and baked; croutons, 1923
Mock candy—ground nuts and fruits pressed together and cut like caramels, 1902

LYNNE M. OLVER

Mock can mean less of a key ingredient, acknowledging a substandard product. Fannie Farmer's 1923 recipe for mock angel food called for two egg whites rather than eight.

Mock can mean a vegetarian alternative. In the 1920s the American vegetarian movement created mock sausage (puréed lima beans) and mock veal cutlets (lentils and peanuts). Tofu burgers were promoted as healthy protein alternatives in the 1970s. American vegetarians in the 1980s celebrated Thanksgiving with "tofurkey" (tofu shaped like turkey).

Mock foods have been known by other names. In 1796, in a recipe for "a tasty indian pudding" in *American Cookery* (considered the first American cookbook) Amelia Simmons substituted cornmeal for wheat flour. In the 1884 edition of the *Boston Cooking-School Cook Book,* Mrs. D. A. Lincoln provided detailed instructions for meat porcupines (molded meat with bacon quills) and mutton ducks (artfully reconstructed bones and meat). Betty Crocker promoted emergency steak (T-bone–shaped meat loaf) during World War II. In the 1950s, residents of Pittsburgh consumed "city chicken" (skewered pork and veal), adopting it as a local favorite.

[See also BETTY CROCKER; COOKBOOKS AND MANUSCRIPTS: AMERICAN COOKBOOKS FROM THE CIVIL WAR TO WORLD WAR I; COOKBOOKS AND MANUSCRIPTS: AMERICAN COOKBOOKS TO 1860; COOKBOOKS AND MANUSCRIPTS: WORLD WAR I AND WORLD WAR II; CRACKERS; NABISCO; THANKSGIVING; VEGETARIANISM.]

BIBLIOGRAPHY

Allen, Ida C. Bailey. *Mrs. Allen on Cooking, Menus, Service: 2500 Recipes.* Garden City, NY: Doubleday, Page, 1924.

Cowles, Florence A. *Seven Hundred Sandwiches.* Boston: Little, Brown, 1929.

Crocker, Betty. *Picture Cook Book,* 2nd ed. New York: McGraw-Hill, 1956.

Crowen, Mrs. T. J. *Mrs. Crowen's American Lady's Cookery Book.* New York: Dick and Fitzgerald, 1847.

Farmer, Fannie Merritt. *Boston Cooking-School Cook Book.* 6th ed. Boston: Little, Brown, 1939.

Greenbaum, Florence Kreisler. *The International Jewish Cook Book.* New York: Bloch, 1918.

Leslie, Eliza. *Miss Leslie's Complete Cookery: Directions for Cookery, in Its Various Branches.* Philadelphia: Baird, 1849.

Lincoln, Mary J. *Boston Cooking School Cook Book: A Reprint of the 1884 Classic.* With a new introduction by Janice Bluestein Longone. Mineola, NY: Dover, 1996.

Randolph, Mary. *The Virginia House-wife.* With historical notes and commentaries by Karen Hess. Columbia: University of South Carolina Press, 1984.

Rombauer, Irma S. *The Joy of Cooking.* New York: Scribner, 1998. Facsimile of 1931 edition.

Webster, Mrs. A. L. *The Improved Housewife or Book of Receipts: Or, Book of Receipts; with Engravings for Marketing and Carving, by a Married Lady.* 5th ed. Hartford, CT: Hobbs, 1844.

Wilcox, Esther Woods. *Buckeye Cookery and Practical Housekeeping, Compiled from Original Recipes.*

Bedford, MA: Applewood, 2000. Facsimile of 1877 edition.

Woman's Home Companion Cook Book. Foreword by Willa Roberts. New York: Collier, 1942.

LYNNE M. OLVER

Molasses

Molasses, like honey, is a liquid sweetener. The term "molasses" has several meanings. In the rural South and in parts of Appalachia, "molasses" refers to a homemade syrup produced from farm-grown sugarcane. The sugarcane is cleaned and then manually crushed by rollers in a mule-powered mill or press. Milling extracts juice and water from the cane. The extracted liquid is boiled down in an open kettle to evaporate some of the water, making a syrup. This very sweet sugary syrup is pure cane syrup or more commonly, "molasses." In Louisiana, this syrup is called *la cuite.* Farther to the north, including most of the Midwest, farm-produced molasses is made from sorghum, a cereal grass, by the same open-kettle technique.

In the refined-sugar industry, molasses is a by-product of the sugar-extraction process. After most of the water is removed from sugarcane juice by evaporation, raw sugar is crystallized from the syrup. These sugar crystals are mechanically removed by first spinning the syrup (centrifugation) and then passing it through very fine screens. The liquid that remains after some or all of the sugar has been removed from the syrup is molasses.

There are three primary types of commercial molasses because the sugarcane juice can be processed three times. After the initial boiling of the juice and the first removal of sugar crystals from the syrup, the remaining liquid is sweet and thick. This by-product is first, or light, molasses. When the syrup is processed a second time and more sugar crystals are removed, the remaining liquid is darker and less sweet. This product is called second, or dark, molasses. The third processing produces blackstrap molasses, a dark, bitter, nonsweet syrup. First or second molasses that has been bleached with sulfur dioxide is called "sulfured" molasses.

Molasses first came to America from the Caribbean. The British started sugarcane cultivation in Barbados in 1646, and by the late 1670s there was a flourishing two-way sea trade between Barbados and the American colony at Rhode Island. The colonists shipped agricultural and forest products, such as pork, beef, butter, cider, barrel staves, and shingles, to the West Indies, and the ships returned with cargoes of cotton wool, rum, molasses, and sugar. The large volume of sugar and molasses going to Rhode Island could not be used there, so much of this cargo was resold in Boston.

The New England colonists used molasses not only as the primary sweetener in cooking and baking but also as an ingredient in brewing birch beer and molasses beer and in dis-

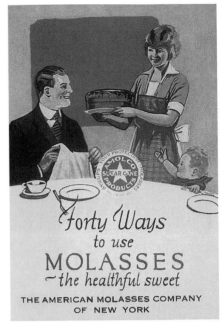

The American Molasses Company published Forty Ways to Use Molasses *in 1923.*

tilling rum. In the early 1700s rum made in New England became an essential element in a highly profitable triangular trade across the Atlantic. The colonists exported rum to West Africa in trade for slaves; the ships brought the slaves from Africa to the French West Indies, trading them for more molasses and sugar; these products were then shipped to New England to make more rum.

Because importation of molasses to New England from the French West Indies seriously harmed British farmers in the Caribbean, the British government passed the Molasses Act in 1733. This law imposed a duty on "foreign" molasses or syrup imported into the American colonies or plantations. In addition, some shipments of American rum were subject to forfeiture and confiscation of the vessel of transport. The Molasses Act of 1733 and the Sugar Act of 1764 caused the price of molasses to rise, leading to the use of less expensive maple sugar as a sweetener. When the cost of refined sugar dropped at the end of the nineteenth century—as a result of increased production from manufacturing advances and huge increases in the amount of imported refined sugar—molasses lost its role as an important sweetener in the American diet.

In the early twenty-first century, molasses is not an important sweetener in cooking. It is, however, an essential flavor ingredient in a number of traditional American baked goods, such as anadama bread, gingerbread, gingersnaps, hermits, Indian pudding, molasses cakes, molasses cookies, and shoofly pie. Molasses is also an important flavor ingredient in Cracker Jack, a popcorn-and-peanuts snack food. Specific regional dishes, such as Boston baked beans and Boston brown bread, require molasses. Because molasses complements pork dishes, it is commonly found in ham glazes and barbecue sauces.

Molasses, like many other food words, has entered American slang. People who are lethargic or not efficient are called "slow as molasses" or "slow as molasses in January." American children are introduced to molasses and its very sticky nature in *Candyland*, a board game for children who have not yet learned to read. *Candyland* is played with gingerbread-men game pieces. The unlucky child whose game piece lands on a certain penalty spot on the way to finding the Lost Castle becomes stuck in the molasses swamp.

[**See also** ANADAMA BREAD; BIRCH BEER; CAJUN AND CREOLE FOOD; CRACKER JACK; GERMAN AMERICAN FOOD, *sidebar on* SHOOFLY PIE; RUM; SORGHUM SYRUP; SUGAR; SWEETENERS.]

BIBLIOGRAPHY

Bienvenu, Marcelle. *Who's Your Mama, Are You Catholic, and Can You Make a Roux? A Family Album, Cajun/Creole Cookbook.* Lafayette, LA: Times of Acadian, 1991.

Farr, Sidney Saylor. *More Than Moonshine: Appalachian Recipes and Recollections.* Pittsburgh, PA: University of Pittsburgh Press, 1983.

Woloson, Wendy A. *Refined Tastes: Sugar, Confectionery, and Consumers in Nineteenth-Century America.* Baltimore: Johns Hopkins University Press, 2002.

ROBERT W. BROWER

Moldy Cheese, *see Cheese, Moldy*

Mondavi, Robert

Robert Mondavi (1913–) is a leading figure in the transformation of the American wine industry, notably the Napa Valley in California. The Robert Mondavi corporation, now a public company, has expanded from its base in the Napa Valley to joint ventures with international wine producers, such as the Frescobaldi in Italy and Eduardo Chadwick in Chile. The best known of Robert Mondavi's strategic partnerships was that with Baron Philippe de Rothschild to create the wine Opus One. This partnership and the quality of the wine gave new cachet to the wines of California, specifically those of the Napa Valley.

The Mondavi dynasty began when Robert's father, Cesare, came to the United States from Italy in 1906. Cesare ran a boarding house in Minnesota and left there in 1922 for the San Joaquin Valley of California. Like the Gallo family, who lived nearby, Cesare became involved in the sale of grapes to home winemakers, a legal enterprise even in the midst of Prohibition. The sale of grapes in limited quantities for personal winemaking was, however, legal. Also like the Gallo family, Cesare Mondavi began to produce wine at the end of Prohibition. He later chose to leave the hot Central Valley, where grapes for sweet wines thrived, for the cooler Napa Valley to concentrate on quality varietal wines. The Gallos remained in the Central Valley and built the world's largest winery, a cornerstone of their empire.

In the cooler climate of the Napa Valley sometime after 1936, Robert Mondavi began to make wine. He worked at the Sunny St. Helena Winery and later was involved in the operation of the Charles Krug Winery, which the Mondavi family acquired in 1943. At the Krug winery, Mondavi became acquainted with the work of Andre Tchelistcheff (1901–1994). Tchelistcheff, a Russian émigré, was an enologist whose work was a major contribution to the California wine industry. Tchelistcheff was working for Georges de Latour of the Beaulieu Vineyard but acted as a consultant to many Napa vineyards. Mondavi and Tchelistcheff's mutual vision was the production of grapes suited to the soil and climate with the goal of making fine wine. Mondavi believed that Cabernet Sauvignon was ideally suited to the region and conducted experiments with the grape. When Cesare Mondavi died in 1959, his brother Peter, whose vision for the winery was at odds with Robert's, cut Robert out of the operation. Family acrimony was not uncommon among the great California winemakers and families such as the Gallos and the Sebastianis had highly publicized disputes. After a difficult legal struggle Robert Mondavi obtained compensation and in 1966 founded his own winery on the Oakville Highway in Napa Valley. Among the first winemakers whom Mondavi consulted was the venerable Andre Tchelistcheff.

Thirteen years after founding his winery, in 1979, Mondavi entered into the historic partnership with Baron Philippe de Rothschild. The wine created was Opus One, a partnership of the old world and the new that was highly regarded. Unlike the Gallo family, who relied on keeping the company private and controlling the many aspects of wine production, Mondavi became a pioneer in joint ventures worldwide and acquired numerous properties. The company expanded to include labels such as Woodbridge, Vichon, and Byron. In 1993 the Robert Mondavi company began selling shares to the public. In his early nineties, Robert Mondavi continues active participation in the company, serving as a goodwill ambassador. Mondavi's children, R. Michael, Timothy, and Marcia manage the company.

[**See also** WINE; LATER DEVELOPMENTS; WINERIES; WINES, CALIFORNIA.]

BIBLIOGRAPHY

Laube, J. "Play or Pass on Mondavi Stock." *Wine Spectator*, 31 July 1993.

Mondavi, Robert. "Scenes from a Life in Wine." *Wine Spectator*, 18 March 1993.

STEVE CRAIG

Monkfish

Monkfish (*Lophius americanus*), nicknamed goosefish and anglerfish, is among the homeliest of edible species caught. It has a huge head and mouth, with lots of sharp teeth, and it feeds on almost anything. Another of the fish eaten by Europeans but not by Americans, it was of virtually no commercial value until after the 1960s; neither was it a common recreational fish. Monkfish was once a bycatch of the ground fisheries but was later caught for its own sake. Since the 1970s, because of the pressure on more favored fish like cod and haddock, monkfish has appeared in seafood markets, and the liver is prized in Asia. Most of the catch is landed on the East Coast from the Middle Atlantic States up through the Canadian maritime provinces.

It is mostly the monkfish's tail with its smooth, solid flesh that is sold for food. When cooked, the flesh hardly flakes apart, and because it resembles lobster meat, it is sometimes called poor man's lobster. It is best used in chowders or other moist heat cookery, such as fish stews or soups. It is not at all suitable for baking or grilling.

SANDRA L. OLIVER

Monte Cristo Sandwich

The Monte Cristo sandwich is composed of white bread, slices of ham, turkey, or chicken, and Swiss cheese. The sandwich is dipped in egg batter, deep-fried in oil or fried in butter, and then dusted with powdered sugar and served with strawberry or raspberry jam for dipping. The Monte Cristo is a variation of the American grilled-cheese sandwich that evolved from the French *croque monsieur*. The sandwich was first mentioned in an American restaurant industry publication in 1923. The origin of the Monte Cristo has been traditionally attributed to California, and it was featured on a 1941 menu in Gordon's, a restaurant once located on Wilshire Boulevard in Los Angeles. Although no explanation of the name has been determined, the sandwich may have been named after the popular movie *The Count of Monte Cristo*, produced in four adaptations between 1908 and 1934. By the early 1950s a Monte Carlo version of the sandwich was being made with sliced tongue, and both sandwiches, cut into small squares for serving with cocktails, were called Monte Benitos.

[**See also** SANDWICHES.]

BIBLIOGRAPHY

Brown, Helen Evans. *West Coast Cook Book.* New York: Knopf, 1991.

Mercuri, Becky. *Sandwiches That You Will Like.* Pittsburgh, PA: WQED Multimedia, 2002.

BECKY MERCURI

Moon Pie

About 1917, the Chattanooga Bakery began selling the Moon Pie, a novel chocolate-coated treat consisting of two large, soft round cookies (similar to graham crackers) with a marshmallow filling in between. Earl Mitchell Sr. claimed to have invented it based on what coal miners said they wanted in a snack. It was also called the marshmallow sandwich. The term *Moon Pie* was not copyrighted until 1930, but its success as a commercial product was immediate. By the 1950s, it was so successful that the Chattanooga Bakery produced nothing else. Chattanooga Bakery has extended the product line with Mini Moon Pies, Double and Single Deckers, and Fruit-Filled Moon Pies. The Moon Pies remain popular in the South, where they are traditionally consumed with RC Cola.

Similar to Moon Pies were Scooter Pies, which were popularized by the television program, *Laverne and Shirley*, and Whoopie Pies popular in Pennsylvania and New England. Similar products, called Wagon Wheels, are manufactured in Canada and the United Kingdom, where they are manufactured by Burtons Biscuits.

BIBLIOGRAPHY
Dickson, Ron, with help from William M. Clark et al. *The Great American Moon Pie Handbook*. Atlanta, Georgia: Peachtree Publishers, 1985.

ANDREW F. SMITH

Moonshine

Moonshine is illicitly distilled liquor. In the rural southern United States, it is most commonly corn whiskey. The word "moonshine" was in use as early as 1785, but at that time it meant smuggled liquor. The current meaning came into use about 1875. Americans were distilling homemade whiskey much earlier than that, of course, for both medicinal and recreational purposes.

Moonshine, also known as angel teat, Kentucky fire, squirrel whiskey, swamp dew, white lightning, or white mule, had its heyday during Prohibition. It is made of water, yeast, malt, sugar or molasses or sorghum, and almost any sugary or starchy edible including, among many other possibilities, cornmeal, hog feed, blackberries, rose hips, potatoes, pumpkins, or raisins fermented in a still. By definition, moonshine is unregulated, so it may be poisoned or unsanitary. It is often cut with water, glycerin, food coloring, extracts, or caustics, and its most dangerous side effect is lead poisoning, which can lead to blindness or death. Unlike regular whiskey, which goes brown from aging in barrels made of charred oak, moonshine is clear and is usually not aged at all.

During Prohibition, moonshiners enjoyed a huge profit margin, making four gallons of whiskey for about $4 and selling them for about $160. The drink is generally tasteless and harsh; many compare its flavor to grain alcohol. There are commercially produced, imitation versions of moonshine available, like Georgia Moon and Platte Valley, packaged in jelly jars and ceramic jugs, respectively.

[**See also** ALCOHOL AND TEETOTALISM; BOURBON; HOMEMADE REMEDIES; PROHIBITION; STILLS; TEMPERANCE; WHISKEY.]

BIBLIOGRAPHY
Kellner, Esther. *Moonshine: Its History and Folklore*. Indianapolis: Bobbs-Merrill, 1971.

Lender, Mark Edward and Martin, James Kirby. *Drinking in America: A History*. Rev. and exp. ed. New York: The Free Press, 1987.

JESSY RANDALL

Mortar and Pestle

Smashing and grinding into fine particles is the job of a mortar and pestle. Mortars are the vessels; pestles are the handheld tools that do the work. The concept and form are probably the earliest of all cookery tools anywhere in the world. The earliest American mortars were probably stone, although other materials—cast iron, cast bronze, and heavy ceramic—would have been brought with immigrants from the beginning. Mortars made of the hardest, densest wood available, *lignum vitae* (wood of life), from a tropical tree, were probably in very early use too. Local hardwoods that resist splintering, such as maple, were also used. Even if set into wooden handles for comfort, the business end of a pestle was made of the same material as its mortar. Since the mid-nineteenth century, most mortars and pestles have been made of thick, white stoneware that resembles marble, with wooden handles for the pestles. Stoneware is impervious to acids and alkalies, and it does not interact with foods. An all-wood implement like a pestle, used with any kind of vessel, is called a beetle.

[**See also** GRINDERS.]

BIBLIOGRAPHY
Franklin, Linda Campbell. *300 Years of Kitchen Collectibles*. 5th ed. Iola, WI: Krause Publications, 2003.

LINDA CAMPBELL FRANKLIN

Moxie

Moxie, which originated in New England, is the oldest carbonated soft drink and outsold Coca-Cola until the 1920s. Aficionados describe Moxie as extremely potent root beer, although it is a cola drink, but detractors find it unappealing and medicinal. Perhaps because of its strong flavor, Moxie became known as a drink with an attitude, and the word "moxie" has come to mean a "can-do" character. Calvin Coolidge is said to have used Moxie to toast his swearing in as president in 1923 (Schlozman, 2001).

Moxie was invented as a patent medicine in 1876 by a pharmacist, Augustin Thompson, who sold it over the counter as Moxie Nerve Food in his Lowell, Massachusetts, drugstore. Thompson claimed that Moxie, made with gentian root, a nerve-calming ingredient, cured everything from upset stomach to dullness of the brain. In 1910, however, the newly formed U.S. Food and Drug Administration put a stop to the claims.

Moxie advertising was aimed at people with discerning taste, such as the "Moxie Man." The Boston Red Sox star Ted Williams promoted the drink with "Make Mine Moxie"

baseball cards. Despite the advertising, Moxie never caught up to Coca-Cola in sales. Nevertheless, every July approximately 25,000 "Moxie heads" gather in Lisbon Falls, Maine, for Moxie Days, which are celebrated with parades, floats, booths of memorabilia, and foods made from Moxie. Although it is considered a New England institution, Moxie is now made by the Monarch Beverage Company, in Atlanta, Georgia.

[**See also** COCA-COLA; NEW ENGLAND; SODA DRINKS.]

BIBLIOGRAPHY
Funderburg, Anne Cooper. *Sundae Best: A History of Soda Fountains*. Bowling Green, OH: Bowling Green State University Popular Press, 2002.
Schlozman, Danny. "Make Mine Moxie." Cambridge, MA: *Perspective* (November 2001).

MARIAN BETANCOURT

Mozzarella

The name mozzarella is derived from the Italian verb, *mozzare* (to cut off), and describes the action that occurs when the cheese is torn into pieces during the production process. Traditionally produced in southern Italy from water-buffalo milk, mozzarella is a fresh pulled or spun curd cheese, also known as *pasta filata*. As early as the thirteenth century, the monks of San Lorenzo in Capua distributed *mozza* and bread to pilgrims. During World War II, the Nazis destroyed much of Italy's water-buffalo herds and although new animals were imported, cow's milk is now also used to produce mozzarella.

Arriving in large numbers on American shores at the turn of the twentieth century, Italian immigrants began to create Italian cheese varieties, including mozzarella. One of the earliest producers was Pasquale Frigo, founder of Frigo Cheese Corporation, who emigrated from Italy to northern Wisconsin, where the climate suited Italian cheese making. During the post–World War II era, mozzarella's popularity soared as it rode the wave of enthusiasm for pizza and other Italian foods that swept the country. By the mid-2000s, mozzarella was the second-best selling cheese in America, where it commanded a 31 percent market share to first-place cheddar's 34 percent.

Processed American mozzarella (also called "pizza cheese") is typically made from cow's milk and is drier than its Italian counterpart. Mass-produced for sale to supermarkets, it is also made for the food service industry as a topping for fresh and frozen pizza, ravioli, and other Italian foods. But even with the advent of factory-made mozzarella, fresh (also called fio di latte) or smoked (provola) mozzarella has traditionally been produced by Italian specialty stores located in areas with substantial concentrations of Italian-Americans. Recently, artisanal American cheese producers have developed their own fresh mozzarella varieties. Layered with ripe tomatoes and basil, fresh mozzarella can be eaten alone with a drizzle of olive oil and a dash of fresh ground pepper.

BIBLIOGRAPHY

American Dairy Association. *Cheese Production, Sales & Consumption Statistics*, http://www.ilovecheese. com/images/newsroom/cheese_facts.pdf.

Jenkins, Steven. *Cheese Primer*. New York: Workman Publishing Company, Inc., 1996.

Mozzarella Company. http://www.mozzco.com/ mozzhisty.html#more.

Selitzer, Ralph. *The Dairy Industry in America*. New York: Dairy and Ice Cream Field and Books for Industry, 1976.

The Food Timeline. http://www.foodtimeline.org.

LAURA WEISS

Mr. Peanut

Planters Peanuts was launched in 1906 by two Italian immigrants, Amedeo Obici and Mario Peruzzi. In 1916, Planters conducted a contest to develop a trademark, offering a prize worth five dollars for the best-designed symbol. The winner was a fourteen-year-old boy named Anthony Gentile, who submitted a drawing of "a little peanut person." With this image as a starting point, Planters hired a Chicago art firm, which commissioned a commercial artist named Andrew Wallach to draw several different caricatures. Planters selected the peanut person with a top hat, monocle, cane, and the look of a raffish gentleman, which was subsequently named "Mr. Peanut." At least, this was the story that Planters circulated. Similar peanut figures, complete with top hat, monocle, cane, and gloves, had illustrated an article in *Good Housekeeping* magazine in 1902.

Whatever the origin of Mr. Peanut, the character was a solid advertising success aimed at America's youth. Planters applied for a trademark on March 12, 1917. During that year, Mr. Peanut made his debut in New England newspapers and on advertising posters in New York City subway trains. This debut was followed by a national advertising campaign in which Mr. Peanut appeared in the *Saturday Evening Post*. These campaigns were so successful that Planters increased its advertising budget for each succeeding year, spending hundreds of thousands of dollars on advertisements in the best newspapers and magazines in the United States. In advertisements, Mr. Peanut proclaimed that peanuts were a perfect food for picnics and baseball games and for use as an ingredient in main dishes served at lunch and dinner. The company used other media as well, including Mr. Peanut paint books.

Planters print promotions moved from commonplace advertising to novel schemes that drew in readers, and the advertising paid off. Sales rose from $1 million in 1917 to $7 million five years later. Within these few years, salted peanuts and confections bearing Mr. Peanut's picture became known all across America. Planters opened a store on the boardwalk in Atlantic City, New Jersey. A man dressed in a Mr. Peanut outfit greeted visitors outside the store and became one of the most memorable figures along the boardwalk. In New York City, Mr. Peanut, complete with hat and cane, appeared on a dazzling sign at Forty-Sixth Street and Broadway, in Times Square. By the mid-1930s, Mr. Peanut had become the symbol for the entire peanut industry.

Since his origin, Mr. Peanut has been on almost every Planters package, container, premium, and advertisement. As a result, the Mr. Peanut caricature has become one of the most familiar icons in advertising history. His likeness graces mugs, pencils, pens, and tote bags, which are available by redemption of product wrappers. Planters offered a variety of premium items with its products: glass jars, charm bracelets, clocks, metal tins, wristwatches, ashtrays, plastic whistles, and display figures with monocles that lit up. At the beginning of the twenty-first century, Mr. Peanut is an American culinary icon known the world over.

[*See also* ADVERTISING; KRAFT FOODS; PEANUTS; SNACKS, SALTY.]

BIBLIOGRAPHY

Lindenberger, Jan, with Joyce Spontak. *Planters Peanut Collectibles 1906–1961*. 2nd ed. Atglen, PA: Schiffer, 1999.

Smith, Andrew F. *Peanuts: The Illustrious History of the Goober Pea*. Urbana: University of Illinois Press, 2002.

ANDREW F. SMITH

Mrs. Fields' Cookies

In August 1977, Debra "Debbi" Fields, a twenty-two-year-old mother with no business experience, and her husband, Randall K. Fields, a Stanford graduate, opened a cookie store called the Mrs. Fields Chocolate Chippery near Stanford University in Palo Alto, California. Her specialty was rich, homestyle chocolate-chip cookies, which were baked throughout the day and sold warm. The company was later renamed Mrs. Fields' Cookies.

Mrs. Fields' began franchising in 1990; in 1993 an economic downturn force Debbi Fields to sell Mrs. Fields' Cookies to private investors in Utah. She was featured on a number of television cooking shows and several cookbooks appeared under her name. Her book, *Mrs. Fields Cookie Book: 100 Recipes from the Kitchen of Mrs. Fields* (1992) sold more than 1.8 million copies and was the first cookbook to top *The New York Times* best-seller list. The company that the Fields created is today part of Mrs. Fields Famous Brands, which also includes the Original Cookie Company, Great American Cookie Company, Pretzel Time, and TCBY Yogurt and Ice Cream. As of 2005, Mrs. Fields' Cookies has more than 450 locations in eleven countries.

BIBLIOGRAPHY

Boyett, Joseph H., and Jimmie Boyett. *The Guru Guide to Entrepreneurship: A Concise Guide to the Best Ideas from the World's Top Entrepreneurs*. New York: Wiley, 2001.

Fields, Debbi, and the editors of Time-Life Books. *Mrs. Fields Cookie Book: 100 Recipes from the Kitchen of Mrs. Fields*. Alexandria, Virginia: Time-Life Books, 1992.

ANDREW F. SMITH

Muffaletta Sandwich

The muffaletta sandwich is composed of a round loaf of crusty italian bread containing layers of mortadella (Italian salami), ham, Genoa salami, mozzarella and provolone cheeses, and olive salad. It reflects the influence of Italian immigrants on the cooking of New Orleans, a city noted for its Cajun and Creole cuisine. Arriving in significant numbers around the turn of the twentieth century, many of the immigrants were from Sicily, and they found employment in the French Quarter's food industry. One such person was Signor Lupo Salvadore, who established Central Grocery in 1906. It is said that Lupo, taking a cue from Italian workers who would scoop broken olives from barrels onto the bread they brought for lunch, created the muffaletta sandwich. It is named for a bread called muffaletta that was first made in New Orleans around 1895 by a baker of Albanian descent from Palermo, Sicily. The bread is still produced, in the early 2000s, by at least one old-fashioned

A muffaletta sandwich at the Nor Joe Import Company in Metairie, Louisiana.

The Planters Peanuts mascot on the cover of a cookbooklet issued by Standard Brands in 1970.

neighborhood bakery in Piano degli Albanese, near Palermo, home of an Albanian colony since the fifteenth century. A signature sandwich of New Orleans, the muffaletta has become so popular that it appears on restaurant menus throughout the United States.

[**See also** HOAGIE; ITALIAN AMERICAN FOOD; PO'BOY SANDWICH; SANDWICHES.]

BIBLIOGRAPHY
Mercuri, Becky. *Sandwiches That You Will Like*. Pittsburgh, PA: WQED Multimedia, 2002.

BECKY MERCURI

Mugs, Beer, *see Beer Mugs*

Mulberries

Three distinct tree fruits are known as mulberries. The white mulberry (*Morus alba*) is a native of western Asia. The two-inch fruits are used dried more commonly than they are fresh. The leaves of the white mulberry are used as feed for silkworms, for which James I of England and his successors offered a subsidy. For this reason, the white mulberry was introduced to America in early colonial times. The plant seeds prolifically, and some of the early trees and their wilding progeny are extant in the Carolinas and Georgia.

The red mulberry (*Morus rubra*), native to the eastern seaboard of North America, bears fruits smaller than those of the white mulberry and appreciated more by Native Americans than by Europeans. The black mulberry (*Morus nigra*), which is unknown in the wild state, was introduced to Europe and then to North America from warmer areas of western Asia. It fruits reliably only in the Pacific Coast states. Popular usage misapplies the names "white," "red," and "black" to the fruits of mulberry trees. In fact, the names indicate the bud-scale colors of the respective species in winter.

Both dark and colorless white forms of white mulberry are grown in the United States. In America, white mulberry is planted as feed for free-range hogs. The high reputation of the flesh of these hogs is attributed to seasonal mulberry and acorn feed. White mulberry also is used to produce feed for free-run chickens. White mulberry is otherwise limited to dooryard culture. Because the pigment of white mulberry fruit causes stains, paler and colorless berries are more popular. The flavor of white mulberry fruits is sweet but never rich, and many find the flavor cloying when the berries are consumed in quantity.

The fruit of the black mulberry is finer for dessert purposes than is that of the white mulberry. Black mulberry fruits are exquisitely fragile and juicy. It is not possible to harvest the fruit without breaking the skin. Highly acid, the juice acquires sugar only in the last day or two before the fruit drops from the tree. For this reason the fruits are highly variable in flavor when harvested. The best berries confirm the reputation of the black mulberry as the richest flavored of all temperate-zone fruits.

Because of the fragility and perishable nature of all mulberries, the market for these fruits is strictly local. Even in California, sales are limited to occasional farmers' market stands. The fruits of the black mulberry are so exquisite that most are consumed fresh. They are unsuited for cooking. There is no American industry for production of mulberry syrup or juice. Such industries do exist in central Asia.

[**See also** DESSERTS; FRUIT.]

BIBLIOGRAPHY
Hedrick, U. P. *Cyclopedia of Hardy Fruits*. New York: Macmillan, 1922.

TODD KENNEDY

Mullet

The term "mullet" (*Mugil cephalus* and *Chaenomugil proboscidens*) applies to both saltwater and freshwater fishes. The saltwater gray, or striped, mullet is found in warm to temperate waters on both the East and West coasts of America and is regarded as a good food fish. Herbivorous, the mullet eats by grazing through mud. The flesh is firm and sweet; however, as it is more perishable than other fish, mullet is best eaten within a day or two of being caught and is found fresh in markets nearest its source, most often in the South. It is not usually frozen but is sometimes smoked or filleted; it can be cooked with almost any dry or wet heat methods.

SANDRA L. OLIVER

Mulligan Stew

Mulligan stew is a hodgepodge combination of available foods, including some meat, potatoes, carrots, onions, and other vegetables; another name for it is Whatchagot Stew. The first print reference to the Mulligan Stew appeared in a 1904 newspaper published in Dawson, Yukon Territory, Canada. The word was adopted in the United States and usually referred to a stew cooked and eaten by hobos or other itinerant people. As there are no set ingredients or cooking procedures, mulligan stew recipes are diverse—it's a given that each version depends on what the cook can round up that day.

BIBLIOGRAPHY
Brown, Helen Evans, and James Beard. *The Complete Book of Outdoor Cookery*. Garden City, NY: Doubleday, 1955.

ANDREW F. SMITH

Mushrooms

"Mushroom" is the colloquial name for approximately 38,000 varieties of fungi that have mycelia (threadlike roots) and often a distinctive cap and stem structure. Most varieties grow only in the wild, although mycologists are increasingly unlocking the mysteries of mushroom cultivation. Mushrooms are marketed fresh, dried, canned, and frozen. Some important families of culinary mushrooms include the *Agaricaceae*, home to *Agaricus campestris*, the field mushroom, and its cultivated "white" or "French" mushroom counterpart, *Agaricus bisporus*; *Boletaceae*, whose most popular member, *Boletus edulis*, travels as the cèpe, or porcini; and *Polyporaceae*, in which the Asian favorites *Lentinus edodes*, or shiitake, and *Grifola frondosa*, or hen-of-the-woods, are grouped.

With such a selection, it may seem surprising that mushrooms entered the American culinary limelight only in the late nineteenth century. Until the 1890s, most mushroom recipes were for ketchups, sauces, and pickles, with occasional stewed mushrooms or French-influenced dishes named "champignons." Few Americans included mushrooms in kitchen gardens, which was understandable given Hannah Glasse's rare and unappetizing instructions for mushroom cultivation in *The Art of Cookery Made Plain and Easy* (1805). Mushroom gathering was

---

How to Raise Mushrooms

Cover an old hot-bed three or four inches thick with fine garden mould, and cover that three or four inches thick with mouldy long muck, of a horse muck-kill, or old rotten stubble; when that bed has lain some time thus prepared, boil any mushrooms that are not fit for use, in water, and throw the water on your prepared bed; in a day or two after, you will have the best small button mushrooms.
Hannah Glasse, The Art of Cookery Made Plain and Easy (1805).

Product	Starting Materials	Microorganism(s)
soy sauce	soybeans and wheat	fungi (*Aspergillus* spp)
		bacteria (*Lactobacillus* spp)
poi	taro	yeast (*Candida* spp)
		bacteria (*Lactobacillus* spp)
kimchi sauerkraut	cabbage or other vegetables	bacteria (lactic acid bacteria, different species)
cured salami	meat	bacteria (*Lactobacillus*, *Pediococcus* spp)
		fungi (*Penicillium* spp) on the casing

fraught with danger, for no reliable American guides distinguished between gustatory pleasure and peril. Typical is *The Kentucky Housewife* (1839) by Lettice Bryan, which simply warns the cook to "be careful to select the esculent mushrooms, as some of them are very poisonous."

Mushroom cultivation began in seventeenth-century France as mushrooms became an important component of France's emerging haute cuisine. The techniques were perfected in the 1870s and spread abroad, just as French cookery became fashionable in America.

By the 1890s, a veritable fungus frenzy was sweeping America, both as a fad food and as a scientific curiosity. Mushrooming clubs, where foragers swapped tips, sprung up quickly. Meticulously illustrated literature educated amateurs and professionals in identifying and cooking mushrooms. The highly technical *Studies of American Fungi* (1911) by George Francis Atkinson contains 250 extraordinary photographs along with recipes by Sarah Tyson Rorer. Rorer differentiates between a dozen genera, each with distinct culinary characteristics. The cultlike adulation of mushrooms is shown by her recipe (similar to others beginning in the 1890s) for baking *Agaricus campestris* on toasts with a bit of cream under a glass bell, "to retain every particle of the flavor. The bell is then lifted at the table, that the eater may get the full aroma and flavor from the mushrooms." This scientific precision in identifying preferred species for different preparations had become common by the early twentieth century, as seen in one of America's first cookbooks devoted exclusively to mushrooms, *One Hundred Mushroom Receipts* (1899) by Kate Sargeant.

The first professional information on mushroom cultivation in America was disseminated on a large scale in the 1890s, mainly through the efforts of William Falconer. Falconer encouraged both hobbyists and industry with detailed explanations of mushroom houses used on successful farms in the vicinity of New York City. By the early twenty-first century, the basics of mushroom cultivation had changed little, although the scale had exploded. There has been some limited success in cultivating mushrooms from families other than *Agaricaceae*, but most of the domesticated industry still grows different strains and hybrids developed in the twentieth century from *Agaricus bisporus*. In 2002, Pennsylvania lead the nation's production with a crop valued at more than $390 million, representing 59.2 percent of the American output.

BIBLIOGRAPHY

The American Mushroom Institute. http://www.americanmushroom.org/.

Falconer, William. *Mushrooms: How to Grow Them: A Practical Treatise on Mushroom Culture for Profit and Pleasure.* New York: Orange Judd, 1891.

CATHY K. KAUFMAN

Muslim Dietary Laws

Islam is a religion that permeates a Muslim's life; and food, recognized as one of God's great gifts, is naturally regulated according to Islamic law. The dietary laws of Islam are based on the Koran, the holy book of Islam, and the Hadith, the collection of the sayings of the prophet Muhammad. Muslims in America, as with Muslims everywhere, are expected to follow these dietary laws. And in a predominantly non-Muslim culture, this can lead to certain problems for Muslims, as well as new opportunities.

Muslim dietary law places most food into two broad categories: halal and *haram*, meaning, in Arabic, permitted (lawful) and prohibited (unlawful). Eating halal essentially means not eating any unlawful or *haram* food.

Haram foods are foods that come into contact with, or are in whole or part:

Pork, or meat from dogs, donkeys, or carnivorous animals, taloned birds, amphibians, reptiles, insects, rats, or other vermin.
Bodies of dead animals that have died due to strangulation, a violent blow, natural causes (carrion), pagan rituals, or being gored or killed by another animal.
Animals not slaughtered in accordance with Islamic law (excepting fish).
Alcoholic beverages, poisonous or narcotic drugs.
Meat cut from a live animal.
Food additives derived from any of the above.

Many *haram*, or prohibited, foods are rarely found in the normal American diet (carnivorous animals, insects, donkeys, dogs, amphibians, taloned birds) and cause no problems for the Muslim eating in the United States; but three aspects of *haram* in particular are of more concern to Muslim Americans.

Pork and alcohol are both *haram*, and thus prohibited; and both are very common in U.S. diets. In addition, most animals are not slaughtered in accordance with Islamic law.

Finally, many products contain additives that may include *haram* items. For example, soy sauce may contain alcohol as a product of fermentation, while muffins or other bread products may include lard from pork. And in general most American food is not prepared in accordance with halal.

Halal foods are those foods that are:

Free from any *haram* component.
Processed, prepared, and stored with apparatus and equipment that has been cleansed in accordance with Islamic law and is thus free from things unclean (*najis*). *Najis* means dirt (such as feces, urine, and blood) that must be cleaned according to Islamic law, generally by clean water.

More specifically, halal foods include:

Milk from cows, sheep, and goats
Honey
Fresh or naturally frozen vegetables
Grains, legumes, and nuts
Fish
Non-*haram* animals (such as beef, sheep, and other hoofed animals, as well as poultry) slaughtered in accordance with Islamic rites, called *Zabidah*.

Zabidah slaughter of animals is an integral part of halal eating. The slaughter must be of live animals or birds, the butcher must be a mature, pious, and knowledgeable Muslim, and the animal's throat must be slit (through the respiratory tract, esophagus, and jugular vein) while the butcher recites in Arabic that this is done "in the name of God, God is most great" (*Bismallah Allahu Akbar*). The knife must be sharp, and the animal must be dead before skinning or dismembering takes place.

All healthy and able Muslims over age twelve are also expected to practice *sawm*, or fasting, during the daylight hours of Ramadan, the ninth lunar month when the Koran was first transcribed. The fast is broken after

A market selling halal meat in Brooklyn, New York.

sunset, with a meal known as *iftar*. During Ramadan especially, the Muslim dietary guidelines of halal and *haram* are most carefully followed.

In addition to these general dietary guidelines, some American Muslims, such as those of the Shia branch of Islam and those from Anatolia, recognize some foods as *makrouh* or doubtful; this category includes shellfish and some birds. But the biggest category of food facing all U.S. Muslims in a predominantly Christian or secular society is what is called *mushbooh* in Arabic, meaning uncertain, doubtful, or suspected. Simply put, the typical American Muslim when shopping in a supermarket or dining out must frequently ask himself or herself: is this food *halal*?

Given these strictures, it is no surprise that halal foods are fast becoming a major social and political issue, as well as a growing industry in the United States. Food has been increasingly labeled as halal. However, there were few regulations concerning these labels, and it was estimated by the California based Minaret Magazine that up to 65 percent of stores in Los Angeles were selling nonhalal foods as halal. But this situation began changing rapidly in the early 2000s.

The U.S. Department of Agriculture has approved an addition to the Standards and Labeling Policy Book on the use of halal labeling on food and poultry products. Several accrediting groups, such as the Islamic Food and Nutrition Council of America (IFANCA) have been authorized. California, Illinois, and New Jersey, among other states with large Muslim populations, have enacted laws making it illegal to sell meat or other foods that are falsely represented as halal. Still, for a Muslim wishing to remain halal, problems persist. Even in 2001, most halal certification was still local; local clerics from nearby mosques certified local foods, leading to questions about reliability and standards. And even more difficult is the problem of food additives. For example, many common foods contain gelatin; the question for the Muslim is from what was the gelatin rendered—a pig or a cow? One Muslim tells of a typical episode while eating in a fast food restaurant. Tempted by the muffins, he ordered some takeout, only to hesitate before eating: were they made with *haram* ingredients such as pork lard? After a series of phone calls to the chain headquarters and the local store, he determined they were not *haram*, only to find another problem: they were now stale.

But, in the early 2000s, books and websites exist listing thousands of common supermarket products and indicating whether they are halal or *haram*. And U.S. restaurants, particularly in Muslim communities, are getting into the picture: McDonald's in Michigan began offering halal McNuggets. Big Boy has begun offering halal hamburgers in the same state. Kroger has begun selling halal chicken. Independent halal butchers have seen a dramatic rise in business as the Muslim population has grown, and national chains are now interested as well. Halal in America, as kosher before it, is becoming big business.

[**See also** AFRICAN AMERICAN FOOD: SINCE EMANCIPATION; JEWISH DIETARY LAWS; MIDDLE EASTERN INFLUENCES ON AMERICAN FOOD.]

BIBLIOGRAPHY

Ali, A. Yusuf. *An English Interpretation of the Holy Qur-an: With Full Arabic Text.* Lahore: Muhammad Ashraf, 1975.

Sakr, Ahmad H. *Understanding Halal Foods: Fallacies and Facts.* Lombard, IL: Foundation for Islamic Knowledge, 1996.

SYLVIA LOVEGREN

Mussels

In most of North America, mussels were almost ignored as a food source until the last half of the twentieth century. Mussels were known in Europe and Great Britain as edible, although some cookery literature pointed out that people sometimes became sick after eating them. As filter feeders, mussels are susceptible to the toxic algae blooms commonly called red tide, and the threat of food poisoning may have discouraged consumers. There was very minor commercial gathering of mussels for the New York market, and an effort was made around the turn of the twentieth century to persuade consumers to use them. In the last few decades of the twentieth century, with clams becoming scarce and expensive and with the public becoming more aware of various ethnic mussel dishes, the shellfish grew in popularity. Mussels are fairly abundant in the wild but are being water-farmed from rafts where cables seeded with juvenile mussels hang, allowing the mussels to feed off naturally occurring plankton until they are a harvestable size.

SANDRA L. OLIVER

Mustard

The mustard plant, an annual belonging to the Cruciferae family, has been one of the most widely grown and used spices in the world. There are three main types of mustard seeds, whose powders are often blended: white or yellow mustard (*Sinapis alba*); brown mustard (*Brassica juncea*), which has a slightly mustier flavor; and black mustard (*Brassica nigra*), the most pungent of all. In addition to the seeds, the leaves of mustard plants are often used in salads and as flavorings.

In ancient Roman times, mustard was made from seeds of a variety of plants in the genus *Brassica*. The word "mustard" in Latin means the "must" of new wine, which suggests that mustard seeds were combined with wine or vinegar. The Romans used the plant for both food and medicine and called it *mustem ardem*, or "burning juice." The French word *moutarde* and the English word "mustard" are derived from Latin. The Romans introduced mustard into France and England. Mustard was manufactured in Dijon at least by the thirteenth century. Mustard was well integrated into French and English cookery by the Middle Ages.

Although several mustard companies flourished in England, it was not until 1814 that Jeremiah Colman, a miller of flour in Norwich, first sold mustard flour. He began to export the flour worldwide around 1830. Coleman's mustard was imported into the United States from a factory in Toronto, Ontario, Canada.

Mustard has been manufactured in America since colonial times. The most important American manufacturer of mustard was Robert Timothy French (1823–1893). French was born near Ithaca, New York, and at the age of twenty-one went to work for a spice merchant and relocated to New York City. In 1883, French and his son, George J. French, purchased a small flour mill and a bakery, creating the R. T. French Company. They moved their operation to Rochester, New York, where they sold spices, including powdered mustard with turmeric. The business became extremely successful after the introduction of their French's cream salad mustard in 1904.

Sold as a condiment is glass jars, French's cream salad mustard was milder than other brands and was used mainly as a salad dressing and as a condiment for hot dogs, a food commonly served in baseball stadiums. The company's association with baseball was symbolized by its adoption of the pennant its official logo in 1915. By this date, French's mustard was America's largest selling prepared mustard, outselling all other brands combined. The competition was not far behind, however, and the R. T. French Company began advertising nationally during the 1920s and published advertising cookery booklets, such as *Made Dishes: Salads and Savories with French's Cream Salad Mustard* (1925). The following year, the R. T. French Company was purchased by Reckitt and Colman, the successor company to Jeremiah Colman's operation in England.

Reckitt and Colman expanded its mustard product line. the French's squeeze package was introduced in 1974, French's Bold 'n Spicy in 1982, and French's Dijon mustard in 1983. In 2000, Reckitt and Coleman merged with Benckiser to form Reckitt Benckiser, Inc. An estimated 80 percent of American households buy mustard each year. By 2002, the total mustard market in America was approximately $280 million.

Mustard advertisement from the January 1921 issue of American Cookery.

French's mustard remains America's largest selling branded mustard, followed by private labels and Kraft Grey Poupon.

[See also Advertising Cookbooks and Recipes; Condiments; Herbs and Spices; Hot Dogs; Ketchup; Salads and Salad Dressings.]

BIBLIOGRAPHY

Jordan, Michele Anna. *Good Cook's Book of Mustard.* Reading, MA: Addison-Wesley, 1994.

Man, Rosamond, and Robin Weir. *The Compleat Mustard.* Bury St Edmunds, Suffolk, UK: St. Emundsbury, 1988.

Roberts-Dominguez, Jan. *The Mustard Book.* New York: Macmillan, 1993.

ANDREW F. SMITH

Mustard Family

The members of the Mustard family contain, in varying amounts, compounds that combine in the presence of water to form Isothiocyanates—esters that provide a distinctive burning taste. If cooked before the enzymes have time to react, no Isothiocyanates are produced, so there is no "heat."

Horseradish (*Armoracia rusticana*) and its Japanese cousin, wasabi (*Wasabia japonica*), are the most pungent members of the family. Only the roots are used.

The seeds of Mustard (*Brassica* species), somewhat milder than those listed above, are used as a spice, and the greens as potherbs.

Watercress (*Nasturtium officinalis*), the most delicate of these species, is used primarily as a salad herb.

[See also Prepared Herb and Spice Mixtures.]

BIBLIOGRAPHY

Allen, Gary. *The Herbalist in the Kitchen.* Champain: University of Illinois Press (forthcoming).

Bailey, L. H. *Hortus Third: A Concise Dictionary of Plants Cultivated in the United States and Canada.* New York: Macmillan, 1976.

GARY ALLEN

Myths and Folklore

Food is central to our physical existence and adds to our emotional and social well-being. It is no surprise, then, that folklore surrounds it, providing ways of expressing identity, value, and meaning through food. Food as folklore helps bind us to one another, gives us connections with past and place, and adds an esthetic dimension to this functional necessity of life.

Myths and Folklore of Food as Traditional Beliefs and Customs

Food myths surround those areas of our lives that tend to worry us, particularly gender and sex; pregnancy, nursing, and parenting; and health and food safety. The saying "real men don't eat quiche" summed up gender expectations during the 1960s and 1970s. Folklore about sex and food refers to how to use foods in a sexually attractive way as well as what foods are best to enhance sexual acts (oysters, ginseng, chili peppers, and chocolate). Food folklore is attached to food during pregnancy, childbirth, and lactation. Unusual food cravings (pickles and ice cream) by pregnant women are fodder for anecdotes. Health concerns around food appear in adages such as "eat like a king in the morning, like a duke in the afternoon, and a pauper in the evening" and "an apple a day keeps the doctor away". Food also appears in folk remedies: chicken soup and oranges for colds; "stuff a cold; starve a fever"; "hair of the dog" for hangovers. Also, there are beliefs concerning the effects of particular foods or ingredients—sugar makes children hyperactive; caffeine stunts their growth. Urban legends surround the fast food industry and ethnic restaurants, warning of unsanitary practices or unappealing substances found in the food (fried rat, finger in soft drink bottle).

Folk Foods and Folk Cookery

Folk foods are those items traditionally associated with specific groups of people. Within the United States, groups are defined by region, ethnicity, and religion: the Amish and the Pennsylvania Dutch with scrapple, shoofly pie, custard, and apple butter; New Englanders with boiled supper, lobster rolls, and clambakes; Cajuns with crawfish and jambalaya; Southerners with grits, biscuits and gravy, salt-cured ham, fried chicken, and pecan pie; Southern Blacks with fried chicken, mashed potatoes, turnip greens, and cornbread; Appalachian mountaineers with cornbread, leather britches (dried green beans), and moonshine (corn whiskey). Any food that is traditional to a group, represents the group's identity, and is used in aesthetic ways to express the interests and values of the group can be considered a folk food. American college students as a folk group are characterized by pizza, ramen noodles, cafeteria food, and beer.

Holiday celebrations tend to have strong food traditions. Christmas includes candy canes, fruitcakes, seafood supper on Christmas Eve for many Italian Americans, brunch on Christmas morning, and turkey dinner on Christmas Day. Easter includes special candy (chocolate rabbits and eggs, jellybeans, and marshmallows in symbolic shapes) along with boiled and decorated eggs, and in some regions, paczki (*paschke*), an eastern European pastry similar to a jelly doughnut. Thanksgiving turkey signifies abundance (as does the cornucopia spilling over with fruits and nuts) and unity and is accompanied by regional and ethnic variations: bread stuffing in New England, oyster stuffing on the Atlantic Coast, and cornbread dressing in the South; mashed potatoes and gravy, vegetables (green beans, peas, carrots, or mashed turnips), breads (dinner rolls, cornbread, muffins, and zucchini or pumpkin bread), and desserts (traditionally pies, particularly pumpkin, apple, pecan, and custard). Ethnic specialties (sauerkraut, lasagna, egg rolls, sushi, or tamales) frequently appear on the table. Halloween is distinguished by pumpkins carved into Jack-o'-lanterns and trick-or-treating, in which children demand candy from strangers. Mass-produced sweets have been developed for this purpose, replacing the more traditional apples, homemade taffy, fudge, and popcorn balls. On New Year's Day, it is common among Pennsylvania Germans and other German Americans to eat pork and sauerkraut. Southerners traditionally eat hoppin' John (black-eyed peas, ham hocks, and rice).

The passing of seasons as well as the seasons themselves are frequently marked by food folklore. The arrival of summer is marked by taking out the grill and setting up for outdoor cooking and picnics and grilling. Fall is marked by chili and hot chocolate.

Foodways

"Foodways" refers "the total cookery complex—the whole range of cookery and food habits in a society." It includes eight components. Procurement is the obtaining of food ingredients and items. Preservation involves strategies used for keeping foods frozen or fresh and storing them until needed. Preparation involves selecting menus and recipes as well as the techniques used to turn raw ingredients into culturally acceptable food. The product is the food itself and includes the actual recipes and ingredients used. Presentation refers to how food is physically displayed, brought to the table, and served to consumers. Consumption refers to how people eat—what utensils they use, what mixtures they create, and the order in which items are consumed. Clean-up includes questions of storage and the use of leftovers. Performance includes the place of foods within the usual meal system and cuisine as well as the symbolic meanings being performed.

"Foodways" suggests the full meaning of food in people's lives and why it carries such significance; the activities surrounding food are integrated into all aspects of daily life. For example, a bagel purchased from the neighborhood deli has an entirely different set of foodways behind it than one purchased from the frozen foods section of a chain supermarket. Similarly, two dinner menus may be identical, but the processes by which they were put together, who cooked them, and who eats them make them two very different experiences.

Food as Artistic Communication (Folklore)

Food as folklore approaches food as "artistic communication in small groups." In this sense, food as folklore is used to communicate feelings, opinions, relationships, social status, relationships, and power. Food folklore appears in three forms: material, oral, and customary. Material foodlore is the actual food itself as a physical object; oral foodlore involves narratives, songs, names, and talking about food; customary foodlore includes the rituals, habits, and patterns of interacting surrounding food. It also emphasizes the aesthetic nature of food—the tastes and textures of foods and how people manipulate food and cooking for aesthetic pleasure. Food carries emotive and symbolic connotations. Garnishes signify a special occasion, as do elaborate dishes requiring sauces and extensive preparation. Raw fruits and vegetables may be carved into artistic designs—radishes into roses, carrots into curlicues, or cucumbers into geometric patterns. Everyday foods may be dressed up with extras to signify a special meal, such as nuts (almonds to green beans), spices (ginger to carrots), and other sauces (pecan butter to brussels sprouts). Gelatin molds can be varied to fit the holiday with the use of appropriate colors (orange or yellow for Thanksgiving, red for Christmas, green for St. Patrick's Day) or fillings (apples and nuts for Thanksgiving molds).

[See also CHRISTMAS; DIETS, FAD; DUTCH INFLUENCES ON AMERICAN FOOD; EASTER; ETHNIC FOODS; FAST FOOD; FOODWAYS; GENDER ROLES; GERMAN AMERICAN FOOD; HALLOWEEN; PICNICS; THANKSGIVING.]

BIBLIOGRAPHY

Counihan, Carole M. and Penny Van Esterik, eds. *Food and Culture: A Reader*. New York: Routledge, 1997.

Gabaccia, Donna R. *We Are What We Eat: Ethnic Food and the Making of Americans*. Cambridge, MA: Harvard University Press, 1998.

Haber, Barbara. *From Hardtack to Home Fries: An Uncommon History of American Cooks and Meals*. New York: Free Press, 2002.

Long, Lucy. "Holiday Meals: Rituals of Family Tradition." In *Dimensions of the Meal: The Science, Culture, Business, and Art of Eating*, ed. Herbert L. Meiselman, 143–160. Gaithersburg, MD: Aspen, 2000.

Long, Lucy, ed. *Culinary Tourism*. Lexington: University Press of Kentucky, 2004.

Yoder, Don. "Food Cookery." In *Folklore and Folklife: An Introduction*, edited by Richard M. Dorson, 325–350. Chicago: University of Chicago Press, 1972.

LUCY M. LONG

Myths and
Folklore

Nabisco

The Nabisco brand is perhaps best known for the cookies and crackers it manufactures and sells, among them Uneeda Biscuits, Oreos, Fig Newtons, Social Tea Biscuits, and Premium Saltines, but the company also contributed to the development of mass marketing in America by making freshness a selling point and distributing products directly to retailers. In 1898, at Adolphus W. Green's urging, the National Biscuit Company (NBC) was incorporated in Jersey City, New Jersey, established through the merger of the American Biscuit and Manufacturing Company, the New York Biscuit Company, and the United States Baking Company. Green's desire was to mass-market. Green sought to maximize profits through high-volume business, an unusual concept at a time when few food manufacturing companies sold nationally. This merger unified much of the biscuit business and led to the creation of a national brand name.

The National Biscuit Company's incorporation in 1898 signaled the end of the cracker barrel as an American institution. When buying from a barrel, it was the first customers who got the freshest crackers from the top of the cracker barrel. As sales proceeded and the barrel emptied, the crackers became broken, soggy, and dirty, sometimes tainted with the odor of an adjacent kerosene tank or befouled by vermin that lived inside the barrel.

To provide the consumer with a crisp, fresh, and sanitary cracker, the National Biscuit Company devised a package that would keep crackers clean and unbroken. A piece of waxed paper was put on a cardboard carton blank, and both were folded into an airtight and moisture-proof box. The packaging was introduced with Uneeda Biscuits, the company's first product. The distinctive packaging's name, *In-er-seal*, was printed on one end of the box. The carton gave wholesomeness and freshness commercial value that consumers began to seek out and did much to destroy confidence in the cracker barrel. As a consequence, many other food products, such as pickles, tea, cheese, flour, and rice, followed suit, moving out of bulk boxes and barrels into clean, convenient packaging. The new approach to packaging started a revolu-

tion that began with a new era of packaged food and self-service markets and ultimately helped pave the way for the emergence of chain stores and supermarkets.

In addition to innovations in packaging, Green's focus on promotion and advertising influenced how food is marketed in the United States. The National Biscuit Company advertised on billboards, sides of buildings, and in newspapers. NBC foods were used in early product placements in movies. With the rise of radio ads in the 1930s, the company started using the word "Nabisco" in its advertising to make its products easier to remember.

NBC acquired the Shredded Wheat Company in 1928 and in 1931 added Milk-Bone dog biscuits. Some thirty years later, in 1962, it bought the Cream of Wheat Company. In 1971 the National Biscuit Company changed its name to Nabisco Inc., and in 1981 merged with Standard Brands Incorporated to become Nabisco Brands Inc. The merger added Planters nuts and snacks to the portfolio. In 1985, RJ Reynolds Industries, Inc., in an attempt to reduce its reliance on tobacco, acquired Nabisco Brands Inc. A year later, in 1986, RJ Reynolds Industries Inc., changed its name to RJR Nabisco Inc., and RJR's Del Monte and Nabisco Brands operations were combined to form Nabisco Brands Inc. In 1999, RJR Nabisco broke up, splitting the U.S. tobacco business off from Nabisco's food division in a bid to shield the food company from liability for smoking-related lawsuits associated with the tobacco side of the company. In 2000, Philip Morris Companies Inc., acquired Nabisco Holdings Corporation; Nabisco Inc.; and its subsidiaries. Nabisco was then integrated into the Kraft Foods business, creating one of the largest food companies in the world.

[**See also** KRAFT FOODS; PACKAGING; WAXED PAPER.]

BIBLIOGRAPHY

Cahn, William. *Out of the Cracker Barrel: The Nabisco Story, from Animal Crackers to Zuzus.* New York: Simon and Schuster, 1969.

Kraft Foods. http://www.kraft.com/newsroom/.

SANDRA YIN

Natchitoches Meat Pies

Natchitoches (pronounced NAK-a-dush), Louisiana is the oldest permanent settlement in Louisiana, predating New Orleans by five years. It is the home of fried turnovers called Natchitoches Meat Pies. Although most of the pie promoters today are Cajun, Natchitoches is well to the north of the traditional Cajun area. It has been cut off from the Mississippi since the late 1830s, when the channel shifted and the Cane River became Cane River Lake. The pies more likely reflect the unusual ethnic history of the early French settlement, in which freed creoles of color, now known as Cane River Creoles, were important plantation owners and even owned their

own slaves. The filling of beef and pork is like French (and Acadian) Christmas pork pies. But the small half-moon pasty shape is like Latino empanadas, and nearby Sabine parish is an old Spanish settlement on the Red River trail from Texas. The Creole seasoning of the filling and the deep fat frying were markers for African American influence generations before the first Cajun reached Louisiana.

Certainly, the main street merchants of the meat pies for the first half of the twentieth century were Cane River Creoles, whose cries of "hotta meat pies!" resounded like the cries of "hot tamales!" elsewhere across the Southern States.

MARK H. ZANGER

Nathan's Famous

In 1915, Nathan Handwerker, a Jewish immigrant from Poland, answered a "help wanted" advertisement and got a job at Charles Feltman's restaurant in Coney Island, New York. Feltman had originated the sausage in a bun concept, charging ten cents for this quick meal. Handwerker worked at Feltman's for a year, then, with $300 savings, he opened a hot dog stand of his own a few blocks from Feltman's.

Handwerker cooked his frankfurters on a twelve-foot grill and sold them for a nickel, but underpricing Feltman was the least of his ploys. At his stand, he installed signs with horns that sounded like fire-engine sirens, and it is said that he hired students, outfitted them in white coats, and had them eat at his stand, giving the impression that his hot dogs were so wholesome that they were eaten by doctors.

When the subway opened in the 1920s, and millions thronged Coney Island in the summer, Nathan's became a local landmark, but Coney Island gradually fell into decline after World War II. Feltman's closed in 1954 and, the following year, the company announced that it had sold its 1955 its millionth hot dog. Nathan's began to expand, opening outlets in other cities. The Nathan's chain had a growth spurt during the 1980s, when investors encouraged the establishment of larger restaurants, but these didn't catch on and the company downsized.

Nathan's Famous Inc., has attempted to promote its operation in a variety of ways. In the 1980s, it published a series of hot-dog cookbooks. More spectacular has been its sponsorship of an Independence Day hot dog eating contest, which has taken place on Coney Island since the stand opened in 1916, according to the company. In 2005, the winner, Takeru Kobayashi of Japan, consumed forty-nine Nathan's Famous hot dogs and buns in twelve minutes.

As of 2001, Nathan's consisted of twenty-four company-owned units and 380 franchised or licensed outlets. Nathan's Branded Products are also sold by more than fourteen hundred independent food-service operators

Hirofumi Nakajima (right) of Kofu, Japan, competes against Ed "The Animal" Krachie of New York City in the 82nd annual Nathan's 4th of July Hot Dog Eating Contest on Coney Island, in Brooklyn.

with outlets at airports, hotels, sports arenas, convention centers, colleges, and convenience stores. In all, the company operates in forty-one states and seventeen foreign countries. Nathan's has also acquired the rights to cobrand with Arthur Treacher's Fish & Chips, and has acquired Kenny Rogers Roasters and Miami Subs. Nathan's Famous hot dogs are also sold in supermarkets.

BIBLIOGRAPHY

Cohen, Gerald Leonard, Barry Popik, and David Shulman, *Origin of the Term "Hot Dog."* Rolla, MO: G. Cohen, 2004.

Handwerker, Murray. *Nathan's Famous Hot Dog Cookbook.* New York: Gramercy Publishing, 1983.

ANDREW F. SMITH

Native American Foods:
Before and after Contact

The ancient history of Native Americans and their food has been dated with certainty from the end of the last ice age—the Clovis people, 11,000 to 6,000 B.C.E.—and very likely before then by forty thousand years. Actually, archaeological evidence strengthens the case of a series of immigrations from Asia. Developed in the Central American-Mexican civilizations, the culture gradually worked its way into North America, where, from a hunting-gathering culture, it formed such large centers as the cultivating, mound-building Hopewell and Adena cultures (1000 B.C.E.-1600 C.E.) of the Eastern Woodlands, changing the early cultivation of numerous wild plants: marsh elder, squash, and sunflowers to domesticated corn and beans.

Precontact dining depended on geography, changing weather systems, and adaptability. The coastal areas, so rich in fish and seafood, offered enough raw material, espe-

cially when supplemented with wild and cultivated plants and occasional trapped small mammals and birds. The salmon cultures of the Northwest continued to feed themselves largely on fish until the modern era. The early hunter-gatherers of the inland areas gradually involved themselves in cultivation of plants—that is, they tended wild plants without moving them. Eventually (ca. 2000 B.C.E.), they settled down into semipermanent areas, where they domesticated corn, beans, squash and pumpkins, sunflower seeds, Jerusalem artichokes, dogs, and turkeys. Some of these were quite sophisticated and were exemplified by domesticated "three sisters"—the system of planting corn, beans, and squash or pumpkins in the same hills. The corn provided poles for the climbing beans, insuring that each had enough sun. The nitrogen-fixing beans carried nitrogen down to the roots, where it was deposited into the soil to fertilize the corn roots. And the pumpkins and squash spread over and between the hills, shading the soil to keep moisture in and weeds out. Precontact cultures also hunted and fished, according to geographical resources.

In most areas, the ratio of meat to vegetative material differed considerably according to time and place. For example, the Prairie-Plains Sioux specialized in buffalo (bison) meats, making seasonal incursions into their grazing areas. Extended periods of rainfall had offered ample moisture to grow rich Southwestern Anasazi gardens, but they later dried up, causing the downfall of their culture.

Food systems grew efficiently and large enough to support the rise and fall of large cities—as large as any in Europe at that time—complete with town centers, large multilevel stone buildings, and roads, although without

the use of iron or the wheel. They covered a long history—thousands of years of adaptation.

Contact

The points of contact varied according to the European movement westward. It began on the Eastern and Southern coast, and moved inland over the Appalachians and Smoky Mountains. At each new point of contact the same things happened: decimation of Indian populations by disease or hostility, voluntary movement of Natives west, and loss of Native American foodways.

At the time the first Spanish arrived in the south, there were five major Indian groups: the Eastern Woodlands, the Southeastern nations, the Southwestern groups, the Northern California-Washington salmon cultures, and the Great Plains and Prairie people. By this time each had familiar landmarks: the Eastern Woodlands had a temperate climate in which the "three sisters" were easily grown and supplemented by hunts. The Southeastern nations were similar, but had more subtropical fruits and vegetables, and more seafoods. The Natives of the Southwest were faced with dry spells and farmed with deeply rooted seeds. The Northwestern salmon tribes maintained fishing and gathering acorn, camas roots, and berries. The Prairie-Plains held the buffalo and were a mixture of Plains hunting and Eastern Woodlands farming.

Distinctive from the coastal tribes, inland people often moved temporarily to the shores of local rivers or lakes in the springtime, when the fish were moving from the lake depths to spawn. This coincided with the "hungry time," when the previous year's supplies of corn, beans, squash and pumpkins, sunflower seeds, and preserved meats were used up. After finishing two hoings, the farmers left to fish, to eat and preserve it, and to consume strawberries and early greens. When the "green corn" (or sweet corn stage) was ready to eat, they returned to their settlements and celebrated the "green corn festival," honoring the first edible crop, and giving thanks for the promise of the dried corn that would take them through the following winter. Similar festivals were celebrated for the first salmon and buffalo.

The first point of contact took place on the Gulf of Mexico where the Spaniard Hernando De Soto, seeking to extend his successful

A Hopi woman grinds corn by hand in Arizona.

colonialization of Mexico, made his early landing in Florida. He crossed the Appalachians and the Mississippi River (1549–1553). Francisco Vázques de Coronado, traveling north from the Southwest (1540–1542), met nomadic Plains Indians, traded with them, and withdrew. The trade was a typical exchange of buffalo robes for the corn of native agriculturists, hides, and salt for axes, hoes, fishhooks, knives, kettles, rum, and beer. The Europeans traded for corn, squash and pumpkin, beans, and sunflower seeds. And the horse became the most important trade item of all—at first serving to enrich the diet of Native Americans of the Plains, and soon thereafter becoming their staple means of transportation. Wheat for trade was grown by the Pueblo people of the Southwest.

Although the Spanish were first to colonize the south, they did not remain. The late-seventeenth-century French took over the Mississippi River and lined its banks with forts all the way to St. Louis, attempting to split the continent and connect with the French in Canada. At the same time, the English colonized the Atlantic coast and the Dutch eastern New York. The patterns were similar to those of the Spanish invasion: European diseases wiped out up to 90 percent of the tribal populations, and the remaining indigenous people were either enslaved, freed, or banded together for survival. Others made good use of the European foods: the Algonquian Mohegans in Connecticut began to grow pigs, beef cattle, and sheep during the 1660s and 1670s, and the Iroquois planted orchards of European apples and pears in their long patterns of adaptation.

Eighteenth Century

By 1700, colonists far outnumbered the Indians of the central Eastern Seaboard. Continued declines were caused by deportations of enslaved Native Americans to the Caribbean and the voluntary moves westward, as people hoped to escape general anti-Indian harrassment and violence. Only a few precontact groups survived on the coasts and maintained their traditions, among them the Pamunkey community in Virginia. Others, such as the Piscataway of coastal New Hampshire, were able to maintain small tracts near their ancestral homes. The strongest tribes and nations (Creek and Iroquois) who had maintained their sovereignty maintained access to their traditional food and foodways.

By the middle of the 1700s, trade was flourishing. There had been a long history of precontact Native American trade; now accommodating Native Americans were producing European foods to sell to the Europeans. Growing trade with Europe had changed the Indian agriculture patterns and hunting equipment, and made them as dependent on them as were Europeans. For example, the Ojibwa of the Great Lakes area harvested more wild rice than they needed and sold the surplus to the French at the rate of one keg of rum for twenty

fawn skins of rice. And they traded with smoked buffalo, rendered bear meat and oil, deer, fish, various melons (introduced earlier), wild fruits berries, and nuts, pumpkins, beans, and corn. Many Native Americans did not immediately embrace European foods.

In general, Native people, having survived generations of contact, disease, and land loss fell into a pattern of transition that included increasing erosion of their foodways. Although many western tribes were still intact on their ancestral land, Indians of the East had been resettled onto reserved lands, such as the town of Mashpee on Cape Cod, Massachusetts, and remote areas on which it was impossible to maintain earlier subsistence economies. Many worked within the Anglo-American communities as laborers, farmhands, servants, fishers, hunters, and trappers. Increasing intimacy with the Anglos wore away traditions. Some children of mixed marriages with the choice of community lost their traditional foodways entirely.

Nineteenth Century

The century began with Meriweather Lewis and William Clark, traversing the area between the Missouri River and the Pacific coast. The explorers passed numerous Native tribes and clans along the way, many of whom had not heard of the Anglo-Americans, and had not changed their diets. The deliberate destruction of the buffalo (forty million to five hundred) decimated the Plains groups, and forced the settlement of previously mobile Apache and Navajo, who turned to sheep-raising in the Southwest. However, by the end of the century, American laws (1830s–1880s) enforced the relocation of most Indians to reservations, drastically changing their diet through government rations distributions, largely wheat flour, lard, beans, sugar, tea, and coffee. This was the start of fry-bread, which grew, into the next century, to become the icon of the pan-Indian movement. The enforced teaching in government schools encouraged new iced layer cakes, home-canned jellies and jams, pork sausage, and milk products. The poverty imposed by reservation life resulted in diets overbalanced with carbohydrates and poor quality fats, supporting high rates of alcoholism, overweight, and diabetes. The Native Americans who resisted "res" life were allowed to hunt deer year round, as opposed to limitations on Anglo-Americans, and the salmon fishers were allowed to leave their reservation homes for three months of fishing.

Twentieth and Twenty-First Centuries

These centuries have struggled to right the many wrongs of the past. A good many urban Native Americans have assimilated, eating the same balance of foods as does most of America. Research into their obesity, diabetes, and alcoholism suggest that a return to precontact eating can reverse the problems. Archaeologists began to write about Native foods, and a few women wrote cookbooks representing

local fare. Some Native products are being sold nationwide, among them Seneca corn products and Hopi Blue Cornmeal products; Apaches conduct hunting and fishing outings on their reservation. Indian museums and restaurants are focusing increasingly on Native cuisines based on archaeological and anthropological research.

[**See also** Beans; Buffalo; Corn; Pumpkins; Squash.]

BIBLIOGRAPHY

Brain, Jeffery P. *Tunica Treasure*. Cambridge, MA: Peabody Museum of Archaeology and Ethnology, 1979.

Dixson, E. James. *Bones, Boats and Bison: Archaeology and the First Colonization of Western North America*. Albuquerque: University of New Mexico, 1999.

Grumet, Robert S. *Historic Contact: Indian People and Colonists in Today's Northeastern United States in the Sixteenth through Eighteenth Centuries*. Norman: University of Oklahoma, 1995.

Kraft, Herbert C. *The Lenape-Delaware Indian Heritage: 10,000 BC–AD 2000*. Stanhope, NJ: Lenape Books, 2000.

Lawrence, Bill. *The Early American Wilderness as the Explorers Saw It*. New York: Paragon, 1991.

ALICE ROSS

Native American Foods:
Spiritual and Social Connections

The Native American worldview conceived of a balance among all forms, including plants, animals, water, wind, earth, stone, and sun. Each had a place in the total scheme, offered spiritual and practical aid to people associated with them, and each needed respect for its contributions. Taking the life of a plant or animal, even though for food, was a serious matter. The spirits of plants and animals presumably offered themselves as food, but only on the condition that they would not be treated cruelly or wastefully. Each food spirit required rituals to express honor and thanks to it and imposed penalties if the gift of itself was abused. These penalties ranged from a species' refusal to make itself available for human sustenance to the punishment of a single offender by the infliction of bad luck or disease. These issues were of paramount importance to people whose welfare depended on the forces of the natural world and they fostered the ideal of a harmonious universe.

Staple foods were central in Native American mythologies. Creation stories focused on the introduction of important foods. Legends described "first people" as hungry, ignorant, and unhappy. They were then transformed by a supreme god or goddess who brought the significant new food and taught its use. Among agriculturists, the Corn Goddess (blonde to represent corn tassels) was a major figure. The northeastern Senecas told of the Earth Mother (also called Corn Mother), whose breasts produced the first corn, and who, in some versions, brought beans, squash, and general fertility. One

COMMON FOODS OF THE COLUMBIAN EXCHANGE, BEGINNING IN 1492

This is not a complete list of indigenous foods, but rather a guide to changing Native American cuisines. The foods brought to America are identified according to those who brought them, not necessarily where they originated.

Foods native to America	Taken to	Foods brought to America	From
Staple grains			
Corn	Universal	Wheat	Europe
Wild rice	Europe	Oats	Europe
		Rye	Europe
		Barley	Europe
		Millet	North Africa
		Rice	Africa, Europe
Staple starches			
Assorted beans, e.g., navy, cranberry, black, kidney, and lima	Universal	Soybeans	Asia
		Adzuki beans	Asia
		Mung beans	Asia
		Fava beans	Europe
		Cowpeas	Africa
Peanuts (South America)	Africa	Peanuts return	Africa (slaves)
Vegetables			
White potatoes (Peru)	Europe	White potatoes	North America
Sweet potatoes	Europe	Yams	Africa
Pumpkins	Europe, Africa	Cucumbers	Europe
Winter squash	Europe	Tomatoes (Mexico)	Spain
Summer squash	Europe	Lettuce	Europe
		Cabbage	Europe
		Turnips	Europe
		Onions	Europe
		Carrots	Europe
		Parsnips	Europe
		Broccoli	Europe
		Collards	Africa
		Okra	Africa
Fruits			
Blueberries, huckleberries	Europe	Apples	Europe
Cranberries	Europe	Pears	Europe
Persimmons		Peaches	Europe
Paw-paws		Citrus fruits	Europe
		Figs	Europe
		Olives	Europe
Strawberries*	Europe	Strawberries	Europe
		Melons	Europe
		Watermelons	Europe, Africa
Cherries*		Cherries	Europe
Grapes		Grapes	Europe
Raspberries,* blackberries		Raspberries, blackberries	Europe
Currants, red and black		Currants	Europe
Mulberries		Mulberries	Europe
Nuts			
Black walnuts		Almonds	Europe
Hickory nuts		English walnuts	Europe

Continued

COMMON FOODS OF THE COLUMBIAN EXCHANGE, BEGINNING IN 1492 (*Continued*)

Foods native to America	Taken to	Foods brought to America	From
Beechnuts		Pistachios	Europe
Hazelnuts	Europe		
Pecans			
Chestnuts	Europe		
Chinquapins			
Pine nuts			

Meat

Foods native to America	Taken to	Foods brought to America	From
Turkey	Universal	Dairy cattle (milk, butter, cheese, cream)	Europe
		Beef cattle	Europe
		Lamb	Europe
		Pig	Europe
		Goat	Europe
		Barnyard poultry (chickens, geese, and ducks and their eggs)	Europe
		Horse (meat, work)	Europe

Beverages

		Tea and coffee	Europe
		Wine and spirits	Europe
		Beer and ale	England
		Cider	Europe

Seasonings

Allspice	Universal	Cinnamon	Europe (colonies)
Juniper	Europe	Cloves	Europe (colonies)
Sassafras	Europe	Nutmeg	Europe (colonies)
Chilies	Universal	Ginger	Europe (colonies)
		Pepper	Europe (colonies)
		Sesame	Africa
		Coconut	Europe

Sweets

Chocolate (Mexico)	Universal	Sugar	Europe
Vanilla (Mexico)	Universal	Honey	Europe
Maple and hickory sugars		Sorghum	Africa
Honey, locust			

*Some considered better quality than European equivalents

Apache benefactor was Turkey, who ended hunger by shaking plant foods out of his feathers, introducing wild fruits, plants, and two varieties of corn. The Ojibwe boy Winaboozhoo found wild rice through a series of visions; Wunzh learned about corn from the god *Mondawmin*.

In addition to the large consumption of these iconographic foods, most tribes followed a series of taboos. These were sometimes related to life stages and gender issues. Many women avoided eating meat for fear of offending hunted animals; during menstruation some avoided all contact with meat lest it spoil. Men, by contrast, ate meat to make themselves more difficult to kill. Sometimes a particular animal was thought to have negative powers; the Iroquois believed that eating a chickadee would make one a liar.

Like so much of Indian culture, mythologies changed with the presence and power of Christian colonists, and the rather vague Creator of precontact myths became a stronger, more personal and immediate figure.

Social and Ritualistic Foods

Socialization was a large part of group living but was often structured by gender. Men and women were divided by complementary work and spiritual roles and developed strong same-sex ties through food. Women spent a good deal of the day in the company of other women, planting and harvesting, cooking for special celebrations, gathering food and fuel, or processing winter provisions. Men worked closely together on extended hunting and fishing trips and the extensive advance preparations needed for them. Men and women sometimes crossed the gender lines to provide help when necessary or to honor male spirits; some men (Osage, for example) cooked meat on special occasions. Certain foods were associated with one gender or another, for example, saskatoon berries (*Amalanchier alnifolia*) of the Blackfoot Indians were a snack food reserved for men. Salmonberry (*Rubus spectabilis*) parties were an event specific to Makah women, who traveled by canoe to the stand of fruit, gathered and pit-steamed it on the beach, and engaged in appropriate women's songs and dances until the fruit was ready.

The taking of animal life also required a ritual in which some part of the animal was returned to the earth, prayers were offered giving thanks, requesting forgiveness, and promising to waste nothing. Some believed that if these rituals were neglected, the spirit of the animal would follow the hunter home and afflict him with disease or poor hunting. Cherokee hunters sacrificed the melt (large fat deposits) of an animal. Sometimes they sacrificed the first animal caught during an extended hunt to express gratitude for recovery from illness or to ensure success in the hunt. Cherokee women routinely threw a piece of fat into the cooking fire before and during meals, as a way of protecting the family from evil and inducing good luck. The northwestern tribes sang to welcome the salmon. The first ritualistic cuts of salmon were made by female shamans. Others burned the salmon heart to prevent it from being defiled by dogs. Dog meat was often used ceremonially, sometimes offered to the god of war to ensure good hunts.

Food taboos and prescriptions were often associated with origin mythologies. One of the injunctions against drinking milk came from the story of the Corn Mother, whose breasts had provided the first corn to the Senecas. Foods to be shunned were often believed to have specific health dangers. The Cherokees avoided eating a number of animals, including dogs, eels, foxes, wolves, snakes and snakelike water eels, and catfish, in the belief that such would bring bodily contamination. The Cayugas believed that the flesh of pregnant animals would produce diarrhea if eaten and avoided allowing the skinned bodies of trapped animals to touch the ground, lest the animal be offended and refuse to offer itself for human use in the future.

In some cases, the foods associated with festivals do not appear to have such strong symbolism. For example, the California Cahuilla use of acorn and meat stews or Iroquois and Chippewa use of blackberry beverages may have more to do with availability and desirable flavor.

Manners

One of the most elusive areas of knowledge about Native American foodways is that of dining etiquette—there is no physical evidence from indigenous records, and most sources come from early European impressions. There is, however, a fair degree of consistency in the descriptions offered by the English in the Chesapeake (1585) and Virginia (1705), the French in Louisiana (early 1700), and the German Moravian John Heckewelder in the northern Eastern Woodlands (1754–1813). Many commented on the principle that it was insulting to thank a host for food, as feeding a guest was considered to be

Food Mythology

Food-related mythologies were part of daily life. Southwestern Zuni women sang the adventures of the Corn Goddesses as they ground corn. Hopi babies were presented to the sun at birth, along with two perfect ears of corn, a reference to the Corn Goddess and the child's two mothers (spiritual and temporal). Lenape men, when hunting deer, or Lenape women, when gathering nuts and firewood in the forests, asked for the approval of *Mësingw*, the bearlike "Keeper of the Game" who was the chief protector of animals and their environment. In addition, annual festivals such as the Corn Dance, the Green Corn Festival, the Strawberry Festival, the First Salmon Ceremony of the Northwest, or the Cheyenne Sun Dance were meant to ensure the survival of humankind and its cultures with sufficient food.

In the areas where hunting predominated, legends tell of creation spirits who brought the game. The Northwest, one of the few regions in which corn was not grown, told creation stories about Salmon Boy and Bear Mother. White Buffalo Woman, of the Lakota Sioux, was the bringer of hordes of buffalo and appropriate instruction. She also taught the women how to make hearth fires, to do stone cooking in buffalo paunches, to make pemmican, corn, and wild turnip, all dishes that were central to Lakota cuisine.

Festivals

Elaborate food preparations with spiritual references were common. The calendar year was punctuated by annual festivals in which plants and animals were asked to provide generously, or thanked for good harvests. For example, the Shinnecock Strawberry Festival was a "first-food" homecoming in which the fruit and gratitude for it were paramount. For agriculturists the most important festival of the year was the Green Corn Festival, a new year celebration of the first edible corn (the often sweet "milk" stage) and the promise of enough food for another year; festivities involved some ten days of feasting and ritual. Similar ceremonies were performed by the eastern foragers of such wild foods as ramps (*alliums*) and strawberries. At the time of the first harvesting of Northwest salmon, men fasted and women and children ate out of sight of the river.

Ceremonies

Key foods were incorporated into ritual dishes for important ceremonials. For example, pit-baked Navajo cake was made for weddings, squaw dances, and womanhood ceremonies. The mixture of roasted cornmeal, raisins and, after contact, European sprouted wheat and brown sugar was precooked, placed on circles of corn husks, sprinkled with cornmeal of four different colors, and pit baked. Colored corn had special meanings. Among the Navajo, white symbolized the East and the rising sun; among the Cherokee it meant happiness and peace. When it was served, the center of the cake, or the "heart," was buried in the ground to feed Mother Earth. In similar fashion, Hopi women making blue corn *piki* threw the first piece of flatbread into the fire to "feed it," asking the baking stone "not to be lazy and to work well." Mooseberry (*Viburnum*) was eaten only at feasts by the Kwakiutl, who also boiled huckleberries mixed with red salmon spawn and oil for their winter ceremony feast.

Potlatch

One of the most unique of Native American feasts was the Kwakiutl potlatch, in which the host family not only fed everyone with ample high-quality food, but also distributed all its accumulated wealth among the guests. In this economic show of power, the quantity and quality of the prepared foods earned commensurate community status.

Robert Beverly on Eating Customs

[They] accustom themselves to no set Meals, but eat night and day, when they have plenty of Provisions, or if they have got any thing that is a rarity. They are very patient of Hunger. . . .
Fashion of sitting at meals is on a mat spread on the ground, with their Legs lying out at length before them, and the dish between their Legs . . . never sit more than two together at a Dish. . . . Spoons which they eat with, do generally hold half a pint; and they laugh at the English for using small ones, which they must be forc'd to carry so often to their Mouths, that their Arms are in Danger of being tir'd, before their Belly.

Robert Beverley, Report on the True State of Virginia, *1705.*

nothing that required extra effort and was simply an everyday interaction.

It would appear that at the time of contact, good manners required that all visitors be offered food soon after arrival, and that guests eat everything offered. People ate sitting on woven grass mats on the ground or floor. Each person owned a bowl and spoon (for soups), brought them to meals, and was responsible for their cleanliness. Most food was eaten with fingers, although there were some ladles and dippers for serving liquid foods. Daily meals were cooked by women for their families, but in their sometimes-communal system much food was also shared, and it was considered quite acceptable for people to help themselves from the cooking pots of other families.

Gluttony was considered reprehensible, in keeping with the proper attitude of respect toward the spirit of the food and a general value on abstemiousness, self-denial, and Spartan strengthening. These general manners were, under certain circumstances, set aside for the greater value of survival. Overeating was common at times of fresh kills (especially when food was scarce or a rarity). It was sometimes a means of surviving periods in which there might be no food at all for days, or it occurred at Iroquois feasts when it was expected that everything placed before a guest, throughout the day, would be completely consumed.

[**See also** MYTHS AND FOLKLORE; NATIVE AMERICAN FOODS: BEFORE AND AFTER CONTACT; NATIVE AMERICAN FOODS: TECHNOLOGY AND FOOD SOURCES.]

BIBLIOGRAPHY

Gill, Sam D., and Irene F. Sullivan, eds. *Dictionary of Native American Mythology.* New York: Oxford University Press, 1994.

Leeming, David, and Jake Page. *The Mythology of Native North America.* Norman: University of Oklahoma Press, 1988.

Storm, Hyemeyohsts. *Seven Arrows.* New York: Ballantine, 1972.

ALICE ROSS

Native American Foods:
Technology and Food Sources

Meals were served in different patterns, according to tribe, season, and occasion. Many observers thought meals were informal affairs, often one-dish preparations like those the Iroquois simmered in large pots and served at noon. By contrast, according to an Onandaga, there was no concept of regular meals but, rather, food was available all day and eaten as one became hungry. The Delaware and Huron scheduled two daily meals, morning and evening. Some meals were described in which a series of separate dishes were served, according to an ethic against mixing foods. At times of seasonal scarcity, sudden availability brought on feasting that may have lasted for days. These feasts may have celebrated fresh meat in wintertime or maple syrup in early spring. The ensuing gorging may have been related to the Indians' genetic ability to store vast quantities of nutrients bodily and to draw on them in later times of hunger.

Many tribes depended chiefly on their basic grains or starches—dishes of corn, acorn, or wild rice. In some regions, these constituted 60 percent of the day's calories, and more in others. They were cooked into breads—steamed, stone baked as flatbreads and

A Papago woman picking cactus fruit with a stick in Arizona, 1907.

bannock, boiled as dumplings, and porridges—and commonly enriched with beans, nuts, seeds, vegetables, and fruit. Appearing in some form at every meal, such "breads" may have constituted an entire meal, and sometimes were simply one component. Dried meat and fish were as important to hunting and fishing tribes as corn was to farmers.

Depending on the season, almost all precontact people roasted and stewed meats, pit-steamed or boiled vegetables and starches, and dressed them with animal fat, nuts and nut oils, and seasonings. Fruits and vegetables were used in and out of season—raw, steamed, or boiled in season and dried to be reconstituted in sauces for meats and fish or as flavorings in grain and starch preparation. Cooked and eaten alone they were frequently dressed in animal fats.

Water was the common beverage, but regional teas were infused with leaves or blossoms, pine needles, fruit, or sap syrup from trees and young corn canes. Fermented alcoholic drinks were rare, although they were used in religious ceremonies in the Southwest. Hot drinks were made from numerous vegetable sources, among them the eastern teaberry (*gaultheria procumbens*) or Oswego tea (genus *Monarda*).

Foods served a variety of purposes. Meat jerkies were combined with parched corn into travel food; dried corn, beans, and pumpkin stored well. Fresh garden produce produced food in times of plenty, and less desirable foods were dried, stored, and held body and soul together in times of scarcity.

Regional differences reflected the foods available in different parts of the country. For example, the Southwest was strong on

Making Bread

A Zuni woman making bread. From In Field and Pasture, *a volume in Dutton's World at Work series, 1906.*

the Mexican corn, beans, squash, pumpkins, sunflower seeds, chilis, cacti, pumpkin seed oil, and tomatoes. In particular, blue corn was used in *piki*, a paper-thin kind of bread; juniper berries were important flavorings. Desert animals were a source of meat and eggs. The vast Eastern Woodlands were characterized by a mixture of rich agriculture, gathering, hunting, and long shorelines of fish and seafood. Their corn-beans-squash/pumpkins were often the basis of the meal, and enriched with whatever was in season or dried: plants, wild fruit, seeds, and nuts, flavored with small mammals, birds, or fish. The Southeast was characterized by much of the Eastern Woodlands, but supplemented with subtropical tomatoes, pawpaws and a strong component of African American foods (black-eyed peas and okra, for example). It also was known for *sofkee*, a liquid version of hominee grits prepared as a beverage enjoyed throughout the day, and wild *Zamia* root flour bread. Stews incorporated alligator and octopus, as well as cabbage palm hearts, fruit, guava products, and sweet potatoes.

The Prairie-Plains people produced similar agricultural products as the Eastern Woodlands, with more hunting of antelope and buffalo on the plains. Those of the Great Lakes areas harvested wild rice, and used it alongside corn in breads, stews, and soups. The dishes were often prepared with fish or small game, including beaver. Roast pumpkin was stuffed with wild rice, rendered fat, venison, buffalo, and sage. The Sioux, originally sedentary farmers of the Prairie, were displaced onto the Plains, achieved ownership of the horse, and became a nomadic buffalo and antelope culture. They maintained trade with the Prairie people, offering hides and dried buffalo for the garden products they had grown earlier. Some of the Sioux continued to garden, but consumed larger proportions of game meats. Typical dishes include *tinpsula*, a complex soup of dried turnips, dried corn, and dried buffalo. *Wahusapa wasna*, fried balls of toasted cornmeal, dried chokecherries or juneberries, and bear grease were a popular old dish, modernized with sugar and frying.

The Pacific Northwest and the Plateau regions ate widely on salmon, halibut, and euchalon (a small oily fish also called candle-fish). The salmon was fished and eaten

Fuels and Fire

Friction was the source of ignition. Bowdrills required the twirling a hard-wood shaft with some pressure against a thin, soft-wood platform. Accumulations of fine sawdust were heated by the friction to the point of glowing. They were placed in "nests" of fine tinder, sometimes Prairie dried grass or the shaved oak of the California Costanoans. There they produced the first flame, to which twigs and branches of graduated sizes were added. Large trunks were rarely burned, as stone axes were inadequate to the job of cutting them up, but modest-sized branches were manageable.

The bow drill was replaced by the European method using *flint and steel*. It produced sparks by striking the steel piece forcefully against the flintstone (sometimes the mineral *chert*). In the 1800s, Native Americans, along with the white population, adopted matches.

Robert Beverly on hearths
"They bake their Bread either in Cakes before the Fire, or in Loaves on a warm Hearth, covering the Loaf first with Leaves, then warm Ashes, and afterwards with Coals over all."
From *The History and Present State of Virginia* (1705)

Clay Cooking Pots

Clay cooking pots and containers were constructed and fired by hand. In many cases, they were handsome, thin-walled, symmetrical, and decorated regionally, characteristically painted in the Southwest and inscribed in the East. They were invariably shaped with round or rounded point-bottoms, sometimes set into loose soil and ringed with fire, sometimes propped and leveled over fire with small easel stones. Those with projecting ears and flaring rims were wrapped with cordage and suspended over the heat. Clay pots were made in all sizes; some, surprisingly large, held over twenty gallons and were used for boiling quantities of festival dishes, for reducing tree-saps into syrup, and as storage containers. They were often admired by Europeans and considered as well-formed and handsome as any being thrown on Europe's potters' wheels of the time.

Broiling, roasting, and drying equipment
"The Indians killed a bear and two does that day . . . they brought the meat of all to the camp that evening, and some of them was busily engaged in cutting the meat off the bones and drying it on a little rod or stick over the fire to make what the Indians call Jerk—*dried meat to carry with them . . . one of the Indians . . . attended . . . continually throughout the night to drying their meat, making Jerk of it so as to carry it with them.*"
Peter Henry, *Accounts of His Captivity and Other Events* (1780)

Basketry

Basketry reached high levels of artistry and craftsmanship, particularly in regions such as the Pacific Northwest, California, and the Great Basin that had neither major clay deposits nor heavy forestation. Such baskets were used as pottery was elsewhere, and were often complex, finely and tightly made baskets of twined and coiled grasses, hazel shoots, or conifer roots. Waterproof baskets were used for stone-boiling such dishes as the staple acorn mush. Others served the largely-nomadic cultures as burden baskets, gathering baskets, storage baskets, trays, water jars, seed beaters, winnowing trays, bottles and bowls.

Indian basketry influenced that of many newcomers, among them Germans of the Eastern central states, Shakers in the Northeast, and British of the Appalachians, and was in turn affected by the work of such newcomers as southeastern African Americans. The adoption of new foods inspired new styles of food baskets, for example, new dairying cheese baskets were adaptations of sifters, but with extremely open weaves for draining. By the late nineteenth century some sifters were replaced with purchased sieves of horsehair or wire mesh. Basketry continues to be a well-developed art form, has continued to represent Native American culture, and is being practiced by regional specialists.

Tools For Grinding

Ginding and pounding apparatuses were made in different sizes, according to the need for transportation and the kind of food being processed. Hard dry corn and acorns required large containers; while small amounts of seed, dried leaf or ash seasonings were easily managed in smaller sizes (which had the additional advantage of portability). A good many dried foods were also pounded, among them pumpkin and sunflower seeds, meats, and nuts.

Storage Containers

With so much of the year's food preserved for lean times, it was essential to use large storage containers, among them large pottery jars, wooden bowls, baskets, and gourds.

The Pomo used large coiled baskets for storing dried blueberries, and Crees kept cranberries in pitch-sealed birchbark. Menominees stored wild rice in containers made from the outer layers of birch or woven from the inner bark of cedar. Eastern Algonkians made grass sacks for corn.

Hunting societies used animal products for their containers. The Apache stored dried pounded acorn and meat mixtures in skins, the Paiute used buckskin bags to hang dried elderberries, and the Menominee stored wild rice in muskrat skins, fawnskins, or raccoon sacks. In some cases, animal bladders were inflated and hung over fire to harden into bottle-shaped containers.

Robert Beverley on salt

[The tribes in his area] "have no Salt among them, but for seasoning use the Ashes of Hiccory, Stickweed, or some other Wood or Plant, affording a Salt ash."
The History and Present State of Virginia (1705)

Fry Bread

Fry bread, made with a dough of wheat flour and milk or water and served with a variety of accompaniment such as honey, maple syrup, and sugar, is perhaps the most symbolic Native American food today. Without question of European origin, it is nevertheless debateable as to where and by whom it was first introduced. One side of the issue suggests that the Spanish made the contribution, as they had a strong deep frying tradition that included a fried, yeast-raised wheat bread called *churros*. A less culinary argument credits the French, particularly noted for their fine yeast-leavened breads, and who, more importantly, maintained influence and contact with tribes throughout the Mississippi area, Canada to Louisiana, and may have spread its use. Still another claim is that fry bread resulted from the creative efforts of inventive reservation women faced with appropriate government rations.

year-round, although consumed in heavier concentrations during spawning time. Also eaten in quantity were acorns, numerous berries, camas and yellow pond lily roots, and the tender buds of pine. The late eighteenth century brought the potato, which became another staple.

California tribes were discovered early, but the relatively late arrival of Spanish missionaries from Mexico (1779) began their catastrophic decimation; it continued with the Gold Rush prospectors (1848). Many Native Americans were lost to disease, conversion, assimilartion, and the newcomers' hunger for land. Relatively little remains of the original tribes of the coastal Southwest, although several small tribes have retained strong cultural identity. The precontact foodways of California locales were substantially different from one another, and included coastal hunting-fishing groups, inland plateau plant-gathering and hunting, and southern desert plant gathering and, to a lesser extent, hunting of large and small mammals. Insects smoked out of trees or taken in "surrounds," were a major source of protein, and often roasted. Acorn-based breads and camas roots provided staple starches, along with cattail roots (from wetlands) and a grassy rice. Pine nuts were not only used as seasonings but also were ground into meal for baking. Southern California showed cacti and other Mexican influences.

Technology

Native Americans mastered the technologies of late Stone Age culture, and efficiently fashioned cooking implements of stone, clay, shell, bone, and leather. They did not use iron, and only occasionally used copper, a softer and more maleable metal. Their cooking technologies and processes were simple and straightforward.

Fire making was the most basic process. The type of fuel was chosen according to its availability and its ability to produce heat, depending on region. Fire drills of hard wood were ground against thin, flat slabs, and the resulting sawdust, heated by friction, glowed and ignited a nest of fine tinder. The fire was built from this first flame by adding gradually larger pieces of wood. A similar process on the Plains used buffalo chips (dried manure) the same way.

Fires were made in shallow fire pits, lined with smooth river rocks, in which tripods of rocks held rounded-bottom clay pots and flat griddles. These hearths held enough heated ash and embers in which to bake foods directly. In the regions where clay pots were not available, the water in containers of basketry was brought to a boil by dropping in small round balls of preheated clay or stone. Some food was hung from twine above the fire and slowly roasted.

In some areas, deeper pit ovens, sometimes lined with stone or heavy green leaves, were dug into the ground; hot glowing coals were placed inside under the foods and covered, to slowly bake or steam leaf-protected foods. In addition to the standard forms of cookery, sun-drying was a common means of preserving food for wintertime eating. Reconstiting with water and sometimes sweetness (first honey and maple sugar, later sugar), they were boiled into sauces, soups, and stews.

Cooking Implements

Wood, basketry, and gourds were common everywhere, and was sometimes replaced by tin articles after contact. They were the source of plates, platters, spoons, dippers, stirrers, spits and skewers, storage containers, and cooking and drying racks. The original shaping tools—beaver teeth, clam shells, and stone—were replaced with traded iron knives soon after contact. Clay bowls and cooking pots were common, rounded-bottomed and fired in hot wood fires. They were replaced, after contact, with brass and iron kettles. Stone pounding and grinding equipment was also common, as were large wooden mortars and pestles for corn. Broiling, roasting, and drying implements held strips of meat in the heat of a fire, sometimes larger portions of fish were splayed between skewers and propped into the smoke to dry. Cutting tools and stone working was flint-knapped by flaking jasper, fine-grained chert, flint, obsidian, and quartzite. Softer stone (steatite or soapstone), was used for carving small bowls or flat griddles. Numerous tools were made from animal parts: bone corn-husking pins, deer jaw scrapers of corn, turtle shell platters, or sinew lashings. The level of craftsmanship and artistry were renowned. The *horno*, a free-standing clay oven, was adopted from the Spanish, and used to roast and bake.

Foodstuffs and Storage

Most tribes used underground caches or protected shelters. In the Northeast, the caches may have been as deep as six feet, and lined with stone, bark, or fragrant grasses. These pits were roofed and made watertight, and then disguised with coverings or soil or brush. Northern tribes sometimes took advantage of the cold, freezing streams: the Washington Makah used them to protect alder-bark cones of elderberry clusters. Above ground, graneries held corn in the north, and acorns in the south. Early practices gave way to nineteenth-century canning and twentieth-century freezing.

BIBLIOGRAPHY

Cox, Beverly and Martin Jacobs. *Spirit of the Harvest: North American Indian Cooking.* New York: Steward, Tabori, and Chang, 1991.
Indian Women's Club of Tulsa, Oklahoma. "The Indian Cook Book," in *Southwest Cookery: Indian and Spanish Influences,* ed. by Louis Szathmary.
New York: Promontory, 1974. Originally published 1933.
Parker, A. C. *Iroquois Uses of Maize and Other Food Plants.* 1910. Ohsweken, Ontario: Iroqrafts, 1983. Originally published 1910.
Raine, Carolyn. *A Woodland Feast: Native American Foodways of the 17th and 18th Centuries.* Huber Heights, OH: Morningstar, 1997.
Stewart, Hilary. *Indian Fishing: Early Methods on the Northwest Coast.* Seattle: University of Washington Press, 1977.
Speth, John C. *Bison Kills and Bone Counts: Decision-Making by Ancient Hunters,* ed. Karl Butzer and Leslie G. Freeman. Chicago: University of Chicago Press, 1983.
Young, Joyce La Fray. *Seminole Indian Recipes.* Tampa, FL: Surfside, 1987.

ALICE ROS

Navajo Tacos

Originating in the southwestern states of Arizona, New Mexico, and Utah, Navajo tacos are a type of Native American snack food served at rodeos, fairs, gatherings, powwows, and even Southwest fast-food restaurants. Instead of using tortillas as in a typical Mexican taco, the Navajo taco starts out with a sopaipilla (also known as Navajo fry bread). A sopaipilla is made from wheat dough that is shaped into a plate-size flat disk and deep-fried in lard. Once fried, the sopaipilla is topped with refried beans, lettuce, tomato, scallion, cheese, avocado, sour cream, and taco sauce or salsa. The origins of the Navajo taco reflect the diversity of southwestern cuisine. The beans, tomato, oregano, and cilantro used in the dish are ingredients brought to the region from Mexico by Spanish conquistadores, while the use of flour and lard is a Spanish contribution. The chilies used to make the salsa for the taco are native to the area, as are the preparation techniques. The Navajo taco is sold throughout the Southwest at the Mexican fast-food restaurant chain Taco Time. The Navajo Nation has not given consent for the use of its name in selling the product.

[See also MEXICAN AMERICAN FOOD; NATIVE AMERICAN FOOD; SOUTHWEST.]

JEAN RAILLA

Nestlé

There are few kitchens in America that do not contain at least one product manufactured by the Nestlé Company. Headquartered in Vevey, Switzerland, Nestlé is the largest food company in the world with almost five hundred manufacturing plants worldwide. The company has had a presence in North America since 1900, when Nestlé opened its first factory in the United States. Nestlé's

Navajo Tacos

410

Nestlé Coffee Products

In 1938, after eight years of experimentation, Nestlé launched Nescafé, a powdered instant coffee superior to previous efforts. It was produced by spraying brewed coffee into heated towers, where it turned to powder almost instantly. The venerable Swiss firm had been founded by Henri Nestlé in 1867, when he invented an infant-feeding formula. With subsidiaries for its chocolate and confectionery products already in place all over the world, Nestlé was ideally situated to promote its new instant coffee, whereas the advent of World War II provided the perfect American market when the U.S. military bought all the instant coffee it could.

In the postwar era, Nestlé tried to sell Nescafé in America with lackluster reason-why ads about no fuss and no coffee grounds, and it lost its lead to instant Maxwell House. In the late 1960s, however, when freeze-drying techniques were introduced that produced a better-tasting coffee, ads for Nestlé's Taster's Choice freeze-dried coffee claimed to offer "all the deep, rich flavor and hearty coffee aroma you used to have to perk up a pot for," and with a $10-million-a-year marketing campaign, Taster's Choice pulled ahead of Maxwell House's Maxim. Nestlé was wise to choose a completely new name for the product so that it was not associated with the low-quality image of Nescafé.

In the 1980s, Nestlé expanded its North American business beyond instant coffee by purchasing once-famous brands, then down on their luck, such as Hills Brothers, MJB, and Chase and Sanborn. Seeking a toehold in the specialty whole-bean market, the firm also purchased California-based Sark's Gourmet Coffee in 1987.

In the early 1990s, Nestlé ran innovative Taster's Choice ads cribbed from its equivalent British brand, Gold Blend. In the serial soap opera–style commercials, suave Tony wooed sexy Sharon by mixing up seductive cups of Taster's Choice in a variety of situations. The commercial in which they finally kissed made the national news.

As the twenty-first century opened, Nestlé was the world's largest coffee company, primarily owing to global sales of instant coffee. In the United States, however, it roasted less coffee than Philip Morris's Maxwell House or Procter & Gamble's Folgers.

BIBLIOGRAPHY

Heer, Jean. *Nestlé: 125 Years, 1866–1991.* Trans. B. J. Benson with Constance Devanthéry-Lewis. Vevey, Switzerland: Nestlé, 1991.
Pendergrast, Mark. *Uncommon Grounds: The History of Coffee and How It Transformed Our World.* New York: Basic Books, 1999.

MARK PENDERGRAST

products are distributed under hundreds of brand names and include Crosse and Blackwell preserves, Stouffer's frozen foods, Poland Springs bottled water, Libby's fruit juices, Carnation Instant Breakfast, and Maggi bouillon cubes.

The history of the company began with Charles Page in 1866. Page had recognized the potential of Gail Borden's condensed milk product, which was first produced in the United States in the decade before the U.S. Civil War. After his experiences as the American consul in Zurich, Page believed that Switzerland, with its central location and abundant milk supply, was the ideal site for developing and marketing a condensed milk product. He called his new business the Anglo-Swiss Condensed Milk Company to make it easier to market his Swiss-made products in England.

In 1867, Henri Nestlé, a pharmacist, was asked by a friend to make something for an infant who could not digest fresh cow's milk. Knowing that the child would die without his intervention, Nestlé created a milk food from crumbs made from baked malted wheat rusks mixed with sweetened condensed milk. This granular brown powder was the first instant infant weaning food. He called his alternative to breastfeeding Farine Lactée Henri Nestlé and adopted his family's coat of arms, a bird's nest, as a trademark. The symbol of the nest suggested maternity, nature, security, and nourishment.

Nestlé sold his company to Jules Monnerat in 1874. The following year another Swiss citizen, Daniel Peter, found a way to combine cocoa powder with milk to create milk chocolate. This company also merged with Nestlé. Five years after opening its first U.S. factory, in 1905 Nestlé merged with Page's Anglo-Swiss Condensed Milk Company. The merger of the two companies made it possible for the new firm to expand.

In 1938, Nestlé added Nescafé, a soluble powdered coffee, to its product line. Nescafé became an American staple after servicemen tasted it in Europe and Asia during World War II. Based on the success of Nescafé, the company developed a freeze-dried coffee in 1966 called Taster's Choice.

During the 1970s, Nestlé aggressively expanded the marketing of its baby formula in developing countries. A boycott against the company started in the United States in 1977; it was claimed that, because of poverty and illiteracy, the company's formula products would be diluted with polluted water, resulting in disease or starvation. The boycott cost Nestlé millions of dollars. In a textbook example of crisis management, the managing director of the company met with the boycotters and agreed to follow the World Health Organization's guidelines for advertising and marketing baby formula in developing countries.

[See also BORDEN; CHOCOLATE; COFFEE, INSTANT.]

BIBLIOGRAPHY

Mirabile, Lisa, ed. *International Directory of Company Histories*. Vol. 2, *Electrical and Electronics—Food Services and Retailers*. Chicago: St. James Press, 1990.
Toussaint-Samat, Maguelonne, et al. *2 Million Years of the Food Industry*. Vevey, Switzerland: Nestlé S.A., 1991.

JOSEPH M. CARLIN

New England

The six New England states—Massachusetts, Rhode Island, Connecticut, Maine, Vermont, and New Hampshire—cover a large enough area to be divided into smaller subregions, some of which have distinctive foodways, distinctions blurred in later times by vast immigrations, mass consumption, and popular culture and possibly retained only by self-conscious effort.

The Colonial and Federal Eras

In New England, early wheat varieties imported from Europe suffered from a rust that greatly limited its production and New Englanders adopted what they called "Indian corn," that is, maize. Rye thrived and was combined with maize to make an everyday bread called "rye and Indian." Mixed crops of grains included oats, rye, barley, and sometimes even wild plant seed to yield "maslin," which was made into bread. When wheat crops did succeed, some homesteads were able to grow enough wheat for the family's consumption. Flour was often reserved for pastry and fine baking.

Cornmeal proved useful for sweet and savory dishes. In addition to bread, grain-based dishes, particularly porridge, were adapted to corn. Cornmeal was used to make a cornmeal mush also called hasty pudding, and to make bannock, a flat, unleavened bread made of grain and water. In Rhode Island this bread was called "jonnycake." A pudding based on milk and cornmeal sweetened with molasses wascalled "Indian pudding."

The colonists also adopted pumpkins. Cooked slowly, pumpkins made a sauce to accompany meat, were put into pastry as apples had been for tarts, or what New Englanders ultimately called "pie." Pumpkins were used in puddings and even baked whole. Native Americans introduced the colonists to the beans well suited to the New England climate. A customary English pottage of slowly stewed peas and meat, often salted meat, gradually gave way to one made of beans. The bean pottage, a substantial dish because of the salted meat, evolved into the region's famous, sweet version of baked beans. The Native American combination of dried beans and corn in a dish called "succotash" sufficiently resembled other familiar pottages that settlers readily adopted it. Beans were boiled as peas were, in a bag suspended in a pot with a piece of boiling salt meat and sometimes with other vegetables. Beans were used fresh in summer and dried for winter use. Early New England colonists cultivated hundreds of varieties of bean, some of which have been preserved as heirlooms.

Apples imported from England took well to the New England soil and climate. In the eighteenth and nineteenth centuries, orchards were established, and hundreds of varieties of apples were cultivated. In some parts of New England, freshly squeezed apple cider was boiled into apple molasses and used in place of the molasses which came from cane sugar. Apple and pear sauces were cooked by the cask-full for household use. Apples dried well, as did pumpkin, for home consumption and later for sale. Cider making took full advantage of New England's apple abundance. Gallons squeezed and fermented provided a family beverage and a way to preserve apples. By the end of the colonial period, an astonishing quantity of alcoholic beverages was being consumed—three or four gallons per capita, the highest level of alcohol consumption in American history.

Molasses became the common sweetener throughout New England and much molasses was distilled into rum. Refined sugar, an expensive import for most of the seventeenth and eighteenth centuries, was reserved for fine cooking, baking, and preserve making. When inland and upcountry people tapped maple trees and boiled sap, they were seeking a locally available version of brown sugar and molasses.

Meat and Fish. For a short time on any frontier, hunting for deer, moose, wildfowl, and small animals helped supplement the diet. By the eighteenth century, meat eating was a significant feature of life in New England. In

Uncle Sam assures John Bull that minced codfish is the American national dish on this late-nineteenth-century advertising card distributed in Boston.

A New England tea room at the Vusper Country Club in Tyngsboro, Massachusetts.

many households, meat was eaten at least twice if not three times a day. Beef was the preferred meat, followed by pork, mutton and lamb, and veal. Fresh meat always was at a premium winter or summer. New England's farms also produced enough meat and cheese for it to be an article of commerce with other colonies and the West Indies.

New Englanders ate eat fish for dinner at least once a week and used fish to accompany other viands at breakfast and supper. Fresh fish was preferred, although New Englanders regularly ate salt cod. Shad and salmon were caught in season, and smaller fish, such as mackerel, alewife, and herring, were salted and smoked. Shellfish, particularly oysters and lobsters, found a ready enough market that oyster harvesting had to be curtailed in the early nineteenth century to prevent overfishing.

Nineteenth and Twentieth Centuries

Once the Erie Canal was completed, connecting the port of New York and southern New England with western New York State and newly settled lands around the Great Lakes, the cost of wheat dropped, and the quantity available increased. New Englanders seemed glad to give up rye-and-Indian as the daily loaf in favor of bread made of wheat. The old combination of rye and Indian with or without wheat flour or meal evolved into a steamed pudding by the middle to late nineteenth century. Sweetened with molasses and mixed with sour milk and baking soda this concoction became known outside the region as "Boston brown bread" and within New England simply as "brown bread." When refined wheat was joined by a more plentiful supply of white sugar, New Englanders took to cake.

A major influence on food habits in New England was food-related commerce and industry. Canneries sprung up in cities and towns close to the growers. Along the coast,

clams, lobster, and sardines joined the list of canned foods. In the late nineteenth century Gloucester and Boston fish producers began selling prepared fish—boneless salt cod, even salt cod shredded and ready for quick freshening in hot water; canned chowder; codfish cakes; and crab and salmon ready for salad or heating in cream sauce.

During the nineteenth century and into the beginning of the twentieth, New England cities, seaports, and industrial centers attracted large numbers of immigrants. The first were Irish fleeing the potato famine, followed by Italians, Germans, Swedes, middle Europeans, Portuguese, freed blacks, and French Canadians. Some ethnic groups were numerous enough to support local grocery stores. Diet reformers took up the cause of teaching immigrants American ways of cookery, which often included meat, potatoes, dairy products, and bread to replace what would, in the late twentieth century, be recognized as a very suitable diet of more fish, more vegetables, small quantities of meat, and fewer sweets.

Two World Wars and a Depression

Three major events disrupted New England foodways in the twentieth century. Two world wars brought periods of rationing of meat, butter, and sugar for most citizens, and the Depression caused hardship for many New Englanders. With meat consumption curtailed during rationing, some families ate more fish than they once had. Many families had victory gardens, and, encouraged by government agencies, patriotically canned fruits and vegetables.

The result seems to have been that with the interruptions caused by hard times, it was easier for New Englanders to forget old ways and to adopt new and, by the 1950s, often commercially introduced foods. In remote

and less prosperous sections of New England, old foodways persisted, but in more affluent urban and suburban areas, national brands and mass distribution overwhelmed many traditions.

Even before the Depression, New England farmers were feeling pressure from the Midwest, where larger farms achieved an economy of scale practically impossible in the northeast. Many smaller canneries in rural areas went out of business by World War II. Dairy farming and fruit growing with some market gardening kept some food production within the region, but rising land values and a growing regional population looking for house lots starting in the 1970s have forced many more farms out of existence. In the early twenty-first century, most food consumed in New England comes from other regions in the United States and the world.

The variety of ethnic fare shared by groups living in New England for decades became absorbed through the influence of mass communication and restaurant offerings. In addition, new immigrants have arrived in the region, introducing their foodways. Even small inland cities are likely to sport a Thai, Mexican, Vietnamese, or Caribbean restaurant.

To provision the dense New England population, food from outside the region continues to supply most of the region's diet. A countervailing impulse comes from regional restaurants featuring locally grown food and from chefs, food writers, and cooking schools who encourage consumers to support regional agricultural by patronizing farmers' markets and community-supported agriculture operations and by demanding locally grown food in supermarkets. Trading on New England's traditional dishes and specialties, locally grown foods, and new cultural influences may freshen the fare of the region.

[**See also** APPLES; BEANS; BOSTON COOKING SCHOOL; BREWING; CAKES; CHEESE; CHRISTMAS; CIDER; CLAMBAKE; CORN; DAIRY; FISH, SALTWATER FLAT; SHELLFISH; ETHNIC FOODS; FOOD FESTIVALS; GRAHAM, SYLVESTER; HASTY PUDDING; JOHNNY APPLESEED; MOLASSES; NATIVE AMERICAN FOOD; RUM; TEMPERANCE; THANKSGIVING; VEGETARIANISM.]

BIBLIOGRAPHY

Conroy, David W. *In Public Houses: Drink and the Revolution of Authority in Colonial Massachusetts.* Chapel Hill: University of North Carolina Press, 1995.

Larkin, Jack. *The Reshaping of Everyday Life, 1790–1840.* New York: Harper and Row, 1988.

Neustadt, Kathy. *Clambakes: A History and Celebration of an American Tradition.* Amherst: University of Massachusetts Press, 1992.

Nylander, Jane. *Our Own Snug Fireside: Images of the New England Home. 1760–1860.* New York: Knopf, 1993.

Oliver, Sandra L. *Saltwater Foodways: New Englanders and Their Food at Sea and Ashore in the 19th Century.* Mystic, CT: Mystic Seaport Museum, 1995.

SANDRA OLIVER

New England Confectionary Company (NECCO)

In 1847, Oliver R. Chase of Boston invented a candy machine called the lozenge cutter. Along with his brother, Silas Edwin Chase, they founded Chase and Company, which later became one of the companies which merged to form the New England Confectionary Company (NECCO). NECCO is considered the oldest continuously operating candy company in America. One of its earliest products was "Conversation Hearts," pastel-colored sugar hearts with romantic mottos printed on them. NECCO renamed them "Sweethearts" in 1902, when they became associated with Valentine's Day. The famous NECCO wafers, disks of various flavored and colored candy sold in rolls, first appeared in 1912; they had previously been called "Peerless Wafers." The "Bolster Bar," peanut crunch covered with milk chocolate, was also manufactured by the New England Confectionery Company. NECCO introduced the "Sky Bar" (a chocolate bar divided into four sections, each with a different filling) in 1937 with a dramatic skywriting campaign.

The company has made a number of acquisitions. In 1990, NECCO acquired Stark Candy Company, which manufactured Mary Jane candies. The NECCO company has since extended this product line to include a wide range of "Mary Jane" products, including Mary Jane Tubs and Mary Jane Peanut Butter Kisses. In 1990, it purchased the Stark Candy Company, which brought to NECCO the Peanut Butter Kiss, Salt Water Taffy, and Mary Jane Candies. NECCO acquired the Clark Bar in 1999. As of the mid-2000s Sweethearts are the best-selling Valentine's Day candy.

BIBLIOGRAPHY

Broekel, Ray. *The Great America Candy Bar Book*. Boston: Houghton Mifflin Company, 1982.

Richardson, Tim. *Sweets: A History of Candy*. New York: Bloomsbury, 2002.

Untermeyer, Louis. *A Century of Candymaking 1847–1947; The Story of the Origin and Growth of New England Confectionery Company*. Boston: The Barta Press, 1947.

ANDREW F. SMITH

New Orleans Syrup

New Orleans syrup is a gold-colored sweetener derived from sugarcane juice. In New Orleans, the product is most commonly known by the brand name, Steen's 100% Pure Cane Syrup or ribbon cane syrup. In southern states, it became known as New Orleans syrup because of the large quantities produced in the New Orleans area.

The sugarcane plant used for syrup production came from India by way of the Caribbean islands. It was first introduced to Louisiana in the mid-eighteenth century and thrives there in the high temperatures and constant moisture required for cultivation. Farmers often raised patches of sugarcane and took their harvests to local sugar mills for processing. During harvest season, the cane is cut down, and its outer leaves are stripped away. At the mill, the stalks are pulverized, and the cane juice is boiled to remove impurities. The resulting syrup is canned and cooled.

Before the prevalence of cane sugar, cane syrup was the primary sweetener. An old-time southern Louisiana desert called "syrup soppin'" consisted of cane syrup poured onto the plate after a finished meal and sopped up with bread. New Orleans syrup is used as a condiment, is poured over biscuits and *pain perdu* (French toast), and is used as a sweetener in baking and other cooking methods. [See also CAJUN AND CREOLE FOOD; SUGAR.]

BIBLIOGRAPHY

Steen, Mrs. J. Wesley, ed. *The Story of Steen's Syrup and its Famous Recipes*. Abbeville, LA: Steen's Syrup Mill.

Gutierrez, Paige C. *Cajun Foodways*. Jackson: University of Mississippi Press, 1992.

JENNIFER MINNICK

An early-twentieth-century advertising card for Weber's bread products depicts a boy pressing apples for New Year's cider.

New Year's Celebrations

Although champagne has become de rigueur as midnight strikes, no single food epitomizes the contemporary New Year's holiday. The menu may be luxurious caviar at a New Year's Eve bacchanalia or sobering hoppin' John on New Year's Day. Celebrations marking the inexorable march of Father Time often involve foods imbued with symbolism, such as in the Pennsylvania Dutch New Year's tradition of sauerkraut (for wealth) and pork—the pig roots forward into the future, unlike the Christmas turkey, which buries the past by scratching backward in the dirt.

Seventeenth-century Dutch immigrants in the Hudson River valley welcomed the New Year by "opening the house" to family and friends. The custom was adapted by English colonists, who used brief, strictly choreographed, January 1 social calls for gentlemen to renew bonds or repair frayed relationships. Ladies remained at home, offering elegantly arrayed collations laden with cherry bounce, wine, hot punch, and cakes and cookies, often flavored with the Dutch signatures of caraway, coriander, cardamom, and honey. Embossed New Year's "cakes," from the Dutch *nieuwjaarskoeken*—made by pressing a cookie-like dough into carved wooden boards decorated with flora and fauna—were a New York specialty throughout the nineteenth century.

Politicians embraced—or were embraced by—the New Year's open house. George Washington inaugurated a custom of presidential New Year's levees in 1791. The levees, which continued until the Franklin D. Roosevelt administration, were a powerful statement in the fledgling democracy: Any properly dressed person with a letter of introduction, could—without an invitation—drink punch and nibble cake with the president. The diarist Philip Hone reported in 1837 that "scamps" with muddy boots stormed the home of the New York mayor, shouting "huzzas" for the mayor and demanding refreshment. The police restored order only after the celebrants had drained the mayor's bottles, devoured his beef and turkey, and wiped their greasy fingers on his curtains.

Heavy drinking, especially among the young and the disadvantaged, was widely reported from the late eighteenth century on, when servants and slaves pounded on doors in the middle of the night demanding New Year's drinks. Alcohol continues to assume a prominent place in New Year's parties, notwithstanding the efforts of nineteenth-century temperance advocates, who pointedly poured effervescent sarsaparilla, coffee, and tea.

The New York custom of open house spread westward in the nineteenth century. Although the Dutch palimpsest continued in the "cold-slaw" found in Eliza Leslie's menus for New Year's dinner in *New Receipts for Cooking* (1854), other influences shaped the holiday, particularly in the South. In the eighteenth and nineteenth centuries, those of French and English backgrounds celebrated the twelve days of Christmas with gifts of food and festive dinners on January 1. Antebellum plantation owners sometimes gave slaves oxen to slaughter on New Year's Day as well as liquor for the slaves' parties. African Americans in the eighteenth and nineteenth centuries made one of the most enduring contributions to the modern holiday. Starting in the Carolinas but extending throughout the South, hoppin' John and greens became traditional New Year's fare, black-eyed peas bringing luck and the rice (which swelled in the cooking) and greens (like money) bringing prosperity. In the early twentieth century, Japanese Americans adopted the open house tradition, serving glutinous rice dishes, soups, boiled lobsters (signifying health and happiness), and fish specially prepared to appear alive and swimming.

[**See also** Christmas; Thanksgiving.]

BIBLIOGRAPHY

Barnes, Donna R., and Peter G. Rose. *Matters of Taste: Food and Drink in Seventeenth Century Dutch Art and Life.* Albany, NY: Albany Institute of History and Art, 2002.

Weaver, William Woys. *America Eats: Forms of Edible Folk Art.* New York: Harper and Row, 1989.

CATHY K. KAUFMAN

New York Food

The Dutch West India Company founded the outpost of New Amsterdam on Manhattan Island in 1624, as the launching point for New Netherland colony. It was not a place of wealth. The colonists initially depended on dried peas and other legumes, salted meat or fish, butter, cheese, beer, salt, and flour, all carried from the Netherlands or other Dutch New World holdings. They drew heavily on the fish and shellfish that were the region's greatest resource, and obtained game and sometimes maize from the Indians, although they also were crowding out the latter from their hunting ranges and extirpating the region's original food resources.

Before and for a generation after the English takeover in 1664, the cooking was largely a replica of the two mother countries' cuisines, which resembled each other as products of damp northern climates with a fairly heavy use of animal fats, reliance of bread and cheese as plain people's everyday fare, and a taste for sugar starting to spread from the elite throughout society. The Caribbean sugar/slave trade became the linchpin of the growing town's economy, with the colonists sending their own wheat, flour, salt meat, and pickled oysters to West Indian plantations in return for sugar and rum. For close to two centuries, New York would be one of America's major sugar-refining towns.

The foundations of Manhattan's restaurant culture did not appear until the early federal era, when residential building started to be pushed away from the concentration of commercial activity at the narrow island's southern tip and business transients began appearing in large numbers. The resulting need for temporary living accommodations and places to take the midday meal gave rise to numerous boardinghouses along with chophouses, coffee shops, confectioners' shops, and oyster houses. Before 1840, imposing hotels and elegant restaurants—the Astor House and Delmonico's being the most famous—were becoming part of the picture.

Before the Civil War, canal and rail transport had made New York into the great national port of entry and exit for commercial food shipments. One result was a rich range of luxury foods from abroad (e.g., Mediterranean and Caribbean fruits). Waves of immigration from Germany from the 1840s on brought the city its first recognizable ethnic cuisine. After the war, the city's growing stature as a hub of finance fostered the rise of a wealthy elite as well as a diverse population of U.S. transplants employed in journalism, book publishing, and the arts; all of these formed diverse clienteles for a varied restaurant scene. Meanwhile, new waves of eastern European Jewish and southern Italian immigrants altered the demographic profile of New York while establishing somewhat hybridized versions of their old foodways that would eventually attract American-born audiences. The same was true of the much smaller Chinese population.

The creation of the present five-borough New York in 1898 ushered in a period of dramatic growth that required a burgeoning labor force and places to feed it. A new component of the workforce was women office workers who frequented popular, inexpensive restaurant chains such as Schrafft's, Childs, and the Horn & Hardart Automats. Despite the disastrous effect of Prohibition on elite dining spots like Delmonico's, the post–World War I era saw a great expansion of eating places from speakeasies and cafeterias to quasi-ethnic restaurants (especially Chinese and Italian) not dependent on wine or liquor sales. By the 1941 début of *Gourmet* magazine, New York also had become the national center of a thriving food-journalist corps who publicized Gotham's glamorous culinary diversity and encouraged a gourmet home-cooking movement.

In the last half of the twentieth century, the New York food story was all too often a tale of two cities: a dynamic, exciting dining and shopping center fueled by a concentration of international corporate headquarters (supporting, for instance, an avid sushi-bar clientele by 1970), and an ex-manufacturing city facing steep blue collar job losses that spelled the end for many inexpensive neighborhood restaurants. The less fortunate among a large influx of southern blacks and Puerto Ricans relied heavily on food stamps, while at the same time a marked cult of restaurants and food fashion (whose adherents were often dubbed "foodies") accompanied the spread of splashy dining spots developed by professional consulting groups, like Restaurant Associates' The Four Seasons. (It should, however, be noted that during the 1980 some noted "foodies" became energetic spearheaders of food-relief efforts such as Citymeals on Wheels and Share Our Strength.) Gourmet home cooking waned somewhat after the late 1970s, making way for an array of gourmet take-out-and-catering shops in the wake of the pathbreaking Silver Palate (founded in 1977).

Meanwhile, the effects of the 1965 Hart-Celler Act, which ended forty years of sharply curtailed immigration and gave rise to vast influxes from many parts of Asia, Africa, and Latin America, went almost unnoticed by the leaders of culinary fashion until the mid-1990s. By then, the brilliant Manhattan restaurant scene owed much to workers from developing countries, whereas immigrant enclaves in Queens, Brooklyn, and nearby New Jersey became new strongholds of home cooking and inexpensive neighborhood eateries.

From the early 1970s on, California increasingly rivaled New York as the nation's glamorous hub of gastronomic innovation. Leaders of elite taste kept proclaiming a series of trends that included high-end Italian cooking, a "New American Cuisine," and—by the late 1980s—an eclectic mix of influences called "fusion food." Eventually, the city food press and the "foodie" community began exploring the culinary contributions

The interior of Delmonico's Restaurant in the late nineteenth century.

Peddler selling pretzels on the sidewalk in New York City, 1917.

Hot dog vendor's cart at Twenty-third Street and Fifth Avenue in Manhattan.

of recent immigrants in growing ethnic neighborhoods. New immigrants in turn became popular street-food sellers in (among other places) the midtown and Wall Street districts of Manhattan, offering fare that ranged from falafel to Chinese roast pork buns.

Before and after the destruction of the World Trade Center on September 11, 2001, the future of high-end gastronomy in New York began to appear somewhat uncertain. The late 1990s and the opening years of the new century were marked by a restless search for new fashions and directions, amid great national and local economic unease.

[See also AUTOMATS; BEER GARDENS; BEER HALLS; BRADY, DIAMOND JIM; CAFETERIAS; CELEBRITY CHEFS; CHINESE AMERICAN FOOD; CLAIBORNE, CRAIG; COFFEEHOUSES; DELICATESSENS; DELMONICO'S; DOUGHNUTS; DUTCH INFLUENCES ON AMERICAN FOOD; ETHNIC FOOD; FARMERS' MARKETS; FUSION FOOD; GERMAN AMERICAN FOOD; INDIAN AMERICAN FOOD; ITALIAN AMERICAN FOOD; JEWISH AMERICAN FOOD; LÜCHOW'S; NOUVELLE CUISINE; PROHIBITION; RESTAURANT CRITICS AND FOOD COLUMNISTS; RESTAURANTS; RESTAURANT CRITICS AND FOOD COLUMNISTS; TAVERNS; TRANSPORTATION OF FOOD; TSCHIRKY, OSCAR.]

BIBLIOGRAPHY

Batterberry, Michael and Ariane Batterberry. *On the Town in New York: The Landmark History of Eating, Drinking, and Entertainments from the American Revolution to the Food Revolution.* 25th Anniversary Edition. New York and London: Routledge, 1999.

Burroughs, Edwin G., and Mike Wallace. *Gotham: A History of New York City to 1898.* New York: Oxford University Press, 1999.

Evans, Meryle. R. "Knickerbocker Hotels and Restaurants 1800–1850." *New-York Historical Society Quarterly* vol. 36 (1952): 377–410.

Rose, Peter G., trans. and ed. *The Sensible Cook: Dutch Foodways in the Old and the New World.*

Syracuse: Syracuse University Press, 1989; paperback, 1998. Contains an annotated translation of the seventeenth-century Dutch cookbook *De Verstandige Kock, of Sorghvuldige Huyshoudster,* Amsterdam, 1683.

ANNE MENDELSON

North American Free Trade Agreement

Entered into on December 17, 1992, the North American Free Trade Agreement, or NAFTA, is a multilateral agreement among the United States, Canada, and Mexico to eliminate barriers to trade, to facilitate cross-border movement of goods and services, and to promote conditions of fair competition in the free trade area. Where food and agriculture are concerned, critics have claimed that NAFTA's free trade provisions present potential risks to the safety of the United States' food supply and significant threats to the existence of America's small farms and small food producers.

NAFTA superseded the 1989 Canada–United States Free Trade Agreement (CUSFTA), an agreement that significantly increased trade between the two countries by reducing and removing certain tariffs and trade barriers. The free trade area was expanded to include Mexico after that country expressed interest in gaining increased access to the Canadian–United States market. NAFTA was ratified by Congress and implemented in the United States when President George H. W. Bush signed the North American Free Trade Agreement Implementation Act on 8 December 1993. It went into effect on January 1, 1994.

Under NAFTA and the NAFTA Implementation Act, trade is not completely free. There are significant limitations on unrestricted free trade among the NAFTA countries concerning

food safety. NAFTA gives each country the right to implement and enforce "sanitary" measures to protect its consumers from unsafe food and food products exported by either of the other countries. The NAFTA Implementation Act definitions of the terms "sanitary measures" (protecting animal and human health) and "phytosanitary measures" (protecting plants) are very broad. They include, in part, any law, regulation, or procedure adopted "to protect human or animal life or health in the United States from risks arising from the presence of an additive, contaminant, toxin, or disease-causing organism in a food, beverage, or feedstuff." Furthermore, the NAFTA Implementation Act states that nothing in the law "may be construed (1) to prohibit a Federal agency or State agency from engaging in activity related to sanitary or phytosanitary measures to protect human, animal, or plant life or health; or (2) to limit the authority of a Federal agency or State agency to determine the level of protection of human, animal, or plant life or health the agency considers appropriate."

This clause means, for example, that under the NAFTA Implementation Act, California retains the right to set its own food safety standards and can test, sample, and inspect at its border all fruits and vegetables imported from Mexico to determine if they comply with California's laws and regulations. Unsafe foods are not allowed to enter the state. Thus, given adequate border inspections, fruits and vegetables imported from Mexico will be as safe as those grown in California. Although there have been some reports of unsafe foods entering the United States from Mexico, it appears that increased food trade under NAFTA has not contributed to the amount of foodborne illness in the United States.

NAFTA's primary impact on food trade has been on the production of food. It is generally agreed that NAFTA has played an important role in the decline of the number of small farms and food producers in the United States. Small farmers, heavily regulated in the United States, cannot compete with the corporations running unregulated, large industrial farms in Mexico. For example, in the United States many farmworkers must be paid more per hour than farmworkers in Mexico earn in a day. Consequently, fruits and vegetables from Mexico can sell in American markets for less than those grown and harvested domestically. As a general rule, however, the maturity and quality of Mexican fruits and vegetables are not comparable to the maturity and quality of those grown by small farmers and food producers in the United States.

It is not a coincidence that since the implementation of NAFTA in 1994 many small farmers and food producers have turned to direct marketing for survival. Such face-to-face marketing at certified farmers' markets or retail food stands near the place of production benefits small farmers by providing a profitable way for them to sell their products, and it benefits American consumers by supplying high-quality agricultural products at reasonable prices. As a result of NAFTA, many Americans can choose between buying low-cost, low-quality imported fruits and vegetables at large chain supermarkets or more expensive, better quality, fresher local produce directly from growers at farmers' markets.

[**See also** DEPARTMENT OF AGRICULTURE, UNITED STATES; FARM SUBSIDIES, DUTIES, QUOTAS, AND TARIFFS; FARMERS' MARKETS; FOOD AND DRUG ADMINISTRATION.]

BIBLIOGRAPHY

McDonald, James H. "NAFTA and Basic Food Production: Dependency and Marginalization on Both Sides of the US/Mexico Border." In *Food in the USA: A Reader*, ed. Carole M. Counihan, 359–372. New York: Routledge, 2002.

ROBERT W. BROWER

North American Vegetarian Society

Every summer, hundreds of people converge on a sylvan campus to hear internationally renowned vegan speakers with deep expertise hold lectures and seminars on various aspects of vegetarian life. Tantamount to a vegetarian university in microcosm, this midsummer conference is known fittingly as Vegetarian Summerfest, and it is organized by the capable staff of the North American Vegetarian Society. Unlike most formal universities, however—where the food is execrable—the food at Vegetarian Summerfest is gourmet vegan fare. It is prepared under the supervision of Ken Bergeron, the first chef in history to win a gold medal for his presentation of vegan cuisine at the International Culinary Olympics in Frankfurt, Germany. Not only do attendees gain knowledge in the lectures and seminars but thanks to the high quality of Chef Ken's cuisine, they may add an inch or two to their girth. But to forestall any unwanted weight gain, Summerfest organizers invite world-class vegan athletes to put weight-conscious attendees through their paces. In 2005 Dr. Ruth Heidrich—a vegan rawfooder, author of *A Race for Life,* and winner of eight gold medals at the Senior Olympics—led morning runs. Brendan Brazier, a vegan Iron-man triathlon champion also conducted vigorous exercise workouts.

Founded by Jay Dinshah (the founder of the American Vegan Society) and a committee of vegetarian activists in 1974, NAVS was initially created to provide the United States with an organization that could host the International Vegetarian Union's world congress in Oronto, Maine in 1975—the first world vegetarian congress held on American soil. After this phenomenally successful World Congress, Brian and Sharon Graff were eventually appointed directors of the organization and through their efforts NAVS has become the North Star in the vegetarian firmament in North America. NAVS publishes a quarterly journal called *Vegetarian Voice,* which features incisive essays, book and product reviews as well as vegan recipes. NAVS staff of advisors incudes nutritional adviser, Dr. George Eisman (*The Most Noble Diet*); food consultant, Chef Ken Bergeron (*Professional Vegetarian Cooking*); historical advisor, Rynn Berry (*Food for the Gods: Vegetarianism and the World's Religions*), and medical advisor, Dr. Michael Klaper, MD (*Vegan Nutrition, Pure and Simple*). From its inception, NAVS has nurtured the growth of local vegetarian groups at the grassroots level and has forged a network of over 150 affiliate groups throughout North America. It was NAVS that originated the concept of observing a world vegetarian day, and thanks to its efforts in promoting it, World Vegetarian Day is celebrated faithfully be vegetarians every year on October 1—the day before Gandhi's birthday.

[**See also** ANIMAL RIGHTS AND FOOD; RAWFOODISM; VEGANISM.]

RYNN BERRY

Nouvelle Cuisine

Perhaps no trend in cookery has incited as much controversy and confusion as nouvelle cuisine, called "one of the splashiest social and artistic events of the postwar period" by the restaurant critic Henri Gault. Developed in France in the early 1960s and exported to America by the 1970s, nouvelle cuisine seemed a bit like pornography: hard to define, but people knew it when they saw it. Although it sounds trite (and a bit pompous) in retrospect, nouvelle cuisine was more an approach to cooking than a tightly structured cuisine. It encouraged each chef to invent personally distinctive dishes, artistically presented, showcasing the best-quality, seasonal ingredients.

Nouvelle cuisine's roots are in the French town of Vienne in the 1950s and the chef Fernand Point's renowned Michelin three-starred restaurant, La pyramide. While largely cooking the classic haute cuisine codified fifty years earlier by the master French chef Auguste Escoffier (1846–1935) in *Le guide culinaire* (1903), the inventive Point (1897–1955) and one of his cooks, Paul Bocuse (1926–), deliberately undercooked the green beans and committed other seeming culinary heresies. When Bocuse opened his own restaurant outside Lyons in 1962, he continued his experiments and soon dubbed his cooking and that of other like-minded French chefs "la nouvelle cuisine française." Cynics viewed the nomenclature as impresario hype, whereas those mesmerized by the cooking (especially Gault and his business partner, Christian Millau) lauded it as revolutionary.

The polemics sparked the famous "Manifesto of Nouvelle Cuisine," published in the October 1973 issue of *Le nouveau guide Gault-Millau*. Aping the Ten Commandments, it identified ten trends in the finest contemporary cooking. The manifesto ignited a firestorm in both France and America, with articles bearing such eye-popping titles as "French Cooking Is Dead; The New French Cooking Is Born," (*Esquire*, June 1975) or "*La Nouvelle Cuisine*: Is It Really New?" (*House Beautiful*, January 1976).

The cognoscenti hailed nouvelle cuisine for breathing life into a moribund French cookery that was suffocating under the dead weight of Escoffier's invariable rules. Detractors lambasted the vaunted rule breaking as a mask for poor technique (undercooking fish so that it was still raw at the bone was a typical nouvelle conceit) and as an excuse for ill-conceived combinations of incongruous ingredients, such as the ubiquitous kiwi paired with veal. They denigrated hamster-sized portions tortuously arranged on Frisbee-sized plates. To add financial injury to gastronomic insult, the food was expensive: one American chef admitted that he charged a lot more for soup simply by following Bocuse's model of crowning it with puff pastry.

Nouvelle cuisine was elitist, targeted to well-heeled, urbane (and urban) audiences. Upscale, fashion-conscious publications such as *Vogue* and *Harper's Bazaar*, as well as the intellectually oriented *New York Review of Books, New Yorker, Natural History,* and *New York Times,* all prepped their readers to sample the cuisine on European vacations or in expensive restaurants in major American cities, such as New York's Dodin-Bouffant, Washington's Jean-Louis, Chicago's Le Perroquet, or Los Angeles's Ma Maison (with the pre-Spago Wolfgang Puck at the stove). Nouvelle cuisine's notoriety led middle-market *Redbook* to publish a "how-to" article in February 1981 (beginning with the phonetic "noo vell kwee zeen"), helping housewives "create a dazzling dinner party" just a few short years after their hip *Vogue*- and *Esquire*-reading siblings. Significantly, the *Redbook* article was the lone middle-market voice: the skilled labor required to prepare a nouvelle meal and the expense and difficulty of procuring many of the ingredients in the 1980s, such as pink peppercorns or foie gras, made nouvelle cuisine all but impossible to reproduce in most homes or find in middle-class, suburban restaurants.

Although no longer the chic cuisine of the moment, nouvelle cuisine has profoundly shaped contemporary American cooking. Its French progenitors, Bocuse, the Troisgros brothers (also Point disciples), and Michel Guérard, published American editions of their cookbooks in the mid-1970s. They toured the United States, teaching and promoting their work as the first cadre of celebrity chefs, influencing a generation of young American cooks. When Guérard opened the Manhattan outpost of Paris's Régine's in 1977, both Larry Forgione and Michael Romano worked under him. They subsequently applied nouvelle cuisine's central tenets of impeccable ingredients, creatively manipulated, to existing American culinary traditions, pioneering "New American Cooking" at Forgione's An American Place and Romano's Union Square Café. Another "New American" pioneer, the Santa Monica–based chef Michael McCarty, trained in France during the height of the nouvelle revolution and incorporated its ideas of "freshness and lightness" into his California riff on new American cooking at the eponymous Michael's.

Nouvelle cuisine's legacy is visible in restaurant presentations of individual plates (rather than the carefully composed platters shown in classic French cookbooks through the 1950s) that have become edible art, often with fragile, almost architectural constructions. Kitchens outfitted with legions of squeeze-bottles holding brightly colored sauces "paint" Jackson Pollock–like squiggles on oversized plates that the Troisgros brothers first used and that the French porcelain maker Limoges now calls "American plates." The American magazine for professional chefs, *Art culinaire* (despite the French name, it covers global cuisine), founded in 1986 at the peak of nouvelle presentations, has never deviated from its luscious high-fashion photographs of plated dishes, now widely and somewhat derisively referred to in the industry as gastro-porn.

Contemporary menus, with their playful culinary puns, such as savory "napoleons," made from layers of carefully grilled vegetables or lobster *navarin* (the classic stew à la Escoffier could only be made with mutton), debuted as nouvelle cuisine. Lengthy descriptions of each offering on the menu are also a nouvelle legacy, as Escoffier's conventional terms no longer adequately communicate the dish. Restaurant reviewers evaluate innovation in addition to skillful cookery, and the demand for innovation has trickled down to the home cook, whose magazines proudly boast of recipes "with a twist," that is, some clever variation on an established dish. That twist may be as minor as substituting cilantro for tarragon in béarnaise sauce, yet it is something that simply was not done prior to nouvelle cuisine.

By prizing creativity above all else, nouvelle cuisine redefined the standards by which great cooking was judged. It uncorked chefs' imaginations and opened the dining public's eyes to experimentation, helping to account for the popularity of fusion cooking. As Christian Millau said in 1983, "The best proof that nouvelle cuisine is not a passing fashion, is that in America you are now trying to create your own." Larry Forgione concurred: "What that movement left was a feeling to pursue our goals without the pressure of conforming. A sense of freedom was felt by every culinary artist throughout the world. That is why nouvelle cuisine should be recognized as one of the most powerful culinary movements of our time."

[See also Celebrity Chefs; French Influences on American Food.]

BIBLIOGRAPHY

Cockburn, Andrew. "Gastro-Porn." *New York Review of Books*, December 8, 1977.

Cooke, Phillip S., ed. *The Second Symposium on American Cuisine.* New York: Van Nostrand Reinhold, 1984.

Gault, Henri. "Nouvelle Cuisine." In *Cooks and Other People: Proceedings of the 1995 Oxford Symposium on Food and Cookery.* London: Prospect Books, 1996.

Urvater, Michele, and David Leiderman. *Cooking the Nouvelle Cuisine in America.* New York: Workman, 1979.

CATHY K. KAUFMAN

Nuevo Latino Cuisine

Nuevo Latino cuisine literally means "new Latin" cuisine. It is a modern interpretation of traditional Latin American dishes. It takes traditional old world dishes and reinvents them using unusual ingredients and European and American culinary techniques. This style of cooking pioneered its way through kitchens in Miami in the late 1980s. It has since exploded on the food scene across the United States.

Chef Douglas Rodriguez is considered the father of Nuevo Latino cooking. His innovative cooking style found its place on the culinary map at Yucca, a restaurant in Miami in the late 1980s. He uses an extraordinary combination of ingredients that result in truly complex and innovative foods. Douglas is a first generation Cuban American. His cooking style originated with the foods he grew up with. Living in Miami, he was surrounded by a melting pot of Latin flavors. He decided to embrace the various Latin traditions that surrounded him by translating them into his own style of cooking. He was able to translate them for the North American palate.

Rodriguez's cuisine was brought to New York in the 1990s, where he became the chef and partner at Patria. It was here that he really introduced this innovative culinary style to the world and where he coined the term Nuevo Latino Cuisine. His approach to cooking has been copied by and has served as inspiration to chefs across the country. His signature dish is guava glazed barbecued ribs. This recipe has been published in numerous cookbooks and appears on restaurant menus across the country.

Nuevo Latino Cuisine does have other alias. In the early days of Nuevo Latino cooking, critics and fans gave this cooking style many labels, "New Caribbean," "New Floridian," "Global Cuisine," and "New Floribbean." Chef Norman Van Aken of Norman's in Coral Gables, Florida, calls it New World Cuisine. He emerged on Florida's food scene at the same time as Douglas Rodriguez. His approach was similar, whereas Douglas Rodriguez approach has more of a Cuban influence; Norman Van Aken's approach is more global. He seems to use Latin flavors to create a huge painters palette, with no limits to the dishes he creates. His signature dishes are Mashed Yucca Stuffed Shrimp with Mojo, Rum and Pepper-Painted Grouper with a Mango-Habanero Mojo and Sweet Fried Plantains.

The beauty of Nuevo Latino cuisine is that it is always changing and evolving. This style of cooking always lends itself to creativity. It certainly differs from traditional Latin American dishes by using finer cuts of meat than the traditional recipe calls for. For example, when making Feijioda, the national dish of Brazil, American chefs will substitute beef tenderloin for beef tongue.

A typical Nuevo Latino menu can consist of mojitos (lime, mint, sugarcane and rum cocktail), Ecuadorian seviches (citrus cured fish salad) with Mexican ingredients, an Argentinean churrascos (steak) with a Peruvian sauce, and a tres leches cake, a Costa Rican dessert made with three types of milk.

Key Nuevo Latino ingredients are chayote (squash), malagna, boniato, purple potatoes (all are root vegetables), cachucha peppers, sugarcane, plantains, garlic, cilantro, lime, mango, guava, papaya, and coconuts. After about ten years, produce suppliers have caught on now stocking most of these items as staples. It takes about ten years for a hot food concept to make its way from a restaurant to stock items you can find in a store.

Leading with Norman Van Aken and Douglas Rodriguez, chefs across the country laid down the groundwork to give this cuisine lasting power. However, demographics and popular culture played a critical role in this cuisine's popularity. According to a 2000 census poll, the number of Hispanics has risen almost 60 percent since 1990 to 35.3 million, making them the largest minority group in the country. That means that more than 12 percent of all Americans are Hispanic in origin. Population demographics have a direct impact on culinary trends. This cuisine benefits from American consumer's growing interest in Latin American culture. In the last ten years, the rise of Latin pop icons, including Marc Anthony, Jennifer Lopez, and Ricky Martin, have helped also.

Nuevo Latino Cuisine becomes somewhat hard to define because it stretches across so many nationalities. While people are always looking for the next new and exciting thing, Nuevo Latino Cuisine has had lasting power and has proven itself here to stay.

BIBLIOGRAPHY

Rodriguez, Douglas. *Nuevo Latino.* Berkeley, CA: Ten Speed Press, 1995.

TRICIA L. WILLIAMS

Nutcrackers and Grinders

Some nutcrackers consist of a small hammer and an anvil; most use levered jaws or screw-clamp jaws to crack nuts. Earliest are cast metal or hardwood, with two hinged arms, corrugated near the hinge to secure the nut before squeezing the handles. Small, silver-plated versions for table use, which cracked small nuts one way and larger nuts when the handles were reversed, came with nutpicks beginning in the 1880s. Corrugations look like animal teeth, and since the 1870s a menagerie of fully figural nutcrackers (including squirrels, dogs, or alligators) has been patented. The lower jaw lever sticks out behind like a tail.

Screw-clamp varieties include handheld nutcrackers with opposing fixed and screwed jaws to crush the shell. Some are strictly utilitarian; some are shaped like nuts. Inventors applied themselves to cracking specific nuts, too: a horizontal screwed cracker on a board was patented in 1914 for pecans. Since the 1930s, small nut grinders with glass jars and cranked teeth in a screw-on hopper have facilitated the chopping of nutmeats for baking. [**See also** GRINDERS; NUTS.]

BIBLIOGRAPHY
Franklin, Linda Campbell. *300 Years of Kitchen Collectibles*. 5th ed. Iola, WI: Krause Publications, 2003.
LINDA CAMPBELL FRANKLIN

Nutmeg Graters

A nutmeg's two usable parts are an outer husk called "mace," which is used in powdered form in baking and cannot be grated, and the inner kernel, the nutmeg, which when dry is hard and easily grated into food or drink. The simplest nutmeg grater is nonmechanical. One type used in Europe and in the early days of America was a portable or pocket-size cylinder with a grating surface and a storage compartment for the nutmeg. The nineteenth-century tin coffin-like grater with hinged compartment and curved grating surface also was simple. This is the only type still made.

So popular had nutmeg become by the mid-nineteenth century, when world trade from Grenada made it easily available, that immediately U.S. inventors started patenting mechanical graters. The first came in 1854; sixteen were patented between 1866 and 1868. Most were cranked devices that held the nutmeg firmly (many with springs) against a grating surface while the grater revolved and scraped the nutmeg. [**See also** GRATERS.]

BIBLIOGRAPHY
Franklin, Linda Campbell. *300 Years of Kitchen Collectibles*. 5th ed. Iola, WI: Krause Publications, 2003.
LINDA FRANKLIN

A nutmeg tree with its flower and fruit from an advertisement for Davis, Sacker & Perkins Importers, Boston, 1878.

Nutrition

For millennia, humans have been aware of the relationship between food and health. At the most basic level, even primitive peoples knew that a lack of food led to sickness or even death and that eating certain plants or animals could bring illness, while other foods could be protective or curative. This collected wisdom was passed down orally, but physicians in ancient Greece, Rome, and China began to assemble this wisdom in herbal manuscripts that were hand-copied for hundreds of years. Herbals were collections of assertions about the relationships between specific foods and health. These assertions were based on contemporary medical theories.

During the late eighteenth and early nineteenth centuries, studies of human digestion began to offer insights into how the body processed food. William Beaumont (1785–1853), an Army surgeon, examined the process of digestion through the examination of a gunshot victim, who had wounds that exposed his stomach. Through this wound, Beaumont was able to observe the operations of the stomach.

By 1840, chemists had classified food into three categories: carbohydrates, fats, and proteins. Carbohydrates, mainly sugars and starches, make up the bulk of the diet of *Homo sapiens* and constitute the chief source of energy. Dietary fats, now generally called lipids, include vegetable oil and animal fat. Lipids are highly concentrated sources of energy, furnishing more calories per gram than either carbohydrates or proteins. Proteins are the major source of building material for the body; they repair and replace worn tissue.

Justus von Liebig of the University of Giessen in Germany is often identified as the father of the scientific approach to nutrition. During the 1820s, he measured and examined foods consumed by animals and the products that were excreted and exhaled. Based on this quantitative research, he proposed theories about intermediate processes in the body in his *Animal Chemistry* (1842).

By the late nineteenth century, many American scientists were focusing on nutritional research. The agricultural chemist Wilbur O. Atwater, who had founded the Office of Experiment Stations for the U.S. Department of Agriculture in 1888, systematically tabulated the caloric compositions of different foods. He calculated the energy yields of carbohydrates, protein, and fat and developed the first American human calorimeter, an apparatus for measuring the amount of calories in food. Using Atwater's methods, other scientists established standards for the energy needs of healthy individuals. Other important work on nutrition was done by Russell Henry Chittenden, head of the Sheffield Scientific School at Yale.

The application of these new findings to the daily diet and home cooking was championed by Ellen Richards, whose *Chemistry of Cooking and Cleaning: A Manual for Housekeepers* (1882), which went through several editions, became a defining work. Food chemistry became an important component of many cooking schools that thrived during the latter part of the nineteenth and early twentieth centuries. Graduates of these schools were often referred to as "dietitians." They applied the principles of nutrition in hospitals, the military, public schools, and other institutional settings. Dietitians became leaders in the home economics movement, and founders of the American Dietetic Association in 1917.

Vitamins and Minerals

The first ailment clearly associated with a specific food was scurvy (caused by a vitamin C deficiency), which was common among sailors on long voyages. By the seventeenth century, it was known, although the reason was not understood, that eating fresh fruit and vegetables could cure scurvy; years later, following scientific studies, British sailors were supplied with lemon juice, and the men remained healthy. During the first decade of the twentieth century, several other diseases, such as beriberi, rickets, and pellagra, were linked to dietary shortcomings. Scientists began to investigate the unknown factors at play in these cases—substances that came to be called vitamins.

Casimir Funk, a chemist at the Lister Institute in London, crystallized an amine substance from rice bran in 1911. Funk used the word "vitamine," constructed from "vital amines," to apply to these previously unknown substances that prevented specific diseases. Because it was soon discovered that many of the substances were not amines, the spelling was changed to "vitamin." Through the course of the century, many other vitamins were isolated and identified. By the early 2000s, seventeen vitamins had been identified as "essential," which meant that the human body could not synthesize them and they had to be ingested for the body to function properly.

Minerals also were found to be essential for the proper functioning of the human body. They had begun to be identified during the late nineteenth century, but it was not until the twentieth century that their functions were determined. Minerals act as catalysts in many biochemical reactions of the body and are also vital to the growth of bones, muscular contractions, digestion, and many other functions. Calcium, for instance, is essential for proper heart rhythm, iron for blood formation, and phosphorus for healthy bones and teeth. Some minerals, such as calcium, iron, and sulfur, are required in relatively large amounts, whereas others, such as zinc, copper, iodine, and fluoride, are required in smaller (trace) amounts. In the early 2000s, twenty-four minerals were identified as essential. One of the first uses of micronutrients to enrich food occurred in the 1920s; once it was determined that dietary iodine could prevent goiter, it was added to commercial table salt and cases of this thyroid disorder dropped markedly.

Nutrition in Public Policy

Before the discovery of vitamins, food processors had concluded that the way to prevent illness caused by food was to sterilize and mill their products to reduce the danger of consumers being exposed to bacteria, mold, and toxins. Beginning in the 1880s, wheat milling removed the bran, germ, and oil from the flour, which was then bleached to a bright white color. But by the 1920s, it was understood that the milling process eliminated much of the nutritional value of the wheat. Nutrition experts attacked flour millers and commercial bakers for white bread's lack of vitamins and minerals. During World War II, the Federal Drug Administration encouraged the enrichment of white bread with vitamins. In 1943, the War Foods Administration temporarily required enriched bread. Most white flour and bread sold in the United States in the early 2000s is enriched with several nutrients.

During World War II, the federal government first published nutritional standards—called Recommended Dietary Allowances (RDA)—for energy, protein, and eight essential vitamins and minerals. These were the levels of nutrients required by the average adult for good health. During the war, the U.S. Department of Agriculture also promoted the "Basic Seven" food groups, which showed people dealing with wartime food shortages how to maintain proper nutrition. These guidelines were modified after the war to the "Basic Four," which stressed dairy products, meats, fruits and vegetables, and grain products. As new research demonstrates additional requirements, RDAs were replaced in the late 1990s with a concept called the Dietary Reference Intakes (DRIs).

A wartime poster advocating good nutrition, 1942.

DRIs are the basis for assessing and planning diets of healthy people. They are also used as a basis for federal nutrition and food programs. The DRIs include: estimated average requirements (EAR), Recommended Dietary Allowance (RDA) and adequate intake (AI). The DRIs are established by the Food and Nutrition Board, the Institute of Medicine, and the National Academy of Sciences.

In the interest of promoting better eating habits among Americans, the Department of Health and Human Services and the Department of Agriculture jointly developed *Dietary Guidelines for Americans* in 1980; it has been regularly updated ever since. Because of an increase in heart disease during the second half of the twentieth century, in 1992 the U.S. Department of Agriculture unveiled the new "Food Pyramid," which broke from the recommendations of previous food-group charts to emphasize more consumption of complex carbohydrates and less consumption of animal protein, fat, and sugar. In 1994, following years of discussion, the Nutrition Labeling and Education Act was passed by

Congress requiring nutrition labels on all processed foods sold in the United States. This measure had been supported for many years by the Center for Science in the Public Interest, which insisted that Americans could not make enlightened food choices—and frequently made the wrong ones—because they did not know the nutritional value of the foods they bought at the supermarket.

The chemist Linus Pauling, the recipient of two Nobel prizes, concluded that huge doses of certain micronutrients—particularly vitamin C—could cure some diseases and prolong life. He published his findings in a 1970 book entitled *Vitamin C and the Common Cold*. Some studies suggested that megadoses of vitamin C could help terminal cancer patients. Based on findings such as these, manufacturers of vitamin and mineral supplements began making claims for the effects of their products. In 1994, the Dietary and Supplement Health and Education Act was passed by Congress, limiting what vitamin manufacturers could claim about abilities of their supplements to prevent or cure diseases.

Developments in Nutrition

During the late twentieth and early twenty-first centuries, the major focus of nutrition has shifted from concern over which foods are required to avoid deficiencies and illness, to what foods and supplements may be consumed to promote health. Nutrition studies are spread over the fields of medicine, biochemistry, physiology, and the behavioral and social sciences, as well as the public health sciences. The issues of special focus among nutritionists include topics related to functional foods, pediatrics, geriatrics, obesity, chronic diseases, malnutrition, and nutritional deficiencies.

[See also ADULTERATIONS; BABY FOOD; CHEMICAL ADDITIVES; COMBAT FOOD; DEPARTMENT OF AGRICULTURE, UNITED STATES; FOOD AND NUTRITION SYSTEMS; EATING DISORDERS; HEALTH FOOD; HUNGER PROGRAMS; MEALS ON WHEELS; PIONEERS AND SURVIVAL FOOD; PRISON FOOD; PURE FOOD AND DRUG ACT; RICHARDS, ELLEN SWALLOW; SCHOOL FOOD; SHIP FOOD; SOUP KITCHENS; VEGETARIANISM; VITAMINS.]

BIBLIOGRAPHY

Beeuwkes, Adelia M., E. Neige Todhunter, and Emma Seifrit Weigley, comps. *Essays of History of Nutrition and Dietetics.* Chicago: American Dietetic Association, 1967.

Cassell, Jo Anne. *Carry the Flame: The History of the American Dietetic Association.* Chicago: The Association, 1990.

McCollum, Elmer Verner. *A History of Nutrition: The Sequence of Ideas in Nutrition Investigations.* Boston: Houghton Mifflin, 1957.

Nestle, Marion. *Food Politics: How the Food Industry Influences Nutrition and Health.* Berkeley: University of California Press, 2002.

ANDREW F. SMITH

Nuts

Tree nuts have been an important part of the human diet since prehistoric times. Although there is extreme diversity among tree nuts, most have in common an edible kernel enclosed in a hard outer shell. (Peanuts, although called "nuts," are actually legumes.)

North America is abundantly supplied with indigenous nut-bearing trees, and their fruit has been gathered and consumed since humans arrived thousands of years ago. Acorns and pine nuts, for instance, were an important constituent of the diet of Native Americans, especially California Indians. Pecans were prized by Native Americans in the Midwest and South, and East Coast Indians used butternuts to thicken their soups. Other Native Americans consumed American chestnuts, filberts, hickory nuts, and black walnuts.

European colonists in North America adopted many indigenous nuts into their diets. The most important of these came from three trees in the walnut family: the pecan, the butternut, and the hickory. The nuts were pressed to make oil and were used in baked goods and confections. Although they were sold well into the twentieth century, only the pecan has survived as a commercial crop. European colonists also introduced into America such old-world nut-bearing trees as the English walnut and the European chestnut. Later, nuts that could not be grown in America, such as cashews and Brazil nuts, were imported and became important additions to the American diet.

By the beginning of the nineteenth century, nut vendors were selling roasted nuts on the streets of major American cities; at the time, few other foods could be so easily produced, transported, distributed, and prepared for sale. By the 1840s, nut vendors appeared at circuses and fairs. At first, children were their main customers.

From 1865 to 1900, nuts made the transition from a snack and dessert food to an important component of the American diet. Clearly, the most influential early work in this field was accomplished by vegetarians such as John Harvey Kellogg. His attempt to produce an alternative to "cow's butter" by grinding various nuts ended in the creation of nut butters, the most famous of which is peanut butter. *Guide for Nut Cookery* (1899) by Almeda Lambert reflects the progress made in nut cookery by vegetarians during the late 1890s. It includes over a thousand nut recipes, most of which had never before been published. It eased nut cookery into the American mainstream and inspired others to include more creative nut recipes in their cookbooks and in cookery magazines. Subsequent vegetarian cookbooks, such as the second edition of *Science in the Kitchen* (1900) by Ella E. Kellogg and *Vegetarian Cook Book; Substitutes for Flesh Foods* (1904) by E. G. Fulton, promoted nut cookery and encouraged its use by nonvegetarians.

Nut cookery was also publicized in the recipe booklets published by commercial nut processors, nut butter manufacturers, and equipment makers. The recipes were often developed by professional cooks, and they represented the pinnacle of nut cookery. These publications helped to bridge the geographically diverse and heterogeneous nut industry, and one of their functions was to encourage nut cookery. Recipes from commercial sources were regularly republished in other magazines and mainstream cookbooks. Specialty cookbooks on specific nuts were published, such as *800 Proved Pecan Recipes* (1925); *A Treasury of Prize Winning Filbert Recipes from the Oregon Filbert Commission* (1973); Carole Bough, *Cooking with Black Walnuts* (1995); Lucy Gerspacher, *Hazelnuts and More* (1995); Jean-Luc Toussaint, *The Walnut Cookbook* (1998); and Annie Bhagwandin, *The Chestnut Cookbook* (2003).

Additional influences on nut cookery were the U.S. Department of Agriculture, the federal and state agricultural experiment stations, and the county extension services, which published recipes and booklets encouraging farmers to grow nut trees and American consumers to eat more nuts. These sources provided thousands of diverse recipes with nuts as ingredients. In addition to roasted nuts served as a snack food, tree nuts appeared as ingredients in recipes for baked goods, beverages, brittle, butters, fudge, ice cream, ketchup, meat substitutes, salads, sauces, and stuffings.

The most important nuts in the United States are almonds, Brazil nuts, cashews, macadamia nuts, pecans, pine nuts, pistachios, and walnuts.

[See also BRAZIL NUTS; CASHEWS; CHESTNUTS; FILBERTS; MACADAMIA NUTS; PEANUTS; PECANS; PINE NUTS; PISTACHIOS; WALNUTS.]

BIBLIOGRAPHY

Bough, Carole. *Cooking with Black Walnuts.* Stockton, MO: Missouri Dandy Pantry, 1993.

Carder, Shirl. *The Nut Lovers' Cookbook.* Berkeley, CA: Celestial Arts, 1984.

MacPherson, Mary. *Completely Nuts: A Cookbook and Cultural History of the World's Most Popular Nuts.* Ontario, Canada: Doubleday Canada, 1995.

Rosengarten, Frederic, Jr. *The Book of Edible Nuts.* New York: Walker, 1984.

ANDREW F. SMITH

O

Oats

The origins of oats (*Avena sativa*) are obscure. They were cultivated in Switzerland and Northern Europe by 2500 B.C.E., and two millennia later they were widely cultivated in Europe by the ancient Romans, Germans, and Celts. The advantage of oats was that they could be grown in higher altitudes and in colder climates than could wheat or other common grains. Oats were mainly used to feed horses, cattle, and other animals, but hulled oats were used in broths, porridges, and gruels. They were particularly important culinarily in Scotland, which led Samuel Johnson to define oats as "a grain which in England is generally given to horses, but in Scotland supports the people" in his *Dictionary of the English Language* (1755).

Oats were introduced into North America by early European explorers including Captain Bartholomew Gosnold, who planted them on Elizabeth Island off the Massachusetts coast. The Dutch grew oats in New Netherland by 1626, and they were cultivated in Virginia prior to 1648. Oats were generally grown throughout colonial America, mainly for animal feed, but Scottish, Dutch, and other immigrants used them in their traditional porridges, puddings, and baked goods. Hannah Glasse's *Art of Cookery Made Plain and Easy* (1747 and subsequent editions), although initially published in England, was one of the most popular cookbooks in colonial America. It included oats in recipes for haggis, flummery, and hasty and other puddings, as well as for cake. Similar recipes were published in America through the nineteenth century. Other oat recipes published in the United States included Scotch burgoo, an oatmeal hasty pudding in which the rolled oats were stirred into boiling water until the mixture thickened; gruel, which was a thinner porridge frequently identified as invalid food; and oatmeal blancmange. Baked goods included Scotch and English oaten cakes baked on a griddle, muffins made from cold cooked oatmeal, and bread and biscuits, for which the oatmeal was usually mixed with flour, because on its own, oatmeal or oat flour does not develop enough gluten to support a rising loaf.

By the nineteenth century, grocery stores sold oat products in bulk. Customers could choose from groats, the whole oat with its outer shell; grits, hulled oat kernels, coarsely ground; and oatmeal, which was milled into several different grades of fineness. In 1877, rolled oats were developed and trademarked by Henry D. Seymour and William Heston, who had established the Quaker Mill Company. The product was packed in cardboard boxes bearing the reassuring image of an elderly Quaker man and promoted via a national advertising campaign, making it the first cereal to advertise nationally. In 1901, the Quaker Mill Company merged with other mills, creating the Quaker Oats Company.

Directions for cooking oatmeal were printed on the outside of the Quaker box. These recipes, in turn, were reprinted in community and other cookbooks, and oatmeal became more popular as a cooking ingredient. During the twentieth century, many new oatmeal recipes were published, including ones for soup, cakes, cookies, wafers, drops, macaroons, quick breads and yeast breads, muffins, scones, and pancakes. Oatmeal also was used as a filler and binder in meatloaf, hamburger, and sausage. The growing interest in healthy diet and vegetarianism in the 1970s saw new interest in oats and other whole grains. Instant oatmeal, which was more finely ground so that it was ready as soon as hot water was added, was introduced in 1966 and made hot cereal as convenient as cold. The announcement in the 1990s that the soluble fiber in oats could reduce cholesterol levels caused a tremendous boom in sales of oatmeal, oat bran, and products made with oats. But by far the most enduring recipe was for oatmeal cookies, which accounted for the most important noncereal use of oatmeal in the early 2000s.

At the beginning of the twenty-first century, the United States was one of the world's largest producers of oats. In 2003, America produced 148 million bushels of oats with the largest production in Minnesota, North Dakota, Wisconsin, South Dakota, and Iowa. [See also BREAD; BREAKFAST FOOD; COOKIES; QUAKER MAN.]

BIBLIOGRAPHY

Hinman, Bobbie. *Oat Cuisine*. Rocklin, CA: Prima, 1989.

Marquette, Arthur F. *Brands, Trademarks and Good Will: The Story of the Quaker Oats Company*. New York: McGraw Hill, 1967.

ANDREW F. SMITH

Obesity

The high rate of obesity in America has attracted much attention. As of 2002, 64.5 percent of adults (120 million people) were overweight, defined as ten to thirty pounds over healthy weight; 33 percent of women and 28 percent of men were obese, defined as thirty or more pounds over healthy weight; and about 15 percent of children age six to nineteen (9 million) were overweight.

Health implications are staggering: a 33 percent rise in type 2 diabetes, a 34 percent higher rate of heart failure in the overweight and 50 percent in the obese. Over the centuries, American culture has moved toward slimmer ideals about weight, but decreasing success in keeping it down.

Cultural Underpinnings

Around the beginning of the twentieth century, social changes forced middle class concern about weight, partly as the result of changing fashions. Scales (1891) were often used publicly at fairs, calling attention to weight. The calorimeter (1894) made it possible to measure calories, the value of foods for producing heat and energy in the body.

A major force in shaping a link between weight and health was life insurance companies actuarial tables. In the 1890s, they started to track heights, weights, life spans, and causes of death based almost exclusively on white, urban, middle-class men. By 1898, the companies dropped the idea that the weights were averages and labeled them "ideals." Actuaries reported that men as little as 10 percent overweight would not live as long as those at ideal weight, whereas men 30 percent or more overweight had a 34.5 percent greater mortality rate. A 1914 insurance association study reported that there should be no weight gain after age thirty-five; above forty, even average weight was excessive.

Remarkably, the medical establishment did not consider health risks reasons for losing weight. Generally, they believed obesity was glandular or hereditary, and little could be done. Only after 1900 did doctors focus on overweight as an adult degenerative disease.

Introduction of a Moral Dimension: 1920s

During the Roaring Twenties, weight consciousness acquired a new intensity. In *Fat History: Bodies and Beauty in the Modern World* (1997), social historian Peter Stearns suggests that the increasing preoccupation was a restraining balance to increased prosperity, consumerism, and sexual permissiveness. For the first time, weight control took on a moral dimension.

Disproportionate attention was paid to women's weight (a trend continuing through the 1950s), partly as a check on women's growing independence, particularly in the sexual area. In the 1920s insurance companies began to require physical exams, focusing attention on weighing by an authority figure, the doctor. More than half of all people over thirty-five were pronounced overweight. This was the beginning of an ever-widening gap between ideal cultural size and actual eating and weight patterns.

National Health Problem

In the 1930s, public health authorities became increasingly convinced that overweight was a national health problem. Physicians determined that the previous recommended daily intake of 3,000 calories for men was too high; it should be 2,400 or lower.

The effects of a weight-loss patent medicine. The illustration is from an advertisement for Richard Hudnut, a New York pharmacist, appeared in Harper's Monthly, August 1894.

loved. When research found that an overweight child had up to an 80 percent greater chance of becoming obese in adulthood, that view changed and plump children were taken to doctors.

Dietary Fat: A New Culprit

In the early 1960s, discussion of weight loss began to focus on dietary fat. Private health organizations—the American Heart Association, American Cancer Society, and American Diabetes Association—set guidelines to limit fat to no more than one-third of daily calories. By the late 1970s, the government added its sanction, promoting a diet based on carbohydrates.

Obesity Epidemic

Despite the low-fat diet, Americans continued to gain weight, and develop heart disease. Apparently, the dietary fat–heart health link applied only to a small subgroup. In the early 1980s, the obesity rate—constant during the 1960s and 1970s—went up by eight points. By the end of the decade, one in four Americans qualified, most of them at the bottom at the socioeconomic scale.

Reasons for the surge of obesity are complex. First, there is failure of the low-fat diet. For 30 to 40 percent of the population, the regimen may be counterproductive, encouraging unlimited consumption of carbohydrates and fat-free products, often made with sugar.

Another factor is too much food and too little exercise. More people eat in restaurants today, where large portions of high-calorie food are the norm. The $112 billion fast food industry provides easy access to inexpensive, calorie-dense, supersize servings. The soft-drink industry—the single major source of added dietary sugar—induced Americans to drink five times as much soda in 2002 as they had in the 1950s. Watching television with its bombardment of food ads encourages simultaneous eating. In terms of culture, the obesity epidemic may simply be the end point of a process in the developed world as food consumption moves from subsistence to abundance.

[**See also** Diets, Fad; Eating Disorders; Fast Food; Food and Nutrition Systems; Nutrition.]

BIBLIOGRAPHY

Powdermaker, Hortense. "An Anthropological Approach to the Problems of Obesity." In *Food and Culture: A Reader*, ed. Carole Counihan and Penny Van Esterik, 203–210. New York: Routledge, 1997.

Rozin, Paul, and C. Fischler, S. Imada, A. Sarubin, and A. Wrzesniewski. "Attitudes to Food and the Role of Food in Life in the U.S.A., Japan, Flemish Belgium and France: Possible Implications for the Diet-Health Debate." *Appetite* 33, no. 2 (1999): 163–180.

Schwartz, Hillel. *Never Satisfied: A Cultural History of Diets, Fantasies, and Fat.* New York: Free Press, 1986.

Doctors began to view excess weight as a character flaw. This was the beginning of the stigmatization of a deviant subculture of the obese.

When Metropolitan Life Insurance revised its tables again in 1942–1943, ideal weights for women were included. The company suggested that a five-foot, four-inch woman weigh between 124 and 132 pounds, and a medium-frame, five-foot, eight-inch man between 145 and 156 pounds.

Throughout the 1950s, pressure to reduce focused on females. Implied rewards for shedding pounds included the mythical belief that all good things would magically be conferred—a glamorous job, wealth, sexual attractiveness, and marriage. By 1959, recommended weights

had pared down to 113 to 126 pounds for women and 138 to 152 pounds for men. African American women escaped these standards with a more liberal definition of obesity at about 50 percent over recommended weights for whites.

National Obsession

By the 1960s, weight loss had become an American obsession; data on heart disease suggested a greater risk for overweight males. Obesity also was linked to some cancers. Anxious dieters placed their faith in behavioral approaches, including weight-reducing chains such as Weight Watchers, Jenny Craig, and fad diet schemes. Through the 1960s, plumpness in children was perceived as evidence of being

Shell, Ellen Ruppel. *The Hungry Gene: The Science of Fat and the Future of Thin.* New York: Atlantic Monthly Press, 2002.

Stearns, Peter N. *Fat History: Bodies and Beauty in the Modern West.* New York: New York University Press, 1997.

Taubes, Gary. "What If It's All Been A Big Fat Lie?" *New York Times Magazine,* July 7, 2002.

LINDA MURRAY BERZOK

Oh Henry!

Stories about the derivation of the name Oh Henry! still circulate today. Perhaps this white fudge and caramel covered log, layered with peanuts and milk chocolate, was named after Hank Aaron, the famous ball player, or William Sydney Porter, the writer whose pseudonym was O. Henry. As it turns out, the Oh Henry! Nut Roll is named after a young man whose visits to the young sales-girls at the Williamson Candy Company in Chicago prompted them to call out "Oh Henry" when they wanted to move large bar-rels of corn syrup (and possibly attract his attention).

Invented in 1920, the Oh Henry! Nut Roll was one of the first candy bars to be launched nationally. The Williamson Candy Company sent twenty-five salesmen out to blanket Chicago with promotional materials (and presumably some candy bars as well). In addition, in 1923, an employee of Williamson, *John Glossinger,* announced that he was going to make the Oh Henry! bar a national best seller. Company officials said it was impossible and denied him the funds for an adver-tising campaign. Glossinger went into the streets and pasted stickers saying merely "Oh Henry!" onto automobile bumpers. People became curious as to what an Oh Henry! was and sales for the bar rose quickly.

In 1965, the company was bought by Warner Lambert and later by Ward Brands. Nestlé acquired the United States rights to the brand in 1984, where it continues to produce the bar; the bar is produced by the Hershey Company in Canada.

RENEE MARTON

Oils, *see Fats and Oils*

Okra

Okra (*Abelmoschus esculentus,* formerly *Hibiscus esculentus*) is an Old World plant that was widely disseminated in Africa and Asia in prehistoric times. Some evidence suggests that it may have originated in Ethiopia. The ridged, seed-filled pods are eaten in a variety of ways. Okra's chief distinction among veg-etables is its mucilaginous nature; when cooked in liquid, it releases a gluey substance that thickens the broth.

The word "okra" clearly derives from West African *nkru ma,* which indicates that the plant was brought to the Americas through the slave trade directly from Africa or indir-ectly through the Caribbean. Slaves grew okra in gardens on southern plantations and

introduced its cookery into mainstream America. The Swedish scientist Peter Kalm reported in his *Travels into North America* (1748) that okra was growing in Philadelphia. Thomas Jefferson, in his *Notes on the State of Virginia* (1785), recorded that okra was culti-vated there. Extensive directions for growing okra were published in Robert Squibb's *The Gardener's Calendar for South Carolina, Georgia, and North Carolina* (1787).

The pod of the okra plant is steamed, boiled, fried, pickled, and cooked in soups and stews, notably gumbo. The seeds are also ground into meal for use in making bread and oil. Southerners used ground okra seeds as a coffee substitute, especially during the Civil War, when coffee was unavailable due to the northern blockade. The leaves and flower buds are also edible and are cooked as greens. The pods and the leaves are dried, crushed into powder, and used for flavoring and thickening soups, in-cluding pepper pot, and stews.

Although recipes for okra appear in early American cookery manuscripts, Thomas Cooper's edition of the *Domestic Encyclopedia* (1821) includes the first published recipe with okra as an ingredient. Mary Randolph's *Vir-ginia House-wife* (1824) offers recipes using okra: Ocra and Tomatoes calls for stewing sliced okra with tomatoes, butter, and onion, and Gumbs A West India Dish, calls for cooking whole pods "in a little water" and serving them with melted butter.

The word "gumbo" or "gombo" is an-other African name for okra. In New Orleans it was applied to both the vegetable and the complex Creole stew made with it. Gumbos frequently contained okra and filé (powdered, dried sassafras leaves), a seasoning and thick-ener thought to have originated with the Choctaw Indians in Louisiana. Okra is just one ingredient in gumbo, which may be based on meat, such as chicken, turkey, squir-rel, or rabbit, or shellfish, such as crabs, oys-ters, or shrimp.

Gumbos migrated quickly throughout America. The first gumbo recipe published in an American cookery book appeared in an edition of Eliza Leslie's *Directions for Cooking* (1838). She identified it as "a favourite New Orleans dish." Will Coleman, the publisher of Lafcadio Hearn's *La cuisine Creole* (1885), de-scribed gumbo as the "great dish of New Orleans." So it remains.

Since the 1960s, okra has entered the American culinary mainstream, although as many writers point out, it is an acquired taste. It is a significant component of soul food and southern cookery in general. Pickled okra is sold in many supermarkets. Okra is generally grown in Florida and Mex-ico and is sold fresh in many grocery stores and farmers' markets. Whereas boiled okra is the norm from Louisiana and points east, in Texas and Oklahoma it is most commonly served fried (usually rolled in cornmeal and flour, often seasoned with cayenne) or

pickled whole with caps intact. Both methods yield products that are devoid of the slimy, viscid quality that some Americans disparage and others love.

[**See also** HEARN, LAFCADIO; JEFFERSON, THOMAS; LESLIE, ELIZA; RANDOLPH, MARY; SOUTHERN RE-GIONAL COOKERY.]

BIBLIOGRAPHY

Raymond, Dick, and Jan Raymond. *The Gardens for All Book of Eggplant, Okra, and Peppers.* Burlington, VT: Gardens for All, 1984.

Smith, Andrew F. *Souper Tomatoes: The Story of America's Favorite Food.* New Brunswick, NJ: Rutgers University Press, 2000.

ANDREW F. SMITH

Old-Fashioned

"Don't muddle with an old-fashioned" could be this cocktail's motto, as the name itself indicates its adherence to tradition. Mud-dling, however, is precisely one of the traditions to which the drink adheres; the old-fashioned is, in fact, probably the best known of the few remaining cocktails whose authenticity depends on the technique, which involves mashing together certain (generally solid) ingredients with a wooden muddler, or pestle, to release their flavors. In this case, orange, lemon, cherries, and sugar are mud-dled with bitters—the storied flavoring agent whose inclusion is another nod to tradition—before the key ingredient, whiskey (typically bourbon), is added. According to legend, the drink was created in the late nineteenth cen-tury at the Pendennis Club in Louisville, Ken-tucky, at the behest of a member, Colonel James Pepper, who must have had a stake in the outcome; Pepper was a distiller of bour-bon under the label "Old 1776." For the record, however, rumors of an even older-fashioned version of the cocktail persist among some rye drinkers. At any rate, eclipsed though it may be by more modern, flashy libations, the old-fashioned shines on through the stout, cylindrical, much-used tumbler that bears its name.

[**See also** BOURBON; COCKTAILS; WHISKEY.]

BIBLIOGRAPHY

Grimes, William. *Straight Up or On the Rocks: The Story of the American Cocktail.* New York: North Point Press, 2001.

Lanza, Joseph. *The Cocktail: The Influence of Spirits on the American Psyche.* New York: St. Martin's Press, 1995.

RUTH TOBIAS

Olestra, *see Fats and Oils*

Olive Oil, *see Fats and Oils*

Olives

The olive (*Olea europea*) is the fruit of a Mediterranean tree that has been cultivated since the dawn of history. The olive tree grows to a great age; the trees in the Garden of Gethsemane, on the Mount of Olives in Jerusalem, are reputed to be two thousand years old. The ripe fruits are more or less oval and are green at first, later turning black. They are extremely bitter because of the glucoside oleuropin. Olives are eaten green and black and are highly nutritious, but they must first be processed to eliminate the bitterness. Processing can be done in several ways, but it always involves steeping the olives in a water solution containing a strong alkali, usually lye or wood ash.

The olive has played a pivotal role in world history, its valuably oily fruit warding off famine in times of want, which is why the three major monotheistic religions—Judaism, Christianity, and Islam—have given it a symbolic significance. Monarchs have traditionally been anointed with olive oil at their coronations.

The olive was brought to California in the late eighteenth and early nineteenth centuries by the Spanish missionaries and grown in the only part of the United States with a suitable climate, the Southwest. The number of olive varieties is enormous, although sometimes the same variety is grown under different names, depending on the country from which it originates.

The Mission olive is still grown in Arizona, New Mexico, and Texas, with a few outposts in Nevada and even Oregon, but the commercial crop comes almost exclusively from Northern California. Southern California land values are now prohibitive (the profitability of an olive grove is only one-tenth that of other fruit trees). The Mission olive is the most widely grown California olive. It is a shiny, wrinkly-skinned fruit, originally planted for processing and canning, though some olives are picked early and processed for oil.

The Sevillano is another olive grown in California. It is eaten green and has thick flesh. It is usually salted and canned—and sometimes pitted, its cavity filled with a blanched almond or red pimiento.

Unlike European olives, commercially grown California olives are almost always sold pitted, and they have a milder flavor than olives imported from the Mediterranean. This flavor results from their being soaked in a ferrous gluconate solution to fix the pigment, then soaked in lye and immediately pickled in brine. Mediterranean olives are normally preserved in olive oil after curing. Olives are imported into the United States from Spain, Italy, and Greece (Kalamata). These olives are sometimes crushed and mixed with spices, such as chili pepper.

Olives are generally eaten as a cocktail snack, but they can be cooked—chicken with olives is a popular Moroccan dish. They are highly nutritious, as is evidenced by their oil content. They contain valuable amounts of protein and trace elements, and their oil (as much as one teaspoon in a serving of seven olives) is monounsaturated and cholesterol free. Ten small olives are said to have the equivalent nutritional value of one hen's egg.

Californians who find olive trees on their property may want to pick and process their olives and make their own olive oil. There is plenty of online help for amateur growers from the Olive Oil Source, which publishes the *California Olive Oil News*.

[**See also** CALIFORNIA; FATS AND OILS.]

BIBLIOGRAPHY

Knickerbocker, Peggy. *Olive Oil: From Tree to Table*. San Francisco: Chronicle Books, 1997.

Rosenblum, Mort. *Olives: The Life and Lore of a Noble Fruit*. New York: North Point Press, 1996.

Taylor, Judith M. *The Olive in California: History of an Immigrant Tree*. Berkeley, CA: Ten Speed Press, 2000.

JOSEPHINE BACON

Onion Family

Members of the Onion family (*Alliaceae*)—part of the order *Liliales* (Lilies)—usually form bulbs or corms, which are parts most often eaten. In a few species, the young foliage is used, alone or in combination with the bulbs (leeks, scallions, chives, and ramps).

The pungency of onions and garlic is a result of compounds (such as Allicin in garlic) that form when the bulbs are cut, and air and enzymes work on sulfur compounds in the cells. Unfortunately, these desirable compounds quickly degrade into Diallyl Disulfide (in garlic)—an unpleasant substance responsible for garlic's bad reputation. Chives (*Allium schoenoprasum*) are the most delicate members of the onion family. Garlic (*Allium sativum*), was regarded by Anglo-Americans as "low class," because it was associated with poor immigrants; today it is, perhaps, the most used seasoning (after salt and pepper) in the United States.

Ramps (*Allium tricoccum*) are the only members of the family that is native to the United States that have become a serious food source (there are other wild onions, but they are only rarely eaten).

[**See also** GARLIC; PREPARED HERB AND SPICE MIXTURES.]

BIBLIOGRAPHY

Allen, Gary. *The Herbalist in the Kitchen*. Champain, IL: University of Illinois Press, forthcoming.

Bailey, L. H. *Hortus Third: A Concise Dictionary of Plants Cultivated in the United States and Canada*. New York: Macmillan, 1976.

GARY ALLEN

Onion Rings

Onion rings are made by cutting a large, mild onion (*Allium cepa*) crosswise into slices that separate into rings. The onion rings are battered (or breaded), deep fried until golden brown and crisp, and served hot.

Some observers claim that onion rings were invented by the Pig Stand restaurant chain of Dallas, Texas, in the 1920s. No primary source evidence supports this claim, however, and recipes for batter-dipped fried vegetables, including onions, were present in American cookbooks well before the twentieth century. However, the Pig Stand did serve onion rings beginning in the 1920s, so it has been credited as possibly the earliest retail seller of this irresistible snack food.

In 1955, frozen breaded onion rings were first commercially packaged by Sam Quigley a food processor in Nebraska, calling them "Sam's Onions." Other companies began manufacturing them for home use and for fast food outlets. Most were prefried and had only to be heated in the oven.

Onion rings did not become a regular item at fast food outlets until the 1970s. Dairy Queen first served them in 1973, followed by Jack in the Box in 1979, and many fast food chains, such as Burger King and Carl's Jr., serve them.

BIBLIOGRAPHY

Rogers, Mara Reid. *Onions: a Celebration of the Onion Through Recipes, Lore, and History*. Reading, MA: Addison-Wesley Pub. Co., 1995.

ANDREW F. SMITH

Onions

Most of America's early settlers brought with them whatever they needed to reestablish their gardens on the new continent. And they always brought onions. Onions could make people weep, but they made any dish taste better. The bulbs were resistant to decay and could last all winter in the root cellar.

Onions are very climate- and soil-sensitive, so European onions had to be adapted selectively to local growing conditions. Kitchen gardens of the eighteenth century tended to rely on imported onions for seed stock because seeds saved from domestically grown onions often deteriorated. After the Revolutionary War, growers started adapting varieties to different American climates. Many of the onion varieties in the eighteenth and nineteenth centuries were derived from the imported English globe onion and were suited for the cooler New England and Mid-Atlantic climates. Other varieties, successful in southern conditions, were developed from Spanish, Portuguese, and Italian stock. A few of these heirlooms are still grown.

Colonists and pioneers also used some of the dozens of onion cousins that grew wild in America. People in the Appalachians discovered the now fabled spring treat, the ramp (*Allium tricoccum*).

American cookbooks were full of onions, first showing up in 1796, when Amelia Simmons published the first American cookbook. She called for roasting the turkey on a spit and serving it up "with boiled onions and cramberry [sic] sauce, mangoes, pickles and celery." And she had other onion advice: "If you consult cheapness, the largest are the best; if you consult taste and softness, the very smallest are the most delicate, and used at the first tables." Few American recipes were specific: people used whatever onions they could grow or buy.

An onion cluster from Reeves & Simonson's Descriptive Catalogue of Choice Selected Seeds, *1874.*

The contemporary onion scene is kaleidoscopic. Onions can be yellow, red, white or brown, as small as a grape or as large as a cabbage. They can be round or oval, or shaped like a torpedo, a spinning top, or a disc. There are slender green onions, or scallions. Although some onions are especially strong, there are sweet onions—Vidalias, Walla Wallas, Mauis, and Texas 1015s—that have so little of those alliaceous or sulfurous compounds that they can be eaten like a peach.

The great breakthrough in the development of all of these varieties was the discovery in 1925 of a male-sterile onion by the botanist Henry Alfred Jones of the University of California. Until then there had been selective breeding of new varieties, but the process was slow. Jones planted sixty-three Italian Red onions to create seed for future propagation. When they bloomed, he put paper bags over each to ensure self-fertilization. One of them did not produce seed; its pollen had failed to develop genetic material. Instead, it produced 136 bulbils, tiny replicas of the sterile plant. Jones used them to propagate the male-sterile specimen, which became the blank canvas on which he could create new cultivars specially adapted to growing conditions like climate, day length, altitude, and soil conditions. If he found a characteristic that might help a variety resist a disease or pest, he could more easily breed it into a new variety. What followed was the explosive development of a great range of onions.

The Americans have been creative with their onions in other ways. The dehydration industry grew up in this country during World War II, and dried and powdered onions were used to spice up the rations being shipped to soldiers abroad. About 7 percent of the American crop is dehydrated for use in the food processing industry. Jerry Bass, a bandleader and businessman in Akron, Ohio, first developed and took to market the precut and prebreaded onion ring that became, for a time, a universal accompaniment to a restaurant steak.

Commercial onion farming dates back to at least 1788, when the Wells Brothers opened their farm in Wethersfield, Connecticut. Farmers in the United States grow 3,350,000 tons of onions on 160,000 acres. California produces more than a quarter of the onions grown in the United States. Idaho and Oregon are also major onion states, and Washington, New York, Michigan, Wisconsin, Nevada, Utah, Nebraska, Ohio, Georgia, and Texas are also important producers. Texas, Georgia, and Washington are especially well known for the so-called sweets, but most of what Americans consume are the pungent, tear-producing storage onions. U.S. onion consumption averages 19.5 pounds per person. The total value of the onion crop in America is approaching $1 billion per year.

There are myriad suggestions for avoiding tears when cutting up a hot onion: chill them first; cut them under water; hold a piece of bread in your mouth; use a food processor; keep your knife sharp; cover the chopped onions with a wet towel; wear goggles. But the best advice is just to grin and bear it with the knowledge that the onions are always worth the tears.

[**See also** GARLIC; SIMMONS, AMELIA.]

BIBLIOGRAPHY

Bacheller, Barbara. *Lilies of the Kitchen.* New York: St. Martin's Press, 1986.

Griffith, Fred, and Linda Griffith. *Onions, Onions, Onions.* Shelburne, VT: Chapters, 1994.

Weaver, William Woys. *Heirloom Vegetable Gardening.* New York: Henry Holt, 1997.

FRED GRIFFITH AND LINDA GRIFFITH

Orange Flower Water

Orange flower water also called orange blossom water is a flavoring distilled from the flowers of sour orange trees, such as Seville and bergamot, usually as a condensed-steam by-product of distilling the oil, known as neroli. It is made primarily in Lebanon and France.

In the nineteenth century, orange flower water flavored many English desserts. It migrated into cake and custard recipes and in *capillaire*, a sugar syrup. Either orange flower water or rose water was a key ingredient in orgeat, originally a beverage and later a syrup used to sweeten other beverages. (In 1828, the cookbook writer Mary Randolph deemed orgeat a "necessary refreshment at all parties.") Orange flower water also piques a boiled orange pudding found in *How To Keep a Husband, or Culinary Tactics* (1872), a cookbook from California.

Except for a star turn in the Ramos gin fizz (the famous cocktail from New Orleans, Louisiana) and Mardi Gras cake, orange flower water in America remains primarily an ingredient of the cuisines of Spain (for example, *turron*, or nougat) and the Middle East (for example, baklava). It is often used interchangeably with rose water.

[**See also** ROSE WATER.]

BIBLIOGRAPHY

Brown, John Hull. *Early American Beverages.* Rutland, VT: C. E. Tuttle, 1966.

ROBIN M. MOWER

Orange Juice

Few Americans drank orange juice before the mid-nineteenth century, mainly because oranges, which were imported from the West Indies, were so expensive. Many of those who did drink orange juice did so in the form of "orangeade" (sweetened, diluted juice, like lemonade). With the completion of the transcontinental railroad in 1869 and the subsequent construction of railroads to Florida, orange growers greatly expanded their groves, and the price of oranges dropped during the late nineteenth and early twentieth centuries.

In the late 1920s, vitamin C was isolated by the Hungarian scientist Albert Szent-Györgyi, and oranges were identified as an excellent source of the vitamin. Although its function was not fully understood at the time, vitamin C is an antioxidant and thus helps prevent disease and encourage healing. Shortly thereafter, orange growers in Florida and California launched a major campaign to promote orange juice as a healthful drink and a breakfast necessity. Orange juice sales skyrocketed as Americans became convinced that their health depended on drinking a glass of the juice every morning. Rarely has a food habit been adopted so quickly by so many people.

Fresh-squeezed orange juice remained a luxury through the early twentieth century, and most Americans consumed less-expensive canned juice. Frozen orange juice was first marketed during the early 1930s, but it was unsuccessful until research showed that concentrating the juice (removing much of the water) before freezing improved the taste. After World War II, frozen foods became big business: grocers devoted more space to freezers, and appliance makers enlarged the freezer compartments of home refrigerators. By the early 1950s, orange juice accounted for 20 percent of the frozen food market.

Orange juice is used as an ingredient in several drinks, including the Orange Julius, the screwdriver (vodka and orange juice), the mimosa (champagne and orange juice), the orange blossom (gin and orange juice), and the tequila sunrise (tequila, orange juice and grenadine).

The largest commercial producers of orange juice in the United States are Minute Maid, owned by Coca-Cola, and Tropicana, owned by PepsiCo. Americans drank on average 4.7 gallons of orange juice in 2003.

[**See also** Citrus; Fruit Juices; Orange Julius; Mimosa; Screwdriver; Tequila Sunrise.]

BIBLIOGRAPHY

Frank, M. G. *Keeping Well with Oranges and Grapefruit.* Tampa: Florida Citrus Exchange, 1931.

McPhee, John. *Oranges.* New York: Farrar, Straus and Giroux, 1967.

Andrew F. Smith

Orange Julius

In 1926, the real estate agent Willard Hamlin helped to secure a downtown Los Angeles storefront for the fresh-squeezed orange juice stand owned by his friend Julius Freed. Hamlin, who had a background in chemistry, thought there might be a market for more interesting orange-based drinks, and he began experimenting with combinations of fresh orange juice and crushed ice blended with various food powders. The result was a fruit drink with a creamy, frothy texture. The formula is proprietary, but published "copycat" recipes for home consumption consist of orange juice blended with such additives as milk, sugar, vanilla, egg whites, powdered whipped topping mix, and vanilla pudding mix. In many ways, the Orange Julius was the forerunner of the smoothie.

Freed adopted Hamlin's recipe, and the business was so successful that Hamlin gave up the real estate business and concentrated on marketing and franchising Orange Julius operations. By 1929, he had opened about one hundred stores from Los Angeles to Boston. The Depression and World War II curtailed expansion, but the company rapidly expanded during the 1950s. In 1967, the company was acquired by International Industries, which also controlled the International House of Pancakes (IHOP) and other restaurant operations. Orange Julius later became part of the Dairy Queen Corporation. By the beginning of the twenty-first century, there were about three hundred Orange Julius outlets in the United States (many in shopping malls), Canada, and other countries.

BIBLIOGRAPHY

Orange Julius of America. http://www.orangejulius.com/en-US/default.htm.

Andrew F. Smith

Oranges, *see Citrus*

Oreos

In 1912, Nabisco introduced the Oreo cookie to compete with Hydrox Biscuit Bonbons, which had been launched by Sunshine Biscuit brand two years earlier. Both brands were round dark-chocolate sandwich cookies with a vanilla cream filling. The origin for the term "Oreo" is unknown, but the name was a good choice for it became one of the most successful cookies in American history.

In 1974, Nabisco officially changed the name of the product to "Oreo Chocolate Sandwich Cookies." During the 1990s, Nabisco introduced a variety of new "Oreo" products,

such as a lower-calorie version of Oreos. The company also introduced Oreos with special coloring for special holidays, such as Halloween and Christmas. In 2000, Nabisco was acquired by Kraft Foods, Inc., which has expanded the Oreo cookie line; there are versions with twice the regular amount of filling ("Doub'l Stuff"), Oreos with different flavored fillings, and chocolate-covered Oreos. Oreos have been used in crumbled format in ice cream and in "Cookies 'n Cream Chess Bars," a southern favorite. Oreos are America's largest selling cookies.

Beginning in the 1960s, the term *Oreo* was used derisively by African Americans for other African American who identified with middle-class white culture.

BIBLIOGRAPHY

Cahn, William. *Out of the Cracker Barrel; From Animal Crackers to Zu Zu's.* New York: Simon and Schuster, 1969.

Andrew F. Smith

Organic Food

The term "organic" has been both a socially and a legally defined category of food that is claimed to be more natural than artificial in both its production and its preparation. Organic foods are now the central element of American health foods and are a rapidly growing market. The Pure Food and Drug Act (1906) and the establishment of the Food and Drug Administration (FDA) were followed by numerous consumer protection laws. Most notable was the Delaney Clause, part of the 1958 food additives amendment to the Food, Drug, and Cosmetic Act (1938). In short, it states that any additive in any amount that is demonstrated to cause cancer in laboratory animals will be banned from the market, with some allowance for "acceptable risks."

This clause introduces an organic food conundrum. If our food is deemed safe by government oversight, then why do we need to have a separate category of organic food distinct from conventional food? The answer represents a complex intersection of traditional perceptions, ideology, and scientific fact.

The history of the organic movement has its early roots in English founders such as Sir Albert Howard (*An Agricultural Testament,* 1940), and Lord Northbourne (*Look to the Land,* 1940), allegedly the first to explicitly use the term "organic farming." Both stressed the concept of the farm as a living and organic entity that must be in balance with humans and the environment.

Emerging from the U.S. dust bowl of the Depression of the 1930s—witness to a failure of soil conservation—the works of individuals including Sir Howard inspired the beginnings of the American organic movement. The movement was popularized most beginning in the early 1940s by the writings and Howard-inspired experiments of Jerome Irving Rodale. In 1942, he began publshing *Organic Farming and Gardening,* and later

Organic and fair-trade stickers on bunches of bananas.

founded *Prevention* magazine. Both became primary sources of information for the American organic health food and agricultural movement.

A crucial impetus to the U.S. organic movement came with the book *Silent Spring* (1962), in which Rachel Carson highlighted the dangers of pesticides in our ecosystems and inevitably on our tables. The mass popularity of her work was quickly incorporated into the counterculture society of the 1960s and 1970s. During this period, organic agriculture and foods became firmly established in U.S. society as an alternative to mainstream agribusiness, which had come to dominate the American food system.

To clarify what "organic" meant to the consumer, several states established their own organic standards for food products and their production in the 1970s and 1980s. In order to provide national uniformity, the Organic Foods Production Act (OFPA) was implemented as Title XXI of the 1990 Farm Bill. It set national standards for how organic food was to be produced, handled, and labeled. It also established the National Organic Standards Board (NOSB), which recommends a list of products that cannot be used in organic production. Those products cannot have a negative effect on human health or the ecosystem and must be compatible with sustainable farming.

With more than a decade of development, the National Organic Rule went into effect on October 21, 2002. Since that time, all standards have been fully implemented with the use of criteria established and modified since OFPA. Under the organic rule producers or handlers who receive more than $5,000 a year in revenue must be certified by a United States Department of Agriculture (USDA) accredited, independent third party. One of the keys to making a product organic is that land used must not have been subjected in the past three years to any of the substances on the NOSB prohibited list of products. For organic plant foods, farmers are to utilize a number of soil and environmentally friendly sustainable methods of production. For the production of animal products, they must be raised in conditions that are open "free-range" natural habitats and excludes the use of antibiotics and growth hormones in healthy animals.

In terms of what the consumer may be eating as organic, the National Organic Rule has very specific labeling parameters. The use of the official USDA organic seal ranges from a product that is "100 percent organic" containing only organic ingredients; to "organic" requiring at least 95 percent organic products.

Again, if both organic and conventional foods must meet federal health and safety standards, why should organic food carry a different label? Perhaps people would rather err on the side of caution than assume the additional risks of unknown factors that might lie in conventional food production and sources coming from around the world. It also becomes an ideological commitment to sustainable food production, for which many are willing to pay the extra cost as an investment in the future.

Although organic farms now produce less than 2 percent of the U.S. food supply and utilize less than 1 percent of American farmland, during the 1990s the organic food market began to grow more than 15 to 20 percent each year. The preoccupation of the aging baby boomers and the children of the 1960s with health and environmental concerns has no doubt contributed to this substantial growth in the organic food market and its appeal to middle-class America.

Whereas this early-twenty-first-century trend (an estimated $10 billion in annual sales and rising) is great news for the organic food industry overall, hard-line organic food advocates are alarmed by a number of changes that are taking place. They feel that as organic foods become more mainstream, many of the traditions of organic farming will be left behind. The traditional small farm is beginning to lose out to the larger corporate farms and food companies. A number of traditional organic food product lines have already been bought up by the major food companies. No longer confined primarily to the natural food stores, organic foods are increasingly more common in large grocery store chains.

In the end, the convenience of the widespread availability of organic foods may compromise the ability to support local organic producers who still advocate for a world in which we "think globally and eat locally."
[See also ORGANIC GARDENING.]

BIBLIOGRAPHY

Lampkin, Nicholas. *Organic Farming*. Alexandria Bay, NY: Diamond Farm Book Publishers, 2000.

Lipson, Elaine Marie. *The Organic Foods Sourcebook*. Chicago: Contemporary Books, 2001.

Nabhan, Gary. *Coming Home to Eat: The Pleasures and Politics of Local Foods*. New York: Norton, 2002.

BARRETT P. BRENTON AND
KEVIN T. MCINTYRE

Organic Gardening

Organic gardening is based on a system of growing food or cultivating plants that maintains and regenerates the fertility of the soil without the use of synthetic pesticides and

Evolutionary Organics, a small farm in the Hudson Valley, sells its produce in Brooklyn and Manhattan from May to December.

fertilizers. Gardening around the world has become a popular pursuit and a thriving industry. By the early twenty-first century, approximately 80 million households were participating in lawn and gardening activities, representing a 40-billion-dollar industry. Roughly 10 percent of this industry is organic.

All gardens and farms remained essentially organic until the early 1800s. In 1840, the German scientist Justin von Liebig sought to produce artificially the major nutrients that plants absorbed naturally from the soil. At the same time, John Bennet Lawes discovered that adding sulfuric acid to phosphate rock would more rapidly release phosphorus to soil for plant use. He opened a fertilizer factory in London in 1842, and within a decade manufacturers had opened similar chemical factories in Baltimore and Boston. This development marked the arrival of chemical fertilizers into soils of farms and gardens in the United States.

During World War I and World War II, the fear of food shortages combined with patriotic impulses and turned many Americans into gardeners. During World War I, Americans were urged to grow "Victory Gardens" and, by the end of the war, such gardens had become a part of everyday life, and many used chemical fertilizers and insecticides. When World War II began, Americans were urged to grow victory gardens once again. In 1942, there were 21 million victory plots in the United States, producing 40 percent of the nation's vegetables. In response to the popularity of gardening and the growing acceptance of garden chemicals, the organic movement began to heat up on both sides of the Atlantic.

The organic movement came to life for the public in the United States via J. I. Rodale's magazine *Organic Gardening and Farming*. He believed that healthy, humus-rich soil would grow healthy crops and improve public health. He had started an

organic gardening experimental farm near Allentown, Pennsylvania.

In 1962, Rachel Carson published *Silent Spring*, which describes the environmental damage caused by the use of synthetic, "toxic" chemicals. Her descriptions sounded an alarm in the hearts of Americans. This unease spurred new interest in alternatives, such as John Jeavons's biointensive approach and David Holmgren and Bill Mollison's permaculture. Robert Rodale (J. I. Rodale's son) believed that nature could heal itself, be productive without chemicals, and meet the needs of both feeding humanity and preserving the land. Robert Rodale called this renewal process "regenerative agriculture," and it has become not only the basis for the methods used by many organic gardeners, farmers, and environmentalists but also a personal way to improve life now and for future generations. These practical organic visionaries saw stewardship of the living world as a sacred duty.

Organic gardeners use plants suited to local weather and soils that are insect and disease tolerant but are not genetically modified or engineered. With heirloom varieties, they can preserve seed for use in the next growing season and protect genetic diversity and crop quality selections for years to come. Regenerating soil means replenishing its nutrients and living systems by subtracting disruptive, unnatural chemical inputs and adding what will feed a healthy living soil community—for example, organic compost, beneficial microbes, enzymes, and earthworms.

Adding compost to soil improves its structure and its ability to retain both air and moisture needed for vigorous plant growth. Organic gardeners recycle their garden material instead of buying compost. Mulching by laying organic materials on the soil surface combats adverse weather by holding in additional moisture and preventing the beating action of heavy rain that compacts the soil and breaks down its structure. Organic mulches also control weeds and add nutrients to the soil while greatly aiding a robust soil biological community. Dried grass clippings, instead of commercial mulch that may contain unwanted coloring or chemicals, are often used by organic gardeners. Crop rotation, cover cropping, and companion planting improve the soil, discourage weeds and unwanted pests, and attract beneficial insects.

Organic growing requires more initial labor input for natural fertilization, pest control, and weed control methods, and it sometimes results in smaller yields. But, as soil improves, the need for input decreases. There are mounting studies on the dangers of garden pesticides—the hidden costs of growing food using chemicals. The U.S. Environmental Protection Agency (EPA) estimates that pesticides contaminate the groundwater in thirty-eight states and pollute the primary source of drinking water for more than half the country's population. The EPA estimates that on average, each American uses over four pounds of chemicals per year on lawns and gardens. These chemicals reduce the diversity of essential soil life, contribute to soil compaction, intensify soil acidity, and increase thatch buildup in lawns. They also lead to an increase in algae growth in lakes, which reduces oxygen levels, killing fish and other organisms. Studies also report an increased incidence of cancer and other health problems among families who use these products.

Studies also showed that 70 percent of Americans listed the higher prices of organic foods as a major factor for not buying organic. As organic production scales up, premiums will narrow, and prices will likely fall as economies grow. The expansion of organics lies in continuing to develop innovative, cost-effective ways to work within the intricate bounds of nature as well as public education programs that will eventually impact perceptions and attitudes toward higher prices that will eventually begin to subside.

[See also ORGANIC FOOD.]

BIBLIOGRAPHY

Dominé, André. *Organic and Wholefoods: Naturally Delicious Cuisine.* Cologne, Germany: Könemann Verlagsgesellschaft, 1997.

Fairbairn, Neil. *A Brief History of Gardening.* Emmaus, PA: Rodale, 2001.

Kuepper, George. "Organic Farm Certification and the National Organic Program." *ATTRA* (October 2002), http://www.attra.ncat.org.

"New and Improved National Organic Standards." Rodale, 2003. *http://www.organicgardening.com/watchdog/food.html.*

"Organic Gardening 1942–2002, 60 Years of OG: Our 60 Greatest Garden Secrets." *OG* (September–October 2002): 26–33.

Rodale, Maria. *Maria Rodale's Organic Gardening.* Emmaus, PA: Rodale Press, 1998.

Stell, Elizabeth P. *Secrets to Great Soil: A Grower's Guide to Composting, Mulching, and Creating Healthy, Fertile Soil for Your Garden and Lawn.* Pownal, VT: Storey Communications, 1998.

ANTHONY RODALE AND SUSAN FEAKES DORSCHUTZ

Orthodox Union and Food

Informally, "kosher" refers to something proper or legitimate, but the word has a very specific and technical meaning. For food to be kosher, in the formal or strict sense, the ingredients and the equipment involved in its preparation must conform to the detailed requirements of Jewish law, set forth in its fundamentals in the Bible and elaborated on in the rabbinical scholarly tradition.

When a kosher-observant Jew sees a product in the market, his or her evaluation of whether the product is kosher is thus informed not only by a familiarity with kosher law but also by an understanding of how the product is made. If the food is a simple ingredient, such as a peanut, kosher law permits a person to presume that it is innocuous. But, in many cases, particularly in highly processed foods that contain a number of ingredients—creamy peanut butter, for example—a contemporary shopper has no idea how the food may have been made and is ill equipped to determine whether it is in fact kosher. In such cases it is necessary to look for kosher *certified* food, which means that a trusted independent agency has visited the manufacturing site and verified that the ingredients and processing adheres to kosher law (it does not mean that the food has been blessed).

The need for such agencies has existed at least since the beginning of the twentieth century, or ever since food preparation became removed from everyday experience. In 1923, the women's division of the Orthodox Union, one of the largest communal Jewish organizations in America, petitioned its parent organization to become involved in the certification of kosher foods. According to the framework the Orthodox Union (OU) eventually developed, the OU would enter into an agreement with a food manufacturing company; OU representatives would audit the site, frequently or less so depending on the sensitivity of the ingredients, to verify that whatever agreed-on ingredients or production considerations are in place. The companies in turn would be authorized to promote their products as kosher, and therefore gain entrance into a new market. The marketing department at Heinz, one of the first companies to become certified under the Orthodox Union, is said to have designed the discreet symbol that would communicate to the consumer a product's kosher certification: Ⓤ

The OU was later courted by other food manufacturing giants—Procter & Gamble, General Mills, and Quaker Oats were some major early accounts. The symbol adorned packages of potato buds and cooking oils, cereals and fruit jellies. The OU symbol became synonymous, in the minds of many Jewish Americans, with kosher food.

Marketing executives of food manufacturers have noticed more recently that other groups in America also purchase kosher certified foods: some, such as those who were lactose intolerant, purchased certified nondairy (*pareve*, in kosher lexicon) foods. Many American consumers apparently also associate kosher with higher quality (although companies with good manufacturing practices also may be kosher certified, there is no inherent or necessary relationship between kosher and quality). This perception has fueled a greater interest in kosher certification.

The Orthodox Union remains the dominant certifying agency, but there are a plethora of national, regional and very local entities that also provide certification. There are differences between elements of the Jewish community on what standards should apply in determining kashruth and these are reflected in personal preferences, community decisions and the certification practices of supervising entities.

GAVRIEL PRICE

Oscar Mayer

Oscar F. Mayer was a German immigrant who started out working in the Chicago stockyards. In 1883, Mayer joined his brother, a sausage-maker and ham-curer, in opening a small retail butcher shop in a German neighborhood on the city's Near North Side. In 1924, the Mayers offered sliced bacon wrapper in a package. Five years later, they took the bold step of putting their own name on their products and began selling America's first brand-name meats, which included bockwurst, liverwurst, bacon, frankfurters, and bologna. In 1929, the Oscar Mayer company further distinguished its products by placing a yellow paper band around retail bundles of hot dogs, a product that until then had been sold in bulk, with no trademark or advertising attached.

Advertising was always an important factor in the company's success. The company began newspaper advertising in 1917. In 1936, the Oscar Meyer Wienermobile hit the road as a traveling ambassador for the company's hot dogs, and later in the twentieth century they ran a succession of television commercials with particularly catchy jingles. "The Oscar Mayer Wiener Jingle," which made its debut in 1963 and "The Oscar Mayer Bologna Song," which first appeared in 1976, became two of America's most famous commercial jingles.

In 1972, Oscar Mayer & Co. began to globalize as kit purchased a company in Japan. Shortly thereafter, the company began selling its products in other Asian countries. Following the death of Oscar F. Mayer (at the age of ninety-five), the company moved its headquarters moved from Chicago to Madison, Wisconsin, in 1955. The Mayer family decided to go public in 1971 and the company was acquired by Kraft Foods North America in 1989.

BIBLIOGRAPHY

Gelbert, Doug. *So Who the Heck Was Oscar Mayer? The Real People behind Those Brand Names.* New York: Barricade Books, 1996.

Oscar Mayer Celebration Cookbook: 1883–1983, 100 Years of Dedication to the Kid in All of Us. Milwaukee, WI: Ideals Pub. Corp., 1983.

ANDREW F. SMITH

Ovens, *see Stoves and Ovens*

Oyster Bars

The shucking and serving of oysters has been a downstairs-upstairs phenomenon in the history of American restaurants. As early as 1763, a cellar on Broad Street in New York City featured half shells, as did a handful of other basement saloons, which were occasionally called parlors or bars. As time passed and the number of these establishments grew, they were recognized by certain distinctive features. A balloon of red muslin, which could be illuminated at night by a candle within, beckoned the oyster aficionado down a short flight of steps. In the nineteenth century, these twenty-five-by-one-hundred-foot cellars were ornately furnished with mirrors, gilded paintings, gaslights or chandeliers, carpeting in the center aisle, and a handsome bar at one end of the room. Oysters became the incentive for consuming alcoholic beverages, and the atmosphere of these clubby, all-male cellars led to the invitation "Let us royster with the oyster—in the shorter days and moister" (*Detroit Free Press*, October 12, 1889). One of the most prestigious of these oyster cellars was Downings at 5 Broad Street in New York. Because of its proximity to the U.S. Custom House, the Merchant's Exchange, banks, and stores, it also became a meeting place of politicians and office-seekers. By 1874, over 850 oyster establishments existed in New York City alone. Not limited to this major, commercial, seaport city, but also located in cities along the Atlantic coast and as far west as the railroads extended, oyster cellars, saloons, and bars displaced coffeehouses as meeting places.

When it became essential for businesspeople to spend the workday away from home, aboveground oyster stalls located in busy market areas and the more leisurely oyster houses and lunchrooms gained in popularity. The stalls offered freshly shucked oysters, instantly prepared stews, and oysters roasted in the wood fire that also kept the vendors warm. The back-of-the-house cooks of the more elaborate oyster houses served oysters in a variety of recipes, with shellfish and fish entrées as well as with steaks and chops. In 1826, the Union Oyster House in Boston,

Oyster stands in New York City's Fulton Market around 1870.

reputed to be the country's oldest restaurant still in operation, introduced a semicircular oyster bar where Daniel Webster was reputed to have eaten three dozen oysters, accompanied by brandy and water, at one sitting. Other cities along the East Coast, as well as Chicago, Pittsburgh, and St. Louis, boasted well-appointed oyster houses decorated with marble and mahogany, offering first-class service and tempting food. In New Orleans, special oyster preparations—Bienville, Roffignac, and Rockefeller—became the distinguishing dishes of famous restaurants, and during the gold rush days, the infamous mining town of Placerville, California, known for its frequent hangings, served an oyster omelet appropriately named the Hangtown fry, later a signature dish of Maye's Oyster House in San Francisco.

The continuing popularity of restaurants like the Grand Central Oyster Bar in New York City, which opened in 1913, proves that the tradition of the oyster bar has not faded. Whether serving a platter of half shells, an oyster stew or panfry, or, in the contemporary mode, offering a selection of shellfish from a pristine raw bar, restaurateurs know that the celebration of the oyster never ends.

[**See also** OYSTERS.]

BIBLIOGRAPHY

Fisher, M. F. K. *Consider the Oyster.* San Francisco: North Point Press, 1988.

Gordon, David G., Nancy E. Blanton, and Terry Y. Nosho. *Heaven on the Half Shell: The Story of the Northwest's Love Affair with the Oyster.* Portland, OR: WestWinds, 2001.

Reardon, Joan. *Oysters: A Culinary Celebration.* Orleans, MA: Parnassus, 1984; rev. ed. New York: Lyons Press, 2000.

JOAN REARDON

Oyster Loaf Sandwich

The oyster loaf sandwich is composed of a hollowed-out loaf of french bread that is buttered and toasted, then filled with oysters that have been lightly breaded in cornmeal and deep-fried. It was created during the late nineteenth century, when oysters, plentiful and cheap, were a popular American food. In New Orleans, Louisiana, husbands who spent the evening carousing in the French Quarter often brought home an oyster loaf in the hope of pacifying a jealous wife; the oyster loaf was thus known as *la médiatrice*, or the mediator. Also laying claim to the oyster loaf is San Francisco, where it is said that Mayes Oyster House, established in 1867, created it. Various versions of the sandwich can typically be found in oyster-harvesting areas throughout the United States.

[**See also** OYSTERS.]

BIBLIOGRAPHY

Mercuri, Becky. *Sandwiches That You Will Like.* Pittsburgh, PA: WQED, 2002.

BECKY MERCURI

Oysters

Oysters are difficult-to-open, rough-shelled bivalves, and once were the most popular of all seafood in America. Since ancient times, Native Americans along the East Coast feasted on oysters, leaving behind large shell heaps. Colonists brought with them a long history of passion for oysters and took to them readily in the New World. Oysters were so popular that they were over-harvested along many parts of the New England coast in the eighteenth century. By the mid-nineteenth century oysters were cultivated with seed oysters brought from the Chesapeake region, where these shellfish abounded.

Oysters were packed and shipped inland all through the eighteenth and nineteenth centuries, each era taking advantage of advances in transportation and packing technology. At home, oysters were used as side dishes, in sauces, and in soups or stews. In inns and taverns oysters were sold as "fast food" to accompany drink. In the nineteenth century, so-called oyster saloons were found in nearly all cities and towns of any size. At these establishments, a bowl of oyster stew could be cooked up quickly or a plate of roasted or raw oysters could be quickly consumed.

[**See also** OYSTER BARS; OYSTER LOAF SANDWICH; PACIFIC NORTHWEST.]

BIBLIOGRAPHY

Gordon, David G., Nancy E. Blanton, and Terry Y. Nosho. *Heaven on the Half Shell: The Story of the Northwest's Love Affair with the Oyster*. Portland, OR: WestWinds, 2001.

Reardon, Joan. *Oysters: A Culinary Celebration*. Orleans, MA.: Parnassus Press, 1984; rev. ed. New York: Lyons Press, 2000.

JOAN REARDON

P

Pacific Northwest

The aboriginal peoples of the Pacific Northwest were the first to feast on an abundance of salmon, halibut, clams, crabs, deer, and venison; young shoots and leaves of green plants (*Heracleum lanatum*, or cow parsnip); root vegetables (camas and wapato); and a variety of berries. The native people who followed migrating animals and the emergence of plants lived on both sides of the Cascades. They cooked with boiling water heated with hot stones in a watertight coiled basket, steamed food in a hot pit filled with grasses and/or dirt and covered with mats, or roasted over a smoldering fire. Seeking food and preparing foods for winter storage were major activities and involved the entire tribe. Over the years, with the arrival of colonists, their foodways began to resemble the predominant culture.

American settlers began arriving in the Pacific Northwest in the 1830s. Beginning in the 1880s, ethnic populations, such as the Chinese, Germans, Irish, Japanese, Jews, Mexicans, and Scandinavians, moved in. Many of the newcomers were skilled farmers eager to provide their families with food as well as make a profit selling the surplus. Although in the beginning shortages forced the family cook to adapt and substitute, the immigrants strove for a customary cuisine and did not familiarize themselves with native cooking.

Agriculture

The settlers missed bread more than any other food and pleaded for merchants to increase the supply of flour. Although by 1846 wheat had become a major crop in the Pacific Northwest, the large influx of immigrants, plus the orders coming from those participating in the California gold rush of 1849, meant supply could not keep up with demand. For homeowners, planting wheat and building a gristmill was as important as constructing a house. The pioneers preferred to plant hard red winter wheat, best suited for breads. Red winter and hard red spring wheat are still grown, but soft white winter wheat, perfect for pasta and pastry, has become the dominant variety.

Most likely, the American Indians obtained potatoes from the Spanish in the eighteenth century. The tuber was successful among the native tribes because it could be harvested and prepared like the camas. Tools used in harvesting the camas root made perfect implements for digging potato holes at planting time and for removing tubers at harvest time. Steaming in pits seemed to be the preferred method of cooking potatoes. In the early twenty-first century, several million acres of well-irrigated land in Washington and Oregon have made the Pacific Northwest one of the largest and finest potato producing areas in the country. Modern, climate-controlled storage facilities ensure the availability of fresh potatoes all year.

Over the years, a profusion of orchards has successfully produced a wide variety of apples. Most of the orchards in Oregon border the Columbia River. The orchards in Washington are nestled in the eastern foothills of the Cascade Mountains and irrigated with cool mountain water. Growers use dwarf trees in high-density plantings to bring new orchards into production faster. Washington leads the nation in apple production and in the percentage of apples going to the "fresh" fruit market. In the nineteenth century, Gravenstein, Winesap, and Northern Spy were the varieties of choice. In the early twenty-first century, Red and Golden Delicious, Fuji, Granny Smith, Gala, and Braeburn head the list.

Native blueberries (*Vaccinium*) and trailing types of blackberries (*Rubus ursinus*) still grow on the western slopes of the Cascade Mountains, but it is the cultivated varieties of caneberries (raspberries, blackberries, marionberries, and boysenberries) that display a cornucopia of colors on northwestern farmlands. Washington is number one in the production of red raspberries, sweet cherries, pears, and Concord grapes. Washington is also one of the top five growing states for apricots, other grapes, tart cherries, prunes, peaches, and plums. Oregon accounts for 95 percent of black raspberries and loganberries (grown mainly for juice, pies, and wine) and is a large producer of wine grapes, pears, and cherries. A new berry, the marionberry, named after Marion County, Oregon, was introduced in 1956 by George Waldo. It was developed from a cross between cultivated and wild blackberries. Bing, Lambert, Royal Ann, and Willamette cherries bursting with flavor began life at the Luelling nurseries in the nineteenth century. Plump, golden Rainier cherries are a more recent variety.

Fish

When the fishing industry is added to agriculture, the importance of the Pacific Northwest to the world's food supply achieves even more fame. The waterways presented a veritable fish market to the native peoples as well as the explorers and settlers who followed them. People might dine on whale meat, trout, sturgeon, smelt, herring, halibut, clams (including geoduck, the largest bivalve along Puget Sound), oysters, crabs, and salmon.

The wild Pacific salmon has had the most "cultural, economic, recreational and symbolic importance" of any food in the Pacific Northwest. Archaeological deposits indicate that salmon have been part of the native diet for at least nine thousand years. Five species of Pacific salmon (*Oncorhynchus*) make their home in the Pacific Northwest. They are chinook (tyee, king), sockeye (red), coho (silver), chum (dog), and pink (humpback). Of the five, chinook is the largest—some reach sixty pounds—and richest in oil. The salmon's incredible life cycle with its regularity—freshwater birth and ocean growth (anadromy) and behavior (homing)—may be why salmon are so venerated and are thought to be magical.

The Hudson's Bay Company began the commercialization of salmon when it began salting and selling the fish in the 1820s. In 1866, Hapgood, Hume, and Company opened a cannery on the lower Columbia River and filled cans with salted chunks of chinook salmon. Spectacular profits drew in other companies, and within twenty years more than fifty canneries had established plants on the Columbia River and its tributaries. With the coming of the railroad and other industrial innovations, such as better refrigeration, Pacific salmon could be found in kitchens all over the world. Unfortunately, the "still abundant salmon population" would be forever altered. Also unfortunately, salmon, native to the Pacific Northwest waterways, are declining in many areas.

The Dungeness crab, a hard-shell crab that is unique to the West Coast, receives much praise. It has been harvested since the late 1800s. Quantities of oysters greeted the early settlers. The tiny native oyster, *Ostrea lurida*, flourished in the pristine waters of Willapa Bay. Portland restaurants featured it

The 1941 salmon run was so huge that the Columbia River Paking Association in Astoria, Oregon, put up more than 125,000 cases in the first five days.

on the menu as early as 1862. Seriously depleted in the 1950s as a result of water pollution, oysters are being reestablished in Hood Canal and other coastal areas. The heartier Pacific oyster is the principal oyster harvested commercially in the Pacific Northwest. Since 1975, oysters, along with clams and mussels, have been farmed at Penn Cove on Whidby Island in Washington. The sweet-tasting Penn Cove mussels (*Mytilus trossulus*) are naturally prevalent from Alaska to Washington.

Beverages

German brewmasters came just in time to take advantage of the heightened popularity of lager beer. Throughout the territory a thirsty population greeted their arrival with joy. Within a few years a burgeoning saloon industry happily opened the tap of wooden kegs filled with local beer. Most of the early breweries were small and soon disappeared or were absorbed by larger concerns. Three—Blitz-Weinhard (1862), Rainier Beer (1878), and Olympia Beer (1896)— achieved national fame, although all are now part of national companies.

Besides benefiting from an abundance of good water, the breweries had quick access to flourishing hop fields, which provided a key ingredient of good lager beer. The Willamette Valley began producing hops in the 1860s, and soon twelve-foot poles all over the territory supported the blossoming green vines of the hop plant. By 1943, Washington had become the leading hop producer in the United States. The proliferation of microbreweries, begun in the 1980s by people looking for beer with character, has once again given rise to numerous small breweries in Oregon and Washington.

Grapes are grown in Washington and in Oregon. Between the two states there are eleven viticultural appellations, each a specific geographic region. Oregon ranks second in the United States for number of wineries; Washington is second in the United States in premium wine production. Chardonnay, Pinot Noir, Cabernet, and Zinfandel grapes generate notoriety for the agricultural industry and enhance the states' revenues.

Starbucks Coffee Company made Seattle a coffee capital when in 1971 it began introducing superior roasted coffee beans. The company rose to fame under the direction of Howard Schultz, who acquired Starbucks in 1985. In 2001, Starbucks sold a variety of coffee beans and coffee drinks at 4,709 locations.

The diversity of products and its high ranking in agriculture production make the Pacific Northwest a special place. In the year 2000, this high-tech territory, especially Washington, ranked number one in the United States in the production of hops, spearmint oil, seed peas, lentils, dry edible peas, apples, hazelnuts, sweet cherries, pears, Concord grapes, processing carrots, sweet corn, and red raspberries. The region also ranks high in production of potatoes, wheat, apricots, tart cherries, prunes, plums, asparagus, strawberries, broccoli, and onions. [See also APPLES; CALIFORNIA; CAMAS ROOT; CHERRIES; COFFEEHOUSES; FISH, FRESHWATER; FISH, SALTWATER FLAT; NATIVE AMERICAN FOOD; PEACHES AND NECTARINES; POTATOES; RASPBERRIES; OYSTERS; SEAFOOD; STARBUCKS; WINERIES.]

Bibliography

Caditz, Mary Houser. *Wandering and Feasting: A Washington Cookbook.* Pullman: Washington State University Press, 1996.

Cone, Joseph, and Sandy Ridlington, eds. *The Northwest Salmon Crisis: A Documentary History.* Corvallis: Oregon State University Press, 1996.

Hibler, Janie. *Dungeness Crabs and Blackberry Cobblers: The Northwest Heritage Cookbook.* New York: Knopf, 1991.

Judson, Phoebe Goodell. *A Pioneer's Search for an Ideal Home: A Book of Personal Memoirs.* Lincoln: University of Nebraska Press, 1984.

Meier, Gary, and Gloria Meier. *Brewed in the Pacific Northwest: A History of Beer-Making in Oregon and Washington.* Seattle, WA: Fjord Press, 1991.

National Agricultural Statistics Service (NASS). http://www.usda.gov/nass.

Schwantes, Carlos Arnaldo. *The Pacific Northwest: An Interpretive History.* rev. ed. Lincoln: University of Nebraska Press, 1996.

Williams, Jacqueline. *The Way We Ate: Pacific Northwest Cooking, 1843–1900.* Pullman: Washington State University Press, 1996.

JACQUELINE BLOCK WILLIAMS

Packaging

Food packages—vessels that facilitate food transportation and trade—began early in human development as shells, gourds, and animal skins. As human societies became more complex, so did packaging. Packages transformed from purely functional to decorative objects and from vessels whose sole purpose was transportation to containers that helped preserve, protect, and increase the appeal of their contents. As the early food packages became more sophisticated, they were made of increasingly diverse materials, including pottery, wood, and cloth.

Similarly, modern food packaging was originally devised as a method for transporting and extending the shelf life of foods. Prior to the later nineteenth century, most food was distributed only in bulk. Bulk foods were commonly associated with spoilage and related sanitation and disease problems.

Toward the end of the nineteenth century, the Industrial Revolution produced key packaging advances, including the use of metal cans for heat-processed foods, the collapsible tube, the folding carton, the corrugated shipping case, the crown closure for sealing bottles, and the ubiquitous paper bag. These advances should not be underestimated in their importance; for instance, the availability of canned and bottled milk is credited with reducing disease and infant mortality.

Advances in food packaging were also key to the growth of the U.S. industry. The commercial success of Quaker Oats beginning in 1886 and Uneeda Biscuits from the National Biscuit Company in 1899 triggered the explosive concept of packaging as a marketing communicator, known as the "silent salesman."

Meat had been canned since the early nineteenth century, and by the beginning of the twentieth century automated machinery turned out thousands of cans per hour. Brand names such as Wilson, Armour, Swift, and Libby, McNeill, and Libby were national in scope. But problems of food safety in the meatpacking industry, revealed in 1906, led President Theodore Roosevelt's administration to create the Food and Drug Administration. The seeds for food packaging regulation were planted.

With World War I came the demand for more preserved goods; the War Department bought three-quarters of all canned goods produced. Early packaging processes and methods were hardly safe, however, and in 1918 the appearance of botulism resulted in the recognition that safer, more scientific methods of preserving in cans were needed.

Meanwhile the demand for more and better packaging was growing, thanks to the advent of supermarkets and readily available refrigeration—and the concomitant expectation of more and better individually packaged goods. The packaging revolution, which Daniel J. Boorstin called "one of the most manifold and least noticed revolutions in the common experience," was now in full force (*The Americans*).

By the late nineteenth century and the early twentieth century, the race was on to win consumer attention with attractive, distinctive containers made of paper, paperboard, glass, and tinplate. Many famous brands arose, from Kellogg's Corn Flakes and Aunt Jemima Pancake Mix in the 1890s to the naturalist-explorer Clarence Birdseye's first frozen foods in 1930, the result of his observations (while on expedition to Labrador) that fish retained its flavor and freshness when frozen.

Major food packaging advances came in 1927, when DuPont perfected waterproof cellophane, and in 1936 with the discovery of polyethylene. These discoveries, combined with the shortages that arose from World War II, led to major advances in plastics, which in turn refocused the way many foods were packaged in the postwar era.

By the 1950s packaged foods of every kind had become commonplace in U.S. households, and by the last decade of the century packaged foods had all but replaced fresh foods in many homes. Packaging became an integral part of a product's profitability, and the marketing component of packaging came under fire as individually packaged portion sizes increased and were suspected of contributing to a national epidemic of obesity.

Food packaging has many functions. At its heart a package is still a vessel by which food is more easily transported, and the package also importantly serves to protect its contents. Packaging is invaluable in helping to sell products and can often cost far more than its contents to produce.

In food packaging four basic materials are used, either alone or in combination: metal, plant (paper and wood), glass, and plastic. Each material has unique characteristics as well as advantages and disadvantages. Metal is strong and creates a good barrier between food and potential spoilage agents such as light, but it is heavy and can corrode. Paper, often an economical choice, is a good medium on which to print manufacturers' messages, but it can disintegrate when it absorbs liquids. Glass is transparent, which can add visual appeal, but it breaks easily. Plastics, which take many forms, are versatile, but they tend to be more costly.

Most packaging is a combination of materials. A milk box, for example, is made of paper, which is economical but which must be lined with a thin layer of plastic in order to create a stable barrier. A peanut butter jar may be glass or plastic, and the lid is usually metal lined with plastic. Most packages such as these are placed in a larger, secondary package or container that facilitates shipment. These secondary containers are often made of paper, but they may also be plastic.

One of the most important challenges facing food packagers is balancing the needs dictated by product characteristics and food safety, the marketing needs of manufacturers, consumer convenience, and the effect the packaging may have on the environment.

Recycling is one approach to the problem of discarded food packages. Aluminum cans make up the largest category of postconsumer recycling. Although most recycled plastics come from the container manufacturing process, postconsumer recycling is growing. Polyethylene terephthalate (PET) products, marked by a triangle on the bottom, are the standard for bottled beverages. Recycling has been instituted by local governments across the United States, but overcoming the traditional American attitude of using and discarding things, for instance, fast food packages, has been difficult.

[**See also** BIRDSEYE, CLARENCE; BOTTLING; CANNING AND BOTTLING; KELLOGG COMPANY; PLASTIC BAGS; PLASTIC COVERING.]

BIBLIOGRAPHY
Beniger, James R. *The Control Revolution: Technological and Economic Origins of the Information Society.* Cambridge, MA: Harvard University Press, 1986.
Boorstin, Daniel J. *The Americans: The Democratic Experience.* New York: Random House, 1973.
Hine, Thomas. *The Total Package: The Evolution and Secret Meanings of Boxes, Bottles, Cans, and Tubes.* Boston: Little, Brown, 1995.

MARGE PERRY

Pale Ale

The origins of pale ale are obscure, but the style has always had hops, so it must have been introduced after the early sixteenth century, when hops were first used in England and the term "ale" was coined to specify a particular style of fermented malt beverage. This was the style of choice for American microbrewers because it was so basic. Pale ale also offers such a range in color, taste, and aroma that brewers felt comfortable when adding their personal touches to the style.

However, the distinct American varieties of hops and the unique fruity-ester aromas created by top-fermenting "ale" yeast mark American-style pale ale as unique. If the United Kingdom can claim Bass Pale Ale as the essential British pale ale, then America can also claim a style defining American pale ale. Garrett Oliver, brewmaster for the Brooklyn Brewing Company, notes on page 288 of *The Brewmaster's Table*:

> American pale ales are deep gold to copper in color and highly aromatic, with a dry, medium-bodied palate supported by relatively light malt flavors. They have snappy bitterness up front and then give way to some fruitiness and malt flavor in the center, leaving a dry, clean finish. Sierra Nevada Pale Ale is a classic version of this style.

According to the Association of Brewers' 2004 Beer Style Guidelines, what differentiates the American-style pale ale from its English cousin is the American variety of hops used to produce higher hops bitterness, flavor, and aroma with stronger fruity-ester flavor and aroma than the English style. The usual alcohol content is 4.5 to 5.5 percent by volume.

[**See also** BEER.]

BIBLIOGRAPHY
Oliver, Garrett. *The Brewmaster's Table.* New York: Ecco, 2003.

PETER LaFRANCE

Pancakes

The basic American pancake (also called flapjack, slapjack, griddle cake, or hotcake) is a flat, round breadstuff made from a simple batter that blends flour, milk, and eggs. The batter is poured onto a lightly greased griddle or skillet, and the cake is flipped over when the underside is done. American pancakes are most commonly made from wheat flour, buckwheat flour, or cornmeal; like other quick breads, they lend themselves to additions such as berries and other fruits. A pat of butter along with maple or another sweet syrup are traditional accompaniments. More elaborate toppings include whipped cream and fresh fruit.

Pancakes are common to many peoples throughout the world. The prototypical American pancakes probably arrived with the earliest English and Dutch settlers, whose pancake traditions dated back to at least the fifteenth century and possibly as far back as prehistoric times. Later immigrants to the United States brought their own pancake recipes, such as Russian blini, French crêpes, eastern European Jewish latkes, Norwegian *lefse*, and Austrian *palatschinken*. Most of these are not breakfast fare but holiday specialties, party foods, or desserts.

The wide appeal of pancakes is attested to by the popularity of pancake restaurants or "pancake houses," such as the International House of Pancakes (IHOP), launched in 1889 in a Los Angeles suburb. These establishments serve pancakes to suit every taste and time of day, from sweet to savory, from breakfast to dinner. Some Episcopal churches hold pancake breakfasts on Shrove Tuesday, even including a British-style pancake race, in which the contestants must flip a pancake in a skillet as they run. Pancake breakfasts are also traditional fund-raisers for nonprofit organizations and other good causes.

Somewhat surprisingly, American inventors saw potential for a convenience food in a recipe as simple as pancake batter. In 1899 Chris L. Rutt and Charles G. Underwood introduced the first ready-mixed commercial food product, which was later renamed Aunt Jemima Pancake Mix. The first located American cookbook focusing exclusively on pancakes is Ruth Ellen Church's *Pancakes Aplenty* (1962); it was followed by Myra Waldo's *Pancake Cookbook* (1963) and many others.

[**See also** AUNT JEMIMA; BREAKFAST FOODS.]

BIBLIOGRAPHY
Messer, Betty, ed. *A Collection of Maple Recipes: Pancakes, and More!!!* From Members of New

Hampshire Maple Producers' Association. Lebanon, NH: Hanover, 2001.

Pappas, Lou Seibert. *Pancakes & Waffles: Great Recipes*. San Francisco: Chronicle Books, 2004.

ANDREW F. SMITH

Pancake Pans

Pancakes are one of the universal foods of the world and were brought to the American colonies early as European crepe-style delicacies. Their preparation at the hearth required flat, cast-iron griddles, usually with legs and swinging bail handles for hanging, or small, flat-bottomed frying pans. They were extremely popular as a colonial French, Dutch American, and English festive food.

Raised American pancakes, an offshoot, became the lighter "flapjack" in the late 1700s, leavened with yeast and later baking soda. Made with wheat flour, cornmeal, or buckwheat, they were also baked on even-cooking soapstone griddles. Earthenware batter jugs with spouts, bail handles, and tin covers for spouts and tops held yeast batters for overnight rising and easy pouring at breakfast time. By the later 1800s the cookstove and the gadget craze provoked the invention of hinged, multiple griddles of cast iron or tin. The batter was poured into individual circlets and flipped, one or all at a time, onto the facing open griddle plate. It is likely that the perfectly circular pancake shape was the attraction.

During this period waves of immigrants also brought pans for their own ethnic pancake versions. The Danes used *ebelskiver* pans (sometimes porcelainized), usually with sets of seven attached cast-iron cups that produced a globular pancake form (flipped with knitting needles); the Swedes and Russians had *plett kakers*—pans with individualized shallow indentations.

Pancake equipment remains in American kitchens. Heavy griddles of iron or soapstone are required for Sunday breakfast treats, and French crepe pans of thin iron produce the delicate wrappings for many sweet and savory fillings.

[See also AUNT JEMIMA.]

ALICE ROSS

Panini

"Panini" is the Americanized version of the Italian word *panino*, which means little sandwich and refers to a class of sandwiches that became popular in the United States in the late 1990s. Flavor is key to panini, which are based on high-quality Italian artisan breads like focaccia or *ciabatta*. The sandwiches are layered, but not overstuffed, with flavorful combinations of cheeses, meats, or roasted vegetables. Various dressings or condiments are added, and the sandwich is pressed and lightly grilled. Panini-style sandwiches are popular in trendy restaurants throughout the United States.

[See also ITALIAN AMERICAN FOOD; SANDWICHES.]

BIBLIOGRAPHY

Mercuri, Becky. *Sandwiches That You Will Like*. Pittsburgh, PA: WQED Multimedia, 2002.

BECKY MERCURI

Pans, *see Pots and Pans*

Parers, *see Apple-Preparation Tools*

Parloa, Maria

Maria Parloa is now nearly forgotten, but in the latter part of the nineteenth century she was well known as a respected cooking authority, teacher and lecturer, author of many popular cookbooks, founder of cooking schools in Boston and New York City, and editor of women's magazines. She was one of the innovative superstars of her field, addressing her material to the training of both cooking teachers and the growing group of urban, middle-class women who had the leisure and desire to improve their cooking and maintain fashion. Parloa's fame was such that her name and recipes were effective endorsements of several commercial products. In her own words, "Having had years of experience as a cook in private families and hotels, I know the wants of the masses and feel competent to supply them."

Parloa was born of English parentage in Massachusetts in September 1843. Although little is known of her early life, she apparently attended school in Maine, and at some point she gained important experience working as a pastry cook in noted New England hotels. Her lifelong association with food and cooking had begun. In 1872 she produced her first comprehensive cookbook, *The Appledore Cook Book, Containing Practical Receipts for Plain and Rich Cooking*. Encouraged by favorable comments on her early fund-raising food demonstrations, she repeated the success in New London, Connecticut (1876).

These activities served as the springboard for Parloa's long, New England–based career as a teacher, lecturer, and author. After only two years in Boston, her reputation was such that she was engaged to teach a series of classes on cooking-teacher training at Tremont Temple in Boston (May 1877). In October of that year she expanded her teaching scope, opening her own cooking school nearby (on the corner of Tremont and Mason streets in Boston). She also began directing the scientific teaching of cooking at Lesell Seminary in Auburndale, Massachusetts, and offered lectures at Miss Morgan's School in Portsmouth, New Hampshire.

Classes and lectures led to additional publications, among them a slim volume called *Camp Cookery: How to Live in Camp* (1878). Intent on expanding her credentials and skills, Parloa traveled abroad, where she studied methods of teaching cooking at the National Training School for Cookery in London and French cuisine in Paris, visiting local schools as she went. Parloa's ambitious training, unusual for a woman at that time, set her apart from many other American cooking authorities.

Once back in the United States, Parloa instituted the first training course in cookery for teachers at the prestigious Chatauqua summer schools (1879). She was one of the first two teachers at the soon to be prestigious Boston Cooking School (1879) and continued to be involved; subsequently she called herself variously the founder or the principal of the school. She taught the school's first normal course, a teacher training program. In that same year she began a lecture tour to such cities as Chicago and Milwaukee, Wisconsin, and she taught at the New York Cooking School. According to William Alexander, writing in *Good Housekeeping*, "Her engagement was a most successful one, the auditorium being crowded every day." A popular figure and a good businesswoman, Parloa commanded an unusually high salary for a woman at that time.

Parloa was also well known as an expert on household management. Once more she traveled abroad, this time for two years, to study Europe's best methods of housekeeping. She again followed her studies with a series of lectures at home. Because many cookbooks of the time included such homemaking instruction, she was able to expand the scope of her own writings. According to Alexander, she gave about seven hundred lectures or public demonstrations in addition to her private instruction. He estimates that she taught courses in forty or fifty towns and cities in a dozen states.

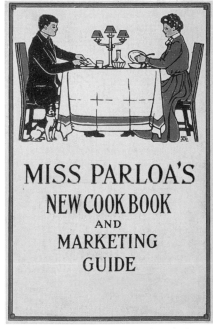

Miss Parloa's New Cook Book and Marketing Guide.

Parloa continued to be active professionally in her later years. As a firm believer in and practitioner of lifelong learning, she attended the first Summer School of Food and Nutrition at Wesleyan University in Middletown, Connecticut. Although she was then close to retirement, she also attended the 1903 Graduate Course in Nutrition. Her valued contributions to the fields of cookery and household management earned her an invitation to participate in the Lake Placid Conferences. As a result of the conferences, the American Home Economics Association was established, and needless to say, Parloa was a charter member.

Parloa retired to Bethel, Connecticut, where she is remembered for her gracious hospitality and generosity to the community. She died there in August 1909 and was buried in Boston.

In addition to those already mentioned, Parloa's publications include *Miss Parloa's Kitchen Companion: A Guide for All Who Would Be Good Housekeepers* (1887); *First Principles of Household Management and Cookery: A Textbook for Schools and Families* (1879); *Miss Parloa's New Cook Book: A Guide to Marketing and Cooking* (1881); *Practical Cookery, with Demonstrations* (1884); *Miss Parloa's Young Housekeeper: Designed Especially to Aid Beginners* (1893); *Home Economics: A Guide to Household Management, Including the Proper Treatment of the Materials Entering into the Construction and Furnishing of the House* (1898); and *Home Economics: A Practical Guide in Every Branch of Housekeeping* (1910). In addition to these voluminous writings, she prepared two widely circulated Farmers' Bulletins for the Office of Experiment Stations of the U.S. Department of Agriculture: *Preparation of Vegetables for the Table* (1914) and *Canned Fruit, Preserves, and Jellies: Household Methods of Preparation* (1917).

As with many prominent cookbook authors and teachers, Parloa's name was considered enough of a draw to feature her work in commercial promotional pamphlets. Notable among these was a series for Walter Baker and Company titled *Choice Receipts* (1893). In some of these she shared authorship with other famous food writers; some booklets are attributed to "Miss Parloa and other Noted Teachers." In at least one the work was entirely her own, "specially prepared for the Walter Baker & Co. Exhibit at the World's Colombian Exposition, 1893." Likewise she contributed to advertising booklets on cocoa, coffee, meat extract, and tableware.
[**See also** COOKBOOKS AND MANUSCRIPTS: AMERICAN COOKBOOKS FROM THE CIVIL WAR TO WORLD WAR I; COOKING MANUSCRIPTS; COOKING SCHOOLS.]

BIBLIOGRAPHY

Shapiro, Laura. *Perfection Salad: Women and Cooking at the Turn of the Century.* New York: Farrar, Straus, and Giroux, 1986.

MARY MOONEY-GETOFF

Parsley Family

The parsleys (Apiaceae) provide many of the most beloved culinary herbs—nearly thirty species. A few species are poisonous, such as hemlock, (*Conium maculatum*), but many are used in the kitchen either as vegetables (carrots, celeriac, celery, fennel bulbs, and parsnips) or as seasonings.

Several parsley family members are used commonly in the United States. The seeds of anise (*Pimpinella anisum*) and fennel (*Foeniculum vulgare*) are used whenever a strong licorice flavor is needed, although licorice (*Glycyrrhiza glabra*) is a member of the unrelated pea family (*Leguminoseae*). Caraway (*Carum carvi*) seeds are used in dishes originally from central Europe and Scandinavia, including rye breads and cabbage dishes such as coleslaw and sauerkraut. Coriander (*Coriandrum sativum*), once grown exclusively for its sweetly aromatic seeds, is now used more for its foliage, which is known as cilantro. Cumin (*Cuminum cyminum*) seeds have a warm, musky scent that is essential to Tex-Mex, Middle Eastern, and Indian cookery. Dill (*Anethum graveolens*) is grown from different cultivars, depending on whether the foliage or the seeds are desired. Parsley (*Petroselinum crispum*), when grown for its foliage, is one of two cultivars, curly or flat-leaf (Neapolitanum) and parsley root or celeriac (Tuberosum).
[**See also** PREPARED HERB AND SPICE MIXTURES.]

BIBLIOGRAPHY

Allen, Gary. *The Herbalist in the Kitchen.* Champaign: University of Illinois Press, forthcoming.

Bailey, Liberty Hyde, and Ethel Zoe Bailey, comps. *Hortus Third: A Concise Dictionary of Plants Cultivated in the United States and Canada.* Revised and expanded by the staff of the Liberty Hyde Bailey Hortorium. New York: Macmillan, 1976.

GARY ALLEN

Parsnips

Parsnips, *Pastinaca sativa*, are creamy white root vegetables that resemble their carrot cousins (*Umbellifera*), but they often taste sweeter and nuttier. Best dug and eaten after the fall frosts, they store well in root cellars or controlled environments, where their starches convert to sugars. They remain alive in the ground during cold winters and are sometimes preferred as early spring vegetables.

Parsnip consumption began with wild plants of the European Stone Age. Cultivated in ancient Greece and Rome, they became central to the medieval diet and (with fava beans) structured many Catholic fast day and Lenten (meatless) meals. The first American seeds were planted in 1609 by the English, followed by German, French, and Dutch settlers. Following ethnic customs, parsnips were served boiled and buttered, baked, mashed, in sweetened rich puddings and fritters, and candied as sweetmeats. European parsnip seeds "escaped" and grew wild in the East; a western wild strain may have

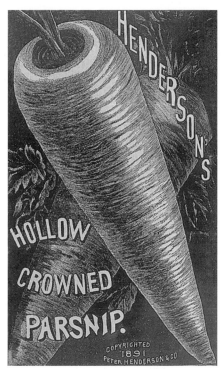

Parsnips shown in the 1894 catalog of Peter Henderson & Co., New York.

been indigenous. Both were dug and eaten by Native Americans and European travelers. Early nineteenth-century hybridization furthered parsnips' already substantial popularity, but by the early 1900s they were largely eclipsed by the carrot and were used mostly as soup flavoring. Experimental cooks have since returned them to fine restaurants and adventurous diners.
[**See also** CARROTS; VEGETABLES.]

BIBLIOGRAPHY

Weaver, William Woys. *Heirloom Vegetable Gardening: A Master Gardener's Guide to Planting, Growing, Seed Saving, and Cultural History.* New York: Holt, 1997.

ALICE ROSS

Partridge

Two varieties of this game bird, the red-legged partridge (*Alectoris rufa*) and the gray partridge (*Perdrix perdrix*), were introduced from England to the thirteen American colonies for sport. They are now farmed for their meat and eggs mainly in Oregon. The chukar partridge (*Alectoris chukar*), native to Turkey, the Mediterranean, and Asia, was introduced to North America in the twentieth century as it is better suited to the warmer U.S. climate. At game bird farms in North America, it is reared by the thousands for hunting and for its meat and eggs. The meat of partridges resembles that of chicken in color and texture, and the bird has a chicken-like shape with plenty of meat but a stronger flavor. All varieties have a similar flavor and are treated the same for culinary purposes. Unlike other types of game, partridges do not need to be hung for more than forty-eight hours to tenderize the flesh. To prevent their flesh from drying out, young birds are first covered with strips of fat pork or bacon, then they are trussed and roasted in a hot oven. Older birds are stewed with root vegetables or with cabbage in the French style. The eggs should be hard cooked and can be served as an appetizer.

[**See also** CHICKEN.]

BIBLIOGRAPHY
Marrone, Teresa. *Cookin' Wild Game: The Complete Guide to Dressing and Cooking Big Game, Small Game, Upland Birds, and Waterfowl.* Minnetonka, MN: Creative Publishing International, 2002.
McClane, A. J., and Donna Turner. *A Taste of the Wild: A Compendium of Modern American Game Cookery.* New York: Penguin, 1991.

JOSEPHINE BACON

Passenger Pigeon

In 1600 the passenger pigeon, *Ectopistes migratorius*, was possibly the most numerous bird in the world, with population estimates of 3 to 5 billion. The birds traveled in vast flocks from northern Mississippi to Nova Scotia and from coastal Massachusetts west to the Great Plains, taking as long as three days to pass over. Hunters did not let this bounty pass unmolested. After a pigeon hunt in 1813, the naturalist John James Audubon said of the slaughter, "The Pigeons were picked up and piled in heaps, until each had as many as he could possibly dispose of, when the hogs were let loose to feed on the remainder."

The dark flesh was good roasted or braised, but the birds were also salted down for later consumption. Another method was described in an 1843 Michigan newspaper: "When I shoot my rifle clear, to pigeons in the skies, I'll bid farewell to pork and beans, and live on good pot pies." Pies filled with squab, the juvenile pigeon, were frequently served when Benjamin Franklin visited Thomas Jefferson at Monticello.

Unfortunately the passion for squabs, the wholesale slaughter of the birds, the destruction of habitat, and perhaps the pigeon's own biological need for large nesting colonies caused a catastrophic collapse of the passenger pigeon population by 1880. The last passenger pigeon died at the Cincinnati Zoo in Ohio in 1914.

[**See also** POULTRY AND FOWL.]

BIBLIOGRAPHY
Niles (Michigan) *Republican*, Apr. 29, 1843. In *Passenger Pigeon Records*, comp. Jon Wuepper, Berrien County, MI, 2001. http://www.ulala.org/P_Pigeon/NewPaper.html.

SYLVIA LOVEGREN

Passover

The Jewish festival of Passover (Pesach) falls in spring, after the first full moon following the vernal equinox. Passover, a weeklong festival, commemorates the flight of the Hebrews from slavery in Egypt. This celebration has special significance in the United States, traditionally a haven from persecution for Jews as for many others. For this reason Passover is the best-known Jewish holiday in the wider community.

Symbolic foods are eaten at all Jewish festivals, but in the case of Passover, they are part of the story. When Pharaoh finally let the Hebrews go, they had to leave so quickly that there was no time to let the bread rise before baking. They carried the dough on their backs, so it baked in the heat of the sun. Therefore only unleavened bread, known as matzo, may be eaten for the eight days of the festival. All leaven (*hametz*) is forbidden during Passover. This directive includes not only yeast-risen and fermented foods but also others that might be liable to ferment. Beer and whisky are banned but not wine. Among Orthodox Jews not only must every food product be kosher for Passover but toothpaste and even cleaning agents, such as pan scourers and detergents, must be guaranteed leaven free.

On the day before the festival, a ceremony is performed called the examination of the leaven (*bedikat hametz*), in which any bread crumbs found are burned. The highlight of Passover is the communal meal of family and friends held on Passover Eve, the first night of the festival, and among Orthodox Ashkenazic Jews also on the second night; the meal is called the seder (order). Certain foods, referred to in the Haggadah, the order of service used for the occasion, must be present on the seder table. These foods include a bitter herb (*maror*), usually horseradish; a roasted lamb or chicken bone (*pesakh*) to symbolize the burned offerings made in the Temple; a roasted egg (*beitza*); a sweet herb, usually parsley; and a paste called *haroset*, made with honey, apples, almonds, and wine, to represent the mortar used by the Hebrew slaves to bind bricks. Three ceremonial pieces of matzo are also on the table symbolizing the three layers of ancient Jewish society: Cohanim (high priests), Leviim (Levites, priests), and Israel (everyone else). Half of the middle cake, known as the *afikoman*, from the Greek word for dessert, is hidden by the organizer of the seder. The other item on the table is a bowl of saltwater to represent the tears shed by the Israelites. At certain points during the seder service, pieces of matzo are passed around, in one case eaten with parsley, in another eaten dipped in saltwater, in a third eaten as a sandwich with horseradish, and in a fourth eaten with *haroset*. Four ritual glasses of wine are drunk. Persian Jews "whip" each other with scallions (green onions) at one point to symbolize the scourges and whips of the Egyptians. Ashkenazic Jews begin the meal with a hard-cooked egg in saltwater. The egg is a sign of mourning and of the spring (renewal and the life cycle). Soup containing *kneidlach*, matzo dumplings or matzo balls, is essential. After the meal, there is a hunt for the *afikoman*. In some families the parents hide it for the children to find, but

This Horowitz Margareten matzo advertisement appeared in the March 13, 1953, newsletter of Congregation Shaare Zedek, New York.

nowadays it is mainly the children who hide it from their parents or the host of the seder. In either case, the adults reward the children with prizes.

A communal seder banquet may also be held at a synagogue or a hotel. As a communal feast celebrating freedom from slavery, the format was loosely adopted by African Americans for the Kwanzaa holiday.

[**See also** JEWISH AMERICAN FOOD; JEWISH DIETARY LAWS; MATZO.]

BIBLIOGRAPHY
Amster, Linda, ed. *The New York Times Passover Cookbook.* New York: Morrow, 1999.
Nathan, Joan. *The Children's Jewish Holiday Kitchen.* New York: Schocken, 1995.

JOSEPHINE BACON

Pasta, *see Italian American Food*

Pasties

Also called "Cornish pasties" or "Cousin Jack pasties," pasties (pronounced PASS-tee or PAHS-tee) are beef-and-vegetable-filled pastries originally eaten by mine workers as a warm noontime meal. They were an ideal food for men working in deep, dark, damp mines. Pasties were brought to America in the mid-nineteenth century from Cornwall, England, by immigrant mine workers. At that time, though depleted tin mines in Cornwall were closing, new mines were opening in America: copper and iron mines in the Upper Peninsula of Michigan, iron mines in northeastern Minnesota, and lead mines in southwest Wisconsin.

Pasties were made at home by hand. First, flour, salt, shortening, and water were mixed to form a piecrust. Some recipes specified using inexpensive ground suet or lard for the shortening, which made a sturdy crust. The piecrust was divided into individual portions, and each portion was rolled out into a circle. Diced beef, sliced potatoes, rutabagas (or turnips), and onions were placed in layers on half of the piecrust and seasoned with salt and pepper. After the filling was dotted with suet or butter, the crust was folded into a semicircle, like a calzone or an empanada, and the edges were crimped. The miner's initials were carved in the crust for easy identification. The pasties were baked in a moderate oven for an hour, timed to finish as a miner left for work. To keep the pasty hot and clean until lunchtime, it was wrapped in oilskins, paper, and cloth. Pasties are primarily a Michigan-Wisconsin-Minnesota regional food. Specialty bakeries make and sell several sizes with various fillings. Pasties not only make good picnic fare but also sell by the thousands at church fund-raisers every month.

Pasties gained national and international recognition in the late twentieth century after they received prominent mention in two best-selling murder mysteries by Lilian Jackson Braun, *The Cat Who Played Brahms* and *The Cat Who Said Cheese*. In these stories, the protagonist prefers tourist-style pasties, ones made with flaky pastry, no turnips, and some juicy sauce.

[See also PASTRIES; PIES AND TARTS.]

BIBLIOGRAPHY

Clayton, Bernard, Jr. *Bernard Clayton's Cooking Across America: Cooking with More Than 100 of North America's Best Cooks and 250 of Their Favorite Recipes.* New York: Simon and Schuster, 1993.

ROBERT W. BROWER

Pastrami

"Pastrami" is a Yiddish word derived from the Romanian *pastram* (a preserved food), in turn from the Latin *parcere* (to save or be thrifty). It is a cured cut of beef, usually brisket, but plate and round are also used. Although not originally a specifically Jewish food, pastrami is exclusively Jewish in the United States (and unknown in other English-speaking Jewish communities). It is rarely home cured but is served in restaurants and available in supermarkets in Jewish neighborhoods. Because it is usually a preprepared dish, it is rarely mentioned in Jewish cookbooks or books about the history of Jewish food. As with so many traditional foods, there are variations in the preparation method in that the meat may be dry cured or soaked for several weeks in brine and spices, as is corned beef. However, in the case of pastrami, after salting, the meat is always smoked. The technique originated in Romania but spread throughout the former Ottoman Empire, where it was also used for curing pork. Indeed throughout the former Ottoman Empire, *pastrama*, *basturma*, or variations of these words can mean cured beef, cured ham, or bacon, depending on whether the community is Muslim or Christian. Pastrami was brought to the United States by Romanian Jews, most of whom immigrated following the Chişinău pogroms of 1903 and 1905.

Pastrami is made from a quality cut of boneless beef brisket, chuck, or round weighing at least three to five pounds. The surface of the meat must be rubbed with kosher (coarse) salt and with a spice mixture that includes brown sugar, garlic, black and white peppercorns, allspice berries, cinnamon stick, hot and mild paprika, bay leaves, and possibly coriander seeds and gingerroot. Naturally there are variations in the mixture. The meat is dry rubbed and refrigerated for seven to ten days; it must be turned frequently and rubbed with more mixture and more coarse salt. Pastrami can also be pickled in brine, flavored with the other pickling ingredients, in which case it should be left for around two weeks in a cool, dark place or in the refrigerator and turned every two days.

When the beef has been cured, it should be left to dry out in a cool, dark place for two days, then placed in a smoker and smoked according to the manufacturer's instructions. When ready, it should be wrapped in plastic wrap or vacuum packaging and refrigerated until ready for cooking.

To serve pastrami, rinse it with cold water to remove excess salt and place in a Dutch oven or casserole. Cover with four inches of unsalted water and bring to a boil. Simmer, but do not allow to boil hard, for two hours or until cooked through. Pastrami is best served hot, straight from the pot, but it can also be served cold. Pastrami is eaten in a sandwich, usually on rye bread, with pickles on the side or on a water or egg bagel with pickles and mustard. It can also be served as an entrée with latkes (potato pancakes) and coleslaw or sauerkraut. As a nod to the current obsession with lower-fat foods, turkey meat is now processed into pastrami.

[See also CORNED BEEF; JEWISH AMERICAN FOOD; JEWISH DIETARY LAWS; MEAT; PICKLING.]

BIBLIOGRAPHY

Bartlett, Jonathan. *The Cook's Dictionary and Culinary Reference: A Comprehensive, Definitive Guide to Cooking and Food.* Chicago: Contemporary Books, 1996.

JOSEPHINE BACON

Pastries

The term "pastry" traditionally denoted any sweet or savory dish that had "paste," a dense dough made from flour, fat, and liquid, as a key ingredient. Nowadays "pastry" loosely embraces most baked or fried sweet foods eaten for breakfasts, desserts, or snacks, regardless of whether paste is an element of the dish.

Classically paste is made only from flour, liquid, and fats such as butter (either melted or solid), lard, suet, and drippings. By the early twentieth century margarine, hydrogenated vegetable shortenings, and occasionally oils could be the tenderizing fat. The proportions of liquid and fat and the techniques for incorporating the fat into the flour determine the paste's flavor and texture. Occasionally pastries are yeasted, giving rise to "Danish,"

Two chefs prepare sweets in a pastry kitchen.

Making tarts at the Institute of Culinary Education.

croissants, and certain doughnuts, or chemically leavened, creating biscuits and scones.

Pastry shops opened in colonial America by the eighteenth century, often under the rubric "confectioner's," and sold sweets to the public as a luxury trade. However, many of the world's earliest pastries were savory. The first known written recipes, cuneiform-incised clay tablets dating to 1700 B.C.E. Mesopotamia, included birds served in pastry. By the Middle Ages, Europe had bustling pie markets, where "pastelers" pieced together "standing" pastes that could be filled with meats and baked, unsupported by a pan. The crust was often inedibly tough, for it was designed to serve as a vessel for cooking, serving, and storing the meats rather than as a crisp contrast to the filling.

Pastry making changed in the seventeenth century as sugar became more available and tenderizing butter entered fancier cookery. Baking dishes, made from earthenware or metal, also became increasingly common, supporting thinner and, importantly, edible crusts. The increasing complexity of pastry making resulted in a cottage industry of pastry teachers, who advertised classes in the colonies as early as 1731, as well as a plethora of pastry recipes in cookery books such as Hannah Glasse's *The Art of Cookery* (London, 1747; Alexandria, 1805). Her pastry recipes included puddings baked or boiled in paste (akin to custard-filled tarts), double-crust meat or fruit pies, and a relatively modern and delicate puff pastry.

Many of Glasse's savory pies reveal medieval roots: the upper crusts were removed during baking; gravy, wine, vinegar, or butter was poured in; and the crusts were replaced, to be removed at the table so the diner could exhume tidbits of venison, goose, oysters, or other savories from the pastry "coffins." These standing pies largely disappeared in nineteenth-century America, although traces linger in the Upper Peninsula of Michigan, where descendants from England's Cornwall continue to bake Cornish meat pasties, notorious for durable crusts that enabled miners to tote them into shafts. *Pâté en croûte*, a medieval holdover in which spiced, ground meat is baked in a dense paste, is still a classic preparation in traditional French restaurants and gourmet shops. By the mid-nineteenth century edible pastes were favored although by no means universal: the *American Home Cook Book* (1854) reminds readers that a particular pastry recipe for lining a meat pie mold "is intended to be eaten."

Less elegant than the molded pies were potpies, where stews were baked in pastry-lined pots and inverted onto a platter for serving. Fruits might replace the meaty stews to make dishes that were a staple of middle-class, working-class, and rural life. *The Kentucky Housewife* (1839) dubbed the inverted peach potpie a "cobbler," explaining it was "not a fashionable pie for company" but "very excellent for family use." Slumps are fruit cobblers that are not inverted but served directly from the baking dish, while pandowdies submerge the pastry crust in the cooking fruit juices, leading to a soft crust.

The great range of pastes sparked creative variations on the potpie theme. Dumplings lightened with eggs or biscuits might replace the paste lining in savory stews; a fruit version is the grunt, which buries fruits under a layer of grunts (an old-fashioned New England term for a dough somewhere between a dumpling and a biscuit) that is then covered and baked. Betties and crisps employ bread crumbs, cookie crumbs, or sweetened oats mixed with a bit of fat and liquid as the paste.

Savory pastries became appetizers and were miniaturized into hors d'oeuvres in the late nineteenth century. New pastries developed, such as the three variations on cheese straws found in *Mrs. Seeley's Cook Book* (1902), ideal for guests standing at twentieth-century cocktail parties who could nibble pastry-wrapped finger foods while holding a cocktail.

Virtually all immigrant groups have contributed pastries to American foodways. Signature ethnic specialties include fried Spanish churros sold as street food in Latino

A Brief Catalog of American Pies

Among pies' many varieties are those made from New World foods and uniquely part of the American repertory, such as pumpkin, squash, sweet potato, green tomato, pecan, blueberry, and cranberry. Florida's Key limes make a revered curd filling. Other pies that have evolved in decidedly American versions include creams (most popularly coconut, banana, and chocolate) and their cousins the chiffons (creams or fruit curds lightened with whipped egg whites); rhubarb (sometimes called "pie plant" and often combined with strawberries); shoofly, crumb, and gravel (Pennsylvania Dutch treats made with molasses, brown sugar, and cake or cookie crumbs); black bottom and Mississippi mud (chocolate custard layered with rum custard or cream cheese, respectively); vinegar and cider (nineteenth-century specialties from the Midwest and New England, respectively, in which egg custards were flavored with a healthy dose of vinegar or cider, used because of the expense of transporting lemons to the hinterland); and President Tyler pie, the most patriotically named of the "transparent" pies, made from a high proportion of sugar or corn syrup, butter, and eggs baked to a translucent gel. Confederate Jefferson Davis pie is a sweetened, spiced custard, sometimes containing dried fruits and nuts, lightened with or covered by meringue. It is similar to the South's beloved chess pie, both of which have discernible British ancestors, although the thick layer of meringue topping is an American tradition. Buttermilk also was thickened into custard and baked in crust.

Mincemeat pies, mixtures of finely chopped meats (often including leftovers or variety meats such as tongue and heart), suet, vegetables, fruits, spices, and brandy, although originating in England, were so ubiquitous and had so many different recipes in the eighteenth and nineteenth centuries that they must be considered an essential American pie. When mince lost its suet and meat in the twentieth century, it was soon exiled to Thanksgiving and Christmas tables as a nostalgic "old-fashioned" dessert. Potato pies also originated in England but found ready acceptance in sweet and savory forms on colonial and nineteenth-century tables.

Boston cream pie and Martha Washington pie are misleadingly named, for they are actually layered cakes filled with pastry cream or raspberry jam, respectively. Angel pies, claimed by James Beard to be one of the most frequently printed pie recipes in the early to mid-twentieth century, take a bit of a nomenclature license as the crust for these "pies" is a meringue shell, which is filled with a lightened fruit curd. Moon pies similarly are cookies sandwiching a marshmallow filling.

[See also APPETIZERS; BREAKFAST FOODS; CRULLERS; DESSERTS; DUMPLINGS; MOON PIE; PASTIES; PIES AND TARTS; PUDDINGS.]

BIBLIOGRAPHY

LeDraoulec, Pascale. *American Pie: Slices of Life (and Pie) from America's Back Roads*. New York: HarperCollins, 2002.

McIntyre, Nancy Fair. *Cooking in Crust*. North Hollywood, CA: Gala Books, 1971. The state of savory pastries in the 1970s.

Time-Life Books. *Pies & Pastries*. The Good Cook series. Alexandria, VA: Time-Life Books, 1981.

Weaver, William Woys. *America Eats: Forms of Edible Folk Art*. New York: Harper and Row, 1989.

CATHY K. KAUFMAN

communities along with savory empanadas, cornmeal turnovers. Pennsylvania Dutch funnel cakes appear at fairs. Central Europeans introduced gossamer strudels, while Greeks use similar phyllo dough in nutty, honey-drenched baklava. French *chou* paste structures éclairs and cream puffs, while puff pastry is deliberately restrained in baking to yield crisp napoleons or allowed to explode for patty shells called vols-au-vents, literally, "soaring on the wind." Italian pastries include fried cannoli and baked *sfogliatelle*.

Pastries' digestibility has long been suspect. Sarah Josepha Hale's *The Good Housekeeper* (1841) intones, "Pies are more apt to prove injurious to persons of delicate constitutions than puddings, because of the indigestible nature of pastry." Warnings about obesity, saturated fats, and refined carbohydrates, the building blocks of calorie-dense pastries, fall on deaf ears: the commercial baking industry valued its annual output of fresh pies and pastries (excluding the large, separate category of frozen product) at over $2.5 billion in the late 1990s.

[See also APPETIZERS; PASTIES; PIES AND TARTS.]

BIBLIOGRAPHY

Belden, Louise Conway. *The Festive Tradition: Table Decoration and Desserts in America, 1650–1900.* New York: Norton, 1983.

Fertig, Judith M. *All-American Desserts.* Boston: Harvard Common, 2003.

LeDraoulec, Pascale. *American Pie: Slices of Life (and Pie) from America's Back Roads.* New York: HarperCollins, 2002.

McIntyre, Nancy Fair. *Cooking in Crust.* North Hollywood, CA: Gala Books, 1971.

Time-Life Books. *Pies & Pastries.* The Good Cook series. Alexandria, VA: Time-Life Books, 1981.

Weaver, William Woys. *America Eats: Forms of Edible Folk Art.* New York: Harper and Row, 1989.

CATHY K. KAUFMAN

Pawpaw

The North American pawpaw (*Asimina triloba*) has a well-established place in folklore and rural culture. "Way Down Yonder in the Pawpaw Patch" is an American folk song that was quite popular once, and fall hunting for pawpaws in the woods is still a cherished tradition for many rural families. Interest has grown in the pawpaw as a gourmet food.

Pawpaws grow wild in the understories of hardwood forests in the eastern United States, ranging from northern Florida to southern Ontario in Canada and as far west as eastern Nebraska. The fruit of the pawpaw can weigh from three or four ounces to a pound and may be borne singly or in clusters. Pawpaws are highly nutritious, with a strong aroma and a unique flavor that resembles a combination of banana, mango, and pineapple. Pawpaws are ripe when soft and are usually harvested from September to October across their native range. When ripe, skin color ranges from green to yellow and flesh color ranges from creamy white to shades of

orange. The fruit should be harvested prior to the first frost.

Pulp from the fruit can be eaten fresh or cooked. The flavor of the fruit can intensify when it is overripe, as with bananas, resulting in pulp that is excellent for use in cooking. The seed and skin are generally not eaten. Local delicacies made from fruit pulp include ice cream, compote, jam, pie, custard, and wine. In the early 2000s most fruits for sale were collected from wild stands in the forest and were sold mainly at farmers' markets, directly to restaurants, or through entrepreneurs on the Internet.

[See also FRUIT; FRUIT WINES.]

BIBLIOGRAPHY

Layne, D. R. "The All-American Pawpaw. Part 1: Revival Efforts May Bear Much 'Fruit.'" *Fruit Gardener* pp.12–14, May–June 1996.

Reich, Lee. "Pawpaw: Banana of the North." *Uncommon Fruits Worthy of Attention: A Gardener's Guide.* Reading, MA: Addison-Wesley, 1991.

KIRK W. POMPER AND
DESMOND R. LAYNE

Peaches and Nectarines

The peach and its smooth-skinned form, the nectarine, were once thought to be native to Persia since the Romans first imported the peach from Persia, giving rise to its botanical name, *Prunus persica*. In fact the fruit originated in China, where as early as 550 B.C.E. it was depicted in art and literature as a symbol of immortality. It still grows wild in eastern Asia, exhibiting many of the variant forms found in modern cultivars, including freestone and clingstone and white-, yellow-, and red-fleshed types. From south China comes the *pen-t'ao*, or flat-shaped peach, as well as the *mi-t'ao*, or honey peach, with its sweet, low-acid flavor. Nectarines were less common in China proper but flourished in

eastern Turkestan, an early extension of the peach's natural range. The Romans spread the peach throughout their empire, especially around the Mediterranean, where warm to hot summers favor ripening.

Introduction of the peach to America occurred during the period of European exploration and colonization in the New World, especially through the Spanish conquest of Mexico and exploration of Florida in the sixteenth century. The peach eventually naturalized and became wild in parts of Mexico, the American South, and the American Southwest, where the Indians cultivated various seedling strains called "Indian peaches," leading botanists several centuries later erroneously to suppose that the peach was a native of the New World. Most of these trees, including clingstones and red-fleshed peaches, were planted as seedlings through the mid-nineteenth century, but several named freestone varieties, such as Early Crawford, Late Crawford, and Oldmixon, also became popular. These peaches and others of their day were noted for their soft, juicy, delicate flesh with a tendency toward bruising. It was not until after the Civil War, when hybrids involving a strain of peach from northern China were introduced, that modern hybridization of peaches began in America.

In 1850 Charles Downing introduced the Chinese Cling variety, which led to the development of many standard American commercial varieties, such as Elberta, J. H. Hale, and Redhaven, all forerunners of modern hybrid peaches characterized by large, round shape; highly blushed skin; and firm, yellow flesh. These kinds of peaches are often harvested when they are not fully ripe so they can be packed and marketed with minimal bruising.

More recently there has been a resurgence of white-fleshed varieties of both peaches and nectarines. In the past white-fleshed fruits were often much too delicate for marketing

Label for Jones Yerkes peaches, circa 1867.

beyond the orchards where they were grown, but firm-fleshed hybrids, initially developed for export and ethnic markets, are showing up more and more in America's mainstream retail markets. These new white-fleshed types are often what are called "subacid" (properly "low-acid") types, having very sweet to mildly sweet flavor with little complementary acidity.

Also increasing in popularity are the so-called "flat" peaches shaped like a doughnut or a bagel; these distinctive fruits actually represent a revival of an ancient form, the favorite of Chinese emperors because they could eat around the pit without suffering the indignity of dripping juice onto their beards.

The clingstone is also a characteristic found among the older strains of peaches. The ripe flesh is often much firmer and less juicy than that of freestone peaches, and for this reason it is preferred by commercial canners because the fruit holds up better after processing. California growers have therefore specialized in the production of cling peaches to supply the state's large canning industry.

The newest trend in developing peaches for the fresh market is to incorporate the cling, or nonmelting, flesh characteristic into market peaches. Fruit breeders in Texas, Georgia, New Jersey, and Florida are developing new varieties that can be tree ripened yet remain firm enough to withstand the rigors of harvesting, shipping, and marketing.

Still others are looking back to the old heirloom varieties of peaches for old-fashioned flavor and juicy texture. Smaller artisanal growers are creating niche markets for these varieties that can be found mostly at fruit stands, farmers' markets, and specialty stores.

It seems that the English invented the word "nectarine" about the middle of the seventeenth century to distinguish the nectarine from the peach. This distinction has sometimes led to the assumption that the nectarine is a unique fruit, perhaps even a cross between a peach and a plum. In fact the nectarine is no more than a smooth-skinned peach, a single recessive gene (homozygous for smooth skin) separating it from the peach. In many Old World cultures there is no distinction beyond making reference to nectarines as "naked" or "hairless" peaches.

The older nectarine varieties imported from Europe to America were not of commercial quality, being smaller, often of poorer flavor, and more prone to rot and insect damage than peaches. It was not until the breeding work of Fred W. Anderson of California, the father of the modern nectarine, that commercial nectarine production was possible. In the 1940s and 1950s Anderson developed many new varieties that were much larger and better in quality for the fresh market. California now leads the nation in the production of the nectarine, and it may overtake the peach in volume of California production because of consumers' preference for fuzzless skin.

While the nectarine finds its special domain in California and in parts of the Northwest and Florida, the peach is adaptable to a wide range of climates, and commercial production exists along the Pacific coast, the eastern seaboard, and the Gulf States from as far north as Michigan to as far south as Florida. Some varieties are extremely cold hardy, while others require little winter chill and can be grown in subtropical climates. Among the minimum requirements for growing peaches, however, are the need for heat during the growing season to ripen the fruit satisfactorily and the need to protect trees from hard freezes and spring frosts, which can destroy a crop or even kill trees.

Both peaches and nectarines are excellent when consumed fresh. They also have many culinary uses, mainly as desserts but also in pickling and in chutneys and preserved in brandy.

Both fruits are high in vitamins A and C and have fewer calories than apples and pears. For dessert, they are great in compotes, ice creams, smoothies, jams, and pastries. Indeed peach cobbler rivals traditional apple pie as the classic all-American dessert.

[See also CALIFORNIA; FRUIT.]

BIBLIOGRAPHY

Janick, Jules, and James N. Moore, eds. *Fruit Breeding*. New York: Wiley, 1996.

Okie, W. R. *A Handbook of Peach and Nectarine Varieties: Performance in the Southeastern United States and Index of Names*. Washington, DC: U.S. Department of Agriculture, Agricultural Research Service, 1998.

ANDREW MARIANI

Peach Melba

Peach Melba is a dessert traditionally composed of fresh peaches, vanilla ice cream, and a sweetened raspberry puree. Its origin is credited to the legendary chef Auguste Escoffier. Various stories have circulated as to how and when he invented it. All versions agree that the dish was named after the Australian opera diva Helen Porter Mitchell, whose stage name was Nellie Melba. She frequently appeared in Covent Garden during the 1890s and the early 1900s and ate at Escoffier's restaurants in London. Escoffier states that he thought up this dessert when the Hotel Ritz was opened in Paris in 1905 but that he first served it at the Carlton Hotel, opened in London in July 1906. However, the first located printed use of the dish dates to 1904, and Edith Wharton mentions "Peches a La Melba" in her novel *The House of Mirth*, first published in 1905. Whatever the date of its origin, it was served in restaurants in the United States during the early twentieth century, and the dish remains the most popular peach dessert in America.

Melba toast, a thin, crisp slice of toasted or baked bread, and Melba sauce, a sweetened puree of fresh raspberries and red currant jelly frequently used on peach Melba, are also credited to Escoffier and are named after Nellie Melba. The circumstances of their inventions also remain confused. Melba toast is manufactured in the United States by many companies, such as Nabisco and Old London Foods. It is served with soups and salads and often as an appetizer topped with melted cheese or other products; it is a favorite of dieters.

[See also DESSERTS.]

BIBLIOGRAPHY

Willan, Anne. *Great Cooks and Their Recipes: From Taillevent to Escoffier*. Boston: Little, Brown, 1992.

ANDREW F. SMITH

Peach Parers and Stoners

Because the immediate pleasure of eating a ripe peach is delayed by peeling, we can sympathize with the words of a certain 1872 editorial writer: "A continuous and urgent inquiry for a machine for Paring Peaches has been ringing in our ears…for five years." He then praised the cast-iron, cranked Lightning Peach Parer, which had been manufactured by an apple-parer company since 1869. A parer that did not waste the fruit was desirable for canneries and home cooks. Merchants' price sheets in the 1860s quoted peeled-peach prices that were twice those for unpeeled.

Also important is removing the pit or stone. Several devices that were available from the 1860s to 1900 pushed the pit out by force with a plunger. Another type, a sort of curved knife, came in different sizes for different pits. With this device, one would first cut the peach in half and then slip the blade around the pit and cut it out. Even in canneries this method was used as recently as the 1930s.

[See also PEACHES AND NECTARINES.]

BIBLIOGRAPHY

Franklin, Linda Campbell. *300 Years of Kitchen Collectibles*. 5th ed. Iola, WI: Krause Publications, 2003.

LINDA FRANKLIN

Peanuts

There is something quintessentially American about peanuts. While people in other areas of the world eat them, nowhere else are they devoured in so many diverse ways or with the same gusto as in the United States. The peanut (*Arachis hypogaea*) originated in the Guarani region of Paraguay, eastern Bolivia, and central Brazil. In pre-Columbian times peanuts were disseminated throughout South America, the Caribbean, and Mexico. When European explorers arrived in the New World, they discovered peanuts and introduced them to Africa, where they were quickly adopted, particularly for use as food in the slave trade. Through the slave trade, peanuts were introduced into the British North American colonies, where they were grown by slaves in

Fig. 1255 (25-28)

A hand-turned peanut roaster and warmer.

culinary potential. Beginning in 1916 George Washington Carver popularized the peanut. His efforts greatly increased peanut consumption in America.

Peanuts are used in soups, salads, and confections as well as in peanut flour, bread, cookies, cakes, and biscuits. Other peanut dishes are local specialties, such as boiled peanuts in some of the U.S. southern states. Finally, peanuts are also a major source of oil, which is a common ingredient in many processed foods.

Modern Peanut Industry

During the late nineteenth century three major peanut companies were launched. The first was started by two Italian immigrants who specialized in roasted peanuts. They named their company Planters Peanuts. In 1917 they created "Mr. Peanut," which became an American culinary icon within a few years. The second company was initiated by John Harvey Kellogg, who popularized peanut butter beginning in 1894. During the early twentieth century peanut butter companies were started in many medium-size cities in the United States. Peanuts are often employed in making candy. Several of the most popular candies include peanuts, such as Baby Ruth bars, Reese's Peanut Butter Cups, Butterfingers, Clark candy bars, and Peanut M&M's.

During the last decade of the twentieth century, American peanut production hovered between 3.6 and 4.9 billion bushels annually. By 2002 peanuts ranked eighth among primary field crops produced in the United States, with an average farm value of $1.2 billion. The American retail market for peanuts and peanut products totaled $2.5 billion annually at the dawn of the 2000s, when consumption had increased 2 to 3 percent over the last few years of the twentieth century.

[See also Candy Bars and Candy; Carver, George Washington; Fats and Oils; Health Food; Kellogg, John Harvey; Mr. Peanut; Peanut Butter; Sandwiches; Snacks, Salty; Vegetarianism.]

BIBLIOGRAPHY

American Peanut Research and Education Association. *Peanuts—Culture and Uses: A Symposium.* Stillwater, OK: American Peanut Research and Education Association, 1973.

Carver, George Washington. *How to Grow the Peanut and 105 Ways of Preparing It for Human Consumption.* Bulletin 31. Tuskegee, AL: Experiment Station, Tuskegee Institute, 1925.

Smith, Andrew F. "Peanut Butter: A Vegetarian Food That Went Awry." *Petits Propos Culinaires* 65 (Sept. 2000): 60–72.

Smith, Andrew F. *Peanuts: The Illustrious History of the Goober Pea.* Urbana: University of Illinois Press, 2002.

ANDREW F. SMITH

Peanut Butter

For centuries peanuts have been ground and consumed by indigenous peoples of South America and by Africans, but peanut butter was not popularized in America until the

Peanut Butter

441

their gardens. Although some white children and teenagers consumed peanuts occasionally at Christmas, they were mainly considered a trash food inappropriate for "genteel" society.

Peanut Cookery and Uses

By the 1830s peanuts had entered mainstream cooking, and recipes featuring them began to appear in cookbooks. Peanut cookery probably was introduced into Philadelphia by French Creole refugees, who had settled there after escaping the 1791 slave insurrection in Haiti. Recipes for peanut cakes and other peanut dishes were featured in cookbooks a few decades later. Eliza Leslie's *Directions for Cookery* (1837), for instance, included a recipe for "Cocoa-nut Maccaroons" with peanuts. Subsequently similar recipes were published by many other authors. The first cookbook printed in the South that contained peanut recipes was Sarah Rutledge's *Carolina Housewife* (1847). Her peanut soup recipe likely derived from African culinary traditions.

The American Civil War (1861–1865) greatly accelerated the adoption of peanuts throughout the United States. When the war broke out, white southerners soon discovered the peanut's value as the northern blockade prevented the importation of goods to the South. Peanut oil was used as a substitute for whale oil in southern industry. At least four factories were established in the South to convert peanuts into oil, which was used as a lubricant for industrial machinery and railroad locomotives. Southern housewives substituted peanut oil for lard as shortening in bread and pastry and for olive oil in salad dressings. Peanuts were ground to make beverages served as a substitute for coffee and chocolate.

When northern armies occupied the peanut-growing areas, Union soldiers were introduced to this "new" food. After the war, peanut cultivation skyrocketed, and peanuts became a fad food throughout the country. Peanuts were mainly consumed roasted in the shell as a snack food at fairs, circuses, and other social events, but cooks and chefs soon began exploring the peanut's broader

Derby Foods in Chicago printed this ad in Peter Pan Peanut Butter in Your Diet.

vegetarian John Harvey Kellogg endorsed it as a substitute for "cow's butter." In the early 1890s Kellogg crushed various nuts between two rollers and claimed the results to be "nut butters." At the time peanuts were less expensive than nuts, and they soon became the most significant "nut" butter. Kellogg was an excellent promoter. He extolled the virtues of peanut butter throughout the nation. To commercialize his discovery, Kellogg created the Sanitas Nut Food Company and placed his brother, Will Kellogg, in charge. Nut butters quickly became a fad among other health-food manufacturers in America. Vegetarians adopted peanut butter, and recipes for making and using it appeared in almost all vegetarian cookbooks from 1899 on.

Dainty tearooms and upper-class restaurants proudly announced that peanut butter was an ingredient in numerous salads, soups, and entrées. Confectioners made candy with peanut butter fillings. Peanut butter recipes filled cookery magazines and cookbooks. Among its earliest and most common uses was in making sandwiches; by 1900 the peanut butter sandwich had quickly spread throughout the United States. Peanut butter sandwiches were also filled with a variety of other foods, such as raisins, jelly, marmalade, cheese, cucumbers, grapefruit, celery, apricots, dates, bacon, and bananas. Peanut butter sandwiches moved down the class structure as the price of peanut butter declined, owing to the commercialization of the industry. They took another leap forward, however, during the Depression, when this low-cost sandwich spread became one of the top luncheon items.

Within two decades of its invention, peanut butter was being manufactured in virtually every large and middle-size city in America. Since the 1920s, however, the peanut butter industry has become centralized, and three companies dominated the peanut butter market by the early 2000s. The first was launched by Joseph L. Rosefield of Alameda, California, in 1922. He developed a process of hydrogenation of peanut butter, which prevented oil separation, made spoilage less likely, and increased the shelf life of peanut butter. Rosefield selected the name Skippy for his new product. The second major peanut manufacturer was the E. K. Pond Company, which began to manufacture peanut butter in 1920. Its sales were limited until the company changed the name of its peanut butter to Peter Pan. The third was Procter and Gamble, which introduced Jif in 1958. In the early twenty-first century Procter and Gamble operated the world's largest peanut butter plant, churning out 250,000 jars every day.

Peanut butter was born at the end of the nineteenth century as a health and vegetarian food, but by the 1920s it was a major mainstream staple used in recipes for many types of food, from soups, salads, and sauces to desserts and snacks of every description. Few other products in American culinary history have achieved such influence in so many ways in such a short period of time. In the early years of the twenty-first century, peanut butter was ensconced in 85 percent of the kitchens of America.

[See also CANDY BARS AND CANDY; HEALTH FOOD; KELLOGG, JOHN HARVEY; SANDWICHES; VEGETARIANISM.]

BIBLIOGRAPHY

Smith, Andrew F. "Peanut Butter: A Vegetarian Food That Went Awry." *Petits Propos Culinaires* 65 (Sept. 2000): 60–72.

Smith, Andrew F. *Peanuts: The Illustrious History of the Goober Pea*. Urbana: University of Illinois Press, 2002.

ANDREW F. SMITH

Pears

The pear is among the several fruits whose origins are attributed to the Caucasus and Elburz mountains of western Asia and that spread in the footsteps of Caucasian civilization to all the temperate zones. Pears arrived in seventeenth-century eastern America chiefly as seeds or seedlings; improved stocks and named varieties as scions and dormant trees did not come to the colonies until the mid-eighteenth century. Thus the American colonies had evolved their own pear varieties for some 150 years, outside the influence of English and Continental sources.

Progress in developing a good eating pear suitable for American conditions was slow, not least because the initial genetic material was most likely perry pear seedlings from the West Country of England. These made up in vigor for what they lacked in fruit quality; the trees grew well despite long tropical summers and arctic winters, not the conditions dessert pears experience in western Europe.

By 1750 the American colonies had evolved numerous pear varieties local to the three chief centers of horticulture: the neighborhoods of Boston, Long Island, and the hinterland of Philadelphia. An industry in perry, the drink of fermented pear juice, had developed, but it was a small trade compared with that in cider, the comparable ferment of apples, which grew much more readily everywhere in the colonies. Perry has never developed any commercial importance in America, which seems odd since the origin of American pear commerce lay in perry pears.

Most notable and still foremost among the early American pears was Seckel, a small fruit that ripens in mid-autumn, originating perhaps from Rousselette or perry pear seed and recovered circa 1780 from the near-wild in Pennsylvania. Seckel has been the parent of many varieties of small pears of quality in America from the early nineteenth century to the present. It is the country's most versatile pear and is suitable for conditions in all the Middle Atlantic states and along the northern Atlantic seaboard.

The variety known as Bartlett is a late-colonial introduction from England by scion or dormant tree. It is the eighteenth-century English variety Williams Bon Crétien and was "discovered" in 1817 in the orchard of Enoch Bartlett in Massachusetts, propagated by many nurserymen in the succeeding decades, and subsequently sold bearing his name. It is known in all the rest of the world under its original and true name. Seckel and Bartlett were the chief pears of the nineteenth-century American market. Other varieties were commercially successful to the degree that they approximated these two, at least in appearance; furthermore, under American conditions, trees of Seckel and to a lesser degree of Bartlett have a survival rate superior to that of European imports. Hence Seckel and Bartlett were the most important parents of modern pears, and introductions of greater merit from Europe never approached their commercial success.

Among the most lasting of nineteenth-century European varieties were Doyenné du Comice and Beurré Bosc—the former a luxury winter fruit, the latter a coarse, sweet fruit resistant to both the insults of machine handling and the climate of the eastern states. Beurré d'Anjou is an undistinguished but nearly indestructible fruit in controlled

Ripe pears.

atmosphere storage, from which it is available nearly year-round.

Fire blight, a bacterial disease first noticed in the Hudson Valley in New York State about 1780, spread rapidly in the United States starting in the 1860s. A ferocious devourer of entire pear trees, especially in climates with warm, humid spring and summer seasons, fire blight devastated the pear orchards of the eastern states. Thereafter commercial pear growing shifted to the three states of the Pacific coast, where the disease was not so destructive.

Modern Production and Uses

In the early twenty-first century, Bartlett pears come from the counties of Sacramento, Mendocino, and Lake in California. The largest production of main-crop pears, however, comes from the high-desert districts of central Washington, chiefly bulk Bartlett, Beurré d'Anjou bound for cold storage, Beurré Bosc, and various red-skinned mutations of common varieties, which have had novelty value. Most sought are the Bartlett and related types from the Hood River district and Doyenné du Comice from the Rogue River district of Oregon. Winter Nelis has vanished from American production, and only Beurré Hardy (under the generic name French Butter Pear) has a limited following among pear fanciers. It is unfortunate that meritorious cultivars such as Gorham, Magness, Beurré Superfin, and Belle Lucrative, though no more costly to produce than Bartlett, are not found in American markets. Purely culinary varieties, such as are sold in Europe for cooking, are unknown in America.

Many, perhaps most, Americans are unaware that pears are to be eaten after softening and indeed treat the pear as an odd-shaped, coarse, and gritty variant of the apple. Thus pears have found no place in institutional feeding or in popular culture. American culinary skill has been applied to preserving pears, however, and tinned Bartlett pears and Bartlett juice are the basis for the truly American invention, the fruit cocktail. Occasional culinary use of whole-pear preserves, chutneys, and dried pears in various forms can be observed in the American home, and there is a small trade in dried Bartlett pears from California. In these uses the pears must be still firm, or they will decompose in processing. Pears appear occasionally in open tarts, according to European principles and recipes. In the early 2000s, the most important industrial use of pears has been for juice, as a highly concentrated syrup to serve as a sweetener of "sugarless" breakfast cereals and confectioneries and as a neutral base for various "all-fruit" beverages.

Nashi and Li

Close relatives of the pear are the *nashi* of Japan and the *li* of China, complex hybrids of several centuries' standing among the species *Pyrus pyrifolia*, *P. ussuriensis*, and *P. bretschneideri*, quite distinct from both pear and apple. The *nashi* are round, coarse, and juicy fruits of late summer and autumn—often with more or less russet skin, which is invariably peeled before consumption of the fruit. The flavor of *nashi* is refreshing but rarely complex and quite ruined by heat, so the fruit has no culinary use except as a canned product. Favorite varieties are Nijiseiki (Twentieth Century), Shinseiki (New Century), and Hosui. Both *nashi* and *li* are produced and common in California, whence they are dispatched to Asian markets elsewhere in America. The fruits of *li* are elongated and pear-shaped with clear green to yellow skin. *Li* are the nearest rivals to apples in the world production of fruits. Practically unknown outside China, where they are ubiquitous, *li* (in the forms Ya Li and Tsu Li) are grown in the Western world chiefly in California. *Nashi* and *li* are unflatteringly called "apple pears" and "sand pears" in the rest of the United States.

Nashi is better appreciated as one parent, with the European pear, of the true Asian pears. These hybrids have inherited resistance to fire blight from *nashi* and are common in the southern states and the Midwest of the United States in the varieties Kieffer, Le Conte, and Pineapple, which are truly impervious, as both tree and fruit, in those climates. The hybrid Asian pears are in common use for home canning while immature, though if they are allowed to ripen on the tree in a long season, the fruits can develop a most extraordinary aroma and a near-melting texture approaching that of the true pear and become a legitimate contribution to the dessert repertoire of American fruits. Indeed these hybrids are among the few truly American contributions to the tree fruits.

[**See also** CONDIMENTS; FRUIT; FRUIT JUICES; PIES AND TARTS; PRESERVES; SWEETENERS.]

BIBLIOGRAPHY

Hedrick, U. P. *The Pears of New York*. Albany, NY: New York Agricultural Experiment Station, 1921.

TODD KENNEDY

Peas

The pea (*Pisum sativum*) is a legume domesticated in prehistoric times in western Asia. Peas can be divided into two categories: sweet or green peas, which can be eaten raw or briefly cooked, and field peas, which are dried for storage and require fairly long simmering to soften and cook them. Peas were widely distributed throughout the Old World in ancient times, and field peas were commonly eaten by the Greeks and Romans.

Peas did not become an important food in England until after the Norman Conquest in 1066. Thereafter, for the lower class, pea soup or gruel was a staple dish for hundreds of years. For the upper class, peas with salt pork was considered a fashionable dish to be consumed at feasts.

Both field and green peas were introduced into America by European explorers and colonists in the early seventeenth century. At first dried peas were used in soups, porridges, and puddings; during the nineteenth century fresh peas were served as a side dish with poultry and meat. Since green peas are among the earliest vegetables picked from the garden, they became a symbol of the advent of summer.

Notably among vegetable recipes in the nineteenth century, instructions for cooking peas often included an admonition not to overcook them. Usually peas were simply boiled and served up with butter, but the French cooked them cloaked in layers of lettuce leaves, and English- and Spanish-style recipes also appeared. Peas were incorporated into omelets, soufflés, dumplings, fritters, and salads. Green peas, with their delicate flavor and short growing season, were popular fodder for home canners. Field peas were dried, and directions were given for converting them into powder. Split peas (they split naturally after drying) became popular for soup making because they cook much faster than whole dried peas.

Bliss's American wonder pea, from Aaron Low's Retail Seed Catalogue and Garden Manual, *1887.*

Peas were among the first vegetables to be canned commercially. By the late nineteenth century peas, along with corn and tomatoes, ranked highest in sales among canned foods. Peas were first frozen in the 1920s, but they did not become popular until the 1950s.

The edible-podded peas, such as snow peas, were introduced to the American table by Asian Americans in the twentieth century and have become mainstream enough that they are now sold frozen. Snow peas are not shelled; rather, both their crisp, flat pods and their diminutive peas are cooked and eaten. Sugar snaps, introduced in the 1970s, have fleshy pods and peas that grow comparatively large while remaining sweet; they are eaten whole, either raw or cooked.

[**See also** CANNING AND BOTTLING; SOUPS AND STEWS.]

BIBLIOGRAPHY
Unwin, Charles W. J. *Sweet Peas: Their History, Development, Culture.* New York: Appleton, 1926.

ANDREW F. SMITH

Pecans

The word "pecan" originated from the Algonquian *paccan*, but its pronunciation is somewhat controversial. In the northern United States it is pronounced "**pee**-kan," with the accent on the first syllable. To southerners this pronunciation evokes a mildly scatological image ("pee can"), and they therefore pronounce it with the accent on the second syllable: "puh-**kahn**" or "puh-**kan**."

Pecan trees (*Carya illinoinensis*) are indigenous to a roughly south-north rectangle extending from the Gulf of Mexico to southern Illinois and Iowa, covering the valley of the Mississippi River, its tributaries, and the major rivers of Texas and Oklahoma. There are also several areas in northern Mexico where pecan trees are indigenous.

Native Americans had been eating pecans and using them as stew thickeners for several millennia before the arrival of Europeans. The first European to encounter pecans was the Spanish explorer Álva Núñez Cabeza de Vaca, who traveled along the northern shores of the Gulf of Mexico and adjacent hinterlands in 1528.

The French colonization of Louisiana at the end of the seventeenth century resulted in a pecan confection called "pralines," which still are sold all over New Orleans. In the eighteenth century pecans were taken to the northeastern colonies by fur traders who obtained them from the Illinois Indians of southern Illinois, Missouri, and Arkansas. The fur traders called these nuts "Indian nuts" or "Illinois nuts." These nuts subsequently came to the attention of F. A. J. Von Wangenheim, a Hessian forester who served with the troops hired by King George III to squelch the rebellious colonists led by George Washington. It was Wangenheim who, in recognition of their common name

"Illinois nuts," gave pecans their species name *illinoinensis*.

Pecans grow on stately trees up to seventy to one hundred feet in height and forty to seventy-five feet wide and have smooth, relatively thin shells, generally ovoid in shape and three-quarters of an inch to two inches long. The kernel somewhat resembles an elongated walnut, but its taste is much milder, with a distinct trace of sweetness.

In the second half of the nineteenth century, pecans were grown primarily in Texas and Louisiana, and trade in pecans was somewhat limited because trees grown from seed yielded unpredictable results, since seedlings are not exact copies of the parent tree. The development of successful cultivars through budding or grafting changed all that. The first grafts were achieved in 1846 or 1847 by a slave named Antoine who was owned by J. J. Roman, a Louisiana plantation owner. While Antoine's success had very little effect on the industry, the work of Emil Bourgeois, starting in 1877 on the Rapidan Plantation in Louisiana, resulted in wide acceptance of the vegetative propagation of pecan trees and laid the foundation for modern pecan orchards.

At the end of the nineteenth century, tree nurseries used Bourgeois's techniques to develop cultivars that combined good taste, large kernel size, high yield, and resistance to insects, diseases, and adverse climatic conditions and, of great importance for economical harvesting, enabled the simultaneous maturing of all the nuts on the tree. It was this development that triggered the start-up of pecan orchards in Georgia and led to that state's twenty-first-century position as the largest producer of pecans from cultivars, with Texas being the largest producer of pecans from the combined harvests of cultivars and seedlings. The main uses for pecans are in raw nut mixtures, confections, and pastries. Pecan pie is a popular and, unlike apple pie, truly all-American dessert.

[**See also** NUTS.]

BIBLIOGRAPHY
Manaster, Jane. *The Pecan Tree.* Austin: University of Texas Press, 1994.
Sparks, Darrell. *Pecan Cultivars: The Orchard's Foundation.* Watkinsville, GA: Pecan Production Innovations, 1992.

EDGAR ROSE

Pennell, Elizabeth

Elizabeth Robins Pennell (1855–1936) could not cook, yet she wrote a newspaper cookery column for five years, authored two books related to cooking, and amassed an extensive collection of rare cookbooks, which is the second largest of the holdings in the Rare Book and Special Collections Division of the Library of Congress.

Pennell, a resident of London from 1884 through World War I, was born in Philadelphia. After the death of her mother, Elizabeth's father sent both Elizabeth and her

sister to a Catholic convent outside Philadelphia. Pennell remained there until her graduation in 1872; she then moved to her father's home and reluctantly acceded to her family's demands to blend into Philadelphia's social milieu. A reacquaintance with her uncle, Charles Godfrey Leland, a journalist with ties to the intellectual community of writers and artists in the United States and Europe, stimulated her imagination and introduced her to a world outside of Philadelphia. Under his tutelage Pennell began to write.

A commission to do a story about Philadelphia led to her introduction to the illustrator and graphic artist Joseph Pennell. Within a few days of their meeting, Elizabeth and Joseph began a lifetime collaboration that led to marriage. A commission in 1884 from *Century Magazine* sent the Pennells to London. They remained there for thirty years, enjoying the company of notable artists and writers and working together on books.

Although Elizabeth Pennell admitted that she could not boil an egg, she agreed to write weekly cookery essays for the *Pall Mall Gazette*, a London newspaper. Her column ran for five years and launched her culinary career. A selection of some of the best essays was published in 1896 as *The Feasts of Autolycus* (later changed to *The Delights of Delicate Eating*). The book broke new ground in venturing beyond the details of recipes to the delights of dining; one reviewer considered it "one of the wisest and wittiest of the literary products of the famous [18]90s." It set the stage for cookery books filled with wit, wisdom, and humor.

Pennell was far ahead of her time in urging women to take pride in mastering their role in the kitchen and, as she wrote in *The Delights of Delicate Eating*, to "be bold, defy convention." *Delights*, with its descriptions of local dishes in Europe and America and tidbits of historical information, gives a unique glimpse into the nineteenth-century world of cookery.

Pennell stumbled into her career as a serious cookbook collector when a friend presented her with a copy of Alexandre Dumas's *Le grand dictionnaire de cuisine*. From its pages Pennell helped herself to dishes and menus that would amuse and instruct her readers. To enhance her essays and not bore her followers with Dumas, Pennell bought a few more cookbooks and began to seriously collect. She recounts her collecting activities and describes the books in *My Cookery Books* (1903).

The large Library of Congress collection, which includes such rarities as *Apicus de re Coquinaria* (1498) and *Acetaria: A Discourse of Sallets* (1699), enables scholars to pursue centuries of culinary cuisine and is a significant contribution to culinary history. Originally comprising over 1,000 books, Pennell's collection suffered water damage during World War I and now includes 433 cookbooks and

299 books on other topics, such as fine printing, bibliography, and literature.

[**See also** Cookbooks and Manuscripts: 1970s to the Present; Cookbooks and Manuscripts: To 1860; Cookbooks and Manuscripts: From World War I to World War II; Library Collections.]

BIBLIOGRAPHY

Beck, Leonard N. *Two Loaf-Givers; or, A Tour through the Gastronomic Libraries of Katherine Golden Bitting and Elizabeth Robins Pennell*. Washington, DC: Library of Congress, 1984.

Pennell, Elizabeth Robins. *The Delights of Delicate Eating*. Originally published as *The Feasts of Autolycus*; reprinted with an introduction to Pennel's life and career by Jacqueline Block Williams. Urbana: University of Illinois Press, 2000.

JACQUELINE BLOCK WILLIAMS

Pennsylvania Dutch Food

The largest non-British ethnic group at the time of the American Revolution was a body of German-speaking citizens who made up about 10 percent of the population of the British North American colonies and as much as one-third of the population of Pennsylvania. The community is usually dated from the 1681 arrival of fourteen Mennonite families to found Germantown, Pennsylvania, but may include some descendants of German speakers from the older New Netherlands colony. The name was an Anglicized version of their "Dietsch" dialect of Deutsch.

The Pennsylvania Dutch came from many parts of the German-speaking world and belonged to many Protestant pietistic sects as well as mainstream Lutheran and Reformed churches. The largest groups came after 1710 from the Palatinate (Rhinepfalz) region of western Germany. They moved into inland valley farms up and down the Appalachians and eventually across them to Ohio and Indiana. They were joined by Moravians settling around Winston-Salem, North Carolina, and Bethlehem, Pennsylvania, and by as many as ten thousand Hessian deserters during the American Revolution. The Pennsylvania Germans were regarded by other colonists and early Americans as thrifty and wise farmers though sometimes caricatured for stinginess, backwardness, and a mixture of Low German and accented English speech. Their food was noted for the quality of the farm produce, dairy products, and baked goods before the American Revolution, and it still is.

Pennsylvania Dutch food includes many items that have become part of the American mainstream (such as casseroles, whoopee pies, pretzels, potato salad, and the chicken noodle soup known in the nineteenth century as *rivvel* soup), others that are widely consumed but still understood as Pennsylvania Dutch or German food (such as apple butter, scrapple, sauerkraut, and shoo-fly pie), and some that have never really crossed over the ethnic line (such as *bouva shenkel*, a kind of ravioli). In addition the typical foods of the Pennsylvania Dutch include pickles and pies that were at one time mainstream American dishes but have been dropped by other populations (such as Montgomery pie and raisin or "funeral" pie).

Like colonial New Englanders, Pennsylvania Dutch cooks had bake ovens and were known to serve pie at every meal and sometimes with every course. Although not every dinner included the proverbial "seven sweets and seven sours," the Pennsylvania Dutch table has always included a number of condiments, such as nicely made preserves and pickles, horseradish, and mustard. The medieval German palate of sweet-and-sour still runs through much Pennsylvania Dutch cooking. Early farmers in the Appalachians made the most of dried apples (*schnitz*) and dried corn, the latter in another chicken soup-stew. Hardworking farm families got their carbohydrates from numerous potato dishes and even more varieties of noodles and dumplings as well as breads, rolls, biscuits, cakes, and pies.

In North America, Pennsylvania Dutch farmers moved from a pig-centric farming system to add dairy and beef cattle culture and developed the smoked Lebanon bologna. Many of the characteristic pies were taken from Anglo-American models. Pretzels came to Pennsylvania from Bavaria in the 1840s, but the ingenious Pennsylvania bakers developed the hard pretzel and developed a national business.

Among the best-known Pennsylvania Dutch dishes are *rivvel* (noodle) soup, chicken soup with sweet corn, *shnitz und knep* (dried apples and dumplings stewed with ham or smoked pork), *bouva shenkel* (beef-stuffed dumplings called "boys legs," much as calzone are named for trousers), Philadelphia scrapple (known as *pan haus* or "pan rabbit" in farm country), hash dishes known locally as *hexel* or *mornix*, red beet pickled eggs, raisin pie, *schnitz* pie, shoo-fly pie, Moravian sugar cake, funnel cakes, and *fastnacht* doughnuts.

German-language cookbooks were published in Pennsylvania and Ohio in the 1840s, joining an already active press of almanacs and periodicals. There are references to Pennsylvania Dutch dishes in *The Kentucky Housewife* (1839), the most explicit being a recipe for vermicelli and noodles: "These are German cookeries, principally used for thickening soups and sauces." By 1866 a recipe for "Snitz and Knep" was published in *Godey's Lady's Book*. Pennsylvania Dutch cookbooks in English began in the early twentieth century with *The Inglenook Cook Book* (1911) which gathers Brethren recipes, and Edith M. Thomas's *Mary at the Farm and Book of Recipes* (1915), which is organized around a running situation comedy about Mary from the city and her Pennsylvania German relatives, who give recipes such as "schnitz and knopf" and an early shoo-fly pie. In the 1930s began the bewildering variety of recipe pamphlets sold to tourists in Pennsylvania Dutch country. Recently the cuisine has been reexplored in popular cookbooks by Marcia Adams, Phyllis Pellman Good, Betty Groff, Edna Eby Heller, and William Woys Weaver, while a number of Amish and Mennonite women have been culinary missionaries via local publication or contribution. There is an old Mennonite colony in Ontario, Canada, where Edna Staebler has popularized the food in books, beginning with *Food That Really Schmecks* (1968).

Although the popular image of the Pennsylvania Dutch is based upon Amish buggies now appearing across Indiana and Ohio and as far as Iowa, 90 percent of Pennsylvania Dutch descendants in the United States are not Amish, and Pennsylvania Dutch cooking, including that of the Amish, has always been innovative. Thus it was possible for Alma Kauffman, who grew up Amish, to write in the 1970s:

> Traditional Amish cooking has not disappeared, it is just a bit overshadowed by new food fashions. To a student like [the Ohio radio broadcaster] Bill Randle the change is an interesting sign because it shows the Amish are a flexible, changing society. To a former Amish girl like me it's regrettable. In *my* cookbook Yumazetti (all sixty dozen variations) will never replace fried ham—or even bean soup.
>
> Bill Randle, *Plain Cookery, Volume II.* Cleveland, c. 1975.

The bean soup was served at Sunday collective meals from at least the mid-nineteenth century. Yummasetti, a pasta casserole, may have entered Amish life as late as the 1960s.

[**See also** Funnel Cakes; Pretzel; Shoo-Fly Pie; Yummasetti.]

BIBLIOGRAPHY

Adams, Marcia. *Cooking from Quilt Country: Hearty Recipes from Amish and Mennonite Kitchens*. New York: Potter, 1989.

Frederick, J. George. *The Pennsylvania Dutch and Their Cookery*. New York: Business Bourse, 1935. Part 2 reprinted as *Pennsylvania Dutch Cook Book*, New York: Dover 1971.

Good, Phyllis Pellman, and Louise Stoltzfus. *The Best of Mennonite Fellowship Meals: More Than 900 Favorite Recipes to Share with Friends at Home or at Church*. Intercourse, PA: Good Books, 1991.

Weaver, William Woys. *Pennsylvania Dutch Country Cooking*. New York: Abbeville, 1993.

Weaver, William Woys. *Sauerkraut Yankees: Pennsylvania-German Foods and Foodways*. Philadelphia: University of Pennsylvania Press, 1983. A translation of the 1851 Pennsylvania Dutch cookbook *Die Geschickte Hausfrau*.

Yoder, Joseph W. *Rosanna of the Amish*. Scottdale, PA: Herald, 1995.

MARK H. ZANGER

Pépin, Jacques

Much like his late colleague and television costar Julia Child, Jacques Pépin has taken his French culinary ambassadorship to all corners of the United States. Pépin has combined techniques acquired over half a century as a professional cook and writing skills that have produced a host of cookbooks, some of them considered landmarks. He is also considered by colleagues to be one of the finest craftspeople of all cooking teachers.

Pépin was born on December 18, 1935, in Bourg-en-Bresse, France. He and his two brothers helped their mother, Jeannette, a self-taught cook, in a series of small restaurants after World War II. At the age of thirteen Pépin left the family business to embark on a formal apprenticeship at the Grand Hotel de L'Europe in the gastronomically rich city of Lyon. Still in his teens, Pépin moved to Paris to work at the Meurice and then the Plaza-Athénée under the renowned chef Lucien Diat. Pépin was assigned to serve as personal chef to three French heads of state, the last being Charles de Gaulle. Eager to expand his knowledge, Pépin immigrated to New York in 1959, speaking no English.

Pépin was welcomed by Chef Pierre Franey into the kitchen of Le Pavillon, considered one of Manhattan's finest restaurants. While working full-time, Pépin passed a high school equivalency test and ultimately earned both a bachelor of arts and a master's degree in French literature at Columbia University. While he was at Le Pavillon, two different patrons courted Pépin to work for them: the family of the presidential candidate John F. Kennedy and Howard Johnson. Pépin accepted Johnson's offer to work in research and development rather than becoming White House chef. During his ten years at Howard Johnson, Pépin learned about mass production, marketing, food chemistry, American food tastes, and how to write lucid detailed recipes, a skill few professional chefs possess. He left Howard Johnson's to open his own restaurant, Le Potagerie, a trendy Manhattan soup restaurant, that was soon a big success. But in 1974 Pépin had a near-fatal car accident, suffering severe injuries that left him unable to keep up the grueling pace in the kitchen.

The event was the catalyst that propelled Pépin into cookbook writing and teaching, traveling the country forty weeks a year at a time when America was ripe for cooking classes. He wrote two groundbreaking step-by-step books on classic French culinary techniques, *La technique* (1976) and *La methode* (1979), that earned him a place in the James Beard Foundation's Cookbook Hall of Fame for their "substantial and enduring impact on the American kitchen."

By 2004, Pépin has authored more than twenty books, some of which also won James Beard Awards, and he has contributed numerous articles to leading food publications and newspapers, including the *New York Times*. In 1989 he began shooting PBS television shows at KQED in San Francisco, later teaming with his daughter Claudine Pépin for a series and ultimately with his longtime friend Child for *Julia and Jacques*

Cook at Home, winning James Beard Awards for his shows and a daytime Emmy Award as well.

To reinforce the importance of cuisine in culture, Pépin teamed with Child to develop and teach a groundbreaking master's degree program in gastronomy at Boston University. In 1988 he became dean of special programs at The French Culinary Institute, where he can often be heard telling his students: "The most important thing is, does it taste good? . . . Food itself and the sharing of food is what sustains the human relationship more than anything."

[**See also** CHILD, JULIA; COOKBOOKS AND MANUSCRIPTS: 1970S TO THE PRESENT.]

BIBLIOGRAPHY

Carlson, Julie. "In the Kitchen with Jacques." *San Francisco Focus*, December 1994, pp. 119–122.

Fenzl, Barbara Poole. "Happy Birthday, Jacques." Food Forum Quarterly (Jan.–Mar. 2006).

Pépin, Jacques. *The Apprentice: My Life in the Kitchen*. New York: Houghton Mifflin Company, 2003.

Seager, Phil. "Jacques of All Trades." *Applause*, April 1991, pp. 25–27.

SCOTT WARNER

Pepper, Black

Black pepper (*Piper nigrum*) is said to have originated on the Malabar Coast of India, where it grew on vines attached to trees. The spice migrated east with Indian traders following the monsoons and thereupon became established as a crop in Java and the Sunda Islands and then in Malaysia, Borneo, Sumatra, Sri Lanka, and Penang. Today it is also grown in Thailand, tropical Africa, the South Sea Islands, and Brazil.

Pepper vines bear white flowers on "spikes" that become peppercorns that look like small clusters of berries. The peppercorns ripen from green to red and then to brown; green

peppercorns become black peppercorns when dried in the sun. Black pepper owes its pungency to a resin and its flavor to a volatile oil. Most of the pungent flavor of the black peppercorn is in its skin. Green peppercorns are picked unripe and sold dry or pickled in vinegar or brine. White pepper is formed by soaking fresh berries in salt water, removing their red shells by hand, and then drying them. Some say white peppercorn is milder than black and is a more favorable spice. Gray pepper is most often a ground mix of black and white peppercorns.

Throughout history pepper has been the most widely used spice. Pepper entered written Western history during the Roman Empire. The Romans established trade routes to India through Alexandria and the Arabian Peninsula. After Portugal's navigations to India in the sixteenth century and for the next two centuries, pepper became a source of economic competition between the Portuguese, the English, and the Dutch.

Pepper was available in the United States in the colonial period, but it was only after the American Revolution that the United States became a player in the global pepper trade. This trade began in 1793, when Jonathan Carnes, a Salem, Massachusetts, sea captain, set sail for the East Indies. He was successful in finding pepper, but on his way home his ship wrecked off Bermuda. He returned from the Indies in 1795 on a new ship, the *Rajah*, with his hold full of peppercorns—which he sold at a 700 percent profit. Others followed, and Salem became the pepper port of note in the new United States—nearly one thousand voyages were completed in one two-year period—and remained so until 1873. By that time other ports such as New York and Boston had grown larger and took in pepper from the British and Dutch. Earlier, Thomas Jefferson's embargo of U.S.

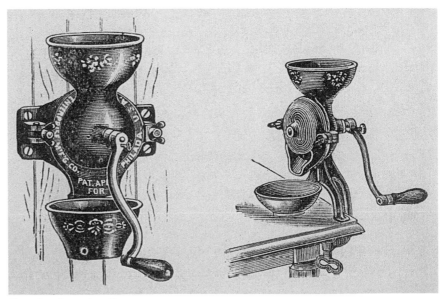

Illustration of two spice mills.

shipping in 1807 greatly hindered the pepper trade, as did the War of 1812. In the early twenty-first century much of the pepper supply arrives through various global importers, such as McCormick.

In the early nineteenth century some regarded pepper as a cause of insanity. Pepper was in any case shunned by food purists, who thought that the spice should be avoided or at least used in moderation. By the post–Civil War period, pepper was considered more acceptable, but it was still to be avoided by children or by those who already had a "sound digestion" and did not need condiments.

Pepper, usually pre-ground, has become, with salt, one of the two basic spices found in American kitchens and on American tables. The three basic types of peppercorns—black, green, and white—have entered American cuisine from other cultures and evolved, in some cases, into unique American dishes.

[**See also** PREPARED HERB AND SPICE MIXTURES.]

FRED CZARRA

Pepperidge Farm

In 1937 Margaret Rudkin of Fairfield, Connecticut, began a small business baking preservative-free, stone-ground whole wheat bread following a doctor's recommendation that it was the best thing for children. She named her company after the family's home, "Pepperidge Farm." Finding a ready market for her breads, Rudkin in 1940 expanded production by opening a bakery in Norwalk, Connecticut. Eventually white bread was added to the product line as well as dinner rolls, stuffing, and more. Rudkin reached an agreement with the venerable Delacre Company in Brussels to produce their cookies in America. In 1955 Pepperidge Farm launched a line of European-style cookies, such as Milano, Bordeaux, Geneva, and Brussels. The company later acquired Black Horse Pastry Company and moved into the frozen food business.

In 1961 Campbell Soup Company acquired Pepperidge Farm. In 1963 Rudkin published *The Margaret Rudkin Pepperidge Farm Cookbook,* which became the first cookbook to make the *New York Times* Best Seller List. Rudkin retired in 1966.

In 1962 the company first produced Goldfish crackers, a small orange-colored cheese-flavored cracker shaped like a fish. It became an instant sensation. Although it was not fat free, it was baked rather than fried like many other salty snack foods. Others tried to duplicate Goldfish. Nabisco reported that it intended to manufacture "CatDog" crackers, orange-colored, cheese-flavored snacks of various shapes sold in a box decorated with the fish cartoon character and the other shapes as background. Pepperidge Farm sued Nabisco for trademark infringement based on the dilution law, which is intended to prevent the diminution of a trademark.

Pepperidge Farm won the case in 1999. Nabisco appealed the decision, and Pepperidge Farm won on appeal.

In the early twenty-first century about one-half of all U.S. households with children under eighteen purchase Goldfish products annually. More than 85 billion Goldfish crackers are consumed each year, which means that Pepperidge Farms manufactures 3,000 Goldfish every second. With the success of Goldfish, Pepperidge Farm has expanded the product line to include other flavors, such as Nacho Flavored Goldfish.

[**See also** SNACKS, SALTY.]

BIBLIOGRAPHY

Rudkin, Margaret. *The Margaret Rudkin Pepperidge Farm Cookbook.* New York: Atheneum, 1963.

ANDREW F. SMITH

Pepperoni

Pepperoni, or peperoni, is essentially a variety of air-dried salami that derives its name from the word "pepper," alluding to the spicy red pepper that is its principal spice. Pepperoni's origins can be traced to ancient Roman times, when butchers chopped and dried mixtures of meat and fat, which had been seasoned with black pepper and other spices, to make a food that was convenient for soldiers to eat during marches. In modern times Italian immigrants introduced pepperoni to the United States, where pepperoni is rarely consumed alone; it is most commonly served on pizzas. In about 1900 pizzerias were established in New York, and pepperoni and cheese were tied as the favorite toppings. More than a century later, pepperoni still heads the list of toppings for pizza.

Pepperoni, like most American foods, is not indigenous to the continent. But no other country has done as much to produce and popularize this highly seasoned salami. The method of making pepperoni had changed little over two millennia, but when pepperoni arrived with the immigrants, American ingenuity introduced several innovations in both manufacturing and ingredients. In the early 1900s Armour and Company in Chicago pioneered automated production of pepperoni. Refrigeration and humidity control technologies enabled year-round manufacture, changing the Old World practice of producing pepperoni only in late fall and early winter.

The traditional recipe for pepperoni included pork trimmings, beef chucks, hearts, cheeks, and pork jowl seasoned with ground red pepper and other spices. These highly seasoned mixtures were stuffed into pig casings and air-dried or smoked at relatively low temperatures (not exceeding 140°F.). The finished product was aged in cool, dry temperatures for a period of six to ten months to help develop its characteristic pepperoni flavor. Americans introduced lactic acid cultures

to help optimize the development of flavor and shorten the curing time from months to days or even hours. Whey and soy-based ingredients helped enhance pepperoni flavor and bind moisture, and they significantly shortened drying and curing processes.

In the 1950s the U.S. Department of Agriculture issued a Standard of Identity for pepperoni and mandated a moisture-to-protein ratio of 1.6 to 1 for retail markets. Pizza makers found that manual peeling and slicing of pepperoni was expensive because of the labor involved—and because of the injuries. Better safety and easier slicing were facilitated first by the invention of slicing machines for pepperoni in the late 1960s and then by the development of edible protein films to replace the traditional pig casings.

Pepperoni is probably the only salami that is heated to help bring out its flavor. Americans use pepperoni as pizza topping, as filling in calzones, and in sauces for pasta. Reduced fat and turkey pepperoni developed by Hormel Foods Corporation are popular with those conscious of fat in their diets. Annually Americans consume twenty-four pounds of pizza, more than two pounds of which is pepperoni. American children rate pepperoni pizza highest of all the foods in the school lunch program, and the general American population loves pepperoni flavor, rating it next to cheese and seasonings as the flavor of choice for savory snacks. Pepperoni popularity is further evidenced by the increasing number of references in treats for pets—Pepperoni Nawsomes and Pupperoni Treats.

[**See also** ARMOUR, PHILIP DANFORTH; DRYING; ITALIAN AMERICAN FOOD; PIZZA; PIZZERIAS; SALAMI; SAUSAGE.]

BIBLIOGRAPHY

Toussaint-Samat, Maguelonne. *A History of Food.* Translated by Anthea Bell. New York: Barnes and Noble, 1998.

KANTHA SHELKE

Pepsi-Cola

Like many other pharmacists at the end of the nineteenth century, Caleb Bradham of New Bern, North Carolina, experimented with various blends of fruit flavors and other extracts, hoping to create a new drink. One of Bradham's concoctions became especially popular with local patrons. This nameless drink eventually became known as Brad's Drink, named after Bradham. As the popularity of Brad's Drink rose, so did the need to give it a proper name. In 1898 Brad's Drink became Pepsi-Cola, and one of the most important beverages in soft-drink history was born. It is believed that the name Pepsi-Cola was chosen because, like pepsin, Pepsi-Cola aids in digestion. At the same time it provides the refreshment of a cola drink.

Over the next few years, demand for Pepsi-Cola spread well beyond New Bern. On December 30, 1902, the Pepsi-Cola Company was formed; the first Pepsi-Cola trademark was registered in 1903. At first Pepsi-Cola was sold exclusively as a fountain drink, but by 1905 it was also available in bottles. At the same time Bradham began offering franchises to bottle Pepsi-Cola. By 1910 there were 280 bottlers in 24 states producing bottled Pepsi-Cola.

The company continued to grow and prosper until the sugar crisis of World War I. Sugar rationing and price controls resulted in an unstable sugar market; since sugar is a primary ingredient in soft drinks, this was a severe blow to the entire soft-drink industry. Pepsi-Cola became desperate to find enough sugar to keep operating. At one point the company tried using sugar substitutes, such as molasses. But the molasses gave Pepsi-Cola an unpleasant taste, which resulted in lower sales. Bradham did not want to take the chance of running out of sugar again. So once the sugar restrictions eased, he purchased a large supply of sugar at a high price. Months later the cost of sugar tumbled to a fraction of what Bradham had paid. Years of sugar rationing and price controls combined with slumping sales were too much for the Pepsi-Cola Company. By 1923 Bradham was forced into bankruptcy.

For the next eight years, the Pepsi-Cola Company was located in Richmond, Virginia, where it struggled through reorganizations and a second bankruptcy before being bought by a Long Island candy company called Loft Candies. By this time the famous Pepsi-Cola trademark had all but disappeared from public view.

In New York, Charles Guth, president of Loft Candies, was embroiled in a dispute over the price of Coca-Cola syrup, which was dispensed at Loft stores in the New York area. Unable to resolve this dispute, Guth decided to purchase the trademark and formula of Pepsi-Cola, which would then be sold in place of Coca-Cola at Loft soda fountains. But the results Guth had hoped for never materialized. The people of New York were not familiar with the Pepsi-Cola name. Furthermore Coca-Cola was filing lawsuits that claimed that Pepsi-Cola was misleading consumers as to which cola drink they were getting.

Finally, in desperation, Guth decided to sell Pepsi-Cola in bottles rather than from the fountain. To make these bottles more distinctive, he decided to use twelve-ounce bottles rather than the standard six-ounce bottle and to sell them for ten cents. This made a bad situation worse. People were not used to paying more than a nickel for a soft drink—even if it was twice the usual size. Faced with the prospect of failure, Guth decided to cut the price of Pepsi-Cola to five cents in a final attempt to revive the drink. His timing could not have been better: in 1934 the country was in the midst of the Great Depression. This new twelve-ounce bottle for a nickel was just what people were looking for. Success came immediately; over the next five years, Pepsi-Cola sales skyrocketed. New

Pepsi bottling franchises were popping up all over the country.

Guth did not share in the success of Pepsi-Cola. Believing he owned the rights to Pepsi-Cola, Guth left Loft and took Pepsi-Cola with him. In a subsequent lawsuit filed by Loft, Guth was forced to give back all rights to Pepsi-Cola. Walter Mack, a financier who had financed the lawsuit against Guth, was now president of the Pepsi-Cola Company.

One of Mack's first actions as CEO was to take control of Pepsi-Cola advertising. Perhaps Mack's greatest contribution to Pepsi advertising history was the popular Pepsi jingle, the first "stand-alone" radio jingle of its day. Mack was also responsible for the creation of "Pepsi and Pete, the Pepsi-Cola Cops," and in 1940 he replaced the plain bottle with a standardized, custom-embossed twelve-ounce bottle. In 1941, to show its support for the war effort, Pepsi changed its bottle crown colors to red, white, and blue. These colors soon became an integral part of the Pepsi logo.

The World War II era was difficult for the Pepsi-Cola Company, which had to deal with everything from raw material shortages to postwar inflation. The inflation issue was the most serious problem because it reduced profits, and it eventually forced Pepsi to raise the five-cent price that had made it famous.

In 1950 Alfred Steele was appointed CEO of Pepsi. Steele's greatest achievement was in modernizing Pepsi-Cola, both in image and in operation. The formula was changed to include less sugar, and a new advertising campaign was launched with the slogan "the Light Refreshment." A new bottle was commissioned, and in 1958 the swirl bottle was introduced to coincide with the "Be Sociable" advertising campaign. Pepsi had moved from the kitchen to the dining room.

The 1960s saw the emergence of the baby boomers. To tap into this market, Pepsi created its most successful advertising campaign to date, "the Pepsi Generation." Pepsi's move into the growing youth market eventually gave it the number one position in soft-drink popularity. In 1965 President Donald Kendall engineered a merger between Pepsi-Cola and Frito-Lay to form PepsiCo.

The 1960s also brought many changes in packaging and products. The American consumer was now more concerned with convenience rather than price. To respond to this new trend, Pepsi introduced nonreturnable bottles and cans. Additionally Pepsi began brand expansion with the introduction of Diet Pepsi and Mountain Dew.

The 1970s and 1980s saw more of the same, with more nonreturnable packaging—especially the two-liter bottle and the twelve-ounce can. The returnable Pepsi bottle was nearly extinct. Brand extension continued with flavors like Pepsi Light, Slice, and Mug Root Beer.

[**See also** COLA WARS; SODA DRINKS; SODA FOUNTAINS.]

BIBLIOGRAPHY

Enrico, Roger, and Jesse Kornbluth. *The Other Guy Blinked: How Pepsi Won the Cola Wars.* New York: Bantam, 1986.

Martin, Milward W. *Twelve Full Ounces.* New York: Holt, Rinehart, and Winston, 1962.

Stoddard, Bob. *Pepsi: 100 Years.* Los Angeles: General Publishing Group, 1997.

BOB STODDARD

Perch

There are several freshwater and saltwater fish called perch. Of the sorts called ocean perch, *Sebastes alutus* comes from the Pacific and *Sebastes marinus* from the Atlantic; the latter is also sometimes called redfish. Perch bones are among the most commonly found fish bones in colonial-era archaeological sites around the Chesapeake.

The best-known food and sport perch in America is yellow perch (*Perca flavescens*). Perch is found mainly in the eastern and midwestern parts of the United States, the range extending south to Florida and Georgia and north to the Great Lakes and into Canada. Perch has been successfully introduced into western lakes. Perch prefers cool water, most often inhabiting lakes, but it also is caught in ponds and slow streams. Perch are small, averaging seven to ten inches, although a historic catch of a four-pound, three-ounce perch was recorded in 1865 at Cross Wicks Creek, New Jersey. Perch are predators, eating minnows, juvenile fish, insects, small crayfish, and snails. Yellow perch has supported a commercial fishery in the lower Great Lakes, but its value comes mainly from sportfishing. Although it is not a fighter, perch is known for feeding frenzies, which make it possible for an angler to catch a large number in a short time.

Because in historical culinary sources the fish is usually called merely perch, it is hard to determine which fish is meant. Most perch seem to have been of medium size and so were poached, baked, or broiled. Small-sized perch are cooked as panfish. It has firm, mild, lean flesh. Ocean perch are often filleted to be broiled, sautéed, or panfried. They are available both fresh and frozen; when frozen they can be marketed simply as "ocean fillets" or under some similar indistinguishable name.

SANDRA L. OLIVER

Periodicals

An integral part of American life, food magazines, with their seductive color photographs, are a ready source of information and pleasure, even though many contemporary cooks admit they never take the magazines into the kitchen. As technological improvements began to reach the kitchen in the nineteenth century, advertisers were quick to take advantage of the magazines that would reach into the homes of prospective buyers. Although editorials declared that their aim was to help their readers perform household tasks more quickly and more efficiently, advertisements frequently blended with editorial content, making it difficult to differentiate one from the other.

Early Magazines

The earliest magazines dealing with food were "educational" periodicals, heavy on fiction, fashion, and needlework with a minimum of cooking and other household information. *Godey's Lady's Book*, founded in 1837 and edited for forty-seven years by Sarah Josepha Hale, set the model for many future publications, featuring generous helpings of advice for young families, fiction, poetry, and fashion plus some food and household hints. Published in 1868, *Berney's Mystery of Living* may have been the first magazine solely of recipes, but it lasted only one issue. By the 1870s more periodicals devoted primarily to food had appeared, some only briefly. In 1886 *Table Talk* began and was edited in its early years by Sarah Tyson Rorer, cooking teacher and writer, who left her own magazine, *Household News*, to take on this new assignment. The final issue appeared in 1920.

Home Economics

In 1896 the *Boston Cooking School Magazine* made its debut. The editor Fannie Farmer, Boston's famous cooking school director, had revolutionized home cooking by standardizing measurements. Her magazine was filled with solid information on stoves, sinks, nutrition, servant problems, health, and sports. The name was later changed to *American Cookery*, edited by Janet McKenzie Hill. Publication ceased after fifty years, leaving a remarkable record of the changes in American society and in women's lives over half a century. In 1894 *New England Kitchen Magazine*, edited by the well-known cooking teacher Mary J. Lincoln, extolled the virtues of cooking schools while lamenting the slow pace of change in cooking techniques and lobbying vigorously for the adoption of scientific principals in the kitchen.

The Big Six

The 1870s witnessed the beginnings of the major service magazines. Called "the Big Six," they included *McCall's*, *Woman's Home Companion*, *Delineator*, *Ladies' Home Journal*, *Pictorial Review*, and *Good Housekeeping*. In 1873 a small fashion sheet designed to advertise clothes was launched, and in 1883 the magazine became *McCall's*, slowly changing its identity, adding fiction by well-known writers and later service features for the homemaker. Television and other opportunities to find information and recreation made serious inroads on all service magazines as they scrambled to meet the needs of a changing population. In 2001 *McCall's* published its last issue.

The *Home*, published in Cleveland, Ohio, also appeared in 1893 and went through several incarnations before becoming the *Woman's Home Companion*, with fiction and articles from some of the country's best writers and food

experts. Corporate financial problems, intense competition, cash flow problems, and declining advertising revenue all served to weaken the *Companion*'s market position, and the January 1957 issue was the last.

In 1873 *Delineator* emphasized fashion, short stories, and serialized novels with increasing information for the homemaker. Over the years the personality of the magazine changed its direction, adding muckraking articles on important social issues, but the Depression cut heavily into advertising revenues, and circulation dropped. In April 1937 *Delineator* merged with *Pictorial Review*.

With the advent of *Ladies' Home Journal* in 1883, serious competition among major service magazines increased. In 1890 the editor Edward Bok shaped the magazine into a service vehicle for the growing middle-class family. Essentially conservative, Bok editorialized against woman suffrage but recommended sex education for women. When he retired in 1919, the *Journal* acquired a series of new editors, each one putting his or her stamp on the magazine. Beatrice Gould, part of a husband-wife team of editors in 1935, set forth the magazine's philosophy in an editorial, declaring that a woman's job was to be as womanly as possible, as pretty as possible, and as loving as possible in order to hold her family together cheerfully with warmth and comfort and good sense. Part of this good sense required skills in the kitchen, and food features still remain in the forefront, reflecting the realities of readers who work outside the home.

The January 1921 cover of American Cookery *featured advice on one-course breakfasts and mock venison.*

Good Housekeeping began publishing in 1885, following the same mix of fiction, recipes, and household advice presented by the other "Big Six" magazines with one major difference: the Good Housekeeping Seal of Approval. In 1902 the publishers offered a money back guarantee on any item advertised in the magazine and began inspecting food products, creating an honor roll of food that passed their tests. The Federal Trade Commission took an interest and determined that the Seal of Approval must go. In its place the magazine introduced a Guaranty Seal, promising to refund the money if an advertised product proved to be unsatisfactory. *Good Housekeeping* has maintained the mix of homemaking and health tips plus information features that appealed to readers from the first issue.

Better Homes and Gardens

In 1924 a new kind of magazine appeared. *Better Homes and Gardens* grew out of *Successful Farming* when the founder and publisher E. T. Meredith decided America needed a broader service magazine addressing middle-class families who were interested in their homes, their kitchens, and their gardens. The formula for providing information and products designed to enhance changing family life continues to prove highly successful.

New Food Magazines

The launching of *Gourmet* in 1941 coincided with World War II, an inauspicious time to begin a magazine dedicated to good food and good living. But the publisher Earl R. MacAusland managed to demonstrate to his readers that despite rationing, his philosophy could benefit America by "a fine appreciation of good food, less waste, and an even smaller expenditure of food" (Endres et al, p. 132). After the war upscale advertising, accomplished writers, and magnificent color photography enhanced the food pages, and circulation increased.

Gourmet's major competitor, *Bon Appetit*, evolved from a liquor store throwaway into a full-fledged magazine in 1956. Aiming for an over-thirty, somewhat affluent audience, the magazine was less sophisticated than *Gourmet* and was among the first to give readers healthy and low calorie menus using easy to find ingredients. *Food and Wine*, published by the American Express Company, follows the pattern of *Gourmet* and *Bon Appetit* but in a more relaxed style, emphasizing consumer information. *Saveur* concentrates on the heritage and tradition of food throughout the world, while *Cuisine at Home* specializes in teaching a culinary technique, then providing several recipes that use that technique. Consumer information is paramount in *Cook's Illustrated*, where reports on kitchen tools, food products, and small appliances share space with details on cooking techniques and basic recipes. One of the newest entries in the Martha Stewart media empire, *Everyday Food* offers recipes for family meals that call for basic supermarket staples rather than the traditional Martha Stewart exotic ingredients.

Supermarket Magazines

In 1932 *Family Circle* began life as a giveaway at Piggly Wiggly stores and was followed in 1937 by *Woman's Day*, which began as a giveaway from the Great Atlantic and Pacific Tea Company. It shortly became a full-fledged magazine, printing features similar to those of its rival.

Diet-Conscious Magazines

The recognition of obesity as a national health problem has proved a challenge to food magazines. In 1950 the first issue of *Prevention: The Magazine for Good Health* was published, and *American Health: Fitness of Body and Mind* arrived in 1982. In 1986 the first issue of *Cooking Light*, an information-filled magazine written in an easy conversational style, was published. *Eating Well* promises to keep its readers informed of new trends in the health field and to help clarify the confusion concerning ever-changing food warnings. First published in 2001, *Light n' Tasty* takes on its competitors by declaring that its goal is to keep calories, fat, cholesterol, and sodium at low levels. In 2003 *A Taste of Home*, a modest, unsophisticated collection of recipes, began, featuring signed recipes solicited from readers and supplemented by a volunteer group of one thousand "field editors" and a small in-house staff.

Impact of Food Magazines on American Cooking

Over several generations, the American lifestyle has changed dramatically. Did food magazines play a leadership role in this change, or did they merely respond to changes already taking place? The answer is inconclusive. One can be certain, however, that America's love affair with food has been sustained by the imagination and enthusiasm of food magazines.

[**See also** BOSTON COOKING SCHOOL; FARMER, FANNIE; GOOD HOUSEKEEPING INSTITUTE; HOME ECONOMICS; RORER, SARAH TYSON; STEWART, MARTHA.]

BIBLIOGRAPHY

Brown, Kathi Ann. *Meredith: The First 100 Years*. Des Moines, IA: Meredith, 2002.

Endres, Kathleen L., and Therese L. Lueck, eds. *Women's Periodicals in the United States: Consumer Magazines*. Westport, CT: Greenwood, 1995.

Langone, Jan. *"Berney's Mystery of Living* and Other Nineteenth Century Cooking Magazines." *Gastronomica: The Journal of Food and Culture* 2, no. 2 (Spring 2002): 97–102.

Mott, Frank Luther. *A History of American Magazines*. 5 vols. Cambridge, MA: Harvard University Press, 1938–1968.

Tebbel, John, and Mary Ellen Zuckerman. *The Magazine in America, 1741–1990*. New York: Oxford University Press, 1991.

Zuckerman, Mary Ellen, comp. *Sources on the History of Women's Magazines, 1792–1960*. New York: Greenwood, 1991.

VIRGINIA K. BARTLETT

Persimmons

The two main persimmon species are *Diospyros virginiana*, native to the American states south of a line from Connecticut to Kansas, and *D. kaki*, indigenous to China. The name "persimmon" comes from the Algonquin word "pessemmin."

The native American persimmon, a round orange fruit that ranges up to the size of a small plum, is fiercely astringent when unripe because of soluble tannins in its flesh but rich, sweet, and custardy when soft. Some improved selections were made in the late nineteenth century and early twentieth century, but traditionally the persimmon is harvested from wild seedlings and used for puddings and breads. Although the fruit is important in American lore, it has been supplanted in commercial cultivation by the larger-fruited Asian kinds.

Of these Asian persimmons there are two main types: the tomato-shaped Fuyu (the common name for several similar varieties), eaten crunchy-hard like an apple, and the acorn-shaped Hachiya, which like the native American species is edible only when soft and gelatinous. Both turn bright red-orange when ripe and are honey-sweet, with mild pumpkiny flavor. The season runs from late September through December. Fuyus are chiefly consumed as fresh fruits; Hachiyas can be eaten fresh, with a spoon, but are mostly used in puddings, ice creams, breads, and cookies.

The cultivation of Asian persimmons, chiefly in central and southern California, began with the importation of grafted trees from Japan in the 1870s and soared to three thousand acres in the 1920s as part of a general boom in subtropical fruits. Plantings later declined, but in the 1970s and 1980s Asian immigration sparked a second boom. The U.S. Department of Agriculture's 1997 census listed 3,459 bearing acres in California.

[See also APPALACHIAN FOOD; SOUTHERN REGIONAL COOKERY.]

BIBLIOGRAPHY

Condit, Ira J. *The Kaki or Oriental Persimmon.* Berkeley: University of California Press, 1919.

Kitagawa, Hirotoshi, and Paul G. Glucina. *Persimmon Culture in New Zealand.* Wellington, New Zealand: Science Information Publishing Centre, 1984.

DAVID KARP

Peter Paul Candy Company (Mounds Bar)

In 1919 Peter Paul Halajian and five associates, all Armenian immigrants, founded the Peter Paul Candy Manufacturing Company in New Haven, Connecticut. One of their first products was a chocolate-covered coconut bar called Mounds, which was released in 1920. In 1922 the company introduced the Mounds bar, consisting of chocolate-covered sweetened coconut. Each package included two bars. Following up this success was Almond Joy, a similar bar with almonds topping the coconut, which was first manufactured in 1946. The company's advertising campaign for Mounds and Almond Joy remains a classic. Its jingle, "Sometimes you feel like a nut, sometimes you don't," was inducted into the Advertising Slogan Hall of Fame in 2002.

In 1972 Peter Paul acquired the York Cone Company, maker of York Peppermint Patties, then a regional confection. Peter Paul expanded production and aggressively promoted the Peppermint Patty nationally beginning in 1975. In

1978 Cadbury acquired the company. Ten years later Cadbury sold the Mounds, Almond Joy, and York Peppermint Patties brands to the Hershey Company, which markets them in the early twenty-first century.

BIBLIOGRAPHY

Richardson, Tim. *Sweets: A History of Candy.* New York: Bloomsbury, 2002.

ANDREW F. SMITH

Philadelphia Cheesesteak Sandwich

The Philadelphia cheesesteak sandwich consists of thinly sliced beefsteak that is grilled with onions and served on an Italian roll with a choice of cheese and a garnish of fried hot or sweet peppers. According to legend, the cheesesteak sandwich was created in 1930 by Pat Olivieri, operator of a hot dog stand at the Italian Market in South Philadelphia. Tired of hot dogs, Olivieri cooked up some thinly sliced beef and onions on his grill and piled it all into a crusty roll. As he was eating his sandwich, a cabdriver and longtime customer arrived and asked for one too. Upon tasting it, the cabbie advised Olivieri to forget hot dogs and sell the new beef sandwich instead. Cheese was added during the 1940s. Pat's King of Steaks, still owned and operated by the Olivieri family, is known for its Philadelphia cheesesteak sandwiches. The sandwich is served by a host of competitors in Philadelphia as well as restaurants and vendors throughout the United States.

[See also SANDWICHES.]

BIBLIOGRAPHY

Mercuri, Becky. *Sandwiches That You Will Like.* Pittsburgh, PA: WQED Multimedia, 2002.

BECKY MERCURI

Philanthropy, *see Fund-Raisers*

Phosphates

Phosphates are a class of soft drink flavored with phosphoric acid, which imparts a distinct but flat sourness. Chemists use various methods to produce phosphoric acid, also called acid phosphate, from phosphorus or phosphate rocks.

Phosphates first appeared in the late 1870s as the result of a patent medicine craze. Companies promoting the healing properties of nostrums like Horsford's Acid Phosphate discovered that consumers liked the powder's sour taste, particularly when mixed with sugar and water. Somebody tried adding it to a fruit syrup soda drink, and the phosphate quickly made the leap from the drugstore's medicine counter to its soda fountain. The chemical was usually added to the soda in the form of a solution of acid phosphate mixed with water.

During the 1880s and 1890s phosphates had a reputation as a "man's" drink (as opposed to "feminine" milk-based concoctions). The basic phosphates were the lemon or

orange phosphate (fruit syrup, phosphate, soda water) and the egg phosphate (a regular phosphate with raw egg added). Soda parlors in the downtown business districts served phosphates mixed with malt extracts for indigestion and with wine for a pick-me-up. After 1900 the sex preferences largely disappeared, and phosphates became one of the most popular soda fountain drinks, generally blended with fruit syrups and soda water. Their heyday lasted until the 1930s, when ice cream–based concoctions began to dominate the soda fountain. In the twenty-first century classic phosphates have all but disappeared except at a handful of "old-time" soda fountains mining the nostalgia craze.

Nevertheless, some of the most popular soft drinks still contain phosphoric acid. Almost all colas are blended with phosphoric acid to impart a hint of flat sourness (while fruit sodas and ginger ales use the more rounded acidity of citric acid). During the 1950s and 1960s some countries, like France and Japan, tried to ban Coca-Cola as dangerous, because phosphoric acid can block the absorption of calcium. These efforts failed when it was shown that the amounts of the acid were too small to have an effect.

[See also HOMEMADE REMEDIES; SODA DRINKS; SODA FOUNTAINS.]

BIBLIOGRAPHY

Fenaroli, Giovanni. *Fenaroli's Handbook of Flavor Ingredients.* Boca Raton, FL: CRC, 2002.

Mitchell, Alan J., ed. *Formulation and Production of Carbonated Soft Drinks.* New York: AVI, 1990.

Woodroof, Jasper Guy, and G. Frank Phillips. *Beverages: Carbonated and Noncarbonated.* Westport, CT: AVI, 1974.

ANDREW COE

Pickerel

Pickerel, a member of family Esocidae, is an elongated fish usually weighing between two and three pounds. The flesh is firm and lean but bony. Most popular with sport anglers are redfin pickerel (*Esox americanus*), also called little pickerel, mud pickerel, grass pickerel, banded pickerel, and red-finned pike, and chain pickerel (*Esox niger*). Pickerel grows less quickly than other pikes. Redfin pickerel, averaging one foot long, is smaller than chain pickerel, which can grow to two feet but usually is smaller. Pickerel seldom weigh more than two pounds, but one record catch was four pounds. The flesh is white, flaky, bony, and sweet but eaten primarily as a sportfishing catch. Small fillets can be steamed or fried.

SANDRA L. OLIVER

Pickles

The word "pickle" derives from the Dutch *pekel* or German *Pökel*; the method of pickling was brought to North America with the arrival of Dutch colonizers from the Netherlands in the early 1600s. Throughout history pickles and other preserved foods have made world exploration possible by providing palatable, mobile foods for sailors to eat. They have helped people survive during winter months when many fresh ingredients were not available.

Pickles date from as far back as ancient Mesopotamia (now Iraq), where a variety of foods were preserved in saltwater brine and regarded as delicacies. In the United States cucumber pickles are the most common pickle, but a variety of fruits, vegetables, meats, and fish have been preserved in a liquid combination of brine or vinegar, herbs, or spices—often in sugar or even oil. Pickles can be sour or sweet, salty, hot, or spicy—even pungent.

Although pickles are a favorite snack all over the country, there are many different recipes and traditions for pickles in America. Since pickles can be sweet or sour, made with vinegar or without, pickle enthusiasts do not necessarily agree on one definition. During the height of immigration into New York City from the late 1800s to the early 1900s, an influx of Jews from eastern Europe brought a specific method of kosher pickling, which was applied mainly to cucumbers but also to sauerkraut (white cabbage), tomatoes, and peppers. The home craft of pickling turned into a lucrative business within the Yiddish-speaking community.

In the practice of koshering (preparing edible foods in compliance with Jewish dietary laws), a rabbi supervises all ingredients and equipment used to make pickles. He or she ensures that the pickling cucumbers are washed, placed in large wooden barrels, and covered with a combination of kosher salt, dill, spices, and finally, clean water. The supervising rabbi also sees that the barrels and equipment are not used for anything else. These "kosher" pickles are covered and sit in a cool, dark place for between a few weeks and several months—until the pickles ferment to the desired flavor, color, and texture. Depending on the length of fermentation, the result will be either "fresh pickles" (bright green and mild—almost like salty cucumbers) or "sour" pickles (dull green and highly flavorful). There is also a "half-sour" or "medium-flavored" pickle, whose fermentation time is halfway between that for fresh and sour pickles. Outside of New York, America refers to all three as "kosher dills."

Before the opening of Hunts Point Market in the Bronx in 1967—now New York City's central port for all fresh food distribution—all cucumbers for the pickle trade used to be sold on Ludlow Street on the Lower East Side, a predominantly Jewish neighborhood. Delicatessens abound in New York City, and a kosher pickle spear is still served alongside deli sandwiches across the city. It remains a strong symbol of New York's culinary heritage.

The English brought with them to America a love for sweet pickles. The cucumbers are first salted, to leech out the bitterness of the peel, then they are rinsed and covered with hot vinegar, sugar, and spice syrup. The Czechs, Poles, Slavs, and Germans brought a passion for mustards, for salt-brined and salt-and-sugar-brined cabbage (sauerkraut and sweetkraut, respectively), and for cucumbers made with spices, herbs, and either salt brine or vinegar. The French brought a passion for cornichons (gherkins)—tiny, delicate cucumber pickles, heavily flavored with vinegar and spices and served with pâtés, cold meats, and cheeses.

In the early twenty-first century pickle varieties from all over the world can be made at home or purchased in specialty stores. Some of the most common international pickles popular in America come from Japan, China, and India, where a variety of pickles are served throughout the day at mealtimes.

Home pickling remains a part of fast-paced American family life, even though it has long been a luxury rather than a necessity. But in the United States most pickles are processed and manufactured commercially and distributed internationally. Pickles are a popular complement to savory foods such as hamburgers, hot dogs, and barbecue; pickled red beets, carrots, cauliflower, and cabbage are also served on their own as appetizers and in salads. In many families, having a plate of pickles at Thanksgiving and Christmas completes a meal.

Although they are not as common as they used to be, homemade pickle prize contests are held annually at county and state fairs across the United States. More than twenty known pickle festivals are held in U.S. cities where pickle farming and manufacturing directly influence the local economy and help maintain cultural stability; some of the more notable festivals are in New York, Arkansas, Pennsylvania, Michigan, and North Carolina. Many of these hometown pickle festivals also include live music and theater performances, 5K running races, baby pageants, pickle-eating contests, and cultural and historical exhibits.

As in many countries around the world, pickles have played a role in the history of American folk medicine and dietary practices. For instance, there seems to be an association between pregnancy and eating pickles: pregnant women in America are believed to crave unlikely food combinations such as "sour pickles and ice cream." Pickle "juice" (brine) has been used to combat dehydration during extremely hot weather, an old remedy brought to national attention in 2000 by the head athletic trainer for the Philadelphia Eagles football team, who used pickle juice—in an elixir he learned from his father, a high school football trainer to help the Eagles combat heat to win a game. Administering pickle juice to football players during extreme heat has

been used by athletic trainers for years, though studies have shown that unless the juice is diluted, dehydration, cramping, and fatigue increase. Too much consumption of pickle juice combined with the stress of competition can also make a person ill or aggravate hypertension and heart disease.

Pickles have gone in and out of fashion in the United States, where many fear the sodium in pickles and hence exclude them from their diet. In other countries, especially in Asia and parts of eastern Europe, pickles became an important accompaniment to meals owing to their historical significance in preventing mass starvation and disease during famines and harsh weather. Pickles provided something rich in vitamins for people to eat with staple foods, and they also pleased the palate. It is no wonder that people's relationship to pickled foods runs deep in those cultures that have relied on them throughout the centuries as a major part of both their diets and their cultural identities.

[See also JEWISH AMERICAN FOOD; JEWISH DIETARY LAWS; PICKLES, SWEET; PICKLING; PRESERVES.]

BIBLIOGRAPHY

Davidson, Alan. *The Oxford Companion to Food.* Oxford: Oxford University Press, 1999.

Norris, Lucy. *Pickled: Vegetables, Fruits, Roots, More; Preserving a World of Tastes and Traditions.* New York: Stewart, Tabori, and Chang, 2003.

Shephard, Sue. *Pickled, Potted, and Canned: The Story of Food Preserving.* London: Headline, 2000.

Ziedrich, Linda. *The Joy of Pickling.* Boston: Harvard Common, 1998.

LUCY NORRIS

Pickles, Sweet

The noun "pickle" applies to that which pickles as well as to that which gets pickled; hence a sweet pickle is both a fruit or vegetable that has been preserved in a sugary solution and the sugary solution in which the fruit or vegetable has been preserved. Known the world over in one form or another—for pickling is an ancient solution to the problems of food storage and spoilage, one that has had a lasting impact on virtually all foodways—sweet pickles reach their peak in condiments like mango chutney from India, northern Italy's *mostarda di frutta*, and *umeboshi*, the exquisitely sour Japanese pickled plum.

In the United States pickles are primarily the products of central European tradition. Pickling begins with vinegar or brine and just about anything deemed edible; American Indians themselves produced a maple-sap vinegar to preserve game in preparation for the winter. Still, the story of American pickles does not really take shape until the early eighteenth century, with the arrival of the Pennsylvania Dutch. These were mostly "plain people" from Germany ("Dutch" is a misnomer) who managed to settle the countryside around Philadelphia with their Mennonite customs largely intact—including a style of cooking that relied heavily on sweet-and-sour flavor combinations. In fact Pennsylvania Dutch cookery fairly rests on the notion of the seven sweets and seven sours thought requisite to any feast; sweet pickles made from small cucumbers, particularly gherkins, are just one of many options but the one Americans have collectively chosen to adopt and to adapt (along with the vocabulary, for both "pickle" and "gherkin" come from the German). Even cursory glances at regional cookbooks reveal a slew of recipes for what are in kind if not always in name sweet pickles, from Refrigerator Pickles, Icicle Pickles, Ripe Pickles, and Chunk Pickles to Candied Dills and curious Garlic Sweet Dills as well as of course Bread and Butter Pickles (so named either for their compatibility with bread and butter or, as the food critic Craig Claiborne has contended, for the income they bring in). Such recipes contain not only copious amounts of sugar but also spices both sweet and savory, including cinnamon, cloves, celery seed, and mustard seed.

There are furthermore numerous variations on the sweet pickle theme more or less popular in American cuisine. Pickled fruits (including strawberries, grapes, and even watermelon rinds) may be less relevant in the twenty-first century than they were in the nineteenth, when home canning and preserving was the norm; elaborate, piquant mixed-vegetable relishes like chowchow (adapted from a Chinese preparation) and piccalilli (a gift from India by way of England) are also less popular. But simpler relishes are crucial to an all-American menu of hamburgers and hot dogs; even ketchup, America's sugary version of yet another Chinese invention, captures the essence of the medium. The production of such condiments built corporate giants like H. J. Heinz Company, which, beginning in the 1870s, was the world's first mass manufacturer of sweet pickles.

[See also CONDIMENTS; CUCUMBERS; H. J. HEINZ COMPANY; KETCHUP; PICKLES; PICKLING; PRESERVES.]

BIBLIOGRAPHY
Shephard, Sue. Pickled, Potted, and Canned: How the Art and Science of Food Preserving Changed the World. New York: Simon and Schuster, 2000.

RUTH TOBIAS

Pickling

Using some sort of liquid or brine—typically a combination of salt, acid, and seasoning—is common to all pickling. It is an old technique for preserving food—older than freezing. Pickling may have begun when people discovered that spice added to salt and vinegar or citrus juice was highly flavorful and could mask foods too bland or rotten to eat.

Pickling is a preservation process that occurs when fresh raw food is introduced into a moderately acidic liquid or brine that denatures fresh foods to the extent that they are no longer raw though not necessarily cooked, thereby temporarily halting spoilage. The acidity in vinegars and citrus juices or that produced naturally by fermentation is what "pickles" a food.

In fermentation safe bacteria in food—for example, Leuconostoc mesenteroides or Lactobacillus plantarum—break apart sugars to create acid (mainly lactic acid). Moderate acid production helps preserve food for an extended time in its partially decomposed form by inhibiting the growth of harmful food-borne pathogens. Too much acid, on the other hand, halts the fermentation process.

Acids from fermentation, citrus juice, and vinegar add flavor but also discourage the growth of harmful microorganisms. Food-borne pathogens, such as Clostridium botulinum (which causes botulism) and Escherichia coli, cannot survive in extreme environments—for example, in pH levels from 2.6 to 4.0.

Refrigeration and freezer storage slow bacteria, often killing them. Canning or processing pickle jars in a hot-water bath with a temperature of 160°F–180°F for ten to twenty minutes also kills bad bacteria. Pickles stored in airtight containers prevent oxidization and the growth of molds in foods, so pickles should be kept covered or tightly sealed. (Nonreactive bowls, glass jars with lids, and sturdy plastic receptacles are best.) Storing pickles in the sunlight activates fermentation in some pickles but is harder to control, while darkness protects foods from overheating and processing.

Salt is an indispensable ingredient in pickling; indeed without salt one can hardly be said to have a pickle. Salt controls fermentation, fosters the progression of good bacteria, draws excess—often bitter—liquid from food, firms the texture of food, and concentrates and balances a host of herbaceous, sweet, and spicy flavors. Without salt, fermentation progresses too quickly, and food never becomes sour enough.

The most common pickles in the United States are either brined or fermented. The acid essential for eliminating harmful bacteria (which cause food to rot) in pickles comes from fermenting with salt or using citrus juice (like lemon juice) or vinegar. Many pickles are salty. Although there are many sweet varieties known in the United States, they still contain a fair amount of salt and nitrites. Pickling retains most of food's original nutrients if they are processed soon after harvesting.

In the twentieth century, during the Great Depression, pickled homegrown food kept many American families from starvation. Home pickling reached its peak of popularity during World War II, when it was people's patriotic duty to grow victory gardens and put away their own canned and pickled foods. The U.S. government even relegated 40 percent of all commercially made pickles to feed the armed forces at home and abroad; those who wanted pickles during this time most likely made their own at home. The decline of home pickling occurred in the last half of the twentieth century because most Americans believed they did not need the skill. It is easier to buy commercially made pickles, though many people claim they are inferior to homemade.

[See also PICKLES; PICKLES, SWEET; PRESERVES.]

BIBLIOGRAPHY
Norris, Lucy. Pickled: Vegetables, Fruits, Roots, More; Preserving a World of Tastes and Traditions. New York: Stewart, Tabori, and Chang, 2003.
Shephard, Sue. Pickled, Potted, and Canned: The Story of Food Preserving. London: Headline, 2000.

LUCY NORRIS

Picnic Kits, see Lunch Boxes, Dinner Pails, and Picnic Kits; Picnics

Picnics

Americans, like other picnickers, prefer the outdoors and hope for that "perfect day for a picnic." Everyone picnics: the rich and the poor, loners and more gregarious folk, old-fashioned couples spooning and modern couples libidinously romancing, parents and children, church congregations and company workers.

Picnic etymology and spelling are uncertain. The English word "picnic" is probably a loan word derived from the French piquenique—appearing in 1692 as a word of unknown origin—that signifies a meal at which each diner pays his or her share for food to be eaten outdoors. Lord Chesterfield, the first to use "picnic" in English, suggests that he means an assembly or salon gathering. Despite this obscurity, Georgina Battiscombe, whose English Picnics (1949) is authoritative, is certain that by the beginning of the nineteenth century English picnics were common events involving an outdoor party during which it was customary to eat a meal of some kind.

The earliest mention in America is of "picnic silk stockings," a satirical phrase used by Washington Irving (or one of his coauthors) in Salmagundi (1807) to signify the silliness of women's fashion. Irving's Wolfert's Roost (1855), a memoir, suggests that lunch breaks at school in the 1790s were picnic like, but Irving does not use the word "picnic." Thomas Cole's eponymous painting Pic-Nic (1846) depicts a customary gathering in the Catskill Mountains. The simplicity of the scene conveys a sense that being out of doors is particularly attractive for dining while suggesting the grandeur of nature and its spiritual impact on the intellect and passions. A picnic in Louisa May Alcott's Little Women (1868) is pleasant and practical: according to Jo, "Mother likes to have us out of doors as much as possible; so we bring our work here, and have nice times. For the fun of it we bring our things in these bags, wear old hats, use poles to climb

A lithographed advertisement for Royal brand canned fish shows a family on a picnic.

the hill, and play pilgrims, as we used to years ago."

Frances Trollope complains that American picnics are too rare and that picnickers are often too rowdy and drunk. Her picnicking described in *Domestic Manners of the Americans* (1832) is a fiasco. In her description of a picnic outside of Cincinnati, Ohio, the day begins well with a hamper packed with sandwiches and books but ends poorly with heat, insects, and a lost forest path. James Fenimore Cooper refers to a June picnic as a "rustic fete" in the novel *Home as Found* (1838). The "customary repast" (whose contents are never divulged) is served by domestics on cloths spread on the ground. Picnic debris discarded without care, the precursor of fast food trash, constitutes the "picnic pots and cans" that Owen Wister complains about in *The Virginian* (1902).

Fourth of July picnics are usually celebrations of the United States' national birthday except in Joyce Carol Oates's novel *Black Water* (1992), in which celebration of the holiday is a backyard barbecue subordinated to a sexual escapade. Labor Day, originally a celebration of the American worker, is often a cause for picnicking that also marks the end of summer. But in William Inge's play *Picnic* (1953), the picnic is not shown, and the food of choice, fried chicken, never gets eaten. When Madge says to Hal, her seducer, that they must get to the picnic, he embraces her and says that the food will have to wait. Juneteenth is celebrated with picnics by African Americans in remembrance of the signing of the Emancipation Proclamation. Angela Shelf Medearis's *The African-American Kitchen: Cooking from Our Heritage* (1997) suggests a picnic menu of jerk pork, potato salad, pickled beets, red rice, roasted potatoes, and pecan cake. "Dinner on the grounds" is a midday picnic meal served during revival meetings of Methodists and Baptists in the

South and Midwest. Usually held in August, the meal is served at tables covered with white cloths and set up outside the church, though twenty-first-century meals are often served indoors in air-conditioned splendor. Two company picnics were held in Henry Louis Gates Jr.'s hometown, one for whites and another for African Americans. In *Colored People: A Memoir* (1994) Gates recalls that there was a traditional meal of fried chicken, and he is nostalgic about corn cooked in a huge, black cast-iron vat set on cinder blocks and fueled by pinewood.

Other occasions for picnics are homecomings, reunions, and grave cleanings, events at which families meet to socialize and pay tribute to the dead, as described in Clyde Edgerton's *The Floatplane Notebooks* (1988). In the South picnickers are served traditional meals, a good selection of which is provided by Edna Lewis in *A Taste of Country Cooking* (1976): baked Virginia ham, southern fried chicken, braised leg of mutton, sweet potato casserole, corn pudding, green beans with pork, sliced tomatoes, various pies and cakes, and lemonade and iced tea. Urban charity picnics for children of the poor were held in post–Civil War New York City in Central Park, and in 1872 the *New York Times* began a series of picnics for the children of the working class in the lower wards of New York at which were served lunches of sandwiches, cake, ice cream, and lemonade.

A "Hoosier barbecue," described by William E. Wilson in Elizabeth L. Gilman's *Picnic Adventures* (1940), was a community picnic. Food was served on wide boards set up on sawhorses that sagged under the weight of roasted corn with butter, potato salad, deviled eggs, ham, cold fried chicken, and burgoo.

A most unusual picnic was W. C. Fields's three-day Southern California picnic binge. As reported by his biographer Robert Lewis Taylor in *W. C. Fields: His Follies and Fortunes*

(1949), the picnic began when Fields had his staff fill big wicker hampers with watercress; chopped olives and nuts; tongue; sandwiches of peanut butter and strawberry preserves; deviled eggs and spiced ham; celery stuffed with Roquefort cheese; black caviar; pâté de foie gras; anchovies; smoked oysters; baby shrimps and crabmeat; tinned lobster; potted chicken and turkey; swiss, liederkranz, and camembert cheeses; a bottle of olives; three or four jars of glazed fruit; angel food and devil's food cakes; and a variety of combination sandwiches. There was a case of Lanson 1928, several bottles of gin, six bottles of sauterne, and a case of beer.

Marian Cunningham's thirteenth edition of the *Fannie Farmer Cookbook* (2000) suggests a picnic basket packed with cold vegetables, scallions, tomatoes, hearts of celery, avocado, cold meat loaf, fried chicken, cold cooked shrimp, and breads.

James Beard's beer party picnic includes sausage board, Westphalian ham, cold meat loaf, deviled eggs, caviar eggs, pungent eggs, coleslaw, dill pickles, emmenthaler cheese, rye bread, pumpernickel, butter, and apple kuchen. This contrasts neatly with tailgating picnics, described by John Madden and Peter Kaminsky in *John Madden's Ultimate Tailgating* (1998), at which sports lovers gather around their trucks and car trunks, even in subzero or heat-scorching weather, to drink beer and enjoy barbecued meats with names like Beer Butt Chicken, Turducken, Pickled Salmon Burgers with Tartar Sauce, and Garlic Gizzards.

Alice Waters begins *The Chez Panisse Menu Cookbook* (1982) with a picnic menu that calls for roasted pepper with anchovies, potato and truffle salad, hard-cooked quail eggs, marinated cheese with olives and whole garlic, roast pigeon with purple grapes, sourdough bread with parsley butter, almond tart, and nectarines, served with red or white Provençal wines and muscatel with dessert.

Once established, picnics became a national fascination, the inalienable right of every American man, woman, and child, according to an anonymous author in *Appleton's Journal* (1869). The democratic impulse to picnic is so ingrained, the author claims, that it is scarcely noticed that when Americans picnic, they reverse the national ethos and carry civilization back to the wilderness.

BIBLIOGRAPHY

Craigie, Carter W. "The Vocabulary of the Picnic." *Midwestern Language and Folklore Newsletter* vol 1–2 (1978–79): 2–6.

Eyre, Karen, and Mireille Galinou. *Picnics*. London: Museum of London, 1988.

WALTER LEVY

Pies and Tarts

The early settlers were well familiar with pies from their native lands and began to bake them as soon as they set up housekeeping in America. The surrounding countryside offered the newcomers a rich array of fillings, not only fruits and berries that were akin to

Beer Garden.
Beer Gardens were introduced to the U.S. by German immigrants in the late 1800s and early 1900s before the age of industrial refrigeration. Brewers planted trees to cool the ground above the cellars where aging lager was kept, and these gardens became popular places to drink and socialize.

Clockwise from top: Fortune Cookies.
*As American as apple pie, fortune cookies were
popularized by Chinese American restaurants after World
War II, and have since spread around the world, including
to China.*

Chinese Fast Food. *According to the* Chinese
Restaurant News, *there are more Chinese restaurants in
America than branches of McDonald's, Wendy's, and
Burger King combined.*

Pizza. *The first Stateside recipe for pizza was printed in
1936 as pizzerias began popping up in cities. Soon after,
the New York Times ran an article explaining this fad as
a pastry which was "savory as opposed to sweet".*

Hamburgers. *The hamburger is the single most popular food item in the United States. Food historians agree that the "Hamburg steak" of spiced ground meat came from Germany, but offer conflicting accounts of its development after that. Though burgers had already been served at fairs by the 1920s, White Castle founders Billy Ingram and Walter Anderson are credited with inducing the burger-in-a-bun phenomenon by making five-cent hamburgers the main item on their menu.*

Margarita. Too many bartenders and restaurateurs to count, in both the U.S. and Mexico, have laid claim to this sweet, tart concoction of equal parts tequila, triple sec, and fresh lime juice, served in a salt-rimmed glass. Whatever its origins, the Margarita spread throughout both countries in the 1960s, and served as an introduction to tequila for American palates at home and on trips south of the border.

Clockwise from top left: Bloody Mary. *Parisian bartender Ferdinand Petiot is said to have first mixed vodka and tomato juice as a hangover remedy in 1921. After moving to the states, he added Worcestershire sauce, hot sauce, lemon juice, and pepper.*

Coca-Cola. *"What's great about this country is... you can be watching TV and see Coca-Cola, and you know that the President drinks Coke, Liz Taylor drinks Coke, and just think, you can drink Coke, too." —Andy Warhol, 1975*

Lemonade. *This hot weather refreshment dates back to Arab recipes from the 1300s. It gained momentum in the U.S. after First Lady "Lemonade" Lucy Webb Hayes, a teetotaler, extolled its strengths during the temperance movement of the 1870s.*

Coffee. *Coffee is the second most valuable traded commodity on earth, after oil. American colonists preferred tea until the Boston Tea Party of 1773, after which it became patriotic to switch to coffee.*

Canned Tomatoes. *In 1889, the Supreme Court reported that the single question in Nix v. The United States was whether tomatoes are fruits or vegetables, and threw the case out because it did not feel confident to rule either way. The tomato importer John Nix had appealed to the Court against having to a pay a tax on importing vegetables.*

Wine Casks. *The legitimization of American wine began to occur in the 1960s, when California vineyards started to create their own new Cabernets, Chardonnays, and Zinfandels rather than attempting weak imitations of French Burgundy and Chianti.*

Facing Page: Lasagna. *Italian food is the most popular ethnic cuisine in the U.S., though an immigrant family of the early 1900s would be unlikely to recognize many of the "Italian" foods that Americans eat today, such as pizza and lasagna.*

Times Square Chocolate Ads. *According to the U.S department of commerce, Americans consumed $17.8 billion worth of candy, which would weigh more than 6.2 billion pounds, in 2004.*

those they knew back home but also unknown vegetables and game they discovered with the help of Indians. The Pilgrims brought apple spurs with them as well, and when they matured into flourishing fruit-bearing trees, apple pie quickly dominated the American table because the abundant fruit was easy to dry and store in barrels during the winter.

Beyond mere preference, however, there was a practical reason for making pies. A piecrust used less flour than bread and did not require anything as complicated as a brick oven for baking. More important, though, was how pies could stretch even the most meager provisions into sustaining a few more hungry mouths.

The Evolution of the American Pie

No one, least of all the early settlers, would be likely to proclaim their early pies as masterpieces of culinary delight. The crusts were often heavy, composed of some form of rough flour mixed with suet that resulted in what one visitor to the colonies reported was a crust that "is not broken if a wagon wheel goes over it" (Benning, p. 3). Real pie refinement had to wait until the arrival of new immigrants—most notably religious sects from Germany who came in search of William Penn's tolerance and aristocratic Frenchmen and their followers fleeing the French Revolution's guillotine.

Recipes contributed by the German Amish and Mennonite immigrants, who were soon lumped together under the misleading designation Pennsylvania Dutch, may be distinguished by their ingenuity and for being not so much sweet as aromatic—and eloquently spiced. The most famous Pennsylvania Dutch pie is the shoo-fly pie, thick with molasses, its crust as dense as a cookie.

The French may be thanked for introducing butter into American piecrusts, thereby turning pies from mere subsistence food into an elegant dessert. In addition, although tarts, galettes, and pâtés were known and enjoyed by many colonists, these variations became more popular with the expatriates' arrival. Tarts are essentially shallow, open-faced pies (though occasionally they may sport a lattice top) with straight instead of sloping sides. More often than not they contain a sweet and delicate filling made of fruit, preserves, or custard (and sometimes all three). In America a galette is often a free-form open-faced rustic tart, but it may also be considered the missing link in the murky evolution of the Boston cream pie, that much beloved half-cake, half-pie mutt comprising a cake topped with vanilla pastry cream and satiny chocolate icing. Pâté is easily defined as any forcemeat devised of meat or fish entirely encased in dough; it is the only French export that has not become completely assimilated into American cuisine.

Pie-Making Tools

Pies are a particularly English form dating back to the Middle Ages. Originating throughout Europe as deep, free-standing meat pies with tough, often inedible crusts that needed no additional support, they came to the colonies as delicate pastry pies that required shaped ceramic pie dishes or pie plates. These were usually dinner plates of a slightly scooped, rounded shape that helped support the shallow, often sweet fillings. With the expansion of tin manufacturing in the eighteenth century, pie plates evolved into pieced-tin flat-bottomed pans with flared straight sides. Little jagging wheels were used to cut zigzag edges for lattice tops, and rolling corrugated crimping wheels sealed and decorated the rims of top and bottom crusts. Small hollow pie funnels, later "pie birds" in the shapes of blackbirds and other birds, were inserted in the top crust to allow steam to escape. Ceramic pie birds have become a popular collectible, and editions of blackbirds, bluebirds, chefs, cartoon characters, and the like have been produced since the 1940s. One-piece rolling pins were fashioned of hardwoods both on lathes and by hand and were either evenly cylindrical or tapered at both ends.

ALICE ROSS

Although mass-produced pie pans have been made for well over one hundred years of stamped tin (then aluminum), enamelware, ceramic, and glass, there has been no need to change their shape. They are still made in shallow and deep-dish versions, usually ranging in diameter between eight and ten inches. Many early to mid-twentieth-century stamped metal pans have embossed advertising; printed underglaze advertising decorates some early twentieth-century spongeware or stoneware pie plates. Inventors have focused on accessories, some of which were meant for the bakeries that began to flourish toward the later 1800s. Inventions included pie markers that marked off segments of a pie and stamped a letter on the top crust ("P" for peach, "H" for huckleberry). Pie cutters and crimpers were patented as early as the 1860s along with "improved" jagging wheels; some crimpers effected the look of pinched or twisted crust edges if the crimper was simply rolled once around the rim of the pie.

Inventors of kitchen tools have taken great interest in rolling pins, constantly seeking the perfect coolness, weight, ease of use, and nonsticky surface. A pin with double rollers was patented in 1867 by Albert Taylor of Vermont, who also in 1867 patented a flour-sprinkling rolling pin, which dusted flour over the dough as you rolled it. Glass pins that could hold ice water were tried, and a number of combination-tool pins were sold widely. Some pins made mostly of tin came apart into components, including a funnel, a doughnut cutter, a nutmeg grater, and a pie crimper. Sets of matching pins and pastry "boards" (made of tin or enameled sheet iron) from the 1890s on were made to hang on the wall between uses. The strangest rolling pin probably ever made was the Magnus, a round-framed red-and-white plastic affair with eight hot dog–like rollers and an arched handle, made in the 1940s by the Magnus Harmonica Company.

LINDA CAMPBELL FRANKLIN

Regional Variations

The common pie continued to sustain people from many different nations as they spread westward over virgin territory. Dried apples played an essential role in both wagon trains and cattle drive mess, and when the apple barrel was empty, canny cooks came up with mock apple pie, the best known being one made from crushed crackers (the makers of Ritz crackers still print the recipe on their boxes). Vinegar-soaked potatoes also made an acceptable apple substitute. Other equally ingenious mock fillings invented on the westward trails included sour green tomatoes (substituted for mincemeat) and soft-shelled river turtles (substituted for everything from oyster to chicken pie).

Once pioneers found a piece of land to call their own, their pies reflected certain regional differences. Some were due to a region's economy, such as the lingering hold of molasses-sweetened pies in southern states, which was influenced by the proximity of molasses and the rum-and-slave trade with the Caribbean Islands, while pies made with maple syrup ruled across the northern states, where Indians taught the newcomers how to tap the syrup from surrounding trees. On the great dairy farms of the Midwest, cream and cheese pies became favorites; blessed with groves of native pecan and black walnut trees, the Southwest won renown for nut pies. Swedish immigrants in the upper plains states made fish and tart berry pies plentiful, while Cornish and Finnish immigrants in Michigan's Upper Peninsula region established a certain reputation for pasties and meat pies. Florida bakers turned native limes into Key lime pie, while those in Kentucky took chess pie, a silky classic of the southern plantation's table, and added bourbon to the rich mix of sugar, cream (or buttermilk), and egg filling. In northern states, where pumpkins have always been plentiful, a preference for pumpkin pie generally holds; below the Mason-Dixon line, where sweet potatoes have been commercially grown since the mid-1600s and were a vital source of nutrition for African American slaves, the populace dreamed of creamy sweet potato pie.

The Diminishment of Pies

The hold that pies had on America's diet began to loosen in the 1870s, coinciding with the growth of the new science of nutrition, which held that consuming so much dough was weighing down the American spirit and which sought to attack the poverty and social ills afflicting both slum dwellers and the hordes of immigrants flooding into the cities by attempting to change how and what they ate. At the same time the new nutritionists, as they came to be called, found a tireless advocate in Sarah Tyson Rorer, a noted cooking teacher and the food editor of the influential *Ladies' Home Journal* who, every chance she got, took pains to warn her middle-class readers about consuming pies because they took a lot of energy to digest.

Industrialization and urbanization also took their toll on pies as the pace of life quickened. Except on farms where their presence remained crucial, women began to join the workforce in record numbers, resulting in the shortening—even the elimination—of weekly pie making to an occasional undertaking.

Pies in the Modern World: A National Emblem Reclaimed

Yet pies lingered on as an abiding symbol of the American home. Through the various world struggles of the twentieth century, popular culture continually invoked pies as the embodiment of the nation's abundant goodness. With the end of World War II and with women, reluctantly or happily, returning to the home, pies experienced a small rebound in fashion.

There was one difference, however. Advances in food science and technology had hatched all manner of ingredients that caused pie making to become less of a challenging art form. Delicate cream and chiffon fillings became foolproof with the availability of instant-pudding mixes. Fruit, in heavy syrup that would readily congeal, was sold in cans. That age-old stumbling block to a flawless pie, the crust, was made easier to achieve as well. Joining the ranks of ready-made crusts already available in stores, frozen in an aluminum tin or sold in a box to be mixed with a little water, women's magazines' and newspapers' "lifestyle" sections divulged recipes for quick crusts constructed out of everything from potato chips and popcorn to canned fried onion rings.

Giant food corporations hired teams of nutritionists to concoct some of the stranger pie creations of the later twentieth century. Thus was born the Jell-O and Cool Whip pie, the Frito-Lay corn chip pie, Bisquik's series of "miracle" pies (the ingredients for the crust and the filling were all mixed together right in the pie pan), and the Hershey Bar pie.

By the early 1980s, when a renewed interest in exploring America's culinary roots took hold, pies were being rediscovered. The overarching theme of pies in the early twenty-first century is their universality, embracing a dizzying array of cross-cultural influences. Pies may no longer play such an essential role in America's diet, but their sublime place in our collective heritage assures that they will always be savored.

[**See also** DESSERTS; PASTIES; PASTRIES.]

BIBLIOGRAPHY

Benning, Lee Edwards. *The Cook's Tales: Origins of Famous Foods and Recipes*. Old Saybrook, CT: Globe Pequot Press, 1992.

Nichols, Nell B., ed. *Farm Journal's Complete Pie Cookbook*. Garden City, NY: Doubleday, 1965.

Purdy, Susan G. *As Easy as Pie*. New York: Ballantine, 1984.

Sokolov, Raymond. *Fading Feast: A Compendium of Disappearing American Regional Foods*. New York: Farrar, Straus, Giroux, 1981.

Willard, Pat. *Pie Every Day: Recipes and Slices of Life*. Chapel Hill, NC: Algonquin Books of Chapel Hill, 1997.

PAT WILLARD

Piggly Wiggly

Clarence Saunders opened the original Piggly Wiggly at 79 Jefferson Street, Memphis, Tennessee, on September 6, 1916. It was the first self-service grocery store in America, and it changed forever the way Americans shopped for food.

Saunders (1881–1953) was born in Virginia and left school at the age of fourteen to clerk at a general store. In those days customers told clerks what they wanted, and the clerks gathered the goods from the shelves. In 1900 Saunders became a traveling salesman for a wholesale grocery distributor, and he observed that many small grocers were suffering because of heavy credit losses and high overhead.

Saunders's patented self-serve invention gave each customer a basket into which he or she placed individually priced items while walking through well-stocked aisles before visiting the checkout counter. Consumers had the benefit of greater variety, lower prices, and quicker shopping.

Saunders enjoyed causing speculation about the source of the name Piggly Wiggly. Some thought the idea may have occurred while he was riding on a train looking out the window and saw several little pigs struggling to squeeze under a fence. Or was it inspired by "this little pig went to market"? Saunders never squealed. When asked why the name Piggly Wiggly, Saunders merely replied, "So people will ask that very question" (Piggly Wiggly Company).

Saunders loved the concept of self-service, and so did his customers. The Piggly Wiggly Corporation issued franchises to hundreds of grocery retailers, who operated stores according to Saunders's rigid specifications on a strictly cash basis. Stores gave shoppers more for their food dollar through high vol-

PIGGLY WIGGLY
San Marcos, Texas

PIGGLY WIGGLY offers within easy reach famous foods from everywhere. Crisp, fresh fruits and vegetables, and the finest quality meats obtainable anywhere. We list only a few of our prices for Friday and Saturday, April 28 and 29.

Banquet—Extra Fancy
TEA, ¼ lb. **15c** ½ lb. **29c**
COCOA, Hershey's 1 lb. can **17c**
Kellogg's
CORN FLAKES, large pkg. **9c**
Stokely's
HOMINY, No. 2½ can **8c**
Premier—Vacuum Can
COFFEE, 1 lb. **26c**
Fancy Peaberry, lb. **20** Fancy Rio **15c**
Libby's
PINEAPPLE, Gallon can **39c**
CATSUP, Ruby, 14 oz. **10c**
P & G or Crystal White
SOAP, 3 giant bars **10c**
Staley's
SYRUP, ½ gal. **25c** Gallon **45c**
PICKLES, quart sour **14c**
MEAT, fresh or cured, **The Best**

The price list from a Piggly Wiggly store in San Marcos, Texas, 1933.

ume, low profit-margin retailing. Refrigerated cases kept produce fresher, employees wore uniforms, and shelves were stocked with Piggly Wiggly's own national brand.

Saunders began issuing stock in his Piggly Wiggly Corporation, and for some time it was successfully traded on the New York Stock Exchange. He began planning the construction of a mansion in Memphis to be built of pink marble from Georgia. In the 1920s, due to unwise investments, Saunders lost control of his Piggly Wiggly stores and declared bankruptcy. He began another chain, Clarence Saunders, Sole Owner of My Name Stores, which enjoyed some success, but the chain closed during the Depression. Saunders chose the brand name Keedoozle (Key-Does-All) for the prototype of an automated grocery store that the indefatigable entrepreneur designed and constructed in 1937. At the time of his death in October 1953, Saunders was working on another automatic store system that he called "Foodelectric." It never opened.

By 1929 Piggly Wiggly was the second-largest group of grocery stores in the nation. The Piggly Wiggly Company was owned by Fleming Companies, Inc., headquartered in Dallas, Texas, at the beginning of the twenty-first century.

The enduring genius of Saunders is most evident in the familiar logo of the happy pig with the jaunty little white cap that, in the early 2000s, smiles beamingly on more than eight hundred Piggly Wiggly stores in twenty-one states. The independent retailers of the Piggly Wiggly family recognize their grocery stores as the dream of an American original.

Saunders's ornate, pink Georgian marble mansion, where the entrepreneur never actually lived, was donated unfinished to the city of Memphis for use as a museum in the late 1920s. The Memphis Pink Palace, Tennessee's most visited museum, features a shrunken head, a hand-carved miniature circus, and a replica of the original Piggly Wiggly supermarket. [**See also** Food Marketing; Grocery Stores.]

BIBLIOGRAPHY

Piggly Wiggly Company. http://www.pigglywiggly.com.
Rath, Sara. *The Complete Pig.* Stillwater, MN: Voyageur, 2000.

Sara Rath

Pigs

Pigs belong to the order Artidactyla, hoofed and even-toed animals, and the family Suidae, subdivided into five genera, nine species, and many subspecies. Only one species is widespread on the American mainland, the European *Sus scrofa* or *Sus domesticus*, the domesticated pig, because pigs are not native animals but immigrants who accompanied human travelers from the Old World. An animal resembling the pig and occupying similar ecological niches already lived in the Americas, the peccary (*Tayassu tajacu*), called javelina in the Southwest.

Pigs were domesticated in the Middle East and Asia sometime in the eighth millennium B.C.E. and have been a major food animal ever since. On his second voyage (1493–1496) Christopher Columbus brought eight pigs to Hispanola, and within a decade pigs had spread to every new Spanish colony in the Caribbean. The first pork-rearing industry was established in the Spanish colony of St. Augustine in Florida (1565) and expanded to settlements in New Mexico around 1600. However, some pigs escaped and became the sleek, swift animals with large tusks later known as razorbacks. French and English colonists brought their own pigs in the seventeenth century. Jamestown, founded in 1607, eventually had so many that attempts were made to sequester them on "Pig Island." Foraging pigs decimated shellfish beds in the Massachusetts Bay Colony's tidal flats, while in New York a wall was built to control feral porkers. Pigs routinely wandered the streets of Boston, Philadelphia, and New York well into the nineteenth century.

Pig Ecology

Pigs were successful in the New World due to their extraordinary adaptability, their fecundity, and their intelligence. Like humans, they are omnivores, eating wide varieties of vegetable material and animal proteins, such as insects, eggs, frogs, mice, snakes, young birds, and carrion. Contrary to popular lore, pigs are picky if voracious eaters (they must eat frequently because they have small stomachs) and only in dire circumstances eat garbage. With only a few predators in the New World, pigs adapted rapidly to New World environments. In the warmer South, with its greater biomass, water, and pine and deciduous forests, pigs flourished; pork became a traditional staple of the regional diet. Even in the North, with cold winters, pigs did well because of their remarkable foraging abilities and herd society.

Wild pigs reproduce rapidly, even more so in farming situations. With individuals living from twelve to fifteen years and producing several litters of three to eight young each year, sometimes more, populations can grow exponentially. Visitors to the United States in the eighteenth and nineteenth centuries often commented on the enormous herds of swine they saw in living in town and country.

Pigs are social animals with a matriarchal social structure, strength in numbers being a key survival strategy. Animal ethologists estimate that among mammals pigs rank fourth in intelligence, at least by human standards. In the wild they are wily and brave, learn rapidly, and have long memories. Anecdotal evidence of pig intelligence from hunters, farmers, and pet pig owners is voluminous.

Pig Breeds

In America semidomesticated pigs were the rule into the nineteenth century, depending on the region, and were dubbed "hogs" once reaching maturity regardless of gender. Living on mast, they were prized for their fatty meat and lard-producing qualities. Purebred pigs, created with specific attributes, such as greater reproduction, or for specific kinds of meat or bacon, appeared in the later eighteenth century; most modern breeds are nineteenth-century creations. Thomas Jefferson may have begun the trend by importing Calcutta pigs (*Sus indicus*) in the early nineteenth century. The same Asians had been imported to England in the 1770s and bred with the native animals to produce the classic Yorkshire. These pigs are lighter and longer and produce leaner meat, and they are considered to be the mother breed from which many others, such as Hampshires, emerged. Yorkshires may have been imported to Pennsylvania before 1812 and appeared in Ohio in the 1830s.

The two breeds in widest use are the Poland China and the Duroc. Poland Chinas are neither Polish nor Chinese but were developed in Ohio supposedly by a farmer of Polish descent. It is a hardy, lean animal that breeds abundantly. The Duroc, developed in New York and New Jersey in the 1830s, may be descended from African pigs brought in the slave trade and from English Berkshires. Both Poland Chinas and Durocs are popular with hog farmers because they gain weight rapidly.

Pigs as Food

Until the mid-twentieth century many farm families who raised hogs did their own slaughtering. Hog-killing time was one of the year's special events. Families and neighbors gathered to share in the festivities and dine on fresh parts, such as brains and pancreas. After slaughtering and debristling, the animal was processed. Various parts, such as hams, were set aside for curing and smoking. Some of the meat was ground and stuffed into cloth sausage bags or made into patties, fried, set into containers, and covered with lard for use during the rest of the year. Lard making was especially important because it was the culinary fat of choice in rural America well into the twentieth century.

Hogs became a commodity in the nineteenth century with the industrialization of slaughtering, rendering, breeding, and rearing. The modern hog industry is an economy of scale with large farms of up to 100,000 animals dominating the market. As farms tried to lower costs and raise production, some became pork producers. Scientific research, often done at land grant universities, has optimized every aspect of pig lives, from

A nineteenth-century engraving of pig butchering.

Raeder on the Pig

Ole Munch Raeder was a jurist sent by the Norwegian government to America to study the jury system in 1847. His observations were sent to an avid Norwegian public in the form of newspaper articles and dispatches. This is one about the glorious pig.

I cannot refrain from saying a few kind words on behalf of the favorite pet of the Americans, the swine. I have not yet found any city, county, or town, where I have not seen these lovable animals wandering about peacefully in huge herds. Everywhere their domestic tendencies are much in evidence, no respectable sow appears in public unless she is surrounded by a countless number of beloved offspring. These family groups are a pleasing sight to the Americans, not only because they mean increasing prosperity, but also because a young porker is a particularly delicious morsel. Besides, the swine have shown certain good traits which are of real practical value; in the country they greedily devour all kinds of snakes and the like, and in the towns they are very helpful in keeping the streets clear "cleaner than men dan do" be eating all kinds of refuse. And then, when these walking sweers are properly filled up they are butchered and provide a real treat for the dinner table.

As with everything else that is typically American, this fondness for pork is most noticeable in the West.

BRUCE KRAIG

comfortable housing to feeding, maximum breeding, disease control, and waste removal. Producers know the chemical and physical properties of pork and can adjust conditions accordingly.

Modern pigs have been engineered, like most modern foods, to be unable to live in the wild. And unlike former days, when farmers knew their animals by personality and name, pigs have become anonymous lumps of protein.

BIBLIOGRAPHY
Horowitz, Roger. *Putting Meat on the American Table; Taste, Technology, Transformation.* Baltimore: Johns Hopkins University Press, 2006.

Horwitz, Richard P. *Hog Ties: Pigs, Manure, and Mortality in American Culture.* Minneapolis: University of Minnesota Press, 2002.

Malcolmson, Robert, and Stephanos Mastoris. *The English Pig: A History.* London: Hambledon, 1998.

Stevens, Betty. "Meat for the Multitudes." *National Provisioner* 185, no. 1, July 4, 1981.

Pukite, John. *A Field Guide to Pigs.* Helena, MT: Falcoln, 1999.

BRUCE KRAIG

Pike

In the family Esocidae are three popular American sport and food fish—pike, pickerel, and muskellunge. Also in this group are walleye and sauger. Pike is the most widely distributed freshwater fish in the world, found in North America, Europe, and northern Asia, usually in lakes and slowly moving streams. Pike have elongated, even serpentine, bodies and flattened heads with duck-billed jaws and sharp back-slanting teeth. Muskellunge (*Esox masquinongy*), nicknamed "muskie" by sport anglers, is the largest of the pikes, averaging between ten and thirty pounds, some trophy fish weighing sixty pounds. Muskellunge occurs naturally in the Great Lakes but has been introduced elsewhere.

Northern pike (*Esox lucius*), also called common pike or American pike, jackfish, northern, and other names, averages eighteen to thirty inches in length and weigh slightly more than one pound to eight pounds, although the largest can measure more than four feet and weigh forty pounds. The Latin species name *lucius* is derived from the Greek *lukos* (wolf) and describes the fish's fierce predatory habit and capacity for fight when caught.

Pike, a favorite with ice fishers, once was part of the Great Lakes commercial fishery and is considered good for eating. One of the fish mentioned by Izaak Walton, pike was recognized by settlers coming to North America as a good food fish, although there is scant mention of pike by name in cookery literature. Depending on size, pike was traditionally baked, poached, or roasted. More recent recipes call for panfrying, stuffing and baking, grilling, or steaming. The mild-flavored fish requires saucing or vegetable accompaniments for flavor interest.

SANDRA L. OLIVER

Pillsbury

Charles A. Pillsbury (1842–1899) bought one-third of the Minneapolis Flour Milling Company in 1869. By the early 1870s, using modernized equipment to process the local spring wheat at several mills, his company was producing two thousand barrels of flour a day. Renamed C. A. Pillsbury and Company in 1872, it adopted the trademark Pillsbury's Best XXXX (the four x's constituting a medieval symbol for top quality).

Pillsbury installed "middlings purifiers" in 1871, implementing a process developed at the Washburn Mills (later to become General Mills) that removed dark specks of hull, producing whiter flour. In the mid-1870s Pillsbury began using a Hungarian innovation that he saw on a visit to Europe, involving sets of iron and porcelain steamrollers that crushed and disintegrated the wheat, replacing traditional millstones; all of the bran and wheat germ was removed, producing an even whiter and longer-lasting flour and boosting production by 3 percent. Pillsbury's brother sold the leftover bran as animal feed.

The company was expanding rapidly, and in 1882 it built a huge new facility, called the "A Mill," which was the largest flour mill in the Western Hemisphere. By 1889 the mill was producing almost seven thousand barrels of flour a day. The company continued to innovate and grow throughout the 1880s, helping Minneapolis become the leading flour-producing city in the United States.

An English financial syndicate acquired C. A. Pillsbury in 1889 along with Washburn Mills, creating Pillsbury-Washburn Flour Mills. Led by Charles Pillsbury, it was the world's largest miller, producing fifteen thousand barrels of flour a day. In 1923 Pillsbury's sons and a nephew bought out the English owners and formed Pillsbury Flour Mills.

The new company began producing cake flours and cereals in 1932. Throughout the 1940s it specialized in kitchen staples, introducing the first convenience baking product, Pie Crust Mix, in 1945 and cake mixes in 1948. To celebrate the company's eightieth birthday, a contest, the Pillsbury Bake-Off, was held in 1949 at the Waldorf Astoria Hotel in New York City.

Pillsbury acquired Ballard and Ballard Flour in 1950 and introduced fresh dough products, followed by refrigerated cookie dough in 1957. The Pillsbury Doughboy was introduced in a television commercial for Crescent Rolls in 1965. In the succeeding decades, Pillsbury made many major acquisitions worldwide: Burger King in 1967, Totino's Pizza in 1975, Green Giant in 1979, the Steak & Ale restaurant chain in 1976, and Häagen-Dazs ice cream in 1983.

After twenty-seven years of steady growth involving over two hundred products in fifty-five countries, losses began to mount in the mid-1980s, particularly in the restaurant sector. Pillsbury was acquired in a $5.75 billion hostile takeover in 1989 by the United Kingdom–based food and spirits company Grand Metropolitan. Pillsbury's fortunes improved under GrandMet (renamed Diageo after a merger in 1997), and acquisitions continued: Country Hearth bread in 1993, Martha White mixes and flours in 1994, and Pet in 1995, including Old El Paso Mexican foods, Progresso, and Pet-Ritz pie crusts.

In October 2002 Pillsbury was sold to General Mills, its long-time rival, for $10.4 billion, creating the world's fifth-largest packaged food company. After a Federal Trade Commission review, several Pillsbury brands, including Martha White, Pillsbury baking mixes, and Softasilk flour, were sold to avoid antitrust concerns.

[**See also** PILLSBURY BAKE-OFF; PILLSBURY DOUGHBOY.]

BIBLIOGRAPHY

"Pillsbury, Charles Alfred." *American National Biography Online*. New York: Oxford University Press, 2000. http://www.anb.org.

Grant, Tina, ed. *International Directory of Company Histories*. Vol. 13. New York: Pillsbury Company, 1996.

JOY SANTLOFER

Pillsbury Bake-Off

Pillsbury's Grand National Recipe and Baking Contest—dubbed the Bake-Off (now a Pillsbury trademark)—was inaugurated in 1949, marking the company's eightieth anniversary and the postwar return to normal home life. Each recipe submitted was required to use a half-cup of Pillsbury's flour, and contestants (mostly women, mostly homemakers) responded with from-scratch pies, cakes, cookies, crisps, cobblers, doughnuts, dumplings, quick breads, and yeast breads. Submissions were winnowed down by a team of home economists, and the finals were held at the Waldorf Astoria Hotel, where one hundred electric stoves filled the ballroom. The winner, for her No-Knead Water-Rising Twists (that is, sweet rolls) was Mrs. Ralph E. Smafield of Detroit; her $25,000 Grand Prize was presented by Eleanor Roosevelt, who also served as a judge. (The Grand Prize became $1 million in 1996.)

In 1951 Jack Meili became the first male prizewinner, taking second place in the junior division with wiener-filled Hot Ziggities. (Creative nomenclature is a Bake-Off tradition.) Over the years the use of Pillsbury convenience products—notably cake, cookie, and frosting mixes and refrigerated dough—was encouraged, and "quick and easy preparation" became a judging standard.

An illustrated booklet published after each Bake-Off affords the winning recipes wide distribution, and early Bake-Off booklets (especially the first one) are sought-after collectibles. Browsing through them yields fascinating insights into a half-century of bak-

Pillsbury Doughboy

459

A bake off winner with Ronald Reagan, who later became President.

ing in America, and quite a few of the winning recipes have become national favorites.

[**See also** PILLSBURY; PILLSBURY DOUGHBOY; RECIPES.]

BIBLIOGRAPHY

Pillsbury, Ann [pseud.]. *Best of the Bake-Off Collection*. Chicago: Consolidated Book Publishers, 1959.

BONNIE J. SLOTNICK

Pillsbury Doughboy

In 1965 Leo Burnett's Chicago ad agency, known for creating many endearing trademark critters to build brands, was assigned the Pillsbury refrigerated-dough account. In search of a character, the creative director Rudy Perz whacked a tube of dough on the table and imagined what might pop out.

A seven-and-one-half-inch-tall Doughboy, weighing the equivalent of two and one-half cups of flour, did. The little fellow was a natural, an outgrowth of the product itself who would go on to become the perfect spokesboy.

But first he needed a voice. Perz auditioned fifty actors before choosing Paul Frees, who also provided the voice of Boris Badenov in *The Adventures of Rocky and Bullwinkle* cartoon series. One of the twelve different dialects Frees used featured the catchy "Hoo, hoo" giggle that, along with the tummy poke, would become the Doughboy's signature.

The Doughboy was soon ready for his first TV commercial. In it he jumped out of a container of Crescent Dinner Rolls and danced a two-step on the kitchen counter.

He introduced himself as "Poppin' Fresh, the Pillsbury Doughboy" and announced Pillsbury's slogan, "Nothin' Says Lovin' Like Something from the Oven, and Pillsbury Says It Best."

Although the Doughboy has become hipper over the years, at times rapping or playing blues harmonica in commercials, his personality has not changed much. He has always been helpful, trustworthy, likable, friendly, charming, and adorable, some might even say irresistible. His appearance too has remained the same—small and plump, with a doughy white complexion. He always sports a large chef's hat, a neckerchief, and a big smile. In addition to having a delightful personality, he is a versatile, multitalented little guy, having appeared as a ballet dancer, singer, musician, painter, rap artist, teacher, poet, cupid, business executive, announcer, skateboarder, and even a cuckoo in a cuckoo clock.

The Doughboy's role, however, has changed over time. Originally envisioned as the ideal homemaker's helper, he was the main character in early commercials. He offered encouraging words and helped out in the kitchen. His job was to convince consumers that Pillsbury's products were as good as those made from scratch. In the 1970s and the early 1980s, when he was considered dated, he made only cameo appearances in commercials, showing up for a belly poke and a giggle at the end of each ad. By the late 1980s, however, he was found at center stage in starring roles, like strumming air guitar for Pillsbury Cinnamon Rolls. His later tasks were more closely focused on the products. He is likely to highlight a product attribute—for example, to close up a resealable package.

The Doughboy quickly captured the hearts of Americans and held onto them. By 1968 he was recognized in a random sampling by nine out of ten Americans, giving him a recognition factor similar to that of the president of the United States. In 1987 he won *Advertising Age*'s Whom Do You Love? contest. *Advertising Age* considers him to be number six of the top ten advertising icons of the twentieth century.

[**See also** ADVERTISING; BISCUIT CUTTERS; PILLSBURY.]

BIBLIOGRAPHY

Pillsbury Company. *Poppin' Fresh Recipes: Appetizers to Desserts; The Doughboy Picks His Favorites.* Pillsbury Classic Cookbooks. Minneapolis, MN: Pillsbury, 1990.

SHARON KAPNICK

Pilsener

This style of beer is a light-straw colored, full bodied, lagered, bottom-fermented beer named after the town of Plzeň (Pilsen) in what was then known as Bohemia, where it was first brewed in 1842. It quickly became a popular unique style because it was so different from the amber brews that were the norm at that time. Pilsner Urquell (literal translationis "original from Plzeň"), named for the town of Plzeň in what is now the Czech Republic, was the first golden colored lager developed in the seventeenth century. Until that time almost all brews, ale and lager, were amber colored or darker.

Unlike the producers of champagne, who legislated on an international level, the use of the word "pilsener" on the label of a beer often has no relation at all to the place of origin of that particular beer. The word "pilsener" has come to mean any bottom-fermented, golden colored, sparkling malt beverage. Even the Association of Brewers' 2004 Beer Style Guidelines has three different pilsener classifications: European-style pilsener, German-style pilsener, and American-style pilsener. They describe the American-style pilsener as a "classic and unique pre-Prohibition American-style Pilsener [that] is straw to deep gold in color. Hop bitterness, flavor and aroma are medium to high, and use of noble-type hops for flavor and aroma is preferred. Up to 25 percent corn in the grist should be used, and some slight sweetness and flavor of corn are expected. Alcohol by volume is between 5–6%."

PETER LAFRANCE

Pimiento Cheese Sandwich

Pimiento cheese has often been called the "comfort food" of the American South, where the sandwich filling is usually homemade in either a cooked or uncooked version and served on white bread. The basic mixture includes grated cheddar or american cheese combined with mayonnaise, chopped canned pimientos, salt, and pepper. Various additions include mustard, cayenne or hot red pepper sauce, garlic, lemon juice, Worcestershire sauce, or horseradish. Researchers have been unable to discover the origin of pimiento cheese, but its popularity has been noted since the availability of hoop cheese in country stores. A recipe for Pimento [sic] Sandwich appeared in the *Up-to-date Sandwich Book* (1909) by Eva Greene Fuller. By the Depression, pimiento cheese sandwiches were served as a popular and economical meal throughout the United States. They were even featured on luncheon menus of some restaurants, including the Hotel Barbara Worth in El Centro, California, where in 1930 the sandwich was priced at thirty cents. Pimiento cheese remains a favorite homemade sandwich filling, and in the South it is also a popular topping for hamburgers and hot dogs.

[**See also** CHEESE; SANDWICHES; SOUTHERN REGIONAL COOKERY.]

BIBLIOGRAPHY

Mercuri, Becky. *Sandwiches That You Will Like.* Pittsburgh, PA: WQED Multimedia, 2002.

BECKY MERCURI

Pineapple

The pineapple (*Ananas comosus*) originated in South America, probably in the area around the Orinoco and Negro river basins. Technically it is not a single fruit but the fruits of a hundred or more separate flowers that grow on a central plant spike. As they grow, they swell with juice and pulp, expanding to become the fruit. There are two major pineapple cultivars: the Smooth Cayenne from Venezuela, which is cultivated for its large, juicy fruit and lack of spines on its leaves, and the Red Spanish from the Caribbean.

In pre-Columbian times pineapples grew widely in Central America and the Caribbean, where they were called *anana*. Caribbean Indians introduced the pineapple to early Spanish explorers, who, noting that it resembled a pinecone, called it *piña*, from whence the English word derives. The Spanish promptly shipped some pineapples back to Spain, where they became an instant sensation. Pineapples were disseminated to Africa and Asia during the sixteenth century. While pineapples thrived in tropical climates, European gardeners had to grow them in hothouses for the wealthy.

In North America, English colonists imported pineapples from the Caribbean beginning in the seventeenth century. The pineapple became a symbol of hospitality in America; pineapple motifs were common in the decorative arts of colonial America, including in architecture, furniture, gateposts, and silverware. Pineapple recipes appeared in English cookbooks during the eighteenth century and in American cookbooks by the early nineteenth century. Mary Randolph's *Virginia House-Wife* (1824), for instance, includes a recipe for pineapple ice cream. Over the decades several attempts were made to cultivate pineapples commercially in Florida and California, but growers were unable to compete with lower-cost production in foreign lands.

Pineapples were also canned in small quantities in Florida and the Caribbean by 1882. The major American pineapple industry started in Hawaii. Pineapples had appeared in Hawaii well before it became a U.S. territory in 1898. Plantations grew pineapples that were shipped to West Coast American cities, but this was expensive. Canning in Hawaii began in 1885 but was of little importance until Jim Dole founded the Hawaiian Pineapple Company in 1901. Pineapple production increased dramatically. By 1911, 95 percent of all Hawaiian pineapples were canned and sent to the mainland. By 1921 pineapple was Hawaii's largest crop and industry.

The vast increase in supply created the need to expand the market, and pineapple growers encouraged publication of pineapple recipes, which soon appeared in cookery magazines and cookbooks. For instance, Riley M. Fletcher Berry's *Fruit Recipes* (1907) included thirty-four pineapple recipes, among them pineapple beer, champagne, muffins, fritters, and omelets. Around 1909 the Hawaii

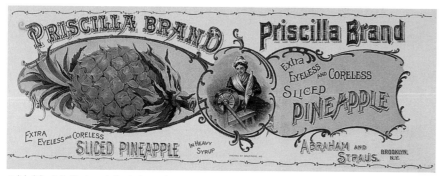

A label for Priscilla brand sliced pineapples.

Pineapple Growers' Association issued its first advertising cookery booklet encouraging Americans to serve pineapple in new ways. During the following decade the cost of canned pineapple decreased until it was affordable to almost all Americans. Cookery magazines and cookbook authors published hundreds of recipes for using canned pineapple, including such dishes as hollowed out pineapple boats for edible presentation of cold salads, vegetables, or fruits; pineapple upside-down cake; and numerous dishes with pork, seafood, and poultry.

Until the 1960s Hawaii supplied almost three-quarters of the world's pineapples, but urbanization and labor costs encouraged Dole and other growers to transfer production to the Philippines, Thailand, and Costa Rica. By 2002 Hawaii produced less than 10 percent of the world's pineapple crops. But pineapple remained a staple in the American diet.

[See also ADVERTISING COOKBOOKLETS AND RECIPES; CANNING AND BOTTLING; FRUIT; RANDOLPH, MARY.]

BIBLIOGRAPHY
Beauman, Francesca. *Pineapple: King of Fruits.* London: Chatto and Windus, 2005.
Hyles, Claudia. *And the Answer Is a Pineapple: The King of Fruit in Folklore, Fabric, and Food.* Burra Creek, New South Wales, Australia: Milner, 1998.

ANDREW F. SMITH

Pinedo, Encarnación

Encarnación Pinedo (1848 1902), cookbook author, wrote the first cookbook by a Hispanic in the United States. *El Cocinero Español* (The Spanish cook) is a landmark, the only contemporary record of what Californios (the original Spanish colonists in California and their descendants) ate and how they prepared it. Through the nineteenth century the Californios lost their social, political, and economic dominance to the Anglo-Americans. Encarnación Pinedo deliberately attempted to keep her cultural foodways from disappearing by compiling this cookbook, printed in San Francisco in 1898.

Encarnación Pinedo's family suffered considerably during the Anglo takeover of California. Her first ancestor in California was her great-grandfather Nicolas Berreyesa,

who arrived in the San Francisco Bay Area with the De Anza expedition in 1775. His son, her grandfather, José Berreyesa, received a land grant for the Rancho San Vicente. It included the valuable New Almaden quicksilver mine, which became a source of tragedy and litigation for the prominent family. José married Maria Bernal, and their daughter, Maria del Carmen, was born in 1811. As the Americans established control over California, they lynched or shot eight Berreyesa men, including Encarnación's namesake uncle. José himself was murdered by Kit Carson in 1846.

Maria del Carmen married an Ecuadoran, Lorenzo Pinedo, and they had two daughters, Dolores, born April 29, 1845, and Encarnación, born May 21, 1848. Lorenzo died suddenly of cholera in 1852, when Encarnación was only four. Encarnación received a secondary education at a well-regarded convent school, the Notre Dame Academy in San Jose, but then, whether or not she ever wanted to marry, she conformed with Mexican custom and devoted her life to caring for her widowed mother. When Maria del Carmen died in 1876, Encarnación was twenty-eight, too old to marry. Her sister, however, had married an Anglo, much against the family's wishes. It is known that by 1880 Encarnación was living in her sister's household and cooking for the family. Her book was published when she was fifty, and on April 9, 1902, she died at fifty-three.

In *El Cocinero Espanol,* Pinedo comments on the insipidity of English food, and one may infer that she feels the same way about the American foodways familiar to her brother-in-law. Her book is one of the most comprehensive cookbooks published in California in the nineteenth century. Most California cookbooks of the period were much smaller. Her book includes some 880 recipes, in which she demonstrates a liberal use of spices, chilies, vinegars, and wines. No American cookbook of the time includes more than a few Mexican (usually called "Spanish") recipes. The sophistication of her recipes is striking, their range remarkable. Pinedo includes recipes not only from Mexico and Spain but from France and Italy as well. The nuns of her convent school may have had a library of cookbooks, and San

Francisco was certainly a bookish city with European connections.

Pinedo was not a professional writer. She took some of her recipes from published sources. Some recipes are detailed, while others are sketchy, and they are written in different and inconsistent voices. Nonetheless, *El Cocinero Español* is a major culinary work, clear evidence that the Mexican community in California harbored cooks of great sophistication showcasing a wealth of flavors that were not widely known in the Anglo community until decades later.

[See also CALIFORNIA; MEXICAN AMERICAN FOOD.]

BIBLIOGRAPHY
Pinedo, Encarnación. *Encarnación's Kitchen: Mexican Recipes from Nineteenth-Century California.* Edited and translated by Dan Strehl. Berkeley: University of California Press, 2003.

DAN STREHL

Pine Nuts

Pine nuts are the seeds of any member of the pine tree family (Pinaceae). Pine nuts were commonly consumed by Native Americans. Piñon nuts (*Pinus edulis*) were particularly important to pre-Columbian Native Americans in the Southwest. They were eaten raw or roasted. Roasted nuts were ground into flour, then mixed with cornmeal to make bread. Pine nuts are an important wild food but have been minimally commercialized. Old World pine nuts have been imported into the United States, and Italian pignoli are the kind most commonly available. Pignoli are sold shelled and are used in pasta dishes and sauces as well as in cakes and cookies.

[See also NATIVE AMERICAN FOODS; NUTS.]

ANDREW F. SMITH

Pinole

Pinole is flour or powder made of toasted maize and also the beverage prepared by dissolving the powder in water or milk. Sugar, other sweeteners, or flavorings such as chocolate, vanilla, or cinnamon may be added. Pinole (from the Nahuatl *pinolli*) belongs to the category of maize-based *atole* gruels used by native peoples in Mexico and the American Southwest. Because pinole requires no cooking, the Aztecs found it ideal for travelers. Spanish explorers quickly adopted it, and pinole became a staple among Hispanic settlers as well as Native Americans. In *Commerce of the Prairies* (1844), a classic account of the Santa Fe trade, Josiah Gregg likened pinole to the "cold flour" of the northern Plains Indians, used by hunters and fur trappers, and noted that some tribes made a similar product from dried mesquite beans. Pinole is still used by elderly people in Hispanic and Native American communities.

[See also CORN; NATIVE AMERICAN FOOD: BEFORE AND AFTER CONTACT; SOUTHWESTERN REGIONAL COOKERY.]

Pinole

461

BIBLIOGRAPHY

Coe, Sophie D. *America's First Cuisines*. Austin: University of Texas Press, 1994.

CHERYL J. FOOTE

Pioneers and Survival Food

From the arrival of the earliest settlers to the closing of the American frontier, pioneers in the wilderness depended on food supplies for their survival. They prepared by bringing staples, seeds, and as much animal stock as they could transport over difficult terrain, and they depended on skills and equipment for foraging, hunting, and fishing. The first stage of life on the frontier often lasted a relatively short time, sometimes only two or three years, before the area's growth could support trade and supplies from the outside. The timing depended largely on available transportation. For example, Ohio River settlements, benefiting from the river's commerce, grew beyond the frontier stage far more quickly than remote areas of the Smoky Mountains.

Survival strategy drove immigrants to arrive at the last possible moment, that is, with enough time to become established before the freezes but not so early as to use up staples needed to get them through the winter. They packed using information from published lists of recommendations. Most brought preserving salt, flours, beans, salt pork, bacon, molasses, and perhaps a little tea and sugar. Those who could also brought draft animals, cattle, pigs, and "dung hill fowl" (poultry). In later years rice, dried apples, and potatoes were added; these were supplemented by foods from the wild.

Good foraging was essential while waiting for field crops, gardens, and herds and flocks to become productive. Hunting, trapping, and fishing were often the major sources of food, but they provided a boring and scurvy-producing diet. Foraged nuts, fruits, berries, greens, and roots added occasional seasonal diversity, dried cattail roots or processed acorns made palatable starches, and English tea was replaced with infusions of monarda or of red sumac berries.

At first frontier fields and gardens on newly worked soils yielded uncertain results. Depending on the time of arrival and plant requirements, northern gardens held corn, beans, squash, pumpkins, and assorted root vegetables that dried easily or stored well. Gardens planted late were limited to short-season plants, such as peas and greens. Cabbages and parsnips, which withstood cold when mulched, were wintered in the ground and dug as needed. Southern settlers found longer growing seasons and had more flexibility in what they planted. Ethnic cuisines were perforce adapted to materials at hand. In emergencies it was sometimes possible to obtain corn or meat from Native Americans; eating one's breeding stock or seed was the last resort.

Cooking utensils were also limited—often a large iron pot, a frying pan, some tinware, and a teakettle, supplemented by home-fashioned implements. With little equipment and heavy demands on time, newcomers cooked simply, frequently making one-dish meals of meats, root vegetables (when at hand), corn, and beans. Improvised cookery made use of hot embers and ash to bake flat breads and ash cakes, root vegetables, and meats. Roasting methods included planking (securing meat or fish to the face of a split log propped before the fire), string roasting (suspending a roast near the heat from a length of twisting homemade string), or spit roasting on a green branch. Foods that were abundant were preserved by drying and smoking; customary preservatives (sugar, vinegar, and salt) were scarce. Although many settlers did not survive this harsh regimen, large numbers of the young and healthy lived to enlarge their holdings and prosper.

[See also FRONTIER COOKING OF THE FAR WEST; HEARTH COOKERY.]

BIBLIOGRAPHY

Stratton, Joanna L. *Pioneer Women: Voices from the Kansas Frontier*. New York: Simon and Schuster, 1981.

ALICE ROSS

Pistachios

The pistachio (*Pistacia vera*) is native to central Asia, where it has been cultivated for over nine thousand years. The ancient Greeks consumed pistachios, and the nuts were introduced to Italy in the first century C.E. The first pistachio seeds were planted in California and several southern states in 1854, but the trees did not thrive. Pistachio nuts were imported and recipes for them published in American cookbooks after the beginning of the twentieth century. In 1929 William E. Whitehouse, an American plant scientist, planted pistachio seeds from Iran in California's San Joaquin Valley, where they thrived. The nuts became popular during the 1930s, when they were largely sold to immigrant groups and distributed through vending machines. In 1976 the first major crop of pistachio nuts was harvested in California, which, in the early 2000s, was the world's second-largest producer. Roasted pistachio nuts in the shell are an addictive snack; the nuts are also used in pastries, cakes, confectioneries, and ice cream, and pistachios appear in some savory dishes as well. The nuts are a good source of protein and several important minerals.

[See also CALIFORNIA; NUTS.]

BIBLIOGRAPHY

Grimes, Gwin Grogan. *Nuts: Pistachio, Pecan, and Piñon*. Tucson, AZ: Rio Nuevo Publishers, 2006.

ANDREW F. SMITH

Pizza

Also called "pizza pie" or "tomato pie," pizza is a flat bread dough made with flour, yeast, salt, olive oil, and water, topped with various combinations of meats, cheeses, and vegetables, and baked in a hot oven. In the United States the combinations of pizza toppings are imaginative and seemingly unlimited.

Pizza came to America at the end of the nineteenth century with immigrants from southern Italy. Italian immigrants built commercial bakeries and backyard ovens to produce breads they had eaten in Italy. In addition Italian bakers used their ovens for flat breads: northern Italians baked focaccia, while southern Italians made pizza. Initially pizza was made by Italians for Italians, but by the late 1930s, after the Great Depression, many Americans were eating pizza in Italian restaurants and pizzerias on the East and West Coasts.

The first American cookbook recipe for pizza appeared in *Specialità Culinarie Italiane, 137 Tested Recipes of Famous Italian Foods*, a fund-raising cookbook published in Boston in 1936. That recipe, for Neapolitan pie or Pizza alla Napolitana, directed that pizza dough be hand-stretched until it was one-quarter-inch thick. The dough was topped with salt and pepper, scamozza (scamorza) cheese, tomatoes, grated parmesan

Two women prepare food over an open fire in a pioneer camp.

cheese, and olive oil in that order. There were no ingredients for the pizza dough itself; instead, the reader was told that the dough "can be purchased in any Italian bake shop."

Over time two basic and distinct styles of American pizza appeared. A thin-crust pizza, commonly called East Coast or New York style, is made with just a few toppings, like *pizze* made in Naples. A common type of thin-crust pie is topped with a light tomato sauce, shredded fresh whole milk mozzarella, and sprinkled dried oregano. After baking, the thin crust should not be too crisp; it should be flexible so that a piece of pizza can be folded in half lengthwise. The crust of thick- or double-crust pizza, also called West Coast style, serves as a foundation for a larger number and amount of toppings. Pizzas with several meats, various vegetables, such as artichoke hearts, zucchini, mushrooms, olives, and onions, with a spicy tomato sauce, and two or three cheeses are not uncommon.

There are several uniquely American pizzas. Deep-dish or Chicago style pizza originated at Pizzeria Uno on East Ohio Street in Chicago in 1943. It is made and baked in a twelve- or fourteen-inch round metal pie pan that has two-inch-deep sides. The pizza dough is placed in the pan, stretched to cover the bottom, and pressed up the sides of the pan. To fill the crust, sliced mozzarella, chunky chopped tomatoes, and sweet Italian sausage are layered on top. Stuffed pizza is a type of Chicago deep-dish. After the bottom crust is filled with chopped spinach and mozzarella and parmesan cheeses, a second, thinner crust is added. The second crust is topped with a spicy crushed tomato sauce.

California or gourmet pizza originated in 1980 at Chez Panisse, a restaurant in Berkeley, California. The Chez Panisse pizzas were lighter; the dough was very thin, often creating a crackerlike crust. Reflecting the philosophy of the restaurant, the pizza toppings were simple combinations of a few fresh ingredients or flavors. Chez Panisse used non-Italian cheeses that came from local suppliers. Many pizzas had no tomatoes and no tomato sauce.

Many Americans make pizza at home. Some people prefer their homemade pizza baked on a square or round thick ceramic tile, called a pizza stone. When a pizza stone is placed in a kitchen oven and preheated, the stone mimics a hearth. For people who do not want to make fresh dough, a premade pizza crust, such as Boboli produces, can be purchased at most food stores. For those who prefer their pizza assembled and ready to bake, most pizzerias sell take-and-bake pizzas, while grocery stores sell unbaked frozen pizzas.

Any doubt about pizza's place in mainstream American culture was erased when pizza was mentioned in an Academy Award–nominated song from the 1953 movie *The Caddy*. "That's Amoré," sung by Dean Martin and Jerry Lewis, included the sing-along line: "When the moon hits your eye like a big pizza pie, that's amoré."

[**See also** FAST FOOD; ITALIAN AMERICAN FOOD; PIZZA HUT; PIZZERIAS; TAKE-OUT FOODS.]

BIBLIOGRAPHY

Bruno, Pasquale, Jr. *The Ultimate Pizza: The World's Favorite Pizza Recipes; From Deep-Dish to Dessert.* Chicago: Contemporary Books, 1995.

Reinhart, Peter. *American Pie: My Search for the Perfect Pizza.* Berkeley, CA: Ten Speed, 2003.

ROBERT W. BROWER

Pizza Hut

Pizza Hut is an international chain of quick-service pizza restaurants founded in Wichita, Kansas, in 1958. Significant in food history, Pizza Hut was primarily responsible for popularizing pizza, bringing a food item previously available only from pizzerias in urban Italian neighborhoods into American standard cuisine. Through extensive franchising, Pizza Hut successfully introduced pizza to consumers in small towns across the United States and eventually throughout the world.

The success of Pizza Hut has more to do with the late-1950s revolution in fast food franchising than with any tradition of Italian immigrant cuisine. With no experience in pizza making but looking for income to pay their college tuitions, the brothers Dan and Frank Carney borrowed $600 from their mother to open their first pizza restaurant in a rented brick building. The brothers needed a name for their restaurant. On a tight budget, they decided that they could afford only to modify the existing sign on their roof; it had room for eight letters, with the first five already spelling "Pizza" left over by the previous tenant. One of their relatives said that their small building resembled a hut and suggested that the word "Hut" be added to the sign. It fit, and the Carneys had their company name. Pizza Hut's success was immediate. With their new restaurant generating sizable profits, the Carneys abandoned their educations, instead expanding their operation and selling franchises. Midwestern consumers loved their pizza, and franchises sold quickly. As their chain grew to eighty-five restaurants by 1965, the brothers established a uniform architecture featuring a sweeping red roof, common marketing strategies, and company-wide standards for customer service. At the peak of their expansion, the Carneys were opening a new restaurant every day.

Though Pizza Huts offered inside seating, over half of their business was done on a take-out basis, enabling them to compete with other types of fast food. The appeal of their pizza, however, had its cultural and regional limitations. Consumers accustomed to authentic pizza from Italian pizzerias did not like Pizza Hut's bland fare. Frank Carney quickly adapted his pizza to suit local tastes, sacrificing product uniformity throughout his chain for the sake of profitability. In addition to regional variations, he soon also offered customers a thin-crust pizza, a thick, Chicago-style pan pizza, sandwiches, and several pasta dishes. Heightened competition from a growing number of pizza chains in the 1970s proved to be a greater threat than regional preferences. California-based Shakey's Pizza Parlors and Omaha's Godfather's Pizza spread quickly, competing for eat-in customers, while the streamlined, low-overhead operations of Domino's and Little Caesars came to dominate the take-out market. Even advances in frozen-food technology undercut the pizza market, providing consumers with a new array of lower-cost pizza choices in grocery store freezer cases.

While still enjoying a comfortable lead in their industry in 1977 with 1,246 company-owned outlets and 1,075 franchisees, the Carneys sold Pizza Hut to PepsiCo, Inc., for over $300 million in PepsiCo stock. PepsiCo retained Frank Carney as head of the company, but he soon resigned, first to become a large-scale franchisee for the Chi-Chi's Mexican food chain and later a franchiser for the competitor Papa John's Pizza. The pizza industry was highly saturated by the late 1980s, but Pizza Hut continued to thrive as a PepsiCo subsidiary by offering such new and innovative pizza products as Super Supreme, Sicilian Pan, Priazzo, Calizza, and Hand-Tossed Traditional Pizza. In the 1990s new products included the Personal Pan, the Bigfoot, Stuffed Crust, Italian Chicken, and Big New Yorker pizzas and spicy chicken wings. Expansion into new markets grew even faster than the menu. Still dominating the domestic United States pizza industry, PepsiCo concentrated on spreading Pizza Hut around the globe in the early twenty-first century.

[**See also** FAST FOOD; FROZEN FOOD; ITALIAN AMERICAN FOOD; PIZZA; PIZZERIAS; TAKE-OUT FOODS.]

BIBLIOGRAPHY

Gumpert, David E. *Inc. Magazine Presents How to Really Create a Successful Business Plan: Featuring the Business Plans of Pizza Hut, Software Publishing Corp., Celestial Seasonings, People Express, and Ben and Jerry's.* Boston: Inc. Publishing, 1996.

Luxenberg, Stan. *Roadside Empires: How the Chains Franchised America.* New York: Viking Press, 1985.

DAVID GERARD HOGAN

Pizzerias

Colloquially called "pizza parlors" or "pizza joints," pizzerias are restaurants that have high-temperature ovens specially designed and constructed to bake pizza. The type of oven significantly influences the pizzeria's products and consequently helps define the restaurant.

Some pizzerias have wood-burning hearth ovens that can attain temperatures of 850°F. These ovens must be manned by skilled pizza makers who by training and experience know how to form a pizza by hand, how to use a pizza peel (a large, long-handled wood or metal paddle) to load the oven, when to rotate the pizza in the oven for even baking, and when to remove the pizza from the oven. An experienced pizza maker can produce up to one hundred pizzas per hour in a single wood-burning hearth oven. Because of the high temperature of the oven, a thin-crust pizza placed on the preheated hearth cooks quickly. The crust of the pizza will be dark and crisp from the high heat of the hearth, and it may have a distinctive wood-smoke taste.

Gas or electric commercial pizza ovens bake at 600–650°F. Although these lower-temperature ovens are easier to use, they retain the advantage of producing a pizza baked on a solid deck of hot baking stone or metal.

High-volume pizzerias use conveyor-belt ovens and mechanically formed pizzas. Dough rounds are formed with a press or rollers, and then the pizzas are placed side by side on a continuous stainless steel belt that moves them through the oven. The pizzas are cooked by a heat source below the belt. Experience is not necessary; anyone can place an unbaked pizza on the belt at one end of the oven and pick up a fully baked pizza at the other end. Conveyor-belt systems also allow pizzas to be baked and served in nontraditional settings, such as snack stands in warehouse discount stores and twenty-four-hour-a-day pizza operations on cruise ships.

Introduction of Pizzas

The first American pizzerias were started by Italian immigrants who built hearth ovens similar to those they had in Italy. On the East Coast immigrants from southern Italy built brick hearth ovens, usually fueled by coal, to bake Neapolitan-style pizza. It is generally agreed that Gennaro Lombardi, an immigrant from Naples, opened the first licensed American pizzeria in New York's Little Italy in 1905. Expansion of the pizza business was slow. Anthony "Totonno" Pero, one of Lombardi's employees, opened Totonno's, a coal-fired brick-oven pizzeria, at Coney Island in 1924. Another Lombardi employee, John Sasso, opened John's Pizzeria in New York's Greenwich Village in 1929.

On the West Coast northern Italian immigrants built hearth ovens to bake Italian breads and the Ligurian specialty flat bread focaccia. Commercial Neapolitan pizza arrived much later. The first West Coast pizzeria, Lupo's, opened in San Francisco in 1936. For non-Italians, Lupo's pizza was called "tomato pie."

In the United States there are two pizzeria business forms, independent and franchise. Independent pizzerias are owned and operated by the same person, family, or company and operate within a small, well-defined urban area. It is not uncommon for an independent chain to have two or three locations. The largest American independent pizza chain in terms of gross sales is Amici's East Coast Pizzeria with seven locations in the San Francisco Bay Area. Founded by two East Coast natives, this independent offers pizza in the styles of New York, Boston, Philadelphia, and New Haven as well as traditional Italian-style thin-crust pizzas baked in gas-fired hearth ovens. The chain's top ranking among independents reflects an efficient and prompt home-delivery system, which includes ordering via the Internet.

Franchise Standards

Franchise pizzerias dominate American pizza. A franchise is a license that grants to one person (the franchisee) the right to own and operate the franchisor's business and sell the franchisor's brand-name product in a limited geographical area. This territorial limit protects the franchisee from competition within the defined market. The franchisee also obtains the right to operate a facility with the brand owner's distinctive design and signage. The owner helps the franchisee in the operation of the business and usually enforces standards of quality. Thus franchise products appear to be uniform regardless of who actually makes them or where they are purchased.

Shakey's was the first pizzeria to franchise in 1954. Fifty years later the leading franchise pizzerias were Pizza Hut, Domino's Pizza, Papa John's, and Little Caesars Pizza. These large franchises had thousands of locations and annual gross sales in the billions of dollars.

Franchise pizzerias from America's Midwest turned Italian pizza into American fast food. Pizza Hut, which originated in Wichita, Kansas, and started franchising in 1959, made pizza into a roadside attraction. Pizza Hut restaurants with uniform architectural style and matching logo signage presented a recognizable image to passing motorists. Although Pizza Hut offered sit-down dining, high-speed pizza production in infrared conveyor ovens contributed to a substantial carryout business. Domino's, which started in Ypsilanti, Michigan, in 1960, refined high-speed pizza production with a limited menu of pizza and Coca-Cola. At one time Domino's promised home delivery within thirty minutes of receiving a telephone order.

Many American pizzerias sell sections or "slices" of a pizza pie, an offering seldom seen in Italy. The pizzeria will bake several different pizzas and cut them into sections. The cut pizzas are placed under heat lamps, and the individual slices are sold as fast food. Since the price of all the slices is greater than the cost of a whole pie, selling pizza by the slice is profitable for the pizzeria. From the customers' point of view, there is no waiting for a whole pie to bake, and a couple of slices of different pizzas make a quick lunchtime meal. The most successful slice operations are located near schools and universities, catering to students' need for fast food.

[See also FAST FOOD; ITALIAN AMERICAN FOOD; PIZZA; PIZZA HUT; ROADSIDE FOOD; TAKE-OUT FOODS.]

BIBLIOGRAPHY

Jakle, John A., and Keith A. Sculle. *Fast Food: Roadside Restaurants in the Automobile Age.* Baltimore: Johns Hopkins University Press, 1999.

Monaghan, Tom, with Robert Anderson. *Pizza Tiger.* New York: Random House, 1986.

ROBERT W. BROWER

PL480, see *International Aid*

Plastic Bags

Polyethylene, the material from which most plastic bags are made, was developed in 1933 by Reginald Gibson and Eric Fawcett at the British industrial behemoth Imperial Chemical Industries. It evolved into two forms, low-density polyethylene (LDPE) and high-density polyethylene (HDPE). LDPE is the most common plastic used to make wraps, films, and packaging materials. The first plastic bags to be widely used were green plastic garbage bags, invented by Harry Wasylyk for hospital use in his native Winnipeg, Manitoba, Canada. Union Carbide Corporation bought the invention from Wasylyk and his partner, Larry Hansen, and the company manufactured the first green garbage bags under the name Glad Bags.

Food spoilage, long known to be accelerated by exposure to the elements, was attacked first by use of Saran plastic film (pioneered by the Dow Chemical Company during World War II) and then by the introduction of plastic food storage bags. Baggies and plastic sandwich bags on a roll were introduced in 1957 to compete with waxed-paper bags then in use. The advent of the folded-lip opening in the 1960s made the use of plastic sandwich bags much more practical. By 1966 plastic produce bags had been introduced in grocery stores.

In 1968 the S. C. Johnson Company test-marketed Ziploc polyethylene food storage bags, which sealed airtight using interlocking grooves and a bead along the bag's opening. The food storage bags were officially launched in 1972, followed by sandwich bags in 1975 and various other specialty Ziploc bags for freezing and fresh vegetables in later years. A different plastic, polyethylene terpthalate (PET), came into use in the 1980s for pouches in which food can be boiled. In 1977 the first plastic grocery bag was introduced to the supermarket as an alternative to paper sacks. At the end of the twentieth century four out of five grocery bags used were plastic.

[**See also** PLASTIC COVERING.]

BIBLIOGRAPHY

Fenichell, Stephen. *Plastic: The Making of a Synthetic Century.* New York: HarperBusiness, 1996.

Heller, Steven, and Anne Fink. *Food Wrap: Packages That Sell.* Glen Cove, NY: Graphic Details, 1996.

Mossman, Susan, ed. *Early Plastics.* London: Leicester University Press, 1997.

JAY WEINSTEIN

Plastic Covering

Plastic covering serves as a barrier against oxygen, moisture, acids, bases, solvents, and odors and can keep foods, both raw and cooked, fresh longer. One of the first plastics to be used to protect food was polyvinylidene chloride (PVDC), which came to the attention of researchers at the Dow Chemical Company in 1933, when Ralph Wiley, a laboratory worker, accidentally found the substance in a vial that he could not scrub clean. Researchers made the PVDC into a greasy film, which Dow named Saran. Initially used to protect fighter jets from salty sea spray and as a stain repellent for car upholstery, Saran was cleared for use in food packaging after World War II. Saran films are best known in the form of Saran Wrap film, the first cling wrap designed for household (1953) and commercial use (1949), introduced by the Dow Chemical Company. Saran Wrap brand plastic film is marketed by the chemical products giant S. C. Johnson Company.

Plastic wrap, which is made of plastics of many kinds, including polyvinyl chloride (PVC), is notable for its ability to cling to almost any material, including glass or ceramic dishes, bowls, pots, and even itself, for an airtight seal. At the grocery it seals in the freshness of foods such as meat, cheese, and cut fruit, making it possible to sell such items days after they have been cut. It is also used to seal prepared foods that go from the grocery shelf or freezer to a home microwave. The wrap made it easier for Americans to cook less often by covering leftovers in plastic and reheating them later.

[**See also** Plastic Bags.]

BIBLIOGRAPHY

American Plastics Council. "Better Living with Plastics." Plasticsinfo.org. http://www.plasticsinfo.org.
American Plastics Council. "Plastics in Your Life." http://www.americanplasticscouncil.org.

SANDRA YIN

Plates

Whether made from wood, metal, ceramic, glass, plastic, or paper, the plate's rich history includes industrial espionage, economic policy, and social competition.

From the Colonial through the Federal Period

The earliest colonists had a surprisingly diverse array of plates. European Maiolica and Chinese porcelain litter the remains of homes for the wealthy in Spanish and English settlements in Florida, California, Jamestown, and Plymouth. But apart from what the immigrants carried, most colonists depended on locally produced dinnerware until well into the eighteenth century. Woodenware, also called treen, was common among the middling classes and could be replaced easily along the heavily wooded Atlantic seaboard. Metal plates and porringers (shallow, rimless

bowls with flat handles, ideal for the ubiquitous gruels of colonial dining and still produced for babies) were common in the English colonies until the eighteenth century for the middling and wealthy. Multiple diners might share pewter plates; the more affluent had individual plates, while the wealthiest had silver. Prized for their durability, beauty, practicality, and inherent value, metal plates were displayed on cupboards in the tradition of a medieval lord.

Local production of earthenwares started by the end of the sixteenth century in Spanish settlements. Glazed wares have been found in the American Southwest, probably produced by expatriate Iberian craftspeople, along with functional unglazed earthenware that was indebted to Native American production techniques. Both Jamestown and Plymouth had potteries by the 1620s, and domestic potteries sprung up wherever a good supply of clay could be found. Plantations often had small, slave-operated kilns where charmingly rustic plates were made; they excelled, however, at utilitarian wares for food preparation, storage, and dairying. Early American efforts to produce elegant tablewares failed, as American clays and glazes were often inferior to their European counterparts.

French, Dutch, and German colonies imported dishware from the homeland through their ports, but England monopolized most colonial trade through its Navigation Acts of 1651 and 1660 and the Staple Act of 1663. This protectionism allowed English delftware in the latter seventeenth century, English salt-glazed stoneware in the early eighteenth century, and English creamware and pearlware by the 1770s to define "good taste" for many in the British colonies. English merchants also imported Chinese porcelain, which became quite popular in affluent circles by the end of the eighteenth century. By this time most modest households could boast a few plates made from of some type of ceramic although not enough to set a fancy table. Treen continued in use through the nineteenth century in poor and frontier areas.

Gentility in a Plate: The Nineteenth Century to the Depression

Owning generous quantities of high-quality ceramics distinguished the elites in the eighteenth century, but during the nineteenth century the middle classes began to fret over whether they ate from fancy, matched dishes or collections inartfully cobbled together. By the end of the nineteenth century even the poor had sets of ceramic dishes, so that mere possession was not enough. One's choice in dishes expressed one's good taste and social standing.

Nineteenth-century etiquette books taught that gentility and self-respect came from using attractive dishware every day. Middle-class housewives were critiqued for using chipped dishes for the family and setting the best por-

Ironstone dinner plates were initially imported from England in the nineteenth century but were later manufactured in the U.S. as they became popular.

Featheredged Leeds creamware plates were imported into the colonies from England in the late eighteenth and early nineteenth centuries.

celain only for guests. In the 1830s middle-class housewives were taught that moderately priced blue and white "India" ware was the wisest, most fashionable purchase. It was made by many manufacturers, so replacements for broken pieces, even if not exactly matching, could be inexpensively integrated, preserving the table's harmony. But fashions changed quickly. By the mid-1840s white dishware was the most desirable, "genteel" tableware, while by the 1870s white china was thought so "ugly and insipid" that a lady should economize on her clothing to afford colorful ware. Domestically produced majolica, riotously colored with fruit, animal, vegetable, and floral motifs, captured the fashions of the late nineteenth century, from precious, three-inch butter pat "pansies" to large serving platters imitating overlapping begonia leaves.

Changes in production and distribution techniques meant that attractive dishware, and lots of it, would penetrate virtually every American household by the late nineteenth century and the early twentieth century. The Great Atlantic and Pacific Tea Company offered majolica and other tablewares as a premium with purchases of teas, spices, and the like in its stores and through its national mail-order business. Decalcoware emerged at the beginning of the twentieth century. It was made by decorating blanks with printed decals in a one-step process that slashed production costs and filled the shelves of the emerging chain stores such as F. W. Woolworth and

Co. that catered to the "shawl trade." These poor and working-class immigrants believed that "pretty dishes" were one indicia of an American lady. Grocery stores offered coupons with purchases that allowed customers to redeem decalcoware premiums, placing cheap plates in even the poorest homes.

Confronting the Modern Market

The Depression killed the demand for fashionable new dinnerware. To make use of the large production capacity, middlebrow American producers such as the Homer Laughlin China Company gave dinner plates to moviegoers at midweek shows. Another big stimulus came in 1936 with Homer Laughlin's introduction of Fiesta, vibrant, monochromatic earthenware priced for the working classes that in the early twenty-first century commands a hefty premium as a collectible. The most popular dinnerware (over 250 million pieces sold between 1939 and 1959) was Russel Wright's American Modern, organically shaped earthenware in muted, natural tones.

New home conveniences changed the composition of everyday dishes. Superficial finishings could not withstand the punishing dishwasher, and metal-based glazes ruined microwaves. Indestructible plastic plates became integral to the efficient mid-twentieth-century home, and increasingly casual entertaining brought guests face-to-face with disposal paper plates.

Individual dinner plates have been slowly increasing in size. An eighteenth-century dinner plate was typically between seven and a half and nine inches in diameter; by the early twentieth century ten-and-a-half-inch plates had become standard. The size continues to increase, with twelve-inch "buffet" plates frequently serving as dinner plates. First popularized in nouvelle cuisine restaurants, these larger plates generally have undecorated eating surfaces. Such plates beg for the artistic plating of individual portions, making decorative food, rather than decorated china, the expression of the twenty-first-century host's good taste.

[See also CHILD, LYDIA MARIA; DINING ROOMS AND MEAL SERVICE; DISHWASHING AND CLEANING UP; MICROWAVE OVENS; NOUVELLE CUISINE.]

BIBLIOGRAPHY

Blaszczyk, Regina Lee. *Imagining Consumers: Design and Innovation from Wedgwood to Corning.* Baltimore: Johns Hopkins University Press, 2000.

Levin, Elaine. *The History of American Ceramics, 1607 to the Present.* New York: Abrams, 1988.

Noël Hume, Ivor. *A Guide to Artifacts of Colonial America.* Philadelphia: University of Pennsylvania Press, 2001.

Quimby, Ian M. G., ed. *Ceramics in America.* Charlottesville: University of Virginia Press, 1973.

CATHY K. KAUFMAN

Plums

Plums are a most diverse group of fruits, varying greatly in size, shape, color, texture, and flavor. Scientists recognize about fifteen species and innumerable varieties grouped according to primary region of origin as American, European, and Asian.

For millennia Native Americans harvested indigenous wild plums, which generally grow on shrubs or shrublike trees. Compared with modern commercial plums, most native fruits are small and tart and have astringent skins; these characteristics are not ideal for fresh fruit but lend character to preserves, sauces, and wines, their chief uses. In the late nineteenth century and early twentieth century, some farmers grew American plums commercially, and fruit breeders used them in hybridizing new varieties because of their adaptation to local environments. Some of the best-known species are the beach plum, *Prunus maritima*, native to the coastal Northeast; the Sierra plum, *P. subcordata*, indigenous to northern California and Oregon; and *P. americana*, native to the central states.

From the colonial era until the early twentieth century, most of the plums cultivated in America were European species, chiefly *P. domestica*, including prunes, greengages, and egg plums, and *P. insititia*, including damsons and bullaces. Although not uncommon, these plums never attained in America the importance they enjoy in Europe, because the plants are less well adapted to American growing conditions. The best European types, such as greengages, have intense, exquisite flavor. However, cultivation of European plums other than prunes faded after the advent of Asian plums, which are generally larger, juicier, and more abundant in bearing.

Prunes—European plums with sufficiently high sugar content that permits them to be dried whole without fermenting—are sold in small quantities as fresh fruits but are primarily dried. The most important variety, Agen, was imported from France in 1854 and intensively grown in California's Santa Clara Valley, near San Jose; cultivation later concentrated in the Sacramento Valley. A convenience food in an age when fresh fruit was less easily available, especially in winter and spring, dried prunes remained a kitchen staple until the mid-twentieth century, when consumption declined as access to cold stored and imported fruit increased. Early in the twenty-first century prune sellers tried to reinvigorate the fruit's image by renaming their product "dried plums."

Luther Burbank, a celebrated plant breeder based in Santa Rosa, California, was the father of the American plum industry, which focuses on Asian and Asian-type plums (*P. salicinia*). Between 1885 and his death in 1926, Burbank imported dozens of plum trees from Japan, crossed them with other species of Asian, Eurasian, and native origin, and introduced more than one hundred varieties. Most fell into oblivion, but about half a dozen, including Santa Rosa, Satsuma, Kelsey, and Elephant Heart, are still grown.

Most Asian plums are quite luscious and flavorful when fully ripe. Growers, however, have dramatically increased production of large, firm, black Asian-type plums, such as Friar and Blackamber, which look ripe even when they are not, do not show bruises, and withstand rough handling and prolonged storage. Virtually all of the commercially available specimens of these plums have a bland flavor, termed "neutral" in the fruit trade.

A private fruit breeder widely regarded as the Luther Burbank of the modern age, Floyd Zaiger of Modesto, California, revolutionized the plum world in the early 1990s by introducing his trademarked Pluots, Asian plum-apricot hybrids in which plum genes and characteristics prevail. Pluots have seized a quarter of the market for plumlike fruits, largely at the expense of traditional plums. The best varieties, such as Flavor Supreme and Flavor King, are superbly sweet and delicious. Most Asian plums and Pluots are consumed fresh, though they are also canned, stewed, and used in desserts such as puddings and tarts.

In 2002 California, by far the largest producing state for Asian-type plums, Pluots, and dried prunes, had 36,000 acres of plums and 73,000 acres of prunes. The leading growing area for fresh prune plums is the Northwest.

[See also APRICOTS; CALIFORNIA; DRYING; FRUIT.]

BIBLIOGRAPHY

Janick, Jules, and James N. Moore, eds. *Fruit Breeding*. New York: Wiley, 1996.

DAVID KARP

Po'Boy Sandwich

Po'Boy sandwiches are based on crusty loaves of Po'Boy-style french bread rarely available outside New Orleans, where long-established bakeries produce loaves noted for their extraordinarily light interior encased in a crusty exterior. Regular french bread is used as a substitute in other areas. Po'Boy fillings range from roast beef with a deep, rich gravy called "debris," to ham, Creole hot sausage, and deep-fried seafood such as shrimp or oysters. Legend credits the creation of the Po'Boy to Benny and Clovis Martin, owners of Martin Brothers Grocery in New Orleans during the 1920s. Some say the Martins developed the Po'Boy as a way to help striking streetcar workers with an inexpensive meal. Others claim that the Martins, unable to resist the pleading of hungry young black boys requesting a sandwich "for a po' boy," would cut their sandwiches into thirds and hand the portions out free to the children. The sandwiches in those days were likely to be filled with french fries and gravy, accounting for the popular french fry Po'Boy still enjoyed in New Orleans. Po'Boys have become well known and appear on sandwich menus throughout the United States.

[See also BREAD; CAJUN AND CREOLE FOOD; SANDWICHES; SAUCES AND GRAVIES.]

BIBLIOGRAPHY

Brown, Cora Lovisa. *America Cooks: Favorite Recipes from the 48 States.* Garden City, NY: Halcyon House, 1949.

Mercuri, Becky. *Sandwiches That You Will Like.* Pittsburgh, PA: WQED Multimedia, 2002.

BECKY MERCURI

Poetry, Food

There have probably been poems that speak about food since there have been poems. Whether frothy doggerel or considered elucidation of the human condition, poems by some of the world's most revered poets have dealt with food. Ancient Roman, Greek, Chinese, and other venerable cultures recorded poetry about food.

Some food poems current in colonial American times were "rhyming receipts" to help an illiterate population remember recipes, and they offered enough detail to cook from. Here is an excerpt from one written in Britain by Sydney Smith (1771–1845) but popular in America. It is called "An Herb Sallad for the Tavern Bowl."

> Of wondrous mustard, add a single spoon.
> Distrust the condiment that bites too soon.
> But deem it not, thou man of herbs, a fault,
> to add a double quantity of salt.
> Fourtimes the spoon with oil of Lucca crown,
> and twice the vinegar procured from town.
> Lastly o'er the flowery compound, toss
> a magic soupspoon of Anchovy sauce.

There were many of these receipts used in the new nation thus continuing the British tradition. Colonials soon developed their own to include New World ingredients. This one, author unknown, is a recipe for "Wheat and Indian Bread," "Indian" meaning corn.

> Two cups Indian, one cup wheat,
> One cup sour milk, one cup sweet,
> One good egg that well you beat.
> Half cup molasses too;
> Half cup sugar add thereto,
> With one spoon of butter new.
> Salt and soda each a teaspoon;
> Mix it up quick and bake it soon.
> Then you'll have cornbread complete,
> Best of all cornbread you'll meet.

Many nursery rhymes originating in England were likewise brought to America and enjoyed great popularity, as many still are.

> Little Jack Horner sat in the corner,
> Eating a Christmas pie:
> He put in his thumb, and pulled out a plum,
> And said, "What a good boy am I!"

Others that mention food prominently are "Little Miss Muffet" and "Jack Sprat." The theme of food appears in what seems the majority of them. Sing-along poems like "Do You Know the Muffin Man" and "Hot Cross Buns" are still common child's fare. Children's play chants often contain food imagery as well. "Pease Porridge Hot" is a dancing or jump-rope chant about a pot of soup, and the baby's clapping game "Patty Cake" comes from the older "Pat-a-Cake."

Poems were often published as broadsides in young America, many for political reasons. When the taxes on tea became oppressive before the Revolutionary War, anti-tea poems appeared. An excerpt from one such poem, "A Lady's Adieu to Her Tea-Table," lamented:

> No more shall my teapot so generous be
> In filling the cups with this pernicious tea,
> For I'll fill it with water and drink out the same,
> Before I'll lose LIBERTY that dearest name,
> Because I am taught (and believe it is fact)
> That our ruin is aimed at in the late act,
> Of imposing a duty on all foreign Teas,
> Which detestable stuff we can quit when we please.
> LIBERTY'S The Goddess that I do adore,
> And I'll maintain her right until my last hour,
> Before she shall part I will die in the cause,
> For I'll never be govern'd by tyranny's laws.

Many sources have created rhymes for some specific purpose, commercial or public-spirited. Here are excerpts from "'Twas the Night after Christmas," a poem published by the U.S. National Park Service promoting kitchen sanitation through graphic doggerel.

> 'Twas the night after Christmas
> And all through the kitchen
> Little creatures were stirring up
> Potions bewitching.
> . . . . .
> Salmonella were working
> In gravy and soup
> In the hopes they could turn it
> To poisonous goop!
> . . . . .

> Clostridia were nestled
> All snug in the ham
> While Hep A virus
> Danced in the yam.

Advertising has had its share of examples as well. Rhymes to sell products or services have a long commercial history. Here is part of an advertising poem from 1859.

> It is the cheap Cash Store, my friends:
> At J. W. Renoud's, please call,
> And find things sold at reason's fee,
> To one, to ten, to all!
> . . . . .
> Yes, find things sold at reason's fee,
> Bread, butter, candles, cheese,
> Salt, Onions, Crackers, Coffee, Brooms,
> And choicest, best of Teas!
> . . . . .
> Sugar and Allspice, Flour and Pork,
> And matches, not the kind
> The young folks often, often make,
> So pleasing to the mind.

As broadcast media took a larger role in advertising, poems set to music—jingles—assumed a more important position. Beginning with early radio efforts and continuing through television advertising, jingles hawk goods and services of all kinds.

There are some rather whimsical settings for food poetry. *Haiku-Sine: 217 Tiny Food Poems by Texans Who Love to Eat and Feed Their Head*, a book by Micki McClelland with Shelby Watson, is a collection of haiku from an annual contest sponsored by Houston's *My Table Dining Guide* (Lazywood Press). It began in 1997 and became a popular annual event. Juvenile literature has its share of food poems as well. Many such volumes exist, and they are generally filled with doggerel, play poems, and tongue twisters.

In serious modern literature, food poetry is a relatively popular area. Many well-known writers have published poetry about food, and there are several published collections. One collection, *O Taste and See: Food Poems*, features the work of more than one hundred authors, including Robert Frost, Gertrude Stein, Louise Bogan, Frank O'Hara, Pablo Neruda, Allen Ginsberg, William Carlos Williams, Diane Wakoski, and Erica Jong. Internet searches for "food poetry" and "food poems" will turn up something over 5 million items, including books, individual poems, and sites to help writers create their own poems.

[See also ADVERTISING; HUMOR, FOOD; LITERATURE AND FOOD; RECIPES; SONGS, FOOD.]

BIBLIOGRAPHY

Garrison, David Lee, and Terry Hermsen, eds. *O Taste and See: Food Poems.* Huron, OH: Bottom Dog, 2003.

Nash, Ogden. *Food.* New York: Stewart, Tabori, and Chang, 1989.

Washington, Peter, ed. *Eat, Drink, and Be Merry: Poems about Food and Drink.* New York: Knopf, 2003.

ROBERT PASTORIO

Poke Salad

Poke salad (*Phytolacca americana*) is a perennial that is native to the eastern United States. It has been suggested that the early white settlers adopted "poke" from the Algonquian name *pocan*. It has also been known as pokeweed, poke salute, pokeberry, inkberry, and numerous other local names. It resprouts early every spring from a tuberous root. By midsummer it has flowered, its main stalk has turned red, and it may be as high as ten feet tall. Grapelike clusters of berries hanging from its limbs turn deep purple by early fall.

When the shoots sprouted in the early spring, they were widely used by the colonists. The young leaves were eaten alone or mixed with other spring greens. The tender, young sprouts were prepared and eaten like asparagus; indeed they are said to taste like asparagus. These would have been welcome additions to the diet following winter meals of cured meat, salted fish, pickled cabbage, and cornmeal.

It has been reported that the native Indians also used various parts of this plant as poultices for arthritic pain, in other medications, and as dyes. Early settlers on the frontier adopted these uses too.

Because of the plant's hardy nature and popularity, it was cultivated in many colonial gardens. It even became popular in Europe for a time, but poke salad's use as a food source dwindled as time passed. Its decline in popularity can be attributed to several factors. The most significant is believed to have been the commercialization of food preservation techniques coupled with a transportation system that makes all foods available at all times, fresh, frozen, and canned.

Another factor that has undoubtedly played a role in poke's passing from the menu is that at a point in its annual growth cycle it becomes poisonous. Although a Dr. Dover was quoted as saying, "Anybody that gets sick from eating poke, I'll treat them free," it has now been scientifically established that the root and the berries are poisonous, as are the stalk and stems after turning red. Dr. Dover to the contrary, there always seems to have been near-universal agreement on the poisonous potential of the plant. Even so, there has been no agreement on the proper preparation technique to avoid the effects of the poison. All of the following directions have been given: never eat a shoot that is more than six inches high; blanch the shoots before eating; boil and discard the water before eating; boil and discard the water twice before eating.

Although there are those who remember that Elvis Presley recorded the song "Polk Salute Annie" in 1973 and although poke salad is still sought as a rite of spring by some natural food enthusiasts, it is now largely remembered as pokeweed in gardening encyclopedias and various treatises of limited interest.

[**See also** GIBBONS, EUELL; HOMEMADE REMEDIES; SALADS AND SALAD DRESSINGS.]

JAMES C. LEE

Polish American Food

Polish immigrants came to the United States in three major waves during the twentieth century. Within cities and towns, they formed communities called "Polonias," where in houses of worship, Polish national homes, restaurants, and food stores many expressions of cultural identity and influence occur. Foodways function as culture identifiers here.

Although new immigrants see widely varied foods in the United States, their diet often bears a striking resemblance to that in Poland. Food resources in various early and mid-century Polonias were consistent with homeland taste preferences; in transplanted households, immigrants raised, cooked, and preserved foods in ways shaped by homeland memories. These included *babka* (egg-rich, yeasted sweet bread), *kapusta* (simmered sauerkraut and fresh cabbage), various soups, pierogi (meat, cheese, potato, *kapusta*, or fruit-filled dumplings), *kluski* (flour and potato noodles), *golubki* (stuffed cabbage), and kielbasa (sausage). In backyards pickling crocks, produce gardens, and occasionally a pig raised for slaughter harkened back to Polish farms.

Many laborious food preparations are available in twenty-first-century Polonia restaurants and groceries. Bakeries sell *chleb* (bread), *paczki* (jam-filled doughnuts), and *makowiec* (poppy seed–filled strudels). Butcher shops offer hams, *boscek* (rib bacon), *kiszka* (blood and groats pudding, although Polish Jews, following Jewish dietary laws, make *kiszka* without blood), and an array of kielbasa. Groceries also sell ready-made convenience foods that are the equivalent of labor-intensive traditional dishes: *golabki* (stuffed cabbage), pierogi (filled dumplings), *flaczki* (tripe soup), and *bigos* (hunter's stew).

Some Polish Food Details

Bigos is a cabbage-based stew. Its history goes back to deep-winter hunting expeditions where, at the evening fire, animal parts were added to a pot containing cabbage and onions.

Pierogi are ubiquitous Polish dumplings filled with savory or fruit fillings. In Poland they may comprise *kolacja*, a casual evening meal. In the United States pierogi are more often homemade for special occasions, in part because of their laborious nature. Hand-rolled dough rounds are filled and pinched shut, then boiled or fried, and if savory, tossed with butter and perhaps sautéed onions. Fillings include sweetened berries, or sauerkraut with mushrooms, or mashed potato and cheese. Pierogi are staples in Polish restaurants and at community events and holiday meals. The dumplings were once made exclusively in Polish American homes, then cottage industries produced them for

sale in local grocery stores, and in the early 2000s they are manufactured and sold frozen in supermarkets nationally.

Kielbasa is a Polish-style sausage with many variations. Meat is ground to different degrees of coarseness, seasoned, and piped into casing. Thin sausage is known as *kabanosy*; kielbasa is thicker and commonly smoked, although "fresh," that is, unsmoked, kielbasa is boiled before serving. Neighborhood butcher shops may have smokehouses for smoking kielbasa and other meats.

Kapusta is the Polish form of sauerkraut. In Poland *kapusta* is typically preserved in autumn for winter consumption by layering shredding cabbage and salt in a crock or wooden barrel. Lore exists about the best way to pack down the cabbage. A wooden mallet is effective but may bruise the cabbage. Better is to tamp the cabbage with the palms of the hands. The best tradition is to hoist a thoroughly scrubbed child into the barrel to pack down the cabbage with bare feet.

Chrusciki, or angel wings, are made from deep-fried dough sprinkled with confectioners sugar. Dough is sometimes cut into diamond shapes and slit in the center with the ends pulled through and fried.

Many of these foods are common to Polish Americans of different faiths, but pork is of course eschewed by Polish American Jews. The Christian church influences foodways, particularly around holidays.

Christian Church Holidays and Foods

Wigilia is the Christmas Eve meal. It is a meatless meal whose number of dishes and attendees is often specifically an odd number. The meal begins with a sharing of wishes and the breaking of the *oplatek*, a blessed wafer.

Swienconka is a ceremony where food baskets containing eggs, meat, bread, salt, and other foods are brought to church for a blessing on the day before Easter Sunday. Each food has a specific symbolic value. Hard-cooked eggs, either plain or dyed, stand for familial strength and for new life. The eggs begin the Easter meal in a ritual called *waletke*. Eggs are tapped with one's neighbor at the dinner table. Broken eggshells symbolize Christ's breaking free from the tomb. The person whose egg remains intact is considered a victor.

Meat at the Easter meal, commonly kielbasa or ham, represents Christ's blood, the Old Testament sprinkling of lamb's blood on doorposts to deter the Angel of Death, and festivity in the Polish diet, marking the absence of a fast day. Yeast-raised bread symbolizes Christ's resurrection. Salt in the basket acknowledges its life-preserving qualities and the flavor that Christ and Christianity added to the world described in Matthew 5:13.

The basket might also include horseradish to represent bitter struggles for faith. Butter, hard sugar, or cake lambs represent the Paschal Lamb. Chocolate, a reward for the hard work characteristic of Polish people, might be added as well as any other item that a person wants blessed. After the blessings by priests, traditional Polish beliefs hold that people consume the sanctified food.

[See also CABBAGE; JEWISH AMERICAN FOOD; JEWISH DIETARY LAWS; SAUSAGE.]

BIBLIOGRAPHY

Hauck-Lawson, Annie. "When Food Is the Voice: A Case Study of a Polish-American Woman." *Journal for the Study of Food and Society* 2, no. 1 (1998): 21–28.

Nowakowski, Jacek, ed. *Polish-American Ways.* New York: Harper and Row, 1989.

Obidinski, Eugene, and Helen Stankiewicz Zand. *Polish Folkways in America: Community and Family.* Lanham, MD: University Press of America, 1987.

ANNIE S. HAUCK-LAWSON

Politics of Food

Most people perceive food as a basic biological need, an indicator of culture, a source of enjoyment, and sometimes a trade commodity or generator of employment but rarely view it as political—an element in the mundane realm of power and manipulation in the interests of commerce. Food and politics, however, are inextricably linked. Politics affect every component of the American food system from production to consumption. Much money is at stake, and the principal stakeholders—the food industry, government regulators, public health officials, nutrition educators, and the general public—have widely varying interests in the food system. Although everyone wants food to be plentiful, safe, environmentally sound, culturally appropriate, affordable, healthful, and palatable, the food industry, which includes any business that produces, processes, makes, sells, or serves foods, beverages, or dietary supplements, has one overriding interest: to sell products. The conflict between the commercial interests of food companies and the concerns of other stakeholders drives the politics of food.

The U.S. food industry produces a food supply so abundant, varied, inexpensive, and independent of geography or season that

The "My Pyramid" food guidance system as it appeared on the USDA website in 2006.

nearly all Americans except the very poorest can obtain enough food to meet biological needs. Indeed the supply is so overabundant that it contains enough calories—3,900 per person per day—to feed everyone in the country nearly twice over, even after exports are considered. This surplus, along with a society so affluent that most citizens can afford to buy as much food as they need, creates a highly competitive marketing environment. To satisfy stockholders, food companies must convince people to buy their products rather than those of competitors or must entice people to eat more food in general, regardless of health consequences.

Companies promote sales through advertising and public relations but also use the political system to convince Congress, federal agency officials, food and nutrition experts, the media, and the public that their products promote health (or at least do no harm) and should not be subject to restrictive regulations. To protect sales, they contribute to congressional campaigns, lobby members of Congress and federal agencies, and when all else fails, file lawsuits. Nearly every food company belongs to a trade association or hires a public relations firm to promote a positive image of its products among consumers, professionals, and the media. Companies form partnerships and alliances with professional nutrition organizations, fund research on food and nutrition, sponsor professional journals and conferences, and make sure that influential groups—federal officials, researchers, doctors, nurses, schoolteachers, and the media—do not criticize their products or suggest eating less of them. To divert attention from health, safety, or environmental concerns, they argue that restrictive regulations overly involve the government in personal dietary choices and threaten constitutional guarantees of free speech. Much of this political activity is an invisible part of contemporary culture that attracts only occasional notice.

In using the political system, food companies behave like any other business—tobacco, for example—in attempting to exert influence. Promoting food raises more complicated issues than tobacco, however. Tobacco is a single product, is unambiguously harmful, and requires simple advice: don't smoke. Food, in contrast, is available in more than 300,000 different products, is required for life, causes problems only when consumed inappropriately, and elicits more complex health messages: eat this product instead of another or eat less in general. The "eat less" message is at the root of much of the controversy over nutrition advice, as it conflicts with food industry interests. Health becomes a goal only when it helps sell food. Therefore government dietary advice is especially subject to political pressure.

The Politics of Dietary Recommendations

The U.S. government has issued dietary recommendations for more than a century, but its advice did not become controversial until the 1970s. In 1900 the leading causes of death were infectious diseases such as tuberculosis and diphtheria, made worse by inadequate dietary intake. To improve public health, government nutritionists advised the public to eat more of a greater variety of foods. The goals of health officials, nutritionists, and the food industry were much the same—to encourage greater consumption of the full range of American agricultural products. Throughout the twentieth century an expanding economy led to nutritional improvements; by the 1970s health officials realized that dietary problems had shifted to those associated with overnutrition, eating too much food or too much of certain kinds of food. Overnutrition causes a different set of health problems; it makes people overweight, disrupts normal metabolism, and increases the risk of "chronic" diseases such as coronary heart disease, certain cancers, diabetes, hypertension, stroke, and others—the leading causes of illness and death among any overfed population. This shift required new dietary recommendations. Instead of advice to "eat more," they needed to advise "eat less." Advice to eat less, however, runs counter to the interests of food producers, hence politics.

The most obvious example comes from food guide pyramids produced by the U.S. Department of Agriculture (USDA). In 1991 the first such pyramid displayed a pattern of food intake in which most servings were to come from the grain, fruit, and vegetable groups, fewer from the meat and dairy groups, and even fewer from foods high in fat and sugar (which are high in energy but relatively low in nutrients). USDA nutritionists intended the pyramid to convey variety (multiple food groups), proportionality (appropriate numbers of servings), moderation (restrictions on fat and sugar), and particularly the idea that it is better to eat some foods than others. Food companies, however, much prefer advice based on different concepts: foods cannot be considered good or bad, and the keys to healthful diets are balance, variety, and moderation. This preference explains why the producers of meat and dairy foods objected to release of the pyramid and induced the USDA to withdraw it from publication. The USDA conducted further research. When this research confirmed the value of the original design, the USDA capitulated and released the pyramid in 1992 with design changes that met some of the industry's objections.

In 2005 the USDA revised the pyramid to eliminate all traces of hierarchy in food groups. The new pyramid depicts bands of different colors, each representing a food group and flanked by a figure climbing a staircase. This pyramid shifts attention away from controversial food to uncontroversial physical activity as a means to promote health; it conveys the message that all foods can fit into healthful diets. This message is correct in principle but avoids indicating that it might be healthier to eat some foods rather than others. Could politics have had something to do with the redesign?

The pyramid is meant to implement federal policy on nutrition and health, expressed in *Dietary Guidelines for Americans*, issued every five years since 1980. The effects of political pressures are most readily observed in the sugar guideline. Sugars contain calories but no nutrients. In diets containing excess calories, advice to eat less sugar makes sense. The 1980 and 1985 guidelines for sugar said so explicitly: "Avoid too much sugar." Since then, in part in response to pressures from sugar trade associations, the guideline has become increasingly complicated and ambiguous. By 2000 the guideline said, "Choose beverages and foods to moderate your intake of sugars." This peculiar wording is explained by politics. Sugar trade associations argued that research on sugar and disease did not support a recommendation to eat less sugar, mainly because studies cannot easily distinguish the health effects of sugar from those of the foods in which it is present or from calories in general. The committee reviewing the guideline at first suggested this wording: "Go easy on beverages and foods high in added sugars." After further discussion, the committee changed the recommendation to say, "Choose beverages and foods that limit your intake of sugars." Sugar lobbyists induced thirty senators, half from sugar-growing states, to demand elimination of this "eat less" suggestion. The USDA changed the word "limit" to "moderate" in the final guideline. By 2005 sugar disappeared as a separate guideline and became a "key recommendation" in a section on carbohydrates: "Choose and prepare foods and beverages with little added sugars or caloric sweeteners, such as amounts suggested by the USDA Food Guide and the DASH [Dietary Approaches to Stop Hypertension] Eating Plan." If dietary guidelines said something as direct as "eat less sugar," the responsible government agencies would be under siege by lobbyists for sugars and every other product whose sales might be jeopardized by that advice.

These examples illustrate why diet is a political issue. Because dietary advice affects food sales and companies demand a favorable regulatory environment for their products, dietary practices raise political issues central to democratic institutions. Thus debates about food issues inevitably involve differences of opinion about the way the government balances corporate against public interests. Despite the overwhelmingly greater resources of food companies, consumer advocates also can and should use the political system to convince Congress, federal agencies, and the courts to take action in the public interest and sometimes are effective in doing so.

BIBLIOGRAPHY

Nestle, Marion. *Food Politics: How the Food Industry Influences Nutrition and Health*. Berkeley: University of California Press, 2002.

U.S. Department of Agriculture. "Steps to a Healthier You." MyPyramid.gov. http://www.mypyramid. gov.

U.S. Department of Agriculture, Economic Research Service. Data Sets: Food Availability. Mar. 3, 2006. http://www.ers.usda.gov/data/foodconsumption/FoodAvailIndex.htm.

U.S. Department of Agriculture and U.S. Department of Health and Human Services. *Dietary Guidelines for Americans*. 6th ed. Washington, DC: U.S. Government Printing Office, 2005. http://www.health.gov/dietaryguidelines/dga2005/document/pdf/DGA2005.pdf.

MARION NESTLE

Pollock

A member of the same Gadidae family to which cod, haddock, hake, cusk, tomcod, and ling belong, pollock (*Pollachius virens*) was caught and used as were the others, all medium to large white-fleshed fish. Pollock could be salted and dried as cod were, but pollock was never considered to be as valuable and was among the salted fish sent to the South for slave food. A blue-gray cast to the flesh earned it the grand name of Boston bluefish in the late nineteenth century and early twentieth century. Pollock has become a candidate for sale as a breaded fillet. Many pollock come from Pacific waters around Alaska. The pollock is caught commercially in the Atlantic and as a sport fish.

SANDRA L. OLIVER

Pomegranates

The pomegranate (*Punica granatum*) originated somewhere in the region from central Asia to Turkey, most likely in Iran, where it has been cultivated for five thousand years. Regally beautiful with its scarlet, leathery skin and turreted crown, it is like a treasure chest inside, with papery white membranes encasing hundreds of glistening garnet gems—seeds embedded in juice sacs. The flavor is sweet-tart and winy, intense but refreshing.

The pomegranate was introduced into Florida by the Spanish no later than the sixteenth century. Almost all of the American crop now comes from the San Joaquin Valley of California, where hot, dry summers mature sweet, attractive fruit. The main commercial variety is the modestly named Wonderful, propagated in 1896 from a Florida cutting. In the late 1990s one huge farm, planted to cash in on the vogue for fruits rich in anthocyanins, tripled California's acreage to 9,500. The season for fresh fruit runs from August through December, peaking in October and November. Pomegranates are used for decoration, eaten fresh (a rather messy affair), and juiced; the juice is used for making jelly, sorbet, cool drinks similar to lemonade, and a kind of wine.

[See also FRUIT; FRUIT JUICES.]

BIBLIOGRAPHY

Mohnan Kumar, G. N. "Pomegranate" In *Fruits of Tropical and Subtropical Origin*, ed. Steven Nagy, Philip E. Shaw, and Wilfred F. Wardowski, 328–347. Lake Alfred: Florida Science Source, 1990.

DAVID KARP

Popcorn

Pre-Columbian Amerindians domesticated maize (*Zea mays*) by 5000 B.C.E. The earliest variety of maize was popcorn (*Zea everta*), which has small, hard kernels. This hard outer covering, or endosperm, makes unpopped kernels difficult to chew or grind. The easiest way to render them edible is to heat the kernel. Heat converts moisture inside the kernel into steam, which puts pressure on the endosperm. When the outer covering can no longer contain the pressure, the kernel pops, or everts, and exposes the tender inner part of the flake.

Popcorn has been found at archaeological sites in the Southwest, but the earliest record of it east of the Mississippi dates to the early nineteenth century. Popcorn was probably imported into New England from South America by whalers. During the 1840s popping corn became a fad in America. Boys sold popcorn at train stations and public gatherings. In Boston wagonloads of popcorn balls were being sold by street vendors by the late 1840s. Popcorn recipes began to appear in American cookbooks during the 1860s. For instance, E. F. Haskell published recipes for "Pop Corn Balls" and "Pop Corn Cakes" in her *Housekeeper's Encyclopedia* (1861). During the 1870s many cookbooks included recipes for "Popcorn Pudding," which was a forerunner of cold breakfast cereal, and popcorn confections.

Technology played an important role in popcorn's expansion. The invention of the popcorn popper in the 1830s made it possible to contain the popped corn. (Before the popper, popcorn was placed near a fire, and when the kernels popped, some fell into the fire, and others fell onto the floor or ground.) The invention of the steam-powered popcorn wagon by Charles Cretors in 1885 allowed vendors to sell hot popcorn on America's streets. By the late nineteenth century popcorn was one of America's most popular snack foods. It was sold regularly at fairs, election rallies, circuses, and other large gatherings. When Americans began popping corn in their homes and at festive affairs such as picnics, sales increased. With the advent of spectator sports, such as baseball, the sales of popcorn and popcorn products—such as Cracker Jack—zoomed even higher.

An advertisement for the American Pop Corn Company, 1929.

At about the time that popcorn wagons disappeared from city streets as the result of zoning restrictions, an unlikely combination of events enhanced the sale of popcorn. The most important was the decision to sell snack foods in movie theaters, which had existed since the late nineteenth century. Early operators, however, had refused to sell popcorn, because it was a mess to clean up. A few independent theaters sold popcorn during the 1920s, but it took the Depression to boost popcorn sales in movie houses dramatically. When Prohibition ended in 1933, cocktail lounges and bars offered complimentary salty popcorn and other salty snacks, which enhanced the sale of alcoholic beverages, thereby greatly improving their profits.

World War II also affected popcorn consumption. Many foods were rationed during the war, but not popcorn. Consuming popcorn became "patriotic" as snack foods made with chocolate or sugar became scarce. During the war the sale of sugar and chocolate was restricted, which further boosted the sale of popcorn. After the war popcorn sales continued to increase. Popcorn remains a significant food in the United States.

[**See also** CRACKER JACK; SNACKS, SALTY; STREET VENDORS.]

BIBLIOGRAPHY

Smith, Andrew F. *Popped Culture: A Social History of Popcorn in America*. Columbia: University of South Carolina Press, 1999.

ANDREW F. SMITH

Popeyes

Al Copeland owned a Tastee Donut franchise in New Orleans, but when Kentucky Fried Chicken started opening outlets in that city, Copeland decided to shift from doughnuts to chicken. He opened a fast food chicken shop, Chicken on the Run, in 1972, serving traditional fried chicken. With nothing distinguished about his product, business was slow, but when Copeland spiced up the recipe, people took notice. He renamed the business Popeyes, supposedly after Popeye Doyle, a character in *The French Connection*, a blockbuster movie of the time. Once he was sure that the operation was a success, Copeland began to franchise it. The first franchise opened in Baton Rouge, Louisiana, in 1976. By 1981 there were more than 300 Popeyes outlets. In 1987 a blind taste test revealed that consumers preferred Popeyes over Kentucky Fried Chicken, and Popeyes advertising proclaimed itself "America's Fried Chicken Champ—The Spicy Taste That Can't Be Beat." Popeyes added buttermilk biscuits to its menu in 1985; Cajun Popcorn Shrimp was introduced four years later and Cajun Crawfish in 1988.

Popeyes bought the Church's Chicken restaurant chain in 1989. Two years later Popeyes opened a restaurant in Kuala Lumpur, Malaysia, and later opened an outlet in Schweinfurt, Germany. In 1993 America's Favorite Chicken Company, now known as AFC Enterprise, Inc., became the new parent company of Popeyes and Church's. The brand's headquarters moved to Atlanta. Popeyes converted many branches of the Pioneer Chicken chain in Los Angeles to Popeyes restaurants and also placed Popeyes outlets in convenience stores and grocery stores.

The brand continued to grow internationally; in 1996 Popeyes opened its one thousandth restaurant worldwide. In 1998 Popeyes acquired sixty-six former Hardee's outlets and converted them into Popeyes restaurants. In 1999 Popeyes opened its first Cajun Kitchen in a Chicago suburb, offering a traditional casual restaurant menu with the speed of a fast food restaurant. In the same year the company initiated the Popeyes Cajun Café format, intended for malls, food courts, and entertainment venues. As of 2005 Popeyes had more than 1,800 restaurants in the United States and 27 international markets, including Puerto Rico, Japan, Germany, Korea, and the United Kingdom.

BIBLIOGRAPHY

Jakle, John A., and Keith A. Sculle. *Fast Food: Roadside Restaurants in the Automobile Age*. Baltimore: Johns Hopkins University Press, 1999.

ANDREW F. SMITH

Popsicle

Street vendors called hokeypokeys sold frozen fruit juices as early as the 1870s on the streets of New York and other American cities, but Frank Epperson, a lemonade sales-

A Popsicle advertisement.

man from Oakland, California, began to manufacture fruit ices commercially in 1923. Epsicles, as he first called them, were ice pops on wooden sticks. He trademarked the name, which was later changed to Popsicle. In 1925 Epperson sold the rights to the product to the Joe Lowe Company of New York. By 1928 more than 60 million Popsicles were sold annually. Consolidated Foods Corporation acquired the company in 1965. Twenty-one years later the Gold Bond Ice Cream Company of Green Bay, Wisconsin, bought Popsicle's American operations. In 1989 Unilever bought Gold Bond. As of 2005 Unilever also owns Good Humor, Dove, Klondike, and Breyers.

BIBLIOGRAPHY

Funderburg, Anne Cooper. *Chocolate, Strawberry, and Vanilla: A History of American Ice Cream*. Bowling Green, OH: Bowling Green State University Popular Press, 1995.

ANDREW F. SMITH

Pork, *see Pigs*

Post Foods

When Charley Post, at the age of thirty-seven, was wheeled into John Harvey Kellogg's Battle Creek Sanitarium in 1891, he had high hopes that finally he would be cured. But the famous doctor's regimen of colon massages, multiple daily enemas, and a severe vegetarian diet were a bust. Frustrated, the man who had seen one enterprise after another sabotaged by his failing digestive tract finally availed himself of a psychic healer. She "vitalized in me the dormant forces," he was to relate later. As a result it was in mesmerism and the related art of marketing that C. W. Post found his métier.

Post used his newfound health to open La Vita Inn, where he instituted a treatment that combined Kellogg's "scientific" methods with a prescription of mental suggestion. When in 1895 the doctor turned down his offer to go into business marketing the sanitarium's coffee substitute, Post holed up in a little horse barn and came up with his own ersatz coffee concocted of toasted wheat, bran, and a little molasses. The resulting Postum was promoted not only as economical, healthy, and natural but also as a builder of nerves, red blood, and all-around health. At the same time Post's copy vilified real coffee for its "poisonous alkaloids" and implicated it as a cause of everything from blindness to heart attacks. "After all," the master mesmerist was once noted saying, "it's not enough to just make and sell cereal. After that you get it halfway down the customer's throat through the use of advertising. Then they've got to swallow it."

Grape Nuts, introduced in 1897, was again based on a Kellogg staple called "granola," made by coarsely grinding a whole-grain cracker and then rebaking the resulting pellets. Post's Grape Nuts was sold in small packages, supposedly because it was "concentrated." It was advertised as an alternative to surgery for an inflamed appendix and was recommended for consumption, malaria, and loose teeth. As a result by 1900 Post was said to be netting $3 million a year. In 1908 one more raid on the sanitarium larder netted Post Toasties cornflakes. Then in 1912 an instant Postum was introduced.

Unfortunately for Post, neither his millions nor his mind-over-matter philosophy provided a cure for his troubles. In 1914 the ailing Grape Nuts magnate shot himself in his California home.

His daughter and sole heir, Marjorie Merriweather Post, steered the company toward further expansion, acquiring over a dozen brands and expanding the product line to some sixty items. The new acquisitions included Baker's chocolate (1927), Maxwell House coffee (1928), and Jell-O gelatin (1925), to name a few. Finally, when the company bought out Clarence Birdseye's frozen food business, Postum was renamed the General Foods Corporation. In 1989 Kraft and General Foods Corporation, now both owned by Philip Morris, were consolidated into Kraft General Foods to form the largest food company at that time in the United States.

Over the years the company's products have veered from cereals like Raisin Bran (1942) that were decidedly in the granola tradition to the likes of Cocoa Pebbles (1971), inspired by the Flintstones, an animated sitcom. C. W. Post would most likely have been thrilled at the idea of cross-promoting a cereal with a television show.

[**See also** BIRDSEYE CORPORATION; BREAKFAST DRINKS; BREAKFAST FOOD; CEREAL, COLD; COFFEE SUBSTITUTES; GENERAL FOODS; HEALTH FOOD; JELL-O; KELLOGG, JOHN HARVEY; KRAFT FOODS; MAXWELL HOUSE.]

BIBLIOGRAPHY

Carson, Gerald. *Cornflake Crusade*. New York: Rinehart, 1957.

Hillwood Museum and Gardens. http://www.hillwoodmuseum.org.

Kraft Foods. Kraftfoods.com. http://www.kraft.com.

Lowe, Berenice Bryant. *Tales of Battle Creek*. Battle Creek, MI: Miller Foundation, 1976.

"Post Healthy Classics and the Eat 2 Lose 10 Plan." Kraftfoods.com. Oct. 4, 2006. http://www.grapenuts.com/postcereals/heritage.html.

MICHAEL KRONDL

Potato-Cooking Tools

Specialized tools for cutting and cooking potatoes have been used at least since the 1870s. Cranked slicers that made continuous curling ribbons of raw potato appeared around the 1860s or 1870s. Peelers similar in design to apple parers came out in about 1874. Chip slicers, dating to the same period, held a raw peeled potato against a revolving cutting blade. Beetles, wooden pestle-like pounders, are the oldest tool for mashing cooked potatoes, undoubtedly in use since Americans first grew potatoes. Other beetles of the 1870s have wire or perforated metal heads. A conical sieve, in which a cooked potato is rubbed with a wooden pestle through the holes, also dates to the 1870s. Potato ricers came in two types: a tabletop style with legs (circa 1900) and a hand-held press (circa 1940) that forced cooked potato through a perforated hopper to create rice-sized potato pellets. An 1890s metal rack had folded prongs that pierced potatoes and directed heat toward their centers to speed the baking. Similarly, about 1950 folding racks with thick aluminum nails began to be used; each rack held four potatoes. Stove-top ovens in the 1940s had a built-in thermometer set directly over the burner and baked potatoes twice as quickly as the stove's oven.

[**See also** POTATOES.]

BIBLIOGRAPHY

Franklin, Linda Campbell. *300 Years of Kitchen Collectibles*. 5th ed. Iola, WI: Krause, 2003.

LINDA CAMPBELL FRANKLIN

Potatoes

Potatoes, which in the 2000s are Americans' favorite vegetable, are botanical varieties of the tuber species *Solanum tuberosum*, which is native to the South American Andes. Europeans brought them first to Europe and from Europe to North America, where potatoes appear to have been introduced multiple times. Thomas Jefferson and other Virginia planters experimented unsuccessfully with potatoes as a field crop. In the Northeast potatoes thrived as a subsistence then a commercial crop. Most sources agree that northeastern potato production was introduced by Presbyterian Scotch-Irish, who settled in Londonderry, New Hampshire (1719), and spread from there across the Northeast and the West.

In 1840 potato commerce entered the U.S. census, which by the mid-1840s chronicled a sharp decline due to blight and then, in the 1850s and 1860s, a recovery based on new varieties and cultivation techniques. The most important new planting material was the Rough Purple Chili variety, an ancestor of the modern Russet Burbank, the variety

A giant potato on a parade float in Aroostook County, Maine, October 1940.

that in the 2000s accounts for the largest share of baking potatoes as well as those processed into fries. Idaho and Washington, specializing in Russet Burbank, are the two largest producers; Wisconsin is a distant third. The Interregional Potato Introduction Station in Sturgeon Bay, Wisconsin, maintains a potato germplasm collection used by researchers and breeders to improve quality characteristics and pest resistance, a continuing challenge because all potato varieties are vulnerable to attacks by viruses, fungi, other microbial blights, and Colorado beetles.

Potato varieties are classified, named, and marketed according to their geographic location of production and intended use; for example, Idaho "baking potatoes" or Eastern "all-purpose" potatoes. Some carry particular varietal names, such as the popular Russet Burbank or the gourmet La Ratte, a small elongated heirloom potato that boasts a nutlike flavor, or descriptive names that denote color and size, as in White Rose. These smaller specialty potatoes offer a counterpoint to larger, more insipid potatoes that, since the 1940s, have been specially bred to be industrially processed into fast and frozen-foods.

Solids content is the most important culinary characteristic: high-starch, floury potatoes are better for baking, frying, and mashing; low-starch, waxy potatoes are better for boiling, roasting, and salads (because they hold their shape); and medium-starch, all-purpose potatoes can be used for many different preparations. In the United States the most common potatoes are low-moisture russets, which contain the highest percentage of solids, so they make good-quality baked potatoes and also yield better fries, which replace moisture with fat. In addition pota-

toes specially bred for standard fries have a long, oblong shape that maximizes the numbers of fries per tuber. Eric Schlosser, in *Fast Food Nation,* describes the slice, wash, cut-into-strips, double-blanch, drag-through-sugar-solution, dry, fry, and freeze steps in fast food potato processing.

Potatoes fulfill three roles in the American diet: (1) co-staple of typical meals (as in "meat and potatoes"), (2) main ingredient in various ethnic foods (as in potato knishes, pancakes, dumplings), and (3) snack food (as in fried chips and crisps). Ground meat and potatoes, in the forms of meat loaf and mashed potatoes (typical "diner" fare) and hamburgers with a bag of fries and a soda (typical "fast food") are among Americans' favorite comfort foods, whether eaten outside or inside the home. Potatoes tend to be more important in the cuisines of regions where the are grown—the Northeast, Midwest, and West. But even in the South, full breakfasts typically include home fried potatoes, dinners of fried chicken bring mashed potatoes, and barbecues serve fried potatoes (chips) or potato salad as sides.

Potatoes are the main ingredient of many complex ethnic American foods, including the "deli" potato knish; Russian, eastern or central European, or Chicago pierogi (potato-filled dough); Pennsylvania potato rolls; Scandinavian flat bread; and Indian *dosi.* They are also a significant ingredient in typical "American" foods, like chowders. In the urban East, potatoes, like other plant foods, are offered as "vegetables" or "side" dishes; at its simplest, the choice is between boiled or mashed or baked or fried. At its most complex, Fleischmann's Restaurant in 1908 offered diners sixteen different potato dishes (boiled, broiled, Saratoga fried, french fried,

sautéed, fried sweet, mashed, lyonnaise, maître d'hôtel, hashed or browned, julienne, au gratin, croquettes, stewed in cream, parisienne, or potato pancakes). New York City restaurants also famously contributed new potato dishes, among them Delmonico potatoes (with butter and lemon juice) and vichyssoise, a chilled potato and leek soup concocted by the Ritz Carlton hotel restaurant. Now consumers face even more numerous choices in the potato frozen food section of their supermarkets.

Nutritionally potatoes, simply boiled, baked, or roasted, offer good value. Their dry mater provides easily digested carbohydrate calories from starch and protein that is high in lysine and low in sulfur-containing amino acids and thus complementary to the protein in cereal grains. Even a small tuber (one hundred grams), boiled in its skin, has sixteen milligrams of ascorbic acid, which is 80 percent of a child's or 50 percent of an adult's daily requirement. Potatoes are also a good source of B vitamins (thiamin, pyridoxine, and niacin) and are rich in potassium, phosphorus, and other trace elements. However, when fried potatoes become the dominant vegetable in diets, they contribute to overweight and related health problems.

In the future two countervailing potato production and consumption trends probably will persist: one favoring uniformity, mass production, and processing and the other favoring a return to greater biodiversity and flavor. The tools of molecular biology will contribute to pest resistance and to potato's nonfood uses for starch, alcohol, pharmaceuticals, and chemical polymers for plastics and synthetic rubbers. Finally, potatoes, historically vilified as the source of the nineteenth-century Irish potato famine, will continue to serve as a model philanthropic crop for gleaners, who recycle some 20 million pounds of potatoes rejected by commercial markets into emergency and supplementary food systems.

[**See also** DINERS; FAST FOOD; FRENCH FRIES; HEIRLOOM VEGETABLES; SALADS AND SALAD DRESSINGS; SOUPS AND STEWS.]

BIBLIOGRAPHY

Bareham, Lindsey. *In Praise of the Potato: Recipes from around the World.* Woodstock, NY: Overlook, 1992.

Marshall, Lydie. *A Passion for Potatoes.* New York: HarperPerennial, 1992.

Woolfe, Jennifer A., with Susan V. Poats. *The Potato in the Human Diet.* New York: Cambridge University Press, 1987.

ELLEN MESSER

Pot Holders

Pot holders, which have existed in the United States probably since the late eighteenth century, both insulate and decorate. In the 1840s needlepoint holders were used for teapots in the parlor. Most surviving nineteenth-century and early twentieth-century examples are of quilted scrap cloth, such as calico and chintz. Some 1880s Pennsylvania holders look like setting hens whose wings fold around an egg cooker's or teakettle's handle. By the 1940s booklets produced by yarn companies gave instructions for crocheting colorful pot holders shaped like animals, faces, and houses. Also in the 1940s weaving kits with pronged frames and bright loops of knitted cotton let children make pot holders. The 1950s brought insulated oven mitts.

BIBLIOGRAPHY

Franklin, Linda Campbell. *300 Years of Kitchen Collectibles.* 5th ed. Iola, WI: Krause, 2003.

LINDA CAMPBELL FRANKLIN

Pots and Pans

Pots and pans of surprising similarity have been used throughout the ancient world and have survived, as basic and necessary cookware, to the twenty-first century relatively unchanged. So common as to be idiomatic, their names combine significantly to mean "assorted essentials." The words themselves signify their universality.

The term "pot," in medieval English, referred to a deep and rounded cooking vessel that was deeper than it was wide, stood on three legs, and had a narrowing top and swinging bail handle. Used for such wet processes as boiling or stewing, pots have since been known as bulge pots, cauldrons, or gypsy kettles. The later, more encompassing sixteenth-century term meant almost any deep container for cooking, including straight-sided, long-handled posnets and pipkins (early saucepans).

Pans, on the other hand, were generally straight-sided and flat-bottomed and tended to be shallow. Often three-legged, they were more likely to be used for dry cooking as drip pans (under the roast), baking pans, frying pans, and preserving pans.

By the time of European settlement in America, the iron pot was perhaps the most important and basic of all possible pieces of hearth equipment, though closely followed by the frying pan and the water kettle. Its round bottom allowed quick and even heat transmission, and the absence of corners made stirring more efficient. Flat-bottom pots, more commonly made from the softer metals, depended on cooking trivets to hold

them high above the hearth's heat. Although they were essential to every kitchen, their numbers, materials, and variations depended on the wealth and social position of their owners.

Immigrants to the New World brought basic pots and pans and re-created them locally. With typical devotion to the food and equipment of their traditional cuisines, the English prepared their stews in stew pots, the French in beloved marmites, and the Spanish in ollas. By the middle of the eighteenth century, the introduction of tin provided a new material for inexpensive cookware, one that would eventually replace earlier ceramics. Increasing availability enabled colonial families to enlarge their stock of pots and pans and to undertake more elaborate cookery.

The American Industrial Revolution (c. 1850), with its new technologies and production techniques, introduced pots and pans adapted to the new cookstoves. Flat-bottomed, short-handled, and legless, these pots and pans made maximum contact with the new cooking surfaces. Cast-iron goods proliferated, and utensils were produced that addressed more decorative and stylish concerns, offering shaped bread pans, such as gem, or muffin pans and cornbread-stick pans. Tinware was also improved stylistically with coatings of colorful baked-on enamel. It filled kitchen shelves until well into the twentieth century, to be superseded by the more durable aluminum and stainless steel.

Americans in the twenty-first century have turned to gourmet, ethnic, and health-oriented cookery, and new pots and pans reflecting these interests and concerns crowd the pantry. Heavy copper pots, once the hallmark of professional chefs, are found in many middle-class kitchens, as are new steamer pots used by the quality conscious and the health conscious. Likewise ethnic cuisines demand that home cooks own such exotica as pasta pots, polenta pots, fondue pots, or paella pans. Looking ahead, pots and pans will continue being adapted to changing food fashion and new fuels, just as they have been adapted to microwaves, magnetic waves, and halogen.

[**See also** COOKING TECHNIQUES; DUTCH OVENS; HEARTH COOKERY; STOVES AND OVENS: GAS AND ELECTRIC; STOVES AND OVENS: WOOD AND COAL.]

BIBLIOGRAPHY

Franklin, Linda Campbell. *300 Years of Kitchen Collectibles.* 5th ed. Iola, WI: Krause, 2003.

Greguire, Helen. *The Collector's Encyclopedia of Granite Ware: Colors, Shapes, and Values,* Vol. 2. Rev. ed. Paducah, KY: Collector Books, 2000.

Smith, David G., and Chuck Wafford. *The Book of Griswold and Wagner.* Atglen, PA: Schiffer, 2001.

Smith, David G., and Chuck Wafford. *The Book of Griswold and Wagner: Favorite Piqua, Sidney Hollow Ware, Wapak.* Atglen, PA: Schiffer, 1995.

ALICE ROSS

Poultry and Fowl

More than twelve thousand species of birds are dispersed throughout the world, and almost all are edible. Early humans likely took eggs from birds' nests and consumed them, and later they figured out how to capture the birds themselves. Fowl had much to offer, as food and otherwise. Birds provided many advantages: eggs were eaten raw or cooked; poultry flesh was consumed; feathers had practical uses on arrows and as personal adornment, clothing, and ceremonial symbols; and birds such as ducks, geese, and storks were religious symbols. Chicken eggs and entrails were used for religious ceremonies, divination, and magic. Cock's combs and other body parts were used in medicines, and roosters were used for gaming and entertainment in cockfights.

Poultry

Domestication of fowl began in prehistoric times in both the Old World and the New World. By far the most important domesticated fowl was the chicken (*Gallus domesticus*), which likely descended from a combination of several species of jungle fowl native to southern and Southeast Asia. Chickens are highly prized because they lay many more eggs than the hens of other fowl and do so throughout the year, providing a steady source of food. In pre-Columbian times, chickens were widely dispersed throughout the Old World and the Pacific Islands. Soon after the beginning of European exploration of the New World in the sixteenth century, chickens were disseminated throughout the Americas. Chickens were kept throughout all the American colonies, and most farms and plantations permitted chickens to roam freely about yards.

Set of Family Copper Saucepans and Boiler

A set of copper saucepans.

Brahma Pootra fowls.

European settlers introduced other poultry into the Americas, including domesticated turkeys, Muscovy and mallard ducks, geese, guinea fowl, and peafowl. By the early nineteenth century chickens and turkeys dominated the poultry yards, and both birds were raised on a large scale for city markets. Little attention was paid to selective breeding of poultry, except for cockfighting purposes, before the 1840s, when traders brought large and exotic chickens, such as the Cochin, Brahma, Shanghai, and Chittagong, from Asia to America. The introduction of exotic fowl contributed to "hen fever," which swept the United States beginning in 1850. Over the next five years poultry prices increased and fortunes were made in breeding and selling exotic fowl. Poultry exhibitions were held, and new breeds, such as the Plymouth Rock, were developed. By the 1870s breeds were standardized, and breeding clubs were formed.

During the following decades the development of refrigerated railway cars allowed producers to ship fresh foods longer distances. Because this system required large amounts of capital, it also led to centralization of the poultry industry in the Midwest. In 1890 2.5 million pounds of dressed fowl were shipped from Kansas City, Missouri, alone. Chickens are the most important form of commercial fowl, followed by turkeys and, a distant third, ducks.

Cookery

Since its introduction in the seventeenth century, the chicken has been America's most important fowl. The mild, neutral flavor of chicken is flattered by any number of different seasonings and companion ingredients. Inexpensive and plentiful, chicken lends itself to an appealing variety of cooking methods and recipes. Chicken—whole or in parts—can be roasted, baked, fricasseed, deviled, fried, hashed, sautéed, made into soups, broths, gumbos, and gravies, and incorporated into pies, puddings, and croquettes. Cold chicken can be served in salads and sandwiches. Poultry can be stuffed with bread, grain, forcemeat, or vegetables or be served with special gravies and sauces, such as oyster and curry sauces. Almost all parts of a chicken, including neck, gizzard, feet, heart, and liver, are consumed in various ways. Recipes for preparing chickens for the table have abounded in cookbooks since the early nineteenth century. These include barbecued chicken, chicken potpie, chicken and dumplings, chicken Maryland, Brunswick stew, jambalaya, gumbo, and chicken à la king.

Chicken was particularly important in the South. Before the Civil War many slaves were permitted to keep chickens, and they elevated the technique of frying chicken to an art form. After the Civil War migrations of African Americans out of the South contributed to making "southern fried chicken" a national dish during the twentieth century.

Poultry was used as inexpensive food for servants and slaves, but domesticated and wild birds also appeared on the tables in America's most elegant restaurants. Nineteenth-century cookbooks provided an abundance of recipes for barnyard fowl and wild duck and goose as well as blackbird, lark, quail, grouse, guinea fowl, peafowl, pigeon, plover, wigeon, and other game birds. There were instructions for buying poultry and for preparing homegrown or purchased birds for the oven or pot. Roasting was a basic method of preparation, but there were also recipes for fricassees, stews, ragouts, potpies, and hashes. The books contained directions for making chicken broth or stock as well as heartier soups and recipes for sauces and stuffings or dressings for specific birds.

Commercialization

Chicken remains the dominant poultry in America and the world. In addition to the traditional ways of preparing chicken in the home, fast food establishments have commercialized specific chicken dishes, such as the fried chicken served at KFC and the chicken McNuggets served at McDonald's. Chicken burgers are served at many hamburger establishments, and "chicken dogs" are sold in supermarkets throughout America. Many manufacturers include chicken in frozen dinners. Turkey remains a distant second in the commercial poultry market, but its sales have extended beyond the traditional Thanksgiving and Christmas periods.

[**See also** AFRICAN AMERICAN FOODS; CHICKEN; DRESSINGS AND STUFFINGS; DUCK; EGGS; GOOSE; SOUTHERN REGIONAL COOKERY; TURKEY.]

BIBLIOGRAPHY

American Poultry Historical Society. *American Poultry History 1823–1973*. Madison, WI: American Poultry History Society, 1974.

Sawyer, Gordon. *The Agribusiness Poultry Industry: A History of Its Development*. New York: Exposition, 1971.

Smith, Page, and Charles Daniel. *The Chicken Book*. San Francisco: North Point, 1982.

ANDREW F. SMITH

Premium Lager

This is perhaps both the broadest and narrowest style of beer. It is broad in that every major brewer as well as midsize and regional brewers label their basic beer as "Premium" at the coaching of their advertising departments. It is narrow in that these same brewers are economically restricted to producing a product that is acceptable to the consumer, at the lowest production cost possible.

The beginnings of this situation can be found in the fantastic economic growth of companies after World War II. At that time the economy of size created megacorporations that produced millions of "affordable" automobiles, appliances, and beer. These products met minimum standards and were sold on price rather than quality. The effect on the American brewing industry was that unique beers became too expensive to produce, promote, and distribute. In the late 1960s there were fewer than one hundred commercial breweries in the United States, and most of them were owned by three corporations. These corporations met an increasing demand for refreshing beverages that were as inexpensive as possible to produce and sold at a low cost to the consumer.

In the early twenty-first century all the major American brewers market their "standard" beers as "premium," and their premium beers are called "super premiums." To try to justify the "premium" appellation, commercial brewers try to ensure that these products contain only 25- to -30 percent rice or corn and often use more expensive malt.

According to the Association of Brewers' 2004 Beer Style Guidelines, American-style premium lager "has low malt (and adjunct) sweetness, is medium bodied, and should contain no or a low percentage (less than 25%) of adjuncts. Alcohol by volume is usually between 4.3–5 percent."

PETER LaFRANCE

Prepared Herb and Spice Mixtures

Countless dry rubs, pickling spices, seasoning salts, and similar mixtures are found in stores' spice aisles. Some are distinctly American, either by birth or by naturalization—through constant use in our kitchens.

Bell's Seasoning was created in 1867 in Newton, Massachusetts, by William G. Bell. Originally intended for making sausage, it has become a Thanksgiving staple. Part of its appeal is the fact that nothing about the product has changed, neither packaging nor ingredients (ginger, marjoram, oregano, rosemary, pepper, thyme, and of course sage).

Chili powder is usually a mixture of ground chilies, cumin, garlic powder, oregano, and sometimes coriander seed. Dewitt Clinton Pendery began selling a mixture of powdered spices he called Chiltomaline in 1890, but the first truly successful chili powder was made by William Gebhardt in San Antonio, Texas, in 1894.

Curry powder is a generic blend of spices, typically chili, cinnamon, cloves, cumin, fenugreek, ginger, nutmeg, turmeric, and others. Cardamom, being more expensive, is included only rarely. Hot Madras Curry Powder contains additional chili. Both curry powders, rarely used in India, are made for export to Europe and the United States.

Italian seasoning is a name for several different commercial mixtures of herbs and spices, often containing basil, bay leaves, oregano, paprika, parsley, pepper, sage, and thyme. It is unlike anything in Italy, where cooks usually prefer only one herb or spice at a time.

Old Bay Seasoning, used with shellfish, especially crabs, around Chesapeake Bay, was invented in Baltimore in 1939 by Gustav Brunn. Its primary ingredient is celery salt, but the mixture includes many other spices—allspice, bay leaves, cardamom, cinnamon, cloves, chili, ginger, mace, mustard, paprika, and black pepper.

Pumpkin pie spice was commonly called mixed spice in Old English cookbooks. Typical blends contain allspice, cinnamon, cloves, ginger, nutmeg, and sometimes cassia and coriander.

[**See also** CHILI; CRAB BOILS; GINGER FAMILY; SWEET SPICES.]

BIBLIOGRAPHY

Allen, Gary. *The Herbalist in the Kitchen*. Champaign: University of Illinois Press, forthcoming.
"Bell's Seasoning Adds the Spice of Life to Thanksgiving Recipes." Valley Breeze, Nov. 17, 2004. http://www.valleybreeze.com/Free/281962755050130.php.

Denker, Joel. *The World on a Plate: A Tour through the History of America's Ethnic Cuisine*. Boulder, CO: Westview, 2003.

GARY ALLEN

Preserves

Preserves are preparations of fruits cooked with sugar until soft and gelled—delicacies that store well for months without refrigeration. They include the familiar jams, jellies, syrups, fruit butters, and marmalades as well as the lesser-known conserves (jamlike but with nuts and raisins and sometimes citrus peels) and preparations of wines, herbs, and spices. Historically the significance of preserves lay in their ability to provide summertime flavors in wintertime, when such luxuries were beyond the reach of most people.

History of Preserves

From antiquity, preserves were made from fruits wherever there was honey or sugar, the essential preservatives. It was not until the medieval period and the introduction of sugar to Europe that the kinds of preserves later known in America were developed. Among the earliest were a series of quince jams, jellies, syrups, marmalades, and preserves. The quince (an applelike but sour fruit), sugar, and rose or perfume flavorings were derivatives of still earlier Middle Eastern preparations, exotic to English palates at the time. In addition to its appealing flavor, quince had the benefit of contributing its own pectin, the gelling factor found in the pulp surrounding its seeds. Many preserves also were based on available orchard fruits, berries, currants, and gooseberries. As many of these lacked their own pectin, long cooking and the addition of high pectin fruits or processed gelatinous animal products (isinglass, hartshorn, or calves' feet) were used to achieve the desired thickening.

These basic recipes were brought to the New World, along with the means to establish sugar and fruit production. At first, because of its scarcity and expense, sugar was used only by the wealthy, who prepared some of their own products and imported others from Europe. Using cookbooks and recipes from their mother countries, seventeenth- and eighteenth-century colonists continued basic preparations, sometimes adapting indigenous American foods to their conserves and marmalades. Thus regional specialties evolved based on northwestern salmonberries and dewberries, southwestern hot and spicy tomato mixtures, and coastal northeastern beach plums.

Colonial preserving usually was the province of the mistress of the house, as sugar work and candying were considered special skills. A gift of preserves clearly honored its recipients. Because of their high status, they were featured components of pyramids of sweetmeats or formal teas. Some

1918 Fruits of Victory poster by Leonebel Jacobs.

accompanied meats: Cumberland sauce of jellied currants served with venison, jellied cranberries paired with turkey, mint jelly with lamb, and wild beach plum jams with ham.

By the end of the nineteenth century, a number of converging factors brought home preserving within the reach of middle-class homemakers. Inexpensive sugar, the new cookstove, glass canning jars with screw-on or clamped lids, and abundant fruits reduced the costs and time-consuming labor; home preserving became integral to the domestic calendar year. A homemaker's reputation rested on her clearest jellies, most flavorful jams and conserves, and most innovative combinations of fruits and spices. Home cooks were inspired and guided by single-themed cookbooks, such as Sarah Tyson Rorer's *Canning and Preserving* (1887) and Gesine Lemcke's *Preserving and Pickling* (1899). Local shops also sold commercially preserved products by companies such as H. J. Heinz and H. K. and F. B. Thurber. Preserves on toast soon became a breakfast standby.

In this era preserving still required long cooking times, which meant a good deal of the fruit's original flavor was lost. Some argued for processing in small quantities. Others shortened cooking times with the introduction of twentieth-century commercial pectins, which were criticized for masking the fruit's flavor. The debate continues. In the early twenty-first century only the occasional home cook fills the pantry with homemade specialties. In an era when lack of time is an issue, it is far easier to buy good-quality products, and a homemaker's reputation now is based on other activities.

Methods of Making Preserves

Historically the standard proportions for preserves were equal weights of fruit and sugar, which were cooked in a shallow brass, bell metal, or enameled iron pan (not uncoated iron, as it darkens the fruit). In some cases the prepared fruit and sugar were allowed to sit overnight before cooking, a process that drew the liquid and maintained a firmer texture. Thickening was achieved by lengthy cooking, often two hours or more. The completed preserve was put up in jelly glasses or stone pots (stoneware), sealed with brandy papers and perhaps melted tallow, and covered with a tied-on paper or cloth. Syrups followed the same procedure, but the fruit was strained and then corked in a bottle.

The cooking time for preserves has been shortened considerably by the use of modern commercial pectin, a product of orange rind. Sealing is accomplished by the use of paraffin, two-piece lids, and sometimes terminal sterilization. Some sweetened, uncooked jams (with wonderfully fresh flavors) are preserved by freezing.

Types of Preserves

Jam is a chunky preservation in which irregular pieces of fruit are cooked in their own juices. This is the most common and simplest form of preserves, in which the fruit preparation involves removing pits and stems (and occasionally peeling) and coarse chopping. Jelly is a clear version of jam. After a brief simmering, the fruit is strained, and the juice is processed as for jam. Preserves are a coarse jam, sometimes mixed with other fruits and spices.

Marmalade was historically a simple jam or jelly, and it became associated with orange and lemon rinds in England before 1700. Thinly sliced rinds sometimes were set with sugar overnight to draw the juice and then cooked until translucent. Early orange marmalades used flavorful but bitter Seville oranges, which may have been presoaked or parboiled to reduce bitterness. Early American marmalades sometimes included sliced pumpkin or American citron (a watermelon variety).

Conserves are more complex jams that combine fruits, nuts, raisins, and spices and are served on bread or with meats. Syrups are jellylike but ungelled flavorings. Fruit butters are dense, long-cooked jams. They are often fortified with cider and spices. Leathers are sheets of chewy, sweetened semidried fruits. They are prepared like jams but cooked longer, spread on papers on a shallow plate or pan, and further dried over a brazier or in a cool oven until leathery. These remain popular snacks.

Preserved whole fruits in syrup were used as decorative and flavorful sweet accompaniments or desserts. Small fruits such as crab apples, cherries, or plums were used as edible garnishes. Preserved whole fruits in brandy were a more elegant form of those preserved in syrup. The brandy itself was a preservative. Despite its historical popularity, the temperance movement helped its demise.

[**See also** CANNING AND BOTTLING; FRUIT; SUGAR.]

BIBLIOGRAPHY

Carey, Nora. *Perfect Preserves: Provisions from the Kitchen Garden.* New York: Stewart, Tabori, and Chang, 1990.

Plagemann, Catherine. *Fine Preserving: M. F. K. Fisher's Annotated Edition of Catherine Plagemann's Cookbook.* Berkeley, CA: Aris, 1986.

ALICE ROSS

President's Day, *see Washington's Birthday*

Pressure Cookers

Cooking food thoroughly using steam under pressure seems modern, but the French scientist Denis Papin invented a pressure cooker in 1679. Called a "digester" or "la marmite," it softened bones and otherwise wasted meat parts. Aware of the potential for explosion, Papin incorporated a valve to let off steam when it reached a level of pressure that was dangerous.

A digester available in America was depicted in the 1854 edition of the *American Home Cook Book.* It shows a squat cast-iron kettle, bowed out at its center, with a swinging handle, and a clamp-on lid. Sizes ranged from one quart to eight gallons. Bones and gristle softened for soup gave thrifty cooks full value for any cut of meat. Almost identical was one manufactured in 1909 for hotels and restaurants, with sealing gaskets and lid clamps.

Cast-aluminum pressure cookers began to appear in the 1920s. Always of prime concern was the danger of pressure building up unrelieved until the cooker exploded, so steam escape valves and pressure gauges were standard. Pressure cookers in the twenty-first century are little changed in form, but safety has been greatly improved.

[**See also** COOKING TECHNIQUES; POTS AND PANS.]

BIBLIOGRAPHY

Franklin, Linda Campbell. *300 Years of Kitchen Collectibles.* 5th ed. Iola, WI: Krause, 2003.

LINDA CAMPBELL FRANKLIN

Pretzel

The original pretzel is the soft kind sold from carts in Philadelphia and New York City. It was probably developed as a Lenten bread in the early Middle Ages in Italy, with the characteristic shape representing arms folded in prayer in the medieval manner. The breads were named by monks either *bracellae* ("little arms") or *pretiola* ("little reward"), which were transmuted into German *Bretzel* or pretzel. Like modern pretzels (and bagels), they were briefly boiled, then baked for a caramelized brown crust, which was usually heavily salted but might also be spiced or sweetened. Pretzels are pictured in Renaissance paintings and may appear on an illustrated manuscript of Virgil's poems from 400 C.E., a pagan manuscript that would contradict the monastery origin story of the pretzel shape.

Soft pretzels may have come to America from Holland with the English Dissenters called Pilgrims, and there is some documentation of them in the New Netherlands colony in the seventeenth century. They were sold on the streets of Philadelphia in the 1820s. The mustard served on soft pretzels

Owner Lewis C. Haines (background) unloads pretzels at the Lititz Springs Pretzel Company while his son, Bob, weighs them and packs them in cans. Lititz, Pennsylvania, was the first town in America to make pretzels.

is an American development, as are all forms of hard pretzels, with the possible exception of pretzel sticks, which developed in Germany as *Saltstangen*. The modern hard-pretzel industry developed in the Pennsylvania Dutch areas of eastern Pennsylvania in the mid-nineteenth century. The small town of Lititz near Lancaster claims the oldest continuously operating pretzel bakery, Sturgis Pretzel House, founded in 1861. Julius Sturgis had probably been baking pretzels already for about ten years, allegedly obtaining the recipe from an immigrant hobo.

The advantage of hard pretzels is shelf life, and they do not have to be reheated for the best flavor as do soft pretzels. They spread around the United States with German beer halls and saloons founded by immigrants from 1848. Machinery to shape hard pretzels came on line in Reading, Pennsylvania, still the "Pretzel City," in 1935. Artisanal pretzels continue to be shaped by hand, often by groups of Amish or Mennonite women, who sing hymns and shape up to forty pretzels per minute.

The hard pretzel became America's favorite snack with beer and was for a time the second most popular of all salted snack foods, after potato chips. It has since slid behind tortilla chips, and popped corn is catching up. Nevertheless, the average American eats almost two pounds per year, and in parts of Pennsylvania the figure is four times that much. Chocolate-covered and yogurt-dipped pretzels have revived the medieval sweet pretzel tradition. However, the Pennsylvania Dutch are still the main people who use pretzels other than as snacks, for example, in a salad, in a soup, in dressing with roasted meats, or hung up as Christmas tree decorations. (The Christmas tree pretzels are sweet cookies decorated with colored sugar.) Pennsylvania Dutch children once wore pretzels for good luck at New Year's. In Europe pretzels were hidden for children to hunt at Easter and were part of a wishbone-like game at weddings.

On January 13, 2002, President George W. Bush choked on a hard pretzel while watching a football play-off game and briefly fainted, falling off the couch he was sitting on and bruising his face.

[See also Pennsylvania Dutch Food.]

BIBLIOGRAPHY
The Lancaster County Farm Cook Book. Whitmer, PA: Applied Arts, 1967.

MARK H. ZANGER

Prickly Pear, *see Cactus*

Prison Food

The goals and challenges of prison food service are similar to those of other institutional food-service operations. Food must be provided to a large, in-house group in a manner that is efficient, cost-effective, and sanitary. The majority of prisons in the United States are run by individual state departments of corrections, which means that prisons differ in their approaches to meeting these goals and challenges. However, on average the cost of feeding an inmate in a U.S. prison in 2000 was $2.42 per day.

Prison menus reflect financial constraints, nutrition and safety concerns, and philosophies of the rights of prisoners. Meals reflect the needs and preferences of the institution rather than those of the inmates. Taste, quality, and variety are not major considerations in correctional facilities.

As American prisons become increasingly crowded, states place increased pressure on prisons to cut food-service costs, resulting in reduced food quality and quantity. In Georgia, for example, prisons cut fried foods from the menu to reduce equipment maintenance, sewage problems, and frying oil expenses. Georgia prisons, in the early 2000s, were adding soy extenders to meat, serving only cold-cut lunches, and preparing only two meals on weekends and holidays. In Texas prisons reduced daily inmate calories from 2,700 to 2,500, and in Iowa prisons replaced orange juice with vitamin-enhanced orange-flavored liquid.

These changes, however, cannot compromise the nutritional value or safety of inmate diets, both of which are guaranteed to the inmates by the Eighth Amendment to the Constitution. All menus must meet basic nutritional requirements and should be monitored by an in-house or consultant dietitian. Guidelines for preparing healthful meals in prisons are outlined in the *Correctional Foodservice and Nutrition Manual* created by Consultant Dietitians in Health Care Facilities and distributed through the American Dietetics Association.

Early twenty-first-century nutritional improvements to inmate meals include the reduction of fatty, red meats and the increased use of lower-fat poultry items. To make foods safer and reduce instances of food-borne illness, some prisons purchase individually portioned packages of meat to control bacterial growth. Other prisons take temperature readings at the time of food delivery to assure that food is served at the proper temperature. Such changes, however, bring challenges. Prisons report that inmates find higher-calorie menus more satisfying than lower-calorie menus and that lower-fat meals are more expensive than meals containing a greater percentage of fat. For example, a meal composed of only 30 percent fat costs 15 percent more than a meal composed of 40 percent fat.

The preparation and service of food in prisons reflects the institution's role as a place of punishment and rehabilitation. Many prison tensions are played out over food; inmates stage hunger strikes and start food riots, corrections officers tamper with food, and kitchens serve tasteless, unappealing food as punishment. Although the content, preparation, and service of prison meals vary by state, all prison meals reflect the American view of prisoners' rights and the role of American penal institutions. Twenty-first-century shifts in prison food service include changes in how food is procured, how it is prepared, and what is served. The most common shift in prison food service is from an internally run operation to one that is contracted out to a private company specializing in institutional food service. Although this shift can mean less control over the dietary department, its benefits include increased cash flow and fewer demands on prison staff. Other states tackle prison food service in more creative ways. In Georgia, for example, the Georgia Department of Corrections' Food and Farm Services Division manages a ten thousand–acre growing, processing, and distribution program. This farm includes vegetable crops, dairy production, and meat production; saves taxpayers millions of dollars; and involves the prisoners in the work of growing, harvesting, processing, and preparing food. In an entirely different approach to feeding prisoners, Victor Valley Medium Correctional Facility in Adelanto, California, implemented the NEWSTART vegan program for approximately half of its inmates. In this program prisoners eat a purely vegan diet (except on weekends) in addition to attending religion and life skill classes. The prison staff at Victor Valley reports that inmates in this program are better behaved and are less likely to become repeat offenders than inmates not enrolled in the program. Regardless of how prisons choose to feed inmates, decisions made reveal the contradictory role of prisons as institutions of punishment, rehabilitation, and guardianship.

[See also NUTRITION; VEGETARIANISM.]

BIBLIOGRAPHY
American Correctional Food Service Association. http://www.acfsa.org.
Consultant Dietitians in Health Care Facilities. http://www.cdhcf.org.

MIMI MARTIN

Prohibition

Prohibition was a period in U.S. history between 1920 and 1933 when federal law forbade the manufacture, importation, and sale of alcohol. Brought on by a century-long temperance movement and imposed by a constitutional amendment, Prohibition was an attempt by temperance advocates to solve the country's social problems. This ban on alcohol successfully reduced drinking, but it also became a divisive political issue and helped a network of organized crime to become entrenched in America. Widespread opposition to the law caused its repeal in 1933.

In the early nineteenth century several Protestant denominations began a national crusade against alcohol abuse. Drinking was a common practice for American men, who often congregated in taverns. Quakers and

Methodists first spoke out against this practice, though they differentiated between distilled spirits, which they cast as evil, and the moderate use of fermented beverages. This movement spread to other denominations, fueled by a resurgence of religious fervor in the 1830s. During this same era, immigrants flooded in from Ireland and Germany, many of them Catholics who habitually drank more than their native-born Anglo-American Protestant neighbors. Feeling culturally and politically threatened by this influx of new immigrants and offended by their drinking habits, the native-born Americans, or "nativists," took steps to preserve the status quo. Protestant leaders formed the American Temperance Society in 1826, urging local and state governments to limit or ban drinking. Women's rights groups and abolitionists added their voices to these demands, viewing alcohol abuse as a major social problem. Several northern states responded by prohibiting alcohol, keeping these laws in force until the 1850s.

These combined efforts did decrease alcohol consumption during this period, but immigrant groups maintained drinking as part of their ethnic cultures. Consumption briefly rebounded during the Civil War with millions of men serving in the military. After the war Protestant temperance groups continued their crusade against drinking, founding new organizations, such as the Anti-Saloon League and the Women's Christian Temperance Union. These groups lobbied legislators, published tracts on temperance, developed a nationwide network of church groups, and gained notoriety by invading saloons and taverns.

Political Action

These temperance organizations continued their fight into the twentieth century, building up political and financial support. The business leaders Sebastian Kresge and John D. Rockefeller funded pro-temperance political campaigns and educational programs. In 1913 the Anti-Saloon League marched on Washington, D.C., delivering to Congress the draft of a constitutional amendment banning alcohol. Their draft soon became the Hobson-Sheppard bill, which was defeated in the Senate. Rebounding from this defeat, temperance leaders heavily funded their "dry" candidates in 1916 elections. Anti-German sentiment during World War I brought public anger against German American–owned breweries. Temperance advocates also argued that grain supplies should be conserved for the war effort, equating sobriety with patriotism. Congress in 1917 responded by passing the Eighteenth Amendment, in principle banning alcohol in the United States, which was ratified within thirteen months. Next Congress passed the National Prohibition Act, commonly called the Volstead Act, which defined the amendment's parameters and en-

forcement measures. Prohibition became law on January 16, 1920, criminalizing the manufacture, sale, importation, or distribution of alcohol in the United States.

The Volstead Act banned most alcohol but allowed exceptions for alcohol used in patent medicines, doctor's prescriptions, sacramental wine, cider, syrups, vinegars, and "near beer" with an alcohol content of 0.5 percent or less. These many exceptions became popular conduits for legally acquiring alcohol. Churches often multiplied their pre-Prohibition wine orders, and drinkers injected toxic rubbing alcohol into near beer to create the more potent though dangerous "needle beer." In addition many drinkers fermented grapes or brewed grain beverages at home, which was not in violation of the law.

Law enforcement authorities became frustrated with Prohibition, since alcoholic beverages were popular, and many Americans continued to drink. Some drinkers stockpiled alcohol before Prohibition began, while others paid exorbitant prices for alcohol. Numerous saloons remained open, becoming illegal "speakeasies," even though distilleries, breweries, and wineries abruptly closed or turned to making other products.

Bootlegging and the Rise of Organized Crime

Illicit suppliers immediately replaced formerly legitimate sources, bringing in Caribbean rum through Florida, Canadian whiskey across the northern border, and higher-priced Scotch whisky and European wines onto Atlantic beaches. Termed bootleggers and rumrunners, these smugglers risked arrest in pursuit of high profits. Domestically beer production often continued in ethnic neighborhoods, and the products were sold to local residents in buckets. Rural producers also distilled grain, selling drinkers their crude but potent "moonshine." The volume of smuggling and illegal sales overwhelmed enforcement agencies, which were often understaffed and poorly funded. To thwart violations, the federal government established the Prohibition Bureau and ordered the Coast Guard to apprehend smugglers, but alcohol flowed into the country unabated.

Smuggling initially was done haphazardly by individuals and small criminal gangs. Once the alcohol had crossed the border, street gangs sold it in their own neighborhoods, closely guarding their territory against intruding gangs. Gangs of similar ethnicity gradually banded together for greater power and profits, controlling even larger areas of their cities. As profits increased, these gangs became increasingly violent, frequently even murdering competitors. Irish, Italian, and Jewish gangs fought each other to dominate the alcohol market, resulting in hundreds of deaths. Infamous among these gang killings was the St. Valentine's Day massacre of 1929,

when Al Capone ordered the murder of seven rival gangsters.

Such violence became commonplace, fighting until a single gang consolidated power in a particular city. Al Capone, for example, emerged from the gang wars as the undisputed crime kingpin of Chicago, enjoying an absolute monopoly over the city's liquor distribution, narcotics, prostitution, and gambling. Gangs often met with little opposition from law enforcement, with police either bribed or from ethnic groups that traditionally prized drinking. Once similar Italian gangs dominated these activities in their own cities, the major crime bosses formed larger syndicates, designed to further increase profits. These intercity connections became the organizational basis for the notorious La Cosa Nostra, which is more commonly known as the Mafia.

Aggressive anti-Prohibition groups began forming in the late 1920s, intent on repealing the Eighteenth Amendment. When the Democratic Party adopted repeal as a major plank in the 1932 campaign, it gained millions of thirsty voters. Besieged by the Depression, many advocates extolled the economic value of restoring jobs in the beer and liquor industries and increasing profits for grain farmers. Democratic candidate Franklin Roosevelt swept into office, partly by promising repeal of Prohibition and a tax on beer to relieve the government's financial problems. Roosevelt kept his promise, officially ending the ban with the Twenty-First Amendment in 1933.

[**See also** Alcohol and Teetotalism; Saloons; Temperance.]

BIBLIOGRAPHY

Kyvig, David E. *Repealing National Prohibition*. Kent, OH: Kent State University Press, 2000.

Rebman, Renne C. *Prohibition*. San Diego: Lucent Books, 1999.

Sinclair, Andrew. *Prohibition: The Era of Excess*. Norwalk, CT: Easton, 1986.

David Gerard Hogan

Prudhomme, Paul

Paul Prudhomme (b. 1940) is the chef and owner of K-Paul's Louisiana Kitchen in New Orleans. He became the face of Cajun cooking during the 1980s, when Cajun became

Paul Prudhomme poses in the kitchen.

widely acknowledged as one of America's distinctive regional cuisines. A familiar national television personality, easily recognized by his formidable size and Acadian accent, Prudhomme introduced Americans to the country-cooking traditions of his native Louisiana, popularizing such dishes as gumbo, jambalaya, and dirty rice. His specialty, blackened redfish, prepared by dusting a fillet with a mix of spices and searing it in a dry, hot cast-iron skillet, was widely copied, and blackening as a cooking technique became a 1980s restaurant trend.

The youngest of thirteen children, Prudhomme was raised on a farm in southern Louisiana, the birthplace of Cajun cuisine. He began his restaurant career early, opening a drive-in at the age of seventeen. After working in a variety of restaurants across the country, Prudhomme returned to New Orleans to head the kitchen at Commander's Palace before opening K-Paul's in the French Quarter in 1979.

His first cookbook, *Chef Paul Prudhomme's Louisiana Kitchen*, published in 1984, shared many of the crowd-pleasing recipes from his restaurant and is still considered to be a standard text on Cajun and Creole cuisine. He has published seven additional cookbooks and hosted four cooking series on public television. In 1982 Prudhomme created a signature line of spices, Magic Seasoning Blends, and was one of the first celebrity chefs to market a consumer product in his own name.

[**See also** CAJUN AND CREOLE FOOD; CELEBRITY CHEFS.]

LYNNE SAMPSON

Puck, Wolfgang

Wolfgang Puck is known as the shy chef who became an industry and the first chef to become a brand name. But there is more to Wolfgang Puck's reputation than just dollars. By showcasing California's bounty of high-quality, locally grown ingredients, Puck helped to create, along with Alice Waters, what is known as "California cuisine." His cookbooks, syndicated food column, Food Network TV show, and restaurant and food-product empire have made Puck as famous as the movie stars he hosts at Spago, his award-winning Los Angeles restaurant.

Born in St. Viet, Austria, in 1949, Puck's first culinary influence was his mother, Maria, who cooked for the dining room of a lakefront hotel. Puck began apprenticing in local restaurants at fourteen, leaving Austria to work in France at seventeen. He eventually became a classically trained French chef in the master kitchens of the Hotel de Paris in Monaco and Maxim's in Paris. His first American stint, in Indianapolis in 1973, taught Puck much about the American eating habits he soon would be influencing. In 1975, after two years in Indianapolis, he moved to Los Angeles, becoming chef and part owner

Master Chef Wolfgang Puck (left) spray paints Oscar-shaped chocolates with gold powder at the annual Academy Governors Ball preview in Hollywood, February 16, 2006.

of Ma Maison, where he cooked classic French food. The bistro became a magnet for the rich and famous, with Puck as the main attraction. In 1981 Puck's star began to rise rapidly after the publication of his first cookbook, *Modern French Cooking*. Capitalizing on this in 1982, Puck opened Spago on the Sunset Strip in Los Angeles. The vividly colored eatery, filled with picnic chairs and patio furniture, was designed by his partner and soon-to-be wife, Barbara Lazaroff. The couple was an early leader in the restaurant-as-theater movement, with Lazaroff creating an open kitchen that put Puck in the spotlight. At the same time Puck also helped pioneer wood-fired gourmet pizza in the United States and is often credited as the father of California-style pizza; his signature pizza is topped with smoked salmon, caviar, and crème fraîche.

In 1983 Puck opened Chinois on Main Street in Santa Monica. At Chinois, Puck began combining French techniques with Asian ingredients, becoming a pioneer with other chefs like Jeremiah Tower in this hybrid cuisine and further changing America's eating habits. Meanwhile Puck's celebrity clientele grew at Spago, and his food came to signify L.A. style. When he began hosting dinners after the Academy Awards, he became a national celebrity himself.

Puck further drew upon his fame by opening other Spago restaurants in Chicago, Hawaii, Tokyo, and Las Vegas, where he was the first star chef to create a fine-dining restaurant. In the 1990s he began opening informal Spago offshoots—Wolfgang Puck Express and Wolfgang Puck Cafes—throughout the United States, after which came a namesake food company, a catering company, and a line of cookware. By 2002 his various companies grossed $375 million annually. Puck also garnered a host of major awards, including the James Beard Outstanding Chef in the United States and Outstanding Restaurant for Spago in Los Angeles.

Although Puck appears happiest when he is cooking in the kitchens of his fine-dining restaurants and kibitzing with guests and staff, he has tied his future to his casual dining eateries and to his packaged supermarket foods like frozen pizzas and canned soups. When asked about his success, Puck says he simply did what he loved and got lucky in between. And, he adds, he learned more from his one restaurant that went bankrupt in 1990 (Eureka, a lavish Los Angeles brasserie) than all his successes.

[See also CALIFORNIA; CELEBRITY CHEFS; FUSION FOOD; WATERS, ALICE.]

BIBLIOGRAPHY
Lubow, Arthur. "Puck's Peak." *New Yorker*, Dec. 1, 1997.
Reichl, Ruth. *Comfort Me with Apples*. New York: Random House, 2001.

SCOTT WARNER

Puddings

Ask Americans to name a pudding, and they might mention chocolate pudding or rice pudding; if the respondent is old enough, perhaps tapioca pudding, bread pudding, or even plum pudding will come to mind. If asked to define "pudding," he or she might say that it is a soft, flavored custard made with starch, eggs, and milk. Few people would mention blood pudding, but in fact it shares the same roots with all the other puddings.

Nathan Bailey's 1776 dictionary defined pudding as "a sort of food well known, chiefly in England, as hog's puddings, etc." Sheridan's Dictionary (1790) described pudding as "a kind of food generally made of flour, milk, and eggs; the gut of an animal; a bowel stuffed with certain mixtures of meal and other ingredients." In James Barclay's Dictionary, published in 1820, pudding was defined as a "kind of food boiled in a bag; or stuffed in some parts of an animal; or baked. The gut of an animal." These descriptions seem far removed from chocolate pudding.

On close examination, our modern idea of pudding is not that far removed from historical reality. Puddings are composed of starch, eggs, milk, and a flavoring of some kind and are cooked in a container. Today pudding would be prepared in a baking dish or tin mold. In the past the pudding preparation would have been stuffed into a length of intestines or the stomach of an animal and boiled until done. Some puddings were wrapped in a piece of cloth (a pudding bag), tied at the top, and submerged in a large pot of simmering water. The pudding cloth was a substitute for an animal's stomach. As refined white sugar, molasses, chocolate, and vanilla became more available, a preference for sweet puddings evolved.

During Roman times blood pudding (Latin, *botellus*) was a sausage made from blood and cereal. The name was altered in Old French to boudin and in Middle English to pudding. In time a mixture of chopped organs, vegetables, and cereals boiled in a sewed-up stomach came to be known as haggis in Scotland. Encased in a pig's stomach, it was called hog maw in Pennsylvania's Lancaster County.

Amelia Simmons's 1796 cookbook *American Cookery*—the first cookbook published by an American in America—contained two recipes for "Pompkin" pudding. We would recognize this dish not as a pudding but as a pie. This is another clue that puddings fall into an extremely broad classification. In America puddings took on regional characteristics. New Englanders preferred hasty pudding, also called Indian pudding (a mush made from cornmeal, molasses, and milk). In the South, African Americans transformed a pudding made from sweet potatoes into sweet potato pie. Puddings traditionally have been made from inexpensive or leftover ingredients, such as stale bread, beef suet, organ meats, or drippings from roasted beef, and then boiled, steamed, or baked. They could be served hot or cold at the beginning of the meal, as the meal itself, or as dessert. One type of pudding called for the ingredients to be tied up in a cloth bag and suspended in a pot of boiling water if the housekeeper did not have a proper tin mold. Another method called for baking the pudding in a pottery basin. In Massachusetts some ceramic pots dated to the early nineteenth century were divided into two compartments, one side for pudding and the other for baked beans.

In the United States in the early 2000s, puddings were still part of the culinary repertoire but as minor players. In the nineteenth century they took center stage. In Mrs. Whitney's 1889 cooking manual *Just How*, the chapter on puddings is larger than the chapter on vegetables. As puddings evolved in both British and American cookery, there was little attempt to provide stabilization or codification of this class of food. In an attempt to bring some semblance of order, Whitney broke down puddings into four general divisions: puddings with crusts, soft-mixed puddings, batter puddings, and sandwich puddings. Puddings with crusts include apple dumplings (boiled, steamed, or baked), Huckleberry hollow, and pandowdy, deep-dish desserts with a crust. Soft-mixed puddings include boiled or baked bread pudding, Indian pudding, plum pudding, and baked rice, tapioca, and lemon pudding.

Whitney defined sandwich puddings as being composed of fruit and bread layered in a dish and baked. She stated that this class of puddings could be "varied and multiplied according to one's own pleasure and ingenuity" and with whatever fruit was in season. The fourth classification included custard puddings and pancakes. Pudding recipes are still found in cookbooks but in fewer numbers.

The phrase "puddingheaded" came into the language with the meaning "one whose head was a sack of boiled haggis, or stupid." Mark Twain named one of his classic novels *Pudd'nhead Wilson* (1894; originally published as *The Tragedy of Pudd'nhead Wilson and the Comedy of Those Extraordinary Twins*), the story of two babies, one slave, one free, switched in their cradles. "Puddinghead," as a disparaging term, seems a little old-fashioned in the early twenty-first century and is seldom heard. One more often hears "mush head" or "meathead," two terms that also trace their roots back to pudding.

[See also CUSTARDS; DESSERTS; HASTY PUDDING; PIES AND TARTS; SAUSAGE.]

BIBLIOGRAPHY
Ciardi, John. *A Second Browser's Dictionary and Native's Guide to the Unknown American Language*. New York: Harper and Row, 1983.
Stone, Robert G., and David M. Hinkley. *The Pudding Book*. Lee's Summit, MO: Fat Little Pudding Boys, 1996.

JOSEPH M. CARLIN

Puerto Rican Food

Puerto Rico is one in a chain of islands called the West Indies. Within this island group, Cuba, Jamaica, Hispaniola (Dominican Republic and Haiti), and Puerto Rico together are known as the Greater Antilles. Puerto Rico, the easternmost and smallest of this group, lies 1,050 miles from the tip of Florida and 1,600 miles from New York. On the north it is bounded by the Atlantic Ocean and on the south by the Caribbean.

Native Foods and Early Immigrant Influences

Since its discovery by Christopher Columbus in 1493, Puerto Rico has been enriched by and in turn has influenced the culinary styles of the various newcomers who have made the island their home. This cuisine has evolved into what is called *cocina criolla* (native cooking).

At the time of Columbus's voyage, the island was inhabited by a tribe of Caribbean Indians known as the Tainos. They were a simple people who had lived for generations on the island they called Borinquen, and they subsisted on what the island provided: fruit, corn, capsicum peppers (especially the large sweet bell peppers known as pimientos), wild birds, and abundant crabs and other seafood. Their primary cooking utensils were made from clay or stone, particularly a vessel called the *caldera*, similar to a kettle.

The new foods discovered on the island (among these cassava bread, native beans, tapioca, and maize) changed the diet of the Old World. But the food exchange between the native and immigrant cultures went both ways. The Spanish introduced pigs, chicken, sheep, and the first horses to the island. They also brought with them sugarcane, wheat, chickpeas, and various vegetables. From this interchange a whole new cuisine emerged, combining Spanish and native Caribbean cooking techniques and foodstuffs.

With the introduction of African slaves to work the sugarcane fields, the cooking styles of Africa were added to the mix. Most likely the Africans brought with them rice, introducing a prime ingredient to Caribbean agriculture and cuisine.

Traditional Dishes and Seasonings

The main difference between Puerto Rican cuisine and that of the North American mainland lies in three words: *sofrito* (a mixture of cilantro, sweet chili pepper, a small leafy plant called *recao,* garlic, onion, and pimientos that serves as the base ingredient for countless dishes), *adobo* (a combination of black peppercorns, oregano, and garlic, which is crushed in a mortar and rubbed liberally into meat, fish, or poultry), and *achiote* (a coloring made of annatto seeds cooked in vegetable oil or olive oil). This basic flavoring, seasoning, and coloring group forms the basis of Puerto Rican cuisine.

Influence of the American Mainland

In 1898 the United States took possession of Puerto Rico during the Spanish-American War, ending 405 years of Spanish rule. With U.S. control came the next social and culinary transition for Puerto Rico. Puerto Ricans were introduced to new foods and cooking styles and adopted them to their needs. They came to savor such dishes as *butifarron* (meat loaf), *hamburgesa* (hamburgers), *carne de pote* (corned beef), *espinaca en crema* (creamed spinach), and even *budin* (bread pudding).

The other transformation in Puerto Rican cooking has been through the Nuyorican influence. "Nuyorican" is short for "New York Puerto Rican." These are Puerto Rican men and women who were either raised or born in New York City.

In a sense Nuyoricans and islanders shared the same palate and ate the same food. But environmental differences soon showed contrasts. Nuyoricans discovered such food items as bagels, bialys, pasta, and milkshakes and Chinese, Italian, and Mexican cuisines, among others. They incorporated these new influences while remaining faithful to the basic concepts of the traditional Puerto Rican cooking style.

In the old days criollo foods were traditionally served with beer or fruit juice. These days the typical accompaniment is a soft drink, another import from the mainland. Rum is also a popular drink in the Puerto Rican culture. Puerto Rican rums are considered among the best in the world; more than 85 percent of all rum consumed in the United States comes from the island.

Those who have ever enjoyed a Puerto Rican family dinner find the dishes unique and healthful, with an emphasis on fresh vegetables and other fresh ingredients. Evolving over more than five hundred years, Puerto Rican cooking is on a par with the world's great cuisines. This is a cooking style that features warmth and sensuality and is infinitely adaptable.

[See also Barbecue; Beans; Caribbean Influences on American Food; Cassava; Chickpeas; Cowpeas; Garlic; Prepared Herb and Spice Mixtures; New York Food.]

BIBLIOGRAPHY

Bender, Lynn Darrell, ed. *The American Presence in Puerto Rico.* Hato Rey, Puerto Rico: Publicaciones Puertorriquenas, 1998.

Davila, Vivian. *Puerto Rican Cooking.* Seacaucus, NJ: Castle, 1988.

Newman, Ross, and Elaine P. Garske. *International Food Flavors of the Home Economics.* Flushing, NY: Queen's College, 1982.

Valldejuli, Carmen Aboy. *Puerto Rican Cookery.* Gretna, LA: Pelican Publishing company, 1985.

OSWALD RIVERA

Pullman, George

George Mortimer Pullman (1831–1897), an American industrialist, invented and manufactured a number of luxury railroad passenger cars, including the Pullman sleeping car and the dining car. He was born in Brocton, New York, and was trained as a cabinetmaker. Having acquired skill at carpentry as an apprentice and at moving buildings from his father's business, he was invited to Chicago (1859) to jack up buildings to a new level as part of a public works project. He invested his earnings from the Chicago project, in partnership with a friend, in the design and construction of the first successful railroad sleeping car, the Pioneer (1865). Pullman, as an experienced rail traveler, had become well acquainted with the deplorable conditions in rail cars of that day and saw the opportunities for improvement. He established the Pullman Palace Car Company (1865) to build his sleeping cars, then went on to introduce hotel cars (1866), sleeping cars outfitted with small kitchens, and dining cars (1868), which were equipped with a kitchen and a dining room and were intended solely for the preparation and serving of food. In 1880 he established the town of Pullman, Illinois, near Chicago, where his cars were then built. Although intended as an industrial utopia, it became the scene of one of the bloodiest strikes in American history in 1894.

Pullman's sleeping cars, with their well-appointed sleeping compartments and sitting areas, drew the well-to-do traveler willing to pay the extra fare for the comfort of riding in them. The addition of dining cars as well as of lounge and buffet cars enabled the railroads that hauled Pullman's cars to offer their passengers both excellent onboard services and faster through trains,

which gave them an advantage in the increasingly competitive railroad industry. The introduction of Pullman's equipment revolutionized rail travel.

In the late 1800s Pullman turned his money-losing dining cars over to the railroads themselves. Nevertheless, the Pullman Company continued to manufacture dining cars for the railroads, culminating in the introduction, in cooperation with the Electro-Motive Division of General Motors (EMD), of the streamlined, all-dome, luxury Train of Tomorrow (1947).

George Pullman and his company can be credited with a number of contributions to American culinary history. Pullman's impact on railroad travel and on dining as a part of that experience was immediate and profound, while his impact on American culinary practices was less direct. First, his dining car kitchens refined and perfected the concept of cooking in a compact kitchen and served as a model for apartment builders in the early twentieth century. The kitchen that features a long and narrow central floor surrounded on both sides by appliances but with little counter space is referred to as a "Pullman kitchen." Among the many space-saving innovations the Pullman Company introduced was the Pullman loaf, popularly known as sandwich bread, wherein baking pans were fitted with lids and produced square, compact loaves. Three of these loaves would fit into a space that could hold only two loaves of bread with crowns.

Second, the practices Pullman instituted to ensure the consistency of food preparation and service that operating a fleet of dining cars required became the prototype for the uniform standards adopted by national restaurant chains later in the twentieth century. And the dining car meal experience itself, with its emphasis on speedy food preparation and delivery to table, and the need to turn over tables quickly so all waiting passengers could eat—as many as three hundred people in a three- or four-hour period—has been noted by fans and critics alike for its role in reinforcing the eat-and-run mentality associated with fast food.

[See also Harvey, Fred.]

BIBLIOGRAPHY

Leyendecker, Liston Edgington. *Palace Car Prince: A Biography of George Mortimer Pullman.* Niwot: University Press of Colorado, 1992.

White, John H., Jr. *The American Railroad Passenger Car.* Baltimore: Johns Hopkins University Press, 1978.

JAMES D. PORTERFIELD

Pumpkin Pie

Enshrined as the dessert most closely associated with Americans' celebration of the Thanksgiving holiday, pumpkin pie is considered a singular American dish. A total of 50 million pumpkin pies are baked and consumed each year, the vast majority during the holiday season beginning with Thanksgiving.

And although apple pie takes top honors during most of the year, pumpkin moves into first place as America's favorite pie during the holidays.

Native Americans baked, broiled, roasted, and dried pumpkins, and European explorers carried pumpkins back home. *The French Cook* by Francois Pierre La Varennne (1653) instructed cooks when making their "pompion" pie to "boile it with good milk" and "put it in your sheet of pate; bake it." Early New England settlers relied on books like *The Accomplisht Cook* by Robert May (1685), whose "pumpion" pie recipe featured marjoram and apples.

The earliest pumpkin "pies" were actually hollowed out pumpkin shells filled with milk and then roasted. *American Cookery* (1796) by Amelia Simmons, the first American cookbook, offered a recipe for the dish. *The Cook Not Mad* (1831), author unknown, tells cooks making the pie to combine a quart of milk or cream, six eggs, and ginger and to sweeten to taste. During the nineteenth century pumpkin pie recipes contained explicit instructions, like those in *Jennie June's American Cookery Book* (1870) by Jane Cunningham Croly to "bake with an undercrust only."

By the mid-century the movement to establish Thanksgiving as a national holiday was gaining momentum. Sarah Josepha Hale, who heavily promoted the holiday, wrote in her 1827 novel *Northwood* that pumpkin pie was an essential component of the true Thanksgiving meal. Women's magazines featured recipes. By the end of the century the totemic pumpkin pie was firmly established as a bulwark of the Thanksgiving meal.

In 1929 Libby's canned pumpkin appeared on grocers' shelves when a Chicago food canning company broadened its product line to include pumpkin. In the early twenty-first century Illinois produces the most pumpkins for processed pie filling. Modern American cooks are as likely to purchase a pie, fresh or frozen, from the grocery store or bakery as to home bake it, but for those who make the pie from scratch, there are literally thousands of recipes to choose from. Traditionally a custard made from pumpkin, evaporated milk, and eggs is flavored with cinnamon, nutmeg, cloves, and ginger, poured into a pie crust, and baked. A popular way to serve the dessert is with a scoop of vanilla ice cream or a dollop of whipped cream.

[**See also** PUMPKINS.]

BIBLIOGRAPHY

Damerow, Gail. *The Perfect Pumpkin: Growing, Cooking, Carving.* Pownal, VT: Storey, 1997.

Tuleja, Tad. "Pumpkins." In *Rooted in America: Foodlore of Popular Fruits and Vegetables,* ed. by David Scofield Wilson and Angus Kress Gillespie, 142–165. Knoxville: University of Tennessee Press, 1999.

LAURA B. WEISS

Pumpkins

The pumpkin (*Curcurbita pepo*) is thought to have originated in Central America about 5500 B.C.E. It was widely disseminated throughout North America in pre-Columbian times. With its thick shell and solid flesh, the pumpkin can be stored through the winter. Native Americans also preserved pumpkin by slicing and drying it.

Pumpkins were introduced into the Old World shortly after the first European explorations of the New World. They are mentioned in European works beginning in 1536. They were originally called *pompions*, or large gourds, and they were cultivated in England by the mid-sixteenth century, well before Thomas Hariot mentioned them in his *Briefe and True Report of the New Found Land of Virginia* (1588). Hence English colonists were familiar with pumpkins prior to settling in North America and immediately began growing them when they arrived. Although pumpkins are related to squash, American colonists carefully distinguished between them and used them culinarily in different ways.

Pumpkins proved easy to cultivate, and they became a common food at all meals, particularly in New England. They were baked, fried, mashed, roasted, and stewed and eaten as an accompaniment to meat. A favorite way of preparing pumpkins was to scoop out their seeds, fill the cavity with sweetened, spiced milk, and cook them near a fire. Pumpkins were also used to make puddings, pancakes, pies, soups, stews, and tarts. Less commonly pumpkins were used as a flavoring in breads, cakes, and muffins and were also employed to make ale. Pumpkin seeds were consumed raw or dried, and pumpkin flower blossoms and buds have been consumed in salads, in sandwiches, and in many other ways.

A recipe for pumpkins was among the first cookery recipes to have originated in what is today the United States. John Josselyn in his *New-England Rarities Discovered* (1672) wrote that pumpkins grown in America were sweeter than those he had tasted in England. The common way to prepare them, Josselyn wrote, was "to slice them when ripe, and cut

Nineteenth-century engraving of a pumpkin patch.

them into dice, and to fill a pot with them of two or three Gallons, and stew them upon a gentle fire a whole day." Butter was then added along with vinegar and spices, such as ginger. The stewed pumpkin was served as a side dish with fish or fowl.

Pumpkin pie recipes appeared in seventeenth-century English cookbooks, such as Hannah Woolley's *The Gentlewoman's Companion* (1675). Culinary fakelore to the contrary, pumpkin pies were not served at the proverbial "First Thanksgiving" and did not become common as a dessert at Thanksgiving dinner until the early nineteenth century. Pumpkin pie recipes frequently appear in American cookbooks beginning in the early nineteenth century. Nineteenth-century cookbooks also offered recipes for baked pumpkin (to be served like mashed potatoes) and pumpkin soup.

The pumpkin is such an important symbol that it frequently appeared in literary works: fairy tales, such as Cinderella and her pumpkin coach, children's nursery rhymes, such as "Peter, Peter, Pumpkin Eater," and poetry, such as John Greenleaf Whittier's "The Pumpkin." In late-nineteenth-century America the pumpkin became associated with Halloween as a jack-o'-lantern, most likely as a result of Washington Irving's headless horseman in the *Legend of Sleepy Hollow*, first published in 1819. In the twentieth century Charles Shulz's *Peanuts* comic strip frequently featured Charlie Brown waiting in a pumpkin patch for the arrival of "the Great Pumpkin." Halloween is celebrated with sweet treats shaped and colored like pumpkins (which are not usually made with pumpkin) as well as baked goods, such as pumpkin cookies, made with canned pumpkin puree.

In the early 2000s farmers invite families to come pick their own pumpkins for Halloween, and the pumpkin is celebrated in seasonal festivals, such as that held in Half Moon Bay, California. A pumpkin weigh-off is usually part of the proceedings, with some specimens weighing more than one thousand pounds.

[**See also** Flowers, Edible; Halloween; Heirloom Vegetables; Snacks, Salty; Squash; Thanksgiving.]

BIBLIOGRAPHY

Damerow, Gail. *The Perfect Pumpkin: Growing, Cooking, Carving*. Pownal, VT: Storey, 1997.

Krondl, Michael. *The Great Little Pumpkin Book*. Berkeley, CA: Ten Speed, 2000.

Tuleja, Tad. "Pumpkins." In *Rooted in America: Foodlore of Popular Fruits and Vegetables*, ed. David Scofield Wilson and Angus Kress Gillespie, 142–165. Nashville: University of Tennessee Press, 1999.

ANDREW F. SMITH

Punch

Over the centuries punch, as a beverage, has had different definitions. Since the early seventeenth century the British, particularly those who were sailors, knew and enjoyed punch. America's founding fathers enjoyed their punch served in Chinese export bowls at their favorite taverns. Throughout the twentieth century nonalcoholic punch was an essential element at every high school prom, dance, graduation, funeral, and social gathering. To every child born after World War II, Hawaiian Punch was one of the most recognizable fruit-juice drinks in America. But for most of its existence a punch was a mixed drink composed of rum, water, a citrus fruit juice and peel, sugar, and a dusting of nutmeg. It was served either hot or cold.

The *Oxford English Dictionary* reports that as early as 1698 the word "punch" was believed to be derived from the Hindustani word for five (*pnch*) because the drink was made from five ingredients. These five ingredients were rum, sugar, lemons, water, and spice. This so-called Rule of Five was also expressed as "One sour; Two sweet, Three strong, Four weak, and spices make Five." Benjamin Franklin celebrated punch in 1737 in his publication *Poor Richard's Almanack*, but he did not mention a spice.

> Boy, bring a Bowl of China here,
> Fill it with Water cool and clear:
> Decanter with Jamaica right,
> And Spoon of Silver clean and bright,
> Sugar twice-fin'd, in pieces cut,
> Knife, Sieve and Glass, in order put,
> Bring forth the fragrant Fruit, and then
> We're happy till the Clock strikes Ten.

Some believe that the name "punch" is not derived from an Indian word but was sailors' talk for a puncheon, the type of cask used for transporting rum at that time. Lending credibility to this theory is that grog, another sailors' drink made by diluting rum with water, was ladled out of a butt, a wooden barrel used for transporting wine. When sailors gathered around the scuttled (full of water) butt to receive their daily allowance of grog, they would pass on gossip, hence the scuttlebutt. "Scuttlebutt" is just one of the many words to enter the English language as a result of sailors' slang. "Punch" could easily be another.

Punch was one of the first mixed drinks served in colonial America. By the early nineteenth century, with the wide availability of mechanically harvested ice, these compound beverages evolved into a separate classification of drinks called cocktails. Punch was usually served in a bowl. For a large gathering it was made in a large bowl and ladled into cups or smaller bowls that were passed from person to person.

A review of punch recipes over the past three hundred years reveals that there is no limit on the number or kind of ingredients that can go into a punch. Some taverns made their punch with rum, brandy, gin, whiskey, wine, tea, sherry, and even milk. Lemons, limes, oranges, pineapples, and guava jelly were frequently added, alone or in combination. Nutmeg was the traditional spice, but sometimes a cordial was substituted. Punches might be named after the person who created them, a town, a historic event, the name of the tavern, or even the name of the tavern keeper. For example, planter's punch, made from fruit juices found in the Caribbean, reportedly originated with Jamaican planters. In time milk punches evolved into eggnog. *The Bar-Tender's Guide* from 1887 listed Mississippi Punch made with bourbon whiskey and Claret Punch made with red wine. When consuming excess, the imbiber was considered "punchy" or "punch-drunk."

Hawaiian Punch, a product of Cadbury Schweppes in the early 2000s, was first concocted in a converted garage in Fullerton, California, and trademarked in 1929. It was created as a blend of seven natural fruits—pineapple, orange, passion fruit, apple, apricot, papaya, and guava juices—to be used as a concentrated tropical fruit topping. It was soon discovered that the concentrate, when mixed with water, made a delicious drink. In 1950 Hawaiian Punch was introduced in the familiar forty-six-ounce can. Punchy, the TV cartoon character, was created in 1961 with the tagline "How about a nice Hawaiian Punch?"

Since colonial times prosperous families have had a punch bowl for entertaining. Eighteenth-century Chinese export porcelain bowls were traditionally made in five sizes holding from less than a quart to several gallons. Larger bowls, often decorated as commemorative or presentation pieces, were frequently commissioned. The larger the bowl a household possessed, the more prominent its status in society was likely to be. During the nineteenth century formal in-home dinner parties were prefaced with a punch. In the twentieth century the punch bowl, made from silver and inscribed, became a trophy piece presented at retirement parties or awarded for sporting accomplishments.

Most American families have a punch bowl, whether a modest one made from glass or plastic for a fruit punch to accompany a backyard cookout or an elegant silver or crystal one for a holiday eggnog.

[**See also** Alcohol and Teetotalism; Drinking Songs; Eggnog; Fruit Juices; Grog; Kool-Aid; Rum; Sangria; Syllabub; Taverns; Temperance; Wine, Hot Spiced.]

BIBLIOGRAPHY

Grimes, William. *Straight-up or on the Rocks: The Story of the American Cocktail*. New York: North Point, 2001.

Lender, Mark Edward, and James Kirby Martin. *Drinking in America: A History*. Rev. ed. New York: Free Press, 1987.

JOSEPH M. CARLIN

Pure Food and Drug Act

The Pure Food and Drug Act of 1906 marked the beginning of effective U.S. federal regulation of food and drug labeling and assurance of a safe food supply. It prohibited the false labeling or adulteration of foods and drugs transported interstate; as such it was limited in scope. Items produced and sold within a state or territory came under only local laws. The Pure Food and Drug Act also did not give the federal government the right to require substantive food labels such as the ones of the early twenty-first century, but it represented the early efforts toward federal protection for food consumers and substantial and effective federal controls on the safety and purity of the U.S. food supply.

Regulation of the food supply was not new, although earlier efforts were fragmentary, subject to intense (and often successful) lobbying by food and drug industry groups, and ineffectively enforced. In the mid-1800s agricultural chemists under Samuel W. Johnson exposed adulteration in the fertilizer industry, which in turn led to attempts to curb adulteration in meat, milk, and other foods. City and state health departments were established, leading to the first general food law, passed in Illinois in 1874. The Pure Foods movement, a grassroots group that formed in the mid-1870s, also began agitating for change. It was originally a trade movement, some of whose members became concerned that the plethora of local laws and the use of mislabeled adulterants were hindering interstate trade and hurting profits. The first national food-adulteration law, the Oleomargarine Act of 1886, was one outcome; then in 1889 the U.S. Department of Agriculture was given the mandate to extend and continue the investigation of the adulteration of foods, drugs, and liquors.

Under the leadership of Harvey Wiley, the jovial and brilliant chief of the department's Bureau of Chemistry, food safety truly reached the public consciousness. Wiley established a "poison squad" of volunteers who ate only foods with measured amounts of chemical additives and preservatives to test the notion that many adulterants were unsafe. He gave numerous public lectures on his findings, and popular magazines such as *Ladies' Home Journal* and *Good Housekeeping* took up his cause. Wiley was opposed in particular by the patent medicine firms, but the "embalmed beef" scandal that erupted in 1898 over the putrid meat shipped to soldiers during the Spanish-American War and the efforts of the writer Upton Sinclair, whose 1906 novel *The Jungle* exposed unsanitary conditions in the meatpacking plants, pushed Congress on June 30, 1906, to pass two measures protecting the public food and drug supply: the Meat Inspection Act and the Pure Food and Drug Act.

The Pure Food and Drug Act specifically prohibited interstate shipping of adulterated or misbranded goods. Administration of the law fell to Wiley's Bureau of Chemistry. For a complicated regulatory subject, the law as passed was terse. It fell to Wiley to elaborate upon the law and to test its enforcement. The first case did not involve food, but the manufacturer of a patent medicine remedy with the unlikely name of Curforhedake Brane Fude; after a precedent-setting trial, the verdict was returned: guilty. The fine was small ($700) compared with the manufacturer's profits (a claimed $2 million), but the precedent was set: the federal government was willing and able to promote food and drug safety.

[**See also** ADULTERATION; DEPARTMENT OF AGRICULTURE, UNITED STATES; SINCLAIR, UPTON; WILEY, HARVEY.]

BIBLIOGRAPHY

Smelser, Neil J., and Paul B. Battles, eds. *International Encyclopedia of the Social and Behavioral Sciences*. New York: Elsevier, 2001.

SYLVIA LOVEGREN

Q

Quaker Oats Man

The Quaker Oats Company Quaker is an internationally known trademark figure that has been representing Quaker Oats products since 1877. The story of the Quaker man is more than simply that of a popular trademark character, however. It is also the story of the emergence of the modern American market system and consumer culture.

As the development of mass production in the nineteenth century increased the number of products rolling off production lines, manufacturers faced the challenge of moving goods as fast as they were made. They turned to advertising to increase demand for specific

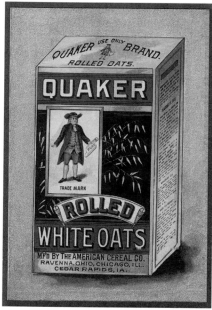

The Quaker Oats man as he appeared in a cookbooklet published by the American Cereal Company in 1894.

products. Oats, for example, had previously been sold only in bulk and were both unbranded and relatively unfamiliar as a food. When new technology made highly efficient, high-volume production possible at the Quaker Mill in Ravenna, Ohio, the owners of the mill, Henry Seymour and William Heston, set out to develop a brand identity for their product in order to establish a national market for it. In 1877 they registered "a figure of a man in 'Quaker garb'" with the U.S. Patent Office, becoming the first to register a trademark for a breakfast cereal. Despite the lack of any actual Quaker connection to their product, they claim to have chosen the figure, a full-length picture of a Quaker man holding a scroll with the word "pure" on it, because they felt that the image represented integrity, quality, and honesty.

In 1881 the mill in Ohio and the name "Quaker" were taken over by Henry Parson Crowell, who continued to work toward establishing a national market for his products by pioneering techniques in packaging, promotion, and advertising. In 1882 Crowell launched the first advertising campaign in national magazines for breakfast cereal. In 1885 he began to use the recently patented folding carton for Quaker Oats packaging. Because it lay flat when unfolded, the carton could be printed with the trademark figure and recipes that helped make the unfamiliar product useful in the lives of new consumers. The Quaker Oats Company remained a leader in national advertising and made the Quaker man a familiar symbol on free samples, billboards, streetcar placards, rural fences, magazines, newspapers, promotional items such as calendars and match strikers, and booths at fairs and expositions.

The Quaker Oats Company Quaker remained a popular trademark figure throughout the twentieth century with just three revisions to his appearance. In 1946 a black-and-white image of the familiar smiling-head portrait was designed by Jim Nash to replace the original standing figure. The image was updated to a full-color figure in 1957 by the artist and illustrator Haddon Sundblom. In 1970 the company adopted a one-color "shadow" image of the Quaker man designed by Saul Bass as the registered trademark of the Quaker Oats Company.

The international presence of the Quaker Oats Company Quaker is nearly as old as the figure itself. Quaker Oats were first shipped to Britain in 1877, and by 1908 the Quaker export catalog claimed that the Quaker trademark was the best-known brand in the world. By the early 2000s the Quaker man was known in nearly every market in the world. [**See also** ADVERTISING; BREAKFAST FOODS; OATS.]

BIBLIOGRAPHY
Marquette, Arthur. *Brands, Trademarks, and Good Will: The Story of the Quaker Oats Company.* New York: McGraw-Hill, 1967.

CHARLOTTE BILTEKOFF

Quince

The quince (*Cydonia oblonga*) is among the minor pome fruits, relatives of the apple and pear, which are practically unknown in modern America. Probably native to the Elburz Mountains of Iran, the quince figures in the traditional cookery of Persia, Armenia, Georgia, and the Middle East in general. In Roman times the quince was brought to southern Europe, and it spread northward during the medieval period. In the United States acquaintance with the quince does not often last beyond the first generation after immigration, and the quince has never been a fruit of much notice.

The quince has suffered in popularity because it is not suited for fresh consumption, being hard, rather dry, low in sugars, and high in tannins. However, the tannins are inactivated by cooking, and the flesh breaks down, often turning pink as it does. It is as a cooked product that the quince excels, for it is a supremely aromatic fruit. Because quince flesh has a pasty quality when cooked, it usually is mixed with apples in pies or sauce or rendered into jellies. A few sorts of quince in central Asia and Turkey are edible when raw, but they are not highly attractive.

Quince plantings have historically been small and scattered, near urban markets; in the early twenty-first century the quince survives only as occasional trees at the edge of orchards. A few commercial plantings exist in the San Joaquin Valley of California, mostly tended by families of Armenian origin. Quinces may sometimes be found in urban greenmarkets in autumn. [**See also** APPLES; PEARS; PIES AND TARTS.]

BIBLIOGRAPHY
Hedrick, Ulysses Prentiss. *Cyclopedia of Hardy Fruits.* New York: Macmillan, 1922.
Meech, William Witler. *Quince Culture.* 2nd ed. New York: Orange Judd, 1919.

C. T. KENNEDY

interviews, she also shared her intense interest in food with her listeners. Advertisers flocked to her program, in part because she rarely presented a conventional commercial, rather giving her personal recommendation to the product.

Local Stars

Many radio stations employed their own local food experts, such as Roy L. Fruit broadcasting over KVBG in Kansas, Marjorie Mills heard throughout New England; and Louise Morgan and Mildred Carson, who broadcast from Boston on WNAC and WBZ. Joe

Carcione's short radio spots as the Green Grocer highlighted fresh produce in the San Francisco markets. Brita Griem began radio broadcasts in 1949 over WTMJ in Milwaukee, Wisconsin, continuing her career in television until 1962.

In more recent years Arthur Schwartz, the Food Maven, broadcast *Food Talk* on WOR, New York, calling himself "the Schwartz Who Ate New York." Minneapolis Public radio's long-running *The Splendid Table*, hosted by Lynne Rossetto Kasper, has brought together the worlds of food in science, history, ecology, health, and diverse cultures.

Radio/TV Food Shows

When General Mills launched Betty Crocker's first radio program in 1924, they could hardly have envisioned the explosion of radio and TV food shows in the twentieth and twenty-first centuries. With an audience presented daily with virtually unlimited ideas for every conceivable style of cuisine and cooking techniques, advertisers were quick to capitalize on the opportunity to reach millions of potential customers, and the friendly, helpful broadcaster became a super salesperson. Betty Crocker was invented as a spokesperson for General Mills in 1926. In 1936 she acquired a face, a portrait blending the features of several "typical" American women that has been updated through the years to reflect perceived changes.

Aunt Sammy

Aunt Sammy, the creation of the U.S. Department of Agriculture, brought information to farm women, many of whom were without modern conveniences such as running water and major appliances and who were often physically isolated, the closest neighbor miles away. Aunt Sammy, the fictional wife of Uncle Sam, was in reality fifty different women, all reading the same script (provided by the Department of Agriculture) over fifty different radio stations. Despite her light-hearted approach with jokes and anecdotes, she never lost sight of her goal to help women cook simple, nourishing food, especially during the difficult Depression days. But as more and more cooking shows appeared, some of them shamelessly cannibalizing Aunt Sammy's, her popularity waned. She "died" in 1944.

Ida Bailey Allen

Known as "the Nation's Homemaker," Ida Bailey Allen also began broadcasting in 1926. She authored several popular cookbooks, and on her tenth anniversary as a broadcaster, twenty thousand fans crowded Madison Square Garden for a celebration.

Mary Margaret McBride

Mary Margaret McBride, one of radio's best salespersons, presented a richly textured picture of American life spanning the Depression, World War II, and the cold war. In addition to her awesome list of celebrity

Advertisements for three broadcasts sponsored by the Pet Milk Co. in the early 1950s. The All Star Revue (originally called The Four Star Revue) ran on NBC television between October 1950 and April 1953. Pet sponsored Fibber McGee and Molly between 1950 and 1952.

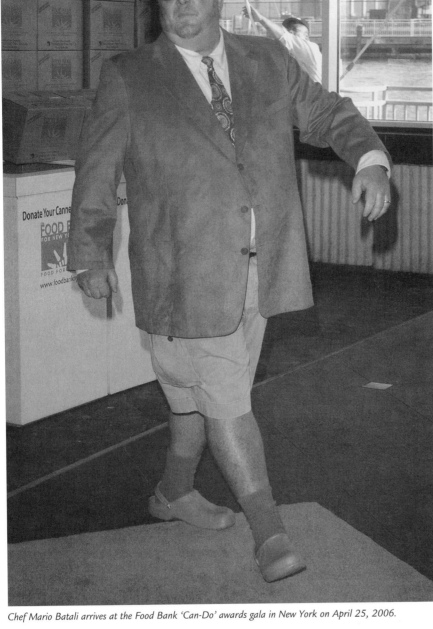

Chef Mario Batali arrives at the Food Bank 'Can-Do' awards gala in New York on April 25, 2006.

asm, each program ending with a display of that day's dishes and her cheerful farewell, "Bon appetit!"

Public Broadcasting

With the great success of Julia Child, Public Broadcasting discovered the appeal of cooking shows and quickly added a variety of quality programs to their schedule. The diminutive Joyce Chen launched the first Chinese cooking show in the 1970s. *The Romagnolis' Table* (1974–1976) featured Margaret and Franco Romagnoli, cookbook writers and restaurateurs. Justin Wilson, a suspender-wearing, down-home Cajun cook, demonstrated *Louisiana Cookin'*. Diana Kennedy shared recipes from all regions of Mexico. Other programs have included Mary Anne Esposito's warm and family-friendly *Ciao, Italia*; Martin Yan's *Yan Can Cook*, a light-hearted demonstration of Chinese cooking; Lidia's *Italian American Kitchen*, starring Lidia Matticchio Bastianich; Pierre Franey's *60 Minute Gourmet*, quick but elegant meals with a French accent; and the suave and knowledgeable Jacques Pépin. *The Frugal Gourmet*, with the casual, comfortable Jeff Wilson as host, appealed to cooks who appreciated his relaxed attitude toward cooking that made it seem like fun rather than a chore.

Food Network

In November of 1993 the Food Network, a new cable channel created by Reese Schoenfeld, began offering twenty-four hour a day programming, creating new food stars, including Emeril Lagasse, who delights his audience not only with his delicious food but also with his ebullient personality.

Foreign Transplants

The Iron Chef from Japan exuded exotic showmanship and ritual, with guest chefs introduced by crashing gongs and pounding drums, as with knives flashing chefs raced against the clock. *Nigella Bites*, starring Nigella Lawson, "the Domestic Goddess," was an instant success imported from Britain, featuring a stunningly beautiful cook leading viewers through deceptively simple food preparations.

Food Shows Turn to Television

Although many food lovers are convinced that Julia Child was the first TV food chef, James Beard's *I Love to Eat* preceded her, premiering in 1946 and lasting only a year. It was followed by Alma Kitchell's *In the Kelvinator Kitchen* and Dionne Lucas's *To the Queen's Taste*, broadcast from the Cordon Blue restaurant in New York (1948–1949).

Julia Child

Living life as an icon, a pioneer, and perhaps the world's most notable cook would faze a less intrepid person than Julia Child, but she managed to withstand the attention and remain focused on her main goal, sharing the pleasures of French cooking. Her distinctive warbling voice, her relaxed manner, and her ability to cope with major and minor crises on camera endeared her to generations of food lovers. Famous for her no nonsense approach to food and its preparation, she delighted her loyal followers with special "Julia moments," such as the day she demonstrated how to flip an omelet and dropped a substantial chunk of it in the fire, remarking that sometimes things were not perfect. Home cooks could relate to these potential kitchen tragedies. Her techniques and recipes were demonstrated clearly and with enthusi-

More to Come?

The first TV food programs appeared shortly after the deprivations of World War II and show few signs of abating. The genre has been primarily left to PBS and the Food Network, cultivating Americans' interest in new cooking styles and techniques as well as in exotic ingredients from other cultures. Advertisers abound on both commercial shows and PBS funder credits, continuing the tradition of radio and TV chefs as super salespersons.

[**See also** ADVERTISING; BETTY CROCKER; CELEBRITY CHEFS; CHILD, JULIA; COOKING TECHNIQUES; PUCK, WOLFGANG; STEWART, MARTHA.]

BIBLIOGRAPHY

Dunning, John. *On the Air: The Encyclopedia of Old-Time Radio*. New York: Oxford University Press, 1998.

Terrace, Vincent. *Radio Programs, 1924–1984: A Catalog of over 1,800 Shows*. Jefferson, NC: McFarland, 1999.

VIRGINIA K. BARTLETT

Radishes

Radishes (*Raphanus sativus*) are mainly cool-weather crucifers grown annually for their swollen roots. Though most radishes that make their way to the American table are small, scarlet globes with crisp, peppery, white flesh, radishes come in an impressive array of sizes and shapes, from small and round to long and tapered, and colors ranging from pink, lavender, red, and purple to black and white. Amelia Simmons's *American Cookery* (1796) lists salmon as her favorite radish. Radishes count as one of the earliest garden vegetables and are among the easiest to grow. Most of the radishes in early America came as seed from England.

Early seed catalogs displayed a tremendous variety of radishes and allowed the farmer three different crops: spring, summer, and fall or winter. Yellow summer radishes, called *jaune hatif*, were popular as a heat-tolerant variety during the eighteenth and nineteenth centuries. Among the most intriguing winter radishes are the pungent black varieties, such as the Long Black Spanish and the Round Black Spanish. Found in America since the seventeenth century, the seed was widely dispersed by the Shakers in the nineteenth century.

Parts other than the root were used in the past. Radish leaf salads, made from immature radishes pulled from beds in the normal thinning processes, were a gourmet treat. Radish pods, particularly from the rat-tail radish introduced from Japan in 1866, were used in pickles and potato salads by the 1880s and were esteemed for enhancing the vibrant green color of pickles. Radishes were occasionally boiled, added to salads, dressed in a dish by themselves, or carved into the ubiquitous flower for use as a garnish. Most connoisseurs consider raw radishes to be the ultimate crudité and pronounce that the best way to eat a radish is to peel off the skin, dip it in salt, and eat it with one's fingers.

[**See also** HEIRLOOM VEGETABLES; SALADS AND SALAD DRESSINGS; VEGETABLES.]

BIBLIOGRAPHY

Bittman, Sam. *The Salad Lover's Garden*. New York: Doubleday, 1992.

Hessayon, D. G. *The New Vegetable and Herb Expert*. London: Expert Books, 1997.

Rubatzky, Vincent E., and Mas Yamaguchi. *World Vegetables: Principles, Production, and Nutritive Values*. 2nd ed. New York: Chapman and Hall, 1997.

Weaver, William Woys. *Heirloom Vegetable Gardening*. New York: Holt, 1997.

KAY RENTSCHLER

Ramps

Ramps (*Allium tricoccum*), also called wild leeks, are members of the onion family. Native to eastern North America, ramps grow in clumps in the rich, moist soil under deciduous trees—sugar maples, birch, and poplar, among others—from New England south to central Appalachia and as far as North Carolina and Tennessee. One of the first spring greens, growing from perennial bulbs in late March and April, ramps have the flavor of sweet spring onions touched with musk and an intense garlic aroma. They are harvested for their young leaves (which resemble lily of the valley) and their small bulbs. Both may be eaten raw—the leaves, for instance, in salads, though the bulbs are frequently fried in smoky fat with eggs or potatoes.

Ramps were part of the Native American diet, valued for their blood-cleansing properties and eaten eagerly at winter's end (ramps are in fact high in vitamin C). Over time the ramp harvest became a rite of spring in many Appalachian communities, giving way to community festivals. Ramp consumption and popularity rose steadily in the last two decades of the twentieth century, threatening the wild populations in the forests from which they are gathered. Up to 85 percent of ramps consumed as food come from wild populations, though efforts are under way in North Carolina and elsewhere to cultivate them.

[**See also** NATIVE AMERICAN FOODS; ONIONS.]

BIBLIOGRAPHY

Elias, Thomas S., and Peter A. Dykeman. *Edible Wild Plants: A North American Field Guide*. New York: Sterling, 1990.

Greenfield, Jackie, and Jeanine M. Davis. *Cultivation of Ramps* (Allium tricoccum *and* A. burdickii). Raleigh: North Carolina State University, 2001.

KAY RENTSCHLER

Randolph, Mary

Mary Randolph was born in 1762 on the Tuckahoe Plantation at Ampthill, Virginia. In 1824 she published *The Virginia House-Wife*, the earliest known southern cookbook in print, regarded by many as the finest work ever to have come out of the American kitchen. Its popularity and influence were such that it had gone through at least nineteen editions by 1860 and only the increasingly general adoption of the kitchen range finally made the work seem old-fashioned. Even so it continued to be massively plagiarized down through the century. After her death in 1828 in Washington, D.C., however, the work was seriously compromised by bowdlerization in an effort to make it seem more up-to-date.

As a member of the Randolph family of Virginia, she might be expected to present an aristocratic cuisine, and there is a great deal of that in her work. Much of it was drawn from the same milieu that produced the great culinary manuscripts of sixteenth- and seventeenth-century England, also seen in *Martha Washington's Booke of Cookery*. In addition many of Randolph's dishes came from the royalist cuisine of France, dishes meticulously described by her cousin Thomas Jefferson in his own hand. Many of her French recipes have entire telltale phrases that are verbatim copies of those attributed to Étienne LeMaire, Jefferson's maître d'hôtel during his years in the President's House (1801–1809), by members of the Jefferson family in their manuscripts. This borrowing was so extensive that she might well be considered the amanuensis of the French aspects of the cuisine of Monticello. But she also presented recipes for more traditional and humble Virginia fare, such as Turnip Tops, boiled with bacon in the Virginia style, Rice Journey or Johnny Cake, and Cat-fish Soup. Perhaps even more significantly, she published early recipes for a number of products indigenous to Africa, such as Gumbs—A West India Dish, Ochra Soup, and Ocra and Tomatoes, all recipes for okra, as well as one for Field Peas, a general term for black-eyed peas, and many other related ones from Africa. Some of these recipes clearly came from African cooks. An interesting fortuitous section contains a number of Spanish recipes, which came to her from her sister, Harriett Hackley, who spent some years in Cádiz. Included among them are directions for To Make an Olla—Spanish, Gazpacha—Spanish, and Ropa Veija—Spanish. (The misspelling of *vieja* was to persist in southern cookbooks pretty much through that century.) All in all this work is wondrously eclectic. It not only recorded the cookery of Virginia but also helped shape the mythic southern cookery of the nineteenth century.

[**See also** COOKBOOKS AND MANUSCRIPTS: TO 1860; FRENCH INFLUENCES ON AMERICAN FOOD; SOUTHERN REGIONAL COOKERY.]

BIBLIOGRAPHY

Randolph, Mary. *The Virginia House-Wife*. With historical notes and commentary by Karen Hess. Columbia: University of South Carolina Press, 1983.

KAREN HESS

Ranhofer, Charles

Charles Ranhofer (b. Nov. 7, 1836, in Saint-Denis, France; d. Oct. 9, 1899, in New York City) was the chef who brought Delmonico's restaurant to greatness, making the name synonymous with American fine dining for more than a century. More important, he was the author of *The Epicurean* (1893), one of the first and perhaps the best of the American encyclopedias of haute cuisine. *The Epicurean* is revolutionary for those who think new American cuisine began in the 1970s. Jeremiah Tower, one of the pioneers of the resurgence of American cooking in the San Francisco Bay Area in the 1970s, described discovering *The Epicurean* after years of exploring other cuisines:

I saw the title of a soup, Cream of Green Corn a la Mendocino. What struck me about the recipe was that it took its name from a town up the coast from San Francisco. Like a bolt out of the heavens, the realization came to me: Why am I scratching around in Corsica when I have it bountifully all around me here in California? It was American food using French cooking principles. I could not contain my exhilaration over what I beheld as the enormous doors of habit swung open onto a whole new vista.

Although Ranhofer has largely been forgotten, his creations have not—two of his signature dishes are lobster Newburg and baked Alaska, which appears under the name "Alaska, Florida" in *The Epicurean.*

Ranhofer was the son and grandson of chefs. He was sent to Paris at age twelve to learn his trade, a generation after the master French chef Marie-Antoine Carême had written his grand treatise on French haute cuisine and during the heyday of Carême's successors, most significantly Urbain François Dubois. At age sixteen Ranhofer went into private service for an Alsatian prince. He moved to New York City in 1856, and his first job was with the Russian consul. Then he went to work in Washington, D.C., and New Orleans, Louisiana. After returning briefly to France in 1860 (where he was in charge of the food for the grand balls of Napoleon III at the Tuileries in Paris), he came back to New York City as chef at the new hot spot, Maison Doree.

When Delmonico's restaurant moved from its original Broadway location to one farther uptown on Fourteenth Street, the owner, Lorenzo Delmonico, hired Ranhofer away. "He was perfect in dress and manner, and his attitude was such as to make me feel that he was doing me a great favor by coming into my employment," Delmonico related. "'You are the proprietor,' he said. 'Furnish the room and the provisions, tell me the number of guests and what they want, and I will do the rest.'"

Ranhofer's "rest" was a combination of exquisite French technique melded with fabulous American ingredients. Many of the rules found in *The Epicurean* come straight from Dubois; indeed, Ranhofer graciously acknowledges his debt to Dubois in the preface. These rules of classic cuisine often sound familiar to modern readers. Sauces and meats should not be repeated within a menu; courses should follow in a sensible order; and "offer on the menus all foods in their respective seasons, and let the early products be of the finest quality.... Only use preserved articles when no others can be obtained."

Even with Ranhofer's classic French background and abundant borrowing from Dubois's masterpiece *La cuisine classique* (1856), what is surprising about *The Epicurean* is how decidedly American so much of the

cooking sounds. Ranhofer describes local ingredients from avocados and cornbread to Virginia ham and striped bass. Game plays a huge role. There are recipes for canvasback, redhead, mallard, and teal ducks as well as prairie hen. Bear steaks are recommended, with the note that "bear's meat when young can be broiled and after it is cooked has much the same flavor as beef."

There is a truly American assortment of cultural influences as well: blini, *kugelhopfen,* jambalaya (spelled "jambalaia"), two gumbos, risotto, and borscht (spelled quasi-Polish fashion as "barsch") made with beets you pickle yourself. There is a detailed description of bird's nest soup (he distinguishes between the nests from the Philippines and those from China) and a recipe for a soy sauce that almost sounds like something out of a modern fusion cookbook—basically a red wine stock reduction finished with soy sauce and butter.

Even so much of the food was just what might be expected from that period. Dishes involved big pieces of meat, usually roasted, and complicated cookery. Consommé Celestine, for example, begins with thin crepes spread with a chicken forcemeat, stacked, pressed, baked, and cut into shapes. The crepes are arranged in the bottom of a bowl with blanched, shredded lettuce, and then hot consommé is poured over them. Sauces and garnishes play important roles. There are flour-thickened sauces, like béchamel, as well as many "essences" (chicken, fish, game, ham, mushroom, root, duck, and truffle) that actually trace their roots to eighteenth- and early nineteenth-century French practice. These sauces are expensive to make, reflecting a time when cost was no object.

Ranhofer's day was indeed the Gilded Age, when it seemed any man could become an instant millionaire and eat just as he chose. (Although Ranhofer was proud that at his restaurant a table of six could enjoy "a very good dinner, with an excellent vin ordinaire" for twelve dollars, there was also the banquet put on by the stock promoter Sir Morton Peto that cost $20,000—at a time when Ranhofer's annual salary was $6,000.)

Ranhofer often sounded quite the kitchen autocrat, lecturing the American dining public on what he considered its ghastly dining habits: "It is a wonder that you have not ruined the nation's digestion with your careless cooking and hasty eating!" One contemporary article reports Ranhofer as saying, "I must teach you something." Yet in reality he was as amenable to his customers' sometimes curious dinner requests as any modern Beverly Hills chef. "It is a mistaken idea that everyone, willy-nilly, is compelled to take or go with the particular style of cooking that commends itself to the chef," Ranhofer complained.

The chef may know more about the proper cooking and serving of dishes than the customer, but should the latter have any particular fancies or weaknesses of his own in the eating line, he

can, provided his purse dances in close attendance upon his whimsicalities of taste, have set before him dishes which fill the sensitive chef's heart with despair.

Ranhofer was not the last American chef to express such sentiments—but he might have been the first.

[**See also** DELMONICO'S; RESTAURANTS; SAUCES AND GRAVIES.]

RUSS PARSONS

Raspberries

The modern raspberry represents the happy commingling of mainly two botanical varieties of raspberry, one from either side of the Atlantic. Fruits of the European variety, *Rubus idaeus vulgatus,* are dark red and conical, whereas those of the North American variety, *R. vulgatus strigosus,* are lighter red, round, and have small glandular hairs. The black raspberry, *R. occidentalis,* which is native to the northeastern United States, also contributes to these hybrids and is a tasty fruit in its own right, being firmer and less prone to rotting than red raspberries. In the past black raspberries were more popular than today.

Raspberries are grown most extensively where summers stay relatively cool, such as in the Pacific Northwest and coastal California. The canes are biennial, typically bearing fruit in midsummer of their second year, but so-called ever-bearing or fall-bearing raspberries begin bearing near their tips toward the end of their first season. This bearing habit has extended the fresh season for this perishable fruit. Frozen berries are sold as such or are used to flavor juices, yogurts, and jams.

[**See also** FRUIT; FRUIT JUICES.]

Raspberries pictured in the 1894 catalog of Peter Henderson & Company, New York.

BIBLIOGRAPHY

McClure, Susan, and Lee Reich. *Fruits and Berries.* Successful Organic Gardening series. Emmaus, PA: Rodale, 1996.

LEE REICH

Rastus

In the late nineteenth century, as large-scale manufacturing took hold, it became apparent that the use of images in advertising would enhance the success of a product. Many producers developed logos, often a personification of qualities judged to be most attractive to the consumer audience. In some cases this was an appeal to middle-class homemakers through upper-class images, suggesting that the wealthy could afford the best and that the middle class could identify itself with the elite by using the same products. In some cases the advertisement reflected the social ideal that middle-class women were efficient and nurturing homemakers, and in others it sentimentalized wholesome and innocent children who would presumably benefit from the product.

Just such a logo was Rastus, who represented Cream of Wheat. Created by Emery Mapes of the budding Cream of Wheat Company of Grand Forks, North Dakota, in 1896, Rastus portrayed a handsome and wise African American chef who symbolized quality cookery, good nutrition (according to the theories of the day), gentility, and geniality. His "portraits" showed him attending to the breakfast table and the children who, presumably, would soon be eating bowlfuls of cooked cereal. Seen within the framework of the overt and common racism of the late nineteenth century, he was the loyal family retainer, someone who could be depended on to guide the family's children with affection, grace, and wisdom.

Alongside the modern view of the political incorrectness of the scene, there is a more noteworthy aspect of the Rastus illustrations. Cream of Wheat used aesthetics innovatively throughout its advertising campaign. In the span between 1902 and 1955, some fifty-eight outstanding artists, each prominent in the new field of illustration, supplied some of the best commercial art of the time. Their steady stream of paintings and drawings appeared in full-color, full-page advertisements in popular periodicals of their time: *Good Housekeeping, Woman's Home Companion, Colliers,* and the *Saturday Evening Post.* Rastus himself most often appeared in the painting but was sometimes seen beneath the picture, accompanied by an enlarged message. Either way, he was the thread that connected the art and identified the product. Sometimes he was the central focus, sometimes he appeared subtly in the background, and sometimes his face, almost incidental, was found as a small painting on the wall or half seen in an open magazine. Finding Rastus in these paintings was sometimes the game that drew the attention of potential buyers.

Throughout the long campaign, Rastus's face never changed, even as the world around him did. As new artists were commissioned, their subject matter and artistic style recorded shifts in social history reflected by the shifting fashions in home decoration and clothing, political and economic events, architecture, and recreation. For example, E. V. Brewer painted Rastus *Standing Back of Uncle Sam* (1918), a recognizable companion piece to his famous Uncle Sam poster of World War I, *I Want You.* The affluence of the later 1920s showed in the well-dressed children of Frederic Kimball Mizen's ice-skating scene *In High Gear.* The Great Depression and its make-do, chin-up motifs were depicted in the simple, rural amusements of Harry Anderson's *Gosh All Fishhooks* (1938) and *Going Down!* (1938). H. H. Sundblom's 1920s impressionistic style could be compared dramatically with the promotional Cream of Wheat cartoon strips (still featuring Rastus) of Al Capp in the 1950s.

[See also ADVERTISING; AUNT JEMIMA; BETTY CROCKER; BREAKFAST FOODS; NABISCO; QUAKER OATS MAN; UNCLE BEN; WHEAT.]

BIBLIOGRAPHY

Kern-Foxworth, Marilyn. *Aunt Jemima, Uncle Ben, and Rastus: Blacks in Advertising, Yesterday, Today, and Tomorrow.* Westport, CT: Praeger, 1994.

Stivers, David. *The Nabisco Brands Collection of Cream of Wheat Advertising Art.* San Diego, CA: Collector's Showcase, 1986.

ALICE ROSS

Ratafia

Ratafia is a homemade brandy-based liqueur made with sour cherries, including the stones, which impart a bitter-almond flavor. The name usually is thought to be derived from the Latin phrase *ut rata fiat* or *res rata fiat* (consider it done), a late-seventeenth-century toast drunk at the conclusion of an accord but eventually transferred to the liqueur itself. However, some sources indicate that ratafia owes its etymology to French Antilles Creole for a sugarcane-based eau-de-vie (*tafia*), perhaps with the addition of the Malay name for the liquor arrack (*araq*).

Early nineteenth-century and Victorian-era American recipes flavored ratafias with considerable imagination: currants, chocolate, quince, juniper berries, angelica, violets, and aniseed. The *Picayune's Creole Cook Book* of 1901 provided extended advice on its preparation. Ratafia has all but disappeared; passing along recipes for cherry ratafia, Louisiana Cajun and Creole families remain the keepers of the flame. Cherry ratafia appears to be indistinguishable from cherry bounce. The food historian William Woys Weaver notes in *America Eats* that "American cherry bounce....is the folk version of the ratafia" (p. 50).

[See also BRANDY; CAJUN AND CREOLE FOOD; CHERRIES; CHERRY BOUNCE.]

BIBLIOGRAPHY

Weaver, William Woys. *America Eats: Forms of Edible Folk Art.* New York: Harper and Row, 1989.

ROBIN M. MOWER

Rawfoodism

In the twentieth century a new vegetarian dietary trend burst upon the culinary scene in the United States. The rawfoods movement eschews enzyme-depleted cooked foods in favor of high-enzyme raw vegetables and fruits. It would be more accurate to say that the trend started back in the 1840s with Sylvester Graham, who recommended living on unfired vegetables and fruits as the optimum diet.

The rawfoods movement was given its greatest public exposure in the modern era by Bernard Macfadden, who during the early decades of the twentieth century ran a successful publishing empire while living ostentatiously on a raw vegetarian diet. Herbert Shelton, a Macfadden employee and protégé, was responsible for systematizing rawfoodism into a health regimen that he referred to as natural hygiene. The central tenet of natural hygiene was that the human body is a self-healing mechanism that thrives best on a diet of uncooked foods. In the event that one contracted a cold or some other malady, Shelton taught that the best way to treat it was through abstaining from food altogether (fasting).

The fact is rawfoodism is not just a transient food fad. The earliest books in America devoted exclusively to the subject of rawfoodism date from the first twelve years of the twentieth century.

Eugene Christian's Uncooked Foods and How to Use Them (1904)

The Christians first attracted the attention of the popular press in 1903, when they threw a gala dinner party in which all the dishes in an elaborate four-course meal were uncooked. For their book *Uncooked Foods and How to Use Them,* Eugene Christian wrote the text,

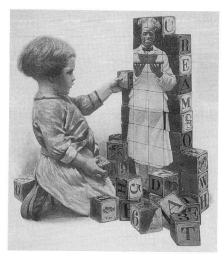

Cream of Wheat advertisement featuring a building block Rastus, 1909.

and his wife Mallis supplied the portfolio of rawfood recipes appended to it. The Christians contend that all the ills that flesh is heir to are due to two things—the eating of cooked foods and the eating of animal flesh. "Civilized man" they say, "can live without cooks."

Otto Carqué's *The Foundation of All Reform* (1904)

California fruit grower and food scientist Otto Carqué developed the Mission Fig and introduced many exotic fruits and nuts to the California food landscape. In his books Carqué argues that a fruitarian diet offers a singular solution to the social and physiological ills that beset "overcivilized" humans.

George Drews's *Unfired Food and Tropho-Therapy (Food Cure)* (1912)

The Chicago nutritionist George J. Drews states that "man's natural foods are fruits, the succulent herbs and roots, the nuts and the cereals, which in their natural (unfired) form appeal to his unperverted sense of alimentation." A Greek scholar, Drews devised a Greek-based nomenclature for rawfoodism that seems to allude to the *apura* ("unfired foods") that Pythagoras enjoined on the members of his order. Drews invited noted rawfood authors like Benedict Lust to hold forth at his Apyrotrophers Society in Chicago.

In fact it was while reading about Lust's Apyrotrophers's lecture and the raw fruit pie served at the banquet following it that John Richter had an epiphany and decided to forswear cooked foods. Richter, who later penned the rawfoods book *Nature: The Healer* (1936), hired Drews to teach him and others how to become a rawfooder. Thus Drews directly influenced Richter and his wife Vera to become "trophes" (Greek for "rawfooder" in Drews lexicon) and to call their rawfood restaurant in Los Angeles The Eutropheon, (Greek for "place of good nourishment").

Although the Eutropheon, America's first rawfoods restaurant, opened in Los Angeles in 1917, until the last years of the twentieth century rawfoods restaurants had been rather sparse on the ground. Suddenly in the early 2000s numerous rawfoods restaurants opened to critical acclaim in America's culinary capitals of New York, Chicago, Los Angeles, and San Francisco. By 2006 there were fifty rawfoods restaurants in the country with multiple rawfood restaurants in each city, and their numbers were growing.

The principal foodstuffs identified closely with the rawfoods movement are sprouted grains, beans, seed and nut cheeses, and wheatgrass juice—all the legacy of Anne Wigmore. Drawing on the knowledge passed on to her by her grandmother, a village healer in her native Lithuania, Wigmore concocted wheatgrass juices and sprouted foods to feed her ailing patients at the Hippocrates Institutes, holistic rawfoods health centers that she opened throughout the United States.

Another immigrant to whom the rawfoods movement owes much is Aris La Tham. A native of Panama, he is considered the father of gourmet ethical vegetarian rawfoods cuisine in America. He debuted his rawfood creations in 1979, when he started Sunfired Foods, a live-foods company in New York City. In the years since, he has trained thousands of rawfood chefs and added innumerable gourmet rawfood recipes to his repertoire.

BIBLIOGRAPHY

Berry, Rynn. *Fruits of Tantalus: A History of Rawfoodism and the Origins of Cooking.* New York: Pythagorean Publishers (forthcoming).

RYNN BERRY

RC Cola, *see Royal Crown Cola*

Recipes

Recipes in America, as in the rest of the world, are the ideas and instructions for handling foods and preparing particular dishes. Although directions for cooking exist in oral form, the historical record is derived mainly from those that are written down, and this account of the development of the recipe in America is based on the written record.

From the times of earliest settlement in the New World, the new immigrants brought their recipes with them. Prominent among the early compilations was a seventeenth-century work, *De Verstandige Kock* (The sensible cook), a book brought by Dutch settlers, whose recipes used the simple, abbreviated forms of the period.

To Make Meatballs. Take veal with veal-fat chopped, add to it mace, nutmeg, salt, pepper, knead it together, then you can make [meatballs] from it as large or as small as you please, also all of it is fried in the pan as one large meatball. Many take a few of the outside peels thinly pared of oranges or lemons, cut very fine. It gives a very good smell and flavor.

The informal, permissive character of the instructions is apparent, based on the assumption that the user of the book was generally knowledgeable about ingredients, about cooking methods, and about the character of a particular dish and the way it should taste. The recipe was basically a set of hints and guidelines, informal in character, often with a suggestion that the reader was being addressed personally—one cook to another. This can also be seen in another major cookbook that immigrants brought with them, Hannah Glasse's legendary *The Art of Cookery Made Plain and Easy* (1747; first American edition, 1805).

To Make an Eel Pie. Make a good crust; clean, gut, and wash your eels very well, then cut them in pieces half as long as your finger; season them with pepper, salt and a little mace to your palate, either high or low. Fill your dish with eels, and put as much water as the dish will hold; put on your cover and bake them well.

In 1796 the first book written by an American-born woman and published in America appeared. Amelia Simmons's *American Cookery* was a conscientious attempt to offer a "treatise . . . calculated for the improvement of Females in America," but the recipes still shared the brisk, simple, cook-to-cook form of address of many of its predecessors:

Baked Custard. Four eggs beat and put to one quart of cream, sweetened to your taste, half a nutmeg, and a little cream—bake.

As long as cooks were familiar with ingredients and the desired outcome, cooking instructions came from an aide-mémoire—a reminder about the food people knew and the observations they had made in their home kitchens as family members and servants cooked. What was called for was good taste and common sense.

By the 1840s and 1850s a number of changes came into play that would have profound impact on the character of the recipe. Many of the household helpers who

> ### 370   *Appendix to the Art of Cookery.*
>
> #### *To make Hamburgh Saufages.*
>
> TAKE a Pound of Beef, mince it very fmall, with half a Pound of the beft Suet; then mix three Quarters of a Pound of Suet cut in large Pieces; then feafon it with Pepper, Cloves, Nutmeg, a great Quantity of Garlick cut fmall, fome white Wine Vinegar, fome Bay Salt, and common Salt, a Glafs of red Wine, and one of Rum; mix all this very well together; then take the largeft Gut you can find, and ftuff it very tight; then hang it up a Chimney, and fmoke it with Saw-duft for a Week or ten Days; hang them in the Air, till they are dry, and they will keep a Year. They are very good boiled in Peas Porridge, and roafted with toafted Bread under it, or in an Amlet.

Eighteenth-century beef sausage recipe.

were actively involved in cooking began to abandon domestic service for opportunities in the outside world, factory work and other jobs generated by the Industrial Revolution, in addition to immigration into the expanding frontier as the new nation surged westward. As domestic servants left, those who drew up menus and supervised the preparation of meals found that they were charged with carrying out the kitchen work themselves, and they were often ill equipped to do so. Increasingly the details of food preparation were no longer self-apparent, and what was called for were more specific, more instructional recipes—recipes that assumed less and left less to chance.

This period also saw the growth of cooking schools to serve the needs of those who could no longer get training at home, and the schools, such as the immensely successful Boston Cooking School incorporated in 1879, committed themselves to produce and teach recipes that "worked"—that were error-free and replicable and that guaranteed uniform quality. This required a distinctly new approach in recipe writing. *Mrs. Lincoln's Boston Cook Book* (1884) by Mrs. D. A. Lincoln, the school's first principal, exemplifies the way in which the cook was now shielded.

Break each egg into a cup, being careful not to break the yolk.... Cut cold meat into... half inch cubes, remove all the gristle and the crisp outside fat.... Mix [ingredients] in the order given and divide the dough into four equal parts.

Many of the recipes provide precise measurements: ¾ cup butter, 2½ cups pastry flour, 1½ teaspoons cream of tartar, white of 8 eggs. This is truly domestic science.

Lincoln's successor at the school, Fannie Farmer, developed these principles even further, adding to her own *Boston Cooking-School Cook Book* (1896) a section called "How to Measure," asserting that "correct measurements are obviously necessary to insure the best results." Her recipes frequently reach a new level of detail. Amelia Simmons's recipe for baked custard was just twenty-one words long; Fannie Farmer's runs more than six times that, not including a preceding ingredient list (itself a user-friendly device introduced gradually during the latter part of the nineteenth century).

Another factor that helped bring about longer, more detailed recipes was the expansion of the cooking repertoire in a country that was growing and diversifying rapidly, exposing its citizens progressively to foods that were new and unfamiliar—foods the "correctness" of whose taste could not be judged by the cook against memory or experience. Recipes under these circumstances could no longer suggest simply "as you please" but had to say, "do it as we tell you," and such works written for immigrants as *The Settlement Cookbook* (1903 and many editions thereafter) provided newcomers with straightforward, no-questions-asked versions

of the mysterious new foods they would be encountering as they made their way in the New World. From the thirteenth edition of the *Settlement* (1924):

Corn Chower

1 can or 2 cups fresh corn,
4 potatoes cut in slices,
2 onions sliced,
2 cups water,
2 tablespoons flour,
3 cups scalded milk,
3 tablespoons fat drippings,
Salt and pepper.

Fry onion in fat, add flour, stirring often, so that the onion may not burn; add 2 cups water and potatoes. Cook until the potatoes are soft; add corn and milk, and cook corn 5 minutes. Season with salt and pepper, and serve.

Equally explicit are recipes for Old World specialties that the immigrants were beginning to lose as their grandparents and parents were no longer present to provide the memories of methods and tastes that had made it possible to cook from the older-style recipes.

Throughout the twentieth century, as cooking and eating habits changed, as more and more women went out to work, as more and more people ate meals outside the home, as the search for new tastes severed reliance on memories of foods "we all know," and as new and unfamiliar ingredients came to the market, those who cooked became progressively unable to rely on instinct to guide their hands and their palates in the kitchen. Recipe writing in books, and in due course in women's magazines and in newspapers, began to cater increasingly to this diminution in knowledge, becoming increasingly specific and in the process rendering the home cooks more and more dependent, undermining their ability to use the recipes as mere guides or reminders.

Recipes at the beginning of the twenty-first century were by far longer and more explicit than ever before. Totally distinct from the personal, permissive suggestions to cooks in seventeenth- and eighteenth-century America are such recipe instructions as:

Lower the heat if the glaze at the bottom of the pan threatens to burn.
In a mortar, crush the peppercorns with a pestle.
Sauté the sage leaves in the butter in a small saucepan over medium-high heat 2 minutes, or until crisp.
Add broth, wine, and saffron. Cook uncovered for 6 minutes. Stir well and cook for 6 minutes more.
Peel the avocados and halve them lengthwise, discarding the pits.
½ teaspoon dried thyme, ¼ cup soft fresh white bread crumbs, 1 ounce dried French chanterelles,

Although it is impossible to know in exactly what direction recipes will develop later in the century, there are some indications that simpler, more intuitive cooking is becoming

attractive to increasing numbers of Americans. If this proves to be the case, there may be movement on the part of food writers and editors to provide their readers with more in the way of inspiration and guidance and less in the way of highly specific prescriptions. Certainly recipes that invite people to explore and to grow in their kitchens will, in the long run, produce better and more innovative cooking, thereby contributing to an overall improvement in the way Americans eat.

[**See also** ADVERTISING COOKBOOKS AND RECIPES; CHILD, LYDIA MARIA; COOKBOOKS AND MANUSCRIPTS: AMERICAN COOKBOOKS FROM THE CIVIL WAR TO WORLD WAR I; COOKBOOKS AND MANUSCRIPTS: AMERICAN COOKBOOKS TO 1860; COOKBOOKS AND MANUSCRIPTS: WORLD WAR I AND WORLD WAR II; COOKBOOKS: WORLD WAR II TO THE 1960S; COOKBOOKS: 1970S TO THE PRESENT; COOKING MANUSCRIPTS; FARMER, FANNIE; LINCOLN, MRS.; SETTLEMENT HOUSES; SIMMONS, AMELIA; RORER, SARAH TYSON.]

BIBLIOGRAPHY

Farmer, Fannie. *Boston Cooking-School Cook Book*. Introduction by Janice Bluestein Longone. Mineola, NY: Dover, 1997.

Glasse, Hannah. *The Art of Cookery Made Plain and Easy*. Introduction by Karen Hess. Bedford, MA: Applewood, 1997.

Kander, Mrs. Simon. *The Settlement Cookbook*. 13th ed. Milwaukee, WI: Settlement Cookbook, 1924.

Lincoln, Mrs. D. A. *Mrs. Lincoln's Boston Cook Book*. Introduction by Janice Bluestein Longone. Mineola, NY: Dover, 1996.

Rose, Peter, trans. *The Sensible Cook* (De Verstandige Kock). Syracuse, NY: Syracuse University Press, 1989.

Simmons, Amelia. *American Cookery*. Introduction by Karen Hess. Bedford, MA: Applewood, 1996.

NAHUM J. WAXMAN

Redenbacher, Orville

Born in 1907 in Brazil, Indiana, Redenbacher grew up on a one-hundred-acre farm. He studied agronomy and genetics at Purdue University and conducted research on the first popcorn hybrids. Upon graduation in 1928, he was hired as a vocational agricultural teacher at a high school, a position he held until May 1929. He was then employed as an assistant county agricultural agent in Terre Haute, Indiana. When the county agent moved to Indianapolis, Redenbacher took over his position and conducted a five-minute radio program beginning in 1930. He was the first county agent in the country to broadcast live from his office and the first to interview farmers in the field with a mobile unit.

In January 1940 Redenbacher began managing a 1,200-acre farm in Princeton, Indiana, that was used for seed farming. He built a hybrid seed corn plant and experimented with popcorn hybrids. Under Redenbacher, Princeton Farms' operations grew by 50 percent. While at Princeton Farms, Redenbacher met Charles Bowman, the manager of the Purdue Ag Alumni Seed Implement

Association, of Lafayette, Indiana. Redenbacher and Bowman went into partnership in 1951 and purchased the George F. Chester Seed Company at Boone Grove, Indiana. Popcorn was part of their hybrid field seed operation, and within a few years Redenbacher and Bowman became the world's largest supplier of hybrid popcorn seed. They also developed new hybrids. In 1965 their popcorn experimentation came up with a new variety, which expanded to nearly twice the size of commercial brands and left almost no unpopped kernels. This new variety was called Red Bow after the first three letters in Redenbacher's and Bowman's last names. For five years Redenbacher tried to sell his new hybrid to the major processors. Unfortunately it cost more to harvest, and yields were smaller, and consequently processors were not interested.

Redenbacher traveled at first to local stores in northern Indiana, hawking his popcorn to anyone who would buy it. In 1970 Redenbacher quit producing popcorn seed for other processors and concentrated on selling Red Bow. Redenbacher and Bowman visited a Chicago public relations firm that persuaded them to change the name from Red Bow to Orville Redenbacher's Gourmet Popping Corn. As the price was higher than that of other popcorn, consumers needed to be convinced that Redenbacher's popcorn was of a better quality than its competitors. The advertising line "The World's Most Expensive Popcorn" emerged. Redenbacher and Bowman achieved regional success through word-of-mouth promotion and virtually no advertising, but they needed assistance to expand nationally. To market their gourmet popcorn, they teamed up in 1973 with Blue Plate Foods, a subsidiary of Hunt-Wesson Foods based in Fullerton, California. This connection permitted national advertising and a widespread distribution system.

When Hunt-Wesson sold Blue Plate Foods in 1974, Redenbacher's gourmet popcorn was so successful that Hunt kept the rights to it. In 1976 Orville Redenbacher's Gourmet Popping Corn business operations and property were sold to Hunt-Wesson, which launched a massive advertising campaign, starring Redenbacher himself, for their newly acquired product. He made hundreds of personal presentations a year and appeared in scores of television commercials. Redenbacher was one of America's most unlikely television stars. His bow tie, dark-framed spectacles, and midwestern accent convinced many that he was just an old country hick. The image worked. Consumers easily recognized the label adorned with Redenbacher's folksy image. Redenbacher's contract for television commercials was not renewed in 1994. While lounging in a hot tub in his home in Coronado, California, Redenbacher suffered a heart attack and drowned on September 19, 1995. His gourmet popping corn stands as his shining legacy.

[**See also** ADVERTISING; POPCORN.]

BIBLIOGRAPHY

Sherman, Len. *Popcorn King: How Orville Redenbacher and His Popcorn Charmed America.* Arlington, TX: Summit, 1996.

Smith, Andrew F. *Popped Culture: A Social History of Popcorn in America.* Columbia: University of South Carolina Press, 1999.

ANDREW F. SMITH

Red Snapper

There are quite a number of fish called red snapper. Generally of the family Lutjanidae, snappers are so called because of their tendency to snap at prey with their sharp upper teeth. In America red snappers, *Lutjanus campechanus*, are found on the southeastern coast, particularly off Florida and in the Gulf of Mexico, where other snappers like mutton, vermilion, mangrove, and yellowtail are also found. The red snapper has firm, white flesh. The smaller fish are panfried; the larger ones are filleted with the skin left on for broiling, grilling, and braising. The red snapper did not achieve important commercial value until the twentieth century.

SANDRA L. OLIVER

Reese's Peanut Butter Cups

Harry Burnett Reese, a former employee of the Hershey Chocolate Company, founded the H. B. Reese Candy Company in 1917 near Hershey, Pennsylvania. Reese experimented at first with molasses and coconut candies called Johnny Bars and Lizzie Bars. In 1928 he came out with chocolate-covered peanut butter cups made with Hershey's chocolate, which were sold wholesale in five-pound packages to be used in boxed candy assortments. Ten years later Reese marketed the confections individually for a penny apiece, and they became known as Reese's Peanut Butter Cups. The public loved the candies, and Reese expanded his factory and became the second largest buyer of chocolate in the United States. During World War II shortages of sugar and chocolate prompted Reese to discontinue his other sweets to concentrate on the Peanut Butter Cups, since peanut butter was not rationed. After the war the Peanut Butter Cup's popularity was such that the company constructed an even larger facility in 1957.

Reese had died in 1956, and his six sons waged a bitter battle for control of the company. With annual sales at $14 million, the company was acquired by Hershey Chocolate Company in 1963 for $23.3 million. The advertising slogan, "Two great tastes that taste great together," was developed by Ogilvie and Mather in 1970 for the Reese's Peanut Butter Cup. In 1976 Hershey put out a new Peanut Butter Cup filled with crunchy rather than smooth peanut butter, and white chocolate Peanut Butter Cups were introduced in 2003. In the early twenty-first century Reese's Peanut Butter Cups remain one of America's most popular candy choices.

BIBLIOGRAPHY

Broekel, Ray. *The Great American Candy Bar Book.* Boston: Houghton Mifflin, 1982.

Richardson, Tim. *Sweets: A History of Candy.* New York: Bloomsbury, 2002.

Smith, Andrew F. *Peanuts: The Illustrious History of the Goober Pea.* Urbana: University of Illinois Press, 2002.

ANDREW F. SMITH

Refrigerators

The mechanical refrigerator was a revolutionary invention that changed life in the United States. No longer were families, restaurants, and businesses inconvenienced by periodic ice deliveries and the necessity of limiting use of the icebox for fear that the ice would melt. Home food costs were reduced because leftovers could be chilled and saved and perishables could be purchased in larger

Loup de mer and red snapper at Citarella's on the Upper West Side of Manhattan.

For the quickest freezing, the metal freezer tray was supposed to be wet on the bottom. Unfortunately this often made the tray itself freeze to the inside of the freezing unit; warm cloths or steam had to be applied to remove the tray. To lower or raise the inside temperature, the dealer had to be called. By the 1960s self-defrosting refrigerators became common. In the 1990s sleek, expensive, built-in refrigerators, pioneered by Sub-Zero, became fashionable. And in 2002 the first combination refrigerator-range was introduced.
[**See also** FREEZERS AND FREEZING; FROZEN FOOD; ICE.]

BIBLIOGRAPHY

Hardyment, Christina. *From Mangle to Microwave: The Mechanization of Household Work*. New York: Basil Blackwell, 1988.

SYLVIA LOVEGREN

quantities. The diet could be more varied as well. With the advent of mechanical refrigerators, frozen and refrigerated foods became a major factor in the American diet, and refrigerator production became big business.

The United States was the first nation to use home refrigerators widely, but refrigeration technology was an international discovery. In both fourteenth-century China and seventeenth-century Italy, it was learned that the evaporation of salt brine absorbed heat and thus storing food in brine would keep food cold. Throughout the nineteenth century attempts were made to further the idea of practical artificial refrigeration based on evaporation. Inventions centered around two basic ideas, a compression system where a cold, volatile liquid, such as ammonia, was circulated by an electric-powered compressor around a container to be kept cold or an absorption system where refrigeration was accomplished by heating the refrigerant (using gas, steam, or some other source) and so causing evaporation and cooling. A series of inventors from France, Germany, Switzerland, and the United States patented various forms of compression and absorption refrigerators throughout the 1800s. Jacob Perkins, a banknote printer, took out the first patent for mechanical refrigeration in the United States in 1834, and by the late 1800s commercial use by shippers and large food businesses became increasingly common.

It was not until the early 1900s in the United States that these artificial refrigeration systems entered the household kitchen, usually using the compression system, powered by newly perfected small electric motors. The Domelre (Domestic Electric Refrigerator) was marketed in Chicago in 1913, but the first large-scale production came from Kelvinator, an early leader in wooden icebox cabinets; the company began selling mechanical refrigerators in 1916. Frigidaire entered the business shortly thereafter, when General Motors purchased a self-contained household refrigerator developed by Alfred Mellowes in 1915.

He called it the "Guardian Frigerator," General Motors changed the name to Frigidaire, and GM not only mass-produced the household appliance but also gave the public a new vernacular name for the refrigerator: "the fridge."

Prices were initially high, at about $900 (at a time when average household income was less than $2,000 per year), so use of the refrigerator was limited. In 1921 about 5,000 mechanical refrigerators were manufactured in the United States; by 1926, 200,000 were sold. With mass production came lowered costs. A 1926 refrigerator sold, on average, for $400. By the mid-1930s home refrigerators were not a luxury but a basic household necessity, even during the height of the Great Depression. In 1935 more than 1.5 million were sold, and the average cost was down to just $170. By 1950 over 80 percent of American farms and over 90 percent of urban and suburban homes had refrigerators.

Refrigerators were initially quite ugly, at least by modern standards, often with the round compressor sitting on top of the refrigerator box, undecorated. General Electric, in 1927, was the first company to seal the motor and sell the box as an integral part of the refrigerator. By the 1930s the fashion of "streamlining" came to refrigerators. Kelvinator led the way in 1932 with bulbous round tops and bowlegs, and GE's sleek model became famous. Soon after even the outline of the compressor was hidden within the steel box surrounding the entire refrigerator, and the familiar rectangular box became the standard. Another standard was introduced in 1939, when GE began mass production of the familiar dual-temperature refrigerator, with one section for chilled food and one for frozen.

Early refrigerators were still rudimentary. The freezing units were small, thin, metal compartments inside the main cabinet of the refrigerator. Instructions were given for the woman who wanted to have both ice cubes (which had to be chipped out of their trays) and a frozen dessert at the same time.

Restaurant Awards and Guides

The first American restaurant guides were produced locally in cities with vibrant restaurant cultures, namely, New York, New Orleans, and San Francisco. Among the earliest was *The Restaurants of New York* (1925) by George Chappell, the architecture critic for the *New Yorker* magazine. The first popular national guide to restaurants across the United States was produced by Duncan Hines, a traveling printing salesman who mailed a list of his 167 favorite restaurants to friends as a greeting card in 1935. The following year he published *Adventures in Good Eating*, which, according to his introduction, "let the public know where they might find decent food, carefully prepared by a competent chef in clean surroundings."

Holiday magazine, founded in 1947, began producing an annual national restaurant guide in 1952 under the tight direction of the magazine's food and restaurant editor, Silas Spitzer. Published in the July issue each year (ceasing in the mid-1980s), the 150 or so restaurant reviews that made up *Holiday*'s Distinctive Dining Awards were ostensibly the opinions of Spitzer, though he relied on input from a network of diners across the country that included Lucius Beebe and James Villas.

During the 1950s American travelers were taking to the road in unprecedented numbers, and several travel guides were produced to help them select hotels and restaurants en route. For large corporations like Mobil Oil—which began rating restaurants in 1958 and published the first *Socony Mobil Guide* in 1960—recommending and rating hotels and restaurants provided a service to consumers, encouraged people to travel by car, and garnered the company respect as an arbiter of taste. In 2002 ten regional Exxon Mobil Travel Guides were produced from a database that included more than eleven thousand restaurant listings; only fourteen received the highest, five-star rating. The American Automobile Association (AAA) began listing restaurants in its travel publications in 1937, but AAA did not rate them until 1988. AAA distinguished its ratings with diamonds (one to five) instead of stars—the 2003 guides contain more than twelve thousand rated restaurants, of which fifty-three received the five-diamond rating.

Arguably the most popular guides are produced and published by Zagat Survey. The founders, Tim and Nina Zagat, were lawyers who began by informally surveying colleagues about where they liked to eat. Their first guide to New York City restaurants was self-published and distributed in 1979; by the early 2000s they were producing some forty-five guides covering the United States and a handful of international cities. Ratings out of thirty for food, service, and decor are compiled from surveys completed voluntarily via the Internet by the general dining public.

Increasing interest in restaurants and chefs has led magazines, newspapers, television food shows, and other media into restaurant rating. Magazine features, such as *Food and Wine*'s annual Best New Chefs award and *Gourmet*'s and *Bon Appétit*'s annual restaurant issues, amount to national restaurant guides, as do reader polls. Also popular are industry awards, such as those given annually by the James Beard Foundation, which *Time* magazine called "the Oscars of the food world." Although they are important for chefs and their colleagues, awards given by trade organizations, such as the American Culinary Federation (ACF), are less well known by consumers and therefore have less of an impact on the seemingly unanswerable question of where to eat.

[See also CELEBRITY CHEFS; HINES, DUNCAN; RESTAURANT CRITICS AND FOOD COLUMNISTS.]

BIBLIOGRAPHY

Chappell, George S. *Adventures in Good Eating.* Bowling Green, KY: Adventures in Good Eating, 1936.

Hines, Duncan. *Adventures in Good Eating: Good Eating Places along the Highways and in the Cities of America.* 7th ed. Bowling Green, KY: Adventures in Good Eating, 1940.

Villas, James. *Between Bites: Memoirs of a Hungry Hedonist.* New York: Wiley, 2002.

MITCHELL DAVIS

Restaurant Critics and Food Columnists

There was plenty written about food in various media during the early and mid-twentieth century. Lucius Beebe, A. J. Liebling, M. F. K. Fisher, and Joseph Wechsberg were among the writers who more than occasionally focused their attention on matters gastronomic in the first half of the twentieth century. *Gourmet* magazine debuted in 1941 and set a new standard for the seriousness with which food and food writing was to be taken. But most of this writing was tailored to a small audience with the financial means and social wherewithal to benefit from advice about which were the best French restaurants in Manhattan and what regional treats to look for while traveling abroad. The alternative was

the type of food writing aimed at housewives—publications such as *Good Housekeeping, Ladies' Home Journal*, and the food pages of most newspapers, for example—which offered recipes and other advice for women burdened with the daily chore of putting dinner on the table.

One person largely responsible for changing the tenor of food writing targeted to the general public was Craig Claiborne, who was hired as the food editor of the *New York Times* in 1957. Trained at the famed École hôtelière de Lausanne in Switzerland, he applied tough standards to the quality of the food about which he wrote, the recipes he developed, and the restaurants he reviewed. As one example of his reach, the standards and format for his restaurant reviews—many anonymous visits; comprehensive consideration of food, service, and decor; and serious evaluation of the taste, presentation, and authenticity of the food—remain in place at the paper and have been copied by other publications around the country. Of his successors in the role of reviewer at the *Times* were Mimi Sheraton, Bryan Miller, and Ruth Reichl, who went on to become editor in chief of *Gourmet*.

Following Claiborne's lead, restaurant critics at other newspapers and magazines asserted themselves as arbiters of taste in important dining centers across the country. Among those who enjoyed the longest tenure and broadest, most loyal readership were Elaine Tait of the *Philadelphia Inquirer*, Phyllis Richman of the *Washington Post*, and Caroline Bates, who was hired by *Gourmet* in 1959 and who began reviewing California restaurants in 1974.

Buoyed by the cooking and dining excitement of the 1960s, various national and local media outlets either enhanced or established food sections and food departments during the 1970s. In 1974 James Beard began writing a series of cooking lessons for *American Way*, the in-flight magazine of American Airlines. That same year Raymond Sokolov's musings on food history began appearing in *Natural History*. Even *Playboy* gave gastronomy serious consideration in a supplement that was eventually spun off to become *Food & Wine* magazine.

Food writers began offering advice in new magazines, such as *Bon Appétit* and *Cuisine*, targeted to a slightly different portion of the food-loving public. By penning cookbooks and narrowly focused articles, experts on specific types of cuisine began to emerge—Paula Wolfert on the food of Morocco and the Mediterranean, Madhur Jaffrey on Indian cooking, Marcella Hazan on Italian food, Richard Olney and Jacques Pépin on French cuisine.

Gourmet Food and Regional Cuisines
As the 1980s approached, the consuming public split into camps to satisfy their developing tastes. There were the high-minded, high-living gourmets with the money to cook with expensive ingredients and to eat at the best restaurants. Sybaritic food writers

such as James Villas satiated their haute hungers in the pages of *Town & Country*. Neo-traditionalists of the sort that celebrated Chez Panisse wanted their prose simmered with locally grown vegetables and cooked in any number of traditional European styles. These were the people that Ed Behr was addressing when he started his *Art of Eating* newsletter in 1986. Novelty seekers preferred their prose doused with raspberry vinegar and garnished with kiwi, and Sheila Lukins and Julee Rosso, the team behind the *Silver Palate*, were primed to give it to them.

For intrepid gourmets, those hunters and gatherers who ferreted out tasty morsels in such unlikely places as rural American backwaters and ethnic immigrant enclaves, a growing body of literature emerged. To this group spoke writers such as the humorist Calvin Trillin, a *New Yorker* staff writer whose "Tummy Trilogy" of books glorified Kansas City barbecue and take-out Chinese food, among other low-brow temptations. The cross-country travelers Jane and Michael Stern took to the highway with *Roadfood* (1976), a celebration of out-of-the-way, regional, hole-in-the-wall eateries. They continued to write for *Gourmet* into the early twenty-first century.

The 1990s saw an ever-increasing number of media outlets for food writing of every type—from the pursuit of authentic ethnic and regional cookery in the pages of *Saveur* to the mastery of home-cooking recipes and techniques in the pages of *Cook's Illustrated* and *Fine Cooking*. Eating healthfully produced its own subgenre of cooking magazines, such as *Eating Well* and *Cooking Light*. Such food columnists as Jeffrey Steingarten in *Vogue* and Alan Richman in *GQ* drew a broad, international audience.

Professionalism in Food Writing
As the cult of celebrity touched the food world during the 1990s, the lines between food writer, chef, cookbook author, entrepreneur, marketer, and television personality blurred. Anthony Bourdain, Emeril Lagasse, Rachael Ray, and Martha Stewart are perhaps the food celebrities who garnered the widest, most varied audiences. The success of their food as entertainment formula even landed them television sitcom and motion picture deals.

Industry recognition for food writing, such as the separate food journalism awards administered by the James Beard Foundation and the International Association of Culinary Professionals, also has contributed to the growing professionalism in the field. Of course it is the quality of the writing that determines the true success of a food writer; the proof of the professionalism of the critic will be in the writing about the pudding.

[See also BEARD, JAMES; CHILD, JULIA; CLAIBORNE, CRAIG; ETHNIC FOODS; FRENCH INFLUENCES ON AMERICAN FOOD; RESTAURANT AWARDS AND GUIDES; RESTAURANTS; STEWART, MARTHA; WHITE HOUSE.]

BIBLIOGRAPHY

Dornenburg, Andrew, and Karen Page. *Dining Out: Secrets from America's Leading Critics, Chefs, and Restaurateurs.* New York: Wiley, 1998.

MITCHELL DAVIS

Restaurant Labor Unions

Most of the better hotel and restaurant kitchens and dining rooms in nineteenth-century and early twentieth-century America were staffed by Europeans. In addition to their expertise in haute cuisine and elegant service, these immigrants imported unionism and the more radical syndicalism, which were emerging in nineteenth-century Europe in the wake of the collapsed guild system. The first American union devoted to the "catering trade" was founded in Chicago in 1866. Representing bartenders and waiters, all of its members were German immigrants.

By the early twentieth century labor unions represented tens of thousands of bartenders, cooks, waiters, and other hospitality workers under the aegis of either the American Federation of Labor or the Industrial Workers of the World (IWW). In addition to German, French, Irish, Italian, and Jewish immigrants, the hospitality unions included significant numbers of African Americans and women. Locals often split along racial and ethnic lines, exacerbated by language barriers. Moreover the different trades within the hospitality industry were compensated differently (wages versus tips) and had competing interests. Finally, members disagreed on tactics to advance their interests: some urged negotiations while others advocated strikes and seizure of the means of production.

The Wobblies were a radical faction that took control of the IWW in New York City in 1912 and staged dramatic strikes. On May 7, at precisely 7:15 p.m., a whistle signaled the walkout of the waiters from an elegant hotel dining room; the waiters bowed and apologized to the tuxedoed and gowned dinner guests for the inconvenience, but the hotel was empty of guests the next day. The mid-service walkout was immediately repeated in other hotels, although unflappable New Yorkers quickly learned to serve themselves from platters of food delivered to the dining room. On May 15 cooks at the Waldorf Astoria joined the waiters' walkout, paralyzing the hotels. Citywide strikes lasted through the end of May, when hotel chains began importing employees from other cities to relieve the labor shortage. The strike was completely broken by the end of June and the Wobblies temporarily discredited.

As an alternative to the strike, other union factions emphasized legal action and increased training for their members as a bargaining tool. Just prior to the 1912 walkouts, the union organizer Joseph Dommers Vehling founded the short-lived newspaper *International Hotel Work* to air many of the issues confronting labor and to urge negotiated, rather than syndicalist, solutions. He was ousted by the Wobblies in the spring of 1912, but his calls for education and reform have echoed through the decades.

Nowadays the most notable of the culinary unions is Local 226 from Las Vegas. Combining both education and negotiation with the tactical possibility of strike, Local 226 advances the interests of its largely immigrant constituency working in restaurant and hotel chains. Wobblies are also trying to organize workers at chains such as Starbucks and Whole Foods. But many food and hospitality workers in small, individually owned restaurants and hotels remain un-unionized in an industry notorious for long hours and few worker benefits.

BIBLIOGRAPHY

Josephson, Matthew. *Union House, Union Bar: The History of the Hotel and Restaurant Employees and Bartenders International Union, AFL-CIO.* New York: Random House, 1956.

Kimeldorf, Howard. *Battling for American Labor.* Berkeley: University of California Press, 1999.

CATHY K. KAUFMAN

Restaurants

The fine-dining restaurants of the Western world originated in eighteenth-century France. They served a highly articulated cuisine to savvy diners aware of the social status implied by public displays of taste. But in the newly formed United States, dining in public for the sake of the food was slow to catch on. Early food service in American inns and taverns catered to hungry travelers and heavy drinkers.

New York City

New York City has always been a trendsetter in American food and dining. The early gatherings at Fraunce's Tavern, established in New York City in 1763, were more notable for the attendees than for any of the food served, which was copious but inferior to food served in private homes. While the quality and variety of raw ingredients were impressive, in the hands of disinterested cooks with minimal training, they were transformed into bland and boring dishes—boiled and roasted meats, overly sweet sauces, and other plain fare. These dishes were served at communal tables, where people of every station sat shoulder to shoulder. As rooms were let on the "American plan," which meant all meals were included in the price of the room, there was little incentive for a person to seek food outside the inn.

The City Hotel in New York was the first modern hotel, where the menu for the three daily meals was large, but the quality was no different from anywhere else. The Tremont Hotel in Boston, opened in 1829, upped the ante in terms of attention to food. New York City countered in 1836 with the opening of Astor House. Tables were laid with dishes, and guests were kept to a strict schedule enforced by a militaristic waitstaff. The New York Hotel provided the first à la carte menu, whereby diners could choose and pay for only the dishes they wanted to eat. It was also the first American hotel to opt for the "European plan," which allowed for separate payment for meals.

By the 1820s the first eating establishments not connected to overnight accommodations began appearing in New York. Early cafeteria-style restaurants known as "eating houses" fit the bill. Speed, a recurring theme in the evolution of American restaurants, was a large part of their appeal. A diner could grab a fixed-price lunch, eat it, pay, and be back in the office in a quarter-hour. Coffeehouses, oyster cellars, and corner liquor stores also began competing for money spent on food consumed outside the home. By the 1840s German beer-hall culture was entrenched in the Bowery's "Little Germany." The 1870s saw prototypical bistros in the French section of Greenwich Village and Chinese restaurants in the same neighborhood as modern-day Chinatown. Spanish and Italian food was available as early as the 1850s.

Drawing of waiters by Randolph Caldecott.

Diners at Café Moutarde are able to experience a bit of Paris in Brooklyn, New York.

Westward and Southern Expansion

In 1869 George M. Pullman debuted his first luxury dining car, fitted with two rows of booths and a kitchen that prepared delectable hot meals. Such finery en route set a standard for dining nationwide. For less affluent travelers, after 1876 Fred Harvey's "refreshment saloons," located in train stations along popular lines, offered mediocre food. In San Francisco the New World Coffee opened in 1850. In 1887 it became the Tadich Grill, and it has remained in operation under that name. Around the same time Chinese immigrants arrived in the San Francisco Bay Area in large numbers and established an early Chinatown with restaurants and food shops to service their needs. The commodity craze brought a wave of prosperity to Chicago. At the center of the country's meat-processing industry, the city's residents took to an enduring form of high-protein dining, the steak house. Areas at the heart of cattle production, such as Kansas City and Oklahoma City, developed local steak house variations. New Orleans, Louisiana, came by its French restaurants naturally as a result of its large French population. The "Big Easy" earned its reputation for fine dining through establishments such as Antoine's, operating since 1840, serving French, Creole, and Cajun cuisines that derive from the city's unique ethnic mix.

Clean, Fair, and Alcohol-Free

At the dawn of the twentieth century, while the upper classes indulged themselves at lobster palaces, steak houses, and fancy French restaurants, those less flush were turning their attention to more mundane matters, such as efficiency, nutrition, hygiene, and temperance. In Chicago and New York growing chains of "luncheonettes" built their reputations on the purity of their ingredients and the cleanliness of their facilities, typified by the Childs chain of cafeteria-style luncheonettes, which opened in 1898. The Philadelphia-based chain of coffee shops founded by Joe Horn and Frank Hardart in 1888 took the idea of efficiency to a new level with the opening of their first automat in 1902. By 1922 the Chicagoan John R. Thompson counted 103 restaurants in his citywide chain of modest, clean, and quick eateries. Built on these same themes, the fast food industry took hold in California during the 1950s with the start of chains like McDonald's (1955) and Carl's Jr. (1956).

Prohibition in 1920 devastated fine-dining restaurants. Until then (as now) the business formula that made restaurants viable relied on the high profit margin on alcohol sales, but other types of restaurants flourished. Soda fountains and luncheonettes took advantage of empty spaces, low rent, and a business model that excluded alcohol. Of course one could still have a drink with a meal if that meal was eaten behind the locked door of a speakeasy. Opened in 1929 in New York City (and still very much in business), Jack and Charlie's "21" was the epitome of the gourmet "speak."

Dining Trends after World War II

The Depression and World War II took further tolls on the restaurant industry. An increased demand for low-cost food was met with advances in food-processing technology. Inexpensive eateries across the country, including chains like Schrafft's and Howard Johnson, increasingly took advantage of these new processed foods, serving canned soups, frozen vegetables, and other prepackaged items that minimized food and labor costs. As the food on menus standardized, American restaurateurs began differentiating themselves with extravagant interior decoration. From Portland, Oregon, to Miami, Florida, Venetian gardens, King Tut's tomb, and other kitsch decor became popular in new restaurants, no matter that the menus invariably included steak, roast chicken, mashed potatoes, and peas.

Meanwhile ethnic dining became fashionable among variety seekers in New York City. Restaurants continued to blossom in the city's immigrant ethnic enclaves, and it was not long before Italian, Jewish, German, Russian, Japanese, and other types of restaurants broke out to other parts of the city. The 1939 World's Fair in the neighborhood of Flushing, Queens, in New York City introduced many Americans to foreign cultures. Among the most popular exhibits was the restaurant in the French pavilion managed by Henri Soulé, who remained in the United States and opened Le Pavillon in 1941. Le Pavillon ushered in a newfound enthusiasm and set the standard for classic French cuisine, prepared by a mostly French staff that included Pierre Franey, who would become chef in 1952. By mid-century much of the country was eating out with a French accent at fancy places like La Caravelle (1960) and Lutèce (1961) in New York City, Maisonette (1949) in Cincinnati, and all sorts of bistros and brasseries between the East Coast and the Midwest.

Simultaneously restaurateurs aspired to create a uniquely American fine-dining experience. Joe Baum merged theatricality, theme, and fine food at the grand restaurants produced by his firm, Restaurant Associates. His Four Seasons project had in understated modern elegance. Opened in the Seagram Building on Park Avenue in 1959, the Four Seasons featured locally

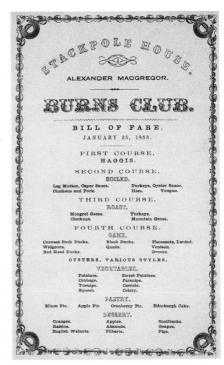

Dishes offered on January 25, 1853, by the Burns Club, Boston.

grown, seasonal American produce. The unabashed ambition of the Four Seasons set in motion a celebration of regional American food that continues in the early twenty-first century.

By the 1970s myriad dining trends were heading off in different directions. Opened in 1971, Chez Panisse in Berkeley, California, celebrated the freshest produce simply prepared, an approach that would come to represent California cuisine. The counterculture found its dining model in the Moosewood vegetarian cooperative, which started in Ithaca, New York, in 1973. Ethnic eateries continued to reflect immigration patterns around the country and were stratified to cater to every class of diner. Even the fast food hamburger model has broadened its offerings to include ethnic specialties and healthful alternatives.

At the beginning of the twenty-first century America experienced an unprecedented economic prosperity that was reflected in a highly diverse dining scene. America has a unique ability to incorporate both strikingly authentic replications of foreign restaurants and what can only be described as bastardized versions of them. This dichotomy means that there are French, Japanese, Chinese, Italian, Mexican, and other types of restaurants that rival the best in the world alongside others that would be unrecognizable anywhere else. Add to this the openness and creativity that has produced a unique American cuisine, which has begun to challenge French cultural hegemony in matters of food. More than just fast food hamburgers, America has exported an inclusive approach to food and dining that has had an extensive impact on restaurant design and operation around the world.

[**See also** AUTOMATS; BARS; BEARD, JAMES; BEER HALLS; BISTROS; CAFETERIAS; CHINESE AMERICAN FOOD; COFFEEHOUSES; DELMONICO'S; ETHNIC FOODS; FAST FOOD; FRENCH INFLUENCES ON AMERICAN FOOD; GERMAN AMERICAN FOOD; HARVEY, FRED; HOTEL DINING ROOMS; ITALIAN AMERICAN FOOD; LUNCHEONETTES; NEW YORK FOOD; OYSTER BARS; PROHIBITION; PULLMAN, GEORGE; RANHOFER, CHARLES; SALOONS; SODA FOUNTAINS; TAVERNS.]

BIBLIOGRAPHY

Batterberry, Michael, and Ariane Batterberry. *On the Town in New York: The Landmark History of Eating, Drinking, and Entertainments from the American Revolution to the Food Revolution.* New York: Routledge, 1999.

Mennell, Stephen. *All Manners of Food: Eating and Taste in England and France from the Middle Ages to the Present.* Urbana: University of Illinois Press, 1996.

Spang, Rebecca. *The Invention of the Restaurant: Paris and Modern Gastronomic Culture.* Cambridge, MA: Harvard University Press, 2000.

Whitaker, Jan. *Tea at the Blue Lantern Inn: A Social History of the Tea Room Craze in America.* New York: St. Martin's, 2002.

MITCHELL DAVIS

The Rise of Restaurants

Americans' relationship with restaurants changed dramatically in the decades following World War II. The economic prosperity of the postwar period increased discretionary income, allowing Americans to lavish their extra dollars on professionally prepared foods outside of the home. In addition the increasing numbers of single-person households, infusion of women into the workforce, decline in cooking knowledge as home economics became a politically incorrect part of high-school curricula, and sheer entertainment, easy availability, and enjoyable sociability of most restaurant experiences all contributed to the waning of at-home dining. Perhaps the most oft-cited reason, proffered in sheepish justification, for the rise in restaurant dining is Americans' popularly bemoaned and irritatingly vague fast-paced lifestyle, which leaves little time, energy, or inclination for cooking. At the turn of the millennium, Americans were on the verge of spending more on food consumed away from home than on food in the family grocery cart.

Since the early 1970s virtually all Americans have spent absolutely and relatively more dollars on food away from home. According to the Food Institute, a trade organization, between 1972 and 1982 American spending at limited menu (fast food) and full menu establishments nearly tripled. Leading the growth in this period were lower-income families. According to the U.S. Department of Labor's Bureau of Labor Statistics, those in the lowest 20 percent of income increased restaurant (including fast food) spending from 18.5 percent of the family food dollar to 24.3 percent. Those in other economic tranches increased their spending as well, with the highest 20 percent of earners spending 37.6 percent of food dollars in restaurants, up from 33.3 percent a decade earlier.

The ratio of spending between fast food and traditional full menu establishments also shifted. In 1972 full-menu restaurants accounted for nearly two-thirds of all restaurant dollars; by 1982 full-menu restaurants had fallen to about 57 percent of restaurant dollars, and this trend continued through 2002, with snack shops and coffeehouses such as the Starbucks chain representing the fastest-growing segment of the restaurant market. In 2002, as frequent restaurant dining for the whole family became a part of American life, so-called fast-casual restaurants, such as Applebee's, Red Lobster, and Olive Garden, represented a faster-growing market in terms of the number of new outlets, than McDonald's and Burger King.

Several conclusions emerge. Spending on food away from home rises with income, regardless of age, gender, or family structure. Higher income households spend disproportionately more on food away from home, reinforcing the discretionary nature of the spending. Single-person households spend more per capita than family units on food away from home, probably due to the diseconomies of small-scale cooking for one and the general dreariness of eating alone. The most important audience for restaurants is the dual-earner household. Although they account for approximately one-third of all households, two-career families control approximately 43 percent of restaurant spending.

BIBLIOGRAPHY

Food Institute. *Menu for Change: Regional Transition in America's Eating and Drinking Places.* Fair Lawn, NJ: Food Institute, 1984.

Mogelonsky, Marcia. *Who's Buying Food and Drink: Who Spends How Much on Food and Alcohol, at and away from Home.* Ithaca, NY: New Strategist Publications, 1996.

CATHY K. KAUFMAN

Reuben Sandwich

The Reuben sandwich is composed of thinly sliced corned beef, swiss cheese, sauerkraut, and russian dressing piled between slices of rye bread and grilled. Three separate camps lay claim to the creation of the Reuben. In New York the sandwich is said to have been introduced in 1914 by Arnold Reuben, owner of Reuben's Restaurant on East Fifty-eighth Street. An out-of-work actress named Annette Seelos arrived at Reuben's and asked for something to eat. Reuben made her an enormous sandwich that consisted of bread, roast beef and other meats, cheese, and spices, and he eventually named it the "Reuben's Special."

In Omaha, Nebraska, legend says that the sandwich, composed of the traditional ingredients, originated in the early 1920s as a snack for a group of hungry poker players at the Blackstone Hotel. Reuben Kolakofsky, a grocer, is credited with its creation, and it was such a hit that the hotel owner Charles Schimmel named it in his honor and put it on the menu. In 1956 a former waitress at the Blackstone Hotel named Fern Snider entered the recipe in a national sandwich competition and won. Finally, it is said that the Reuben was created in 1937 at the Cornhusker Hotel in Lincoln, Nebraska. A menu from that establishment, listing the proper ingredients and dated the same year, has been submitted as proof. To date this menu is the only evidence that has surfaced to substantiate any of the three claims. The Reuben sandwich is a standard offering on delicatessen and restaurant menus throughout the United States.

[**See also** CORNED BEEF; DELICATESSENS; SANDWICHES.]

BIBLIOGRAPHY
"Reuben and His Restaurant." *American Life Histories: Manuscripts from the Federal Writers' Project, 1936–1940*. American Memory. http://memory.loc.gov/ammem/amhome.html.
Mercuri, Becky. *Sandwiches That You Will Like.* Pittsburgh, PA: WQED Multimedia, 2002.

BECKY MERCURI

Rhubarb

Rhubarb (*Rheum rhabarbarum*), related to sorrel, grows in a form typical of vegetables, but the U.S. Customs Court at Buffalo, New York, ruled in 1947 that it is a fruit, since that is how it is usually used. A hardy perennial and a pleasant harbinger of spring, rhubarb is also called "pie plant" in the United States. American commercial production of rhubarb is concentrated in Washington, Oregon, and Michigan but also exists in other northern states. About a quarter of the crop is sold fresh; most of the rest is frozen.

Rhubarb originated in Asia over five thousand years ago and was introduced to Maine at the end of the eighteenth century when

Rhubarb advertisement.

a gardener obtained seeds or roots from Europe. Cultivation soon flourished in Massachusetts, and by 1822 rhubarb was sold in New England produce markets. In the late nineteenth century the great plant breeder Luther Burbank developed a mild variety with a long growing season well suited to California.

Early Americans used rhubarb extract and syrup for dyspepsia and a variety of bowel complaints. Most mid-nineteenth-century medical guides recommended the use of rhubarb extracts (an 1866 medical book suggested fifteen drops be given to a constipated child), and tinctures of rhubarb were a standard in medicine chests.

Nineteenth-century American cookbooks carried rhubarb recipes for sweet pies, cobblers, conserves, and tarts. In her *American Frugal Housewife* (1833, twelfth edition), the New England author Lydia Maria Child wrote, "Rhubarb stalks, or the Persian apple, is the earliest ingredient for pies, which the spring offers." But she mourned, "These are dear pies, for they take an enormous quantity of sugar" (p. 69). However extravagant the pies may have been, eating rhubarb in spring was considered a "broom for the system," and pioneer women took rhubarb seeds west with them on the Overland Trail, where they were eventually sowed beside log cabins and sod houses. Some rhubarb beds dating back a century or more still thrive in the West, although the dwellings they stood by have long disappeared.

Rhubarb leaves contain large amounts of oxalic acid, which makes them inedible. The stalks also contain this poisonous substance, but only in amounts equal to that found in spinach and chard.

[**See also** CHILD, LYDIA MARIA; HOMEMADE REMEDIES; PIES AND TARTS; SORREL.]

BIBLIOGRAPHY
Child, Lydia Maria. *American Frugal Housewife* twelfth edition. Boston: Carter, Hendee And Co., 1832.
Morse, J. E. *The New Rhubarb Culture.* New York: Orange Judd, 1909.
Schneider, Elizabeth. *Vegetables from Amaranth to Zucchini: The Essential Reference.* New York: Morrow, 2001.

SARA RATH

Rice

A staple food for more than two-thirds of the world's population, rice is one of the most important grains in the world. There are two domesticated species: Asian rice (*Oryza sativa*), which has been cultivated for at least 7,000

years in Southeast Asia, China, and India, and African rice (*Oryza glaberrima*), which was cultivated in West Africa for 3,500 years. In the sixteenth century *O. sativa* was introduced into West Africa, probably by the Portuguese, and it largely replaced indigenous African rice, mainly because of its higher yields.

Asian rice, the major modern commercial rice, has two major subspecies: *japonica*, a short-grain rice, and *indica*, a long- or medium-grain rice that thrives in hot climates. *Indica* takes longer to mature and is less starchy and mushy when cooked. Historically *indica* types were first grown in the southern states, while *japonica* types were initially cultivated in California in the twentieth century.

Rice Cultivation

The earliest record of rice cultivation in the English colonies dates from Virginia in 1647. Rice cultivation expanded southward to the Carolinas and later Georgia. From the beginning, it was considered an export crop. As tobacco was more profitable, rice growing was generally limited to the swampy lowlands, where tobacco could not be grown. Asian rice (*O. sativa indica*) was probably first introduced to South Carolina from Madagascar in the 1680s. "Carolina rice" came to be a generic term for long-grain rice of high quality. It was named for the golden color of the ripe grain in the field. It was frequently mentioned in British cookbooks and won medals at European agricultural fairs and expositions.

Commercial rice production—difficult and brutal work—required a large labor force that was supplied through the importation of slaves from rice-growing areas of West Africa. Slaves prepared the fields, constructed the canals and dikes, planted and cultivated the crops, flooded and drained the fields, and harvested, winnowed, and polished the rice. Rice cultivation in the South expanded until 1860. Without a cheap labor source, it declined after Civil War. By the 1920s rice was no longer was milled in South Carolina.

Rice was also grown in small quantities in French settlements in Louisiana during the eighteenth century. Just before the Civil War planters along the Mississippi River began to expand rice production, and cultivation exploded after the war. Rice production began in Arkansas and Texas in the 1880s, and it began in California during the early twentieth century. In 2002 rice production in the United States was concentrated primarily in Arkansas, which produced almost half of

Hoppin' John, a common Southern rice dish.

the rice grown in the nation, followed by California, Louisiana, Mississippi, Missouri, and Texas. The United States ranked third among nations with the largest rice exports.

Rice Cookery

The South was the birthplace of American rice cookery. Beginning in the early nineteenth century, recipes for rice appeared in many American cookbooks. Many immigrants and residents of newly acquired territories came from rice-consuming cultures. For instance, rice was integrated into the diets of those of Mexican heritage in the Southwest, as among Puerto Ricans and Hawaiians. Many Italian immigrants who arrived during the late nineteenth century and early twentieth century were also familiar with rice as were Chinese immigrants.

As Hispanic and Asian immigration to the United States increased, so did the importance of rice in the American diet. Asian immigrants have introduced sticky rice into the mainstream American diet. But it was not until after World War II that cookbooks focusing on rice were regularly published in the United States.

Commercial Rice Products

Numerous commercial products made from rice have been manufactured in America. One of the early successful products was Puffed Rice, a cereal developed by Alexander P. Anderson. The Kellogg Company first marketed Rice Krispies, a cold breakfast cereal, in 1928. Three gnomelike characters, originally drawn by Vernon Grant, were its mascots. "Snap!" first appeared in 1933 while "Crackle!" and "Pop!" were introduced in 1941. Eight years later the characters were changed to look more elfin and appealing. The recipe for Kellogg's Rice Krispies Treats, made by mixing the cereal with melted marshmallows, was introduced in 1933. Uncle Ben's Rice was developed in the 1940s by Gordon Harwell of Texas, who used a British process of treating rice with pressurized steam to drive minerals and vitamins into the kernel. Minute Rice was developed by an Afghan inventor, Ataullah K. Ozai-Durrani, who sold the process to General Foods Corporation in 1941. The process precooked rice, then dried it so that only brief boiling was needed to reconstitute it. General Foods first marketed Minute Rice in 1946.

Yet another product was Rice-A-Roni, composed of rice, pasta, and a dry seasoning mix, created by Vince DeDomenico of the Golden Grain Company in San Francisco.

Later Developments

Many varieties of rice are available in American supermarkets, each slightly different in texture and flavor. In addition to regular white and brown rice, converted rice, and quick-cooking rice, many stores carry fragrant types, such as Indian basmati rice (both brown and white) and Thai jasmine rice; American-grown fragrant rice varieties, called Calmati and Texmati, are less expensive alternatives to the imported products. Chinese and Japanese rice varieties, imported or grown domestically, are also available. Americans' consumption of rice doubled during the last two decades of the twentieth century, and it will likely continue to grow in the twenty-first century.

[See also African American Food: To the Civil War; Cajun and Creole Food; Cereal, Cold; Chinese American Food; Hawaiian Food; Japanese American Food; Kellogg Company; Mexican American Food; Southeast Asian Food; Southern Regional Cookery; Southwestern Regional Cookery.]

BIBLIOGRAPHY

Carney, Judith A. *Black Rice: The African Origins of Rice Cultivation in the Americas.* Cambridge, MA: Harvard University Press, 2001.

Dethloff, Henry C. *A History of the American Rice Industry, 1685–1985.* College Station: Texas A&M University Press, 1988.

Hess, Karen. *The Carolina Rice Kitchen: The African Connection.* Columbia: University of South Carolina Press, 1992.

Smith, C. Wayne, and Robert H. Dilday, eds. *Rice: Origin, History, Technology, and Production.* Hoboken, NJ: Wiley, 2003.

Andrew F. Smith

Rice Dishes

The sustaining combination of rice and peas—black-eyed peas, cowpeas, or whatever legume is available—is an African dish that took various forms in the Americas, such as Brazilian *feijoada* and Cuban *Moros y Cristianos*. The only specifically American versions of this dish are the hoppin' John of South Carolina and red beans and rice of New Orleans, Louisiana. Hoppin' John may have as its leguminous component cowpeas, or black-eyed peas (*Vigna unguiculata*), and Congo peas, or pigeon peas (*Cajanus cajan*), but green or yellow field peas (*Pisum sativum*) are not used. A recipe for hoppin' John is in *The Carolina Housewife* (1847) by Sarah Rutledge, and it is a signature dish of South Carolina cookery.

Pilau, also known as pilaf, polo, or pullow (there are still more spellings), is long-grain rice that has been washed and presoaked. The rice is briefly browned in fat, and then a flavorful broth is added, usually in the proportion of two parts liquid to one part rice by volume. Other ingredients, such as chicken or seafood, may be added to the rice as it simmers. Pilau likely originated in Iran, and it traveled to Europe and South Asia after the expansion of Islam. A number of dishes related to pilaf, including arroz con pollo (chicken and rice), paella (a complex dish made with chicken and several types of shellfish), and jambalaya (a spicy dish from New Orleans, Louisiana, that might also contain ham, sausage, chicken, or shellfish with vegetables) are all enjoyed in the United States.

Recipes called "rice soup" had been published in England by the late eighteenth century and in America by 1805. Many other soup recipes contain rice, including ones for pepper pot, okra soup, gumbo, and mulligatawny soup.

Rice bread has been consumed for millennia in Europe and Asia. These breads are mainly flat breads; unlike wheat, rice develops no gluten to support rising dough. These recipes were brought from Europe to America in colonial times. The rice breads, cakes, and cookies of the Carolina lowlands were largely made with rice flour. Rice bread without the addition of flour was dense, even when made with boiled rice flour, which produces a superior loaf. Rice bread was popular in England in the late eighteenth century, and recipes were regularly published in the United States during the nineteenth century. It was mainly used as a substitute for wheat flour in the South. When the price of wheat flour dropped in the nineteenth century, the making of rice bread declined. During World War I it became patriotic to add rice flour to bread so that more wheat could be shipped to European allies and the American armed forces.

Rice cakes and other baked goods were based on traditional English recipes for other grains, such as wheat. Colonists brought them to America and adapted them. Johnnycakes, breads, pancakes, and fritters were all of European origin. In rice-growing areas of America, rice was substituted for oats or wheat.

Sweet rice dishes, classified as puddings, evolved from English and French recipes for blancmange. In rice-growing areas of America, colonists substituted rice for other grains used in these recipes. Many sweet rice dishes died out in the twentieth century, with the exception of rice pudding, which remains a favorite.

Andrew F. Smith

Rice Cookers

Toshiba of Japan claims to have released the first electric rice cooker in 1955, but Japan's Ministry of Trade and Technology asserts that the devices first emerged in 1946, around the same time as the Japanese constitution. The earliest automatic rice cookers bear a resemblance to slow cookers used for stewing, with an electric element in a cylindrical base applying heat to a removable cooking vessel. A thermostat triggers a power shutoff when the vessel temperature exceeds the boiling point of water, ensuring that the cooked rice does not scorch. Before the introduction of electric cookers, steamed rice, which requires slow cooking under a tight-fitting lid, was generally made in pots designed for the purpose, heated over fire. Photographic records exist of large, lidded, iron "rice cookers" found by U.S. troops on the Marshall Islands at the end of World War II; they had been used as defensive shields by the Japanese.

America's adoption of the electric devices, which have a 90 percent market penetration in urban China and are ubiquitous in Japan, came with the rising popularity of Asian foods like sushi (Japanese vinegared short-grain rice, usually served with raw fish known as sashimi) in the late twentieth century. The advantage over conventional rice cookery methods in commercial sushi preparation is gained through keeping the rice warm, important to the formation of the traditional sushi shapes. Technological improvements in rice cookers, such as nonstick linings, computerized timing and temperature control, and childproof safety features, have made the devices more versatile, allowing for preparation of complex dishes like paella and vindaloo with little or no attention from start to finish.

[**See also** Japanese American Food; Rice; Slow Cookers.]

JAY WEINSTEIN

Richards, Ellen Swallow

Ellen Henrietta Swallow Richards (1842–1911), American chemist, educator, and first president of the American Home Economics Association, was born in Dunstable, Massachusetts. She graduated from Vassar in 1870 and that year was the first woman to be admitted to the Massachusetts Institute of Technology (MIT), as "a special student" pursuing an advanced degree in chemistry. In 1876, with the help of the Boston Women's Education Association, she was instrumental in organizing the Woman's Laboratory at MIT to offer scientific education for women. She served as an instructor in sanitary chemistry at the laboratory, and her first book, *The Chemistry of Cooking and Cleaning*, was published during this period. In 1884, when women were first admitted to the university as regular students, Richards became a member of the MIT faculty, a position she held until her death in 1911.

Richards devoted her life to helping women gain access to scientific education and to the field of chemistry at a time when it was closed to them. By focusing scientific principles on roles that women already filled, she was able to ease the entry of women into applied chemistry laboratories and academic departments in the sciences. She felt that the scientific theories that revolutionized late-eighteenth-century and early nineteenth-century industry could improve the health, happiness, and productivity of the American family if women had access to that information and applied it to their work in the home. With the help of several wealthy Bostonians, Richards founded the New England Kitchen, a cooking laboratory in which recipes for basic New England foods were scientifically formulated and distributed to neighborhood people when they came to purchase the nourishing, low-cost foods that were produced there. A second center was established in Boston and one in New York, but the experiment failed to attract and reeducate the immigrant homemakers of the two cities.

In 1899 Richards organized the first Lake Placid Conference for people working in the field of home science. The group included educators in chemistry, biology, physics, bacteriology, economics, sanitary science, hygiene, domestic science, and the emerging fields of psychology and sociology. The conferences continued to be held annually in Lake Placid, and in 1903, at a joint session with the National Education Association's manual training session, the group developed a four-year college curriculum in home economics. At the 1908 meeting the Lake Placid Conference became the American Home Economics Association with Richards as president, a position she held until 1910.

Near the end of her career Richards became interested in the new field of nutrition and wrote some of the first government pamphlets on the subject. She also fostered euthenics, the science of controlled environment, a discipline that dealt with the development of human well-being by the improvement of living conditions. A supporter of the Muckrakers and their campaign to clean up the American food supply, Richards had her students analyze foods for safety and advocated that they do similar tests in their own homes. The theories that she formulated throughout her life came together in the writing of *Euthenics* (1910) and *Conservation by Sanitation* (1911).

[**See also** Food and Nutrition Systems; Home Economics; Nutrition.]

BIBLIOGRAPHY

Shapiro, Laura. *Perfection Salad: Women and Cooking at the Turn of the Century.* New York: Holt, 1986.

Vare, Ethlie A. *Adventurous Spirit: A Story about Ellen Swallow Richards.* Minneapolis, MN: Lerner, 1992.

JOANNE LAMB HAYES

Roadhouses

The roadhouse, as it is popularly conceived in B movies and country ballads, is a rustic saloon where trouble eternally brews. Whether it is a honky-tonk with sawdust on the floor, a seedy neighborhood dive, or even a brothel and whether the colorful characters within are cowboys, showgirls, or Hells Angels, one thing is certain: the roadhouse is a transgressive space—quite literally in that such establishments are often found on the lawless outskirts of town. Technically, however, the term "roadhouse" is rather more prosaic, referring simply to an establishment located on the side of the road to provide some combination of refreshment, lodging, and entertainment; in that sense, it may apply equally well to a colonial tavern, gold rush–era boardinghouse, touristy clam shack, or desolate motel café.

Roadhouses before the Age of Automobiles

The tavern is the clear forerunner of the roadhouse, complete with generally unsavory reputation—although its legality as such, far from being questionable, was actually guaranteed in the seventeenth and eighteenth centuries by ordinances binding many a community to the upkeep of some form of public accommodation. It often served many other municipal functions as well, from post office to meetinghouse. Essentially, though, it was an alehouse; patrons intending to dine as well as drink had better be prepared to do so as, when, where, and if the proprietor saw fit, for the restaurant would not come fully into its own until the dawn of the nineteenth century. Flexible hours, waitstaff, menus, and room service in these times were still amenities of the future.

More clearly influential than the coming of the restaurant upon the modern roadhouse was that of rail (and, later, auto) transport; the railroads supplied at once the impetus, the site, and even the model—two in fact—for its evolution. Depots, after all, were surfacing in the middle of nowhere, with eating places springing up of necessity right alongside them; these soon developed personalities of their own. For instance, there was the Harvey House, a late-nineteenth- to mid-twentieth-century chain of in-station eateries conceived by Fred Harvey to make traveling more palatable through the employment of well-trained chefs, tasteful decor, and comely waitresses known as Harvey Girls. Then there was the dining car of the train itself; the very symbol of luxury for its time, it became in turn the inspiration for the kitschy diner, which in its rural rather than urban form is one of the main types of roadhouse today.

Roadhouses after the Advent of Automobiles

Connoting a casual atmosphere and down-home fare, the word "diner" may apply to a variety of roadside venues, many of them veritable warehouses of pop-culture icons, from chrome to Formica, neon jukebox to wise-cracking waitress with beehive hairdo, bottomless cup of joe to mile-high slice of pie. As the twentieth century picked up speed and automobiles progressed from rich man's novelty to everyman's exigency, as highways were constructed and the American way of life became synonymous with mobility, so eateries began to dominate the scenery. At their most basic, they were simply stands or shacks selling a limited number of snacks, such as hamburgers or hot dogs—memorable, especially in the period before World War II, not for their food but for their fanciful architecture, sometimes resembling the very items they served, such as giant coffeepots or cups, frankfurters, and ice cream cones.

More permanent structures, featuring full-service dining—diners in fact—began appearing too. Truck stops in their mid-century heyday were considered oases of respectable, if meat-heavy, cookery for respectable, if meat-heavy, truckers. The roadhouse in all its forms, like the tavern before it, has been largely the domain of men, just as the travel opportunities that occasioned it were granted primarily to men. Wives and children may sometimes have come along, but they would never, barring unusual circumstances, have set foot on such premises alone. (The exception to this rule was the tearoom of the 1920s, which emerged as a safe country haven precisely for the gentlewoman traveler.) The surprisingly decent truck stop of old has long since made way for the anonymous, corporate-run service plaza.

Coffee shops, whether freestanding or set on the grounds of motor inns or motels, are another manifest roadside destination. From this category have emerged some particularly successful chains, such as Howard Johnson, or "Ho-Jo," which spread westward from Massachusetts beginning in the 1930s, making its mark with bright-orange roofs, and Denny's, a round-the-clock operation that extended eastward from California beginning in the 1950s. Appealing above all to the virtue of consistency, the menus of such places are generally of a piece: all-day breakfasts feature eggs, bacon, sausage, pancakes, home fries, and hash brown potatoes; lunch items include soups, salads, and sandwiches; and dinner, almost without exception, is a meat-and-potatoes affair.

Of course for all their notorious homogeneity, even these roadside eateries have been out-systemized, not to mention outnumbered, by fast food franchises. Convenience (even to the point of kitchen mechanization), on the one hand, and familiarity (even to the point of monotony), on the other, are the factors most commonly cited to explain the industry's dominance over all other types of road-accessible venues. In response, however, many an American gastronome has made a point of celebrating, or at least commemorating, the roadhouse in print. In books like *Roadfood and Goodfood*

and *A Taste of America*, for instance, Jane and Michael Stern have chronicled their years of experience on the nation's byways and back roads, engaged in a never-ending search for the consummate slice of meat loaf or flawless buffalo wing—the very stuff of roadhouse cuisine (along with beer). The last decades of the twentieth century also gave rise to countless books devoted to roadside architecture, some purely picture books and others scholarly forays into art history and sociology. The American roadhouse may have nothing on, say, the Roman Colosseum, but those judging by the enthusiasm for the literature on the topic would never be the wiser.

[See also BOARDINGHOUSES; DINERS; FAST FOOD; HARVEY, FRED; HOWARD JOHNSON; ROADSIDE FOOD; SALOONS; TAVERNS.]

BIBLIOGRAPHY

Jakle, John A., and Keith A. Sculle. *Fast Food: Restaurants in the Automobile Age*. Baltimore: Johns Hopkins University Press, 1999.

Mariani, John. *America Eats Out: An Illustrated History of Restaurants, Taverns, Coffee Shops, Speakeasies, and Other Establishments That Have Fed Us for 350 Years.* New York: HarperCollins, 1991.

Pillsbury, Richard. *From Boarding House to Bistro: The American Restaurant Then and Now*. Boston: Routledge, 1990.

Salinger, Sharon V. *Taverns and Drinking in Early America*. Baltimore: Johns Hopkins University Press, 2002.

Stern, Jane, and Michael Stern. *American Gourmet*. New York: HarperCollins, 1991.

RUTH TOBIAS

Roadside Food

Roadside food developed in response to the fast-growing American market of hungry travelers. Unlike its culinary cousin known as "fast food," roadside food typically involves a measure of hands-on craftsmanship in its preparation and presentation; though it is still rather fast, the cuisine also requires a modicum of patience from the customer. Fast food, as the saying goes, "waits for you."

America's ability to produce almost anything on an assembly line served it well in the development and adoption of fast food as the unofficial national cuisine. The country's vast expanse cultivated an obsession with travel, facilitated first by the railroads and then by the automobile. Eating habits would necessarily have to conform to this quicker pace of life, now precisely measured by mechanical clocks rather than the sun's passage. Industrialization provided the necessary improvements in food transport, packaging, and storage that would become an absolute requirement for any successful food service operation.

America's roadside food owes much of its existence to the efforts of Fred Harvey, an English-born restaurateur credited with establishing the first chain restaurant. His

Harvey Houses greeted railroad passengers traveling through America's Southwest. Harvey's ability to serve hot meals fast in familiar and friendly surroundings made his concept a hit with the itinerant public, who had to adhere to the strict railroad timetables. Harvey enhanced the experience by hiring young, attractive, and wholesome women as servers. The "Harvey Girls" became as much a trademark of the operation as any special on the menu.

As railroad dining became a popular component of rail travel, the design of the railcar kitchens in such cramped quarters would soon play a role on the roadsides as well. The railroads' ability to cook hot meals efficiently for its passengers bode well for the hurried pace of passing motorists. The roadside diner car not only mimicked the style of its railroad counterpart but also shared much of its functional efficiency.

The spread and improvement of the national road network that began in the 1920s inspired thousands of enterprising individuals to set up some of the earliest roadside businesses designed specifically for the automobile trade. In the early years of this trend, spaces between major cities consisted primarily of farms. Resident farmers were the first to seize upon this opportunity to profit from hungry motorists. Already possessing the necessary raw materials—property, beef, pork, and dairy—farmers could easily diversify into this new business, adding a new source of revenue. These early attempts at serving food at the roadside adhered to local culinary traditions, adapted to the quicker pace of this new mobile market.

At about the same time the White Castle and White Tower restaurant chains opened their first outlets in midwestern cities. Their distinctive buildings clad in white porcelain enamel were designed to counter the negative image of roadside stands as unhealthy greasy spoons, an appellation that many places probably deserved. The chains also capitalized on the rapidly developing efficiency of the meatpacking industry. Able to serve hamburgers at a price of only five cents each, these chains and others promoted their purchase "by the bag."

Though enormously popular in its own right, the ubiquitous hot dog resisted a national restaurant standard and therefore a national chain specializing in them. Easy to prepare and eat, though ever mysterious in its ingredients, the hot dog has become an iconic American meal. While a hamburger has few varieties, hot dogs acquired many regional identities, methods of preparation, and corresponding monikers, such as Coneys, franks, wieners, hots, pups, and tube steaks.

Other popular roadside food alternatives vary in availability. In the Northeast the proximity of the fishing industry means a broader availability of seafood, usually deep-fried, while fried chicken and barbecue stands have greeted motorists in the South. Barbecue's labor-intensive preparation makes it ill suited for chain restaurants but provides one of the most savory roadside experiences. Barbecue comes in three general regional styles, known as Southern, Kansas City, and Texas, which are distinguished by the use of rubs, sauces, and cooking methods. The Pig Stand in Texas became one of the nation's first drive-in restaurants in the 1920s.

By the 1930s the symbiosis of architecture and advertising hit its stride. Roadside restaurant owners built highly distinctive structures to lure passing motorists, often in the image of their signature product or their name. The Pig Stand venues looked like giant pigs, while an ice cream stand might take the shape of a giant cone. Operators distracted travelers still more with bright neon signs standing sentry over buildings covered with the restaurant's menu. Often-outlandish architectural gimmickry abounded as the owners strove to outdo their competition.

Following the typical American economic business model, the roadside stand spread quickly across the landscape in its early years. The low barrier of entry attracted anyone with cooking abilities willing to work hard. Those staking out the better locations and having savvier marketing and management abilities trumped the competition. Consolidation of the industry followed as people like Howard Johnson perfected the family restaurant concept and its duplication. Other founders of the industry, such as Colonel Harlan Sanders (Kentucky Fried Chicken) and Ray Kroc (McDonald's) famously followed. By the 1950s the industry would set and maintain a standard for family-friendly dining: clean, consistent, inexpensive, and homey.

In terms of dollars, the hamburger chain rules American roadside dining. McDonald's became the world's largest restaurant chain by selling billions of them, and its market dominance has dictated the structure of the entire American food-processing industry, particularly those sectors that supply beef, potatoes, and chicken. Its practice of marketing heavily to children, acknowledged as the real decision makers for family dining, has also skewed American eating habits toward a preference for faster, easy-to-serve finger foods.

By the early 2000s American roadside food had lost little of its actual variety though much of its ubiquity. Local variations of roadside food have become much harder to find thanks to extremely relentless competition and stricter government regulations. Yet the cuisine still thrives in more remote locations or where operators have upheld high standards of quality and value.

[**See also** BARBECUE; DINERS; DRIVE-INS; FAST FOOD; HARVEY, FRED; HOT DOGS; HOWARD JOHNSON; KENTUCKY FRIED CHICKEN; MCDONALD'S; ROADHOUSES; SANDERS, COLONEL; WHITE CASTLE.]

BIBLIOGRAPHY

Anderson, Will. *Where Have You Gone, Starlite Café? America's Golden Era Roadside Restaurants.* Portland, ME: Anderson, 1998.

Gutman, Richard J. S. *American Diner: Then and Now.* 2nd ed. Baltimore: Johns Hopkins University Press, 2000.

Pillsbury, Richard. *From Boarding House to Bistro: The American Restaurant Then and Now.* Boston: Unwin Hyman, 1990.

RANDY GARBIN

Roasters, Coffee, see *Coffee Makers, Roasters, and Mills*

Robert Mondavi Co.

In 1966, one year after he left Charles Krug Winery, his family's business, Robert Mondavi founded his eponymous company on the Oakville Highway in the Napa Valley of California. The Charles Krug Winery had been purchased by his father, Cesare, in 1943, and Robert was associated with it until his brother Peter, having a different vision for its future, removed him from active participation. The result of this was lengthy litigation finally awarding compensation to Robert Mondavi, after which he decided to form his own winery. His company became known for its research and production of wines based on European grapes, notably, Cabernet Sauvignon. It also was one of the first California producers to recognize the importance of wood and conducted many experiments on the variations of barrel size, manufacture, and wood type on its wines.

In 1979 the company formed a partnership with Philippe de Rothschild to produce a wine in the Napa Valley; the success of that wine, Opus One, is now legendary. This success came despite the fact that Mondavi, in a break with the tradition of using estate-grown grapes for ultra-premium wines, used sourced grapes to produce their wine. The company built its own winery at a cost of $17 million in 1992. Since 1992 all grapes used to make Opus One have been estate-grown from Opus-designated vineyards. This strategic partnership set the stage for other international alliances with prestige producers around the globe—notably, with the Frecobaldi family in Italy to produce the Super-Tuscan Luce and with the Chadwick family in Chile to produce Sena, one of South America's most expensive wines. While these partnerships gave the winery more prestige, it was the lower-end wines, particularly those of the Woodbridge label, that were the financial workhorses providing the most revenue and profit in the last decade of the twentieth century.

In 1993 the Robert Mondavi Company was producing about 500,000 cases of wine in the Napa Valley. Mondavi's substantial landholdings there were estimated at 1,500 acres, and the winery also acquired the Byron and Vichon properties in the Santa Maria Valley of California and in the Langue-doc region of France, respectively. Nonetheless, the company was struggling with a massive debt load, and in 1993 Mondavi went public, selling stock at $13.50 per share; this offering raised $70 million for 28 percent of the company. Little changed in management, however; Robert Mondavi remained as chairman, and his two sons shared the responsibilities of chief executive officer. But the offering gave the public a rare look into the books of a prestige producer, and many were surprised that the aforementioned Woodbridge line accounted for 85 percent of sales and 65 percent of net revenues. Since then the winery, while reaping substantial publicity for its luxury wines, has expanded its relationship with the Chadwick family of Chile to include inexpensive wines marketed under the Caliterra label (in addition to the premium Sena, mentioned above). Mondavi also discontinued the Vichon Napa line in favor of operating as a negocient (or middleman) in France's Languedoc region, where in 1995 the company began buying bulk "unfinished" wine that had matured to a certain point and finishing the maturation process in California. It later arranged to produce the wine entirely in France and purchased its own vineyards for a percentage of the label's wines. The company also created the La Familiglia line of Italian varietals and began to make "district" wines under the Robert Mondavi label.

The Robert Mondavi Company continues to innovate and was among the first in America to use a capsule-less bottle design and synthetic stoppers for some of its labels. Unlike its neighbor in California's Central Valley, the privately held and secretive Gallo wine empire, the Mondavi clan has risked its future on public markets, global ventures, and strategic partnerships. Whatever the future may bring, Mondavi is an American success story that has had an effect on the global wine industry through its innovations and quality wine making and marketing.

[**See also** GALLO, ERNEST AND JULIO; MONDAVI, ROBERT; WINE: CALIFORNIA WINES; WINE BARRELS; WINE BOTTLES; WINE CASKS.]

STEVE CRAIG

Rolling Pins, see *Pies and Tarts*

Rombauer, Irma

Irma von Starkloff Rombauer (1877–1962), a leading twentieth-century American cookbook author, was born in St. Louis, Missouri, during the city's nineteenth-century economic and cultural heyday. Rombauer belonged to prominent German American social circles and until middle age had only the knowledge of food to be expected of a sophisticated, well-traveled hostess and club woman. When she was widowed in 1930, she decided to support herself by writing a cookbook. *The Joy of Cooking*, published at her own expense in 1931, was initially a modest, fairly conventional recipe collection with assorted contributions from family and friends, but she shortly began planning an expanded version.

Rombauer was able to interest the Bobbs-Merrill Company of Indianapolis and New York in her idea, which featured a recipe-writing format of her own devising, with ingredients introduced in the order of their use rather than as an initial list. The first Bobbs-Merrill edition appeared in 1936. Both Rombauer and the publishers (though they soon fell to quarreling) thought that it might eventually challenge the established kitchen manuals of the day, *The Boston Cooking-School Cook Book* and *The Settlement Cook Book*. Like the first version, it presented a miscellaneous array of recipes (standard American dishes like baked beans and corned beef, German Christmas cookies, and many shortcut canned-soup dishes and gelatin salads). It was, however, about twice as long, with more about cooking basics (for example, making soup stocks and working with yeast dough) and new kitchen appliances, such as electric mixers. Rombauer also differentiated her work from others by stressing an informal, chatty personal tone—present but less conspicuous in the first edition—that was at the time unorthodox in a cookbook.

The first commercial *Joy of Cooking* was moderately successful, but the book did not become a best seller until 1943, when Rombauer revised it to incorporate the contents of her shorter 1939 work *Streamlined Cooking* (a collection of hurry-up recipes mostly based on canned and preprocessed foods) and a small selection of recipes meant to help cooks cope with World War II meat and sugar rationing. The resulting version cemented her national reputation and made her highly individual "voice" known to a wide and demographically diverse audience, including people who ordinarily detested cooking and cookbooks but gained confidence through her breezy encouragement.

By the time of this success Rombauer was in her mid-sixties. It was clear that a serious updating of *The Joy of Cooking*, possibly requiring the contributions of a younger cook, would eventually be needed in order to address rapid changes on the food scene—for example, new appliances such as home freezers, new fashions like Swiss-style fondue and chilled cream soups, and postwar economic adjustments like meat-price inflation. A stopgap revision appeared in 1946, with the wartime-rationing material replaced by a section of one-bowl cakes but little other change; in the same year Rombauer published her fairly successful *A Cookbook for Girls and Boys*.

In the late 1940s Rombauer invited her daughter Marion Rombauer Becker (1903–1976) to work with her on the next revision. The Cincinnati-based Becker had been involved with the production of the 1931 version and was familiar with *Joy* as it had developed. Her participation caused some

adjustment of priorities, beginning with the far-reaching revision that appeared in 1951. Reflecting Becker's bent for serious instruction and interest in nutrition and "natural" foods, the new edition somewhat downplayed the earlier emphasis on shortcuts and prepackaged foods; included such new material as meats "roasted" in foil, aspic base made "from scratch," and whole-grain breads (with expanded information on flours); and sought to bolster coverage of weak areas, such as fish.

After 1955 illness prevented Rombauer from further work on the book. Her daughter (assisted by her husband, John W. Becker) prepared two large, ambitious revisions that would long earn *Joy* the reputation of an inexhaustible reference work equally suited to state-of-the-art kitchens and desert islands. The first of these appeared in a garbled version in 1962 (during a battle with the publishers) and in corrected form in 1963. It sought to preserve the lively, personal Rombauer voice while trimming many old convenience-food recipes, broadening the international range of coverage, and greatly increasing the amount of space given to information about ingredients and cooking processes. In 1966 Becker published a small limited-edition history of *Joy* titled *Little Acorn*; in 1975 she completed her last and most ambitious edition of *Joy*. For at least a generation Becker's two revisions of her mother's cookbook would be the best general source of knowledge about many culinary matters, including unusual herbs and formerly exotic fruits and vegetables.

Becker was succeeded as author by her son Ethan Becker. After some years of uncertainty during the publishing mergers and acquisitions of the 1980 and 1990s, a new publisher, Scribner, issued a dramatically transformed version in 1997. Prepared by a large stable of contributors under the direction of the well-known editor Maria Guarnaschelli, it replaced nearly all of the earlier contents with an up-to-date, eclectic mix of recipes. Guarnaschelli also oversaw a 1998 reprint of the original 1931 edition.

In Rombauer's and, to a certain extent, Becker's lifetimes, *The Joy of Cooking* was exceptional among American cookbooks as a midwestern rather than an East Coast production, as the work of culinary amateurs rather than professional recipe developers, and as a family affair. Its example probably encouraged other cookbook writers to cultivate a certain conversational stance marked by informal asides and anecdotes, but no one (not even her daughter) has managed to duplicate Rombauer's idiosyncratic appeal. The first success of her book had little to do with directing American taste in any particular culinary path. Rombauer's achievement was rather to spontaneously embody or bring to life the state of mid twentieth-century American taste—in all its extremes and inconsistencies—across many

social and culinary fault lines, without lapsing into mere shapelessness. Under Becker the book retained a modicum of its irreverent, inclusive, person-to-person quality while at the same time replicating many aims of the sober early twentieth-century kitchen bibles, to which, ironically, Rombauer's first efforts had been at least partly meant as an antidote.

[**See also** Boston Cooking School; Cooking Techniques; Recipes.]

BIBLIOGRAPHY

Becker, Marion Rombauer. *Little Acorn: The Story behind "The Joy of Cooking," 1931–1966.* Indianapolis, IN, and New York: Bobbs-Merrill, 1966. Reissued as *Little Acorn: Joy of Cooking; The First Fifty Years, 1931–1981* in 1981.

Mendelson, Anne. *Stand Facing the Stove: The Story of the Women Who Gave America "The Joy of Cooking."* New York: Scribner, 2003.

ANNE MANDELSON

Ronald McDonald

In 1960 the McDonald's franchise in Washington, D.C., decided to sponsor a local children's television program called *Bozo's Circus*. Bozo was played by Willard Scott, who later gained fame as a television meteorologist and writer. Scott subsequently was asked to play Bozo at the grand opening of another McDonald's outlet in the area. Sales in Washington grew by a whopping 30 percent per year during the next four years. In 1963 the television station decided to drop *Bozo's Circus*, which lagged in the ratings. The local McDonald's franchise chose to produce their own television commercials starring another clown. Previously McDonald's franchisees had not independently developed television commercials. The owners of this establishment wondered what to name the clown, and an advertising agency proposed "Archie McDonald," which offered an allusion to McDonald's golden arches symbol. But there was a sportscaster in the Washington area named Arch McDonald, so another name had to be found. Using a simple rhyme, Willard Scott came up with the name Ronald McDonald. Scott played Ronald McDonald in the first television commercials, which were broadcast in October 1963.

The national McDonald's Corporation decided to sponsor the broadcast of the Macy's Thanksgiving Day Parade in 1965. They chose to feature Ronald McDonald, but they replaced Willard Scott with Coco, a Hungarian-speaking clown from the Barnum and Bailey Circus. Until then no fast food chain had advertised on national television; it was considered a risk, especially in autumn, since major sales were achieved largely in summertime. Likewise Ronald McDonald appealed to children, who were not thought to be an important target of fast food promoters at the time. Nonetheless, the Thanksgiving Day advertisement produced immediate nationwide results, which persuaded McDonald's to expend more funds to target children, thus giving McDonald's an edge in the children's market.

Ronald McDonald became McDonald's official spokesman in 1966. He also became the centerpiece of numerous other advertising activities: his image appeared on television commercials and a vast array of products, including book covers, coloring books, comic books, cups, dolls, masks, Frisbees, games, calendars, mugs, napkins, postcards, puppets, records, toy parachutes, trains and trucks, and the famous "Flying Hamburger," a cartoon McDonald's hamburger with wings.

In addition McDonald's Playlands, children's recreational spaces designed as part of the restaurant, featured Ronald McDonald and a cast of other fictional characters. While none of the other "McDonaldland" characters achieved the prominence of Ronald McDonald, the Playlands strengthened McDonald's dominance in the children's fast food market. When McDonald's signed a contract to open three hundred outlets at military bases, Ronald McDonald posed for pictures in front of an aircraft carrier. The first Ronald McDonald House, a residence located adjacent to a hospital to provide free or low-cost room and board for families with children requiring extended hospital care, was set up in Philadelphia in 1974. Since then two hundred more have been constructed in the United States and eleven in other countries. All are sponsored by local McDonald's operations. Ten years later Ronald McDonald's Children Charities was founded in honor of Ray Kroc, the man who started McDonald's. It is still one of the largest organizations financially devoted to the welfare of children. In 1997 McDonald's published a book "authored" by Ronald McDonald, *The Complete Hamburger: The History of America's Favorite Sandwich.*

As McDonald's expanded to other countries, so did Ronald McDonald. In some countries adjustments were necessary. In Japan, for instance, the name was changed to Donald McDonald owing to the difficulty the Japanese had in pronouncing the "r" in Ronald. By the early 2000s Ronald McDonald was among the most popular children's characters in the world. Ninety-six percent of American children recognize Ronald McDonald, about the same percentage of children who recognize Santa Claus.

[See also ADVERTISING; MCDONALD'S.]

BIBLIOGRAPHY

Losonsky, Terry, and Joyce Losonsky. *McDonald's Happy Meal Toys around the World.* Atglen, PA: Schiffer, 1995.

Losonsky, Joyce, and Terry Losonsky. *McDonald's Pre–Happy Meal Toys from the Fifties, Sixties, and Seventies.* Atglen, PA: Schiffer, 1998.

Love, John F. *McDonald's behind the Arches.* Rev. ed. New York: Bantam, 1995.

ANDREW. F. SMITH

Root Beer

Now a sweet soft drink flavored with a mixture of herbal essences, root beer was originally a real beer and a tonic health drink. Small beers, or low-alcohol beers carbonated by the action of yeasts, had been traditional and nutritious drinks for children, women, and old people in England and Europe for centuries. Although many of these small beers were flavored with ginger or lemon, another common flavoring and one popular for its antiscurvy properties was that of the bark of spruce or birch trees. When colonists arrived in North America, they found new varieties of the traditional spruce and birch for their beers but discovered Native Americans using such novel flavorings as the roots of sarsaparilla (*Smilax ornata*) and sassafras (*Sassafras albidum*) as well. Both of these were similar to spruce and birch in taste, and the colonists soon learned to use them in their small beer, often with molasses as a sweetener and fermenting agent.

Exactly when sweetened small beer made with various roots was first called "root beer" is unknown. One of the earliest mentions is in *Dr. Chase's Recipes* from 1869. The doctor's typical recipe calls for the roots of burdock, yellow dock, sarsaparilla, dandelion, and spikenard along with the oils of spruce and sassafras and says that "families ought to make it every Spring, and drink freely of it for several weeks, and thereby save, perhaps, several dollars in doctors' bills."

In 1876 Charles E. Hires, who claimed to have invented root beer, began marketing packets of the herbal ingredients necessary to make "the Greatest Health-Giving Beverage in the World" at the Centennial Exposition in Philadelphia. This kit for making root beer was supposed to contain sixteen roots, herbs, barks, and berries, including sassafras, the dominant flavoring, and required home fermentation with yeast. In 1884 Hires decided consumers would be more interested in an easier-to-use product and began selling a liquid concentrate and soda fountain syrup as well as bottled root beer. By 1892 he was selling 3 million bottles a year. His success, along with the growing temperance movement, brought many others into the marketplace, including Barq's in 1898, A&W in 1922, and Dad's in 1937. The author Tom Morrison has documented over 831 brands since Hires's modest beginnings in 1876. Yet as popular as root beer has always been, it accounts for less than 3 percent of the total American soft-drink market.

The root beer industry was considerably shaken in 1960, when the key flavor component in sassafras, safrole, was found to be carcinogenic and banned by the FDA. Although sassafras treated to remove the toxic safrole is available, most bottlers have substituted other ingredients, such as anise, wintergreen, lemon and orange oils, cloves, molasses, and vanilla, which gives root beer its creamy taste.

Hires Root Beer

A Philadelphia pharmacist, Charles E. Hires, was on his honeymoon in New Jersey in 1875 when he found a recipe for "herb tea" that reportedly contained at least eight different ingredients. When he returned to Philadelphia, he began to experiment with the formula and finally produced Hires' Rootbeer Household Extract, to be used for making root beer at home. The new product was exhibited at the Centennial Exposition in Philadelphia in 1876.

Hires's root beer, being nonalcoholic, was promoted as a health beverage. Advertising for the new product encouraged coal miners to switch from hard drinks to his root beer, which was advertised as "the National Temperance" drink and "the Greatest Health-Giving Beverage in the World."

In 1884 advertisements for Hires's root beer appeared in *Harper's Weekly* and *Harper's Monthly Magazine.* Two years later Hires began selling bottled root beer, but the company continued to encourage home brewing of Hires's extract until 1983. By the early 1890s over 3 million packages were sold annually, in addition to 3 million bottles of ready-made root beer. In 1936 Hires's operations expanded; branch plants were established in several cities.

In 1962 Crush International acquired Charles E. Hires Co. In 1980 Crush International, along with Hires Root Beer, was sold to Procter and Gamble, who sold it in 1989 to Cadbury Schweppes Americas Beverages (CSAB), a subsidiary division of Cadbury Schweppes. Hires Root Beer, along with Vernor's Ginger Ale, are considered the oldest continuously marketed soft drinks in the United States.

BIBLIOGRAPHY

Enkema, L. A. *Root Beer: How It Got Its Name, What It Is, How It Developed from a Home-Brewed Beverage to Its Present Day Popularity.* Indianapolis, IN: Hurty-Peck, 1952.

Morrison, Tom. *Root Beer Advertising: A Collector's Guide.* Colorado Springs, CO: Morrison, 1990.

Yates, Donald, and Elizabeth Yates, eds. *American Stone Ginger Beer and Root Beer Heritage, 1790 to 1920.* Homerville, OH: Donald Yates, 2003.

ANDREW F. SMITH

Old-fashioned-style root beer was coming back into popularity at the beginning of the twenty-first century, and the number of small, local brewers had increased dramatically. Home brewing of root beer was again becoming fashionable as well. At a 1998 taste test sponsored by the *Chicago Tribune*, fifty different root beers were evaluated, nowhere near a complete sampling of the many root beers on the market.

[**See also** Birch Beer; Brewing; Homemade Remedies; Sarsaparilla; Sassafrasses; Soda Drinks; Soda Fountains; Temperance.]

BIBLIOGRAPHY

Brown, John Hull. *Early American Beverages*. New York: Bonanza Books, 1966.

Morrison, Tom. *Root Beer: Advertising and Collectibles*. West Chester, PA: Schiffer, 1992.

SYLVIA LOVEGREN

Rorer, Sarah Tyson

Sarah Tyson Heston Rorer (1849–1937) was a nineteenth-century American culinary superstar—a nationally recognized, respected, and beloved source of kitchen expertise who made her mark well before the advent of mass communication media. Rorer was born in Richboro, Pennsylvania. As a young wife she countered suburban boredom by attending lectures at the Woman's Medical College of Pennsylvania. Rorer considered becoming a pharmacist or a physician but instead became the first American dietician.

In 1879 Rorer began attending cooking classes at the New Century Club, a women's club founded in 1877 in Philadelphia. Rorer devoted herself to the classes, becoming the star pupil. When the instructor resigned, Rorer took over teaching duties, which included lecturing at the Woman's Medical College. Apprehensive about her qualifications, Rorer devoured nutrition texts and became convinced of the importance of diet in health and disease. Rorer also continued to attend lectures in chemistry, physiology, anatomy, and hygiene.

Rorer's lessons were well received, and over the years she taught a wide range of students: finishing-school girls, residents of a home for wayward children, physicians from prestigious Philadelphia hospitals, professional cooks, society matrons (who were required to do the post-lesson cleanup themselves), and at a city mission, poor immigrant women—who broadened her palate when they taught her to love garlic.

In 1883 Rorer opened the Philadelphia Cooking School, which operated until 1903. Her husband, an unambitious bookkeeper, came to work for her, and before long Rorer was the sole support of her family—a situation almost unheard-of among women of her class at the time. Rorer's lecture-demonstrations attracted audiences of up to five thousand, and Rorer put her recipes and theories in print in 1886 in *Mrs. Rorer's Philadelphia Cook Book*. Between its waterproof and greaseproof covers lay prescient admonitions: "Green

vegetables should be freshly gathered, washed well in cold water, and cooked in freshly-boiled water until tender, *no longer*." "Macaroni... is the bread of the Italian laborer. In this country, it is a sort of luxury among the upper classes; but there is no good reason... why it should not enter more extensively into the food of our working classes."

Also in 1886 Rorer began conducting a question-and-answer column in *Table Talk*, a culinary magazine. Soon she was writing five features, including one on "dietetics." Eight years later, along with two doctors interested in food chemistry and dietetics, Rorer founded *Household News*, which featured articles on pure food, healthy diet, and household sanitation. In its pages Rorer continued (as she had in *Table Talk*) to endorse commercial products ranging from shredded wheat, coffee, and cheese to waffle irons and meat choppers. In

1896 *Household News* folded, and Rorer became domestic science editor of the *Ladies' Home Journal*, a post she held through October 1911.

For a series of pure food expositions held in Philadelphia beginning in 1889, Rorer gave wildly popular cooking demonstrations. Impeccably dressed in silk and lace (to show how mess-free cooking could be) Rorer extolled the virtues of plain, as opposed to "fancy," food, daily eating of salads, and well-made bread and condemned—even as she prepared them—puddings, pies, and candies. At the World's Columbian Exposition in Chicago in 1893, Rorer presided over the "corn kitchen," where myriad manners of cooking corn were demonstrated six days a week.

Rorer wrote more than fifty books and booklets, including promotional publications for, among others, Cottolene shortening, Wesson oil, Cream of Maize cereal,

"There is nothing in a cake to give you brain and muscle unless you get the latter from beating the cake," proclaimed Sarah Rorer, widely recognized as the first American dietician.

Tabasco sauce, Cleveland baking powder, and the Enterprise meat chopper. Among her books are *Mrs. Rorer's New Cook Book* (1902); *Bread and Bread-Making; Home Candy Making; Hot Weather Dishes; How to Use a Chafing Dish; Ice Creams, Water Ices, Frozen Puddings; Made Over Dishes; Sandwiches; Salads; New Ways for Oysters;* and the temptingly titled *Dainties.*

[**See also** ADVERTISING COOKBOOKLETS AND RECIPES; COOKBOOKS AND MANUSCRIPTS: FROM THE CIVIL WAR TO WORLD WAR I; COOKING SCHOOLS: NINETEENTH CENTURY.]

BIBLIOGRAPHY

Rorer, S. T. *Mrs. Rorer's Philadelphia Cook Book.* Philadelphia: Arnold, 1886.

Weigley, Emma Seifrit. *Sarah Tyson Rorer: The Nation's Instructress in Dietetics and Cookery.* Philadelphia: American Philosophical Society, 1977.

BONNIE J. SLOTNICK

Rose Water

Introduced to Europe from Arab cuisine by the Crusaders in such dishes as marzipan and Turkish delight, rose water is the distillate of rose petals, most famously from the damask rose. Substitutes for the distillate have been made by adding attar of rose, which is the oil extracted from crushed roses, to water.

Colonial Americans used rose water as a flavoring, similar in purpose to the later-introduced vanilla, in confectionery and dessert recipes inherited from Europe and in syrups used to flavor beverages. Rose water also flavored savories, such as chicken pies and creamed spinach. Some housewives, even as late as the 1880s, distilled their own. Others purchased it, perhaps as "Double Distilled Damask Rose Water" from the Shakers, a religious sect respected for the quality and purity of their products and for their rose water apple pie.

Twenty-first century use is most common in the cuisines of Middle Eastern, Indian, or Sephardic heritage, flavoring desserts and drinks, such as baklava, sorbets, and *lassi.* Rose water is sometimes used interchangeably with orange flower water and may be sprinkled on fresh fruits.

[**See also** FLAVORINGS; ORANGE FLOWER WATER.]

ROBIN M. MOWER

Royal Crown Cola

In 1905 Claud A. Hatcher, a pharmacist, established the Union Bottling Works in the basement of his family's grocery store in Columbus, Georgia. Chero-Cola was the first of his Royal Crown line of beverages; it was followed by ginger ale, strawberry soda, and root beer. In 1912 Hatcher changed the name of the company to the Chero-Cola Company. The company struggled through the sugar rationing of World War I and suffered financial difficulties during the early 1920s, but in 1924 Hatcher was able to launch a new brand, Nehi, with orange and grape sodas leading the new line. No one seems to know what the name Nehi meant.

By 1925 the Chero-Cola Company had 315 plants located primarily in the southern states. In 1928 Hatcher changed the name of the company to the Nehi Corporation. Hatcher died in 1933, and his successor, H. R. Mott, streamlined operations, reformulated Chero-Cola, and shortened the brand name, Royal Crown Cola, to RC. By 1940 the company's products were available in all states but one. The company continued to expand and aggressively advertised in national publications, including the *Saturday Evening Post* and *Good Housekeeping.*

The Nehi Corporation was a major innovator in the soft drink world. In 1954 it was the first to nationally distribute soft drinks in cans. Four years later the company introduced the sixteen-ounce bottle, which made Coca-Cola's eight-ounce bottle look puny. In 1958 the company released the first diet cola, called Diet-Rite, on a local basis; Diet-Rite went national in 1962. At this time the company changed its name to the Royal Crown Company. In 1980 the company released RC 100, the first caffeine-free cola, and Diet Cherry RC, the first diet cherry cola. In the same year Royal Crown bought the Arby's fast food chain.

In 1998 the company introduced RC Edge, the first maximum-power cola containing a "synergistic blend" of Indian spices and caffeine. In 2000 the RC Cola brand was acquired by Cadbury Schweppes America Beverages, located in Plano, Texas.

BIBLIOGRAPHY

Jakle, John A., and Keith A. Sculle. *Fast Food: Roadside Restaurants in the Automobile Age.* Baltimore: Johns Hopkins University Press, 1999.

ANDREW F. SMITH

Roy Rogers

In 1967 Roy Rogers, beloved cowboy star of the large and small screens, licensed his name to the Marriott Corporation for use on a fast food chain. The following year the first Roy Rogers Western Roast Beef Sandwich restaurant opened in Falls Church, Virginia. The chain quickly grew through franchising, and the menu was expanded to include chicken and hamburgers.

In 1982 the Marriott Corporation bought Gino's, another fast food chain, and converted many of the restaurants into Roy Rogers outlets. Three years later Marriott bought Howard Johnson's restaurants and converted some of them into Roy Rogers outlets. By 1990 the Roy Rogers chain had 894 restaurants. In that year Imasco, the parent company of Hardee's, bought the Roy Rogers chain from Marriott. Hardee's converted 220 Roy Rogers outlets into Hardee's restaurants but then reconverted them into Roy Rogers two years later. Other Roy Rogers outlets were sold to Boston Chicken (later renamed Boston Market), Wendy's, and McDonald's. Only thirteen Roy Rogers franchisees survived. In 2002 Imasco sold the Roy Rogers trademark to Plamondon Enterprises,

Inc., one of the few remaining franchisees, which then created a new company called Roy Rogers Franchise, Inc. The remaining franchises are scattered on the East Coast from Connecticut to Virginia.

BIBLIOGRAPHY

Jakle, John A., and Keith A. Sculle. *Fast Food: Roadside Restaurants in the Automobile Age.* Baltimore: Johns Hopkins University Press, 1999.

ANDREW F. SMITH

Rum

Rum is a consumable spirit derived from sugarcane. Either fresh cane juice or water added to cane syrup or molasses is used as a base, which is then fermented and distilled to an alcohol ranging from 80 to 150 proof (roughly 40 percent to 75 percent alcohol). Unlike spirits made from other sources, such as grains, the conversion of starch to sugar (critical for fermentation to occur) is not necessary when making rum. Rum is also unique in that it can be made either as a white (colorless) spirit, like vodka or gin, or as a brown spirit, like brandy or scotch. Consequently rum is the most versatile of liquors and is the top-selling distilled spirit in the world.

Rum Varieties

Rum comes in many varieties. Some of the terminology describes the beverage's color or weight (for example, white, light, silver, gold, dark, or black). Other terms, like "overproof" (150, 151, or full strength), "premium distilled," "aged," *añejo* (Castilian for aged), "single marks," "select," "reserve," and "rare," are used to describe alcohol content, age, and quality levels. Fuller-flavored, more complex rums tend to be darker and somewhat heavier and can range in color from light amber to the color of strongly brewed tea. These darker, traditional styles typically start with molasses and are fermented more slowly and aged in charred oak casks to impart deep, rich flavors and color prior to blending. Light (colorless) rum—originally developed in Cuba in the mid-1800s by the Bacardi brand founder Don Facundo, who was seeking to refine the spirit—undergoes faster fermentation in stainless steel tanks and is not aged. This process produces rum that is not only lighter in weight and color but is also drier (less sweet) and more delicately flavored—a style that is considered ideal for mixing into cocktails and that accounts for most modern rum production.

Technological advances in how rum has been made over the centuries are reflected in the traditional copper pot stills (still used by conventional distillers) to the more modern continuous distillation method (enabling production of fine rum at a faster pace). Caramel or another coloring agent is sometimes added for greater color and consistency in certain dark varieties. Rums flavored with spice, vanilla, or fruit essences (like citrus, banana, coconut, or pineapple) are growing in both production and popularity. Other spirits distilled from sugarcane include *arrak* from the East Indies and *cachaca* from Brazil.

Most commercial rum is produced in the Caribbean, and nearly 80 percent of rum consumed in the United States is from Puerto Rico, the largest exporter and the primary base for Bacardi. While many places produce both dark and light rums, the majority of dark rum varieties (which are in the oldest style) are made in Jamaica, and most light rum is produced in Puerto Rico. A range of such varieties is widely emulated in nearly every part of the Caribbean. Centuries-old formulations and secret family recipes, many of which have never been written down, vary among regions and makers. Hawaii is also a producer and exporter of rum, as are other climates hospitable to the growth of sugarcane, including some southern states in the United States (such as Florida and Louisiana).

Fermenting and distilling beverages from sugarcane dates back thousands of years to China, Egypt, India, Syria, Southeast Asia, and the South Pacific. The Moors introduced sugarcane distillation to Europe via the Spanish and the Portuguese, who later cultivated the tall, weedlike crop on Atlantic islands west of the Iberian Peninsula (Azores). Sugarcane cuttings arrived in the Americas with Christopher Columbus in 1493.

These few initial transplants not only grew into the dominant crop but also became the central economic engine throughout Central America and South America, especially Brazil and the Caribbean Islands, which came to be known as the "sugar islands." This New World industry and its offshoots, the molasses and rum trades, depended entirely on the exploitation of human labor. The arduous toil of millions of captive, relocated Africans was deemed essential for the intense cultivation required for such crops and generated great profits for Europe and the new American colonies. Accordingly the sugar and rum trade generated the transatlantic slave trade that endured from the fifteenth century through the late nineteenth century.

The Rum Trade

Rum also played a significant role in early American economic and political development. Imported molasses, primarily from the West Indies, was converted into rum in New England and New York, where distilleries churned out rums described as heavy and full flavored. Small quantities are still produced in some parts of New England. Eventually rum became the most popular distilled beverage during the colonial American era. It was drunk straight, diluted with water, and used in many beverages, including the flip, the sling, the swizzle, the toddy, punch, and grog—a daily ration of which was long served on American naval ships.

This early American rum was also used as a successful trading medium. Some was traded with Native Americans for goods and land, but most was exported to Europe and exchanged along the west coast of Africa to supply the constant stream of slaves working the massive Caribbean and South American sugar plantations. Rum was thus a key component of the "triangular trade"; it was especially important to the economies of Massachusetts, New York, Philadelphia, and Rhode Island and was the top American export well into the early nineteenth century. This heavy maritime trade significantly increased sea traffic and illustrates why barrels of rum have long been associated with pirates, buccaneers, and other swashbucklers sailing the high seas during the seventeenth and eighteenth centuries. "Rum-running" brought easy wealth not only for legitimate shipping companies but also for privateers as well as those engaged in pure piracy.

American rum production was an integral factor in America's independence from England. British duties and taxes on molasses imported into American colonies from non-British territories (Molasses Act of 1733 and Sugar Act of 1764) fueled colonial unrest that ultimately culminated in the Revolutionary War and later the War of 1812. The latter led to the demise of the early U.S. rum industry and gave rise to spirits made from locally grown grains (such as whiskey and bourbon). During Prohibition (1919–1933) "rum" often synonymously referred to all alcohol and hard liquor in such terminology as "demon rum" and "rum riots." State- and county-run "rum rooms" were designated to hold any type of alcohol seized by the government from bootleggers. During Prohibition a jet-set crowd, including Hollywood's elite, artists, bohemians, and writers, flocked to Cuba, where there was an established American military presence and where drinking was legal. The original rum and Coke, called a Cuba libre (free Cuba), made and garnished with the juice from a squeezed lime wedge, was first introduced at an American military bar in Havana in 1899.

Despite the repeal of Prohibition, spirits production took a while to return to full swing, delayed in part by the Great Depression. By the dawn of World War II, the then-Cuban brand Bacardi was the most readily available spirit imported in bulk to an American public reembracing its cocktail culture. This availability, along with the popularity of the Andrews Sisters' song "Rum and Coca-Cola" (1944), helped establish this drink duo as the official cocktail of America.

Soldiers returning after World War II from Hawaii and the South Pacific brought a Polynesian pop culture known as "tiki," featuring rum as the main spirit in drinks decorated with paper parasols, flowers, and leis. Later, as tourism to places like Hawaii and the Caribbean became accessible to more Americans, so did a seemingly infinite assortment of rum-based concoctions combining both dark and light varieties blended with any combination of tropical fruit juices. Rum continues to be the preferred spirit in colorful cocktails sipped by Americans vacationing in warm locales the world over.

Well-known rum drinks include the blue whale, the daiquiri, the hurricane, the mai tai, the piña colada, rum punch, the yellow bird, and the zombie. Libations mixed with rum are most often paired with Caribbean and nuevo Latino cuisine, with beverages like Jamaican rum punch and the resurgent Cuban *mojito* available on drink menus of many American restaurants serving such fare. Rum is also used as a cooking ingredient for both sweet and savory sauces, cakes, other desserts, and candies.

[See also Caribbean Influences on American Food; Cocktails; Cuba Libre.]

BIBLIOGRAPHY

Barty-King, Hugh, and Anton Massel. *Rum, Yesterday and Today.* London: Heinemann, 1983.

DeGroff, Dale. *The Craft of the Cocktail.* New York: Clarkson Potter, 2002.

McCusker, John J. *Rum and the American Revolution: The Rum Trade and the Balance of Payments of the Thirteen Continental Colonies.* New York: Garland, 1989.

TONYA HOPKINS

Russian American Food

Russian American food reflects its two origins, the lowly shtetl and the noble estate. The bulk of immigrants from Russia fled either religious or political persecution; fewer came to America purely for economic opportunity. The demographics of the various groups that immigrated in the wake of Russia's social and political upheavals determined the nature of the foods they brought with them.

Immigration Patterns

The first Russian immigrants to contribute significantly to American food culture were Jews escaping the pogroms of 1881–1884 and 1903–1906. They brought foods that Americans now identify more closely with Russia than with Jewish cuisine, namely borscht (beet soup), black bread, and stuffed cabbage.

The so-called "first wave" of ethnic Russian immigration to the United States occurred following the Russian Revolution of 1917. These immigrants consisted largely of aristocrats, and the foods they introduced thrilled the American palate. Sophisticated diners appreciated elegant dishes like blini (raised pancakes) with caviar, Nesselrode pudding, and beef Stroganoff.

The "second wave" of immigration occurred in the wake of World War II. These Russians did not bring aristocratic ways. The restaurants they established tended to offer daily fare, such as piroshki (little pies filled with ground meat or vegetables), *pelmeni* (boiled Siberian dumplings), and a range of baked goods.

Russian restaurants along the boardwalk in Brighton Beach, Brooklyn, New York.

The "third wave" arrived in the 1970s and 1980s, when Jewish "refuseniks" who had been denied permission to leave the Soviet Union were finally allowed to emigrate. The tastes of this community resembled those of the larger Soviet society. Delicatessens specialized in sausages, smoked fish, and prepared foods. A new influx arrived after the collapse of the Soviet Union in 1991. More entrepreneurial in spirit than the preceding immigrants, most of these Russians came to the United States for economic advantage rather than as refugees. Their foodways do not differ from those of the earlier Soviet groups.

Dissemination of Russian Food in America

Of the foods brought by the early Jewish immigrants, borscht and kasha (buckwheat groats) became the most popular. Although borscht is widespread in Russia, this soup, which Americans consider quintessentially Russian, is actually Ukrainian in origin. By contrast, kasha is deeply Russian, yet most Americans consider kasha part of Jewish cuisine.

Other Russian foods were introduced to Americans through restaurants. The restaurant that for over seventy years defined Russian cuisine for Americans was the Russian Tea Room, located next to Carnegie Hall in New York City. Thanks to the Russian Tea Room's extravagant menu—not least its legendary caviar and blini—Russian food in America came to epitomize luxury. The Russian Tea Room's allure lasted until 2002, when its doors finally closed. By then Russian food had lost its cachet.

Cookbooks also helped acquaint Americans with Russian cuisine. In 1941 the Colt Press of San Francisco published a limited-edition volume of *The Epicure in Imperial Russia* by Marie Alexandre Markevitch, a noblewoman whose purpose was to present "the essential character of the culinary art of Imperial Russia." Like the Russian Tea Room, this cookbook represented the glories of an era long past and perpetuated the image of an extravagant table. Far more influential was Princess Alexandra Kropotkina's *How to Cook and Eat in Russian*, published in 1947. Written at the beginning of the cold war, this book sought not only to make Russian food accessible, it also attempted to familiarize Americans with the Russian character in order to make "Ivan" seem less formidable and more friendly.

Russian Dishes in America

By the mid-twentieth century Americans were familiar with a few of the mainstays of Russian cuisine at both the high and low ends: blini and borscht, caviar and cabbage. The allure of Russian food continued into the 1960s, when one of the era's most popular hostess dishes was beef Stroganoff, which began to appear on the menus of "continental" restaurants throughout the United States. Another popular restaurant dish was chicken Kiev. Unknown in czarist times, this dish was actually a Soviet-era innovation. During the 1970s and 1980s it was served at the most elegant catered events in America. A third dish that Americans readily adopted is strawberries Romanoff, which bears the name of the royal family even though it is not a traditional Russian dessert.

Like strawberries Romanoff, other dishes that Americans associate with Russia carry Russian names but are not part of the traditional cuisine. These include Russian dressing, a mixture of mayonnaise and chili sauce, and Russian tea cakes, cookies similar to Mexican wedding cakes and likely called "Russian" in the United States because of their association with tea. The image of a samovar and tea cookies is in fact Russian and might also account for the name Russian tea, for which recipes are found in many community and southern cookbooks. Russian tea is simply tea spiced with cinnamon and allspice and often flavored with lemon.

No discussion of Russian American food would be complete without a mention of vodka. More than any foodstuff or dish, vodka may be the item most closely associated in American minds with Russia. For many years the industry standard was Smirnoff, produced by a noble family that fled to France after the revolution. In 1980 PepsiCo signed an exclusive agreement with Stolichnaya vodka to sell Pepsi in the Soviet Union and promote "Stoli" in the United States. Stoli did not dominate the market for long, however; by the 1990s non-Russian companies had made inroads into the premium vodka market. Vodka cocktails continue to be popular. One American favorite is the Black Russian, a mixture of vodka and Kahlúa, which later gave birth to the White Russian. The latter also contains a splash of cream and plays on the name for the monarchist aristocracy at the time of the Russian Revolution.

At the beginning of the twenty-first century Russian food is no longer considered chic in America. The popular conception is of a bland, heavy diet. Americans who traveled to Russia during the Soviet era invariably returned with stories of bad food and even worse service, and this impression has not easily been dispelled. Even so Americans continue to enjoy the borscht, blini, caviar, and vodka with which Russian cuisine is still most closely identified in this country.

BIBLIOGRAPHY

Goldstein, Darra. *A Taste of Russia.* 2nd ed. Montpelier, VT: Russian Life Books, 1999.

DARRA GOLDSTEIN

S

Saint Patrick's Day

American Saint Patrick's Day has been described as "Eiresatz: a sentimental slur of imagined memories, fine feeling and faux Irish talismans and traditions" (Dezell, *Irish America*, 17). It is a festival of soda bread, corned beef and cabbage, cardboard shamrocks, green hats, bagels, and beer. In Ireland, Saint Patrick's Day is a religious holiday, but in America it has become a spectacle.

The Irish emigrated to the United States in two distinct waves. In the early eighteenth century a relatively small number of Scotch-Irish, mostly Presbyterians from Ulster, settled in the agricultural green hills and valleys of the Appalachian region. From 1845 to 1850 Ireland lost 2 million people to starvation and to emigration to the United States. Over the next fifty years, half a million Irish, mostly Roman Catholic, emigrated each decade.

Perhaps because of their experiences in the potato famine and owing to prohibitively expensive farmland near U.S. cities, many immigrants chose not to return to country life. They created new lives in the port cities of the Northeast and Midwest. Saint Patrick's Day evolved in urban America. Like most immigrant groups, the Irish lost some of their traditions as they assimilated American culture. But as they did for many other immigrant groups, poverty and repression led to maintenance as well as modification of holidays that preserve group identity. Simple nostalgia for the "old sod" turned a minor religious event into a major holiday. Saint Patrick's Day evolved from being a feast as in "religious celebration" to being a feast as in "secular celebration, party." Traditional Irish symbols—such as the harp and Celtic cross—were replaced by clichés, like leprechauns and shillelaghs often promoted by non-Irish Americans, that made it easy for all Americans to participate in what a century before had been a parochial event.

The Irish adapted their traditional foodways to their changed circumstances. If there was a national dish in Ireland, it was probably colcannon: boiled potatoes, cabbage, and leeks in buttermilk flavored with wild garlic. Another Irish dish was brown soda bread, made with whole-grain flour. These dishes are recognizable relatives of "authentic" Irish American dishes. Corned beef and cabbage and soda bread made with white flour and currants or caraway seeds replaced colcannon and brown bread as Saint Patrick's Day foods in America. The Irish in nineteenth-century Ireland rarely ate corned beef. For political and economic reasons, the meat was produced primarily for export to England. The immigrants chose to celebrate their holiday in their new country with a food not available to them in the old country. In Ireland white soda bread was reserved for special occasions. It may be that when they arrived in the United States, poor immigrants appropriated the "higher status" bread as their own, adding currants or caraway as signs of their new affluence. These "improved" foods were adopted by the non-Irish in an attempt to "play" at being Irish. Corned beef and cabbage is to authentic Irish cooking as chili con carne is to authentic Mexican food. Both are American dishes in the imagined style of other countries.

[**See also** CABBAGE; CHRISTMAS; CORNED BEEF; FOURTH OF JULY; NEW YEAR'S CELEBRATIONS; PASSOVER; THANKSGIVING; VALENTINE'S DAY; WASHINGTON'S BIRTHDAY.]

BIBLIOGRAPHY

Cole, Rosalind. *Of Soda Bread and Guinness: An Irish Cookbook, and a Picture of Ireland as Seen through Its People, Its Places, Its Traditions, and Its Cooking Lore.* Indianapolis, IN: Bobbs-Merrill, 1973.

Dezell, Maureen. *Irish America: Coming into Clover.* New York: Doubleday, 2000.

FitzGibbon, Theodora. *Irish Traditional Food.* London and Basingstoke, U.K.: Macmillan London, 1983.

GARY ALLEN

Salads and Salad Dressings

European colonists brought the concept of salad to the New World. Salad was considered a survival food by many, because salad ingredients were gathered in the early spring before crops matured. Colonial middle- and upper-class Americans enjoyed salads. Most kitchen gardens included salad ingredients, such as lettuce, cabbage, watercress, kale, cucumbers, carrots, parsley, leeks, shallots, onions, spinach, garlic, and chives. In addition wild greens were collected from fields. In the southern colonies wider arrays of kitchen garden plants and vegetables were grown. Salad dressings varied, including single ingredients, such as salt or sugar or vinegar or melted butter, or combinations, such as vinegar and egg yolks or salt, vinegar, and sugar or molasses. Occasionally dressings included olive oil, which was an expensive commodity in colonial and early America, as it had to be imported. It was also frequently adulterated and prone to turning rancid easily.

While the main definition of salad revolved around the leafy green plants, such as lettuce, immigrants and other groups had concepts of salad that did not necessarily have any greens in them at all. German immigrants brought potato salad. The Shakers had long made fruit salads. French cookbooks and French immigrant chefs introduced mayonnaise into the United States. It was one of the sauces of classical French cookery, and its use introduced chicken and lobster salads to America.

Occasionally fruits and vegetables were considered unhealthy by some medical authorities. City councils also occasionally prohibited the sale of fruits and vegetables during cholera epidemics. But by the 1840s the reputations of fruits and vegetables were rehabilitated by many medical professionals, who considered them healthy edibles, although some remained concerned about eating vegetables in their raw state.

The American upper class enjoyed European-style salads throughout the nineteenth century. This enjoyment increased as new restaurants opened in the large cities during the early nineteenth century. In New York, for instance, Delmonico's restaurant specialized in salads and salad dressings. Its 1838 menu included six salads based on lettuce, endive, celery, anchovies, lobster, and chicken, and several of them included a dressing of mayonnaise. After the Civil War salad experimentation began in earnest in America. Middle and upper classes consumed lettuce salads and others made of potatoes, tomatoes, and cabbages. For balls, evening parties, or formal afternoon teas, lobster, oyster, crab, and turkey salads were highly rated. Chicken salad was a particular favorite. The upper class also served green salads with vinegar and olive oil. Garlic was generally not employed, but it was a frequent component in dressings served in French and other restaurants in America.

This new emphasis on salads appeared in cookbooks by the late 1870s. The first American cookbook devoted solely to salads was Emma Ewing's *Salad and Salad Making* (1883), which was a manual for students in cooking school. Ewing believed that salads were highly nutritious and easy to make. Her goal was to demystify and simplify salad construction. She included thirty-four recipes, dividing the salads into five categories: fruit salads, vegetable salads, fish salads, meat salads, and mixed salads.

Salads had become important enough by the 1870s that salad dressings were commercially bottled and sold by grocers. The most important nineteenth-century manufacturers were the E. R. Durkee Company of New York City and Curtice Brothers of Rochester, New York. Chicago's Tildesley and Company manufactured Yacht Club salad dressing. Durkee began issuing advertising cookbooklets featuring its products by 1875. Other salad dressing manufacturers followed at a later date.

Iceberg lettuce was developed in 1894. The sturdiness of this green made it easier to transport lettuce long distances. As the price of iceberg lettuce dropped during the early twentieth century, it became the base of most American salads, with romaine lettuce coming in a distant second. By the beginning of the twentieth century, molded or congealed salads, made with gelatin or aspic, had burst onto the culinary mainstream. Frozen salads followed. The ubiquitous lettuce and tomato salad did not appear in cookbooks until 1890 but was not commonly served in restaurants until decades later.

Commercial salad plants grew easily in California, and it is no surprise that a late-nineteenth-century visitor to California found it the "land of salads." California was the inspiration for a great number of famous salads, such as the green goddess salad and Caesar salad. So pervasive was the California influence that salad has become a common main-course item in itself, called "chef's salad" and including ham and hard-boiled eggs, on many restaurant menus as well as at many private tables.

During the twentieth century warm salads, such as potato salad, were introduced. Awareness of salads from other countries, continents, and cultures was growing. Although the tomato was the queen of the vegetable market in the United States by the mid-nineteenth century, Italian immigrants made the tomato a popular ingredient in salads. Cold pasta salads, particularly those made with tortellini, mayonnaise, and dill, became fashionable.

In 1939 the Boston Oyster House of the Morrison Hotel in Chicago opened what it called a "salad bar" at which customers arranged their own salads. It consisted of thirty glass bowls, packed in ice, containing greens and a variety of cooked and fresh vegetables in season that could be used to make up combination salads. Also on the bar were bowls of julienne chicken, ham, fresh crab flakes, beef, anchovies, tuna, shrimp, and eight varieties of dressing. During the 1970s salad bars became a fixture of medium-priced and family restaurants throughout the United States.

Origins of Specific Salads and Salad Dressings

Caesar salad is a combination of romaine lettuce, garlic, olive oil, croutons, parmesan cheese, Worcestershire sauce, and often anchovies. It was purportedly created by Caesar Cardini, an Italian immigrant who opened a series of restaurants in Tijuana, Mexico, just across the border from San Diego. In 1924 Cardini concocted the salad as a main course, arranging the lettuce leaves on a plate with the intention that they would be eaten with the fingers. Later Cardini shredded the leaves into bite-size pieces. The salad became particularly popular with the Hollywood movie in-crowd who visited Tijuana. The salad was later featured at restaurants in Los Angeles. Cardini insisted that the salad be subtly flavored and therefore opposed the introduction of anchovies. He also decreed that only Italian olive oil and imported parmesan cheese be used. In 1948 he established a patent on the dressing, which in the early 2000s was still packaged and sold as Cardini's Original Caesar dressing mix, distributed by Caesar Cardini Foods, Culver City, California.

Cobb salad was introduced by Robert Cobb, owner of the Brown Derby restaurant in Los Angeles. It consists of avocado, tomato, watercress, lettuce, bacon, chicken, Roquefort cheese, and a hard-boiled egg arranged in a striped pattern in a flat bowl topped with french dressing.

Green goddess dressing, consisting of many ingredients, including mayonnaise, cream, vinegar, parsley, onion, anchovies, and garlic, was introduced by the Palace Hotel in San Francisco in the early 1920s. It was inspired by the British actor George Arliss, who was a hit in the play *The Green Goddess* then playing in San Francisco.

Lettuce and tomato salad did not become common until the mid-twentieth century. Although tomatoes had been used in salads for decades, their combination into the ubiquitous lettuce and tomato salad first appeared in the United States in the late nineteenth century. It was popularized by Fannie Merritt Farmer's *Boston Cooking-School Cook Book*.

Potato salad is a cold or hot side dish made with potatoes, mayonnaise, and seasonings. It became popular in the second half of the nineteenth century and is a staple of both delicatessens and home kitchens. Hot potato salad, usually made with bacon, onion, and vinegar dressing, was associated with German immigrants and is therefore often called German potato salad.

Salade niçoise is generally a mixture of lettuce, tomatoes, french beans, anchovies, tuna, olives, and hard-boiled eggs with vinaigrette dressing.

Thousand island dressing is a mayonnaise-based salad dressing flavored with tomatoes, chilies, and green peppers, among other things. The name presumably comes from the Thousand Islands between the United States and Canada in the St. Lawrence River.

Waldorf salad is a combination of apples, celery, and mayonnaise that dates from 1896. Its invention is credited to Oscar Tschirky, who was in charge of a dining room at Delmonico's before he moved to the Waldorf-Astoria. Walnuts were added during the first decade of the twentieth century.

Ranch dressing, consisting in part of soybean oil, buttermilk, vinegar, sour cream, egg yolk, garlic, and sugar, was introduced in the mid-1970s by Hidden Valley Ranch in a dry dressing mix and later in bottled form. Competitors followed suit, and in the early 2000s ranch-style dressing reigned as America's favorite dressing flavor, followed in order by italian, creamy italian, thousand island, french, and caesar.

Dressings have ranged from the simple oil and vinegar, called french (or italian) dressing, to elaborate sauces that might contain orange slices and marshmallows. International hotel cuisine, under American influence, in the twenty-first century offers three dressings: oil and vinegar, thousand island, and Roquefort or blue cheese.

[See also DELMONICO'S; FLOWERS, EDIBLE; FRUIT; JELL-O; JELL-O MOLDS; LETTUCE; MAYONNAISE; POKE SALAD; RANDOLPH, MARY; RORER, SARAH TYSON; TOMATOES; VEGETABLES.]

BIBLIOGRAPHY

The Salad and Cooking Oil Market. New York: Packaged Facts, 1991.

Shapiro, Laura. *Perfection Salad: Women and Cooking at the Turn of the Century.* New York: Holt, 1987.

ANDREW F. SMITH

Salami

Originally from Italy, salami is a type of sausage made with ground pork and cubes of fat seasoned with garlic, salt, and spices. The name "salami," from the Italian *salare*, meaning "to salt," refers to the salting process used to make highly seasoned dry sausages with a characteristic fermented flavor.

Salami is usually approximately three to four inches in diameter and often named after the city or region of origin. Salami varies according to country or region of origin, coarseness or fineness of the meat blend, size, and seasonings. Kosher salami is made from kosher ingredients under rabbinical supervision.

Italian immigrants introduced salami to the United States in the mid to late nineteenth century. At the beginning of the twentieth century, the immigrants identified the temperate climate of northern California as best suited for dry-curing salami. San Francisco emerged as the leader in salami production and continues to be regarded as the salami capital of America.

In the early eighteenth century Armour and Company, in Chicago, started the first automated commercial production of salami. Salami, in accordance with Old World customs, was traditionally made in late fall and early winter and cured during the cooler season for consumption throughout the year. Refrigeration and humidity control technologies did away with the seasonality of salami production and allowed for salami production throughout the year. Salami manufacture initially required five to ten days to ensure optimum curing and flavor development. When lactic acid cultures became available commercially, curing time decreased from days to hours. With advances in ingredient technologies, egg whites and sodium caseinate were used to bind moisture in the product and significantly reduce drying time. Smoke flavoring further helped reduce production time to a matter of hours.

The basic salami-making process—whether the sausage is batch- or mass-produced—consists of stuffing a cured meat mixture into casings and air-drying or smoking the sausages at a relatively low temperature (not exceeding 140°F.). Smoking stops fermentation and adds flavor while drying the product. The finished

A selection of salami and other cured meats at Blue Apron foods in Brooklyn, New York.

product is rinsed with water or brine to prevent mold growth and then is chilled or aged.

Salami is consumed without being heated. Salami made from mildly cured fresh meats and cooked before air drying is known as "cooked salami." Cooked salami, such as *cotto* salami, which contains whole peppercorns, is softer than dry and semidry salami and must be refrigerated.

Convenience, versatility, and low cost helped cooked salami become a staple of snacks and meals among the less affluent and working class of America. Targeted advertising further helped the easy-to-digest and mild-tasting salami and bologna become favorites with children in America.

Salami production and consumption continue to grow in the United States. A high-protein and low-carbohydrate profile makes salami ideal for the popular Atkins and South Beach carbohydrate-restricted weight loss diets. Innovative packaging technologies are adding to the popularity of salami. For example, miniature salami is becoming increasingly popular as a handheld food.

[**See also** CALIFORNIA; ITALIAN AMERICAN FOOD; MEAT; PEPPERONI; SAUSAGE; VIENNA SAUSAGE.]

BIBLIOGRAPHY
Dowell, Philip, and Bailey, Adrian. *Cook's Ingredients.* New York: Bantam, 1980.

KANTHA SHELKE

Sally Lunn

Sally Lunn is a delicate, fairly rich bread made with yeast, eggs, milk, wheat flour, butter, and a little sugar, much like the French brioche. Sally Lunn is popular in England, Canada, and New Zealand, where it is served hot as a tea cake or fork-split and toasted. In the United States it has many variations, some made with yeast and others with baking powder. Still other variants include cornmeal,

sour cream, or buttermilk. It can be baked in a shallow cake pan, a ring mold, a Turk's head mold, a bread pan, a bundt or tube pan, or even in muffin tins. One recipe makes a light corn bread, baked as a dropped batter on a baking sheet. Whatever the form, Sally Lunn is generally cut into wedges, slices, or squares and served hot with butter and jam. It is a favorite Virginia hot bread and is claimed by colonial Williamsburg, where visitors can dine on Sally Lunn in the museum's taverns and take home bags of Sally Lunn bread mix.

The origins of Sally Lunn are unclear but perhaps date to the 1670s in Bath, England, when Bath buns were served in the Pump Room. Over time Bath buns acquired spices and lemon, while Sally Lunn remained a plain and simple kind of bun. Sally Lunn buns were served with morning coffee in the fashionable Bath Pump Room during the eighteenth century. *The Oxford English Dictionary* dates the first citation to 1798, "a certain sort of hot rolls, now, or not long ago, in vogue at Bath." A dictionary published in 1898 also placed the first use of the term "Sally Lunn" at the close of the eighteenth century.

Legend has it that Sally Lunn herself was a seventeenth- or eighteenth-century pastry cook who first sold these buns from a basket in the streets of Bath. Nineteenth-century sources credit Dalmer, a baker and musician, who bought her business, made a song about Sally Lunn, and made the bread famous. (The song has been lost.) The Sally Lunn Museum and Restaurant in Bath, England, portrays Sally Lunn as a young French refugee who arrived in England in 1680 and baked the buns to support herself. The bun became a popular delicacy in Georgian England and was enjoyed with either sweet or savory accompaniments. It can be used as a base for Welsh rabbit, sliced for sandwiches, or used for bread pudding.

Another theory is that the bread's name is a corruption of the French phrase *soleil et lune* (sun and moon), referring to the bread's golden top and white bottom. It is also possible that the name comes from a French word, such as *solimeme* or *solilemme*, for a type of brioche. Proponents of the theory of a French origin believe that the originator of the buns in Bath may have been a French Huguenot who fled from France to escape persecution sometime after the revocation of the Edict of Nantes in 1685.
[**See also** BREAD.]

BIBLIOGRAPHY
Perl, Lila. *Red-Flannel Hash and Shoo-Fly Pie: American Regional Foods and Festivals.* Cleveland, OH: World Publishing, 1965.

VIRGINIA SCOTT JENKINS

Salmon

Salmon consumed in America comes from both the Atlantic and the Pacific and is caught wild as well as farm raised. The Atlantic salmon (*Salmo salar*) and its Pacific counterparts—sockeye (*Oncorhynchus nerka,*; chinook (*O. tshawytscha*), chum (*O. keta*), coho or silver (*O. kisutch*), and pink or humpback (*O. gorbuscha*)—are all anadromous. Salmon ranks among the most favored of finfishes of the past and present. Salmon are eaten fresh and are available as fillets, as steaks, and in the round. They are poached, baked, and grilled. The rich flesh accepts salt and smoke; can be made into uncooked but cured products, such as gravlax and *lomi* salmon; and is used in sushi and sashimi. Tlingit people caught salmon on its way to spawning and dried the flesh.

Landlocked salmon is generally indistinguishable from its saltwater counterparts. Freshwater salmon are mostly harvested for sport. On the Great Lakes, however, where coho and chinook salmon were introduced in the 1960s, there is a valuable commercial fishery as well as a sport fishery. Salmon is a fine food fish.

In past times the reddish flesh of salmon and its rich flavor meant that the fish was sometimes regarded as "red blooded" and was included on the list of "royal" fish, those presented to royalty. A version of this tradition continued in the United States until 1992 as the first salmon caught each year on the Penobscot River in Maine was traditionally sent to the president.

For centuries there have been both commercial and recreational salmon fisheries. Salmon have been caught by weirs along the shores of bays and inlets that the fish must pass to reach their spawning sites, with dip nets at the fall line where the fish must jump upstream, and by hook and line. Trollers uses baited hooks in open seas to catch particular species of salmon, while seiners select individual schools of sockeye, pink, and chum salmon; gillnetters fish for sockeye and chum. Native American fishing employs nearly all of these methods plus hooks and spears, sometimes by special governmental arrangements for tribal food and ceremonial salmon use.

Salmon were plentiful for Native Americans and colonists and were taken in large numbers. When those streams had been heavily fished, dammed for power in the 1800s, or polluted by industry, subsequent catches were greatly limited, especially on the East Coast. By the start of the twentieth century, West Coast salmon fisheries had greatly exceeded the East Coast catches, with most of the western fish canned and shipped all across the country. Evidence of the nationwide availability of salmon is apparent in early twentieth-century inland cookbooks with their recipes for salmon loaf and salmon salad.

Salmon are at the center of much controversy. On the West Coast migratory salmon are caught by both U.S. and Canadian fishermen, but managing the stocks and developing workable treaties have become extremely difficult because once the fish are at sea, it is impossible to discern whether they originated in Canadian or American territorial waters. On both coasts there is considerable discussion as to whether there are any genetically pure, indigenous salmon stocks left. For years hatchery-raised salmon were released into streams to replenish lost wild stocks, and farmed salmon are escaping and intermixing with the wild stocks. Salmon farming's intensive growing promotes disease among the fish, and fish farms are not always welcome neighbors as they upset local ecological balances and obstruct scenery.

Still, farmed salmon as a globally traded product is among the least expensive fish in markets. Organizations seeking to protect various fish caution against consuming farm-raised salmon from the Pacific Northwest, Chile, and Great Britain, and they advise that the Alaskan wild stocks are the strongest and most sustainable. However, alternative points of view are equally easy to find.

SANDRA L. OLIVER

Saloons

Swinging doors, player pianos, gunfights, and the wild west are some of the images that the word "saloon" conjures up. Others think of skid row, red-light districts, drunkenness, and wasted lives when they hear the word. At one time the word embraced all of these ideas and many more. Long before the saloon became associated with debauchery and the wild west, saloons were watering holes for both the privileged and the poor.

Saloons in America evolved from the public taverns and ordinaries of the eighteenth century and early nineteenth century. During the colonial period taverns generally served a broad cross section of society. It was during the federalist period that these public drinking spaces started to serve a more restricted clientele. The wealthiest found haven in private clubs, and merchants and businessmen

Two signs behind a mixologist at work in New York City advertise hot punch and Tom & Jerry, a warm holiday cocktail.

retreated to coffeehouses and restaurants. The traveler frequented hotel bars, which had the attributes of both the club and saloon. At first the saloon (from the French salon) catered to wealthy native-born Americans. These saloons, decorated with handsome furniture, woodwork, large mirrors, and carpets, created an ambience of luxury and were associated with the poshest hotels (Boston's Parker House and the Palmer House in Chicago) and restaurants (Delmonico's in New York) in America. It was in the environment of this kind of saloon that the cocktail, a uniquely American invention, had its origins.

After the Civil War the saloon evolved to meet the needs of urban working-class males. Saloons dominated poor working-class neighborhoods, serving both low-cost food and drink to factory workers. These establishments were mostly frequented by male patrons, who spent many of their nonworking hours drinking beer and cheap whiskey and in some cases eating free food, providing they purchased a sufficient quantity of beer. The food was heavily salted to encourage thirst, and the saloon "bouncer" kept an eye on those with too hearty an appetite. Saloons made no pretense of serving fine food.

Because so many of these working-class men were immigrants, saloons have been called "ethnic spaces" and in cities have often been identified with the Irish. It was the saloon that men turned to as a place to meet, eat, take a bath, use a restroom, receive credit, gamble, locate pornography, meet a prostitute, or buy narcotics. In some cities political bosses recruited saloon regulars to stuff ballot boxes. In Chicago and San Francisco, centers of organized prostitution, the red-light districts coexisted with the saloon culture. It was also in saloons that unions found their strikebreakers. Fraternal organizations frequently met in the back room or on second-floor halls. Jack London found that in a saloon "life was different. Men talked with great voices, laughed great laughs, and there was an atmosphere of greatness."

Saloons located near factories and places that employed large numbers of men were frequented at lunch, during work breaks, and by apprentices sent to fetch pails of beer for millworkers. Breweries owned many saloons and put pressure on managers to meet quotas. To do this they frequently had to break blue laws (local closing ordinances, such as those forbidding the serving of drink on Sundays) and promote gambling and other underworld activities. The increase in drinking by the poor was identified with the increase in the rise of skid rows in many urban areas. The term "skid" comes from the track made by Seattle's lumbermen to "skid" timber downhill. As Seattle grew, the area around where the lumbermen worked filled up with seedy bars and quarters for unemployed workers, derelicts, and transients. Skid rows developed in other urban areas including New York's Bowery district.

The temperance movement had been concerned with the problem of alcoholism even before the Civil War, but after the war the excesses of saloon culture brought matters to a head. Because of the abuse of alcohol, particularly in saloons, the Woman's Christian Temperance Union (WCTU) made the saloon the target of its hatred, finding in this institution the symbol of women's fears of abandonment. Saloons were associated with drunkenness, prostitution, unemployment, wastefulness, crime, and disease in the minds of many Americans.

The saloon disappeared, except in the form of illegal speakeasies, during the period of Prohibition that lasted from 1920 until 1934. The word is sometimes used in the eary twenty-first century in association with the name of a restaurant or drinking place that attempts to evoke a Victorian, late-nineteenth-century feel or a western frontier ambience.

[See also Alcohol and Teetotalism; Alcoholism; Bars; Beer Halls; Boardinghouses; Cocktails; Coffeehouses; Delmonico's; Drinking Songs; Lüchow's; Prohibition; Roadhouses; Temperance.]

BIBLIOGRAPHY

Grimes, William. *Straight Up or on the Rocks: The Story of the American Cocktail*. New York: North Point, 2001.

Lender, Mark Edward, and James Kirby Martin. *Drinking in America: A History*. Rev. ed. New York: Free Press, 1987.

Murdock, Catherine Gilbert. *Domesticating Drink: Women, Men, and Alcohol in America, 1870–1940*. Baltimore: Johns Hopkins University Press, 1998.

JOSEPH M. CARLIN

Salsa

Salsa is condiment made from a variety of ingredients, raw or cooked, usually served at room temperature as a dip for fried corn tortilla chips and as a garnish for other dishes, savory or sweet. Salsas are typically colorful in appearance, chunky in texture, and often (but not always) hot and spicy in taste. In many ways the salsas eaten in the United States are similar to coarsely textured condiments in other parts of the world, such as the *sambals* of Southeast Asia and the chutneys of India and Pakistan as well as the relishes of America's own Deep South.

"Salsa" is the Spanish word for sauce—an indication of this condiment's origin in Spanish-speaking countries of the Western Hemisphere, particularly Mexico and Central America. In these countries the word "salsa" encompasses a wide range of culinary concoctions, from sauces that are smooth, cooked, and served warm or hot to condiments that are chunky, raw, and served at room temperature.

In the United States the consumption of condiment salsas began to expand beyond the local Hispanic communities during the 1940s, initially in those parts of the American Southwest where Mexican food was traditionally eaten. The most common type of salsa was and still is a version of Mexican *salsa cruda* (raw sauce), also known as *salsa fresca* (fresh sauce) or *salsa mexicana* (Mexican sauce), made with chopped tomatoes, onions, and fresh green jalapeño or serrano peppers, their colors a reflection of the red, white, and green of the Mexican flag. Chopped cilantro (fresh coriander leaves) and a little lemon or lime juice or salt are often added to the mixture to enhance the flavor.

Salsas made at home or in restaurants can be raw, cooked, or made with a combination of both raw and cooked ingredients. Fresh salsas containing raw ingredients are usually eaten shortly after they are made. Bottled salsas, typically sold in widemouthed jars, are always cooked to preserve their ingredients. The first commercially bottled salsas were made in Texas in the late 1940s, and by 1992 salsa had become America's most popular commercial condiment, outselling in dollars the country's other longtime favorite, tomato ketchup.

Salsa's popularity nationwide is generally attributed to Americans' increasing consumption of hot and spicy foods during the second half of the twentieth century—first in the Southwest and later throughout other parts of the country, at home, for snacks, in Mexican-food restaurants, and more recently in restaurants featuring fusion foods that combine ingredients and cooking techniques from many places around the globe. Salsas are also perceived as healthy foods, because many of them are low in calories, high in fiber, and full of vitamins. Salsas have become such an accepted part of American cuisine that since 1995 the International Chili Society has hosted hundreds of local, state, and regional salsa cook-offs, where cooks compete for cash prizes and ultimately a world champion title for salsas made from their own personal recipes.

Red, tomato-based salsas are the most common in the United States, followed by green salsas made with tomatillos, green peppers, avocados, and cilantro or other green herbs. But salsas can be made from a wide range of ingredients, including vegetables, fruits, berries, grains, herbs, spices, oils, vinegars, sugars, nuts, seeds, mushrooms, and occasionally even seafood. The chunky texture of salsas comes from their solid ingredients, which can be coarsely or finely chopped. And their piquant, distinctive taste comes from the combination of contrasting flavors—usually hot and spicy, often salty, occasionally sour, and sometimes even sweet.

Almost all salsas in the United States contain mild to hot capsicum peppers, which can be fresh, pickled, or dried and chopped, crumbled, or ground into powder. Although salsa in the United States was originally a hot-and-spicy condiment, the increasing demand for salsas with milder flavors has resulted in the development of new varieties of peppers. These provide the taste of naturally hot peppers, such as jalapeños and habaneros, without the accompanying high levels of capsaicin, an alkaloid present in hot peppers that produces the characteristic burning sensation in the mouth and on the skin.

Salsas turn up on the table as condiments with courses from appetizers to main dishes to desserts. Spicy, hot red or green salsas, typically served as dips for tortilla chips at the beginning of a Tex-Mex meal, are also often used as garnishes for a number of dishes of Mexican origin, including enchiladas, tacos, and tamales. Savory salsas—spicy or mild, with a wide range of flavors and colors—are served as accompaniments to grilled, baked, broiled, or fried meats, fish, and poultry. Some cooks use salsas as an ingredient in marinades, salad dressings, soups, stews, and cooked sauces and even as a topping for baked potatoes, pizzas, and pastas. In the early 2000s an emerging trend was to make sweet salsas from fruits, berries, sugars, and spices paired with fruity-flavored peppers, such as habaneros, Scotch bonnets, and *datils*, to serve with pound cakes, cheesecakes, and frozen desserts.

[See also Chili; Condiments; Frito-Lay; Mexican American Food; Southwestern Regional Cookery.]

BIBLIOGRAPHY

Hearon, Reed. *Salsa: Musica for Your Mouth*. San Francisco: Chronicle Books, 1993.

Miller, Mark. *The Great Salsa Book*. Berkeley, CA: Ten Speed, 1994.

Schlesinger, Chris, and John Willoughby. *Salsas, Sambals, Chutneys, and Chowchows*. New York: William Morrow, 1993.

SHARON HUDGINS

Salsify

Salsify (*Tragopogon porrifolius*) is also known as oyster plant because the pleasant flavor is said to resemble that of an oyster, although it has the firm texture of all root vegetables. The roots of this European vegetable, which can be up to twelve inches long, are grayish-black or brown and the flesh is white. There is a variety with a black skin known as *scorzonera*. Marion Harland, the pen name of Mary Virginia Terhune (1830–1922; née Hawes), who wrote many cookbooks and books on domestic economy, was fond of oyster plant and had several recipes for it. It can be cooked like any root vegetable in soups, stews, and so forth. It is in season from early summer through the winter but is most likely to be found in markets in the fall.

[See also Soups and Stews.]

JOSEPHINE BACON

Salt and Salting

The chlorine ion bound with a sodium ion forms the chemical compound sodium chloride (NaCl), known as common salt. NaCl is chemically composed of 60 percent chlorine, a gas, and 40 percent sodium, a metal. Purity of salt is dependent on its source and its method of production. For instance, mined rock salt typically ranges between 95 percent and 99.9 percent NaCl, and evaporated salt from purified brine is nearly 99.9 percent pure.

Salt is an essential nutrient. Humans and animals need salt for musculature balance, digestion of food, and proper functioning of the nervous system; salt is lost daily through urination and perspiration. The human body, containing about eight ounces of salt, strives to maintain its optimal saline balance.

Salt enhances flavor. The human tongue readily detects four main taste sensations: salty, sweet, bitter, and sour. Harold McGee, in *On Food and Cooking: The Science and Lore*

Nineteenth-century salt bag.

Kinds of Salt

Salt is available in varying particle gradations and forms and consequently varies in utility. Sea salt has a coarse flake texture. Sea salt may contain impurities, most notably trace amounts of minerals from evaporated seawater. Its mineral content may impart a slight flavor or discolor food, and it is thus unsuitable for preserving foods.

Kosher salt has a coarse flake texture. Sold in its unaltered crystal form, kosher salt's large surface area allows for absorption of more moisture than a similarly sized cubic salt crystal. It usually contains an anticaking agent and is free of iodine. Many cooks champion kosher salt for its flavor and texture. Kosher salt is generally pure salt suitable for preservation techniques, such as canning, pickling, and meat curing. Like other coarse salts, it can be used in recipes that call for a salt crust. It is to be noted that kosher salt is itself not kosher but is used in the process of koshering meat.

Table salt or refined granulated salt is the most versatile salt and is widely used for cooking and as a condiment. Some critics of the taste of refined salt claim it leaves a bitter and unpleasant taste on the back of the tongue and mouth when compared to salt in a purer form. Table salt contains an anticaking agent and is available with or without iodine.

Fine grain salt, such as canning and pickling salt, is used to make brines for preserved foods like pickles and sauerkraut. Such salt is free of additives, which can cause discoloration or darkening if used for pickling. Popcorn salt has fine grains, granulated specifically to adhere to popcorn.

Unrefined salt, such as rock salt or water-conditioning salt or agricultural salt, is not food grade and is sold in large chunky crystals. Its grayish cast suggests retention of minerals and harmless impurities. Rock salt and halite are used on roads to melt snow and ice. Rock salt is also used to freeze ice cream by combining it with ice in crank-style ice cream makers. When salt dissolves in water, the freezing point of the resulting solution is lowered, and its boiling point is raised. Rock salt commonly serves as a bed for serving baked oysters and clams.

Salt in the United States

Salt is an essential commodity. Establishment of early American settlements and demographic shifts of population were determined by continuous and reliable supplies of salt. For instance, along the Kanawha River in West Virginia or near Onondaga, New York, deer and buffalo traveled to salt springs to lick salt. Native Americans followed the animal trails in search of a salt supply. Upon discovery of salt and brine springs, Native Americans set up kettles and boiled brines to produce salt.

According to the Salt Institute, the U.S. salt industry formally began in 1614, when the colonists established solar saltworks on Smith's Island, Virginia. Abundant sources of salt in a region typically led to innovations in search and production methods. Large-scale salt production from brine springs was under way in America by 1800, and within a few years drilling for more concentrated brine had begun. Solar evaporation methods were systemized in New England during the early 1800s. Mechanical evaporation in multiple-effect open "grainer" pans began in about 1833, along with methods to purify the brine before evaporation. Full-scale production in open pits or quarries began in 1862, during the Civil War. By 1869 the first underground salt mine was in operation.

Abundant salt supply also spawned adjunct industries in the area, such as fishing and cattle industries. Further, massive quantities of salt produced often translated to an upgrade in infrastructure in order to transport the salt. For instance, the Erie Canal was opened in 1825 with salt as its principle cargo. Salt-producing towns have thus enriched local history, and many American cities and landmarks memorialize the importance of salt.

Salt production was so important to the growth and prosperity of America that patents and subsidies were granted to anyone who could produce vast quantities of salt cheaply. Since the advent of the salt industry, continuous supply of pure salt has remained the goal. Before 1776 salt could be procured from Massachusetts, Europe, and the West Indies at reasonable rates. During the American Revolution part of the British war strategy was to deny Americans access to salt. If the salt supply was cut, American soldiers, horses, medical community, fisheries, furriers, and households would invariably suffer.

Americans thus have a long history of boiling saltwater during salt scarcities. In fact salt production came to be known as a downright patriotic activity. The coarse salt was produced by boiling during the War of 1812 and again during the Civil War. During lean times, alternative methods for curing meat and preserving foods were experimented with, and salt conservation was a hot topic among neighbors. Making salt for domestic use was deemed as commonplace and necessary as making soap from ash and grease or gathering firewood and lumber from forests.

Salt as a By-product, By-products of Salt

On occasion salt manufacturing was a by-product of the lumbering industry, or salt was accidentally discovered while in pursuit of another resource, such as oil or petroleum. Brine is a source material for the chemical industry. Rock salt or brine serves as a basic component for an array of materials, including plastics, glass, synthetic rubber, cleansers, pesticides, paint adhesives, metal coatings, and chlor-alkali chemicals. World War I brought a demand for chlorine, caustic acid,

---

of the Kitchen, explains: "Concentration of salt in a food helps determine chemically how many of the other flavors components are going to behave; that is, how available they are to our senses." For instance, salt firms the textures of pickles and concentrates and balances a host of herbaceous, spicy, and sweet flavors.

Cooks are partial to their favorite salt. The texture and flavor of different salts determine their best usage. For purified salt, such additives as iodine (an important preventative for hypothyroidism), fluoride, and anticaking agents influence usage, especially for preservation techniques like curing, brining, and pickling. In unpurified salt, organic remains could potentially react with proteins in the foods being preserved and cause spoilage.

Salt is an excellent food preservative. High concentrations of salt preserve food by drawing water out of the cells and destroying bacterial and fungal cells. Salt controls fermentation, wherein the safe, "good" bacteria already existing in the food breaks apart sugars to create an acid. The acid helps preserve the food for extended periods, thereby preserving nutrients.

The United States is the world's largest salt producer 45 million tons a year. The basic methods of producing salt have not changed for centuries—boiling, evaporation, and mining. The modern salt industry cites fourteen thousand distinct uses for salt in countless industries, most notably in the manufacture of chemicals, preservation of meats and food products, curing of hides, and deicing of roads.

Harper's Weekly *published Frederick Ray's drawing of salt works at Syracuse, New York, on November 13, 1886.*

and other chemical products, which could be obtained from salt brine.

In the twenty-first century exotic salt is considered chic. Gourmet markets sell the rock in all colors and gradations from the world over. Modern food preservation methods, such as refrigeration, pasteurization, pressure cooking, and hygienic food packaging, have eliminated the need to preserve food with salt. Nevertheless, the United States, with its variety of ethnic groups, continues to employ corning, pickling, and brining, the time-honored salting techniques. Bacon, ham, pickles, anchovies, and other salty foods remain enduring classics in America.

[See also CONDIMENTS; DRYING; FLAVORINGS; JEWISH DIETARY LAWS; PICKLING; SNACKS, SALTY.]

BIBLIOGRAPHY

Eskew, Garnett Laidlaw. *Salt: The Fifth Element.* Chicago: Ferguson, 1948.

Jorgensen, Janice. *Encyclopedia of Consumer Brands.* Vol. 1, *Consumable Brands.* Detroit, MI: St. James, 1994.

Kurlansky, Mark. *Salt: A World History.* New York: Penguin, 2002.

McGee, Harold. *On Food and Cooking: The Science and Lore of the Kitchen.* New York: Scriber, 2004.

Norris, Lucy. *Pickled: Preserving a World of Tastes and Traditions.* New York: Stewart, Tabori, and Chang, 2003.

Steingarten, Jeffrey. *It Must Have Been Something I Ate.* New York: Knopf, 2002.

HYON JUNG LEE

Saltwater Taffy

Saltwater taffy is a uniquely American candy made and sold at seaside resorts on the east and west coasts and in Salt Lake City, Utah. Also known as "saltwater kisses" or "seaside taffy," saltwater taffy is in the class of sweet, chewing candies, along with toffees, nougats, caramels, and other taffies. The bite-size pieces of pastel-colored candy are sold loose by the pound or packed in decorative boxes or tins. A one-pound box of assorted flavors of saltwater taffy is a traditional gift from someone who has vacationed at the seashore.

Saltwater taffy originated in 1883 in Atlantic City, New Jersey. It was merely a saltwater version of hand-pulled molasses taffy, which had existed in America since the 1840s. Initially molasses was the only flavor of saltwater taffy. Vanilla and chocolate flavors soon followed.

Saltwater taffy is made by boiling sugar, corn syrup, salted water, and butter to a syrup at the hard-ball stage (250°–268°F). The final temperature of the syrup determines the taffy's texture. Syrup cooked to a low temperature is soft and chewy, whereas high-temperature taffy is hard. When the syrup reaches the desired temperature, the hot syrup is poured onto a marble slab or a metal table to cool. Then the candy is aerated and expanded by pulling and twisting. Flavor and color are added. When satiny, opaque, and light, the taffy is cut into small pieces and individually wrapped in waxed paper.

Since the early 1900s these operations have been performed by specialized machines.

[See also CANDY BARS AND CANDY; MOLASSES.]

BIBLIOGRAPHY

Levi, Vicki Gold, ed. *Atlantic City: 125 Years of Ocean Madness; Starring Miss America, Mr. Peanut, Lucy the Elephant, the High Diving Horse, and Four Generations of Americans Cutting Loose.* 2nd ed. Berkeley, CA: Ten Speed, 1994.

ROBERT W. BROWN

Sanders, Colonel

Colonel Harland David Sanders was born on September 9, 1890, in Henryville, Indiana, the son of an impoverished butcher. An internationally recognized icon in the twenty-first century, he is famous for founding and developing Kentucky Fried Chicken, an achievement that helped change the way America eats.

When Harland was six years old, his father died. To make ends meet, his mother worked in a tomato-canning plant, leaving the boy to fend for his siblings. Every night Harland cooked and fed them—nurturing, legend has it, his talent as a truly good cook. "The one thing I always could do was cook," he would say years later (Pearce). The rest of Sanders's early life was spent doing a variety of jobs as farmhand, streetcar conductor, private in the military in Cuba, and railroad fireman. Always he dreamed of making it big. He settled with his wife in Kentucky, seizing on business opportunities as a lawyer, an insurance salesman, and a ferry operator, alternating between going up in the world and slipping down. By 1930 Sanders was operating a service station on Highway 25 in Corbin, Kentucky. Noting the lack of anywhere decent to eat, he started cooking traditional southern fare—including fried chicken—for passersby out of a small room in his filling station. Despite the Depression, the Sanders Café did well, even attracting the praise of Duncan Hines in *Adventures in Good Eating* (1939), a book designed to inform Americans where they could eat well on the road.

Though already in his late forties, Sanders still yearned to make real money. He began experimenting, finding a way to make fried chicken faster (and tastier) by using the newly invented pressure cooker. A few years later he added seasonings—eleven herbs and spices—to the standard eggs, milk, and flour that formed the base of the traditional fried chicken crust. People raved about the chicken, and business grew. In 1949 the governor of Kentucky conferred on Sanders the honorary title of colonel in recognition of his work. Sanders liked the idea. He began to refer to himself as "Colonel," donning a white suit and a black string tie and growing a white goatee to match his hair. The creation of an icon had begun.

In 1952 Sanders had a meeting that changed his life. Pete Harman, a restaurateur in Salt Lake City, was a fellow attendee at the National Restaurant Association convention in Chicago. Between them they came up with the idea of franchising the Colonel's recipe, and before long Harman had opened the first franchise. Seeing great potential in Sanders as a marketing image, Harman named the franchise Colonel Sanders' Kentucky Fried Chicken and painted the Colonel's face on the signboard above his Utah store.

Helped by frequent radio advertising, the franchise was a great success. But the following year the Colonel faced downfall: Highway 25 was rerouted away from his Corbin café, removing all his potential customers. Undeterred, the Colonel took to the road himself, relentlessly selling his recipe to roadside eateries. His larger-than-life image and his love of self-promotion worked wonders. By 1960 two hundred franchises were selling Kentucky Fried Chicken; three years later the number had soared to some six hundred.

Colonel Sanders sold his company in 1964 but remained inseparable from his chicken. "He was our ace," said the new owner, the future Kentucky governor John Y. Brown. "He wasn't just a trademark. He wasn't just someone an adman had made up. . . . He was a real, live human being, and a colorful, attractive, persuasive one. My job was to get him before the American people and let him sell his own product" (Pearce). In the late 1960s the Colonel appeared in national advertising, TV shows, celebrity events, and even a movie. A nationally recognized symbol, he became the emotional connection between the brand and consumers. To the public he was Kentucky Fried Chicken.

Colonel Sanders died in 1980, and for a while his image receded from view. But his power as a brand icon was undeniable. In 1990 a look-alike actor was used in TV commercials. The ads fell flat. The Colonel, it appeared, could not be imitated. Eight years later he came back more convincingly in an animated format, dancing onto TV screens. In 2002 commercials had the actor Jason Alexander, known for his role on *Seinfeld*, declaring he was on "a mission from the Colonel."

Harland David Sanders entered into the restaurant business in 1930 when he opened a café at the gas station he owned in Kentucky.

As the twenty-first century opened, KFC was a vast, multimillion-dollar global corporation with nearly twelve thousand outlets worldwide. The Colonel's face embellished every one of them. KFC has kept him as an icon –in residence quite intentionally. As a company KFC sells chicken as part of a logistically complex process of mass production and mass-marketing. But by using Colonel Sanders as an icon, the company could at least present the face of a bygone age, when times were good and the chicken really was home fried.

[See also Chicken; Fast Food; Hines, Duncan; Roadside Food; Pressure Cookers.]

BIBLIOGRAPHY

Jackle, John A., and Keith A. Sculle. *Fast Food: Roadside Restaurants in the Automobile Age*. Baltimore: Johns Hopkins University Press, 1999.

Pearce, John Ed. *The Colonel: The Captivating Biography of the Dynamic Founder of a Fast-Food Empire*. Garden City, NY: Doubleday, 1982.

CORINNA HAWKES

Well-dressed women prepare sandwiches for needy children.

Sandwiches

The fourth earl of Sandwich was probably not the first person to place food between two pieces of bread and consume it by holding it in his hand, but his doing so launched a culinary revolution that has gained momentum ever since. Sandwiches became popular in London and were first mentioned in 1762.

The British introduced sandwiches into the United States. Sandwich recipes were first published in American cookbooks in 1816. Early published sandwich fillings included a wide variety of fillings, such as shellfish, meats, fish, poultry, cheese, eggs, fruit, nuts, mushrooms, tongue, jelly, and jam. After the Civil War sandwiches were extremely common in the United States. Some were dainty pieces consumed at upper-class luncheons, teas, suppers, and picnics. For the working class, sandwiches were much less dainty. Large rolls were often used to house diverse fillings. These substantial sandwiches were served at taverns and bars.

At the end of the nineteenth century, sandwiches acquired specific names. Multi-layered one were called club or triple-deckers by the 1890s, while others took the names of specific individuals, although the referents are greatly debated, such as the original creator of the Reuben sandwich.

During the 1890s sandwiches took another leap forward. In 1893 Mrs. Alexander Orr Bradley published her *Beverages and Sandwiches*. This included twenty-seven sandwich recipes, including recipes for unusual sandwiches filled with woodcock, imported Italian tuna, tuna roe, and imported Roquefort, gruyère, brie, and neufchâtel cheeses. By the end of the nineteenth century, salads and sandwiches had become closely associated. Many salads, among them those for chicken, egg, and lobster, became sandwich

fillings. From the earliest sandwich recipes, condiments and fillings were listed as ingredients. The most common early sandwich flavoring was butter. Other early fillings and condiments included lettuce, ketchup, mustard, curry powder, pickles, and mayonnaise.

Hot Sandwiches

Until the early twentieth century most sandwiches were served cold. Sandwiches were usually served in the home on thin slices of bread that could not easily contain the juices from hot meat or sausage. The solution was to use large rolls or buns, but these were not considered delicate enough to be consumed easily in polite company. Virtually all large and hot sandwiches were first sold by vendors or delicatessens. This innovation was followed by the appearance of toasted or fried sandwiches, such as the ever-popular toasted cheese sandwich. Sausages and ground meat were another matter. Hot sausages were sold in buns by vendors by the mid-nineteenth century. The first located mention of the hamburger sandwich occurs in 1890s, but like the hot dog, hamburger sandwiches were not common until the early twentieth century. Other hot or large sandwiches, such as grinders, po'boys, Philadelphia cheesesteaks, sloppy joes, and submarine sandwiches, were created by vendors about this time.

Sandwich Revolutions

Several major changes revolutionized sandwich making in America. The first was the removal of the germ in the bread. Rancidity in bread was caused mainly by lipids in the wheat germ. Without the germ, bread stayed fresh tasting longer. The second was the use of chemical leavening agents, which greatly reduced the time necessary to make bread, and the introduction of chemical preservatives that prevented commercial bread from

turning stale quickly. The invention of the continuous conveyor oven also made possible the production of bread at a faster pace. Finally, Gustav Papendick invented a process for slicing and wrapping bread in the late 1920s. That each of these changes reduced the taste and nutritional quality of bread was less important than the mass production and national distribution of low-cost bread, rolls, and buns the changes facilitated.

Perhaps the greatest impact of these changes was felt by America's youth and the nation's working class. Sandwiches had been recommended for school lunches as early as 1884. The relationship between children and sandwiches was cemented with the production of commercial sliced bread. Sliced bread meant that young children could make sandwiches themselves without needing to use potentially dangerous knives for cutting through bread loaves. As a consequence of lowered costs, new ease of assembling, and infinite potential variety, sandwiches became one of the top luncheon foods consumed by the nation's working class beginning in the early 1900s. Brought in lunch bags to work or bought in company cafeterias, from street vendors, or at fast food establishments, sandwiches remain one of America's favorite lunch foods in the twenty-first century.

By 2005 this had increased to an estimated two hundred sandwiches per American. Through the American military and American fast food establishments, the Anglo-American sandwich went global during the second part of the twentieth century. Sandwiches in the twenty-first century are consumed in some form in almost every country in the world.

[See also Bread, Sliced; Club Sandwich; Dagwood Sandwich; Denver Sandwich; Gyro; Hamburger; Hoagie; Hot Brown Sandwich; Hot Dogs; Italian Sausage Sandwich with

PEPPERS AND ONIONS; MONTE CRISTO SANDWICH; MUFFALETTA SANDWICH; OYSTER LOAF SANDWICH; PHILADELPHIA CHEESESTEAK SANDWICH; PIMIENTO CHEESE SANDWICH; PO'BOY SANDWICH; RANHOFER, CHARLES; REUBEN SANDWICH; RORER, SARAH TYSON; SANDWICH TRUCKS; STREET VENDORS; WAXED PAPER; WRAPS.]

BIBLIOGRAPHY

Beverages and Sandwiches for Your Husband's Friends by One Who Knows. New York: Brentano's, 1893.

Marton, Renée. "Say 'Cheese!' How the Grilled Cheese Sandwich Evolved in American Culinary History." *ASFS: Association for the Study of Food and Society* 15 (Fall 2002): 5–8.

Mercuri, Becky. *Sandwiches That You Will Like.* Pittsburgh, PA: WQED Multimedia, 2002.

ANDREW F. SMITH

Sandwich Trucks

Sandwich trucks are a type of catering truck, or mobile food unit, and are referred to in the industry as mobile industrial caterers. They are designed to cover a route and sell lunch to people working at construction sites, industrial parks, or other areas without many food options nearby.

The idea of taking lunches to where the workers were employed arose in the early twentieth century, when people began to travel to work in centralized locations, such as factories, and were unable to go back to their homes to eat lunch. Local food companies began packing box lunches in commissary kitchens. These boxes contained all-inclusive meals that typically included a sandwich, piece of fruit, cold beverage, dessert, and stick of gum. The food companies would send workers out to take these lunches to factories and work sites and have them wait outside for the noon bell to ring. The factory hands would come out and purchase box lunches from them.

By the 1940s the food companies began refining the process by delivering lunches in holding boxes that had hot charcoal on the bottom so that hot sandwiches could be served. Thermoses were used to provide hot coffee. Eventually the food companies found that selling lunches from trucks was more convenient than selling them from holding boxes. This was how the sandwich truck evolved.

The California truck, or cold truck, became popular in the 1950s. It originated in California and is basically a pickup truck with a stainless steel body. Its primary purpose is to serve prewrapped sandwiches and simple foods, like hot dogs, that can be prepared on a steam table. Throughout the years mobile catering trucks have been constantly refined and updated. In addition to cold trucks, there are hot trucks, which are kitchens on wheels that contain everything from coffee urns to ovens and grills.

According to the executive director of the Mobile Industrial Caterer's Association (MICA), sandwich trucks offer "everything you can imagine" in the way of food choices. The most popular items are sandwiches, chips, candy, and soda. Most sandwiches are premade by specialized companies such as Landshire, Bridgeford, and White Castle. However, some trucks are equipped to prepare and sell foods on the spot. These items might range from grilled cheese and burgers to popular Mexican food products.

All mobile food units must be assigned to certified kitchens or wholesale supermarkets called commissaries. The trucks are cleaned, stocked, and stored there overnight. Most of the food for sale on the truck is purchased at the commissary. Individual states have their own regulations, usually guided by the Department of Health Services. California, for example, has strict rules regarding the purchase of food for trucks, requiring that it all be obtained from an approved vendor, facility, or commissary.

The ways of bringing meals to workers have evolved through the years. The type of truck and the variety of food choices available may have changed with the times, but sandwich trucks have remained a mainstay for employees in need of convenient food choices at lunchtime.

[See also FAST FOOD; STREET VENDORS; TAKE-OUT FOODS; WHITE CASTLE.]

COLLEEN JOYCE PONTES

Sangria

Sangaree—from the Spanish word *sangría*, which literally means "bloody"—was a common drink in the colonial period of American history, continuing in popularity through the late nineteenth century. It was a punch made of sweetened, diluted red wine spiced with nutmeg. Americans most likely acquired the drink from the Caribbean, where it had been made since at least the late seventeenth century. In North America sangaree was served either cold or hot, depending on the season. It largely disappeared in the United States during the early twentieth century.

In the twentieth century sangria became the national iced drink of Spain, and it remained popular in the Caribbean, where American tourists sipped the cool beverage in the tropical heat. During the late 1940s sangria reemerged in the United States, where it was consumed by Hispanic Americans and was served in Spanish restaurants. In 1964 it captured the attention of other Americans when it was featured at the Spanish pavilion at the New York World's Fair. Sangria's popularity soared in America during the following decade, and Yago Sant'Gria, a commercial type of sangria, was imported from Spain in the 1970s.

Sangria is traditionally made with a full-bodied red wine (such as a Spanish rioja), sweetened with a little sugar, and flavored with orange juice. Sliced lemons and oranges are added and left to macerate in the wine. Still or sparkling water and ice are added when the sangria is served. White sangria is an innovation made using white wine. Some American recipes replace the sparkling water with a lemon-lime soft drink and increase the sugar, thus creating a sweet, bubbly, alcoholic beverage. Americans have also served sangria with a vast array of other fruit (apples, cherries, mangoes, or peaches, for instance), and occasionally brandy is added. Sangria's popularity was most likely the inspiration for the commercial wine coolers, made of white wine and fruit juice, that came on the market in the early 1980s.

ANDREW F. SMITH

Sara Lee Corporation

Sara Lee Corporation is one of the world's largest manufacturers and packagers of branded (as opposed to private-label) goods. Operating in some two hundred countries, its product lines include clothing, household products, and foods—its core business. Sara Lee's corporate history is an example of how aggressive acquisition, combined with technological innovations and keen marketing strategies, succeeded in the new post–World War II global economy.

Sara Lee bears the name of its most celebrated bakery division. Founded in 1950 by Charles Lubin and Arthur Gordon, Lubin's brother-in-law, the Kitchen of Sara Lee was a wholesale baker of high-quality products, such as its celebrated All Butter Pound Cake and All Butter Pecan Coffee Cake introduced in 1952. Sara Lee herself was Lubin's only daughter, who had earlier given her name to either a fruitcake or a cheesecake. As the business expanded in the Chicago area, Lubin realized that frozen products could extend the company's reach. Together with Ekco, a housewares manufacturer, Sara Lee developed the first aluminum foil packages with laminated lids as well as new formulas for frozen products to go inside them in 1954. Products were shipped nationwide.

This success attracted Nathan Cummings, president of Consolidated Foods. A Canadian, Cummings had built various businesses and in 1939 entered the U.S. market by purchasing a food distribution company in Baltimore, Maryland. Soon other companies were added, including the packager of the well-known Richelieu brand, as Cummings developed an ongoing corporate philosophy—expansion through acquisition both at home and abroad. At one time Consolidated owned Piggly Wiggly and Eagle supermarkets, long since divested under Federal Trade Commission orders. In the middle 1960s Consolidated began to purchase nonfood companies, and by 1975 about two-thirds of company profits came from these entities.

In 1956 Sara Lee was brought in, with Lubin remaining as president until his retirement in 1965. In 1965 Sara Lee built the largest and most modern baking facility in the country in Deerfield, Illinois (closed in 1990). To go with the increased production and growth in retail and institutional sales, the company hired Mitch Leigh, composer of the hit Broadway show *Man of la Mancha*, to write a new advertising jingle. The result became a part of American popular culture: "Nobody doesn't like Sara Lee."

With John H. Bryan's presidency beginning in 1975, Consolidated Foods saw a huge expansion of sales, a growing presence worldwide, and a new name. In 1985, after considerable market research, the company's name was changed to its most recognizable high-quality brand, Sara Lee Corporation. Bryan came from Bryan Brothers Packing of West Point, Mississippi, the Southeast's best-known meat packager. By judicious cutting and purchasing, Sara Lee became a profitable company, which, as the twenty-first century began, had never failed to pay shareholders a dividend. Nor should it be surprising that by the 1990s Sara Lee had become America's largest packaged-meat producer. Among its meat brands were Hillshire Farms, Ball Park, Jimmy Dean, Bryan, Kahns, State Fair, Rudy's Farm, Briar Street Market, Trail's Best, Galileo, and Bil Mar. Baked goods, however, remained critical to the company in the form of Sara Lee Bakery, International, Mr. Pita, Manhattan Deli (bagels), Wolferman's English Muffins, and Earthgrains, a newly acquired whole-grain bread company.

[**See also** BAKERIES; CAKES; FREEZERS AND FREEZING; MEAT.]

BIBLIOGRAPHY

Brinson, Carroll. *A Tradition of Looking Ahead: The Story of Bryan Foods.* Jackson, MS: Oakdale, 1986.

Grant, Tina, ed. *The International Directory of Company Histories.* Detroit, MI: St. James, 1996.

Knoch, Joanne. "Turning out Sweets a Science at Sara Lee." *Chicago Tribune,* Dec. 2, 1959.

BRUCE KRAIG

Sarsaparilla

The word "sarsaparilla" may evoke images of languid belles and parched cowboys, but its etymology is decidedly less romantic. An Anglicization of *zarzaparilla*, it refers at once to various New World plant species of the genus *Smilax*, the roots of these vinelike plants, the extracts derived from the roots, the drinks flavored by the extracts—and the subjugation of American indigenes by the Spanish conquistadores who named it. The Spanish deferred to the native populations, however, in their approach to the plant as a promising medical find (and as an antisyphilitic first and foremost). Meanwhile their North American counterparts did the same.

In the nineteenth century, as a developing craze for restorative mineral waters slowly took its toll on the long-standing custom of home brewing, apothecaries in Philadelphia and elsewhere began to invent and dispense flavored soda waters that were of course the first soft drinks. Among them was sarsaparilla, which became a favorite at the pharmacy–cum soda fountain not only as a soft drink in itself but also as an ingredient in root beer

and ice cream sodas. (One creation myth among many links sarsaparilla to the world's first Black Cow.) Increasingly, however, flavors such as sassafras, licorice, and wintergreen were employed to soften the bitterness of sarsaparilla until all that was finally left was the name. In the twentieth century that too disappeared, perhaps not coincidentally as the medical establishment began mounting challenges to sarsaparilla's therapeutic reputation.

[**See also** HOMEMADE REMEDIES; ROOT BEER; SODA DRINKS; SODA FOUNTAINS; SASSAFRASSES.]

BIBLIOGRAPHY

Funderburg, Anne Cooper. *Sundae Best: A History of Soda Fountains.* Bowling Green, OH: Bowling Green State University, 2002.

Kiple, Kenneth F., and Kriemhild Coneè-Ornelas, eds. "History, Nutrition, and Health." In *The Cambridge World History of Food,* vol. 2. Cambridge, U.K. Cambridge University Press, 2000.

RUTH TOBIAS

Sarsaparilla and Wintergreen

These species are botanically unrelated but have similar usage: birch beer, root beer, and sarsaparilla were once flavored with them. Sassafras (*Sassafras albidum*) is a deciduous tree in the laurel family (Lauraceae), the same family as allspice, bay leaves, and cinnamon, and shares their sweet, warmly aromatic character.

Sarsaparilla (*Smilax ornata*), a woody vine of the lily family (Liliaceae), has a mild anise flavor, and provides root beer's foamy head. Wintergreen (*Gaultheria* species) is an evergreen perennial in the heath family (Ericaceae). Its distinctive spicy flavor, also found in sweet birch (*Betula lenta*), comes from methyl salicylate, which is now made synthetically.

[**See also** ROOT BEER; SASSAFRASSES; SWEET SPICES.]

BIBLIOGRAPHY

Allen, Gary. *The Herbalist in the Kitchen.* Champain: University of Illinois Press, forthcoming.

Bailey, L. H. *Hortus Third: A Concise Dictionary of Plants Cultivated in the United States and Canada.* New York: Macmillan, 1976.

GARY ALLEN

Sassafrasses

The sassafras tree (*Sassafras albidum*) is a New World tree. All parts of the tree are pleasantly aromatic, and its bark and roots can be steeped as a beverage and for medicinal purposes. Large leaves on a single branch of the sassafras tree appear in three different shapes. Sassafras was so prized for a time that it was used as a medium of exchange and offered to guests at weddings.

Before the Civil War, Native Americans and East Coast settlers made sassafras each spring by boiling new maple sugar sap, then adding sassafras roots and simmering for a time. The bark and roots contain the highest concentration of oil. These are steeped to

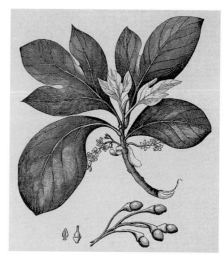

A sassafras illustration from the Cyclopedia of Useful Knowledge, *1890s.*

make a deep red sassafras tea given as a diuretic to treat sickness caused from drinking polluted water. It could also be used as a yellow-orange dye. In later years sassafras flavoring became a useful ingredient in the making of root beer and as a scent in perfumes and soaps.

The Choctaw of Louisiana's bayou country discovered that young sassafras leaves and stems, once dried and reduced to a powder, added rich flavor as well as thickening to Creole and Cajun dishes, especially as filé (FEE-lay) powder in gumbos. The filé must be added at the end of cooking to prevent it from becoming tough or stringy.

Sassafras oils have been found to contain a carcinogenic substance called safrole. The U.S. Food and Drug Administration has banned many forms of sassafras for human consumption.

[**See also** FOOD AND DRUG ADMINISTRATION; HOMEMADE REMEDIES; ROOT BEER.]

BIBLIOGRAPHY

Clepper, Henry. "The Singular Sassafras: Fact, Folklore, and Fantasy about This Unique Understory Tree with the Mitten Leaves." *American Forests* 95, nos. 3–4 (Apr. 1989): 33.

Peeples, Edwin A. "Native Sassafras." *Country Journal* 17, no. 1 (Jan.-Feb. 1990): 18.

MARTY MARTINDALE

Sauces and Gravies

An eighteenth-century French visitor allegedly sniped that America was a nation of many religions but only one sauce. Sarah Josepha Hall, in *The Good Housekeeper* (2nd ed., 1841), agreed: "The French have a much greater variety of gravies than the English or Americans, who copy the English mode of cookery. Melted butter is with us the gravy for most meats" (p. 62).

The seventeenth-century colonists continued the late-medieval English tradition of thickening broth, wine, vinegar, and fruit juices with bread crumbs and seasoning those sauces with dried fruits and sweet spices. By the end of the seventeenth century, however, dairy products were becoming more plentiful in the colonies and could follow the new English styles of butter- and cream-based sauces. The signature American sauce was "drawn" or "melted" butter, comprised of a spoonful of water, a dusting of flour, and lots of butter gently swirled into an emulsion. But woe to the inattentive cook who overheated the butter, causing it "to oil." Frequent, unappetizing descriptions of sauces "composed of little else than liquid grease" (Hamilton 29) confirm the exasperation of Mary Randolph in *The Virginia House-Wife* (1824) that no sauce is "so generally done badly" (112–13).

Another option for eighteenth- and nineteenth-century Americans was to take or mix sauces at the table from an assortment of pots, cruets, and casters containing "store sauces." While a few store sauces might be commercially made (and thus "store-bought"), the term referred to sauces with long shelf lives such, as homemade ketchups, mustards, chutneys, Worcestershires, and flavored vinegars. Catharine Beecher's *Domestic Receipt-Book* (1858) explains, "Soy is a fashionable sauce for fish, which is mixed on the plate with drawn butter" (245–46). Miss Beecher's "soy" is a homemade concoction of caramelized sugar, salt, anchovies, and flavorings. Her schematic of a properly set table shows a set of castors, but others loathed the practice because spices quickly staled and olive oil turned rancid in the poorly sealed table ornaments. Castors had fallen from fashion by the early twentieth century, although jars of mustard, ketchup, and commercial steak sauce still appear on the table.

The French Influence

Direct French influences on American cooking date from Huguenot settlements in the late seventeenth century. Yet except for rarified tables with cooks skilled enough to use Louis Eustache Ude's *The French Cook* (Philadelphia, 1828) or Eliza Leslie's *Domestic French Cookery* (Philadelphia, 1832), French sauces were thought impossibly complex. According to Sarah Rutledge's *The Carolina Housewife* (1847), most French cooking "require[d] an apparatus either beyond our reach or too complicated for our native cooks" (iv).

One reason for this daunting reputation is that many French sauces require an ever-bubbling stockpot. Many cookery books of the first half of the nineteenth century eschewed the preparation of meat stocks as a "superfluous waste." Lettice Bryan's *The Kentucky Housewife* (1839) disapproved of the "practice of some cooks to fry pieces of coarse meat for the purpose of making brown gravies" and urges the cook "to avoid expense and trouble" (p. 164) by storing the "white gravy" from boiled meats for her few recipes requiring meat gravy as an ingredient. This barebones approach undoubtedly appealed to overworked frontier housewives. But in fashionable urban restaurants and homes, French cookery and sauce making was expected by the late nineteenth century, encouraged by two ex-patriot French chefs living in New York, Pierre Blot and Charles Ranhofer. Both wrote cookbooks touting extensive sauce repertories. Ranhofer's *The Epicurean* (1893) contained over 250 sauce recipes, many taken directly from the best examples of French haute cuisine. It became the bible for sauce cookery.

Middle-class housewives in the early twentieth century were guided by several simpler American cookery books devoted exclusively to sauces. Yet only one sauce was widely prepared: the roux-based white sauce, or simplified béchamel, that was the darling of Fannie Farmer and the home economics movement. Frequently reduced to a formulary chart for "Thin, Medium, or Thick" sauces in works such as the Good Housekeeping Institute's *Good Meals and How to Prepare Them* (1927), connoisseurs likened them to "library paste gone wrong." Housewives also relied on convenient, finished sauces, marketed under brands such as Chef Boiardi, Escoffier, Heinz, and Maison Petitjean. The ever-practical Julia Child in *Mastering the Art of French Cooking* (1961) offered tricks for doctoring canned bouillon when the ambitious home cook did not have time to prepare stock from scratch. Although she gave recipes for the classic French béchamel, hollandaise, and velouté, Child omitted any recipe for the traditional brown mother sauce, demi-glace, explaining that it takes "several days to accomplish and the result is splendid, but as we are concerned with less formal cooking, we shall discuss it no further" (1:66). Given her involved recipes for baguettes with three risings and beef stuffed with foie gras and truffles, this omission echoes the American fear of fancy sauces.

Recent Developments

Nouvelle cuisine may have killed the flour-thickened béchamels, but it reinvented the rich, emulsified butter sauces of the eighteenth and nineteenth centuries under the name beurre blanc. Moreover home chefs cooking for recreation make laborious demi-glace or purchase it frozen from gourmet purveyors. It differs from the commercial sauces of an earlier generation by providing the foundation to the hobbyist cook, who creatively finishes the sauce.

Greater familiarity with ethnic cuisines supports a growing market for purchased sauces. The availability of formerly exotic ingredients allow more ambitious home cooks to assemble Chinese stir-fries with hoisin, raw Latin American salsas spiked with jalapeños, or pan-Asian dipping sauces redolent of cilantro, fresh ginger, lime, and fermented fish sauce.

Gravy

Gravy is a subset of sauces, identified in most eighteenth- and nineteenth-century American cookbooks as broth or meat essences. Gravy formed the base for the more complicated sauces and was essential to the intimidating French cuisine. But Americans have also made quick gravies by binding the meat

Making a sauce at the Institute of Culinary Education, New York.

juices and fatty drippings left in the roasting pan with flour. Quirky variations include the cream gravy for fried chicken or steak that mixes the leftover frying fat with flour and water and the white gravy label given to fricassees popular in the South. Italian American spaghetti gravy refers to tomato sauce with ground meat.

BIBLIOGRAPHY

Child, Julia, Louisette Bertholle, and Simone Beck. *Mastering the Art of French Cooking* (updated, vol. 1), New York: Knopf, 1985.

Lehmann, Gilly. "The Rise of the Cream Sauce, 1660–1760." In *Milk: Beyond the Dairy; Proceedings of the 1999 Oxford Symposium on Food and Cookery.* Totnes, UK: Prospect Books, 2000, 225–31.

Peterson, James. *Sauces.* New York: Van Nostrand Reinhold, 1991.

Weaver, William Woys. "White Gravies in American Popular Diet." In *Food in Change: Eating Habits from the Middle Ages to the Present Day,* ed. Alexander Fenton and Eszter Kisbán. Edinburgh: J. Donald Publishers, 1986, 41–52.

CATHY K. KAUFMAN

Sauger

Sauger (*Stizostedion canadense*) is similar to walleye and walleye pike and has some of the same nicknames, such as jackfish, jack salmon, pike perch, and gray pike. Sauger is smaller than walleye and does not usually grow beyond two to four pounds. Sauger occupies most of the same waters as walleye. Sauger is a game fish and supports a commercial fishery in Canada.

SANDRA L. OLIVER

Sausage

Sausage was invented as an economical means of preserving and transforming into more palatable forms the less-desirable cuts of meat and components, such as blood and internal organs, that could not be consumed fresh at slaughter. The word "sausage" is derived from the Latin *salsisium*, from *salsus*, meaning "salted" or "preserved meat." Although the etymology indicates that sausage can be made from any kind of salted meat, the term traditionally applies to chopped pork stuffed into a casing.

The origin of sausage making is lost in history. Sausages probably resulted when early cultivators discovered that salt could preserve easily perishable surplus meat. Sausages were reportedly produced from pigs as long ago as 5000 B.C.E. in Egypt and the Far East. One of the earliest documentations of sausage making and consumption is Homer's *Odyssey* (800 B.C.E.). Consumed by the Romans but outlawed by Constantine the Great and forbidden by the early Christian Church because of an association with many pagan festivals, sausages became highly sought after and even gave rise to a black market for distribution.

The history of sausages in the United States is a history of the immigrants who introduced them. American sausages reflect Old World traditions adapted to the prevailing climatic conditions and locally available ingredients. The simple process of salting, smoking, and drying meats to preserve what could not be consumed immediately has evolved into a modern process providing Americans with hundreds of sausage varieties, more than anywhere else in the world.

Early sausage-making directions were clear. "Sausage skins"—the intestines, uterus, stomach, or bladder preserved at butchering time—were used to encase the "stuffing"—meat, scraps, and chopped organs mixed with herbs, seasonings, and fat. The sausages were dried or smoked, and the resulting links were suspended from iron hooks over a fire.

Advances in microbiology and processing technology have transformed the art of sausage making into a precise science. Refrigeration allows flexible production schedules and ingredient choices. Processing innovation and novel ingredient technologies contributed to improvements in both high-speed, large-scale production and small batch-type operations. Modern mass production transforms prime cuts of meat, along with less tender cuts, into delicious sausages

that contain seasonings, other ingredients, and extra preservatives, such as sodium metabisulfite and ascorbyl palmitate.

Sausages traditionally are classified as fresh, cured, or heat processed. Fresh sausages are intended for immediate cooking. Cured and heat-processed sausages may be kept and eaten cold or heated before consumption. Because of their convenience and versatility, heat-processed sausages are particularly popular among Americans.

Fresh sausages are made by seasoning and usually, but not always, stuffing into a casing fresh meats that are not cured, smoked, fermented, or cooked. These products, such as fresh Italian sausages, require refrigerated storage and cooking before consumption. Cured sausages, primarily salami, cervelat, and pepperoni, are made from cured meats that are not heat processed but may be smoked. Also known as summer sausages, these products are classified as semidry or dry, depending on the extent of drying. Characteristically tangy from fermentation, these products are generally stored at room temperature and can be refrigerated for extended shelf life. Heat-processed sausages are further classified as precooked, emulsion type, or cooked. Precooked sausages include knockwurst and some types of bologna. The nonfermented stuffing is cured (brined) and heat treated for reduction of moisture for better keeping quality. These sausages may be eaten as such or further cooked. Emulsion-type sausages, such as wieners and frankfurters, are products of cured meats homogenized with fat, water, and seasonings. These sausages may be pasteurized and may be eaten as such or scalded before consumption. Cooked sausages are ready-to-serve products, prepared from fresh meats that may sometimes be cured or smoked and cooked after stuffing. Some cooked sausages, such as liverwurst and knockwurst, are not stuffed into casings but are molded and therefore are not always considered sausages. In the United States sausages also are classified by primary ingredient—pork, beef, chicken, turkey, or veal. Pork sausage was predominant because beef was more expensive. Beef and veal sausages, introduced when beef became plentiful at low prices, are not as common elsewhere in the world as they are in the United States.

The introduction of mass manufacturing led to inexpensive production of sausages. Small sausage manufacturers, facing immense competition from industry titans, resorted to distinguishing their sausages from mass-manufactured products as a way of maintaining or increasing market share. The small manufacturers added poultry meats to sausages and marketed the products as tasty and more healthful versions of traditional sausage products. When American consumers embraced turkey as a part of a healthful diet, sausage manufacturers introduced turkey sausages. Artisanal sausages abound, incorporating chicken and

The John Wagner sausage stuffer pictured in the McArthur, Wirth catalog of equipment for butchers, packers, and sausage makers, 1900.

other exotic game and fowl. Dehydration technologies allowed for the addition of dried fruits and vegetables to produce uniquely American sausages with unprecedented variety and texture. Around 1990 vegetarian imitations appeared. Made of soybeans and textured vegetable protein, these sausages were fashioned to mimic the original product in taste and texture. Americans, aware of the health benefits of soybeans, welcomed soy sausages.

Sausages are usually bought already prepared. Although specialty sausages, such as andouille, blood sausage, *bockbier* sausage, bratwurst, chorizo, head cheese, kielbasa, knockwurst, and mortadella, are available in the United States, Americans have consumed more than 20 billion hot dogs in recent years. Alternating between decadent and healthful foods, Americans consume sausages as part of meals and as snacks and have even created a similar product, called "Snausages," for their dogs. The sausage in one form or another is a staple in the average American diet.

[See also Chorizo; Hot Dogs; Meat; Pepperoni; Salami; Vienna Sausage.]

BIBLIOGRAPHY
Kinsella, John, and David Harvey. *Professional Charcuterie*. New York: Wiley, 1996.

KANTHA SHELKE

Sazerac

The Sazerac is a whiskey-and-bitters drink in the tradition of the earliest cocktails. In the early nineteenth century, the owner of a New Orleans apothecary, Antoine Amédée Peychaud, developed a product called Peychaud's Bitters. He mixed it with cognac and enjoyed serving it to his friends. Sewell Taylor, who owned the Sazerac Coffeehouse, put the drink on the map by mixing it with a popular cognac named Sazerac de Forge et Fils and serving Peychaud's concoction as his house cocktail, calling it the Sazerac.

In 1870 Thomas Handy bought the coffeehouse and the rights to Peychaud's Bitters. He changed the recipe of the Sazerac to appeal to the rye whiskey–drinking crowd of the day. The Sazerac recipe of the mid-nineteenth century was a more complex affair with many layers of flavor. The serving glass was seasoned with a splash of the absinthe, an anis-based spirit, and then the rye whiskey was dashed with bitters and slightly sweetened with sugar.

Thomas began to purchase the rights to other spirit brands and market them. Eventually an employee of Thomas's, C. J. O'Reilly, created the company known in the early 2000s as the Sazerac Company, Inc.

[See also Cocktails; Whiskey.]

BIBLIOGRAPHY
The Sazerac Company, New Orleans, LA. www.sazerac.com.

DALE DEGROFF

Sbarro

In 1959 Gennaro and Carmela Sbarro opened a *salumeria Italiana*—an Italian grocery store—in Brooklyn. They sold fresh mozzarella, imported cheeses, sausages, and salamis and later added ready-to-eat foods, such as pastas, salads, and sandwiches, but their biggest seller was pizza. Pizza by the slice was not a new concept in New York, but it was unknown in other parts of the country. They focused on their pizza and opened additional locations in the New York City area and then throughout the Northeast. Unlike other fast food operations, Sbarro featured thirty-five-foot cafeteria-like counters, rather than tables, at their outlets, making them more like the familiar urban pizza parlor.

As of 2005 Sbarro operated 960 restaurants in 48 states and 26 countries, including the United Kingdom, Puerto Rico, Canada, Russia, and Israel. Sbarro is the largest shopping mall–based restaurant chain in the world and has grown to include locations in airports, hospitals, travel plazas, movie theaters, highway rest stops, universities, and train stations. Its corporate headquarters is in Melville, New York.

ANDREW F. SMITH

Scallops

In early times scallops were not favored the way other shellfish were. In more recent times a substantial commercial fishery for scallops has developed on the East Coast and in the Pacific Northwest. Scallops are increasingly the object of aquaculture. The fishery usually is conducted in winter, and scallopers refit their boats for that purpose. Two types of scallop, the large sea scallop and the smaller bay scallop, are preferred for eating. Although the whole scallop is edible, the American market prefers only the muscle that enables the scallop to scoot around the seabed. This preference dates to the nineteenth century, when scallops were cleaned and sold shelled. Scallops are cleaned at sea, and most are sautéed quickly for entrées, incorporated into fish stews and chowder, or skewered and grilled. Scallops also can be eaten raw.

SANDRA L. OLIVER

Scandinavian and Finnish American Food

Scandinavian food has the reputation of being simple, hearty, and somewhat colorless, with a "meat and potatoes" stereotype. Most of the immigrants to America came from a rural rather than a cosmopolitan background and became farmers and laborers, who were not inclined to become restaurateurs. This is why there are not many Scandinavian restaurants in the United States. The best Scandinavian food has always been found in the home kitchen. It was the woman's job to feed hungry laborers on farms and in logging and mining camps.

Between 1830 and 1930, 2.5 million people emigrated from the Nordic countries to North America. Although the emigrants made up a small part of the total European emigration, the number amounted to one-third of the total population of the five countries—Iceland, Sweden, Norway, Denmark, and Finland. (Although Finns are technically not Scandinavians, their food and culture are similar to those of Sweden, Norway, and Denmark. Eastern Finnish food, however, bears resemblance to Russian, particularly the fish and meat pies.) This large-scale emigration was driven by famines in Scandinavia and the dwindling of family farms, which had been traditionally passed down from one generation to another and divided among the sons of the family until they were too small. Those who left their homeland were attracted to the upper Midwest by the offer of free land.

Settling in America

The more to the north the emigrants had originally come from, the more to the north they tended to settle in America. Icelanders settled in Canada, with a few in northern Minnesota. Finns mostly settled in the north and became small farmers, loggers, and miners in Michigan, Minnesota, and Ontario. They retained their heritage, including food traditions and language, longer than did most other Scandinavians.

Swedish settlers were numerous in Minnesota, Illinois, New York, Massachusetts, Washington, and the Canadian prairies. Norwegians settled the prairies to the west and the south and are known for growing high-quality wheat, potatoes, and other grains in the rich soils of the Red River Valley of Minnesota and the Dakotas. This became the foundation of the milling industry that grew in Minneapolis and St. Paul. At the same time, the Danes were spread in small groups over larger areas in Wisconsin, Iowa, Nebraska, Kansas, and California. Danes were dairy farmers and important in the dairy industry in Wisconsin, southern Minnesota, and Iowa.

Contributions to Cuisine

Finnish women, who trained in home economics schools before emigrating, commonly worked as cooks and maids until they married. They were aided by a bilingual cookbook, *Mina Wallin Keitokirja* (Mina Valli's Cookbook), published in New York in the early 1900s in both Finnish and English. The book includes recipes for classic European preparations, from soups to desserts, few of which were common fare in Finland.

The Finns and the Cornish worked together as miners in northern Minnesota and the Upper Peninsula of Michigan. They found common ground in the "pasty," an oval-shaped pie filled with a mixture of beef, potatoes, onions, and sometimes rutabaga, turnips, or carrots, which they carried in their lunch boxes into the mines. The Finns have claimed pasties as their own because

A Scandinavian feast at an outdoor festival near Madison, Wisconsin, 1870s.

of their similarity to the meat pies traditional in eastern Finland. In the twenty-first century pasties are still sold in bakeries throughout the Iron Range of Minnesota and the Upper Peninsula of Michigan. They make great picnic food, and every baker has a personal variation.

The Swedish "smorgasbord" has come to mean a buffet consisting of a variety of foods both simple and elaborate. The American version, however, bears little resemblance to the authentic Scandinavian table. In Sweden and all of Scandinavia "smorgasbord" (or *koldt bord* in Danish, Norwegian, and Icelandic and *voilepapoyta* in Finnish) refers to a bread and butter table. The smorgasbord meal follows a definite pattern. It starts with cold meats, fish, and salads and ends with hot foods. Smorgasbord is served in several courses, and guests never pile their plates high, as is commonly done in America.

Swedish meatballs are often found on the smorgasbord and have become a popular appetizer item on American menus. Authentically they are made of a blend of ground beef, pork, and veal with onions, bread, egg, and seasonings. The mixture is formed into small, one-half-inch balls and sautéed in butter. They are served in a pale brown cream sauce made by combining the pan drippings with cream or milk.

Danes contributed Danish pastry, a yeast pastry that is rolled out and layered with butter in a fashion similar to puff pastry. Known simply as "Danish," they contain a variety of fillings, such as fruit, cream cheese, almond paste, and nuts. In Denmark this pastry is known as "Viennabread."

Norwegian contributions to the cuisine of America are not widely known. *Lefse*, a flat bread that is cooked on a dry griddle, comes from an area in Norway that is small but significant because of the large number of people that emigrated from there. Lutefisk, another contribution of Norwegians, is also known but in a more limited way by Swedes, Danes, and Finns. Lutefisk translates as "lye fish" and is an air-dried cod, so dehydrated that it resembles a thin slice of firewood. It can be kept without refrigeration until it is ready to be reconstituted. The dried cod is soaked first in a solution of lye and water to open the pores. Then the fish is soaked in fresh water for several days until it is reconstituted into a partially gelatinous consistency. Originally lutefisk (*lutfisk* in Swedish and *lipeakala* in Finnish) was the food of poor people and was eaten throughout the winter. Immigrants brought with them supplies of the dried cod. Because it takes so many days of preparation, the precious store became a special Christmas dish. American fish companies, especially in the upper Midwest, import tons of dried cod from Norway, largely during the holiday season.

Baking is an important part of the Scandinavian kitchen. Crispbreads, flat breads, spiced coffee breads, cakes, and cookies are universal among Swedes, Norwegians, Danes, Icelanders, and Finns. Butter, sugar, flour, and eggs are the basic ingredients. Swedes and Finns bake saffron-flavored Lucia bread and the spicy *Pepparkakor* cookies for St. Lucia's Day celebrations on December 13.

Butter cookies, such as Swedish *Vaniljhorn, Mandelkakor, and Spritz Sandbakelser*, can be found in Scandinavian bakeries during the Advent season and sometimes throughout the year. Many cookies are known by other names as well; for example, Swedish *Klenater* is also known by the Norwegian name *Fattigman*.

Generally the Scandinavian contribution to the food traditions of the United States is basic: Finns cleared farmland out of the forests, Norwegians and Swedes tilled the prairie and grew grains, and Swedes and Danes developed food-related businesses, including the all-important dairy and milling industries. [**See also** DAIRY INDUSTRY.]

BIBLIOGRAPHY

Barton, Arnold H. "Introduction." In *Scandinavian Roots—American Lives*. Copenhagen: Nordic Council of Ministers, 2000.

Kaplan, Anne R., Marjorie A. Hoover, and Willard B. Moore. *The Minnesota Ethnic Food Book*. St. Paul: Minnesota Historical Society Press, 1986.

Norman, Hans, and Runblom Harald. *Transatlantic Connections: Nordic Migration to the New World after 1800*. London: Norwegian University Press, 1987.

Ojakangas, Beatrice. *The Great Scandinavian Baking Book*. Minneapolis: University of Minnesota Press, 1999.

BEATRICE OJAKANGAS

School Food

Most of the millions of school meals served daily in the United States are provided through breakfast and lunch programs supported by the Food and Nutrition Service (FNS), a branch of the U.S. Department of Agriculture (USDA). The FNS provides a tiered cash subsidy for school meals that meet certain nutritional criteria. The USDA provides further support with donated commodity foods. These contributions seldom cover expenses, and most urban areas supply additional funds to cover higher labor and distribution costs associated with city provisioning.

As designed by the government, school meals provide an opportunity to use targeted farm products and work as a defense against the problems of poverty. For schools, providing meals is both an administrative burden and an essential element of educational success. Studies have found that children who eat in the School Breakfast Program have significantly higher scores on standardized tests; improved math grades; less hyperactivity, depression, and anxiety; fewer absences; less tardiness; and improved social behavior. Studies have also demonstrated that low-income children in particular do better in schools with meal programs and that early school success and good childhood nutrition have dramatic, long-range impact on later need for government assistance, cost of health care, employment, and overall health and productivity.

History

The first school lunch programs in the United States were charitable efforts to feed the hungry poor. In 1853 the Children's Aid Society of New York supplied the first recorded school lunches in America. Boston, Philadelphia, Cleveland, Milwaukee, and Chicago had meal programs by the early 1900s.

Federal Subsidy

In 1933 Congress set aside 30 percent of import tax revenue to increase domestic consumption and remove farm surplus from the market. Until 1946 allocations for school lunch were granted on a year-to-year basis and addressed clear, immediate needs. The 1946 National School Lunch Act established school lunch as an ongoing government program, permanently authorizing funds "as may be necessary" for school lunch on a matching basis with states. Congress also established the Special Milk Program, a subsidy (three cents) for each half-pint of milk consumed outside of meal programs, to increase the amount of milk drunk in schools and to lessen USDA farm support purchases.

Special Assistance

A major shift in the School Lunch Act program came in the 1960s, beginning with the launch of a pilot special assistance program that consisted of free lunches for children of families whose incomes were at USDA poverty-level rates and reduced-price lunches for children of families whose incomes were 125 percent below poverty level in low-income areas. The program was permanently authorized by the National School Lunch Act and the Child Nutrition Act of 1966.

Though created to help the poor, the administration of the special assistance program created problems. Family income levels determined eligibility for the increased subsidy and marked students as being in "poverty" or "near poverty"; many children felt stigmatized by participating. In addition the stigma meant that those who could pay full price frequently dropped out, greatly reducing the available operating cash and thereby lowering the quality of the programs. Perhaps the biggest burden for schools was the dramatic increase in paperwork required to document eligibility of children receiving free meals.

Child nutrition was brought to the fore in the public mind by the 1969 CBS television documentary *Hunger USA*. Throughout the 1970s the USDA expanded and experimented with programs to address the issues of poverty in the United States, including permanent authorization of school breakfast in 1975 and pilot summer meals and snack programs.

1980s Budget Cuts

The federal budget cuts of the 1980s had the single greatest impact on the availability and quality of school meals since the program's inception in 1946. The Omnibus Budget Reconciliation Acts cut school lunch funding by one-third, raising income levels for assistance; lowering subsidies, especially for reduced-price meals; reducing child care food supplements; freezing the milk subsidy; and removing the Special Milk Program from public schools serving lunch and from most private schools. As a result an estimated 3 million low-income children were forced out of the school lunch program.

Ongoing Issues

The discussion of school lunch has always been multifaceted, touching on the effect of satiety on learning, the direct contribution of good childhood nutrition to lifelong health, the importance of good health to national defense, the debate over food cost and quality, and direct service to America's poor. Views on all these issues determine program funding.

Privatization

Corporations have contracted with some public school districts to take over food service on site. Although privatization has actually led to short-term improvements in the worst lunch programs, studies show that in the long term neither the cost ratio nor the quality is much improved, and in many cases quality and food choice and taste diminish, as does the student participation rate. School meals are a big, profitable market for catering companies, who still seek meal service contracts.

Vending and Nonnutritious Foods

Vending companies and soft-drink manufacturers offer educational perks and money for exclusive rights to sell drinks. This money is often used by schools to fund clubs, activities, and even core curricula. Some contracts give schools money up front, based on projected sales in the lunchrooms, student lounges, and hallways, and have asked for it back if projections are not met, creating a situation in which children and parents actively promote the products outside of school. School districts have become "Pizza Hut districts" or "Coke districts" based on contracts with school boards. These foods frequently replace meals with nutritional value.

Milk

Milk is a source of protein, calcium, and vitamins A and D. Using milk and cheese in school meals supports prices for dairy farmers, and this support played a major part in establishing the lunch program in 1946. Milk also has a high amount of bacteria when compared with soybean milk and can spoil in a matter of hours. Most milk served in schools comes from cows treated with hormones and antibiotics, the use of which has been a major health concern since the beginning of these controversial practices. In addition, when proper precautions are neglected, large contracts for milk and other commodity foods can be used as a dumping ground for tainted or low-quality products.

Multiculturalism

As classrooms become more ethnically diverse, meal programs must pay more attention to varied religious and cultural taboos. Though most dietary requirements can be met with minor shifts in supplies, state-wide food purchases and donated commodities are not as responsive and create additional work for local administrators. Agencies also report the difficulties of filling out assistance eligibility forms for undocumented or non-English-speaking immigrants. Both issues may discourage immigrant participation.

Twenty-first-Century Programs

Meal programs are seeing innovations. A few schools serve organic and non-genetically modified or locally grown and seasonal foods. Student, parent, and staff nutrition committees collaborate, and salad bars and more food choices are appearing. But the very existence of meal programs remains extremely vulnerable to local administration and funding cuts at every level.

[**See also** CAFETERIAS; FARM SUBSIDIES, DUTIES, QUOTAS, AND TARIFFS; HUNGER PROGRAMS; MILK; NUTRITION; POLITICS OF FOOD.]

BIBLIOGRAPHY

American School Food Service Association. Your Child Nutrition eSource. http://www.asfsa.org.

Center for Science in the Public Interest. http://www.cspinet.org.

Food and Nutrition Service, U.S. Department of Agriculture, School Meals Program. http://www.fns.usda.gov/cnd.

Schlosser, Eric. *Fast Food Nation: The Dark Side of the All-American Meal.* Boston: Houghton Mifflin, 2001.

NANCY RALPH

Schrafft's

William F. Schrafft a Bavarian confectioner—founded his candy company in Boston in 1861, selling gum drops and candy canes. Schrafft's sons joined the firm, and in 1927 Schraffts and Sons had built the largest chocolate and candy production factory in the world in Charlestown, Massachusetts.

In 1929 the Frank G. Shattuck Company bought Schrafft's to operate the company's retail stores. Frank G. Shattuck had been the best salesman in the Schrafft family's candy business. The Schrafft's chain of restaurants began as a concept to promote candy sales. The luncheon or tearoom, with its soda fountain, genteel decor and feminine touches, became popular quickly. One outlet in 1898 in Boston led to twenty restaurants by 1915, mostly in New York City. Women were hired as cooks, waitresses, and managers, and many

women spent their entire careers at Schrafft's, which provided bonuses and paid vacations. Efforts to unionize the chain in 1953 were voted down by the employees despite the occasional need of the Labor Relations Board to negotiate pay raises. "Many of our customers are secretaries and stenographers . . . who must watch their pocketbooks," Shattuck was quoted as saying. During World War II sugar rationing restricted customers to two lumps per cup of coffee or tea. Schrafft's also sponsored contests for Girl Scouts to promote the use of victory garden vegetables. Winning entries received a $100 War Bond.

Despite efforts to attract more men as customers with the addition of cocktail bars at many "stores," as they were known, Schrafft's remained known primarily as a women's emporium, where hot fudge sundaes, lobster Newburg, and creamed chicken on toast could be had in an atmosphere of middle-class gentility. In 1948 the company celebrated its fiftieth anniversary with the opening of a Schrafft's restaurant in Rockefeller Center in New York City. The Shattuck family controlled the company until 1967, when it was broken into various divisions. Helme Products, Inc., a tobacco, snacks and candy firm, bought Schrafft's in 1967, and Gulf and Western acquired it in 1974, later selling it to American Safety Razor Company. Declining sales, the burgeoning health food movement, increased costs of ingredients, outdated machinery in the factory, and the seasonal nature of the candy business were factors that contributed to a steady decline in sales that had started in the 1970s. The final part of the Schrafft's empire to be sold was the candy factory in Charlestown, which closed in 1984.

RENEE MARTON

Scrapple

Scrapple, or Philadelphia scrapple, is a spiced pork breakfast sausage refried or regrilled in slices and served with ketchup or syrup. It is most common in the Pennsylvania Dutch region of eastern Pennsylvania and the nearby parts of New Jersey, Delaware, and Maryland. But it is shipped as a commercial product across America and is sometimes made in rural homes in a number of variations with beef or game substituting for the pork.

Scrapple is the distinctively American descendant of a variety of European slaughtering-day recipes for puddings of pork parts made by simmering them into a gelatinous gruel that is then thickened with meal, spiced, and cooled into a loaf. What makes scrapple American is the substitution of a mixture of buckwheat and cornmeal for European grains, the omission of blood, and the standard use of sage and pepper as seasonings.

The Pennsylvania Dutch name *pawnhas* (or *pawnhoss, panhas, pan hoss*) is recorded earlier than the name "scrapple," even in English-language sources, so its immediate

ancestors are most likely black puddings called *panhas*, which are still popular in Germany. But the buckwheat is strongly associated with the New Netherland colony (which briefly included Delaware), and there are similar English recipes as early as 1390.

The name *pan hoss* is usually understood as a variation of *pan haas*, meaning pan rabbit, by analogy with German terms like "false hare" for meat loaf. But William Woys Weaver has traced *panhas* in Germany back to the 1500s and suggests that it derives from *panna*, the name of a Celtic vessel, in the same way that dishes like chowder, terrine, and potpie are named for the vessels in which they are cooked. The word "scrapple" is not recorded as naming this food until the 1820s and is usually traced to the English "scrap" and Holland Dutch *scrabbel* as applied to kitchen leftovers, but Weaver has argued that "scrapple" came from *"panha-skröppel"* (literally, a slice of *panhas*) in the Krefelder dialect of the original 1680 Germantown settlers, which was conflated with the English word "scrapple," locally applied to leftovers and three similarly shaped tools: a kitchen scraper, a grubbing hoe, and an ash rake. Supporting this explanation is the fact that scrapple was not originally made from kitchen scraps and quite early became a commercial by-product of slaughterhouse activity. (One explanation of why scrapple went from a black blood pudding to a white pudding, unlike the German *panhas*, is that the blood was being diverted to other industrial uses.)

But Weaver also notes that scrapple was sometimes made from scrapings of meat and sometimes scrapings of bread, and the word "scrapple" had been used for stone or wood chips in medieval Latin and as a verb for dressing timber in Middle English. The 1390 English manuscript *Forme of Curye* has a recipe for a saffron-flavored scrapple under the title "For to make grewel forced."

Although European preparations range from hot soups and loose hashes to puddings, pâtés, and sausages, American scrapple is now almost always sliced and panfried as a breakfast meat. Scrapple was originally made and traded by farm families in winter and became a commercial product in the early nineteenth century as improved roads and railroads increased the size and scope of slaughterhouses and urban markets. The introduction of the home-size meat grinder in the late nineteenth century meant that scrapple could be made for family consumption in home kitchens and also produced a number of fanciful (and short-lived) recipes as well as more enduring tastes for meat loaf and peanut butter. In the early twenty-first century, scrapple is again a primarily industrial product with some old and new artisanal producers.

[**See also** BREAKFAST FOOD; GERMAN AMERICAN FOOD; GOETTA; SAUSAGE.]

BIBLIOGRAPHY

Weaver, William Woys. *Country Scrapple: An American Tradition*. Mechanicsburg, PA: Stackpole, 2003.

MARK H. ZANGER

Screwdriver

There is much lore surrounding the cocktail known as the screwdriver. In one story American oilmen in the Middle East concocted the drink from vodka and canned orange juice, calling it a screwdriver after the one tool on their belts appropriate for use as a stirring stick. The Norwegians—especially the makers of Finlandia vodka—claim that the screwdriver was first concocted in Norwegian oil fields, not the Middle East. Ian Wisniewski and Nicholas Faith in *Classic Vodka* state that a gin drink commonly known as the orange blossom became the first screwdriver during Prohibition, when bootleggers added canned orange juice to bathtub gin to mask its awful flavor. A screwdriver was needed to pierce the orange juice cans, hence the cocktail's name.

All of these stories aside, John G. Martin, president of Heublein, Inc., in the 1940s, used the screwdriver (and the Moscow mule, Bloody Mary, and vodkatini) to promote the introduction of Smirnoff vodka to gin-drinking Americans. It worked. By 1967 vodka sales had pulled ahead of gin sales in the United States.

The screwdriver consists of a shot of vodka mixed with about five ounces of orange juice, over ice, in a highball glass. Notwithstanding the origins of the cocktail, fresh orange juice makes a superior drink. The most famous screwdriver variation was concocted to promote an Italian liqueur, Galliano. A standard screwdriver was topped with a float of Galliano and called a Harvey Wallbanger after an imaginary character, a surfer, who was said to have bumped into walls after consuming several drinks.

[**See also** COCKTAILS; PROHIBITION; VODKA.]

BIBLIOGRAPHY

Wisniewski, Ian, and Nicholas Faith. *Classic Vodka*. London: Prion, 1997.

DALE DEGROFF

Seafood

Fish and shellfish are notorious for their propensity to spoil, the presence of small and pesky bones or tough-to-penetrate exterior shells, and the perceived difficulty of cooking them. The sooner fish can be eaten or preserved after capture, the better. A premium has always been placed on fish sold fresh or even alive.

Salting and drying were the simplest ways of preserving fish. When the canning industry had developed sufficiently in the nineteenth century to have an impact on the food supply, fish and shellfish joined the seasonal cycle of products being preserved, often, in larger canneries, alternating with fresh vegetable crops.

Canned fish and shellfish seem to have found a more ready market than many fresh fish because they answered questions of freshness and often solved the problem of cooking

Photograph of Fisherman's Wharf in San Francisco taken in 1943.

method. Many late-nineteenth-century and early-twentieth-century canned fish and shellfish producers promoted their products with cookery books replete with recipes for salmon loaf, shrimp wiggle, clam chowder, and tuna or lobster salad.

In the nineteenth century, when middle-class eating habits were becoming more refined, thoughtful hostesses did not serve fish from which a guest would be obliged to pick bones. Oysters and lobsters were served already shucked or picked, suitable for eating with a fork, so that the diner never had to handle the shell.

Commercial filleting also helped move through market the great number of fish caught by steam-powered otter trawl, a new fishing technology introduced in the United States around 1900. This technology caught many more fish than consumers wanted.

Wartime Spikes in Seafood Consumption

The fisheries experienced a discernible spike in fish consumption during the meat rationing of World War I, but a slump immediately followed the war. Marketing efforts and industry organization attempted to overcome this consumer resistance. Many households turned to fish—always a low-cost source of protein—during the Depression. During World War II fish consumption rose again until rationing was over and the prosperity of the 1950s once again eased people into eating more red meat.

Seafood as Insufficient Fare

Fish had a long association with the practice of fasting. In spite of being an animal food, fish occupied a middle ground between red-blooded animals and vegetables and grains. Many found pleasure and satisfaction eating

red meat, while eating the relatively blander and low-calorie fish was less satisfying or, as some thought, less nutritious unless enriched. In the American past small fish were pan-fried, and larger fish were served with butter, oyster or lobster sauce, or sometimes a butter or cream sauce containing mashed, boiled egg. Salt pork fat, cream, or butter added considerable calories, while horseradish, mustard, vinegar, and other sharp ingredients gave fish a livelier flavor. New Englanders served fish sprinkled with small pieces of fried salt pork and drizzled with the rendered pork fat. Consumers still often prefer deep-fried breaded fish or shellfish. The breading absorbs enough oil to give the fish caloric substance besides adding a crunchy texture.

In the early twentieth century medical and nutrition experts were much less likely to make the distinction among various forms of animal protein and so did not attempt to dismiss fish as less nutritious. The greatest criticism of fish was that it was less interesting than meat. In the 1970s the medical establishment became concerned about a possible correlation between cholesterol and heart disease. Seafood, as a naturally low-cholesterol food, gained sudden popularity.

Prepared Seafood

Public desire for precooked seafood has helped the aquaculture industries find a market for their products. Fish processors, who keep their products frozen for sale anywhere in the country or even abroad, buy large quantities of farm-raised catfish, tilapia, and salmon, among others. Some seafood products, particularly the breaded fillets, can be produced from whatever whitefish is most plentiful. Consumers buying fish described only as "breaded fillets" or "fish fingers" or "fish nuggets" might be hard-pressed to distinguish between tilapia, Alaskan pollock, and even catfish.

Since the 1970s fish and poultry have become rivals for the low-fat, low-cholesterol market, with precooked fish products competing with ready-to-eat chicken products. Fish processors label breaded fish products as "fingers" or "nuggets" with the understanding that the public will compare them favorably to chicken products of the same name. This marketing ploy was used earlier in the twentieth century for canned tuna, which was styled as "chicken of the sea," interchangeable with canned chicken in popular casseroles, salads, and sandwiches.

Seafood, Leisure, and the Exotic

In the nineteenth century clambakes and chowder parties were common seaside leisure activities that usually entailed the participants catching the fish or digging the clams, which they then cooked outdoors. At the mid-nineteenth century skilled individuals were hired as chowder- or bake-masters by groups making an event of it. In some seaside towns so-called shore dinners consisting of steamed clams, lobster, corn, and other comestibles were offered in an informal restaurant-like establishment. Lobster and clam festivals have since cropped up along the coast in summer, mostly for tourists.

In the late nineteenth century and early twentieth century vacationers looking for a rustic experience in New England, where lobstering is done, would go to the pounds and eat lobsters on site. The pounds, which had been used as storage for lobsters about to be transported live to market, also became eateries where lobsters were boiled to order. In the twenty-first century lobster pounds are sometimes found at a distance from water, but they remain part of leisure-time seafood consumption.

Similarly along the Chesapeake Bay in Maryland and Virginia and the coasts and estuaries of North Carolina, South Carolina, Georgia, Florida, and the Gulf states, blue crab boils are a leisure activity. In the Deep South shrimp and crawfish boils are held seasonally. Socializing around jambalaya in Louisiana relies on enthusiasts installing large cooking pots in their fishing camps or summer cottages for the purposes of making large quantities for friends and family. The Mississippi Delta, now famous for catfish farming, has individuals and establishments famous for their fried catfish.

On the Great Lakes and other freshwater lakes and rivers where whitefish and catfish abound, boils and fish fries fill a role similar to the fish and shellfish events elsewhere, and small roadside stands featuring local fish appear in some areas. Door County on Lake Michigan in Wisconsin is famed for its white-fish boils, which some report are derived from the habit of fishermen, who used steam vessels for fishing, cooking whitefish on their steam engines. As in other places and with other seafood, there is a mixture of commercial and private boils and fries that supply locals and tourists.

Independence, Industry, and Wild Food

Fishing, like most wild-food hunting, is speculative and depends on luck, experience, and intuition. Compared with farming, it seemed risky to the English settlers in New England when they established the cod fishery that ultimately built fortunes. But the men who preferred to fish liked it because of the independence that working on the water afforded them.

Since the mid-nineteenth century fisheries have endeavored to even out the highly seasonal nature of the work, guarantee catches, and provide year-round work for fishermen. In the nineteenth century vessels were refitted to take advantage of seasonal variations in the fish stocks. Some fishermen worked on vessels in northern waters until winter and then went to work in the southern fisheries. Fisheries in the twenty-first century have employed a range of technologies and sophisticated equipment that nearly unerringly find fish, scoop them up, and even process them on board. In only a few days on the water, one vessel can catch what formerly took a season's worth of vessels to harvest. However, older, lower-tech fishing methods, including trolling and long-lining, have been revived to reduce by-catch and also to improve the quality of the product. Improvements in equipment efficiency have almost always meant that a favored species soon will be overfished. When one stock is reduced, a similar fish replaces it until it also becomes scarce.

While seafood still does not rank near to meat in frequency of consumption, more people are eating fish more often than ever, and with wild stocks under stress from American and foreign fishing fleets, a wider variety of fish is taken and eaten than earlier. Further, Americans consume a greater-than-ever amount of farm-raised fish. America ranks third in world consumption of fish in the early 2000s.

[See also Clambake; Fish; New England; Oyster Loaf Sandwich; Oysters; Salt and Salting; Tuna.]

BIBLIOGRAPHY

Davidson, Alan. *North Atlantic Seafood.* New York: Viking, 1979.

German, Andrew. *Down on T-Wharf: The Boston Fisheries as Seen through the Photographs of Henry D. Fisher.* Mystic, CT: Mystic Seaport Museum, 1982.

Oliver, Sandra L. *Saltwater Foodways: New Englanders and Their Food at Sea and Ashore in the Nineteenth Century.* Mystic, CT: Mystic Seaport Museum, 1995.

SANDRA L. OLIVER

Sea Mammals

Seals, dolphins, and porpoises do not figure largely in the diets of most modern Americans, though among the Inuit seals and whales are harvested for food and ceremonial purposes as part of the preservation of Inuit culture. In the Canadian maritime provinces, seal is captured and eaten, particularly in Newfoundland and Labrador. Historically seal meat sustained explorers and adventurers in the Arctic and Antarctica.

At sea American sailing ships caught dolphins and porpoises, and sailors cooked them for all the crew to eat, often in a dish called sea pie. The liver, often described as being much like beef liver, was apportioned to the captain's cabin. Porpoise is sometimes caught and marketed in Japan, though America regards this trade as illegal.

SANDRA L. OLIVER

Sea Turtle

The green sea turtle is not the only edible turtle, but for the purposes of describing American seafood, this is the most exploited species. The taste and fashion for turtle soup probably traveled from the Caribbean to England and thence to North America. For much of the last half of the eighteenth century and into the early nineteenth century, turtle soup was so stylish that a mock version was developed to replace it. Some American sailing ships captured turtles for fresh meat, but sailors did not often welcome it.

Sea turtle was said to resemble veal and lobster. The edible portions—the flipper meat, called calipee, and the meat from the lower shell, called calipash—have a gelatinous characteristic, largely out of favor with modern people. There was a small commercial fishery of green turtles for canning in the late nineteenth century. Turtle eggs were also harvested. Sea turtles are now largely protected.

SANDRA L. OLIVER

Sea Urchins

Sea urchins were of no historical interest as a food fishery in America until the last decades of the twentieth century, when they were fished commercially for a high-value global market, most going to Japanese buyers for use in sushi. Urchins are gathered by diving. Because there is no regulation over the numbers taken, the sea urchin population has been seriously depleted.

SANDRA L. OLIVER

Seaweed

Historically few seaweeds in American waters had much commercial culinary value, though to make a blancmange, some people in the nineteenth century gathered Irish moss, which they steeped in hot milk to obtain the carrageenan, a gelatin-like substance.

In the late twentieth century, as Americans learned about Asian, particularly Japanese, foods they were introduced to the use of a wider variety of edible seaweeds. Among the seaweeds that are gathered and sold in the United States are alaria, kelp, dulse, laver, and red and green algae.

Some seaweeds are dried and pulverized to create seasonings or are added to other ingredients to make crackers or chips. Commercially, much seaweed is used in food production, particularly the products carrageenan, agar, and algin; these products probably account for the average American's seaweed consumption.

SANDRA L. OLIVER

See's Candies

See's Candies began in Los Angeles, California, when Charles See arrived from Canada with his wife Florence and mother Mary; they opened their first shop in 1921. From thirty shops in the late 1920s the business grew to the more than two hundred independent shops, including locations in Hong Kong and Tokyo, and airport and department store kiosks of the early twenty-first century. The black and white design of the store became part of the company's well-known style. The two "candy kitchens" (that is, factories) in which the candies and chocolates are manufactured are located in San Francisco and Los Angeles, California. See's Candies Company was sold to Berkshire Hathaway in 1972. While primarily a West Coast phenomenon, the company has a shop in Chicago and in 2005 set up more than ninety-five holiday kiosks for the period from Thanksgiving through Christmas, from Florida to Maine.

Chocolate truffles, caramels, and toffees are manufactured, and kosher candies were introduced in 1995. Several specific confections are associated with the See's Candies name. See's old-fashioned rectangular lollipops, are made with heavy cream from a recipe in use for more than sixty years. Eighty million of these slow-melting lollipops sold in 2005. Flavors include chocolate raspberry, sassafras, butterscotch, and café latte as well as more traditional flavors. Toffee-ettes (bite-size brittles), Awesome Bars, Milk Chocolate Bordeaux (made with white and brown sugar, butter, and cream), chocolate buttercreams, and Almond Royales are other popular items. See's Candies sold 30 million pounds in 2005.

RENEE MARTON

Segmenters, see Apple-Preparation Tools

Seltzer

Seltzer water is artificially carbonated water to which no flavorings have been added. In the New York City area, seltzer water is often synonymous with soda water. Aside from the bubbles, seltzer's distinct quality is a slightly sour taste caused by the reaction of water with carbon dioxide gas.

Seltzer water takes its name from the German town of Niederselters, the site of a naturally carbonated mineral water spring. With low amounts of minerals and high carbonation, so-called Selters water earned

a reputation as a popular table water. In the eighteenth century Niederselters began exporting its water to North America, where it the name became "seltzer" water. The expense of imported mineral waters led American businesspeople to concoct their own domestic water using artificial carbonation, added salts, and other chemicals. By 1810 artificial soda water, including locally made Selters water, was a popular refreshment in New York and Philadelphia. In the late nineteenth century, however, many soda bottlers stopped adding minerals to their seltzer water. Seltzer became simple tap water that had been filtered and carbonated before being bottled.

Locally made soda bottles occasionally exploded under the pressure of carbonated water. In the 1860s manufacturers, such as Carl H. Schultz of New York, began importing heavy glass bottles from France and central Europe. These were topped with metal siphons that dispensed the liquid without reducing the carbonation left in the bottle. Due to their cost, the siphon bottles remained the property of the seltzer manufacturer, whose name was usually etched or painted onto the glass. Once emptied, the bottles were taken back to the plant for refilling. Because siphons did not work with flavored sodas, the bottles became known as seltzer bottles.

Deliverymen carrying wooden cases of seltzer were common in most American cities and towns. Seltzer water kept people cool in summertime; the wealthy could imitate the English, who drank their whiskey with carbonated water; and immigrants could have mineral water on their dinner tables just as they had back in the old country. They called it *Belchwasser* in German or *greps-wasser* in Yiddish because of the way it aided digestion. Big city seltzer manufacturers tended to be of central European origin, and by the 1920s many German and east European Jews had entered the business. Seltzer's ubiquity in Jewish neighborhoods made it an essential part of the American Jewish experience. On movie screens the siphon bottle appeared on drink trolleys in elegant drawing room scenes and in the raucous fights of slapstick comedies. In homes seltzer gained a reputation as a stain remover and as the secret ingredient in the lightest matzo balls.

After 1945 the market for seltzer water began to shrink, as customers moved to the suburbs and women were less often at home to accept deliveries. Supermarkets began to sell carbonated water in throwaway containers. Seltzer water became a novelty, and bottlers either moved into more lucrative lines or were forced out of business. By the 1970s the refillable seltzer bottle had disappeared from all but a big few cities.

In the early 2000s there remained less than a dozen bottlers nationwide who still refilled the old seltzer siphons. In the Northeast supermarkets sold various brands of

seltzer water in disposable plastic bottles. There have been attempts to revive the old-style seltzer trade, but except for a diehard group of customers who enjoy its distinct qualities, seltzer water remains part of the past.

[**See also** EGG CREAM; SODA DRINKS; SODA FOUNTAINS; WATER; WATER, BOTTLED.]

BIBLIOGRAPHY

Funderburg, Anne Cooper. *Sundae Best: A History of Soda Fountains.* Bowling Green, OH: Bowling Green State University Popular Press, 2002.

Kuhnigk, Armin. *Niederselters und das Selterswasser in historischen Darstellungen.* Camberg, Germany: M. Neumann, 1972.

McKearin, Helen. *American Bottles and Flasks and Their Ancestry.* New York: Crown, 1978.

ANDREW COE

Settlement Houses

Settlement houses were part of a broad endeavor to preserve human values in changing industrial times. The first settlement house, Toynbee Hall, was formed in 1884 by Samuel A. Barnett in the slums of East London. Barnett's idea was to "settle" university men in a working-class neighborhood, where they could apply their intelligence and skills to help relieve poverty while also experiencing the "real world." Barnett's model influenced several Americans who imported ideas from Toynbee Hall to their local communities. The first settlement house in the United States was Neighborhood Guild, formed in 1886 in New York City by Stanton Coit. Three years later College Settlement opened, also in New York City; simultaneously Jane Addams and Ellen Starr founded Hull-House in Chicago.

Activities of the Houses

By 1918 more than four hundred settlement houses thrived in both urban and rural communities across the country. In their early years settlements were financed exclusively through charitable donations and reflected their origins in England, with its state church, by virtue of religious affiliations. Settlement houses became significant facilitators in easing immigrants' adjustment to living in a new culture. Yet immigrants did not escape ethnic stereotypes or prejudice, and most settlements were segregated by ethnicity. Throughout the settlement system the notion of "general welfare"—the conception, associated with emerging social policy of that time, that individuals had a right to basic assistance, regardless of their religious affiliation—replaced that of charity. The objective was to help each immigrant group become part of the mainstream, to realize the American dream.

In the early twentieth century some settlement houses began to play important roles in the reform movements of the Progressive Era. Settlement houses themselves provided some of the first opportunities for women to become influential leaders in society. Jane Addams and Frances Perkins both carved their way into national affairs through their management of settlement houses. Most settlement activities started with clubs, classes, lectures, and art exhibitions. Settlement house workers pioneered in the kindergarten movement, taught English, and established theaters, courses in industrial education, and music schools.

Food Reforms

The best-known commercial product of the settlement house system was *The Settlement Cook Book: The Way to a Man's Heart*, published for the first time in 1903 by Mrs. Simon Kanter. The cookbook was a response to the need for educational materials to complement the cooking classes Kanter taught at the settlement in Milwaukee, Wisconsin. She believed that if students could take home printed recipes of the dishes they made in class, they would be more likely to utilize them. The settlement board refused the eighteen dollars required to print the books, but the women were undaunted. They solicited advertisements to defray these costs, a form of financing that soon became a model for the multitude of giveaway cookbooks that began to surface with the advent of cooking tools and advanced food product technology in the 1920s.

Accounts of food reform, as told through recipes, instructions, and anecdotes spanning several decades of cookbook publication, tell stories of class, gender, domestic science, and "new philanthropy" movements. (New philanthropy at that time was defined as "an age in which scientific information coupled with social science research suggested cures for a myriad of social ills.") These recipe histories offer a unique perspective on the Americanization of immigrants in the late nineteenth century and early twentieth century, as traditional recipes were adapted to local ingredients and new dishes were introduced that were thought to be definitively American.

The University Settlement Society, for example, was concerned with Americanizing the home. Domestic scientists attempted to replace the supremacy of the palate with the rule of scientific law. The rigorous methods of science could bring order to the diversified cultural approaches of immigrants to food preparation. For the reformers, eating was a distasteful but necessary biological function. Food could be civilized only by being controlled, limited, and changed through cooking. The totality of the immigrant homemakers' foodways came under the scrutiny of the reformers. In 1889 a report titled "Food Stores and Purchases in the Tenth Ward" exemplified the scientific observation of culinary habits. Reformers followed the path of food from production to postconsumption, tracing food's place of purchase; its storage, preparation, and consumption in the home; and its removal from the home as waste.

Distributing food to children at the Five Points Mission in New York, 1880s.

Immigrant women, in their traditional roles as homemakers and mothers, were relied on to achieve the reformers' intended results, but cooking classes for boys and specific classes on hygiene were also held. Reformers encouraged the use of new tools, which were designed for measuring ingredients precisely. Each food item was rigorously analyzed for its properties. The nutritional value of foods could be newly measured in calories and then subdivided further into new categories of protein and carbohydrate. Reformers studied the chemistry of digestion and concluded that the biological process was eased by cooking vegetables until they lost all texture, color, and flavor. Whereas taste was subjective, nutrition was objective and could be strictly prescribed.

Because the settlement movement was defined in the United States by its nonreligious stance, teaching kashruth, the dietary law of religious Jews, was intentionally left out of cooking instruction at many Jewish settlement houses. The purpose of the cooking classes was to teach American cooking, which consisted of American methods used on American foods. Efforts were made, via recommended menus, to proclaim what foods were American. The nutritionally sound yet benign and bland diet of rural New England was elevated.

The literature of early-twentieth-century Jews in America voices deep resentment and cynicism about attempts to change Jewish food habits. Still, *The Settlement Cook Book*

became one of the most popular texts in Jewish immigrant and second-generation kitchens. As the temperance movement spread, further emphasis was placed on the importance of food reform within all settlement houses. Domestic scientists, missionaries, and temperance workers promoted good meals as the solution to what they saw as the drinking problem of the poor.

After World War II settlement house activities shifted to being more recreational in nature, while the food programs became more service- or convenience-oriented. For example, during this time settlement houses provided the unmarried working woman with an acceptable alternative to living alone or with family. Maid services and the settlement house's public kitchen freed women in the workforce from the need to keep house as well.

The approximately eight hundred settlement houses that exist at the beginning of the twenty-first century continue to provide environments of hope in times of need for new Americans. Settlements provide housing targeted to particular ethnic groups, advocate for policy reform, and facilitate the delivery of government programs as all or part of this ideal. Food continues to be a primary service component, with settlement food programs that include meals-on-wheels for the homebound elderly and after-school and summer meal programs for children, most of which are funded through state and federal sources. The original *Settlement Cook Book* continues to be revised and reprinted.

[**See also** Cookbooks and Manuscripts: From the Civil War to World War I; Cookbooks and Manuscripts: From World War I and World War II; Cooking Schools; Ethnic Foods; Jewish American Food; Jewish Dietary Laws.]

BIBLIOGRAPHY

Blank, Barbara Trainin. "Settlement Houses: Old Idea in New Form Builds Communities." *New Social Worker* 55, no. 3 (Summer 1998).

Bryan, Mary Lynn McCree, and Allen F. Davis, eds. *One Hundred Years at Hull-House*. Bloomington: Indiana University Press, 1991.

Trolander, Judith Ann. *Professionalism and Social Change: From the Settlement House Movement to Neighborhood Centers, 1886 to the Present*. New York: Columbia University Press, 1987.

KAREN KARP

7 UP

7 UP is a soft drink created by Charles Leiper Grigg of St. Louis, Missouri. Grigg created his first soft drink, called Whistle, in 1919. Following a dispute with his employers, Grigg quit his job, leaving Whistle behind, and obtained a new position developing soft-drink flavoring agents for the Warner Jenkinson Company. There he developed his second orange-flavored drink, called Howdy. Deciding to seek his fortune, Grigg formed a partnership with the financier Edmund D. Ridgway and established the Howdy Corporation in 1920.

Competition from Orange Crush, which dominated the orange soda market, motivated Grigg to develop a new, lemon-lime-flavored drink. By 1929, after testing eleven formulas, Grigg introduced Bib-Label Lithiated Lemon-Lime Soda. At the time it actually did include lithium, which was sometimes found in natural spring water and was thought to have curative health

effects. The new soft drink, introduced only two weeks before the stock market crash of October 1929, was costly compared with the more than six hundred lemon-lime beverages already on the market, and it bore an unwieldy name; nevertheless, it sold well.

It was not long, however, before Grigg changed the name of his soft drink to 7 UP. The origin of the name is unknown, but various theories have been proposed. At the time 7 UP contained seven ingredients and was sold in seven-ounce bottles. Another popular St. Louis soda, called Bubble Up, may have inspired the "UP" portion of the name. Some speculate that Grigg named his new soda after a card game; others claim that its name is based on a cattle brand that caught Grigg's attention.

The Howdy Corporation fought hard to gain a place for 7 UP in a national market severely affected by the Depression. Lacking national distribution, Grigg instituted a clever marketing strategy by selling 7 UP to the speakeasies that had sprung up as a result of Prohibition, and it quickly became a popular mixer for alcoholic beverages. After the repeal of Prohibition in 1933, Grigg lost no time in openly advertising 7 UP as a mixer. In 1936 the Howdy Corporation became the Seven-Up Company, and by 1940 the product had become one of the most popular soft drinks in the United States.

Early 7 UP advertising featured a winged 7 UP logo and the slogan "Seven natural flavors blended into a savory, flavory drink with a real wallop." In 1967 the "UNCOLA" advertising campaign was launched, followed by "No Caffeine" in 1982 and the cartoonlike character of Spot in 1987. In 2002, 7 UP got a new look with Godfrey, the 7 UP Guy who personifies the "Make 7 UP Yours" campaign.

In 1986 the Seven-Up Company merged with the Dr Pepper Company; in 1995 Dr Pepper/Seven Up Companies Inc. was acquired by Cadbury Schweppes of London. In the 1990s the introduction of Diet 7 UP and various new flavors was geared toward increasing 7 UP's market share. In the United States 7 UP is still widely used as a beverage mixer, and home cooks utilize it as an ingredient in a variety of dishes, including cakes and desserts, molded salads, marinades, and pancakes.
[**See also** Cola Wars; Soda Drinks.]

BIBLIOGRAPHY

Morgan, Hal. *Symbols of America: A Lavish Celebration of America's Best-Loved Trademarks and the Products They Symbolize*. New York: Viking, 1986.

Rodengen, Jeffrey L. *The Legend of Dr Pepper/7-Up*. Fort Lauderdale, FL: Write Stuff Syndicate, 1995.

7UP.com. http://www.7up.com.

BECKY MERCURI

Shad

Like alewives, the anadromous shad are found running up freshwater rivers in the spring, originally along the East Coast from the South to the North and, after their introduction in 1871, along the West Coast as well. Although shad are bony and oily, their great plenty in colonial times and the relative ease of catching them during their upstream migration made them welcome. Particularly prized was the roe from the females, and cookbooks from the 1800s provide many recipes for preparing roe. Some early sources say that buck (male) shad were thrown back as unmarketable.

There were commercial shad fisheries in the South and in the North, with southern-caught shad sent north by rail early in the spring until the fish appeared in northern rivers later in the season. A combination of overfishing, industrial damming, and pollution caused a great decline to near disappearance of shad in many East Coast rivers. Conservation efforts in the second half of the twentieth century were rewarded by the fish reappearing in greater numbers, though still not enough to support a commercial fishery.

Shad, introduced to California waters in 1871, have grown in numbers and spread from Monterey Bay to the Columbia River and Alaska. Mostly a sport fish on the West Coast, shad have not been a substantial commercial fishery there, except for a small fishery on the Columbia River, because there is a small market for them as well as a desire to avoid bycatch of protected salmon.

Shad were eaten fresh (often planked) and salted or sometimes smoked for later use. In the nineteenth century outdoor bakes accounted for recreational shad consumption mostly in the South and Middle Atlantic regions. As with all fish, shad cooked with bones in are tastier, but by the late twentieth century a filleting method nicknamed the "x, y, z cut" was being used. This method calls for removing most of the bones, but it shreds the flesh, obliging the fish sellers to wrap the fish in plastic wrap to hold the fillet together.

SANDRA L. OLIVER

Shakey's

In 1954 Sherwood Johnson and Ed Plummer opened the first Shakey's pizza parlor restaurant in Sacramento, California. Johnson's nickname was "Shakey," because he had suffered a case of malaria while serving during World War II; Johnson and Plummer decided to use this name for the restaurant. He encouraged other franchisees to hire banjo players, and this became one of the chain's trademarks. The second Shakey's pizza parlor opened in Portland, Oregon, in 1956, and two years later Shakey's began franchising the restaurant. The chain had more than 272 outlets by 1967. The first franchise in Canada was established in 1968, and by 1975 outlets reached Japan and the Philippines. Johnson was a banjo player, and he sometimes played at the restaurants to entertain the customers.

Advertisement on the back cover of a 1957 cookbooklet containing recipes that used 7 UP.

Shakey's was the first franchise pizza chain, although it was not truly a fast food restaurant because most customers ate inside the restaurant—there was little carry-out business and no home delivery. Responding to stiff competition, Shakey's added a hot and cold salad buffet to its pizza menu in 1978.

Johnson retired in 1967 and sold his half of the company to the Colorado Milling and Elevator Company, which acquired Plummer's half the following year. The company changed hands several times thereafter and suffered as a result. In 2004 Shakey's was sold to Jacmar Companies of Alhambra, California. At that time there were only 63 Shakey's restaurants in the United States and about 350 in the Philippines.

BIBLIOGRAPHY

Jakle, John A., and Keith A. Sculle. *Fast Food: Roadside Restaurants in the Automobile Age.* Baltimore: Johns Hopkins University Press, 1999.

ANDREW F. SMITH

Shellfish

For much of American culinary history, shrimps or prawns, crayfish, scallops, mussels, and clams have had a minor role, whereas oysters, lobster, and crab were popular. Shellfish were used in stews, soups, and sauces, and later in salads. Once harvested in New England to be used as bait, some species of clams are eaten raw; others, however, are good only after being chopped for soup or chowder. Some shellfish are popular for outdoor recreational cookery, such as crab, shrimp, and crayfish boils and clambakes. Many shellfish are farm raised and hold a more important place in cuisine, especially in ethnic cookery, than they once did. Abalone and sea urchins go almost unmentioned in early cookery sources.

Oysters, relished by the aboriginal Americans, were joined by lobster and crab to find favor in America from the time of the first settlers and are the most frequently mentioned shellfish in cookbooks. Early on, commercial fisheries existed to harvest them, but these shellfish also were a subsistence food for those who could gather them. Thus these creatures were simultaneously of high and of low value. Of these three shellfish, oysters are the only one commonly eaten raw.

A disadvantage in eating any shellfish is that once the hard exterior is opened, only small pieces of meat are found. For this reason, the value of shellfish often lay in their use in sauces, soups, and, mixed with a binding ingredient, cakes and croquettes. Cooked lobster and crab became popular for salads in the mid-nineteenth century, and they became marketable as canned products. The larger the shellfish, the greater the meat reward for the effort required to pick it out of the shell. Thus, the large Pacific Coast crabs are extremely popular.

[See also CLAMBAKE; CLAMS; CRAB BOILS; FISH: FRESHWATER FISH; FISH: SALTWATER FLAT FISH; OYSTER BARS; OYSTER LOAF SANDWICH; OYSTERS; SEAFOOD.]

BIBLIOGRAPHY

Davidson, Alan. *North Atlantic Seafood.* New York: Viking, 1980.
Davidson, Alan, ed. *The Oxford Companion to Food.* 2nd ed. Oxford: Oxford University Press, 2006.
Lipfert, Nathan, and Kenneth R Martin. *Lobstering and the Maine Coast.* Bath: Maine Maritime Museum,1985.
Warner, William. *Beautiful Swimmers: Watermen, Crabs, and the Chesapeake Bay.* New York: Penguin, 1987.

SANDRA L. OLIVER

Sherry

Sherry, the afternoon drink of doddering grandmothers and grandaunts, the choice companion to tapas for dedicated Andalusia admirers, and the inspiration for a short story by Edgar Allan Poe, has a deeper past. Sherry was one of the sweet wines referred to as sack, a commodity that had been heavily traded to the Americas from colonial times. Sack was popular for three reasons. It was inexpensive compared with French wine, it had a high alcohol content because of its fortification with brandy (a practice no longer followed), and it was palatably sweet; all these traits led to its being drunk often by all classes, either alone or as part of a mixed drink. Sherry was used to make a type of American sangria, colloquially called sangaree, and was also the main ingredient of sack posset, a concoction of sherry, sometimes mixed with ale, cooked with sugar, eggs, and cream or milk, and finished off with spices, usually nutmeg or mace, and drunk at weddings in all of the colonies.

Sherry's popularity waned as more whiskeys, jacks, and beers were created in America, but sherry was still used as a mixer as late as the 1867 World Exposition, during which the American pavilion featured sherry cobblers. The twentieth century saw the evolution of two types of sherry. America developed cooking sherry to circumvent the Prohibition laws. Its flavor was created through cooking or by artificial means, and it was then salted to prevent its being drunk as a beverage. Cheap, fortified sherries were also marketed as inexpensive and potent wines that were often sold in gallon jugs, mainly from California. In contrast, Spanish sherry transformed itself from a fortified wine to one made almost exclusively with the *solera* system, an aging process that blends several vintages, with distinctions among the four basic styles (in order of dry to sweet, Fino, Manzanilla, Amontillado, and Oloroso). Fino is made with Palomino grapes, is light yellow in color, crisp and dry, and best with savory foods. Manzanilla is Fino aged in Sanlúcar de Barrameda, which, given the proximity to the Mediterranean Sea, lends the sherry a particular (some say salty) taste. Amontillado is oxidized Fino. It is dark brown, nutty, and slightly sweet, and it perfectly balances salted foods like spiced nuts, olives, and other appetizers. Olorosos are made with Ximenez grapes, which are then fortified and sweetened; they complement desserts, cheeses, fruits, and roasted nuts.

[See also PROHIBITION; SANGRIA; WINE: HISTORICAL SURVEY; WINE: LATER DEVELOPMENTS.]

BIBLIOGRAPHY

Gordon, Manuel M. González. *Sherry.* London: Cassell, 1972.

LISA DELANGE

Ship Food

The centuries-long practice of carrying hard bread, salted meat (both beef and pork), and staple legumes (peas or beans) formed the baseline of American shipboard food. Besides water, many vessels supplied spirits or beer and cider. Other fare depended a great deal on era and place and included dried fruits, dried fish, rice, cornmeal, wheat flour, cheese, sweetening, and some vegetables to be consumed as long as they lasted. After the 1740s it was understood that fresh fruits and vegetables, particularly citrus, prevented debilitating scurvy, although at the time no one knew that it was specifically vitamin C that sailors needed. By the end of the eighteenth century, responsible shipowners took aboard antiscorbutics, usually citrus juice, sauerkraut, and vinegar.

In the early nineteenth century basic legal scales of provision on average allowed a pound of beef or pork a day, from fourteen to sixteen ounces of bread, a half pint of spirits, a half-pound of rice or flour, an ounce of coffee or cocoa, and a quarter ounce of tea a day per person. Other items like a half pint of peas or beans might be allowed three times a week, with cheese, pickles, dried fruit, and the like specified once or twice a week. These ingredients were organized into daily menus, or mess bills, repeated weekly. A sailor could practically tell what day of the week it was by the combination of food that appeared.

Rations and Hierarchy

Generally the finest and freshest food was accorded the individuals at the top of the hierarchy: the captain, first officers, and cabin passengers. If, for example, there was any fresh meat, either purchased or newly killed from one of the small animals often carried alive—as pigs, sheep, goats, chickens often were—that meat was prepared for the cabin, while the sailors before the mast only enjoyed such fare on special occasions. Similarly fresh vegetables, if in short supply, were cooked for the first officers and passengers, and the fo'mast hands made do with dried peas or beans to go with the salt meat. For sweetening, the occupants of the cabin enjoyed white sugar, while the seamen received the cheaper molasses. The cabin was accorded freshly baked bread, while the rest of the crew ate hardtack.

Niceties, such as preserves, butter, canned fruits or vegetables, and ham, were carried aboard for the cabin, although sometimes the common seamen themselves brought nicer foods from home, received them as gifts, or when and if they could afford it, bought them in port or from locals in small craft who swarmed newly arriving vessels looking for buyers of fresh produce.

Technology and Nutritional Change

With increased use of steam power, voyages were shorter, and ships were reprovisioned more often. At the same time artificial refrigeration, using either ice or cold generated by other means, enabled vessels to store certain foods longer. Food-processing technology made canned fruits, vegetables, and meat both available and cheaper.

Once it was technologically possible to provide better food for all hands, the expectation of better fare rose as well, as the legal scale of provisions enacted in 1898 revealed. With this scale, canned meat, canned tomatoes, more dried fruit, a greater variety of grains, seasonings, such as pepper and mustard, and butter, cheese, lard, and fresh bread, in addition to hardtack, became minimum requirements.

Food in Fishing Fleets

The best food for working seafarers was surely that provided in the offshore fishing fleets in the later 1800s and in the 1900s. Fishing vessels were often owned and outfitted by the fishermen's families and neighbors. Part of the food was provided by the vessel, the rest paid for by the crew. Additionally the cooks hired were well-paid and skilled individuals, in contrast to the cooks aboard many merchant and whaling ships of the same era, who might have had little or no prior experience. Fishermen's fare was notably egalitarian. All hands ate alike, from captain to newest crew member, in kind, quantity, and manner. (Interestingly the same rule applied aboard vessels engaged in piracy.) Fishermen ate well three times a day, with snacks in between.

Passengers' Food

In the seventeenth and eighteenth centuries, passengers traveling by sea were expected to provide much of their own food, even when they were served in the cabin in the same manner as the captain and first officers. When transatlantic packet service began in the 1800s, passengers were sorted into a hierarchy according to their accommodations, usually designated by class. Each classification ate at a different time and had its own menu. Passengers' food often resembled hotel fare, increasingly so as the nineteenth century wore on.

Many poorer immigrant passengers, occupying steerage, could not have had a more different experience. Responsible for bringing their own provisions, they prepared food for themselves in a usually insufficient cooking area provided for them. Agents recruiting

them for passage too often misrepresented the length of the voyage.

Sea Cooks

Sea cooks in working vessels in earlier years could be young boys, especially on small fishing or coasting vessels. On naval vessels a disabled seaman sometimes was given the berth, if he was still fit for service though unable to clamber in rigging or man guns. In larger American merchant and whaling vessels, particularly as the nineteenth century progressed, the cook was most often a black or Asian man, hardly ever trained at cookery.

On modern working vessels, most of the old distinctions regarding food have diminished among the crew. Modern food technology and relatively short voyages mean fresh refrigerated and frozen food, making possible even shipboard salad bars and fresh meat or fish every day with vegetables. Cooks are professionally trained for cooking at sea.

[See also Hardtack; Ice; Salt and Salting.]

BIBLIOGRAPHY

Carpenter, Kenneth J. *The History of Scurvy and Vitamin C.* Cambridge, U.K.: Cambridge University Press, 1986.

Oliver, Sandra L. *Saltwater Foodways: New Englanders and Their Food, at Sea and Ashore, in the Nineteenth Century.* Mystic, CT: Mystic Seaport Museum, 1995.

SANDRA L. OLIVER

Shoat, *see Pigs*

Shoo-Fly Pie

This sugar pie topped with streusel is the canonical dessert of Pennsylvania Dutch cuisine. Thrifty molasses pies hearken back to English treacle tarts, and the crumb topping is from German *streuselkuchen*, translated as "crumb cake" in Pennsylvania manuscripts since at least the 1860s. Despite the obvious folk etymology, the "shoo-fly" name is not likely older than the 1870s, when "shoo fly" was what (English-speaking) baseball players said instead of swearing when they missed a play. The phrase might have become attached to a pie that was so easy to make as a kind of "aw shucks" pie.

The name spelled "shoe fly cake" appears in a Pennsylvania manuscript of the 1890s. A published Mt. Carmel Church cookbook of about the same era has a "Shoo Fly Cake" made in pie pans and a "Shoo-Fly Cake" made in a piecrust. The 1904 *Inglenook Cook Book* has a crumb pie as well as the cake. A 1915 Reading collection has "shoo-fly pie." Edna Eby Heller in the mid-twentieth century differentiated between "wet" and "dry" versions of shoofly pie, the latter for dunking in breakfast coffee. In Pennsylvania Dutch country one is as likely to find apple, cherry, or blueberry crumb pies as the original sugar base. A lemon base with a crumb topping is Montgomery pie.

[See also Pennsylvania Dutch Food.]

MARK H. ZANGER

A package of Old Fashioned Shoofly Pie Mix.

Shrimp and Prawns

The terms "shrimp" and "prawn" are used almost interchangeably. Americans primarily use the word "shrimp" for large and small crustaceans in the Penaeidae and Pandalidae families. Elsewhere in the world "prawn" usually describes a smaller creature. In America shrimp were harvested mostly in the South, where they were more abundant than in the North, and so appear with greater frequency in older southern cookbooks. In the North canned shrimp from states on the Gulf of Mexico became available after the 1870s.

Mostly used in earlier times in sauces, soups, and stews, shrimp seemed to be interchangeable with other crustaceans and shellfish. Toward the end of the nineteenth century shrimp became popular in salads and sandwiches. In the twentieth century shrimp, often served alone with a cocktail sauce, became an important item on appetizer menus. In the early twenty-first century shrimp is used in Asian and fusion cookery. Shrimp also is a staple of the fast food industry. It is battered and deep-fried and served as one of several shellfish on seafood platters, in baskets with french fries, or as so-called popcorn shrimp, small shrimp eaten like popcorn, with the fingers.

Until the 1940s shrimp were harvested along the Gulf of Mexico with seines set close to shore and hauled by men and horses. Shrimpers used trawlers thereafter, fishing in deeper waters of the gulf. Use of bottom-trawling gear helped create a commercial shrimp fishery on the Pacific coast of Canada after the 1960s.

Many species of shrimp are eaten in America—from small cold-water shrimp harvested in winter in the Gulf of Maine; to the larger shrimp of the Gulf of Mexico variously called pink, white, gray, and green tailed; to large, imported tiger shrimp of the Indo-Pacific, which are common on restaurant menus. The United States is a shrimp-catching country, but it imports much more than it catches.

Pink shrimp are considered abundant in the United States. The shrimp fishery bycatch includes sea turtles and juvenile populations of many other favored food fishes, such as red snapper and red drum, and trawling damages the seabed. Although shrimp can be farm raised, that business is underdeveloped in America, because shrimp can be imported inexpensively from South American and Asian countries willing to exploit their mangrove forests for shrimp aquaculture.

SANDRA L. OLIVER

Sieves, Sifters, and Colanders

Utensils with meshes or perforations of different sizes are used for straining solids from liquids, washing and draining fruit, forcing lumpy materials, such as gravy, into smooth homogeneity, pulping ripe fruit, and sifting dry foods into batters. Benjamin Gilbert of Redding, Connecticut, invented wire screening about 1835, after years of making horsehair sieves. Horsehair had to be washed and sorted, woven, set into bentwood frames, and sewed securely with waxed thread. Wire screen was made on special looms and held in metal frames. Gilbert prospered from making screening for meat-safe doors, sieves, and dairy strainers.

Flour sifters differ mostly in the scraper that pushes the flour through the fine screen and in how it moves. Scrapers of revolving wires might be cranked or moved by squeeze action or shaking. Some flour sifters had lids at both ends, making it easy to double- or triple-sift flour for light pastries.

Colanders were first made of copper or tin, then of sheet iron that was enameled to keep the metal from reacting with acidic food, and then of aluminum by 1900. Colanders may be designed like saucepans, or they may have round bottoms that rest in a separate or an attached ring foot. They might also stand on tab feet. Plastic has been used for colanders since the 1960s. In the early 2000s metal wire screen was still used for strainers and flour sifters.

[**See also** FLYTRAPS AND FLY SCREENS; FRYING BASKETS.]

BIBLIOGRAPHY
Franklin, Linda Campbell. *300 Years of Kitchen Collectibles*. 5th ed. Iola, WI: Krause, 2003.

LINDA FRANKLIN

Sifters, *see Sieves, Sifters, and Colanders*

Silverware

Americans use the word "silverware," which properly defines objects fashioned from silver or silver plate, synonymously with "flatware" or "cutlery." This speaks to silver's enduring popularity and historical importance at the table. Ancient hosts wowed their guests with impressive banqueting silver (which could, however, be melted down for cash in difficult times).

Colonial America
To be "born with a silver spoon" in colonial America meant real privilege. Most people owned pewter, latten (a copper alloy similar to brass), or wood. As late as 1750 roughly one in five American households lacked forks and knives.

Without local mines, New England silversmiths created wares from coins or outmoded objects. By 1800 approximately 2,500 silversmiths were employed in the United States. Styles copied English fashions until the nineteenth century, and imported silverware continued to be popular.

Innovations and the Gilded Age
T. Bruff registered the first American silverware patent in 1801. Numerous others soon followed. Britannia metal manufacturers then began to produce flatware in inexpensive white alloys.

Electroplating, patented in England by G. R. and H. Elkington in 1840, revolutionized the industry. The Philadelphian John O. Mead was the first of many Americans to imitate the process. Hotels, restaurants, railway cars, and steamboats spread awareness of these new wares.

Between 1875 and 1915 American silverware production almost quadrupled. The discovery of vast silver deposits in the American West and mass production methods made cheap silverware widely available.

When the French fashion for dining à la russe, with numerous individual courses served consecutively, became stylish in America in the latter nineteenth century, new silverware forms proliferated. Specialized implements had already existed, however, Gilded Age Americans purchased, among other items, ice cream saws, aspic slicers, and servers for macaroni, fried oysters, and Saratoga chips, later called potato chips.

Escalating production costs for these innumerable pieces proved burdensome. Regulations implemented in 1926 limited their introduction. Three years later Emily Post decreed that no more than three forks and two knives should be set on the table at one time, adding, "NO rule of etiquette is of less importance than which fork we use."

Stainless steel, discovered early in the twentieth century, and plastic brought cutlery to even the humblest households in the boom years after World War II.

Spoons
The word "spoon" is derived from the Celtic *spon*, meaning wood chip, the commonest material for early spoons. Primitive societies made them by attaching shells to makeshift handles. The earliest American examples, called "slip-end" spoons, had fig-shaped bowls and slender handles. Later colonial spoons came in three basic sizes: porridge, table, and tea. Ladles, pierced spoons, and versions for basting, marrow, mustard, and sugar also existed.

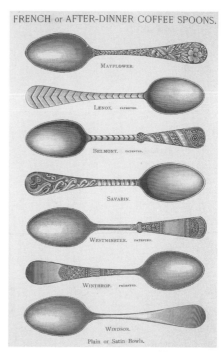

Examples of French or after-dinner coffee spoons.

Spoons resonate with symbolic meaning. In the Old Testament, God commanded Moses to make gold spoons for the tabernacle containing the Ark of the Covenant. The ancient Egyptians buried ivory spoons in the tombs of pharaohs. The English coronation ceremony has utilized a spoon since the twelfth century. Traditionally spoons are gifted to godchildren at their christenings. Welsh brides received them for their betrothals, which led to the colloquial term "spooning" for making love.

New Amsterdam silversmiths created fanciful "monkey spoons" to commemorate significant occasions. New England silversmiths invented coffin-end spoons to memorialize death. Spoons are the stuff of nursery rhymes, "The dish ran away with the spoon," and distance us from others: "Marry, he must have a long spoon that must eat with the devil" (Shakespeare, *The Comedy of Errors*).

By 1800 spoons for salt, dessert, and tea caddies appeared. Ice cream, afternoon tea, after-dinner coffee, and chocolate spoons became fashionable mid-century. Service à la russe introduced versions for sorbet, bouillon, chowder, cream soup, preserves, jam, jelly, eggs, lemonade (later iced tea), and grapefruit and ladles for cream, mayonnaise, and oyster stew.

As spoon forms multiplied, diners were entreated to use them less—by 1887 only for stirring tea or eating soup. Paradoxically, spoon collecting steadily accelerated. "Keepsake," berry and Renaissance-revival "Apostle" spoons anticipated the late Victorian craze for commemorative souvenir spoons with themes including the battle of Gettysburg, Tampa strawberries, and Dumbo the elephant. World War I decimated the

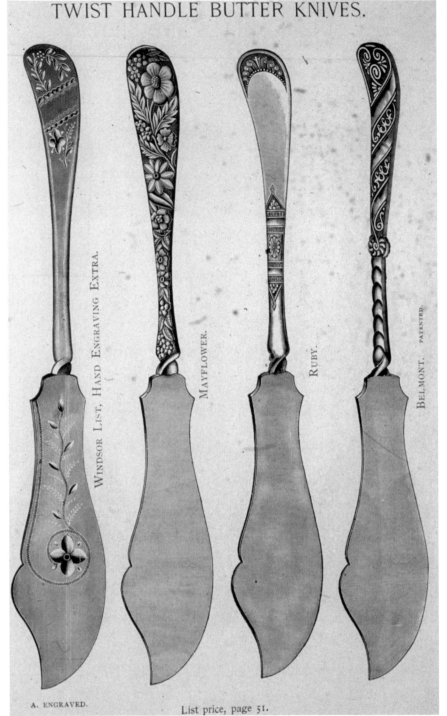

TWIST HANDLE BUTTER KNIVES.

WINDSOR LIST, HAND ENGRAVING EXTRA.

MAYFLOWER.

RUBY.

BELMONT. PATENTED.

A. ENGRAVED.

List price, page 51.

Twist handle butter knives.

souvenir spoon business. However, spoon use made a comeback at that time.

Knives

Knives were among humankind's first tools. They have also featured in ritual sacrifice and meat distribution since the earliest recorded banquets of ancient Sumer. Medieval carving was an honorific service performed by noblemen. Personal knives long served as the West's primary dining utensil. In northern Europe they retained that preeminence until the early eighteenth century.

As late as 1837, Eliza Ware Farrar maintained that Americans could eat, "armed with a steel blade . . . provided you do it neatly." However, the 1852 *Art of Pleasing* told diners to "eat always with a fork or spoon." The sociologist Norbert Elias argued that the table knife's importance diminished as society deemed it disturbingly violent. The nineteenth-century inventions of fish, butter, and salad knives all have blunt blades. Conversely, sharp steak knives are used only when required.

Forks

Homer described roasting forks, and rare, delicate Roman forks survive. However, the ancient world used forks primarily as cooking tools or weapons—Poseidon's trident and the devil's pitchfork. The earliest known dinner fork belonged to a Byzantine princess who married the doge of Venice circa 1060. The ecclesiastics cursed her for using one, but her habit gradually spread through Italy.

People in northern Europe resisted what they considered an effeminate affectation. As late as 1515 the Protestant reformer Martin Luther purportedly declared, "God protect me from forks." And though his courtiers used them, King Louis XIV (r. 1643–1715) never did.

Most known colonial examples were made for cooking or to spear candied sweetmeats. Although two-tined forks for steadying meat became popular, three- and four-tined dinner forks remained rare in America until the mid-nineteenth century. By 1860 they were considered essential. Late-nineteenth-century Americans developed fork fanaticism. They invented versions not only for pastry, salad, and fruit but also for strawberries, sandwiches, bread, and ice cream. Etiquette books declared, "Never use a knife or spoon when a fork will do." In the era of fast food, people often forego all three.

[**See also** COOKING EQUIPMENT, SOCIAL ASPECTS OF; DINING ROOMS AND MEAL SERVICE; ETIQUETTE BOOKS.]

BIBLIOGRAPHY

Goldberg, Michael J. *Collectible Plastic: Kitchenware and Dinnerware, 1935–1965.* Atglen, PA: Schiffer, 1995.

Heritage Plantation of Sandwich. *A Cubberd, Four Joyne Stools and Other Smalle Thinges: The Material Culture of Plymouth Colony and Silver and Silversmiths of Plymouth, Cape Cod, and Nantuckett.* Catalog to the Heritage Plantation of Sandwich Exhibition, 8 May–23 October 1994. Sandwich, MA: Trustees of the Heritage Plantation of Sandwich, 1994.

Hood, William P., Jr., with Roslyn Berlin and Edward Wawrynek. *Tiffany Silver Flatware: 1845–1905, When Dining Was an Art.* Woodbridge, Suffolk, U.K.: Antique Collectors' Club, 1999.

Newman, Harold. *An Illustrated Dictionary of Silverware.* London: Thames and Hudson, 1987.

Philips, John Marshall. *American Silver.* Mineola, NY: Dover, 2001.

Stutzenberger, Albert. *American Historical Spoons: The American Story in Spoons.* Rutland, VT: Charles E. Tuttle, 1971.

Venable, Charles L. *Silver in America, 1840–1940: A Century of Splendor.* New York: Abrams, 1995.

Visser, Margaret. *The Rituals of Dinner: The Origins, Evolution, and Meaning of Table Manners.* New York: Grove Weidenfeld, 1991.

CAROLIN C. YOUNG

Simmons, Amelia

Amelia Simmons was the author of *American Cookery*, which first appeared in Hartford, Connecticut, in 1796. The work appears to be the earliest extant published cookbook written by an American. Previously published cookbooks in the colonies had simply been reprints of English works. What is described on the title page as "the second edition" was published in Albany, New York. No date is given, but Eleanor Lowenstein (*Bibliography of American Cookery Books*) cited an advertisement for the work in the *Albany Gazette*, 31 October 1796. Lowenstein listed thirteen appearances of the work; there were also pirated editions.

Considering the importance of *American Cookery*, little is known about Amelia Simmons except that she was "an American orphan" and that she wrote the second edition not only because "the call was so great" but also to free the work "from those egregious blunders, and inaccuracies, which attended the first: which were occasioned either by the ignorance, or evil intention of the transcriber for the press." Simmons clearly had been forced by necessity to earn her living as a domestic worker, but her home of origin is not known. It has often been suggested that she must have been from Connecticut, but in some respects a more persuasive case can be made for the Hudson River valley. Evidence of the latter likelihood is the early published use in English of a number of words of Dutch origin. The most notable is "slaw" specifically referring to cabbage salad, that is, "coleslaw" or "cole slaw" (from Middle Dutch *kool* and *sla*, meaning "cabbage salad"). Another word of Dutch derivation is "cookie" (from *koekje*, meaning "cookie") rather than either of the corresponding English terms "small cake" or "biscuit." Although it took some time, both of those Dutch terms came to be quintessentially American.

Most of the recipes in *American Cookery* are English. Seven recipes, beginning with "To make a fine sullabub from the cow," are taken verbatim from *The Frugal Housewife*, by Susannah Carter, which had appeared in American editions beginning in 1772. Even Simmons's famous "election cake," the recipe for which did not appear until the Albany edition and so cannot be directly associated with Hartford, as it often is, was simply a "great cake" from historical English baking. Recipes for this cake abound in sixteenth- and seventeenth-century English cookbooks and manuscripts.

Despite the English influence in *American Cookery*, there was a distinctively American use of elements, such as serving "cramberry-sauce" with roast turkey and using "Indian meal" (cornmeal) in place of other types of meal, most typically oatmeal. The book contains three recipes for "a tasty Indian pudding" that describe a strictly traditional English method for puddings made with other types of meal. Likewise, although various hearth cakes made with Indian meal had been made by the colonists from the beginning of settlement and are often cited in literature, Simmons's three recipes for "johny cake, or hoe cake" may be the earliest to actually see print. The very word "johny" comes from *jonniken*, a term from northern England meaning oaten bread. Simmons also provided recipes for gingerbread made light with pear lash, a precursor of baking soda, a type of gingerbread that came to be the American style. Simmons's work demonstrates that the use of alkali for leavening in baking must have been a long-standing technique in America.

[**See also** CAKES; COOKBOOKS AND MANUSCRIPTS: TO 1860; COOKING MANUSCRIPTS; MIDDLE ATLANTIC STATES.]

BIBLIOGRAPHY

Simmons, Amelia. *American Cookery*. 2nd ed. Albany, NY: Webster, 1796. In facsimile with an introduction by Karen Hess. Bedford, MA: Applewood, 1996.

Simmons, Amelia. *American Cookery: Or, the Art of Dressing Viands, Fish, Poultry, and Vegetables, and the Best Modes of Making Puff-Pastes, Pies, Tarts, Puddings, Custards, and Preserves, and All Kinds of Cakes, from the Imperial Plumb to Plain Cake*. Hartford: Hudson and Goodwin, 1796. In facsimile, *The First American Cookbook*, with an essay by Mary Tolford Wilson. New York: Oxford University Press, 1958; New York: Dover, 1984.

KAREN HESS

Sinclair, Upton

Before the summer of 1905, food safety was monitored by just two men who made up the Department of Agriculture's entire Bureau of Chemistry. The Senate had contemplated a

Upton Sinclair published The Jungle *when he was just 27.*

pure food and drug bill for three years with little enthusiasm until a novel by Upton Sinclair (1878–1968), in serial form, was published in the socialist magazine *Appeal to Reason*. Sinclair's depiction of conditions in Chicago's stockyards and packing plants aroused the wrath of the meat-consuming public and forced the creation of the Pure Food and Drug Act of 1906, the Beef Inspection Act, and ultimately the Food and Drug Administration. The serial was published in book form in 1906 as *The Jungle*. The book, filled with disturbingly squalid details, was typical of the muckraking journalism of the day. Sinclair had been a student in New York City in the 1890s, and his book was an emotionally charged and convincing extension of Jacob Riis's 1890 exposé of tenement conditions, *How the Other Half Lives*.

The popularity of *The Jungle* caused meat sales to decline so sharply that President Theodore Roosevelt empowered the Neill-Reynolds Commission to investigate conditions in the nation's food industry. The commission confirmed all but one of Sinclair's observations. Nevertheless, influential industry lobbyists succeeded in hamstringing the resulting regulations.

The Pure Food and Drug Act, which was concerned primarily with adulteration, contained only one sentence about food quality (other than issues of undesirable additives). According to section 7, a food was considered impure "if it consists in whole or in part of a filthy, decomposed, or putrid animal or vegetable substance, or any portion of an animal unfit for food, whether manufactured or not, or if it is the product of a diseased animal, or one that has died otherwise than by slaughter." While superficially in the best interest of consumers, the act's penalties for industry violators were light: either a maximum of one year's imprisonment or a maximum fine of $500 per violation or both.

Sinclair was a lifelong defender of lost causes and ethical living and, consequently, an exposer of corruption, writing on slavery, Nicola Sacco and Bartolomeo Vanzetti, and the Teapot Dome scandal as well as the healthy alternative diet of vegetarianism. He wrote more than eighty books, including novels, nonfiction, an autobiography, a collection of letters, articles, essays, reviews, and poems, and countless other works under pseudonyms. He received the Pulitzer Prize in 1946 for a historical novel in his Lanny Budd series. Sinclair tried to manifest his utopian ideals by founding Helicon Hall in Englewood, New Jersey, with royalties from *The Jungle*. The experiment in communal living lasted only one year, collapsing when its building burned in 1907. Sinclair ran unsuccessfully for governor of California in 1934 using the slogan "End Poverty in California." It was five years before John Steinbeck's *Grapes of Wrath* drew attention to the plight of California's migrant farmworkers.

Sinclair had gone to the stockyards to expose brutal working conditions, not the quality of the foods produced there. He com-

plained, at the end of his life, that he had "aimed at the public's heart, and by accident hit it in the stomach."

[**See also** Armour, Philip Danforth; Butchering; Food and Drug Administration; Pure Food and Drug Act.]

BIBLIOGRAPHY

Sinclair, Upton. *The Jungle*. New York: Heritage, 1965.
Sinclair, Upton. *My Lifetime in Letters*. Columbia: University of Missouri Press, 1960.

GARY ALLEN

Singapore Sling

The first recorded definition of the cocktail, in the May 13, 1806, edition of the *Balance and Columbian Repository* of Hudson, New York, defined the cocktail as a "bittered sling." The sling therefore is an older category of mixed alcoholic drink than the cocktail, so what exactly is a sling? The definition offered in the periodical mentioned is "a stimulating liquor, composed of spirits of any kind, sugar, water, and bitters—it is vulgarly known as a bittered sling." A sling, then, includes sugar, water, and spirits, which corresponds perfectly with the recipe for the sling published by Jerry Thomas in his groundbreaking book *How to Mix Drinks; or, The Bon Vivant's Companion* (1862). The slings and toddies are listed together in Thomas's book; Thomas explains that the gin sling is made with the same ingredients as the gin toddy, except with a little grated nutmeg on top. The gin toddy recipe, as listed in Thomas's book, is gin, water, sugar, and ice.

The Singapore sling was created in 1915 by Ngiam Tong Boon, a bartender at the Long Bar in the Raffles Hotel in Singapore. The original recipe has been lost. The recipes published in the 1920s and 1930s simply replace the sugar with cherry brandy or liqueur (specifically cherry Heering), replace the water with soda water, and add lemon juice. There is a recipe from 1922 called the straits sling, touted as the "well-known Singapore drink," in *Cocktails and How to Mix Them*, a book by Herbert Jenkins that introduces bitters and Benedictine to these recipes.

The recipe that the head bartender at Raffles provided in 1990 was gin, Cointreau, Benedictine, cherry Heering, bitters, lime, and pineapple juice with a splash of soda. That recipe has been poured at the Rainbow Room in New York City and has become the modern standard.

[**See also** Cocktails; Gin; Hot Toddies.]

DALE DEGROFF

Skillets, *see Frying Pans, Skillets, and Spiders*

Slang, Food

American food slang can claim a proud heritage and a truly golden age in the 1930s and 1940s. Food neologisms abound thanks to culinary globalization and the insatiable appetite of Americans for new tastes. However, these new terms are typically loan words or standard register, not slang. To be sure, food

metaphors abound in idiomatic American speech—"American as apple pie" (thoroughly American), "bring home the bacon" (earning the wages that support a family), "baloney" (nonsense), "go bananas" (lose your temper), "bread" and "dough" (money), "cheesecake" (a pretty, scantily clad woman), and "toss your cookies" (to vomit) are examples.

For actual food slang, forsake the white tablecloths and head for the greasy spoon on the other side of the tracks. Popular culture, not high culture, produces slang. Common food eaten by common people, not haute cuisine eaten by highbrows, has inspired America's culinary slang.

Western and Military Slang

An early example of culinary slang is found in the American cowboy. As Ramon Adams wrote in *Cowboy Lingo* (1936), "The cowboy did not slight his slang when it came to his 'chuck,' the unpoetic name he gave to food"(p. 147). We can thank the cowhand for such slang terms as "Mexican strawberries" (dried beans), "mountain oysters" (cattle testicles), "son-of-a-gun stew" (a medley of calf brain, organs, and parts), and "belly cheater" (camp cook).

A similar flair for slang is found in the language of the lumberjack. Loggers enjoyed what they claimed were the best "eats" in the world, but their culinary slang was cynical. Onions were "fruit," the assistant camp cook was a "crumb chaser," oleomargarine was "ole," butter was "salve," and eggs were "hen fruit."

The pinnacle of sarcasm in American food slang is found in the armed forces. In *Chow* (1978), Paul Dickson notes that "like the slang of prisoners, hoboes, college students, summer campers and their counselors, the cant which has emerged to describe military food is fundamentally negative, graphic and colorful" (p. 259). "Armored cow" (condensed milk), "army strawberries" (prunes), "battery acid" (coffee), "blood" (ketchup), "bug juice" (powdered fruit drink), "dog food" (corned beef hash), and "SOS" (creamed corned beef on toast) are all colorful examples.

1930s and 1940s Slang

The finest examples of American food slang were heard at the lunch counters, diners, and soda fountains of the 1930s and 1940s. In *Hash House Lingo* (1941), Jack Smiley observes that there was no limit "to the lengths to which the bright boys behind the marble counters have extended themselves to outdo the other fellow with fantastic, grotesque or witty labels for food combinations from the kitchen" (p. 5). Their witty use of fabricated slang was unprecedented and has not been matched since. "Adam's ale" (water), "cow paste" (butter), "guess water" (soup), "hounds on an island" (frankfurters with beans), "one from the Alps" (swiss cheese sandwich), "raft" (slice of toast), and "yum-yum" (sugar)—the humor and creativity are striking.

Soda Fountain and Diner Slang

Adam and Eve on a raft: poached eggs on toast
angels on horseback: oysters rolled in bacon, served on toast
axle grease: margarine
bad breath: onions
baled hay: Shredded Wheat cereal
bark: a frankfurter
belly busters: baked beans
belly warmer: a cup of coffee
bilge water: soup
board: a slice of toast
Bossy in a bowl: beef stew
break it and shake it: add an egg to a drink
brick: a biscuit
cackle berries: eggs
choker: a hamburger
city juice: water
dogs and maggots: crackers and cheese
drag one through Georgia: a glass of Coca-Cola with chocolate syrup
first lady: spare ribs
glue: tapioca pudding
gold dust: sugar
hash: food
hot top: chocolate sauce
Irish cherries: carrots
jamoka: coffee
looseners: prunes
lumber: a toothpick
maiden's delight: cherries
mug of murk: a cup of black coffee
nervous pudding: Jell-O
O'Connors: potatoes
pause: a glass of Coca-Cola
punk: bread
radio sandwich: a tuna fish sandwich
rush it: Russian dressing
salt horse: corned beef
shimmy: jelly
sinker: a doughnut
squeeze: orange juice
squeal: ham
take a chance: hash
twist it, choke it, and make it cackle: a chocolate malted milk shake with an egg
virgin juice: cherry syrup
wet mystery: beef stew
yard bird: chicken
yum-yum: sugar

TOM DALZELL

An equally clever slang was used by the young men who worked behind soda fountains. The soda jerk's slang served several functions. It could communicate complicated orders in several words; it was a code understood by insiders only; most importantly it established the soda jerk as a remarkable fellow. A glass of Coca-Cola was an "Atlanta special," to serve a scoop of ice cream was to "dip a snowball," a banana split was a "houseboat," and to add ice cream to a slice of pie was to "put a hat on it."

In the early twenty-first century, while food metaphors abound, food slang does not. Some slang terms for food may be heard in the speech of young people ("za" for pizza is a fixture of modern youth speech), in the armed forces ("Meals Refused by Ethiopians" for the ready-to-eat meals issued by the military with the official title of MREs), and upscale coffee bars ("why bother" for a decaffeinated, nonfat latte), but the modern idiom is a weak shadow of the glory days.

Drink Slang

Turning to drinking, the slang of drink is extensive and creative. Types of alcohol ("grape" for wine, "dago red" for cheap red wine, "brewski" for beer, and the all-encompassing "hooch" for alcohol) require slang names. This is also the case with the places where we drink (a "gin mill" or a "beer emporium"), with those who serve the drinks ("beer jerker," "doctor," or "mixologist"), and with the actual act of drinking, from "name your poison" for the "antifogmatic," "booster," or "eye-opener" (the first drink of the day) to the "sundowner" or "settler" (the last drink of the night).

No physical condition can boast more slang synonyms in American English than inebriation. Benjamin Franklin, who is reported to have known something about intemperance, was so impressed with the number of slang expressions meaning "drunk" that in 1733 he compiled the *Drinker's Dictionary*, a glossary of some 228 slang terms for "intoxicated." Drinkers have continued to invent new adjectives to use for those under the influence of adult beverages. The language writer Paul Dickson published a list of 2,231 terms in *Dickson's Word Treasury* (1992) and has since added several hundred entries.

The most ingenious alcohol slang is that of the bootlegger and moonshiner. The criminal status bestowed on alcohol by the U.S. Constitution from 1919 until 1932 guaranteed an imaginative vernacular. The moonshiner has always boasted a rich slang, drawing on the expressive language in the rural, southern Appalachian hills where moonshining is practiced—"Johnny Law" (any law enforcement official), "kitchen" (an illegal still), and the many variations on the end product, from "balm of Gilead" to "panther piss" or "white lightning."

Drinking has always been part of the social fabric of the United States, and the slang vocabulary of drinking is constantly expanding. This imperative to name anew simply reveals the manifest destiny of humans to create new ways of saying old things.

[**See also** BEER HALLS; COFFEEHOUSES; COMBAT FOOD; DRINKING SONGS; SODA FOUNTAINS; TAVERNS.]

BIBLIOGRAPHY

Abel, Ernest L. *Alcohol Wordlore and Folklore: Being a Compendium of Linguistic and Social Fact and Fantasy Associated with the Use and Production of Alcohol as Reflected in the Magazines, Newspapers, and Literature of the English-Speaking World.* Buffalo, NY: Prometheus, 1987.

Adams, Ramon F. *Cowboy Lingo.* Boston: Houghton Mifflin, 1936.

Dalzell, Tom. *The Slang of Sin.* Springfield, MA: Merriam-Webster, 1998.

Dickson, Paul. *Chow*. New York: New American Library. 1978.

Dickson, Paul. *The Great American Ice Cream Book*. New York: Atheneum, 1972.

Jones, Michael Owen. "Soda-Fountain, Restaurant, and Tavern Calls." *American Speech* 42 (1967): 58–64.

Keller, Mark, Mairi McCormick, and Vera Efron. *A Dictionary of Words about Alcohol*. New Brunswick, NJ: Rutgers Center of Alcohol Studies, 1982.

Smiley, Jack. *Hash House Lingo*. Easton, PA: Self-Published, 1941.

Spears, Richard A. *The Slang and Jargon of Drugs and Drink*. Metuchen, NJ: Scarecrow, 1986.

TOM DALZELL

Slicers, *see Apple-Preparation Tools*

Sloppy Joe

The all-American sloppy joe sandwich is typically composed of ground beef that is browned with chopped onions, green pepper, and garlic; combined with tomato sauce and seasonings of choice; and served hot on a hamburger bun. Although it is not known when the sandwich was first called the "sloppy joe," similar ground beef concoctions have been recorded in American cookbooks since the beginning of the twentieth century. Some food historians believe that, with the addition of ketchup or tomato sauce, it evolved from the popular Iowa loose meat sandwich introduced by Floyd Angell, the founder of Maid-Rite restaurants, in 1926. During the Great Depression and World War II, ground beef provided an economical way to stretch meat and ensured the popularity of the sandwich. As for the name sloppy joe, some say it was inspired by one of two famous bars named Sloppy Joe's in the 1930s—one in Havana, Cuba, and the other in Key West, Florida. The name caught on throughout the United States, and based on the number of establishments that subsequently became known as Sloppy Joe's by the late 1930s, it is likely that the messy-to-eat sandwich was named after restaurants that commonly served it. By 1948 the sloppy joe was firmly established in America's sandwich culture.

[**See also** SANDWICHES.]

BIBLIOGRAPHY

Mercuri, Becky. *Sandwiches That You Will Like*. Pittsburgh, PA: WQED Multimedia, 2002.

BECKY MERCURI

Slow Cookers

The Rival Company introduced the Crock-Pot Slow Cooker in 1971. According to company records, Rival had acquired a smaller company, Naxon Utilities, which manufactured an electric ceramic bean cooker called the Beanery. It consisted of a glazed brown crock liner housed in a white steel casing. After experimenting with the Beanery, Rival added more wire to the metal housing, found a factory to manufacture the ceramic crocks, came up with the name Crock-Pot, and started selling the appliance with the slogan "Cooks all day while the cook's away."

The slow cooker's emergence in the 1970s coincided with a simultaneous upsurge in American interest in cooking and an economic need to find attractive ways to cook less expensively. Tough stewing meats could be turned into gourmet delights in the slow cooker with the addition of wine and a few herbs. Eager cooks also discovered that a can of condensed Campbell's soup could be used to make a quick and easy sauce base in the cooker. By 1981 Rival was reporting over $30 million in sales for the homely Crock-Pot. Although "Crock-Pot" is commonly used to mean any electrified ceramic slow cooker, it is still Rival's trademark.

BIBLIOGRAPHY

Crock-Pot under "Links" at http://www.rivalproducts.com/.

Lovegren, Sylvia. *Fashionable Food: Seven Decades of Food Fads*. New York: Macmillan, 1995.

SYLVIA LOVEGREN

Slow Food U.S.A.

Slow Food U.S.A. is a nonprofit educational organization with 12,000 members that is divided into 140 local "convivia," or chapters. It is dedicated to preserving endangered foodways, celebrating local food traditions, such as animal breeds and heirloom varieties of fruits and vegetables, and promoting artisanal products. It advocates economic sustainability and biodiversity through educational events and public outreach programs. Created in 2000, it is the U.S. branch of the international Slow Food organization, which began in 1986 in Italy with a protest against the "fast food" way of life. When a McDonald's opened in Rome near the Piazza di Spagna, the Italian journalist Carlo Petrini organized a demonstration using bowls of penne pasta for weapons. By 2006, the international organization had grown to encompass a collection of nonprofit and commercial entities, including a university and a hotel, and had amassed a membership of 83,000 worldwide. The first U.S. convivium was started in 1991 in Portland, Oregon, by Pastaworks owner Peter de Garmo, who is currently on the Slow Food U.S.A. Board of Directors.

In the early twenty-first century Petrini, who still leads the international organization, describes Slow Food as an eco-gastronomic movement. The democratic nature of Slow Food means that each country and convivium may concentrate on those aspects it chooses. But broadly speaking, Slow Food reminds the world that food is more than fuel, that the rituals of cooking and eating bind humanity in ineffable ways, and that it is important to know where food comes from, who produces it, and how these actions impact the world. Slow Food embraces the art of food production, from field to table. Its advocacy has sometimes been characterized as virtuous or compassionate globalization. Slow Food U.S.A. emphasizes the camaraderie of taking meals together, an activity endangered by America's "speed eating" culture. It also views reconnecting with pleasure as a way to preserve food heritage. Slow Food's symbol is a snail, because "it moves slowly and calmly eats its way through life."

Slow Food started as a loose federation of like-minded enthusiasts in Italy, who formally created Arcigola Slow Food in July 1986. ("Arcigola" was a made-up word combining ARCI, an acronym for a recreational-cultural organization and also the word "arch," with *La Gola*, a culinary magazine to which many original members had a connection.) In December 1989 the International Slow Food movement was founded in Paris, where the protocol was signed by representatives from fifteen nations. At that first meeting the magazine *Il Gambero Rosso* introduced the *Almanaco dei golosi*, an inventory of Italian foods produced using traditional methods that was compiled with the help of Arcigola. This was the beginning of Slow Food's substantial commitment to preserving traditional foods and foodways. Since 2000 Slow Food's Foundation of Biodiversity has recognized outstanding achievements in this arena with its Slow Food Award for the Defense of Biodiversity. American recipients have included Dale Lasater, a Colorado rancher who pioneered the revival of sustainable practices in raising grass-finished beef cattle, and the American Chestnut Foundation in Bennington, Vermont, which is working to restore the chestnut in eastern forests after it was decimated by a blight.

The nonprofit Foundation of Biodiversity was created in cooperation with the region of Tuscany and is dedicated to saving and promoting endangered heritage foods around the globe. It started with the Ark of Taste, which was launched at the first Slow Food Salone del Gusto gathering in 1996. The Ark, with its symbolic name, rescues gastronomic products that, according to the organization, are threatened by industrial standardization, hygiene laws, the regulations of large-scale distribution, and environmental damage. Ark products in the United States range from the Olympia native oyster to New Mexico's Navajo-Churro sheep, from California's Meyer lemon to Louisiana heritage strawberries. The Presidia, whose creation followed the Ark, works hand in hand with the Ark to give these products economic viability through promotion and marketing as well as providing direct support to some projects. In the United States, Presidia projects have included heritage turkey breeds and American raw milk cheeses. The Foundation for Biodiversity, created in 2003, now oversees both the Ark and Presidia.

Besides the foundation, five other major nonprofit and commercial entities come under the Slow Food umbrella, which is based in Petrini's hometown of Bra, Italy.

These are the Slow Food International Association; the Slow Food National Associations, which includes Slow Food U.S.A.; the University of Gastronomic Sciences; Slow Food Italy Promotion; and Slow Food Italy Editore. The national and international associations oversee the convivia. Besides the United States, countries with national associations include Italy, Germany, Switzerland, France, Great Britain, and Japan. The University of Gastronomic Sciences opened in 2004 in the town of Pollenzo, south of Turin. Its mission is renewing farming methods, protecting biodiversity, and building an organic relationship between gastronomy and agriculture science. In addition the complex houses a hotel and a restaurant as well as a wine vault. Slow Food Italy Promotion and Slow Food Italy Editore are commercial branches of Slow Food Italy.

Since 1996 Slow Food has hosted the Salone del Gusto every two years in Turin. Like so many Slow Food projects, it began as an experiment with local food producers and has grown to take on a life of its own. The Salone in 2004 attracted more than 140,000 visitors and inaugurated the first Terra Madre: A World Meeting of Food Communities, attended by 5,000 artisanal producers from around the world, including 629 from North America. Terra Madre featured a closing address by His Royal Highness Charles, Prince of Wales, long an advocate of sustainable agriculture.

BIBLIOGRAPHY
Petrini, Carlo. *Slow Food: The Case for Taste.* New York: Columbia University Press, 2001.
Slow Food. www.slowfood.com.
Slow Food U.S.A. www.slowfoodusa.org.

KIM PIERCE

Smelt

A member of the family Osmeridae, silvery, small true smelt is both freshwater and anadromous (spends part of its life in saltwater). Often abundant, smelt is harvested commercially both for human food and for fertilizer. Smelt also is used by sportfishers as bait for larger fish. Mostly carnivorous, smelt feeds on zooplankton, other small fish, and invertebrates. Schooling smelt can be harvested thousands at a time in nets. Smelt is a popular ice-fishing catch—shacks are erected close to the freshwater or brackish end of estuaries and rivers. Their small size and somewhat oily flesh make smelt ideal for frying. The heads and sometimes the tails are removed, and the fish are dipped in batter, fried quickly, and eaten whole.

SANDRA L. OLIVER

Smoking

Smoking is an age-old process used to preserve foods. Smoking was employed to aid preservation of meats, fish, and poultry in conjunction with salting and drying and to develop flavor. Preservation techniques have advanced significantly, but smoking is still used to preserve, impart flavor, and add texture to different foods. The basic process and tools for smoking foods have remained unchanged through the millennia.

Smoking originated in prehistoric times, most likely in several regions of the world independently. That smoke could impart a pleasant flavor and improve the keeping quality of meats and fish was probably discovered in conjunction with dehydration techniques and the use of wood-fueled fire to cook foods. Wood smoke helps dehydrate and sterilize foods and introduces characteristic flavors. The flavor and color of the smoked product depend considerably on whether the wood used is hard or soft, wet or dried, in the form of chips or sawdust. Hardwoods are used predominantly; softwoods are added to enhance color.

Wood selection is a regional preference and is as unique to each region as the smoking technique. Foods may be smoked simply by suspension over an open wood fire or in enclosures that collect the smoke. And the smoking enclosures themselves may be as simple as buckets and barrels or as elaborate as specially built kilns and smokehouses.

The principle of smoking involves exposing food to fat- and water-soluble molecules, steam, and other particles released from burning wood. Foods absorb these compounds, lose moisture, and develop characteristic "smoked" flavors. Wood smoke components, including acids, aldehydes, and phenols, have distinct roles in the preserving, texturing, and flavoring processes. Smoke acids influence protein coagulation and texture, aldehydes help create networks and influence texture, and phenols contribute to the development of aroma and taste. Smoking temperature and humidity govern the degree to which these reactions occur and thereby the extent of cooking, drying, and flavor. Hot smoking also cooks the food, while cool smoking (below 90°F) primarily enhances flavor. The length of smoking also affects the texture and extent of drying.

An important step in the smoking process involves brine—a mixture of sugar, salt, and spices—to cure meats, poultry, and seafood before they are smoked. The mixture may be applied dry as a surface rub, used as a solution for soaking, or injected directly into the food.

Producing the desired smoke flavor, a side effect of a food preservation process, has evolved into an art and a science. In the United States indigenous hardwoods—hickory (genus *Carya*) and mesquite (genus *Prosopis*)—are used for smoking. Mesquite and hickory smoke flavors are acknowledged universally to be uniquely American and have evolved as popular flavors for potato chips, cheese, nuts, beer, wine, and even chocolates. American ingenuity is further demonstrated in a product called Wright Liquid Smoke based on E. H. Wright's (Kansas City, Kansas) patent in 1910. It is a water-based solution of smoke flavors and is used extensively as an antimicrobial and to add flavor, color, and texture to commercially processed foods. As the twenty-first century opened, concerns about the carcinogenic effect of some components of wood smoke were discouraging consumption of heavily smoked foods and favoring lighter smoking and liquid smoke usage.

[**See also** DRYING; MEAT; SALT AND SALTING.]

BIBLIOGRAPHY
Toussant-Samat, Maguelonne. *History of Food.* Translated by Anthea Bell. New York: Barnes and Noble, 1998.

KANTHA SHELKE

Smorgasbord

Literally translated from Swedish, smorgasbord means "buttered bread board." It came to mean a table filled with an assortment of cold hors d'oeuvres, including sandwiches; cheese; cold cuts; pickled, smoked, cured, or salted fish; meatballs; potato salad; breads; and many other delicacies.

The smorgasbord tradition was brought to the United States by Swedish immigrants at the beginning of the twentieth century. The first cookbook published in the United States that has smorgasbord in the title was Inga Norberg's *Good Food from Sweden, including the Smörgåsbord* (1939). Smorgasbord did not become a popular part of the American food scene until the 1950s. It was adopted, at least in name, by some "all you can eat" restaurants, and numerous cookbooks have been published on how to prepare and serve smorgasbord dishes. In the early twenty-first century smorgasbord can be a bountiful prelude to a meal, or it can be a meal in itself. American smorgasbord frequently includes hot dishes as well as the traditional cold ones.

BIBLIOGRAPHY
Norberg, Inga. *Good Food from Sweden, including the Smörgåsbord.* New York: M. Barrows, 1939.

ANDREW F. SMITH

Snacks, Salty

At the beginning of the twentieth century Americans were likely to choose fruit, unsalted nuts, or bread and cheese if they wanted a snack between meals. At the time few commercial snacks were available. During the 1950s salty snacks were promoted on television, and sales skyrocketed. By the end of the century Americans annually consumed almost $22 billion in salted nuts, popcorn, potato chips, pretzels, corn chips, cheese snacks, and other salty snacks.

Nuts and Peanuts

Nuts require little preparation, are relatively inexpensive, and can easily be transported. Historically nuts were roasted and salted by vendors and homemakers, but the commercial processes of how to salt nuts so that the salt remains on the nut after packaging was not learned until the early twentieth century. The most important nuts grown and sold in

In 2004 snack food giant Frito Lay Canada announced that it was eliminating trans fat from its popular potato chip brands.

America are almonds, walnuts, and pecans followed by chestnuts, pistachios, and macadamias. In addition cashews and Brazil nuts are imported. The most important snack nut is the peanut, which technically is a legume. Peanuts were relatively unimportant as a snack food until after the Civil War, when vendors began selling them on streets in cities. One peanut vendor was Amedeo Obici, an Italian-born immigrant who created Planters Peanuts, which became a national snack food company in less than two decades and remains America's most popular nut brand.

Popcorn

The popcorn industry began in the latter part of the nineteenth century, when vendors sold popcorn on the streets and at fairs, circuses, and sporting events. Popcorn was not sold in movie theaters until the Great Depression, when owners found that they could make more money on popcorn and other snack food sales than they did on theater admissions. The selling of ready-to-eat popcorn in large bags began before World War II, and sales have increased ever since. The invention of the microwave oven increased popcorn sales and profits to even greater heights.

Potato Chips

Home recipes that called for fried "shavings" of raw potatoes had appeared in American cookery books beginning in 1824. As a home and restaurant treat, they became popular at the end of the nineteenth century. Early commercial potato chips were often stale due to poor packaging. In 1933 the Dixie Wax Paper Company introduced the first waxed glassine bag, which made it possible for manufacturers to print brand names and other information on the outside of the bag. This mode of packaging promptly became the standard in the salty snack world. Potato chip sales increased throughout World War II, and advertising increased sales even more when the war ended.

The postwar period also saw the introduction of several new potato chip products, such as Ruffles, which were introduced in 1958. In the 1960s Procter and Gamble introduced Pringles, much to the chagrin of the potato chip industry. Pringles were made from dehydrated potato flakes that were reconstituted, formed, and flash fried. All chips were identical, making possible the packaging of Pringles in a long tube.

Pretzels

Pretzels are salted biscuits twisted into a knot or sticks. The Dutch probably first introduced pretzels into America, and pretzels were made and sold by street vendors. Early pretzel manufacturers were concentrated in Pennsylvania, and pretzels did not emerge as a national snack until the 1960s.

Corn Chips

The success of potato chips created a market for corn chips, which originated as a Mexican snack—cut up, fried, or hardened tortillas. Elmer Doolin was in San Antonio snacking on *friotes*, which were made from fried masa, or corn flour. He manufactured them under the name "Fritos." In 1945 Doolin met the potato chip manufacturer Herman Lay, who agreed to distribute Fritos. When Doolin died in 1959, the two companies merged, creating Frito-Lay, Inc., which continued to grow and acquired other snack foods. In 1965 Frito-Lay was acquired by the Pepsi-Cola Company. The newly merged company launched many new snack foods, such as Doritos, which almost overnight became one of America's most popular snacks. By the end of the twentieth century the corn chip industry was dominated by Frito-Lay, with the top sellers being Doritos and Tostitos.

Cheese Snacks

The process of extruding was invented by accident during 1930s. The first popular extruded snack was Chee-tos which were invented in the late 1940s by the Frito Company and were marketed by Herman Lay in 1948. Similar products were manufactured by other companies. By the beginning of the twenty-first century Chee-tos dominated the puffed snack market with sales twice as much as all the other top fifteen sales combined.

Modern Salty Snack Food

As the twentieth century progressed the quantity and diversity of salty snack foods proliferated until nearly every grocery store, kiosk, newsstand, and corner shop in America was heavily stocked with bags and packets of chips, crackers, pretzels, and much more. During the 1950s the term "junk foods" came to mean snack foods, convenience foods, sodas, and fried fast foods that were high in sugar, fat, salt, and calories and low in nutritional value. Health advocates were concerned with the relationship between the increase in consumption of these snack foods and an increase in heart disease, high blood pressure, cancer, and obesity. This problem is especially of concern for young Americans, whom snack food manufacturers have targeted in their advertising. While nutritionists properly complain about the consumption of snack foods, there is no sign that Americans are decreasing their consumption of salty snacks.

[**See also** ALMONDS; BRAZIL NUTS; CASHEWS; DIPS; FAST FOOD; FRITO-LAY; MACADAMIA NUTS;

Nachos

Nachos, a combination of tortilla pieces with melted cheese and jalapeño peppers, are credited to Ignacio Anaya, the chef at the old Victory Club in Piedras Negras across the border from Eagle Pass, Texas. He assembled the first nachos for some Eagle Pass ladies who stopped in during a shopping trip in the 1940s. Nachos became popular in Texas and throughout the United States during the 1960s. Nacho and other spicy flavorings took the snack food industry by storm, and nacho-flavored corn chips and spicy potato chips were soon on the market. Nachos were also at the spearhead of a national interest in ethnic flavors that were soon applied to corn chips, including jalapeño, cheese, nacho cheese, and other spicy seasonings.

ANDREW F. SMITH

MEXICAN AMERICAN FOOD; MR. PEANUT; NUTS; PEANUTS; PECANS; PISTACHIOS; POPCORN; WALNUTS.]

BIBLIOGRAPHY

50 Years: A Foundation for the Future. Alexandria, VA: Snack Food Association, 1987.

Hess, Karen. "The Origin of French Fries." Petits Propos Culinaires 68 (November 2001): 39–48.

Jacobson, Michael F., and Bruce Maxwell. What Are We Feeding Our Kids? New York: Workman, 1994.

Smith, Andrew F. Peanuts: The Illustrious History of the Goober Pea. Urbana: University of Illinois Press, 2002.

Smith, Andrew F. Popped Culture: A Social History of Popcorn in America. Columbia: University of South Carolina Press, 1999.

ANDREW F. SMITH

Snapple

Snapple was introduced to the soft drink market in 1972, when Leonard Marsh, Hyman Golden, and Arnold Greenberg, three childhood friends from Brooklyn, New York, formed the Unadulterated Food Corporation and began selling all-natural juices in Greenwich Village in New York City. Appealing to the health market, Marsh, Golden, and Greenberg used the best ingredients—real fruit flavors and real tea—without preservatives, chemical dyes, or artificial flavorings. At the time no other major soft drink producer could make that claim, and Snapple set the standard for those that followed. The name came from a carbonated apple soda that was part of the original beverage line.

Distributors initially worried that Snapple would not sell or, if it did, would have a limited market. They were wrong. Good nutrition and quirky names, such as Mango Madness and Amazing Grape, which were uncommon in food marketing at the time, intrigued consumers who did not mind paying nearly twice the price of an ordinary soft drink. Snapple was a new age product that was extremely popular by the second year of production. Stores had begun to call distributors before their next scheduled delivery because they had run out. When stores wanted large orders to stock up, the company refused, because it did not want to limit distribution.

Competitors began to make similar types of fruit juice and tea drinks that eventually cut into the Snapple market. But Snapple had already established itself with a solid name. When the personable and bubbly "Snapple lady" began appearing in television commercials in 1991, more people became fans. As the Snapple lady, Wendy Kaufmann, who had been "discovered" when she worked in the company's order department, received hundreds of letters a week, including marriage proposals.

In 1992 the original owners sold the Snapple company to a Boston-based investment firm that took Snapple public and in three months tripled the value of the stock.

Snapple became one of the most popular stocks in the United States. When Quaker Oats Company bought Snapple in 1994, the Snapple lady was dismissed as the commercial spokesperson, and because Quaker Oats had other priorities, Snapple declined. In 1997 Triarc bought Snapple from Quaker Oats for $300 million and brought the company back to the forefront of the market by repairing distributor relationships and appealing to young drinkers. Triarc also returned the Snapple lady to television commercials, claiming that "Wendy is the essence of the brand." In 2000 Snapple was sold to the world's third-largest soft drink maker, Cadbury Schweppes, a company that also handles Mistic, Orangina, Stewart's Root Beer, and Yoo-hoo. By the beginning of the twenty-first century Snapple had regained its place as the leader in the noncarbonated beverage market.

Snapple offers juice drinks, teas, lemonades, and diet drinks in more than thirty flavors. The highest-selling flavors are lemon tea, peach tea, diet peach tea, kiwi strawberry, diet lemon tea, raspberry tea, diet raspberry tea, Mango Madness, fruit punch, and diet cranberry raspberry. Snapple is available all over the world and claims 28 percent of the premium beverage market in the United States.

[See also FRUIT JUICES; SODA DRINKS.]

MARIAN BETANCOURT

Snickers

The Snickers candy bar, produced by Mars, Inc., built upon the success of earlier peanut and chocolate candies, including the Goo Goo Cluster (1913), Goldenberg's Peanut Chews (1922), and Reese's Peanut Butter Cups (1928). Snickers was created in 1929 by Frank Mars and his family. It was first sold to the public the following year. Named for the Mars family horse, the Snickers bar was composed of peanut butter, nougat, peanuts, and caramel encased in milk chocolate. Snickers were hand wrapped until 1944, at which time wrapping was automated.

Snickers quickly became the most popular candy bar in America, a position it has held ever since. Snickers sponsored the *Howdy Doody Show* on television from 1949 until 1952. Building upon the success of Snickers, Mars has introduced variations. In 1984 it introduced Snickers Ice Cream bars, and since then Snickers Cruncher and Snickers Almond have been added to the line.

When the Center for Science in the Public Interest targeted junk food as "empty calories" in the 1990s, consumption of many snack foods declined. Mars, Inc. responded with an advertising campaign boasting that "Snickers really satisfies." According to another ad campaign, eating a Snickers bar relieves tension and helps people enjoy life: "A Snickers a day helps you work, rest, and play." The company also used creative opportunities to promote its product. For instance, during the Gulf War frozen Snickers bars were sent to the American military. On Thanksgiving Day 1990 Snickers bars were given to every American soldier in the Middle East.

Snickers are now sold throughout the world, although in the United Kingdom its name was changed to Marathon Bar, because "snickers" sounds like "knickers," a British slang term for underpants. Subsequently Mars, Inc., made the decision to use uniform product names throughout the world, and the United Kingdom's Marathon Bar became Snickers despite resistance (and giggles) from some consumers. The candy bar is popular in other areas, particularly Russia and eastern Europe. Snickers has remained America's largest selling chocolate candy bar for almost seventy years.

BIBLIOGRAPHY

Brenner, Joël Glenn. The Emperors of Chocolate: Inside the Secret World of Hershey and Mars. New York: Broadway Books, 2000.

Pottker, Janice. Crisis in Candyland: Melting the Chocolate Shell of the Mars Family Empire. Bethesda, MD: National Press Books, 1995.

Richardson, Tim. Sweets: A History of Candy. New York: Bloomsbury, 2002.

ANDREW F. SMITH

Soda Drinks

Soda drinks encompass all carbonated nonalcoholic beverages. At the end of the twentieth century they were the fastest-growing segment of the U.S. beverage market.

The thirst for soda drinks began with the popularity of naturally carbonated mineral waters, which were thought to have medicinal properties. During the eighteenth century European scientists, such as Joseph Priestley, developed processes for artificially carbonating water. In 1806 a Yale chemistry professor named Benjamin Silliman purchased an apparatus for impregnating water with carbon dioxide. Within three years he owned soda parlors in New Haven, Connecticut, and New York City that sold his mineral water by the glass and by the bottle. Although the use of these waters was at first strictly therapeutic, soon people realized that these shops could be gathering spots for more than sick people. Everybody seemed to enjoy the refreshing qualities of carbonated water. By 1820 soda makers had started adding flavored syrups to their waters, and a whole new industry was born.

Dispensing

Soda "fountains" dispensed their carbonated water into glasses from urns or pipes. They concealed the machinery for carbonating and cooling water beneath elaborate marble and metal trimmings. To these were added pumps for dispensing syrups, sometimes in dozens of flavors. In addition to being impressive sights, these machines allowed employees to mix and serve their concoctions with minimal effort. Soda parlors soon became centers of urban social life, and temperance advocates promoted them as alternatives to saloons. By 1895 there were an estimated fifty thousand soda fountains across the nation.

Soda drinks were also sold by the bottle, to be enjoyed at home or in restaurants. However, the technology of soda bottling took many years to perfect. Bottles were all handblown and often exploded while being filled. The capping devices, mainly internal stoppers or wire clamps over corks, tended to leak both liquid and carbonation. It was not until the 1890s that American bottle manufacturers invented the technology for producing strong, inexpensive, and standardized glass soda bottles. In 1891 William Painter of Baltimore invented the "crown" metal bottle cap whose corrugated edge crimped around the bottle top. These advances paved the way for the giant soda companies of the twentieth century.

Flavors

Except for seltzer water, all soda drinks contain added flavoring. Artificial mineral waters were manufactured with blends of salts and other chemicals to duplicate the flavors of natural waters. The earliest sweet flavors were mixtures of sugar syrup and fresh fruit juices (lemon, raspberry, and strawberry) or plant extracts, such as sarsaparilla and spruce beer. By the 1880s syrup manufacturers had concocted hundreds of often unusual flavors, including allspice, cayenne pepper, champagne, maple, pistachio, and white rose. These were mixed into the glass at the fountain and had to be made almost daily because they tended to ferment quickly. For bottling purposes, the first flavors with shelf life were lemon and ginger ale, joined later by sarsaparilla, root beer, and cream soda.

Through the early 1900s ginger ale was by far the most popular bottled soda flavor. However, soda makers realized that there was more money to be made in proprietary brands than in generic flavors. Their recipes closely guarded, these new syrups were often made from more than a dozen natural and synthetic flavorings. Charles Elmer Hires began in 1876 by selling Hires Root Beer flavorings for mixing at home; through aggressive marketing, the drink was soon being sold at soda fountains nationwide. In the mid-1880s pharmacists in Waco, Texas, and Atlanta, Georgia, concocted recipes for medicinal tonics that were respectively called Dr Pepper and Coca-Cola. Their therapeutic properties were quickly forgotten as they found a market as soda fountain specialties. Coca-Cola and other companies began selling their syrups to franchised bottlers, and the modern soft-drink industry was born.

Big Business

Between 1899 and 1970 the yearly national consumption of soft drinks rose from 227 million to 72 billion 8-ounce servings. Bottling plants used new mechanized production lines to produce far greater quantities of soda and transported their products on motorized trucks riding along newly paved roads. Manufacturers realized early the value of advertising, first in newspapers and then on the radio. While regionally distributed sodas boomed (many of them fruit flavors like orange, grape, and cherry), the most phenomenal growth occurred in the cola sector. By 1920 cola drinks had overtaken ginger ale as the most popular flavor. Ten years later over seven thousand bottling plants were producing six billion bottles of soda a year.

After struggling through the Great Depression and then World War II–era shortages of raw materials, the soda drink industry took advantage of postwar prosperity. Indeed soft drinks became symbols of that prosperity and of the nation's growing role in the world. Wherever American soldiers traveled around the globe, they were sure to bring American-made sodas, Coca-Cola in particular. At home the big bottlers greatly expanded their plants and began concentrating on fewer, higher-volume brands. They found new outlets in suburban supermarkets, drive-up fast-food restaurants, and improved automatic vending machines. To meet demand from dieters, they developed low-calorie drinks using cyclamates or saccharin as artificial sweeteners. (Cyclamates were eventually banned because they were believed to increase cancer risks, and aspartame became the most widely used artificial sweetener.) Bottlers also broadened their markets with new flavor lines; Pepsi-Cola introduced Diet Pepsi, Teem, Patio, and Mountain Dew. The soda drink industry became big business, causing thousands of smaller bottlers either to sell out or to close. Hundreds of local soft-drink brands disappeared from store shelves forever.

Soda drink packaging evolved rapidly during this era. After supermarkets complained about processing returnable bottles, manufacturers introduced inexpensive "one-way" bottles and, beginning in 1953, metal cans. The popularity of cans skyrocketed after the introduction of pull tabs, and the containers soon littered roadsides across America (eventually leading to laws mandating returnable cans and bottles). Cans are by far the most popular soda container, followed by plastic bottles made of polyethylene terephthalate (PET).

From the 1960s to the 1990s soda manufacturers tapped into a vast and constantly renewing market through advertising campaigns that effectively linked soft-drink consumption to youth culture. Consumption rose steadily every year, and soda bottles and cups grew ever larger to feed this phenomenal thirst. In the 1980s manufacturers received a further boost to profits when they replaced sugar with inexpensive high-fructose corn syrup. In 1998 the rate of consumption peaked at a phenomenal fifty-six gallons per person and then began to decline slightly every year. The main culprits are saturation—carbonated drinks have penetrated every possible market—and competition from bottled waters and other forms of noncarbonated beverages.

Americans drink more than fifty-two gallons of soda drinks per person every year, with the highest consumption among consumers between the ages of eighteen and twenty-four. Most sodas are purchased in cans or bottles, while about 25 percent are dispensed in bars and restaurants. The number of bottlers is down to approximately 300, producing 450 brands of soda. While these brands include many generics and the remaining regional drinks, major manufacturers like Coca-Cola, Pepsi-Cola, and Cadbury Schweppes still command the market. Although profits may no longer be as high, it is likely that soda drinks will be a large part of Americans' diets for years to come.

[**See also** BOTTLING; CANNING AND BOTTLING; COCA-COLA; COLA WARS; CREAM SODA; DR PEPPER; GINGER ALE; PEPSI-COLA; ROOT BEER; SARSAPARILLA; SELTZER; 7-UP; SODA FOUNTAINS; SWEETENERS.]

BIBLIOGRAPHY

Funderburg, Anne Cooper. *Sundae Best: A History of Soda Fountains*. Bowling Green, OH: Bowling Green State University Popular Press, 2002.

Riley, John J. *A History of the American Soft Drink Industry: Bottled Carbonated Beverages, 1807–1957*. New York: Arno, 1972.

ANDREW COE

Soda Fountains

The soda fountain originated in the early 1800s and lasted through the 1960s. It was a gathering place for both sexes and all ages within walking distance of home or work. At a time when more women were working and did not eat in restaurants unescorted, the soda fountain provided a pleasant, inexpensive dining place.

Take the Waters

From ancient times people have recognized the healing properties of natural springs, and scientists have tried to re-create these waters. They were considered medicines, touted for curing everything from obesity and dysentery to fevers and scurvy. "Soda water" came to be the generic term for sparkling waters.

In the early nineteenth century one of the first Americans to produce mineral waters was Philip Physick (aptly named) of Pennsylvania. Another was Benjamin Silliman of Connecticut, who bottled and sold soda water. Within a fairly short time, it became a common beverage.

Though waters were initially sold as medicines, their sales as a pleasurable beverage soon outpaced their sales as medicine due to the addition of flavored syrups, which occurred in the late eighteenth century. Early flavorings were made by the apothecary, but by the late 1800s many manufacturers of soda fountains also sold soda water and syrups.

Soda Fountains and the Drug Stores

The drug store soda fountain is of long standing since early on the druggist produced soda waters. One of the earliest apothecary shops in America selling waters was opened in Philadelphia in 1825 by the French émigré Elias Durand. His apothecary has often been termed the first modern drug store with its ornate marble and mahogany fixtures. His store became a gathering place for intellectuals, the forerunner of the community social center of later soda fountains.

Fountains

The earliest "fountain" was a small boxlike apparatus for generating carbonated water. The fountain sat on the counter, connected by tubes to the apparatus set under the counter or in the cellar. There was a spigot on the fountain, shaped like a gooseneck, to draw the water. The water was then poured into a glass with or without syrup. These early fountains evolved into much more elaborate ones made of marble and costing from a few hundred to thousands of dollars.

One of the first to manufacture a soda water apparatus was John Matthews of New York City, who began manufacturing apparatuses in the early 1830s. Matthews produced 25 million gallons of soda water by combining sulfuric acid with the marble scraps from the construction of Saint Patrick's Cathedral. He later added the sale of syrups and carbonated water to his business. Matthews compared a young person's first sip of soda water to the first experience of love.

Another important manufacturer was Gustavus Dows of Massachusetts. In the 1850s he manufactured a cottage-shaped fountain of marble. The addition of marble, adding an ornate touch, was an innovation, as was the device within the fountain to shave ice. Dows's fountains had silver-plated spigots for drawing syrups, with the name of the syrup engraved on each. These early fountains were placed against a wall, but in 1903 the counter soda fountain was introduced. Customers sat at the counter facing the soda jerk as he manipulated the various spigots to create sodas, banana splits, and so forth.

After the Civil War concoctions like ice cream sodas became fountain staples. In their heyday fountains offered malted milk drinks, flips, phosphates, egg drinks, sundaes, banana splits, milkshakes, ice cream floats, and fizzes. Many of these concoctions had fanciful names, such as the Knickerbocker glory sundae and black cow.

Soda Jerk and Soda Fountain Calls

The soda fountain was also a theater with the major role played by the dispenser, also called a "soda jerk," "the professor," "thrower," and in one place "licensed fizzician," who by the 1920s was an American folk figure. He dispensed sundaes, sodas, and entertainment. Becoming a good dispenser took years of practice and often ensured a good salary. To help

him in his task, the International Association of Ice Cream Manufacturers held a series of seminars called "Sundae Schools," the purpose of which was to share information on the latest treats. This was important for the industry since the soda fountain was the major point of sale for ice cream at a time when most homes had no refrigeration other than an ice box.

In addition to creating soda fountain concoctions and entertaining customers with their artistry, soda jerks provided linguistic entertainment through the use of soda fountain calls. Soda fountain lingo was a type of shorthand used to speed up orders and provide a bit of fun. The lingo also served as a memory aid. Most calls were plays on words. Anything with strawberry flavoring was a "patch," milk was "cow juice," and an order for three of anything was a "crowd."

Prohibition

Soda fountains benefited considerably during the late nineteenth century, when the temperance movement was gaining ground and there was a need for an alternative to the saloon. Fountain operators eliminated concoctions containing alcohol and began promoting rich beverages like egg drinks and malted milk that would appeal to men.

Soda fountains began adding lunches around the beginning of the twentieth century. These eventually evolved into luncheonettes, which provided full meals. Initially these meals were intended to draw female customers, but when men could no longer get the free lunch to which they were accustomed in the saloon, menu items were geared to drawing male customers. The soda fountain lunch was quick and inexpensive enough to maintain business even during the years of the Great Depression.

Decline of the Soda Fountain

As America emerged from World War II, soda fountains were still a strong presence. Several things worked together to bring about the soda fountain's decline. There was a move to the suburbs, drive-in restaurants opened, and supermarkets began to gain a larger share of ice cream sales once refrigerators and freezers were available for homes. Now the old-time soda fountain is more memory than reality.
[**See also** COCA-COLA; ROOT BEER; ICE CREAM SODAS; LUNCHEONETTES; MOXIE; PROHIBITION; SODA DRINKS; TEMPERANCE.]

BIBLIOGRAPHY

Dickson, Paul. *The Great American Ice Cream Book.* New York: Atheneum, 1972.

Funderburg, Anne Cooper. *Sundae Best: A History of Soda Fountains.* Bowling Green, OH: Bowling Green State University Popular Press, 2002.

Kelly, Patricia M., ed. *Luncheonette: Ice-Cream, Beverage, and Sandwich Recipes from the Golden Age of the Soda Fountain.* New York: Crown, 1989.

Riley, John J. *A History of the American Soft Drink Industry: Bottled Carbonated Beverages, 1807–1957.* New York: Arno, 1972.

Weir, Robin. " 'One Leg of a Pair of Drawers': The American Soda Fountain Lingo." In *Disappearing Foods,* ed. Harlan Walker, 215–220. Devon, England: Prospect Books, 1995.

PATRICIA M. KELLY

Songs, Food

Americans had songs and nursery rhymes with mentions of food before there was an America. "Hot Cross Buns," "The Muffin Man," and "Pease Porridge Hot" are nursery rhymes that still survive. Humpty Dumpty was an egg. Yankee Doodle sticking a feather in his cap and calling it macaroni was a food reference once removed. It referred to the practice of calling English dandies in the eighteenth century who affected foreign mannerisms "macaronis."

The colonists, in the folk tradition, adapted the song lyrics to be both a bit of cheerleading and a political prod. Just before the beginning of the American Revolution, the song printed below scolded England. Note the inclusion of coffee and tea to imply weakness of character. Some of the verses as printed in the *Virginia Gazette* in November 1774 were:

> *When good Queen Elizabeth sat on the throne,*
> *Ere coffee and tea, and such slip-slops were known,*
> *The world was in terror if ere she did frown.*
>
> *Our nobles had honour in records of fame;*
> *Their sons are but shadows, and know but the name,*
> *Their fathers eat beef, their sons whore and game.*
>
> *With beef and their charters, how happy and free!*
> *Their sons, if they've charters, must live upon tea,*
> *and cringe to a venal majority.*

Through the colonial period, tavern songs and other songs sung at fairs and markets enjoyed great popularity. The melody of a drinking song was used for many patriotic songs around the time of the War of 1812, including America's anthem, "The Star-Spangled Banner," by Francis Scott Key (1779–1843).

In the early eighteenth century many songs extolled the beauty or bounty of the lands beyond the frontier as the nation was expanding westward. "Hunt the Buffalo" in several variations was popular in America and even enjoyed some acclaim in London. It offered this view of the far lands:

> *There are fishes in the river*
> *That is fitting for our use,*
> *And high and lofty sugar-canes*
> *That yield us pleasant juice,*
> *And all sorts of game, my boys,*
> *Besides the buck and doe.*

In the turbulent period before and during the American Civil War, songs that contained apparent food references were common. "Follow the Drinking Gourd" gave instructions for runaway slaves and referred to the Big Dipper constellation. It had nothing to do with food. Other songs reflected the black humor that can often emerge in difficult times. "Eating Goober Peas" was popular with the Confederate military and mentioned that uniquely southern crop, peanuts:

Just before the battle, the General hears a row
He says "The Yanks are coming, I hear their rifles now."
He looks down the roadway and what d'you think he sees?
The Georgia Militia cracking goober peas.

In the early twentieth century American life was sharply changed by a world war, a dust bowl, a depression, and a general shifting away from the steady life of an agrarian society. That was a perfect setting for a song like "Big Rock Candy Mountain," a traditional hobo ballad that appears in many slightly different versions over the years. Burl Ives popularized his variation in the 1940s and 1950s. It uses food as metaphor for the comfortable life, as in the chorus:

Oh the buzzin' of the bees
In the cigarette trees
Near the soda water fountain
At the lemonade springs
Where the bluebird sings
On the big rock candy mountain.

Sometimes songs speak code to the initiates, as in so many sly blues songs where the food references are actually about anatomical parts (jelly roll for female privates), sexual activities, or other sociosexual recognitions, like "That Chick's Too Young to Fry." On occasion the songs maintain both the food and the sexual reference as in "It Must Be Jelly ('Cause Jam Don't Shake like That)."

Some songs like "Beans and Cornbread" and "Saturday Night Fish Fry" by Louis Jordan (1908–1975) are almost chants against a lively background and can often just be foils for the instrumental work of the artists. The lyrics do mention food, but as novelties or euphemisms. "Beans and Cornbread" has an infectious rhythm, a rather flat melody line, and a lyric that makes little sense:

Beans and Cornbread,
Beans and Cornbread had a fight.
Beans knocked Cornbread out of sight.
Cornbread said, "Now, that's all right,
meet me at the corner tomorrow night."
"I'll be ready, I'll be ready tomorrow night,"
That's what Beans said to Cornbread.
"I'll be ready tomorrow night."

Most often songs use food as metaphors for other elements of life. They can include political urgings as noted above, glancing blows of serious romance, like "You're the Cream in My Coffee," and the plaintive note struck by the impecunious boyfriend, "Banana Split for My Baby; Glass of Plain Water for Me."

Other songs, most notably parodies, go into food in some detail but are often funny primarily because of the contrast with the original, as in the many contemporary food songs of Weird Al Yankovic, like "My Bologna," which parodies a top-forty song called "My Sharona," or "Eat It" to parody "Beat It" by Michael Jackson.

Often food songs have simply been novelty ditties. Their hallmarks have been slyness and broad wit. They enjoyed a great vogue during the heyday of radio with such notables as Spike Jones (1911–1965) and his strange recordings of songs like "Cocktails for Two" and "Yes, We Have No Bananas." Songs from the 1940s through the 1960s like Louis Prima's (1910–1978) "Please No Squeeza Da Banana" are novelty songs specifically done for a grin. More recently "Junk Food Junkie" by Larry Groce has kept alive that style.

The popular song by George Gershwin (1898–1937) and Ira Gershwin (1896–1983) "Let's Call the Whole Thing Off," from the 1937 film *Shall We Dance?* about lovers being too different to stay together, wittily exploited food pronunciations in verses like this:

You like potato and I like potahto
You like tomato and I like tomahto

Once in a great while the songs are actually about food, as in many folk songs, like "Shortnin' Bread" and "Bile That Cabbage Down," but most of the time they are about something else. Food in songs can be metaphor, euphemism, code word, or diversion from the real meaning. Virtually everybody sings about the basic human needs and satisfactions. Food references are a socially acceptable substitute for the taboo ones.

[**See also** Myths and Folklore.]

Robert Pastorio

Sonic

In 1954 Troy Smith of Shawnee, Oklahoma, opened a root beer and hot dog stand called the Top Hat Drive-In. He installed a speaker system for orders and used the slogan "Service with the Speed of Sound." He also offered carhop service. In 1956 Smith franchised his first operation to Charlie Pappe of Woodward, Oklahoma, who became Smith's partner, and they changed the company's name to Sonic Drive-In.

When Pappe died in 1967, Sonic had 41 outlets, which expanded to 165 stores within 6 years. In 1973 the company was restructured into Sonic Systems of America (the name was later changed to Sonic Industries). Ownership of the company shifted to its franchisees, and Sonic became a publicly traded company. By 1978 Sonic expanded to more than eight hundred outlets in thirteen southern and southwestern states.

Sonic confronted many problems in the early 1980s. As its profits fell, underperforming outlets were closed. The chain survived mainly because its strength was in small towns, where real estate costs were lower and competition less intense.

The first Sonic television commercial appeared in 1977. By 2000 Sonic's media spending approached $64 million. Sonic's "retro-future" logo was introduced, and the entire system adopted a consistent new look and menu. With almost three thousand Sonic Drive-Ins across the United States, Sonic is the only national fast-food chain that still has carhops as an integral part of its operation.

Andrew F. Smith

Sorghum Flour

Historical records trace the sorghum plant, *Sorghum bicolor* (L.) Moench, to Africa. Benjamin Franklin was thought to have introduced sorghum to the United States in the late 1700s. Sometimes known as one of the "4F" plants, it can be used for fuel, food, forage, and feed. The diversity of the crop has led to many uses: as broomcorn; in building materials, breads, porridges, and alcoholic beverages; for renewable fuel production; and as animal feed. Worldwide, grain sorghum is used for food, and because the plant is drought resistant, it is a predominant cereal in many developing countries, especially in parts of Africa and Asia. In the United States most sorghums are cultivated for animal feed. Sorghum's popularity as a food item is growing because of its unique nutritional profile and the efforts of several sorghum researchers and marketers.

The whole grain can be cooked liked rice or ground into meal or flour. Unlike wheat, sorghum is gluten free, which is beneficial to people with intolerance to gluten. Some sorghums are even high in antioxidants and can be used in making healthy, whole-grain breads. Not readily available, sorghum can be found in some health food markets and through the Internet.

[**See also** Sorghum Syrup.]

BIBLIOGRAPHY

Bumgarner, Marlene Anne. *The New Book of Whole Grains: More than 200 Recipes Featuring Whole Grains, Including Amaranth, Quinoa, Wheat, Spelt, Oats, Rye, Barley, and Millet.* New York: St. Martin's Griffin, 1997.

Cheryl Forberg

Sorghum Syrup

The sorghum syrup plant, *Sorghum bicolor* (L.) Moench, shares the nomadic heritage of its sister, sorghum grain. Syrup-making techniques came into prominence in the United States around the mid-1800s. Because of the scarcity of sugar during wartime, sorghum syrup was the principal sweetener in many parts of the country. By 1920 the annual U.S. production was nearly 50 million gallons. After World War II less expensive refined sugar became available, and sorghum syrup use declined. The bulk of production remains in the southeastern United States, Kentucky and Tennessee being the leading producers.

While molasses is a by-product of sugarcane processing, pure sorghum syrup is the goal (and only) product of sorghum cane processing. Like sugarcane, the sorghum plant is harvested and fed into a mill, which crushes the stalks, extracting clear juices. Impurities are removed before the liquid is simmered in an evaporating pan. It is slowly reduced to a viscous amber syrup, which is milder in flavor than molasses and less sweet than honey. Nutritionally it is rich in antioxidants and minerals.

In the South sorghum syrup is also referred to as "sorghum molasses." This versatile sweetener is used in beverages, confections, and baking. In the South too it is most commonly found on top of hot biscuits. In substituting sorghum for sugar, the general rule is to increase the amount of sorghum by one-third over the amount of sugar and decrease the liquids by the same amount.

[See also MOLASSES; SORGHUM FLOUR; SWEETENERS.]

BIBLIOGRAPHY

University of Georgia College of Agricultural and Environmental Sciences. "Growing Sweet Sorghum for Syrup." Athens: University of Georgia, 1999, http://:www.ces.uga.edu/Agriculture/agecon/pubs/sweetsorg.htm.

Sweet Sorghum Production and Processing. Poteau, OK: Kerr Center for Sustainable Agriculture, 1992.

CHERYL FORBERG

Sorrel

Sorrel (genus *Rumex*) is a perennial herb that originated in Asia and became naturalized throughout Europe and North America. Closely related to rhubarb, sorrel shares with rhubarb a bright astringency, which comes from a high oxalic acid content (binoxalate of potash). Unlike rhubarb, which is harvested for its stalks but has leaves that are considered poisonous, sorrel is most treasured for its pointed green leaves. Consumed throughout the ancient world, particularly in Egypt, for its tonifying and culinary properties, sorrel in modern times is perhaps most revered by the French.

The name "sorrel" comes from the Old French *surele*, which means "sour." Both major species of cultivated sorrel, the true French sorrel (*Rumex scutatus*) and broadleaved or garden sorrel (*Rumex acetosa*), have a lemony tartness, but French sorrel is less acidic. Other sorrel species, *Rumex hymenosepalus* (like rhubarb, used for its tart stalks) and *Rumex patientia* (used for its mild leaves), are naturalized in North America. Sorrel is most frequently used in salads, sauces, soups, and pies and alone as a vegetable. None of the varieties has found lasting popularity in American gardens or on American tables.

There is some mystery surrounding the introduction of sorrel to America. Few early American cookbooks contained recipes for sorrel. Mary Randolph, in *The Virginia House-Wife* (1824), is an exception, and Thomas Jefferson noted the appearance of sorrel in Washington, D.C., markets. It is possible that Jefferson grew sorrel. Sorrel began to appear more regularly in cookbooks in the last third of the nineteenth century. Most of these books were written by French or French-trained chefs, who viewed sorrel as one of the most "recent additions to our lists of esculent plants." Sorrel's lasting public relations problem was aptly summarized by Mary Henderson in *Practical Cooking and Dinner-Giving* (1877): sorrel "would be popular in America if it were better known."

[See also FRENCH INFLUENCES ON AMERICAN FOOD; JEFFERSON, THOMAS; RANDOLPH, MARY; SALADS AND SALAD DRESSINGS; VEGETABLES.]

BIBLIOGRAPHY

Hessayon, D. G. *The Vegetable and Herb Expert*. London: Sterling, 1998.

McEwan, Barbara. *Thomas Jefferson, Farmer*. Jefferson, NC, and London: MacFarland, 1991.

Schneider, Elizabeth. *Uncommon Fruits and Vegetables*. New York: Harper and Row, 1986.

Spencer, Colin. *Vegetable Book*. London: Conran Octopus, 1995.

KAY RENTSCHLER

Soul Food, *see African American Food*

Soup Kitchens

The earliest references to soup kitchens, in 1826, describe communal areas within cultural venues, such as theaters and charity balls, where meals were served to staff as payment for their services. The term was popularized in 1839 to denote establishments serving minimum dietary essentials to needy people. In 1847 the British government passed the Temporary Relief Act, also known as the Soup Kitchen Act, which replaced public works as the main form of relief to the Irish during the potato famine. As the name implies, the act was to be provisional for the summer months, ending at harvest.

The Soup Kitchen Act contrasted sharply with earlier relief schemes in Britain, which incorporated various "tests" of need and required labor or internment in return from their recipients. Soup kitchens were initially financed by the government, but many areas did not take advantage of the legislation, which required that funds be paid back, and instead opened private soup kitchens, which were less expensive to run.

Because of the poor quality of the soup served, recipients were not fond of soup kitchens, yet the establishments were heavily depended upon, serving more than 3 million people per day during their peak in July 1847. Despite a significant decrease in mortality while the soup kitchens operated and the hardships of subsequent seasons, soup kitchens in Ireland closed permanently in the autumn of 1847.

In the United States during the nineteenth century and early twentieth century, food assistance, like welfare, was dominated by private and religious organizations whose social concepts were based on the Protestant ethic and liberal values. By the beginning of the twentieth century new kinds of welfare organizations had emerged with a more scientific and complex way of seeing poverty and its causes; this work was based within neighborhood assistance. New food programs emerged within the expanding settlement house system, at workers' union halls, and through voluntary political organizations.

For more than a decade, beginning in the mid-1900s, welfare capitalism was popular, but the Great Depression, which started at the end of the 1920s, had proved that business could not solve the problems of poverty, including hunger alleviation. Local governments tried to help the needy, but expenditures, which averaged $8.20 per month per person, did nothing to help the thousands more who required federal aid. Thus, following the stock market crash of 1929, organizations like the Red Cross and the Salvation Army provided help through soup kitchens and breadlines: 13 million people—25 percent of the population—were unemployed and hungry.

After the Depression the United States enjoyed many decades of economic growth and affluence, and the need for emergency food declined except among the poorest citizens. Federal food relief programs were established, including the Food Stamp program (1964); Women, Infants, and Children (WIC; 1974); and the National School Lunch, School Breakfast, Special Milk, Child and Adult Care Food, and Summer Food Service programs (all 1969), with the intention of meeting the food and nutrition needs of every citizen.

In the early 1980s another great resurgence of private food programs, including soup kitchens, occurred as a direct result of several factors: a sharp economic recession, interest rate hikes, and cuts in social programs. In the late twentieth century food assistance transformed from the realm of "emergency" to "supplemental." The number of people considered "food insecure"—those who have limited or uncertain availability of food—grows each year. Nearly 11 percent of U.S. households were food insecure during the 2001 calendar year. That year nearly 3 percent of the population, including 19 percent of households deemed food insecure, received food from a soup kitchen, food pantry, or other program.

The majority of soup kitchens, thousands nationwide, are run by religious organizations. Most of the other agencies that run soup kitchens are private, nonprofit organizations with no religious affiliation. Direct contact between soup kitchen workers—who are mostly volunteers—and guests appeases a natural inclination to help those less fortunate than oneself. This personal contact provides both physical and emotional support to soup kitchen guests.

Food banks, which distribute government commodities, are the principal source of food, providing 43 percent of food resources for soup kitchens. Other food comes through food rescue organizations, private donations, or discount purchases from farmers and commercial distributors. Menus attempt to provide basic nutritional needs but cannot effectively be planned because of the unpredictability of food available and the prevalence of volunteer labor.

More than 58 percent of soup kitchens in major metropolitan areas have seen an increase in patrons since 1998. The kitchens, which have historically served the homeless, also serve poor working families with children. In New York City more than one in five soup kitchen clients is a child. There is no federal standard or procedure for determining recipients' eligibility to receive emergency or supplemental food: patrons are presumed needy if they seek food.

Several political factors indicate that food assistance programs will continue to grow; these include the lack of jobs paying a living wage, the shrinking safety net of federal assistance programs, an emphasis on farming subsidies and food exports, the development of an underclass, the rising cost of housing, and the general acceptance of poverty within an otherwise affluent society. Soup kitchens and other food assistance programs—and the organizations that support them—are anticipating this increasing need by becoming more professional and by accepting their role as permanent providers of ongoing, supplementary sources of food for a growing percentage of the population.

[**See also** Food Stamps; Hunger Programs; Settlement Houses.]

BIBLIOGRAPHY

Ohls, James, Fazana Saleem-Ismail, Rhoda Cohen, Brenda Cox, and Laura Tiehen. *The Emergency Food Assistance System—Findings from the Provider Survey.*, Volume 2: *Final Report.* Economic Research Service Food Assistance and Nutrition Research Report no. 16-2. Washington, DC: U.S. Department of Agriculture, 2002.

KAREN KARP

Soups and Stews

Boiling was not a commonly used cooking technique until the invention of waterproof and heatproof containers about five thousand years ago. Boiling has several advantages over roasting. Water turns to steam at 212°F at sea level. Compared to hot air over a fire, boiling water is denser and comes more fully in contact with the entire surface of submerged foods. Hot water easily and quickly imparts its energy to the food. In addition to consistency, boiling permits the fuller use of animal and plant products for food and expands the range of potential edibles. Many animal parts could not otherwise be eaten.

By definition soups usually have a predominance of liquids and are served in bowls or mugs. Stews tend to have less water and are frequently cooked in covered containers over low heat for an extended period of time. Stews are often thicker and contain more and larger solids than soups. In a stew the liquids are frequently boiled down and employed as sauces for the stew Stews are usually served on plates. But even with these loose definitions, boundaries between soups and stews remain fluid.

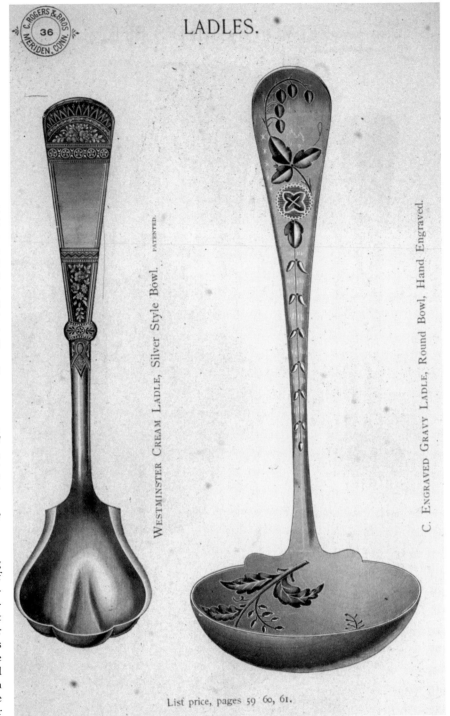

LADLES.

WESTMINSTER CREAM LADLE, SILVER STYLE BOWL. PATENTED.

C. ENGRAVED GRAVY LADLE, ROUND BOWL, HAND ENGRAVED.

List price, pages 59 60, 61.

A Westminster cream ladle and engraved gravy ladle.

Early American Soups and Stews

The American upper class followed English fashion and adopted the custom of serving soup with their meals. While American culinary traditions were largely based on English cookery, many other national and cultural groups influenced the culinary life of the new nation. Pennsylvania Germans liked soups and were particularly famous for those based on potatoes. Soup was a symbol of community, religious fellowship, and even communion. In two-course meals, soup was the first course; in one-pot meals, soup was the only dish. The French also influenced American views about soup. In 1784 Jean Baptiste Gilbert Payplat dis Julien, for instance, opened a public eating house in Boston that was famous for his soups and stews, and he was nicknamed the "Prince of Soups." He is credited with introducing to America the julienne soup, a composition of vegetables in long, narrow strips. Julien specialized in making turtle soup.

Bouillons were produced by slowly simmering bones, aromatics, and usually some flesh and were frequently augmented by herbs, vegetables, and cereals. Bouillons were

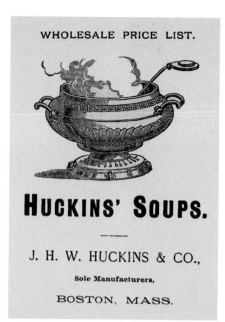

The cover image for a canned soup price list sold by J.H.W. Huckins and Co., 1880s.

considered healthful. Many bouillon recipes originated in New Orleans, Louisiana, which had once been a French colony. Recipes for consommé were first published in the United States during the 1830s. Consommé came to be defined as a rich, clear broth that has been boiled down, skimmed, and strained. Its base was meat or fish but not bones. During the nineteenth century the term was also applied to soup made with vegetables. Fricassee usually involves stewing chicken, veal, or small game, which is cut into pieces and fried. Ragout is a rich stew containing meat or fish and vegetables in a thick sauce. Ragout recipes were published in the United States beginning in 1828.

By the late nineteenth century America's most famous chefs featured soup on their menus. Thomas J. Murrey, a professional restaurateur in Philadelphia and New York City, believed that the selection of the right soup for the right occasion presented an excellent opportunity for the cook to display good taste and judgment. Arranging and harmonizing a bill of fare was an art form, Murrey believed, and soup was the pivot upon which the meal harmony depended. The famous chef Charles Ranhofer also published many soup recipes in his monumental work *The Epicurean* (1894). Ranhofer recommended serving two soups, a clear soup and a cream soup, at each meal. His guide to professional cookery includes more than two hundred soup recipes.

As the nineteenth century progressed, recipes for soup making increased in cookbooks. The first known American cooking pamphlet that focused solely on soups was written by Emma Ewing: *Soups and Soup Making* (1882). As an article of diet, soup ranked second in importance only to bread, proclaimed Ewing. Soup was an important part of most Americans' diets by the end of the nineteenth century.

Stewing referred to gentle boiling with a small amount of water at a moderate heat for a long time. Recipes for stewing particular foods, such as beef, lamb, poultry, fish, and seafood, regularly appeared in American cookery books. Specific stews, however, are usually defined as including two or more solid products. Early stews, such as beef stew and Irish stew, were common throughout the early United States. Regional stews, such as gumbos, bouillabaisse, Brunswick stew, and burgoo, emerged during the nineteenth century. Stews were more common in twentieth-century cookbooks, although many recipes were composed of ingredients at hand, such as mulligan stew, which is made from odds and ends.

Commercial Soup

The first known commercial soup manufacturer was James H. W. Huckins of Boston, who began canning soup about 1858. The soups were sold in two-quart cans, and all the consumer needed to do was to heat the contents and serve. Huckins began advertising his soup nationally during the 1880s due to the emergence of a major competitor headed by Alphonse Biardot, who had been a soup maker and canner in France. About 1880 Biardot immigrated to the United States, and in 1886 he incorporated the Franco-American Food Company in Jersey City, New Jersey. The company trademarked the phrase "French Soups," which undoubtedly increased the soups' snob appeal. The soup cost almost twice as much as some competitors' soup. Biardot was so successful that in 1916 the company was acquired by the Campbell Soup Company of Camden, New Jersey.

Twentieth-Century American Soups and Stews

Many twentieth-century soups and stews derived from non-English culinary traditions that entered the United States with immigrants. Many of these dishes straddled the line between soups and stews; these include minestrone, a thick Italian vegetable soup, and *menudo*, a thick, spicy Mexican tripe-based soup or stew. Others were clearly soups, such as eastern European borscht, generally a beet-based soup; the Mexican *sopa de alb digas*, or meatball soup; Japanese miso soup, made with miso (a paste made from soybeans and rice), tofu, and occasionally vegetables; and Chinese hot and sour soup, composed of various ingredients, including tofu, cornstarch, soy sauce, mushrooms, chili sauce, and meats. These stews and soups proliferated with the success of Hungarian, Italian, Mexican, Japanese, Jewish, and Chinese restaurants.

While there are eighty major soup manufacturers in the United States, the American soup market is dominated by the Campbell Soup Company, which accounts for 60 percent of all soup sales. It boasts four of the five best-selling soups.

Specific Soups and Stews

Turtle and Mock Turtle Soup. Turtles were found in abundance in the New World, and they were eaten from the beginning of European settlement. Terrapin turtles were particularly prized. Female turtles, or cow turtles, were treasured for their meat. The male, or bull turtles, had little value and were generally used for making soup. As turtle meat used in soup making was bland, it was usually spiced with red pepper. Turtles were easy to transport long distances and were held in pens until sold. Prior to the Civil War they were so plentiful as to be considered slave food in the South.

In the North turtle meat and turtle soup were prized. From the earliest American cookbooks, directions for making turtle soup were included. For instance, the longest and most complicated recipe in Amelia Simmon's *American Cookery* (1796) is for dressing turtles. She also includes a simpler recipe for preparing calf head in the fashion of a turtle.

Turtle soup was difficult to prepare at home. As soon as turtles were killed, they had to be cooked. Because many turtles were extremely large, frequently weighing three hundred pounds, they were sold to cafés, taverns, and restaurants that had a high volume of business. Eliza Leslie omitted a recipe for turtle soup in her *Directions for Cookery* (1837) because, she reported, it was a costly, complicated, and difficult dish to prepare: if a family wanted turtle soup, she advised hiring a first-rate cook or buying it at a turtle soup house. Most cookbooks offered recipes for mock turtle soup, usually made from calves brains or calves feet, which were thought to have the same texture as turtle meat.

Turtle and terrapin soups were among the first to be commercialized. By 1882 canned turtle soup was regularly sold in grocery stores. This commercial production finally depleted the abundant stock of turtles, and prices soared during the early twentieth century. By 1911 turtle had become one of the highest priced foods in America. This shortage led to the creation of turtle farms, on which turtles were bred and raised for market. Turtle and mock turtle soup had gone out of fashion by the early twentieth century.

Okra Soup and Gumbos. Okra (*Hibiscus esculentus*) originated in Africa. The slave trade brought okra to the Caribbean, where it was cultivated by 1707. From the Caribbean, okra migrated north. Although okra could be prepared in many ways, the early recipes are for okra used as an ingredient in soup. The first published recipe for okra soup appears in 1824, and subsequently okra soup became a common ingredient listed in American cookbooks.

Similar to okra soups were the gumbos of New Orleans. At first gumbos contained okra and filé (dried sassafras leaves), a seasoning thought to have originated with the Choctaw Indians in Louisiana. In addition to okra, cooks prepared gumbos with many other principal ingredients, such as chicken, turkey, squirrel, rabbit, crab, oyster, shrimp, or even cabbage. The main common element at this stage was the filé powder.

Gumbos migrated throughout America during the early nineteenth century. Ingredients in early recipes included okra, tomatoes, and onions seasoned with pepper and salt. The first gumbo recipe published in an American cookery book, in Eliza Leslie's *Directions for Cooking* (1837), identified gumbo as a New Orleans dish. Her recipe included okra but not filé. Gumbo delighted many admirers. Will Coleman, the publisher of Lafcadio Hearn's *La Cuisine Creole* (1885), described it as the great dish of New Orleans, and it remains so.

Bouillabaisse. Bouillabaisse is somewhere between a soup and a stew. In America, New Orleans was famous for its bouillabaisse, the classic French fish stew, which was a specialty of Marseilles, France. Bouillabaisse was a fisherman's soup based on fish from the Mediterranean but also sea bass, bonito, conger eel, and other fish and seafood. During the nineteenth century bouillabaisse became the rage in Europe. Recipes for bouillabaisse appeared in several British cookbooks in the 1850s. The American cookbook writer Pierre Blot admitted that the real bouillabaisse was made in Marseilles. Imitations, claimed Blot, were inferior to the real one. However, he offered a recipe based on fish that could be procured in the United States. By the end of the nineteenth century bouillabaisse was firmly ensconced in fashionable American restaurants and clubs.

Chowders. Whether chowders were introduced into New England by French, Nova Scotian, or British fishermen is undocumented, but chowders had become important dishes by the beginning of the eighteenth century in America. The earliest known American recipe for chowder was published in Boston in 1751. Chowders were quite distinct from broths and soups. Chowders, originally stews, were composed of fish, seafood, and vegetables of various proportions. The object was to prepare a thick, highly seasoned dish without reducing the ingredients to the consistency of a puree.

Several twentieth-century cookbooks presented recipes for vegetable chowder, vegetable clam chowder, and corn chowder. The first located recipe titled "Manhattan Clam Chowder" was published in Virginia Elliot and Robert Jones's *Soups and Sauces* (1934). This recipe substitutes tomatoes for milk. Despite detractors, Manhattan clam chowder survived and thrived.

Borscht. Borscht was originally a soup from Ukraine based on cow parsnips, a plant belonging to the carrot family. Like many other foods, borscht evolved: beets became its defining ingredient. The first located American recipe for borscht, or polish soup, was published in 1895. In America borscht was initially an ethnic food particularly associated with Jewish immigrants. So associated were Jewish immigrants with borscht that during the 1930s Jewish-owned resorts in the Catskill Mountains were referred to as the Borscht Belt.

Gazpacho. Gazpacho originated in Spain, where it was a considered a peasant soup. Consequently recipes for it were not published in early Spanish cookbooks, which were written mainly for the upper middle class. Mary Randolph's *The Virginia House-Wife* (1824) includes the first known recipe for gazpacho. As the culinary historian Karen Hess has noted, Randolph probably acquired this recipe from her sister, Harriet Randolph Hackley, who had lived in Cadiz, Spain. Gazpacho may have gained general acceptance in Anglo-American high society before it was generally accepted in Spain. Reports of its excellence had filtered back to the United States. In Spain great diversity exists among gazpacho recipes, but in America the only ones that thrive are those that are tomato based. As gazpacho is served ice-cold, it may have been one of the first popular chilled soups. Gazpacho became popular in the United States during the 1960s. Recipes for gazpacho appear in many cookery books and magazines.

Tomato Soup. Tomatoes have been grown in the United Kingdom since the late sixteenth century, but they did not become popular as a food until the late eighteenth century. The early culinary use of tomatoes in Britain was as an ingredient in soups. Tomatoes provided coloring and an acidic flavor unmatched by other fruits or vegetables. While references to tomatoes in soups appeared in English medical, agricultural, and botanical works, early recipes titled "Tomato Soup" were really vegetable soups of which tomato was an ingredient. As the nineteenth century progressed, the amount of tomatoes increased, and other vegetables decreased, so that by mid-century tomatoes had become the major ingredient.

In America tomato soup recipes commonly appeared in cookbooks in the mid-nineteenth century. New types of tomato soup emerged at the close of the nineteenth century and beginning of the twentieth century: cream of tomato and the combination of tomato soup with other ingredients, such as rice. Milk or cream became an ingredient in tomato soup during the early 1880s. Tomato soup was canned after the Civil War. By the beginning of the twentieth century tomato soup was America's favorite soup, a position

it retained for the next eighty years. Tomato soup remains among the top five soups sold commercially in America.

Brunswick Stew. Brunswick stew emerged in the mid-nineteenth century and is claimed to have originated in both Georgia and Virginia. It was commonly made with leftovers or whatever was available, such as squirrel, chicken, or other meats along with bacon, green corn, tomatoes, lima beans, potatoes, and other vegetables. The first known recipe for Brunswick stew appeared in Marion Harland's *Common Sense in the Household* (1871). She reported that it derived from Brunswick County, Virginia. Brunswick stew remains a regional southern stew, and many different recipes claim to be authentic.

Irish Stew. In the eighteenth century Irish stew was traditionally made of mutton (usually neck), potatoes, onions, and parsley, although some cooks added turnips or parsnips, carrots, and barley. Mutton was the dominant ingredient because of the economic importance of wool and sheep milk in Ireland. Only old sheep ended up in the stew pot, where it needed hours of slow boiling before it was palatable. This stew was recognized as an Irish national dish about 1800.

In America, Irish stew evolved. As sheep were not plentiful, other meats were substituted. When made in the traditional manner, Irish stew is cooked so long that the individual ingredients break down, and the result is a thick and hearty broth. Not everyone was pleased with Irish stew. Mark Twain in his *American Claimant* (1892) proclaimed that Irish stew was composed of leftovers. Lamb has become the predominate meat in Irish stew.

Pepper Pot. Pepper pot was a savory West Indian stew made with juice of the bitter cassava root with seasoning. This recipe changed in the eighteenth century to include meat, fish, or vegetables spiced with red pepper. Recipes for pepper pot had been published in British cookbooks by the mid-eighteenth century, and some of these recipes were reprinted in America. However, pepper pot may have been brought to America previously by African slaves who had lived in the Caribbean. American pepper pot was composed of a variety of ingredients, such as fish, mutton, pork, vegetables, lobster, and crab, but all recipes were highly seasoned with crushed peppercorns or red pepper. Pepper pot recipes had been published in America by the early nineteenth century. Traditional West Indian pepper pot employed tripe and veal spiced with red pepper. Two other recipes are common, the first of which is made from spinach, onions, potatoes, lettuce, bacon, suet, dumplings, and cayenne pepper; the second includes beef, ham, onions, potatoes, fowl, pork, and lobster, then considered a hunger food. Pepper pot generally disappeared in the twentieth century but lives on in culinary fakelore, which purports that this dish was first made at Valley Forge, Pennsylvania, by George Washington's army.

Burgoo. Burgoo is a thick stew that originated in Kentucky and Tennessee during the nineteenth century but quickly spread throughout the South and the Southwest. It could contain almost any combination of meats and vegetables. Squirrel, wild turkey, pigeons, and fish were frequently ingredients, and the vegetables might include tomatoes, celery, turnips, and corn.

Frogmore Stew. Frogmore stew, a combination of sausage, corn, crabs, and shrimp with seasoning, is attributed to Richard Gay of Gay Seafood Company. Gay claimed to have invented frogmore stew around 1950, when he was on national guard duty in Beaufort, South Carolina, while preparing a cookout of leftovers for his fellow guardsmen. According to Gay, the Steamer Restaurant on Lady Island near Beaufort was the first establishment to offer frogmore stew commercially.
[**See also** Brunswick Stew; Cajun and Creole Food; Campbell Soup Company; Dumplings; Native American Foods.]

BIBLIOGRAPHY

Peterson, James. *Splendid Soups: Recipes and Master Techniques for Making the World's Best Soups.* New York: Bantam Books, 1993.

Smith, Andrew F. *Pure Ketchup: A History of America's National Condiment.* Columbia: University of South Carolina Press, 1996.

Smith, Andrew F. *Souper Tomatoes: The Story of America's Favorite Food.* New Brunswick, NJ: Rutgers University Press, 2000.

ANDREW F. SMITH

South American Food, *see Iberian and South American Food*

Southeast Asian Food

Much food of Southeast Asia—Brunei, Cambodia, Indonesia, Laos, Malaysia, Myanmar (formerly Burma), the Philippines, Singapore, Thailand, and Vietnam—is represented in the United States, but primarily Thai and Vietnamese food have become mainstream. Although Southeast Asian foods share a flavor profile—a balance of hot, salty, sour, sweet, and sometimes bitter—individual cuisines of countries are distinctive. In some, fish sauce supplies the salty; in others, salt is used. Palm sugar may provide sweetness and lime the sour. Chilies from the Americas were not added until the sixteenth century. Some cultures eat mostly jasmine rice, others sticky. A typical meal is based on a large serving of rice with a modest topping of stir-fried meat or fish, vegetables, seasonings, and sometimes coconut milk. Noodles made of rice flour, eggs, or mung beans may be substituted for rice. Leaf wrappers, often banana or pandanus, are used to package some foods. Soup is essential. Dessert often consists of fresh fruit or sticky rice with bits of fruit.

In immigrant communities in the United States, there is an attempt to re-create the food of the homeland. When adapted to Western tastes, chili content is decreased, and portions of toppings are large over small amounts of rice—the reverse of the traditional.

Thai

The bold, contrasting flavors of Thai food have had the greatest visibility in a thriving restaurant business, although the numbers of Thai Americans—approximately 113,000 according to the 2000 census—is small. Thai is a fusion of Chinese and Malay food ideas with some influences from India (*massaman* curry) and even Portugal (deep-fried appetizers). During the early 1960s, during the Vietnam War, the American military "discovered" this cuisine. In Boston and New York during the 1970s and 1980s, a penchant for spicy Szechwan (Chinese) food paved the way for Thai flavors. In the 1980s millions of Americans began to visit Thailand, promoted as a gourmet paradise.

Thai flavor is produced by a balance of fish sauce, lemongrass, lime, coriander, ginger or galangal, garlic, sweet Thai basil, chilies, sometimes coconut milk, and peanut sauce made with chilies. The most familiar Thai dishes are pad thai—pan-seared rice noodles with pieces of salty dried shrimp, cooked egg, pork, and sweet preserved turnip; *mee krob*, a crispy noodle dish; *satay*, marinated meat threaded on skewers and served with peanut chili dipping sauce; salad with peanut dressing; various chili-based curries mixed with coconut milk, the most popular being green and red curries; Thai jasmine rice; and Singha beer.

In the early twenty-first century approximately 575 Thai cookbook titles can be found in American libraries. Ingredients are available from Asian markets, mail-order and online sources, and local supermarkets for home cooking.

Vietnamese

With the fall of Saigon (renamed Ho Chi Minh City) to the North Vietnamese in 1975, refugees began arriving in the United States, reaching a population of 1,112,528 by 2000, including children born in the United States. Most live in Southern California, while others have settled in Houston, Texas; Boston; Massachusetts; Denver, Colorado; the Pacific Northwest; and Florida.

Vietnamese cuisine is more restrained than Thai, featuring beef and salads that are closer to American. There is a strong vegetarian tradition with an herbaceous trait—basil, mint, and cilantro. Shaped by French colonization, the cuisine includes Vietnamese bouillabaisse and sizzling, savory rice-flour crêpes filled with shrimp, pork, and bean sprouts. The blending of fresh and cooked flavors and the combination of meat, fruits, and vegetables in salads are hallmarks.

The most familiar Vietnamese foods are spring rolls wrapped in transparent rice flour paper; nuoc mam, fish sauce; carrot and daikon pickled salad; *pho bo*, beef broth aromatic with star anise, cinnamon, and ginger slowly simmered and then poured over rice noodles, thinly sliced beef, and fresh basil leaves; *banh mi*, sandwiches of strong-tasting meats, French Vietnamese pâté, pickled carrots, and fresh coriander on French-style baguettes with butter and mayonnaise; strong, dark coffee layered over condensed milk; *nuoc leo*, peanut *satay* sauce; *nuoc cham*, a dipping sauce of diluted fish sauce, garlic, chilies, lime juice, and sugar; and *mam tom*, fishy dipping sauce.

Vietnamese restaurants appeared in the late 1970s. The site of many early eateries was Little Saigon in Orange County, California. Even though the Vietnamese population in the United States is approximately seven times that of the Thai, it was not until the 1990s that Vietnamese cuisine began to become mainstream. Emotional and political issues surrounding the Vietnam War were an issue. By 1999 a franchise of fifty-five noodle shops had been launched in predominantly Vietnamese communities.

Filipino

Filipinos are unique among Southeast Asian settlers, having arrived first and in greatest numbers. As residents of a U.S. colonial territory since 1902, Filipinos held American passports and traveled freely. In 1992 Filipinos accounted for 20 percent of the total Asian American population. Yet Filipino cooking has had the least penetration. Some social scientists believe the many years of colonial rule—first by Spain, then by the United States—eroded cultural identity.

Hmong wedding reception in Saint Paul, Minnesota.

Indonesian

In the late 1950s, after Indonesian independence, a number of Dutch Indonesians came to America as refugees. Most Indos (Indonesian Europeans) arrived after the 1965 changes in the immigration quota system. Of these immigrants, 60 percent live in Southern California and San Francisco, with smaller numbers in New York City, Houston, Chicago, and Washington, D.C. Between 1980 and 1990 the number of Indonesian immigrants more than tripled, but the total is small, only about forty thousand according to the 2000 census. One dish commonly thought to be Indonesian, rijsttafel, is actually a Dutch elaboration of a native tradition—a buffet in which a rice dish is surrounded by small condiments.

Other dishes include *nasi goreng* (fried rice), beef *rendang*, *saté* (skewers of meat served with dipping sauces), and several forms of hot *sambal*, made from Indonesian chilies. *Sambal oelek* is a paste of chilies and salt used both for cooking and as a condiment. Other common ingredients are sweet dark soy sauce, coriander, and *blachan* (shrimp paste).

[**See also** CENTRAL ASIAN FOOD; CHINESE AMERICAN FOOD; COCONUTS; INDIAN AMERICAN FOOD; JAPANESE AMERICAN FOOD; KOREAN AMERICAN FOOD.]

BIBLIOGRAPHY

Alejandro, Reynaldo. *The Philippine Cookbook.* New York: Putnam, 1985.

De Monteiro, Longeine, and Neustadt, Katherine. *The Elephant Walk Cookbook.* Boston: Houghton Mifflin, 1998.

Mowe, Rosalind, ed. *Southeast Asian Specialties: A Culinary Journey.* Cologne, Germany: Konemann, 1999.

Zanger, Mark. *The American Ethnic Cookbook for Students.* Phoenix: Oryx, 2001.

LINDA MURRAY BERZOK

Southern Regional Cookery

In 1607 the first English colony in America was established at Jamestown, Virginia. The colonists brought cattle, pigs, chickens, and sheep; grains, such as wheat and oats; fruit trees, root vegetables, and cabbages to supplement the New World corn, beans, pumpkins, squash, and greens; berries, plums and wild grapes; and wild game and seafood, such as turkeys, deer, rabbits, squirrels, duck, quail, turtles, oysters, shrimp, crabs, catfish, trout, herring, shad, and sturgeon. From Virginia, English colonies were established in the Carolinas and finally Georgia. Other Europeans—German and French—settled in different areas, and some of their culinary traditions can be seen in southern cookery.

African American Influences

Perhaps the greatest culinary tradition to influence southern food was from Africa. Slaves were imported into Jamestown beginning in 1619. With the slave trade came African foods, such as okra, black-eyed peas, collards, yams, and melons. In the low country,

Shoppers purchase produce at a French vegetable market in New Orleans.

enslaved peoples worked in rice plantations. African cooks in plantation and town house kitchens prepared hearty one-pot meals, such as gumbo and rice dishes, including shrimp pilau and hoppin' john (a bean and rice pilau).

African-style soups, stews, rice dishes, and other one-pot meals with little bits of meat (often smoked or cured) came to be more typical of the southern table. Brunswick stew, burgoo (a stew containing mixed game, particularly squirrel meat), pilau, okra soup, and country captain (a tomato-based curried rice dish) are southern dishes that are now beloved beyond the region. Plants such as tomatoes and eggplant were grown on southern plantations decades before they were accepted in other colonies. African words remained attached to certain foods, such as yams, benne (sesame seeds), okra, and gumbo.

Antebellum South

The antebellum wealth of the southern planters, with their unlimited slave labor, gave rise to a privileged society that entertained often. The grand style of plantation hospitality mimicked European royalty, with elaborate dishes, particularly desserts, reflecting the neoclassical tastes of the wealthy.

A hallmark of southern tables both rich and poor is the condiment. From its beginnings, the South developed a taste for chutneys. Every large southern seaport claims country captain as a dish of its own. It is served with an assortment of mixed pickles, grated coconut, roasted peanuts, and the sweet-and-sour tang of a homemade chutney made with peaches, pears, or green tomatoes.

Barbecue sauces change hue and tone across county lines: some are little more than vinegar and hot pepper, others are mostly prepared mustard and ketchup. Gravies are offered with both fried and baked meats as well as with breakfast breads and casseroles. Red-eye gravy, made with coffee and the pan drippings of fried country ham, is common throughout the region.

Beans are served over rice in South Carolina; a spicy relish of sweetened and pickled ground vegetables or fruits is served alongside the dish. Served with buttered cornbread and a simple salad of sliced tomatoes with a dollop of homemade mayonnaise and thick sorghum syrup as the requisite sweet drizzled over the cornbread, beans become a midsummer meal. Relishes are made from green tomatoes (piccalilli), cabbage (chow chow), pears, sweet peppers, Jerusalem artichokes, and corn. A variety of tomato and pepper sauces, both raw and cooked, is common. Vinaigrettes and mayonnaise-based sauces, such as tartar sauce, are common on the Atlantic and the Gulf Coast. Gravies made with a little of the fat left over from frying chicken, pork chops, or cube steak (called chicken-fried steak, mothered steak, or country-fried steak, with flour and water, milk, or stock, are legion in the South, where they are poured on meats, biscuits, rice, and mashed potatoes.

An example of a Southern cookbook.

Poultry

Southern fried chicken is perhaps the best-known dish of the area, and it too is a legacy of African cooks in plantation kitchens. Most of the pan-fried versions are succulent home-made dishes made to be served hot, but many southern cooks now leave the deep-fried versions to the many fast food franchises that were begun in the South, among them, Kentucky Fried Chicken, Bojangles', and Hardee's.

Regional poultry dishes include country captain, chicken bog (a rice dish from South Carolina), chicken pilau, and chicken pie. Barbecued chicken is favored in some areas. Chicken and duck are often simmered and added to a world of soups and stews; a gumbo made with duck and sausage is common. In the late twentieth century the deep-frying of whole turkeys spread from southern hunters' camps across America. Peanut oil has replaced lard as the preferred oil for deep-frying.

Pork

In the early South pigs were often allowed to roam the woods to forage. They were hunted as game and killed in the fall and early winter. Much of the hog has traditionally been cured by either smoking or salting. Some form of pork was served at most country tables, but it was used as flavoring more than substance. The country hams of Virginia, Tennessee, Kentucky, and the Carolinas are salted, smoked, and hung to cure for a year. On New Year's Day hoppin' john is eaten for good luck. It is traditionally cooked with a smoked ham hock and served with greens, which are cooked with smoked hog jowl. Most of the pork eaten at home in the South is lean meat cut from lean hogs and sold in supermarkets. Barbecue restaurants, however, are popular. Pork slowly cooked over smoldering hickory or oak, then often

pulled from the bones, is one of the South's great culinary achievements. The smoked meat is chopped, sliced, left on the ribs, and mopped with thick or thin sauces that might be tomato, vinegar, or mustard based. The sauces can be fiery hot or sticky and sweet. The meat might be piled on plates, served with rice, served on a bun, or topped with pickles; accompanied by coleslaw, potato salad, or baked beans; or simply sucked from the rib bones; but nearly every county in the South has its version of barbecue in which it takes pride. A rich stew is served alongside barbecued pork in some areas: burgoo is offered in Kentucky; Brunswick stew (similar to burgoo) is claimed by Virginians, North Carolinians, and Georgians.

Seafood

Along the eastern seaboard, oyster stew is a simple dish of oysters warmed with milk or cream. In colonial and antebellum days, oysters were more plentiful than meat along the coast; they were added to sausages and stuffings. Oyster dressing is still a favorite holiday dish. Oysters and clams are eaten raw and steamed at roasts along the shore. Oysters are fried and served with cocktail or tartar sauce or added to po'boys. They are stirred into jambalayas and gumbos. Shrimp are boiled, steamed, fried, grilled, baked in pies, served atop pasta and grits, ground into pastes, pickled, and added to pilaus and soups. Crabs are steamed and eaten at outdoor tables, or the picked meat, usually cooked with hot spices, is added to soups and salads or transformed into crab dips, deviled crab, crabmeat casseroles, and pan-fried crab cakes. Fishing is a popular pastime for young and old of both sexes. Pan fish from freshwater ponds, lakes, streams, and rivers are fried by the ton each year; they are invariably served with hush puppies.

Moon Pie

The Moon Pie is not a pie at all but a cellophane-wrapped snack consisting of two cookies, four inches in diameter, sandwiched with marshmallow filling and coated in either chocolate, vanilla, or banana-flavored coating. The Chattanooga Bakery in Chattanooga, Tennessee, is the exclusive manufacturer of Moon Pies. The bakery originally started as a business to use excess flour produced at the nearby Mountain City Flour Mill. In the early 1900s the bakery produced more than two hundred different baked goods, but by the late 1950s the Moon Pie was so popular that the bakery's capacity could not handle anything else. The Moon Pie remains the only product the Chattanooga Bakery makes.

According to company lore, Earl Mitchell, a salesman for the Chattanooga Bakery, was the originator of the now famous snack. In the early 1900s he called on a Tennessee country store that catered to coal miners and asked them what kind of snacks they would like in the lunch boxes they took into the mines. One man replied that they needed a solid, filling snack. Mitchell asked the man how big it should be, and the man, pointing to the sky where a full moon looked down, said, "About that big." With this concept in mind, Mitchell went back to the bakery, where he saw workers dipping cookies into marshmallow. The idea occurred to him to sandwich the marshmallow between the cookies and then coat the whole thing in chocolate. The bakery eventually mastered the technique of making a snack from Mitchell's original idea, and the first Moon Pies were produced and sold in 1917.

Making Moon Pies is a simple process: the dough for the cookies is made in large sheets, then cut into circles and baked. Marshmallow filling is sandwiched between two cookies and then covered in a coating that hardens while the Moon Pie passes through a refrigerated room on a conveyor belt. The Moon Pies are individually wrapped, boxed, and shipped all over the United States, Canada, and Mexico.

The phrase "RC and a Moon Pie" is a traditional reference to a convenient and inexpensive snack combination in the South. It is a holdover from the 1920s and 1930s, when a ten-cent lunch meant a nickel for an RC Cola and a nickel for a Moon Pie. In Bell Buckle, Tennessee, the RC and Moon Pie pairing is celebrated with an annual festival that features a Moon Pie toss, a craft fair, and the crowning of the RC and Moon Pie queen. The combination is even recognized in a tune called "RC Cola and a Moon Pie," recorded by the singer Tom Waits in 1986.

The Chattanooga Bakery keeps up with the times, adding microwave instructions to the package (no more than fifteen seconds); producing a smaller, snack-size Moon Pie; and occasionally trying out new flavors. For nearly a century southerners have enjoyed the handy, cheap, and tasty marshmallow treat, making it, as the Moon Pie package logo says, "the only one on the planet."

[**See also** COOKIES; MARSHMALLOW FLUFF.]

BIBLIOGRAPHY

Dickson, Ron. *The Great American Moon Pie Handbook*. Atlanta, GA: Peachtree Publishers, 1985.

Schmidt, William E. "Moon Pie, Staple of the South." *New York Times*, April 30, 1986.

JACKIE MILLS

Side Dishes

Vegetables and side dishes are favorites in the South. Most vegetables grow well in the South, with its long growing season. Eggplant, okra, hundreds of varieties of beans, leafy green vegetables, squash, melons, sweet potatoes, and corn are favored. Sweet Vidalia onions, grown in southern Georgia, became a popular and successful crop in the 1970s.

Side dishes include baked casseroles, such as cheese grits, fried apples, numerous sweet potato concoctions, braised greens, corn puddings, succotash, stewed okra and tomatoes, pole beans and new potatoes, baked stuffed tomatoes, red rice, dirty rice (with bits of chicken gizzard and liver), red beans and rice, and salads that include avocados, benne seeds, pecans, country ham, or bacon.

Beverages

Iced tea (usually sweet) is often the beverage of choice at many meals, but southerners are also fond of sweetened drinks of many types, from elaborate alcoholic punches to lemonade, sangria, and soft drinks. Most of the major soft drink producers began their operations in the South: Coca-Cola, Pepsi-Cola, RC Cola, and Gatorade. Bourbon is from Kentucky; sour mash whiskey is from Tennessee. Mint juleps and other cocktails and punch remain popular.

Desserts

The desserts, candies, pastries, cakes, puddings, pies, cobblers, cookies, creams, ices, meringues, fruits, and nuts of the South have differed from the sweets in more urban settings because they are made by home bakers. Until the end of the twentieth century, many southern cookbooks devoted fully half their pages to sweets, especially cakes.

Modern South

Television and other media contributed to the homogenization of the South. Home cooking is still found in rural communities and small towns, at church socials, and at bake sales. In the 1980s and 1990s cookbook authors and chefs throughout the region began, however nostalgically, to call for a return to traditional southern fare.

[See also AFRICAN AMERICAN FOOD; BARBECUE; CARIBBEAN INFLUENCES ON AMERICAN FOOD; CHIPPED BEEF; CONDIMENTS; FISH: FRESHWATER; FISH: SALTWATER; FRENCH INFLUENCES ON AMERICAN FOOD; PEPSI-COLA; SEAFOOD.]

BIBLIOGRAPHY

Dabney, Joseph E. *Smokehouse Ham, Spoon Bread, and Scuppernong Wine.* Nashville, TN: Cumberland House, 1998.

Egerton, John. *Southern Food.* New York: Knopf, 1987.

Taylor, John. *The New Southern Cook.* New York: Bantam Books, 1995.

JOHN MARTIN TAYLOR

Southwestern Regional Cookery

New Mexico, Texas, and Arizona share a culinary heritage though the foodways of the three states are not identical. New Mexico's is the oldest and most deeply rooted, Texas boasts several culinary traditions, and Arizona's cuisine is closely linked to that of the Mexican state of Sonora.

New World corn, beans, and chili furnished the basis for the southwestern diet, but European imports and cooking techniques added important influences. When the Spanish colonized New Mexico in 1598, they were already familiar with the corn and chilies of Mexico. Where Pueblo Indians raised corn, beans, squash, dogs, and turkeys, the Spanish introduced chili from Mexico and European crops and animals including cattle, sheep, goats, pigs, chickens, wheat, lentils, vegetables, herbs, and fruits. The Spanish also brought metal cooking implements and built the dome-shaped ovens known as *hornos*.

At the center of New Mexican cookery was corn, ground for gruels like *atole* or treated with lye to remove the hull for posole and masa for tamales or tortillas, used in enchiladas and tacos. *Bolita* beans and later pinto beans provided a second dietary staple, and chili became the preeminent vegetable and seasoning; fresh green chili appeared in stews or sauces or stuffed for chiles rellenos. Dried red chili pods were made into sauce, and meat was added for chili con carne. Mutton, goat, beef, and dried buffalo were used in stews, while less-plentiful pork was marinated in red chili and baked as *carne adobada*. Medieval Spanish influences lingered in roast chicken stuffed with meat, raisins, and spices.{tc "At the center of New Mexican cookery was corn, ground for gruels like atole or treated with lye to remove the hull for posole and masa for tamales or tortillas, used in enchiladas and tacos. Bolita beans and later pinto beans provided a second dietary staple, and chile became the preeminent vegetable and seasoning; fresh green chiles appeared in stews or sauces, or stuffed for chile rellenos. Dried red chile pods were made into sauce, and meat was added for chile con carne. New Mexicans also raised wheat because the Roman Catholic Church required wheaten wafers for Holy Communion. Wheat flour yielded tortillas, bread, hardtack, and sopaipillas. A sweet Lenten pudding, penuche, was made from sprouted wheat, and another Lenten dessert, *capirotada* or *sopa*, used bread, raisins, and cheese. Desserts based on eggs or cheese included *arroz con leche*, *chongos*, and *natillas*. Settlers crushed grapes for wine and brandy and cornstalks for corn syrup and sugar. They relied on local *tesquesquite* (sodium bicarbonate) for leavening. The only food preservation technique New Mexicans used was drying, employed for everything from meat to melons. After the American annexation of the Southwest in 1846, Anglo food preferences influenced the production of more beef, pork, and potatoes, and by 1900 Fabian Garcia of New Mexico State University had developed milder chilies, which appealed to newcomers who welcomed the first New Mexican cookbook in 1916.

Two hundred years earlier, Spain had established settlements in Texas, home to nomadic Indian tribes but lacking an agricultural Indian population. Thus early colonists relied heavily on game and cattle, which led to the development of a vigorous livestock industry. Beef predominated in the Tejano diet even as settlers cultivated corn, chili, beans, pumpkins, fruits, and sugarcane. Corn tortillas, *atole*, pinole, tamales, and frijoles became common dishes in Texas as in New Mexico, though wheat was scarce.

After 1821 Americans from Kentucky, Tennessee, and Arkansas, who lived on bacon, ham, cornbread, and biscuits, migrated to Texas. From their interactions with Tejanos, Tex-Mex cuisine emerged. By the 1870s "chili queens" in San Antonio sold a dish of beef, red chili, and cumin known as chili con carne. Chili became a hallmark of Texas cookery, inspiring convenience foods such as William Gebhardt's chili powder and canned chili. Gebhardt was one of thousands of German immigrants who contributed sausages and other pork dishes and a variety of beers to Texas cuisine. Czech migrants added *kolac* and other pastries, while Louisiana dishes like gumbo journeyed west. However, few ethnic specialties were included in the first Texas cookbook in 1883, which primarily reflected Anglo-American food preferences. Only one recipe included chili.

After the Civil War the beef bonanza in West Texas created a distinctive ranching culture. Charles Goodnight lashed a cook box to a wagon for the chuck wagon, which

Qahatika harvesting a giant cactus in southwestern Arizona, 1907.

Advertisements for two Texas specialties: Mexene Chile Powder and Walker's Red Hot Chile Con Carne.

dispensed pinto beans, sourdough biscuits, and freshly butchered beef. From this tradition three favorite Texas dishes emerged, chicken-fried steak, son-of-a-bitch (son-of-a-gun) stew, and barbecued beef brisket.

As Texas grew, Arizona remained sparsely occupied. Tucson had been founded in 1776 as the northernmost outpost of Sonora, where cattle raising constituted the most important enterprise and beef played a starring role at the table. Sheep, chickens, corn, beans, lentils, pumpkins, and chilies also grew there, and as in New Mexico and Texas, settlers ate frijoles, posole, *atole*, tortillas, and various chili stews. After the American annexation, Anglos slowly settled in Arizona, but the population grew slowly until 1910, when the Mexican Revolution of 1910 sent thousands of Mexicans across the border with their preferences for large, thin wheat tortillas, tamales made of green corn, and *carne seca*, beef strips dried in the sun, then pounded and shredded for *machaca*.

In modern southwestern cuisine, *machaca* often appears in chimichangas, a popular Arizona dish. Another Arizona speciality is cheese crisps, made from flour tortillas baked with cheese. In Arizona dishes often feature more beef, milder chilies, and greater amounts of cheese and sour cream than in other parts of the Southwest. In Texas significant Mexican immigration also followed the Mexican Revolution and continues to add new influences, such as fajitas and barbecued *cabrito* or beef head, to Texas cuisine. Meanwhile some Tex-Mex foods have become national favorites, including fritos, nachos, and salsa.

In New Mexico chili remains central to the cuisine, appearing in everything from enchiladas to bagels. Families observe a fall tradition of roasting and freezing bushels of green chilies even though the product is commercially available. Throughout the Southwest, people buy mass-produced foods from tortillas to frozen entrees, and regional foodways are blurred. Still, traditions endure as chili cook-offs and barbecues draw crowds in Texas, harvesttime brings green corn tamales in Arizona, and *bizcochitos* signal the Christmas season in New Mexico. Proud of their culinary heritage, Texans designated chili the state dish. New Mexicans honor chili and pinto beans as state vegetables, and the *bizcochito* is enshrined as the first state cookie in the nation.

[**See also** BARBECUE; CHILI; FRITO-LAY; MEXICAN AMERICAN FOOD; PINOLE; SOUTHERN REGIONAL COOKERY.]

BIBLIOGRAPHY

Coe, Sophie D. *America's First Cuisines*. Austin: University of Texas Press, 1994.

Gabaccia, Donna R. *We Are What We Eat: Ethnic Food and the Making of Americans*. Cambridge, MA: Harvard University Press, 1998.

Gilbert, Fabiola Cabeza de Baca. *The Good Life: New Mexico Traditions and Food*. Santa Fe: Museum of New Mexico Press, 1982.

Jamison, Cheryl Alters, and Bill Jamison. *Border Cookbook: Authentic Home Cooking of the American Southwest and Northern Mexico*. Boston: Harvard Common, 1995.

Jamison, Cheryl Alters, and Bill Jamison. *Texas Home Cooking*. Boston: Harvard Common, 1993.

Jaramillo, Cleofas M. *The Genuine New Mexico Tasty Recipes*. Santa Fe, NM: Ancient City, 1981.

Jones, Oakah L. *Los Paisanos: Spanish Settlers on the Northern Frontier of New Spain*. Norman: University of Oklahoma Press, 1996.

Linck, Ernestine Sewell, and Joyce Gibson Roach. *Eats: A Folk History of Texas Foods*. Fort Worth: Texas Christian University Press, 1989.

Pilcher, Jeffrey M. "Tex-Mex, Cal-Mex, New Mex, or Whose Mex? Notes on the Historical Geography of Southwestern Cuisine." *Journal of the Southwest* 43 (Winter 2001): 659–679.

CHERYL FOOTE

Soybeans

The soybean, *Glycine max*, is an annual summer legume that ranks as one of the world's most nutritious, economical, and protein-rich food sources. Although the soybean is used primarily for animal and human food, it also finds industrial applications in such diverse products as printer's ink, biodiesel fuel, paints, varnishes, plastics, and adhesives. The soybean plant—a close relative of peas, clover, and alfalfa—is an erect, hairy plant, ranging from two to five feet in height. Also called "soy" or "soya beans," the spherical seeds, which develop in pods, are usually a creamy beige with a black, brown, or yellow hilum (seed scar).

Each bean is composed of about 38 percent protein and 18 percent oil, making the soybean the world's leading source of both edible oil and high-protein feed supplements for livestock. When processed, each sixty-pound bushel of soybeans yields eleven pounds of soybean oil and forty-eight pounds of soybean meal, used to feed livestock. The soybean is one of the few plant foods that supplies all of the essential amino acids, important protein building blocks needed for human growth and tissue repair. The soybean's slight deficiency in one of these components, methionine, can easily be offset with the addition of grains to the diet.

Soybeans are also rich in phytonutrients, the naturally occurring substances that serve as hormones, enzymes, pigments, and growth regulators and that give plant foods their distinctive flavors and colors. Phytonutrients help protect plants from assaults by parasites, bacteria, viruses, and insects. When humans eat plants containing these nutrients, especially the ones known as "isoflavones," some of the benefits are passed on and may help protect the consumer against certain cancers, heart disease, and osteoporosis.

One of the oldest crops raised by humans, soybeans are believed to have been cultivated first in China some five thousand years ago by farmers who planted the small brown seeds of a wild ancestor. Through careful selection over thousands of years of domestication, the plant grew more upright, and the pods bore larger seeds.

Although the soybean, when merely boiled, lacks appeal for the human consumer, the Chinese and later the Japanese ingeniously transformed the legume into myriad appetizing, protein-rich foods, including miso, soy sauce, tempeh, and tofu. So well disguised was the soybean in the Asian diet that the first Europeans who visited the Orient, including Marco Polo, did not realize that the foods they tasted were derived from the soybean.

The merchant Samuel Bowen introduced the soybean to the New World when he brought back seeds from China in 1765. For the next century and a half, American farmers grew soybeans primarily as a forage crop, either baled as hay or preserved as silage. The plant also served as pasture for grazing hogs and sheep. When shipping was disrupted during the American Civil War, ground soybeans slipped briefly into the tin cups of Union soldiers as a substitute for the coffee bean.

In 1904 George Washington Carver discovered that the soybean contained valuable protein and oil. With the onset of World War I, fats and oils became scarce, and America turned to the soybean for these precious commodities. Research soon brought soybean oil into the kitchen in the form of cooking oil, salad oil, and shortening. Shortly after the war the soybean began its industrial career as an oil with many useful properties. The American Soybean Association lists more than 350 industrial products containing soybean-derived materials.

Soybean protein was fed almost exclusively to livestock until World War II, when the powder was used as an extender in sausages and other ground meat products. Research documenting the health benefits of the soybean has boosted American consumption of soybean products.

By the end of the twentieth century some 2,500 soybean products appeared on the American grocery shelf. Soybeans are transformed into tofu (bean curd), soybean milk, soybean butter and cheese, infant formula, roasted and frozen whole bean products, meat substitutes, breakfast cereals, sprouts, and many other foods. In the year 2000 in the United States 1 billion pounds of soybean products were produced for human consumption. This amounts to about four pounds per person.

In 2000 American farmers planted 74.5 million acres (30.2 million hectares) of soybeans, an area roughly the size of Colorado, harvesting 2.77 billion bushels (75.39 million metric tons) of the legume. The trifoliate plants produce white or purple flowers and short pods usually containing two to three seeds. In the fall the leaves turn yellow and drop, and the dry pods can be harvested and shelled with a combine.

Like other legumes, the soybean plant supports colonies of microorganisms that live in root nodules. These specialized microorganisms are able to "fix," or capture, nitrogen from the air, making the addition of nitrogen fertilizer unnecessary in a soybean field. A significant portion of this fixed nitrogen, which is an essential plant nutrient, remains in the soil after harvest. Most of the U.S. soybean crop is grown in the midwestern Corn Belt. The typical farmer will alternate soybeans with corn, taking advantage of the nitrogen contribution of the bean plant to help fertilize the next year's corn crop.

Soybeans can produce more than 33 percent more protein from an acre of land than any other crop and ten times more protein than cattle grazing on a comparable area. Despite the soybean's protein advantage, less than 2 percent of U.S. grown soybeans are processed for human consumption. This figure is 10 percent worldwide.

The bulk of the soybean crop is converted into feed for cattle, hogs, and poultry. Processors clean and dehull the beans and then run them through giant rollers to crush them into flakes. The addition of a hexane solvent extracts the oil, leaving defatted soybean meal that is used for feed. Cycling soybean meal through animals to produce human food results in a net energy loss because it takes from seven to twenty-one pounds of soybean protein to produce one pound of livestock protein.

[See also BEANS; FATS AND OILS; SOY SAUCE; VEGETARIANISM.]

BIBLIOGRAPHY

Endres, Joseph G., ed. Soy Protein Products: Characteristics, Nutritional Aspects, and Utilization. Rev. ed. Champaign, IL: AOCS, 2001.

Liu, KeShun. Soybeans: Chemistry, Technology, and Utilization. New York: Chapman and Hall, 1997.

Shurtleff, William, and Akiko Aoyagi. The Book of Tofu: Protein Source of the Future—Now! Berkeley, CA: Ten Speed, 1998.

PEGGY L. HOLMES

Soy Sauce

Soy sauce is a brown, salty liquid produced from a mixture of fermented soybeans and roasted grain, such as wheat or barley. During the production process, the soybean and grain mixture is injected with a yeast mold, and salt is added. Following a period of aging, the mixture is strained and bottled for sale.

Soybeans (Glycine max) originated in tropical Asia and in prehistoric times were widely disseminated to China, Japan, India, and Southeast Asia. Fermented soybean products were common throughout Asia. British sailors, traders, and colonial administrators encountered soy sauce in the late seventeenth century.

By the seventeenth century Japan had specialized in manufacturing soy sauce and has been the dominant producer ever since. The Japanese recognize five major types of soy sauce: dark, which dominates the market; light, used for cooking white fish and vegetables; tamari, very dark, used for sashimi; saishikomi, twice fermented, darker and thicker, used for sushi and sashimi; and white, used for white fish and vegetables. From Japan, soy sauce was exported to Asia, England, and eventually the United States.

Soy sauce was imported into the United States in small quantities during the early nineteenth century. It appeared in cookbooks published in the United States by 1814 and was important enough in the second half of the nineteenth century to be sold occasionally in grocery stores. Because imported soy sauce was expensive, manufacturers counterfeited it, and several nineteenth-century scientists offered the means of distinguishing imitation soy sauce from the real thing. Manufacturers also used soy sauce to make other commercial sauces. For instance, soy sauce was a component in Worcestershire sauce, which originated in Britain in the 1820s but was imported and later manufactured in the United States. Soybeans were later used in the commercial manufacture of ketchup.

Soybeans were promoted by the U.S. Department of Agriculture during the early twentieth century but were mainly considered an animal feed crop. The shift to human consumption of soybeans began during World War II, when the U.S. government recommended soybean products as a meat substitute. After the war health and nutrition advocates, such as Clive McCay of Cornell University, recommended greater use, as did Ancel and Margaret Keys in Eat Well and Stay Well (1959). Probably more significant was the rise in America of Chinese and Japanese restaurants, which featured soy sauce. It became an important American condiment by the 1980s.

In the United States soy sauce is used in cooking and as a table sauce. Kikkoman, a Japanese food conglomerate, is the largest producer of soy sauce in the world. It also manufactures soy sauce in the United States, as do several other companies.

[See also CONDIMENTS; SOYBEANS.]

BIBLIOGRAPHY

Smith, Andrew F. Pure Ketchup: A History of America's National Condiment. Columbia: University of South Carolina Press, 1996.

ANDREW F. SMITH

Space Food

On February 20, 1962, John Glenn became the first American to orbit the Earth and the first human to eat in space. On his five-hour flight, Glenn carried a menu of freeze-dried powders and spaghetti, applesauce, and roast beef reduced to semiliquids and crammed into aluminum tubes. He also carried a variety of solid foods reduced to bite-size cubes. The food was far from perfect. It lacked taste and texture, and the cubes flaked into crumbs that floated around Glenn's capsule, threatening to jam delicate equipment.

The two-person Gemini program began in 1965 with a revised approach to space food. Gemini astronauts ate bite-size cubes now coated with an edible gelatin to prevent crumbing. They also carried freeze-dried foods packaged in special containers to allow better reconstitution. To rehydrate food, the astronauts injected water into the pack through the nozzle of a device that looked like a water pistol. After the contents were kneaded, the food became a puree, which was squeezed through a one-way valve into the astronaut's mouth. Menus included shrimp cocktail, chicken and vegetables, butterscotch pudding, and applesauce. Astronauts were allowed to select their meal combinations as long as the calorie count added up to 2,800 per day. However, the food was still largely unappetizing.

In the Apollo moon program of the late 1960s, the quality and variety of space food was greatly improved. Hot water was available for rapid reconstitution of freeze-dried foods, and the taste of the foods was much better. The astronauts carried "spoon bowls," pressurized plastic containers that could be opened with a plastic zipper and the contents eaten with a spoon. Because it had a high moisture content, the food clung to the spoon, making eating seem closer to the earthbound experience. A pantry stocked with more than one hundred food items (including strawberry and peanut cubes, spaghetti that could be rehydrated, salmon salad, and seventy-five drinks) helped stay the boredom of repetitious menu choices. Freeze-dried ice cream was provided on one flight but was abandoned because it was not at all like real ice cream.

One of the great myths of the Apollo program is that it brought the world Teflon nonstick coating, Tang drink mix, and Velcro fasteners. Actually Tang mix, first developed for the army, was purchased for the Apollo astronauts by NASA employees in a supermarket. Teflon fluorocarbon resin was invented by accident in 1938 in the laboratories of the DuPont chemical company. Teflon coating became a commercial product in 1948. The Velcro fastener was invented in 1948 by George de Mestral, a Swiss engineer.

The Skylab program in 1973 and 1974 had larger spacecraft and vast culinary improvements. Unlike previous space vessels, Skylab had enough space for a dining table, essentially a pedestal on which food trays were mounted. When dining, the three-astronaut teams sat using foot and thigh restraints and ate in an almost-normal manner. Conventional utensils were used, as was a scissors for cutting open plastic seals. Because it was relatively large, *Skylab* had an ample pantry, which included a refrigerator for fresh fruits and vegetables and a freezer for such foods as filet mignon and real ice cream. Results of *Skylab* experiments showed a need to change the nutritional content of space foods. After long periods in space, astronauts lose calcium and other vital minerals, so all future menus reflected these needs.

Since the first flight in 1976, space shuttle astronauts have been offered a wide array of food items and allowed to choose a standard menu designed around a typical seven-day mission. They also have been allowed to substitute items to accommodate their own tastes. The astronaut-designed menus are checked by a dietitian to ensure that a balanced supply of nutrients is consumed. This flexibility stems in part from the fact that approved foods are commercially available on grocery store shelves. NASA calls these products "natural form foods." They are low in moisture and include nuts, cookies, candy bars, and crackers. Drinking water is provided by shuttle fuel cells. Chemical reactions between hydrogen and oxygen produce electricity for the shuttle, and water is a by-product of the reaction. Nearly two gallons of water per hour are available for drinking, eating, and washing. This is more than enough, so the remainder is released overboard.

[**See also** CONDIMENTS; COOKING CONTAINERS; FREEZE-DRYING; FREEZERS AND FREEZING; IRRADIATION; REFRIGERATORS; SODA DRINKS; TANG.]

BIBLIOGRAPHY
National Aeronautics and Space Administration. http//:www.nasa.gov.

PAUL DICKSON

Spam

Spam is a canned luncheon meat manufactured of pork shoulder and ham by the Hormel Foods Corporation. Spam is popular in Hawaii and Guam and among many families in the American heartland but is viewed by many others as the symbol of everything that is wrong with American processed food. Spam, a pink block of fatty, salty pork, became a subject of derision during World War II, when its durability and affordability made it a favorite of armed forces food-purchasing offices. Spam became infamous to baby boomers thanks to a skit performed in 1970 on the popular British comedy television program *Monty Python's Flying Circus*. The skit, which was about a restaurant with an all-Spam menu, inspired the Internet term for ubiquitous and unwanted e-mail messages. Spam is as familiar to people who eat it as it is to those who do not. Those who do

not eat Spam may wear Spam T-shirts or enter Spam-carving contests.

A Way to Peddle Pork Shoulder

Spam was invented in 1937 by Jay Hormel—the son of George Hormel, the founder of the meat company—as a way to peddle the then-unprofitable pork shoulder. The Hormel company, based in Austin, Minnesota, was a pioneer in producing canned pork products. The company introduced canned ham in 1926, and Hormel spiced ham and pork luncheon meats quickly followed. The new product had hardly reached delicatessen cases, however, before competitors produced their own versions. Jay Hormel determined that his company's pork luncheon meat would have to be sold in cans sized conveniently for consumers and with a name that could be trademarked. In late 1936, at a naming party at Jay Hormel's house, Kenneth Daigneau, an actor and the brother of a Hormel vice president, won the top prize of $100 for "Spam," a portmanteau word that stood for either "spiced ham" or "shoulder of pork and ham" (company sources disagree). Sales were slow at a time when most meat was sold either fresh or cured. Housewives had trouble believing that canned meat could be safe to eat.

Spam and World War II

The U.S. armed forces quartermaster's office had no reservations about the safety of the canned meat. Nutritious, filling, affordable, and shelf stable, Spam was a nearly perfect mess-tent food. Before the war was over, the army alone received 150 million pounds of pork luncheon meat. The result was a chorus of complaints, cartoons, poems, and jokes about Spam. In letters to Hormel and in the military newspapers *Yank* and *Stars and Stripes*, soldiers called the product "ham that didn't pass its physical," "meat loaf without basic training," and "the real reason war was hell." Some of the "Spam" served to soldiers was generic luncheon meat made to government specifications. But because it was the most famous brand before the war, Spam received all the blame. Spam even became part of the language of the war: Uncle Sam became "Uncle Spam," the European invasion fleet was called the "Spam fleet," and the United Services Organizations (USO) toured the "Spam circuit."

England and Russia received Spam as part of American aid packages. In Russia, Nikita Khrushchev was grateful. "We had lost our most fertile lands—the Ukraine and the Northern Caucasus...Without Spam we wouldn't have been able to feed our army," Khrushchev recalled in his autobiography. In Italy and England a can of Spam was a prized commodity that could be traded for manual labor, intelligence, and even the services of a prostitute.

In the United States, Hormel company executives worried that Spam would become a wartime casualty. But Spam sales increased after World War II. Although

many former soldiers had tired of it, many more who had been introduced to Spam during the war soon had their families eating it.

Spam is popular in parts of the world where U.S. troops were stationed, including Guam, Hawaii, and Okinawa. Hawaiian restaurants serve Spam in ramen noodle soup, in box lunches called *bento*, fried with eggs and rice for breakfast, but most commonly in sushi. Made by topping a fried slice of Spam with a block of sticky rice and wrapping them together with a belt of seaweed, Spam sushi, or *musubi*, is as common in convenience stores and take-out stands in Hawaii as hot dogs are in these establishments on the mainland. The world's Spam-eating capital is Guam. Annual per capita consumption in this U.S. territory is eight pounds. Automobile dealers in Guam use trunkfuls of Spam as sales promotions.

Selling Spam

After World War II, Hormel hired former servicewomen to sell Spam and other products. That group grew into a traveling sales force of sixty musically talented women who starred in a radio show as the Hormel Girls. In 1953 Hormel returned to the more conventional and economical sales approach of magazine advertisements featuring Spam recipes. The most popular recipe—Spam glazed with brown sugar and studded with cloves in the manner of baked ham—was featured on the can for fifty years. In 1997 that image was replaced by a Spamburger—a quarter-pound slice of Spam grilled and served on a hamburger bun. This serving suggestion was designed to position Spam as an alternative to fast food hamburgers. The Hormel Spamburger television advertising campaign in 1992 sent Spam sales soaring.

At a time when fresh and natural foods are extremely popular, Hormel is the only American meat company that advertises processed canned meat on national television. It is also one of few companies whose advertising addresses criticisms of its product, albeit humorously. Hormel's "Surprise" campaign in 1980 recorded the surprisingly positive reactions of people who did not know they were eating Spam. "Okay, so the name's funny. But there's nothing funny about the taste," was the copy in the Spam advertising campaign in 1997. Hormel has addressed concerns about the fat and sodium content of Spam by introducing lower-salt and lower-fat varieties, such as Spam Less Sodium (1986), Spam Lite (1992), and Turkey Spam (2000).

Since 1991 Hormel has sponsored Spam recipe contests at state fairs throughout the United States. Entrants are encouraged to extend their efforts beyond the most popular uses in sandwiches and fried and served with eggs. Grand prize–winning recipes have included Spam-stuffed peppers, Spam manicotti, Spam fritters, and Spam potato cupcakes. Spam dishes served at Spamarama in Austin, Texas, include Spam tequila, Spamores, and ice cream Spamwiches. Spamarama is a fan-sponsored Spam cook-off and athletic event that attracts as many as eight thousand people annually. Spamarama is the oldest and largest of dozens of grassroots Spam celebrations held across the United States every year.

The World Wide Web has many Spam sites, including the Spam Haiku Archive, the mock-religious Church of Spam, and the Spam Cam, which focuses a real-time camera on a decaying brick of Spam. Spam continues to be the butt of jokes in movies and on television by comedians such as Jay Leno. Hormel has joined the fun (or tried to defuse the unauthorized kind) with its own Spam website, annual festival, and merchandise catalog and a 16,500-square-foot Spam museum, which is visited by almost 100,000 persons annually.

[See also Breakfast Foods; Canning and Bottling; Combat Food; Food Festivals; Hawaiian Food; Historical Overview: World War II; International Aid; Pig.]

BIBLIOGRAPHY

Corum, Ann Kondo. *Hawai'i's 2nd SPAM Cookbook.* Honolulu, HI: Bess, 2001.

Talbott, Strobe, ed. *Khrushchev Remembers.* Boston and Toronto: Little, Brown and Company, 1970.

Wyman, Carolyn. *Spam: A Biography.* San Diego, CA: Harcourt, 1999.

CAROLYN WYMAN

Spiders, *see Frying Pans, Skillets, and Spiders*

Spinach

Spinacia oleracea is a leafy vegetable with many cultivars ranging from light to dark green and from smooth-textured to highly crinkled leaves. Spinach tastes slightly bitter (owing to the presence of oxalic acid), reduces dramatically in volume when cooked, requires several washings before being eaten, delivers few calories, and contains a nutritional powerhouse of beta-carotene, minerals, fiber, protein, and vitamins B, C, and E. Cultivated as early as the A.D. fourth century in Persia, the country to which it owes both its name (from the Persian *aspanākh*) and its highest accolade ("prince of vegetables"), spinach traveled east to China before reversing direction to Europe and thence to America in the seventeenth century.

John Winthrop Jr., the governor of the Massachusetts Bay Colony, bought "spynadge" seed in 1631—perhaps not to universal applause. Bert Greene (1984) referred to a Pilgrim child's prayer to ward off "unclean foreign leaves," that is, "sandy spinach." By the eighteenth century spinach flourished in colonial Williamsburg gardens as one of many potherbs, round and prickly seed varieties assuring year-round harvests. Grown predominantly in the gardens of the well-to-do, spinach long retained the aura of luxury shared by cucumbers and shelling peas. Improved varieties, appearing in the late 1800s, broadened the appeal of spinach. Nonetheless, spinach has remained a stranger to most American tables. American annual per capita consumption, only 0.4 pounds by 1977, increased to 1.3 pounds by 2002—lower than that of all other vegetables except artichokes, asparagus, and eggplant.

Recipes from the eighteenth century through the mid-twentieth century show that spinach was invariably served cooked, sometimes unappealingly overcooked by modern standards. Its juice was used as a food coloring. Although salads became popular around the end of the nineteenth century, the spinach salad of 1915—a cooked spinach mold—would be unrecognizable to aficionados of the raw leaves wilted with bacon dressing that became popular in the 1960s.

An emphasis on nutrition in the early 1900s spooned spinach into children's nurseries, where the vegetable met with much resistance. Carl Rose, a cartoonist for the *New Yorker*, drew a child unhappily faced with a plate of broccoli. E. B. White captioned the 1928 cartoon, "I say it's spinach, and the hell with it!"

Improvements in refrigerated rail transportation, Clarence Birdseye's development in 1929 of a commercial frozen food process, and claims made by the Depression-era cartoon character Popeye encouraged spinach consumption. At the height of Popeye's popularity, children ranked spinach as their third-favorite food—behind turkey and ice cream. The cookbook authors Mollie Gold and Eleanor Gilbert wrote: "No one has yet been able to crystallize the slanderous rumors concerning spinach.... Nevertheless, spinach cooked properly, and in moderation, is a highly delectable dish." Cooked properly means steamed for five minutes without water, chopped, and cooked for five minutes in butter.

Spinach stars in famous American dishes, including some versions of oysters Rockefeller and Joe's special hash, a San Francisco specialty. Botanically unrelated New Zealand spinach, Malabar spinach, and wild spinach (also known as mountain spinach and orache) are often substituted for *S. oleracea.*

[See also Birdseye, Clarence; Salads and Salad Dressings; Transportation of Food; Vegetables.]

BIBLIOGRAPHY

Gold, Mollie, and Eleanor Gilbert. *The Book of Green Vegetables.* New York: Appleton, 1928.

Greene, Wesley. "Salad Greens." Williamsburg, VA: Colonial Williamsburg Foundation, 2004, http://www.history.org/.

Hebert, Malcolm. "Popeye's Vegetable Remains Popular." *San Jose Mercury News,* August 31, 1988.

ROBIN M. MOWER

Spoons, *see Silverware*

Sprouts

"Sprout" is the colloquial name for sprouted seeds and young shoots that are used in raw and cooked salads or as vegetable garnishes; they are also juiced. Sprouts cover many plant genera, including beans, peas, grasses, and bulbs; the most common in America are sprouts from aduki, alfalfa, buckwheat, clover, garlic, garlic chive, radish, sunflower, kaiware, mung bean, soybean, and pea. Growers have also developed a stunning array of sprout blends for the commercial market. Adaptable to a range of climates, sprouts have become a relatively common supermarket staple nationwide. Associated with Asian cuisines as well as health food faddists, sprouts are integral to modern California cookery.

Much of the credit for familiarizing Americans with sprouts must go to the grocer Wallace Smith of Detroit, Michigan, and his Korean partner, Ilhan New, college chums who developed a fresh bean sprout business in the 1920s. The business matured into La Choy Food Products, selling canned and jarred sprouts.

Notwithstanding their contemporary image, sprouts occasionally show up in the culinary patrimony. Lettice Bryan's unusual recipe for "sprouts and other young greens" in *The Kentucky Housewife* (1839) calls for blanching the sprouts and serving them with a hot bacon and vinegar dressing.

[See also Health Food; Salads and Salad Dressings.]

CATHY K. KAUFMAN

Spruce

Ancient Scandinavians and their Viking descendants brewed beer from young shoots of Norway spruce, drinking the beer for strength in battle, for fertility, and to prevent scurvy on long sea voyages. Introduced to spruce beer by the Vikings, European colonists were familiar with the beverage when they arrived in North America. Recipes for spruce beer are in the first American cookbooks. To prevent scurvy, eighteenth-century navies brewed the beer at sea using the decoction essence of spruce.

Native Americans and native Alaskans were the first Americans to use the inner bark, green tips, and new shoots of spruce for medical and culinary purposes. They chewed spruce resin for dental hygiene. In the early twenty-first century native Alaskans harvest spruce tips as an indigenous vegetable. Alaska exports spruce-tip jelly and syrup as specialty food items.

In the Northeast sugar maple sap was added to spruce beer for flavor and fermentation. In 1848 John Curtis began selling spruce gum. Sweetened paraffin gum debuted in 1850, and its popularity reduced spruce gum to the status of New England curiosity. Commercial breweries reduced spruce beer to another regional rarity after World War I. The emergence of microbreweries in the late twentieth century reintroduced spruce beer to mainstream consumers.

[See also BEER, CORN AND MAPLE; BIRCH BEER; HISTORICAL OVERVIEW: COLONIAL PERIOD TO THE REVOLUTIONARY WAR; HOMEMADE REMEDIES; NATIVE AMERICAN FOOD; SCANDINAVIAN AND FINNISH FOOD.]

ESTHER DELLA REESE

Squash

The early European explorers of the New World were delighted to find what they thought were melons growing wild wherever they went. These were not melons but squashes, members of the same family (*Cucurbita pepo* sp.), which also includes pumpkins, cucumbers, gourds, loofahs, zucchini, and chayotes. Remains of squash dating from 7000 B.C.E. have been found in Central and South America.

The word "squash" is believed to derive from the Algonquian words "*askoot asquash*," meaning "eaten green." New varieties of squash are constantly being bred or evolve naturally. That is because squash blossoms can be either male or female and are pollinated by bees and other insects. Squashes are subdivided into summer and winter squashes. Both types are now available throughout the year, but summer squashes are picked at a younger stage. In general the seeds are smaller, and the whole vegetable, including seeds and skin, may be eaten.

Winter squashes are tougher and more fibrous. They are peeled before or after cooking, and larger specimens are cut into chunks and the seeds removed before cooking. Winter varieties include the banana squash; butternut squash, a bulbous, pale-yellow variety with orange flesh; the acorn or Des Moines squash, a small green or yellow, rounded variety; and spaghetti squash, whose flesh falls into narrow spaghetti-like strands when cooked. The magnificently colored red and yellow turban squash is similar to the acorn squash; Hubbard squash is a warty variety, eaten at the unripe green stage as well as in its mature orange stage. There are also cabocha, delicata, and sweet dumpling squashes.

Summer squashes include the crookneck, an ocher-yellow squash with a long curved neck, and pattypan, a small white squash that is given a variety of names in different locations, including Peter Pan, scallops, and scallopini. A miniature version is known as baby boo. In the South this squash is variously known as simlin, symbling, or cymling.

Squash and pumpkin seeds are salted and sun-dried and eaten as a snack in the Southwest and in Mexico, where they are known as *pepitas*, and are also sold unsalted and skinned in health food stores. The Mexican and southwestern drink known as *horchata* is made by mixing the ground seeds with sugar, cinnamon, and water. Squashes are cooked in stews, pureed and added to soups, or boiled, baked, or broiled and served as a side dish with a white sauce. Stuffed squash blossom is a popular dish in the Southwest and in Mexico. These flowers are always some shade of yellow or orange-yellow and are generally filled

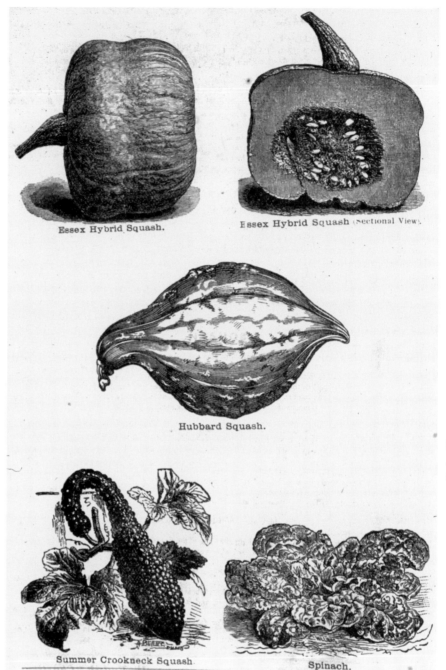

Essex Hybrid Squash.

Essex Hybrid Squash (Sectional View).

Hubbard Squash.

Summer Crookneck Squash.

Spinach.

Illustrations of various types of squash.

with a savory mixture. Zucchini blossoms are cooked in the same way.

[See also CUCUMBERS; FLOWERS, EDIBLE; MELONS; PUMPKINS; SNACKS, SALTY; VEGETABLES.]

BIBLIOGRAPHY

Bacon, Josephine. *Exotic Fruits and Vegetables*. London: UPSO, 2004.

McNair, James. *James McNair's Squash Cookbook*. San Francisco: Chronicle Books, 1995.

National Gardening. *Book of Cucumbers, Melons, and Squash*. Edited by the staff of *National Gardening*. Rev. ed. New York: Villard, 1987.

Tarr, Yvonne. *The Squash Cookbook: How to Grow and Cook All Kinds of Squash, from Acorn to Zucchini, Including Pumpkins and Gourds*. New York: Wings Books, 1995.

JOSEPHINE BACON

Squid

A mollusk, squid (families *Ommastrephidae* and *Loliginidae*) more often appears on menus and in the market by its Italian name, calamari. The ommastrephids are the major commercial species around the world, but the American market depends mostly on squid caught off the New England and California coasts. That modern Americans know calamari at all is owed to immigrants from the Mediterranean who introduced its use in the twentieth century and provided recipes for its preparation. Battered and deep-fried calamari rings cut from the tube-shaped body are common fare in seafood restaurants, and prepared and frozen calamari is available for salads, stews, and stir-fries. The fishery for wild calamari is still abundant.

SANDRA L. OLIVER

Starbucks

Starbucks has become a symbol of the modern American specialty coffee movement. Starbucks coffee bars are opening in small towns and major cities alike. Starbucks began in 1971 as one of many grassroots batch-roasting firms started by idealistic, dedicated baby boomers rediscovering the joys of coffee made from freshly roasted, high-quality arabica beans. Jerry Baldwin, Gordon Bowker, and Zev Siegel, three Seattle friends, modeled the first Starbucks store on the Peet's Coffee and Tea shop in Berkeley, California. By the time Siegel sold out in 1980, Starbucks had six retail outlets and was selling beans wholesale to restaurants and supermarkets. By early 2003 there were approximately 5,000 stores in continental North America and 1,500 elsewhere. Consolidated net revenues were approximately $4 billion annually.

In 1983 Starbucks purchased Peet's. Four years later, frustrated by the commute between Berkeley and Seattle, Jerry Baldwin decided to focus on Peet's, selling Starbucks to Howard Schultz, his former head of marketing. Schultz, a Brooklyn native, was inspired by a 1983 trip to Italy, where he loved the theatrical and communal feeling of espresso bars.

Schultz set about transforming Starbucks into a coffeehouse chain specializing in espresso-based milk drinks, such as cappuccino and latte. The coffee bars spread throughout the Northwest then to Chicago and Los Angeles. The company went public in 1992 and continued to advance throughout the United States and Canada. With hardly any advertising, Starbucks became a cultural icon, its green-and-white mermaid logo appearing in movies and its lingo ("That'll be an unleaded grande latte with wings") mocked by comedians. Schultz, the company's chief global strategist, envisions Starbucks as a world brand comparable with Coca-Cola and Disney. The company is opening outlets in Europe, Asia, and Latin America.
[See also COFFEE; COFFEEHOUSES.]

BIBLIOGRAPHY

Pendergrast, Mark. *Uncommon Grounds: The History of Coffee and How It Transformed Our World.* New York: Basic Books, 1999.

Schultz, Howard, and Dori Jones Yang. *Pour Your Heart into It: How Starbucks Built a Company One Cup at a Time.* New York: Hyperion, 1997.

MARK PENDERGRAST

Stewart, Martha

Martha Stewart (1941–) is a domestic enhancement industry magnate who began her career as a caterer. Born Martha Kostyra, Stewart was the second of six children of Polish American parents in Nutley, New Jersey. After an education at Barnard College and early careers as a model and a stockbroker, she first entered the realm of professional domesticity as a private caterer. By 1982, with the publication of her first book, *Entertaining*, Stewart had begun her transformation from the white, ethnic, middle-class Martha Kostyra to her trademark persona, the Greenwich, Connecticut, Yankee Martha Stewart. She went on to build a phenomenally successful domestic enhancement empire, Martha Stewart Living Omnimedia, Inc., with cookbooks, magazines, newspaper columns, television and radio appearances, mail-order catalog, and website, all offering material goods and advice on home beautification, including the production, preparation, and proper display of food both for entertaining and for everyday family meals. A controversial figure who evokes strong feelings among fans as well as detractors, as evidenced in a widely reported trial and conviction in 2004 on charges of obstruction of justice and securities violations, Stewart is the latest in a long line of famous American women domestic advice givers, including Sara Josepha Hale, Eliza Leslie, and Catharine Beecher.

The extraordinarily polished appearance of Martha Stewart food belies a class-specific aura that transcends ethnicity and becomes accessible by cultivation rather than by heritage. Martha Stewart food is enveloped in a high-Protestant, New England Yankee gloss. Stewart's upper-middle-class taste provides those who aspire to it a kind of cultural capital that has helped shape ideals of modern American food. Not only is the preparation of Martha Stewart food a sign of one's status, but Stewart's food itself is prescriptive, class conscious, and authoritarian, as if she has taken upon herself the task of being a strict arbiter of proper American taste. Appearance is more important than taste, to which the carefully constructed and controlled food photography in Martha Stewart publications attests.

Martha Stewart food lends itself to elaborate, conspicuous consumption and is based upon an invented artisan ethos fully realized only by those who have the luxury to perform the work—whipping cream by hand, for example, or making crackers from scratch. Though many criticize Stewart as an elitist perfectionist with a notorious reputation for demanding and rude treatment of her staff and household help, many home cooks are fiercely loyal, seeing her as transforming their lives for the better. Many (women in particular) find the intricate world of Martha Stewart food most gratifying for infusing a sense of pleasure into the daily, often mundane activities of procuring and preparing food, and these home cooks derive a sense of accomplishment and pleasure from cooking à la Martha Stewart, to whatever limited extent. While Stewart's handcrafted approach evokes such positive notions as conservation and recycling, in actuality many of these projects (and recipes) are quite complex, require a fair amount of money, and can be wasteful of resources.

The Martha Stewart empire is not all cast in this mold, however. Stewart has produced a range of household goods, including an expanding panoply of "everyday" kitchen and dining implements, for Kmart, a middle- to lower-middle-class shopping venue (although research suggests that people of all economic levels shop at Kmart at least occasionally). Martha Stewart Kmart products, however, are never featured and are infrequently advertised in the magazine *Martha Stewart Living* or on the television program *From Martha's Kitchen*. This disjuncture may be poised to change, however, given that in 2003 Martha Stewart Living Omnimedia launched a monthly periodical of recipes, *Everyday Food*, designed for a much broader audience than *Martha Stewart Living*. *Everyday Food*, which does not feature Stewart's photograph or even her name prominently, is designed to be sold at the grocery store checkout counter. Given her conviction and prison sentence, Martha Stewart's title as preeminent domestic advice-giver, as well as the fate of her company, remains to be decided.

BIBLIOGRAPHY

Bentley, Amy. "Martha's Food: Whiteness of a Certain Kind." *American Studies* 42, no. 2 (2001): 89–100.

Leavitt, Sarah Abigail. *From Catherine Beecher to Martha Stewart: A Cultural History of Domestic Advice.* Chapel Hill: University of North Carolina Press, 2002.

AMY BENTLEY

Stills

Two types of stills are used for making alcoholic beverages. The pot still appeared approximately five thousand years ago in India. The column still is less than two hundred years old. Stills were originally tools in two basic human desires: to get rich and to live forever. Just as alchemists tried to transmute base metals into gold, they also tried to transmute plant materials into cure-alls. Scented oils for medicinal use and perfumes made by distillation were the results.

The most basic still consists of three parts: a vessel in which to boil a liquid, a lid that has a tube or "beak" that runs from the top of the vessel slanting downward to channel vapor away from the boiler and help the vapor condense, and a vessel for catching the condensing vapor as it drips. (The word "distill" comes from the Latin *destillare*, meaning "to drip.") American colonists made distilled spirits with small pot stills. They bartered their whiskeys freely until a tax on whiskey was imposed in 1791. The tax triggered the Whiskey Rebellion of 1794, which was quelled by President George Washington.

Farm produce is perishable. Surplus corn could not be held after it was picked, and it was too bulky to be transported economically. Fermenting, distilling, and bottling surplus corn solved both problems. Bourbon shipped from Bourbon County, Kentucky, around 1780 emerged as the unique American whiskey. Bourbon was distilled from corn to eighty proof and aged in new charred-oak barrels. For another half century or so, the pot still reigned supreme. The inherent disadvantage of the pot still, however, is that it is a single-run processor. The liquid to be distilled, called the "wash," is put into the pot and boiled. The distillate is captured, and the pot must then be emptied and cleaned. The still can then be recharged to repeat the process. The newly distilled wash, called "low wine," often has to be distilled again to result in a substance with a more concentrated alcohol level, called "high wine."

The column still was a nineteenth-century design that allowed uninterrupted feeding of the wash and provided a continuous output of distillate that could complete distillation in one process, directly from wash to high wine. Until the advent of the column still, distilling was done in small quantities, and the start-up cost was small. Column stills, on the other hand, were expensive to build and complex to operate, and they needed considerably larger amounts of raw materials to justify their operation. The result was a new kind of distiller who produced high volumes of marketable spirits at low cost.

Early in the twentieth century Prohibition was enacted, and distilling by commercial producers ceased almost entirely. New categories of distillers were born: bootleggers and their country cousins, moonshiners. After Prohibition ended, the spirits industry rebounded through the last third of the twentieth century, when a downward trend in consumption began. Americans are consuming less distilled spirits than in the past, replacing them with beer and wine. In the early twenty-first century most American commercial spirits are made with column stills. A small movement of artisanal distillers uses the old methods, much as in baking, cheese making, and other culinary arts.

[See also ALCOHOL AND TEETOTALISM; ALCOHOLISM; BOURBON; BREWING; CORN; DISTILLATION; GIN; PROHIBITION; RUM; TEMPERANCE; VODKA; WHISKEY.]

ROBERT PASTORIO

Stoners, Fruit, see Cherry Pitters or Stoners; Peach Parers and Stoners

Stores, see Grocery Stores

Stout

The style of beer called "stout" is a variation of a unique style of malt beverage called "porter." The style was developed as a result of the need to manufacture a brew that would meet the demand for a particular mixture popular in England in the early 1700s that consisted of beer, ale, and "two penny" (a pale small beer). When a customer ordered this popular libation, the publican had to draw from three different casks. Ralph Harwood, of the Bell Brewhouse in Shoreditch, East London, England, in 1722 conceived of a brew in which the three elements were already mixed. It was first called Mr. Harwood's Entire Butt or Entire Butt, and was first dispensed at a pub called the Blue Last, on Great Eastern Street in Shoreditch. The publican began calling the brew "porter," after the occupation of most of the Blue Last customers.

The popularity of the brew extended into the London market, where demand soon made the product popular with other brewers. Irish laborers, a large percentage of them porters, began demanding the brew when they returned to their native land, and the style of brew slowly spread in popularity to Ireland. In Dublin in 1778 Arthur Guinness began brewing a stronger version of the drink, calling it "stout porter." Both the Irish and English versions of stout porter were imported into the American colonies almost as soon as regular trade was established.

A number of stouts are produced, all varying only slightly from the original. The most common product is called "dry classic Irish stout"(3.8–5.4 percent alcohol by volume) and is represented by the Guinness brand. In the United States stout is one of the most popular styles of beer made by small breweries. It is a style that is easy to identify, and its unique flavor profile can be forgiving in the hands of small-batch brewers. Examples of stout brewed in the United States are Alaskan Stout, made by Alaskan Brewing Company; Anniversary Stout, Ithaca Brewing Company; Black Hawk Stout, Mendocino Brewing Company; Brooklyn Dry Stout, Brooklyn Brewing Company; Cadillac Mountain Stout, Bar Harbor Brewing Company; Dominion Oak Barrel Stout, Old Dominion Brewing Company; Heart of Darkness, Magic Hat Brewing Company; Shakespeare Stout, Rogue Ales; Sierra Nevada Stout, Sierra Nevada Brewing Company; Ipswich Oatmeal Stout, Mercury Brewing Company; and more than one hundred other stouts brewed by as many breweries.

[See also BEER; BREWING.]

BIBLIOGRAPHY

Foster, Terry. Porter. Boulder, CO: Brewers, 1992.
LaFrance, Peter. Beer Basics. New York: Wiley, 1995.
Rhodes, Christine P., ed. The Encyclopedia of Beer. New York: Holt, 1995.
Van Wieren, Dale E. American Breweries. West Point, PA: East Coast Breweriana Association, 1995.

PETER LAFRANCE

Stoves and Ovens: Gas and Electric

For almost three centuries, most Americans cooked before an open fireplace or hearth. In the nineteenth century, Americans shifted to wood- or coal-burning ovens, ranges, and stoves. An oven was simply a metal box used for baking, whereas a range was a flat surface with two or more holes into which pots could be fitted and used for boiling or frying. The word "stove" frequently meant a combination of oven and range.

Coal- and wood-burning stoves had definite advantages over an open fireplace, but they also had disadvantages. Wood did not furnish sustained heat, which made baking difficult. Coal filled the kitchen with dust and ashes. Both coal and wood stoves generated considerable external heat, which was desirable during the winter, but in hot weather the extreme heat made the kitchen almost unbearable. For these reasons alternative fuels, such as gas and electricity, were explored as possible substitutes for coal and wood.

Gas Ranges

Natural gas (methane) was used in many places in the world, but until the mid-nineteenth century it was difficult to recover and store the gas. In the late eighteenth century William Murdoch, a Scottish engineer, pioneered a technique for manufacturing gas from coal. After further experimentation, he developed a system that could fuel street lights. Beginning in 1800 Murdoch and others designed and built gasworks for mills and factories. In the United States in 1816 Baltimore chartered the first gas-manufacturing plant, and other American cities followed soon thereafter. Until the late nineteenth century gas was used almost exclusively for street illumination.

The first known use of gas for cooking is credited to a Moravian chemical manufacturer who in 1802 prepared a meal on a gas cooker, the British term for a small gas range. The gas cooker was not commercialized until James Sharp of Northampton, England, developed the first experimental gas stove in 1826. Ten years later he opened a factory to manufacture gas stoves.

By the 1850s gas ranges were available in the United States. Many early ranges were simply burners placed on tabletops for cooking. One of the first models to appear on the market was Morrill's Evaporator Cooking Stove, which was advertised in Boston in 1858. The allure of gas stoves was obvious. Gas burned cleaner than either wood or coal and required less preparation (wood chopping, coal carrying) and cleanup (ash removal). Compared with gas stoves, wood and coal stoves took a long time to heat up, and they required constant attention to maintain a specific temperature. Gas stoves required a simple turn of a knob for instant heat. Coal and wood ranges required constant replenishment and a large storage area for fuel. Gas was supplied through a pipe or in a "reservoir," a tank filled with gas. Gas stoves produced much less external heat and were therefore more pleasant to use in hot weather.

Despite all these advantages, the adoption of gas cookery occurred slowly in the United States. Early gas stoves were plagued with problems. Gas from municipal systems produced a low-temperature flame useful for gas lighting but too low for heating food. In addition the gas supply experienced a

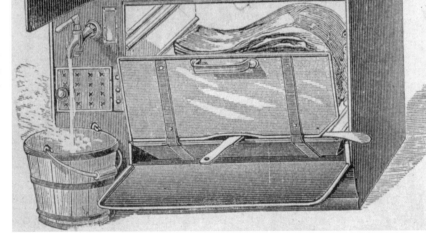

This drawing of a gas stove shows its many uses.

Thomas Edison invented the incandescent light bulb in 1879. More important, he invented the system that supplied electricity to homes and businesses. Edison opened the first central electricity generating plant in 1882. Like natural gas, electricity was initially used for lighting streets and homes. Beginning in the early 1890s experiments with electric cooking appliances attracted considerable attention. The first electric stove is credited to the Carpenter Electric Heating Manufacturing Company. The organizers of the 1893 Columbian Exposition in Chicago constructed an electrified home equipped with an electrified marble slab intended to heat food. On June 30, 1896, William Hadaway was issued the first patent for an electric stove.

Despite auspicious beginnings, the electric stove remained a novelty well into the twentieth century, in part because few American houses were wired for electricity. By 1907 only 8 percent of American homes were on the power grid, and the price of electricity was high compared with that of coal, wood, and gas. Even homes supplied with electricity had serious problems with electric stoves. The incoming current was weak, and it took an hour to heat an oven for baking. There often was not sufficient amperage to power the stove burners while the oven was heating.

Experimentation with prototype electric stoves continued, and three models, including stoves developed by General Electric and Westinghouse, appeared on the market in 1908. However, these stoves were beset with problems because the heating elements frequently burned out, and the stoves were in constant need of service. In 1920 cooking by electricity was still a novelty.

In the 1920s important changes were made to electric stoves. The first changes were technological improvements. New heating elements, first installed by Hotpoint, decreased problems related to the burning out of heating elements. The introduction of the electromechanical thermostat kept the temperature constant in ovens. The second set of changes related to fashion. Electric ranges available in the early 1920s were constructed on tall legs, and the boxlike oven compartment rose above the burners. In new stoves the oven was below the burners. This configuration made possible level countertops and work surfaces throughout the kitchen. Then Westinghouse and other manufacturers dazzled consumers by offering electric ranges in a variety of colors. Despite these improvements, only 875,000 American households had switched to electric stoves by 1930.

In the 1930s electric stoves began to effectively compete with gas ranges. The cost of electricity dropped, particularly after the construction of major hydroelectric projects, such as the Tennessee Valley Authority and

considerable loss of pressure during times of heavy use, making it impossible to heat ovens when they were most needed. Although reservoirs were used, they frequently ran out of gas before cooking was finished. In winter gas lines occasionally froze. In addition gas stoves were more expensive than coal and wood stoves, and natural gas was generally more expensive than wood or coal. Early gas stoves constantly needed repair, and maintenance costs added to their expense. Many Americans were frightened by the possibility of gas leaks, which could cause gradual asphyxiation or a sudden explosion.

As gas companies struggled along, some began to manufacture their own stoves and other appliances. Trade associations subsidized firms interested in developing improved models. As the gas delivery system improved, the advantages of the gas stove increased, and the price of natural gas decreased. As improvements were made in design, gas stoves gained wider acceptance. The 1895 Montgomery Ward catalog offered gas ranges with reservoirs, which increased sales in rural areas. In 1915 the American Stove Company sold the first models with oven thermostats, ushering in the era of steady, reliable baking temperatures. Gas stoves with top burners and ovens were found in most households by the 1920s.

Early gas ranges, like their coal- and wood-burning forebears, were black. In 1923 Hotpoint introduced a white enamel range, and within four years color in the kitchen was becoming fashionable. By 1930 twice as many U.S. households cooked with gas as did with wood or coal.

Hoover Dam. By 1941, 80 percent of all houses were wired for electricity, and the shift to electric ranges had begun. By the 1950s electric ovens were outselling gas models. By the end of the twentieth century twice as many American homes cooked with electricity as did with gas.

Gas and electric stoves equipped with thermostats made accurate, standardized temperature control possible, and cookbooks began to include exact cooking times and temperatures in recipes. The introduction of gas and electric stoves meant that new cooking techniques were required. To help educate American consumers, utility companies offered cooking demonstrations, and many stove companies produced cookery booklets to promote their products.

Later in the twentieth century accessories and improvements were added to kitchen ranges, including timers, storage drawers under the oven, windows in the oven door, interior lights in the oven, self-cleaning functions, preheating signals, and an automatic shutoff function for turning off the oven at a programmed time. Broilers have been added for radiant-heat cooking, and gas stoves have electronic ignitions, which obviate pilot lights. In the late twentieth century a new competitor arose—the microwave oven. The microwave oven initially had problems with image and function similar to those exhibited by primitive gas and electric ovens.

[**See also** MICROWAVE OVENS; STOVES AND OVENS: WOOD AND COAL.]

BIBLIOGRAPHY

Brewer, Priscilla. *From Fireplace to Cookstove: Technology and the Domestic Ideal in America*. Syracuse, NY: Syracuse University Press, 2000.

Cowan, Ruth Schwartz. *More Work for Mother: The Ironies of Household Technology from the Open Hearth to the Microwave*. New York: Basic Books, 1983.

Franklin, Linda Campbell. *300 Years of Kitchen Collectibles*. 5th ed. Iola, WI: Krause, 2002.

Plante, Ellen M. *The American Kitchen: 1700 to the Present*. New York: Facts on File, 1995.

ANDREW F. SMITH

Stoves and Ovens:
Wood and Coal

American cast-iron cookstoves had their earliest origins in the kitchens of the wealthy in Europe after the Middle Ages. These early ranges were large boxes that held a fire. Flat-bottomed pots placed on the range absorbed sufficient heat for cooking. In some kitchens a sheet-iron oven with hinged doors was set flush in the wall above its own "fireplace" alongside the main hearth. The heat from the fire below circulated around the oven before entering the flue leading to the main chimney. These adjuncts to hearth cooking heated more quickly than large brick ovens but were apparently limited to more affluent homes. It was from such precedents that the American cookstove evolved. The rapid rise in popularity and use of cookstoves coincided

A woman stands in front of a cast-iron stove in the 1870s.

with the beginnings of the nineteenth-century American Industrial Revolution. Embraced by middle- and upper-class householders in growing cities, cookstoves played a role in changing American home life and American cuisine.

The development of the capacious multiple-oven cookstove owed much to the experiments and inventions of the American-born physicist Benjamin Thompson (1753–1814), later Count Rumford. While living in Germany, Thompson designed a massive though rudimentary range for cooking meals on a large scale at a Munich workhouse. The large metal structure was built around a fireplace. The heat of the fire was conducted into an oven and into a series of "wells" that held deep cooking pots. Thompson also designed a small, portable iron stove that held a single large pot placed in a well over a fire. Thompson's investigations into the physics of heat conduction and convection were the basis of subsequent cookstove development.

Philo Penfield Stewart (1798–1868), who helped found Oberlin College in Ohio in 1833, was one of the men responsible for bringing Rumford's ideas to fruition in America. One of his most important contributions was slanting the sides of the firebox to concentrate the fuel as it burned down. Sales of the "Oberlin" stove, which was patented in 1834, profited the college.

Early American cookstoves were small and low (the cooking surface was usually about two feet off the floor). Only small amounts of food could be cooked at one time, and the cook had to bend to use either the oven or the stovetop. As larger stoves were made, they were raised on legs, and the oven was elevated, often in a stepped or "horseblock" configuration in relation to the cooking surface. As the stove continued to evolve, the waist-high cooktop became the norm, and cooks could stand upright as they worked.

Internationally renowned for their inventive spirit, Americans secured nearly eight hundred patents for cookstoves and attachments between 1840 and 1864. There seemed to be a mania for improving the stove, whether the innovations changed the efficiency and convenience of stoves or merely their appearance. Patents were issued for ongoing improvement in the design of grates, flues, warming ovens, hot-water reservoirs, and ventilating apparatuses. Stoves also became more decorative. Scrollwork, flowers, and other patterns were molded into the black iron, and contrasting shiny nickel or steel was used for trim. Some stoves were made so that they could be taken apart annually for cleaning and for removal to and reassembly in a summer kitchen. However, over time some iron stoves were constructed in such monstrous proportions that once in place, they were not moved.

The closed stove, although it changed the American cooking style, turned out not to be such a labor-saving device. Someone had to cut wood to short lengths to fit the firebox, stack it, and carry it into the house, and the cook had to keep on hand a supply of finely split tinder and kindling. However, the quantity of wood used was far less than that consumed by an open hearth or brick oven. When coal became a common fuel, the wood-supply chores diminished, but the burned-out coal clinkers—heavier than wood ash and not as useful—had to be carried out.

To fire the stove, the user laid wood on the grate inside the firebox (a small chamber at one side of the stove) and then lit it enough in advance of cooking time to let the stove heat up. Cookstoves were equipped with a system of dampers that controlled the flow of air into the fire and of smoke up the chimney. At first a damper was opened in the smokestack, producing a strong draft that encouraged the fire to grow. Once a good blaze was in progress, that damper was closed, and the heated air and smoke were redirected through passages between the inner and outer walls of the oven, thus heating the oven, and then up through the stack to the chimney. Other vents controlled airflow into the firebox, supplying more oxygen for a stronger fire or limiting the air supply to slow the fire.

Because even a small fire concentrated its heat efficiently, preheating was accomplished with less fuel and time than had been necessary in a hearth or brick oven. Within twenty minutes, an experienced cook might be setting up coffee water for breakfast and within forty minutes have a pan of rolls or biscuits baking. Keeping the temperature steady long enough to bake a cake was a matter of experience. To determine the heat level, cooks held a hand in the oven for as long as tolerable and judged the temperature by time. (Some authorities recommended thirty-five to forty-five seconds as the time indicative of a "moderate" oven.) This system was highly individual, because it depended on the peculiarities of the oven itself and the heat tolerance of the cook. Another method was to put a piece of writing paper or a cube of bread in the oven to see how long it took to brown. Once the initial temperature was established, the drafts and dampers had to be skillfully manipulated to keep the fire at a steady heat. If the oven overheated, the cook opened the door a bit and then closed it when the heat was judged right. Trial and error, aided by sensory memory, were the cook's learning tools. After the day's cooking, ashes and cinders were swept out. From time to time the stove was taken apart so the flues and drafts could be cleaned of soot, the iron surfaces blacked, and the bright trim polished.

As the price of wood continued to increase, anthracite coal, which burned more steadily and less smokily than wood, became less expensive and more widely available and thus more popular as a fuel. Because coal burns hotter than wood, cooks had to adjust their tried-and-true skills in regulating stovetop and oven heat. To accommodate variations in the availability of fuel, some manufacturers began to supply stoves built to burn either wood or coal.

For those who grew up cooking at the hearth, the cookstove represented great progress. Cooking required less time, because the heating was accomplished more quickly. The range top and the oven allowed the development of a more complex cuisine. Cooks prepared more dishes for each meal, because they had the time and technology. They followed the changing cuisine through magazines and newspapers as literacy and communication media grew. Women enjoyed special meals—teas and luncheons—focused on entertaining other women, and homemakers specialized in growing numbers and kinds of baked desserts. Home canning became prodigious, and reputations were made on the quantity and quality of homemade pickles and preserves. Although it was not the only factor in these changes, the cookstove played a substantial role in enabling.

Despite their many advantages, iron cookstoves were far from an ideal solution to all cooking problems. The stoves were notoriously unpredictable and difficult to control. Each stove had its idiosyncrasies, and the cook had to be sensitive to its needs and knowledgeable in responding to them. The fire, hidden from sight in the firebox, could flare up or die down quickly, requiring the cook to check it every few minutes and make appropriate adjustments. Ovens were drafty, especially because the heat was controlled by opening the oven door. Delicate dishes such as angel food cake and soufflés, which require steady and draft-free conditions, were so challenging as to be almost impossible. Roasted meats were not nearly as good as those cooked on a hearth over fire, and breads baked in the cookstove oven were inferior to those from a brick oven. The great back saver of the waist-high cooking surface was countered by arduous weekly cleaning and blacking necessary to prevent rust.

By the 1920s gas ranges had largely replaced solid-fuel cookstoves in cities and towns, but wood- and coal-burning stoves were still used in many rural and remote areas. In the 1970s wood stoves enjoyed a small renaissance because of fuel shortages, a growing interest in family food traditions, the attraction of simple, basic living, and romanticism regarding country kitchen decor. In the early twenty-first century air-quality regulations and standards of convenience and household efficiency limit the use of wood as fuel.

[**See also** Kitchens: 1800 to the Present; Stoves and Ovens: Gas and Electric.]

BIBLIOGRAPHY

Brewer, Priscilla. *From Fireplace to Cookstove: Technology and the Domestic Ideal in America*. Syracuse, NY: Syracuse University Press, 2000.

Cowan, Ruth Schwartz. *More Work for Mother: The Ironies of Household Technology from the Open Hearth to the Microwave*. New York: Basic Books, 1983.

Smallzreid, Kathleen Ann. *The Everlasting Pleasure: Influences on America's Kitchens, Cooks and Cookery, from 1565 to the Year 2000*. New York: Appleton-Century-Crofts, 1956.

BONNIE J. SLOTNICK

Strawberries

The modern strawberry (*Fragaria* x *ananassa*) originated in the early eighteenth century in a garden near Brest, France, as a chance cross of two American species. One, the Chilean strawberry (*F. chiloensis*), is native to the Pacific beaches of North and South America; the other, the Virginia strawberry (*F. virginiana*), is native to eastern North America. Deliberate improvement began in 1817 with the work of Thomas Knight in England. The ensuing two centuries have given rise to numerous strawberry cultivars differing not only in fruit characteristics but also in disease resistance and adaptability to various soil types and climatic conditions.

The twentieth century saw the development of ever-bearing varieties of strawberries. The first types of ever-bearing plants, developed early in the twentieth century, bore two crops each season, one in spring and one in fall. True ever-bearing strawberries—varieties that fruit continuously through the growing season—have been available since approximately 1980.

The strawberry is a woody plant with a much foreshortened stem, from which arises a whorl of leaves. Plants send out runners, at the tips of which new plants develop, and these plants can give rise to more runners and daughter plants. The plants' habit of strewing may have led to the name "strewberry," which became "strawberry." An alternative explanation is that the name arose from the straw traditionally used for mulching the plants. Although strawberry plantings can remain productive for a few years before disease and weeds make inroads, the trend has been toward planting and cropping the plants for one season and then removing them. Strawberries are an intensively grown, high-value crop.

Commercial strawberries are extensively grown in warm winter areas, such as California and Florida. Although strawberries were once a springtime treat, varieties bred to withstand the rigors of shipping are available year-round, at some sacrifice to texture and flavor.

Not to be overlooked are two old-fashioned species of strawberry. Alpine strawberries (*F. vesca*) are ever-bearing wood strawberries that do not produce runners. This species also is known by the French name *fraise de bois* and is native to North and

Strawberries as seen in the 1894 catalog of Peter Henderson & Company, New York.

South America, Europe, northern Asia, and Africa. Alpine strawberry fruits are tiny but highly colored (except for white-fruited sorts) and are intensely flavored. Cultivated forms of musk strawberry (*F. moschata*), which is native to northern Europe and Siberia, date to the sixteenth century. These strawberries also have been called "hautbois strawberries." Although the fruit is borne only in spring and is very soft and only dull red, the flavor of musk strawberries is intense and delectable, a commingling of the flavor of strawberry with those of raspberry and pineapple.

Botanically, the fruit of the strawberry is what most people consider its seeds. These achenes, as such hard, dry fruits are called, stimulate growth of associated receptacles, which swell together to become the juicy, red "fruits." Strawberries are rich in vitamin C. Although they usually are used fresh, strawberries can be frozen and are frequently processed into preserves, jelly, extracts and flavorings, and pie filling.

[**See also** Fruit; Preserves; Transportation of Food.]

BIBLIOGRAPHY

Darrow, George M. *The Strawberry: History, Breeding, and Physiology.* New York: Holt, Rinehart, and Winston, 1966.

Wilhelm, Stephen, and James E. Sagen. *A History of the Strawberry: From Ancient Gardens to Modern Markets.* Berkeley: University of California Division of Agricultural Sciences, 1974.

Lee Reich

Street Vendors

Street vending has been a vital part of meeting physical and emotional needs throughout America's history. Street vending is a poor family's way of supplementing meager income, keeps cultural traditions alive, and supplies customer's needs for variety, sustenance, and sociability. Opposition to this informal practice, however, has consistently produced restrictive regulations as well as complaints from businesses and the public. Street vendors reflect their countries of origin while responding to climates and resources in the United States.

Traditions of peddling food in streets and markets have existed worldwide throughout the ages. Drawings in an Egyptian tomb exhibit at the Field Museum depicted a market of four thousand years ago with vendors selling fruits, vegetables, and fish. In biblical times peddlers carried produce from countryside to towns and returned with wares and crafts needed by the rural people. Despite their role in satisfying needs, these traders were often viewed with suspicion. In Europe market squares surviving from Roman times are still used for the purchase and bartering of food.

By the Middle Ages, Jews, forbidden land of their own, became the main link between East and West as they traded grains, spices, dates, and nuts. In nineteenth-century eastern Europe, as Jews were persecuted and barred from peddling in cities, thousands of poorer Jews were driven to seek their livelihoods in America. Economic betterment and escape from oppression have motivated successive waves of immigrants who came to America not as slaves but of their own volition from South and Central America, Africa, and Asia.

Immigrants brought with them the food cultures of their native lands and adapted them to the resources and conditions they found in their new home. For example, street cries of Britain were distinctive and called attention to the peddlers' wares, so these cries became a feature of colonial America. Vendors, new arrivals themselves, communicated in immigrants' languages and delivered familiar foods directly to customers. Fresh, daily food was delivered to immigrant populations who lacked refrigeration. Elderly persons still recall the "delicious" fresh fish, "lovely" crisp fruit, and hot roasted potatoes sold in winter from mobile, charcoal-burning metal carts.

A consistent goal of street vendors in America was upward mobility. With scant English language skills or financial resources, vendors moved from carrying their wares on their backs to carts, stands, small shops, horses and wagons, and finally trucks. Beginning vendors aspired to becoming their own bosses, despite the long hours and physical hardship. Future businesses followed familiar ethnic trajectories. For example, many Greek peddlers went into the restaurant business, whereas Italian food vendors progressed to the wholesale trade of fruit, vegetables, and nuts.

With differing religious and cultural traditions, the role of women vending on the streets varies. Women hawk food in many parts of the world, and immigrants from these areas continue the practice. If culturally restricted, women and children participate in the family business by home tasks such as cultivation and preparation of fruits and vegetables.

Many vendors come from countries where unions are a familiar solution to obstacles, but in America language problems often form barriers. Also vendors tend to possess an independent, enterprising spirit, so they often prefer to solve their problems independently.

Municipal regulation of street vending in America is diverse, complex, and often confrontational. Restrictions on vending is worldwide, but in the third world regulations have been tempered by the sheer numbers of people who depend on vending for their livelihoods. Officials in America have been heavily influenced by health and hygiene reforms and by the power of fixed location business owners.

Vendor restrictions may mean stringent requirements for storage, hot and cold running water on a cart, tent over the food, health permit, forbidden foods, and attendance at classes. Chicago is widely known for its restrictions, whereas New York is celebrated for the variety and quantity of food available from street vendors. Midsize cities often appreciate food vendors for ambiance but carefully restrict the activities and appearances of food carts.

Many city regulations target arbitrary locations for prohibition. Food vendors often are cited as being threats to "public safety" when the actual issue is that they are considered threats to the profits of fixed-location businesses. Studies have shown that vendors may actually increase customer traffic and enhanced safety in the area.

Food vendors are sometimes forced from main selling streets and are barred from selling to schoolchildren or to factory or downtown business workers, common sources of customers outside America. Other restrictions limit hours of selling so that selling is prohibited during hours that will generate the greatest customer volume. Similarly city councils have argued heatedly about street cries, some officials citing noise nuisance and others pointing out that this is the only way vendors can make their presence known in neighborhoods.

Buyers appreciate street food for reasons of ethnic taste, nostalgia, and the opportunity to eat quickly obtained, reasonably priced, and flavorful food in a sociable setting. Vendors respond to these needs by presenting food that is ethnic but also satisfies American tastes for the new. Vendors barred from central business districts make up the loss by selling their wares in neighborhoods and market streets. Peddlers sell sweetened, shaved ice cones across the street rather than in front of schools and provide tamales and steamed corn on the cob after Spanish-language Mass. Every neighborhood has its own version of the hot dog, and in many cities customers can take their pick of Middle Eastern foods.

As heritage food festivals become popular in America, street vendors may lose some of their independence but gain ready-made customers. In Washington State, Asian food is offered by Buddhists, Vietnamese, and Indians. Midwesterners promote rhubarb and strawberry festivals, and Russian Jewish immigrants in Florida vend pastries stuffed with meat, carrots, and potatoes. The Feast of

Andy Russo and Tony Maldonado sell fruit from their truck in Brooklyn, New York.

San Gennaro in New York attracts customers with traditional Italian food. A relatively new street festival in Illinois, Juneteenth, celebrates the Emancipation Proclamation, with vendors selling southern-style and African food.

[See also Farmers' Markets; Food Festivals.]

BIBLIOGRAPHY

Cross, John. "Introduction to Special Issue on Street Vending in the Modern World." *International Journal of Sociology and Social Policy* 21 (2000): 1–4.

Eastwood, Carolyn. *Chicago's Jewish Street Peddlers.* Chicago: Chicago Jewish Historical Society, 1991.

CAROLYN EASTWOOD

Strong Pale Ale

This strong (high alcohol) brew is particular for its dark (almost opaque) color and a sweet flavor that masks the heat of an alcohol content that, in some cases, can reach 6 to 8 percent by volume. American-style strong pale ale has its origins in what is known as Indian Pale Ale (IPA), an English beer style developed in the early nineteenth century. It was brewed with a high alcohol content and high hop flavor in order to survive shipping to English colonies, particularly those in India, where large numbers of civil servants and troops thirsted for fondly remembered English brew. In the early twenty-first century IPAs are sold as premium beers, and those brewed outside the Burton area treat their water to simulate that of the gypsum salts of Burton water.

American microbrewers adopted this style of brew early on because it took a relatively short time to brew and the flavor profile (heavy on the hops) was much in demand. Many craft-brewers, or microbrewers, are also drawn to the intrinsically high alcohol content of this beer and the inherent challenge of brewing a high alcohol beer that is balanced with both massive sweet malt flavor and almost astringent hops flavor. For brewers, achieving this balance is a challenge that is irresistible.

According to the Association of Brewers' 2004 Beer Style Guidelines, this style is characterized by American-variety hops used to produce high hops bitterness, flavor, and aroma, and has medium body with low to medium maltiness. Alcohol content is usually between 5.5 percent and 6.3 percent by volume.

PETER LAFRANCE

Stuckey's

Stuckey's, a multimillion-dollar chain known for selling pecan candy, was founded by Williamson Sylvester Stuckey, an entrepreneur and self-taught marketing expert who was a pioneer in the convenience store and fast food concept. Born in Dodge County, Georgia, on March 26, 1909, Stuckey dropped out of the University of Georgia in 1929 because of a lack of funds and went home to plow a mule (the lowest form of farm employment in the South during the Great Depression). In the early 1930s, after his grandmother lent him thirty-five dollars, Stuckey began buying and selling Georgia pecans. In 1936 he built a roadside stand on a two-lane highway near Eastman, Georgia. There he sold pecans and later added pralines made at home by his wife, Ethel Mullis Stuckey. The first Stuckey's Pecan Shoppe opened in Eastman, Georgia, in 1937, selling pecan log rolls, pralines, divinity, and pecans. The store later added souvenirs and food and beverage service. Gasoline pumps were installed as other stores opened.

Much of Stuckey's success is attributed to the founder's uncanny business and marketing sense. He offered one-stop shopping years before convenience stores appeared, adopted a universally recognizable store design, and used franchisees to manage his stores. Long before integration in the South, blacks were welcome in Stuckey's stores. A framed copy of Stuckey's customer service philosophy, "The Friendship of a Traveler Means a Great Deal to Us," hung in every store. A parrot or mynah bird greeted customers in many stores. The locations for stores and billboards were carefully selected on the basis of results of traffic studies. Stuckey lived the American dream and saw his name become a household word.

There were 160 Stuckey's stores by 1964, when Stuckey's merged with Pet, Inc., the consumer food giant that also owned Whitman's chocolates. Stuckey became a vice president and member of the board of Pet, Inc., and remained president of the Stuckey's division until his early retirement in 1970. During the time he managed the division (1964–1970), the number of Stuckey's stores increased from 160 to approximately 350 coast to coast.

After Stuckey's death in Eastman, Georgia, on January 6, 1977, Pet, Inc., was bought by Illinois Central Industries, a Chicago conglomerate, after Pet fought the merger and lost. Williamson Sylvester Stuckey Jr. had worked with his father in Stuckey's before he became congressman for the Eighth District of Georgia in the U.S. House of Representatives, where he served from 1966 to 1976. On May 1, 1985, Stuckey Jr. and his partners, Charles "Chip" Rosencrans and Gregory Griffith, repurchased Stuckey's from Illinois Central Industries, ending seventeen years during which the company had not been under Stuckey family ownership. When co-branding became popular, the Stuckey's Express franchise, a store-within-a-store concept, was established.

In late 2002 Stuckey's had two hundred franchises in nineteen states from Pennsylvania to Florida and as far west as Arizona along interstate highways in convenience stores and travel plazas. Stuckey's capitalizes on its nostalgic appeal to travelers who remember the familiar stores from the 1950s through the 1970s. Stuckey's pecan candies, nuts, and souvenirs inside stores along America's highways continue the Stuckey's legend.

[See also Nuts; Pecans; Restaurants; Roadside Food.]

BIBLIOGRAPHY

Drinnon, Elizabeth McCants. *Stuckey: The Biography of Williamson Sylvester Stuckey, 1909–1977.* Macon, GA: Mercer University Press, 1997.

ELIZABETH MCCANTS DRINNON

Stuffed Ham

Stuffed ham is a corned or smoked ham that has been stuffed with vegetables and spices. Slits or holes are cut into the ham, and the ingredients are packed in. Traditionally the stuffing consisted of differing amounts of cabbage, kale, and onions. Variations may include celery, watercress, turnip, mustard seed, and spinach. Spicy elements are celery seed, mustard seed, ground red pepper, black pepper, and salt.

Stuffed ham is thought to have originated in southern Maryland, specifically in St. Mary's County, where it is a specialty dish. St. Mary's, dating from 1634, was Maryland's first settlement and is located southeast of Washington, D.C., off the Potomac River. Hogs were available to Maryland settlers in the mid-seventeenth century. There are no references to stuffed ham in the seventeenth or eighteenth centuries in Maryland, nor are there written references in the nineteenth. However, there are references to vegetable- and parsley-stuffed hams in Maine in 1786 and in Virginia and Kentucky in the early eighteenth century.

Twentieth-century cookbooks contain various recipes, and serving the ham, especially at Christmas and Easter, is a tradition at both African American and white church suppers in St. Mary's. Before the twentieth century, oral traditions of St. Mary's County residents can trace stuffed ham to the post–Civil War period. Legends include those that say it originated in England or was brought from Africa by slaves. Some say the slaves used the lower jaw, or the jowl, of the pig as the base, stuffing it with vegetables, such as kale, cabbage, "greasy greens" (wild watercress), or turnip tops.

BIBLIOGRAPHY

Oliver, Sandra L. "Maryland Stuffed Ham for the Holiday." *Food History News* 6, no. 2 (Winter 1999): 1, 10–11.

Tilp, Frederick. "Potomac Stuffed Ham—A Culinary Art." *Chronicles of St. Mary's* 22, no.4 (April 1974), pp. 349–53.

FRED CZARRA

Stuffing, *see Dressings and Stuffings*

Sturgeon

Strange and rare, sturgeon (family Acipenseridae) were highly esteemed in the past for their reddish flesh; their cartilaginous external plates that meant fewer internal bones;

their large size, with some individuals growing to six hundred or more pounds; and the sturgeon caviar, which was favored over other sorts. Sturgeon are found in the Northern Hemisphere, with seven species in North America, caught in both lakes and saltwater. Lake sturgeon (*Acipsenser fulvescens*, family Acipenseridae) are found in North American lakes. By the beginning of the twentieth century sturgeon had been almost entirely eliminated from the Great Lakes because it was believed that sturgeon were eating the eggs of favored species, particularly walleye. Sturgeon has been fished commercially, mostly in Canadian waters. The fish can live to be 150 years old and grow to great size. In 1968 a 162-pound fish was caught in the Rainy River in Minnesota. At one time fish weighing more than 250 pounds were pulled from the Great Lakes. Sturgeon ranges from most waters that empty into Hudson Bay to Louisiana. Sturgeon flesh and roe are valuable and bring a higher price than do those of any other freshwater species. The flesh is richly flavored, white, and firm. Smoking is the most common method of preparation. The eggs are prized as caviar.

Few modern people will have eaten sturgeon, whose flesh is said to resemble veal in flavor; in most places the fish is a protected, endangered species. It was plentiful in America into the nineteenth century, heavily fished in the Hudson and Delaware rivers and even nicknamed "Albany beef." It was mentioned slightly more often in southern cookbooks than in northern ones, and toward the end of the nineteenth century much of the commercial catch was smoked and sold wherever there was a large German population.

Since Atlantic sturgeon is anadromous, the fishery is now mostly conducted on the Hudson River. On the West Coast there are two species of sturgeon, the green and the white, but the green is not considered good for eating. There is a small commercial fishery of sturgeon on the Columbia River. Some efforts are being made to farm raise sturgeon. The main object of sturgeon fishery worldwide is the caviar, but the beluga sturgeon is so overfished and poorly managed that conservationists list beluga caviar among seafood to avoid.

SANDRA L. OLIVER

Submarine Sandwiches

Hearty sandwiches made on loaves of Italian bread became popular in a number of American cities during the late nineteenth century. In Philadelphia street vendors known as hokeypokey men sold a variety of foods, including ice cream. During the early twentieth century they began selling sandwiches made with sliced meats, cold cuts, cheese, fish, and vegetables on a long oval roll and seasoned with oil and vinegar. They called the sandwich a "hoagie."

In New Orleans, Clovis Martin, the owner of Martin Brothers Grocery, asked his cook to come up with a five-cent sandwich that would keep the "poor boys"—locals who were unemployed during the Depression—satisfied for an entire day. The sandwich, which came to be called "the po'boy," is a hefty cross section of French bread stuffed with roast beef and cheese. In the early twenty-first century po'boys may contain a fried fish filet, thinly sliced roast beef, or cold cuts. If lettuce, tomatoes, or chopped cabbage is added, the sandwich is referred to as "dressed." A variation is *la mediatrice* or "the peacemaker," a loaf stuffed with fried oysters.

In Chicago, Italian beef sandwiches were sold by street vendors after World War I. Thin shavings of roasted beef along with mozzarella and roasted peppers were stuffed into Italian bread, which was then drenched in a beef broth flavored with garlic and oregano. This sandwich is still popular in Chicago, with many variations to choose among. They can be still be bought from street vendors and in most Italian restaurants in the city. Similar sandwiches are sold in other America cities, such as the French dip sandwich.

The first fast food chain featuring these sandwiches was launched in 1964 by Tony Conza, Peter DeCarlo, and Angelo Baldassare in Hoboken, New Jersey. They called it a Blimpie. The second submarine sandwich chain was created in 1965 by Frederick DeLuca and Peter Buck of Bridgeport, Connecticut, who called their shop Subway; it is the nation's largest sub chain in the early twenty-first century. These were followed Quiznos Sub restaurant, launched in 1981, which quickly became the second largest sandwich chain.

BIBLIOGRAPHY
Jakle, John A., and Keith A. Sculle. *Fast Food: Roadside Restaurants in the Automobile Age.* Baltimore: Johns Hopkins University Press, 1999.

ANDREW F. SMITH

Subway

In 1965 seventeen-year-old Frederick DeLuca of Bridgeport, Connecticut, borrowed $1,000 from a family friend, Dr. Peter Buck, and opened Pete's Submarine Sandwiches in Milford, Connecticut. The first shop floundered, but DeLuca tried again, and when a second shop did well, the partners began expanding their operation. The flagship product was the "submarine" sandwich composed of a variety of cold cuts, including ham and turkey, and salad vegetables. They changed the name of the restaurant to Subway (its corporate name is Doctor's Associates, Inc.). DeLuca and Buck began franchising in 1974. Subway expanded its operation through "development agents," who sold Subway franchises—a system that has led to abuses and numerous lawsuits. The costs of setting up a Subway outlet, however, are comparatively low, as are the franchising fees. By 1979 Subway had one hundred stores. A large number of franchisees are immigrants, who work long hours to make their businesses succeed.

In 1993 Subway began opening outlets in convenience stores, truck stops, and Walmart stores and also opened outlets abroad in the 1990s. The chain changes its menu choices to reflect changing tastes, stressing low-fat options and adding sandwiches such as Sweet Onion Chicken Teriyaki and Southwest Chipotle Cheese Steak. In 1999 Jared Fogle, an Indiana University student, claimed to have lost 245 pounds by eating mostly the lower-fat Subway sandwiches and adopting a walking regimen to burn calories. He has become a spokesperson for Subway, promoting their "healthy" image. As of 2005 Subway was the largest sub chain in America and the second largest fast food franchise in the world, with more than 24,000 locations in the United States and 82 other countries.

BIBLIOGRAPHY
Jakle, John A.. and Keith A. Sculle. *Fast Food: Roadside Restaurants in the Automobile Age.* Baltimore: Johns Hopkins University Press, 1999.
Mercuri, Becky. *American Sandwich: Great Eats from All 50 States.* Layton, UT: Gibbs Smith, 2004.

ANDREW F. SMITH

Succotash

Most contemporary accounts of the Pilgrim-Indian diplomatic conference called "the first Thanksgiving" describe succotash, and it is likely that succotash was eaten there. But it was not the succotash most Americans know as a stew of lima beans and sweet corn in a cream sauce. Nor did it have decorative red and green bell peppers chopped in. All of these vegetables were unknown to the Native New Englanders and the Plymouth colonists at that time.

The succotash that might have gone around the table in the seventeenth century was later described as "Plymouth succotash" or "winter succotash." It would have been the typical standing dish of all the eastern Native tribes, a stew of field corn or lye hominy with shell beans and either fresh or preserved meat or fish or both. By the mid-nineteenth century Plymouth succotash was a winter dish of lye hominy, dried beans, and corned beef. It was made in large quantities, and leftovers were sometimes frozen for future use. In Native homes this stew was constantly on or near the fire, added to as needed or possible, and taken from as people were hungry. It got its English name from the Narragansett *msíckquatash*, "boiled whole kernel corn." An early reference in English is the 1769 menu for the Plymouth "Founder's Day" dinner, at which men commemorated the Indian foods eaten by their ancestors. The word appears more often around the turn of the nineteenth century for a stew of fresh shell beans and corn. The most widely read early reference was a somewhat garbled one in James Fenimore Cooper's 1826 novel *The Last of the Mohicans*.

Native lima beans and butter beans did not grow north of the Carolinas and are not described in English until the early eighteenth century. Sweet corn arose as a mutation of field corn but may not have been collected and developed by Native farmers until around the time of the American Revolution and was not widely available in seed catalogs until after the Civil War. Thus while our contemporary vegetarian succotash probably was an Indian dish, it would have been in southern tribes in the nineteenth century.

An early printed recipe for "succatosh" from *Miss Beecher's Domestic Receipt-Book* (1846) suggests boiling the (unspecified) beans for thirty to forty-five minutes, implying fresh shell beans, and boiling with the cobs. This last direction is common in old recipes and would have added a little more sweetness to a stew of starchy field corn. An 1852 New England cookbook specifies corn cut from the cob and shell beans, dressed with butter and salt. The recipe in the 1876 *National Cookery Book* again boils corn on -the cob with beans, later cutting the corn off the cobs, but adds the modern improvements of a butter-flour thickener and tomato ketchup. A fifty-year-old Plymouth recipe, published in the 1880s, specifies white beans, white hominy, salt pork, corned beef, fresh chicken, turnips, and potatoes. An early recipe for succotash with butter beans (still using corn cobs) was published by Annabella P. Hill of Georgia in 1872 and may reflect antebellum southern practice. She also mentioned a winter version made of dried beans and corn. As late as 1896 the southern-born Marion Harland specified string beans with corn in a succotash.

MARK H. ZANGER

Suet, see Fats and Oils

Sugar

Supporting early colonial empires of the Dutch, French, and English, sugar was the most significant commodity coming from the tropics, emerging as the dominant plantation crop of Barbados by the 1640s and Jamaica by the early 1700s. It was Britain's most important colonial import in the eighteenth century. With sugar as its anchoring crop, the Caribbean formed the center of a growing Atlantic commerce that involved three continents: Africa supplied slave labor for sugar plantations; North America provided raw materials, including shipbuilding timber, to transport the commodity; and Europe generated goods for its own and export markets. The success of Britain's Caribbean colonies during the seventeenth and eighteenth centuries helped fuel economic growth and influence the American colonies. How sugarcane was processed provided a template for the cultivation of similarly labor-intensive crops in the South, particularly the use of slave labor for cotton and tobacco production.

Sugar Production

Performed by man or machine, sugar production is a labor-intensive process. Three key processes transform cane, a tropical grass growing up to three inches in diameter and twenty feet high, into refined sugar: extraction, purification, and crystallization. Extraction separates sucrose (sugar) from bagasse (leftover vegetable material). Purification removes waste products. Crystallization gives sugar its characteristic granularity. Once refined, the sugar is then cooled and dried. In the eighteenth and nineteenth centuries, refined sugar was packed tightly in hollow conical clay molds to cure. Early sugar varied from dark brown to white in color, and from syrupy to completely dry in texture. Highly refined sugar reaching American kitchens in the eighteenth century and early nineteenth century was separated into chunks using sugar snips and then grated into dissolvable granules.

An alternative to cane, profitable beet sugar production began in American in the 1880s, increasing sugar's production rate and decreasing its price. Processed like cane, sugar beets benefit from more temperate climates and a shorter growing season. Domestic sugarcane cultivation is limited to parts of Hawaii, Louisiana, Florida, and Texas. Key beet sugar regions, much larger, include the Dakotas, the Upper Midwest, the Plains, and the Far West.

Sugar and the Economy

Since 1789 the government has placed tariffs on sugar to protect domestic refining industries and generate revenue. From 1842 on policies became protectionist in nature, favoring domestic refineries and sugar producers. The McKinley Act of 1890 changed the tariff schedule for imported sugars, ultimately decreasing the price and boosting consumption further. The Sugar Trust (organized under the name the Sugar Refineries Company and renamed the American Sugar Refining Company) was formed in 1887, a consolidated and powerful group of the country's top sugar refiners. During the Great Depression, the Sugar Act of 1934 established price controls, set production quotas, and determined equitable distribution of profits among large and small processors. In the 1980s the U.S. Department of Agriculture (USDA) became directly involved in protective measures, giving price supports to domestic growers and establishing import quotas for foreign sugar sources. In 2000, six companies comprised the American refining industry, operating ten refineries in seven states; they marketed their products nationally, with about 60 percent of raw sugar supplies coming from domestic sources.

Sugar in the Diet

Sugar was initially considered a precious spice; like saffron, cinnamon, and cumin, it was kept under lock and key. Physicians considered sugar a powerful medicine, prescribing it for a variety of maladies. In the eighteenth and nineteenth centuries sugar, still expensive, was considered a status

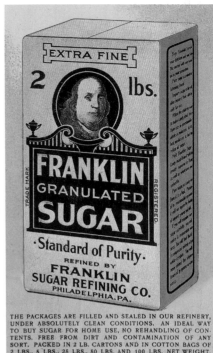

A box of Ben Franklin granulated sugar, circa 1890.

symbol. Its material versatility, along with its "neutral" flavor, appealed to Americans. In the nineteenth century apothecaries used sugar-coated lozenges to conceal the bitter drugs inside; from those medicinal products came hard candies.

Sugar's uses are numerous. Individuals buy it in five-pound bags and use it in their homes for baking, sweetening beverages, enhancing the taste of fresh fruits and cereals, making confections, and as a preservative in home canning. Brown sugar, moister and less refined, is incorporated in baked goods. For professional bakers and confectioners, sugar is a key ingredient for making cakes and their decorative icing, pastries, and doughnuts. Candy manufacturers use a combination of sugar and other sweeteners (including glucose, dextrose, and high-fructose corn syrup) for producing candy bars, lollipops, hard candies, licorice, and other confectionery. Ice cream manufacturers combine sweeteners with cream, eggs, and flavorings to make frozen treats. Soft drink makers, who once exclusively used refined sugar, no longer use it for manufacturing carbonated beverages. Molasses (a by-product of sugar refining) is used as a liquid sweetener in baked goods. Rum (fermented molasses) counted as an important colonial good (traded with Native Americans for furs, skins, and horses) and remains a popular kind of alcohol.

For centuries available only to the rich—its value was once almost equal to gold—sugar became a mainstay in elite diets and social rituals. It tempered the bitter taste of other luxurious imported substances, such as coffee, chocolate, and tea. Sweetened imported dainties, such as candied nuts and preserved fruits, comprised the bulk of a confectioner's stock. The accessories of sweetness—sugar bowls, tongs, spoons, and graters—were often fashioned of elaborate materials, such as gilt porcelain or pure silver.

As sugar became more affordable, its integration into popular rituals became more common. Beginning in the 1870s wedding cakes became popular and by the turn of the century had become an essential part of the marriage ceremony. Molded gelatins became the inspiration for middle-class desserts around the same time. Instant dessert preparations, such as granulated gelatin and ice cream powder, in addition to promotional pamphlets and tin molds democratized upper-class deserts, making them cheaper and easier to prepare for those of all classes.

On a larger scale sugar came to play an important role in American holidays. Imported sweetmeats were treats enjoyed during early Christmas celebrations in upper-class homes. In the nineteenth century the range of holidays incorporating confections expanded to include Valentine's Day and Easter. In the twentieth century candy had become central to the ritual of trick-or-treating on Halloween.

Sugar became so elemental in the America diet that its absence represented hard times. Its scarcity was a noted issue during the Civil War, especially in the South. While there were some sugar rationing during World War I and supplies of candy for the soldiers became a priority (it was a quick and portable energy source and did not go bad), women on the home front especially felt the shortages during World War II. It was the first commodity to be put on the ration list and the last to be taken off (in 1947).

Although Americans embraced sugar from the time it entered the marketplace, its consumption has also aroused controversy for political, social, and dietary reasons. Beginning in the 1790s, abolitionists called for boycotts on commodities produced with slave labor, offering maple sugar as a substitute for cane sugar. Because sugar has no nutritional value and is something that brings pleasure, many nineteenth-century Americans identified it as a source of various societal maladies. Victorian medical advisers and reformers alike, preoccupied with personal respectability and good conduct, believed that sugar was slightly addictive and would lead to other vices, such as gambling and drinking. In the late twentieth century people blamed hyperactivity, obesity, attention deficit disorder, diabetes, and other debilities (especially among children) on sugar consumption.

Despite its critics, sugar retained its popularity. Consumption rates rose steadily from the eighteenth through the twentieth centuries. The average annual per capita consumption for the 1790s was about 8 pounds and in the 1970s was about 120 pounds. Although sugar consumption peaked in the late twenti-

A 1917 poster by Ernest Fuhr urges conservation of sugar during wartime.

eth century, total intake for sweeteners continues to rise from increased consumption of liquid and chemical sugar substitutes.

The addition of both natural and chemical sweeteners has made the American diet of the early twenty-first century much sweeter than it was in the past (when sugar was scarce), changing the flavor of foods not ordinarily considered sweet, such as pizza dough, gravy mixes, and ketchup. According to the USDA, in the year 2001 the intake of caloric sweeteners alone totaled over 150 pounds per capita. This figure did not include the noncaloric chemical sweeteners, such as aspartame and saccharin. In the 1950s few people consumed saccharin (the only artificial sweetener on the market at the time). Twenty years later each American annually ingested on average 7.1 pounds of it, and by 1984 its consumption topped out at 10 pounds. In the same year aspartame (trademarked as Nutri-Sweet) accounted for 5.8 pounds of sweetener consumed per person for the year.

Cyclamates, aspartame, and saccharin are not only sweeter than sugar—thirty, two hundred, and three hundred times, respectively—but are also cheaper to produce. Identified as cancer causing, cyclamates were permanently banned by the Food and Drug Administration in 1969 and saccharin temporarily in 1977. Because it is so cheap to produce and can be made from domestic crops, high-fructose corn syrup (entering commercial production in 1972) has been substituted for sugar in soft drink beverages and other foods. Candies, ice cream, cookies, and other confections contain not only refined sugar but also high-fructose corn syrup and dextrose.

Sugar Symbolism

The qualities of sugar are highly symbolic in American culture. Associated with refinement and sweetness, sugar has come to represent stereotypical feminine qualities. Phrases such as "Home Sweet Home," "eye candy," and "sugar and spice" (what girls are made of) have entered the vocabulary. When it first appeared on the market, refined sugar represented a "modern" sweetener to Americans, because, white and highly processed, it offered an alternative to traditional sweeteners such as honey and maple sugar. At the start of the twenty-first century those sweeteners are coming back in vogue, and refined sugar has been replaced by the more modern-seeming chemical sweeteners.

BIBLIOGRAPHY

Galloway, J. H. *The Sugar Cane Industry: An Historical Geography from Its Origins to 1914.* Cambridge, U.K.: Cambridge University Press, 1989.

Mancall, Peter C. *Deadly Medicine: Indians and Alcohol in Early America.* Ithaca, NY: Cornell University Press, 1995.

Mintz, Sidney W. *Sweetness and Power: The Place of Sugar in Modern History.* New York: Viking, 1985.

Polopolus, Leo C., and Jose Alvaraz. *Marketing Sugar and Other Sweeteners.* Amsterdam: Elsevier, 1991.

Woloson, Wendy A. *Refined Tastes: Sugar, Confectionery, and Consumers in Nineteenth-Century America.* Baltimore: Johns Hopkins University Press, 2002.

WENDY A. WOLOSON

Sugar Beets

American botanists categorize the sugar beet as a modern cultivar of the ancient group *Beta vulgaris* var. *crassa*, native to western Europe and the Mediterranean. In Europe, where the original research and experimentation with

Mexican sugar beet workers near Fisher, Minnesota, 1937.

sugar beets took place, horticulturalists distinguish members of the species *B. vulgaris* by the significantly different uses to which the plants are put: *B. vulgaris* var. *esculenta* denotes the common red, golden, or white table beet; *B. vulgaris* var. *rapa* indicates the fodder beet; and *B. vulgaris* var. *altissima* identifies the light beige-colored root resembling a parsnip, which for the past two hundred years has been harvested primarily for processing into sugar.

The demand for luxurious, expensive sugar exploded in the seventeenth century, when Europe fell in love with the hot beverage troika of chocolate, tea, and coffee. Dependence on tropical cane for table sugar left Europe and America subject to the vagaries of trade, transportation, and war. By contrast, the beet thrives in the temperate climates found in much of continental Europe and America. In 1747 the German chemist Andreas Margraf first discovered that beets contain small amounts of sucrose, the chemical component of table sugar, which can be extracted in crystalline form. Fifty years later Margraf's student Franz Karl Achard successfully cultivated *altissima* Silesian beets with a higher sugar content than *esculenta* beets, making extraction potentially feasible. From these sugar-rich beets, he refined the first loaf of beet sugar. The process was improved in France in the early nineteenth century under pressure from the British blockade of French ports during the Napoleonic Wars, although beet sugar remained expensive. During the 1820s French manufacturers further improved the process, bringing down the cost of beet sugar.

The technology quickly spread to the United States, brought by Americans who had seen the process firsthand in France. In the 1830s the Beet Sugar Society of Philadelphia was organized to promote practical knowledge for cultivating and processing sugar beets. Early industry crusaders saw beet sugar as a weapon in the fight to abolish slavery. Didactic literature linked the consumption of cane sugar with support for slavery and urged consumers to purchase beet sugar instead, thereby undermining the cane sugar plantations.

But early efforts to manufacture beet sugar in the United States, in Pennsylvania, Michigan, New York, and Utah, ended poorly. Most notably Brigham Young's Church of Jesus Christ of Latter-day Saints (the Mormons) toiled for five years to establish a beet sugar industry in Utah but never produced palatable sugar because of technical gaffes and poor growing conditions around the Great Salt Lake.

California was home to the first successful U.S. sugar beet industry in the 1870s, with factories in Alvarado and Watsonville. Throughout the country others followed suit, buoyed by the tariff act of 1890, which paid a bounty to domestic beet sugar producers. In 1891 a plant financed and operated largely by the Mormons opened in Lehi, Utah. This time, with improved technology, they were successful and soon built additional factories in Utah. They attracted the attention of New York's cane sugar magnate Henry Havemeyer, who purchased a controlling interest in 1902. He financed additional factories, which matured into the Utah-Idaho Sugar Company. After Havemeyer was bloodied in battles involving the new antitrust laws, the Mormons repurchased Havemeyer's interest, just in time to enjoy the escalating sugar prices brought about by World War I.

The boom was short-lived. The market collapsed in 1921, the insatiable beet leafhopper devoured crops, and the Great Depression continued the industry's economic woes. By World War II increasing mechanization became the only solution to efficient beet cultivation. Cooperative postwar ventures through the U.S. Sugar Beet Association, West Coast Beet Seed Company, Western Seed Production Corporation, and Beet Sugar Development Foundation all continue to assist modern growers and refiners, who rank second to cane growers in supplying sugar both in America and worldwide. Federal subsidies and price supports intervened throughout the twentieth century to protect the industry.

Sugar beets are grown primarily in western and midwestern states, with a crop valued in excess of $1 billion annually. Significantly Utah has had no sugar beet industry since the 1980s, although in 2002 its state legislature named the sugar beet Utah's historic state vegetable. The concentrated sweetness of the sugar beet (a good harvest can reach up to 20 percent sugar) prevented its acceptance as a table vegetable in the eighteenth and nineteenth centuries. Amelia Simmons's *American Cookery* (1796) critiques the "white" beet that "has a sickish sweetness, which is disliked by many." More recently it is grown as a specialty vegetable by gardeners whose sweet tooth extends throughout the meal.
[**See also** SUGAR.]

BIBLIOGRAPHY

Arrington, Leonard J. *Beet Sugar in the West: A History of the Utah-Idaho Sugar Company, 1891–1966*. Seattle: University of Washington Press, 1966.

Clauson, Annette L., and Frederic L. Hoff. *Structural and Financial Characteristics of U.S. Sugar Beet Farms*. Washington, DC: U.S. Department of Agriculture, Economic Research Service, 1988.

Schmalz, Charles L. "The Failure of Utah's First Sugar Factory." *Utah Historical Quarterly* 56, no. 1 (Winter 1988): 36–53.

CATHY K. KAUFMAN

Sunfish

The sunfish family (Centrarchidae) is large and includes crappie and bass, but the word "sunfish" generally refers to bluegill (*Lepomis macrochirus*) and redear or shellcracker (*Lepomis microlophus*). Both bluegill and redear are popular sport fishes, and both are farm raised to stock recreational fisheries. There are many regional and colloquial names for sunfish, including paper mouth, silversides, calico bass, white perch, speck, speckled perch, slab, and among Cajuns *sac-a-lait* ("bag of milk"), which describes the white flesh. Sunfish also include pumpkinseeds (*Lepomis gibbosus*) and long-eared sunfish (*Lepomis megalotis*). Sunfish is widely distributed, being found in lakes all over America. Bluegill is a favorite for sportfishers and is a good panfish. Pumpkinseed also is regarded as a good sport fish, but it is generally too small for use as food. To be useful as panfish, sunfish have to weigh two pounds or less. The meat can be fried, baked, or broiled.

SANDRA L. OLIVER

Sunflowers

Agricultural historians cannot agree on where the sunflower, *Helianthus annuus*, originated: Peru, Central America, or what is now the southwestern United States are all candidates. Everyone agrees, however, that the sunflower spread through the New World in pre-Columbian times, reaching what is now the eastern United States before the Spanish landed. It was one of two food plants (the other being its botanical cousin, the Jerusalem artichoke) domesticated by Native Americans in central North America between 3000 and 900 B.C.E..

Indigenes extracted oil by crushing the seeds, boiling them, and skimming off the separated oil; the leftover seed mash formed a high protein cake. Native Americans chewed stems like gum and cooked the petioles, or the immature seed receptacles. Seeds made purple and black dyestuffs, and the brilliant golden petals were (and still are) salad fodder. Thomas Hariot's *A Brief and True Report of the New Found Land of Virginia* (1588) described broths and "breads" made from seeds as well as careful interplanting techniques with maize, beans, and squashes that resulted in enormous yields.

Spanish conquistadores had exported sunflowers to Europe as an ornamental by 1510; the plant eventually reached greatest prominence as the major source of food oil in Russia and eastern Europe. Post-Columbian Americans made comparatively little use of the sunflower, although the 1881 *Household Cyclopedia of General Information* encouraged copying the Native American interplanting techniques to stimulate other crops; the sunflowers themselves were demoted to use as animal fodder and were suggested for home-based oil extraction as a substitute for olive oil.

The sunflower's nutritional profile, high in protein, mono- and polyunsaturated fats, fiber, and certain vitamins and minerals, made it a darling of health food enthusiasts in the later twentieth century. At the same time a relatively small domestic oil industry had started, and sunflower seeds were marketed as a healthy snack and ground into "sunbutter," competing with peanut butter. The brightly named "sunchoke," originally a cross of the sunflower and the Jerusalem artichoke, was commercially unsuccessful; the name has cheerily marketed the Jerusalem artichoke since the late twentieth century.

[See also ARTICHOKES; FATS AND OILS; FLOWERS, EDIBLE; HEALTH FOOD.]

BIBLIOGRAPHY

Couplan, François. *The Encyclopedia of Edible Plants of North America: Nature's Great Feast*. New Canaan, CT: Keats, 1998.

Heiser, Charles B., Jr. *Seeds to Civilization: The Story of Food*. New ed. Cambridge, MA: Harvard University Press, 1990.

CATHY K. KAUFMAN

Supawn

Supawn was a Native American porridge made of cornmeal and water and introduced to European colonists very early. Transliterated by different Europeans in an age when spelling was inconsistent, the name of the dish appeared variably in print as "suppawn," "sepawn," "sipawn," "sepan," "supon," "sepon," "suppaen," "supporne," and "soupaan." Settlers adopted supawn almost universally as a staple, because corn agriculture and milling were particularly reliable and culinary preparation was simple. Among newcomers and those on the frontier, supawn often represented survival.

Europeans varied New World versions of the dish by boiling cornmeal in milk and adding butter, cream, or molasses (depending on economic station) and serving it either hot or cold. There were a few ethnic variations. The English ate cornmeal in the tradition of mush and hasty pudding. The Dutch, who were partial to sour flavors, drowned cornmeal in buttermilk. Supawn was prepared for any meal of the day but was a common supper dish. The eighteenth-century Old Albany Dutch Church customarily rang what was called the "suppawn bell," a signal for supper and bed.

Supawn maintained its central place in changing American cuisine but gradually gave way to new fashions. Patriotic centennial celebrations remembered its original names and role in American history. The dish continues to appear on Native American tables and at powwows.

[See also CORN; DUTCH INFLUENCES ON AMERICAN FOOD; NATIVE AMERICAN FOOD.]

BIBLIOGRAPHY

Parker, A. C. *Iroquois Uses of Maize and Other Food Plants*. Albany: University of the State of New York, 1910. Repr. Ohsweken, Ontario: Iroqrafts, 1983.

JONATHAN REES

Supermarkets, *see Grocery Stores*

Supper, *see Meal Patterns*

Swanson

Swanson, the company whose name is synonymous with TV dinners, began as Jerpe Commission Company, a wholesale grocery firm, in 1899 in Omaha, Nebraska. The founders, Carl A. Swanson, Frank D. Ellison, and John P. Jerpe, specialized in the sale of poultry, eggs, and butter. In 1945 the company, which since 1928 had been owned solely by Swanson, changed its name to Swanson and Sons and began producing a line of canned and frozen chicken and turkey products.

When they took over the business in the early 1950s, Swanson's sons realized that postwar America had changed. The most important difference was that record numbers of women were working outside the home. The brothers, seeing an opportunity, in 1951 began selling easy-to-prepare frozen beef, chicken, and turkey potpies. Their efforts met with instant success.

By 1952 television sets, with their eight-inch, black-and-white screens, were becoming the preferred type of home entertainment, and the Swanson brothers were determined to capitalize on this phenomenon. Inspiration came the next year in the form of 520,000 pounds of surplus post-Thanksgiving turkey, which the company had no room to warehouse. Gerald Thomas, a Swanson executive, had the idea for a frozen prepared meal. He presented the idea, along with an initial sketch of an aluminum tray with three compartments, to the Swanson brothers. In December 1953 Swanson introduced on television the first TV dinner, which had been created by Betty Cronin, director of product development. The ninety-eight-cent dinner, which featured turkey with cornbread stuffing and gravy, sweet potatoes, and peas, created a new food category. The decision to call the meals "TV dinners" was the result of research showing that people were already eating Swanson potpies in front of the television. Fried chicken dinners were introduced in 1955 and were followed soon after by Salisbury steak. Almost as soon as the products were launched, the company was blamed for ruining the family dinner, because the variety allowed each member to reach for a different meal.

Campbell Soup Company acquired Swanson in 1955. Under the Campbell auspices, Swanson grew rapidly. Dessert was added to meals in 1960; a breakfast line was launched in 1969; Hungry-Man dinners debuted in 1973 in a television commercial featuring the athlete Mean Joe Green; the entire line was reworked to accommodate microwave cooking in 1986; Fun Feast dinners intended for children were introduced in 1991; and potato-topped potpies entered the market in 1999.

By the end of the 1990s Campbell had shifted its focus away from frozen foods and moved the Swanson brand to the newly formed Vlasic Foods International, which eventually went bankrupt. In 2001 Pinnacle Foods Corporation bought the Vlasic and Swanson brands out of bankruptcy.

Regardless of ownership, the Swanson TV dinner is such a beloved icon of American food that its aluminum tray was inducted into the Smithsonian Institution—placed alongside the leather jacket worn by Henry Winkler as Fonzie in the popular situation comedy *Happy Days*. Swanson even received a star on the Hollywood Walk of Fame.

[See also CAMPBELL SOUP COMPANY; FROZEN FOOD; TURKEY; TV DINNERS.]

DAVID LEITE

Sweeteners

Sweeteners are plant-derived materials that owe their sweet taste to simple carbohydrates called sugars. Sugars are produced in plants during photosynthesis and serve as the standard currency of chemically stored energy for all living animals and plants. Sucrose,

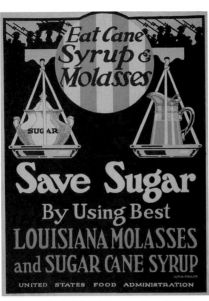

A U.S. Food Administration poster from 1918 advocates the use of molasses instead of sugar.

fructose, and glucose are most predominantly used sweeteners. Sucrose, also known as common sugar or table sugar, is found in sugarcane and sugar beets and is composed of a molecule each of glucose and fructose. Glucose and fructose occur naturally in fruits and vegetables and are the major components of honey.

Sweeteners may be classified as caloric, noncaloric, natural, and artificial. Sugar, corn syrups, honey, molasses, and maple syrup are caloric sweeteners, which upon digestion yield four calories per gram. In addition to sweetening, they help preserve jams and jellies, enhance flavor in various processed foods, such as meats and juices, provide the basis for fermentation and flavor in the production of breads, wines, liquors, and pickles, depress the freezing point of frozen foods, such as ice creams, and contribute to the viscosity of beverages.

Sweeteners in History

The description of sugarcane, syrup, and foods sweetened with sugarcane in the Sanskrit epic of the *Ramayana* (ca. 1200 B.C.E.) is one of the earliest documented references to sweeteners. The technology of making sugar by squeezing sugarcane and boiling the juice down into crystals for later use was developed in India around 500 B.C.E.

Sugarcane and the technique for extracting sweeteners were carried westward from India to Persia by the Persians around the sixth century C.E. and to northern Africa, Syria, and Spain by the Arabs who conquered Persia around 640 C.E. Sugar was introduced to Christian Europe during the twelfth-century Crusades to the Holy Land. Europeans used sugar and honey as flavoring and as medicine. Apothecaries composed "confections" (Latin *conficere*, "to put together") with

sugar as the predominant ingredient or as an additive to mask the taste of other ingredients in the preparation.

Christopher Columbus may have introduced sugarcane to the West Indies in 1493. The Native peoples of North America had used honey and maple tree sap to sweeten their foods. The immigrants taught them to concentrate sap into syrup and introduced a kind of molasses, which they used for baked goods, baked beans, and meats, such as pork and ham, and for producing rum. Molasses was an important sweetener until sugar prices plummeted after World War I, making sugar more economical to use.

One of the greatest innovations in the food industry was the production of the various types of corn syrups, or maltodextrins, and high-fructose corn syrup from cornstarch. A new category of major commercial products emerged and significantly influenced food manufacturing practices and Americans' food consumption pattern. It all began in 1747 with the Prussian chemist Andreas Margraf's demonstration of sugar production from sugar beets (*Beta vulgaris*) and the Frenchman Benjamin Delessert's commercialization of the technology into sugar-beet factories. In 1811 Konstantin Kirchhof laid the foundations of sweetener production using enzymes.

Enzyme technologies made corn syrup production economical, and the production of fructose-based syrups of varying fructose levels became increasingly popular because corn crops, the raw material source, were more predictable than sugarcane or sugar beet crops. HFCS or high-fructose corn syrup was significantly cheaper since fructose is sweeter than sucrose and maltose. HFCS became the sweetener of choice for the food industry in the United States when technological advances allowed for tailoring of sweetness and physical properties of syrups.

Noncaloric Sweeteners

Noncaloric sweeteners include substances—such as saccharin, cyclamate (not on the market since 1970), acesulphame-K, aspartame, sucralose, sorbitol, mannitol, and xylitol—that gained importance as economical and healthy alternatives to sugar in processed foods because they provide sweet taste without contributing any calories. These are generally chemically processed materials and are therefore known as artificial sweeteners.

When it became clear that consuming large amounts of sugar was associated with various health issues, such as dental caries, diabetes, and obesity, science provided a solution in the form of nonsugar and noncaloric sweeteners. The German chemist Constantin Fahlberg discovered saccharin in 1879 and named the new, intensely sweet compound "saccharin" (*saccharum*, Latin for "sugar"). He also developed a process for manufacturing the compound in bulk.

Saccharin consumption increased dramatically during the two world wars, when sugar became scarce. Although numerous studies clearly show that saccharin, in the dosages consumed, does not cause cancer in humans, labels on products with saccharin must carry a statement saying that saccharin has caused cancer in laboratory animals.

Cyclamate was discovered in 1937 by Ludwig Audrieth and Michael Sveda, chemists at the University of Illinois. Cyclamate was subjected to extensive scientific investigations and, despite being declared safe in the mid-1950s, never gained popularity in the United States.

Aspartame, discovered in 1965 by the scientist James Schlatter at G. D. Searle and Company, was approved soon after by the Food and Drug Administration (FDA) for use in foods and beverages that do not undergo heating. Acesulfame-K, although discovered at the same time as aspartame, was approved for use in the United States by the FDA about twenty years later. Sucralose, developed in 1976 from sucrose, has rapidly gained acceptance as the noncaloric sweetener of choice in the United States.

A commercial class of sweeteners called polyols, or sugar alcohols, emerged in the early 2000s. Polyols, such as erythritol, sorbitol, maltitol, isomalt, lactitol, and xylitol, have gained popularity because they contribute fewer calories than sugars, are diabetic-friendly, and do not contribute to dental caries. Polyols are present in fruits, mushrooms, and fermentation-derived foods like wine, soy sauce, and cheese and have been part of the human diet for thousands of years.

Several other new commercial sweeteners are emerging, including plant-derived materials such as stevia, stevioside, agave syrup, Lo Han, mogroside, glycyrrhizin, dihydrochalcones, and thaumatin. These range in sweetness from thirty to three thousand times that of sucrose and have been known to humans since prehistoric times. They are being explored for commercial viability in the early 2000s.

BIBLIOGRAPHY

Mintz, Sidney W. *Sweetness and Power: The Place of Sugar in Modern History.* New York: Viking, 1985.

KANTHA SHELKE

Sweet Potatoes

The sweet potato (*Ipomoea batatas*) is a root that comes in a variety of shapes, sizes, and colors. Its flavor is largely based on starch and sugar. The plant originated in the tropical areas of Central America and northwestern South America. The earliest archaeological evidence of the sweet potato, however, was found in Peru and dates to 2000 B.C.E. Domestication may have occurred as early as 8000 B.C.E.

In pre-Columbian times sweet potatoes were disseminated throughout much of South America, Central America, and the Caribbean. Spanish explorers in the Caribbean ran across them and called them by the Taino name, *batatas*. The Spanish shipped sweet

Harvesting sweet potatoes at Claflin University, Orangeburg, South Carolina, circa 1899.

potatoes back to Europe, where they became a sensation. Sweet potatoes were among the earliest New World foods adopted in Europe. At approximately the same time as the Spanish exploration, Portuguese explorers encountered sweet potatoes in Brazil and transported them to Africa, where they were grown to provision Portuguese ships headed to and from Asia and slave ships headed to the New World. A linguistic imbroglio arose when the Spanish encountered the white potato (*Solanum tuberosa*) in South America in 1529. They called the white potato *batata* and later *patata*, which led to confusion between white potato and sweet potato. The shipping activity among South America and Africa and Europe led to confusion between the sweet potato and the yam (*Dioscorea*), another large tuberous root of which many varieties were native to tropical regions of the Old World. Varieties of sweet potatoes and yams are similar in appearance, and sweet potatoes in the United States are frequently misidentified as yams.

Although sweet potatoes were not cultivated in England as a commercial crop, the British esteemed them in the sixteenth and seventeenth centuries. Sweet potatoes were imported from Spain and Portugal, and they became popular, in large part owing to their purported aphrodisiac qualities, as noted by Shakespeare in *The Merry Wives of Windsor*. In America sweet potatoes were grown extensively in Virginia, Georgia, and the Carolinas, but they were a luxury in the North before 1830.

From a culinary standpoint, sweet potatoes are extremely versatile. They can be boiled, broiled, baked, roasted, fried, stewed, and mashed. The orange and yellow varieties can be eaten raw, for example, by being grated into a salad. Sweet potatoes have been used as an ingredient in pie, bread, and pudding. They can be juiced and made into a drink and can be fermented for use as an alcoholic beverage. In the United States sweet potatoes are served with a variety of foods, and they are favorites at Thanksgiving.

Sweet potatoes are highly nutritious, containing protein, fiber, vitamins A and C, calcium, folic acid, magnesium, and potassium. They are one of the most important root tubers in the world, and they are the sixth principal food crop worldwide. Approximately 85 percent of the world's sweet potato crop is grown in China. In the United States, North Carolina, Louisiana, and California

produce three-fourths of the nation's sweet potato crop.

[**See also** Caribbean Influences on American Food; Potatoes; Thanksgiving.]

BIBLIOGRAPHY

Martin, Franklin W., Ruth M. Ruberte, and Jose L. Herrera. *The Sweet Potato Cookbook*. North Fort Myers, FL: Educational Concerns for Hunger Organization, 1989.

Woolfe, Jennifer A. *Sweet Potato: An Untapped Food Resource*. Cambridge, U.K: Cambridge University Press, 1992.

ANDREW F. SMITH

Sweet Spices

The sweet spices, along with the ginger family, are mostly tropical in origin, and almost all of them are from the Old World. They are primarily used in baking, although they sometimes appear in savory dishes.

The first three are members of the laurel family (Lauraceae). Allspice (*Pimenta dioica*), a New World species, contains several of the essential oils found in cinnamon and cloves. Bay leaves (*Laurus nobilis*) are the only European natives in this category. Technically an herb (since its leaves are used), it is treated like a spice because its warm sweet aroma is derived from a broad range of compounds usually found in tropical spices, like allspice. Cinnamon (*Cinnamomum zeylanicum*) and cassia (*Cinnamomum aromaticum*), the bark of South Asian trees, are used interchangeably, although cassia is hotter and less expensive so is found in more commercial applications.

A cinnamon tree with its flower and fruit from an advertisement for Davis, Sacker & Perkins Importers, Boston, 1878.

Cloves (*Syzygium aromaticum*) are dried flower buds of an evergreen tree of the myrtle family (Myrtaceae), originally from Indonesia. Mace and nutmeg (*Myristica fragrans*), another evergreen tree from Indonesia, is of the nutmeg family (Myristicaceae). Vanilla (*Vanilla planifolia*) "beans" are pods of a tropical vine in the orchid family (Orchidaceae). Like allspice, it is native to the New World tropics.

[**See also** Ginger Family; Prepared Herb and Spice Mixtures.]

BIBLIOGRAPHY

Allen, Gary. *The Herbalist in the Kitchen*. Champain: University of Illinois Press, forthcoming.

Bailey, L. H. *Hortus Third: A Concise Dictionary of Plants Cultivated in the United States and Canada*. New York: Macmillan, 1976.

GARY ALLEN

Swift, Gustavus Franklin

Gustavus Franklin Swift (1839–1903) was the eponymous founder of one of America's largest and best-known meat-processing companies. He is credited with introducing refrigeration to food transportation networks, but his greater importance lay in the organizational concepts and methods he created. Swift was a father of America's modern food-processing and distribution systems.

Born and reared on hardscrabble Cape Cod, Massachusetts, and with little formal education, Swift went to work as a butcher's apprentice at age fourteen. Not long after, he began his own business, buying cattle, butchering them, and selling the meat door-to-door. Over the next twenty years he built a successful wholesale business with James A. Hathaway and operated a modern market in Clinton, Massachusetts. The lessons of frugality and resource management that he learned in these years were the foundations for his future role as America's "dressed beef king."

Swift's main obsession was expansion of business opportunities. Seeing that Chicago had become the meat-processing center of the nation, he moved to that city in 1875. There he hit upon the formula that would change the production of fresh meats. Companies such as Armour and Morris canned and preserved meats, but the nation was hungry for steaks and roasts. At the time fresh beef was shipped on the hoof via rail to the great eastern markets. Swift reasoned that since only 60 percent of the animal would become food, he would slaughter and process meat in Chicago and ship only the high-profit carcasses. The extra animal parts became a profit center for the company, hence his phrase, "now we used all of the hog except his grunt."

To use his facilities economically, Swift had to ship meat year-round and keep it at a stable temperature. During the previous decade, refrigeration systems had been introduced to market facilities and were experimentally used on a railcar by the Chicago packer G. H. Hammond in 1874. After tinkering with several devices, Swift had his

An ad for Chicago's Swift packing plant.

engineer friend Andrew J. Chase build the first successful refrigerated car using ice blocks (mechanical refrigeration came later). Swift and company undersold all the eastern competition, made huge profits, and became the country's leading beef producer by the later 1880s. He then set up processing facilities in Kansas City and St. Joseph's, Missouri, to be even nearer his raw ingredients. Later he turned to mutton and then pork, outstripping all his competition.

Swift's innovations appeared at exactly the same time that new machines were making mass production of meat and other foods possible. Perhaps anticipating Frederick W. Taylor's time and motion studies, Swift developed an efficient "disassembly" line for food animals, with each station along it devoted to one task, such as debristling hogs. Hooked to an overhead traveling belt, the carcasses were processed and fed directly into the waiting boxcars for transportation. Swift also established separate plants for each element of the company, from lard and oleomargarine manufacture to marketing. Each division reported to a central office whose watchword was "efficiency." Swift's organization was the model of the modern factory system. It was this system that Henry Ford observed when visiting Chicago's meat plants and then applied to the manufacture of automobiles.

[See also ARMOUR, PHILIP DANFORTH; BUTCHERING; ICEBOXES; MEAT; SINCLAIR, UPTON; TRANSPORTATION OF FOOD.]

BIBLIOGRAPHY

Wade, Louise Carroll. *Chicago's Pride: The Stockyards, Packingtown, and Environs in the Nineteenth Century.* Urbana: University of Illinois Press, 1987.

BRUCE KRAIG

Switchel

Switchel (also called haymaker's switchel, harvest drink, haymaker's drink, and ginger water) is a beverage usually made with molasses, water, vinegar, and spices (most often ginger) and occasionally with rum. Switchel, thought to be of New England origin, was drunk by fieldworkers to quench their thirst during harvesttime and is frequently mentioned in nineteenth-century accounts of whaling expeditions and merchant ship voyages. Although few recipes for switchel appear in nineteenth-century cookbooks, L. B. Abell included the following recipe in *The Skilful Housewife's Book* (1852):

Harvest Drink—*Mix with five gallons of good water, half a gallon of molasses, one quart of vinegar, and two ounces of powdered ginger. This will make not only a very pleasant beverage, but one highly invigorating and healthful.*

The addition of ginger was thought to have prevented stomach cramps. Recipes for similar refreshing beverages may appear in cookbooks under the name of raspberry (or other fruit) vinegar or raspberry "shrub." The following modern adaptation of the period recipe calls for similar ingredients:

One tablespoon of vinegar (either cider vinegar or raspberry wine vinegar but not distilled white vinegar); one tablespoon of one of the following sweeteners: honey, molasses, maple syrup, or brown or white sugar; and one cup of cool water. Mix thoroughly. Add one-eighth teaspoon of powdered ginger to taste if raspberry vinegar is not used. Do not use a metal container to mix or store the switchel.

[See also CIDER; GINGER ALE; KVASS; PUNCH; RATAFIA; SYLLABUB.]

BIBLIOGRAPHY

Lanzerotti, B. *Parting Glass: An American Book of Drink.* Wheaton, IL: Twin Willows Publishers, 1998.

VIRGINIA MESCHER

Swordfish

Swordfish (family Xiphiidae) were not a significant food fish until the late nineteenth century, though they were apparently harpooned and consumed by people on Nantucket and Martha's Vineyard in the early 1800s; these people also salted the swordfish for trade to the West Indies. In American cookbooks swordfish were virtually ignored until the later 1800s, though the fish appeared in the market. Swordfish has meaty flesh and large bones, which helped it gain popularity, and it is enjoyed grilled and baked.

There is a substantial sport fishery around swordfish and marlin as well, which also has a swordlike bill. Swordfish were killed by harpoon in the early days of the fishery on the East Coast as well as on the West Coast in the early 1900s. Where the swordfish is still pursued, longlines are usually used. The Atlantic sword fishery is managed but is still considered stressed, and many restaurants will not offer swordfish on menus; it also appears on many lists of species to avoid eating. The Pacific sword fishery is considered by some to be stable and healthy, but it is not managed.

SANDRA L. OLIVER

Syllabub

Syllabub was a popular drink in England from the sixteenth century until the mid-nineteenth century. In America the popularity peaked in the eighteenth century, when syllabub was a fashionable evening beverage or dessert served at card parties, ball suppers, and public entertainments. Syllabub was prepared by beating warm milk with sweetened, spiced wine, cider, or ale. The froth that formed was set aside to drain. The resulting clear liquid was poured into glasses, and the froth was placed on top. For dramatic effect, a cow might have been milked into the bowl of sweetened alcohol so that the mixture would froth. When the concoction was left to sit for several hours, a honeycombed curd formed on top. Sometimes a layer of thick fresh cream was poured over the curd, providing a rich drink for country parties and festivals. A solid dessert syllabub was made by reducing the ratio of alcohol and sugar to cream and adding beaten egg white or gelatin. The dessert was flavored with citrus or ginger and eaten with a spoon. The first cookbook to be printed in America (*The Compleat Housewife*, 1727) contained a recipe for everlasting syllabubs that would remain in perfect condition for nine or ten days, although they were at their best after three or four. Syllabub has retained seasonal popularity as an alternative to eggnog, especially in parts of the South, where bourbon, rum, or brandy is substituted for wine or ale. Colonial Williamsburg sells packaged syllabub mix.

[See also CIDER; DESSERTS; EGGNOG; KVASS; PUNCH; RATAFIA; SWITCHEL.]

BIBLIOGRAPHY

David, Elizabeth. *An Omelette and a Glass of Wine.* New York: Lyons and Burford, 1997.

VIRGINIA SCOTT JENKINS

Szathmary, Louis

Louis Szathmary (1919–1996) was once referred to as "a man for all seasonings" (Johnson and Wales). This Hungarian-born chef brought much flavor and color to America's culinary legacy. A pioneer in frozen food technology, Szathmary helped elevate the official status of all U.S. chefs, influenced American fine-dining standards, became one of the first U.S. "celebrity chefs," and established one of the premier culinary archives in the United States.

Born on a cattle car en route from Transylvania to Budapest as his parents fled the onslaught of World War I, Szathmary never stopped moving, at least not when it came to accomplishments. He earned a master's degree in journalism and a doctorate in psychology from the University of Budapest and then was drafted into the Hungarian army during World War II and became an officer. Szathmary immigrated to the United States in 1951. At the time he spoke no English and had only $1.10 in his pocket.

Szathmary took a job as a short-order cook, learned, and kept moving up, soon catering to the rich and famous on the East Coast. Through his catering company, Szathmary began developing numerous dishes for companies pioneering the field of frozen prepared entrees. In 1959 Szathmary moved to Chicago to work for Armour and Company, where he developed a number of frozen food lines for Armour and for many other companies, including Stouffer. The frozen spinach soufflé Szathmary created for Stouffer became a classic. Szathmary also became increasingly involved in the tremendous changes taking place in food-service technology in the 1950s, such as freeze-drying and boil-in bags. Some of the food the astronauts took into space had Szathmary's stamp on it through his work with the U.S. National Aeronautics and Space Administration (NASA).

Szathmary began to see his real niche as a restaurateur. In 1963, with his wife and partner Sadako Tanino, Szathmary opened The Bakery on the near north side of Chicago. In the first year, more than two hundred articles were written about The Bakery. Many restaurant critics across the nation gave rave reviews. Of those who did not, Szathmary observed, "They don't know shiitake from shinola" (Warner, "Remembering Chef Louis"). Guests came from Tokyo, Japan, Sydney, Australia, New York, and Montreal. Szathmary hosted almost every celebrity who visited Chicago. The chef Charlie Trotter celebrated his high

school prom night at The Bakery. Trotter was so overcome by the sight of Szathmary's grand entrance that he knew at that moment he too would be a chef one day. "It was a decisive moment for me," Trotter recalled (Warner, "Remembering Chef Louis").

When Szathmary opened The Bakery, the standard for fine dining in Chicago was typically a meal of shrimp cocktail, iceberg lettuce with thousand island dressing, prime rib of beef, asparagus with hollandaise sauce, and baked Alaska. Szathmary, however, served such "exotic" fare as grated celery root salad, *paprikás csirke* (also called chicken *paprikash*) drizzled with sour cream, and his signature dish, beef Wellington with Cumberland sauce. Desserts included mocha pecan torte laced with rum and filled with apricot preserves and enrobed in butter-rich icing and eclairs puffed with banana and whipped cream filling and anointed with bourbon-scented chocolate sauce. Szathmary called his cuisine continental with American undertones and soon had diners waiting weeks for reservations.

It mattered little to the public that the 117-seat restaurant was in an old and rickety building in a then-seedy neighborhood, that Szathmary had filled his three dining rooms with secondhand silverware and furniture he described as "early restaurant and late Salvation Army," (Warner, "Remembering Chef Louis") or that some of the food was being prepared in full view on a table in one of the dining rooms because the kitchen was not large enough. All diners saw were the cheery red-and-white candy-striped awning outside, the clean white tablecloths, the spotless wooden floors, and Szathmary's family greeting and seating them.

The showstopper at The Bakery was the entrance of Chef Louis. All eyes turned to the large mustachioed figure who would suddenly stride through the swinging kitchen door. Looking like Santa Claus with a towering chef's toque, Szathmary would visit each table, becoming one of the first chefs in America to "work" the dining room of his restaurant and interact with customers. "I treat everyone like a king I know," he said (Warner, "Remembering Chef Louis"). Szathmary was one of the first chef food personalities, "long before Alice Waters and Wolgang Puck," wrote the former *Chicago Sun-Times* food editor Bev Bennett in her obituary of Chef Louis. "His real contribution was in developing the chef as a cult figure," Bennett continued.

Szathmary wrote seven cookbooks. His first one, *The Chef's Secret* (1972), made the *Time* magazine best seller list for nonfiction. Szathmary made guest appearances on more than 150 network and local television shows across the United States and made more than 1,000 appearances on radio shows. Szathmary also appeared in television commercials and magazine advertisements for Sears, Lipton Tea, Christian Dior, and Jim Beam. For more than ten years he wrote a food column for the *Chicago Sun-Times*. The "Chef Louis" column he wrote for a wire service appeared in more than one hundred newspapers. Szathmary wrote more than five hundred articles on food service for scientific and educational journals. He kept three secretaries busy full time answering fans' cooking questions and coordinating his touring schedule. Szathmary lectured at hotel schools throughout the United States. Although he downplayed his involvement in the evolution of the profession of chef, Szathmary was one of several industry figures who in the late 1970s successfully petitioned the U.S. Department of Labor to elevate "executive chef" in the *Dictionary of Occupational Titles* from the services category to the professional, technical, and managerial occupations category. No longer would executive chefs be listed with maids and butlers.

Szathmary kept thirty-one apartment rooms upstairs of The Bakery filled with his historical and eclectic collection of food books. When he retired in 1989, Szathmary donated thirty thousand of the books to establish the Culinary Archives and Museum at Johnson and Wales University in Providence, Rhode Island. The collection also included 400,000 culinary items, including a baker's ring found on a skeleton in the ruins of Pompeii and presidential papers about entertaining in the White House. Szathmary was named chef laureate at the university and commuted there regularly until his death at age seventy-seven. The museum is referred to as the "Smithsonian" of food archives.

[**See also** CELEBRITY CHEFS; FREEZE-DRYING; FROZEN FOOD; RESTAURANT CRITICS AND FOOD COLUMNISTS; RESTAURANTS; SPACE FOOD; TROTTER, CHARLIE.]

BIBLIOGRAPHY

Clarke, Paul. "Third Millennium Chefs: A Conversation with Chef Louis Szathmary." *Chef*, January 1996.

SCOTT WARNER

T

Tacos

In Mexico the word "taco," which means a bite or snack, came to refer to a particular genre of edibles—a tortilla wrapped or folded around a filling, the whole meant to be eaten with the hands. Standard taco fillings include beef (shredded or ground), chicken, pork, sausage, eggs, cheese, roasted peppers, and refried beans, singly or in combination, seasoned with a variety of sauces. (The traditional Mexican taco is made with a soft, fresh corn tortilla; "hard shell" tacos, made with tortillas fried in a basket to give them a sturdy "U" shape, are a creation of Mexican restaurants in the United States.) The first known English-language taco recipes appeared in California cookbooks beginning in 1914.

In American cookbooks, the names of taco recipes often refer to their "hometowns." For instance, Puebla-style tacos are filled with sausages, eggs, tomatoes, onions, peppers, and cream cheese; San Cristobal tacos, served as a dessert, are filled with eggs, flour, sugar, and butter. Other taco recipes are identified by their fillings. *Tacos de rajas* contain strips of roasted sweet peppers. Seafood tacos originated in coastal Mexico and were transplanted first to California and later throughout the Southwest.

Until the 1960s tacos were mainly served in California and the Southwest at small roadside taco stands run by Mexican Americans. This changed when Glen Bell launched the first Mexican American fast food franchise in 1962 in Downey, California, Taco Bell had to overcome vast distrust and prejudice among many American consumers against Mexican restaurants. The new chain's advertising emphasized that these were American restaurants that just happened to serve Mexican-style food. Taco Bell assured the public that its tacos and other offerings were no more spicy or "foreign" than hamburgers.

While these "Mexican" foods were new to many Americans, their ingredients were not. Tacos, for instance, were similar enough to hamburgers (both made with ground beef, cheese, tomatoes, lettuce, and sauce) to be easily accepted. The main difference was the tortilla, which customers could comprehend as a substitute for the hamburger bun.

Other fast food chains tried to imitate Taco Bell, and few strayed far from this traditional American combination. Although it took liberties with the original recipes, Taco Bell helped popularize tacos and other foods based on Mexican culinary traditions in the United States.

BIBLIOGRAPHY

Pilcher, Jeffrey M. *¡Que Vivan los Tamales! Food and the Making of Mexican Identity*. Albuquerque: University of New Mexico Press, 1998.

Smith, Andrew F. "Tacos, Enchiladas, and Refried Beans: The Invention of Mexican-American Cookery," in Mary Wallace Kelsey and ZoeAnn Holmes, eds., *Cultural and Historical Aspects of Foods*. Corvallis: Oregon State University, 1999. pp. 183–203.

ANDREW F. SMITH

Taco Bell

During the early 1950s few Americans outside California and the Southwest knew what a taco was. In the early twenty-first century Mexican American food is one of America's fastest-growing cuisines. Although there are many reasons for this change, one was the Taco Bell fast food chain launched by Glenn Bell.

Bell operated a one-man hamburger and hot dog stand in San Bernardino, California, but he liked eating Mexican take-out food. Taco stands dotted the Southern California landscape, but none offered fast food. Bell developed ways to improve the efficiency of preparation of Mexican food. At the time taco shells were made by frying soft tortillas for a few minutes. Bell invented a prefabricated hard taco shell, which did not have to be fried, thus saving time on each order. Bell also developed procedures for accelerating service.

Bell decided to test his new ideas. Bell opened the Taco Tia restaurant in 1954 in San Bernardino, California, the same year and the same city in which Richard and Maurice McDonald opened their revolutionary fast food establishment. Like the McDonald brothers, Bell quickly opened more restaurants in the surrounding area. Bell sold his interest in Taco Tia, and with new partners launched another chain, El Taco. The first outlet was opened in 1958 in Long Beach, California.

In 1962 Bell sold his share in El Taco to his partners and opened the first Taco Bell in Downey, California. The menu consisted mainly of tacos and burritos plus beverages. This small outlet was quickly followed by eight stores in the Long Beach, Paramount, and Los Angeles areas. These establishments generated $50,000 per year, and Bell decided to franchise the operation. The resulting Taco Bell chain used the symbol of a sleeping Mexican sitting under a sombrero, and the buildings had a California mission style.

By 1978 Taco Bell had 868 restaurants, which specialized in selling tacos, burritos, and a few other food items. Glen Bell sold the company to PepsiCo, and management was placed in the hands of John Martin, who had worked for several fast food companies. Martin made Taco Bell's Mexican-style dishes popular throughout the United States by means of heavy discounting and value meals, which combined foods and drinks for cost savings. By 1980 Taco Bell had 1,333 outlets and was rapidly expanding. One reason for the expansion was the continuing introduction of new products, such as fajitas, wraps, gorditas, and chalupas.

Taco Bell has had both success and failure in its promotional efforts. The original sleepy Mexican symbol was thought to be a negative stereotype, and it was immediately replaced by a mission bell when PepsiCo took over. On the success side were commercials that starred a talking Chihuahua, who squealed "*Yo quiero* Taco Bell!"

Taco Bell is the leading Mexican-style quick-service restaurant chain in the United States, with more than $4.9 billion in system-wide sales. Taco Bell serves more than 55 million consumers each week in 6,400 restaurants in the United States. In 1997 Taco Bell was spun off from PepsiCo and became a division of Yum! Brands, Inc., which also owns KFC, Pizza Hut, Long John Silver's, and A&W restaurants.

[**See also** ADVERTISING; FAST FOOD; MEXICAN AMERICAN FOOD; TACOS; TAKE-OUT FOOD.]

BIBLIOGRAPHY

Baldwin, Debra Lee. *Taco Titan: The Glen Bell Story*. Arlington, TX.: Summit, 1999.

Smith, Andrew F. "Tacos, Enchiladas, and Refried Beans: The Invention of Mexican-American Cookery." In *Cultural and Historical Aspects of Foods*, ed. Mary Wallace Kelsey and ZoeAnn Holmes. Corvallis: Oregon State University Press, 1999.

ANDREW F. SMITH

Taffy

Taffy is a chewy candy made with sugar, molasses or corn syrup, butter, and assorted flavorings. Unlike its British cousin toffee, which is allowed to set before being cut into pieces, American taffy is stretched, by hand or by machine, so that it aerates and assumes a lighter color and more supple consistency.

During the first half of the nineteenth century, taffy appeared in home kitchens and at fairs in the eastern and midwestern states. By the middle of the century the taffy pull, in which young people gathered with buttered hands to tug ropes of homemade candy, was a popular pastime and courtship ritual. In the 1880s the competing entrepreneurs Joseph Fralinger and Enoch James began packaging saltwater taffy as a souvenir for tourists in the burgeoning seaside resort of Atlantic City, New Jersey, and it quickly caught on in waterfront destinations around the country. Fralinger's and James's companies have since merged but maintain their distinct recipes, in which seawater never was an ingredient.

While saltwater taffy remains a nostalgia item marketed to adults, the candy industry continues to appeal to children with square or bar-shaped chews in bright colors and intense fruit and sour flavors. Among the most popular brands of this type are Perfetti Van Melle's Airheads and Nestle's Laffy Taffy and Tangy Taffy.

BETH KRACKLAUER

Taffy, Saltwater, *see Saltwater Taffy*

Tailgate Picnics

Tailgate picnics are meals served out of doors close to an automobile. A car's tailgate—or rear door—need not be used to assemble a tailgate picnic. The term refers to a form of dining that has followed the evolution of the automotive industry.

Tailgate picnics became popular in the United Kingdom around 1919 as a result of the rise of "woodies," wood-paneled cars and small trucks designed and manufactured to conserve steel, a valuable commodity for the production of war materials. Many of the earliest woodies came equipped with a small trailer, commonly referred to as a "teardrop" because of its elliptical shape. These lightweight wooden trailers contained all of the equipment necessary to create thrifty and savory meals along the roadside: a gas or charcoal stove, cold-storage containers, a folding table, and sometimes chairs.

In the United States woodies were used primarily as service vehicles for lodges, clubs, and inns. Before World War II these vehicles were status symbols among the wealthy. By the 1930s, with the improvement of roads and a surge in automobile travel, Americans embraced woodies and teardrops as a means of affordable travel. By the late 1940s and early 1950s, tailgate picnics enjoyed even greater popularity as parents creating a postwar baby boom searched for affordable family entertainment and leisure activities. With the advent of motel chains during the 1960s, tailgating began to decline. A new generation of enthusiasts and nostalgic baby boomers, however, has revived this form of dining and entertainment.

The cultural, ethnic, and regional culinary palate of America can be found in tailgate picnics throughout the United States: in the parking lots of large sports arenas before sporting events or rock concerts, along beachfronts, in national parks, at highway rest stops, and at antique fairs where old woodies are showcased. Tailgate picnics may have reached their culinary apex with the development of state-of-the-art portable gas stoves and cooling facilities that make it possible to prepare dishes that represent the diversity of the American palate, such as sausage and peppers, chili, barbecued spare ribs, and sauerbraten.

[See also HISTORICAL OVERVIEW; WORLD WAR II TO THE EARLY 1960s; PICNICS.]

JANE C. OTTO

Take-Out Foods

The term "take-out" describes both a style of eating and a growing list of prepared foods that consumers purchase from a restaurant or food stand and eat in another location. Delivery format, packaging, and types of food vary greatly, ranging from hamburgers to expensive gourmet fare, but all may be categorized as take-out because of this off-premise consumption. In the United States take-out food is often viewed as synonymous with fast food. Fast food, however, is not always eaten on a take-out basis; fast food restaurants often provide an on-site dining area for their patrons. Other terms for take-out food include "carryout" and "take-home" food. This take-out style of eating, marketed by American restaurant chains, had become popular throughout the world by the late twentieth century.

The concept of take-out food and the practice of buying prepared foods for consumption elsewhere date to early civilization. Roadside stands and food stalls in busy urban markets were commonplace in ancient Greece and Rome, providing hungry travelers and workers with quick and inexpensive food items. Almost every culture in every era has had its version of take-out foods, which were often popular yet mundane types of foods. Notable among these foods was the famed British fish and chips, deep-fried then wrapped in old newsprint for takeout.

Urban industrial workers in nineteenth-century America further popularized take-out foods. Food vendors sold various sausages and stews from carts outside factory gates, catering to workers with little time or money. Many of these food vendors grew their businesses into neighborhood diners, serving the workers on premises or with take-out items. Fast food hamburger restaurants became a specialized variation of these urban diners. Beginning with the White Castle system, founded in Wichita, Kansas, in 1921, hamburger restaurants usually offered a few stools for on-premises seating but sold most of their food on a take-out basis. White Castle even adopted the slogan, "Buy 'em by the sack," encouraging the purchase of a take-out bag of ten hamburgers. White Castle devised insulated paper bags for keeping the food warm. The competing chains White Tower and Steak n Shake followed the White Castle approach, advertising to "Buy 'em by the bag" and "TakeHomaSak." Serving take-out food proved successful for restaurateurs, who could provide greater convenience to customers and sell a larger volume of food than their dining areas could accommodate.

In many urban areas ethnic Italian and Chinese restaurants competed with early hamburger outlets for take-out customers. Small storefront pizzerias and "chow chow houses" sold inexpensive pizzas and Americanized Chinese foods on a primarily take-out basis. Using broad, flat white cardboard boxes for pizzas and small, waxy paper cartons for chow mein and chop suey, these ethnic restaurants standardized distinctive take-out packaging that became synonymous with their foods. Although popular in city neighborhoods, ethnic restaurants long composed only a small share of the take-out food market.

Automobiles revolutionized the take-out food industry, requiring larger-volume production and specialized delivery systems. Drive-in restaurants made early accommodations for patrons by offering carhop service, servers bringing meals directly to the cars of diners. Although they served car patrons foods often associated with take-out restaurants, drive-ins encouraged on-premise consumption, albeit in their parking areas. Closer to true take-out format was the walk-up window featured by the burgeoning franchised hamburger chains of the late 1950s and early 1960s. Built at the crossroads of busy suburban thoroughfares, McDonald's and Burger King first sold their hamburgers, milkshakes, and french fries to walk-up customers. Because dining areas were not provided, the explicit message from fast food purveyors was that the sale of the food would be the only service given. Burger King stores were emblazoned with the words "Self Service." Customers drove to the restaurants, walked up to the front service window, bought their food, and then drove away. This format of walk-up window service of strictly take-out hamburgers was the norm for the fast food industry for much of the 1960s.

By the end of the 1960s fast food restaurants began offering dining areas to customers. Although these dining areas were an alternative to eating the food off premises, fast food companies also began selling food from convenient drive-through windows. Fast food restaurants had experimented with drive-up service off and on since the 1920s, constantly searching for better and faster ways to serve customers. The drive-up format did not become a fast food industry standard until the late 1960s, when most of the major chains adopted it. In 1969 Wendy's built its first restaurants complete with car-service windows and special lanes for motoring customers.

The late 1960s also brought advances in take-out food packaging. Earlier take-out fast food was usually wrapped in waxed paper or light foil and then placed in a paper bag. When the technology became available, restaurants began packaging take-out foods in plastic foam cartons. Plastic foam packaging retained heat well and protected items from being crushed when stacked in bags. Plastic foam continued to be the favored type of take-out packaging for more than two decades, until environmental activists successfully pressured restaurant chains first to recycle the plastic and then to use more environmentally friendly paper wrappings.

Take-out foods became considerably more diverse during the 1960s and 1970s. Tacos, roast beef sandwiches, gyros, chicken, and fish joined hamburgers, pizza, and Chinese carryout food as favorite American take-out offerings. Modern take-out foods extend even farther beyond the fast food hamburger industry, encompassing a variety of ethnic, heartland, and gourmet fare. Pizzerias and Chinese restaurants became mainstream and suburban while selling much of their food for off-premise consumption. In the 1980s and 1990s national chains such as Boston Market featured complete "home-cooked" entrées, side dishes, and desserts on a take-out basis. Many large specialty markets and grocery stores sell hot, prepared meats and complete meals on a take-out basis.

[**See also** Burger King; Chinese American Food; Diners; Drive Ins; Ethnic Foods; Fast Food; McDonald's; Packaging; Pizza; Pizza Hut; Pizzerias; Street Vendors; Wendy's.]

BIBLIOGRAPHY

Belasco, Warren, and Philip Scranton, eds. *Food Nations: Selling Taste in Consumer Societies*. New York: Routledge, 2001.

DAVID HOGAN

Tamale Pie

Tamale Pie is a casserole or savory pie with the ingredients of a tamale rearranged for easy assembly, baking, and eating. Into a cornmeal "crust" goes meat or a meat stew, cheese, some chili powder or other Mexican seasonings, and possibly tomatoes, beans, or salsa. And there may be a top crust. Because of the ingredients and flavor, tamale pie is thought of in the United States as "Mexican food," even though it has never been popular among Mexican Americans, who value the collective labor and festival abundance of traditional Mexican tamales.

Tamale pie was invented around the beginning of the twentieth century and by the teens was widely taught in high school home economics classes. At least one World War I cookbook includes it as a substitute for saving wheat. An early recipe contributed to the 1899 *The Capitol Cook Book* (Austin, Texas) is a potpie with a wheat-flour crust on top. But by 1905, *The* [Los Angeles] *Times Cook Book No. 2* had the now-classic casserole with cornmeal crusts above and below. The Los Angeles contributor describes it as "better than tamales. Improves by warming over the second or third day." A thick bottom crust of cornmeal and lard became standard by the teens. The dish persists to the present day in contributed cookbooks, especially in California.

MARK H. ZANGER

Tamales

Tamales originated in Central America in pre-Columbian times and have remained popular ever since. They consist of a filling, such as shredded beef, pork, chicken, turkey, vegetables, or fruit, encased in a handful of cornmeal dough that is then wrapped in a cornhusk or banana leaf and boiled or steamed. Tamales are usually served with salsa and beans.

Tamales were an important part of the Aztec diet, and Spanish and Mexican colonists introduced this ancient delicacy into Texas, California, and the Southwest beginning in the late seventeenth century. By the 1890s Mexican cookery had penetrated as far north as Chicago and New York City, where "Tamaleros" plied the streets, calling "Fresh hot tamales!" By the early twentieth century, canned tamales were available in the United States.

The traditional recipe for tamales, in which the dough is wrapped in leaves, may have been daunting to U.S. cooks, thus the invention of tamale-like foods in America's beloved casserole form. Tamale pies, for instance, substituted simple layering for the more labor-intensive technique: a layer of cornmeal mush, then cooked chicken, pork, or beef, a chili-spiked tomato sauce, and another layer of cornmeal mush, which baked into a thick top crust. The high point of tamale pie and tamale loaf cookery may have been achieved in 1950s with the publication of nineteen recipes in Willow Borba's *Loyalty Cook Book: Native Daughters of the Golden West* (1956).

Mexican American fast food chains introduced tamales to a broader cross section of Americans in the late twentieth century. The popularity of Mexican restaurants in the United States has made them fairly standard fare, although they remain most popular in places with substantial Mexican American populations.

BIBLIOGRAPHY

Pilcher, Jeffrey M. *¡Que Vivan los Tamales! Food and the Making of Mexican Identity*. Albuquerque: University of New Mexico, 1998.

Smith, Andrew F. "Tacos, Enchiladas, and Refried Beans: The Invention of Mexican-American Cookery." In *Cultural and Historical Aspects of Foods*, ed. Mary Wallace Kelsey and ZoeAnn Holmes, 183–203. Corvallis: Oregon State University, 1999.

ANDREW F. SMITH

Tang

Tang, made by General Foods, is a sweetened drink powder artificially colored and flavored orange. It is one of America's most celebrated chemically created foods. Tang is almost synonymous with space travel. Tang went to space on the Gemini and Apollo missions. The mix was delivered to the astronauts in silver pouches. When water was added, the pouches yielded a sweet, slightly tangy, orange-flavored drink that provided an entire day's worth of vitamin C. By the first Gemini flight in 1965, Tang had been languishing on supermarket shelves for six years. Then General Foods dubbed it "the drink of the astronauts," and the new Tang, with a prominent picture of a launchpad on the outside of the canister, soon was rocketing upward in sales and consumption. General Foods also marketed the newly popular Tang as an instant, nutritious, and drinkable breakfast. Children influenced by television demanded the sugary drink, and parents, believing it was healthful, bought it. At the peak of Tang's popularity in the 1960s and 1970s, American households consumed the "instant breakfast" on a regular basis. Sales of Tang declined after the novelty of human travel in space subsided. In 1998 Tang received a much-needed boost in popularity when John Glenn, the first person to orbit Earth and the first human to eat in space, insisted on taking the powder with him on his return to space on the shuttle *Discovery*.

[**See also** Breakfast Drinks; Breakfast Foods; General Foods; Space Food.]

JEAN TANG

Tastee-Freez

In 1950 Leo Maranz invented a small freezer to make soft serve ice cream. He approached Harry Axene, who had previously helped franchise Dairy Queen, and they formed a new Chicago-based chain, which they named Tastee-Freez. The company sold its freezers at cost to franchisees and made its profits on the sale of the ice cream mix. In addition to soft serve ice cream, Tastee-Freez introduced other foods, such as its Big Tee Burgers. By 1956 the chain had 1,500 outlets.

One early finance executive was Harry Sonneborn, who gained a great deal of experience in franchising while working with Tastee-Freez. Later Sonneborn teamed up with Ray Kroc, and many consider Sonneborn to be the cofounder of the McDonald's chain.

In 1982 the DeNovo Corporation of Utica, Michigan, bought the Tastee-Freez brand and launched a program of store modernization. The majority of franchises serve a complete menu of fast food—breakfast, lunch, and dinner. In 2003 Tastee-Freez became a part of Galardi Group, Inc., of Newport Beach, California, which also owns the hot dog chain Wienerschnitzel. It has about ninety-five outlets in twenty-two states nationwide and two in Panama. In addition Tastee-Freez desserts are now served in many Wienerschnitzel outlets.

BIBLIOGRAPHY

Funderburg, Anne Cooper. *Chocolate, Strawberry, and Vanilla: A History of American Ice Cream*. Bowling Green, OH: Bowling Green State University Popular Press, 1995.

ANDREW F. SMITH

Tastykake

The name Tastykake is synonymous with individually wrapped baked snack cakes, pies, and donuts produced in the Philadelphia area. The Tastykake was born in 1914 when Phillip J. Bauer, a baker, and

Herbert T. Morris, an egg salesman, decided to join forces and sell individual prepackaged cakes made from fresh and natural ingredients. As samples were prepared, Mrs. Morris was attributed to describing the cakes as "tasty" and thus the unique name Tastykake and Tasty Baking Company. On the first day of operation in 1914, the bakery produced 100 cakes, and Morris sold $28 worth the first day at ten cents a cake. By the end of 1914, gross sales were $300,000.

Chocolate Junior, an iced cake slice, was the first new product developed; then electric ovens were added for cupcakes. By 1918 sales reached $1 million. With the introduction of Butterscotch Krimpets, a cake iced with creamy butterscotch, in 1927, sales increased to $6 million. Krimpets and cupcakes were the two best sellers at two packs for a nickel. Individual handheld pies were introduced to the market in 1930. The first pie was apple, then peach, then lemon and blueberry, and now there are thirteen different pies with the newest additions, Tasty Grahams Pudding Pies. Donut making began in 1985 with Premium large, mini donuts, and donut holes. The most popular of the product line is Kandy Kakes, cakes topped with creamy peanut butter and covered with a chocolate candy shell. The newest of the product line Tastykake Sensables has been the ninety-year-old company's response to the carbohydrate revolt with a sugar free, low net carbohydrate product. In September 2004 Tastykakes received the highest kosher designation and became certified kosher by the Orthodox Union (OU). Now the over one hundred products under the Tastykake brand name can display the OU symbol.

SUSAN MCLELLAN PLAISTED

Taverns

Taverns were an integral and favored part of British and Dutch culture. Samuel Johnson, the eighteenth-century English author and lexicographer, declared, "There is nothing which has yet been contrived by man, by which so much happiness is produced, as by a good tavern or inn." In the seventeenth century places that sold intoxicating liquors were called "ordinaries," "taverns," "inns," or "public houses." In 1656 the General Court of Massachusetts made towns liable to a fine for not operating an ordinary. Taverns were frequently located close to the meetinghouse so the congregation could warm and refresh themselves after long services. The terms "tavern," "inn," and "ordinary" did not mean the same thing throughout the colonies. In New England and New York "tavern" was usually used, in Pennsylvania "inn" was more common, and in the South "ordinary" was the general term. Small establishments that did not offer lodging, stable, or other services but sold only alcohol were called tippling-houses or petty ordinaries.

In 1714 Boston had a population of ten thousand and supported thirty-four taverns. As the population grew during the eighteenth century and people moved west, there was an enormous increase in turnpikes and stagecoach routes. This growth resulted in an increase in the number of inns and taverns along every major road. By 1809 there were 265 taverns in Albany, New York, alone.

Taverns not only served travelers as places for eating, sleeping, and pasturing horses but also served communities as central meeting places. The tavern was the town's post office—a center for receiving and passing on news. Before and during the Revolution it was in taverns that the political future of the colonies was debated. In the absence of a courthouse, a tavern was where the court met and town selectman came together to regulate the community. Taverns were the first stop for traveling musicians, actors, animal acts, and magicians. If a tavern had a hall or large room, it was used for balls, assemblies, and dancing. During the Revolution taverns were used for military trials, prisons, hospitals, and officers' quarters. Numerous existing taverns from Washington, D.C., to Maine justly claim that "Washington slept here!"

During the Revolutionary War many tavern keepers in Manhattan were Tories, who controlled this strategic location. The signs hanging in front of taverns declared the keepers' allegiance: The Sign of Lord Cornwallis, The King's Arms, and The Prince of Wales. In Boston the names of the taverns were less political: the Punch Bowl, the Green Dragon, and the Golden Ball.

Taverns were everywhere in colonial America because they filled the needs that hotels, motels, bars, lounges, restaurants, and clubs filled later. Taverns were an integral part of the social fabric of both cities and towns, and they dotted the rural landscape wherever a change of stagecoach horses was necessary, such as at highway junctions or ferry landings. Many seventeenth- and eighteenth-century taverns have been converted into private homes and bed and breakfast inns or have been relocated to historical sites, such as Old Sturbridge Village in Massachusetts. The taverns at Williamsburg, Virginia, Fraunces Tavern Museum in New York City, and the City Tavern in Philadelphia are open to the public. The 1640 Hart House Restaurant in Ipswich, Massachusetts, may be the oldest structure in America that has a tavern on the premises.
[See also BEER HALLS; BOARDINGHOUSES; ROADHOUSES; SALOONS.]

BIBLIOGRAPHY

Batterberry, Michael, and Ariane Batterberry. On the Town in New York. New York: Routledge, 1999.
Larkin, Jack. The New England Country Tavern. Sturbridge, MA: Old Sturbridge, 2000.
Rice, Kym S. Early American Taverns: For the Entertainment of Friends and Strangers. Chicago: Regnery Gateway. 1983.

JOSEPH M. CARLIN

Tea

Tea has a dual significance as both a beverage and a social occasion. Dutch colonists in New Amsterdam introduced it to America in the 1650s. By the 1750s tea drinking was established among the wealthy, gradually spreading to households of modest means. After the British imposed duties on tea in the 1760s and 1770s, boycotts organized against it, however, after the Revolution it resumed in popularity. Until the 1820s, when coffee drinking grew, tea remained the most popular hot beverage.

All tea is grown from an evergreen of the camellia family (Camellia sinensis). The three basic kinds of tea—green, oolong, and black—result from the degree of fermentation the leaves undergo after picking. Green is unfermented, oolong is partially fermented, and black is fully fermented. The tea tree will grow in any nonarid climate, but it flourishes best in warm, wet environments. Historically China and Japan produced mostly green tea, Formosa (now Taiwan) produced mostly oolong, and India, Ceylon (now Sri Lanka), Java, Sumatra, and a few other countries produced mostly black tea. Most of the black tea imported into the United States in the early twenty-first century comes from Argentina. There have been several small-scale experiments in tea growing in the United States.

Although black tea was available in the colonial period, green tea from China dominated the American market then and up until the twentieth century. Japanese green tea came onto the American market during the Civil War and Formosa oolong shortly thereafter. Less expensive black teas grown by the British on large estates in India and Ceylon were introduced at the World's Columbian Exposition in Chicago in 1893. By 1930 green tea from China had fallen to 8 percent of tea importations. Although health concerns have renewed interest in green tea, black tea holds about 95 percent of the market.

Until the 1890s teas were marketed unblended, just as they came from Asian tea gardens. As packaged brand-name black teas became popular, teas of varying quality and flavor were blended to produce a distinctive, uniform, and profitable product. The widely advertised name "orange pekoe," found on packaged black teas in America, took on an aura of high quality even though orange pekoe refers only to the size and shape of tea leaves, and teas of this grade can run the gamut of cup quality.

Iced tea accounts for about 80 percent of tea consumed in the United States. The custom of drinking tea with ice dates back at least to the 1860s. By the 1870s it was

Publicity booklet for the Tea Room Institute of the Lewis Hotel Training Schools, Washington, D.C., early 1920s.

Tea drinking has always been full of ceremony, much of it requiring the careful handling of delicate and expensive tea wares. Chinese tea ware was popular in the colonies. A full tea set around 1790 contained a teapot, twelve cups without handles, twelve saucers, a cream jug, a sugar bowl, and a slop bowl for pouring out dregs before refilling a cup. Until prices fell and tea was stored in tin canisters, precious tea was kept fresh in airtight caddies made of fine wood, china, or silver.

Evening and afternoon tea parties in private homes or public halls were fashionable social affairs during the late eighteenth century and throughout the following century. Often women organized tea parties to raise funds for their churches or charities or for restoration of patriotic properties such as Mount Vernon.

Despite the propriety associated with tea, tea parties have historically been occasions in which participants relaxed, traded gossip, and escaped the formalities of dinner parties. Like picnics, tea parties represented a break in ordinary routines and conventions. Small collapsible tea tables could be set up anywhere with ease, permitting tea gatherings to take place before parlor fireplaces, on porches, and in gardens.

In the early twentieth century the afternoon tea custom spread to hotels, department stores, and small tearooms. Tearooms, many run by women, peaked in popularity in the 1920s, a decade in which the national outlawing of alcoholic beverages stimulated both tea and coffee drinking in public eating places. The Depression and the end of Prohibition in the 1930s dampened the tearoom business, but in the 1990s tearooms and tea drinking experienced a revival.

[**See also** CHINESE AMERICAN FOOD; COFFEE; PREPARED HERB AND SPICE MIXTURES; JAPANESE AMERICAN FOOD; PROHIBITION.]

BIBLIOGRAPHY

Hooker, Richard J. *Food and Drink in America: A History.* Indianapolis, IN: Bobbs-Merrill, 1981.

Whitaker, Jan. *Tea at the Blue Lantern Inn: A Social History of the Tea Room Craze in America.* New York: St. Martin's, 2002.

Williams, Susan. *Savory Suppers and Fashionable Feasts. Dining in Victorian America.* New York: Pantheon Books, 1985.

JAN WHITAKER

served in hotels and on railroads. Especially popular in hotter parts of the country, it has recently become a year-round beverage sold in cans and bottles.

From colonial days, sugar has been the most important addition to tea, whether hot or cold. Two teaspoons to each cup was considered a restaurant industry standard in the 1890s when inexpensive granulated white sugar became available. By the 1940s over two-thirds of all tea was drunk with sugar. Milk and cream have been added to hot tea throughout the centuries, but in the eight-eenth century cream was preferred. Lemon was not used much until later in the nineteenth century, when transcontinental railroads made citrus fruit affordable.

Food served with tea is usually lighter than that at mealtimes. Eighteenth-century selections could include cold meats, nuts, preserved fruits, candies, and cakes. In the succeeding century salads and dainty sandwiches appeared on tea tables. In New England, where "tea" was another word for supper, the repast included less meat and fewer items than the midday dinner.

Temperance

Temperance was a movement combining social, religious, and political efforts to ban the consumption of alcohol in the United States. Convinced that alcohol was the root cause of most social problems, antialcohol crusaders lobbied and protested throughout much of the nineteenth and into the early twentieth century, their efforts culminating in 1920 with the federal government's prohibition against the manufacture, importation, and sale of alcohol. Although temperance

Boston Tea Party

Tea, introduced in New York in the early 1600s by the Dutch, was even more popular in colonial America than in England. When Parliament wanted to punish the Americans for rebelling against taxes imposed under the Townshend Act, it enacted a heavy tea tax in 1767. The result was smuggling, and a brisk illicit trade developed between the Americans and the Dutch. The East India Company, which controlled the legal tea trade, saw its profits slide and pressured the British government to take action. In 1773 Parliament enacted the Tea Act, mandating that all tea going to America must pass through English ports. The British hoped that the American desire for tea, coupled with the fact that tea was less expensive in the colonies than in Britain, would minimize anger over trade restrictions. Instead, American resentment flared.

On the evening of December 19, 1773, fifty to sixty men, including Samuel Adams and John Hancock, dressed up as Indians and stole onto the tea ships in Boston Harbor. They hacked open the tea chests, threw the tea overboard, and then melted away into the night. Instead of arresting the lawbreakers, Massachusetts authorities condoned their actions, which infuriated the British. Immediately Parliament passed four bills designed to punish Massachusetts's insubordination, part of the "Intolerable Acts" that lead to the formation of the Continental Congress and thence to the Declaration of Independence. It can easily be argued that the Boston Tea Party was the first overt act of the American Revolution.

BIBLIOGRAPHY
Chitwood, Oliver Perry. *A History of Colonial America.* 2d ed. New York: Harper, 1948.
"A History of Tea." Stash. http://www.stashtea.com.

SYLVIA LOVEGREN

In "Woman's Holy War," a lithograph published by Currier and Ives in 1874, members of the Temperance League smash barrels of alcohol.

Temperance

584

advocates succeeded in winning Prohibition, overwhelming popular sentiment restored America's right to drink in 1933.

The origins of temperance are difficult to ascertain, but many Protestant denominations in the British colonies long prohibited the use of alcohol. Ministers railed against "strong drink" while many in their congregations continued to imbibe. Colonists commonly brewed their own beer and drank rum, port, and corn whiskey. Due to the copious production of grain, distilled spirits were abundant and inexpensive. Benjamin Franklin was infamous for his fondness of alcohol, and George Washington purportedly won his first election to the Virginia House of Burgesses in 1758 by distributing brandy, rum, and beer to voters at the polls. Though opposed by the clergy, drinking alcohol remained an important if discreet part of mainstream colonial and post-Revolution culture.

Alcohol consumption became a more contentious public issue in the first half of the nineteenth century as non-Anglo immigrants flocked to East Coast cities. The population of the United States tripled between 1790 and 1830, threatening the balance of political power and the conventions of society. Centuries-old hatred between British Protestants and Irish Catholics rekindled in America, sparked by the great influx of Irish immigrants. British Americans viewed the Irish as inferiors who would undermine American society. Exacerbating these biases was the Irish love for alcohol. Long at the center of Irish ethnic culture, the drinking of cheap ale and whiskey became a popular pastime for urban Irish workingmen and street gangs. Protestants condemned Irish drinking as proof of their immorality, laziness, and violent tendencies and tried to contain alcohol consumption. A wave of Protestant religious revivals in the early nineteenth century strengthened temperance sentiments, spawning the American Temperance Society (1826) and the Washingtonian Movement (1840), which attracted 200,000 members. In addition temperance became part of both the early women's movement and abolitionism, often tied together as the pressing moral issues of that era. Notable feminist leaders, including Susan B. Anthony and Frances Willard, were also outspoken temperance advocates.

In cities still controlled by native-born Protestant elites, city councils enacted ordinances limiting saloons and grog shops. Massachusetts briefly banned the sale of alcohol between 1838 and 1840, Maine outlawed its manufacture and sale in 1851, and many towns in New York State voted themselves dry. Following Maine's lead, twelve other northern states adopted prohibition laws between 1852 and 1854. Southern states rejected this trend, viewing it as a further cultural difference between North and South. In 1854 the nativist Know-Nothing Party pushed to make prohibition federal policy but ran into political opposition, especially from immigrant groups. In 1855 a Know-Nothing mayor of Chicago attempted to close saloons on Sundays, causing a violent backlash, known as the Lager Riot, by German immigrants. That same year the mayor of Portland, Maine, ordered the state militia to fire on a crowd of Irish workers protesting the strict laws. The temperance movement stalled, however, at the start of the Civil War, as Americans moved on to more pressing issues. The federal government even tacitly encouraged drinking during the war, because a tax on alcohol helped finance the war.

Temperance efforts rekindled after the war, as the American Temperance Union reorganized into the National Temperance Society. Massachusetts restored prohibition in 1865, hiring war veterans as state constables whose sole responsibility was the enforcement of alcohol laws. Maine founded its state police force that year to combat prohibition violators. Other states banned Sunday alcohol sales, mandating enforcement by local officials. German and Irish immigrants formed opposition groups that actively protested against restrictions on drinking. The temperance issue was at the center of the political and economic struggle between old-line Anglo-Protestant groups and immigrant interests. Demographic changes at that time threatened the status quo, which favored those holding social and political power. Although many temperance advocates held sincere beliefs, historians question the extent to which prohibition crusades were a means of preserving control over a changing society.

Temperance efforts accelerated in the late nineteenth century with the creation of the Women's Christian Temperance Union (WCTU) in 1873 in Fredonia, New York, and the Anti-Saloon League in 1893 in Oberlin, Ohio. WCTU members crusaded against saloons, often invading them, and advocated that workingmen drink cold water instead of alcohol. With the motto "The Saloon Must

"The Bar of Destruction," a drawing by Thomas Nast, appeared in Harper's Weekly, on March 21, 1874.

Go," the Anti-Saloon League vowed to close every saloon in America. In addition to endorsing temperance candidates of the Prohibition Party and lobbying legislators, they formed a nationwide network of chapters at local churches. The Anti-Saloon League renamed itself the National Anti-Saloon League in 1895, creating the American Issue Publishing Company, which published forty tons of temperance periodicals every month. Funded by the benefactors John D. Rockefeller and Sebastian Kresge, the league became more politically active with its 1913 protest march on Washington and its support for temperance legislation. Though their first legislative initiative, the Hobson-Sheppard Bill (1916), was defeated in the Senate, a pro-temperance Congress enacted a constitutional amendment outlawing alcohol in 1917. In 1919 thirty-six states ratified the Eighteenth Amendment, which prohibited the manufacture, sale, and distribution of alcohol in the United States. After ratification, Congress passed the National Prohibition Act, commonly referred to as the Volstead Act, which outlined the parameters of the law and its enforcement measures.

The temperance movement continued throughout Prohibition, constantly advocating stricter enforcement of the Volstead Act. Despite often ineffective enforcement efforts and an ongoing national debate between "wets" and "drys," Prohibition remained the law of the land throughout the 1920s. Alcohol became legal again under federal law in 1933, soon after Franklin D. Roosevelt and an influx of Democratic legislators reclaimed Washington. The repeal of Prohibition marginalized temperance as a national issue, but temperance remained a lingering controversy in several states.

[**See also** Alcohol and Teetotalism; Alcoholism; Beer Halls; Prohibition; Saloons; Taverns.]

BIBLIOGRAPHY

Blocker, Jack S. *Retreat from Reform: The Prohibition Movement in America, 1890–1913.* Westport, CT: Greenwood, 1976.

Pegram, Thomas D. *Battling Demon Rum: The Struggle for a Dry America.* Chicago: Ivan R. Dee, 1998.

DAVID GERARD HOGAN

Tequila

Tequila, the spirit of Mexico, is made nowhere else in the world, and its origins date to pre-Columbian times. Before the Spanish conquered Mexico, the indigenous people made a naturally fermented beverage called pulque from maguey plants. The Spanish transformed the fermented drink into a distilled one and created mescal (also spelled "mezcal"), the general category that includes tequila.

For years tequila was not widely known outside Mexico and adjacent areas of the United States. That situation changed after the Mexican government established the Norma Oficial Mexicana (called the Normas) in 1978 to regulate tequila quality and consistency. According to the Normas, tequila must be made from the blue agave plant, a variety of the maguey plant called *Agave tequilana* Weber (for the German botanist who first classified it). The plants must be grown on the volcanic soil of Jalisco Province, which includes the town of Tequila, and designated nearby areas. Tequila must contain at least 51 percent blue agave juice. The other 49 percent can be cane or corn syrup or juices from other varieties of agave. Tequila made from 100 percent blue agave is so labeled.

Blue agave plants can take ten years to mature and at maturity weigh as much as 150 pounds. The heart, or *piña*, is harvested, cooked, and crushed so that the juice can be extracted. The juice, called *aguamiel*, or honey water, is fermented and then distilled twice. After distillation, tequila may or may not be blended, and it may or may not be aged. Tequila is bottled in Mexico or is shipped in tanker trucks for bottling in the United States.

There are three styles of tequila. Silver, also known as white or *blanco*, is bottled less than sixty days after distillation. *Reposado* ("rested") has been aged for up to one year. *Añejo* ("aged") tequila is aged in barrels for at least one year and up to four. Both the *reposado* and *añejo* styles take on a golden hue as a result of aging. So-called "gold" tequila is simply silver tequila with caramel coloring added. Although often described as fiery, tequila is generally bottled at eighty proof, making it no more potent than gin or vodka.

First exported to the United States in 1873, tequila enjoyed a brief popularity surge during World War II owing to the scarcity of whiskey and other liquors. In the 1970s several factors, including the Normas, the industry's marketing efforts, and the growing popularity of Mexican and Tex-Mex cuisines accompanied by margaritas, spurred the growth of tequila. In 1975 the United States consumed 2.5 million cases of tequila; by 2000 consumption had increased to 7.3 million cases. Tequila's share of the spirits market has gone from less than 2 percent to nearly 5 percent, making it one of the few spirits showing growth.

There are many ways to drink tequila. Some people bolt down shots in a ritual consisting of licking their hands between the thumb and forefinger, sprinkling the wet spot with salt, licking it off, downing a shot of

---

Mescal

All distilled maguey juices are mescals, a word derived from *mexcalmetl*, the Nauhuatl word for the agave plant. Tequila is mescal from the state of Jalisco. Oaxaca, in southern Mexico, is the production center for the liquor called "mescal" (also spelled "mezcal"). Much mescal is produced locally in the old-fashioned way. Maguey *piñas* are placed in pits, covered with heated rocks and layers of fiber matting, and then allowed to cook for several days. The process gives mescal its distinctive smoky, earthy flavor. Once cooked, the maguey is placed in wooden barrels and allowed to ferment for up to a month. The resultant mixture of fiber and liquid is distilled twice, sometimes with a chicken breast, in small stills. Like tequila, mescal is classified as aged or not. Three types are unique, among them the ninety-six proof *tobala*, a rare maguey distilled in black ceramic containers and often sold in ceramic bottles, and *minero*, named for miners who wanted strong triple-distilled liquor. Probably the best known outside Mexico is mescal *con gusano*, sold with a "worm" in the bottle. The "worm" is really the larva of a moth that lives in the base of the maguey plant. Highly prized for their flavor and texture, *gusanos* are sold in markets and eaten out of hand. *Sal de gusano*, dried *gusanos* ground together with salt and chilies, is used with mixed drinks and as a condiment. *Gusanos* are not traditional additions to mescal bottles but are a marketing ploy dating to the 1950s, along with invented folklore stories about macho qualities imparted to those who dare to eat them.

tequila, and then biting a lime wedge. Gourmetship in tequila has increased dramatically, some versions costing $300 and more a bottle. Aficionados sip good 100 percent blue agave *añejo* tequilas in elegant brandy snifters. The most popular tequila drink is the margarita, one of most popular mixed drinks in the United States.

[**See also** Cocktails; Margarita; Mexican American Food; Tequila Sunrise.]

BIBLIOGRAPHY

Cutler, Lance. *The Tequila Lover's Guide to Mexico and Mezcal*. Vineburg, CA: Wine Patrol, 2000.

Kretchmer, Laurence. *Mesa Grill Guide to Tequila*. New York: Black Dog and Leventhal, 1998.

Quinzio, Jeri. "Vino de Tequila." *Massachusetts Beverage Price Journal*, April 1996, pp. 4–5, 16.

Walker, Ann, and Larry Walker. *Tequila: The Book*. San Francisco: Chronicle, 1994.

Jeri Quinzio

Tequila Sunrise

During the 1970s the tequila sunrise was a trend-setting new drink. It was so popular that a Hollywood film, several restaurants, a hit song, a quilt pattern, and at least three yellow and red flowers—a rose, a snapdragon, and a coreopsis—came to be named after it. The tequila sunrise was one of the emblematic drinks in Cyra McFadden's 1976 novel *The Serial*, a parody of the California lifestyle. No one knows for sure who invented the tequila sunrise, but it is thought to have originated in California. The tequila sunrise was considered the perfect "morning-after" drink, a cure for hangovers brought on by tequila shots or margaritas drunk the night before.

The first published recipes for tequila sunrises, in bartenders' guides of the 1960s and early 1970s, had little resemblance to the sunny orange juice drink bartenders later came to serve. The tequila sunrise originally was made with tequila, lime juice, grenadine, crème de cassis, and club soda and served in a tall glass. The popularity of the cocktail inspired imitation. In Oaxaca, Mexico, restaurateurs who catered to tourists created the Donaji cocktail and used the local mescal rather than tequila. The Donaji is named after a mythical indigenous princess who sacrificed her life for her people. Except for the addition of *sal de gusano*—a mixture of dried agave "worms," chilies, and salt—the Donaji is a sunrise. The Berta, a drink that likely predates the Donaji, was originally served at Berta's, a bar founded around 1930 in Taxco, Mexico. The Berta is made with tequila, limes, soda water, and honey rather than grenadine.

[**See also** Cocktails; Margarita; Tequila.]

BIBLIOGRAPHY

Blue, Anthony Dias. *The Complete Book of Mixed Drinks*. New York: HarperCollins, 1993.

Jeri Quinzio

Terrapin

While the terrapin is a reptile, cookbooks traditionally categorize it as seafood. Like its seagoing relatives, the freshwater or brackish-water turtle, particularly the diamondback terrapin (*Malaclemys terrapin*) and its eggs, have long been esteemed as food. Terrapin is found in salt marshes and in waters along the East Coast from Massachusetts to the Gulf of Mexico. In 1918 Fannie Farmer's *Boston Cooking-School Cook Book* specifically mentioned that the terrapin of the Chesapeake Bay is the best, fetching the highest prices, but that terrapin from Florida and Texas was what northeasterners could expect to find in the market from November to April. Female terrapins are larger than males and average six to nine inches long. The meat of females is generally considered more tender and thus better for cooking.

A nineteenth-century fad for turtle dishes, particularly soup, considerably reduced turtle populations. The fact that turtle dishes have fallen out of favor has protected turtle species. Loss of habitat has become the most serious threat, although conservation efforts are being made to protect the habitat. Some cookbooks in the early twentieth century described ways of preparing chicken and veal in terrapin style. Turtle meat can be found frozen and canned in specialty stores, sparing cooks from having to follow Farmer's advice to cook terrapin live.

Sandra L. Oliver

Thanksgiving

Thanksgiving was observed in many communities during the seventeenth century. Thanksgiving proclamations have survived, most of which were issued by ministers and governors in various colonies, particularly in New England. These observances were usually selected in response to specific events, such as a military victory or a good harvest, but no specific thanksgiving day was observed on an annual basis. A Puritan thanksgiving was a solemn religious day celebrated with attendance at church and prayer.

The "First Thanksgiving"

None of the previously mentioned Thanksgiving proclamations mentioned the first Thanksgiving or the Pilgrims, a term that was first used in 1799 to refer to the colonists who landed at Plimoth Plantation in 1621. The first association between the Pilgrims and Thanksgiving appeared in print in 1841, when Alexander Young published a copy of a letter dated December 11, 1621, from Edward Winslow, who described a three-day event held after the crops were harvested. They acquired fowl, and Native Americans brought deer. In a footnote to the letter Young claimed that this was "the first Thanksgiving." Whatever happened in 1621, the Puritans did not have special memories of it. They made no subsequent mention of the event and did not observe it in later years. The event described by Winslow included no prayer, and it had many secular elements. The Puritans would not have considered it a day of thanksgiving.

Not much is known about early Thanksgiving dinners, if there were any. From the eighteenth century only few descriptions of Thanksgiving dinners have survived. One description dated 1784 mentions drinking and eating in general and implies that pigs, geese, turkeys, or sheep were served. By comparison, many descriptions of Thanksgiving dinners date to the nineteenth century. Two-course Thanksgiving meals were common. The first course consisted of roast turkey, chicken pie, ham, beef, sausage, and duck supplemented with sweet potatoes, yams, succotash, pickles, sweetbreads, turnips, and squash. The second course consisted of pies, tarts, puddings, creams, and

Best Wishes for a Happy Thanksgiving

A Thanksgiving greeting.

586

Tequila Sunrise

other sweets. Wine, rum, brandy, eggnog, punch, coffee, and tea were served with the meal.

Although Thanksgiving Day church services continued to be observed, the religious character of the observance gave way to the family dinner. At its core were foods considered to have originated in America. The central main course was turkey. Other traditional components include stuffing, cranberry sauce, potatoes, and pumpkin pie.

Hale's Tale

The driving force behind making Thanksgiving a national holiday was Sarah Josepha Hale, who was born in 1788 in Newport, New Hampshire. After her husband's death, Hale turned to writing to generate money. Her novel *Northwood: A Tale of New England* (1827) included an entire chapter devoted to a Thanksgiving dinner. Its publication brought Hale fame, and she ended up as editor for *Godey's Lady's Book*, the most influential women's magazine in the pre–Civil War era. For seventeen years Hale campaigned to proclaim the last Thursday in November Thanksgiving Day. Hale encouraged other magazines to join the quest of making Thanksgiving a national holiday, and many published Thanksgiving-related stories, poems, and illustrations. During the Civil War, Hale redoubled her efforts. A few months after the North's military victories at Gettysburg and Vicksburg in the summer of 1863, President Abraham Lincoln declared the last Thursday in November a national day of thanksgiving. Every president since has proclaimed Thanksgiving Day a national holiday.

Hale's pre-1865 letters and editorials promoting Thanksgiving Day made no mention of the Pilgrims or the first Thanksgiving feast. There were several good reasons for this. Jamestown had been settled before Plymouth, and colonists in Jamestown had observed days of thanksgiving before Plymouth was settled. Hale made the connection between the Pilgrims and the first Thanksgiving holiday in an 1865 editorial in *Godey's Lady's Book*. This connection was picked up by newspapers and by other magazines. By 1870 school textbooks contained the story of the "first Thanksgiving."

By the late 1880s the concept of the Pilgrim-centered Thanksgiving had blossomed in popular books. Thanksgiving plays were produced annually, and many schools offered special dinners based on fictional visions of life in Plymouth in 1621. This curriculum spawned a large body of children's literature focused on the Pilgrims and the "first Thanksgiving." These myths were enshrined in books, magazines, and artworks during the twentieth century.

The rapid adoption of the Pilgrim Thanksgiving myth had less to do with historical fact and more to do with the hundreds of thousands of immigrants from southern and eastern Europe flooding into the United States. Because the immigrants came from many lands, the American public education system needed to create an easily understood history of America. The Pilgrims were an ideal symbol for America's beginning, so they became embedded in the nation's schools, as did the Thanksgiving feast.

President's Thanksgiving Day Proclamation, 2005

Thanksgiving Day is a time to remember our many blessings and to celebrate the opportunities that freedom affords. Explorers and settlers arriving in this land often gave thanks for the extraordinary plenty they found. And today, we remain grateful to live in a country of liberty and abundance. We give thanks for the love of family and friends, and we ask God to continue to watch over America.

This Thanksgiving, we pray and express thanks for the men and women who work to keep America safe and secure. Members of our Armed Forces, State and local law enforcement, and first responders embody our Nation's highest ideals of courage and devotion to duty. Our country is grateful for their service and for the support and sacrifice of their families. We ask God's special blessings on those who have lost loved ones in the line of duty.

We also remember those affected by the destruction of natural disasters. Their tremendous determination to recover their lives exemplifies the American spirit, and we are grateful for those across our Nation who answered the cries of their neighbors in need and provided them with food, shelter, and a helping hand. We ask for continued strength and perseverance as we work to rebuild these communities and return hope to our citizens.

We give thanks to live in a country where freedom reigns, justice prevails, and hope prospers. We recognize that America is a better place when we answer the universal call to love a neighbor and help those in need. May God bless and guide the United States of America as we move forward.

Now, therefore, I, George W. Bush, President of the United States of America, by virtue of the authority vested in me by the Constitution and laws of the United States, do hereby proclaim Thursday, November 24, 2005, as a National Day of Thanksgiving. I encourage all Americans to gather together in their homes and places of worship with family, friends, and loved ones to reinforce the ties that bind us and give thanks for the freedoms and many blessings we enjoy.

In witness whereof, I have hereunto set my hand this eighteenth day of November, in the year of our Lord two thousand five, and of the Independence of the United States of America the two hundred and thirtieth.
GEORGE W. BUSH

Challenges to Thanksgiving

Historians have debunked the myths surrounding the Pilgrims and the "first Thanksgiving." Businesses have commercialized Thanksgiving Day as the launch date for the Christmas season. Illustrators, filmmakers, and television producers have generated new Thanksgiving images. Immigrant groups have added new ingredients to the Thanksgiving culinary stew. Native Americans have proclaimed Thanksgiving Day the National Day of Mourning as a reminder of spiritual connection and in protest of oppression experienced. Vegetarians have campaigned against the consumption of turkey and other meat products. And those concerned with poor and homeless people have served special dinners for the needy. But the significance of Thanksgiving dinner has not faded. [**See also** CRANBERRIES; PIES AND TARTS; POTATOES; SWEET POTATOES; TURKEY; VEGETARIANISM.]

BIBLIOGRAPHY

Appelbaum, Diana Karter. *Thanksgiving: An American Holiday, an American History.* New York: Facts on File, 1984.

Siskind, Janet. "The Invention of Thanksgiving: A Ritual of American Nationality." *Critique of Anthropology* 12 (1992): 182–183, 186.

Smith, Andrew F. "The First Thanksgiving." *Gastronomica*, Fall 2003, 79–85.

Smith, Andrew F. *The Turkey: An American Story.* Urbana: University of Illinois Press, 2006.

ANDREW F. SMITH

"Give everyone a chance to have a piece of the pie," Thomas said of success. "If the pie's not big enough, make a bigger pie."

Thomas,
Dave

Thomas, Dave

R. David Thomas (1932–2002) was born in Atlantic City, New Jersey; he was adopted shortly afterward and raised in Kalamazoo, Michigan. His adopted family moved around. At the age of twelve Thomas was hired for a restaurant job at a barbecue restaurant in Knoxville, Tennessee. Four years later he dropped out of high school to work at the Hobby House Restaurant in Fort Wayne, Indiana. After a stint in the army, he returned to Hobby House. In 1954 he married Lorraine Buskirk, and their daughter Melinda Lou was nicknamed "Wendy." Over the next few years Thomas worked at many restaurants, including an Arthur Treacher's outlet. He later became the operations manager for three hundred regional Kentucky Fried Chicken (KFC) restaurants, and he met Harland Sanders (according to Thomas's autobiography, *Dave's Way*, published in 1991, Colonel Sanders was one of his greatest influences).

In 1962 Thomas took over four failing Kentucky Fried Chicken restaurants in Columbus, Ohio. He acquired additional KFC outlets but sold them back to the company in 1968. Thomas used his profits to open the first Wendy's restaurant the following year. Wendy's intentionally targeted young adults for sales of the Old Fashioned Hamburger, with a large square patty and a round bun, and the Frosty, a combination of milk, sugar, cream, and flavorings. Thomas relinquished day-to-day control over Wendy's International in 1982, when he became "senior chairman." In 1989 Thomas began appearing in Wendy's advertisements, and he became an instant, if unlikely, media star. In 1993 Thomas went back to school; he completed his GED three years later. Thomas wrote two inspirational books, *Dave's Way* (1991) and *Dave Says—Well Done!* (1994). From the profits he earned through Wendy's, Thomas and his wife gave large sums to charity. Thomas died in 2002 at age sixty-nine.

BIBLIOGRAPHY

Thomas, R. David. *Dave's Way: A New Approach to Old-fashioned Success.* New York: Putnam, 1991.

Thomas, R. David. *Dave Says—Well Done! The Common Guy's Guide to Everyday Success.* Grand Rapids, MI: Zondervan, 1994.

ANDREW F. SMITH

Tilapia

Tilapia (*Oreochromis niloticus*) is a member of the family Cichlidae, which includes many species kept as pets in aquariums. Tilapia is a native of Africa but has become an important farm-raised, freshwater food fish in America. Like perch, tilapia grows rapidly, requiring less feed than many other fish; spawns frequently; and tolerates high population density. Most tilapia farms, many of which are in the southwestern United States, use enclosed systems and so have less environmental impact than other forms of fish farming, because there is almost no water pollution or fish escape. Tilapia has firm, white, and relatively bland flesh, which can be broiled, fried, or baked and then sauced for flavor. Tilapia is a key fish for prepared battered fish products, such as fillets, fingers, and nuggets.

SANDRA L. OLIVER

Timers, Hourglasses, Egg Timers

Measuring how long it takes for sand (or other fine granular substances, including ground eggshells) to flow from one blown glass bulb through a narrow neck to another glass bulb has been used for centuries as an accurate way of determining the passage of time. Most famously hourglasses measure an hour. Short times, especially for cooking eggs, have been measured with similar, smaller hourglass-shaped timers since the 1800s, maybe earlier. Three minutes is a standard. A "three-minute egg" has a cooked white and soft yolk. These glass timers typically are set in a decorative wooden cylinder with windows or are protected by dowels connecting a flat bottom and top, so the device can be flipped to double the time or start over. Other timers revolved within a decorative frame. One such device struck a bell after sufficient sand tipped the glass. Around 1910 one kitchen supply company, Silver's, sold a wall-mounted timer. Marked on a plaque behind the rotatable timer were levels denoting "hard boiled," "well done," "medium cooked," and "soft boiled." Clockwork bell timers were introduced in the early twentieth century. Dials could be set for 1 to 60 minutes, even 120 on some models. By the 1990s many clockwork timers came in whimsical shapes, including various kitchen utensils. Electric timers that could be wired to ovens were introduced around 1930, electronic ones sixty years later.

[**See also** EGG-PREPARATION TOOLS; EGGS.]

BIBLIOGRAPHY

Franklin, Linda Campbell. *300 Years of Kitchen Collectibles*. 5th ed. Iola, WI: Krause Publications, 2003.

LINDA CAMPBELL FRANKLIN

Toast

Bread becomes toast in the course of a complex series of chemical reactions to dry heat that includes the caramelization of sugars and the breakdown of starches, known collectively as the Maillard reaction. The ancient Egyptians are credited with the discovery of yeast leavening, and they are assumed to have been the first to brown the resulting loaves in a fire—that is, to make toast. The English have made the most extensive use of the practice in their cookery. In medieval times, toast frequently appeared at the table in the form of sops and sippets—relatively small pieces of toast used for dipping, mopping, and topping with various meats and sauces. In the Victorian era "toast water" was used as a folk tonic. Although it is a dish unto itself at breakfast and teatime, toast plays a supporting role in classics of home cooking, such as creamed tuna or chipped beef on toast, the restorative milk toast, with fricassee or stew, and in the shape of garnishing points or croutons.

As the heirs to such tradition, Americans rely on toast as a mealtime staple. Historically crops such as corn and oats eclipsed wheat in terms of availability, yielding breads with a crumb not generally associated with toast. In the nineteenth century wheat and wheat products began to dominate. In the early twenty-first century a traditional American breakfast of bacon or sausage and eggs almost inevitably includes toast with butter and jelly. Common alternatives range from cinnamon toast (an English hand-me-down) to Texas toast, which is served in grilled slabs rather than slices and is topped with gravy or honey. French toast, which technically is not toast at all, is day-old bread dipped in egg, sautéed in butter, and sprinkled with powdered sugar. At lunchtime toasted bread is the key to many sandwiches, including the club sandwich; bacon, lettuce, and tomato; peanut butter and jelly; and grilled cheese. Hamburger and hot dog buns are properly browned as well.

But if the taste for toasting is Anglo-bred, it was a typically American thirst for convenience that spurred the revolutionary invention of the electric toaster at the beginning of the twentieth century. Before that time the world, the English in particular, made do with hearth implements such as long-handled forks and ornate swiveling irons that held the bread upright. Tin and wire racks served the same function on early wood-burning stovetops. Between 1904 and 1909 the first electric models were patented and put on the market with varying degrees of success. General Electric had the most models, although Hotpoint

and Simplex were also industry pioneers. Note that "electric" does not automatically mean "automatic." The early toasters were manual, meaning the user was no less responsible than before for determining doneness by empirical observation. In 1926 toasters became fully automatic. A bell heralded the end of the toasting cycle, and there was a mechanism for dislodging the toast. This "pop-up" toaster led to the development of sliced, packaged bread. As electricity entered more homes, this method of toasting became a way of life in American kitchens.

RUTH TOBIAS

Toasters

The complexity of colonial hearth toasters reflected the culinary importance of toast, particularly among colonists from Great Britain. Set before the fire, the most elaborate toaster held several pieces of bread in an open, four-legged, wrought iron rack. Kick toasters were used for browning both sides of bread. The cook used a toe to nudge the device around on a central swivel. Long-handled drop toasters were lifted and turned manually. Simpler models required the cook to pick up and turn slices by hand. Cooks of modest means speared a slice of bread on a large, forged-iron fork and held it to the fire.

In the 1890s stovetop toasters were made of perforated sheet iron and had wire supports for bread on four pyramidal sides. The chimney-like effect of these toasters caused rising heat to toast bread one side at a time. Electric heating elements similar to those used in twenty-first century toasters were known in the 1890s, but a functioning electric toaster did not come about until approximately 1910. This toaster was essentially a heavy wire rack on which two slices of bread were positioned near a central mica-insulated heating element. Refinements of many kinds followed, including enclosures for toasting both sides simultaneously; automatic, adjustable timing; warming racks; and pop-up mechanisms. Since the 1940s styling has been largely cosmetic; the essential heating elements have changed little.

[**See also** BREAD; BREAD, SLICED; BREAKFAST FOODS; HEARTH COOKERY.]

BIBLIOGRAPHY

Artman, E. Townsend. *Toasters, 1909–1960: A Look at the Ingenuity and Design of Toaster Makers*. Atglen, PA: Schiffer, 1996.

Franklin, Linda Campbell. *300 Years of Kitchen Collectibles*. 5th ed. Iola, WI: Krause Publications, 2003.

Greguire, Helen. *Collector's Guide to Toasters and Accessories: Identification and Values*. Paducah, KY: Collector Books, 1997.

LINDA CAMPBELL FRANKLIN

Toasts

Toasting was well established elsewhere when the United States became a country, but America gave its own twist to the custom of saying something clever when glasses were

raised. During the American War of Independence, toasts tended in the direction of curses, such as "To the enemies of our country! May they have cobweb breeches, a porcupine saddle, a hard-trotting horse, and an eternal journey." After the war, no official dinner or celebration was complete without thirteen toasts, one for each state. The origin of the thirteen toasts appears to date from the series of banquets held in honor of George Washington on his retirement. For many years the thirteen toasts were obligatory at local Fourth of July celebrations. At such times each toast was followed by an artillery salute, three cheers from the crowd, and a song. Although they differed somewhat from locale to locale, the thirteen toasts were generally patriotic, proud, and nonpartisan. Those honored ranged from the holiday itself—"May it ever be held in grateful remembrance by the American people"—to the nation's former presidents—"In the evenings of well-spent lives pleased with the fruits of their labors, they cheerfully await the summons that shall waft them to brighter abodes." Invariably there was a toast to the signers of the Declaration of Independence.

Toasting not only transferred easily to North America but also was enhanced by the skill of various practitioners, including some of America's early leaders. If not the best, Benjamin Franklin certainly ranked with them. A number of Franklin's toasts have been recalled but none more often than one he delivered at Versailles while American emissary to France. On this occasion the toasting was led by the British ambassador, who said, "George the Third, who, like the sun in its meridian, spreads a luster throughout and enlightens the world." The next toast came from the French minister, who said, "The illustrious Louis the Sixteenth, who, like the moon, sheds his mild and benevolent rays on and influences the globe." Franklin finished the round, "George Washington, commander of the American armies, who, like Joshua of old, commanded the sun and the moon to stand still, and both obeyed."

Although quite popular through the colonial period and beyond, toasting fell out of "polite society" by the mid-nineteenth century, when etiquette writers considered toasts not gentlemanly and deemed them appropriate only in taverns. This proscription probably was related to the increase in formal, mixed-sex dining in the nineteenth century. Ladies eschewed what they considered the vulgar custom of "drinking healths." Toasting never disappeared entirely, however. Americans tended away from Old World floweriness to give toasting its own utilitarian spin by getting right down to business. The following are a few examples.

*A drop of whiskey
Ain't a bad thing right here.*

Bret Harte

Here's to Prohibition,
The devil take it!
They've stolen our wine,
So now we make it.

Toast to the Volstead Act

Here's to today!
For tomorrow we may be radioactive.

Cold War toast, circa 1955

Here's to Hollywood—
A place where people from Iowa
Mistake each other for movie stars.

Fred Allen

[**See also** DRINKING SONGS.]

BIBLIOGRAPHY

Dickson, Paul, ed. *Toasts: Over 1,500 of the Best Toasts, Sentiments, Blessings, and Graces.* New York: Crown, 1991.

PAUL DICKSON

This Anderson Canning Company label celebrates the size of their beefsteak tomatoes.

Tomatoes

The tomato plant (*Lycopersicon esculentum*) originated in South America but was domesticated in Central America in pre-Columbian times. When Europeans arrived, tomatoes were being consumed only in Central America. The lack of widespread diffusion suggests that tomatoes were a late addition to the culinary repertoire of Mesoamerica. The Spanish first encountered tomatoes after their conquest of Mexico began in 1519. They disseminated tomato plants to the Caribbean and then into Europe, where the fruit was consumed in southern Italy and Spain by the mid-sixteenth century.

The first published record of tomatoes appeared in an Italian herbal in 1544. By the late seventeenth century, tomatoes were being eaten in the eastern Mediterranean region and North Africa. Tomato cookery flourished in southern France late in the eighteenth century. Tomatoes were cultivated in England by 1597; however, there is little evidence of British consumption before the mid-eighteenth century.

Spanish colonists introduced tomatoes in their settlements in what became the states of Florida, New Mexico, Texas, and California. English colonists in South and North Carolina were using tomatoes by the mid-eighteenth century. From the South tomato culture slowly spread up the Atlantic coast and the Mississippi River system. By the early nineteenth century tomatoes were consumed in all regions of the United States, and tomato recipes appeared in American cookery manuscripts.

In pre-Columbian times tomatoes were used by the Aztecs and other indigenous peoples of Central America for making sauces, particularly in combination with chilies and ground squash seeds. After the Spanish Conquest, vinegar was added to the tomato and chilies to produce what came to be called salsa. Numerous other uses of the tomato were developed in Mexico and Central America.

Since the mid-nineteenth century American cookbooks have regularly published recipes for tomatoes. In these recipes tomatoes were stuffed, fried, hashed, pickled, baked, scalloped, broiled, chopped, or preserved. Tomatoes were added to soups and gumbos and cooked with poultry, veal, ham, pork, beef, calves feet, or sweetbreads. Tomatoes also were used in sweets, including marmalade and jellies, as well as in and on macaroni, fish, and shrimp.

Tomatoes were first canned in New Jersey during the 1840s, and the tomato canning industry accelerated during and after the Civil War. Cans were fashioned by hand, and the seams and lids were soldered on. The cans were then boiled in water. The cans were hand filled, and the cappers soldered on the lids one at a time.

The Civil War greatly stimulated the growth of tomato canneries. These wartime effects were small, however, compared with the dramatic expansion in tomato consumption after the war. Many northern soldiers ate canned vegetables for the first time while they were in the army. After the war the demand for canned products soared. By 1870 tomatoes were among the main three canned vegetables, along with peas and corn. With the completion of the transcontinental railroad, fresh tomatoes were shipped from California to New York. Commercial production of tomatoes began in northern Florida in 1872, and within ten years Florida tomatoes were sold on the Chicago market.

In 1883 Congress passed the Tariff Act, levying a 10 percent duty on imported vegetables. In the spring of 1886 John Nix imported tomatoes into New York from the West Indies. Maintaining that they were a fruit rather than a vegetable, Nix paid the duty under protest. In February 1887 he brought suit in New York against the collector, Edward L. Hedden, to recover the duties. After six years of winding through courts and appeals courts, the case of *Nix v. Hedden* was argued before the U.S. Supreme Court. The opinion of the Supreme Court was delivered by Justice Horace Gray, who reported that the single question in this case was whether tomatoes, considered as provisions, were classed as vegetables or as fruit within the meaning of the Tariff Act of 1883.

The tomato canning and bottling processes were automated during the second half of the nineteenth century, when devices for capping, filling, scalding, topping, wrapping, and boxing came into use. This equipment was integrated and interconnected by the 1920s, and tomato canning was fully automated.

Another automation revolution occurred in the harvesting of tomatoes. Before World War II, California produced 20 percent of the nation's tomatoes. The mechanical harvester caught on in California during the late 1940s.

Hoop training of tomatoes, from Reeves & Simonson's Descriptive Catalogue of Choice Selected Seeds.

By 1953 California growers cultivated 83,000 acres and produced 50 percent of all tomatoes in the United States. The acreage had reached 130,000 by 1960. The harvester reduced by two-thirds the cost of processing tomatoes. At the same time, yields have increased greatly. In 1967 California growers harvested between seventeen and twenty tons of tomatoes per acre. By the 1990s they averaged thirty-four tons per acre. Hence total production of tomatoes for processing increased from 2.25 million tons in 1960 to more than 9 million tons in 1990. At the beginning of the twenty-first century 90 percent of all American processed tomatoes are grown in California.

Nutritional Information

Tomatoes have considerable vitamin C and some vitamin A. Tomatoes rank thirteenth among other commonly consumed fruits and vegetables as a source of vitamin C and sixteenth as a source of vitamin A. Overall tomatoes rank sixteenth nutritionally behind other vegetables. Despite this comparatively low ranking, tomatoes contribute more vitamin A and C and other nutrients to the American diet than do other fruits and vegetables because so many more tomatoes are consumed. In addition medical researchers believe that tomatoes may be an anticancer weapon. Tomatoes contain lycopene, the plant pigment that makes the fruits red. Results of research have demonstrated that people with more lycopene in their blood have lower rates of certain forms of cancer.

In the United States tomatoes are second only to potatoes in annual vegetable consumption. Since the late 1990s annual per capita use of tomatoes and tomato products in the United States has increased nearly 30 percent, reaching an annual total fresh-weight equivalent of ninety-one pounds per person by 1999. The United States is one of the world's largest tomato producers.

[See also CANNING AND BOTTLING; CHILD, LYDIA MARIA; MEXICAN AMERICAN FOOD; KETCHUP; RANDOLPH, MARY; SALSA; TRANSPORTATION OF FOOD.]

BIBLIOGRAPHY
Smith, Andrew F. Pure Ketchup: The History of America's National Condiment. Columbia: University of South Carolina Press, 1996.
Smith, Andrew F. Souper Tomatoes: The Story of America's Favorite Food. New Brunswick, NJ: Rutgers University Press, 2000.
Smith, Andrew F. The Tomato in America: Early History, Culture, and Cookery. Columbia: University of South Carolina Press, 1994.

ANDREW F. SMITH

Tombstone Pizza

The siblings Joseph, Ronald, Frances, and Joan Simek owned the Tombstone bar, a small country tavern across the street from a cemetery in Medford, Wisconsin. In 1962 they began serving pizzas in the tavern and also started packaging frozen pizzas in a small factory next door for distribution to other bars and taverns. As demand grew, they opened factories in Medford and nearby Sussex. Kraft Food bought the operation from the Simek family in 1986. During the 1990s Tombstone Pizza became America's top-ranked frozen pizza, partly thanks to memorable commercials, such as the 1995 ad in which an eighteenth-century French aristocrat, about to be guillotined, requests a Tombstone pizza (with cheese and pepperoni) for his last meal. The guillotine blade is shown falling…only to slice the pizza. In 2001 Kraft extended its Tombstone pizza line with a Mexican-style pizza.

ANDREW F. SMITH

Tom Collins, see Cocktails; Collins

Toothpicks

The humble toothpick likely has been around since the about the time of the discovery of the wheel. Christy G. Turner, an anthropologist at Arizona State University, was quoted as follows in Smithsonian magazine in 1997: "As far as can be empirically documented, the oldest demonstrable human habit is picking one's teeth." In America the toothpick is mentioned in the rules that have become known as "George Washington's Rules of Civility" (adopted from Francis Hawkins's Youth's Behaviour; or, Decencie in Conversation amongst Men, which appeared in 1664): "Cleanse not your teeth with the Table Cloth Napkin Fork or Knife, but if Others do it let it be done w/t Pick Tooth." Washington's preference was a toothpick made from goose quill. Until 1870 toothpicks were made of bone, quill, ivory, gold, or silver. They were often displayed as signs of personal wealth but were considered an American vulgarity when used in public, as Charles Dickens observed in the 1840s.

America gave the world the throwaway, mass-produced wooden toothpick. Working as an exporter's agent in Brazil in the late 1860s, Charles Forster saw young boys selling "wooden slivers" carved from Spanish willow. He sent some home to his wife in the United States, and she gave them away to friends, who found them a pleasure to use. Forster returned to the United States determined to get into the business. He developed a machine for manufacturing toothpicks out of white birch, "a wood that was easily carved and left no aftertaste." In January 1870 in Boston, Forster opened his first factory and began to produce toothpicks in huge numbers: one birch tree produced millions of toothpicks. Within weeks Forster realized that he had to establish a demand for his product and hit on a bit of inspired marketing. He recruited Harvard students to work for him in return for free meals. A student would go to one of the best restaurants in Boston, purchase a meal, and then loudly demand a wooden toothpick. When none was forthcoming, the diner would inform the restaurant management that toothpicks could be obtained from Forster. The scheme worked, and soon almost every restaurant and many dining rooms featured toothpicks in holders designed for the purpose. Forster moved his operation to Maine to be close to a ready supply of birch.

Toothpicks became elements of dental hygiene and were sold door to door by children working for prizes. In the mid-1920s every youngster selling one hundred boxes of Velvet toothpicks received a baseball and bat. Advertisements for Velvet toothpicks proclaimed: "Tooth picks should be used as regularly as a tooth brush. They save the teeth and preserve the health." The advent of widespread flossing and the decline in the custom of public tooth picking led the Wall Street Journal to proclaim in a 1985 headline, "End of an Era: Toothpicks Fall Out of Favor." The versatility of toothpicks, however, has provided their salvation. Toothpicks are used for purposes ranging from dental hygiene to structural integrity for club sandwiches. In the early twenty-first century the Forster plant in Strong, Maine, which had been purchased by Diamond and then the Jarden Corporation, was supplying the United States with 85 to 90 percent of its toothpicks. According to one estimate, toothpicks are present in more than 90 percent all American households.

[See also DINING ROOMS AND MEAL SERVICE.]

PAUL DICKSON

Tootsie Roll

In the late nineteenth century the word "tootsie" was a slang word for a girl or sweetheart. In 1896 Leo Hirschfield, an immigrant from Austria, began making the small, log-shaped, chewy chocolate caramel in his candy store in New York City. In 1905 he named the candy after his daughter Clara, who was nicknamed "Tootsie." Hirschfield began manufacturing Tootsie Rolls, which became the first penny candy to be individually wrapped. The company was named Sweets Company of America, and in 1917 it began advertising nationally. In 1931 the Tootsie Pop was introduced—a spherical lollipop with a soft Tootsie Roll center. During World War II, Tootsie Rolls were placed in ration kits, mainly because the candy could survive various climatic conditions. After the war the company targeted its advertising to children, sponsoring popular television shows such as Howdy Doody, Rin Tin Tin, and Rocky and Bullwinkle.

The company's name was changed to Tootsie Roll Industries, Inc., and the firm began to expand its operations abroad, first into the Philippines and Southeast Asia and later into Canada and Mexico. In 1991 Tootsie Roll Industries acquired Charms Company, America's largest lollipop manufacturer and the maker of the Charms Blow Pop. Two years later it acquired Warner-Lambert's chocolate and caramel division, which included Junior Mints, Sugar Daddy, Sugar Babies, and the Charleston Chew! In the early twenty-first century Tootsie Roll Industries is headquartered in Chicago.

BIBLIOGRAPHY

Brenner, Joël Glenn. *The Emperors of Chocolate: Inside the Secret World of Hershey and Mars.* New York: Broadway Books, 2000.

Broekel, Ray. *The Great America Candy Bar Book.* Boston: Houghton Mifflin, 1982.

Richardson, Tim. *Sweets: A History of Candy.* New York: Bloomsbury, 2002.

ANDREW F. SMITH

Train Food, *see Dining Car*

Transportation of Food

The transportation of food marked the beginning of the colonization of North America. Legend has it that cattle and hogs were transported to Florida by a Spaniard in 1521. A century later the first groups of English settlers brought seeds with them to Massachusetts and Virginia to plant parsnips, cabbages, wheat, and apples. Potatoes arrived in the 1620s, vines, broccoli, chives, and strawberries arrived with Thomas Jefferson in the 1700s.

By the middle of the eighteenth century agriculture was thriving, and America began to develop as an international trading force. Hundreds of thousands of Atlantic codfish were shipped to the world market. Hams and apples went from Virginia to England. In return, food was imported: molasses and rum came from the West Indies, produced by slaves fed by American codfish. A veritable feast crisscrossed the ocean. Combined with native crops, seeds and breeds originally transported from afar became the basis of a unique American diet. But once the foods had taken root, they did not travel far. On North American soil, the degree of food transportation was relatively small. Roads were bad or nonexistent; the cost of transportation was astronomical; and the spoilage rate was high. This all changed with the advent of canals, railroads, highways, and air travel.

First came the steamboats, tested successfully on the Delaware River in 1787. Then came the canals. The 363-mile-long Erie Canal connecting the Great Lakes with New York City was completed in 1825, becoming the principal transportation route for midwestern agricultural commodities to the burgeoning eastern markets. The Midwest became America's breadbasket, shipping corn and oats to feed eastern livestock and wheat and flour for humans. Freight costs were just five to ten dollars per ton by canal, relative to a hundred dollars by land. After the canal opened, the cost of flour fell to four dollars in eastern cities, down from around sixteen dollars. The economic attractions of the Erie Canal started a frenzy of further building. By 1850 U.S. canals covered 3,600 miles, and freight rates were as low as one cent per ton per mile. More farmers and ranchers could now transport more food to more places over more miles, but vast swaths of forests had been cut, Native peoples were displaced, and many of the canal builders (largely Irish immigrants) died on the job. Still, canals remained an imperfect method of transporting food. In winter canals could freeze for long periods, and it took almost three weeks to transport salt pork from Cincinnati to New York. Food shippers needed something faster, a system that would operate year-round. For that they turned to what would eventually supplant the canals—the railroads.

Railroads appeared in America in 1826 and subsequently developed alongside the steam engine. In 1830 the Baltimore and Ohio Railroad began carrying goods on the first American-built steam engine. From then on, railroads were built at a remarkable rate, from 3,000 miles of track in 1840 to a peak of 254,000 miles in 1916. Freight rates declined precipitously, allowing relatively inexpensive shipment of food to almost every community in the United States. Meat distribution was particularly affected. Regional railroads focused on Chicago, leading to its development as the nation's meatpacking center. In 1885 the Missouri, Kansas, and Texas Railroads reached the heart of cow country, ending cattle drives for good.

The next major development was the refrigerated railroad car. Starting in 1842 cars packed with ice were used on the Erie Railroad to ship milk to New York and fresh butter from New York to Boston. Seafood was shipped in the opposite direction, from the coast inland. In 1867 the first patented refrigerator car transported strawberries on the Illinois Central Railroad. Later application of mechanical refrigeration made it possible to transport perishable foods over long distances without spoilage. The development revolutionized the American fruit and vegetable industry, as apples, peaches, and oranges extended along the pathways cut by the railroads. For example, the Georgia peach industry was saved by the expansion of the northern railroad network, which allowed a new breed of longer-lasting peaches to reach northern cities.

Railroads changed the way Americans ate. No longer did people have to rely largely on food that was locally available. Food quality also changed. Fruits and vegetables were no longer partially rotten on arrival, dairy products were not half-rancid, and beef became more tender because cattle no longer walked but rode to market. The cost of food decreased. In 1898, compared with 1872, one dollar could buy 62 percent more fresh mutton, 25 percent more fresh pork, 60 percent more lard and butter, and 42 percent more milk. But the railroads had cut deep scars through the landscape, contaminating their routes with noise and smoke. This process of environmental change continued with the next great transportation revolution—the highways.

Construction of a national highway system in the United States began in 1883. In 1956 the Federal-Aid Highway Act authorized the 41,000-mile interstate highway system. With these new roads, trucks could carry foodstuff shipments once reserved for railroads. At the same time gasoline prices fell, and scientists developed technologies to extend the shelf life of perishables. Ethylene allowed tomatoes to ripen during transport rather than on the plant; iceberg lettuce could be vacuum cooled in transit, becoming almost indestructible in any form of transportation. Roads also changed the functioning of the food economy, encouraging migration to the cities, the spread of the suburbs onto farmland, and the enlargement of farms. The numbers of people producing America's food fell. In 1930 the farm population (30.5 million) was approximately one-fourth of all persons living in the United States. By 1980 less than 3 percent (6.1 million) of the population were farmers. The advent of road transport also contributed to the changing organization of food retailing. Before World War II, farmers generally delivered their crops to a shipping point such as a produce auction, where buyers paid for the food and then graded, packed, and transported it to wholesalers in terminal markets. With the roads, supermarkets and food processors could have greater control over the system, sourcing directly through large-volume centralized buying operations from almost anywhere in the country.

In the latter part of the twentieth century, food transported from other countries, by sea and air, became more important. Although pineapples and bananas had been arriving in the United States since the nineteenth century, transportation of more tender foods, such as grapes and tomatoes, took the development of more sophisticated technology. The arrival of grapes from Chile in the late 1970s inaugurated what is known as "global cool chains," an integrated system of refrigeration from farm to fork. The process changed America's eating habits, allowing consumption of fruits and vegetables after the U.S. seasons end. The rise of processed foods also created new transportation patterns, with each multiple component sourced from all over the world. By way of what has been termed "food miles," food in the United States typically travels between 1,550 and 2,480 miles from field to fork, with consequent environmental costs.

A result of the food transportation revolution in the United States is that Americans can eat food from practically anywhere. Food transportation means that the U.S. food economy is more national and international than ever before, while international food trade means that more people are eating U.S. food. The United States is the largest food exporter in the world. However, in the face of the long distance between food and consumer, there is a "local food" movement in favor of transporting food less. This change would be a progressive one but ironically would take Americans a little closer to the old way of obtaining food—before the rise of trains, planes, and automobiles.

[**See also** CALIFORNIA; DAIRY INDUSTRY; FARMERS' MARKETS; FRUIT; ICE; LETTUCE; MEAT; MILK; SWIFT, GUSTAVUS FRANKLIN; VEGETABLES.]

A drawing of the New York Central and Hudson River Railroad's massive grain elevator by W. P. Snyder, published by Harper's Weekly on December 22, 1877.

Loading oranges onto a refrigerator car, 1943.

BIBLIOGRAPHY

Halweil, B. *Home Grown: The Case for Local Food in a Global Market*. Washington, DC: Worldwatch, 2002.

Pillsbury, R. *No Foreign Food: The American Diet in Time and Place*. Boulder, CO: Westview, 1998.

Pirog, R., T. Van Pelt, K. Enshayan, and E. Cook. *Food, Fuel, and Freeways: An Iowa Perspective of How Far Food Travels, Fuel Usage, and Greenhouse Gas Emissions*. Ames, IA: Leopold Center for Sustainable Agriculture, 2001.

CORINNA HAWKES

Trencher

"Trencher" comes from the French, *tranchoir*, to slice. Originally referring to slices of stale bread used in the Middle Ages as disposable plates, by the sixteenth century trenchers denoted carved wooden plates or platters, frequently with a small niche to hold salt. They were often reversible: one could flip the trencher between main and dessert courses to provide a clean surface. In the earliest American settlements, two or more diners often shared trenchers, a practice imported from England, hence the term "trenchermate"; "trencherman" refers to someone with a hearty appetite. Trenchers could be quite elegant. One seventeenth-century Plymouth inventory lists a

A wooden trencher typical of plates used in the early eighteenth century.

dozen small fruit trenchers designed for the dessert course, each of which was decorated with an image of one of the twelve months.

CATHY K. KAUFMAN

Trotter, Charlie

The chef and restaurateur Charlie Trotter has been quoted as saying, "If it isn't broken, then break it." Trotter made his reputation on a cuisine in which, according to Molly O'Neill (*New York Times*), "the complexity of his recipes pushes the outer limits of culinary sanity." The cuisine, however, has won Trotter international acclaim and almost every major culinary award for his namesake restaurant, his books, and his television series.

Trotter was born in 1959 and was reared in the northern Chicago suburb of Wilmette. His family was not food oriented, and Trotter never had ambitions of becoming a chef. However, on his prom night in 1976, while dining at The Bakery restaurant in Chicago, Trotter had an epiphany. Seeing the dramatic persona of the impeccably toqued chef Louis Szathmary, Trotter declared that one day he too would be a chef.

In college at the University of Wisconsin, Madison, where he majored in political science, Trotter began his quest by cooking for friends. After graduation he pursued a culinary career full time. With no formal experience, Trotter was given his first break at Sinclair's, a restaurant owned by Gordon Sinclair and Marshall Field IV in Lake Forest, Illinois, a northern suburb of Chicago. After several months at Sinclair's, training under the chef Norman Van Aken, Trotter began a self-styled apprenticeship, working in restaurants in Florida and San Francisco and reading every cookbook he could get his hands on. Trotter moved to France and ate out frequently at Michelin-rated three-star restaurants.

When he returned to the United States, Trotter catered elaborate dinner parties for prominent business and social leaders to hone his skills. In 1987, with his father's financial backing, Trotter purchased a 1908 Victorian house on the north side of Chicago. Trotter remodeled the building into the elegant, wood-paneled fine-dining establishment that bears his name. Trotter's cuisine, superbly paired with wines, quickly earned stellar reviews.

Likening his food to improvisational jazz, Trotter changes menus daily and never repeats a dish. The cuisine is based on classical French techniques, but Trotter freely uses Asian influences, as have other innovative American chefs, including Wolfgang Puck and Jeremiah Tower. Trotter incorporates other international touches in his tasting menu of, typically, fifteen courses. The chef relies on natural vegetable juices and stocks, purees, and infused oils instead of cream and butter-rich sauces, which Trotter believes neutralize flavors. Trotter emphasizes freshness, using organically grown grains and vegetables, meats from free-range animals, and line-caught fish.

To communicate his legacy of cuisine and service, Trotter has published ten books and teaches cooking on his award-winning PBS TV show. He regularly invites inner-city schoolchildren to experience fine dining at his restaurant and awards culinary scholarships through his philanthropic foundation. He has won numerous awards, among them the James Beard Foundation Award for Outstanding Chef in the United States (1999). *Wine Spectator* magazine cited Charlie Trotter's as the best restaurant in the world for wine and food. Trotter also received the dubious distinction of being named one of the meanest bosses in Chicago by a local magazine. He was cited for overseeing every dish that leaves the kitchen "and often bringing cooks and servers to tears." Trotter has said, "You basically give up your life to the pursuit of perfection."

[See also CELEBRITY CHEFS; PUCK, WOLFGANG; SZATHMARY, LOUIS.]

BIBLIOGRAPHY

Brown, Rochelle. *The Chef, the Story, and the Dish.* New York: Stewart, Tabori, and Chang, 2002.

Lawler, Edmund. *Charlie Trotter's.* New York: Lebhard Friedman, 2000.

SCOTT WARNER

Trout

Trout is a legendary freshwater fish, both as a sport fish and as food. Trout has long been highly valued in lore and literature. Fly-fishing for trout has been richly described in terms of technique, equipment, and stories of memorable fishing experiences. As happens with other favored fishes, many names are applied to the same fish, causing much confusion. Most species of trout are in the genus *Salmo*, which also includes some species of salmon. Trout is found nearly everywhere in the world, occurring either naturally or because of introduction. Trout was among the earliest fish to be farm raised. It is widely raised both for food and for stocking lakes and ponds for sport. Trout is a good sport fish, prefers cool water, and has flavorful flesh. Each type of trout has its adherents among anglers, who equip themselves for catching their favorite type and travel to spots where they are likely to yield a catch.

Rainbow trout (*Salmo gairdneri*) is native to the mountains of the western United States but, beginning in the 1870s, has been introduced nationwide. Where the water is clear and cold, rainbow trout reproduce naturally after introduction. A good fighter, rainbow trout prefers streams but also lives in lakes if there are streams to which the fish can migrate to spawn. Rainbow trout is the most widely grown trout for stocking and food, because the fish grow quickly and seem able to adapt to nonnatural feed. Because of its abundant cold water, Idaho is a center for farm-raised rainbow trout, which needs temperatures less than 70°F. In the Great Lakes rainbow trout can grow to two to almost three feet in length, sometimes being mistaken for coho or chinook salmon. Smaller fish are more usual outside the Great Lakes. Pond-raised rainbow trout usually reaches two to five pounds.

Brown trout (*Salmo trutta*) is an introduced fish. It is native to Germany and was brought to America in the 1880s. The U.S. Fish Commission first stocked the Pere Marquette River in Michigan with brown trout, and the fish spread to almost every other state. Because brown trout does not naturally reproduce in most places where it has been introduced, the best way to maintain populations is restocking. Brown trout has become established in the upper Great Lakes. Like rainbow trout, brown trout prefers cooler water but can tolerate temperatures up to 75°F. Lake-caught brown trout can weigh as much as eight pounds and are predominantly silver, whereas stream-dwelling brown trout are spotted.

The cutthroat trout (*Oncorhynchus clarki clarii*) is native to America. The Latin name honors William Clark of the Lewis and Clark expedition, during which, on June 13, 1805, the fish was found and identified near the Great Falls of the Missouri River, Montana. Montana has named the cutthroat trout its state fish, partly to draw attention to the scarcity of this fish. Clark's cutthroat trout were sixteen to twenty-three inches in length and were described as being similar to speckled trout in the East. Cutthroat trout hybridizes with rainbow trout.

Lake trout (*Salvelinus namaycush*) and brook trout (*Salvelinus fontinalis*) are popular sport and food fishes, both have many regional names and nicknames, and both are char. Lake trout, called togue, salmon trout, forktail trout, and mackinaw, usually is one and one-half to two feet long and weighs three to nine pounds. This trout is a native of the Great Lakes, where it was part of the gill net fishery, but has been introduced elsewhere in America. Lake trout thrives in cool, deep water. Brook trout, also called brookie, speckled trout, square tail, and common or eastern brook trout, among other names, often is ten to twelve inches long when caught and weighs less than one to two pounds. Brook trout is native to eastern North America and has been widely introduced nationwide. Brook trout prefers cold water and can be found in small, cold streams and lakes at high altitudes. Brook trout is smaller than other species and so is not as popular with sportfishers, although the flesh rivals that of other trout for flavor. Also called trout is steelhead (*Oncorhynchus mykiss*, formerly *Salmo gairdneri Richardson*), an anadromous form of rainbow trout. Steelhead is large, often averaging five to ten pounds, and is a good sport fish. Steelhead, like many freshwater sport fish, has a large following of enthusiasts. Trout meat is generally oilier and more flavorful than meat of other fish, making small trout excellent panfish. Trout also is good filleted and prepared in any number of ways. It is excellent smoked.

SANDRA L. OLIVER

Tschirky, Oscar

Oscar Tschirky (1866–1950), better known as "Oscar of the Waldorf," was maître d'hôtel of the Waldorf-Astoria Hotel in New York City from 1893 to 1943. Tschirky emigrated from Switzerland in 1883, and with the help of his elder brother Brutus, who was a chef in New York, he landed a job as busboy at the Hoffman House, the best hotel in the city, the same day he landed in the United States.

From the moment of his arrival, Tschirky worked only at the finest places. In 1887 he was hired by Delmonico's, the most prestigious restaurant in New York City at the time. There Tschirky advanced to become headwaiter for the private dining rooms. Ever ambitious, when he heard about the $10 million Waldorf Hotel (the Astoria came later, with the addition of the Astoria wing in 1897) being built at Thirty-third Street and Fifth Avenue, Tschirky applied for a position. He wrote himself a letter of recommendation on Delmonico's stationery and encouraged the restaurant's well-known patrons to sign it. Four days after he mailed his impressive ten-page list, which resembled a who's who of New York, Tschirky was hired as the hotel's first employee.

Tschirky's management skills, attention to detail—he made a point of remembering what important guests liked to eat and drink—tact, class, good nature, and plain old hard work were some of the qualities that helped him thrive at the Waldorf and become the most influential American maître d'hôtel in his day. Tschirky established standards of service and grace that contributed to making the Waldorf the home away from home of celebrities, society, royalty, and presidents. Although Tschirky married and had three children, the hotel was his home away from home too.

Guests always assumed that Tschirky prepared and supervised all meals at the Waldorf. He was besieged by requests for recipes, especially after 1896, when he wrote *The Cook Book by "Oscar" of the Waldorf*, a hefty 900-page tome that included recipes from the most famous chefs of the day. But Tschirky admitted that he never cooked anything more difficult to prepare than scrambled eggs. The Waldorf chronicler James Remington McCarthy wrote in his book *Peacock Alley*, "His fame…has rested upon the condition that the public—erroneously…—regards him—as an artist who has composed sonatas in soups, symphonies in salads, minuets in sauces, lyrics in entrees." Tschirky's art, however, was orchestrating the score to create a harmonious meal. In 1902 Tschirky shared his art in a booklet titled "Serving a Course Dinner by Oscar of the Waldorf-Astoria." In the booklet he explained in simple terms the intricacies of serving a modern course dinner to legions of eager hostesses who wanted to re-create at home the elegance of a meal served under Oscar's guidance.

Tschirky is perhaps best remembered for the Waldorf salad, which he did create, but only with apples, celery, and mayonnaise. The salad has become a classic American dish, and there are as many versions of it as there are chefs. It is ironic that Tschirky hated the walnuts that somehow became standard in the salad.

Legend around the Waldorf had it that, as a joke, Oscar's wife phoned the hotel one day and asked for Mr. Tschirky, who was paged throughout the hotel but did not answer the call. It seems Tschirky had forgotten his last name. The surname may be forgettable, but the legend of Oscar of the Waldorf lives on. [See also COOKBOOKS AND MANUSCRIPTS: FROM THE CIVIL WAR TO WORLD WAR I; HOTEL DINING ROOMS; NEW YORK FOOD.]

BIBLIOGRAPHY
McCarthy, James Remington, with John Rutherford. *Peacock Alley*. New York: Harper, 1931.

SHARON KAPNICK

Tuna

At the beginning of the twentieth century, few Americans ate tuna. Within a few decades tuna rose from obscurity to become America's most consumed fish. At the end of the twentieth century high-priced tuna was ranked among America's finest culinary delicacies. Tuna is an oceanic fish in the Scombridae family related to mackerel and bonito. Historically tuna has been consumed for hundreds of years in the Mediterranean, Latin America, Asia, and Polynesia. Although tuna was abundant off North American shores, it was rarely consumed. Beginning in the 1870s sportsfishermen were enthralled with catching tuna. By 1898 tuna fishing was so popular that the Avalon Tuna Club was organized on Santa Catalina Island off mainland California.

Canned Tuna

Tuna was canned in France and Italy, and small quantities of *thoun* or *tonno* were imported into the United States by the early 1880s. The first American tuna cannery was established by Albert P. Halfhill, a grocer who moved to Los Angeles in the 1880s. Halfhill began canning albacore in 1908. The depletion of other traditionally consumed fish stocks, coupled with Halfhill's modest success, encouraged more tuna canners.

In 1910 salmon fishermen, who supplied the Columbia River Packers Association, began tuna fishing. The association later adopted the brand name Bumble Bee. Another packer was Van Camp Seafood, which operated under the brand names Chicken of the Sea and White Star. The promotional campaign, which likened tuna to chicken, greatly increased sales of tuna in America. By 1920 thirty-six tuna canneries dotted the West Coast landscape. One new packer was the French Sardine Company, which created StarKist Seafood. Decades later Bumble Bee, Van Camp Seafood, and StarKist became America's and for a time the world's largest tuna canners.

By 1925 the albacore had largely disappeared from California waters, and the tuna packing industry almost collapsed. By this time tuna had become wildly popular in mainstream America. So the tuna industry shifted to yellowfin, which had a higher percentage of dark meat. Because Americans expected white albacore meat, only the white meat was selected from yellowfin, and it was marketed as "light meat tuna." Americans made the shift to yellowfin and demanded even more tuna. As tuna fishermen increased in number and expanded their catch to meet demand, yellowfin stocks disappeared along the California coast, and tuna fishermen traveled farther south. This movement required a change in the vessels used to catch tuna. Small fishing boats gave way to the tuna clipper, which was equipped to carry live bait and was fitted with an ice system that allowed retention of the catch for long periods. By 1937 these large vessels fished off Central and South America and in subsequent years fished for tuna in the South Pacific.

Tuna Cookery

Once Americans concluded that tuna was palatable, the abundance of tuna off America's east and west coasts assured easy access to the fish. As demand for tuna increased, technological improvements in catching and processing meant that supply expanded faster than demand. The result was a decline in the price of tuna. When the Depression hit during the 1930s, low-cost, healthful tuna became America's most highly consumed fish.

Tuna recipes were not published regularly in cookery magazines and American cookbooks until the early twentieth century. The first located tuna advertising cookbooklet was published by a canner in 1913, Avalon Tuna, and other companies followed suit. Early tuna recipes were surprisingly diverse. Recipes were published for canapés, fish cakes, salads, soufflés, loafs, rolls, fish balls, tuna melts, savory pies, cream tuna, croquettes, omelets, puddings, and sandwiches. Two major uses of tuna emerged from this diversity: tuna salad, which was considered healthful and dietetic, and tuna sandwiches, which became a mainstay in children's lunch boxes. The third major use, tuna noodle casserole, made its debut during the 1930s but became emblematic of American foodways in the 1950s.

Tuna Challenges and Prospects

Despite tuna's rapid rise to stardom, several major challenges confronted the American tuna industry. The first was related to health. Tuna was considered a healthful food and was mentioned as a diet food by the 1920s. Indeed tuna is an excellent low-fat source of protein, contains B vitamins and omega-3 fatty acids, and has half the fat and cholesterol of an equal portion of chicken. However, problems emerged related to mercury, an industrial by-product dumped into America's rivers. Coastal fish ingested the mercury, and when they fed on these fish, tuna became contaminated with mercury, which is toxic. Testing procedures have been improved, greatly decreasing the possibility of mercury contamination in processed tuna.

Beginning in the 1950s increased foreign competition with lower labor costs and fewer environmental controls led to the most serious challenge to confront the American tuna industry. Tuna companies began to migrate outside the continental United States, and many tuna boats were reflagged or sold to companies in other countries. By 1989 there was only one surviving tuna cannery in the continental United States, and the tuna fleet, once the world's largest, had declined to only sixty-three boats.

The bases of the American tuna industry became American Samoa and Puerto Rico. Both had access to a lower-paid labor pool than did operations on the U.S. mainland, and both had tax laws supportive of the tuna industry. Despite these changes, the American tuna industry has declined since 1989. Correlated with this decline have been the rise of imported tuna and the establishment of foreign tuna operations in the United States. More than 60 percent of the tuna eaten in America is imported.

Whatever the source of the catch, tuna remains America's most important fish. In addition to its sale in the inexpensive canned form, tuna has emerged as a gourmet food. Beginning in the 1980s the sale of fresh tuna expanded. It is served in restaurants as grilled or sautéed steaks. Simultaneously Japanese restaurants serving sushi and sashimi have become popular, and these two raw fish dishes are sold regularly in fish markets and supermarkets. Tuna is estimated as being only 5 percent of the total fish catch worldwide, but economically it is one of the most important fishes in the world.

BIBLIOGRAPHY
Black, Andy. *A Can of Tuna: The Complete Guide to Cooking with Tuna*. Santa Rosa, CA: Prism, 1995.
Block, Barbara A., and E. Donald Stevens, eds. *Tuna: Physiology, Ecology, and Evolution*. San Diego, CA: Academic, 2001.
Bonanno, Alessandro, and Douglas Constance. *Caught in the Net: The Global Tuna Industry, Environmentalism, and the State*. Lawrence: University Press of Kansas, 1996.
Joseph, James, Witold Klawe, and Pat Murphy. *Tuna and Billfish: Fish without a Country*. La Jolla, CA: Inter-American Tropical Tuna Commission, 1988.
Smith, Bill. *Tuna*. Short Hills, NJ: Burford, 2000.

ANDREW F. SMITH

Tupperware

Tupperware is the registered trademarked name for all products of the Tupperware corporation. Most famous are the lightweight, odorless, reusable plastic containers with patented airtight lids that epitomize American postwar suburban culture. Tupperware embodies the era of convenience foods and home refrigeration, the age of plastic and industrial production. Perhaps most important, its home-selling plan, the Tupperware party, promulgated the distinctively American form of entertaining at which hostesses sell consumer products.

Earl Silas Tupper (1907–1983), a twentieth-century Benjamin Franklin, established Tupper Plastics Company in 1939 and developed the first Tupperware prototype around 1942. A home inventor who was raised on a New England farm, Tupper held traditional Yankee values of thrift and self-improvement and believed that industrial innovation could improve everyday life. Tupper's breakthrough came with a milky white, injection-molded plastic "bell tumbler," which launched the Tupperware line. The product reached stores in 1946. Three years later Tupper published his first mail-order catalog, introduced the brand name Tupperware, and proclaimed his dream for the "Tupperization" of every home in America. That same year Tupper received the patent for his airtight Tupper seal, which he issued "standard" with all containers beginning in 1948.

Almost indestructible, Tupper's containers were made from a refined polyethylene plastic, which he trademarked as Poly-T: Material of the Future. Tupperware's domestication of an avant-garde material previously used by industry and aviation was revolutionary. Although others sold functional kitchen plastics, Tupperware had no direct competition.

The industrial design movement quickly embraced Tupperware's clean lines and intrinsic utility. To the avant-garde, Tupperware married form and function on an industrial scale, the ideal set forth by the Bauhaus school of design and architecture that arose in Germany in the 1930s. *House Beautiful* magazine described Tupperware as "fine art for 39 cents." In 1947 the Detroit Institute of Arts displayed stacks of Tupperware in its Exhibition for Modern Living. In 1956 the Museum of Modern Art in New York featured the Wonderlier bowl in its exhibition on outstanding twentieth-century design. The museum later singled out Tupperware for its "ingenious hinges, handles and stopper." The curator wrote that "the carefully considered shapes are marvelously free of that vulgarity which characterizes so much household equipment" (quoted in Drexler and Daniel, 75).

Tupperware used a Fifth Avenue showroom to foster the image of its containers as sleek, modern conveniences, but the products failed to sell. Brownie Wise, a divorced mother from the suburbs of Detroit, among other top distributors, reported to Tupper that his wares lent themselves perfectly to home demonstration. Wise had sold Stanley Home Products through home parties, a practice introduced by Wearever Aluminum Cooking Products in the 1920s and promoted by Stanley during the 1930s as an alternative to door-to-door selling. Starting in 1948 Wise organized a team of saleswomen to hold "patio parties" at which Tupperware was sold along with other branded house-

wares and cosmetics. Gift incentives and a weekly sales bulletin motivated her band of dealers. In 1951 Tupper appointed Wise vice president of Tupperware Home Parties. The product was withdrawn from all stores and sold exclusively through home party distribution.

Tupperware and its selling method ideally suited the burgeoning culture of suburbia. The critical demonstration technique became known as the Tupperware burp. "Tupperware ladies" demonstrated the product's indispensability within the comfort of a friend's home while household tips and gossip were exchanged over coffee and cake. Elsie Mortland, billed by the company as an "ordinary housewife" turned "expert hostess," provided dealers with recipes and entertaining ideas that incorporated the product. The 1958 catalog included recipes for Tropicana salad, made of drained pineapple bits, maraschino cherries, and cottage cheese, and sandwich spreads of canned deviled ham spread and mayonnaise. Fruity colors of orange, lemon, raspberry, and lime and an expanding range of forms fueled consumer demand. The Party Susan, a sectioned hors d'oeuvres server, appealed to the taste for casual postwar entertaining. In 1955 Tupperware introduced TV Tumblers, which the catalog promised were "the perfect answer to beverage serving when watching your favorite TV program." From its inception, the Tupperware corporation actively sought co-branding alliances with food producers, such as Red Rooster cheese and Betty Crocker. Tupperware products such as the Giant Canister, which could hold ten-pound bags of flour, a large milk container, or eight king-size Coca-Cola bottles, were designed to fit commercial food packaging.

By 1952 party plan sales had become so indispensable that Tupperware purchased a 1,000-acre site on the Orange Blossom Trail in Orlando, Florida. Top dealers attended conferences that approximated evangelical revivals, praising the glory of Tupperware and the capitalist economy that saw it thrive. By 1954 tourist buses arrived in droves to visit the headquarters, where they toured the "Magic Kitchen" to watch product testing and demonstrations. Corporate songs and rituals reinforced the mystique of "Tupper Magic," while select participants were "baptized" at Poly Pond. In 1954 the annual jubilee bringing thousands of managers and distributors together included a "Big Dig" at which six hundred members of the Tupperware sales force vied to unearth more than $48,000 worth of buried prizes—including toasters, radios, diamond rings, mink stoles, and even a toy car that was traded in for a full-size Ford.

Feminists have accused the Tupperware company of reinforcing the stereotype of the happy housewife and of contributing to the homogenization of American suburban culture. Nevertheless, the Tupperware corporation provided career opportunities for women after those epitomized by Rosie the

Riveter relinquished factory jobs to war veterans. Other companies soon imitated the hostess party model that Tupperware made famous. By the end of the 1950s it was estimated that more than three-quarters of a million women were involved in direct selling.

Although in 1954 *Business Week* magazine featured her as the first woman ever on its cover, Wise was fired by Tupper in 1958, purportedly because of her extravagant spending. That same year Tupper sold the company and its subsidiaries, believing the company's peak of success had passed.

A 1960 marketing report concluded that the Tupperware party plan could not be successfully exported to England, where guests would be offended at the pressure to buy. Similar complaints circulated in parts of the United States, where some also thought the product distastefully lower middle class. Yet Tupperware and its home-selling method flourished, extending through Europe, South America, Africa, and Japan. Despite a mixed reception by the press, England adored the shiny wares emblematic of modern American culture. By 1965 Japanese housewives were buying twice as many pieces as their American counterparts. By the late 1970s catalogs transformed the image of the Tupperware hostess from a housewife into a career woman, who might hold parties at the office instead of at home.

In 1998 Tupperware expanded its sales strategy to include mall kiosks, abandoning the exclusivity of the home party plan for the first time since 1951. In the early twenty-first century the company offers products online, on home-shopping television networks, and in selected retail stores. Nevertheless, home parties continue to account for 90 percent of company sales. Tupperware has become a billion-dollar multinational company with a range of products from special containers for cooking in microwave ovens to children's toys to seasoning mixes. The bowls and lids that first made the company famous, however, continue to define Tupperware.

[See also CONTAINERS; GENDER ROLES; HISTORICAL OVERVIEW: WORLD WAR II TO THE EARLY 1960s; JELL-O MOLDS; RECIPES.]

BIBLIOGRAPHY

Clarke, Alison J. *Tupperware: The Promise of Plastic in 1950s America*. Washington, DC: Smithsonian Institution Press, 1999.

Drexler, Arthur, and Greta Daniel. *Introduction to Twentieth Century Design from the Collection of the Museum of Modern Art, New York*. Garden City, NY: Doubleday, 1959.

CAROLIN C. YOUNG

Turkey

In pre-Columbian times wild turkeys were plentiful from Honduras to the eastern coast of North America. When the Spanish arrived in Mexico in 1519, they found an abundance of wild and domesticated turkeys. The Spanish introduced domesticated turkeys into the

An illustration of wild turkeys.

Caribbean by 1520 and into Spain soon thereafter. From Spain turkeys disseminated rapidly throughout western Europe and the Mediterranean. Turkeys reached England before 1550. Turkey was an extremely important food for European colonists in North America. Because domesticated turkeys were plentiful in England by 1570, British colonists were familiar with turkey well before their ships landed in North America. Turkeys were also an important food source on the western frontier. Domesticated turkeys were imported from England into British North America soon after the establishment of English colonies.

Along river valleys, wild turkeys wandered in flocks of five thousand or more birds. The historian Remington Kellogg believed that had it not been for the supply of meat from deer and turkeys, the westward expansion of America would have been long delayed. Success was accompanied by problems, however. Wild turkeys were depleted in many areas during colonial times. However, wild turkeys were among the first wild animals to be successfully reintroduced, and they abound in New England in the early twenty-first century.

Turkey Cookery

The first American to publish a cookbook, Amelia Simmons, had five turkey recipes in her *American Cookery* (1796). Most subsequent cookbooks published additional recipes. In general cookbook instructions fell into five categories: how to select turkeys; how to roast, boil, fry, steam, or bake them; how to stuff them; foods to accompany them; and what to do with turkey leftovers. In the South where Christmas was celebrated, the turkey became the centerpiece of the Christmas dinner. In the North the turkey was a common feature at Thanksgiving meals. The phrase "Turkey Day" did not become a synonym for Thanksgiving until the late nineteenth century.

Turkey Breeding

Soon after the introduction of domesticated turkeys into the British North American colonies, domesticated birds bred with wild turkeys, and new turkey varieties emerged. During the mid-nineteenth century poulterers deliberately bred turkeys to produce specific traits. Several turkey varieties were elevated to breeding status; the two most important commercial varieties were the medium-sized White Holland, which could be raised close to population centers and sold directly to nearby customers, and the large Bronze, which could be raised at great distances from population centers and then frozen for transportation.

In 1927 Jesse Throessel, an Englishman, bred large birds that had exceptionally wide breasts but lacked other important qualities. As the breasts of the new turkeys became larger and the legs shorter, it became difficult for turkeys to mate, so artificial insemination became standard practice.

Turkey Production

Until the early twentieth century turkeys were raised on family farms and were marketed locally. After World War II growers began to expand the size of their operations. In 1961 the turkey market crashed, and many growers lost their businesses. Those who remained had to lower their costs to survive. One way of lowering costs was vertical integration, in which all aspects of turkey farming were combined into one operation to eliminate middlemen. This system tended to concentrate the turkey industry in fewer hands, and most small farmers dropped out of the turkey business. Centralization of the turkey industry has continued since the 1960s. Among the larger American turkey businesses are Jennie-O Turkey Store, Cargill Turkey Products, and the Butterball Turkey Company. All are controlled by major food conglomerates.

Starting in the early twentieth century, turkey meat has consistently been presented as a nutritious, low-calorie alternative to beef and pork. Turkey has the smallest amount of saturated and unsaturated fat of any commercial meat and the highest percentage of protein. Yet health concerns related to turkey have regularly been reported. The U.S. Centers for Disease Control and Prevention (CDC) has regularly reported that at least 13 percent of raw U.S. turkey carries salmonella, a bacterium that can cause serious health problems if the meat is not properly handled and thoroughly cooked. A more serious problem is *Listeria monocytogenes* contamination, which can cause death.

Turkey in the Early Twenty-first Century

To attract year-round buyers, new products were created, such as turkey roll, which many consumers claimed did not taste like turkey, and ground dark turkey meat, which required considerable research. The industry launched a promotional campaign encouraging consumers to substitute turkey meat in traditional chicken and beef dishes. Turkey consumption has increased throughout the year, but the major reasons for this change have been the consumption of turkey sandwiches and the increase in the sale of frozen dinners that contain turkey.

North Carolina and Minnesota are the two main turkey-producing states, followed by Arkansas, Missouri, Virginia, California, Indiana, and South Carolina. In the United States annual consumption of turkey increased from 8.1 pounds in the early 1980s to more than 13.8 pounds per person in 2001. Regardless of how much is consumed, the turkey is a powerful culinary and social symbol in the United States.

[**See also** Christmas; Club Sandwich; Dressings and Stuffings; Food Safety; Fowl; Sandwiches; Simmons, Amelia; Swanson; Thanksgiving.]

BIBLIOGRAPHY

Davis, Karen. *More than a Meal: The Turkey in History, Myth, Ritual, and Reality.* New York: Lantern, 2001.

Schorger, A. W. *The Wild Turkey: Its History and Domestication.* Norman: University of Oklahoma Press, 1966.

Small, M. C. "Turkeys, Once Only a Holiday Festivities Dish, a Great Industry Has Been Developed," In *American Poultry History 1823–1973,* ed. John L. Skinner. Madison, WI: American Poultry History Society, 1974.

Smith, Andrew F. *The Turkey: An American Story.* Urbana: University of Illinois Press, 2006.

ANDREW F. SMITH

Turnips

The turnip (*Brassica rapa, Brassica campestris*) is a root vegetable in the Cruciferae, or mustard, family and is closely related to the rutabaga (*Brassica napobrassica*). Turnips were brought to the North American colonies in the seventeenth century but were not widespread until the eighteenth. By the nineteenth century turnips were well established for two purposes—culinary use and farm animal fodder. The latter was popularized by the English politician and land improver Charles Townshend,

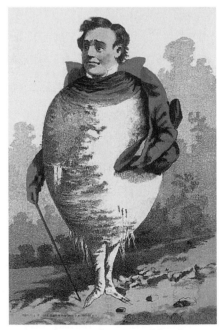

A nineteenth-century advertising card featuring a strange turnip person.

called "Turnip Townshend," who in approximately 1730 developed a system of rotating grain crops with turnips. Because they are a cool weather crop and have a high protein content, turnips are perfect for fattening cattle during the autumn and winter. Forage turnips appear in early farmer's manuals along with the traditional advisory jingle to sow the seeds "before the Twenty-Fifth of July, whether it be wet or dry."

Until the twentieth century most culinary turnips were garden crops. Early recipes in America appear in cookery books such as *The Art of Cookery* by Hannah Glasse (1748) and *The Virginia House-Wife* by Mary Randolph (1824). Glasse recommended treating turnips like potatoes, boiling and mashing them. She also suggested making wine from turnips. Randolph called for the same treatment but also gave a classic southern recipe, boiled turnip greens with bacon "in the Virginia style." The amount of turnips eaten by humans remains regional. Turnip greens, often cooked with diced turnip root, are a part of the standard southern menu and often are considered "soul food." Turnip roots, cooked in the Glasse style, are more appreciated in the Northeast than elsewhere. The bland-tasting and low-fiber turnip, however, remains a barely tolerated visitor to most traditional American tables. Turnips usually are boiled and served with fat or corned meats and are used in vegetable soups.

[**See also** AFRICAN AMERICAN FOOD: SINCE EMANCIPATION; VEGETABLES.]

BIBLIOGRAPHY

Vaughan, J. G., and C. Geissler. *The New Oxford Book of Food Plants.* Oxford: Oxford University Press, 1997.

BRUCE KRAIG

Turnspit Dogs

Spits for roasting large joints of meat at the hearth had to be turned constantly. Small servant boys were used in European kitchens, slaves in America. In the eighteenth century, and probably long before, a specially bred short-legged, large-chested dog called a "turnspit dog" was placed into a caged wheel that was mounted to a wall or suspended from joists. The dog then was made to run, sometimes for hours, like a hamster in its wheel. A long leather belt encircled the wheel and turned the smaller wheel of the spit. The English writer Thomas Hone in 1850 wrote that "[in England] the turnspit-dog and apparatus for cooking are now nearly out of use." It is believed that these dogs were used in the United States well into the 1870s. The breed has died out, at least in name, but certain stocky mixed terriers resemble the short-eared, curly-tailed dog seen in old prints.

[**See also** HEARTH COOKERY; KITCHENS: EARLY KITCHENS; MEAT.]

BIBLIOGRAPHY

Franklin, Linda Campbell. *300 Years of Kitchen Collectibles.* 5th ed. Iola, WI: Krause, 2003.

LINDA FRANKLIN

TV Dinners

Swanson introduced the frozen TV dinner in 1954 in a package designed to resemble a television set. The three-section aluminum tray containing turkey and gravy, peas, and sweet potatoes required only reheating—a hallmark of convenience. It was also a hallmark of changing American cooking and eating habits. Critics judged TV dinners and their imitators guilty of promoting bland uniformity on a grand scale, the same judgment they leveled against television. A potent symbol of social change, the original aluminum tray, replaced by a plastic one with the advent of the microwave oven, is housed in the Smithsonian Institution.

MATT MCMILLEN

TV Dinners: A Firsthand Account

C. A. Swanson and Sons' signature product was turkey, and in 1951 the company possessed a record crop of Ute turkeys that had been produced from California to Minnesota. Credit for this plenitude could be attributed to the system established by Carl Swanson of Omaha, Nebraska, founder of the company, who had been dubbed the "Turkey King of America" by *Fortune* magazine. In order to stabilize the production of turkeys, each year he guaranteed a purchase price for turkeys grown for Swanson and delivered in prime condition. This generous contractual arrangement assured Swanson of an abundance of birds each year, but they had to be sold prior to Thanksgiving, since in those years ninety percent of all turkeys were sold for that holiday. The unsold inventory was so great in February 1952 that an emergency meeting was convened to discuss the matter. Thanksgiving had long since passed, and the next "season" was nine months away. At the meeting we learned that we had over twenty refrigerated train carloads of turkeys— 52,000 pounds in each car—going back and forth across the country because there was no market. There wasn't enough static cold storage space, so they had to remain in the refrigerated cars, on the track and moving.

Driving my Plymouth home from the meeting, slowly, on those snow-rutted Omaha streets, I remember thinking that I'd been passionately involved in the frozen food business ever since being hired by Swanson in 1948. Every day anticipated some kind of discovery. World War II was just concluded, and it was a time of great optimism and adventure. Hell, I nearly tap-danced to work every day, I was that eager to get on the job.

There are similarities, I think, between the frozen food technology of the 1940s and 1950s and the digital technology of the 1980s and 1990s. The technology is far different, of course, but both industries offered rewards for creativity featuring value-added products. We received the same siren call then that men and women in the digital age heard in the 1980s and 1990s. It was seductive, compelling, and exciting.

The Monday after the February 1952 meeting, I inspected a frozen food warehouse with one of our distributors in Pittsburgh. I noticed some shipping cartons holding foil-wrapped products. The distributor said the cartons belonged to Pan Am Airlines. They had just ordered new jet passenger planes for overseas flights, featuring, for the first time, hot meals prepared on board in convection ovens. With a mental "flicker of a light bulb," I slipped a product into my overcoat pocket for the flight back to Omaha. At a follow-up meeting the following Saturday morning, ideas for turkey sales were conventional commodity oriented, then I showed the group the experimental consumer product I'd discovered. It was a single-compartment aluminum tray holding mashed potatoes, a slice of beef, and gravy. I had noodled with an idea on the DC-3 returning from Pittsburgh via Chicago to Omaha, drawing diagrams of three-compartment trays, suggested to me by my negative experience in World War II with single-compartment mess gear, which resulted in stew for every meal. I suggested that we might consider a prepared "meal," because our success in 1950 with frozen chicken pies had generated public expression of wanting everything faster with more convenience.

We reviewed the pros and cons of such an undertaking. Clarke and Gilbert Swanson had been raised in the price-driven commodity business by their father and were born gamblers. They were more than willing to take risks. They also, at the time, happened to be up to their eyeballs in turkeys.

Without blinking, Clarke said, "Hell, Gil, let's do it."

Once the idea had been mutually embraced by the Swanson brothers, everyone on the small staff proceeded to move with haste—each in their own field of expertise—to create an environment for success.

Marketing was my field of expertise. When I joined Swanson in 1948 the company had scant interest and no education in product names or branded consumer packaging. In fact, except for annual calendars sent to suppliers, there had been no expenditures for advertising. I was hired by Clarke and Gilbert, with my freshly earned University of Nebraska BS degree in Marketing, to fill that void in management.

Continued on following page.

Twinkies

Twinkies, oblong sponge cakes with a cream filling, were created in 1930, during the Depression. James A. Dewar, manager of the Continental Baking Company in Schiller Park, Illinois, was looking for a way to use the pans used to bake shortbread fingers, which were used only during the summer strawberry season. The original sponge cakes were sold without cream filling for use in strawberry shortcakes. Dewar injected the cakes with a banana filling, creating a year-round item that sold two for a nickel. A banana shortage during World War II prompted Continental to substitute vanilla cream for the original banana-cream filling. The vanilla filling continues to be used in Twinkies. According to Hostess, the division of Continental that produces Twinkies, the name for the cakes came from a billboard advertising "Twinkle Toe" shoes that Dewar saw on a business trip to St. Louis. Continental was purchased by Interstate Bakeries Corporation, headquartered in Kansas City, Missouri, in 1995.

Twinkies have added to the American lexicon. In the late 1970s the attorney for Dan White, a San Francisco city councilman, said his client's overindulgence in sugary food rendered him momentarily insane and was to blame for the killing of the city's mayor and another councilman. The jury convicted White of manslaughter rather than murder, and the phrase "Twinkie defense" was coined. Another coinage was "Twinkie tax," after a proposal in 1997 for placing a tax on high-fat foods and soft drinks. The intention was to curb Americans' consumption of "junk" food and to combat obesity.

[**See also** BAKERIES; BANANAS; CAKES; DESSERTS.]

BIBLIOGRAPHY

Jackson, Susan. "How about a Big, Fat Tax on Junk Food?" *BusinessWeek*, June 26, 1997.

KARA NEWMAN

TV Dinners: A Firsthand Account (Continued)

A brainstorming session of key management players generated significant decisions on packaging and finalized the side dishes for a turkey and gravy entrée—corn bread dressing, mashed sweet potatoes, and petite peas. Both the potatoes and petite peas would be topped with a pat of 92 score Swanson butter. At the session's conclusion, Clarke fixed cool blue eyes on me and in his warm but husky voice added, "One more thing, Gerry, this is your baby, what are you going to call it?"

I'd given the subject a lot of thought. The juxtaposition of letters, the forming of words and acronyms, had been my preoccupation since childhood. In the army in World War II my specialty had been cryptography and cryptanalysis. This revolutionary new product demanded a unique personality. My thoughts went to the most popular entertainment attraction happening in America—television. By marrying the word "television" to a frozen meal, the "issue" would automatically become contemporary. The name would be easy to say and remember . . . and it was "cool."

The name I coined was "TV dinner."

In society, a perverse dichotomy was at work. Women, fresh from the liberation of working outside the home during World War II, were eager to embrace a product that permitted them to provide satisfying meals for their family and still work part time. On the negative side, there were few home freezers, limited equipment in stores for display and storage, no equipped delivery trucks, and little knowledge of frozen food preparation. In this environment success was questionable.

Within two years we had a line of products that included fried chicken, roast beef, and filet of haddock, each variety with appropriate side dish components. We were selling turkey dinners at a rate of 13 million a year by 1954. Then in April of 1955, Campbell Soup Company, recognizing the leading edge of a dynamic new industry, frozen heat-n-serve dinners, acquired C. A. Swanson and Sons . . . and the "TV dinner."

GERRY THOMAS

Twinkies, Deep-Fried

Deep-fried Twinkies are a relatively recent addition to the Twinkie canon. Restaurateur Christopher Sell is credited with concocting this delicacy in early 2001. The native of Rugby, England, is the proprietor of the fish-and-chips restaurant Chipshop, in Brooklyn, New York. The shop was selling fried candy bars such as Mars Bars and Snickers, a longtime treat in Scotland. To pass the time one evening, Sell and his coworkers began tossing random junk food items into the shop's industrial deep fryer and found that the Twinkie worked well as a fried treat.

The result, which can resemble a beignet or a soufflé, is crispy outside and has a soft, pudding-like inside. The deep-fried Twinkie has become a regular on the fair food circuit, alongside other fried snacks such as funnel cake and curly fries. Interstate Bakeries, which makes Hostess Twinkies, is active in promoting the concept of fried Twinkies to vendors at state and county fairs.

KARA NEWMAN

Uncle Ben

Uncle Ben was a poor African American rice farmer who produced top-quality, high-yield rice near Beaumont, Texas, in the early 1940s. Legend has it that his crops were held in high regard and that local farmers tried to produce rice "as good as Uncle Ben's." Little else is known about him; even his last name is lost to history. He died never knowing that his name would be associated with rice and a line of food products.

During World War II a Texas produce broker named Gordon Harwell and an English food chemist named Eric Huzenlaub developed a process for pressure boiling long-grain rice before it was milled. Traditional milling lost all but 5 percent of the nutritional value of rice. The new process retained 80 percent of the vitamins and minerals, representing the first change to rice in more than five thousand years. Pressure boiling also dramatically increased the storage life of rice, making it a practical staple for the U.S. military to ship to troops fighting overseas. The product was sold exclusively to the armed forces under the name "Converted rice" until the war ended.

After the war Harwell and his business partner, Forrest E. Mars, introduced the product to the American public. They renamed it "Uncle Ben's" after the Texas farmer. The model for the product trademark was a Chicago maître d'hôtel named Frank C. Brown. His likeness continues to be used. In response to complaints that the name "Uncle Ben" and Brown's picture depicted slavery stereotypes, the logo with Brown's likeness was withdrawn in the 1980s. Sales plummeted, and the logo returned two years later. The size of the logo and its placement on packaging have changed over the years, but the picture has remained the same since 1947.

Uncle Ben's Converted rice was one of the first convenience foods introduced in America. It also marked the acceptance of rice as an alternative to potatoes. An advertising theme of "perfect every time" and "each grain salutes you" expanded steadily for more than fifty years. Over time various grain products, including wild rice, brown rice, and a quick-cook product known as "instant rice," were added to consumers' tables. Basmati, arborio, and jasmine rice have been joined by a no-cook brand of Converted rice for commercial kitchens. Consumers are targeted with more than sixty products associated with rice and pasta plus a line of stir-fry and skillet sauces. Uncle Ben's products are sold in more than twenty countries in North America, Europe, and Asia.

Uncle Ben's Converted rice is the world's top-selling Converted brand. Uncle Ben's, Inc., which is owned by the privately held Mars, Inc., has expanded to include food for every meal. Brand extensions moved to the freezer aisle with the introduction of a bowl category. Uncle Ben's sales strategy has broadened from selling side dishes to one-dish meals while markedly increasing frozen food sales in supermarkets. Uncle Ben's soups and rice puddings are other additions to grocery aisles. Trademark applications indicate that snack products and more desserts will be added, all bearing the familiar Uncle Ben's logo.

[**See also** Combat Food; Mars; Rice.]

BIBLIOGRAPHY

Kern-Foxworth, Marilyn. *Aunt Jemima, Uncle Ben, and Rastus: Blacks in Advertising, Yesterday, Today, and Tomorrow.* Westport, CT: Greenwood, 1994.

Maryanne Nasiatka

USDA, *see Department of Agriculture, United States*

Utensils, *see Silverware*

V

Valentine's Day

The feast of Saint Valentine is observed on February 14—a day set aside by the Roman Catholic Church to honor two martyred saints: Valentine of Rome and Valentine of Termi. Some saints' days have long-standing connections with food, such as Saint Patrick's Day with corned beef and cabbage. There are, however, no historic or modern food associations with Saint Valentine. Over time "Saint" was dropped from Saint Valentine's Day, and the feast evolved into a day on which gifts are given to demonstrate love and affection.

Initially lovers merely sent decorated cards to their "valentine's." Later, flowers became appropriate as well as desired gifts. Food, especially candy, joined the Valentine's Day gift trilogy after the Civil War. This phenomenon was apparently due to a decrease in the price of sugar and the rise of America's commercial confectionery. Candy manufacturers created heart-shaped boxes of chocolates decorated in the style of hand-decorated Victorian Valentine's Day cards.

Valentine's Day food occupies a seasonal promotional food niche from January 2 to mid-February, when stores are overstocked with chocolates and sweets. The quintessen-

tial Valentine's Day candy gift is a small box of assorted Sweethearts Conversation Hearts candy. These small, heart-shaped pastel wafers—printed with such Valentine's Day messages as "Be Mine," "Kiss Me," and "Sweet Talk"—have been made by the New England Confectionery Company since 1902.

Most other Valentine's Day food is also heart shaped or heart related. Popular Valentine's Day salads include artichoke hearts, hearts of palm, or hearts of romaine as essential ingredients. Cookies, cakes, and tarts are heart shaped and usually are filled with red raspberry jam. Some adult Valentine's Day dinner menus feature foods that are popularly believed to be aphrodisiacs, such as oysters, champagne, and chocolate.

[See also Candy Bars and Candy; Chocolate; Christmas; Fourth of July; Molasses; New Year's Celebrations; Passover; Saint Patrick's Day; Thanksgiving; Washington's Birthday.]

BIBLIOGRAPHY

Cohen, Henning, and Tristam Potter Coffin, eds. *The Folklore of American Holidays: A Compilation of More Than 400 Beliefs, Legends, Superstitions, Proverbs, Riddles, Poems, Songs, Dances, Games, Plays, Pageants, Fairs, Foods, and Processions Associated with over 100 American Calendar Customs and Festivals*. 3rd ed. Detroit, MI: Gale, 1999.

Woloson, Wendy A. *Refined Tastes: Sugar, Confectionery, and Consumers in Nineteenth-Century America*. Baltimore: Johns Hopkins University Press, 2002.

ROBERT W. BROWER

Vanilla

The genus *Vanilla*, a member of the enormous orchid family, includes about one hundred species, all of which are tropical vines with trailing stems that attach themselves to nearby trees. All species of vanilla produce elongated pods filled with tiny seeds, but only two species of vanilla (*planifolia* and *tahitensis*) are used for commercial purposes.

Vanilla is native to southern Mexico, Central America, and the West Indies. The source of its distinctive flavor is the "bean"—the long, flat, slender seedpod, which is odorless when picked. The distinctive vanilla aroma develops only when the pod is properly cured. In pre-Columbian times the Totonac people discovered that beans left in the sun became fragrant, and they sold great quantities of the beans to the Aztecs, who called them *tlilxochitl*, or black flower.

The first European to make mention of vanilla was Bernal Díaz, a soldier in the army of the explorer Hernán Cortés, who conquered Mexico in the early sixteenth century. Díaz noted that vanilla beans were added to ground cocoa beans to make a frothy and fragrant (though bitter) drink that was the delight of the Aztec nobility. The Spanish called the newly discovered product *vania*, which means a sheath or pod.

Cortés sent vanilla and cocoa beans to Spain, where they were among the first New World foods to be adopted in the Old World. Large quantities of vanilla beans were shipped

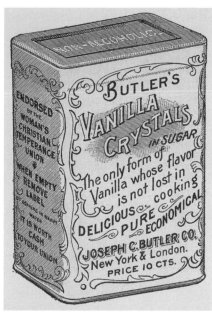

An advertisement for Butler's Vanilla Crystals, 1898.

to Europe, where people readily took up the habit of drinking chocolate beverages flavored with vanilla. Vanilla was in such demand that repeated unsuccessful attempts were made to grow the plants in greenhouses in Europe. The reason for the failure, which was not understood until the nineteenth century, is that vanilla's natural pollinators are the *Melipona* bees and other insects native to Mexico. These insects did not thrive outside of southern Mexico, which was the only supplier of vanilla beans until the nineteenth century.

Charles Morren of Liège, Belgium, succeeded in artificially fertilizing vanilla in 1836. The French grew vanilla on their islands in the Indian Ocean. Five years after Morren's discovery, Edmond Albius, a former slave on the island of Réunion, discovered a better way of pollinating the flowers that greatly increased productivity. Vanilla growing expanded to other tropical French islands, including Madagascar and Tahiti.

Although vanilla was used extensively in French cookery, it was not an important flavoring in colonial America, although small quantities of vanilla beans were imported into the United States prior to 1800. Thomas Jefferson imported vanilla beans and used them in making ice cream, but vanilla remained a rare flavoring in America until the mid-nineteenth century, when the vast increase in world production greatly decreased its cost.

Joseph Burnett, a Boston chemist, figured out how to make extract from vanilla beans, and he began bottling and selling the product in 1847. The extract was easier to ship and store than the whole beans, and the extract was pale brown, making it useful for flavoring white or light-colored sauces. In 1874 German chemists synthesized vanillin, the dominant flavor component of vanilla beans. While synthetic vanillin does not have the

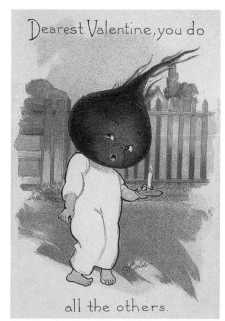

A valentine card published by Raphael Tuck and Sons in 1907.

Dearest Valentine, you do

all the others.

full flavor of natural vanilla, its production did greatly lower the cost of vanilla-like flavoring for home and commercial use.

By the late nineteenth century vanilla was an important ingredient in American recipes for sauces, ice cream, baked goods, and beverages. Aside from the Joseph Burnett Company, vanilla extract was produced by many other firms, including the C. F. Sauer Company of Richmond, Virginia, and the J. R. Watkins Company of Winona, Minnesota.

As the prices of vanilla and vanillin declined, the flavoring was used in a much wider range of foods and dishes, including custards, puddings, cakes, candies, cookies, meringues, macaroons, and pies. In the 1870s soda fountain proprietors began using vanilla as a flavoring, and the cream soda was invented. In addition to cookery, vanilla also became an important ingredient in making perfume and other scent-based commercial products.

Vanilla manufacturers produced cookbooklets filled with recipes to encourage the use of their products. The first noncommercial vanilla cookbook was published in 1986 by Patricia Rain. She has subsequently promoted vanilla cookery throughout the United States and has been referred to as the "Vanilla Queen."

The largest culinary use of vanilla is in the making of ice cream. Until the mid-twentieth century vanilla was America's favorite ice cream flavor, followed by chocolate. Although no longer America's favorite flavor of ice cream, vanilla remains an important ice cream flavor. The largest American manufacturer of vanilla extract and vanillin is McCormick and Company, which was founded in Baltimore in 1889.

BIBLIOGRAPHY

Coe, Sophie D. *America's First Cuisines*. Austin: University of Texas Press, 1994.

Rain, Patricia. *Vanilla: The Cultural History of the World's Most Popular Flavor and Fragrance*. New York: Tarcher/Penguin, 2004.

ANDREW F. SMITH

Veganism

In 1944 in Leicester, England, Donald Watson (1910–2005) and his wife Dorothy coined the word "vegan," which they formed from the first three and last two letters of "vegetarian." With this new term the Watsons wanted to encompass the meaning of "vegetarian" imparted by the Pythagoreans and Buddhists—one who, for reasons of compassion, abstain from consuming all foods and other products of animal origin. When asked in an interview what had impelled him to coin the term "vegan," Watson said, "Veganism originated from the thought that any sentient creature has rights" (Connelly 2005, p. 23). From this it is clear that veganism—grounded as it is in compassion for other beings—is a corollary of the animal rights movement. Vegans do not consume honey, for instance, because it is the work product of the bee, and honey cannot be harvested without causing the death of some

Vegetable advertising cards from the nineteenth century.

bees. Nor do vegans wear clothing from animal sources. Shoes made from leather, dresses made from silk, or jackets made from wool are verboten to vegans, because their manufacture may result in the discomfort or death of animals. Pharmaceuticals and medicines extracted from animals or that contain animal ingredients are also studiously avoided.

It took time for the word "vegan" to catch on in the United States, but now it has become almost a competing term with "vegetarian." To help win recognition for the vegan concept in America, H. Jay Dinshah started

the American Vegan Society in 1960. Dinshah, of Parsee descent, infused American veganism with the Jain and Buddhist doctrine of ahimsa, nonviolence to all living beings. In fact *Ahimsa* was the name of the journal (latterly the *American Vegan*) that Dinshah and his wife published quarterly for forty-one years. Dinshah's wife Freya wrote the first ethical vegetarian or vegan cookbook in the United States, *The Vegan Kitchen* (1966), which remains a steady seller. Despite the seeming hardships that a vegan diet imposes on its practitioners, veganism is a burgeoning movement, especially among younger Americans. In the endurance sports, such as the Ironman triathlon and the Ultramarathon, the top competitors are vegans who consume much of their vegan food in its uncooked state. Even young weight lifters and body-builders are gravitating to a vegan diet, giving the lie to the notion that eating animal flesh is essential for strength and stamina. Brendan Brazier, a young athlete who regularly places in the top three in international triathlon events and who formulated Vega a line of whole food, plant-based performance products, said of his fellow vegan athletes, "We're beginning to build a strong presence in every sport" (Connelly 2006, p. 24).

Indeed Carl Lewis, who holds the record for the number of gold medals won in track and field events, is a vegan. The tennis star Martina Navratilova, who was still winning tennis championships in her fifties, adopted a raw foods vegan diet late in middle age and credits the diet with helping prolong her career. Dennis Kucinich, the first vegan to run for the American presidency, attributed his stamina on the grueling campaign trail to his vegan diet. The film actors Woody Harrelson and Alicia Silverstone are vegan activists, as is Sir Paul McCartney of Beatles fame. McCartney is such a staunch vegan that he insists that only vegan foods be sold by concessionaires at his concerts.

Vegan cuisine reached its apotheosis in 1992 and 1995, when two American vegan chefs, Ken Bergeron and his mentor Brother Ron Pickarski, a Franciscan friar, won gold medals for their presentations of vegan cuisine at the International Culinary Olympics in Frankfurt, Germany. A spate of glossy new vegan cookbooks with too-clever titles—*How It All Vegan* (1999), *The Garden of Vegan* (2003), and *La Dolce Vegan* (2005)—are being devoured by young health enthusiasts, environmentalists, and animal-rights activists throughout North America. New York City now boasts so many vegan restaurants and emporia that there is even a *Vegan Guide to New York City* (Rynn Berry and Chris Abreu-Suzuki), now in its fifteenth year of publication. Doubtless it is a harbinger of many such Baedekers as vegan goes mainstream.

BIBLIOGRAPHY

Connelly, Joseph. "The Donald," *Veg-News* 45 (September–October 2005).

Connelly, Joseph. "Lean, Clean Vegan Machine," *Veg-News* 47 (January–February 2006).

Stepaniak, Joanne. *The Vegan Sourcebook.* Los Angeles: Lowell House, 1998.

RYNN BERRY

Vegetable Oils

At first the only oil regularly available to colonial Americans was olive oil. Yet only in the most elite enclaves within the Spanish colonies was this expensive import used for cooking. In the English and French settlements, it was reserved almost exclusively for salad dressings.

This only changed with advent of new processing methods in the late eighteenth century and the nineteenth century. Among the first new oils to come to market was peanut oil. George Brownrigg developed a process for extracting "a well tasted" oil from peanuts in North Carolina around 1768, and the oil came to be used as a substitute for olive oil, at least in the South. Due to its low price, it was often used as an adulterant in much more expensive olive oil. By the 1840s peanut oil was used in the southern states as a cooking fat in its own right, but by the end of the Civil War peanut oil production had ceased. Grocers had to turn to Europe to stock their shelves with peanut oil. Not until World War II did government efforts light a fire under the domestic peanut industry, resulting in an improved oil used not only for cooking and the manufacture of other compound fats but also numberless industrial uses. In 1930 the Planters Peanuts company harnessed its considerable marketing acumen to promote its own brand of oil, resulting in its familiar packaging.

After the Civil War cottonseed oil production largely replaced peanut oil in the cotton-producing states. Cottonseed processing on a commercial scale began in New Orleans and in Providence, Rhode Island, in 1855. Most processing plants were located wherever cotton was grown in quantity, and not until the railroads were expanded to many parts of the South around 1880 did the business take off. Demand increased further when cottonseed oil was sold under the Wesson brand as of 1900. Crisco was largely composed of hydrogenated cottonseed oil as well. With the decline of American-grown cotton in the late twentieth century, cottonseed oil has largely been replaced by less expensive oils.

In the early twentieth century new chemical techniques were devised to extract and refine oils from plants with a relatively low fat content. One of these new oils was first refined from corn at the Corn Products Refining Company in 1910 and marketed under the label Mazola. Increasingly the new oil that came to dominate American and overseas production was processed from soybeans. The increase in output was particularly notable after World War II. Between 1939 and 1986 world soybean oil production increased fifteenfold.

Perhaps the most notable addition to supermarket shelves since the 1980s has been the introduction of rape seed oil, an oil long used for industrial purposes in Europe. In the United States it was reformulated and renamed "canola" oil and touted for its healthier profile. Olive oil has also seen a remarkable renaissance both for its purported health benefits and for its snob appeal. Some brands are now marketed much like fine wine, with price tags to match. The early colonists would have understood.

MICHAEL KRONDL

Vegetables

A vegetable is defined as any herbaceous crop grown for parts that can be eaten fresh or processed. Native Americans grew beans, squash, and flint corn (not the modern sweet corn), and European settlers adopted these "three sisters" early and avidly, bringing them into their kitchen gardens to grow among the English and European transplants. Onions might have been the first vegetable planted in the colonies—they enlivened the drab monotony of a daily porridge. Other sturdy specimens, such as cabbages, and roots—from skirrets (a relative of the carrot) and swedes (or rutabagas, so called by virtue of their popularity in Scandinavia) to turnips, beets, parsnips, and carrots—took residence in the root cellar without withering. Cucumbers and radishes also counted among the first of the Old World crops cultivated in the colonies, and both culinary and medicinal herbs were planted in vegetable gardens.

With the arrival of potatoes, circuitously returned to the New World by eighteenth-century Scottish and Irish immigrants after this South American native was introduced into Europe, vegetables in North America largely mirrored the vegetables found on English and European tables. The first American cookbook—*American Cookery*, published in 1796 by Amelia Simmons—mentions all of these vegetables as well as asparagus, peas, lettuce, and herbs (any of which could be found in an English cookbook of the same period); she also mentions American crops such as corn, Jerusalem artichokes, pumpkins, and several varieties of string beans.

Annual vegetable varieties of the late seventeenth century and the eighteenth century, handed down from year to year as seeds, almost certainly no longer exist, whereas perennial vegetables, such as artichokes and asparagus, and perennial herbs as well as self-pollinating annuals like beans have suffered fewer changes. The latter have, in some cases, survived unchanged. Actual plant breeding for specific qualities, and with it the creation of new varieties, did not begin until the early nineteenth century, but it quickly took off. By the mid-nineteenth century companies produced, sold, and marketed seeds in the United States. New varieties were available for purchase, able to move from place to place, and many old varieties were, as a result, simply forgotten.

From 1850 to World War II

In the nineteenth century, with the rise of market gardens and truck farms, commercial vegetable growing advanced to the level of a skilled profession. Market gardeners, occupying high-rent acreage on the outskirts of major cities, used interplanting, cold frames, and other production practices to grow a broad variety of vegetables—including valuable perishable specimens—in relatively small spaces. Horse manure, collected from city liveries, was the preferred fertilizer, and

A nineteenth-century engraving of a vegetable market.

newly arrived immigrants provided the labor. Truck farmers, on the other hand, grew less-perishable vegetables, often only one or two kinds, on land several miles from market and transported them to market or to nearby canneries or pickle packers by truck. Refrigerated railcars, developed in the late nineteenth century, made even longer shipping distances possible. Around this time southern farmers began taking advantage of their early spring to ship vegetables north, and southern Florida became a major center for vegetable production. The gold rush hastened California's drive toward statehood, and the completion in 1869 of the transcontinental railroad linked the new state with the rest of the nation, poising the Central Valley—a 400-mile-long fertile pocket between the coastal and the Sierra Nevada mountains—to become

the most dynamic agricultural region in the world.

The pace of change quickened in the first half of the twentieth century, driven in no small measure by the needs and requirements of two great wars. Vegetables went from glass jars into cans and then into thick, dried wafers for soldiers on the front lines. During World War I vegetable producers were mobilized to counteract food shortages at home and abroad. A grassroots movement of community gardens, including both private gardens and those planted on urban lots to supply vegetables to poor neighborhoods, experienced renewed vitality as individuals "planted for freedom." At the end of World War I, Clarence Birdseye, a field naturalist working for the U.S. government in the Arctic, discovered that quick-frozen fish, when thawed, retained characteristics of freshness. The same proved true for vegetables.

Although community gardening was largely unsustained in the period between the wars, it made a comeback during World War II as part of the national "victory garden" program. In an effort to reduce demand for commercial produce, as well as the demand for the metal in commercial cans, and to leave the railroads free for munitions transport, Americans were asked to plant gardens and preserve their own vegetables. Nearly 20 million Americans planted victory gardens during World War II; not to do so was considered unpatriotic.

Postwar Period

In the years immediately after World War II, Americans grew in numbers and affluence, while the proportion of farmers in the labor force declined to about 15 percent. Farming became big business; as farming grew, the bulk of vegetable production shifted to just a few states, and regional vegetable selection

and variety fell dramatically. Agriculturally this period was characterized by a rise in the use of pesticides and the development of hearty vegetable hybrids that could travel long distances.

By the 1960s the contentment and prosperity of postwar America were giving way to a mass movement that came to be called the counterculture. Among the ecologic and environmental concerns of this movement was the charge that manufacturers had lost contact with the process and had forfeited responsibility for how food made its way to the consumer. Over the next several decades increased foreign travel, a new health consciousness, and shifting demographics created demands for different vegetables, segmenting and diversifying the American market. Mainstream Americans were no longer wholly satisfied with the convenience of frozen vegetables—they wanted fresh vegetables at their service year-round. Technology had the ways and the economy had the means to deliver. The vegetables that used to wind up in cans or freezers now found themselves on trucks—spared from processing.

Although the development of new products occurred at a record rate after 1980 and fresh vegetable consumption rose, the vegetables themselves often left much to be desired. New varieties, developed to extend the vegetables' seasons, left many worthy cultivars behind, and the traveling schedule of even generic vegetables made proper ripening impossible—even undesirable.

Eating Habits in the Early Twenty-first Century

In the early twenty-first century Americans on the whole are eating only about 17 percent more vegetables—fresh and processed—than they were twenty-five years ago. This stems in part from the fact that food consumption in countries with low population growth and generally high incomes, like the United States, remains relatively stable. Because the demand for produce is considered inelastic, growth in one area of consumption tends to predict decline in another. Processed vegetables continue to outsell fresh, though by a narrow margin. According to the U.S. Department of Agriculture (USDA), head lettuce tops the list of most-consumed vegetables, followed by frozen potatoes, fresh potatoes, canned tomatoes, potatoes for chips, and dried beans. Dark yellow and green vegetable consumption comes in at around 5 percent. California is the dominant producer of vegetables in the United States, followed by Florida. The balance of vegetable production is dispersed among other states, among them Arizona, Oregon, Washington, and New York.

Vegetable sales show significant gains, however, in the so-called niche markets. First, greater numbers of Americans in various ethnic groups in the United States and Americans who travel abroad have heightened awareness of ethnic or exotic vegetables and have created a demand for them in

An advertisement for White House brand vegetables.

supermarkets. The examples are numerous. Italian cooking, for instance, has added dark, leafy greens to the American repertoire in the form of escarole and lacinato kale. Americans eat salads brightened with radicchio, arugula, and shaved fennel. Southeast Asian cuisine has brought the stir-fry and its many vegetables to the American table. Americans frequently cook bok choy, or Chinese cabbage, and broccoli, snow peas, and bean sprouts. Even pea shoots are becoming more and more available in supermarkets. Mexican cuisine has opened a world of incendiary sauces made with their chilies. Jalapeño and serrano peppers are used fresh, and many others (chipotle, ancho, pastillo, and serrano) are used dried. Avocados, jicama, and tomatillos find their way into cooling salsas, chayote into stews, and yucca into the deep fryer. Cooking with these vegetables used to require a trip into ethnic neighborhoods. They have become common in large urban supermarkets. Mainstream Americans buy 75 percent of all ethnic vegetables sold in the United States.

The second major area of growth is in organic produce. The organic movement may have found its footing in health food stores and green markets, but it has worked its way slowly into supermarkets. Beginning on October 21, 2002, producers and handlers were required to have USDA accreditation for all organic products. The national standards replace what was a tangle of certification systems run by individual states. Vegetables may carry the USDA organic label if they are 95 to 100 percent organic based on current regulations, which dictate that organic food be produced without the use of conventional pesticides, petroleum- or sewage sludge–based fertilizers, bioengineering, or ionizing radiation. Research suggests that average consumers show growing interest in organic produce but are more likely to purchase organic produce when it is comparably priced to conventional produce and when it is available in supermarkets or mainstream stores. In the early twenty-first century 9 to 19 percent of Americans report that they buy organic produce at least once a week.

[See also BIRDSEYE, CLARENCE; CALIFORNIA; CANNING AND BOTTLING; COMMUNITY-SUPPORTED AGRICULTURE; COOKBOOKS AND MANUSCRIPTS: TO 1860; DEPARTMENT OF AGRICULTURE, UNITED STATES; HEALTH FOOD; ITALIAN AMERICAN FOOD; JEFFERSON, THOMAS; MEXICAN AMERICAN FOOD; NATIVE AMERICAN FOOD; NOUVELLE CUISINE; ORGANIC FOOD; ORGANIC GARDENING; SOUTHEAST ASIAN FOOD; VITAMINS; WATERS, ALICE; *entries for individual vegetables*.]

BIBLIOGRAPHY

Bachmann, Janet, and Richard Earles. *Post Harvest Handling of Fruits and Vegetables*. 2000. http://attra.ncat.org/attra-pub/PDF/postharvest.pdf.

Cook, Roberta L. *The U.S. Fresh Produce Industry: An Industry in Transition*. Davis: Department of Agricultural and Resource Economics, University of California at Davis, 2001. http://www.agecon.ucdavis.edu/facultypages/cook/articles.htm.

Dauthy, Mircea. *Fruit and Vegetable Processing*. Rome, Italy: Food and Agriculture Organization of the United Nations, 1995.

Leighton, Ann. *American Gardens in the Eighteenth Century*. Boston: Houghton Mifflin, 1976.

U.S. Department of Agriculture, Agricultural Research Service. Food and Nutrition Research Briefs. "Antioxidant capacity of vegetables." http://www.ars.usda.gov/is/np/fnrb.

Weaver, William Woys. *Heirloom Vegetable Gardening*. New York: Holt, 1997.

Weaver, William Woys. *100 Vegetables and Where They Came From*. Chapel Hill, NC: Algonquin, 2000.

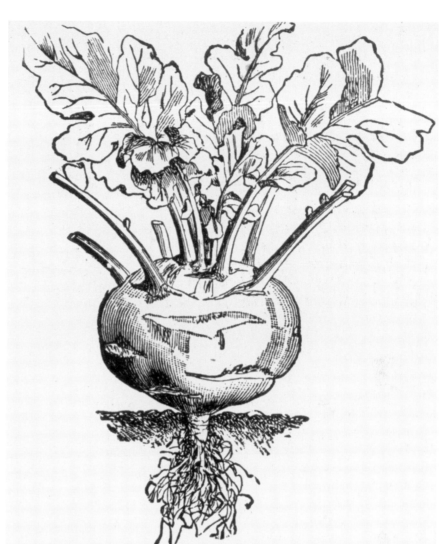

An illustration of a kohlrabi, a cabbage with a turnip-like stem.

Vegetarianism

The writings of the German mystic Jakob Böhme were instrumental in converting a young English rustic with a literary bent, Thomas Tryon, to a Pythagorean diet. (Before the coining of the terms "vegetarian" and "vegan" in the nineteenth and twentieth centuries, respectively, Americans and Europeans who ate a fleshless diet were widely known as Pythagoreans.) In numerous works Tryon advocated a Pythagorean diet on practical and moral grounds. One of his books, *Wisdom's Dictates* (1691), which was a digest of Tryon's voluminous *The Way to Health, Long Life, and Happiness* (1683), found its way into the hands of the young Benjamin Franklin in the 1720s. For three years, during his late adolescence, the young printer's apprentice embraced the Pythagorean system. In his *Autobiography* (1791), Franklin acknowledges his debt to Tryon and, in the same passage, makes it plain that his reasons for adopting a fleshless diet were chiefly pecuniary. By not eating flesh, he found that he could cut his food expenses in half, enabling him to acquire more books for his library. Pythagoreanism arrived in America as a fledgling social movement only in 1817. In this year the Reverend William Metcalfe and forty-one other members of the Bible Christian Church (a vegetarian church founded by

The ancient Greek sage and religious teacher Pythagoras was the namesake of nineteenth-century American vegetarians. Portrait by Glory Brightfield from Famous Vegetarians and Their Favorite Recipes.

the Reverend William Cowherd in 1807) left England for the United States. On March 29, 1817, they set sail from Liverpool in the *Philadelphia Packet*, and eighty days later they arrived in Philadelphia. Not all of these vegetarian pilgrims survived the rigors of the voyage as vegetarians. Half in fact had succumbed to the lure of the meat rations. But Metcalfe and his wife Susanna came through the hardships unscathed and untainted to found the North American branch of the Bible Christian Church, the first vegetarian church planted on American soil. Despite its detractors' prophecies of a speedy demise, the church survived into the early twentieth century.

Although his reception in Philadelphia by the orthodox Swedenborgian Church and other denominations was decidedly chilly, Metcalfe was undaunted. The first public vegetarian advocate in the United States, Metcalfe continued to preach vegetarianism from the pulpit and to write essays on moral dietetics in newspapers. In 1821 Metcalfe penned a pamphlet, *On Abstinence from the Flesh of Animals (Echoing Porphyry)*, that won to the cause two converts who played an indispensable role in launching the vegetarian movement in America.

The first convert was America's first vegetarian physician, William A. Alcott, cousin to the transcendentalist philosopher and teacher Bronson Alcott; William in turn converted Bronson. In the course of his long career William Alcott wrote numerous works advocating a vegetarian diet, including his best-known book, *Vegetable Diet* (1838). Bronson Alcott, father of the novelist Louisa May Alcott, founded the first ethical vegetarian commune in America, Fruitlands, near Harvard, Massachusetts, which was financed by Alcott's neighbor, Ralph Waldo Emerson, another transcendentalist. Metcalfe's other illustrious convert was himself a Protestant minister and no mean pulpit orator—the Reverend Sylvester Graham. Although his nutritional theories, as set forth in his books *A Treatise on Bread, and Bread-Making* (1837) and *Lectures on the Science of Human Life* (1839), were derided by the medical establishment of his time, his theory that dietary fiber is a vital force in human health was vindicated by medical researchers in the twentieth century.

Sometime in the early 1840s in England the term "vegetarian" was coined. No one knows exactly when or by whom. The story that it was first coined by a vegetarian classical scholar from the Latin word *vegetus* is apparently apocryphal. What is historically attested is that on September 29, 1847, at a hydropathic clinic in Ramsgate, the first vegetarian society was formed. The outmoded term "Pythagorean" was officially replaced by the neologism "vegetarian."

In 1850, three years after the vegetarian society in England had begun to call its diet "vegetarian," Graham, Metcalfe, William Alcott, and Russell Trall founded America's first secular vegetarian society, the American Vegetarian Society, at Clinton Hall in New York City. Now defunct, the society continued to hold meetings until 1922.

Cornflake Crusaders

Through Ellen White, founder of the Seventh-Day Adventists, the early Adventists became acquainted with the latest in health-care procedures. Sister White, as she was affectionately dubbed by her followers, absorbed her immense health knowledge partly through divine revelation and partly through a close reading of the works of food reformers like Graham and James Caleb Jackson. She was an avid reader of Jackson's *Water-Cure Journal*. She also saw, in one of her visions, that God had fashioned the human body as his temple, so that any abuse of the body was a violation of God himself. Alcohol, tobacco, and meat were detrimental to the body, so she roundly denounced them and declared them proscribed foods. Eventually, through her prophecies and teachings, the Seventh-Day Adventists became strong advocates of a vegetarian diet.

As sedulously as White had studied Jackson's methods, so did her protégé, John Harvey Kellogg. In the kitchen of his wife Ella, Kellogg and his brother Will discovered the cereal-flaking process that yielded Granose Flakes, the precursor of cornflakes—those golden flakes that gave rise to the modern breakfast cereal industry and the uniquely American practice of eating cold cereal for breakfast. Kellogg was a Promethean inventor of an array of other food products that helped many Americans effect a smooth transition to a vegetarian diet. Among these foods was America's first meat analogues. Kellogg in fact claimed to be the inventor of peanut butter. Whether or not he actually concocted this goober pâté is still a matter for conjecture, but there is no doubt that he was instrumental in its adoption as a vegetarian food all over the country.

Modern American Vegetarianism

Although Kellogg carried his vegetarian crusade into the 1940s, during the early decades of the twentieth century a triumvirate of self-appointed food authorities was helping to change the way Americans viewed the meat on their plates. The first of these was Upton Sinclair. A novelist and social reformer, Sinclair became a food reformer quite by accident. His novel *The Jungle* (1906), which he had intended to be a diatribe against capitalism, was so vivid in its portrayal of the horrors of the meatpacking industry that it gave the country a case of national dyspepsia. It was influential in the passage of the Pure Food and Drug Act (1906), and one year after its publication the U.S. Food and Drug Administration was formed (1907). Sinclair

A portrait of Bronson Alcott by Glory Brightfield from Famous Vegetarians and Their Favorite Recipes.

himself became a vegetarian, albeit for only three years; however, there is no doubt that many Americans were stirred by his book to swear off meat eating altogether.

The next was Horace Fletcher. A corpulent American businessman, Fletcher lost weight by devising a system of repetitive chewing. When Fletcher found that meat offered the greatest resistance to being liquefied through chewing, the Great Masticator stopped eating meat and recommended that earnest followers of his regimen (who were legion) do likewise.

The third reformer, Bernarr Macfadden, was a rags-to-riches physical culturist turned publishing magnate and a charismatic public health figure. As one of America's richest young tycoons, he could have indulged his appetite on a Lucullan scale, but he lived chiefly on raw vegetables and fruit. (Later in his life he became a bit of a backslider and included some meat in his diet, but in his heyday he lived mainly on raw vegetarian food.) On rare occasions when he fell ill, he cured himself through fasting. In 1902 he opened one of New York's first vegetarian restaurants, Physical Culture (named after his fitness magazine), where for a nickel one could dine on an entrée like "hamburger steak," which was made from nuts and vegetables. By 1911 twenty vegetarian Physical Culture restaurants had sprung up in Philadelphia, Chicago, and sundry other locations.

In 1927 America's longest continuously running vegetarian society, the Vegetarian Society of the District of Columbia, was founded in Washington, D.C., by Milton Trenham with strong Seventh-Day Adventist backing. On July 28, 1947, at the Commodore Hotel in New York, a vegetarian political party, the American Vegetarian Party, was formed with the object of putting up a presidential candidate for the 1948 election. The party's candidate was John Maxwell, a naturopathic doctor and restaurateur from Chicago. To oppose General Dwight D. Eisenhower in the 1952 election, the party nominated General Herbert C. Holdridge, a vegetarian

West Point alumnus of the class of 1917. In every subsequent quadrennial election until 1964 (by which time the party had faded away) a candidate ran for the presidency on the vegetarian ticket.

A Paradigm Shift

In freezer cases across America, one can find a vast array of vegetarian entrées, from the sophisticated to the ordinary. Supermarkets are stocking more and more vegetarian food products. Vegetarian restaurants in such cities as New York, Seattle, and San Francisco continue to proliferate. All of this suggests that the popular image of vegetarianism as an eccentric, cranky, fringe movement has undergone a paradigm shift. Among younger Americans it is very much in vogue to be vegetarian if not vegan.

BIBLIOGRAPHY

Berry, Rynn. *Famous Vegetarians and Their Favorite Recipes.* New York: Pythagorean Publishers, 1994.

Berry, Rynn. *Food for the Gods: Vegetarianism and the World's Religions.* New York: Pythagorean Publishers, 2001.

RYNN BERRY

Velveeta

In *The Joy of Cooking*, Irma S. Rombauer sniffs, "We can only echo Clifton Fadiman when he declares that processed cheese represents the triumph of technology over conscience." In 1915 the chemist Elmer E. Eldredge, employed by Phenix Cheese Company in Lowville, New York, invented Phen-ett, a processed cheese containing whey protein, cheese (american, swiss, or camembert), and sodium citrate, an antioxidant. Meanwhile scientists for J. L. Kraft Brothers were formulating NuKraft, a similar product. Kraft patented its tinned cheese in 1916, and it was included in the rations of soldiers going overseas during World War I.

Phenix and Kraft agreed to share patent rights to their processed cheeses, and in 1928 Velveeta was born. Kraft's brand name reflects the velvety texture of the product when melted.

By law Velveeta must contain at least 51 percent cheese; Velveeta blends colby, swiss, and cheddar. The ingredients are heated to incorporate more moisture, rendering the product easier to spread and melt. Pasteurization prevents ripening, so Velveeta has a remarkable shelf life. Velveeta was originally packaged in a wooden box with a tinfoil lining; it does not require refrigeration. In 1937 a Kraft salesperson suggested combining Velveeta with a box of macaroni noodles; the product became Kraft Macaroni and Cheese Dinner. Over a million boxes were sold each day in 2002.

BIBLIOGRAPHY

Harte, Tom. "The Power of (Pasteurized and Prepared) Cheese." *Southeast Missourian,* January 22, 2003.

SARA RATH

Vending Machines

The first American vending machine appeared in 1888, when the Thomas Adams Gum Company (American Chicle, Pfizer) placed a machine selling Tutti-Frutti chewing gum on a platform of the elevated train in New York City. The following year a penny vending machine was developed that could dispense handfuls of candy and peanuts. Round, bubble-topped penny gumball machines were introduced in 1907. Because vending machines were still quite unreliable, most sold only penny items until the 1920s. One exception was the Horn and Hardart Baking Company, which opened the first coin-operated Automat restaurant in Philadelphia in 1902, where diners selected their menu choices for prepared food displayed behind a wall of small glass windows.

In 1908 the Public Cup Vendor Company (Dixie Cup Company), devised a machine that served cooled water in a paper cup for a penny; later machines sold just the cup (the water was free). Sodamats, forerunners of the modern soda machine, were installed in amusement parks in 1926; grouped together to use the same compressors and pumps, the machines had attendants to keep them running.

In the 1930s vending machines began to offer a variety of candy bars. Movie theaters, popular sites for candy machines, displayed large, ornately designed versions. In 1935 the first cup-type soft-drink vending machine, made by Vendrink Corporation, appeared in Chicago, and Coca-Cola introduced the first standardized coin-operated bottled soda machines selling nickel Cokes. By 1950, 25 percent of all Cokes were sold through vending machines. There were approximately 1.2 million soft-drink machines in 1964, and soda cans, introduced in 1961, made up a large percentage of the sales. Using dry ice for cooling, ice cream vendors became available in 1933, followed by milk machines in 1938. Refrigerated machines were perfected in the early 1950s.

The War Production Board stopped the production of vending machines in 1942 because of the need for metal to support the war effort. Still, vending machines sustained the war effort, feeding factory workers during their long shifts, which led to the later acceptance of vending machines in the workplace.

By 1960 some companies, schools, and colleges abandoned their cafeterias and replaced them with banks of the less expensive vending machines. Sandwiches, desserts, hot coffee, and soup created a growing market in factories and plants, one of the largest categories for vending-machine sales in the early twenty-first century. This period also saw the introduction of machines that exchanged coins for dollar bills and the arrival of vending machines on college campuses and in public schools. Hot coffee machines were invented in 1945 and remained unchanged until the 1980s, when new innovations allowed coffee beans to be ground

Vending machines offer cheap snacks at rest stops, offices, and school campuses.

within the machine as needed. This innovation produced the 1990s explosion of gourmet coffee and espresso machines.

Advances in payment systems during the 1990s included the use of debit or credit cards and cell phones, helping allay the problem of slugs, the fake coins that have plagued the industry from its infancy. In 2002 a supersized sidewalk "convenience store," an idea that had been tried unsuccessfully in past decades, was opened in Washington, D.C. The wall of two hundred vended products, ranging from motor oil to roast beef sandwiches, has raised hopes for a new era in vending.

[See also AUTOMATS; CAFETERIAS; CANDY.]

BIBLIOGRAPHY

National Automatic Merchandising Association. http://www.vending.org.

Segrave, Kerry. *Vending Machines: An American Social History*. Jefferson, NC, and London: McFarland, 2002.

JOY SANTLOFER

Venison

Deer was by far the most important game animal in colonial and early American times. It was plentiful throughout North America and was relatively easy to hunt. Because of this intensive hunting, the common deer actually became scarce in some colonies even before the American Revolution. For settlers migrating west, deer meat was a major food source, particularly while settlers built homes and prepared land for farming. By the mid-nineteenth century venison had became rare in eastern markets, and by 1900 deer were scarce even in many western states. The twentieth century saw the virtual elimination of venison from the American diet.

In the nineteenth century the haunch, the largest and meatiest cut of venison, was roasted, broiled, fried, or cut into slices (collops). Currant sauce was a popular accompaniment. Bonier parts of the animal, such as the neck, shoulder, and saddle (the ribs and loin), were used in soups, stews, sausages, pies, and pasties. Deer tripe was considered a delicacy by

some. Venison was also potted and jerked for future use. Most nineteenth-century cookbooks included at least a few recipes for venison; some offered a dozen or more. In addition to home consumption, venison was served as a luxury in fashionable restaurants throughout the nineteenth century.

During the early twentieth century laws protecting deer and other game were passed and enforced, and hunting declined. Where deer were more numerous, particularly in the South, venison remained on the menu. Deer began to proliferate throughout many states by the late twentieth century, and in addition deer began to be raised on farms. Venison was again seen on the American table. Accompanying this resurgence of the deer were cookbooks instructing hunters how to prepare venison. More than a dozen such cookbooks were published during the early twenty-first century, including Don Gulbrandsen's *501 Venison Recipes* (2005) and Rick Black's *Deer Burger Cookbook* (2005).

BIBLIOGRAPHY

Black, Rick. *Deer Burger Cookbook: Recipes for Ground Venison—Soups, Stews, Chilis, Casseroles, Jerkies, and Sausages*. Mechanicsburg, PA: Stackpole Books, 2005.

Gulbrandsen, Don, ed. *501 Venison Recipes*. Iola, WI: KP Books, 2005.

ANDREW F. SMITH

Vermouth

Originating in the late eighteenth century in Italy and served in France and Italy as an aperitif or digestif, vermouth is better known in America as the mixer that makes Manhattans, Rob Roys, French kisses, and martinis. Vermouth can be dry, bitter, or sweet and white or red. A wine fortified with brandy, vermouth gets its name from the German word for the bitter root wormwood, *Vermut*. Some vermouth is still made with wormwood (now known to be hallucinogenic), but it is more often made with other herbs and botanicals, giving it a distinctive aromatic taste.

American production is centered in California, where several brands make this complex wine. Grape varietals used to make the wine include Orange Muscat, Colombard, Picpoul, and Valdepenas. The wine from these grapes is made and then fortified with brandy and infused with dried herbs or essential oils, depending on the producer. The mixture of botanicals creates a distinctive type of vermouth, and each maker's vermouth is proprietary. The selection of botanicals used can range widely, including angelica, coriander seed, sage, quinine, linden, cloves, juniper, rosemary, mace, marjoram, citrus rinds, and other pungent spices.

The origins of vermouth are as murky as the recipes for making it. Undisputed is that it was first produced in the Piedmont region of northern Italy—Turin is the greatest producer. Although the truth is yet to be discovered, three beliefs predominate as to its

creation: first, to balance the taste of astringent wines; second, as a medicinal tincture (the botanicals were considered healing); and third, as a replacement for polluted water. According to *The Dictionary of American Food and Drink*, the word "vermouth" was first printed in 1806. The alcohol content hovered around 15 percent, somewhat higher than wine and about the same as port.

As a mixer vermouth adds complexity to drinks—the aromatics create layers of flavor, while the wine and brandy add fruitiness. This complexity was particularly effective during the era of Prohibition, when most of the alcohol being drunk in America was gin, easily and quickly distilled and comparatively crude by present-day standards. The martini was created many years earlier, but its popularity bounded when vermouth was added to the crude gin.

Although the origins of the first martini are obscured, there is consensus among cocktail connoisseurs that both the vermouth and the gin were sweeter then than is popular in the early twenty-first century. Consequently the term "dry" martini may not mean that there is less vermouth but that dry vermouth, rather than sweet vermouth, is used. American vermouth production has divided into two camps: those vintners who use lesser-quality grapes and wine for large vermouth production, to be used as mixers and for cooking, and smaller and boutique producers who make vermouth to be tasted on its own or as a complex mixer.

[See also BRANDY; COCKTAILS; GIN; MARTINI.]

BIBLIOGRAPHY

Grimes, William. *Straight up or on the Rocks: The Story of the American Cocktail*. New York: North Point, 2001.

Vya. "Vermouth Contents and Production." http://www.vya.com.

LISA DELANGE

Vichyssoise

This dish of cold cream of potato-leek soup garnished with chives was on the menu of every "authentic" French restaurant in American from the late 1950s to the early 1980s. But it was invented in the United States and has never become popular in France. Crème vichyssoise glacée was invented at the New York Ritz-Carlton Hotel by the French chef Louis Diat, and the recipe was published in 1941. Diat took a humble French potato-leek soup, *potage bonne-femme*, pureed and chilled it, added rich cream, and presented it over ice. Despite the association of Vichy with a collaborationist French government during World War II, this made an easy and impressive dish for American dinner parties, and Irma S. Rombauer and Marion Rombauer Becker's *The Joy of Cooking* (1975) has two versions (one using both a blender and a pressure cooker and adding cucumber) and carefully warns that the final *s* should be pronounced despite the tendency for many Americans to drop the *s* in "genteel" fake

French. One of the few French writers to take note of it, Raymond Olivier, compares it to Russian chilled soups. Julia Child, coming upon it late in her life, labeled it correctly as Diat's and opined her preference for his simple cream base over canned chicken broth.

Mark H. Zanger

Vienna Sausage

The Vienna sausage is one of those foods brought to America by immigrants and then naturalized into an iconic item. Hailing from German-speaking Europe, it has several incarnations. One is the wiener, from *Wienerwurst*, or Vienna sausage (from Wien, the German spelling of Vienna), originally made mainly from pork and appearing in bundles of links. In late-nineteenth-century and early-twentieth-century America, the name "wiener" came to be used interchangeably with "hot dog" and sometimes "frankfurter," a different formulation of beef and pork. Properly speaking, the Vienna or Vienna-style sausage is a linked sausage, often with a frankfurter-style mixture of meats. It was sold in braided links, but in America it transformed into something else: canned sausage. In this form it became an early example of convenience food.

Home sausage canning is a preservation technique associated with the winter slaughter of hogs on farms across America. Commercial canning of sausage had appeared by the mid-nineteenth century and became more popular with the introduction of mechanized meat processing and canning production in the 1860s. The term "Vienna" or "Vienna-style" seems to have appeared around 1903. The term meant a sausage (skinless after the 1950s) cut into two-inch lengths and then canned. Small, one- or two-inch "cocktail sausages" at times have been touted as the origin of the canned variety, but they are different products.

By the end of the century such Chicago-based companies as Armour, Swift, and Libby (Libby, McNeill, and Libby) as well as Hormel in Minnesota dominated the market for canned sausages. Armour, with its pop-top aluminum can, remains the industry sales leader. In the South, where canned meats appeared in the 1890s, one company became synonymous with canned sausages, the first commercial meat canner in Mississippi, Bryan Packing Company of West Point. Beginning in 1938 Bryan packed Vienna sausages in oil, unlike most northern products, and the product achieved such renown that it was identified with southern regional food. Canned bologna, produced in the United States only at the Plumrose plant in Booneville, Missouri, is a variation on the Vienna canned sausage.

Although the product is still widely sold, famously to hikers and fishermen, Vienna sausage consumption has declined since its heyday from the 1940s to the 1970s. At its height the sausage seeped into international cuisines through U.S. military bases. The sausages are used in Filipino *pancits*, and there is even a popular Cuban dish consisting of Viennas cooked with rice and flavored with Cuban spices, no doubt courtesy of Guantánamo Bay.

[**See also** Sausage.]

Bibliography

Loebel, Leon, and Stanley Loebel. *All about Meat.* New York: Harcourt, 1975.

Bruce Kraig

Vitamins

Vitamins are a group of organic substances that are essential for human growth and normal metabolism. They occur naturally in small amounts in most foods and beverages and can be produced synthetically. The lack of certain vitamins in the diet can bring about specific diseases. Although research into the link between diet and some of these diseases had been going on for well over a century, vitamins did not gain widespread public attention until the period between World Wars I and II.

History of Vitamins

By the mid-eighteenth century the problem of scurvy on shipboard had led some doctors to suspect that a mysterious "element" in fresh fruits, vegetables, wine, and malted barley was necessary for life, even though most scientists still believed that only fats, carbohydrates, proteins, and salts were essential for adequate nutrition. Early advances in the search for this unknown element came from unexpected field trials associated with tragic circumstances. In 1747 James Lind was caring for sailors on the British ship *Salisbury* during a scurvy epidemic and selected twelve subjects for an experiment. He administered six different antiscorbutic diets to pairs of the sick men, and the two who received citrus fruits recovered dramatically. The study, which Lind reported in *A Treatise of the Scurvy* (1753), led his pupil, Sir Gilbert Blane, to introduce citrus fruits to the required rations on British sailing ships.

In 1871 J. B. A. Dumas wrote of the German siege of Paris, during which nutritionists created artificial milk from pure fat and sugar syrups for the children. The mixture did not sustain the children, and Dumas concluded that though the liquid was pure, something was lacking that exists in natural milk. Laboratory studies in the late nineteenth century and early twentieth century began to shed light on the existence of these organic compounds.

In 1890 the Dutch physician Christiaan Eijkman, working in Java, discovered and extracted a "protective factor" in the germ and pericarp of rice that kept domestic fowl from exhibiting symptoms resembling those of beriberi (which occurred when they were fed polished rice). This factor was eventually named "thiamine."

In 1905 animal studies at the University of Utrecht, conducted by C. A. Pekelharing, proved that a diet of pure fats, carbohydrates, proteins, and salts was not adequate for survival. When he added small amounts of milk to the diet, the animal's health was restored. Sir Frederick Gowland Hopkins of Cambridge University reported briefly in 1906 and fully in 1912 on experiments that showed that there must exist in certain foods "accessory food factors" not previously known but essential.

The year 1912 became a turning point in the search for these essential factors. Casimir Funk, at London's Lister Institute, wrote in *Die Vitaminen* that beriberi, rickets, pellagra, and sprue might be caused by the lack of special substances in the diet. Believing that the unknown substances must be coenzymes that provide the transfer site for biochemical changes catalyzed by the recently discovered enzymes, and therefore would be amines, he combined the prefix "vita," meaning life, and "amine" (at the time it was thought that all coenzymes were amines, or derivations of ammonia) to name these unknowns "vitamines." In 1913 two groups of Americans, T. B. Osborne and L. B. Mendel and E V. McCollum and M. Davis, extracted from butter and cod liver oil the missing growth factors that the latter workers called "fat-soluble A." It later came to be called simply vitamin A. McCollum wrote that there might be important differences between adequate and optimal quantities of vitamins in nutrition and that just a small amount of milk or of certain fruits and vegetables made the diet adequate.

As soon as the existence of vitamins was confirmed, biochemists started work to isolate them, trying to find out how much of each of these compounds exists in different foods and ascertain whether there is an optimal intake of each in human nutrition. In 1920 the name "vitamine" was changed to "vitamin" through the efforts of J. C. Drummond, who suggested that not all coenzymes had to be amines. In addition to the fat-soluble vitamin A, a water-soluble vitamin B (the anti-beriberi substance) and the antiscorbutic vitamin C had been identified by that time. Vitamins are still distinguished as water soluble or fat soluble; the vitamin B complex and vitamin C are water soluble, and the rest are fat soluble. Although by 1938 all thirteen vitamins considered essential had been isolated and some had been synthesized, research on the importance of vitamins in human and animal health continued at many American university and government research centers.

Vitamin Properties

Vitamin A was the first vitamin to be isolated. It is obtained from carotene and occurs in green and yellow vegetables, egg yolk, butter, and cod liver oil and other seafood products. It is essential to growth, protects the skin, and prevents night blindness. Because it is fat soluble, it can build up in the body and be toxic if taken in excess.

Vitamin B at first was thought to be just one coenzyme. The isolation of what became known as thiamin, or B_1, in 1926 showed that vitamin B had to have more than one factor, because the anti-beriberi factor was heat sensitive and other factors were thought to be heat stable. The second factor discovered, riboflavin or vitamin B_2, promotes healthy skin and good vision. As more related substances were identified, the group was renamed the "vitamin B complex." Vitamin B_3, also known as niacin or nicotinic acid, functions in the prevention of pellagra, a disease marked by gastrointestinal disorders and dermatitis. Vitamin B_6, or pyridoxine, aids in nutrient metabolism. Folic acid, or folacin, once known as vitamin B_9, has a role in human reproduction and promotes the production of red blood cells. Vitamin B_{12}, or cobalamin, has been found to prevent pernicious anemia and certain nervous system disorders. Pantothenic acid and biotin, also factors of the B complex, function in the metabolism of nutrients.

Vitamin C got its name in 1920, although as the "antiscorbutic substance" it already had the longest history of research. In 1928 ascorbic acid was isolated but not recognized; in 1932 it was isolated and identified and, within months of that discovery, was synthesized. In 1937 researchers thought that it should be renamed "ascorbic acid," and both names are now used.

Vitamin D includes any of several fat-soluble compounds that can be produced in the skin by the action of the sun or supplied by fortified foods. A deficiency of this compound causes rickets, a disease in which insufficient calcium and phosphate are deposited in the bones. In 1918 Sir Edward Mellanby showed that rickets was a nutritional disease that could be remedied by a substance present in cod liver oil. In 1922 scientists at Johns Hopkins distinguished the "anti-ricketic factor" from vitamin A. This fourth discovered nutrient was named vitamin D. In 1923 it was discovered that irradiating foods stimulated the provitamins (substances that are converted to vitamins) in them so that the body could turn them into vitamin D more easily. Although the natural concentration of vitamin D in milk varies considerably, milk is the only product that the government has allowed to be fortified with vitamin D. The first vitamin D–fortified milk was sold in 1933.

Vitamin E, or alpha-tocopherol, is a fat-soluble vitamin abundant in vegetable oils, whole-grain cereal, butter, and eggs. It is important as an antioxidant in the deactivation of free radicals and in the maintenance of the body's cell membranes. Although natural deficiency is rare, when deficiency is produced in a laboratory it causes reproductive failure. Vitamin E sometimes is used as a food supplement and, because it is not eliminated by the body, can cause toxicity if taken in doses larger than recommended.

Vitamins K_1 and K_2 are fat-soluble vitamins found in leafy vegetables, brown rice, bran, and pork liver. They increase the content of the plasma protein, prothrombin, in the blood, thereby promoting blood clotting. The Danish biochemist Henrik Dam described the condition caused by a deficiency of this factor and suggested calling the factor vitamin K, from the German word *Koagulation*. [**See also** BARLEY; BUTTER; CITRUS; EGGS; FATS AND OILS; FRUIT; IRRADIATION; MILK; RICE; VEGETABLES.]

BIBLIOGRAPHY

McCollum, Elmer Verner. *A History of Nutrition.* Boston: Houghton Mifflin, 1957.
Wardlaw, Gordon. *Contemporary Nutrition: Issues and Insights.* New York: McGraw-Hill, 2002.

JOANNE LAMB HAYES

Vodka

Scholars debate the beginnings of vodka. Most agree that vodka has been made for one thousand years or so. Some believe it was distilled first in the area that became Russia. The word "vodka" comes from the Russian *zhizenennia voda* (water of life). Others think that vodka was born a little west of Russia, in present-day Poland. Still other scholars stake claims for other European nations and even the British Isles.

The great difficulty in identifying the origins of vodka comes from its ill-defined nature. The U.S. Bureau of Alcohol, Tobacco, and Firearms (BATF) defines vodka as a colorless, odorless, tasteless spirit. But vodka does have flavor and aroma—few are likely to mistake it for water. The way to make sense of this apparent contradiction is by understanding that vodka (except those types that are labeled "flavored") is not made flavorful by being aged in barrels (like whiskey) or infused with herbs (like gin) or syrups (like liqueurs). It is distilled, filtered, and then bottled.

Unlike other spirits, vodka is not classified by the materials from which it is distilled. (Bourbon, for instance, is mostly corn.) Vodka is made from grains, like wheat and rye, and nongrains, such as potatoes, sugar beets, and even mare's milk (the Mongolian *kumiss*). Whereas many spirits are defined in part by where they are made (for example, Scotch whisky can be made only in Scotland), vodka can be made anywhere. Thus vodka is produced in England, France, Italy, and many other nations, including of course America.

It is entirely possible that vodka existed in America in the nineteenth century. Anyone who distilled moonshine and softened it through filtration would have been making vodka. However, vodka did not appear as vodka until 1934. In 1933 Rudolph Kunett, a Russian émigré to the United States, visited France. There he met Vladimir Smirnoff. The Smirnoff family's fortunes had been hurt when the Bolsheviks took over Russia and seized their factories in 1917. The Smirnoffs had looked around Europe for new places to distill their family spirit. Smirnoff licensed Kunett to make an American version. The next year Kunett began producing Smirnoff vodka in Connecticut. Kunett struggled in the distilling business and sold out to the Heublein Company in 1939.

By 1946 Americans bought thirty thousand cases of Smirnoff a year. In 1955 Smirnoff sales in America topped one million cases per year. Vodka's immediate popularity was largely a function of its near absence of flavor. This made it inoffensive and easy to mix into cocktails (among them, the Moscow mule, screwdriver, and Bloody Mary). Heublein's advertisements, which reminded consumers that vodka is odorless on the breath ("Smirnoff—It will leave you breathless!"), also helped.

The booming American economy of the late twentieth century invited an enormous influx of vodka brands. Many of them are made in the United States, and even more are imported, especially from nations where state-subsidized distilleries have been privatized. Clever marketing of vodka in print periodicals and as chic cocktails (such as the vodka martini and cosmopolitan) helped draw many consumers to vodka. The result has been soaring quality and wide-ranging product diversification. Numerous "boutique" brands have appeared, fetching $25 or more per one 750-milliliter bottle. There also are more flavors of vodka than ever: apple, peach, lemon, ginseng, vanilla, and chocolate to name just a few. [**See also** COCKTAILS; DISTILLATION.]

BIBLIOGRAPHY

Emmons, Bob. *The Book of Gins and Vodkas.* Peru, IL: Open Court, 2000.

KEVIN R. KOSAR

Waffle, Wafer, and Pizelle Irons

Waffles and wafers were festive delicacies baked on the hearth on flat, hinged, wrought, and cast-iron plates worked with long, scissor-action handles. Originally communion wafers, they were sometimes incised with pictorial references to saints or holidays; they were later secularized. Brought to the American colonies, the waffle and wafer irons produced thin, crisp, and meltingly tender Dutch *hard waffels*, English wafers, Swedish *krumkaga*, Italian *pizzele*, and French *gaufrettes*.

Waffle irons that originated in the Netherlands and Belgium were similar but had deeper waffle patterns. Fifteenth-century offshoots of wafer irons, they were used in the American colonies in the same way—propped or held over fires or embers, one at a time.

Handles were shortened to adapt cast-iron waffle irons to the nineteenth-century cookstove. The hinged irons now rested in supporting frames and required less work to swivel and turn. In 1854 the plates of a large, round "waffle furnace" were scored to break the waffle into four wedges; others were rectangular with demarcated lines for cutting. By 1900 most were of cast iron and a few were of aluminum, some having decorative waffling patterns that included hearts, diamonds, squares, Xs, or crosses. By 1917 or 1918 electric waffle irons were popular for use right at the breakfast table.
[See also BREAKFAST FOODS.]

BIBLIOGRAPHY

Franklin, Linda Campbell. *300 Years of Kitchen Collectibles*. 5th ed. Iola, WI: Krause Publications, 2003.

Smith, David G., and Chuck Wafford. *The Book of Griswold and Wagner: Favorite Pique, Sidney Hollow Ware, Wapak; With Revised Price Guide*. Rev. 2nd ed. Atglen, PA: Schiffer, 2000.

ALICE ROSS AND LINDA
CAMPBELL FRANKLIN

Walleye

Walleye (*Stizostedion vitreum*) has many alternative names that can lead to misidentification. Not to be confused with saltwater walleye of the Pacific coast, walleye, or walleyed pike, is a freshwater fish of the Great Lakes and central Canada. It is sometimes called green, blue, gray, or yellow pike. Other names include dory (from the French *doré*), jack salmon, jackfish, white eye, glass eye, and sauger, even though there is another fish properly called sauger. Walleye sometimes is called perch—pike perch, walleyed perch, yellow pike perch—and in fact it is the largest in the Percidae (perch) family.

Walleye, so-called because of its odd, large eyes, which help the fish locate their food, is a game fish, favored only over largemouth bass. A sport fishery for walleye has existed since the late nineteenth century. Because it is so important, walleye has been introduced to lakes and streams around the Great Lakes and even in southern and western lakes. There is a limited farm-raising effort for walleye, mostly for stocking, because even though it is a favored food fish, walleye is a carnivore and once it approaches adult size is prone to cannibalism when confined. Most walleyes caught weigh between one and three pounds and are filleted. The firm, white flesh is used in many recipes for baking, broiling, poaching, or frying. The fish often is stuffed and prepared with other, more flavorful ingredients.

SANDRA L. OLIVER

Walnuts

Walnuts are common to both the New World and the Old World. The black walnut (*Juglans nigra*) is native to eastern North America. Black walnuts were consumed by Native Americans, but as the nuts are small, the yield is low, and black walnuts never became a major commercial crop. The black walnut is highly sought after as a hardwood and has become scarce. Old-world walnuts (*J. regia*) were domesticated at an early date, probably in central Asia. Walnuts have been found in many archaeological sites in Europe, Persia, and China. The Greeks and the Romans were fond of them. European (also called English) walnuts were brought to New England by early settlers. Franciscan missionaries from Spain also introduced walnuts to California in the eighteenth century. Walnuts have been made into ketchup and preserves, pressed for their oil, and made into candies, cakes, and cookies, including American favorites like fudge, penuche, Toll House cookies, and brownies. Green walnuts are made into vinegar, and the leaves of the tree have been used to make tea. California produces the vast majority of commercial walnuts, and the United States is leading world producer of these popular nuts.
[See also CALIFORNIA; NUTS.]

BIBLIOGRAPHY

Toussaint, Jean-Luc. *Walnut Cookbook*. English edition by Betsy Draine and Michael Hinden. Berkeley, CA: Ten Speed, 1998.

ANDREW F. SMITH

Washington's Birthday

George Washington was born on February 12, 1732. In 1752 Britain adopted the metric system of the eighteenth century, the Gregorian calendar, recalculating February 12 to February 22 and setting the stage for a great deal of confusion. This ambiguity

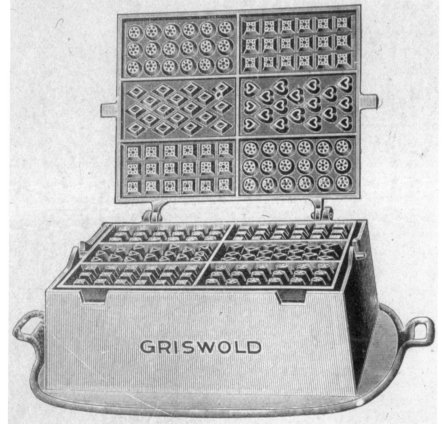

A waffle iron featuring several different patterns.

An embossed postcard of Washington and cherries from the early twentieth century.

was finally settled by an act of Congress in 1968, which moved the official celebration of Washington's Birthday to the third Monday of February.

The first recorded celebration of Washington's Birthday took place during the Revolutionary War; the occasion was marked by a military band at Valley Forge in 1778. Food first entered into the festivities three years later, at a dinner hosted by America's French allies in honor of Washington and his officers. By 1782 Americans were celebrating the occasion with similar public and private parties. These patriotic dinners grew into the "birth-night balls" of the new Republic, where the eating of "American" foods like turkey and turtle were accompanied by round upon round of toasts from glasses filled with "domestic" spirits.

Washington's death in 1799 furthered his iconic status in a young nation in search of its identity on the world stage. Parson Mason Locke Weems capitalized on the hunger for American heroes by writing a spurious biography of Washington, *A History of the Life and Death, Virtues and Exploits of General George Washington* (1800). The most enduring "tall tale" invented by Weems is the confession of the young Washington that he "chopped down" a cherry tree because he could not "tell a lie." In the spirit of the allegorical age, cherries immediately featured on the menu for Washington's Birthday celebrations.

Perhaps because fresh cherries were rare and difficult to procure in February, pie made from sweet cherry preserves quickly became the featured dish of holiday celebrations. Menus from modern-day magazines and popular cooking shows use the featured

cherries in various forms, from fresh to frozen to canned, in every course, including the traditional pie.

[**See also** CHERRIES.]

BIBLIOGRAPHY

Douglas, George William. *The American Book of Days: A Compendium of Information about Holidays, Festivals, Notable Anniversaries and Christian and Jewish Holy Days with Notes on Other American Anniversaries Worthy of Remembrance.* 8th ed. Revised by Helen Douglas Compton. New York: Wilson, 1970.

Imbornoni, Ann Marie. "Presidents' Day or Washington's Birthday?" http://www.factmonster.com/spot/washington1.html.

ESTHER DELLA REESE

Water

Bountiful supplies of potable water were touted as wonders of the New World in a Renaissance Europe troubled by large-scale pollution and water scarcity. But within one hundred years of the establishment of colonies in America, contamination and excessive exploitation of water resources led to disease and crises. Modern public water systems evolved from a need to make the nation's abundant resources safe and accessible. The experience in New York is emblematic of the chain of events leading to creation of regulated municipal water systems in all major cities across the United States.

Early Systems of Water Supply

In the original Dutch colony of New Amsterdam (now New York), poor sanitation resulted in the pollution of the available freshwater and in disease. In 1639, when there were only a few hundred settlers, water was drawn from local streams, ponds, and springs. While plans for a public well were drawn up in 1658, they were never carried out, and residents began to dig wells in their yards. The English captured New Amsterdam in 1664 largely because the Dutch leader, Peter Stuyvesant, surrendered after determining that there was not a sufficient water supply in the fort to maintain a lengthy defense. The English later dug a well in the fort, which provided sufficient potable water, much to the astonishment of the Dutch.

Wells, hand pumps, and springs provided inconsistent but adequate supplies for the next hundred years, though it is known to have been of poor quality. Travelers to New York City remarked that even horses balked at the quality of water offered them. By the dawn of the American Revolution, plans were being made for construction of a storage reservoir in lower Manhattan. A large well was dug, and water was pumped by a steam engine to the reservoir in the settled lower part of the island through a system of wooden pipes made of pine logs. The system was abandoned during occupation by the British army in September 1776.

The years after the Revolutionary War saw the rise of private water supply companies, many of them disreputable. One such venture, the Manhattan Company, started by

Aaron Burr (soon to become vice president of the United States) and his friends in April 1799, constructed a system much like the one scuttled by the Revolution, using hollow logs to transmit water from a well to a reservoir and then to customers' houses. The firm used its ostensible mission—establishment of a supply of wholesome drinking water—as a ruse to cement unlimited banking privileges. The company survives as the Chase Manhattan Bank.

By 1830 the city's population had reached 200,000, and supplies of water were poor and clearly inadequate. An epidemic of yellow fever underscored the need for new sources, and the growing city reached north to Westchester County's Croton River for an infusion of 80 million gallons of water per day. A diverting dam was built, and water was piped thirty-four miles via aqueducts to the nearby city of Yonkers, from where it was piped through the Bronx to distributing reservoirs. One reservoir was between Seventy-ninth and Eighty-sixth streets, in the area that is now Central Park, and the other was at Forty-second Street and Fifth Avenue, the site of the present-day New York Public Library. The Croton supplies were quickly outgrown, and as the population swelled with waves of immigrants in the late 1800s, stopgap measures were added to harness more water from Croton tributaries.

Severe droughts in the 1880s highlighted the need for additional works; a ten-year water-tunnel construction project resulted in a thirty-one-mile underground aqueduct to a terminus at 135th Street. A series of forty-eight-inch pipes conveyed a daily supply of 336 million gallons into a new distribution reservoir in Central Park. The reservoir still exists, though it was dropped from the city's water supply system in the mid-1990s. The separate municipalities of the Bronx and Brooklyn sourced their water separately, with the Bronx also tapping the Croton supplies and Brooklyn piping in from underground aquifers beneath Long Island. Most American cities followed a similar pattern of exploiting local supplies to the point of extinction and then reaching out to outlying areas for more.

Interstate treaties were enacted in the West, such as one in the 1870s diverting plentiful California river water to newly founded cities in Arizona. No one at the time could have predicted that, a century later, cities like Phoenix would be battling Golden State farmers for the precious resource that had once seemed inexhaustible. Eastern regions early on had established systems of water-usage trading, whereby some amount of water must be returned to the source after use (runoff, for example). Western states allowed a more first-come, first-served usage system, which has fueled agriculture and aquaculture development but led to more contentious water disputes in those areas.

Solutions of the Twentieth Century and Beyond

In New York the twentieth century brought the greatest immigration surge in American history, taxing the water supply to its limit. The city undertook the most massive urban public water project in history, to create a secondary series of reservoirs in the Catskill Mountains northwest of the city. By 1917, 571 square miles of mountainous land was designated a "watershed" region, protected as a system of collection basins for New York's water supply. The construction of dams along the Esopus Creek and aqueducts forming the Ashokan Reservoir guaranteed a supply of at least 500 to 600 million gallons per day, even in times of drought.

The system is based on gravity. The water flows on its three-day journey to the city without pumping through aqueducts constructed of various materials (some of which consist of tunnels blasted through mountains, while other sections are massive underground channels made of poured concrete). The 1940s saw even greater water demand, and the city then expanded its watershed system to include sources from the headwaters of the Delaware River and other Catskill tributaries. The Delaware system was placed in service in stages: The Delaware Aqueduct was completed in 1944, Rondout Reservoir in 1950, Neversink Reservoir in 1954, Pepacton Reservoir in 1955, and Cannonsville Reservoir in 1964.

Per capita water consumption in the city, which was approximately one hundred gallons per day in 1900, reached a peak of more than two hundred gallons a day in the late 1980s and has settled down, thanks to conservation, migration of businesses, and improved technology, to 155 gallons a day. The city consumes 1.184 billion gallons per day. By the early 2000s two major water tunnels supplied all of New York's water from the Croton and Catskill watersheds. A third water tunnel, conceived in 1960, has been under construction since the 1970s and will provide the city with flexibility in maintenance and supply.

In the years immediately preceding World War II, science became aware of the hygienic benefits of a naturally occurring element in groundwater, fluoride. Dental experts determined that it strengthens tooth enamel and is the most effective defense against tooth decay, and in 1945 the city of Grand Rapids, Michigan, became the first water system to add fluoride to drinking water. Once the beneficial results of the Grand Rapids experiment became known, other cities and smaller municipalities proposed that solutions of fluoride be added to water supplies to promote general dental health. By the late 1950s the vast majority of municipal water supplies incorporated some degree of fluoride treatment, added at treatment plants along the route from source to consumer. Another element, chlorine, is also added to inhibit the growth of harmful microbes. No national standard exists for water treatment, and the U.S. Centers for Disease Control and Prevention is examining levels and setting parameters, which may be instituted nationally.

While America is still blessed with an abundance of naturally occurring freshwater, the country has followed the European pattern of overexploitation and pollution, limiting possibilities for future contingency usage. Contamination by industry and agriculture has led to "dead" rivers, streams, and lakes, which ultimately must be cleaned up at great public expense. Two of the most notable (and successful) waterway cleanups were those of Lake Erie and the Hudson River, both in the 1970s and 1980s.

BIBLIOGRAPHY

Steuding, Bob. *The Last of the Handmade Dams: The Story of the Ashokan Reservoir.* Fleischmanns, NY: Purple House, 1989.

JAY WEINSTEIN

Water, Bottled

Bottled water is defined as water that is sealed in food-grade bottles and intended for human consumption. Thus bottled water is classified as food and regulated by the Food and Drug Administration. In the late 1970s the bottled-water industry began to make an unprecedented climb toward its top position as purveyor of the world's fastest-growing bottled-beverage choice. Two main factors explain this growth: awareness of the real problems with the quality of public drinking water supplies and the growing preference among Americans for bottled water over sugar-laden soft drinks as a thirst quencher (with no fat and no preservatives). The demand for clean, fresh water is everywhere, and quite apart from the question of taste, more Americans are now drinking bottled waters because they think they have true therapeutic value.

There are several types of bottled water. Sparkling water is carbonated, and water without carbonation is called still water. Bottled still water is the type of water most frequently used to substitute tap water. Bottled water can come from a large variety of sources; it can be groundwater from a well, water from a protected spring, or water from a public supply.

The bottled water industry saw significant mergers and acquisitions in the last years of the twentieth century. Among the major U.S. companies are Nestlé Waters North America, Inc. (Poland Springs, Perrier, Arrowhead, Deer Park, Zephyrhills, Ozarka, Ice Mountain, Calistoga, and Great Bear brands), Danone Waters of North America (Evian, Dannon, AquaPenn, Volvic, and McKesson brands), PepsiCo (Aquafina), Coca-Cola (Dasani), Suntory Water Group (Crystal Springs, Sierra Springs, Hinckley Springs, Kentwood Springs, and Belmont Springs brands), Crystal Geyser (Alpine Spring), and U.S. Filter (Cullinan). In 2001 consumers spent about $6.4 billion on bottled water, making it the fastest-growing beverage category for the tenth year in a row. Although U.S. bottled water consumption more than doubled from about 1993 to 2003, when compared with other countries (for example, European countries), it is still low. This implies that there is significant potential for expansion and that the industry will continue to grow into the twenty-first century.
[**See also** FOOD AND DRUG ADMINISTRATION; WATER; WATER, IMPORTED.]

BIBLIOGRAPHY

International Bottled Water Association. http://www.bottledwater.org.

ALFREDO MANUEL DE JESUS OLIVEIRA COELHO

Water, Imported

Until the late 1970s bottled water was imported for health concerns and in response to a fashionable trend. With the growing globalization of firms and consumption patterns, more and more foreign companies started to export their own brands. As a result the volume of bottled water tripled in the last decade of the twentieth century from 55.6 million gallons in 1989 to 151.1 million of gallons in 1999. The prestige of imported waters seems to justify the considerable transport costs. The leading imported bottled water brands are Evian, Aberfoyle Springs, Naya, Perrier, San Pellegrino, Avalon, Fiji, Apollinaris, Volvic, and Vittel. Perrier is the foremost imported spa water in the growing U.S. market.

Bottled water imported into the United States is regulated at three levels, through federal and state agencies and trade associations. In addition all bottled waters imported from countries outside the United States must meet the regulatory requirements established by their own countries as well as comply with all U.S. regulations.
[**See also** FOOD AND DRUG ADMINISTRATION; WATER; WATER, BOTTLED.]

BIBLIOGRAPHY

International Bottled Water Association. http://www.bottledwater.org/.

ALFREDO MANUEL DE JESUS OLIVEIRA COELHO

Watermelon

Watermelon (*Citrullus lanatus*) is a member of the gourd family (Cucurbitaceae) and is native to central Africa. Watermelons were disseminated to Asia in prehistoric times and were widely distributed throughout the Old World by the time the Americas were colonized. The Spanish introduced watermelons into the Caribbean and Florida and later into the American Southwest. Early French explorers and trappers planted watermelon seeds in Canada and subsequently in the Midwest and along the Mississippi River system. The first known references to watermelons in the English colonies are from Massachusetts, dated 1629. John Josselyn, in

Watermelon Cake

A popular nineteenth-century conceit was the watermelon cake, which imitates the appearance of the fruit without including it as an ingredient. Baked in a round or oval pan, the cake had an outer layer made from white batter; the batter for the center was tinted a bright pink and studded with raisins. With the outside sprinkled with green sugar after baking, it resembled a ripe watermelon.

New-England's Rarities Discovered (1672), reports that these melons grew well in Massachusetts. Watermelons also grew easily in other colonies; they were a field crop in many places and were commonly consumed throughout colonial America.

Amelia Simmons published a watermelon recipe in her *American Cookery* (1796), and most nineteenth-century cookbooks included directions for serving them cold and recipes with watermelons as ingredients. With its refreshing juiciness and sherbet-like texture, chilled watermelon was a favorite picnic food; the fruit was eaten as a snack and incorporated into salads, desserts, and preserves (marmalade, jelly, and spicy pickled rind served as a condiment with meats). Watermelons also were used to flavor ice cream and other frozen desserts. As watermelons contain considerable amounts of sugar, their juice has been used as a sweetener in cooking. It also has been fermented to make wine and other alcoholic beverages, which became a specialty in the South. Watermelon juice is sold as a specialty item in natural food stores, and it is served occasionally in restaurants, blended with lemonade.

Beginning in the 1830s medical professionals proclaimed that watermelons were deleterious to health, a view that survived for decades. The cookbook writer Pierre Blot pronounced in his *Hand-Book of Practical Cookery, for Ladies and Professional Cooks* (1867) that watermelons were "considered very unwholesome by the great majority of doctors, chemists, and physiologists." Most Americans continued eating watermelons despite the warnings.

The wide availability of commercial frozen desserts has pushed watermelon out of the summer-dessert spotlight. "Ice-cold" is no longer a novelty. In 2002, however, Americans still consumed about fourteen pounds of watermelon per capita, and the United States ranked fourth in production worldwide. The states with the largest production are Florida, Texas, California, and Georgia. There are more than 1,200 varieties of watermelon, but only about fifty are popular in the United States. Most varieties are grown regionally. Breeders have developed "baby" varieties, designed to fit in a modest-sized refrigerator, and seedless varieties, which are taking over the market from seeded kinds.

[See also CONDIMENTS; DESSERTS; FRUIT JUICES; FRUIT WINES; ICE CREAMS AND ICES; PRESERVES.]

BIBLIOGRAPHY

Maynard, Donald N., ed. *Watermelons: Characteristics, Production, and Marketing*. Alexandria, VA: ASHS, 2001.
Turner, Patricia A. "Watermelons." In *Rooted in America: Foodlore of Popular Fruits and Vegetables*, ed. David Scofield Wilson and Angus Kress Gillespie. Nashville: University of Tennessee Press, 1999.

ANDREW F. SMITH

Waters, Alice

Alice Waters was born in Chatham, New Jersey, in 1944. During the summer of 1965, while a student at the University of California, Berkeley (UC Berkeley), Waters visited France as part of her studies. She was so taken with the country, and particularly with its food, that when the class was scheduled to return to the United States, she stayed behind. Upon her return to Berkeley in the fall of 1965, Waters began to experiment with cooking in the French fashion in her home, serving meals to her friends engaged in the Free Speech movement and those protesting the Vietnam War. In 1967 she graduated from UC Berkeley with a degree in French cultural studies. On a trip to London she visited the cookware shop run by the writer Elizabeth David, who became a major influence on Waters's culinary development. Waters's favorite cookbook was David's *French Country Cooking* (1952). Waters returned to Berkeley, where in 1971 she opened a small restaurant, Chez Panisse. The menu, which in the French tradition was changed every day, was based on the cuisine of Provence.

Observing that she simply could not make the dishes taste like they did in France, Waters concluded that she should focus on northern California's own local, seasonal produce and seafood and local wines. She headed out to nearby farmers' markets and farms in search of the best produce, artisanal cheeses, and organic meats. She encouraged local farmers to grow fresh herbs and heirloom vegetables, and a network of organic farmers and ranchers grew up around the San Francisco Bay Area. The restaurant served a number of dishes that came to be identified with "California cuisine," like grilled fish and vegetables, green salads topped with grilled meat or warm goat cheese, and grilled pizza with nontraditional toppings. In 1972 Waters hired a then-unknown chef named Jeremiah Tower; she later hired Paul Bertolli, Lindsey Shere, Mark Miller, and others who helped revolutionize the American palate.

The food served at Chez Panisse astonished the public. James Beard, who first dined at the restaurant in 1973, reported that the fare was not nouvelle cuisine but "Alice Waters cuisine." In 1975 *Gourmet* magazine featured Chez Panisse, and subsequently Beard and many others wrote about the restaurant, raising it to national prominence.

A more casual upstairs café was opened at Chez Panisse in 1980. A year later Waters met Stephen Singer; their daughter Fanny was born in 1983. The following year Waters opened a stand-up café called Café Fanny a few miles from Chez Panisse. In 1996 she created the Chez Panisse Foundation to help fund programs such as the Edible Schoolyard, which allows school children to experience the rewards of planting, harvesting, cooking, and eating their own vegetables. Waters has authored or coauthored eight cookbooks, from *The Chez Panisse Menu Cookbook* (1982) to *Chez Panisse Fruit* (2002).

BIBLIOGRAPHY

Reardon, Joan. *M. F. K. Fisher, Julia Child, and Alice Waters: Celebrating the Pleasures of the Table*. New York: Harmony Books, 1994.

African Americans and Watermelon

The stereotypical association between African Americans and watermelons is a post–Civil War phenomenon. Slaves grew and ate watermelons in the South, as did most other Americans. After the Civil War, Negro minstrels sang songs, such as "The Watermelon Song" and "Oh, Dat Watermelon," in their shows. These songs were first published in the 1870s and were mainstream America's first printed evidence of an association between African Americans and watermelons. When film came along in the 1890s, African Americans' association with watermelons moved into mainstream culture. During the early twentieth century and up to about 1940, the association between African Americans and watermelons was cemented through print caricatures (postcards, posters, and advertisements) and as a decorative theme for household goods, especially kitchen accessories. The most common caricature depicts a man with a wide, open-mouthed smile, the deep red interior of his mouth paralleling the color of the watermelon. Many African Americans deeply resented the caricature. When the 1893 Columbian Exhibition tried to attract African Americans to the world's fair, a special "Colored People's Day" was planned, which included African American entertainers and the distribution of free watermelons. The African American community in Chicago boycotted the day, as did many of the scheduled performers. In 1939 the actress Butterfly McQueen, playing Scarlett O'Hara's slave, refused to eat watermelon in the film *Gone with the Wind*.

Waters, Alice, with Alan Tangren and Fritz Streiff. *Chez Panisse Fruit*. New York: HarperCollins, 2002.

Waters, Alice, with Linda P. Guenzel. *The Chez Panisse Menu Cookbook*. New York: Random House, 1982.

ANDREW F. SMITH

Waxed Paper

For much of the twentieth century waxed paper was found in nearly every kitchen. At the beginning of the twenty-first century it could be found in one of every two American homes, particularly in the homes of people who grew up with the product and knew how useful it can be in the kitchen.

Waxed paper is also called "glassine" because of its clarity. Glassine is made by passing paper through a device called a supercalender (alternating chilled cast iron and paper or cotton rolls). The result is a paper that is translucent and smooth and glossy on both sides. When coated with paraffin, a petroleum-based wax, it is resistant to oils, grease, and odors.

In 1926 Laura Scudder reportedly invented the first potato chip bag. She took sheets of waxed paper, cut them to size, and ironed them into bags. After they were filled by hand, the tops were sealed with a warm iron. Prior to this innovation, potato chips were sold fresh or packed into five-gallon metal cans with removable lids. Once the cans were empty, they were returned to the store to be refilled. In 1933 the Dixie Wax Paper Company of Dallas, Texas, introduced the first preprinted waxed glassine bags, using inks that did not fade or bleed. Some potato chip companies did not switch from glassine to foil bags until the 1970s.

In the home waxed paper has many kitchen uses, such as wrapping sandwiches, lining baking pans, rolling out piecrust, wrapping cheese, and catching crumbs. In 1932 Nicholas Marcalus, a self-taught engineer and a mechanical designer, received a patent for a continuous roll of waxed paper packaged in a dispenser box with a serrated cutter. He called his new invention Cut-Rite waxed paper. Marcalus reportedly got the idea after watching his wife prepare for a Sunday picnic. She had a hard time separating the waxed paper sheets because of the summer heat. At that time waxed paper was precut, folded, and placed in envelopes.

Glassine paper was used by the Hershey Chocolate Company as an inner wrap for its milk chocolate bars as far back as the 1940s. Besides the hundreds of uses of waxed paper in the kitchen, it is reported that in 1938 Chester Floyd Carlson made the first xerographic copy in Queens, New York, when he pressed waxed paper against an electrostatically charged plate covered in dark powder. Generations of children have used a piece of waxed paper and a comb to make an improvised kazoo. Waxed paper is an essential element for hundreds of craft projects constructed at the kitchen table.

[**See also** PACKAGING.]

BIBLIOGRAPHY

Stohs, Nancy. "Waxing on about Rolls of Paper, Foil, and Plastic." *Milwaukee Journal Sentinel*, March 12, 2002.

JOSEPH M. CARLIN

Weddings

It is difficult to overestimate the role of food in weddings and associated events. Celebratory eating and drinking is central to the engagement party, bridal shower, bachelor party, rehearsal dinner, and wedding reception. The marriage ceremony may include consecration with wine or sacramental communion. Despite such significance, there are surprisingly few food rites specific to American weddings.

In precolonial times weddings were linked more to food security than to romance. For many Native Americans marriage was a way to extend families and solidify clan relationships, providing a safety net during times of scarcity. Furthermore a potential spouse might be evaluated on his ability to hunt or her skill at grinding corn. Elder tribal women arranged Cherokee marriages, though approval of the couples was sought. The girl demonstrated acceptance by preparing a bowl of hominy, and the boy indicated agreement by eating it. In some Hopi villages a girl took the initiative by bringing a piki (thin blue cornmeal cake) to her intended. If he took a bite, they were engaged. In Navajo marriages the bride's mother would prepare cornmeal porridge and place it in a basket woven with designs symbolizing the union of Sky Father and Earth Mother. Corn pollen, representing fertility and the cardinal directions, was sprinkled across the top. The couple concluded the ceremony by eating small amounts of the mush, sharing the rest with guests. In the early twenty-first century Native American weddings were frequently Christian based; however, traditions such as the basket of cornmeal porridge might be incorporated into the service.

The colonists brought marriage customs from their countries of origin and various faiths to the United States. The food traditions most associated with American weddings are of European Christian derivation, including celebration of the Eucharist (in some denominations), tossing of rice at the couple as they leave the church, and a reception meal with an elaborate cake and a champagne toast. Both the rice and cake originated from the ancient practice of tossing wheat to ensure fertility. The Romans modified the concept, throwing small wheat cakes at the couple or crumbling cakes over the bride's head. Over time the wedding cake was served rather than thrown, and rice was substituted for tossing. The cake usually included fruit (another symbol of fecundity), and it was this type that was introduced by British settlers. With the development of white cakes in the nineteenth century, the fruitcake was relegated to duty as a smaller groom's cake. The champagne toast also has a long history, dating to a time when the bell-like chime of clinking glasses was believed to frighten away evil spirits and bring good luck. While champagne is the customary drink, owing to its association with celebration, other beverages sometimes are used.

Beyond the standard cake and champagne (rice is losing favor at modern weddings and often is prohibited by churches and other venues), numerous variations on American wedding food practices exist. In the Jewish tradition the betrothal benediction is read over a glass of wine, which the couple then drinks. At the end of the ceremony the glass is shattered by the groom with his foot. The meaning of this custom is obscure: it may commemorate the destruction of the Temple in Jerusalem (70 C.E.), or it may represent the marriage relationship, in which only the

The wedding banquet of Rabbi David Matt and Lena Friedman in Minnesota, 1913.

couple can partake. In Eastern Orthodox weddings the bride and groom take three sips of wine from a common cup, symbolic of a shared life.

Muslim marriage is considered a religious duty but a civil contract. Thus Muslim American traditions are more dependent on nationality than faith; for example, molded sugar cones traditionally are grated over the heads of Iranian American couples as an expression of best wishes, and jordan almonds are served to symbolize sweetness in marriage at Pakistani American weddings. Hindu wedding ceremonies are also diverse. Hindu American couples may make a fire offering of rice or ghee (clarified butter) to ask for blessings, or they may feed each other five mouthfuls of sweets, signifying the bride's duty to care for her husband and the groom's obligation to provide for his wife.

African Americans may add pan-African elements to their ceremony or offer African, Brazilian, Caribbean, or soul food dishes at the reception. In Latino weddings the reception may feature traditional items, such as a Mexican heart-shaped piñata, a Jamaican rum-soaked fruitcake, or a Peruvian wedding cake with ribbons inserted between layers. In the last tradition unmarried women each pull an end of ribbon, and the one who finds a ring attached will be the next to marry. Japanese Americans may incorporate the *san san kudo* ritual, bonding the couple and their families through the ceremonial sipping of sake (rice wine). Traditional elements are common in Chinese American weddings, such as drinking wine from two cups tied together with red string during the vows or serving auspicious foods at the reception, including whole fish (for abundance) and lotus seed desserts (for fertility). Korean Americans may add the *pyebaek* ritual to their ceremony, in which the bride formally greets her parents-in-law, who in turn pelt her with chestnuts and jujubes (a datelike fruit) to ensure wealth and the birth of sons.

[**See also** CAKES; CHAMPAGNE.]

BIBLIOGRAPHY

Fuller, Robert C. *Religion and Wine: A Cultural History of Wine Drinking in the United States.* Knoxville: University of Tennessee Press, 1996.

Gourse, Leslie. *Native American Courtship and Marriage Traditions.* New York: Hippocrene Books, 2000.

Mordecai, Carolyn. *Weddings: Dating and Love Customs of Cultures Worldwide.* Phoenix, AZ: Nittany, 1999.

PAMELA GOYAN KITTLER

Wendy's

The restaurant chain Wendy's was significant in changing the public's perception of fast food, challenging conventional wisdom by successfully offering upscale menu items to consumers at prices far higher than its major competitors. Under the direction of the founder, Dave Thomas, Wendy's became the third-largest fast food chain in the United States

---

Wedding Cakes

The modern American wedding cake emerged from various religious and cultural traditions dating back centuries. The Romans crumbled cakes made of barley or wheat over a bride's head to symbolize fertility and abundance. Displaying their economic power and social status, the extremely wealthy of the Middle Ages arranged lavish banquets featuring highly decorative food made of exotic ingredients, including towering sculptures formed of almond paste. French chefs employed by King Charles II during his seventeenth-century reign took to coating pyramids of English spice cakes with sugar icing, a practice adopted on a smaller scale at weddings of the general populace.

The elite of England and its colonies in the eighteenth century celebrated marriages with one-tiered cakes incorporating prized ingredients of the time, such as sugar, imported spices, fresh butter and eggs, nuts, and dried fruits. The surfaces of the dense cakes often were brushed with thin layers of sugar glaze or sprinkled with rose water. In the 1830s recipes for cakes covered in layers of almond paste began appearing in American cookbooks. Later in the century fancy confectioners added sculpted marzipan and sugar piping to their repertoires of cake decoration.

Well into the nineteenth century these special cakes, like the ceremonies they accompanied, remained accessible only to the rich, emphasizing the economic and social status of the bride and groom as much as symbolizing communal sanction of the marriage. The extremely wealthy commissioned skilled bakers (often immigrant German "sugar bakers") to create custom cakes and often had two—a lighter "bride's" cake and a darker, fruitcake-like "groom's" cake. Both were festooned with personalized ornaments of molded sugar and marzipan. Others had their own cooks create the ceremonial cakes. Still others, who could afford the ingredients but not the labor, made their own cakes.

By the end of the nineteenth century technological improvements helped democratize the wedding cake. Cheaper and more accessible ingredients, including refined flour and sugar, more reliable ovens, and mass-produced cake ornaments helped bring the wedding cake's basic ingredients to more people of the middle classes. Bakers themselves were able to profit from selling prebaked, pre-ornamented cakes and offered different sizes and models. At the same time the groom's cake fell out of fashion, leaving the bride's cake as the ceremony's culinary focal point. The improved quality of baking powder, baking soda, refined sugar, and flour allowed the most fashionable cakes to grow ever lighter, whiter, and taller by the end of the nineteenth century.

By the early twentieth century the highly decorated white cake had become the norm for most American weddings of all but the lowest classes. Those who could afford it added more tiers and embellishments, and after the advent of domestic freezers, it became common for couples to save the top tier and eat it on their first anniversary. Cutting the cake, a practice that first appeared in the mid-nineteenth century, had by the 1930s become a significant part of the ritual, involving both the bride and the groom and witnessed by all the guests. These practices remained fairly unchanged until the end of the twentieth century, when more couples opted for personalized wedding cakes in idiosyncratic shapes and incorporating exotic combinations of ingredients. What had not changed, however, was the necessity of a ceremonial cake to mark the occasion, serve as a personal expression of the bride and groom, and foster community solidarity through its collective consumption.

BIBLIOGRAPHY

Charsley, Simon. *Wedding Cakes and Cultural History.* London: Routledge, 1992.

Woloson, Wendy A. *Refined Tastes: Sugar, Confectionery, and Consumers in Nineteenth-Century America.* Baltimore: Johns Hopkins University Press, 2002.

WENDY A. WOLOSON

---

within a decade of its inception, behind only McDonald's and Burger King, and a leading innovator in the American restaurant industry.

Thomas learned the restaurant trade early in life, having escaped an unhappy home at the age of twelve by working the night shift at a local diner. He was living on his own by age fifteen. Thomas worked in several restaurants, gaining experience and honing his ideas about product quality and customer service. At age seventeen he enlisted in the army as a cook, soon gaining a reputation for crafty resourcefulness, which led to positions of quickly increasing responsibility.

Recognized for his competence, Thomas, just two years later, was hired to manage an enlisted men's club in Germany, where he improved the menu offerings and increased food sales from $40 each day to more than $700.

After his army service, Thomas returned to Indiana to manage a Hobby Ranch House restaurant in Fort Wayne. There he met "Colonel" Harlan Sanders, an elderly restaurateur from Kentucky who was traveling from state to state trying to sell franchises for restaurants to sell his fried chicken recipe. Colonel Sanders convinced Thomas and his employer that his "Kentucky Fried Chicken" would be a popular item. Chicken soon became the mainstay of their business, and Thomas's career thrived. He took over four failing Kentucky Fried Chicken restaurants in Columbus, turned them around, and then with his partner sold them back to the parent company and became a millionaire as well as a senior executive with Kentucky Fried Chicken. When Thomas finally left the company in 1968, he was wealthy and still young at thirty-seven years old. He soon became restless, however, and began supervising the national operations of the Arthur Treacher's Fish and Chips chain.

The late 1960s was a bleak time for the fast food industry; a saturation of hamburger restaurants was causing many major chains to fail. Entering this industry at that time defied all conventional wisdom and logic. Acting against the advice of friends and restaurant-industry analysts, Thomas left Arthur Treacher's in 1969 to open a fast food hamburger restaurant in downtown Columbus, Ohio, featuring large, made-to-order burgers, each selling at more than twice the price of those at the major chains. Borrowing his youngest daughter's nickname, he called his restaurant Wendy's Old Fashioned Hamburgers. To differentiate his restaurant from other hamburger chains, he chose an upscale motif, with hanging Tiffany lamps, carpeting, and bentwood chairs. Workers wore aprons and bow ties, and males wore chef's hats. Although Thomas offered a streamlined menu similar to those of the major chains, he stressed an "old-fashioned" approach, grilling each burger to order and serving it with the precise condiments selected by the customer. Accompanying these fresh-made burgers, he offered customers french fries; a thick, milkshake-like "Frosty"; and chili. His premise in founding Wendy's was that customers would happily pay more for higher-quality food and service, and he proved to be correct.

Thomas saw a net profit in less than six weeks, and his business boomed. Success in downtown Columbus spawned additional locations within a year, all featuring automobile pickup windows to enhance sales volume. For the next two years Thomas expanded his company throughout Ohio before opening his first out-of-state restaurant in Indianapolis, Indiana, in 1972. Selling franchises to eager investors for $200,000 each, he had blanketed the United States with more than one thousand Wendy's by 1976.

Responding to enthusiasm from Wall Street, that same year Thomas took Wendy's public, offering one million shares of stock, each at an initial price of twenty-eight dollars. Remaining as majority stockholder and company chairman, he oversaw further fast food industry innovations, such as the introduction of a salad bar; an assortment of chicken sandwiches; and eventually, such diverse items as baked potatoes, stuffed pitas, and caesar salads. Primarily marketing to a middle-class customer base, Wendy's captured and retained a consistent third-place position in the fast food industry and by 1990 had opened more than five thousand units worldwide.

By the late 1980s Thomas had relinquished control of the company while still remaining active as Wendy's highly recognizable television pitchman, making more than 800 commercials over a 13-year period. In his quasi-retirement, he volunteered in philanthropic causes, focusing on children's issues and becoming a national advocate for the cause of adoption. He founded the Dave Thomas Foundation for Adoption with the goal of finding a permanent home for every child in US foster care. Thomas died on January 8, 2002, but the company he founded continues to be a major force in the American restaurant industry.

[See also BURGER KING; DRIVE-INS; FAST FOOD; KENTUCKY FRIED CHICKEN; MCDONALD'S; ROADSIDE FOOD; SANDERS, COLONEL.]

BIBLIOGRAPHY

Thomas, R. David. *Dave's Way: A New Approach to Old Fashioned Success*. New York: Putnam's, 1991.

Jakle, John A., and Keith A. Sculle. *Fast Food: Roadside Restaurants in the Automobile Age*. Baltimore: Johns Hopkins University Press, 1999.

DAVID GERARD HOGAN

Whale Meat and Whale Oil

Whale meat and whale oil are significant foods for the Inuit people of Alaska. The Inuits have hunted whales for hundreds of years, and whale meat may account for up to 60 percent of the Inuit diet. Whale hunting, with its attendant ceremonies, helps perpetuate the culture and ethnic identity of Inuits, who are permitted by the International Whaling Commission to harvest a limited number of bowheads annually. Still, the practice is controversial and is under fire from those interested in whale conservation.

The Inuit hunt for bowhead from the middle of April through the middle of June. The mammal grows to about sixty feet long and can weigh up to sixty tons. A whaling crew who catches a whale hosts a thanksgiving celebration, named Naluqatak, usually held in mid-June, and the meat is shared among members of their community. The daylong celebration is observed with a feast that includes a dish called *mikigaq*, or fermented whale meat, as well as other wild foods.

Among non-Inuit Americans, however, whale meat and oil as food products have had a limited use and no appreciable commercial fishery. Whale oil was used for lighting and as an industrial lubricant in the late eighteenth century and the nineteenth century, when a substantial fishery was established for it. Some nineteenth-century whale men were known to eat portions of the flesh, but it was uncommon, and whale oil was used to fry doughnuts for the crew in an observance of the one-thousandth barrel of whale oil filled on any given voyage.

SANDRA L. OLIVER

Wheat

Wheat used for making raised bread has a higher level of glutenin and gliadin, two proteins that, when moistened and stirred or kneaded, combine to create gluten. Gluten, while possessed by other grains, is found in high enough concentrations to make raised bread only in wheat. Gluten provides a bubble that traps carbon dioxide and steam, thus creating small pockets when baked, resulting in a light, porous loaf.

European settlers introduced wheat into their North American colonies. It was grown extensively in the middle colonies from New York to Delaware. Because of their prodigious wheat production, New York, New Jersey, Pennsylvania, Delaware, and Maryland became known as the "bread colonies."

Inventions

In colonial times wheat was ground between two flat millstones, which removed the outer husks but ground the remaining portions of the grain so finely that they could not be separated. Mills operated on a toll system in which the miller took a portion of the flour in payment. The wheat was usually not bolted (sifted), so the bran remained in the flour. By the late eighteenth century finer flour was being produced, but mills were much more labor intensive.

In 1782 the wheelwright Oliver Evans built a mill near Wilmington, Delaware. He studied existing mills and improved the traditional design, connecting the different machines through the use of elevators, conveying devices, and mechanical devices. This meant that wheat could be ground without the intervention of a human operator, except as adjustments to the machinery became necessary. Evans's mill, which began operation in 1785, ground grain more finely and consistently than did earlier mills. His inventions revolutionized mills in Europe and the United States.

The Erie Canal, which was to connect Lake Erie with Albany, was begun in 1817, and even before it was completed eight years later, its beneficial effect on transportation had already begun to affect the price of flour. New mills using Evans's technologies were constructed

Tewa Indians winnowing wheat near San Juan, New Mexico.

A nineteenth-century engraving of a wheat harvest.

Wheat is one of the most widely produced and consumed cereal grains in the world. The United States has been consistently the largest exporter of wheat for decades. About 60 million acres of wheat are harvested each year in the United States. In 2001 America produced 2.6 billion bushels of wheat, of which 1.1 billion bushels were exported. America's wheat belt extends north from Texas through Oklahoma and Kansas, which is the largest producer, and from eastern Washington to central Montana. [**See also** BREAD; CEREAL, COLD; GENERAL MILLS; NABISCO; PILLSBURY.]

BIBLIOGRAPHY

Ferguson, Eugene S. *Oliver Evans: Inventive Genius of the Industrial Revolution.* Greenville, DE: Hagley Museum, 1980.

Ham, George E., and Robin Higham, eds. *The Rise of the Wheat State: A History of Kansas Agriculture, 1861–1986.* Manhattan, KS: Sunflower University Press, 1987.

Storck, John, and Walter Dorwin Teague. *A History of Milling Flour for Man's Bread.* Minneapolis: University of Minnesota Press, 1952.

ANDREW F. SMITH

along the route of the Erie Canal. Wheat growing and flour milling greatly expanded around Lake Erie. By the 1830s wheat grown in western New York was much less expensive than wheat grown in New England, even after transportation was calculated. Consequently many eastern farmers, particularly New Englanders, moved to the Midwest and established new farms on more productive land.

Until the nineteenth century wheat was cut by hand with sickles and scythes. In 1834 Cyrus McCormick, an American inventor, patented a reaping machine. A threshing machine was also invented in 1834 by two brothers from Maine. The development of these machines allowed farmers to do in only a few hours the work that once took several days. Another invention was the steel plow with a highly polished moldboard, which scoured itself as it turned furrows. This development made plowing easier and faster. Yet another invention was the thresher, which could process twenty to twenty-five bushels of wheat per hour.

Wheat and the Civil War

Because of the abundance of grain during the Civil War, northern soldiers and sailors were comparatively well fed, as were northern civilians. Just as important, England and France had poor grain harvests just before the war and needed increased imports. Grain exports from the North increased during the war, and the need for these exports was one reason why England and France did not recognize the Confederacy.

After the war mechanization continued on the farm. The stationary baler or hay press was invented in the 1850s. Mechanical mowers, crushers, windrowers, and other machines came into widespread use during the twentieth century. The combine, which performed virtually all these functions, revolutionized the speed at which wheat was harvested. As the combine was expensive and

worked better on flat land, wheat farms on the Great Plains became the center of American grain growing. By the beginning of the twentieth century, wheat production and milling had become a mechanized, standardized, large-scale industry. American farmers and millers worked for quantity and sought the qualities that customers wanted: a bright white color and a low price.

American Roller Mills

Roller mills were costly to build, and most millers did not have the capital or the right conditions to apply these technologies. As the flour produced by roller mills was much cheaper than flour ground by millstones, most small mills closed because they could not compete. The milling industry became increasingly centralized. In the mid-1800s there were an estimated 25,000 mills in America; by 1900 there were only 13,000 mills; by 2000 there were a mere 100 flour milling companies. In 2001 the Pillsbury Company was acquired by General Mills, and a handful of companies, including General Mills and Nabisco, controlled the vast majority of American flour milling. With the advent of roller mills, hard wheat could be milled with complete removal of the bran. Virtually all American bread is made from hard wheat, while soft wheat is used for making cakes, pastries, crackers, and similar products, which require less gluten.

Modern Wheat

Wheat has many uses in America, and it is found in more foods than any other cereal grain. There are thousands of varieties of bread on the market and tens of thousands of different types of rolls, buns, crackers, cookies, biscuits, and other baked goods. Wheat flour is also used in pasta, noodles, packaged goods, sauces, canned goods, frozen foods, and many other products.

Whiskey

American whiskey is a group of distinct alcoholic products made only in the United States, produced by fermenting then distilling "mash," a mixture of barley, rye, wheat or corn and water and yeast. While whiskey is made in other countries, there are several types made only in America: rye, corn, American blended whiskey, Tennessee whiskey, bourbon, and now wheat.

The word "whiskey" comes from the ancient Gaelic word *uisqebeatha or uisebaugh*, pronounced OOS-kee-baa or whis-kee-BAW (water of life). When the word refers to the product made in Scotland, Scotch whisky, it is spelled without the *e*.

When the fledgling American government needed to raise revenue in 1791 to retire its Revolutionary War debt, it turned to taxing liquor production. Angry farmers in the western portion of the new country, who made whiskey from their surplus grain, revolted and refused to pay the tax. For the first time in U.S. history, President George Washington mustered fifteen thousand federal troops, an enormous army at the time. By 1794 the Whiskey Rebellion had been quelled, and the new federal government had withstood its first test of centralized power.

Both the production and consumption of American whiskey rose annually until Prohibition in 1919. Not only did this federal law decrease consumption dramatically, but it also irrevocably changed consumers' tastes. Imbibers grew accustomed to the lighter taste of "bathtub" gin and other illegal alcoholic beverages. When Prohibition was repealed in 1933, consumers did not return to their former high levels of whiskey consumption.

Blended American whiskey had a great sales boost during and after World War II, extending into the late 1960s. Since the 1960s, however, lighter goods, such as vodka, have become the largest sellers in distilled beverages.

Whiskey-Making Process

The taste and quality of whiskey depends on many factors: the type of grain used, (corn, rye, wheat, or barley—the exact mix is part of the proprietary recipe of each distillery), how the grain is processed, whether the wort (the mixture of crushed grain, yeast, and malted grain in warm water) is distilled in copper pot stills or column stills, how the spent yeast is handled, in what container and under what conditions the whiskey is stored, how long it is aged, and if and how the whiskey is blended. The distiller is looking for a finished product with just the right combination of "congeners," substances that contribute whiskey's distinct aroma, taste, and color.

For sour mash whiskey, the sour residues of the spent yeast from the last batch of wort made are added to the new wort of the next batch. A sweet mash whiskey is made with new yeast in every new batch.

Most whiskey is aged after distillation, an exception being corn whiskey, which is immediately bottled. To age, whiskey is pumped from the still into wooden barrels that are then placed in rows in warehouses. The insides of these barrels have been charred by putting an open flame into the barrel and burning the wood evenly on all sides of the barrel for a light, medium, or heavy toast. Charring gives the whiskey its color and additional caramel, toasty flavors from the natural sugars in the oak. As the temperature and humidity change in the warehouse where the barrels are aging, the whiskey passes in and out of the walls of the oak barrel, collecting the toasted oak's characteristics.

If the whiskey is to be blended, a master distiller tastes samples of many barrels. The distiller then combines the whiskeys to attain a consistent taste for the brand and ends by adding distilled water to lower the proof (expressed in degrees and double the amount of beverage alcohol in the spirit) of the final product. Thus the taste of an American blended whiskey will be consistent over time. By contrast, if the whiskey is to be "single barrel," or "straight," the barrel is opened, water is added, and the product is then bottled.

Types of American Whiskey

Corn whiskey, an unaged product, is a rough drink with a harsh taste. Illegally produced whiskey, called "moonshine" or "white lightning" because of its colorlessness, is made with corn because of corn's ready availability and ease in fermenting. Bourbon is the most famous corn whiskey and is a true American innovation. Legally bourbon must contain at least 51 percent corn, be distilled at less than 160 proof, and be aged for a minimum of two years in new white oak charred barrels.

Straight whiskey is American whiskey, aged at least two years in new white charred oak barrels. The addition of water brings the alcohol down to no lower than 80 proof.

Rye, a grain similar to wheat, makes a full-bodied, pungent whiskey. Very little rye whiskey is bottled. Most of its production is incorporated into American blended whiskey. American blended whiskey is a product of at least 20 percent straight whiskey mixed with neutral spirits. This category generally has a lighter flavor and body than a straight whiskey. If the final product does not have the rich brown tones of straight whiskey, coloring from natural caramel can be used to darken the product.

Tennessee whiskey is made using the same process used in making bourbon with an added step. Before bottling, the whiskey is filtered through thick beds of sugar maple charcoal. This filtration removes some of the congeners and creates a smooth, mellow taste.

Contemporary Trends

To fight their decreasing market share, whiskey distillers have introduced two high-end line extensions. A master distiller chooses a "single barrel" of whiskey to bottle in limited quantity, usually three hundred bottles. "Small Batch" refers to a limited bottling of a few barrels of whiskey specially blended by the master distiller. Specially chosen for their richer, distinctive taste, these elite bottlings are often in elaborate packaging. A Kentucky bourbon distiller created the first new whiskey category in years, releasing a wheat whiskey in 2005 that contains at least 51 percent wheat.

[**See also** BOTTLING; BOURBON; COCKTAILS; DISTILLATION; FERMENTATION; RUM; SAZERAC.]

BIBLIOGRAPHY

Dikty, Alan S., ed. *The Beverage Testing Institute's Buying Guide to Spirits*. New York: Sterling, 1999.

Jackson, Michael. *The World Guide to Whiskey*. Topsfield, MA: 1988.

Murray, Jim. *Classic Bourbon, Tennessee, and Rye Whiskey*. London: Prion Books, 1998.

"Spirits Remain High." *Beverage Industry*, June 2002.

MARK C. GRUBER

Whiskey Sour

The making of a whiskey sour and sour drinks in general is an art form that distinguishes amateur bartenders, who like to toss an occasional cocktail party in the den, from professionally trained bartenders. For that reason, the whiskey companies that wanted to promote this popular classic cocktail had to come up with a ready-mix product that would aid the home bartender in preparing sour drinks. The whiskey sour traditionally calls for fresh lemon juice and a sweetener, and the balance between sweet and sour is critical and difficult to achieve. Fresh lemon juice is so concentrated that adding too much produces an overly sour, undrinkable cocktail. The downside of the premade sour mixes is

flavor; unfortunately, the flavor of fresh fruit cannot be re-created with modern chemistry.

The whiskey sour has just three main ingredients: whiskey, usually blended American but sometimes a straight whiskey (like bourbon or rye); fresh lemon juice; and some form of sugar. Over the years bartenders have played with the ingredients to achieve certain effects, for example, adding a small amount of egg white to give the drink a handsome layer of foam on top. Somewhere along the line a bartender added a splash of orange juice to the mix and called it a California, or stone, sour. In the nineteenth century, when the technology to inject gas into water was perfected, sours were doused with sparkling water; the results were Collins-style drinks.

The tradition of combining lemon juice with spirits and other alcoholic beverages probably dates back to ancient times, when wine was flavored with flowers and other additives to make it more palatable. The Italians, who were pioneers in infusing spirits with fruit and herbal and spicy ingredients, were making a *limoncello*-style infusion five hundred years ago by combining spirits with lemon juice and lemon oil from the rind. But the custom that led to the modern use of lemon in cocktails was probably the punch craze that Americans went through in colonial times. English tea traders brought back the punch recipe from trips to India, along with the mnemonic for remembering the five ingredients: strong, sweet, sour, spicy, and weak. In order, the ingredients were rum; sugar; lemon juice; a mixture composed of nutmeg, cinnamon, mace, and other spices; and tea, juice, or water.

The modern sour evolved between 1862 and 1880. The early cocktail book *How to Mix Drinks* (1862), by Jerry Thomas, does not have a sour recipe under that name. But just after the short cocktail section Thomas lists the "Whiskey Crusta," a drink made with lemon juice, whiskey, and gum syrup that was shaken and served in a glass with a sugared rim and a large peel of lemon. To make a simple sour cocktail, start with 1½ to 2 ounces of the base liquor. Add ¾ ounce of the sour ingredient (e.g., fresh lemon juice) and 1 ounce of one or more sweet ingredients (e.g., a simple syrup). Shake hard while slowly counting to ten. Dale DeGroff says in *The Craft of the Cocktail* that adding egg white to a sour can leave behind an offensive flavor. Foam also can be produced simply by shaking the drink harder.

[**See also** COCKTAILS; FLAVORINGS; WHISKEY.]

DALE DEGROFF

White Castle

White Castle, through its founder Edgar "Billy" Ingram, successfully popularized the hamburger sandwich; created a uniform company standard of architecture, menu, and quality among its many outlets; and introduced consumers to a carryout style of eating. Many of White Castle's culinary and corporate innovations later became fundamental to both the American diet and modern business operations.

Partnering with Walter Anderson, a fry cook, in Wichita in 1921, Ingram founded the White Castle System of Eating Houses. The premise of Ingram's White Castle operation was simply to sell inexpensive hamburger sandwiches in large volume. To accomplish this goal, however, he had to convince hungry consumers that ground beef was a safe and healthy food, that his restaurants were clean and hygienic establishments, and that his products were a good value. The buying public distrusted the meat industry in the early twentieth century and held ground meat in particularly low regard. The popular perception during this era was that butchers routinely ground up meat when it began to spoil, giving them a few additional days to sell it. Compounding this public disregard for ground meat, small sandwich shops customarily carried a stigma of being both transient and unsanitary.

The White Castle System

In creating his White Castle restaurants, Ingram countered these negative stereotypes by grinding choice cuts of fresh beef directly in front of his customers, constructing his buildings out of gleaming stainless steel and white enamel, and adopting a crenellated roof design that resembled a castle. Even his choice of name was a marketing tactic, stressing that "white" would symbolize purity and cleanliness and that the "castle" image would signify strength and permanence. His message to consumers was that White Castles were clean, healthy, and here to stay. Ingram's marketing strategies, combined with an affordable price of five cents for a hamburger, made his White Castle restaurants an overnight success in Wichita.

White Castle saturated the Wichita market in less than two years, and Ingram expanded to other cities in the region. He spread his chain to Omaha in 1923, to Kansas City the following year, and to St. Louis in 1925. Similar success in these cities led to even further expansion, with new White Castles opening in Chicago, Minneapolis, Louisville, Indianapolis, Columbus, Cincinnati, and New York City by the end of the decade. Ingram stressed consistency in standards and menu throughout his growing chain and purchased company biplanes to allow senior managers greater access to their expanding territory. Friends suggested to Ingram that he sell franchises of his business rather than fund the expansion with his own capital. He opposed this approach, however, believing that franchising would lead to his losing control over standards and practices, undermining uniformity of quality.

As Ingram opened restaurants in new cities, he placed advertisements in local papers with coupons that offered customers their initial ten hamburgers at the half price of only twenty-five cents. These discount coupons led to huge lines of hungry coupon-holders and to an almost instant customer base. As White Castle spread from city to city, popular enthusiasm for its hamburger sandwich continued to grow.

Soon the White Castle name and crenellated architecture became synonymous with the product itself. Hundreds of enterprising restaurateurs in the 1920s capitalized on White Castle's success by selling White Castle–style hamburgers in small, white buildings, often featuring a confusingly similar name, such as White Tower, Red Castle, or White Palace. One leading competitor even borrowed White Castle's "Buy 'em by the Sack" slogan, changing it only slightly to "Buy 'em by the *Bag.*" For the next two decades, until after the end of World War II, the vast majority of restaurants featuring hamburgers remained close to Ingram's system in architectural style, image, and food products. In fact the fast food king Richard McDonald later publicly credited White Castle as being the original model for his successful chain. If imitation is truly the highest compliment, restaurant entrepreneurs in the 1920s and 1930s accorded Ingram great respect. White buildings and catchy slogans, however, were relatively insignificant in comparison to Ingram's real success. In 1929 the president of the American Restaurant Association declared the hamburger and apple pie to be "America's favorite foods." The cumulative effect of White Castle's success, and the successes of its competitors and imitators, elevated the hamburger sandwich from disgrace and obscurity in 1921 to a position of respect and prominence by the close of the decade.

Changes and Challenges

The 1930s brought changes to White Castle. In 1934 Ingram moved his corporate headquarters to Columbus, Ohio, in order to be more centrally located in the middle of his Kansas to New York territory. This was also a decade of extreme economic hardship. White Castle survived the Depression, while most of its competitors went bankrupt. Realizing that his predominantly working-class customer base had fewer nickels to spend on hamburgers, Ingram redirected his marketing emphasis to attract more of a middle-class clientele. After studying the success of Betty Crocker and other fictional "corporate hostesses," Ingram hired a real woman to serve as White Castle's company spokeswoman. Operating under the pseudonym Julia Joyce, Ingram's spokeswoman visited garden clubs and women's groups in order to convince middle-class women that White Castle hamburgers were good, healthy family fare. Supported by the findings of company-sponsored scientific studies—one such study fed a student only water and White Castle hamburgers for sixty days—Julia Joyce taught these women how a sack of hamburgers could be a proper family entrée, served side-by-side with potatoes and vegetables. Her marketing efforts, in conjunction with an intensive ad campaign depicting middle-class families dining on hamburgers, succeeded in attracting the middle class to White Castle. This additional customer base helped the company weather the economic downturn of the 1930s. It ended the decade even larger and more profitable than it had been before the Depression began.

White Castle's continued prosperity, however, came to an abrupt halt with the beginning of World War II. Civilian workers quickly became soldiers, draining the domestic labor force and driving up wages. Available workers flocked to higher-paying factory jobs, leaving White Castle's counters unmanned. Unable to fully staff his restaurants and often unable to purchase rationed food supplies, such as meat, sugar, and coffee, Ingram curtailed hours of operation and ultimately had to shut down half of his White Castles. Ravaged by the wartime shortages, he struggled to keep his company afloat throughout the rest of the 1940s. Exacerbating this already bleak situation, burgeoning postwar suburbs lured away a large segment of young adults, leaving Ingram's remaining restaurants to sell hamburgers in less-populated and deteriorating urban neighborhoods.

Still profitable in its reduced form, White Castle remained in these city locations while the giant franchised fast food hamburger chains appearing in the 1950s and 1960s focused their building and marketing efforts on the developing suburbs. Without the capital to build new locations and still averse to the concept of franchising, Ingram could not afford to compete in suburbia. In many ways Ingram's White Castle system was left behind for several decades, stagnating while its franchised competitors dominated the new markets. Later, in the late 1960s and 1970s, the company rebounded under the direction of Ingram's son, Edgar Ingram, and grandson, Bill Ingram, eventually opening successful outlets in the suburbs while also usually retaining its traditional locations and customers in city neighborhoods.

Still small in size in the early 2000s compared to the multinational fast food giants, the White Castle chain operated restaurants in fourteen American cities and enjoyed a loyal customer following. Often serving hamburgers to the great- and great-great-grandchildren of its original customers, White Castle's popularity and success are perhaps based more on its longevity and mystique than its burgers.

[See also Drive-Ins; Fast Food; Hamburger; McDonald's; Take-Out Food.]

BIBLIOGRAPHY

Hogan, David. *Selling 'Em by the Sack: White Castle and the Creation of American Food.* New York: New York University Press, 1997.

Langdon, Philip. *Orange Roofs and Golden Arches: The Architecture of American Chain Restaurants.* New York: Knopf, 1986.

David Gerard Hogan

Whitefish

Whitefish (*Coregonus clupeaformis*), which is related to the salmon family, is found in cold lakes and streams across the northern states and Canada and is fished commercially in the Great Lakes. Whitefish is plentiful in Lake Superior and in northern Huron and Michigan. The flesh is firm and white, which makes whitefish popular for eating, and is available year-round. Whitefish is often caught in gill nets in summer and through ice in winter, although it is not considered a great sport fish. Whitefish roe is salted and sold as golden caviar. Whitefish can be cooked in almost any way—broiled, grilled, baked, steamed, fried, or poached.

Around Lake Michigan outdoor whitefish boils are popular traditional events, likely derived from the practice of boiling the fish onboard the gill netters that caught them. The fish, cut in chunks, is put into a pot with small potatoes and onions and allowed to boil. Kerosene is added to the fire at the end of cooking, and the resulting flare-up causes the pot to boil over, a process that drives off the accumulated fish oil. The fish and potatoes are served with butter and, often, coleslaw. Pie is served for dessert. Civic organizations host fish boils in the summer and early fall, and the region's restaurants and lodges offer whitefish boil on their menus. Whitefish is also called chub, cisco, lake herring, and tullibee, although these are different fish.

SANDRA L. OLIVER

White House

From the Founding Fathers' continental tables, through the gargantuan meals of Ulysses S. Grant and William H. Taft, to Dwight Eisenhower's "common man" TV tray dinners and Richard Nixon's spartan cottage cheese and ketchup, the First Table reflects both presidential personality and political exigencies. The dour Calvin Coolidge scrutinized White House food bills and claimed that the greatest disappointment of his presidency was the White House hams. after carving slices from a large joint to serve President and Mrs. Coolidge, the butler whisked the ham away. Coolidge could never learn what happened to the leftovers.

The Public versus the Private Table

George Washington understood the need to balance the formality and dignity suitable to a head of state on the international stage with the competing demands of host to the nation's constituents. He introduced open houses at which any respectable citizen—that is, one with a proper letter of introduction and suitably dressed—could be admitted to enjoy light refreshments such as tea, coffee, cakes, and ice creams. These levees continued until the Civil War.

Martin Van Buren and the "Gold Spoon" Speech (1840)

Martin Van Buren's enjoyment of French food and fine tableware may have cost him a second term. Representative William Ogle's famous "Gold Spoon" speech on the floor of Congress grossly misrepresented Van Buren's expenditures on White House furnishings, falsely accusing him of profligate spending on gold silverware that had been purchased by his predecessors, especially James Monroe. Coming on the heels of the populist Andrew Jackson and running against William Henry Harrison, whose log cabin homestead (itself a bit of a myth) was depicted on souvenir glass and ceramics, the patrician Van Buren was painted as hopelessly effete and out of touch:

> How delightful it must be to be . . . to eat his *pâté de foie gras, dinde desosse* and *salade à la volaille* from a silver plate with a golden knife and fork. And how exquisite to sip with a golden spoon his *soupe à la Reine* from a silver tureen. What will honest Loco Focos [a political group] say to Mr. Van Buren for spending the People's cash in foreign Fanny Kemble green finger cups, in which to wash his pretty, tapering, soft, white lily fingers after dining on *fricandeau de veau* and *omelette souffle*? How will the friends of temperance relish the foreign "cut wine coolers" . . . ?

Esther Singleton, The Story of the White House (2 vols.), New York: McClure, 1907, vol.1: 256, quoted in Jane Shadel Spillman, White House Glassware: 200 Years of Presidential Entertaining (Washington, DC: White House Historical Association, 1989), 44–45.

The smear was successful. Van Buren took the bait, grousing that Harrison was content with a barrel of hard cider. Harrison won, and his brief tenure was marked by dinner parties where the liquor was reported to flow freely.

French cooking was the language of culinary diplomacy at state and political receptions. Starting with the John Adams and Thomas Jefferson administrations, many of the White House chefs and stewards were French or French trained. Nineteenth century chroniclers judged the White House table against French standards. Dolley Madison was known for her brilliant, unpretentious parties, described as "always abundant and sumptuous, more, however, in the Virginian style than in the European." Contrary to his corncob pipe image, Andrew Jackson loved French food and was complimented for his "gorgeous supper table shaped like a horse-shoe, covered with every good and glittering thing French skill could devise."

By the latter half of the nineteenth century, much of the cooking for official functions was delegated to outside caterers, usually ex-patriot French cooks. The private table, however, was customized to each president. Grover Cleveland maintained Chester A. Arthur's French chef, one M. Fortin, for political dinners but imported his female cook from his days as the governor of New York for his private table. Elizabeth Jaffray, the White House housekeeper from the William Howard Taft through the Calvin Coolidge administrations, described the miserly salaries paid to the women cooks hired for the presidents' private tables and the cost-cutting measures of having the private staff prepare official receptions, aided only in extreme cases by caterers.

Part of this economy was prompted by the expense of living in the White House. Until the Coolidge administration, all food costs, including staff meals, were paid for by the president personally. Starting in the mid 1920s the president was given an entertaining budget for

---

Buy American, or at Least Decorate American

An 1826 federal law required that "all furniture purchased for the use of the President's House [the name "White House" was adopted only during Theodore Roosevelt's presidency] shall be as far as practicable of American or domestic manufacture." This legislation helped promote the fledgling domestic glass industry; virtually all glassware since then has been purchased from American manufacturers. Not so with porcelain. American porcelain manufacturers were judged inferior to their European competition. Thus artists created designs, most commonly incorporating the seal of state, for European manufacturers to place on high-quality blanks. A striking exception to this motif was Rutherford B. Hayes's state china. Designed and signed by the artist Theodore R. Davis, each piece depicted American flora and fauna; executed by the French company Haviland, the service is unparalleled. First Lady Caroline (Mrs. Benjamin) Harrison was accomplished at china painting, a genteel hobby in the nineteenth century; she designed dishes incorporating the indigenous goldenrod and maize in the border, executed by the French company Tressemannes and Vogt in 1892. It was not until 1918 that a complete set of American porcelain (termed "fine china" by its producer, the Lenox China Company) was purchased as the official state dinner service.

CATHY K. KAUFMAN

---

official functions. The costs of private dinners for family and personal guests still come out of the president's salary. Rosalynn Carter was stunned by a food bill over $600 for Jimmy Carter's first ten days as president.

Even with an entertaining budget, Franklin Roosevelt's public and private tables were reportedly atrocious. Some have claimed Eleanor Roosevelt was indifferent to food and expediently hired the inexperienced but politically loyal Henrietta Nesbitt as housekeeper to superintend all meals. Nesbitt's job may simply have been impossible, for she had to contend with Franklin Roosevelt's poor health and the politics of Depression-era mores and World War II rationing.

Gourmet dining reemerged when Jacqueline Kennedy chose the Frenchman René Verdon as White House chef for both the public and private table, flaunting the tradition of having a "plain" private cook. Sensing a political storm, the White House expedited Verdon's naturalization papers so that an American would bring haute cuisine to the White House. The Clintons broke new ground in hiring an American-trained chef to run the public table.

The White House Table as Bully Pulpit

Many mid- to late-nineteenth-century presidents banned hard liquor from the White House, either from personal conviction or as a nod to the growing temperance movement. Rutherford B. Hayes, influenced by his wife "Lemonade Lucy" Hayes, banned even wine except when entertaining foreign dignitaries. Hayes personally liked wine, and the decision was political; he claimed in his diary that it was "wise and useful as an example" as well as a reward to his temperance supporters. Although menus from the Hayes administration include frozen punches normally spiked with alcohol, Hayes's diary (and the White House purchase receipts) suggest that nonalcoholic flavorings were used in the kitchen.

President Arthur ignored vigorous temperance lobbying. His dinners were Gilded Age extravaganzas of fourteen courses with eight different wines, capped by brandy and cigars. Warren G. Harding's official dinners were dry, but notwithstanding Prohibition, "Duchess" Lillian Harding freely poured "medicinal" liquor in the family quarters to wash down knockwurst and sauerkraut at late-night poker games.

The most controversial meal ever at the White House was Theodore Roosevelt's October 1901 impromptu invitation to Booker T. Washington to join a family dinner to discuss southern politics. Whether Roosevelt had misgivings about being the first president to invite a black man to an intimate meal in the White House or felt the invitation was perfectly natural is unclear, but the dinner ignited a firestorm. Conservative newspapers labeled the dinner "the most damnable outrage," while liberal voices called the meal "splendid in its recognition of the essential character of the presidential office." The dinner is believed to have sparked race riots in Louisiana a few weeks later in which eleven people died.

White House cachet sells cookbooks. The earliest and most influential was *The White House Cookbook*, first published in 1887 by Hugo Ziemann, Cleveland's White House Steward, and Frances Gillette. Revealing the White House kitchen to be much like its private middle-American counterparts, the book was more a didactic cookery manual, complete with home remedies and housekeeping tips, than a repository of elite dining. The voyeuristic instructions for serving a state dinner were its one concession to rank. The most recent edition (1996) bears little firsthand connection to the White House.

Closer to the first table are newspaper and magazine features that highlight the holiday meals the first family will enjoy. These recipes emphasize the regional background, family traditions, and preferences of the president or first lady, creating a vogue for clam chowder and *poulet à l'estragon* during the Kennedy years and endless variations on barbeque for much of the past forty.

BIBLIOGRAPHY

Haber, Barbara. *From Hardtack to Home Fries*. New York: Free Press, 2002.

Klapthor, Margaret Brown. *The First Ladies Cook Book*. Helen Duprey Bullock, consulting ed. New York: Parents Magazine Enterprises, 1982.

Klapthor, Margaret Brown. *The Official White House China: 1789 to the Present*. 2nd ed., with additions and revisions by Betty C. Monkman, William G. Allman, and Susan Gray Detweiler. New York: Abrams, 1999.

Spillman, Jane Shadel. *White House Glassware: 200 Years of Presidential Entertaining*. Washington, DC: White House Historical Association, 1989.

CATHY K. KAUFMAN

Whoopie Pie

The Whoopie pie is not a pie at all but two typically large, cake-like chocolate cookies that are sandwiched together with a fluffy white filling. It is considered both a New England and a Pennsylvania Amish country traditional comfort food. Both geographical areas claim to be the birthplace of the whoopie pie, and there are several theories of origin. There is some agreement that the special treat traces back to the Depression era. The Amish traditional explanation is that a cook had some leftover cake batter and dropped it in generous rounds to bake. And according to legend, children would find these cream-filled cakes in their lunch bags and shout "whoopie." While the dough does seem to have evolved from a cake batter, a commercial baker may have created the cake-like product that could be individually packaged and eaten by hand. The Berwick Cake Company of Boston has been given the credit as the first to make them in 1926. The Lebadies Bakery in Maine claims to be the first to make the original Maine Whoopie Pie since 1925. Whoopie pie's popularity in New England is the result of the Durkee Mower Company sponsoring a weekly radio show *Flufferettes* in the 1930s. The program, broadcast to twenty-one stations in New England, promoted the *Yummy Book*, a recipe book featuring marshmallow fluff as an ingredient, which included a recipe for whoopie pie. In the early twenty-first century whoopie pies are found in different flavors—molasses, peanut butter, and pumpkin—but chocolate continues to be the traditional and most popular flavor.

SUSAN MCLELLAN PLAISTED

Wieners, *see Hot Dog*

Wienerschnitzel

John Galardi, a commissary manager for a small chain of Mexican restaurants called El Taco in Long Beach, California, decided to launch his own fast food chain based on hot dogs. One of the owners of the chain, Glen Bell, invested in Galardi's chain and helped develop the idea. Martha Bell, Glen's wife, supplied a name: Der Wienerschnitzel. The name comes from the traditional Austrian veal cutlet, Wiener schnitzel, which has nothing to do with hot dogs, but Galardi liked the sound of the name. ("Der" was removed from the name in 1977.)

In 1961 the first outlet, featuring hot dogs, corn dogs, and chili dogs, opened in Newport Beach, California. Galardi's first stand was flat-roofed, but he switched to an A-frame in which customers actually drove through the building. The chain's mascot is a hot dog that runs away from people who want to eat him. Wienerschnitzel remains privately owned; its parent company, the Galardi Group Franchise and Leasing, Inc., is headquartered in Newport Beach. Wienerschnitzel is the largest hot dog chain in the world, with more than 360 outlets in 10 states. In 2005 the company co-branded with Tastee-Freez, so its menu now includes Tastee-Freez items.

BIBLIOGRAPHY

Jakle, John A., and Keith A. Sculle. *Fast Food: Roadside Restaurants in the Automobile Age*. Baltimore: Johns Hopkins University Press, 1999.

Langdon, Philip. *Orange Roofs, Golden Arches: The Architecture of American Chain Restaurants*. New York: Knopf, 1986.

ANDREW F. SMITH

Wild Rice

Wild rice (*Zizania aquatica*), not a true rice, is the long, brownish-black seed of a wild grass indigenous to North America and Asia. In America it grows in lakes and rivers primarily in areas west and north of the Great Lakes as well as in isolated pockets from New Jersey to Florida and Texas. It was consumed in pre-Columbian times by Native Americans, who harvested it from canoes, beating the grain from the plants with sticks; some wild rice is still harvested in this fashion, and its price reflects the labor-intensive method. As befits its wild origins, the rice is commonly served with game, but it is also served with domestic poultry. Cultivated varieties of wild rice were developed in the 1960s, and California is the largest producer.

BIBLIOGRAPHY

Hauser, Susan Carol. *Wild Rice Cooking: Harvesting, History, Natural History, and Lore with 80 Recipes*. New York: Lyons, 2000.

ANDREW F. SMITH

Wiley, Harvey

Harvey Washington Wiley, MD, is generally considered the father of pure food and drug legislation and the U.S. Food and Drug Administration. He was a central figure during the passage of the Pure Food and Drug Act of 1906, called by some the Wiley Act, and its successor, the 1938 Federal Food, Drug, and Cosmetic Act.

Wiley was born in 1844 in Indiana, served as a corporal in the Civil War, received his MD from Indiana Medical College, and later completed a bachelor's degree at Harvard. In 1874 Wiley joined the faculty of Purdue University as its first professor of chemistry. There he turned his attention to the study of sugar. In 1883 he left Purdue to become head of the Division of Chemistry at the U.S. Department of Agriculture (USDA), a position he held until 1912.

From an early date Wiley identified himself with the pure food movement in the United States and used it as a springboard to expand his department. One of the more controversial things Wiley did was to set up the infamous human feeding study on the safety of food preservatives. Twelve young, able-bodied men, all employees of the USDA, volunteered to let the government lace all of their meals with borax, salicylic acid, sulfuric acid, sodium benzoate, and formaldehyde. They consumed their meals in the basement of the Department of Agriculture for at least six months. George Rothwell Brown of the *Washington Post* dubbed the volunteers the "Poison Squad," and they became a national sensation. The study ended because the chemicals made some of the volunteers so sick from nausea, vomiting, and stomachaches that they could not do productive work.

The study was seriously flawed scientifically since there was no control group and no norms with which to compare the findings. In addition the experiment as conceived by Wiley reflected his bizarre and unusual notions about digestion. He believed in the archaic idea that digestion and spoilage were the same thing. He reasoned that if preservatives prevent foods from spoiling, they must also interfere with digestion. While the government never followed up with the men on the long-term effects of the chemicals they consumed, anecdotal evidence suggests that no one was harmed. William O. Robinson, one of the original human guinea pigs, lived to the age of ninety-four.

Because of Wiley's many dealings with business interests (he worked for a time for and accepted gifts from Arbuckle, the coffee company) and his commercial favoritisms, he was frequently in conflict with other government officials, especially the secretary of agriculture. After leaving the USDA Wiley became director of the Bureau of Foods, Sanitation, and Health at *Good Housekeeping* magazine, where he wrote a monthly column and established the Good Housekeeping Seal of Approval. He died in 1930 and is buried at Arlington National Cemetery.

[**See also** DEPARTMENT OF AGRICULTURE, U.S.; FOOD AND DRUG ADMINISTRATION; GOOD HOUSEKEEPING INSTITUTE.]

BIBLIOGRAPHY

Coppin, Clayton A., and Jack High. *The Politics of Purity: Harvey Washington Wiley and the Origins of Federal Food Policy*. Ann Arbor: University of Michigan Press, 1999.

Lewis, Carol. "The 'Poison Squad' and the Advent of Food and Drug Regulation." *FDA Consumer Magazine*, November–December 2002.

JOSEPH M. CARLIN

Willan, Anne

In addition to being considered one of the world's authorities on French cooking, cookbook author Anne Willan is a pioneer in the development of the modern cooking school and has influenced modern food writing.

Born January 26, 1938, in Newcastle, England, Willan earned a master's degree in economics from Cambridge University but decided to follow her love of cooking by earning a diploma from the Cordon Bleu in Paris in 1963. Willan then taught cooking in Paris and in London before moving to the United States and becoming an associate editor of *Gourmet*. She became a U.S. citizen in 1973.

With the encouragement of Julia Child, Willan opened Ecole de Cuisine La Varenne in Paris in 1975 with her husband, the economist Mark Cherniavsky. The school drew many Americans with English-speaking classes that provided a solid French culinary background.

Willan was one of the first to use an overhead mirror in her classes. Willan also drafted students to help her write her cookbooks in exchange for tuition, providing them intensive training in recipe writing. Her students went on to become editors and writers for most of the leading food publications, prominent cookbook authors, and cooking school teachers. Willan herself has been prolific, writing more than a dozen cookbooks, including the landmark culinary reference *La Varenne pratique* (1989); the Look and Cook series, a companion to her 26-episode PBS TV cooking show that aired in 1992–1995; and *From My Chateau Kitchen* (2000), which chronicles the foods and history of her seventeenth-century Château du Fey in Burgundy, where she moved her cooking school in 1991. Her books have been published in two dozen countries and translated into more than twenty languages. Her articles have appeared in numerous publications, such as the *Washington Post*, the *Los Angeles Times*, and *Travel and Leisure*. Willan has been active as a leader in various food organizations, serving as president of the International Association of Culinary Professionals (1990–1991), and she is a founder and former trustee of the American Center for Wine, Food, and the Arts (COPIA). An avid culinary historian, Willan and her husband have amassed one of the world's largest private collections of antique cookbooks. In naming her Cooking Teacher of the Year (2000), *Bon Appétit* cited Willan for helping "broaden cooking careers for food professionals, particularly for women, and she has influenced the technical writing of recipes."

[**See also** CELEBRITY CHEFS.]

BIBLIOGRAPHY

Willan, Anne. *From My Chateau Kitchen*. New York: Potter, 2000.

Willan, Anne. *La Varenne Pratique*. New York: Crown, 1989.

SCOTT WARNER

Wilson, Mary Tolford

Mary Tolford Wilson (b. 1899 in Wisconsin; d. 1998 in Connecticut) is known for her scholarly work in culinary history. Her admirable essay "The First American Cookbook" served as the introduction to a 1958 facsimile edition of *American Cookery* (1796) by Amelia Simmons; the essay stands as a model study of culinary Americana. Later Wilson wrote a scholarly account concerning *The Pocumtuc Housewife* (1897), which was falsely claimed by the publisher to have originally been published in 1805, giving rise to numerous phantom citings of a spurious work in certain august lexicons.

[See also COOKBOOKS AND MANUSCRIPTS: TO 1860; SIMMONS, AMELIA.]

BIBLIOGRAPHY

Simmons, Amelia. *American Cookery*. A facsimile of the first edition with an essay by Mary Tolford Wilson. New York: Oxford University Press, 1958.

Wilson, Mary Tolford. "To Lay a Ghost." *Harvard Library Bulletin* 28, no. 1 (January 1980).

KAREN HESS

Wine:

Historical Survey

From the beginnings of settlement the American colonists hoped to make wine. The abundant native grapes (for example, *V. riparia, V. labrusca, V. aestivalis*), however, were at once found to be unsuited to wine making. The European vine (*V. vinifera*) was then imported but would not grow; the experiment was repeated again and again in all of the colonies for two centuries to unvarying failure. Not until the nineteenth century was some understanding of the reasons reached. The New World, which abounded in grapes, also abounded in pests and diseases unknown in Europe. The chief were black rot, powdery mildew, downy mildew, phylloxera, and Pierce's disease, which, singly or in combination, were lethal to vinifera.

In the first two centuries of settlement there was no understanding whatever of these things. Thus futile effort followed futile effort in monotonous succession. Germans in Pennsylvania, French in South Carolina, English in Virginia and Georgia, Dutch in New York, Greeks and Italians in Florida tried and failed. Official encouragement was of no avail. Nearly all of the leading figures in early American history were among the countless would-be wine growers doomed to frustration: Governor William Bradford, General James Edward Oglethorpe, Benjamin Franklin, George Washington, Thomas Jefferson.

The breakthrough came with the discovery of accidental hybrids, crosses of vinifera with a native grape. The first such hybrid cultivated was the Alexander or Cape grape, followed by

> ## Phylloxera
>
> All of the grapes grown in Europe were of the species *Vitis vinifera*, and until the nineteenth century they were not exposed to diseases and insects that could threaten their existence. Beginning in the 1860s vine cuttings from the United States introduced powdery mildew into the French vineyards. Shortly afterwards *Phylloxera vastatrix*, a plant louse that could attack the roots of the vinifera, was accidentally imported from America and was responsible for devastating hundreds of thousands of acres of grapes throughout Europe. This was followed by yet another fungal disease, downy mildew.
>
> There were two responses to the phylloxera crisis in France. One was to find phylloxera-resistant rootstocks onto which the classic vinifera varieties could be grafted, and it was discovered that the rootstocks of American varieties could be used successfully because they were strongly resistant to phylloxera. A second response came from private French hybridizers such as Albert Seibel who made hundreds of thousands of crosses. Some of these with the potential for making dry table wines eventually found their way into the United States. Among those that found a permanent place in the East were Seyval Blanc, Vidal, Maréchal Foch, and Chambourcin.
>
> HUDSON CATTELL

Catawba, Isabella, and a host of others. The first successful commercial wine making was carried out by Swiss colonists growing the Alexander in Indiana in the first decade of the nineteenth century; they were followed by Nicholas Longworth in Cincinnati with the Catawba. From these beginnings wine making developed in Missouri, northern Ohio, upstate New York, and New Jersey. In the South, the home of Pierce's disease, the resistant muscadine grapes, of which scuppernong is the best-known variety, were the main dependence. Wine making in the eastern states, led by New York, continued on the basis of native hybrids down to Prohibition.

In California, from the beginning of the missions in 1769, it was found that vinifera would grow; the mission vineyards showed the way, and from the 1820s a small but growing industry was established in and around Los Angeles. This was transformed after the gold rush of 1849 and California statehood. Commercial wine making spread throughout the state; by 1920, when Prohibition shut it down, the California wine industry was producing nearly 40 million gallons of wine annually and dominated the national trade, as it still does. The business was largely in the hands of a combine called the California Wine Association, created after the financial disasters of the panic of 1893. The vineyards of the state suffered serious losses from phylloxera, introduced in the 1870s; growers were slow to respond to the danger but ultimately did as the French had done and grafted their vinifera vines to resistant American rootstocks.

The period of national Prohibition (1920–1933) devastated the wineries of the country, most of which went out of business. Home wine making was legally permitted, with the result that the nation's vineyard acreage doubled between 1920 and 1925. Overplanting was followed by the Great Depression; when repeal of Prohibition came at the end of 1933, things were in a sorry state. Through the next thirty years most American wine was sweet and fortified and made from inferior varieties in wineries operating on an industrial scale. Efforts to improve this situation, led by university scientists and a handful of dedicated fine wine producers, began to take effect by the 1960s. They were helped by two trade developments. Wines were now bottled at the winery instead of being shipped out in bulk to regional bottlers. And so-called "varietal" labeling slowly became the standard practice; wine was now named for the grape it was made from—Cabernet, or Chardonnay, or Zinfandel—rather than being called something it was not—Burgundy, Chablis, Chianti, and the like.

Sales of dry table wine passed those of fortified wines in 1967. Vineyard acreage grew steadily, and vineyards were now planted to superior varieties. New wineries appeared by the hundreds, and wine makers aimed higher than ever before. In California in 1970, 240 wineries made 212 million gallons of wine 30 years later 847 wineries made 565 million gallons, most of it table wine. There had been a wine revolution.

The East was similarly changed. The old native hybrids began to be replaced, first by the French hybrids (for example, Chambourcin, Vidal) promoted by Philip Wagner, and then by vinifera, especially following the work of Konstantin Frank. Modern understanding of plant pathology at last allowed successful vinifera cultivation over many regions of the eastern states. The renewed interest in wine growing was greatly encouraged in many states by the passage of "farm winery" legislation, designed to promote wine growing by lowering fees and enabling retail sales direct from the winery. By this means many new, small enterprises were created, some in states that already had some wine growing history but others in places where it was a new thing.

By the beginning of the twenty-first century all fifty of the states had at least one functioning winery, and production on a considerable scale was carried on in, for example, Pennsylvania, Virginia, North Carolina, and Texas. In the Northwest, Washington and Oregon showed remarkable growth; Oregon had more than 200 wineries; Washington's

Wilson, Mary Tolford

626

growth was such that it ranked second in wine production to California, displacing New York from the position that it had long held.

The Twenty-first Amendment repealing Prohibition in 1933 had also given the states full authority over liquor control, with the result that fifty different sets of regulation were created and the interstate commerce in wine severely hampered. A Supreme Court decision in 2005 struck down certain discriminatory practices that had developed and at least opened the possibility for a less impeded traffic in wine among the states. The states still guarded their authority in this matter, however, and the effect of the Court's decision is not yet known.

BIBLIOGRAPHY

Adams, Leon. *The Wines of America.* 4th ed. New York: McGraw-Hill, 1990.

Gohdes, Clarence. *Scuppernong: North Carolina's Grape and Its Wines.* Durham, NC: Duke University Press, 1982.

Husmann, George. *American Grape Growing and Wine Making.* 4th ed. New York: Orange Judd, 1896.

Muscatine, Doris, Maynard A. Amerine, and Bob Thompson, eds. *The University of California/Sotheby Book of California Wine.* Berkeley: University of California Press; London, Sotheby, 1984.

Peninou, Ernest P., and Gail Unzelman. *The California Wine Association and Its Member Wineries, 1894–1920.* Santa Rosa, CA: Nomis, 2000.

Pinney, Thomas. *A History of Wine in America: From the Beginnings to Prohibition.* Berkeley: University of California Press, 1989.

Pinney, Thomas. *A History of Wine in America: From Prohibition to the Present.* Berkeley: University of California Press, 2005.

Sullivan, Charles. *A Companion to California Wine.* Berkeley: University of California Press, 1998.

THOMAS PINNEY

Wine:
California Wines

Viticulture arrived in Alta California, the region that is the state of California today, with the Franciscan fathers, who established a string of missions, beginning with San Diego in 1769. But the first grapes were not planted until 1778. In 1834 the Mexican government began secularizing mission lands, a process that brought more settlers, who in turn planted more vineyards. In 1846 Alta California was conquered almost bloodlessly by American forces. In 1849 gold was discovered in the Sierra Nevada foothills, and the world rushed in.

By the early 1860s a tiny wine industry was operating in California. Although production began in Los Angeles, it was northern California that was destined to be the center of the state's wine industry. The market was there, as were the best soils and climate. The new centers were the Santa Clara Valley (now Silicon Valley) and the northern San Francisco Bay counties of Sonoma and Napa. The leader in Sonoma was Agoston Haraszthy, whose Buena Vista estate was the largest wine operation in California in the 1860s. In the Napa Valley the most important pioneers were Charles Krug and George Belden Crane. There

---

Philip Wagner

Philip Marshall Wagner (1904–1996) moved to Baltimore, Maryland, to begin what was to be a 34-year career with the *Baltimore Sun* papers, becoming editor of the *Evening Sun* in 1938 and editor of the *Sun* in 1943. He began making wine in 1931 and in 1933 bought property in Riderwood, Maryland, where he began planting vines. In May of that year he finished writing his first book, *American Wines and How to Make Them*, which at that time was the only book in English on wine making.

After his book was published, Wagner began experimenting with an increasing number of grape varieties in his search for the right ones that would make European-style table wines. In 1939 he imported twenty-five vines of Baco No. 1 from France, the first shipment of French hybrid vines into American viticulture for wine production. He and his wife Jocelyn started their grapevine nursery in 1940 and opened their winery Boordy Vineyard in 1945. In that same year Philip Wagner published *A Wine-Grower's Guide*, a book on grape growing that included information on growing the French hybrids.

Wagner met other needs as well. In those days it was difficult to obtain grape growing and wine making equipment suitable for small operations, and in 1950 Boordy Vineyard began selling hardware.

Satisfactory inexpensive wine glasses were also hard to find. What was needed were good-size glasses of clear glass or crystal with a simple shape that were sturdy enough to put into a dishwasher. In 1950 Jocelyn Wagner located an eight-ounce glass of the classical tulip shape in New York made by Morgantown Glassware Guild in West Virginia. Boordy Vineyard had Morgantown adapt the glass to their specifications, and for many years Boordy was a major supplier of wine glasses in the East and California. Throughout the 1950s Boordy was the only commercial nursery selling French hybrid vines, and the combination of Wagner's knowledge and the services he could provide made him a major influence throughout this period.

HUDSON CATTELL

---

were also many vineyards and small wineries in the Sierra foothills, but they were isolated and had to wait long for their glory days.

Boom and Bust

In the 1870s large-scale wine growing began in the lower Central Valley, particularly in Fresno County. Several large operations attempted to produce table wines, but their quality was not high. Gradually it became clear that fortified wines, mostly sherry and port, were to be the main products in this hot land. The wine boom lasted from the late 1870s to the late 1880s. Although much of this expansion resulted from massive corporate investment, a large number of enthusiastic entrepreneurs were attracted to the world of wine growing. This was most obvious in Napa, Livermore, and along the East Bay around the town of Mission San Jose, south of Oakland. More than the industrial producers, these men were attracted to the lighter-

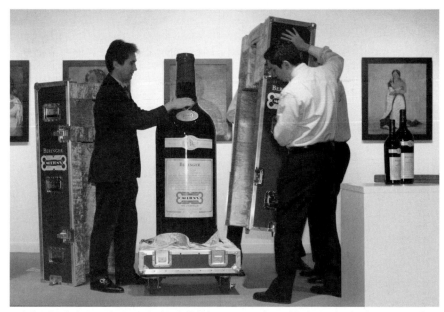

Sotheby's head of wine sales Jamie Ritchie (left) helps to remove the world's largest bottle of wine, a 130-liter "Maximus" of Beringer Cabernet Sauvigon Private Reserve 2001, from its protective case in New York.

An advertisement for Germania Wine Cellars that appeared in Harper's Monthly, August 1894.

yielding wine varieties associated with world-class wines, particularly those of Bordeaux. A few experimented with Pinot Noir, Chardonnay, and Syrah but with little success. There was also a strong ethnic character to these enthusiasts.

In 1880 the California legislature appropriated money for the Agriculture Department at the University of California, Berkeley, earmarked for viticulture and wine-making research. Under Professor Eugene Hilgard, the university began a series of programs to promote better wine making. Hilgard was also a leader in the fight against the phylloxera, the plant louse that had devastated European vineyards, which had been spotted in Sonoma in 1873 and was slowly spreading. By the 1890s urban consumers in virtually all parts of the United States were able to buy California wine, which was almost always bottled locally.

By 1888 it was clear that far too many acres of grapes had been planted in California during the boom. A huge oversupply of wine was the result, followed by steeply falling prices. When the nation was hit in 1893 by its most devastating economic depression to that time, the California wine industry was beaten to its knees. Meanwhile the phylloxera root louse had become a deadly infestation throughout the northern California coastal valleys.

The oversupply and falling prices led to cutthroat competition among the California wine merchants. Wine producers and vineyardists could hardly cover their expenses. A result of this chaos was the creation in 1894 of the California Wine Association (CWA), dubbed the "wine trust" by its opponents. The CWA was made up of most of the large wine merchants of San Francisco, many of whom also owned large wineries and vast acreages of vineyards. Thereafter most wine produced and sold in California was controlled by the CWA. As individual producers and merchants were able to keep their own brand identity, the consumer rarely had a glimpse of the "trust" at work. The CWA had brought relative stability to the California wine industry.

Prohibition

With the prosperity and stability of the period before World War I, the wine industry faced its greatest threat ever, that of national prohibition of the production of alcoholic beverages. The Eighteenth Amendment, which banned the production and sale but not necessarily the consumption of alcoholic beverages, was submitted to the states in 1917 and rode to victory on a wave of patriotic rhetoric in 1919.

Most California wineries went out of business. Because sacramental and medicinal wines were not legally considered beverages, a few wineries maintained some production. Beaulieu Vineyards (Napa) and Wente Brothers (Livermore) were the leading examples. Other California vineyardists struck gold by selling their grapes all over the country to home wine makers. The Volstead Act, enforcing the amendment, drew the line on a legal beverage at 0.5 percent alcohol, but it allowed "fruit juices" to be made by the heads of households. A family could legally make two hundred gallons, or about four barrels, of homemade wine per year. Between 1920 and 1930 Americans consumed approximately 5 billion bottles of homemade wine, most of it red. So great were the profits from the "fresh grape deal," as it was called, in the early 1920s that California's vineyards grew in size to an acreage that was not surpassed until the boom years of the 1970s.

Repeal and the Doldrums

Repeal of Prohibition in 1933 came to the nation in the depths of the Great Depression. The only wines that sold well in the years to come were fortified sweet wines, ports, sherries, and muscatels. And these were attractive mostly for their high alcohol content and their low price.

From the 1930s through the 1950s cheap fortified wines manufactured in huge wine factories in the Central Valley and Southern California were overwhelmingly the chief product of California wineries. As late as 1950 more than 70 percent of California production consisted of fortified rather than table wines.

In the late 1930s there was a small movement to produce fine wine that could be identified by the grape variety in California. Such varietal production would do away with the use of generic labels, which told the consumer little about what went into the bottle. By 1943 one could find such varietal California wines in hotels and restaurants all over the United States, although generic wines were still popular and cheaper.

One unforeseen wartime situation changed the California wine industry forever. Few tank cars could be spared from the war effort to haul wine. This forced the wineries to bottle their own wines on site. Happily this led to better control of quality and a more uniform and dependable product.

Another plus for California wine during these years came from the work of the Viticulture and Enology Department of the University of California, Davis, whose professors went out into the field to bring practical assistance to the state's wine makers. They worked to get growers to plant better wine varieties that were more suited to the soils and climate situations.

The Second Wine Boom

By the late 1950s California table wines were clearly on the rise. By the mid-1960s they had passed fortified wines in total gallons produced, and there were scores of wineries, large and small, in a race to attract those consumers whose tastes were now focused on fine Continental cuisine and the proper wines to accompany it. By the early 1970s it was clear that California, and America as a whole, was experiencing a second wine boom. There were wine-tasting clubs, consumer wine publications, and wine columns in leading newspapers. There was even a rush of interest in home wine making using top varieties. Wine-grape acreage in California rose 120 percent between 1969 and 1975.

The question of whether California was capable of producing truly world-class wines was answered in Paris in 1976. A blind tasting was put together there by the wine merchant Steven Spurrier. He matched fine California Chardonnays with five top white Burgundies and fine California Cabernet Sauvignons with five *grand cru* red Bordeaux. The tasters represented the height of the French wine establishment. When the results were announced, they were shocked to learn that they had picked a 1973 Chateau Montelena Chardonnay and a 1973 Stag's Leap Wine Cellars Cabernet Sauvignon, both of Napa, as winners, California's best on a level with the best of France. The American wine-drinking public was made well aware of the outcome by the press and often reminded of it thereafter. This second California wine boom began leveling off in the mid-1980s, with American per capita consumption of wine peaking in 1986, having more than doubled since 1969.

The 1990s and After

Consolidation and growth have typified the California wine industry since 1990. In the early 2000s big corporations controlled a large percentage of the most popular and, in some cases, the most prestigious brands. As the twenty-first century opened, sales had continued to rise every year since 1992. And in that period the retail value of these sales had climbed 74 percent, to almost $20 billion annually. The greatest part of this growth was in the wines from the world-class varieties.

BIBLIOGRAPHY

Baldy, Marian W. *The University Wine Course*. San Francisco: Wine Appreciation Guild, 1993.

Gallo, Ernest, and Julio Gallo. *Ernest and Julio: Our Story*. New York: Random House, 1994.

Lapsley, James. *Bottled Poetry: Napa Winemaking from Prohibition to the Modern Era*. Berkeley: University of California Press, 1996.

Mondavi, Robert. *Harvest of Joy: How the Good Life Became Great Business*. New York: Harcourt Brace, 1998.

Peninou, Ernest P. *History of the Sonoma Viticulture District*. Santa Rosa, CA. Nomis Press: 1998.

Pinney, Thomas. *A History of Wine in America: From the Beginnings to Prohibition*. Berkeley: University of California Press, 1989.

Robinson, Janis. *The Oxford Companion to Wine*, 3rd. Ed. Oxford and New York: Oxford University Press, 2006.

Sullivan, Charles L. *A Companion to California Wine: An Encyclopedia of Wine and Winemaking from the Mission Period to the Present*. Berkeley, University of California Press, 1998.

Sullivan, Charles L. *Like Modern Edens: Winegrowing in the Santa Clara Valley and Santa Cruz Mountains, 1798-1981*. Cupertino, CA: California History Center, 1982.

Sullivan, Charles L. *Napa Wine: A History from Mission Days to the Present*. San Francisco: Wine Appreciation Guild, 1994.

Sullivan, Charles L. *Zinfandel: A History of a Grape and Its Wine*. Berkeley: University of California Press, 2003.

Thompson, Bob. *The Wine Atlas of California and the Pacific Northwest*. New York: Simon and Schuster, 1993.

CHARLES L. SULLIVAN

Wine:
Eastern U.S. Wines

The North American continent east of the Rocky Mountains forms a unique wine region marked by difficult conditions for growing grapes. As opposed to the Mediterranean climate in California, the continental mass east of the Rockies has extreme weather conditions in many areas, including winter temperatures that can fall well below zero, damaging late spring and early autumn frosts, high humidity that provides ideal conditions for fungus diseases, hurricanes that can bring heavy rains during harvest, extended droughts, hail, and sometimes intense bird pressure.

Another unifying factor in this huge region with its diverse soils and climates is the similarity of the grape varieties grown in this region, some of which are not grown anywhere else in the world. Winter hardiness and the ability to resist diseases and insect pests have been determinants in the choice of varieties to grow.

There are three broad categories of grapes grown in the East. The native American varieties such as Concord and Niagara are primarily members of the species *Vitis labrusca*; the varieties originating in Europe such as Chardonnay and Cabernet Sauvignon belong to the species *Vitis vinifera*; and hybrid grapes for the most part are crosses between these two species.

Charles Fournier

Charles Fournier (1902–1983) was born in Reims, France, and in 1926 became the wine maker at the French champagne house of Veuve Cliquot Ponsardin as his uncle had been before him. In 1933 he was offered the job of wine maker and production manager at Gold Seal Vineyards, then called the Urbana Wine Company, in Hammondsport, New York. When he arrived at Gold Seal in 1934 he found that the Finger Lakes region could produce traditional champagne flavors by using the right combination of soil and grapes. Catawba was particularly useful when it was made sparkling and aged in the bottle on the sediment. In 1950 his Charles Fournier Champagne won a gold medal at the California State Fair when the competition was opened for the first time to wines from outside California. Gold Seal's champagnes and sparkling wines were sales triumphs along with Catawba Pink, a fruity rosé.

Fournier is best remembered for his decision in 1953 to hire Konstantin Frank to develop a vinifera program at Gold Seal. Commercial plantings began at Gold Seal in 1957, and 60 acres of vinifera were planted by 1966 and 150 by 1977.

HUDSON CATTELL

Classic European vinifera varieties could not be grown in the East until after World War II because they lacked cold hardiness and had no natural immunity to diseases and insects prevalent in the East but not found in Europe. In contrast to the relatively subtle European-style table wines, the wines made from the American varieties were stronger and often had a grapy flavor, which some wine drinkers found objectionable. These varieties were lower in sugar and higher in acid and were better suited for making fortified wines and champagnes than dry table wines.

Early History

The quest to grow vinifera in the East began as early as 1619, when the first vinifera vines were brought to the English colonies along the eastern seaboard. For more than three hundred years all attempts to grow vinifera in the East were unsuccessful, and it was only with the development of modern sprays and new viticultural techniques since World War II that the vinifera could be grown in favorable microclimates in the East.

In the nineteenth century the eastern wine industry was based on native American grapes such as Catawba, which was discovered growing near Asheville, North Carolina, about 1802. Ohio's wine production of 570,000 gallons in 1859 made it the largest wine-producing state in the nation. This was more than one-third of the national total and more than twice the amount produced in California. Wines from Ohio, New York, and Missouri dominated the eastern wine scene in the years before 1900. They competed directly in the best restaurants with wines from Europe and won international recognition. At the Vienna Exposition in 1873 a Great Western champagne from New York State became the first American champagne to win a gold medal in Europe. This was followed by many other gold medals won at various world's fairs by wines from eastern wineries.

The supremacy of eastern wines began to fade in the late 1880s, when many vineyards started to succumb to diseases for which sprays had not yet been invented. Another factor was the boom period in California, which began in the 1880s and led to California becoming the leading wine-producing state by the end of the century. The final blow came on January 17, 1920, when Prohibition ended the commercial wine industry in the United States.

Prohibition was repealed on December 5, 1933, and each state was given the right to regulate its alcoholic beverage industry. In some states wine was tightly controlled as if it were a distilled spirit; in others the wine industry was given relative freedom. Quite often pressure had to be brought on state legislatures to pass laws permitting the existence of small wineries.

Growth of the Modern Industry

The years following Prohibition marked a turning point in the search in the East for grapes that would make dry table wines. Several pioneering individuals were instrumental in laying the foundation for the modern grape and wine industry. Philip Wagner, a journalist, learned about the French hybrids in 1936 while working as the London correspondent for the *Baltimore Sun*. On his return to Riderwood, Maryland, he began searching for French hybrid varieties to plant in his vineyard. He made wines from the hybrids and soon became convinced that the French hybrids were the most promising path to pursue in the difficult climates of the East. In 1940 he and his wife Jocelyn established a wine grape nursery, Boordy Nursery, and by 1944 they were selling vines to half the states in the country. In August 1945 they opened a small commercial winery, Boordy Vineyard, and their 1945 Baco Noir was the first commercial varietal French hybrid wine to be produced in the East.

In September 1945 Wagner took some of his French hybrid wines to a tasting in Fredonia, New York. One of those attending was Adhemar de Chaunac, the wine maker at Brights Wines in Niagara Falls, Ontario. He was so impressed with the wines that Brights immediately ordered twenty French hybrid varieties and three vinifera varieties from France. They arrived in 1946 and were planted in the winery's vineyard. Together with a similar order placed by the Horticultural Research Institute of Ontario at Vineland a year later, these two shipments to Canada were the first large plantings of the French hybrids in the East.

The person in charge of viticultural research at Brights, George Hostetter, was given the job of supervising their care. Hostetter had a theory that applying sprays before disease symptoms became evident could be a key to controlling diseases. This theory proved successful not only for the hybrids but also for the vinifera. The vinifera vines planted by Brights in 1946 became the start of the first successful vinifera vineyard in the East, and the first commercial vinifera wines to be produced in the East were a Brights Pinot Champagne in 1955 and a Pinot Chardonnay in 1956.

Another pioneer in the search for dry table wines was Charles Fournier at Gold Seal Vineyards in Hammondsport, New York. Fournier left the champagne house of Veuve Clicquot Ponsardin in France in 1933 to become the wine maker at Gold Seal. In the mid-1950s he established a successful vinifera program that began by hiring Konstantin Frank to run it. Frank was a Russian-born viticulturist who had settled in Geneva, New York, after immigrating to the United States in 1951. He had had long experience growing the vinifera in the cold climates of Russia and convinced Fournier to grow the vinifera in New York State. It took five years of experimentation before the right combination of rootstocks and viticultural approaches led to commercial plantings in 1957. Gold Seal's 1960 Pinot Noir and 1960 Pinot Chardonnay were the first commercial vinifera wines to be released in New York State.

With French hybrid grapes and vinifera varieties available, wineries opened with increasing rapidity in the 1960s and 1970s. Many factors contributed to the growth of the industry. The need for information on how to grow grapes and make wine resulted in more assistance being provided by state extension services. New research projects at universities included field trials to determine which varieties of grapes were appropriate for various areas, methods of disease control, types of yeasts to use in wine making, and vineyard and winery economics.

Grower and wine making conferences were established. Organizations such as the American Wine Society and the Eastern Section of the American Society of Enologists brought people together to share and learn. Trade shows and the founding of industry newsletters and magazines were all part of the eastern scene by the mid-1970s.

One of the major reasons for the increase in the number of small wineries was the passage of farm winery legislation in many eastern states, starting in Pennsylvania in 1968. This legislation, although it varied in detail from state to state, permitted grape growers to make and sell wine on the premises where the grapes were grown. Farm winery license fees were made affordable, and excise taxes on wine produced in the state were often reduced. Common provisions were a requirement that wineries use only grapes grown in that state for making wine and a cap placed on the amount of wine a farm winery could make each year. The passage of farm winery bills made it easier to pass other legislation, such as permitting Sunday sales or opening sales outlets away from the winery.

By 1976 there were approximately 140 wineries in 22 states and Canadian provinces east of the Rockies. That number passed 1,000 in the early 2000s, and when 2 wineries were licensed in North Dakota in 2001, all 50 states had wineries in operation for the first time.

In several important ways the industry reflects its past. Wines are made from a wider variety of grapes and fruits than elsewhere in the world. Thanks to advances in viticulture and technology, the classic vinifera varieties can be grown in areas where it would not have been possible a few decades ago. The French hybrids and newer hybrid varieties such as Cayuga White and Traminette developed at the New York State Agricultural Experiment Station and elsewhere are grown not only because of limitations of climate but also out of choice. Native American varieties remain popular for making sweeter wines. In many parts of the East, fruit wines have a strong following, as do ice wines where the winters are cold enough to naturally freeze the grapes before harvest. Also reflecting the past, eastern wines are winning top medals in national and international competitions where they are entered against some of the best wines in the world.

If the eastern wine industry reflects its past, the past has also built a solid base for the future. It is because of its past that the East has become an important and unique wine region of the world.

BIBLIOGRAPHY

Cattell, Hudson, and Lee Miller. *Wine East of the Rockies.* Lancaster, PA: L&H Photojournalism, 1982.

Cattell, Hudson, and Linda Jones McKee. *Eastern Wines since Prohibition.* Forthcoming.

Morton, Lucie T. *Winegrowing in Eastern America: An Illustrated Guide to Viniculture East of the Rockies.* Ithaca, NY: Cornell University Press, 1985.

Pinney, Thomas. *A History of Wine in America: From Prohibition to the Present.* Berkeley: University of California Press, 2005.

Pinney, Thomas. *A History of Wine in America: From the Beginnings to Prohibition.* Berkeley: University of California Press, 1989.

HUDSON CATTELL

Wine:
Later Developments

For the American wine industry, the 1990s were a period of consolidation, marketing innovation, technological advances, hype, and speculation. There is little doubt that by the beginning of the twenty-first century the American wine industry was providing a better quality product at a lower cost than ever before, but America's largely unregulated production has limited the global success of its wines.

In 1997 the United States had approximately 778,000 acres designated as vineyard area, whereas France, Italy, and Spain had a combined total of more than 7 million acres. Per capita wine consumption in America, although rising, is still miniscule when compared with Europe. In 1996 the annual per capita wine consumption in France and Italy was more than 15 gallons; in the United States consumption was 2.03 gallons, a modest increase from 1.88 gallons in 1991. Australia, whose wines have taken the world by storm, has approximately 222,000 vineyard acres and, at 4.78 gallons, a per capita consumption more than twice that of the United States.

The potential market for increased wine consumption in the United States, with its relatively affluent population, is perhaps the single most important factor related to the majority of later developments. It is little wonder that major corporations from around the world are investing in American land and production facilities to take advantage of this attractive situation. Another attraction could be the relative lack of production regulation. To produce an appellation wine in France or in most European Union (EU) countries, a wine maker must adhere to numerous regulations, including limitations on additives. The American system, which establishes approved vinicultural areas (AVA), requires only that 85 percent of the grapes come from the district of the AVA (75 percent of the variety if the wine is a varietel) and imposes no regulatory structure on the wine maker for providing this information. This laissez-faire style of production has drawbacks and is one of the major reasons why even premium wines from the United States have not penetrated the European market to any great extent.

Wine consumers in the United States have been gratified by a number of court rulings allowing vineyards to sell directly to consumers across state lines. The removal of these sales restrictions, remnants of Prohibition, is important for the survival of the small vineyard owner in a market increasingly dominated by a few distributors. Vineyard owners of all sizes face questions about ground pollution and water usage, issues that could result in major consequences and costs to producers throughout the country. New techniques and technologies will continue to be developed to meet these and other challenges.

One important resource to the industry is the University of California, Davis (UC Davis), one of the premier training schools in the scientific aspects of wine making. The ascendancy of wine making as a science has allowed graduates of such schools as UC Davis to become important executives at some of the largest producers in the United States, much in the way that technocrats have replaced entrepreneurial operators in other evolving industries.

One of the least desirable later developments is the establishment of many small AVA vineyards that produce inferior products. These wines take on a local cachet (Martha's Vineyard has AVA status) that becomes more important than the wine itself. In many cases these small vineyards would seem to exist to take advantage of the tax credits available, giving prestige to their owners, who may be speculating that urban sprawl will increase land value. Another unfortunate trend is the purchase of brands for market share by large conglomerates that do little to improve the product. The exception is the Gallo family, with their investment in premium wines and dedication to producing a better product at a fair price. Gallo, which already has America's largest market share of table wine, has proven that big is not always bad.

It is the consumer who will decide the future of the American wine industry. The interest in wine is growing. Wine educators conduct classes and wine tastings in almost every major city; wine tours are often sold out, be they on Long Island, New York, or in Napa Valley, California; and books on wine meet with a substantial readership. Wine auctions have expanded into a multimillion-dollar business, and there are buyers who are investing in wine based on the knowledge that even a slight change in the demographics of drinkers will catapult the demand for high-quality wine from great vineyards. Research suggesting that wine, when taken in moderation, may be healthful has helped create a new group of health-conscious consumers. The transition of America to a wine-drinking nation may be slow to develop, but an increasingly knowledgeable public bodes well for the future of an industry that barely survived Prohibition.

[See also GALLO, ERNEST AND JULIO; MONDAVI, ROBERT; ROBERT MONDAVI CO.; WINERIES.]

BIBLIOGRAPHY

Adams, Leon. The Commonsense Book of Wine. New York: McGraw-Hill, 1986.

Gallo, Ernest, and Julio Gallo, with Bruce B. Henderson. Ernest and Julio: Our Story. New York: Times Books, 1994.

Mondavi, Robert, with Paul Chutkow. Harvests of Joy: My Passion for Excellence. New York: Harcourt Brace, 1998.

STEVEN M. CRAIG

Wine, Fruit, see Fruit Wines

Wine, Hot Spiced

Hot spiced wine, often called "mulled wine," is typically made by simmering red and occasionally white wine with a mixture of citrus (juice, slices, or zest from lemons or oranges) and virtually any combination of spices, including cinnamon, clove, allspice, ginger, cardamom, nutmeg, or mace. Wines ranging from dry table wines to sweet ports or fortified wines (strengthened with additional alcohol) are used. Brandy, liqueurs, or other spirits and water are sometimes added.

This beverage has an ancient history, stemming from early civilizations of 5000 B.C.E. (Mesopotamia and Egypt) and subsequent Greece and Rome. Wines were sometimes infused with herbs and spices for a range of gastronomic, hallucinogenic, medicinal, religious, and preservation purposes. In medieval Europe wine was customarily consumed as a safer, healthier alternative to often-contaminated water. In colder climates wine and other fermented beverages were sometimes heated to create longed-for and much-needed warmth. At the same time local substances, such as tree bark, resin, leaves, flowers, roots, and seeds, were often added for preservation, to mask bad tastes in deteriorating wine, or for their perceived healing properties. For those who could grow or buy them, it was also possible to use European bay leaf, caraway and coriander seed, saffron, myrtle, wormwood, and such sweeteners as raisins and honey.

The introduction of tropical spices to medieval Europe opened the door to a wide

---

Hybridization

Hybridization is an important tool in agriculture used to create new or different varieties of plants, flowers, vegetables, or fruits with a desired quality or set of characteristics. For grapes, particularly for those grown in the East, the goal is to create varieties that will be disease resistant and cold tolerant while at the same time bearing fruit that will make a European-style table wine.

Seeds are nature's way of reproducing grapevines. Grape growers, however, prefer to propagate vines by planting cuttings, pieces of the canes of one-year-old shoots cut into six- to eighteen-inch lengths. This assures that the new vines will be identical to the vines from which the cuttings were taken.

Creating new varieties, or hybridizing, requires the use of seeds. The hybridizer pollinates the flowers of one variety with pollen from another so the resulting berries will have the characteristics of both parents. These seeds are planted and the seedlings allowed to bear fruit. Over a period of years wine is made from the strongest and healthiest of these new vines. The vines with the best wine making potential are kept and the remainder discarded. Eventually the new grape variety will be given a name if it is to be used commercially.

Hybridization is synonymous with improving the breed, and no one questions the term "hybrid" when it is used in connection with corn or tea roses. For no justifiable reason, there are those who find the term "hybrid" objectionable when applied to grapes.

HUDSON CATTELL

"Champagne" or "Sparkling Wine"?

In the wake of Prohibition, the Federal Alcohol Administration (later to become part of the Bureau of Alcohol, Tobacco, and Firearms) was set up in the U.S. Treasury Department to create licensing and permit requirements and establish regulations. Charles Fournier of Gold Seal Vineyards in Hammondsport, New York, became involved in the promulgation of federal regulations to legalize use of the term "champagne" in the United States. The regulations as drawn up stated that an American champagne must be "a type of sparkling light wine which derives its effervescence solely from the secondary fermentation of the wine within glass containers of not greater than one gallon capacity, and which possesses the taste, aroma, and other characteristics attributed to champagne as made in the Champagne district of France." A sparkling wine not having these characteristics can only be called a sparkling wine.

The French and the European Union (EU) have long claimed that the producers in the Champagne district of France should have the exclusive rights to the term "champagne," and they also claim exclusive rights to *méthode champenoise*, the French term for the secondary fermentation in the bottle. Other countries in the EU have been required to use other terms; the Spanish, for example, use the term *cava*. Some producers in the United States respected the French position and voluntarily chose to use the term "sparkling wine" instead of "champagne." In 2005, as the result of a trade agreement between the United States and the EU, the term "champagne" was restricted in the United States to wineries using the term prior to the time of the agreement. New brands are now prohibited from using the term "champagne."

Fournier, who had been the wine maker at Veuve Cliquot Ponsardin in France, felt strongly that the champagnes he made in New York State were worthy of the great French name "champagne" and proudly used the term on the label. His sparkling wines that did not meet that standard were called "sparkling wine." Throughout his career, Fournier stated his strong opposition to those who would use the term "champagne" on the label of inferior foaming wine.

In the early twenty-first century Konstantin Frank's son Willy Frank is president of Chateau Frank Champagne Cellars in Hammondsport, New York, and he adamantly insists on using the term "champagne" on his Finger Lakes Champagnes for exactly the same reasons that Fournier did. He makes them by the *méthode champenoise*, keeps them for at least four years, and makes them from all three classic grape varieties, Pinot Noir, Chardonnay, and Pinot Meunier. Only when he is emulating the French does he place the word "champagne" on the label.

HUDSON CATTELL

Dickens. Hot spiced wine was frequently served alongside or in lieu of eggnog enjoyed at middle-class tables, sometimes with appropriate temperance substitutions of fruit juice. At this time tropical citrus fruits were becoming more common in local shops, and packaged ground spices were more affordable and available.

Like many foods resulting from the American amalgam of heritages, adult Americans of diverse backgrounds and cultures consume hot spiced wines during the winter months. Still centered on the Christmas season at holiday parties, caroling, and family gatherings, it has also become integral to the hospitality at many American ski resorts. Recipes for hot spiced wine and its many namesakes are usually included in special holiday issues of contemporary American food and wine publications as well as in popular cookbooks. With increasing focus on good quality and tradition, they sometimes highlight early techniques that include manual grinding and the individualistic creation of spice and fruit blends. For those with less time, premixed mulling sachets and spice blend packets dissolve instantly in warmed wine. Some modern American recipes call for the substitution or addition of fruit juices, such as cranberry or apple, making the drinks more appropriate for youngsters.

[See also CHRISTMAS; FRUIT WINES.]

BIBLIOGRAPHY

Brown, John Hull. *Early American Beverages*. Rutland, VT: Tuttle, 1966.

McGovern, Patrick E. *Ancient Wine: The Search for the Origins of Viniculture*. Princeton, NJ: Princeton University Press, 2003.

TONYA HOPKINS

range of flavors. Wildly expensive and exotic at the time, they were available only to the wealthy and were used to enrich the libation hippocras, the descendant of an ancient Roman drink. Hippocras was made from wine heated with honey, pepper, and many other spices, such as galingale (similar to ginger), and it was often consumed as an elixir at the end of a large feast. Although it occasionally appeared later in seventeenth-century cookbooks, it had lost most of its high status and popularity by then.

By the latter part of the seventeenth century, European trade with India and the Indonesian Spice Islands had begun to flourish. The trade brought in substantial quantities of spice at somewhat lower prices, but products were still not available economically to all. These tropical spices (such as cinnamon and nutmeg) began to replace earlier European flavorings in heated wines and dramatically changed the taste and character of the wines. In addition the British in India encountered a local spiced "paunch" (later called "punch"), a warmed beverage consisting of a fermented drink, sugar, water, citrus, and spices. Taken back to En-

gland, it became a favorite drink; the elite substituted their own wine or spirits and served it hot or cold at large social gatherings. Other European nations involved in the spice trade (France, Germany, the Netherlands, Norway, and Sweden) enjoyed their own versions. These appeared in the American colonies as mulled wine, sometimes made with thickening raw eggs or yolks, which would be cooked by the hot wine. The resultant curdling was reminiscent of such other period concoctions as possets, caudles, and syllabub.

Many English, German, Dutch, and Scandinavian emigrants who came to America brought these long-held traditions and prepared heated and spiced libations for winter festivals, in particular Christmas. Somewhat varied, they were served under such names as Swedish glogg, German *Glühwein*, and English wassail or mulled wine. Successive waves of European immigration brought others. By the late 1800s these warmed spiced wines had become an integral part of the American Christmas menu, largely because of the strong influence of the mid-nineteenth-century novel *A Christmas Carol* by Charles

Wine Barrels

Wine barrels have a long history and are essential to the making of many wines. The American wine industry is the largest user of imported French oak barrels, employing them in concert with domestic oak barrels. The importance of these wooden barrels lies in the flavors the wood imparts during wine's maturation process. The woods used come from various sources, but the most important is oak. American oak, *Quercus alba*, or European oak, *Q. rubur* and *Q. sesslis*, are the most sought after; they are, however, processed in entirely different ways and impart very distinct flavors. Most American oak is kiln-dried from sawn wood, which lends strong flavors to wine. European oak is split wood and, for the most part, air-dried, ideally for three years, which gives wine a softer flavor that changes with the age of the wood used. This processing method also imparts a higher tannin level to the wine. It is essential that wine makers know the source and age of the woods they are using. For example, tannins are more evident in wood that is harvested in summer than in spring, and each wooded area may have a goût de terroir (or taste of the earth) that makes its flavor unique; thus a mistake in the selection of wood can lead to difficulties as the wine matures.

In the United States many wooden barrels still come from whiskey industry cooperages, which produce about 800,000 barrels; of this total, a scant 50,000 are for the wine trade. The standard American barrel, which holds fifty gallons, is made from domestic oak, accounting for about 3 percent of the annual oak harvest. Unlike the European trade, there does not seem to be the demand for specificity in wood by the American wine maker, perhaps because of the stronger initial flavors American oak imparts. Several prominent French coopers are experimenting in the United States with specific wood sources and plan to produce barrels in the European manner. [**See also** WINE CASKS.]

STEVEN M. CRAIG

Wine Books

The earliest books on wine in America were either practical (John Adlum, *A Memoir on the Cultivation of the Vine in America*, 1823) or promotional (Agoston Haraszthy, *Grape Culture, Wines, and Wine-Making*, 1862). Such encyclopedic books of European origin as André Jullien's *The Topography of All the Known Vineyards* (1824) and Cyrus Redding's *A History and Description of Modern Wines* (1833) were influential authorities. Their tradition continues in the present day through such works as Frank Schoonmaker's *Encyclopedia of Wine* (1964) and Alexis Lichine's *Encyclopedia of Wines and Spirits* (1967). The discussion and appreciation of wine for the general reader rather than for the wine maker or merchant was begun by the Englishman George Saintsbury, in his *Notes on a Cellar-Book* (1920). What he started was carried on by other English writers such as Warner Allen and Maurice Healy and by the Anglo-French André Simon, who wrote more than a hundred books on food and wine between 1905 and 1973. Saintsbury himself enjoyed all sorts of wines, but his followers took a narrower view: for them, wine meant the *grands vins* of Bordeaux, Burgundy, and Champagne, and that view powerfully influenced American ideas about wine for many years.

They were succeeded by other generations of English writers, of more catholic tastes, who continue to have a large American readership. Cyril Ray, Hugh Johnson, Gerald Asher, Jancis Robinson, and Oz Clarke are the best known. Johnson's *World Atlas of Wine* (1971) gave a new detail to the study of wine, and Jancis Robinson's *Oxford Companion to Wine* (1994) comes first among the works of general reference.

American writers in this English mode appear rather late and irregularly, beginning with Frank Schoonmaker and Tom Marvel, whose *Complete Wine Book* (1934) is still a readable and instructive book. They collaborated again on *American Wines* (1941), a book that had no predecessor and is still import-

ant. Rather different, but widely influential, were the books of Philip Wagner. His *American Wines and How to Make Them* (1933) was meant to instruct the home wine maker under Prohibition but managed to convey much general information; a later version is called *Grapes into Wine* (1976). Wagner belongs to the tradition of practical literature, but he was read for general interest as well. *Wine: An Introduction for Americans* (1965), by the University of California scientists Maynard Amerine and Vernon Singleton, was published when the American boom in wine was beginning, and it profited from that coincidence; it is now seriously out of date. The first coffee-table book about California wine is by M. F. K. Fisher and Max Yavno, *The Story of Wine in California* (1962). It has had many imitators.

Many, if not most, living American writers on this topic are journalists turning out immediate copy or compiling guides that tell readers what to buy. But substantial and original books reflecting the new status of American wines have been written, among them, Leon Adams's *The Wines of America* (1973), Ruth Teiser and Katherine Harroun's *Winemaking in California* (1983), and Charles Sullivan's *A Companion to California Wine* (1998).

[**See also** WINE: HISTORICAL SURVEY.]

THOMAS PINNEY

Wine Bottles

The modern wine bottle, a bottle capable of being laid on its side, probably dates to the early 1700s in Europe. Prior to this, wine bottles were often flask shaped and stood upright. Some, because of their rounded appearance, are referred to as "onions" or "bladders." In ancient times wine was stored in standing containers; the Romans were known to have transferred the liquid into smaller glass containers when it was served.

The development of the modern bottle came about with the desire to age and store wine effectively while using as much of the storage area's space as possible. This resulted in the development of a bottle that could be laid horizontally, in row upon row, a system called "binning." Laying bottles horizontally would not have been possible without a change in their stoppers from glass and attached string to cork. Although cork had been used in ancient times, it was not widely used again until its attributes were rediscovered in the 1700s. Cork was ideal for complementing the new bottle design. It was economical and provided a tight seal, and its ability to breathe allowed for an aging process that enhanced the wine. The capacity of cork to maintain the stability of the wine's condition while the bottle rested on its side altered the storage and aging process.

The standard modern wine bottle is 750 milliliters, although bottles are made in a variety of sizes, the largest being the Nebuchadnezzar, which is the equal of 16 bottles

and usually is used only by sparkling wine producers. More common large-format bottles are the magnum, 1.5 milliliters, or the equivalent of 2 bottles; the double magnum, 3 liters; and the Imperiale, 6 liters. There is a cachet to the large bottle. Some argue that because of the large size the wine will mature more slowly and age with finer attributes. There is by no means unanimous agreement on this, but the theory has done much to enhance the collectibility and price of these limited edition behemoths when they are released by prestige producers.

Since the early 1990s some subtle changes in bottle shape have occurred that allow for the elimination of the capsule covering the stopper. And a variety of synthetic stoppers have also been developed. American wine producers, such as Robert Mondavi, have been involved in the research and creation of these innovations but have been slow to adopt the changes for their premium wine brands.

[**See also** BOTTLING; CORKS; MONDAVI, ROBERT; ROBERT MONDAVI CO.; WINE BARRELS; WINE CASKS; WINE CELLARS.]

STEVE CRAIG

Wine Casks

"Wine cask" is a term for a cylindrical wooden container; it is often used in the same context as "wine barrel" but can indicate any form of wooden container used in the wine making process, such as an open vat. Wooden casks have been used to ferment, store, and ship wine for well over two thousand years. A major change in modern wine making techniques with respect to wooden casks centers on the use of stainless-steel tanks during the initial fermentation process and then transfer of the wine into wooden casks.

The wooden cask still has an important part to play in the wine making process: if wine were made entirely in stainless steel, it would display strong elements of the fruit and have a less tannic quality, making the aging process difficult and long-term aging almost impossible. The character of the wine would also be completely different, as wood is an essential part not merely of aging but also of adding flavor. Robert Mondavi, one of America's premier vintners, conducted extensive experiments with different wooden casks and the same base wine, confirming the major

Casks of aging wine in Sonoma County, California, January 1942.

effect of wood and, specifically, of aging in casks in the creation of desired flavors in wine. The wooden cask may not be as important as the grape, but great red wines cannot be created without it, and knowledge of wood is essential for a competent wine maker.

[**See also** MONDAVI, ROBERT; WINE BARRELS.]

STEVE CRAIG

Wine Cellars

The wine cellar is where wine is often stored by the producer, the merchant, or the consumer. In all cases the desire is the same: to allow the wine to mature and to protect it from deterioration. Cellars, or wine storage areas, can be traced to the ancient world, where it became known that the aging of some wines would bring about positive changes. Cellars were often just that, below-ground areas, but since the twentieth century they may be any area where it is possible to control temperature, humidity, light, and vibration.

Wine does not thrive in extreme or changing temperatures. A constant 45°F to 60°F is often recommended along with a relatively high humidity of 70 percent or more to ensure the cork's stability as the wine rests on its side, a position that allows the liquid to keep the cork damp. Light also changes the aging process, so the environment should be dark as well as free from vibration. This is of course the ideal and is rarely achieved in most private cellars. Consequently many wine drinkers are increasingly relying on commercial storage cellars for their fine wines.

The condition of the wine when it is cellared is of critical importance. Unless purchased by the consumer at the estate or winery, it is impossible to ascertain every step of a wine's shipping and storage process. A wine may be subject to any number and manner of abuses before it is even received by the local distributor, at which point it still may have several steps to go before it reaches its initial buyer, who may then in turn sell it at auction. Although it is possible to discover certain characteristics—the fill, clarity, and cork integrity among others—of a poorly stored wine by looking at the bottle, the only real test is to taste it. A cellar, no matter how ideal its conditions, will not reclaim a poorly handled wine. It is therefore strongly recommended that a wine be sampled before putting it in long-term storage.

There have been numerous experiments in the storage of wine, including changing the stopper material from natural cork to man-made material and even storing the wine under water (which seems to delay the aging process). However, be it a closet adapted to create a controlled environment in a city apartment or a historic cellar at a fine estate, the purpose is the same—to age, preserve, and store wine.

[**See also** WINE: HISTORICAL SURVEY; WINE: LATER DEVELOPMENTS; WINE BOTTLES.]

STEVE CRAIG

Wine Coolers

Wine coolers, low-alcohol (5 percent) beverages made with wine, sweetened fruit juices, and carbonation, are similar to the wine-based cocktails and "coolers" historically prepared in saloons, taverns, and bars across America. These prepackaged drinks successfully entered the retail market on a small scale in 1981, when two entrepreneurs from Santa Cruz, California, created the California Cooler. Concurrent with an escalating American fondness for convenience and portability, the coolers were sold chilled in colorful four-packs of single-serving bottles through widespread distribution channels. Positioned as a beer alternative, they appealed primarily to young social drinkers and to female consumers.

Many manufacturers followed with similar brands, such as E. and J. Gallo's Bartles and Jaymes and Seagram's Coolers. Sizable advertising expenditures of these larger companies elevated consumer awareness and fueled significant growth in this new alcoholic beverages category. Wine coolers reached peak popularity in the mid-1980s with flavors like strawberry, peach, and tropical fruit, which proved enjoyably refreshing to a generation weaned on soft drinks. This welcome spike for then-declining alcohol sales was seen as promising; it was thought to offer the possibility to cultivate future wine consumers.

Changing market dynamics, consumer preferences, and plummeting sales rendered wine coolers a fad by the early 1990s. The term is still used in reference to a category now comprising mostly fruit-flavored, malt liquor–based brews more appropriately called "malternatives" or "hard beverages."

[**See also** COCKTAILS; FRUIT WINES.]

BIBLIOGRAPHY

"Prepared Cocktails." In *Adams Liquor Handbook*, 195–206. Norwalk, CT: Adams Business Media, 2002.

Lender, Mark Edward, and James Kirby Martin. *Drinking in America: A History*. Rev. ed. New York: Free Press, 1987.

"Wine Coolers." In *Adams Wine Handbook*, 49–61. Norwalk, CT: Adams Business Media, 2002.

TONYA HOPKINS

Wine Glasses

Wine through the ages has been consumed from every kind of vessel imaginable: pottery bowls, bejeweled gold goblets, fine Venetian glass, and ordinary glass containers. It is known that the ancient Romans drank and served from glass containers and that the Venetians in the sixteenth century perfected a specialized form of glassmaking, but it was in the seventeenth century that the British developed a lead and flint glass that revolutionized the industry. This new glass was further adapted by designs and shapes for different wines and spirits into the eighteenth century.

Although no one can say with certainty what the ideal glass form is from which to drink wine, certain standards are universal. The glass should be clear with an unobstructed view of the contents, and the bowl should be large enough to allow the release of the aroma when the wine interacts with the air. It should have a stem long enough that it is possible to hold the glass without warming the liquid in it. The International Standards Organization (ISO) set the basic standard for a tasting glass at a total capacity of 215 milliliters for a tasting of 50 milliliters. The tasting glass should be tulip shaped with the bowl at its widest diameter being 65 millimeters and with a top diameter of 46 millimeters, giving it a modest chimney effect. The height of the glass should be 155 millimeters with a bowl height of 100 millimeters. This glass would serve for the drinking of almost any kind of wine, including sparklers.

The preferred style for sparkling wines is the flute, which gives maximum opportunity to view the bubbles while affording them a longer life as the wine is consumed. The coup glass, which according to legend was modeled from the breast of Marie Antoinette, is not desirable because it does not show the bubbles rising and it dissipates the bouquet over too wide an area. Variations to the classic tasting glass include a larger bowl for Pinot Noir, a more enhanced chimney for Cabernet Sauvignon and Merlot, and a less enhanced chimney for Chardonnay and other white wines.

Georg Riedel, an Austrian manufacturer, has designed glasses for dozens of different varietals, including a tasting glass of just 26 milliliters, or five-eighths of an ounce, that allows for 35 portions from the standard 750 milliliter bottle. They range in price from several hundred dollars for the finest crystal glass in its own leather carrying case to less than ten dollars for an everyday potash-based glass. Riedel has even designed glasses for specific appellations and ages of wine. The basics are the same, however, and no one needs a dozen different glass styles to appreciate wine.

[**See also** DINING ROOMS AND MEAL SERVICE; GLASSWARE; WINE: HISTORICAL SURVEY; WINE-TASTING ROOMS.]

STEVEN M. CRAIG

Wineries

Wineries are the physical establishments where wine and brandies are made from grapes as well as other fruits (such as berries and peaches). The wine-making process involves many stages, from grape growing, harvesting, and crushing to fermentation, filtering, blending, aging, bottling, and storing. This process places wineries at the heart of production and manufacturing for the U.S. wine industry. Many American wineries grow and harvest grapes from vineyards on their own estates, and a large number purchase grapes from independent growers, later applying their wine-making techniques. A more elastic and virtual definition of the term is frequently used to refer to wine producers without traditional facilities who may rent space or produce wines at various locations.

Wineries range in types and sizes from smaller boutiques utilizing artisanal methods to larger industrial enterprises producing more mass-market products. While the majority of American wineries are small, family-owned operations, the four largest U.S. wineries account for nearly 50 percent of the nation's entire wine storage capacity. California is home to more than half of the wineries in America, but there is at least one winery in each of the fifty states (wineries in Alaska and North Dakota are the most recent additions). Nearly all wineries are in rural areas, close to their grape or fruit crops.

Wine making has long been part of American history and has connections to early settlers, colonists, and subsequent waves of European immigrants who brought long-held traditions of making and drinking wine. Spanish missionaries are considered the first to have brought the art of wine making to the Americas, to parts of Texas and California. By the last quarter of the eighteenth century the missionaries had successfully planted vineyards to make sacramental wines at the twenty-one California missions they founded, stretching from as far south as San Diego to as far north as Sonoma. Some of the nation's earliest wine making experiments took place in the oldest states along the eastern seaboard (Virginia is among the best-known early but failed attempts of the French wine enthusiast Thomas Jefferson). In the early to mid 1800s states such as Indiana, Kansas, Missouri, Ohio, North Carolina, New Jersey, and New York were all successful grape-growing and wine-making regions. In the 1840s Nicholas Longworth, regarded the founding father of American wine, produced the country's first successful commercial wines using the native American Catawba grape, grown near Cincinnati, Ohio.

Aside from the phylloxera that led to the closing of several California wineries that had successfully grown European vines (*Vitis vinifera*), by the late nineteenth century there was a vibrant, thriving American wine industry. But it would soon all come to an end. The temperance movement and later Prohibition, a massive disruption for American wineries and the industry as a whole, was firmly in place in many states by 1912 and full scale by 1919 via the Eighteenth Amendment to the Constitution, which outlawed the production and sale of all alcoholic beverages throughout the nation. Thousands of acres of vineyards were uprooted, and many wine-making facilities were demolished or converted to other commercial use. Some California wineries remained legal to make sacramental wines, and home wine making flourished in large part due to a loophole in federal law allowing families to make up to two hundred gallons of fruit juice a year for personal use. The repeal of Prohibition in 1934 led to new laws granting individual states (and counties within states) legislative power over the distribution and sale of wine and spirits.

The subsequent road to rebuilding the wineries and the industry overall was paved by a number of visionaries and pioneering scientists, both homegrown and from abroad. After World War II many American wineries were in the habit of producing cheap, sweet, fortified wines that were popular at the time. Eventually, as American tastes in food changed with growing interest in more sophisticated fare, so did the desire for better-quality table wines. On course with this trend the first completely new facility since Prohibition was built in the mid-1960s in Napa, California, by the Mondavi family, followed shortly thereafter by the opening of the largest winery in the United States (Ernest and Julio Gallo). In 1975 there were approximately six hundred federally bonded, licensed wineries in the United States. Since then the numbers have grown substantially each decade, amounting to more than three thousand by the early twenty-first century. The most significant growth (more than a third) took place after 1990. New wineries continue to open nationwide along with an expanding American interest in and consumption of wine.

Scientific advancement, technology, academic (enological) knowledge, innovation, and shared international techniques have ushered in an era of modern wine making, dramatically changing the way most wineries have traditionally operated. The resulting increases in quality control, sterile environs, automation, and the ability to offset seasonal weather uncertainties have also led to greater volume increases and product consistency.

Wine grapes are now among the fastest-growing agricultural crops in the country and the highest-valued American fruit crop. This phenomenon, along with the increasing number of trade groups dedicated to supporting and growing the business, signals the increasing importance of regional U.S. wineries to the overall American economy. Some wineries are now becoming part of big businesses, being purchased by large brewing and liquor companies that in turn invest in agricultural and wine-making technology as well as in growing marketing budgets to assist with the increasingly competitive global wine market.

American wineries are a key part of state and county tourism, offering increasingly popular packages of "agri-tourism" for those seeking agrarian landscape getaways. Promoting destination wineries, many convention and visitors bureaus link prospective visitors to wineries and local attractions like harvest festivals and jazz concerts. Many American vintners compete to open the most lavish hospitality centers, complete with high-profile draws like celebrity chef appearances, cooking classes, picnic areas, and fine restaurants—in addition to traditional cellar tours. Winery gift shops offer accessories, gift baskets, gourmet foods (with cheeses and other products often made with the facility's wines), and on-premise wine. The winery tasting room, virtually nonexistent in earlier times, has emerged as an important marketing tool representing a multimillion-dollar industry and often exists in urban centers far from the related winery. In quintessential American fashion, Robert Mondavi and Disney together opened the Golden Vine Winery in February 2001 as a major attraction at the Disneyland theme park in Anaheim, California.

[**See also** GALLO, ERNEST AND JULIO; ROBERT MONDAVI CO.; WINES: CALIFORNIA WINES.]

BIBLIOGRAPHY

Folwell, Raymond J. "The Changing Market Structure of the USA Wine Industry." *Journal of Wine Research* 14, no. 1 (April 2003): 25–30.

Lukacs, Paul. *American Vintage: The Rise of American Wine*. Boston: Houghton Mifflin, 2000.

Peters, Gary L. *American Winescapes: The Cultural Landscapes of America's Wine Country*. Boulder, CO: Westview, 1997.

Pinney, Thomas. *A History of Wine in America: From the Beginnings to Prohibition*. Berkeley: University of California Press, 1989.

TONYA HOPKINS

Wine-Tasting Rooms

The first tasting rooms were probably established by the Greeks and Phoenicians in their trading settlements along the Mediterranean during the period 1500 to 500 B.C.E. and quite possibly even earlier by wine sellers in the ancient world. Tasting rooms, whether they are attached to a winery, an estate vineyard, or a merchant's business, are simply showrooms to display, taste, and sell wine.

The physical plant of a tasting room can be as simple as a few folding chairs and a card table in a wine cellar or as elaborate as antique furnishings and old master paintings at a wine merchant. Many tasting rooms are an integral part of modern wineries, which use them not only as sales points but also to establish brand loyalty. Some have restaurants (the laws permitting) and sales areas for a variety of items, from locally produced foodstuffs to souvenirs. In California many wineries have extensive tasting areas, and some sell their wine across the country directly to the consumer. While this sales method is traditional in Europe, it can run afoul of some states' laws. If this situation, which is yet to be resolved, is decided in favor of the wine makers, it could have a dramatic effect on the way small-production wines are sold. Many distributors and retailers fear that luxury wineries will take their tasting rooms on tour, leaving them with only the large commercial wines to sell. Such retailers have lobbied against any out-of-state liquor sales, citing grievances ranging from the loss of tax revenue to the illegal purchase of spirits by children. Whatever the resolution of this issue, the tasting-room experience enhances the understanding of the product as much in the early twenty-first century as it did in ancient times.

[See also WINE: HISTORICAL SURVEY; WINERIES.]

STEVEN M. CRAIG

World's Fairs

World's Fairs are expositions in which nations and corporations feature their foods, cultures, consumer goods, and technological advancements. Beginning in the 1850s, these expositions became the forum for introducing new inventions, such as the telephone, medical x-rays, and television, and new, often futuristic architectural designs. While being part entertainment fair, part international diplomacy, and part marketplace, world's fairs have always stressed innovation and the diversity of world cultures while allowing fairgoers to sample new foods from around the globe and visit exhibits featuring scientific and mechanical innovations. Similar to seeking the opportunity to hold the modern Olympic Games, cities competed to host fairs to enhance their civic reputation and boost local economies. World's fairs remained extremely popular during the nineteenth century and much of the twentieth century but declined in attendance, status, and commercial importance by the end of the twentieth century.

Early History

Fairs and events that celebrate national pride and commercial success began in medieval times. Large-scale markets developed at the intersections of major trade routes, expanding into commercial fairs during the 1700s. The first recorded "universal and international" exhibition was held in London in 1851, widely known as the Crystal Palace Exhibition for its immense nineteen-acre glass and iron pavilion but formally titled the Great Exhibition of the Works of Industry of All Nations. The Crystal Palace Exhibition attracted 6 million visitors, making it an enormous political and financial success.

Fairs in the United States

Observing London's 1851 success, promoters in the United States held the New York Crystal Palace Exhibition in Manhattan between 1853 and 1854. Modeled on the London fair, the New York exhibition introduced new consumer products, including George Crum's "potato chip" snack food, but failed overall due to poor planning, faulty construction, and an increasingly tense pre–Civil War political climate.

Civil War production stimulated America's industrial economy. To display this new industrial might and to commemorate the signing of the Declaration of Independence, Philadelphia held the Centennial International Exhibition in 1876. The event introduced new and exotic foods to fairgoers in addition to pavilions featuring German,

French, and American regional fare. Soda water stands were popular, as were a Vienna Model Bakery, which sold items made with Goff, Fleischmann, and Company's compressed yeast products. The Centennial International Exhibition succeeded beyond the hopes of its promoters, with over 10 million people in attendance.

Witnessing Philadelphia's successful exhibition, other cities sought recognition by holding their own fairs. Chicago led the way with the World's Columbian Exposition in 1893, belatedly celebrating the four-hundredth anniversary of Christopher Columbus's voyage. Planners erected magnificent-looking imitation marble buildings and featured George Ferris's 264-foot wheel ride on the midways of the fairgrounds. The 27 million people who attended saw new technological innovations and tasted many new and different foods. Canada advertised its cheese industry with a eleven-ton block of cheese. Schlitz and Pabst, competing American breweries, served their beers, while the Pittsburgh-based Heinz Company made a map of the United States with its pickles. Americans tasted a wide range of ethnic foods for the first time in addition to domestic favorites such as baked beans, pumpkin pie, and clam chowder. Many also tried a new combination of caramelized popcorn and peanuts introduced at the fair as Cracker Jack.

The Columbian Exhibition earned a $1.4 million profit, demonstrating the value of hosting major exhibitions. Encouraged by Chicago's success, Buffalo hosted the Pan-American Exposition in 1901. Though well-attended by 8 million visitors, Buffalo's exposition lost $3 million and became the tragic site of President William McKinley's assassination. Undaunted by this tragedy and Buffalo's losses, several other cities mounted expositions into the early twentieth century. The Louisiana Purchase Exposition opened in St. Louis in 1904, featuring several new American foods, including iced tea, sliced bread, prepared baby foods, and purportedly hot dogs, hamburgers, and ice cream cones. Legend holds that ice cream cones came into being there when the midway ice cream vendor Joseph Menches ran out of bowls, substituting *zalabia*, a Middle Eastern wafer-like pastry to sell his ice cream. His customers loved the consumable "bowl," and the popular ice cream cone was born. St. Louis's fair proved equally popular, effectively showcasing their city and earning huge profits.

Their success spawned subsequent expositions in Norfolk, Virginia (1907), and San Francisco (1915), but due to World War I and its aftermath, no other American fairs were held until 1933. In the interim host fair countries founded the Paris-based Bureau of International Expositions in 1928 to regulate the locations and frequency of world's fairs and to outline the obligations of exhibitors and organizers.

The Maillard chocolate company constructed a chocolate pavilion at the 1893 World's Columbian Exposition in Chicago.

Despite the hardships of the Great Depression, Chicago held the Century of Progress World's Fair in 1933. In addition to many scientific and industrial exhibits, fairgoers sampled Moroccan, Asian, and Middle Eastern dishes and feasted on German sausages and beer. Kraft unveiled its new Miracle Whip salad dressing, which became an American staple. Chicago's fair attracted 48 million visitors and made a modest profit.

Not to be outdone by its midwestern rival, New York City planned an even greater fair for 1939. Constructed in Queens and billed simply as the New York World's Fair, it featured food as a central theme. Visitors met Borden's Elsie the Cow, tasted varieties of doughnuts, and could choose to dine at numerous ethnic restaurants. In spite of generous funding by huge commercial and government investments, New York's fair suffered from the growing turmoil in Europe and bad weather, ultimately losing $18.7 million.

Owing to the devastation of World War II, no major fairs were held until 1962, when Seattle opened its Century 21 Exposition. Seattle's fair featured futuristic architecture and meals from the Food Circus, which offered an assortment of ethnic dishes, or from innovative vending machines. Following soon after Seattle's success, New York City attempted another exposition, the New York World's Fair of 1964–1965, constructed on its 1939 fairgrounds. Though a financial failure, losing over $20 million, the 1964–1965 fair helped popularize many new foods, including Korean kimchi, tandoori chicken, hummus, and Turkish coffee. Though less exotic, the most popular food vendors were Van Dam's Belgium waffles, the Chunking Inn, offering 99-cent Chinese meals, and Mastro's Pizza. The fair was also the first round of the famed "cola wars," with Coca-Cola and Pepsi openly competing for customers. This array of food, however, could not compensate for poor attendance and faltering revenues, causing some exhibitors to leave before the fair's second season.

Ultimately the financial failure of New York's 1964–1965 fair ended the era of the grand expositions in America. Popular enthusiasm for such major events waned by the end of the twentieth century due to permanent

The Wonder Bakery pavilion on the back cover of The Wonder Book of Good Meals, *distributed by the Continental Baking Company at the Century of Progress Exposition in Chicago, 1933–1934.*

entertainment venues such as Disney's Epcot Center, a proliferation of varied ethnic restaurants, and an increased familiarity with other cultures via television. Smaller cities held lesser expositions during the late 1960s through the early 1980s, but promoters throughout the United States scrapped further plans after the New Orleans fair lost $121 million in 1984.

[See also AMUSEMENT PARKS; COLA WARS; CRACKER JACK; ICE CREAMS AND ICES.]

BIBLIOGRAPHY

Allwood, John. *The Great Exhibitions.* London: Cassell and Collier Macmillan, 1977.

Benedict, Burton, ed. *The Anthropology of World's Fairs.* London: Scolar, 1983.

Rydell, Robert W. *All the World's a Fair: Visions of Empire at American International Exhibitions, 1876–1916.* Chicago: University of Chicago Press, 1984.

Rydell, Robert W. *Fair America: World's Fairs in the United States.* Washington, DC: Smithsonian, 2000.

DAVID GERARD HOGAN

Wraps

During the 1990s wraps became a popular new form of sandwich in the United States. Flour tortillas, plain or flavored, or various flat breads are used as a base on which imaginative pairings of ingredients, often reflecting international cuisines, such as Asian, Latin American, or Mediterranean, are layered. Fillings typically include thinly sliced meats and cheese and greens like spinach, basil, or cilantro. Onion, roasted red pepper, avocado, or hot peppers along with a variety of flavored dressings provide additional taste. The tortilla or flat bread is then folded in at one or both ends and rolled up from one edge. Wraps originated in northern California based on the concept of the burrito, which utilizes a flour tortilla in the same fashion to hold various combinations of Tex-Mex food.

Breakfast burritos have become one of the most popular forms of wraps in the United States. They are made from a variety of American breakfast favorites, like sausage, eggs, potatoes, and cheese, folded into flour tortillas and accompanied by salsa. Fusion cooking often incorporates the wrap concept in such dishes as duck breast, hoisin sauce, and scallion in Mandarin pancakes or flour tortillas. International cousins of the American wrap include Mexican tacos, Italian calzone, and Asian specialties like spring rolls and *moo shu* pork or Peking duck wrapped in thin pancakes called *bao bing*. Wraps are popular menu items in restaurants and as take-out food from sandwich shops throughout the United States.

[See also FUSION FOOD; MEXICAN AMERICAN FOOD; SANDWICHES; TAKE-OUT FOOD.]

BIBLIOGRAPHY

Mercuri, Becky. *Sandwiches That You Will Like.* Pittsburgh, PA: WQED Multimedia, 2002.

BECKY MERCURI

Yan, Martin

"If Yan can cook, so can you," says the television personality and cookbook author Martin Yan on virtually every one of his shows. With his rapid-fire cleaver and quick wit, Yan is considered one of the single greatest influences in bringing Asian cuisine and culture to the American public. Julia Child once referred to him as "the premiere exponent of Chinese cuisine."

Born on December 2, 1948, in Guangzhou, formerly known as Canton, Yan was raised in the culinary world. His father was a restaurateur and his mother operated a grocery store. Yan began cooking when he was twelve and at thirteen apprenticed at his uncle's restaurant in Hong Kong, where he later received a diploma from the Overseas Institute for Cookery. Yan emigrated to the United States and pursued an MS in food science at the University of California, Davis, moving to Calgary to become an instructor at the school's extension program. Discovering that he had a flair for teaching, Yan opened a cooking school in Calgary and in 1978 was approached by a local television station to host 130 cooking shows; his *Yan Can Cook* series became one of the first cooking shows on TV. Yan has hosted more than two thousand shows that have been broadcast in sixty countries, including in the Middle East and India; he has written more than twenty-five cookbooks and numerous articles for food publications. His TV shows and books have earned several James Beard Awards.

In 1985 Yan founded the Yan Can International Cooking School in San Francisco, and more recently he established a chain of Asian restaurants in California. While some detractors have accused Yan's TV presentation, which combines his colorful Cantonese accent with comic behavior, of perpetuating an Asian stereotype for entertainment value, Yan is nonplussed. He prefers to focus on dispelling the mysteries of Asian cooking. "My mission is to get people excited," he says.

BIBLIOGRAPHY

Yan, Martin. *Martin Yan's Chinatown Cooking.* New York: Morrow, 2002.

Yan, Martin. *The Yan Can Cook Book.* Toronto, Ontario: Doubleday Canada, 1981.

SCOTT WARNER

Yeast

Yeast is the great transformer, the catalyzing agent that converts boiled grains into beer, fruit juice into wine, and dense, sticky dough into light and airy bread and cake. Yeast is a single-celled fungus. It is found everywhere—in the air we breathe, on the surfaces of fruits and grains, and in the soil. Yeasts of interest to cooks are those that digest sugars to produce alcohol, carbon dioxide, and a number of other compounds that affect the flavor and character of the finished beverage or food.

Five thousand years ago Egyptian bakers are known to have leavened bread with yeast. In the early Middle Ages, around 1000, the word "yeast" was introduced into English. By the time European settlers arrived in North America in the early seventeenth century, they had wide experience working with yeasted beverages, breads, and cakes. The yeast they preferred, although at the time unnamed by science, was the robust *Saccharomyces cerevisiae* (*S. cerevisiae*), called "baker's" or "brewer's" yeast in cookbooks.

Colonists usually fermented beer and herbal wines with yeast reserved from a previous brewing. For fruit wines they relied on spontaneous fermentation—the action of wild yeasts, already present on the fruit, revived by contact with nutrients in a moist and warm environment. Early American baking practices were the same as those described in seventeenth- and eighteenth-century English cookbooks, such as Gervase Markham's *The English Hus-wife* (1615). Colonial bakers knew how to balance conditions and ingredients to make recipes work. They understood that temperature extremes, and an excess of salt or sugar, retarded the growth of yeasts. Most colonial bakers preferred leavening bread and some cakes with the yeasty sediments left behind by the brewing process. When brewer's yeast was not available, home bakers used either previously dried brewer's yeast, fermented dough held back from the previous baking, or wild yeasts in a spontaneously fermented starter.

The nineteenth-century American cookbook literature reveals a vibrant tradition of leavening breads with yeast starters, many of which included a tea made of dried hops flowers (*Humulus lupulus*), an herb added to discourage souring but that also contributed its own distinctive flavor. *The Home Cook* (1882) includes a rich array of recipes for these starters.

Until the late nineteenth century American bread bakers often multiplied their yeast by adding it to a batter of flour and water. When this "sponge" had risen, which took some hours, they added the remaining ingredients, which then fermented for several more hours. Bread dough sometimes was started the afternoon or evening before the actual baking day. Long rising contributes to the texture and flavor of the loaf. Commercially produced yeast first appeared in the United States in the 1860s. Charles and Maximillian Fleischmann, immigrants from Austria-Hungary, with the financial backing

An advertisement for Fleischmann's yeast.

of James Gaff, patented and sold standardized cakes of compressed yeast (*S. cerevisiae*) produced in their factory in Cincinnati. By the early twentieth century factory-produced yeast was widely available. Cookbook recipes began specifying that commercial yeast be added directly to bread dough in sufficient quantities to leaven it in less than two hours. Bread changed in texture, becoming lighter and softer, and its flavor turned blander. (Bread leavened quickly has a lighter texture than does bread leavened slowly.)

In the early nineteenth century American cooks began widely substituting chemical leavening agents—initially pearlash—for the yeast called for in English cake recipes. By the early twentieth century chemical leavening, such as baking soda and baking powder, was widely available to home cooks. The English tradition of yeasted dessert cakes had passed completely out of favor. Cookbooks, such as Fannie Farmer's *Boston Cooking-School Cook Book* (1896), specified chemical agents, sometimes supplementing them with eggs, as the primary leaven. This remains the customary practice. These chemical leavenings contributed to changes of texture and flavor.

Ginger ale, root beer, and other refreshing and so-called medicinal beverages had been fermented with brewer's yeast. However, with the growing influence of the temperance movement in the nineteenth century, chemicals like baking soda increasingly were used to produce the fizz. These temperance beverages became the basis of the huge American soft drink industry in the twentieth century.

The last third of the twentieth century saw a revolution in American food culture, which included a revival in the arts of wine making, brewing, and baking. Wine makers and brewers transformed their industries by taking a scientific approach to managing selected strains of *S. cerevisiae*. Artisanal bakers looked to European bread making methods to improve their breads' flavor, texture, and character. They slowed the fermentation process, employed the older sponge system, often used spontaneous ferments, and frequently dispensed with baking tins.

Historically, aside from some German rye breads and San Francisco sourdough, American sourdough breads were made in a way that minimized or eliminated sourness. In the late twentieth century, for the first time, Americans as a whole began to appreciate sourness in their bread, a flavor that is common in many artisanal and homemade loaves. At this same time "fast rising" yeast strains were developed for home cooks who felt they did not have time to let bread rise slowly. By the end of the twentieth century cookbooks, such as *The Joy of Cooking* by Irma S. Rombauer, Marion Rombauer Becker, and Ethan Becker (1997), reflected these changes in the American artisanal bread-baking style.

[**See also** BREAD; BREWING; FRUIT WINES.]

BIBLIOGRAPHY

David, Elizabeth. *English Bread and Yeast Cookery.* New York: Viking, 1977.

WILLIAM RUBEL

Yum! Brands, Inc.

Beginning in the 1970s PepsiCo acquired several fast food restaurant chains, including Kentucky Fried Chicken, Pizza Hut, and Taco Bell, as adjuncts to its soft-drink business. It required that those chains serve only Pepsi-Cola. Other fast food chains, such as McDonald's, saw PepsiCo as a competitor and stopped selling PepsiCo products. PepsiCo finally concluded that it made sense to spin off its restaurant businesses. Accordingly in 1997 Tricon Global Restaurants, Inc., was founded as an independent, publicly traded company, with headquarters in Louisville, Kentucky. In 2002 Tricon announced the acquisition of Yorkshire Global Restaurants with its two brands, Long John Silver's and A&W All-American Food. Tricon changed its name to Yum! Brands, Inc., in 2003. As of 2005 Yum! Brands operated 33,000 restaurants in more than 100 countries. It is the world's largest fast food company.

BIBLIOGRAPHY

"Special Report: Yum! Brands—Fast Food's Yummy Secret." *Economist* 376, no. 8441 (2005): 61.

ANDREW F. SMITH

Yummasetti

Yummasetti (also Yumazetti) is a baked casserole of cooked spaghetti or noodles, ground meat, tomato sauce, canned or fresh vegetables, two different canned cream soups, sometimes sour cream and usually topped with breadcrumbs. An early printed recipe was called "smack" during World War II. Yummasetti is now an omnipresent Amish recipe. Although casserole dishes are characteristic of Pennsylvania Dutch cooking, Yummasetti may not have entered Amish kitchens until the 1960s. This illustrates both that the Amish are as ingenious and innovative with factory foods as less conservative Americans but also the extent of culinary conformity within a closed culture.

BIBLIOGRAPHY

Randle, Bill. *Plain Cooking: Low-Cost, Good-Tasting Amish Recipes.* New York: Quadrangle, 1974.

MARK H. ZANGER

Yum!
Brands, Inc.

Zombie

The zombie was the brainchild of the talented bartender Ernest Raymond Beaumont-Gantt, nicknamed "Donn Beach." He and his business-savvy wife Cora Irene Sund, a former schoolteacher turned cocktail waitress, opened Don the Beachcomber in 1937 in Hollywood, California. Their timing was flawless. The country was a few short years past Prohibition, and many of the Hollywood stars had spent that dry time in the playground of Havana, Cuba, where rum drinks were the order of the day. The famous Trader Vic, Victor Bergeron, was inspired by the success of the Beachcomber to reinvent Hinky Dinks, his saloon in Oakland, California, as Trader Vic's. Tiki was definitely the order of the day.

The recipe for the zombie takes advantage of the unique quality that rum possesses. Unlike other spirits, rum is best when combined with other kinds of rum. When different rums are mixed together, the individual rums synergistically produce spectacular results. Gantt and Bergeron both mastered this blending technique in their recipes. They created a library of rum recipes that is still consulted. The original zombie recipe, like all of Donn Beach's recipes, was a closely guarded professional secret throughout his lifetime. Twenty-three years after his death in 1978 his widow Phoebe Beach and her second husband Arnold Bitner decided to tell the Donn Beach story in their book *Hawai'i Tropical Rum Drinks and Cuisine by Don the Beachcomber*. The original zombie recipe illustrated Beach's genius for blending five different rums to make the base for the zombie.

ZOMBIE

¾ ounce lime juice
½ ounce grapefruit juice
1/2 ounce Falernum
1/2 ounce simple syrup
1¼ ounce Ramirez Royal Superior rum (substitute Captain Morgan rum)
1 ounce Lemon Hart Demerara rum 151°
1 ounce Palau 30-year-old Cuba rum (substitute 30-year-old Ron Zacapa Centenario rum)
1 ounce Myers's dark rum
1 ounce Treasure Cove 32-year-old Jamaican (substitute Appleton Estate Rum)
2 dashes each Angostura bitters and Pernod
3 dashes grenadine
¾ ounce maraschino liqueur

Pour ingredients into a blender. Add a handful of small cracked ice. Blend at medium speed. Pour into a fourteen-ounce glass with three or four cubes of ice. Decorate with a spear of fresh pineapple juice, orange slice, cherry, and sprig of mint. Serve with a straw. Sip with eyes half closed.

[**See also** COCKTAILS; RUM.]

BIBLIOGRAPHY

Bitner, Arnold, and Phoebe Beach. *Hawai'i Tropical Rum Drinks and Cuisine by Don the Beachcomber*. Honolulu, HI: Mutual Publishing, 2001.

DALE DEGROFF

Food
Bibliography

General Histories

Bower, Anne L., ed. *Recipes for Reading: Community Cookbooks, Stories, Histories*. Amherst: University of Massachusetts Press, 1997.

Carson, Barbara G. *Ambitious Appetites: Dining, Behavior, and Patterns of Consumption in Federal Washington*. Washington, DC: American Institute of Architects Press, 1990.

Haber, Barbara. *From Hardtack to Home Fries: An Uncommon History of American Cooks and Meals*. New York: Free Press, 2002.

Hooker, Richard J. *A History of Food and Drink in America*. Indianapolis: Bobbs-Merrill, 1981.

Levenstein, Harvey A. *Paradox of Plenty: A Social History of Eating in Modern America*. New York: Oxford University Press, 1993.

Levenstein, Harvey A. *Revolution at the Table: The Transformation of the American Diet*. New York: Oxford University Press, 1988.

Shapiro, Laura. *Perfection Salad: Women and Cooking at the Turn of the Century*. New York: Holt, 1987.

Shapiro, Laura. *Something from the Oven: Reinventing Dinner in 1950s America*. New York: Penguin Group, 2004.

Williams, Susan. *Savory Suppers and Fashionable Feasts: Dining in Victorian America*. Knoxville: University of Tennessee Press, 1996.

Bibliographies

Bitting, Katherine. *Gastronomic Bibliography*. San Francisco: Halle-Cordis Composing Room/Trade Freeroom, 1939.

Brown, Eleanor, and Bob Brown. *Culinary America: Cookbooks Published in the Cities and Towns of the United States of America during the Years from 1860 through 1960*. New York: Roving Eye, 1961.

Cagle, William R., and Lisa Killion Stafford. *American Books on Food and Drink*. New Castle, DE: Oak Knoll, 1998.

Cook, Margaret. *America's Charitable Cooks: A Bibliography of Fund-Raising Cook Books Published in the United States (1861–1915)*. Kent, OH: n.p., 1971.

Longone, Janice B., and Daniel T. Longone. *American Cookbooks and Wine Books, 1797–1950*. Ann Arbor, MI: Clements Library/Wine and Food Library, 1984.

Lowenstein, Eleanor. *Bibliography of American Cookery Books, 1742–1860*. Worcester, MA: American Antiquarian Society, 1972.

Cookbooks: Reprints and Facsimiles

Benson, Abraham Benson, ed. *Penn Family Recipes: Cooking Recipes of William Penn's Wife Gulielma*. York, PA: Shumway, 1966.

Blot, Pierre. *Hand-Book of Practical Cookery*. New York: Appleton, 1869. Facsimile, New York: Arno, 1973.

Bryan, Lettuce. *Kentucky Housewife*. Cincinnati, OH: Shepard and Stearns, 1839. Reprint, Columbia: University of South Carolina Press, 1991.

Davidis, Henriette. *Pickled Herring and Pumpkin Pie: A Nineteenth-Century Cookbook for German Immigrants to America*. Edited by Louis A. Pitschmann. Madison: University of Wisconsin, 2002.

Estes, Rufus. *Good Things to Eat as Suggested by Rufus*. Chicago: Published by the Author, 1911. Reprinted as edited by D. J. Frienz. Jenks, OK: Howling at the Moon Press, 1999.

Eustis, Celestine. *Cooking in Old Creole Days*. New York: Russell, 1904. Reprint, New York: Arno, 1973.

Farmer, Fannie Merritt. *Boston Cooking-School Cook Book*. Boston: Little, Brown, 1896. Facsimile, New York: Weathervane, 1986.

Fisher, Mrs. Abby. *What Mrs. Fisher Knows about Old Southern Cooking*. San Francisco: Women's Co-operative Printing Office, 1881. Reprinted with historical notes by Karen Hess. Bedford, MA: Applewood, 1995.

Glasse, Hannah. *Art of Cookery Made Plain and Easy*. London. First edition published by the Author in London, 1796. Facsimile, Schenectady, NY: United States Historical Research Service, 1994.

Hearn, Lafcadio. *La Cuisine Creole: A Collection of Culinary Recipes from Leading Chefs and Noted Creole Housewives, Who Have Made New Orleans Famous for Its Cuisine*. New York: Coleman, 1885. Reprint, Baton Rouge, LA: Pelican/Moran, 1967.

Hill, Mrs. A. P. *Mrs. Hill's New Cook Book*. New York: Carleton, 1872. Reprinted with *The Confederate Receipt Book*. Birmingham, AL: Oxmoor, 1985.

Hooker, Richard J., ed. *A Colonial Plantation Cookbook: The Receipt Book of Harriott Pinckney Horry, 1770*. Columbia: University of South Carolina Press, 1984.

Josselyn, John. *New-England Rarities Discovered*. London: Widdowes, 1672. Reprint, Boston: Massachusetts Historical Society, 1972.

Kander, Mrs. Simon, and Mrs. Henry Schoenfeld, comps. *The "Settlement Cookbook": The Way to a Man's Heart*. Milwaukee, WI, 1903. Facsimile, New York: Grammercy Publishing Co., 1987.

Lea, Elizabeth Ellicott. *A Quaker Woman's Cookbook: The Domestic Cookery of Elizabeth Ellicott Lea*. Edited with an introduction by William Woys Weaver. Philadelphia: University of Pennsylvania, 1982.

Lee, N. K. M. *The Cook's Own Book*. Boston: Munroe and Francis, 1832. Reprint, New York: Arno, 1972.

Leslie, Eliza. *Directions for Cookery: Being a System of the Art, in Its Various Branches*. 10th ed. Philadelphia: Carey and Hart, 1848. Reprint, New York: Arno, 1973.

Leslie, Eliza. *Indian Meal Book*. Reprinted under title *Corn Meal Cookery: A Collection of Heirloom Corn Meal Recipes Dating from 1848*. Hamilton, OH: Burns, 1998.

Levy, Esther. *Mrs. Esther Levy's Jewish Cookery Book*. Philadelphia, 1871. Reprint, Cambridge, MA: Applewood, 1988.

Lincoln, Mrs. D. A. *Boston Cooking School Cook Book*. Boston: Roberts, 1887. Reprinted with an introduction by Janice Longone. Mineola, NY: Dover, 1996.

Midwestern Home Cookery. Facsimile of three cookbooks, New York: Arno, 1973.

[Moss, Maria J.]. *A Poetical Cook-Book*. Philadelphia: Caxton Press of C. Sherman, 1864. Reprint, New York: Arno/New York Times, 1972.

Pennell, Elizabeth Robins. *The Delights of Delicate Eating*. Introduction by Jacqueline Block Williams. Urbana: University of Illinois Press, 2000.

Pinckney, Eliza Lucas. *Recipe Book*. Charleston: Committee on Historic Activities of the South Carolina Society of the Colonial Dames of America, 1969.

Porter, M. E. *Mrs. Porter's New Southern Cookery Book*. Philadelphia: Potter, 1871. Reprinted with an introduction and suggested recipes by Louis Szathmáry. New York: Arno, 1973.

Presbyterian Cook Book, Compiled by the Ladies of the First Presbyterian Church. Dayton, OH: Thomas, 1875. Reprinted with an introduction and suggested recipes by Louis Szathmáry. New York: Arno, 1973.

Randolph, Mary. *The Virginia House-Wife*. Washington, DC: Davis and Force, 1824. Facsimile edited by Karen Hess. Columbia: University of South Carolina Press, 1984.

Ranhofer, Charles. *The Epicurean*. New York: Ranhofer, 1893. Reprint, New York: Dover, 1971.

Rombauer, Irma S. *The Joy of Cooking*. 1931. A facsimile of the first edition. New York: Scribners, 1998.

Rose, Peter. *The Sensible Cook: Dutch Foodways in the Old and the New World*. Syracuse, NY: Syracuse University Press, 1989.

Simmons, Amelia. *American Cookery*. A facsimile of the first edition with an essay by Mary Tolford Wilson. New York: Oxford University Press, 1958.

Simmons, Amelia. *American Cookery*. 2nd ed.. Albany, NY: Webster, 1796. A facsimile with an introduction by Karen Hess. Bedford, MA: Applewood, 1996.

Thornton, P. *The Southern Gardener and Receipt Book*. Newark, NJ: Denis, 1845. Reprint, Birmingham, AL: Oxmoor, 1984.

Ude, Louis Eustache. *The French Cook*. Philadelphia, 1828. Reprint, New York: Arco, 1978.

[Washington, Martha] *Martha Washington's Booke of Cookery*. Edited by Karen Hess. New York: Columbia University Press, 1981.

Weaver, William Woys. *Sauerkraut Yankees: Pennsylvania German Foods and Foodways*. Philadelphia: University of Pennsylvania Press, 1983.

Wilcox, Estelle Woods, comp. *Centennial Buckeye Cook Book*. Reprinted with an introduction and appendices by Andrew F. Smith. Columbus: Ohio State University Press, 2000.

Women's Centennial Executive Committee. *National Cookery Book Compiled from Original Receipts for the Women's Centennial Committees of the International Exhibition*. Philadelphia: Women's Centennial Executive Committee, 1876. Reprint. Introduction by Andrew F.

Smith. Bedford, Mass.: Applewood Books, 2005.

Ziemann, Hugo, and Mrs. F. L. Gillette. *The White House Cookbook.* New York: Saalfield, 1903. Reprint, Old Greenwich, CT: Devin Adair, 1983.

Encyclopedias

Katz, Solomon, ed. *Encyclopedia of Food and Culture.* 3 vols. New York: Scribners, 2003.

Kiple, Kenneth F., and Kriemhild Conèe Ornelas, eds. *The Cambridge World History of Food.* 2 vols. New York: Cambridge University Press, 2000.

Ethnic Food

Gabaccia, Donna R. *We Are What We Eat: Ethnic Food and the Making of Americans.* Cambridge, MA: Harvard University Press, 1998.

Zanger, Mark H. *The American Ethnic Cookbook for Students.* Phoenix, AZ: Oryx, 2001.

Regional Histories

Luchetti, Cathy. *Home on the Range: A Culinary History of the American West.* New York: Villard, 1993.

Williams, Jacqueline B. *The Way We Ate: Pacific Northwest Cooking, 1843–1900.* Pullman: Washington State University Press, 1996.

Restaurants

Thomas, Lately. *Delmonico's: A Century of Splendor.* Boston: Houghton Mifflin, 1967.

Specific Foods and Food Products

Brenner, Joël Glenn. *The Emperors of Chocolate: Inside the Secret World of Hershey and Mars.* New York: Broadway, 2000.

Carson, Gerald. *Cornflake Crusade.* New York: Rinehart, 1957.

Jenkins, Virginia Scott. *Bananas: An American History.* Washington: Smithsonian, 2000.

Smith, Andrew F. *Peanuts: The Illustrious History of the Goober Pea.* Urbana: University of Illinois Press, 2002.

Smith, Andrew F. *Popped Culture: A Social History of Popcorn in America.* Columbia: University of South Carolina Press, 1999.

Smith, Andrew F. *Pure Ketchup: A History of America's National Condiment.* Columbia: University of South Carolina Press, 1996.

Smith, Andrew F. *The Tomato in America: Early History, Culture and Cookery.* Columbia: University of South Carolina Press, 1994.

Wilson, David Scofield, and Angus Kress Gillespie, eds. *Rooted in America: Foodlore of Popular Fruits and Vegetables.* Nashville: University of Tennessee Press, 1999.

Woloson, Wendy A. *Refined Tastes: Sugar, Confectionery and Consumption in Nineteenth-Century America.* Baltimore: Johns Hopkins University Press, 2002.

Wyman, Carolyn. *Spam, A Biography: The Amazing True Story of America's "Miracle Meat"!* New York: Harcourt Brace, 1999.

Wyman, Carolyn. *Jell-O, A Biography: The History and Mystery of "America's Most Famous Dessert."* San Diego: Harcourt, 2001.

Special Topics: Reform and Counterculture

Belasco, Warren J. *Appetite for Change: How the Counterculture Took on the Food Industry 1966–1988.* New York: Pantheon, 1989.

Crump, Nancy Carter. *Hearthside Cooking: An Introduction to Virginia Plantation Cuisine, Including Bills of Fare, Tools and Techniques, and Original Recipes with Adaptations for Modern Fireplaces and Kitchens.* McLean, VA: EPM, 1986.

Davis, Adelle. *Let's Eat Right to Keep Fit.* New York: Harcourt, Brace, 1954.

Hess, John, and Karen Hess. *The Taste of America.* New York: Grossman, 1977.

Lappé, Frances Moore. *Diet for a Small Planet.* New York: Friends of the Earth/Ballantine, 1977.

Schlosser, Eric. *Fast Food Nation: The Dark Side of the All-American Meal.* Boston: Houghton Mifflin, 2001.

Other

Franklin, Linda Campbell. *300 Years of Kitchen Collectibles.* 5th ed. Iola, WI: Krause, 2002.

Funderburg, Anne Cooper. *Sundae Best: A History of Soda Fountains.* Bowling Green, KY: Bowling Green State University Popular Press, 2002.

Gutman, Richard J. S. *American Diner, Then and Now.* Baltimore: Johns Hopkins University Press, 2000.

Inness, Sherrie A., ed. *Kitchen Culture in America: Popular Representations of Food, Gender and Race.* Philadelphia: University of Pennsylvania Press, 2001.

ANDREW F. SMITH

Drink Bibliography

General Histories

Barr, Andrew. *Drink: A Social History of America.* New York: Carroll and Graf, 1999.

Brown, John Hull. *Early American Beverages.* Rutland, VT: Tuttle, 1966.

Conroy, David. *In Public Houses: Drink and the Revolution of Authority in Colonial Massachusetts.* Chapel Hill: University of North Carolina Press, 1995.

Hooker, Richard J. *A History of Food and Drink in America.* Indianapolis: Bobbs-Merrill, 1981.

Lender, Mark Edward, and James Kirby Martin. *Drinking in America: A History, The Revised and Expanded Edition.* New York: Free Press, 1987.

Salinger, Sharon V. *Taverns and Drinking in Early America.* Baltimore: Johns Hopkins University Press, 2002.

Thompson, Peter. *Rum Punch and Revolution: Taverngoing and Public Life in Eighteenth-Century Philadelphia.* Philadelphia: University of Pennsylvania Press, 1999.

Bibliographies

Gabler, James M. *Wine into Words: A History and Bibliography of Wine Books in the English Language.* Baltimore: Bacchus, 1985.

Noling, A. W., comp. *Beverage Literature: A Bibliography.* Metuchen, NJ: Scarecrow, 1971.

Beer and Cider

Baron, Stanley. *Brewed in America: A History of Beer and Ale in the United States.* New York: Arno, 1972.

LaFrance, Peter. *Beer Basics: A Quick and Easy Guide.* New York: Wiley, 1995.

Orton, Vrest. *The American Cider Book: The Story of America's Natural Beverage.* New York: Farrar, Straus, and Giroux, 1973.

Cocktails

Bullock, Tom. *173 Pre-Prohibition Cocktails.* Jenks, OK: Howling at the Moon Press, 2001.

Harwell, Richard Barksdale. *The Mint Julep.* Charlottesville: University Press of Virginia, 1975.

Coffee

Pendergrast, Mark. *Uncommon Grounds: The History of Coffee and How It Transformed Our World.* New York: Basic Books, 1999.

Milk

Dillon, John J. *Seven Decades of Milk: A History of New York's Dairy Industry.* New York: Orange Judd, 1941.

Soda

Pendergrast, Mark. *For God, Country and Coca-Cola.* New York: Scribners, 1993.

Riley, John J. *A History of the American Soft Drink Industry: Bottled Carbonated Beverages 1807–1957.* Washington, DC: American Bottlers of Carbonated Beverages, 1958.

Prohibition and Temperance

Asbury, Herbert. *The Great Illusion: An Informal History of Prohibition.* Garden City, NY: Doubleday, 1950.

Spirits

Brander, Michael. *The Original Scotch: A History of Scotch Whisky from the Earliest Days.* New York : Potter/Crown, 1975.

Carson, Gerald. *The Social History of Bourbon: An Unhurried Account of Our Star Spangled American Drink.* New York: Dodd, Mead, 1963.

Furnas, J. C. *The Life and Times of the Late Demon Rum.* London: Allen, 1965.

Tea

Roth, Rodris. *Tea Drinking in 18th-Century America: Its Etiquette and Equipage.* Paper 14. Contributions from the Museum of History and Technology, 1961.

Wine

Fuller, Robert C. *Religion and Wine: A Cultural History of Wine Drinking in the United States.* Knoxville: University of Tennessee Press, 1996.

Gabler, James M. *Passions: The Wines and Travels of Thomas Jefferson.* Baltimore: Bacchus, 1995.

Pinney, Thomas. *A History of Wine in America from the Beginnings to Prohibition.* Berkeley: University of California Press, 1989.

Pinney, Thomas. *A History of Wine in America: from Prohibition to the Present.* Berkeley: University of California Press, 2005.

Sullivan, Charles L. *Napa Wine: A History.* San Francisco: Wine Appreciation Guild, 1994.

Other

Lathrop, Elise. *Early American Inns and Taverns.* New York: Tudor, 1937.

Weiss, Harry B. *The History of Applejack or Apple Brandy in New Jersey from Colonial Times to the Present.* Trenton, NJ: New Jersey Agricultural Society, 1954.

ANDREW F. SMITH

Food Festivals

American Royal Barbecue, Kansas City, MO. First weekend in October. Invitational and open barbecue competition for pork, ribs, chicken, and brisket; other competitions include side dishes, sausage, dessert, and the International Sauce, Baste, and Rub Contest for professionals.
http://www.americanroyal.com

Apple Butter Festival, Berkeley Springs, WV. Columbus Day weekend. A celebration of old-fashioned mountain cooking with cider making, fresh apple butter, an apple-baking contest, apple butter contest, and country ham and chicken.
http://www.berkeleysprings.com/apple

Asian Moon Festival, Milwaukee, WI. Father's Day weekend. The diverse traditions of more than a dozen Asian cultures are celebrated with music, dance, sports, handicrafts, and foods presented by Asian restaurants.
http://www.asianmoonfestival.com

Beef Empire Days, Garden City, KS. First two weeks in June. Promotes Kansas's beef industry with rodeos, sports events, cowboy poetry, and a variety of food events featuring beef.
http://www.beefempiredays.com

Breaux Bridge Crawfish Festival, Breaux Bridge, LA. First full weekend in May. The Crawfish Capital of the World celebrates Cajun cooking and heritage with music, traditional crafts, a crawfish-eating contest, and crawfish étouffée cook-off.
http://www.bbcrawfest.com

Burgerfest, Hamburg, NY. Third Saturday in July. Honors the all-American hamburger, reportedly introduced at the Hamburg Fair in 1885, with a burger contest and a variety of entertainment.
http://www.hamburg-chamber.org/index.php?BurgerFest

California Strawberry Festival, Oxnard, CA. Third weekend in May. Promotes California's strawberry industry with entertainment, arts and crafts, strawberry-shortcake-eating contest, strawberry foods, and a recipe contest.
http://www.strawberry-fest.org

Castroville Artichoke Festival, Castroville, CA. A weekend in September. The Artichoke Capital of the World promotes the local artichoke crop with exhibits, music, arts and crafts, a parade, cooking demonstrations, and artichoke cuisine.
http://www.artichoke-festival.org

Central Maine Egg Festival, Pittsfield, ME. Fourth Saturday in July. Promotes Maine's major export with a traditional ham and egg breakfast, a cheesecake contest, cheesecake dessert luncheon, and a chicken barbecue.
http://www.pittsfieldmaine.com/eggfestival

Chocolate Fest, Burlington, WI. Weekend following Mother's Day. Promotes Burlington's chocolate industry with exhibits, a chocolate-tasting tent, music, parade, carnival, exhibits, and a chocolate cook-off.
http://www.chocolatefest.com

Deutsch Country Days, Marthasville, MO. Third Weekend in October. Historic Luxenhaus Farm preserves and celebrates nineteenth-century German American heritage with exhibits, crafts demonstrations, and food preparation.
http://www.deutschcountrydays.org

Eastport Salmon Festival, Eastport, ME. First Sunday after Labor Day. Promotes Maine's salmon-farming industry with music, educational displays, farmers market, crafts, and barbecued salmon dinners.
http://www.eastportme.net

Feast of San Gennaro, New York, NY. Eleven days including September 19. Vendors and restaurants in Little Italy celebrate this religious holiday and fair with multicultural foods, a cannoli-eating contest, music, and processions featuring the statue of San Gennaro, Patron Saint of Naples.
www.sangennaro.org

Feast of the Hunter's Moon, West Lafayette, IN. A weekend in October. Re-creation of an eighteenth-century French and Native American trade gathering along the Wabash River featuring eight thousand costumed participants, traditional craft demonstrations, and over sixty French and Native American foods prepared on open fires.
http://www.tcha.mus.in.us/feast.htm

Festival of American Folklife, Washington, DC. Last week of June and first week of July. Smithsonian Institution annually focuses on folkways, music, dancing, and arts and crafts of specific American cultural groups, regions, or states with emphasis on ethnic makeup and foodways, including cooking demonstrations and samples.
http://www.folklife.si.edu/center/festival.html

Fiesta Day, Tampa, FL. Second Saturday in February. Historic Ybor City celebrates Cuban and Latin heritage with music, a parade, arts and crafts, and food specialties, including the world's largest Cuban sandwich.
http://www.ybor.org/events/fiestaday.asp

Finger Lakes Wine Festival, Watkins Glen, NY. A weekend in July. Tasting of five hundred wines from sixty Finger Lakes wineries.
http://www.flwinefest.com

Georgia Peanut Festival, Sylvester, GA. Third weekend in October. The Peanut Capital of the World promotes peanut farming and peanut butter manufacturing with parades, arts and crafts, street dances, and peanut-related foods.
http://www.gapeanutfestival.com/

Gilroy Garlic Festival, Gilroy, CA. Last full weekend of July. Growers promote garlic with children's entertainment, dancing, garlic products and food, and a cook-off.
http://www.gilroygarlicfestival.com

Goleta Lemon Festival, Goleta, CA. Third weekend in October. Promotes local lemon and citrus crops with a farmers' market, musical entertainment, arts and crafts, a lemon pie–eating contest, a pie-baking contest, and lemon-flavored food and drink.
http://lemonfestival.com/

Great American Beer Festival, Denver, CO. Last weekend in September. A public tasting of twelve hundred beers from three hundred American breweries.
http://www.gabf.org

Great Taste of the Midwest, Madison, WI. Second Saturday in August. A public tasting of four hundred beers from one hundred breweries and brewpubs.
http://mhtg.org

Great Wisconsin Cheese Festival, Little Chute, WI. First full weekend in June. Promotes Wisconsin's cheese industry with a parade, sporting events, contests, cheese-carving demonstrations, a cheese omelet breakfast, and cheesecake contest.
http://www.littlechutewi.org/calendar_events/cheesefest.html

Gumbo Festival, Bridge City, LA. Second weekend in October. The Gumbo Capital of the World celebrates Louisiana's famous Cajun gumbo with a champion gumbo-cooking contest and regional specialty foods.
http://www.hgaparish.org/gumbofestival.htm

Hatch Chile Festival, Hatch, NM. Labor Day weekend. The Chile Capital of the World promotes chiles and celebrates New Mexico culture with music, crafts,

dancing, a chile cook-off, jalapeno-eating contest, and southwestern cuisine.
http://www.nmchili.com/hatch_chile_fest.htm

Hot Dog Festival, Frankfort, IN. Last weekend in July. Celebrates the all-American hot dog with a flea market, farmers' market, parade, sports tournaments, music, and arts and crafts.
http://mainstreet.accs.net/HDF.aspx

Indio International Tamale Festival, Indio, CA. First weekend in December. Celebrates Hispanic culture and cuisine with sporting events, a parade, sports competitions, music, dancing, and a tamale-tasting contest.
http://www.tamalefestival.net

International Chili Society World's Championship Chili Cookoff, Reno, NV. First weekend in October. Winners of ICS sanctioned cook-offs compete in four contests: Last Chance Red Chili, World's Championship Salsa, World's Championship Chili Verde, and World's Championship Traditional Red Chili.
http://www.chilicookoff.com

International Dutch Oven Championship Cookoff, Sandy, UT. Annually in March. Ten qualifying teams compete for the world championship by cooking a main dish, bread, and dessert.
http://www.idos.com

International Horseradish Festival, Collinsville, IL. First weekend in June. The Horseradish Capital of the World promotes horseradish with sports events, a horseradish-eating contest, and a horseradish recipe contest.

Contact: International Horseradish Festival, P.O. Box 766, Collinsville, IL 62234
http://www.horseradishfestival.com/

International Pancake Day Race, Liberal, KS. Shrove Tuesday. Traditional competition with Olney, England, in which married women race while flipping pancakes in skillets; includes pancake breakfast, parade, and eating contest.
http://www.swdtimes.com/pancakeday/index2.html

International Ramp Cook-Off and Festival, Elkins, WV. Last weekend in April. Spring ramp harvest is celebrated with a traditional ramp dinner, a ramp cook-off, and public tasting.
http://www.randolphcountywv.com/FestivalsandEvents/RampFestival.htm

Jack Daniel's World Championship Invitational Barbeque, Lynchburg, TN. Fourth weekend in October. An invitational event involving fifty competition teams that have won a major contest the previous year.
http://jackdaniels.com

Jambalaya Festival, Gonzales, LA. Memorial Day weekend. The Jambalaya Capital of the World holds its championship jambalaya cooking contest accompanied by music, dancing, and regional Louisiana foods.
http://www.jambalayafestival.org/

J. Millard Tawes Crab and Clam Bake, Crisfield, MD. Third Wednesday in July. The Soft-shell Crab Capital of the World celebrates the harvest with an all-you-can-eat feast.
http://www.crisfieldchamber.com/clambake.htm

Kentucky Bourbon Festival, Bardstown, KY. A weekend in September. Promotes American bourbon including a food court, seminars, and cooking demonstrations.
http://www.kybourbonfestival.com

Kona Coffee Cultural Festival, Kailua-Kona, HI. First week in November. Promotes Hawaii's cultural heritage and coffee industry with tours, exhibits, parades, a farmers' market, cooking demonstrations, and coffee recipe contests.
http://www.konacoffeefest.com

Kutztown Pennsylvania-German Festival, Kutztown, PA. Fourth of July week. Celebrates Pennsylvania Dutch life with traditional crafts demonstrations, pageants, a quilt sale, farmers market, and foods.
http://www.kutztownfestival.com/about/food.shtml

Louisiana Sugar Cane Festival and Fair. Last weekend in September. Promotes the state's sugar industry with concerts, art shows, the blessing of the crop, a street fair, boat parade, and sugar cookery contest.
http://www.hisugar.org

Louisiana Yambilee, Opelousas, LA. Last weekend in October. Promotes Louisiana yam industry with arts and crafts, a parade, sweet potato auction, and yam cooking contest.
http://www.yambilee.com/

Maine Lobster Festival, Rockland, ME. First weekend in August. Promotes Maine's lobster industry with boat rides, marine exhibits, Maine crafts and products, a carnival, and lobster culinary competition.
http://www.mainelobsterfestival.com

Marion Popcorn Festival, Marion, OH. Weekend after Labor Day. Largest popcorn festival in the world celebrates Ohio popcorn manufacturing with a parade, sports events, musical entertainment, midway, beer gardens, and popcorn treats.
http://www.popcornfestival.com

Monterey Wine Festival, Monterey, CA. A weekend in April. America's oldest wine festival; wine tasting, seminars, cooking demonstrations.
http://www.montereywine.com

Morro Bay Harbor Festival, Morro Bay, CA. First weekend in October. Promotes California's seafood industry with maritime heritage exhibits, an oyster-eating contest, entertainment, seafood cuisine, and albacore barbecue.
http://www.mbhf.com/

Morton Pumpkin Festival, Morton, IL. Second week in September. Promotes the Pumpkin Capital of the World with a carnival, parade, entertainment, sports events, arts and crafts, the Punkin' Chuckin' Contest, a pumpkin cooking contest, and pumpkin foods.
http://www.pumpkincapital.com

Mushroom Festival, Kennett Square, PA. Second weekend in September. Honors the birthplace of the American mushroom industry with exhibits, mushroom sampling, a parade, mushroom auction, arts and crafts, mushroom farm tours, mushroom cooking demonstrations, and cook-off.
http://www.mushroomfest.com

Napa Valley Mustard Festival, Napa Valley, CA. February to April. Promotes the agriculture, food, and wines of the region with entertainment, an array of casual and black-tie events, and cooking demonstrations by renowned chefs.
http://www.mustardfestival.org

National Apple Harvest Festival, Arendtsville, PA. First two weekends in October. The Apple Capital of the U.S.A. promotes apple production with apple products, heritage demonstrations, apple pancake breakfast, apple pie–eating contest, and baking contest.
http://www.appleharvest.com

National Asparagus Festival, Hart and Shelby, MI. Second weekend in June. Celebrates the asparagus harvest with a parade, food show, sports events, asparagus lunch and bake sale, fish boil dinner, and asparagus and roast beef smorgasbord.
http://www.nationalasparagusfestival.org/index.html

National Buffalo Wing Festival, Buffalo, NY. Labor Day weekend. Celebrates chicken wings, created at the Anchor Bar in Buffalo, with a wing-eating contest, a wing sauce contest, and entertainment.
http://www.buffalowing.com

National Cherry Festival, Traverse City, MI. Eight days beginning the first Saturday after July 4. The Cherry Capital of the World promotes cherries with parades, sporting events, arts and crafts, a midway, air shows, concerts, cherry orchard tours, cherry products, and a cherry pie–eating contest.
http://www.cherryfestival.org

National Cornbread Festival, South Pittsburg, TN. Last weekend in April or first weekend in May. Celebrates southern cornbread with music, a car show, arts and crafts, a working gristmill, southern barbecue, and a cornbread-baking contest.
http://www.nationalcornbread.com

National Date Festival, Indio, CA. Third weekend in June. Promotes local date production with entertainment based on an Arabian theme, exhibits, cooking demonstrations, and recipe contest.
http://www.datefest.org

National Shrimp Festival, Gulf Shores, AL. Second full weekend in October. Promotes local shrimp industry with music, a boat show, sailboat regatta, arts and crafts, and shrimp culinary specialties.
http://www.nationalshrimpfestival.com

Nebraska Czech Festival, Wilber, NE. First weekend in August. The Czech Capital of the United States honors its heritage with a kolache-eating contest and traditional Czech dinners.
http://www.ci.wilber.ne.us/festival_events.asp

North Beach Festival, San Francisco, CA. Third weekend in June. California's Little Italy honors Italian heritage with a street fair, including a book sale, arts and crafts, music, dancing, blessing of neighborhood pets, and food from local restaurants and vendors.
http://www.sfnorthbeach.org/festival/

North Carolina Seafood Festival, Morehead City, NC. First weekend in October. Promotes the state's seafood industry with the blessing of the fleet, exhibits, demonstrations, entertainment, ship tours, arts and crafts, sporting events, dances, and seafood sampling.
http://www.ncseafoodfestival.org

North Carolina Turkey Festival, Raeford, NC. Third weekend in September. Promotes North Carolina's turkey industry with musical entertainment, children's activities, car show, arts and crafts show, sports events, dog show, Stompin' Turkey Dinner and Dance, Turkey Hoagie Brunch, and turkey cooking contest.
http://www.ncturkeyfestival.com/

Oktoberfest-Zinzinnati, Cincinnati, OH. Third weekend in September. The world's second-largest, authentic Oktoberfest, modeled on that in Munich, celebrates German heritage with German food, beer, games, a parade, and music.
http://www.oktoberfest-zinzinnati.com

Oregon Brewers Festival, Portland, OR. Last weekend in July. A public tasting of handcrafted beers from seventy top American craft breweries.
http://www.oregonbrewfest.com

Original Terlingua International Frank X. Tolbert-Wick Fowler Memorial Championship Chili Cookoff, Behind the Store, Terlingua, TX. First weekend in November. Competitions include the Terlingua International Chili Cookoff Championship, World's Championship Margarita Mixoff, and Brisket BBQ, Bean, and Black-eyed Pea Cookoffs.
www.abowlofred.com

Parke County Maple Syrup Festival, Rockville, IN. Last weekend in February and first weekend in March. Promotes maple syrup production with tours of sugar camps and covered bridges, pancake feeds, and maple products.
http://www.mansfieldvillage.com/maple.php

Persimmon Festival, Mitchell, IN. Last weekend in September. Celebrates the American persimmon and Hoosier cooking with sports events, a parade, carnival, dinners, and a persimmon pudding contest.
http://www.mitchell-indiana.org/persimmon.htm

Phelps Sauerkraut Festival, Phelps, NY. First weekend in August. Promotes the local cabbage industry with arts and crafts, bands, a parade, and sauerkraut cuisine.
http://www.phelpssauerkrautfestival.com/

Pie Town Festival, Pie Town, NM. Second Saturday in September. Pie-eating and pie-baking contests, pie sale, breakfast, pit barbecue, fiddling contest, and hot air balloons.
http://www.pietown.org

Polish Fest, Milwaukee, WI. Third weekend in June. The largest Polish festival in the country features folk dancing, polka bands, a cultural village with crafts, and traditional foods.
http://www.polishfest.org

Reynoldsburg Tomato Festival, Reynoldsburg, OH. Weekend after Labor Day. Celebrates Reynoldsburg as the birthplace of the tomato, developed commercially by resident Alexander W. Livingston, with a parade, car show, rides, exhibits, and tomato cookery.
http://www.reynoldsburgtomatofestival.org

St. Mary's County Oyster Festival, Leonardtown, MD. Third weekend in October. Celebrates the opening of the Chesapeake's fall oyster season with oysters, entertainment, a carnival, arts and crafts, exhibits, the National Oyster Shucking Championship, and the National Oyster Cook-Off.
http://www.usoysterfest.com

Staunton's Annual African-American Heritage Festival, Staunton, VA. Third weekend in September. African American heritage is honored with music, dance, arts and crafts, exhibits, children's activities, and traditional foods.
http://www.staunton.va.us

Swedish Festival, Stromsburg, NE. Third weekend in June. The Swede Capital of Nebraska celebrates its heritage with sporting events, parades, dancing, a band concert, smorgasbord, and Swedish pancake breakfast.
http://www.stromsburgnebraska.com/festival.asp

Terlingua International Chili Championship, Chili Appreciation Society International, Rancho CASI de los Chisos, Terlingua, TX. First weekend in November. Winners of CASI sanctioned cookoffs compete in the TICC International Chili Championship Cookoff; other competitions include wings, beans, and salsa.
http://www.chili.org/terlingua.html

Texas Folklife Festival, San Antonio, TX. Second weekend in June. Celebrates the heritage of over forty Texas ethnic groups with pioneer crafts demonstrations, entertainment, and Texas ethnic and regional foods.
http://www.texancultures.utsa.edu/tff/tff2006/index.html

Texas Rice Festival, Winnie, TX. Last weekend in September. Promotes Texas rice with livestock shows, farm equipment displays, competitions, music and dancing, exhibits, a parade, BBQ and fajita cook-offs, and rice cooking contest.
http://www.texasricefestival.org

Trigg County Ham Festival, Cadiz, KY. A weekend in October. Promotes Kentucky country hams with a ham judging and giveaway, a horse and mule pull, parade, the world's largest ham and biscuit sandwich, canning contest, and baking exhibit.
http://www.hamfestival.com

United Tribes International Powwow, Bismarck, ND. Weekend after Labor Day. A celebration of Native American culture with drumming, singing, and dancing competitions, traditional foods, and Sunday dinner, Native American–style.
http://www.unitedtribespowwow.com

Vidalia Onion Festival, Vidalia, GA. Last weekend in April. Promotes Georgia's sweet Vidalia onion industry with entertainment, an onion-eating contest, cooking demonstrations, and cooking contest.
http://www.vidaliaonionfestival.com/

Vintage Virginia Wine Festival, The Plains, VA. A weekend in June. Virginia's oldest and largest wine festival features 45 wineries pouring 350 selections, seminars, and cooking demonstrations.
http://www.atwproductions.com/vintageva/

Warrens Cranberry Festival, Warrens, WI. Third weekend in September. The Cranberry Capital of Wisconsin promotes its

crop with antique vendors, a flea market, farmers market, cranberry marsh tours, cranberry pie sales, cranberry foods, and cranberry recipe contest.
http://www.cranfest.com

West Virginia Black Walnut Festival, Spencer, WV. Second weekend in October. Promotes Spencer's black walnut crop with a parade, carnival, flea market, sports events, Civil War encampment, and the Black Walnut Bake-Off.
http://www.wvblackwalnutfestival.org

Wild Blueberry Festival, Machias, ME. Third weekend in August. Promotes Maine wild blueberries with sports events, quilts, a pie-eating contest, blueberry pancake breakfast, and blueberry dessert bar.
http://www.machiasblueberry.com

World Catfish Festival, Belzoni, MS. First or second Saturday in April. Promotes Humphreys County as the Catfish Capital of the World with music, arts and crafts, the South's Largest Catfish Fry, a catfish-eating contest, and celebrity chef's cook-off.
http://www.catfishcapitalonline.com

World Championship Barbecue Cooking Contest, Memphis, TN. Third weekend in May. Part of Memphis in May, this contest is billed as the "Superbowl of Swine" because the emphasis is on pork barbecue.
http://www.memphisinmay.org

World Chicken Festival, London, KY. Last weekend in September. Honors Colonel Sanders and Kentucky-style fried chicken

with parades, magic shows, rides, musical entertainment, a chicken wing–eating contest, and fried chicken dinners.
http://www.chickenfestival.com

World Grits Festival, St. George, SC. A weekend in April. Celebrates grits as southern heritage food with dancing, music, a parade and carnival, and contests, including a grits cooking competition.
http://www.worldgritsfestival.com/

BIBLIOGRAPHY

Carlson, Barbara. *Food Festivals: Eating Your Way from Coast to Coast.* Detroit, MI: Visible Ink Press, 1997.

Mercuri, Becky. *Food Festival U. S. A.: 250 Red, White and Blue Ribbon Recipes from All 50 States.* San Diego, CA: Laurel Glen Publishing, 2002.

BECKY MERCURI

Food Festivals

Food-Related Museums

These food and beverage museums or collections are only a small number of the total existing throughout the United States. They are listed in the following order: A. food and drink in general (alphabetized by state); B. specific foods; C. nonalcoholic beverages, brewed beverages, fermented products, and distilled spirits; and D. food containers.

I. Food and Drink in General

1. Copia, the American Center for Wine, Food, and the Arts, Napa Valley, CA; 707-257-3603; www.theamericancenter.org

An education center rather than a museum but with a curator of food; three half-acre outdoor gardens of organic edibles; and frequent exhibits on food and wine in its exhibit galleries. Galleries, classrooms, a rare book library, a theater for films and lectures, and a demonstration kitchen total eighty thousand square feet. Opened in November 2001; nonprofit with the American Institute of Wine and Food, the University of California at Davis, and Cornell University School of Restaurant and Hotel Administration as partners in its efforts.

2. Smithsonian Institution's National Museum of American History, Washington, DC; 202-357-2700; www.americanhistory.si.edu

Food-related objects are on view in almost every exhibition: agricultural implements from the eighteenth through the twentieth centuries; fishing industry objects; tableware of silver, ceramics, plastic, aluminum, earthenware, and glass belonging to presidents, ordinary citizens, and the Santa Fe Rail Road; small electrical appliances and large kitchen equipment; food containers from canning jars to rice-harvesting baskets and a grape crate; sections of the Stohlmann Confectionery, a 1902 Automat, and the Greensboro, North Carolina, lunch counter where the first civil rights sit-in took place; Julia Child's entire kitchen; mess kits for soldiers from George Washington to World War II fighters; the role of Americans in the battls for pure food and water; and the role of chemistry in developing saccharin and genetically engineered tomatoes. Not currently on exhibit, but available to see by appointment, are the museum's vast holdings in the collections of the Division of Cultural History, the Division of Social History, the Division of the History of Technology, and the Archives Center, with its collections of papers, photos, and other materials related to the production, packaging, and marketing of many foodstuffs, as well as the collections of the Wine History Project.

3. Farmers' Museum Inc., Cooperstown, NY; 888-547-1450; www.farmersmuseum.org

This living history museum's emphasis, with its heritage plants and breeds of livestock and more than 23,000 objects, is on mid-nineteenth-century upstate New York. The land has been farmed since 1813 when James Fenimore Cooper was its owner. The museum, with close links to the New York State Historical Association, is privately funded and nonprofit.

4. Culinary Archives and Museum at Johnson and Wales University, Providence, RI; 401-598-2805; www.culinary.org

Exhibits of the late chef Louis Szathmary's collection of food-related items from many parts of the world and from 3000 B.C.E. to the present, plus objects from other donors. Its more than 300,000 objects include cooking utensils and equipment, large and small appliances, menus, cookbooks, and a myriad of other culinary materials.

II. Specific Foods

1. Candy Americana Museum (Chocolate), Lititz, PA; 888-294-5287; Website not operational.

History, manufacturing, and advertising of candy; re-created 1900s candy kitchen, antique implements, molds, containers, and chocolate pot collection. Modern working candy kitchen.

2. Hershey Museum, Hershey, PA; 717-534-8940; www.hersheymuseum.org

A variety of exhibits, original working machinery, and unique artifacts relate the story of Milton Hershey, the candy empire he created, and the model town he founded. Old-time candy kitchen.

3. Mystic Seaport, Mystic, CT; 860-572-0711; mysticseaport.org

Oystering, lobstering, and salmon-fishing exhibits; fishing industry vessels and equipment.

4. Chesapeake Bay Maritime Museum, St. Michaels, MD; 410-745-2916; www.cbmm.org

Exhibits on oystering, crabbing, and extensive collection of seafood industry objects.

5. Mount Vernon Gristmill, Mount Vernon, VA; 703-780-2000; www.mountvernon.org

George Washington's 1771 gristmill: rebuilt stone mill with a working waterwheel.

6. Jell-O Gallery, LeRoy, NY; 585-768-7433; www.jellomuseum.com

History and technology of Jell-O in town where the product was invented in 1897. Permanent exhibition: "There's Always Room for Jell-O." Part of LeRoy Historical Society site.

7. Wyandot Popcorn Museum, Marion, OH, 740-387-4255; www.wyandotpopcornmus.com

Large collection of restored antique poppers, popcorn vending trucks, wagons, and carts.

8. Rice Museum, Georgetown, SC; 843-546-7423; www.ricemuseum.com

Rice culture in early South Carolina, a society based on one crop; dioramas, tools, equipment, maps, and graphics. In 1842 Old Market Building. Opened in 1970.

III. Beverages

1. World of Coca-Cola Atlanta, Atlanta, GA; 404-676-5151; www.woccatlanta.com

Coca-Cola's history from its 1886 beginnings, through exhibits featuring advertising, promotional, and packaging materials, especially from the 1950s onward; re-created 1930s soda fountain, ten-minute film, and self-guided tours.

2. Dr Pepper Free Museum and Free Enterprise Institute, Waco, TX; 817-757-1024; www.drpeppermuseum.com

Collection of objects in renovated original bottling plant of Dr Pepper; focused on the story of the entire soft drink industry; includes a functioning 1930s soda fountain. Opened 1991.

IV. Food Containers

1. Tupperware Museum of Historic Food Containers, Kissimmee, FL; 407-826-5050; www.Tupperware.com

Large collection of food containers, varying in size, shape, function, materials, and age, from a six thousand-year-old Egyptian jar to today's American plastics. At Tupperware headquarters.

SHIRLEY E. CHERKASKY

Food Periodicals

Art of Eating, The. 1986-. http://www.Artof Eating.com.

Bon Appetit. 1956-. http://www.bonappetit. com.

Chile Pepper. 1987-. http://www.chilepepper. com.

Chocolatier. 1984-. http://www.bakingshop. com/magazine/chocolatierhtm.

Cooking Light. 1986-. http://www.cooking light. com.

Cook's Illustrated. 1993-. http://www.cooksil-lustrated.com.

Cuisine. 2000. Name changed to *Cuisine at Home,* 2001.

Cuisine at Home. 2001-. http://www.cuisine. com.

Eating Well. 1980-. http://www.eatingwell. com.

Everyday Food. 2003-. http://www.everyday food. com.

Fiery Foods and Barbecue Magazine. 1997-. http://www.fieryfoods.com.

Fine Cooking. 1994-. http://www.taunton. com/finecooking.

Food and Wine. 1983-. http://www.foodand wine.com.

Food History News (newsletter). 1989-. http:// www.foodhistorynews.com.

Gastronomica. 2001-. http://www.gastronomica. com.

Gourmet. 1941-. http://www.gourmet.com.

Healthy Exchange Food (newsletter). 1992-. http://www.healthyexchanges.com.

Herb Quarterly. 1979-. http://www.herbquar-terly.com.

Light n' Tasty. 2001-. http://www.lightntasty. com.

Pasta. 2000-. http://www.inlandempiremaga-zine.com/pastafallo1.html.

Quick Cooking. 1998-. http://www.quickcoo-king.com. Also titled *Taste of Home's Quick Cooking'.*

Saveur. 1994-. http://www.saveur.com.

Simple Cooking. Newsletter. 1980-. http:// www.outlawcook.com.

Taste of Home. 1993-. http://www.tasteofhome. com.

Vegetarian Times. 1978-. http://www.vegetar-iantimes.com.

Veggie Life. 1993-. http://www.veggielife.com.

Weight Watchers. 1988-. http://www.weight-watchers.com/shop/h_sh_mag.asp.

Service Magazines

Backwoods Home. 1989-. http://www.back-woodshome.com.

Better Homes and Gardens. 1924-. http:// www.bhg.com.

Coastal Living. 1997-. http://www.coastalli-ving.com.

Country Living. 1980-. http://www.magazines. ivillage.com/countryliving.

Essence. 1970-. http://www.essence.com.

FDA Consumer. 1972-. http://www.fda.org.

Good Housekeeping. 1885-. http://www.good-housekeeping.com.

Health. 1981-. http://www.health.com.

Healthy Exchanges Food Newsletter. 1992-.

House Beautiful. 1896-. http://www.house-beautiful.com.

Ladies' Home Journal. 1883-. http://www.lhj. com.

Martha Stewart's Living. 2000-. http://www. marthastewart.com.

Midwest Living. 1987-. http://www.midwestli-ving.com.

New Mexico Magazine. 1974-. http://www.nmma-gazine.com.

Northwest Palate. 1998-. http://www.nwpalate. com.

Prevention. 1950-. http://www.prevention. com.

Real Simple. 2000-. http://www.realsimple. com.

Southern Living. 1966-. http://www.southern-living.com.

Sunset. 1898-. http://www.sunset.com.

Weight Watchers. 1988-. http://www.weight-watchers.com/shop/h_sh_mag.asp.

Wine Country Living. 2002-. http://www.wine-countryliving.com.

Woman's Day. 1937-. http://www.womans-day.com.

Working Woman. 1970-. http://www.working-woman.com.

Yankee Magazine. 1935-. http://www.Yankee-Magazine.com.

VIRGINIA K. BARTLETT

Food-Related Organizations

The first food-related society established in America was the Massachusetts Society for Promoting Agriculture. It was founded in Boston, Massachusetts, in 1792 with a charter membership of twenty-eight people. By 1820 membership had grown to over six hundred individuals, some from as far away as China. The organization's logo was "The Source of Wealth" set into a seal emblazoned with a yoke of oxen working a furrowed field. Ever since, professional dietitians, chefs, food technologists, and flavor chemists have formed professional societies to develop their skills, share information among their membership, and monitor high ethical standards within their profession.

Besides professional societies, a slew of marketing associations, focused on one particular food or product, developed during the twentieth century to promote the industry. Whether they go by the name of association, board, commission, or institute, their primary mission is to promote increased consumption of their particular agricultural product (such as potatoes, raisins, or walnuts) or processed food (such as biscuits or candy). Many of these trade associations are located close to where their product is harvested or manufactured. For example, the American Mushroom Institute is located in Pennsylvania, and the Cranberry Institute is in Massachusetts, places long associated with the production and marketing of these products. In recent years, trade associations have opened offices in or around Washington, DC, in order to lobby their interests before Congress and to interact with government agencies that monitor, evaluate, or regulate their industries.

This list of associations will serve as a valuable resource for students researching a particular product or industry. For writers, newspaper food editors, and journalists, these associations can open the door to experts in every facet of the food and culinary industry.

This list is divided into two sections: associations for professionals and trade associations.

Professional Associations

American Dietetic Association
120 S. Riverside Plaza, Ste. 2000
Chicago, IL 60606-6995
800-877-1600
http://www.eatright.org
In the early twenty-first century, the world's largest organization of food and nutrition specialists with nearly seventy thousand members.

American Institute of Wine and Food
304 W. Liberty St., Ste. 201
Louisville, KY 40202
502-992-1022
800-274-2493
F: 502-589-3602
http://www.aiwf.com
Educational organization devoted to improving the appreciation and understanding of food and drink.

American School Food Service Association
700 S. Washington St., Suite 300
Alexandria, VA 22314
703-739-3900
F: 703-739-3915
http://www.asfsa.org

Association of Food Journalists
38309 Genesee Lake Rd.
Oconomowoc, WI 53066
http://www.afjonline.com
Networking organization for journalists who devote most of their working time to planning and writing food copy for news media.

Institute of Food Technologists
525 W. Van Buren, Ste. 1000
Chicago, IL 60607
312-782-8424
F: 312-782-8348
http://www.ift.org
Membership includes researchers, academicians, regulators, scientists, and technologists in the food industry.

International Association of Culinary Professionals
304 W. Liberty St., Ste. 201
Louisville, KY 40202-3011
502-581-9786
F: 502-589-3602
http://www.iacp.com
Provides continuing education and development for members who are engaged in the areas of culinary education, communication, or preparation of food and drink.

Research Chefs Association
5775 Peachtree-Dunwoody Rd.
Bldg. G, Ste. 500
Atlanta, GA 30342
404-252-3663
F: 404-252-0774
http://www.culinology.com

Trade Associations

American Association of Meat Processors
P.O. Box 269
Elizabethtown, PA 17022
717-367-1168
F: 717-367-9096
http://www.aamp.com
North America's largest meat and poultry trade organization.

American Cheese Society
304 W. Liberty St., Ste. 201
Louisville, KY 40202
502-583-3783
F: 502-589-3602
http://www.cheesesociety.org
Upholds the traditions and preserves the history of American cheesemaking.

American Dairy Products Institute
116 N. York St.
Elmhurst, IL 60126
630-530-8700
F: 630-530-8707
http://www.americandairyproducts.com
http://www.adpi.org
Membership organization of manufacturers of evaporated and dry milks, cheese, and whey products.

American Egg Board
1460 Renaissance Dr.
Park Ridge, IL 60068
847-296-7043
F: 847-296-7007
http://www.aeb.org
Organization of egg producers to increase markets for eggs through promotion, research, and education.

American Meat Institute
1700 N. Moore St., Ste. 1600
Arlington, VA 22209
703-841-2400
F: 703-527-0938
http://www.meatami.com
Represents the interests of packers and processors of beef, pork, lamb, veal, and turkey products and their suppliers.

American Peanut Council
1500 King St., Ste. 301
Alexandria, VA 22314
http://www.peanutsusa.com
Forum for all segments of the peanut industry to discuss issues impacting the production, utilization, and marketing of peanuts.

American Spice Trade Association
2025 M St. NW, Ste. 800
Washington, DC 20036
202-367-1127
202-367-2127
http://www.astaspice.org
Founded in 1907 to serve members in over thirty-four spice-producing nations around the world.

Center for Science in the Public Interest
1875 Connecticut Ave. NW, Suite 300
Washington, DC 20009
202-332-9110
F: 202-265-4954
http://www.cspinet.org

Nutrition and food safety policy advocacy group.

Grocery Manufacturers of America
2401 Pennsylvania Ave. NW, 2nd Floor
Washington, DC 20037
202-337-9400
F: 202-337-4508
http://gmabrands.com
World's largest association of food, beverage, and consumer product companies.

Independent Bakers Association
1223 Potomac St. NW
Washington, DC 20007
202-333-8190
F: 202-337-3809
http://www.independentbaker.org
Association of over four hundred mostly family-owned wholesale bakeries and allied industry trades.

National Aquaculture Association
111 W. Washington St.
Charles Town, WV 25414-1529
304-728-2167
F: 304-876-2196
http://aqua.ucdavis.edu/organizations/organizations.NAA.html
Works with aquaculture community to create a U.S. infrastructure capable of supporting a profitable, competitive, and environmentally responsible industry.

National Association for the Specialty Food Trade
120 Wall St., 27th Floor
New York, NY 10005
212-482-6440
F: 212-482-6459
http://www.specialtyfood.com
Founded in 1952 to foster trade and interest in the specialty food industry. Publishes *Specialty Food* magazine.

National Association of Flavors and Food-Ingredient Systems
3301 Rte. 66, Ste. 205, Bldg. C
Neptune, NJ 07753
732-922-3218
F: 732-922-3590
http://www.naffs.org

National Cattlemen's Beef Association
9110 E. Nichols Ave., #300
Centennial, CO 80112
http://www.beef.org

National Chicken Council
1015 Fifteenth St. NW, Ste. 930
Washington, DC 20005-2622
202-296-2622
F: 202-293-4005
http://www.nationalchickencouncil.com
Represents companies that produce, process, and market 95 percent of the chickens and chicken products sold in the United States.

National Coffee Association of U.S.A.
15 Maiden Ln., Ste. 1405

New York, NY 10038
212-766-4007
F: 212-766-5815
http://www.ncausa.org
Founded in 1911 as the first trade association for the U.S. coffee industry.

National Confectioners Association
8320 Old Courthouse Rd., Ste. 300
Vienna, VA 22182
703-790-5750
F: 703-790-5752
http://www.candyusa.org

National Fisheries Institute
1901 N. Fort Myer Dr., Ste. 700
Arlington, VA 22209
703-524-8880
F: 703-524-4619
http://www.nfi.org

National Food Processors Association
1350 I Street NW, Ste. 300
Washington, DC 20005
202-639-5900
F: 202-639-5932
http://www.nfpa-food.org
Voice of the 500-billion-dollar food industry on scientific and public policy issues.

National Frozen and Refrigerated Foods Association
4755 Linglestown Rd., Ste. 300
Harrisburg, PA 17112
717-657-8601
F: 717-657-9862
http://www.nffa.org

National Grocers Association
1005 N. Glebe Rd., Ste. 250
Arlington, VA 22201-5758
703-516-0700
F: 703-516-0115
http://www.nationalgrocers.org

National Meat Association
1970 Broadway, Ste. 825
Oakland, CA 94612
510-763-1533
F: 510-763-6186
1400 16th St. NW, Ste. 400
Washington, DC 20036
202-667-2108
http://www.nmaonline.org
Association represents meatpackers and processors.

National Milk Producers Federation
2101 Wilson Blvd., Ste. 400
Arlington, VA 22201
703-243-6111
F: 703-841-9328
http://www.nmpf.org

National Restaurant Association
1200 Seventeenth St. NW
Washington, DC 20036-3097
202-331-5900
800-424-5156
F: 202-331-2429

http://www.restaurant.org
Represents and promotes the restaurant and hospitality industry.

National Soft Drink Association
1101 Sixteenth St. NW
Washington, DC 20036
202-463-6732
F: 202-463-8277
http://www.nsda.org
Founded in 1919 as the American Bottlers of Carbonated Beverages. Represents beverage manufacturers, distributors, and support industries.

Organic Trade Association
P.O. Box 547
Greenfield, MA 01302
413-774-7511
F: 413-774-6432
http://www.ota.com
Founded in 1985 to cultivate a strong organic industry.

Refrigerated Foods Association
2971 Flowers Rd. S, Ste. 266
Atlanta, GA 30341-9717
770-452-0660
F: 770-455-3879
http://www.refrigeratedfoods.org
Association of manufacturers and suppliers of refrigerated foods, such as wet salads, home meal replacement options, refrigerated entrées, desserts, ethnic foods, and side dishes.

Salt Institute
700 N. Fairfax St., Ste. 600
Fairfax Plaza
Alexandria, VA 22314-2040
703-549-4648
F: 703-548-2194
http://www.saltinstitute.org
Source of authoritative information about salt (sodium chloride) and its more than fourteen thousand known uses.

Seafood Choices Alliance
1731 Connecticut Ave. NW, Ste. 450
Washington, DC 20009
866-732-6673
http://www.seafoodchoices.com
Promotes sustainable seafood on the international level.

Snack Food Association
1711 King St., Ste. One
Alexandria, VA 22314
703-836-4500
F: 703-836-8262
http://www.sfa.org

Sugar Association
1101 Fifteenth St. NW, Ste. 600
Washington, DC 20005
202-785-1122
F: 202-785-5019
http://www.sugar.org

JOSEPH M. CARLIN

Food Websites

Long before there was a World Wide Web, the Internet was already a major gathering place for food information. Listervs, Usenet, telnet, gopher sites, and bulletin boards were filled with recipes, and dozens of databases of food information were available by subscription. The Web has become the dominant form of Internet publishing, and thousands upon thousands of websites are dedicated to food—and not just recipe and commercial sites either.

This small, and by no means comprehensive, appendix deals only with American food, but with an even narrower focus. Most of these sites are at least partially historical in nature, although some manage to convey their historical information in a casual fashion. The web is, however, a very fluid and changeable place, and many of the sites listed may have already moved or morphed into something else by the time this book goes to press. There is little that can be done to avoid that, but sometimes a little judicious searching, through whatever search engine is most effective at the time, can discover the new location of these peripatetic sites.

American Indian Ethnobotany Database
http://www.umd.umich.edu/cgi-bin/herb

The Boston Cooking-School Cook Book (text of Fannie Farmer's 1918 edition)
http://www.bartleby.com/87

The Boston Cooking-School Magazine: The First Seven Volumes, 1896–1902
http://students.washington.edu/bparris/bcsm.html

The Civil War Cookbook
http://www.civilwarinteractive.com/cookbook.htm

Coca-Cola Advertisements
http://memory.loc.gov/ammem/ccmphtml/colahome.html

Common Sense in the Household: A Manual of Practical Housewifery (Marion Harland's 1872 book)
http://www.hti.umich.edu/cgi/t/text/text-idx?c=moa;idno=AEL7637

A Complete Guide to Cooking in the Civil War Era
http://www.civilwarinteractive.com/cookbook.htm

Cookery Collection
http://www.lib.msu.edu//coll/main/spec_col/cookery

The Culinary Collection
http://www.tulane.edu/~wc/text/culinary.html

Culinary History: A Research Guide
http://www.nypl.org/research/chss/grd/resguides/culryla.html

Emergence of Advertising in America: 1850–1920
http://scriptorium.lib.duke.edu/eaa

Feeding America: The Historic American Cookbook Project
http://digital.lib.msu.edu/cookbooks

Food and Drug Administration (FDA) Center for Food Safety and Applied Nutrition
http://www.foodsafety.gov/list.html

Food and Nutrition Publications
http://extension.usu.edu/publica/foodpubs.htm

Food Dictionaries
http://www.1000dictionaries.com/food_dictionaries_1.html

Food History News
http://foodhistorynews.com

Food History Yellow Pages
http://foodhistorynews.com/linkmain.html

The Food Museum
http://www.foodmuseum.com

Food Network
http://www.foodtv.com

The Food Reference Website
http://www.foodreference.com

Food Review
http://www.ers.usda.gov/publications/foodreview/archives

Food Timeline
http://www.gti.net/mocolib1/kid/food.html

Gallery of Regrettable Food (food advertisements from the 1950s and 1960s)
http://www.lileks.com/institute/gallery

A Guide to Pillsbury Cookbooks and Premiums 1869–1969
http://www.friktech.com/pills/pills1.htm

Hardtack
http://www.kenanderson.net/hardtack/index.html

Healthy School Meals
http://schoolmeals.nalusda.gov:8001

History Notes
http://www.gti.net/mocolib1/kid/foodfaq3.html

History of Household Technology
http://www.loc.gov/rr/scitech/tracer-bullets/householdtb.html

The History of Rations
http://www.qmfound.com/history_of_rations.htm

The Inglenook Cook Book
http://www.foodreference.com/html/recipe-singlenookcookbook.html

Institute of Food Science and Technology (IFST)
http://www.easynet.co.uk/ifst

The International Federation of Competitive Eaters (IFOCE)
http://www.ifoce.com

It's Spam
http://www.SPAM.com

Jell-O Museum Web Site
http://www.jellomuseum.com

Key Ingredients-Smithsonian Institution
www.museumsonmainstreet.org

also
http://www.MOMA/KI.asp

The Kitchen—History of Kitchen Appliances
http://inventors.about.com/library/inventors/blkitchen.htm

The Magic of Fire (hearth cookery)
http://www.williamrubel.com

Making of America
http://moa.umdl.umich.edu

Manuscript Collections—Agricultural Technology to Viticulture and Enology
http://www.lib.ucdavis.edu/specol/html/manu_idx.html

Moonpie.com
http://moonpie.com

The Moxie Collectors Page
http://www.xensei.com/users/iraseski

Newspaper Food Columns Online
http://www.recipelink.com/newspapers.html

Not by Bread Alone
http://rmc.library.cornell.edu/food/default.htm

Nutrition and Food Science Links
http://www.science.wayne.edu/~nfs/nfslinks.htm

Pennsylvania Dutch Life, Tales, and Cooking
http://midatlantic.rootsweb.com/padutch/life.html

Peppers: History and Exploitation of a Serendipitous New Crop Discovery
http://www.hort.perdue.edu/newcrop/proceedings1993/v2-132.html

Professional Cooking Schools
http://www.sallys-place.com/food/chefs-corner/schools_pro_usa.htm

Professional Food Organizations
http://www.sallys-place.com/food/chefs-corner/organizations.htm

Records of the Food and Drug Administration
http://www.archives.gov/research_room/federal_records_guide/food_and_drug_administration_rg088.html

Salt Institute
http://www.saltinstitute.org

Southern Foodways Alliance (SFA)
http://www.southernfoodways.com

Special Collections in the Library of Congress: Joseph and Elizabeth Robins Pennell Collection
http://lcweb.loc.gov/spcoll/183.html

USDA Food Composition Data
http://www.nal.usda.gov/fnic/foodcomp/Data

BIBLIOGRAPHY

Allen, Gary. *The Resource Guide for Food Writers.* New York: Routledge, 1999

GARY ALLEN

Index

Page numbers in **boldface** refer to the main entry on the subject. Page numbers in *italics* refer to illustrations, figures, and tables.

A&P, 265, 266, 450
A&W, 1, 640
A&W Root Beer, 234
A&W Root Beer Stands, **1**
abalone, **1**
Abell, L. B., 576
abolitionism
    and sugar beets, 116
    and temperance movements, 12
Absolut vodka, 259
ABZ of Human Nutrition (Fletcher), 225
Acadians, 81–82
Accomplished Cook, The (May), 237, 483
acesulfame-K, 574
Achard, Franz Karl, 572
achiote, 482
Acme Can Company, 60
Adams, Leon, 633
Adams, Ramon, 540
Adams, Thomas, 267
Adams Confectionary, 80
A Date with a Dish (De Knight), 152
additives. *See* chemical additives; flavor additives; food additives
Ade, George, 152
ades, 245
Adlum, John, 633
adobo, 177, 482
adulteration, **1–2**, 228. *See also* contamination; Pure Food and Drug Act
    beef, 485
    bread, 64, 262
    butter, 227
    candy, 89
    canned and bottled foods, 93
    chocolate, 122
    coffee, 23, 139
    fertilizer industry, 485
    ground meat, 271
    laws against, 353
    milk, 387
    in mixes, 109
    of moonshine, 394
    near beer, 479
    powdered milk, 388
    whiskey, 266
Adventures in Good Eating (Hines), 497, 520
advertising, **2–5**, 287, 290. *See also* advertising cookbooklets and recipes; advertising icons; jingles
    baby food, 5
    Beech-Nut, *41*, 42
    Bloody Mary, 56
    breakfast cereals, 2, 4, 102, 255
    Campbell Kids, 88
    Campbell's, 87, 88–89
    candy and candy bars 32, 77, 261, 451, 496, 5, 545
    children as target of, 5, 7, 102, 173, 507–8, 591
    coffee, 23, 137, 138, 227, 369, 410

in community cookbooks, 143
    Cracker Jack, 173
    Crisco, 176, 231
    Dunkin' Donuts, 201
    fast food, 325, 579
    food festivals, 228–29
    Fritos, 240
    Good Humor man, 262
    and government, 5
    health claims, 4
    H. J. Heinz Company, 298
    Horn and Hardart Automat, 28
    Hostess, 302–3
    Hunt Foods, 308
    illustrators, 42, 47, 134, 328, 395, 487, 493
    industrial promotion films, 186
    Jell-O, 328
    Karo Syrup, 339
    Keebler, 339–40
    ketchup, 186
    Klondike Bar, 347
    Kraft, 349, 370
    Lipton dips, 195
    Lipton Tea, 4
    magazine, 448–49
    Manischewitz, 369
    as marketing tool, 231
    Miller Lite Beer, 390
    movie tie-ins, 497
    Nabisco, 401
    Orville Redenbacher's Gourmet Popping Corn, 496
    Oscar Mayer, 304, 428
    Ovaltine, 5
    Pillsbury, 459–60
    print, 2, 5, 6, 231
    Quaker Oats Company, 487
    radio, 5, 28
    radio and television, 231
    and sex, 5
    Smirnoff, 612
    soda drinks, *134*, 140, 448, 197, 292, 394, 508, 534, 546
    Spam, 559
    sponsorship, 5
    spot ads, 5
    television, 5, 28
    television, Budweiser, 73
    Uneeda biscuits, 173
    and vitamins, 4
    wine coolers, 634
    women, targeted to, 4–5
    Wonder Bread, 65
advertising cookbooklets and recipes, **5–8**, 149. *See also* advertising; cookbooks and manuscripts
    Agate Iron Ware, 6
    Appalachian food, *17*
    avocados, 28, *29*, 195
    bananas, *34*
    Betty Crocker, 117
    blenders, 55
    cakes, *84*, *85*
    Campbell Soup Company, 88
    canapé, *19*
    cauliflower, 98
    and children, 7, 117
    and cookery equipment, 6
    Crisco, 176
    Del Monte, 186
    distribution, 7–8
    Fairbanks Company, 6
    Farmer, Fannie, 6–7
    Franklin Baker Company, *135*
    Genesee Pure Food Company, 6
    Granit Iron Ware, 6
    Hunt Foods, 308
    ingredient-based, 6–7
    Jell-O, 6, 328
    Karo Syrup, 339

    Kraft, *84*
    Liebig Company, 6
    Marvelli Company, 6
    patent medicine, 6
    Perfection Stove Company, 6
    Pillsbury Company, 117
    pineapple industry, 460–61
    product, 6
    Rorer, Sarah Tyson, 6
    R.T. French Company, 398
    Shredded Wheat Company, 6
    Sun-Maid raisins, *85*
    tuna, 596
    vanilla, 604
    Walter Baker and Company, 435
    Westinghouse, 117
advertising icons, 26
    Aunt Cora, 369
    Aunt Jemima, 5, 7, 26–28
    Betty Crocker, 7, 47, 117, 255, 392, 489
    Campbell Kids, 88–89
    Captain Midnight, 5
    Colonel Sanders, 520–21
    Elsie the Cow, 58, 59
    Gerber Baby, 31
    Jolly Green Giant, 336–37
    Keebler Elves, 339–40
    La Belle Chocolatiere, 5
    Marlboro Man, 337
    Mr. Peanut, 395
    Mrs. Olson, 227
    Pillsbury Doughboy, 458, 459–60
    Quaker Oats man, 7, 487
    Rastus, 493
    Ronald McDonald, 337, 371, 507–8
    Snap! Crackle! Pop!, 341
    Snapple lady, 545
    Thomas, Dave, 619
    Tony the Tiger, 5, 341
    Toucan Sam, 341
    Uncle Ben, 601
A. E. Staley Manufacturing Company, 170, 218
AFC Enterprises, 128–29, 471
Afghan food. *See* central Asian food
afikoman, 436
African American cooks, 8–10, 87, 111
African American food, **8–11**, 82, 87, 311, 352, 482, 554
    Chesapeake region, 111
    chicken, 475
    chitterlings, 122
    to the Civil War, **8–10**
    cookbooks, 143, 147, 151, 152, 153, 154, 179
    coush-coush, 171
    cowpeas, 171–72
    desserts, 188
    development in America, 8–11
    dietary reform, 11
    ethnic revival, 10–11
    fried chicken, 239
    hush puppies, 309
    Kwanzaa, 349–50
    in literature, 359–60
    Natchitoches meat pies, 401
    New Year's celebrations, 413–14
    origins in Africa, 8
    picnics, 454
    since Emancipation, **10–11**
    tribal foods, 8
    watermelon, 616
    weddings, 618
African-American Kitchen, The: Cooking from Our Heritage (Medearis), 454
afternoon tea, 583
Agate Iron Ware, 6
agave, 585
agribusiness
    Archer Daniels Midland, 23–24
    Armour, 24
    concerns about, 216, 278

Agricultural Adjustment Act, 214
agricultural exports, 319–20
agricultural workers, 213–14
agriculture. *See also* family farms; fruit; organic
    farming; sustainable agriculture
    aquaculture, 22, 239
    California, 85–86
    community-supported, 143–44
    concerns about, 22, 170–71, 216
    dairy industry, 182–84
    government policies, 214
    Pacific Northwest, 431
Agriculture, Department of. *See* Department of
    Agriculture, United States
Agriculture, Food and Human Values Society,
    179
Agrilink Foods, 51
agrobiotechnology companies, 49
aguduk, 12
Ahwahnee Hotel, 127
aioli, 369
airan, 101
airplane food, **11**
Airy Fairy cake mix, 23
akara, 85
Aken, Norman Van, 248
Alaska, **11–12**, 33
    Russian influences, 12
    whale meat and whale oil, 619
Alaska Florida, 33, 492
Alaska king crab, 172
albacore. *See* tuna
Albala, Ken, 297
Albius, Edmond, 603
alcohol and teetotalism, **12–13**. *See also*
    temperance
Alcohol Dependence Syndrome. *See* alcoholism
alcoholic beverages. *See also* cider, hard; cocktails
    applejack, 19–20
    barley wine ale, 36
    beer, 12, 14, 15, 36, 42–43, 44–45, 71, 357–58,
      361, 368, 433, 460, 475–76, 560–61, 563. *See*
      also breweries
    bitters, 526
    brandy, 12, 19, 20, 52, 61, 62–63, 110, 195,
      305
    brunch, 373
    Civil War, 286
    in colonial America, 282, 411
    cordials, 167
    from fruit juices, 245
    gin, 258–59, 540
    hot drinks, 320
    kvass, 349
    moonshine, 394, 621
    perry, 442
    punch, 484
    rum, 195, 266, 305, 392, 510–11
    sangria, 522
    tequila, 585–86
    toddy, 136
    vermouth, 610
    vodka, 512, 612
    whiskey, 60–62, 195, 258, 305, 390, 423, 526,
      620–21
    wine, 103–4, 245, 535, 626–31
    wine coolers, 634
Alcoholics Anonymous, 13, 14
alcoholism, **13–14**
    treatment for, 14
Alcott, Bronson, 16, 263, 608
Alcott, Louisa May, 20, 453–54
Alcott, William, 144, 147, 608
Alderton, Charles, 197
ale, brown, 71
ale boot, 14
ale slipper, **14**
Aleuts, 12
alewives, 223, 265
Alexander, Jason, 520

Alexander cocktail. *See* brandy Alexander
Alford, Jeffrey, 155
Alice's Restaurant Cookbook, The (Brock), 153
All about Coffee (Ukers), 23
All-Bran, 4, 102, 340
Allen, Ida Bailey, 151, 152, 489
Allen, Lucy, 163, 194
Allen, Roy, 1
Allied Domecq, 201
Allied Lyons, 201
allspice, 575
Alluring Avocado, The: Recipes Hot and Cold (Hicks
    and Thompson), 29
almanacs, 149
Almond Joy, 89, 451
almonds, **14**
Alphabet for Gourmets (Fisher), 224
Alpine Confections, 213
Amadama bread. *See* Anadama bread
amber lager, **14**, 15
amber red ale, **15**
Amelung, John Frederick, 260
America Eats (Weaver), 247, 493
American Airlines, 11
American and His Food, The (Cummings), 296–97
American Automobile Association travel guides,
    497–98
American Beverage Corporation, 196
American Breakfast Cereals, *102*
American Can Company, 45, 60
American Center for Wine, Food, and the Arts,
    625
American cheese, 105, 272, 460
American Chestnut Foundation, 542
American chop suey, **15**
American Cookery (Beard), 71
American Cookery (magazine), 449
American Cookery (Simmons), 538–39
    apple pie, 20
    on asparagus, 26
    baked custard recipe, 494
    on beets, 572
    on blackfish, 55
    on carrots, 95
    on chicken, 113
    on cookies, 156
    on cucumbers, 178
    on dressing turtles, 551
    on geese, 262
    mock foods, 392
    on pumpkin pie, 483
    on pumpkin pudding, 481
    on radishes, 491; recipe for Election Cake, 207
    on turkey, 598
    on vegetables, 605
    and Wilson, Mary Tolford, 626
American Cooking (Brown), 153
American Culinary Federation, 163, 294, 498
American Federation of Labor (AFL), 213–14,
    499
American Food: The Gastronomic Story (Jones), 154
American Frugal Housewife, The (Child, L.), 502
    on cucumbers, 178
American Gardener's Calendar, The (M'Mahon), 100,
    178
American Glucose Company, 170
American Health (magazine), 450
American Home Economics Association, 299, 300,
    435, 504
American Institute of Wine and Food, 116, 294
American Issue Publishing Company, 585
American Licorice Company, 356
American Personal Chef Association, 294
American plan, 304, 499
American Poulterer's Companion (Bement), 113
American Regional Cookery (Hibben), 152
American Safety Razor Company, 529
American Society of Enologists, 630
American Style Amber Lager, 15
American Temperance Society, 479, 584

American Temperance Union, 584
American Vegan Society, 604
American Vegetarian Party, 609
American Vegetarian Society, 275, 608
American Wines (Schoonmaker and Marvel), 633
American Wines and How to Make Them (Wagner),
    633
American Wine Society, 630
American Woman's Cook Book (Berolzheimer),
    151
American Woman's Home, The (Beecher), 41, 180,
    345
America's Cook Book, 151
America's First Cuisines (Coe), 39, 179
America's Founding Food (Stavely and Fitzgerald),
    318
Amerine, Maynard, 633
Amici's East Coast Pizzeria, 464
Amish foods, 159, 445, 624, 640. *See also*
    Pennsylvania Dutch food
Among Friends (Fisher), 224
Amos, Wally, 156, 213
Ams, Charles M., 92, 368
Amtrak, 192
amusement parks, **15–16**
Anadama bread, **16**
Anaya, Ignacio "Nacho", 209–10, 544
Anchor Bar, 74
Anchor Brewing Company, 44
Anchor Steam Brewery, 379
anchos, 117
anchovies, **16**, 200, 223, 226
Anderson, Abraham, 87
Anderson, Alexander P., 102, 503
Anderson, Fred W., 440
Anderson, Harry, 493
Anderson, Jay, 280
Anderson, Jean, 154
Anderson, Walter, 216, 271, 622
Andoh, Elizabeth, 154
Andreas, Dwayne, 23–24
Andreas, Lowell, 23–24
angel cake, 84
Angell, Floyd, 542
angel pies, 438
Anglo-Swiss Condensed Milk Company, 411
Angostura bitters, 135
Anheuser, Eberhard, 73
Anheuser-Busch, 43, 390
    Budweiser, 73
anhydration, 51
Animal Crackers, 156
Animal Liberation (Singer), 16–17
animal rights, **16–17**
    and veganism, 604
animals. *See also* meat
    buffalo, 73–74
    butchering, 75–76
anise, 435
Annales school, 297
anorexia nervosa, 204
antipasto, 19
Anti-Saloon League, 479, 584–85
Antoine's (New Orleans), 500
Appalachian food, **17–18**, 491
Appert, Nicolas, 54, 91
*Appetite for Change: How the Counterculture Took on
    the Food Industry* (Belasco), 171, 179
appetizers, **18–19**
    Buffalo chicken wings, 74
    canapé, 89
    celery, 100
    clams casino, 133
    deep-fried, 553
    hummus, 115
    Indian, 316, 317
    Japanese, 318
    Melba toast, 440
    nachos, 210
    partridge eggs, 436

pickled foods, 452
savory pies, 438
shrimp cocktail, 536
Stilton cheese, 106
Swedish meatballs, 527
Appetizing; or, The Art of Canning (Bitting, A.), 54
Appledore Cook Book (Parloa), 434
Bangor Cake, 72
applejack, **19–20**
Applejack: The Spirit of Americana, 20
apple parer, *20*
apple pie, **20**
mock apple pie, 20, 391
apples, 20, **21–22**, 243, 381, 487. *See also* applejack;
cider
apple-preparation tools, **20–21**
food festivals, 230
and Halloween, 270
Johnny Appleseed, 334–35
Midwestern, 384–85
in New England, 411
in Pacific Northwest, 431
Red Delicious, 21
varieties, 21–22
Appleseed, Johnny. *See* Johnny Appleseed
appliances, electric. *See* electric appliances
approved vinicultural areas, 104, 631
apricots, **22**
aquaculture, **22**
carp, 94
catfish, 97
environmental concerns, 22
freshwater, 239
salmon, 22
shrimp, 22
Arab American food. *See* Middle Eastern
influences on American food
Arbuckle, John, 23
Arbuckles', **23**, 136
Arby's, **23**, 217
Archer Daniels Midland, **23–24**
Archibald, H. Teller, 213
Archibald Candy Corp., 213
Architecture, 28, 199
Argyle sparklers, 104
Ariosa coffee, 23, *86*, 136
Arizona cookery, 557. *See also* Southwestern
regional cookery
Arkell, Bartlett, 41, 42
Ark of Taste, 542
Armour, 76, 144, 304, 447, 514, 577, 611
advertising, *24*
lard, 353
Armour, Philip Danforth, **24–25**, 75
Arnaud's (New Orleans), 82
Arnold Bread Company, 16
aromas, 70
Art culinaire (magazine), 417
Arthur, President, 624
Arthur Bryant's barbecue, 384
Arthur Treacher's Fish & Chips, 224, 402, 619
Artichoke Cookbook , The (Rain), 25
artichokes, **25**
food festivals, 230
artificial sweeteners, 361, 571, 574
in gum, 267
and soda drinks, 546
artisanally produced foods, 33, 105
baked goods, 33, 66, 434, 640
cheese, 105–6, 107, 394
chocolates, 123–24
pretzels, 478
and Terra Madre, 542–43
Art of Cheese-Making, The (Johnson), 149
Art of Confectionary, The, 151
Art of Cookery Made Plain and Easy, The (Glasse),
237
broccoli, 70–71
eel pie recipe, 494
on fricassee, 239

on oats, 421
pastry recipes, 438
on raising mushrooms, 396
on turnips, 599
Art of Eating, 498
Art of Food Photography, The (Custer), 320
Art of German Cooking and Baking (Meier), 257
Art of Good Living (Simon), 152
Art of Preserving (Appert), 91
ascorbic acid, 612
aseptic packaging, **25**
ketchup, 342
milk, 388
ashcakes, 18, 67
ash cooking, 276
Asian Americans, 639. *See also* individual cuisines
cookbooks, 154–55
frontier, 242
Asian pears, 443
asparagus, **25–26**
aspartame, 571, 574
aspic, 383
Association for Living History, Farm and
Agricultural Museums (ALHFAM), 280, 294,
297
Association for the Study of Food and Society,
179
Association of Brewers, 380
Association of Brewers' 2004 Beer Style
Guidelines, 14, 15, 36, 71, 358, 361, 368, 433,
460, 476, 568
Astor House, 499
Astor House (New York), 304
Atha, Frank, 227
Athabascans, 12
At Home on the Range, 143
Atkins, Robert C., 275
Atkins diet, *231*, 275
Atkinson, George Francis, 397
atole, 317, 461
Atwater, Wilbur O., 418
Atwood, Margaret, 359
aubergine. *See* eggplants
Audot, Louis, 149, 238
Audrieth, Ludwig, 574
Audubon, John James, 436
Augustin, Peter, 94
Aunt Cora, 369
Aunt Jemima, 5, 7, **26–28**
Aunt Jemima Pancake Mix, 5, 26, 27, 28, 69, 433
Aunt Sammy, 489
Aunt Sammy's Radio Recipes, 152
Auster, Louis, 205
Authentic Mexican (Bayless and Bayless), 38, 154
automats, **28**, 80, 137, 500, 609
avena, **28**
avocados, **28–29**
advertising cookbooklets and recipes, 7, 28, *29*,
195
Axene, Harry, 184, 234, 581

Babcock, Orville E., 61
Babcock test, 182
Babe Ruth Home Run Bar, 32
babka, 331
baby food, 5, **31**, 42. *See also* infant formula
Baby Ruth, **31–32**
Bacardi, 511
Back to the Table: The Reunion of Food and Family
(Smith), 155
bacon, 376
bagels, **32**, 48, 69, 176
Bagels and Yox, 32
Baggies, 464
baked Alaska, **33**, 492
baked beans, 39, 411
baked goods, 33, 65. *See also* bread; cakes
bran muffins, 63
and corn syrup, 170
croissants, 65

crullers, 176–77
pastries, 437–39
prepackaged, 447, 581–82
Baker, Franklin, 136
Baker, Harry, 84
Baker, James, 122, 124
Baker, Walter, 122
bakeries, **33**, 64, 66
artisanal, **33**
emergence of commercial, 289
Pepperidge Farm, 447
Tastykake, 581–82
Baker's chocolate, 189, 472
Baker's Weekly Recipes, 72
baker's yeast, 73, 639
bakeware. *See* pots and pans
baking. *See also* baked goods; bakeries; home
baking
bread-making tools, 67
Scandinavian and Finnish American food, 527
yeast, 639–40
baking powder, 13, 64, 109–10. *See also* chemical
leavening
baking soda, 109
Baldassare, Angelo, 55, 569
Baldwin, Jerry, 562
Ballard and Ballard Flour, 458
bananas, **33–35**
advertising cookbooklets and recipes, *34*
banana bread, 35
banana pudding, 35
genetically modified, 49
puree, 35
banana split, 35
Bangor Brownies, 71–72
Bangor Cake, 72
bannocks, 337
Banquet Foods Company, 144
baozi, 121
barbacoa, 35
barbecue, **35–36**, 165, 384, 505–6
contests, 158–59
Fourth of July, 234
grills, 165, 253
Midwestern, 385
political feasts, 142
Barber, Benjamin, 371
bar code scanners, 266
barding, 165
barley, **36**, 70
barley bread, 66
barley wine ale, **36**
Barlow, Arthur, 317
Barr, Terry, 220
barrel pork, 375, 376
barrels and kegs, 146
applejack, 19
beer, 45
cracker barrel, 401
whiskey, 621, 633
wine barrels, 632–33
wine casks, 633–34
bars and drinking establishments, **36–37**, *43*,
516–17, 582
bar food, 37, 74
juice bars, 245, 337–38
oyster bars, 429
salad bars, 514
Basic Four, 419
Basic Seven, 291, 419
basil, 390
baskets, 146
Native American, 408, 409
Baskin, Burt, 37
Baskin-Robbins, 37
Basques, 311
bass, **37–38**
Bastianic, Lidia Matticchio, 490
Bastianovich, Lidia, 255
Bates, Caroline, 498

batidos, **38**
Battiscombe, Georgina, 453
Battle Creek, Michigan, 102, 190, 275
Battle Creek Sanitarium, 340, 472
Battle Creek Toasted Corn Flake Company, 102, 275, 340
Bauer, Phillip, 581
Baum, Joe, 500
Bavarian creams, 176
bay leaves, 575
Bayless, Rick, **38–39**, 154
Bazore, Katherine, 152
Beach, Donn, 363, 641
Beach, Rex, 12
beans, 8, 9, 17, **39**, 57. *See also* baked beans; legumes; peas; soybeans
    adzuki, 274
    African American food, 8, 9
    in Alaska gold rush, 12
    and barbecue, 35, 292
    black, 178, 210
    as boardinghouse food, 57
    in Brunswick stew, 72
    in burritos, 75
    in Chesapeake diet, 111
    chickpeas, 115
    in chili, 118, 128, 378
    in *cholent*, 331
    in colonial America, 411
    combat food, 141, 241, 283, 285
    and counterculture, 171
    cowpeas, 85, 171–72
    in dips, 195
    dried, with savory, 390
    fava, 435
    in fireless cookers, 221
    frontier cooking, 241
    green, 97, 293
    in Iberian and South American food, 311
    in Italian cooking, 295
    in jambalaya, 81
    in kitchen gardens, 343
    lima, 391, 392, 552, 569
    and Mexican American foods, 379
    in Native American diet, 402, 405, 408, 605
    and nitrogen fixation, 49
    overnight beans, 202
    pioneer food, 241, 462
    red beans and rice, 503
    refried, 69, 210, 410
    shell 569, 570
    as ship food, 535
    slang, 141, 540, 541
    in Southern regional cookery, 554, 556
    in southwestern cooking, 295
    in succotash, 209, 302, 569–70
    and tamales, 581
bear, 252
Beard, James, **40**, *99*
    and Alice Waters, 86, 616
    on boardinghouses, 57
    cookbooks and food writing, 89, 152, 154, 498
    on Denver sandwich, 187
    and garlic, 253
    and Helen Evans Brown, 71
    picnics, 454
    TV cooking show, 98–99, 490
Beatrice, **40–41**, 76, 144, 349
Beaulieu Vineyards, 628
Beaumont, William, 418
Beck, Simone, 116
Becker, Ethan, 507
Becker, Marion Rombauer, 155, 507, 610
Bed-Book of Eating and Drinking (Wright), 152
Beebe, Lucius, 55–56, 497, 498
Beecher, Catharine, 12, **41**, 180, 194, 254, 345, 524
Beech-Nut, **41–42**, 357
    advertising, *41*, 42
    baby food, 31, 42
beef, 375. *See also* hamburger.

adulteration, 485
    bully beef, 74
    chicken fried steak, 114
    chipped, 122
    Cincinnati chili, 129–30
    corned, 169, 513
    European Union ban, 214
    ground beef, 292, 542, 622
    pastrami, 437
beef Stroganoff, 103, 292, 511, 512
beer, 12, 36, **42–44**, 71, 368. *See also* breweries; microbreweries
    ale, brown, 71
    amber lager, **14**, 15
    amber red ale, **14–15**
    barley, 36
    barley wine ale, 36
    barrels, **45**
    boilermaker, 58
    bottling, 60
    brewing, 42, 70
    Budweiser, 73
    cans, **45**, 166
    corn, **44–45**
    drinking songs, 197–98
    early American, 42–43, 44
    light beers, 357–58, 361
    light lager, 357–58
    maple, **44–45**
    Märzen/Oktoberfest, 368
    mugs, **46**
    pale ale, 433
    pilsener, 460
    porter, 563
    premium lager, 475–76
    spruce beer, 560–61
    stout, 563
    Vienna style, 14
    and yeast, 639, 640
beer gardens, 16, **45**, 46
beer halls, **45–46**. *See also* bistros
beetles, 472
beets, sugar. *See* sugar beets
Behr, Ed, 498
beignets, 69
Beijing food, 121–22
Belasco, Warren, 171, 179
Bell, Glen, 86, 579, 625
Bell, Martha, 625
Bell, William G., 476
Belle tablets, 301
Bellissimo, Teressa, 74
Bell's Seasoning, 476
Ben & Jerry's, **46–47**
Benedictine, 167
Benihana, 294
Bennett, John William, 233
Benny, Jack, 328
Bent, Josiah, 173
Bent Company, 173
Bentley, Amy, 179
Bent's water crackers, 173
Beranbaum, Rose Levy, 85
Bergen, Polly, 140
Bergeron, Ken, 416, 605
Bergeron, Victor, 363, 366, 641
Berghoff Brewing Company, 45
Berkshire Hathaway, 184, 532
Berlanga, Friar Tomas de, 34
Berney's Mystery of Living, 449
Berolzheimer, Ruth, 151
berries, 180
    blackberries, 54–55
    blueberries, 56
    cranberries, 174
    in Pacific Northwest, 431
    raspberries, 492–93
    strawberries, 566–67
Berry, Riley M. Fletcher, 460
Berry, Rynn, 416

Berta, 586
Bertha, Doña, 366
Bertholle, 116
Berwick Cake Company, 624
Best, Frederick Charles, 389
Best Foods mayonnaise, 370
Better Homes and Gardens (magazine), 450
Better Homes and Gardens Cookbook, The, 154
betties, 438
Betty Crocker, 7, 47, 117, 255, 392, 489
Betty Crocker Cooking School of the Air, 47
beverages. *See also* alcoholic beverages; milkshakes, malts and floats; phosphates; punch; soda drinks
    bubble tea, 72–73
    chocolate, 122
    coffee, 136–38
    and cream, 175
    iced tea, 582–83
    lemonade, 354–55
    pinole, 461–62
    post-Revolutionary War food, 284
    switchel, 576
    syllabub, 576
    Tang, 581
    tea, 582–83
    water, bottled, 615
Beverages and Sandwiches (Bradley), 521
Beverley, Robert, 406, 408, 409
Bhagwandin, Annie, 420
bialy, **48**, 331
Biardot, Alphonse, 551
Bible Christian Church, 607–8
bicarbonate of soda, 64, 65
bierocks, **48**
Big Boy, **50–51**, 86, 216, 271, 398
bigos, 468
Billings, C. K. G., *193*
Bill Neal's Southern Cooking, 154
Biltmore Estate Brut, 104
binge-eating disorder, 204
biodiversity. *See* Foundation of Biodiversity; heirloom vegetables
bioproducts, 23
biotechnology, **48–50**, 182, 278
birch beer, **51**, 523
Birds Eye, 51, 236, 242, 472
Birdseye, Clarence, 11, **51**, 236, 242, 606
Birdseye Corporation, **51**
Birdseye Seafood Company, 51
birthday cake, 52–53
birthday pudding, 41
birthdays, **51–53**
biscochos, 32
biscuits, 69
    biscuit cutters, **53**
bison. *See* buffalo
Bisquick, 7, 69, 192
bistros, **53–54**
bitters, 135, 364, 367–68, 423, 526
Bitting, Arvil, 54
Bitting, Katherine, **54**
BK Veggie, 75
Black, Rick, 610
blackberries, **54–55**, *63*
blackfish, **55**
Black Hunger (Witt), 179
Black Muslims. *See* Nation of Islam, dietary laws
black pepper. *See* pepper, black
Black Russian, 512
blackstrap molasses, 392
Blane, Gilbert, 611
Blank, Les, 220
Blanke, Cyrus, 138
Blanton's Bourbon, 61
blenders, 38, **55**, 231, 389, 611, 641
Blimpie International, Inc., **55**, 569
blintzes, 69, 331
Blizzard, 184
Blob's Park, 45

blood pudding, 284, 481
Bloody Mary, 56
Bloody Mary and Virgin Mary, **55–56**
Blot, Pierre, 162, 227, 238, 240–41, 524, 552, 616
Blount, Roy, Jr., 72, 349
blueberries, **56**, *243*
Blue Book of Social Usages, The (Post), 194
blue cheeses, 107
blue crabs, 111, 172
Blue Moon beers, 166
Blue Plate Foods, 496
Blue Plate mayonnaise, 370
boardinghouse reach, 57
boardinghouses, **56–58**, 254
Boar's Head Provision Company, 185
Bob's Big Boy. *See* Big Boy
Bob's Pantry, 50
Boca Burgers, 24
Bocuse, Paul, 248, 416
Böhme, Jakob, 607
boilermaker, 58, **58**
boiling, 164, 550
Bok, Edward, 449
Bombay gin, 259
Bon Appetit (magazine), 450, 498
Booke of Cookery, A (Washington, M.), 25, 133, 161, 167, 179, 352
Booker's, 61
Book for All Households, The (Appert), 54
Boon, Ngiam Tong, 540
Boordy Nursery, 629
Boordy Vineyard, 627
Boost, 68
bootleggers, 479
booyah, **58**
Borba, Willow, 581
Borden, **58**
  baby food, 31
  Elsie the Cow, 58–59
Borden, Gail, 58, 411
Born, Samuel, 338
borscht, 511, 512, 552
Boston, 16, 64, 412
Boston Beer Company, 379
Boston Chicken, 59–60
Boston Cooking School, 6, **59**, 162–63, 215, 254, 358, 434, 494
Boston Cooking-School Cook Book, 6, 149
Boston Cooking-School Cook Book (Farmer), 59, 149, 151, 155, 162, 215, 494, 639
  brownie recipes, 71
  casserole recipe, 97
  on frappes, 235
  mock foods, 391–92
  terrapin, 586
Boston Cooking-School Cook Book (Lincoln), 162, 392
Boston Cooking-School Cook Book (Perkins), 151
Boston Cooking-School Magazine, 6, 59, 449
Boston cream pie, 455
Boston Market, **59–60**, 580
Boston Oyster House, 514
Boston School Kitchen Text-Book (Lincoln), 162
Bottled-in Bond Act, 61
bottled water. *See* water, bottled
bottling, **60**, 92–93. *See also* canning and bottling
  ketchup, 342
  milk, 388
  soda drinks, 133, 139–40, 448, 546
  wine, 628, 633
Bottoms Up (Saucier), 367
botulism, 432, 453
Bough, Carole, 420
bouillabaisse, 552
bouillon, 550–51
Boulder (microbrewery), 379
bourbon, **60–62**, 195, 390, 562–63, 621
Bourgeois, Emil, 444
Bournville, 80
Bowen, Samuel, 557

Bowker, Gordon, 562
Bowman, Charles, 495–96
boxes, 146
box lunches, 522
Boyd, Lewis R., 368
Boylan's, 50
Bracebridge dinners, 127
bracero program, 213, 214
Brach's, 89, 270, 329
Bracken, Peg, 153
Bradham, Caleb, 140, 447–48
Bradley, Alice, 19, 127, 151, 163
Bradley, Mrs. Alexander Orr, 521
Brad's Drink, 447
Brady, Diamond Jim, **62**, 186
branding, 5, 6, 216, 287, 290
  in amusement parks, 16
  fast food, 216
  and packaging, 433
  Quaker Oats, 4
  Sara Lee Corporation, 522–23
brandy, **62–63**, 195
  applejack, 19–20
  in cordials, 167
  hot toddies, 305
brandy Alexander, **63**
bran muffins, **63**
brass, 157
bratwurst, 386
Brauhaus, 46
Braun, Lilian Jackson, 437
Brazier, Brendan, 416, 605
Brazil nuts, **63**
bread, **63–66**. *See also* bakeries; baking; flatbreads
  additives, 108
  adulteration, 64, 262
  Anadama bread, 16
  bagels, 32
  bakeries, 33
  barley, 36, 66
  bialy, 48
  bierocks, 48
  challah, 66, 331
  corn breads, 169
  Dutch, 201
  muffaletta, 395–96
  Native American, 337
  pan de muertos, 248
  Parker House rolls, 65
  Po'Boy, 467
  Portuguese sweet bread, 66
  Pullman loaf, 482
  pumpernickel, 65
  rye and Indian bread, 411
  Sally Lunn, 515
  and sandwiches, 521
  soda bread, 65
  sourdough bread, 65, 640
  toast, 589
  white, enriched, 419
  Wonder Bread, 65
bread, sliced, 65, **66**, 521
Bread and Bread-Making (Rorer), 510
Bread Bakers Guild of America, 66
Bread-Givers (Yezierska), 359
bread machines, **66–67**
bread-making, commercial. *See* bakeries
bread-making tools, **67**
bread sauce recipe, 524
bread starters, in frontier cooking, 241
Breakfast, Dinner and Supper (Harland), 127
breakfast bars, 103
breakfast burrito, 69, 637
breakfast cereals, 2, 69. *See also* cereal, cold
  and bananas, 35
  Cream of Wheat, 69
  Malt-O-Meal, 69
  oatmeal, 421
  Quaker Oats, 2, 69
breakfast drinks, 28, **67–68**, 581

breakfast foods, **68–70**. *See also* breakfast cereals; breakfast drinks; cereal, cold
  apple pie, 20
  colonial American, 372
  coush-coush, 171
  croissants, 65
  Denver sandwich, 187
  Easter, 203
  eggs, 69, 207
  goetta, 261
  pancakes, 433–34
  Quaker Oats, 487
  scrapple, 261, 529
  toast, 589
  twentieth century, 373
breast-feeding, 31
Bredenbek, Magnus, 167
Brenham Creamery Company, 56
Brer Rabbit, 7, 8
breweries, 42–44, 45, 475–76
  Anheuser-Busch, 73
  Berghoff Brewing Company, 45
  Bridgport Brewing Company, 45
  Chesapeake region, 111
  Coors Brewing Company, 14, 166, **166–67**
  G. Heilemann Brewing Company, 45
  Hofbraühaus, 46
  Kaltenberg Castle Brewery, 46
  Michelob, 73
  microbreweries, 379–80
  Pabst Brewing Company, 73
  in Pacific Northwest, 432
  Pennsylvania Brewing Company, 46
  Weeping Radish, 46
brewer's yeast, 639
brewing, **70**
  beer barrels, 45
  Budweiser, 73
  yeast, 639–40
Brewmasters Table, The (Oliver), 15, 36, 433
brewpubs, 379
Breyer, William A., 70
Breyers, **70**
brick cheese, 105
Bridge Luncheon Food, **70**
bridge mix, 70
Bridgport Brewing Company, 45
Brights Wines, 629–30
brine, 543
brisket, 331, 437
Bristow, Benjamin Helm, 61
Brix, 144
broccoflower, 98
broccoli, **70–71**
Brock, Alice May, 153
Brock, Robert L., 127
Brock Candy Company, 267
broiling, 165
Broma, 124–25
Bronin, Betty, 573
Brooks, Martin, 177–78
Brooks Tropicals, 177–78
Brown, Dale, 153
Brown, Diva, 139
Brown, Frank C., 601
Brown, Helen Evans, **71**
Brown, John I., 6
Brown, John Y., 341, 520
Brown, Marion, 153
Brown Ale, **71**
brown cow, 389
Brown Derby, 220, 514
brownie pizza, 72
brownies, **71–72**
Brownrigg, George, 605
Bruckman, Frederick, 315
brunch, 372–73
Brunckhorst, Frank, 185
Brunn, Gustav, 172, 476
Brunswick stew, **72**, 142, 552

Bryan, John H., 523
Bryan, Lettice, 114, 175, 180, 397, 524, 560
Bryan Brothers Packing, 523
Bryan Packing Company, 304, 611
Bryant, Arthur, 384
Bryant, Charlie, 384
bubble and squeak, 79–80
bubble gum, 267
bubble tea, **72–73**
Buck, Peter, 569
Buckley, T. H., 190
Buck's fizz, 390
buckwheat, and scrapple, 529
Buddha's Delight, 121
Budweiser, **73**
buffalo, **73–74**, 252, 403
Buffalo Chicken wings, **74**, 230, 240, 383
Bugialli, Giuliano, 154
bulgur, 384
bulimia, 204
bulk foods, 166, 401, 432
Bullock, Tom, 368
bully beef, **74**
Bumble Bee, 596
bundt cake, **74**, 85
bundt pan, 74
Burbank, Luther, 244, 466, 502
burek, 331
Burger Chef, 217
Burger King, 28, **74–75**, 217, 235, 272, 292, 580
burgoo, 553
Burnett, Joseph, 603
Burnett, Leo, 336, 459
Burns, Jabez, 136
burrito, 39, 69, **75**, 86, 378, 579, 637
Burt, Harry, 262, 314
Busch, Adolphus, 73
Busch, August A., Sr., 73
Bush, George W., and pretzels, 478
Bushnell, Nolan, 127
butchering, **75–76**, 454
    hogs, *457*
    Muslim dietary laws, 397
butcher shops, 76
butter, **76**, 365–66
    adulteration, 227
    Blue Bell, 56
    clarifying, 133
    packaging, 41
    margarine as substitute for, 365–66
    tools for making, 77
butter cakes, 85
butter cracker, 173
Butterfinger, **77**
Butterflies in My Stomach (Taylor), 319
butter-making tools and churns, **77**
buttermilk, 31, **77**
Butterscotch Krimpets, 582
buying clubs, 165, 166
Byce, Lyman, 206

cabbage, **79**
    kale, 339
cabbage cutters and planes, **79–80**
cabbage palm, 277
cabinet, 389
Cabinet-Maker's and Upholsterer's Guide, The
    (Hepplewhite), 192–93
cacao beans, 122, 123
cactus, **80**, *556*
Cadbury, John, 80
Cadbury Beverages, Inc., 1
Cadbury Schweppes, 1, **80**, 197, 484, 508, 534
    and Peter Paul Candy Company, 451
    and Snapple, 545
Cadbury Schweppes Americas Beverages, 508, 510
    brands, 80
Caesar salad, 16, 355, 514, 619
café brulôt, 62
cafeterias, **80–81**

caffeine, 136, 137–38
Cajun and Creole food, **81–83**, 237–38, 295,
    479–80
    coush-coush, 171
    crayfish, 174
    frogs' legs, 241
    jambalaya, 325
    Natchitoches meat pies, 401
    New Orleans syrup, 413
    peanuts, 441
    Po'Boy sandwich, 467
    ratafia, 493
    sassafras, 523
Cajun Kitchen, 471
Cake Bible, The (Beranbaum), 85
cake decoration, 53
cake mixes, 53
    Airy Fairy, 23
    Duncan Hines, 279, 280
cakes, **83–85**, 112
    advertising cookbooklets and recipes, 84, 85
    and birthdays, 52–53
    bundt cake, 74
    cheesecake, 107
    Chesapeake region, 111
    Devil's Food, 188–89
    Election Cake, 207
    jelly rolls, 329
    Lady Baltimore Cake, 351
    lady fingers, 351
    post-Revolutionary War food, 284
    watermelon cake, 616
    weddings, 618
calamari, 561–62
calas, 69, **85**, 200
Calavo, 7, 28, *29*, 195
calcium propionate, 109
California, **85–87**
    almonds, 14
    apricots, 22
    artichokes, 25
    asparagus, 26
    avocados, 28
    brandy industry, 63
    celery, 100
    cooking, 461
    dairy industry, 182
    dates, 184
    drive-ins, 199
    figs, 219
    food festivals, 230
    fruits, 244–45
    garlic, 253
    grapes, 263–64
    lettuce, 86
    olives, 86, 424
    peaches and nectarines, 440
    pistachios, 462
    plums, 466
    pomegranates, 470
    prickly pears, 80
    salad greens, 514
    state laws, 353
    sugar beets, 572
    tomatoes, 590–91
    vegetables, 606
    vermouth, 610
    walnuts, 613
    wines, 86, 379, 627–29
California Cookbook, The (Callahan), 152
California Cooler, 634
California cuisine, 294, 480, 616
California dip, 293
California Fruit Canners Association, 186, 308
California Fruit Growers Exchange, 245
California Packers Association. *See* CalPak
California Pizza Kitchen, **87**
California roll, 326
California truck, 522
California Wine Association, 626, 628

Callahan, Genevieve, 152
Cal-Mex cooking, 378
caloric composition of foods, *175*, 418
calorimeter, 418, 421
CalPak, 186
calvados, 20
camas root, **87**, 241
Campbell, Joseph, 87–88
Campbell, Tunis G., 8, 9, **87**, 147
Campbell Soup Company, 86, **87–88**, 89, 93, 383,
    551
    advertising cookbooklets and recipes, 8, 88
    brands, 88
    Pepperidge Farm, 447
    Swanson, 573, 600
    tomato juice, 55, 88
    V8 juice, 88
Campbell Soup Kids, **88–89**
Camp Coffee, 138
camp cook, 128
Camp Cookery: How to Live in Camp (Parloa), 434
Canada Dry Bottling Company, 197
canals, 592
canapé, *19*, **89**, 210
Canapé Book, The (Maiden), 89
Candler, Asa, 133, 139
candy and candy bars, **89–91**, *90*. *See also* candy
    companies
    adulteration, 89
    advertising, 5, 32, 77, 261, 451, 496, 545
    Babe Ruth Home Run Bar, 32
    Baby Ruth, 31–32
    Butterfinger, 77
    children as target of marketing, 90
    chocolate, 122–24, 279
    Conversation Hearts, 90, 413
    and corn syrup, 170
    Easter, 203
    fudge, 246–47
    Halloween candy, 270
    insects, 319
    jelly bean, 329
    Just Born, 338
    Kandy Kate bar, 31
    licorice, 356–57
    LifeSavers, 357
    M&M milk chocolate candies, 364
    Mars Bar, 389
    Mary Jane candies, 413
    Milky War, 389
    NECCO wafers, 413
    Oh Henry!, 423
    peanut, 441
    Reese's Peanut Butter Cups, 496
    saltwater taffy, 520, 579–80
    Snickers, 545
    Sweethearts, 413, 603
    taffy, 579–80
    Tootsie Roll, 591
    Valentine's Day, 603
    vending machines, 609
    York Peppermint Patties, 451
candy canes, 90
candy companies
    Fannie May, 89, 213
    Hershey Chocolate Company, 122–23, 261, 279,
        451, 496, 617
    Mars, 89, 123, 364, 366, 389, 545
    New England Confectionery Company
        (NECCO), 90, 413
    Peter Paul Candy Company (Mounds Bar), 451
    See's Candies, 532
    Stuckey's, 568
candy corn, 270, 329
candy drops, 77
Candyland, 393
Canfield, Richard, 133
CanLit Foodbook, The (Atwood), 359
canned foods, 91, 92, 286. *See also* canning and
    bottling

baby food, 31
Campbell's, 88
chili, 119
crab, *223*
frontier, 241
meat, 75, 432, 559
tuna, 595–96
Vienna sausage, 611
Cannery and Agricultural Workers Industrial
  Union, 213
canning and bottling, 60, **91–93**, 368. *See also*
  bottling; canned foods; home canning
  Armour, 24
  beer, 45
  canning in Pacific Northwest, 431
  Chesapeake region, 111
  Del Monte, 186
  fruits, 245
  Hunt Brothers, 308
  peas, 444
  pickles, 453
  pineapple, 460–61
  preserves, 476–77
  soups, 551
  tomatoes, 590
Canning and Preserving (Rorer), 91, 476
canola oil, 218, 605
can openers, **93**
can sealer, *92*
cantaloupes, 377
Cantonese food, 121
Capitol Cook Book, The, 581
capons, 113–14
Capp, Al, 493
Capper-Volstead Act, 76, 182, 387
capsaicin, 117
caquelon, 227
caramel, 84, 246
caraway, 435
carbohydrates, 289, 300, 418, 422, 470, 611
  light (low-carbohydrate) beers, 357, 361, 390
  low-carb diets, 190
  and Native American diet, 405
carbonated water, 545, 615. *See also* seltzer; soda
  drinks; soda water
cardamom, 259
Cardini, Caesar, 514
CARE, 320
Carême, Marie-Antoinette, 492
carhops, 1, 198, 199, 292, 548, 580
Caribbean influences on American food, **93–94**,
  296
  bananas, 34
  batidos, 38
  cassava, 96–97
  molasses, 392
  New York food, 414
  sugar, 570
Carlisle, John G., 61
Carl Karcher Enterprises (CKE), 94, 339
Carl's Jr., **94**, 272, 339
Carnation's Instant Breakfast, 69
Carnes, Jonathan, 446
Carney, Dan and Frank, 463
Carolina Housewife, The (Rutledge), 85, 147, 302,
  441, 524
Carolina Rice Kitchen, The (Hess), 179, 302
carp, **94–95**
Carpenter Electric Heating Manufacturing
  Company, 564
Carqué, Otto, 494
carrot cake, 85
carrots, **95**
Carson, Rachel, 426, 427
Carter, Jimmy, and Coca-Cola, 134
Carter, Rosalynn, 624
Carter, Susannah, 539
Carvel, 53
Carvel, Thomas, 95
Carvel Corporation, **95**

Carver, George Washington, **95–96**, 441, 557
Case, Frank, 152
cashews, **96**
cassareep, 97
cassava, **96–97**
cassava bread, 96–97
Casserole Cookery (Tracy and Tracy), 152
casseroles, 15, **97**, 257. *See also* soups and stews
  as funeral food, 247
  tamale pie, 581
  yummasetti, 640
cassia, 575
cast-iron pans, 157, 169
  Dutch ovens, 202
catalogs, Arbuckles', 23
catering, and African Americans, 9–10
Catering for Special Occasions (Farmer), 215
catfish, **97**, 239
Cather, Willa, 360
Cat Who Played Brahms, The (Braun), 437
Cat Who Said Cheese, The (Braun), 437
cauliflower, **97–98**
caves, 313
caviar, 569
Cazenave, Arnaud, 82
CEC Entertainment, Inc., 127
Cedar Point (Sandusky, Ohio), 16
celebration cakes, 83
celebrations. *See also* holidays
  birthdays, 51–53
  Native American, 406
  weddings, 617–18
celebrity chefs, **98–100**
  Beard, James, 40, 57, 71, 86, 89, 98–99, *99*, 152,
    154, 187, 253, 454, 490, 498, 616
  Chen, Joyce, 99, 490
  Child, Julia, 98–99, **115–16**, 115–16, 153, 154,
    238, 254, 293, 446, 490, 524, 611, 639
  Claiborne, Craig, 57, 99, 131, **131–32**, 131–32,
    154, 253, 293, 453, 498
  cookbooks, 155
  cooking classes, 163
  cooking schools, 162
  Kerr, Graham, 99
  Lagasse, Emeril, 100, 351
  nouvelle cuisine, 416–17
  Pépin, Jacques, 154, 445–46
  Prudhomme, Paul, 99, 154, 295, 479–80
  Puck, Wolfgang, 86, 99, 239, 248, 480–81
  Ranhofer, Charles, 33, 149, 186, 238, **491–92**,
    524, 551
  Rick Bayless, 38–39
  Romagnoli, Margaret and Franco, 99, 490
  Szathmary, Louis, 296, 336, 577, 594
  Trotter, Charlie, 577, 594–95
  Waters, Alice, 86, 99, 249, 254–55, 258, 278,
    294, 454, **616–17**
  Willan, Anne, 625–26
  Yan, Martin, 490, 639
celery, **100**
  in American chop suey, 15
  with Buffalo chicken wings, 74, 383
  in burgoo, 553
  cocktail food, 293
  in culinary gardens, 343
  and dips, 195
  in etouffée, 82
  as hors d'oeuvres, 19
  in jambalaya, 325
  in lobster roll, 360, *382*
  and parsley family, 435
  and picnics, 454
  in roux, 230
  in stuffed ham, 568
  in Waldorf salad, 328, 514, 595
  wild, and ducks, 111, 252
celery glasses, 100
celery salt, 100, 172, 476
celery seed, 435
celery soda, 196

Celestial Seasonings, 171
cellarettes, 359
cellophane, 433
Cel-Ray, 196
Centennial Buckeye Cook Book, 143, 207
Centennial International Exhibition, 636
Center for Science in the Public Interest, 46, **100**,
  171, 419, 545
central Asian food, **100–101**
Century 21 Exhibition, 636
Century of Progress World's Fair, *67*, 636
ceramics. *See also* earthenware; redware; stoneware
  dishware, 157, 465
  and food storage, 25, 146
ceramics definitions, **101**
cereal, cold, **101–3**, 255
  advertising, 2, 4, 102, 255
  All-Bran, 4, 102, 340
  Cheerios, 102, 255
  Cocoa Pebbles, 69, 472
  Cocoa Puffs, 69
  corn flakes, 2, 102, 190, 275, 340, 608
  Elijah's Manna, 102, 255
  fortified, 103
  Frosted Flakes, 69
  Fruit Loops, 69
  Fruity Pebbles, 69
  Granose Flakes, 69
  Granula, 69, 190
  Grape-Nuts, 2, 69, 102, 190, 255, 258, 472
  Kellogg Company, 340
  Kix, 102
  organic, 103
  Post Toasties, 102, 472
  Puffed Rice, 102
  Ranger Joe Popped Wheat Honnies, 102
  Rice Krispies, 69, 102
  Shredded Wheat, 102
  sweetened, 102
  Wheaties, 69, 102, 255
cereals. *See* breakfast cereals; cereal, cold
certification
  halal foods, 398
  kosher foods, 428
  of milk, 182, 387
  of organic foods, 426, 607
chafing dish, **103**
  and fudge, 246
Chafing Dish Possibilities (Farmer), 215
challah, 66, 248, 331
Champagne, **103–4**, 632
  as aphrodisiac, 603
  bottles, 60
  bridge luncheon food, 70
  champagne grape, 264
  champagne toast, 617
  and Charles Fournier, 629
  at Delmonico's, 186
  Eastern U.S., 629
  ginger champagne, *259*
  in mimosa, 390, 425
  Mumm's and Perrier-Jouet, 291
  and New Year's, 413
  versus sparkling wines, 632
  and weddings, 617
champagne bottle, 60
Chao, Buwei Yang, 152, 153
Chapman, John, 334–35
Chappell, George, 497
charity fund-raisers, 247
Charles Krug Winery, 506
Charlie Brown, 484
Charlie Trotter's (Chicago), 164
Charmat bulk processing, 104
Charms Company, 591
Chartreuse, 167
Chase, Andrew J., 576
Chase, Caleb, 137
Chase, Oliver R., 413
Chase, Silas Edwin, 413

Chase and Company, 413
Chastity; or, Our Secret Sins (Lewis), 144
Chateau Frank Champagne Cellars, 632
Chattanooga Bakery, 393–94, 555
Chavez, Cesar, 214
cheddar cheese, 104
Cheek, Joel, 137, 369
Cheerios, 102, 255
cheese, **104–6**, 181
    American cheese, 105, 272, 460
    cheddar cheese, 104
    cream cheese, 175–76
    fondue, 227
    food festivals, 230
    and genetic modification, 49
    goat's milk, 181
    historical overview, **104–5**
    Kraft, 349
    moldy, **106–7**
    mozzarella, 105, 394–95
    pimiento cheese sandwich, 460
    processed, 105, 609
    recent developments, **105–6**
    tools, 107
cheese baskets, 107
cheesecake, **107**, 176, 257
cheesecloth, 226
cheese drainers, 107
cheese-making tools, **107–8**
cheese press, 107
cheese snacks, 544
cheese straws, 438
Chee-tos, 240, 544
Cheez Whiz, 105, 349
Chef Paul Prudhomme's Louisiana Kitchen, 154, 480
chefs, 10, 254, 255. *See also* celebrity chefs
Chef's Collaborative, 39
Chef's Secret, The (Szathmary), 577
chemical additives, 1–2, **108–9**, 485
    and baby food, 31
    flavorings, 225
    and health, 625
    to salt, 518
chemical fertilizers, 427, 428
chemical leavening, **109–10**, 639
    and doughnuts, 196
    pearlash, 639
chemical preservatives, 1–2
Chemistry of Cooking and Cleaning (Richards), 418
Chen, Joyce, 99, 490
Chernin, Kim, 359
Chero-Cola Company, 510
cherries, 107, **110**, 245, 358, 368, 385, 536, 546
    food festivals, 230
    and George Washington, 614
    Midwestern, 385
cherries jubilee, 110
cherry bounce, 110, 282, 413, 493
cherry pitters or stoners, **110**
Chesapeake Bay (microbrewery), 379
Chesapeake region, food and drink of the, **110–12**
    crab, 172–73
chess pie, 112, 339, 455
Chester Cheetah, 240
Chesterfield, Lord, 453
Chestnut Cookbook, The (Bhagwandin), 420
chestnuts, **112**, 197, 277, 404, 432, 542, 544, 618
Chew, William, 335
chewing gum. *See* gum
Cheyenne diner, *191*
Chez Panisse, 86, 238–39, 249, 255, 278, 294, 463, 501, 616
Chez Panisse Menu Cookbook, The (Waters), 454
Chicago world's fair. *See* World's Columbian Exposition
Chi-Chi's Mexican, 463
chicken, **112–13**, 474. *See also* chicken cookery; eggs
    Buffalo Chicken wings, 74
    Church's Chicken, 128–29

fried, 239–40
    Kentucky Fried Chicken, 341–42, 520–21
Chicken à la King, 113
chicken cookery, **113–14**
chicken divan, 292
chicken fried steak, **114**
chicken industry, 113, 114
chicken Kiev, 512
Chicken McNuggets, **114–15**, 371
Chicken on the Run, 471
chickpeas, **115**
chicle, 267
chicory, 207–8
    roots, and coffee, 139
chiffon cake, 84
Child, Julia, 98–99, **115–16**, 153, 154, 238, 254, 293, 446, 490, 524, 611, 639
Child, Lydia Maria, **116**, 147, 178, 502
children as target of advertising, 5, 7, 102, 117, 173, 507–8, 591
Children's Aid Society, 528
children's cookbooks, **116–17**
Childs. *See* diners
Childs, Samuel and William, 80
chile, **117–18**, 184, 378
chile (New Mexico), 118–19
chile powder, 295–96
chili, **118–19**, 378, 384, 556
    Cincinnati, 129–30
    contests, 159
    Frito pie, 240
chili jargon, 129
chili mac, 118
chili parlors, 118, 130
chili powder, 117, 119, 476
Chinese American food, **119–21**, 209, 292, 293–94
    appetizers, 19
    chop suey, 15
    cookbooks, 153
    dim sum, 19
    fortune cookies, 233
    funeral food, 248
    in Hawaii, 274
    restaurants, 500
    take-out foods, 580
    weddings, 618
Chinese Exclusion Act, 119
Chinese New Year, **121**
    dumpling soup, 200
Chinese regional foods, **121–22**
Chinois, 480
Chipotle Mexican Grill, 60, 75, 117
chipotles, 117
chipped beef, **122**
chitlins. *See* chitterlings
Chittenden, Henry, 418
chitterlings, **122**
chives, 424
chlorine, 615
chocolate, 89, **122–24**, 388, 411
    adulteration, 122
    advertising, 4
    boxed, 213
    brownies, 71–72
    Cadbury, 80
    cookies, 156
    Devil's Food, 188–89
    in egg cream, 205
    fudge, 246–47
    and health, 124
    Hershey Foods Corporation, 279
    historical overview, **122–23**
    M&M milk chocolate candies, 364
    packaging, 617
    recent developments, **123–24**
    technology, 124
    and Valentine's Day, 603
chocolate chip cookie, 156
chocolate drinks, 122, **124–25**
Chocolate Junior, 582

Chocolate Manufacturers Association, 89
cholent, 331
chopping knives and food choppers, **125**
chop suey. *See* American chop suey
chorizo, 19, **125**, 177, 311, 526
Chow (Dickson), 540
chowderfish, 55
chowder party, *132*
chowders, 552. *See also* clam chowder; corn chowder recipe
Christian, Eugene, 493–94
Christian Science, and temperance, 13
Christmas, **125–27**, 196, 200, 230, 239, 262, 399
    candy, 90, 329
    Christmas dinner, 126–27, 203, 286, 350, 468
    Christmas pudding, 52
    Christmas pear salad, 127
    doughnuts, 196
    drinks, 205, 266, 632
    lutefisk, 527
    plum cake, 83
    pretzels, 478
    Polish American, 468
    turkey, 413, 598
Christmas Carol, A (Dickens), 52, 126, 127, 632
chrusciki, 468
Chuck E. Cheese Pizza, **127**
chuck wagons, **127–28**, 556–57
    Denver sandwich, 187
Chunking Inn, 636
Church, George W., Sr., 128
Church, Ruth Ellen, 433
Churchill, Winston, 104
Church's Chicken, **128–29**, 292, 471
churns, 77
Chy-Max chymosin, 49
Ciao, Italia, 490
cider, 12, 13, 14, **129**, 243, 282
    home brewing, 43
    Midwestern, 385
    in pies, 438
    production, 21, 381, 385, 411
    ship food, 535
cider, hard, 68, **129**, 244. *See also* applejack
ciderkin, 129
cider oil, 19
cider press, *413*
Cincinnati chili, 118, **129–30**
cinnamic aldehyde, 225
cinnamon, 145, 575
    in apple dumplings, 200
    artificial, 225
    in avena, 28
    in babka, 331
    in cherry bounce, 110
    in chili, 118, 129
    cinnamon rolls, 69, 257, 333, 460
    in fruit punch, 348
    in haroseth, 331
    in hot toddy, 305
    in prepared herb and spice mixtures, 476
    Red Hots, 89–90
    in Russian tea, 512
    in *Schnecken*, 333
    in Smart Start, 341
    toast, 589
    in whiskey sour, 621
cisco, **130**
citral, 225
citrus, **130–31**, 243–44. *See also* lemons; oranges
    citrus industry, 245
City Hotel, 304, 499
Civil War, 286
Civil War reenactments, 281
Clabir Corporation, 347
Claiborne, Craig, 57, 99, **131–32**, 154, 253, 293, 453, 498
Claire, Mabel, 152
clambake, **132**
clambakes, 531

clam chowder, 142
clams, **132**, 133, 306, 535. *See also* clambake
    in Chesapeake region, 111–12
    clam chowder, 142, 335, 552
    clam dip, 293
    clam frappé, 235
    clamshells as pot scrapers, 195
    in Korean American food, 348
    in Pacific Northwest, 431–32
clams casino, **133**
clarifying, **133**
Clark, David L., 89
Clark Bar, 89, 413
Clarke, Alison J., 297
Classic French Cooking (Claiborne), 154
Classic Italian Cook Book, The (Hazan), 154
Classic Vodka (Wisniewski and Faith), 530
Clemson blue cheese, 107
Cleveland, Grover, 623
Cleveland, Ruth, 32
Clinton, Bill and Hillary, 624
closed pit barbecue, 35
cloves, 575
club sandwich, **133**
Coalition for Food Aid, 320
Cobb, Robert, 514
cobblers, 438
Cobb salad, 514
Coca-Cola, 2, 93, **133–35**, 234, 292, 394, 425, 448,
    546
    acquisition of Minute Maid, 144, 245
    advertising, 5
    cola wars, 139–40
    and corn sweeteners, 214
    and corn syrup, 339
    flavorings, 225
    health claims, 50
    health criticisms, 451
    and IsoSweet, 170
    kashruth certification, 334
    in mixed drinks, 177, 511
    vending machines, 609
cocaine, and Coca-Cola, 133
cocktail hour, 19
cocktail parties, 293
cocktails, 13, **135**
    Berta, 586
    bitters, 135
    Black Russian, 512
    Bloody Mary and Virgin Mary, 55–56
    brandy Alexander, 62
    Buck's fizz, 390
    Collins, 140
    Cuba Libre, 94, 177, 511
    daiquiri, 94
    Donaji, 586
    Gibson, 368
    and ginger ale, 259
    grasshopper, 264
    Harvey Wallbanger, 530
    lime rickey, 358
    mai tai, 363–64
    Manhattan, 135, 364
    margarita, 366, 585, 586
    Martinez, 367
    martini, 135, 167, 259, 367–68, 610
    mimosa, 390, 425
    mint julep, 61, 62, 390
    mojito, 178
    old-fashioned, 61, 423
    orange blossom, 425
    origins, 81, 516
    piña colada, 94
    planter's punch, 484
    punch, 484
    Ramos gin fizz, 425
    rum and Coke, 511
    rum drinks, 511
    rum punch, 94
    Sazerac, 526

screwdriver, 425, 530
sidecar, 62
Singapore sling, 540
stinger, 62
tequila sunrise, 425, 586
tiki drinks, 511
and use of cordials, 167
whiskey sour, 621
White Russian, 512
zombie, 641
Cocktails and How to Mix Them (Jenkins), 540
cocoa, *124*
Cocoa Pebbles, 69, 472
cocoa powder, 122
Cocoa Puffs, 69
coconut cream, 136
coconut milk, 136
coconuts, **135–36**
coconut water, 136
cod, 223, 224, 527
Cody, William F., 252
Coe, Sophie D., 39, 179, 301
coffee, **136–37**
    adulteration, 23, 139
    advertising, 23, 137, 138, 227, 369, 410
    Ariosa coffee, 23
    café brulôt, 62
    health concerns, 137–38
    Irish, 320
    Maxwell House, 137, 138, 255, 369
    Nestlé, 410, 411
    Starbucks, 432, 562
    vending machines, 609–10
coffee, decaffeinated, **137–38**
coffee, instant, 137, 138, **138**, 369, 410
coffee bars, 562
coffee gelatin, 137
coffee grinders, 265
coffeehouses, **138**, 562
coffee makers, roasters, and mills, **138**
coffee pots, *136*, *137*, *139*
coffee shops, 505
coffee substitutes, **138–39**
    Grain-O, 327
    ground okra seeds, 423
    Postum, 255, 472
Cohen, Ben, 46
cola drinks, competitors to Coca-Cola, 139
colanders, 537
cola wars, **139–40**, 636
colby cheese, 105
Cole, Thomas, 453
Coleman, Will, 423, 552
cole slaw, 79, 201, 539
collard greens, 339
Collet, Joseph, 238
Collins, **140**
Colman, Jeremiah, 398
Colonel Sanders. *See* Sanders, Colonel
colonial American food, 281–83
    applejack, 19–20
Colonial Williamsburg, 280
Colorado Milling and Elevator Company, 535
Colored People: A Memoir (Gates), 454
Colquitt, Harriet Ross, 152
Columbia River (microbrewery), 379
Columbus, Christopher, 117, 122, 377, 457
column stills, 196, 562, 563
combat food, 140, **141–42**. *See also* C ration; D
    ration; K ration; Lurp (Long Range Patrol
    Ration); MCI (Meal, Combat, Individual);
    MRE (Meal, Ready-to-Eat)
    bully beef, 74
    carrots, 95
    chipped beef, 122
    Civil War, 285–86
    coffee, instant, 138
    condensed milk, 58
    frontier, 241
    hardtack, 272–73

M&M milk chocolate candies, 364
    powdered onions, 425
    processed cheese, 105, 609
    Revolutionary War, 283
    Spam, 559
    Tootsie Rolls, 591
    Uncle Ben's Converted rice, 601
comfort food, 295
    macaroni and cheese, 363
    pimiento cheese sandwich, 460
    Whoopie pie, 624
Commerce of the Prairies (Gregg), 461
commissaries, 28, 522
Common Sense in the Household (Harland), 552
communal gatherings and integration, **142**
community cookbooks, **142–43**, 207, 246, 247
community gardens, 344, 606
community-supported agriculture, **143–44**, 171
Companion to California Wine, A (Sullivan), 633
company lunchroom, 81
Compassionate Cook, The: Please Don't Eat the Animals
    (PETA), 17
Compleat Housewife, The (Smith), 147, 237, 576
Complete Wine Book (Schoonmaker and Marvel),
    633
compressed yeast, 173, 636, 639
ConAgra, 41, 76, **144**, 309
Conair Corporation, 232
concentrated orange juice, **144**, 425
condensed milk, 58, 411
condensed soups, 88
condiments, **144–46**
    dips, 195
    H. J. Heinz Company, 297–98
    ketchup, 342
    mayonnaise, 369–70
    mustard, 398–99
    opposition to use of, 144
    pickled cauliflower, 98
    relishes, 453
    salsa, 517
    Southern regional cookery, 554
    soy sauce, 558
cone-top cans, 60
Coney Island, 15–16, *303*, 401, *402*
coneys, 129, 386
confectionary. *See* candy and candy bars
Conner Prairie Settlement, 281
Conrad, Barnaby III, 367
Conrad, Carl, 73
conscience joint, 80
conserves, 477
Consider the Oyster (Fisher), 152
Consolidated Foods, 472, 522–23
Consolidated Fruit Jar Company, 368
consommé, 551
conspicuous consumption, 62
consumption of, in colonial times, 411
Contadina, 186
containers, **146**. *See also* barrels and kegs; cooking
    containers; pots and pans
    casseroles, 97
    Dutch ovens, 202
    lunch boxes, dinner pails, and picnic kits,
    361–62
    Native American, 408–9
    Tupperware, 596–97
contamination, 182, 228, 614, 615
contests. *See* cooking contests
contests, hot dog eating, 401
Continental Baking Company, 65, *67*, 302, 600
Continental Can Company, 45
convection oven, 11, 165
convenience foods
    frozen foods, 243
    hot dogs, 304
    pancake batter, 433
    Uncle Ben's Converted rice, 601
    Vienna sausage, 611
convenience stores, **146–47**

Conversation Hearts, 90, 413
converted rice, 601
Conza, Tony, 55, 569
Cook, Margaret, 143
Cook at Home in Chinese (Low), 152
Cook Book for Boys and Girls (Crocker), 117
Cookbook for Girls and Boys, A (Rombauer), 507
cookbooklets. *See* advertising cookbooklets and
    recipes
Cook Book of Oscar of the Waldorf (Tschirky), 238,
    595
cookbooks and manuscripts, **147–55**, 327. *See also*
    cooking manuscripts
    to 1860, **147–49**
    1970s to the present, **154–55**
    African American, 9
    African American food, 147, 151, 152, 153, 154
    alcohol-free recipes, 13
    applejack, 20
    artichokes, 25
    Asian food, 154–55
    Beard, James, 40
    Betty Crocker, 47
    broccoli recipes, 70–71
    cakes, 84, 85
    canapé, 89
    Catharine Beecher, 41
    celebrity, 152
    celebrity chefs, 155
    charity, 149
    children's, 116–17
    chocolate recipes, 122, 123
    Christmas, 125–27
    from the Civil War to World War I, **149–51**
    classics, 147
    collections, 361
    collections of, 54, 355–56, 444–45, 577, 625
    community, 142–43
    Creole food, 85
    delicatessens, 185
    desserts, 151
    duck recipes, 200
    eggplants, 205–6
    encyclopedias, 147–49, 151
    ethnic, 149, 210
    fairs and expositions, 149–51
    foreign cuisines, 152
    French, 149, 154, 238
    French food, 238, 239
    German American food, 257
    health food, 153
    Italian food, 154
    Jewish American food, 152
    and measurements, 374
    Mexican American food, 38, 39, 154, 378–79
    niche, 151–52
    nuts, 420
    promotional, 4
    regional, 147, 151, 152, 153, 154
    Russian American food, 512
    Scandinavian and Finnish American food, 543
    Southern regional cookery, 154
    sweets, 155
    and temperance, 12–13
    vegetarian, 16–17, 99
    White House, 624
    from World War II to the 1960s, **152–53**
    from World War I to World War II, **151–52**
Cookerie as It Should Be, 162
cookie cutters, **155–56**, 196
cookies, **156**, 188, 201, 539
    chocolate-chip, 395
    fave dei morti, 248
    fortune cookies, 233
    Girl Scout cookies, 259–60
    hermit, 278–79
    Mrs. Fields cookies, 395
    osso dei morti, 248
    rugelach, 333
    Whoopie pie, 624

Cooking à la Ritz (Diat), 152
cooking as a hobby, 293
Cooking Club of Tu-Whit Hollow (Pratt), 116
cooking containers, **157–58**
cooking contests, **158–59**
    barbecue, 35–36
    pickle, 452
    Pillsbury Bake-Off, 459
    salsa, 517
    Spam, 559–60
cooking equipment, 344–45. *See also* cooking
    containers; cooking equipment, social
    aspects of; electric appliances; stoves and
    ovens
    and advertising cookbooklets, 6, 7
    kosher, 334
    Native American, 410
    pressure cookers, 477
cooking equipment, social aspects of, **159–61**
Cooking for Two (Hill), 151
Cooking Light (magazine), 99, 450, 498
cooking magazines. *See* periodicals
*Cooking Manual of Practical Directions for Economical
    Every-Day Cooking* (Corson), 162
cooking manuscripts, 107, **161**. *See also* cookbooks
    and manuscripts
Cooking Mexican, 38
Cooking of Italy, The (Root), 153
Cooking of Provincial France, The (Fisher), 153, 224
Cooking of Vienna's Empire, The (Wechsberg), 153
cooking schools, 255, 494
    Boston Cooking School, 59, 215, 358, 434, 494
    celebrity chefs, 162
    collegiate, 163
    Cordon Bleu, 151–52
    Culinary Institute of America, 163
    Culinary School of Design, 162
    Ecole de Cuisine La Varenne, 625
    French, 238
    James Beard Cooking School, 40
    Johnson and Wales, 335–36
    L'Ecole des Trois Gourmandes, 116
    military, 141
    Miss Farmer's School of Cookery, 163, 215
    New York Cooking School, 149, 162
    nineteenth century, **161–63**
    Philadelphia Cooking School, 149, 162, 509
    twentieth century, **163–64**
    Yan Can International Cooking School, 639
Cooking School Text Book and Housekeeper's Guide
    (Corson), 162
cooking sherry, 535
cooking shows. *See* radio/TV food shows
cooking techniques, **164–65**
    barbecue, 35–36
    boiling, 550
    casseroles, 97
    hearth cookery, 276–77
    stewing, 551
cooking utensils. *See also* cooking equipment
    Africa, 8
    Alaskan, 12
    ale slipper, 14
    shalivka, 32
cooking wine, 13
Cooking with Black Walnuts (Bough), 420
Cooking with Master Chefs (Child), 154
Cooking without Mother's Help (Judson), 117
Cooking with the New American Chefs, 99–100
Cook It Outdoors (Beard), 152
Cook Not Mad, The, 483
Cook's Illustrated, 450, 498
Cook's Own Book, The (Lee), 25, 113, 147, 200
cookstoves. *See* stoves and ovens
cookware, 157–58
Coolidge, Calvin, 623
Coolidge, Mrs. Calvin, *260*
coonie, 128
Cooper, James Fenimore, 454
Cooper, Thomas, 423

cooperatives, **165–66**, 171
    community-supported agriculture, 144
    dairy, 76, 104, 182, 387
co-ops. *See* cooperatives
Coors, Adolph, 166
Coors Brewing Company, 14, 45, *164*, **166–67**
Coors Light, 166
Copeland, Al, 471
copper, 157
Coppola, Francis Ford, 219
copyright infringement. *See* intellectual property
    rights
cordials, **167**
    Benedictine, 167
    cherry bounce, 110, 493
    ratafia, 493
cordials, historical, **167**
Cordon Bleu, 151–52, 489
Cordon Bleu Cook Book, The (Lucas), 151–52
Cores, Arthur, 59
coriander, 435
corks, 60, 92, **167–68**, 633, 634
corn, **168–69**
    beer, 44–45
    and bread, 63–64
    coush-coush, 171
    in Cuban American food, 177
    federal subsidies, 214
    grits, 301–2
    Midwestern, 384
    pinole, 461
    popcorn, 470–71
    succotash, 569–70
    tamales, 305
    types of, 168
cornbread, 169, 230. *See also* johnnycakes and
    hoecakes
cornbread baking pans, **169**
corn chips, 544
corn chowder recipe, 494
corned beef, **169**, 513
    bully beef, 74
    Reuben sandwich, 501–2
corned beef slang, 74
corn flakes, 2, 102, 190, 275, 340, 608
Corning Glass Works, 261
cornmeal, 10, 18, 147, 286, 411. *See also* cornbread;
    johnnycakes and hoecakes
    in Anadama bread, 16
    breads, 350
    cooking contests, 158
    coush-coush, 94, 171
    cush, 286
    Granola, 101
    hasty pudding, 68, 273, 317
    hush puppies, 309
    Indian pudding, 317–18, 392
    in Injun 'n' Rye, 64, 68
    mamaliga, 333
    mush, 69, 171, 202, 309, 317, 337
    and Native American weddings, 617
    Navajo cake, 406
    in New England, 411
    scrapple, 69, 261, 529
    supawn, 573
    tamale pie, 581
    tamales, 305
corn oil, 169, 605
corn pones, 337
corn-preparation tools, **169–70**
Corn Products Refining Company, 339
cornstarch, 169, 170, 339
corn syrup, 169, **170**, 339, 574
Coronado National Memorial, 281
Correctional Foodservice and Nutrition Manual, 478
Corson, Juliet, 149, 162
Cortés, Hernán, 122, 124
cottage cheese, 181
cottonseed oil, 605
counterculture, food, **170–71**, 606

Country Kitchen, The (Lutes), 152
coup glass, 634
coupons, and Ariosa coffee, 23
couscous, 384
Couscous and Other Good Food from Morocco (Wolfert), 154
coush-coush, 94, **171**
Coville, Frederick, 56
cowboy cuisine, 127–28, 136, *241*
Cowboy Lingo (Adams), 540
cowboy slang, 540
cowpeas, 85, **171–72**, 302
Cox, Palmer, 71
Coyote Café (Santa Fe), 86
crab, 172, 535
    in Chesapeake region, 111, 476
    cookbooklet, *223*
    in frogmore stew, 553
    mock crab, 391
    in Pacific Northwest, 431
    in Southern regional cookery, 555
crab boils, **172**, 531
crab cakes, **172–73**
crab houses, 172
cracker barrel, 401
Cracker Jack, 89, **173**, 392, 636
crackers, **173–74**
    Animal Crackers, 156
    and barbecue, 35
    CatDog crackers, 447
    as chili garnish, 118, 129
    cocktail food, 293
    crackers and cheese, 106
    filler in crab cakes, 173
    Goldfish crackers, 88, 447
    Graham crackers, 263
    hardtack, 272
    in mock foods, 391
    Nabisco, 401
    oyster crackers, 97, 129
    in puddings, 112
    Ritz crackers, 20, 349, 391, 455
    and seaweed, 532
    slang, 541
    as snack food, 544
    and soft wheat, 620
    as space food, 559
    Tam Tam crackers, 369
craft brewing, 13
cranberries, **174**
Crane, Clarence, 357
Crane, George Belden, 627
crappie, **174**
C ration, 141
crawfish. *See* crayfish
crayfish, 82, **174**, 239
cream, **174–75**
    in barley berry (dessert), 36
    in Black Russian, 512
    in brandy Alexander, 63
    and butter production, 76, 77
    in candies, 532
    coconut, 136
    consumption, 181, 182, 387
    creamed chicken, 69, 113, 529
    creamed chipped beef, 69, 122
    creamed corn, 170
    creamed corned beef, slang, 540
    cream gravy, 9, 69, 114, 525
    cream sauces, 293, 524, 527, 530, 569
    cream soups, 97, 247, 257, 551, 552, 610–11, 640
    in custards, 180, 494
    and egg creams, 204–5
    in eggnog, 205
    in grasshopper, 264
    in green goddess dressing, 514
    homogenization, 388
    in ice cream sodas, 316
    in lime rickey, 358

liqueurs, 167
    in martinis, 367
    mock, 391
    in oyster stew, 555
    in pumpkin pie, 483
    in Roquefort dressing, 107
    in sack posset, 535
    separators, 76, 182
    in supawn, 573
    and syllabub, 576
    and tea, 583
    Twinkies filling, 302, 600
    utensils, 537, *550*
    whipped, 137, 315, 320, 433
cream cheese, **175–76**, 181, 257
creameries, 76
cream liqueurs, 167
cream of tartar, 64, 109, 176
Cream of Wheat, 69, 493
creams, dessert, **176**, 188, 438, 455
cream soda, **176**, 604
crème brûlée, 180
Creole Cookery, 85
Creole food, 94, 275–76. *See also* Cajun and Creole food
Cretors, Charles, 470
Crisco, 6, **176**, 218, 231, 353, 605
crisps, 438
Crocker, Betty. *See* Betty Crocker
Crocker, William G., 47
Crock-Pot Slow Cooker, 542
croissants, 65
Croly, Jane Cunningham, 329–30
Crosby, John, 255
Cross Creek Cookery (Rawlings), 152
Crowell, Henry Parson, 487
Crown Cork and Seal Company, 60
crown cork cap, 60
Crown Soda Machine, 60
Crowntainer, 60
crudités, 98, 491
crullers, **176–77**
Crum, George, 636
Crush International, 508
Crystal Palace Exhibition, 636
Crystal's, 271
Cuba Libre, 94, **177**, 511
Cuban American food, 94, **177–78**
cucumbers, **178**. *See also* pickles
cudighi, 386
Cuisinart, 232
Cuisine (magazine), 498
Cuisine at Home, 450
Cuisine Creole, La (Eustis), 85
Cuisine Creole, La (Hearn), 151
Cuisine Créole, La (Hearn), 275, 276
Cuisine Française, La (Tanty), *237*
Cuisines of Mexico, The (Kennedy), 154
Culinary Archives and Museum, 577
culinary associations, 294–95
culinary historians, 161, 178–79, 625, 626
Culinary Historians of Ann Arbor, 296
Culinary Historians of Boston, **178–79**, 296
Culinary Historians of Hawaii, 296
Culinary Historians of Southern California, 296
Culinary Historians of Washington, D. C., 296
culinary history, history of, 296–97
culinary history associations, 295–96, 297
culinary history vs. food history, **179–80**
Culinary Institute of America, 163, **180**, *180*
Culinary School of Design, 162
Culinary Trust, 320
Cullen, Michael, 266
Cullen Bill, 43
Cumberland Farms, 147
cumin, 435
Cummings, Nathan, 522
Cummings, Richard Osborn, 296–97, *297*
Cunningham, Marion, 155, 454
cupboards and food safes, **180**

cup cake, 84
cupcakes, 302–3, 582
curaçao, 135
curd, 107
curing, 169
currants, **180**, 264
curry powder, 476
Curtice Brothers, 513
Curtis, Jeremiah, 6
Curtis, John, 560
Curtiss Candy Company, 31–32, 77
custards, **180**, 481, 494
Custer, Delores, 320
cutlery. *See* silverware
Cut-Rite waxed paper, 617
cutters, biscuit, 53
cyclamates, 571, 574

Dabney, Ted, 127
Daft, Douglas, 134
Daggett, Ezra, 91
Dagwood sandwich, **181**
Daigneau, Kenneth, 559
Dainties (Rorer), 510
dainty dishes, 19
daiquiri, 94
dairy, 56, **181–82**
    butter, 76, 77
    buttermilk, 77
    cheese, 104–7
    churns, 77
    cream, 174–75
    health concerns, 181
    how-to guides, 149
    milk, 386–88
dairy industry, 175, **182–84**, *183*
    Beatrice, 40–41
    Borden, 58
    butter, 77
    buttermilk, 77
Dairy Queen, **184**, 234, 424, 426
Dairy Queen National Trade Association, 184
Dakota Inn Rathskeller, 46
Daley, Regan, 155
Dalquist, H. David, 74
Dalton Poultry Company, 144
D'Aluisio, Faith, 319
Dam, Henrik, 612
Danish pastry, 527
Darden, Norma Jean and Carole, 154
Darden Restaurants, 255
D'Ascenzo, Nicola, 28
dates, **184**
Date with a Dish, A: A Cookbook of American Negro Recipes (De Knight), 152
datil chile, 117, **184**
Dave Says—Well Done! (Thomas), 588
Dave's Way (Thomas), 588
David, Elizabeth, 616
David Ransom and Company, 6
Davidson, Alan, 179
Davies, Jack, 104
Davis, Adelle, 171, 275
Davis, Fletcher, 271
Davis, Karen, 17
Davis, R. G., 26
Davis, Theodore R., 623
Davis and Company, 87
de Alba, Felipe, 366
Decalcoware, 465–66
DeCarlo, Peter, 55, 569
de Chaunac, Adhemar, 629
DeDomenico, Vince, 503
deep-fat frying, 245–46
    fried candy bars, 600
    hush puppies, 309
    Twinkies, 600
Deep Foods, 243
deer, 251–52, 609
Deer Burger Cookbook (Black), 610

Deetz, James, 280
de Garmo, Peter, 542
dehydration, of food, 51
Dekafa, 137
De Knight, Freda, 152
Delaney Clause, 426
Delaplane, Stanton, 320
Delaware, 383
Deleboe, Franz, 258–59
delicatessens, **184–85**
Déliée, Felix, 200, 238
Delights of Delicate Eating, The (Pennell), 444
Delineator, 449
Delmonico, John, 185–86
Delmonico, Lorenzo, 186, 492
Delmonico's, 149, **185–86**, 238, *414*, 491–92, 513,
    595
    baked Alaska, 33
    Delmonico potatoes, 473
    Hamburg Steak, 270–72
Del Monte, 86, 93, **186**, 298
    advertising cookbooklets and recipes, 186
    baby food, 31
    ketchup, 342
DeLuca, Frederick, 569
Denny's, 191, 505
DeNovo Corporation, 581
dent corn, 168
Denver omelet, 69
Denver sandwich, **186–87**
De Palma, Al, 298–99
Department of Agriculture, United States, 49,
    187, 227, 419
    Aunt Sammy, 489
    food pyramid, 5, 469–70
    food stamps, 232
    international aid, 319–20
    pamphlets, 5
    publications, 435
    school lunches, 528
Depth Charge, 58
dessert drinks, 205
desserts, **187–88**, 295. *See also* cakes; pies and tarts
    baked Alaska, 33
    Chesapeake region, 112
    cookbooks, 151
    crème brûlee, 180
    dessert creams, 176
    dumplings, 200
    ice cream molds, 314
    Jell-O, 327–29
    lady fingers, 351
    Peach Melba, 440
    post-Revolutionary War food, 284
    puddings, 481
    syllabub, 576
    Twinkies, 600
    watermelon, 616
Devereaux, Elizabeth, 162
De Verstandige Kock, 494
Devil's Food, **188–89**
DeVoe, Thomas, 151
DeVoto, Bernard, 367
Dewar, James A., 600
dewberries, 55
Diageo, 74, 459
Diamond, 591
Dias, Isaac, 206
Diat, Louis, 152, 610
Dickens, Charles, 25, 127, 186 , 591
    Christmas Carol, A, 52, 126, 127, 632
Dickinson, R. S., 144
Dickson, Paul, 540
dietary guidelines, sugar, 470
Dietary Guidelines for Americans, 182, 419, 470
dietary laws. *See* Jewish dietary laws; Muslim
    dietary laws
Dietary Reference Intakes. *See* DRIs
Dietary Supplement Health and Education Act, 5

Diet Coke, 134
diet drinks, 68
diet foods, 239
Diet for a Small Planet (Lappé), 154, 168, *170*, 171
Diet-Rite, 510
diets, fad, 68, 90, **189–90**, 275. *See also* weight-loss
    diets
dill, 435
dim sum, 19, 120
Diner, Hasia, 179
diners, **190–91**, 216, 504–5
    slang, 187, 540–41
dining car, *191*, **191–92**, 239, 273, 482, 504, 505
dining rooms and meal service, 87, **192–94**,
    210–11. *See also* table settings
    hotel dining rooms, 304–5
*Dining with Friends: The Art of North American Vegan
    Cuisine* (Friends of Animals), 17
dinner pails, 361–62
Dinner Roles (Inness), 179
dinnerware, 157–58, 159. *See also* plates
Dinshah, Freya, 604
Dinshah, Jay, 416, 604
Dionne Quintuplets, 32, 339
dips, 145, **194–95**
Directions for Cookery (Leslie), 26, 273, 423, 441,
    551, 552
direct selling
    farmers' markets, 215–16
    Tupperware, 597
    wines, 631
discos, 36
Disease Concept of Alcoholism, The (Jellinek), 14
diseases and illnesses, 301. *See also* vitamins *and*
    phylloxera.
    dietary deficiencies, 418–19
    food-borne, 197, 228, 320
    of grapes, 263, 626.
    and milk, 387, 388
    of pears, 443
    water-carried, 614
dishwashing and cleaning up, **195**
Disneyland, 16, 27, 635
distillation, 60–62, 135, **195–96**
    applejack, 19–20
    brandy, 62, 63
    rum, 510
    stills, 562
    vodka, 612
    whiskey, 620–21
distribution, food. *See* food distribution systems
divinity, 246
Dixie Wax Paper Company, 544, 617
Dlugosch, Sharon, 194
DNA. *See* biotechnology
Dock Street Brewing Company, 379
Dods, Matilda Lees, 162
doh, 101
Dole, Jim, 460, 461
Domaine Ste. Michelle, 104
Domestic Cook Book, A (Russell), 151
Domestic Encyclopedia (Cooper), 423
domestic enhancement, 562. *See also* Beecher,
    Catharine; Hale, Sarah Josepha; Leslie, Eliza
Domestic French Cookery (Leslie), 238, 524
Domestic Manners of the Americans (Trollope), 210,
    454
Domestic Receipt Book (Beecher), 41, 133, 194
Domestic Receipt-Book (Beecher), 524, 570
Domino's Pizza, 74, **196**, 463, 464
Donaji, 586
Donato's, 60
Don the Beachcomber, 641
Doolin, Elmer, 240, 379, 544
Doritos corn chips, 240, 544
Dorney Park (Allentown, Pennsylvania), 16
Dorrance, Arthur, 87–88
Dorrance, John T., 88
*Doubleday Cookbook: Complete Contemporary
    Cooking* (Anderson and Hanna), 154

doughnut-making tools, **196**
doughnuts, **196**. *See also* crullers
    beignets, 69
    Dunkin' Donuts, 200–201
    Dutch oliebollen, 69
    frying baskets, 246
    frying in whale oil, 619
    jumbles, 188
    Krispy Kreme, 349
    malasadas, 274
    origins, 258
    paczki, 468
    sufganiyot, 333
Downing, Charles, 439
Downings, 429
Dows, Gustavus, 547
dragon fruit, 80
D ration, 141–42
Dr. Atkins' Diet Revolution, 275
Drayton, Grace, 88
Dr. Brown's, **196–97**
Dreher, Anton, 14, 368
dressings and stuffings, **197**
Drews, George, 494
drinking chocolates. *See* chocolate drinks
drinking establishments. *See* bars and drinking
    establishments
drinking songs, **197–98**, 547–48
drinking vessels, 46, 260
Drinks (Straub), 368
drink slang, 541
DRIs, 419
drive-ins, 1, **198–99**, 292, 580
drive-through windows, 199, 318, 325, 580
Dr Pepper, 50, 139, **197**, 546
Dr Pepper Museum and Free Enterprise Institute,
    197
Dr Pepper/Seven Up, Inc., 1, 197, 534
Dr. Physick's Soda Water, 60
drugs, in chicken, 114
drum method for instant coffee, 138
Drummond, J. D., 611
drunk driving, 13
drying, **199**
Dubois, Urbain François, 492
duck, **199–200**, 252, 475
Duff's, 74
Duffy, Patrick Gavin, 279
Duguid, Naomi, 155
Dull, Henrietta, 152
Dumas, J. B. A., 611
Dumpling Cookbook (Polushkin), 200
dumplings, **200**
    hush puppies, 309
    pierogi, 468
Duncan Hines, 144, 279, 280
Dungeness crab, 172, 431
Dunkin' Brands Inc., *38*
Dunkin' Donuts, 196, **200–201**, 292
DuPont, 433
Dupree, Nathalie, 154
Durand, Elias, 547
Durgin-Park, 137
Durkee, 513
Durkee, H. Allen, 367
Dutch chocolate, 122
Dutch influences on American food, **201–2**, 381.
    See also Pennsylvania Dutch food
    cookies, 156
    crullers, 176–77
    doughnuts, 196
    funnel cakes, 248
    New Year's celebrations, 413
    pickles, 451–53
Dutch ovens, **202**
dyspepsia, 101, 263, 502

earthenware, 101, 465
Easter, **203**
    food traditions, 399

jelly beans, 329
Polish American, 468
sweet breads, 207
Easy Steps in Cooking (Fryer), 116–17
Eat-a-Bug Cookbook (Gordon), 319
eating disorders, **203–4**
eating establishments. *See* bistros; diners; hotel
dining rooms; luncheonettes; restaurants
Eating for Victory (Bentley), 179
Eating Right in the Renaissance (Albala), 297
Eating Well (magazine), 450, 498
Eat My Words (Theophano), 179
Eaton, Nathaniel, 43
Eat Well and Stay Well (Keys), 558
Eat Your Heart Out (Hightower), 371–72
eco-friendliness, Ben & Jerry's, 46
Ecole de Cuisine La Varenne, 625
Edgar H. Hurff Company, 186
Edgerton, Clyde, 454
Edgerton, David, 74
Edison, Thomas, 564
eel, **204**, 223, 494
Egerton, John, 154
eggbeaters, 206
egg cream, 125, 175, **204–5**
Egg McMuffin, 69
eggnog, **205**, 266, 484
eggplants, **205–6**
egg-preparation tools, 85, **206**. *See also* timers,
hourglasses, egg timers
egg production, technology, 206
eggs, **206–7**, 474. *See also* Breakfast Burrito;
Denver sandwich; Egg McMuffin; eggnog
in Appalachian diet, 17
and breakfasts, 69
in brownies, 71–72
in cakes, 83, 84, 85, 280
in Chinese diet, 120
clarifying butter, 133
and coffee, 23, 138
in custards, 180, 438, 481, 494
in dessert creams, 176
deviled, 454
in dumplings, 200
Easter, 203, 468
egg phosphate, 451
as funeral food, 248
in grasshopper, 264
Hangtown fry, 241
in mayonnaise, 369
in mock foods, 391, 392
nutritional value, 113, 611, 612
partridge, 435, 436
and Passover, 436
production, 112–13, 114
safety regulations, 353
in salads and salad dressings, 513, 514
slang, 141, 540, 541
terrapin, 586
in whiskey sour, 621
egg timers, 588–89
Egli, Konrad, 227
800 Proved Pecan Recipes, 420
Eijkman, Christiaan, 611
Eisenhower, Dwight, and Coca-Cola, 134
Eisman, George, 416
E. K. Pond Company, 442
El Cocinero Español (Pinedo), 461
Elderly Nutrition Program, 373
Eldredge, Elmer E., 609
Election Cake, **207**, 539
electric appliances, 345–46
blenders, 55
bread machines, 66–67
food processors, 231–32
refrigerators and freezers, 236, 312–13,
496–97
rice cookers, 504
stoves and ovens, 564–65
testing of, 261

toasters, 65, 589
electroplating, 537
Elijah's Manna, 102, 255
Ellet, Elizabeth, 149, 194
Ellison, Frank D., 573
Ellwanger, George H., 151
El Pollo Loco, 75
Elsie Presents James Beard in "I Love to Eat", 40,
98–99, 490
Elsie the Cow, 40, 58, 59, 636
El Taco, 579, 624
Embury, David, 367
Emerson, Ralph Waldo, on pie, 20
Empire Cheese Factory, 176
emulsifiers, 108
enchilada, **207**
Encyclopaedia of Domestic Economy (Webster), 149
Encyclopedia of Wine (Schoonmaker), 633
Encyclopedia of Wines and Spirits (Lichine), 633
encyclopedias, culinary, 147–49, 151
endive, **207–8**
Enfamil, 31
English Hus-wife, The (Markham), 639
English Picnics (Battiscombe), 453
enriched flour, 66
Enrico, Roger, 140
entertaining, 192–94, 210–11
books on, 152
etiquette, 210–11
Gilded Age, 84
home selling, 596–97
informal, 103, 261
punch bowls, 484
table settings, 466
White House, 623–24
Entertaining with Insects (Taylor), 319
entomophagy, 318–19
environmental concerns, 60, 217
Environmental Protection Agency, 49
Epcot Center, 16
Epicurean, The (Ranhofer), 33, 149, 186, 238,
491–92, 524, 551
Epicure in Imperial Russia, The (Markevitch), 512
Epperson, Frank, 471–72
E. Prichard Company, 308
Epsicles, 472
Erewhon, 171
Erie Canal, 619–20
escarole, 207–8
Escoffier, Auguste, 238, 416, 417, 440
Eskimo pie, 262, 347
Eskimos, 12
Espanola Valley Cookbook, 143
Esposito, Mary Anne, 490
essence of lockjaw, 19
Essen House, 46
esters, 70
Estes, Rufus, 10, 351
ethanol production, 24
ethical vegetarianism, 16–17
ethnic foods, **208–10**. *See also* individual
ethnicities
community cookbooks, 143
condiments, 145
desserts, 188
fusion food, 249
potato-based, 473
restaurants, 500
vegetables, 606–7
ethrog, 331
etiquette, 193–94, 406–7
Etiquette (Post), 70, 210
etiquette books, **210–11**
étouffée, 82
European plan, 304, 499
euthenics, 504
Eutropheon, 494
Evans, Oliver, 619–20
Every Bodys Cook and Receipt Book (Hardin), 147
Everybody's Cook Book (Lord), 151

Everyday Food, 450, 562
Ewing, Emma, 513
Ex-Cell-O Corporation, 388
Experiments on the Spoilage of Tomato Ketchup
(Bitting, A.), 54
Exxon Mobil Travel Guides, 497

Facundo, Don, 510
Fahlberg, Constantin, 574
Fairbanks Company, 6
fairs and expositions. *See also* food festivals
cookbooks, 149–51
cooking contests, 158
World's Fairs, 636–37
Faith, Nicholas, 530
falafel, 384
Falconer, William, 397
Family and the Householder's Guide, The (Storke), 210
Family Circle (magazine), 450
family farms, 171
Family Receipts (Barnum), 147
Famous Amos, 156, **213**
Famous Amos Story, The (Amos), 213
Fannie Farmer Cookbook, 454
Fannie Farmer Cookbook, The, 154, 155
Fannie May, 89, **213**
Farewell to Arms, A (Hemingway), 360
farinha, 96, 97
farm aid. *See* price supports
Farm Animal Reform Movement (FARM), 17
farm bills, 214, 232, 426
Farmer, Fannie, 59, 97, 149, 151, 162, **215**, 235,
358, 391, 449, 494, 586
advertising cookbooklets and recipes, 6
bran muffin recipe, 63
brownie recipes, 71
cookbooklets, 6
and fudge, 246
organization of, 18–19
farmers' markets, 171, **215–16**
farm labor and unions, **213–14**
Farm Labor Organizing Committee (FLOC), 214
farm raising fish, 239
bass, 38
carp, 94–95
catfish, 97
farms, small, and farmers' markets, 215–16
Farm Sanctuary, 17
farmstead cheese, 105
farm subsidies, duties, quotas, and tariffs, **214**
farm winery bills, 630
farm workers, 213–14
fast food, **216–18**. *See also* sandwich shops
in amusement parks, 15–16
Arby's, 23, 217
Arthur Treacher's Fish & Chips, 224, 402, 619
Big Boy, 50–51, 86, 216, 271
Boston Market, 59–60, 580
Burger King, 28, 74–75, 75, 217, 235, 272, 292,
580
cafeterias, 80–81
in California, 86
Carl's Jr., 94, 272, 339
Chuck E. Cheese Pizza, 127
Church's Chicken, 128–29, 292, 471
Cincinnati chili, 129
criticisms of, 371–72
Dairy Queen, 184, 234, 424, 426
diners, 190–91, 216
Domino's Pizza, 196, 463, 464
drive-ins, 198–99
and franchising, 234–35
French fries, 237
fried chicken, 471
hamburgers, 270–72
Hardee's, 235, 272, 339, 471, 510
Horn and Hardart Automat, 28
hot dogs, 304
In-N-Out Burger, 318
Jack in the Box, 86, 292, **325**, 325, 424

fast food (Contd).
   Kentucky Fried Chicken, 217, 239, 292, 341–42, 520–21, 588, 619, 640
   ketchup, 342
   Little Caesars, 360
   Long John Silver's, 224, 640
   McDonald's. *See* McDonald's; Mexican American food, 379
   and obesity, 422
   pizza, 463–64
   Popeyes, 128–29, 471
   regional, 216, 217
   roadside food, 505
   Taco Bell, 75, 86, 117, 217, 341, **579**, 579, 640
   vs. take-out foods, 580
   use of catfish, 97
   Wendy's, 217, 272, 580, 588, 618–19
   White Castle, 216, 271, 505, 580, 621–22
   Wienerschnitzel, 624–25
Fast Food Nation (Schlosser), 371, 473
fasting, 190, 203, 204, 493
   and fish, 530
   Muslim dietary laws, 397-98
Fat History: Bodies and Beauty in the Modern World (Stearns), 421
fats and oils, **218**. *See also* lard and shortening; salads and salad dressings; vegetable oils
   butter, 76
   Crisco, 176
   margarine, 76, 365–66
   in pastries, 437
   peanut oil, 441
   schmaltz, 333
   soybean oil, 557
   sunflower oil, 573
   whale oil, 619
Faust Instant Coffee, 138
fave dei morti, 248
Favorite Recipes: A Columbian Autograph Souvenir, 151
Favorite Recipes of the Movie Stars cookbooklet, 7
Fawcett, Eric, 464
FDA. *See* Food and Drug Administration
Feast Made for Laughter (Claiborne), 131
Feasts of Autolycus (Pennell), 444
Federal Agriculture Improvement and Reform Act, 214
Federal Food, Drug and Cosmetic Act (1938), 108
Federal Food, Drug, and Cosmetic Act of 1938, 2, 228, 353, 625
federal regulations, 1–2, 353. *See also* Department of Agriculture, United States; Food and Drug Administration
   meat, 75
   Pure Food and Drug Act (1906), 484–85
Fee Brothers bitters, 135
Feeding the Lions: An Algonquin Cookbook (Case), 152
Feltman, Charles, 16, 65, 303, 401
fennel, 435
fermentation, 70, 104, **218**
   and bread, 64
   cider, 129
   in Korea, 348
   pickling, 453
   and salt, 518
Fernandez-Armesto, Felipe, 249
fertilizer industry, and adulteration, 485
Field, Carol, 154
Field, Eugene, 20
Fields, Debbi, 156, 395
Fields, W. C., and picnics, 454
Fiesta, 466
Fifteen Cent Dinners for Workingmen's Families (Corson), 149
Fig Newton, 156
figs, **218–19**
filberts, **219**
filé, 81, 423, 523, 552
Filipino food, 553
Filippini, Alessandro, 186

film, food in, **219–21**
   9-1/2 Weeks, 220
   Affair with a Stranger, 28
   Alive, 220
   American Pie, 219
   Avalon, 220
   Babette's Feast, 219
   Big Night, 219
   Chocolat, 220
   Chulas Fronteras, 220
   Crimes and Misdemeanors, 220
   Eating , 220
   E.T., The Extra Terrestrial, 5, 497
   Five Easy Pieces, 220
   Fortune Cookie, The, 233
   Freshman, 219
   Garlic Is as Good as 10 Mothers, 220
   Godfather, The, 219, 220
   Godson, 219
   Good Humor Man, The, 262
   Grande Bouffe, Le, 219
   Heavy, 220
   Just This Once, 28
   Like Water for Chocolate, 219
   Matrix, The, 219
   Modern Times, 219
   Off the Menu: The Last Days of Chasen's, 220
   Pulp Fiction, 220
   Silence of the Lambs, 219
   Soul Food, 219
   Soylent Green, 219
   Tampopo, 219
   Teenage Mutant Ninja Turtles II, 302
   That Touch of Mink, 28
   Tom Jones, 220
   What's Eating Gilbert Grape?, 220
   When Harry Met Sally, 220
   Who Is Killing the Great Chefs of Europe?, 219
Fine Art of Mixing Drinks, The (Embury), 367
Fine Cooking (magazine), 498
fine grain salt, 518
finnan haddie, 269
Finnish American food. *See* Scandinavian and Finnish American food
fire and fuel, Native American, 408, 409–10
fire blight, 443
firehouse cooking, **221**
fireless cookers, **221–22**
Firmenich, 225
fish, 530
   anchovies, 16
   aquaculture, 22
   bass, 37–38
   blackfish, 55
   carp, 94–95
   catfish, 97
   Chesapeake region, 111
   cisco, 130
   crappie, 174
   flounder, 226
   freezing, 51
   freshwater fish, **222**
   grunion, 267
   haddock, 269
   halibut, 269
   herring, 279
   mackerel, 363
   Midwestern, 385
   monkfish, 393
   mullet, 396
   in New England, 412
   in Pacific Northwest, 431
   perch, 448
   pickerel, 451
   pike, 458
   pollock, 470
   red snapper, 496
   salmon, 332–33, 431, 515–16
   saltwater flat fish, **222–23**
   sardines, 279

   sauger, 525
   shad, 534
   smelt, 543
   sole, 226
   sturgeon, 568–69
   sunfish, 572
   swordfish, 576
   tilapia, 588
   trout, 595
   tuna, 595–96
   walleye, 613
   whitefish, 623
fish and chips, **223–24**, 383–84
fish boils, 385, 623
Fisher, Abby, 9–10, 151, 239
Fisher, M. F. K., 152, 153, **224**, 498, 633
fisheries, 1, 222, 265, 531
fish farms. *See* aquaculture
fish fries, 531
fish kettle, 164
Fitzgerald, Kathleen, 318
501 Venison Recipes (Gulbrandsen), 610
flapjacks. *See* pancakes
flatbreads. *See also* ashcakes; barley bread; crackers
   cassava bread, 96–97
   lefse, 527
   matzo, 368–69
   rice breads, 503
flatware. *See* silverware
flavonoids, 124
flavor additives, 109, 135
Flavor and Fortune, 297
flavor chemistry, 225
flavored syrups, for ice cream, 315–16
flavor industry, 225
flavorings, **224–25**
   banana, 35
   fruit, 245
   rose water, 510
   smoke, 543
   in soda drinks, 546
   vanilla, 603–4
Flavr Savr tomato, 49
Flax, Larry, 87
Fleischmann, Charles and Maximillian, 639
Fleming Companies, 456
Fletcher, Horace, 225–26, 609
Fletcherism, **225–26**
flint corn, 168
Floatplane Notebooks, The (Edgerton), 454
floats, 389
Florida, and vegetables, 606
Florida Foods Corporation, 245
flounder and sole, **226**
flour, 2, 66, 548. *See also* milling, flour
flour corn, 168
flowers, edible, **226**
fluoride, 615
flute glass, 634
fly screens, 226
flytraps and fly screens, **226**
FOCUS Brands, 95
Folger, James, 136, 226–27
Folger, James III, 227
Folgers, 137, **226–27**
folic acid, 108
folk foods, 399
folklore. *See* myths and folklore
fondant, 246
fondue, 103, 195, **227**, 293
Fondue Cookbook, The (Callahan), 227
fondue pot, **227**
Food & Wine (magazine), 498
Food: A Culinary History (Sonnenfeld), 249
Food Additive Amendment (1958), 108, 225
food additives, 31, 398, 426. *See also* chemical additives
Food Administration, 289, 290
Food and Cookery for the Sick and Convalescent (Farmer), 63, 215

Food and Culinary Professionals, 294
Food and Drink in America: A History (Hooker), 297
Food and Drug Administration, 49, 68, 108, 187, 196, 225, **227–28**, 275, 319, 540, 608, 625
Food and Fuel Control Act, 289
Food and Nutrition Service, 187, 528
food and nutrition systems, **228–29**
Food and Wine (magazine), 99, 450
food assistance, 319–320, 549–50. *See also* hunger programs
food banks, 549
Food Channel, 5
food chemistry, 418
Food Control Law, 43
food cooperatives. *See* cooperatives
food counters, 362
food distribution systems, 106, 245, 231, 575–76. *See also* transportation of food
food festivals, 158, **229–30**, 567–68, 646–49
    advertising, 228–29
    fund-raisers, 230
    Moon Pie, 555
    pickle, 452
    regional, 230
Food for Peace Act, 319
Food for the Gods: Vegetarianism and the World's Religions (Berry), 416
Food Forum, 320
Food Guide Pyramid, 187
food gums, 108
food historians, 178–79
Food History News, **230**, 297
food magazines. *See* periodicals
Foodmaker, Inc., 325
food marketing, **230–31**, 287. *See also* branding; food distribution systems
    to children, 90
    and cooperatives, 166
    farmers' markets, 215–16
    fruits, 245
    grocery stores, 265–66
    small farms, 415
food museums. *See* museums
Food Network, 100, 490
food processing, 286–87, 575–76
    Beech-Nut, 41
    butchering, 75–76
    ConAgra, 144
food processors, 55, **231–32**
food pyramid, 5, 419, 469–70
food riots, 283
food safes, 345
food safety, 100, 227–28, 287, 353–54. *See also* law
    irradiation, 320–21
    standards, 187, 228, 415
food service
    African American, 9–10
    in amusement parks, 16
food shortages, 289
    wartime, 283
Foods of Our Forefathers in the Middle Colonies (Thomas), 117
Foods of the World (Time-Life), 153, 154
Foods of Vietnam, The (Routhier), 154
food stamps, 187, **232**, 307
food storage. *See* containers; cupboards and food safes; storage
food taboos, Native American, 405, 406
Food That Really Schmecks (Staebler), 445
foodways, **232–33**, 399
Foodways Group of Austin, 296
Foodways Section of the American Folklore Society, 294
food writers
    Beard, James, 40
    Claiborne, Craig, 131–32
    Fisher, M. F. K., 224
    Pennell, Elizabeth, 444–45
    Pépin, Jacques, 446
    Pinedo, Encarnación, 461

Rombauer, Irma, 506–7
Rorer, Sarah Tyson, 509–10
Willan, Anne, 625–26
food writing, 71, 498
foraging, 258
Ford, Gerald, 367
Forgione, Larry, 99, 416–17
forks, 538
formal dinners, 210
Forster, Charles, 591
For the Love of Food (Griswold), 320
fortified wines, 627, 628, 629
fortune cookies, **233**
Forum of the Twelve Caesars, 40
Foundation of Biodiversity, 542
Four Hundred, at Delmonico's, 186
Fournier, Charles, 629, 630, 632
Four Seasons, 414, 500–501
Fourth of July, **233–34**
    ice cream and Indian pudding, 318
    Japanese American celebrations of, 326
    picnics, 454
    toasts, 589
fowl, 474–75. *See also* chicken; poultry and fowl
    goose, 262
    partridge, 435–36
    passenger pigeon, 436
    turkey, 597–98
    wild, 252
Fox, John M., 144
Fralinger, Joseph, 579
Francatelli, Charles, 238
Franchise Associates Inc., 306
franchising, 217, **234–35**
    7-Eleven, 146
    A&W Root Beer, 1, 234
    in amusement parks, 16
    Arby's, 23
    Baskin-Robbins, 37
    Big Boy, 50
    Burger King, 74, 235
    Carl's Jr., 94, 339
    Carvel, 95
    Church's Chicken, 128–29
    Coca-Cola, 234
    Dairy Queen, 184, 234
    Domino's Pizza, 464
    Dunkin' Donuts, 201
    grocery stores, 456
    Hardee's, 235
    Howard Johnson, 234, 306
    Jack in the Box, 325
    Kentucky Fried Chicken, 341, 520
    McDonald's, 234–35, 371
    Orange Julius, 426
    Pepsi-Cola bottling, 448
    Pig Stand, 199
    Pizza Hut, 463, 464
    pizzerias, 464
    Popeyes, 471
    Roy Rogers, 234
    Shakey's Pizza, 464, 534–35
    Southland Ice Company, 146
    Stuckey's, 568
    Tastee-Freez, 581
    Wendy's, 619
Franco-American Cookery Book (Déliée), 200, 238, 262
Franco-American Food Company, *238*, 551
Franey, Pierre, 131, 154, 306, 446, 490, 500
Frank, Konstantin, 629, 630
Frank, Willy, 632
frankfurters, 129, 303
Franklin, Benjamin
    and alcohol, 584
    and cooperatives, 166
    and drink slang, 541
    toasts, 589
    and vegetarianism, 607

Franklin Baker Company, *135*
Franklin Infant Food, 31
frappes, **235**, 389
fraud, 1–2, 232, 235. *See also* adulteration
Fraunces, Samuel, 94
Fraunce's Tavern, 499
Freed, Julius, 337, 426
free lunch, 37
Frees, Paul, 459
free trade. *See* North American Free Trade Agreement (NAFTA)
freeze-drying, 199, **235–36**
freezers and freezing, **236**, 242, 497
French, George J., 398
French, Robert Timothy, 398
French bakeries, 33
French Chef, The, 98–99, 115–16, 238, 293
French Chef Cookbook, The (Child), 153
French Cook, The (LaVarenne), 240, 354, 483
French Cook, The (Ude), 238, 524
French Cook, The (Utrecht-Friedel), 149
French Cookery: The Modern Cook (Francatelli), 149, 238
French Country Cooking (David), 616
French cuisine, 292
French Culinary Institute, 238
french dip, **236**
French Domestic Cookery (Audot), 149, 238
French fries, **236–37**, 371
    at Burger King, 75, 580
    at Church's Chicken, 128
    and condiments, 145
    fish and chips, 223
    with fried shrimp, 536
    as frozen food, 243
    at Hardee's, 272
    at Jack in the Box, 325
    at McDonald's, 370, 371, 580
    at Nathan's, 303
    and Po'Boy, 467
    at Wendy's, 619
French influences on American food, 81, **237–39**
    appetizers, 18–19
    bistros, 53
    French fries, 236–37
    frogs' legs, 240–41
    nouvelle cuisine, 416–17
French service, 193, 194
French's mustard, 398
Freshel, Curtis, 16
Freshel, Emarel, 16
freshwater aquaculture, **239**
Fresnaye, Louis, 363
fricassee, 114, 239, 551
fried candy bars, 600
fried chicken, **239–40**
    and African American food, 11, 111
    airplane food, 11
    Chicken McNuggets, 114
    Church's Chicken, 128
    Kentucky Fried Chicken, 341–42, 520–21, 618–19
    Popeyes, 471
    funeral food, 247
    and hush puppies, 309
    and picnics, 454
    in southern regional cookery, 113, 352, 399, 475, 555
    TV dinners, 573, 600
fried ice cream, 33
fried oysters, **240**
Friends of Animals, 17
Frigidaire, 312, 497
Frigo, Pasquale, 394
Frigo Cheese Corporation, 394
Frisch Company, 50
Frito Bandito, 240
Frito Kid, 240
Frito-Lay, **240**, 448, 544
Frito pie, **240**

Fritos, 240
Fritos corn chips, 240, 544
Fritsch, Albert, 100
Fritsche, John, 28
fritters, 200, 248
frogmore stew, 553
frogs' legs, **240–41**
from fruit juices, 245
Frontera foods, 39
Frontera Grill, 38–39
frontier cooking of the far west, 73, **241–42**. *See also* pioneers and survival food
frozen food, 51, 236, **242–43**, 577. *See also* ice creams and ices; TV dinners
    freeze-drying, 235
    juices, 245
    orange juice concentrate, 144
    pizza, 591
fructose, 574. *See also* high fructose corn syrup
Frugal Gourmet, The, 490
Frugal Housewife, The (Carter), 539
Frugal Housewife, The (Child, Lydia), 116, 147
fruit, **243–44**
    apples, 21–22
    apricots, 22
    avocados, 28–29
    bananas, 33–35
    blackberries, 54–55
    blueberries, 56
    brandy, 62
    cherries, 110
    citrus. *See* grapefruit; lemons; lime; mandarins; oranges; in colonial America, 282
    cranberries, 174
    currants, 180
    dates, 184
    figs, 218–19
    kiwis, 346
    melons, 377–78
    Mexico as supplier, 214
    mulberries, 396
    olives, 423–24
    pawpaw, 439
    pears, 442–43
    persimmons, 450–51
    pineapple, 460
    plums, 466–67
    pomegranates, 470
    preserves, 476–77
    quince, 487
    and railroads, 592
    watermelon, 615–16
    wine grapes, 635. *See also* wine
fruitarianism, 190
fruit butters, 477
fruit cake, 83
fruit drier, *244*
fruit drinks, 38, 245
fruit juices, **244–45**
    frozen, 471–72
    juice bars, 337–38
    lemonade, 355
    orange juice, 425–26
    Snapple, 515
Fruitlands, 16, 608
Fruit Recipes (Berry), 460
fruit wines, **245**, 634
Frusen Gladje, 269
fry bread, 209, 403, 409
Fryer, Jane, 151
frying baskets, **245–46**
frying pans, skillets, and spiders, **246**
fudge, **246–47**, 367
Fuller, Eva Greene, 460
Fulton, E. G., 420
Fulton Fish Market, *222*
fund-raisers, 230, 247, 254
funeral biscuits, 247
funeral food, **247–48**
funeral pie, 247

funeral potatoes, 247
Funk, Casimir, 418
funnel cakes, **248**
fur, and animal rights, 17
fusion food, **248**, 296, 311, 637
Fussell, Jacob, 314
fuyus, 451

Gabaccia, Donna, 179
Gaff, James, 639
Gaige, Crosby, 152
Galardi, John, 624–25
Galardi Group, 581, 625
galette, 455
Galliano, 530
Gallo, Ernest and Julio, **251**, 631, 635
Galloping Gourmet, The, 99
game, **251–53**, 435–36
Gardener's Calendar for South Carolina, Georgia, and North Carolina (Squibb), 423
gardening. *See* kitchen gardening
Gardner, James Carson, 272
garlic, **253**, 424
Garrett, Eleanor, 51
Gary's Brewing, 176
gas grill, **253**
gas liquid chromatography (GLC), 225
gas ranges, 563–64, 565, 566
Gastronomica (magazine), 297
Gastronomical Me, The (Fisher), 152, 224
Gastronomic Bibliography (Bitting, K.), 54
Gates, Henry Louis, 454
Gault, Henri, 238, 416
Gay, Richard, 553
gazpacho, 552
Gebhardt, William, 476, 556
geese, 475
gefilte fish, 95, 331
gelatin, 176, 267, 284, 327
Gemme, Charlie, 190
gender roles, 2, 247, 253–55, 405
General Agreement on Tariffs and Trade, 214
General Electric, 497, 564, 589
General Foods, 51, 102, 122, 137, 236, 242, **255**, 328, 347, 472, 503
    Arbuckles', 23
    Birds Eye, 47
    brands, 255
    Maxwell House, 137, 369
    Tang, 581
General Mills, 102, **255–56**, 620
    and Betty Crocker, 47
    brands, 255
    breakfast cereals, 69
    Cheerios, 102, 255
    Cocoa Puffs, 69
    cookbooklets, 7
    cookie mixes, 156
    granola bars, 69, 90
    Harmony, 103
    Kix, 102
    and kosher foods, 428
    and Pillsbury, 459
    Sunrise, 103
    Trix, 102
    Wheaties, 69, 102, 255
General Motors Corporation, 236
General Seafoods Corporation, 51, 242
generic products, advertising, 7
Genesee Pure Food Company, 6, 7, 328
genetically modified organism (GMO). *See* biotechnology
genetic engineering. *See* biotechnology
Gentile, Anthony, 395
Gentlewoman's Companion, The (Woolley), 484
geoduck, 132
George H. Ruth Candy Co., 32
George Killian's, 14, 166
Gerber, Dorothy, 31
Gerber Baby, 31

Gerber Company, 31
German American food, **255–58**
    beer gardens and beer halls, 45–46
    bierocks, 48
    delicatessens, 184–85
    goetta, 261
    hot dogs, 303
    Jewish, 330
    Lüchow's, 361
    scrapple, 529
    Vienna sausage, 611
Gerspacher, Lucy, 420
G. F. Heublein and Company, 56
G. Heilemann Brewing Company, 45
Ghirardelli, Domenico, 124
Gibbons, Euell, 153, **258**
Gibson, 368
Gibson, Reginald, 464
Gilbert, Benjamin, 537
Gilbert, Eleanor, 560
Gillette, Frances, 624
Gilman, Elizabeth, 454
Gilman, George F., 265
gin, 258–59, 540
    dry gin, 258
    excessive use in England, 13
    martini, 367–68
    Old Tom, 258
    toddy, 540
    Tom Collins, 140
ginger, 259
ginger ale, 50, **259**, 546
ginger beer, 259
gingerbread, 156, 188, **258–59**, 539
ginger family, **259**
gingersnaps, 156
Gino's, 292, 510
gin toddy, 540
Girl from Rector's (Rector), 152
Girl Scout cookies, **259–60**, 340
Giuliano Bugialli's Classic Techniques of Italian Cooking, 154
Giuliano Bugialli's Foods of Italy, 154
Givaudan, 225
Glad Bags, 464
Gladstone, William, 225
Glasse, Hannah, 237, 239, 273, 396, 421, 438, 494, 599
Glassie, Henry, 280
glassine bags, 544, 617
glassware, 157–58, **260–61**, 279, 305, 623, 627, 634
Glenn, John, 558, 581
Glenora, 104
global cool chains, 592
globe artichokes. *See* artichokes
glogg, 632
Glossinger, John, 423
glucose, 574
gluten, 64, 619
glyphosate, 49
GMOs, 278. *See also* biotechnology
Godey's Lady's Book, 149, 445, 449, 587
Godfather's Pizza, 463
Goelitz, Gustav, 270, 329
Goelitz Candy Company, 267, 329
Goelitz Confectionary Company, 270
goetta, 258, **261**, 385
go-go clubs, 36
Goizueta, Roberto, 134, 140
Gold, Mollie, 560
Gold Bond-Good Humor Ice Cream Company, 70
Gold Bond Ice Cream Company, 472
Golden, Hyman, 545
Golden Arches East: McDonald's in East Asia (Watson), 372
Goldenberg's Peanut Chews, 545
golden cake, 83
Golden Restaurant Operations, 60
Golden Rule Cookbook, The (Freshel), 16

Golden Vine Winery, 635
Goldfish crackers, 447
Goldman, Sylvan, 266
Goldman Sachs Trading Company, 242
Gold Medal flour, 255
Gold Seal Vineyards, 629, 630, 632
Gone with the Wind, 220
Goobers, 89
Good & Plenty, **261**, 356
Goode, George Brown, 174, 269
Goodfellow, Elizabeth, 162, 238
Good Food from Sweden (Norberg), 152
Good Form Dinners, Ceremonious and Unceremonious,
    and the Modern Methods of Serving Them
    (Longstreet), 19
Good Housekeeper, The (Hale), 113, 167, 439, 523
Good Housekeeping (magazine), 4, 26, 151, 190, 450,
    625
Good Housekeeping Cook Book, 151
Good Housekeeping Institute, 228, **261–62**
Good Housekeeping Seal of Approval, 450, 625
Good Humor, **262**, 314
Good Humor-Breyer's Ice Cream Company, 70
Good Humor man, 262
Good Maine Food (Mosser), 152
Goodnight, Charles "Chuck", 127, 128, 556
Good Things to Eat (Estes), 351
Goo Goo Cluster, 545
goose, **262**
Gordon, Arthur, 522
Gordon, David George, 319
Gorman, Marion, 366
Gottfried, Ruth A. Jeremiah, 152
Gottfried Krueger Brewing Company, 45
Gould, Beatrice, 449
Gourmet (magazine), 292, 414, 450, 498, 616
gourmet cooking, 293
Gourmet Dinners (Fougner), 152
government pamphlets, 5
government regulations, 5, 227–28, 353–54. *See*
    also Department of Agriculture, United
    States; federal regulations; Food and Drug
    Administration
    on biotechnology, 49
    dairy industry, 182
    on street vendors, 567
Graff, Brian and Sharon, 416
grafting, 334
Graham, Sylvester, 63, 147, 190, **262–63**, 274–75,
    608
    boardinghouses, 57
    and bread, 64
    and condiments, 144
    and rawfoodism, 493
Graham bread, 64
graham cracker, 173
Graham hotels, 263
Graham societies, 263
grains. *See also* beer
    barley, 36
    corn, 63, 168–69
    oats, 421
    rice, 502–3
    wheat, 619–20
    wild rice, 625
Grand Central Oyster Bar, 429
Grand Metropolitan PLC 74, 459
Grand Union Company, 265
Granit Iron Ware, 6
granola, 69, 101, 340, 472
granola bar, 69, 90
Granose Flakes, 69, 101, 340, 608
Grant, Bert, 379
Grant, Ulysses S., 61
Granula, 69, 190
Grape Culture, Wines, and Wine-Making (Haraszthy),
    633
grapefruit, 130
    California, 244
    in film, *219*

grapefruit salad, 127
    honey, 302
    in mai tai, 363
    in zombie, 641
Grape-Nuts, 2, 69, 102, 190, 255, 258, 472
grapes, 243, 245, **263–64**. *See also* wine
    brandy, 63
    Champagne, 103
    eastern U.S. wines, 629
    varieties, 263–64
    wine, 635
Grapes into Wine (Wagner), 633
grasshopper, **264**
grasshopper pie, 264
grasshoppers, 319
graters, **264**, *265*, 418
gravy, 524–25
grazing, 19
Great American Meatout, 17
Great Atlantic and Pacific Tea Company. *See* A&P
great cake, 83, 207
Great Lakes Commercial Fishery, The, **265**
Greek food, 248, 267, 384
Greeley, Horace, 263
Green, Adolphus W., 401
Green, Charles, 175–76
Green, Nancy, 26
Green, Robert, 316
Greenberg, Arnold, 545
Green Burrito, 94, 339
Greenfield, Jerry, 46
Green Giant Company, 337
green goddess dressing, 514
greenmarkets. *See* farmers' markets
Green Tavern, 138
Gregg, Josiah, 461
Gregory, Dick, 11
griddles, 434
griebenes, 331
Griffith, Gregory, 568
Grigg, Charles Leiper, 534
grilling, 164, *165*. *See also* barbecue
    African, 8
    Brazilian, 311
    and California cuisine, 616
    cookbooks, 152
    and hearth cookery, 276–77
    hibachi, 274, 326
    Italian sausage, 322
    Korean American food, 347, 348
    Native breads, 337
    panini, 434
    Philadelphia cheesesteak sandwich, 451
    Reuben sandwich, 501
    Sheboygan bratwurst, 386
    Spamburger, 559
grills, 253, 292
Grimes, William, 248
grinder (hoagie), 298
grinders, **265**, 299
    meat, 265, 303
    mortar and pestle, 394
    Native American, 408
    nut, 417–18
Griswold, Madge T., 320
grits, 169, 230, 301–2
groats, 421
Grocer's Encyclopedia, The (Ward), 151
grocery stores, **265–66**, 287, 456–57
grog, **266–67**, 484
grogshops, 266
Groom, Barbara, 380
Gross, Fritz A., 380
ground beef, 292, 542, 622. *See also* hamburger
ground meat, adulteration of, 271
Ground Round, 306
grouper. *See* bass
gruel, 421
Gruet, 104
grunion, **267**

grunts, 438
guacamole, 28, 195
Guarnaschelli, Maria, 507
Guérard, Michel, 416
Guide Culinaire (Escoffier), 152, 238
Guide for Nut Cookery (Lambert), 420
Guide to Cooking Schools, The, 164
Guide to Easier Living (Wright), 193
Guide to Modern Cookery (Escoffier), 238
Guinness, 563
Guittard Chocolates, 124
Gulbrandsen, Don, 610
Gulf and Western, 529
gum, 80, 89, **267**, 560
gumballs, 609
gumbo, 81, 230, 423, 552
gummy candy, **267**
gusanos, 585
Guth, Charles, 448
gyro, **267**

Häagen-Dazs, **269**, 315
Haas, Eduard, 90
habaneros, 117, 184
Haber, Barbara, 179
hachiyas, 451
Hadaway, William, 564
Hagiwara-Nagata, Sumiharu, 233
Haida. *See* Northwest Coast Indians
Haiku-Sine: 217 Tiny Food Poems (McClelland and
    Watson), 467
Halajian, Peter Paul, 89
halal foods, 333–34
Hale, Sarah Josepha, 167, 439, 449, 483, 523, 587
half-and-half, 175
Halfhill, Albert P., 596
halibut, **269**
Hall, William M., 380
Halloween, **269–70**, 399, 484
ham, 375, 376, 568
Hamantaschen, 331
hamburger, 216–17, 258, **272**, 292, 318, 521,
    621–22
hamburger buns, 65
    sloppy joe, 542
    and Spam, 559
    tenderloin sandwich, 385
    tortillas, as substitutes for, 579
Hamlin, Bill, 337
Hamlin, Willard, 426
Hammond, G. H., 575
Hamwi, Ernest, 315, 384
Hancock Shaker Village, 281
Hand-book of Practical Cookery (Blot), 227, 240–41,
    616
Handwerker, Nathan, 16, 401
Handy, Thomas, 526
Hangtown fry, 241, 429
Hanna, Elaine, 154
Hannon, John, 124
Hansen, Larry, 464
haram foods, 333–34
Haraszthy, Agoston, 627, 633
Hardart, Frank, 28
Hardee, Wilbur, 272
Hardee's, 235, **272**, 339, 471, 510
Harding, Lillian, 624
Harding, Warren G., 624
hardtack, 33, 141, 173, 241, **272–73**
Haribo, 267
Hariot, Thomas, 483, 573
Harland, Marion, 79, 552
Harman, Pete, 520
haroseth, 331
Harper, Michael, 144
Harrelson, Woody, 605
Harriot, Thomas, 96–97
Harris, Jessica, 154
Harrison, Mrs. Benjamin, 13

Harroun, Katherine, 633
Harry's Bar, 55, 62
Hart-Celler Act, 414
Hartford, George H., 265
Hart House Retaurant, 582
Hartshorne, Henry, 151
Harvey, Fred, **273**, 500, 504, 505
Harvey Girls, 504, 505
Harvey Houses, 273, 504, 505
Harvey Wallbanger, 530
Harwell, Gordon, 503, 601
Hash House Lingo (Smiley), 540
Haskell, E. F., 151
Haskell, George, 40
Haskins, Creed, 72
hasty pudding, 209, **273–74**, 481
Hatch Act, 287
Hatcher, Claud A., 510
Hathaway, James A., 575
Havemeyer, Henry, 572
Hawaiian and Pacific Foods (Bazore), 152
Hawaiian food, **274**
   and Japanese, 326
      macadamia nuts, 363
      pineapple industry, 460–61
Hawaiian Pineapple Company, 460
Hawaiian punch, 484
Hawley, Adelaide, 47
hay box, 222
Hayden, H. W., 343
Hayes, Mrs. Rutherford B., 13
Hayes, Rutherford B., 623, 624
Hazan, Marcella, 154
hazelnuts. *See* filberts
Hazelnuts and More (Gerspacher), 420
Hazen, Chester, 104
H. B. Reese Candy Company, 496
health claims for foods, 2–4, 67–68
   advertising, 4
   bananas, 34
   broccoli, 71
   carrots, 95
   cereal, cold, 101
   chocolate, 124
   citrus, 245
   ginger ale, 259
   ice cream sodas, 316
   mineral water, 125
   soda drinks, 50
   tuna, 596
health concerns about foods
   butter and margarine, 365–66
   canned goods, 92
   desserts, 188
   eggs, 114, 207
   fast food, *209*, 217
   fats and oils, 218
   salmonella, 207
   salty snacks, 544
   turkey, 598
   watermelon, 616
health food, 263, **274–75**, 293
   cookbooks, 153
   and juice bars, 337
Healthy Choice, 144
Hearn, Lafcadio, 151, **275–76**
hearth cookery, 14, 159, **276–77**, 344, 599
hearts of palm, **277**
Heater, Maida, 333
Heidrich, Ruth, 416
Heinz. *See* H. J. Heinz Company
Heinz, Henry J., 297–98
Heirloom Vegetable Gardening (Weaver), 205
heirloom vegetables, **277–78**, 344. *See also* heritage
   foods
Helfrich, Ella, 74
Hellman, Richard, 185
Hellmann's mayonnaise, 370
Helme Products, 529
Hemingway, Ernest, 360

hemp, **278**
Henderson, Mary F., 194, 549
Henry, Peter, 408
Henry Heide, Inc., 90, 91
herbal teas, 171
herbicide resistance, and Roundup Ready
   soybean, 49
herbs and spices, 109, 225. *See also* chile; garlic;
   ginger family; mint family; mustard family;
   onion family; parsley family; pepper, black;
   prepared herb and spice mixtures; sweet
   spices
Herbs for the Kitchen (Mazza), 152
Here Let Us Feast (Fisher), 153, 224
heritage breeds, 280
heritage foods, 542. *See also* heirloom vegetables
hermit cookies, **278–79**
hero, 298, 299
herring and sardines, **279**
Hershey, Milton, 89, 122, 125, 279, 388
Hershey Chocolate Company, 4, 122–23, 261, 279,
   451, 496, 617
Hershey Foods Corporation, 91, 261, **279**, 356
Hershey Trust, 279
Hess, Karen, 161, 179, 302, 317–18, 552
Heston, William, 421, 487
Heublein Inc., 341, 530, 612
Hibben, Sheila, 152
Hidden Valley Ranch, 514
highball, **279**
high fructose corn syrup, 23, 170, 176, 197, 571,
   574
Hightower, Jim, 371–72
Hildegard, and beer, 42
Hilgard, Eugene, 628
Hill, Annabella, 151
Hill, Janet McKenzie, 6, 71, 149, 151, 152, 163,
   246, 449
Hines, Duncan, **279–80**, 341, 497, 520
hippocras, 632
Hires, Charles E., 60, 508, 546
Hires Root Beer, 60, 508, 546
Hirsch, Harold, 139
Hirshfield, Leo, 89, 591
Historical Cookbook of the American Negro, 143
historical dining reenactment, **280–81**, 297
historical overview
   1960s to the present, **293–96**
   Civil War and Reconstruction, **285–86**
   colonial period to the Revolutionary War,
      281–83
   Revolutionary War food, **283–84**
   Revolutionary War to the Civil War, **284–85**
   Victorian America to World War I, **286–89**
   World War I, **289–90**
   World War II, **291–92**
   World War II to the early 1960s, **292–93**
   World War I to World War II, **290–91**
Historic Foodways Society of the Delaware Valley,
   296
historiography, **296–97**
History and Description of Modern Wines (Cyrus), 633
History and Methods of the Fisheries (Goode), 269
Hitchcock, Alfred, 390
H. J. Heinz Company, 93, *218*, **297–98**, 342, 636
   advertising, 298
   baby food, 31
   Boston Market, 60
   horseradish, 145
   and kosher foods, 428
   pickles, 453
   tomato juice, 55
hoagie, 181, **298–99**, 569
hochepot, 58
hoecakes. *See* johnnycakes and hoecakes
Hofbraühaus, 46
Hoffman House Bartender's Guide, 368
hogs, 457
hokeypokey men, 569
Holdridge, Herbert C., 609

Holiday magazine, 497
holidays
   and candy, 90
   Chinese New Year, 121
   Christmas, 125–27
   Easter, 203
   Fourth of July, 233–34
   Halloween, 269–70
   Kwanzaa, 349–50
   New Year's celebrations, 413–14
   Passover, 436
   Saint Patrick's Day, 169, 513
   and sugar, 571
   Thanksgiving, 586–88
   Valentine's Day, 603
   Washington's Birthday, 613–14
Holiday World (Santa Claus, Indiana), 16
Holstein cows, 106, 107, 175
Holt, Vincent, 319
Home, 449
Home as Found (Cooper), 454
home baking, 33, 52, 64, 66
Home Candy Making (Rorer), 510
home canning, 91, 92, 291, 368
   and cookstoves, 566
home delivery, and Domino's Pizza, 196
home economics, 41, 116, 117, 143, 254, **299–301**,
   374, 504
Home Helps: A Pure Food Cook Book (Lincoln), 358
Homemade Ice Cream Company, 184
homemade remedies, **301**, 502
homemakers, 254, 299–300, 329–30
home pickling, 453
home preserving, 476
Home Queen Cookbook, The, 189
Homer Laughlin China Company, 466
Home Science Cookbook, The (Lincoln), 358
home wine making, 626, 628, 635
hominy, 169
hominy grits, **301–2**
homogenization, 388
Hone, Philip, 193
honey, **302**
   and artichokes, 25
   and avena, 28
   and baklava, 439
   and barley, 36
   and beer, 42, 166
   components of, 574
   and fruitarianism, 190
   and fry bread, 409
   halal foods, 397
   in *hangwa*, 348
   and haroset, 436
   honey cake, 126, 332
   and hot spiced wine, 632
   in hot toddies, 305
   and no-heat cookery, 165
   as preservative, in preserves, 476
   in *Schnecken*, 333
   slang, 329
   in sofkey, 317
   as sweetener, 68, 145, 282, 574
   in *taiglach*, 333
   and veganism, 604
honeydew melon, 377
Hong Kong Noodle Company, 233
Honigman, John, 233
Hooker, Richard J., 297
Hoosier barbecue, 454
Hoosier cabinet, 345
Hooter's, Buffalo Chicken wings, 74
Hoover, Herbert, 289
Hopkins, Frederick Gowland, 611
hoppin' John, 94, 172, **302**, 503
hops, 42, 70, 432, 433
horchata, 561
Horlick, William, 389
Hormel, Jay, 559
Hormel Foods Corporation, 447, 559

Hormel Girls, 559
Horn, Joe, 28
Horn and Hardart Automat, 28
Horn and Hardart Baking Company, 609
Horn and Hardart Children's Hour, 28
Hors d'Oeuvre and Canapés, with a Key to the Cocktail Party (Beard), 89, 152
hors d'oeuvres. *See* appetizers
horseradish, 144, 145, 203, 399
Horsford Cook Book, The (Farmer), 6
Hostess, **302–3**, 600
Hostetter, George, 630
Hot, Sour, Salty, Sweet: A Culinary Journey through Southeast Asia (Alford and Duguid), 154–55
Hot Brown sandwich, **303**
hot chocolate, 122, 124, 125, 189, 367
    fondue, 227
hot cross buns, 203
hot dog buns, 65, 360
hot dogs, 16, 258, 292, **303–4**, 401, 505
    coneys, 386
    Howard Johnson, 305
    Wienerschnitzel, 624–25
hotel dining rooms, 87, **304–5**
    Waldorf-Astoria Hotel, 595–96
Hotel Keepers, Head Waiters, and Housekeepers Guide (Campbell), *8, 9*, 87, 147
Hotel Monthly Press, 149
hot peppers, 517. *See also* chile
Hotpoint, 564, 589
hot sauces, 117
hot tamales, **305**
Hot Tamales, 338
hot toddies, **305**
Hot Weather Dishes (Rorer), 510
hourglasses, 588–89
House Book, The (Leslie), 210
Household Cyclopedia of General Information Containing over Ten Thousand Receipts (Hartshorne), 151
Household News, 449, 509
Household Searchlight Recipe Book, 114
Housekeeper's Encyclopedia, The (Haskell), 151, 470
Housekeeping in Old Virginia (Tyree), 151
House of Mirth (Wharton), 359
House Servant's Directory, The (Roberts), 9, 147, *150*, 167
Howard, Albert, 426
Howard, Maria Willett, 71, 72
Howard Johnson, 280, **305–6**, 335, 446, 505, 506, 510
Howdy, 534
How I Became Young at 60 (Fletcher), 225
How to Cook and Eat in Chinese (Chao), 152, 153
How to Cook and Eat in Russian (Kropotkina), 512
How to Cook a Wolf (Fisher), 152, 224
How to Keep a Husband, or Culinary Tactics, 425
How to Mix Drinks; or, The Bon Vivant's Companion (Thomas), 135, 167, 258, 390, 540
How to Use a Chafing Dish (Rorer), 510
Huckins, James H. W., 551
Hudson, Henry, 62
huevos rancheros, 69
human rights abuses, 124
hummus, 115, 384
humor, food, **306–7**, 548
Humphrey, Hubert, 319
Hungering for America (Diner), 179
hunger programs, **307–8**, 319–20
    food stamps, 232
    Meals on Wheels, 373–74
    school lunches, 528–29
    soup kitchens, 549–50
Hungry Hearts (Yezierska), 359
Hungry Self, The (Chernin), 359
Hunt, Joseph and William, 308
Hunt Foods, 308
Hunt's, 86, 342,, **308–9**
Hunt-Wesson, 41, 308–9, 496
Hurtz, Gene, 1

hush puppies, **309**
Husted, Marjorie, 47
Hutchinson closure, 60
Hutton, Edward F., 255
Huzenlaub, Eric, 601
hybridization, 631
hydrogenation, 442
Hydrox cookie, 156, 340, 426
Hygrade, 304

Iberian and South American food, **311–12**
ice, 236, **312–13**, 314
iceboxes, 312, **313**
ice cream cone, 314–15, 384, 636
ice cream makers, 254, **313**, 314
ice cream molds, 313, **314**
Ice Creams, Water Ices, Frozen Puddings (Rorer), 510, 633
ice creams and ices, 188, **314–15**
    Alaskan, 12
    baked Alaska, 33
    Baskin-Robbins, 37
    Ben & Jerry's, 46
    and birthdays, 52
    Blue Bell, 56
    Breyers, 70
    Carvel, 53, 95
    and corn syrup, 170
    Dairy Queen, 184
    flavorings, 225
    floats, 389
    frappes, 235
    Frusen Gladje, 269
    Good Humor, 262
    Häagen-Dazs, 269
    Howard Johnson, 234, 305, 335
    Klondike Bar, 146–47, 346
    milkshakes, 235
    Popsicles, 471–72
    post-Revolutionary War food, 284
    soft serve, 184, 581
    Tastee-Freez, 581
    vanilla, 604
ice cream sodas, 314, **315–16**, 389
iced tea, 582–83
icehouses, 312
Ice Screamers, 235
ice tongs, *159*
Ida Bailey Allen's Modern Cook Book, 151
Ida Bailey Allen's Wine and Spirits Cook Book, 152
Ideal Bartender, The (Bullock), 368
I Hate to Cook Book, The (Bracken), 153
Ilitch, Mike and Marian, 360
Ilitch Holdings, 360
Illinois Central Industries, 568
illness. *See* diseases and illnesses
illustrators
    advertising, 42, 47
    Anderson, Harry, 493
    Capp, Al, 493
    Mizen, Frederic Kimball, 493
    Nash, Jim, 487
    O'Neill, Rose, 328
    Parrish, Maxfield, 328
    Rockwell, Norman, 7, 328
    Sundblom, Haddon, 134, 487, 493
    Wallach, Andrew, 395
Imasco, 272, 510
immigrants. *See also* specific nationalities
    and alcohol, 584
    boardinghouses, 57
    and butchering industry, 76
    and settlement houses, 532–33
    soups and stews, 551
    street vendors, 567
    in the West, 239
immigration laws, 119, 213
Imperial Group, 306
Imperial Packing Company. *See* Beech-Nut
in colonial America, 282

incubators, 206
Indian American food, **316–17**
Indian Pale Ale, 568
Indian pudding, **317–18**, 481
Indonesian food, 554
Industrial Designers, Inc., 11
Industrial Luncheon Services, 201
industrial promotion films 186
Industrial Revolution, 2
Industrial Workers of the World (IWW), 213, 499
infant botulism, 302
infant formula, 31
    Borden's condensed milk, 31
    Enfamil, 31
    Mellin's Food, 31
    Nestlé, 411
    Similac, 31
Inge, William, 454
Ingle, John Stuart, 47
Inglenook Book Book, The, 445
Ingram, Bill (grandson), 622
Ingram, Edgar "Billy", 65, 271, 621–22
Ingram, Edgar (son), 622
Injun 'n' Rye, 64, 66
Inness, Sherrie, 179
In-N-Out Burger, **318**
insects, **318–19**
instant hot cocoa, 125
Instead of Chicken, Instead of Meat (Davis), 17
Institute of Culinary Education, *163, 164*, 223
Institute of Food Technologists, and aseptic packaging, 25
institutional food. *See also* prison food; school lunches
    school food, 528–29
intellectual property rights
    Beech-Nut, 42
    Coca-Cola, 139, 149
    copyright infringement, and Baby Ruth, 32
    and genetic modification, 49
    trademark infringement, 42
    international aid, **319–20**
International Association of Culinary Professionals, 116, 294–95, **320**
International Beigel Bakers' Union, 32
International Chili Society, 517
International Culinary Olympics, 605
International Dairy Queen, 184
International Flavors and Fragrances, 225
International Hotel Workers Union, 163
International House of Pancakes, 69, 433
International Industries, 426
International Longshoremen's and Warehousemen's Union, 213–14
internment camps, and Japanese Americans, 326–27
Interstate Bakeries Corporation, 302–3, 600
In the Sweet Kitchen: The Definitive Baker's Companion (Daley), 155
invalid cooking, 301, 355, 421
invasive species, 265
Iowa Agricultural School, 163
Iowa Beef Processing, 76
Irish American foods, 513
Irish coffee, **320**
Irish soda bread, 65, 513
Irish stew, 552
Iron Chef, 490
Iron Horse, 104
irradiation, **320–21**
Irving, Washington, 484
    Bracebridge dinners, 127
    on picnics, 453
Isaly Dairy Company, 346
Isaly family, 146–47, 346
Islam, 333–34. *See also* Muslim dietary laws
Islamic Food and Nutrition Council of America, 398
Islamic law. *See* Muslim dietary laws
isoflavones, 557

IsoSweet, 170
Israel Coe and Company, 343
Israeli food, 384
Italian American food, *209*, 292, 293, 295, **321–22**,
  381
  antipasto, 19
  artichokes, 25
  broccoli, 70
  cookbooks, 154
  Italian beef sandwiches, 386, 569
  Italian sandwiches, 299
  Italian sausage sandwich with peppers and
    onions, **322–23**
  muffaletta sandwich, 395–96
  pizza, 462–63, 464
  salami, 514
Italianmerican: The Scorsese Family Cookbook, 220
Italian seasoning, 476
Ivester, Doug, 134

Jack in the Box, 86, 292, **325**, 424
Jackson, Andrew, *105*, 623
Jackson, James C., 190
Jackson, James Caleb, 608
Jackson, Reuben W., 198
Jacmar Companies, 535
Jacobson, Michael, 100
Jaffray, Elizabeth, 623
J. A. Folger and Company, 226–27
Jägermeister, 167
jalapeños, 117
jam, 477
Jamaican pepper pot stew, 94, 97
Jamba Juice Company, 337
jambalaya, 81, **325**
James, Enoch, 579
James Beard Awards, 39, 100, 446, 639
James Beard Cookbook, The, 40
James Beard Cooking School, 40
James Beard Foundation, 295, 498, 595
James Beard's American Cookery, 40, 71, 154, 187
James Beard's Theory and Practice of Good Cooking,
  40
Japanese American food, 292–93, 294, **325–27**
  in Hawaii, 274
  seaweed, 531–32
  soy sauce, 558
  weddings, 618
Jarden Corporation, 591
Jean-Louis, Cooking with the Seasons (Maroon), 155
Jefferson, Thomas, 97, **327**, 491, 592
  and apricots, 22
  and eggplants, 205
  and French cooking, 238
  and French fries, 237
  and grapes, 263
  and ice cream, 314
  and Italy, 321
  and pasta, 363
  and pigs, 457
  and potatoes, 472
  and sorrel, 549
  and vanilla, 603
Jeffries, James Jackson, 58
Jellinek, E. M., 14
Jell-O, 4, 255, *292*, **327–28**, 472
  advertising cookbooklets and recipes, 6, 7, 328
  flavorings, 225
  molds, **328–29**
Jell-O Girl, 328
jelly, 477
jelly bean, 90, **329**
Jelly Belly, 329
jelly cake, 84. *See also* jelly rolls
jelly rolls, **329**
Jenkins, Herbert, 540
Jennie June, **329–30**
Jennie June's American Cookery Book, 329, 483
jerked meat, 241
Jerpe, John P., 573

Jerrico, Inc., 224
Jersey lightning, 19
Jessel, George, 55–56
Jewish American food, **330–33**, 436, 511–12
  bagels, 32
  bialy, 48
  in community cookbooks, 143
  cookbooks, 152
  and Crisco, 176
  dairy, 181
  delicatessens, 185
  doughnuts, 196
  Dr. Brown's, 196
  egg cream, 205
  and film, 220
  funeral food, 247–48
  knish, 347
  matzo, 368–69
  pastrami, 437
  pickles, 452
  seltzer, 532
  weddings, 617–18
Jewish dietary laws, 32, 330, **333–34**, 353, 428. *See
  also* kashruth
J. Hungerford Smith Company, 1
Jif, 442
Jiffy, 69
Jigglers, 328
Jihad vs. McWorld (Barber), 371
Jim Beam Brands, 61
jingles, 467, 523
  Coca-Cola, 5
  Jell-O, 328
  Oscar Mayer, 428
  Pepsi-Cola, 448
  Sara Lee Corporation, 523
J. Lyons & Co., 37
Joe Booker stew, 200
Joe Lowe Company, 472
John Collins, 140
John Madden's Ultimate Tailgating (Madden and
  Kaminsky), 454
Johnny Appleseed, **334–35**, 385
Johnny Bars, 496
johnnycakes and hoecakes, 65, 67, 230, **337**, 539
Johnson, Gertrude I., 335
Johnson, Howard, 234, 315, **335**
Johnson, Howard Brennon, 306, 335
Johnson, Howard Deering, 305–6, 335
Johnson, Hugh, 633
Johnson, Joshua, 149
Johnson, Nancy M., 313, 314
Johnson, Robert Gibbon, and the tomato, **335**
Johnson, Sherwood, 534–35
Johnson and Wales, **335–36**, 577
John's Pizzeria, 464
Jolly Green Giant, **336–37**
Jones, Evan, 154
Jones, Henry Alfred, 425
Jones, Samuel Messer, 190
Jordan Company, 213
Joseph Campbell Preserve Company, 88
Joseph Fry & Son, 89
Josselyn, John, 317, 483, 615–16, 616
Joyce, Julia, 622
Joy of Cooking, The (Rombauer), 71, 151, 152, 154,
  155, 210, 257, 506–7, 609, 610–11
J. S. Fry and Son, 80
Judson, Clara Ingram, 117
juice bars, 245, **337–38**
juice boxes, 25
juicers, **338**
juicing machine, 245
Jujubes, 90
Jullien, André, 633
jumbles, 156, 188, 196
June Platt's Party Cookbook, 152
Juneteenth, 454
Jung, David, 233

Jungle, The (Sinclair), 2, 75, 108, 187, 271, 275, 485,
  540, 608
Junior's (New York), 107
junk foods, 544
Just Born, 329, **338**

ka'ak, 32
kale, **339**
Kalm, Peter, 319, 360, 423
kalo, 274
Kaltenberg Castle Brewery, 46
Kander, Mrs. Simon, 152, 533
Kandy Kate bar, 31
Kappeler, George J., 140
kapusta, 468
Karcher, Carl, 94, **339**
Karenga, Malauna, 349, 350
Karo Syrup, **339**
kasha, 331–32, 512
kasha varnishkes, 331–32
kashruth, 330–31, 333–34
Kasper, Lynne Rossetto, 154
Kato, Sartori, 138
Katzen, Mollie, 255
Kaufmann, Wendy, 545
Keebler, **339–40**, 341
Keebler, Godfrey, 339
Keebler Company, 213
Keedoozle, 456
Keller, Julius, 133
Kellogg, Ella, 420
Kellogg, John Harvey, 69, 101–2, 190, 263, 275,
  340, 441, 442, 608
  and Fletcherism, 226
  nut butters, 420
Kellogg, Will K., 4, 101–2, 263, 275, 340, 442, 608
Kellogg Company, 69, 190, 213, **340–41**, 503
  acquisition of Keebler, 340
  advertising, 4
  All-Bran, 4, 102, 340
  Bran-Flakes, 340
  Corn Flakes, 2, 340
  Frosted Flakes, 69, 102
  Fruit Loops, 69
  granola bars, 69
  Granose Flakes, 69, 340
  Pop-Tarts, 69
  Raisin Bran, 340
  Rice Krispies, 102
  Smart Start, 103
  Special K, 340
  Sugar Corn Pops, 102
Kelvinator, 497
Kemp, John, 55
Kemp, Ralph, 55
Kendall, Donald, 448
Kennedy, Diana, 154, 490
Kennedy, Jacqueline, 624
Kennedy, John F., and coconuts, 136
Kennedy Biscuit Company, 156
Kenny Rogers Roasters, 402
Kensett, Thomas, 91
Kent, Louis Andrews, 152
Kentucky Fried Chicken, 217, 239, 292, **341–42**,
  520–21, 619, 640
  and Dave Thomas, 588
Kentucky Housewife, The (Bryan), 147, 175
  on barbecue, 165
  broccoli, 71
  on burnt custard, 180
  on carrots, 95
  on chicken, 114
  on cordials, 167
  on gravies, 524
  on mushrooms, 397
  sprouts, 560
Kerr, Alexander H., 368
Kerr, Graham, 99
Kersands, Billy, 26
Kessler (microbrewery), 379

ketchup, 144, 145, 297–98, **342**, 558
　advertising, 186
　bottles, 297–98
　Del Monte, 186
　Hunt's, 308
　preservative-free, 54
Ketchup: Methods of Manufacture (Bitting, A.), 54
kettles, **342–43**
Key Fortune Cookie Company, 233
Key lime pie, 455
Keys, Ancel, 142, 558
Keys, Margaret, 558
KFC. *See* Kentucky Fried Chicken
kielbasa, 468
Kikkoman, 558
kimchi, 348
King Cole Bar, 55
King Kullen, 266
King Ranch Casserole, 97
Kingsford Chemical Company, 292
Kinney, Alva, 144
Kiradjieff, Athanas "Tom" and John, 129
Kirby, Jessie G., 198
Kirchhof, Konstantin, 574
kishke, 332
Kitchell, Alma, 490
KitchenAid, 232
Kitchen Fun: Teaches Children to Cook Successfully (Bell), 117
kitchen gadgets, 345
kitchen gardening, **343–44**
kitchens, 290
　1800 to the present, **345–46**
　cooking equipment. *See* cooking containers; cooking equipment, social aspects of; electric appliances; stoves and ovens; cupboards and food safes, 180
　in dining cars, 192, 482, 505
　dishwashing and cleaning up, 195
　early kitchens, **344–45**
　firehouse kitchens, 221
　hearth cookery, 276–77
　historical reenactments, 280, 281
　professional kitchens, 163–64, 499
　sandwich trucks, 522
　summer kitchens, 92
　test kitchens, 261
kiwis, **346**
Kix, 102
Klaper, Michael, 416
Klink's Baking Company, 16
Klondike Bar, 146–47, **346–47**
kluski, 200
knaidlach, 332
Knight, Gladys, 27
Knight, Thomas, 566
knish, 200, 332, **347**
knives, 125, 195, 538
Kobayashi, Takeru, 401
Koch, Jim, 379
Koeppler, Jack, 320
Kohlsaat, H. M., 362
Kolakofsky, Reuben, 502
koliva, 248
Kolow, Steven, 59
Konstantin Frank Vinifera Winery, 104
Kool-Aid, **347**
Korean American food, **347–48**
　in Hawaii, 274
　weddings, 618
kosher food, 331, 333, 428, 436
　beef boycott, 334
　hot dogs, 303–4
　pickles, 452
　Tastykake, 582
kosher salt, 518
Kossar's, 48
Kosuth Cake, 112
Koziol, Walter, 253
K-Paul's Louisiana Kitchen, 479

Kraft, James, 105, 349, 370
Kraft Cheese Company, 105
Kraft Foods, 93, 176, 255, 347, **348**, 357, 363, 401, 426, 429, 472, 609
　advertising, 349, 370
　advertising cookbooklets and recipes, *84*
　Breyers, 70
　brownie pizza, 72
　mayonnaise, 370
　Tombstone Pizza, 591
Kraft General Foods, 472
K ration, 42, 142
kreplach, 200, 332
Kresge, Sebastian, 479, 585
Kretchmer, Martin, 357
Krispy Kreme, 41, 196, **349**
Kroc, Ray, 217, 234–35, 292, 371, 506, 508
　and Dairy Queen, 184
Kroger, and halal foods, 398
Kroger, Bernard H., 265
Kropotkina, Alexandra, 512
Krueger Special Beer, 45
Krug, Charles, 627
krupnik, 330
Kruse, E. F., 56
Kucinich, Dennis, 605
kugel, 332
Kuhnau, Steve, 337
Kunett, Rudolph, 612
Kutztown Soda Company, 50
kvass, 349, **349**
Kwanzaa, 11, **349–50**

Labor Day picnics, 454
labor unions. *See* unions
La Choy Food Products, 41, 560
Ladies' Handbook, The, 143
Ladies' Home Journal (magazine), 4, 26, 88, 149, 151, 449, 509
ladles, *550*
Lady Baltimore (Wister), 351
Lady Baltimore Cake, 111, **351**
lady cake, 83
lady fingers, **351**
La Fonda del Sol, 40
Lagasse, Emeril, 100, **351**
lager beer, 14, 15, 43, 45, 46, 73, 475–76
Laird and Company, 20
La Leche League, 31
Lam, Tom, 179
lamb and mutton, 101, **351–52**
　Easter lamb, 203
Lambert, Almeda, 420
Lambrinides, Nicholas, 130
lampreys, 265
Lancaster Caramel Company, 122, 279
Land Grant Education Act, 187
Land O'Lakes, 76
Lantern Festival, 121
Lappé, Frances Moore, 154, 171
lard and shortening, **352–53**
larding, 165
largemouth bass, 38
Las Americas Restaurant, *177*
Lasater, Dale, 542
Lassen, Louise, 270–71
Latin American foods
　avena, 28
　avocados, 28–29
　Nuevo Latino cuisine, 417
　weddings, 618
latke, 332
La Varenne, Francois Pierre, 240, 354, 484
La Varenne pratique (Willan), 625
La Vita Inn, 472
law, **353–54**. *See also* dietary laws; Food Additive Amendment (1958); Food and Drug Administration; Food Control Law; immigration laws; Meat Inspection Act (1906); North American Free Trade

Agreement (NAFTA); Prohibition; Public Law 480; Pure Food and Drug Act; trademark infringement
commercial weights and measures, 374
Elderly Nutrition Program, 373
and maple syrup, 365
and molasses, 392
and processed cheese, 609
and sugar content of melons, 377
and wine, 63, 245
Lawes, John Bennet, 427
Lawrence, William A., 175–76
Lawson, Nigella, 490
Lay, Benjamin, 16
Lay, Herman W., 240, 544
layer cake, 84
Lazaroff, Barbara, 480
Lazenby, Robert S., 197
lazy Susan, 58, 346
Leaf North America, 91
leathers, fruit, 477
leavening agents, 83, 109, 436. *See also* baking powder; bicarbonate of soda; chemical leavening; cream of tartar; yeast
Lebadies Bakery, 624
LeBeau, Joe, 349
Le Bernardin (New York), 164
Lectures on the Science of Human Life (Graham), 144
Lee, Archie, 134
Lee, Joseph, 66
Lee, N. K. M., 25, 200
leeks, **354**, 424
　in colcannon, 513
　ramps, 491
lefse, 527
legal issues. *See* law
Legal Seafoods, 223, 360
legumes. *See* beans; peas; soybeans
　and nitrogen fixation, 49
Leigh, Mitch, 523
lekakh, 332
Le Magimix, 231–32
LeMaire, Étienne, 491
Lemcke, Gesine, 476
lemonade, **354–55**
Lemonade Lucy, 13, 354, 624
lemons, 130, 621
　California, 244
　in hot spiced wine, 631
　juice, 244, 245
　in kvass, 349
　in punch, 484
　in sangria, 522
　substitutes, 438
Lender, Murray, 32
Lender's, 32
Lenox, Walter Scott, 466
Lenox China Company, 466, 623
lentils, 383. *See also* beans
　funeral food, 248
　and mock foods, 391, 392
　in Pacific Northwest, 432
Leong, William T., 233
Le Pavillon, 446, 500
Le Potagerie, 446
Le Robot-Coupe, 231–32
Leslie, Eliza, 26, 133, 147, 162, 210, 238, 273, **355**, 413, 423, 441, 524, 551, 552
　on hotel dining rooms, 304
　list of cookbooks, 355
　southern sources, 10
Lester Milk Jar, 388
Let's Eat Right to Keep Fit (Davis), 275
lettuce, 86, **355**
　boycott, 214
　California, 86
　in club sandwich, 133
　in Consommé Celestine, 492
　consumption, 606
　cooked with peas, 443

lettuce (*Contd.*)
    in fast food hamburgers, 271, 272
    in Gold Rush, cure for scurvy, 241
    in hoagies, 298
    in Hot Brown sandwich, 303
    iceburg, 86, 362, 513–14, 577, 592
    in Navajo taco, 410
    in pepper pot, 552
    in salads, 253, 513–14
    sandwich condiment, 521
    slang, 141
    in tacos, 579
lettuce and tomato salad, 514
levees, 413, 623
Levenstein, Harvey, 179
Lewis, Aylene, 27
Lewis, Carl, 605
Lewis, Dio, 144
Lewis, Edna, 154, 454
li, 443
liberty cabbage, **355**
liberty gardens, 344
library collections, **355–56**, 444–45
Library of Congress, cookbook collection, 444
Lichine, Alexis, 633
licorice (liquorice), **356–57**, 435
Lidia's Italian American Kitchen, 490
Liebig Company, 6
Liebling, A. J., 498
Life, 88
LifeSavers, 42, 90, **357**
Liggett, Robert, 50
light beers, 357–58, 361, 389–90
light lager, **357–58**
Light n' Tasty, 450
lime, 130
lime rickey, **358**
Lincoln, Abraham, 61
    and apple brandy, 19
    and Thanksgiving, 587
    and USDA, 187
Lincoln, D. A., 494
Lincoln, Mary, 59, 149, 151, 162, 358, 392, 449
Lincoln, Mrs., **358**
Lind, James, 611
Linden Hills (Naylor), 359
Lindt, Ruldolphe, 89
Lindy's (New York), 107, 501
linseed oil, 23
Lipe, Walter, 41
lipids, 418
Lipton, 293
    french onion dip, 145, 195
    tea, 4
Lipton dips, 195
Lipton Tea, 4
liqueurs, 167. *See also* cordials
    coffee, 72
    at Delmonico's, 186
    Galliano, 530
    in hot spiced wine, 632
    and Irish coffee, 320
    maraschino, 364, 367, 641
    Ratafia, 493
    strawberry, 367
    use in foods, 63
liquid diets, 68
liquor cabinets, **359**
Listeria monocytogenes, 598
Lite Beer, 361
literature and food, **359–60**
Little Acorn (Becker), 507
Little Caesars, **360**, 463
Little Tavern, 271
Litton, 380
Lizzie Bars, 496
lobster, **360**, 530, 535
    antebellum, 284
    canning, 92
    clambakes, 132

food festivals, 230
lobster Newburg, 37, 186, 492, 529
lobster pounds, 531
    New England, 412
    and New Year's, 414
    poor man's lobster, 393
    salads, 513
    shore dinners, 531
lobster roll, 248, **360**
Lobster Roll Restaurant, 360
locusts, 319
Loft Candies, 448
lokshen, 332
Lolliard Tobacco Company, 42
lollipops, 338, 532
Lombardi, Gennaro, 464
Long John Silver's, 224, 640
Longstreet, Abby Buchanan, 19
Longworth, Nicholas, 635
Lord, Isabel Ely, 151
Lorna Doone, 156
Lost Coast Brewery & Café, 380
Lotus Fortune Cookie Company, 233
Louie, Edward, 233
Louisiana Cookin', 490
Louisiana Purchase Exposition, 315, 636
Louis' Mixed Drinks with Hints for the Care and Service of Wines (Muckensturm), 364, 368
Low, Henry, 152
low-calorie syrup, **361**
low-carb diets
    Atkins diet, 275
    salami, 515
low-carbohydrate light lager, **361**
Lowenstein, Eleanor, **361**, 539
Lowney, Walter M., 122
Lowney's Brownies, 71–72
lox, 332–33
Loyalty Cook Book: Native Daughters of the Golden West (Borba), 581
lu'au, 274
Lubin, Charles, 522
Lucas, Dione, 151–52, 490
Lüchow, August Guido, 361
Lüchow's (New York), **361**
Lukins, Sheila, 155, 498
lunch boxes, dinner pails, and picnic kits, **361–62**
luncheonettes, **362**, 500, 547
    diners, 190–91
    Horn and Hardart Automat, 28
    Schrafft's, 529
luncheons, bridge, 70
Lunch Room, The (Richard), 113
Lupo's, 464
Lurp (Long Range Patrol Ration), 142
Lust, Benedict, 494
lutefisk, 527
Lutes, Della T., 152
lycopene, 591
Lydia Pinkham, 301
lye hominy, 301–2
Lyman, Joseph B. and Laura E., 345
Lynes, Russell, 253

M&M milk chocolate candies, 89, **364**, 366
macadamia nuts, **363**
macaroni and cheese, 349, **363**, 363, 609
macaroon, 156
MacAusland, Earl, 450
MacDonaldization Revisited, 372
mace, 418, 575
Macfadden, Bernarr, 190, 609
machinery, farm, 620
machines. *See also* electric appliances
    bread making, 66–67
    bread slicer, 66
    ice cream makers, 313
    juicers, 338
Mack, Walter, 140, 448
mackerel, **363**

MacPherson, John, 152
macrobiotics, 171, 190
Macy's Cook Book for the Busy Woman (Claire), 152
Madeira, 62
Made Over Dishes (Rorer), 510
Madison, Dolley, 623
Magarrell, Don, 11
magazine advertising, 448–49
magazines. *See* periodicals
Magic Seasoning Blends, 480
Magic Yeast, 4
magret, 200
Maid-Rite restaurants, 542
Maillard Corporation, 338
Maillard reaction, 589
mai tai, **363–64**
maize. *See* corn
majolica, 465
makrouh foods, 398
Malin, Joseph, 223
malted milk powder, 389
malteds. *See* malts
malting, 70
maltodextrin, 108
Malt-O-Meal, 69
malts, 389
Ma Maison (Los Angeles), 86, 239, 480
mamaliga, 333
mandarins, 130
M and F Worldwide, 356
Man Eating Bugs: The Art and Science of Eating Insects (Menzel and D'Aluisio), 319
Manhattan (cocktail), 135, **364**
Manhattan Brewing Company, 379
manioc, 96
Manischewitz, 369
Manischewitz, Dov Ber, 369
Manners and Social Usages (Sherwood), 210
manoc starch, 97
Mansfield Pure Milk Company, 146, 346
Manual for Army Cooks, 15
Man with No Name (Amos), 213
Mapes, Emery, 493
maple beer, 45
maple syrup, 145, 230, **364–65**
Maranz, Leo, 581
maraschino cherries, 110
marble cake, 84
Marcalus, Nicholas, 617
March beer, 14
Marchiony, Italo, 315
Mardi Gras cake, 425
Margareten, Regina and Ignatz, 369
Margaret Rudkin Pepperidge Farm Cookbook, The, 447
margarine, 76, 108–9, 218, 292, **365–66**
margarita, **366**, 585, 586
Margraf, Andreas, 572, 574
Mario, Thomas, 367
marionberry, 431
Marker's Mark, 62
Market Assistant, The (DeVoe), 151
Market Book, The (DeVoe), 151
market gardens, 605–6
marketing. *See* food marketing
Marketing Hall of Fame, 88
markets. *See* convenience stores; farmers' markets; grocery stores; markets
Markevitch, Marie Alexandre, 512
Markham, Gervase, 639
Marlboro Man, 337
marmalade, 477
Maroon, Fred J., 155
Marriott, J. Willard, 234
Marriott Corporation, 234, 306, 510
Marryat, Frederick, 390
Mars, 89, 123, 364, **366**, 389, 545
    3 Musketeers, 89
    M&M milk chocolate candies, 89
    Mars Bar, 89, 366, 389

Milky Way Bar, 89
  Peanut M&Ms, 89
  Snickers, 89
  Uncle Ben's, 601
Mars, Forrest, 89, 364, 366, 389, 601
Mars, Frank, 89, 366, 389, 545
Marsh, Leonard, 545
marshmallow, 7
  fudge, 246
  and Jell-O salads, 327, 329
  mock, 391
  Moon Pie, 383, 438, 555
  Peeps, 90, 203, 338
  Rice Krispies Treats, 503
  sandwiches, 393
Marshmallow Fluff, **366–67**, 624
Marshmallow Peeps, 338
Martha Stewart Living Omnimedia, Inc., 562
Martin, Benny, 467
Martin, Clovis, 467, 569
Martin, John, 530, 579
Martin, Judith, 210
Martinez, 367
Martinez, Mariano, Jr., 366
martini, 135, 259, **367–68**, 610
Martini, The (Conrad), 367
Marvel, Tom, 633
Marvelli Company, 6
Mary at the Farm and Book of Recipes (Thomas),
  445
Mary Frances Cook Book, The (Fryer), 151, *155*
Mary Jane candies, 413
Märzen/Oktoberfest, 14, **368**
marzipan, 14
mash, 620
mashing, 70
mash tuns, 70
Mason, John L., 92, 368
Mason jars, 92, **368**
Massey, Jack, 341
Mastering the Art of French Cooking (Child), 55, 99,
  116, 153, 154, 238, 254, 293, 524
Mastro's Pizza, 636
Matchell, Leonard Jan, 361
Mathieu, Philippe, 236
Matthews, John, 547
Matthews, "Uncle" Jimmy, 72
Mattus, Reuben, 269, 315
matzo, 333, **368–69**, 436
matzo balls, 200
Maude, John, 38
Maxim, 369, 410
Maxson Company, 11
Maxwell, John, 609
Maxwell House, 137, 255, **369**, 410, 472
May, Robert, 237
May Breakfasts, 230
Mayer, Oscar F., 428
Mayfield, J.C., 139
Mayflower, 42
mayonnaise, 144, 145, 185, **369–70**, 513
Maytag, Fritz, 44, 107, 379
Maytag blue, 107
Mazola, 605
Mazza, Irma Goodrich, 152
McAuliffe, Jack, 44, 379
McBride, Mary Margaret, 489
McCall's (magazine), 449
McCann-Erickson, 390
McCarthy, James R., 152
McCartney, Paul, 605
McCarty, Michael, 417
McClelland, Micki, 467
McCormick, Cyrus, 620
McCormick and Company, 172, 225, 604
McCullough, H. A. "Alex", 184
McCullough, John F., 184
McDonald, John, 61
McDonald, Maurice, 86, 234, 292, 371–72, 622
McDonald, Richard, 86, 234, 292, 371–72, 622

McDonaldization, **371–72**
McDonaldization of Society, The (Ritzer), 371, 372
McDonald's, 86, 216, 217, 218, 272, **370–71**,
  580, 640
  apple pie, 20
  Boston Market, 60
  Breakfast Burrito, 75
  Chicken McNuggets, 114–15
  criticisms of, 371–72
  diners, 191
  Egg McMuffin, 69
  franchising, 234–35
  French fries, 237
  Golden Restaurant Operations, 60
  halal foods, 398
  Playlands, 508
  Ronald McDonald, 507–8
McFadden, Cyra, 586
MCI (Meal, Combat, Individual), 142
McIlhenny's Tabasco Bloody Mary Mix, 56
McKinley Act, 570
McLamore, James W., 74
McLamore, Jim, 217
McMein, Neysa, 47
mead, 302
Mead Johnson, 31, 68
Meadow Gold butter, 41
meal patterns, **372–73**
  boardinghouses, 57
  in colonial America, 282
  Native American, 407
meal service, 192–94
Meals on Wheels, 307, **373–74**
meal trays, and airplane food, 11
measurement, **374–75**
  in African American cooking, 10, 87
  barrels as measures, 146
  in cake baking, 84
  of calories, 418, 421
  in cookbooks, 117, 161
  standardization of, 117, 215, 315, 358, 449,
    495, 533
  of sugar content, 377
  Sumerian, 36
  of temperature, 246, 374, 472, 566
  of time. *See* timers, hourglasses, egg timers
meat, **375–77**. *See also* beef; pork
  barbecue, 35–36
  buffalo, 73–74
  butchering, 75–76
  canned, 432
  chipped beef, 122
  in colonial America, 282
  consumption, 292, 376
  corned beef, 169
  game, 251–53
  and kosher kitchens, 334
  lamb, 101
  lamb and mutton, 351–52
  in New England, 411–12
  sausage, 525–26
  venison, 610
  whale, 619
meatballs recipe, 494
meat distribution, 592
meat grinders, 265, 303, 529
Meat Inspection Act (1906), 1, 2, 75, 108, 187,
  353, 485
meatpacking industry, 75–76, 286, 376, 575–76.
  See also butchering
  criticisms of, 2, 540, 608
  processing line, 24, 75, 576
  and refrigeration, 375
meat pies
  bierocks, 48
  Jamaican, 10, 94
  Jewish, 331
  medieval, 180, 455
  Natchitoches meat pies, 311, 401
  pasties, 386, **436–37**, 526–27

tamale pie, 581
mechanical cream separator, 76
Medearis, Angela Shelf, 454
medicinal alcohol, 167, 195, 301
medicinal whiskey, 61
medicine, 301
Mediterranean Culinary Historians of Houston,
  296
Meehan, Michael J., 262
Megargel, Roy, 140
Meier, Lina, 257
Meili, Jack, 459
Meister Brau, 361, 389
Melba, Nellie, 440
Melba toast, 440
Mellanby, Edward, 612
Mellin, Gustav, 31
Mellin's Food, 31
Mellowes, Alfred, 497
melons, 214, 245, **377–78**. *See also* watermelon
Memoir on the Cultivation of the Vine in America, A
  (Adlum), 633
Memorable Meals (Claiborne), 131
Menches, Frank, 271
Menches, Joseph, 636
Mendel, Gregor, 48
men's roles. *See* gender roles
Menu-Cook-Book (Bradley), 19
Menzel, Peter, 319
Meredith, E. T., 450
mescal, 585, 586
mesclun, 355
Metcalfe, William, 607–8
méthode champenoise, 103, 104, 632
methylmercaptan, 26
Metrecal, 68
Metzelthin, Pearl V., 152
Mexican American food, 311, **378–79**
  avocados, 28, 29
  in California, 86, 461
  cookbooks, 38
  enchilada, 207
  Frito pie, 240
  funeral food, 248
  nachos, 209–10
  pork fat, 353
  and Rick Bayless, 38–39
  salsa, 195, 517
  tacos, 579
  tamale pie, 581
  tamales, 581
Mexico—One Plate at a Time, 39
Meyers, Perla, 154
mezze, 19
Miami Subs, 224, 402
Michel Guérard's Cuisine Minceur, 154
Michelob, 73
microbreweries, 44, **379–80**
  and beer barrels, 45
  and Coors, 166
  in Pacific Northwest, 432
  and spruce beer, 560–61
  strong pale ale, 568
Microscopic Examination (Bitting, K.), 54
microwave ovens, 11, 236, 243, 295, **380**
Middle Atlantic states, **380–83**
Middle Eastern influences on American food,
  383–84
  appetizers, 19
  beer, 42
  coffeehouses, 138
  mezze, 19
  weddings, 618
Midwest, 73, 592
Midwestern regional cookery, **384–85**, 455
Mike and Ike, 338
Milbank, Jeremiah, 58
military provisions. *See* combat food
military rations. *See* combat food
military slang, 540

milk, 181, **386–88**
  additives, 108
  adulteration, 387
  buttermilk, 77
  in Indian pudding, 317, 318
  and kosher kitchens, 334
  packaging, 25, 41, 58, **388**, 388
  powdered, **388**
  and school lunches, 528–29
  and vitamin D, 612
milk marketing order system, 182, 387
milkshakes, malts and floats, 38, 235, **389**
Milky Way, 89, 366, **389**
Milla Handley, 104
Millar, Bryan, 498
Millau, Christian, 238, 416, 417
Millennium Guild, 16
Miller, David, 179
Miller, Frederick, 389
Miller, Mark, 86, 99
Miller Brewing Company, 43, 361, **389–90**
Miller Lite Beer, 390
milling, flour, 26, 64, 66, 255, 458, 619, 620
Millstream (microbrewery), 379
Millville Manufacturing Company, 147
mimosa, **390**, 425
mincemeat pie, 126, 438
minerals, 419
miners' food, 436–37, 555
Minnesota Valley Canning Company, 336
mint, 390. *See also* mint family; mint julep
  crème de menthe, 264
  desserts, 264
  in kvass, 349
  LifeSavers, 357
  Mint Meltaways, 213
  mint sauce and jelly, 352, 476
  mojito, 178, 417
  Thin Mints, 259
  in Vietnamese food, 553
mint family, **390**
mint julep, 61, 62, **390–91**
Mint Products Company, 357
mints, 357
Mintz, Sidney, 179
Minute Maid, 144, 245, 425
Minute Rice, 503
Miracle Whip, 349, 370, 636
Miss Farmer's School of Cookery, *60*, 163, 215
Miss Manners, 210
Mister Donut, 201
Mitchell, Earl, 393, 555
mixed drinks. *See* cocktails
mixers, 67
  7 UP, 534
  ginger ale, 259
  sherry, 535
  vermouth, 610
mixes, prepackaged, 85, 109. *See also* Aunt Jemima
    Pancake Mix
  adulteration of, 109
  Airy Fairy, 23
  biscuit, 69
  cake, 53
  cookie, 156
  Duncan Hines, 280
mix-ins, 46
Mizen, Frederic Kimball, 493
M'Mahon, Bernard, 178
Mobil Oil restaurant guides, 497
mock foods, **391–92**, 455
  apple pie, 20, 391
  turtle soup, 531
mock turtle soup, 551
Modern American Drinks (Kappeler), 140
Modern French Cooking (Puck), 239, 480
Modern French Cooking for the American Kitchen
    (Puck), 239
Modern Home Products (MHP), 253
mojito, 178, 417, 511

molasses, 7, 170, **392–93**, 411, 574, 576
  brownies, 71–72
  hermit cookies, 278–79
  Indian pudding, 317–18
  and rum, 511
  taffy, 520
molds
  butter, *77*
  cake, *83*
  ice cream, 314
  Jell-O, 328–29
Mole Poblano, 117
Molson Inc., *164*
Monaghan, Thomas S., 196
Monarch Beverage Company, 394
Mondavi, Cesare, 393, 506
Mondavi, Robert, **393**, 506, 633–34
Mondavi family, 635
Monell Chemical Senses Center, 224
monkfish, **393**
Monnerat, Jules, 411
Monsanto, 49, 278
Monte Cristo sandwich, **393**
Moon Pie, **393–94**, 438, 555
moonshine, **394**, 479, 621
Moores and Ross Milk Company, 31
Moosewood, 501
Moosewood Cookbook (Katzen), 99, *154*
Morales, Pancho, 366
More Classic Italian Cooking (Hazan), 154
Morgantown Glassware Guild, 627
Mormon Church, 13, 209, 572
Morren, Charles, 603
Morris, Herbert T., 582
Morrison, Wade B., 197
mortar and pestle, **394**
  and African cooks, 8, 85
  and *haroseth*, 331, 436
  and Native Americans, 63, 302, 410
Mortland, Elsie, 597
Morton's, 220
Mosser, Marjorie, 152
Most Noble Diet, The (Eisman), 416
Mott, H. R., 510
Mounds Bar, 89, 451
moussaka, 384
Moveable Feast, A (Hemingway), 360
movies, food in. *See* film, food in
movie tie-ins, 497
Mower, Fred L., 367
Moxie, 50, 139, **394**
mozzarella, 105, 182, **394–95**
MRE (Meal, Ready-to-Eat), 142, 541
Mr. Peanut, **395**, 441
Mrs. Allen on Cooking, Menus, Service, 151
Mrs. Allen's Cook Book, 151
Mrs. Appleyard's Kitchen (Kent), 152
Mrs. D. A. Lincoln's Boston School Kitchen Text-Book,
    358
Mrs. Fields cookies, 156, **395**
Mrs. Hill's Southern Practical Cookery, 151
Mrs. Lincoln's Boston Cook Book, 151, 358, 494
*Mrs. Lincoln's Cook Book: What to Do and What Not to
    Do in Cooking*, 358
Mrs. Olson, 227
Mrs. Rorer's New Cook Book, 510
Mrs. Rorer's Philadelphia Cook Book, 162, 509
Mrs. Smith's pies, 20
Mrs. Winslow's Domestic Receipt Book, 6
Muckensturm, Louis, 364
muffaletta sandwich, **395–96**
muffin method, 85
muffins, bran, 63
mulattos, 117
mulberries, **396**
mulled wine, 631–32
mullet, **396**
mulligan stew, **396**
Multimixer, 371
Murdoch, William, 563

Murrey, Thomas J., 178, 551
Murrie, Bruce, 364
museums, 297, 650
  Culinary Archives and Museum, 577
  Dr Pepper, 197
  Jell-O, 328
  Memphis Pink Palace, 457
mush, 273
  cornmeal, 317–18, 337
  mamaliga, 333
mushrooms, **396–97**
  black, 120
  in Chicken a la King, 113
  cloud ear, 121
  cream of mushroom soup, 70, 97
  enokidake, 295
  gathering, 258, *382*
  gravy, 239
  in mock oysters, 391
  morels, 17
  polyols, 574
Muslims, 11, 101, 397–98
mussels, **398**
mustard, **398–99**
  in baked beans, 292
  barbecue sauce, 35, 554
  condiment, 144, 145, 272, 298, 347, 370, 386,
    437, 445, 521, 524
  Dijon, and tariffs, 214
  hot sauces, 117
  in Indian American cookery, 317
  In-N-Out Animal Style burger, 318
  in mock crab sandwich, 391
  mustard sauce, 9, 122
  and pickles, 452, 453
  on soft pretzels, 477–78
mustard family, **399**
mutton, 351–52
My Ántonia (Cather), 360
My Cookery Books (Pennell), 444
Mystery Chef, 152
Mystery Chef's Own Cook Book, The (MacPherson),
    152
My Table Dining Guide, 467
myths and folklore, **399–400**
  Johnny Appleseed, 334–35
  Native American, 403, 406
  Robert Gibbon Johnson and the tomato, 335

Nabisco, 156, 173, 339, 357, 391, **401**, 426, 447,
    620
nachos, 209–10, 544
Nadaff, George, 59–60
NAFTA. *See* North American Free Trade
    Agreement (NAFTA)
Nagreen, Charlie, 271
Napa Valley, 393, 506
napkins, 88, 194, 508
Nash, Jim, 487
Nash, Ogden, 367
nashi, 443
Natchitoches meat pies, 311, **401**
*Nathalie Dupree's Southern Memories: Recipes and
    Reminiscences*, 154
Nathan's Famous, 16, 224, 303, *303*, **401–2**
Nation, Carrie, 43
National A&W Franchisees Association (NAWFA),
    1
National Biscuit Company. *See* Nabisco
National Confectioners Association, 89, 90
National Cook Book (Hibben), 152
National Cookery Book, 151
National Council on Alcohol and Drug
    Dependence, 13
National Dairy Products Corporation, 70
National Institute on Alcohol Abuse and
    Alcoholism, 14
National Labor Relations Act, 213
National Licorice Company, 356
National Organic Program, 50

National Organic Rule, 426, 427
National Organic Standards Board, 426
National Temperance Society, 584
Nation of Islam, dietary laws, 11, 209
Native American foods, 81, 301–2, 311
  before and after contact, **402–5**
  Appalachian food, 18
  authenticity, 209
  beans, 39
  boiled leaf breads, 305
  bread, 63–64
  buffalo, 73
  camas root, 87
  cassava, 96–97
  Chesapeake region, 111
  chocolate, 124
  clams, 132
  corn, 68, 168
  cornmeal, 273
  desserts, 188
  fish, 265
  fruits, 243
  game, 251
  Indian pudding, 317–18
  insects, 319
  johnnycakes and hoecakes, 337
  maple syrup, 364–65
  Middle Atlantic states, 380–81
  Midwestern, 384
  mulberries, 396
  nuts, 420
  oysters, 429
  pecans, 444
  pine nuts, 461
  Plimoth Plantation, 280–81
  plums, 466
  pumpkins, 483
  ramps, 491
  salt, 518
  sassafras, 523
  spiritual and social connections, **403–7**
  spruce, 560
  succotash, 569
  sunflowers, 573
  supawn, 573
  technology and food sources, **407–10**
  weddings, 617
Native Americans, and Thanksgiving, 586, 587
Naudin, Charles, 377
Navajo tacos, **410**
Navratilova, Martina, 605
Naylor, Gloria, 359
Neal, Bill, 154
Neal, John, 369
Near a Thousand Tables (Fernandez-Armesto), 249
near beer, 13, 479
Nebraska Consolidated Mills (NCM), 144
NECCO wafers, 413
nectarines, 139, 140
needle beer, 479
Negrete, Daniel, 366
Nehi Corporation, 510
Neil, Marion Harris, 186
Nero Wolfe mysteries, 152
Nesbitt, Henrietta, 624
Nescafé, 137, 138, 410, 411
Nestlé, 31, 58, 137, **410–11**, 423
  $100,000 Bar, 89
  acquisition of Squibb, 31
  Butterfinger, 77
  Crunch bar, 89
  Milk Chocolate Bar, 89
  Taster's Choice, 137
Nestlé, Henri, 58, 89, 388, 411
Neufchatel, 175–76
New, Ilhan, 41, 560
New Albion Brewery, 44
New American Cook Book (Wallace), 151
New American Cookery, 20
New American cooking, 417

"new and improved", 6
New Book of Cookery, A (Farmer), 63, 215
New Coke, 134, 140
New England, **411–12**
  boiled dinner, 169
  clambake, 132
  maple syrup, 364–65
  molasses, 392
  Moxie, 394
  Whoopie pie, 624
New England Breakfast Breads (Swett), 151
New England Confectionery Company (NECCO),
  90, 413, **413**, 603
New England Economical Housekeeper (Howland),
  147
New England Kitchen, 504
New England Kitchen Magazine, 449
New Haven Restaurant Institute, 163, 180
New Jersey, 380–83, 381–83
  applejack, 19, 20
  Atlantic City, 298, 395, 520, 579
  Blimpie, 55, 569
  blueberries, 56
  cabbage, 79
  Central Asian immigrants, 100
  Cuban immigrants, 177
  diners, 191
  flavor companies, 225
  glass-blowing industry, 157, 260
  Howard Johnson, 306, 335
  Neufchatel, 175
  Revolutionary War food, 283
  tomato canning, 590
  wheat production, 619
  wine-making, 626, 635
New Mexican cookery, 556, 557. *See also*
  Southwestern regional cookery
New Orleans Culinary History Group, 296
New Orleans syrup, **413**
New Recipes for Cooking (Leslie), 413
newsletters and journals, food history, 297
New Ways for Oysters (Rorer), 510
New World Coffee, 500
New Year's celebrations, 399, **413–14**. *See also*
  Chinese New Year
  eggnog, 205
  Japanese American, 326, 327
New York City. *See also* Coney Island
  A&P, 265
  Astor House, 304, 499
  automats, 28
  bars, *37, 43*
  beer gardens, 45, 46
  Caribbean influences on American food, 94
  Central Asian immigrants, 100–101
  charity picnics, 454
  City Hotel, 304, 499
  culinary collections, 356
  delicatessens, 185, 196, 452
  fairs and expositions. *See* Crystal Palace
    Exhibition *and* New York World's Fair;
    firehouse cooking, 221
  flavor companies, 225
  flavorings companies, 225
  food writing, 151
  hotels, 37
  and ice, 312
  invention of ice cream cone, 315
  Korean American food, 348
  luncheonettes, 500
  New York Hotel, 499
  New York style pizza, 463
  and pigs, 284, 457
  restaurant guides, 497, 498
  settlement houses, 532, *533*
  street vendors, *323, 362, 415*, 471, 477, 567–68
  taverns, 582
  Waldorf-Astoria Hotel, 595–96
  water supply system, 614–15
  World's Fair. *See* New York World's Fair

New York Condensed Milk Company, 58
New York Cooking School, 149, 162, 434
New York Dairy Company, 388
New York food, **414–15**
  bagels, 32, 176, 181
  bialys, 48
  cheesecake, 107, 176, 181, 257
  clams casino, 133
  delicatessens, 185
  Dr. Brown's, 196–97
  egg cream, 125, 175, 204–5
  hero, 299
  knish, 347
  lox, 332
  Nuyorican influence, 482
  pickles, 452
  Reuben sandwich, 501–2
  seltzer water, 532
  soft pretzels, 477
New York Hotel, 499
New York restaurants
  Aquavit, 248
  Benihana, 294
  Brawta Café, *93*
  Café Moutarde, *500*
  Chalet Suisse, 227
  cheesecake, 107
  Cheyenne diner, *191*
  Delmonico's, 33, 149, 185–86, 238, 241, 270,
    321, 352, *414*, 491–92, 513, 595
  Exchange Buffet, 80
  Fraunce's Tavern, 499
  Italian, 322
  La Caravelle, 500
  Le Bernardin, 164
  Le Pavillon, 446, 500
  Lüchow's, 361
  Lutèce, 500
  oyster bars, 429
  Park Slope Ale House, *379*
  Patria, 417
  potato dishes, 473
  Rector's, 62
  Russian Tea Room, 512
  Schrafft's, 529
  Tontine Coffee House, 315
  21 Club, 500
  vegan, 605
  Vong, 249
New York State. *See also* Buffalo Chicken wings
  Anchor Bar, 74, 230
  asparagus, 26
  Beech-Nut, 41–42
  beef, 381
  canning, 91
  cheese, 104, 106
  Chinese American food, 121
  Culinary Historians of New York, 296
  currants, 180
  dairy industry, 76, 77, 175, 181, 182, 365, 381
  duck raising, 199
  Dutch influences on American food, 79, 109,
    177, 188, 201, 381, 413
  fire blight, 443
  grapes, 243, 263
  Jell-O museum, 328
  rum, 511
  salt works, *519*
  Shakers, 383
  wheat, 381, 412, 619, 620
  wine, 104, 257, 263, 383, 626, 627, 629, 630, 632
New York Times Cook Book, The (Claiborne), 253,
  293
New York World's Fair, 500, 522, 636
  cookbooks, 152
  Elsie the Cow, 59
  Wonder Bread, 65
*New York World's Fair Cook Book: The American
  Kitchen* (Gaige), 152
niacin, 108, 612

Nigella Bites, 490
nightclubs, 36
nitrogen fixation, 49, 558
Nix, John, 590
nixtamalization, 301, 302
Noble, Edward, 357
Noble, Sherb, 184
No Foreign Food (Pillsbury), 179
Nomenclature of the Apple (Ragan), 21
noncaloric sweeteners. *See* artificial sweeteners
nopalitos, 80
Norberg, Inga, 152
Nordic Ware, 74
Norfolk dumpling, 200
North American Free Trade Agreement (NAFTA), 214, 339, **415–16**
North American Vegetarian Society, **416**
Northbourne, Lord, 426
Northwest Coast Indians, 12
Northwood (Hale), 483
Norworth, Jack, 173
Notes on a Cellar-Book (Saintsbury), 633
Notes on the State of Virginia (Jefferson), 97
Not Now But Now (Fisher), 224
nouvelle cuisine, 154, 238, 248, 294, **416–17**, 524
Novartis, 31
Nuevo Latino cuisine, **417**
nursery rhymes, 467, 547
nut butters. *See* peanut butter
nutcrackers and grinders, **417–18**
nutmeg, 575
nutmeg grinders, **418**
nutraceuticals, 23
Nutrament, 68
Nutrasweet, 56, 218
nutrition, 170–71, 299–300, 373, **418–20**, 469–70, 504
  additives, 108
  Center for Science in the Public Interest, 100
  child, 528
  criticisms, 100
  prison food, 478
Nutrition Labeling and Education Act, 100, 419
nuts, **420**
  almonds, 14
  Brazil nuts, 63
  cashews, 96
  chestnuts, 112
  coconuts, 135
  filberts, 219
  and Halloween, 270
  macadamia nuts, 363
  nutcrackers and grinders, 417–18
  peanuts, 96
  pecans, 444
  pine nuts, 461
  pistachios, 462
  as snacks, 543–44
  walnuts, 613

Oates, Joyce Carol, 359, 454
oatmeal, 421
  cookies, 156, 421
  in goetta, 261
  in Granola, 101
  gruel, 301
  krupnick, 330
oats, **421**. *See also* oatmeal; Quaker Oats
  avena, 28
  in bread, 589
  in early America, 282, 284
  in goetta, 385
obesity, 190, 204, **421–23**. *See also* overnutrition
  and film, 220
  and food magazines, 450
  and packaging, 433
Obici, Amedeo, 395, 544
Ocean of Flavor, An: The Japanese Way with Fish and Seafood (Andoh), 154
Of Cabbages and Kings Cookbook (Turgeon), 98

Official Mixer's Manual, The (Duffy), 279
Ogilvy and Mather, 496
Ogle, William, 623
Ogura, Keishi, 380
Oh Henry!, **423**
Ohsawa, George, 190
oil cakes, 85
oils. *See* fats and oils; vegetable oils
okra, **423**
okra soup, 551
Oktoberfest, 45, 368. *See also* Märzen/Oktoberfest
Oktoberfest beer, 14
Old Bay Seasoning, 172, 476
Old Doc's Soda Shop, 197
old-fashioned (cocktail), 61, **423**
Old Sturbridge Village, 281
Old-Time Saloon, The (Ade), 152
Olean, 218
Oleomargarine Act, 485
Olestra, 218
oliekoecken, 196, 202
Olive Garden, 255
olive oil, 218, 513, 605
Oliver, Garrett, 15, 36, 433
Oliver, Marion, brownie recipes, 71–72
olives, 36, 86, **423–24**
  as appetizers, 18, 19, 535
  California, 86
  mock olives, 391
  in muffaletta sandwich, 395
  and picnics, 454
  in *salade Niçoise*, 514
Olivier, Raymond, 611
Olivieri, Pat, 451
Oltz, Harry M., 184
O'Mahoney, Jerry, 190–91
One Hundred Four Prize Radio Recipes (Allen), 152
O'Neill, Rose, 328
onion family, **424**
onion rings, **424**, 425
onions, 253, **424–25**, 605. *See also* leeks; ramps
  bialys, 48, 331
  and bratwurst, 386
  and chili, 118, 129
  and clarifying butter, 133
  cocktail onions, 368
  French onion dip, 145, 195, 293
  French onion soup, 292
  Georgia crop, 556
  home remedies, 301
  in Indian American cookery, 317
  Italian sausage sandwich with peppers and onions, 322–23
  in jambalaya, 325
  and Philadelphia cheesesteak sandwich, 451
  slang, 128, 540, 541
open pit barbecue, 35
Opus One, 393, 506
orange blossom (cocktail), 425
orange flower water, **425**
orange juice, 244, 337, 373, **425–26**. *See also* concentrated orange juice
  in California sour, 621
  frozen, 69, 236, 245
  in grasshopper, 264
  juice bars, 337, 426
  in mimosa, 390
  packaging, 25
  powdered, 245
  in sangria, 522
  in screwdriver, 530
  slang, 264
  sodas, 534
  Tang, 581
Orange Julius, 184, 337, 425, **426**
oranges, 130. *See also* concentrated orange juice; orange juice
  in ambrosia, 188
  bitter oranges, 135
  blood oranges, 295

California, 243–44, 353
  in marmalade, 241, 477
  orange bitters, 367
  orange-flavored cordials, 167
  orange flower water, 425
  orange rind, 477
  in punch, 484
  in sidecar, 62
  Sunkist, 2
  symbolism, 121, 248
oregano, 390
  in *adobo*, 482
  in chili, 118, 119, 129, 378
  in Italian beef sandwiches, 569
  in Navajo taco, 410
  in prepared seasonings, 476
O'Reilly, C.J., 526
Oreos, 156, 340, **426**
organic farming, 124, 144, 170–71, 245
organic farms, 427
organic food, **426–27**, 607
  and cooperatives, 166
  and genetic modification, 50
  Sunrise, 103
  and USDA, 187
Organic Foods Production Act, 426
organic gardening, 171, 344, **427–28**
Organic Gardening and Farming, 427, 429
organizations, 652–54
orgeat, 425
Origin Diet, The (Somers), 275
Orthodox Union and food, **428**
Orville Redenbacher's Gourmet Popping Corn, 496
Oscar Mayer, 303, 304, **428–29**
Oscar of the Waldorf, 595–96
Osius, Frederick, 55
osso dei morti, 248
O Taste and See: Food Poems, 467
Out of Our Kitchen Closets: San Francisco Gay Jewish Cooking, 143
Ovaltine, advertising, 5
ovens, 84, 344, 563. *See also* microwave ovens; stoves and ovens
  for bread, 67
  cracker bakers, 173
  Dutch ovens, 202
  pizza, 463–64
  tin reflecting, 345
  wood and coal, 565–66
ovenware, 158
overnutrition, 469
Owades, Joseph L., 361
Oxford Companion to Wine (Robinson), 633
oyster bars, **429**
oyster loaf sandwich, **429**
oyster plant. *See* salsify
oysters, 172, 284, **429–30**, 431–32, 535
  Chesapeake region, *111*
  food festivals, 230
  fried, 240
Ozai-Durrani, Ataullah K., 503

Pabst Brewing Company, 43, 44, 73, 636
Pabst Park, 45
Pace, Dave, 195, 379
Pace Foods, 195
Pacific Northwest, 55, 87, **431–32**
packaging, **432–33**. *See also* canning and bottling; milk, packaging; TV dinners
  aseptic packaging, 25
  and branding, 4
  butter, 41
  canning and bottling, 368
  fish, frozen, 51
  frozen foods, 242–43
  glassine bags, 544
  glass jars, 41–42
  ketchup, 342
  meats, 523

and microwave ovens, 380
milk, 388
preservatives, 109
Sara Lee Corporation, 522
soda drinks, 546
take-out foods, 580
tin, 242
waxed paper, 617
paczki, 386
Page, Charles, 58, 411
Page, David, 155
pain perdu, 69
Painter, William, 60, 546
Palace Hotel, 514
pale ale, 433, *433*, 568
Paleolithic Prescription, The (Eaton, Shostak, and
     Konner), 275
Palladin, Jean-Louis, 155
palm, hearts of, 277
Palmer, Charles H., 190
palmetto, 277
Palombo, Ruth, 179
Pan American Airways, 11
Pan-American Exposition, 636
Pancake Cookbook (Waldo), 433
pancake flour, 26
pancake pans, 201, **434**
pancakes, 25, **433–34**. *See also* johnnycakes and
     hoecakes; pancake pans
     Aunt Jemima Pancake Mix, 5, 26, 27, 28, 69
     blini, 511
     blintzes, 69, 331
     buckwheat, 69
     buttermilk, 77
     Dutch influences on American food, 201
     and Peking duck, 121, 637
     potato, 332, 437, 473
     and syrups, 365
Pancakes Aplenty (Church), 433
Pancakes for Breakfast (de Paola), 117
pan de muertos, 248
panhas, 529
panini, **434**
panocha, 246
Pan-Pacific Cook Book, 151
pans. *See* pots and pans
Papa John's Pizza, 463
Papendick, Gustav, 65, 66, 521
Papin, Denis, 477
Pappe, Charlie, 548
paprikas, 117
Paradox of Plenty (Levenstein), 179
Paramount's Kings Island (Kings Island, Ohio), 16
pareve, 428
Parker House rolls, 65
Parker's Tonic, 301
Parloa, Maria, 59, 72, 162, **434–35**
Parrish, Maxfield, 328
parsley, 435
     in American chop suey, 15
     and bread sauce, 524
     in fried chicken, 239
     and Irish stew, 552
     in Italian seasoning, 476
     parsley dumplings, 200
     parsley-stuffed hams, 568
     at Passover, 436
     in tabbouleh, 384
parsley family, **435**
parsnips, 95, **435**
partridge, **435–36**
pashka, 107
pasillas, 117
passenger pigeon, 252, **436**
Passover, 369, **436**
Pasteur, Louis, 64
pasteurization, 181, 387
     and cheeses, 106
     and processed cheese, 609
pasties, 386, **436–37**, 526–27

Past Masters in Early American Domestic Arts, 281
pastrami, **437**
pastries, **437–38**
     pasties, 436–37
patent barley, 36
patent medicine, 2, 108, 151, 301, 327, 485
     advertising cookbooklets and recipes, 6
     Coca-Cola, 2, 133
     drinks, 67–68
     Moxie, 394
     phosphates, 451
pathogens, 453
Pat's King of Steaks, 451
Pauling, Linus, 275, 419
pawpaw, **439**
PBS, 625
peaches and nectarines, **439–40**
Peach Melba, 440
peach parers and stoners, **440**
Peacock Alley (McCarthy), 152
peanut butter, 340, 420, **441–42**, 608
     Reese's Peanut Butter Cups, 496
peanut oil, 605
peanuts, 95, 395, **440–41**
     Baby Ruth, 31–32
     and George Washington Carver, 96
     as snacks, 543–44
pearl ash, 83, 109, 147, 639
pearled barley, 36
pearl tapioca, 97
pears, **442–43**
peas, **443–44**. *See also* beans; hoppin' John;
     legumes
     advertising, 336–37
     black-eyed, 9, 10, 39, 111, 350, 554.
     chickpeas, 115
     cowpeas, 171–72.
     goober peas, 547–48. *See also* peanuts
     Jolly Green Giant, 336–37
     and rice dishes, 503
     ship food, 535
     and TV dinners, 599, 600
pecan pie, 339
pecans, **444**, 568
pectin, 476, 477
peelers, 472
Peeps, 203
Peet's Coffee and Tea shop, 562
Peking Duck, 121
pellagra, 301
Pemberton, John S., 133, 139
pemmican, 241, 263
Pendennis Club, 61
Pendery, Dewitt Clinton, 476
Penick and Ford, 8
Pennell, Elizabeth, **444–45**
Pennsylvania Brewing Company, 46
Pennsylvania Dutch Cooking (Weaver), 179
Pennsylvania Dutch food, 257, **445**
     New Year's celebrations, 413
     pickles, 453
     pretzels, 478
     scrapple, 261, 529–30
     yummasetti, 640
penny candy, 90, 591, 609
People for the Ethical Treatment of Animals
     (PETA), 17
Pépin, Jacques, 154, 306, **445–46**
pepper, black, 145, **446–47**
Pepper, James E., 61
Pepperidge Farm, **447**
pepperoni, **447**
pepper pot, 94, 97, 381, 552–53
peppers, hot, 117, *118*. *See also* chile
PepsiCo, 93, 341, 425, 512, 640
     formation of, 448
     and Pizza Hut, 463
     Taco Bell, 579
Pepsi-Cola, 134, **447–48**
     acquisition of Frito-Lay, 544

cola wars, 139–40
flavorings, 225
perch, **448**
Perdue Farms, 114
periodicals, **448–50**, 651
Perkey, Henry, 101–2
Perkins, Cora, 72, 151
Perkins, Edwin, 347
Perkins, Jacob, 497
Perkins, Wilma Lord, 151
Pero, Anthony "Totonno", 464
perry, 442
Perry, Henry, 384
Persian foods. *See* central Asian food
persimmons, **450–51**
Peruzzi, Mario, 395
Perz, Rudy, 459
pesticides, 426, 428
pestle, 394
Pet, Inc., 568
petcha, 333
Peter, Daniel, 411
Peter Pan, 442
Peter Paul, 91
Peter Paul Candy Company (Mounds Bar), **451**
Peterson, Robert O., 86, 325
Petiot, Ferdinand "Pete", 55
petite cuisinere habile, La (Utrecht-Friedel), 238
Peto, Morton, 492
Petrini, Carlo, 171, 542
pewter, 157
Peychaud, Antoine Amédée, 81, 305, 526
Peychaud's bitters, 135
Pez, 90
Pfizer, and Chy-Max chymosin, 49
pharming, 49
Phenix Cheese Company, 349, 609
Philadelphia, 33, 381
Philadelphia cheesesteak sandwich, 381, **451**
Philadelphia Cooking School, 149, 162, 509
Philadelphia Cream Cheese, 176, 333
Philadelphia pepper pot, 381
Philadelphia soft pretzel, 381, 477–78
Philadelphia world's fair. *See* Centennial
     International Exhibition
Philip Morris, 255, 349, 389, 401, 472
     Maxwell House, 137
     purchase of General Foods, 369
Philippe the Original, 236
Philippines Packing Corporation, 186
Philosophy of Housekeeping, The (Lyman), 345
phosphates, **451**
phylloxera, 263, 626, 628, 635
Physical Culture, 609
Physick, Philip, 546
phytonutrients, 557
Picayune Creole Cook Book, 85, 200
Pickarski, Ron, 605
Pickett, Anne, 104
pickle juice, and athletes, 452
pickerel, **451**
pickles, 178, **451–52**. *See also* condiments; pickles,
     sweet; pickling
     and delicatessens, 185
     and hamburgers, 272, 370
     and H. J. Heinz Company, 297
     kimchi, 348
     okra, 423
     pastrami, 437
     in Pennsylvania Dutch food, 445
     and picnics, 454
     in saloons, 257
     and salt, 518
pickles, sweet, **452–53**
pickling, 169, 424, **453**
Picnic Adventures (Gilman), 454
picnics, 16, *289*, **453–54**
     and bratwurst, 386
     and casseroles, 97

picnics (*Contd.*)
  clambake, 132
  crab boils, 172
  Fourth of July, 233, 234, 326
  and grilling, 399
  and ice, 313
  as inspiration for waxed paper, 617
  and lemonade, 354
  and pasties, 437
  and peanuts, 395
  picnic kits, 361–62
  picnic parks, 15–16
  tailgate picnics, 580
  watermelon, 616
Pictorial Review (magazine), 449
pie birds, 455
pie-making tools, 455
pierogi, 200, 333, 468
pie safes, 180
pies and tarts, 188, 438–39, **454–56**
  chess pie, 339
  Midwestern, 385
  pasties, 436–37
  pecan pie, 339
  pies as funeral food, 247
  shoo-fly pie, 536
pigeon, 252, 436
Piggly Wiggly, 266, 290, 450, **456–57**
pigs, **457–58**
Pig Stand, 198–99, 424, 506
pike, **458**
pilafs, 101, 114, 383, 503
Pillsbury, 255, **458–59**
  acquired by General Mills, 459
  acquired by Grand Metropolitan, 459
  advertising, 459–60
  and Ben & Jerry's, 46
Pillsbury, Charles, 255, 458
Pillsbury, Richard, 179
Pillsbury Bake-off Contest, 74, 158, 458, **459**
Pillsbury Company, 269, 620
  advertising cookbooklets and recipes, 117
  Burger King, 74, 458
  cookie mixes, 156
  Green Giant, 458
  Häagen-Dazs, 238, 269, 458
  refrigerated cookie dough, 156
  Steak & Ale, 458
  Totino's Pizza, 458
Pillsbury Cookbook, The, 154
Pillsbury Doughboy, 458, **459–60**
Pillsbury Flour Mills, 458
Pillsbury-Washburn Flour Mills, 458
pilsener, 460, **460**
pimiento cheese sandwich, **460**
piña colada, 94
pineapple, **460–61**
Pinedo, Encarnación, **461**
pine nuts, **461**
Pinkham, Lydia, 6
Pinnacle Foods Corporation, 573
pinole, **461–62**
Pioneer Chicken, 471
pioneers and survival food, 222, **462**, 502
pistachios, 86, 420, **462**, 544
pita, 66, 209, 267, 384
pizza, 322, **462–63**
  California-style brick-oven, 86, 480
  frozen, 243
  frozen foods, 591
  pepperoni and, 447
Pizza Hut, 74, 196, 292, 341, **463**, 464, 640
Pizza Time Theatre, 127
pizzerias, **463–64**
  California Pizza Kitchen, 86
  Chuck E. Cheese Pizza, 127
  Domino's Pizza, 196, 463, 464
  Little Caesars, 360
  Pizza Hut, 196
  Pizzeria Uno, 463

  Sbarro, 526
  Shakey's Pizza, 534–35
  Tombstone Pizza, 591
Pizzeria Uno, 463
PL 480, 319–20
plank cookery, 165, 223
Planters Peanuts, *99*, 395, 441, 544, 605
planter's punch, 484
plastic bags, **464**
plastic covering, **465**
plastics, 433
  Tupperware, 596–97
plastic wrap, 465
plates, **465–66,** 594
Platina, 18
Platt, June, 152
Playboy's Host and Bar Book (Mario), 367
Pleasures of the Table (Ellwanger), 151
pledge cards, and temperance, 13
Plimoth Plantation, 280
plum cake, 83
Plummer, Ed, 534–35
plums, 244, **466–67**
plum wine, 245
pluots, 466
Plymouth succotash, 569
poaching, 164
poblanos, 117
Po'Boy sandwich, **467**, 569
pocket soup, 241
pod corn, 168
Poetical Cook-Book, A, 149
poetry, food, 283, 367, **467**, 483, 484
poi, 274
Point, Fernand, 416
poisons 468, 502
Poison Squad, 2
poke salad, **468**
Polish American food, **468–69**
  bagels, 32
  bialy, 48
  bouja, 58
politics of food, **469–70**
Polk administration, 624
pollock, **470**
Polushkin, Maria, 200
polyethylene, 433, 464, 597
polyols, 574
polyvinyl chloride, 465
polyvinylidene chloride, 465
pomace, 129
pome, 56
pomegranates, **470**
popcorn, 168, 173, **470–71**, 495–96, 544
popcorn wagon, 470, 471
Popeye, and spinach, 560
Popeyes, 128–29, **471**
Poplawski, Stephen, 55
Popsicles, **471–72**
Pop-Tarts, 69
pop wines, 245
porcelain, 101, 623
pork, 375–76, 457–58. *See also* bacon; barrel pork;
  ham; pigs; salt pork
  American chop suey, 15
  in antebellum America, 284
  in Appalachian diet, 17
  barbecue, 11, 35, 158–59, 385
  blood pudding, 284
  bratwurst, 230, 386
  in Brunswick stew, 72, 142
  in Chesapeake diet, 111
  in Chinese diet, 119, 120, 121, 293
  chitterlings, 122
  chorizo, 125
  Christmas dinner, 127
  "city chicken", 258, 392
  in colonial America, 282
  in Cuban diet, 94, 178
  and dietary laws, 11, 350, 397

  French dip, 236
  fried pork rinds, 94
  goetta, 258, 261, 385
  in Hawaiian diet, 274
  and hoppin' John, 39, 172
  hot dogs, 303
  and irradiation, 320
  Italian sausage, 323
  in the Midwest, 385
  in mock foods, 391
  in Natchitoches meat pies, 401
  in pasties, 386
  in pepper pot, 552
  pepperoni, 447
  and picnics, 454
  Pig Stand, 198
  and sauerkraut, 399, 413
  sausages, 525
  salami, 514
  scrapple, 69, 529
  in slave diet, 285
  soul food, 9
  in Southern regional cookery, 555
  in Southwestern regional cookery, 556
  Spam, 559
  in tacos, 579
  in tamales, 581
  Vienna sausage, 611
pork fat, 352–53
port, 62
porter, 563
porter bottle, 60
Portuguese foods, 311
Portuguese influences on American food. *See*
  Iberian and South American food
Portuguese sweet bread, 66
Post, Charles William, 69, 102, 139, 190, 255, 275, 472
Post, Emily, 70, 194, 210, 537
Post, Marjorie Merriweather, 51, 255, 472
Post Foods, **472**
  Cocoa Pebbles, 69, 472
  Fruity Pebbles, 69
  and General Foods, 472
  Grape-Nuts, 2, 69, 102, 190, 255, 258, 472
  Raisin Bran, 102, 472
  Sugar Crisp, 102
  Toasties, 102, 255, 472
post-Revolutionary War food, 284–85
Postum, 69, 255, 328, 472
Postum Company, 51, 102, 139, 242, 255
potash, 109
potassium bicarbonate, 109
potassium carbonate, 109
potato chips, 195, 237, 543, 544, 636
  Lay's, 240
  and Olestra, 218
  packaging, 617
potato-cooking tools, **472**
  Idaho, 192
  potato steamers, 164
potatoes, 311, **472–73**, 605. *See also* French fries;
  pancakes, potato; potato chips; potato-
  cooking tools; sweet potatoes
  casseroles, 15, 97
  in corn chowder, 495
  in early America, 282, 311, 431
  funeral potatoes, 247
  and genetic modification, 49
  Irish potato famine, 278, 412, 513, 549
  knish, 200, 332, 347
  in Mulligan Stew, 396
  Ore-Ida, 298
  in Pacific Northwest, 431
  and picnics, 454
  pierogi, 200, 333
  potato salad, 513, 514
  slang, 541
  soups and stews, 550, 552, 610
  U.S. consumption, 591, 606

pot cheese, 77
pot holders, **473–74**
potlatch, 406
potpies, 438
pots and pans, 157, 159, *283*, *285*, 345, **474**
  ale slipper, 14
  bundt pan, 74
  chafing dish, 103
  cleaning, 195
  cornbread baking pans, 169
  Dutch ovens, 202
  fondue pot, 227
  hearth cookery, 276–77
  jelly-roll pans, 329
  kettles, 342–43
  Native American, 408
  pancake, 434
  pancake pans, 201
  pie pans, 455
  sheet pans, 329
pot stills, 196, 562–63
poultry and fowl, **474–75**. *See also* chicken
  sanctuary, 17
  Southern regional cookery, 555
poultry industry, 475
Pound, Wendy, 380
pound cake, 83
powdered drinks. *See also* coffee, instant
  Kool-Aid, 347
powdered milk, 388
power bars, 90
Practical Cooking and Dinner Giving (Henderson), 194
  sorrel, 549
Practical Home Economics, 15
Practical Housekeeper, The (Ellet), 149
  on napkins, 194
pralines, 82, 246, 444, 568
prawns. *See* shrimp and prawns
premium beers, 568
premium lager, **475–76**
Premium saltine, 173
prepared herb and spice mixtures, **476**
preservation of food
  in Alaska, 12
  canning and bottling, 91–93
  of cream, 175
  drying, 199
  fermentation, 218, 348
  freeze-drying, 235
  freezers and freezing, 236
  of fruits, 245
  in Korea, 348
  pickling, 451–53
  refrigeration, 312–13
  salt and salting, 169, 348, 517–20
  of sausage, 525–26
  smoking, 543
preservatives, 1–2., 625 *See also* chemical additives
preserves, **476–77**
Preserving and Pickling (Lemcke), 476
President Baking Company, 213
Presidia, 542
pressed glass, 260
pressure cookers, **477**, 520
pretzel, **477–78**, 544
Pretzel Boy, 240
Prevention (magazine), 275, 426, 450
price controls, 291
price-fixing, Archer Daniels Midland, 24
price supports, 187, 214, 290, 570
pricing, 231
prickly pears, 80
Prim, Sam Houston, 197
Prime Motor Inns, 306
Princeton Famrs, 495
Pringles, 544
print advertising, 2, 5, 6, 231
prison food, **478**

Procedures for the Appraisal of the Toxicity of Chemicals in Food, 108
  processed foods, 105, 349, 559, 609
processing line, Armour, 24
Procter & Gamble, 176, 218, 227, 442, 508, 544
  Crisco, 6, 176
  Folgers, 137
  and kosher foods, 428
Product 19, 340
product placement, 5
Professional Vegetarian Cooking (Bergeron), 416
Prohibition, 12–13, 36, 37, 43, 61, 251, 258–59, 286, 290, 359, 379, **478–79**, 516–17, 583–85
  and Anheuser-Busch, 73
  and bars, 37
  and Cuba, 511
  and fruit wines, 245
  and ice cream sales, 315
  moonshine, 394
  and restaurants, 500
  and soda fountains, 547
  and whiskey, 620
  and wine industry, 626, 627, 628, 629, 635
promotions, 32
propylene glycol, 108
Protein Power (Eades and Eades), 275
proteins, 418
Prudhomme, Paul, 99, 154, 295, **479–80**
prunes, 466
Public Cup Vendor Company, 609
Public Enemy, The, 219
public health, 387, 421–22, 469. *See also* nutrition; obesity; Pure Food and Drug Act
Public Law 480, 319–20
pubs. *See* bars and drinking establishments
Puck, Wolfgang, 86, 99, 239, 248, **480–81**
puddings, 188, **481**
  scrapple, 529
Pudgie's Famous Chicken, 224
Puerto Rican food, **481–82**
Puffed Rice, 102, 503
Pullman, George M., 192, 482, 500
Pullman car, 192, 482
Pullman kitchen, 482
Pullman loaf, 482
pumpernickel, 65
pumpkin pie, 455, **482–83**, 484
pumpkin pie spice, 476
pumpkins, **483–84**
  Halloween, 269
  in New England, 411
punch, 484, **484**, 632
  sangria, 522
  whiskey sour, 621
punch bowl, 484
punch-top cans, 60
Punchy, 484
Pure Food Act, 1, 2
Pure Food and Drug Act, 5, 6, 75, 93, 187, 228, 261, 275, 287, 301, 353, **484–85**, 540, 608, 625
  Food Additive Amendment (1958), 108, 225
Pure Food Manufacturers Association, 308
pure food movement, 2, 485, 625
Pure-Pak, 388
Puritans, 126
Purvis, William, 363
push-top can, 60
Puzo, Mario, 219
Pyrex, 158, 261
Pythagoreans, 607, 608

quahogs, 132
Quaker City Confectionary Company, 261, 356
Quaker Mill Company, 421
Quaker Oats, 2, *67*, 421, 432, 487
  advertising, 4, 5, 7, 487
  Aunt Jemima, 27–28
  breakfast oats, 69
  Cream of Wheat, 69

  and kosher foods, 428
  and oatmeal cookies, 156
  Puffed Rice, 102
  and Snapple, 545
Quaker Oats man, **487**
Quakers, 381, 478–79
Quaker Woman's Cookbook, A, 179
Queen of the Kitchen, Old Maryland Receipts (Tyson), 151
quenelles, 200
Query, Archibald, 367
queso de tuna, 80
Questing Cook, The (Gottfried), 152
quiche, 180
quick freezing, 51, 242
quick-service food. *See* fast food
Quigley, Sam, 424
quince, 476, **487**
Quiznos Sub, 569
quotas, 214

Race for Life, A (Heidrich), 416
Radcliffe Culinary Friends, 295
radio, 5, 28, 231, 369
radio jingles. *See* jingles
radio/TV food shows, 41, 47, 98–100, **489–91**, 625
  60 Minute Gourmet, 490
  Betty Crocker Cooking School of the Air, 47
  Ciao, Italia, 490
  Cooking Mexican, 38
  Elsie Presents James Beard in "I Love to Eat", 40, 98–99, 490
  French Chef, The, 98–99, 115–16
  Frugal Gourmet, The, 490
  fusion food, 248
  Galloping Gourmet, The, 99
  Iron Chef, 490
  James Beard, 40
  Lidia's Italian American Kitchen, 490
  local radio stars, 489
  Louisiana Cookin', 490
  Mexico—One Plate at a Time, 39
  Mystery Chef, 152
  To the Queen's Taste, 490
  Romagnolis' Table, The, 490
  Yan Can Cook, 490, 639
radishes, 297, **491**, 605
Raeder, Ole Munch, 458
Raffel, Forrest, 23
Raffel Brothers, Inc., 23
Raffles Hotel, 540
ragout, 551
railroad chefs, 10
railroads, 284–85, 287, 592. *See also* refrigerated cars, rail; transportation of food
  dining cars, 191–92, 482
  and Harvey Houses, 273
Rain, Patricia, 604
Raisinets, 89
raisins, 247
  ants on a log, 100
  in apple pie, 20
  in babka, 331
  in brownies, 72
  in cakes, 83, 85
  California crop, 86
  in chess pies, 112
  conserves, 476, 477
  in fruit wines, 245
  in funeral pie, 247
  funeral pie, 445
  in hermit cookies, 278
  in hot spiced wine, 632
  in *koliva*, 248
  in kvass, 349
  in moonshine, 394
  in Navajo cake, 406
  in oatmeal cookies, 156
  in oliekoecken, 202
  Raisin Bran, 102, 340, 472

raisins (*Contd.*)
  Raisinets, 89
  raisin grapes, 264
  Salzburger raisin bread, 257
  in *schnecken*, 333
  in scrumpy, 129
  in watermelon cake, 616
Raklos, John, 362
Ralston Purina, 325
Ramos gin fizz, 80, 425
ramps, 424, **491**
ranch dressing, 514
Randolph, John, 70
Randolph, Mary, 20, 97, 147, 205–6, 239, 309,
  327, 354, 363, 374, 423, 425, 460, **491**, 524,
  549, 552, 599
Ranger Joe Popped Wheat Honnies, 102
ranges, 345, 346
Ranhofer, Charles, 33, 149, 186, 238, **491–92**, 524,
  551
Ransom's Family Receipt Book, 6
rapeseed, 218
rapeseed oil, 605
raspberries, **492–93**
Rastus, **493**
ratafia, **493**
rationing, 289, 290, 291–92
Rausing, Ruben, 25
raw food cookery, 165
rawfoodism, **493–94**
raw foods movement, 226
Rawlings, Marjorie Kinnan, 152, 277
Rawls, J. Leonard, 272
Raytheon Corporation, 380
RC Cola, 555
RDAs, 300, 419
ready-mix foods. *See* mixes, prepackaged
ready-to-eat cereals. *See* cereal, cold
recipes, 5–8, **494–95**. *See also* advertising
  cookbooklets and recipes; cookbooks and
    manuscripts
  African American, 9
  in magazines, 4
  in poetry, 467
Recipes from Home (Page and Shinn), 155
Reciprocal Trade Agreements Act, 214
Reckitt and Colman, 398
Reckitt Benckiser, Inc., 398
recombinant bovine growth hormone, 182
recombinant DNA technology. *See* biotechnology
Recommended Dietary Allowances. *See* RDAs
Rector, George, 152
Rector Cook Book, The (Rector), 152
Rector's, 62
Rector's Marine Café, 62
recycling, 433
red beans and rice, 39, 81
Red Coach Grills, 306
Redding, Cyrus, 633
Redenbacher, Orville, **495–96**
Red Hots, 89–90
Red Lobster, 255
red pepper, 145
red snapper, **496**
redware, 157, 159
Reese, Harry Burnett, 496
Reese's Peanut Butter Cups, **496**, 545
Reese's Pieces, 497
refrigerated cars, rail, 287, 312, 575–76, 592
  Armour, 24–25
  and meatpacking, 75
  and vegetable shipping, 606
refrigeration, 24–25, 51, 56, 284–85, 312–13
  and food transport, 575–76
  and meatpacking, 24–25, 375
refrigerators, 236, **496–97**
regional cooking, and dining cars, 192
regional foods, 209, 239
Reichl, Ruth, 498
religious beliefs about eating, 159, 181, 203, 209

religious food restrictions. *See* Jewish dietary laws;
  Muslim dietary laws
Research Chefs Association, 295
reservations, and Native Americans, 403
Restaurant Associates, 40
restaurant awards and guides, 279, 280, **497–98**
restaurant critics and food columnists, **498–99**
Restaurant Institute of Connecticut, 180
restaurant labor unions, **499**
restaurants, 290, **499–501**. *See also* bistros;
  cafeterias; diners; fast food; hotel dining
    rooms; luncheonettes; New York restaurants;
    oyster bars; pizzerias
  Arnaud's, 82
  The Bakery, 577, 594
  Chez Panisse, 86
  Durgin-Park, 137
  Eutropheon, 494
  German American, 257, 361
  Howard Johnson, 305–6, 335
  Indian, 316–17
  Italian, 322
  Le Potagerie, 446
  Ma Maison, 86
  Physical Culture, 609
  Sinclair's, 594
  Spago, 86
Restaurants of New York, The (Chappell), 497
restaurateurs. *See* celebrity chefs
Retail Confectioners International, 89
Reuben, Arnold, 501
Reuben sandwich, 169, **501–2**
Revolutionary War food, 283–84
Revolutionary War reenactments, 281
Revolution at the Table (Levenstein), 179
Rheingold Breweries, 361
Rhodes 101 Stops, 147
Rhodes Companies, 147
rhubarb, **502**
  food festivals, 567
  household remedy, 301
  rhubarb pie, 385, 438
  and sorrel, 549
  strawberry-rhubarb pie, 112
ribbon cane syrup, 413
riboflavin, 108, 612
rice, **502–3**. *See also* hoppin' John; wild rice
  breakfast cereals. *See* Puffed Rice; Rice Krispies;
    Special K; *calas*, 69, 85, 200
  and casseroles, 97
  in Chinese food, 119, 120, 121
  cookbooks, 147, 179
  dirty rice, 556
  in early America, 283–84
  in Indian American cookery, 317
  in jambalaya, 81, 325
  in Japanese American food, 326, 327
  in Korean American food, 348
  and Kwanzaa, 350
  and nutrition, 611, 612
  pilafs, 101, 383
  pressure boiling, 601
  red beans and rice, 39, 81
  slang, 128
  in Southeast Asian food, 553, 554
  in Southern regional cookery, 554, 555
  Uncle Ben, 601
  and weddings, 617, 618
Rice-A-Roni, 384, 503
rice bread, 286, 503
rice cookers, 326, **504**
Rice Krispies, 69, 102, 340, 503
Rice Krispies Treats, 503
rice soups, 503
Richards, Ellen Swallow, 179, 299, 418, **504**
Richman, Phyllis, 498
Richter, John, 494
rickets, 612
Riedel, Georg, 634
Riegel, Hans, 267

Riley, C. V., 187
Riley-Lyon (microbrewery), 379
rising agents. *See* chemical leavening
Ritz-Carlton Hotel, 473, 610
Ritz crackers, 20, 173, 391
Ritzer, George, 371, 372
Rival Company, 542
RJ Reynolds Industries, 186, 341, 401
RJR Nabisco, 77, 341
road food, 240. *See also* roadhouses; roadside food
Roadfood (Stern), 498, 505
roadhouses, **504–5**
roadside cafés, 254
roadside food, **505–6**. *See also* cafeterias; diners;
  drive-ins; fast food; luncheonettes;
    roadhouses; take-out foods
  Carvel, 95
  clam shacks, 132
  Howard Johnson, 306, 335
  Stuckey's, 568
road transport. *See* transportation of food
Roark Capital Group, 95
roasting, 164–65, 599
Robbins, Irvine, 37
Robert, Ann, 179
Robert Mondavi, 393
Robert Mondavi Co., **506**
Roberts, Leonard E., 10
Roberts, Robert, 9, 10, 87, 147, 167
Robinson, Anna, 27
Robinson, Frank, 133
Robinson, Jancis, 633
Robinson, William O., 625
Rochdale Pioneers Equitable Society, 165–66
rock crab, 172
Rockefeller, John D., 479, 585
rockfish, 38
rock salt, 518
Rockwell, Norman, 7, 328
Rodale, Jerome, 170, 275, 426, 427
Rodale, Robert, 427
Rodriguez, Douglas, 417
Rohwedder, Otto, 66
Rold Gold, 240
rolled oats, 373, 421
rolling pins, 455
rolls. *See* bread
Romagnoli, Margaret and Franco, 99, 490
Romagnolis' Table, The, 490
Romano, Michael, 416–17
Rombauer, Irma, 151, 152, 155, **506–7**, 609, 610
Ronald McDonald, 337, 371, **507–8**
Ronald McDonald House, 508
Ronald McDonald's Children Charities, 508
Roosevelt, Eleanor, 624
Roosevelt, Franklin, 624
Roosevelt, Theodore, 2, 624
Root, Waverley, 153
root beer, 1, 60, **508–9**, 523
Roquefort, 106, 107
Rorer, Sarah Tyson, 6, 91, 149, 162, 397, 449, 456,
  476, **509–10**
Rose, Peter, 109
Rosefield, Joseph L., 442
Roselius, Ludwig, 137
rosemary, 390
  in Bell's Seasoning, 476
  and Dutch colonists, 201
  and honey, 302
  in vermouth, 610
Rosenberg, William, 200–201
Rosencrans, Charles "Chip", 568
Rosenfield, Rick, 87
rose water, 425, **510**
Rosso, Julee, 155, 498
Rothschild, Philippe de, 393, 506
Rotisserie Grill, 60
Rotolactor, 59
rouladen, 257
Roundup Ready soybean, 49

Routhier, Nicole, 154
Royal Baking Powder, 4
Royal Crown Cola, 23, 140, **510**
Royal Farms Convenience Stores, 147
Royal gelatin, 328
Roy Rogers, **510**
R.T. French Company, 398
Rudkin, Margaret, 447
Rudolph, Vernon, 349
Rueckheim, Frederick, 173
Rueckheim, F. W., 89
Rueckheim, Louis, 173
Ruffles, 240, 544
rugelach, 333
Rules of Civility & Decent Behaviour in Company and Conversation (Washington), 210, 591
rum, 12, 195, 266, 392, **510–11**
    Cuba Libre, 177
    hot toddies, 305
    lime rickey, 358
    mai tai, 363–64
    Puerto Rican, 482
    punch, 484
    zombie, 641
rum and Coke, 511
Rumford, Count, 33
Rumford Chemical Works, 6
rum punch, 94, 167
runzas, 48
Russell, Lillian, 62, 186
Russell, Malinda, 151
Russian American food, **511–12**
    in Alaska, 12
    appetizers, 19
    zakuska, 19
Russian service, see *service á la Russe*
Russian tea, 512
Russian Tea Room, 512
rutabaga, 598
Ruth, Babe, 32
Rutledge, Sarah, 302, 441, 524
Rutt, Chris, 26, 433
rye and Indian bread, 411
rye bread, 64
rye 'n' injun, 68
rye whiskey, 111, 621

S&W, 186
SABMiller, 390
Sabrett, 304
saccharin, 571, 574
sack, 535
sack posset, 535
Safford, Anson, 207
safrole, 508, 523
sage, 390
    in Bell's Seasoning, 476
    in dressings and stuffings, 126, 197
    in honey, 302
    in Italian seasoning, 476
    in pot cheese, 77
    in roast pumpkin, 408
    in scrapple, 529
    in vermouth, 610
Saint Patrick's Day, 169, **513**
Saintsbury, George, 633
Sala, George Augustus, 33
Salad and Salad Making (Ewing), 513
salad bars, 80, 514
Salads (Rorer), 510
salads and salad dressings, 145, 355, **513–14**
    Jell-O, 328–29
    mayonnaise, 369–70
    poke salad, 468
    salade niçoise, 514
    Valentine's Day, 603
Salads and Sauces (Murray), 178
salami, **514–15**
    and curing, 218, 396
    Genoa salami, 395

mortadella, 395
    pepperoni, 447
sal de gusano, 585, 586
saleratus, 64, 109
Sally Lunn, 69, **515**
salmon, 11, 22, 223, 239, 431, **515–16**
    in boardinghouses, 57
    lox, 332–33
salmonella, 114, 598
Salone del Gusto, 543
saloons, **516–17**
    and temperance, 584–85
salsa, 145, 195, **517**
salsify, **517**
salt and salting, 145, **517–20**
    in colonial America, 282
    iodized, 108–9
    and pickling, 453
    as preservatiion method, 169
salt pork, 9, 24, 68, 241, 285
    in Chesapeake diet, 111
    and sauerkraut, 443
    scrapple, 530
    ship food, 535
saltwater taffy, **520**, 579–80
Salvadore, Lupo, 395
Salvation Army, 307
sambusak, 333
Sames, Margarita, 366
Samuelson, Marcus, 248
San Antonio chili, 378
Sanborn, James, 137
Sanders, Colonel, **520–21**
Sanders, Harland, 239, 341–42, 506, 618–19. *See also* Sanders, Colonel
Sandoz, 31
sandwiches, **521–22**
    club sandwich, 133
    Dagwood sandwich, 181
    Denver sandwich, 186
    French dip, 236
    gyro, 267
    hamburgers, 621–22
    hoagie, 298–99
    Hot Brown, 303
    Italian, 321
    Italian beef, 386
    Italian sausage sandwich with peppers and onions, 322–23
    lobster roll, 360
    Monte Cristo, 393
    muffaletta, 395–96
    oyster loaf sandwich, 429
    panini, 434
    peanut butter, 442
    Philadelphia cheesesteak, 451
    pimiento cheese, 460
    Po'Boy, 467
    Reuben, 501–2
    sloppy joe, 542
    submarine sandwiches, 569
    tenderloin, 385
    wraps, 637
Sandwiches (Rorer), 133, 510
sandwich puddings, 481
sandwich shops, 55, 236
sandwich trucks, 522
San Francisco Professional Food Society, 295
sangaree, 535
sangria, 522, **522**
sanitary can, 92, 368
sanitary fairs, 142, 247
Sanitas Nut Food Company, 442
Santa Ana, Antonio de, 267
Santa Barbara Recipes, 207
Sara Lee Corporation, 137, **522–23**
Saran plastic film, 464, 465
Saran Wrap, 465
sardines, **279**
    canning, 412

in Dagwood sandwich, 181
    sardine openers and shears, 93
sarsaparilla, 50, **523**
sarsaparilla and wintergreen, **523**
sassafrasses, 50, 81, 508, 523, **523**
Sasso, John, 464
Saturday Evening Post (magazine), 26, 88
sauces and gravies, **523–25**
Saucier, Ted, 367
sauerbraten, 257
sauerkraut, 79, 80, 111, 257, 355, 468
sauerkraut balls, deep-fried, 386
Sauerkraut Yankees (Weaver), 179
sauger, **525**
Saugus Mill, 246
Saunders, Clarence, 265–66, 456
sausage, **525–26**
    bratwurst, 386
    chorizo, 125
    hot dogs, 303–4
    Italian, 322–23
    kielbasa, 468
    pepperoni, 447
    salami, 514–15
    scrapple, 529–30
    Vienna sausage, 611
Savannah Cook Book, The (Colquitt), 152
Saveur (magazine), 450, 498
Savoring the Past (Wheaton), 179
Savoy Cake, 83
Sazerac, 80, **526**
Sbarro, **526**
Sbarro, Gennaro and Carmela, 526
scallops, **526**
scandals, 24, 61
Scandinavian and Finnish American food, 19, **526–27**
Scarsdale Diet, The (Tarnower), 275
Scharffen Berger, 124
Schimmel, Charles, 502
Schimmel, Yonah, 347
Schlatter, James, 574
Schlitz Brewing Company, 43, 45, 636
Schlitz Palm Gardens, 45
Schlorer Delicatessen company, 370
Schlosser, Eric, 371, 473
schmaltz, 333
Schmidt, Carl, 28
Schmidt, Fred K., 303
Schmidt, Herman B., 24
schnapps. *See* cordials
schnecken, 333
Schnering, Otto Y., 31–32, 77
Schoenfeld, Reese, 490
Schoneberger & Noble, 196
School Breakfast Program, 528
school food, 81, **528–29**
school lunches, 187, 307, 447, 521
Schoonmaker, Frank, 633
Schrafft, William F., 529
Schrafft's, **529**
Schramsberg, 104
Schrumpf, Mildred Brown, 71
Schueler, Jacob, 166
Schultz, Carl H., 532
Schultz, Howard, 432, 562
Schweppes, Jacob, 259
Schweppes, Jean Jacob, 80
Schweppes Company, 80
Science in the Kitchen (Kellogg), 420
S. C. Johnson Company, 464
Scorsese, Catherine, 220
Scorsese, Martin, 220
Scotch bonnets, 117
Scotch burgoo, 421
Scott, Walter, 190
Scott, Willard, 507–8
scrapple, 381, **529–30**
screw cap, 92, 168
screwdriver, 425, **530**

Index

685

scrumpy, 129
Scudder, Laura, 617
scurvy, 241, 418, 535, 611
seafood, 530–31. *See also* fish; shellfish; shrimp
    and prawns
    abalone, 1
    Chesapeake region, food and drink of the,
      110–12
    crayfish, 174
    eel, 204
    lobster, 360
    sea urchins, 531
    Southern regional cookery, 555
    squid, 561–62
sea mammals, **531**
Seaman's Beverages, 358
Sean O'Farrell, 58
sea salt, 518
Sea Shepherd Conservation Society, 17
Seasonal Kitchen, The (Meyers), 154
Seattle world's fair. *See* Century 21 Exhibition
sea turtle, **531**
sea urchins, **531**
seaweed, **531–32**
2nd Ave. Deli, *185*
Second Harvest, 307
Secrets of the Great Whiskey Ring (McDonald), 61
seder, 333, 436
Sedgwick, Robert, 42
Sedlmayr, Gabriel, 14, 368
See, Charles, 532
seed-saving organizations, 278
See's Candies, **532**
Seibel, Albert, 626
Seikatsu Club, 144
Selected Receipts of a Van Rensselaer Family, 133
selective breeding of chickens, 112
*Selective Guide to Culinary LIbrary Collections in the
    United States* (Griswold), 320
self-service grocery stores, 266, 290, 456
Sell, Christopher, 600
seltzer, 60, **532**
Señor Pico, 366
Sensuous Artichoke, The (Castelli), 25
Serve It Forth (Fisher), 152, 224
service á la Russe, 160, 193–94
Settlement Cookbook, The (Kander), 143, 151, 152,
    257, 494, 533
settlement houses, 373, **532–34**
7-Eleven, 146, 267
Seventh-Day Adventism, 13, 190, 275, 340, 608
Seventy-five Receipts for Pastry, Cakes, and Sweetmeats
    (Leslie), 133, 147, 162
7 UP, **534**
Seven-Up Company, 197, 534
sex, in advertising, 5
Seymour, Henry D., 421, 487
shad, 223, **534**
Shaffer, Irv and Jack, 338
Shakers, 159, 355, 383, 510
Shakey's, 292, 463, 464, **534–35**
shalivka, 32
Shanghainese food, 121
Sharp, James, 563
Shattuck, Frank G., 529
sheep, 351–52
shellfish, 530, **535**
    abalone, 1
    aquaculture, 22
    clams, 132
    crab, 172
    Dungeness crab, 431
    mussels, 398
    oysters, 429–30, 431–32
    scallops, 526
Shelton, Herbert, 493
Sheraton, Mimi, 498
sherbet, 245
Sheridan, Joe, 320
sherry, 62, **535**

Sherwood, Mary Elizabeth Wilson, 210
Shinn, Barbara, 155
ship food, **535–36**
    chipped beef, 122
    hardtack, 272–73
    ship bread, 33
shish kebab, 384
shoofly pie, 257, 455, **536**
shopping carts, 266
shore dinners, 531
shortening, 352–53
shoyu hot dogs, 325
shredded coconut, 136
Shredded Wheat, 6, *67*, 102
shrimp and prawns, 22, 239, **536–37**
shrubs, 245, 576
Sibley, John, 140
Sichuan food, 121
Sickler, Joseph S., 335
sickroom cookery, 215. *See also* invalid cooking
sidecar, 62
Sidway, Henry, 53
Siegel, Zev, 562
Sierra Nevada Brewery, 379–80
sieves, sifters, and colanders, **537**
sifters, 537
signboards, 2
Silent Spring (Carson), 426, 427
Silliman, Benjamin, 545, 546
Silver Palate, 414, 498
Silver Palate Cookbook, The (Rosso and Lukins), 155
Silverstone, Alicia, 605
silverware, *194*, **537–38**
Simek siblings, 591
Similac, 31
Simmons, Amelia, 13, 20, 26, 55, 95, 147, 156, 178,
    207, 253, 254, 262, 392, 481, 491, 494,
    538–39, 551, 572, 598, 605
Simon, André, 152
Simon, Norton, 308
Simonds, Nina, 179
Simplesse, 218
Simplex, 589
Sinclair, Upton, 2, 75, 108, 187, 271, 275, 485,
    539–40, 608–9
    and Fletcherism, 226
Sinclair's, 594
Singapore sling, **540**
Singer, Peter, 16–17
single-barrel bourbon, 61
single-malt scotches, 61
Singleton, Vernon, 633
siphon bottles, 532
Sitting Bull, 285
60 Minute Gourmet, 490
skid rows, 516
Skilful Housewife's Book, The (Abell), 576
skillets, 246
Skinny's, 147
Skippy, 442
Skyline Chili, *129*
slang, food, **540–42**
    molasses, 393
    Oreo, 426
    puddinghead, 481
    sailors', 484
    soda fountains, 389
    soldiers', 285
slaughterhouses, 75–76
Slaughtery, John, 279
slavery
    Aunt Jemima, 26–27
    chicken, 239
    cooks, 285
    diet, 285
    and hoppin' John, 302
    and kitchen gardening, 343
    peanuts, 440–41
    and sugar, 570, 571
slave trade, 311, 511, 554

Slim-Fast, 68, 190
sloppy joe, **542**
slow cookers, 504, **542**
    fireless cookers, 221–22
slow food movement, 171, 258, 542–43
Slow Food U.S.A., 295, **542–43**
slumps, 438
Smafield, Ralph E., 459
small-batch bourbon, 61–62
small-batch brewers, 563
small beers and ales, 259, 508
small farms, 415
smallmouth bass, 38
Smarties, 90, 364
Smart Start, 340–41
smelt, **543**
Smiley, Jack, 540
Smirnoff, Vladimir, 612
Smirnoff vodka, 56, 512, 530, 612
Smith, Art, 155
Smith, E., 237
Smith, Eliza, 147
Smith, Grace and Beverly, 152
Smith, Richie, 269
Smith, Sidney, 467
Smith, Troy, 548
Smith, Wallace, 560
Smith, Wally, 41
Smithfield, 76
smoked fish, 385
smoking, **543**
Smoot-Hawley Tariff Act, 214
Smoothie King Franchises Inc., 337
smoothies, 245, 337
smorgasbord, 19, 80, 527, **543**
snack foods, 240, 373, **543–45**. *See also* crackers
    dips, 195
    Goldfish crackers, 447
    Moon Pie, 393–94
    Native American, 410
    olives, 424
    onion rings, 424
    peanuts, 441
    pickles, 452
    popcorn, 470
    potato, 473. *See also* potato chips; pretzels, 478
Snake River (microbrewery), 379
Snap! Crackle! Pop!, 503
snapper soup, 381
Snapple, **545**
Snickers, 89, **545**
Snider, Fern, 502
snow crab, 172
snow peas, 444
Snyder, Harry and Esther, 318
Society for Creative Anachronism, 281
soda bread, 65
soda cans, 546
soda cracker, 173
soda drinks, 80, **545–46**
    advertising, 546
    birch beer, 50
    and blenders, 55
    Cadbury Schweppes, 80
    chocolate, 125
    Coca-Cola, 133, *134*, 140, 292
    cream soda, 176
    Diet-Rite, 510
    Dr. Brown's, 196–97
    Dr Pepper, 197
    egg cream, 204–5
    Hires Root Beer, 508
    ice cream sodas, 316
    lime rickey, 358
    Moxie, 394
    and obesity, 422
    Pepsi-Cola, 140, 447–48
    root beer, 508–9
    Royal Crown Cola, 510
    sarsaparilla, 523

seltzer, 532
7 UP, 534
vending machines, 609
soda fountains, 197, 235, 259, 305, 315–16, 335, 389, 500, 545, **546–47**
egg cream, 205
phosphates, 451
slang, 540–41
soda jerks, 205, 547
slang, 540–41, 547
Sodamats, 609
soda water, 60, 532, 546
sodium aluminosilicate, 108
sodium bicarbonate, 109
sodium metabisulphite, 108
sodium propionate, 109
sofkey, 302, 317
sofrito, 177, 482
soft candies, 246
soft drinks, 615
soft-shell clams, 111–12
soft-shell crabs, 111, 172
Sokolov, Raymond, 498
sole, 226
songs, food, 57, 272, **547–48**, 616
Sonic, **548**
Sonneborn, Harry, 235, 581
Sonnenfeld, Albert, 249
Sontheimer, Carl G., 231–32
sopaipilla, 410
sorbetière, 313, 314
sorghum flour, **548**
sorghum syrup, **548–49**
sorrel, **549**
Soulé, Henri, 500
soul food, 9, 10, 11, 122, 153, 301–2
soup kitchens, 247, 307, 308, **549–50**
soups, **550–53**. *See also* stews.
in Alaska, 12
condensed, 88
cream soups, 97, 247, 257, 551, 552, 610–11, 640
vichyssoise, 610–11
sour cream, 175
sourdough bread, 65, 218, 640
South African Breweries, 390
South American Cook Book (Brown), 152
South American food. *See* Iberian and South American food
South Beach Diet, The (Agatston), 275
Southeast Asian food, **553–54**, 618
Southern Cook Book, The (Brown), 153
Southern Cooking (Dull), 152
Southern Food: At Home, on the Road, in History (Egerton), 154
Southern Foodways Alliance, 295
Southern Gardener and Receipt Book (Thornton), 147
Southern regional cookery, 302, **554–56**
barbecue, 35–36
breakfasts, 69
chicken, 475
cookbooks, 153, 154, 491
funeral food, 247
Karo Syrup, 339
New Year's celebrations, 413–14
okra, 423
pies and tarts, 455
Southern Tenants Farmers' Union, 213
Southland Ice Company, 146
Southwestern regional cookery, 295, **556–57**
barbecue, 35–36
breakfasts, 69
pies and tarts, 455
pinole, 461
salsa, 517
tacos, 579
tamales, 581
soybean oil, 23, 557, 605
soybeans, 39, 289, **557–58**
business, 23

and genetic engineering, 48, 49
and international aid, 319
and ketchup, 342, 558
in Korean foods, 348
in miso, 551
in mock sausages, 526
sacred in China, 36
and soy sauce, 396, 558
in World War II, 289
soy lecithin, 23
soy protein, 23
soy sauce, **558**
space food, **558–59**
Tang, 581
spaetzle, 200
Spago (Hollywood), 86, 220, 480
Spam, 292, **559–60**
Spanish influences on American food, 311. *See also* Iberian and South American food
tapas, 19
sparkling water, 615
sparkling wine, 103–4, 629, 632
sparrow grass. *See* asparagus
speakeasies, 36, 500, 516, 534
Speakman, Townsend, 60
Special K, 340
Speedee Service System, 371
Spencer, Percy, 380
spice boxes, 146
spice cabinets, 146
spice grinders, 265
spices. *See also* herbs and spices
in wine, 631–32
spiders (frying pans), 246
spinach, **560**
in colonial America, 282
coloring for ice cream, 314
creamed spinach, 482, 510
frozen, 236, 242
frozen spinach soufflé, 577
and Gerber, 31
in knishes, 347
in pasta, 295
in pierogi, 200
in southern kitchen gardens, 343
in stuffed ham, 568
in stuffed pizza, 463
in West Indian pepper pot, 552
Spira, Henry, 17
spits, 599
Spitzer, Silas, 497
spokespersons. *See* advertising icons
sponge, in bread baking, 639
sponge cake, 83
Spoonbread and Strawberry Wine (Darden and Darden), 154
spoon breads, 169
spoons, 537–38
spray-drying, 199
sprouts, **560**
spruce, **560–61**
spruce beer, 560–61
Spurrier, Steven, 628
squab, 436
squash, **561**
Squibb, 31, 42
Squibb, Robert, 423
squid, **561–62**
in Hawaiian cooking, 274
ink, as pasta colorant, 295
in paella, 325
squirrel stew, 72
stack cake, 18
Staebler, Edna, 445
Stalking the Wild Asparagus (Gibbons), 153, 258
Standard Brands, 32, 137
standardization, 192
of measuring cups and spoons, 215, 358, 374
Standard Manual of Soda and Other Beverages, The, 205

Starbucks, 137, 432, **562**
Stark Candy Company, 413
StarKist Seafood, 596
Stars (San Francisco), 86
Star Wars Cookbook, The, 220
Statesmen's Dishes and How to Cook Them, 13
Stavely, Keith, 318
steak house, 500
Steak n Shake, 580
steamboats, 592
steaming, 164
Stearns, Peter, 421
steel, 157
Steele, Al, 140
Steele, Alfred, 448
Steinwand, Joseph, 105
Stellar, 218
Stephen F. Whitman Company, 89
Stern, Jane and Michael, 498, 505
Stewart, Martha, **562**
Stewart, Philo Penfield, 565
stew dogs, 72
stews, 15, **550–53**. *See also* Soups.
bigos, 468
Booyah, 58
Brunswick stew, 72, 552
burgoo, 553
chili, 118–19
chop suey, 15
étouffée, 82
frogmore stew, 553
Irish stew, 552
Joe Booker stew, 200
mulligan stew, 396
pepper pot, 552–53
pilafs, 101
son of a bitch stew, 128
succotash, 569–70
Stiegel, Henry William, 260
stills, 196, **562–63**
still water, 615
stinger, 62
stink fish, 11
St. Louis world's fair. *See* Louisiana Purchase Exposition
Stolichnaya vodka, 512
stoneware, 101, 146, 157
Stop and Smell the Rosemary, 143
stoppers, 633, 634
storage. *See also* containers
coonie, 128
liquor cabinets, 359
Native American, 410
plastic bags, 464
wine, 634
Storey, Walter, 363
Stork Club Bar Book (Beebe), 55
Storke, E.G., 210
Story of Wine in California, The (Fisher and Yavno), 633
Stouffer, 577
stout, 563, **563**
Stout, Rex, 152
stoves and ovens, 84, 159, 160, 164
gas and electric, **563–65**
wood and coal, **565–66**
straight whiskey, 621
Straub, Jacques, 368
strawberries, **566–67**
on brownie pizza, 72
cheesecake topping, 107
and chocolate fondue, 227
in colonial America, 281, 592
food festivals, 406, 567
forks, 538
and freezing, 242
frontier food, 241
ice cream flavor, 305, 315, 335
jam, 393
Jell-O flavor, 327

strawberries (*Contd.*)
    in juice, 244
    Kool-Aid flavor, 347
    licorice candy flavor, 357
    Marshmallow Fluff flavor, 367
    Mexico as supplier, 214
    milkshakes, 389
    in Native American diet, 111, 188, 243, 402, 406
    in Pacific Northwest, 432
    pickled, 453
    slang, 141, 540, 547
    soda, 510, 546
    strawberries Romanoff, 512
    strawberry liqueur, 367
    strawberry margarita, 366
    strawberry-rhubarb pie, 112, 438
    strawberry shortcake, 302, 317, 600
    transportation of, 592
    wine coolers, 634
strawberries Romanoff, 512
street foods. *See* street vendors
street vendors, 567–68, 580. *See also* sandwich trucks
    African American, 10
    bread, *323*
    bubble tea, 72
    frozen juices, 471
    gyro, 267
    hokeypokey men, 471, 569
    hot dogs, 304, *415*
    Indian, 316
    Italian, 321–22
    Italian beef sandwiches, 569
    limonadiers, 354
    Natchitoches meat pies, 401
    popcorn, 470
    pretzels, *415*, 477, 544
    tamales, 305
    wagons, 190, 362
Streit's, 369
strikes, 499
striped bass. *See* bass
Strite, Charles, 66
Strong Ale, 36
strong pale ale, **568**
Stuckey, Ethel Mullis, 568
Stuckey, Williamson Sylvester, 568
Stuckey's, **568**
Studies of American Fungi (Atkinson), 397
stuffed ham, **568**
stuffings, 197
sturgeon, **568–69**
Sturgis, Julius, 478
Sturgis Pretzel House, 478
Stutchkoff, Nahum, 369
sublimation, 235
submarine, 298, 299
submarine sandwiches, **569**
subsidies, 24, 214
Subway, **569**
Successful Farming (magazine), 450
succotash, 39, 209, 302, 411, **569–70**
sucralose, 574
sucrose, 574
sufganiyot, 333
sugar, *89*, 302, 392, 411, **570–71**
    and bread, 64
    in breakfast cereals, 102
    and candy, 89
    and Coca-Cola, 140
    as condiment, 145
    criticisms of, 571
    federal quotas, 214
    health concerns, 470
    in preserves, 476
    rationing, 134, 289
    and soft drinks, 448
    sugar beets, 570, 571–73, 574
    and tea, 583

Sugar Act, 570
sugar alcohols, 574
sugar beets, 570, **571–72**, 574
    and antislavery reform, 116
sugar biscuit, 173
sugarcane, 570
sugar content of melons, 377
sugar prices, and Coca-Cola, 133–34
sugar snap peas, 444
sugar substitutes, 170
Sugar Trust, 570
Sullivan, Charles, 633
Sullivan, Jim, 100
sultanas, 264
summer savory, 390
Sun Also Rises, The (Hemingway), 360
sunchoke, 573
Sundblom, Haddon, 134, 487, 493
Sunfired Foods, 494
sunfish, **572**
sunflowers, **572–73**
Sunkist, 2, 245
Sun-Maid raisins, 85
Sunset All-Western Cook Book (Callahan), 28, 132
Sunshine Biscuits, 156, 426
Sunshine brand, 340
Sunsweet, 86
supawn, **573**
supermarkets, 228, 229, 266, 290, 296, 306
    and coffee, 369
    and food transport, 592
    and GMOs, 49
    and ice cream, 315, 547
    and mesclun, 355
    and Mexican American foods, 379
    and milk packaging, 388
    origins, 146, 166, 290, 401
    and packaging, 5, 25, 32, 432
    and plastic grocery bags, 464
    and seltzer, 532
    and soda packaging, 546
    supermarket magazines, 450
    vegetable availability, 606–7
supplements, 419
sushi, 325, 327, 504
    bagel sushi, 331
    California rolls, 326
    and Chinese dominance, 316
    and Koreans, 348
    salmon, 515
    sea urchins, 531
    and soy sauce, 558
    Spam sushi, 559
    sushi bars, 294, 414
    tuna, 596
sustainable agriculture, 86, 216
    Chef's Collaborative, 39
    chocolate, 124
    and cooperatives, 166
    and slow food movement, 542–43
Sveda, Michael, 574
swamp cabbage, 277
Swanson, 243, 293, **573**, 599–600
    TV dinners, 236
Swanson, Carl A., 573
Swedish meatballs, 103, 527
Sweeney, Joanna, 59
SweeTarts, 90
sweet corn, 168
sweeteners, **573–74**. *See also* artificial sweeteners
    in colonial America, 282
    corn syrup, 170
    honey, 302
    Karo Syrup, 339
    maple syrup, 364–65
    molasses, 170, 392–93
    New Orleans syrup, 413
    in soda drinks, 546
    sorghum syrup, 548–49
    sugar, 302, 570–71

watermelon, 616
Sweethearts, 413, 603
Sweetness and Power (Mintz), 179
Sweetose, 170
sweet potatoes, 9, **574–75**
    in early America, 311
    in Hawaiian diet, 274
    and mock foods, 391
    slang, 128
    sweet potato pie, 455–56, 456, 481
    and TV dinners, 599
sweets. *See also* cakes; candy and candy bars; cookies; desserts; pies and tarts
    chrusciki, 468
    cookbooks, 155
    fudge, 246–47
    Twinkies, 600
Sweets Company of America, 591
sweet spices, **575**. *See also* allspice; bay leaves; cinnamon; cloves; mace; nutmeg; vanilla
Sweet Success, 190
Swett, Lucia Gray, 151
Swift, 304
Swift, Gustavus Franklin, 24, 312, **575–76**
Swiss rolls. *See* jelly rolls
switchel, **576**
swordfish, **576**
syllabub, 175, 205, **576**
Sylvia's, 10
syrups, 477. *See also* corn syrup; low-calorie syrup; maple syrup; molasses; New Orleans syrup; sorghum syrup
Szathmary, Louis, 296, 336, **577**, 594
Szent-Györgyi, Albert, 425

Tabasco Company, 143
Tabasco pepper, 117
Tabasco sauce, 145, *145*
tabbouleh, 384
Table, The (Filippini), 186
table grapes, 263
table manners, 210
table salt, 518
Table Service (Allen), 194
Table Setting Guide (Dlugosch), 194
table settings, 193–94, 210
    glasses, 260–61
    plates, 465–66
    silverware, 537–38
    White House, 623
    wine glasses, 634
Table Talk, 149, 449, 509
table wines, Eastern, 629
Taco Bell, 75, 86, 117, 217, 341, **579**, 640
tacos, **579**
Taco Tia, 579
Tadich Grill, 500
taffy, *89*, **579–80**
    saltwater taffy, 520
Taggart Baking Company, 65, 302
taiglach, 333
tailgate picnics, **580**
Taino Indians, 177, 481
Tait, Elaine, 498
take-out foods, **580–81**. *See also* fast food; sandwiches
    wraps, 637
tamale pie, **581**
tamales, **581**. *See also* hot tamales
    food festivals, 230
Tang, 69, 558, **581**
tapas, 19
tapioca pearls, in bubble tea, 73
Tappan Company, 380
taprooms, 37
Tariff Act, 590
tariffs, 214, 570
taro, 274
tartaric acid, 64
tarts. *See* pies and tarts

Tastee-Freez, **581**, 625
Taste of America, The (Hess), 317
Taste of Country Cooking, The (Lewis), 154, 454
Taste of Home, A (magazine), 450
Taster's Choice, 137, 138, 410, 411
tasting glass, 634
Tasty Grahams Pudding Pies, 582
Tastykake, **581–82**
Taubman, A. Alfred, 1
taverns, 504, 516, **582**
  colonial, 36, 37
Taylor, Albert, 455
Taylor, Edmund Haynes, Jr., 61
Taylor, Ronald, 319
Taylor, Sewell, 526
tea, 265, **582–83**
  bubble tea, 72–73
tea parties, 583
tearooms, 505, 583
  Schrafft's, 529
Technique, La (Pépin), 154, 446
Teflon, 558
teiki ventures, 144
Teiser, Ruth, 633
television advertising. *See also* advertising icons;
    radio/TV food shows
  advertising, 5, 28
  Budweiser, 73
  frozen foods, 242–43
  Mars, 364
  Maxwell House, 369
television food shows. *See* radio/TV food shows
temperance, 43, 87, 262–63, **583–85**
  and baking powder, 13
  and Christian Science, 13
  and cookbooks, 12–13
  and Mormon Church, 13
  and pledge cards, 13
  and saloons, 584–85
  and Seventh-Day Adventism, 13
  and yeast, 13
temperance drinks, 639–40
  birch beer, 50
  grasshopper, 264
  lemonade, 354
  malted milk, 389
  punch, 13
  root beer, 508
  Welch's Grape Juice, 245
temperance movements, 12–13, 478–79
  anti-drinking songs, 198
  and Quakers, 478–79
  and saloons, 516
  and soft drinks, 197
temperance organizations
  American Temperance Society, 479, 584
  American Temperance Union, 584
  Anti-Saloon League, 584–85
  National Temperance Society, 584
  Women's Christian Temperance Union, 13, 43,
    479, 584
tenderloin sandwich, 385
Tennessee whiskey, 62, 621
tequila, **585–86**
Tequila Book, The (Gorman and de Alba), 366
tequila sunrise, 425, **586**
terminator seeds, 278
terrapin, **586**
terrapin soup, 551
Tested Recipe Cook Book, 151
test laboratories, 54
Tetra Pak, 25
Texas chili, 118
Texas cookery, 35, 556. *See also* Southwestern
    regional cookery
Tex-Mex cuisine, 556
textured soy protein, 23
T.G.I. Friday's, and brandy Alexander, 63
Thai food, 553
Tham, Aris La, 494

Thanksgiving, **586–88**
  Bell's Seasoning, 476
  dinners, 586–87
  food traditions, 399
  and Native Americans, 586, 587
  Plimoth Plantation, 280
  pumpkin pie, 482–83
  turkey, 598
The Bakery, 577, 594
theme parks, 16
Theophano, Janet, 161, 179
The Phenix Cheese Corporation, 176
thermoses, 361
thermostats, 564
thiamine, 108, 611, 612
thirteen toasts, 589
Thistle Eaters Guide (Scammell), 25
Thomas, Benjamin, 133
Thomas, Dave, 217, **588**, 618–19
Thomas, Gerald, 573
Thomas, Jerry, 135, 167, 258, 390, 540
Thomas Adams Gum Company, 609
Thomas J. Lipton Company, 194–95, 262
Thompson, Augustin, 394
Thompson, Benjamin, 565
Thompson, John R., 500
Thorne family, 213
thousand island dressing, 514
3 Musketeers, 89
Throessel, Jesse, 598
Through the Kitchen Door (Smith and Wilson), 152
Thunderbird, 251
thyme, 390
Tierney, Patrick, 190–91
tiki drinks, 511
tilapia, 239, **588**
Tildesley and Company, 513
timers, hourglasses, egg timers, **588–89**
tin, 157
  artifacts, 345
  boxes, 146
  canning, 91, 92
  cans, 111
  cookie cutters, 155–56
  packaging, 242
Tinkham, Guy L., 312
T. J. Cinnamons Classic Bakery, 23
Tlingit. *See* Northwest Coast Indians
toast, **589**
toasted ravioli, 386
toaster pastries, 69
toasters, 65, 66, **589**
toasts, **589–90**
toddy, 136
To Have and Have Not (Hemingway), 360
Toklas, Alice B., 278
Toll House Cookies recipe, 4
Toll House Inn, 156
Toll House Tried and True Recipes (Wakefield), 72,
  156
tomato aspic, 292
tomatoes, 335, **590–91**
  beefsteak, 87
  food wars, 214
  genetically engineered, 49
  Hunt's tomato sauce, 308
  ketchup, 54, 342
  soup, 552
  tomato juice, 55, 88
Tombstone Pizza, **591**
Tom Collins, 140
tools
  bread-making, 67
  butter-making, 77
  cabbage cutters and planes, 79–80
  cheese-making, 107
  cherry pitters or stoners, 110
  coffee makers, roasters, and mills, 138
  cookie cutters, 155–56
  corn-preparation, 169–70

  doughnut-making, 196
  egg-preparation, 206
  graters, 264
  grinders, 265
  mortar and pestle, 394
  pie-making tools, 455
  potato-cooking, 472
Toomre, Joyce, 178, 179
toothpicks, **591**
Tootsie Pop, 591
Tootsie Roll, 89, **591–92**
Top Hat Drive-In, 548
Topography of All the Known Vineyards, The (Jullien),
  633
Topolobampo, 39
tortillas, 207, 379, 637
Toshiba, 504
To the Kelvinator Kitchen, 490
To the Queen's Taste, 490
Totonno's, 464
Toussaint, Jean-Luc, 420
Tower, Jeremiah, 86, 239, 491–92, 616
Town & Country Food Stores, 147
Townshend, Charles, 598–99
Tracy, Marian and Nino, 152
trade associations, 89, 104
trademark infringement, 447. *See* intellectual
  property rights
Trader Vic, 363, 641
Trall, Russell Thacher, 173
trans fats, 100, 218, 260, 365
transfer method, 104
transgenic organisms. *See* biotechnology
transportation of food, 111, 284–85, 287, 312,
  592, **592–94**
  bananas, 33
  Erie Canal, 619–20
  meat, 24–25
  railroads, 111
tray-boys and tray-girls, 1
*Treasury of Prize Winning Filbert Recipes from the
  Oregon Filbert Commission*, 420
Treatise on Bread and Bread-Making (Graham), 64,
  147
Treatise on Domestic Economy (Beecher), 41, 345
Treatise on Gardening by a Citizen of Virginia
  (Randolph, J.), 70
Tremont Hotel, 499
Tremont House, 304
trencher, 36, **594**
Trenham, Milton, 609
Triarc, and Snapple, 545
trick-or-treating, 270
Tricon Global Restaurants, 224, 342, 640
Trillin, Calvin, 74, 384, 498
triple sec, 167
Troisgros brothers, 416, 417
Trollope, Frances, 210, 151
Tropicana, 425
Trotter, Charlie, 577, **594–95**
trout, 239, **595**
truck farms, 278, 605, 606
truck stops, 505
Tryon, Thomas, 607
Tsai, Ming, 248
Tschelistcheff, Andre, 393
Tschirky, Oscar, 238, 253, 514, **595–96**
tsimmes, 333
Tsimshian. *See* Northwest Coast Indians
Tudor, Frederick, 312
tuna, 223, **595–96**
  creamed tuna, 589
  marketing, 531
  in mock chicken, 391
  in *salade niçoise*, 514
  sandwiches, 521
  slang, 541
  StarKist, 298
  tuna-potato chip casserole, 97
  tuna salad, 185, 362, 530

tunas, 80
Tupper, Earl Silas, 597
Tupper Plastics Company, 597
Tupperware, **596–97**
Tupperware: The Promise of Plastic in 1950s America (Clarke), 297
turkey, *75*, 475, **597–98**. *See also* wild turkeys
   Christmas, 126–27
   and Swanson's TV dinners, 599–600
Turkish foods. *See* central Asian food
turmeric, 259
Turner, Christy G., 591
Turner, Fred, 114
turnips, **598–99**
turnspit dogs, **599**
turtles. *See* sea turtle; terrapin
turtle soup, 531, 551
TV dinners, 236, 243, 293, 573, **599**, 600
21 Club, 55, 500
Twinkie defense, 600
Twinkies, 302, **600**
Twizzlers, 356
Tyree, Marion Cabell, 151
Tyson, M. L., 151
Tyson Foods, 76, 114

Ude, Louis Eustache, 238, 524
Ukers, William, 23
Unadulterated Food Corporation, 545
Uncle Ben, **601**
Uncle Ben's, 503
Underwood, Charles, 26, 433
Underwood, William, 91
Uneeda biscuits, 173, 401, 432
Unilever, 147, 261, 347, 370, 472
   Ben & Jerry's, 46
   Breyers, 70
   Good Humor, 262
Union of Orthodox Jewish Congregatons, 334
Union Oyster House, 429
unions, 213–14, 499
   and fast-food companies, 217
   International Beigel Bakers' Union, 32
   International Hotel Workers Union, 163
   Schrafft's, 529
   United Packinghouse Workers Union, 76
Union Sugar Company, 170
United Airlines, 11
United Biscuit Company, 339
United Brands Company, 1
United Farm Workers (UFW), 214
United Fruit Company, 1
   bananas, 34
   Baskin-Robbins, 37
United Packinghouse Workers Union, 76
United Poultry Concerns, 17
United States Sanitary Commission, 247
University of California, Berkeley, and wine industry, 628
University of California, Davis, and wine industry, 628, 631
University Settlement Society, 533
unrefined salt, 518
Up-to-date Sandwich Book (Fuller), 460
urbanization, and bread distribution, 64
USDA. *See* Department of Agriculture, United States
utensils, 159–60
   apple corers, 20
   apple-paring tools, *20*
   biscuit cutters, 53
   can openers, 93
   cherry pitters or stoners, 110
   eating, 193–94
   graters, 264
   grinders, 265
   knives, 125
   waffle irons, 613
   wood, 157
utopian visions, 279
Utrecht-Friedel, Mme, 238

V8 juice, 88
vacuum evaporator, 58, 144
Valentine's Day, 90, 413, **603**
Val Vita Food Products, 308
Van Aken, Norman, 417, 594
Van Buren, Martin, 623
Van Camp Seafood, 596
Vancouver, George, 17
Van Dam's Belgian Waffles, 636
van En, Robyn, 144
Van Houten, Coenraad, 122
vanilla, 176, 575, **603–4**
vanillin, 225
Van Mons, Jean Baptiste, 334
Van Wormer, John, 388
varietal labeling, 626, 628
Vega, 605
veganism, 17, 190, 416, **604–5**
Vegan Kitchen, The (Dinshah), 604
Vegan Nutrition, Pure and Simple (Klaper), 416
Vegetable Compound, 6
Vegetable Diet (Alcott), 147
vegetable oils, **605**
vegetables, **605–7**
   artichokes, 25
   asparagus, 25–26
   broccoli, 70–71
   cabbage, 79
   carrots, 95
   cassava, 96–97
   cauliflower, 97–98
   celery, 100
   in colonial America, 281–82
   as condiments, 145
   cucumbers, 178
   eggplants, 205
   endive, 207–8
   heirloom, 277–78
   kale, 339
   lettuce, 355
   mushrooms, 396–97
   okra, 423
   onions, 424–25
   parsnips, 435
   peas, 443–44
   potatoes, 472–73
   pumpkins, 483–84
   radishes, 491
   and railroads, 592
   rhubarb, 502
   salsify, 517
   seaweed, 531–32
   soybeans, 557
   spinach, 560
   sprouts, 560
   squash, 561
   sweet potatoes, 574–75
   tomatoes, 590–91
   turnips, 598–99
Vegetarian Book Book; Substitutes for Flesh Foods (Fulton), 420
vegetarianism, 171, 190, 226, 262–63, 275, 340, 416, **607–9**. *See also* ethical vegetarianism; veganism
   and animal rights, 16–17
   and juice bars, 337
   mock foods, 392
   peanut butter, 442
   prison food, 478
   rawfoodism, 493–94
   sausages, 526
Vegetarian Voice, 416
Vehling, Joseph Dommers, 163, 499
Velcro, 558
Velveeta, 105, 349, **609**
vending machines, 28, **609–10**
venison, **610**. *See also* deer
Verdon, René, 98, 624
Verdun, Pierre, 232
vermouth, 135, 364, 367–68, 610, **610**

Vernon, Edward, 266
Vernor's, 259, 508
vichyssoise, 473, **610–11**
victory gardens, 290, 291, 344, 427, 606
Vienna Beef, 304
Vienna sausage, **611**
Vienna style beer, 14
Vietnamese food, 553
Villas, James, 497, 498
Vinifera Wine Cellars, 630
Vinylite, 60
Virgin Coke, 140
Virginia, 20
Virginia Cookery—Past and Present, 143
Virginia House-Wife, The (Randolph), 97, 147, 179, 309, 327, 374, 491
   baked apple pudding, 20
   on eggplants, 205–6
   fried chicken, 239
   gazpacho, 552
   lemonade, 354
   okra recipes, 423
   pineapple, 460
   on roasting, 165
   on sauces, 524
   sorrel, 549
   on turnips, 599
Virginian, The (Wister), 454
Virgin Mary. *See* Bloody Mary and Virgin Mary
viscolizer, 55
vitamin A, 108, 611–12
vitamin B, 611
vitamin B complex, 612
vitamin C, 275, 419, 425, 611, 612
vitamin D, 108, 612
vitamin E, 612
vitamin K, 612
vitamins, 275, 418–19, **611–12**
   additives, 108
   and advertising, 4
   advertising, 4
Vlasic Foods International, 573
vodka, 55–56, 259, 512, 612, **612**
   martini, 367–68
   screwdriver, 530
   Smirnoff, 530
Vogel, A. H., 53
Vol-Pak, 342
Volstead Act, 290, 479, 585, 628
Vongerichten, Jean-Georges, 248, 249
von Liebig, Justin, 427
von Liebig, Justus, 418
von Tilzer, Albert, 173

waffle, wafer, and pizelle irons, **613**
Waffle House, 69
waffle syrup, 339
Wagner, Philip, 627, 629, 633
Wait, Pearle, 327
Wakefield, Ruth, 72, 156
Waldo, Myra, 433
Waldorf-Astoria Hotel, 61, 595–96
Waldorf salad, 514, 595–96
Wales, Mary T., 335
Walker, Norman, 245
walk-up window, 580
Wallace, Lily Haxworth, 151
Wallach, Andrew, 395
walleye, **613**
Walnut Cookbook, The (Toussaint), 420
walnuts, 420, **613**
   in brownies, 72
   in California, 85, 86
   in chess pies, 112
   coffee substitutes, 139
   as dessert, 188
   Halloween traditions, 270
   in *haroseth*, 331
   in ketchup, 342
   maple walnut pie, 365

in Native American diet, 18, 111, 281
  as snacks, 544
  in Waldorf salad, 514, 596
Walter Baker and Company, 122, 123, 435
Walter Baker Company, 246
Wangenheim, F. A. J., 444
Ward, Artemas, 151, 185
Ward Brands, 423
Warhol, Andy, 59
Waring, Fred, 55
Waring Blender, 55
Warner-Lambert, 423, 591
Washburn, Cadwallader, 255
Washburn-Crosby Company, 47
Washburn Mills, 458
Washington, Booker T., 624
Washington, George, 61, 210, 413, 613–14,
    623
  and alcohol, 584
  and apple brandy, 19
  favorite breakfast, 337
  and ice cream, 314
Washington, George (Belgian), 138
Washington, Martha, 25, 133, 167, 239, 350
Washingtonian Movement, 584
Washington's Birthday, 51, 613–14
wassail, 632
Wasylyk, Harry, 464
water, 12, 532, 614–15
Water, Alice, 238–39
water, bottled, 60, 532, 615
watercress, 399
watermelon, 615–16
  from Africa, 111, 311, 343, 350
  and African Americans, 616
  pickled, 453
  tall tales, 307
  watermelon cake, 616
Waters, Alice, 86, 99, 249, 254–55, 258, 278,
    294, 454, 616–17
water supply systems, 614–15
Watson, Donald and Dorothy, 604
Watson, James. L., 372
Watson, Paul, 17
Watson, Shelby, 467
Wawa, 147
waxed paper, 617
Way to a ... Man's Heart, The, 143
Way to a Man's Heart, 257
Way to Cook, The (Child), 154
We Are What We Eat (Gabaccia), 179
Weaver, William Woys, 179, 205, 247, 493, 529
Web sites, 655
Wechsberg, Joseph, 153, 498
weddings, 617–18
Wedgwood, Joseph, 101
Weems, Parson Mason Locke, 614
Weeping Radish, 46
weight-loss diets, 190, 275, 513
weights and measures. *See* measurement
Welch, Charles, 245
Welch, Mary B., 163
Welch, Thomas, 13, 245
*Welcome Table, The: African-American Heritage
    Cooking* (Harris), 154
Wells Brothers, 425
Wendy's, 217, 272, 580, 588, 618–19
Wente Brothers, 628
West Coast Cook Book (Brown), 71
Western sandwich, 186
West India Company, and beer, 43
Westinghouse, 117, 564
whale meat and whale oil, 619
Wharton, Edith, 359, 440
What Mrs. Fisher Knows about Old Southern Cooking
    (Fisher), 9, 151
What Shall We Drink? (Bredenbek), 167
What to Have for Dinner (Farmer), 215
What to Have for Luncheon (Lincoln), 358
wheat, 36, 64, 381, 431, 619–20

wheat germ, 64
Wheaties, 69, 102, 255
Wheaton, Barbara Ketchum, 178–79, 296
When Mother Lets Us Cook (Judson), 117
whey, 107
Whirlwind Oven, 11
whiskey, 195, 258, 423, 526, 620–21
  adulteration, 266
  American, 12
  barley, 36
  boilermaker, 58
  bourbon, 60–62, 195, 390, 423, 621
  in cordials, 167
  and flavorings, 225
  highball, 279
  hot toddies, 305
  John Collins, 140
  Manhattan, 364
  moonshine, 394
  substitute for rum, 266
whiskey barrels, 633
Whiskey Rebellion, 60–61, 562, 620
Whiskey Ring, 61
whiskey sour, 621
whisks, wire, 206
Whistle, 534
White, Elizabeth, 56
White, Ellen G., 275, 608
White Castle, 216, 271, 505, 580, 621–22
white cuisine, 181
whitefish, 623
Whitehead, Joseph, 133
White House, 623–24
Whitehouse, William E., 462
White House Cookbook, The (Ziemann and Gillette),
    624
White Russian, 512
white sauces, 524
White Tower, 271, 505, 580
Whittier, John Greenleaf
  on Lydia Maria Child, 116
  on pumpkins, 483, 484
whole-hog barbecue, 35
Wholesome Meat Act (1967), 75
Wholesome Poultry Act (1967), 75
Whoopie pie, 624
Whopper, 74, 272
Who Says We Can't Cook, 143
Why Not Eat Insects? (Holt), 319
Wian, Robert, 50, 271
Widmer, Joe, 105
wieners, 303, 611
Wienerschnitzel, 624–25
Wigmore, Anne, 494
Wildes, Harry Emerson, 335
wild rice, 384, 403, 405, 407, 408, 409, 625, 625
wild turkeys, 252
Wiley, Harvey, 625
Wiley, Harvey W., 1–2, 133, 187, 228, 261, 485
Wiley, Ralph, 465
Willan, Anne, 625–26
Williams, E. W., 242
Williams, Roger, 209, 317
Williamson Candy Company, 423
William Underwood Company, 91
Wilson, Bill, 14
Wilson, Charles Morrow, 152
Wilson, Edith, 27
Wilson, Jeff, 490
Wilson, Justin, 490
Wilson, Mary Tolford, 626
Wimpy, 74
wine, 626–31
  California wines, 86, 627–29
  Champagne, 103–4
  eastern U.S. wines, 629–30
  fruit, 245
  grapes, 629
  historical survey, 626–27
  later developments, 630–31

sack, 535
sangria, 522
sherry, 535
sparkling wine, 103–4
and yeast, 639, 640
wine, hot spiced, 631–32
Wine: An Introduction for Americans (Amerine and
    Singleton), 633
wine barrels, 632–33. *See also* wine casks
wine books, 633
wine bottles, 633
wine casks, 633–34
wine cellars, 634
wine coolers, 522, 634, 634
wine glasses, 260, 261, 627, 634
wine grapes, 263
Winemaking in California (Teiser and Harroun),
    633
wineries, 104, 263, 626, 628, 634–35
  fruit wines, 245
  Gallo, 251
  in Pacific Northwest, 432
  Robert Mondavi, 393
  wine barrels, 632–33
  wine-tasting rooms, 635–36
Wines of America, The (Adams), 633
wine-tasting rooms, 635–36
Winning of a Peach, The, 186
Winterfest, 166
wintergreen, 523
winter melons, 377
Wisconsin
  and cheese, 104–5
  dairy industry, 182
  food festivals, 230
  production of cabbage, 79
Wise, Brownie, 597
Wisniewski, Ian, 530
Wistar, Caspar, 260
Wister, Owen, 351, 454
With Bold Knife and Fork (Fisher), 224
Witt, Doris, 179
W. K. Kellogg Foundation, 341
Wobblies, 499
Wolf, Fred W. Jr., 312
Wolfert, Paula, 154
Woman's Day, 450
Woman's Exchange movement, 247
Woman's Glory: The Kitchen, 143
Woman's Home Companion, 449
Woman's Home Companion Cook Book, 151
Woman Suffrage Cook Book, The, 143
(Woman) Writer (Oates), 359
women
  activities, 149
  and advertising, 4–5
  and homemaking, 41
  issues, 41, 161
  roles, 293. *See also* gender roles
Women's Christian Temperance Union, 13, 43,
    479, 584
Women's Educational Association, 59
Women's Education Association, 162
Women's Home Companion, 4, 151
women's magazines, 151
women's rights, and community cookbooks,
    143
Wonder Bread, 65, 66
Wonton Food, Inc., 233
wood, 157
Woodbridge wines, 506
Woodruff, Ernest, 133–34
Woodruff, Robert, 134, 140
Woodward, Orator, 327–28
Woolley, Hannah, 484
Woolworth, 240
Worcestershire sauce, 558
workers' housing, 80, 279
workers' rights, 213–14
World Atlas of Wine (Johnson), 633

World Food Program, 320
World's Columbian Exposition, 636
  Aunt Jemima, 5, 26
  Brady, Diamond Jim, 62
  cookbooks, 151
  sanitary can, 92
World's Fairs, **636–37**
World's Fair Souvenir Cook Book (Rorer), 151
World Wide Cook Book (Metzelthin), 152
wort, 70, 621
wraps, **637**
Wright, Frank, 1
Wright, Mary, 193
Wright, Richardson L., 152
Wright, Russel, 193, 466
Wright Liquid Smoke, 543
Wrigley, William, Jr., 89
Wrigley Company, 267, 357
writers. *See* food writers; literature and food
Wunderle Candy Company, 270
Wyeth, N. C., 26
Wyld, Federico Lehnhoff, 138

Xinjiang, 101

Yakima Brewing and Malting Company, 379
yam, 575
Yan, Martin, 490, **639**
Yan Can Cook, 490, 639
Y and S Candies, 356
yang foods, 120
Yankee Oyster Pie, 97
Yavno, Max, 633
yeast, **639–40**
  advertising, *4*
  and ale, 43
  and beer, 73
  and bread, 64
  compressed yeast, 636, 639
  and crackers, 173
  and lager, 43
  and temperance, 13
yeast powders, 109
Yezierska, Anzia, 359
yin foods, 120
Yoder, Don, 233
yogurt, 101
York Cone Company, 451
York Peppermint Patties, 451

Yorkshire Global Restaurants, 224, 640
Young, James Webb, 26
Young, John, 74
Young, Murat "Chick", 181
Yuban, 23
yucca, 96
Yum! Brands, Inc., 224, 342, 579, **640**
yummasetti, **640**

Zabar's, *66*
Zagat, Tim and Nina, 498
Zagat Survey, 498
Zaiger, Floyd, 466
zakuska, 19
Zbikiewicz, Henry, 55
Zerbe, Jerome, 367
Ziemann, Hugo, 624
Zima, 166
Ziploc, 464
zip-tab can, 60
Zojirushi Corporation, 66
zombie, **640**
Zone, The (Sears), 275

Picture Credits